The Victoria History of the Counties of England

EDITED BY WILLIAM PAGE, F.S.A.

A HISTORY OF
BUCKINGHAMSHIRE

VOLUME IV

View of the Vale of Aylesbury from Whitchurch.

Engraved by Wm Byrne, F.S.A.

THE
VICTORIA HISTORY
OF THE COUNTIES
OF ENGLAND

BUCKINGHAMSHIRE

PUBLISHED FOR

THE UNIVERSITY OF LONDON
INSTITUTE OF HISTORICAL RESEARCH

REPRINTED FROM THE ORIGINAL EDITION OF 1927

BY

DAWSONS OF PALL MALL

LONDON

1969

Published by
the St. Catherine Press
in 1927

Reprinted for the University of London
Institute of Historical Research
by
Dawsons of Pall Mall
16 Pall Mall, London, S.W. 1
1969
ISBN: 07129 0373 9

HAMPSHIRE COUNTY LIBRARY

R942
89

0712903739

C008790906

Reprinted by Stephen Austin and Sons Ltd., Caxton Hill, Hertford

INSCRIBED
TO THE MEMORY OF
HER LATE MAJESTY
QUEEN VICTORIA
WHO GRACIOUSLY GAVE
THE TITLE TO AND
ACCEPTED THE
DEDICATION OF
THIS HISTORY

THE
VICTORIA HISTORY
OF THE COUNTY OF
BUCKINGHAM

EDITED BY WILLIAM PAGE, F.S.A.

VOLUME FOUR

PUBLISHED FOR
THE UNIVERSITY OF LONDON
INSTITUTE OF HISTORICAL RESEARCH
REPRINTED BY
DAWSONS OF PALL MALL
LONDON

CONTENTS OF VOLUME FOUR

CONTENTS OF VOLUME FOUR

CONTENTS OF VOLUME FOUR

LIST OF ILLUSTRATIONS

LIST OF ILLUSTRATIONS

xiv

LIST OF ILLUSTRATIONS

LIST OF ILLUSTRATIONS

xvi

LIST OF ILLUSTRATIONS

LIST OF ILLUSTRATIONS

LIST OF MAPS

EDITORIAL NOTE

As stated in the Editorial Note to the third volume, the history of Buckinghamshire was so far advanced when the work upon it fell into abeyance on the outbreak of war, that it has been found necessary to publish the remaining two volumes, then in hand, without bringing them up to date.

The Editor desires specially to acknowledge the help he received from Sir Lancelot Aubrey-Fletcher, Sir Laurence Gomme, Mr. F. W. Bull, Mr. A. C. Chibnall, Rev. James H. Harvey, Mr. John N. Knapp, Mr. Arthur H. Kerr, Mr. E. S. Roscoe, Rev. J. Maurice Turner, Mr. W. Andrews Uthwatt and Mr. Thomas Wright, who by lending manuscripts and notes materially assisted in the compilation of the manorial descents given in this volume.

The Editor has again to thank the clergy and others who have read the proofs of their parishes and made corrections. He would mention in this respect the help he has received from Rev. A. C. Alford, Rev. J. T. Athawes, Rev. T. Appleton, Rev. C. Bass, Rev. R. C. Bailey, Rev. F. W. Bennitt, Rev. H. A. G. Blomefield, Rev. C. Bolden, Rev. J. L. Bowley, Mr. W. Bradbrook, Rev. A. F. Q. Bros, Rev. R. M. G. Browne, Rev. G. A. Browning, Rev. P. L. Cantley, Rev. C. Sydney Carter, Rev. W. K. Clay, Rev. H. J. M. Clements, Rev. C. H. Coles, Rev. W. H. Davis, Rev. G. Dangerfield, Rev. C. C. Dawson-Smith, Rev. G. D. Dunlop, Rev. W. S. Eaton, Rev. U. J. Easson, Rev. E. S. Elwell, Rev. F. E. G. Farmer, Rev. and Hon. W. S. Fiennes, Rev. F. Fisher, Rev. A. F. G. Fletcher, Rev. C. W. Fullmer, Rev. L. E. Goddard, Lt.-Col. A. W. H. Good, Rev. B. G. Goodrich, Rev. A. Gordon, Rev. H. B. M. Gorham, Rev. C. Greaves, Rev. A. N. Guest, Rev. W. J. Harkness, Rev. E. J. Harper, Rev. G. Hawke Field, Rev. F. M. Higgins, Mrs. Napier Higgins, Lt.-Col. Hobart, Mrs. Hood, Rev. J. F. Hoyle, Rev. A. H. James, Rev. St. J. B. James, Rev. H. J. Johnson, Rev. L. Jones, Rev. O. J. Jones, Mrs. Longuet-Higgins, Rev. H. Mare, Rev. J. Martin, Rev. E. R. Massey, Rev. A. Matheson, Rev. A. G. Mildmay, Rev. G. F. Moore, Rev. W. O'Reilly, Rev. E. Paine, Rev. A. A. Pargiter, Rev. R. J. Pearce, Rev. B. H. A. Philpotts, Rev. C. O. Phipps, Rev. C. R. Prideaux, Rev. N. R. Ramsay, Rev. P. E. Raynor, Rev. W. B. Rickards, Rev. G. G. Roworth, Rev. R. F. Rumsey, Rev. G. F. Sams, Mrs. Richard Selby-Lowndes, Rev. C. J. Senior, Rev. E. R. Sill, Rev. J. Skinner, Rev. A. B. Smith, Rev. H. W. Smith, Rev. B. Staley, Rev. J. L. Starling, Rev. M. Stevens, Rev. B. E. Symonds, Rev. T. W. Tidmarsh, Mr. J. D. Tomes, Rev. J. Turnbull, Rev. R. Usher, Rev. J. R. Vincent, Rev. R. R. Vyvyan, Rev. B. H. C. Wafsberger, Rev. H. F. Wilson, and Rev. A. B. Wright.

A HISTORY OF

BUCKINGHAMSHIRE

TOPOGRAPHY

THE HUNDRED OF ASHENDON

CONTAINING THE PARISHES OF

ASHENDON
ASTON SANDFORD
BOARSTALL
BRILL
CHEARSLEY
CHILTON
EAST CLAYDON
MIDDLE CLAYDON
LONG CRENDON
DORTON
GRANDBOROUGH
GRENDON UNDERWOOD

HOGSHAW
ICKFORD
ILMER
KINGSEY
LUDGERSHALL WITH
 KINGSWOOD
FLEET MARSTON
NORTH MARSTON
OAKLEY
OVING
PITCHCOTT

QUAINTON WITH
 SHIPTON LEE
QUARRENDON
SHABBINGTON
TOWERSEY
WADDESDON WITH WEST-
 COTT AND WOODHAM
LOWER OR NETHER
 WINCHENDON
UPPER WINCHENDON
WORMINGHALL
WOTTON UNDERWOOD

Until the late 13th or early 14th century the hundred of Ashendon was divided into the three hundreds of Ashendon, Ixhill and Waddesdon.[1] The hundred of Ashendon contained Ashendon, Chearsley, Grendon Underwood, Hogshaw, Ludgershall, Oving, Quainton, Winchendon and Wotton Underwood. The hundred of Ixhill comprised Aston Sandford, Boarstall, Brill, Chilton, Long Crendon, Dorton, Ickford, Ilmer, Kingsey, Oakley, Shabbington, Towersey and Worminghall. The hundred of Waddesdon included the Claydons, Grandborough, Fleet Marston, North Marston, Pitchcott, Quarrendon, Waddesdon and Woodham. In 1086 Ashendon Hundred was assessed at 112 hides 1 virgate,[2] Ixhill[3] (Tichesele) at 116 hides 3 virgates,[4] and Waddesdon Hundred at 89 hides 3 virgates.[5] The distinctive names of the hundreds of Ixhill and Waddesdon gradually became obsolete, and only four references to them have been found in the 16th and 17th centuries, the latest occurring in 1665.[6]

Of the names given in the list of parishes and hamlets, those of Hogshaw, Fulbrook, Kingswood, Boarstall, Kingsey, Pitchcott, Westcott and Woodham are not found in the Domesday Survey. Towersey occurs as Eie, and Boarstall, Kingsey and Kingswood were later subdivisions of the royal domain of Brill. The following places mentioned in Domesday are not

---

[1] *Hund. R.* (Rec. Com.), i, 23, 25, 45 ; *Feud. Aids,* i, 113, 121.

[2] Including 2½ hides in Quainton, where the hundred heading is omitted (*V.C.H. Bucks.* i, 272).

[3] Surviving in Ixhill in Oakley parish.

[4] Including 2 hides 3 virgates in Waldridge, part of Dinton parish, which extended into this hundred (*V.C.H. Bucks.* ii, 246), and excluding 2 hides in Lesa in Beckley parish, Oxfordshire (ibid. i, 268), and 1¾ hides held by Alvered of Thame under Giles (ibid. i, 273), probably also in Oxfordshire. The 5 hides 3 virgates given for Oakley are afterwards said to be 8 hides (ibid. 258).

[5] Excluding 10 hides in Creslow and Hoggeston (ibid. i, 255, 263) in Cottesloe Hundred.

[6] Lay Subs. R. bdles. 78, no. 114 ; 79, no. 209 ; Pat. 14 Chas. II, pt. xix, no. 6 ; 17 Chas. II, pt. ix, no. 1.

included in the list: Beachendon in Waddesdon parish, Sortelai formerly in Shipton Lee, Addingrove in Oakley. Most of the names of the thirty-one parishes occur in 16th-century assessment lists,[7] and all are enumerated in some belonging to the 17th century.[8]

The court leet of the bailiwick was held twice yearly usually at Towersey. All actions under 40s. might be tried and determined at the court held every three weeks at Brill.[9]

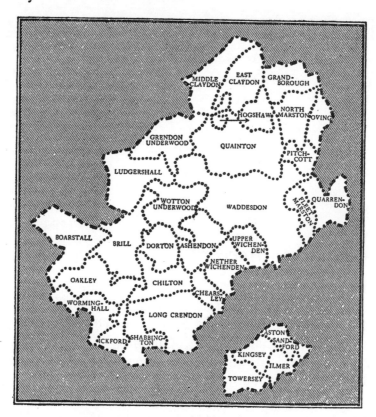

INDEX MAP TO THE HUNDRED OF ASHENDON

In 1665 a grant of the Ashendon Hundreds was made to Queen Katherine subject to a thirty-one years' lease granted to Robert Dormer[10] in 1662.[11]

---

[7] Lay Subs. R. bdles. 78, no. 141 ; 79, no. 164, m. 5 ; 79, no. 232.
[8] Ibid. bdles. 79, no. 275 ; 80, no. 309.   [9] Parl. Surv. Bucks. no. 2.
[10] Pat. 17 Chas. II, pt. ix, no. 1.   [11] Ibid. 14 Chas. II, pt. xix, no. 6.

ASHENDON

Assedone, Assedune (xi cent.) ; Essendon (xiii cent.) ; Aysshyndon, Ashendon, Essundon (xiv cent.).

This parish includes more than 2,127 acres, of which about one-eighth is arable, while the rest, except 11 acres of woodland,[1] is pasture.[2] The soil is loam and clay on a subsoil of Kimmeridge Clay and Corallian.[3] The land rises from 300 ft. above the ordnance datum in the north-west to 500 ft. near the village, whence it sinks to about 300 ft. at Lower Pollicott.

The village, which is small and consists of farmhouses and thatched or tiled cottages grouped irregularly on high ground, lies in the west of the parish on a road which enters it from Westcott on the north. The church stands on a hill at the south-west extremity of the village. East Farm, about 250 yards in a north-easterly direction from the church, and the farm 50 yards further on, are both of late 17th-century origin, but much altered and restored. About a quarter of a mile south-west of the church is the hamlet of Upper Pollicott (Policote, xi cent.; Polikote, xiii cent.), south of which Lower Pollicott lies in a hollow a little distance from the main road.[4] Lower Pollicott farm-house,[5] about three-quarters of a mile south of the church, was built late in the 16th or early in the 17th century. It was originally timber-framed, but has been partly refaced in later times with stone rubble and brickwork. Three of the original chimney stacks survive, and some original oak panelling remains internally.

An early inclosure of 60 acres in this parish made by the Abbot of Nutley before 1503 rendered twenty persons homeless.[6] Towards the end of that century Thomas Palmer, lord of the manor, was accused by his tenants of taking in the better half of the manor and inclosing it in his own demesnes.[7] In 1738 1,700 acres were inclosed by Act of Parliament.[8] Some place-names of that date were Launders Mead, Barkham Hill, Mollets Haynes Hill, Overgoose Bath, and Neither Landhurst.[9] A

few Anglo-Saxon remains have been found in Ashendon.[10]

MANORS The manor of *ASHENDON*, which three brothers held before the Conquest, belonged to Walter Giffard in 1086,[11] and was held of the honour of Giffard until the second half of the 13th century.[12] The overlordship descended with the manor of Long Crendon (q.v.) until between 1247 and 1255 it came to William de Valence on his marriage with Joan daughter of Warin de Monchensy by Joan sister and co-heir of Anselm Earl of Pembroke.[13] Between 1302, when Joan widow of William de Valence held it alone,[14] and the death of their son Aymer in 1324,[15] this overlordship apparently passed to the Argentein family, who had enjoyed a mesne lordship here since 1255. Giles de

LOWER POLLICOTT FARM, ASHENDON

Argentein, of whom the manor of Ashendon was held at that date,[16] was succeeded by his son Reynold,[17] mesne lord in 1284 and 1302.[18] At the death of John son and heir of Reynold[19] it was found that Ashendon was held of him by the service of one knight's fee and 40s. rent, payable to his manor of Little Wymondley, Hertfordshire.[20] The overlordship then descended[21] in the Argentein family and their

---

[1] A part of Pollicott Bucktot (see below) was afforested by Richard I and included in Bernwood Forest in the 13th century (Boarstall Chart. fol. 114).

[2] Statistics from Bd. of Agric. (1905).

[3] Geol. map in *V.C.H. Bucks.* i.

[4] These hamlets correspond to the two manors of Pollicott.

[5] This is probably the farm-house of Little Pollicott mentioned in 1738 (Priv. Act, 11 Geo. II, cap. 20).

[6] Leadam, *Dom. Incl.* 1517 (Royal Hist. Soc.), i, 159–60.

[7] Chan. Proc. (Ser. 2), bdle. 285, no. 7.

[8] Slater, *Engl. Peasantry and Encl. of Com. Fields*, 271.

[9] Priv. Act, 11 Geo. II, cap. 20.

[10] *V.C.H. Bucks.* i, 197 ; *Rec. of Bucks.* (Bucks. Arch. and Archit. Soc.), ii, 117.

[11] *V.C.H. Bucks.* i, 248.

[12] Misc. Bks. (Exch. K.R.), vi, fol. 168 ; *Hund. R.* (Rec. Com.), i, 23.

[13] *Hund. R.* (Rec. Com.), i, 23 ; G.E.C. *Peerage*, vi, 204–5.   [14] *Feud. Aids*, i, 95.

[15] *Cal. Inq. p.m.* (Edw. II), vi, 314.

[16] *Hund. R.* (Rec. Com.), i, 55.

[17] *Cal. Inq. p.m.* (Edw. I), ii, 275.

[18] *Feud. Aids*, i, 75, 95.

[19] *Cal. Inq. p.m.* (Edw. II), v, 11.

[20] Ibid. vi, 105, 103.   There was probably a further mesne lordship held by John de Adingrave (ibid.).

[21] *Cal. Close*, 1323–7, p. 81 ; *Cal. Inq. p.m.* (Edw. III), vii, 446–7 ; Clutterbuck, *Hist. and Antiq. of Herts.* ii, 541–4 ; *Cal. Pat.* 1416–22, p. 215 ; Chan. Inq. p.m. 6 Hen. V, no. 13 ; 2 Hen. VI, no. 27 ; 6 Hen. VI, no. 53 ; 7 Hen. VI, no. 8 ; 38 & 39 Hen. VI, no. 42 ; 20 Edw. IV, no. 58 ; (Ser. 2), cxx, 11 In 1623 Ashendon was said to be held of Wymondley, Cambridge (ibid. cccxcix, 149) ; G.E.C. *Peerage* (new ed.), i, 106–9 ; Feet of F. Div. Co. Mich. 1656 ; Mich. 10 Will. III.

successors,[22] and Sir Robert Grosvenor had rights in Ashendon as lord of Wymondley as late as 1738.[23]

Nothing seems to be known of Richard, sub-tenant of Walter Giffard in 1086.[24] Thomas St. Andrew, owner of a free tenement here in 1213,[25] was succeeded in a few years by Henry St. Andrew, lord in 1236.[26] In 1255 the manor belonged to another Thomas,[27] possibly the Thomas St. Andrew accused in 1276 of having obstructed the king's highway.[28] He seems to have been succeeded, though perhaps not immediately, since John St. Andrew enjoyed rights here in 1267,[29] by his son Walter, lord from 1284 to 1316.[30] In 1317 the manor was settled on Thomas St. Andrew, with contingent remainders to John son of Walter St. Andrew, Isabel sister of John, and Walter son of Thomas St. Andrew.[31] Another settlement was made about 1322 on Thomas and his wife Alice,[32] who held Ashendon in dower from her husband's death until possibly after 1346.[33] The marriage of their daughter Gille was granted when Thomas died in or before 1334 to John de Moleyns, who transferred his interest to Thomas Frembaud.[34] In 1343 Thomas and Gille, then husband and wife, made a settlement of Ashendon,[35] which was held by Thomas alone in 1361. A lease of the manor, which he then granted to Sir Richard de la Vache, and which was ratified by his son Thomas,[36] was followed two years later by the final quitclaim of the younger Thomas.[37] From 1363 until 1407-8 Ashendon descended with the manor of La Vache in Chalfont St. Giles (q.v.) and Vaches Manor in Aston Clinton.[38] After the death of Sir Philip de la Vache in 1407-8 Ashendon Manor appears to have passed with the Aston Clinton property, since it reappears in 1503 in the possession of Edmund Lord Grey de Wilton and his wife Florence.[39] In 1508 they made a settlement of Ashendon Manor,[40] possibly a preliminary to its alienation to the Fawconer family. From Henry Fawconer, lord about that date and in 1517,[41] the manor seems to have passed to William Fawconer, who died seised in 1558,

ARGENTEIN. *Gules three covered cups argent.*

ST. ANDREW. *Gules six voided lozenges or.*

DE LA VACHE. *Gules three lions argent with crowns or.*

FAWCONER. *Paly argent and azure a bend gules with three trefoils or thereon.*

leaving a son and heir William.[42] Anne, a daughter of the second William, held Ashendon with her husband Benedict Winchcombe in 1610, a year after her father's death,[43] and in 1623, when Benedict died.[44] She was childless, and the remainder of her inheritance had been settled not two years before Benedict's death on his nephew and heir Benedict Hall,[45] who, with his mother Mary Hall and his brother Henry, quitclaimed to her in 1623.[46] In 1626, however, Benedict Hall still retained his interest here.[47] He was alive when Anne died in 1630, leaving Ashendon to his younger brother Thomas, generally known as Thomas Hawles,[48] for twelve years from her death.[49] Two years later William Fawconer, son of her father's younger brother Ralph,[50] with his wife Catherine and sons William and Robert, sold or mortgaged the manor of Ashendon to Roger Nicoll and William Aston.[51] They were probably agents for Richard Grenville of Wotton, who acquired the manor at this date, at first for ninety-nine years but later in fee, and settled it on trustees for the use of his son and heir Richard in 1663.[52] It has since followed the descent of Wotton Underwood (q.v.), Algernon Earl Temple of Stowe being now lord.

Lands of the yearly value of 30s., held in 1367 of Philip de la Vache, lord of Ashendon Manor,[53] were assigned in 1325 to Lawrence son of John Hastings, kinsman and co-heir of Aymer de Valence,[54] and included in the dower of his mother Juliana from 1327 to 1367.[55] From 1367 to 1400, when the last separate mention of them seems to occur, they descended with the Hastings manor in Long Crendon[56] (q.v.).

William Goley, who owned land in Ashendon in 1241,[57] fourteen years later was returned as holding 2 hides here, one as forester of the woods in Bernwood Forest of the honour of Giffard, the other

[22] See account of Great and Little Wymondley, *V.C.H. Herts.* iii, 183.

[23] Priv. Act, 11 Geo. II, cap. 20.

[24] *V.C.H. Bucks.* i, 248.

[25] *Abbrev. Plac.* (Rec. Com.), 92.

[26] Misc. Bks. (Exch. K.R.), vi, fol. 168; *Testa de Nevill* (Rec. Com.), 259, 261.

[27] *Hund. R.* (Rec. Com.), i, 23.

[28] Ibid. 42.

[29] Feet of F. Bucks. 52 Hen. III, no. 6.

[30] *Feud. Aids*, i, 75, 95, 113; De Banco R. 211, m. 297 d.

[31] Feet of F. Bucks. 11 Edw. II, no. 21.

[32] Chan. Inq. p.m. Edw. III, file 41, no. 18.

[33] Feet of F. Bucks. 7 Edw. III, no. 8; *Feud. Aids*, i, 120.

[34] *Cal. Inq. p.m.* (Edw. III), vii, 447.

[35] Feet of F. Bucks. 7 Edw. III, no. 8.

[36] *Cal. Close*, 1360-4, pp. 265, 276.

[37] Ibid. 550. [38] *V.C.H. Bucks.* ii, 314.

[39] De Banco R. Mich. 19 Hen. VII, m. 136.

[40] Ibid. East 23 Hen. VIII, m. 264.

[41] Leadam, l c. cit.

[42] Chan. In q. p.m. (Ser. 2), cxx, 11.

[43] Feet of F. Bucks. East. 8 Jas. I; Lipscomb, *Hist. and Antiq. of Bucks.* i, 16.

[44] Chan. Inq. p.m. (Ser. 2), cccxcix, 149.

[45] Ibid.

[46] Ibid. ; Feet of F. Bucks. Mich. 21 Jas. I.

[47] Recov. R. Hil. 2 Chas. I, m. 62.

[48] Lipscomb, loc. cit.

[49] P.C.C. 74 Scroope.

[50] G. W. Marshall, *Visit. of Wilts.* (1623), 11.

[51] Feet of F. Bucks. East. 8 Chas. I.

[52] P.C.C. 58 Mico.

[53] Chan. Inq. p.m. 41 Edw. III (1st nos.), no. 34.

[54] *Cal. Close*, 1323-7, pp. 288, 360; 1327-30, pp. 12, 75.

[55] Chan. Inq. p.m. 41 Edw. III (1st nos.), no. 34.

[56] An inquisition of 1397 on the forfeited lands of Richard Earl of Arundel describes this tenement as the manor of Ashendon rented at 32s. (Chan. Inq. Misc. file 266, m. 5).

[57] Feet of F. Bucks. 25 Hen. III, no. 15.

by serjeanty of the same honour.[58] In 1316 Thomas Golde (? Goley) was one of the lords of Ashendon.[59] The name survived in 'Gollyes Farm,' held, with 7½ virgates of land, by Richard Franklin in the 17th century.[60]

Two hides in Ashendon were owned by Miles Crispin at the Survey, and held of him by Wichin, their former lord.[61] The overlordship of this land, which was in the honour of Wallingford,[62] descended from 1284[63] until 1575 with the manor of Eythrope in Waddesdon (q.v.), whose lords of the family of Darches enjoyed a mesne lordship here in the 13th and 14th centuries.[64] Of the early sub-tenancy little is known. The fee was divided between the St. Andrew and Bernard families and the Abbot of Nutley in the 13th century,[65] and from 1552 to 1580 descended as a so-called manor of Ashendon with Wing Manor (q.v.). It seems to have been alienated not long after the latter year, lands in Ashendon purchased of Robert Dormer of Wing being held at his death in 1615 by Richard Franklin,[66] ancestor possibly of George Franklin, a landowner here in 1738.[67]

The manor of *POLLICOTT*, which consisted of 10 hides, 5 of which had been held before the Conquest by Alric son of Godinge, whilst the rest belonged to three brothers, was amongst the possessions of Walter Giffard in 1086.[68] As part of the honour of Giffard the overlordship followed the descent of Long Crendon (q.v.) probably until William de Valence acquired the overlordship of Ashendon.[69] It seems then to have been shared between William and Eleanor Countess of Leicester, widow of the younger William Marshal,[70] William holding Little Pollicott, the countess holding Great Pollicott.[71] No part of Eleanor's rights seems to have descended to her heirs. After her death Great Pollicott was held of the Crown in chief by William and his heirs until 1609,[72] Little Pollicott being held of William and his heirs until 1346,[73] after which their overlordship seems to have lapsed.

The pre-Norman division of this manor, which also prevailed after the Conquest, two knights holding of Walter Giffard in 1086,[74] survived to the middle of the 19th century,[75] if not later. It is probable that Alric's share was the manor of *GREAT POLLICOTT*, also called *POLLICOTT CRESSY* and *POLLICOTT VALENCE*, which was doubtless included in the fee held in this county of the honour

of Giffard by Hugh de Cressy in 1166.[76] He had also Chearsley (q.v.), with which Pollicott Cressy descended[77] until the death of Aymer de Valence in 1324,[78] when Pollicott was assigned to his niece Elizabeth Comyn,[79] on whom with her husband Richard Talbot, afterwards Lord Talbot, the manor was settled in 1327.[80] They made a life grant of it five years later to James of Woodstock,[81] and another in 1343 to Aline widow of Robert de Sapy.[82] In 1352 Richard, who had been returned as lord in 1346,[83] obtained licence to enfeoff his son Gilbert and Parnel Butler of the manor of Pollicott.[84] From Gilbert Pollicott descended to his son by

TALBOT. *Gules a lion and an engrailed border or.*

Parnel, another Richard Talbot,[85] who in 1387 and 1394 sued Sir Nicholas Stafford and others for this manor.[86] Gilbert his son and heir was betrothed to Joan second daughter of Thomas Duke of Gloucester,[87] and it is supposed that Pollicott was included in their marriage settlement and transferred at Joan's death to her sister Anne.[88] In 1425 Humphrey Earl of Stafford, Anne's son and heir by her second husband, was lord of Pollicott,[89] of which six years later Sir Lewis Robsart, husband of Elizabeth Bourchier, a relative

STAFFORD. *Or a cheveron gules.*

of Anne through her third husband Sir William Bourchier,[90] died seised.[91] The remainder of the manor after the death of Elizabeth, who survived Sir Lewis, belonged to Humphrey, Anne retaining a mesne lordship during the Robsart tenure.[92] Humphrey, then Duke of Buckingham, was lord in 1457–8.[93] He also held Newton Blossomville Manor (q.v.), with which Pollicott descended until the attainder and execution of Edward Duke of Buckingham in 1521.

In 1522 Henry VIII granted the manor of Pollicott to his servant Thomas Palmer[94] for life,[95] giving the reversion, also for life, five years later to Henry[96]

---

[58] *Hund. R.* (Rec. Com.), i, 23.

[59] *Feud. Aids*, i, 113.

[60] See below.

[61] *V.C.H. Bucks.* i, 261.

[62] *Hund. R.* (Rec. Com.), i, 23, 42 ; Chan. Inq. p.m. 2 Ric. II, no. 57 ; Ct. R. (Gen. Ser.), portf. 212, no. 5.

[63] *Feud. Aids*, i, 75.

[64] Ibid. 113 ; Rentals and Surv. (Duchy of Lanc.), bdle. 14, no. 3.

[65] *Feud. Aids*, i, 75. For the abbot's portion, 1 hide, see below.

[66] Chan. Inq. p.m. (Ser. 2), cccxlix, 166.

[67] Priv. Act, 11 Geo. II, cap. 20.

[68] *V.C.H. Bucks.* i, 248.

[69] See above.

[70] See in Long Crendon.

[71] *Hund. R.* (Rec. Com.), i, 42.

[72] *Feud. Aids*, i, 75, 95, 121. See below for later references. In 1460 it was said to be held of the heirs of William de Valence, in 1475 of William himself

(Chan. Inq. p.m. 38 & 39 Hen. VI, no. 59; 15 Edw. IV, no. 44).

[73] *Feud. Aids*, i, 75, 95, 121. In the 13th century Fulk de Coudray enjoyed a mesne lordship here (*Testa de Nevill* [Rec. Com.], 247 ; *Hund. R.* [Rec. Com.], i, 23 ; *Feud. Aids*, i, 75).

[74] *V.C.H. Bucks.* i, 248.

[75] Lipscomb, op. cit. i, 33.

[76] *Red Bk. of Exch.* (Rolls Ser.), 312.

[77] See also Feet of F. case 16, file 37, no. 98.

[78] *Cal. Inq. p.m.* (Edw. II), vi, 340.

[79] *Abbrev. Rot. Orig.* (Rec. Com.), i, 287.

[80] *Inq. a.q.d.* (P.R.O. Lists and Indexes), i, 262 ; *Cal. Pat. 1327–30*, p. 9 ; Feet of F. case, 288, file 35, no. 1.

[81] *Cal. Pat. 1330–4*, p. 304 ; De Banco R. 291, m. 117 ; Feet of F. case 19, file 79, no. 26.

[82] *Cal. Pat. 1343–5*, p. 14 ; Feet of F. case 19, file 85, no. 17.

[83] *Feud. Aids*, i, 121.

[84] *Cal. Pat. 1350–4*, p. 327.

[85] G.E.C. *Peerage*, vii, 359.

[86] De Banco R. 507, m. 561 d. ; 532, m. 72 d.

[87] G.E.C. loc. cit.

[88] Ibid. 211–12.

[89] Ibid. ; Chan. Inq. p.m. 3 Hen. VI, no. 29.

[90] G.E.C. loc. cit. ; Blomefield, *Topog. Hist. of Co. Norf.* vii, 187.

[91] Chan. Inq. p.m. 9 Hen. VI, no. 52.

[92] Ibid.

[93] Feet of F. case 293, file 73, no. 431.

[94] This Thomas, afterwards Sir Thomas Palmer, cannot be the better known Sir Thomas Palmer, executed in 1553, to whom this grant has been ascribed (*Dict. Nat. Biog.*), as he was dead in 1544 (Pat. 36 Hen. VIII, pt. xxi, m. 23).

[95] Pat. 14 Hen. VIII, pt. i, m. 9.

[96] Ibid. 19 Hen. VIII, pt. ii, m. 26.

son of Sir Edward Palmer of Angmering, Sussex, elder brother of Thomas.[97] From Thomas, described in 1540 as 'old Master Pawmer of Buckinghamshire,'[98] Pollicott descended to Henry Palmer in or before 1544, when the grant of 1514 was renewed in perpetuity.[99] He leased the manor in 1548 for seventy-one years to Thomas King, whose son and successor William complained four years later that the ancient rights of the copyholders had prevented his father from occupying it.[100] In 1599 the tenants sued Sir Henry's son and heir Thomas Palmer and his son

PALMER of Wingham, baronet. *Or two bars gules each charged with three trefoils argent and a greyhound sable running in the chief.*

of the same name[1] for their oppressive and extortionate practices.[2] The younger Sir Thomas died in 1608, in his father's lifetime, leaving a son, also named Thomas,[3] who in 1624 succeeded his grandfather in his lands and the baronetcy he had acquired in 1621.[4] His tenure lasted until 1656,[5] when Pollicott passed to his son Henry, lord in 1658.[6] At Sir Henry's death without issue in 1706 he was succeeded by his nephew Thomas, son of his younger brother Herbert, who died in 1723, leaving four daughters.[7] The three elder of these—Mary wife of Daniel Earl of Winchilsea and Nottingham, Elizabeth wife of Charles Fielding, and Anne—held three-quarters of the manor in 1739.[8] The youngest sister Frances Palmer, her mother Elizabeth, and Thomas Hey, second husband of Elizabeth, made a settlement of the other quarter about three years later,[9] and in 1744 joined with the Earl of Winchilsea and his wife Mary, Charles Fielding and Anne Palmer in the sale of the manor to Richard Grenville.[10] Since that time Pollicott has descended with Ashendon and Wotton Underwood (q.v.).

Early in the reign of Henry III the other half of the manor, *LITTLE POLLICOTT* or *POLLICOTT BUCKTOT*, was held by Thomas Bucktoft as half a knight's fee.[11] He or his heir of the same name acquired land here in 1236.[12] In 1255, 1284 and 1302 the lord was again called Thomas Bucktoft.[13] Ellen, widow of the last Thomas, with her son Philip, received in 1325 from Walter St. Andrew a release

of his rights in lands in Ashendon and Pollicott Bucktot which he held by gift of her late father, Philip Horton.[14] Philip Bucktoft was lord in 1346.[15] The manor seems to have remained in this family until the reign of Henry VI, when it was held by John Bucktoft, clerk,[16] son of another Philip Bucktoft, who granted it to Lincoln College, Oxford, in 1451.[17] John was dead in 1452, when his kinswoman and heir, Thomasine, with her husband John Ascote, surrendered her rights in the manor to John Beck, rector of Lincoln College.[18] Pollicott Bucktot was retained by Lincoln College, which had manorial rights here in the middle of the 19th century.[19]

In 1255 the Abbot of Nutley, through the gifts of Walter Bernard and an ancestor of Walter de Berk, owned a hide in Ashendon,[20] which belonged to the honour of Wallingford.[21] One of his successors owed suit to the court of this honour in 1422,[22] and in the 16th century another was tenant of 40 acres by lease from Henry Fawconer.[23]

Land in Pollicott Bucktot acquired in 1279 by John Grenville[24] is said to have passed by marriage to Reynold Hampden and to have been held by his descendants as part of Ashendon until the forfeiture of Sir Edmund Hampden,[25] after which Edward IV granted it to Richard and Thomas Croft.[26]

In 1334 the manor of Ashendon had a capital messuage, a dovecote and a windmill,[27] and a windmill was one of its appurtenances in the 17th century.[28] A capital messuage, 'well-built and fitly roofed,' belonged to the manor held of Simon Darches in 1392.[29] From the 13th to the 18th century view of frankpledge was reckoned amongst the liberties of the lords of Ashendon and Pollicott,[30] and the grants of Pollicott to Thomas and Henry Palmer made especial mention of court leet, view of frankpledge and free warren.[31]

CHURCH The church of *ST. MARY*, built of stone rubble, consists of a chancel measuring internally 28 ft. 6 in. by 16 ft., nave 47 ft. 6 in. by 16 ft. 6 in., south aisle 9 ft. 6 in. wide, west tower 8 ft. 6 in. by 8 ft., and south porch.

The church dates from about 1120, and, as first built, consisted of the eastern part of the present nave, a south aisle, and probably a small chancel. About the end of the 12th century the nave and aisle were lengthened westwards, while at the end of the 13th century the chancel and aisle were rebuilt and the

[97] Jenyns, *Ped. of the Palmers.*
[98] *L. and P. Hen. VIII*, xv, 1030 (31).
[99] Pat. 36 Hen. VIII, pt. xxi, m. 23.
[100] Ct. of Req. bdle. 18, no. 46.
[1] G.E.C. *Baronetage*, i, 165–6.
[2] Chan. Proc. (Ser. 2), bdle. 285, no. 7.
[3] Chan. Inq. p.m. (Ser. 2), cccv, 112.
[4] G.E.C. loc. cit. ; Feet of F. Bucks. Mich. 22 Jas. I ; Recov. R. Mich. 21 Jas. I, m. 106.
[5] Feet of F. Bucks. Mich. 4 Chas. I ; Recov. R. Trin. 11 Chas. I, m. 72 ; G.E.C. loc. cit.
[6] Feet of F. Div. Co. Trin. 1658.
[7] G.E.C. loc. cit.
[8] Feet of F. Div. Co. East. 12 Geo. II; Recov. R. East. 12 Geo. II, m. 244.
[9] Feet of F. Div. Co. Hil. 15 Geo. II.
[10] Ibid. Bucks. East. 17 Geo. II. According to the pedigree of the Palmer family (G.E.C. loc. cit.) Anne was twice married, Charles Fielding being her second husband, and died in 1742–3, whilst Elizabeth was the wife of Charles Finch.

[11] *Testa de Nevill* (Rec. Com.), 247.
[12] Feet of F. Bucks. 20 Hen. III, no. 55.
[13] *Hund. R.* (Rec. Com.), i, 23 ; *Feud. Aids*, i, 75, 95.
[14] *Cal. Close*, 1323–7, p. 366.
[15] *Feud. Aids*, i, 121.
[16] John also owned land in Ashendon (Feet of F. Bucks. 9 Hen. VI, no. 40 ; 11 Hen. VI, no. 56 ; Early Chan. Proc. bdle. 19, no. 2, 405).
[17] Lipscomb, op. cit. i, 32.
[18] Feet of F. Bucks. 31 Hen. VI, no. 3. Between 1450 and 1465 John Ascote and his wife brought a suit in Chancery against the trustees of John Bucktoft for the possession of the manor of 'Pollicott the little' (Early Chan. Proc. bdle. 28, no. 332). From the 17th century onwards Little Pollicott was generally held on lease by the lord of Great Pollicott (q.v.) (Lipscomb, op. cit. i, 33).
[19] *Valor Eccl.* (Rec. Com.), ii, 239 ; Lipscomb, op. cit. i, 31.
[20] *Hund. R.* (Rec. Com.), i, 23.

[21] *Feud. Aids*, i, 75.
[22] Ct. R. (Gen. Ser.), portf. 212, no. 2.
[23] Leadam, op. cit. i, 159.
[24] Feet of F. Bucks. 7 Edw. I, no. 7.
[25] Lipscomb, op. cit. i, 13, with which cf. Feet of F. Bucks. 18 Edw. II, no. 13, and *Hist. MSS. Com. Rep.* v, App. i, 562.
[26] *Parl. R.* v, 589*b*. Lipscomb (loc. cit.) explains the title of Little Pollicott by the alleged transference of this land from Pollicott Bucktot to Ashendon.
[27] Chan. Inq. p.m. Edw. III, file 41, no. 18.
[28] Feet of F. Bucks. East. 8 Jas. I ; East. 8 Chas. I.
[29] Rentals and Surv. (Duchy of Lanc.), bdle. 14, no. 3, fol. 62 d.
[30] *Hund. R.* (Rec. Com.), i, 23 ; Feet of F. Bucks. Mich. 22 Jas. I ; East. 17 Geo. II ; Div. Co. Hil. 15 Geo. II.
[31] Pat. 14 Hen. VIII, pt. i, m. 9 ; 19 Hen. VIII, pt. ii, m. 26 ; 36 Hen. VIII, pt. xxi, m. 23.

ASHENDON CHURCH FROM THE SOUTH-WEST

ASTON SANDFORD CHURCH FROM THE SOUTH-WEST

latter widened. The nave clearstory and the tower were added about 1480, and the fabric appears to have been restored in the 16th century and again in the 18th century, while early in the following century the chancel was again rebuilt.

The chancel is lighted from the east by a square-headed window of three lights and from the south by two square-headed windows of two lights, all of which probably date from the 16th century, but have been restored later, and were reset in the walls when the chancel was rebuilt. In the north wall is a low 15th-century recess with a moulded arch and crocketed label, and on the south is a trefoiled piscina, which probably dates from the 13th century. The pointed chancel arch is of the late 13th century, but the capitals and bases of its responds have been restored.

On the south side of the nave is an arcade of two pointed bays supported by a central octagonal pillar and responds with moulded capitals and bases; this dates from the rebuilding of the aisle late in the 13th century. The pointed arch to the west of it is contemporary with the extension of the nave and aisle at the end of the 12th century. A chapel existed at the north-east of the nave in the 15th century, and the arch opening from it to the nave as well as the line of the low-pitched roof can still be traced; further west is a plain 12th-century doorway, now blocked, and at the west end of the wall is a 13th-century lancet. The clearstory is lighted by late 15th-century traceried windows of two trefoiled lights; the window at the north-east contains in its head some contemporary glass. The upper doorways of the rood-loft can be traced at the east end of both walls, though both doorways are blocked; a corbel for the support of the loft remains on the south. The open low-pitched roof probably dates from the 17th century.

The south aisle is lighted from the west by twin lancets, one of which is of the 13th century, but the other is probably an 18th-century addition. The easternmost of the two windows in the south wall, of about 1300, is of three lights with tracery in the head; the lowered sill forms a sedile, and near it is an early 14th-century trefoiled piscina. The other window, which dates from the first half of the 14th century, is of two lights, with the head and tracery cut out of a single stone. The moulded doorway between them, which is also of the same period, retains an old door with its hinges. The aisle is covered by a 15th-century lean-to timber roof.

The west tower, which is crowned by a plain parapet, is of two stages, and has diagonal buttresses at the western angles; its moulded west doorway and two-light window and the pointed tower arch are all original. The bell-chamber has a small opening in each wall filled with a pierced oak shutter.

The circular font probably dates from the 12th century, but has been retooled at a later period; it has a tapering bowl with a roll at the bottom and a 17th-century wood cover. In the chancel are a communion table and a chair, both of the 17th century, and above the recess in the north wall are two small oak shields which are said to have belonged to the rood screen and have palimpsest heraldry, the lower coats being probably of the 15th century and the upper of about 1600. The pulpit dates from about 1700, but has a modern base. In the south aisle are preserved a chest and a stool of the 17th century. In the vestry is a similar stool, and a washing stand which is placed here contains some re-used 17th-century panelling.

In the recess on the north side of the chancel is a late 13th-century Purbeck marble effigy of a knight in chain mail and surcoat carrying a shield charged with a cheveron, possibly for Chenduit; the legs are crossed and the feet rest on a lion. On the north side of the nave is a floor slab to Ann wife of Samuel Bampton, who died in 1697. The lead rain-water pipes and heads on the outside of the clearstory may be of the 17th century.

There are three bells and a sanctus: the first is by Robert Atton, 1633, and the second, the third, and the sanctus are by Henry Bagley, 1658.

The plate consists of a plated cup, flagon and paten. The registers begin in 1732.

ADVOWSON The church was given by Walter Giffard, the founder, to Nutley Abbey,[32] and remained in its possession until its surrender.[33] In 1542 and 1546 it was granted by Henry VIII to Christ Church, Oxford,[34] and the dean and canons were patrons until 1881.[35] Since 1882 the advowson has descended with the manor[36] (q.v.). The living, which was a perpetual curacy, was united to that of Dorton (q.v.) on 30 October 1847 under the Act of 1 & 2 Victoria.[36a]

Half a virgate in the park of Pollicott belonged to the rectory in the 16th century,[37] when the rent of a cottage given for keeping an obit in this parish was valued at 2s.[38] In 1738 there was a rectory-house here known as the 'Priest's Lodging.'[39] A pension of 3s. 4d. from the revenues of the manor of Little Pollicott was paid by Lincoln College for the preaching of the 'divine word' in the church there, presumably the parish church of Ashendon, in the 16th century.[40]

CHARITIES John Hart, by his will proved in the P.C.C. 15 May 1665, demised (*inter alia*) an annual rent-charge of £2 issuing out of Easington Manor, Oxfordshire, for apprenticing a poor boy. A sum of £73 Great Eastern Railway 4 per cent. stock, arising from accumulations, is also held by the official trustees in trust for this charity.

By a scheme of the Charity Commissioners, dated 30 March 1904, the annuity of £2 (less land tax) and the annual dividends, amounting to £2 18s. 4d., are made applicable in apprenticing or in providing outfits for poor boys entering upon a trade or occupation.

[32] *Cal. Chart. R.* 1300–26, p. 210.
[33] *Valor Eccl.* (Rec. Com.), iv, 233.
[34] *L. and P. Hen. VIII*, xvii, g. 881 (26); xxi (2), g. 648 (25).
[35] Priv. Act, 11 Geo. II, cap. 20; Bacon, *Liber Reg.* 506; *Cler. Guide*, 1817–81.
[36] *Clergy List*.
[36a] *Accts. and Papers*, 1850, xlvii, no. 524.
[37] *L. and P. Hen. VIII*, xxi (2), g. 648 (25).
[38] Chant. Cert. 5, no. 55.
[39] Priv. Act, 11 Geo. II, cap. 20.
[40] *Valor Eccl.* (Rec. Com.), ii, 239.

ASTON SANDFORD

Estone (xi cent.) ; Astun Samford (xiii cent.).

Aston Sandford contains an area of 678 acres, of which by far the greater part is pasture land.[1] It is watered by the Standbridge Brook, a tributary of the Thames. The land has only a variation of some 10 ft. in level, being about 255 ft. above the ordnance datum. The soil is gault and sandstone, the subsoil clay and limestone. The chief crops are wheat, oats, and beans. The village, with the church, lies in the south-west of the parish. The rectory-house, which was built by the Rev. Thomas Scott on his appointment as rector in the early 19th century,[2] stands to the south-east and the manor-house to the south-west of the church. Part of a homestead moat lies a mile north-east from the church on the site of Aston Court.[3]

In 1086 ASTON [SANDFORD] alias MANOR COLD ASTON (xvi, xvii cent.) MANOR, previously held by Sotiny, one of Earl Tosti's men, was assessed at 4½ hides and held by Manno the Breton.[4] In common with his other holdings the overlordship of this manor, which was held in 1328 by the service of half a knight's fee and 10s. yearly towards the ward of Northampton Castle,[5] descended in the barony of Wolverton [6] (q.v.). It is last mentioned in 1618.[7]

Before the Domesday Survey Manno had subinfeudated Aston Manor to Odo,[8] probably the ancestor of the family from whom it appears to have derived its distinguishing name of Sandford. John de Sandford held lands in Aston in 1199,[9] 1219, and 1220.[10] Nicholas de Sandford had succeeded before 1234.[11] His descendants had mesne overlordship rights in Aston Sandford [12] during the next two centuries, Nicholas de Sandford being mentioned in 1349 [13] and 1350,[14] and his heirs in 1351[15] and 1439.[16]

In the middle 13th century Aston Sandford was held by the Countess of Warwick (Philippa widow of Henry de Newburgh) [17] for life.[18] Robert de Vere, son of the Earl of Oxford and Alice his wife, daughter and co-heir of Gilbert de Sandford,[19] was holding it in 1284.[20] Robert appears to have given Aston Sandford Manor (probably on succeeding to the earldom) to his younger brother Alphonso, who was

holding it in the early 14th century.[21] He died seised about 1328, when his heir was his son John.[22]

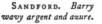

SANDFORD. Barry wavy argent and azure.

VERE. Quarterly gules and or with a molet argent in the quarter.

He in 1331 succeeded to the earldom, and Aston Sandford descended with Whitchurch to Edward Earl of Oxford,[23] who in 1578 sold it to William Fleetwood,[24] owner of Missenden Abbey.[25] His widow's life interest in Aston Sandford [26] appears to have been purchased by Sir David Fowles, who married Fleetwood's daughter Cordelia [27] in 1604.[28] In 1610 he agreed to purchase the estate from his brother-in-law, Sir William Fleetwood,[29] and obtained a grant in confirmation of his title,[30] but being unable apparently to raise the purchase-money, transferred it again to Sir William Fleetwood,[31] who left it to his younger children for life.[32] In 1711 the manor had reverted to John Fleetwood of Great Missenden Manor.[33] He sold the Aston Sandford estate about 1737 to Charles Price,[34] sheriff for the county in 1743.[35] His son Sir Charles Price, kt., sold it in 1771 to Henry Hurt,[36] who left it in trust by his will, proved in 1785, to his granddaughter Susannah Gines.[37] She and her husband John Barber settled

FLEETWOOD. Party wavy azure and or six martlets countercoloured.

---

[1] Statistics from Bd. of Agric. (1905).
[2] Scott, Life of Rev. Thomas Scott, 366.
[3] V.C.H. Bucks. ii, 29.
[4] Ibid. i, 270.
[5] Chan. Inq. p.m. Edw. III, file 10, no. 11.
[6] Testa de Nevill (Rec. Com.), 248 ; Cal. Close, 1272–9, p. 350 ; Feud. Aids, i, 84, 95 ; Cal. Close, 1349–54, p. 169.
[7] Chan. Inq. p.m. (Ser. 2), ccccclxxx, 131.
[8] V.C.H. Bucks. i, 270.
[9] Feet of F. Bucks. 1 John, no. 11.
[10] Pipe R. Bucks. and Beds. 3 Hen. III, m. 5.
[11] Testa de Nevill (Rec. Com.), 248.
[12] Hund. R. (Rec. Com.), i, 25.
[13] Chan. Inq. p.m. 23 Edw. III, pt. i, no. 35.
[14] Cal. Close, 1349–54, p. 169.
[15] Chan. Inq. p.m. 25 Edw. III (1st nos.), no. 6.
[16] Ibid. 17 Hen. VI, no. 38.
[17] G.E.C. Complete Peerage, viii, 54.

[18] Hund. R. (Rec. Com.), i, 25.
[19] G.E.C. Complete Peerage, vi, 164. Gilbert de Sandford was a contemporary of Nicholas de Sandford (Testa de Nevill [Rec. Com.], 266b), probably his brother, and a son of John de Sandford of Great Hormead, Hertfordshire (Nichols, Coll. Topog. et Gen. v, 199). He died about 1248, when the wardship and marriage of his daughter Alice were granted to Hugh Earl of Oxford (Dugdale, Baronage, i, 191).
[20] Feud. Aids, i, 84.
[21] Ibid. 95, 114.
[22] Chan. Inq. p.m. Edw. III, file 10. no. 12.
[23] V.C.H. Bucks. iii, 445.
[24] Feet of F Bucks. Mich. 20 & 21 Eliz. ; Chan. Inq. p.m. (Ser. 2), ccxxxviii, 69.
[25] V.C.H. Bucks. ii, 351.
[26] Chan. Inq. p.m. (Ser. 2), ccxxxviii, 69.
[27] Lipscomb, Hist. of Bucks. i, 45.
[28] Ibid. ii, 377, quoting Reg. of Great

Missenden, but here he confuses her with her niece Cordelia, sister of Marian, daughter of Sir William Fleetwood (ibid. i, 48).
[29] Close, 8 Jas. I, pt. ix.
[30] Pat. 8 Jas. I, pt. xxxv, no. 1.
[31] Chan. Inq. p.m. (Ser. 2), ccccclxiv, 99 ; Feet of F. Bucks. Hil. 8 Jas. I.
[32] Chan. Inq. p.m. (Ser. 2), ccccclxiv, 99 ; ccccxci, 88. Three of his daughters lived at the manor-house in the middle 17th century (Lipscomb, op. cit. i, 45, quoting letter from the rector to Willis).
[33] Recov. R. Mich. 10 Anne, m. 58. Settlements in respect of the reversion were made in 1655 (Recov. R. Mich. 1655, m. 203 ; Feet of F. Bucks. Mich. 1655) and 1681 (Recov. R. Mich. 33 Chas. II, m. 160).
[34] Lysons, Mag. Brit. i (3), 501.
[35] P.R.O. List of Sheriffs, 10.
[36] Com. Pleas Recov. R. East. 11 Geo. III, m. 78.
[37] P.C.C. 604 Ducarel.

the property in 1798.[38] He died in 1809,[39] his widow surviving till 1846.[40] Before 1862 Aston Sandford Manor had passed to John and William Dover,[41] and in 1873 the former was sole owner.[42] His heir, Mr. J. Guy Dover, in 1909 sold the manorial rights and the major portion of the land to Mr. Percy Fisher, the present owner.

The right of view of frankpledge appurtenant to this manor before 1254[43] is named in the trust deed of 1798. A grant of free warren in Aston Sandford was made to John de Vere in 1329[44] and confirmed in 1424.[45]

CHURCH The church of *ST. MICHAEL*, one of the smallest in the kingdom, consists of a chancel, measuring internally 18 ft. 6 in. by 12 ft., nave 38 ft. by 14 ft., north vestry, south porch and west bellcote. It is built of limestone and roofed with tiles.

The building was so considerably restored in 1878, its details being retooled and reset, that it is now difficult to assign accurate dates to its parts. The nave probably dates from the 12th century, the chancel from the 13th century, and the south porch from the 18th century, while the vestry and bellcote are modern.

The chancel is lighted by three lancets in the east wall, two windows in the south wall, and a single cinquefoiled light in the north wall; all are modern except the last, which, though much retooled, is probably of the 14th century. In the north wall is an old locker. Some late 13th-century painted glass, representing a seated figure, is placed in the central lancet in the east wall. The chancel arch has been replaced by a modern wood truss, below which

on both sides are twin shafts with carved capitals, one of the southern pair having a grotesque head; these are probably of 13th-century date, though considerably restored.

The nave is lighted by two windows in the north wall and two in the south wall, while in the west wall is an early window blocked by a 15th-century buttress. The north-east window of two uncusped lights, and the blocked north doorway, though considerably modernized, probably date from the 14th century. The south doorway and the two south windows are modern, but the tracery of the south-east window is set in an old opening. On the western buttresses outside are some incised circles. The nave has an old collar-beam roof.

There are three bells : the treble, with an unfinished inscription 'Sancte Toma Oř,' and the tenor, inscribed 'Sancte Clemes Ora Pro Nobis,' are both from the Wokingham foundry, and date from the first half of the 15th century ; the second, dated 1675, is by Ellis & Henry Knight.

The communion plate consists of a chalice and cover paten of 1661, an old pewter flagon and a modern plated flagon.

The registers date from 1615.

ADVOWSON The church of Aston Sandford, which is a rectory, was valued at £4 13s. 4d. in 1291[46] and at £13 6s. 8d. in 1535.[47] The advowson has descended with the manor until recently,[48] when it was sold to Mrs. A. A. Pargiter of Towersey vicarage, the present patron.

There do not appear to be any endowed charities subsisting in this parish.

BOARSTALL

Burchestala, Burcestala, Burcstal, Burchestal, Burkestall, Borkestaw (xii cent.) ; Borgstall, Burstale, Borestall, Borstall (xiii cent.) ; Boarstall (xvi cent.).

Boarstall contains 3,078 acres, of which 6 are water, on a soil of gravel and stiff blue clay and subsoil of Corallian and Oxford Clay. There are 330 acres of arable land where wheat, barley and beans are the chief crops, 2,202 of permanent grass, and 186 of woods and plantations.[1] The land rises from about 200 ft. above the ordnance datum in the north and west to about 330 ft. at the village in the centre, and reaches 600 ft. on the east boundary.

From the 11th to the 17th century Boarstall was included in the royal forest of Bernwood.[2] A 15th-century map of the site of the manor[3] shows woodland except in the south-east, where lay the arable

land known as le Derehyde, or la Derhyde (Deerhyde),[4] a name which survived until 1611,[5] though it was partially superseded in 1444 by La Vente,[6] and in 1602 by Hillwood.[7] All three have vanished from modern maps, which still mark the Panshill farms, situated on some part of Pauncehall, Paunsale, or Pawncell, at one time the king's demesne wood.[8] South-east of these farms are Oriel Wood, representing the 8 acres of 'woode ground' owned by Oriel College in 1586,[9] and Old and New Arngrove Farms, once part of the Arnegrave field which lay between Panshill and the ancient village.[10] Before 1577 a large common called Stonehurst, together with 100 acres in 'the Quarters' which fell within the boundaries of this parish, had been inclosed by the lord of the manor.[11] The inhabitants petitioned the queen for

[38] Feet of F. Bucks. East. 38 Geo. III.
[39] Gent. Mag. lxxix (1), 989.
[40] Tablet in church ; cf. Lipscomb, op. cit. i, 45.
[41] Sheahan, Hist. and Topog. of Bucks. 333.
[42] Ret. of Owners of Land (1873), Bucks. 7.
[43] Hund. R. (Rec. Com.) i, 25.
[44] Chart. R. 3 Edw. III, m. 15, no. 30.
[45] Cal. Rot. Chart. et Inq. a.q.d. (Rec. Com.), 162.
[46] Pope Nich. Tax. (Rec. Com.), 34, 41b.
[47] Valor Eccl. (Rec. Com.), iv, 236.
[48] Cal. Pat. 1327–30, p. 420 ; Harl. MS. 6952, fol. 63 ; Inst. Bks. (P.R.O.) ; Bacon, Liber Regis. 503.

[1] Statistics from Bd. of Agric. (1905).
[2] V.C.H. Bucks. ii, 131–2, 137.
[3] Boarstall Chartul. (penes Sir Lancelot Aubrey Fletcher containing transcripts of deeds relating to the possessions of Edmund Rede made in 1446), fol. 1.
[4] Ibid. fol. 2 ; Hund. R. (Rec. Com.), i, 36.
[5] Pat. 8 Jas. I, pt. lix, no. 134.
[6] Boarstall Chartul. fol. 1b. Fifty acres which bore this name in 1347 were part at least of the Derhyde (Cal. Close, 1346–9, p. 446).
[7] Chan. Inq. p.m. (Ser. 2), cclxviii, 149. This must be the wood called Hullwod which lay close to the Derhyde

and was part of the Confessor's grant (Boarstall Chart. fol. 1).
[8] Cal. Close, 1231–4, pp. 345, 504 ; Abbrev. Rot. Orig. (Rec. Com.), i, 216 ; Lansd. MS. 47, fol. 3 ; Boarstall Chartul. fol. 115b ; Pat. 8 Jas. I, pt. lix, no. 134. In 1586, however, much of Panshill belonged to the lord of Boarstall Manor (Lansd. MS. 47, fol. 3). [9] Lansd. MS. 47, fol. 3.
[10] Boarstall Chartul. fol. 1, 54b ; Cal. Close, 1346–9, p. 446 ; Pat. 8 Jas. I, pt. lix, no. 134.
[11] Pat. 19 Eliz. pt. vi, m. 1. The Quarters were here described as 2,000 acres of woody and waste ground belonging to divers manors.

the restoration of their rights,[12] but, apparently, without success, as more inclosures were made within the next few years.[13] The 'New Park,' which still gives its name to a farm in Boarstall, seems to have been an earlier inclosure,[14] while a pasture called Lachemede had been inclosed before 1437.[15]

The parish is crossed by the main road from Bicester to Thame. A branch road leads south-west into the little village to the turreted gate-house called Boarstall House, which is all that is left of the fortified mansion

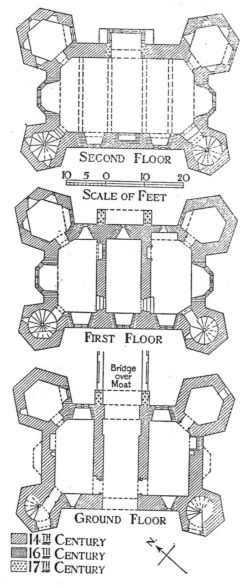

SECOND FLOOR

10 5 0   10   20

SCALE OF FEET

FIRST FLOOR

Bridge over Moat

GROUND FLOOR

14TH CENTURY
16TH CENTURY
17TH CENTURY

PLAN OF GATE-HOUSE, BOARSTALL TOWER

and tower of the ancient lords of the manor. This is a rectangular stone building of three stories with hexagonal corner turrets dating from the 14th century; it was probably built when a licence to crenellate or fortify his house was granted to John Handlo in 1312,[16] and is a charming and well-preserved example of its

period, though some alterations were made and new windows were inserted in the 16th and 17th centuries. The site of the mansion is surrounded by a moat, originally crossed at the gate-house by a drawbridge, but this was replaced in 1735 by the present stone structure. The gateway itself, which was protected by a portcullis, the grooves for which can be seen on the inside, has a wide segmental arch, and is inclosed by a 17th-century porch-like projection formed by two flanking buttresses surmounted by a connecting round arch; the central passage into which it opens has a room on either side and a similar gateway at the other end. The entrance faces north-east, and the flanking turrets on this side, which have small chambers on all floors, are pierced by original cross loopholes, some of which are blocked, larger windows having been inserted in the 16th century. On the other side the turrets have small loop lights and contain newel stairs; the uppermost light of the south turret has a trefoiled head, and in the upper stage of the west turret are a clock and louvred openings for the bell. All the turrets have embattled parapets and original gargoyles. The porch on the entrance front supports a mullioned bay window, and the wall between the turrets is surmounted by a 17th-century cornice and balustraded parapet. The other front has an original plain parapet, and near the centre are two 17th-century stone chimneys, while 16th-century windows have been inserted on all floors of this front and on the lower floors of the entrance front. Both end walls have in the centre an oriel window, which rises from moulded corbelling and is surmounted by a balustraded parapet.

The north-west room on the ground floor has an old wide fireplace, and in the opposite room is a moulded stone fireplace of the 16th century. The first floor is divided into three rooms, and retains some original pointed doorways with old battened doors; the second floor, which forms one large apartment, has an old low-pitched ceiling with heavy beams, original doorways to all the turrets, and a fine 16th-century moulded fireplace. The bay window over the entrance archway contains a considerable amount of 17th-century heraldic glass, including shields of Aubrey quartering Mansel, Basset and South, with the motto 'Solem fero'; Aubrey impaling Lewis, dated 1692; and Ap Gwyllym; in the east turret window are two shields, one being Basset quartering de la Bere. The bell in the west turret is inscribed 'Richard Keene made me 1661.' There is a stone underground passage to the south-west of the gate-house which probably led to the moat from the mansion cellars, while on the south a 17th-century brick wall with a moulded stone doorway separates the grounds from the churchyard.

In 1644 Boarstall House gave much trouble to the Parliamentarian generals as a Royalist stronghold,[17] Sir William Waller leaving it unattempted, after a futile summons to surrender,[18] whilst Fairfax, to whom the Commissioners had written, 'We desire that you would not amuse yourself about Boarstall House,' was 'beaten from thence with considerable loss' the next year.[19] A little beyond stands the church of St. James with

[12] *Acts of P.C.* 1575–7, pp. 296, 323.
[13] Lansd. MS. 47, fol. 3, 5.
[14] Harl. Chart. 79, G 13; Chan. Proc. (Ser. 2), bdles. 224, no. 11; 57, no. 37.
[15] Chan. Inq. p.m. 16 Hen. VI, no. 38.
[16] *Cal. Pat.* 1307–13, p. 493.
[17] *Cal. S. P. Dom.* 1644, pp. 216, 320, 325–7, 330, 334, 341, 394–5.
[18] Ibid. 362–3; *Hist. MSS. Com. Rep.* vii, App. i, 448a.
[19] Clarendon, *Hist. of the Rebellion,* bk. ix, par. 34, 36; *Cal. S. P. Dom.* 1644–5, p. 567; 1645–7, pp. 99, 147, 431–2; *Hist. MSS. Com. Rep.* vi, App. i, 121a, 124b.

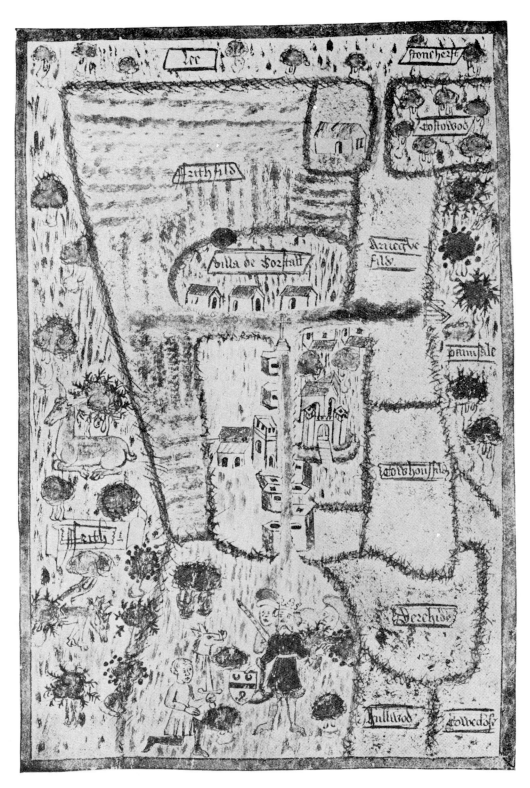

Boarstall Manor: Plan of about 1444, from the Boarstall Chartulary

Boarstall Tower

the remains of a fine old stone cross in its church-yard.[20]

Tower Farm is a 16th-century building retaining much original work, and among the other buildings in the parish, dating from the 16th and 17th centuries, may be mentioned Upper Panshill Farm, Old Arngrove Farm, and Pasture Farm.

A few place-names among many, some of them occurring from the 13th to the 17th century, but now unknown, are Frith, Quechenwell, Geyreswode, Bardolfes, Wolvesdeham, Wolvenhurst, Coppidthorne, Yakyndonesfurlong, Wulfendene, Guildenheirdene, and le Ridg.[21]

Domesday Book does not mention *MANOR BOARSTALL*, which was a member of the royal manor of Brill until 1213,[22] and possibly for a century after.[23] The nucleus of the manor was a hide of land called the Derhyde, always associated with the serjeanty of Bernwood Forest[24]; it was held of the Crown in chief with the forest bailiwick for a rent of 50s.[25] Manorial rights seem always to have belonged to this fee, which, described in 1347 as consisting of the site of the manor and about 135 acres of land and the bailiwick,[26] was for nearly a hundred years afterwards regarded as the main part of the manor.[27] Another part of Boarstall held of Brill Manor from 1289 to 1527[28] may perhaps be identified with certain lands granted by the Empress Maud from her demesne here before 1158.[29] In 1347 this consisted of 2 hides, which apparently with later additions were described in 1489 as the actual manor.[30] Before the middle of the 14th century another hide, which seems to have been included in Oakley Manor in 1302,[31] had been taken into the manor of Boarstall, and in 1346 bore its name.[32] From 1563 until 1634 the manor of Boarstall was merely said to be held of the Crown, no distinction of its component parts being made.[33]

According to tradition the Derhyde and the custody of Bernwood Forest were granted by Edward the Confessor to Niel, the ancestor of the lords of Boarstall, in reward for slaying a formidable boar,

the supposed evidence of the grant being the horn preserved by his heirs.[34] This story is partially corroborated by the confirmation in 1266 by Henry III to the heir of the Fitz Niels of the bailiwick and Derhyde, the former being described as held by his ancestors from the Conquest.[35]

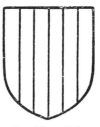

FITZ NIEL. *Paly argent and gules.*

It seems that Niel's heirs were dispossessed by the Lisures until Fulk de Lisures and his son William after him restored to William Fitz Niel the land and office which had been his father's.[36] This was perhaps the William Fitz Niel who in 1167 made a payment for this township.[37] He or another of the same name was tenant in chief of the Derhyde between 1210 and 1212.[38] John Fitz Niel, William's son,[39] was keeper of Bernwood Forest in 1255[40] and 1264,[41] and received a formal grant of its bailiwick with the Derhyde in 1266.[42] His death took place about 1289,[43] and Boarstall descended to his son and heir John,[44] who ten years later obtained licence to enfeoff Robert de Harwedon of the lands he held of the Crown with the intention that they should be re-settled on himself with remainder to his son-in-law John, son of Richard Handlo, and his daughter Joan, John's wife.[45] Before the completion of this settlement John Fitz Niel died, and his lands passed to John Handlo and Joan.[46] A grant of land in Bernwood Forest was made to John in 1305,[47] and in 1310 he acquired from John son of Benet le Vilur tenements in Boarstall, some held of Brill Manor, others of the honour of Wallingford.[48] The licence of 1312 to crenellate his dwelling-house of Boarstall[49] and the fresh grant of 1315 from the royal forest[50] were followed by a temporary seizure of John Handlo's manor and peel tower here, which were restored to him by royal command in 1322,[51] a year marked by violent attacks upon his dwellings and lands.[52] Richard, John's son

[20] Clement Shorter, *Highways and Byways in Bucks.* 49, 50; *Rec. of Bucks.* iii, 155.

[21] Boarstall Chartul. fol. 6, 39, 56, 61, 76–7, 79, 89; *Cal. Inq. p.m.* (Edw. I), ii, 438; *Hen. VII*, i, 233; Chan. Inq. p.m. (Ser. 2), cclxviii, 149; dxii, 7; *L. and P. Hen. VIII*, xx (2), g. 1068 (50); Pat. 31 Eliz., pt. xiii, m. 21; 8 Jas. I, pt. lix, no. 134; Chan. Proc. (Ser. 2), bdle. 57, no. 37.

[22] *V.C.H. Bucks.* i, 227; Lipscomb, *Hist. and Antiq. of Bucks.* i, 97; *Chart. R.* 1 John, pt. ii, m. 5, no. 180; *Abbrev. Plac.* (Rec. Com.), 91.

[23] *Feud. Aids*, i, 114.

[24] See below.

[25] *Red Bk. of Exch.* (Rolls Ser.), ii, 537; Pat. 51 Hen. III, m. 33, no. 101; *Cal. Inq. p.m.* (Edw. I), ii, 438; *Cal. Pat.* 1299–1301, p. 430; *Cal. Close*, 1346–9, p. 446; Chan. Inq. p.m. 20 Edw. III (1st nos.), no. 51; 7 Hen. V, no. 63; 10 Hen. VI, no. 23; *Cal. Inq. p.m. Hen. VII*, i, 197; *Plac. de Quo Warr.* (Rec. Com.), 91.

[26] *Cal. Close*, 1346–9, p. 446.

[27] Chan. Inq. p.m. 7 Hen. V, no. 63; 10 Hen. VI, no. 23; 16 Hen. VI, no. 38.

[28] *Cal. Inq. p.m.* (Edw. I), ii, 438; *Cal. Close*, 1346–9, p. 446; Chan. Inq. p.m. 7 Hen. V, no. 63; 10 Hen. VI,

no. 23; *Cal. Inq. p.m. Hen. VII*, i, 197; Exch. Inq. p.m. (Ser. 2), file 22, no. 7.

[29] Hunter, *Gt. R. of the Pipe* 2–4 *Hen. II* (Rec. Com.), 139.

[30] *Cal. Inq. p.m. Hen. VII*, i, 197.

[31] *Feud. Aids*, i, 94.

[32] Chan. Inq. p.m. 20 Edw. III (1st nos.), no. 51.

[33] Exch. Inq. p.m. (Ser. 2), file 22, no. 7; Chan. Inq. p.m. (Ser. 2), cclxviii, 149; dxii, 7.

[34] Kennet, *Paroch. Antiq.* i, 70; Boarstall Chartul, fol. 1*b*; *Arch.* iii, 15. By his will dated 7 Apr. 1487 Sir Edmund Rede left to William Rede his heir a little register 'clapsed' with silver and a great black horn 'hamsal' with silver and gilded, which horn was the first charter of office of the forest of Bernwood and given by the king to a certain Niel *cum corta tunica*, his ancestor, long before the conquest of England. P.C.C. 32 Milles.

[35] *Cal. Pat.* 1266–72, p. 15.

[36] Boarstall Chartul. fol. 1*b*. As Fulk de Lisures was living in 1167, William Fitz Niel cannot have been, as Lipscomb says, son of the original Niel (Lipscomb, op. cit. i, 66). It is evident also that the horn which Fulk de Lisures wore as the symbol of his office was connected

with his office of forester in Northants, not Bucks. (*Red Bk. of Exch.* [Rolls Ser.], i, 333).

[37] *Pipe R.* 22 *Hen. II* (Pipe R. Soc.), 21. Richard Fitz Niel who paid scutage in Bucks. between 1161 and 1168 may have been of the same family (ibid. 7 *Hen. II*, 11; 8 *Hen. II*, 42; 11 *Hen. II*, 23; 14 *Hen. II*, 11).

[38] *Red Bk. of Exch.* (Rolls Ser.), ii, 537. In 1346 the grant of the serjeanty of Bernwood Forest was ascribed to King John (Chan. Inq. p.m. 20 Edw. III [1st nos.], no 51).

[39] Boarstall Chartul. fol. 2.

[40] *Hund. R.* (Rec. Com.), i, 26.

[41] *Cal. Pat.* 1258–66, p. 307.

[42] Pat. 51 Hen. III, m. 33, no. 101.

[43] cf. *Plac. de Quo Warr.* (Rec. Com.), 91.

[44] *Cal. Inq. p.m.* (Edw. I), ii, 438.

[45] *Cal. Pat.* 1292–1301, p. 430.

[46] *Parl. R.* ii, 215*b*, 216*a*.

[47] *Cal. Pat.* 1301–7, p. 310.

[48] Feet of F. Bucks. 3 Edw. II, no. 1; Chan. Inq. p.m. 21 Edw. I, no. 20, 40; *Cal. Close*, 1288–96, p. 290.

[49] *Cal. Pat.* 1307–13, p. 493.

[50] *Cal. Fine R.* 1307–19, pp. 228–9; Boarstall Chartul. fol. 39.

[51] *Cal. Pat.* 1321–4, p. 78.

[52] Ibid. 163, 319.

and heir by wife Joan, died in his father's lifetime,[53] and in 1345 John settled the manors she had brought him on trustees for his own use, with remainder to Richard's son Edmund and his wife Alice.[54] He died the next year,[55] and Boarstall was shortly afterwards seized by the king's officers on the pretext of his grandson's minority, the settlement of 1345 being declared invalid on the ground that John had enjoyed no independent rights in the property.[56] On the petition made in the interest of the heir, then about seven,[57] an order was issued after inquiry[58] for the restitution of certain parts,[59] but the 2 bovates or Derhyde, and the bailiwick of Bernwood Forest always associated with them, seem to have been retained by the Crown until Edmund's death in 1355.[60] His lands came to his sisters and heirs, Elizabeth wife of Edmund de la Pole and Margaret wife of Gilbert Chastellyn,[61] Margaret and her second husband John Appleby receiving Boarstall in 1362.[62] Four years later, by a fresh partition, this manor was assigned to Elizabeth and her husband Edmund de la Pole.[63] They had two daughters, one of whom, Elizabeth, with her husband Ingelram Bruyn, in 1394 conveyed her right to the reversion of a moiety of Boarstall Manor to her sister Katherine, wife of Robert James.[64] Four years before Robert and Katherine had obtained licence to settle their share in the reversion for the use of themselves and their heirs.[65] Elizabeth died before her father, who enjoyed a life interest in this manor until 1419, when he was succeeded by Robert and Katherine James.[66] Katherine was doubtless dead in 1428, when Robert settled her inheritance on himself, with remainder to their daughter Christine and her husband Edmund Rede.[67] He died in 1432, and Christine, then widowed, held Boarstall[68] until her death three years later, with the exception of one-sixth, which she granted to her stepmother Maud in exchange for other dower lands.[69] Edmund son and heir of Edmund Rede and Christine enjoyed his mother's share of the manor from 1435,[70] and inherited the rest when Maud died in 1437.[71] At his death in 1489 his possessions, largely increased by various purchases,[72] descended to his grandson William, son of his late son William Rede,[73] Katherine his widow holding some lands in Boarstall in dower until 1498.[74] William Rede settled the manor of Boarstall on himself and his heirs in 1511,[75] and in or before 1527 it passed to his son Leonard,[76] lord in 1547,

when he conveyed the remainder, after the death of himself and his wife Anne, to his daughter Katherine and her husband Thomas Dynham.[77] Thomas and Katherine were in possession in 1552.[78] At Thomas's death eleven years later Boarstall descended to his son and heir John,[79] who obtained licence to enter on his father's manors in 1570[80] and in 1576 conveyed the Derhyde and bailiwick of Bernwood Forest to Alexander Denton of Hillesden in exchange for an Oxfordshire manor.[81] Alexander died the next year, after settling this part of the manor of Boarstall on trustees till the majority of his infant son Thomas.[82] His executors afterwards agreed to restore the Boarstall lands and bailiwick to John Dynham for the rest of Thomas Denton's minority on condition that the fee simple should be conveyed to John Dynham by Thomas when he came of age.[83] Two suits in Chancery brought by John on the ground of non-fulfilment of this agreement[84] were followed by the settlement of the Derhyde and bailiwick by Thomas Denton on John Dynham and his son and heir John in 1596.[85] To the younger John Dynham, who was aged sixteen at his father's death in 1602,[86] a full grant was made by the king in 1611 of his ancestors' lands in Bernwood Forest with others once held there by religious houses.[87] The manor of Boarstall was settled by John and his second wife Penelope, daughter of Sir Richard Wenman,[88] on themselves, with remainder to their eldest daughter Mary and her husband on her marriage in 1632 with Lawrence Banaster.[89] Two years later Sir John died, leaving besides Mary two younger daughters.[89a] Penelope Lady Dynham was living at Boarstall, then a Royalist stronghold,[90] in 1645, when she certified that Stephen Soame, her daughter Mary's second husband, had been with her there at a time when he was reported to be in arms against the Parliament.[91] To Lawrence Banaster, Mary had borne one child Margaret,[92] who held Boarstall with her husband William Lewis in 1651[93] and as his widow in 1661.[94] Edward her son and heir died without issue in 1672,[95] and two years later his sister Mary and her husband William Jephson were in possession.[96] Mary, who was the wife of Sir John Aubrey, bart., in 1693,[97] had no child by him.[98] In accordance with the settlement made on her second marriage, Boarstall came on her death in 1717 to her step-son Sir John Aubrey, whose second wife was her daughter Frances Jephson.[99]

[53] Boarstall Chartul. fol. 47.
[54] *Cal. Pat.* 1343–5, p. 436; Feet of F. Bucks. Trin. 19 Edw. III, no. 15.
[55] Chan. Inq. p.m. 20 Edw. III (1st nos.), no. 51.
[56] *Cal. Close*, 1346–9, pp. 101, 327, 385–6.
[57] *Parl. R.* ii, 215b, 216a; *Cal. Pat.* 1348–50, p. 69.
[58] *Cal. Close*, 1346–9, pp. 445–6; *Abbrev. Rot. Orig.* (Rec. Com.), ii, 187.
[59] *Abbrev. Rot. Orig.* (Rec. Com.), ii, 196.
[60] Ibid. 193; *Cal. Close*, 1354–60, pp. 137–8, 592; Chan. Inq. p.m. 32 Edw. III (1st nos.), no. 36.
[61] Chan. Inq. p.m. 32 Edw. III (1st nos.), no. 36.
[62] *Cal. Close*, 1360–4, pp. 386–7; *Abbrev. Rot. Orig.* (Rec. Com.), ii, 265.
[63] *Cal Close*, 1364–8, pp. 229, 230.
[64] Feet of F. Div. Co. 18 Ric. II, no. 268.
[65] *Cal. Pat.* 1388–92, p. 334; Feet of F. Div. Co. Mich. 19 Ric. II, no. 285.

[66] Chan. Inq. p.m. 7 Hen. V, no. 63.
[67] *Cal. Pat.* 1422–9, p. 458; Feet of F. Div. Co. 6 Hen. VI, no. 65.
[68] Chan. Inq. p.m. 10 Hen. VI, no. 23.
[69] Ibid. 13 Hen. VI, no. 38.
[70] Ibid.
[71] Ibid. 16 Hen. VI, no. 38.
[72] Boarstall Chartul. fol. 54b, 89, 94b, 97.
[73] *Cal. Inq. p.m. Hen. VII*, i, 197.
[74] Ibid. 233; Chan. Inq. p.m. (Ser. 2), xiii, 132.
[75] Exch. Inq. p.m. (Ser. 2), file 22, no. 7.
[76] Ibid.; Lipscomb, op. cit. i, 166.
[77] Feet of F. Div. Co. East. 1 Edw. VI; Harl. Chart. 79, G 13.
[78] Feet of F. Div. Co. East. 6 Edw. VI.
[79] Chan. Inq. p.m. (Ser. 2), cxxxvi, 2; W. and L. Inq. p.m. x, 48.
[80] Pat. 12 Eliz. pt. viii, m. 9.
[81] Chan. Proc. (Ser. 2), bdle. 57, no. 37.
[82] Chan. Inq. p.m. (Ser. 2), clxxvi, 4.
[83] Chan. Proc. (Ser. 2), bdles. 224, no. 11; 57, no. 37.

[84] Ibid.
[85] Chan. Inq. p.m. (Ser. 2), cclxviii, 149.
[86] Ibid.
[87] Pat. 8 Jas. I, pt. lix, no. 134.
[88] Lipscomb, op. cit. i, 66. His first marriage with Elizabeth daughter of Sir John Dormer of Long Crendon was childless.
[89] Ibid.; Feet of F. Divers Co. Mich. 8 Chas. I; Chan. Inq. p.m. (Ser. 2), dxii, 7.
[89a] Chan. Inq. p.m. (Ser. 2), dxii, 7.
[90] See p. 10.
[91] *Cal. S. P. Dom.* 1645–7, p. 69.
[92] Lipscomb, loc. cit.
[93] Parl. Surv. Bucks. no. 16.
[94] Feet of F. Div. Co. Hil. 13 & 14 Chas. II. [95] Lipscomb, loc. cit.
[96] Feet of F. Div. Co. Mich. 26 Chas. II.
[97] Ibid. Hil. 4 & 5 Will. and Mary.
[98] G.E.C. *Baronetage*, iii, 94.
[99] Ibid.

Sir John, was holding in 1733,[100] and was succeeded ten years later by his elder son John, who, dying unmarried in 1767, left his estates to his younger brother, afterwards Sir Thomas Aubrey.[1] In 1766, however, Richard Aubrey, younger son of Thomas,[2] seems to have been the lord of Boarstall and Brill.[3] From his elder brother John, who succeeded his father in 1786, both manors descended forty years later to Sir John Digby Aubrey, Richard's son and heir.[4] Sir Thomas left no child at his death in 1856,[5] and his estates descended under his uncle's will to his cousin Elizabeth Sophia, daughter of his uncle Colonel Thomas Aubrey and then wife of Charles Spencer Ricketts.[6] Mrs. Ricketts, who was married to the Rev. George Chetwode in 1868,[7] was succeeded in 1874 by her son Charles Aubrey Ricketts, known as Charles Aubrey Aubrey.[8] He died in 1901, and his lands passed under the same will to Sir Henry Fletcher, grandson of Sir Henry Fletcher of Ashley Park, who was great-grandson through the female line of the Sir John Aubrey who died in 1743.[9] Sir Henry, who assumed the name of Aubrey-Fletcher in 1903,[10] was succeeded

AUBREY. *Azure a cheveron between three eagles' heads razed or.*

FLETCHER. *Argent a cross engrailed between four roundels sable each charged with a pheon argent.*

in 1911 by his brother Sir Lancelot Aubrey-Fletcher, who transferred the property to his son Mr. Henry L. Aubrey-Fletcher in 1913.

From the 11th to the 13th century a considerable part of Boarstall remained in the Crown. The Empress Maud, who held this land in demesne, granted it before 1158 to her clerk, Adam de Ely,[11] tenant until 1166.[12] It was in the hands of William de Rochelle from 1167 to 1179,[13] and leased to Walter Bustard in 1200.[14] Before 1213 Thomas de Fekenham, son and heir of Thomas de Hereford, Adam de Ely's heir, recovered from Walter his inheritance in Boarstall,[15] which was again in the Crown

in the next reign.[16] The greater part, however, seems to have been acquired before 1289 by John Fitz Niel,[17] whose heir, John Handlo, in 1310 added to it a little land formerly held of the Crown through a mesne lord, William Belet.[18] As late as 1316, however, Boarstall was classed with Brill amongst the 'burghs' of the king,[19] possibly on account of the large part which fell within the bounds of the royal forest of Bernwood. Grants from this were made to John Handlo in 1305 and 1315[20] and later and descended with the manor, but many hundred acres remained in the Crown at the close of the 16th century.[21]

Assize of bread and ale belonged to the manor of Boarstall in 1275.[22] In 1286 its lord was called upon to make good his claim to view of frankpledge which his ancestors had held in the Derhyde from time immemorial,[23] and his heirs still held in 1527.[24] There was a capital messuage here in 1289,[25] probably the dwelling-house which John Handlo afterwards obtained licence to crenellate,[26] and the 'peel and manor' of 1322.[27] The site alone was mentioned in 1347.[28] Two centuries later there was a dwelling called the Hall End or Master Rede's lodging,[29] presumably the lodge in the 'New Park' of 1597,[30] and the capital messuage of 1602 and 1634,[31] which has its place in history.[32]

From the reign of Henry II until 1275 the abbey of Godstow reckoned among its possessions Lachemede,[33] which two centuries later as 65 acres of pasture was held by the lord of Boarstall Manor of the king.[34] The abbey also enjoyed half the wood called Hildesdene by gift of King John,[35] confirmed by Henry III,[36] until 1314, when Maud of Upton, then abbess, granted it to John Handlo.[37] The other moiety belonged in 1275 to Oseney Abbey,[38] as at one time did the common called Stonehurst, which came after the Dissolution from the Crown to Lord Williams of Thame, then to Lord Norreys and finally to John Dynham.[39]

CHURCH The church of *ST. JAMES* is a small stone building consisting of chancel and nave with a bellcote at the junction containing one small bell. It was rebuilt in the Perpendicular style on the old foundations in 1818 by Sir John Aubrey, and contains some fittings re-used from the old church. The building was restored in 1884. The panelled pulpit and sounding-board are of the late 17th century. At the east end of the nave is some 17th-century panelling, and in a vestry at the west end is a communion table with a carved upper rail dated 1615. On the south side of the chancel is a late 15th-century rectangular tomb with a panelled

[100] Recov. R. Hil. 7 Geo. II, m. 30.
[1] G.E.C. *Baronetage*, iii, 94.
[2] Ibid. 95.
[3] Recov. R. Trin. 6 Geo. III, m. 291.
[4] G.E.C. loc. cit.; Recov. R. Mich. 54 Geo. III, m. 392.
[5] G.E.C. loc. cit.
[6] Burke, *Landed Gentry* (1886), i, 57.
[7] Burke, *Peerage* (1911).
[8] Burke, *Landed Gentry* (1886), i, 57.
[9] G.E.C. *Baronetage*, v, 219.   [10] Ibid.
[11] Hunter, *Gt. R. of the Pipe* 2-4 Hen. II (Rec. Com.), 139.
[12] Pipe R. 5 Hen. II (Pipe R. Soc.), 18; 6 Hen. II, 11; 8 Hen. II, 40; 9 Hen. II, 14; 10 Hen. II, 29; 11 Hen. II, 22; 12 Hen. II, 11.
[13] Ibid. 13 Hen. II, 102; 14 Hen. II, 6, 7; 25 Hen. II, 73.

[14] Chart. R. 1 John, pt. ii, m. 5, no. 180; Rot. de Oblatis et Fin. (Rec. Com.), 52.
[15] Cur. Reg. R. 59, m. 4; Abbrev. Plac. (Rec. Com.), 91.
[16] Testa de Nevill (Rec. Com.), 245.
[17] Cal. Inq. p.m. (Edw. I), ii, 438.
[18] Feet of F. Bucks. 3 Edw. II, no. 1; Chan. Inq. p.m. 21 Edw. I, no. 20; Cal. Close, 1288-96, p. 290.
[19] Feud. Aids, i, 114.
[20] Cal. Pat. 1301-7, p. 310; Cal. Fine R. 1307-19, pp. 228-9; Lansd. MS. 47, fol. 3.
[21] Lansd. MS. 47, fol. 3.
[22] Hund. R. (Rec. Com.), i, 35.
[23] Plac. de Quo Warr. (Rec. Com.), 91.
[24] Exch. Inq. p.m. (Ser. 2), file 22, no. 7.

[25] Cal. Inq. p.m. (Edw. I), ii, 438.
[26] Cal. Pat. 1307-13, p. 493.
[27] Ibid. 1321-4, p. 78.
[28] Cal. Close, 1346-9, p. 446.
[29] Harl. Chart. 79, G 13.
[30] Chan. Proc. (Ser. 2), bdle. 57, no. 37.
[31] Chan. Inq. p.m. (Ser. 2), cclxviii, 149; dxii, 12.
[32] Cal. S. P. Dom. 1645-7, p. 69.
[33] Hund. R. (Rec. Com.), i, 22, 37.
[34] Chan. Inq. p.m. 16 Hen. VI, no. 38.
[35] Hund. R. (Rec. Com.), i, 37.
[36] Pat. 8 Jas. I, pt. lix, no. 134.
[37] Ibid.; Boarstall Chartul. fol. 38b, 139.
[38] Hund. R. (Rec. Com.), i, 37.
[39] Pat. 19 Eliz. pt. vi, m. 1. It seems, however, to have been first granted to Christ Church, Oxford, as was also Gyres Wood (ibid. 8 Jas. I, pt. lix, no. 134).

front having three plain brass shields and a Purbeck marble covering slab with the matrices for two shields and an inscription. There is also a monument to Sir John Aubrey, who died in 1826, besides tablets to other members of the Aubrey family. The church-yard cross has been restored, but the lower part of the shaft and the octagonal base with broached stops date from the 15th century.

The communion plate was stolen in 1812. The present plate includes a silver-gilt cup given to the church in 1824, the date letter of which is illegible, and a stand paten of 1615; the cup is inscribed, 'This cupe and cover wayeth 28 oz. 3 dwt.,' and bears representations in repoussé work of the Annunciation and the Nativity.

The registers begin in 1640.

ADVOWSON   The church of Boarstall, dedicated in honour of St. John the Evangelist in 1391,[40] and of St. James from 1417 to the present day,[41] was a chapel of Oakley in the 12th century.[42] Its descent has been in the main identical with that of Oakley and Brill Churches (q.v.), and it is now held with Brill. In 1449, however, the Prior of St. Frideswide granted the nomination of the perpetual chaplain of Boarstall to Edmund Rede and his heirs, retaining for himself and his successors the admission of their nominees.[43] It was probably in consequence of this concession that the lords of Boarstall manors claimed some right to the church more than a century later, Leonard Rede in 1547 including the advowson in his sale of the manor to Thomas Dynham,[44] and Thomas making a settlement of both in 1552.[45]

Indulgences were offered for the repair of Boarstall chapel in 1391 and for the building of its bell-tower.[46] In 1417 the right of burial here was conceded,[47] and chapel and cemetery were consecrated the following year.[48] The inhabitants of Boarstall, however, were still expected to contribute to the repair of Oakley Church, and the dispute which arose on this matter was not settled until 1430.[49] In 1450 Edmund Rede granted his perpetual chaplain a messuage called 'Prestys House' with land in the parish.[50] This Edmund Rede, by his will dated 7 April 1487, left directions for his burial in the chapel of the Holy Trinity on the south of the church.[50a]

CHARITIES   Dame Penelope Dynham, by her will proved 11 December 1672, devised a yearly rent-charge of £8 issuing out of lands in Boarstall. By a scheme of the Charity Commissioners of 6 May 1913 the income of the charity is made applicable in apprenticing poor children to some useful trade or occupation, or in assisting persons under twenty-one years of age upon entering such trade or occupation.

Edward Lewis, by his will proved 26 February 1674, directed a sum of £300 to be laid out in the purchase of a yearly rent for the benefit of the poor. The endowment consists of a rent-charge of £12 issuing out of lands in Boarstall, which is applied in gifts of money.

The lands out of which the annuities of £8 and £12 are payable now belong to Mr. Henry Lancelot Aubrey-Fletcher.

Charles Aubrey Aubrey, by his will proved 17 March 1902, bequeathed £200 consols, the annual dividends, amounting to £5, to be applied in repairing the Aubrey family monuments in the church and the grave of Sir John Aubrey outside the church. The income, when not required for such purposes, is paid to the account of the school, erected by the testator.

The stock is held by the official trustees, who also hold a sum of £600 consols bequeathed by the same testator, producing £15 a year, for the repairs of the school buildings in this parish and the parish of Chilton.

BRILL

Brunhelle (xi cent.); Breohilla, Brohill (xii cent.); Bruhulle, Brihull, Brehull (xiii cent.).

This parish, which, like Boarstall, lay within Bernwood Forest, and in the 13th century gave the alternative name of the forest of Brill to part if not the whole of it,[1] extends over nearly 2,940 acres, of which 307 are arable, 207 woodland, and the rest pasture.[2] The surface soil varies, but the subsoil is Kimmeridge Clay and Portland Beds. At Muswell Hill, which is partly in Oxfordshire, where there are traces of Roman occupation,[3] and at the village, the land rises to 600 ft., but elsewhere it rises to 400 ft. At the town of Brill, which was ravaged by the Danes in 914,[4] Edward the Confessor is said to have had a house.[5] At least one charter of Henry I is dated from Brill,[6] and the early Plantagenet sovereigns were not infrequently resident here.[7] In the 13th century timber from Bernwood Forest was constantly in demand for the repair of the houses of the king's manor of Brill,[8] and several records survive of the replenishing of the royal cellars before the king's arrival.[9] The site of the royal palace is thought to have been near the church.[10]

The village, placed on the summit of a high hill, consists of a long, wide street from which smaller roads diverge. The church of All Saints stands at the south-east end, with the almshouses and the Wesleyan chapel, dating from 1841, close by. The Congregational chapel a little further on was built in

---

[40] *Cal. of Papal Letters,* iv, 406.
[41] Linc. Epis. Reg. Memo. Repingdon, fol. 169 d.
[42] Chart. R. 1 Edw. III. m. 45, no. 87.
[43] Boarstall Chartul. fol. 115.
[44] Feet of F. Div. Co. East. 1 Edw. VI; Harl. Chart. 79, G 13.
[45] Feet of F. Div. Co. East. 6 Edw. VI.
[46] *Cal. of Papal Letters,* iv, 406.
[47] Linc. Epis. Reg. *ut supra.*
[48] Boarstall Chartul. fol. 114b.
[49] Ibid. fol. 126b.   [50] Ibid. fol. 126.

[50a] P.C.C. 32 Milles.
[1] *Cal. Close,* 1227–31, pp. 49, 59, 217, 472–3; 1231–4, p. 489; *Cal. Pat.* 1272–81, p. 241; 1258–66, p. 293.
[2] Statistics from Bd. of Agric. (1905).
[3] *V.C.H. Bucks.* ii, 5.
[4] Camden, *Brit.* (ed. Gough), i, 314.
[5] Kennet, *Paroch. Antiq.* i, 57.
[6] Round, *Anct. Charters* (Pipe R. Soc.), 4.
[7] Kennet, op. cit. i, 161, 164; Lipscomb, *Hist. and Antiq. of Bucks.* i, 97; *Rot. de Oblatis et Fin.* (Rec. Com.), 503–5,

524–5; *Cal. Close,* 1234–7, p. 101; 1272–9, p. 93.
[8] *Rot. Lit. Claus.* (Rec. Com.), i, 492, 498b; *Cal. Close,* 1231–4, p. 76; 1272–9, pp. 19, 24, 175, 536; 1279–88, p. 459; 1288–96, pp. 25, 67; 1307–13, pp. 380, 389; 1313–18, pp. 271, 290.
[9] *Rot. Lit. Claus.* (Rec. Com.), i, 28b, 69b, 100b, 471b, 507, 598; *Cal. Close,* 1234–7, p. 101; 1272–9, pp. 93, 528.
[10] Sheahan, *Hist. and Topog. of Bucks* 341.

1839. In 1644 Brill was selected as the winter quarters for a thousand Parliamentarian foot-soldiers.[11] A strong rampart and ditch north of the church and another line of defence further down the hill were probably constructed about this time.

The village contains a number of buildings dating from the 17th century, including Manor Farm, the Swan[12] and Red Lion Inns, and the windmill, but most of them have been considerably restored and altered in later years.

The manor-house, at the south end of the village, appears to have been developed from a half-timber house of the late 15th century. The structure, as it now stands, is mainly of the late 16th century, and the walls are of brick with stone dressings, the original timber portion having been encased. Although it has been a good deal altered and added to subsequently, much original detail remains, including several panelled rooms.

Coldharbour Farm, about a mile north, and a farm-house about a mile south of the village, are both of 17th-century date; at Little London, a hamlet near the south-west boundary of the parish, are several cottages of the same period, but all have been more or less altered at subsequent dates. There is also a Congregational chapel here, built in 1847.

Pottery and tile-making were mediaeval industries at Brill,[13] and continued to the latter half of the 19th century. About a mile north of the village, beyond the old brickfields and the common with its old wooden mill, is Brill station, on the Brill and Quainton Road branch of the Metropolitan and Great Central Joint railway. Not far off lies Rushbeds Wood, of which more than 100 acres were inclosed about 1575,[14] a part, called Upper Rushbeds Coppice, being still Crown land in 1651, when the Parliamentary commissioners reported that a sufficient number of acres from it should have been given to the late Sir John Dynham to compensate him for the office of forester.[15] Other inclosures, against which the people of Brill petitioned Queen Elizabeth, were made at Clere Fields and Poole Trees,[16] names still surviving in the north-east of the parish, Hale Hill, Mollens, once probably Moleyns Wood and Godstow or Costow Park.[17] At Godstow, part of which with Clere Fields and Hale Hill had belonged to the lords of Boarstall Manor since 1305,[18] it was said that Mr. Dynham had inclosed 140 acres of the queen's ground to make a park.[19] Another petition was

presented in 1610 against the inclosure of Godley Common or Brill Hills.[20] In 1632 part of Godstow was allotted to the poor of Brill and Oakley in lieu of Cartbridge Waste.[21] Leap Hill, Hercumdean, Leatherslade, Parkpale Farm and Well House, which lie in the south-east of the parish, are names known there since the 16th and 17th centuries.[22] Rid's Hill, north-east of the village, is probably the Red's Hill of 1634,[23] whilst Chinkwell Wood, to the east of it, dates from 1681[24]; the Hutwood or Outwood of 1255 and later[25] does not occur in modern maps.

There seems to be no doubt that a **BOROUGH** royal borough at one time existed at Brill, but by the mid-13th century it had been merged in the manor. At the eyre of 1241 the borough of Brill came by twelve men, and the town (villata) made fine of 20s. before judgement.[26] At an eyre of uncertain date, probably not much later, Brill again appeared by twelve men, but they had nothing more to present than had been said elsewhere by the representatives of the hundred.[27] As late, however, as the year 1316 Brill and Boarstall were returned as royal boroughs.[28] These indications are strengthened by the 13th-century extents, which show half-acre and acre plots of 'land built upon' (terra edificata), which may represent the early burgages.[29] The growth of the borough was arrested early, though in the reign of John we hear of the 'legales' or 'probi homines' of Brill.[30]

BRILL, formerly one of the manors of **MANORS** Edward the Confessor, belonged to the Conqueror in 1086,[31] and until the 14th century remained in the Crown,[32] of which it was held in chief as one knight's fee from 1337 to 1634.[33]

Grants of the whole or part of the manor, generally during the royal pleasure or for a term of years, were made by Henry II and his successors.[34] Certain lands here of the king's gift were held by William de Rochelle from 1168 to 1178,[35] and in 1204 John granted the manor of Brill to Walter Bustard, servant of his chapel, in fee farm.[36] Many other grants of custody were made during the reign of Henry III.[37] The Bishop of Bath and Wells was tenant for seven years from 1266,[38] and in 1275 the manor of Brill was assigned to Queen Eleanor in dower.[39] Other grants of short duration[40] were followed by one made in 1317 to Richard Lovel and his wife Muriel, in return for a manor exchanged.[41] Richard, who

[11] Cal. S. P. Dom. 1644–5, p. 141.
[12] Preserving the name of a 15th-century messuage (Early Chan. Proc. bdle. 123, no. 68).
[13] Sheahan, op. cit. 339.
[14] Pat. 19 Eliz. pt. vi, m. 1; Lansd. MS. 47, fol. 5; Chan. Inq. p.m. (Ser. 2), dxii, 7.   [15] Parl. Surv. Bucks. no. 16.
[16] Pat. 19 Eliz. pt. vi, m. 1; Lansd. MS. 47, fol. 6.
[17] Ibid.; Exch. Dep. Mich. 22 & 23 Eliz. no. 16; East. 26 Eliz. no. 5; Exch. Spec. Com. no. 434.
[18] Cal. Pat. 1301–7, p. 310.
[19] Lansd. MS. 47, fol. 6.
[20] Cal. S. P. Dom. 1603–10, p. 606.
[21] Exch. Spec. Com. no. 5169, 6670; Chan. Inq. p.m. (Ser. 2), dxii, 7.
[22] Exch. Dep. Trin. 27 Eliz. no. 3; Hil. 1655–6, no. 10; East. 33 Chas. II, no. 2; Chan. Inq. p.m. (Ser. 2), cccxlvii, 84; dxii, 7; W. and L. Inq. p.m. x, 48;

L. and P. Hen. VIII, xv, g. 612 (7); Harl. Chart. 79, G. 13; Chan. Proc. (Ser. 2), bdle. 224, no. 11; Pat. 8 Jas. I, pt. lix, no. 134; Chan. Enr. Decr. no. 1408, m. 3.
[23] Chan. Inq. p.m. (Ser. 2), dxii, 7.
[24] Exch. Dep. East. 33 Chas. II, no. 2.
[25] Hund. R. (Rec. Com.), i, 21; Cal. Pat. 1345–8, p. 407.
[26] Assize R. 55, m. 23.
[27] Ibid. 62, m. 5.
[28] Feud. Aids, i, 114. Boarstall was apparently included loosely as formerly a member of Brill.
[29] Hund. R. (Rec. Com.), i, 35.
[30] Rot. Lit. Claus. (Rec. Com.), i, 8, 189.
[31] V.C.H. Bucks. i, 322.
[32] Feud. Aids, i, 114; Hund. R. (Rec. Com.), i, 35.
[33] Cal. Pat. 1334–8; p. 464; Chan. Inq. p.m. 13 Hen. VI, no. 35; (Ser. 2), cxxxv, 2; cccxviii, 149; dxii, 7.

[34] Pipe R. 14 Hen. II (Pipe R. Soc.), 7; Cal. Pat. 1216–25, p. 117; 1225–32, p. 52; 1313–17, p. 53.
[35] Pipe R. 14 Hen. II (Pipe R. Soc.), 17; 15 Hen. II, 87; 16 Hen. II, 25; 17 Hen. II, 55; 18 Hen. II, 47; 19 Hen. II, 69; 20 Hen. II, 81; 21 Hen. II, 48; 22 Hen. II, 16; 23 Hen. II, 156; 24 Hen. II, 91.
[36] Chart. R. 5 John, m. 7, no. 47; Cart. Antiq. Q 13; BB 21; Rot. Lit. Claus. (Rec. Com.), i, 216b, 246.
[37] Cal. Pat. 1247–58, pp. 153, 651; 1258–66, p. 392.
[38] Ibid. 1258–66, p. 626.
[39] Cal. Chart. R. 1257–1300, p. 192. It was in the king's hands earlier in the year (Hund. R. [Rec. Com.], i, 35).
[40] Abbrev. Rot. Orig. (Rec. Com.), i, 39, 203, 238; Cal. Close, 1323–7, p. 229; Cal. Pat. 1313–17, p. 53.
[41] Cal. Pat. 1313–17, p. 662.

petitioned the king, about four years later, against the malicious withholding of his dues in Brill by 'le Mestr' de Smityngfeld,[42] retained possession until 1337, when, on a grant of the manor in fee by Edward III to John de Moleyns, he released his rights to the new lord.[43]

The manor of Brill then descended with Stoke Poges (q.v.), with a few divergencies noticed below, until Francis Earl of Huntingdon sold it to Thomas Dynham in 1554.[44] Since then it has followed the descent of Boarstall Manor, Mr. Henry L. Aubrey-Fletcher being now lord.

The custody of Brill Manor was committed in 1358 to Gilbert Chastellyn,[45] and the bailiwick in 1384 to Richard Wilcocks,[46] a John Wilcocks farming the manor in 1397.[47] A settlement of Brill appears to have been made on Thomas Chaucer, said in 1435 to have been seised of the same.[48] Mortgages of the manor were made in 1539 and 1549 by the Earl of Huntingdon.[49] Frideswide daughter of Eleanor de Moleyns by her second husband Sir Oliver de Mannyngham[50] apparently brought Brill to her husband Sir Thomas Oxenbridge, who held in 1489,[51] but in 1493 they surrendered all claim, for a life annuity of £10 to Frideswide, to Sir Edward Hastings and Mary his wife, daughter and heir of Thomas Hungerford.[52] Frideswide's daughter and heir Dorothy, wife of Sir Thomas Digby, afterwards unsuccessfully sued the trustees of Edward and Mary for the recovery of Brill,[53] and her grandson Everard Digby of Long Stratton revived the claim c. 1565[54] against Thomas Dynham's trustees.[55] In 1592 a grant of Brill Manor was made to the fishing grantees Tipper and Dawe.[56]

There appears to have been a rectory manor of Brill, the rector holding assize of bread and ale for his tenants in 1276.[57]

The manor had a mill in 1086.[58] Two centuries later a windmill was built here of timber from Bernwood Forest,[59] probably on the site on which John de Moleyns, about 1345, constructed another with oaks felled in his demesne woods.[60] From that time until 1733 a windmill appears amongst the appurtenances of the manor,[61] of which the ancient windmill now standing may be the survival. Assize of bread and ale was a liberty granted to John

de Moleyns in 1338, when he also received view of frankpledge.[62] According to a later record, free warren and the right of erecting gallows on his land were included in the grant of the manor to him.[63] The tolls of a market and fair held at Brill at the beginning of August were accounted for by John Norton about 1317.[64] In 1347 John de Moleyns was authorised to hold a fair at his manor of Brill on the eve, day and morrow of the Translation of St. Thomas the Martyr[65] (7 July). One or more dovecotes were amongst the appurtenances of the 16th and 17th centuries.[66]

In 1563 there was a capital messuage on the lands called Harehill,[67] Halehill,[68] or the Hall Hill.[69] The site of the manor and lands were sold by John Dynham to William Belson in 1587,[70] and he and his heirs had a capital messuage here in the 17th century.[71]

An appurtenance of Brill Manor in the 13th and 14th centuries was a bowl of honey due from the Abbot of Woburn for land in Swanbourne.[72] Before 1535 this had been commuted for an annual payment of 13s. 4d.[73]

In 1305 Edward I granted John de Handlo 138 acres in Les Clers, on the borders of if not within the boundaries of Ludgershall parish.[74] This seems to have been the nucleus of what was known from 1362 to 1527 as the manor of CLERESPLACE or CLEREFIELD, and descended with Boarstall (q.v.), being held in the 16th century of the lord of Brill as of his manor of Brill.[75]

In the 16th century the Abbot of Nutley, to whose house King Henry II had given two cartloads of fuel a day from Bernwood Forest,[76] a grant rescinded by Edward III,[77] held a considerable property in Brill.[78] The promise of a lease of a valuable part of this, Brill Closes or Wellfields, was obtained from the abbot for Richard Cromwell by Sir Robert Dormer in 1536.[79] In 1540 they were granted, with other lands formerly of Nutley Abbey, to John Williams,[80] whose possessions in the parish were augmented by another grant six years later.[81] All were left under the title of the manor of Brill by John, then Lord Williams, at his death in 1559 to his servant John Place for life,[82] and at the beginning of the 17th century were held by the heirs of his daughter Margery wife of Henry Lord Norreys.[83]

[42] Parl. R. i. 395. Smityngfeld should be Santingfeld (see p. 17).
[43] Cal. Pat. 1334–8, pp. 464, 527–8; Cal. Close, 1337–9, p. 238.
[44] Feet of F. Bucks. East. 1 Mary.
[45] Abbrev. Rot. Orig. (Rec. Com.), ii, 247.
[46] Cal. Pat. 1381–5, p. 515.
[47] Chan. Misc. Inq. file 266, no. 6a.
[48] Chan. Inq. p.m. 13 Hen. VI, no. 35.
[49] Feet of F. Bucks. Hil. 30 Hen. VIII; Mich. 3 Edw. VI; Com. Pleas D. Enr. Mich. 32 Hen. VIII, m. 3.
[50] Early Chan. Proc. bdle. 304, no. 26.
[51] Cal. Inq. p.m. Hen. VII, i, 197.
[52] Feet of F. Bucks. 8 Hen. VII, file 127; De Banco R. 923, m. 21.
[53] Early Chan. Proc. bdle. 304, no. 26; De Banco R. 975, m. 345.
[54] After Thomas Dynham's death in 1563 and during the minority of his son, aged fourteen in 1563 (Chan. Inq. p.m. [Ser. 2], cxxxvi, 2).
[55] Chan. Proc. (Ser. 2), bdle. 57, no. 16.
[56] Pat. 1385, m. 10.
[57] Hund. R. (Rec. Com.), i, 36.
[58] V.C.H. Bucks. i, 232.
[59] Cal. Close, 1272–9, p. 102; 1288–96, p. 58.
[60] Chan. Misc. Inq. file 157, no. 35; Cal. Pat. 1345–8, p. 407.
[61] Chan. Inq. p.m. 4 Ric. II, no. 38; 13 Hen. VI, no. 35; (Ser. 2), ccclix, 132; Pat. 29 Eliz. pt. xi, m. 5; Feet of F. Div. Co. Mich. 26 Chas. II; Hil. 13 & 14 Chas. II; Recov. R. Hil. 7 Geo. II, m. 30.
[62] Chart. R. 12 Edw. III, m. 4, no. 3; Chan. Inq. p.m. 18 Hen. VI, no. 31; Feet of F. Bucks. East. 1 Mary.
[63] Chan. Inq. p.m. 18 Hen. VI, no. 31.
[64] Boarstall Chartul. fol. 138. John Norton was then keeper of the manor (Cal. Fine R. 1307–19, p. 325).
[65] Chart. R. 21 Edw. III, m. 1, no. 26. In the 18th century a fair was still held on the Wednesday after Old Michaelmas Day (Lysons, Mag. Brit. i [3], 523), and this was revived before 1862 (Sheahan, op. cit. 339).
[66] Feet of F. Bucks. East. 1 Mary; Chan. Inq. p.m. (Ser. 2), cclxviii, 149.
[67] W. and L. Inq. p.m. x, 48.
[68] Exch. Spec. Com. no. 434. In 1305 it was called Hallehalle (Cal. Pat. 1301–7, p. 310).
[69] Lansd. MS. 47, fol. 5.
[70] Pat. 29 Eliz. pt. xi, m. 5; Feet of F. Bucks. Trin. 29 Eliz.
[71] Chan. Inq. p.m. (Ser. 2), cccxlvii, 84; ccclix, 132.
[72] Hund. R. (Rec. Com.), i, 21; Boarstall Chartul. fol. 128; Cal. Pat. 1340–3, p. 42.
[73] Valor Eccl. (Rec. Com.), iv, 213.
[74] Cal. Pat. 1301–7, p. 310.
[75] Cal. Close, 1360–4, pp. 386–7; 1364–8, p. 229; Exch. Inq. p.m. (Ser. 2), file 22, no. 7.
[76] Cal. Chart. R. 1300–26, p. 210; Dugdale, Mon. vi, 278.
[77] Cal. Close, 1346–9, p. 312; Cal. Pat. 1345–8, p. 375; 1354–8, p. 20.
[78] Valor Eccl. (Rec. Com.), iv, 232.
[79] L. and P. Hen. VIII, x, 20, 95.
[80] Ibid. xv, g. 612 (7).
[81] Ibid. xxi (1), g. 717 (5).
[82] P.C.C. 11 Melhershe.
[83] Ibid.; Fine R. 44 Eliz. pt. i, no. 44; Chan. Inq. p.m. (Ser. 2), cccxiv, 127.

BRILL: THE MANOR HOUSE

BRILL CHURCH FROM THE SOUTH

The brothers of the hospital of Santingfeld, near Wissant in Picardy, paid 60s. a year into the royal exchequer for lands in Brill from 1154 to 1199.[84] These were perhaps part of the 3 hides in the neighbouring parish of Ludgershall granted by Henry II to this house, for which the Master of Santingfeld owed suit at the court of Brill.[85]

CHURCH The church of ALL SAINTS consists of a chancel measuring internally 18 ft. by 15 ft., nave 58 ft. 6 in. by 21 ft. 6 in., north aisle 13 ft. 6 in. wide, south aisle 14 ft. wide, west tower 11 ft. by 11 ft. 6 in., and a timber south porch. The walling is principally of rubble and the roofs are tiled.

The chancel and nave date from the early 12th century. Beyond the addition of the tower in the early 15th century and the insertion of windows at various dates in the Middle Ages, the plan of the fabric remained practically unchanged till 1839, when the north aisle was added. In 1889 the south aisle and porch were built, and the chancel, which had been reroofed in the early 17th century, was extended eastwards about 6 ft.

The east window of the chancel is modern, and has three lights under a traceried head. Above it is a reset and retooled two-light window of about 1400. In the north wall are a late 13th-century trefoiled light and a small blocked window of about 1120, and in the south wall a pointed doorway and a two-light window, both probably of the 13th century, the latter much restored and altered. The fine 17th-century roof is supported by three trusses and plastered below the collar-beams. The middle truss has an elaborate arch above the tie-beam filled with pierced balusters radiating from a central pendant; the eastern truss, which stands away from the wall and marks the position of the original east end, has curved struts, while the tie-beam of the western truss has been cut away and only the ends remain. The pointed chancel arch dates from the 13th century, the label on the east side and the north abacus being re-used from the 12th-century arch. On the north side are notches for the rood screen, and the arch is rebated on the east, doubtless for a wood tympanum; the south jamb has been considerably restored. On the soffit are 14th-century paintings of St. Peter holding a book and a key, and St. Paul holding a book and a sword.

In the west wall of the nave is a 15th-century pointed arch opening to the ground stage of the tower; the inner order rests upon corbels, and above

it is a round-headed light of the 12th century. The arcades and the clearstory are modern, but the north and south doorways, though restored, are both of the early 12th century, and, with some windows and fittings taken out of the original side walls of the nave, have been rebuilt in the walls of the modern aisles. The doorways are alike, each having a round head of two orders supported by detached shafts. In the east wall of the north aisle is a late 13th-century window of four uncusped lights with tracery, while the south aisle has an early 16th-century window of two cinquefoiled lights in the east wall, a three-light window, probably of the same period, in the west

BRILL CHURCH : THE CHANCEL ROOF

wall, and in the south wall a two-light traceried window of about 1320, from which many of the modern aisle windows have been copied. A round-arched recess, and a moulded pillar piscina, the shaft of which is modern, have also been re-used. Some old white glass in the head of the 14th-century window is probably original.

The low tower, which hardly rises above the ridge of the nave roof, is of two stages, the upper being slightly diminished in size, and has diagonal buttresses at the western angles. On the south side is a

84 Hunter, Gt. R. of the Pipe 2–4 Hen. II (Rec. Com.), 21 ; Red Bk. of Exch. (Rolls Ser.), ii, 670, 793; Pipe R. 5 Hen. II (Pipe R. Soc.), 18 et seq.

85 Cal. Chart. R. 1300–26, p. 414 ; Dugdale, Mon. vi, 639 ; Boarstall Chartul. fol. 128 ; Hund. R. (Rec. Com.), i, 21.

clock dial. The lower stage has a two-light traceried window on the west, and there are traces of a late doorway, now blocked, on the north. The bell-chamber is lighted from each side by an original window of two lights, the western one being repaired in oak, and there are original gargoyles on the string-course below the parapet.

The font, which dates from the 14th century, has a traceried panel on each of the seven sides of the bowl, and an octagonal stem and base, the base being prolonged to form a step. The communion table dates from the 17th century. In the chancel and nave are six mediaeval oak benches and in the tower is a rail supported by 17th-century balusters. On the south wall of the chancel is an early 16th-century brass inscription to John Hood and his wife Maud.

The tower contains a ring of six bells recast by William & John Taylor of Oxford in 1825, and a sanctus by James Keene, 1624, inscribed round the lip ‘ Pe Newman Ier Sergeant.’

The communion plate includes a silver cup and cover paten of 1569, the latter inscribed ‘ B 1570 ’ ; a cup and cover paten of 1689 given by Robert Hart ; a flagon given by Sir Thomas Snell in 1751 ; a small modern pewter chalice and paten ; and a modern silver-gilt chalice, paten, and pyx.

The registers begin in 1569.

ADVOWSON The church of Brill from the 12th to the 16th century was a chapel of Oakley Church[86] (q.v.), with which it seems always to have descended. According to a charter of Stephen it had belonged to the priory of St. Frideswide, Oxford, since the time of Edward the Confessor.[87] In the 13th century and the early years of the 14th, presentations, which included Oakley, were made to the church of Brill,[88] the importance of the latter parish as containing a royal manor and residence and the position of Oakley Church within its boundaries[89] apparently obscuring the real relationship between the mother church and its chapel.

Brill had two other chapels in the 13th century. For the service of one, ‘ the chapel of the king’s court,’ John in 1205 granted Robert the hermit of St. Werburgh and his successors 50*s.* a year and the site of the hermitage.[90] A single chaplain seems to have been in charge of the hermitage or ‘ priory of St. Werburgh ’[91] and the royal chapel[92] until the annexation of the former to Chetwode Priory in 1251.[93] The prior was then required to supply two chaplains, one for the chapel of St. Werburgh at the hermitage, the other for the royal chapel, receiving in lieu of the 50*s.* formerly paid him for the latter 21 acres of the king’s assart in Brill.[94] The service of both had probably been long intermitted before the middle of the 15th century, when it was proposed to resume certain lands in Brill held by the Prior of Chetwode on the unfulfilled condition of maintaining a chaplain to celebrate there on Sundays, Wednesdays, and Fridays.[95] In 1460 the advowsons of the chapels of St. Edmund and St. Werburgh were included in the surrender made by the prior to the Bishop of Lincoln,[96] which was followed the next year by the annexation of his house and possessions to Nutley Abbey.[97]

In the 16th century there were lands in Brill devoted to the maintenance of certain lamps in the church, and the rent of a close supported an obit.[98]

CHARITIES Eleemosynary Charities. — The charity formerly known as the Poor Folks’ Pasture, which was founded in or about the year 1623, is regulated by a scheme of the Charity Commissioners of 26 April 1912. The trust estate consists of 149 acres, or thereabouts, in Boarstall, known as the Pasture Farm, and 29 acres of allotment land, producing £126 yearly. The income, augmented by the letting of the shooting rights thereon, is applicable under the scheme for the general benefit of the poor in one or more of the modes therein specified. In 1912 the sum of £3 was given to each of thirty-four recipients.

Alice Carter’s almshouse charity, stated in the Parliamentary Returns of 1786 to have been founded by deed in 1591 for poor widows, consists of the almshouse, close, cottages and gardens containing about 3 acres, let to various tenants, producing about £30 a year.

John Hart, by his will proved in the P.C.C. 15 May 1665, devised (*inter alia*) an annual rent-charge of £5 issuing out of Easington Manor, Oxfordshire, for binding one poor boy to some good trade. In 1912 a premium of £10 was paid for apprenticing a boy.

Edward Lewis, by his will proved 26 February 1674, directed a sum of £300 to be laid out in the purchase of a yearly rent for the benefit of the poor. The endowment consists of a yearly rent-charge of £8 issuing out of lands belonging to Mr. Henry L. Aubrey-Fletcher, which is applied in the distribution of coal.

Miss Mary Elliott, by her will 1864, bequeathed £100 consols, the annual dividends of £2 10*s.* to be applied in the distribution at Christmas of gowns, flannel and calico among three poor women members of the Established Church.

Samuel Turner, by his will proved at London 14 November 1873, bequeathed £400, the income to be distributed annually at Christmas in money, food, fuel, or clothing to the poor. The legacy, less duty, is represented by £360 consols, producing £9 yearly.

The sums of stock are held by the official trustees.

Educational Charities.—In 1637 John Pym by deed gave an annuity of £10 to be paid to a school-master for teaching ten poor children. In 1710 a

---

[86] Chart. R. 1 Edw. III, m. 45, no. 87 ; *Pope Nich. Tax.* (Rec. Com.), 34 ; Linc. Epis. Reg. Memo. Sutton, fol. 217 d ; *Valor Eccl.* (Rec. Com.), iv, 233.

[87] Coxe and Turner, *Cal. Chart. in Bodl.* 301.

[88] *Rot. Lit. Claus.* (Rec. Com.), i, 631 ; *Cal. Pat.* 1247–58, p. 471 ; 1317–21, pp. 120, 195.

[89] Exch. Dep. Mixed Co. Trin. 1650, no. 2.

[90] Chart. R. 7 John, m. 7, no. 55. There was a hermitage at Muswell Hill,

but presumably within the borders of Piddington parish, Oxfordshire, in the 12th century (Boarstall Chartul. fol. 30).

[91] *Cal. Close*, 1231–4, p. 392 ; *Hund. R.* (Rec. Com.), i, 21.

[92] *Cal. Close*, 1231–4, p. 392.

[93] *V.C.H. Bucks.* i, 380.

[94] *Cal. Pat.* 1247–58, pp. 117, 464 ; *Cal. Chart. R.* 1257–1300, p. 20 ; *Hund. R.* (Rec. Com.), i, 37. Henry III gave 1 carucate of land to assure these services, but the prior complained of receiving no

profit therefrom on account of the entrance of the king’s fair on that land. Licence was accordingly granted in 1256 for the inclosure of the arable land, and the prior was to have five cartloads of palings yearly from the forest for the upkeep of the inclosure, with an old oak for the hearth (*Cal. Pat.* 1247–58, p. 464).

[95] Memo. R. (Exch. L.T.R.), Mich. 31 Hen. VI, m. 14.

[96] Chan. Misc. Inq. file 317, no. 69.

[97] *Cal. Pat.* 1461–7, p. 137.

[98] Chant. Cert. 5, no. 58.

sum of £300, representing arrears of the annuity, was laid out in the purchase of 12 acres called Spar Closes, which are let at £20 a year. By a scheme of the Charity Commissioners of 1 February 1895 the income is made applicable in the maintenance of evening classes and in prizes and exhibitions.

In 1825 Sir John Aubrey gave £2,200 stock, the dividends, subject to the payment of 20s. to the parish clerk and of £5 yearly for keeping in repair the family monuments in the church, to be applied for educational purposes. In 1904 there was set aside with the official trustees a sum of £240 consols as the ecclesiastical branch, to provide the annual sum of £6 for the clerk and repair of the monuments, and

£1,960 consols as the educational branch of the charity. In 1910 the sum of £980 consols, part of the last-mentioned sum of stock, was sold out to provide the cost of altering and improving the Church of England schools, for the replacement of which a sum of £660 consols, further part thereof, was set aside and accumulated, leaving a sum of £320 consols with the official trustees on current account. The dividends of £8 a year are applied towards the upkeep of the school premises. The stock on the investment account amounts to £715 6s. 7d. consols.

Church Acre.—There is in the parish an acre of land, so called, let at £2 5s. a year, which is carried to the churchwardens' account.

CHEARSLEY

Cerdeslai, Cerleslai (xi cent.) ; Chaddesle (xiv cent.) ; Chardesle Valence, Chardislee Molyns (xv cent.) ; Cheardesley, Chersley (xvii–xix cent.).

Chearsley covers 942 acres, 322 of these being arable land, 476 permanent grass, and 18 woods and plantations.[1] The soil is clay and loam, with a subsoil of clay and limestone ; the chief crops are wheat, barley and turnips. The southern boundary of the parish is the River Thame. Here and in the west the land is low-lying, averaging about 250 ft. above the ordnance datum. Towards the north-east, however, the ground reaches a height of 407 ft. The small and somewhat scattered village lies at the foot and on the slope of this hill, the church of St. Nicholas being at the southern end.

The village contains a good number of 17th-century timber-framed houses, most of which have been altered and added to in later times. Remains of a moat exist near the church.

An Inclosure Act for Chearsley was passed in 1805.[2] There is a small Baptist chapel in the village, built in 1854.

Chearsley has been thought to be identical with ' Cerdicesleah,' at which Cerdic and Cynric fought with the Britons in 527.[3]

There is a tradition that the lord's gallows formerly stood on the hill near the cross-roads ; the discovery of several skeletons close by tends to bear out the story.[4]

A few details concerning the land of the parish, given during legal proceedings in the 17th century, help us to form some idea of the local conditions at that date.[5] It appears that the meadows lying near the river and other brooks being frequently ' flotten and utterly spoiled ' by floods, and ' being exceeding fruitful, mellow and tender,' were often so overstocked with cattle that many rotted. The manor lay in open fields and was ' a champion place ' with a very fertile

and fruitful soil which was ' oftentimes hurtful and very casual ' for sheep but excellent for other animals, although there was no convenient cow pasture save among the corn and grain which ' by reason thereof is much spoiled.'

MANORS Six thegns held a manor in Chearsley before the Conquest, and in 1086 it formed part of Walter Giffard's lands.[6] Since the manor was parcel of the honour of Giffard,[7] the overlordship passed to the Earls of Pembroke[8] and descended with the manor of Pollicott in Ashendon[9] (q.v.), the lords of this manor retaining rights in Chearsley as late as 1739.[10]

The tenants at the time of the Survey were Ernulf and Geoffrey.[11] In 1166 Hugh de Cressy held a fee in this county of the Giffard Honour.[12] His son Roger[13] died in 1246, leaving a son and heir Hugh,[14] who in 1255 held Chearsley in demesne.[15] Stephen de Cressy, brother of this Hugh, inherited about 1263,[16] and in 1268 Richard de St. Denis, Stephen's heir, sued for his right in the manor against William de Valence, who was at that time overlord (see Pollicott), and who claimed the manorial rights by a grant from his brother, the king.[17] As a result of the suit Richard quitclaimed all right, and for some time after this the chief lord appears to have held the manor in demesne.[18] Aymer de Valence, son of William, succeeding in 1296,[19] made a life grant of Chearsley to Peter de Carbonel, Isabel his wife, and John their son in survivorship, for an annual rent of £4.[20] After the death of Aymer in 1324,[21] the partition of his inheritance gave rise to disputes, but eventually the annual rent and the reversion of the manor were assigned to David de Strabolgi, Earl of Athole, and Joan his wife,[22] niece and co-heir of Aymer.[23]

Their son David, a rebel, forfeited his lands to the king, who made a grant in fee of the manor,[24] after the Carbonels should die, to Sir Walter Mauny, kt.,

[1] Statistics from Bd. of Agric. (1905).
[2] Priv. Act, 45 Geo. III, cap. 86.
[3] *Angl.-Sax. Chron.* (Rolls Ser.), i, 26.
[4] Lipscomb, *Hist. and Antiq. of Bucks.* i, 122.
[5] Chan. Proc. (Ser. 2), bdles. 333, no. 1; 398, no. 110.
[6] *V.C.H. Bucks.* i, 248.
[7] *Hund. R.* (Rec. Com.), i, 23.
[8] *Testa de Nevill* (Rec. Com.), 247.
[9] *Feud. Aids,* i, 121 ; Chan. Inq. p.m. 3 Hen. VI, no. 39 ; 8 Hen. VI, no. 38 ; Feet of F. Bucks. Mich. 22 Jas. I.

[10] Com. Pleas Recov. R. East. 12 Geo. II, m. 20. [11] *V.C.H. Bucks.* i, 248.
[12] *Red Bk. of Exch.* (Rolls Ser.), 312.
[13] Dugdale, *Baronage,* i, 108.
[14] Fine R. 30 Hen. III, m. 4.
[15] *Testa de Nevill* (Rec. Com.), 247 ; *Hund. R.* (Rec. Com.), i, 23.
[16] *Cal. Inq. p.m.* (Hen. III), i, 170 ; *Excerpta e Rot. Fin.* (Rec. Com.), ii, 398.
[17] *Cal. Chart. R.* 1257-1300, p. 92 ; *Abbrev. Plac.* (Rec. Com.), 208.
[18] *Feud. Aids,* i, 75.
[19] Chan. Inq. p.m. 24 Edw. I, no. 56 ;

Cal. Close, 1296-1302, p. 3 ; *Feud. Aids,* i, 95, 113.
[20] Chan. Inq. p.m. 17 Edw. II, no. 75.
[21] Ibid.
[22] *Cal. Close,* 1323-7, p. 446 ; 1330-3, pp. 456, 584 ; Chan. Inq. p.m. 20 Edw. II, no. 60.
[23] G.E.C. *Peerage,* i, 182.
[24] The reversion of the manor was stated in 1328 to belong to Elizabeth Comyn, another co-heir of Aymer de Valence (see Pollicott) (Chan. Inq. p.m. 2 Edw. III [1st nos.], no. 35).

in 1335.[25] Sir Walter granted the reversion to Sir John de Moleyns, kt., in 1339.[26] Peter de Carbonel died about 1328,[27] and Isabel de Carbonel, who obtained a confirmation of her right in 1329,[28] still held in 1346.[29] Both she and her son John were dead by 1353,[30] when Sir John de Moleyns obtained full possession, and from this date Chearsley descended with the manor held by this family in Stoke Poges [31] until 1537, when George son of Edward Lord Hastings and Mary Baroness de Moleyns [32] joined with his son Sir Francis Hastings in conveying the manor to Sir John Baldwin, kt.[33] He was lord of Danvers in Little Marlow (q.v.), with which Chearsley descended until 1594–5, when William Borlase alienated it to John Dormer.[34] He already held Long Crendon Manor (q.v.), with which Chearsley descended, until the Cottrell-Dormers alienated the former about the middle of the 18th century.[35] Sir Charles Cottrell-Dormer made a settlement of Chearsley in 1745,[36] and by his will, proved in October 1779, left it to his son Clement,[37] lord of the manor in 1805.[38] On his death three years later [39] his son Charles succeeded him and was dealing with Chearsley in 1822.[40] From him the manor appears to have passed between 1844 and 1854 to Captain Wyndham,[41] who was still lord in 1864. By the following year the property had come to Richard Roadnight.[42] The trustees of Mr. Richard Roadnight are now among the principal landowners in the parish and his executors hold the Manor Farm.

The lord of the manor held view of frankpledge in Chearsley in 1254–5,[43] and it was still among his rights in 1594–5, when he was also stated to hold free warren, return of writs, goods and chattels of felons and fugitives and other privileges,[44] which had been granted in extenso to John de Moleyns in 1339.[45] A windmill is mentioned among the appurtenances of the manor in 1296 [46] and in later inquisitions.[47] A deed of 1822 mentions two windmills and two water corn-mills here.[48]

In 1254–5 Hugh de Cressy claimed a common fishery in the waters of Chearsley against John de Columbars; the latter gave up all his claim, receiving in return from Hugh certain fishery rights.[49] Free fishery was held by subsequent lords until 1627 or later.[50]

In 1356–9 the Prior of Rochester, holding the manor of Haddenham, adjacent to Chearsley, complained that his free fishery in the Thame was greatly interfered with by five weirs which Sir John de Moleyns had raised ; the sheriff, having made a survey, caused the weirs to be thrown down.[51] In 1363 Sir William de Moleyns brought a suit for trespass in his fishery against the Abbot of Nutley.[52]

The manor afterwards known as *BUCKTOFTS* probably originated in the half-fee held here of the honour of Giffard in 1254–5 by John de Columbars.[53] It was held by William de Columbars in 1284–6,[54] and in 1294–5 Joan daughter of William conveyed a messuage, land and rent in Chearsley to Michael de Drokensford.[55] John de Drokensford, probably the son of Michael,[56] held part of a fee here in 1302.[57] In 1325 Ellen de Boketot or Bucktoft, widow of Thomas de Bucktoft,[58] held a tenement consisting of a messuage, garden, land, rents of free and customary tenants and works.[59] Philip de Bucktoft her son [60] held in 1346 [61] a part of Chearsley which had formerly belonged to the Drokensfords.[62] The manor seems to have passed to Sir Edmund Hampden, kt., before 1465,[63] and was granted, after his attainder, to Richard Croft and Thomas Croft for life,[64] but there is no further record of it.

The Domesday Survey shows that 1½ hides of land which Alden, a man of Earl Harold, had held belonged in 1086 to Miles Crispin.[65] It afterwards belonged to the honour of Wallingford, passing with it to the Earls of Cornwall,[66] the last mention of this overlordship occurring in 1469.[67] The sub-tenant in 1086 was Richard,[68] who also held 4 hides in Ickford [69] (q.v.), and these two holdings were assessed together in the 13th century as a fee in Ickford and Chearsley.[70] In the early part of that century Walter son of John held the Chearsley portion for half a fee, and the Ickford portion, also accounted half a fee, was held by Thomas de Appleton.[71] He was in possession of the whole fee in 1235,[72] but subinfeudated half a fee consisting of the Chearsley portion and 2 virgates in Ickford,[73] and later, in 1270, alienated the overlordship rights in this part to Denise de Stokes.[74] There was some doubt as to the validity of the conveyance, for in 1284 the heir of Thomas de Appleton was said to be overlord of this half-fee,[75] and an inquisition was held in 1292 as to alienation of lands in Chearsley and Ickford, at that time held by Denise de Stokes and her son Robert.[76] The Stokes's claims were evidently overruled, as Walter son of Thomas de Appleton was stated to be overlord of this half-fee in 1302.[77]

[25] *Cal. Pat.* 1334–8, p. 89.
[26] Ibid. 1338–40, p. 348 ; Feet of F. Bucks. Mich. 13 Edw. III, no. 15.
[27] Chan. Inq. p.m. 2 Edw. III (1st nos.), no. 35.
[28] *Cal. Pat.* 1327–30, p. 382.
[29] *Feud. Aids,* i, 121.
[30] *Cal. Pat.* 1350–4, p. 437.
[31] See Stoke Poges.
[32] *G.E.C. Peerage,* iv, 287.
[33] Recov. R. Trin. 28 Hen. VIII, m. 505 ; Feet of F. Bucks. Mich. 29 Hen. VIII ; Hil. 29 Hen. VIII ; Com. Pleas D. Enr. East. 29 Hen. VIII.
[34] Feet of F. Bucks. Mich. 37 Eliz.
[35] Ibid. Mich. 15 Jas. I.
[36] Ibid. Div. Co. East. 18 Geo. II.
[37] P.C.C. 408 Warburton.
[38] Priv. Act, 45 Geo. III, cap. 86.
[39] Burke, *Landed Gentry* (1906).
[40] Recov. R. East. 3 Geo. IV, m. 9.
[41] Lipscomb, op. cit. i, 118 ; Sheahan, *Hist. and Topog. of Bucks.* 347.

[42] *Ret. of Owners of Land,* 1873, Bucks. 17.
[43] *Hund. R.* (Rec. Com.), i, 23.
[44] Feet of F. Bucks. Mich. 37 Eliz.
[45] *Cal. Chart. R.* 1327–41, p. 463.
[46] Chan. Inq. p.m. 24 Edw. I, no. 56.
[47] Ibid. 17 Edw. II, no. 75.
[48] Recov. R. East. 3 Geo. IV, m. 9.
[49] Feet of F. case 16, file 33, no. 1.
[50] Chan. Inq. p.m. 24 Edw. I, no. 56 ; 4 Ric. II, no. 38 ; 17 Hen. VI, no. 52 ; (Ser. 2), ccccxxxv, 112.
[51] Chan. Inq. p.m. 33 Edw. III (2nd nos.), no. 84 ; *Cal. Pat.* 1358–61, p. 247.
[52] De Banco R. 414, m. 157.
[53] *Hund. R.* (Rec. Com.), i, 23 ; *Testa de Nevill* (Rec. Com.), 247.
[54] *Feud. Aids,* i, 75.
[55] Feet of F. case 17, file 53, no. 9.
[56] Wrottesley, *Ped. from Plea R.* 41.
[57] *Feud. Aids,* i, 95.
[58] Feet of F. Bucks. Hil. 6 Edw. III, no. 1.

[59] Chan. Inq. 17 Edw. II, no. 75.
[60] *Cal. Close,* 1323–7, p. 366.
[61] *Feud. Aids,* i, 121.
[62] Ibid. 95.
[63] Chan. Inq. p.m. 4 Edw. IV, no. 43.
[64] *Cal. Pat.* 1461–7, p. 473 ; *Parl. R.* v, 589.
[65] *V.C.H. Bucks.* i, 261.
[66] *Testa de Nevill* (Rec. Com.), 261 ; *Hund. R.* (Rec. Com.), i, 23.
[67] Chan. Inq. p.m. 21 Edw. I, no. 28a.
[68] *V.C.H. Bucks.* i, 261.
[69] Ibid.
[70] *Testa de Nevill* (Rec. Com.), 258.
[71] Ibid. 247.
[72] Ibid. 258.
[73] *Feud. Aids,* i, 76.
[74] Feet of F. Div. Co. Hil. 54 Hen. III, no. 43.
[75] *Feud. Aids,* i, 76.
[76] Chan. Inq. p.m. 21 Edw. I, no. 28a.
[77] *Feud. Aids,* i, 95.

CHEARSLEY CHURCH FROM THE SOUTH-EAST

CHEARSLEY CHURCH: THE INTERIOR LOOKING EAST

The subinfeudation had taken place before 1254, when Walter Knight was holding.[78] In 1284[79] and 1292 John Knight was in possession.[80] This estate had passed by 1302 to Thomas de Zouche,[81] who was probably a relative of the Knights, as it was held in 1346 by a member of this family, Walter,[82] whose name occurs in connexion with Chearsley in 1324[83] and in 1342.[84] The property seems to have come into possession of the Brightwell family by the 15th century. William Brightwell of Chearsley is mentioned in 1434,[85] and Walter Brightwell, who died before 1468, was seised of six messuages and about 250 acres of land in Chearsley, Warmeston and Quainton, which

BRIGHTWELL of Chearsley. *Argent a cross sable with five quatrefoils argent thereon.*

he had granted to feoffees with intent to defraud the king of the custody and marriage of the heir, Walter's son Nicholas.[86] The king granted the custody to Richard Fowler in 1469.[87] In 1616 John Brightwell made a settlement of this land on the marriage of his son Thomas with Ann Lamborne.[88] Thomas died in 1633, the property being called by the name of *BRIGHTWELL'S FEE* in his inquisition.[89] His heir was his son John, a minor,[90] who in 1666 was complainant in a dispute over the conversion of arable land into pasture for his cattle.[91] No later reference to this estate has been found.

CHURCH   The church of *ST. NICHOLAS* consists of a chancel measuring internally 20 ft. 6 in. by 14 ft., north vestry, nave 44 ft. 6 in. by 18 ft. 6 in., west tower 12 ft. by 11 ft., and south porch, the last being built of brick, while the other parts are of stone rubble roofed with tiles.

The nave dates from about 1300, the tower from the early part of the 15th century, and the chancel, which was probably erected at the same time as the nave, was rebuilt about 1480, when it seems to have been widened towards the north. The porch and vestry are modern.

The chancel is lighted from the south by two late 15th-century windows of two lights under square heads, and on the north are two similar windows, but the westernmost has been blocked. The east window is modern. A pointed doorway with moulded jambs, in the north wall, and a similar one in the south wall, both probably dating from the end of the 13th century, have been reset in the walls, and the chancel arch, which is of the same period, has also been rebuilt, and now centres neither with the chancel nor the nave. In the south wall is a piscina with a sexfoil bowl. The timber roof dates from the late 15th century, but has been restored.

The north and south doorways of the nave, which have pointed heads and moulded jambs, and a lancet window in each of the north and south walls, are all probably original; in each side wall there are also a modern window and a 15th-century window of three lights under a square head, while at the south-east is a two-light window of about 1600, near the square head of which a head corbel has been reset in the wall. The north doorway has been partly blocked and the upper part glazed. The pointed tower arch on the west appears to have been rebuilt about 1480. The nave has a fine timber roof, with curved braces and foliated struts, which probably dates from the late 14th century; it appears to have been somewhat altered about 1500, and has been repaired at a modern period. The original pitch can be traced on the tower wall.

The tower is of two stages with a stair turret at the south-east rising above the embattled parapet. The west window, of two cinquefoiled lights with tracery in a pointed head, is original, and retains in its head some fragments of painted glass. In each wall of the bell-chamber is a window of similar character, also original.

In the chancel is a brass with the inscription, 'Her lyth John Frankeleyn & Margarete hys wyff which ordeyned [ ]stowe to this chirch & divine service to be doone every day in the [ye]r. A°.M.CCCC.LXII. on whos soules god have mercy Amen.' Above the inscription are their figures, and below are groups of three sons and four daughters.

The font has an early 13th-century circular bowl, with a cable mould round the rim and a band of foliated ornament; it stands upon a later octagonal stem and moulded base.

In the churchyard is the octagonal base and part of the stem of a mediaeval churchyard cross.

There is a ring of three bells in the tower: the first, inscribed 'Sancte Paule Ora Pro Nobis. W.H.,'[91a] is of about 1500; the second is by Thomas Lester of London, 1741, and the third by Henry Knight, 1616. There is also a sanctus, with no inscription.

The communion plate consists of a silver cup of 1569, with a cover; a modern silver paten; and a modern plated flagon.

The registers begin in 1570.

ADVOWSON   The church of Chearsley, anciently a chapel to Crendon, formed part of the original endowment of the abbey of Nutley, founded in the early 12th century by Walter Giffard.[92] The grant was confirmed by later deeds,[93] and the abbey continued to hold until the Dissolution.[94] In 1535 the rectory was valued at £10 10s. annually, from which sum an annual pension of 22s. was paid to the rector of Ickford.[95] Henry VIII granted the rectory and advowson of the vicarage to the Dean and Canons of Christ Church, Oxford, in 1542.[96] In 1579 both were granted to Nicholas

[78] *Hund. R.* (Rec. Com.), i, 23.
[79] *Feud. Aids*, i, 76.
[80] Chan. Inq. p.m. 21 Edw. I, no. 28a.
[81] *Feud. Aids*, i, 95.
[82] Ibid. 121.
[83] *Cal. Close*, 1323–7, p. 321.
[84] Feet of F. case 19, file 84, no. 2.
[85] *Cal. Pat.* 1429–36, p. 398.
[86] Chan. Inq. p.m. 8 Edw. IV, no. 23.
[87] *Cal. Pat.* 1467–77, p. 152.

[88] Chan. Inq. p.m. (Ser. 2), ccccxciv, 8.
[89] Ibid.
[90] Ibid. Thomas's widow, Ann, held in 1635 (Chan. Proc. [Ser. 2], bdle. 398, no. 110).
[91] Chan. Proc. (Bridges Div.), bdle. 594, no. 109.
[91a] Probably by William Hasylwood of Reading (Cocks, *Church Bells of Bucks.* 340).
[92] *V.C.H. Bucks.* i, 377, 379; *Cal. Rot. Chart.* 1199–1216 (Rec. Com.), 46.

[93] *Cal. Chart. R.* 1300–26, p. 210; *Cal. of Papal Letters*, v, 508.
[94] About the middle of the 15th century a quarrel arose between the abbot and his Crendon parishioners as to the right of burial in Chearsley churchyard (Linc. Epis. Reg. Memo. Chedworth, fol. 31).
[95] *Valor Eccl.* (Rec. Com.), i, 232. This pension was 20s. in 1291 (*Pope Nich. Tax.* [Rec. Com.], 34).
[96] *L. and P. Hen. VIII*, xviii, g. 881 (26).

Clerke, Helen Towers, widow, and William Fitz William, jun., to be held in turn by each.[97] The Fitz Williams held in 1595[98] and conveyed to Sir Robert Dormer in 1598,[99] and the property then followed the descent of the manor until after 1864.[100] Since that date the right of presentation has several times changed hands. It was held by J. Oades in 1870 and by D. Bradley in 1877. It is now in the hands of Col. F. T. H. Bernard.

In the Chantry Returns made in the reign of Edward VI it was found that the annual rent of 12*d.* from a rood of meadow in Chearsley was given for the maintenance of a lamp within the church.[101] This rood, lying in the west of the parish, was granted to John Howe and John Broxholme in 1549.[102]

CHARITIES

John Hart, by his will proved in the P.C.C. 15 May 1665, devised (*inter alia*) an annual rent-charge of £2 issuing out of Easington Manor, Oxfordshire. A sum of £97 0*s.* 3*d.* consols, arising from accumulations, is also held by the official trustees in trust for this charity. By a scheme of the Charity Commissioners of 14 April 1905 the annuity of £2 (less land tax) and the annual dividends, amounting to £2 8*s.* 4*d.*, are made applicable for apprenticing a boy or girl, or in defraying the cost of an outfit of an apprentice.

Church Land.—There are in the parish 5 acres of land so called, the rents of which are applied for purposes connected with the church.

CHILTON

Ciltone (xi cent.) ; Chiltone (xii cent.) ; Schelton (xiii cent.).

This parish, which lies 3½ miles south-east of Brill, contains 2,067 acres. About 404 of these are arable, 19

CHILTON HOUSE

woodland and the rest laid down in permanent grass,[1] the soil being loam and clay on a subsoil of Kimmeridge Clay. Most of the parish is rather over 300 ft. above the ordnance datum, but a central ridge rises to 450 ft. The village lies on the road from Long Crendon and contains several brick and timber houses of the 16th and 17th centuries. The vicarage, though cased with later brick, is of the latter date, while the post office is probably of mediaeval origin. All, however, have been much altered and added to in later times. Chilton Park Farm, in the north-west corner of the parish and about 1½ miles from the village, is an interesting example of a late 16th-century house, much altered, but retaining several original features. This is 'the lodge in the park of Chilton' of 1607.[2]

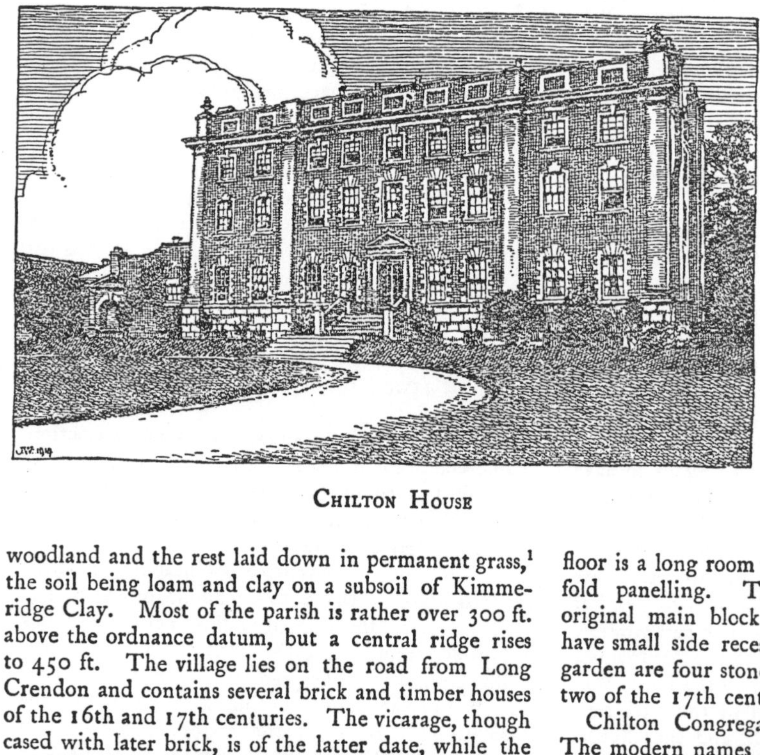

Chilton House, which stands to the east of the church, is a rectangular building of red brick with stone dressings, three stories in height, with an attic. Though it was practically rebuilt in 1740, remains of the house erected here in the 16th century survive in the north and south fronts and the cellars. The plan seems to have been originally ⌐-shaped with the wings projecting westward, but the space between the wings was inclosed in 1740 when the east and west fronts were rebuilt. There is an original four-centred doorway on the south front with a contemporary four-light window above it, and on the north front, besides traces of blocked windows, there are two old chimney stacks of brick surmounted by diagonal shafts. There is an early 17th-century moulded fireplace in one room on the first floor, and three other rooms have re-used panelling of the same period, while on the second floor is a long room with re-used 16th-century linenfold panelling. The cellars which lie under the original main block are barrel-vaulted in brick and have small side recesses. In the walls of the north garden are four stone doorways, two of the 16th and two of the 17th century.

Chilton Congregational chapel dates from 1887. The modern names of Chilton Grove and Hornage Farm recall 'Le Grove' of 1316[3] and 'Harnage' of 1607[4] and probably mark the site of the farms bought by the Deloraine family in the reign of Queen Anne.[5] About 1544 140 acres of waste called Fyppenhoe or Phippenhoo were inclosed by John Croke with the consent of the lords and tenants of Brill and Dorton who had right of pasture there,[6] and were known henceforward as Chilton Park.[7] Place-names of the 14th century are Le

[97] Pat. 30 Eliz. pt. xv, m. 1.
[98] Feet of F. Div. Co. Trin. 37 Eliz.
[99] Ibid. Bucks. Trin. 40 Eliz. ; Recov. R. Trin. 40 Eliz. m. 33.
[100] See manor.

[101] Chant. Cert. 5, no. 57.
[102] Pat. 3 Edw. VI, pt. ii, m. 27.
[1] Statistics from Bd. of Agric. (1905).
[2] P.C.C. 50 Dorset.
[3] Chan. Inq. p.m. 9 Edw. II, no. 55.

[4] P.C.C. 50 Dorset.
[5] Sheahan, *Hist. and Topog. of Bucks.* 351.
[6] Exch. Dep. East. 26 Eliz. no. 5.
[7] Ibid. ; Lansd. MS. 47, fol. 3.

Grascrofte and Leverecheshanger,[8] of the 17th Worland, Beanyfield or Benyfields and Duas Lawnes.[9]

MANORS The manor of *CHILTON*, which Alric, son of Goding, a king's thegn, had held before the Conquest, belonged to Walter Giffard in 1086.[10] As parcel of the honour

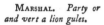

MARSHAL. *Party or and vert a lion gules.*

CLARE. *Or three cheverons gules.*

of Giffard[11] it came to William Marshal, Earl of Pembroke, by his marriage with Isabel de Clare.[12]

After the death of Anselm, the last Earl of Pembroke of this house, his rights here descended to his sisters Isabel and Joan.[13] Gilbert de Clare, Earl of Gloucester, Isabel's grandson,[14] entered the chief manor of Chilton, presumably as overlord, on the death of the sub-tenant in 1272,[15] and it was held of his son and heir of the same name in 1314[16] and of Hugh Audley, Earl of Gloucester, in 1347.[17] From 1387 to 1399, however, at least some part was held of the Earls of Stafford.[18] In 1265, 1284, 1302, and 1323 the overlordship was ascribed to the Crown,[19] of which this manor was held by the service of one-twentieth of a knight's fee from 1488 to 1640.[20]

William de Valence, husband of Anselm Marshal's niece Joan,[21] seems to have been overlord of a half-fee in Chilton at the end of the 13th century,[22] as was his son Aymer in 1302[23] and 1324,[24] his great-great-grandson Richard Talbot in 1397.[25] Eleanor de Lucy, mesne lord here in 1284,[26] was followed in the 14th century by Adam and John Fitz Piers and their heirs successively.[27]

No record of the subinfeudation of Chilton before the 13th century survives. It was in the hands of Walter Giffard himself in 1086,[28] in the keeping of

the guardian of the honour of Giffard a hundred years later.[29] In the reign of Henry III the sub-tenant was Robert Grenville,[30] under whom Walter de Burgh held in 1236 and 1237.[31] Robert's tenure had ceased by 1244, when the king gave his possessions in Chilton to Paul Pever as escheat of the lands of the Normans.[32] In 1247 Paul's holding was further augmented by a gift of land here, similarly forfeited, which had belonged to Eustace Grenville.[33] Paul died in 1251,[34] when his widow Joan sold the marriage of their son Paul to John de Grey, who married him to his daughter.[35] Shortly afterwards Joan made a runaway match with John de Grey to avoid marriage with a foreigner,

PEVER. *Argent a cheveron gules with three fleurs de lis or thereon.*

Stephen de Salines, the king's choice.[36] The younger Paul Pever evidently died without issue before his mother Joan's death in 1256, when the custody of the heir, his brother John, was given to Master Peter Pever.[37] In 1261 this John son of Paul Pever was in possession of his inheritance[38] and died before Michaelmas 1267, when the custody of his lands was committed to the queen.[39] Emma, the widow, survived until 1272, when their son John was still a minor.[40] He afterwards acquired part of Marsworth Manor (q.v.), with which Chilton descended until 1429, when at the death of Thomas Pever it passed to Alice daughter of his daughter Mary by her second husband Richard Lord St. Maur and wife of William Lord Zouche.[41] A year after her maternal grandfather's death, when his heir, her step-brother John Broughton, was twenty-two,[42]

ZOUCHE. *Gules bezanty with a quarter ermine.*

a release was granted to her and her husband by John Pever of Chilton and other Buckinghamshire manors formerly of Thomas Pever.[43]

[8] Chan. Inq. p.m. 9 Edw. II, no. 55.

[9] Ibid. (Ser. 2), dcxiv, 76 ; P.C.C. 50 Dorset ; Exch. Dep. East. 3 Jas. II, no. 20. [10] V.C.H. Bucks. i, 248.

[11] Red Bk. of Exch. (Rolls Ser.), i, 69.

[12] G.E.C. Peerage, vi, 196-8 ; Testa de Nevill (Rec. Com.), 257.

[13] G.E.C. Peerage, vi, 203-4. [14] Ibid.

[15] Cal. Inq. p.m. (Edw. I), ii, 66.

[16] Ibid. (Edw. II), v, 342 ; Cal. Close, 1313-18, p. 134.

[17] Chan. Inq. p.m. 21 Edw. III (1st nos.), no. 59.

[18] Ibid. 10 Ric. II, no. 38 ; 16 Ric. II, pt. i, no. 27 ; 22 Ric. II, no. 46.

[19] Abbrev. Plac. (Rec. Com.), 166 ; Feud. Aids, i, 84, 94 ; Cal. Inq. p.m. (Edw. II), vi, 360. In the last Chilton is held of the king as of the honour of Gloucester as of the purparty of Hugh Audley. The forfeiture of the Grenvilles (see below) was perhaps the origin of the royal rights.

[20] Pat. 3 Hen. VII, pt. i, m. 22 ; Chan. Inq. p.m. (Ser. 2), cccxvi, 11 ; ccclxxxiii, 81 ; dcxiv, 76. In 1468 and 1471 the tenure was unknown (Chan.

Inq. p.m. 8 Edw. IV, no. 53 ; 11 Edw. IV, no. 40). A mesne lordship here was enjoyed by Joan widow of Gilbert de St. Owen in 1316 (Cal. Inq. p.m. [Edw. II], v, 377). It is possible that her husband had held in trust here for the earl (cf. Cal. Pat. 1307-13, p. 526). See also in Easington. [21] G.E.C. Peerage, vi, 203-4.

[22] Feud. Aids, i, 84 ; Lipscomb, Hist. and Antiq. of Bucks. i, 127.

[23] Feud. Aids, i, 94.

[24] Cal. Inq. p.m. (Edw. II), vi, 314. In 1314, however, and in 1347 the overlordship was the same as in the chief manor (see above).

[25] Chan. Inq. p.m. 20 Ric. II, no. 51.

[26] Feud. Aids, i, 84.

[27] Cal. Inq. p.m. (Edw. II), vi, 314 ; Feud. Aids, i, 120 ; Chan. Inq. p.m. 20 Ric. II, no. 51.

[28] V.C.H. Bucks. i, 248.

[29] Red Bk. of Exch. (Rolls Ser.), i, 69.

[30] Misc. Bks. (Exch. K.R.), vi, 168.

[31] Cal. Close, 1234-7, pp. 353, 423.

[32] Close, 28 Hen. III, m. 9. Between 1238 and 1242 Paul was guardian of the see of Winchester and Sheriff of Beds.

and Bucks. (Cal. Close, 1237-42, pp. 62, 285, 463).

[33] Cal. Chart. R. 1226-57, p. 328.

[34] Matt. Paris, Chron. Maj. (Rolls Ser.), v, 242.

[35] Ann. Mon. (Rolls Ser.), iii, 182-3.

[36] Ibid. ; Excerpta e Rot. Fin. (Rec. Com.), ii, 119, 167 ; Cal. Pat. 1247-58, p. 104.

[37] Ann. Mon. (Rolls Ser.), iii, 202 ; cf. ibid. 333 ; Assize R. 68, m. 9 d. ; and Feet of F. Bucks. Trin. 42 Hen. III, no. 11.

[38] Assize R. 58, m. 11 d.

[39] Abbrev. Plac. (Rec. Com.), 166 ; cf. ibid. 180, 184.

[40] Chan. Inq. p.m. 2 Edw. I, no. 65 ; Cal. Fine R. 1272-1307, p. 37.

[41] Chan. Inq. p.m. 10 Hen. IV, no. 38 ; Close, 2 Hen. VI, m. 12.

[42] Chan. Inq. p.m. 8 Hen. VI, no. 21.

[43] Close, 8 Hen. VI, m. 1. A settlement of Chilton had been made by Thomas Pever and his wife Margaret about 1390, probably on the marriage of their daughter Mary with her first husband John Broughton (Feet of F. Bucks. Trin. 13 Ric. II, no. 6).

As no other mention of this John Pever occurs, it is possible that John Broughton had assumed his grandfather's surname. He bore his father's, however, in a suit of 1434 touching land in Cornwall.[44] From William and Alice Zouche, Chilton descended to their son, another William Zouche.[45] He died in 1468, leaving a son John, aged eight,[46] and Katherine his widow held Chilton in dower with a second husband Sir Gilbert Debenham.[47] John Zouche was lord in 1485, when he fought at Bosworth on the side of Richard III,[48] and the manor was granted two years later to Sir John Risley, who had enjoyed the profits since the battle.[49] It was probably restored on the reversal of his attainder in 1495 to Lord Zouche,[50] whose son and heir, another John Lord Zouche, sold it in 1529 to John Croke,[51] or Le Blount, one of the six clerks, and afterwards a master, in Chancery.[52]

From this lawyer, lord in 1535,[53] Chilton descended to his son and heir Sir John Croke, who held his first court in 1554 after his father's death,[54] and died seised in February 1608–9.[55] His eldest son and heir of the same name, then a judge of the King's Bench,[56] settled the manor the same year, when his son John married Rachel daughter of Sir William Webb, on himself, after the death of his mother,

CROKE. *Gules a fesse between six martlets argent.*

Dame Elizabeth Croke, with successive remainders to his wife Katherine and John and Rachel.[57] He was seised at his death in January 1619–20, when Chilton descended to his son and heir the third Sir John Croke,[58] lord until 1640.[59] In 1642 his son and heir, another John Croke, was created a baronet by Charles I,[60] for whose service he had raised a troop.[61] The greater part of his inheritance, already impaired by the expenses of office incurred by his grandfather the judge[62] and further diminished by his loyalty,[63] was given up to his creditors a few years after the Restoration and his manor leased by the Crown to one of their number, Mrs. Ann Andrews.[64] In 1667

the false accusation of robbery brought by Sir John against Robert Hawkins, vicar of Chilton, completed his ruin.[65] The sales or mortgages of the park and small holdings in lands and tithes begun by his father were continued by himself and his son,[66] and he died a prisoner in the Fleet, March 1678–9.[67] He left the manor, manor-house, and park of Chilton to his daughter Margaret Hyde for the payment of his debts,[68] but his son and heir Sir Dodsworth Croke, bart., disputed the will in 1682.[69] In 1695 Jane Mathew, widow, conveyed to John Limbrey her right in the manor of Chilton,[70] which is said to have passed from Richard Limbrey to Edward Hervey six years later.[71] Another Edward Hervey in 1739 conveyed his rights here to Sir John Aubrey and Thomas Blackall,[72] who were probably acting on behalf of Richard Carter,[73] with whom both were connected by marriage.[74] On Richard's death in 1755 his estates descended to his son George Richard Carter.[75] He died in 1771, leaving two daughters and co-heirs,[76] the survivor of whom, Martha Catherine, brought Chilton to her husband John, afterwards Sir John, Aubrey.[77] On her death without issue Sir John is said to have given this manor to the Hon. Henry Grey Bennet, son of Earl Tankerville by Emma sister of Sir John's first wife Mary Colebrooke,[78] with remainder to Mrs. Ricketts.[79] Chilton has since followed the descent of Boarstall (q.v.), and Mr. Henry L. Aubrey-Fletcher is now lord of the manor.

A dovecote which belonged to the manor in 1626[80] had been succeeded by two dove-houses by 1739, when there was also a malt-house here.[81] View of frankpledge, an appurtenance from 1609 to 1640 with free warren,[82] in 1785 mentioned alone,[83] was held in this manor about 1547 of the king as parcel of the honour of Gloucester.[84]

Half a knight's fee in Chilton, probably once part of the undivided Grenville manor,[85] was in the possession of William Grenville in 1255,[86] of his son John[87] in 1284, 1301, and 1302,[88] and came afterwards to Sir Reginald Hampden through his marriage with Nichola, one of John's daughters and co-heirs.[89] From that date until 1553 it descended with the manor of Great Hampden[90] (q.v.). On the death

---

[44] Wrottesley, *Ped. from Plea R.* 351.
[45] Chan. Inq. p.m. 8 Edw. IV, no. 53.
[46] Ibid.
[47] Ibid. 11 Edw. IV, no. 40. In 1471 Gilbert was sued by Robert Duplage, tailor of London, who claimed 'Zouches manor' in Chilton in payment of debts (Early Chan. Proc. bdle. 34, no. 58).
[48] G.E.C. *Peerage*, viii, 224.
[49] Pat. 3 Hen. VII, pt. i, m. 22 ; Chan. Inq. p.m. (Ser. 2), xxiii, 57.
[50] G.E.C. *Peerage*, viii, 224. Chilton was not found amongst John Zouche's lands at his death in 1511 (Chan. Inq. p.m. [Ser. 2], lxix, 190).
[51] Feet of F. Bucks. Trin. 21 Hen. VIII; Croke, *Gen. Hist. of Croke Fam.* i, 401.
[52] *Dict. Nat. Biog.*
[53] *Valor Eccl.* (Rec. Com.), iv, 232.
[54] Chan. Proc. (Ser. 2), bdle. 68, no. 2.
[55] Chan. Inq. p.m. (Ser. 2), cccxvi, 11.
[56] P.C.C. 50 Dorset.
[57] Feet of F. Div. Co. Trin. 7 Jas. I ; Chan. Inq. p.m. (Ser. 2), ccclxxxiii, 81.
[58] Chan. Inq. p.m. (Ser. 2), ccclxxxiii, 81.
[59] Ibid. dcxiv, 76 ; Feet of F. Bucks. East. 2 Chas. I ; Mich. 10 Chas. I ; Mich. 13 Chas. I.

[60] G.E.C. *Baronetage*, ii, 241.
[61] Croke, op. cit. i, 488.
[62] Ibid.
[63] *Cal. Com. for Comp.* 68. He had trouble with tenants in 1656 (Chan. Proc. [Bridges Div.], bdle. 27, no. 28).
[64] Exch. Dep. Hil. 21 & 22 Chas. II, no. 6.
[65] *Dict. Nat. Biog.* ; Croke, op. cit. i, 488–96.
[66] Feet of F. Bucks. East. 2 Chas. I ; Trin. and Hil. 16 Chas. I ; East. 14 Chas. II ; Hil. 15 & 16 Chas. II ; Mich. 23 Chas. II ; Hil. 24 & 25 Chas. II ; Chan. Proc. (Bridges Div.), bdles. 460, no. 134, 181 ; 493, no. 72.
[67] G.E.C. loc. cit.
[68] P.C.C. 82 Cottle.
[69] Chan. Proc. (Bridges Div.), bdle. 503, no. 85 ; cf. Exch. Dep. East. 3 Jas. II, no. 20.
[70] Feet of F. Div. Co. Mich. 7 Will. III.
[71] Lipscomb, op. cit. i, 132.
[72] Feet of F. Bucks. Mich. 13 Geo. II.
[73] Lipscomb, loc. cit.
[74] Thomas Blackall was Richard Carter's step-son and Richard's daughter Mary married Thomas son of Sir John Aubrey (P.C.C. 36 Paul).

[75] Ibid. ; Lipscomb, op. cit. i, 133.
[76] P.C.C. 148 Trevor.
[77] Lipscomb, loc. cit.
[78] Ibid.
[79] See Boarstall.
[80] Feet of F. Bucks. East. 2 Chas. I.
[81] Ibid. Mich. 13 Geo. II.
[82] Ibid. Div. Co. Trin. 7 Jas. I ; Bucks. Mich. 10 Chas. I ; Chan. Inq. p.m. (Ser. 2), cccxvi, 11 ; dcxiv, 76.
[83] Feet of F. Bucks. Mich. 26 Geo. III.
[84] Ct. R. (Gen. Ser.), portf. 155, no. 13.
[85] See p. 23.
[86] *Hund. R.* (Rec. Com.), i, 25.
[87] Lipscomb, op. cit. i, 599.
[88] *Feud. Aids*, i, 84, 94 ; Feet of F. Bucks. 29 Edw. I, no. 3.
[89] Lipscomb, op. cit. ii, 231–4 ; *Cal. Inq. p.m.* (Edw. II), v, 377. In 1314 he is called Roger (*Cal. Inq. p.m.* [Edw. II], v, 342 ; *Cal. Close*, 1313–18, p. 134).
[90] Thomas Hampden who died in 1486 provided for some of his younger children from his manors of Chilton and Easington, one-third of which was claimed by his widow in dower in 1487 (Chan. Inq. p.m. [Ser. 2], xxiii, 47 ; P.C.C. 27 Logge ; De Banco R. Mich. 3 Hen. VII, m. 501).

of John Hampden in 1553 Chilton passed to his granddaughter Anne, wife of William Pawlet. In 1608 her granddaughter Elizabeth, and her husband, Oliver St. John, conveyed their rights in Chilton and Easington to Sir John Croke and other members of his family.[91] As no later mention of this manor occurs in public records it is probable that it was afterwards merged in the chief manor of Chilton.

Land in Chilton given in the 13th century to the abbey of Nutley[92] was the nucleus of the manor owned here by that house in 1535.[93] In 1542 this was granted under the title of *CANNON FARM* or *CANNON COURT* to John Croke,[94] who had begged Cromwell's mediation with the king in the matter three years before.[95] Having passed through various hands after the breaking up of the Croke estates it was finally purchased by Sir John Aubrey.[96]

EASINGTON (Hesintone, Essintone, Easyngdon), a manor which Alric, son of Goding, held before the Conquest, belonged to Walter Giffard in 1086, when it was assessed at 5 hides.[97] It was held of the Crown in chief until 1590,[98] from 1387 to 1523 as of the honour of Gloucester.[99]

Like Chilton (q.v.), Easington, of which Roger was sub-tenant in 1086,[100] came from the Giffards to the Marshals and from the Marshals to the Clares.[1] It does not seem to have been permanently subinfeudated by either family. Geoffrey de St. Martin held it of William Marshal in the reign of Henry III.[2] Gilbert de Clare, Earl of Gloucester, lord in 1284 and 1302,[3] granted Easington to Ralph de Badlesmere for life, and on Ralph's death, Joan, Gilbert's widow, gave a life interest in the manor to her husband's brother Guy, who died seised.[4] By her son Gilbert,[5] the last Earl of Gloucester of the house of Clare, who succeeded his mother in 1307,[6] Easington was settled in 1313 on Gilbert de St. Owen and his wife Joan, with reversion to himself should they die without issue.[7] In 1316 Joan was seised alone.[8] She seems afterwards to have married Nicholas de la Beche, who with his wife Joan, in 1318, called on the sisters and heirs of Earl Gilbert with their husbands, Hugh le Despencer the younger, Hugh Audley, and Roger Dammory, to warrant their possession of Easington against Maud, Gilbert's widow, who claimed a third of the manor in dower.[9] In 1346 Hugh Audley held Easington,[10] which came on his death, the

next year, to his daughter Margaret and her husband Ralph Lord Stafford.[11] Ralph, who obtained licence in 1350 to make a life grant of the manor to Edmund Mortayn, clerk,[12] was succeeded, since his eldest son was dead, by his second son Hugh.[13] He died seised in 1386,[14] and his title and lands descended to his son Thomas, after whose death in 1392[15] one-third of Easington was granted to his widow Anne, while the custody of the rest of the estate was given to Thomas, Duke of Gloucester, until William Stafford, his brother and heir,

STAFFORD. *Or a cheveron gules.*

should come of age.[16] William Stafford was succeeded at his death in 1395 by his brother Edmund[17] who died in 1403, leaving an infant son and heir Humphrey,[18] Duke of Buckingham from 1444 until his death in 1460 on the battlefield of Northampton.[19] His grandson Henry Duke of Buckingham was executed by Richard III in 1483,[20] when Easington was granted to Christopher Wellesbourne for life.[21]

On the reversal of the duke's attainder the manor was restored to his son Edward Duke of Buckingham,[22] in possession in 1505.[23] He was beheaded in 1521,[24] and Easington was granted to Sir Henry Marney, who was already enjoying the profits, in the following year,[25] and he died seised in 1523.[26] At the death without male issue of his son and heir John Lord Marney, in 1525,[27] Easington reverted to the Crown and was granted to William Cary in 1526.[28] He was succeeded in 1528 by his son and heir Henry,[29] who completed his sale of the manor to John Croke, lord of Chilton Manor, and his wife Prudence, in 1553.[30] John Croke was seised at his death the following year.[31] In 1587 his son and heir Sir John settled Easington on himself for life with remainders to his wife Elizabeth and their eldest son John.[32] This settlement was followed four years later by the sale of the manor by the younger John to his brother George,[33] to whom he conveyed it again in 1601.[34] Sir George disregarded his brother's request to allow his son and heir to redeem Easington,[35] and his widow, Mary, to whom he left the manor

[91] Feet of F. Bucks. Trin. 6 Jas. I.
[92] Boarstall Chartul. fol. 7; Sheahan, loc. cit.
[93] *Valor Eccl.* (Rec. Com.), iv, 232; Dugdale, *Mon.* vi, 280.
[94] *L. and P. Hen. VIII,* xvii, g. 220 (49).
[95] Ibid. xiv (2), 790.
[96] Sheahan, loc. cit.
[97] *V.C.H. Bucks.* i, 48.
[98] *Feud. Aids,* i, 84, 94, 120; Chan. Inq. p.m. 35 Edw. I, no. 47; (Ser. 2), lxxxi, 217; xlviii, 70; Pat. 33 Eliz. pt. i, m. 13.
[99] Chan. Inq. p.m. 10 Ric. II, no. 38; 4 Hen. IV, no. 41; (Ser. 2), xxxvi, 10.
[100] *V.C.H. Bucks.* i, 48.
[1] Misc. Bks. (Exch. K.R.), vi, 168; *Feud. Aids,* i, 84.
[2] Misc. Bks. (Exch. K.R.), vi, 168.
[3] *Feud. Aids,* i, 84, 94.
[4] Chan. Inq. p.m. 35 Edw. I, no. 47.
[5] *Cal. Fine R. 1272–1307,* p. 517.
[6] Chan. Inq. p.m. 35 Edw. I, no. 47.

[7] Feet of F. Div. Co. case 285, file 29, no. 83; De Banco R. 198, m. 97.
[8] *Feud. Aids,* i, 116.
[9] De Banco R. 230, m. 101; 231, m. 19 d.; 234, m. 107 d.
[10] *Feud. Aids,* i, 120.
[11] Chan. Inq. p.m. 21 Edw. III (1st nos.), no. 59.
[12] *Cal. Pat. 1348–50,* p. 570.
[13] G.E.C. *Peerage,* vii, 210.
[14] Chan. Inq. p.m. 10 Ric. II, no. 38.
[15] Ibid. 16 Ric. II, pt. i, no. 27.
[16] Close, 16 Ric. II, m. 20. Some of this property, including Little Brickhill, was accounted among the duke's possessions at his death in 1397 (Chan. Misc. Inq. file 266, no. 6b).
[17] Chan. Inq. p.m. 22 Ric. II, no. 46.
[18] Ibid. 4 Hen. IV, no. 41.
[19] G.E.C. *Peerage,* ii, 63–4; Chan. Inq. p.m. 38 & 39 Hen. VI, no. 59.
[20] G.E.C. *Peerage,* vii, 212.
[21] *Cal. Pat. 1476–85,* p. 418.
[22] G.E.C. loc. cit.
[23] Mins. Accts. Hen. VII, no. 1476.

[24] Chan. Inq. p.m. (Ser. 2), xxxvi, 10; Mins. Accts. Hen. VIII, no. 5808.
[25] Chan. Inq. p.m. (Ser. 2), xxxvi, 10; *L. and P. Hen. VIII,* iii (2), g. 2145 (18).
[26] Chan. Inq. p.m. (Ser. 2), xl, 7.
[27] Ibid. lxxxi, 217.
[28] *L. and P. Hen. VIII,* iv (1), g. 2002 (20); iv (2), 3087; Orig. R. (Exch. L.T.R.), 18 Hen. VIII, m. 23.
[29] Chan. Inq. p.m. (Ser. 2), xlviii, 70; see also *Acts of P.C.* 1552–4, p. 88; Orig. R. (Exch. L.T.R.), 6 Edw. VI, pt. ii, m. 71.
[30] Recov. R. Mich. 2 Edw. VI, m. 322; *Acts of P.C.* 1552–4, p. 88; Feet of F. Bucks. Hil. 6 & 7 Edw. VI.
[31] Memo. R. (Exch. L.T.R.), Mich. 1 & 2 Phil. and Mary, pt. i, m. 44.
[32] Feet of F. Div. Co. Trin. 29 Eliz.; Pat. 32 Eliz. pt. xxi.
[33] Pat. 33 Eliz. pt. i, m. 13; Feet of F. Bucks. East. 33 Eliz.
[34] Feet of F. Bucks. Mich. 43 & 44 Eliz.
[35] P.C.C. 17 Soame.

for life,[36] conveyed it to their son Thomas in 1646.[37] She appears, however, to have been in possession when she died in 1657,[38] possibly having survived Thomas, who is said to have left no issue.[39] The manor seems to have then descended to the daughters of Sir George Croke.[40] In 1686 it was sold by Richard Sherrard, Sir John and William Brownlow, and the daughters and heirs of John Green, Alice widow of Francis Johnson, Sybil wife of Adrian Gamlyn, and Jane Green, to Thomas Parsons.[41] Margaret, widow of Thomas, held in 1709.[42]

Forty years later Samuel Horne bought Easington of Gilbert Jackson and his wife Elizabeth, the younger Gilbert Jackson, and Richard Nevill Aldworth.[43] His son and heir, Edward Horne, sold the manor to John Aubrey in 1782,[44] and it has descended with Chilton (q.v.) from that time, Mr. Henry L. Aubrey-Fletcher being now lord.

There was a capital messuage in Easington in 1307.[45] View of frankpledge, which, with assize of

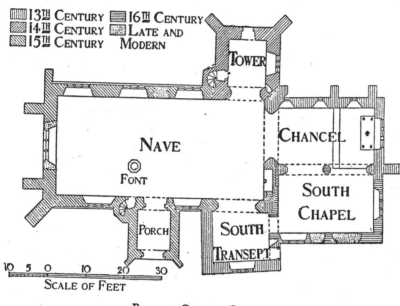

13TH CENTURY ▨ 16TH CENTURY
14TH CENTURY ▨ LATE AND
15TH CENTURY ▨ MODERN

TOWER

NAVE
FONT

CHANCEL

SOUTH CHAPEL

PORCH

SOUTH TRANSEPT

10 5 0 10 20 30
SCALE OF FEET

PLAN OF CHILTON CHURCH

(Adapted from the Inventory of the Historical Monuments of Buckinghamshire with the permission of the Royal Commission and the consent of the Controller of H.M. Stationery Office)

period was rebuilt about 1520. The tower dates from about 1350, and the porch was added in the 15th century when the nave was widened on the south side and practically rebuilt, perhaps incorporating a south aisle. The whole fabric was restored in 1907.

The chancel has a three-light, pointed window in the east wall and three lancets in the north wall, all dating from the late 13th century. On the south side is a 16th-century arcade of two four-centred arches with a central octagonal column; this has replaced a 13th-century arcade, the responds of which have been retained with the original bases and one original capital. In the north wall is a plain locker. The pointed chancel arch dates from about 1280, but seems to have been rebuilt in the 15th century when the bases of the responds were renewed. The high-pitched chancel roof, though much repaired, probably dates from the 15th century. The chapel is lighted by two windows, one in the east wall and one in the north wall, each of three cinquefoiled lights under a four-centred head, while a similar window and a doorway in the south wall are now blocked; in the west wall is a semicircular arch to the transept. Some fragments of 16th-century glass remain in the east window.

The nave has three traceried windows in the north wall and two in the south wall, all of three lights and dating from about 1480; a modern window has replaced one of the same period in the west wall, traces of which can be seen on either side. The north and south doorways, the former now blocked, are also of the late 15th century, as is a small doorway beside the latter admitting to the parvise stair; the south doorway has a pointed head and moulded jambs, and below the west window are traces of another doorway, now blocked. On the east side of the south doorway is a square-headed stoup. Opening into the tower at the east end of the north wall is a 14th-century pointed arch of three orders, and opposite to it on the south another pointed arch of about 1480, with responds having moulded capitals and bases, opens into the south transept. At the south-east of the nave is a 15th-century rood-loft stairway with the original upper and lower doorways. Adjoining the lower doorway on the north, and communicating with the stairway, is a contemporary arched recess which may have been constructed for the pulpit. The low-pitched nave roof probably dates from about 1580, but has been considerably repaired; on the wall

bread and ale, formed part of the grant to William Cary,[46] was an appurtenance of the manor in 1387.[47]

The church of *ST. MARY THE CHURCH VIRGIN* consists of a chancel measuring internally 25 ft. 6 in. by 14 ft., south chapel 25 ft. 6 in. by 15 ft., nave 54 ft. 6 in. by 25 ft. 6 in., north tower 12 ft. by 10 ft., south transept 15 ft. 6 in. by 13 ft., and a south porch. It is built of rubble and roofed with lead and tiles.

The north and east walls of the nave may be built on parts of the foundations of a 12th-century church, but the only detail of this period now surviving is a fragment reset in the south transept doorway. The chancel and south transept date from the late 13th century, and a south chapel erected at the same

[36] Croke, op. cit. i, 601.
[37] Recov. R. Mich. 22 Chas. I, m. 35; Com. Pleas D. Enr. Mich. 22 Chas. I, m. 15 d.   [38] Lipscomb, op. cit. i, 155.
[39] Ibid. 132.   [40] Ibid. 155.
[41] Close, 2 Jas. II, pt. xi, no. 21; Feet of F. Bucks. Mich. 2 Jas. II.
[42] Recov. R. East. 8 Anne, m. 73.
[43] Feet of F. Bucks. Trin. 22 & 23 Geo. II.
[44] Close, 22 Geo. III, pt. xvi, no. 11.
[45] Chan. Inq. p.m. 35 Edw. I, no. 47.
[46] Orig. R.(Exch. L.T.R.), 18 Hen. VIII, m. 23.
[47] Chan. Inq. p.m. 10 Ric. II, no. 38.

CHILTON : THE VILLAGE

CHILTON CHURCH : THE INTERIOR LOOKING EAST

CHILTON CHURCH FROM THE NORTH-WEST

CHILTON CHURCH FROM THE SOUTH

above the chancel arch can be seen the lines of an earlier roof of high pitch.

In the east wall of the south transept are a partly blocked 13th-century lancet and a small doorway in which some 12th-century work has been re-used. The window in the south wall, of three pointed lights with internal jamb shafts, probably dates from the 13th century. The tower is of two stages with diagonal buttresses on the north, a stair-turret at the south-west, and a plain parapet. The lower stage has a three-light traceried window on the east and one of two trefoiled lights on the north, both of about 1350, while below the latter is a doorway now covered with cement. The walls of the bell-chamber are pierced by small trefoiled lights. The south porch has a barrel vault divided by moulded ribs into five traceried compartments, and is entered through a richly-moulded archway flanked by diagonal buttresses. The parvise above the porch, approached by a stair-turret on the north-west, has a two-light window over the archway, and is surmounted by a plain parapet. The turret doorway retains an original traceried door.

The font is of the 15th century, and has an octagonal bowl on a moulded round stem and base. Incorporated in the quire stalls are two 16th-century bench-ends with poppy-heads and some traceried panels from a screen of the same period. Between the chancel and chapel is a 16th-century traceried screen, the uprights of which have been replaced by 17th-century balusters. On the east wall of the nave is a 17th-century wrought-iron hour-glass stand, and on a bracket in the chapel is a funeral helm of about 1500. There are some old encaustic tiles on the tower floor, while below the floor of the transept are some stone slabs which are probably mediaeval coffin lids.

In the south chapel are brass inscriptions to John Croke 'the ealder,' master in Chancery, who died in 1554, with a shield of Croke quartering Haynes; to Sir John Croke, judge of the King's Bench, who died in 1619; and to Edward Croke, who died in 1626, with a shield of Croke. Against the south wall of the chapel, surrounded by an iron railing, is an elaborate marble monument to Sir John Croke, who died in 1608, and his wife Elizabeth (Unton), who died in 1611, with their recumbent effigies, the knight wearing the armour of the period. They lie upon a rectangular tomb in a round-headed recess flanked by Corinthian columns supporting an entablature and pediment, and below are the kneeling figures of eight sons and three daughters. Above the kneeling figures are the shields of Croke and its alliances, and a shield over the pediment has the Croke crest, two swans' heads coming out of a crescent and holding a ring in their beaks. In the south transept is a marble monument to Elizabeth (Croke), wife of Sir John Tyrell of Heron, who died in 1631. Her kneeling figure with a chrisom child is placed in a recess flanked by Ionic

columns with a pediment above. In the chancel is a floor slab to Jane (Tryon), wife of John Croke, who died in 1636. There are also 18th-century monuments to the Carter family, besides later memorials to members of the Croke family. Outside in the east gable of the nave is set a cross-legged effigy of a knight of about 1280 in chain mail and long surcoat.

The tower contains a ring of three bells, all by Richard Keene, 1686, and a sanctus, which is probably by the same maker though it has no inscription.

The communion plate includes a chalice and cover of 1569, the latter being inscribed 'Chilton 1570.'

The registers begin in 1730.

ADVOWSON The church was granted by Walter Giffard to the abbey of Nutley and remained in its possession until the Dissolution,[48] when the church came to the Crown. It was granted by Henry VIII in 1542 to Christ Church Cathedral, Oxford.[49] Five years later the church of Chilton with the tithes of Easington came to Sir Anthony Lee and John Croke, the latter of whom was already tenant.[50] It has descended with the manor (q.v.) from that time.[51]

Half an acre of land given to find a lamp in this church and included in 1574 in a grant to Christopher Fenton and Bernard Gilpin seems to have lain in Dorton parish.[52]

CHARITIES In 1628 Nicholas Almond by deed conveyed to trustees a messuage with the appurtenances situate in the High Street of New Thame, Oxfordshire, upon trust to apply the rents for the benefit of the poor. The property is let at £35 a year, which is distributed in coal.

John Hart, by his will proved in the P.C.C., 15 May 1665, devised (*inter alia*) an annual rent-charge of £3 issuing out of the manor of Easington, Oxfordshire, for binding apprentice one poor boy.[53] The annuity (less land tax) is applied as occasion arises.

For the charity of Charles Aubrey Aubrey for keeping in repair the school buildings in this parish and Boarstall, see under the parish of Boarstall.

The Clerk's Close, the origin being unknown, consists of a furlong called Mill Way in a close containing 25 acres, in respect of which 10s. a year is paid to the clerk.

This parish has a share in the Studley Almshouses' Charity in Beckley, Oxfordshire, founded about 1640 by Sir George Croke. The charity is regulated by a scheme of the Charity Commissioners, 23 January 1880, whereby £20 a year is paid to the officiating minister at Horton (Oxon.), £10 to the vicar of Chilton and the residue of the net income for the benefit of the almshouses. The number of inmates is fixed at four; whereof two are men not less than sixty years of age and two are women not under fifty years. They are selected from Chilton, Waterstock or Beckley, or some place within six miles of the almshouses.

48 *Cal. Rot. Chart.* 1199-1216 (Rec. Com.), 46; Dugdale, *Mon.* vi, 278; *Valor Eccl.* (Rec. Com.), iv, 233.
49 *L. and P. Hen. VIII,* xvii, g. 881 (26).

50 Pat. 37 Hen. VIII, pt. xvi, m. 23.
51 Bacon, *Liber Regis.* 505; *Cler. Guide*; Crockford, *Cler. Dir.*

52 Pat. 16 Eliz. pt. xiv, m. 11.
53 P.C.C. 161 Hyde.

EAST CLAYDON

Claindone (xi cent.) ; Estcleydone (xiii cent.).

This parish contains 2,395 acres, including 1,936 acres of permanent grass and 181 acres of arable land.[1] The slope of the land above the ordnance datum varies from 295 ft. in the east of the parish to 407 ft. in the south-west, the soil being rich clay loam ; the subsoil clay and gravel. Wheat, beans, roots and oats are grown, but the chief industry is dairy farming. Pillow-lace was still made by women and children in East Claydon in 1862.[2] Grandborough Road station on the Metropolitan Extension railway and Winslow Road station on the Metropolitan railway are within the borders of this parish.

The village of East Claydon is situated on rising ground towards the north-west of the parish. White House Farm, the old manor-house, stands on a moated site near the church to the north. The oldest

house of about the same date, to which a stone front was added in 1675, the date being on a stone panel over the south doorway, with the initials $_E{}^V{}_M$ and a shield. A wing was added at the back of the house in the 18th century. At the corner of the road leading to Botolph Claydon is a picturesque L-shaped house of about 1600, timber framed, with later brick facing. The upper story of the east gable end overhangs, the projecting beams having curved brackets beneath.

Half a mile south-west of East Claydon is the village of Botolph Claydon (Botteclaydon, xiii cent. ; Botteleclaydon, xiv cent.), with Botolph House, a substantial brick and stone manor-house, the residence of Mrs. Verney, at its east end. Botyl Well, commonly corrupted into St. Botolph's Well, is reached by steps at its south-west end.

In this village are a number of small 17th-century timber-framed houses, mostly with red brick chimney-stacks, the most interesting one being at Bernwood Farm. It has closely set upright timbers, and is probably not later than about 1600; a wing was added in the 18th century. Claydon Mill appears to have stood in Botolph Claydon.[3]

THE WHITE HOUSE, EAST CLAYDON

MANORS In 1086 Miles Crispin held 7 hides 3 virgates of land in *EAST CLAYDON* as one manor.[4] This land was attached to the honour of Wallingford,[5] and with it transferred to the honour of Ewelme.[6] The last reference to this overlordship in East Claydon occurs in 1572.[7]

Miles Crispin had subinfeudated his manor in Claydon[8] before 1086 to Geoffrey.[9] This mesne overlordship had passed before 1234 to Peter

part dates probably from the end of Elizabeth's reign. The house stands east and west, with a wing at right angles at the south-west, in which is a good stone bay window with moulded mullions and transoms. The walls are in part of half-timber work and in part of brick and stone. The south front has an overhanging story with a plastered cove and moulded beams, and an added stone-faced porch of 17th-century date with a flat-arched entrance under a square head, flanked by fluted pilasters. The inner doorway is of oak with a moulded frame, and retains its old door. In one of the rooms is a stone arched fireplace. To the north-west of the church is a

de la Mare,[10] before 1302 to Robert de la Mare,[11] and by 1312 to Robert's son and heir Peter.[12] In 1346 it was appurtenant to the manor of Aylesbury,[13] and later in the century it was held by the Earl of Warwick, the last reference to it occurring in 1375.[14] Part of the Crispin manor in Claydon was split up and descended with neighbouring manors ; the remainder corresponds to the land which passed in the later 12th century in marriage with Maud de la Mare.[15] In 1199 her second husband, Giles de Pinkeny, surrendered his claim to hold it for life to her son William de Englefield.[16] This land was evidently the half-fee held in the middle 13th

[1] Statistics from Bd. of Agric. (1905).
[2] Sheahan, *Hist. and Topog. of Bucks.* 355.
[3] Chan. Inq. p.m. 6 Edw. II, no. 44 ; Rentals and Surv. (Gen. Ser.), portf. 5, no. 20. [4] *V.C.H. Bucks.* i, 261.
[5] *Feud. Aids,* i, 85, 93 ; Chan. Inq. p.m. (Ser. 2), v, 32 (*b*) ; xxxiv, 20 ; Ct. R. (Gen. Ser.), portf. 212, no. 18.

[6] Ct. R. (Gen. Ser.), portf. 212, no. 20, 21, 25.
[7] Chan. Inq. p.m. (Ser. 2), clx, 15.
[8] More frequently called Botolph Claydon in the 13th century.
[9] *V.C.H. Bucks.* i, 261.
[10] *Testa de Nevill* (Rec. Com.), 257*b*, 261. His ancestor Peter de la Mare held three fees of the honour of Wallingford

in the time of Henry II (*Liber Niger* [ed. 1771], i, 185).
[11] *Feud. Aids,* i, 93.
[12] Chan. Inq. p.m. 6 Edw. II, no. 44.
[13] *Feud. Aids,* i, 119.
[14] Chan. Inq. p.m. Edw. III, file 143, no. 8 ; 49 Edw. III (1st nos.), no. 59.
[15] Hunter, *Pedes Finium* (Rec. Com.), 181. [16] Ibid.

THE VILLAGE, EAST CLAYDON

BOTOLPH CLAYDON VILLAGE

century by Robert de Wimbervill,[17] since his kinsman, Roger de Wimbervill, was exempted from this service in 1248 by William de Englefield in exchange for a yearly rent of 46s. 8d.[18] Part of this land must have passed to Thomas de Valognes and formed part of the 13 virgates held by Robert de Grey in East Claydon in 1284.[19] His widow Joan de Valognes was holding the half-fee with a separate estate of 2 hides (see below) in 1302.[20] These, with 4 virgates of land of the honour of Peverel (see below) formed *CLAYDON* or *EAST CLAYDON MANOR*, of which Joan's grandson and heir John, Lord Grey of Rotherfield, died seised in 1359.[21] Until 1477 it descended with the manor of Shabbington, and afterwards with the secondary overlordship there, until 1543,[22] when it was sold by Henry Parker, Lord Morley, to Thomas King.[23] Thomas Lee of Moreton died seised of East Claydon Manor in 1572.[24] His son and heir Thomas,[25] afterwards Sir Thomas Lee, kt., sold it in 1624 to William Abel.[26] His son William Abel[27]

LEE of Moreton. *Azure two bars or with a bend checky or and gules over all.*

ABEL. *Argent a saltire engrailed azure.*

succeeded before 1659,[28] and died while sheriff for the county in 1661.[29] His daughter and heir Mary married Edmund Verney, eldest son of Sir Ralph Verney, the first baronet.[30] She survived her husband and their children, and on her death in 1715[31] East Claydon Manor passed to a cousin, William Abel.[32] In 1722 his children, Richard and Bridget Abel,[33] surrendered their interests in it to Messrs. Paltock & Snow,[34] and in 1728 it was purchased by

Ralph Viscount Fermanagh.[35] It has since passed with Middle Claydon (q.v.), and Sir Harry Calvert Verney, bart., is the present owner.

A manor of 7 hides in East Claydon, *CLAYDON* or *BOTOLPH CLAYDON MANOR*, was held before the Conquest by Suen, a man of Ansgar the Staller.[36] In 1086 it was held by Geoffrey de Mandeville.[37] The overlordship in the earldom of Hereford is traceable in the 13th century.[38] A mesne overlordship descended in the Fitz John (Fitz Geoffrey) family,[39] and was appurtenant in 1346 to the manor of Aylesbury[40] (q.v.).

Botolph Claydon had been subinfeudated to Thomas de Valognes in the middle 13th century,[41] and passed by the marriage of his daughter and heir Joan to Robert de Grey.[42] It descended with East Claydon Manor (q.v.), but its identity as a second manor was not recognized in the confirmation of the sale in 1624. A grant of free warren in East Claydon and Botolph Claydon was made to John de Grey in 1330.[43]

In 1086 William Peverel held 3 hides 1 virgate of land in [East] Claydon as a manor which had been formerly held by Alwin, one of King Edward's thegns.[44] The overlordship belonged to the honour of Peverel and is traceable in East Claydon until the end of the 14th century.[45]

William Peverel's manor in East Claydon was subinfeudated to Ralph in 1086.[46] In the middle 13th century Ralph son of Ralph de Quarrendon held the land by the serjeanty[47] of finding a horse, haversack and pack-saddle for the king when on expedition to Wales, and transferred it to Thomas de Argentein.[48] Subinfeudation had already begun. Nine virgates held at this time by Ralph de Quarrendon,[49] traceable in part as descending in his family and that of the Wades,[50] correspond to the land in East Claydon alienated in 1345 to Studley Priory by John Frelond and William atte Wood.[51] The priory lands here, valued at 40s. yearly in 1535,[52] were granted in 1540 to John Croke,[53] who did not retain them.[54] They, together with a messuage called Pontifex, were purchased from Arthur King by Simon Love, who died seised in 1574 (see advowson). In the 17th century the priory farm, evidently part of this estate, was under the same ownership as East Claydon Manor.[55] The

[17] *Testa de Nevill* (Rec. Com.), 245.

[18] Feet of F. Bucks. Mich. 32 Hen. III, no. 6.

[19] *Feud. Aids*, i, 85.

[20] Ibid. 93.

[21] See Shabbington. In 1312, John de Grey's property in East Claydon extended at £13 19s. 7d. yearly was granted in custody to John de Handlo during Grey's minority (*Abbrev. Rot. Orig.* [Rec. Com.], i, 194).

[22] See Shabbington. Sir Edward Howard and Alice his wife (Feet of F. Div. Co. Hil. 21 Hen. VII; De Banco R. 975, m. 308) were seised of East Claydon Manor in 1506 to the use of Henry and Alice Parker and their issue (Chan. Inq. p.m. [Ser. 2], xxxiv, 20).

[23] Com. Pleas D. Enr. Mich. 35 Hen. VIII, m. 1; Feet of F. Bucks. Hil. 35 Hen. VIII.

[24] Chan. Inq. p.m. (Ser. 2), clx,, 15.

[25] Ibid.

[26] Recov. R. Mich. 22 Jas. I, m. 87; Feet of F. Bucks. Hil. 22 Jas. I; Com. Pleas Recov. R. Trin. 1 Chas. I, m. 6 (confirmation of sale).

[27] M.I. in church.

[28] Com. Pleas Recov. R. Trin. 1659, m. 4.

[29] M.I. in church.

[30] *Verney Memoirs of the 17th cent.* ii, 23. His name occurs in a settlement of the manor in 1658 (Recov. R. East. 1658, m. 197). A shield of their arms impaled is over the south doorway of the old manor-house.

[31] *Verney Memoirs of the 17th cent.* ii, 487.

[32] M.I. in church.

[33] Ibid.

[34] Feet of F. Bucks. Mich. and Hil. 9 Geo. I.

[35] *Verney Memoirs of the 17th cent.* i, 24.

[36] *V.C.H. Bucks.* i, 259.

[37] Ibid.

[38] *Testa de Nevill* (Rec. Com.), 245.

[39] Ibid.; *Feud. Aids*, i, 85; Chan. Inq. p.m. 25 Edw. I, no. 50 b; *Cal. Close*, 1296–1302, p. 284.

[40] *Feud. Aids*, i, 119.

[41] *Testa de Nevill* (Rec. Com.), 245.

[42] *Feud. Aids*, i, 85.

[43] Chart. R. 4 Edw. III, m. 18, no. 44.

[44] *V.C.H. Bucks.* i, 253.

[45] *Testa de Nevill* (Rec. Com.), 245; Chan. Inq. p.m. 6 Edw. II, no. 44; *Cal. Pat.* 1321–4, p. 134; 1343–5, p. 544; Chan. Inq. p.m. Edw. III, file 245, no. 3, m. 7.

[46] *V.C.H. Bucks.* i, 253.

[47] *Testa de Nevill* (Rec. Com.), 245.

[48] Ibid. 257.

[49] Ibid.

[50] Chan. Inq. p.m. Hen. III, file 47, no. 6; Feet of F. Bucks. Mich. 1 Edw. I, no. 5; *Cal. Pat.* 1281–92, p. 29; Chan. Inq. p.m. 3 Edw. II, no. 28; 5 Edw. II, no. 2; *Cal. Pat.* 1321–4, p. 134.

[51] Chan. Inq. p.m. 18 Edw. III (2nd nos.), no. 47; *Cal. Pat.* 1343–5, p. 544.

[52] *Valor Eccl.* (Rec. Com.), ii, 186; the priory's estate in Botolph Claydon was assessed at this sum.

[53] *L. and P. Hen. VIII*, xv, g. 282 (109).

[54] Croke, op. cit. i, 436.

[55] Com. Pleas Recov. R. Trin. 1 Chas. I; Trin. 1659, m. 4.

EAST CLAYDON CHURCH FROM THE WEST

EAST CLAYDON CHURCH: THE INTERIOR LOOKING EAST

remaining 4 virgates of land, part of which was held by Richard de Argentein in the 13th century,[56] and conveyed by him in 1250 to Thomas de Valognes,[57] appear in 1359 as part of East Claydon Manor (q.v.).

Miles Crispin held 2 hides of land in Claydon in 1086, retaining as tenants two Englishmen formerly Harning's men.[58] This land was held by Thomas de Valognes in the middle 13th century, and afterwards formed part of East Claydon Manor[59] (q.v.).

The church of *ST. MARY THE VIRGIN* consists of a chancel 26 ft. by 14 ft. 6 in., with a modern north vestry, a nave 47 ft. 6 in. by 22 ft., with a south chapel 18 ft. 6 in. by 9 ft. 6 in., and a modern north aisle and south porch, and a west tower 11 ft. by 10 ft. These measurements are all internal.

The earliest part of the church, which at the beginning of the 13th century consisted of an aisleless nave and chancel, is the western half of the south wall of the nave. No details, however, of earlier date than the 13th century are to be seen. The south chapel was added to the nave about 1230, and the chancel was rebuilt about 1350. Towards the end of the 15th century, or a little later, the nave was widened northwards, thus being thrown out of centre with the chancel, while the tower, which is on the same axis as the nave, seems to have been added at the same time. The clearstory of the nave also belongs to this time, but owing to the rebuilding of the north wall when the modern north aisle was added, only the south side now remains.

The chancel is ashlar-faced and has a modern east window and two windows in the north wall, of which the western is much-repaired 14th-century work of two trefoiled lights with tracery, and the eastern a modern copy of it, retaining only a few old stones in its jambs to show that it represents an original window. Between them is a 14th-century doorway with four-leaved flowers in the head and jambs, now opening to the modern vestry, which overlaps the western window. The two windows in the south wall of the chancel are modern copies of the others. In the north wall of the chancel is a modern recess, containing the 14th-century jambs of what was doubtless a piscina, ornamented with rosettes and four-leaved flowers. The weathering of a steep-pitched roof, coeval with the chancel, shows on the east face of the east gable of the nave, but the present chancel roof is of low pitch, having a wagon-headed ceiling with egg and tongue ornament of the 17th century on its ribs. The chancel arch, which is of the date of the chancel, is of two chamfered orders, the inner order springing from corbels carried by grotesque winged figures.

The nave has a modern north arcade of three bays, but in the wall to the west of it is a much-restored lancet window, of which part is doubtless of 13th-century date, and the wall in which it is set, like the south wall of the nave, may be older. In the modern north aisle a late 15th-century doorway has been

reset near the east end of the north wall; it has a four-centred head and tracery in the spandrels. At the south-east angle of the nave the upper doorway of the rood-stair remains, with part of the stair, opening from the south chapel; the shouldered head of the doorway is not original. The south chapel opens to the nave by a plain pointed 13th-century arch with an indented label, and to the east of it is an opening from the chapel, of 15th-century date, made for the double purpose of giving a view of the chancel from the chapel and of lighting the nave altars; its west jamb is splayed outwards to command a wider view to the eastward. The chapel is lighted by five lancet windows, two on the east, two on the south, and one on the west, all with internal rebates for the glazing frames. In the south wall is an original piscina recess with a shouldered head. The south doorway of the nave is plain 13th-century work of a single order, and west of it is an uncusped two-light window, nearly all modern. Of the nave clearstory only the south side remains, with two square-headed windows of three cinquefoiled lights. The nave roof, of contemporary date, is low pitched and of plain character.

The tower is of three stages, ashlar-faced, with a stair turret at the south-west; the tower arch is of two chamfered orders, the inner order dying at the springing. The west doorway has a four-centred arch under a square head, and over it is a window of three cinquefoiled lights. In the second stage there is only one opening, a round-headed light in the north wall, while in each face of the third stage are two uncusped openings with square heads. There is an embattled parapet and flat leaded roof.

The plain octagonal font is of the 15th century. There are no other ancient fittings, but a small 17th-century communion table is preserved in the vestry.

In the chancel floor is the grave slab of William Abel, 1661, lord of the manor and sheriff in the year of his death. In the churchyard is a slab with the indent of a cross-brass.

There is a ring of five bells, all by Abel Rudhall, 1752. The sanctus bell, dated 1657, is probably by Anthony Chandler.

The plate includes a cup and cover of 1569.

The registers begin in 1584.

ADVOWSON The church of East Claydon, valued at £6 13s. 4d. in 1291,[60] is mentioned in 1312[61] as appurtenant to the land afterwards distinguished as Botolph Claydon Manor (q.v.). It descended in the Greys,[62] and was granted by John Lord Grey of Rotherfield[63] in 1371 to Bisham Priory, with licence to appropriate the church.[64] The Crown grant was ratified in 1409,[65] and a vicarage was ordained in 1421.[66] In the next century the advowson, valued at £8 yearly in 1535,[67] had passed with the rectory to the Knights Hospitallers.[68] The advowson was granted in 1551 to Lord Clinton[69] and transferred to William King,

[56] *Testa de Nevill* (Rec. Com.), 257.
[57] Feet of F. Bucks. Trin. 34 Hen. III, no. 9.   [58] *V.C.H. Bucks.* i, 261.
[59] *Testa de Nevill* (Rec. Com.), 245.
[60] *Pope Nich. Tax.* (Rec. Com.), 34. Deducting a pension of 10s. yearly to Wallingford Priory. This was increased to 16s. in 1369 (*Cal. Chart. in Bodl.* 6, quoting Wallingford Priory Charter). It was granted in 1532 to the trustees of

St. George's Chapel, Windsor (*L. and P. Hen. VIII*, v, 1351).
[61] Chan. Inq. p.m. Edw. II, file 29, no. 11.
[62] *Cal. Pat.* 1317-21, p. 409.
[63] Inq. a.q.d. file 378, no. 17; *Abbrev. Rot. Orig.* (Rec. Com.), ii, 323. Licence for him to alienate a messuage and 64 acres of land in East Claydon to Bisham Priory.

[64] *Cal. Pat.* 1408-13, p. 84.
[65] Ibid. Other particulars of the appropriation are given in *V.C.H. Berks.* ii, 83.
[66] Harl. MS. 6952, fol. 63.
[67] *Valor Eccl.* (Rec. Com.), iv, 236.
[68] Pat. 3 Edw. VI, pt. ix, m. 1, 2; W. and L. Inq. p.m. xvii, 19; Rentals and Surv. portf. 5, no. 72.
[69] Pat. 5 Edw. VI, pt. vi, m. 2.

who presented in that year.[70] Later in the century it was sold by Arthur King to Simon Love, who died seised in 1574 during the minority of his son and heir John.[71] Pardon for alienation to his executors in trust was granted in 1579.[72] His widow married John Morgan Wolfe, and they with John Love, who attained his majority in 1587,[73] sold East Claydon advowson in the same year to Robert Hoveden[74] (or Hovenden). Robert Hoveden was succeeded by his nephew Robert Hoveden in 1613.[75] After 1680[76] East Claydon advowson passed to two daughters and co-heirs,[77] one of whom, Diana, married Count Fieschi.[78] They conveyed it in 1726 to Ralph Verney,[79] who retained it.[80] From 1752, when he succeeded as Earl Verney, this advowson has descended with Middle Claydon[81] (q.v.), and the present owner is Sir Harry Calvert Williams Verney, bart.

In 1821 the vicarage of East Claydon was united with that of Steeple Claydon to the rectory of Middle Claydon,[82] and this union has continued in respect of East Claydon.

The rectory of East Claydon was granted in 1549 to George Wright and Eustace Moon.[83] Sir Robert Lane was seised of it in 1568, when he leased it to William King for twenty-one years.[84] Six years later

he sold the reversion to Alexander Denton,[85] and some of the tithes descended to his son Sir Thomas Denton.[86] In 1666 the rectory is named as in the possession of John Duncombe.[87]

William Spyrke, of Botolph Claydon, in his will dated 10 January 1451, left two sheep for the lights of St. Mary and the Holy Cross in the church of East Claydon.[88] A light was maintained in 1548 from the rent (2d. yearly) of half an acre of land in East Claydon.[89] This land was granted in 1586 to John Walton and John Cresset.[90]

CHARITIES
The following charities were consolidated by a scheme of the Charity Commissioners of 17 January 1913, namely : William Abel's charity, founded before 1721, consisting of a rent-charge of £4 ; Maurice Griffiths' charity, will 1673, consisting of a rent-charge of £2 ; and the Town stock, being an annuity of £1 12s. supposed to represent a gift of £34 by a donor unknown. These annuities, amounting together to £7 12s., are paid out of an estate at East Claydon now in the possession of Sir Harry Verney, bart., and are applied in the distribution of money among poor families, poor labourers, and a portion for the benefit of the sick and needy. (See also under Middle Claydon.)

MIDDLE CLAYDON

Claindone (xi cent.) ; Little Claydon (xiii, xiv cent.).

This parish has an area of nearly 2,640 acres, of which more than half is arable land, the remainder being divided between meadow and woodland.[1] The height of the land above the ordnance datum varies from 287 ft. to a maximum height of about 410 ft. at Runt's Wood in the south-east of the parish. The ancient Three Points Lane, running north-west to north of Runt's Wood, is part of the eastern boundary of the parish, and Claydon Brook bounds it on the north-west. The soil is clay loam with beds of sand and gravel ; the subsoil is clay. The chief feature of this parish is Claydon Park. Centrally situated, it covers over 300 acres, including three fine pieces of water. In it stands Claydon House, the seat of Sir Harry Calvert Williams Verney, bart., who owns the whole of the parish except the Glebe and a small portion belonging to the railway. Claydon House was originally built in the time of Henry VII, probably by Roger Gifford (or Giffard), lessee under the first Sir Ralph Verney.[2] Known as Gifford's Farmhouse in 1732,[3] it was enlarged by the first Viscount Fermanagh, and almost entirely rebuilt on a grand

scale from Adam's designs in the middle 18th century by Ralph, the second Earl Verney.[4] His successor, Mary Baroness Fermanagh, pulled down the greater part of the new building, retaining only the south front.[5] Considerable alterations and repairs were carried out in the mid-19th century.[6]

In its present state Claydon House, as far as external appearance goes, is a fine 18th-century building, but although retaining much 17th-century internal detail, it is probably of 16th-century construction. It is of three stories with an attic, the principal front looking westwards. The oldest detail is some panelling of early 17th-century date in an attic room, while on the ground floor are some ceiling beams of the middle of the 17th century, with a chimneypiece of the same date bearing the arms of Verney. A fine room on the first floor has chimneypiece, doorways and low panelling of the time of Charles II, and there is also some good later woodwork of the beginning of the 18th century, and an iron fireback dated 1664. The muniment room here contains many early documents and a large collection of letters chiefly of the 17th and 18th centuries.[7] The church stands to the south-west of Claydon House. The village of Middle

[70] Lipscomb, *Hist. and Antiq. of Bucks.* i, 171.

[71] W. and L. Inq. p.m. xvii, 19. Before the subsequent sale John Love secured his title against Arthur King and his wife Anne (Feet of F. Bucks. Mich. 29 Eliz.).

[72] Pat. 22 Eliz. pt. viii, m. 31. Reference to a grant in 1356 occurs in this document.

[73] Fine R. 30 Eliz. pt. ii, no. 22.

[74] Feet of F. Bucks. Hil. 30 Eliz. ; Pat. 33 Eliz. pt. viii.

[75] Chan. Inq. p.m. (Ser. 2), cccxliii, 152.

[76] Inst. Bks. (P.R.O.).

[77] Lipscomb, op. cit. i, 170, quoting

letter of Rev. F. Greene, then vicar, to Willis.

[78] Feet of F. Bucks. Trin. 12 Geo. I.

[79] Feet of F. Bucks. East. and Trin. 12 Geo. I.

[80] Inst. Bks. (P.R.O.).

[81] Bacon, *Liber Reg.* 505 ; Inst. Bks. (P.R.O.).

[82] Lipscomb, op. cit. i, 170, 189.

[83] Pat. 3 Edw. VI, pt. ix, m. 1, 2.

[84] Chan. Proc. (Ser. 2), bdle. 105, no. 65.

[85] Ibid. ; Feet of F. Bucks. Mich. 17 & 18 Eliz.

[86] Chan. Inq. p.m. (Ser. 2), clxxvi, 4.

[87] Recov. R. Hil. 18 Chas. II, m. 15 ;

Chan. Proc. (Bridges Div.), bdle. 420, no. 81.

[88] Lipscomb, op. cit. i, 173, quoting Willis MS.

[89] Chant. Cert. 5, no. 5.

[90] Pat. 28 Eliz. pt. xiv, m. 12, no. 4.

[1] Statistics from Bd. of Agric. (1905).

[2] Lipscomb, *Hist. and Antiq. of Bucks.* i, 186.

[3] Close, 6 Geo. II, pt. x, no. 15.

[4] Lipscomb, op. cit. i, 186.

[5] Ibid.

[6] Sheahan, *Hist. and Topog. of Bucks.* 361.

[7] *Hist. MSS. Com. Rep.* vii, App. i, 433b, 509a.

Claydon lies to the north of the park with the rectory[8] and the almshouses, which originally stood to the north-west of the churchyard, but were removed by Ralph, second Earl Verney, to their present position.[9] North-east of the village is Townsend Farm and the cemetery, dating from 1877. West of the park are brick and tile works. Glebe Farm lies in the north-west of the parish, and Muxwell Farm, a 17-century brick house with a thatched roof, just within its eastern borders; Knowlhill Farm, another 17th-century brick and timber house with a thatched roof, is near Home Wood.

Under King Edward the Confessor, *MANOR* Alwin, one of his thegns, held [*MIDDLE*] *CLAYDON MANOR*, which was held in 1086 by William Peverel.[10] It formed two knights' fees of the honour of Peverel,[11] held of the king in chief,[12] the last direct reference to the honour in this connexion occurring in 1517.[13] In 1525[14] and 1559 the overlordship was vested in the Earls of Rutland.[15]

Two of the three fees held by Ralph de Gresley of the honour of Peverel in 1211 correspond to Middle Claydon.[16] He presented to the church in 1231.[17] His daughter and heir Agnes married Hugh Fitz Ralph,[18] who was holding in 1234.[19] His son Ralph held the manor before 1258, since he presented to the church in that year,[20] but apparently died before his father.[21] In 1261 Ralph's daughter and heir Eustacia and her husband Nicholas Cauntlow[22] (de Cantilupe) granted [Middle] Claydon Manor to his widow Joan for life, who in return gave up all claim to Hugh's estates.[23] By 1268 the manor had reverted to Eustacia, whose second husband William de Ros[24] was holding in

VERNEY of Middle Claydon. *Azure a cross argent charged with five pierced molets gules.*

1284.[25] They apparently enfeoffed Eustacia's son William Cauntlow[26] before 1302.[27] On his death in 1308 one-third of this manor was assigned to his widow Eva,[28] and two-thirds passed with his son and heir William into the custody of Hugh le Despencer.[29] In 1320 William Cauntlow granted Middle Claydon Manor to his brother Nicholas,[30] who soon afterwards succeeded him in Ellesborough. Middle Claydon then descended with Ellesborough in the Cauntlows[31] and Zouches to William la Zouche, a minor at his father's death in 1416.[32] In 1431 he and his wife Alice conveyed Middle Claydon to John Brockley, William Edy and other feoffees,[33] and they in 1434 bought up outstanding interests in it[34] arising out of previous feoffments.[35] In 1460 William Edy was sole owner.[36] Sir Ralph Verney advanced him money on the security of Middle Claydon,[37] and his son and heir John, afterwards Sir John Verney, died seised in 1505.[38] In 1514 Sir Ralph Verney obtained livery of this manor as his father's heir,[39] and died in 1525, in the minority of his son Ralph,[40] who did homage for Middle Claydon in 1536.[41] Dying in 1546,[42] he left Middle Claydon among five sons, so that on the death of the eldest, Sir Edmund Verney, without issue in 1558, the next brother, Edmund (afterwards knighted, and, to prevent confusion, often called junior), had the largest interest.[43] He died seised of the whole manor in 1600.[44] It had been settled by Act of Parliament, in 1597,[45] on his widow Mary until their son Edmund had attained his majority.[46] In 1620 he purchased from Martin Lister the remainder of a lease formerly made to Roger Gifford,[47] and was the first of the Verneys to reside at Middle Claydon. He was knight marshal and standard bearer to Charles I and was killed at Edgehill in 1642.[48] His son and successor Sir Ralph Verney, kt., at first sympathized with the Parliament,[49] but refused to take the Covenant in 1643, and, obtaining a licence of protection for his estates, went into voluntary exile.[50] His property was, however, sequestered by Parliament in 1644,[51] but the sequestration was

---

[8] The 'new parsonage house' of 1675 built by Sir Ralph Verney was rebuilt in 1825 (Lipscomb, op. cit. i, 189, quoting church terrier; Sheahan, op. cit. 364).

[9] Lipscomb, op. cit. i, 197.

[10] *V.C.H. Bucks.* i, 253.

[11] Pipe R. (Oxon. Notts. Derby), 12 Hen. III; *Testa de Nevill* (Rec. Com.), 245; Inq. a.q.d. file 61, no. 4; Chan. Inq. p.m. 49 Edw. III, pt. i, no. 18; 6 Hen. IV, no. 17; Exch. Inq. p.m. (Ser. 2), file 5, no. 15.

[12] *Feud. Aids*, i, 85, 93, 119; Pat. 4 Eliz. pt. ix, m. 29.

[13] Leadam, *Dom. Incl.* 1517 (Royal Hist. Soc.), i, 174.

[14] Chan. Inq. p.m. (Ser. 2), xliv, 91.

[15] Ibid. cxx, 4.

[16] *Red Bk. of Exch.* (Rolls Ser.), 180.

[17] *Reg. of Hugh of Wells* (Cant. and York Soc.), ii, 81.

[18] Pipe R. (Oxon. Notts. Derby), 12 Hen. III.

[19] *Testa de Nevill* (Rec. Com.), 245. Hugh son of Richard held one fee at this time (ibid. 259b).

[20] Harl. MS. 6950, fol. 123.

[21] Chan. Inq. p.m. Hen. III, file 45, no. 7. This inquisition on Hugh Fitz Ralph is undated, and the writ is missing.

[22] Ibid.

[23] Feet of F. Bucks. Mich. 45 Hen. III, no. 9.

[24] *Abbrev. Plac.* (Rec. Com.), 171–2. He had to pay a heavy fine for marrying her without licence.

[25] *Feud. Aids*, i, 85. Sir John Beauchamp was then lessee and had been for at least six years, since he presented to the church in 1279 (Harl. MS. 6950, fol. 126).

[26] *V.C.H. Bucks.* ii, 332.

[27] *Feud. Aids*, i, 93.

[28] Chan. Inq. p.m. 2 Edw. II, no. 51; *Cal. Close*, 1307–13, p. 82.

[29] *Cat. of Anct. D.* i, 9.

[30] Inq. a.q.d. file 145, no. 17.

[31] *V.C.H. Bucks.* ii, 333.

[32] Ibid. 332.

[33] Feet of F. Bucks. Trin. 9 Hen. VI, no. 6.

[34] Ibid. Mich. 13 Hen. VI, no. 6.

[35] *V.C.H. Bucks.* ii, 332. Feet of F. Bucks. East. 3 Hen. VI, no. 4; East. 6 Hen. VI, no. 3.

[36] Close, 38 Hen. VI, m. 14.

[37] Bruce, *Verney Papers*, 22. He appears to have purchased it, since he presented to the church, in 1463 (Lipscomb, op. cit. 190), but no mention of Middle Claydon is made in his inquisition (Chan. Inq. p.m. 18 Edw. IV, no. 23), or in his will (P.C.C. 1 Logge).

[38] Exch. Inq. p.m. (Ser. 2), file 5, no. 15. See Fleet Marston.

[39] *L. and P. Hen. VIII*, i, 5514.

[40] Chan. Inq. p.m. (Ser. 2), xliv, 91.

He is called Sir Ralph Verney, jun., to distinguish him from his uncle.

[41] Memo. R. Hil. 28 Hen. VIII, m. 23.

[42] Chan. Inq. p.m. (Ser. 2), lxxiv, 2.

[43] Ibid. cxx, 4.

[44] Ibid. cclxii, 126. An alienation of the manor by him to John Hastings and Francis Darrell, in 1562 (Pat. 4 Eliz. pt. ix, m. 29), appears to have been only a temporary arrangement.

[45] *Lords Journ.* ii, 222.

[46] Bruce, op. cit. 82. Edmund's elder half-brother Sir Francis Verney petitioned against this Act of Settlement (ibid. 93), but lost his suit in 1606 (*Commons Journ.* i, 277, 290), and surrendered his claims on Middle Claydon and Mursley to his step-mother in 1608 (Feet of F. Bucks. Mich. 6 Jas. I).

[47] Bruce, op. cit. 134. This purchase necessitated various settlements of the manor (Feet of F. Bucks. East. 21 Jas. I; Hil. 22 Jas. I; Trin. 11 Chas. I).

[48] *Hist. MSS. Com. Rep.* vii, App. i, 433b; M.I. in Middle Claydon Church.

[49] *Hist. MSS. Com. Rep.* vii, App. i, 442. His father's death necessitated fresh settlements of this manor (Recov. R. Hil. 18 Chas. I, m. 2; Feet of F. Bucks. Hil. 18 Chas. I).

[50] *Hist. MSS. Com. Rep.* vii, App. i, 434. [51] Ibid.

removed in 1647.[52] Sir Ralph Verney returned to England before 1653,[53] was imprisoned for some months in 1655,[54] and created a baronet in 1661.[55] He died in 1696,[56] and his son and successor Sir John Verney, who authorized a settlement of Middle Claydon made shortly before his father's death,[57] became Viscount Fermanagh in 1703.[58] His son Ralph, the second viscount, was given the higher title of Earl Verney in 1743.[59] In 1752 he was succeeded by his second son and heir Ralph, second Earl Verney, who was buried at Middle Claydon in 1791.[60] His niece the Hon. Mary Verney succeeded to the family estates and was raised to the peerage as Baroness Fermanagh.[61] She, the last of the Buckinghamshire Verneys, died unmarried in 1810 and was buried at Middle Claydon.[62] She bequeathed all her estates to her maternal half-sister Catherine, directing her and her husband, the Rev. Robert Wright, to take the name and bear the arms of Verney.[63] He died in 1820 and she in 1827.[64] Middle Claydon then passed to her cousin Captain Sir Harry Calvert, bart., who

CALVERT. *Paly ermi-nois and pean a bend engrailed countercoloured.*

VERNEY. *Azure a cross argent fimbriated or with five molets gules thereon.*

soon afterwards by royal licence took the name and arms of Verney.[65] Middle Claydon has since descended in his family, and his grandson [66] Sir Harry Calvert Williams Verney, bart., is the present owner.

In 1517 Roger Gifford or Giffard was lessee of Middle Claydon Manor, apparently from 1495.[67] He was buried at Middle Claydon in 1542,[68] leaving the premier right in the lease, which had been renewed for about 100 years, in 1535, to his second son George.[69] He acquired his brothers' rights in the lease in 1545,[70] and died in 1557.[71] His daughter

Lettice[72] married Urian Verney,[73] who presented to Middle Claydon Church in 1571, apparently in right of this lease.[74] In 1620 the leasehold rights were vested in Martin Lister, who surrendered them in that year to Edmund Verney, afterwards knight marshal.

The right of view of frankpledge appertained to Middle Claydon Manor in the 17th century.[75] Middle Claydon Wood was granted to King John by Ralph de Gresley in exchange for Willey Wood in Nottinghamshire, but the Crown failed to perform its part of the bargain.[76] In 1336 Middle Claydon Wood was restored to his descendant Nicholas Cauntlow, after frequent applications to Parliament.[77] A windmill on the manor is mentioned in 1308.[78]

CHURCH The church of *ALL SAINTS* has a chancel measuring internally 29 ft. by 14 ft. 6 in., a nave 34 ft. by 23 ft. 6 in. and a west tower 10 ft. 6 in. by 9 ft.; the vestry and south porch are modern additions.

The nave dates from the beginning of the 14th century and the west tower from the end of the 15th. The date of the chancel is fixed by an inscription over the north door, 'Rogerus Giffard et Maria uxor ejus hanc cancellam fieri fecerunt anno dñi 1519.' It is an interesting piece of work, of very good masonry, but shows a dryness of detail characteristic of the last phase of English Gothic. The east window is four-centred and has five lights under a traceried head, and there are two three-light windows in each side wall with uncusped lights, the south-east window being carried down to serve as sedilia, while under the south-west window is an arched recess with panelled soffit, originally the canopy of a tomb, but now pierced with a modern doorway. The chancel is full of monuments of Giffards and Verneys, but has no old fittings; there is, however, a 17th-century communion table in the vestry. The chancel arch is of the date of the nave, and in it stands a screen probably coeval with the rebuilding of the chancel; it has a wide four-centred doorway and four narrower traceried bays on either side, with a moulded cornice, a good deal repaired, and capped with a modern embattled moulding.

The nave has two windows in the north wall of about 1300, of two pointed uncusped lights with a pierced spandrel, and in the south wall are a like pair, but almost entirely modern. West of each pair

[52] *Cal. Com. for Comp.* 68, 3243.
[53] *Hist. MSS. Com. Rep.* vii, App. i, 434. He wrote an account of the surrender of the House of Commons to Cromwell, and his notes of the proceedings of the Long Parliament, in which he sat as member for Aylesbury (ibid. 433*b*), have been published by the Camden Society. For a complete list of Verney members of Parliament and the constituencies represented by them, see *Verney Memoirs of the 17th cent.* i, 195-6.
[54] *Verney Memoirs of the 17th cent.* ii, 11.
[55] G.E.C. *Baronetage*, iii, 177.
[56] M.I. in church.
[57] Recov. R. East. 7 Will. and Mary, m. 80; Feet of F. Bucks. Mich. 8 Will. III.
[58] G.E.C. *Baronetage*, iii, 178; *Complete Peerage*, iii, 325.
[59] G.E.C. *Complete Peerage*, iii, 326. He and his eldest son John (whose only child Mary was afterwards Baroness

Fermanagh) made a settlement of Middle Claydon Manor in 1732 (Close, 6 Geo. II, pt. x, no. 15; Recov. R. Mich. 6 Geo. II, m. 247).
[60] G.E.C. *Complete Peerage*, iii, 326.
[61] Ibid.; Tablet in Middle Claydon Church.
[62] Ibid.
[63] Tablet in church.
[64] Ibid.
[65] Inscr. on mural monum. of his father in the church. His second wife Frances Parthenope was Florence Nightingale's sister (Burke, *Peerage* [1906]). The *Verney Memoirs of the 17th century* were edited after her death from a MS. compiled from her research work at Claydon.
[66] Burke, *Peerage* (1906).
[67] Leadam, *Dom. Incl.* 1517 (Royal Hist. Soc.), i, 174.
[68] Brass in church.
[69] P.C.C. 2 Pynnyng.
[70] Bruce, op. cit. 50, quoting deed of surrender for £300 and in consideration

of expenses of repairs to the chancel and manor-house.
[71] Chan. Inq. p.m. (Ser. 2), cxx, 1; P.C.C. 2 Noodes.
[72] Ibid.
[73] Inscr. on mural monum. in chancel.
[74] Lipscomb, op. cit. i, 186, 190. He was still alive on 4 July 1608, but died before the following January (M.I. in chancel). On the former date his nephew Sir Francis Verney, who in 1605 had leased to him reversionary rights in Middle Claydon (including the advowson) for 1,000 years (Feet of F. Bucks. Mich. 3 Jas. I), gave him authority before going abroad to act for him in all business matters (Bruce, op. cit. 95).
[75] Feet of F. Bucks. Hil. 4 Jas. I; Mich. 6 Jas. I; East. 21 Jas. I; Trin. 11 Chas. I; Hil. 18 Chas. I; Trin. 26 Chas. II.
[76] *Cal. Pat.* 1334-8, p. 196.
[77] Ibid. 195-6.
[78] Chan. Inq. p.m. 2 Edw. II, no. 51.

MIDDLE CLAYDON : CLAYDON HOUSE, THE SOUTH-WEST FRONT

MIDDLE CLAYDON CHURCH : THE INTERIOR LOOKING EAST

are doorways, that on the north of about 1350, that on the south of about 1300. In the north wall west of the doorway are two more windows, entirely modern. In the sill of the south-east window is a piscina, but all other fittings are new except the Jacobean hexagonal pulpit of oak, a good specimen with 'perspective' arches on each panel, and a moulded cornice; the base is modern.

The tower is of three stages, with a north-east staircase and a west doorway, which has in one of its external spandrels the words 'Ihc merci' cut to read backwards, probably by an illiterate mason. Over the doorway is a three-light window, and in the belfry stage are uncusped two-light windows under square heads. The tower arch springs from half-octagonal responds, with moulded capitals and bases.

The church contains a very fine series of monuments, the earliest being a brass in the chancel to Isabella Giffard, 1523, with figure and inscription, and the next a figure of a priest, Alexander Anne, 1526. A third brass is to Roger Giffard, 1542, the builder of the chancel, and his wife Mary [Nansicles], with their thirteen sons and seven daughters, and has the arms of Giffard : three lions passant, impaling a cheveron between three lapwings with three stars on the cheveron. The brass is palimpsest on one to Walter Bellingham, 1487, Ireland King of Arms. The most interesting monument in the church is an altar-tomb in the chancel with the alabaster effigy of Margaret Giffard, 1539, a beautiful piece of late Gothic and Italian Renaissance detail. The effigy is of alabaster, and in general design follows the fashion of English effigies of the time, but with a freedom and mastery of detail which give evidence of the new influence. The tomb itself has shields of the Gothic type, but Italian baluster shafts at the angles, and the marginal inscription is in capital letters of mixed Gothic and Italian character. The heraldry gives the arms of Giffard and of Bradfield : three fleurs de lis on a bend quartered with quarterly a border ermine. On the north wall of the chancel is an uninscribed monument with the Giffard arms, of fine Italian detail and about contemporary with Margaret Giffard's monument. There are a number of monuments of the Verneys, who succeeded the Giffards, the earliest being that of Urian and Lettice Verney (d. 1608). Others are Col. Henry Verney (d. 1671), Sir Edmund Verney (d. 1642), Sir Ralph Verney (d. 1696), John Verney (d. 1694) and Mary Verney (d. 1694).

There is a ring of three bells : the treble, 1674, and second, 1664, are probably by Richard Chandler ; the tenor bears no date or inscription. There is also a saunce bell, which is blank.

The plate includes a standing paten of 1663, and a paten of 1667.

The registers begin in 1630.

ADVOWSON The advowson of the rectory of Middle Claydon has always descended with the manor[79] (q.v.).

William Cauntlow in 1306 gave the rectors of Middle Claydon a rent-charge of 13s. 4d. yearly on land in the parish for the maintenance of two wax-lights, weighing 12 lb. each, to burn daily at the elevation of the Host.[80] A grant of 2s. from this yearly rent was made to Christopher Denton and Bernard Gilpin in 1573[81] and of 9 acres of pasture called the 'Torch-land,' worth 3s. 4d. yearly, to John Walton and John Cresset in 1586.[82]

CHARITIES The charities founded by Sir Ralph Verney by deeds, dated respectively 16 December 1691 and 24 May 1694, consist of six almshouses in Middle Claydon, a rent-charge of £15 12s. issuing out of an estate now belonging to Sir Harry Verney, bart., 19 a. 2 r., known as Poor's Piece, and a house and 4 a. 2 r. situate in Steeple Claydon, let at £48 a year, and £47 19s. 10d. India 3 per cent. stock with the official trustees, arising from the sale of timber, producing £1 8s. 8d. yearly.

The charities are administered under the provisions of schemes of the Charity Commissioners, dated respectively 10 August 1883 and 29 October 1909, whereby the net income is applied in payment of stipends to the almspeople. In 1912 the sum of £45 10s. was so applied.

The charities of Elizabeth Verney, endowed with £858 10s. 2d. consols, producing £21 9s. yearly, and that of Mary Verney Baroness Fermanagh, endowed with a rent-charge of £12 issuing out of lands in Steeple Claydon, are under a scheme of the Charity Commissioners, dated 16 August 1883, applicable in apprenticing children to a trade or profession, or in exhibitions at any place of higher education.

The sum of stock is held by the official trustees, who also hold £65 1s. 2d. India 3 per cent. stock, arising from accumulations, producing £1 19s. yearly.

The Cottage Hospital Fund, arising under the will of Mrs. Emily Caroline Freemantle, proved at London 20 September 1877, consists of the following sums of stock held by the official trustee, namely :—

£1,012 5s. 10d. consols, £137 7s. 8d. India 3 per cents. and £526 15s. 6d. India 3 per cents. (constituting a building fund), producing together in annual dividends £45 4s. 4d. yearly.

By the will of the Very Rev. William Robert Freemantle, dated in 1892, it was directed that the income of the trust should be applied towards the maintenance of any cottage hospital existing in any of the three parishes of Middle Claydon, East Claydon and Steeple Claydon. In 1912 the income was paid to the Claydon District Nursing Association.

---

[79] Harl. MS. 6952, fol. 36 ; Inst. Bks. (P.R.O.) 17th and 18th cent. ; Bacon, *Liber Reg.* 504. Hugh son of Richard who had manorial rights in Claydon in the early 13th century (*Testa de Nevill* [Rec. Com.], 259b) gave two parts of the tithes to Lenton Priory (Notts.) equivalent to a pension of 10s. yearly (*Pope Nich. Tax.* [Rec. Com.], 34). This grant was confirmed in 1319 and 1382 (*Cal. Pat.* 1381–5, p. 187).

[80] Inq. a.q.d. file 61, no. 4 ; *Cal. Pat.* 1301–7, p. 468.
[81] Pat. 16 Eliz. pt. xiv, m. 11.
[82] Pat. 28 Eliz. pt. xiv, no. 4.

LONG CRENDON[1]

Crendone (xi cent.); Craendon, Creindon (xii cent.); Grandone (xiii cent.); Grendon-by-Tame, Croyndon (xiv cent.); Creedonia (xv cent.); Cryndon, Credendon, Long Crendon (xvi cent.).

This parish covers 3,348 acres, of which about 1,413 are arable, 1,587 permanent grass, and 2 woods.[1a] The soil is loam and clay on a subsoil of Kimmeridge Clay, Portland Beds and Gault. The level of the land varies from rather over 200 ft. above the ordnance datum in the south by the Thames to about 400 ft. in the north, near the Chilton boundary.

great extent absorbed in a substantial modern mansion, the property and residence of Mr. H. Reynolds.

The existing remains of the abbey are built of stone and include parts of the south and west cloister ranges dating from the 13th century, and an L-shaped building, probably the guest-house, on the north-west, dating from the 15th and early 16th centuries. The church, which stood on the north side of the cloister, and the whole of the eastern range of the cloister have been destroyed, while of the south and west ranges little remains except those walls adjoining the

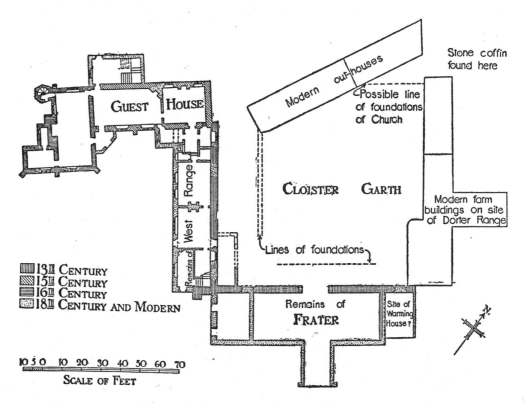

PLAN OF NUTLEY ABBEY, LONG CRENDON

(*Adapted from the Inventory of the Historical Monuments of Buckinghamshire with the permission of the Royal Commission and the consent of the Controller of H.M. Stationery Office.*)

In the 16th century Leland entered Long Crendon over Crendon Bridge of four stone arches and journeyed thence 'by some hilly and aftar great pasture ground and grounds fruitfull of benes.'[2] The bridge or its successor, now bearing the name of Thame Bridge, still carries the road to Bicester across the Thame. Some distance north-east of the bridge it flows past the site of Nutley Abbey, a house of Austin Canons, the remains of which are now to a

cloister which are now incorporated into comparatively modern structures.

The buildings on the south consisted of the frater, with the common room or warming-house on the east, and probably the kitchen on the west. At the west end of the original north wall is a moulded 13th-century doorway with jamb shafts which doubtless admitted from the cloister to the screens at the west end of the frater, while a similar doorway at the

[1] Sir Laurence Gomme states that 'Long Crendon represents in a special degree that untouched portion of English village life which is now becoming increasingly difficult to discover. Surnames which appear in the 16th-century church books are still the surnames of villagers, and there is ample evidence of unbroken descent through many generations of these families. There is also a distinctive character in the physique and craniology of the oldest inhabitants. An almost classical beauty is apparent in many cases, and the dialect, separated, as it appears to be, from surrounding dialects, points to a specialized racial distinction in this hill village on the borders of Buckinghamshire and Oxfordshire.'

[1a] Statistics from Bd. of Agric. (1905).

[2] Leland, *Itin.* (ed. L. Toulmin Smith), v, 110.

Long Crendon : Nutley Abbey, The East View, Drawn by S. and N. Buck, 1730

Long Crendon : Nutley Abbey

Long Crendon Manor

east end opened into the warming-house ; both are now blocked and a wide gateway has been opened in the north wall of the frater. The wall between the frater and warming-house is also original and retains a blocked 14th-century doorway which formed an entrance to the cellar under the frater ; high in the wall is a richly moulded corbel table with an arcade of trefoiled arches. The site of these buildings is now occupied by a barn, stables and coach-house, the other inclosing walls being comparatively modern. Of the west range, which was probably the cellarer's building, the east and part of the south walls are original, while the north end abuts upon the guest-house, which was entered from these buildings by a 15th-century doorway, now blocked. In the east wall are a richly moulded doorway from the cloister and traces of another doorway further north which has been built up.

The guest-house, which, having been converted into a dwelling-house, has been well preserved though somewhat altered, consists of a 15th-century block with an early 16th-century wing built at right angles to it on the west, and a modern projection on the north containing the staircase ; the west cloister range, which has been partly rebuilt and converted into kitchen offices, forms an additional wing at the south-east. The house is of two stories with tiled roofs and forms a picturesque group of buildings. The hall, on the ground floor of the 15th-century block, is lighted from the south side by two original windows, each of two cinquefoiled lights with tracery under a square head, and above them on the first floor are two similar windows. In one of the rooms of the first floor is a 15th-century fireplace with carved spandrels, and the heavy oak beams supporting this floor are of the same period. The 16th-century wing has a hexagonal stair turret projecting from its north-west angle, and behind the fireplace in the main apartment on the ground floor is a closet entered from a small room projecting at the south-west. A large stone dovecote with a tiled roof to the north-east of the house, which is probably of pre-Suppression date, contains a very large number of cells, its accommodation being increased by short celled projections from its internal walls. A stone coffin has been unearthed on the site of the east cloister range, which is now occupied by modern farm buildings, while foundations of old walls have been disclosed about the cloister garth.

The village, built on high ground to the west, consists of irregular narrow streets branching off from the high road to Thame, and along these are many 17th-century buildings and some of earlier date. Not far from the church at its north-east end is Cop Hill, which must have given its name to the Copt Close of the 17th century.[3] An ancient cemetery with remains of Roman date was discovered close by in 1824.[4]

To the west of the churchyard stands the Court House,[5] once known as Old Staple Hall, which dates at least from the 15th century. It is a long rectangular timber-framed building of two stories, the upper story projecting on the south and west sides. The east end seems originally to have formed one narrow but lofty apartment, reaching from the ground floor to the roof, and is distinguished in the upper part externally by a break in the line of projection of the wall of the upper story, the wall-plate, which is continued without break, being trussed by straight struts. A large fireplace at this end, with a 16th-

THE COURT HOUSE, LONG CRENDON

century moulded wood lintel, occupies the full width of the building, while near it on the south is a round brick oven, which projects beyond the outer face of the wall ; the arrangement of the rest of the lower stage has been somewhat altered for domestic purposes. The upper story is divided by the main uprights into five bays, four of which form one large apartment with an open timber roof, while the east bay, originally the upper part of the lofty room already mentioned, has been formed into a separate apartment by the insertion of a floor. The house has a tiled roof, at the east end of which is a rectangular chimney stack, which has been rebuilt with the old bricks. This interesting building is now in the hands of the National Trust.[6]

Immediately south-east of the church is the Manor House, a square two-storied stone building with brick quoins and a classical wood cornice, dating from about

[3] Close, 1649, pt. xxiii, no. 23.
[4] V.C.H. Bucks. ii, 6.

[5] There was a house for holding courts belonging to the Bohun manor in 1420

(Rentals and Surv. [Duchy of Lanc.], bdle. 14, no. 4). [6] See Country Life, 17 Feb. 1912.

1680, but considerably altered early in the 19th century; it has a tiled hipped roof containing attics, and retains some original moulded panelling and a staircase with twisted balusters.

Long Crendon Manor, to the south-west of the village, is a timber-framed house of two stories with attics. It appears to have been originally an early 15th-century H-shaped building having a large central hall, now converted into the kitchen, with wings at either end. The west wing was rebuilt in the 16th century and contains some moulded fireplaces of that date, one of which has carved spandrels; the whole building has been considerably altered at subsequent periods and is now entirely coated with rough-cast. A courtyard before the house is entered through a mediaeval gate-house, the southern archway of which has been rebuilt, while the floor to the story over, which appears to have been approached by a stairway on the east, has been removed, but traces of the original vaulting remain.

The Mound, at Lower End, a timber-framed house of two stories with a thatched roof, is probably of mediaeval date, though it has been considerably altered and enlarged at subsequent periods. It retains some wood mullioned windows of late 16th-century date, and a stone moulded fireplace, while in an old external stone wall, now incorporated in the house, is a wide doorway with moulded jambs. An old timber and brick stable, to the south-east, with an original timber roof, was formerly a cottage, but the first floor has been removed. This house, once known as Emertons, has lately been bought and restored by Sir Laurence Gomme.

Long Crendon Baptist chapel dates from 1810; the Wesleyan chapel built in 1840 replaces an earlier building. Since 1866 the Primitive Methodists have had a place of worship here.[7]

The inhabitants of Long Crendon are now almost entirely engaged in agriculture, but there was formerly a considerable trade in the manufacture of needles. One of the factories where this industry was carried on still survives.[8]

Tittershull (Tudreshull, xiv and xv cent.; Totterell, xvii cent.[9]) Wood, an outlying part of Long Crendon, between the parishes of Ludgershall and Wotton Underwood, the woodland for a hundred swine of 1086,[10] was formerly shared in equal portions by the lords of the manor. Other place-names are Rodewellefeld, Prestosleyen, Frychhegh, Harlagesforlond, Stubforlond and Wasshefordweye (xiv cent.), and Charlons Close, Putney Plott, Priestleyes and Crooxhams Close (xvii cent.).[11]

HONOUR In 1086 there was a park for beasts of the chase at Long Crendon,[12] and since the manor was later the caput of the honour of Giffard,[13] an important house of the lord must have existed here. Tradition calls it a castle

and places it in the neighbourhood of Cop Hill. When the park was granted with other property for the foundation of Nutley Abbey, in the 12th century, it is likely that Long Crendon ceased to be the chief residence of the lord. In 1233 the king ordered the houses and gardens of Richard Earl Marshal at Crendon to be destroyed,[14] but in the following year Gilbert, his brother and heir, received a grant of timber from Bernwood Forest, 'ad se hospitandum apud Crendon.'[15]

GIFFARD. *Gules three lions passant argent.*

The honour of Giffard represented the Domesday fief of Walter Giffard, which comprised lands in Akeley, Ashendon, Aston Abbots, Beachampton, Bradwell, Bow Brickhill, Broughton, Buckingham, Chearsley, Chilton, Long Crendon, Dorton, Edgcott, Fawley, Hardmead, Hartwell, Hillesden, Great Horwood, Great Kimble, Lavendon, Leckhampstead, Lenborough, Lillingstone Dayrell, Linford, Loughton, Maids' Moreton, Milton Keynes, Missenden, Moulsoe, Mursley, Newton Longville, Oakley, Pitstone, Ravenstone, Stewkley, Stone, Swanbourne, Whaddon, Whitchurch, Lower Winchendon, Little and Great Woolstone and Wotton Underwood,[16] with some manors in Bedfordshire[17] and Berkshire.[18] The descent of the honour seems to have been identical with that of the manor of Long Crendon[19] until the partition, in 1191, of the Giffard inheritance between William Marshal Earl of Pembroke and Richard de Clare Earl of Hertford,[20] who between 1201 and 1212 each held forty-two knights' fees as a moiety of the honour of Giffard.[21] The later history is obscure. Most of the Giffard manors of Domesday were included in William Marshal's liberty as part of the honour of Giffard in the early years of Henry III,[22] and after the partition of the Pembroke lands in 1275 the honour seems to have been merged in the barony of the marshalcy, of which Crendon itself was held in 1284.[23]

MANORS The manor of *LONG CRENDON*, once of Seric, son of Alveva, was held of the Crown in chief in 1086 by Walter Giffard,[24] probably son of the Walter Giffard who fought at the Conquest.[25] From the second Walter Giffard Crendon descended to his son and heir of the same name,[26] who died without issue in 1164.[27] It seems to have remained in the Crown until the partition of the Giffard inheritance in 1191,[28] when the manor came to William Marshal, afterwards Earl of Pembroke, by his marriage with Isabel de Clare.[29] William Marshal held the greater part of Crendon, then head of the honour of Giffard,[30]

[7] cf. Sheahan, *Hist. and Topog. of Buck.* 373.

[8] *V.C.H. Bucks.* ii, 127; *Home Counties Mag.* vi, 181–6.

[9] Chan. Inq. p.m. 45 Edw. III (1st nos.), no. 22; 23 Hen. VI, no. 33; Close, 1649, pt. xxiii, no. 20.

[10] *V.C.H. Bucks.* i, 248.

[11] Chan. Inq. p.m. 45 Edw. III (1st nos.), no. 22; Rentals and Surv. (Duchy of Lanc.), bdle. 1, no. 8; Close, 1649, pt. xxiii, no. 20.

[12] *V.C.H. Bucks.* i, 223.

[13] *Testa de Nevill* (Rec. Com.), 247.

[14] Close, 18 Hen. III, m. 35 d.

[15] Ibid. m. 10.

[16] *V.C.H. Bucks.* i, 247–52.

[17] Ibid. *Beds.* i, 231–2.

[18] *Testa de Nevill* (Rec. Com.), 123.

[19] See below.

[20] G.E.C. *Peerage*, vi, 197–9.

[21] *Red Bk. of Exch.* (Rolls Ser.), 136, 138, 535.

[22] *Testa de Nevill* (Rec. Com.), 247.

[23] *Feud. Aids*, i, 84. Buckingham, which alone of all the Domesday holdings

of Walter Giffard preserved its connexion with the honour at this date, being described as part of the honour of Giffard and held of the Earl of Gloucester, was held of the Earl without further qualification in 1346 (ibid. 85, 126).

[24] *V.C.H. Bucks.* i, 248.

[25] Ibid. 212. [26] G.E.C. *Peerage*, ii, 62.

[27] *Pipe R. 9 Hen. II* (Pipe R. Soc.), 16; G.E.C. loc. cit.

[28] G.E.C. *Peerage*, vi, 199.

[29] Ibid. ii, 267; vi, 196–8.

[30] *Misc. Bks.* (Exch. K.R.), vi, 168.

in demesne until his death, when regent of the kingdom, in 1219.[31] From his widow Isabel[32] it passed to their second son Richard, who leased it in 1228 to John de Wilenhale, citizen of London,[33] tenant in 1233,[34] when the custody of this manor was committed to Richard Earl of Cornwall.[35] Gilbert, younger brother and heir of Richard Marshal, in the next year assigned the issues of the manor of Crendon to Eleanor Countess of Pembroke,[36] the king's sister, widow of his eldest brother the younger William Marshal.[37] Eleanor, whose second husband Simon de Montfort was returned as lord in 1255,[38] died seised in 1275, and Crendon was divided between the co-heirs of Eva wife of William de Braose,[39] youngest sister and co-heir of Anselm Marshal, the last survivor of the regent's sons.[40]

Maud, the only surviving child of Eva de Braose in 1275, when she was wife of Roger Mortimer,[41]

Roger on his son Edmund and his wife Elizabeth,[47] then passed to the widowed Elizabeth,[48] afterwards wife of William de Bohun, Earl of Northampton, on

BRAOSE. *Azure crusily and a lion or.*

MORTIMER. *Barry or and azure a chief or with two pales between two gyrons azure therein and a scutcheon argent over all.*

THE VILLAGE, LONG CRENDON

granted her third of Crendon Manor to her younger son William. He died childless in or before 1297,[42] and the manor reverted to his mother,[43] descending in 1301 to her eldest son Edmund Lord Mortimer of Wigmore.[44] After Edmund's death in 1304 Crendon was held by his widow Margaret.[45] She survived by about four years her son and heir Roger Mortimer, Earl of March, who died in 1330.[46] Crendon, the reversion of which had been settled in 1316 by

whose behalf an extent of the manor was made in 1336.[49] She died seised in 1356,[50] and two years later her son and heir Roger Mortimer, Earl of March, granted his manor of Crendon to William Lord Ferrers of Groby in exchange for half the manor of Ludlow.[51] William was seised at his death in 1371, when part of Crendon was assigned in dower to his widow Margaret.[52] Henry their son and heir also left a third of his estate in this parish to his

[31] Stubbs, *Constitutional Hist. of Engl.* ii, 31.

[32] *Rot. Lit. Claus.* (Rec. Com.), i, 392*b*.

[33] *Cal. Chart. R. 1226–57*, p. 142.

[34] Richard was then in arms against the king (Stubbs, op. cit. ii, 48–50).

[35] *Cal. Close, 1231–4*, pp. 273, 281.

[36] *Cal. Pat. 1232–47*, p. 125.

[37] G.E.C. *Peerage*, vi, 200–3.

[38] *Hund. R.* (Rec. Com.), i, 26.

[39] *Cal. Close, 1272–9*, p. 190; *Cal.*

Fine R. 1272–1307, p. 58; Chan. Misc. bdle. 88, file 4, no. 70.

[40] G.E.C. loc. cit.

[41] *Cal. Close, 1272–9*, p. 190.

[42] Ibid. *1296–1302*, p. 73; Chan. Inq. p.m. 25 Edw. I, no. 36.   [43] Ibid.

[44] Chan. Inq. p.m. 29 Edw. I, no. 53.

[45] Ibid. 32 Edw. I, no. 63*a*; *Cal. Close, 1302–7*, p. 175.

[46] Chan. Inq. p.m. 8 Edw. III (1st nos.), no. 19; *Cal. Close, 1333–7*, p. 237; G.E.C. *Peerage*, v, 243.

[47] *Cal. Pat. 1313–17*, p. 491.

[48] Chan. Inq. p.m. 8 Edw. III (1st nos.), no. 19.

[49] Rentals and Surv. (Duchy of Lanc.), bdle. 1, no. 8.

[50] Chan. Inq. p.m. 30 Edw. III (1st nos.), no. 13; *Cal. Close, 1354–60*, p. 271.

[51] *Cal. Pat. 1358–61*, pp. 40–1, 44, 56; *Cal. Close, 1354–60*, p. 507.

[52] Chan. Inq. p.m. 45 Edw. III (1st nos.), no. 22.

widow Joan, who died in 1394.[53] From her son William Lord Ferrers the manor descended in 1445 to Elizabeth daughter of his son Henry and wife of

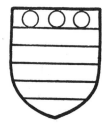

FERRERS of Groby.
Vairy or and gules.

GREY de Ruthyn.
Barry argent and azure with three roundels gules in the chief.

Sir Edward Grey,[54] a younger son of Reginald Lord Grey de Ruthyn.[55] Elizabeth settled Crendon in 1447,[56] and again in 1462, in conjunction with her second husband Sir John Bourchier.[57] This was after the death of the son of her first marriage, Sir John Grey, whose widow Elizabeth Woodville became the wife of Edward IV.[58] Thomas Grey, the eldest son of Sir John Grey and Elizabeth, afterwards Marquess of Dorset,[59] died in 1500 seised of the manor of Crendon,[60] which his son and heir Thomas sold twenty years later to Michael Dormer.[61] At his death in 1545 Sir Michael left this part of Crendon to his son Geoffrey with contingent remainder to his son William.[62] William, who was already owner by his father's will of several smaller holdings in this parish,[63] acquired the Dorset manor of Geoffrey in 1552.[64] In 1563 he conveyed it to John Piers,[65] by whom and his wife Alice it was mortgaged to Simon Egerton in 1569.[66] Simon acquired from Henry Yonge and his wife Alice[67] their interest in this manor in 1574,[68] and died seised in 1576, when he was succeeded by his brother Richard.[69] Within five years, however, John Piers and his wife Alice had recovered possession and settled Crendon on their daughter Thomasine and her husband John Brewster.[70] John and Thomasine obtained licence in 1584 to alienate this property to John son and heir of William Dormer aforesaid,[71] who was lord

until his death in 1627.[72] From his son and heir Robert, who was dead in 1641,[73] Crendon passed to his son Robert Dormer.[74] He was succeeded in 1689 by Robert Dormer, his eldest son by his first wife Katherine Bertie.[75] The younger Robert survived his father about four years,[76] and was succeeded by his half-brother John Dormer, the eldest of his father's seven sons by his second wife Anne Cottrell,[77] lord in 1705[78] and 1706, and in the latter year holding with his wife Diana.[79] In his will, proved in 1719, John left his Buckinghamshire manors to his younger brother, another Robert Dormer,[80] from whom it passed to another younger brother, Lieutenant-General James Dormer.[81] He died unmarried in 1737,[82] leaving his landed estates to his first cousin Sir Clement Cottrell, who took the additional surname of Dormer.[83] Charles, his eldest son and heir-apparent, in 1744 settled Crendon,[84] which he apparently parted with before his death in 1779.[85] It is said to have been sold to George Grenville of Wotton,[86] whose grandson Richard Grenville, Duke of Buckingham and Chandos, was lord in 1824.[87] His grandson of the same name and title held it in 1887,[88] and was succeeded in 1889 by his daughter Lady Kinloss,[89] who still has rights in the parish.

Another of the co-heirs of Eva de Braose was Humphrey de Bohun, son and heir of her daughter Eleanor by Humphrey, son and heir of Humphrey de Bohun Earl of Hereford.[90] From Humphrey, Eleanor's son, who was returned as lord about 1284,[91] the manor descended in 1298 to his son Humphrey.[92] John, son and heir of the last Humphrey,[93] in 1330 settled on Peter Favelore the remainder of his manor here which Walter de Finchingfield then held for life.[94] John's heir in 1336 was his brother Humphrey, who died in 1361.[94a] He was succeeded by his nephew Humphrey, son and heir of his younger brother William Earl of Northampton,[95] who died in January 1372-3, leaving two daughters Eleanor and Mary.[96] His manor of Crendon was held by his widow Joan until she died in 1419,[97] nearly twenty years after the death of their daughter Eleanor.[98] Mary their second daughter was represented at Joan's death by her eldest son, then Henry V,[99] who was found to be co-heir of his grandmother with Anne daughter of the late Duke of Gloucester and Eleanor.[100] In

[53] Chan. Inq. p.m. 17 Ric. II, no. 24; Close, 18 Ric. II, m. 37.
[54] Chan. Inq. p.m. 23 Hen. VI, no. 33.
[55] G.E.C. *Peerage*, iii, 340-1.
[56] Feet of F. case 293, file 71, no. 323.
[57] Ibid. case 294, file 74, no. 7; G.E.C. loc. cit.
[58] G.E.C. loc. cit.
[59] Ibid.
[60] Exch. Inq. p.m. (Ser. 2), file 5, no. 10.
[61] Feet of F. Bucks. Trin. 12 Hen. VIII.
[62] P.C.C. 38 Pynnyng.
[63] Chan. Inq. p.m. (Ser. 2), lxxiii, 10.
[64] Memo. R. (Exch. L.T.R.), Trin. 6 Eliz. m. 8.
[65] Ibid. The family of Piers or Fitz Piers held lands in this parish in the 13th and 14th centuries (see p. 42).
[66] Feet of F. Bucks. Trin. 11 Eliz.
[67] The origin of their interest in this manor, of which Henry was at one time lord (Chan. Proc. Eliz. H 7, no. 2), is obscure. Perhaps Alice was the widow of John Piers and the John Piers of 1581 their son.
[68] Feet of F. Bucks. Hil. 16 Eliz.
[69] Chan. Inq. p.m. (Ser. 2), clxxvi, 3.

[70] Feet of F. Bucks. Mich. 24 & 25 Eliz. Richard Egerton, however, had still some rights here in 1584 (Chan. Proc. [Ser. 2], bdle. 241, no. 5).
[71] Pat. 27 Eliz. pt. viii, m. 27; Chan. Proc. (Ser. 2), bdle. 241, no. 5; Recov. R. Mich. 27 Eliz. m. 84.
[72] Chan. Inq. p.m. (Ser. 2), ccccxxxv, 112.
[73] Cal. S. P. Dom. 1640-1, p. 335.
[74] Ibid. 1661-2, p. 152; Recov. R. Mich. 1650, m. 104.
[75] P.C.C. 78 Ent.
[76] Ibid. 44 Box.
[77] Ibid. 78 Ent.; 44 Box.
[78] Recov. R. Hil. 4 Anne, m. 137.
[79] Feet of F. Div. Co. East. 5 Anne.
[80] P.C.C. 80 Browning; 78 Ent. In 1689 there were three other brothers, Charles, William and Philip, between John and the second Robert.
[81] P.C.C. 78 Ent.
[82] Dict. Nat. Biog.
[83] P.C.C. 83 Trenley.
[84] Recov. R. Mich. 18 Geo. II.
[85] Long Crendon is not named in his will (P.C.C. 408 Warburton).

[86] Lipscomb, *Hist. and Antiq. of Bucks.* i, 206.
[87] Priv. Act, 5 Geo. IV, cap. 6.
[88] *Rec. of Bucks.* (Bucks. Arch. and Archit. Soc.), vi, 272.
[89] G.E.C. *Peerage*, iv, 409.
[90] *Cal. Close*, 1272-9, p. 190; G.E.C. *Peerage*, iv, 213-14.
[91] *Feud. Aids*, i, 84; see also *Cal. Pat.* 1292-1301, p. 84.
[92] G.E.C. op. cit. iv, 214.
[93] Ibid.
[94] Feet of F. Bucks. 4 Edw. III, no. 1; De Banco R. 346, m. 289; 348, m. 570 d.; 350, m. 202.
[94a] G.E.C. loc. cit.
[95] Chan. Inq. p.m. 37 Edw. III (1st nos.), no. 10; G.E.C. loc. cit.
[96] Chan. Inq. p.m. 46 Edw. III (1st nos.), no. 10.
[97] Rentals and Surv. (Duchy of Lanc.), bdle. 14, no. 4; Chan. Inq. p.m. 7 Hen. V, no. 59.
[98] Chan. Inq. p.m. 1 Hen. IV, pt. 1, no. 50, 51.
[99] G.E.C. *Peerage*, iv, 215.
[100] Chan. Inq. p.m. 7 Hen. V, no. 59.

the partition of the Bohun inheritance Crendon fell to the king, to whose widow Queen Katherine it was assigned in dower in 1422.[1] It belonged to the Crown fifteen years later,[2] but before or in 1449 was

BOHUN. *Azure a bend argent cotised or between six lions or.*

ALL SOULS COLLEGE, OXFORD. *Or a cheveron between three cinqfoils gules.*

granted to the college of All Souls, Oxford,[3] and has remained in its possession to the present day.[4]

In 1483 Crendon was one of the Buckinghamshire manors claimed by Henry Duke of Buckingham as a descendant of Humphrey de Bohun.[5]

The last third of the manor was divided between the two heirs of Eva, second daughter of Eva de Braose, who had married William Cantelow.[6] One of these, John, afterwards Lord Hastings, son of her daughter Joan by Sir Henry Hastings,[7] was a minor and the king's ward in 1275.[8] In 1313 he left his share in the manor to his son John,[9] at whose death in 1324 it descended to his son Laurence, aged six, afterwards Earl of Pembroke.[10] Laurence, in or before 1342, granted Crendon for life to Theobald de Mounteny,[11] who died in 1362.[12] The reversion belonged to John, son and heir of Laurence, but the king resumed the wardship in 1363.[13] Agnes widow of Laurence was dowered in 1364,[14] and John died seised eleven years later.[15] His son and heir John died without issue in 1389.[16] Crendon, which was amongst his possessions,[17] is not mentioned in the claims on the Hastings inheritance in 1391.[18] In that year one of the claimants, Reynold Lord Grey de Ruthyn, apparently placed the manor in trust for the benefit of Philippa, the last earl's widow.[19] Her second husband, Richard Earl of Arundel, who was executed in 1397, died seised of a quarter of a knight's fee in Crendon in right of his wife.[20] Philippa died in 1400,[21] and Reynold Grey, who was then found to hold the reversion of other

Buckinghamshire lands which she held in dower from John Hastings,[22] again settled,[23] and in 1405 further put Crendon in trust[24] for the use of Joan wife of William Beauchamp, Lord of Bergavenny and daughter of Richard Earl of Arundel by his first wife Elizabeth, daughter of William Bohun, Earl of Northampton.[25] She died seised of a quarter of a knight's fee in Crendon in 1435, when her heir was her granddaughter Elizabeth wife of Edward Nevill, younger son of Ralph first Earl of Westmorland.[26] It is uncertain whether Crendon came to the Crown before Elizabeth's death in 1448, but her husband was living in 1467,[27] when it was granted for life to Elizabeth queen of Edward IV,[28] who surrendered it in the next year.[29] Katherine, Dowager Duchess of Norfolk, a daughter of Ralph Nevill first Earl of Westmorland,[30] enjoyed a life interest in this manor in 1475, when the king settled his remainder of it on the queen.[31] The duchess was dead before 1480,[32] in which year Edward IV granted the manor of Crendon to the Dean and Canons of St. George's, Windsor.[33] It remained among their possessions, except for a temporary alienation in 1649,[34] until 1867,[35] and has since been held by the Ecclesiastical Commissioners.[36]

ST. GEORGE'S, WINDSOR. *Argent a cross gules.*

The other half of the purparty of the heirs of Eva Cantelow[37] came in 1275 to her daughter Milicent and her husband Eudo la Zouche.[38] Milicent, who held alone between 1284 and 1286,[39] in 1296 made a settlement in favour of her son William and his wife Maud.[40] This William la Zouche, one of the lords of Crendon in 1302 and 1316,[41] apparently conveyed his rights to John second Lord Hastings, whose share, a sixth in 1316,[42] had increased to a third before his death in 1324.[43]

At the beginning of the 14th century William de Warmodeston held land in Crendon of the Hastings and Bohun lords,[44] some of which was settled on him and his wife Alice by John de Warmodeston in 1311.[45] This or another John de Warmodeston held with his wife Alice in 1335.[46] Alice de Warmodeston, sole tenant in 1346,[47] was succeeded by a second or third John de Warmodeston, whose daughter and heir Katherine, a minor in 1361,[48] was in 1367 the wife

[1] Duchy of Lanc. Misc. Bks. xviii (2), m. 49 d.
[2] *Cal. Pat.* 1436–41, pp. 32, 44.
[3] *Rec. of Bucks.* (Bucks. Arch. and Archit. Soc.), vi, 361.
[4] *Valor Eccl.* (Rec. Com.), ii, 234; Chan. Inq. p.m. (Ser. 2), ccxxiv, 4; ccxliv, 13; Priv. Act, 5 Geo. IV, cap. 6.
[5] Dugdale, *Baronage*, i, 168–9.
[6] G.E.C. *Peerage*, vi, 204; iv, 179.
[7] Ibid.
[8] *Cal. Fine R.* 1272–1307, p. 58; cf. *Feud. Aids*, i, 84.
[9] *Cal. Inq. p.m.* (Edw. II), v. 233. John Segrave had a life interest in a sixth of the manor (ibid.) and was sued in 1316 for destroying a grange and cutting down 300 oaks (De Banco R. 215, m. 92).
[10] *Cal. Inq. p.m.* (Edw. II), vi, 386.
[11] *Cal. Pat.* 1340–3, p. 517.
[12] Chan. Inq. p.m. 38 Edw. III (1st nos.), no. 26.

[13] Ibid.; *Cal. Pat.* 1361–4, p. 350.
[14] *Cal. Close*, 1364–8, pp. 27–8.
[15] Chan. Inq. p.m. 49 Edw. III (1st nos.), no. 70. [16] Ibid. 14 Ric. II, no. 147.
[17] Ibid.; Rentals and Surv. (Duchy of Lanc.), bdle. 14, no. 3.
[18] Chan. Misc. bdle. 88, file 4, no. 71.
[19] Feet of F. Div. Co. Mich. 2 Hen. IV.
[20] Chan. Inq. p.m. 21 Ric. II, no. 2.
[21] Ibid. 2 Hen. IV, no. 54. [22] Ibid.
[23] Feet of F. Div. Co. Mich. 2 Hen. IV.
[24] De Banco R. 576, m. 1d.
[25] G.E.C. *Peerage* (new ed.), i, 26.
[26] Chan. Inq. p.m. 14 Hen. VI, no. 35.
[27] G.E.C. *Peerage* (new ed.), i, 27–30.
[28] *Parl. R.* v, 628 a.
[29] Close, 8 Edw. IV, m. 14.
[30] G.E.C. *Peerage*, vi, 42.
[31] Feet of F. case 294, file 76, no. 104.
[32] *Cal. Inq. p.m.* (Rec. Com.), iv, 338.
[33] Duchy of Lanc. Misc. Bks. xix, fol. 12.
[34] This was a sale by the Long Parlia-

ment to Henry Cannon (Close, 1649, pt. xxiii, no. 20).
[35] Ct. of Req. bdle. 61, no. 72; Chan. Enr. Decr. 1201, no. 4; Priv. Act, 5 Geo. IV, cap. 6.
[36] *Lond. Gaz.* 28 June 1867, p. 3630.
[37] See above.
[38] *Cal. Fine R.* 1272–1307, p. 58.
[39] *Feud. Aids*, i, 84. She then bore the name of her first husband John de Montalt (G.E.C. *Peerage*, viii, 222–3).
[40] *Cal. Pat.* 1292–1301, p. 184.
[41] *Feud. Aids*, i, 94, 114.
[42] De Banco R. 215, m. 92.
[43] *Cal. Inq. p.m.* (Edw. II), vi, 386.
[44] Feet of F. Bucks. 30 Edw. I, no. 5; 35 Edw. I, no. 1; 9 Edw. II, no. 12; *Feud. Aids*, i, 94.
[45] Feet of F. Bucks. 5 Edw. II, no. 13.
[46] Ibid. 9 Edw. III, no. 6.
[47] *Feud. Aids*, i, 120.
[48] *Abbrev. Rot. Orig.* (Rec. Com.), ii, 270.

of Thomas de Loveden,[49] a descendant probably of the Thomas de Loveden who had held half a knight's fee in Crendon in 1330.[50] Their combined lands formed the so-called manor of *LOVEDENS*, sold by Thomas Loveden of Crendon to Michael Dormer in 1517.[51] William, Sir Michael's son, sold it in 1554 to Nicholas Bethune.[52] In 1568 James Braybrook held an estate in Crendon of All Souls College, Oxford,[53] which, as the manor of Lovedens or Loveday, descended on his death in 1590 to his son William,[54] whose son Richard was seised from 1592 to 1648.[55]

A so-called manor in Crendon, held by John Barton and his wife Isabel between 1432 and 1473,[56] was probably part of the manor of All Souls College, from the revenues of which two priests were paid to celebrate for the souls of Isabel and John.[57]

Other sub-tenants of the divided manor of Crendon in the 13th and 14th centuries belonged to the families of Fitz Piers, Ellis, and Craven.[58]

Clarice widow of Peter Morel, who held $1\frac{1}{2}$ hides of land in Crendon of her own inheritance in 1179 and 1185,[59] was succeeded by John Morel, probably her son,[60] tenant of a quarter of a knight's fee here of the old enfeoffment under William Marshal in the reign of Henry III.[61] At the latter date Robert son of William Revel, a minor, held land of William Marshal of the new enfeoffment.[62] Robert or his heir of the same name was a landowner in Crendon in 1277, when half his possessions were assigned to his creditor Benedict the Jew.[63]

A weekly market on Thursday, which was allowed to William Marshal in 1218,[64] does not appear to have survived the partition of the manor. In 1276 free warren was claimed.[65] Courts leet and views of frankpledge were held for the manor.[66] There is evidence of a windmill in the manor from 1297.[67] Robert Revel owned a capital messuage in 1277[68]; the Mortimer and Hastings lords had theirs rather later[69]; in 1554 there was a capital messuage on the manor of Lovedens which the Dormers owned,[70] and the Dean and Canons of Windsor owned a mansion-house here in 1706.[71]

NUTLEY MANOR, which owed its origin to Walter Giffard's grant of the park of Crendon, an important appurtenance of the manor in 1086,[72] to the house which he founded there, and which was often called accordingly St. Mary of the Park of Crendon,[73] belonged to Nutley Abbey until its surrender[74] in 1538.[75] The wardenship was given in 1542 to Sir John Williams,[76] who received a life grant of the demesne the next year.[77] In 1547 this with the site of the monastery was granted to Sir William Paget.[78] The estate afterwards came to Sir John Williams, and as the manor of Nutley was left by him in 1559 to his widow in dower,[79] passing at her death to his daughters and heirs, Isabel wife of Richard Wenman, and Margery wife of Henry Norreys.[80] In 1579 Isabel, with her second husband Richard Huddleston,[81] alienated her moiety to Bartholomew Wyld and William Bower,[82] probably with a view to its transference to her sister, whose son John, afterwards Sir John Norreys, was lord of the whole in 1585 and 1590 and mortgaged it in 1592.[83] From Sir John Norreys Nutley descended in 1597 to his nephew Francis Lord Norreys, son and heir of his elder brother William,[84] who was engaged three years later in a suit for its recovery from the trustees of his uncle's mortgagee.[85] As Earl of Berkshire he died seised in 1623-4,[86] and his manor of Nutley passed to his daughter Elizabeth, wife of Edward Wray.[87] She and her husband leased the site in 1625 for twenty-one years to Edward Lenton,[89] who was living there at the close of this term.[89] The manor, which was included in a settlement of 1628-9,[90] afterwards came to Bridget, only child of Edward and Elizabeth Wray.[91] Bridget held it with her second husband, Montagu

LENTON. *Azure a bend ermine between two dolphins or.*

[49] *Cal. Close*, 1364-8, p. 319.
[50] Duchy of Lanc. Knights' fees, bdle. 1, no. 6. From the later connexion of Lovedens with the college of All Souls, it would seem that this half-fee, though held immediately of the Duke of Lancaster in 1330, was part of the Bohun third. In 1336 the Mortimer manor, in 1392 the Hastings manor, in 1420 the Bohun manor was ascribed to the Duchy of Lancaster (Rentals and Surv. [Duchy of Lanc.], bdles. 1, no. 8; 14, no. 3, 4).
[51] Close, 9 Hen. VIII, no. 22.
[52] Com. Pleas D. Enr. Mich. 1 & 2 Phil. and Mary, m. 11. Nicholas was not seised of this land at his death in 1557 (Chan. Inq. p.m. [Ser. 2], cxii, 131), though he is called of 'Crendon' (P.C.C. 22 Wrastley).
[53] Chan. Inq. p.m. (Ser. 2), ccxxiv, 4.
[54] Ibid. ccxliv, 113.
[55] Feet of F. Bucks. Mich. 10 Jas. I; Trin. 8 Chas. I; Hil. 18 Chas. I; Mich. 24 Chas. I.
[56] Early Chan. Proc. bdle. 11, no. 522. Nicholas Barton sold land in Crendon in 1315 (Feet of F. Bucks. 9 Edw. II, no. 12).
[57] *Valor Eccl.* (Rec. Com.), ii, 234.
[58] Feet of F. Bucks. 14 Edw. I, no. 1, 9, 10; 7 Edw. III, no. 2, 11; 9 Edw. III, no. 6; 15 Edw. III, no. 6, 7; *Feud. Aids*, i, 94, 120; Rentals and Surv.

(Duchy of Lanc.), bdle. 1, no. 8; *Cal. Inq. p.m.* (Edw. II), vi, 612.
[59] Pipe R. 25 Hen. II (Pipe R. Soc.), 80; Stacey Grimaldi, *Rot. de Dominabus*, 22.
[60] A son and heir of Peter and Clarice was aged fifteen in 1185 (Stacey Grimaldi, loc. cit.).
[61] Misc. Bks. (Exch. K.R.), vi, 168.
[62] *Testa de Nevill* (Rec. Com.), 247.
[63] *Cal. Close*, 1272-9, p. 395. A William Revel of Crendon was living in 1341 (Inq. Nonarum [Rec. Com.], 339).
[64] Rot. Lit. Claus. (Rec. Com.), i, 363b.
[65] *Hund. R.* (Rec. Com.), i, 45.
[66] Rentals and Surv. (Duchy of Lanc.), bdle. 14, no. 3; Close, 1649, pt. xxiii, no. 20; Chan. Inq. p.m. 23 Hen. VI, no. 33.
[67] Chan. Inq. p.m. 25 Edw. I, no. 36; 29 Edw. I, no. 53; Rentals and Surv. (Duchy of Lanc.), bdle. 1, no. 8; Chan. Inq. p.m. 18 Edw. II, no. 83; Com. Pleas D. Enr. Mich. 1 & 2 Phil. and Mary, m. 11; Memo. R. (Exch. L.T.R.), Trin. 6 Eliz. m. 8; Feet of F. Bucks. Trin. 11 Eliz.; Hil. 16 Eliz.; Mich. 24 & 25 Eliz.; Pat. 27 Eliz. pt. viii, m. 27.
[68] *Cal. Close*, 1272-9, p. 395.
[69] Chan. Inq. p.m. 25 Edw. I, no. 36; 18 Edw. II, no. 83.
[70] Com. Pleas D. Enr. Mich. 1 and 2 Phil. and Mary, m. 11.
[71] Chan. Enr. Decrees, 1201, no. 4.

[72] *V.C.H. Bucks.* i, 248.
[73] *Cal. Rot. Chart.* 1199-1216 (Rec. Com.), 46; *Cal. Chart. R.* 1300-26, p. 210.
[74] *Cal. Chart. R.* 1327-41, pp. 84, 327; *Cal. Pat.* 1396-9, p. 380; *Pope Nich. Tax.* (Rec. Com.), 46b; *Valor Eccl.* (Rec. Com.), iv, 234; Dugdale, *Mon.* vi, 280.
[75] *L. and P. Hen. VIII*, xiii (2), 1014.
[76] Ibid. xvii, p. 691.
[77] Ibid. xviii (1), p. 555.
[78] Pat. 1 Edw. VI, pt. ii, m. 43; 4 Edw. VI, pt. viii, m. 34.
[79] P.C.C. 11 Mellershe.
[80] Chan. Inq. p.m. (Ser. 2), cxxvi, 150.
[81] Lee, *Hist. and Antiq. of the Church of Thame*, 433.
[82] Pat. 21 Eliz. pt. v, m. 43; Feet o F. Bucks. Hil. 21 Eliz.
[83] Pat. 27 Eliz. pt. viii, m. 47; 32 Eliz. pt. xvi, m. 37; Recov. R. Trin. 27 Eliz. m. 6.
[84] Chan. Inq. p.m. (Ser. 2), ccxciii, 13.
[85] *Cal. S. P. Dom.* 1598-1601, p. 217; Chan. Proc. Eliz. Nn 4, no. 46.
[86] Chan. Inq. p.m. (Ser. 2), cccxcix, 153.
[87] Ibid.; Feet of F. Div. Co. East. 21 Jas. I.
[88] Feet of F. Bucks. Mich. 1 Chas. I.
[89] *Cal. S. P. Dom.* 1645-7, p. 502.
[90] Feet of F. Div. Co. Hil. 4 Chas. I.
[91] G.E.C. *Peerage* (new ed.), i, 45.

Long Crendon Church from the South-West

Long Crendon Church: The Interior looking East

Earl of Lindsey, in 1648[92] and in 1650, when they renewed the lease of 1625 to Norris Lenton.[93] In 1689 Henry, one of their younger sons, was lord.[94] He died in 1734, having had by his wife Philadelphia a son James, whose son Norris seems to have been the last of his line.[95] By 1765 the manor had come to Peregrine Bertie, eldest son of Peregrine Bertie of Lincoln's Inn,[96] a great-grandson of Bridget Wray's husband by his first wife, Martha Cockayne.[97] Albemarle Bertie, who succeeded his brother Peregrine in 1782,[98] sold Nutley in 1791 to Henry Reynolds,[99] whose ancestors had long been tenants here and whose descendant, Mr. Henry Reynolds, is still in possession.[100]

Later gifts of Walter Giffard from the township of Crendon itself, the whole wick (*wykam*) with the men and their holding (*tenura*), the garden once of Robert the chaplain, the site of the kitchen where the earl's dogs afterwards lay, the site of the grange for which the monks of Newton Longville paid rent,[1] passed under the style of Crendon Manor[2] with Nutley until 1648,[3] if not later. In 1731 it belonged to Willoughby Bertie,[4] son and heir of James Bertie, grandson of Bridget Wray and the Earl of Lindsey.[5] Willoughby Bertie still held in 1745,[6] when he had succeeded his uncle Montagu in the earldom of Abingdon.[7] His son and heir, another Willoughby Earl of Abingdon,[8] who succeeded in 1760,[9] is said to have sold the estate before or in 1799 to George Spencer Duke of Marlborough,[10] whose youngest son, Francis Almeric Lord Churchill, owned it in 1824.[11] He was succeeded in 1845 by his son and heir Francis George Lord Churchill,[12] whose estate in Long Crendon had passed before 1862 to Mr. John Dodwell,[13] and is now held by Mr. Herbert Dodwell.

Lands in Crendon called *SPERLINGS MANOR* at the close of the 15th century, when they belonged to the chantry or gild of St. Christopher in Thame,[14] were granted in 1552 to Sir John Williams,[15] and leased by his daughter Margery and her husband Henry Norreys to John Ketill in 1567.[16]

The water-mill mentioned in Domesday Book[17] was possibly identical with the mill which, about a century later, the third Walter Giffard granted to Nutley Abbey.[18] A water-mill adjoining the abbey[19] was included amongst the appurtenances of the manor of Nutley in the 17th century.[20] In 1862 this was represented by the ' very ancient water-mill ' situated to the left of the abbey ruins.[21] One or possibly two windmills, and dovecotes varying in number from one to three, belonged to the manors of Nutley and Crendon in the 16th and 17th centuries.[22] Court leet, view of frankpledge and free warren came to Sir William Paget with the site of the manor of Nutley in 1547.[23]

The church of *ST. MARY THE VIRGIN* consists of a chancel measuring internally 29 ft. by 16 ft., central tower 17 ft. square, north transept 24 ft. by 17 ft., south transept 23 ft. 6 in. by 16 ft. 6 in., nave 40 ft. by 19 ft., north aisle 15 ft. wide, south aisle 9 ft. 6 in. wide, and north, south and west porches. It is built of limestone and roofed with lead and tiles.

The church dates from the 12th century, but the only remains of this period are the lower parts of the lateral walls at the west end of the nave, and the head of a small window reset in the west wall. The chancel, tower, transepts and aisles, with the nave arcades, were built during the 13th century. The north aisle was widened, the north part of the north transept rebuilt, and the north porch added in the first half of the 14th century. The south porch dates from the 15th century, when the south transept was rebuilt. About 1510 the west porch and the upper stages of the tower were added and the west wall of the nave was rebuilt. The fabric was restored by Sir Arthur Blomfield in 1890–1, and the transepts have since been repaired.

The chancel is lighted by two original lancets on the north, three on the south and a modern five-light window on the east, while in the south wall are a square-headed doorway, which is probably original, and a trefoiled piscina with a sexfoil bowl. On the east wall is a 15th-century bracket, and in the east jamb of the middle window on the south is a mask corbel. The upper part of the north wall is thinner than the lower part, the offset occurring externally at a line midway in the height of the lancets. The central tower opens by four 13th-century arches to the chancel, nave and transepts, and is of three stages with an embattled parapet ; the tower arches were restored in the 16th century, when the upper stages were built, and again in 1632 and 1633, these last dates being carved on the piers. The bell-chamber, which is reached by a stair turret on the north-west, is lighted from all sides by pairs of 16th-century windows, each of two transomed lights with tracery in the head.

The north transept has a large 14th-century traceried window in the north wall of five cinquefoiled lights, two 13th-century lancets in the east wall, one of which is blocked, and a 14th-century arch to the aisle on the west ; the walls were raised in the 15th century and finished with a plain parapet. Under the large window is a moulded tomb recess. The south transept is lighted from the east by two 17th-century square-

---

[92] Feet of F. Div. Co. Hil. 24 Chas. I.
[93] Ibid. Bucks. Mich. 1650.
[94] Ibid. Mich. 1 Will.and Mary;Recov. R. Mich. 1 Will. and Mary, m. 54.
[95] Lee, op. cit. 443.
[96] Com. Pleas D. Enr. Trin. 5 Geo. III, m. 207 ; Recov. R. Trin. 5 Geo. III, m. 251.
[97] Lee, op. cit. 447-51. This Peregrine Bertie also held Wooburn Manor (*V.C.H. Bucks.* iii, 108).
[98] Lee, loc. cit.
[99] Ibid. 617-18 ; Lipscomb, op. cit. i, 237 ; *Rec. of Bucks.* (Bucks. Arch. and Archit. Soc.), vi, 358.
[100] Lee, loc. cit.
[1] Dugdale, *Mon.* vi, 278 ; *Cal. Chart.*

R. 1300-26, p. 210 ; cf. *Pope Nich. Tax.* (Rec. Com.), 46 *b.*
[2] *Valor Eccl.* (Rec. Com.), iv, 234 ; L. *and P. Hen. VIII,* xvii, p. 702 ; xx (1), g. 621 (7).
[3] Feet of F. Div. Co. Hil. 24 Chas. I.
[4] Recov. R. Mich. 5 Geo. II, m. 56.
[5] G.E.C. *Peerage* (new ed.), i, 45-8.
[6] Recov. R. Mich. 19 Geo. II, m. 485.
[7] G.E.C. loc. cit.
[8] Ibid.
[9] Ibid.; Recov. R. Hil. 1 Geo. III, m. 156.
[10] Lipscomb, op. cit. i, 214. The duke, however, presented to the church in 1774 (Inst. Bks. [P.R.O.]).

[11] Priv. Act, 5 Geo. IV, cap. 6; G.E.C. *Peerage,* ii, 248.
[12] G.E.C. loc. cit.
[13] Sheahan, op. cit. 368.
[14] De Banco R. Trin. 15 Hen. VII, m. 351.
[15] Pat. 6 Edw. VI, pt. iv, m. 32 (20).
[16] Feet of F. Bucks. Hil. 9 Eliz.
[17] *V.C.H. Bucks.* i, 248.
[18] Dugdale, *Mon.* vi, 278.
[19] Aug. Off. Misc. Bks. ccccvi, fol. 12, 13 ; Pat. 1 Edw. VI, pt. ii, m. 43.
[20] Feet of F. Div. Co. Mich. 1650 ; Bucks. Mich. 1 Will. and Mary.
[21] Sheahan, op. cit. 375.
[22] See under manors.
[23] Pat. 1 Edw. VI, pt. ii, m. 43.

headed windows, and from the west by a 15th-century traceried window of three lights. In the south wall is a 15th-century window of four lights, now blocked by the Dormer monument. The present roof of this transept dates from the 15th century, but above the tower arch can be seen the lines of the original high-pitched roof.

The nave has on either side a 13th-century arcade of two arches, the north arcade having a quatrefoil pillar and responds with moulded bell capitals, and the south similar responds, but an octagonal pillar with a capital of the same character. High in the wall on the south are traces of circular clearstory windows. In the west wall is an early 16th-century doorway with moulded jambs, and above it a contemporary window of four lights under a four-centred head. The jambs of this window are continued to the floor, and the recess so formed is flanked by two

entrance arch of two orders, the inner order springing from corbels, and the west porch has a moulded archway with foliated spandrels, and a quatrefoil light in each side wall.

The octagonal font dates from about 1380 ; the sides of the bowl have quatrefoil panels, and at the angles are angel-heads with outspread wings, which form a rich band round the rim ; the base is enriched with foliated panels and lions' heads. In the south transept is a 17th-century communion table with rails. Below the northern tower arch are parts of a 16th-century screen, and in the south transept is an open screen of about 1680. The stand of the wood lectern is of the late 17th century.

On the east wall of the north transept is a brass with figures commemorating John Canon, who died in 1460, and Agnes his wife, 1468, with groups of three sons and eight daughters. There are also 18th-

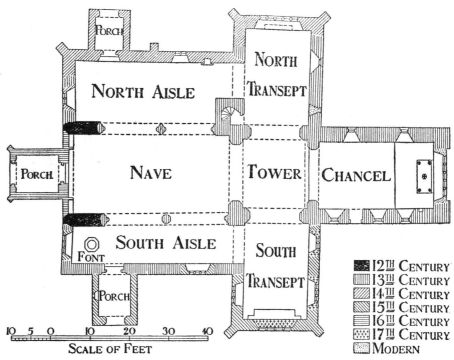

PLAN OF LONG CRENDON CHURCH

Adapted from the Inventory of the Historical Monuments of Buckinghamshire with the permission of the Royal Commission and the consent of the Controller of H.M. Stationery Office

other recesses, the jambs of which fall upon stone benches. Above the west window is the head of the 12th-century light already mentioned. The north aisle is lighted by two 14th-century windows, one in the north wall and the other in the west wall, both of two trefoiled lights with tracery, and in the north wall is a doorway of the same period, while at the north-east are a low blocked window and a 14th-century trefoiled niche with a crocketed label. The north porch, though considerably restored, retains the original entrance archway. The south aisle has a 13th-century doorway with jamb shafts and a richly moulded arch, above which are traces of a gable ; to the east of it is a 15th-century traceried window, and there is a similar window in the west wall. The roofs of the nave and aisles, though much repaired, retain a considerable amount of 15th and 16th-century work. The south porch has an original

century monuments to the Canon family. In the south transept, surrounded by an iron railing, is a large monument commemorating Sir John Dormer (d. 1627) and Jane his wife, daughter of John Giffard of Chillington, Staffordshire (d. 1605). The inscription records that they had four sons (Robert, John, Gyfford and William) and two daughters (Elizabeth and Dorothy). Their recumbent figures, the knight in armour, are placed in a panelled recess flanked by Tuscan columns and surmounted by an entablature and shield of arms. In the chancel are floor slabs to Jane wife of John Burnham (d. 1686) and William Langbaine (d. 1672).

The tower contains a ring of eight bells, all by Lester & Pack of London, 1768, and a small bell by George Chandler, 1719. Five of this ring are said to have been brought from Nutley Abbey about 1540,[24] three were added in 1632, and the whole ring was recast in 1768.[25]

[24] Lysons, *Mag. Brit.* i (3), 489. [25] *Rec. of Bucks.* (Bucks. Arch. and Archit. Soc.), vi, 280.

The plate consists of a cup of 1590 and a flagon and plate of the 18th century.

The registers begin in 1559.

ADVOWSON The church of Long Crendon, now dedicated in honour of St. Mary the Virgin,[26] appears to have been originally granted by the second Walter Giffard to St. Faith Longueville,[27] but later resumed and given by his son to the abbey he had founded at Nutley,[28] remaining in its possession until the Dissolution.[29] The church afterwards followed the descent of the manor of Crendon, once of Nutley Abbey[30] (q.v.), remaining in Lord Churchill's gift after he had parted with the manor. He was patron until 1883 ; from 1884 to 1888 the advowson belonged to the executors of R. Cottman, from 1889 to 1891 to D. B. Chapman. The Rev. F. E. Ogden, vicar from 1887 to 1901, was also patron from 1892 ; from 1901 to 1903 the living was in the gift of Miss Ogden and Mrs. Barclay Chapman ; from 1904 to 1906 of Mr. W. Toone, since which year the Bishop of Oxford has been patron.[31]

Lands given for the keeping of lights in the church of Crendon and for the maintenance of an obit were included in a grant to Sir Edward Bray and others made in 1552.[32]

CHARITIES The following charities are regulated by a scheme of the Charity Commissioners, dated 24 July 1906, namely :—

Charity of Sir John Dormer, founded by deed 1 May 1620, consisting of a rent-charge of £30 (less land tax) issuing out of land at Piddington, Oxfordshire.

Thomas Westbrooke's charity, will 1630, being an annuity of 15s. issuing out of Downe Lane Close at Littlemore, Oxfordshire.

Thomas Canon's charity, deed 23 December 1648,

trust fund £40 2½ per cent. annuities, arising from the redemption in 1902 of rent-charge of £1.

John Hart's charity, will proved in the P.C.C. 15 May 1665, being a rent-charge of £5 (less land tax) issuing out of land at Easington, Oxfordshire ; and

Trott's charity, being an annuity of 10s. issuing out of North Down Field, date of foundation unknown, but mentioned in the Parliamentary Returns of 1786.

It is directed by the scheme that out of the income of Sir John Dormer's charity the yearly sum of £2 10s. shall be applied in keeping in repair the tomb and monument of the founder and the aisle of the church in which it is situated, and payment of a yearly sum of 12s. to the person so employed ; also a sum not exceeding £6 to be applied every third year towards the cost of a dinner on the day kept as the court day for the lord of the manor, with 15s. to the steward.

The income of John Hart's charity is to be applied in apprenticing or in prizes or exhibitions for children attending a public elementary school, the residue of the income of the charities being applicable for the benefit of the poor of not less than sixty years of age during the winter season. The distribution is usually made in coal.

The church lands, the origin of which is unknown, consist of 16 acres, let at £15 a year, which is applied in aid of the general church expenses.

The poor's allotment, also known as Deiman's charity, consists of 12 acres, let at £12 a year, which is applied in the distribution of coal.

The Wesleyan Methodist chapel, comprised in deed 2 July 1829, was by an order of the Charity Commissioners, 6 January 1911, vested in trustees thereby appointed upon the trusts of the Skircoat Model Deed, dated in 1832.

DORTON

Dortone (xi cent.) ; Durton (xiii cent.).

This parish contains 1,477 acres, of which 122 are arable land and 1,108 permanent grass.[1] The land, of which the surface is clay on a subsoil of Kimmeridge Clay and Portland Beds, varies from about 250 ft. above the ordnance datum on the eastern boundary to over 450 ft. at Dorton Hill.

In the west of Dorton, on the borders of Brill, is a chalybeate spring, and a pump room and baths, now demolished, were erected here about the middle of the 19th century.[2] The village, approached by a road from Chilton, is of small size. At its south end, on low ground, are the church of St. John Baptist and the parsonage built in 1849. Near them Dorton House, the seat of Mr. Henry Aubrey-Fletcher, stands surrounded by 18 acres of pleasure grounds in which there is a lake. The house, a brick building of the half-H type with stone quoins and tiled roofs, dates from 1626, though it was much altered in the 18th

century and has been restored at a modern period. The screens, placed in the centre of the main block, are entered from the forecourt on the east, through an 18th-century portico which forms the main entrance. To the north of the screens are the original hall, the main staircase opening off the hall and projecting into the forecourt, and the library and Queen Elizabeth's room, the last two being in the north wing. To the south of the screens are the morning room, a corridor leading to a second staircase, the offices and the dining room, the latter, which is in the south wing, being the original kitchen. Above the hall is the drawing room, with two small rooms and an ante-room to the north of it, the latter entered from the main staircase, while the whole of the first floor of the north wing is occupied by the long gallery. The north front, with its three bay windows, has been little altered, and elsewhere many original mullioned windows remain. The hall has a panelled dado

[26] Bacon, *Liber Regis.* 505 ; Crockford, *Cler. Dir.*
[27] *Cal. Doc. of France,* 77.
[28] Cart. Antiq. E 7 ; *Cal. Rot. Chart.* 1199–1216 (Rec. Com.), 46; *Cal. Chart. R.* 1300–26, p. 210.
[29] *Cal. of Papal Letters,* v, 508 ; *Valor Eccl.* (Rec. Com.), iv, 233.
[30] See also Feet of F. Div. Co. Hil. 8 Chas. I ; *Cal. S. P. Dom.* 1655, p. 132 ; Inst. Bks. (P.R.O.) ; Bacon, loc. cit. ; *Cler. Guide,* 1817–36.
[31] *Clergy Lists,* 1864–1914.
[32] Chant. Cert. 9, no. 52 ; Pat. 6 Edw. VI, pt. ix, m. 8.
[1] Statistics from Bd. of Agric. (1905).
[2] Sheahan, *Hist. and Topog. of Bucks.* 376–80.

and a wide moulded fireplace with an overmantel enriched with strapwork, in the centre of which is a modern shield, incorrectly painted, showing the quartered coat of Sir John Aubrey, sixth baronet (1786–1826), with those of his two wives, Mary Colebrooke and Martha Catherine Carter, in pretence. Above is the eagle's head, the crest of Aubrey. The screen, at the south end of the hall, is an elaborate piece of Jacobean work. It is pierced by two doorways and the panelled bays are divided by fluted Ionic pilasters, the whole being surmounted by an entablature and open-work cresting. Opening into the main staircase is a round-headed stone doorway with a panelled soffit. The principal stairway, which bears the date 1626 on one of the plaster soffit panels and rises by easy flights from an oak screen in the staircase hall, is of the dog-legged type, and has chamfered newels with urn-shaped finials, moulded handrails and turned balusters ; the staircase hall has a plaster frieze with grotesque and foliated ornament in relief and a rich plaster ceiling. The room over the morning room is panelled and has a moulded fireplace with an elaborate overmantel, and both this and the drawing-room have rich coved ceilings, the latter displaying the Dormer badge, an eye with rays issuing from it. The ceiling over the long gallery is plain, but of barrel form. The staircase to the south of the hall rises in easy flights and has square newels with moulded finials and square balusters, the mouldings of which follow the rake of the stairs. The Boarstall horn, a black silver-mounted cow-horn, 1 ft. 10 in. long, dating from the 15th century, is preserved in the house, as well as the private chartulary of the manor of Boarstall and other manors belonging to Edmund Rede. The stables, which are contemporary with the house, were considerably repaired about the end of the 18th century.

Park Farm, in the north-east of the parish, was probably part of the Dorton Woods inclosed by the Dormers in the 16th century.[3] On the summit of Dorton Hill in the south are traces of an ancient encampment.[4]

DORTON, held by Alric before the
MANORS Norman Conquest, and by Walter Giffard in 1086,[5] came from the Giffards through the Marshals[6] to the Earls of Gloucester.[7] After 1284, when the whole fee belonged to Gilbert Earl of Gloucester,[8] the overlordship seems to have been divided between the descendants of Isabel and Joan, the sisters of Anselm Marshal,[9] one half-fee being retained by the Earls of Gloucester and their heirs of the house of Stafford until 1459,[10] the other belonging to Aymer de Valence in 1302 and 1324,[11] and to Richard and Gilbert Talbot respectively in

1346 and 1419.[12] Both, however, were held of Thomas Earl of Stafford in 1392, and of his brother and heir Edmund ten years later.[13] From 1545 to 1627, when the last mention of its overlordship occurs, the manor of Dorton was held of the king as of the honour of Gloucester.[14]

No certain record of the sub-tenancy of Dorton before the 13th century survives, though possibly the knight's fee which Pain de Dorton held of Walter Giffard in 1166 was in this parish.[15] By 1255 the manor had been divided into two parts.[16] One of these, then owned by Sibyl de Birmingham,[17] came afterwards to William de Birmingham and followed the descent of the manor of Hoggeston (q.v.) until 1383, when the manor was either mortgaged or conveyed in trust by Sir John de Birmingham and his wife Elizabeth to Richard de Piriton, clerk, and others.[18] Sir John and Elizabeth had no children.[19] In 1419 Elizabeth, then widow of another husband, John Lord Clinton, held the manor as half a knight's fee in Dorton,[20] but it was not accounted for amongst her lands at her death four years later.[21] Her heirs were the descendants of Thomas de Birmingham, younger brother of John, who had died before him leaving a daughter Elizabeth. She married Thomas Roche and had two daughters and co-heirs,[22] between whom the manor was divided. Ellen the elder, wife of Edmund Lord Ferrers in 1423,[23] with her second husband, Sir Philip Chetwynd, granted her moiety of Dorton to her younger son, John Ferrers, who surrendered his right to it in 1443,[24] probably to the trustees of his elder brother, William Lord Ferrers.[25] William was seised the following year and at his death in 1450, when he left an only child Anne, then wife of Walter Devereux.[26] In 1544 their grandson, another Walter Devereux Lord Ferrers,[27] who had included Dorton in a settlement more than thirty years before,[28] sold his moiety to Sir Michael Dormer.[29]

The other moiety of the Birmingham inheritance in this parish came through Elizabeth, younger granddaughter of Thomas de Birmingham and wife of George Longville,[30] to Richard son of their son Richard,[31] passing at his death in 1458 to his infant son and heir, John Longville,[32] lord in 1497.[33] By the said John, then Sir John Longville, and his son Arthur[34] it was sold in 1541 to Michael Dormer and his son Geoffrey.[35] Sir John was dead a year later,

BIRMINGHAM. *Party indented argent and sable.*

[3] Lansd. MS. 47, fol. 3 ; Exch. Dep. East. 26 Eliz. no. 5 ; Mich. 21 Jas. I, no. 2.
[4] Sheahan, loc. cit.
[5] *V.C.H. Bucks.* i, 248.
[6] Misc. Bks. (Exch. K.R.), vi, fol. 168.
[7] *Feud. Aids*, i, 84.
[8] Ibid.
[9] See Chilton.
[10] *Feud. Aids*, i, 94, 120 ; *Cal. Close,* 1364-8, pp. 435-6 ; Chan. Inq. p.m. 16 Ric. II, pt. i, no. 27 ; 4 Hen. IV, no. 41 ; 37 Hen. VI, no. 28.
[11] *Feud. Aids*, i, 94 ; *Cal. Inq. p.m.* (Edw. II), vi, 328. In 1322 and 1323 John de Somery was overlord (*Cal. Inq.*

p.m. [Edw. II], vi, 257; *Cal. Close,* 1318-23, p. 631).
[12] *Feud. Aids,* i, 120 ; Chan. Inq. p.m. 7 Hen. V, no. 68.
[13] Chan. Inq. p.m. 16 Ric. II, pt. i, no. 27 ; 4 Hen. IV, no. 41.
[14] Ibid. (Ser. 2), lxxiii, 10 ; ccccxxxv, 112.
[15] *Red Bk. of Exch.* (Rolls Ser.), i, 312.
[16] *Hund. R.* (Rec. Com.), i, 26.
[17] Ibid.
[18] Feet of F. Bucks. 6 Ric. II, no. 4.
[19] Chan. Inq. p.m. 2 Hen. VI, no. 36.
[20] Ibid. 7 Hen. V, no. 68 ; G.E.C. *Peerage,* ii, 304, where Elizabeth is said to have married Sir John de Birmingham

after Lord Clinton's death. Her last husband was Sir John Russell.
[21] Chan. Inq. p.m. 2 Hen. VI, no. 36.
[22] Ibid. [23] Ibid.
[24] Close, 22 Hen. VI, m. 32.
[25] G.E.C. *Peerage,* iii, 331.
[26] Chan. Inq. p.m. 28 Hen. VI, no. 22.
[27] G.E.C. loc. cit.
[28] Feet of F. Mixed Co. East. 4 Hen. VIII.
[29] Feet of F. Bucks. Trin. 36 Hen. VIII.
[30] Chan. Inq. p.m. 2 Hen. VI, no. 36.
[31] Ibid. 36 Hen. VI, no. 36.
[32] Ibid. 37 Hen. VI, no. 28.
[33] De Banco R. 942, m. 352.
[34] *Visit. of Bucks.* (Harl. Soc.), 83.
[35] Feet of F. Bucks. Trin. 33 Hen. VIII.

DORTON HOUSE FROM THE SOUTH-EAST

Dorton Church from the South

Dorton Church: The Interior looking East

when John Cheyne, son and heir of his daughter Anne, wife of Drew Cheyne, renounced all right to his grandfather's estate in Dorton.[36]

The manor thus united was settled by Sir Michael Dormer in 1545 on his second son William and his wife Elizabeth,[37] to whom it passed the same year.[38] In 1552 William Dormer made a life settlement of Dorton on Henry Grey and his wife Anne, who then leased the manor to him for ninety years. The remainder of this lease was granted by William to Hugh Hollingshed in 1561 and his reversion of the manor itself mortgaged to Henry Reynolds shortly after.[39] William Dormer died two years later, having settled Dorton on his wife Elizabeth, with contingent remainder to Michael son of his brother Ambrose.[40] In 1565 his son and heir John[41] agreed that Henry Grey should hold the manor for life with remainder, also for life, to Elizabeth wife of Hugh Hollingshed and remainder to Hugh himself after the death of the longer survivor of these two for seven years.[42] All these interests had expired or been bought out by 1594, when John Dormer, being sued in Chancery for payment of an old debt of his father's, was able to say that his inheritance in Dorton had come to him ' for great sums of money and for good considerations.'[43] He was lord in 1616[44] and 1617, and settled Dorton in the latter year on the marriage of his son Robert with Mary daughter of Thomas Read.[45] Dorton henceforward descended with the Dormers' manor of Long Crendon[46] (q.v.) until the death, probably early in 1694, of Robert Dormer, who by his will left land and rent to the value of £200 a year from his estates in Dorton and Brill to each of his step-brothers, Charles, Robert, William, Philip, James, and Clement Dormer, settling the residue in equal proportions on his three uncles, Peregrine, Charles and Henry Bertie, and Henry Cane.[47] Peregrine Bertie in 1695 sold his quarter to Richard Harvey and Richard Adams to be disposed of by them according to his directions.[48] In 1713 a settlement of a quarter and half another quarter of the manor of Dorton on John Burgh was made by Charles Bertie and Henry Bertie and his wife Mary,[49] but Charles Bertie was still lord of one quarter a year later.[50] One part of the Bertie property in Dorton is said to have been acquired by the Mitchell family,[51]

DORMER. *Azure billety or and a chief or with a demi-lion sable therein.*

whilst another came into the possession of Sir Clement Cottrell Dormer.[52] Both were purchased between 1773 and 1783 by John, afterwards Sir John, Aubrey,[53] who seems to have made Dorton House his seat from 1774.[54] The manor has followed the descent of Boarstall (q.v.) from that time, the present lord being Mr. Henry Aubrey-Fletcher.

The other part of the original manor of Dorton[55] belonged to Robert Beauchamp of Hatch in Somerset in 1255.[56] He was succeeded by his son John,[57] whose son and heir, another John Beauchamp,[58] was intrusted to the custody of Peter Corbet, a connexion by marriage of this family,[59] in 1284.[60] In 1302, however, and in 1316 the Beauchamp half-fee in Dorton was held by Simon de Aston,[61] whether by marriage with the elder John's widow or as trustee does not appear. It was again in the hands of the

BEAUCHAMP of Hatch. *Vair.*

Beauchamps in 1327, when William younger son of the above John Beauchamp was engaged in litigation with his late bailiff here.[62] John Beauchamp was succeeded in 1336 by his son and heir John Beauchamp,[63] whose widow Margaret received her dower in Dorton in 1343.[64] Margaret and her tenants were holding in 1346.[65] She died fifteen years later,[66] and in 1362 Dorton passed from her son John Beauchamp, who had survived her only a few months,[67] to Cecily, one of his sisters and heirs.[68] In 1392, when Cecily, then widow of Richard Turbeville, was lately dead,[69] licence was granted for the alienation of the reversion of her moiety of Dorton Manor, which Sir John Clinton and his wife Elizabeth then held for the life of Elizabeth, to the Warden and scholars of St. Mary's College of Winchester in Oxford.[70] There does not seem to be any evidence for the completion of this alienation and the subsequent history of the Beauchamp fee is obscure.

A manor in Dorton called *COTESMORES* was settled in 1456 by Matthew Haye and John Cotesmore on Robert Danvers and his wife Katherine with reversion to Matthew and John and the heirs of John on Katherine's death.[71] Another John Cotesmore was seised of this property in 1490 and 1491, when he claimed as his villein and imprisoned one Simon Mascall, a freeman.[72]

A windmill was an appurtenance of the manor in the 16th century, one or more dovecotes in the 18th century.[73] In 1616 Sir John Dormer and his heirs

[36] Com. Pleas D. Enr. Mich. 34 Hen. VIII, m. 4 d.
[37] Chan. Inq. p.m. (Ser. 2), cxli, 24.
[38] Ibid. lxxiii, 10.
[39] Ibid. cxli, 24 ; Feet of F. Div. Co. Trin. 6 Edw. VI ; Bucks. Hil. 4 Eliz.; Com. Pleas D. Enr. Mich. 1 & 2 Phil. and Mary, m. 11 d.; Chan. Proc. (Ser. 2), bdle. 241, no. 5.
[40] Chan. Inq. p.m. (Ser. 2), cxli, 24.
[41] Ibid.
[42] Feet of F. Div. Co. Mich. 7 & 8 Eliz. Here also there was a contingent remainder to Michael son of Ambrose Dormer.
[43] Chan. Proc. (Ser. 2), bdle. 241, no. 5.
[44] Pat. 13 Jas. I, pt. iv, no. 37.
[45] Chan. Inq. p.m. (Ser. 2), ccccxxxv,
112.

[46] Ibid. See also Recov. R. Trin. 1 Will. and Mary, m. 24. Michael Dormer and his wife Dorothy seem to have had an interest in the manor until Michael's death in 1624. [47] P.C.C. 44 Box.
[48] Close, 7 Will. III, pt. ix, no. 19.
[49] Feet of F. Bucks. Trin. 12 Anne.
[50] Recov. R. Trin. 13 Anne, m. 43.
[51] Lipscomb, *Hist. and Antiq. of Bucks.* i, 242.
[52] Lysons, *Mag. Brit.* i (3), 352, see Chearsley. [53] Lysons, loc. cit.
[54] MSS. of J. B. Fortescue (Hist. MSS. Com.), i, 267, 561 ; Paterson, *Descr. of Roads* (1826), 176. [55] See p. 46.
[56] *Hund. R.* (Rec. Com.), i, 26.
[57] Dugdale, *Baronage*, i, 252.
[58] G.E.C. *Peerage*, i, 275.

[59] Wrottesley, op. cit. 289–90.
[60] *Cal. Pat.* 1281–92, pp. 115, 175 ; *Feud. Aids*, i, 84.
[61] *Feud. Aids*, i, 94, 114.
[62] De Banco R. 267, m. 10 d.
[63] G.E.C. loc. cit.
[64] *Cal. Close*, 1343–6, p. 181 ; *Cal. Pat.* 1343–5, p. 123. [65] *Feud. Aids*, i, 120.
[66] G.E.C. loc. cit. [67] Ibid.
[68] *Abbrev. Rot. Orig.* (Rec. Com.), ii, 269 ; *Cal. Close*, 1364–8, pp. 435–6.
[69] Chan. Inq. p.m. 15 Ric. II, pt. i, no. 103. [70] *Cal. Pat.* 1391–6, p. 62.
[71] Feet of F. Bucks. 35 Hen. VI, no. 36.
[72] De Banco R. 917, m. 401 ; 918, m. 105.
[73] Feet of F. Bucks. Hil. 4 Eliz.; Trin. 12 Anne.

received a grant of park, liberty of park and free warren here, with licence to stock the park with all kinds of game.[74]

The church of *ST. JOHN BAP-*
CHURCH TIST consists of a chancel measuring internally 16 ft. 6 in. by 15 ft., nave 46 ft. by 18 ft. 6 in. at the east end and 16 ft. 6 in. at the west end, south aisle 17 ft. 6 in. by 7 ft. 6 in., south porch, and timber bell-turret. It is built of stone and roofed with tiles.

The chancel and nave are probably of the 12th century; the south porch was added in the following century, and in the middle of the 14th century a small aisle was thrown out on the south side. The aisle was restored towards the close of the 15th century and the porch was partly rebuilt at the same time. In the 16th century the south wall of the chancel was rebuilt further to the south, and about a century later the bell-turret was erected. In 1904 the north wall of the nave was partially renewed and the whole fabric was restored.

The chancel has a two-light east window, and a wide light in the south wall with a pointed inner and square outer head; both windows are of the 16th century, while the two-light window inserted in the north wall is probably of the same period. The responds and moulded bases of the chancel arch date from the 14th century, but the arch and a portion of the north respond are modern.

On the south side of the nave is a 14th-century arcade of two pointed arches with a restored octagonal pillar and responds. To the west of the arcade, opening to the porch, is a moulded 15th-century doorway, on the east side of which is a stoup with a pointed head and round bowl; near the doorway, which retains the old studded oak door, is a 13th-century lancet window. The north wall was partially rebuilt in 1904, and has two modern windows with wood lintels made from old beams. In the west wall is a restored 15th-century window of two lights. The south wall of the aisle is gabled, and is pierced by a square-headed two-light window of about 1480, the label of which forms part of an external string course. In the east wall is a restored 14th-century window of two trefoiled lights, and on the south is a trefoiled piscina of the same period, part of the bowl of which has been cut away. In the east wall of the porch, now looking into the aisle, is a blocked 13th-century

window; the entrance archway, which dates from the 15th century, has a pointed head of two orders, and semi-octagonal responds with moulded capitals. The bell-turret is supported by three wood arches which project into the nave and spring from moulded corbels and two heavy posts; it is weather-boarded and covered with a pyramidal tiled roof.

The font has a 12th-century circular bowl placed on a 15th-century octagonal base; the cover, which has a finial and scroll-work brackets, bears the inscription, 'A gifte to butyfie the house of God Francis Harryson anno domnie 1631.' Some 17th-century panelling remains at the west end of the nave, and the chancel has a panelled dado of the same period which was brought from Dorton House when the church was restored in 1904. The communion rails also date from the 17th century, as do two legs re-used in the credence table and two panels in the pulpit, while a seat at the west end of the nave may be of the 16th century.

There is a ring of three bells, and a small bell, the latter undated; the treble is by Taylor & Sons, 1828, the second by Robert Atton, 1626, while the tenor, by Bartholomew Atton, is inscribed 'God save King James 1604.'

The communion plate consists of a chalice and cover paten with the date letter of 1568, and the date 1569 inscribed on the paten, and a chalice, paten and large flagon in Sheffield plate.

The registers begin in 1694.

ADVOWSON   The church was originally a chapel of Chilton, with which it was given by Walter Giffard to Nutley Abbey.[75] It belonged to that house until its surrender,[76] and in 1542 and 1546 was granted by Henry VIII to the Dean and Chapter of Christ Church, Oxford,[77] since which time it has descended with the church of Ashendon (q.v.), Earl Temple being now patron.[78]

The tithes of the demesne of Dorton, granted by Walter Giffard to Longville Priory,[79] descended after the suppression of the alien priories with the manor of Little Pollicott in Ashendon (q.v.).

In 1586 two roods in Dorton fields, which had been given for the maintenance of light and lamp in this church, were granted to John Walton and John Cresset.[80]

There do not appear to be any endowed charities subsisting in this parish.

GRANDBOROUGH

Greneburga, Grenesberga (xi cent.); Greneburne (xiii cent.); Grenesbyri, Greneborewe (xiv cent.); Granborough (xvi cent.).

This parish covers 1,580 acres, of which 139 are arable and 1,223 permanent grass,[1] and is well watered by Claydon Brook and another stream which joins it. The soil is clayey loam with gravel, with a subsoil of clay and marl, the chief crops being wheat, oats, and beans. The borders of the parish lie from 300 ft. to 350 ft. above the ordnance datum, but at the

centre the ground is somewhat higher, and the village stands on this ridge. It is built around the main road in rather a straggling fashion; part of it, on a road branching off at right angles towards Swanbourne, is known as Green End. At the south-east of the village stands the church. There is a Wesleyan chapel dating from 1871.

Several of the cottages have 17th-century brick chimney stacks and large open fireplaces. The Sovereign Inn may date from c. 1600; its best

[74] Pat. 13 Jas. I, pt. iv, no. 37.
[75] Dugdale, *Mon.* vi, 278; cf. *Pope Nich. Tax.* (Rec. Com.), 34.
[76] *Cal. Chart. in Bodl.* 27; *Valor Eccl.* (Rec. Com.), iv, 233; Dugdale, *Mon.* vi, 280.
[77] *L. and P. Hen. VIII*, xvii, g. 881 (26); xxi (2), g. 648 (25).
[78] Bacon, *Liber Regis.* 506; *Cler. Guide*; Crockford, *Cler. Dir.* In 1817 and 1822 Sir John Aubrey was patron (*Cler. Guide*).
[79] *Cal. Doc. of France*, 75-7.
[80] Pat. 28 Eliz. pt. xiv.
[1] Statistics from Bd. of Agric. (1905).

feature is the large chimney stack, and several rooms have old ceiling beams.

It may be noted that in the parish is a mound called Millknob Hill, about 4 ft. high by 60 ft. in diameter. Whether it was made for a mill, or is a tumulus adapted to such a use, can only be settled by excavation.

Bigging Farm, taking its name from the manor, was standing near the bridge joining the Grandborough and Winslow fields as late as 1861.[2] A chapel near the farm is said to have been pulled down about 1680. In a large hollow in one of its beams was carved a cross before which the parish processions halted on Rogation Monday.[3]

An Inclosure Act for the parish was passed in 1796.[4]

MANORS During the reign of Edward the Confessor, Leofstan, Abbot of St. Albans, obtained 5 hides at *GRANDBOROUGH* from Egelwyn Niger, or Egelwyn 'ye Swarte,' and Wynflaeda his wife.[5] In 1086 these were held as a manor by the abbot and belonged to the demesne of the monastery,[6] the descent being identical with that of Winslow[7] (q.v.), which was likewise held by the

ST. ALBANS ABBEY.
Azure a saltire or.

LOWNDES. *Argent fretty azure with bezants at the crossings of the fret and a quarter gules charged with a leopard's head or.*

abbey in 1086. The present lord is Mr. W. Selby-Lowndes.

As in Winslow the question on what tenure the abbey held Grandborough was debated in the 14th century and settled in favour of the abbot.

The first mention of *BIGGING* (La Bygginge, xiv cent.) occurs in 1302–3, when the Abbot of St. Albans held half a knight's fee in 'Biggeng cum Greneborewe,'[8] but it seems to have had a separate identity as a manor as early as 1330 when it was demised by the abbot to Simon Fraunceys.[9] In 1491 this manor was granted[10] on a fifty-year lease to Richard Empson for an annual rent of 100s., and later leased in 1533 to John Duncombe, his heirs and assigns for thirty-one years.[11] It was included in

the life grant made of Grandborough, Winslow and other manors to Richard Breme and Margery his wife after the Dissolution,[12] but it seems that John Duncombe and, afterwards, Benedict Lee, who was apparently his assignee, continued to farm Bigging under these grantees.[13] In 1557 the reversion of the manor was granted to Benedict Lee and his heirs.[14] It was held in 1582 by John Arden, who granted it in that year to Thomas Lee, and later to Peter Dormer, his brother-in-law, to be held in trust for four years, the profits to go to the payment of Arden's debts.[15] Soon after, Dormer having died, John Arden brought a suit against the executor, John Chester. He stated that his brother-in-law before his death, finding that he had enough money in hand for the discharge of all debts, had, before the four years were up, allowed Arden to enter the manor. John Chester, however, denied that the entry was made with Dormer's permission and stated, moreover, that the debts were not yet settled, offering to show the Court all his accounts in proof of this.[16] It is not clear how Bigging came again to the Lees, but it was held in 1624 by Sir Thomas Lee, kt.,[17] and sold by him in that year to William Abel,[18] from whom it passed in 1628 to Emanuel Scrope, Earl of Sunderland.[19] He held Hambleden Manor (q.v.) with which Bigging descended[20] until 1678, in which year it was conveyed to Sir Robert Clayton and John Morris.[21] There is no further record of this manor, but Lipscomb states that it came to the Lowndes family with the main manor,[22] in which it was apparently absorbed.

CHURCH The church of *ST. JOHN BAPTIST* consists of a chancel measuring internally 20 ft. 6 in. by 14 ft. 6 in., a nave 43 ft. by 21 ft., and a west tower 9 ft. 6 in. by 9 ft.

The nave, dating from early in the 14th century, is the oldest part of the church; the chancel was rebuilt at the end of the same century by Abbot John de la Moote of St. Albans (1396–1401) and the tower, which is faced with ashlar, dates from c. 1500, the walls of the nave having been heightened at the same time. The church was restored in 1881 by Sir Gilbert Scott.

The east window of the chancel dates from the rebuilding, and has three cinquefoiled lights with tracery over, and the north-east and south-east windows, of two lights, are of the same work. In the north wall is a 15th-century doorway, while at the south-west is a low-side window, a single trefoiled light of earlier style than the rest of the nave, and probably contemporary with the nave. The chancel arch also is of this period, but its moulded half-octagonal capitals and bases have been reworked about the time of the rebuilding of the chancel. The piscina recess, with a cinquefoiled head, is

[2] Sheahan, *Hist. and Topog. of Bucks.* 382.

[3] Ibid.

[4] Priv. Act, 36 Geo. III, cap. 36.

[5] Cott. MS. Nero, D vii, fol. 89*b*; Kemble, *Cod. Dipl.* iv, 296; *Gesta Abbat.* (Rolls Ser.), i, 39.

[6] *V.C.H. Bucks.* i, 242.

[7] See Winslow; see also *Testa de Nevill* (Rec. Com.), 245; *Feud. Aids*, i, 84, 94, 113, 119; Priv. Act, 36 Geo. III, cap. 36.

[8] *Feud. Aids*, i, 94.

[9] *Cal. Pat.* 1327–30, p. 497; *Chron. Mon. S. Albani* (Rolls Ser.), ii, 71.

[10] Exch. Inq. p.m. (Ser. 2), file 6, no. 15.

[11] Ld. Rev. Misc. Bks. clxxxviii, fol. 188.

[12] *L. and P. Hen. VIII*, xv, p. 541.

[13] Ld. Rev. Misc. Bks. clxxxviii, fol. 188, 189; Pat. 3 & 4 Phil. and Mary, pt. vii, m. 5.

[14] Pat. 3 & 4 Phil. and Mary, pt. vii, m. 5.

[15] Chan. Proc. (Ser. 2), bdl. 203, no. 37.

[16] Ibid.

[17] Recov. R. Mich. 22 Jas. I, m. 87; Feet of F. Bucks. Mich. 22 Jas. I.

[18] Ibid.; Com. Pleas Recov. R. Trin. 1 Chas. I, m. 6.

[19] Feet of F. Bucks. Trin. 4 Chas. I.

[20] Ibid. East. 28 Chas. II. Martha James *alias* Sandford, the mother of the earl's children, compounded for her estate in Grandborough in 1647 (*Cal. Com. for Comp.* 67).

[21] Feet of F. Bucks. Trin. 30 Chas. II.

[22] Lipscomb, *Hist. and Antiq. of Bucks.* i, 248.

original, and in the north wall is a locker closed by an oak door dated 1735. The communion table is inscribed 'Annis Hopper, 1625,' and has turned legs and moulded rails; there is also a good 17th-century chair in the chancel. The roof is probably of late 15th-century date, with trussed rafters and a moulded plate.

The nave is lighted from the north-east and south-east by three-light windows of late 15th-century date, inserted to give more light to the nave altars. Both replace original early 14th-century windows, of which a west jamb is left in the north wall, and an east jamb, with an angle piscina set in it, in the south wall. The second window in the south wall retains its original early 14th-century design, though its stonework is nearly all modern or retooled. There are north and south doorways in the nave of original date with moulded jambs and heads, but much repaired, and to the west of them are windows, that in the north wall, c. 1450, of two trefoiled lights under a square head, and that in the south wall of the same type, much restored. The roof is of low pitch, dating from the time when the walls were heightened, and has a moulded tie-beam.

The tower is of three stages, with a south-west stair and square-headed belfry windows of two trefoiled lights below an embattled parapet. There is a west doorway and over it a two-light window, all details being very plain, and the tower arch is of two chamfered orders with square jambs.

The church possesses a much-weathered alabaster panel of the Crucifixion, of 15th-century date; it was formerly built into the gable of a house in the village. A far more unusual possession is a leaden chrismatory, a rectangular case 6 in. long by 2 in. deep by 2⅜ in. wide, containing round receptacles for the three oils, 'oleum sanctum,' 'oleum infirmorum,' and 'chrisma.' Two of the three retain their lids, to which are fastened hooks to lift the tow on which the oil was administered; pieces of tow remain in each receptacle. The case stood on small feet modelled as lions, and had a gabled cover with open-work cresting, of which only fragments are preserved. The chrismatory was found built into the east wall of the nave, south of the chancel arch. On the floor of the chancel is deposited a fragment of the head of a late 15th-century fireplace. This was dug up in Bigginfield. A black-letter Bible of 1615 is preserved in a chest at the vicarage.

There are five bells and a sanctus; the treble by Ellis Knight, 1637; the second, originally by Richard Chandler, 1636, recast in 1887 by Mears & Stainbank; the third by Robert Atton, 1623; and the fourth of 1628 by the same founder. The tenor is a 15th-century bell, perhaps by Roger Landon, inscribed 'In multis annis resonet campana Iohannis,' and the sanctus is blank, and of 17th-century date or later.

The plate consists of a silver cup of 1569, a modern silver-gilt chalice and paten, and a modern plated cruet.

The registers begin in 1538.

ADVOWSON The church of Grandborough was held with the manor by the abbey of St. Albans. In 1291 it is mentioned as a chapel appurtenant to the church of Winslow.[23] The church was assessed at £8 in 1535,[24] and a rent of £3 6s. 8d. was received from the vicarage, the vicar being allowed a rebate of 20s. for purposes of hospitality; he was, moreover, entitled to the tithes of grain.[25] The rent from the vicarage was paid after the Dissolution to the Crown,[26] in whom the patronage was vested from that time until after 1865.[27] Between that date and 1870 it passed to Sir Harry Verney, bart., of East Claydon,[28] who was already impropriator of the great tithes and whose grandson Sir Harry C. W. Verney, bart., is the present patron.

A life grant of the rectory was made to Richard Breme and Margery in 1540.[29] A twenty-one years' lease was made to Thomas Awdley, 'valet of the wet larder,' in 1567, and in 1573 the reversion of the rectory was granted in fee to Henry Wellby and George Blythe and their heirs.[30] It had passed before 1613 to Robert Hoveden, whose nephew and heir inherited the property at his death in 1614.[31] This family also held the advowson of East Claydon, with which property the rectorial tithes of Grandborough appear to have since descended.[32]

In 1585-6 Queen Elizabeth granted to John Walton and John Cresset two small closes in this parish which had been formerly given for the maintenance of an obit in Grandborough Church.[33]

CHARITIES It is recorded in the Parliamentary Returns of 1786 that a donor unknown gave 8s. yearly for the benefit of poor widows. The annuity is received from the rector of Middle Claydon and distributed on 21 December in each year.

Poor's Allotment.—In 1797, under the Inclosure Act of this parish, 5 a. 2 r. 22 p. were awarded for the poor in lieu of their right of cutting furze. The land produces about £6 a year, the net income being distributed in gifts of money.

Church Land.—The churchwardens are possessed of about an acre of land, the rent of which, amounting to £2 13s. 6d., is applied towards the church expenses.

GRENDON UNDERWOOD

Grennedone (xi cent.); Grenedon, Crenedon (xii cent.); Grendun, Grandon (xiii cent.); Grendon Underwode (xvi cent.).

This parish covers 2,565 acres, of which 129 are arable, 2,014 permanent grass and 21 woods and plantations.[1] The soil is clay. The River Ray flows westward across the parish and also forms part of the western border. On the south the boundary follows the line of the Akeman Street, which crosses a tributary of the Ray at Gallows Bridge. This well-watered

[23] Pope Nich. Tax. (Rec. Com.), 37.
[24] Valor Eccl. (Rec. Com.), 231.
[25] Exch. Spec. Com. no. 435.
[26] Ibid.
[27] Inst. Bks. (P.R.O.); Bacon, Liber

Regis. 512; Lipscomb, op. cit. i, 249; Clergy Lists.
[28] Clergy Lists.
[29] L. and P. Hen. VIII, xv, p. 541.
[30] Pat. 16 Eliz. pt. iv, m. 1.

[31] Chan. Inq. p.m. (Ser. 2), cccxliii, 152.
[32] See East Claydon advowson; Sheahan, op. cit. 382. [33] Pat. 28 Eliz. pt. xiv, m. 12.
[1] Statistics from Bd. of Agric. (1905).

GRANDBOROUGH CHURCH FROM THE SOUTH-EAST

GRANDBOROUGH CHURCH: THE INTERIOR LOOKING EAST

GRENDON UNDERWOOD CHURCH FROM THE SOUTH-EAST

GRENDON UNDERWOOD CHURCH: THE INTERIOR LOOKING EAST

western district averages little over 200 ft. in height, but the ground rises towards the east to a height of over 400 ft. above the ordnance datum.

The church of St. Leonard stands at the west end of the village, which straggles along the main road of the parish. Two homestead moats lie about a quarter of a mile from the church. In the village are a number of picturesque thatched cottages, built chiefly of timber with brick in-fillings; they date probably from the early part of the 17th century, as a general rule, and have red brick chimney stacks and wide fireplaces. Shakespeare Farm is a larger building of late 16th and 17th-century dates, principally of timber construction with red brick fillings. It was formerly known as the Ship Inn. Some of the old oak-mullioned lattice windows remain, and there are arched fireplaces on the ground and first floors, and a staircase with turned finials to the newel posts; only part of the house is now inhabited. Rookery Farm is in a better condition, and retains some panelling on the ground floor and a stone-arched fireplace on the first floor.

On the hill which rises to the north of the village is Grendon Park, containing about 160 acres, in which stands Grendon Hall, a building in the Elizabethan style, the property of Mr. A. E. Skinner. Beyond it lies Greatmoor, an open district which is crossed by the Great Central railway. Grendon Wood and part of Doddershall Wood, on the east, include about 21 acres. The woodland was more than double this as late as 1840,[2] while earlier extents,[3] as far back, indeed, as the Survey of 1086,[4] show that no small proportion of the manor was wooded. Part of it lay within the king's forest of Bernwood, having been afforested by Henry II.[5] The land so included amounted to about 100 acres in 1310,[6] the 200 acres of thorn-wood referred to in an inquisition taken about twenty years later apparently comprising the whole of the woodland on the manor.[7] From the part lying in Bernwood Forest the lord of the manor was not apparently entitled to receive any profits.[8] He seems, however, to have received certain grants in compensation.[9]

Kingswood, to the south of Doddershall Wood, on the border of the parish, is mentioned in a perambulation of 1298.[10] There is a small hamlet there consisting of a few cottages and a Baptist chapel built in 1851.

It is commonly supposed that Grendon Underwood, which lay on the forest tracks used by gipsies and strolling players, was visited more than once by Shakespeare, who stayed at the house above-mentioned, formerly an inn, now known as Shakespeare Farm. Aubrey says: 'The humour of . . . the constable in A Midsummer Night's Dream he happened to take at Grendon in Bucks. . . . and there was living that constable about 1642 when I first came to Oxon.'[11]

It is possible Aubrey had in mind the character of Dogberry in *Much Ado about Nothing*, since there is no constable in the play he mentions.

An Inclosure Act for this parish was passed in 1769.[12]

MANOR Boding the constable held, and could sell, the manor of *GRENDON* before the Conquest. In 1086 it formed one of the two manors held in this county by Henry de Ferrers.[13] No further record of the latter's lordship is evident, however. It is probable that the overlordship belonged to the honour of Wallingford in the 12th century,[14] being attached to it possibly by Henry II, when the manor was in the Crown. Later the overlordship rights were certainly exercised by the Earl of Cornwall,[15] though whether the manor was attached to his honour of Wallingford or to that of St. Valery appears to have been very imperfectly known, as various 14th-century documents ascribe it to one or other indiscriminately.[16] The confusion may have been partly due to the similarity of service by which Grendon and an Oxfordshire manor were held of the Earl of Cornwall. Both manors were held

CORNWALL. *Sable bezanty.*

TYES. *Argent a chevron gules.*

by the same tenant, Henry Tyes, some time in the 13th century,[17] and after he lost Grendon he retained the Oxfordshire manor, for which in 1300 he rendered to the honour of St. Valery an ebony bow and three barbed arrows or 12d. yearly.[18] This identical service was also due from Grendon from the 13th to the end of the 15th century,[19] and it seems likely that similarity of overlord, tenant and service may have caused confusion as to which particular honour the manor was attached. It belonged to the honour of Wallingford as late as 1520[20] and in 1559 was held of the queen as of her honour of Ewelme,[21] this being the last mention of the overlordship.

Henry de Ferrers himself held the manor in 1086,[22] but by the time of Henry II it had come into the king's hands. In 1162–3 the Sheriff of Buckinghamshire rendered account of 1 mark from Grendon.[23] During the years 1176–9 land here was held for 60s. yearly by Henry the king's 'cytharist' or harpist,[24] whose descendants may have been the

² Lipscomb, *Hist. and Antiq. of Bucks.* i, 252.

³ Chan. Inq. p.m. 4 Edw. II, no. 42; Edw. III, file 35, no. 33.

⁴ *V.C.H. Bucks.* i, 265.

⁵ Boarstall Chartul. fol. 114.

⁶ Chan. Inq. p.m. 4 Edw. II, no. 42.

⁷ Ibid. Edw. III, file 35, no. 33.

⁸ Ibid. 4 Edw. II, no. 42.

⁹ *Cal. Close,* 1227–31, pp. 472–3; 1231–4, pp. 536, 540.

¹⁰ *V.C.H. Bucks.* ii, 132.

¹¹ Aubrey, *Letters by eminent men* (ed. 1813), ii (2), 538.

¹² Priv. Act, 9 Geo. III, cap. 28.

¹³ *V.C.H. Bucks.* i, 265.

¹⁴ *Pipe R.* 23 *Hen. II* (Pipe R. Soc.), 165; 24 *Hen. II,* 97; 25 *Hen. II,* 100. It seems most likely that these entries refer to Grendon Underwood, as apparently no part of Long Crendon belonged to this honour.

¹⁵ *Hund. R.* (Rec. Com.), i, 24; Chan. Inq. p.m. 4 Hen. IV, no. 40.

¹⁶ Chan. Inq. p.m. 28 Edw. I, no. 44 (27); 4 Edw. II, no. 42; Edw. III, file 35, no. 33; Mins. Accts. (Gen. Ser.), bdle. 1096, no. 6.

¹⁷ *Cal. Close,* 1231-4, p. 540; *Testa de Nevill* (Rec. Com.), 120.

¹⁸ Chan. Inq. p.m. 28 Edw. I, no. 44 (27).

¹⁹ *Hund. R.* (Rec. Com.), i, 24; Chan. Inq. p.m. 4 Edw. II, no. 42; Edw. III, file 35, no. 33; *Cal. Inq. Hen. VII,* i, 363.

²⁰ Chan. Inq. p.m. (Ser. 2), cxxii, 11.

²¹ Ibid.

²² *V.C.H. Bucks.* i, 265.

²³ *Pipe R.* 9 *Hen. II* (Pipe R. Soc.), 16.

²⁴ Ibid. 23 *Hen. II,* 165; 24 *Hen. II,* 97; 25 *Hen. II,* 100; see n. 14.

William le Harpur and Henry le Harpur who held half a virgate here in 1234.[25] At some period during the 12th century the main part of Grendon was held by Robert de Tyboville or Tibeville, a Norman, and valued in 1205, after his forfeiture, at £6, the stock consisting of eight oxen and two plough-horses.[26] Geoffrey le Sauser received the manor before 1210–12,[27] and afterwards demised it to John Marshal.[28] In 1228 the king promised that he would not disseise John as long as he should be in Ireland on the king's service.[29] The following year the king granted the manor to Thomas Basset 'to sustain himself in the service of the king for as long as pleased him,' on condition that as long as he held it he should pay 100s. rent annually from the land to Geoffrey le Sauser.[30] At the same time John Marshal was allowed to reserve his stock and the corn he had sown on the land.[31] Thomas Basset, however, had either died or given up the land before the end of 1230, when it was granted to Henry Tyes (Teutonicus),[32] who was to hold it until the king should restore it to the right heirs by a peace or by his free will.[33] Henry was still in possession in 1234,[34] but it was held soon after this date by Ralph de St. Amand,[35] who died in 1245–6.[36] His son Aumary de St. Amand,[37] who succeeded him in the manor,[38] was 'amerced in the Court of King's Bench as a Baron' in 1279–80[39] and died about 1285, leaving a son and heir Guy.[40] The latter died soon after, while still a minor,[41] and his widow Lucy received a grant as dower in 1287.[42] His heir was his brother Aumary, to whom Grendon was restored, Lucy receiving another manor in exchange.[43]

The manor then followed the descent of the barony of St. Amand [44] until its abeyance in 1402, when the heirs of Aumary Lord St. Amand were his younger daughter Ida who died without issue and Gerard Braybroke, son of his elder daughter Eleanor.[45] His widow died in 1426, when the daughters and heirs of Gerard Braybroke inherited.[46] Of these Maud, wife of John Babyngton, died in the same year, leaving her two sisters as co-heirs to her portion.[47] One of these, Eleanor Braybroke, died unmarried two years later.[48] The other, Elizabeth, married William Beauchamp [49] and held the manor [50] until her death in 1491.[51] Her son and heir Richard Beauchamp,[52] who, like his father, bore the title of Lord St. Amand, was attainted in 1483, but was restored in 1485, by Henry VII.[53] He had no lawful issue, but at his death in 1508 left

this manor to his illegitimate son Anthony.[54] In 1520 Anthony St. Amand conveyed the manor to John

ST. AMAND. *Or fretty sable and a chief sable charged with three bezants.*

BEAUCHAMP, Lord St. Amand. *Gules a fesse between six martlets or with the difference of a border argent.*

Cheyne and others,[55] trustees of Thomas Pigott of Whaddon,[56] who died later in that year. Grendon was then held by the trustee, Sir Richard Sacheverell, kt.,[57] and after the death of Elizabeth Pigott, the widow, about 1549 [58] it passed, by the terms of Thomas's will, to their eldest son Thomas.[59] Doddershall in Quainton (q.v.) also came to this son, and the two manors then descended together until about the middle of the 19th century,[60] when William Pigott sold the manor of Grendon to one of the Jervoise family,[61] presumably George Purefoy Jervoise, whose father, the Rev. George Huddleston Purefoy Jervoise, had already in 1796 bought a large part of the Pigotts' lands here and left them at his death in 1805 [62] to his son the above George Purefoy Jervoise.[63] At the death of the latter in 1847 his estates devolved on his sister and heir Mary Purefoy Jervoise, whose husband, the Rev. Francis Ellis, assumed the additional name of Jervoise in 1848.[64] Their son Francis Jervoise Ellis-Jervoise was lord of the manor in 1869.[65] Before 1873, however, the manor had returned to the Pigott family, being held then and afterwards by the Rev. R. H. Pigott.[66] Mrs. R. H. Pigott is now lady of the manor.

JERVOISE. *Sable a cheveron between three eagles close argent.*

[25] *Rot. Lit. Claus.* (Rec. Com.), i, 61, 64.
[26] *Rot. Norman.* (Rec. Com.), 131; *Cal. Rot. Pat.* (Rec. Com.), 11.
[27] *Red Bk. of Exch.* (Rolls Ser.), 538.
[28] *Cal. Close,* 1227–31, p. 184.
[29] *Cal. Pat.* 1225–32, p. 185.
[30] *Cal. Close,* 1227–31, p. 184.
[31] Ibid. 184, 205.
[32] Ibid. 377.
[33] *Cal. Chart. R.* 1226–57, p. 132.
[34] *Cal. Close,* 1231–4, p. 540.
[35] *Testa de Nevill* (Rec. Com.), 245. The land at this date, as in 1086, amounted to 2 hides.
[36] Dugdale, *Baronage,* ii, 20.
[37] Ibid.
[38] *Hund. R.* (Rec. Com.), i, 24.
[39] G.E.C. *Peerage,* vii, 8.
[40] *Cal. Inq. p.m.* (Edw. I), ii, 350.
[41] G.E.C. *Peerage,* vii, 8.
[42] *Cal. Close,* 1279–88, pp. 462, 504.
[43] Ibid. 1288–96, pp. 62, 68.
[44] G.E.C. *Peerage,* vii, 8; *Cal. Close,*

1288–96, p. 391; 1307–13, p. 284; 1360–4, p. 546; Chan. Inq. p.m. 28 Edw. I, no. 44 (27); 4 Edw. II, no. 42; *Cal. Inq. p.m.* (Edw. III), vii, 364; *Feud. Aids,* i, 113; De Banco R. 211, m. 51; 207, m. 91; 538, m. 1; *Cal. Pat.* 1354–8, p. 587.
[45] G.E.C. *Peerage,* vii, 9; Chan. Inq. p.m. 4 Hen. IV, no. 40.
[46] Chan. Inq. p.m. 4 Hen. VI, no. 17.
[47] Ibid. 5 Hen. VI, no. 18.
[48] Ibid. 7 Hen. VI, no. 39–40.
[49] Ibid.; G.E.C. *Peerage,* vii, 9.
[50] Feet of F. Div. Co. East. 16 Hen. VI.
[51] *Cal. Inq. p.m. Hen. VII,* i, 305. Her second husband Sir Roger Tocotes died the following year (ibid. 363).
[52] Ibid. 305.
[53] G.E.C. *Peerage,* vii, 10.
[54] Ibid. P.C.C. 16 Bennett.
[55] Feet of F. Bucks. Hil. 12 Hen. VIII.
[56] Chan. Inq. p.m. (Ser. 2), xxxv, 1.

[57] Ibid.   [58] P.C.C. F. 41 Populwell.
[59] Ibid. 26 Ayloffe.
[60] See Doddershall, also Ct. of Req. bdle. 67, no. 10; Recov. R. Mich. 22 Eliz. m. 450; Chan. Proc. (Ser. 2), bdle. 291, no. 8; Feet of F. Bucks. Trin. 6 Jas. I; Recov. R. Trin. 6 Jas. I, m. 42; East. 7 Geo. II, m. 289; Hil. 11 Geo. III, m. 298; Feet of F. Bucks. Hil. 11 Geo. III; Priv. Act, 9 Geo. III, cap. 28. At the death of John Pigott in 1751, however, Grendon passed at once to his nephew, and was not held in dower by his widow Christobella, who received £1,000 charged on this estate (P.C.C. 316 Bushey).
[61] Sheahan, *Hist. and Topog. of Bucks.* 384.
[62] Burke, *Landed Gentry* (ed. 5).
[63] Ibid.; Sheahan, loc. cit.; Local and Pers. Act, 41 Geo. III, cap. 110.
[64] Burke, loc. cit.   [65] Ibid.
[66] *Ret. of Owners of Land* (1873), Bucks. 16.

A messuage appurtenant to the manor was recorded to be worth 5*s.* per annum with a curtilage in 1285.[67] In 1310 it was valued at 2*s.* only because the house was falling down,[68] but by 1333 it had evidently been rebuilt, as it was then worth 6*s.* 8*d.* annually.[69]

In 1234 the king's officer was ordered to let Henry Tyes take thirty logs in Grendon Wood to make a windmill,[70] and this, or its successor, was included among the appurtenances of the manor in the 17th and 18th centuries.[71] In 1333 mention is made of a certain tallage called 'Cristmesseyelde' payable by the lord of the manor at Christmas.[72]

As early as the 13th century the Abbot of Reading held land in Grendon in free alms of the gift of John de Hannay, chaplain, who had granted to the monastery a small estate here.[73] Henry de Scaccario afterwards held this land under the abbot, paying 5*s.* annually,[74] and in 1253 Ralph de Scaccario sub-infeudated this estate to Robert of Grendon, clerk,[75] son of Henry Tyes,[76] who held it as 1 hide in 1254-5.[77] In 1271 Robert for 20*s.* yearly granted his interest in a messuage and 6 virgates to Geoffrey le Fraunceys and Margery his wife, who were to hold after the donor's death of the chief lords.[78] In 1291 the abbey's lands here were still valued at 5*s.*,[79] but there is no trace of them at the Dissolution.

READING ABBEY.
Azure three scallops or.

CHURCH The church of *ST. LEONARD* has a chancel measuring internally 33 ft. 6 in. by 16 ft., with modern north vestry, a nave 45 ft. by 22 ft. 6 in., and a west tower 10 ft. by 9 ft. 6 in.

The nave is probably in part of the 12th century, though having no details earlier than c. 1230 ; the chancel, which is set out on an axis inclining northwards from that of the nave, dates from early in the 14th century, and the tower is of c. 1460. The church was restored in 1866, when the east window was renewed and the chancel reroofed. In 1902 various structural defects which had developed in the intervening period were remedied, the north-east angle of the nave being rebuilt.

The chancel has a modern east window of five lights, but two original north windows and three on the south, all of two uncusped lights with plain pierced spandrels in the head ; a moulded string-course runs below the sills, but has been cut away on the north wall, and there is a plain chamfered north doorway of two orders, originally external, but now opening to the modern vestry. The piscina is of more ornamental detail than the rest of the chancel, having a trefoiled head under a gabled label, inclosing a sunk trefoil, flanked by panelled and crocketed shafts, of which the eastern has been cut back to make room for a wall monument. In the recess over the basin is a moulded stone shelf. The chancel

arch has two orders with plain continuous chamfers and broach-stops at the base, and shows remains of mediaeval painted ornament on its soffit. All the seating is modern except for a 17th-century chair within the altar rails.

The nave is lighted by four windows, one at the north-east being like the chancel windows, but almost entirely renewed. The north-west window is of 15th-century date, of two cinquefoiled lights under a square head, and both windows on the south are of three cinquefoiled lights, the eastern of late 15th and the western of 16th-century date, with a straight-sided pointed head. It is to be noted that the eastern half of the south wall is some 6 in. thicker than the western half, the latter being the later in date. There is no north doorway to the nave, but a break of masonry in the north wall may point to its former existence. The south doorway is the best piece of detail in the church, though much damaged ; it is of two moulded orders, of c. 1230, with remains of foliated capitals and shafts to the outer order, which had in the arch large undercut foliated dog-tooth ornaments. The mouldings in both orders consist of rolls and deeply-cut hollows, those of the inner order continuing down the jambs. There are marks of the former existence of a south porch, and within the doorway is a 15th-century holy water stoup. Replaced at the south-east of the nave is a cinquefoiled piscina recess with a stone shelf, of late 14th-century date, which was moved in 1868 to the north-west corner of the nave. The hexagonal oak pulpit is in part of c. 1620, with carved panels set on a modern base. The nave roof is of late 15th-century date, of low pitch, with moulded tie-beams, under which are curved braces with traceried spandrels ; it has undergone alteration and repair, and the western tie-beam and one purlin in the west bay of the roof are of different detail from the rest.

The tower is embattled, of three stages, with a stair-turret at the south-east, and has pointed two-light belfry windows with tracery ; in the second stage are plain trefoiled lights on the north and south, and in the west wall of the ground stage is a window of three cinquefoiled lights above a four-centred west doorway. The latter has a square label and trefoiled spandrels. The tower arch is of the full internal span of the tower, of three moulded orders, and two-centred.

The octagonal font is plain 15th-century work retooled and the nave seating is modern, but a few pieces of 15th-century bench-ends, formerly in the church, are now at the rectory. In the tower is an oak chest, probably of Elizabethan date. There are no monuments of importance, but in the chancel are 18th-century mural monuments to the Pigott family and to Richard Lord Saye and Sele (d. 1781), and another to his widow Christobella (d. 1789). There are also a certain number of late 17th-century headstones still remaining in the churchyard. Several incised sundials are to be seen on the south walls of the nave and chancel, and an incised cross on the south doorway.

67 Chan. Inq. p.m. 14 Edw. I, no. 20.
68 Ibid. 4 Edw. II, no. 42.
69 Ibid. 7 Edw. III (1st nos.), no. 33.
70 *Cal. Close,* 1231–4, p. 536.
71 Recov. R. Trin. 6 Jas. I, m. 42 ; Hil. 9 Geo. II, m. 225.

72 Chan. Inq. p.m. 7 Edw. III (1st nos.), no. 33.
73 Harl. MS. 1708, fol. 93 d.
74 Ibid.
75 Feet of F. Bucks. Hil. 37 Hen. III, no. 1.

76 Ibid. East. 55 Hen. III, no. 3.
77 *Hund. R.* (Rec. Com.), i, 24.
78 Feet of F. Bucks. East. 55 Hen. III, no. 3.
79 *Pope Nich. Tax.* (Rec. Com.), 46.

There are three bells, the treble by Robert Atton, 1621, the second and third, of 1677 and 1664 respectively, from the Chandlers' foundry at Drayton Parslow.

The plate includes a covered communion cup of 1569, the cover being of 1570, and a plated paten and flagon. The registers begin in 1653.

ADVOWSON The first mention of the church, which is a rectory, occurs in 1223, when the Bishop of Lincoln collated Robert Haldein of Banbury to the church, which had been vacant one and a half years ; the right of any patron was then reserved.[80] In 1285 Aumary de St. Amand was patron,[81] and the advowson remained the property of the lord of the manor until the 19th century.[82] At the sale of the manor to the Jervoises the advowson was retained by the Pigotts of Doddershall,[83] and has descended with that manor in the direct line to Vice-Admiral W. H. Pigott, the present patron. Samuel Clarke, annotator of the Bible, was rector of Grendon at the Restoration, but was ejected by the Act of Uniformity of 1662.[84]

CHARITIES In 1665 John Hart, by his will proved in the P.C.C., devised (*inter alia*) an annuity of £3 for apprenticing a poor boy, issuing out of Easington Manor, Oxfordshire. The rent-charge (less land tax) is accumulated and applied in apprenticing as occasion requires.

For the charities of Dame Anne Pigott, founded in 1672, and of Thomas Pigott, founded by deed poll 1704, for the education and apprenticing respectively of poor children of Grendon and Quainton, see under the parish of Quainton.

The charity of Christobella, Viscountess Saye and Sele, founded by will dated 8 December 1787, is possessed of school buildings at Grendon and at Quainton, and is endowed with a sum of £14,041 14s. 7d. consols, transferred out of the Court of Chancery to the official trustees, producing £351 0s. 8d. yearly. The official trustees also hold a sum of £247 7s. 3d. consols on an investment account towards replacement of a sum of £500 by instalments of £12 10s. yearly. By a scheme of the Charity Commissioners of 17 August 1900 two-thirds of the net income is made applicable for the advancement in life of poor boys of Grendon and Quainton and one-third in the advancement of the education of children in the same parishes. The educational branch is regulated by a scheme of the Board of Education of 23 December 1908.

HOGSHAW

Hocsaga (xi cent.) ; Hogseagh (xii cent.) ; Horkeshawe (xiii cent.) ; Hoggeshagh, Hogshawe (xiv cent.) ; Folebroc, Fulebroc (xii cent.).

This parish covers nearly 1,322 acres, of which 115 are arable and 1,205 permanent grass.[1] There are only six scattered farm-houses and a few cottages. The slope of the land varies from 311 ft. above the ordnance datum on the northern border to 600 ft. in the southeast of the parish. The soil is clay and sand, the subsoil clay, and the chief crops are wheat, barley and beans. The church of St. John Baptist[2] no longer exists, but human remains have been found near its reputed site in the west of the parish.[3] To the northeast is Upper Hogshaw Farm with a moat close by.[4] The farm was called Hill House in the middle of the 19th century, and in it the manorial courts were formerly held.[5] Fulbrook Farm, once the manor-house of Fulbrook Huett,[6] is in the east of the parish on a moated site. The house, originally of late 16th-century date, is stone built with an ashlar-faced 17th-century wing and later additions. An original four-light stone-mullioned window remains on the south, and the brick chimney stack of the 16th-century house is also preserved.

MANORS Before the Conquest *HOGSHAW MANOR* was held by Alwin, one of King Edward's thegns,[7] and in 1086 by William Peverel.[8] In the middle 13th century the overlordship appertained to the honour of Peverel,[9] which was afterwards vested in the Crown.[10]

William son of William Peverel[11] in the time of Henry II gave Hogshaw Manor to the Knights Hospitallers as part of the original endowment of their commandery of Hogshaw.[12] They retained this manor, which included 2 virgates of land in Fulbrook,[13] until the Dissolution.[14] In 1543 Hogshaw Manor was granted in fee to Dame Maud Lane, widow of Sir Ralph Lane, who in 1512 acquired a lease from the Knights Hospitallers for ninety years,[15] and died in 1540.[16] His widow died in 1558, leaving Hogshaw Manor to her younger sons Ralph and William Lane.[17] In

THE KNIGHTS HOS-PITALLERS. *Gules a cross argent.*

---

[80] *Reg. of Hugh of Wells* (Cant. and York Soc.), ii, 65.

[81] *Cal. Inq. p.m.* (Edw. I), ii, 350. The church was valued at £6 13s. 4d. in 1291 (*Pope Nich. Tax.* [Rec. Com.], 34, 41), and at £15 17s. 4d. in 1535 (*Valor Eccl.* [Rec. Com.], iv, 236).

[82] See manor and Inst. Bks. (P.R.O.).

[83] *Clergy Lists.*

[84] *Dict. Nat. Biog.*

[1] Statistics from Bd. of Agric. (1905).

[2] Bacon, *Liber Regis.* 506.

[3] O.S. Bucks. (25 in.).

[4] *V.C.H. Bucks.* ii, 30.

[5] Sheahan, *Hist. and Topog. of Bucks.* 387.

[6] A capital messuage is mentioned in 1305 (Chan. Inq. p.m. Edw. I, file 118, no. 17) and in 1618 (ibid. [Ser. 2], ccclxxvi, 99).

[7] *V.C.H. Bucks.* i, 253.   [8] Ibid.

[9] *Hund. R.* (Rec. Com.), i, 24.

[10] *Feud. Aids,* i, 121 ; Leadam, *Dom. Incl.* 1517 (Royal Hist. Soc.), i, 193 ; Orig. R. (Exch. L.T.R.), 35 Hen. VIII, pt. v, m. 15 ; Chan. Inq. p.m. (Ser. 2), cxviii, 6.   [11] Dugdale, *Baronage,* i, 437.

[12] *V.C.H. Bucks.* i, 390 ; see also

Hunter, *Pedes Finium* (Rec. Com.), i, 197 ; *Abbrev. Plac.* (Rec. Com.), 62.

[13] *Hund. R.* (Rec. Com.), i, 24.

[14] *Testa de Nevill* (Rec. Com.), 245 ; *Hund. R.* (Rec. Com.), i, 24 (Hugh is named as tenant) ; *Feud. Aids,* i, 96, 113, 121 ; Early Chan. Proc. bdle. 304, no. 76; *L. and P. Hen. VIII,* ii, 4370.

[15] *L. and P. Hen. VIII,* xviii (1), g. 981 (88). See also Leadam, op. cit. i, 193, 490; *L. and P. Hen. VIII,* iv, g. 3142 (18).

[16] Exch. Inq. p.m. (Ser. 2), file 35, no. 1.

[17] Chan. Inq. p.m. (Ser. 2), cxviii, 6.

1573 their elder brother, Sir Robert Lane,[18] with his wife Mary and their son William, alienated it,[19] with the exception of certain pastures (see below), to Thomas Pigott the younger, of Doddershall, with warranty against all claimants through Maud Lane.[20] Litigation ensued,[21] but in 1603 Pigott settled the manor,[22] and it subsequently descended with Doddershall in Quainton (q.v.) to Richard Pigott, who was involved in money difficulties in 1624.[23] He with his son Richard sold Hogshaw Manor about 1626[24] to Fulk, Lord Brooke of Beauchamp Court.[25] Shortly before his death in 1628 he settled it in successive tail-male on his son and successor Robert, on another son William, and on Fulk son of Sir Edward Greville.[26] Hogshaw Manor descended with the barony[27] to George, second Earl Brooke and Earl of Warwick,[28] who in 1786 mortgaged it,[29] and in 1788 sold it to Mrs. Du Pré.[30] This estate has since descended with

Du Pré. *Azure a chevelon or between two molets in the chief and a lion passant in the foot all argent with a pile or over all.*

Greville. *Sable a cross and a border both engrailed or with five roundels sable on the cross.*

Wooburn[31] to Mr. William Baring Du Pré, M.P., the present owner.

The estate exempted from the sale of Hogshaw Manor in 1573 included certain lands called Newick and Woodfield, with pasturage for 320 sheep in Copsley Hills. It was sold in 1576 and 1577 by Sir Robert and William Lane to Paul Wentworth and his wife Ellen.[32] She was living at his death in 1594, but their son Paul[33] made a settlement of the estate in 1616.[34] In 1626 Richard Pigott the younger and Alban Pigott with Thomas Wentworth the younger sold it to Fulk, Lord Brooke,[35] and it was included in the sale to Mrs. Du Pré in 1788.

The Knights Hospitallers had view of frankpledge.[36]

In 1338 there were a windmill and a dovehouse in the manor.[37] Fishing rights appertained to the manor.[38]

Fulbrook, which formed one vill with Hogshaw in the early 14th century,[39] is not named in the Survey of 1086. Seven virgates of land here,[40] afterwards *FULBROOK alias FULBROOK HUETT MANOR,* were held in chief in the 14th century of the honour of Wallingford by the service of a quarter of a knight's fee.[41] In 1549 the tenure was unknown to the jury,[42] and in 1618 the overlordship rights were vested in the Crown.[43]

A mesne overlordship in this manor as a member of Cublington appertained to the Earl of Gloucester and is last mentioned in 1346.[44]

In the middle 13th century Fulbrook Manor was held by Geoffrey Lucy,[45] and descended in his family with Cublington (q.v.) until the end of the 14th century,[46] when it appears to have passed in marriage with Katherine, sister of Sir Geoffrey and aunt of Sir Reginald Lucy, to Robert Bolour.[47] In 1430 their son Thomas released all right in Fulbrook Manor to John Burbache and his wife Thomasine,[48] who in 1424 had granted it during Thomasine's life to Edmund Rede and Richard Sturgeon.[49] Probably before the end of the century, when he was farming Fulbrook Eynsham (q.v.), this manor had been acquired by Roger Gifford, lessee of Middle Claydon, who made some settlement respecting it in 1522.[50] On his death in 1542 (see Middle Claydon) the estate passed under a settlement to his son George,[51] afterwards Sir George Gifford, and in 1557 to the latter's widow Philippa.[52] In 1584 their son Thomas[53] with George Gifford conveyed this manor, under the name of Fulbrook Huetts (distinguishing it from Fulbrook Eynsham until the early 19th century[54]), to George, afterwards Sir George Throckmorton.[55] He died seised in 1612,[56] and was buried at Hogshaw.[57] The manor passed by a settlement of 1606 to his widow Jane for her life.[58] In 1616 their son Sir George Throckmorton, kt., with his wife Jane and his brother Henry, sold it to Sir Ralph Winwood, with remainder to

Lucy. *Gules three luces argent.*

[18] Chan. Inq. p.m. (Ser. 2), cxviii, 6.
[19] Egerton Chart. 291.
[20] Feet of F. Bucks. Mich. 15 & 16 Eliz. ; Memo. R. Mich. 16 Eliz. m. 67.
[21] Egerton Chart. 297 ; Chan. Proc. Eliz. Pp 6, no. 56.
[22] Egerton Chart. 303 ; Feet of F. Bucks. Hil. 45 Eliz.
[23] Chan. Proc. (Ser. 2), bdle. 340, no. 8.
[24] Recov. R. East. 2 Chas. I, m. 163.
[25] Close, 28 Geo. III, pt. xxv, no. 4, enumerating former purchase.
[26] Chan. Inq. p.m. (Ser. 2), dcxxiv, 63. References to this settlement occur in 1636 (Recov. R. Trin. 12 Chas. I, m. 46 ; Feet of F. Div. Co. Trin. 12 Chas. I).
[27] Recov. R. Mich. 12 Chas. II, m. 192; Mich. 2 Geo. I, m. 309 ; Hil. 14 Geo. II, m. 240 ; Feet of F. Div. Co. Hil. 14 Geo. II ; Recov. R. Hil. 12 Geo. III, m. 325.
[28] G.E.C. *Complete Peerage,* ii, 32–4.

[29] Feet of F. Bucks. Trin. 26 Geo. III.
[30] Close, 28 Geo. III, pt. xxv, no. 4.
[31] *V.C.H. Bucks.* iii, 108–9.
[32] Egerton Chart. 294, 296 ; Feet of F. Bucks. Hil. 19 Eliz. ; Chan. Inq. p.m. (Ser. 2), ccxl, 84.
[33] Chan. Inq. p.m. (Ser. 2), ccxl, 84.
[34] Feet of F. Bucks. Mich. 16 Jas. I.
[35] Close, 2 Chas. I, pt. iii, no. 32.
[36] *Hund. R.* (Rec. Com.), i, 24 ; *Plac. de Quo Warr.* (Rec. Com.), 90.
[37] Larking, *Knights Hospitallers in Engl.* (Camd. Soc.), 68.
[38] Feet of F. Bucks. Hil. 3 Chas. I ; Close, 28 Geo. III, pt. xxv, no. 4.
[39] *Feud. Aids,* i, 113.
[40] *Hund. R.* (Rec. Com.), i, 24.
[41] *Feud. Aids,* i, 96, 121.
[42] Chan. Inq. p.m. (Ser. 2), cxx, 1.
[43] Ibid. ccclxxvi, 99.
[44] Ibid. Edw. I, files 39, no. 1 ; 118, no. 17 ; Edw. III, file 81, no. 10 ; *Feud. Aids,* i, 101, 126.

[45] *Testa de Nevill* (Rec. Com.), 245. Roger de Wimbervill was his tenant.
[46] See also *Hund. R.* (Rec. Com.), i, 24. Walter of Fulbrook is named as tenant (Feet of F. Div. Co. Trin. 2 Edw. III, no. 29 ; *Feud. Aids,* i, 96, 121).
[47] Close, 8 Hen. VI, m. 2.
[48] Ibid.
[49] Feet of F. Bucks. Hil. 2 Hen. VI, no. 2.   [50] Ibid. Mich. 14 Hen. VIII.
[51] Ibid. East. 33 Hen. VIII.
[52] Chan. Inq. p.m. (Ser. 2), cxx, 1.
[53] Ibid.
[54] Recov. R. Mich. 5 Geo. IV, m. 44.
[55] Feet of F. Bucks. Mich. 26 & 27 Eliz. ; Hil. 27 Eliz. (in bdle. Hil. 37 Eliz.).
[56] Chan. Inq. p.m. (Ser. 2), cccxxxv, 18 ; ccclxxvi, 99.
[57] Lipscomb, *Hist. and Antiq. of Bucks.* i, 271, quoting Quainton Reg.
[58] Chan. Inq. p.m. (Ser. 2), cccxxxv, 18 ; ccclxxvi, 99.

himself six months after the death of his mother.[59] It had reverted to him before 1636, at which date

GIFFORD. *Gules three lions passant argent.*

THROCKMORTON. *Gules a cheveron argent charged with three gimel bars sable.*

he appears to have sold it to Richard Winwood,[60] who three years earlier had acquired interests in the manor from Michael and Jane Constable.[61] It has since descended with Quainton (q.v.), forming with Fulbrook Eynsham the Fulbrook estate,[62] now owned by George Godolphin Osborne, tenth Duke of Leeds.

Free warren in Fulbrook was granted to Geoffrey Lucy and his heirs in 1332.[63]

Wigan of Wallingford in the middle 12th century granted 2 hides of land in Fulbrook in free alms to Eynsham Abbey, Oxfordshire, with North Marston Church (q.v.). The abbey retained its estate in Fulbrook, known as *FULBROOK* or *FULBROOK EYNSHAM MANOR*, until the Dissolution.[64] This property was granted in 1539[65] to Sir George Darcy, and by arrangement with him in 1543 to Sir Edward

OSBORNE, Duke of Leeds. *Quarterly ermine and azure a cross or.*

North.[66] He immediately alienated it to George Gifford,[67] owner of Fulbrook Huett (q.v.). The reversion of the manor of Fulbrook Eynsham (probably in reference to some lease) was acquired from Francis Power and others in 1573 by Thomas Gifford and his wife Margaret, and settlements were made in 1578.[68] In 1602 Thomas Gifford and Francis Power conveyed it to George Throckmorton.[69] This estate has since descended with Fulbrook Huett (q.v.).

During the time the manor was held by Eynsham Abbey it was frequently leased,[70] the last tenant being Roger Gifford.[71]

Richard Tochwick, the abbey's bailiff, claimed in 1286 to have view of frankpledge, but admitted that there were only three or four tenants on the manor and that he had no means of punishing criminals.[72]

The church of *ST. JOHN BAPTIST CHURCH* has long since been destroyed, and its site is only approximately known, the foundations having been dug up in the 18th century for road material.[73] Some 15th-century stones on Hogshaw Farm, partly built into a modern cow-house, appear to be relics of the church. In the last century the font was used at Fulbrook Farm as a cistern, and afterwards as a garden flower-vase.[74] The church is said to have been injured during the Commonwealth, but was still used for divine service in 1650.[75] It was in ruins at the end of the 17th century, when the parish was consolidated with that of East Claydon.[76] The last interment at Hogshaw took place in 1683.[77] The church was part of the original endowment of the commandery of Hogshaw,[78] and was appropriated by the Knights Hospitallers,[79] one of their order serving as chaplain there in the middle 14th century.[80] The descent of the advowson[81] and rectory followed that of Hogshaw Manor (q.v.), and the rectory and all tithes were included in the sale of 1788.

There do not appear to be any endowed charities subsisting in this parish.

ICKFORD

Iforde (xi cent.); Ycford, Hicford, Hitford, Ikeford, Ickeforde (xii–xiv cent. and after).

The parish of Ickford covers 1,249 acres, of which 146 are arable and 817 permanent grass.[1] The chief crops grown are wheat and beans. The soil and subsoil are clay. The entire parish lies low, the highest part, which is very little over 200 ft. above the ordnance datum, being in the north. The village lies

mainly round the junction of the chief roads, which meet a little south of the centre of the parish. The central portion is sometimes known as Great Ickford or Church Ickford, while the part lying further eastward is Little Ickford. The first name occurs in the 14th century,[2] but that of Church Ickford does not appear until the 16th century.[3] The church of St. Nicholas stands at the west end of the village, which

[59] Feet of F. Bucks. Mich. 14 Jas. I; Chan. Inq. p.m. (Ser. 2), ccclxxvi, 99. Between 1626 and 1639 Sir George Throckmorton filed a bill in Chancery against his brother Henry and his wife Sarah with respect to payments under this sale (Chan. Proc. [Ser. 2], bdle. 416, no. 65).
[60] Recov. R. Trin. 12 Chas. I, m. 10.
[61] Feet of F. Bucks. Hil. 8 Chas. I.
[62] Recov. R. Mich. 5 Geo. IV, m. 44.
[63] Chart. R. 6 Edw. III, m. 20, no. 35.
[64] *Testa de Nevill* (Rec. Com.), 245; *Hund. R.* (Rec. Com.), i, 24; *Pope Nich. Tax.* (Rec. Com.), 46*b*; Leadam, op. cit. i, 193; *L. and P. Hen. VIII*, ii, 4370; *Valor Eccl.* (Rec. Com.), ii, 208.
[65] *L. and P. Hen. VIII*, xiv (1), g. 904 (4).

[66] Ibid. xviii (1), g. 802 (10); g. 981 (81).
[67] Ibid. (2), g. 449 (72); Chan. Inq. p.m. (Ser. 2), cxx, 1.
[68] Pat. 20 Eliz. pt. v, m. 1, 2, enumerating earlier deed (Kynsham instead of Eynsham in the document must be a clerical error); Feet of F. Bucks. Trin. 20 Eliz.
[69] Feet of F. Bucks. Trin. 44 Eliz.
[70] *Eynsham Cartul.* (Oxf. Hist. Soc.), i, 133, 200, 249, 380; Feet of F. case 14, file 2; case 15, file 22; Bucks. Mich. 4 John, no. 23; Trin. 57 Hen. III, no. 4; *Cal. Close*, 1231–4, p. 568; Harl. Roll E. 31.
[71] Leadam, op. cit. i, 193; Early Chan. Proc. bdle. 503, no. 37.
[72] *Eynsham Cartul.* (Oxf. Hist. Soc.), i, 312; Dugdale, *Mon.* iii, 17, 18.

[73] Lipscomb, op. cit. i, 269.
[74] Ibid. 274; Sheahan, op. cit. 389.
[75] *V.C.H. Bucks.* i, 329.
[76] Lysons, *Mag. Brit.* i (3), 581, quoting Browne Willis.
[77] Lipscomb, op. cit. i, 269, quoting East Claydon Reg.
[78] *V.C.H. Bucks.* i, 390.
[79] Bacon, op. cit. 506.
[80] *V.C.H. Bucks.* loc. cit.
[81] This may have been retained by the Crown after the Dissolution. The only provision for the curate still traceable in the middle 19th century was a rent-charge on the manor of £10 yearly (Lipscomb, op. cit. i, 284).
[1] Statistics from Bd. of Agric. (1905).
[2] Feet of F. Bucks. Mich. 19 Edw. II.
[3] *L. and P. Hen. VIII*, xv, g. 613 (23).

contains a few buildings of the 16th and 17th centuries, mostly of timber and brick with thatched or tiled roofs. The rectory, which is mainly of brick with a tiled roof, is possibly of late 16th-century date, but seems to have been much altered in the next century. Church Farm is an 18th-century house incorporating some fragments of an earlier building.

At Little Ickford, which lies to the south-east of the village, are several other old houses and cottages. Manor Farm is a half-timber building of the late 16th century, added to and altered in 1675 and again about 1700; many original features remain, including two panelled rooms. A Baptist chapel, dating from 1825, stands in the road leading to Little Ickford. The outlying fields of the parish are liable to floods both from the River Thame and the stream which forms the north and west boundary of the parish. A bridge across the Thame existed here as early as 1237, since in that year Walter de Burgh was ordered to provide the keeper of Ickford Bridge with an oak from Brill (Brohull) Wood for repairs.[4] The present bridge, which carries the road from Ickford to Tiddington, is a stone structure of three elliptical arches. The triangular starlings on each side of the northern pier continue upwards to the parapets and form recesses. In the recess on the east side of the bridge are two stones, the southern one inscribed '1685, Here ends the county of Oxon,' and the northern one 'Here beginneth the county of Bucks, 1685.' Wodebrugge and Widebrugge are mentioned in the 13th century.[5]

The dramatic poet William Joyner *alias* Lede lived at Ickford 'in a devout condition' in the 17th century[6]; his great-nephew, Thomas Phillips, biographer of Cardinal Pole, was born here in 1708.[7]

There is no Inclosure Act for the parish.

The following 13th-century place-names occur in Ickford: Stanfordpons, Brokforlang, Penygkoke, Dol-

mede, Goce, Holewebroc, Holerodacres, and Maseforlang.[8]

MANORS

In 1086 Miles Crispin held 4 hides in *ICKFORD*; the name of the owner before the Conquest does not appear.[9] The manor afterwards formed part of the honour of Wallingford,[10] and this overlordship is last mentioned in 1627.[11] The tenant in 1086 was Richard,[12] who also held of the same overlord in Chearsley (q.v.), with which this part of Ickford descended for some time. In 1226 the guardians of Geoffrey de Appleton seem to have held Ickford,[13] and his name appears as witness to a charter here,[14] apparently before the year 1235, when Thomas de Appleton held a fee in Ickford and Chearsley[15] (q.v.). The Ickford portion, assessed at half a fee, passed at the death of Thomas de Appleton before 1284[16] to his son Walter,[17] who held as late as 1302–3.[18] In 1313 William son of John de Appleton was lord.[19] Soon after this date—

THE RECTORY, ICKFORD

before 1316, in fact[20]—the rights of lordship appear to have been ceded to the atte Water family, who were under-tenants of the Appletons here[21] as early as 1284–6.[22]

William atte Water, who held this land at his death in 1313,[23] also held other lands in Ickford, to the value of half a fee, of another overlord (see Grestein Abbey Manor), and both estates evidently amalgamated to form *GREAT ICKFORD MANOR*,[24] which was alienated before 1346 by his son and heir

[4] *Cal. Close*, 1234–7, p. 475; cf. ibid. 1364–8, p. 497.

[5] Wigram, *Cartul. of St. Frideswide* (Oxf. Hist. Soc.), ii, 174–89.

[6] *Dict. Nat. Biog.*   [7] Ibid.

[8] *Cartul. of St. Frideswide*, loc. cit.

[9] *V.C.H. Bucks.* i, 261.

[10] *Testa de Nevill* (Rec. Com.), 247; *Hund. R.* (Rec. Com.), i, 25, and see manor.

[11] Chan. Inq. p.m. (Ser. 2), ccccxxxviii, 123.

[12] *V.C.H. Bucks.* loc. cit.

[13] Lipscomb, *Hist. and Antiq. of Bucks.* i, 282; see account of advowson.

[14] Misc. Bks. (Exch. K.R.), xx, fol. 64.

[15] *Testa de Nevill* (Rec. Com.), 258, 261.   [16] *Feud. Aids*, i, 76.

[17] Ibid.; Chan. Inq. p.m. 21 Edw. I, no. 28a.   [18] *Feud. Aids*, i, 94.

[19] Chan. Inq. p.m. 6 Edw. II, no. 29.

[20] *Feud. Aids*, i, 114.

[21] Chan. Inq. p.m. 6 Edw. II, no. 29.

[22] *Feud. Aids*, i, 83; Chan. Inq. p.m. 21 Edw. I, no. 28a. In 1312 William atte Water granted an annual rent of 6d. 'of his own free will' to the Earl of Cornwall (Chan. Inq. p.m. 6 Edw. II, no. 29). As no reference was made to the mesne lords, the de Appletons, of whom

he also held in Ickford at that time (Chan. Inq. p.m. 6 Edw. II, no. 29), it seems possible that the atte Waters held a tenement of the earl direct, especially as this rent was still paid to the honour of Wallingford by Nicholas atte Water in 1377 (Mins. Accts. [Gen. Ser.], bdle. 1096, no. 6), long after the family had alienated the main manor. For the early history of the atte Water or de Ickford family see the Grestein Abbey Manor in this parish.

[23] Chan. Inq. p.m. 6 Edw. II, no. 29.

[24] Ibid. 33 Edw. III (1st nos.), no. 38; 2 Ric. II, no. 57.

John atte Water[25] to John, Lord Grey of Rotherfield.[26] The latter made a life grant of a messuage and 47 acres in Ickford, to be held for the annual rent of a rose, to John atte Water, with reversion to the Greys.[27] In 1379 the manor was held by the heirs of John de Grey,[28] son of the above.[29] It is not very clear which members of the family enjoyed the property for the next hundred years, but apparently, after the failure of the male heirs of John de Grey in 1400–1,[30] it reverted to a younger branch, descendants of a younger son of Robert de Grey, kt.,[31] grandfather of the John de Grey who obtained Ickford Manor. Their representative, Thomas Danvers,[32] certainly held in Ickford in 1489[33]; his heir was his brother William, afterwards Sir William Danvers, kt., who died seised of Ickford Manor in 1504, leaving his son John as heir.[34] At the death of the latter in 1508 the manor, which was then worth £5 10s. per annum, passed to his son John,[35] who died a minor in 1517, leaving four sisters as heirs.[36] One of these, Mary, died unmarried soon after.[37] Another, Elizabeth, with her husband Thomas Cave,[38] afterwards held land in Ickford,[39] but the main manor evidently came to the youngest sister Dorothy, who held it with her husband Nicholas Hubaud in 1532.[40] She survived her husband and died in 1559, leaving a son John.[41]

It does not appear that she held Ickford at the time of her death, and it may have passed before that date to Thomas Tipping,[42] who in 1585 made a settlement of it on his son George, then about to marry Dorothy Borlase.[43] Thomas died in 1601.[44] George held until his death in 1627,[45] when he was succeeded by his grandson Thomas, son of John Tipping.[46] Thomas, who was afterwards knighted, held the estate[47] until he died in 1693.[48] His son Thomas was created a baronet in 1698,[49] and in 1703 obtained an Act of Parliament to enable him to sell the manor of Ickford.[50] After this date various portions of the manor were enfranchised or the reversions sold, the main part with the demesne lands becoming the

TIPPING. *Or a bend engrailed vert with three pheons or thereon.*

property of Sir Edmund Harrison, kt.,[51] who died in 1712.[52] In 1733 his son Fiennes Harrison died also.[53] His sisters and heirs were Cecilia wife of William Snell, Sarah wife of Joel Watson, Jane wife of Matthias King, and Mary wife of Samuel Read[54]; the two latter families sold their share to the two former.[55] In 1754 a fine of the manor was levied[56] by William Snell and Cecilia, John Hood, husband of their daughter Cecilia,[57] Joel Watson, Sir John Danvers, bart., and Mary his wife, daughter of Joel and Sarah Watson,[58] Cecilia Watson, another daughter, and Mary King. Mary King appears to have quitclaimed her share, and Cecilia Watson, who married Thomas Delavale, bequeathed hers to her niece Mary Danvers.[59] This Mary Danvers, daughter and heir of Sir John Danvers and Mary, married the Hon. Augustus Richard Butler,[60] and in 1792–3 they levied a fine of the 'manor' of Ickford,[61] though they did not apparently hold the entire property. They conveyed their estate to Henry Woolhouse Disney Roebuck,[62] who died in 1796,[63] and whose son Henry Disney Roebuck[64] held about 273 acres in 1831, at which date William Hood, son of John and Cecilia, held about 250 acres with the manor and a fishery, a division of the estate between himself and Roebuck having been made.[65] The Roebuck family retained lands in the parish as late as 1869,[66] but Hood's share seems to have passed to the Jacomb family, who were his cousins, his mother's sister Mary having married William Jacomb.[67] Thomas Jacomb was lord in 1862–9,[68] and his trustees held in 1873.[68a] It passed before 1877 to J. W. Stephenson, who sold it after 1895 to Arthur Parsons Guy. At his death in 1912 his brother Mr. Frederick Parsons Guy succeeded.

Before the Conquest Ulf, a man of Earl Harold, held a second manor which in 1086 belonged to the Count of Mortain.[69] In 1377 overlordship rights here were held by William Montagu, Earl of Salisbury,[70] who succeeded to some of the Mortain lands.[71]

In 1086 this manor was held of the count as 6 hides by the monks of his abbey of Grestein in Normandy.[72] A later confirmatory charter to the abbey states that Ickford had been given to them by Maud Countess of Mortain.[73] The abbey continued to hold until the 14th century.[74] In 1359 lands here are said to have been held of the priory of Wilming-

[25] Chan. Inq. p.m. 6 Edw. II, no. 29.
[26] *Feud. Aids*, i, 119; Feet of F. Bucks. Trin. 21 Edw. III, no. 7.
[27] Feet of F. Bucks. Trin. 21 Edw. III, no. 8.
[28] Chan. Inq. p.m. 2 Ric. II, no. 57.
[29] G.E.C. *Peerage*, iv, 104.
[30] Ibid.
[31] See account of advowson. Lee, *Hist. and Antiq. of the Church of Thame*, 291–4.
[32] Ibid.
[33] *Cal. Inq. p.m. Hen. VII*, i, 197.
[34] Chan. Inq. p.m. (Ser. 2), xxiv, 62 (2).
[35] Ibid. 18.
[36] Ibid. xxxii, 43.
[37] Ibid. lxxix, 235.
[38] *Visit. of Oxon.* (Harl. Soc.), 1; Lee, op. cit. 91.
[39] *L. and P. Hen. VIII*, iv, g. 4896 (18).
[40] Chan. Inq. p.m. (Ser. 2), xxxii, 43; *Visit. of Oxon.* (Harl. Soc.), 1; Lee, op. cit. 91; Feet of F. Div. Co. Trin. 24 Hen. VIII.

[41] Chan. Inq. p.m. (Ser. 2), cxcii, 139.
[42] cf. suit recorded Ct. of Req. bdle. 42, no. 88.
[43] Pat. 27 Eliz. pt. viii, m. 21.
[44] Chan. Inq. p.m. (Ser. 2), cclxiv, 162, 163; P.C.C. 63 Woodhall.
[45] Recov. R. Hil. 11 Jas. I, m. 75; Feet of F. Div. Co. Trin. 16 Jas. I.
[46] Chan. Inq. p.m. (Ser. 2), ccccxxxviii, 123.
[47] Recov. R. Trin. 14 Chas. I.
[48] G.E.C. *Baronetage*, iv, 172.
[49] Ibid.; Recov. R. Hil. 11 Will. III, m. 30; see also Com. Pleas Recov. R. Hil. 11 & 12 Will. III, m. 9.
[50] Priv. Act, 2 & 3 Anne, cap. 11.
[51] Lipscomb, op. cit. i, 279.
[52] Musgrave, *Obit.* (Harl. Soc.), iii, 155; P.C.C. 11 Leeds. [53] Ibid.
[54] Ibid.; Lipscomb, op. cit. i, 279–80; G.E.C. *Baronetage*, v, 91.
[55] Lipscomb, loc. cit. Mary King, daughter of Jane and Matthias (ibid.), appears to have retained some interest as late as 1754 (see below).

[56] Feet of F. Bucks. Hil. 27 Geo. II; ibid. (K.S.B.).
[57] Lipscomb, loc. cit.; P.C.C. 650 Rockingham.
[58] G.E.C. loc. cit.
[59] Lipscomb, op. cit. i, 279.
[60] G.E.C. loc. cit.
[61] Feet of F. Bucks. Mich. 33 Geo. III.
[62] Lipscomb, loc. cit.
[63] P.C.C. 214 Harris.
[64] Ibid.
[65] Lipscomb, loc. cit.
[66] Sheahan, op. cit. 390.
[67] P.C.C. 650 Rockingham.
[68] Sheahan, loc. cit.
[68a] *Ret. of Owners of Land* (1873), *Bucks.* 11.
[69] *V.C.H. Bucks.* i, 243.
[70] *Cal. Pat. 1391–6*, pp. 117, 118.
[71] *V.C.H. Bucks.* ii, 355.
[72] Ibid. i, 243.
[73] Dugdale, *Mon.* vi, 1090.
[74] *Cal. Close, 1234–7*, p. 182; *Hund. R.* (Rec. Com.), i, 25; *Feud. Aids*, i, 84, 94; Chan. Inq. p.m. 6 Edw. II, no. 29.

ton in Sussex,[75] the English cell of the Norman abbey.

Towards the end of the 12th century Bartholomew de Ickford held lands in the parish,[76] probably as tenant of Grestein, since his descendants certainly held of the abbots.[77] Bartholomew was succeeded by his son William.[78] Thomas de Ickford, son of William,[79] was sued by the abbot in 1235 for customs and services.[80] In 1254–5 the same Thomas was found to hold the 6 hides of the abbot for a pair of gauntlets.[80a] Thomas, who still held in 1284–6,[81] was succeeded by his son John, tenant in 1302–3.[82] About this date the family appear under the name of atte Water.[83] In 1313 William atte Water died seised of a messuage, lands, and a fishery, which he held of the abbot for half a knight's fee.[84] He was also in possession of the Wallingford Honour lands, and the two holdings appear to have been amalgamated, descending henceforth to the same lords.

Members of the Ickford and Appleton families gave lands in Ickford to the abbey of Godstow[85] and the priory of St. Frideswide.[86] In the 14th century the atte Waters gave to the priory of Bisham lands,[87] afterwards called a manor, granted in 1540 to William Burt.[87a] This estate passed in marriage to the Tipping family, who, from 1585 onwards, held the 'manors of Great and Little Ickford.'[87b] The abbey of Bradwell also claimed lands in Ickford by grant from the atte Waters.[88]

The church of *CHURCH ST. NICHOLAS* consists of a chancel measuring internally 26 ft. 6 in. by 13 ft., nave 41 ft. by 13 ft., north aisle 6 ft. 6 in. wide, south aisle 5 ft. 6 in. wide, south porch, and west tower 10 ft. 6 in. square.

The present building dates in the main from about 1210, but the north and south aisles do not seem to have been added till some twenty years later. The width of the south aisle appears to have been governed by a south porch to the original nave, the outer wall of which is preserved in part on either side of the south doorway. The upper stage of the tower assumed its present form in the 14th century, and the east wall of the chancel was rebuilt about the same time, probably on account of some failure at the north-east angle. The south porch, though much altered about 1600, is probably of the 15th century. Restorations were undertaken in 1856 and 1875, and in 1907 the south side of the chancel was rebuilt and other repairs done. The walling generally is of limestone rubble and the principal roofs are tiled.

The chancel is lighted from the east by a three-light 14th-century window, with a traceried pointed head and image brackets on either side, and from the north by two original lancets, the western of which has been reset further west to give room for the large Tipping monument, removed from the north aisle in 1906. At the south-east is a square-headed window of two trefoiled lights of about 1350 said to have been brought from elsewhere. To the west of the central buttress of the south wall is an original lancet, and between this and the west end of the wall are a 13th-century doorway, and a cinquefoiled 15th-century light with a depressed head. The lower part of this last window apparently formed a low-side window and has two sills inside, much restored. Beneath the western lancet on the north side is a blocked low-side window, and east of this a recess which seems to indicate the former existence of a squint. In the south wall, in the usual position, is a 13th-century piscina with a credence shelf. The communion table is of the 17th century, but now supports a mediaeval altar slab found at the east end of the north aisle. The chancel arch is pointed and of two moulded orders towards the nave. It is of original early 13th-

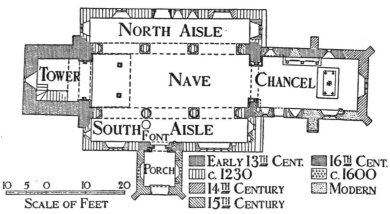

PLAN OF ICKFORD CHURCH

century date, but appears to have been considerably altered at a later period; the south jamb has been cut away on the east side, apparently to make room for the aumbry between it and the south-east window of the chancel, and a moulded corbel inserted to carry the arch. The jambs have attached circular shafts with early 13th-century capitals, that on the north being scalloped. Externally there are string-courses of original date on the north and south walls, which leap the heads of the lancets and form their labels; these have been cut for the later windows, and beneath the sills of the lancets in each wall is a second string-course, interrupted by the low-side windows.

[75] Chan. Inq. p.m. 33 Edw. III (1st nos.), no. 38.

[76] Dugdale, op. cit. iv, 364; Misc. Bks. (Exch. K.R.), xx, fol. 64. [77] See n. 74.

[78] Misc. Bks. (Exch. K.R.), xx, fol. 64.

[79] Cartul. of St. Frideswide (Oxf. Hist. Soc.), ii, 174.

[80] Cal. Close, 1234–7, p. 182.

[80a] Hund. R. (Rec. Com.), i, 25.

[81] Feud. Aids, i, 84.

[82] Ibid. 94; Misc. Bks. (Exch. K.R.),

xx, fol. 64 d.; Chan. Inq. p.m. 21 Edw. I, no. 28a.

[88] Cartul. of St. Frideswide (Oxf. Hist. Soc.), ii, 183–4.

[84] Chan. Inq. p.m. 6 Edw. II, no. 29.

[85] Misc. Bks. (Exch. K.R.), xx, fol. 64, 64 d.; Feud. Aids, i, 94, 119; Dugdale, op. cit. iv, 373.

[86] Cartul. of St. Frideswide (Oxf. Hist. Soc.), ii, 174–9, 180–4; Feud. Aids, loc. cit.

[87] Cal. Pat. 1391–6, pp. 117, 118; Close, 1 Hen. IV, pt. i, m. 35 d.; L. and P. Hen. VIII, xii (2), g. 1311 (22).

[87a] L. and P. Hen. VIII, xv, g. 613 (23); xix (1), p. 384; Close, 32 Hen. VIII, pt. iii, no. 34.

[87b] Pat. 27 Eliz. pt. viii, m. 21; Lipscomb, op. cit. i, 450.

[88] Lipscomb, op. cit. i, 277 (quoting Chan. Inq. p.m. 4 Ric. II, no. 101, now missing).

The nave arcades are each of three bays, and are contemporary with the aisles, with the exception of the eastern arch on the south, which appears to have been rebuilt. The arches are of two orders supported by circular columns and responds, all having plain capitals, except the western column of the south arcade, which has a foliated capital.

The north aisle is lighted from the north by a mid-14th-century square-headed window of three cinquefoiled lights, which has been altered at a later date, a narrow 13th-century lancet with 16th-century rear-arch, possibly re-used from the original nave, a round-headed lancet set high in the wall, also perhaps re-used, and a 13th-century coupled lancet repaired in the 16th century. In the east and west walls are coupled lancets, that on the east probably a 16th-century insertion, while that on the west, though originally of the 13th century, has been much restored. Between the third and fourth windows is an original round-headed doorway with a continuous chamfer.

The south aisle is lighted from the south by a four-light square-headed window, probably of the 16th century, near the east end of the wall, the head of which has been much restored, and by a modern three-light window at the opposite end of the wall, above which in the roof is a modern dormer window. The east and west windows are single lancets; the west window is modern, but the head, which was found in the south wall during the restoration of 1906, is of original 13th-century date. Above it is a small 13th-century quatrefoil. Between the two windows in the south wall is the south doorway, which is probably contemporary with the building of the chancel and nave, and once formed the outer doorway of a south porch. The head has been rebuilt in the 15th century; the inner order is four-centred, and the outer order, which is pointed, rises above its apex. The original pointed head has apparently been re-used as the head of the outer doorway of the porch added in the 15th century. The jambs are of two orders with detached shafts having moulded bases and annulets and carved and moulded capitals. The portion of walling in which the doorway is set is probably the south wall of the first porch; two fragments of the weather-mould of its roof can still be seen over the doorway. At the south-east is a damaged piscina contemporary with the aisle, and to the east of the south doorway is a stoup, much renewed, but partly of the 14th century. A niche at the east end with a trefoiled head probably dates from the 15th century.

The tower, which is crowned by a saddleback roof, contains three stories, but is divided externally only by the string-course beneath the windows of the bell-chamber. The tower arch is pointed and of two chamfered orders with small detached jamb shafts, having a scalloped capital on the north and a foliated capital on the south; the base of the southern jamb shaft has been patched with part of an octagonal column. In the west wall of the ground story is an original lancet. The story above was originally lighted by round-headed lights on the north, west, and south, but only that on the north now remains unblocked. In the east wall is a modern loop formed in a doorway

which must have originally opened into the nave roof. The topmost stage is lighted on the west by a pair of tall lights with trefoil heads and jambs of two orders externally, the outer orders having acutely pointed heads inclosed by labels and rising considerably above the apices of the inner heads. In each of the remaining three sides are pointed 14th-century windows of two trefoiled ogee lights with traceried heads; on the south and east the original 13th-century windows can be traced. Three fragments of worked stones preserved in the chancel probably belonged to these windows.

The chancel roof is of the 14th century and has trussed collar-beams and rafters. The nave roof, which is modern, has been lowered, but the weathering of the original roof is visible on the east side of the tower. The pitch of the roof and gable of the south porch has been raised in modern times. The timbers are mostly ancient; a boss on the southern tie-beam is carved with a Tudor rose, while reset on the modern northern tie-beam is another original boss carved as a lion's face.

The font has a plain round bowl and may be of the 13th century. The pulpit and sounding board, the latter enriched with a guilloche ornament, are of the 17th century. In the nave are some plain 16th-century seats. The gallery at the west end has a front of 17th-century panelling. Some 14th-century glass with foliated patterns remains in the tracery of the east window of the chancel. There are some modern shields and one ancient shield bearing the following charge: barry or and azure over all a bend gules. Some quarries of the same date survive in a north aisle window.

There is a large monument on the north side of the chancel to Thomas Tipping (d. 1601) and Margaret his wife. It is of chalk or clunch with columns painted in imitation of black marble, and contains kneeling figures of their four sons and five daughters. At the south-west of the chancel is a floor slab to Edmund Lawrence (d. 1645), and at the west end of the nave is a slab to Ann wife of Thomas Coles (d. 1695). A mural tablet in the south aisle commemorates Thomas Phillips (d. 1704) and Mary his wife (d. 1681).

There are three bells and a sanctus. The treble has letters selected at random cast upon it by way of an inscription[89]; the second is inscribed 'Chandler made me 1716'; and the tenor 'Let your hope be in the Lord 1623.' The sanctus bell is by W. Taylor, 1847.

The plate includes a cup of 1661 and a standing paten of the same date, the cup inscribed, 'Ex dono Gilberti (Sheldon) Episcopi Londini nup. Rectoris de Ickford in Com. Bucks'; and an 18th-century paten.

The registers begin in 1561.

ADVOWSON Reference to Ickford Church occurs first in 1194–5, when Helias son of Goce, in the tithing of William son of Goce, was accused of robbing the 'priest of Ickford,' for which offence he was fined.[90] It appears to have been attached to Miles Crispin's land, as it was held by the Appletons in 1226.[91] In 1262 Thomas de Appleton granted the advowson to Thomas de

[89] Mr. A. H. Cocks suggests that this bell is by John Appowell of Buckingham, who died in 1577 (*Church Bells of Bucks.* 188). [90] *R. of the King's Ct.* 1194–5 (Pipe R. Soc.), 145. [91] Lipscomb, op. cit. i, 282.

ICKFORD CHURCH FROM THE SOUTH-EAST

ICKFORD CHURCH: THE INTERIOR LOOKING EAST

Valognes and his heirs to be held of the Appleton heirs for 1*d.* rent and foreign service.[92] The advowson descended with the manor of Shabbington (q.v.) to Thomas de Valognes's daughter and heir Joan, wife of Robert de Grey, kt., and passed at her death, about 1313, to Joan, the daughter and heir of their dead son Thomas, upon whom a settlement had been made by Robert de Grey and confirmed by Joan his widow in 1297.[93] The younger Joan married Guy de Breton,[94] who presented to the church in 1318 and again in 1333.[95] In 1387 the advowson was held by Thomas Merington, William Wolfe and others, who had purchased it of John son and heir of William de Breton.[96]

Presentation was made by the king in 1405,[97] and in 1412 by John Clayrell,[98] who apparently left daughters as heirs, as in 1419 Thomas Wodelawe and Margaret his wife quitclaimed a moiety of the advowson, subject to a life interest to be retained by Margaret, to Richard Quartermain.[99] This Richard was the grandson of Thomas Quartermain, who died in 1342, by Katharine his wife, daughter and heir of Guy de Breton and Joan above mentioned.[100] Richard Quartermain presented to the church in 1458,[1] and after his death the advowson probably passed to his sister and co-heir Maud, wife of John Bruley, or her descendants.[2] Their daughter and heir Joan had married John Danvers, whose eldest son Thomas became his grandmother's heir,[3] and held property in Ickford in 1489.[4] His brother, Sir William Danvers, died seised of the advowson and the manor,[5] with which the advowson descended until the sale by the Tipping family in 1703.[6] After this date it was held

separately from the manor by various persons, presentation being made by John Beauchamp in 1728, by Evans Pitt in 1737, and by Hester or Esther Newell, widow, in 1747 and 1775.[7] The patronage was obtained before the end of the 18th century by Richard Townsend,[8] in whose family it remained until after 1890, when it passed to the Turner family, who still present to the rectory.[9]

Thomas de Valognes received half a virgate of land with the advowson in 1262,[10] and five messuages, 3 virgates 19 acres of land and 5 acres of meadow were held with this property in 1313.[11] In 1316 Guy de Breton is recorded as holding Ickford[12] with John atte Water, lord of the manor, from which account it seems possible that a manor of the rectory at one time existed.

In 1430 William Hebbenge, the rector, received a papal dispensation to hold for five years another benefice with Ickford.[13]

Among other rectors of Ickford may be named Gilbert Sheldon, who later became Bishop of London in 1660 and Archbishop of Canterbury in 1663.[14] The incumbent in 1632 was Calibute Downing, author of several treatises and sermons, advocating amongst other things the taking up of arms against the king in defence of religion.[15]

CHARITY Thomas Phillips, by deed poll 6 January 1697, charged lands in the parish of Tetsworth, Oxfordshire, with the yearly payment of £10. By a scheme of the Charity Commissioners of 3 March 1911 the annuity is used to provide clothing for three poor men and three poor women.

ILMER

Imere (xi cent.); Ymmere, Ylemere, Hilmere, Illmire (xiii–xiv cent.).

The parish of Ilmer, having an extent of a little over 753 acres, lies low, to the north-west of the Chiltern Hills. The land is lowest, under 200 ft. above the ordnance datum, in the south, where two streams cross the parish flowing in a north-westerly direction. Towards the north and east the land rises, especially in the latter district, in which the village is situated and where a height of 282 ft. is reached. The village itself is small and compact, the church of St. Peter standing to the north-east. Near by is the manor-house, now occupied as a farm.

A considerable part of the parish is pasture land; in 1905, 172 acres were arable land, while 580 acres were permanent grass.[1] It is interesting to note that at an early date the parish was apparently ill-provided

with pasture.[2] Royal licence to inclose the woods of Ilmer and La Sale and to make a park was granted to John de Moleyns in 1336.[3]

On the arable land of the parish wheat, barley and beans are the chief crops grown. In 1602 the lord of the manor sued a tenant for refusing to render, besides his money payment, an annual rent of two bushels of 'sweet and clean and dry beans' at the lord's house at Ascott.[4]

Fourteenth-century place-names in Ilmer include Middlefurlong benorth, Middlefurlong undertown,[5] and in the 15th century Shrobbes pasture, Brookfurlong, Groveditch, and Kingslake are mentioned.[6]

MANOR Before the Conquest Godwin, a man of Earl Leofwin, held in *ILMER* a manor which he could sell; in 1086 it was of the land of Odo of Bayeux, whose tenant Robert held

[92] Feet of F. Bucks. Hil. 46 Hen. III, no. 10. The church was valued at £6 13*s.* 4*d.* in 1291 (*Pope Nich. Tax.* [Rec. Com.], 34). The Appleton interest was held in 1313 by the atte Waters (*Cal. Inq. p.m.* [Edw. II], v, 222).

[93] See Shabbington and Feet of F. Bucks. East. 25 Edw. I, no. 3.

[94] *Visit. of Oxon.* (Harl. Soc.), 22.

[95] Lipscomb, loc. cit.

[96] Ibid. [97] Ibid. [98] Ibid.

[99] Feet of F. Div. Co. Hil. 6 & 7 Hen. V, no. 72.

[100] *Visit. of Oxon.* loc. cit.; Lee, op. cit. 291–4.

[1] Lipscomb, loc. cit.

[2] Lee, loc. cit. [3] Ibid.

[4] *Cal. Inq. p.m.* Hen. *VII*, i, 197.

[5] Chan. Inq. p.m. (Ser. 2), xxiv, 62 (2).

[6] See manor; Inst. Bks. (P.R.O.). Grants of the advowson were occasionally made by the family (Inst. Bks. [P.R.O.]; Lipscomb, op. cit. i, 282–4).

[7] Inst. Bks. (P.R.O.).

[8] Lipscomb, op. cit. i, 284; Sheahan, loc. cit.

[9] *Clergy Lists.* Presentation appears to have been made by Stephen Hemsted between the years 1869 and 1883.

[10] Feet of F. Bucks. Hil. 46 Hen. III, no. 10.

[11] *Cal. Inq. p.m.* (Edw. II), v, 222.

[12] *Feud. Aids*, i, 114.

[13] *Cal. of Papal Letters*, viii, 165. The church was assessed in 1535 at £11 6*s.* 8*d.*, in which sum was included a pension of 22*s.* paid by Nutley Abbey from Chearsley rectory (*Valor Eccl.* [Rec. Com.], iv, 234, 235).

[14] *Dict. Nat. Biog.* [15] Ibid.

[1] Statistics from Bd. of Agric. (1905).

[2] Chan. Inq. p.m. 34 Edw. I, no. 53; 2 Edw. IV (1st nos.), no. 27; De Banco R. 411, m. 52; Chan. Inq. p.m. 4 Ric. II, no. 38; 8 Hen. VI, no. 38.

[3] *Cal. Chart. R.* 1327–41, p. 353.

[4] Chan. Proc. (Ser. 2), bdle. 273, no. 2.

[5] *Cal. Close*, 1349–54, p. 58.

[6] Mins. Accts. (Gen. Ser.), bdle. 761, no. 2.

61

it as 4 hides.[7] In the 12th century it was in the possession of the family of Rumenel (Romney),[8] who also held, as a member of it, Aston Bernard or Aston Mullins in Dinton.[9] Aston is not, however, invariably mentioned among the Fitz Bernards' lands here,[10] and in 1371 it was found that the manor of Aston was, and always had been, parcel of the manor of Ilmer.[11] They were finally separated in the 16th century, when George Earl of Huntingdon and his son and heir Francis Lord Hastings sold Aston in 1537 to Michael Dormer and Ilmer in 1538–9 to Sir Robert Dormer, kt.[12] Sir Robert held also the manor of Wing, with which Ilmer then descended, passing to the Earls of Carnarvon and Chesterfield, and being held by the latter until the 19th century.[13] At some period, probably about the middle of that century, Ilmer was sold by the Stanhopes to Moreton John Edwin Frewen, who was lord of the manor in 1862.[14] He and Mrs. Raper held the manor jointly in 1869 and until some time after 1880, and he and General Raper in 1887. General Raper's share appears to have been Upper Farm, sold by the Raper family in 1909 to Mr. A. Goodchild, the present owner. The greater part of Ilmer, however, consisting of the Manor, Lower and Coldharbour Farms, belonged to Mrs. Moreton Craigie, after whose death a life interest was enjoyed by Miss Moreton. She died in 1912, when the property passed to Mrs. Carter, by whom it was immediately sold, the Manor and Lower Farms being purchased by Mr. W. Hill and Mr. A. A. Kingham, while Mr. A. Fisher bought Coldharbour.

The lord of the manor enjoyed the same rights and privileges in Ilmer as in Aston.[15]

The capital messuage of the manor is mentioned in 1238, when the sheriff was ordered to assign either it or the one in Aston to Ralph Fitz Bernard's widow Joan.[16] It is again referred to in 1306.[17]

A mill was included among the appurtenances of the manor in 1086.[18] In 1306 there was a windmill, out of repair.[19] In 1328 the water-mill was also found to be broken down and valueless,[20] but it was repaired in 1342–3.[21] Later inquisitions, however, include no mention of either mill. There are interesting surveys of the manor taken in the 14th and 15th centuries, with particulars concerning the economic conditions of the time.[22]

The office of marshal and keeper of the king's hawks and other birds was held in the 12th century by the Rumenel family, lords of Ilmer, who seem at first to have held the marshalship as their personal right and not as appurtenant to their manor, for in 1204 the king, at the petition of Aubrey de Rumenel, widow of William de Jarpenville, who had with Aubrey 'all her inheritance and the marshalship of our birds,' granted the office to Thomas Fitz Bernard and his wife, the heir of the Jarpenvilles, and to their heirs for ever.[23] Afterwards, however, the office came to be actually the serjeanty by which the manor was held,[24] as was also the case with the Rumenels' manor of 'Effeton' in Kent.[25] In 1338 Sir John de Moleyns, who acquired Ilmer about twenty years after it left the Fitz Bernard family, petitioned the king for a grant of the office with the fees and wages, asserting that it was parcel of the manor, although neither he nor his immediate predecessors in the manor, including Ralph Fitz Bernard, had been seised thereof for some time. It having been found that William Fitz Bernard had held Ilmer by this serjeanty, it was granted to Sir John, 'because the manor is said to have been held by such service and in consideration of his long service to him (the king) and as well of his great charges and grave perils therein both beyond the seas and within.'[26]

In 1610 Sir Robert Dormer received a confirmation of the serjeanty.[27] A claim was made for the same office in respect of the manor of Aston.[28] Charles Earl of Carnarvon, as seised of the manor of Ilmer, claimed to be marshal of the king's hawks in England at the coronation of James II in 1685, but the claim was not allowed, 'because not respecting the coronation,' but the earl was 'left to take his course at law if he thought fit.'[29]

It is stated in 1306 that the marshal might if he wished send another to fill the office.[30] He held the post at the king's expense.[31] By a later account the marshal was found to have the 'superior custody of the king's falcons and other hawks from the game of the river, and the office of surveyor of all the services of the custody or mewing of the falcons, goshawks and other hawks, due to the king by any persons and of rivers preserved'; he had also full power of punishing delinquents in rivers preserved so far as such punishments belonged to the king by right.[32] The marshal also claimed the right of nominating his under-officers.[33]

The alienations of parts of this serjeanty in the 13th century have been referred to under Aston.[34] One portion, a messuage and 34 acres, was held by three tenants of the Abbot of Missenden.[35] In the reign of Henry III the abbot, with the consent of the tenants, agreed to pay a yearly rent of 7s. 6d. to the Crown in lieu of the serjeanty due for that portion.[36] In 1585–6 these lands were granted by the Crown to John Walton and John Cresset.[37]

[7] V.C.H. Bucks. i, 236.
[8] Rymer, Foedera, i (1), 90; Feet of F. Bucks. Hil. 6 Hen. III, no. 9; Testa de Nevill (Rec.Com.), 260, and see advowson.
[9] V.C.H. Bucks. ii, 274 et seq.; Feet of F. Bucks. 15 Hen. III, no. 2; Cal. Close, 1382–7, p. 419; Cal. Pat. 1327–30, p. 75; 1334–8, pp. 195, 222; Feud. Aids, i, 120. For a further account of the de Moleyns, Hungerford and Hastings families see Stoke Poges.
[10] Testa de Nevill (Rec. Com.), 254, 255.
[11] Memo. R. (Exch. L.T.R.), East. 45 Edw. III.
[12] Recov. R. Hil. 29 Hen. VIII, m. 151; Feet of F. Bucks. East. 30 Hen. VIII; Com. Pleas D. Enr. Mich. 31 Hen. VIII, m. 2.

[13] See Wing, under manor, and Com. Pleas Recov. R. Hil. 16 Chas. I, m. 36.
[14] Sheahan, Hist. and Topog. of Bucks. 392.
[15] V.C.H. Bucks. ii, 274–6; Cal. Chart. R. 1327–41, pp. 399, 430, 457.
[16] Cal. Close, 1237–42, p. 68.
[17] Chan. Inq. p.m. 34 Edw. I, no. 53.
[18] V.C.H. Bucks. i, 236.
[19] Chan. Inq. p.m. 34 Edw. I, no. 53.
[20] Ibid. 2 Edw. III (1st nos.), no. 27.
[21] Mins. Accts. (Gen. Ser.), bdle. 761, no. 2.
[22] Chan. Inq. p.m. 34 Edw. I, no. 53; 4 Ric. II, no. 38; 8 Hen. VI, no. 38.
[23] Rymer, op. cit. i (1), 90.
[24] Red Bk. of Exch. (Rolls Ser.), 537.
[25] See Round, The King's Serjeants,

303–10, for a detailed account of the marshalship.
[26] Cal. Pat. 1338–40, pp. 47, 156; Cal. Close, 1337–9, p. 322.
[27] Cal. S. P. Dom. 1603–10, p. 580.
[28] Chan. Inq. p.m. (Ser. 2), cccxliii, 143; Cal. S. P. Dom. 1660–1, p. 49.
[29] Sandford, Coronation of Jas. II, 130.
[30] Chan. Inq. p.m. 24 Edw. I, no. 53.
[31] Ibid. 2 Edw. III (1st nos.), no. 27.
[32] Cal. Pat. 1338–40, p. 156.
[33] Sandford, loc. cit.
[34] V.C.H. Bucks. ii, 276.
[35] Testa de Nevill (Rec. Com.), 254, 257.
[36] Ibid.
[37] Pat. 28 Eliz. pt. xiv, m. 12.

Ilmer Church from the North-East

ILMER CHURCH: THE INTERIOR LOOKING EAST

CHURCH The church of *ST. PETER* consists of a chancel measuring internally 17 ft. by 14 ft., nave 39 ft. 6 in. by 16 ft., north porch and west bellcote; it is built of stone rubble and roofed with tiles.

The earliest part of the building is the nave, which dates from the 12th century. The chancel seems to have been rebuilt in the 14th century, when a small transept, destroyed in 1662,[37a] was added on the south side of the nave. In the 16th century the timber bellcote at the west end of the nave was built, and in 1890 the whole fabric was restored and the porch added.

The chancel, which is divided from the nave by an oak screen on a low stone wall, has two single-light windows in each lateral wall and a two-light window with modern tracery in the east wall. The north-west window is a 14th-century trefoiled light, but on its inner jambs are two late 15th-century sculptured groups, one representing the Holy Trinity with angels, and the other St. Christopher. The south-east window, which has a trefoiled head and traceried external spandrels, is probably of about 1380; the other windows have been considerably restored. In the south wall is a 14th-century trefoiled piscina.

On the south side of the nave is a blocked 12th-century doorway with a round head springing from chamfered abaci, and near the east end is a blocked 14th-century arch of two orders which opened to the transept mentioned above; a late 18th-century window of two lights has been inserted in the blocking. In the north wall are a square-headed two-light window of about 1500 and a 13th-century pointed doorway with moulded abaci. The west wall, which is much thicker than the lateral walls, is pierced by a trefoiled light, which appears to have been reset in the 16th century. The nave has a 16th-century collar-beam roof with a plastered ceiling. The bellcote, which is supported by moulded posts at the west end of the nave, is weather-boarded, and is surmounted by an oak shingled spire.

The font is of mediaeval date, but the sides of its plain octagonal bowl have been recut; the oak cover is of the 17th century. The chancel screen, of ten traceried bays on either side of a central doorway with a four-centred head, dates from about 1500.

There are three bells: the treble inscribed 'Henri Knight made mee ano 1618'; the second 'Gloria in excelcuc (*sic*) deo 1586,' by William Knight; and the tenor 'Sancta Margareta Ora Pro Nobis. W. H,' probably by William Hasylwood of Reading, c. 1500.

The communion plate includes a chalice and cover paten of 1569.

The registers begin in 1660.

ADVOWSON The church of Ilmer was granted to the priory of Studley in Oxfordshire about 1203 by Aubrey daughter of David de Rumenel.[38] The vicarage, which was ordained before 1235, was in the gift of the prioress.[3] Ralph Fitz Bernard, grandson of the original benefactor, claimed the advowson and part of the land against the prioress in 1229,[40] but as he could not prove his right was obliged to quitclaim all interest to her and her successors.[41] In 1535 the annual value of the benefice was £7 exclusive of an annual pension of 6s. 8d. paid by the vicar to the prioress.[42] After the dissolution of Studley the rectory and advowson of Ilmer were granted to John Croke,[43] who received licence later in the same year—1540—to alienate to Sir Robert Dormer and others.[44] Sir Robert also held the manor (q.v.), with which the rectory and advowson were held[45] until 1858, when the Rev. W. E. Partridge bought the advowson from the Earl of Chesterfield.[46] Before this date the incumbents had not infrequently held other livings simultaneously with Ilmer. Thus the vicar at the time of the Commonwealth was also rector of Aston Sandford; Cornish, presented in 1700, was curate of Princes Risborough and Kingsey, while a later vicar was also rector of Radnage.[47] The Rev. W. E. Partridge at the time of the sale above mentioned was not only the incumbent at Ilmer, but also rector of Horsenden, and these two livings were united by an Order in Council in 1865, the patronage passing, at the death of the Rev. W. E. Partridge in 1886, to his daughter and heir Mrs. Leonard Jaques,[48] with whom it still remains.

In 1349 Sir Richard Gladwin, the vicar, resigned the living; the lord of the manor then granted him for life a plot of the garden of the manor measuring 100 ft. by 50 ft., with permission to root up trees, to 'bring it into culture and otherwise to do his pleasure therein,' with a further gift of 7½ acres of arable land to be held for a yearly render of a rose at Midsummer, so that he should have the lord and his wife in memory both in masses and orisons.[49]

CHARITIES The Church Close, containing 1 a. 1 r. 20 p., was given, on a date not stated, by Earl Stanhope for the repair of the church. The land is let in allotments, producing £3 12s. 6d. yearly, which is applied towards the general church expenses.

Mrs. Sarah Maria Clotilda Raper by her will, proved at London 25 May 1881, bequeathed one-nineteenth part of her residuary personal estate for the benefit of the poor. The legacy is represented by £617 17s. 3d. consols with the official trustees. The annual dividends, amounting to £15 8s. 8d., are applied mainly in the distribution of coal and other articles in kind.

KINGSEY

Eie, Kingesie (xii cent.); Kingsley (xv cent.); Kingeshay (xvii cent.).

Kingsey is a parish with an area (including the liberty of Tythrop) of 1,431 acres, of which 7 acres are covered by water.[1] The greater part (1,022 acres) is in permanent grass, while only 315 acres are arable

---

[37a] Lipscomb, *Hist. and Antiq. of Bucks.* i, 292.   [38] Dugdale, *Mon.* iv, 249.
[39] Gibbons, *Liber Antiq.* 15.
[40] *Cal. Pat.* 1225–32, p. 301.
[41] Feet of F. Bucks. 14 Hen. III, no. 2; 15 Hen. III, no. 1.
[42] *Valor Eccl.* (Rec. Com.), iv, 236.
[43] *L. and P. Hen. VIII,* xv, g. 282 (109).
[44] Ibid. g. 436 (3).
[45] Inst. Bks. (P.R.O.).
[46] Sheahan, op. cit. 393.
[47] Lipscomb, op cit. i, 291–2.
[48] *Clergy Lists*; *V.C.H. Bucks.* ii, 254.
[49] *Cal. Close,* 1349–54, p. 58.
[1] *Census Rep. Oxon.* 1901, p. 18.

land and 45 acres woods and plantations.[2] The soil is heavy loam, the subsoil clay, and the chief crops are wheat and beans. The land is level, the height generally being about 240 ft. above the ordnance datum. The parish was transferred to Oxfordshire for civil purposes in 1894.[3]

The village stands in a central position on the London road, the church being in the middle, with the manor-house and school on the south-east and the vicarage a quarter of a mile to the north-west. A stream feeding a decoy pond forms a part of the northern boundary of the parish.

The following place-names have been found: Parisham,[4] Rudanache[5] (xv cent.), Fornyfield and My lord of Essex's ground (20 acres including a vineyard of 5 a. 20 p.) (xvi cent.).[6]

Tythrop (Duchitorp, xi cent. ; Tuphrop, Twythrop, xiii cent. ; Titethrop, xiv cent.) is a liberty in the west of Kingsey parish which was assessed in 1086 under Lewknor Hundred, Oxfordshire.[7] References to it under this hundred have been found to the middle 16th century.[8] Tythrop House stands in a park of 120 acres. It is a fine stone house and is the seat of Mr. Philip Digby Wykeham, owner of the whole of Tythrop and the greater part of Kingsey.

Saxon antiquities have been found in the parish.[9]

MANORS   Kingsey is not mentioned in the Domesday Survey, but was included under the royal manor of Brill[10] (q.v.). Henry I granted the land of Kingsey, afterwards *KINGSEY MANOR*, to William de Bolebec,[11] and it was held of the barony of Bolebec[12] by the service of a knight's fee,[13] last mentioned in 1349.[14]

Herbert de Bolebec died seised of Kingsey in the time of Henry I,[15] and his son Gilbert was holding under Henry II.[16] He died about 1180,[17] and his son, who in 1185 was in the custody of William de Jarpenville (Charpunville),[18] is probably the Herbert de Bolebec who was lord of Kingsey about 1197[19] and was living in 1210.[20] William de Bolebec is named later in the century[21] and Gilbert de Bolebec in 1236.[22] Gilbert died seised about 1247, when his

heir was his son Herbert.[23] He died about 1268, and was succeeded by his brother Gilbert de Bolebec,[24] who held Kingsey[25] until his death, about 1298. His son Simon was said to be his heir,[26] but judgement was afterwards given in favour of another son Henry,[27] and his widow Agnes had dower.[28] In 1304 Henry de Bolebec granted Kingsey Manor to Eleanor de Ewelme and her nephews Geoffrey and William Neyrnut, sons of Sir John Neyrnut.[29] Geoffrey and William Neyrnut both died,[29a] apparently, before 1316,[30] and Eleanor in 1347 enfeoffed Sir Robert Marny, who thereupon granted it to her for life.[31] It reverted to him on her death in

BOLEBEC. *Vert a lion argent.*   MARNY. *Gules a leopard rampant or.*

1349.[32] Kingsey Manor was in the king's hands in 1351 with other lands belonging to Sir Robert Marny,[33] but it was restored to him in 1352, a temporary grant to William of Salop in that year[34] being cancelled.[35] Marny leased it for ten years in 1363 to John of Newport, Thomas Young and Edmund Barnabe.[36] In 1376–7 the manor was settled on Sir Robert Marny, Alice his wife and their heirs in tail-male,[37] and in 1383 their title was confirmed to them by John Neyrnut, great-nephew and heir of Eleanor de Ewelme.[38] Kingsey descended to Sir William Marny, who died seised in 1414, leaving a son Thomas.[39] He died about 1424,[40] and later in this year, on the death of his infant daughter Margaret, his brother John Marny succeeded,[41] dower being assigned to the widow Margaret, afterwards the wife of Sir Thomas Echingham.[42] In 1469 Sir John

[2] Statistics from Bd. of Agric. (1905).

[3] Loc. Govt. Bd. Order, 27 Oct. 1894.

[4] Early Chan. Proc. bdle. 222, no. 123.

[5] Ct. R. (Gen. Ser.), portf. 155, no. 18.

[6] Rentals and Surv. (Gen. Ser.), portf. 5, no. 73, part of a terrier of the time of Hen. VIII.

[7] *Dom. Bk.* (Rec. Com.), i, 155*b.*

[8] *Hund. R.* (Rec. Com.), i, 43; ii, 784; Ct. R. (Gen. Ser.), portf. 212, no. 1, 4, 7, 12, 15, 19, 20, 25.

[9] *V.C.H. Bucks.* i, 198, 205.

[10] *Hund. R.* (Rec. Com.), i, 35. It was probably originally known as Eye (Stacey Grimaldi, *Rot. de Dominabus,* 22 ; *Testa de Nevill* [Rec. Com.], 259*a*), but from its connexion with the Crown appears as Kingsey from the 12th century onward, and was thus distinguished from the neighbouring parish of Eye, later called Towersey.

[11] *Hund. R.* loc. cit.

[12] *Liber Niger* (ed. 1771), i, 197; Inq. a.q.d. file 286, no. 5.

[13] *Testa de Nevill* (Rec. Com.), 245; *Hund. R.* (Rec. Com.), i, 25, 35 ; *Feud. Aids,* i, 84, 120.

[14] Chan. Inq. p.m. 23 Edw. III, pt. ii, no. 63.

[15] *Liber Niger,* loc. cit.   [16] Ibid.

[17] Stacey Grimaldi, loc. cit

[18] Ibid.

[19] Feet of F. case 14, file 1, no. 10. He granted one-third in dower to Richent de Lorinton.

[20] *Red Bk. of Exch.* (Rolls Ser.), 536.

[21] *Testa de Nevill* (Rec. Com.), 245.

[22] Ibid. 259*a* ; *Cat. of Anct. D.* ii, 500.

[23] Chan. Inq. p.m. Hen. III, file 5, no. 2. His death was apparently ignored by the jurors in 1254 (*Hund. R.* [Rec. Com.], i, 25).

[24] Chan. Inq. p.m. Hen. III, file 35, no. 7.

[25] *Hund. R.* (Rec. Com.), i, 35 ; *Feud. Aids,* i, 84 ; *Plac. de Quo Warr.* (Rec. Com.), 90.

[26] Chan. Inq. p.m. Edw. I, file 82, no. 15.

[27] *Abbrev. Plac.* (Rec. Com.), 238. Final judgement was not given until 1302 (Chan. Misc. bdle. 49, file 2, no. 25), and Kingsey was in the king's hands earlier in that year (*Feud. Aids,* i, 95).

[28] *Cal. Close,* 1296–1302, p. 147.

[29] *Cat. of Anct. D.* ii, 257 ; Inq. a.q.d. file 48, no. 4 ; *Cal. Pat.* 1301–7, p. 291 ; De Banco R. 155, m. 205 ; Feet of F. Bucks. Trin. 33 Edw. I, no. 4.

[29a] Assize R. 1494, m. 2.

[30] *Feud. Aids,* i, 114, 120 ; Ct. R. (Gen. Ser.), portf. 155, no. 15. Eleanor's

name occurs on several deeds in connexion with Kingsey about this time (*Cat. of Anct. D.* ii, 466 ; Feet of F. Bucks. Trin. 34 Edw. I, no. 7 ; Hil. 5 Edw. II, no. 2 ; *Abbrev. Rot. Orig.* [Rec. Com.], i, 227).

[31] Inq. a.q.d. file 286, no. 5 ; *Cal. Pat.* 1345–8, p. 426 ; De Banco R. 352, m. 609 ; *Cat. of Anct. D.* i, 510.

[32] Chan. Inq. p.m. 23 Edw. III, pt. ii, no. 63.

[33] Mins. Accts. (Gen. Ser.), bdle. 761, no. 7.   [34] *Cal. Pat.* 1350–4, p. 222.

[35] *Cal. Close,* 1349–54, p. 435.

[36] Ibid. 1360–4, p. 512.

[37] *Abbrev. Rot. Orig.* (Rec. Com.), ii, 348 ; Inq. a.q.d. file 388, no. 20 ; Close, 51 Edw. III, m. 23 ; Feet of F. Bucks. Hil. 51 Edw. III ; Assize R. 1494, m. 2 ; Chan. Misc. bdle. 49, file 2, no. 28, giving particulars of the descent of the manor from 1304.

[38] *Cat. of Anct. D.* i, 483 ; Close, 7 Ric. II, m. 24 d.

[39] Chan. Inq. p.m. 2 Hen. V, no. 29.

[40] Ibid. 2 Hen. VI, no. 15.

[41] Ibid.

[42] These dower lands were exempted in a lease of Kingsey Manor made by John Marny in 1440 to John Hobbs and his sons John and Richard (*Cat. of Anct. D.* i, 396).

Marny, kt., was fined £800 as a Lancastrian, and he and his wife Joan were allowed to grant his two parts of this manor to Sir Thomas Tyrell, his sister's husband,[43] and other feoffees for purposes of settlement.[44] On the death of Sir John Marny in 1477 his feoffees obtained a licence to grant Kingsey Manor to his widow Joan for life with remainder to the son and heir Henry.[45] He succeeded his mother in 1478,[46] was knight both of the Bath and of the Garter,[47] and became the first Lord Marny[48] shortly before his death in 1523.[49] His son and successor John Lord Marny[50] died in 1525 leaving two daughters and co-heirs, Katherine and Elizabeth, both minors,[51] but Elizabeth finally got all the manor of Kingsey. About 1542 she married Lord Thomas Howard, who in 1559 became Viscount Howard of Bindon.[52] She died before 1565,[53] and in 1576 her husband with their son Henry Howard obtained leave from Parliament to sell Kingsey Manor in order to defray debts to the Crown.[54] It was purchased by William Wright in 1577.[55] He or his son granted it to his mother and her second husband, named Gamage, for their lives, and in 1589 applied to the Privy Council for redress against her action in making a deed of gift of the estate to a third person contrary to their agreement.[56] In 1610 he settled the manor in tail-male,[57] and his will was proved in January 1610–11 by his widow Elizabeth.[58] Further settlements were made by his son William,[59] who sold it in 1615 to Sir John Dormer.[60] It appears to have passed in marriage with his daughter Elizabeth to Sir Robert Spiller,[61] who owned it in 1627.[62] At this time, apparently on a second marriage, he seems to have sold Kingsey Manor to his father, Sir Henry Spiller, subject to a payment of £3,000 to his daughter Jane at the age of eighteen.[63] In 1646 she petitioned for the allowance of her portion from her grandfather's sequestered estate, and in consequence some reduction was made in 1648 in the heavy fine

SPILLER. *Sable a cross voided between four pierced molets or.*

which he had incurred.[64] In 1650 the claim of her husband James Herbert as heir-at-law in right of his wife to Sir Henry Spiller (with certain exceptions) was allowed.[65] He settled the manor in 1667[66] and died in 1677, his wife surviving him.[67] Kingsey Manor passed to two of their sons in succession, Thomas, who was buried at Thame in 1702,[68] and James,[69] who was one of the members for Aylesbury in that year,[70] and died in 1709.[71] His son James,[72] who succeeded him,[73] died in 1721,[74] and left a son, another James Herbert,[75] who died when member of Parliament for Oxford in 1740.[76] Philip, brother of the last James,[77] died without issue in 1749.[78] One moiety of Kingsey Manor passed to his sister Sophia, wife of Philip sixth Viscount Wenman,[79] and descended to their son the seventh viscount, who died without issue in 1800.[80] His nephew and heir William Richard Wykeham[81] died a few months later.[82] His daughter and heir Sophia[83] sold her moiety about 1813[84] to her uncle Mr. Philip Thomas Wykeham, who in 1810 had inherited the other moiety from his great-aunt Anne Herbert,[85] the other sister and co-heir of Philip Herbert.[86] Mr. Philip Thomas Herbert Wykeham succeeded his father in 1832,[87] and on his death in 1879 bequeathed Kingsey Manor to his younger nephew, Mr. Philip Digby Wykeham of Tythrop House,[88] who is the present owner.

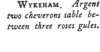

WYKEHAM. *Argent two cheverons sable between three roses gules.*

Gilbert de Bolebec claimed view of frankpledge in 1286,[89] and in the early 17th century this right is referred to as pertaining to the manor.[90]

Manorial Court Rolls are extant for the years 1318–24,[91] 1351–67, for 1414 and 1460,[92] also some Ministers' Accounts of the middle 14th[93] and 15th centuries.[94] A water-mill appertained to Kingsey Manor.[95]

An estate in Kingsey extending into Towersey was also called *KINGSEY MANOR.* Part of it appertained in the middle 14th century to Ewelme Manor, Oxfordshire,[96] and the whole was held in the early

[43] *Cal. Pat.* 1476–85, p. 13.
[44] Ibid. 1467–77, pp. 151–2, 344; Feet of F. Div. Co. Trin. 9 Edw. IV, no. 69.
[45] *Cal. Pat.* 1476–85, p. 13.
[46] Chan. Inq. p.m. 18 Edw. IV, no. 44.
[47] Shaw, *Kts. of Engl.* i, 144, 20.
[48] G.E.C. *Complete Peerage,* v, 259.
[49] Chan. Inq. p.m. (Ser. 2), xl, 7.
[50] Ibid.
[51] Ibid. xliv, 92.
[52] G.E.C. *Complete Peerage,* iv, 261.
[53] Ibid.
[54] W. and L. Inq. p.m. xxiii, 153.
[55] Recov. R. East. 19 Eliz. m. 507.
[56] *Acts of P.C.* 1588–9, p. 196.
[57] Feet of F. Div. Co. Hil. 7 Jas. I; Close, 7 Jas. I, pt. xv.
[58] P.C.C. 2 Wood.
[59] Feet of F. Bucks. Hil. 6 Jas. I.
[60] Ibid. Div. Co. Mich. 13 Jas. I.
[61] Lipscomb, *Hist. and Antiq. of Bucks.* i, 298.
[62] Recov. R. East. 3 Chas. I, m. 101.
[63] Ibid.; Feet of F. Div. Co. East. 3 Chas. I; *Cal. Com. for Comp.* 1146. In 1642 Giles son and heir of William Wright petitioned the House of Lords with

respect to the purchase of this manor by Sir Henry Spiller (*Hist. MSS. Com. Rep.* v, App. i, 64).
[64] *Cal. Com. for Comp.* 1146.
[65] Ibid. 1147. Particulars about Jane Spiller's marriage and Henry Spiller's claim to the manors of Kingsey, Tythrop and Haddenham are given in *V.C.H. Bucks.* ii, 283.
[66] Feet of F. Div. Co. East. 19 Chas. II.
[67] P.C.C. 49 Hale.
[68] Lee, *Hist. and Antiq. of the Church of Thame,* 570.
[69] *Topog. and Gen.* iii, 268.
[70] *Ret. of Memb. of Parl.* i, 600.
[71] Musgrave, *Obit.* (Harl. Soc.), iii, 196.
[72] Lee, loc. cit.
[73] Recov. R. Mich. 9 Anne, m. 240.
[74] Musgrave, loc. cit.
[75] P.C.C. 110 Buckingham; Recov. R. East. 10 Geo. II, m. 11, 12.
[76] Musgrave, loc. cit.
[77] P.C.C. 110 Buckingham; 321 Browne. His brother Peregrine named in these wills appears to have been dead.
[78] Musgrave, *Obit.* (Harl. Soc.), iii, 197; inscr. in Thame Park Chapel; P.C.C. 284 Lisle.

[79] Inscr. in Thame Park Chapel; Feet of F. Oxon. Trin. 24 & 25 Geo. II.
[80] G.E.C. *Complete Peerage,* viii, 93.
[81] Ibid.; Recov. R. Trin. 40 Geo. III, m. 29. [82] *Gent. Mag.* lxx (2), 700.
[83] *V.C.H. Bucks.* ii, 283.
[84] Recov. R. Mich. 54 Geo. III, m. 263.
[85] *Gent. Mag.* lxxx (1), 287; P.C.C. 83 Collingwood.
[86] Lysons, *Mag. Brit.* i (3), 589.
[87] Burke, *Landed Gentry* (1906), under Wykeham-Musgrave.
[88] Ibid. under Wykeham.
[89] *Plac. de Quo Warr.* (Rec. Com.), 90.
[90] Feet of F. Div. Co. Mich. 13 Jas. I; East. 3 Chas. I; Recov. R. East. 3 Chas. I, m. 101.
[91] Ct. R. (Gen. Ser.), portf. 155, no. 15.
[92] Ibid. no. 16, 17, 18.
[93] Mins. Accts. bdles. 1240, no. 19–21; 761, no. 8. [94] Ibid. bdle. 1120, no. 7.
[95] Chan. Inq. p.m. Edw. I, file 82, no. 15; Mins. Accts. (Gen. Ser.), bdle. 1120, no. 7; Feet of F. Div. Co. Hil. 7 Jas. I; Recov. R. East. 3 Chas. I, m. 101; Mich. 9 Anne, m. 240.
[96] Chan. Inq. p.m. 30 Edw. III (1st nos.), no. 42.

15th century of the heirs of Sir John Neyrnut,[97] in 1473 of the king,[98] and in 1486 of Sir William Norris.[99]

Edmund Bacon held the land in Kingsey pertaining to Ewelme Manor at his death in 1336.[100] It had been settled in remainder on his heirs by his first wife Joan.[1] Their daughter Margaret had married William de Kerdeston,[2] and he was granted custody of these lands in 1337 during the minority of his daughter Maud.[3] She afterwards married John Burghersh, who died in 1349,[4] and in 1362, on a final partition of Edmund Bacon's estates, Kingsey Manor was awarded to their son John Burghersh, then a minor.[5] He was granted seisin in 1366[6] and died about 1392.[7] On the death of his widow Ismania in 1420 this manor passed by agreement with Thomas and Maud Chaucer in 1418[8] to John and Margaret Arundell, Maud and Margaret being the daughters and co-heirs of John and Ismania Burghersh.[9] John Arundell died in 1423,[10] and in 1472 his son and heir Sir John Arundell conveyed the estate to John Henton and other feoffees[11] for the use of Geoffrey Dormer of Thame, an arrangement which was still holding later in the century.[12] In 1502 Geoffrey and Alice Dormer quitclaimed it for themselves and the heirs of Alice to their son Peter[13] and his wife Agnes.[14] This land does not reappear as a separate entity.

In 1086 Tythrop was assessed at 5 hides as part of the land of the Bishop of Bayeux.[15] Half this land, afterwards known as *TYTHROP KINGSEY alias ROSE KINGSEY MANOR*, had been subinfeudated by the bishop to Wadard.[16] It was afterwards attached to the barony of Arsic in Oxfordshire,[17] and paid 21s. 8d. yearly for the ward of Dover Castle.[18] The last reference to this overlordship occurs in 1602.[19]

In the middle of the 13th century Robert de la Rose held this half of Tythrop,[20] and he or another Robert de la Rose was holding it in 1261.[21] His daughter and heir married William Saunderton,[22] who was holding in 1279.[23] This land descended with Saunderton St. Mary to William Saunderton,[24] who in 1449 and 1450, with John and Alice Logge and others, conveyed Tythrop Manor to John Norris,[25] who made a settlement including it in 1462.[26] It does not appear, however, to have descended in his

family. It is not included in the lands held by him at his death in 1467[27] nor by his son William, who died about 1509,[28] although John, the latter's grandson and heir,[29] may be identical with the John Norris who, holding Tythrop Manor in right of his wife Elizabeth, quitclaimed it in 1523 to Sir Henry Marny.[30] From that time it descended with the principal manor of Kingsey [30a] (q.v.) to Mr. Philip Digby Wykeham of Tythrop House, who is the present owner.

The other half of Tythrop, distinguished from Rose Kingsey in the early 17th century as *WASE-COURT alias BAYLIES HEYS MANOR*, had been subinfeudated in 1086 by the Bishop of Bayeux to Ilbert Lacy,[31] and later appertained to the fee of Pontefract[32] and the earldom of Lincoln.[33] No

WASE. *Barry argent and gules a quarter gules with a pierced molet argent therein.*

CAMOYS. *Or a chief gules with three roundels argent therein.*

LEWKNOR. *Azure three cheverons or.*

reference to this overlordship has been found after the end of the 13th century.[34]

A mesne lordship in Tythrop was connected with Little Haseley, Oxfordshire. It was held by

[97] Chan. Inq. p.m. 8 Hen. V, no. 114.
[98] Ibid. 13 Edw. IV, no. 26.
[99] Ibid. (Ser. 2), i, 58.
[100] Ibid. 30 Edw. III (1st nos.), no. 42.
[1] Ibid.
[2] Ibid. 35 Edw. III, pt. i, no. 22.
[3] Cal. Pat. 1334–8, p. 495. Eleanor de Ewelme (see principal manor) held part of this estate for life by grant of John Bacon, father of Edmund (Chan. Inq. p.m. 35 Edw. III, pt. i, no. 22).
[4] Chan. Inq. p.m. 24 Edw. III (1st nos.), no. 94.
[5] Cal. Close, 1360–4, p. 337.
[6] Ibid. 1364–8, p. 259.
[7] Chan. Inq. p.m. 15 Ric. II, pt. i, no. 8.
[8] Feet of F. Div. Co. East. 6 Hen. V, no. 66.
[9] Chan. Inq. p.m. 8 Hen. V, no. 114.
[10] Ibid. 2 Hen. VI, no. 29.
[11] Ibid. 14 Edw. IV, no. 37. They were dispossessed for a short time on the death of Sir John Arundell in 1473 by Sir James Tyrell and his wife Anne,

Sir John's daughter, on the finding of an earlier inquisition (ibid. 13 Edw. IV, no. 26).
[12] Chan. Inq. p.m. (Ser. 2), i, 58; Early Chan. Proc. bdles. 76, no. 116; 197, no. 66.
[13] Lupton, *Hist. of Thame and Hamlets,* 80.
[14] Feet of F. case 294, file 80.
[15] Dom. Bk. (Rec. Com.), i, 155.
[16] Ibid.
[17] Testa de Nevill (Rec. Com.), 100, 106; Hund. R. (Rec. Com.), i, 43; ii, 785.
[18] Hund. R. (Rec. Com.), i, 43; ii, 785.
[19] Chan. Inq. p.m. (Ser. 2), ccxcv, 63.
[20] Testa de Nevill (Rec. Com.), 100, 106.
[21] Red Bk. of Exch. (Rolls Ser.), 709.
[22] Hund. R. (Rec. Com.), ii, 785.
[23] Ibid.
[24] cf. under Saunderton; Cat. of Anct. D. ii, 446; Feud. Aids, iv, 171.
[25] Feet of F. case 191, file 28, no. 33.
[26] Ibid. case 294, file 74, no. 8.

[27] Chan. Inq. p.m. Edw. IV, file 22, no. 1.
[28] Ibid. (Ser. 2), xxiv, 76.
[29] Ibid.
[30] Feet of F. Div. Co. Hil. 14 Hen. VIII.
[30a] Tythrop Kingsey was held for some time by Edmund Wright and his son Edmund of Wasecourt Manor (Chan. Proc. [Ser. 2], bdle. 295, no. 7; Feet of F. Oxon. Hil. 42 Eliz.; Chan. Inq. p.m. [Ser. 2], ccxcv, 63) with which it was granted to Sir Henry Spiller in 1610 (Pat. 7 Jas. I, pt. xxix, no. 5; Feet of F. Div. Co. Mich. 13 Jas. I). For later descent see Recov. R. East. 10 Geo. II, m. 12; Feet of F. Oxon. Hil. 18 Geo. II. (A quitclaim by Henry Reynell Spiller).
[31] Dom. Bk. (Rec. Com.), i, 155. The fee of Lacy is named as one of the fees of the Bishop of Bayeux in 1133 (Red Bk. of Exch. [Rolls Ser.], 686).
[32] Testa de Nevill (Rec. Com.), 106.
[33] Hund. R. (Rec. Com.), i, 43.
[34] Ibid. ii, 784.

William de Brug and his wife Olive in her right in the early 13th century,[35] and apparently corresponds to that held later in the century by William de Stalebroc[36] and in 1279 by Robert son of Henry.[37] The Barantines or Barentynes held Little Haseley Manor for over two centuries,[38] and in 1478 Dru Barantine owned mesne lordship rights in Tythrop.[39]

Richard de Parco was tenant in Tythrop in the early 13th century,[40] Gilbert Wase (or Wace) later in the same century,[41] and William Wase in 1254.[42] He or another William Wase was holding this half of Tythrop in 1279[43] and his son William[44] in 1346.[45] On the death of his son Sir Gilbert Wase in the early 15th century the Wase lands passed to a distant relative, Sir Richard Camoys.[46] His feoffees in 1416 granted TYTHROP MANOR to his widow Joan for life, with remainder successively in tail-male to his sons John, Ralph, and Hugh, and to his own right heirs.[47] On the death of Hugh second Lord Camoys, son of Sir Richard Camoys, in 1426,[48] his sisters and co-heirs were Margaret wife of Ralph Radmylde and Eleanor wife of Roger, afterwards Sir Roger Lewknor.[49] Ralph Radmylde died seised of half this manor in 1443, his wife having predeceased him.[50] Their son Robert, then a minor,[51] obtained a licence in 1448 to enter into his heritage without suing livery from the king.[52] It has not been found possible to trace the descent of this part of the original manor further.

On the death of Sir Roger Lewknor in 1478 the heritage of his wife Eleanor, including Tythrop Manor in Kingsey, passed to their son Thomas.[53] An Act of attainder and forfeiture against him was reversed in 1485.[54] His son Sir Roger Lewknor[55] after 1498 granted this property under the name of Kingsey Manor to Edmund Dudley for life.[56] Owing to his attainder it was taken into the king's hands in his lifetime.[57] In 1538 Sir Roger and Elizabeth Lewknor, with the concurrence apparently of their son-in-law William, afterwards Sir William Barantine,[58] conveyed this manor to Sir John Harecourt,[59] probably in trust, since Sir Roger Lewknor, in his will dated January 1542, left it 'as much as in me lyeth' to

Roger Lewknor for life.[60] This property evidently passed later in the century into the same hands as Rose Kingsey (q.v.), and the farm of Wasecourt alias Baylies Heys about 1581 was leased by William Wright to his brother Edmund and transferred to the latter in 1591.[61] He settled it in 1594 in jointure on his second wife, Mary Norrington, who after his death in 1602 married James Fairborne and defended this property against her husband's son Edmund Wright.[62] In 1617 Mary Fairborne, then a widow, with Vincent Wright sold it to Sir Thomas Elliott and Edward Penn.[63] This property, as mentioned under Rose Kingsey (q.v.), had been previously granted by the Crown to Sir Henry Spiller, and is not afterwards distinguishable from the modern estate of Tythrop Manor.

At his death in 1349 Sir John Burghersh was tenant of part of the Wase lands in Tythrop,[64] corresponding apparently to the Tythrop Manor held by his son John's widow Ismania and their son-in-law Sir John Arundell

KINGSEY CHURCH FROM THE SOUTH-WEST

in addition to the second manor in Kingsey (q.v.). Some property in Tythrop was included in the conveyance of that manor in 1502.

A small property in Tythrop, called in the early 17th century ROLLES alias ROLVES, originally parcel of Kingsey Manor, was acquired in fee from Gilbert de Bolebec by Nicholas son of Adam de Risborough, and descended to his son Ralph and to Edmund son and heir of Ralph's son described as Gilbert Rolves.[6]

[35] Feet of F. case 187, file 2, no. 79.
[36] Testa de Nevill (Rec. Com.), 106.
[37] Hund. R. (Rec. Com.), ii, 784.
[38] Davenport, Lords Lieutenant and High Sheriffs of Oxon. 19, 32-5.
[39] Chan. Inq. p.m. 18 Edw. IV, no. 37.
[40] Feet of F. case 187, file 2, no. 79.
[41] Testa de Nevill (Rec. Com.), 106.
[42] Hund. R. (Rec. Com.), i, 43.
[43] Ibid. ii, 784.
[44] Davenport, op. cit. 21.
[45] Feud. Aids, iv, 176.
[46] Davenport, op. cit. 21 ; cf. Boarstall Chartul. fol. 28b.

[47] Harl. Chart. 54 I, 34.
[48] G.E.C. Complete Peerage (new ed.), ii, 508.
[49] Chan. Inq. p.m. 5 Hen. VI, no. 26.
[50] Ibid. 21 Hen. VI, no. 34.
[51] Ibid.
[52] Cal. Pat. 1446-52, p. 125.
[53] Chan. Inq. p.m. 18 Edw. IV, no. 37.
[54] Parl. R. vi, 245b, 273a.
[55] Sussex Arch. Coll. iii, 96.
[56] Exch. Inq. p.m. (Ser. 2), file 784, no. 16.
[57] Ibid.
[58] Sussex Arch. Coll. loc. cit.

[59] Recov. R. Mich. 30 Hen. VIII, m. 447 ; Feet of F. Div. Co. Mich. 30 Hen. VIII.
[60] P.C.C. 18 Spert.
[61] Chan. Proc. (Ser. 2), bdle. 295, no. 7.
[62] Ibid. ; Chan. Inq. p.m. (Ser. 2), ccxcv, 63.
[63] Feet of F. Div. Co. Mich. 15 Jas. I.
[64] Chan. Inq. p.m. 24 Edw. III (1st nos.), no. 94.
[65] Cal. Pat. 1350-4, p. 526. Sir John Burghersh at his death in 1349 held land of Gilbert Rolves (Chan. Inq. p.m. 24 Edw. III [1st nos.], no. 94).

Edmund Rolves and his wife Maud are referred to in 1353,[66] and the former died seised in 1361 and was succeeded by his son and heir John.[67] Rolves, then in the tenure of John Elmes or his assigns, was included in the grant to Sir Henry Spiller in 1610.[68]

CHURCH The church of *ST. NICHOLAS*, consisting of chancel, nave, organ chamber, vestry, and south-west tower with spire, is a modern building in the style of the 15th century, erected in 1892–3, to replace a late 18th-century church, much of the old material being re-used.

The tower contains a ring of three bells : the first, inscribed 'Feare God 1632,' is by Ellis Knight ; the second, 1625, and the third, 1628, are both by James Keene ; there is also a small bell undated.

The plate consists of a silver cup, two patens and a flagon, all given by James Herbert in 1710.

The registers begin in 1538.

ADVOWSON The advowson of Kingsey Church was alienated from the manor and given to Rochester Priory by Gilbert de Bolebec in the time of Henry III.[69] The church was then a chapel to Haddenham,[70] but in 1231 a vicar was instituted to it.[71] Kingsey Church was valued at £6 13s. 4d. yearly in 1291[72] and at £8 13s. 4d. in 1535.[73] The advowson of the vicarage and also the rectory (leases excepted) have descended with that of Haddenham,[74] and

belong to the Dean and Chapter of Rochester Cathedral.

Leases of the rectory were held by Thomas Boller in 1490 and 1517,[75] and by the Herberts of Kingsey and Tythrop (q.v.), who were also lessees of the advowson[76] in the 17th and 18th centuries.[77]

Lights in the church were maintained from lands called the Park and Foxhills.[78] Foxhill Close and the Lamplands were included in the grant of 1610 to Sir Henry Spiller.[79] Foxhills survives as the name of a farm.

CHARITIES Philip Herbert, by his will proved in the P.C.C. 14 July 1722, bequeathed £300 for the benefit of the poor ; Ann Herbert, by her will proved in the P.C.C. 22 February 1810, bequeathed £100 ; and Philip Thomas Wykeham, by his will proved in the P.C.C. 29 October 1832, also bequeathed £100 for the poor. These legacies are now represented by £573 1s. 4d. consols.

Philip Thomas Herbert Wykeham, by his will proved at Oxford 12 July 1879, bequeathed £200 for the benefit of the poor, which was invested in £204 1s. 7d. consols. The sums of stock are held by the official trustees, the annual dividends of which, amounting together to £19 8s. 4d., are applied in the distribution of coal at Christmas among all the cottagers in the village, each receiving about 15 cwt.

LUDGERSHALL WITH KINGSWOOD

Lotegarsar, Lotegarser (xi cent.) ; Lotegarsale, Lutgarshale, Luttegareshale (xiv cent.) ; Lurgesall, Lutgersall (xvi cent.) ; Ludgershall (xviii cent.).

This parish covers an area of 2,732 acres, of which 2,347 acres are permanent grass and 199 acres arable.[1] The land rises from about 200 ft. above the ordnance datum in the north to an average of 300 ft. in the south of the parish. The soil is loam and clay, the subsoil clay. Two brooks, rising in Muswell Hill, across the Oxfordshire border, water the north-west of the parish. Akeman Street passes through the north of Ludgershall, forming part of the boundary.

The low-lying village, which is situated in the south-east of the parish, is irregular. The cottages, of which several are of 17th-century origin, are scattered along either side of the so-called High Street, which leads to a large village green. The Wesleyan chapel built here in 1844 is now disused, a new brick chapel having been opened in the High Street in 1904. To the north and east of the village are numerous outlying farms. Close to it, on the south-west, is a station called Brill and Ludgershall, on the Birmingham section of the Great Western railway.

The church stands at the south end of the village, at the junction of three main roads ; to the north of it is the school, and the rectory grounds are separated by the road from the west end of the churchyard. The house was rebuilt in brick at the end of the 18th century.[2] There is no manor-house, but there is evidence that the capital messuage in Ludgershall was habitable at the end of the 16th century.[3] South-west of the church is a small moated[4] site with which the traditional name of King Lud's Hall[5] was still connected at the end of the 18th century.[6]

Bury Court, from which a portion of the tithes were payable to Bermondsey Priory (see advowson), stood on the north-east of the church in the middle 19th century, by which date it had been divided into small tenements. It was then in the hands of an Oxfordshire family named Coles,[7] and stood on a small estate owned by John Harris in 1777.[8]

The Five Bells and White Hart Inns in the High Street are 17th-century buildings of timber and brick ; on the ground floor of the latter is a large open fireplace. On the Piddington road are several cottages and farm-houses of the same date, the most noteworthy

---

[66] *Cal. Pat.* 1350–4, p. 526.

[67] Chan. Inq. p.m. 36 Edw. III, pt. ii, no. 26.

[68] Pat. 7 Jas. I, pt. xxix, no. 5.

[69] *Hund. R.* (Rec. Com.), i, 35 ; *Abbrev. Plac.* (Rec. Com.), 269.

[70] *V.C.H. Bucks.* ii, 286.

[71] *Reg. of Hugh of Wells* (Cant. and York. Soc.), ii, 84.

[72] *Pope Nich. Tax.* (Rec. Com.), 34.

[73] *Valor Eccl.* (Rec. Com.), iv. 236.

[74] *V.C.H. Bucks.* ii, 286 ; see also Linc. Epis. Reg. Inst. Bk. fol. 112 ; Bacon, *Liber Reg.* 503 ; Inst. Bks. (P.R.O.), late

18th and early 19th century ; Lysons, *Mag. Brit.* i (3), 589.

[75] Leadam, *Dom. Incl.* 1517 (Royal Hist. Soc.), i, 207.

[76] Inst. Bks. (P.R.O.) ; Bacon, loc. cit.

[77] Feet of F. Div. Co. East. 19 Chas. II; Lysons, loc. cit.

[78] Pat. 21 Eliz. pt. vi, m. 16 ; cf. ibid. 28 Eliz. pt. xiv, m. 20 ; 34 Eliz. pt. iv, m. 34 ; Chant. Cert. 5, no. 63.

[79] Pat. 7 Jas. I, pt. xxix, no. 5.

[1] Statistics from Bd. of Agric. (1905).

[2] Sheahan, *Hist. and Topog. of Bucks.* 400.

[3] Chan. Inq. p.m. (Ser. 2), ccxxxvii, 121.

[4] *V.C.H. Bucks.* ii, 32.

[5] Kennet says that Brill Castle was generally considered to have been one of the seats of this British king, but his derivation of the name of this parish from Ludswell (*Paroch. Antiq.* ii, 428) does not agree with the earlier forms.

[6] Lipscomb, *Hist. and Antiq. of Bucks.* i, 305, referring to map made by the inclosure surveyors.

[7] Ibid. 311.

[8] Priv. Act, 17 Geo. III, cap. 43.

of which is Home Farm, a building of half-timber with modern brick repairs and refacings, two stories in height with an attic. Originally T-shaped on plan, with the tail of the T projecting from the north side, a small wing was added at the south-west of the southern limb of the plan in the 18th century, as recorded by the date 1738 on a dormer window, and modern additions have also been made to the central wing. Some original doors remain on the first floor.

Tetchwick (Tochingewick, xi cent. ; Togwick, xiii cent.; Touchewyk, xiv cent.) is a hamlet 1¼ miles north-east from Ludgershall, containing three farms. On the one known as Tetchwick Farm there is an irregular quadrangular moat.[9] The house is a late 17th-century building of stone.

Kingswood is another hamlet, covering 261 acres,[10] and extending into the neighbouring parish of Grendon Underwood. It lies about three-quarters of a mile further to the north-east from Tetchwick. One of the two farms within its borders, Mercers' Farm, was owned for nearly two centuries before 1829 by the Mercers' Company of London. Kingswood Lane Farm is a two-storied 17th-century house, much altered during the last two centuries. Kingswood, formerly forest land, is traditionally connected with Fair Rosamund, and in an old map of part of Bernwood Forest a lane between the woods appears as 'Rosiman's Waye.'[11] Kingswood is included as Crown property in the royalty of Brill.

Sharp's Hill Farm, in the extreme north-east of the parish of Ludgershall, probably derives its name from John Sharp, who paid £1 in tithes in 1659.[12] During the 19th century it was occupied by members of the Holt family, whose representatives are still living in Tetchwick.[13]

John Wycliffe was rector of Ludgershall from 1368[14] to 1374, when he was presented to Lutterworth (Leics.).[15]

Ludgershall was inclosed by Act of Parliament in 1777, but there is no mention of Tetchwick or Kingswood.[16]

Among place-names in Ludgershall proper there are found Coston, the Portway, Brutine, Dylingsham[17] (xiii cent.); Hallehulle,[18] la Wecche,[19] la Breche (a wood which John de Moleyns was licensed in 1339 to impark with 100 acres of land adjoining)[20] (xiv cent.) ; pastures called Shippbridge and Tittersall[21]

(xvi cent.) ; Wellfield[22] (xvii cent.) ; Room of the Rush Piece, Illoem Piece[23] (xviii cent.); and Lady Brown's Yard,[24] Gallows Lane and Bridge[25] and Dove House Field[26] (xix cent.).

MANORS — *LUDGERSHALL MANOR*, which before the Conquest had been held of Queen Edith by Eddeva, in 1086 was held by the Bishop of Coutances.[27] The overlordship afterwards appertained to the honour of Gloucester.[28]

Ludgershall Manor had not been subinfeudated by the Bishop of Coutances in 1086,[29] but before 1190 [30] it was held by the de Traillys of Yelden in Bedfordshire as part of their barony.[31] It was evidently included in the four fees held by Walter de Trailly of the honour of Gloucester in the early 13th century.[32] Waleran Tyes was holding later in this century,[33] apparently as husband of Walter's widow Sybil de Huntingfield, who on her death in 1251 held it in dower.[34] It reverted to Walter's grandson John de Trailly,[35] who was succeeded

TRAILLY. *Or a cross between four martlets gules.*

in 1272 by his son Walter.[36] He was holding[37] Ludgershall in 1284, and shortly afterwards enfeoffed William de Louth, afterwards Bishop of Ely, and his heirs, subject to a payment of £40 yearly during William's life.[38] William de Louth died seised about 1298, when his heirs were William, afterwards Sir William, Touchet, his nephew, and Isabel wife of Roger de Morteyn,[39] his sister, who surrendered her right to William Touchet.[40] He recovered seisin in 1301 against John, son and heir of Walter de Trailly, who, attaining his majority, had disseised him on the ground that the manor had only been leased to William de Louth.[41] After retaining it at least seven years[42] Sir William Touchet granted Ludgershall Manor to the elder Sir Hugh le Despencer,[43] who before 1316[44] had transferred it to John de Handlo for life.[45] Walter son of John de Trailly unsuccessfully claimed the manor against John de Handlo in 1327–39.[46] In the meantime the reversion forfeited by Hugh le Despencer was granted

[9] *V.C.H. Bucks.* ii, 32.

[10] *Census Rep. Bucks.* (1901), 18.

[11] Lipscomb, op. cit. i, 313. An engraving reduced from the original survey (ibid. between pp. 50 and 51), which, dated 1530, was then (1847) in possession of Col. Pigott of Doddershall (ibid. 605).

[12] Lipscomb, op. cit. i, 322, quoting from notes by the rector on the cover of the parish register of 1659.

[13] Ibid. 316; Sheahan, op. cit. 398; *Ret. of Owners of Land*, 1873, *Bucks.* 11.

[14] Linc. Epis. Reg. Inst. Buckingham, fol. 419.

[15] Pat. 48 Edw. III, pt. i, m. 23.

[16] Priv. Act, 17 Geo. III, cap. 43.

[17] Kennet, op. cit. i, 369.

[18] *Cal. Pat.* 1301–7, p. 310.

[19] *Abbrev. Rot. Orig.* (Rec. Com.), i, 216. [20] *Cal. Pat.* 1338–40, p. 429.

[21] Exch. Dep. Mich. 22 & 23 Eliz. no. 16.

[22] Chan. Inq. p.m. (Ser. 2), cccxiv, 127. An old well still remained to the

south of the village in the middle 19th century (Lipscomb, op. cit. i, 311), but was afterwards filled up (Sheahan, op. cit. 398).

[23] Exch. Dep. Mich. 12 Geo. I, no. 5.

[24] Lipscomb, op. cit. i, 322.

[25] Ibid. 307. [26] Sheahan, loc. cit.

[27] *V.C.H. Bucks.* i, 239.

[28] *Testa de Nevill* (Rec. Com.), 245*a* ; *Hund. R.* (Rec. Com.), i, 42 ; Chan. Inq. p.m. Edw. I, file 2, no. 5 ; *Feud. Aids*, i, 75, 95, 121 ; Chan. Inq. p.m. 8 Edw. II, no. 68 ; Ct. R. (Gen. Ser.), portf. 155, no. 13. [29] *V.C.H. Bucks.* i, 239.

[30] *Ann. Mon.* (Rolls Ser.), iii, 447.

[31] *V.C.H. Beds.* iii, 175–6.

[32] Ibid. where a further account of the Traillys will be found.

[33] *Cal. Close*, 1227–31, p. 540 ; *Testa de Nevill* (Rec. Com.), 248*b*.

[34] *Excerpta e Rot. Fin.* (Rec. Com.), ii, 100.

[35] Ibid. 105 ; *Hund. R.* (Rec. Com.), i, 24 ; Chan. Inq. p.m. Hen. III, file 20, no. 8.

[36] *Cal. Inq. p.m.* (Edw. I), ii, 13; *Cal. Fine R.* 1272–1307, p. 3.

[37] *Feud. Aids*, i, 75.

[38] Kennet, op. cit. i, 431.

[39] Chan. Inq. p.m. Edw. I, file 86, no. 6; Assize R. 1323, m. 9 d.

[40] Assize R. 1323, m. 9 d.

[41] Ibid. Walter de Trailly had died about 1289 (*Cal. Inq. p.m.* [Edw. I], ii, 482).

[42] *Feud. Aids*, i, 95 ; Chan. Inq. p.m. Edw. II, file 7, no. 9.

[43] *Cat. of Anct. D.* i, 6. The grant included the reversion of a rent held for life by Mabel, widow of William Grimbald (Chan. Inq. p.m. 30 Edw. I, no. 31 ; *Abbrev. Rot. Orig.* [Rec. Com.], i, 123 ; Add. Chart. 41569; *Cal. Fine R.* 1272–1307, p. 463).

[44] *Feud. Aids*, i, 113.

[45] De Banco R. 279, m. 155; *Cal. Close*, 1330–3, p. 350.

[46] De Banco R. 270, m. 43 ; 274, m. 42 d. ; 279, m. 155 ; *Cal. Close*, 1330–3, p. 350 ; 1339–41, p. 80 ; Feet of F. Bucks. East. 13 Edw. III, no. 5.

by the Crown to John de Moleyns in 1335.[47] After the death of John de Handlo in 1346[48] Ludgershall Manor reverted to John de Moleyns,[49] and it descended in his family with their manor in Stoke Poges[50] (q.v.) until 1537, when George Earl of Huntingdon and his son Sir Francis Hastings conveyed Ludgershall with Chearsley (q.v.) to Sir John Baldwin, lord of Danvers in Marlow. This manor then descended with Danvers[51] (q.v.), and later also with Little Marlow (q.v.) to Sir John Borlase Warren, bart.,[52]

DE MOLEYNS. *Sable a chief or charged with three lozenges gules.*

who sold it in 1784 to Mrs. Martyn, widow of John Martyn, formerly professor of botany at Cambridge.[53] She was buried at Ludgershall in 1786, and was succeeded by her only son, the Rev. Claudius Martyn,[54] who had shortly before become rector of the parish on his mother's presentation.[55] Ludgershall Manor descended in his family[56] to his great-granddaughter Miss Martyn,[57] the owner in 1911. Shortly afterwards she sold all her house property in Ludgershall to various purchasers, retaining only the village green, which now belongs to Lady Mary Jane Skrine.

In the mid-13th century John de Trailly held view of frankpledge in Ludgershall,[58] but apparently without due warrant. In 1338 this right was granted to John de Moleyns with the assize of bread and ale.[59] A grant of the return of writs and other regalities was made to John de Moleyns in 1337.[60] The manorial court was held every three weeks in the middle 15th century,[61] and a reference to it occurs in 1725.[62] In the mid-19th century courts leet and baron had not been held in Ludgershall for many years.[63] Free warren in this manor was granted in 1318 to Hugh le Despencer, John de Handlo and Hugh's heirs,[64] and in 1337 to John de Moleyns.[65]

A windmill is mentioned in the middle of the 15th century.[66]

A second manor of *LUDGERSHALL* evidently emerged later from the Domesday royal manor of Brill

(q.v.). Overlordship rights in Ludgershall were appurtenant to Brill Manor,[67] and are still traceable in the mid-16th century.[68]

The capital messuage of this manor in the wood of Brill appears to have been retained by Henry II after his grant to the brethren of the Holy Trinity, St. Inglevert (see below). In the 13th century this capital messuage was held by the lords of the principal manor of Ludgershall[69] (q.v.).

Three hides of land and 10 acres of wood in his manor of Ludgershall had been granted by Henry II to the brethren of the Holy Trinity, St. Inglevert (Santingfeld), near Wissant in Picardy, before 1156.[70] A hospital subordinate to that of Farley in Luton, Bedfordshire, was apparently built on this land, three oaks from the forest of Brill being granted by the king in 1236 to the master for the repair of his houses which had been burnt.[71] In 1238 Walter, son of Romanus of Ludgershall, increased the endowment,[72] and the royal grants were inspected and confirmed in 1285.[73] During the later war with France John de Felmersham obtained a life grant of the St. Inglevert lands from Edward III,[74] but after an inquiry in 1347 the master was reinstated.[75] In 1348 Richard de Cotyngham was sent to Ludgershall Hospital for maintenance during his life.[76] The estate of the hospital in Ludgershall,[77] called in the 16th and 17th centuries *LUDGERSHALL MANOR*, was after the Dissolution granted in fee in 1547 to Sir Thomas Palmer,[78] and after his attainder in 1554 to George Rotherham,[79] son of the George Rotherham[80] to whom in 1521 George Caron, then master of St. Inglevert, had granted a ninety years' lease.[81] On the death of the grantee in 1593 Ludgershall Manor passed by settlement to his second wife Anne for life.[82] In 1595 their son Isaac Rotherham sold the reversion to William, afterwards Sir William, Borlase and his wife Mary,[83] who in 1596 obtained a release from Isaac's half-brother George Rotherham.[84] Sir William Borlase died seised in 1629,[85] and this manor became merged into the principal manor of Ludgershall (q.v.).

The hamlet of *TETCHWICK*, formerly held by Alwin, one of King Edward's thegns, was in 1086 assessed as a manor at 2 hides, and included under

---

[47] Chart. R. 9 Edw. III, m. 1, no. 1 ; *Cal. Pat.* 1334–8, p. 173.
[48] Chan. Inq. p.m. 20 Edw. III (1st nos.), no. 51.
[49] *Cal. Close,* 1346–9, p. 98 ; *Feud. Aids,* i, 121 ; *Cal. Pat.* 1345–8, pp. 207–8 ; 1334–8, p. 462 ; *Cal. Close,* 1337–9, p. 273 ; Cal. 24 Edw. III, pt. i, m. 26 (a quitclaim from John son and heir of Walter de Trailly).
[50] *V.C.H. Bucks.* iii, 305–6.
[51] Ibid. 82.
[52] Ibid. 80–1 ; Priv. Act, 17 Geo. III, cap. 43.
[53] Lysons, *Mag. Brit.* i (3), 598.
[54] Lipscomb, op. cit. i, 311. She died intestate, letters of administration being granted in 1787 (P.C.C. Major).
[55] Inst. Bks. (P.R.O.).
[56] Lipscomb, loc. cit. ; *Ret. of Owners of Land,* 1873, *Bucks.* 13.
[57] Lipscomb, loc. cit.
[58] *Hund. R.* (Rec. Com.), i, 24.
[59] Chart. R. 12 Edw. III, m. 4, no. 3. An enumeration of all the liberties granted to John de Moleyns about this time occurs in 1440 (Chan. Inq. p.m. 18

Hen. VI, no. 31). See also Chan. Inq. p.m. 17 Hen. VI, no. 52 ; (Ser. 2), cccclix, 48.
[60] Inq. a.q.d. file 241, no. 24 ; *Cal. Chart. R.* 1327–41, pp. 399, 430.
[61] Chan. Inq. p.m. 17 Hen. VI, no. 52.
[62] Exch. Dep. Mich. 12 Geo. I, no. 5.
[63] Lipscomb, loc. cit.
[64] Chart. R. 11 Edw. II, m. 3, no. 6.
[65] Ibid. 11 Edw. III, m. 27, no. 56.
[66] Chan. Inq. p.m. 17 Hen. VI, no. 52.
[67] Kennet, op. cit. i, 323 ; *Hund. R.* (Rec. Com.), i, 24, 35, 37, 46 ; Chan. Inq. p.m. Hen. III, file 20, no. 8 ; Edw. I, file 2, no. 5 ; *Cal. Close,* 1296–1302, p. 184 ; 1346–9, p. 98.
[68] Feet of F. Bucks. East. 1 Mary.
[69] *Hund. R.* (Rec. Com.), i, 35, 46 ; *Cal. Close,* 1296–1302, p. 184 ; 1346–9, p. 98. [70] *V.C.H. Bucks.* i, 395.
[71] *Cal. Close,* 1234–7, p. 252.
[72] Feet of F. case 15, file 23, no. 3.
[73] *Cal. Chart. R.* 1257–1300, p. 295. The lands being possessions of the Count of Flanders and not of the King of France were not seized in 1324 and 1327 (Mins. Accts. bdle. 1127, no. 18, m. 17).

[74] *Cal. Pat.* 1345–8, p. 439.
[75] Chan. Inq. p.m. 21 Edw. III, no. 99 (a grange in Ludgershall is mentioned, but the document is half obliterated) ; *Cal. Pat.* 1345–8, p. 439. The charter of 'Henry, sometime King' granting these lands for chantries for his soul and those of his heirs and others and its confirmation by Edward II is mentioned.
[76] *Cal. Close,* 1346–9, p. 420.
[77] The supposed site of the hospital is Friars Mead on land granted to the poor of Bicester (Lipscomb, op. cit. i, 312).
[78] Pat. 1 Edw. VI, pt. vi, m. 1.
[79] Ibid. 1 Mary, pt. xiii, m. 19.
[80] *V.C.H. Beds.* ii, 358.
[81] Pat. 1 Mary, pt. xiii, m. 19.
[82] Chan. Inq. p.m. (Ser. 2), ccxl, 90 ; Chan. Proc. Eliz. Rr 2, no. 58.
[83] Close, 37 Eliz. pt. ix. Anthony Willoughby had leasehold rights for several years under a twenty-one years' lease (Feet of F. Bucks. East. 37 Eliz.).
[84] Cal. of F. Bucks. Mich. 38 & 39 Eliz.
[85] Chan. Inq. p.m. (Ser. 2), ccccli, 107. The purchase from Isaac and George Rotherham is named.

the lands of William Peverel.[86] The overlordship was afterwards attached to the honour of Peverel, but no reference to it has been found after the mid-13th century.[87]

Tetchwick had been subinfeudated to a tenant named Payn before 1086.[88] It was given to the Knights Hospitallers by William Peverel, son of the Domesday holder, probably with Hogshaw Manor (q.v.), of which manor it was held,[89] and confirmed to them by King John in 1199.[90]

Henry of Chequers (de Scaccario) was tenant under the Knights Hospitallers of 1 hide of land in Tetchwick[91] before 1222, when he received ten oaks from the king for rebuilding and repairs.[92] The heirs of his son Ralph[93] held the whole of Tetchwick in fee in 1254.[94] One of these, Ralph's daughter Katherine, married William Hawtrey (de Alta Ripa, Haut-rive),[95] and in 1286-7 a moiety of a messuage and lands in Tetchwick was conveyed to them by their son William,[96] probably the William Hawtrey who was holding Tetchwick in 1302.[97] His son Thomas succeeded before 1346,[98] and from his second son Nicholas[99] Tetchwick descended through three generations to Thomas Hawtrey,[100] who held before 1490.[1] He died in 1522, having settled this manor on the marriage of his son Thomas with Sybil daughter and co-heir of Richard Hampden of

HAWTREY. *Azure a fesse indented argent.*

JENKINSON. *Azure a fesse wavy argent with two stars or in the chief and a cross formy gules on the fesse.*

Great Kimble.[2] Thomas Hawtrey, the son, died in 1544[3] and was succeeded by his grandson William,

son of another Thomas Hawtrey, who had predeceased his father.[4] He transferred Tetchwick Manor in 1589 to his son William, afterwards Sir William Hawtrey, kt., and his wife Winifred.[5] She survived her husband, who died in 1591, leaving as co-heirs his daughters Mary, Bridget and Anne.[6]

Bridget afterwards married Sir Henry Croke, and they sold her portion in 1615 to Robert Jenkinson,[7] who died seised in 1618.[8] His son and heir Robert[9] was knighted and died in 1645.[10] His son Robert, created a baronet in 1661,[11] was succeeded in 1677 by his son Sir Robert Jenkinson, bart.,[12] ancestor of the Earls of Liverpool.[13] He sold his Tetchwick estate about 1703 to Edward Mitchell,[14] and it passed in succession to his sons John and Stafford, to Stafford's son Edward and to the latter's uncle Walter Mitchell.[15] John Hollier, who afterwards purchased this property and owned all manorial rights in Tetchwick at the end of the 18th century,[16] sold it to Thomas Bett.[17] His nephew John Bett succeeded in 1819, and was owner in the mid-19th century.[18]

Sir William Hawtrey's youngest daughter and co-heir Anne carried her third of Tetchwick Manor in marriage to John Saunders, and it descended with their moiety of Fleet Marston (q.v.) to their daughter Elizabeth and her husband Sir Walter Pye in 1631.[19] The share of the eldest daughter Mary, wife of Sir Francis Wolley, who died without issue,[20] appears to have reverted to them before 1639, when their estate in Tetchwick is described as a moiety of the manor.[21] They owned this moiety at Elizabeth's death in 1640,[22] but it was evidently sold after 1647, when there were difficulties about the restoration of Sir Walter Pye's estates, which had been confiscated for delinquency.[23] John Irons was owning in Tetchwick later in the century.[24] His property appears to have been transferred before 1697 to John Deacle,[25] who owned a farm here at his death in 1723, Thomas Holton being lessee.[26] He was dispossessed with difficulty in 1727 by the succeeding owner, William Deacle.[27] This property had presumably been purchased before 1777 by George Grenville,[28] and has since descended with other land which he afterwards bought in Ludgershall[29] with Stowe (q.v.) to Algernon, fifth Earl Temple of Stowe, the present owner.

[86] *V.C.H. Bucks.* i, 253*a*.
[87] *Hund. R.* (Rec. Com.), i, 24.
[88] *V.C.H. Bucks.* i, 253.
[89] *Testa de Nevill* (Rec. Com.), 245; *Hund. R.* (Rec. Com.), i, 24, 42. The last reference shows that the Knights Hospitallers held view of frankpledge in Tetchwick once a year in the mid-13th century and urged their claim to this right in 1276.
[90] *Cal. Rot. Chart.* 1199-1216 (Rec. Com.), 16*b*.
[91] *Testa de Nevill* (Rec. Com.), 245.
[92] *Rot. Lit. Claus.* (Rec. Com.), i, 488.
[93] *Visit. of Bucks.* (Harl. Soc.), 172.
[94] *Hund. R.* (Rec. Com.), i, 24. A family named de Tetchwick appear to have had some estate as tenants between 1292 and 1336 (Feet of F. case 17, file 54, no. 14; case 18, file 73, no. 11; case 19, file 81, no. 1).
[95] *Visit. of Bucks.* loc. cit.; Croke, *Gen. Hist. of Croke Family*, i, between pp. 500 and 501.
[96] Feet of F. Div. Co. Mich. 14 & 15 Edw. I, no. 43.
[97] *Feud. Aids*, i, 95. [98] Ibid. 121.
[99] He made a settlement with his

brother William in 1364 securing the descent of the family lands in Ellesborough to himself and his heirs (Feet of F. Bucks. Mich. 38 Edw. III, no. 10).
[100] *Visit. of Bucks.* loc. cit.; Croke, loc. cit.
[1] Leadam, *Dom. Incl.* 1517 (Royal Hist. Soc.), 168.
[2] Chan. Inq. p.m. (Ser. 2), xl, 18.
[3] There is a brass to him and his wife Sybil in Ellesborough Church (*V.C.H. Bucks.* ii, 337).
[4] Ibid.; Chan. Inq. p.m. (Ser. 2), lxxiii, 4.
[5] Feet of F. Bucks. East. 31 Eliz.
[6] Chan. Inq. p.m. (Ser. 2), ccxliii, 75.
[7] Close, 14 Jas. I, pt. vii, no. 37. Minute details are given of the property, which included the north part of the chief mansion-house with certain other rights of entry.
[8] Chan. Inq. p.m. (Ser. 2), dcxlvii, 31.
[9] Ibid.
[10] *Misc. Gen. et Her.* (Ser. 2), v, 13.
[11] G.E.C. *Baronetage*, iii, 197.
[12] Ibid. [13] Burke, *Peerage* (1907).
[14] Lysons, *Mag. Brit.* i (3), 598.
[15] Lipscomb, op. cit. i, 315.

[16] Lysons, loc. cit. A transfer of a small parcel of Tetchwick Manor is dated 1777 (Feet of F. Bucks. East. 17 Geo. III), and is the last documentary reference to the manor that has been found.
[17] Lipscomb, loc. cit. [18] Ibid.
[19] Fine R. 7 Chas. I, pt. iii, no. 47.
[20] *V.C.H. Bucks.* ii, 336.
[21] Feet of F. Bucks. Hil. 14 Chas. I; Recov. R. Trin. 15 Chas. I, m. 42.
[22] Chan. Inq. p.m. (Ser. 2), dcclxviii, 12.
[23] *Cal. Com. for Comp.* 68.
[24] Lipscomb, op. cit. i, 322, quoting cover of parish register for 1659.
[25] Ibid. 316, quoting MS. of an Exch. Tithe Suit of 1720 brought by the rector against Thomas Holton.
[26] Exch. Dep. East. 13 Geo. I, no. 8.
[27] Ibid.; Hil. 3 Geo. II, no. 17. His wife Catherine and their children John, William and Susannah were joint complainants with him in the latter suit in 1729 against Martin Sandys and Thomas Chetle, apparently trustees.
[28] Priv. Act, 17 Geo. III, cap. 43.
[29] Lipscomb, op. cit. i, 312. A small estate held in 1777 by Richard Drope-Gough.

Two hides of land in Ludgershall, previously held by Alvric, King Edward's chamberlain, were held in 1086 as a manor by William son of Manne.[30] It was held of Brill Manor.[31]

This estate having reverted to the Crown, Henry I granted it to Gerard de Cauz subject to the serjeanty of keeping one of the king's hawks.[32] It descended in the Cauz family and in that of the Lords Grey de Wilton with the manors of Water Eaton and Bletchley[33] (q.v.). View of frankpledge was appurtenant to the manor.[34]

The hamlet of Kingswood corresponds to that part of the forest of Bernwood which extended into Ludgershall and Grendon Underwood and in which the inhabitants of the former parish had agistment rights in 1373.[35] These they claimed in 1577, when they petitioned the Crown against the inclosure of Kingswood by Sir John Dynham, as from time immemorable.[36]

Some coppices in Kingswood called Carwell Hill, Staple (or Stample Hill) and Copywell Hill were held by Sir John Fortescue at his death in 1607.[37] These, with others, were sold in 1613 by Peter Fyge of Winslow and his wife Elizabeth to Richard More and Timothy Wagstaff.[38] Richard More's estate, afterwards the Mercers' Farm, was sold by him to George Garth, and later, in 1639, by William Honeywood and others to the Mercers' Company of London.[39] They exchanged it for other property about 1829 with Richard, first Duke of Buckingham and Chandos.[40] It has since descended with his estate at Stowe (q.v.) to Earl Temple of Stowe.

Timothy Wagstaff's estate is now represented by Kingswood Lane Farm. It had been purchased by the Borlases before 1659,[41] and has presumably since[42] descended with the principal manor of Ludgershall (q.v.).

The church of *THE ASSUMPTION CHURCH OF THE BLESSED VIRGIN* consists of a chancel measuring internally 26 ft. 6 in. by 18 ft., organ chamber, nave 42 ft. by 15 ft., north aisle 7 ft. wide, south aisle 5 ft. 6 in. wide, south porch, and a west tower 9 ft. by 8 ft. 6 in.

A church apparently existed here in the 13th century, consisting of a chancel and nave. The chancel was rebuilt early in the 14th century, while the nave was lengthened and the aisles thrown out about fifty years later. Early in the 15th century the tower, which encroaches upon the west bay of the nave, was erected, and in the following century the south porch was added. In 1889 the organ chamber on the north side of the chancel was built and the church restored. With the exception of the rubble walls of the chancel and porch the whole exterior is rough-casted; the roofs of the nave, aisles and porch are covered with lead, but that of the chancel is tiled.

The chancel is lighted from the east by a modern window of three lights with tracery in a pointed head, and from the north and south by two 15th-century windows on each side with tracery in depressed heads, those on the north being of two lights and those on the south of three. Between the windows on the north side is a modern opening to the organ chamber. The priest's doorway on the south, which is pointed and continuously moulded, is of the 15th century, but the label on the outside appears to be of the 13th century, reset. The piscina, in the usual position, is of the 14th century and has a square head, the jambs being ornamented with four-leaved flowers. The openings of squints from the aisles may be seen at the west ends of the side walls. The roof is of the 15th-century hammer-beam type. In the floor on the north side are some mediaeval tiles. The chancel arch is low and wide and dates from the 14th century. It is pointed and of two orders, the inner order springing from engaged shafts and the outer being continuous.

The 14th-century arcades which separate the nave from the aisles are each of four bays with pointed arches of two orders springing from octagonal columns and responds. The capital of the second column on each side has peculiarly bold carving representing the busts of men wearing capes with liripipe hoods; the capital of the third column on the north side has a dog-tooth pattern on the abacus, while that of the corresponding column on the south has carved heads. The other columns have bell capitals without carving, that of the first column on the south having been recut in the 15th century. The roof of the nave is of flat pitch and dates from the 16th century. At the rafter feet are angels with shields.

The north and south aisles are each lighted from the side by three square-headed windows with uncusped lights, dating from the 16th century. The easternmost windows are of two lights and the middle of three lights. The westernmost window of the north aisle is of two lights and the corresponding window of the south aisle is a single light. The east window of the south aisle is also a single light of the same period, but that of the north aisle is a 14th-century window of three trefoiled lights with tracery in a pointed head. In its upper lights are some fragments of contemporary coloured glass, comprising a Majesty. At the east end of the south wall is a 15th-century piscina with a flat head and quatrefoil bowl. The north doorway is now blocked; both it and the south doorway are pointed and of the 14th century. The south porch has a parvise reached by a vice on the west side, which is entered by a pointed doorway in the south aisle. The parvise is lighted by a single light on the south side. The entrance arch to the porch is pointed. Over the east gable is a small and much-restored 15th-century bellcote for a sanctus bell, with a finial and pinnacles.

The tower is of two stages and is crowned by an embattled parapet. There is a vice at the southwest, and the tower is strengthened by square buttresses at each angle, which finish at the top of the first stage. The ground stage opens to the body of the church by three 15th-century pointed arches, each of three orders. The west window was apparently the west window of the 14th-century lengthened nave. It is pointed and has three lights under a traceried

---

[30] V.C.H. Bucks. i, 267a.

[31] Hund. R. (Rec. Com.), i, 21, 35. In 1396 and 1442 its tenure was unknown (Chan. Inq. p.m. 19 Ric. II, no. 29; 20 Hen. VI, no. 23).

[32] Hund. R. (Rec. Com.), i, 24, 35.

[33] Testa de Nevill (Rec. Com.), 245a;

Hund. R. (Rec. Com.), i, 21, 24; Mins. Accts. (Gen. Ser.), bdle. 1119, no. 3.

[34] Hund. R. (Rec. Com.), i, 24; Chan. Inq. p.m. 19 Ric. II, no. 29; 20 Hen. VI, no. 23.   [35] Kennet, op. cit. ii, 139.

[36] Acts of P.C. 1575–7, p. 323.

[37] Chan. Inq. p.m. (Ser. 2), cccv, 132.

[38] Add. Chart. 53785.

[39] Lipscomb, op. cit. i, 313, quoting these transactions from a printed report to which he had access.   [40] Ibid.

[41] Ibid. 322, quoting from the cover of the Parish Register of 1659.

[42] Close, 31 Chas. II, pt. iii, no. 4.

LUDGERSHALL CHURCH : THE INTERIOR LOOKING EAST

LUDGERSHALL CHURCH FROM THE SOUTH

Fleet Marston Church from the South-East

Fleet Marston Church: The Interior looking East

head. The upper stage is lighted from the north and south by pointed two-light windows with pierced spandrels.

The font is of the late 12th century and has a circular bowl enriched with foliage of the acanthus type. In the tower is a plain mediaeval chest.

In the chancel is a table tomb with brasses commemorating Anne wife of Michael (Mihill) English, Sheriff of London, who died in 1565, aged ninety-five ; Anne (English), wife of John Gyfford, and her daughter Anne Neele. There are mural monuments to the Spiers family.

There is a ring of five bells : the treble is without date or inscription, but is perhaps by Richard Keene ; the second is by Messrs. Taylor, 1892, and replaces a bell by Richard Keene, 1658 ; the third is by Thomas Lester of London, 1745 ; the fourth by Richard Keene, 1658 ; and the tenor, by Messrs. Taylor, 1892, replaces a bell by Richard Keene, 1662.

The plate, consisting of a chalice and two patens, was presented in 1853.

The registers begin in 1538.

ADVOWSON The rectory church of Ludgershall appertained to the Knights Hospitallers before the middle 13th century.[43] It was valued in 1291 at £6 13s. 4d. yearly,[44] and in 1535 at £18 4s. yearly.[45] The advowson remained with the Knights Hospitallers[46] certainly until 1511[47] and apparently until the Dissolution.[48] It was granted in 1554 as parcel of the possessions of Henry late Duke of Suffolk to John Petty and William Winlove.[49] Later it came into the possession of Thomas Rede, who sold it in 1581 to Henry Poole.[50] He died in 1593, and his son Henry, then a minor,[51] obtained freedom of his inheritance in 1606.[52] In the same year he with his wife Dorothy and Robert and Cecily Ruffyn conveyed the advowson of Ludgershall to Sir William Borlase,[53] lord of the principal manor of Ludgershall. It descended with this manor[54] (q.v.), from which it was alienated on the death of the Rev. Thomas Martyn, in 1869,[55] to Messrs. Philip Rose (afterwards Sir Philip Rose, bart.) and H. E. Norton.[56] After a few years they transferred it to Lady Anna Gore-Langton,[57] who died in 1879.[58] The advowson of Ludgershall has since belonged to her third son, the Hon. Edward Grenville Gore-Langton.[59]

In 1588 William Knight, then rector of Ludgershall, leased the rectory for ninety-nine years to the queen, who immediately transferred her interest in it to Christopher Freeman.[60] In 1606 John Dynham conveyed it to George Woodward and John Freston,

to hold for seventy-six years at a peppercorn rent.[61] The remainder of the lease was afterwards purchased by Sir John Borlase, bart., probably in the later 17th century.[62]

The tithe on inclosures in Ludgershall is stated in 1517 to have declined from £6 8s. 4d. to 40s. yearly.[63] An allotment, now represented by the 300 acres of glebe, was made to the rector in lieu of tithes at the inclosure of the parish in 1777.[64]

Two-thirds of the tithes of Ludgershall, afterwards known as a portion of the Bury Tithes,[65] were granted in 1190 to Geoffrey de Trailly in 1190 to Bermondsey Priory.[66] This portion, estimated at £1 yearly in 1291,[66a] was retained by the priory until the Dissolution.[67] It was granted in 1553 to Thomas Reve and George Cotton,[68] but later was included in the grant in 1581 to Henry Poole of the advowson (q.v.), with which it descended until the early 18th century, when the tithes on Bury lands appear to have been commuted.[69]

In 1548 1 acre of land, worth 2d. yearly, maintained a light in Ludgershall.[70] It was probably half of this land, called the Rood-land, which in 1553 was granted to Sir Edmund Bray, John Thornton and John Danby.[71]

CHARITIES John Hart, by will proved in the P.C.C. 15 May 1665, devised (inter alia) a yearly charge of £3 issuing out of the manor of Easington, Oxfordshire, for apprenticing a poor boy. In 1809 William Spiers, by deed, charged land in this parish known as Brown Yards with an annuity of £8. These charities are administered under a scheme of the Charity Commissioners of 14 July 1908. The annuity of John Hart's charity (less land tax) is applied in apprenticing as occasion requires, and five-eighths of the income of William Spiers' charity is applicable in providing coats for old men and three-eighths in gowns for old women.

Elizabeth Cole, by her will proved 22 January 1871, bequeathed £50, the interest to be applied in coals for the poor, and preference to be given to widows and persons having large families. The legacy was invested in £53 15s. 1d. consols with the official trustees, producing £1 6s. 8d. yearly.

The National school, founded by deed 10 April 1847, is possessed of £310 consols, given by William Barker by deed 24 June 1847, and of £100 consols derived under the will of the same donor proved at London 27 October 1862, held by the official trustees, producing £10 5s. yearly ; also of an annual rent-charge of £10, charged upon a farm in the parish by Robert Morrell, by deed dated 1 October 1847.

[43] Kennet, op. cit. i, 312 ; Harl. MS. 6950, fol. 79.
[44] Pope Nich. Tax. (Rec. Com.), 34.
[45] Valor Eccl. (Rec. Com.), iv, 236.
[46] Harl. MS. 6952, fol. 22.
[47] Ibid. 6953, fol. 28.
[48] Valor Eccl. (Rec. Com.), iv, 236. When a pension of 6s. 8d. mentioned in the middle of the 14th century (Larking, Knights Hospitallers, 68) was still paid from this church. No other evidence has been found to confirm the statement of 1593 that this advowson had belonged to Nutley Abbey (Chan. Inq. p.m. [Ser. 2], ccxxxiv, 45).
[49] Pat. 1 Mary, pt. vi, m. 32.
[50] Chan. Inq. p.m. (Ser. 2), ccxxxiv, 45.
[51] Ibid.
[52] Fine R. 4 Jas. I, pt. iii, no. 17.

[53] Feet of F. Bucks. Trin. 4 Jas. I.
[54] Inst. Bks. (P.R.O.) ; Bacon, Liber Reg. 503.
[55] He was rector from 1821 to 1869 (Clergy Lists, 1865, 1870).
[56] Ibid. 1870-5.
[57] Ibid. 1880 (giving the owner for the previous year).
[58] Burke, Peerage (1907), under Earl Temple of Stowe.
[59] Ibid. He obtained a patent of precedence as son of an earl in 1890, his elder brother having succeeded their uncle Richard third Duke of Buckingham in 1889 as fourth Earl Temple of Stowe.
[60] Pat. 30 Eliz. pt. xiv, m. 18.
[61] Feet of F. Bucks. East. 4 Jas. I.
[62] Exch. Dep. Mich. 12 Geo. I, no. 5.
[63] Leadam, Dom. Incl. 1517 (Royal

Hist. Soc.), i, 169. Noted as quite an exceptional mention.
[64] Priv. Act, 17 Geo. III, cap. 43.
[65] The rector's share in these tithes in 1659 was £2 10s. 8d. (Lipscomb, op. cit. i, 322, quoting notes on cover of the Parish Register).
[66] Ann. Mon. (Rolls Ser.), iii, 447.
[66a] Pope Nich. Tax. (Rec. Com.), 34.
[67] Abbrev. Plac. (Rec. Com.), 281 (recording a suit in which the parson of Ludgershall was found guilty of taking the prior's corn for two years) ; Mins. Accts. bdle. 1125, no. 1 ; Chan. Inq. p.m. (Ser. 2), ccxxxiv, 45.   [68] Pat. 846, m. 15.
[69] Lipscomb, op. cit. i, 317, quoting MS. of a tithe suit of 1720.
[70] Chant. Cert. 5, no. 62.
[71] Pat. 850, m. 31.

FLEET MARSTON

Merstone (xi cent.); Flettemerstone (xiii cent.).

Fleet Marston is a small parish of three farms and several cottages with an area of 934 acres,[1] which, with the exception of about 24 acres of arable land, is low-lying pasture land of an average height of 250 ft. above the ordnance datum. Both soil and subsoil consist of heavy clay. The church stands in the east of the parish between Akeman Street and the Metropolitan and Great Central Joint Railway. The parsonage accommodation being inadequate, the rector has been non-resident for a long time. A mansion, possibly the site of the manor mentioned in 1517,[2] formerly stood near the church on Chapel Ground, and was taken down in 1772.[3] In Akeman Street, near the church, is a 17th-century house, partly refaced with brick, with original chimney, ceiling beams, and oak newel staircase. Fleet Marston Farm, which has plastered walls and a tiled roof, stands to the north of the church; part of the building is of the 17th century and retains some moulded ceiling beams and a portion of the original oak staircase.

MANORS Under Edward the Confessor Turgot, Earl Lewin's man, held and could sell *FLEET MARSTON MANOR*.[4] In 1086 it was assessed at 3 hides and held by Walter Vernon.[5] Early in the 13th century the overlordship appertained to the honour of Wallingford.[6] It continued in this honour[7] and afterwards in that of Ewelme,[8] being last mentioned in 1639.[9]

Fleet Marston Manor was held by the Bellewes in the 12th century, and was divided into moieties at the death of Geoffrey Bellewe, about 1200.[10] One moiety, afterwards the principal manor, called Fleet Marston Manor and including the doubtful 16th-century manors of Neyrnuts Grove and Hartshorn, passed through the marriage of his daughter Maud to the Neyrnuts and descended with Pitstone Neyrnut (q.v.) to the sisters of the last John Neyrnut, Margaret wife of John Harvey, and Elizabeth wife of John Hartshorn.[11] Margaret's share in the estate descended to her grandson George,[12] afterwards Sir George Harvey, and was conveyed by him in 1513 to Robert Lee of Quarrendon,[13] to whom he had leased it ten years previously.[14] Elizabeth's share descended in the Hartshorns, as did Pitstone Neyrnut.[15] Mary, widow of John Colt and then the wife of Richard Higham, sold it in 1540 to Sir Anthony Lee.[16] The whole Neyrnut manor in Fleet Marston thus descended with Quarrendon [17] (q.v.) to Charles Lee-Dillon, twelfth Viscount Dillon, who sold it to John Tirel-Morin early in the 19th century.[18] Morin died in 1807,[19] and his only child, Jane Elizabeth, died in the following year. In 1809 the manor was sold by the trustees under an Act of Parliament [20] to William Williams of Wandsworth.[21] In 1862 Miss Williams and Sir Astley Cooper, bart., owned Fleet Marston,[22] but all manorial rights have apparently lapsed.

The second moiety of the original manor in Fleet Marston, afterwards also called *FLEET MARSTON MANOR*, passed in 1200 to Geoffrey Bellewe's daughter and co-heir Alice, wife of Thomas son of Richard.[23] She sold it to Ralph Verney [24] in 1223.[25] On his death about 1226 his widow Mabel held it for two years by special grant,[26] and his son John did homage for it in 1229,[27] and was still living in 1234.[28] Ralph Verney had succeeded his father John [29] before 1246,[30] and his son Robert was holding in 1283,[31] and was succeeded in 1322 by his son John.[32] His immediate successors appear to have been two other John Verneys in the direct line,[33] Fleet Marston Manor then passing to the last John Verney's brother Edward,[34] or his son Ralph, father of the first Sir Ralph Verney.[35] The latter, who was Lord Mayor of London in 1465 and member of Parliament for that city in 1472,[36] died seised of Fleet Marston Manor in 1478, when his heir was his son John.[37] From this date the manor follows the descent of Middle Claydon (q.v.) till 1559,[38] when Edmund and Francis Verney conveyed it to William, afterwards Sir William Hawtrey and his wife Agnes.[39] By 1612

---

[1] Statistics from Bd. of Agric. (1905).

[2] Leadam, *Dom. of Incl.* 1517 (Roy. Hist. Soc.), i, 170.

[3] Lipscomb, *Hist. and Antiq. of Bucks.* i, 328, quoting the parochial returns of 1826.

[4] *V.C.H. Bucks.* i, 265. [5] Ibid.

[6] *Rot. de Oblatis et Fin.* (Rec. Com.), 232.

[7] *Rot. Lit. Claus.* (Rec. Com.), ii, 138; *Feud. Aids,* i, 84, 93; Mins. Accts. bdle. 1096, no. 6; Ct. R. portf. 212, no. 5; Chan. Inq. p.m. 18 Edw. IV, no. 23; (Ser. 2), xxiii, 67.

[8] Ct. R. (Gen. Ser.), portf. 212, no. 20, 21, 25; Chan. Inq. p.m. (Ser. 2), xc, 2; cxx, 4; cccxx, 139.

[9] Chan. Inq. p.m. (Ser. 2), dxcii, 89.

[10] *Rot. de Oblatis et Fin.* (Rec. Com.), 63.

[11] cf. under Pitstone; *Feud. Aids,* i, 93; Feet of F. Bucks. Mich. 14 Edw. II; East. 12 Edw. III.

[12] Lipscomb, op. cit. i, 326.

[13] Feet of F. Bucks. Trin. 5 Hen. VIII.

[14] Marcham, *Cat. of Bucks. Deeds,* i, 15.

[15] cf. under Pitstone. In 1517 it was in lease to Robert Lee (Leadam, loc. cit.).

[16] Close, 32 Hen. VIII, pt. iii, no. 32.

[17] William Hawtrey as grandson of Elizabeth Hartshorn disputed Sir Henry Lee's right to the Hartshorn moiety of this manor, involving him in at least two Chancery suits, one in the later 16th century (Chan. Proc. [Ser. 2], bdle. 83, no. 4) and the other in 1603 (ibid. bdle. 117, no. 31).

[18] Com. Pleas Recov. R. Hil. 44 Geo. III, m. 95.

[19] Local and Pers. Act, 49 Geo. III, cap. 165.

[20] Ibid.

[21] Lipscomb, op. cit. i, 328.

[22] Sheahan, *Hist. and Topog. of Bucks.* 401.

[23] *Rot. de Oblatis et Fin.* (Rec. Com.), 63, 232.

[24] *Rot. Lit. Claus.* (Rec. Com.), ii, 138.

[25] Feet of F. Div. Co. case 282, file 8, no. 20. Apparently in subinfeudation, but her grandson Thomas son of Geoffrey in 1233 refused warranty to John Verney on the ground that he had withdrawn his services from Alice and rendered them directly to Earl Richard (Maitland, *Bracton's Note Bk.* ii, 560).

[26] *Rot. Lit. Claus.* (Rec. Com.), ii, 138.

[27] *Excerpta e Rot. Fin.* (Rec. Com.), i, 188.

[28] *Testa de Nevill* (Rec. Com.), 257b, 261b.

[29] Bruce, *Verney Papers* (Camden Soc.), 5, quoting here and elsewhere Fleet Marston charters *penes* Mr. Thoms, then (1853) secretary of the society.

[30] Feet of F. Bucks. Hil. 30 Hen. III, no. 12.

[31] De Banco R. 51, m. 63 d.; cf. *Feud. Aids,* i, 84, 93; Chan. Inq. p.m. 28 Edw. I, no. 44.

[32] Mins. Accts. bdle. 1090, n°. 12.

[33] *Verney Papers,* 5.

[34] Ibid.

[35] Verney descent recorded on brass in Middle Claydon Church.

[36] *Verney Memoirs of the Seventeenth Century,* i, p. xvii.

[37] Chan. Inq. p.m. 18 Edw. IV, no. 23.

[38] It was held for about twenty years in jointure by Elizabeth widow of Sir Ralph Verney, jun. (Ct. of Req. bdle. 2, no. 65).

[39] Recov. R. Mich. 1 Eliz. m. 728; Feet of F. Bucks. Mich. 1 Eliz.

it had been divided between two of his daughters and co-heirs, Anne wife of John Saunders, and Bridget wife of Henry, afterwards Sir Henry Croke,[40] who made settlements in this year.[41] Anne Saunders died in widowhood in 1624, and her daughter and heir Elizabeth,[42] with her husband Sir Walter Pye, obtained her mother's moiety in 1631.[43] In 1640[44] she died seised of this moiety, and probably Sir Henry Croke held the other. Their lands were split up and sold during the Civil War.[45] Some of them came to Richard Hampden, and in 1730 were sold by his trustees to Sarah Duchess of Marlborough.[46] The duchess had purchased other lands in Fleet Marston, including Putlowe's Farm, from the representatives of Sir Richard Anderson, bart.,[47] in 1729, and the whole estate thereupon descended with Upper Winchendon Manor (q.v.) until after the death of George Duke of Marlborough in 1817,[48] when it was sold to William Williams,[49] owner of Fleet Marston Manor (q.v.).

LITTLE alias WRETCHED MARSTON MANOR corresponds to the land in Little Marston (a district lying apparently chiefly in Fleet Marston parish and extending into Quarrendon) held by John Fitz Geoffrey in the middle 13th century,[50] and to the Marston Manor held by his son John in 1264.[51] It reappears among the estates of Sir Henry Lee in 1577,[52] when it consisted of a great pasture called Little Marston and some meadows.[53] It is distinguished from Fleet Marston in the enumeration of the Lee estates[54] until 1660,[55] probably on account of its association by tenure with Quarrendon.[56]

Medmenham Abbey owned some lands in Fleet Marston granted to it in 1349 by Hugh de Berewic.[57] After the Dissolution these lands, then in lease to Robert Lee, were granted in 1545 to John Lord Russell,[58] who sold them to Sir Anthony Lee,[59] and they became incorporated with his other lands.

The church of *ST. MARY THE VIRGIN* consists of a chancel measuring internally 19 ft. by 13 ft. 6 in., nave 39 ft. by 14 ft., north porch and west bellcote; it is built of stone and roofed with tiles.

The church seems to have been considerably altered during the 14th century, and the earliest existing details are of that period, but traces of two small windows in the chancel, now blocked, indicate that the fabric was built at an earlier date. The church was restored in 1868-9, and the porch and bellcote are modern.

The chancel has in each side wall a 14th-century trefoiled light, and at the south-east is a two-light square-headed window of the same period, which retains some fragments of contemporary glass and has a sexfoil piscina bowl in its sill. The southern windows have been restored. The east wall, which seems to have been rebuilt, is pierced by a trefoiled light, mostly modern. In the south wall is also a 14th-century pointed doorway, and in the north wall is a square locker. The roof is modern. The chancel arch, the jambs of which retain traces of a former stone screen, and have ball-flower capitals, dates from the early 14th century; the pointed arch is now somewhat distorted.

In the south wall of the nave is a square-headed window of four cinquefoiled lights of about 1380, and in the north wall are two much-restored windows and a 14th-century doorway. The eastern window, which is of the late 14th century, is of two cinquefoiled lights with tracery, and the other is a wide single light with a 14th-century rear-arch. At the north-east is a corbel, probably for the rood-loft; on the jambs of the north-east window and the doorway are traces of old colour. Externally there is a sundial on the south wall of the nave, and at the north-west is a projection which supported a former bell-turret. The nave has a 15th-century open-timber roof, with queen-post trusses and curved wind-braces. The porch has been rebuilt, but a 14th-century trefoiled light has been reset in each of the lateral walls; above the nave doorway is a moulded trefoiled niche of the same period.

The font, which probably dates from the 13th century, though since retooled, has a rough tapering bowl with an edge-roll at the bottom, and a plain round stem. On the south wall of the chancel is a monument to Agnes wife of John Hoffman, rector of the parish, who died in 1639, and her two daughters. There are also mural monuments to members of the Markham family.

There is one bell, inscribed 'John Woodman. C.W. E.H. 1746,' by Edward Hall of Drayton Parslow.

The plate is modern.

The registers begin in 1630.

ADVOWSON The church of Fleet Marston, which is a rectory, was appurtenant to the manor. A presentation was made by the bishop in 1223.[60] In 1246 Geoffrey Neyrnut made good his claim to the right of presentation for that turn against Ralph Verney,[61] who afterwards sold his moiety to John Neyrnut.[62] The right of John Neyrnut was established in law against Robert Verney in 1283.[63] The church was valued at £4 6s. 8d. in 1291[64] and at £10 in 1535.[65] The

---

[40] cf. under Wendover.

[41] Feet of F. Bucks. East. and Trin. 10 Jas. I.

[42] Chan. Inq. p.m. (Ser. 2), ccccvii, 99.

[43] Fine R. 7 Chas. I, pt. iii, no. 47.

[44] Chan. Inq. p.m. (Ser. 2), dccxlviii, 12. Settlements in 1638 (Feet of F. Bucks. Hil. 14 Chas. I) and 1639 (Recov. R. Trin. 15 Chas. I, m. 42).

[45] Fleet Marston is named in 1647, not among the confiscated estates of Sir Walter Pye, but among those of Sir Edmund Pye (*Cal. Com. for Comp.* 68).

[46] Close, 5 Geo. II, pt. vii, no. 17.

[47] Ibid. 3 Geo. II, pt. x, no. 16. Early in the 17th century this property had been conveyed by Frances Countess of Essex to George Throckmorton (Marcham, op. cit. i, 16).

[48] Lipscomb, op. cit. i, 325. [49] Ibid.

[50] *Testa de Nevill* (Rec. Com.), 245.

[51] *Cal. Pat.* 1258–66, p. 475.

[52] Feet of F. Bucks. Hil. and East. 19 Eliz.

[53] Ct. of Req. bdle. 32, no. 112. The parish of Little Marston referred to in this document is assumed to be Fleet Marston. [54] cf. under Quarrendon.

[55] Recov. R. Trin. 12 Chas. II, m. 120. Here again the name Little Marston is evidently used as an alternative for Fleet Marston.

[56] Chan. Inq. p.m. (Ser. 2), dxcii, 89. Its tenure is apparently intended to be included with that of Fleet Marston in an earlier inquisition (ibid. cccxxii, 139).

[57] Inq. a.q.d. file 293, no. 2; Cal. Pat. 1348–50, p. 409.

[58] *L. and P. Hen. VIII*, xx (2), g. 496 (56).

[59] Ibid. g. 1068 (52); Add. Chart. 19541, 17355.

[60] *Reg. of Hugh of Wells* (Cant. and York Soc.), ii, 61.

[61] Feet of F. Bucks. Hil. 30 Hen. III, no. 12; Harl. MS. 6950, fol. 80.

[62] *Verney Papers*, 5, giving copy of original deed. [63] De Banco R. 51, m. 63 d.

[64] *Pope Nich. Tax.* (Rec. Com.), 34, 41b. It paid a pension of £2 13s. 6d. yearly to the rector of Chalgrove, Oxon. (ibid. 10).

[65] *Valor Eccl.* (Rec. Com.), iv, 236. £1 6s. 8d. was paid to Thame Abbey as impropriator of Chalgrove (ibid. ii, 213). This seems to be the portion of the tithes granted to Oxford Cathedral in 1542 (*L. and P. Hen. VIII*, xvii, p. 491) and afterwards resumed and granted to Sir Antony Lee and John Croke in 1546 (ibid. xxi [1], g. 504 [12]).

advowson descended with the principal manor of Fleet Marston (q.v.) (presentations being made by agreement between the owners of the moieties during the period of subdivision)[66] until its sale in 1805 by John Tirel-Morin[67] to Mr. Dobree, whose son the Rev. John Gale-Dobree, rector of Fleet Marston, owned it in the middle of the 19th century.[68] The advowson has since been frequently purchased by successive rectors.[69] Mr. W. Brimblecombe has, however, owned it since 1903.[70]

There do not appear to be any endowed charities subsisting in this parish.

NORTH MARSTON

Merstone (xi cent.) ; Normerstone (xiii cent.) ; Merston *alias* Marskton, Northmerstone (xiv cent.).

The parish of North Marston covers an area of 1,983 acres, of which the greater part (1,771 acres) is permanent grass and only some 68 acres arable.[1] The land varies from 334 ft. above the ordnance datum in the north of the parish to 452 ft. in the south-east, where the hills average 400 ft. in height. The soil is loam and clay, the subsoil clay,

and vicarage to the south-east and the school to the north-west. Manor Farm lies further to the west of the church. It is a good example of the better class of house, dating from the 16th century, with a 17th-century wing and later additions. The Wesleyans and the Primitive Methodists have each a chapel in the village. Near the latter, to the south-east, is the Shorne Spring, a chalybeate spring of very pure cold water which supplies the town well. It is

NORTH MARSTON VILLAGE

and the chief crops are wheat and beans. The village in the centre of the parish is nearly 1 mile in length. A fire is said to have destroyed many houses in 'the High Street' in 1700[2]; nevertheless, there still remain a number of old cottages and small houses, mostly of half-timber with brick fillings and thatched or tiled roofs. A few retain their wattle and daub fillings. These date from the 16th century and later, and there is a good deal of brickwork of the 17th century onwards. Some of the red brick chimney stacks are, however, of 16th-century date. The church stands conspicuously at the north-east end of the village, on rising ground, with the glebe farm

said to have been blessed by the venerated rector of the parish, Sir John, St. John, or Master John Shorne, who died at North Marston in 1314, and continued to be one of the most popular local saints in England until the Reformation.[3] Two or three miles west of the village there are two homestead moats.[4]

This parish was inclosed in 1778.[5]

William Fitz Ansculf in 1086 held **MANORS** *NORTH MARSTON MANOR*, assessed at 6½ hides.[6] It was afterwards held of the honour of Dudley,[7] and attached to the manor of Newport Pagnell[8] (q.v.), the last reference to the overlordship occurring in 1615.[9] Ranulf was

[66] Lipscomb, op. cit. i, 330. (List of institutions with a gap between 1373 and 1433). Inst. Bks. (P.R.O.), xvii, xviii cent. ; Bacon, *Liber Reg.* 503.

[67] Lysons, *Mag. Brit.* i (3), 603.

[68] Lipscomb, op. cit. i, 329.

[69] *Clergy Lists.*

[70] Ibid.

[1] Statistics from Bd. of Agric. (1905).

[2] Lipscomb, *Hist. and Antiq. of Bucks.* i, 338.

[3] *V.C.H. Bucks.* i, 288–9. See also *Rec. of Bucks.* ii, 60–74. [4] *V.C.H. Bucks.* ii, 32.

[5] Priv. Act, 18 Geo. III, cap. 48. Two pieces of land, the Tithe Pieces and the Bull and Boar Piece, were given up at the inclosure. They were formerly held by the Dean and Canons of St. George's,

Windsor, in lieu of certain tithes and for keeping a bull and a boar for the use of the parishioners. [6] *V.C.H. Bucks.* i, 254.

[7] *Plac. de Quo Warr.* (Rec. Com.), 88 ; Chan. Inq. p.m. Edw. I, file 59, no. 12 ; *Feud. Aids,* i, 93 ; see Oving.

[8] *Feud. Aids,* i, 119, 121 ; Chan. Inq. p.m. (Ser. 2), cxlii, 109.

[9] Chan. Inq. p.m. (Ser. 2), cccxlvii, 64.

tenant in 1086,[10] and the manor passed before 1154 to Wigan of Wallingford, who was succeeded about 1156 by his brother Meinfelin of Oving. Meinfelin was followed shortly after by his sister's son Alan de Penros.[11] North Marston after this was incorporated with Oving (q.v.).

In 1346, in addition to his fee in Oving with North Marston, Thomas Tochwick held half a fee in North Marston with his tenants.[12] This estate appears to have been disintegrated, but probably formed part of the small estate extending into Oving called in the middle of the 16th century *NORTH MARSTON MANOR.* It was held by Oliver Vachell, who on his death in 1564 was succeeded by his son Stephen.[13] He sold it in 1573 to Richard Saunders,[14] who added to his property in North Marston in 1579.[15] He died in 1602, and was buried at North Marston.[16] His widow Elizabeth held the manor for life, surviving their son Richard, who died seised of the reversion in 1615.[17] His son Richard obtained livery of the manor in 1629.[18] Another Richard Saunders was owner in 1679,[19] and his

SAUNDERS. *Party cheveronwise sable and argent three elephants' heads razed and counter-coloured.*

nephew, also Richard Saunders, in the mid-18th century.[20] He died in 1757,[21] and part of his estate probably formed the property owned by Mary Gibbard, widow, in 1778.[22] She shortly afterwards sold it to Francis Wastie, who in 1779 was awarded an allotment in respect of possible manorial rights,[23] and died in 1816.[24] His daughter and heir Mary Gilkes-Wastie had married in 1804 John Ingram Lockhart,[25] who purchased other lands held by Richard Watkins in 1778.[26] His successor of the same name held here in the middle of the 19th century property[27] which appears to have been owned later by John Clarke.[28]

The estate in North Marston sometimes called *NORTH MARSTON MANOR,* belonging to the President and Fellows of St. Mary Magdalen's College, Oxford, originated in a hide of land held before the Conquest by Alwi, Brictric's man.[29] In 1086 Bernard held it under William Fitz Ansculf.[30] In the middle of the 13th century Robert Chetwode was tenant,[31] and in 1264 his son William alienated it to

St. John's Hospital, Oxford.[32] A grant of other land in North Marston was also made to this hospital by Nicholas Dewey in 1272.[33] In 1456 its possessions

MAGDALEN COLLEGE, OXFORD. *Lozengy ermine and sable a chief sable with three garden lilies proper therein.*

OSENEY ABBEY. *Azure two bends or.*

were given to William Waynflete for the endowment of St. Mary Magdalen's College, Oxford.[34]

Oseney Abbey held lands in North Marston granted to it in free alms by William de Thoreny before 1320, when his charter was confirmed.[35] In 1535 Randolph Bell leased the greater part of this land from the abbey.[36] Oseney Abbey surrendered in 1539,[37] and its lands in North Marston were granted first in 1542 to the new cathedral,[38] and afterwards in 1545 to the Dean and Canons of Christ Church, Oxford.[39]

In 1086 Miles Crispin held a hide of land in [North] Marston,[40] and 5 virgates were held in 1284 as a quarter of a fee of the honour of Wallingford.[41] This overlordship continued in North Marston,[42] being transferred in the mid-16th century to the honour of Ewelme,[43] and rights appertained to George Earl of Macclesfield in respect of it in the middle of the 19th century.[44] Seric, formerly Brictric's man, was tenant in 1086[45] and John Carbonel in 1284.[46] Part of his holding passed with Beachendon in Waddesdon (q.v.), with which it formed one fee in 1346.[46a]

In 1086 the Bishop of Bayeux also held a hide of land in [North] Marston which he had subinfeudated to Robert.[47] Three virgates of this land were apparently held in chief in 1284 by St. Albans Abbey, the other virgate having been absorbed into the honour of Wallingford.[48] Land in North Marston was granted with the other possessions of this abbey in Buckinghamshire in 1540 to Richard and Margery Breme.[49]

[10] *V.C.H. Bucks.* i, 254.

[11] See under advowson.

[12] *Feud. Aids,* i, 119.

[13] Chan. Inq. p.m. (Ser. 2), cxlii, 109.

[14] Close, 15 Eliz. pt. viii; Recov. R. East. 15 Eliz. m. 808; Feet of F. Bucks. East. 15 Eliz.

[15] *Cat. of Anct. D.* iii, 214.

[16] Inscr. on brass in the church.

[17] Chan. Inq. p.m. (Ser. 2), cccxlvii, 64.

[18] Fine R. 4 Chas. I, pt. iii, no. 1.

[19] Recov. R. Trin. 31 Chas. II, m. 35.

[20] Lipscomb, *Hist. and Antiq. of Bucks.* i, 336.

[21] Ibid. 346. He left 2 acres of land to the vicar and his successors on condition that his private vault should not be opened.

[22] Priv. Act, 18 Geo. III, cap. 48. The names of sixteen other owners of land in North Marston are given.

[23] Com. Pleas Recov. R. East. 20 Geo. III, m. 218. He took down the house formerly inhabited by the Saunders family (Lipscomb, op. cit. i, 335).

[24] *Gent. Mag.* lxxxvi (2), 467.

[25] Ibid. lxxiv, 86.

[26] Lipscomb, loc. cit.   [27] Ibid.

[28] Sheahan, *Hist. and Topog. of Bucks.* 403; *Ret. of Owners of Land* (1873), *Bucks.* 5.

[29] *V.C.H. Bucks.* i, 255.   [30] Ibid.

[31] *Testa de Nevill* (Rec. Com.), 248.

[32] *Cal. Chart. R.* 1257–1300, p. 50; Feet of F. Bucks. Mich. 49 Hen. III, no. 10; cf. *Hund. R.* (Rec. Com.), i, 45; *Feud. Aids,* i, 84.

[33] Feet of F. Bucks. Mich. 57 Hen. III, no. 6.

[34] *Cal. Pat.* 1452–61, p. 343; *Parl. R.* vi, 351.

[35] *Cal. Chart. R.* 1300–26, p. 425.

[36] *Valor Eccl.* (Rec. Com.), ii, 219. Five shillings yearly was paid for freedom from suit of court of Newport Pagnell.

[37] *V.C.H. Oxon.* ii, 92.

[38] *L. and P. Hen. VIII,* xvii, g. 881 (26).

[39] Harl. MS. 4316, fol. 60; cf. Priv. Act, 18 Geo. III, cap. 48; Com. Pleas Recov. R. East. 20 Geo. III, m. 218.

[40] *V.C.H. Bucks.* i, 261.

[41] *Feud. Aids,* i, 84.

[42] Ibid. 93, 119; Ct. R. (Gen. Ser.), portf. 212, no. 5.

[43] Ct. R. (Gen. Ser.), portf. 219, no. 20, 21, 25.

[44] Lipscomb, op. cit. i, 336.

[45] *V.C.H. Bucks.* i, 261–2.

[46] *Feud. Aids,* i, 84.

[46a] Ibid. 121.

[47] *V.C.H. Bucks.* i, 237.

[48] *Feud. Aids,* i, 84.

[49] *L. and P. Hen. VIII,* xv, p. 541.

A virgate of land in [North] Marston held in 1086 by the Bishop of Coutances,[50] and under him by Ranulf, sub-tenant of the manor (q.v.), afterwards passed to the honour of Dudley, as did his land in Oving (q.v.), and, being absorbed into North Marston Manor, does not reappear.

The church of ST. MARY THE CHURCH VIRGIN is a fine building, doubtless owing the excellence of its later developments to the fame of one of its rectors, Master John Shorne, who died here in 1314. On account of the many miracles worked at his shrine, it was carried off to St. George's Chapel by the Dean and Canons of Windsor in 1478.[51] The church has a chancel 40 ft. by 20 ft., with a two-storied north vestry, and nave 35 ft. by 18 ft., with north aisle 6 ft. 6 in. wide, south aisle 10 ft. wide, and south porch, and a west tower 9 ft. 6 in. square, all measurements being internal.

The nave is the oldest part of the building,

once contained a figure of John Shorne. The head of the window is filled with good tracery, and in the north wall are two three-light windows, and in the south wall three of similar detail but plainer design. The middle bay of the north wall, against which the vestry is built, has stone panelling of the same design as the windows, pierced only by a small square-headed opening to the upper floor of the vestry. The vestry door is below this, opening to the ground floor of the vestry, which has a three-light east window and a much-restored square-headed fireplace in the north wall. The stair from the upper floor is at the south-west, contained in an octagonal turret, but this floor is reached by a modern wooden stair. There is in its north wall a fireplace, as below, and single-light windows in the north and west walls, with a two-light window on the east, all rebated for wooden shutters. The chancel has a south doorway corresponding to that on the north, and at the south-

NORTH MARSTON CHURCH : THE NAVE LOOKING EAST

representing in plan an aisleless structure, to which a north aisle was added in the middle of the 13th century and a south aisle about 1320. The east end of this aisle was rebuilt c. 1350, and a south porch added, and it is possible that the cult of Master John Shorne may have been the cause of this, and that his shrine may have stood at the east end of the south aisle. The chancel with its vestry is good 15th-century work, and the west tower is of much the same period, the clearstory of the nave having been added at the end of the century, and some alterations made to the two west bays of the south arcade.

The chancel is of excellent detail, built of ashlar with well-designed moulded plinths, strings, cornices and embattled parapets ; the buttresses are surmounted by tall crocketed pinnacles with panelled shafts. The pitch of the roof is low, and over the five-light east window is a niche, which, it has been suggested,

east a fine set of sedilia, unfortunately a good deal damaged, and a piscina in two stages, the upper having a stone shelf under a cinquefoiled crocketed head ; in the vestry is another similarly arranged. The sedilia have projecting canopies with vaulted soffits flanked by pinnacled buttresses. The chancel retains six stalls at the west end, of 15th-century date, with good misericordes, panelled fronts and carved poppy heads, while on the north and south walls the old back panelling remains, but the fronts, seats and desks are represented by modern benches only. The external niche over the east window is unusually elaborate, being treated as a pinnacle carried forward on a carved corbel flanked by angels holding scrolls ; the soffit of the canopied recess is vaulted. The chancel roof is modern, but rests on the original corbels, four of which are carved with the evangelistic symbols. The chancel arch is plain, of two chamfered orders, the outer continuous, the inner springing from moulded corbels.

[50] V.C.H. Bucks. i, 239.
[51] Ibid. 288–9 ; Lipscomb, op. cit. i, 346.

North Marston Church from the South

The nave has a north arcade of three bays, with pillars of four engaged rounded shafts, moulded bell capitals and plain chamfered pointed arches with indented labels, of c. 1250. The north aisle has two two-light north windows, the one of c. 1450, the other of somewhat later and coarser detail, having large shield-stops to its external label ; on one shield is a cross and a ring, on the other some roughly cut heraldry, quarterly, two quarters containing a wreath and two being blank. Between the windows is a 14th-century doorway and in the west wall a single 14th-century light. The south arcade, of three bays, has an east bay of c. 1350, with an octagonal pillar with moulded angles alternating with flat fillets, a moulded bell capital carved with four-leaved flowers, and a segmental pointed arch of two moulded orders and a hollow. The east respond has a similar half-pillar, pierced with a contemporary opening to the aisle, with a cinquefoiled head and carved flowers in the jambs and sill. The other two bays of the arcade have arches of c. 1320, with moulded inner orders, but the octagonal pillar and west respond have concave faces and are clearly rebuildings of the end of the 15th century or later. The clearstory has three four-light square-headed windows on each side, of late 15th-century date, with cinquefoiled lights. The south aisle has a three-light east window of c. 1350, with tracery and carved flowers in the jambs ; it is flanked by contemporary image niches, cinquefoiled, and below runs an enriched string-course returning along the north wall. At the north-east is a squint to the chancel, now blocked, and at the south-east a cinquefoiled piscina, with a crocketed head and flanking buttresses. There are two south windows, both of three lights and of 16th-century date, and the south doorway between them is of c. 1350, with a moulded arch of three orders. The south porch, of the same date, has an outer arch of two orders, and the south door, though of modern woodwork, has old wrought-iron hinges, which are probably mediaeval.

The roofs of nave and aisles are plain, low-pitched work of 16th-century date, with moulded timbers, and tracery in the spandrels of the wall brackets in the nave ; the corbels are angels holding shields.

There are a number of plain late mediaeval benches in the nave, and in the south aisle an Elizabethan poor-box. The 15th-century font has an octagonal panelled bowl, three of the panels containing shields much defaced, and the other five foliated ornament ; on the stem are five angels.

The tower is of three stages, with a south-west staircase, and has a west doorway with a two-light window over it with cinquefoiled lights and tracery. The second stage is lighted by a single square-headed window, and the belfry windows are square-headed,

each of two trefoiled lights, under an embattled parapet. The tower arch is of two chamfered orders dying out at the springing.

There are three brasses, one in the nave to John Ingram (Yngrame) (d. 1459), and two in the chancel to Richard Saunders (d. 1602), and Elizabeth his widow (d. 1615). There is also on the north wall of the chancel a curious tablet to John Virgin, minister of North Marston (d. 1694), with a hand pointing to his burial-place, and the words 'He lise just doune thare.' In the vestry are kept several books belonging to the church, Erasmus's *Paraphrases*, in three volumes, undated ; Jewell's *Sermons*, 1609 ; *Homilies*, 1600 ; a Bible of 1603 ; and the *Commentaries* of D. Wolfgangus Musculus, 1578. There is also a chest in the vestry of early 16th-century date, with a shaped lock plate and iron straps.

On the nave clearstory are several old rain-water heads, probably of mid-16th-century date ; one has the figure of a bishop in mass vestments, and seems to be an unusually early example.

There are five bells and a sanctus : the treble, second and third by James Keene, 1627 ; the fourth by Richard Chandler, 1699 ; and the tenor by Lester & Pack, 1763. The sanctus is blank.

The communion plate includes a cup and cover paten of 1569.

The registers begin in 1587.

ADVOWSON North Marston Church was granted about 1154 to Eynsham Abbey, Oxfordshire, by Wigan of Wallingford and his brother Meinfelin.[52] Henry II confirmed the gift soon after his accession,[53] as did also Robert Bishop of Lincoln,[54] and later Alan de Penros, Wigan's nephew,[55] and Archbishops Theobald,[56] Richard[57] and Hubert.[58] An agreement made between Eynsham Abbey and Dunstable Priory[59] proving unsatisfactory, the abbey surrendered its rights to the Knights Hospitallers,[60] who granted them to the priory in 1185.[61] It made a presentation to North Marston Church in 1223[62] and obtained a licence to appropriate it in 1306,[63] and a papal mandate to that effect in 1332.[64] In 1334 Dunstable Priory alienated a pension of 26s. 8d. from this church to the see of Lincoln,[65] and a vicarage was ordained in 1335.[66] The advowson and rectory were conveyed in 1480 by Dunstable Priory to the collegiate church of Windsor.[67] The dean and canons have since retained both. In 1778 their lessee of the impropriate rectory, consisting of the tithes and three yardlands with right of common, was the Rev. James Cutler.[68] James Neild of Chelsea, memorable as a visitor of prisons,[69] and his son John Camden Neild, who on his death in 1852 left his large property to Queen Victoria,[70] were afterwards lessees.[71] The lease was next held by Sir Thomas Fremantle, bart.,[72] afterwards

52 H. E. Salter, *Eynsham Cartul.* (Oxf. Hist. Soc.), i, 101–2.
53 Ibid. 55. 54 Ibid. 42–3.
55 Ibid. 102.
56 Ibid. 57–8.
57 Ibid. 58.
58 Ibid. 59, 60.
59 Ibid. ii, 157.
60 Ibid. i, 64.
61 Cott. MS. Nero, E vi, fol. 286. One silver mark yearly was to be paid to the incumbent for his life and four yearly to the Hospitallers after his death.

62 R. of Hugh of Wells (Cant. and York. Soc.), i, 91.
63 Inq. a.q.d. 34 Edw. I, file 57, no. 10 ; Cal. Pat. 1301–7, p. 459 ; Abbrev. Rot. Orig. (Rec. Com.), i, 149.
64 Cal. of Papal Letters, ii, 369, when the church was valued at over 20 marks yearly, 4 being payable to the Knights Hospitallers. The net value without the pension was estimated at £6 13s. 4d. in 1291 (Pope Nich. Tax [Rec. Com.], 41 b).
65 Cal. Pat. 1330–4, p. 567. After-

wards payable by Windsor Collegiate Church (Bacon, Liber Reg. 505) ; 6s. 8d. is given in Valor Eccl. (Rec. Com.), iv, 9.
66 Linc. Epis. Reg. Inst. Burghersh, fol. 347.
67 Cal. Pat. 1476–85, pp. 170, 181 ; Black, Cat. of Ashmolean MSS. Oxf. 876.
68 Priv. Act, 18 Geo. III, cap. 48.
69 Gent. Mag. lxxxvii (1), 305.
70 Sheahan, op. cit. 404.
71 Lipscomb, op. cit. i, 342.
72 Sheahan, loc. cit.

Lord Cottesloe, and his son Thomas Lord Cottesloe[73] now holds it.

Joan Ingram in her will dated 1519 is said to have left small sums of money for the rood light and for the lights of St. Katherine, St. Christopher, St. John, St. Margaret, and St. Anne in the church of North Marston, in addition to 1 lb. of wax for Master Shorne's light, and also for the sepulchre light, and 5 marks for the parish highways.[74]

CHARITIES The Clock Land, comprised in a decree of Commissioners of Charitable Uses, 28 August 1600, consists of

14 acres in the parish, let to various tenants, and producing £13 a year or thereabouts.

By a scheme of the Charity Commissioners two-thirds of the net income is applicable towards the maintenance and repair of the parish church and one-third for the benefit of the poor.

The Poor's Allotment, under the Inclosure Act of 1778, consists of 12 acres in Long Marston, producing £5 a year or thereabouts, which is applicable under the same scheme for the benefit of the poor.

In 1910 the sum of £8 8s. was distributed in blankets.

OAKLEY

Achelei (xi cent.); Akeley (xii cent.); Aclei, Acle, Ocle (xiii cent.); Ocle iuxta Brehull (xiv cent.); Whokeley (xvi cent.).

This parish, which with its neighbours Boarstall and Brill was formerly part of Bernwood Forest and contained woodland sufficient for 200 swine at the

Brill.[8] The parish boundary of Oakley, however, here forms a salient, skirting the churchyard, vicarage garden and orchard, and returning nearly to the point whence it starts. The Manor Farm, with its remains of a moat, probably on the site of the capital messuage of the 17th and 18th centuries,[9] and the Congregational chapel, first built in 1845, are a little distance west of the church.

The village contains many 17th-century half-timber buildings, several of which are thatched. On the east side of the Worminghall road is a brick farmhouse with a tiled roof, on the west front of which are two stone-mullioned bay windows, and upon the gable above is a tablet bearing the date 1660. To the north of this is a brick and timber

OAKLEY VILLAGE

Domesday Survey,[1] has still 468 acres of woods and plantations in its area of 2,806 acres.[2] Not quite 300 are arable, and nearly all the rest are laid down in pasture.[3] The land is generally 300 ft. above the ordnance datum. Here, as in Boarstall and Brill, some unauthorized inclosures were made before 1577, the offender in this parish being Richard Leigh, who, holding some 200 acres in right of his wife, the widow of George Tyrrell,[4] inclosed 'all their woody grounds.'[5] Oakley was formally inclosed by a Private Act of 1819.[6]

The village, which is small and scattered, lies in a wide-spreading valley close to the hamlet of Little London.[7] The church, at its east end on the high road from Bicester to Thame, was reputed in the 17th century to stand within the borders of the parish of

farm-house of the same century with an original chimney stack. The Sun Inn, on the north side of the road to Oakley Common, is a late 17th-century brick building of two stories with a central chimney stack. The village school, on the north side of the Bicester road, is a 17th-century building of brick and timber, much altered to suit its present use.

Near the south-east angle of the parish is Addingrove, which has for many years consisted of only two farms.[10] Another farm, Ixhill, once the site of a Roman building,[11] was probably part of the royal demesne meadow and forest in this parish from the 12th to the 17th century,[12] and had as late as 1707 a dwelling known as Ixhill Lodge.[13] In 1623 the keeper of the king's 'fee-hay' of Ixhill received instructions to publish in the parish churches of the

[73] cf. under Hardwick.
[74] Lipscomb, op. cit. i, 348–9, quoting Willis MS.
[1] V.C.H. Bucks. i, 258.
[2] Statistics from Bd. of Agric. (1905).
[3] Ibid.
[4] See under Thornton.
[5] Pat. 19 Eliz. pt. vi, m. 1.

[6] Priv. Act, 59 Geo. III, cap. 78 (not printed).
[7] See Brill.
[8] Exch. Dep. Mixed Co. Trin. 1650, no. 2.
[9] Com. Pleas D. Enr. Hil. 21 & 22 Chas. II, m. 1; East. 7 Will. and Mary, m. 12; Close, 6 Anne, pt. viii, no. 22; 4 Geo. II, pt. vii, no. 20.

[10] Sheahan, Hist. and Topog. of Bucks. 408.
[11] V.C.H. Bucks. ii, 10.
[12] Pipe R. 32 Hen. II (Pipe R. Soc.), 121; Hund. R. (Rec. Com.), i, 21; Cal. Pat. 1345–8, p. 407; Lansd. MS. 47, fol. 3.
[13] Close, 6 Anne, pt. viii, no. 22.

neighbourhood an order for the protection of the deer preserved there for the prince's buckhounds.[14]

Before the Norman Conquest 2 hides *MANORS* in *OAKLEY* belonged to Alwid the maid, who also held a half hide of the demesne 'ferm' granted her by Godric the sheriff for the term of his shrievalty on condition that she taught his daughter embroidery.[15] These with other lands, presumably formerly of King Edward, by 1086, when the whole amounted to 5 hides and 3 virgates, had come to Robert Doyley,[16] and were later held of the honour of Wallingford.[17]

One of the successors of Robert son of Walter, tenant in 1086,[18] was Luvet de Brai, lord in the reign of Henry I,[19] who accounted for the taxes of the royal forest in this county in 1131.[20] He left Oakley to Basilia his wife in dower.[21] Basilia married, apparently after 1163,[22] Osmund Bassett, who had been enfeoffed by Brian Fitz Count of this manor before 1166.[23] After Osmund's death Oakley came to John Bassett, his son by Basilia, but his title was disputed by Fulk son of Luvet.[24] In 1182 it was in the hands of Gilbert Bassett,[25] guardian possibly of William Bassett, John's son, who held Luvet de Brai's land in Boarstall three years later.[26] The Bassett tenure lasted until 1194, when Emma de Peri,[27] daughter of Fulk, made good her claim to one knight's fee in Oakley as her inheritance from her grandfather Luvet.[28] She was represented in this suit by William Fitz Ellis, her son,[29] who was in possession in 1217. In that year William Bassett, to whom King John had confirmed in 1208 the knight's fee in Oakley which his grandfather Osmund had held by charter of Brian Fitz Count,[30] renewed his claim without success.[31] William Fitz Ellis, William Bassett's rival, died about 1229, leaving a son William, who did homage in that year

FITZ ELLIS. *Argent a bend between six fleurs de lis gules.*

for one fee in Oakley,[32] and a widow, Rose de la Rokell, who was still alive in 1235.[33] This fee, as the records of 1235,[34] 1236 [35] and 1258 [36] show, was the manor of Oakley.

The Bassett claim seems to have expired in 1230, when Alan Bassett, perhaps William Bassett's son, conveyed to William son of William Fitz Ellis 2 carucates of land in Oakley.[37] The younger William Fitz Ellis had been dead at least three years in 1275, when his lands were occupied by John Fitz Niel.[38] John, who was still in possession between 1284 and 1286, holding a knight's fee in Oakley for term of life with reversion to the heirs of Thomas Fitz Ellis,[39] may have owed his interest here to his sister Joan, widow of Thomas,[40] who was dead by 1277,[41] the heir and probably great-nephew of William Fitz Ellis.[42] Robert his son, a minor in 1279,[43] had been succeeded before 1290 by a son of the same name,[44] whose son and heir, another Robert Fitz Ellis, was ward of Roger de Beaufoe in 1302.[45] The third Robert, lord in 1316,[46] with his wife Margaret in 1339 made a settlement of the manor with contingent remainders to his brothers John, Thomas and William, and to John de Bruly and his wife Bona.[47] He was living in 1341,[48] but in 1346 his widow Margaret held alone.[49] At her death in 1375 her heir was found to be John Duyn, son of Elizabeth daughter of William the third brother of Robert Fitz Ellis.[50] No evidence of John's tenure survives, and the manor afterwards came to John Fitz Ellis, son of another John Fitz Ellis,[51] who in 1413 settled it on Thomas Chaucer in trust for John's wife Joan and their heirs, with contingent remainders to his sister Maud and Robert James.[52] John Fitz Ellis must have died without issue before 1418, when William Bruly, probably heir of John Bruly and his wife Bona, released to Robert James his right in the manor of Oakley called Fitz Ellis.[53] After Robert's death in 1432 [54] Oakley was held by his widow Maud,[55] presumably the sister of John Fitz Ellis. Although at her death in 1437 it was said to be the inheritance of the Redes[56] (Boarstall, q.v.), it must have reverted to the Fitz Ellis family, for Robert Fitz Ellis settled it on

[14] *Cal. S. P. Dom.* 1623–5, p. 68.

[15] *V.C.H. Bucks.* i, 258. It has been suggested that Alwid may be the Leuiede of Wiltshire who was still the royal embroideress in 1086 (Ellis, *Introd. to Dom.* i, 267).

[16] *V.C.H. Bucks.* i, 258.

[17] *Red Bk. of Exch.* (Rolls Ser.), i, 309 ; *Feud. Aids,* i, 83, 94, 120 ; Chan. Inq. p.m. 28 Edw. I, no. 44 ; 2 Ric. II, no. 57 ; (Ser. 2), xxiv, 20 ; cvii, 2 ; clxiii, 3 ; ccxciv, 92 ; cccxc, 165.

[18] *V.C.H. Bucks.* i, 258.

[19] *Rot. Cur. Reg.* (Rec. Com.), i, 22, 23.

[20] Hunter, *Mag. Rot. Scacc.* 30 Hen. I (Rec. Com.), 100.

[21] *Rot. Cur. Reg.* (Rec. Com.), i, 22, 23.

[22] *Pipe R.* 9 *Hen. II* (Pipe R. Soc.), 16.

[23] *Red Bk. of Exch.* (Rolls Ser.), i, 309 ; *Cal. Rot. Chart.* 1199–1216 (Rec. Com.), 175.

[24] *Rot. Cur. Reg.* (Rec. Com.), i, 22, 23. The 'common stock' acknowledged by both sides in the suit of 1194 implies that Basilia was mother both of Fulk son of Luvet and of John Bassett.

[25] *Pipe R.* 28 *Hen. II* (Pipe R. Soc.), 121.

[26] Stacey Grimaldi, *Rot. de Dominabus,* 22 ; Pipe R. 34 Hen. II, m. 1 d.

[27] Emma and her husband William Fitz Ellis are mentioned in 1199 (*Cartul. of St. Frideswide* [Oxford Hist. Soc.], ii, 49).

[28] Pipe R. 6 Ric. I, m. 2 ; *Rot. Cur. Reg.* (Rec. Com.), i, 22, 23, 362 ; *Abbrev. Plac.* (Rec. Com.), 7. In or before 1199 Emma granted land in Oakley to Ellis son of William, probably her younger son (Pipe R. 1 John, m. 8 d.).

[29] *Rot. Cur. Reg.* (Rec. Com.), i, 22, 23, 362.

[30] *Cal. Rot. Chart.* 1199–1216 (Rec. Com.), 175.

[31] Maitland, *Bracton's Note Bk.* iii, 309.

[32] Fine R. 13 Hen. III, m. 4 ; *Topog. and Gen.* i, 273.

[33] Parker, *Archit. Antiq. of Oxford,* 257 ; *Cal. Close,* 1234–7, p. 105.

[34] *Testa de Nevill* (Rec. Com.), 261*b*.

[35] Ibid. 257*b*, 258.

[36] *Hund. R.* (Rec. Com.), i, 21.

[37] Feet of F. Bucks. 14 Hen. III, no. 4.

[38] *Hund. R.* (Rec. Com.), i, 36.

[39] *Feud. Aids,* i, 83.

[40] Boarstall Chartul. fol. 25.

[41] Feet of F. Hil. 5 Edw. I, no. 3.

[42] Boarstall Chartul. fol. 86, where William Fitz Ellis in 1262 confirms a

grant of his brother Ellis. See also *Hund. R.* (Rec. Com.), ii, 725–6. The Boarstall Chartulary, however (fol. 86), contains various references to Ellis son of William, who seems from the context to be William Fitz Ellis.

[43] *Hund. R.* (Rec. Com.), ii, 725.

[44] Assize R. 1292, m. 5 d. ; *Abbrev. Rot. Orig.* (Rec. Com.), i, 80.

[45] *Feud. Aids,* i, 94.

[46] Ibid. 114.

[47] Feet of F. Div. Cos. case 287, file 40, no. 259.

[48] Chart. R. 14 Edw. III, m. 2, no. 4.

[49] *Feud. Aids,* i, 120.

[50] Chan. Inq. p.m. 49 Edw. III (1st nos.), no. 54 ; cf. Wrottesley, *Ped. from Plea R.* 90. Elizabeth is called Marjory in a later inquisition (Chan. Inq. p.m. 5 Ric. II, no. 24).

[51] Close, 10 Hen. IV, m. 25. The eldest of Robert's three brothers was named John (Feet of F. Div. Cos. case 287, file 40, no. 259), but there is no evidence that this John Fitz Ellis was his son.

[52] Boarstall Chartul. fol. 52.

[53] Ibid. fol. 53.

[54] Chan. Inq. p.m. 10 Hen. VI, no. 23.

[55] Ibid. 16 Hen. VI, no. 38.

[56] Ibid.

his daughter and heir Margery at her marriage with Thomas Billing. Their daughter and heir Sibyl, aged six, the wife of George Ingleton, inherited Oakley at the death of her grandmother, Margaret Fitz Ellis, in 1470.[57] George Ingleton inherited Thornton Manor on the death of his father Robert in 1472 or 1473, and Oakley henceforward descends with Thornton (q.v.) until the death in January 1605–6 of Sir Edward Tyrrell, who left Oakley to his widow Margaret with successive remainders to his three younger sons.[58] Timothy, the eldest of them, in 1613 settled or mortgaged the manor,[59] of which he was lord at his death twenty years later.[60] In 1646 his son and heir, another Sir Timothy Tyrrell,[61] gentleman of the Privy Chamber,[62] paid his first fine for bearing arms against the Parliament.[63] He made a settlement of Oakley Manor on the marriage in 1669 of his son and heir James, an historical writer,[64] with Mary only daughter and heir of Sir Michael Hutchinson,[65] and twenty-six years later James with his son and heir the younger James Tyrrell barred the entail.[66] A mortgage made by father and son in 1701[67] was followed in 1707 by the sale of the manor to William Cadogan, afterwards Lord Cadogan of Oakley,[68] whose brother and heir Charles Lord Cadogan sold it in 1730 to Sarah Dowager Duchess of Marlborough.[69] Her great-grandson George Duke of Marlborough,[70] lord in 1760,[71] in 1812 conveyed Oakley to trustees, by whom it was sold in parcels.[72] Robert Polhill of Chipstead, who bought the manor and some land,[73] was succeeded in 1817 by his brother Edward,[74] who held in 1822.[75] Not long afterwards Oakley was acquired by Sir John Aubrey.[76] It has followed the descent of Boarstall (q.v.) to the present day, the lord of the manor being now Mr. Henry L. Aubrey-Fletcher.

Free warren granted to Robert Fitz Ellis in 1341[77] still belonged to the manor in 1707, when court leet and view of frankpledge were also reckoned amongst its appurtenances.[78]

TYRRELL. *Argent two cheverons azure in a border engrailed gules.*

A so-called manor in Oakley, of which the nucleus seems to have been a little land held of the heirs of William Fitz Ellis by John Fitz Niel at his death in or before 1289,[79] belonged to John Handlo in 1316,[80] and was held of the Fitz Ellis manor by the lords of Boarstall (q.v.) until Robert James became lord of all Oakley in 1418.[81] The two manors being then in the same hands, the Fitz Ellis overlordship naturally fell into abeyance, but reappeared again after their separation, Edmund Rede holding lands here in the 15th century of George Ingleton, lord of the Fitz Ellis manor.[82] In 1527, 'after dyvers varyances stryves and debates,' this, with the manor of Addingrove, was settled on Dame Anne Rede as her jointure by her son Leonard.[83] It seems to have passed to a younger branch of the Dynhams as the capital messuage or farm called Allnetts, of which Edward Dynham died seised in 1595 and his son John in 1632.[84]

Some land here was also held with Boarstall by the serjeanty of the custody of Bernwood Forest.[85]

Land in Oakley belonged to Nutley Abbey from the 13th to the 16th century.[86]

ADDINGROVE (Eddingrave, Adegrave, Adingrave, xi–xv cent.). This manor, held by Ulward, a man of Queen Edith, in the reign of Edward the Confessor, was part of the lands of Walter Giffard in 1086, and then assessed at 3½ hides.[87] It was still attached to the honour of Giffard in 1256,[88] when the overlordship had come to William de Valence, Earl of Pembroke,[89] by marriage with Joan, lineal descendant of the first Walter Giffard through the houses of Clare and Marshal.[90] After the death of their son Aymer the fee of Addingrove descended to their granddaughter, Elizabeth Comyn,[91] of whose husband, Richard Talbot, it was held in 1346 as of his manor of Pollicott,[92] in Ashendon. From Elizabeth's grandson Richard the overlordship came to his son Gilbert Talbot,[93] and was assigned at his death in 1419 to his widow Beatrice,[94] Addingrove being then and in 1432 and 1446 held of Pollicott Manor[95] (q.v.), a connexion of which no later trace appears.[96]

A mesne lordship over Addingrove originating in the tenure of Hugh de Bolebec, subfeudatory of Walter Giffard in 1086,[97] followed the descent of the manor of Whitchurch (q.v.) until 1635.[98]

Other mesne lords here holding under the Earls of Oxford, heirs of Hugh de Bolebec,[99] were Gilbert

---

[57] Chan. Inq. p.m. 9 & 10 Edw. IV, no. 22. [58] Ibid. (Ser. 2), ccxciv, 92.
[59] Feet of F. Bucks. Mich. 11 Jas. I.
[60] Chan. Inq. p.m. (Ser. 2), ccccxc, 165.
[61] Ibid.
[62] In 1645 he was governor of Cardiff under Lord Gerard (*Dict. Nat. Biog.*). His wife was daughter of Archbishop Ussher (ibid.).
[63] Cal. of Com. for Comp. 67, 1563–4.
[64] Dict. Nat. Biog.
[65] Com. Pleas D. Enr. Hil. 21 & 22 Chas. II, m. 1; Recov. R. Hil. 21 & 22 Chas. II, m. 51.
[66] Com. Pleas D. Enr. East. 7 Will. III, m. 12; Recov. R. East. 7 Will. III, m. 33.
[67] Feet of F. Bucks. Hil. 12 Will. III.
[68] Ibid. East. 6 Anne; Close, 6 Anne, pt. viii, no. 22; Recov. R. East. 6 Anne, m. 50; G.E.C. Peerage, ii, 101.
[69] Close, 4 Geo. II, pt. ii, no. 20.
[70] G.E.C. Peerage, v, 255–6.
[71] Recov. R. Hil. 33 Geo. II, m. 166.
[72] Lipscomb, *Hist. and Antiq. of Bucks.* i, 354.

[73] Sheahan, op. cit. 408.
[74] Berry, Co. Gen. Suss. 266.
[75] Feet of F. Bucks. Hil. 2 & 3 Geo. IV.
[76] Lipscomb, loc. cit.
[77] Chart. R. 14 Edw. III, m. 2, no. 4.
[78] Feet of F. Bucks. East. 6 Anne; Recov. R. East. 6 Anne, m. 50.
[79] Cal. Inq. p.m. (Edw. I), ii, 438.
[80] Feud. Aids, i, 114. [81] See p. 81.
[82] Cal. Inq. p.m. Hen. VII, i, 197.
[83] Close, 19 Hen. VIII, no. 22.
[84] Chan. Inq. p.m. (Ser. 2), ccxliii, 13; dcxxx, 52. In a lawsuit brought by Edward, son and heir of John Dynham, in 1645 it is stated that Jane his mother spent much money on repairing the dwelling-house at Allnetts (Chan. Proc. [Bridges Div.], bdle. 389, no. 38).
[85] Cal. Inq. p.m. (Edw. I), ii, 438; Chan. Inq. p.m. 20 Edw. III (1st nos.), no. 51; 10 Hen. VI, no. 23; Cal. Close, 1346–9, pp. 101, 335.
[86] Boarstall Chartul. fol. 114; Valor Eccl. (Rec. Com.), iv, 232; Pat. 8 Jas. I, pt. lix, no. 134.
[87] V.C.H. Bucks. i, 248.

[88] Testa de Nevill (Rec. Com.), 61; Hund. R. (Rec. Com.), i, 25.
[89] Hund. R. (Rec. Com.), i, 26, 42; Feud. Aids, i, 84, 94.
[90] G.E.C. Peerage, ii, 62; vi, 196–207.
[91] Ibid. 208–9; Cal. Close, 1323–7, p. 273; G.E.C. Peerage, vii, 359.
[92] Chan. Inq. p.m. 20 Edw. III (1st nos.), no. 51; Feud. Aids, i, 120.
[93] Chan. Inq. p.m. 20 Ric. II, no. 51.
[94] Ibid. 8 Hen. V, no. 127.
[95] Ibid. 7 Hen. V, no. 63; 10 Hen. VI, no. 23; Boarstall Chartul. fol. 94.
[96] The king was declared to be overlord in 1435, whereas two years later the tenure was unknown (Chan. Inq. p.m. 13 Hen. VI, no. 38; 16 Hen. VI, no. 38).
[97] V.C.H. Bucks. i, 248.
[98] Misc. Bks. (Exch. K.R.), vi, 168; Feud. Aids, i, 84; Cal. Close, 1323–7, p. 273; Chan. Inq. p.m. 20 Ric. II, no. 51; (Ser. 2), cxxxvi, 2; dviii, 15; Exch. Inq. p.m. (Ser. 2), file 22, no. 7; Feet of F. Bucks. East. 26 Eliz.; Boarstall Chartul. fol. 11b.
[99] G.E.C. Peerage, vi, 163.

Pippard in 1185,[100] and from 1255 to 1302 Ralph Pippard.[1]

A family called Morel were sub-tenants of Addingrove in the 12th century. Peter Morel, who died in or before 1173,[2] left a wife Clarice and a son,[3] who was probably the John Morel to whom Clarice in 1197 surrendered her claim to dower in Addingrove.[4] John Morel or a son of the same name, lord in 1236[5] and 1255,[6] in 1257 granted land in Oakley and Addingrove to John Fitz Niel,[7] who afterwards acquired from John Morel's daughters and co-heirs the rest of his manor here.[8] From that time until 1563 Addingrove descended with the manor of Boarstall (q.v.). John Croke of Chilton held the farm of Addingrove by lease in 1554, when he bequeathed his interest here to his son and heir John.[9] The term had not expired in 1607, a rent of £10 being then payable to Sir John Dormer,[10] whose son Sir Robert Dormer is said to have conveyed Addingrove to the family of Mitchell.[11] From Richard Mitchell the estate passed in the 18th century to John Aubrey, afterwards sixth baronet of that family,[12] and again descended with Boarstall (q.v.).

CHURCH The church of *ST. MARY* consists of a chancel 26 ft. by 13 ft., nave 45 ft. 6 in. by 14 ft. 6 in., north aisle 9 ft. 6 in. wide, south transept 21 ft. 6 in. by 13 ft., and a west tower 10 ft. by 9 ft. 6 in. These measurements are all internal.

The plan of the present building has been developed from that of a 12th-century church consisting probably of a chancel and nave, of which only the nave remains. The first stage in its evolution was the addition of a short north aisle about 1200, but about 1325 both the aisle and the arcade opening to it from the nave were reconstructed, and at the same time the chancel was rebuilt and the south transept was added to the nave. A small building, perhaps a bell-turret, seems to have been built at this period at the west end of the aisle, but this was removed later in the century when the west tower was erected and the aisle was extended westwards. The last alteration to the fabric in the middle ages was the construction in the 15th century of the nave clearstory. In 1885–6 the church was thoroughly restored, when the chancel was practically rebuilt. There were further restorations in 1889 and in 1909. All the walls are of rubble with wrought dressings.

The western of the two windows on both the north and south sides of the chancel are old. They are each of two lights under a square head, that on the north being of the 16th century and that on the south of the 15th century. The other windows on each side, and the three-light east window, are modern. The chancel arch, which has an inner order dying into the jambs and a continuous outer order, belongs to the period of the early 14th-century reconstruction. At the south-west of the chancel is a squint from the south transept.

At the north-east of the nave is a 14th-century piscina niche with a trefoiled head and a restored basin. The north arcade is of five bays of unequal width. The fact that the second and third columns, both of which are circular, are evidently re-used work of the end of the 12th century, though their capitals have been recut, indicates that an arcade of that date was replaced by the four eastern arches early in the 14th century, to which period the octagonal eastern column and respond with their clumsily moulded capitals belong. As only two earlier columns are made use of, it may also be reasonably inferred that the arcade of which they formed part was of three bays only. The arches of this portion of the arcade are pointed and of two orders, the two eastern being narrower than the pair next to the west, and in their reconstruction the 14th-century builders appear to have made considerable use of the earlier material. The western column, which has apparently been formed from the west respond of the arcade as first rebuilt, is square with chamfered angles, and has a rudely executed capital unmoulded on the north. The fifth and westernmost bay is the narrowest of the whole arcade and the arch is lower. The west respond has a capital like that of the western column and is octagonal in shape. On the south side of the nave, above the opening to the transept, is the upper doorway to the rood-loft. The arch into the south transept dates from the 14th-century reconstruction and is of two chamfered orders dying into the jambs. In the east jamb are a piscina with a mutilated projecting basin, and a plain opening, communicating with the squint between chancel and transept, which is rebated for a door. The south wall of the nave is pierced by two windows; the eastern window is of the 16th century, and is of three plain lights under a traceried four-centred head, while the western window, which is placed high in the wall, is also of three lights with tracery. The clearstory is lighted by three 15th-century cinquefoiled lights on the north and two on the south. Over the east gable is a stone bellcote.

There is a 14th-century pointed window with a traceried head in each of the three walls of the transept; that in the south wall is of three lights, but the others are of two; all have been restored. In the east window is an ancient stained glass shield of arms, Quarterly or and gules a bend sable, and in the west window is a shield with the arms, Or a cross engrailed sable. On the outside of the south wall is a 14th-century tomb recess with a cinquefoiled head containing a plain slab.

The first of the three windows in the north wall of the north aisle is square-headed, with two trefoiled lights, and dates from the 15th century. The next is a pointed window of two trefoiled lights with a traceried head, and dates from the 14th century. The westernmost is a square-headed late 14th-century window of two trefoiled lights. In the east wall is a pointed window of two lights with a traceried head and in the west wall is a single trefoiled light with an ogee head; both are of the 14th century. The original north doorway is pointed and continuously moulded. In recesses in the north wall are two 14th-century stone coffin lids with carved and incised crosses.

The tower is of two stages with western diagonal buttresses, and has a stair turret at the south-east

[100] Stacey Grimaldi, loc. cit.
[1] *Hund. R.* (Rec. Com.), i, 25; *Feud. Aids,* i, 84, 94; Boarstall Chartul. fol. 20.
[2] *Pipe R.* 19 *Hen. II* (Pipe R. Soc.), 71.
[3] Stacey Grimaldi, loc. cit.

[4] *Pedes Fin.* 9 *Ric. I* (Pipe R. Soc.), 65.
[5] *Testa de Nevill* (Rec. Com.), 61, 258.
[6] *Hund. R.* (Rec. Com.), i, 25.
[7] Boarstall Chartul. fol. 7, 11 *b.*
[8] Ibid. fol. 12–17; Feet of F. Bucks.

[3] Edw. I, no. 2; [4] Edw. I, no. 3; [6] Edw. I, no. 2.
[9] P.C.C. 33 More.
[10] Ibid. 50 Dorset.
[11] Lipscomb, op. cit. i, 365; Sheahan, op. cit. 409.   [12] Ibid.

angle entered by a small doorway in the south wall. The tower arch is of three orders, the inner order dying into the jambs and the outer order continuous. The ground stage is lighted by a west window of two lights with tracery in a pointed head. The bottom of the window has been encroached upon by the modern doorway below it. Above the window is a small trefoiled ogee light, and there are similar lights at the same level in the north and south walls. The bell-chamber is lighted from the west by a square-headed window of two trefoiled lights, and from the north and south by single lights of the same type.

The roofs are modern, but some old timbers have been made use of in that of the nave. On a part of a tie-beam preserved in the south transept are traces of a painted shield : Party cheveronwise gules and argent three unicorns' heads razed and countercoloured.

The circular font is of the early 13th century. The communion table, which has turned legs, is of the early 17th century. The pulpit is modern.

In the north aisle is a mural tablet to Ann, the wife of John Clarke and daughter of John Farrington, who died in 1693. In the south transept is a tablet to Margaret daughter of Sir Timothy Tyrrell of Shot-over, who died in 1686. In the pavement are slabs commemorating the following members of the Tyrrell family : Mary wife of James Tyrrell, who died in 1687; John son of Sir Timothy Tyrrell, who died in 1692; Elizabeth daughter of the famous James Ussher, Archbishop of Armagh, and wife of Sir Timothy Tyrrell, who died in 1693 ; and Sir Timothy Tyrrell, who died in 1701. The inscription states that Sir Timothy was governor of Cardiff Castle and master of the buckhounds to Charles I. There are also some later monuments to this family.

There is a ring of three bells : the treble and second by Henry Knight, 1622 and 1621 respectively, both inscribed 'Henri Knight made me,' with the date ; and the tenor by Joseph Carter, inscribed 'This Bell was made 1601.' There is also a sanctus bell bearing the date 1664.[13]

The plate consists of a stand paten, probably of 1700, but the date letter is much worn ; a secular tasting dish with handle, of 1686, bearing the initials EWE on the handle ; and a cup and cover paten of 1764.

The registers begin in 1704.

ADVOWSON It is possible that the church of Oakley[14] belonged before the Conquest, with its chapels of Brill, Boarstall, and Addingrove, to the church and canons of St. Frideswide, Oxford.[15] All were formally granted

to their house by the Empress Maud, with confirmation from Henry II.[16] In or before 1218, however, the patronage was claimed for the Crown, in whose favour the temporal courts pronounced.[17] The prior appealed to the pope, who sent bulls in defence of his right.[18] The king also appealed,[19] and his nominee was admitted to the church in 1222,[20] and he and his successors continued to present [21] until 1318, when the controversy was renewed and the case submitted to the decision of the king's justices.[22] It was still unsettled in 1325, when the prior again petitioned for judgement.[23] His right was established by 1327, when the charters of the Empress Maud and her son were confirmed together with the licence of appropriation granted by the Bishop of Lincoln at the empress's instance.[24] In or shortly before 1339 another appropriation of the church, with its chapels of Brill and Boarstall, was granted to the priory of St. Frideswide.[25] The vicarage mentioned in 1349[26] was ordained in 1343.[27] In 1525, the year after the suppression of the priory,[28] the rectories of Oakley, Brill, and Boarstall were included in a grant of its possessions to Wolsey,[29] and the licence granted him in 1526 to appropriate them for 'Cardinal's College'[30] was followed the next year by their settlement on the dean.[31] After Wolsey's fall they were surrendered to the king,[32] who granted them to the use of 'King Henry the Eighth's college' in 1532[33] and confirmed their incorporation with it five years later.[34] It would appear, however, that this grant was revoked before 1545, when the rectory and advowson of Brill, held in 1318 and 1650 to have been identical with Oakley from time immemorial,[35] were granted to John Pollard and George Rythe.[36] Sir John, afterwards Lord Williams, then tenant,[37] was owner in 1559, when he left the rectories and parsonages of Brill, Oakley and Boarstall in trust for the foundation of a free school at Thame.[38] Here, too, as in the case of the Oxford college, the connexion was not of long duration, John Dynham, lord of the manors of Boarstall and Brill, dying seised of the rectories of all three churches and the advowsons of Oakley and Boarstall in 1602.[39] The comprehensive grant made to John's heir in 1614 of the possessions of his ancestors included the rectory and church of Brill,[40] and from that date to the present day the advowsons of Oakley, Brill and Boarstall have descended with the manor of Boarstall.[41]

The gift of Oakley Church by the Empress Maud to the church of St. Frideswide included a chapel at Addingrove,[42] which was still existing in 1318.[43]

[13] This is inscribed in the small set of figures used by Richard Keene of Woodstock (A. H. Cocks, *Church Bells of Bucks.* 168). [14] Bacon, *Liber Regis.* 505.
[15] *Cal. Chart. in Bodl.* 301.
[16] Chart. R. 1 Edw. III, m. 45, no. 87.
[17] *Cal. of Papal Letters*, i, 60 ; Dugdale, *Mon.* ii, 135.
[18] Ibid. ; *Abbrev. Plac.* (Rec. Com.), 328, 330. [19] *Cal. Pat.* 1216–25, p. 311.
[20] *Reg. of Hugh of Wells* (Cant. and York. Soc.), ii, 260.
[21] *Abbrev. Plac.* (Rec. Com.), 328, 330 ; *R. of Hugh of Wells* (Cant. and York. Soc.), ii, 260 ; *Cal. Pat.* 1247–58, p. 471 ; 1258–66, p. 9 ; 1292–1301, p. 339 ; 1317–21, p. 195 ; *Cal. Close*, 1318–23, p. 7.
[22] *Abbrev. Plac.* (Rec. Com.), 328, 330 ; *Cal. Close*, 1313–18, p. 527.

[23] *Parl. R.* i, 438.
[24] Chart. R. 1 Edw. III, m. 45, no. 87. See also De Banco R. Mich. 1 Edw. III, m. 16. In 1338, however, the advowson of Oakley was included in a settlement made by John de Moleyns (Feet of F. Bucks. 12 Edw. III, no. 12), who quitclaimed his right to Oakley Church with the chapels of Brill and Boarstall to the prior the same year (Kennet, *Parochial Antiq.* ii, 76–7).
[25] *Cal. Chart. in Bodl.* 304.
[26] *Cal. Pat.* 1348–50, p. 329.
[27] Kennet, op. cit. ii, 80.
[28] Dugdale, *Mon.* ii, 138.
[29] *L. and P. Hen. VIII*, iv (1), 1468.
[30] Ibid. 2167 (2).
[31] Notes of F. Div. Co. Mich. 18 Hen. VIII.
[32] *L. and P. Hen. VIII*, v, 47 (6).

[33] Ibid. g. 1370 (23).
[34] *Cal. Chart. in Bodl.* 312.
[35] *Abbrev. Plac.* (Rec. Com.), 330 ; Exch. Dep. Mixed Co. Trin. 1650, no. 2.
[36] *L. and P. Hen. VIII*, xx (2), g. 910 (3).
[37] Ibid. [38] P.C.C. 11 Mellershe.
[39] Chan. Inq. p.m. (Ser. 2), cclxviii, 149.
[40] Pat. 8 Jas. I, pt. lix, no. 134.
[41] Chan. Inq. p.m. (Ser. 2), dxii, 7 ; Inst. Bks. (P.R.O.) ; Recov. R. Mich. 8 Chas. I, m. 226 ; Hil. 7 Geo. II, m. 30 ; Mich. 54 Geo. III, m. 392 ; Bacon, *Liber Regis.* 504–5 ; Feet of F. Div. Co. Hil. 13 & 14 Chas. II ; Hil. 4 & 5 Will. and Mary ; *Cler. Dir.*
[42] Chart. R. 1 Edw. III, m. 45, no. 87.
[43] *Abbrev. Plac.* (Rec. Com.), 328 ; *Cal. Close*, 1313–18, p. 527. In 1339 it seems to have been no longer used (*Cal. Chart. in Bodl.* 304).

OAKLEY CHURCH FROM THE SOUTH

OAKLEY CHURCH: THE INTERIOR LOOKING EAST

OVING CHURCH FROM THE SOUTH-WEST

OVING CHURCH: THE INTERIOR LOOKING EAST

A virgate in Oakley, which belonged to the church in free alms, was granted in 1224 by Ralf de Norwich, the parson, to Robert de Pollicott and Joan his wife for life at a rent of 5s., with reversion to the parson of the church.[44]

Land in Oakley, appropriated in the 16th century to the maintenance of a light,[45] is probably identical with the acre given by John Brande of Worminghall to find a wax candle or taper ' in the storey called the aisle of St. Nicholas,'[46] which Queen Elizabeth granted to Christopher Fenton and Bernard Gilpin in 1574.[47]

CHARITIES Eleemosynary Charities. — The Poor Folks' charity, founded in or about the year 1623-4, is regulated by a scheme of the Charity Commissioners of 26 April 1912. The trust estate consists of 112 a. 2 r. 32 p. in Boarstall let at £128 a year, augmented by the letting of the sporting rights thereon. · The income is applicable for the general benefit of the poor under one or more of the modes specified in the scheme.

The Poor's Allotment, containing 4 acres, was allotted to the poor under the Inclosure Act. The land is let at £8 a year, which is applied in the distribution of calico and coats.

John Hart's Charity.—This parish is entitled to a rent-charge of £3 (less land tax) issuing out of Easington Manor, Oxfordshire, charged by will proved in the P.C.C. 15 May 1665. The charity is applied, as required, in apprenticing a poor boy.

Ecclesiastical Charities.—The Church Land, derived from a gift of Richard Turpin and Ralph Beall by deed dated 12 March 1562, consists of 6 acres let at £12 10s. a year, which is applied towards the general church expenses.

John Clark, who died in 1678, bequeathed—as appeared from an inscription on his tombstone—an annuity of £1 towards the repair of the parish church. The annuity is received out of land belonging to the Manor Farm, Oakley.

A sum of 4s. yearly is received from the churchwardens of the parish of Brill and 4s. yearly from the churchwardens of Boarstall. These sums are also carried to the churchwardens' accounts under the title of the Brill and Boarstall Tribute, being considered as an acknowledgment that Oakley is the mother church.

OVING

Olvonge (xi cent.) ; Ovunges, Eeunges, Vuinges (xii cent.) ; Owynge, Oking (xiii cent.).

The parish of Oving has an extent of 990 acres, in which are included 138 acres of arable land, 803 acres of permanent grass, and 2 acres of woods and plantations.[1] The pasture land, which thus forms the bulk of the parish, is of an excellent quality and is well watered, since Oving is bounded on the east and west by streams which meet at the northern point of the parish, while various smaller springs rise in the higher land in the centre. The pasture was always important. In the 16th century the lords of the manors and some of their freeholders had laid together 100 acres from their respective lands in Oving, to be called the cow pasture and to be used as common for their mutual benefit. This land was later claimed as common of the manor of North Marston.[2] In 1607 a forty years' lease of this land, then reckoned at 120 acres lately ditched and hedged, was made to Silas Tyto.[3]

The soil of this parish is a sandy loam, on a limestone stratum in the higher parts and stiff clay in the valleys. The low land near the borders of the parish is from about 350 ft. to 400 ft. above the ordnance datum, save in the south-east corner, where it is higher. Towards the middle of Oving, more particularly in the south, the land rises considerably, and the village, standing on a hill, is about 500 ft. above sea-level. On the crest of the hill (529 ft.) is the meeting-place of five roads. The main part of the village lies around the road leading south down the hill ; it is, however, rather scattered and much intersected by roads and lanes.

The church of All Saints is in the north-west ; a Primitive Methodist chapel, rebuilt in 1809, lies beyond the village to the north. On the south of it is Oving House, a fine building dating from the 18th century, when it was built by Charles Pilsworth, M.P. for Aylesbury ; it has been altered and enlarged by subsequent owners.[4] It was leased to Sir Digby Aubrey, bart., in the 19th century, and after his death in 1856 to G. H. Brettle.[5] Col. Caulfield Pratt was a tenant for some years.[6] It is now in the possession of Mr. Henry Yates Thompson.

South-west of the church is the manor-house, a timber building with brick infilling, of late Elizabethan date in its earliest parts ; the brickwork is set in herring-bone pattern, and inside the house the old ceiling beams and framework are to be seen. In the hall is a large open fireplace. The Black Boy Inn is of similar construction, but perhaps a little later in date, and there are several smaller houses in the village of 17th-century date.

There is no Inclosure Act for the parish.

MANORS Edwin, a thegn of King Edward, held the manor of *OVING* before the Conquest ; it was afterwards part of the lands of the Bishop of Coutances and was held of him in 1086 by two knights, being then assessed at 10 hides and having woodland for 200 swine.[7] After the forfeiture of the bishop's lands this manor became part of the honour of Dudley,[8] belonging in the 12th

---

[44] *Rot. Lit. Claus.* (Rec. Com.), i, 631 ; Feet of F. case 14, file 15, no. 10.

[45] Chant. Cert. 5, no. 60.

[46] 'In Stadio vocat' the Ile Sci Nichi' (Pat. 16 Eliz. pt. xiv, m. 11).

[47] Ibid.

[1] Statistics from Bd. of Agric. (1905).

[2] Chan. Proc. Eliz. Mm 2, no. 22. Robert Carter, a tenant of North Marston, was accused of taking ' in some sort of outrageous behaviour . . . the grass growing upon the same ground with the mouths of his beasts.'

[3] Pat. 4 Jas. I, pt. ix, m. 3.

[4] Sheahan, *Hist. and Topog. of Bucks.* 412.

[5] Ibid.

[6] Kelly, *Dir. of Bucks.* 1869, 1877.

[7] *V.C.H. Bucks.* i, 239.

[8] *Testa de Nevill* (Rec. Com.), 248.

century to the Paynel family,[9] to whose manor of Newport Pagnell it became attached,[10] the successors of the Paynels claiming to hold view of frankpledge in Oving in the 13th century.[11] The last mention of the overlordship occurs in 1611.[12]

Towards the middle of the 12th century Wigan of Wallingford had an estate here,[13] as in North Marston. He died about 1156,[14] and was succeeded by his brother Meinfelin[15] of Oving, who held here in 1167.[16]

Robert of Oving, who held two fees here about the middle of the 13th century[17] and was still seised as late as 1273,[18] may possibly have been a member of the same family, as, although Oving was held as one fee by Robert le Lord in 1284–6,[19] it had passed by 1302 to William Penros, who held it as 'Oving with North-merston,'[20] and who may have been a descendant of Wigan of Wallingford's nephew, Alan Penros.[21] In 1316 a portion of Oving was held as dower by William's mother, Sara widow of Robert Penros.[22] William Penros still held in 1323.[23] In 1332 he granted his lands here to Thomas Tochwick and his heirs, making an agreement with Thomas and with Jane his wife (probably the daughter of William) whereby the grantees were to allow to William Penros during his life such meat and drink as they themselves used, and to find him a robe, 2 pairs of breeches of the price of 2s. 8d., 2 new shirts of the price of 3s., 4 pairs of shoes and a suitable bed.[24]

The Tochwicks were seised in 1346,[25] and in 1361 they settled the manor of Oving on themselves for life with reversion to their daughter and heir Jane, wife of Nicholas son of Richard Darches, and the heirs of Jane and Nicholas, the remainder, in default, being to Richard brother of Nicholas and his heirs.[26] Richard Darches, probably the son of the last-mentioned Richard, left a daughter and heir Joan, who married Sir John Dynham, kt.,[27] afterwards Lord Dynham. The latter died in 1458 seised of a messuage and a carucate of land in Oving, held in his wife's right and worth 40s. yearly.[28] His son John died in 1501 seised of the manor of Oving and leaving as co-heirs his two nephews Sir Edmund Carew, kt., and Sir John Arundel, kt., sons of his sisters Margaret and Catherine respectively, and his two remaining sisters Lady Elizabeth Fitzwarren and Lady Joan Zouche.[29] The manor retained his name, however, and was known after this date as the manor of *DINHAMS* or *DYNHAMS*. In 1512–13 Sir Edmund Carew granted his fourth share to Sir Robert Throckmorton and others,[30] feoffees of Sir William Compton, who died seised of this portion

in 1528.[31] In 1576 Sir William's grandson Lord Henry Compton[32] conveyed it to Ralph Redman,[33] who obtained the Arundel fourth from Sir John Arundel, kt., and Anne his wife in the following year.[34] Elizabeth Fitzwarren, who afterwards married Sir Thomas Brandon, kt., died seised of a quarter of the manor in 1516, leaving as heir her son John Bouchier[35]; the Zouche family were still seised of their share in 1531.[36] Which of these portions passed to the Dormer family and which to the Westons is not clear, but in 1554 Ambrose and John Dormer conveyed a fourth to Thomas Redman,[37] father of Ralph,[38] who inherited it before 1559,[39] and in 1579 Jeremy Weston and Mary his wife conveyed their fourth, which was held in Mary's right, to Ralph Redman also,[40] thus completing his possession of the entire manor. The

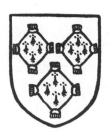

REDMAN. *Gules three cushions ermine having fringes and tassels or.*

manor, which in Redman's time was estimated at 6½ virgates,[41] was settled on Owen Westall and Jane his wife, apparently the daughter and heir of Ralph Redman and Bridget his wife.[42] Jane survived both her husband Owen and her eldest son Ralph, and, afterwards marrying — Bosse, died in 1609, leaving her second son Thomas Westall as her heir[43]; the latter still held Dynhams Manor in 1612,[44] but its further descent is uncertain.

The family which held Oving in the 12th and 13th centuries, taking their name from the place, appear to have subinfeudated a part of their holding while retaining the rest—probably one of the two fees which they had held at first. At the close of the 12th century this holding became divided into sevenths. In 1218–19 Castelusa, widow of William Cratard, quitclaimed a virgate of land here to Hugh Juvenis[45] and another virgate to John de Cruce or de la Croye,[46] and in 1270 William Juvenis and Hugh de la Croye held part of the demesne lands which had formerly belonged to Wigan of Wallingford in Oving.[47]

The Abbot of St. Albans received a grant of land here from Maud de Estuna,[48] probably one of the co-heirs, as in 1254–5 Niel de Chaucon held a seventh part of Oving of the abbot.[49]

In 1254–5 Robert 'Austin' (probably Justin, *vide infra*) held a seventh part of the Abbot of Cirencester,[50] and this family still held land here in 1292.[51]

[9] See Newport Pagnell.
[10] Chan. Inq. p.m. 1 Edw. I, no. 15; 36 Hen. VI, no. 39; (Ser. 2), xxxi, 21; xlviii, 167.
[11] *Plac. de Quo Warr.* (Rec. Com.), 88.
[12] Chan. Inq. p.m. (Ser. 2), cccxxiii, 45.
[13] Feet of F. Bucks. Mich. 52 Hen. III, no. 10; East. 54 Hen. III, no. 3; see V.C.H. Bucks. iii, 123.
[14] Salter, *Eynsham Cartul.* (Oxf. Hist. Soc.), i, 101.
[15] Ibid.
[16] *Red Bk. of Exch.* (Rolls Ser.), 269; Pipe R. 13 Hen. II (Pipe R. Soc.), 110.
[17] *Testa de Nevill* (Rec. Com.), 248; Hund. R. (Rec. Com.), i, 23.
[18] Chan. Inq. p.m. 1 Edw. I, no. 15.
[19] *Feud. Aids,* i, 75.
[20] Ibid. 96.
[21] Salter, op. cit. i, 102.

[22] Feet of F. Bucks. 10 Edw. II, no. 30.
[23] *Feud. Aids,* i, 113; Chan. Inq. p.m. 16 Edw. II, no. 72; *Cal. Close,* 1318–23, p. 623.
[24] Lipscomb, *Hist. and Antiq. of Bucks.* i, 372 (quoting from private deeds).
[25] *Feud. Aids,* i, 121.
[26] Lipscomb, loc. cit. (quoting from deeds of the Arundel family at Wardour Castle).
[27] Dugdale, *Baronage,* i, 514.
[28] Chan. Inq. p.m. 36 Hen. VI, no. 39.
[29] Ibid. (Ser. 2), xv, 58.
[30] Feet of F. Bucks. East. 4 Hen. VIII.
[31] Chan. Inq. p.m. (Ser. 2), xlviii, 167.
[32] G.E.C. *Peerage,* ii, 340.
[33] Feet of F. Bucks. Trin. 18 Eliz.
[34] Ibid. Hil. 19 Eliz.
[35] Chan. Inq. p.m. (Ser. 2), xxxi, 21; Feet of F. Div. Co. Mich. 1 Hen. VIII.

[36] Feet of F. Div. Co. Trin. 23 Hen. VIII; Recov. R. Trin. 23 Hen. VIII, m. 156.
[37] Feet of F. Bucks. Mich. 1 & 2 Phil. and Mary.
[38] *Visit. of Bucks.* (Harl. Soc.), 203.
[39] Recov. R. East. 1 Eliz. m. 159; Feet of F. Bucks. Mich. 18 Eliz.
[40] Feet of F. Bucks. East. 21 Eliz.
[41] Chan. Inq. p.m. (Ser. 2), dcxlvii, 29.
[42] Ibid.; cccxxiii, 45.
[43] Ibid.
[44] Feet of F. Bucks. Mich. 10 Jas. I.
[45] Ibid. 3 Hen. III, no. 35.
[46] Ibid. no. 34.
[47] Ibid. East. 54 Hen. III, no. 3.
[48] Cott. MS. Nero, D vii, fol. 90 d.
[49] *Hund.* R. (Rec. Com.), i, 23.
[50] Ibid.
[51] Feet of F. Bucks. Trin. 20 Edw. I, no. 6.

Again, at the former date the Abbot of Oseney held a seventh part, of which he had been enfeoffed by William de Toreney or Torence,[52] son of Robert, confirmation of this gift having been made by William de Beauchamp, the overlord, and Ida his wife.[53] In 1291 it included a mill.[54] Half of a seventh part was held by the Abbot of Medmenham in 1254–5 of the gift of Godfrey de Gibwen.[55] At that date two at least of the tenants were definitely stated to owe various services to Robert de Oving, described as the 'lord of the said vill.'

About 1267–70 these seven parts were in the immediate possession of Walter Champion, Robert son of Robert, John de Bedford, Ralph de Sanford and Isabel his wife, Robert Justin, William Juvenis and Hugh de la Croye[56] (the three latter families having evidently retained their portions from the 12th century), who were all sued during those years by the Masters of the hospitals of Wycombe and Crowmersh. The Masters claimed the tenth shock of corn coming from 'the demesne lands which were of Wigan of Wallingford in Oving,' parts of which were held by the seven defendants, after the usual tithe had been paid to the parish church, according to Wigan's charter.[57] As a result of the suits the defendants agreed to pay the tithe or the equivalent.[58]

Ralph de Sanford and Isabel his wife, who had their own manorial court,[58a] conveyed their part to Walter de Wimberville and Damerond his wife in 1271.[58b] Walter afterwards granted it to the Abbot of Oseney,[59] when it became united to the abbot's other holding here. This composite estate, retained by the abbey until the Dissolution,[59a] was granted as a manor in 1542 to the Dean and Chapter of Christ Church, Oxford,[59b] and afterwards, in 1546, to Sir Anthony Lee and John Croke.[60] There is no further trace of it.

The moiety of a seventh part held in 1254–5 by the Abbot of Medmenham must have been augmented at a later date. In 1474 it was described as a manor and held directly of the manor of Newport Pagnell[61] by Maud widow of Robert Bothe and formerly wife of John Enderby, who died in that year. Her son and heir Sir Richard Enderby, kt.,[62] died in 1487, holding the manor of the Abbot

of Medmenham.[63] John Enderby, son of Richard, conveyed the manor in 1507 to the trustees of Thomas Pigott,[64] whose son Francis had married Enderby's daughter Eleanor,[65] and in 1510–11 the manor was quitclaimed to Pigott by Sir Edmund Lucy, kt., and Eleanor his wife,[66] who was probably the widow of John Enderby.[67] Thomas Pigott, who was a serjeant-at-law and held property in Whaddon (q.v.), died in February 1519–20 holding Oving,[68] which he left by will to his third[69] son Roger[70] ; Roger leased it in 1542 for ninety-nine years to his brother Thomas, whose son Thomas afterwards held the lease.[71] Roger Pigott died in 1562 and was succeeded by his son Francis,[72] who conveyed the manor in 1580[73] to Henry Manfield.[74] From the latter the manor passed to Arthur Claver in 1594.[75] In 1623–4 Claver settled the manor[76] on the occasion, probably, of the marriage of his son Marmaduke with Simon Harborne's daughter Joan.[77] In 1675 the manor was held by Marmaduke's son Arthur,[78] who apparently conveyed it in that year to John Smith, Francis Nourse and others.[79] In 1677 Francis Nourse, John Nourse and Ralph Smith sold to Gerard Langbaine all their lands in Oving amounting to about 80 acres, for £1,240.[80] Langbaine died in 1692.[81] It was probably this manor which was held in 1714 by William Bennett, who conveyed it in that year to George Collins.[82] Henry Lovibond died seised of a manor here in 1727,[83] and his son Henry[83a] and his nephew Henry Lovibond-Collins afterwards held. The latter sold in 1735 to Francis Tyringham,[84] whose sister and heir Parnell married Charles Pilsworth, who inherited Oving at her death in 1741.[85] Pilsworth, dying in 1748, left all his property at Oving to his second wife Elizabeth and her heirs.[86] She left it by will, proved in 1755, to her brother Sir Thomas Cave, bart.,[87] and he sold it in 1756 to Richard Hopkins and Anne Maria Hopkins, widow.[88] Richard Hopkins died in 1799, bequeathing this property to his nephew Richard Northey, who afterwards assumed the name of Hopkins.[89] He attained the rank of lieutenant-general in 1809, and still held in 1842,[90] being succeeded by his son William Hopkins Northey.[91] The latter's daughter married George Ives Irby, Lord Boston,[92] and in 1861 Lord Boston's

[52] *Hund. R.* loc. cit.
[53] *Cott. MS. Vitell.* E. xv, fol. 24 d.
[54] *Pope Nich. Tax.* (Rec. Com.), 46.
[55] *Hund. R.* loc. cit.
[56] Feet of F. Bucks. Mich. 52 Hen. III, no. 10; East. 54 Hen. III, no. 3.
[57] Ibid.
[58] Feet of F. Bucks. Mich. 52 Hen. III, no. 10; East. 54 Hen. III, no. 3.
[58a] Ibid. 54 Hen. III, no. 7.
[58b] Ibid. East. 55 Hen. III, no. 6. This part consisted of three messuages, 4½ virgates of land, 12 acres of meadow, the seventh part of 12 acres of wood and 22s. 11½d. rent, and probably constituted the whole of the Sanford's holding as in 1317 Walter received a quitclaim for all arrears of wheat which he owed Crowmersh Hospital (*Hist. MSS. Com. Rep.* vi, App. i, 581).
[59] *Cott. MS. Vitell.* E. xv, fol. 24 d.
[59a] *Cal. Chart. R.* 1300–26, p. 425.
[59b] *L. and P. Hen. VIII,* xvii, g. 881 (26). [60] Ibid. xxi (1), g. 504 (12).
[61] Chan. Inq. p.m. 13 Edw. IV, no. 46. See Ledburn Manor in Mentmore (*V.C.H. Bucks.* iii, 399).

[62] Chan. Inq. p.m. 13 Edw. IV, no. 46.
[63] Exch. Inq. p.m. (Ser. 2), file 2, no. 1.
[64] De Banco R. Trin. 22 Hen. VII, m. 447 d. ; Mich. 12 Hen. VII, m. 1 d. ; Chan. Inq. p.m. (Ser. 2), xxxv, 1.
[65] *V.C.H. Beds.* ii, 224 ; *Visit. of Beds.* (Harl. Soc.), 132.
[66] Feet of F. Bucks. East. 2 Hen. VIII.
[67] John Enderby had died in 1509 (Chan. Inq. p.m. [Ser. 2], xxiii, 308).
[68] Ibid. xxxv, 1.
[69] Ibid.; Feet of F. Bucks. Hil. 4 Edw. VI ; East. 5 Edw. VI.
[70] P.C.C. 26 Ayloffe. He apparently alienated part of the Oving lands before his death, as a 'manor of Oving' afterwards passed with Ledburn Manor in Mentmore (q.v.), which had also descended from the Enderbys to Thomas Pigott, to William Byllyng, Edmund Peckham, Joan Brook and Thomas Duncombe between the years 1529 and 1547 (see Mentmore in *V.C.H. Bucks.* iii, 399). After the latter date there is no mention of this 'manor.'
[71] Chan. Inq. p.m. (Ser. 2), cxlii, 110.
[72] Ibid. 110, 111 ; cxxxviii, 3.

[73] Recov. R. Trin. 21 Eliz. m. 711 ; Feet of F. Bucks. Trin. 21 Eliz.
[74] Feet of F. Bucks. Mich. 22 Eliz.
[75] Ibid. Hil. 36 Eliz.
[76] Ibid. Hil. 21 Jas. I.
[77] *Visit. of Bucks.* (Harl. Soc.), 28.
[78] Ibid. ; Feet of F. Div. Co. Trin. 27 Chas. II.
[79] Ibid. ; Lipscomb, op. cit. i, 375.
[80] Close, 29 Chas. II, pt. xv, no. 29.
[81] Musgrave, *Obit.* (Harl. Soc.), iv, 13.
[82] Feet of F. Bucks. East. 13 Anne.
[83] Lipscomb, loc. cit. ; Musgrave, *Obit.* (Harl. Soc.), iv, 94.
[83a] Ibid.
[84] Lipscomb, loc. cit.
[85] Ibid.
[86] P.C.C. 52 Lisle.
[87] Ibid. 53 Paul.
[88] Feet of F. Bucks. Trin. 29 & 30 Geo. II.
[89] Lipscomb, op. cit. i, 377.
[90] Ibid. ; Recov. R. Trin. 51 Geo. III, m. 324.
[91] Ibid. ; Sheahan, op. cit. 411.
[92] G.E.C. *Peerage,* i, 381.

property here, called the 'Oving House Estate,' was sold by auction for £20,324.[93] Baron de Rothschild was a purchaser to the extent of £13,120,[94] and Mr. Leopold de Rothschild is still an extensive landowner in the parish. Other buyers were J. Parrott, R. Paxton, Sir T. Fremantle, bart., and — Vines.[95] It seems, however, that the manorial rights have lapsed, as a dispute as to the right of lordship of the manor was opened at the beginning of the 19th century and has never been settled.

The church of *ALL SAINTS* has a
CHURCH chancel measuring internally 26 ft. by 16 ft., a nave 33 ft. 6 in. by 16 ft. 6 in., with north transept, south aisle and chapel 9 ft. 6 in. wide, and south porch and a west tower. A north aisle to the nave formerly existed. The proportions of the nave and chancel, and the fact that the latter bends southward from the axial line of the former, suggest that the chancel is a rebuilding. It dates from early in the 13th century, so that the plan of the nave is probably of the 12th century, though no details of that date are now to be seen. The church underwent a restoration in 1867.

The chancel has three lancet windows at the east and two in each side wall, all having original 13th-century stonework on their inner faces, while the external faces have been everywhere renewed in modern times. The south-east chapel of the nave overlaps the chancel, from the south-west angle of which an arch of c. 1330 opens to the chapel. The chancel arch is plain 13th-century work of two chamfered orders, but the jambs are apparently of later date and are of coarser workmanship, probably altered at the time of the insertion of the rood screen, which still remains in an imperfect condition. It is of 15th-century date, with three open traceried bays on each side of the four-centred doorway. The whole is a good deal repaired, but retains traces of old red and green colour ; it is finished with a modern cornice.

The nave has in its north wall evidences of a former north aisle of late 13th-century date, in the remains of the arcade which opened to it ; the aisle seems to have been destroyed in the 17th century and the arcade blocked, but the eastern bay has been reopened and forms the entrance to a modern north transept. The existing pillar of the arcade is octagonal, with moulded capital and base, and the arch of two chamfered orders. The blocked north doorway, of 13th-century date, has been reset on the line of the arcade when the outer wall of the aisle was pulled down, and to the west of it is a single trefoiled 14th-century light, similarly reset ; it formerly had tracery in the head. The south arcade is of three bays, the two eastern of which, of similar date and character to the north arcade, are separated from the western bay by a blank wall. The latter bay is of late 15th-century date, showing a probable lengthening of the south aisle at this time. The nave has a clearstory of late 15th-century date, with one two-light window in the north wall and two in the south ; externally their stonework is modern. The nave roof dates from the same period and is of three bays, low-pitched, with tie-beams, purlins, ridge, and moulded wall-plates. In the 17th century (1657

according to a date on the roof) braces were added below the tie-beams, springing from scrolled corbels, and one of the tie-beams is of this time. On the soffits of the second and third tie-beams are carved bosses, one with a lion's face and the other with a shield of the Passion, both contemporary with the beams.

The chapel at the east end of the south aisle has an east window of three trefoiled lights with net tracery, c. 1330, and on either side of it an image bracket. At the south-east is a contemporary trefoiled piscina recess with the broken remains of a projecting basin, and to the west of it a wide tomb recess with an ogee arch, trefoiled and moulded, in the head of which a small window opening of later date has been cut. Between the piscina and the tomb recess is a three-light window of 16th-century date, and to the west of the recess is a similar four-light window, of which only the trefoiled heads of the lights are old. A third south window is modern, and between it and the second window is the south doorway, of plain 13th-century work, having a pointed head of one chamfered order. Over it is a 14th-century porch, the moulded outer arch being original work on restored jambs, while above the arch is the date 1717, recording repairs at that time. There is a holy-water stoup, of 14th-century date, to the east of the inner jambs of the south doorway, and the door itself is old, with vertical chamfered fillets and wrought-iron strap hinges of the 15th century.

The tower is of three stages, with a south-east stair-turret and diagonal buttresses at the western angles. The whole appears to be of early 16th-century date, but there is a good deal of modern work, including the embattled parapets. The belfry windows are single lights with round heads under square frames, and the cornice over them has gargoyles at the centres and angles of each face. In the ground stage is a three-light west window, nearly all modern, over a west doorway, both having low straight-sided arches, and the tower arch is four-centred, of two chamfered orders, dying out at the springing.

The font has a plain round bowl, which may be of the 13th century. The pulpit is of stone and modern. In the west end of the south aisle are four oak benches with panelled standards, of 15th-century character. No other old fittings remain, but in the east wall of the nave, south of the chancel arch, is part of an old wall-painting with a seated figure of Christ.

There are three bells and a sanctus : the treble and second of 1627, by James Keene, and the tenor by Robert Atton, 1617.

The communion plate includes a cup and cover paten of 1569, a paten of 1708 on a stand, and a plated flagon.

The registers begin in 1678.

The church of Oving was in exist-
ADVOWSON ence in the 12th century.[96] It was held, from an early date until the Dissolution, by the priory of St. John of Jerusalem in England, the priors of that foundation presenting rectors to the living as early as 1222 and until 1523.[97] The church was valued at £4 6s. 8d. in 1291,[98] and in 1535 at £11 1s. 10d., from which an annual pension of 53s. 4d. was paid to the Prior of St. John.[99]

[93] Sheahan, op. cit. 412.
[94] Ibid. [95] Ibid.
[96] Feet of F. Bucks. Mich. 52 Hen. III, no. 10. See account of manor.
[97] Lipscomb, op. cit. i, 379.
[98] *Pope Nich. Tax.* (Rec. Com.), 34.
[99] *Valor Eccl.* (Rec. Com.), iv, 235. This pension was afterwards acquired by the lords of the manor, with which it was alienated in 1675 (Feet of F. Bucks. Hil. 21 Jas. I ; Div. Co. Trin. 27 Chas. II).

After the Dissolution the living came to the Crown, in whom it has since remained,[100] presentation to the rectory being made by the Lord Chancellor. In 1902 the rectory of Pitchcott was annexed,[101] and since then the presentation has been alternately in the Lord Chancellor and the patron of Pitchcott, who is at present Mr. H. Yates Thompson of Oving House.

After an ecclesiastical visitation made in 1635 the commissioners returned that Oving parish had no copy of Bishop Jewell's works and no flagon to put wine in at the sacrament of the Lord's Supper.[102]

The Chantry Returns show that certain lands, of the annual value of 12d., had been given for the maintenance of a light in the church.[103] It was probably these lands which were granted by Queen Elizabeth in 1571 to Richard Hill and William

James as 1 acre and 1 rood in North Marston, formerly given for the maintenance of a light burning before the image of St. Nicholas in the chancel of Oving Church, half an acre near Fulwell Hill given for keeping a light before the image of the Virgin Mary, also in Oving Church, and 1½ acres in Oving in the occupation of Edward Nicholls and Edward Meyer, churchwardens [104]

CHARITIES

Clock Money.—An annual sum of 8s. 2d. issuing out of 5 acres in North Marston, now belonging to Captain Henry Aubrey Cartwright, is applied towards the upkeep of the parish clock.

For the charity of William Hill, founded by will 1723, see Bierton.[105] The annual sum of £1 received from the trustees is distributed among the poor, and one overcoat is also given to each one old man each year.

PITCHCOTT

Pichecote (xiii cent.).

Pitchcott is a small parish with an area of 925 acres, including only 32 acres of arable land, the rest, some 887 acres, being all pasture land.[1] The slope of the land drops from 500 ft. above the ordnance datum on Pitchcott Hill, in the north of the parish, to 267 ft. in the south-east. The soil is loam and the subsoil clay. The village is situated on the south-east of Pitchcott Hill, and from it there is a fine view over the Vale of Aylesbury. The church stands to the north-west of the village, with the rectory, built in the middle of the 19th century, to the south-east. There are no houses of importance in the parish, but the Manor Farm appears to date in part from the 17th century; the older parts of the building are, however, covered with cement, and little can be said of them. A panel of moulded brickwork, with pediment and pilasters, on the north-east wall, is said to be dated 1797, but, from its style, should be of considerably earlier date. The 'long causeway,' towards the repair of which John Perott in 1524 left a rent-charge,[2] is supposed to have been a line of stepping-stones used as a foot-road from Oving to Pitchcott churchyard.

In 1086 PITCHCOTT, though not named, was apparently assessed under Miles Crispin's land in Waddesdon Hundred,[3] since it was held as one fee of the honour of Wallingford in 1225.[4] The overlordship continued in this honour,[5] and was merged with it in that of Ewelme,[6] the latest reference to it in this connexion occurring in 1550.[7]

Pitchcott was probably one of the seven fees held of the honour of Wallingford in 1166 by William and Robert Pipard,[8] as in 1225 it was held in mesne

MANOR

by Roger Pipard.[9] This overlordship had passed by 1284 to Ralph Pipard.[10] In the next century it was vested in the earldom of Hereford, and in 1377 was held by the heirs of Humphrey Bohun, Earl of Hereford,[11] as an appurtenance of the manor of Haseley, Oxfordshire.[12] This manor passed in marriage with the earl's granddaughter Anne to Edmund Earl of Stafford,[13] who was holding the mesne lordship in Pitchcott in 1400.[14] No later reference to it has been found.

In 1225 William son of Richard Vernon of Haddon, Derbyshire,[15] was holding two-thirds of Pitchcott as Roger Pipard's tenant,[16] and the whole fee in 1235[17]

PIPARD. *Argent two bars gules and a quarter azure with a cinqfoil or in the quarter.*

VERNON. *Argent a fret sable.*

and 1236 [18] apparently as guardian of Hawise daughter of his half-brother Robert Vernon,[19] whom he seems to have married to his son Richard. The latter was holding both in Pitchcott and Haddon in the mid-13th century.[20] Hawise afterwards married Gilbert Francis,[21] who, surviving her, died in 1278.[22] His son and heir Richard married the daughter of Michael de

---

[100] Inst. Bks. (P.R.O.) ; Bacon, *Liber Regis.* 504.
[101] *Accts. and Papers* (1903), l, 595.
[102] *Cal. S. P. Dom.* 1635, p. 345.
[103] Chant. Cert. 5, no. 59.
[104] Pat. 14 Eliz. pt. ii, m. 23.
[105] *V.C.H. Bucks.* ii, 327.
[1] Statistics from Bd. of Agric. (1905).
[2] Lipscomb, *Hist. and Antiq. of Bucks.* i, 386, quoting Willis MSS.
[3] *V.C.H. Bucks.* i, 261.
[4] *Rot. Lit. Claus.* (Rec. Com.), ii, 15.
[5] *Testa de Nevill* (Rec. Com.), 248 ; *Feud. Aids,* i, 84, 93 ; Chan. Inq. p.m.

30 Hen. VI, no. 8 ; Exch. Inq. p.m. (Ser. 2), file 13, no. 1 ; Ct. R. (Gen. Ser.), portf. 212, no. 5, 7.
[6] Ct. R. (Gen. Ser.), portf. 212, no. 20, 21.
[7] Ibid. no. 25.
[8] *Red Bk. of Exch.* (Rolls Ser.), 309.
[9] *Rot. Lit. Claus.* (Rec. Com.), ii, 15.
[10] *Feud. Aids,* i, 84.
[11] Duchy of Lanc. Royal Char ers, no. 349 ; Chan. Inq. p.m. 1 Ric. II, no. 165.
[12] Chan. Inq. p.m. 1 Ric. II, no. 38.
[13] Dugdale, *Baronage,* i, 163.
[14] *Cat. of Anct. D.* ii, 494.

[15] *Derb. Arch. and Nat. Hist. Soc. Journ.* xv, 179.
[16] *Rot. Lit. Claus.* (Rec. Com.), ii, 15.
[17] *Testa de Nevill* (Rec. Com.) 261b.
[18] Ibid. 259.
[19] Wrottesley, *Ped. from Plea R.* 534. Matilda Vernon, Robert's mother, held part of Pitchcott in dower in the time of King John.
[20] *Testa de Nevill* (Rec. Com.), 248, 4b, 9.
[21] Wrottesley, loc. cit.
[22] Chan. Inq. p.m. Edw. I, file 18, no. 9.

A HISTORY OF BUCKINGHAMSHIRE

Hartcla,[23] and took the name of Vernon.[24] In 1290 he enfeoffed his son Richard and Eleanor daughter of Giles Fenes of Pitchcott Manor,[25] and in 1292 it was granted to her father in custody during their minority.[26] Richard Vernon, the father, regained seisin of this manor, however, before 1302,[27] and in 1323 was sued by Maud, the widow of his son Richard, who claimed a third of it in dower.[28] A grant of free warren in Pitchcott was made to Richard Vernon in 1328.[29] His grandson William Vernon[30] had succeeded early in 1331, when Isabel widow of his grandfather and Maud widow of his father claimed dower in Pitchcott.[31] William died before 1346, when two-thirds of Pitchcott was in the custody of the Earl of Northampton[32] during the minority of Richard,[33] afterwards Sir Richard Vernon, kt. He died in 1376, and, his son Richard being a minor,[34] the custody of Pitchcott Manor was granted to Thomas of Woodstock, son of Edward III.[35] In 1378 dower was assigned to the widow Juliane Vernon.[36] In 1400 this manor was granted by Edmund Earl of Stafford to Nicholas Bradshaw during the minority of Richard son of the last heir.[37] Sir Richard Vernon died in 1451, having a year previously granted Pitchcott Manor for life to his son Thomas subject to a rent-charge during his own life to Roger Palmer.[38] In 1453 Sir Richard's elder son Sir William Vernon[39] granted it to Thomas and Elizabeth his wife for life.[40] Sir William Vernon died in 1461,[41] and later in the century this manor reverted to his son[42] Sir Henry Vernon of Haddon, who at his death in 1515 had settled it in trust for his son and heir Richard.[43] He died in 1518, leaving as successor a young son George,[44] afterwards Sir George Vernon, kt., who died in 1566.[45] Pitchcott was assigned to his daughter and co-heir Margaret wife of Thomas Stanley,[46] and after various settlements, detailed under Adstock (q.v.), came to their son Edward Stanley, who mortgaged it in 1588 to Richard Saunders.[47] He died seised about 1602,[48] his son John obtaining livery of this manor in 1612.[49] In 1637 his daughter Elizabeth with her husband Sir Walter Pye conveyed this estate to her uncles[50]

Sir Thomas and Francis Saunders,[51] who five years earlier had interests in it.[52] By mutual agreement[53] Pitchcott Manor descended in their families in moieties, one of which passed apparently in the direct line from Sir Thomas Saunders through his son Thomas[54] to Thomas Saunders, a distinguished naval officer,[55] who was sheriff for the county in 1733[56] and was buried at Brill in 1741.[57] His son Thomas[58] made a settlement of his estate in 1749,[59] and in 1773 purchased the other moiety of the manor. On his death in 1775 Pitchcott Manor passed to his son Thomas,[60] who was sheriff in 1785.[61] His successor about 1798, in accordance with a settlement under his father's will,[62] was his uncle Captain Richard Saunders, whose son, another Thomas Saunders,[63] had succeeded in 1813[64] and died in 1831.[65] A quarter of Pitchcott Manor went to his sister Elizabeth Lyster,[66] the other co-heirs being another sister, Mary Wheeley, and the heirs of their two sisters Martha Smith and Jane Wilson.[67] Their representatives sold this manor in 1852 to Baron Mayer de Rothschild, who in the following year exchanged it for property in Mentmore with the Dean and Chapter of Christ Church, Oxford,[68] who are the present owners.

The other moiety of the manor passed before 1665[69] to Thomas son and heir of Francis Saunders,[70] who was buried at Pitchcott in 1690.[71] His lands here, which in 1675 were settled on his wife Hester,[72] had reverted by 1708 to Thomas Saunders,[73] probably their son. He was knighted in 1714 as one ' of the honourable band of gentleman pensioners,'[74] and was living in 1727.[75] His moiety of the manor was owned by Francis Saunders in 1742.[76] Before 1773 it had passed to Ann Mead, widow, and Richard Mead, who conveyed it in that year to Thomas Saunders,[77] owner of the other moiety.

References to the manorial courts of Pitchcott occur in the 15th[78] and 16th centuries.[79]

CHURCH The church of *ST. GILES* has a chancel measuring internally 20 ft. by 14 ft., a nave 42 ft. by 15 ft., with south porch, and a west tower 8 ft. by 8 ft. 6 in. There

[23] Chan. Inq. p.m. Edw. I, file 18, no. 9. In 1314, as Richard Vernon, he made some agreement with his brother-in-law, Andrew de Hartcla, afterwards Earl of Carlisle (G.E.C. *Peerage*, ii, 150), concerning Pitchcott Manor (De Banco R. 204, m. 103 d.; Feet of F. Bucks. East. 7 Edw. II).
[24] De Banco R. 204, m. 103 d. In the 1284-6 assessment for feudal aids he is entered as Richard Fraunceys under Adstock (*Feud. Aids*, i, 81), but his father Gilbert is erroneously returned as lord of Pitchcott (ibid. 84).
[25] *Abbrev. Plac.* (Rec. Com.), 223.
[26] *Cal. Pat.* 1281-92, p. 470.
[27] *Feud. Aids*, i, 93; see also De Banco R. 178, m. 218; 204, m. 103 d.; *Feud. Aids*, i, 113.
[28] De Banco R. 248, m. 127; 250, m. 114 d.; 252, m. 151; 253, m. 227 d.
[29] Chart. R. 2 Edw. III, pt. i, no. 36.
[30] *Cal. Inq. p.m.* (Edw. II), vi, 238.
[31] De Banco R. 286, m. 348 d.
[32] Evidently by grant of the Earl of Hereford, his father (G.E.C. *Complete Peerage*, vi, 67).
[33] *Feud. Aids*, i, 119.
[34] Chan. Inq. p.m. 1 Ric. II, no. 38.
[35] *Cal. Pat.* 1377-81, p. 67; Duchy of Lanc. Royal Charters, no. 349.

[36] Close, 2 Ric. II, m. 23; Chan. Inq. p.m. 2 Ric. II, no. 52.
[37] *Cat. of Anct. D.* ii, 494.
[38] Chan. Inq. p.m. 30 Hen. VI, no. 8.
[39] Ibid.
[40] Feet of F. case 22, file 124, no. 2.
[41] Chan. Inq. p.m. (Ser. 2), xix, 129.
[42] Ibid.
[43] Ibid. xxx, 73.
[44] Exch. Inq. p.m. (Ser. 2), file 13, no. 1.
[45] Chan. Inq. p.m. (Ser. 2), cxliv, 170.
[46] Ibid.
[47] Recov. R. Trin. 29 Eliz. m. 23; Close, 29 Eliz. pt. xxv. Certain leases and rents granted by Sir George Vernon, Margaret Stanley, and her second husband, William Mather, were excepted.
[48] Chan. Inq. p.m. (Ser. 2), cclxx, 129.
[49] Fine R. 10 Jas. I, pt. iii, no. 8.
[50] *Visit. of Bucks.* (Harl. Soc.), 10.
[51] Feet of F. Bucks. Trin. 13 Chas. I.
[52] Ibid. Mich. 8 Chas. I, two settlements, one with Sir William and Elizabeth Rowe, the other between Sir Thomas Saunders and Sir David Watkins.
[53] Feet of F. Bucks. Mich. 24 Chas. I.
[54] *Visit. of Bucks.* (Harl. Soc.), 10.
[55] *Gent. Mag.* xi (2), 665.
[56] P.R.O. *List of Sheriffs*, 10.

[57] Lipscomb, op. cit. i, 385; P.C.C. 31 Trenley.
[58] Lipscomb, loc. cit.
[59] Feet of F. Bucks. Trin. 22 & 23 Geo. II.
[60] P.C.C. 493 Alexander.
[61] P.R.O. *List of Sheriffs*, 10.
[62] P.C.C. 493 Alexander.
[63] Lipscomb, loc. cit.
[64] Recov. R. Trin. 53 Geo. III, m. 262.
[65] *Gent. Mag.* ci (2), 92.
[66] Recov. R. East. 2 Will. IV, m. 297.
[67] Lipscomb, loc. cit.
[68] Sheahan, *Hist. and Topog. of Bucks.* 413.
[69] Feet of F. Bucks. East. 17 Chas. II.
[70] *Visit. of Bucks.* (Harl. Soc.), 10; Marcham, *Cat. of Bucks. Deeds*, ii, 32.
[71] Lipscomb, op. cit. i, 389, quoting Par. Reg.
[72] Marcham, loc. cit.
[73] Recov. R. Hil. 7 Anne, m. 208.
[74] Shaw, *Kts. of Engl.* ii, 280.
[75] He presented to the church in that year for his turn (Lipscomb, op. cit. i, 387).
[76] Recov. R. East. 15 Geo. II, m. 382.
[77] Feet of F. Bucks. Trin. 13 Geo. III.
[78] Ct. R. (Gen. Ser.), portf. 212, no. 2.
[79] Ibid. no. 18.

is a modern vestry north of the chancel. The church was restored in 1864.[80]

The chancel dates from the first half of the 13th century, and the nave is of earlier date, though none of its original windows or doorways has survived. The west tower was added in the 15th century, but its upper part is of early 16th-century date.

The east wall of the chancel has been rebuilt in modern times, with the east window, but in the south wall are two 13th-century lancet windows, much restored, the eastern of the two having its sill carried down to serve as a sedile. The western lancet is interesting as having in its east splay a stone book-desk, apparently in position, and part of the 13th-century work. Between the lancets is a priest's doorway of c. 1340. The north wall of the chancel retains no old features except a plain locker, and the chancel arch is also modern.

The nave is lighted from the south by two square-headed two-light 15th-century windows, and from the north by modern copies of them. The north doorway is of plain detail of c. 1400, and is now blocked, while the south doorway, of similar character, is the principal entrance, and has over it a trefoiled niche, now empty. The south porch has a four-centred outer doorway, above which is a stone with the date 1662, perhaps recording a repair of damage done during the Civil War. There are stone benches on both sides of the porch and modern single-light windows.

The tower has diagonal buttresses and a south-west staircase. There is a

PITCHCOTT CHURCH FROM THE SOUTH-EAST

four-centred west doorway with a two-light window over it, and in the belfry stage, which, as already noted, appears to be later than the rest of the tower, are single trefoiled lights under square heads. The stonework is a good deal decayed, and has been made up with cement.

There is no old woodwork in the church, except some of the timbers in the tower.

There are three bells and a sanctus : the treble, of 1686, by Chandler of Drayton Parslow, and the second inscribed 'Sent Luke Apostel, 1590,' said by Mr. A. H. Cocks[81] to be the work of Robert Newcombe and Bartholomew Atton. The tenor, of 1717, is by George Chandler.

The communion plate includes a cup and cover paten of 1569, a chalice of 1871 with cover paten of 1884, a pewter paten and pewter flagon.

The registers begin in 1680.

ADVOWSON The advowson of the rectory of Pitchcott was appurtenant to the manor (q.v.). Presentations were made by Malvern Priory during the 13th century,[82] but in 1310 Richard Vernon proved his right to the advowson,[83] and it descended with the manor. In 1291 it was valued at £5 6s. 8d.[84] and in 1535 at £10 10s. 8d.[85] The owners of the moieties of the manor in the 17th and 18th centuries presented by turns.[86] The heirs of Captain Saunders retained the advowson until the later 19th century.[87] It has since belonged successively to the Rev. Peter Aubertin and his trustees,[88] to the Rev. C. L. Banister[89] and the Rev. C. J. Banister,[90] and has lately been acquired by Mr. H. Yates Thompson, the present owner.

In 1902 the rectory of Pitchcott was united with that of Oving,[91] and the owners of the advowsons have the right of presenting to the benefice alternately.

There do not appear to be any endowed charities subsisting in this parish.

---

[80] The church was in a most dilapidated condition in 1817. The walls were cracked, the roof falling in, and the chancel boarded off from the main body of the church (Lipscomb, op. cit. i, 388).

[81] *Ch. Bells of Bucks.* 549.

[82] Wrottesley, loc. cit.

[83] Ibid.

[84] *Pope Nich. Tax.* (Rec. Com.), 41b. This was exclusive of 6s. yearly paid to the priory.

[85] *Valor Eccl.* (Rec. Com.), iv, 235.

[86] Inst. Bks. (P.R.O.) ; Bacon, *Liber Regis.* 504.

[87] *Clergy List,* 1879.

[88] Ibid. 1889–1900.

[89] Ibid. 1901–5.

[90] Ibid. 1906–11.

[91] *Accts. and Papers,* 1903, l, no. 595.

QUAINTON with SHIPTON LEE

Chentone (xi cent.); Quinton (xiii cent.); Coynton, Qwenthon (xiv cent.).

Sibdone (xi cent.); Schibdone, La Lee (xiv cent.); Sibdon, Shibdon or Shipdon Lee (xviii cent.).

The parish of Quainton covers an area of 5,346 acres, including 452 acres of arable, 4,444 of permanent grass and 305 acres of woods and plantations.[1] The slope of the land gradually falls from 610 ft. above the ordnance datum on Quainton Hill in the north-east of the parish to 247 ft. near Binwell Lane Farm in the south-west. The soil is stiff clay, the subsoil loam and clay. There are old stone-pits to the north-east of Quainton Hill, from the summit

THE MARKET CROSS, QUAINTON

of which the view is said to extend over seventeen counties.

The large and scattered village of Quainton occupies a fairly central position in the parish. Approached from the south-east along the Vale of Aylesbury, the houses appear to be nestling among trees. A street leads from each angle of a large open oblong space on the highest ground in the village called the square. At its north end, near the centre, stand the remains of the market cross, dating probably from the 15th century, consisting of the lower part of an octagonal shaft with a square base elevated on three much worn steps. The house on Cross Farm, now owned by

Mr. M. J. Gibbs, bears the date 1723, and was built by Sir Robert Dormer,[2] apparently on the site of Quainton Farm-house, mentioned as Dormer property in 1639.[3] A short distance westward from the cross is the boundary mark on the causeway leading to Lee and Doddershall, at which by ancient custom the clergyman used to meet funerals from these hamlets.[4]

The rectory, to the north-west of the church, is a 16th-century building of two stories with attics, originally of L-shaped plan, but enlarged and refaced with brick in the 17th and 18th centuries. The original hall and kitchen, now the drawing room and study respectively, are in the east block, and the main staircase is at the back of the hall; the present entrance is in the south wing. The old hall has a panelled ceiling with moulded beams and 16th-century wall panelling, while the fireplace, which is flanked by 17th-century round-headed recesses, has an overmantel of re-used 16th-century work. At the north end of the hall is a moulded oak screen with linen-fold panels, dating from the beginning of the 16th century and said to have been brought here from the old manor-house; it has two late 16th-century doors, and above the panels is the inscription 'G de Neil' in fanciful characters, and the shields of Brudenell of Stoke Mandeville impaling Croke of Chilton, Brudenell impaling Englefield, Brudenell impaling another coat, Iwardby of Quainton impaling Brudenell, Pigott of Doddershall impaling Iwardby, Verney of Claydon impaling Iwardby, and Clifford impaling Iwardby, while between the first two letters of the inscription is a shield carried by a bird pierced with an arrow. Some of the other rooms have panelling of the 16th and 17th centuries, and the original kitchen has a wide fireplace, now partially blocked, to the south of which is an old winding staircase. The main staircase dates from the end of the 16th century and is of oak with square newels, flat shaped balusters and moulded handrails, the newels having moulded finials and pendants.

To the west of the churchyard are the Winwood almshouses, built in 1687, which form a picturesque row of eight cottages contained in one brick building. The roofs are gabled and the windows retain their leaded lights, while the chimneys are grouped into four stacks surmounted by diagonal shafts. Stone panels over the two north porches record the foundation by Richard son and heir of Sir Ralph Winwood,[5] principal Secretary of State to James I. Two of the chimney stacks have been rebuilt. The village contains a disused windmill and several 17th-century timber cottages, more or less restored, with tiled or thatched roofs. Upper South Farm, about a mile south-west, and a farm-house in Station Road, half a mile from the village, date from the same period.

There are Baptist and Primitive Methodist chapels. A mile south-west from the village is Quainton

---

[1] Statistics from Bd. of Agric. (1905).
[2] Lipscomb, *Hist. and Antiq. of Bucks.* i, 401.
[3] Chan. Inq. p.m. (Ser. 2), dcclxix, 54. On the death of Robert Dormer (see

Shipton Lee Manor), who was buried at Quainton in 1791, this property passed by the marriage of his sister and heir Mary to the Trelawny, afterwards the Trelawny-Brereton, family, who owned

it in the mid-19th century (Lipscomb, op. cit. i, 400-1).
[4] Lipscomb, op. cit. i, 401.
[5] P.C.C. 43 Exton.

Road station on the Metropolitan and Great Central joint railway.

The hamlet of Shipton Lee, a mile north-west from the village, was united to Quainton in 1886.[6] It comprises several farms. Lee Grange, formerly the manor-house of the Abbots of Thame and afterwards the residence of the Dormers, was taken down in the middle of the 18th century by John Dormer, when a large sum of money was found in a cavity in a beam.[7] Later in the century Grange House, now a farm, was built on the site,[8] but remains of the older building exist.

WINWOOD. *Argent a crosslet sable.*

The hamlet of Denham with its dairy farms is half a mile north-east from Quainton. The mansion erected on the site of the original manor-house of Dundon or Dundon Court[9] and inhabited by Richard Winwood and his widow Anne was partly taken down after her death, and the remainder converted early in the 18th century into the farm-house known as Denham Lodge.[10] It is a stone and brick building of about 1620, with later side wings, built on the site of the manor-house, and entirely surrounded by a moat, which was probably crossed by a draw-bridge at the spot where the old gate-house still stands to the south of the house. The moat is fed by springs from the hill behind the house called Church Hill, whence the foundation stones of the church, according to village tradition, were repeatedly removed by an unseen power to its present site. On Wood Hill, to the north-west, human remains were found in 1878.[11]

Doddershall House (Dodereshill or Dodereshull, xiii–xiv cent. ; Dodershill, xvi cent.), beautifully situated in a large park about 1½ miles west of Quainton, is the seat of Vice-Admiral William Harvey Pigott, and has been in his family for over 400 years. It is a two-storied brick building coated with roughcast, and was originally surrounded by a quadrangular moat, of which only fragments remain. The plan consists of a main block and north-east wing, built probably by Thomas Pigott, serjeant-at-law, about 1510, to which a south-west block containing some principal rooms and the main staircase was added late in the 17th century. A former north-west wing was destroyed after the death of Christobella Viscountess Saye and Sele in 1789,[12] and the house, which is now ⌐-shaped with the wings projecting north-west, has been somewhat altered and enlarged since that date.

The hall, which occupies the centre of the main block and has been subdivided, has an original panelled ceiling with moulded beams, and a moulded stone fireplace with a four-centred arch. Projecting from the south-east front is a fine early 16th-century chimney-stack with a rusticated panel above the eaves line and two octagonal shafts with moulded bases and capitals ; built into this chimney-stack and into the south front are several stones carved with heads and foliage. On the north side facing the courtyard is a gabled two-storied porch with a four-centred doorway. To the east of the hall is a 17th-century winding staircase with square newels, turned balusters, and moulded handrail. The apartment to the east of this, originally the kitchen, is now subdivided, and the present kitchen and offices are in the north-east wing. The main staircase is of oak with large panelled newels, twisted balusters, and heavy moulded handrails. Panelling of the 16th and 17th centuries, incorporating some 15th-century carving, has been refixed in the

THE RECTORY, QUAINTON

staircase hall, and there is some 15th-century tracery in the frieze and on the door, while the stair newels are ornamented with 17th-century figures and have finials formed from 15th-century poppy-heads halved and placed round a central nucleus ; it is supposed that this mediaeval woodwork came from the old church at Hogshaw. The fireplace has a 17th-century panelled overmantel, and on the panelling of the staircase are three shields of Pigott impaling Iwardby, while in the window glass is a quartered shield of Holt dated 1577. The arms of Pigott are represented on two wood shields on the south front of the house and in some fragments of old glass in the north-west window of the hall. The drawing room and room above are panelled, and there is a panelled overmantel in a first-floor room on the south-west. Two rain-water heads on the south-east are inscribed 'T.L. 1689.'

Doddershall Wood, a mile to the west of Doddershall House, extends into the parish of Grendon Under-

6 Loc. Govt. Bd. Order 19623. The hamlet formerly maintained its own poor.
7 Lipscomb, op. cit. i, 416.
8 Ibid.
9 Chan. Inq. p.m. (Ser. 2), ccclxxv', 99.
10 Lipscomb, op. cit. i, 403.
11 O.S. Bucks. (25 in.).
12 Lipscomb, op. cit. i, 411 ; *Gent. Mag.* lix (2), 764.

wood. Finemere Wood, in which there was formerly a hermitage and later a chapel, is situated in the north-west of the parish. Quainton Meadow, in the south-east, formed part of the race-course maintained during the late 17th and early 18th centuries by Thomas Earl of Wharton and by his son Philip.[13]

Dr. Richard Brett the Orientalist, and one of the translators of the Authorized Version of the Bible, was rector of this parish from 1595 until his death in 1637.[14] It was the birthplace in 1773 of George Lipscomb, the historian of Buckinghamshire,[15] whose parents were buried in the churchyard.

Quainton was inclosed in 1840, when provision was made for a recreation ground of between 3 and 4 acres.[16]

MANORS The land which afterwards became the vill of Quainton was assessed in 1086 at 10 hides. Of these, 7½ hides were held by Miles Crispin, the successor of Wigod of Wallingford, as one manor,[17] known as *QUAINTON* or *QUAINTON MALET*,[18] or later as *QUAINTON DUNDON* or *DUNDON alias DONINGTON*. It was held of the honour of Wallingford,[19] by the service of sending two armed men to Wallingford Castle in time of war, and paying the expenses of one for forty days and of the other for twenty[20]; in the 16th and 17th centuries it was attached to the honour of Ewelme.[21]

The lands of Miles Crispin in Quainton were held by Rowland Malet in 1162[22] and a few years later by his son[23] Hervey.[24] He or another of the same name represented the family in 1201,[25] and was living in 1224.[25a] Robert Malet had succeeded before 1234.[26] He or his successor Robert[27] was steward of Wallingford Castle in 1254,[28] and another Robert Malet, probably his son, held Quainton in 1284[29] and died seised of it about 1295.[30] His son Robert succeeding,[31] settled the manor in 1319 on Robert Malet, his son, his wife Isabel, and their issue.[32] In 1348 this manor was split up among co-heirs. William Beauvoir and his wife Alice and Robert atte Hull and his wife Joan were holding a half of two parts, with equal rights in the reversion of a third of a third held by Richard Talbot in right of his wife Joan, widow of John Malet. In that year their rights were purchased by Thomas de Missenden and his wife Isabel,[33] who also bought Richard Talbot's lands in Quainton[34] and came to an agreement with Thomas Lambin in respect of a half of two parts and two parts of a third of the manor.[35] Further conveyances were made to the Missendens of a third of the manor in 1351 by William de Heure and his wife Joan,[36] and in 1352 by Aylmer Fitz Warin and Isabel his wife,[37] and finally in 1356 of a half of two parts by John Poignant and his wife Alice.[38] The whole manor thus acquired

MALET. *Azure three scallops or.*

follows the same descent as that of Overbury in Great Missenden (q.v.) until the death in 1485 of John Iwardby,[39] whose widow Joan held it in 1525.[40] Owing to the death in 1509 of his second daughter Margery, first wife of Sir Ralph Verney, the reversion passed to their son Ralph,[41] who died seised in 1546.[42] On the death after 1559[43] of his widow Elizabeth it passed to his son Sir Edmund Verney, heir of his brother Edmund.[44] Sir Edmund died seised in 1600, having settled this manor on his wife Mary and his elder son Francis.[45] Francis Verney and his stepmother sold the Quainton estate in 1607 to Richard Abraham and others.[46] In 1615 Richard Abraham and his wife Judith, with Thomas and Mary Johnson, conveyed Quainton Dundon to Sir Ralph Winwood.[47] Richard Winwood succeeded his father in 1617,[48] and from the death of his mother in 1659 this manor descended with Ditton Park in Stoke Poges (q.v.) until 1718,[49] and afterwards with Chalvey[50] (q.v.). No other manor is mentioned in Quainton in 1840.[51] The present owner is George Godolphin Osborne, tenth Duke of Leeds.

A grant of free warren in Quainton was made to Thomas de Missenden in 1354.[52] The right of view of frankpledge with pleas and return of writs belonged to Richard Earl of Cornwall in 1254.[53] References to a mill occur in the 16th and 17th centuries.[54]

---

[13] Lipscomb, op. cit. i, 390. Lord Roos paid in 1696 £5 2s. 3d. for men and horses at Quainton and 2s. 6d. for music at the ra e (*MSS. of the Duke of Rutland* [Hist. MSS. Com.], iv, 557).

[14] M.I. in Quainton Church.

[15] *Dict. Nat. Biog.*

[16] Priv. Act, 3 & 4 Vict. cap. 15.

[17] *V.C.H. Bucks.* i, 261.

[18] This name has been found as late as 1630 (Feet of F. Bucks. Trin. 6 Chas. I).

[19] *Hund. R.* (Rec. Com.), i, 25; *Feu'. Aids*, i, 96; Chan. Inq. p.m. 2 Edw. IV, no. 10; Ct. R. (Gen. Ser.), portf. 212, no. 5, no. 7, m. 13; Chan. Inq. p.m. (Ser. 2), xliv, 91.

[20] Chan. Inq. p.m. 23 Edw. I, no. 53.

[21] Ct. R. (Gen. Ser.), portf. 212, no. 20, 21, 25; Chan. Inq. p.m. (Ser. 2), cxx, 4; ccclxxvi, 99.

[22] Kennet, *Paroch. Antiq.* i, 164.

[23] *Cal. Chart. in Bodl.* 13.

[24] Hearne, *Liber Niger* (ed. 1771), i, 186; *Red Bk. of Exch.* (Rolls Ser.), 310. A Hervey Malet gave 1 virgate of land in Quainton to Northampton Priory and 1 virgate to Wallingford Priory (*Hund. R.* [Rec. Com.], i, 24).

[25] *Rot. de Oblatis et Fin.* (Rec. Com.), 166.

[25a] *R. of Hugh of Wells* (Cant. and York Soc.), ii, 63.

[26] *Testa de Nevill* (Rec. Com.), 258. Roger de Wimbervill (ibid. 245, 251) and William Cervoise (ibid. 245) were tenants. The latter made an exchange of land with Robert Malet in 1250 (Feet of F. Bucks. East. 34 Hen. III, no. 5).

[27] *Hund. R.* (Rec. Com.), i, 25.

[28] Ibid. i, 43.   [29] *Feud. Aids*, i, 75.

[30] Chan. Inq. p.m. 23 Edw. I, no. 53.

[31] Ibid.; *Cal. Fine R.* 1272–1307, p. 354; *Abbrev. Rot. Orig.* (Rec. Com.), i, 88; *Feud. Aids*, i, 96, 113.

[32] Feet of F. case 18, file 71, no. 4; cf. file 72, no. 3.

[33] *Cal. Close*, 1346–9, p. 556; Feet of F. case 20, file 89, no. 16, 17; De Banco R. 355, m. 86, 140 d.

[34] *Cal. Close*, 1346–9, pp. 556, 558; De Banco R. 355, m. 86.

[35] De Banco R. 356, m. 332 d.; Feet of F. Bucks. Mich. 22 Edw. III, no. 22.

[36] Feet of F. case 20, file 90, no. 7.

[37] Ibid. case 20, file 91, no. 4.

[38] Ibid. file 93, no. 6.

[39] *V.C.H. Bucks.* ii, 349; See also Chan.

Misc. bdle. 49, file 2, no. 32; *Cal. Inq. p.m. Hen. VII*, i, 4.

[40] Chan. Inq. p.m. (Ser. 2), xliv, 91.

[41] Ibid.; M.I. in church.

[42] Ibid. lxxiv, 2.   [43] Ibid. cxx, 4.

[44] Ibid. He made a settlement regarding it in 1592 (Feet of F. Bucks. Trin. 34 Eliz.).

[45] Chan. Inq. p.m. (Ser. 2), cclxii, 126.

[46] Feet of F. Bucks. Trin. 4 Jas. I; Hil. 4 Jas. I; Recov. R. Trin. 4 Jas. I, m. 13; Mich. 5 Jas. I, m. 19; *Verney Memoirs*, i, 47.

[47] Feet of F. Bucks. Mich. 13 Jas. I.

[48] Chan. Inq. p.m. (Ser. 2), ccclxxvi, 99; Feet of F. Bucks. Trin. 6 Chas. I; Recov. R. East. 12 Chas. I, m. 6.

[49] *V.C.H. Bucks.* iii, 308; Chan. Decr. R. Div. iii, pt. i, no. 1645.

[50] *V.C.H. Bucks.* i.i, 316.

[51] Priv. Act, 3 & 4 Vict. cap. 15.

[52] Chart. R. 28 Edw. III, m. 3, no. 12.

[53] *Hund. R.* (Rec. Com.), i, 24; cf. Ct. R. (Gen. Ser.), portf. 212, no. 5; no. 7, m. 13; no. 20, 21, 25; Recov. R. Hil. 3 Anne, m. 228.

[54] Feet of F. Bucks. Trin. 34 Eliz.; Hil. 4 Jas. I; Recov. R. Trin. 6 Chas. I, m. 7; East. 12 Chas. I, m. 6.

The remaining 2½ hides in Quainton previously held by Azor, son of Toti, housecarl of King Edward, were held as one manor in 1086 of Hascoit Musard.[55] The overlordship remained attached to the Musard barony, the head of which was at first Miserden Castle in Gloucestershire,[56] and afterwards Staveley Castle, Derbyshire,[57] the last reference to it occurring in 1254.[58]

Eudo was Hascoit Musard's tenant in 1086.[59] In the middle 13th century the greater part of his land in Quainton was held by Geoffrey Neyrnut, the remainder in free alms by the Knights Hospitallers.[60] John Neyrnut had succeeded his father[61] before 1270[62] and the Knights Hospitallers claimed view of frankpledge in their land in Quainton and Donington in 1286.[63] Robert Malet, at his death about 1295, held the whole of this land partly of John Neyrnut for the rent of a clove pink at Christmas, partly of the Knights Hospitallers. No trace of the Neyrnuts in Quainton has been found after 1303,[64] and their land was apparently retained by the Malets and absorbed into their manor, but the land of the Hospitallers appears in 1525 as the manor of *QUAINTON*, later *QUAINTON VERNEYS*, when it was held of their manor of Hogshaw,[65] the overlordship being vested in the Crown in 1618.[66] It was settled in jointure in 1523 on Elizabeth widow of John Breton on her marriage with Sir Ralph Verney, who died in 1525.[67] On her death it reverted to his son Sir Ralph, and descended with the principal manor of Quainton (q.v.), retaining its distinctive name into the first quarter of the 19th century.[68]

SHIPTON, later *SHIPTON GRANGE* or *SHIPTON LEE MANOR*, before the Conquest was held by Boding the 'constable'; in 1086, when it was assessed at 7 hides, by Henry Ferrers.[69] Later it was held as one knight's fee of the honour of Tutbury,[70] which descended in the Ferrers, Earls of Derby,[71] and in the duchy of Lancaster.[72]

The Ferrers' land in Shipton was given by William Fitz Otho before 1146 to Thame Abbey, his brother Everard being the first abbot.[73] Shipton Lee remained with the abbey[74] until its surrender in 1539,[75] a lease for ninety-nine years having been granted in 1534 to Peter and Agnes Dormer.[76] In 1576 the manor was granted subject to the terms of this lease to John Dudley and John Ayscough,[77] and in 1609 to George Salter and John Williams.[78] The latter sold their estate in it in 1617 to Sir William Garaway,[79] who transferred it in 1622 to Sir Fleetwood Dormer, then holding the manor[80] as grandson of the original lessee.[81] He died seised in February 1638–9.[82] His son and successor John Dormer[83] made a settlement of Shipton Lee Manor in 1648[84] and in 1662, on the marriage of his son John,[85] who had been created baronet in the previous year.[86] John the son died at Leghorn in 1675, but was buried at Quainton.[87] The baronetcy became extinct on the death of his son and heir Sir William Dormer, bart., who was buried at Quainton in March 1725–6.[88] Shipton Lee passed by entail[89] to his uncle Sir Robert

DORMER. *Azure billety or a chief or with a demi-lion sable therein.*

Dormer, justice of the Common Pleas.[90] He also died in 1726, his only son Fleetwood, whose name occurs in settlements of the manor in 1717[91] and 1726,[92] having predeceased him by a few months.[93] Elizabeth, one of the daughters and co-heirs of Sir Robert Dormer, had married Sir John Fortescue-Aland, justice of the King's Bench, afterwards Lord Fortescue of Credan,[94] and the other co-heirs, Ricarda wife of John Parkhurst and Katherine Dormer, joined in confirming his title to the whole of the Shipton Lee estate in 1730.[95] John Dormer claimed it as next male heir in 1732, and obtained a judgement in his favour in 1740.[96] He died in 1747,[97] and his son Robert Dormer[98] sold the manor in 1764[99] to John Calcraft.[100] He died about 1772, when his heir was his son John,[1] who sold Shipton Lee Manor about 1786[2] to Thomas Quintin of Hatley St. George, Cambridgeshire,[3] and sheriff for

---

[55] *V.C.H. Bucks.* i, 272.

[56] *Cal. Close,* 1227–30, p. 359; *Testa de Nevill* (Rec. Com.), 19; Chan. Inq. p.m. Hen. III, file 40, no. 17.

[57] Chan. Inq. p.m. Hen. III, files 5, no. 18; 31, no. 16.

[58] *Hund. R.* loc. cit.

[59] *V.C.H. Bucks.* i, 272.

[60] *Hund. R.* loc. cit. Roger de Wimbervill and William Cervoise were tenants of the Knights Hospitallers in Quainton in 1235 (*Testa de Nevill* [Rec. Com.], 245).

[61] *Cal. Gen.* i, 170.

[62] Feet of F. case 16, file 41, no. 2.

[63] *Plac. de Quo Warr.* (Rec. Com.), 90.

[64] Feet of F. Bucks. Hil. 31 Edw. I, no. 2.

[65] Chan. Inq. p.m. (Ser. 2), xliv, 91.

[66] Ibid. ccclxxvi, 99.

[67] Ibid. xliv, 91.

[68] Recov. R. Mich. 5 Geo. IV, m. 44.

[69] *V.C.H. Bucks.* i, 265.

[70] *Hund. R.* (Rec. Com.), i, 24; *Feud. Aids,* i, 96, 121.

[71] G.E.C. *Complete Peerage,* iii, 64–7.

[72] *Feud. Aids,* v, 15; G.E.C. *Complete Peerage,* iii, 67; *Cal. Pat.* 1391–6, p. 112.

[73] *V.C.H. Oxon.* ii, 83, 84; cf. *Chart. R.* 11 Hen. III, pt. i, m. 26.

[74] *Hund. R.* (Rec. Com.), i, 24; *Feud.*

[Aids,] i, 96, 121; *Pope Nich. Tax.* (Rec. Com.), 46b; *Inq. Non.* (Rec. Com.), 338; *Valor Eccl.* (Rec. Com.), ii, 214. It was leased in 1388 to John Beck, who absconded for felony (*Cal. Pat.* 1391–6, p. 112), retained by the king on the finding of an inquisition in 1391 (Chan. Inq. p.m. 14 Ric. II, no. 98), and granted to John Verdon (*Cal. Pat.* 1388–92, p. 456). The abbey regained seisin in 1392 by bringing a suit of *scire facias* (ibid. 1391–6, p. 112).

[75] *V.C.H. Oxon.* ii, 85.

[76] Ld. Rev. Misc. Bks. clxxxviii, fol. 37; cxcvii, fol. 124.

[77] Pat. 18 Eliz. pt. xii, m. 21.

[78] Ibid. 7 Jas. I, pt. xvi, no. 1.

[79] Chan. Proc. (Ser. 2), bdle. 343, no. 3.

[80] Ibid.

[81] Lipscomb, op. cit. i, 415. His father, Peter Dormer, died in 1583 (Chan. Inq. p.m. [Ser. 2], ccx, 89), and his guardian during minority was John Chester (Ct. of Req. bdle. 31, no. 7). Shipton Lee was leased in 1606 to Sir William Borlase for seven years at a peppercorn rent (Feet of F. Bucks. Mich. 4 Jas. I).

[82] Chan. Inq. p.m. (Ser. 2), dcclxix, 54.

[83] Ibid.

[84] Feet of F. Div. Co. Hil. 23 Chas. I.

[85] Recov. R. Mich. 14 Chas. II, m. 17;

Com. Pleas Recov. R. Trin. 12 Geo. I, m. 3; cf. Chan. Proc. (Bridges Div.), bdle. 47, no. 14.

[86] G.E.C. *Baronetage,* iii, 223.

[87] Ibid.

[88] Lipscomb, op. cit. i, 416, quoting Quainton Reg.

[89] Com. Pleas Recov. R. Trin. 12 Geo. I, m. 3.

[90] *Dict. Nat. Biog.*

[91] Recov. R. Hil. 4 Geo. I, m. 46.

[92] Feet of F. Bucks. East. 12 Geo. I; Com. Pleas Recov. R. Trin. 12 Geo. I, m. 3.

[93] Musgrave, *Obit.* (Harl. Soc.), ii, 198; Monum. in the church tower.

[94] G.E.C. *Complete Peerage,* iii, 399; Feet of F. Bucks. Hil. 13 Geo. I.

[95] Feet of F. Bucks. East. 3 Geo. II.

[96] Lipscomb, loc. cit., quoting notes from Judge Fortescue's pocket-book; Recov. R. Trin. 14 & 15 Geo. II, m. 52.

[97] Musgrave, *Obit.* (Harl. Soc.), ii, 199.

[98] P.C.C. 308 Potter.

[99] Recov. R. Hil. 4 Geo. III, m. 181; Feet of F. Bucks. Hil. 5 Geo. III.

[100] Lipscomb, loc. cit.

[1] P.C.C. 288 Taverner.

[2] Recov. R. Mich. 27 Geo. III, m. 152.

[3] P.C.C. 160 Pitt.

that county in 1795.[4] He died in 1806,[5] and his son and heir John[6] in 1833.[7] He was succeeded by his only son Thomas Quintin,[8] owner of the family estates both in Hatley St. George and Shipton Lee in 1862.[9] The property now belongs to Corpus Christi College, Oxford.

The mill and the court of Shipton Lee are both named as pertaining to Thame Abbey in 1291,[10] and a grant of free warren was made to it in 1365.[11]

Four hides of land in 'Sortelai' (Sotelehe, xiii cent.)[12] were held in the time of Edward the Confessor by Wlward, a man of Queen Edith. She gave them in marriage with Wlward's daughter to Alsi,[13] who was holding them in 1086 as one manor,[14] called *DODDERSHALL MANOR* in 1286.[15] In the 12th century this land was held with 2 hides in Shipton as a knight's fee of the barony of Clifford,[16] to which Doddershall remained attached as late as the 14th century.[17] The overlordship was vested in the Crown in 1520,[18] but later in the century appertained to the Lees of Quarrendon[19] (q.v.), the last reference to it occurring in 1637.[20]

In the early 13th century Roger Cramford, who held Doddershall, agreed that Robert de Baskerville was to hold 1 hide of Roger and his heirs.[21] In 1208 Richard and Agnes Fitz Osbert quitclaimed to Roger Cramford the yearly rent due to them from half this land.[22] Roger was holding Doddershall in 1235,[23] but was succeeded before 1254 by Robert Cramford.[24] He or another of the same name was holding in 1284,[25] and was succeeded by his son Walter,[26] who was living in 1332.[27] Robert Cramford, who was holding Doddershall in 1346,[28] was alive in 1361.[29] William Cramford represented the family in 1429[30] and Richard Cramford later in the century.[31] Margaret, his widow, was to hold Doddershall Manor for life, and brought it to her second husband, John Goldwell.[32] He claimed over four years' rent after her death from her son Richard Cramford, who stated that his mother had surrendered the manor to him for an annuity.[33] The manor appears to have passed to Thomas Pigott

of Whaddon, serjeant-at-law, about 1495.[34] He died in February 1519–20, and his widow, Elizabeth, by marriage settlement held Doddershall Manor for her life with remainder to their son Thomas and other sons in fee-tail.[35] She died about 1549,[36] and Thomas Pigott settled the manor in 1551.[37] He was sheriff for the county in 1552 and 1557,[38] and died in 1559.[39] His son and heir Thomas Pigott[40] met with various difficulties in the settlement of his father's estate,[41] and in 1580 secured his title to Doddershall Manor.[42] He died in 1606,[43] and his son and successor, Sir Christopher Pigott,[44] was member of Parliament in 1604,[45] but expelled in 1606 for a violent speech against the Scots.[46] He died in 1613, and was succeeded by his brother Richard.[47] At his death in 1637 his heir was his son Richard,[48] afterwards Sir Richard Pigott, who died without issue and was buried in Quainton Church in 1685.[49] His wife Ann was also buried there in 1686,[50] and his nephew and heir Thomas Pigott in 1704.[51]

Thomas Pigott was the last of the Whaddon branch of the Pigott family, and his widow Lettice held Doddershall Manor[52] in dower until her death in 1735,[53] when John Pigott, second son of Robert Pigott of Chetwynd in Shropshire,[54] secured his title in law.[55] His will was proved in 1751 by his widow Christobella, upon whom he had settled Doddershall Manor for life,[56] and she survived her third husband, Richard last Viscount Saye and Sele.[57] On her death in 1789[58] this estate passed by

PIGOTT. *Ermine a fesse indented of three points sable.*

John Pigott's will to his nephew William Pigott,[59] who made a settlement of it in tail-male in 1794.[60] He died in 1802,[61] and the manor has descended in the direct line[62] to his great-grandson Vice-Admiral William Harvey Pigott,[63] the present owner.

[4] P.R.O. *List of Sheriffs*, 16.
[5] *Gent. Mag.* lxxvi (1), 186.
[6] P.C.C. 160 Pitt.
[7] Lipscomb, loc. cit.
[8] Ibid. By grandfather's settlement (P.C.C. 160 Pitt).
[9] Sheahan, *Hist. and Topog. of Bucks.* 420.
[10] *Pope Nich. Tax.* (Rec. Com.), 46b.
[11] Chart. R. 39 & 40 Edw. III, m. 7, no. 20; cf. Feet of F. Bucks. Hil. 21 Jas. I; East. 12 Geo. I; Hil. 5 Geo. III; Ld. Rev. Misc. Bks. clxxxviii, fol. 37–8; cxcvii, fol. 121–4.
[12] Southlee appeared as a place-name in Shipton Lee in a very ancient map extant in the middle of the 19th century (Lipscomb, op. cit. i, 417).
[13] *V.C.H. Bucks.* i, 275.
[14] Ibid. 274.
[15] *Abbrev. Plac.* (Rec. Com.), 211.
[16] Hunter, *Pedes Finium* (Rec. Com.), i, 243.
[17] *Testa de Nevill* (Rec. Com.), 261b; *Hund. R.* (Rec. Com.), i, 24; *Feud. Aids*, i, 76, 96. In 1254 John son of Niel claimed a hen at Christmas and six eggs at Easter from every house in Doddershall, the Lee and Quainton and some other places in the hundred (*Hund. R.* [Rec. Com.], i, 25).
[18] Chan. Inq. p.m. (Ser. 2), xxxv, 1.
[19] Ibid. cxxii, 11.

[20] Ibid. dccxlviii, 20.
[21] Hunter, loc. cit. Roger was the son of Beatrice sister of Agnes mother of Robert (Cur. Reg. R. 42, m. 2).
[22] Feet of F. Bucks. 10 John, no. 1. He was their sub-tenant for half the fee in 1205 (Cur. Reg. R. 42, m. 2).
[23] *Testa de Nevill* (Rec. Com.), 245, 258b.
[24] *Hund. R.* (Rec. Com.), i, 24.
[25] *Feud. Aids*, i, 76.
[26] *Abbrev. Plac.* (Rec. Com.), 211; *Feud. Aids*, i, 96, 113.
[27] Lay Subs. R. bdle. 242, no. 102a.
[28] *Feud. Aids*, i, 121.
[29] *Cal. Close*, 1360–4, p. 276.
[30] Feet of F. Bucks. Mich. 8 Hen. VI, no. 4.
[31] Early Chan. Proc. bdle. 204, no. 51.
[32] Ibid.
[33] Ibid.
[34] Leadam, *Dom. Incl.* 1517 (Royal Hist. Soc.), 162. Richard Cramford was connected with Doddershall in 1499 (Feet of F. case 22, file 128) and John Pigott was feoffee of the manor in 1501 (De Banco R. 957, m. 356).
[35] Chan. Inq. p.m. (Ser. 2), xxxv, 1; P.C.C. 26 Ayloffe. William son of Thomas Pigott and his first wife Agnes disputed this settlement (Early Chan. Proc. bdle. 554, no. 19), but apparently without success.
[36] P.C.C. F. 41 Populwell.

[37] Feet of F. Bucks. Hil. 4 Edw. VI; East. 5 Edw. VI.
[38] P.R.O. *List of Sheriffs*, 3.
[39] Chan. Inq. p.m. (Ser. 2), cxxii, 11.
[40] Ibid.
[41] Chan. Proc. (Ser. 2), bdles. 84, no. 58; 142, no. 68.
[42] Recov. R. East. 22 Eliz. m. 758.
[43] Chan. Inq. p.m. (Ser. 2), dccxlviii, 20.
[44] Ibid.
[45] *Ret. of Memb. of Parl.* i, 442.
[46] *Com. Journ.* i, 336, 344.
[47] Chan. Inq. p.m. (Ser. 2), dccxlviii, 20.
[48] Ibid. [49] M.I. [50] Ibid.
[51] Ibid. Reference to him in connexion with Doddershall (Feet of F. Bucks. Mich. 12 Will. III).
[52] Feet of F. Bucks. Mich. 6 Anne.
[53] Musgrave, *Obit.* (Harl. Soc.), v, 41.
[54] Lipscomb, op. cit. i, 409, quoting pedigree at Doddershall.
[55] Close, 9 Geo. II, pt. xvi, no. 3; Recov. R. Hil. 9 Geo. II, m. 225.
[56] P.C.C. 316 Busby.
[57] G.E.C. *Complete Peerage*, vii, 69.
[58] *Gent. Mag.* lix (2), 764.
[59] Com. Pleas Recov. R. Mich. 35 Geo. III, m. 67.
[60] Ibid. [61] *Gent. Mag.* lxxii (1), 467.
[62] Com. Pleas Recov. R. Trin. 57 Geo. III, m. 87; *Ret. of Owners of Land* 1873, *Bucks.* 16.
[63] Burke, *Landed Gentry* (1906).

References to the manorial courts occur in the 15th and 16th centuries.[64]

In 1086 Alsi also held 2 hides in Shipton which he had acquired by the same means as the 4 hides in Sortelai,[65] with which they were held later as Doddershall and Southlee[66] and Doddershall and La Lee.[67] They descended in the Cramford family, but were subinfeudated by Roger Cramford to Thame Abbey,[68] which held them of Richard Cramford in the middle of the 13th century.[69] They formed the estate known as the *LEE* or *LEE GRANGE*, which, descending with the abbey's manor of Shipton (q.v.), gave it the additional name of Lee.

One hide of land in Sortelai formerly held by two thegns, Brictric's men, was held in 1086 by Miles Crispin, and, under him, by two tenants.[70] This does not reappear in Quainton, and probably passed with Waddesdon Manor (q.v.), where Miles Crispin succeeded Brictric.

Alwin, a thegn of King Edward, held a hide of land in Shipton, which in 1086 formed part of the lands of William Peverel.[71] This evidently passed with Hogshaw Manor (q.v.) to the Knights Hospitallers, who in 1254 made an agreement with Thame Abbey for the mutual convenience of their tenants for pasturage in Shipton.[72] The Knights Hospitallers also held Quainton Verneys, and this estate probably amalgamated with it.

Henry II confirmed to Nutley Abbey the hermitage of Finemere, in Rowland Malet's fee of Quainton,[73] in 1162,[74] and his charter was confirmed in 1328.[75] Later in this century it is mentioned as one of the abbey holdings in connexion with which Bishop Bek appointed a commission of inquiry.[76] The abbey was dissolved in 1529,[77] and in 1535 4s. was paid in pension to the former abbot out of 20s. which went to Quainton Church yearly from offerings at Finemere Chapel.[78] The abbey lands in Quainton and Grendon Underwood were granted in fee in 1540 to Michael,[79] afterwards Sir Michael Dormer, who in 1543 obtained a licence to alienate them to Peter Dormer[80] of Shipton Lee Manor (q.v.), into which they were apparently absorbed.

CHURCH The church of *ST. MARY THE VIRGIN AND HOLY CROSS* consists of a chancel 43 ft. 6 in. by 19 ft. 6 in., north vestry, north chapel 26 ft. 6 in. by 12 ft., nave 61 ft. by 21 ft., north and south aisles each 7 ft. wide, south porch, and a west tower 13 ft. 6 in. by 13 ft. These measurements are all internal. The tower is faced with ashlar, but the rest of the building is of rubble. The nave and chancel roofs are tiled, the other roofs being lead-covered.

No part of the existing building appears to be earlier than the first half of the 14th century, to which date the nave and aisles belong. About 1353 the patrons, Thomas and Isabel de Missenden, proposed to make the church collegiate,[81] and with this end in view they probably rebuilt the chancel, lengthening it eastward, widening it on the north, and adding a vestry on this side. Considerable alterations were made in the 15th century, when the arcades were heightened and the clearstory added, and the west tower, north chapel and south porch were built. In 1877 it was found necessary to take down and rebuild the chancel and vestry, both the 14th-century nave aisles, and the south porch, the new walls being built on the old foundations and most of the old detail re-used. The nave arcades, which were leaning seriously, were at the same time brought back to the perpendicular and the clearstory was rebuilt. At the time of its demolition the chancel is said to have been in a very ruinous condition ; apparently it had been in part rebuilt in the 16th century, and almost every trace of the old windows had disappeared, but the doorway to the vestry and a piscina still remained *in situ*. The nave clearstory had been built or rebuilt in the 18th century, probably during a restoration of about 1772, vertically upon the leaning walls.[82]

All the chancel windows are modern. The original 14th-century doorway to the vestry, in the eastern half of the north wall, has a pointed head and moulded jambs, all scraped and retooled. A four-centred arch of the 15th century occupies most of the remainder of the wall. The chancel arch, which survived the reconstruction of the chancel about 1353, is of earlier 14th-century date than the vestry doorway. It springs from half-octagonal responds with moulded capitals and bases and is of two pointed orders ; in the north respond of the arch is a recess with a four-centred cinquefoiled head, probably the reredos of a nave altar.

The north or Winwood chapel is lighted from the north by two restored late 15th-century windows ; the eastern window has a four-centred head with tracery and is of three lights. The western window is similar, but almost round-headed. The doorway in the east wall, communicating with the vestry, and the arch to the aisle, are entirely modern, but the doorway to the churchyard at the north-west is of original 15th-century date, though renewed externally.

The nave arcades are each of five bays, with octagonal columns having moulded capitals and restored bases, and pointed arches of two orders. There are five square-headed clearstory windows on either side, each of two trefoiled lights.

A square-headed doorway, rebated for a door, opens from the north aisle to the rood-stairs, some of the steps of which remain. The three windows in the north wall of this aisle are of the 15th century and are each of three cinquefoiled lights under a square traceried head, but the westernmost has been almost wholly renewed. The pointed north doorway is of the original date of the aisle. A gallery was erected in this aisle in 1828.

The south aisle is lighted from the east by a two-light window with modern tracery, but original 14th-century inner jambs and rear-arch, and from the south by three much-restored square-headed 15th-

[64] Ct. R. (Gen. Ser.), portf. 212, no. 2, 5, 18, 20.
[65] *V.C.H. Bucks.* i, 275.
[66] Hunter, op. cit. i, 243.
[67] *Feud. Aids,* i, 113, 121. This vill was assessed at £28 8s. 2d. for the payment of one-fifteenth in 1322 (Lay Subs. R. bdle. 242, no. 102a).
[68] *Hund. R.* (Rec. Com.), i, 24. [69] Ibid.
[70] *V.C.H. Bucks.* i, 261.
[71] Ibid. 253.
[72] Feet of F. Bucks. Mich. 39 Hen. III, no. 14.
[73] Harl. Roll O. 26, no. 3.
[74] Kennet, op. cit. i, 164.
[75] Ibid. ii, 3.
[76] Linc. Epis. Reg. Memo. Bek, fol. 64.
[77] *V.C.H. Bucks.* i, 379.
[78] *Valor Eccl.* (Rec. Com.), iv, 235.
[79] *L. and P. Hen. VIII,* xvi, g. 379 (2).
[80] Ibid. xviii (2), g. 529 (30).
[81] See below under advowson.
[82] Report by Mr. William White, the architect, who was responsible for the restoration of 1877 (*Rec. of Bucks.* v, 26). In the east wall was formerly a medallion of Charles I (Lipscomb, op. cit. i, 428).

century windows, each of three lights with tracery. In the east jamb of the south-east window, the opening of which appears to be of the 14th century, is an angle piscina of that date with a sexfoiled basin and trefoiled ogee head. At the east end of the south wall is a second piscina, quite plain, with a similar basin. The pointed south doorway is contemporary with the aisle. The 15th-century porch has a pointed outer doorway and square-headed windows of three lights in the east and west walls. At the south-east corner is a 15th-century stoup with a round basin.

The tower is of three stages with a stair-turret at the south-west and western angle buttresses stopping midway between the second and third stages, above which are diagonal buttresses of slight projection. The walls of the tower are crowned by an embattled parapet, as are also those of the stair-turret, which rises above the tower parapet. In the west wall of the ground stage is a reset 14th-century window of two trefoiled ogee lights under a traceried and pointed head, and beneath it is a pointed doorway of the same date with elaborately moulded jambs. The tower arch is of three pointed and chamfered orders with plain responds. The intermediate stage is lighted by small loops on the north and west, and there is a similar loop on the south, now blocked. On all four sides of the bell-chamber are traceried 15th-century windows of two lights with pointed heads. There is a clock, a successor to one existing here in 1682.[83] The roofs are modern, but a few old timbers have been made use of in the aisle roofs.

The font is of the 15th century and has an octagonal bowl panelled on all sides but one. At the east end of the north aisle are fragments of a late 15th-century screen, comprising four panels with traceried heads, the mouldings being painted white and red, and the panels with figures of saints, each holding a book, upon backgrounds of brown and red sprinkled with roses. In the south aisle is an early 17th-century oak communion table, and upon it is a carved oak desk, bearing the date 1682 with the names of the churchwardens.

On the north wall of the chancel are placed five interesting brasses which were taken up from the floor when the church was restored. The earliest, which is undated, is probably of the mid-14th century and has a French inscription to Joan 'Plessi' with a demi-figure of a young girl with long hair. Next in date is a brass with a kneeling figure of John Lewys, rector of the parish, who died in 1422. A later rector, John Spence, who died in 1485, is commemorated by a brass with a marginal inscription and a figure in processional vestments. The two latest brasses are to Margery wife of Sir Ralph Verney and daughter of John Iwardby, who died in 1509, with figures of herself and her children (one son and three daughters) and two shields of arms, and to Richard son of Nicholas Iwardby, who died in 1510, with his figure in civil costume, and two shields of arms.

Against the north wall of the north aisle is a large and elaborate marble monument to Sir Richard Pigott of Doddershall, who died in 1685, and his wife Ann daughter of Sir Edward Harrington, who

died in the following year; later members of the same family are also commemorated. The monument was the work of I. Leoni, whose name is inscribed upon it. In front, included in the design, is a floor slab to Lettice daughter of the Hon. Thomas Cooke of Doddershall, who died in 1693. On the west wall is a monument commemorating Susan (Brawne) wife of Sir John Dormer of Lee Grange, Quainton, who died in March 1672–3, and her husband, who died in 1675. Richard Brett, who died in 1637, is commemorated by an elaborate monument of black marble and alabaster on the south wall of the south aisle, with kneeling figures of himself, his wife Alice (who erected the monument) and his sons and daughters. At the west end of the same aisle is a table tomb with recumbent effigies, erected by Anne Winwood, to Richard Winwood, who died in 1688, and Ann, daughter of Sir Thomas Read, his wife, who died in 1693. The inscription records that Richard Winwood, one of the deputy-lieutenants of the county in the reign of Charles II, was the son and heir of Sir Ralph Winwood, principal Secretary of State to Charles I. Elizabeth, Susan and Martha Rachael, daughters of Sir Gilbert Cornwall of Burford, Salop, nieces of Ann Winwood, are also commemorated upon the monument. Against the south wall of the tower is a large marble monument to Fleetwood Dormer of Lee Grange, who died in 1638, his son John, who died in 1679, and Fleetwood Dormer, who died in 1696. Against the opposite wall of the tower is a large and elaborate marble tomb, designed by Roubiliac, to Robert Dormer, a justice of the Court of Common Pleas, who died in 1726, Mary his wife, who died in 1728, and Fleetwood their son, who died in 1726. On the monument is represented the effigy of the judge in his robes with figures of his wife and son. Behind is an entablature supported by Corinthian pilasters, and in the tympanum is a shield with the Dormer arms. On the walls and floor are slabs to other members of the Dormer and Pigott families.

There is a ring of five bells: the treble inscribed 'Thinke no cost to much. H.K. 1621' (for Henry Knight); second, 'That you bestow of all. H.K. 1621'; third, 'To bring to pas. H.K. 1621'; and the fourth, 'So good a thing. H.K. 1621'; and the tenor, 'I. Eeles & W. Tomes Ch Wardnes 1745. T. Lester of London made me.' The inscription is incised, and it appears likely that the original inscription has been cut off. There is also a sanctus inscribed in small black letter 't e.'[84]

The plate includes a cup and cover paten of 1569, a flagon of 1669 and a paten of 1672, the two latter pieces given by Dame Ann Pigott.

The registers begin in 1599.

There is in the church a black-letter Bible recently restored. It bears the date 1658 on an embossed leather cover.

ADVOWSON   In 1223 Hervey Malet secured his claim to the advowson of Quainton Church against the Knights Hospitallers and Roger de Wimbervill.[85] It descended with the manor of Quainton Malet (q.v.), being valued at £20 in 1291[86] and at £31 6s. 8d. in

[83] Lipscomb, op. cit. i, 425.
[84] Probably for Thomas Eldridge, the first bell-founder of the Eldridge family, who is known to have cast bells in 1565

for Bray and Winkfield in Berks. and probably for Great Marlow in 1592 (A. H. Cocks, *Church Bells of Bucks.* 242, 552).
[85] Cur. Reg. R. 84, m. 20 d. He pre-

sented in 1224, when reference is made to the previous suit (*R. of Hugh of Wells* [Cant. and York. Soc.], ii, 63).
[86] *Pope Nich. Tax.* (Rec. Com.), 34.

QUAINTON: DENHAM LODGE

QUAINTON CHURCH FROM THE SOUTH-EAST

QUARRENDON: REMAINS OF CHAPEL OF ST. PETER

SHABINGTON CHURCH FROM THE NORTH-EAST

1535,[87] until the early 18th century,[88] when it was alienated by John Duke of Montagu.[89] Benjamin Alicock presented in 1732,[90] and soon afterwards the advowson belonged to the Elkins of Barton Seagrave, Northamptonshire,[91] and descended in that family or their assigns until after 1862.[92] After several transfers it was purchased about 1890 by the present owner, Captain H. Cautley.

In 1353 Thomas and Isabel de Missenden obtained a licence to endow a college of priests with a messuage and a carucate in Quainton and the advowson of the church and also to appropriate the church to the uses of the college,[93] but their purpose appears never to have been effected. An allotment for glebe to the rector was made in 1840.[94]

There was formerly a chapel at Shipton Lee, and Ingram Berenger endowed a chantry in it in 1312 with 2 virgates of land.[95] It appertained to Lee Grange and had been destroyed before the end of the 18th century.[96]

Shipton Lee was tithe-free in common with the other lands of Thame Abbey,[97] the Cistercian Order being freed from such payments in the early 13th century.[98] In the middle of the 19th century £8 yearly was paid from the hamlet of Denham to the rector of Quainton for exemption from tithes.[99]

CHARITIES The almshouses founded and endowed by will of Richard Winwood, dated 20 January 1686–7,[100] are administered under the provisions of a scheme of the Charity Commissioners of 14 October 1910. The trust estate consists of eight almshouses in Church Street, a farm at Quainton containing 156 acres let at £174 a year, other pieces of land containing 5 acres or thereabouts, and cottages and gardens producing about £40 a year, and £1,372 7s. 8d. consols, and £167 Metropolitan Railway 3½ per cent. stock arising from sales of land from time to time, and producing £40 2s. 10d. a year. The sums of stock are held by the official trustees, who also hold a sum of £315 16s. 9d. consols, derived under the will of Alice Bett, proved at London 13 June 1873, the annual dividends of which, amounting to £8 19s. 8d., are applicable in providing coal or warm clothing for the inmates. By the scheme the net income is applicable in providing stipends for the inmates at a rate of not more than 5s. a week, and any surplus may be applied in providing a nurse to attend the inmates, also any sick or infirm persons of the parish. Provision is also made in the scheme for the building of cottages out of surplus income to be let at a low rent, which is in course of being carried into effect.

Distributive Charities.—Matthew Nash, as recorded on a tablet in the church, by his will in 1667 devised certain properties at North End for the distribution of twelve sixpenny loaves to the poor of Quainton every Good Friday and 1s. to be given to the overseer for his trouble, and the same for the poor of Waddesdon and Westcott. The charge of 7s. yearly, being the share of Quainton, was redeemed in 1887 by the transfer to the official trustees of £11 16s. 8d. consols, now producing 5s. 8d. yearly, which is expended in the distribution of fourteen loaves to fourteen widows on Good Friday (see also under parish of Waddesdon).

In 1776 John Eeles charged his land in Quainton with forty sixpenny loaves for distribution at the church the Sunday after Christmas Day.

Mary Eeles, widow of the said John Eeles, by her will in 1777 gave £1 10s. yearly out of land in Quainton to be distributed in sixpenny loaves in the like manner.

It is understood that the owners of the lands charged provide a hundred sixpenny loaves in respect of these legacies.

Educational Charities.—It was recorded on tablets in the church that in 1692 Susannah Booth and Helen Plydwell gave £20 for educating poor children, which was laid out in land in 1724 ; also that in 1691 Patrick Symmer, rector, gave £50 for the same purpose, which was also invested in land. The endowment of these charities now consists of 11 a. 1 r. 11 p. let at £11 a year, which is applied for the benefit of the National school.

It was further recorded that in 1672 Dame Ann Pigott laid out £160 in land at Ambrosden, Oxfordshire, to educate children of Quainton and Grendon Underwood and buy them Bibles. The endowment consists of 7 acres called the Pix, comprised in deed 13 December 1678, which is let at £8 a year, one moiety of which is applied in each of the two parishes.

In 1704 Thomas Pigott by deed gave £300 for apprenticing poor children of Quainton and Grendon Underwood. The principal sum, with accumulations, is now represented by £484 2s. 2d. consols with the official trustees, producing £12 2s. yearly. The charity is regulated by a scheme of the Charity Commissioners of 4 September 1908, a moiety of the dividends being applied in each of the two parishes.

For the endowments of the charity of Christobella Viscountess Saye and Sele, founded by will dated in 1787, see under parish of Grendon Underwood.

Church Land or Bridge Land.—It was further recorded on a church tablet that a person unknown gave a parcel of land, now called Church Land, to repair the causeways and bridges leading to the church. The land comprises about 6 acres and is let at £6 a year, which is duly applied.

[87] Valor Eccl. (Rec. Com.), iv, 235.
[88] Particulars of various suits in 1313 and 1314 arising out of a disputed right to a third turn in the presentation granted to William of Eton by Juliane Malet, who was then holding one-third of the manor in dower, are given in De Banco R. 196, m. 162 d. ; 198, m. 2 d., 12 d., 180, 189 ; 199, m. 11 d., 19, 24, 128 ; 204, m. 34 d., 244 d. George Evelyn presented in 1691 (Inst. Bks. [P.R.O.]) by grant of Richard Winwood (Lipscomb, op. cit. i, 422). See also Cal. Pat. 1391–6, p. 505 ; 1396–9, pp. 12, 191.
[89] Lipscomb, op. cit. i, 419.
[90] Inst. Bks. (P.R.O.) ; Bacon, Liber Regis. 504.
[91] Lipscomb, loc. cit.
[92] Inst. Bks. (P.R.O.) ; Lysons, Mag. Brit. i (3), 623 ; Sheahan, op. cit. 420.
[93] Cal. Pat. 1350–4, p. 493.
[94] Priv. Act, 3 & 4 Vict. cap. 15.
[95] Cal. Pat. 1307–13, p. 511.
[96] Lysons, op. cit. i (3), 622.
[97] Lipscomb, op. cit. i, 414.
[98] Cal. of Papal Letters, i, 78.
[99] Lipscomb, op. cit. i, 405.
[100] P.C.C. 43 Exton.

QUARRENDON

Querndon (xiii, xiv cent.); Quoryndon (xiv cent.).

Quarrendon (or Quarrington) is a small and secluded parish with an area of 1,948 acres, of which 54 acres are arable ; practically all the remainder is permanent grass,[1] the grazing lands ranking as the finest in the county. The pasture known as Berryfield is named in the middle 17th century as letting for £800 yearly, the tenant not complaining of his bargain.[2] Quarrendon is situated in the Vale of Aylesbury, and the land varies in height only from 238 ft. above the ordnance datum on Akeman Street in the south-west of the parish to 290 ft. in the east. The subsoil is Kimmeridge Clay. The Metropolitan railway crosses the south-west corner of the parish. There is no village and the inhabitants are few in number ; as far back as 1636 Quarrendon is referred to as 'an ancient enclosure depopulated.'[2a]

The ruins of the church or chapel of St. Peter stand in a small field surrounded by an iron railing in the south-east of the parish.[3] The church, which dated from the latter half of the 13th century, consisted of a chancel, nave and north and south aisles, but the eastern part of the nave and the whole of the south aisle except two angle buttresses have been destroyed, while all that remains of the chancel is the north-east corner. The remaining part of the east wall of the chancel retains the north jamb of a 15th-century window and a stone corbel, and the north-east angle is supported by a diagonal buttress. The nave had on each side an arcade of three pointed arches of late 13th-century date, but only the westernmost bay on the north and the two western bays on the south now remain ; these have octagonal pillars and responds, moulded capitals, and labels with shield stops. In the west wall are the jambs and arch of a large 15th-century window. The north aisle, which is fairly complete with the exception of the east wall, has on the north two 14th-century square-headed windows, originally of two lights, but now wanting both mullions and tracery. The church was altered and decorated by Sir Henry Lee at the end of the 16th century,[4] but in the early part of the 19th century it was allowed to fall into decay.[5] The roof was taken to repair the farm-house and cottages near, and the beautiful Lee monuments, which were still extant, although much defaced, in 1817, had disappeared with the remaining fittings of the interior before the middle of the century.[6]

There are two moats of quadrangular form at Quarrendon,[7] one at Church Farm, a 17th-century house, the other at the site to the south of the ruined church. Here formerly stood the mansion of the Lees, where Sir Henry Lee entertained Queen Elizabeth for two days in 1592.[8] It was taken down in the early 18th century.[9] Upping's Farm, which is referred to in the middle 16th century,[10] is situated in the extreme north-east of the parish. The present house dates from the 17th century. Leland states that the well of St. Osyth, who is said to have been born at Quarrendon, stood between it and Aylesbury.[11] Quarrendon suffered severely in the great storm of 1570, when Sir Henry Lee is said to have lost 3,000 sheep besides a great number of cattle and horses.[12]

Some earthworks east of Church Farm are said to have been thrown up at the time of the Civil War.

BARONY The lands held in Buckinghamshire by the Fitz John (Fitz Geoffrey) family in the middle 13th century formed a barony with Quarrendon as its head.[13] Peter Carbonel of Mandeville's Manor, Addington, Thomas de Valognes of Botolph Claydon, in East Claydon, and Robert Passelewe of Swanbourne were tenants of this honour. At the death of Richard Fitz John in 1297 his lands were split up among his heirs : Maud Countess of Warwick, his eldest sister ; Robert Clifford, son of Isabel daughter of Isabel Vipont, his second sister ; Idonea daughter of Isabel Vipont ; Richard de Burgh Earl of Ulster, son of Aveline, his third sister ; and Joan widow of Theobald Butler, his fourth sister ;[14] and Quarrendon Honour does not reappear after this date.

FITZ JOHN. *Quarterly or and gules a border vair.*

MANOR Under Edward the Confessor Suen, one of Asgar's men, held QUARRENDON MANOR, but could not sell without his lord's consent.[15] In 1086 it was assessed at 10 hides, and was held of the king in chief by Geoffrey de Mandeville.[16] The overlordship follows the same descent as Amersham until the death of Humphrey last Earl of Hereford and Essex in 1373.[17] It evidently formed part of the inheritance of Mary Bohun, his younger daughter and co-heir,[18] and was brought by her in marriage to Henry Earl of Derby.[19] She died in 1394, and three years later her husband was created Duke of Hereford, a title which became merged in the Crown on his accession as Henry IV.[20] A reference to Henry V as his mother's heir occurs in 1421.[21] This accounts for the apparent inclusion of Quarrendon towards the end of the 15th century under the duchy of Lancaster.[22] Between 1499 and

---

[1] Statistics from Bd. of Agric. (1905).

[2] Fuller, *Worthies of Engl.* (ed. 1811), i, 133.

[2a] *Cal. S.P. Dom.* 1636-7, p. 110.

[3] Land for the churchyard was provided by Robert de Tinchebrai, whose charter was confirmed by Stephen and again in 1329 (*Cal. Chart. R.* 1327-41, p. 103).

[4] *Gent. Mag.* lxxxvii (2), 107, quoting epitaph then in the chancel.

[5] Ibid. 105-8, descriptive of the church in 1817. Views taken in 1815 are given between pp. 488 and 489.

[6] *Rec. of Bucks.* i, App. 8.

[7] *V.C.H. Bucks.* ii, 32.

[8] Nichols, *Progresses of Queen Eliz.* iii, 125.

[9] Lysons, *Mag. Brit.* i (3), 623.

[10] Chan. Inq. p.m. (Ser. 2), lxi, 25 ; cccclxxix, 97 ; Marcham, *Cat. of Bucks. Deeds,* i, 33.

[11] Leland, *Itin.* (ed. L. Toulmin Smith), ii, 111.

[12] Holinshed, *Chron.* iii, 1223.

[13] *Testa de Nevill* (Rec. Com.), 3, 245, 246.

[14] Chan. Inq. p.m. Edw. I, file 80, no. 6.

[15] *V.C.H. Bucks.* i, 259.

[16] Ibid.

[17] Ibid. iii, 146.

[18] Ibid.

[19] G.E.C. *Complete Peerage,* iv, 215.

[20] Ibid.

[21] *Cal. Pat.* 1416-22, p. 381.

[22] Mins. Accts. (Duchy of Lanc.), no. 10348, 10353. The tenure is stated as unknown to the jurors in 1401 (Chan. Inq. p.m. 2 Hen. IV, no. 58, m. 6) and 1446 (ibid. 24 Hen. VI, no. 43).

1512 it was held by lease from the Crown,[23] and afterwards in socage.[24]

The descent of Quarrendon Manor is the same as that of Amersham (q.v.) until 1232,[25] when temporary seisin of it was given to Roger de Dantes, second husband of Maud Countess of Essex.[26] She gave it to her half-brother John Fitz Geoffrey[27] about 1234,[28] and he later obtained a confirmation from her son Humphrey de Bohun.[29] The descent of the Fitz Geoffrey or Fitz John family has been traced under Whaddon[30] (q.v.), and in 1316 Robert Montalt was holding Quarrendon[31] and Whaddon in right of his wife Emma, widow of Richard Fitz John. In 1332, after Emma's death, Quarrendon passed to Thomas Beauchamp, Earl of Warwick,[32] to whose grandmother, Maud Countess of Warwick,[33] the reversion had been assigned in 1299 as eldest sister and co-heir of Richard Fitz John.[34] The descent of this manor then became identical with that of Hanslope (q.v.) until 1499, when a Crown lease of Quarrendon was granted to Richard Lee,[35] who had farmed the manor for several years,[36] and whose family had been connected with Quarrendon for a century.[37] He died soon afterwards, leaving instructions in his will to be buried in Quarrendon Church before the image of St. George, and his son[38] and successor Robert, afterwards Sir Robert Lee, on the death of his mother Joan,[39] obtained a grant of the manor in 1512.[40] He was sheriff for the county in 1534,[41] and died in 1539.[42] His son Anthony, who had been knighted in the previous year,[43] succeeded,[44] and on his death in 1549[45] was buried at Quarrendon.[46] He was succeeded by his son Henry,[47] later Sir Henry Lee, M.P. for the

LEE of Quarrendon.
Argent a fesse between three crescents sable.

county in 1558[48] and 1572,[49] and champion to Queen Elizabeth,[50] who gave him a confirmation of Quarrendon Manor in 1602.[51] He died without issue in 1611 and was succeeded by his cousin Henry Lee,[52] who was created a baronet in the same year.[53] He died in 1631, when his son and heir Francis Henry was a minor.[54] He had attained his majority in 1637[55] and died in 1639.[56] His son Henry had come into his inheritance[57] in 1657,[58] and died a year later.[59] His brother Francis Henry succeeding,[60] died in 1667.[61] His son and heir Sir Edward Lee, bart.,[62] was created Earl of Lichfield in 1674, with the second title of Viscount Quarrendon.[63] This manor remained in the earldom of Lichfield[64] until the death in 1776 of Robert, the last earl.[65] It then passed with the Lee estates to his niece Charlotte, widow of Henry Viscount Dillon.[66] She died in 1794,[67] and her son and heir Charles twelfth Viscount Dillon,[68] who had adopted the additional surname of Lee,[69] conveyed Quarrendon Manor in 1802 to James Du Pre.[70] His grandson Mr. William Baring Du Pre, M.P.,[71] is the present owner.

View of frankpledge[72] and free warren[73] were among the liberties appertaining to this manor. In 1276 John Fitz John, by virtue of a grant from Henry III, made a park at Quarrendon within the forest bounds.[74]

ADVOWSON

Most of the particulars relating to Quarrendon Church have been already given under Bierton, to which it was an appendant chapel in 1535.[75] It was included in the list for exemption from the payment of two-tenths in 1419.[76] Regular services ceased during the 18th century,[77] though the church was still used occasionally,[78] a burial taking place there as late as 1803.[79] The vicarage of Quarrendon is annexed to that of Bierton, and the Dean and Canons of Lincoln have been patrons of the living since 1266.[80]

The great tithes were commuted in 1847 for £555 yearly and leased to the lord of the manor by the

[23] Pat. 15 Hen. VII, pt. id.; *L. and P. Hen. VIII*, i, 3268.

[24] Pat. 4 Hen. VIII, pt. i, m. 19; Chan. Inq. p.m. (Ser. 2), xc, 2; cccxxii, 139; ccclxxix, 97; Pat. 44 Eliz. pt. iv, m. 22.

[25] *V.C.H. Bucks.* loc. cit.; Anct. D. (Duchy of Lanc.), L 1490.

[26] Close, 16 Hen. III, m. 8, 5.

[27] Add. MS. 28024, fol. 56a. Copy of the original charter, which is undated.

[28] A suit was pending in this year (*Cal. Close*, 1231–4, p. 550), and a grant of timber for building at Quarrendon was made by the king to John Fitz Geoffrey (ibid. 521).

[29] Anct. D. (Duchy of Lanc.), L 1579.

[30] See also *Testa de Nevill* (Rec. Com.), 245; *Hund. R.* (Rec. Com.), i, 28–43; *Feud. Aids*, i, 84; *Plac. de Quo Warr.* (Rec. Com.), 95.

[31] *Feud. Aids*, i, 114.

[32] *Cal. Close*, 1330–3, p. 429.

[33] G.E.C. *Complete Peerage*, viii, 56, 57.

[34] *Cal. Fine R.* i, 422; *Cal. Close*, 1330–3, p. 429.

[35] Pat. 15 Hen. VII, pt. id.; *L. and P. Hen. VIII*, i, 3268.

[36] Mins. Accts. Hen. VII, no. 24; (Duchy of Lanc.), no. 10353.

[37] *Rec. of Bucks.* i, 150, traced through the Court Rolls at Ditchley, Oxon. His father, Benet Lee, died in 1476 and left

him 'his place in Quarrendon' (P.C.C. 26 Wattys). See also *Gen.* (new ser.), viii, 226 et seq.

[38] P.C.C. 4 Moone.

[39] She held two-thirds of her husband's estate in Quarrendon for life (ibid.).

[40] Pat. 4 Hen. VIII, pt. i, m. 19.

[41] *L. and P. Hen. VIII*, vii, 80.

[42] Ibid. xiv (1), 388.

[43] Shaw, *Kts. of Engl.* ii, 51.

[44] Chan. Inq. p.m. (Ser. 2), lxi, 25.

[45] Ibid. xc, 2.

[46] *Gent. Mag.* lxxxvii (2), 107–8, quoting inscription as far as legible in 1817.

[47] Chan. Inq. p.m. (Ser. 2), xc, 2.

[48] *Ret. of Memb. of Parl.* i, 400.

[49] Ibid. 407.

[50] *Dict. Nat. Biog.*

[51] Pat. 44 Eliz. pt. iv, m. 22. There seems to have been some doubt as to the title (Recov. R. East. 25 Eliz. m. 93; Trin. 1 Jas. I, m. 21).

[52] Chan. Inq. p.m. (Ser. 2), cccxxii, 139.

[53] G.E.C. *Baronetage*, i, 78; cf. Recov. R. Mich. 13 Jas. I, m. 73.

[54] Chan. Inq. p.m. (Ser. 2), ccclxxix, 97.

[55] Recov. R. Trin. 13 Chas. I, m. 56; Feet of F. Div. Co. Trin. 13 Chas. I.

[56] Chan. Inq. p.m. (Ser. 2), dxii, 89.

[57] Ibid.

[58] Recov. R. Hil. 1657, m. 109.

[59] G.E.C. *Baronetage*, i, 78.

[60] Ibid.; Recov. R. Trin. 12 Chas. II, m. 120.

[61] G.E.C. loc. cit.

[62] Ibid.

[63] G.E.C. *Complete Peerage*, v, 75.

[64] Com. Pleas Recov. R. Mich. 6 Geo. I, m. 17; Recov. R. Mich. 6 Geo. I, m. 267.

[65] G.E.C. *Complete Peerage*, v, 76.

[66] Ibid. iii, 104.

[67] Musgrave, *Obit.* (Harl. Soc.), ii, 185.

[68] Recov. R. Hil. 39 Geo. III, m. 287.

[69] G.E.C. *Complete Peerage*, iii, 124.

[70] Feet of F. Bucks. Trin. 42 Geo. III.

[71] Burke, *Landed Gentry* (1906).

[72] *Hund. R.* (Rec. Com.), i, 28; *Plac. de Quo Warr.* (Rec. Com.), 95; Chan. Inq. p.m. Edw. III, file 11, no. 5; (Ser. 2), lxi, 25; xc, 2.

[73] *Hund. R.* (Rec. Com.), i, 43; Chart. R. 26 Edw. III, m. 10, no. 23 (special grant in 1352 to Thomas Beauchamp, Earl of Warwick).

[74] *Hund. R.* (Rec. Com.), i, 45.

[75] *V.C.H. Bucks.* ii, 326. See also *Pope Nich. Tax.* (Rec. Com.), 33.

[76] *Cal. Pat.* 1416–22, p. 179.

[77] Lysons, loc. cit.

[78] *Rec. of Bucks.* ii, 27, as proved by Bierton Regs.

[79] Ibid. i, App. 12.

[80] *V.C.H. Bucks.* ii, 326.

Dean and Canons of Lincoln,[81] who are also holders of the small tithes.

In 1392 John de Farnham, John Smith and John Herbert obtained a licence to endow a chantry in Quarrendon chapel.[82] The advowson of the chantry belonged to the lords of the manor.[83]

There do not appear to be any endowed charities subsisting in this parish.

SHABBINGTON

Sobintone (xi, xiv cent.) ; Shobindon (xv, xvi cent.).

The parish of Shabbington has an area of 1,637 acres, including 7 acres covered by water,[1] 305 acres of arable land and 1,296 acres of permanent grass.[2] The slope of the land varies between 237 ft. above the ordnance datum in the north-east and 190 ft. in the south of the parish, where it is divided from Oxfordshire by the River Thame. The soil is loam and clay, the subsoil clay, three-quarters of the area being pasture. The chief crops raised are wheat and beans. The west of the parish is marshy and in parts liable to floods. The village is situated towards the south of the parish and is very irregular. The Thame flows past the south-east end of the village, under a narrow bridge by the Old Fisherman Inn, on the road to Thame. The church stands beyond the inn to the north-west ; the vicarage, a modern building, stands to the north of the churchyard, and the school to the north-west of the cross-roads. There are two much altered early 17th-century timber-framed cottages. A Wesleyan chapel was built in 1864. The old manor-house is supposed to have stood in a field on the south of the churchyard, in which foundations of buildings and encaustic tiles have been dug up.[3] Manor Farm is about half a mile south-west from the village, and other farms lie to the north and west of it.

Before the Conquest the manor of *MANOR SHABBINGTON* was held by Wigod of Wallingford,[4] and by 1086 it had descended to Miles Crispin.[5] The overlordship remained in the honour of Wallingford,[6] and from the middle of the 16th century in that of Ewelme.[7]

Shabbington Manor represents the two knights' fees held by Alan de Valognes of the honour of Wallingford in the early 13th century.[8] In 1210 his brother and heir Robert paid 100 marks and two palfreys for livery of this land.[9] Thomas de Valognes had succeeded before 1234.[10] His heir was his daughter Joan wife of Robert de Grey,[11] who was holding in 1284.[12] He died in 1295,[13] and in 1299 his widow alienated Shabbington Manor in free alms to the Knights Hospitallers, of whom she afterwards held it for life.[14] On her death in 1312 it reverted to the Knights Hospitallers,[15] who held it[16] for some years, but in 1326–9 Joan's grandson and heir John de Grey[17] successfully disputed their right[18] on the ground that Thomas de Valognes had given it to Robert and Joan de Grey and their issue.[19] John de Grey, later Lord Grey of Rotherfield,[20] died in 1359 seised of the manor jointly with his son and heir John,[21] to whom the Knights Hospitallers released all right in 1360.[22] John died in 1375, and his son and successor Bartholomew[23] in the following year.[24] The other son Robert, fourth Lord Grey of Rotherfield, died without male issue in 1388.[25] In 1401 his only daughter Joan married John Lord Deyncourt,[26] and Shabbington Manor descended with Wooburn Deyncourt (q.v.) until 1474,[27] when it passed by a settlement made in 1466[28] to William Lovel, Lord Morley.[29] He released it in 1474, subject to a fee-farm rent of 50 marks (£33 6s. 8d.), to Richard Pigott and others,[30] who transferred it to other feoffees, of whom the principal was Richard Fowler, who died in 1477.[31] His son Richard, then a minor, was knighted in 1501,[32] and in 1507 settled the manor[33] and sold it in 1515 to John, later Sir John, Clerke,[34] the final transfer taking place

GREY of Rotherfield. *Barry argent and azure with the difference of a baston gules.*

---

[81] Sheahan, *Hist. and Topog. of Bucks.* 741.

[82] *Cal. Pat.* 1391–6, p. 160.

[83] Chan. Inq. p.m. Ric. II, file 266, m. 4 ; 24 Hen. VI, no. 43 ; *Cal. Pat.* 1446–52, p. 37.

[1] *Census Rep.* 1901, *Oxon.* 18. Shabbington comes under Thame in Oxfordshire for civil administration.

[2] Statistics from Bd. of Agric. (1905).

[3] Sheahan, *Hist. and Topog. of Bucks.* 425.

[4] *V.C.H. Bucks.* i, 261.

[5] Ibid.

[6] *Cal. Close,* 1227–31; p. 515 ; *Testa de Nevill* (Rec. Com.), 261 ; *Hund. R.* (Rec. Com.), i, 25 ; *Feud. Aids,* i, 94, 119 ; Mins. Accts. (Gen. Ser.), bdle. 1095, no. 3 ; Ct. R. (Gen. Ser.), portf. 212, no. 5, 7.

[7] Ct. R. (Gen. Ser.), portf. 212, no. 20, 21, 25.

[8] *Red Bk. of Exch.* (Rolls Ser.), 145.

[9] Pipe R. 12 John, m. 2 d.

[10] *Testa de Nevill* (Rec. Com.), 257b.

[11] Chan. Inq. p.m. Edw. II, file 29, no. 11 ; *Cal. Close,* 1307–13, p. 491.

[12] *Feud. Aids,* i, 84.

[13] *Cal. Fine R.* 1272–1307, p. 353.

[14] *Cal. Chart. R.* 1257–1300, p. 476 ; *Cal. Pat.* 1292–1301, p. 408 ; Chan. Inq. p.m. Edw. II, file 29, no. 11 ; *Cal. Close,* 1307–13, p. 491 ; Feet of F. Div. Co. Trin. 27 Edw. I, no. 45. A third was at this time still held in dower by Joan widow of Thomas de Valognes (Feet of F. case 285, file 24, no. 247).

[15] *Cal. Close,* 1307–13, p. 491.

[16] *Feud. Aids,* i, 114 ; Cott. MS. Nero, E vi, fol. 906.

[17] *Cal. Fine R.* 1307–19, p. 151.

[18] De Banco R. 264, m. 1 ; 275, m. 194 d.

[19] Ibid. 279, m. 18 d. The judgement also dispossessed Richard of Jarpenville and John Cok de Edrope, small holders in the manor (ibid. 274, m. 3).

[20] *G.E.C. Complete Peerage,* iv, 103 ; *Feud. Aids,* i, 119.

[21] Chan. Inq. p.m. Edw. III, file 143, no. 8 ; *Cal. Close,* 1354–60, p. 598.

[22] *Cal. Close,* 1360–4, pp. 123, 139.

[23] Chan. Inq. p.m. 49 Edw. III, pt. i, no. 59.

[24] *G.E.C. Complete Peerage,* iv, 104.

[25] Ibid.   [26] Ibid.

[27] *V.C.H. Bucks.* iii, 107–8.

[28] Feet of F. Div. Co. Trin. 6 Edw. IV, no. 39 ; Chan. Inq. p.m. 13 Edw. IV, no. 64.

[29] Chan. Inq. p.m. 13 Edw. IV, no. 64.

[30] Close, 14 Edw. IV, m. 25 ; Feet of F. Bucks. East. 14 Edw. IV. The fee farm remained in the family of Lord Morley till sold by Edward Parker, Lord Morley, to John Lacy (Com. Pleas D. Enr. 1360, m. 20 ; Feet of F. Bucks. Hil. 21 Eliz.). In the 17th century it was payable to the Savoy Hospital and later to the Crown (Lipscomb, op. cit. i, 446 ; *V.C.H. Lond.* i, 548 ; Close, 5 Geo. I, pt. x, no. 1).

[31] Chan. Inq. p.m. 17 Edw. IV, file 62, no. 6. He left to his widow Joan all household stuff, &c., except the cattle upon Shabbington Manor (P.C.C. 32 Wattys).

[32] Shaw, *Kts. of Engl.* i, 147.

[33] De Banco R. 979, m. 370 ; Feet of F. Bucks. Hil. 22 Hen. VII.

[34] Close, 7 Hen. VIII, no. 38.

in 1518.[35] Sir John Clerke died about 1540 [36] and his son and successor Nicholas [37] in 1551.[38] His heir William,[39] afterwards Sir William Clerke, inherited Hitcham Manor on the death of his mother in 1598, and the descent of Shabbington follows that of Hitcham (q.v.) until 1660,[40] when it was retained by Sir John Clerke, bart. Shabbington then became the principal seat of the Clerke family, and descended with the baronetcy until 1716,[41] when Sir John Clerke, great-grandson of the last-mentioned Sir John, sold it to Francis Heywood.[42] He was succeeded in 1739[43] by his son Francis, whose heir in 1747 was his brother William.[44] On his death in 1762 his sisters, Mary wife of John Wright,[45] and Elizabeth Fonnereau, widow, and their nephew John Crewe, purchaser of Bolesworth Castle, Cheshire, in 1763,[46] became joint owners.[47] By a settlement in 1788 Shabbington Manor became the sole property of John Crewe,[48] and on the death of his widow Elizabeth it passed to their son-in-law George, fourth Viscount Falmouth.[49] After his death in 1808 [50] the Shabbington estates were sold in lots.[51] The manor with some 446 acres was purchased in 1815 by William Beasley, and sold in 1827 to Edward Blount.[52] In 1830 he settled the manor on his son Walter Aston,[53] who succeeded his father in the middle of the 19th century.[54] His nephew, Sir Walter de Sodington Blount, bart.,[55] is the present owner.

A grant of view of frankpledge in Shabbington was made to the Knights Hospitallers in 1299.[56] When they lost the manor the right appears to have been resumed by the honour of Wallingford, whose officers held the courts for Shabbington and other vills in the 15th century at Ickford [57] and in the 16th century at Shabbington.[58] This right with court leet was granted to Sir William Clerke in 1619 [59] and included in the later transfers of the manors, a court leet being held by Mr. Edward Blount in October 1828.[60] A grant of free warren in Shabbington was made to

CLERKE, baronet.
Argent a bend gules between three roundels sable with three swans argent on the bend and a sinister quarter charged with a demi-ram argent and in the chief two fleurs-de-lis or and over all a baston or.

John de Grey in 1330.[61] There are various references to the water-mill [62] valued at 10s. yearly in 1086[63]; the site only is named in 1683.[64] It is noted in the Domesday Survey that 100 eels came from the fishery at Shabbington,[65] and fishing rights in the Thame have descended with the manor.[66]

An estate in Shabbington was conveyed in 1731 by Dame Katherine, widow of Sir William Clerke, her son Sir William and her daughters Elizabeth and Mary to Sarah Duchess of Marlborough.[67] It descended with the dukedom until the early 19th century, when it was sold by George Spencer-Churchill, the fourth duke, to William Rowland.[68] It has since remained in his family,[69] the Rev. W. C. Rowland being the present owner.

The property known as Shabbington Wood, which was transferred from Shabbington to Oakley for civil purposes in 1886,[70] was owned at his death in 1822 by John Atkins-Wright, a descendant in the female line of the Wrights, part owners of the manor in 1763.[71] It was shortly afterwards purchased by Mr. Joseph Henley, of Waterperry House, Oxfordshire,[72] and his son, the Rt. Hon. Joseph Warner Henley, owned it in 1862.[73] It is now held in trust for Commander J. Henley, R.N.

The church of *ST. MARY MAGDALENE* consists of a chancel measuring internally 21 ft. by 16 ft. 6 in., nave 43 ft. by 22 ft. 6 in., north porch and a west tower 11 ft. 6 in. by 10 ft. 6 in.

The walls of the nave and chancel, which are of rubble incorporating herring-bone work, are partly of late 11th-century date, but no contemporary detail survives, new windows and doorways having been inserted in the 14th century, when the chancel arch was rebuilt, while the west tower was added in the succeeding century. The north porch is a modern addition. The church was restored in 1882.

The chancel is lighted from the east by a three-light window with cusped intersecting tracery, and from the north by a two-light window with flowing tracery, to the west of which is a small square-headed

BLOUNT, baronet.
Barry wavy or and sable.

[35] Feet of F. Bucks. Mich. 10 Hen. VIII.
[36] Exch. Inq. p.m. (Ser. 2), file 33, no. 4.
[37] Ibid.; Close, 32–6 Hen. VIII, m. 9, no. 9. In 1542 Sir John Williams was holding a sixty years' lease of this manor (Harl. Chart. 80, I 35).
[38] V.C.H. Bucks. iii, 232.
[39] Harl. Chart. 79, G 29. He took various steps to secure his title in 1570 (ibid. E 40; 80, I 40; 77, G 11; 75, H 15; Recov. R. Trin. 12 Eliz. m. 519).
[40] V.C.H. Bucks. iii, 232–3. See also Feet of F. Bucks. Hil. 1 Chas. I; East. 22 Chas. I.
[41] G.E.C. Baronetage, iii, 80; Recov. R. East. 35 Chas. II, m. 175.
[42] Recov. R. Trin. 2 Geo. I, m. 86; Close, 3 Geo. I, pt. x, no. 1; Feet of F. Bucks. Hil. 3 Geo. I; East. 3 Geo. I.
[43] Musgrave, Obit. (Harl. Soc.), iii, 208.
[44] P.C.C. 97 Potter.
[45] Feet of F. Bucks. Trin. 2 Geo. III.
[46] Ormerod, Hist. of Cheshire, ii, 678.

[47] Lipscomb, Hist. and Antiq. of Bucks. i, 447.
[48] Ibid.
[49] Lysons, Mag. Brit. i (3), 628. He married Elizabeth Anne Crewe in 1784 at St. George's, Hanover Square (Reg. Mar. of St. George's, Hanover Sq. [Harl. Soc.], 362). Her will was proved in 1794 (P.C.C. 138 Holman).
[50] G.E.C. Complete Peerage, iii, 314.
[51] Lipscomb, op. cit. i, 448.
[52] Ibid.
[53] Recov. R. East. 11 Geo. IV, m. 133; Com. Pleas Recov. R. Trin. 11 Geo. IV, m. 133.
[54] Sheahan, Hist. and Topog. of Bucks. 425.
[55] Walford, Co. Families (1912). His mother Mary married her cousin, the eighth baronet.
[56] Cal. Chart. R. 1257–1300, pp. 476–7.
[57] Ct. R. (Gen. Ser.), portf. 212, no. 7, m. 14.
[58] Ibid. no. 19, 20.

[59] Pat. 16 Jas. I, pt. ix, no. 3.
[60] Lipscomb, op. cit. i, 448.
[61] Chart. R. 4 Edw. III, m. 18, no. 44.
[62] Chan. Inq. p.m. Edw. II, file 29, no. 11; Feet of F. Bucks. Hil. 22 Hen. VII; Mich. 10 Hen. VIII; Ct. R. (Gen. Ser.), portf. 212, no. 19.
[63] V.C.H. Bucks. i, 261.
[64] Recov. R. East. 35 Chas. II, m. 175.
[65] V.C.H. Bucks. loc. cit.
[66] Chan. Inq. p.m. Edw. II, file 29, no. 11; Feet of F. Bucks. Mich. 10 Hen. VIII; Hil. 3 Geo. I; Close, 3 Geo. I, pt. x, no. 1; Recov. R. East. 11 Geo. IV, m. 133.
[67] Close, 5 Geo. II, pt. vii, no. 8.
[68] Lipscomb, op. cit. i, 449, quoting from deeds at Woodstock.
[69] Sheahan, loc. cit.; Ret. of Owners of Land, 1873, Bucks. 17.
[70] Local Govt. Bd. Order, no. 19618.
[71] Lipscomb, op. cit. i, 448.
[72] Ibid.
[73] Sheahan, loc. cit.

low-side window with a modern shutter. The two windows on the south are each of two lights, the eastern window having flowing tracery, while the western has a plain spandrel in the head. Except the low-side window, all have pointed heads and date from about the middle of the 14th century. On the south, in the usual position, is a 15th-century piscina with a cinquefoiled head and stone shelf, and in the east wall is some badly formed arcading of uncertain date. The pointed chancel arch, which is of two continuous orders, is of the same date as the windows.

The nave has been so much restored that the details, though incorporating fragments of the old work, which are of 14th-century character, are practically modern. There are north and south pointed doorways, each between two windows of two lights. The jamb shafts of the north-east window are old, and some 12th-century stones have been used in the relieving arch of the south doorway. To the east of the north-east window the east jamb of the doorway to the rood-stairs can be traced. The roof is of the 15th century, and has trusses of the queen-post type with moulded wall plates ; the narrower eastern bay, which was over the rood-loft, is ceiled with boards below the level of the western bays, and is treated with greater elaboration. The modern north porch has a pointed entrance arch and open sides. Reset in its west wall is an early 14th-century coffin-lid with a marginal inscription in Norman French, now nearly indecipherable, but apparently commemorating one Isobel de Swell.

The tower, which is covered with ivy, so that much of its detail is hidden, is of the 15th century, apparently without external divisions, and is crowned by an embattled parapet. It has a stair-turret at the south-west angle, and has been strengthened by massive western buttresses at some time subsequent to the date of its erection. In the ground stage is a pointed west window of three lights with a traceried head, and beneath it a pointed doorway of two continuous orders. The tower arch is pointed and has plain jambs, into which its two orders die. The intermediate stage has small square-headed windows, and on the north side is a clock dial. The bell-chamber is lighted by square-headed windows of two plain lights, and the stair-turret has small quatrefoil lights. In each side wall of the tower is a shallow square-headed niche with a projecting sill.

The font is probably mediaeval, but has been so scraped that it is impossible to date it with certainty. The bowl is plain and octagonal, and stands upon a tapering stem. The pulpit bears the date 1626, and is hexagonal in plan with moulded panels. A tablet on the west wall of the chancel commemorating Sir William Clerke, bart., who died in 1678, is the only monument of interest, but there are 18th-century slabs to members of the Spencer and Burnard families.

There is a ring of six bells, the treble by Mears & Stainbank, London, 1881, and the others by Abraham Rudhall of Gloucester, 1718. There is also a small bell bearing the date 1794, probably by Thomas Mears.[74]

The plate includes a cup and cover-paten of 1683 and a flagon of 1758.

The registers begin in 1715.

ADVOWSON A vicarage was ordained in Shabbington in 1221, the advowson and the rectory then belonging to Wallingford Priory,[75] by whom it was retained[76] until its dissolution in 1525.[77] Both advowson and rectory, with a hide of land in Shabbington, were granted by the Crown in 1528 to Cardinal Wolsey,[78] the advowson only in 1532 to trustees for St. George's Chapel, Windsor,[79] and both in 1541 to Sir John Williams.[80] He at once transferred the property to William Burt, the tenant, reserving the advowson.[81] This was afterwards acquired by the Burts or the Tippings. Agnes Burt, niece and eventual heir of William Burt, married William Tipping, and their son Thomas inherited the Shabbington property.[82] He appears to have given it with the advowson to his second son Bartholomew,[83] who made a settlement of both in 1610[84] and a later detailed settlement in 1620,[85] cited in the inquisition after his death in 1632.[86] His sons Thomas and John Tipping[87] appear to have given up their interests in favour of their nephew Bartholomew[88] in 1646,[89] and he also acquired his father's claim in 1654.[90] His elder brother John[91] owned the advowson in 1688.[92] His widow, or the widow of his son Bartholomew, Prudence Tipping, presented to Shabbington in 1728 and 1736,[93] but the advowson had descended to John's grandson or great-grandson Bartholomew Tipping[94] before 1768.[95] His son Bartholomew succeeded in 1775,[96] presented to Shabbington in 1777 and 1782,[97] and died unmarried in 1798.[98] His heir was his niece Mary Anne,[99] wife of the Rev. Philip Wroughton.[100] She survived her husband many years and died in 1841.[1] The advowson of Shabbington remained in her family,[2] but was purchased about 1882 by the Rev. A. F. Q. Bros, who has been vicar of Shabbington from 1892, and is the present owner.

CHARITY William Burnard, by his will proved in the P.C.C. 13 August 1828, bequeathed £100 consols, the interest to be applied in the distribution of woollen clothes on 24 December yearly. The stock is held by the official trustees, the annual dividends of £2 10s. being duly applied.

[74] A. H. Cocks, *Church Bells of Bucks.* 560.

[75] *Reg. of Hugh of Wells* (Cant. and Yorks Soc.), ii, 49. It was valued at £8 in 1291 (*Pope Nich. Tax.* [Rec. Com.], 34). It had risen in value to £11 in 1535 (*Valor Eccl.* [Rec. Com.], iv, 235).

[76] It obtained a confirmation of the appropriation in 1320 (Coxe and Turner, *Cal. Chart. in Bodl.* 14).

[77] *Cat. of Anct. D.* ii, 165 ; Chan. Inq. p.m. (Ser. 2), v, 76, m. 4 ; Bacon, *Liber Reg.* 504.

[78] *L. and P. Hen. VIII,* iv (2), 4471.

[79] Ibid. v, 1351.

[80] Ibid. xvi, g. 779 (2).

[81] Close, 33 Hen. VIII, pt. iii, no. 7.

[82] Wroughton MSS. Woolley, 38.

[83] Ibid.; *Visit. of Oxon.* (Harl. Soc.), 274.

[84] Feet of F. Div. Co. Mich. 8 Jas. I.

[85] Recov. R. Trin. 18 Jas. I, m. 54.

[86] Chan. Inq. p.m. (Ser. 2), cccclxxxix, 134.

[87] Ibid.

[88] His father Bartholomew was the second son (*Visit. of Oxon.* loc. cit. ; *Gen.* vi, 99).

[89] Feet of F. Div. Co. Hil. 22 Chas. I.

[90] Ibid. Bucks. Trin. 1654.

[91] *Visit. of Oxon.* loc. cit. ; *Gen.* vi, 99.

[92] Inst. Bks. (P.R.O.).

[93] Ibid.

[94] Lipscomb, op. cit. i, 451.

[95] Inst. Bks. (P.R.O.).

[96] Lipscomb, loc. cit.

[97] Inst. Bks. (P.R.O.).

[98] Lipscomb, loc. cit.

[99] Burke, *Landed Gentry* (1906).

[100] P.C.C. 151 Howe.

[1] Burke, *Landed Gentry* (1906).

[2] Sheahan, op. cit. 426.

TOWERSEY

Eie (xi cent.) ; Toureseye (xiii cent.).

Towersey is a parish on the borders of Oxfordshire with an area of 1,380 acres, including 320 acres of arable land and 911 of permanent grass.[1] The slope of the land is from the south-east (271 ft. above the ordnance datum) to the north-west (219 ft.). The soil is strong loam, the subsoil gravel, clay, and limestone, the chief crops being wheat, beans, barley, clover and grasses. The Wycombe, Thame, and Oxford branch of the Great Western railway runs through the south of the parish from south-east to north-west.

The village is situated on the Thame Road in the west of the parish. There are many 16th and 17th-century half-timbered houses, several of which have thatched roofs. The church stands at the west of

belonging to Thame Abbey, is a 16th-century half-timber house with brick nogging, altered and enlarged. Attached to it is the ancient tithe barn probably built about 1500. It is a stone building of five bays with aisles having original blocked doorways, on the jambs of one of which are three sundials. The roof, which is a fine specimen of its kind, is supported by two rows of oak posts. Upper Green Farm and Lower Green Farm are both 17th-century houses with thatched roofs. There is a Baptist chapel in the village, and in the north-west of the parish is a windmill.

The parish was inclosed in 1822.[2]

MANORS Before the Conquest seven of King Edward's thegns held *EYE MANOR*.[3] In 1086 it was assessed at 9 hides 1 virgate

TOWERSEY VILLAGE

the village, with the vicarage, built in 1845, on the north-west and the school on the south-west. At the side of the road on the south of the church are the remains of the village stocks. The 16th-century house known as the Church Farm, to the north of the church, may represent the old manor-house. It is a timber-framed building, much altered, and the portion which contained the hall is now a ruin. The present manor-house, at the other end of the village, was built in the Italian style by Mr. Edward Griffin in 1858. In 1899 it was sold by Mr. J. Whitehouse Griffin, to the Hon. Paulyn F. C. Rawdon Hastings, by whom it was largely rebuilt and sold in 1911 to Mr. G. J. C. Harter. It has since then been unoccupied. The Grange Farm, probably on the site of the grange

among the lands of Niel Daubeny,[4] and was attached to his barony of Cainhoe, Bedfordshire.[5]

Niel Wast was sub-tenant in Eye in 1086,[6] and by the middle of the 13th century Ralph Pirot was holding the mesne lordship in Towersey,[7] which continued in his family[8] and was still held by his descendant, another Ralph Pirot, in 1337.[9] No later reference to it has been found.

In the middle of the 13th century Richard, son of Robert Towers (de Tours), probably a descendant of John Towers, whose name occurs in the late 12th century,[10] was holding the greater part of Eye Manor[11] corresponding to land which was afterwards distinguished by the name of this family as *TOWERSEY MANOR*. He and his descendants bearing the same

[1] Statistics from Bd. of Agric. (1905).
[2] Priv. Act, 3 Geo. IV, cap. 14.
[3] *V.C.H. Bucks.* i, 268.
[4] Ibid.
[5] *Liber Niger* (ed. 1771), i, 202. Evidently included in Ralph Pirot's five fees

(*Testa de Nevill* [Rec. Com.], 250*b*). For the descent of this barony see *V.C.H. Beds.* ii, 324.
[6] *V.C.H. Bucks.* loc. cit.
[7] *Testa de Nevill* (Rec. Com.), 250*b*.
[8] *Hund. R.* (Rec. Com.), i, 25 ; *Feud.*

Aids, i, 94. Ralph Pipard was holding in 1284, apparently as guardian of an heir of the Pirots (ibid. 84).
[9] Inq. a.q.d. file 240, no. 5.
[10] Add. Chart. 20376.
[11] *Testa de Nevill* (Rec. Com.), 250*b*.

name were holding later in the century,[12] and in 1302[13] and 1316.[14] Richard Towers was living in 1329[15] and died before 1337 when his son Richard granted the reversion of a third of Towersey Manor then held in dower by his father's widow Agnes, and of lands in Towersey held for life by Henry Towers, to Thame Abbey.[16] At the same time this abbey also received a grant of the remaining two-thirds of this manor from Edmund de Berford.[17] A rent-charge on the manor of £10 yearly was surrendered by Richard Towers' wife Agnes and his daughter Elizabeth and her husband Richard de Leming in 1338.[18] Towersey Manor remained with Thame Abbey, which received a grant of free-warren there in 1365,[19] until the Dissolution.[20] In 1542 it was granted to the Dean and Chapter of the cathedral of Christ and St. Mary, Oxford,[21] and afterwards in 1545 to Christopher Edmunds and others[22] with rights in the manor extending into Oxfordshire. It was afterwards apparently acquired by Sir John Williams, Lord Williams of Thame,[23] and was conveyed in 1566[24] by Daniel Snow to Edward Lord Windsor.[25] Towersey Manor descended with Bradenham[25] (q.v.) to Thomas, Viscount Wentworth,[27] who sold it in 1788 to George Bowden of Radford, Oxfordshire.[28] His son George who succeeded in 1791[29] left three daughters Mary Elizabeth, Elizabeth, and Anne Frances,[30] who were ladies of the manor in 1822.[31] About the middle of the 19th century it was purchased by Mr. Edward Griffin,[32] who died in 1879.[33] His son and successor, Mr. James Whitehouse Griffin,[34] is the present owner of Towersey Manor.

The remainder of the Domesday Eye Manor estate corresponding to that part of the vill of Towersey called *LITTLE EYE* was held of Ralph Pirot in 1254 by John de Morton.[35] In 1265 he, with his wife Sarah, alienated this estate in free alms to Thame Abbey, for the service of a pair of white gauntlets or 1d. at Easter.[36] This abbey continued to hold Little Eye,[37] which is not distinguishable from the principal manor in Towersey after 1346.[38]

THAME ABBEY. *Sable a chief argent with two croziers.*

The 11 hides at which Towersey was assessed in 1254 comprised, besides the Domesday Eye Manor, an estate of 7 virgates,[39] apparently part of one of Gilbert Pinkney's fees in Buckinghamshire and held of him in 1166 by Robert de Wauci.[40] In 1254 Muriel de Weston held it in socage and by the service of 20s. yearly for ward of Windsor Castle of Robert's descendant, Robert de Wauci.[41] Henry de Weston, probably her son, granted it in 1275 to Thame Abbey,[42] when it became absorbed in the principal manor.

A small estate called *BRITTONS MANOR* appears in Towersey in the later 16th century, when it was held of the President and scholars of Magdalen College, Oxford.[43] In 1564 Nicholas and Alice Collingridge conveyed it to John Goodwin[44] and Richard Belson died seised of it in 1569.[45] His wife Elizabeth held it for life and was alive in 1575, when her eldest son Bartholomew died.[46] Thomas Belson, another son, claimed it in 1585 against his elder brother Augustine under their father's will[47] and obtained judgement in 1586.[48]

In 1623 John, Thomas and Richard Porter with Mary and Robert Whitfield surrendered their interests in Brittons Manor to John Harman and his heirs.[49] John Harman of Towersey, deceased, is mentioned in 1646,[50] but the later descent has not been traced.

A small estate in Towersey called in the later 16th century *PARAGE MANOR* corresponds to the property conveyed in 1341 by Walter, son of William Audlaf of Stoke, to Edmund Parage and his wife Agnes.[51] This property reappears in 1577 when Parage Manor was conveyed by Francis and Katherine Bertie to William Fleetwood and John White,[52] but no other reference to it has been found.

The church of *ST. CATHERINE CHURCH* consists of a chancel measuring internally 17 ft. 6 in. by 13 ft., nave 56 ft. by 24 ft. with north transeptal recess 12 ft. wide by 4 ft. deep, and south tower; it is built of rubble with tiled roofs.

The chancel dates from the early 13th century and the nave from about the middle of the 14th century. The tower added in 1854 replaced a 14th-century porch, the archway of which was re-used in the lower stage. The church was restored in 1850 and again in 1877.

---

[12] *Hund. R.* (Rec. Com.), i, 25 ; *Feud. Aids,* i, 84.
[13] *Feud. Aids,* i, 94.
[14] Ibid. 114.
[15] Feet of F. Bucks. Trin. 3 Edw. III, no. 7. Other deeds in reference to settlements between him and his wife Agnes and the Thomas of Aylesbury mentioned in this fine are Feet of F. Bucks. East. 18 Edw. II, no. 7 ; Trin. 1 Edw. III, no. 6 ; De Banco R. 269, m. 79. Agnes was living in 1340 (Feet of F. Bucks. East. 14 Edw. III, no. 5).
[16] Inq. a.q.d. file 240, no. 5 ; *Cal. Pat.* 1334–8, p. 491.
[17] Ibid. ; Feet of F. Bucks. case 19, file 81, no. 6.
[18] *Cal. Pat.* 1338–40, p. 92 ; Feet of F. case 19, file 82, no. 16–18.
[19] Chart. R. 39 & 40 Edw. III, m. 7, no. 20.
[20] *Valor Eccl.* (Rec. Com.), ii, 214.
[21] *L. and P. Hen. VIII,* xvii, g. 881 (26).
[22] Ibid. xx (2), g. 1068 (50).
[23] William Goodwin had also applied

for a grant in 1545 (Aug. Off. Partic. for Grants, 498), when Joan widow of Robert Belson was still holding a lease of the manor originally granted by Thame Abbey (*Valor Eccl.* [Rec. Com.], ii, 214).
[24] Pat. 8 Eliz. pt. i.
[25] It was in 1637–47 held by Sir Edmund Pye (Feet of F. Bucks. Trin. 13 Chas. I ; *Cal. Com. for Comp.* 68).
[27] *V.C.H. Bucks.* iii, 36 ; Feet of F. Bucks. Trin. 41 Eliz. ; Trin. 4 Jas. I.
[28] Lee, *Hist. and Antiq. of the Church of Thame,* 286, from information supplied by Mr. Griffin in 1882.
[29] Admon. P.C.C. Bevor.
[30] Lee, loc. cit.
[31] Priv. Act, 3 Geo. IV, cap. 14. The youngest was then an infant, so only two names appear in 1821 (Recov. R. Trin. 2 Geo. IV, m. 381).
[32] Lee, loc. cit.
[33] Burke, *Landed Gentry* (1906).

[34] Ibid.
[35] *Hund. R.* (Rec. Com.), i, 25.
[36] Feet of F. case 16, file 39, no. 1.
[37] *Feud. Aids,* i, 84, 94 ; Feet of F. case 17, file 49, no. 30.
[38] *Feud. Aids,* i, 120.
[39] *Hund. R.* (Rec. Com.), i, 25.
[40] *Red Bk. of Exch.* (Rolls Ser.), 317.
[41] Chan. Misc. Inq. file 33, no. 5 ; *Hund. R.* (Rec. Com.), i, 25.
[42] Chan. Misc. Inq. file 33, no. 5 ; *Cal. Close,* 1272–9, p. 187.
[43] Chan. Inq. p.m. (Ser. 2), clviii, 29.
[44] Feet of F. Bucks. Mich. 6 & 7 Eliz.
[45] Chan. Inq. p.m. (Ser. 2), clviii, 29.
[46] Ibid. clxxiv, 60.
[47] Chan. Proc. Eliz. Bb 25, no. 18.
[48] Feet of F. Bucks. Trin. 28 Eliz. ; Recov. R. East. 28 Eliz. m. 1.
[49] Feet of F. Bucks. East. 20 Jas. I.
[50] *Cal. S. P. Dom.* 1645–7, p. 501.
[51] Feet of F. case 19, file 84, no. 5. Walter and John Parage are mentioned.
[52] Notes of Fines Bucks. Mich. 19 & 20 Eliz.

TOWERSEY CHURCH FROM THE SOUTH

TOWERSEY CHURCH: THE INTERIOR LOOKING EAST

WADDESDEN MANOR: THE SOUTH FRONT

The chancel has in each side wall an early 13th-century lancet, the rear arch of which, originally round, has been subsequently made roughly pointed. In the east wall is a two-light traceried window of the mid-14th century, and at the south-west is a late two-light window. Under the lancet in the north wall is a round-headed recess, and in a square recess on the south is a 12th-century piscina formed in a scalloped capital. The chancel arch, which dies into the side walls, dates from the 14th century. The high-pitched roof over the chancel, with curved wind-braces and moulded wall-plates, is of the 15th century.

In the east wall of the nave, on either side of the chancel arch are two traceried 14th-century windows each of two lights with labels linked to that of the arch. In each side wall are two windows of the same number of lights, all renewed, except the heads, which date from the 14th century. In the west wall, which appears to have been rebuilt, is a modern three-light window with a 14th-century label and a contemporary outer order, reset, to the external jambs. The north and south doorways, with arch mouldings continuous with the jambs, are also of the 14th century, and the strap hinges on the south door are probably of the same period. The transeptal recess has been considerably restored and its north wall, which contains a three-light window with a 14th-century rear arch, may have been rebuilt inside the line of the original wall; the archway in the nave wall is similar to the chancel arch. The tower is of three stages surmounted by pinnacles and an embattled parapet; its lower stage forms a porch in which the 14th-century archway of the former porch has been reset.

The font is of a plain cylindrical shape with no detail by which its date can be determined, though it is probably ancient. The panelled hexagonal pulpit, which is enriched with foliage and scroll ornament, dates from the early 17th century; the sounding-board support is original though the sounding-board itself is modern. There are also four 16th-century bench ends with poppy heads.

The tower contains a ring of four bells : the treble by Richard Keene 1695; the second and third, inscribed 'This bell was made 1627,' and the tenor 'Prayes

the Lord. 1627,' by Ellis Knight; and a small bell undated.

The communion plate includes a late 16th-century cup, the date letter of which is partially obliterated, and also a modern chalice and paten.

The registers begin in 1589.

ADVOWSON Towersey was a chapelry appendant to the church of Thame, Oxfordshire,[53] and as such the advowson appertained to the prebend of Thame, founded by Bishop Grosteste in Lincoln Cathedral in the middle of the 13th century.[54] The prebend of Thame was alienated to Edward Duke of Somerset in 1547,[55] and sold by him in 1561 to Sir John Thynne.[56] It descended in his family to Thomas, third Viscount Weymouth.[57] His brother Henry Frederick Thynne, Lord Carteret,[58] sold the advowson of Thame with the chapel of Towersey in the early 19th century to John Blackall,[59] who owned it in 1822.[60] His heir-at-law Walter Long,[61] with his wife Mary Long, conveyed it about 1830 to Richard Harrison,[62] apparently agent for Dr. Slater of High Wycombe. He vested the advowson of the vicarage of Towersey, which was separated from Thame in 1841,[63] in trustees,[64] and their successors, known as the Peache Trustees,[65] are the present owners.

In 1822 the great tithes of Towersey were in the hands of Henry Bowden, George and William Frith, and other assignees of the estate of George Bowden, and all other tithes in the parish belonged to the vicar of Thame.[66] Land given for the maintenance of lights in Towersey Church was granted to Edward Downing and John Walker in 1578.[67]

CHARITIES The charity of Christopher Deane, founded by will proved in the P.C.C. 16 March 1695, is regulated by a scheme of 28 October 1879, made under the Endowed Schools Acts. The endowment consists of 20 acres, or thereabouts, at Gayton (co. Lincoln), let at £30 a year. Under the scheme £5 a year is payable to the minister of Towersey, £20 for educational purposes, and the residue of the income for apprenticeships.

This parish is entitled to a share of the charity of Mrs. Katherine Pye, founded by deeds of lease and release, dated respectively 13 and 14 November 1713.[68]

WADDESDON WITH WESTCOTT AND WOODHAM

Votesdone (xi cent.) ; Woddesdon (xiv cent.).

Waddesdon is a large parish covering, with Westcott (1,411 acres) and Woodham (838 acres), an area of 7,252 acres, including 5,890 acres of permanent grass, 470 acres of arable land, and 364 acres of woods and plantations.[1] The slope of the land varies from 231 ft. above the ordnance datum in the south-west of the parish to 476 ft. near Waddesdon Hill Farm. The hills in the west and centre of the parish average from 300 ft. to 400 ft. The soil is clay, the subsoil varies. A small silk factory, founded

at Waddesdon in 1843 as a branch establishment from Aylesbury,[2] provided work for a certain number of the inhabitants for nearly fifty years. In 1862 pillow-lace making was carried on by many of the women, and about forty were still employed in hand loom-weaving.[3] The Metropolitan and Great Central Joint railway passes through the north-east of this parish, and has a station called Waddesdon Manor. A branch line from Quainton Road to Brill has two stations, Waddesdon Road and Westcott. The large village of Waddesdon, now one of the

[53] Bacon, *Liber Reg.* 509.
[54] Lee, op. cit. 132.
[55] Ibid. 138–9, quoting deeds and notes from documents belonging to the Marquess of Bath at Longleat (Wilts).
[56] Feet of F. Oxon. East. 3 Eliz.
[57] Ibid. Mich. 3 Jas. I; Chan. Inq. p.m. (Ser. 2), dcclxv, 47 ; Feet of F. Oxon. Mich. 1653 ; Lupton, *Hist. of Thame and*

Hamlets, 64. Thomas, first Viscount Weymouth, repaired the chancel of Towersey Church in 1707 (Lupton, op. cit. 84). [58] G.E.C. *Complete Peerage*, ii, 170.
[59] Lupton, loc. cit.
[60] Priv. Act, 3 Geo. IV, cap. 14.
[61] Lupton, op. cit. 100.
[62] Feet of F. Oxon. Hil. 10 & 11 Geo. IV.

[63] *Accts. and Papers*, 1872, xlvi, 6.
[64] Lee, op. cit. 148.
[65] *Clergy Lists.*
[66] Priv. Act, 3 Geo. IV, cap. 14.
[67] Pat. 21 Eliz. pt. vi, m. 16.
[68] *V.C.H. Bucks.* ii, 267.
[1] Statistics from Bd. of Agric. (1905).
[2] Sheahan, *Hist. and Topog. of Bucks.* 429. [3] Ibid.

model villages of the county, is situated in the north-west of the parish, on the Akeman Street, which here forms the main road from Aylesbury to Bicester. The church, approached through a lych-gate and by an avenue, stands in a large churchyard on rising ground to the north-west of the village, with the modern rectory to the north-east of it. The chief mansion-house in Waddesdon formerly stood to the south of the church, on Philosophy Farm, the original endowment of the Sedleian Professorship of Natural Philosophy at Oxford University (see p. 110). Near the farmhouse in 1862 was a square piece of ground of about three-quarters of an acre in extent, surrounded by a deep moat, and in that year an old stone building supported by pillars with 13th-century capitals, which formerly stood in the farm-yard and had long been used as a stable, was taken down.[4] The village hall, on the south side of the High Street, was built in 1897 by the late Baron Ferdinand de Rothschild, who in 1883 had provided a club and reading-room for working-men. The Goodwin almshouses, which were erected in the 17th century by Arthur Goodwin, were rebuilt in 1894 by Baron Rothschild. He also rebuilt the Five Arrows Hotel at the western end of the village. One of the two elementary schools in the village belongs to the Church of England, and was built by Miss Alice de Rothschild in 1910, when the old school premises were adapted into the Waddesdon Institute for the use of tradesmen and farmers in the district. The Primitive Methodists, Wesleyans and Baptists have each their chapel. The Baptists have also a chapel and cemetery on Waddesdon Hill given by Francis Cox of Cranwell, who was buried there in 1803.[5]

Waddesdon Manor, the seat and property of Miss Alice de Rothschild, stands in grounds extending over 800 acres on Lodge Hill, half a mile south-west of the village. The house, overlooking the Vale of Aylesbury, was built by the late Baron Ferdinand de Rothschild, who housed here his art treasures, which since 1900 have been exhibited at the British Museum in the Waddesdon Bequest Room.[6] To the south-west of Waddesdon Manor is Windmill Hill Farm,[7] near which is an ancient windmill.

Eythrope (Herope, Ethorp, xiii cent.; Edrope, xiv cent.), in the south-east of the parish, which is now part of the Waddesdon Manor estate, was formerly distinct from it. Eythrope House, once a favourite country seat of the Dormers and Stanhopes, stood in a well-wooded valley close to the north bank of the Thame, which was there expanded into a lake for decorative purposes.[8] It was enlarged in the middle of the 16th century by Sir William Dormer (who built an armoury, and apparently a large picture gallery),[9] and in 1610 by his widow Dame Dorothy.[10]

In 1616 Robert Lord Dormer obtained a licence to impark and to stock with game,[11] and a later owner, Sir William Stanhope, who died in 1772,[12] added to the house and erected fanciful buildings in the grounds and plantations.[13] The Earl of Chesterfield was living at Eythrope in 1786,[14] but the house was afterwards dismantled,[15] and finally taken down in the early 19th century.[16] The original wall, inclosing 5 acres of private grounds, was intact in 1862.[17] Some twenty years later Miss Alice de Rothschild had a pavilion erected by the lake.

Beachendon (Bichedone, xi cent.; Bichindon, xiv cent.), formerly a manorial estate, is now represented by a single 17th-century farmhouse, about three-quarters of a mile south-west from Eythrope. A rockery in the grounds of the house is formed of carved stones, which are said to have come from Eythrope chapel.

Cranwell (Crendewelle, xiii, xiv cent.; Cranewell, xvi cent.), the name of two estates, formerly manorial, similarly survives in Cranwell Farm, to the north of Eythrope Park.

There are two farms at Blackgrove, in the north-east corner of the parish, representing two former manorial estates.

The hamlet of Westcott is $1\frac{3}{4}$ miles west of Waddesdon, and contains several 17th-century brick and timber thatched cottages. The church of St. Mary stands in the west of the hamlet, with the school to the north-east. The woodland called Gipsy Bottom lies in the south of the hamlet, and Windmill Hill Plantation in the south-east.

There are two moated sites in Westcott, one in a field called the Bury, with traces of a fish-pond, the other in Whitchurch Close West, with a large circular fish-pond; also traces of a third moat in Farm Close.[18]

The hamlet of Woodham lies to the north-west of Westcott. It was originally part of the forest of Bernwood, and is still well wooded. There are an inn and some cottages at Ham Green, which extends into the neighbouring parish of Wotton Underwood. To the south of this hamlet is Colwick or Collett, now the name of a farm only, but formerly a small manorial estate.

The inclosure of Westcott with certain lands in Waddesdon was authorized in 1765,[19] and the award was made in 1766.[20] Waddesdon was inclosed in 1774.[21]

MANORS   Brictric, one of Queen Edith's men, held *WADDESDON MANOR* before the Conquest.[22] In 1086 it was assessed at 27 hides, and held by Miles Crispin.[23] During the next century this land was divided into the manors of Waddesdon and Eythrope. The overlord-ship of Waddesdon Manor descended with the honour of Wallingford,[24] afterwards with that of Ewelme,[25]

---

[4] Sheahan, op. cit. 432.
[5] Lipscomb, *Hist. and Antiq. of Bucks.* i, 512.
[6] In accordance with his will (*Times*, 22 Feb. 1899).
[7] There are memorial slabs in Waddesdon Church to the Greens of this farm between 1767 and 1810.
[8] Lipscomb, op. cit. i, 482.
[9] Lysons, *Mag. Brit.* i (3), 655.
[10] Ibid. The date with her arms and initials was over the chimneypiece in one of the rooms.
[11] Pat. 14 Jas. I, pt. xi, no. 12.

[12] *Visit. of Oxon.* (Harl. Soc.), 340.
[13] Lysons, loc. cit. One remained in 1862 (Sheahan, op. cit. 431).
[14] *Hist. MSS. Com. Rep.* xiii, App. iii, 266–7.   [15] Lysons, loc. cit.
[16] Lipscomb, op. cit. i, 483. Some of the panelling and a door are said to be at Winchendon Hill Farm.
[17] Sheahan, loc. cit.
[18] Sheahan, op. cit. 432. Ellis of Whitchurch held half a virgate in West-cott in 1224 (Feet of F. case 14, file 15, no. 6).   [19] Priv. Act, 5 Geo. III, cap. 7.
[20] Com. Pleas Recov. R. Trin. 6

Geo. III, m. 165. The award mentions an ancient public bridle road from the Water gate in the North Field to Binwell Lane Farm to the north-west of Colwick.
[21] Priv. Act, 14 Geo. III, cap. 24.
[22] *V.C.H. Bucks.* i, 261.   [23] Ibid.
[24] *Testa de Nevill* (Rec. Com.), 247 *b*; Hund. R. (Rec. Com.), i, 45; Chan. Inq. p.m. 28 Edw. I, no. 44; 2 Ric. II, no. 57; Ct. R. (Gen. Ser.), portf. 212, no. 5, 7; Leadam, *Dom. Incl.* 1517 (Royal Hist. Soc.), i, 172.
[25] Ct. R. (Gen. Ser.), portf. 212, no. 20–22, 25, 27, 28.

the last reference in this connexion occurring in 1665.[26]

Henry II granted Waddesdon Manor to Henry of Oxford,[27] and after the latter's death before 1167,[28] to Reynold Courtenay,[29] who is said to have come over to England in his train in 1151.[30] He married between 1173[31] and 1178[32] Hawise, elder co-heir of the Earl of Devon, and appears to have settled Waddesdon Manor in dower on his wife's half-sister Maud on her marriage to a near relative of his in France.[33] After the death of her husband she came to England about 1214,[34] and died about 1224,[35] when Waddesdon Manor reverted to Robert Courtenay, elder son and heir of Reynold and Hawise.[36] He was buried at Ford Abbey in 1242,[37] when Waddesdon Manor was assigned to his widow Mary in dower.[38] She appears to have survived his son and heir John,[39] who died in 1273.[40] This manor reverted to the latter's son and heir Hugh,[41] who died seised in 1292.[42] In 1293 it was granted in dower to his widow Eleanor,[43] who afterwards married Stephen de Haccumbe.[43a] Hugh son of Hugh Courtenay[44] was holding in 1316,[45] and was created Earl of Devon in 1335. On his death in 1340 he was succeeded by his son Hugh.[46] He settled Waddesdon Manor

COURTENAY. *Or three roundels gules and a label azure.*

on Maud daughter of Thomas Holand Earl of Kent and her issue by his grandson Hugh, and the latter held it in right of his wife at his death in 1374.[47] His grandfather arranged with the widow Maud to hold this manor of her during her life,[48] and on his death in 1377[49] dower in it was assigned to his widow Margaret,[50] who died in 1392.[51] The successor to the earldom of Devon, Edward son of

the last earl's third son Edward,[52] was holding Waddesdon Manor in 1378,[53] and in 1380 granted it during Maud's life (she being then the wife of the Count of St. Paul) to her brother John Holand and other feoffees.[54] Edward Earl of Devon died seised of this manor in 1419,[55] and it descended with the other estates of his earldom[56] to his great-grandson Thomas Earl of Devon, who in 1461 was beheaded as a Lancastrian after the battle of Towton.[57] Edward IV granted a licence to his brother and heir Henry Courtenay to enter into some of the estates of his heritage, including Waddesdon Manor, without proof of age,[58] but on his brother's attainder later in the year they were forfeited to the Crown.[59] In 1462 this manor was granted for life to George Nevill Bishop of Exeter, afterwards Archbishop of York,[60] and in 1465 he obtained the fee simple.[61] He helped to place Henry VI again on the throne in 1470, and surrendered him to Edward IV on the latter's entrance into London in 1471.[62] A hollow reconciliation was effected after a short imprisonment; but in 1472 the archbishop was arrested and his lands confiscated.[63] In 1474 Waddesdon Manor was granted to Henry Earl of Essex and his wife Isabel, aunt of Edward IV, and the heirs of their bodies.[64] He died seised in 1483[65] and she in 1485, during the minority of their grandson and heir Henry.[66] Later in this year, on the accession of Henry VII, Sir Edward grandson of Sir Hugh Courtenay, a younger brother of Edward Earl of Devon,[67] was granted the title and estates of the former earls.[68] In 1490 Waddesdon Manor, however, was granted to Sir Hugh Conway and his wife Elizabeth,[69] sister of Thomas Earl of Devon, who had been attainted in 1461.[70] He retained it[71] until his death in 1518, when it reverted to Katherine Countess of Devon with remainder to her issue by William, late Earl of Devon,[72] in accordance with an agreement between the king and her husband in 1511 and a royal grant in 1512, after his death.[73] Waddesdon Manor was delivered to the countess in 1518,[74] and

[26] Ct. R. (Gen. Ser.), portf. 212, no. 29.
[27] *Testa de Nevill* (Rec. Com.), 115.
[28] *Red Bk. of Exch.* (Rolls Ser.), 36.
[29] *Testa de Nevill,* loc. cit.
[30] Cleaveland, *Hist. of Courtenay Family,* 118.
[31] When her mother died and he was granted the custody and marriage of Hawise and of her half-sister Maud then an infant (Dugdale, *Mon.* v, 377).
[32] *Hist. MSS. Com. Rep.* ix, App. ii, 406. Transcript of a bull of Pope Alexander III to Reynold and his wife Hawise.
[33] She appears to have married William Courtenay, sometimes said to have been Reynold's son by a former wife, sometimes his brother. The evidence is discussed by Cleaveland, op. cit. 120–1. In 1220 she is styled widow of Reynold Courtenay (Cur. Reg. R. Trin. 4 Hen. III, A m. 12, B m. 6 d.), but he may have been a second husband.
[34] *Rot. Lit. Pat.* (Rec. Com.), 122; see also ibid. 44, 106.
[35] Kennet, *Paroch. Antiq.* i, 277. It was possibly after her death that Simon de Pateshall was holding this manor at the king's pleasure (*Testa de Nevill,* loc. cit.).
[36] Dugdale, op. cit. v, 378; *Excerpta e Rot. Fin.* (Rec. Com.), i, 38; Wrottesley, *Ped. from Plea R.* 482.
[37] Dugdale, op. cit. v, 379. Monum. in Ford Abbey Chapel.

[38] *Cal. Close,* 1237–42, p. 476.
[39] *Excerpta e Rot. Fin.* (Rec. Com.), i, 388.
[40] Dugdale, loc. cit.; Chan. Inq. p.m. Edw. I, file 6, no. 1.
[41] Chan. Inq. p.m. Edw. I, file 6, no. 1.
[42] Ibid. file 62, no. 7.
[43] *Cal. Close,* 1288–96, p. 236. A lease granted by her in Waddesdon is extant (Add. Chart. 13912).
[43a] De Banco R. 211, m. 95; Feet of F. Div. Co. Mich. 9 Edw. II, no. 114.
[44] Chan. Inq. p.m. Edw. I, file 62, no. 7.
[45] *Feud. Aids,* i, 113.
[46] G.E.C. *Complete Peerage,* iii, 102–3.
[47] Chan. Inq. p.m. 48 Edw. III (1st nos.), no. 14.
[48] Ibid. 51 Edw. III (1st nos.), no. 6.
[49] Ibid. 1 Ric. II, no. 12.
[50] Close, 1 Ric. II, m. 38.
[51] Chan. Inq. p.m. 15 Ric. II, pt. i, no. 16.
[52] Ibid. 51 Edw. III (1st nos.), no. 6; 1 Ric. II, no. 12; G.E.C. *Complete Peerage,* iii, 104.
[53] Chan. Inq. p.m. 2 Ric. II, no. 57.
[54] Add. Chart. 13917.
[55] Chan. Inq. p.m. 7 Hen. V, no. 75.
[56] Ibid. 10 Hen. V, no. 29; Mins. Accts. (Gen. Ser.), bdle. 1118, no. 6; Chan. Inq. p.m. 36 Hen. VI, no. 38.
[57] G.E.C. loc. cit.
[58] *Cal. Pat.* 1461–7, p. 70.
[59] Ibid. 118.

[60] Ibid. 105.
[61] Ibid. 105, 477. See also Chan. Inq. p.m. 1 Edw. IV, no. 29, dated 1465.
[62] *Dict. Nat. Biog.* [63] Ibid.
[64] *Cal. Pat.* 1467–77, p. 480.
[65] Chan. Inq. p.m. 1 Ric. III, no. 31.
[66] Ibid. 2 Ric. III, no. 25.
[67] G.E.C. *Complete Peerage,* iii, 105.
[68] Pat. 1 Hen. VII, pt. i, m. 28.
[69] L. and P. Hen. VIII, i, 2080.
[70] G.E.C. *Complete Peerage,* ii, 386.
[71] Chan. Inq. p.m. (Ser. 2), xiv, 57; Leadam, *Dom. Incl.* 1517 (Roy. Hist. Soc.), i, 172; Chan. Inq. p.m. (Ser. 2), xxxiii, 38. Inquisitions in 1511 and 1512 stated that Waddesdon Manor had formerly belonged to Thomas Earl of Devon (Chan. Inq. p.m. [Ser. 2], lxxviii, 8; lxxix, 215).
[72] Chan. Inq. p.m. (Ser. 2), xxxiii, 38.
[73] L. and P. Hen. VIII, loc. cit. William, son and heir of Edward Courtenay, Earl of Devon, was imprisoned by Henry VII for marrying before 1495 the Lady Katherine Plantagenet, sixth daughter of Edward IV, was attainted for alleged conspiracy in 1504 and so disabled from inheriting the earldom on his father's death in 1509. He was received into favour by Henry VIII, who created him Earl of Devon shortly before his death in 1511 (G.E.C. *Complete Peerage,* iii, 106).
[74] L. and P. Hen. VIII, ii (2), 4341.

passed on her death in 1527 to her son Henry Earl of Devon,[75] afterwards Marquess of Exeter, but on his attainder in 1539 escheated to the Crown.[76] It was granted in 1540 to John Goodwin,[77] and afterwards descended with Upper Winchendon (q.v.)[78] to John seventh Duke of Marlborough. He sold his Buckinghamshire estates in 1874 to Baron Ferdinand de Rothschild,[79] who built Waddesdon Manor and died there in 1898.[80] He was succeeded by his sister Miss Alice de Rothschild,[81] the present owner.

ROTHSCHILD. *Quarterly: 1, Or an eagle sable; 2 and 3, Azure a bent and naked arm issuing from the side of the shield, the hand grasping a sheaf of arrows argent; 4, Or a lion proper; and over all a scutcheon gules charged with an ancient shield proper.*

References to a mill on the manor occur from the 11th to the 15th century.[82]

The chief mansion-house at Waddesdon with its appurtenances, which in 1477 had included a park,[83] was leased by the Crown in 1539 for twenty-one years to Edward Lamborne.[84] He died in the same year[85] and his successor John Lamborne conveyed the lease to Thomas Palmer and John Dormer, who obtained the fee simple, which they sold in 1547 to Ralph Palmer, then lessee.[86] His son, William Palmer,[87] in 1577 settled it on his wife Joyce, who survived him at his death in 1595.[88] It continued for some time in the tenure of Joyce or her son Peter Palmer,[89] and in 1622 was sold by George Croke and Gregory Hirst, probably trustees, to Sir John Sedley, bart., of Aylesford, Kent.[90] As executor of his father, Sir William Sedley, bart., who left £2,000 for this purpose, he transferred it in trust to the chancellor, masters and scholars of Oxford University towards the endowment of a lectureship in natural philosophy.[91] In 1774 they were authorized

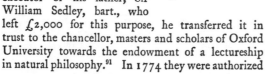

PALMER. *Azure a cheveron engrailed between three crescents argent.*

to inclose 4 yard lands and 4 acres in Waddesdon.[92] This property, covering 339 acres in 1873,[93] and long known as Philosophy Farm, yields about £200 yearly at the present time towards the stipend of the Sedleian Professor of Natural Philosophy.[94]

A dovecote was included in the transfers of 1547 and 1622.

The remainder of the Domesday estate in Waddesdon was held as three fees of the honour of Wallingford, certainly from the later 12th century.[95] This was originally held as one estate known as *EYTHROPE MANOR*, a name which during the 14th century began to be limited to a part held by service of one and a half fees,[96] the remainder splitting up into the sub-manors of Cranwell, Blackgrove and Ham.

Eythrope Manor corresponds to the three fees held by William Darches in 1196[97] and in the early 13th century.[98] He was living in 1218[99] and had been succeeded in Eythrope before 1235 by Jordan Darches,[100] probably his son. Richard Darches, who was holding in 1284,[1] died about 1308[2] and was followed by his son Simon.[3] He died in 1316, when the custody of his son Richard was granted to John de la Haye.[4] Richard Darches attained his majority in 1333[5] and was holding in 1346,[6] but Simon Darches had succeeded before 1378.[7] He died between 1382[8] and 1396[9] and was followed by another Simon Darches,[10] who was living in 1425.[11]

Eythrope Manor descended through the marriage of Joan, daughter and heir of Richard, presumably grandson of the last-mentioned Richard Darches, with Sir John Dynham to their son John, Lord Dynham, who died in 1501 (see Dynham's Manor, Oving).[12] By agreement with his heirs in 1499[13] he had enfeoffed John Newport and others in trust of Eythrope Manor for the use after his own death of Thomas Lowe or Lawe, apparently an illegitimate son, and his heirs in tail male.[14] He was usually known as Sir Thomas Dynham,[15] and in 1502 granted John's widow, Elizabeth, dower in this manor.[16] His wife, who had a life interest in the manor,[17] afterwards married Sir William Fitz William, who about 1529 leased it to John,[18] son and heir of Sir Thomas Dynham.[19] Being involved in money difficulties he sold the reversion in fee of the manor in 1532 to Richard Sparre[20] with the right of pre-emption for his heirs.[21] In 1533 he and Richard Sparre conveyed

[75] G.E.C. *Complete Peerage*, iii, 106, 107.
[76] Chan. Inq. p.m. (Ser. 2), xxxiii, 6.
[77] *L. and P. Hen. VIII*, xv, g. 611 (7); Add. Chart. 6032.
[78] Recov. R. Hil. 12 Eliz. m. 335; East. 16 Chas. I, m. 44; Feet of F. Bucks. Hil. 4 Chas. I; East. 16 Chas. I; Priv. Act, 14 Geo. III, cap. 24; cf. Upper Winchendon.
[79] *Times*, 20 Aug. 1874.
[80] Ibid. 19 Dec. 1898.
[81] Ibid. 22 Feb. 1899.
[82] *V.C.H. Bucks.* i, 261; Chan. Inq. p.m. 48 Edw. III (1st nos.), no. 14; Mins. Accts. (Gen. Ser.), bdle. 1118, no. 6. [83] *Cat. of Anct. D.* iii, 401.
[84] *L. and P. Hen. VIII*, xiv (1), g. 1056 (21).
[85] Ibid. xiv (2), g. 435 (14).
[86] Close, 38 Hen. VIII, pt. i, no. 9. The manor-house was held of Eythrope Manor in 1596 (Chan. Inq. p.m. [Ser. 2], ccl, 77).
[87] *Visit. of Bucks.* (Harl. Soc.), 193.
[88] Chan. Inq. p.m. (Ser. 2), ccl, 77.

[89] Ibid.
[90] Close, 20 Jas. I, pt. iii, no. 16.
[91] Ibid.
[92] Priv. Act, 14 Geo. III, cap. 24.
[93] *Ret. of Owners of Land*, 1873, Bucks. 20.
[94] *Hist. Reg. of Oxf. University*, 1900, p. 54.
[95] Pipe R. 8 Ric. I, m. 15 d.; *Testa de Nevill* (Rec. Com.), 258; *Feud. Aids*, i, 84; Chan. Inq. p.m. 28 Edw. I, no. 44; Edw. II, file 53, no. 25.
[96] *Feud. Aids*, i, 93, 118, 134.
[97] Pipe R. 8 Ric. I, m. 15 d.
[98] *Rot. de Oblatis et Fin.* (Rec. Com.), 150; *Red Bk. of Exch.* (Rolls Ser.), 145.
[99] Feet of F. Bucks. Trin. 2 Hen. III, no. 2.
[100] *Testa de Nevill* (Rec. Com.), 258.
[1] *Feud. Aids*, i, 84; See also Chan. Inq. p.m. 28 Edw. I, no. 44; *Feud. Aids*, i, 118; Chan. Inq. p.m. Edw. II, file 88, no. 10; *Abbrev. Rot. Orig.* (Rec. Com.), i, 290.
[2] Chan. Inq. p.m. Edw. II, file 9, no. 7.
[3] Ibid.; *Feud. Aids*, i, 134, 114.

[4] Chan. Inq. p.m. Edw. II, file 53, no. 25.
[5] Ibid. Edw. III, file 37, no. 1.
[6] *Feud. Aids*, i, 118.
[7] Chan. Inq. p.m. 2 Ric. II, no. 57.
[8] Ibid. 5 Ric. II, no. 62.
[9] Ibid. 19 Ric. II, no. 52.
[10] *Cal. Pat.* 1401–5, p. 358; Chan. Inq. p.m. 3 Hen. V, no. 96.
[11] Chan. Inq. p.m. 3 Hen. VI, no. 8.
[12] Feet of F. case 293, file 73, no. 446; cf. Dynham's Manor.
[13] De Banco R. 950, m. 21; Feet of F. case 22, file 128 (2 doc. Mich. term).
[14] De Banco R. 948, m. 142 d.; Chan. Inq. p.m. (Ser. 2), xv, 58.
[15] G.E.C. *Complete Peerage*, iii, 126.
[16] De Banco R. 962, m. 114.
[17] Chan. Inq. p.m. (Ser. 2), xxxiv, 61.
[18] *L. and P. Hen. VIII*, ix, 1114.
[19] Chan. Inq. p.m. (Ser. 2), xxxiv, 61; P.C.C. 25 Ayloffe; Nichols, *Coll. Topog. et Gen.* vii, 257.
[20] *L. and P. Hen. VIII*, ix, 1114.
[21] Com. Pleas D. Enr. Trin. 27 Hen. VIII, m. 1 d.

the manor to Sir Thomas More and others on behalf of Giles Heron,[22] who immediately transferred it to Sir Francis Bryan and other trustees to the use of Robert Dormer.[23] On the death of John Dynham in 1535,[24] Robert entered the manor[25] by virtue of a lease granted to him by Sir William Fitz William, who had died in 1534.[26] Giles Heron, to whom John Dynham had left his lands for three years,[27] unsuccessfully disputed the validity of this lease.[28] Dame Jane Fitz William died about 1542,[29] and in the following year George, brother of John Dynham, brought a suit against Robert then Sir Robert Dormer,[30] which was continued by George, son of George Dynham, against Sir William, son of Sir Robert Dormer.[31] A settlement securing possession to Sir William Dormer was finally effected in 1560.[32] On his death in 1575 Eythrope was held as dower by his widow Dorothy, daughter of Anthony Catesby.[33] She survived her second husband, Sir William Pelham,[34] and dying in 1613, was buried at Wing.[35] Eythrope reverted to Robert Lord Dormer,[36] who had made a settlement respecting it in 1580.[37] It descended with Wing[38] to George, sixth Earl of Chesterfield,[39] who owned it in the mid-19th century. Eythrope was acquired about the same time as Waddesdon Manor (q.v.) by Baron Ferdinand de Rothschild and is now the property of Miss Alice de Rothschild.

A dovecote and fishery were appurtenant to the capital messuage of Eythrope in the early 14th century,[40] and some rents were still payable in kind in 1458.[41] Free warren was granted to Robert Lord Dormer in 1616 with his liberty of park.[42]

A water-mill in Eythrope was held by Wallingford Priory before 1291[43] and at the Dissolution,[44] when it was included in the grant of the possessions of this priory in 1528 to Cardinal Wolsey[45] for his proposed college at Oxford.[46] The lord of Eythrope Manor was tenant of two-thirds of this mill in the early 14th century,[47] and the whole was held as parcel of this manor by Robert Earl of Carnarvon in the middle of the 17th century.[48]

That part of Eythrope afterwards called CRANWELL MANOR had acquired its distinctive name by the early 13th century.[49] It descended with

Eythrope Manor[50] (q.v.), preserving its identity as a manor into the 19th century[51] and its name in Cranwell Farm.

An estate in Cranwell, called in the early 16th century *CRANWELL MANOR*, remained in a branch of the Darches of Eythrope, descendants possibly of the Alan Darches who held 4 virgates of land in Eythrope and Cranwell before 1289[52] (by grant of Richard Darches for life) until his death in 1325,[53] or more probably of Robert Darches of Cranwell,[54] son of the Richard Darches[55] who was holding Eythrope (q.v.) in 1346. Ralph Arches was seised before 1495,[56] and in 1512 he settled the manor to certain uses.[57] He was succeeded before 1517 by his son William,[58] who sold the manor to Sir Edward Grenville.[59] About 1529 a suit was brought against the trustees of the settlement of 1512 by John Welch and his wife Margaret, sister and heir of William Arches.[60] Cranwell Manor came later into the possession of Sir Richard Anderson, who died seised of it in 1632.[61] His son Henry[62] was created a baronet in 1643.[63] Sir Richard Anderson, his son, the second baronet,[64] settled the manor in 1680[65] and died in 1699.[66] His second wife Mary afterwards married Brownlow Sherard,[67] and in 1703 they conveyed this manor to Simon Harcourt,[68] husband of Sir Richard's daughter Elizabeth.[69] It descended with Pendley in Tring and Wigginton, Hertfordshire, to their grandson Richard Bard Harcourt,[70] who is named as owner in the early 19th century.[71] It has not been found possible to trace the later descent of this property.

ANDERSON, baronet. *Argent a cheveron between three crosslets sable.*

The distinction between Eythrope proper and Blackgrove is traceable from about the middle of the 13th century,[72] and the principal estate thereof, called later *BLACKGROVE MANOR*, descended with Eythrope Manor (q.v.) to Philip fourth Earl of Chesterfield, who owned it in 1717.[73] This

[22] Recov. R. Trin. 25 Hen. VIII, m. 310; Feet of F. Bucks. Trin. 25 Hen. VIII. Dynham's wife was Joan, daughter of Sir John Heron (Chan. Inq. p.m. [Ser. 2], xxxiv, 61).

[23] Com. Pleas D. Enr. East. 26 Hen. VIII, m. 1.

[24] He was living in June (ibid. Trin. 27 Hen. VIII, m. 1 d.) and his will was proved by Giles Heron in October (P.C.C. 28 Hogen).

[25] Ct. of Req. bdle. 3, no. 359.

[26] L. and P. Hen. VIII, vii, 1120.

[27] P.C.C. 28 Hogen.

[28] L. and P. Hen. VIII, ix, 1114.

[29] P.C.C. 10 Spert.

[30] Ct. of Req. bdle. 3, no. 359.

[31] Chan. Proc. (Ser. 2), bdle. 55, no. 15; cf. Wing.

[32] Recov. R. Mich. 2 & 3 Eliz. m. 139; Feet of F. Bucks. Mich. 2 & 3 Eliz.

[33] Chan. Inq. p.m. (Ser. 2), clxx, 2; xcv, 5.

[34] Ibid. ccxvii, 120; ccl, 77. In his will proved in 1587 he left her all his personal effects at Eythrope (P.C.C. 12 Rutland).

[35] P.C.C. 104 Capell. Dormer monum. in Wing Church.

[36] Chan. Inq. p.m. (Ser. 2), ccclviii, 99.

[37] Feet of F. Bucks. East. 22 Eliz.

[38] cf. under Wing; Hist. MSS. Com. Rep. xiii, App. iii, 266, 267.

[39] Recov. R. Mich. 7 Geo. IV, m. 295. It was held in 1645 by Lady Alice Dormer, mother of the first Earl of Carnarvon, for life, or an unexpired term of thirty years (Chan. Inq. p.m. [Ser. 2], dcclxxvii, 105).

[40] Chan. Inq. p.m. Edw. II, file 9, no. 7.

[41] Ibid. 36 Hen. VI, no. 39.

[42] Pat. 14 Jas. I, pt. xi, no. 12.

[43] Pope Nich. Tax. (Rec. Com.), 46b. It owned a yearly rent there of 6s. 8d. evidently due from this mill.

[44] Chan. Inq. p.m. (Ser. 2), lxxvi, 4.

[45] L. and P. Hen. VIII, iv, 4471.

[46] V.C.H. Berks. ii, 315.

[47] Chan. Inq. p.m. Edw. II, file 9, no. 7.

[48] Ibid. (Ser. 2), dcclxxvii, 105.

[49] Feet of F. Bucks. Trin. 2 Hen. III, no. 5; Mich. 3 Hen. III, no. 35.

[50] Ibid.; East. 14 Edw. I, no. 22; Leadam, op. cit. i, 174.

[51] Recov. R. Mich. 7 Geo. IV, m. 295.

[52] Feet of F. Bucks. Trin. 17 Edw. I, no. 5.

[53] Chan. Inq. p.m. Edw. II, file 88,

no. 10; Abbrev. Rot. Orig. (Rec. Com.), i, 290. [54] Cal. Close, 1349–54, p. 377.

[55] Feet of F. Bucks. Trin. 16 Edw. III, no. 3.

[56] Leadam, op. cit. i, 175. The 'd' is dropped in this branch of the family.

[57] Chan. Misc. bdle. 49, file 2, no. 36; Arundel MS. xxvi, fol. 68b–70b.

[58] Leadam, loc. cit.

[59] Early Chan. Proc. bdle. 594, no. 1.

[60] Ibid. Partly illegible.

[61] Chan. Inq. p.m. (Ser. 2), dxxvi, 156; Visit. of Herts. (Harl. Soc.), 109.

[62] Ibid.

[63] G.E.C. Baronetage, ii, 211.

[64] Ibid.

[65] Feet of F. Div. Co. East. 32 Chas. II.

[66] M. I. at Aldbury (Herts.); P.C.C. 43 Noel.

[67] Feet of F. Bucks. Hil. 1 Anne.

[68] Ibid. Div. Co. East. 2 Anne.

[69] V.C.H. Herts. ii, 315. Both named in the settlement of 1680.

[70] Ibid.; Recov. R. Trin. 19 & 20 Geo. II, m. 30.

[71] Lysons, op. cit. i (3), 656.

[72] Hunter, Pedes Finium (Rec. Com.), i, 229.

[73] Recov. R. East. 3 Geo. II, m. 81.

property was afterwards sold, and passing through various hands, came into the possession of Charles Shaw Lefevre, who owned it as a farm in the early 19th century.[74]

A hide of land in Blackgrove was held as a fifth of a fee of Jordan Darches by Geoffrey Neyrnut at his death[75] between 1263 and 1272.[76] This estate, called in the later 15th century *BLACK-GROVE* or *BLAGROVE MANOR*[77] (probably augmented in the middle 16th century by a small property formerly appertaining to Wallingford Priory[78]), descended in the Neyrnut family with Pitstone Neyrnuts Manor and afterwards with Fleet Marston Manor (q.v.) to Charles twelfth Viscount Dillon. He in 1802 sold it to Robert Lord Carrington,[79] and it has since descended with Moulsoe Manor (q.v.) to the Marquess of Lincolnshire, the present owner.

A mill in Blackgrove was released by Biddlesden Abbey in the time of Henry III to Gilbert de Finemere, son of William son of Gregory.[80]

A district called Ham extended into the parishes of Waddesdon and Wotton Underwood. The part in Waddesdon was situated in Eythrope and called the manor of Ham or Woodham,[81] and that in Wotton Underwood was called Ham, Fieldham, or Ham cum Wotton. The manor of *HAM* or *WOODHAM* was held by the service of a pair of gilt spurs and suit of court of the manor of Eythrope (q.v.).[82]

Ham was held by the Cantlows and passed, like Ellesborough[83] (q.v.), through Millicent, heiress of that family, to the Zouches. William la Zouche of Haryngworth seems to have given a life interest in the manor to Thomas, one of his younger sons, with remainder to William la Zouche of Totnes, another son.[84] William la Zouche of Haryngworth, the father, died in 1352, and was succeeded in the barony of Zouche of Haryngworth by his grandson William, son of Eudo, who had predeceased his father.[85] This William eventually became possessed of Ham and died seised of it in 1382.[86] His son William died seised of it in 1396,[87] and was succeeded by his son William la Zouche, who conveyed it for life to Robert Isham in 1412.[88] After the death of Robert Isham in 1424[89] it reverted to William fifth Lord Zouche and was held by his widow Elizabeth in 1468.[90] It was afterwards held by John seventh Lord Zouche till his attainder after the battle of Bosworth Field in 1485. A reversal of the attainder was obtained by John la Zouche in 1495, and in 1497 he conveyed this manor to trustees,[91] who sold it to Sir Henry Colet. His son John Colet, Dean of St. Paul's, succeeded in 1505,[92] and granted it in trust to the Mercers' Company as part of the endowment of St. Paul's School.[93] The Mercers' Company still own the manor, which has been held under leases renewed from time to time by the Grenville family.[94]

Two small holdings were assessed in 1086 under Beachendon as distinct from Waddesdon, one at 2 hides held by Miles Crispin,[95] the other at a virgate held by the Bishop of Bayeux.[96] Both holdings with some land in North Marston,[97] probably the virgate of the bishop's holding there which did not go to St. Albans Abbey (see North Marston), formed by the later 12th century a fee of the honour of Wallingford.[98]

THE MERCERS' COMPANY. *Gules a demivirgin coming out of clouds all proper with her clothing and her crown or and a wreath of roses about her head all in a border of clouds argent.*

The tenants in Beachendon in 1086 were two Englishmen, the former holders, one of whom had been Brictric's, the other Azor's, man.[99] One of the Carbonels was evidently holding about 1166,[100] possibly Richard Carbonel, in whose family Beachendon descended with Carbonels Manor, Addington[1] (q.v.), to John Carbonel, who was holding in 1284.[2] John de Lyndhurst, holder in the early 14th century,[3] quitclaimed his right in *BEACHENDON MANOR* in 1306 to Peter Carbonel, at the same time enrolling a charter by which Robert de Lyndhurst had surrendered his right in it to Aymer de Valence,[4] afterwards Earl of Pembroke,[5] who held it at his death in 1324.[6] In 1326 Beachendon Manor was assigned to David de Strabolgi, Earl of Athole, and his wife Joan,[7] niece and co-heir of Aymer de Valence.[8] In 1332 their son and heir David[9] succeeded to the manor[10] and leased it for three years to John de Pulteney,[11] who in 1335, on account of the rebellion and forfeiture of the Earl of Athole,[12] obtained protection for his goods at Beachendon.[13] The manor was granted in this year first to Queen Philippa,[14] but afterwards to Sir Walter Mauny,[15] to whom John de Pulteney released it.[16]

[74] Lysons, loc. cit.

[75] Chan. Inq. p.m. Hen. III, file 46, no. 16.

[76] cf. under Pitstone.

[77] Chan. Inq. p.m. (Ser. 2), xxiii, 67.

[78] *Pope Nich. Tax.* (Rec. Com.), 46*b*; L. and P. Hen. VIII, iv, 4471.

[79] Marcham, *Cat. of Bucks. Deeds*, ii, 39.

[80] Harl. Chart. 85 D 51, called simply Blagrave Mill, Bucks.

[81] Probably so called from being in Bernwood Forest and to distinguish it from Fieldham.

[82] Chan. Inq. p.m. 5 Ric. II, no. 62.

[83] *V.C.H. Bucks.* ii, 331.

[84] Feet of F. Bucks. Mich. 25 and Hil. 26 Edw. III, no. 1. For the children of William la Zouche who died in 1352, see *Cal. Pat.* 1324-7, p. 254.

[85] Chan. Inq. p.m. 26 Edw. III (1st nos.), no. 51.

[86] Ibid. 5 Ric. II, no. 62.

[87] Ibid. 19 Ric. II, no. 52.

[88] Ibid. 3 Hen. V, no. 46.

[89] Ibid. 3 Hen. VI, no. 8.

[90] Ibid. 8 Edw. IV, no. 53.

[91] De Banco R. 941, m. 84.

[92] Chan. Inq. p.m. (Ser. 2), xix, 36.

[93] cf. Bury Manor, in Rowsham, Wingrave.

[94] Priv. Act, 15 Geo. II, cap. 39.

[95] *V.C.H. Bucks.* i, 261.   [96] Ibid. 237.

[97] *Feud. Aids*, i, 95, 121.

[98] *Liber Niger* (ed. 1771), i, 186; cf. *Red Bk. of Exch.* (Rolls Ser.), 145, 599; *Hund. R.* (Rec. Com.), i, 23; *Cal. Inq. p.m.* (Edw. I), iii, 481; Chan. Inq. p.m. Edw. III, file 45, no. 24.

[99] *V.C.H. Bucks.* i, 237, 261.

[100] *Liber Niger*, loc. cit.

[1] *Red Bk. of Exch.* (Rolls Ser.), 145, 599; *Testa de Nevill* (Rec. Com.), 257*b*; Feet of F. case 15, file 24, no. 5; *Hund. R.* (Rec. Com.), i, 23.

[2] *Feud. Aids*, i, 75.

[3] *Cal. Inq. p.m.* loc. cit.; *Feud. Aids*, i, 95.

[4] De Banco R. 159, m. 257.

[5] G.E.C. *Complete Peerage*, vi, 207.

[6] *Cal. Inq. p.m.* (Edw. II), vi, 315; cf. *Feud. Aids*, i, 113.

[7] *Cal. Close*, 1323-7, p. 446; 1330-3, pp. 456, 584 (Résumé to 1332).

[8] G.E.C. *Complete Peerage*, i, 182.

[9] Chan. Inq. p.m. Edw. II, file 104, no. 1.

[10] *Cal. Close*, 1330-3, p. 457.

[11] *Cal. Pat.* 1338-40, p. 348; Chan. Inq. p.m. Edw. III, file 45, no. 24.

[12] Chan. Inq. p.m. Edw. III, file 45, no. 24; G.E.C. *Complete Peerage*, i, 182.

[13] *Cal. Pat.* 1334-8, p. 81.

[14] Ibid. 61.

[15] Ibid. 89; *Cal. Close*, 1333-7, p. 392.

[16] *Cal. Pat.* 1338-40, p. 348.

A further grant was made in 1336 of the custody during the minority of the Earl of Athole's heir,[17] and dower in the manor was assigned in 1337 to the widow Katherine.[18] In 1339, however, Sir Walter Mauny conveyed Beachendon Manor to Sir John de Moleyns,[19] to whom it was confirmed in tail by the Crown after an inspection of the previous charters.[20] It descended with his manor in Stoke Poges,[21] except that Thomas Chaucer held it at his death in 1434[22] apparently on lease or in trust for Anne Lady Moleyns,[23] to George Hastings, first Earl of Huntingdon. In 1538, with the assent of his son Sir Francis Hastings, the earl sold Beachendon and Ilmer Manors to Robert Dormer.[24] Beachendon has since followed the descent of Eythrope[25] (q.v.), and Miss Alice de Rothschild is the present owner.

In 1339 Sir John de Moleyns obtained a grant of view of frankpledge and free warren in Beachendon Manor[26] with all the other manorial liberties which he had already secured in his Ludgershall manor (q.v.). Fish ponds and a dovecote were appurtenant to the capital messuage in 1327.[27] A water-mill is mentioned in 1198[28] and 1324.[29]

A hide of land in Beachendon afterwards known as *COLLETT*, and in the 17th century as *COLWICK GRANGE*, had been subinfeudated before the middle of the 13th century.[30] It was held of Beachendon Manor by the service of a quarter of a fee,[31] and after the Dissolution of the Crown in chief.[32] Under an early grant from William and Maud Carbonel of lands at Shoteley by Colwick,[33] the manor passed to Woburn Abbey in Bedfordshire and was held by that house in the 13th century.[34] Colwick Manor remained with this abbey[35] until the Dissolution, at which time Laurence Faircliff was lessee.[36] In 1538 this estate was included in a grant in exchange to Charles, Duke of Suffolk.[37] By 1539 it was vested in Elizabeth Pigott of Doddershall Manor in Quainton (q.v.), who gave it to her son Robert Pigott and his heirs.[38] He died

WOBURN ABBEY.
Azure three bars wavy argent.

in 1587,[39] when Colwick (with the exception of a close owned by Thomas Pigott of Doddershall) passed to his son Francis,[40] who in 1608 settled Colwick Grange, the principal messuage, on the marriage of his son Alban with Martha Wolley.[40a] Colwick Grange was afterwards acquired by Thomas Cripps, who died seised of it about 1627.[41] His daughter and heir Elizabeth,[42] with her husband John Wilkinson, obtained livery in 1634.[43] John died in 1664,[44] and his son John[45] left Colwick Grange in 1684 to his wife Elizabeth for life, with remainder to his brother Henry and his heirs.[46] In 1694 Henry Wilkinson was dead and his son and heir Robert sold his remainder, on the death of Elizabeth, then wife of John Grubb, to Joseph Garthwait.[47] Colwick was afterwards acquired by John Deacle,[48] who died in 1723, and his successor William Deacle (see Tetchwick in Ludgershall) owned it as Colwick Manor in 1739.[49] A later co-heir of the Deacle family carried it in marriage to Mr. Griffith, who owned it early in the 19th century.[50] Before 1828 the manor had been acquired by Joseph Hulston,[51] but does not reappear.

No later reference has been found to the Colwick mills mentioned in 1337,[52] but fish-ponds were appurtenant to the Grange in 1627.[53] There was a dovecote on the manor in 1587.[54]

BINWELL LANE FARM corresponds to that part of Colwick Manor which extended into Doddershall or the second of the two messuages mentioned in 1587[55] and 1608.[56] Lipscomb says that this farm was sold by Alban Pigott about 1640 to Sir Thomas Reade, kt.[57] He died in 1650,[58] and his grandson and heir Compton Reade of Barton, Berkshire, and afterwards of Shipton Court, Oxfordshire was created a baronet in 1661.[59] In 1766 Binwell Lane Farm was owned by his descendant Sir John Reade, the fifth baronet.[60] He sold it in 1788 to Samuel Athawes,[61] from whom it passed in 1822[62] by bequest to the Rev. John Athawes,[63] who became rector of Loughton in 1833.[64] His son the Rev. John Thomas Athawes succeeded his father as rector in 1883.[65]

A *RECTORY MANOR* was attached to each of the three portions of Waddesdon rectory (see advowson). Each had a residence and a plot of land of

[17] *Cal. Pat.* 1334–8, p. 276.
[18] *Cal. Close,* 1337–9, pp. 27, 116.
[19] *Cal. Pat.* 1338–40, p. 348.
[20] Ibid.
[21] *V.C.H. Bucks.* iii, 305–6.
[22] Chan. Inq. p.m. 13 Hen. VI, no. 35.
[23] It is not named in the inquisition on the death of her husband Sir William Moleyns in 1429 (Chan. Inq. p.m. 8 Hen. VI, no. 38), but is included in 1441 in her jointure and dower lands (Mins. Accts. [Gen. Ser.], bdle. 761, no. 3).
[24] Com. Pleas D. Enr. Mich. 31 Hen. VIII, m. 2.
[25] Recov. R. Mich. 7 Geo. IV, m. 295. A settlement in respect of this manor was made in 1586 (Feet of F. Bucks. Mich. 28 & 29 Eliz.).
[26] *Cal. Chart. R.* 1327–41, p. 463.
[27] Chan. Inq. p.m. Edw. II, file 104, no. 1.
[28] Hunter, op. cit. i, 61.
[29] Chan. Inq. p.m. Edw. II, file 83, no. 1.
[30] *Hund. R.* (Rec. Com.), i, 24.
[31] *Feud. Aids,* i, 95, 121.

[32] Chan. Inq. p.m. (Ser. 2), ccxiv, 224 ; cccxlviii, 143.
[33] *Cal. Chart. R.* 1300–26, p. 286. An *inspeximus* and confirmation in 1315 of a grant in free alms by Aymer de Valence of his rights in the lands of the original grant.
[34] *Hund. R.* loc. cit. See also ibid. 42, 45.
[35] *Feud. Aids,* loc. cit.
[36] *Valor Eccl.* (Rec. Com.), iv, 212.
[37] *L. and P. Hen. VIII,* xiii (2), g. 1182 (18*l*).
[38] Ibid. xiv (2), g. 780 (19).
[39] Chan. Inq. p.m. (Ser. 2), ccxiv, 224. No date on the memorial slab in the chancel of Waddesdon Church.
[40] Ibid.; Recov. R. Mich. 17 & 18 Eliz. m. 922 ; Fine R. 30 Eliz. pt. i, no. 22.
[40a] Feet of F. Bucks. Trin. 6 Jas. I ; Chan. Inq. p.m. (Ser. 2), cccxlviii, 143.
[41] Chan. Inq. p.m. (Ser. 2), ccccxxviii, 76.
[42] Ibid.
[43] Fine R. 10 Chas. I, pt. i, no. 50.
[44] Lipscomb, op. cit. i, 501, quoting Par. Reg.

[45] *Visit. of Bucks.* (Harl. Soc.), 130.
[46] Close, 6 Will. and Mary, pt. viii, no. 31.
[47] Ibid.
[48] Lipscomb, op. cit. i, 487.
[49] Recov. R. Trin. 13 Geo. II, m. 43.
[50] Lysons, op. cit. i (3), 656.
[51] Recov. R. East. 9 Geo. IV, m. 243.
[52] *Cal. Pat.* 1334–8, p. 493. The second mill appears to have stood on a small stream at Binwell Lane Farm (Lipscomb, op. cit. i, 418).
[53] Chan. Inq. p.m. (Ser. 2), ccccxxviii, 76.
[54] Ibid. ccxiv, 224.
[55] Ibid.
[56] Feet of F. Bucks. Trin. 6 Jas. I.
[57] Lipscomb, loc. cit.
[58] G.E.C. *Baronetage,* iii, 172.
[59] Ibid. 173.
[60] Com. Pleas Recov. R. Trin. 6 Geo. III, m. 165.
[61] Lipscomb, loc. cit.
[62] *Gent. Mag.* xcii (1), 572.
[63] Lipscomb, loc. cit.
[64] Ibid. iv, 240.
[65] *Clergy List,* 1914.

about 2½ acres called Priest's Acre.[66] In addition *BENTHAMS MANOR*, appertaining to the first portion, had about 26 acres of land, two closes adjoining the residence and ten houses; *RASING*[67] or *MOTONS MANOR*, appertaining to the second portion, had five houses; *AT THE GREEN*[68] or *GREEN END MANOR*, belonging to the third portion, comprised about 20 acres of land (chargeable with straw and hay to litter the church), £12 yearly from Pitchcott rectory[69] and five houses.[70] The three manors were leased by royal licence in 1571 for twenty-one years at a yearly rent of £15 each to Richard Senhouse.[71] Since there is now only one rector of Waddesdon, he is lord of the three manors. The Court Rolls in his possession date from 1595.[72]

The hamlet of *WARMSTONE*, in Waddesdon, was held in the 13th and 14th centuries as one-fifth of a fee of the honour of Wallingford.[73]

A mesne lordship there was held by the lords of Waddesdon Manor (q.v.) from the later 13th century to 1409,[74] when Edward Courtenay Earl of Devon with his wife Maud surrendered his rights as mesne lord.[75] Yearly rents of 25s. 4d. and 2 lb. of pepper were payable in 1501[76] to the lord of Eythrope.

Robert de Rival was holding Warmstone in 1235,[77] and John le Brut and his tenants (apparently including six sub-tenants of the Courtenays)[78] early in the 14th century.[79] John le Brut had been succeeded by Henry le Brut before 1346.[80] In 1409 Thomas Kerdington, tenant of the greater part of Warmstone, obtained the reversion of the remainder on the death of William Cowper with a release of mesne rights from Edward Courtenay Earl of Devon and his wife Maud.[81] In 1415 John and Thomasine Burbache settled the manor,[82] and in 1429 they conveyed it to William Puxstede, sen.[83] It passed later to Walter Brightwell, and descended with Brightwell's fee in Chearsley (q.v.) to Nicholas Brightwell. In 1502 he and his wife Emma conveyed it to Edward Saunders.[84] Eventually it came to the Goodwins, being apparently included with Waddesdon Manor in the grant of 1540. A settlement between Sir Edward Saunders

and John Goodwin and his son John respecting lands in Waddesdon was made in 1557,[85] and may refer to Warmstone, which in any case has since descended as a part of the Waddesdon Manor estate (q.v.).

The hamlet of Westcott was originally part of the Courtenay Waddesdon Manor (q.v.). Reynold Courtenay evidently settled certain lands in Waddesdon and Westcott, afterwards known as *WESTCOTT MANOR*, on his daughter Egeline and her husband Gilbert Basset,[86] who granted them late in the 12th century to Bicester Priory, Oxfordshire.[87] This manor was retained by this house until the Dissolution.[88] In 1540 it was granted to John Goodwin,[89] and has since descended with Waddesdon Manor (q.v.)[90] to Miss Alice de Rothschild.

A small estate described in 1230 as 11 librates of land in Waddesdon[91] appears later as *WESTCOTT MANOR*. Previously held of the honour of Wallingford,[92] by the accession of Henry IV it became attached to the Duchy of Lancaster,[93] and was so held in 1544.[94]

This estate was granted in 1230 in marriage with his daughter Hawise, by Robert Courtenay to John Nevill.[95] In 1246 the custody of the latter's lands and heirs was given to John Courtenay.[96] Hawise Nevill did not long survive her second husband John de Gatesden,[97] who died in 1269.[98] In 1357 when Margaret de la Warde was holding Westcott Manor for life of the heritage of Robert de Teye, a conveyance was made of Robert's reversionary rights to John Nevill of Essex[99] for life, with remainder to William Bohun Earl of Northampton and his heirs.[100] In 1380 land in Westcott was included in the estates of the latter's son[1] Humphrey Bohun last Earl of Hereford and Essex.[2] His son-in-law Henry of Lancaster[3] about 1396 granted Westcott Manor for life to Thomas Duke of Gloucester,[4] who died in the following year.[5] Livery was granted in 1398 to Henry of Lancaster,[6] who in 1403, after his accession as Henry IV, leased Westcott Manor for twelve years to John Burbache.[7] It was part of the dower of Katherine widow of Henry V,[8] and in 1475 was

[66] Lipscomb, op. cit. i, 494, quoting from an old terrier among the Willis MSS. in the Bodleian Library.

[67] *Cal. of Papal Letters*, ii, 89. William of Withington was allowed to retain Rasing in 1311. He was succeeded as rector of the second portion in 1318 by Eustace Moton (Lipscomb, op. cit. i, 499), from whom the manor derived its later name.

[68] *Cal. of Papal Letters*, viii, 387.

[69] In 1349 John son of Richard le Spenser, of Fleet Marston, recovered seisin with Richard de Stoke of Bicester of 1 messuage and 21 acres of land and meadow in Pitchcott against Henry de Chaddesden, rector of the third portion of Waddesdon (*Abbrev. Rot. Orig.* [Rec. Com.], ii, 199).

[70] Lipscomb, op. cit. i, 494, quoting from the old terrier.

[71] Pat. 13 Eliz. pt. vii, m. 8.

[72] *Rec. of Bucks.* (Bucks. Arch. and Archit. Soc.), x, 98; other rolls at the B. M. are Add. R. 47356–7, 47361 (A–Ð), 47364–7; Add. Chart. 18145–6, 18148–9, 47358–60, 47363.

[73] *Testa de Nevill* (Rec. Com.), 261b; *Feud. Aids*, i, 94, 119; cf. Ct. R. (Gen. Ser.), portf. 212, no. 5, 7.

[74] *Cal. Inq. p.m.* (Edw. I), iii, 26; *Cal.*

Close, 1288–96, p. 237; Chan. Inq. p.m. 1 Hen. VI, no. 63.

[75] Feet of F. Bucks. East. 11 Hen. IV, no. 3.

[76] Chan. Inq. p.m. (Ser. 2), xv, 58; cf. Feet of F. Bucks. Mich. 2 & 3 Eliz.

[77] *Testa de Nevill* (Rec. Com.), 258, 261b.   [78] *Cal. Inq. p.m.* loc. cit.

[79] *Feud. Aids*, i, 94.

[80] Ibid. 119.

[81] Feet of F. Bucks. East. 11 Hen. IV, no. 3.

[82] Ibid. Hil. 3 Hen. V, no. 1.

[83] Ibid. East. 8 Hen. VI, no. 3.

[84] Ibid. Hil. 17 Hen. VII.

[85] Com. Pleas D. Enr. Mich. 4 & 5 Phil. and Mary. This document is now unfit for production.

[86] Kennet, op. cit. i, 268.

[87] Add. Chart. 10597; cf. Maitland, *Bracton's Note Bk.* iii, 355; *Cal. Pat.* 1216–25, p. 489; Feet of F. case 14, file 15, no. 6. The names of several tenants each holding half a virgate are given.

[88] Mins. Accts. (Gen. Ser.), bdle. 763, no. 15; Ct. R. (Gen. Ser.), portf. 155, no. 28; *Valor Eccl.* (Rec. Com.), ii, 189.

[89] *L. and P. Hen. VIII*, xv, g. 282 (111).

[90] Priv. Act, 5 Geo. III, cap. 7. Some Court Rolls still exist (Ct. R. [Gen. Ser.],

portf. 155, no. 28; Add. Chart. 18147; 18150).

[91] Cur. Reg. R. 104, m. 24.

[92] Chan. Inq. p.m. 3 Ric. II, no. 12.

[93] Duchy of Lanc. Misc. Bks. xvi, fol. 33; xix, fol. 22 d.; Mins. Accts. (Duchy of Lanc.), bdle. 660, no. 10661.

[94] Duchy of Lanc. Misc. Bks. xxii, fol. 193.

[95] Cur. Reg. R. 104, m. 24.

[96] *Excerpta e Rot. Fin.* (Rec. Com.), i, 461.

[97] Chan. Inq. p.m. Hen. III, file 45, no. 14.

[98] *Cal. Inq. p.m.* (Hen. III), i, 223.

[99] He died without issue in 1358 (G.E.C. *Complete Peerage*, vi, 14).

[100] Feet of F. Div. Co. Mich. 31 Edw. III, no. 28; Chan. Inq. p.m. 32 Edw. III (1st nos.), no. 30.

[1] G.E.C. *Complete Peerage*, vi, 68.

[2] Chan. Inq. p.m. 3 Ric. II, no. 12.

[3] G.E.C. loc. cit.

[4] *Cal. Pat.* 1396–9, p. 13.

[5] Chan. Inq. p.m. 21 Ric. II, no. 29.

[6] Close, 21 Ric. II, pt. ii, m. 20.

[7] Duchy of Lanc. Misc. Bks. xvi, fol. 33.

[8] *Cal. Pat.* 1436–41, p. 32; Mins. Accts. (Duchy of Lanc.), bdle. 653, no. 10565.

granted to Elizabeth wife of Edward IV.[9] This manor in 1519 was leased for seven years to John Lamborne,[10] and in 1544 was granted to John Goodwin,[11] owner of the other manor of Westcott, into which it was absorbed.

A small property in Westcott was held by service of one-fifth of a fee by Richard le Mount in 1292,[12] and it appears to have been held by members of his family[13] until it escheated to Hugh Courtenay Earl of Devon, who held it at his death in 1422.[14] It corresponds to the land in Westcott and Waddesdon held by Richard Nash long before his death in 1499, when he was succeeded by his son Thomas.[15] It is possibly the property purchased from Sir Francis Goodwin and Thomas Googe by William Deane shortly before his death in 1615 when his son and heir William was a minor,[16] and may be the spurious Westcott Manor conveyed in 1725 by John and Elizabeth Street and others to John Ashwell, jun.[17]

to the east. A little later, about 1340, the north arcade was formed and the north aisle added to the nave, and towards the end of the century the chancel was widened on the north and a west tower was erected. The chancel was again altered in the latter part of the 15th century, the eastern half of the south wall being rebuilt ; at the same time the clearstory was added to the nave, the three eastern bays of the south wall of the south aisle were taken down and widened, and part of the north wall of the north aisle, to the west of the north doorway, appears to have been renewed, probably on account of some structural failure. The south porch, since rebuilt, is also an addition of the same period. The church has been much restored, the first restoration being completed in 1877 ; the tower, with the western walls of the aisles, was entirely rebuilt in 1891–2, and the exterior was extensively repaired in 1902. With the exception of the walls of the tower and the new walls

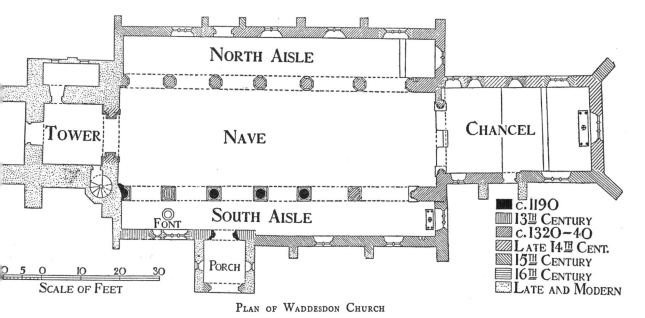

PLAN OF WADDESDON CHURCH

Adapted from the Inventory of the Historical Monuments of Buckinghamshire with the permission of the Royal Commission and the consent of the Controller of H.M. Stationery Office

CHURCHES

The church of *ST. MICHAEL* consists of a chancel 37 ft. by 21 ft., nave 81 ft. 6 in. by 23 ft., north aisle 9 ft. 6 in. wide, south aisle 9 ft. wide at the east and 7 ft. wide at the west, south porch, and west tower 15 ft. square. These measurements are all internal.

The three middle columns of the south arcade of the nave, and the west respond, which are of the late 12th century, are the earliest details in the building. The nave and the south aisle were lengthened some 12 ft. westwards in the 13th century, and early in the 14th century the nave was further lengthened eastward by about 20 ft., entailing the entire rebuilding of the chancel on a new site

of the aisles, all the building is rough-casted ; the roofs are lead-covered.

The east window of the chancel belongs to the reconstruction of the late 14th century. It is of three cinquefoiled lights, acutely pointed, with cusped intersecting tracery in a pointed head ; the rear arch is four-centred, a peculiar feature. The north-east window, a square-headed insertion of the late 15th century, is of three cinquefoiled lights ; to the west of it are two 14th-century trefoiled lights, and at the extreme west end of the wall is a pointed two-light window with a plain spandrel in the head, which has probably been reconstructed in the 17th century. The rood stairs were entered from the chancel by a

[9] Feet of F. Div. Co. Trin. 15 Edw. IV, no. 103. A grant of £50 yearly from the issues of several manors, including Westcott, was granted by the Crown in 1481 to her brother, Sir Edward Wydvill (Duchy of Lanc. Misc. Bks. xix, fol. 22 d.).

[10] Mins. Accts. (Duchy of Lanc.), bdle. 660, no. 10661.
[11] Duchy of Lanc. Misc. Bks. xxii, fol. 193.
[12] Chan. Inq. p.m. 20 Edw. I, file 62, no. 7 ; *Cal. Close*, 1288–96, p. 237.
[13] *Hist. MSS. Com. Rep.* ix, App. ii, 405a. Agnes, widow of John de Mon-

tibus, is named in two conveyances of property in 1294.
[14] Chan. Inq. p.m. 1 Hen. VI, no. 63. Said to have been formerly held by Richard le Mount.
[15] Ibid. (Ser. 2), xiv, 57.
[16] Ibid. cccxlviii, 110.
[17] Feet of F. Bucks. Hil. 11 Geo. I.

pointed doorway in the north respond of the chancel arch, which has been since blocked. The south-east window is like the corresponding window in the north wall. A break in the south wall about 18 ft. from the east end marks the extent of the 15th-century rebuilding ; immediately to the west of the break is a small priest's doorway contemporary with the earliest rebuilding of the chancel, and to the west of the doorway is a pointed window of two cinquefoiled lights with tracery of the same period. The chancel arch, which is chamfered towards the chancel and elaborately moulded towards the nave, is also of the 14th century ; the responds are half-octagonal and have moulded capitals and bases. Within the arch is a modern chancel screen.

The nave arcades are each of six bays, the two eastern bays on either side being wider than the western bays. The 14th-century north arcade has pointed arches of three orders and octagonal columns and responds with moulded capitals and bases. The two eastern arches of the south arcade date from the 14th century and are pointed, having two orders, the outer chamfered and the inner moulded. The east respond is like those of the chancel arch, and the eastern column, from which both arches spring, is octagonal and has a moulded capital and base. The late 12th-century columns of the next three bays are circular and have scalloped capitals, broken out on the nave face to form the capitals of small attached shafts supported by corbels about 1 ft. below the necking. Upon these capitals originally stood small shafts with scalloped capitals and moulded bases, which must have supported the wall-posts of a former timber roof. Two of these shafts remain in position, but the easternmost has disappeared. The three arches of this portion of the arcade are pointed and of two moulded orders, and have labels on the nave face moulded with a hollow containing dog-tooth and pellet enrichment, the labels on the aisle face being plain rolls. These arches appear to have been rebuilt in the 14th century. The 13th-century western-most arch is of two chamfered orders, and springs from a circular column with a moulded capital and a restored base ; on the nave face of the arch is a plain label similar in section to the adjoining labels. The west respond is that of the original 12th-century arcade re-used. It is semicircular and like the contemporary columns of the three middle bays, except that the wall-post shaft is continued to the ground. Over each arcade are six late 15th-century square-headed clearstory windows, each of two cinquefoiled lights.

In the east wall of the north aisle is a pointed window with modern two-light tracery in an original 14th-century opening. In the easternmost bay of the north wall is a square-headed, late 15th-century window of three cinquefoiled lights. The windows in the next two bays are like the east window, having modern tracery of the same type in original 14th-century openings. In the fourth bay is a pointed doorway of the same date. The window in the westernmost bay is of the same date and design as the easternmost window, but has been considerably restored. There is a 14th-century piscina with a trefoiled head and round basin in the north face of the east respond of the nave arcade for the use of the north aisle altar.

The two eastern windows in the south wall of the widened eastern portion of the south aisle are of late 15th-century date, each having two cinquefoiled lights under a depressed head, while that in the east wall is of three similar lights under a straight-sided, pointed head. To the west of the break in the wall which marks the junction of the later building with the work of the 13th century is a reset late 12th-century doorway with a pointed head, enriched with the cheveron, and jambs of two orders, the outer order being shafted. In the bay to the west of the door-way is a square-headed three-light window of 16th-century date, and immediately adjoining its western jamb, but lower in the wall, is a 15th-century cin-quefoiled light with a square external head. In the usual position is a piscina for the south aisle altar with a depressed head and circular bowl. Over the door-way externally is a square-headed recess of 14th-century date. The modern south porch has a pointed and moulded outer arch, partly reset 15th-century work, and square-headed single-light windows.

The rebuilt tower is of three stages, with a stair-turret at the south-east angle and a vestry on its north side. All the details are modern except the late 14th-century arch to the ground stage, which is pointed and continuously moulded, and the bell-chamber windows, which have original square heads of the 15th century. On the south side is a clock. The roofs are all modern, but some old timbers have been made use of in the porch roof.

The octagonal font is of c. 1400 ; the sides have quatrefoil panels with shields. At the west end of the south aisle is placed an oak chest with a high-backed seat upon it having a carved canopy with an entablature, and arms at the sides with carved standards. It has been much restored, but is probably French work of the early 16th century. At the east end of the south aisle is a sepulchral slab of the late 13th century with a sunk quatrefoil containing the bust of a priest. In the floor of the chancel are four 16th-century glazed tiles with a pattern in relief.

On the north side of the chancel is a large effigy of a man in armour of the style of the first half of the 14th century with a sword and misericord. Hung on his left arm is a broken heater-shaped shield. The feet rest on a lion. On the slab has been cut by some later hand the date 1330.[17a] At the south-east of the nave is the fine brass of Sir Roger Dynham, who died in 1490. This, with the coffin con-taining his remains, was brought from Eythrope, where it was discovered, in 1887, and the remains were re-interred on the east side of the south porch. The brass contains the figure of the knight, who wears plate armour covered by a tabard charged with his arms, a fesse indented. The head rests on a tilting helm with mantling, hat of estate, and part of a crest, and the feet on a stag. Inclosing the figure is a triple canopy, and at the corners were originally four shields, two of which have been lost ; the shields which remain are Dynham, and Dynham impaling a cross with five roundels thereon. Framing the whole is a brass marginal inscription with the symbols of the Evangelists. On the south side of the chancel is the brass of Richard Huntyndon, a former rector, who died in 1543 ; he is represented in mass vestments, holding the chalice

[17a] The effigy may be that of Richard Darches who held the manor of Eythrope and died in 1316 or of his son Richard who died after 1346.

and Host. In the same part of the church is a brass with a shrouded figure and rhyming inscription, commemorating Hugh Bristowe, who died in 1548. A third brass in the chancel is to Robert Pigott and his wife Mary. The inscription is undated, but Robert Pigott died in 1587 and his wife probably predeceased him. Robert Pigott is represented in plate armour, and his wife in a gown with puffed sleeves. Originally there appear to have been brasses of his children, but only part of the brass of his sons and the indent of the figures of his daughters now remain. There were also two shields, one of which, charged with the arms of Pigott of Colwick in Waddesdon, impaling Yate of Lyford, still remains. Round the whole is a marginal inscription. Under the eastern arch of the north arcade of the nave is a brass to Mary the wife of Cuthbert Raynolds, who died in 1602, with a quartered shield of Raynolds.

On the north wall of the chancel is a tablet commemorating Guy Carleton, who died in 1608, and at the east end of the south wall are tablets to Christian Wake, daughter of Sir William Wigson of Wolston, Warwickshire, who died in 1609, and to Henry Wilkinson, a former rector, 1647. A second monument on the north wall commemorates John Ellis, a former rector, who died in 1681, and his wife Susan, who died in 1700. Externally, on the south buttress of the chancel, are set tablets to Henry Batterson, who died in 1682, his wife Anne, 1689, and their sons Henry and Michael, 1680 and 1696, and to 'E. B. uxor W. B.' of Warmstone in Waddesdon, who died in 1699. There are also 18th-century slabs to the Green family.

There is a ring of six cast steel bells by Naylor, Vickers & Co., of Sheffield, 1861–2, and a clock bell bearing the date 1806.

The plate consists of a chalice and paten of 1715, a standing paten of the same date, a flagon of 1709 and a modern chalice.

The registers begin in 1538.

The church of *ST. MARY*, Westcott, was erected in 1867 by Richard, last Duke of Buckingham and Chandos, from designs by G. E. Street. It consists of chancel, nave, north and south aisles, and bell-turret. It is a chapel of ease to Waddesdon Church.

ADVOWSON By the early 13th century Waddesdon Rectory was a prebend[18] in Lincoln Cathedral held in three portions, each portion being estimated at £10 yearly in 1291[19] and at £15 net in 1535.[20] The advowson of each portion descended with Waddesdon Manor[21] (q.v.) until 1874, when it was retained by John Duke of Marlborough, and has since descended with the title to the present owner, Charles, the ninth duke. In 1876 the three portions, subject to the next voidance of the first and second portions, were consolidated into one rectory.[22]

In 1765 an annual payment of £105 was secured to the rectors of Waddesdon from the Duke of

Marlborough's estate in lieu of all tithes from Westcott and ancient inclosures.[23] In 1774 an allotment was awarded to each in lieu of small tithes in Waddesdon and 7 acres in Lot Meadow which they had held from time immemorial in redemption of tithes there.[24]

There was formerly a chapel at Eythrope Manor. By the will of Roger, brother of John, Lord Dynham, who died in 1490, Eythrope Chapel, then being built, was to be 'consecrated anew' as a chantry chapel, to which his body was to be removed from its temporary resting-place in Waddesdon Church.[25] In 1491 Lord Dynham made arrangements with Fotheringhay College for a yearly payment of £6 13s. 4d. to the chantry priest.[26] This was continued until the suppression of the chantries in 1548,[27] when the chapel was reported as of no great use except for the household of Sir Robert Dormer, who supplied the ornaments for the chapel and a lodging for the priest.[28] Lysons states on the authority of Browne Willis that Sir William Stanhope had Eythrope Chapel fitted up for divine service in 1728, but that in 1738 he caused it to be taken down and used the stones for a bridge over the Thame near his house.[29]

In the latter part of the 14th century there was a chapel of the Holy Trinity at Westcott for the maintenance of which an indulgence was granted by Bishop Buckingham.[30]

In 1549 4s. 4d. from land in Westcott, in the occupation of John Gurney with land there, for which he paid half a pound of pepper yearly; land in the occupation of John Edwards, and land in Waddesdon, formerly parcel of the possessions of the fraternity of Aylesbury; also half an acre one rood in Prior's furlong in the north field of Waddesdon, formerly given for the maintenance of a lamp in Waddesdon Church, were granted to Henry Tanner and Thomas Boches.[31]

CHARITIES Arthur Goodwin by a codicil to his will proved in 1644,[32] reciting his intention of erecting six almshouses, requested Lord Wharton, so soon as the distractions of the times would permit, to complete the same; and the testator charged the manor of Waddesdon with an annuity of £30, to be divided equally among the inmates. Each of the six inmates receives £2 10s. half yearly.

Charity of Matthew Nash:—See under parish of Quainton. The payments due to Waddesdon and Westcott were redeemed in 1887 by the transfer to the official trustees of £23 13s. 4d. consols, now producing 11s. 8d. yearly, which is expended in the distribution on Good Friday of twenty loaves to twenty widows.

In 1724 Lewis Fetto by his will directed £140 to be laid out in land, the rents to be applied as to 40s. yearly for putting four poor children to school, and the residue for putting out apprentices. The property consists of about 12 acres in Westcott, let partly in

[18] *Reg. of Hugh of Wells* (Cant. and York Soc.), ii, 49.

[19] *Pope Nich. Tax.* (Rec. Com.), 34.

[20] *Valor Eccl.* (Rec. Com.), iv, 235.

[21] *Reg. of Hugh of Wells* (Cant. and York Soc.), ii, 49, 79; Harl. MS. 6950, fol. 79, 80, 123, 126; 6951, fol. 36, 71, 72, 99, 106, 107, 118; 6952, fol. 22,

26, 36, 56, 57, 69, 96, 107; 6953, fol. 26, 27; Inst. Bks. (P.R.O.) of 17th cent.; Bacon, *Liber Regis.* 504.

[22] *Lond. Gaz.* 1830–83, p. 667.

[23] Priv. Act, 5 Geo. III, cap. 7.

[24] Ibid. 14 Geo. III, cap. 24.

[25] P.C.C. 27 Milles.

[26] Chant. Cert. 4, no. 5.

[27] *Valor Eccl.* (Rec. Com.), iv, 235; Chant. Cert. 5, no. 54.

[28] Chant. Cert. 4, no. 5.

[29] Lysons, op. cit. i (3), 655.

[30] Linc. Epis. Reg. Buckingham Memo. 31 d.   [31] Close, 3 Edw. VI, pt. vi, m. 13.

[32] P.C.C. 1 Rivers. Codicil to will dated 30 Aug. 1642.

allotments, producing in the whole about £24 a year. The annual sum of 40s. is applied in prizes to children attending the elementary schools under the title of 'Fetto's Educational Foundation,' and the residue in premiums for apprenticing, usually of £15.

The official trustees also hold a sum of £167 consols, arising from the sale in 1883 of land purchased with a legacy of £30 by will of one John Beck for apprenticing. The dividends of £4 3s. 4d. yearly are applied with Fetto's charity.

William Turner by his will proved in the P.C.C. in 1784 bequeathed his residuary personal estate for the benefit of the poor. The bequest is now represented by £3,265 11s. 6d. consols, with the official trustees. The annual dividends, amounting to £81 12s. 8d., are distributed half-yearly in gifts of money, the clerk receiving £2 a year for managing the charity.

The schools, known as the British Schools, comprised in deed, 17 October 1846, consist of 1 rood of ground with the school erected thereon, and a piece of land containing 30½ perches, formerly the site of the school, but now a plantation.

Nonconformist Charities :—The Particular Baptist Chapel was founded by Francis Cox by indentures of lease and release dated respectively 7 and 8 September 1792. Francis Cox by his will proved in the P.C.C., 16 July 1803, bequeathed £1,000 for the support of the minister and £100 for the benefit of poor members. The legacies, less duty, are now represented by a sum of £1,034, which is secured on mortgage of a farm at Owlswick in Monks Risborough at 4 per cent., producing £41 6s. 8d. yearly, which is applied proportionately for the benefit of the minister and for the poor.

In 1825 Henry Cox by deed conveyed to trustees two messuages in Waddesdon and a building adjoining. The trust property was sold in 1889 for £300, which has been placed on mortgage of houses in Watford (Herts.) at 4½ per cent. The annual income of £13 10s. is applied towards the expenses of the chapel, repairs, &c.

LOWER or NETHER WINCHENDON

Wichendone, Witchende (xi cent.) ; Winchendona, Wichintona (xii cent.) ; Winchedon, Winchende, Wynchedon, Wynchedone Desous, Nether Wynchedon (xiii cent.) ; Wychydone Inferior (xiv cent.) ; Lower Wynchindon, Wynchenden le Neyther (xvi cent.); Nether Winchingdon (xvii cent.); Little Winchenden (xix cent.).

The area of this parish is 1,553 acres, of which 469 are arable land, where wheat, barley and turnips are grown, about 1,026 permanent grass, and 2 woods and plantations.[1] The soil is limestone and clay on a subsoil of Kimmeridge Clay and Portland Beds. In the greater part of Lower Winchendon the land stands about 300 ft. above the ordnance datum, rising to more than 400 ft. at the summit of a ridge which runs from north-east to south-west across the parish. The south-eastern boundary follows approximately the course of the River Thame and the north-western boundary that of a tributary of the same.

The village, which still contains some interesting 17th-century timber and brick cottages, is situated in a well-wooded valley at the base of hills. South of the church, on low ground, stands the manor house, known as Winchendon Priory since the middle of the 19th century,[2] and now the seat of Mrs. Napier Higgins. The present house, which consists of a central block and two wings, was probably built by William Goodwin before 1571, when he conveyed it to Thomas Tyringham as 'all that parte of my mansion howse' which he had lately built.[3] The house is stuccoed and was considerably altered about 1800. The old hall in the central block, now the dining room, has

an original arched doorway with foliated spandrels, and a stone mantelpiece, the frieze of which is enriched with foliated and grotesque ornament. Over the doorway is the name John Danvers. The drawing-room has 16th-century panelling of linen-fold pattern and an arched stone fireplace. Some of the windows contain 17th-century glass, probably foreign. On the south side of the house are two fine original chimneys with groups of twisted and moulded shafts.

The water-mill standing east of the park doubtless marks the site of the mill mentioned in 1086[4] and later.[5] There are several 17th-century farm-houses scattered over the parish. The house called the Manor Farm, a building of ⌐-shape, constructed mainly of brick with windows having brick mullions, has an oak door bearing the date 1620. This may be the capital messuage which Richard Mills held in the 17th century,[6] and which came to the Knollys family through the marriage of his daughter Ellen.[7]

Winchendon Hill Farm, another 17th-century house, is built of stone with a tiled roof and contains some 17th-century panelling ; a door preserved here is said to have been brought from Eythrope House. Marsh Farm is a stone house bearing on a tablet the date 1687. Bakers Farm is an early 17th-century house of brick and timber, and Muskhill Farm is a brick building of the latter part of the same century.

MANOR This manor, which Eddeda held of Queen Edith before the Norman Conquest, was owned by Walter Giffard in 1086,[8] and was granted before 1164 by his son Walter to the abbey of his foundation in Long

---

[1] Statistics from Bd. of Agric. (1905).
[2] Sheahan, *Hist. and Topog. of Bucks.* 436-8.   [3] Close, 13 Eliz. pt. vi.
[4] *V.C.H. Bucks.* i, 248.
[5] *Valor Eccl.* (Rec. Com.), iv, 232 ; Pat. 1 Eliz. pt. x, m. 23 ; 13 Eliz. pt. ii, m. 20 ; 16 Eliz. pt. xiii, m. 10 ; Feet of F. Bucks. East. 13 Eliz. ; Hil. 16 Eliz. ; Trin. 38 Eliz. ; Mich. 20 Jas. I ; East. 1650.

[6] Chan. Inq. p.m. (Ser. 2), ccccxviii, 99. His widow Ellen afterwards married Thomas Tyringham (Lipscomb, *Hist. and Antiq. of Bucks.* 1, 519).
[7] Chan. Inq. p.m. (Ser. 2), ccccxviii, 99. The connexion of the Knollys family with Lower Winchendon was, however, of earlier date. Lettice, daughter of Sir Francis Knollys, courtier of Edward VI and Elizabeth, and wife of two of

Elizabeth's favourites, was born in the parish (C. Shorter, *Highways and Byways in Bucks.* 37 ; *Dict. Nat. Biog.*). There were Knollyses of Lower Winchendon until the 18th century (Feet of F. Div. Co. Mich. 6 Geo. I ; *Cal. Com. for Advance of Money*, 972-3 ; *Cal. S.P. Dom.* 1694-5, p. 136).
[8] *V.C.H. Bucks.* i, 248, 249.

WADDESDEN CHURCH FROM THE SOUTH-EAST

WADDESDEN CHURCH: THE INTERIOR LOOKING EAST

LOWER WINCHENDON CHURCH FROM THE SOUTH-EAST

Crendon.[9] The Abbot of Nutley held the manor of *LOWER WINCHENDON* of the honour of

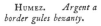

HUMEZ. *Argent a border gules bezanty.*

WAKE. *Or two bars gules with three roundels gules in the chief.*

Giffard in 1255,[10] and of the marshalsy in 1302.[11] In the 16th century it was held in chief.[12]

It is said that during Earl Walter's absence his seneschal resumed the manor,[13] which seems to have reverted to the Crown on Walter's death in 1164.[14] In 1175 Richard de Humez, Constable of Normandy, held half of Lower Winchendon by virtue of a grant from the king,[15] and in 1180 his son William de Humez had succeeded him.[16] Before the end of the reign of Henry II William gave his possessions in this parish to his daughter Agnes in marriage with Baldwin Wake.[17] The abbey made an unsuccessful claim to the manor in the reign of Richard I, and again about 1205.[18] In 1207 Agnes Wake obtained a charter from King John empowering her to hold her land in Winchendon of him in chief and forbidding the Abbot and canons of Nutley to vex or molest her.[19] She was enjoying her moiety of the manor undisturbed in 1210,[20] but eight years later an

action was brought against her by the abbot,[21] which was still pending in 1221, when its conclusion was deferred until the king's majority.[22] Possibly some compromise was effected privately, for Agnes and her son Baldwin gave a messuage in this parish to Nutley Abbey.[23] In 1234 this long dispute was ended by a grant made by Hugh Wake, grandson and heir to Agnes,[24] of the moiety of the manor of Lower Winchendon to the Abbot of Nutley for a yearly rent of £16.[25]

The other moiety came into the possession of Robert de Briencourt and was forfeited by him in the reign of Richard I. The abbot offered the king 100 marks for its recovery, but the king's absence on the crusade prevented the completion of this transaction. In 1205 an offer of £100 and two palfreys was accepted by King John.[26] Five years later the abbot owned 15 librates of land, once of Robert de Briencourt, forfeited as land of the Normans,[27] and

THE VILLAGE, LOWER WINCHENDON

from 1234 to the surrender of his house he and his successors were lords of all Lower Winchendon.[28] Lands in this parish were alienated to the abbey in the 13th and 14th centuries by Walkelin de Ardern, Robert Pepir, John Dering and other donors.[29]

---

[9] Dugdale, *Mon.* vi, 278 ; G.E.C. *Peerage*, ii, 62. The gift was in free alms (Cur. Reg. R. 80, m. 1 ; *Plac. de Quo Warr.* [Rec. Com.], 89 ; *Feud. Aids*, i, 121), but in the 12th century one moiety was held by Richard de Humez, and his son William after him in serjeanty, as Constable of Normandy (see below).

[10] *Hund. R.* (Rec. Com.), i, 23.

[11] *Feud. Aids*, i, 96.

[12] Pat. 2 Eliz. pt. iv, m. 45 ; 20 Eliz. pt. iii, m. 26 ; Memo. R. (Exch. L.T.R.), Mich. 16 Eliz. m. 73.

[13] *Rot. de Oblatis et Fin.* (Rec. Com.), 271-2. [14] G.E.C. loc. cit.

[15] Pipe R. 21 Hen. II (Pipe R. Soc.), 56 ; 22 Hen. II, 27.

[16] Ibid. 26 *Hen. II*, 46 ; Dugdale, *Baronage*, i, 631.

[17] Cur. Reg. R. 79, m. 7 ; 80, m. 1 ; Pipe R. 9 John, m. 15 ; Dugdale, loc. cit.

[18] *Rot. de Oblatis et Fin.* loc. cit.

[19] Cur. Reg. R. 79, m. 7 ; 80, m. 1 ; *Cal. Rot. Pat.* (Rec. Com.), 2 ; Pipe R. Bucks. & Beds. 7 John, m. 15.

[20] *Red Bk. of Exch.* (Rolls Ser.), 538.

[21] *Rot. Lit. Claus.* (Rec. Com.), i, 378b.

[22] Maitland, *Bracton's Note Bk.* iii, 416 ; Cur. Reg. R. 79, m. 7 ; 80, m. 1.

[23] Dugdale, loc. cit.

[24] Ibid.

[25] Feet of F. Bucks. East. 18 Hen. III, no. 4. This rent granted by Hugh to Isabel

de Hogthon in 1240 (Feet of F. Div. Co. Hil. 24 Hen. III, no. 36) was still paid in 1255, when Hugh enjoyed a mesne lordship here (*Hund. R.* [Rec. Com.], i, 23), but seems to have lapsed before the 14th century (*Feud. Aids*, i, 96, 121).

[26] *Rot. de Oblatis et Fin.* (Rec. Com.), 271-2, 242 ; Pipe R. 7 John m. 6.

[27] *Red Bk. of Exch.* (Rolls Ser.), 537 ; *Cal. Rot. Pat.* (Rec. Com.), 11.

[28] *Hund. R.* (Rec. Com.), i, 23 ; *Feud. Aids*, i, 96, 113, 121 ; *Pope Nich. Tax.* (Rec. Com.), 46b ; Dugdale, *Mon.* vi, 280 ; *Valor Eccl.* (Rec. Com.), iv, 232-4 ; *Plac. de Quo Warr.* (Rec. Com.), 89.

[29] *Cal. Pat.* 1281-92, p. 417 ; 1391-6, p. 104 ; 1461-4, p. 469.

In 1535 Lower Winchendon was held by Sir John Dauncey on a lease from the abbot,[30] and it remained in the Crown until his death.[31] Edward VI granted it in 1547 to John Lord Russell and his wife Anne,[32] who sold it to William Goodwin, citizen and mercer of London, twelve years later.[33] The sale was confirmed by the Crown in 1560 to William and his son Blaise.[34] In 1571 Francis Earl of Bedford, son and heir of Lord Russell,[35] and William Goodwin and his wife Margaret alienated the site of the manor, with the capital messuage and lands, to Jerome Weston,[36] on behalf of Thomas Tyringham of Tyringham,[37] who bought of William a few weeks later other land which Goodwin and his son had purchased of the Crown.[38] In the next year a further 300 acres were added to Thomas's holding in Lower Winchendon.[39] Various legal processes followed,[40] and the purchase was finally completed early in 1574.[41] In 1578 the manor was settled on Thomas Tyringham's younger son Thomas and his wife Elizabeth,[42] who were holding it in 1596[43] and 1622.[44] Thomas their son and heir-apparent, on whom Lower Winchendon was settled in 1650 by his brother-in-law and nephew Christopher and Walter Horton,[45] died without issue in 1656 or 1657. He was succeeded by his brother Francis,[46] whose sons John and Francis held after him in turn.[47] Francis died in 1727, leaving a son of the same name, lord in 1728.[48] At his death without issue in 1735[49] Lower Winchendon descended to his sisters, Parnel wife of Charles Pilsworth, and Mary

TYRINGHAM. *Azure a saltire engrailed argent.*   BERNARD. *Argent a bear rampant sable with a muzzle or.*

Tyringham.[50] Mary the survivor left the manor in 1745 to her cousin Jane, daughter of John Tyringham

and wife of Christopher Beresford,[51] who died childless in 1771,[52] after making her cousin Sir Francis Bernard, bart., only son of her mother's sister Margaret daughter of Richard Winlowe, her heir.[53] From Sir Scrope Bernard-Morland, third son and ultimate heir of Sir Francis,[54] who took part in a settlement of the manor in 1819,[55] Lower Winchendon descended in 1830 to his younger son Thomas Tyringham Bernard.[56] He had succeeded to the baronetcy before his death in 1883,[57] when his daughter Mrs. Napier Higgins, the present lady of the manor, inherited his estates.[58]

In the 11th century fourscore eels were an appurtenance of Lower Winchendon Manor,[59] to which fisheries belonged in 1535[60] and later.[61] A dovecote is mentioned in connexion with the capital messuage of the 16th century.[62] View of frankpledge, held by the Abbot of Nutley in 1255[63] and in 1286, when he also claimed tumbrel,[64] was, with court leet, amongst the liberties of the lord of the manor 300 years later,[65] and again in 1622.[66] Assize of bread, wine and ale, included in the grant of 1560,[67] probably also belonged to the abbot.[68]

Land in this parish, of which the rent came to the Abbot of Warden in an exchange with Aumary de St. Amand in 1374, when it was valued at £10 4s. 4½d.,[69] was owned by his successor Abbot Augustine in 1499 as his manor of Lower Winchendon.[70] It seems to have afterwards come to the Abbot of Nutley, who paid the Abbot of Warden a pension of this amount in the 16th century.[71] The Prior of Chicksand acquired in 1242 from Isabel Daubeny the half of a rent of £4 8s. 10d. in Winchendon,[72] and in 1291 he owned rent here of considerable value.[73] The possessions of another religious house, Studley Priory, probably in both Winchendons, were granted in 1540 to John Croke, who alienated them to Sir Robert and Michael Dormer and John Goodwin.[74]

CHURCH The church of *ST. NICHOLAS* consists of a chancel measuring internally 25 ft. 6 in. by 16 ft., nave 52 ft. by 22 ft. 6 in., south porch and west tower; it is built of limestone rubble, the chancel being roofed with tiles and the nave with lead.

The chancel and nave were rebuilt in the first half of the 14th century, but the existence of an

[30] *Valor Eccl.* (Rec. Com.), iv, 232.
[31] Pat. 1 Edw. VI, pt. i, m. 14.
[32] Ibid.
[33] Pat. 1 Eliz. pt. x, m. 23. There are discrepancies in the pedigrees showing the relationship of William to the Goodwins of Upper Winchendon. According to one, he was father of the elder John Goodwin (Lipscomb, loc. cit.), whilst another makes his son Blaise son of the same John (Berry, *Bucks. Gen.* 71).
[34] Pat. 2 Eliz. pt. iv, m. 45.
[35] Burke, *Peerage* (1907).
[36] Pat. 13 Eliz. pt. ii, m. 20; Feet of F. Bucks. East. 13 Eliz.
[37] His wife was Parnel daughter of John Goodwin of Upper Winchendon (Lipscomb, loc. cit.).
[38] Close, 13 Eliz. pt. vi. This can hardly be other than part at least of the lands acquired of the Earl of Bedford.
[39] Feet of F. Bucks. Hil. 14 Eliz. This was the land acquired by William, of Thomas Rede (Close, 4 & 5 Phil. and Mary, pt. xii).
[40] Memo. R. (Exch. L.T.R.), Mich. 16 Eliz. m. 73; Pat. 16 Eliz. pt. xiii, m. 10.

[41] Close, 16 Eliz. pt. xxvii; Feet of F. Bucks. Hil. 16 Eliz.
[42] Pat. 20 Eliz. pt. iii, m. 26.
[43] Feet of F. Bucks. Trin. 38 Eliz.
[44] Ibid. Mich. 20 Jas. I.
[45] Feet of F. Bucks. East. 1650; P.C.C. 137 Ruthen.
[46] P.C.C. 137 Ruthen; Lipscomb, op. cit. i, 519–20.
[47] Lipscomb, loc. cit. John left a daughter (see below) but the manor was entailed on his brother.
[48] Lipscomb, loc. cit.; Recov. R. Trin. 2 Geo. II, m. 296.
[49] P.C.C. Ducie Admon.
[50] Lipscomb, loc. cit. It appears from Mary's will, made in 1740 when Parnel was still alive, that she was then sole possessor of the manor (P.C.C. 193 Edmunds).
[51] P.C.C. 193 Edmunds; Lipscomb, loc. cit.
[52] G.E.C. *Baronetage*, v, 150–1.
[53] P.C.C. 38 Taverner; Lipscomb, loc. cit. Sir Francis obtained his baronetcy by his services to the Crown as Governor of Massachusetts Bay (G.E.C. loc. cit.).

[54] G.E.C. loc. cit.
[55] Recov. R. East. 59 Geo. III, m. 269. Earl Temple was nominal lord at this date.
[56] G.E.C. loc. cit.   [57] Ibid.
[58] Ibid.; Walford, *Co. Families* (1913).
[59] *V.C.H. Bucks.* i, 249.
[60] *Valor Eccl.* (Rec. Com.), iv, 232.
[61] Pat. 1 Eliz. pt. x, m. 23; 13 Eliz. pt. ii, m. 20; Close, 16 Eliz. pt. xxvii.
[62] Feet of F. Bucks. East. 13 Eliz.; Trin. 38 Eliz.
[63] *Hund. R.* (Rec. Com.), i, 23.
[64] *Plac. de Quo Warr.* (Rec. Com.), 89.
[65] Pat. 2 Eliz. pt. iv, m. 45; Close, 16 Eliz. pt. xxvii.
[66] Feet of F. Bucks. Mich. 20 Jas. I.
[67] Pat. 2 Eliz. pt. iv, m. 45.
[68] Ct. R. (Gen. Ser.) portf. 155, no. 31.
[69] Inq. a.q.d. file 385, no. 6; *Cal. Pat.* 1377–81, pp. 10–11.
[70] De Banco R. Hil. 14 Hen. VII, m. 339.
[71] *Valor Eccl.* (Rec. Com.), iv, 234.
[72] Feet of F. Bucks. 26 Hen. III, no. 7.
[73] *Pope Nich. Tax.* (Rec. Com.), 46b.
[74] *L. and P. Hen. VIII*, xv, g. 282 (109), g. 436 (3).

earlier building is shown by the late 13th-century chancel arch. The porch belongs to the reconstruction of the 14th century, while the tower was added in the second half of the 15th century. In 1891 the chancel was partially rebuilt, and the whole fabric has been restored.

The east window of the chancel, of three trefoiled lights with tracery in the head, and the two traceried windows in the north wall, each of two lights, all date from the 14th century, though restored and apparently reset. Some 15th-century glass remains in the north-west window, including a shield of Stafford and a leopard's head, and the east window also contains a few fragments. On the south are two 15th-century two-light windows with tracery under four-centred heads, an ogee-headed piscina of the same period, and a restored priest's doorway of the 14th century; the sill of the easternmost window is carried down to form sedilia. The chancel arch, which dates from about 1280, is of two orders springing from semi-octagonal responds with moulded capitals and bases.

There is a 14th-century pointed doorway with continuous mouldings on the south side of the nave, and a straight joint in the walling on the north may indicate a north doorway, long since blocked. The nave windows, of which there are two on either side, date from about 1480; the north-west and south-east windows are alike, each having three cinquefoiled lights under a four-centred head; the north-east window is of two lights with tracery in a head of the same form, while that at the south-east is of three lights with tracery in a square head. The 15th-century tower arch in the west wall has semi-octagonal responds with moulded capitals. The north-west and south-west windows retain some mediaeval glass, that in the latter window including an excellent figure of St. Peter and a shield of arms, Sable three boars' heads argent severed at the neck. The porch, which contains the remains of a holy-water stoup, is lighted from each side by a trefoiled window of about 1320, and has a pointed archway of the same period.

The tower is of two stages with an embattled parapet, and has a pointed west doorway of about 1450, enriched with flower ornament. Above the doorway is a traceried window of two cinquefoiled lights, also original. The bell-chamber, which was completed later in the 15th century, is pierced by plain two-light windows.

The font, dating from the 15th century, has an octagonal bowl and a moulded base. In the chancel is a brass figure of a man in plate armour of the early 15th century; another of a lady in head-dress and fur-trimmed robe of the same period; and a brass, with figures, to John Barton *alias* John Bayle (d. 1487) and Margaret his wife. In the chancel and nave are various monuments to the Tyringham family. There are floor slabs in the nave to Dorothy

Tyringham (d. 1603), to Thomas Tyringham (d. 1609) and to Elizabeth Tyringham (d. 1639), and a tablet in the chancel to Francis Tyringham (d. 1684) and Elizabeth his wife, daughter of John Chelsham of Kingston upon Thames, clerk of the Jewel House 'for King Charles the Martyr,' who died in 1682. There are later slabs to the Tyringham and Dewberry families. The communion table and hexagonal pulpit with canopy date from the first half of the 17th century, and there is a chair in the chancel of the same period. Incorporated in the nave seating are parts of mediaeval benches and four traceried panels from a 16th-century screen.

The tower contains a ring of five bells : the treble by John Briant of Hertford, 1796 ; the second inscribed ' Prayes God. 1640,' the third, ' Hope in God 1640,' the fourth, ' Feare God 1640,' and the tenor, ' Love God 1651,' are all by Ellis Knight. There is also a small bell by Robert Atton, 1622.

The plate consists of a paten dated 1697, and a chalice, with paten and flagon, presented by Mrs. Jane Beresford in 1770.

The registers begin in 1563.

ADVOWSON The church was granted with the manor (q.v.) to Nutley Abbey,[75] and descended with it until the surrender of that house.[76] In the 12th and 13th centuries it was described as a chapel of the church of Long Crendon.[77] It remained in the Crown from the Dissolution until 1542, when it was granted to Christ Church, Oxford.[78] About three years later a fresh grant brought it to Sir Richard Long and Christopher Edmonds.[79] Sir Richard within a few weeks relinquished his right to Christopher,[80] by whom the advowson was sold in 1547 to Lord Williams of Thame.[81] He sold it in 1555 to Thomas Rede,[82] who in 1558 alienated it to William Goodwin.[83] In 1572 Thomas Tyringham bought the church from Goodwin.[84] From that time until 1735 the advowson followed the descent of the manor (q.v.). One moiety is said to have then passed to Parnel, sister and co-heir of the last Francis Tyringham, and to have been left, after her death without issue, by her husband Charles Pilsworth[85] to his second wife Elizabeth, daughter of Sir Thomas Cave, bart.[86] From Elizabeth it came to her brother, Sir Thomas Cave, bart.,[87] to whom the advowson of Lower Winchendon belonged in 1756.[88] After his death it was settled in 1780 on his younger son the Rev. Charles Cave, who succeeded to the title in 1792.[89] Sir William Cave Brown Cave, bart., cousin and heir of Charles,[90] was patron from 1822 to his death in 1838.[91]

The other moiety seems to have remained with the manor, Scrope Bernard-Morland, afterwards baronet and lord, being patron in 1817.[92] Since 1845 the whole advowson has followed the descent of the manor [93] (q.v.), the living, a perpetual curacy,[94] being now vested in Mrs. Napier Higgins.

[75] Dugdale, *Mon.* vi, 279.
[76] Feet of F. Bucks. 18 Hen. III, no. 4 ; *Valor Eccl.* (Rec. Com.), iv, 233.
[77] Dugdale, loc. cit. ; *Pope Nich. Tax.* (Rec. Com.), 34.
[78] *L. and P. Hen. VIII*, xvii, g. 881 (26).
[79] Ibid. xx (2), g. 266 (5).
[80] Close, 4 & 5 Phil. and Mary, pt. xii.
[81] Ibid.
[82] Ibid.

[83] Ibid. ; Orig. R. (Exch. L.T.R.), 4 & 5 Phil. and Mary, pt. iv, m. 93. Early in 1573 William Goodwin and Blaise were found to own nothing here (Memo. R. [Exch. L.T.R.], Mich. 16 Eliz. m. 73).
[84] Feet of F. Bucks. Hil. 14 Eliz.
[85] P.C.C. 193 Edmunds.
[86] Lipscomb, op. cit. i, 530–1.
[87] Ibid.
[88] Feet of F. Bucks. (K.S.B.), Trin. 29 & 30 Geo. II.

[89] Feet of F. Bucks. Hil. 20 Geo. III ; G.E.C. *Baronetage*, ii, 94.
[90] G.E.C. loc. cit.
[91] *Clerical Guide* ; *Clergy List* ; G.E.C. loc. cit.
[92] *Clerical Guide.* The entries here for 1822 and 1829 are evidently erroneous, the Duke of Marlborough being described as patron of Lower instead of Upper Winchendon for these years.
[93] *Clergy List.* [94] Bacon, *Liber Reg.* 506.

A tenement called 'le churche house,' in 1548 held by the wardens at the will of the lord,[95] was granted to William Goodwin with the manor,[96] and came afterwards to Thomas Tyringham.[97]

In and before 1558 there was also a house called 'the Prestes Chamber.'[98]

There do not appear to be any endowed charities subsisting in this parish.

UPPER WINCHENDON

Uvere Wincedona (xii cent.) ; Upwynchendon (xiii cent.) ; Over Winchendon (xiv cent.).

The area of this parish is 1,202 acres, of which 288 are arable land where wheat, barley, turnips, beans and mangold are grown, and 835 permanent grass.[1] The soil is of limestone and clay on a subsoil of Kimmeridge Clay and Portland Beds. The land stands generally 400 ft. above the ordnance datum, falling in some parts to 300 ft.

The village, which is small, is built on high ground with the church in a beautiful situation commanding fine views. On the brow of a hill south-east of the

England,[7] but scattered by the second Duke of Marlborough, who pulled down the greater part of the house.[8] The fragment of the house which now survives, called the Wilderness, is a two-storied building with attics dating from about 1650. A part of a moulded arch now in an outhouse dates from the 16th century, and is probably a portion of an arched fireplace. In the remaining spandrel is a leaf ornament and a shield of arms charged with a cheveron with a cock between three roundels thereon and a chief with a rose between two leopards' heads. The house retains an original staircase and some open ceilings.

THE WILDERNESS, UPPER WINCHENDON, FROM THE NORTH

In the early years of the 16th century some arable land in this parish was turned into pasture by John Goodwin,[9] and doubtless formed part of the 'goodly pasture containing by estimation 400 acres' which Cromwell noted in 1531.[10] A tract of arable land called Cokestyle belonged to the messuage during the tenancy of John Goodwin,[11] and he or his descendants must have made the inclosures known in the next century as the New Close, Water Mead, Bulls Water Mead, Stony Down,[12] le Combe, le Nashe, le Pitts Mead, le Nether ground with Clott Mead, le Moor Close, and Googesground.[13] Another inclosure of the same date, Mainesground,[14] perhaps the modern Mainshill,[15] recalls the connexion with Upper Winchendon of the family of Mayne in the neighbouring parish of Dinton.[16] Three years before his death in 1617,[17] Simon Mayne bought this with other land from Sir Francis Goodwin,[18] and his widow Coluberry[19] was engaged in a chancery suit against Sir Francis touching this property in 1623.[20] There was at this time a fishpond in Bulls Water Mead and the fishing of which Sir Francis retained a moiety in the sale to Simon[21] may have been here. The River

church stood the ancient mansion of the Goodwins,[2] probably the messuage which John Goodwin allowed to fall into such decay that it was uninhabitable in 1517,[3] and which a memorandum of Thomas Cromwell described fourteen years later as 'a manor-place somewhat in ruins.'[4] After the Goodwins the Whartons made it their home.[5] Here Philip Lord Wharton, husband of Jane Goodwin,[6] had a collection of Vandykes and Lelys said to be the finest in

[95] Ld. Rev. Misc. Bks. clxxxviii, fol. 150.
[96] Pat. 2 Eliz. pt. iv, m. 45.
[97] Ibid. 16 Eliz. pt. xiii, m. 10.
[98] Close, 4 & 5 Phil. and Mary, pt. xii.
[1] Statistics from Bd. of Agric. (1905).
[2] Sheahan, Hist. and Topog. of Bucks.440.
[3] Leadam, Dom. Incl. 1517 (Royal Hist. Soc.), i, 175-6.
[4] L. and P. Hen. VIII, v, 47 (6).
[5] Rec. of Bucks. (Bucks. Arch. and Archit. Soc.), vii, 250-1 ; Cal. S. P. Dom. 1673-5, p. 481.

[6] See p. 123.
[7] Rec. of Bucks. (Bucks. Arch. and Archit. Soc.), vii, 250.
[8] C. Shorter, Highways and Byways in Bucks. 38.
[9] Leadam, loc. cit.
[10] L. and P. Hen. VIII, loc. cit.
[11] Leadam, loc. cit.
[12] Chan. Proc. (Ser. 2), bdle. 352, no. 25.
[13] Chan. Inq. p.m. (Ser. 2), dxxv, 128 ; dcclxxvii, 104.

[14] Chan. Proc. loc. cit. ; Chan. Inq. p.m. (Ser. 2), ccclxxvi, 98.
[15] Bucks. 6 in. O.S.
[16] Dict. Nat. Biog.
[17] Chan. Inq. p.m. (Ser. 2), ccclxxvi, 98.
[18] Chan. Proc. loc. cit.
[19] Sister of Sir Richard Lovelace (Chan. Inq. p.m. [Ser. 2], ccclxxvi, 98). Simon, son of Simon and Coluberry, was one of the regicides (Dict. Nat. Biog.).
[20] Chan. Proc. loc. cit.
[21] Ibid.

Thame, however, touches the parish of Upper Winchendon in the south and has been one of its boundaries since the 11th century.[22]

The house of Samuel Clarke of 'Winchingdon,' licensed in 1672 for Presbyterian worship, must have stood in Upper or Lower Winchendon.[23]

The manor of *UPPER WINCHENDON MANOR DON* belonged to the priory of St. Frideswide before the Norman Conquest and was reckoned amongst the lands of the canons of Oxford in 1086.[24] It was held by the same house of the Crown in chief,[25] and in frankalmoign,[26] until its suppression in 1524,[27] and afterwards of the Crown in socage until 1645.[28]

Charters were granted by Henry I, John, and Henry III, to the Prior and Convent of St. Frideswide confirming their possessions here.[29] In 1518 a lease of manor, advowson and rectory for sixty years was granted to John Goodwin and Parnel Nashe, widow,[30] the former of whom had been the prior's tenant-at-will for a considerable amount of land in the parish for some years previously.[31] Upper Winchendon, which came to the Crown on the suppression of St. Frideswide, was granted to Cardinal Wolsey in 1525[32] and settled by him in the next year on the college of his foundation at Oxford.[33] On Wolsey's fall the manor was once more in the king's hands. Though it was reckoned for some years amongst the possessions of Cardinal's College,[34] later the college of Henry VIII in Oxford,[35] it does not appear that it was actually reappropriated to that foundation, and in 1531 Cromwell was evidently appraising it for sale.[36] The next year John Williams[37] received a grant of the rent of £27 reserved by the prior on the lease of 1518 and of the reversion of the property included in that lease,[38] and another rent from the manor of Upper Winchendon and certain churches in the neighbourhood was bestowed on the Bishop of Lincoln a few weeks later.[39] Sir John Williams must have surrendered his rights here in or before 1546 when John Goodwin, the tenant of 1518, was granted the reversion of all that he held by lease in Upper Winchendon with the rent reserved.[40] He bought land here of Sir Edward Saunders in 1557[41] and was lord of the manor at his death in the following year.[42]

By his son and heir, Sir John Goodwin,[43] who was sheriff in 1587,[44] it was settled about 1574 on the marriage of his son and heir of the same name with Anne, daughter of Sir Richard Baker.[45] The younger John died before his father,[46] and Upper Winchendon descended in or before 1597 to Sir John's younger son Francis.[47] A dispute which arose in that year with Elizabeth Goodwin, widow of Sir John, already re-married to Thomas Stukeley,[48] concerning the inheritance of Francis in Upper Winchendon and other parishes, seems to have been settled in 1600, Thomas and Elizabeth then relinquishing Elizabeth's claim on the manor to Francis,[49] who mortgaged it later in the same year.[50] Sir Francis Goodwin was knight of the shire in 1586 and 1597,[51] but though elected in 1604 the chancellor stated that he was an outlaw at the time and thereby disabled.[52] The House of Commons reversed the chancellor's decision, and although at the king's suggestion a new writ was issued, the result was really a victory for the Commons.[53] In 1614, 1621, 1625 and 1626 he was returned without opposition,[54] and was sheriff for the county in 1623.[55]

GOODWIN. *Party or and gules a lion between three fleurs de lis all countercoloured.*

Sir Francis Goodwin settled the manor of Upper Winchendon on the marriage of his son and heir, Arthur, with Jane, daughter of Sir Richard Wenman, afterwards Viscount Wenman, in 1618,[56] and obtained five years later a grant from the king of the whole of his inheritance in this parish.[57] Arthur Goodwin, who succeeded his father in 1634,[58] had been member for Chipping Wycombe in 1621 and 1624, for Aylesbury in 1626,[59] and was returned as knight of the shire to the Long Parliament of 1640.[60] He died in 1643 leaving an only daughter and heir Jane, then wife of Philip Lord Wharton.[61] Lord Wharton, like his father-in-law a strong Puritan, and a commander in the Parliamentarian army,[62] and afterwards a member of Cromwell's House of Lords,[63] held Upper

[22] Kemble, *Cod. Dipl.* iii, 328.
[23] *Cal. S. P. Dom.* 1672, pp. 153, 199, 377.
[24] *V.C.H. Bucks.* i, 243; Kemble, loc. cit. (This charter is probably spurious.)
[25] *Feud. Aids*, i, 96, 121; *Cal. Pat.* 1334-8, p. 90.
[26] *Testa de Nevill* (Rec. Com.), 245.
[27] Dugdale, *Mon.* ii, 152-3.
[28] Pat. 21 Jas. I, pt. xxvi, no. 2; Chan. Inq. p.m. (Ser. 2), dxxv, 128; dcclxxvii, 104.
[29] Dugdale, *Mon.* ii, 145, 147-8; *Cal. Rot. Chart. et Inq. a.q.d.* (Rec. Com.), 4; *Plac. de Quo Warr.* (Rec. Com.), 93.
[30] *L. and P. Hen. VIII*, v, g. 1370 (8); xxi (1), g. 1383 (6); Exch. Inq. p.m. (Ser. 2), file 20, no. 14. Parnel was perhaps John's mother, widowed a second time (Langley, *Hist. and Antiq. of Hund. of Desborough*, 442.)
[31] Leadam, loc. cit.
[32] *L. and P. Hen. VIII*, iv (1), 1468.
[33] Feet of F. Div. Co. Trin. 18 Hen. VIII.
[34] *L. and P. Hen. VIII*, v, 47 (6).

[35] *Valor Eccl.* (Rec. Com.), ii, 250.
[36] *L. and P. Hen. VIII*, v, 47 (6).
[37] Later Sir John Williams, and finally Lord Williams of Thame. See Long Crendon.
[38] *L. and P. Hen. VIII*, v, g. 1370 (8).
[39] Ibid. (23).
[40] Ibid. xxi (1), g. 1383 (6).
[41] Com. Pleas D. Enr. Mich. 4 & 5 Phil. and Mary.
[42] Chan. Inq. p.m. (Ser. 2), cxviii, 2.
[43] Berry, *Bucks. Gen.* 71.
[44] P.R.O. List of *Sheriffs*, 9.
[45] Chan. Inq. p.m. (Ser. 2), cclxii, 140; Close, 16 Eliz. pt. xxiv.
[46] Ct. of Req. bdle. 30, no. 44.
[47] Chan. Inq. p.m. (Ser. 2), cclxii, 140. Theophilus Adams and Thomas Butler, to whom a grant of lands in Upper Winchendon was made in 1585 (Pat. 27 Eliz. pt. iv, m. 29), were probably 'fishing grantees,' as no record of their tenure survives.
[48] Ct. of Req. bdle. 30, no. 44. She is styled Elizabeth Goodwin in this case, but Francis in his deposition speaks of her husband 'Mr. Stukeley.'

[49] Feet of F. Bucks. Hil. 42 Eliz.
[50] Ibid. Mich. 42 & 43 Eliz.
[51] *Ret. of Memb. of Parl.* i, 417, 432.
[52] Ibid. 442; T. Carew, *Rights of Elections* (1755), i, 100.
[53] Langley, op. cit. 445-6; *Rec. of Bucks.* (Bucks. Arch. and Archit. Soc.), vii, 252.
[54] *Ret. of Memb. of Parl.* i, 450, 462, 468, App. p. xxxvii.
[55] P.R.O. List of *Sheriffs*, 9.
[56] Chan. Inq. p.m (Ser. 2), dxxv, 128; Com. Pleas D. Enr. Trin. 16 Jas. I, m. 16 d, 17; Recov. R. Trin. 16 Jas. I, m. 19.
[57] Pat. 21 Jas. I, pt. xxvi, no. 2.
[58] Chan. Inq. p.m. (Ser. 2), dxxv, 128.
[59] *Ret. of Memb. of Parl.* i, 450, 456, 468.
[60] Ibid. 485.
[61] Chan. Inq. p.m. (Ser. 2), dcclxxvii, 104.
[62] *Dict. Nat. Biog.*; G.E.C. *Peerage*, viii, 126. Neither met with much success in arms. Arthur Goodwin tried ineffectually to storm Brill, and his son-in-law's regiment fled from the field of Edgehill.
[63] G.E.C. loc. cit.

Winchendon [64] till his death in 1695–6, when he was succeeded by his third but eldest surviving son Thomas,[65] who had represented the county in Parliament many times since 1679.[66] From Thomas Wharton, created a marquess in February 1714–15,[67] the manor passed a few weeks later to his son, the brilliant and eccentric Philip Wharton, created Duke of Wharton in January 1717–18.[68] He held Upper Winchendon with his wife Martha when he attained his majority in 1719,[69] and mortgaged it to his creditors the same year.[70] Four years later, the greater part of his inheritance having been squandered,[71] a decree in Chancery ordered the sale of the manor of Upper Winchendon to the Duchess of Marlborough and other trustees of the late Duke of Marlborough, into whose possession it passed shortly afterwards.[72] Winchendon then descended with the title to John Winston, seventh Duke of Marlborough, who alienated it in 1874 to Baron Ferdinand de Rothschild.[73] His sister Miss Alice de Rothschild succeeded him in 1898,[74] and is now lady of the manor.

WHARTON. *Sable a sleeve argent and a border or charged with eight pairs of lions' legs razed gules and crossed saltire-wise.*

CHURCHILL, Duke of Marlborough. *Sable a lion argent and a quarter of St. George.*

View of frankpledge belonged to the Prior of St. Frideswide in 1255 and remained appurtenant to the manor until the 17th century.[75] In 1286 tumbrel and gallows were also appurtenances.[76] There was a dovecote near the capital messuage in 1645.[77]

The church of *ST. MARY MAG-DALENE* consists of a chancel measuring internally 24 ft. by 14 ft. 6 in., nave 41 ft. by 16 ft. 6 in., north aisle 8 ft. 6 in. wide, west tower 11 ft. by 9 ft. and south porch ; it is built of stone and roofed with tiles.

The earliest detail which can be dated with certainty is the mid-12th-century south doorway of the nave, but the plain north arcade suggests the addition of an aisle at an earlier period to an already existing nave. At the end of the 12th century the chancel was reconstructed, and in the middle of the 14th century the north aisle was apparently rebuilt and the south porch erected. The west tower was added about 1420. In modern times the church has been completely restored.

The chancel is lighted by three original lancets in each of the lateral walls and two in the east wall, all having round-headed rear arches. On the south are a blocked priest's doorway, a pointed sedile, and a round-headed piscina, while below the south-west lancet are the remains of a low-side window ; at the north-west corner is a squint connecting the chancel with the north aisle. There is a bracket on the east wall, and another on the south wall, indented for a beam ; they are both probably original and retain traces of colour. The chancel arch, which is of late 12th-century date, though restored, is of a single order springing from plain responds with moulded abaci ; over the arch is hung a funeral helm and crest.

The north arcade is of three bays, each having a round arch of one plain order springing from square jambs ; in the absence of detail, the whole being covered with plaster, it is impossible to assign an exact date to this arcade. The mid-12th-century south doorway has a round head of two moulded orders springing from jamb shafts enriched with twisted and lozenge ornament and having scalloped capitals ; a cross potent has been scratched on the east jamb. The holy-water stoup is placed on the nave wall inside. East of the doorway are two square-headed windows of about 1480, each of three cinquefoiled lights, and at the east end of the wall is a pointed recess, probably of original late 12th-century date, containing a small round-headed light. The upper doorway to the rood loft remains at the north-east of the nave. On the west is the pointed tower arch, which dates from about 1420, and is of three orders dying into plain responds.

The north aisle is lighted by two traceried windows in the north wall, each of two lights, a similar window on the west, and one of three lights on the east, all dating from the 14th century, though the east window appears to have been reset. The continuously-moulded north doorway is of the same period. The south porch, which is of timber on a stone base, has been very much restored.

The 15th-century tower is of two stages, and is surmounted by an embattled parapet, and supported by diagonal buttresses on the west. At the south-east is a stair turret which changes from a square to an octagonal plan at the commencement of the upper stage of the tower, and is crowned by a pyramidal stone roof. The continuously-moulded west doorway and two-light traceried window above are of the original date of the tower, as are also the windows of the bell-chamber, which are each of two trefoiled lights with tracery under a pointed head.

The font has a plain round bowl, dating probably from the 12th century, on a modern stem, and an early 17th-century cover constructed from a pulpit canopy. On the floor of the chancel is a brass figure of a priest in the habit of an Austin canon, and below is the inscription ' Syr John Stodeley and hys mother Emmot lyyn under thys marbyll stone have mynde of us forget us nat we pray to you frendys everychone that our soulis in blys may be say a pater noster wyth an ave huic ecclesie perpetuus prefuit iste vicarius a deo sit benedictus amen. anno domini xv°05.' At the north-east of the chancel is a mural monument

[64] Recov. R. Mich. 25 Chas. II, m. 69.

[65] Dict. Nat. Biog. ; G.E.C. Peerage, viii, 127.

[66] Ret. of Memb. of Parl. i, 534, 540, 546, 551, 557, 564, 572.

[67] G.E.C. Peerage, viii, 127.

[68] Ibid. 128–9 ; Rec. of Bucks. (Bucks. Arch. and Archit. Soc.), vii, 256 :

' Wharton the scorn and wonder of our days,
Whose ruling passion was the love of praise.'
(Pope, Epistle, 1).

[69] Recov. R. Hil. 6 Geo. I, m. 51.

[70] Chan. Enr. Decr. 1751, no. 1.

[71] G.E.C. loc. cit.

[72] Chan. Enr. Decr. 1751, no. 1.

[73] Times, 20 Aug. 1874.

[74] Burke, Peerage (1907).

[75] Hund. R. (Rec. Com.), i, 23 ; Plac. de Quo Warr. (Rec. Com.), 93 ; Pat. 21 Jas. I, pt. xxvi, no. 2 ; Recov. R. Mich. 11 Chas. I, m. 100.

[76] Plac. de Quo Warr. loc. cit.

[77] Chan. Inq. p.m. (Ser. 2), dcclxxvii, 104.

Upper Winchendon Church from the South-East

Upper Winchendon Church: The Interior looking East

with three beautifully drawn brass shields of Goodwin, Goodwin impaling Blondesden, and Goodwin and Blondesden impaling Bladlow ; below is a verse commemorating John Goodwin, who died 11 May 1558, and Katherine his wife. They had eighteen children. There are three 17th-century floor slabs in the aisle. The pulpit, which has traceried panels and an embattled cornice, dates from the 14th century, and is cut from a single block of wood. Below the chance arch is a 15th-century traceried screen, and there are some 16th-century benches incorporated in the seating of the nave. The communion table and rails date from the 17th century, and in the north aisle there is a plain chest which probably dates from the 13th century.

The tower contains a ring of three bells, all inscribed 'Richard Chandler made me 1675,' and a small bell dated 1827.

The plate consists of a chalice and paten of 1689.

The registers begin in 1606.

ADVOWSON The church, which belonged to the priory of St. Frideswide in the 12th century [78] and probably from its foundation,[79] followed the descent of the manor [80] (q.v.), but was not alienated to Baron Ferdinand de Rothschild, the present Duke of Marlborough being now patron.[81] The vicarage was ordained by Bishop Hugh of Wells, and consisted of all the altar offerings, of the tithes of sheaves from half a hide which Robert son of Gervase held, and tithes of sheaves and hay from half a virgate which Walter Tresboen held together with a suitable house.[82]

CHARITY This parish participates in the distribution of Bibles and religious books from Lord Wharton's general charity.

WORMINGHALL

Wermelle (xi cent.) ; Wormehale (xii, xiii cent.) ; Wrmehale (xiii, xiv cent.) ; Worminghale (xiv, xv cent.) ; Wornall (xviii cent.).

The parish of Worminghall with the hamlet of Thomley is contained within an area of nearly 2,075 acres, including 1,366 acres of permanent grass, 420 acres of arable land, and 200 of woods and plantations.[1] The soil is loam and clay, the subsoil clay, and the chief crops are wheat and beans. The land slopes from 244 ft. above the ordnance datum in the north of the parish to 195 ft. west of Court Farm. The south of the parish bordering on the River Thame is liable to floods. The village, with numerous outlying farms, is situated in the east of the parish. It contains several 17th-century buildings a good deal altered and restored. The almshouses founded by the will proved 15 April 1671 of John King,[1a] son of Henry King, Bishop of Chichester and grandson of John King, Bishop of London, are of brick and stone. The buildings with their stone-mullioned windows, stone cornice, and tiled roofs form a picturesque group. The school stands to the east, and the vicarage to the south-east, of the almshouses. The church is about a quarter of a mile south-east of the vicarage, with Court Farm to the west of the churchyard. The farm-house is a plain, unpretentious building, formerly the manor-house. The old vicarage-house south-west of the church had been turned into two cottages before 1862.[2]

Wood Farm, an 18th-century building in the north-western part of the parish, contains some re-used 17th-century panelling ; a stone barn attached to the farm may be mediaeval.

The forest of Bernwood in the 13th century stretched 'between the field of Worminghall and the field of Thomley.'[3] In 1235 Rose de la Rokell was ordered to make a trench in her wood of Worminghall for the security of passers-by, under the superintendence of the king's forest officials.[4] As late as 1610 Sir George Tipping claimed certain lands in Bernwood Forest as part of his Worminghall estate.[5]

The hamlet of Thomley (Tubele, xi cent. ; Tumele, xii cent. ; Thornele, Thumele, xiv cent.) forms a low-lying marshy district to the west of Worminghall, and lies partly in this parish and partly in that of Waterperry, Oxfordshire. It contains one farm, sometimes called Thomley Hall, and a few cottages, and is part of the Worminghall estate, now in the hands of Lord Annaly as trustee for Leopold fifth Viscount Clifden.

The following place-names occur in Worminghall in the 12th century : Bradeput, Brancesbeg, Hangerforlong,[6] Boggeburg, Garbrode[7] ; and in the 13th century in Worminghall, la Porteweye,[8] and in Thomley : Bremor, Gorstilond, Evedeburn, Tunestowe,[9] la Leaweye, Monk's Water,[10] la Bidelonde, Hemestreme, la Longorstilond, la Shortorstilond, la Ockestubbe, Waterilonde,[11] Etwerdesbegge, Stewescrubbes,[12] Boche, Esturbroderode, Harse (lake), Widenden,[13] and Mora.[14]

MANORS WORMINGHALL, which before the Conquest had formed part of Queen Edith's lands, in 1086 was held by the Bishop of Coutances as one manor assessed at 5 hides.[15] It was afterwards one of the fees of the honour of Gloucester.[16] The overlordship of Worminghall passed through his mother Margaret, granddaughter of Hugh Audley, Earl of Gloucester, to Hugh second

[78] *Cartul. of St. Frideswide* (Oxf. Hist. Soc.), i, 14, 21, 29 ; *Cal. Rot. Chart. et Inq. a.q.d.* (Rec. Com.), 4.

[79] A suit of 1227–8 between Walter son of Robert and Roger de Verly for the moiety of the advowson of the church of 'Wychinton' (Assize R. 54, m. 14) may refer to Upper Winchendon.

[80] Dugdale, *Mon.* ii, 147–8 ; Cart. Antiq. EE. 15 ; *Cal. Pat.* 1348–50, p. 329 ; Feet of F. Bucks. Hil. 4 Chas. I ; *Cal. Chart. in Bodl.* 26 ; Inst. Bks. (P.R.O.) ; Bacon, *Liber Reg.* 505 ; *Clerical Guide.*

[81] *Clergy List.*

[82] Gibbons, *Liber Antiq.* 14 ; *Reg. of Hugh of Wells* (Cant. and York Soc.), i, 182, 199 ; ii, 38, 72, 87.

[1] Statistics from Bd. of Agric. (1905).

[1a] P.C.C. 48 Duke.

[2] Sheahan, *Hist. and Topog. of Bucks.* 443.

[3] Kennet, *Paroch. Antiq.* i, 458.

[4] *Cal. Close,* 1234–7, p. 105.

[5] *Cal. S. P. Dom.* 1603–10, p. 606.

[6] *Cartul. of St. Frideswide* (Oxf. Hist. Soc.), ii, 143.

[7] Ibid. 147.

[8] Ibid. 159.

[9] Ibid. 158.

[10] Ibid. 159.

[11] Ibid. 163.

[12] Ibid. 164.

[13] Ibid. 165.

[14] Ibid. 167.

[15] *V.C.H. Bucks.* i, 239.

[16] *Testa de Nevill* (Rec. Com.), 245a ; Assize R. 1292, m. 5 d ; *Cal. Inq. p.m.* (Edw. I), iii, 249 ; *Feud. Aids,* i, 83, 94, 119.

Earl of Stafford.[17] It was eventually merged in the duchy of Lancaster,[18] apparently passing in 1397 with some of the forfeited estates of Thomas of Woodstock, Duke of Gloucester,[19] to Henry Earl of Derby, afterwards Henry IV. Reference to the Crown rights in Worminghall occurs in 1562.[20]

DUCHY OF LANCASTER. *ENGLAND with a label of FRANCE.*

Robert was tenant in Worminghall under the Bishop of Coutances in 1086.[21] Geoffrey son of Robert, who was holding six fees of the honour of Gloucester in the early 13th century,[22] was probably his descendant, since Thomas, Geoffrey's son, was holding Worminghall in fee later in the century.[23] He or his successor was identical with Thomas de Doynton, Gloucestershire, who was holding similarly in 1254[24] and 1284.[25] Amice de Doynton, probably his widow, held Worminghall before 1290,[26] and his heirs were holding six fees of the honour of Gloucester in 1295, of which Worminghall was one.[27] In 1302 the latter had passed to John de la Rivere[28] (de Ripariis), who died seised about 1315.[29] In 1333 his son and heir John proved his majority[30] and obtained livery of Worminghall Manor[31] (half the original estate, the other half having been subinfeudated long before). Thomas Darches was holding in 1346,[32] Denise, widow of John de la Rivere, who was still alive in 1340,[33] retaining dower in the manor[34] until her death in 1347.[35] Before 1363 Worminghall Manor had passed to William Durant,[36] and in 1367 Ralph Stodeye and his wife Edith surrendered her dower interests in it to Sir John Tracy.[37] William Tracy, his descendant in the direct line,[38] was holding this manor in 1455, apparently in right of his wife Margery,[39] daughter of Sir John Pauncefote.[40] They conveyed it in this year to William Browne,[41] who died in 1461, in the minority of his son and heir Robert.[42] He succeeded to his father's property in 1480, on the death of his mother Agnes,[43] who had survived her second husband Sir Geoffrey Gate nearly four years.[44] Christopher son and heir of Robert Browne proved his age in 1498,[45] and died seised of

the Worminghall estate in 1509,[46] when an assignment in dower there was made to his widow Sybil.[47] The custody of the son and heir John was granted in 1510 to Edward Grevill.[48] In 1550 John Browne sold Worminghall Manor to William Birt,[49] Sir John Browne and his wife Margaret and Christopher Browne and his wife Eleanor surrendering their interests.[50] A settlement of this manor was made in 1552 by which Leonard Chamberlain was seised to the use of William Birt and his heirs and assigns.[51] In 1556 William Dunche was enfeoffed to William Birt's use for life, with reversion in a year after Birt's death to Thomas Tipping,[52] who had succeeded before 1562.[53] In this year he also acquired the other manor of Worminghall (q.v.), and the whole estate descended as one manor in his family with Ickford Manor (q.v.) to Sir Thomas Tipping, bart.,[54] who died in 1718.[55] His widow Anne, with their daughters and co-heirs Letitia wife of Samuel Sandys and Katherine wife of Thomas Archer,[56] conveyed Worminghall Manor in 1727 to John Rudge.[57] He seems to have been succeeded soon afterwards by Edward Rudge of Wheatfield, Oxfordshire,[58] probably his son, and he or his successor sold this manor about 1772 to Samuel Horne[59] of Clapham, who died in 1777.[60] The next owner was his son Edward Horne[61] of the Leasowes, Halesowen, who was living in the early 19th century.[62] His son and heir Edward died in 1824,[63] and on the death of his widow in 1827[64] the trustees appointed under his father's will conveyed the Worminghall estate, covering the whole parish except about 50 acres and including the hamlet of Thomley, to Henry second Viscount Clifden.[65] It descended with the title to Leopold fifth viscount,[66] who died in 1899,[67] and is at present in the hands of his surviving trustee, Luke Lord Annaly.

AGAR-ROBARTES, Viscount Clifden. *Azure three stars and a chief wavy or.*

Thomas de Doynton was accustomed to hold view of frankpledge in his manor of Worminghall in 1254,[68] and the right was included in the transfer

---

[17] G.E.C. *Complete Peerage*, vii, 209-10 ; Chan. Inq. p.m. 5 Ric. II, no. 24.
[18] Chan. Inq. p.m. (Ser. 2), xxiv, 17. No reference has been found to confirm the statement of 1462 that Worminghall was held of John Earl of Oxford (Exch. Enr. of Inq. no. 556).
[19] G.E.C. *Complete Peerage*, vii, 211.
[20] Memo. R. (Exch. L.T.R.), Hil. 4 Eliz. m. 53. [21] *V.C.H. Bucks*. i, 239.
[22] *Rot. de Oblatis et Fin*. (Rec. Com.), 159 ; *Red Bk. of Exch*. (Rolls Ser.), 607.
[23] *Testa de Nevill* (Rec. Com.), 245a.
[24] *Hund. R*. (Rec. Com.), i. 25.
[25] *Feud. Aids*, i, 83. William de St. Odone is named as tenant apparently through some temporary arrangement.
[26] Assize R. 1292, m. 5 d.
[27] *Cal. Inq. p.m.* loc. cit.
[28] *Feud. Aids*, i, 94.
[29] Chan. Inq. p.m. 8 Edw. II, no. 27.
[30] Ibid. 6 Edw. III (1st nos.), no. 48b.
[31] *Cal. Close*, 1333-7, p. 31. He was holding in 1336 (ibid. 674).
[32] *Feud. Aids*, i, 119.

[33] Inq. a.q.d. file 253, no. 4.
[34] De Banco R. 348, m. 234. With reversion to William Darches.
[35] Chan. Inq. p.m. Edw. III, file 83, no. 12. [36] Inq. a.q.d. file 348, no. 16.
[37] Feet of F. case 20, file 98, no. 2.
[38] Lipscomb, *Hist. and Antiq. of Bucks.* i, 576.
[39] Feet of F. case 22, file 124, no. 6.
[40] Rudder, *A New Hist. of Gloucs*. 771.
[41] Feet of F. case 22, file 124, no. 6.
[42] Exch. Enr. of Inq. no. 556. Henry Tracy is said in this document to have released this manor to William Browne and his wife Agnes.
[43] Chan. Inq. p.m. 21 Edw. IV, no. 36 (Oxon. Inq.).
[44] Ibid. 16 Edw. IV, 50.
[45] Ibid. (Ser. 2), xii, 88.
[46] Ibid. xxiv, 17.   [47] Ibid. 103.
[48] *Cat. of Anct. D*. v, 396.
[49] Recov. R. Mich. 4 Edw. VI, m. 664.
[50] Feet of F. Div. Co. Hil. 4 & 5 Edw. VI.
[51] Close, 6 Edw. VI, pt. i, no. 33.

[52] Ibid. 2 & 3 Phil. and Mary, pt. ii, no. 18.
[53] Memo. R. (Exch. L.T.R.), Hil. 4 Eliz. m. 53.
[54] *Cal. S. P. Dom.* 1603-10, p. 606.
[55] G.E.C. *Baronetage*, iv, 172.
[56] Ibid. 173.
[57] Feet of F. Bucks. East. 13 Geo. I.
[58] He presented to Wheatfield Church in 1737 (Inst. Bks. [P.R.O.]), the Tipping estate in this parish (*Visit. of Oxon*. [Harl. Soc.], 274-5) having been sold by Anne Lady Tipping to John Rudge in 1726 (Feet of F. Oxon. East. 12 Geo. I).
[59] Lysons, *Mag. Brit*. i (3), 672.
[60] Musgrave, *Obit*. (Harl. Soc.), iii, 252.
[61] P.C.C. 21 Collier.
[62] Lysons, loc. cit.
[63] *Gent. Mag*. xciv (2), 571.
[64] Ibid. xcvii (1), 477.
[65] Lipscomb, op. cit. i, 577.
[66] G.E.C. *Complete Peerage*, ii, 289 ; *Rec. of Bucks*. (Bucks. Arch. and Archit. Soc.), iv, 78 ; Sheahan, loc. cit.
[67] Burke, *Peerage* (1907).
[68] *Hund. R*. (Rec. Com.), i, 25.

of 1727.[69] In the 14th century there is mention of a fishery and a windmill.[70] A grant of free warren[71] and two grants of a weekly market and a yearly fair in Worminghall were made to John de la Rivere in 1304. In the first grant the market was to be held on Fridays and the fair on the eve and day of the Invention of the Holy Cross[72] (2 and 3 May), and in the second the market was to be on Thursdays and the fair on the eve, day and morrow of St. Peter[73] (28, 29, 30 June). No other documentary reference has been found, but Sheahan says in 1862 that the market and fair had long been discontinued.[74] A village 'feast' is still held annually.

The lords of Worminghall appear to have subinfeudated half a fee, afterwards called *WORMING-HALL MANOR*, before the mid-12th century (see advowson). The overlordship descended with the principal manor[75] (q.v.).

Luvet de Brai, lord of Oakley, was presumably tenant in the middle of the 12th century, and this manor descended with that of Oakley (q.v.), through the Fitz Ellis and Ingleton families, to Sir George Tyrrell.[76] He sold the latter in 1562 to Thomas Tipping,[77] owner of the principal manor (q.v.), into which it was afterwards absorbed.

William Fitz Ellis held view of frankpledge for his tenants in Worminghall in 1254,[78] and a grant of free warren there was made to Robert Fitz Ellis in 1341.[79]

A small property in Worminghall held by St. Frideswide's Priory, Oxfordshire,[80] was gradually absorbed into the rectory (q.v.).

The hamlet of *THOMLEY* was assessed in 1086 at 4¼ hides and formed part of the lands of the Bishop of Bayeux.[81] It afterwards appertained to the honour of Pontefract,[82] which passed in succession to the earldom of Lincoln[83] and the earldom[84] and duchy of Lancaster.[85] This overlordship is last mentioned in connexion with Thomley in 1375.[86]

Hervey was tenant of Thomley under the Bishop of Bayeux in 1086.[87] In 1206 a mesne lordship there was held by William de Brug in right of his wife Olive,[88] in 1254 by William Foliot,[89] and in 1279[90] and 1311 by William de Scalebroc.[91] The latest reference to this lordship that has been found

occurs in 1361, when Sir Roger Gateford was mesne lord.[92]

A second mesne lordship in Thomley appertained in 1279 to Henry de Bruly, lord of Waterstock, Oxfordshire,[93] but in 1284 he released all rights in it to William de Scalebroc and his heirs.[94]

The representatives of a family afterwards taking its name from Thomley appear to have been lords of this hamlet from at least the middle of the 12th century. Ruald and his brother Jordan were succeeded by Jordan's son Henry, who about 1185 confirmed a grant made by his uncle and father of a hide of land in Thomley to Stratford Langthorne Abbey in Essex,[95] making a final transfer in 1192.[96] The connexion between Henry de Thomley and William Fitz Ellis of Worminghall is not forthcoming, but the latter had rights in Thomley in 1199.[96a] Robert de Thomley, probably one of his sons,[97] made grants of land in Thomley about 1235.[98] His son Ellis[99] had succeeded before 1254,[100] and Robert son of Thomas son of Ellis,[1] lord of Thomley in 1279,[2] corresponds to Robert heir of Thomas Fitz Ellis, whose son Robert afterwards held Oakley Manor (q.v.). Thomley Manor was included in the settlement made by Robert Fitz Ellis in 1339.[3] His widow Margaret seems to have made some arrangement with her brother John, who attained his majority as lord of Thomley in 1344.[4] He apparently died about 1347, when the Fitz Ellis property in Thomley, reduced by the numerous grants to religious houses,[5] was entrusted by the Crown to Thomas North.[6] He was still in charge at the death of Margaret Fitz Ellis in 1375,[7] and in 1381 his heir, William North, was his executor.[8] It has not been found possible to trace the later descent of this property.

In the latter part of the 13th century Oseney Abbey, Oxfordshire, held an estate in Thomley called in the 16th century *THOMLEY MANOR*. It consisted of half a hide of land held in fee for 1s. yearly of Goring Priory, Oxfordshire. It was confirmed by Ellis de Thomley, together with other small plots of land acquired by the abbey from Robert and Ellis de Thomley.[9] This estate was retained by Oseney Abbey[10] until the Dissolution, the lessee in 1535 being Sir John Browne.[11] It was granted in fee in 1542 to Richard Andrews,[12]

[69] Feet of F. Bucks. East. 13 Geo. I.
[70] Chan. Inq. p.m. 8 Edw. II, no. 27.
[71] Chart. R. 32 Edw. I, m. 5, no. 87.
[72] Ibid.
[73] Ibid. m. 1, no. 10.
[74] Sheahan, loc. cit. The fair is not mentioned in the list of 1792 (*Rep. of Royal Com. on Market Rts. and Tolls*, i, 139).
[75] Chan. Inq. p.m. 49 Edw. III, pt. i, no. 54; see also Feet of F. case 16, file 44, no. 3; Assize R. 1292, m. 5 d.; Chan. Inq. p.m. (Ser. 2), xxiv, 20.
[76] *Cartul. of St. Frideswide* (Oxf. Hist. Soc.), ii, 152; *Testa de Nevill* (Rec. Com.), 245a; Assize R. 1292, m. 5 d.; *Feud. Aids*, i, 94, 114; Feet of F. Div. Co. Hil. 1 & 2 Phil. and Mary; East. 2 & 3 Phil. and Mary. Robert de Leytone was holding in 1284, apparently during a Fitz Ellis minority (*Feud. Aids*, i, 83). The James family did not acquire any interest in Worminghall.
[77] Feet of F. Bucks. Hil. and East. 4 Eliz.; Close, 4 Eliz. pt. x, no. 44.
[78] *Hund. R.* (Rec. Com.), i, 26.
[79] Chart. R. 14 Edw. III, m. 2, no. 4.
[80] *Cartul. of St. Frideswide* (Oxf. Hist.

Soc.), i, 489; ii, 145, 152–3; *Feud. Aids*, i, 119; *Pope Nich. Tax.* (Rec. Com.), 46b. [81] *Dom. Bk.* (Rec. Com.), i, 156a.
[82] *Hund. R.* (Rec. Com.), ii, 38; *Cal. Inq. p.m.* (Edw. II), v, 156; Chan. Inq. p.m. 49 Edw. III, pt. i, no. 54.
[83] *Hund. R.* (Rec. Com.), ii, 714; *Cal. Inq. p.m.* loc. cit.
[84] *Cal. Inq. p.m.* loc. cit.
[85] Chan. Inq. p.m. 35 Edw. III, pt. i, no. 122.
[86] Ibid. 49 Edw. III, pt. i, no. 54.
[87] *Dom. Bk.* loc. cit.
[88] Feet of F. case 187, file 2, no. 79.
[89] *Hund. R.* (Rec. Com.), ii, 38.
[90] Ibid. 725.
[91] *Cal. Inq. p.m.* loc. cit.
[92] Chan. Inq. p.m. 35 Edw. III, pt. i, no. 122.
[93] *Hund. R.* (Rec. Com.), ii, 714.
[94] Feet of F. case 188, file 11, no. 6.
[95] *Cartul. of St. Frideswide* (Oxf. Hist. Soc.), ii, 154.
[96] Ibid. 156; Parker, *Archit. Antiq. of Oxf.* 256.
[96a] *Cartul. of St. Frideswide* (Oxf. Hist. Soc.), ii, 149.
[97] Nichols, *Topog. and Gen.* iii, 273;

Ellis, *Notices of Ellises of France and Engl.*, 57.
[98] *Cartul. of St. Frideswide* (Oxf. Hist. Soc.), ii, 164–5; *Hund. R.* (Rec. Com.), ii, 714.
[99] *Cartul. of St. Frideswide* (Oxf. Hist. Soc.), ii, 166–7; *Hund. R.* loc. cit.
[100] *Hund. R.* (Rec. Com.), ii, 38.
[1] Ibid. 725. [2] Ibid. 714.
[3] For particulars see Oakley.
[4] *Cartul. of St. Frideswide* (Oxf. Hist. Soc.), ii, 173.
[5] *Hund. R.* (Rec. Com.), ii, 714. Robert de Thomley was only holding a virgate of land directly in 1279.
[6] Mins. Accts. (Gen. Ser.), bdle. 961, no. 34.
[7] Chan. Inq. p.m. 49 Edw. III, pt. i, no. 54.
[8] Mins. Accts. (Gen. Ser.), bdle. 961, no. 34. [9] *Hund. R.* (Rec. Com.), ii, 714.
[10] Add. Chart. 20379 (an acquittance for 6s. rent paid in 1338 to Goring Priory); *Valor Eccl.* (Rec. Com.), ii, 218, noting the payment of 10s. yearly still continued in 1535.
[11] *Valor Eccl.* (Rec. Com.), ii, 217.
[12] *L. and P. Hen. VIII*, xvii, p. 261.

but was acquired before 1550 by Sir John Browne,[13] who conveyed it in that year to William Birt,[14] a transfer confirmed by royal grant in 1551.[15] In 1553 William Birt sold Thomley Manor (with the glebe land in Thomley of Worminghall Rectory and the tithes appertaining to it), chargeable with the customary services and a yearly rent of 5s. to Magdalen College, Oxford,[16] to William Gardiner of Grove Place, Chalfont St. Giles.[17] It was inherited by his son John, who with his wife Rhoda[18] conveyed it in 1570 to Thomas Tipping and his wife Margaret.[19] Thomley has since descended with Worminghall Manor[20] (q.v.), excepting that Anne Lady Tipping sold it to John Rudge in 1726,[21] a year before Worminghall. It is at present held in trust by Lord Annaly.

A small estate called *THOMLEY MANOR* in the latter half of the 14th century[22] was held by Edmund Handlo at his death in 1355,[23] and descended with Boarstall Manor (q.v.) to Edmund Rede (with that part of the manor which reverted to him in 1437).[24] It does not appear, however, among his possessions at his death in 1489,[25] and is not at present otherwise traceable.

Stratford Langthorne Abbey, which acquired an estate of 1 hide of land in Thomley about the middle of the 12th century, retained rights in it into the 13th century.[26] The latest reference found to this abbey in connexion with Thomley occurs in 1229,[27] but its rights there appear to have been acquired by Oseney Abbey some time previous to 1279.[28]

The estate itself was granted about 1185 by Stratford Abbey to St. Frideswide's Priory for a yearly rent of 18s.[29] The priory continued to hold this land,[30] which was still traceable as a separate entity in the first half of the 14th century.[31] During the first half of the 13th century St. Frideswide's Priory retained a virgate of this estate in Thomley and distributed the remainder in equal portions to three tenants, whose names are enumerated in 1229.[32] Later William Oliver, one of these tenants, was holding half of it,[33] and had been succeeded by Nicholas Oliver before 1279.[34] At this date the remainder was held by John Gamel,[35] who about 1325 quitclaimed two parts of the whole estate with other land in Thomley to the priory.[36] It presumably corresponds to the messuage and land in Thomley leased by the priory in 1532 to Sir John Browne, and of which he was Crown lessee in 1535.[37] It was apparently afterwards acquired by him with Thomley Manor, formerly belonging to Oseney Abbey (q.v.), and absorbed into it.

St. Frideswide's Priory held 1½ hides of land in Thomley granted with Worminghall Church in 1199 (see advowson). This property descended as part of the rectory (q.v.), except between 1552 and 1570, when it passed with Thomley Manor formerly appertaining to Oseney Abbey (q.v.).

An estate of over 1 hide of land in Thomley was held by Dorchester Abbey, Oxfordshire, of Robert de Thomley in 1279 by the service of rendering a rose at Midsummer.[38] After the Dissolution the reversion of this abbey's farm in Thomley was granted in fee in 1537, on the expiration of a lease held by Sir John Browne, to Sir Thomas Pope.[39] A further grant of the rent then reserved was made to him in 1545.[40] This property must have been afterwards absorbed into Thomley Manor, since it does not reappear.

Studley Priory, Oxfordshire, was holding half a virgate of land in Thomley in 1279 for a small yearly rent of Robert de Thomley.[41] Its possessions in Thomley and Worminghall were granted in fee in 1540 to John Croke.[42] He sold them to Sir John Browne, who was pardoned in 1544 for acquiring them without royal licence.[43]

The church of *ST. PETER AND CHURCH ST. PAUL* consists of a chancel measuring internally 22 ft. by 11 ft. 6 in., north vestry, nave 38 ft. 6 in. by 18 ft., south porch, and west tower 10 ft. 6 in. square.

The nave is probably of the latter half of the 12th century, but the chancel appears to have been rebuilt in the 14th century, while the tower is an addition of the 15th century. In 1847 an extensive restoration was undertaken; the north wall and part of the south wall of the nave were taken down and rebuilt, the north vestry was added, and the old timber south porch removed and replaced by the present one. The walling generally is of rubble.

In the east wall of the chancel is a 15th-century window of three cinquefoiled lights with vertical tracery in a four-centred head. The two-light window and vestry doorway on the north are modern, but the two south windows, each of two trefoiled lights with flowing tracery in a pointed head, retain a few old stones, though the tracery has been renewed. At the south-east of the chancel is a 14th-century piscina with a trefoiled head, a credence shelf, and a circular basin. The chancel arch, which is of a single round-arched order, unmoulded, with angle shafts having carved capitals and moulded bases towards the nave and plain square jambs towards the chancel, is of the original date of

[13] Recov. R. Mich. 4 Edw. VI, m. 664.
[14] Feet of F. Div. Co. Hil. 4 & 5 Edw. VI. [15] Pat. 5 Edw. VI, pt. ii, m. 15.
[16] This college held land in Thomley farmed at 3s. yearly in 1535 (*Valor Eccl.* [Rec. Com.], ii, 275).
[17] Close, 7 Edw. VI, pt. ii, no. 2. See *V.C.H. Bucks.* iii, 189.
[18] Chan. Proc. (Ser. 2), bdle. 71, no. 7.
[19] Feet of F. Oxon. Hil. 12 Eliz. Perhaps with a view to this subsequent purchase Thomley Manor was included in the Birt-Dunche-Tipping settlement of 1556 (see Worminghall Manor). See also Feet of F. Oxon. Trin. 2 & 3 Phil. and Mary.
[20] Feet of F. Div. Co. Mich. 13 Chas. I.
[21] Ibid. Oxon. East. 12 Geo. I.
[22] *Cal. Close,* 1360–4, p. 386; 1364–8, p. 229.

[23] Chan. Inq. p.m. 32 Edw. III, no. 36. Illegible as regards Thomley, which is called a manor in the Record Commission Calendar.
[24] Chan. Inq. p.m. 16 Hen. VI, no. 38.
[25] *Cal. Inq. p.m. Hen. VII,* i, 197.
[26] *Cartul. of St. Frideswide* (Oxf. Hist. Soc.), ii, 161–3.
[27] *Reg. of Hugh of Wells* (Cant. and York Soc.), ii, 75.
[28] *Hund. R.* (Rec. Com.), ii, 714.
[29] *Cartul. of St. Frideswide* (Oxf. Hist. Soc.), ii, 154.
[30] Ibid. 161–3; *Hund. R.* loc. cit.
[31] *Cartul. of St. Frideswide* (Oxf. Hist. Soc.), ii, 170–1.
[32] *Reg. of Hugh of Wells,* loc. cit. Bishop Godfrey, one of the tenants, should be Godfrey Bishop (*Cartul. of St. Frideswide* [Oxf. Hist. Soc.], ii, 161). References

to earlier tenants of his land occur (*Cartul. of St. Frideswide* [Oxf. Hist. Soc.], ii, 157–60).
[33] *Cartul. of St. Frideswide* (Oxf. Hist. Soc.), ii, 162–3.
[34] *Hund. R.* (Rec. Com.), ii, 714.
[35] Ibid.
[36] *Cartul. of St. Frideswide* (Oxf. Hist. Soc.), ii, 170–1.
[37] Exch. Inq. p.m. (Ser. 2), file 806, no. 5.
[38] *Hund. R.* (Rec. Com.), ii, 714.
[39] Augm. Off. Partic. for Grants, no. 881; *L. and P. Hen. VIII,* xii (1), g. 539 (19).
[40] *L. and P. Hen. VIII,* xx (1), g. 465 (47).
[41] *Hund. R.* (Rec. Com.), ii, 714.
[42] *L. and P. Hen. VIII,* xv, g. 282 (109).
[43] Ibid. xix (1), p. 385.

the nave, but has been very much restored. A modern opening, communicating with the pulpit, has been pierced in the north respond.

The two north windows of the nave, each of two trefoiled lights with vertical tracery under a square head, are modern copies of their predecessors in the wall which was taken down in 1847. Close to one of these windows, previous to the restoration, traces of a plain opening, said to have been 'Norman,' could be seen.[44] The north doorway has a round-arched external order, filled by a tympanum forming a square head to the opening itself. Though substantially of the 12th century, it has been very considerably renewed. The south-east window is modern and of two lights in a traceried head; at the west end of the south wall is a wide lancet window, originally an insertion of the 13th century, but almost completely renewed at the restoration. The same fate has also overtaken the 12th-century south doorway between the two windows, which has a round head of two orders, the outer moulded with the billet, and nook shafts in the jambs. In this wall is also a piscina with a pointed head and circular basin, probably of the 13th century, on either side of which are set upright in the wall short pieces of roll-moulding; three painted crosses are also visible on the face of the piscina. At the west end of the nave there was formerly a gallery, which was taken down in 1847.

The tower rises in two stages, and is crowned by an embattled parapet. There is a vice-turret at the south-east angle, entered from the ground stage by a doorway with an elliptical head. The tower arch has square jambs, from which spring two pointed and chamfered orders. In the west wall of the ground stage is a window of three cinquefoiled lights with a traceried head. The ringing chamber, which is contained in the upper part of the lower stage, is lighted from all sides except the east by small cinquefoiled lights; the bell-chamber has restored square-headed windows of two lights, that in the east wall being probably a 16th-century insertion.

The cylindrical font is possibly of the 13th century. Some early 16th-century plain benches remain in the western portion of the nave, and these have been copied in deal for the remainder of the seating. In the vestry is an iron-bound oaken chest, probably of the 17th century.

At the south-east of the chancel is a brass to Philip King, who died in 1592. He is represented with his wife Elizabeth kneeling in prayer, with the figures of his five sons and six daughters and a chrisom child. Below the figures is an inscription in English verse, and below this again a Latin inscription stating that he was educated by his uncles, Robert King, Bishop of Oxford, and John Lord Williams of Thame, and that he died after forty years of married life with his wife Elizabeth, who survived him and caused the brass to be set up. On the north wall of the chancel are the arms of the see of London impaling King, evidently for John King, son of the above Philip King, who was consecrated Bishop of London in 1611. In the chancel are also floor slabs to Edmund King, who died in 1577; to Winifred Littlepace, who died in 1686, and her daughter Elizabeth Price, 1685; to Francis Price, a former vicar, who died in 1701, and his first wife Jane, 1662; and to Thomas Stevens, who died in 1687, Elizabeth his daughter, 1685, and Thomas Philips, 1686; there is also a floor slab, partly covered by the organ, which hides the date, to a second Thomas Philips.

There is a ring of three bells and a sanctus bell, all cast by Taylor at Oxford in 1847, partly from the old bells.

The plate includes a cup and cover paten of 1629. The registers begin in 1538.

ADVOWSON Worminghall Church is mentioned about 1158 in a general confirmatory charter of Pope Adrian IV to St. Frideswide's Priory,[45] and in a bull issued later in the century by Pope Alexander III in favour of this priory.[46] It was granted in free alms at the end of the century by William Fitz Ellis with the consent of his wife Emma.[47] This gift was confirmed in 1199 by King John;[48] early in the 13th century by William Bishop of Lincoln,[49] by the original grantors William and Emma Fitz Ellis[50] and other members of his family;[51] in 1218 by Pope Honorius;[52] and in the 14th century by Edward II and Edward III.[53] A vicarage was ordained in 1229,[54] and the advowson, valued at £4 13s. 4d. in 1291[55] and in 1480[56] and at £7 1s. 10d. in 1535,[57] with the rectory, followed the same descent as that of Oakley (q.v.) from 1339 (when the latter was finally secured to St. Frideswide's Priory) to 1546. In that year John Pollard and George Rythe obtained a licence to alienate them to William Birt.[58] In 1552 he sold them, with the exception of the glebe land in Thomley to which reference has already been made, to Thomas Tipping.[59] Both descended with Worminghall and Oakley Manors (q.v.) until 1627, when, on the death of Sir George Tipping, they passed by a settlement made in 1618 to his younger son Samuel.[60] He appears to have sold them in 1652 to William Codrington.[61] The owners in 1682 were Dorothy and Katherine Stoughton.[62] Settlements were made later in this year after Dorothy's marriage to Simon Brittiff.[63] Her moiety had presumably reverted before 1700 to her sister Katherine, then wife of John Burton,[64] who presented in 1703.[65] Sir Isaac Shard, who was

[44] *Rec. of Bucks.* (Bucks. Arch. and Archit. Soc.), iv, 79.

[45] *Cartul. of St. Frideswide* (Oxf. Hist. Soc.), i, 29.

[46] Ibid. ii, 95–6.

[47] Ibid. 149.

[48] Ibid. i, 43; ii, 153; Chart. R. 1 John, pt. i, m. 8.

[49] *Cartul. of St. Frideswide* (Oxf. Hist. Soc.), i, 46; ii, 153.

[50] Ibid. ii, 151, 152.

[51] Ibid. 150, 152.

[52] Ibid. 164.   [53] Ibid. 150.

[54] *R. of Hugh of Wells* (Cant. and York Soc.), ii, 75; Gibbons, *Liber Antiq.*

Hugonis Wells, 14. The endowment of the vicarage valued at 5 marks is set forth.

[55] *Pope Nich. Tax.* (Rec. Com.), 34.

[56] *Cartul. of St. Frideswide* (Oxf. Hist. Soc.), i, 488.

[57] *Valor Eccl.* (Rec. Com.), iv, 235. The rectory, worth £10 yearly, of which £4 was paid to the vicar (ibid. ii, 250), had been leased to John Daves for forty years in 1517 (Rentals and Surv. [Gen. Ser.], portf. 23, no. 59), a tenure which had been changed before 1545 for one on three lives, i.e., his own and those of his wife and daughter Joan (*L. and P. Hen. VIII*, xx [2], g. 910 [3]).

[58] *L. and P. Hen. VIII*, xxi (2), p. 347.

[59] Close, 6 Edw. VI, pt. i, no. 34.

[60] Chan. Inq. p.m. (Ser. 2), ccccxxxviii, 123; Recov. R. Trin. 4 Chas. I, m. 39.

[61] Recov. R. Mich. 1652, m. 162; Feet of F. Bucks. Mich. 1652.

[62] Recov. R. Mich. 34 Chas. II, m. 214.

[63] Feet of F. Bucks. Hil. 34 & 35 Chas. II. Two documents, one conveying to John Weston and the other to Walter Cave, in the second case Dorothy's moiety only.

[64] Feet of F. Bucks. Trin. 12 Will. III.

[65] Inst. Bks. (P.R.O.).

owner before 1726,[66] died in 1739.[67] His son Isaac Peccatus Shard, who presented in 1754,[68] died in 1766.[69] His property in Worminghall had been purchased before 1783 by Edward Horne,[70] who thus re-united the advowson and rectory to the manorial estate (q.v.), with which they descended[71] to Lord Annaly, in trust for Leopold fifth Viscount Clifden. Subscribers from the rural deanery of Waddesdon purchased the advowson of Lord Annaly in 1912 and presented it to the Bishop of Oxford, who is thereby patron of the living.

The tithes in Worminghall had been commuted before 1862.[72]

CHARITIES The following charities are administered by a scheme of the Charity Commissioners of 13 August 1912 under the title of 'The United Charities,' namely:

The Almshouse charity, founded by will of John King, dated 24 May 1670, for the benefit of six old men and four old women. The trust estate consists of ten almshouses in hand, house and land known as Pepper's Hill at Shabbington containing 67 a. 3 r. 8 p. let at £84 a year, and 11 a. at Oakley let at £8 10s. a year. Eight of the almshouses only are at present occupied ; each of the inmates receives 3s. 3d. a week with an allowance for coal and clothing.

The Bread charities, founded by Henry King, Bishop of Chichester, by his will, dated 14 July 1653 and proved 16 November 1669,[73] and by others. The following properties are included under this head, namely—12 a. 1 r. 32 p. at Oakley purchased with £100 given by Bishop King, let at £7 a year ; 7 a. 1 r. 27 p., part of 'Gentlemen's Ground' at Worminghall, let in allotments, producing about £14 a year ; two cottages and gardens at Worminghall let at £4 18s. a year, and an allotment of 15 p. at Oakley let at 8s. a year.

In 1912 twenty-five persons received weekly half a quartern loaf, with an additional quartern and a sum of 1s. each at Easter.

WOTTON UNDERWOOD

Ottone (xi cent.) ; Vittona, Wtton (xii cent.) ; Wotton next Brehill (xiii cent.) ; Wotton juxta Bernewode, Wotton subtus Bernewode (xiv cent.) ; Wotton Underwood (xvi cent.).

This parish, called Underwood from its proximity to Bernwood Forest, has always been well wooded.[1] Of the 2,600 acres comprised within its borders, 360 are still covered with woods and plantations, 193 are arable land, and 1,937 permanent grass.[2] The soil is of clay on a subsoil of Kimmeridge Clay and Portland Beds. The average height is 300 ft. above the ordnance datum. In the 16th century some lands in this parish were inclosed by Edward Grenville,[3] whose descendant and heir Richard Grenville in 1742 joined with other landowners here in the inclosure of 1,668 acres.[4]

The northern boundary is formed by Akeman Street, from which runs Kingswood Lane in a southerly direction skirting the park of Wotton House. The only remaining parts of the house erected by Richard Grenville in 1704[5] are the detached wings containing the kitchen and stables. The principal portion, which was of brick with stone dressings and pilasters, was burnt out in 1820, and was rebuilt,[6] the main features of the old elevations being to a certain extent preserved. The kitchen and stable wings are pleasant examples of the freer manner of the period ; each is of one story with a modillion cornice and a tiled hipped roof containing an attic floor lighted by dormer windows. The principal windows have wood mullions and transoms with leaded casement lights, and each roof is crowned by a clock and cupola. The railings and gates of the forecourt are particularly good examples of early 18th-century wrought-ironwork.

South-east of the house are the church, school, and vicarage in the little village which contains a few buildings of 17th-century date. In 1862 it was described as consisting of cottages, each with a plot of garden ground, built by the Marquess of Buckingham in the second decade of the 19th century.[7] Windmill Hill, north-east of the large lake in the grounds of Wotton House, is probably the site of the mill which belonged to the manor in the 16th and 17th centuries.[8] In the south of the parish Grenvilles Wood, known by this name from the 17th century,[9] adjoins Rushbeds Wood in Brill. Both are skirted by the Oxford and Aylesbury tramroad, which has a station at the south-east end of Wotton Underwood. Lawn Farm, which stands near, probably preserves the name of Wotton Lawnd, a common in 1580[10] and until its inclosure in 1742, when it contained 500 acres.[11] The Kingswood branch of the Wotton tramway runs in a northerly direction. Moat Farm, which stands east of the village, is a 17th-century house considerably restored, with vestiges of a moat,[12] once, it is said, part of the manor of Ham and owned by the Mercers' Company.[13]

There are now stations on the Great Central railway and the Brill and Quainton Road branch of the Metropolitan and Great Central railway.

[66] Feet of F. Bucks. East. 12 Geo. I.
[67] Musgrave, *Obit.* (Harl. Soc.), iii, 258. [68] Inst. Bks. (P.R.O.).
[69] Musgrave, *Obit.* (Harl. Soc.), iii, 258.
[70] A presentation was made by Edward Horne in this year (Inst. Bks. P.R.O.).
[71] Inst. Bks. (P.R.O.), 1795 ; *Clergy Lists.*
[72] Sheahan, loc. cit.
[73] P.C.C. 136 Coke.
[1] *V.C.H. Bucks.* i, 249 ; Feet of F. Bucks. East. 24 Eliz. ; Chan. Inq. p.m. (Ser. 2), ccclxxxv, 14.

[2] Statistics from Bd. of Agric. (1905).
[3] Lansd. MS. 47, fol. 3 ; Pat. 19 Eliz. pt vi, m. 1.
[4] Priv. Act, 15 Geo. II, cap. 39.
[5] Lipscomb, *Hist. and Antiq. of Bucks.* i, 603. The house which it succeeded is mentioned in 1618, and was left by Richard Grenville by his will dated 30 Dec. 1665 to his wife Eleanor (Chan. Inq. p.m. [Ser. 2], ccclxxvi, 92 ; P.C.C. 58 Mico).
[6] Sheahan, *Hist. and Topog. of Bucks.* 449 ; Paterson, *Descr. of Roads* (1826), 176.

[7] Sheahan, op. cit. 446.
[8] Feet of F. Bucks. East. 24 Eliz. ; Chan. Inq. p.m. (Ser. 2), ccx, 136 ; ccxvi, 45 ; Recov. R. East. 13 Chas. I, m. 78.
[9] Chan. Inq. p.m. (Ser. 2), ccclxxvi, 92 ; cccxxxv, 14.
[10] Exch. Dep. Mich. 22 & 23 Eliz. no. 16 ; Chan. Inq. p.m. (Ser. 2), cccxxxv, 14.
[11] Priv. Act, 15 Geo. II, cap. 39.
[12] *V.C.H. Bucks.* ii, 32.
[13] Lipscomb, op. cit. i, 605. See p. 132 for this manor.

MANORS

The manor of *WOTTON*, later GRENVILLE'S MANOR, which Eddeva wife of Ulward held before the Norman Conquest with right to sell, was amongst the lands of Walter Giffard in 1086,[14] and belonged to the honour of Giffard.[15] The overlordship of the whole followed the descent of Long Crendon (q.v.) until the death of the elder William Marshal, of whom two knights' fees in Wotton were held.[16] One of these descended with Long Crendon[17] until 1275, when William de Valence became overlord.[18] There appears to have been some doubt as to the overlordship rights, the tenants of the manor asserting it to be within the liberty of William de Valence and not in that of the Earl of Gloucester, whose bailiffs restored to William de Scobingdon some cattle wrongfully taken by Eustace de Grenville, tenant of Wotton.[19] Eustace lost his case, but the overlordship rights of William de Valence did not suffer, and this fee descended with the manor of Pollicott Cressy in Ashendon[20] (q.v.), of which it was held from 1346 to 1618.[21]

Though the tradition that a Grenville was lord of Wotton before the close of the 11th century seems to be without foundation,[22] it is likely that the connexion of this family with the parish began at an early date. Gerard de Grenville, who held three knights' fees of the honour of Giffard in 1166,[23] died in or before 1184, when 100 marks were due from his nephew for his lands in Buckinghamshire.[24] This nephew was probably Eustace de Grenville,[25] who was succeeded by Richard de Grenville mentioned in connexion with Wotton in 1213[26] and alive in 1236.[26a] His son Eustace de Grenville was in possession[26b] in 1255 and in 1284.[27] He was succeeded in or before 1302 by his son Richard,[28] who was returned as sole lord of the parish in 1316,[29] and held in 1324.[30] In 1329 the manor was settled on Richard for life with remainder to his son William, and contingent remainders to a younger son Edmund and daughters Margery, Nichola and Agnes.[31] Richard

GRENVILLE. *Vert a cross argent with five roundels gules thereon.*

de Grenville died before Michaelmas 1336, when his widow Joan transferred her rights in Haddenham to his son William.[32] In the spring of 1346 William with his wife Margaret made a settlement of lands in Haddenham.[32a] He may have died shortly afterwards, as the names of John Sergeant, evidently a trustee, and his tenants Agnes and Nichola de Grenville, William's sisters, are returned for the feudal assessment of that year in Wotton and Haddenham.[33] William de Grenville was certainly dead by 1351.[33a] Agnes de Grenville, whom he must have married after the death of Margaret between 1346 and 1351,[34] received in 1365 a quitclaim from William Freysel and his wife Margery.[35] Sixteen years later it was settled on Agnes by her son Thomas de Grenville.[36] Thomas, who was living in 1400,[37] was succeeded by his son Richard,[38] lord in 1419 and 1420,[39] whose widow Christina was described as late of Wotton under Bernwood in 1452, when she was in money difficulties.[40] From Eustace, their son and heir,[41] one of the gentlemen of Buckinghamshire whose names were returned by the Commissioners of 1433,[42] Wotton descended to his son and heir Richard,[43] lord until 1518, when he was succeeded by his son Edward.[44] Another Edward Grenville, eldest son of the last, inherited Grenville's Manor, first so-called, in 1536,[45] and was entrusted to the guardianship of John Josselyne about two years later.[46] In 1548 he was of age, and entered into possession.[47] He and his wife Alice held together in 1582,[48] and until his death in 1585.[49] As wife, or more probably, widow of Walter Dennis[50] Alice was still seised in 1604 when Richard Grenville, her first husband's brother and heir, was succeeded by his son of the same name.[51] Fourteen years later the second Richard died lord of Wotton Underwood, leaving by his widow Frances another Richard, then aged six,[52] at whose death in January 1665–6 the manor descended to his son, also Richard Grenville.[53] He died in 1719, leaving a son, another Richard,[54] who married Hester Temple,[55] by whom his will was proved in March 1726–7.[56] Richard, their eldest son,[57] who was lord of Wotton Underwood in 1733[58] and 1742,[59] became Earl Temple at his mother's death in 1752.[60] She had succeeded to the estate of her brother Richard, Viscount Cobham, at Stowe, which henceforth became the family's chief seat, and with which

[14] *V.C.H. Bucks.* i, 249.
[15] *Hund. R.* (Rec. Com.), i, 24.
[16] *Testa de Nevill* (Rec. Com.), 247.
[17] *Hund. R.* (Rec. Com.), i, 24.
[18] See in Ashendon.
[19] *Abbrev. Plac.* (Rec. Com.), 265.
[20] *Feud. Aids,* i, 75, 95.
[21] Ibid. 121 ; *Chan. Inq. p.m.* (Ser. 2), xlix, 52 ; ccx, 136 ; cccxxxv, 14, 15 ; ccclxxvi, 92.
[22] Lipscomb, op. cit. i, 586.
[23] *Red Bk. of Exch.* (Rolls Ser.), 312.
[24] *Pipe R.* 30 *Hen. II* (Pipe R. Soc.), 118.
[25] Lipscomb, op. cit. i, 591. A Gerard de Grenville witnessed a charter of Nutley Abbey concerning Winchendon Manor in 1205 (*Rot. de Oblatis et Fin.* [Rec. Com.], 242).
[26] *Abbrev. Plac.* (Rec. Com.), 92.
[26a] *Cal. Close,* 1234–7, p. 373.
[26b] *Visit. of Bucks.* (Harl. Soc.), 65.
[27] *Hund. R.* (Rec. Com.), i, 24 ; *Feud. Aids,* i, 75.

[28] *Feud. Aids,* i, 95 ; *Visit. of Bucks.* loc. cit.
[29] *Feud. Aids,* i, 113.
[30] *Cal. Inq. p.m.* (Edw. II), vi, 328.
[31] *Feet of F. Bucks.* 3 Edw. III, no. 11.
[32] Ibid. case 19, file 81, no. 119.
[32a] Ibid. file 87, no. 3. For other references to William Grenville see *Cal. Close,* 1333–7, p. 654 ; *Cal. Pat.* 1334–8, p. 219 ; 1338–40, p. 348 ; 1340–3, p. 233.
[33] *Feud. Aids,* i, 121, 122.
[33a] *Cal. Close,* 1349–54, p. 378.
[34] Lipscomb, op. cit. i, 594, 612.
[35] *Feet of F. Bucks.* 39 Edw. III, no. 4. Margery may have been one of Richard de Grenville's daughters.
[36] *Feet of F. Bucks.* 4 Ric. II, no. 4.
[37] *Cal. Pat.* 1399–1401, p. 168.
[38] *Visit. of Bucks.* loc. cit.
[39] *Chan. Inq. p.m.* 7 Hen. V, no. 68 ; 8 Hen. V, no. 127.
[40] *Cal. Pat.* 1452–61, p. 6.
[41] *Visit. of Bucks.* loc. cit.
[42] Fuller, *Worthies of Engl.* i, 147 ; cf. *Cal. Pat.* 1429–36, p. 398.

[43] *Visit. of Bucks.* loc. cit.
[44] *Exch. Inq. p.m.* (Ser. 2), file 13, no. 3.
[45] *Chan. Inq. p.m.* (Ser. 2), xlix, 52.
[46] *L. and P. Hen. VIII,* xiii (1), g. 384 (30).
[47] *Fine R.* 2 Edw. VI, no. 31.
[48] *Feet of F. Bucks.* East. 24 Eliz.
[49] *Chan. Inq. p.m.* (Ser. 2), ccx, 136 ; ccxvi, 45 ; cccxxxv, 15.
[50] Lipscomb, loc. cit. ; *Cal. S. P. Dom.* 1591–4, p. 403.
[51] *Chan. Inq. p.m.* (Ser. 2), cccxxxv, 14.
[52] Ibid. ccclxxvi, 92 ; *Recov. R.* East. 18 Chas. I, m. 78.
[53] P.C.C. 58 Mico. ; Lipscomb, op. cit. i, 612.
[54] Lipscomb, op. cit. i, 599.
[55] G.E.C. *Peerage,* ii, 324.
[56] P.C.C. 62 Farrant.
[57] G.E.C. loc. cit.
[58] *Recov. R.* Trin. 6 & 7 Geo. II, m. 200.
[59] Priv. Act, 15 Geo. II, cap. 39.
[60] *Dict. Nat. Biog.*

Wotton descended until the death of the last Duke of Buckingham and Chandos in 1889.[61] The title of Earl Temple and the estate at Wotton then passed to his nephew William Stephen Gore-Langton, whose son Algernon, now Earl Temple, has been lord of the manor of Wotton Underwood since 1902.[62]

GORE-LANGTON, Earl Temple. *Quarterly sable and or a bend argent.*

A dovecote belonged to the manor in 1618.[63]

The second knight's fee in Wotton, held of the honour of Crendon in the early 13th century (see Wotton Manor), corresponds to *FIELDHAM, HAM, HAM-CUM-WOTTON*, or from the later 15th-century *WOTTON MANOR*. Before 1276[64] the overlordship was attached to the honour of Gloucester,[65] and descended with Easington Manor (see Chilton) to Edward Duke of Buckingham, who held it in 1510.[66]

Robert de la Rokele[67] was holding this fee early in the 13th century.[68] William de la Rokele,[69] who was holding Ham Mill of the Templars in 1185, probably held it before him. Robert de Tattershall enfeoffed the heirs of William Cantelow, holders in 1255.[70] From the Cantelow heirs Fieldham descended with Ellesborough Manor to William la Zouche,[71] who was holding in 1299.[72] He granted Fieldham before 1302 to one of his younger sons, John la Zouche,[73] for life.[74] He was living in 1325, when William la Zouche made a settlement of this manor in remainder on another son William.[75] The latter appears, however, to have died before his father, for in 1346 John, a descendant of John la Zouche, the former tenant for life, was holding Fieldham.[76] This manor had reverted before 1370[76a] to William grandson and heir of William la Zouche, who died in 1352.[77] Except for certain settlements,[78] this manor followed the descent of the manor of Ham in Waddesdon (q.v.) from this date.

The manorial court mentioned at the end of the 13th century[79] used to be held by the Mercers' Company at Moat Farm.[80]

Two virgates of land in Ham, on which stood a mill, were granted by Gerard de Grenville to the Knights Templars, who were holding in mesne in 1185[81] and 1255 of the honour of Giffard.[82]

Their tenant at the earlier date was William de la Rokele, at the later the heirs of William Cantelow, then lords of Fieldham Manor (q.v.). Richard de la Rokele was probably the Cantelows' sub-tenant in respect of this property.[83] At least three representatives of his family had holdings in Wotton in 1284,[84] but no later reference to the mill has been found except that a pasture in Ham called 'the mill' was leased in 1521 for twenty-one years to Christopher Wren.[85]

An estate in Wotton, known from the 15th century as *BEREWELLS MANOR*, was held of the manor of Pollicott Cressy in Ashendon,[86] the last reference to this overlordship occurring in 1548.[87] In 1518 it was said to be attached to the Grenvilles' manor in Wotton, which was similarly held of the Pollicott fee,[88] and was probably an integral part of that manor until 1308, when John de Grenville and Jane his wife granted lands in Wotton to Richard son of Humphrey de la Rokele and Basilia his wife and the issue of Basilia, in default of which, remainder to Richard son of the said Richard de la Rokele.[89] It has not been found possible to trace the connexion between the various members of this family, who held until the 14th century.[90] In 1284 the heirs of Humphrey de la Rokele, Peter and John de la Rokele were returned as lords, but probably in connexion with Ham Manor.[91] Peter and John de la Rokele four years later brought an action to recover their common pasture in Wotton of which they had been disseised.[92] Eustace de la Rokele is mentioned in 1311,[93] and in 1328 his son Peter was sued for debt on two different counts.[94] There is no further trace of the Rokeles in Wotton, and the estate passed to the Berewell family, from whom it acquired its distinctive name. In 1358 Nicholas Berewell bought a small property in Wotton from William Freysel and his wife Margery,[95] and John Berewell bought a considerable amount of land in this parish from Sir William Wakelyn and his wife Gille twenty-eight years later.[96] This may be the John, son of Richard Berewell, whose son and heir William acquired additional lands in Wotton of the fee of Easington, otherwise Gloucester fee, by his marriage with Joan daughter of Thomas Langport.[97] In 1463 Annis or Agnes, daughter of William and Joan, and her husband Ralph Ingoldsby, sued Edmund Rede and other of her father's trustees in Chancery for the recovery of the manor of Berewells. It was urged in

[61] See also Recov. R. Trin. 57 Geo. III, m. 11.

[62] G.E.C. *Peerage*, vii, 374.

[63] Chan. Inq. p.m. (Ser. 2), ccclxxvi, 92.

[64] *Hund. R.* (Rec. Com.), i, 42.

[65] Chan. Inq. p.m. Edw. I, file 90, no. 2 ; *Feud. Aids*, i, 93, 121.

[66] Chan. Inq. p.m. (Ser. 2), xxv, 160.

[67] *Red Bk. of Exch.* (Rolls Ser.), 583 ; *Rot. de Oblatis et Fin.* (Rec. Com.), 596.

[68] *Testa de Nevill* (Rec. Com.), 247.

[69] *Red Bk. of Exch.* (Rolls Ser.), 89, 115, 120, 151, 740.

[70] *Hund. R.* (Rec. Com.), i, 24.

[71] *V.C.H. Bucks.* ii, 331 ; *Cal. Close,* 1272-9, p. 115 ; *Cal. Fine R.* 1272-1307, p. 18 ; *Hund. R.* (Rec. Com.), i, 42 ; *Feud. Aids*, i, 75.

[72] Chan. Inq. p.m. Edw. I, file 90, no. 2.

[73] *Feud. Aids*, i, 95, 113 ; *Cal. Pat.* 1324-7, p. 254.

[74] Feet of F. case 286, file 32, no. 246.

[75] Ibid. ; De Banco R. 255, m. 111.

[76] *Feud. Aids*, i, 121.

[76a] Harl. Chart. 58, D 47.

[77] *V.C.H. Bucks.* ii, 332.

[78] Harl. Chart. 58, D 47. Symond Ward, to whom a life grant of the manor was made by the deed, may have been a relative of Richard Ward, who appears to have previously held it (Feet of F. Bucks. Mich. 2 Edw. II, no. 20 ; Chan. Inq. p.m. 46 Edw. III [1st nos.], no. 62). Roger Ward, perhaps as Symond's executor, was subsequently in possession (ibid. 16 Ric. II, pt. i, no. 27).

[79] Chan. Inq. p.m. Edw. I, file 90, no. 2. [80] Lipscomb, op. cit. i, 604.

[81] Dugdale, *Mon.* vi, 823.

[82] *Hund. R.* (Rec. Com.), i, 24.

[83] He paid half a quartern of corn and ½d. yearly to Brill Manor to be quit of tonnage (*Hund. R.* [Rec. Com.], i, 24) and Fieldham included a piece of wood in Bernwood Forest (Chan. Inq. p.m. Edw. I, file 90, no. 2).

[84] *Feud. Aids*, i, 75. See below.

[85] *L. and P. Hen. VIII*, iii (2), g. 1451 (13).

[86] Early Chan. Proc. bdle. 27, no. 129-34.

[87] Fine R. 2 Edw. VI, no. 31.

[88] Exch. Inq. p.m. (Ser. 2), file 13, no. 3.

[89] Feet of F. case 18, file 16, no. 23.

[90] Ibid. case 17, file 47, no. 4 ; case 18, files 60, no. 21 ; 69, no. 34.

[91] *Feud. Aids*, i, 75.

[92] *Abbrev. Rot. Orig.* (Rec. Com.), i, 59.

[93] *Cal. Close*, 1307-13, p. 353.

[94] De Banco R. East. 2 Edw. III, m. 257 d. ; Mich. 2 Edw. III, m. 159 d.

[95] Feet of F. Bucks. 32 Edw. III, no. 4. She was probably a Grenville (see Wotton Manor).

[96] Ibid. 9 Ric. II, no. 7, 8.

[97] Early Chan. Proc. bdle. 27, no. 129-34.

WOTTON UNDERWOOD : WOTTON HOUSE, THE EAST FRONT

WOTTON UNDERWOOD CHURCH FROM THE SOUTH

WOTTON UNDERWOOD CHURCH : THE INTERIOR LOOKING EAST

the defence that William had granted half Berewells by nuncupatory will to his second wife, another Joan, and the other half to his son Thomas, who was to inherit the whole on Joan's death.[98] The issue of the suit has not been recorded. In course of time Berewells seems to have come into the possession of Edmund Hall, who towards the close of the 15th century acquired land in Wotton of Harry Harper *alias* Tyes.[99] In 1509 Isabel widow of Edmund and sister of William Temple, was seised of a manor in Wotton [100] which from its later history must be identified with Berewells. This was settled by William on Isabel at her marriage with Walter Wilcocks,[1] and two years later Walter and Isabel sold it to Robert Dormer.[2] In 1515 Robert granted it to Richard Grenville in exchange for an Oxfordshire manor,[3] and it is probable that after 1548, when the last mention of Berewells in public records occurs,[4] it was absorbed once more in Grenville's Manor.[5]

CHURCH   The church of *ALL SAINTS* consists of a chancel measuring internally 28 ft. by 16 ft., north vestry, nave 41 ft. 6 in. by 21 ft., south aisle and west tower; it is built of stone rubble and roofed with lead.

The chancel was probably built about 1320, but the whole fabric has been so much restored and enlarged that precise dates cannot be assigned to either chancel or nave. The south aisle, founded originally for a chantry in 1343 by William Grenville, was rebuilt in 1710 and became a mortuary chapel for the Grenville family. It was extensively repaired in 1800 by George Marquess of Buckingham, and again practically rebuilt in 1867 by the last Duke of Buckingham and Chandos. The tower dates from about 1800, and the vestry is modern.

The chancel has in each side wall a 14th-century trefoiled light considerably restored. Modern arches open to the north vestry and the east end of the aisle or chapel. In the east wall is a modern three-light window with an original 14th-century rear-arch. In the south wall is a modern piscina recess with a medieval sexfoil bowl. The pointed chancel arch, though much restored, probably dates from the 14th century.

The nave is lighted by three 15th-century windows on the north and a modern window at the south-west, all of two lights with traceried heads. In the north wall is also a 15th-century doorway with a four-centred head. A modern doorway to the tower on the west preserves a 12th-century lintel, enriched with diaper ornament, perhaps a relic of an earlier church on this site. On the south an arcade of three pointed arches, dating from 1867, opens to the mortuary chapel. It is designed in the early 14th-century manner and has clustered pillars and responds with moulded capitals and bases, the two western bays being filled with unglazed tracery supported by slender shafts.

The tower, which is of two stages, is lighted by wide pointed windows with wood frames and is surmounted by an embattled parapet and lead spire. On the parapet is the inscription 'Thomas A Beckett hujusce ecclesiae presbyter MDCCC.'

The mortuary chapel contains several monuments to members of the Grenville family. At the east end is a marble slab with the brass figures of Edward 'Greneveile' (d. 1585), and of Alice his wife, daughter of William Haselwood, the figure of a chrisom child, an incised marginal inscription, and matrices for three shields. On the south wall are tablets to Richard Grenville (d. 1665–6) and Eleanor daughter of Richard Grenville (d. 1688); on the north wall are two stone shields of Grenville. In a modern recess in the west wall is a 16th-century recumbent effigy of a lady in ruff and veil, with a modern and obviously erroneous inscription commemorating Agnes de Wightham, wife of William de Grenville, who died in 1386. On the same wall are two kneeling figures, a man in plate armour and lady in full skirt and ruff, also of the 16th century. There are also monuments to Richard, last Duke of Buckingham and Chandos (d. 1889), Anna Eliza, Duchess of Buckingham and Chandos (d. 1836), and Caroline, Duchess of Buckingham and Chandos (d. 1874), besides several tablets and slabs to other members of the Grenville family. In the tower is a plain oak chest.

The tower contains a ring of six bells: the treble and tenor are by Thomas Mears of London, 1800; the third, fourth and fifth by Edward Hemins, of Bicester, 1728; and the second, recast by Hemins in 1728, bears the additional inscription, 'Alicia Dennis vidua dedit me huic parochiae. 1615.' There is also a small bell, with no inscription.

The communion plate includes a chalice and cover paten of 1589.

The registers begin in 1599.

ADVOWSON   The church, a peculiar of Canterbury,[6] belonged to the priory of St. Gregory, Canterbury.[7] It is said to have formed part of the endowment of Bentley Priory, a cell of that house, and to have reverted, on the suppression of the smaller religious houses in the early years of Henry VIII, to St. Gregory,[8] whose prior was seised in 1535 of lands and rent in Wotton [9] which had belonged to the Prior of Bentley in 1291.[10] After the Dissolution the possessions of the priory of St. Gregory were granted in an exchange to the see of Canterbury,[11] to which the advowson of Wotton Underwood belonged[12] until the archbishop granted it to the Marquess of Buckingham in 1805,[13] from which date it has followed the descent of the manor (q.v.). The rectory descended with the advowson until 1742, when Richard Grenville acquired it in exchange for Muswells Farm in Brill and Boarstall.[14]

Tithes granted before 1102 by Walter Giffard to the abbey of St. Faith in Longueville and enjoyed by its cell, the alien priory of Newton Longville,[15] came

[98] Early Chan. Proc. bdle. 27, no. 129–34; De Banco R. 810, m. 365 d.
[99] Early Chan. Proc. bdle. 235, no. 65.
[100] Close, 1 Hen. VIII, no. 19.
[1] Ibid.; Feet of F. Bucks. Mich.
1 Hen. VIII.
[2] Feet of F. Bucks. East. 3 Hen. VIII.
[3] Close, 7 Hen. VIII, no. 34.
[4] Fine R. 2 Edw. VI, no. 31.

[5] In 1704 John Dormer had rights in the manor of Wotton Underwood (Recov. R. East. 3 Anne, m. 163).
[6] Bacon, *Liber Reg.* 505; *Clerical Guide.*
[7] Bacon, loc. cit.; Priv. Act, 15 Geo. II, cap. 39.   [8] Lipscomb, op. cit. i, 606.
[9] *Valor Eccl.* (Rec. Com.), i, 25.
[10] *Pope Nich. Tax.* (Rec. Com.), 46b.

[11] Dugdale, *Mon.* vi, 616; *Statutes of the Realm* (Rec. Com.), iii, 712.
[12] Exch. Dep. East. 25 Chas. II, no. 10; Bacon, loc. cit.   [13] Lipscomb, loc. cit.
[14] Priv. Act, 15 Geo. II, cap. 39.
[15] Round, *Cal. Doc. of France*, 77; Dugdale, *Mon.* vi, 1036; *Pope Nich. Tax.* (Rec. Com.), 34; *Valor Eccl.* (Rec. Com.), ii, 259.

in 1441, with other possessions of that house, to New College, Oxford.[16] These, under the name of Longville's Portion, were the subject of a dispute between the archbishop's lessee and the warden and scholars in 1673.[17] In 1742 Richard Grenville acquired the Longville tithes from New College, in exchange for an annuity of £5 from his lands in Brill called Little London.[18]

CHARITIES John Hart, by his will proved in the P.C.C. 15 May 1665, demised (*inter alia*) an annual rent-charge of £3 issuing out of Easington Manor, Oxfordshire, for apprenticing a poor boy. The annuity, less land tax,

has from time to time been accumulated by reason of there being no applicants for apprenticing. By a scheme of the Charity Commissioners of 28 January 1913 it was provided that, in so far as the trustees cannot apply the income in apprenticing, it may be applied in the assistance of poor boys or girls in outfits and advancement in life.

Richard Smith, by his will proved in the Archdeacon's Court at Oxford 15 April 1725, bequeathed £5, the income to be distributed in bread. The principal sum is in the hands of the parish, in respect of which 5s. is distributed among ten of the most needy persons.

[16] *Cal. Pat.* 1436–41, p. 558.   [17] Exch. Dep. East. 25 Chas. II, no. 10.   [18] Priv. Act, 15 Geo. II, cap. 39.

THE HUNDRED OF BUCKINGHAM

CONTAINING THE PARISHES OF

ADDINGTON	HILLESDEN	SHALSTONE
ADSTOCK	LECKHAMPSTEAD	STEEPLE CLAYDON
AKELEY	LILLINGSTONE DAYRELL	STOWE
BARTON HARTSHORN	LILLINGSTONE LOVELL [1a]	THORNBOROUGH
BEACHAMPTON	LUFFIELD ABBEY	THORNTON
BIDDLESDEN	MAIDS' MORETON	TINGEWICK
CAVERSFIELD [1]	MARSH GIBBON	TURWESTON
CHETWODE	PADBURY	TWYFORD WITH CHARNDON
EDGCOTT	PRESTON BISSETT	AND POUNDON
FOSCOTT	RADCLIVE	WATER STRATFORD
	WESTBURY	

All the names given above are mentioned in the Domesday Survey,[2] except Luffield Abbey and Poundon; the latter was probably included under Charndon. Evershaw in Biddlesden, Dadford and Lamport in Stowe, and a hide of land called Hasley were described separately in 1086.[3]

Buckingham Hundred comprises the three ancient hundreds of Stodfald, Rovelai and Lamva,[4] which appear grouped as the three hundreds of Buckingham in the later 13th century.[5] The hundred of Stodfald, assessed in 1086 at 101 hides,[6] contained the parishes of Akeley, Biddlesden, Foscott, Leckhampstead, Lillingstone Dayrell, Maids' Moreton, Radclive, Shalstone, Stowe, Turweston, Water Stratford and Westbury. The hundred of Rovelai was assessed in 1086 at 105 hides and included the parishes of Barton Hartshorn, Beachampton, Caversfield, Chetwode, Edgcott, Hillesden, Preston Bissett, Thornton and Tingewick.[7] The hidage of Lamva Hundred, under which the parishes of Addington, Adstock, Marsh Gibbon, Padbury, Steeple Claydon, Thornborough and Twyford were assessed in 1086, covered 122 hides.[8] Edgcott and Thornton were transferred later from Rovelai to Lamva Hundred.[9]

In 1625 the royal hundreds of Buckingham (the old names surviving as Stotford, Roulawe and Meanes)[10] were leased for three lives to Sir

---

[1] Caversfield was transferred to Oxfordshire by Statutes 2 & 3 Will. IV, cap. 64 (1832), 7 & 8 Vict. cap. 61 (1844).

[1a] Lillingstone Lovell is in the hundred of Ploughley, Oxfordshire; it was transferred to Buckinghamshire by Statute 7 & 8 Vict. cap. 61.   [2] V.C.H. Bucks. i, 231–77.   [3] Ibid.

[4] Ibid. Willis connects Rovelai with lands called Rowley Hills in Lenborough, Buckingham (Hist. and Antiq. of Buckingham, 2).   [5] Feud. Aids, i, 89.

[6] V.C.H. Bucks. i, 231–77. Total of the hidage under this hundred, including 9 hides 2 virgates assessed in error under Mursley in Cottesloe Hundred (ibid. 269).

[7] Ibid. i, 231–77. The total hidage includes a hide in Bourton, a hide in Gawcott, and 7 hides in Lenborough, places which have been described under Buckingham Borough (ibid. iii, 481–4).

[8] Ibid. i, 231–77. The total includes 9 hides 1 virgate from three places in this hundred which are unnamed in the Survey.

[9] Hund. R. (Rec. Com.), ii, 351; Feud. Aids, i, 109 ; Lay Subs. R. bdles. 78, no. 109 ; 79, no. 261.

[10] Meanes is called Buckingham Hundred in two Lay Subsidy Rolls (bdles. 78, no. 109 ; 79, no. 261).

Thomas Denton.[11] In 1651 the rents or certainty money were valued at £23 1s. 1d. yearly ; the general perquisites at £10.[12] These were claimed by Edmund Denton of Hillesden, who did not, however, produce any proof in support of his claim.[13] In 1661 a petition was made to the Crown for the protection of the rights in this respect of his infant heir, Alexander Denton.[14] In 1665 the Crown rents from the Buckingham hundreds were granted in dower to Queen Katherine.[15]

In the middle of the 17th century the court leet was held at the usual

INDEX MAP TO THE HUNDRED OF BUCKINGHAM

times and the ordinary court every three weeks at any convenient place in the hundreds at the will of the lord or his steward.[16]

[11] Pat. 1 Chas. I, pt. xxiv, no. 11.
[14] Cal. of Treas. Bks. i, 166.
[16] Parl. Surv. Bucks. no. 3.

[12] Parl. Surv. Bucks. no. 3.
[15] Pat. 17 Chas. II, pt. ix, no. 1.

[13] Ibid.

ADDINGTON

Edintona, Eddintone (xi cent.).

Addington covers 1,303 acres, of which 147 acres are arable and 1,008 acres permanent grass.[1] The soil is mixed clay and gravel. Claydon Brook bounds the parish on three sides. The slope of the land varies from 346 ft. above the ordnance datum in the south-east to 289 ft. in the north-west. The greater part of the area is taken up by the Addington Manor estate, which was inclosed during the ownership of Dr. Busby in 1710.[2]

The village, consisting of a few houses and the parish church of St. Mary, lies some little distance south of the main road from Buckingham to Winslow, near the entrance to the manor. West of the church is the rectory, which was built in 1868 on the site of an older house. The old manor-house, now known as Addington House, a rectangular two-storied building of brick and stone, standing to the north of the church, is part of a larger house, formerly a story higher. It now faces south and was reduced to its present form in 1859, when the walls were partly refaced, a floor was added to the middle part, which was originally of one story, and the farm buildings at the north end were converted into domestic offices. The windows and stone quoins at the south end of the eastern front are original work of the 17th century. There is a good deal of original oak panelling of that date in the older rooms. To the north-west of the house is a barn of the 16th century, built of brick and lighted by two tiers of narrow loops splaying inwards. It is about 60 ft. long in five bays,

ADDINGTON MANOR HOUSE

and is placed with its greatest length from north to south, the central bays on each side projecting from the main block, and is entered by a doorway in the gabled eastern projection. Opposite to the barn are the stables dated 1642. Near the garden gates are still to be seen the old village stocks. The present Addington Manor was built in 1854–6 by the first Lord Addington. It is designed in the French château style; the fireplace in the hall and parts of the main staircase were brought from the old manor-house. A farm in the south-east of this parish is known as Seven Gables. Addington has always been small in size and population. On the occasion of a general taxation in the middle of the 14th century the inhabitants claimed a low assessment, because

they said 4 virgates of land were uncultivated, there was very little live stock, and no traders there.[3]

A terrier of 1517 giving the 'Butments and Boundings of the Parsonage Lands' furnished the following place-names, Attwell Hole, Harcot, Edwards Way, Flexmore Path, Millfield, Windmill Furz, Hallwell Close, Leetfurlong, Dunway and Wipas.[4]

In the south of the parish Gallows Gap is supposed to mark the site of an ancient gallows, the privilege of maintaining which was acquired by the lord of Addington Manor in 1338.[5]

During the Civil War Addington was twice the headquarters of Parliamentarian troops. On 15 January 1643–4 Captain Thomas Shelburne is found addressing a letter to the Earl of Essex 'from my quarters at Addington,'[6] while on 5 March of the

following year the same address is given by Jecamiah Abercromby.[7]

The name of Robert Whitehall (1625–85), the poetaster, is connected with Addington, where his father was rector.[8] Luke Heslop was also rector here from 1792 to 1804.[9]

The overlordship of *ADDINGTON MANORS MANOR* was vested in the Bishop of Bayeux at Domesday.[10] After his death the manor is found held by the grand serjeanty of acting as king's falconer.[11] No reference has been found to this serjeanty later than 1432.[12]

Robert de Rumenel was tenant of this 6-hide manor at Domesday,[12a] and its subsequent descent until the 16th century in the families of Jarpenville, Fitz Bernard,

[1] Statistics from Bd. of Agric. (1905).
[2] Willis, *Hist. and Antiq. of Buckingham*, 113.
[3] *Inq. Nonarum* (Rec. Com.), 330.
[4] Willis, op. cit. 115.
[5] Ibid. See Manor.
[6] *Hist. MSS. Com. Rep.* xiii, App. i, 166.   [7] Ibid. 214.
[8] *Dict. Nat. Biog.*
[9] Ibid. See Adstock.
[10] *V.C.H. Bucks.* i, 239.
[11] Rymer, *Foedera*, i (1), 90; *Hund. R.* (Rec. Com.), i, 28; Chan. Inq. p.m. 24 Hen. III, no. 3; 1 Edw. II, no. 25; 3 Edw. III (1st nos.), no. 27; 4 Ric. II, no. 38; *Feud. Aids*, i, 81.
[12] Chan. Inq. p.m. 11 Hen. VI, no. 34.
[12a] *V.C.H. Bucks*, i, 239.

Blaket, Moleyns and Hastings, has already been traced under Aston Mullins[13] (q.v.). In 1254–5 Thomas Fitz Bernard claimed to be free from suits at both the hundred and county courts, and to have the right of holding a view in Addington.[14] John de Moleyns, who was lord of the manor in 1335, obtained in that year a grant of free warren,[15] and between that date and 1338 received grants and confirmations of further privileges, namely, return of writs, precepts and summonses within the manor, infangenthef, outfangenthef, view of frankpledge, and assize of bread and ale.[16]

Various members of the house of Moleyns appear to have made life grants of the manor in the 14th and 15th centuries, it being found in the family of Barton for two generations between 1375 and 1432.[17]

Addington was finally separated from the Aston Mullins estate in 1534, when George Hastings, Earl of Huntingdon, sold the manor to Richard Curzon,[18] whose father, Walter Curzon,[19] had already acquired Carbonels Manor in this parish. Richard Curzon died in 1549, and by his will left to his widow Agnes 'twoo and twentie score of my Shepe goyng or pasturyng in and uppon my londes, tenements and hereditaments in Addyngton.'[20] His eldest son, Vincent Curzon,[21] succeeded to the Addington estate, which

CURZON. *Argent a bend sable with three popinjays or thereon.*

he settled by fine in 1575.[22] He died in 1585, when he was succeeded by his son, Francis Curzon,[23] who held till his death in 1610.[24] His widow Anne appears to have been heavily fined as a recusant, for in the year following his death the manor was granted by the Crown for a term of forty-one years to Sir John Dormer and John Symonds at the nomination of Walter Toderick, to whom her recusancy had been granted.[25] Apparently some composition was arrived at, for in 1628 her son, Sir John Curzon, kt., was in possession of the manor, which he then alienated to Robert Busby.[26] Robert Busby made a settlement of the manor in 1639,[27] and died and was buried at Addington in 1652.[28] He was succeeded by his son and heir, John Busby, who was knighted in 1661[29] and died in 1700, leaving his eldest son Thomas as his executor.[30] Thomas Busby, LL.D., who made a settlement of the manor in 1701,[31] was both rector

and patron of the church, and held the living till his death in 1725,[32] when his daughters Jane and Anne succeeded to the paternal estate.[33] They suffered a recovery of Addington in 1734,[34] and three years later Anne became the wife of Sir Charles Kemeys Tynte, bart.[35] He died in 1785,[36] and his widow's name is found as plaintiff in settlements of the manor in the following year[37] and in 1787.[38] Lady Tynte died without issue in 1798,[39] and her sister Jane, who never married, did not long survive her.[40] Under the terms of their wills Addington then passed to Vere Poulett, second

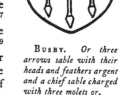

BUSBY. *Or three arrows sable with their heads and feathers argent and a chief sable charged with three molets or.*

son of the third Earl Poulett,[41] who held it in 1801.[42] Together with his son John Poulett he settled the estate in 1809,[43] while the latter held it in 1830.[44] It shortly after passed to John Gellibrand Hubbard, a London merchant, who, when raised to the peerage in 1887, took the title of Baron Addington of Addington.[45] He died two years later, and was succeeded by his son, Egerton Hubbard, who died in 1915. His son John Gellibrand is the present lord of the manor.[46]

A second overlordship in Addington at the Domesday Survey was that of Miles Crispin, whose tenants had half a hide here worth 10s.,[47]

HUBBARD, Lord Addington. *Vert a cheveron engrailed and couple-closed between three eagles' heads razed argent each having flowered collars gules.*

and known later as *ADDINGTON* or *CARBONELS MANOR.* This half-hide became attached later to the honour of Quarrendon, and is so described from the 13th to the 16th century.[48] Lewi, a man of Edwi, was tenant of this manor during the Confessor's reign, and was succeeded by Eddulf, who held at the time of the Survey. He was followed some time in the 12th century by a family of the name of Carbonel, the earliest member of whom mention has been found being Richard Carbonel, whose widow Maud in 1198 claimed dower of her brother-in-law 'Hamudum' Carbonel from 5 virgates in Addington.[49]

[13] *V.C.H. Bucks.* ii, 275. A great many general references under this manor refer to Addington. See also Assize R. 68, m. 14 d.; *Hund. R.* (Rec. Com.), ii, 353; *Cal. Pat.* 1327–30, pp. 75, 77, 281. For detailed account of the Moleyns see Stoke Poges.
[14] *Hund. R.* (Rec. Com.), i, 28.
[15] Chart. R. 9 Edw. III, m. 7, no. 31.
[16] *Cal. Chart. R.* 1327–41, pp. 342, 354, 399, 430, 457.
[17] Chan. Inq. p.m. 11 Hen. VI, no. 34.
[18] Recov. R. Trin. 26 Hen. VIII, m. 155.
[19] *Visit. of Oxon.* (Harl. Soc.), 131.
[20] P.C.C. 5 Coode.
[21] Ibid. Willis has gone astray here in the Curson pedigree.
[22] Feet of F. Bucks. Hil. and East. 17 Eliz.

[23] Chan. Inq. p.m. (Ser. 2), ccxi, 154.
[24] Ibid. cccxv, 169.
[25] Pat. 9 Jas. I, pt. xii; *Cal. S. P. Dom.* 1611–18, p. 84; Memo. R. East. 10 Jas. I, m. 113.
[26] Feet of F. Bucks. Mich. 4 Chas. I.
[27] Ibid. Trin. 15 Chas. I.
[28] Willis, loc. cit.; Lipscomb, *Hist. and Antiq. of Bucks.* ii, 511, quoting monument in church.
[29] Le Neve, *Pedigrees of the Knights* (Harl. Soc.), 144; Marcham, *Cat. of Bucks. Deeds,* no. 3.
[30] P.C.C. 33 Dyer; M. I. in church.
[31] Recov. R. Hil. 13 Will. III, m. 14.
[32] P.C.C. 168 Romney.
[33] G.E.C. *Baronetage,* iv, 62.
[34] Recov. R. Trin. 7 & 8 Geo. II, m. 39.
[35] G.E.C. loc. cit.
[36] *Musgrave's Obit.* (Harl. Soc.), vi, 142.

[37] Feet of F. Bucks. Mich. 26 Geo. III.
[38] Ibid. Mich. 27 Geo. III.
[39] G.E.C. loc. cit.
[40] Lysons gives the date of the sisters' deaths as 1800 and 1801 (*Mag. Brit.* i [3], 495), but see charities, p. 140.
[41] Lysons, loc. cit.
[42] Feet of F. Bucks. Trin. 41 Geo. III.
[43] Recov. R. Mich. 50 Geo III, m. 42.
[44] Ibid. Trin. 11 Geo. IV, m. 317.
[45] G.E.C. *Complete Peerage* (ed. 2), ii, 57.
[46] Ibid.
[47] *V.C.H. Bucks.* i, 263.
[48] *Testa de Nevill* (Rec. Com.), 244, 252; *Hund. R.* (Rec. Com.), i, 28; Chan. Inq. p.m. 25 Edw. I, no. 50b; 2 Edw III (1st nos.), no. 35; Exch. Inq. p.m. (Ser. 2), file 22, no. 6.
[49] Feet of F. 9 Ric. I (Pipe R. Soc.), 130.

In the middle of the 13th century Peter Carbonel was said to hold 4 hides in this parish.[50] The Fitz Johns at this time represented the honour of Quarrendon in Addington,[51] and in 1265, after Evesham, 16 virgates in Addington, which Sir John Fitz John held as guardian of John Carbonel, were seized by the Earl of Gloucester, Sir John Fitz John being a rebel.[52] The land was almost immediately recovered by John Carbonel,[53] who held half a knight's fee here in 1284–6.[54] Robert le Wolf, possibly acting as guardian for a Carbonel during his minority, is returned for one-fourth of a fee in 1302–3.[55] The next owner was Peter Carbonel, who died seised in 1328, when an inquisition states that he held the site of a certain 'manor' and 75 acres of land, 10 acres of meadow and rents in Addington by suit at Quarrendon.[56] He also held 3 virgates in the same place by service of a sore sparrow-hawk, or of 3s. yearly, to the Earl Marshal.[57] He was also seised of Burston Manor in Aston Abbots, with which Carbonels descended,[58] like it dividing into moieties on the death of John Kentwood in 1487. All trace of the Swafield half is lost, but the Fettiplace purparty passed with their part of Burston to William Fettiplace,[59] who in 1526 alienated 'half of the manor of Carbonel' (here so-called for the first time) to Walter Curzon.[60] He died in 1527, and his son Richard Curzon[61] seven years later acquired Addington Manor in which this manor is henceforward absorbed. It appears under its own name in a document of 1575,[62] and in 1628 the whole estate is called Addington alias Carbonels Manor,[63] but no later mention has been found.

CARBONEL. *Gules a cross argent with a border engrailed or.*

According to Willis the ancient manor-house is said to have been built by the family of Windsor, whom he mentions as tenants under the Earls of Huntingdon.[64] In support of this statement may be quoted an entry in the baptismal registers of Edward son of Walter and Margaret Windsor, who was baptized here in 1559.[65] This carries their tenancy on to the time of the Curzons, and certainly Anne Windsor,

widow, held the manor for life, while it was in the possession of Francis Curzon, the third of his family to hold.[66]

The church of the *ASSUMPTION CHURCH OF THE BLESSED VIRGIN* consists of a chancel 22 ft. by 14 ft., with vestry, a nave 33 ft. by 16 ft., with north and south aisles and south porch, and a western tower 12 ft. by 9 ft., with a vice at its south-western angle. All the measurements are internal.

A 12th-century capital and shaft now preserved in the vestry suggests that there was a church here at that date probably consisting of a chancel and nave only. In the 14th century the aisles were thrown out and the tower built. About 1490 the tower was restored. In 1858 the chancel and aisles with the porch were rebuilt and the vestry added. The walls are of rubble, and the nave roof is of lead, while that of the chancel is tiled.

The modern chancel is lighted by pointed windows

ADDINGTON CHURCH FROM THE SOUTH

with traceried heads, designed in the style of the 14th century. The pointed chancel arch is of the 14th century, having two orders springing from semi-octagonal responds with moulded capitals and bases.

The nave has on either side a 14th-century arcade of three pointed arches; each arch is of a single order springing from octagonal piers without capitals. The circular clearstory windows have modern tracery, but the openings may be of original 14th-century date. The aisles have modern windows in the 14th-century style. Both these windows and those of the chancel contain Flemish glass of the 16th and early

[50] *Hund. R.* (Rec. Com.), i, 28; *Testa de Nevill* (Rec. Com.), 252.

[51] *Hund. R.* (Rec. Com.), ii, 353; Chan. Inq. p.m. 25 Edw. I, no. 50*b* and *c*.

[52] Chan. Misc. Inq. file 25, no. 25.

[53] Ibid.

[54] *Feud. Aids*, i, 81.

[55] Ibid. 100.

[56] Chan. Inq. p.m. 2 Edw. III (1st nos.), no. 35.

[57] Ibid. This service, which the Earl Marshal had by grant of the king, may be part of the serjeanty by which Addington Manor was held.

[58] *Feud. Aids*, i, 125.

[59] Leadam, *Dom. Incl.* 1517 (Royal Hist. Soc.), 200–1.

[60] Feet of F. Bucks. Mich. 18 Hen. VIII.

[61] Exch. Inq. p.m. (Ser. 2), file 22, no. 6.

[62] Feet of F. Bucks. Hil. and East. 17 Eliz.

[63] Ibid. Mich. 4 Chas. I.

[64] Willis, op. cit. 114.

[65] Ibid. 121.

[66] Ct. of Req. bdle. 94, no. 11.

17th centuries, illustrating various subjects from the Bible.

The tower, which is overlapped by the aisles, is of three stages, and is crowned by an embattled parapet. The ground stage opens into the church by pointed arches of the original date of the tower on the east, north and south. The west window, a 15th-century insertion, is of two cinquefoiled lights under a four-centred head. Beneath it is a moulded doorway of similar date. The bell-chamber is lighted by two-light windows.

The furniture is all modern. In the south aisle are monuments to Elizabeth Busby (d. 1651) and to Sir John Busby (d. 1700), the latter with a portrait-bust. There are many other later tablets to the Busby family. In the vestry are preserved a fragment of a mediaeval altar slab and the 12th-century capital and shaft above-mentioned, which are now used as a pillar piscina. The communion table has a miniature altar slab of slate inserted in it ; this was discovered during the rebuilding of 1858, walled up in the church. At the same time six books were found bearing dates of publication between 1519 and 1571, and initialled with the name of Thomas Andrewes, who was rector from 1559 to 1587 ; also eighty-seven pieces of window glass and a piece of metal, possibly part of a sacring bell.

There is a ring of three bells : the treble, recast by Warner of London in 1870 ; the second by Anthony Chandler, dated 1656 ; the tenor by Robert Atton, with the date 1626. There is also a small bell uninscribed, which is perhaps the sanctus mentioned in the visitation of 1553.

The plate consists of a silver-gilt chalice with cover paten of 1858 ; also a credence paten of silver-gilt, and glass cruets with silver-gilt mounting of the same date, and a silver-gilt spoon of 1857.

The registers begin in 1558.

ADVOWSON The church of Addington was granted to the Prior of St. John of Jerusalem by the lord of the manor before 1220,[67] in which year Ralph and Robert Fitz Bernard renounced their claim in favour of the hospital, whose prior continued to present down to the Dissolution. The church paid a pension of 40s. yearly to the Hospitallers at their preceptory of Hogshaw in the same county.[68] In 1535 the rectory was worth £12.[69] The Crown did not for long retain the advowson, but granted it in 1543 to Richard Andrews and Nicholas Temple,[70] the former of whom in the following year alienated it to Richard Curzon,[71] lord of Addington Manor. Its descent henceforward follows that of the manor,[72] the present patron being Lord Addington.[73]

In 1726 a private Act was passed for exchanging tithes and glebe lands of the rectory of Addington for other lands in Addington, settling the latter on the rector and his successors.[74]

At the dissolution of the chantries half an acre in Addington, situated on St. Agnes' Hill,[75] was devoted to keeping a light within the parish church.[76]

CHARITIES Anne Tynte, by her will proved in the P.C.C. 12 April 1798, bequeathed £200, the interest to be applied in teaching poor children to read, and for apprenticing ; and Jane Busby, by her will proved in the P.C.C. 8 August 1800, bequeathed £200 for the poor. The two legacies, with accumulations, are now represented by £720 consols with the official trustees, producing £18 a year, which in 1909–10 were applied in the payment of £1 to a convalescent home, £7 in the distribution of money, and the balance for educational purposes.

Church Property.—The churchwardens received £1 yearly from an estate in the parish, which was carried to their account.

ADSTOCK

Edestocha (xi cent.) ; Adestoca, Adestocha (xii cent.) ; Adestok, Haddestok (xiii cent.).

Adstock covers 1,166 acres, of which 138 are arable, 898 permanent grass, and 15 woods and plantations.[1] The soil is clay. The parish is watered by Padbury Brook, which joins Claydon Brook, and forms the southern and eastern boundaries. The slope of the ground varies from over 370 ft. above the ordnance datum in the centre of the parish to 285 ft. in the south of the village. In the east of the parish are old gravel-pits, and at the time of the inclosure in 1798 allotment was made for them.[2]

The village of Adstock stands off the high road from Buckingham to Winslow in the south-west of the parish, the few houses of which it consists being grouped round the parish church of St. Cecilia. Several half-timber cottages of the 17th century, with roofs of tiles and thatch, still remain. A little distance to the north-east of the church is a half-timber house formed out of several tenements, and completely remodelled internally, which contains much re-used old woodwork. On the east side of the main road is an L-shaped 16th-century house with heavy timber framing. The present Adstock Manor in the south of the village was built in the middle of the last century. A Wesleyan chapel was erected here in 1889, a thatched barn having been previously used as a chapel since 1834.

The parish has always been purely agricultural, and is stated to be so in a 14th-century assessment for taxation, when Benet Berner claimed allowance on account of the failure of his bean and pea crops.[3] During the time of the Great Plague in the 17th century there is a tradition that, so greatly were Buckingham and Winslow infected, a market was held here for some time.[4]

Robert Sharrock (1630–84), 'accounted learned in divinity, in the civil and common law, and very

[67] R. of Hugh of Wells (Cant. and York Soc.), ii, 58.
[68] Larking, Knights Hospitallers in Engl. (Camd. Soc.), 68.
[69] Valor Eccl. (Rec. Com.), iv, 239.
[70] L. and P. Hen. VIII, xviii (1), g. 981 (20).

[71] Ibid. xix (1), g. 812 (114).
[72] Inst. Bks. (P.R.O.).
[73] Clergy List (1914).
[74] Priv. Act, 13 Geo. I, cap. 27.
[75] Willis, op. cit. 121.
[76] Chant. Cert. 5, no. 2.

[1] Statistics from Bd. of Agric. (1905).
[2] Com. Pleas Recov. R. Trin. 39 Geo. III, m. 118.
[3] Inq. Nonarum (Rec. Com.), 330.
[4] Willis, Hist. and Antiq. of Buckingham, 125.

knowing in vegetables,' was the son of the rector of Adstock.[5] Luke Heslop, who wrote on inclosures and their effect at the end of the 18th century, was rector from 1778 to 1803.[6] Charles Neate (1806–79), political economist, was born here.[7]

Adstock was inclosed in 1798, and the Award, with map, is preserved at the Public Record Office.[8] From it the following place-names have been abstracted: Mile Bridge *alias* Addington Planks, Darrell's Gate, Harrups Towns End, Fishers ford, Beggar Lane Close, Bootem Close, Haskell field, Pilch Common.

Previous to the Survey *ADSTOCK MANORS MANOR* was held by Gethe,[9] whose husband Ralph, apparently Earl of Hereford under Edward the Confessor, was degraded from his earldom by William I.[10] The manor belonged to William Peverel in 1086,[11] and was held in chief as of the honour of Peverel until 1518,[12] after which date no reference has been found to the honour in this manor. Adstock appears to have been the chief manor of the honour in this county, for in 1289 Alice de Luton owed suit for her two manors, to be paid 'at the king's court of the honour of Peverel at Haddestok.'[13]

Ambrose was the tenant of Adstock Manor at Domesday,[14] but after 1086 it was held by the lords in demesne. William Peverel was succeeded by a son or grandson of the same name, who took Stephen's side in the Civil War. In 1153 (that is, before ascending the throne) Henry of Anjou granted Peverel's lands to Ranulph Earl of Chester, who died the same year from poison administered, it is said, by Peverel.[15] After his accession to the throne Henry again confiscated the lands of William Peverel, who is not heard of after 1155.[16] Adstock Manor was granted to William Avenel, as appears from a document of the time of Henry II preserved among the

Adstock thus became divided into two portions, the more important part, that which included the 'capital mansion' with two orchards, falling to Richard Vernon.[18] A few years later Richard and his wife Avis, together with William their son and heir, are found confirming to Azo son of Niel a virgate of land in Adstock, formerly belonging to Aluwi.[19] Richard Vernon was dead in 1195, when Simon Basset, Avis' brother-in-law, gave 100 marks to acquire Vernon's lands as the inheritance of his wife.[20] The Vernons, however, made good their claim, and in an undated charter of King John's reign William Vernon granted Adstock to his half-brother Robert,[21] though he, William, was acknowledged to hold half a knight's fee here in 1229.[22] At this date William Vernon also held Pitchcott (q.v.), with which Adstock descended[23] to George Vernon, who died in 1566 leaving daughters and co-heirs, Margaret wife of John Stanley and Dorothea wife of John Manners.[24] Two years later Henry Vernon brought a suit against Henry Vernon for the detention of the will of the Henry Vernon who had died in 1515.[25] These two Henrys must have represented a younger branch of the family, the defendant being possibly, as plaintiff states, heir male.[26] Adstock Manor went to Margaret Stanley, and during the next twenty years various settlements are found in her or her husband's name. In 1568 they made a settlement on Edward Armstrong and others,[27] in which settlement John Manners and Dorothea his wife joined them.[28] In 1577 Margaret, who was by this time a widow, appears to have received a quitclaim from Henry Vernon, probably the defendant of the case quoted above.[29] She shortly after married William Mather,[30] and in 1579, together with him, settled the manor on Edward Stanley, her son by her first husband.[31] Margaret Stanley died in 1596,[32] and in accordance with the settlement

AVENEL. *Argent a fesse between six rings gules.*

VERNON. *Argent fretty sable.*

STANLEY. *Argent a bend azure with three harts' heads caboshed or thereon.*

FORTESCUE. *Argent a bend engrailed argent cotised or.*

Duke of Rutland's manuscripts, by which William Avenel granted Addington to Richard Vernon and Simon Basset, who had married his daughters.[17]

Adstock passed to Sir Edward Stanley, kt., of Tong Castle in Shropshire,[33] and the same year he with

[5] *Dict. Nat. Biog.*
[6] Ibid.
[7] Ibid.
[8] Com. Pleas Recov. R. Trin. 39 Geo. III, m. 118.
[9] *V.C.H. Bucks.* i, 253.
[10] G.E.C. *Complete Peerage*, iv, 210.
[11] *V.C.H. Bucks.* loc. cit.
[12] *Red Bk. of Exch.* (Rolls Ser.), 122; *Testa de Nevill* (Rec. Com.), 244; Close, 13 Hen. III, m. 6; *Hund. R.* (Rec. Com.), i, 28; ii, 353; *Feud. Aids*, i, 81, 125; *Cal. Close*, 1288–96, p. 28; Chan. Inq. p.m. (Ser. 2), xxx, 73; xiii, 1.
[13] *Cal. Close*, loc. cit.
[14] *V.C.H. Bucks.* loc. cit.

[15] *Dict. Nat. Biog.*
[16] Ibid.
[17] *MSS. of the Duke of Rutland* (Hist. MSS. Com.), iv, 23.
[18] Ibid.
[19] Ibid. 24.
[20] Pipe R. Bucks. 6 Ric. I, m. 14.
[21] *MSS. of the Duke of Rutland* (Hist. MSS. Com.), iv, 25; Wrottesley, *Ped. from Plea R.* 534.
[22] Close, 13 Hen. III, m. 6.
[23] *Feud. Aids*, i, 81, 100, 109, 125; Star Chamb. Proc. Hen. VIII, ii, fol. 273. No reference to this manor in Adstock has been found between 1346 and 1451.
[24] Chan. Inq. p.m. (Ser. 2), cxliv, 170.

[25] Chan. Proc. (Ser. 2), bdle. 184, no. 86. [26] Ibid.
[27] Feet of F. Div. Co. East. 10 Eliz.
[28] Memo. R. (Exch. L.T.R.), Hil. 11 Eliz. m. 44.
[29] Feet of F. Div. Co. East. 19 Eliz.; Recov. R. East. 19 Eliz. m. 519.
[30] P.C.C. 92 Drake.
[31] Feet of F. Bucks. Mich. 21 Eliz.; Chan. Inq. p.m. (Ser. 2), cclix, 36.
[32] P.C.C. 92 Drake; Chan. Inq. p.m. (Ser. 2), cclix, 36.
[33] Adstock is not mentioned in her will, and William Mather appears to have given up claim to it as early as 1591 (Pat. 33 Eliz. pt. i).

Lucy his wife made a settlement of the manor on Sir Francis Fortescue of Salden and Grace (Manners) his wife,[34] whose son John had married Frances daughter and co-heir of Sir Edward Stanley.[35] Francis and Grace Fortescue settled the manor in 1614,[36] and he died seised in 1624, his son John surviving him.[37] Previous to his death, according to Willis, he sold his demesne to six of the principal tenants of Adstock in fee, reserving to himself the titular manor.[38] Shortly after his father's death John Fortescue sold it to Thomas Egerton, then rector of Adstock, whose grandson conveyed it c. 1675 to Sir Ralph Verney.[39] Ralph Verney, Viscount Fermanagh, grandson of the above Ralph, held at the time Willis was writing.[40] Nothing further has been found about this manor, which, as above shown, was titular only, save Lysons's suggestion that it had amalgamated with the second manor in Adstock.[41]

That portion of the Adstock estate which passed to Elizabeth daughter of William Avenel on her marriage with Simon Basset [42] is sometimes known as *HAUSTED* or *ADSTOCK MANOR*. Like Adstock, it continued to be attached to the honour of Peverel, last mention of which in this manor is found in 1626.[43]

Simon Basset died in or about the year 1205, when his widow Elizabeth paid a fine to the Crown.[44] In 1238 Robert Basset acknowledged the right of William Basset to one-fourth of a knight's fee and the rent of 3*d.* and 1 lb. of cummin in Adstock, which William had received from 'Elizabeth Avenel,' grandmother of Robert Basset.[45] About the same date William Basset is described in the *Testa* as holding half a fee of Robert here.[46] In 1245 a settlement on William Basset of one-fourth of the 'manor' is found, with reversion to Elizabeth daughter and heir of Reynold Basset.[47] In 1249 William Basset died holding half a knight's fee in Adstock, a court with a close, a messuage, 1 carucate of land, 5½ acres of meadow, rents of freemen, customary rents and works and aids, worth in all £7 7*s.* 8½*d.* here.[48] It would therefore appear that the whole property had come into his ownership. His heir was his nephew Robert, son of John Basset,[49] who in 1252 obtained a grant of free

BASSET. *Barry wavy argent and azure.*

warren in his demesne lands of Adstock,[50] but in 1280 the manor appears as the property of Robert Bardolf and Lora his wife, who then made a settlement by fine with their overlord, by which the third of Adstock, then held in dower by Regina wife of John la Chambre, was to revert to the Bardolfs, instead of to Roger Bozun.[51] Four years later Robert Bardolf was assessed for half a fee in Adstock, and mention is there found of an extraordinary number of intermediary lords, for he is said to hold of Roger Bozun, who held of Richard son of John, who held of Agnes Gryke, who held of Peter Basset, who held of Robert father of Peter, who held of the king in chief as of the honour of Peverel.[52] In 1305 Robert Bardolf died seised of Adstock Manor, his heir being Avis, then aged thirty years.[53] From her it passed to John de Hausted, who held in 1316.[54] He was made Seneschal of Gascony in 1327, and from 1332 until his death was summoned to Parliament as a baron.[55] In 1335 he made a settlement of Adstock on his son John de Hausted and his heirs, with reversion to himself.[56] John de Hausted, jun., appears to have predeceased his father, on whose death in 1336 the heir to Adstock was declared to be his son William de Hausted, then aged thirty.[57] In 1337 Fina, widow of John de Hausted, received a messuage, 120 acres of land, 4 of meadow, a plot of pasture, £8 11*s.* 2½*d.* rent and a windmill in Adstock as dower.[58] William de Hausted died without issue before 1346, and his lands passed to his sister Elizabeth.[59] Joan de Den, who may possibly be her daughter, held this fee in 1346.[60] In 1393 John Cope and Elizabeth his wife held Adstock Manor (here called Hausted for the first time),[61] and it seems likely that it had passed to the Cope family by marriage, for Adstock certainly follows the same descent as Denshanger (Northants), which John Cope held by the courtesy of England in 1397.[62] At this latter date he bought all rights in the reversion of Denshanger,[63] a third of which came to him on the death of Amy widow of William Hausted in 1400,[64] and, though no record has been found, a similar transaction appears to have taken place with regard to Adstock, which is now found in the Cope family for several generations. John Cope died in 1417 and was succeeded by his son John Cope,[65] whose widow Joan Cope held the manor till her death in 1434.[66] Stephen Cope, her son, next became lord of the manor, which on his death in 1445 passed to his son John Cope,[67] mentioned in connexion with Adstock in 1489.[68]

---

[34] Feet of F. Bucks. Hil. 39 Eliz.; Recov. R. Trin. 39 Eliz. m. 42.

[35] *Visit. of Bucks.* (Harl. Soc.), 58. Grace Fortescue was the daughter of John Manners of Nether Haddon, Derby, and therefore perhaps cousin to Edward Stanley.

[36] Feet of F. Bucks. East. 12 Jas. I.

[37] Chan. Inq. p.m. (Ser. 2), ccccvii, 105.   [38] Willis, op. cit. 123.

[39] Ibid. loc. cit. There is certainly a fine of 1674 which bears out this statement, Daniel Reading and others acknowledging the right of Sir Ralph Verney to view of frankpledge in Adstock (Feet of F. Bucks. Trin. 26 Chas. II).

[40] Willis, loc. cit.

[41] Lysons, *Mag. Brit.* i (3), 495.

[42] *MSS. of the Duke of Rutland* (Hist. MSS. Com.), iv, 23.

[43] *Testa de Nevill* (Rec. Com.), 244; Chan. Inq. p.m. 33 Hen. III, no. 17; 33 Edw. I, no. 21; 13 Hen. VI, no. 19; (Ser. 2), dccxl, 118; *Feud. Aids,* i, 81, 125.

[44] *Rot. de Oblatis et Fin.* (Rec. Com.), 307.

[45] Feet of F. Bucks. case 15, file 23.

[46] *Testa de Nevill* (Rec. Com.), 244.

[47] Feet of F. Bucks. case 15, file 27.

[48] Chan. Inq. p.m. Hen. III, file 7, no. 17.   [49] Ibid.

[50] *Cal. Chart. R.* 1226–57, p. 385. He also made a settlement of the manor in this year (Feet of F. Div. Co. 36 Hen. III, no. 59).

[51] Feet of F. Div. Co. 8 & 9 Edw. I, no. 33.   [52] *Feud. Aids,* i, 81.

[53] Chan. Inq. p.m. 33 Edw. I, no. 21; other references to Robert Bardolf's

tenure are Feet of F. Bucks. Hil. 26 Edw. I, no. 1; *Feud. Aids,* i, 108.

[54] *Feud. Aids,* i, 109.

[55] G.E.C. *Complete Peerage,* iv, 193.

[56] *Cal. Close,* 1333–7, p. 325.

[57] Chan. Inq. p.m. 10 Edw. III (1st nos.), no. 48.

[58] *Cal. Close,* 1333–7, p. 642.

[59] G.E.C. loc. cit.

[60] *Feud. Aids,* i, 125.

[61] Feet of F. Bucks. case 21, file 108; 16 Ric. II, no. 4.

[62] *Cal. Pat.* 1396–9, p. 210.

[63] Ibid.

[64] Chan. Inq. p.m. 2 Hen. IV, no. 23.

[65] Ibid. 2 Hen. V, no. 20.

[66] Ibid. 13 Hen. VI, no. 19.

[67] Ibid. 24 Hen. VI, no. 8.

[68] De Banco R. Mich. 5 Hen. VII, m. 152.

Adstock Manor is next heard of in 1511, when it was settled by Benedict Lee and Isabel his wife on John Clark and other trustees.[69] Isabel was possibly an heir of the Copes, and certainly seems to have had some special connexion with Adstock, for Benedict Lee, who survived his wife and married again, directs in his will, dated 21 February and proved 17 April 1545, that a yearly obit shall be made in Adstock Church for the soul of his wife Isabel.[70] In 1568 Robert son of Benedict Lee made a settlement of the manor on Valentine and George Pigott.[71] Three years later further settlements took place, which resulted in the final alienation, through Anthony Jackson, of the manor to Thomas Smythe.[72] Christopher Smythe, whose relationship to Thomas has not been traced, held Adstock in 1576.[73] He settled it on Thomas Smythe in 1583,[74] and he with his wife Ellen alienated it to Robert Tomlyns in 1586.[75] Robert Tomlyns held the manor at his death in 1622, when it passed to William Tomlyns, his son and heir.[76] Other members of this family subsequently held Adstock. Richard Tomlyns held a court baron for the manor here in 1647,[77] and in 1676 Jonathan and Samuel Tomlyns finally sold it to William Greaves.[78] His daughter married a member of a family called Whitehale,[79] and the manor continued to remain with the Whitehales, of whom Charles Whitehale and Hester his wife combined with Matthew Shelswell and others in a settlement of Adstock in 1707.[80] This family were still holding in 1735,[81] but by the end of the century had been displaced by the Turneys, of whom John Clark-Turney held in Lysons' day.[82] In 1798 John Clark-Turney and Elizabeth Goodman, widow, are returned as joint lords of the manor.[83] In the middle of the 19th century James Hawley was lord of the manor,[84] which at the present day belongs to Mr. Charles Matthew Prior.

The church of ST. CECILIA THE CHURCH VIRGIN consists of a chancel measuring internally 25 ft. 6 in. by 15 ft., nave 38 ft. 6 in. by 21 ft. 6 in., south porch 6 ft. 6 in. square, and a west tower 10 ft. by 9 ft.

The nave walls, up to the sills of the windows, belong to a 12th-century church, the chancel of which was rebuilt about 1330, when the north porch was added. The upper part of the nave walls was taken down and erected anew late in the 15th century, the date of the addition of the tower. The building was restored throughout in 1875. The walls of the body of the church are of rubble, but the tower is faced with ashlar.

The chancel is lighted from the east by a window of three trefoiled lights with tracery in a pointed head, and from each side wall by two pointed two-light windows of the same type. The westernmost window on each side is transomed to form a low-side window, the lower portion retaining the staple of the shutters with which it was fitted. All these windows are of 14th-century date, though much restored. Between

the two north windows is a contemporary doorway with a pointed head, now blocked, and in the south wall is an original piscina niche with a trefoiled head. The chancel arch is pointed and of three chamfered orders recessed only on the nave side, the innermost order springing from modern corbels. The chancel roof retains a truss bearing the date 1597.

The four windows lighting the nave, two in each side wall, are each of three transomed cinquefoiled lights with a pointed and tracered head, and are contemporary with the late 15th-century rebuilding. Between them are the north and south doorways, both of which, though partly reset, are substantially of the 12th century. The former is now blocked; it has a round-arched external order, the head enriched with foliated ornament in beaded semicircles, and inclosed by a label with 15th-century head-stops. The jambs are chamfered and the imposts are ornamented with the indented moulding. The head of the doorway itself has been brought to an ogee form by cutting out part of the tympanum which originally filled the head of the external order. The south doorway has 12th-century shafted jambs with curiously sculptured abaci and capitals to the jamb shafts, but the pointed head is of the 15th century. The jambs of both doorways have several incised crosses. The roof of the nave, which is dated 1599, is an interesting example of late 16th-century work. The trusses have pierced pendants and tracery in the spandrels of the wall brackets.

The outer doorway of the south porch has a pointed head of two orders moulded continuously with the jambs ; the window in the east wall is modern.

The tower is crowned by an embattled parapet and is of two stages with a vice at the south-west and diagonal buttresses at the western angles. The west window of the ground stage is of two cinquefoiled lights with a pointed and tracered head, and the tower arch is of three pointed orders. The bell-chamber is lighted by louvred two-light windows, that in the south wall being apparently a re-used window of c. 1400. The other windows have square heads and are of the same date as the tower.

The font is of the 15th century and is octagonal with panelled sides to the bowl. The altar table is of about 1600. Three tracered heads worked into the panels of the pulpit appear to be remains of screenwork. The plain south door bears the date '17xx2' (1722) scratched upon it, though the workmanship looks earlier. Inserted in the gable over the outer entrance of the porch is a sundial with the date 1581 and the initials T.E.

There is a mural monument dated 1720 to the third of three Thomas Egertons, who were rectors of the parish, and another to Alexander Burrell, rector, who died in 1771.

There are two bells and a sanctus. The first, inscribed in Gothic small with crowned capital initials, 'Sancta Anna Ora Pro Nobis,' is by John Sturdy,[85] the second is inscribed 'Richard Chandler made me

[69] Feet of F. Div. Co. Mich. 3 Hen. VIII.

[70] P.C.C. Alen, F 42.

[71] Ibid. ; Feet of F. Div. Co. East. 10 Eliz.

[72] Feet of F. Bucks. East 13 Eliz. ; Hil. 14 Eliz.

[73] Ibid. Trin. 18 Eliz. ; Recov. R. East. 18 Eliz. m. 818.

[74] Feet of F. Bucks. Hil. 25 Eliz.

[75] Ibid. Mich. 28 Eliz.

[76] Chan. Inq. p.m. (Ser. 2), dccxl, 118.

[77] Willis, loc. cit.

[78] Feet of F. Bucks. Mich. 28 Chas. II.

[79] Willis, loc. cit.

[80] Feet of F. Bucks. Hil. 5 Anne.

[81] Willis, loc. cit.

[82] Lysons, loc. cit.

[83] Com. Pleas Recov. R. Trin. 39 Geo. III, m. 118.

[84] Sheahan, Hist. and Topog. of Bucks. 255.

[85] A. H. Cocks, Church Bells of Bucks. 296.

1676,' and the sanctus, probably by Mears, bears the date 1826.[86] On the frame is cut the date 1618 with the name IOHN IEFS.

The plate includes a cup and cover paten of 1569, a pewter paten and flagon, and a modern plated almsdish.

The registers begin in 1538.

ADVOWSON The church of Adstock, together with a carucate of land, formed part of the grant of William Avenel to the Abbot and convent of St. Mary de Pré, Leicester.[87] In 1221 Robert Vernon, clerk, under age, was presented by the convent and admitted by dispensation of the bishop, who ordered a perpetual vicarage of 5 marks to be instituted and a fixed pension reserved to the abbey.[88] If the vicar so appointed died within seven years, and while Robert was studying at the schools, he (Robert) was to appoint another, but if later Robert might take the whole church.[89] Six years later the abbot and convent presented Robert de Eddeshoure,[90] who was accordingly instituted, but subsequent presentations are to rectors. In 1282 the Bardolfs unsuccessfully tried to wrest the presentation from the abbot.[91] Adstock was taxed at £6 13s. 4d. in 1291.[92] In 1423 Thomas Thowe, rector of Adstock and of 'noble birth,' received a dispensation to hold another living in conjunction with this one, the value of the two not to exceed 30 marks.[93] This dispensation was renewed in 1427.[94] He was the last rector presented by the abbey, which seems to have come to some arrangement with the lords of the manor, by which the latter resumed

the right of presentation.[95] At the Dissolution the rectory was said to be worth £18 6s. 8d.[96] In 1609 Sir Francis Fortescue, lord of the manor, conveyed the advowson to Peter Fige for a turn.[97] The lord of the manor retained the right of presentation until about the year 1635, when Sir John Fortescue alienated the advowson to Robert Sharrock, rector of Drayton Parslow,[98] from whom a turn was purchased in 1671 by Thomas Egerton, then lord of the titular manor.[99] In 1707 Robert, grandson of the above Robert Sharrock, bequeathed the advowson to the Bishop of Lincoln and his successors,[100] by whom the right of presentation was exercised till the 19th century.[101] By the middle of the last century it had passed to the Hart family,[102] of whom Edward Hart owns the advowson at the present day.

At the inclosure of the parish the rector received 300 acres allotted in lieu of tithes.[103]

In 1456 licence was granted to one priest to serve the neighbouring churches of Adstock and Addington, the issues of which were said to be sufficient for only one chaplain, who was to say mass daily in each.[104]

CHARITIES The church lands, containing 4 a. 2 r. 4 p., were allotted to the churchwardens by the Inclosure Award of 13 August 1798 in lieu of several dispersed parcels of land in the open fields. The land is let at £7 a year, which is applied towards general church expenses.

The Emily Bayne's charity of 1911 yields annually from consols £7 13s. 4d., which is distributed in coals on St. Thomas's Day to the aged and deserving poor.

AKELEY

Achelei (xi cent.); Aqueleie, Akeleia (xii cent.); Acle (xiii cent.); Akle juxta Bukyngham, Ocle under Whittilwode (xiv cent.); Akeley-cum-Stockholt (xviii cent.).

This parish, lying on the road from Towcester to Buckingham, covers 1,325 acres, most of which is laid down as permanent grass, only 195 acres being arable land.[1] Both soil and subsoil are clay. The ground rises slightly from about 300 ft. above the ordnance datum in the north-east to about 400 ft. in the south.

The village lies 3 miles north of Buckingham station on the Verney Junction and Banbury branch of the London and North Western railway. The church of St. James stands on high ground with the rectory, a modern building, to the south. In 1639 the parsonage-house is described as a building of two bays.[2]

There are several 17th-century cottages and houses in the village, some timber-framed and some of stone, with thatched or tiled roofs. About a quarter of a mile east of the rectory is the manor-house. It is a

17th-century house, originally built of stone, but it has now been refronted in brick. Some of the original mullioned windows remain.

There is a Wesleyan chapel, built in 1828, at Duck End, close to the church of St. James, and a little south of the church is the school, built in 1854, and subsequently enlarged for 100 children.

North of the village is Akeley pottery, and the industry is evidently an ancient one, since Pottery Hooke is one of the closes mentioned in the early 18th century.[3] To the south-east of the pottery are brickworks.

About half a mile north-west of the village lies Stockholt Farm, all that remains of the once important manor and district of Stockholt (Stotholt, Stockholt, xiii cent.; Stockholt next Ocle, Stokholtbernes, xiv cent.; Stokholt Barnes, xvi cent.; Stockholte Barnes *alias* Stockholt *alias* Stockwell, xvii cent.). The name does not occur before the early 13th century (see below), but by the 18th century the parish was known as Akeley-cum-Stockholt,[4] and a chapel of ease

[86] A. H. Cocks, *Church Bells of Bucks.* 296.
[87] *Cal. Chart. R.* 1300–26, p. 380, which recites the charter.
[88] *R. of Hugh of Wells* (Cant. and York Soc.), ii, 52.
[89] Ibid.   [90] Ibid. 70.
[91] De Banco R. 47, m. 58.
[92] *Pope Nich. Tax.* (Rec. Com.), 41.
[93] *Cal. Papal Letters*, vii, 273.
[94] Ibid. viii, 17.

[95] Lipscomb, *Hist. and Antiq. of Bucks.* ii, 515; Willis, op. cit. 124.
[96] *Valor Eccl.* (Rec. Com.), iv, 239.
[97] Feet of F. Bucks. East. 7 Jas. I; Memo. R. Mich. 11 Jas. I, m. 292.
[98] Willis, op. cit. 124.
[99] Inst. Bks. (P.R.O.); Lipscomb, op. cit. 516.
[100] Willis, loc. cit.
[101] Inst. Bks. (P.R.O.); Bacon, *Liber Regis.*; Lysons, loc. cit.

[102] Sheahan, loc. cit.
[103] Com. Pleas Recov. R. Trin. 39 Geo. III, m. 118.
[104] Linc. Epis. Reg. Memo. Chedworth, m. 22.
[1] Statistics from Bd. of Agric. (1905).
[2] Lipscomb, *Hist. and Antiq. of Bucks.* ii, 521.
[3] Exch. Dep. Mich. 9 Anne, no. 9.
[4] Ibid.; Inst. Bks. (P.R.O.).

ADSTOCK CHURCH FROM THE SOUTH-EAST

ADSTOCK CHURCH: THE INTERIOR LOOKING EAST

BARTON HARTSHORN CHURCH FROM THE NORTH-WEST

to the parish church apparently existed at Stockholt at that date.[5] As its name would imply, it was that wooded part of Akeley which extended into Whittlewood Forest,[6] and was probably included in the woodland for 806 swine which appertained to Akeley Manor in 1086.[7] In 1279 the Prior of Newton Longville brought an action for trespass against William de Brewes for taking wood from Stockholt Wood in Whittlewood Forest,[8] at that time assessed at 21 acres.[9] The inclosure of this wood began with the grant to Ralf Briton (see below), who in 1228 had licence to inclose 4 acres with ditch and fence, and to cultivate the same[10]; and in 1412 Thomas Linford, lord of Stockholt Manor, was permitted to add to Stockholt Park by inclosing an adjoining field called Homfeld *alias* Mansherdfeld and Coppedmorfeld, containing 200 acres, and a wood of 100 acres with a fence adjoining the same, and a park called Kingsshrobfeld.[11] Further extensive inclosures were made about 1660, and among the names of closes mentioned in a dispute as to tithes in 1710 are Swannells Grounds, Waking Slade, Parson's Hooke, Bam and Cockley Leas, Kill and Netherway Closes, and Chadwells.[12] The Inclosure Act for the parish was passed in 1794, the Award being dated 1796.[13] An allotment of land was then made for the poor in lieu of furze, and compensation was made for tithes, the *modus* or composition for the Marquess of Salisbury's property of Stockholt Farm remaining, however, as before.[14] There is very little wood now left in the parish, only 75 acres being covered by woods and plantations.[15] Akeley Wood, referred to as an inclosure in the suit of 1710,[16] covers about 200 acres of well-timbered grass land in the west of the parish, with Akeley Wood Farm at the north-western end, and at the southern Akeley Wood House.

MANORS Before the Conquest Alric son of Goding held 3 hides at *AKELEY*, which he could sell.[17] By 1086 this estate was held by Robert of Walter Giffard,[18] who bestowed it, together with Newton Longville (q.v.), on the priory of St. Faith at Longueville in Normandy.[19] Like Newton Longville it was part of that division of the honour of Giffard or Gloucester which went to the earls of Gloucester and Stafford,[20] and though the prior of Newton Longville was said in the 13th century to hold in free alms,[21] in the 14th century the service of a half fee was demanded from Akeley, the prior paying 20s. at the assessment of 1346.[22] The manor can never have been of much importance, the prior's possessions here being rated at only £4 2s. 4d. in 1291,[23] and it was deemed to be part of Newton Longville Manor, with which it was granted in 1441 to the Warden and Fellows of New College, Oxford,[24] who have remained in possession ever since.

In the 17th century Robert Smyth, whose father

Sir William had been a Fellow of New College, 1558–71,[25] obtained a lease for a thousand years of the manor.[26] He was slain in 1645 fighting for the king,[27] and his widow Martha compounded in 1647 for the estate, which was sequestered for her husband's delinquency in leaving his habitation and residing in Oxford, and because her son William Smyth, M.P., joint purchaser with his father, had adhered to the king.[28] She obtained leave to compound on the ground that her son had no right to the estate except as trustee, and that her husband had

NEW COLLEGE, OXFORD. *Argent two cheverons sable between three roses gules.*

directed in his will, of which he had appointed her executrix, that the lease should be sold by her.[29] The estate, however, ultimately passed to her son William, a captain in the king's army, who compounded in 1647 for his delinquency,[30] and was made a baronet as of Radclive in 1661,[31] when he was member of Parliament for Buckingham.[32] At his death in 1696 he was succeeded by his son Sir Thomas Smyth, bart.,[33] who held in 1711,[34] and at whose death unmarried in 1732[35] the Akeley property, freehold and leasehold, passed to his cousin William Smyth (see Wavendon), according to the terms of the first baronet's will.[36] William Smyth, described as a baronet in his will, proved in 1741, left his lands in Akeley to William, Thomas and John King, sons of Margaret the daughter of the first baronet,[37] by whom they were

SMYTH of Radclive, baronet. *Sable a cheveron between six crosses formy fitchy argent with three fleurs de lis azure upon the cheveron.*

probably alienated, for there is no later record of this family in Akeley.

The estate known in the 13th century and subsequently as the manor of *STOCKHOLT*, and from the 14th century more usually called *STOCKHOLT BARNES*, appears to have been included in Akeley at the date of the Domesday Survey, and to have been granted by Walter Giffard as parcel of that manor to the priory of Longueville, whose prior made various grants in Stockholt early in the 13th century.[38] In 1235 Gilbert Marshal, Earl of Pembroke, the overlord, included Stockholt among other Buckinghamshire manors, the issues of which were granted by him to his sister, Eleanor Countess of

[5] Carlisle, *Topog. Dict.* (1808) ; Lewis, *Topog. Dict.* (1849).
[6] *V.C.H. Bucks.* ii, 131.
[7] Ibid. i, 250.
[8] *Abbrev. Plac.* (Rec. Com.), 197.
[9] *Hund. R.* (Rec. Com.), ii, 339.
[10] Cart. Antiq. PP 58.
[11] *Cal. Pat.* 1408–13, p. 425.
[12] Exch. Dep. Mich. 9 Anne, no. 9.
[13] *Blue Bk. Incl. Awards*, 10.
[14] Priv. Act, 34 Geo. III, cap. 176.
[15] Statistics from Bd. of Agric. (1905).
[16] Exch. Dep. Mich. 9 Anne, no. 9.
[17] *V.C.H. Bucks.* i, 250.

[18] Ibid.   [19] *Cal. Doc. of France*, 74–7.
[20] See Newton Longville.
[21] *Testa de Nevill* (Rec. Com.), 247 ; *Hund. R.* (Rec. Com.), i, 32 ; ii, 339 ; *Plac. de Quo Warr.* (Rec. Com.), 96.
[22] *Feud. Aids*, i, 100, 125.
[23] *Pope Nich. Tax.* (Rec. Com.), 47.
[24] *Cal. Pat.* 1436–41, pp. 516, 558.
[25] G.E.C. *Baronetage*, iii, 191.
[26] *Cal. Com. for Comp.* 1770.
[27] G.E.C. loc. cit.
[28] *Cal. Com. for Comp.* 1770.
[29] Ibid. ; Reg. Bucks. Archdeaconry 1646, fol. 32.

[30] *Cal. Com. for Comp.* 1770.
[31] G.E.C. loc. cit.
[32] *Ret. of Memb. of Parl.* i, 519.
[33] G.E.C. loc. cit. Sir William left instructions for his burial in the chapel of the chancel of Akeley Church under the great stone where his grandfather Sir William Smyth lay (P.C.C. 40 Pyne).
[34] Exch. Dep. Mich. 9 Anne, no. 9.
[35] G.E.C. loc. cit.
[36] P.C.C. 40 Pyne.
[37] P.C.C. 319 Spurway.
[38] Cart. Antiq. PP 58 ; *Cal. Close*, 1227–31, pp. 261, 268.

Pembroke, to hold until the payment of £400 which he owed to her was complete.[39] It was accounted parcel of the manor of Akeley, and was held of New College as late as 1627.[40]

The nucleus of the manor appears to have been 4 acres of wood in Stockholt granted to Ralf Briton in 1228 by the Prior of Longueville.[41] These he received licence to inclose, and in the following year acquired from the priory 12 acres of land in Stockholt 'in augmentum terre sue de Stocholt.'[42] In 1242 John de Ferentin had apparently acquired this property, a grant of Stockholt being made by him on 1 February to John de Gatesden,[43] between whom and Thomas de Aldham a fine was levied of the manor of Stockholt in the time of Henry III.[43a] John de Gatesden's daughter Margaret held the manor with her husband John de Cameys in 1279, when other property was granted for life by them to Thomas de Aldham's widow Isabel and her then husband Richard de Pevenes.[44] The manor had passed to Stephen de Trafford and Elizabeth his wife, apparently as the inheritance of Elizabeth, before 1332, in which year Edmund de Ayete surrendered to them all right which he had in the manor under a lease at 8 marks yearly which they had made to him.[45] In the same year Stephen and Elizabeth granted a messuage and land in Akeley to Thomas de Useflete, clerk, for life, to hold at a rent of 10 marks, with reversion to themselves and the heirs of Elizabeth,[46] and in 1345 Stephen son of Stephen de Trafford granted the manor for 100 marks to the same Thomas de Useflete,[47] who in 1347, being then Dean of St. Martin le Grand in London, conveyed the manor to John Giffard, canon of St. Peter's, York, and to John Holt, parson of Althorp Church, and the heirs of John Giffard.[48] In 1352 John Holt granted the manor, then first called Stockholt Barnes, to Adam le Lorymer of Leominster and Agnes his wife,[49] to whom in 1358 John son of Roger Giffard, kinsman and heir of the late canon, released all his right in the manor.[50] For more than a century the history of the manor is obscure. It was held in 1412 by Thomas Linford,[51] who had been succeeded in 1473 by Thomas Littleton, by whom it was granted in that year to Richard Fowler.[52] His son Sir Richard Fowler was lord in 1507,[53] but Akeley had passed before 1540 to George Baldry, who died seised of it on 14 February of that year,[54] when he was succeeded by Elizabeth, his year-old daughter and heir, who about 1555 married Robert, second Lord Rich.[55] Robert Lord Rich died in 1581,[56] and his widow, at her marriage with her second husband Robert Forthe, settled the manor in 1585 on herself and

her husband for life, with remainder successively in tail-male to her second son Edwin Rich, and to her grandsons Robert and Henry, sons of her eldest son Robert Lord Rich.[57] She died on 1 December 1591,[58] and six years later the manor was sold by Sir Edwin Rich and his wife Margaret to John Lambert, or Lambard,[59] of the Castle House in Buckingham. He held Barton or Lambards Manor in Buckingham (q.v.), with which Stockholt descended to his grand-daughter and eventual heir, Mary Lambert.[60] She made a settlement of the manor in 1641 on her marriage with her second husband Edward Bagot,[61] who succeeded his father as baronet in 1660.[62] In 1670 they settled the manor on their son and heir-apparent Walter,[63] who succeeded his father in the estate and title in 1673.[64] Three years later he conveyed Stockholt Barnes to Simon Bennett of Beachampton,[65] and from this date it descended with Beachampton[66] (q.v.), until sold c. 1800 by James Marquess of Salisbury to Robert Lord Carrington,[67] by whom it was conveyed to the Duke of Buckingham.[68] The Duke sold it c. 1850 to Mr. A. J. Robarts, whose grandson, Mr. Abraham Robarts, now owns it.

CHURCH The church of *ST. JAMES*, consisting of a chancel, nave, and a tower, with a spire, on the south side, was rebuilt in 1854 in stone in the style of the 14th century and restored in 1901. The churchyard was enlarged by gift of Mr. George Attwood in 1903.

The church has two bells, one modern, and the other by Richard Chandler, 1674.

The plate includes a cup and cover paten with date-mark 1569.

The registers begin in 1682, the early volumes having been burnt.[69]

ADVOWSON The church was granted with the manor by Walter Giffard to Longueville Priory,[70] the presentation being made by the Norman prior,[71] who had a pension of £1 13s. 4d. in the church,[72] by the Prior of Newton Longville, or by the king when the temporalities of the English cell were in his hands by reason of war with France,[73] until the grant of the manor to New College. The advowson was held by New College until 1873,[74] when it was transferred to Mr. C. Pilgrim, who held it until 1892.[75] In 1893 and 1894 it was held by Mr. E. A. Mounsey, and from 1895 to 1897 by the trustees of Mr. C. Pilgrim. From 1898 to 1911 it was vested in Mrs. Pilgrim, and is now in the Church Association Trust.[76]

The church was returned as worth £6 13s. 4d. yearly in 1535.[77]

[39] *Cal. Pat.* 1232–47, p. 125.
[40] Chan. Inq. p.m. (Ser. 2), ccccxxix, 118.
[41] Cart. Antiq. PP 58 ; *Cal. Chart. R.* 1226–57, p. 79. Ralf was permitted to assart, cultivate, and inclose, but not to sell to Jews or any religious house.
[42] *Cal. Close*, 1227–31, pp. 261, 268 ; Close, 14 Hen. III, pt. i, m. 22.
[43] *Cal. Chart. R.* 1226–57, p. 265.
[43a] Feet of F. Div. Co. Mich. 7 & 8 Edw. I, no. 19.
[44] Ibid.
[45] De Banco R. 288, m. 1.
[46] Feet of F. case 19, file 79, no. 4.
[47] Ibid. file 86, no. 11.
[48] Ibid. case 20, file 88, no. 10.
[49] Ibid. file 91, no. 10.

[50] *Cal. Close*, 1354–60, p. 537.
[51] *Cal. Pat.* 1408–13, p. 425.
[52] Feet of F. case 22, file 125, no. 1.
[53] De Banco R. Mich. 23 Hen. VII, m. 619. See Lambard's Manor, Buckingham.
[54] Chan. Inq. p.m. (Ser. 2), lxii, 71.
[55] G.E.C. *Peerage*, vi, 341.
[56] Ibid.
[57] Recov. R. East. 27 Eliz. m. 96 ; Feet of F. Div. Co. East. 27 Eliz. ; Chan. Inq. p.m. (Ser. 2), ccxxxii, 56.
[58] Chan. Inq. p.m. (Ser. 2), ccxxxii, 56.
[59] Feet of F. Bucks. Trin. 39 Eliz.
[60] Chan. Inq. p.m. (Ser. 2), ccccxxix, 119 ; Recov. R. Hil. 16 Chas. I, m. 15.
[61] Feet of F. Bucks. Mich. 17 Chas. I.
[62] G.E.C. *Baronetage*, ii, 23, 24.

[63] Feet of F. Bucks. East. 22 Chas. II.
[64] Ibid. Mich. 25 Chas. II ; G.E.C. loc. cit.
[65] Feet of F. Bucks. Hil. 28 & 29 Chas. II.
[66] Priv. Act, 34 Geo. III, cap. 176.
[67] Lysons, *Mag. Brit.* i (3), 499.
[68] Lipscomb, op. cit. ii, 518.
[69] Ibid. 521.
[70] *Cal. Doc. of France*, 75–6.
[71] *R. of Hugh of Wells* (Cant. and York Soc.), ii, 97.
[72] *Pope Nich. Tax.* (Rec. Com.), 32.
[73] *Cal. Pat.* 1396–9, p. 8.
[74] Inst. Bks. (P.R.O.) ; *Clergy Lists.*
[75] *Clergy Lists.*
[76] Ibid.
[77] *Valor Eccl.* (Rec. Com.), iv, 240.

In 1279 Robert, rector of the church, held 1 virgate of land, with which the church was endowed.[78]

CHARITIES   The poor's allotment, containing 12 a. 2 r. 9 p., was allotted for the benefit of the poor on the inclosure in 1794. The land is let in allotments, producing about £12 a year. The net income is distributed in money gifts to the poor.

Sir William Smyth, by his will proved in the P.C.C. 10 February 1696–7, bequeathed £100 for the benefit of the poor. The sum of £66 13s. 4d., part of the legacy, was invested in an annuity of £2 13s. 4d. payable out of the rectory of Oving, and the balance was placed out on a mortgage. The mortgage, with considerable arrears of interest, was paid off and invested in 1874 in £196 7s. 10d. consols with the official trustees, producing £4 18s. yearly. The income of the charity is by a scheme of 31 July 1874 made applicable in supplying clothes, bedding, fuel, &c., to the poor, in giving pecuniary aid, and in aiding provident associations. The distribution is usually made in coal.

BARTON HARTSHORN

Bertone (xi cent.) ; Barton Hertishorne (xv cent.) ; Beggers Barton, Little Barton (xvi cent.).

This parish covers 891 acres, of which 165 are arable and 694 permanent grass.[1] The soil is clay. The south of the parish is watered by two streams, and the land here is lowest—about 300 ft., rising in the north beyond the Great Central railway to nearly 400 ft. above the ordnance datum. The church of St. James, a few farms and other buildings stand near the centre of the parish, on its chief road, and a smaller road branching off to the south leads to the manor-house, which till the latter half of the 19th century was a farm, but is now occupied by Lieut.-Col. C. W. Trotter. It is built of stone, and the date 1635, which with two letters, perhaps T.L. for Thomas Lisle, is inscribed on a stone in the west gable, probably gives the date of the original building and the name of the builder. The house has, however, been much altered and modernized, though it still retains some of its mullioned windows, an original fireplace, staircase, and 17th-century panelling. In the grounds is a much-altered cottage which seems to have formed part of a 16th-century house, possibly an earlier manor-house. Some of the windows have their original mullions. The King's End Farm, near the church, is a 17th-century stone house, and belonging to it is a stone barn of the same date with a thatched roof.

In the middle of the 16th century the tenants accused the lord of the manor of wrongfully inclosing some 30 acres of ground near the church, called Porter's Lees, which should have been common for half the year and through which, at all times, there was a common highway to drive cattle and for carriage to and from the village or town of Barton Hartshorn, and a passage to and from the church. As a result of this wrongful inclosure, the tenants were forced to use ' a fowle and myrie lane ' next adjoining the said land, to their great ' dyscomodytie and anoyance.' The lord of the manor, whom the complainants variously stated to be ' a gentleman of a covetous and envyous mynde,' of an ' obstinate and presumptuous mynde ' and of ' a dyvellishe and myschevous mynde,' was also accused of having wounded one of the complainants in an affray which had occurred on the lees, but he stated that he had been at some distance off, standing near his house and, having a bow and arrows under his girdle merely to shoot at coneys near the house, he had shot an arrow in defence of his son when he saw him attacked.[2]

An Act for inclosing the lands of the parish was passed in 1812.[3]

MANORS   Wilaf, a thegn of Earl Lewin, held the manor of BARTON before the Conquest, but it passed before 1086 to the Bishop of Bayeux, of whom it was held at that date by Ernulf de Hesding.[4] After the forfeiture of Odo's possessions, this overlordship appears to have come into the possession of the Earls of Pembroke, being held by William de Valence in 1284–6,[5] and in the 14th century by his heirs, the Talbots, Earls of Shrewsbury.[6] Barton was held under these overlords by the family of Dyve of North Witham, Lincolnshire. John Dyve is mentioned in 1254–5,[7] and again in 1284–6, when he was found to pay for his holding here 12s. per annum to Rochester Castle for ward.[8] In 1328 Geoffrey Dyve as mesne lord was successfully sued by his under-tenant for quittance of services demanded of him by the Talbots.[9] Thomas Dyve held in 1365.[10] In 1585 a special inquiry was made as to the tenure of the manor, and it was then found that it was held in chief, there being no mesne lord between the queen and the lord of the manor.[11]

The early lords of Barton took their name from the place. It seems probable that the half hide in ' Burton ' held by the daughter and heir of Walter de Burton in 1185 for serjeanty of dispenser (dispensarie)[12] refers to land here. Ivo de Barton was certainly lord here before 1198, at which time, and later, his son John confirmed various grants made to Biddlesden Monastery by the father.[13] Henry son of Ivo de Barton succeeded his brother and held land here in the early years of the reign of Henry III.[14] John de Barton was lord in 1254–5,[15] and another Henry in 1284–6.[16] Roberga, widow of Henry, held in 1302–3,[17] but had been succeeded by Henry de Barton, probably her son, before 1316.[18] He was still holding in 1327–8,[19] but Thomas de Barton was lord in 1346.[20] In 1421 John de Barton,

[78] Hund. R. (Rec. Com.), ii, 339.
[1] Statistics from Bd. of Agric. (1905).
[2] Star Chamb. Proc. Phil. and Mary, bdle. 5, no. 8.
[3] Priv. Act, 52 Geo. III, cap. 51.
[4] V.C.H. Bucks. i, 238.
[5] Feud. Aids, i, 88.
[6] Ibid. 124 ; G.E.C. Peerage, vi, 208–9.
[7] Hund. R. (Rec. Com.), i, 30.

[8] Feud. Aids, i, 89.
[9] De Banco R. 274, m. 46 ; 275, m. 248 d., 257 d.
[10] Chan. Inq. p.m. (Ser. 2), ccvi, 38.
[11] Ibid.
[12] Stacey Grimaldi, Rot. de Dominabus, 19, 22.
[13] Harl. Chart. 84, D 14, D 20, H 33 ; Harl. MS. 4714, fol. 306-8.

[14] Harl. Chart. 84, H 13, 34 ; Harl. MS. 4714, fol. 307 ; Feet of F. Bucks. 9 Hen. III, no. 9.
[15] Hund. R. (Rec. Com.), i, 30.
[16] Feud. Aids, i, 88.
[17] Ibid. 99.
[18] Ibid. 108.
[19] De Banco R. 274, m. 46.
[20] Feud. Aids, i, 124.

jun., Margaret, sister of Henry de Barton, and others, probably trustees, granted *BARTON HARTSHORN MANOR*, first so called, to Henry de Barton and Alice his wife.[21] It was held in 1498 by John Porter and Joan his wife,[22] who was the heir of the Barton family.[23] John and Joan settled the manor in that year on Thomas Porter and Agnes his wife, with remainder, in default of issue, to George brother of Thomas, and Joan their sister.[24]

PORTER. *Gules three bells or.*

The manor continued in possession of this family. John Porter was lord about the middle of the 16th century, and had a son of the same name.[25] In 1577 Edward Porter died seised of the manor, leaving a son Richard,[26] who attained his majority in 1590.[27] At his death, which occurred in 1629, he was succeeded by his son Edward.[28] At about this date, according to Willis, the manor was sold to Thomas Lisle,[29] whose heir, Fermor Lisle, held it at his death in 1742, when he left it to trustees to the use of his sister and heir Elizabeth, wife of the Rev. Thomas Bowles, and her heirs.[30] Elizabeth's son, the Rev. William Thomas Bowles, died in 1786, leaving the manor to his wife Bridget for life with the remainder to all his sons as tenants in common.[31] Two of the sons, the Rev. William Lisle Bowles and Charles Bowles, were lords of the manor in 1812,[32] and the family still held about 1840.[33] By 1862 the manor was in possession of the Rev. J. Athawes,[34] whose family retained possession as late as 1899. Soon after this date it was acquired by Major, now Lieut.-Colonel, Charles William Trotter, who is the present lord of the manor.

A second manor of *BARTON* had its origin in lands here granted to the priory of Chetwode in 1246 by Ralph de Norwich[35] and Sibyl de Caversfield.[36] The latter held her lands by grant of John de Barton.[37] They passed with the priory's lands to Nutley Abbey, and were granted in 1540 as the 'Manor of Barton Hartshorn' to William Risley.[38] Thenceforward they descended with the priory manor of Chetwode (q.v.). No mention of it, as a manor, occurs after 1840,[39] but the owners of the priory estate in Chetwode have continued to hold land in this parish.

By 1254–5 the abbey of Oseney was seised of land in Barton[40] which was afterwards known as the manor of *BARTON HARTSHORN alias BEGGARS BARTON*, and held it until the Dissolution.[41] In 1541 it was granted in fee to John Wellesbourne,[42] who died in 1548.[43] His son John conveyed the manor in 1569–70 to Edmund Packson or Paxton,[44] who died seised in 1596.[45] His son William succeeded him,[46] and died in 1628, leaving a son Thomas.[47] After this date it passed, according to Willis, to the Butterfield family, a member of which had married the heiress of the Paxtons.[48] About 1716 Eleanor Butterfield married George Southam, to whom she brought this estate, which he held in 1735.[49] There is no further trace of it after this date, but Sheahan, in 1862, refers to an ancient stone house in the parish then occupied as a farm by Mr. Henry Paxton.[50]

CHURCH The church of *ST. JAMES* consists of a continuous chancel and nave 63 ft. 6 in. by 14 ft., north and south transepts, north and south porches, a western bellcote for two bells surmounted by a cross,[51] and north vestry. The walls are of stone rubble and the roofs are tiled.

The chancel was rebuilt in the 19th century, and the transepts were added in 1841 by the patron, Mr. W. H. Bracebridge, the only ancient part of the church now left being the nave, which is probably of 13th-century date. The two square-headed windows in the south wall, each of two lights, are of the 14th century, and between them is a pointed south doorway of 13th-century date reset. In the north wall are two 16th-century square-headed windows, the eastern of two lights and the western a single light ; the north doorway, between the two windows, has a reset segmental head, and chamfered jambs which may be of original 14th-century date. The blocked west doorway is of late 15th or early 16th-century date ; above it is a 13th-century lancet, with rebated jambs. The north porch is modern, but the south porch may be of the 17th century.

The font is modern. The communion table is of the 17th century and has turned legs. There are some 15th-century tiles in the vestry.

The two bells are possibly of the 14th century, and are inscribed respectively 'Jacobus est nomen ejus' and 'Jhesu pie flos Marie.'

The plate includes a cup of 1570 and modern paten and flagon. The registers begin in 1582.

ADVOWSON The church of Barton is thought to have formed part of the endowment of Chetwode Priory about 1245,[52] and was confirmed to that house by Bishops of Lincoln in 1268 and 1303.[53] Presentation was made to the vicarage from 1276 onwards,[54] the church being served by canons of the priory.[55] The 'church of the Blessed Mary at Barton' is mentioned

<hr>

[21] Add. Chart. 1984.
[22] Feet of F. Div. Co. Mich. 14 Hen. VII.
[23] *Visit. of Bucks.* (Harl. Soc.), 198.
[24] Feet of F. Div. Co. Mich. 14 Hen. VII.
[25] Star Chamb. Proc. Phil. and Mary, bdle. 5, no. 8.
[26] Chan. Inq. p.m. (Ser. 2), clxxxiv, 4; ccvi, 38.
[27] Fine R. 32 Eliz. pt. i, 52.
[28] Chan. Inq. p.m. (Ser. 2), dxxiii, 78.
[29] Willis, *Hist. and Antiq. of Buckingham*, 134.
[30] P.C.C. 302 Trenley.
[31] Ibid. ; 501 Norfolk.
[32] Ibid. ; Priv. Act, 52 Geo. III, cap. 51.
[33] Lipscomb, *Hist. of Bucks.* ii, 523.
[34] Sheahan, *Hist. and Topog. of Bucks.*

258. See also *Ret. of Owners of Land*, 1873, *Bucks.* I.
[35] Feet of F. Bucks. Hil. 30 Hen. III, no. 9.
[36] Ibid. no. 10.
[37] Ibid.
[38] *L. and P. Hen. VIII*, xv, g. 831 (58).
[39] Feet of F. Bucks. Mich. 56 Geo. III ; Lipscomb, loc. cit.
[40] *Hund. R.* (Rec. Com.), i, 30.
[41] *Pope Nich. Tax.* (Rec. Com.), 47 ; *Valor Eccl.* (Rec. Com.), ii, 220 ; *Feud. Aids*, i, 99, 108, 124.
[42] *L. and P. Hen. VIII*, xvi, g. 1226 (30).
[43] Chan. Inq. p.m. (Ser. 2), lxxxvii, 56.
[44] Memo. R. (Exch. L.T.R.), Hil. 14 Eliz. m. 60.

[45] Chan. Inq. p.m. (Ser. 2), ccl, 80.
[46] Ibid. ; Fine R. 40 Eliz. pt. i, 54.
[47] Chan. Inq. p.m. (Ser. 2), dccxli, 172.
[48] Willis, loc. cit.
[49] Ibid.
[50] Sheahan, op. cit. 259. The manor-house answers to Sheahan's description.
[51] Willis describes this in the early part of the 18th century as a little turret lathed and plastered over and tiled at the top, in which hung two small bells (op. cit. 135).
[52] *V.C.H. Bucks.* i, 380.
[53] Linc. Epis. Reg. Inst. Dalderby, fol. 177.
[54] Willis, op. cit. 135–6.
[55] *V.C.H. Bucks.* loc. cit.

in the deed of the priory's surrender in 1460 [56] before it was annexed to Nutley Abbey. In 1540 the advowson of the vicarage and the rectory of Barton were granted, with the possessions of the late priory of Chetwode, to William Risley,[57] and the property has since passed with the priory estate in Chetwode (q.v.), the advowson being at present held by Major G. F. Green. After the Dissolution the living was presented to as a curacy only in 1525 and 1542.[58] Since the latter date the same incumbents have served both Chetwode and Barton; the living is now a vicarage with Chetwode annexed to it.

CHARITIES The poor's allotment, containing 2 a. 2 r. 35 p., was allotted for the benefit of the poor by an award made under the Inclosure Act. The land is let in allotments, producing about £4 5s. yearly, which is distributed in coal.

BEACHAMPTON

Becentone, Bechentone (xi cent.); Becchamton (xii cent.); Bechehampton (xiii cent.).

This parish covers 1,528 acres, of which 1,229 acres are permanent grass, 229 arable and 28 woods and plantations.[1] The soil is clay, the subsoil limestone. The chief crops are wheat, oats, beans and barley. The parish is well-watered, and the low-lying land in the north-west, where the Ouse forms the boundary, is liable to flood. A stream which enters the parish on the south-east runs through it in a north-westerly direction, finally joining the River Ouse. Closely parallel to this stream is the road along which straggles the village, its north end bounded by a cross-road, on the far side of which stands the church of St. Mary. The land near the river lies low, usually less than 200 ft. above the ordnance datum, but on each side of the village it rises to over 300 ft. Hill Farm and Beachampton Grove also stand high.

Hall Farm, a little distance to the north of the church, on the south bank of the Ouse, is all that remains of Beachampton Hall,[2] long the residence of the lords of the manor. It is a two-storied house of stone with tiled roofs, and dates in its present state principally from the first quarter of the 17th century. The plan is irregular, the main block being placed north and south, and having wings at the north-west and south-east. The latter wing probably occupies the position of the solar and undercroft of a late 15th-century house, the gable at the west end of the south wall of this wing probably marking the site of the north end wall of the hall to which the solar and undercroft were attached. The surviving portion of the plan, with this exception, is entirely of the 17th century, and contains, at the south end of the principal block, a very fine staircase leading to the upper floor of the solar block. The mediaeval house to which the greater part of the present building formed an addition was removed in the 18th century, and some of its stones have been re-used in the outbuildings of the farm.

The southern portion of the house, which is no longer inhabited, remains very much in its original state. The staircase, on the south, rises in four flights, the solar or great chamber on the first floor of the south-east wing being entered by a doorway opening off the landing at the head of the two lower flights. Both these and the third flight have heavily moulded and carved strings and handrails, with turned balusters, and square carved newel-posts surmounted by square baluster-shaped finials supporting heraldic beasts holding shields, a lion, two unicorns with collars and chains, and a griffin. In the east wall of the great chamber is a large bay window with five mullioned and transomed lights in the principal face, and one in each return. Some heraldic glass of the 16th century still remains in the window. The walls have 17th-century oak panelling, now covered with paint and crowned by a later deal frieze. The stone fireplace on the south is now blocked and two of the windows on the north are hidden by the panelling. Below this portion of the house is a basement containing two rooms. The elevations are characteristic of the period, and many of the original mullioned windows survive, the gabled end of the south-east wing with the bay window lighting the great chamber being especially noteworthy. Fragments of a wall with gate piers, to the south of the house, appear to be of the early 17th century, and in a ruined wall to the north-west of the house is a reset doorway of the late 15th century.

To the south-east of the village lies the farmhouse known as Elmer School, a stone building of the last half of the 17th century, two stories in height with an attic, and having wood-mullioned windows and tiled roof, and an entrance porch with a round-headed outer doorway on the principal front. The building has undergone alteration in the succeeding century, the roof, which is surmounted by a cupola, having been reconstructed with the present dormer windows. The plan is rectangular and the end walls are gabled. On the south side of the lane, opposite Elmer School, is the Grange, a two-storied farmhouse of stone, with a timber-framed upper story, dating from the first half of the 17th century.[2a] On the south-west front is a projecting two-storied timber porch, with open balustered sides to the ground stage, and a gabled upper story with a mullioned window projecting on shaped brackets. Later additions have been made at the north-west and a wing has been added at the south-east.

Seventeenth-century field-names include Poor Man's Plot, Bridge Meade,[3] Shrives Close and Queen's Close,[4] the last-named recalling the fact that the Queens of England once held lands here as part of their dower.

Willis states that the parish was inclosed in 1579–80.[5] There is no Inclosure Act.

[56] Chan. Inq. p.m. 38 & 39 Hen. VI, no. 69.
[57] L. and P. Hen. VIII, xv, g. 831 (58).
[58] Willis, op. cit. 136.
[1] Statistics from Bd. of Agric. (1905).
[2] According to tradition it was at one time inhabited by Catherine Parr, but of this no documentary evidence exists.
[2a] The Grange, 'where I now dwell,' is mentioned in the will of William Elmer dated 3 Jan. 1648–9. The trustees carried out his instructions as to the building of the school opposite his house in the close called Saffords (P.C.C. 62 Brent).
[3] Parl. Surv. Bucks. no. 7.
[4] Com. Pleas Recov. R. Mich. 7 Jas. I, m. 82.
[5] Willis, Hist. and Antiq. of Buckingham, 144.

MANORS Before the Conquest Alric, a man and thegn of King Edward, held and could sell a manor in *BEACHAMPTON* which was in the possession of Walter Giffard in 1086.[6] It thus formed a parcel of the honour of Giffard, and the overlordship descended with that of Lillingstone Dayrell (q.v.). As in the case of this latter parish, Walter's Domesday tenant Hugh was succeeded by the Earls of Oxford, to whom a mesne lordship of both manors belonged,[7] their rights in Beachampton being mentioned as late as 1634.[8]

The first under-tenant recorded was Osmer de Beachampton, mentioned in 1175–6,[9] and the names occur in 1202 of Richard de Beachampton and Avis his wife.[10] Richard appears to have been identical with the Richard son of Roger de Beachampton who in the early 13th century granted his son Richard land in Beachampton, which included a virgate which Osmer had held.[11] Sir William de Beachampton, kt., son of Richard, was lord of this part of Beachampton by 1218.[12] He was probably the elder son of the younger Richard.[13] William, or a son of the same name, continued seised of the manor as late as 1254–5,[14] but John son of William succeeded before 1284–6.[15] In 1289 John de Beachampton conveyed to John Wolf and Amice his wife two-thirds of the manor, with the reversion of the remaining third after the death of William's widow Margery[16]; this conveyance was made in favour of the heirs of Amice.[17] By 1302 Philip de Hardreshull was lord of the manor,[18] which he held in the right of his wife Amice,[19] evidently the widow of John Wolf. She died in 1332,[20] but Philip was still lord in 1333.[21] Robert Wolf, son of John,[22] however, held in 1346.[23] William Wolf was apparently lord in 1349,[24] but in the following year the estate was in the hands of guardians owing to the minority of the heir,[25] evidently the Philip Wolf who with Elizabeth his wife made a settlement of the manor in 1357.[26] Philip and Elizabeth Wolf still held in 1407, in which year mention is also made of their son John and Joan his wife.[27] Five years later John was seised of the manor.[28] A Roger Wolf of Beachampton was alive in 1414,[29] but there seems to be no definite evidence concerning the manor for the next forty years. In 1455 it was held by John Cornwall and Elizabeth his wife in the right of Elizabeth,[30] who may thus have been the daughter and heir of John

Wolf. The Cornwalls quitclaimed the manor in that year to John Mody,[31] who had received a quitclaim in 1453 from William Joyntour,[32] probably a trustee. Beachampton passed within the next few years to Richard Pigott, who was slain at the battle of Wakefield in 1460.[33] His son John inherited the manor, and his widow Joan, who afterwards married Richard or William Forster, also held a share.[34] In 1490 Agnes, widow of John Mody, petitioned against both Joan and John for her dower of a third of the manor and of five messuages and 35 acres in Beachampton,[35] but the result of the suit is not apparent. The Pigotts, however, remained seised of the manor. John was followed by his son Robert, and he by his son Thomas.[36] In 1585, on the marriage of his eldest son Valentine with Eleanor Fortescue, Thomas Pigott made a settlement of the manor by which, after various provisions, it was eventually to remain to the sons of Valentine and Eleanor, and, in default of such, to the other children of Valentine.[37] Valentine died in 1590, during his father's lifetime; his heirs were his three daughters by a former marriage, Mary, Ursula and Judith, who shortly after married respectively Thomas Waterhouse, Christopher Pigott and William Tresham.[38]

PIGOTT. *Sable three picks argent.*

Each heiress dealt with a third of the manor by fine in 1591–2,[39] but as Thomas Pigott was still alive at the time it was he, not they, who by the terms of the settlement was actually in seisin of the manor.[40] In June 1592 the heiresses and their husbands brought a suit in Chancery[41] in which they complained that their uncle, George Pigott, eldest surviving son of Thomas, was attempting to defraud them of the reversion of the manor after the death of Thomas, who was 'very old, and weak in his mind.' Both Ursula and Thomas Pigott died at the end of the year 1592.[42] Probably there were some further difficulties between George Pigott and his nieces, as in 1593–5 he received quitclaims of their shares,[43] and soon afterwards made a settlement of the whole manor.[44] A further settlement was made in 1599.[45]

---

[6] *V.C.H. Bucks.* i, 250.

[7] See Lillingstone Dayrell; also *Feud. Aids*, i, 88, 124.

[8] Chan. Inq. p.m. (Ser. 2), dviii, 15.

[9] *Pipe R.* 22 *Hen. II* (Pipe R. Soc.), 27.

[10] Hunter, *Pedes Finium* (Rec. Com.), 32.

[11] Add. MS. 37068, fol. 33 d.

[12] Ibid. fol. 34; *R. of Hugh of Wells* (Cant. and York Soc.), i, 68; see account of church.

[13] Richard son of Richard married Cecilia and died before 1230, when his son Richard granted a hide in Beachampton to Snelshall Priory (Feet of F. case 15, file 18; Add. MS. 37068, fol. 34, 75 d.). This grant was confirmed by William, and by Cecilia, who had married Alexander de Drayton or de Tattenhoe by that time (ibid.).

[14] *Testa de Nevill* (Rec. Com.), 247, 258, 259, 261; *Hund. R.* (Rec. Com.), i, 29.

[15] *Feud. Aids*, i, 88.

[16] Feet of F. case 17, file 50.

[17] Ibid.

[18] *Feud. Aids*, i, 99.

[19] Feet of F. case 18, file 65.

[20] *Cal. Inq. p.m.* (Edw. III), vii, 304.

[21] De Banco R. 205, m. 219; 252, m. 24 d.; 253, m. 83; Trin. 1 Edw. III, m. 106 d.; *Feud. Aids*, i, 108; *Rentals and Surv.* (Gen. Ser.), R. 800.

[22] Baker, *Hist. and Antiq. of Northants,* i, 124.

[23] *Feud. Aids*, i, 124.

[24] Lipscomb, *Hist. and Antiq. of Bucks.* ii, 530.

[25] Lipscomb, loc. cit.

[26] *Cal. Close,* 1354–60, pp. 427–8.

[27] Feet of F. case 21, file 113. See also Chan. Inq. p.m. 34 Edw. III (1st nos.), no. 84; 45 Edw. III (1st nos.), no. 45.

[28] Lipscomb, loc. cit.

[29] *Cat. of Anct. D.* i, 498.

[30] Feet of F. case 22, file 124.

[31] Ibid.

[32] Close, 35 Hen. VI, m. 23.

[33] Lipscomb, op. cit. ii, 528.

[34] Ibid.; *Cal. Pat.* 1467–77, p. 524; Linc. Epis. Reg. Chadworth Memo. fol. 102 d.

[35] De Banco R. 913, m. 112; 916, m. 150 d., 350 d.

[36] *Visit. of Bucks.* (Harl. Soc.), 195 et seq.

[37] Feet of F. Bucks. Mich. 27 Eliz.; Chan. Inq. p.m. (Ser. 2), ccxxxiv, 38.

[38] Chan. Inq. p.m. (Ser. 2), ccxxxiv, 38.

[39] Feet of F. Bucks. Hil. 33 Eliz.; East. 34 Eliz. (two).

[40] Chan. Inq. p.m. (Ser. 2), ccxxxiv, 38.

[41] Chan. Proc. (Ser. 2), bdle. 252, no. 3.

[42] Chan. Inq. p.m. (Ser. 2), ccxxxiv, 38; ccxliii, 2.

[43] Feet of F. Bucks. Mich. 36 Eliz.; Mich. 37 Eliz.

[44] Ibid. Mich. 38 Eliz.

[45] Ibid. Trin. 41 Eliz.; Recov. R. Trin. 41 Eliz. m. 36.

Sir Thomas Pigott, kt., George's son, was seised in 1609, in which year he conveyed Beachampton to Sir Thomas Bennett, kt.[46] The latter made a settlement in 1613 in favour of his second son Simon,[47] who also inherited Calverton (q.v.), with which Beachampton descended until the early 19th century.[48] It was then sold by the Marquess of Salisbury, the sale being completed in August 1807, to George Brooks, trustee of the will of Ann Brooks, to the use of her nephew, John Harrison of Shelswell, Oxfordshire, for life, with contingent remainder to her cousin James Walker.[49] John Harrison died in or about September 1834, without issue male, whereupon Beachampton passed to James Walker of Sand Hutton, Yorkshire, son of the above James Walker, who had died in 1829.[50] James Walker was created a baronet in 1868,[51] and the property has since continued in his family, Sir Robert James Milo Walker, the fourth baronet, being the present lord.

BENNETT. *Gules a bezant between three demi-lions argent.*

A considerable portion of land in the parish is owned by the Marquess of Lincolnshire, whose ancestor, according to Lipscomb, obtained it about 1806.[52]

A manor-house was in existence in 1333.[53] Record of it is again found in 1592, when it was apportioned to Valentine Pigott's widow after the death of Thomas.[54] It was included in the conveyance of 1609.[55]

A water-mill stood on this manor in 1086 and was valued at 10s.[56] In 1285 there were two water-mills in Beachampton, which were conveyed in that year to Ellis de Tingewick and his heirs.[57] This conveyance was made by the lord of the second manor in Beachampton, but in 1324 Ellis de Tingewick's widow petitioned the lords of both manors for her dower in the two mills.[58] They were among the appurtenances of the united manor in 1593,[59] and 'the water-mill called the Upper Milne' was conveyed to Sir Thomas Bennett with the manor in 1609.[60]

A second manor in Beachampton, known afterwards as *WHITYNGHAM'S MANOR*, was held by Lewin of Nuneham (Courtenay) both in the time of King

WALKER of Sand-Hutton, and of Beachampton, baronet. *Argent a cheveron gules charged with three rings or between three crescents azure.*

Edward and in 1086.[61] It passed to the Fitz Niel family with Lewin's manors in Mursley and Salden

CECIL, Marquess of Salisbury. *Barry of ten pieces argent and azure six scutcheons sable each charged with a lion argent differenced with a crescent.*

(q.v.), and followed the descent of these and of Whityngham's Manor in Great Kimble[62] until 1499, in which year Richard Whityngham sold his manor in Beachampton to Richard Emson.[63] Two years later Richard Emson sold it to John Pigott,[64] lord of the other moiety of Beachampton, with which this was doubtless amalgamated after that date, as no separate mention of it occurs again.

There were tenants holding this manor of the Fitz Niels in the 13th and 14th centuries. Robert de Bray, who is mentioned in 1277,[65] held 'half the vill of Beachampton' of Robert Fitz Niel in 1284–6.[66] He quitclaimed the manor in 1291–2 to Ralf de Bray[67] and died before 1298 leaving a widow Juliana.[68] Robert de Bray, son of Ralf, held in 1302–3,[69] and Ralf de Bray, possibly a younger son of Ralf, in 1316.[70] The second Ralf married Maud, and their son John was lord in 1346.[71] The return of Ralf's name as tenant in 1349[72] is obviously erroneous, for the son, John de Bray,[73] continued to hold and is mentioned as late as 1360.[74] There is no further record of these tenants.

A third holding in Beachampton in 1086 consisted of a hide, previously held by Levric, a man of Azor, which at this date was held by Lewin of Roger de

[46] Com. Pleas Recov. R. Mich. 7 Jas. I, m. 82.

[47] Ibid. ; Feet of F. Bucks. Trin. 11 Jas. I ; Chan. Inq. p.m. (Ser. 2), cccclxxx, 105.

[48] Lysons, *Mag. Brit.* i (3), 508.

[49] Beachampton Title Deeds ; Lipscomb, op. cit. ii, 530.

[50] Beachampton Title Deeds ; *Post Office Dir.* (1847, 1854, &c.) ; Sheahan, *Hist. and Topog. of Bucks.* 260.

[51] Burke, *Peerage.*

[52] Lipscomb, loc. cit.

[53] Rentals and Surv. (Gen. Ser.), R. 800.

[54] Chan. Inq. p.m. (Ser. 2), ccxxxiv, 38.

[55] Com. Pleas Recov. R. Mich. 7 Jas. I, m. 82.

[56] *V.C.H. Bucks.* i, 250.

[57] Feet of F. case 17, file 47.

[58] De Banco R. 253, m. 83 d. ; 256, m. 2.

[59] Chan. Inq. p.m. (Ser. 2), ccxxxiv, 38.

[60] Com. Pleas Recov. R. Mich. 7 Jas. I, m. 82.

[61] *V.C.H. Bucks.* i, 275.

[62] Ibid. ii, 300 ; *Rot. de Oblatis et Fin.* (Rec. Com.), 132 ; *Testa de Nevill* (Rec. Com.), 244, 252, 262 ; *Feud. Aids,* i, 124 ; *Excerpta e Rot. Fin.* (Rec. Com.), ii, 35 ; Feet of F. case 16, file 34, no. 3.

[63] De Banco R. 950, m. 309, 361.

[64] Ibid. 958, m. 2.

[65] Feet of F. case 16, file 44.

[66] *Feud. Aids,* i, 88.

[67] Feet of F. case 17, file 51.

[68] *Cal. Close,* 1296–1301, p. 201.

[69] *Feud. Aids,* i, 99 ; Feet of F. case 18, file 60.

[70] *Feud. Aids,* i, 108 ; Feet of F. case 18, file 60.

[71] Feet of F. case 18, file 69 ; *Feud. Aids,* i, 124.

[72] Chan. Inq. p.m. 23 Edw. III (1st nos.), no. 85.

[73] *Cal. Close,* 1349–54, p. 614.

[74] Ibid. 1354–60, p. 622.

Iveri.[75] The latter's possessions were afterwards known as the honour of St. Walery,[76] and in 1254–5 it was found that Robert Fitz Niel had a hide of land in Beachampton which usually paid 2s. hidage per annum to the sheriff, but that this sum had during the past year been seized for the honour of St. Walery.[77]

The priory of Snelshall also held lands here, granted by the lords of both moieties in the 13th century.[78] In 1535 the prior paid an annual rent of 7s. 5d. to the Pigotts.[79] A terrier of 1581 belonging to the Beachampton free school mentions the 'houses and closes, lands and meadows belonging to the grange in Beachampton being now the lands of John Fortescue Esq. formerly belonging to the Priory of Snelshall and now in the tenure of William Elmer.'[80] This Elmer was no doubt the ancestor of the founder of the free school ; the trustees of the Elmer charity still own land here.

The church of the ASSUMPTION CHURCH OF ST. MARY THE VIRGIN consists of a chancel 28 ft. by 14 ft., with modern north vestry and organ chamber, nave 33 ft. by 14 ft. 6 in., north aisle 8 ft. 6 in. wide, south aisle 8 ft. wide with south porch, and west tower 6 ft. by 5 ft. 6 in. These measurements are all internal.

No detail survives of an earlier period than the north arcade of the nave, which is of the first half of the 14th century ; the aisle then added was probably the first of a series of additions to a previously existing church consisting of a chancel and an aisleless nave. Further alterations and additions seem to have been undertaken a few years later, the chancel being rebuilt and an aisle thrown out on the south side, while the clearstory was added to the nave and a tower built at the west end. In the early part of the 15th century both aisles were much altered. The church was restored in 1873–4, and again more recently. The chancel and the wooden bell-chamber and spire of the tower have been rebuilt, while the north vestry and the organ chamber and the south porch are modern. The walling generally is of rubble.

No original features remain in the east and north walls of the chancel ; the windows at the east and north-east are modern, and a modern archway opens to the north organ chamber. At the east end of the south wall of the chancel is a much-restored 14th-century window of two lights with uncusped tracery in a pointed head. To the west of this is a pointed doorway of the same date, and at the west end of the wall is a square-headed two-light window of c. 1600,[81] both features, as in the case of the south-east window, having been reset and restored. The chancel arch is of two pointed and chamfered orders springing from moulded capitals supported by carved corbels, that on the north having a grotesque head, and that on the south large leaved foliage. In the east wall of the vestry is a reset 15th-century window.

The 14th-century north and south arcades of the nave are each of three bays with pointed arches of two chamfered orders carried by clustered columns having moulded capitals and bases, the mouldings of the capitals in the south arcade being of a slightly later section. The east and west responds continue the outer order, the inner order being carried by foliated or grotesque corbels with moulded capitals. The nave roof is of low pitch, and on the tie-beam of the eastern truss is the date 1622.

The north and south aisles are each lighted from the side by two square-headed early 15th-century windows in the north and south walls, the eastern windows being of three lights and the western of two. At the east end of the north aisle is a modern archway to the vestry, and at the east end of the south aisle is a pointed late 15th-century window of three transomed and cinquefoiled lights with a traceried head, on either side of which are plain image brackets, the southern one being a restoration. The window in the west wall of the north aisle and the north doorway are modern. To the east of the latter is a stoup recess with a round head, the basin being destroyed, and in the same wall is a square-headed aumbry. The pointed south doorway, which is of two continuous chamfered orders, is of the 14th century, but has been much restored. At the east end of the south aisle is a 15th-century piscina with a trefoiled head and round basin. The outward thrust of the north wall has necessitated the erection of a flying buttress spanning the aisle.

The tower is of three stages, crowned by a plain parapet, above which rises the timber bell-chamber and shingled spire, originally built in 1680, but much altered in the last century. The western angles are strengthened by diagonal buttresses, stopping below the third stage. The tower arch is of two orders, both chamfered, the outer brought to the square of the plain jambs by broach-stops and the inner carried by roughly-worked corbels. The two-light west window of the ground stage has modern tracery. The uppermost of the stages in the stone portion of the tower has a rectangular 14th-century opening with tracery, placed low down. The remains of a flight of steps to the intermediate stage of the tower can be seen against the west wall of the north aisle.

The font and fittings are modern.

On the south wall of the chancel is a curious and elaborate monument with a figure in grave-clothes and an inscription on a brass plate commemorating Matthew Pigott, a former rector (d. 1598). A modern slab in the north aisle contains the brass, with figure, of William Bawdyn of Beachampton, blacksmith (d. 1600). In the south aisle is a brass to Alice wife of George Baldwyn, and daughter of William Mathew of Calverton (d. 1611). The brass is engraved with her figure and those of her two sons and two daughters. At the east end of the nave is a brass to William Elmer (d. 1652), a benefactor to the parish. A modern recess in the north wall of the chancel contains a monument commemorating Simon Bennett (d. 1682), Grace his wife, and their children. The monument is of marble and of elaborate design, consisting of a black marble pedestal, on which stands a white marble bust under a classical canopy, supported by Ionic columns and bearing the arms and crest of Bennett. A floor slab in the chancel commemorates Sir Simon Bennett, bart. (d. 1631).

There is a ring of five bells which were recast from three old bells in 1912, and a sanctus. The

[75] V.C.H. Bucks. i, 269.
[76] Ibid. 214.
[77] Hund. R. (Rec. Com.), i, 29.
[78] Add. MS. 37068, fol. 34–9 ; Feet of F. case 15, file 18.
[79] Valor Eccl. (Rec. Com.), iv, 229.
[80] Willis, op. cit 143.
[81] At the visitation of 1519 the chancel was said to be ruinous (Bp. Atwater's Visit. in Alnwick Tower, Lincoln).

BEACHAMPTON: HALL FARM FROM THE EAST

BEACHAMPTON: THE VILLAGE

BEACHAMPTON CHURCH FROM THE SOUTH-EAST

BEACHAMPTON CHURCH: THE INTERIOR LOOKING EAST

original treble, inscribed 'Sancta Margareta Ora Pro Nobis,' bore the initials of Johane Sturdy, the widow of John Sturdy, and must have been cast between 1458 and 1461, the years of her widowhood[82]; the second was probably of the 14th century, and bore the inscription, in Gothic capitals, ' + Nos : prece : sanctorum : defendas : Xpe : tuorum'; the tenor was inscribed 'Robert Atton made me 1633 W.E.' The sanctus is dated 1695 and is probably by Richard Chandler.

The older plate consists of a chalice, paten and flagon and two large plates. There are also a modern chalice, two patens and a flagon.

The registers begin in 1628.

ADVOWSON The church of Beachampton was held at an early date in separate moieties by the two lords of the vill. Richard Fitz Niel granted his moiety to the priory of Luffield[83] probably in the 12th century.[84] The priors from that time until 1470 presented a rector to their moiety.[85] The other half was held by the Beachampton family and their successors, the earliest presentation recorded being made in 1218 by Sir William de Beachampton.[86] Their incumbent appears to have ranked as a chaplain.[87] In 1470 an agreement was come to by the Pigotts and the prior by which the two moieties were united under one incumbent,[88] who was presented by the priors and the lords of the manor alternately.[89]

The manorial portion always descended with the manor.[90] That held by Luffield was granted after the Dissolution, with the site of the priory, to Sir Nicholas Throckmorton,[91] and continued to be held by this family and their heirs the Temples as late as 1701.[92]

In 1687 both Viscountess Baltinglass, the granddaughter and co-heir of Sir Arthur Throckmorton,[93] and Mrs. Bennett were returned as presenting to the living.[94] Willis states that this was the result of a claim to the patronage set up by Lady Baltinglass,[95] but that all the Luffield right had been sold to the Pigotts about 1610.[96] The latter statement does not appear to be correct, but it is possible that some agreement was afterwards come to between the Temple heirs and the lords of the main manor, as the latter continued sole patrons as late as 1798.[97] In 1811 William Palmer presented William Jocelyn Palmer,[98] who vacated the living and presented the next rector in 1815.[99] By 1827 the patronage was vested in the Master and Fellows of Gonville and Caius College, Cambridge,[100] by whom it is still held.

An annual rent from half a yardland was paid for the maintenance of a light in the church.[101]

CHARITIES For the charity of Sir Simon Bennett, bart., founded by will, 1631, see under parish of Calverton in Newport Hundred. The share of this parish in 1910 amounted to £16 15s. 10d., of which £12 was applied in clothing and £4 15s. 10d. was carried to the churchwardens' general account.

Charity of Simon Bennett, or the Bradwell estate (see under parish of Calverton). In 1911 the share of this parish amounted to £9 10s., being five twenty-first parts of the net income, which was distributed in coal.

The following charities were founded by will of William Elmer, proved at Westminster 3 May 1653, namely :

(1) The school, for which see article on Schools.[102] The charity is now administered under a scheme of the Board of Education of 19 January 1906. A sum of £352 17s. consols is held by the official trustees, producing £8 16s. 4d. yearly.

(2) Charity for clothing sixteen poor men and women. The trust property consists of a messuage called The Grange and several parcels of land, containing together about 60 a. and two cottages, producing together about £50 a year. The official trustees also hold £69 18s. 5d. consols, producing £1 14s. 8d. yearly. The will directs that three of the men and three of the women should belong to Beachampton, one man and one woman to Maids' Moreton, one man and one woman to Nash, two men and two women to Whaddon, one man and one woman to Calverton. After providing coats and gowns to the sixteen beneficiaries, the net income is paid proportionately to the parish officers of the five parishes specified, and applied for the benefit of poor families.

(3) Charity for apprenticing, consisting of 4 a. 1 r. 24 p., formerly known as Water Close, now as 'Five Pound Meadow,' let at £5 a year.

(4) Bridge Trust, endowed with 2 a. 2 r. in Calverton of the rental value of £3 a year, and £5 0s. 6d. consols with the official trustees.

(5) Charity for the trustees, consisting of 3 a. 1 r. 17 p. in Side Meadow, let at £2 18s. a year.

(6) Charity for the poor of Beachampton, endowed with 3 a. 1 r. in Whaddon, let at £3 a year.

(7) For charity for the poor of Whaddon and Nash see under Whaddon parish in Cottesloe Hundred.

BIDDLESDEN

Betesdene, Bechesdene (xi cent.); Bethlesdene, Betlesden (xii cent.).

The area of Biddlesden parish, which was formerly 1,630 acres,[1] increased to 2,052 acres between 1871 and 1881,[2] probably under the Divided Parishes Acts of 1876 or 1879.[3] A further extension, which gave the parish its present area, 3,201 acres, was made before 1891, doubtless under the Local Government

---

[82] A. H. Cocks, *Church Bells of Bucks.* 312.

[83] Cott. MS. Cleop. C iii, fol. 350 ; Dugdale, *Mon.* iv, 350.

[84] See Salden and Mursley.

[85] Willis, op. cit. 147.

[86] See account of manor ; *R. of Hugh of Wells* (Cant. and York Soc.), i, 68.

[87] Add. MS. 37068, fol. 36 d., 38 ; Willis, loc. cit.

[88] Linc. Epis. Reg. Memo. Chadworth, fol. 102 d.

[89] Willis, loc. cit.

[90] See under manor ; Inst. Bks. (P.R.O.).

[91] Pat. 5 Edw. VI, pt. iii, m. 31.

[92] See Luffield ; Recov. R. Mich. 25 Eliz. m. 21 ; Inst. Bks. (P.R.O.) ; G.E.C. *Peerage*, i, 228.

[93] G.E.C. loc. cit.

[94] Inst. Bks. (P.R.O.).

[95] Willis, op. cit. 149.

[96] Ibid. 139.

[97] Inst. Bks. (P.R.O.).

[98] Ibid.

[99] Lipscomb, op. cit. ii, 531.

[100] Ibid.

[101] Chant. Cert. no. 5.

[102] *V.C.H. Bucks.* ii, 218.

[1] According to Browne Willis, *Hist. and Antiq. of Buckingham*, 156, the parish contained 1,700 acres and about twenty houses in 1755.

[2] *Pop. Ret. sub annis.*

[3] *V.C.H. Bucks.* ii, 94.

Act of 1888.[4] A 16th-century account of the bounds of the manor shows that the extensions have been made in the east of the parish; it contains many field-names still to be found. The bounds ran by Homewood, Earlswood, Briary Coppice, Newridinge, Whitfield Wood, Evershaw, Westbury Corner, Smallye mead, Walkemeade, Evershaw Bridge, and along the banks of the Ouse.[5]

The River Ouse forms part of the western boundary, separating Biddlesden from Northamptonshire. The land is lowest in this part, under 400 ft. Towards the middle it rises slightly and reaches a height of a little over 500 ft. in the north-east. There are 560 acres of arable land with 2,215 acres laid down in grass [6] on a soil of gravel with a subsoil of limestone, and agriculture forms the main employment of the population. The numerous woods and coppices still existing, about 337 acres in extent, are evidence of the time when the woodland in the parish was probably far more extensive than at present, since the

which covers about 150 acres in the west of the parish. It is the property of the lord of the manor and the residence of General F. J. and Mrs. Heyworth. A pond in the grounds, fed by a small stream which the road crosses at Beggar's Bridge, probably marks the site of the old fish-ponds.

Some 16th and early 17th-century accounts of the manor-house, which must have incorporated at least part of the old abbey, state that it contained sixteen bays, a brew-house, stable, 'colehouse,' dovecots, orchard, hop-yard, and three fisheries.[9] The abbey church was destroyed by Sir Robert Peckham about the middle of the 16th century; its five large bells are supposed to have been given to Denham parish, where in 1683 they were melted down and run into eight.[10] Browne Willis, when he visited Biddlesden in 1712, found the ruins of both church and Abbey House in good part standing; there were then to be seen the walls of the east side of the cloister and a part of the tower, together with a small chapel and the chapter-house, which was a handsome arched room about 40 ft. square supported by four pillars. In the chapel lay a broken alabaster effigy of a figure in armour, from the tomb of one of the Lords Zouche.[11] The remains of other tombs were also to be seen. Another figure, of Christ, had been destroyed about 1704 by the lord of the manor, John Sayer. His successor, Henry Sayer, was still more destructive. Willis coming to the parish again in 1737 found that Sayer had so 'totally demolished the footsteps of the Abbey that not the least appearance remains of the site of any ancient building.'[12] Sheahan speaks of a doorway in the garden to the west of Biddlesden House and a bit of wall still existing in 1862 [13]; nothing, however, now remains above

BIDDLESDEN PARK

royal forest of Whittlewood in the next county lay on its northern borders. Certain woods in the manor belonged to the king as part of the forest, and he had the right of fowling and hunting throughout the manor.[7] In 1536 Sir Francis Brian, anticipating the suppression of the foundation, desired to have the abbey of Biddlesden for himself, 'as it adjoins the forest and the king's game might be injured by another man.'[8]

The chief historical interest of the parish attaches to the abbey founded here in 1147, which owned nearly all the land and held its markets and fairs within the manor. The neighbourhood seems to have been less prosperous after the Dissolution. The abbey site is now occupied by an 18th-century house standing in a well-wooded estate, Biddlesden Park,

ground but some stones belonging probably to a 13th-century arch. Sayer built the present house about 1731.[14] Having also destroyed the old chapel of St. Margaret, 'a little tiled fabric with a bell in a turret,'[15] which stood, according to an early document, 'at the gate of the Abbey,'[16] and which, since the demolition of the abbey church, had probably served as a parish church, he fitted up a chapel on the left wing of the house as a place of worship for the parish.[17] Sheahan, writing c. 1862, speaks of it as then forming part of the stable, though detached from the house, and as yet unconsecrated.[18] It continues to be the parish church. The churchyard of St. Margaret's Chapel was likewise desecrated by the same Sayer, who told Willis he had had the coffins

---

[4] V.C.H. Bucks. ii, 94 ; Pop. Ret.
[5] Ld. Rev. Misc. Bks. ccx, fol. 15.
[6] Statistics from Bd. of Agric. (1905).
[7] Ld. Rev. Misc. Bks. ccx, fol. 14, 15.
[8] L. and P. Hen. VIII, x, 572.

[9] Ld. Rev. Misc. Bks. ccx, fol. 2 ; Pat. 7 Jas. I, pt. xx, no. 2.
[10] Willis, op. cit. 152.
[11] Ibid.   [12] Ibid. 155.
[13] Sheahan, Hist. and Topog. of Bucks. 263.

[14] Lipscomb, Hist. and Antiq. of Bucks. ii, 545.
[15] Willis, op. cit. 153.
[16] Harl. MS. 4714, fol. 43.
[17] Willis, loc. cit.
[18] Sheahan, op. cit. 264.

dug up, 'and several thousand human bones removed and thrown away, as he gloried in, to level ground, together with the rubbish, with great indecency.'[19] Finally, however, he caused a low arch to be turned over some of the graves.[20]

Biddlesden Farm, now called the Abbey Farm, is a 17th-century stone house, to which belongs a stone barn of the same date.

Evershaw (Eversel, xi cent.; Euersache, xii cent.; Evereshag, Eversschawe, Evirsaw, xiii–xiv cent.; Hevershay, xv cent.), now the name only of a farm and adjoining lands, was described as a village of three or four houses in 1755,[21] and seems to have ranked as a separate parish as late as the 15th century.[22] A church or chapel, dedicated to the honour of St. Nicholas, formerly stood here, but no traces of it remained in the 18th century.[23] Sheahan, however, speaks of the Upper and Lower Chapel Fields (still so called) near Evershaw Farm, where signs of a moat and foundations of buildings had been discovered.[24] An early 17th-century record of Evershaw Close of 110 acres and of Evershaw Bridge, which apparently crossed the Ouse at what is now the south-west corner of Biddlesden,[25] suggests the extent and locality of the former parish. Browne Willis also speaks of Gorral or Gorhall or Gorrell, now a farm, as a 'decayed hamlet' in this parish.[26]

MANORS   Before the Conquest Azor son of Tored, a thegn of King Edward, held this manor, but the Conqueror afterwards gave it to Earl Aubrey.[27] It was, however, held by King William in 1086 as 4 hides and 1 virgate.[28] In the reign of Henry I Robert son of William de Meppershall was lord of *BIDDLESDEN*.[29] According to a 16th-century story he was threatened with disgrace at court for having stolen a hound, and gave the land to Osbert or Geoffrey de Clinton, chamberlain of the king and a royal favourite, in order to obtain his protection.[30] Robert afterwards married a kinswoman of Osbert de Clinton, and so obtained the land again,[31] but in the reign of Stephen he forfeited it for default of service due. It was thereupon given to the Earl of Leicester, whose steward, Arnold de Bois,[32] being subinfeudated,[33] founded the abbey here, as has been already related,[34] endowing it with all his land in the parish. Confirmations of this grant were made to the abbey by Arnold's son, grandson and great-grandson, all bearing the same name, by John de Bois, son of the last, and in the 14th century by Stephen de Bois.[35] The abbey continued to hold the manor until its dissolution in 1538.[36] A little

before this the site of the abbey and its lands here had been leased for ninety-nine years by the abbot to Edmund Clerke,[37] who in December 1538 transferred his interest to Sir Thomas Wriothesley, kt., by whom it was conveyed in 1539 to Robert, afterwards Sir Robert, Peckham.[38] In October 1540 Wriothesley obtained from the king the reversion in fee of the site,[39] which he conveyed in the following month for £700 to Edmund Peckham, cofferer, afterwards knighted and father of Sir Robert.[40] Sir Edmund died in 1564[41] and his son Robert in 1569.[42] He was succeeded by his brother, Sir George Peckham,[43] who in 1577 conveyed Biddlesden to Arthur Lord Grey de Wilton,[44] lord of Giffards Manor in Whaddon (q.v.), with which it afterwards passed to the Duke of Buckingham. In 1651, when the duke's estates were held by the Commonwealth, Biddlesden Manor was granted to John Thurloe and Nathaniel Waterhouse in trust for the widow and children of Henry Ireton, late Lord Deputy of Ireland. Hugh Royell was authorized to receive the rents, and disputes arose with the tenants.[45] About 1681, when the second Duke of Buckingham had regained his estates,[46] he sold Biddlesden to Henry Sayer,[47] who died soon after. His son, John Sayer, was murdered in 1712 by John Notle, an attorney who had intrigued with his wife.[48] Henry Sayer succeeded to Biddlesden, and held until about 1755,[49] when he conveyed it to Ralph, second Earl Verney.[50] His niece and successor, Mary, created Baroness Fermanagh,[51] sold it about 1791 to the Rev. George Morgan,[52] in whose family the manor has since remained.[53] Major Luis F. H. C. Morgan, son of Lieut.-Col. George Manners Morgan, married Lady Kinloss in 1884, and in 1890 they assumed her family name of Grenville.[54] Their son, the Hon. Richard G. Morgan-Grenville, was killed in action in 1914, and was succeeded by his brother Robert.

In 1086 two mills valued at 28d. belonged to the manor.[55] They are mentioned in 1278–9 as standing one within and one without the abbey.[56] By the 13th or 14th century there was also a windmill here,[57] later apparently called 'Walkermyll.'

Among the 17th-century appurtenances is included a rabbit warren.[58] A grant of a weekly Monday market and of an annual eight-day fair to be held at the feast of St. Margaret the Virgin in their manor of Biddlesden was made to the abbot and monks in 1315,[59] but there is no later reference to them. The first Sunday in August, as next but one after St. Margaret, is still called Feast Sunday.

---

[19] Willis, loc. cit.   [20] Ibid.
[21] Ibid. 156.   [22] See below.
[23] Ibid.   [24] Sheahan, op. cit. 265.
[25] Ld. Rev. Misc. Bks. ccx, fol. 15.
[26] Willis, loc. cit.
[27] *V.C.H. Bucks.* i, 232.
[28] Ibid.
[29] Harl. Chart. 85, G 48.
[30] Harl. MS. 4714, fol. 1.
[31] Ibid.; Dugdale, *Mon. Angl.* v, 364.
[32] Ibid.
[33] *Hund. R.* (Rec. Com.), ii, 343.
[34] See *V.C.H. Bucks.* i, 365.
[35] Harl. Chart. 84, H 50–7; Harl. MS. 4714, fol. 1*b*, 2.
[36] *Hund. R.* (Rec. Com.), ii, 343; Chart. R. 8 Edw. II, m. 16, no. 32; *Valor Eccl.* (Rec. Com.), iv, 237.
[37] Pat. 32 Hen. VIII, pt. iii, no. 26; Harl. MS. 4714, fol. 353.

[38] Chan. Inq. p.m. (Ser. 2), cxxxviii, 2.
[39] Pat. 32 Hen. VIII, pt. iii, no. 26; L. and P. Hen. VIII, xvi, g. 220 (3).
[40] Harl. MS. 4714, fol. 358; Close, 32 Hen. VIII, pt. ii, no. 19, 20; L. and P. Hen. VIII, xvi, 222.
[41] Chan. Inq. p.m. (Ser. 2), cxxxviii, 2.
[42] Ibid. cliii, 1.
[43] Ibid.; Feet of F. Div. Co. Hil. 13 Eliz.; East. 15 Eliz.; Willis, op. cit. 155.
[44] Feet of F. Div. Co. Hil. 19 Eliz.
[45] *Cal. Com. for Comp.* 658. See also Chan. Proc. (Bridges Div.), bdle. 409, no. 38.
[46] See under Whaddon; see also *Hist. MSS. Com. Rep.* xii, App. iii, 42; Recov. R. Trin. 13 Chas. II, m. 133; Feet of F. Bucks. Trin. 22 Chas. II.
[47] Willis, loc. cit.

[48] Ibid.; *Trials, Speeches, Confessions and Broadsides, 1691–1718,* p. 32.
[49] Feet of F. Bucks. Trin. 12 Geo. I; Trin. 11 & 12 Geo. II.
[50] Ibid. Trin. 28 Geo. II.
[51] G.E.C. *Peerage,* iii, 326.
[52] Lipscomb, loc. cit.
[53] Sheahan, op. cit. 262; *Ret. of Owners of Land,* 1873, *Bucks.* 14.
[54] G.E.C. *Peerage,* iv, 409; Walford, *County Families.*
[55] *V.C.H. Bucks.* i, 232.
[56] *Hund. R.* (Rec. Com.), ii, 343.
[57] Harl. MS. 4714, fol. 35. For later references see Pat. 32 Hen. VIII, pt. iii, no. 26; 7 Jas. I, pt. xx, no. 2; Land Rev. Misc. Bks. ccx, fol. 5, 13; Recov. R. Trin. 13 Chas. II, m. 133.
[58] Pat. 7 Jas. I, pt. xx, no. 2.
[59] Chart. R. 8 Edw. II, m. 16, no. 32.

A second entry in the Survey concerning Biddlesden shows that 3 virgates there, held before the Conquest by Alric, a man of Alwin son of Goding, formed part of the lands of the Count of Mortain ; the land, sufficient for one plough, had been laid waste.[60] It does not appear to have any further separate history. Nicholas de Stunteville held half a fee in 'Briddischame' in this county in the time of Henry III.[61]

In the time of Edward the Confessor 'a certain bandy-leg' held *EVERSHAW* as 1 hide, and in 1086 the same man still retained it holding 'in almoin of the king,' although the land was reckoned as part of Lewin of Nuneham's holding.[62] In the 12th century it belonged to the fee of the Beauchamps of Bedford, being held by Pain de Beauchamp,[63] and the overlordship was still in this family at the end of the 13th century.[64]

The family who held under the Beauchamps took its name from the place. William de Evershaw, called lord of Evershaw, flourished in the 12th century, and gave half a hide here to the priory of Luffield.[65] Pain de Beauchamp confirmed this gift,[66] which must thus have been made before 1155-6.[67] In 1200 the prior claimed against Simon de Beauchamp the service of Hugh de Evershaw for a whole hide of land, but his right to only half this amount—4s. 8d.—was allowed.[68] The priory continued to hold this part of Evershaw until it was annexed with its possessions to Westminster Abbey in 1504.[69] In 1535 the abbey received £3 16s. 8d. per annum for its demesne lands in Evershaw from Biddlesden Abbey.[70] This part of Evershaw apparently descended in part with the site of Luffield Priory and its manor of Thornborough to the Temple family, who held land here in the 18th century,[71] and in part with the priory's manor in Whitfield, Northamptonshire, with which it was purchased in 1720 by Worcester College, Oxford, who still hold.[72]

WORCESTER COLLEGE, OXFORD. *Or two cheverons gules between six martlets sable.*

Pain de Beauchamp is recorded to have given his other half hide to Biddlesden Abbey.[73] In this case the original total of land in Evershaw—1 hide—must have been considerably added to, for William de Evershaw, called lord of Evershaw, son of Hugh,[74] held half a fee of William de Beauchamp in the reign of Henry III.[75] The Evershaw family made extensive grants of lands to Biddlesden Abbey during this time. Hugh de Evershaw and his sons William, Ralph, Osbert, Philip, Henry and Walter gave lands amounting to over 100 acres to the abbey.[76] William de Evershaw also granted the monks his 'free park' and his 'free court to receive fines from malefactors and to do justice.'[77] Henry, his brother and heir, a chaplain, granted them his capital messuage with the rents of all his free tenants, ward, reliefs, escheats, &c., saving only foreign service to the king and 4s. 8d. annually to the priory of Luffield.[78]

Biddlesden continued to hold its portion of Evershaw, which included a mill,[79] until the Dissolution,[80] after which date it apparently became merged in the manor of Biddlesden.[81] According to the conveyance of 1540 the Biddlesden estate comprised Evershaw Park.[82]

GORRAL was apparently among the lands granted to Biddlesden by the Evershaw family.[83] In 1232 the abbot was granted twenty oaks in Whittlewood Forest to repair his grange of Gorral which was burnt.[84] It appears to have lain partly in Dadford Manor in Stowe parish,[85] with which it was assessed in the 13th century.[86] In 1540 it was granted to Sir George Giffard, kt.,[87] whose son Thomas[88] conveyed it to John Temple in 1570.[89] He died in 1603 seised of Gorral and also of the manors of Dadford and Stowe,[90] with which it was held as late as 1819.[91] Lands called Gorral woods, however, remained appurtenant to Biddlesden Manor.[92]

The church of *ST. MARGARET CHURCH* was built by Henry Sayer about 1730.

It is a plain brick building with stone dressings, having a turret with one bell. In the churchyard is a gravestone of 14th-century date, from Biddlesden Abbey.

The plate consists of a silver-gilt cup inscribed 'The guift of Mrs. Philadelphia Sayer to ye Church of Bidlesden 1702'; a small paten (also silver-gilt, as is the rest of the church plate), probably part of the same gift, inscribed 'P.S. 1702'; a large paten bearing the inscription 'This and the guilding the cup and cover the gift of Henry Sayer, esq. to the Church of Bidlesden 1735'; and a flagon and alms-dish presented in 1880.

The registers begin in 1686.

ADVOWSON The church of St. Mary at Biddlesden was confirmed to the monastery there by the Archbishop of Canterbury between the years 1147 and 1160,[93] and it seems to have become the conventual church

---

[60] *V.C.H. Bucks.* i, 245.

[61] *Red Bk. of Exch.* (Rolls Ser.), 746.

[62] *V.C.H. Bucks.* i, 275.

[63] *Abbrev. Plac.* (Rec. Com.), 26 ; *Hund. R.* (Rec. Com.), ii, 343.

[64] Harl. MS. 4714, fol. 41 d.

[65] *Hund. R.* loc. cit.

[66] *Abbrev. Plac.* loc. cit. This record states that Pain had given a hide, but this appears to be a mistake.

[67] *V.C.H. Beds.* iii, 9.

[68] *Abbrev. Plac.* loc. cit. The prior had a house in Evershaw (Harl. MS. 4714, fol. 38).

[69] *Feud. Aids,* i, 100, 108, 126 ; Early Chan. Proc. bdle. 11, no. 395 ; *V.C.H. Northants,* ii, 97.

[70] *Valor Eccl.* (Rec. Com.), iv, 238.

[71] See Thornborough ; Willis, op. cit. 156, 279, 289 ; Feet of F. Bucks. Mich. 6 Anne ; Trin. 13 Will. III.

[72] Cf. Willis, op. cit. 156.

[73] *Hund. R.* loc. cit.

[74] Harl. MS. 4714, fol. 28, 30.

[75] *Testa de Nevill* (Rec. Com.), 249. His name is mentioned several times during this reign in connexion with lands in Evershaw (Feet of F. Bucks. 12 Hen. III, no. 20 ; Hil. 25 Hen. III, no. 13).

[76] Harl. MS. 4714, fol. 28-44.

[77] Ibid. fol. 43b.   [78] Ibid. fol. 36b.

[79] *Hund. R.* (Rec. Com.), i, 33 ; ii, 343 ; *Pope Nich. Tax.* (Rec. Com.), 47.

[80] *Feud. Aids,* i, 100, 108, 126 ; *Valor Eccl.* (Rec. Com.), iv, 238.

[81] Pat. 7 Jas. I, pt. xx, no. 2 ; 14 Jas. I, pt. xxi, no. 16 ; cf. Harl. MS. 4714, fol. 28 et seq.

[82] Close 32 Hen. VIII, pt. ii, no. 19, 20.

[83] Harl. MS. 4714, fol. 28 d.

[84] Close, 16 Hen. III, m. 9.

[85] *Pope Nich. Tax.* loc. cit.

[86] Ibid. 47b.

[87] Pat. 31 Hen. VIII, pt. iv.

[88] Chan. Inq. p.m. (Ser. 2), cxx, 1.

[89] Pat. 12 Eliz. pt. ix ; Feet of F. Bucks. Mich. 13 Eliz.

[90] Chan. Inq. p.m. (Ser. 2), cclxxxi, 93.

[91] See also Stowe.

[92] Pat. 32 Hen. VIII, pt. iii, no. 26.

[93] Harl. Chart. 84, C 41.

BIDDLESDEN CHURCH FROM THE SOUTH-WEST

of that foundation.[94] After the Dissolution the patronage followed the descent of the manor, and is now vested in the Hon. Robert Morgan-Grenville. The benefice is a perpetual curacy.[95] The lord of the manor in the 16th century had to pay an annual stipend of £6 to the curate.[96] This was reduced to £4 in the early part of the 17th century,[97] but the incumbent was then said to have a little house of one bay adjoining the church, with tithes and oblations amounting to 20s. per annum.[98] Willis, however, states that in 1631 the stipend amounted to £20 per annum, with 40s. from lands, &c.[99] In 1720 the living was augmented by William Freind, a divine, and Alexander Denton, who gave £200 to enable it to obtain a grant from Queen Anne's Bounty.[100]

About 1293 the Bishop of Lincoln consecrated three altars in the church of Biddlesden.[101] Bishop Burghersh (1320–40) granted an indulgence for fabric, lights and ornaments therein.[102]

The chapel of St. Margaret, which served as the parish church in the 17th century after the destruction of the abbey building, existed as early as the 13th century, when Robert son of Osbert Carpenter granted a messuage and half an acre for the support of the said chapel.[103]

William lord of Evershaw in the 12th century gave the church of Evershaw to the priory of Luffield.[104] The name of 'Oliver, priest of Euersache' occurs as witness to a charter of the reign of Henry II.[105] In a later charter the names of Ralf, vicar of Evershaw, and Richard, chaplain of Evershaw, occur.[106] The church is mentioned as belonging to Luffield in 1291, when it was taxed at 13s. 4d.[107] In 1341–2 the value of the ninth in the 'parish of Evershaw' was again 1 mark only, as there was very little land in the parish.[108] A suit occurred towards the end of the 15th century between the prior and others concerning tithes due to Evershaw parsonage, which the prior farmed out; this document again mentions Evershaw as being a parish.[109] After Luffield Priory passed to Westminster its possessions were leased in 1513 to William Tyler and included the advowson of the chapel of St. Nicholas in Evershaw, with a cottage, 10½ acres of land and a rood of pasture in Evershaw.[110] In the grant of these Luffield possessions to Sir Nicholas Throckmorton in 1551 the chapel is not specifically mentioned, although 'Evershaw' is included among the long list of advowsons.[111] There is no later reference to this chapel, and it probably fell into disuse with the general decay of the parish.

There do not appear to be any endowed charities subsisting in this parish.

CAVERSFIELD

Cavrefelle (xi cent.); Kaueresfuld, Chauresfeld, Caffresfeld, Caueresfeud, Kaveresfeld (xii–xiii cent.); Catesfield (xviii cent.).

The parish of Caversfield, although entirely detached, was included in the county of Buckingham until the 19th century, when, by Acts of 1832[1] and 1844,[2] it was transferred to Oxfordshire. A detached portion of Caversfield was added to Stratton Audley by a Local Government Board Order dated 24 March 1888.[3] The entire parish has an area of 1,497 acres, of which 651 acres are arable land, 326 acres permanent grass and 5 acres are covered by woods and plantations.[4] The soil is cornbrash with a stony subsoil. The land in the north-west of the parish is about 360 ft. above the ordnance datum, and falls gradually about 100 ft. towards the south. The parish is crossed by the road from Banbury to Bicester and is bounded on the east by the Roman road from Bicester. There is no village, the buildings in the parish being mainly farms. Near the centre of the parish is Caversfield House, a large modern building, the seat of Mrs. Herbert Phillips, the lady of the manor. The church and old rectory-house lie to the west of it. The Home Farm, immediately south of the church on the west side of the road to Bicester, is a two-storied stone house dating from the 16th century, with original stone-mullioned windows on the south front. The windows of the upper story are of two lights with moulded jambs and mullions, and the ground-floor windows are also moulded and have square labels; they were originally of three lights, but the mullions have been removed and wood frames inserted. The house is now divided into tenements and the interior has been modernized. Near the house are two 16th-century stone barns lighted by narrow loopholes and roofed with thatch; one of these has been added to, somewhat altered and converted into a stable.

An Inclosure Act for the parish was passed in 1780.[5]

MANOR Edward, a man of Earl Tosti, held and could sell the 5-hide manor of CAVERSFIELD before the Conquest, but in 1086 it was among the possessions of William de Warenne.[6] The overlordship of the Earls Warenne lasted until the beginning of the 14th century,[7] but had passed before 1317 to Aymer de Valence, Earl of Pembroke,[8] at whose death in 1324 it was

---

[94] There is no record of it as a parish church until after the Dissolution. The episcopal registers, however, for 1312–13 show a licence granted to the abbot and convent in that year for 'the dedication of their convent church' (Linc. Epis. Reg. Memo. Dalderby, fol. 241 d.).

[95] One mention occurs in 1650 of the 'vicar of Biddlesden' (Cal. Com. for Comp. 191), but he is referred to in a general way with other incumbents, and probably the curate only was meant.

[96] Harl. MS. 4714, fol. 353, 357 d.

[97] Ld. Rev. Misc. Bks. ccx, fol. 13; Pat. 14 Jas. I, pt. xxi, no. 16.

[98] Ld. Rev. Misc. Bks. ccx, fol. 13.

[99] Willis, loc. cit.

[100] Dict. Nat. Biog.

[101] Linc. Epis. Reg. Memo. Sutton, fol. 97 d.   [102] Ibid. Burghersh, fol. 40.

[103] Harl. MS. 4714, fol. 43. Possibly it was originally a family chantry for the Evershaws. Hugh Carpenter, father of Osbert, is described as the son of John de Evershaw (Harl. MS. 4714, fol. 32, 36). It stood outside the abbey precincts (ibid. fol. 43).

[104] Hund. R. (Rec. Com.), ii, 343; Dugdale, Mon. Angl. iv, 350.

[105] Harl. Chart. 84, H 47.

[106] Ibid. 85, D 22.

[107] Pope Nich. Tax. (Rec. Com.), 32b.

[108] Inq. Nonarum (Rec. Com.), 330.

[109] Early Chan. Proc. bdle. 11, no. 395.

[110] Willis, op. cit. 224, quoting documents now at Westminster.

[111] Pat. 5 Edw. VI, pt. iii, m. 11.

[1] Stat. 2 & 3 Will. IV, cap. 64.

[2] Stat. 7 & 8 Vict. cap. 61.

[3] Loc. Govt. Bd. Order 21435.

[4] Statistics from Bd. of Agric. (1905).

[5] Priv. Act, 20 Geo. III, cap. 43.

[6] V.C.H. Bucks. i, 253.

[7] Harl. MS. 3688, fol. 126b, 127b; Feud. Aids, i, 87; Cal. Pat. 1317–21, p. 150.

[8] De Banco R. Mich. 11 Edw. II, m. 419; Chan. Inq. p.m. 17 Edw. II, no. 75.

inherited by his second sister's daughter and co-heir Joan wife of the Earl of Athole.[9] Their son and grandson held it,[10] but after the death of the latter in 1375, notwithstanding a claim to the fee put in by his daughter and co-heir Philippa, then wife of Sir John Halsham,[11] it passed to the heirs of Aymer de Valence's eldest sister.[12] Joan, widow of Lord Bergavenny, died seised of the overlordship in 1435,[13] and though the names of the overlords are not afterwards mentioned, this connexion can be

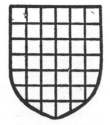

WARENNE. *Checky or and azure.*

traced until the 17th century in the attachment of Caversfield, from the 14th century onwards, to the fee of Castle Acre, Norfolk, one of the manors held by William de Warenne in 1086.[14] In 1559 the manor was said to be held of the queen at fee farm,[15] but this statement obviously applies only to that part of Caversfield formerly belonging to Bicester Priory.

William de Warenne's tenant in 1086 was Brienz.[16] Caversfield was probably held in the 12th century by the Gargate family, who owned lands in Northamptonshire, in connexion with which the names of Hugh and Robert Gargate occur in 1181–2.[17] Roger Gargate appears to have been tenant in Caversfield about the end of that century,[18] and was succeeded by Hugh Gargate or Hugh de Caversfield,[19] son of Roger Gargate and Agnes.[20] He was alive in 1216,[21] but died before 1220, in which year his widow Sibyl attempted to regain possession of lands once her husband's.[22] She was plaintiff in an agreement made in 1227 with Osmund son of Robert about a virgate in Caversfield[23] and was still alive in 1244.[24] Hugh and Sibyl's daughters and co-heirs, Isabel wife of Gerard son of Roger de Munbury (?) and Muriel widow of William de Ros, inherited the land here,[25] but 1236 appears to be the last date in which mention is found of either. They endowed the priory of Bicester with lands here amounting to half the entire vill (see below). The remaining part was held apparently between 1236 and 1254 by Walter de Norton and William Hay, the former's immediate overlord being 'Garin fil' Keroldi' (Gerold ?).[26]

In 1254–5 William Hay held 2½ hides, the whole of the moiety of Caversfield which was not in ecclesiastical hands,[27] and by 1284–6 his interest had passed to William de Wynncote, who held direct of Earl Warenne.[28] Already at this date William de Wynncote had subinfeudated Simon de Wynncote in the manor,[29] but rights of overlordship were retained by his heirs as late as the 17th century.[30] In 1622, during a Chancery suit concerning this manor (with which the second manor of Caversfield had by then become amalgamated), the defendant stated that although the lord of the manor claimed that a moiety of it was held of the heirs of William de Wynncote, yet 'the said tenure is to no purpose as well for the uncertainty what moiety was so held as for the name of the heirs of William de Wynncote.'[31]

Simon de Wynncote, who held, as had been said, in 1284,[32] received in 1286–7 a quitclaim of a carucate of land from John le Bret on behalf of Sarah his wife,[33] and a Simon was still seised in 1316.[34] John de Wynncote succeeded to the manor by an arrangement made in 1312 with Simon whereby the latter was to hold nineteen messuages, 2 carucates and 7 virgates of land, 10s. rent and half a mill in Caversfield of John for life at a rose rent, with reversion to John.[35] John de Wynncote died in or before 1317, as Eleanor, probably his widow, wife of John Hampton, claimed dower at the end of the year; it was found that John de Wynncote's heir was a minor.[36] A John de Wynncote held in 1324[37] and in 1346.[38] By 1350 the manor was in possession of John de Peyto, who conveyed it in that year to Fulk de Birmingham.[39] In 1386 John de Birmingham, son of Fulk,[40] and Elizabeth his wife conveyed Caversfield to John Tame,[41] but whether for purposes of settlement or not is not recorded. Caversfield afterwards came to the Langstons, and an inquisition taken in 1435, after the death of John Langston, lord of Bucknell in Oxfordshire, speaks of him as 'of Caversfield.'[42] His son and heir John, then aged six,[43] on attaining his majority sued Robert Gilbert, Bishop of London, and others whom his father had enfeoffed to the uses of his will for their refusal to make him an estate of Caversfield.[44] John Langston married Amice daughter of John Danvers, and in 1449 a settlement was made on them and their heirs.[45] By his will, dated 16 February 1499–1500, John Langston desired to be buried in the chancel of St. Laurence, Caversfield, and left instructions for two priests to celebrate mass for seven years for the souls of himself and his wife Elizabeth,[46] whom he had evidently married after the death of Amice. At his death in 1506 he was succeeded by his son and heir Richard, aged forty,[47]

---

[9] Chan. Inq. p.m. 17 Edw. II, no. 75 ; 1 Edw. III (1st nos.), no. 85.

[10] Ibid. 50 Edw. III (1st nos.), no. 93 ; 14 Ric. II, no. 139b.

[11] Ibid. 50 Edw. III (1st nos.), no. 93.

[12] G.E.C. *Peerage,* i, 17 ; vi, 208, 211.

[13] Chan. Inq. p.m. 14 Hen. VI, no. 35.

[14] *Feud. Aids,* i, 124 ; Exch. Inq. p.m. (Ser. 2), file 5, no. 13 ; Chan. Inq. p.m. (Ser. 2), xlv, 31 ; Chan. Proc. Eliz. M 3, no. 45.

[15] Chan. Inq. p.m. (Ser. 2), cxxii, 12.

[16] *V.C.H. Bucks.* i, 253.

[17] *Pipe R.* 28 *Hen. II* (Pipe R. Soc.), 119.

[18] Harl. MS. 3688, fol. 126b (see advowson).

[19] Ibid.   [20] Ibid.

[21] *Red Bk. of Exch.* (Rolls Ser.), 619 ; *Rot. Lit. Claus.* (Rec. Com.), i, 288b. There is reference to him in 1207–8 (*Rot. de Oblatis et Fin.* [Rec. Com.], 460).

[22] *Excerpta e Rot. Fin.* (Rec. Com.), i, 43.

[23] *Feet of F.* Bucks. 12 Hen. III, no. 25.

[24] Aug. Off. Misc. Bks. xlv, fol. 258. See also Harl. MS. 3688, fol. 126b, 127b ; *Cat. of Anct. D.* iii, 537.

[25] Harl. MS. 3688, fol. 126b, 127b ; Maitland, *Bracton's Note Bk.* ii, 615.

[26] *Testa de Nevill* (Rec. Com.), 243.

[27] *Hund. R.* (Rec. Com.), i, 29.

[28] *Feud. Aids,* i, 87.

[29] Ibid.

[30] Chan. Inq. p.m. 1 Edw. III (1st nos.), no. 85 ; 14 Hen. VI, no. 35 ; (Ser. 2), xlv, 31 ; Chan. Proc. Eliz. M 3, no. 45.

[31] Chan. Proc. (Ser. 2), bdle. 388, no. 16.

[32] *Feud. Aids,* i, 87.

[33] Feet of F. case 17, file 55.

[34] *Feud. Aids,* i, 99, 109.

[35] Feet of F. case 18, file 64.

[36] De Banco R. Mich. 11 Edw. II, m. 419.

[37] Chan. Inq. p.m. 17 Edw. II, no. 75. A messuage and 2 virgates in Caversfield were held of the Wynncotes by the Chastillons of Thornton in the 14th century (ibid. 11 Edw. III [1st nos.], no. 33 ; 21 Edw. III [2nd nos.], no. 74).

[38] *Feud. Aids,* i, 124.

[39] Feet of F. case 287, file 44.

[40] *Gen.* (New Ser.), xvi, 44.

[41] Feet of F. case 21, file 106.

[42] Chan. Inq. p.m. 14 Hen. VI, no. 38.

[43] Ibid.

[44] Early Chan. Proc. bdle. 14, no. 29.

[45] Pat. 27 Hen. VI, pt. i, m. 20.

[46] P.C.C. 12 Adeane.

[47] Exch. Inq. p.m. (Ser. 2), file 5, no. 13.

though another son Thomas was made executor of the will.[48]

Richard Langston made a settlement of the manor in 1508,[49] and in 1511 leased it to Thomas Denton for a term of twenty years at an annual rent of £26.[50] About 1525 he brought a suit against the lessee, who 'of his subtle and crafty mind, being expert in making of writings,' had forged a new lease granting himself a further term in the manor.[51] Richard Langston died in December 1525, leaving a son John as heir.[52] Joan, Richard's widow, held the manor in dower,[53] and married John Harman,[54] whose second wife, Dame Dorothy Guido, was afterwards sued by the lord of the manor for retaining in her possession deeds and other evidences concerning the title.[55] John Langston meanwhile made a settlement of the manor in 1554,[56] and died in 1558, when his heir was his nephew, Thomas Moyle,

LANGSTON. *Gules a cheveron ermine between three hinds or.*

MOYLE. *Gules a mule passant argent.*

son of his sister Amy.[57] Langston, however, made more than one will attempting to dispose of the property as he pleased, and the manor was the subject of several lawsuits during the next few years. By a will of 1556 he had bequeathed Caversfield to his godson, Thomas Denton.[58] A later will, dated 1558, is mentioned in the inquisition, giving the manor to Thomas Pigott of Doddershall and his heirs.[59] Directly after Langston's death Thomas Denton and John his father resisted the claim of Thomas Pigott, declaring the will of 1558 to be a forgery.[60] The Dentons' suit succeeded; the second will was disallowed, and Thomas Denton appears to have held the manor until his death, which occurred before 1563.[61] In that year Denton's brother and heir John was sued for the manor by Thomas Moyle, Langston's heir-at-law, who declared that, as Thomas Denton had died without issue, the manor under the terms of the will should revert to him, Moyle.[62] He was apparently successful in proving this claim, and in 1587 obtained a quitclaim from the Pigott family

also.[63] In the same year he demised the manor (*inter alia*) for twenty-one years at an annual rent of £77 6s. 8d. to Walter Moyle, whose interest and term of years were after his death conveyed in 1595–6 by his executor to Edward Ewer.[64] Meanwhile Thomas Moyle died without issue in 1592, bequeathing the manor to his second cousin, Thomas Moyle of Molash, Kent, with remainder to his sons John and Thomas in tail-male.[65] Thomas Moyle in 1598 settled the manor on his son John and regained possession from the lessee, Ewer, who had committed waste on the lands.[66] Afterwards, according to the father's evidence in a lawsuit,[67] John promised that if his father would 'be good unto him,' pay his debts and keep him he would renounce all claim to the manor. Thomas paid the debts, amounting to about £1,000, but his son 'matched himself to a gentlewoman that brought him no portion' without the consent of his father, who could have married him to a lady having £1,500 as portion, and did not mend his ways in other directions. In consequence of his behaviour Thomas determined in 1614 to settle the manor finally on his second son Thomas, who, 'taking better courses of life,' had married Mary daughter of Sir Henry North, kt., the heiress of his father's choice.[68] John Moyle in 1621–2 claimed the manor under the deed of 1598.[69] The father offered to give him sufficient lands for his support if he would renounce his life interest.[70] Thomas Moyle, who died in 1622, in his will bitterly complains of the conduct of his son John, and continues: 'I am in doubt to him what to give because he dealt so lewedly with me . . . He also married a wife against my will. However because he made over the manor of Caversfield to me again . . . though I bought it of him at a dear rate.' Thomas nevertheless settled on John and his male issue the mansion and site of Caversfield with the dove-house, 'fishpools and islands in the said site being the old walls' and other premises.[71] The two sons, John and Thomas Moyle, made a joint settlement of the manor in 1624,[72] and dealt with it again in 1634.[73] In that year a conveyance was made to Sir Cecil Trafford and Humphrey Davenport,[74] probably in settlement on the marriage of James Davenport, son of Humphrey, with Mary daughter and co-heir of Thomas Moyle.[75] Thomas Moyle died in 1649,[76] and James Davenport sold the manor in 1653 to Maximilian Bard,[77] who died in 1690.[78] Thomas Bard, his son, succeeded him,[79] and joined with his sons in 1704 in selling Caversfield to William Vaux,[80] who was lord of the manor in 1735.[81] By his will, proved 19 July 1737, William Vaux left his real and personal estate, subject

[48] P.C.C. 12 Adeane. This Thomas, to whom his father bequeathed 2,000 sheep, was sheriff of the county in 1496 and 1523 (P.R.O. *List of Sheriffs*, 2, 3).
[49] Chan. Inq. p.m. (Ser. 2), cxxii, 12.
[50] Early Chan. Proc. bdle. 538, no. 5.
[51] Ibid.
[52] Chan. Inq. p.m. (Ser. 2), xlv, 31.
[53] Ibid. cxxii, 12.
[54] Close, 32 Hen. VIII, pt. ii, no. 56.
[55] Chan. Proc. (Ser. 2), bdle. 130, no. 7.
[56] Chan. Inq. p.m. (Ser. 2), cxxii, 12.
[57] Ibid.
[58] Chan. Proc. (Ser. 2), bdle. 50, no. 83.
[59] Chan. Inq. p.m. (Ser. 2), cxxii, 12.
[60] Chan. Proc. (Ser. 2), bdle. 50, no. 83.

[61] Ibid. bdle. 130, no. 6.
[62] Ibid.
[63] Feet of F. Bucks. Trin. 29 Eliz.
[64] Chan. Proc. (Ser. 2), bdle. 388, no. 16.
[65] Ibid. Eliz. M 3, no. 45; Chan. Inq. p.m. (Ser. 2), ccxxxviii, 78.
[66] Chan. Proc. (Ser. 2), bdle. 388, no. 16.
[67] Ibid.
[68] Ibid.; Feet of F. Bucks. Trin. 9 Jas. I; Trin. 12 Jas. I; *Visit. of Notts.* (Harl. Soc.), 173.
[69] Chan. Proc. (Ser. 2), bdle. 388, no. 16.
[70] Ibid.
[71] P.C.C. 108 Savile; Chan. Inq. p.m. (Ser. 2), ccccxix, 35.

[72] Feet of F. Bucks. East. 22 Jas. I; Recov. R. East. 22 Jas. I, m. 53.
[73] Feet of F. Bucks. Trin. 10 Chas. I; Recov. R. Trin. 10 Chas. I, m. 105.
[74] Feet of F. Div. Co. Trin. 10 Chas. I.
[75] *Visit. of Notts.* loc. cit.
[76] P.C.C. 147 Fairfax. He speaks of Humphrey Davenport as his son-in-law.
[77] Recov. R. Hil. 1653, m. 6; Feet of F. Div. Co. 1653; Recov. R. Mich. 1656, m. 254.
[78] *Coll. Topog. et Gen.* iv, 60; P.C.C. 155 Vire.
[79] *Coll. Topog. et Gen.* iv, 60; Feet of F. Div. Co. Mich. 2 Jas. II; Recov. R. Mich. 9 Will. III, m. 26.
[80] Willis, *Hist. and Antiq. of Buckingham*, 166.
[81] Ibid.

to certain bequests, to his son John,[82] who died without issue in 1740. His instructions to his sister Abigail Gregory to sell Caversfield and pay his debts[83] were carried out in the following year, when Sir James Harington, bart., acquired the property for £3,000, Abigail's sister, Cecilia wife of Richard Serjeant, renouncing any claim to the manor.[84] Ten years later Richard Harington, representative of Sir James, sold it for the same amount to John Southcote.[85] In 1764 the latter sold to Joseph Bullock for £3,400 and the payment of a £40 life annuity to his brother George Southcote *alias* Parker.[86] Bullock, who was sheriff of the county in 1781,[87] at his death in 1806 left a daughter and heir Amelia Frances wife of Canon the Hon. Jacob Marsham.[88] She died in 1836, her husband surviving her four years, and Caversfield passed to their son, Robert Bullock-Marsham, D.C.L., warden of Merton College, who held until his death in 1880.[89] His son Charles Jacob Bullock-Marsham

BULLOCK. *Gules a cheveron ermine between three bulls' heads cabossed argent with horns or.*

MARSHAM. *Argent a lion passant bendways gules between two bends azure.*

alienated the manor about 1897 to Mr. Herbert E. Phillips, whose widow is the present owner.

The property of the Gargates in Caversfield in the 13th century included a windmill and water-mill and 'the capital court of Caversfield.'[90] In the 16th and 17th centuries the manor-house was included in the Moyle property.[91] A lease made of it in 1588-9 excepted to the use of Thomas Moyle a chamber over the kitchen and inner chamber over the larder and the gallery over the said chamber, the stable near the brew-house with ingress and egress.[92] It is mentioned in the sales in the manorial property in the 18th century, at which time a close called the Park, containing 21 acres, was also included.[93]

In the 13th century Muriel de Ros, daughter of Hugh Gargate, granted land here to the priory of Bicester in Oxfordshire.[94] Isabel, the other daughter, also made a grant in 1236,[95] and both gifts were confirmed by John de Warenne, Earl of Surrey, in 1308.[96] In 1254-5 the prior held 2½ hides here, a

moiety of the whole fee,[97] and continued to hold it until the Dissolution,[98] when the farm of the manor was worth 53s. 4d. annually.[99] The property was held at farm by the Langston family, to one of whom, John Langston, the prior had demised it in 1487 as the 'moiety of the manor of Caversfield.'[100] The Langstons and their heirs held the rest of Caversfield in fee-tail (see above), a circumstance which led to numerous disputes in the 16th century, since they evidently tried to amalgamate both the estate held at farm and that held in fee as one manor held in fee.

In 1563 the queen granted the manor of the late priory in Caversfield to Robert Hitchcock and his heirs.[1] Suits at law between Hitchcock and Thomas Moyle followed[2]; the former's interest was vested in Edward Ewer before 1602, and disputes between Ewer and the Moyles continued,[3] both as regards this estate, which Ewer claimed to hold in fee of the Crown, the Moyles being only the lessees of it, and the other estate in which he was the lessee and the Moyles the real owners.[4] His right in the priory manor seems to have been upheld, since the Crown made a regrant to him and his heirs in 1604.[5] In 1610 the annual rent of 53s. 4d. received by the Crown for this manor was granted to Anthony Aucher and Thomas Hardres, kts.,[6] but it seems probable that the estate was afterwards obtained by the Moyles, since in the somewhat lengthy lawsuit between Thomas Moyle and his son John in 1621-2 it certainly appears that the family were seised in fee of both properties and held them as one manor.[7]

The church of *ST. LAURENCE* consists of a chancel measuring internally about 27 ft. 9 in. by 13 ft. 10 in., north vestry and organ chamber, nave 29 ft. by 13 ft. 6 in., north and south aisles each 6 ft. 4 in. wide, and a west tower 11 ft. 2 in. by 10 ft. 6 in.

CHURCH

The ground stage of the tower, which retains two original windows in the north and south walls, is probably of pre-Conquest date. The walls are of small limestone rubble, but the quoins have all been renewed. The tower arch, though entirely restored, represents in all probability a late 12th-century enlargement of the original opening, and the west window may have been inserted at the same date, when the upper part of the tower appears to have been first rebuilt; the 12th-century doorway reset in the north wall of the present north aisle affords evidence that some considerable repair of the fabric was undertaken at that period. Early in the 13th century the bell-chamber of the tower was rebuilt or added, the chancel reconstructed, and north and south aisles were added to the nave. The doorway in the north wall of the chancel leading to the present vestry, which

---

[82] P.C.C. 172 Wake.

[83] Ibid. 158 Browne.

[84] Close, 15 Geo. II, pt. xii, no. 3 ; Feet of F. Bucks. Trin. 14 & 15 Geo. II.

[85] Close, 25 Geo. II, pt. viii, no. 1.

[86] Ibid. 4 Geo. III, pt. xviii, no. 9 ; this annuity had been settled on George Southcote *alias* Parker (Feet of F. Div. Co. East. 25 Geo. II), who evidently had some rights in the manor, in 1755 (Close, 6 Geo. III, pt. xiii, no. 11), and was renounced by him to Bullock in 1766 (ibid.).

[87] P.R.O. *List of Sheriffs*, 10.

[88] Mural tablet in church.

[89] *Ret. of Owners of Land*, 1873, Bucks. 13 ; Lipscomb, *Hist. and Antiq. of Bucks.* ii, 596.

[90] *Cat. of Anct. D.* (i, 304 ; iii, 537). A mill is mentioned in 1312 (Feet of F. case 18, file 64).

[91] Chan. Proc. Eliz. Ee 3, no. 63 ; P.C.C. 108 Savile.

[92] Chan. Proc. Eliz. Ee 3, no. 63.

[93] Close, 15 Geo. II, pt. xii, no. 3, &c.

[94] *Cat. of Anct. D.* i, 304.

[95] Ibid. iii, 537.

[96] *Cal. Pat.* 1317-21, p. 150.

[97] *Hund. R.* (Rec. Com.), i, 29.

[98] *Pope Nich. Tax.* (Rec. Com.), 47 ;

Feud. *Aids*, i, 87, 99, 109, 124 ; Mins. Accts. (Gen. Ser.), bdle. 957, no. 11-16.

[99] Dugdale, *Mon. Angl.* vi, 432 ; *Valor Eccl.* (Rec. Com.), ii, 188.

[100] *Var. Coll.* (Hist. MSS. Com.), ii, 3.

[1] Pat. 5 Eliz. pt. v, m. 9.

[2] Chan. Proc. Eliz. Mm 3, no. 45.

[3] Ibid.

[4] Ibid. ; Ee 3, no. 63.

[5] *Cal. S. P. Dom.* 1603-10, p. 97.

[6] Pat. 8 Jas. I, pt. xliii, no. 5. A lease of the manor had been made to Archibald Napper in 1608 (ibid. 5 Jas. I, pt. xxix, m. 1).

[7] Chan. Proc. (Ser. 2), bdle. 388, no. 16.

has a shouldered head and jambs with the rebate on the vestry side, suggests the addition of a north vestry about 1300, but it is possible that it was not adapted to its present use till the restoration of the church in the last century. The arch to the organ chamber at the west end of the north wall of the chancel is probably that which is referred to by Parker in *A guide to the architectural antiquities in the neighbourhood of Oxford* (1846) as being then the chancel arch, and was moved here in 1874. As they now stand, the vestry and organ chamber date from 1874, when the nave aisles, which had been pulled down, probably in the 18th century, were rebuilt, the chancel arch renewed, and the whole building, with the exception of the tower, reroofed.

In the east wall of the chancel is a pair of early 13th-century lancets with plain wide internal splays, and labels on both faces. The internal labels intersect at their junction and are original, but the linked external labels appear to have been restored. At the east end of the north wall is a small aumbry, to the west of which, within the present sanctuary, is a recess with a two-centred head, all of modern stonework and probably made in 1874 for the Langston tomb which now stands in it. The remaining features in this wall are the doorway to the vestry and the arch to the organ chamber referred to above; the latter is two-centred and of two chamfered orders with responds worked to a single wide chamfer on each face. At the south-east is a rough trefoil-headed piscina with a quatrefoil basin, and immediately to the west of it is an early 14th-century window of two acutely pointed cinquefoiled lights with a quatrefoiled spandrel in a two-centred head. Near the centre of the wall is an original lancet and at the south-west is a square-headed early 15th-century window of two cinquefoiled lights. All these windows have been very much restored, their rear arches being modern. The present chancel arch was built at the general restoration in 1874 and is constructed almost entirely of modern stonework. The walling of the chancel is of limestone rubble and the original window dressings are of a yellow sandstone. Limestone is used for the later insertions, the south-east window being of a dark brown stone of a ferruginous nature. The north window of the organ chamber is of three lights, and has original leaf tracery of about 1360 reset, but its original position is doubtful.

The early 13th-century nave arcades are each of two bays with two-centred arches of two orders supported by a central circular column and semicircular responds. The work has been very much patched and restored, the capitals having been considerably damaged by the blocking inserted in the bays when the aisles were pulled down. The south arcade is of slightly earlier character than the north arcade, and has spurred bases of a pronounced Attic type, standing upon square plinths with roll-moulded sub-plinths. The bases of the north arcade are also spurred, but the hollow has become a water table, and the projecting sub-plinths have their upper edges plainly chamfered. The capitals of both arcades are foliated and have volute leaves at the angles, with human heads or leaves on each face, their moulded

abaci being square. The arches are roll-moulded and the outer orders are enriched by a band of dog-tooth, while the inclosing labels are ornamented with the nail-head. The walls pierced by the arcades are only 2 ft. 1 in. in thickness, and, if not actually of pre-Conquest date, are most probably built on the foundations of the original nave. Reset in the north wall of the modern north aisle is a good doorway of the last half of the 12th century, recessed in two round-arched orders, the outer order having shafted jambs. The head of this order is moulded with a keel inclosed by 'dentelle' ornament, and has a roll-moulded label with head-stops; the inner order has a roll enriched with leaves. No other original detail remains in the aisles, which are designed in the 13th-century manner.

The tower rises in three stages marked by slight set-offs, and is crowned by a saddle-back roof gabled east and west. The restored tower arch has square jambs with chamfered abaci, and a plain arch slightly pointed with a chamfered label. The early windows lighting the ground stage on the north and south have heads roughly semicircular in form, and are set near the middle of the wall with wide splays on both

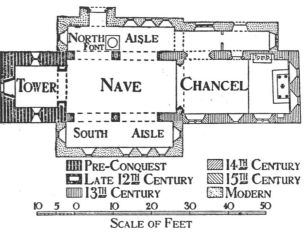

PRE-CONQUEST   14ᵀᴴ CENTURY
LATE 12ᵀᴴ CENTURY   15ᵀᴴ CENTURY
13ᵀᴴ CENTURY   MODERN

SCALE OF FEET

PLAN OF CAVERSFIELD CHURCH

faces. The actual opening in each case is about 6 in. wide and 1 ft. 2 in. high, and appears to be perforated in a block of tufa-like stone. Internally the openings are increased by the splaying of the jambs, head and sill to a width of about 2 ft. 4 in. and a height of 3 ft. 10 in., while they are splayed to about the same dimensions externally, where the radiation of the stones forming their heads interrupts the coursing of the limestone rubble for some distance round. The round-headed window in the west wall is entirely modern externally, though one or two original stones remain in the internal jambs. A slight difference in the walling marks the later work of the two upper stages. In the west wall of the ringing chamber is a modern window of two round-headed lights with old internal jambs, probably of the late 12th century. The bell-chamber is lighted on the east and west by tall lancets with modern external stonework. The gables to the saddle-back roof have been renewed, but the internal jambs of the windows and the timbers in the roof show much of the work to be of the early 13th century.

The font has a modern base supporting an early 12th-century tub-shaped bowl about 2 ft. 3 in. in diameter and 1 ft. 8½ in. deep, encircled by a roughly carved intersecting arcade.

On the nave floor near the chancel arch is a marble slab with three brass scrolls issuing from a heart held by two hands ; the heart bears the word 'credo,' and the scrolls are inscribed respectively 'heu michi domine quia pecavi nimis in vita mea,' 'quid faciam miser ubi fugiam nisi ad te deus meus,' and 'miserere mei dum veneris in novissimo die.' The inscription below has been lost, but at the foot of the slab is a shield of Denton impaling a cross moline, presumably that of John Denton, father-in-law to the Richard Langston mentioned below. Affixed to the wall at the south-east of the north aisle are the brass figures of a man in a fur-lined cloak with head uncovered and a lady in a long cloak and gabled head-dress. There are also groups of twelve sons and ten daughters with two shields of Langston and one of Langston quartering Danvers ; these brasses, now detached from the slab in which they were originally placed, are to John Langston, who died in 1506, and Amice his wife. A fragment 'Deus Amen.' near this group is doubtless the end of the upper inscription given in full by Lipscomb [8] ; and the lower inscription, which remains in full and is now placed near the table tomb in the chancel, runs as follows : 'O pater excelse miserere precor miserere | Johannis langston et conjugis amisie | Atque sue sobilis (sic) que te in terra coluere | Hosce velis oro jungere celicolis.' The table tomb already referred to doubtless commemorates Richard Langston, son of the above John Langston, who married Joan daughter of John Denton. It stands in the modern recess on the north side of the chancel, and has a Purbeck marble top slab with moulded edges ; the sides are divided into traceried panels, three in front and one at either end, in the centre of each of which is a shield painted with the arms of Langston impaling Denton, some of the coats being very indistinct. On the wall at the south-east of the north aisle is a brass inscription to Raulf Heydon (d. 1592), in the nave before the chancel arch is a floor slab with arms to Maximilian Bard (d. 1690), and there is another floor slab at the east end of the south aisle to Thomas Bard (d. 1719), while in the tower are tablets to Rebecca Meggott (d. 1782), Christian Walter (d. 1789), and William Ellis, vicar of the parish (d. 1795).

The tower contains a ring of three bells. The treble is a most interesting bell, the date of which, about 1200, can be established by the inscription on the sound-bow ; this has been reversed in the casting, and reads from right to left. Some of the letters are now illegible, and q's are used in place of g's, but the following reading has been prepared with great probability [9] : 'Hug(h) Gargat Sibillaq(ue) u(x)or h(aec) ti(m)ppana fecerunt e(x)poni.' On the waist is the inscription in plain characters, 'In honore Dei et Santi Laurencii.' The second was recast by

J. Taylor & Co. of Loughborough in 1874 from a 14th-century bell inscribed 'In honore Beati Laurencii,' and the tenor was recast by the same firm in 1876 from a companion bell to the treble.

The plate consists of a cup of 1657 inscribed on the foot, 'The communion cup of Caversfeild in the county of Buckingham,' a large salver of 1783 inscribed, 'In honore Dei et Sancti Laurentii,' a flagon of 1874, a plated flagon, and two plated patens.

The registers before 1812 are as follows : (i) baptisms 1640 to 1769, marriages 1650 to 1753, burials 1658 to 1762 (one entry 1796) ; some leaves of this book have been extracted and parts of others torn off ; (ii) baptisms 1764 to 1810, burials 1769 to 1811 ; (iii) marriages 1754 to 1810.

ADVOWSON   The church of Caversfield was given to the Abbot and convent of Missenden in the 12th century by Roger Gargate to be held, together with an acre of his demesne, in free alms.[10] Guy, parson of the church, is mentioned in the charter,[11] and his predecessors in that position are also referred to.[12] Hugh son of Roger confirmed the gift.[13] A vicarage was ordained during or before the early years of the 13th century, when the vicar, presented by the abbot, received all small tithes and half the tithes of 6 virgates in Stratton, and had a suitable house with 2 acres of land [14] ; it was found that one chaplain sufficed for the cure.[15] In 1291 the church was valued at £6 13s. 4d.[16] and at £6 in 1535.[17] The abbey continued to hold until the Dissolution.[18] In 1545 a grant in fee of the rectory and advowson was made to Richard Ingram and Anthony Foster.[19] Their interest appears to have passed within a year to Thomas Denton, who conveyed in 1545–6 to John Langston,[20] lord of the manor, with which the advowson has since been held,[21] the patronage of the vicarage, which has been annexed to Stoke Lyne, being now in the possession of Mrs. Phillips. John Langston's widow afterwards married Robert Hitchcock, who was sued by Thomas Moyle for retaining possession of all deeds and evidences relating to the title of the rectory [22] ; Moyle's claim to the latter was questioned by Hitchcock, who thought that as John Langston left no issue the property should revert to the Dentons.[23] The Moyles, however, successfully upheld their right, and the rectory afterwards passed with the manor.[24]

Roger Gargate also granted to Missenden half a hide of land here for which the proper service was to be rendered to him and his heirs.[25] These heirs afterwards released their overlordship rights to the abbey, which then held the half hide direct of the Earl Warenne for the service due from a tenth part of the whole vill of Caversfield.[26] The value of this property was given as only 11s. 11d. in 1291,[27] but nevertheless in 1302 the abbot, at the instigation of Walter Agmondesham, was granted free warren in

---

[8] Op. cit. ii, 599.

[9] V.C.H. Bucks. ii, 116.

[10] Harl. MS. 3688, fol. 126b.

[11] Ibid.

[12] Ibid.

[13] Ibid.

[14] Liber Antiq. Hugonis Wells, 13 ; R. of Hugh of Wells (Cant. and York Soc.), ii, 66.

[15] R. of Hugh of Wells (Cant. and York Soc.), i, 196.

[16] Pope Nich. Tax. (Rec. Com.), 32.

[17] Valor Eccl. (Rec. Com.), iv, 238.

[18] Cal. Papal Letters, v, 435.

[19] L. and P. Hen. VIII, xx (1), g. 621 (7).

[20] Chan. Proc. (Ser. 2), bdle. 129, no. 74.

[21] Chan. Inq. p.m. (Ser. 2), cxxii, 12 ; Inst. Bks. (P.R.O.).

[22] Chan. Proc. (Ser. 2), bdle. 129, no. 74.

[23] Ibid.

[24] Feet of F. Bucks. Trin. 7 Chas. I.

[25] Harl. MS. 3688, fol. 126b.

[26] Ibid. fol. 126b, 127b.

[27] Pope Nich. Tax. (Rec. Com.), 47. The Master of Farley, Bedfordshire, had lands worth 14s. at this date. Earlier in the century the Master granted to Muriel, widow of William de Ros, a messuage in Caversfield which Roger de Cublington, clk., had bestowed upon the hospital (Aug. Off. Misc. Bk. xlv, fol. 280).

his demesne lands at Caversfield among other places,[28] and the charter was confirmed in 1426.[29]

CHARITIES Thomas Mansfield, by deed of 22 January 1874, gave £150, the interest thereof to be divided among eight of the oldest deserving poor. The gift was invested in £162 12s. consols with the official trustees, the annual dividends of which, amounting to £4 1s. 4d., are equally divided among the eight beneficiaries.

CHETWODE

Cetwuda (x cent.); Ceteode (xi cent.); Chettewuda (xii cent.); Chetwod, Chetewode, Chetwode (xiii-xiv cent.); Chytwood (xvi-xix cent.).

This parish covers 1,171 acres, of which 983 are permanent grass and 138 arable land; there are 14 acres of woods and plantations.[1] The land falls gradually from about 383 ft. above the ordnance datum in the north to a little under 300 ft. in the south, where the ground is liable to flood from a tributary of the Ouse. The Great Central railway crosses the parish.

There is no actual village, but several scattered farms, among them Sunflower Farm, a stone building dating from the 17th century. On the gable of a staircase wing on the north side is the inscription 'T.B.C. 1662, P.H.' Priory House, built on the site of the small house of Austin Canons established here in 1245 by Ralph de Norwich,[2] stands about the centre of the parish. The only traces of the old priory are found in the church, which superseded the parish church in 1480, the fish-ponds and moats. In 1285 the priory buildings, except the church which 'contained the Host,' were burnt by 'certain malevolent persons,'[3] and the canons were thereupon granted protection whilst collecting alms for their relief.[4] After the Dissolution the house built here was for many generations the home of the Risleys, but the present house dates only from about 1833.[5]

In 1290 the prior and canons were granted an annual three-day fair to be held at their priory on the feast of the Nativity of the Blessed Mary.[6]

Half a mile north-east of the church is the Manor House, with the site of the old parish church and graveyard near by. A long avenue of trees leads to the road near which, and at a little distance from the gates, is the site of the hermitage of St. Stephen and St. Lawrence.

The house is a brick and stone building of two stories with an attic, consisting of a T-shaped house of about 1600 with substantial 18th-century and modern additions on the east. The original part retains its stone-mullioned windows, some of which are now blocked, and two old chimney stacks, one with diagonal shafts. The kitchen on the south-west has a wide-arched fireplace, and there is a stone moulded fireplace with a four-centred head in a passage on the first floor. Over the kitchen is an oak panelled room with moulded panels, carved frieze, and oak fireplace and overmantel, all dating from the first half of the 17th century. The fireplace is flanked by columns of Doric type supporting a mantelpiece enriched with conventional ornament and lions' heads, and the overmantel consists of a large panel

CHETWODE MANOR HOUSE

with an heraldic achievement of Chetwode flanked by Corinthian columns and surmounted by an entablature and cornice.

Willis states that in his time the mansion had been neglected for many generations, as the principal residence of the Chetwode family was at Oakley in Staffordshire.[7]

The Chetwode family enjoyed considerable rights and privileges in Chetwode, the most interesting of which is that known as the Rhyne toll. Tradition asserts that this toll originated in consequence of a Chetwode having killed a huge and very ferocious wild boar, which had long been the terror of the inhabitants, at a date when this district was to a great extent uncleared forest and on the outskirts of the

---

[28] *Cal. Chart. R.* 1300-26, p. 24.
[29] *Cal. Pat.* 1422-9, p. 344.
[1] Statistics from Bd. of Agric. (1905).
[2] *V.C.H. Bucks.* i, 380.

[3] *Cal. Rot. Pat.* (Rec. Com.), 51; *Cal. Pat.* 1281-92, p. 194; *Cal. Close,* 1279-88, p. 341.
[4] *Cal. Pat.* loc. cit.

[5] Sheahan, *Hist. and Topog. of Bucks.* 267.
[6] *Cal. Chart. R.* 1257-1300, p. 370.
[7] Willis, *Hist. and Antiq. of Buckingham,* 174.

forest of Bernwood. A discovery which certainly bears out this story was made about 1810. There formerly stood in Barton Hartshorn less than a mile from Chetwode manor-house a large mound surrounded by a ditch locally known as Boar's Pond. The tenant of this property, on levelling the mound, discovered the remains of a wild boar of enormous size ; some of the bones were well preserved, and were taken possession of by the Chetwodes.[8] There appears to be no documentary evidence concerning the toll before the 16th century, but in 1577 a suit was instituted between the widow of one of the Chetwodes and her son concerning their respective rights in the manor and in the rhyne toll, and in the records of the suit there occurs a very full and interesting account of the toll.[9]

It was found that the common of the manor consisted of 2,000 acres in Chetwode, Barton, Tingewick, Gawcott, Preston, Hillesden, Prebend End in Buckingham, and Lenborough, and that the lord had, for three days yearly, between Michaelmas and Martinmas, 'a drift of all cattle that should be found in those three days within the said commons, called the Rhyne, in the manner following : In the begining of the said drift of the common or Rhyne, first at their going forth they shall blow a welke-shell or horn immediately after the sun rising at the mansion house of the manor of Chetwode ; and then in their going about they shall blow their horn a second time in the field between North Purcell and Barton Hartshorn in the said county ; and shall also blow their horn a third time at a place near the town of Finmere in the county of Oxfordshire ; and they shall blow the fourth time at a certain stone in the market town of Buckingham and there give the poor 6d., and so going forward in this manner about the said drift shall blow the horn at several bridges called Thornborough bridge, King's bridge and Bridge Mill. And also they shall blow their horn at the Pounde Gate called the Lord's Pounde in Chetwode. The lord of the manor has all the time been used, by officers and servants, to drive away all foreign cattle that shall be found within the said three days within the parishes and fields aforesaid, to impound the same in any pound in the said towns and to take for every beast 2d. for the mouth and 1d. for a foot for every one of them.' Further details follow concerning the claiming of the cattle during the next three days ; if unclaimed at the end of that time they became the property of the lord.

The nature of the toll has changed slightly since that date. During the 19th century the custom has been, after the blowing of horns at 9 A.M. on 30 October, to levy a tax of 2s. per score on all cattle or swine driven through the said districts

between that time and midnight on 7 November. The local farmers usually compound for immunity for 1s. per annum. The right of the lord to collect has more than once been upheld legally against those refusing to pay. The proceeds of the tax, amounting earlier in the century to £20, greatly diminished after the advent of the railway. It was rented at 25s. per annum in 1863.[10] It appears to have lapsed for a period about the year 1884,[11] but was afterwards renewed.[12]

Place-names include la Breche and Hocroft[13] (xiii cent.), Boysterwode[14] (xv–xvi cent.), and Damsells Meade[15] (xvi cent.).

An Inclosure Act for this parish was passed in 1812.[16]

The first mention of land at CHET- MANORS WODE occurs in a charter of 949, in which it was stated that Ælfstan had sold to Æthelflede 20 'manentes' at Chetwode and Hillesden.[17] At the date of the charter the land appears to have been held by Eadred, King of Northumbria.[18] The boundaries of this land are given ; they began at the 'holy oak,' and stretched towards Chieveley in Berkshire.[19]

Later Chetwode was held as a manor by Alnod Chentisc, a thegn of Edward the Confessor, and in 1086 it was among the possessions of Odo of Bayeux.[20] In the 13th century the overlordship belonged to the Say family,[21] and was held by them as late as 1531,[22] when the last mention of it occurs.

Robert de Thame was the bishop's tenant at the time of the Survey.[23] In 1166–7 'Robert,' possibly Robert de Chewod or Chet- wode mentioned in 1199,[24] rendered account of half a mark for Chetwode.[25] This was probably the father of Robert de Chetwode, who held the manor in 1224, in which year, his son Robert having predeceased him, he settled half the manor on Annora, the widow, as dower.[26] He appears to have still held in 1234–5 [27] ; between 1235 and 1247 Ralph de Chetwode was lord.[28] Robert de Vitteney held Chetwode in wardship in 1254–5,[29] and in 1284 Robert de Chetwode was lord.[30] John de Chetwode, who was knight of the shire in 1298 and 1302,[31] had succeeded before 1302–3.[32] He married Amice, and made a settlement of the manor in 1313.[33] Apparently he married a second wife Jane, as John de Chetwode, sen., and Jane his wife held the manor in 1324.[34] He was succeeded by another John

CHETWODE of Chet- wode. *Quarterly argent and gules four crosses formy countercoloured.*

[8] *Rec. of Bucks.* (Bucks. Arch. and Archit. Soc.), ii, 155.

[9] Ibid. 153 (quoting from MSS. in possession of the vicar of Buckingham, 1863).

[10] *Rec. of Bucks.* (Bucks. Arch. and Archit. Soc.), ii, 151–2.

[11] Tucker, *Chetwode of Chetwode*, 74.

[12] *N. and Q.* (Ser. 9), viii, 403.

[13] Feet of F. Bucks. East. 25 Hen. III, no. 37.

[14] Chan. Inq. p.m. 38 & 39 Hen. VI, no. 69 ; *L. and P. Hen. VIII*, xv, g. 831 (58).

[15] Com. Pleas D. Enr. Mich. 6 Edw. VI, m. 8 d.

[16] Priv. Act, 52 Geo. III, cap. 51 (not printed).

[17] Kemble, *Cod. Dipl.* no. 424.

[18] Ibid.   [19] Ibid. vi, 233.

[20] *V.C.H. Bucks.* i, 238.

[21] *Testa de Nevill* (Rec. Com.), 243 ; Hund. R. (Rec. Com.), i, 29 ; *Feud. Aids*, i, 87.

[22] *Feud. Aids*, i, 124 ; Chan. Inq. p.m. (Ser. 2), lii, 20.

[23] *V.C.H. Bucks.* i, 238.

[24] *Rot. Cur. Reg.* (Rec. Com.), ii, 116. The pedigree given by Tucker in *Chetwode of Chetwode* (1884), taken from a parchment roll in possession of Sir George

Chetwode, bart., does not entirely agree with the above evidence.

[25] Pipe R. 13 *Hen. II* (Pipe R. Soc.), 109.

[26] Feet of F. Bucks. 8 Hen. III, no. 9.

[27] *Testa de Nevill* (Rec. Com.), 262.

[28] Ibid. 252 ; Harl. MS. 6950, fol. 163.

[29] Hund. R. (Rec. Com.), i, 29.

[30] *Feud. Aids*, i, 87.

[31] *Ret. of Memb. of Parl.* i, 8, 15. He was also coroner for the county (*Cal. Close*, 1302–7, p. 415 ; 1307–13, p. 511).

[32] *Feud. Aids*, i, 99.

[33] Feet of F. Bucks. East. 6 Edw. II.

[34] Ibid. East. 17 Edw. II.

before 1346.[35] Later in the reign of Edward III Nicholas de Chetwode, son of John, was lord of the manor.[36] He married Elizabeth de Lyons, and was followed by his son John,[37] who was knight of the shire in 1386 and 1395,[38] and by his grandson Thomas,[39] the last-named being alive in the reign of Henry VI.[40] His two daughters died without issue,[41] and the manor passed to his sister Elizabeth, wife of Thomas de Wahull or Wodhull, kt.[42] She died holding it in 1475 and was succeeded by her grandson John, son of Thomas.[43] John was followed by a son Fulk and grandson Nicholas.[44] At the death of the latter in 1531 Chetwode became the property of his son Anthony,[45] who married Ann Smith and died in 1542, leaving a daughter and heir, Agnes, aged only seventeen days.[46] She married Richard Chetwode, a distant relation, a younger son of the Chetwodes of Oakley in Staffordshire, a younger branch of the original family,[47] whose name thus became again associated with the place.

A statute passed in 1558–9 for restoring to the Crown its ancient ecclesiastical and spiritual jurisdiction has a proviso by which Richard and Agnes Chetwode—who had appealed to Rome against Cardinal Pole's decision that their marriage was invalid—were allowed to abide by the decision of the papal court, 'any lawe, costume, usage, canon, to the contrary notwithstanding.'[48] After the death of Richard his widow married Sir George Calveley; at her death in 1576 her heir was her son Richard Chetwode, a minor.[49] In 1613 the latter presented a petition to the king claiming the ancient barony in fee of Wahull, as sole lineal heir of the Wahull barons; a full account of this claim and of similar ones made later by his descendants is given in the history of Odell in Bedfordshire.[50] Richard Chetwode's son Richard married Ann Knightley, but died during the lifetime of his father.[51] Valentine Chetwode, grandson and heir of the latter, held the manor in 1634–49.[52] He did not die until 1685, but before this time the manor appears to have been sold to the Chetwodes of Oakley, descendants of the elder brother of Agnes Wodhull's husband Richard Chetwode.[53] John Chetwode of Oakley and Eleanor his wife held this manor by 1666,[54] and were succeeded by their son Philip, who married Hester Touchet.[55] John Chetwode, son of Philip and Hester, was created a baronet in 1700.[56] He dealt with the manor by fine in

1728[57] and died in 1733.[58] His descendants continued to hold Chetwode,[59] and the seventh baronet, Sir Philip Walhouse Chetwode, is now lord of the manor.

A mill worth 30d. was among the appurtenances of the manor in 1086,[60] and is again mentioned in 1223.[61] No further record of it appears until the 16th century, when Robert Harris and James Bradshaw were successively millers of Chetwode.[62] The latter achieved some notoriety in his time, being implicated in an intended rising of the people in Oxfordshire in 1596.[63] The plans were discovered, and Bradshaw, as one of the ringleaders, was sent up for examination—his hands pinioned, his legs bound under his horse's belly, speech forbidden, and guarded at night at the inns where they lodged. He, 'being a miller and travelling the county,' had undertaken to persuade others to join in the riot, the cause of which appears to have been mainly the high price of wheat, so that he 'wondered what poor men would do,' and with his comrades, judging that 'it would never be well till the gentlemen were knocked down,' he had proposed attacking Lord Norreys' house and securing the armour and two field pieces which stood there.[64] The water-mill was still held by the lord of the manor in 1641, and is mentioned as late as 1785.[65]

In 1226–7 Ralph de Norwich acquired the following parcels of land in Chetwode: 1 virgate from William le Nenu,[66] 4½ virgates from Sibyl Gargate of Caversfield,[67] and 2 virgates 2 acres from Robert de Easington and Sibyl his wife, to be held for a pair of gauntlets.[68] In 1231–2 he acquired, further, 1 virgate from William son of Ralph to be held for a pair of white gloves or 1d.[69] and 1 virgate from William Perdun (?).[70] In 1235 he received a life exemption from suit at the county and hundred courts, and from sheriffs' aids and hidages due from his lands here.[71] In 1241 Sibyl Gargate quitclaimed to him a further 4½ virgates.[72] In 1245 he received licence to found the priory of Chetwode,[73] and in 1246 conveyed to the prior 10 virgates of land in Chetwode and elsewhere,[74] which probably included the main part of the above grants, and which became known later as the *MANOR OF CHETWODE PRIORY*. Ralph reserved to himself for life a capital messuage, paying annually 2 lb. of wax, with reversion to the prior at his death, the whole to be held by the priors of Ralph

[35] *Feud. Aids*, i, 124.
[36] Tucker, op. cit. 25.
[37] Ibid. 26; Close, 18 Hen. VI, m. 23 d.
[38] *Ret. of Memb. of Parl.* i, 228, 249.
[39] Tucker, loc. cit.
[40] Wrottesley, *Ped. from Plea R.* 354; Tucker, op. cit. 7, 13.
[41] Tucker, op. cit. 7, 8.
[42] Ibid.; *V.C.H. Beds.* iii, 71; Chan. Inq. p.m. 9 Hen. V, no. 33.
[43] Chan. Inq. p.m. 15 Edw. IV, no. 21.
[44] Ibid. (Ser. 2), vi, 68; *Visit. of Beds.* (Harl. Soc.), 69.
[45] Chan. Inq. p.m. (Ser. 2), lii, 20.
[46] Ibid. lxv, 6; lxvi, 57.
[47] Tucker, op. cit. 9; *Statutes of the Realm* (Rec. Com.), iv (1), 350, 355.
[48] *Statutes of the Realm* (Rec. Com.), iv (1), 355.
[49] Chan. Inq. p.m. (Ser. 2), clxxiii, 7; Feet of F. Div. Co. Trin. 3 Eliz.
[50] *V.C.H. Beds.* iii, 72.

[51] Tucker, loc. cit.; *Misc. Gen. et Her.* (Ser. 2), i, 85–91.
[52] Feet of F. Bucks. Hil. 9 Chas. I; Recov. R. Hil. 17 Chas. I, m. 34; Feet of F. Bucks. Hil. 1649.
[53] Willis, op. cit. 173; Tucker, op. cit. 9, 10.
[54] Feet of F. Div. Co. Hil. 17 & 18 Chas. II. By a deed of 1654 this John Chetwode purchased the water-mill in Chetwode from Arthur and Henry Chetwode, sons of his brother Henry. The latter had bought it from Thomas Packer of Derbyshire (Close, 1654, pt. iv, no. 41; *Cal. Com. for Comp.* 2438; Tucker, op. cit. 32. See also Recov. R. Hil. 3 Will. and Mary, m. 99; Mich. 7 Will. III, m. 125).
[55] *Misc. Gen. et Her.* (Ser. 2), i, 88.
[56] G.E.C. *Baronetage*, iv, 183.
[57] Feet of F. Bucks. East. 1 Geo. II.
[58] G.E.C. *Baronetage*, iv, 183.
[59] Recov. R. Hil. 29 Geo. II, m. 181; Trin. 25 Geo. III, m. 249; East. 2 Geo. IV, m. 203.

[60] *V.C.H. Bucks.* i, 238.
[61] Feet of F. Bucks. 8 Hen. III, no. 9.
[62] Star Chamb. Proc. Phil. and Mary, bdle. 2, no. 21.
[63] *Cal. S. P. Dom.* 1595–7, pp. 318–19, 343.
[64] Ibid.
[65] Recov. R. Hil. 17 Chas. I, m. 34; Hil. 3 Will. and Mary, m. 99; Mich. 7 Will. III, m. 125; Trin. 25 Geo. III, m. 249.
[66] Feet of F. Bucks. 11 Hen. III, no. 1.
[67] Ibid. no. 2.   [68] Ibid. no. 3.
[69] Ibid. 16 Hen. III, no. 4.
[70] Ibid. no. 5.   In four of the above five transactions a mewed sparrow-hawk was given as fine.
[71] *Cal. Pat.* 1232–47, p. 133.
[72] Feet of F. Bucks. East. 25 Hen. III, no. 37.
[73] Linc. Epis. Reg. Rolls, Grosteste (10th year).
[74] Feet of F. Bucks. Hil. 30 Hen. III, no. 9.

and his heirs.[75] In the same year Sibyl Gargate quit-claimed 4 virgates, saving to herself for life the capital messuage, for which she gave the prior 4 lb. of wax annually.[76] In 1254–5 the priory lands in Chetwode amounted to 2 hides and half a virgate[77]; in 1284 the prior was found to hold the site and 8½ virgates of Robert de Chetwode.[78] In 1540, after the dissolution of Nutley Abbey, to which the priory and its possessions had been annexed,[79] the site of the priory was granted as a manor to William Risley and his wife Alice in fee.[80] He died in 1552, leaving as heir his son William,[81] who died in 1603, his son Paul succeeding to the manor.[82] Paul married Dorothy Temple and died seised in 1626, his eldest son and heir being William.[83] William, however, did not succeed to the property. His father, by deeds of 1623 and 1626, had provided out of the estate for his younger children, Anne, Dorothy, Mary, Elizabeth, Crescens, Paul and Peter, and had granted an annuity to William. The remainder was held by trustees to the use of his son Thomas in tail,[84] and Thomas afterwards held the manor.[85] He was sheriff of the county in 1666[86] and died in 1671, his son and heir being John, who married Cristiana.[87] John's only child, a daughter, died young, and as his cousin and heir Henry, son of his uncle Paul, mentioned in the settlements of 1623 and 1626, was alien born, as were Henry's two sons, John Risley at his death in 1682 left Chetwode to trustees until the heirs were naturalized, when Henry was to hold for life and his sons in tail-male.[88] Paul son of Henry Risley[89] was in possession by 1696[90] and still held in 1735,[91] but had been succeeded four years later[92] by his sister's son Risley Brewer, who took the surname of Risley.[93] He made a settlement of the manor in 1741,[94] was sheriff of the county in 1744,[95] and died in 1755,[96] when letters of administration were granted to his widow Anne, since his father Thomas Brewer, whom he had made his sole executor and universal legatee by a will of 1739, had predeceased him.[97] In 1767 the manor was held by William Jesson and Hannah his wife and William Wither.[98] William Jesson was the grandson of the granddaughter and

RISLEY. *Argent a fesse azure between three crescents gules.*

heir of the Anne Risley mentioned in the deeds of 1623 and 1626,[99] and apparently by this date the heir of the Risley family. His daughters and heirs were Hannah Freeman, wife of William Pearson, and Elizabeth Pudsey, wife of Thomas Grosbeck Lynch.[100] Ann Jesson, spinster, probably a third daughter, quit-claimed a moiety of the manor to the former couple in 1788,[1] and later in the same year both co-heirs and their husbands quitclaimed a moiety to Abraham Bracebridge, husband of Mary Holte, niece of William Jesson.[2] William Jesson Pearson, son of William and Hannah,[3] held a fourth part in 1805[4] and 1808,[5] and Henry Gratian Lynch was seised of a like portion in 1816.[6] Before 1829, however, the whole manor had become the property of Walter Henry Bracebridge and Mary Holte Bracebridge his wife,[7] nephew and daughter respectively of Abraham Bracebridge.[8] They had held a part at least of the manor in 1812.[9] The priory estate was held by the Bracebridge family as late as 1883,[10] after which it passed to its present possessor, Major G. F. Green.

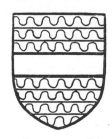

BRACEBRIDGE. *Vairy argent and sable a fesse gules.*

The church of *ST. MARY AND CHURCH ST. NICHOLAS* consists of chancel and nave in one rectangular building, measuring internally 57 ft. 6 in. by 24 ft., north chapel 21 ft. by 16 ft. and north-west tower 8 ft. 6 in. by 8 ft.; it is built of stone rubble and roofed with slate.

The chancel and nave, which formed the quire of the priory church founded here in the 13th century, date probably from about 1250,[11] and the north chapel was added during the first half of the 14th century. The priory was dissolved in 1460, and while the quire and north chapel were preserved as the parish church, the nave and other conventual buildings have since disappeared. A rough sketch plan of the buildings, made during the reign of Elizabeth and preserved in the Bodleian library at Oxford,[12] shows a transeptal church with the cloister and conventual buildings on the south and a church-yard on the north, a nave about the same length and width as the quire, and a tower at the north-west of

[75] Feet of F. Bucks. Hil. 30 Hen. III, no. 9.
[76] Ibid. no. 10.
[77] *Hund. R.* (Rec. Com.), i, 29.
[78] *Feud. Aids,* i, 87. It has been suggested that Ralph de Norwich was identical with the Ralph de Chetwode who flourished 1235–47 (see above account of manor of Chetwode). There appears to be no conclusive proof of this, but the fact that the prior held his demesne here of Ralph de Norwich and heirs in 1246, and of Robert de Chetwode in 1284, decidedly supports the probability.
[79] *V.C.H. Bucks.* i, 381.
[80] *L. and P. Hen. VIII,* xv, g. 831 (58).
[81] Chan. Inq. p.m. (Ser. 2), xcv, 3; Pat. 1 Eliz. pt. i; Memo. R. (Exch. L.T.R.), East. 10 Eliz. m. 16. In 1557 William Risley had trouble with his tenant farmers as to the boundaries of their lands (Star Chamb. Proc. Phil. and Mary, bdle. 2, no. 21).

[82] Chan. Inq. p.m. (Ser. 2), cclxxx, 47; Fine R. 2 Jas. I, pt. iii, no. 19; Feet of F. Bucks. Mich. 20 Jas. I.
[83] Chan. Inq. p.m. (Ser. 2), ccccxlii, 25.
[84] Ibid.
[85] Feet of F. Bucks. Mich. 5 Chas. I; Mich. 10 Chas. I; Recov. R. Mich. 10 Chas. I, m. 59.
[86] P.R.O. *List of Sheriffs,* 9.
[87] Willis, op. cit. 174–5; Recov. R. Trin. 32 Chas. II, m. 140.
[88] P.C.C. 154 Cottle; Willis, loc. cit.
[89] Willis, op. cit. 175.
[90] Recov. R. East. 8 Will. III, m. 207.
[91] Willis, loc. cit.
[92] P.C.C. 325 Paul.
[93] Lipscomb, *Hist. and Antiq. of Bucks.* iii, 3.
[94] Feet of F. Bucks. Trin. 14 & 15 Geo. II.
[95] P.R.O. *List of Sheriffs,* 10.
[96] *Musgrave's Obit.* (Harl. Soc.), v, 146.

[97] P.C.C. 325 Paul.
[98] Feet of F. Bucks. East. 7 Geo. III.
[99] Lipscomb, loc. cit.
[100] Ibid.
[1] Feet of F. Div. Co. East. 28 Geo. III.
[2] Ibid. Trin. 28 Geo. III; Lipscomb, loc. cit.   [3] Lipscomb, loc. cit.
[4] Recov. R. Trin. 45 Geo. III, m. 83.
[5] Ibid. Mich. 49 Geo. III, m. 6.
[6] Feet of F. Bucks. Trin. 56 Geo. III.
[7] Ibid. Hil. 9 & 10 Geo. IV.
[8] P.C.C. 575 Machan; Lipscomb, loc. cit.
[9] Priv. Act, 52 Geo. III, cap. 51 (not printed); Feet of F. Bucks. Mich. 56 Geo. III.
[10] Sheahan, op. cit. 267.
[11] In 1285 the king granted ten oaks for the construction of the church (*Cal. Close,* 1279–88, p. 341). This must refer to works westward of the quire, the details of which can hardly bear so early a date.
[12] Browne Willis MSS. xxii.

CHETWODE CHURCH FROM THE NORTH-WEST

CHETWODE CHURCH: THE INTERIOR LOOKING EAST

the nave. After the Dissolution a wall was built across the west end of the original quire and the present tower was added at a later period. The church was very considerably restored and partly rebuilt early in the 19th century, and has since been further restored.

Practically the whole of the east wall is occupied by a graceful group of five tall lancets of the original date of the quire,[13] with internal jamb shafts having moulded capitals and bases, edge rolls with foliated capitals, and richly moulded rear arches; the lancets increase in height to the centre, and as the capitals are all on the same level the central arches are stilted. In each of the north and south walls, near the east end, is a triplet of similar lancets, the shaft capitals of which are enriched with foliage and grotesques. Below the southern group is an arcade of four richly moulded arches of the same period. The eastern recess probably contained the piscina, while the other three formed the sedilia; the divisions and responds are formed of grouped shafts with moulded bases and foliated capitals, and, like the arches, are enriched with dog-tooth ornament. The third arch from the east, which is wider than the others, has been repaired, and the back has been opened out to form a doorway. At the west end of the south wall, in that part of the old quire now used as the nave, are two windows of about 1300, placed close together and high in the wall, each of two lights with tracery under a pointed head; in the north wall opposite is a two-light window of about the same period, the traceried head of which has been replaced by a modern lintel. Between the latter and the north-east lancets are a 14th-century pointed arch to the chapel and a 13th-century pointed recess, the former being of two orders, the outer continuous and the inner springing from crowned head corbels. At the back of the recess there is some contemporary painting. The tower arch at the north end of the west wall springs from 17th-century moulded corbels, and is coated with plaster; south of it are a two-light window of about 1300, with interlacing tracery, which has been reset in the wall, and another two-light window, which is probably modern. In the south-east window is some fine mediaeval glass, removed here from the east window and restored. The central lancet is filled with 13th-century grisaille, including two vesicae, one a beautiful panel of St. John Baptist on a blue background, holding an Agnus Dei, and the other inclosing the figure of an archbishop in mass vestments; at the foot of the light is a shield of England. The upper part of the eastern lancet is filled with 13th-century grisaille, including a green and red cross, and in the lower part is a 14th-century figure of a saint in an architectural setting; the west light is similarly divided, the upper including a circular panel representing the Crucifixion and the lower three 14th-century figures—the Blessed Virgin, St. Peter, and a bishop, the latter being at the foot of the light with the fragmentary inscription 'Amicus dei Nicholaus.'

The north chapel has an original two-light traceried

window in the west wall, but the east window, of two square-headed lights, is modern. Both the east wall and the north wall, which is pierced by a modern doorway, have been rebuilt.

The low tower is of two stages, coated with roughcast, and is surmounted by a pyramidal tiled roof. The ground stage has a modern west doorway and a late two-light window above with a square head. The bell-chamber is lighted by square-headed windows similar to that on the ground stage.

On the north wall of the chancel is a mural monument, flanked by weeping figures and surmounted by an urn, to Mary daughter of Paul Risley, who died in 1668, and on the chancel floor are a 15th-century marble slab with matrices for brasses, and three 17th-century slabs to members of the Risley family. Below a door, in the wood floor near the organ and at the original floor level, is a stone slab of about 1350 with an incised foliated cross and the following marginal inscription, now somewhat indistinct: 'Sir Jon Giffard gist icey De sa alme Dieu pur pyte ait mercy.'

A table in the north chapel, part of another in the

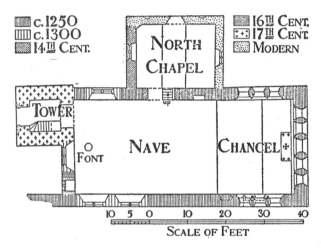

PLAN OF CHETWODE CHURCH

tower, and an oak chest in the chapel, all probably date from the 17th century, while some panelling of the same period has been re-used in the chapel.

There are two bells. One inscribed in Lombardic characters, 'me tibi xpe dabat i chetwode quem peramabat,' probably dates from about 1350, and the other is a small bell with no inscription, but apparently of 18th-century date.

The plate consists of a modern chalice and paten and a modern flagon and bread-box.

The registers begin in 1756.

ADVOWSON The church of Chetwode is mentioned in 1223, at which date the advowson was held by Robert de Chetwode.[14] The dedication to St. Martin is mentioned in an institution of 1234–5.[15] It remained appurtenant to the manor[16] until the end of the 14th century. The Prior and convent of Chetwode obtained licence in 1349 to acquire the church in

[13] Lipscomb (op. cit. iii, 8) states that these lancets were erected in 1842 by Walter Henry Bracebridge. Doubtless he referred to some restoration of them or the insertion of the glass, as the work seems to be of the 13th century.
[14] Feet of F. Bucks. 8 Hen. III, no. 9.
[15] R. of Hugh of Wells (Cant. and York Soc.), ii, 96.
[16] Feet of F. Bucks. East. 6 Edw. II; East. 17 Edw. II.

mortmain and to appropriate it [17]; the appropriation, however, did not take place until 1389-91, when a further licence from the Crown [18] and from the bishop [19] was obtained; a conveyance of the advowson from John de Chetwode to the prior was made in the latter year. [20] It was surrendered with the priory to Nutley Abbey in 1460. [21] In 1480, owing to the state of decay into which St. Martin's Church had fallen, an agreement was made between the Abbot of Nutley and the parishioners by which the priory church was finally given to the inhabitants of Chetwode for parochial use, save fourteen times a year, when service was to be held in the old parish church. [22] Since that time the priory church has been regarded as the parish church, and the advowson has descended with the priory estate, being at present held by Major G. F. Green and annexed to the living of Barton Hartshorn.

By the agreement of 1480 [23] the bishop decreed that the old church of St. Martin was to be regarded as a chapel depending on the sometime conventual, now parochial, church as long as the said chapel should be kept in repair by the parishioners. The Abbot of Nutley, however, was at liberty to remove to the parish church, for which he was responsible, the font of St. Martin's, with timber, lead, &c., for repairs, 'leaving enough to inclose the east end of the said chapel.' Neither party was to cut down trees in the old churchyard; the lord of the manor was to keep it in repair and have profits of grass there, while he and all the parishioners were to have right of way through the abbot's 'Church-breche close' and Town-breche, by which dwellers in the manor of Chetwode had been wont to come to the priory.

These arrangements led to disputes after the Dissolution. About the middle of the 16th century, after the Risleys had obtained the possessions of Nutley Abbey in Chetwode, the inhabitants of the parish lodged a series of complaints against the family. [24] It was alleged that the Risleys had entered the old church and had 'rased and plucked down all the stones, timber, iron, glass, lead and bells and all trees in the churchyard and taken it to their own use.' On a recent occasion, moreover, they had come upon the complainants, who were sitting listening to divine service in the parish or priory church and had driven them out so that 'now they durst not come to

the said cell or priory as their parish church, but go to other towns instead.' They also complained that William Risley had made a well-house in the said cell and had 'appointed well-winders there to wind his well to the nuisance of your said orators during divine service.' He had also built a lime-house in the church and had put his cattle in the churchyard, making it very dirty. Risley, in his defence, denied the riot and said that it was the parishioners themselves who had desecrated St. Martin's by removing materials, but that, in any case, he had a right to it since, by the deed of 1480, St. Martin's, a much smaller building than the priory church, had become a chapel at the disposal of the abbot, and thus was now his property. He also claimed that the bigger church was, similarly, his private property, and as a result of this or a later quarrel appears to have taken part of the south cross aisle or transept into his house. [25] It was at this time probably that the nave and transepts were destroyed.

The north cross-aisle or transept belonged in Willis's time to the Chetwode family. [26] In 1480 the abbot guaranteed to the lord of Chetwode that the abbot and his successors should cause mass to be said daily for the souls of the Chetwodes in the parish church, in place of the canon whom the family claimed to have continually 'found singing in the said Priory of Chetwode.' [27] This right may have originated when the Chetwode hermitage or chapel fell into disuse. There is, however, no other connexion between it and the priory. [28]

The hermitage of St. Stephen and St. Lawrence was founded by Robert de Chetwode in the 12th or early 13th century, [29] and presentation was made by the lords of Chetwode until 1359. [30] In the register of Bishop Grostestè (1235-52), when presentation was made to the 'hermitage and chapel,' it was stated that the said hermitage had afterwards been properly dedicated and was now only called a hermitage by the laity on account of its solitude, and not because a hermit had ever lived there; but the chaplain serving there was wont to wear secular dress and live there with his family, having 24 acres of land to sow. [31] After the presentation of 1359 there is no further mention of the foundation.

There do not appear to be any endowed charities subsisting in this parish.

EDGCOTT

Achecote (xi cent.); Hecchecota (xii cent.); Hachekote, Achecot (xiii cent.); Eggecote, Attchecott (xvi cent.).

The parish of Edgcott contains 1,140 acres, of which only 82 are arable land, the rest being permanent grass. [1] The soil is clay with a subsoil of clay. The parish is bordered on the west and south-

east by branches of the River Ray. The land here and in the north-west is little over 200 ft. in height, but rises in the centre and in the north-east to about 310 ft. above the ordnance datum. The village lies at the foot and on the lower slopes of Perry Hill, and contains some 17th-century cottages with thatched roofs. A few more houses straggle along the road

[17] *Cal. Pat.* 1348-50 p. 274

[18] Ibid. 1388-92, p. 89.

[19] Linc. Epis. Reg. Memo. Buckingham, fol. 377.

[20] Feet of F. Bucks. Mich. 15 Ric. II; Chan. Inq. p.m. 12 Ric. II, no. 133; 15 Ric. II, no. 85.

[21] Chan. Inq. p.m. 38 & 39 Hen. VI, no. 69.

[22] Willis, *Hist. of the Mitred Abbies*, ii,

19; Star Chamb. Proc. Phil. and Mary, bdle. 8, no. 42.

[23] Willis, loc. cit. The bishop decided the conditions 'according to a decree made by John Chadworth, my predecessor.'

[24] Star Chamb. Proc. Phil. and Mary, bdle. 8, no. 42.

[25] Willis, *Hist. and Antiq. of Buckingham*, 1, 78.

[26] Ibid. 177.

[27] Willis, *Hist. of the Mitred Abbies*, ii, 17-22.

[28] *V.C.H. Bucks.* i, 381.

[29] Harl. MS. 6950, fol. 163.

[30] Feet of F. Bucks. East. 6 Edw. II; East. 17 Edw. II; Linc. Epis. Reg. Dalderby, fol. 187 d.; Willis, *Hist. and Antiq. of Buckingham*, 177-8.

[31] Harl. MS. 6950, fol. 163.

[1] Statistics from Bd. of Agric. (1905).

leading south out of the village, and there are one or two farms in the outlying parts of the parish.

The Manor Farm, which stands near the church, and was formerly the Manor House, is a late 17th-century building of brick with a tiled roof. Near it is the old Rectory, an early 17th-century house of brick and timber with a thatched roof, much modernized. There is a small Congregational chapel in the village dating from 1825.

Before the Conquest *EDGCOTT* was MANOR held in four several parts by four thegns. One, Alwin, had 2½ hides as one manor, a second had a hide and a virgate also as a manor, Almar held half a hide, and Thori, a house carl of King Edward, 3 virgates.[2] All these portions were held of Walter Giffard in 1086 as one manor,[3] which thus became a parcel of the honour of Giffard,[4] and the overlordship descended with that of Whaddon Manor in Cottesloe (q.v.), being vested in the Duke of Buckingham in 1514.[5] After his attainder in 1521[6] Edgcott was held of the Crown, at first as of the duchy of Buckingham for a pair of gilt spurs or 6d.,[7] and afterwards as of the manor of East Greenwich in 1627.[8]

Ralf was the tenant of Walter Giffard at the time of the Survey.[9] Possibly a family taking its name from the place were tenants in Edgcott in the 12th and early 13th centuries. Alan de Englefield certainly held the manor before 1219,[10] but a deed of 1226 records the acknowledgement by Henry de Edgcott to Alan de Englefield of rent and service for the 'vill' of Edgcott held on lease for nine years.[11] The Englefield family afterwards obtained full possession. Their chief seat was at Englefield, Berkshire,[12] and the references to their connexion with Edgcott are few. William de Englefield, son of Alan,[13] leased land here to Henry de Edgcott in 1235,[14] and held the vill in demesne as one knight's fee.[15] He acquired rights in half a hide in 1243,[16] and was succeeded by his son John,[17] whose son William granted the manor to Roger Bishop of Coventry and Lichfield before 1277,[18]

ENGLEFIELD. *Barry gules and argent a chief or charged with a lion passant azure.*

when the latter was sued by John's widow Burgia, who claimed dower.[19] At this date the bishop was said to hold the manor on a life grant,[20] but in 1284–6 it was stated that he held as guardian to William's heir,[21] Roger, who was seised in 1302–3.[22] He retained Edgcott until some time after 1316,[23] but his son Philip[24] was in possession in 1318.[25] Philip was still alive in 1346,[26] but little is known of the history of the manor between that date and 1398, when his descendant John Englefield held the manorial rights.[27] His mother had married as her second husband Thomas Prior,[28] which may account for the name of Julian Prior being returned as lord of Edgcott in 1418.[29] A Richard Prior was interested in the settlement made upon Gerard Braybrook in 1422 by Philip Englefield.[30] The Braybrooks retained some right in Edgcott for several years,[31] but in 1453 Richard Prior quitclaimed his interest to Robert Englefield, who with John Englefield appears to have mortgaged the manor for £4,000 to William Brook of London.[32] Robert Englefield held until his death in 1469,[33] when he was succeeded by his grandson Thomas, his son John having died in 1466.[34] Thomas Englefield was returned as lord in 1493[35] and died seised of the manor in 1514[36]; his son, also called Thomas,[37] died in 1537.[38] Sir Francis Englefield, son of the latter, held Edgcott until his attainder in 1585.[39] In 1601 the manor was granted by the Crown to Robert Wright and Henry Maye and their heirs.[40] It passed before 1607 to Sir William Dormer and Sir John Dormer,[41] in whose family it descended, with Long Crendon Manor (q.v.), until 1716, when John Dormer sold Edgcott to Sir Samuel Garth,[42] the fashionable physician and poet. He died in 1719,[43] leaving the manor in trust for Henry Boyle, son of his daughter Martha Beaufoy by William Boyle.[44] Henry died unmarried in 1756.[45] His sisters, Beaufoy, Elizabeth and Harriet, had married respectively John Wilder, Matthew Graves and William Nicholas.[46] Under the terms of Sir Samuel's will the manor passed to them and their heirs as tenants in common, and Edgcott was therefore held, after Henry's death, by Beaufoy Wilder,[47] Henry Boyle Graves[48] and Robert Boyle Nicholas.[49] In 1795 William Graves conveyed his third of the manor to Joseph Bullock,[50] who obtained the remainder of the estate from Henry Wilder,[51] Beaufoy's son.[52] After that date Edgcott was held with Caversfield (q.v.), being, however,

[2] *V.C.H. Bucks.* i, 251.
[3] Ibid.
[4] *Testa de Nevill* (Rec. Com.), 247; *Hund. R.* (Rec. Com.), i, 28; Ct. R. (Gen. Ser.), bdle. 155, no. 13.
[5] Chan. Inq. p.m. (Ser. 2), xxix, 79.
[6] G.E.C. *Peerage*, ii, 64.
[7] Chan. Inq. p.m. (Ser. 2), lx, 124.
[8] Ibid. ccccxxxv, 112.
[9] *V.C.H. Bucks.* loc. cit.
[10] *R. of Hugh of Wells* (Cant. and York Soc.), i, 51.
[11] Add. Chart. 19276.
[12] See *V.C.H. Berks.* iii, 406–7.
[13] Wrottesley, *Ped. from Plea R.* 493.
[14] Add. Chart. 19277.
[15] *Testa de Nevill* (Rec. Com.), 247.
[16] Feet of F. case 15, file 26.
[17] *Cat. of Anct. D.* iii, 44.
[18] *Hund. R.* (Rec. Com.), ii, 352.
[19] De Banco R. 21, m. 45 d.
[20] *Hund. R.* loc. cit.
[21] *Feud. Aids*, i, 81.
[22] Ibid. 99.

[23] *Cal. Close*, 1313–18, p. 134; *Feud. Aids*, i, 109.
[24] *Cal. Inq. p.m.* (Edw. II), vi, 260.
[25] Feet of F. case 18, file 71.
[26] *Feud. Aids*, i, 125.
[27] Chan. Inq. p.m. 22 Ric. II, no. 46.
[28] Cherry, 'Prosapiae Bercherienses,' i, 412–13; *Cat. of Anct. D.* iii, 564.
[29] Chan. Inq. p.m. 7 Hen. V, no. 68.
[30] Add. Chart. 20288.
[31] Chan. Inq. p.m. 4 Hen. VI, no. 17; 5 Hen. VI, no. 18; 7 Hen. VI, no. 39–40.
[32] Feet of F. case 293, file 72; Close, 33 Hen. VI, m. 12.
[33] Chan. Inq. p.m. 38 & 39 Hen. VI, no. 59; 13 Edw. IV, no. 24.
[34] Ibid. 13 Edw. IV, no. 24.
[35] *Cal. Inq. p.m. Hen. VII*, i, 362.
[36] Chan. Inq. p.m. (Ser. 2), xxix, 79.
[37] Ibid.
[38] Ibid. lx, 124.
[39] Ibid.; Pat. 43 Eliz. pt. xiv, m. 25.

[40] Pat. 43 Eliz. pt. xiv, m. 25; by a Patent of 30 Eliz. (pt. xviii, m. 12) a grant of all the woods in the manor had been made to Robert Wright, Thomas Crompton, and Gelly Merrick.
[41] Lipscomb, *Hist. of Bucks.* iii, 10–12; Chan. Inq. p.m. ccccxxxv, 112.
[42] Exch. Dep. Mich. 11 Anne, no. 16; Lipscomb, op. cit. iii, 12; P.C.C. 8 Browning.
[43] *Dict. Nat. Biog.*
[44] P.C.C. 8 Browning.
[45] Ibid. 97 Glazier.
[46] Ibid.; Lipscomb, op. cit. iii, 11.
[47] Recov. R. Trin. 4 Geo. III, m. 261.
[48] Ibid. East. 32 Geo. II, m. 311; Feet of F. Bucks. Mich. 6 Geo III.
[49] Recov. R. Mich. 9 Geo. III, m. 34.
[50] Feet of F. Bucks. East. 35 Geo. III.
[51] Lipscomb, loc. cit. This authority states that Henry Wilder or his representatives conveyed the whole manor to Bullock, but this seems to be inaccurate.
[52] Berry, *Berks. Gen.* 154.

retained by the Bullock-Marshams when they alienated Caversfield, the present lord of the manor being Mr. Charles John Bullock-Marsham.

The site of the manor, mentioned in 1576,[53] was held by Sir Francis Englefield at his attainder.[54] Leases of it were granted by the Crown in 1591 and 1596 to Carew Reynolds and John Wineard respectively,[55] but it was nevertheless included with the manor in the grant of the latter made in 1601.[56]

CHURCH The church of *ST. MICHAEL* consists of a chancel 23 ft. by 12 ft. 6 in. with modern vestry on the north side, nave 28 ft. by 20 ft. and western tower 9 ft. square, all measurements being internal.

The plan of the present building is probably the result of the gradual rebuilding of a 12th-century church consisting of a chancel and nave. The first stage in its evolution, so far as can now be traced, was the rebuilding of the chancel in the middle of the 14th century. About a century later the nave was in turn partially rebuilt, and the west tower was added, new windows, doorways and roof being constructed. The church was restored in 1604 and again in 1875, when the north vestry was added.

In the east wall of the chancel is a modern pointed window of three lights. In the north wall are two 14th-century windows, the western of which is transomed to form a low-side window, the sill being prepared for a shutter. In the south wall is a 14th-century single light, to the east of which is a modern doorway to the vestry incorporating parts of a 14th-century window formerly in the same wall. The chancel arch is of the 14th century, though much restored, and has remains of painted scrollwork on the inner order.

On the south side of the nave are two 15th-century windows, one of two, and the other of three, trefoiled lights, and between them is a 15th-century doorway with a 17th-century door. The windows on the north side are modern except part of the sills and jambs. The 15th-century staircase to the rood-loft with contemporary upper and lower doorways still remains at the south-east of the nave. Over the latter doorway are the remains of a 12th-century window, and above the doorway to the loft is a small trefoiled light. The flat nave roof is of the 15th century, but has been considerably restored.

The tower is of two stages; in the west wall of the ground stage is an original pointed doorway with a two-light traceried window above it. The upper stage is lighted by two-light windows, also of original detail. In the north wall of the tower is a corbel with a curiously carved head. Part of the 16th-century rood screen has been used to form the back of the return stall on the north side of the chancel, and other parts of the stalls here, and some of the seating in the nave, are of the same date.

The plain octagonal font is of the 15th century.

There are three bells: the treble, by John Danyell, is of the 15th century, and is inscribed 'Sancta Katerina ora pro nobis'; the second is by R. Taylor & Son, and is dated 1829; and the tenor is inscribed 'James Keene made me 1626.' The sanctus is by Edward Hemins of Bicester, 1730.

The plate consists of a cup and paten of 1569, a flagon of the early 18th century, and a more modern plated flagon.

The registers begin in 1539.

In the churchyard is a stone which may be the base of a churchyard cross.

ADVOWSON The earliest recorded presentation to the church was made between 1209 and 1219 by the lord of the manor,[57] to which the patronage has ever since remained attached.[58] The church was valued at £12 10s. in 1535.[59]

The chantry returns show that a rent of 6d. was received from lands in the parish, given for the maintenance of a 'lampe light' in the parish church.[60]

CHARITIES Gang Monday Land.—This charity dates from 1582, when an acre of land was left by Isabel Ledbrook, widow, to the poor of Edgcott, the proceeds to be distributed in cakes and ale at the perambulation of the parish every Rogationtide. The rent-charge was redeemed in 1862 by the transfer of £66 13s. 4d. consols to the official trustees, now producing £1 13s. 4d. yearly, which, with money added by the squire, Mr. C. J. Bullock-Marsham, is distributed in coal.

FOSCOTT

Foxescota (xi cent.); Foxcota (xii cent.); Foscote (xv cent.); Foxcott, Foscott (xvi cent.).

The parish of Foscott or Foxcott covers 718 acres, of which 501 are permanent grass, 157 arable and 47 woods or plantations.[1] The land falls from over 400 ft. above the ordnance datum in the north-west to about 260 ft. in the south and south-east. The Ouse with one of its tributaries and the Grand Junction Canal form a portion of the county boundary. In the middle of the parish stands Foscott Manor House, a large stone building with a tiled roof, the property of the trustees of the late Mrs. Lawrence Hall. There was a capital messuage here in 1333.[2] Edward Grenville is said to have built the present house about 1656,[3] and it was considerably restored by Lawrence Hall in 1868.[4] The garden front is divided into three bays by Doric pilasters. There is an original staircase, but perhaps not in its original position.

The soil is clay and gravel. Roman remains have been found in the parish.[5]

MANOR Leit, a thegn of King Edward, held and could sell the manor of *FOSCOTT* before the Conquest. At the date of the

[53] Add. Chart. 39946 (15).
[54] Pat. 43 Eliz. pt. xiv, m. 25.
[55] Ibid.
[56] Ibid.
[57] R. of Hugh of Wells (Cant. and York Soc.), i, 51.
[58] See under manor; Inst. Bks.(P.R.O.).
[59] Valor Eccl. (Rec. Com.), iv, 239.
[60] Chant. Cert. 5, no. 1.
[1] Statistics from Bd. of Agric. (1905).
[2] Chan. Inq. p.m. 7 Edw. III (1st nos.), no. 20.
[3] Willis, Hist. and Antiq. of Buckingham, 188.
[4] Sheahan, Hist. and Topog. of Bucks. 275. In Sheahan's time it was occupied by a farmer.
[5] V.C.H. Bucks. ii, 7; Sheahan, loc. cit.

Edgcott Church from the South-West

Edgcott Church: The Interior looking East

FOSCOTT CHURCH FROM THE SOUTH-EAST

FOSCOTT CHURCH: THE INTERIOR LOOKING EAST

Survey it was assessed at 6 hides, and belonged to Odo, Bishop of Bayeux.[6] His tenant was Turstin, who as Turstin de Giron held of the bishop in Dunton (q.v.). The overlordship of Foscott descended with Dunton Manor, ward at Dover Castle being owed for both manors by the Giron or Gerunde and the Chalfont families.[7] It was attached to the honour of Grafton after 1542.[8] Hamo de Gerunde and Hugh his son subinfeudated their land in Foscott to Walter de la Hay in 1194–7.[9] A fine was levied in the latter year by which Walter agreed for himself and his heirs to render the service of one knight's fee for the land, and for this agreement he gave Hamo de Gerunde 5 marks of silver and a black and white horse (*nigrum equum bausein*).[10] In 1215 Walter de la Hay was numbered among the king's enemies, and the sheriff was ordered to give his lands to his brother Roger de la Hay.[11] They were, however, afterwards restored to Walter, who held as late as 1226–7.[12] Stephen de la Hay succeeded to Foscott not long afterwards.[13] In 1278–9, when he was still lord, his son, also called Stephen, was one of his free tenants.[14] One of the two held in 1284–6,[15] but John de la Hay was seised of the manor by 1302–3[16] and still held in 1308.[17] In 1316 and 1323 Robert Kynne held Foscott,[18] apparently as second husband of Agnes widow of John de la Hay,[19] who died seised of the manor before June 1333, leaving her son Thomas de la Hay as heir.[20] Thomas was holding in 1348,[21] and had a son named Simon,[22] of whom, however, there is no trace after 1346, and the Thomas de la Hay who was holding in 1364[23] was probably his father. In 1371 the manor was held by John Kynne, subject to the life interest of Agnes wife of Alan Aete or Ayote,[24] and, possibly, the widow of Thomas or Simon de la Hay. Alan Aete held as late as 1400.[25] In the early 15th century John Barton, jun., was seised of Foscott, which he granted to feoffees to the use of his wife Isabel and her heirs for conveyance to All Souls College, Oxford.[26] Possibly

DE LA HAY. *Argent a sun gules.*

Isabel was the daughter and heir of John Kynne, since two of the feoffees were also feoffees of John Kynne in 1371. After the death of John Barton, Isabel brought a suit against John Dayrell and Eleanor his wife, who had entered the manor so that the feoffees were unable to perform the deceased's will.[27] The nature of the Dayrells' claim is not evident, but apparently Isabel came to terms with them, since the conveyance of the manor to All Souls was never carried out. By 1457 Foscott was held by William Purfrey or Purefoy,[28] whose wife Marian was the daughter and heir of Alan Aete,[29] although it is not apparent that he held the land in his wife's right.[30] In 1464 he conveyed the manor to Thomas Waldyve,[31] whose brother and heir Nicholas Waldyve of London, mercer, sold it in 1475 to John Denton of 'Shirford' in Warwick.[32] John Denton died seised of Foscott in 1497, leaving a son Thomas,[33] who was holding in 1525.[34] In 1542 John Denton surrendered the manor to the Crown in exchange for other lands,[35] and in 1557 it was granted in fee to Thomas Smythe, who died in the same year.[36] By his will he left the 'manor of Foscote or bargayne of Foscote' to his wife Agnes to sell or give at her pleasure for the payment of his debts and legacies.[37] She married Thomas Westwick in 1558,[38] and in the following year they conveyed two-thirds of the manor to Nicholas and Joan West, who conveyed immediately to Marmaduke and Elizabeth Claver and Matthew Claver their son.[39] In 1570 Edmund or Edward Smythe, son and heir of Thomas, came of age and received the remaining third of the manor,[40] but the Clavers appear to have held the entire property by 1587, about which date, on the marriage of Matthew, it was settled on him and his wife Jane Tyrell and their issue male.[41] Matthew died in 1605,[42] and Jane afterwards married John Phillips,[43] who held her life interest in Foscott, and who in 1620 acquired from John Claver, son and heir of Matthew Claver and Jane,[44] his reversionary interest in the manor.[45]

CLAVER. *Sable a gimel bar between three castles argent.*

---

[6] *V.C.H. Bucks.* i, 238. The bishop also held Ospringe Manor in Kent (Hasted, *Hist. of Kent*, ii, 790), to which the overlordship of Dunton and Foscott belonged in the 14th century (see also Dunton).

[7] See also Dunton; *Testa de Nevill* (Rec. Com.), 343; *Feud. Aids*, i, 79, 108, 127.

[8] Ct. R. (Gen. Ser.), bdle. 195, no. 27; Chan. Inq. p.m. (Ser. 2), cxi, 3.

[9] Pipe R. 6 Ric. I, m. 14 d.; 7–9 Ric. I; *Rot. Cur. Reg.* (Rec. Com.), i, 55.

[10] Feet of F. Bucks. 9 Ric. I, no. 32.

[11] *Rot. Lit. Claus.* (Rec. Com.), i, 242.

[12] Ibid. ii, 162.

[13] *Testa de Nevill* (Rec. Com.), 343; *Hund. R.* (Rec. Com.), i, 32.

[14] *Hund. R.* (Rec. Com.), ii, 339.

[15] *Feud. Aids*, i, 79.

[16] Ibid. 100. This entry states that John de la Hay held the 'manor of Foxcot with Dunton for one fee.' At the same time Hugh de Gerunde held 'Dunton with Foxcot one fee' (ibid. 101).

Possibly the de la Hays were for a period tenants under the Gerundes in Dunton also. [17] *Cal. Inq. p.m.* (Edw. II), v, 45.

[18] *Feud. Aids*, i, 108.

[19] Willis, op. cit. 189.

[20] Chan. Inq. p.m. 7 Edw. III (1st nos.), no. 20; *Abbrev. Rot. Orig.* (Rec. Com.), ii, 76.

[21] *Feud. Aids*, i, 126; *Cal. Close*, 1346–9, p. 591.

[22] *Cal. Close*, 1346–9, p. 165.

[23] *Cal. Pat.* 1361–4, p. 487.

[24] Feet of F. Div. Co. Hil. 44 Edw. III, no. 65.

[25] Chan. Inq. p.m. 48 Edw. III (1st nos.), no. 18; Willis, op. cit. 190.

[26] Early Chan. Proc. bdles. 11, no. 522; 38, no. 225.

[27] Ibid.

[28] Willis, loc. cit.

[29] *Visit. of Leics.* (Harl. Soc.), 12.

[30] Feet of F. Bucks. Mich. 4 Edw. IV, no. 1.

[31] Ibid.

[32] Early Chan. Proc. bdle. 56, no. 241.

[33] Chan. Inq. p.m. (Ser. 2), xii, 42.

[34] Ibid. lxxx, 125.

[35] *L. and P. Hen. VIII*, xvii, 1012 (53).

[36] Orig. R. (Exch. L.T.R.), 4 & 5 Phil. and Mary, pt. xiv, m. 1; Chan. Inq. p.m. (Ser. 2), cxi, 3.

[37] Chan. Inq. p.m. (Ser. 2), cxi, 3.

[38] Memo. R. (Exch. L.T.R.), Hil. 9 Eliz. m. 85.

[39] Feet of F. Bucks. Hil. and East. 1 Eliz.; East. 1 Eliz.; Pat. 1 Eliz. pt. x, m. 16.

[40] Chan. Inq. p.m. (Ser. 2), cxi, 3; Fine R. 12 Eliz. no. 6.

[41] Pat. 32 Eliz. pt. xiv; Feet of F. Bucks. East. 32 Eliz.; Chan. Inq. p.m. (Ser. 2), cclxxxviii, 132.

[42] Chan. Inq. p.m. (Ser. 2), cclxxxviii, 132. [43] Ibid. dlxxiii, 65.

[44] Ibid. cclxxxviii, 132.

[45] Com. Pleas Recov. R. Trin. 18 Jas. I, m. 16; Feet of F. Bucks. Trin. 18 Jas. I; East. 19 Jas. I. John Claver had become bankrupt shortly before his death in 1622, and the commissioners made a sale of the manor in 1623 to John Anthony and others. It was found, how-

At the death of John Phillips, in 1630, the manor was worth only 33s. 4d., because, according to the inquisition, 'a great part of the manor was alienated by Phillips to certain persons'[46]; it had been valued at £13 2s. in 1557.[47] Thomas Phillips, son and heir of John, conveyed the manor to Thomas Hunt in 1635,[48] and in 1638 it was held by the latter and by Ralph Hunt and Frances his wife,[49] she being the daughter and heir of John Phillips by a former marriage.[50] The Hunts mortgaged the manor to Edward Grenville, son of Richard Grenville of Wotton Underwood, to whom they were finally obliged to convey it.[51] A fine of the manor was levied in 1650 between Ralph and Frances Hunt and Richard Grenville and others, trustees for Edward Grenville.[52] The latter died in 1661; his sons Edward and George were both minors, their guardian being their uncle Richard Grenville.[53] Edward, the elder, died in the same year as his father.[54] George died without issue in 1693,[55] and the Foscott estate passed, according to the terms of a previous settlement, to the elder branch, the descendants of Richard Grenville,[56] in which it remained until the sale of the second Duke of Buckingham's estates in 1848,[57] after which date it passed to Lawrence Hall, who held in 1862.[58] His son Lawrence succeeded him in 1866 and died in 1891; the trustees of his widow are now lords of the manor and sole landowners.

A free fishery in the Ouse is mentioned among the appurtenances of the manor in the 16th century.[59]

CHURCH The church of ST. LEONARD consists of a chancel 19 ft. by 15 ft. 6 in., nave 32 ft. 6 in. by 18 ft., and south porch, all measurements being internal.

The church was apparently built in the middle of the 12th century. About 1350 the chancel was enlarged and the chancel arch rebuilt. The south porch was added and other alterations were made in the following century, and in 1887 the church was restored. The walling is of rubble and the roofs are tiled.

The chancel has a 15th-century east window of three cinquefoiled lights in a pointed traceried head and two two-light windows on the south side, both probably of the 14th century, but much altered and restored. Only the opening of the eastern window, which is pointed and of two plain lights, is original, while the western window, the rear arch of which is at the same level, has two square-headed lights placed low down. The former contains some fragments of 16th-century coloured glass showing the head of a woman and what appear to be bones. The 14th-century priest's doorway between the windows

has a pointed head and a label on the outside with carved stops representing the heads of a man and a woman with head-dresses of the period. In the same wall is a 15th-century cinquefoiled piscina. The chancel arch is of three orders with plain jambs, the innermost order springing from corbels ornamented with the ball flower.

The eastern of the two south windows of the nave is probably of the 14th century, though much altered; the western window is of the 15th century and is of two trefoiled lights. The south doorway is of the 12th century and has a round moulded head and moulded label. At the east end of the north wall is a much-altered window, which appears to have been originally similar to that opposite to it. On the same wall are remains of texts, possibly of the time of Edward VI. The north doorway is now blocked, but the arch is apparently of the 15th century and the jambs and imposts of the 12th century. The staircase to the rood-loft, which projects slightly externally and is lighted by a small loop, remains with its upper and lower doorways at the south-east angle of the nave. The porch has a 15th-century outer entrance, and there is a stoup with a four-centred head, probably of the same date, on the east side of the south doorway. The communion table bears an inscription recording its presentation in 1633 by Samuel Wastel. The rails are probably of a slightly later date. The pulpit is made from 17th-century panelling.

There is a brass to Edward Grenville (d. 1661) with a shield of arms, a cross with five roundels thereon, and there is also a monument to Richard Major (d. 1705) and Anne his wife (d. 1708).

A bell, probably of the early 14th century,[60] now hangs in an upper window at the west end of the nave. There was formerly a small wooden bell-turret at the west end.

The plate consists of a cup and cover paten of 1632.

The registers begin in 1664.

ADVOWSON Presentation to the church at Foscott was made in 1220 by Walter de la Hay, lord of Foscott.[61] The advowson has always remained appurtenant to the manor,[62] the living, a rectory, being now in the gift of the trustees of the late Mrs. L. Hall. In 1535 the annual value was £10.[63] In 1639 the terrier of the parsonage showed that the dwelling-house had three rooms—parlour, kitchen and dairy—with three chambers over them, while outside there were the usual farm-buildings with 20 acres of arable land and pasture and 8 acres of orchard and close.[64]

There do not appear to be any endowed charities subsisting in this parish.

ever, that as the commission had not been sued out until three months after Claver's death, the sale was not good, and the indenture of 1620 was quoted and adhered to (Chan. Proc. [Ser. 2], bdle. 408, no. 16). Some settlement of the manor was arrived at between Claver and Phillips as early as 1613 (Feet of F. Bucks. Mich. 11 Jas. I).

[46] Chan. Inq. p.m. (Ser. 2), dlxxiii, 65.

[47] Ibid. cxi, 3.

[48] Feet of F. Bucks. Trin. 11 Chas. I. Edward brother of John Claver was a party to this conveyance.

[49] Ibid. Mich. 14 Chas. I.

[50] Willis, op. cit. 188.

[51] Chan. Proc. (Bridges Div.), bdle. 1, no. 64. The first conveyance seems to have taken place in 1640, when there was trouble with Arthur Claver, uncle of John Claver, to whom he had lent £1,500. He had been paid back from the proceeds of the sale to John Phillips in 1620, but, as he had retained the title-deeds, he refused to acknowledge the validity of Phillips' title, and was supported by Edward and other younger brothers and sisters of John Claver, then dead (ibid. no. 61).

[52] Feet of F. Bucks. Trin. 1650; P.C.C. 91 May.

[53] Rec. of Bucks. (Bucks. Arch. and Archit. Soc.), ii, 294; P.C.C. 91 May.

[54] Willis, loc. cit.

[55] P.C.C. 185 Coker.

[56] P.C.C. 91 May; Willis, loc. cit.

[57] Recov. R. Hil. 10 Geo. II, m. 32; Edmondson, Baronagium Gen. iii, 277; G.E.C. Peerage, ii, 61 n.; Recov. R. East. 59 Geo. III, m. 269.

[58] Sheahan, op. cit. 274.

[59] Feet of F. Bucks. East. 32 Eliz.

[60] A. H. Cocks, Church Bells of Bucks. 387.

[61] Willis, op. cit. 189.

[62] Ibid.; see under manor; Inst. Bks. (P.R.O.).

[63] Valor Eccl. (Rec. Com.), iv, 239.

[64] Willis, loc. cit.

HILLESDEN

Hildesdún (x cent.) ; Ulesdone, Ilesdone (xi cent.). The parish of Hillesden has an area of about 2,600 acres, of which the greater part is laid down in permanent grass ; there are 310 acres of arable land and 12 acres woods and plantations.[1] The soil is clay. A small branch of the Ouse forms the boundary on the south and south-east, in which district the land is lowest (about 260 ft. to 280 ft. above the ordnance datum). Towards the centre and the west of the parish the ground is undulating and rises gradually, but the highest part (from 360 ft. to 380 ft.) is in the north. The village is divided into three parts, known as Church End, Barracks and Lower End.[2]

At Church End stand the church, the vicarage and the school. Little of secular architectural interest remains in the parish beyond a 17th-century brick house to the south of the church and a small half-timber cottage of c. 1600 at the Barracks. The chief point of interest is Hillesden House, the site of which is still to be traced to the east of the church, where irregularities in the ground indicate the lines of its foundations, while the remains of three terraces, the brick walls of the garden, and the fish-pond suggest the lay-out of the grounds.

The Dentons, who held Hillesden [3] for more than 200 years, were a family of considerable local importance.[4] Sir Alexander Denton, the head of the house at the time of the Civil War, had married a cousin of John Hampden,[4a] but his Royalist sympathies were well known. In 1642 a Parliamentary soldier, Nathaniel Wharton, boasted of having, with a file of men, 'marched to Sir Alexander Denton's park, who is a malignant fellow, and killed a fat buck.' [5]

In January 1643–4, when the Parliamentary forces held Aylesbury and Newport, Captain Jecamiah Abercromby and a troop of Parliamentarians occupied Hillesden House, the Royalist men in the neighbourhood having retreated before them.[6] A contemporary record, with Parliamentary sympathies, states that the taking of the house was 'much to the ease and comfort of the poor inhabitants of the almost wasted county of Buckingham,' which was oppressed by the owners of the great house.[7] Less than a month later, however, Abercromby, making a sortie, was captured by Captain Peter Dayrell and his party defeated.[8] It was after this, early in February, that Col. William Smith was sent from the king's forces at Oxford with a small troop to garrison Hillesden House, which, lying nearly midway between Oxford and Newport, might prove a strong support to the king's operations in the former city.[9] At this time there were in the house, besides Sir Alexander's children, several other relatives, his sisters and nieces, and some of the Verney family.[10] He afterwards wrote to Sir Ralph Verney that he himself had only come accidentally to Hillesden House, to remove his family, the king having placed a garrison there.[11] The actual garrison appears to have amounted to about 263 men.[12]

Col. Smith assumed command. He built additional accommodation for men and horses, had a trench dug inclosing the house and the parish church, and made foraging expeditions in the district. One of these led to a dispute with the owner of some cattle taken ; the man appealed to the governors at Newport and Aylesbury, who thereupon awoke to the growing danger of the garrison at Hillesden. A force was dispatched thither from Aylesbury, but, finding the garrison fully prepared, retired without accomplishing anything. Between this and the second attack the defenders at Hillesden replenished their ammunition and summoned the countryside under penalty of a fine to come and keep garrison and continue the work of fortification.[13] But the enemy moved with great promptitude. An order made by the committee of both kingdoms to Col. Oliver Cromwell, about this date, instructs him, his forces being about Hillesden, to stay in those parts and 'to be as active to the prejudice of the enemy as with your safety you may.' [14] He advanced on Hillesden, encamping in Claydon at the spot known as Camp Barn, the night before the siege. Sir Samuel Luke, governor of Newport, advanced also, and the besiegers, amounting to about 2,000 strong, appeared before Hillesden House, which was unprepared for such a rapid approach, before nine o'clock on the morning of 4 March 1643–4.[15]

According to Luke's own dispatch the house at once sounded a parley and Col. Smith sent out to ask for terms. An unconditional surrender was demanded, and this being refused the assault commenced. From the first the defenders were overpowered. Their fortifications and entrenchments were incomplete and proved inadequate ; a retreat was made to the church and house, and in a second assault the church was taken, whereupon Col. Smith surrendered on a promise of quarter. Luke states that his men 'in less than a quarter of an hour were masters of the house and works.' He seems, however, having made prisoners of the defenders, to have violated his promise, many

---

[1] Statistics from Bd. of Agric. (1905). There is mention of Burchelade and Portway coppices in the 16th century (Pat. 1 Edw. VI, pt. ii, m. 4).

[2] Sheahan, *Hist. and Topog. of Bucks.* 275.

[3] When the house came into their possession in 1547 what was used as the capital messuage appears to have been Raphael Moore's farm (Com. Pleas D. Enr. Mich. 6 Edw. VI, m. 8 d. ; Chan. Inq. p.m. [Ser. 2], clxxvi, 4 ; dxliii, 11).

[4] Willis, *Hist. and Antiq. of Buckingham*, 195–6 ; *Dict. Nat. Biog.* ; *Mem. of Verney*

Family (ed. 1904), *passim* ; P.R.O. *List of Sheriffs*, 9.

[4a] Chan. Proc. (Bridges Div.), bdle. 3, no. 21.

[5] *Cal. S. P. Dom.* 1641–3, p. 379.

[6] *Rec. of Bucks.* (Bucks. Arch. and Archit. Soc.), ii, 228.

[7] John Vicars, 'God's ark overtopping the world's waves,' *Parl. Chron.* pt. iii, 133.

[8] *Rec. of Bucks.* (Bucks. Arch. and Archit. Soc.), ii, 229 ; Captain Abercromby, during the later operations at Hillesden, fell in love with and married a sister of Sir Alexander Denton, Susan Denton (*Mem. of Verney Family*, i, 318).

[9] *Mem. of Verney Family*, i, 316.

[10] Ibid. cap. xxi.   [11] Ibid. 316.

[12] *Rec. of Bucks.* (Bucks. Arch. and Archit. Soc.), ii, 96.

[13] The main facts of the following account are taken from *Rec. of Bucks.* (Bucks. Arch. and Archit. Soc.), ii, 93–7, 229–33, and *Mem. of Verney Family*, i, cap. xxi.

[14] *Cal. S. P. Dom.* 1644, p. 33.

[15] This is the date usually given. In a letter of Thomas Verney, written shortly after he was taken prisoner at Hillesden House, the date is given as 3 March (*Hist. MSS. Com. Rep.* vii, App. 447a.).

of the garrison being slain without mercy. He also speaks in his dispatch of the spoils gained—thirteen barrels of powder with match and ball proportionable, the cellars full of good beer, the stables full of horses, and yards full of oxen and beasts. The day after the siege a soldier discovered a large sum of money and treasure hidden in the wainscoting. A rumour that the king's troops were advancing from Oxford created great panic, and for this and other reasons the captors evacuated Hillesden the day after the siege, setting fire to the house, which was entirely destroyed.[16]

The casualties during the siege amounted to about forty on the side of the defenders and not above six of the attacking side, which included 'no officer killed or hurt save onely Col. Pickering and that onely a little chocke under the chin with a musquet balle.'

As regards the inhabitants of the house, the women and children were left in a beggared condition, though not molested by the enemy, and some of them at least found a refuge in the Verneys' house at Claydon.

Sir Alexander Denton and Col. Smith with other officers were taken prisoners and subsequently removed to the Tower.[17] In a letter of about this time Sir Alexander says, 'You may see what I suffered in two dayes cannot but be allmost every man's fortune by degrees, if these most unhappe tymes continue but a short tyme.' Ralph Verney also wrote to Edmund Denton, 'Suffer me to tell you how much I am afflicted for the ruin of sweet Hilesdon, and the distreses that hapened to my aunt and sisters.'

Sir Alexander bade his steward cause a view to be taken of the house that he might have some certain information of the ruin caused by the fire, whether it would be possible to rebuild the walls that remained standing 'if the distraction of the times should settle,' adding that he was 'yet in health notwithstanding these many misfortunes are fallen upon me, and my comfort is I knowe myself not guilty of any faulte.' But his accumulated misfortunes told upon him; his eldest son Col. John Denton was killed in August 1644, and at the end of the year his health gave way and he died without regaining his liberty on New Year's Day 1644–5.

The house was afterwards rebuilt; a letter of 1648 contains the information that 'they are building there again and intend to set up a little house where the old one stood.'[18] In the following century it is described as a 'good old house,' and became famous as the house of Mr. Justice Denton, the contemporary and friend of Browne Willis. After the sale of the estate by Thomas Coke, afterwards Earl of Leicester, it was pulled down about the second decade of the 19th century.[19]

MANORS Land at *HILLESDEN* is mentioned in the Anglo-Saxon charter of 949,[20] to which reference has been made in Chetwode (q.v.). Before the Conquest Alric, a thegn of King Edward, held a manor here; in 1086 it was assessed at 18 hides as part of the lands of Walter Giffard, first Earl of Buckingham.[21] It was afterwards held by the third Walter Giffard, second earl,[22] who died without issue in 1164, and when his inheritance was finally divided in 1191 between William Marshal, Earl of Pembroke, and Richard de Clare, Earl of Hertford,[23] the overlordship of Hillesden, which amounted to a half fee, passed to the latter,[24] and descended with the earldoms of Hertford and Gloucester until the death of Gilbert de Clare in 1314,[25] when it became the portion of his sister Margaret, wife of Hugh Audley,[26] and so passed through heiresses to the Earls of Stafford.[27] It was held by Humphrey Earl of Stafford and Duke of Buckingham in 1460,[28] but is not afterwards mentioned.

Walter Giffard's tenant in 1086 was Hugh,[29] probably Hugh de Bolebec, who held of Walter elsewhere in the county.[30] Walter de Bolebec held Hillesden in the reign of Henry II.[31] His daughter and co-heir married Robert de Vere, third Earl of Oxford,[32] and inherited Hillesden.[33] The fourth earl subinfeudated it towards the middle of the 13th century, but a mesne lordship here continued to be held by the Earls of Oxford,[34] and is last mentioned in 1584.[35]

Hugh de Vere, the fourth earl, granted the manor to his daughter Isabel on her marriage with John de Courtenay of Okehampton.[36] He had inherited

VERE Earl of Oxford. *Quarterly gules and or with a molet argent in the quarter.*

COURTENAY Earl of Devon. *Or three roundels gules and a label azure.*

Waddesdon Manor (q.v.), with which Hillesden descended for nearly 300 years. It was bestowed in dower on Isabel in 1274,[37] and was later held by her second husband, Oliver de Dinham.[38] Eleanor,

[16] See also *Hist. MSS. Com. Rep.* vii, App. 446, 447, 69.
[17] Col. Smith afterwards married Sir Alexander's daughter Margaret.
[18] *Mem. of Verney Family*, i, 323.
[19] *Rec. of Bucks.* (Bucks. Arch. and Archit. Soc.), ii, 97–8.
[20] Kemble, *Cod, Dipl.* no. 424.
[21] *V.C.H. Bucks.* i, 251.
[22] Dugdale, *Mon.* vi, 278; see under church.
[23] G.E.C. *Peerage*, vi, 199 n. (d.); *Cal. Rot. Chart.* 1199–1216 (Rec. Com.), 47.
[24] *Testa de Nevill* (Rec. Com.), 247; another entry in the *Testa* (244) states that this part of Hillesden was 'of the fee of the Marshal,' but this appears to be a mistake, as there is no other record

of this overlordship being in the Earls of Pembroke; a possible explanation of the confusion may be found in the fact that a mesne lordship in the other part of Hillesden (see below) seems to have been held by the Marshal family.
[25] Chan. Inq. p.m. 8 Edw. II, no. 68.
[26] Ibid. 21 Edw. III (1st nos.), no. 59.
[27] Ibid. 46 Edw. III (1st nos.), no. 62; 10 Ric. II, no. 38; 16 Ric. II, no. 27; 22 Ric. II, no. 46; 4 Hen. IV, no. 41.
[28] Ibid. 38 & 39 Hen. VI, no. 59.
[29] *V.C.H. Bucks.* i, 251.
[30] Ibid. 213.
[31] Maitland, *Bracton's Note Bk.* ii, 484–5; *Pipe R.* 13 *Hen. II* (Pipe R. Soc.), 109.

[32] G.E.C. *Peerage*, i, 367.
[33] *Testa de Nevill* (Rec. Com.), 247.
[34] *Feud. Aids*, i, 87, 124; Chan. Inq. p.m. 20 Edw. I, no. 133; 8 Edw. II, no. 68; 46 Edw. III (1st nos.), no. 62, &c., as in note 27; 36 Hen. VI, no. 38.
[35] Feet of F. Bucks. East. 26 Eliz.; in 1420 and 1422, however, the manor was said to be held by the Courtenays as tenants in chief (see below), so possibly by this date the rights of the Earls of Oxford were merely nominal.
[36] *Hund. R.* (Rec. Com.), i, 29; Chan. Inq. p.m. 2 Edw. I, no. 27; Close, 2 Edw. I, m. 7.
[37] *Cal. Close*, 1272–9, p. 89.
[38] *Cal. Inq. p.m.* (Edw. I), ii, 141; *Feud. Aids*, i, 87.

the next dowager countess, held Hillesden in 1316,[39] and it formed part of the portion of Anne, widow of Hugh Earl of Devon, reverting at her death in 1441 to their son Thomas Earl of Devon.[40] After the attainder of his son Thomas in 1461 it was granted by Edward IV in 1462 to Walter Devereux, Lord Ferrers,[41] but was afterwards restored like Waddesdon to the Earls of Devon.[42]

At the attainder of the Marquess of Exeter in 1539 the history of the two manors diverges, Hillesden being granted by Edward VI in 1547 to Thomas Denton and Margaret his wife and their heirs.[43] Thomas was Treasurer of the Temple and M.P. for Buckinghamshire in 1554.[44] Margaret survived her husband, who died in 1558, when their son Alexander was sixteen years of age.[45] Alexander died in January 1576–7.[46] His son Thomas was sheriff of the county in 1600,[47] received the honour of knighthood at Salden House in 1603,[48] and was member for Buckingham Borough from 1604 to 1628.[49] He died in 1633.[50] His son Alexander, who inherited Hillesden,[51] was made a knight in 1617,[52] and he, too, represented the borough, being a member of the Long Parliament until, being 'disabled to sit,' John Dormer was elected in his place.[53] He was the defender of Hillesden House during the siege and died in prison in 1645.[54] Hillesden was afterwards held by Alexander's second but first surviving son Edmund, who in 1651 begged discharge of this manor on the grounds that it had been granted him by Parliament.[55] Sir Alexander, before his death, had been greatly involved in debt, and there appears to have been some question of selling part of his estate to satisfy his creditors.[56] Hillesden was retained by the family, however, although Edmund, succeeding to an impoverished estate and a ruined house, appears to have done little towards retrenchment.[57] He died in 1657, having by his will, dated 17 October 1657,

DENTON of Hillesden.
Argent two bars with three cinqfoils gules in the chief.

made provision for his wife and children out of Hillesden Manor.[58] His son Alexander was M.P. for the borough of Buckingham in 1690–8,[59] dying seised of Hillesden in 1698, when his eldest son Edmund succeeded.[60] He was created a baronet in 1699,[61] but died without issue in 1714, when his brother Alexander inherited the property.[62] Alexander, who was also a member of Parliament,[63] was in addition Recorder of Buckingham, a justice in the court of Common Pleas, and chancellor of the Prince of Wales.[64] He died in March 1739–40,[65] leaving no issue, his heir being his sister's son, George Chamberlayne, whom he had adopted and who afterwards took the name of Denton,[66] under which name he was returned to Parliament on 4 May 1741 as member for Buckingham Borough.[67]

The descent of Hillesden Manor is identical at this time with that of Buckingham, under which account their joint history for the next 100 years is given (q.v.). The Duke of Buckingham and Chandos was lord of Hillesden Manor as late as 1847,[68] but it had passed before 1854 to Mr. James Morrison of Basildon Park, Berkshire,[69] from whom it descended to Mr. Hugh Morrison of Fonthill House, Fonthill Gifford, Wiltshire, grandson of James Morrison by his second son Alfred.[70] He sold the estate in October 1910, some of the tenants purchasing the farms held by them, while others were acquired by Christ Church, Oxford.

The capital messuage of the manor is first mentioned in 1274,[71] and is invariably included in all extents of the manor as given in inquisitions down to the 16th century.

A mill belonged to the manor in 1086,[72] and in 1279–80 Roger de Martinall quitclaimed two mills in Hillesden to John Giffard.[73] A 17th-century deed records the existence of a mill in the parish.[74]

Land in Hillesden was held of the Earls of Oxford by other sub-tenants than the Courtenays in the 13th and 14th centuries. In 1203 Ralf Triket granted 15s. in lieu of dower in certain lands here to Agnes daughter of Maud, who renounced her right in them to the Knights Templars.[75] In 1207 Simon Pateshull made a life grant to Ralf of 9 virgates in Hillesden, retaining to his own use a capital messuage with fishpond and garden.[76] Walter Pateshull is mentioned

[39] *Feud. Aids*, i, 109.

[40] Chan. Inq. p.m. 19 Hen. VI, no. 40.

[41] *Cal. Pat.* 1461–7, p. 153.

[42] John Conway, great-nephew and heir of the Hugh Conway who held both Waddesdon and Hillesden for a time, sued William Weston, Prior of the Hospital of St. John of Jerusalem, for deeds relating to property in Hillesden (Early Chan. Proc. bdle. 494, no. 56). Thomas Docwra, the former prior, was one of the executors of Hugh, who died in 1518 (*L. and P. Hen. VIII*, ii [2], 4184).

[43] Pat. 1 Edw. VI, pt. ii, m. 4 ; the grant was made in accordance with the last will of Henry VIII, and in performance of an indenture between Edward VI, his father's executors and Denton.

[44] Verney, *Bucks. Biog.* 115 ; *Ret. of Memb. of Parl.* i, 389.

[45] Chan. Inq. p.m. (Ser. 2), cxx, 2.

[46] Ibid. clxxvi, 4. See also Recov. R. Hil. 1566, m. 517.

[47] P.R.O. *List of Sheriffs*, 9.

[48] Shaw, *Kts. of Engl.* ii, 111.

[49] *Ret. of Memb. of Parl.* i, 442, 450, 474 ; App. p. xxxvii.

[50] Chan. Inq. p.m. (Ser. 2), dxliii, 11.

[51] *Cal. S. P. Dom.* 1637–8, p. 567 ; Recov. R. East. 14 Chas. I, m. 48.

[52] Shaw, op. cit. ii, 166.

[53] *Ret. of Memb. of Parl.* i, 462, 468, 480, 485.

[54] *Mem. of Verney Family*, i, 321.

[55] *Cal. Com. for Comp.* 2878 ; *Mem. of Verney Family*, i, 567.

[56] Ibid.

[57] *Mem. of Verney Family*, i, *passim*.

[58] Willis, op. cit. 195 ; P.C.C. 269 Pell. He is called Edward in the will.

[59] *Ret. of Memb. of Parl.* i, 564, 572, 579.

[60] Willis, loc. cit. See also Feet of F. Bucks. Trin. 28 Chas. II ; Recov. R. Trin. 28 Chas. II, m. 155 ; Mich. 10 Will. III, m. 236. By his will dated 4 June 1698 he desired his trustees to sell all manors save Hillesden in payment of his debts (P.C.C. 57 Pett). Hillesden was mortgaged to his brother and sister Edmund and Dorothy Denton (Chan. Proc. [Bridges Div.], bdle. 605, no. 83).

[61] G.E.C. *Baronetage*, iv, 180.

[62] Willis, op. cit. 195, 199 ; Feet of F. Bucks. Hil. 2 Geo. II.

[68] *Ret. of Memb. of Parl.* ii, 9, 37, 50.

[64] Willis, op. cit. 196.

[65] *Musgrave's Obit.* (Harl. Soc.), ii, 171.

[66] P.C.C. 291 Browne (this was in accordance with his uncle's will) ; Lipscomb, *Hist. and Antiq. of Bucks.* iii, 18 ; G.E.C. *Peerage*, v, 52.

[67] *Ret. of Memb. of Parl.* ii, 85.

[68] *Dir. of Bucks.* 1847.

[69] Ibid. 1854.

[70] Burke, *Landed Gentry*.

[71] Chan. Inq. p.m. 2 Edw. I, no. 27.

[72] *V.C.H. Bucks.* i, 251.

[73] Feet of F. case 17, file 46.

[74] Recov. R. East. 14 Chas. I, m. 48.

[75] Hunter, *Pedes Finium* (Rec. Com.), i, 218–19.

[76] Feet of F. Bucks. Hil. 8 John ; in this deed the land is said to be held of three overlords—the smallest portion of the Knights Templars, the rest of William de Hastings, and Ellis de Beauchamp and Constance his wife. The Prior of St. John of Jerusalem had rights in Hillesden as late as 1518 (Early Chan. Proc. bdle. 494, no. 56), but probably only as executor of Hugh Conway (see n. 42). William de Hastings's name appearing may be due

in 1221,[77] and in 1254–5 Simon Pateshull held 2½ hides, apparently of the Earls of Oxford.[78] In 1284 Eustace de la Hesche held,[79] but the land had passed before 1302 to Nicholas Trimenel,[80] who is returned as lord in 1316.[81] He was sued by John Trimenel and Elizabeth his wife for this property, called a manor, the case lasting from 1314 to 1317.[82] John Trimenel, kt., held in 1346[83] and in 1360,[84] and Roger Trimenel in 1371,[85] but no further record of it appears.

One hide of land in Hillesden was held before the Conquest by Alric son of Goding,[86] and was included in 1086 among the lands of the Count of Mortain.[87] With the count's other lands it afterwards formed part of the honour of Berkhampstead, belonging to the little fee of Mortain,[88] and was so held by the Earls of Cornwall with that honour as late as the 15th century.[89]

The count's tenant in 1086 was Rannulf.[90] An entry in the Pipe Roll of 1166–7, 'Hildeston-Marescaldi,'[91] may refer to this part of Hillesden, as Ralf Marshal held a carucate of land here in 1234,[92] and in 1284–6 Ralf Marshal held 2 hides, for a third of a fee, of the honour of Berkhampstead.[93] The tenants under the Marshals at that date were the Abbots of Nutley,[94] who were already seised earlier in the 13th century,[95] and so remained[96] as late probably as the Dissolution. It is difficult to trace the subsequent history with any certainty. The abbots also held land in Hillesden of the Earls of Oxford in the 13th century.[97] In 1535 the abbot's estate in Hillesden consisted of the rectory lands only,[98] to which, however, manorial rights appear to have been attached.[99] Possibly, therefore, the entire Nutley property had been amalgamated into this one holding, the descent of which is given below.

The origin of the *RECTORY MANOR* is probably to be found in the lands granted with the church to Nutley by Walter Giffard.[100] In 1291 the abbey's lands pertaining to the church property amounted in value to £3 18s. 9d. per annum, including rent, courts, escheats and value of works.[1] In 1535 the annual value of the rectory at farm was £19 8s.[2] In 1538 a complaint was made against Roger Giffard of Claydon and his sons for having persuaded the abbot to falsify a lease of the parsonage made some time before to Thomas Giffard of Twyford (Berks.), and for having personally injured the latter.[3] After the Dissolution the rectory was granted in 1542 to the Dean and Chapter of Christ Church, Oxford,[4] the present owners of the tithes and of about 200 acres of land.

In 1555 the dean and chapter granted an eighty-year lease of the parsonage and mansion-house to Roger Giffard, whose efforts to sublet the property led to considerable litigation.[5] The tithes were afterwards held on lease by the Dentons.[5a]

CHURCH The church of *ALL SAINTS* consists of a chancel 30 ft. 6 in. by 18 ft., north chapel of the same length, 18 ft. 6 in. in width, a two-storied vestry at the north-east of the chapel 15 ft. 6 in. by 9 ft., nave 46 ft. 6 in. by 18 ft. 6 in., north and south transepts each 13 ft. 6 in. by 12 ft. 6 in., north aisle 8 ft. 6 in. wide, south aisle 8 ft. wide, west tower 10 ft. square, and a north porch. These measurements are all internal.

The present building is a very fine and complete example of the style of the late 15th century, having been rebuilt, with the exception of the tower, shortly after the year 1493.[6] The church which it replaced was probably a 12th-century cruciform building, and fragments of the west walls of its transepts are perhaps incorporated in the short west walls of the existing transepts, which are considerably thicker than the other walls. The unequal settlement of the south wall of the south transept at its junction with the west wall affords additional evidence, as no material settlement has occurred elsewhere. Prior to the entire rebuilding, the still surviving west tower, which is of mid-15th-century date, appears to have been added or reconstructed. In the last century a thorough restoration, completed in 1875, was carried out by Sir Gilbert Scott.

The north side of the chancel is almost entirely occupied by an arcade of two bays opening to the north chapel; the arches are of three moulded orders and spring from a central pier of lozenge plan with attached shafts at the cardinal points and in the centre of each face, all having moulded octagonal capitals and independent bases of the same form standing upon double plinths about 2 ft. 6 in. in height. The responds repeat the half plan of the pier. The east window is of five lights, divided by a transom and cinquefoiled in both tiers, the depressed four-centred head being filled by vertical tracery descending some distance below its springing. The glass line is placed at the middle of the wall and the jambs are elaborately moulded on both faces, while the head, like those of all the other windows of the body of the church, has an external label. Below the sill internally is a moulded string-course, stopped and returned upon itself for the high altar, and continued upon the north wall on either side of the arcade. The two south windows, the jambs of which are moulded like those of the east window, are each of four transomed and cinquefoiled lights, rising without other tracery into a flat four-centred head; below their sills is a bold string-course, deeper, and placed at a slightly lower

to the fact that about this time he was impleading against the Marshal family (*Cal. Rot. Chart.* 1199–1216 [Rec. Com.], 46), and may have laid claim to their fees.

[77] Feet of F. case 14, file 13.

[78] *Hund. R.* (Rec. Com.), i, 29; the Courtenays' holding amounted to 14½ hides (ibid.).

[7] *Feud. Aids,* i, 87.

[80] Ibid. 99.

[81] Ibid. 109.

[82] De Banco R. 211, m. 5; 212, m. 231 d.; 214, m. 13; 216, m. 3 d.; 217, m. 221.

[83] *Feud. Aids,* i, 124.

[84] Chan. Inq. p.m. 34 Edw. III (1st nos.), no. 84.

[85] Ibid. 45 Edw. III (1st nos.), no. 45.

[86] *V.C.H. Bucks.* i, 245.

[87] Ibid.

[88] *Feud. Aids,* i, 77, 99, 107, 133.

[89] Chan. Inq. p.m. 2 Ric. II, no. 57 (23); Ct. R. (Gen. Ser.), bdle. 177, no. 14. [90] *V.C.H. Bucks.* i, 245.

[91] *Pipe R.* 13 *Hen.* II (Pipe R. Soc.), 109.

[92] Feet of F. case 15, file 20.

[93] *Feud. Aids,* i, 77.

[94] Ibid.

[95] *Testa de Nevill* (Rec. Com.), 244; *Hund. R.* (Rec. Com.), i, 29.

[96] Chan. Inq. p.m. 2 Ric. II, no. 57 (23).

[97] *Testa de Nevill* (Rec. Com.), 251.

[98] *Valor Eccl.* (Rec. Com.), iv, 233.

[99] Chan. Proc. (Ser. 2), bdle. 23, no. 20.

[100] Dugdale, *Mon. Angl.* vi, 278–9.

[1] *Pope Nich. Tax.* (Rec. Com.), 47.

[2] *Valor Eccl.* (Rec. Com.), iv, 233.

[3] *L. and P. Hen. VIII,* xiii (1), p. 579.

[4] Ibid. xvii, p. 491; xxi (2), 648 (25).

[5] Chan. Proc. (Ser. 2), bdles. 23, no. 20; 173, no. 53.

[5a] Ibid. (Bridges Div.), bdles. 3, no. 21; 5, no. 57.

[6] Willis, op. cit. 198.

level than that below the east window. Above the string-courses the whole of the blank surface of the east and side walls of the chancel is richly panelled in three stages, the two lower having compartments with cinquefoiled and traceried heads, while the uppermost stage, a mere frieze, has smaller and narrower cinquefoiled compartments, cut into by the heads of the windows and the arches of the north arcade. Crowning the whole, immediately below the roof, is a band of sculptured angels in high relief, those upon either side of the east window, which extends the whole height of the chancel, bearing instruments of music, an organ, a guitar, a harp, and a violin, while the rest hold scrolls of music. The chancel arch is of two pointed and moulded orders separated by casements, and has responds with attached shafts to each order, the curves of the shafts of the outer orders finishing flush with the wall faces. The roof is concealed by a modern flat-pitched plaster ceiling, said to be of the same design as the original ceiling ; it is divided by moulded oak ribs into small squares, and each square is again divided saltirewise by subsidiary ribs. At the east end of the south wall is a shallow piscina niche having leaf-carved spandrels and a projecting semi-octagonal basin. Immediately over the niche is a credence recess half covered by the monument of Dr. William Denton described below. On either side o the east window are semi-octagonal image brackets, that on the north having circular quatrefoiled panels on each face, while the southern bracket is plainly moulded. The lower stage of panelling is omitted on this wall, and immediately below the second stage are sculptured angels, one over each bracket, holding shields with the emblems of the Passion. Externally the walls rise from a moulded plinth, and are crowned by a cornice surmounted by elaborately panelled battlements, with pinnacles at the eastern angles and at the centre of each side wall. A moulded string-course runs round the exposed walls below the sills of the windows, and there is a buttress of two stages between the south windows, the south-eastern angle having a pair of buttresses of the same type. The plinth and string-course are continued round the whole church, interrupted only by the north-east vestry and the tower.

The walls of the north chapel have stone panelling in two stages divided by an embattled transom, the upper panels having cinquefoiled ogee heads with tracery, while the lower panels have heads of the same form without tracery. The flat-pitched ceiling is modern, and of the same type as that of the chancel. The east window is of four lights with an embattled transom, the lights being cinquefoiled in both stages, while the depressed four-centred head is filled with

quatrefoil tracery. On either side are semi-octagonal image brackets, that on the north having cinquefoiled panels in each face. In the north wall is a four-light window with an embattled transom, but in other respects like the south windows of the chancel, though less lofty, and placed like the east window at a lower level. To the east of it is an elaborately moulded doorway with a four-centred head and traceried spandrels opening to the vestry. At the south-east is a piscina niche with a cinquefoiled ogee head and carved leaf spandrels, but all trace of the drain has now disappeared. On the west an arch like the chancel arch, but smaller, opens to the north transept. The walls of the chapel are treated externally like those of the chancel, but the battlements are plain.

The two-storied vestry adjoining the chapel has an octagonal turret at the north-east containing the stairs to the upper floor, and the walls rise to the same height as those of the north chapel. The room on the ground floor has an external doorway with a four-centred head at the south-east, and is lighted by

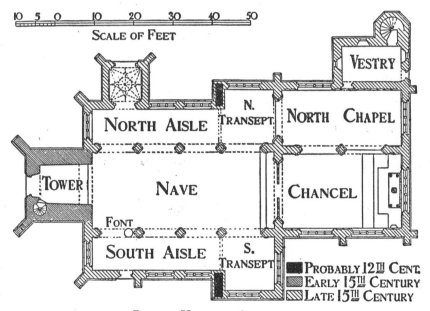

SCALE OF FEET

PLAN OF HILLESDEN CHURCH

single lights with four-centred heads on the east, north, and west. At the north-east is a doorway opening to the stair-turret. The upper room has a blocked doorway in the east wall, which was probably a private entrance from Hillesden House, and must have been approached by a bridge. In the east wall is a square-headed cinquefoiled light, and on the north and west are two-light windows of the same type. All have external labels, and a bold string-course, continued round the north-east turret, runs beneath their sills. A doorway with plain rebated jambs and a four-centred head leads to the stair-turret. In the south wall is a series of seven radiating loopholes, four now blocked, with a larger opening, also blocked, towards the east end. The stairs in the turret, which is lighted by loops, are continued upwards to the roof, upon which they open by a doorway with a four-centred head ; the central newel is surmounted by a column with a moulded base and capital supporting a plain vault of fan form. The turret rises above the embattled parapet of the vestry, and is crowned by a moulded cornice and panelled battlements, from the pinnacled angles of which spring cusped flying buttresses meeting in the centre, where they are strengthened by an octagonal column and support a central crocketed pinnacle.

The nave arcades are each of four bays with pointed arches of two hollow-chamfered orders separated by casements. The piers have each four attached shafts with octagonal capitals, and stand upon high octagonal plinths. The arches opening to the transepts are of the same width, but are raised higher by lifting the eastern halves of the eastern piers. The responds repeat the half plan of the piers, and are like those of the chancel arch. The upper entrance to the rood-loft still remains above the south-east respond,

HILLESDEN CHURCH : NORTH DOORWAY AND STONE PANELLING OF THE NORTH CHAPEL

and has in its western jamb a pocket which received the end of the top-rail of the loft. The clearstory is lighted by three square-headed windows of five cinquefoiled lights on either side, placed so close together as to form almost a continuous wall of glass. The north transept is lighted on the north by a transomed window of four uncusped lights under a four-centred head, and the south transept has a window of the same design in its south wall, but the east window is like the south windows of the chancel. Each aisle has two windows in its side wall and one in the west wall, all of three uncusped lights under four-centred heads. The north doorway has a four-centred head moulded continuously with the jambs, and a flat rear arch ; the smaller and less elaborate

south doorway has a head of the same form. Flat segmental arches, about 9 in. in thickness, divide the ceilings of the aisles and transepts and form the only separation between them. Both transepts have embattled parapets, and follow the general exterior treatment of the eastern portion of the church, the north transept being designed externally as a continuation of the north chapel ; the aisles are also embattled, but the parapet of the three western bays of the nave is plain, the embattled parapet of the chancel being continued over the eastern bay only. The nave, transepts, and aisles have modern flat-pitched plaster ceilings with oak ribs, copied from their predecessors of the late 15th century.

The mid-15th-century west tower is of three stages with a south-west stair-turret, western diagonal buttresses and an embattled parapet. The tower arch is pointed and of two orders, the outer moulded with a chamfer continued down the meeting angles of the nave and tower walls, while the inner order, which is moulded with a sunk chamfer, dies into the side walls of the tower. The arch is inclosed on the nave side by a label with head-stops. In the west wall of the ground stage is a doorway with moulded jambs and a depressed head, and above it is a pointed window of two cinquefoiled lights with tracery in the head. The ringing stage is lighted from the west by a plain opening, while the bell-chamber has pointed and traceried windows of two cinquefoiled lights on all four sides. All the detail is of the original date of the tower.

The north porch, an extremely rich piece of work, has a low-pitched gable and a moulded cornice surmounted by panelled battlements. At the angles are buttresses with panelled upper stages. The porch is ceiled by a modern fan-vault, the original vault, if ever completed, having gone by the date of Scott's restoration.[7] The vaulting shafts remain in each angle, and the shape of the wall ribs is shown by the form of the panelling upon the side walls. The north doorway is inclosed on the porch side by narrow trefoiled panels, and above the head is fine tracery work. The outer doorway, which is inclosed by similar panelling on the inner side, has a four-centred head within a square external labelled head, and is most elaborately wrought with panelled jambs and soffits. Above the doorway externally is a richly carved niche with a projecting semi-octagonal canopy crowned by a finialled cupola. The base of the niche is elaborately moulded and the whole is flanked by pinnacled flying buttresses worked on the wall-face of the porch.

Below the present altar table is a 15th-century stone altar slab with two consecration crosses remaining upon it. The font is circular and stands upon an octagonal stem of later date than the bowl, which is of the 13th century ; the oak cover is of the 17th century. Twelve consecration crosses, two now hidden, still survive on the walls of the chancel, chapel, transepts and aisles, each consisting of a cross formy inclosed within a circle about $10\frac{1}{2}$ in. in diameter.

[7] *Rec. of Bucks.* (Bucks. Arch. and Archit. Soc.), iv, 313.

The rood screen, which is contemporary in date with the rebuilding of the church, remains in a very perfect condition, only the parapet of the loft having gone. It is divided into three bays with pointed heads by posts with small attached shafts having foliated capitals, from which spring the ribs of the vaulted coves beneath the projecting loft. The lower portion of each bay has four linen-fold panels with moulded styles supporting a rail enriched with running foliage, and the upper portion has four open lights with ogee heads and foliated cusping, above which, filling the pointed head, is tracery of mixed vertical and flamboyant character. The middle bay opens in two leaves, the tracery in the head being fixed, while the mullions detach themselves immediately below the springing of the heads of the lights. The face of the western beam of the loft above the vaulted cove is enriched with a bold vine-pattern, but the eastern beam is plain. In the chancel are two late 15th-century desk-fronts, with two tiers of linen-fold panelling, moulded rails and buttressed muntins. Nine benches with panelling of the same date remain in the nave. A low screen, made up with fragments of desk-fronts like those in the chancel, separates the north chapel from the adjoining transept. The doorways from the stair-turret to the upper and lower rooms in the vestry building retain their original batten doors, that to the upper room having a moulded framing planted upon it, and a lozenge pattern scratched on the battens, with nails at the intersections; the strap hinges to both doors are also original, and form good examples of the ironwork of the period. The door in the north doorway, on the external face of which is an almost obliterated carving of the sun, moon and stars, is also of original late 15th-century date. It has been considerably damaged by bullet holes, probably during the Civil War. In the north transept is a fine mid-17th-century pew having on the front and sides carved bolection moulded panels in two ranges, the lower range of panels being pedimented. In the north chapel is a 17th-century communion table, and in the vestry is preserved a chest of the same date.

The remains of late 15th-century glass are important and valuable. The finest is that in the four upper lights of the east window of the south transept, illustrating eight legends of St. Nicholas. Each light contains two subjects, and under each subject is a descriptive Latin hexameter inscribed in black letter. The upper panel in the northernmost light and the corresponding panel in the next light illustrate the legend of the cups. In the first is represented a three-masted ship at sea, from which the boy is seen falling overboard with the golden cup in his hand. Upon the ship are two sailors lowering the sail, while the father looks on, leaning his elbows on the rail of the poop. The hull of the ship is of a yellow colour and the figures wear bright colours, but the faces are almost white. Underneath is inscribed 'Cadit puerulus quem mox sal(va)t Nicholaus.' In the second panel the father and mother are seen kneeling at the altar of St. Nicholas, whose seated figure, wearing episcopal vestments, is placed at the north end of the altar. Behind his parents stands the boy holding the gold-covered cup; below is the inscription 'Tunc offert cyphum grates (sic) pro mun(er)e reddens.' The third panel, continuing from north to south, illustrates the relief of the famine at Myra by St. Nicholas.

The saint is shown in the foreground standing by the shore without nimbus or vestments to indicate that the event occurred in his lifetime. Near him are sailors pouring out corn into sacks, while in the background is a large three-masted ship with figures. Underneath is inscribed 'Multiplicat frugem presul quam nave recepit.' The next three panels illustrate the legend of St. Nicholas and the Jew of Calabria. In the foreground, helping themselves to the Jew's treasure, are seen the robbers, truculent ruffians, armed with sword and axe, and wearing bright-coloured clothes, the northern of the two nearer figures being clad in a crimson tunic with green hose, while the southern figure has a purple tunic with slashed sleeves. In the background is the Jew setting out on his journey, staff in hand, and threateningly warning the figure of St. Nicholas to keep guard over his wealth in his absence. He wears a crimson cloak trimmed with gold, and has a flowing white beard. Below the panel is inscribed 'Que tulerant (fures) bona cogit reddere presul.' The next panel shows St. Nicholas appearing to the robbers, and in the background the Jew attacking the saint's image with his staff, the subject being thus described: 'Auro furato baculo flagellat amicum.' In the remaining panel of the series is shown the restitution of the treasure to the Jew, who is drawn in the foreground, receiving back from the robbers a gold casket, which appears in the two former panels. In the background is a gate-house with trees and foliage. Below is inscribed 'Restituit rursus latro quod sustulit aurum.' The last two panels illustrate the restoration to life of the boy strangled by the devil disguised as a pilgrim. In the foreground of the first panel the devil is seen strangling the boy, whom he has forced to a half-kneeling position, while the food which had been brought out to him drops from the dish in the boy's hands. In the background is a house with a half-gable, and above its walls is seen the father, who clasps his hands in horror, with two guests beside him. The incident is described by the line: 'Strangulat hic (demon) puerum (pul) menta ferentem.' In the last panel the boy lies dead on the ground with his parents kneeling by him, and in the doorway of the house, from which the guests are looking out, appears St. Nicholas. Beneath is the inscription, 'Mortuus ad vitam rediit precibus Nicholai.'

In the heads of the lower lights of the windows are fragments of other panels which probably illustrated further legends of St. Nicholas, as in the head of the fourth light is the fragmentary inscription in black letter 'eledgite (eligite ?) Nicholaū ī episcopum.' In nine of the ten lights of the tracery of the east window of the chancel are fragments of canopied figures, that in the second light from the north having been entirely destroyed. The remaining figures, taken from north to south, are as follows: in the first light, a pope, perhaps St. Gregory; in the third light, St. Peter; in the fourth, a figure with a book, perhaps St. Paul; in the fifth, a figure with a nimbus, probably St. John Baptist; in the sixth, St. John the Evangelist; in the seventh, St. George; in the eighth, St. Christopher; in the ninth a bishop, perhaps St. Augustine; and in the tenth a second bishop, perhaps St. Ambrose. Fragments of canopy work also remain in the two south windows. Other fragments also survive in the east and north windows of the north chapel, including an Annunciation and a Majesty. In the south-east window of the south aisle are two heads of bishops, with part of the figure of an archbishop holding a crozier, and in the next window to the west is a third bishop's head.

In the upper room of the vestry are preserved some fragments of moulded stone from the former church, a carved female head of the 14th century, and some worn 15th-century tiles. A sundial set in the south buttress of the nave bears the date 1601 and the name 'Georg . . . de Fraisne,' with the inscription 'Sic transit gloria mundi.' In the churchyard on the north side of the church is the base, stem, and fragment of the head of a fine 14th-century cross. The shaft is octagonal, and the remaining portion of the head is carved with the ball-flower.

Against the north wall of the north chapel is an elaborate alabaster monument to Thomas Denton, who died in 1558. The monument is of the table type and has a pilastered base with shields of arms, and upon the top are the recumbent effigies of Thomas Denton and his wife, both considerably damaged. He is wearing plate armour with a tabard of his arms, and his head rests on his crested helm. At the north-east of the chapel is a beautifully designed monument to Alexander Denton, who died in 1576, and his second wife Mary, who died in 1574; the inscription states that she was the daughter of Sir Roger Martyn. Upon the same wall is also a monument to Thomas Isham, who died in 1676. At the south-east of the chancel is a monument to Dr. William Denton, physician to Charles I and Charles II, who died at an advanced age in 1691. Two other monuments of interest remain on the south side of the chancel; one is a large and elaborate monument of marble with portrait busts commemorating Sir Alexander Denton, one of the justices of the court of Common Pleas, who died in 1739, and his wife Agnes, who died in 1753. The other, a mural tablet, commemorates George Woodward, 'Envoy Extraordinary from the King of Great Britain to the King and Republic of Poland,' who died at Warsaw in 1735, at the age of thirty-eight. He was the son of George Woodward of Stratton Audley and of his wife Anne, daughter of Alexander Denton.

There is a ring of six bells: the treble and second, by Henry or Matthew Bagley, both inscribed 'Alexander Deanton E^q S 1681'; the third inscribed 'Prayse ye the Lord M.B. (Matthew Bagley) 1681'; the fourth 'Henricus Bagley me fecit'; the fifth recast by Mears & Stainbank in 1893 and bearing the inscription of the bell which it replaced, 'W. Hall made me 1756'; and the sixth, also recast by Mears & Stainbank, bearing the inscription of the former bell, 'Pro rege et ecclesia Alexander Denton Robert Corbett Church Warden Henry Bagley made me 1721.'

The plate consists of a silver cup of 1811; a paten without marks or inscription; a fine silver flagon inscribed, 'The Gift of the Honble Alexander Denton one of the Justices of His Majesty's Court of Common Pleas, and Chancellor to his Royal Highness Frederick Prince of Wales, to ye Parish of Hillesden in the County of Bucks, 1737,' and bearing the marks of the year 1736; and a plated caudle-cup, the base of which may be silver, though without marks.

The registers begin in 1594.

ADVOWSON The church of Hillesden was granted to Nutley Abbey before 1164 by Walter Giffard and Ermengard his wife,[8] and confirmed to the monastery by subsequent charters of kings and popes.[9] A vicarage is mentioned in the early part of the 13th century,[10] but no presentations to it are found in the episcopal registers, the church being served by a canon of Nutley. After the Dissolution the vicarage was granted with the rectory in 1542 to the Dean and Chapter of Christ Church, Oxford,[11] but the living was only held as a perpetual curacy from that time until 1868–9,[12] at which date a vicarage was formed, presentation to which is still made by the dean and chapter.

A complaint was made against Nutley Abbey in 1344 that this and other of their churches were destitute of vicars,[13] and in the next century it was found that the abbey had allowed the chancel and other parts of the church to become very ruinous.[14]

At the time of the Dissolution an annual stipend of £4 was paid to the incumbent, which sum was afterwards continued by the rectors. In 1680 the churchwardens certified at a visitation that there was no house, glebe or endowment saving 40*s.* which Alexander Denton paid to the churchwardens. This allowance was augmented by the college to £20 per annum, which the lessee tenants, the Dentons, on being permitted to nominate a minister, increased to £30; in addition, they gave the ministers very generous entertainment at their house.[15] Further augmentations to the curate's stipend were made during the 19th century.[16]

In 1548 the commissioners returned that land in the parish to the annual value of 2*s.* had been given for the keeping of an obit in the church.[17]

CHARITIES Francis Clarke, by his will proved 27 July 1910, bequeathed £500 consols, the dividends to be distributed among the deserving sick and aged poor. The stock is held by the official trustees, and the annual dividends, amounting to £12 10*s.*, are duly applied.

LECKHAMPSTEAD

Lechamstede (xi cent.).

The parish of Leckhampstead, on the borders of Northamptonshire, has an area of 2,570 acres, of which 348 are arable land, 1,796 permanent grass and 179 woods and plantations.[1] The soil is clay and gravel; the subsoil various. The undulating surface, about 300 ft. above ordnance datum, rises to 350 ft. in the east and north. The Ouse, which here

[8] Dugdale, *Mon. Angl.* vi, 278.

[9] Ibid. 278–9; *Cal. Chart. R.* 1300–26, p. 210; *Cal. Papal Letters,* v, 509.

[10] *Liber Antiq. Hugonis Wells,* 14.

[11] *L. and P. Hen. VIII,* xvii, p. 491; xxi (2), 648 (25).

[12] *Clergy Lists.*

[13] Willis, loc. cit.

[14] Ibid.

[15] Ibid.; the lease of the rectory is mentioned in the wills of Alexander Denton, 1698, and of Alexander Denton, 1739 (P.C.C. 57 Pett, 291 Browne).

[16] Sheahan, op. cit. 278.

[17] Chant. Cert. 5.

[1] Statistics from Bd. of Agric. (1905).

HILLESDON CHURCH FROM THE NORTH

HILLESDON CHURCH: THE INTERIOR LOOKING EAST

LECKHAMPSTEAD CHURCH FROM THE NORTH

LECKHAMPSTEAD CHURCH: THE INTERIOR LOOKING EAST

flows in an easterly direction, forms the southern boundary. The Grand Junction Canal intersects the south of the parish, and is crossed at Cattleford Bridge by the road from Buckingham to Stony Stratford. Leckhampstead Wharf is about a quarter of a mile west of the bridge.

The village lies near the centre of the parish on a road branching north-west from the Buckingham road. It is divided into Church End at the north, where are the church of St. Mary and the schools, Middle End and South End, and is watered by a stream called the Leck, which rises in Whittlebury Forest, and is spanned here by South End Bridge. About a quarter of a mile east of Church End is Limes End with Limes End Bridge, formerly the manor of Little Leckhampstead, Great Leckhampstead occupying the north of the parish, and the space between being called Tween Towns.[2]

A large manor-house, the seat of the lords of Great Leckhampstead, described by Browne Willis as 'moated about antiently,' formerly stood west of the church, adjoining the churchyard ; but according to this authority it was 'good part of it pulled down' by Lady Wentworth in the first half of the 18th century, and 'made a Tenants' house.'[3] The present house, a plain stone building of the 17th century, is occupied as a farm-house by Mr. Henry George Hurst. 'A newly built house in Nast End,' referred to among the possessions of Sir Edward Tyrell of Little Leckhampstead at his death in 1606,[4] was probably the Toy, built in 1603 at a cost of £3,000. Browne Willis describes it as 'a lofty house of good freestone,' but in a bad state of repair, and converted into a farm-house long before 1735.[5] Toye Court or Lower Farm is a modern house about half a mile south-east of the church, but it has two early 17th-century windows, which probably came from the Toy above referred to.

Home Farm at South End is a 17th-century house, and retains its original staircase with twisted balusters and moulded handrail. A wing at the back is dated 1762, and built into the east wall are two stone windows with moulded jambs and mullions, said to have been brought from a house which stood near the farm.

The Rectory, about a quarter of a mile north-east of the church, is a handsome house, pleasantly situated on a hill, and surrounded by shrubbery and meadow.

The extreme north of the parish is occupied by Leckhampstead Wood, with Notamore Copse, Libby Wood and part of Wicken Wood. South of these woods are Hill Farm Wood House, Brook House and Lodge Farm.

Among place-names have been found Nutthrop End[6] (xvii cent.), Fishwater Meadow and the Harriotts[7] (xviii cent.).

MANORS At the date of the Domesday Survey 18 hides in *LECKHAMPSTEAD* were included among the lands of the Bishop of Bayeux.[8] This manor Earl Lewin had previously held,[9] and after the confiscation of the bishop's fief this holding, like those of his other chief tenants,[10] became a barony, called the barony of Maminot (Mamisnot),[11] after the Domesday tenant Maminot,[12] held of the Crown in chief, and owing ward to Dover Castle.[13] Maminot was probably soon displaced by Geoffrey de Mandeville, lord of another manor in Leckhampstead at the Survey, since this 18-hide manor was held for one fee of Geoffrey's heirs, the Says,[14] in the 13th[15] and 14th centuries,[16] Geoffrey de Say renouncing any claim in the advowson, doubtless as overlord, before 1219.[17] At the death of Elizabeth Baroness Say in 1399, and the partition of her property among her co-heirs, the three sisters of her father William de Say, the overlordship of this fee appears to have passed to Mary and Maud, the daughters and co-heirs of the second sister Elizabeth and of her husband Thomas de Aldon.[18] Sir William Heron, the second husband of Elizabeth Baroness Say, who held the overlordship rights here with her in 1396,[19] styled himself Lord Say, and possessed himself of many of his wife's estates after her death in 1399. In the following year he obtained a release of all her right in this fee from Thomas de Aldon's daughter Maud, wife of Thomas Bosenho,[20] and died seised of it in 1404.[21] A century later his interest appears to have come into the possession of the descendants of William de Say's third sister and co-heir Joan, wife of Sir William Fiennes, as the overlordship was stated in 1511 to be vested in John Fiennes, Lord

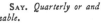
SAY. *Quarterly or and sable.*

FIENNES. *Azure three lions or.*

Saye,[22] and in 1520 in Edward Fiennes, son and heir of Thomas Fiennes, Lord Clinton and Saye.[23]

[2] Sheahan, *Hist. and Topog. of Bucks.* 282.

[3] Willis, *Hist. and Antiq. of Buckingham,* 207.

[4] Chan. Inq. p.m. (Ser. 2), ccxciv, 92.

[5] Willis, op. cit. 208.

[6] Chan. Inq. p.m. (Ser. 2), ccxciv, 92.

[7] Com. Pleas D. Enr. Mich. 10 Geo. III, m. 4.

[8] *V.C.H. Bucks.* i, 238.

[9] Ibid.

[10] Ibid. 211.

[11] *Red Bk. of Exch.* (Rolls Ser.), 617, 710, 721.

[12] He was probably the nephew and namesake of Gilbert Maminot, Bishop of Lisieux (*V.C.H. Bucks.* i, 211).

[13] *Red Bk. of Exch.* loc. cit. ; *Hund. R.* (Rec. Com.), ii, 338.

[14] G.E.C. *Complete Peerage,* vii, 62.

[15] *Testa de Nevill* (Rec. Com.), 243, 252; *Hund. R.* (Rec. Com.), i, 33 ; ii, 338 ; Chan. Inq. p.m. 9 Edw. I, no. 18 ; *Feud. Aids,* i, 79.

[16] *Feud. Aids,* i, 125.

[17] *R. of Hugh of Wells* (Cant. and York Soc.), i, 109, 110.

[18] G.E.C. *Peerage,* vii, 63.

[19] Feet of F. Div. Co. Hil. 19 Ric. II, no. 110.

[20] Close, 2 Hen. IV, pt. ii, m. 19 d.

[21] Chan. Inq. p.m. 6 Hen. IV, no. 21.

[22] Ibid. (Ser. 2), xxvi, 112.

[23] Ibid. xxxv, 60. There seems to have been some confusion in these returns between representatives of the Say co-heirs, and there was no such person as John Fiennes, Lord Saye, at that date. The

eldest son of Sir William Fiennes, son of Joan de Say and Sir William Fiennes, was Roger Fiennes, whose only son and heir Richard became Lord Dacre by his marriage with Joan *suo jure* Baroness Dacre in 1458, and their son Thomas Fiennes, Lord Dacre, would be heir to Joan de Say's property at these dates. Edward Fiennes, Lord Saye and Sele, the descendant of James Fiennes, the younger brother of Roger Fiennes, was holding the estates of the younger branch from 1501 till his death in 1528 (G.E.C. *Complete Peerage,* iii, 3 ; vii, 66). Thomas Lord Clinton, who died in 1517, leaving a son Edward as his heir, was not a Fiennes, though his great-grandmother was Elizabeth daughter of Richard Fiennes, Lord Dacre, and he may have held under some settle-

By the end of the 12th century the manor had been subinfeudated to Hugh Chastillon, who in 1199 levied a fine of lands here with Richard Chastillon,[24] probably identical with his son and heir Richard, whose widow Parnel, daughter of Ralph Pirot, received in 1205 from her father-in-law Hugh Chastillon a third of the vill in dower, with the advowson of the church.[25] Hugh seems to have been succeeded by his son Hugh, to whom Parnel Pirot and Hugh son of Richard, apparently her son, released the advowson before 1219,[26] and who as Hugh son of Hugh granted land in Leckhampstead in 1219 to Richard Chastillon.[27] Hugh Chastillon obtained a verdict from the bishop in 1223 that he was lawfully married to Gunnora de Bray,[28] and was dealing with land in Leckhampstead in 1228 and 1229.[29] Sir Hugh Chastillon presented to the church in 1251,[30] and was returned as lord of Leckhampstead in 1254.[31] He was alive in 1260-1,[32] but had been succeeded by his son Richard Chastillon before 1279, in which year Richard died seised of the manor, which then passed to his son Hugh.[33] Hugh Chastillon held Leckhampstead during the reigns of Edward I and Edward II,[34] and was knight of the shire for 1300 and 1301.[35] Between 1316 and 1323 he was succeeded by Richard Chastillon,[36] his son,[37] who was sued for debt in 1327[38] and 1330.[39] He, who was knight of the shire in 1331 and again ten years later,[40] in 1332 settled two-thirds of the manor and the reversion of the third held by Hawise widow of Hugh in dower on himself for life, with remainder to his son Hugh and the latter's wife Margaret.[41] In 1344 he settled messuages, land and rent in Great Leckhampstead and Foscott on himself and his wife Elizabeth, with remainder to their son Richard and his heirs male,[42] and was still holding the manor in 1346.[43] He was succeeded probably before 1356 by his son Hugh, who was Sheriff of Bedfordshire and Buckinghamshire in that year,[44] and presented to the church in 1359.[45] In 1366 a commission of array was issued to this Hugh,[46] and he was still alive in 1379.[47] His son Richard had a daughter and heir Elizabeth, who with her husband William Gernon was plaintiff in an action concerning Clanfield Manor, Oxfordshire, in 1396.[48] In 1434 William and Elizabeth Gernon settled Leckhampstead on themselves and issue,[49] but were obliged to sue the trustees for refusing to re-enfeoff them.[50] Their son and heir Thomas was succeeded by a son William, who put in a claim to

Thornton Manor (q.v.) in 1464,[51] and died in 1479, leaving a son William, aged fourteen.[52] The Gernon line ended in an heir Joan, who brought the manor to her husband Ralph Tylney, citizen and alderman of London, with whom in 1488 she inspected the settlement of 1434, Elizabeth Hill, widow, being also a party to the proceedings.[53] Ralph's son Reginald Tylney died in 1506,[54] before his mother Joan, who by her will, dated and proved in 1509, left a legacy to her daughter and heir Elizabeth.[55] Elizabeth died in January 1510-11, her heir being her father's brother John Tylney.[56] He, who was twice married —his first wife's name being Lucy and that of his second Margaret—died on 15 May 1518. His will, made four days earlier, appointed his wife Margaret his executrix, and settled the manor on her and his heirs by her.[57] Margaret later instituted proceedings against John Mylborne, citizen and alderman of London, and other feoffees, who refused to make an estate to her,[58] and died in London on 15 January 1518-19, a week after the birth of a daughter and heir Joan.[59] Joan married Richard Greenway of Dinton,

TYLNEY. *Argent a cheveron between three griffons' heads gules having beaks or.*

GREENWAY. *Gules a cheveron between three griffons' heads razed argent with three anchors sable on the cheveron.*

lord of Woodrow Manor in Amersham (q.v.), with which Leckhampstead descended until the end of the century. Joan's second husband, Michael Harcourt, was ordered in 1587 to appear before the council on the complaint of Marmaduke Claver (of Foscott Manor),[60] who had instituted proceedings against him as to right of intercommon between the two manors,[61] but with whom he finally promised to be 'good neighbours,' and not to unjustly molest nor vex him.[62] His daughter Winifred married his stepson Anthony Greenway, with whom and with their

ment by her. He represented the eldest branch of co-heirs, being descended from William de Say's eldest sister, Idonea de Say (G.E.C. *Peerage,* ii, 305).

[24] *Rot. Cur. Reg.* (Rec. Com.), ii, 37 ; see also ibid. ii, 239 ; i, 222, 255, 432.

[25] Feet of F. case 14, file 8, no. 1.

[26] *R. of Hugh of Wells* (Cant. and York Soc.), i, 109-10. The entry is made 'before the 10th year.'

[27] Pipe R. 3 Hen. III, m. 51.

[28] *R. of Hugh of Wells* (Cant. and York Soc.), ii, 204.

[29] *Cal. Close,* 1227-31, pp. 15, 237.

[30] Harl. MS. 6950, fol. 163.

[31] *Hund. R.* (Rec. Com.), i, 33 ; see also *Testa de Nevill* (Rec. Com.), 243, 252.

[32] *Cal. Pat.* 1247-58, p. 433 ; *Red Bk. of Exch.* (Rolls Ser.), 710.

[33] Chan. Inq. p.m. 7 Edw. I, no. 9 ; 9 Edw. I, no. 18. See also *Hund. R.* (Rec. Com.), ii, 338.

[34] *Feud. Aids,* i, 79, 100, 108.

[35] *Ret. of Memb. of Parl.* i, 10, 13.

[36] Willis, op. cit. 209.

[37] Wrottesley, *Ped. from Plea R.* 408.

[38] De Banco R. Hil. 1 Edw. III, m. 21.

[39] *Cal. Close,* 1330-3, p. 120.

[40] *Ret. of Memb. of Parl.* i, 94, 133.

[41] Feet of F. case 19, file 79, no. 3.

[42] Ibid. file 86, no. 502. The father was described as Richard Chastillon the elder of Great Leckhampstead in 1345 (*Cal. Close,* 1343-6, p. 643). The younger Richard, as Richard Chastillon of Leckhampstead, granted 18s. rent in Westbury to the priory of Catesby in 1363 (*Cal. Pat.* 1361-4, p. 325).

[43] *Feud. Aids,* i, 125.

[44] *Gesta Abbat.* (Rolls Ser.), ii, 351 ; P.R.O. *List of Sheriffs,* 2.

[45] Willis, loc. cit.

[46] *Cal. Pat.* 1364-7, p. 365.

[47] *Cal. Close,* 1377-81, p. 181.

[48] *Gen.* (New Ser.), xiv, 250.

[49] Feet of F. Div. Co. East. 13 Hen.VI, no. 59 ; De Banco R. Trin. 3 Hen. VII, m. 427.

[50] Early Chan. Proc. bdle. 11, no. 269.

[51] Wrottesley, loc. cit. The pedigree given in the pleadings omits Richard and makes Elizabeth Gernon daughter of Hugh Chastillon.

[52] Chan. Inq. p.m. 19 Edw. IV, no. 50.

[53] De Banco R. Trin. 3 Hen. VII, m. 427.

[54] See church.

[55] P.C.C. 23 Bennett.

[56] Chan. Inq. p.m. (Ser. 2), xxvi, 112.

[57] Ibid. xxxv, 60.

[58] Early Chan. Proc. bdle. 449, no. 25.

[59] Chan. Inq. p.m. (Ser. 2), xxxv, 60.

[60] *Acts of P.C.* 1587-8, p. 241.

[61] Chan. Proc. Eliz. C 18, no. 39.

[62] *Acts of P.C.* 1587-8, p. 247.

son Richard he was dealing with the manor in 1595.[63] He died in 1597,[64] and in the year following his death John Chowe of Leckhampstead instituted proceedings in Chancery, claiming that when Michael Harcourt had been sheriff (which was in the year 1594–5)[65] he as under sheriff had made payments and borrowed money on his account.[66] In 1599 Anthony Greenway, in conjunction with his mother Joan Harcourt and his wife Winifred, made a settlement of Leckhampstead after the death of his mother, wife and himself, on his son Richard and the latter's wife Elizabeth, in tail-male.[67] He died on 28 January 1618–19 and was succeeded by Richard,[68] who died in the following August, when the manor passed to Richard's son Anthony.[69] Anthony, then just under twenty-one, appears to have been in money difficulties within a few years of his father's death. He was dealing with the manor in 1624 in conjunction with Beale Sapperton,[70] with whom and with John Pollard he and his wife Amphillis conveyed messuages and lands in Leckhampstead to Edmund Pye in that year.[71] In 1626 proceedings were instituted against Anthony Greenway and Amphillis by Thomas Packington of Shoelands in Puttenham (co. Surrey), who claimed the chief messuage and lands as security for £600 paid to them by him to purchase an annuity from the manor.[72] In 1628 Anthony Greenway and Amphillis his wife, Thomas Packington and Anne his wife, and John Pollard and Katherine his wife conveyed the manor to Edmund Pye (of St. Martin's, Ludgate, London) and his son and heir Edmund.[73] The elder Edmund was still alive in 1635,[74] in which year the younger Edmund married Katherine, sister of John first Lord Lucas of Shenfield.[75] The son was made a baronet as Sir Edmund Pye of Leckhampstead in 1641, and knighted four days later.[76] In 1646 he compounded on the Articles of Oxford; he had lived at Oxford for three years, his fine, a tenth, being set at £3,865.[77] He died in 1673, and was survived by

PYE of Leckhampstead, baronet. *Or a pile azure with three scallops or thereon.*

LOVELACE. *Gules a chief indented argent with three martlets sable therein.*

his wife Dame Katherine and his two daughters and co-heirs—Martha, who married John third Lord

Lovelace, of Hurley, and Elizabeth wife of the Hon. Charles West. Sir Edmund Pye's widow died in 1701, and the manor passed to Elizabeth West, at whose death it descended to Martha Lovelace, only surviving child of Martha Pye and John Lord Lovelace, Baroness Wentworth in her own right.[78] She married Sir Henry Johnson, who died in 1719, and, after nearly pulling down the old manor-house, she died childless in 1745.[79] Under her will the manor passed to Martha, sister of the last Lord Lovelace, who had married Lord Henry Beauclerk, fourth son of the first Duke of St. Albans.[80] She, being then a widow, with her son and heir-apparent the Rev. Henry Beauclerk, then of Christ Church, Oxford, barred the entail on the manor on 17 November 1769.[81] At her death in 1788 she was succeeded in the manor by her son Henry, then incumbent.[82] He was holding the manor in 1793 with his son John Beauclerk,[83] and was lord in 1811.[84] He was succeeded by his son John Beauclerk, whose son Henry William Beauclerk succeeded in 1840,[85] and was lord until his death in 1894.[86] Before 1899 the manor had passed to its present owner, Mr. Lawrence James Baker of Brambridge Park, Eastleigh (Hants).

BEAUCLERK. *The royal arms of King Charles II with the difference of a sinister baston gules cut off at the ends and charged with three silver roses.*

Two hides included among the lands of Walter Giffard in 1086 and previously held by Suartin, a man of Asgar the Staller,[87] with 3 hides previously held by Suartin, and included among the lands of Geoffrey de Mandeville at that date,[88] were afterwards held for half a fee and two-thirds of a fee respectively, and though these 5 hides had amalgamated under the same tenant by 1225, when they were held for one and a sixth fee,[89] the distinction between the amount of service due from each portion was maintained during the 13th century.[90] The greater amount was wrongly assigned to the 2-hide holding in 1254,[91] but the mistake was rectified in 1279.[92] The total service due from the combined estate was given in 1284–6,[93] but after that date, with the disappearance of the Mandeville overlordship, the military service rendered by his part of Leckhampstead fell into abeyance, and the manor continued to be held for half a fee only until the abolition of feudal tenure in the 17th century.[94]

The 2 hides of Walter Giffard united with the rest of his lands to form the honour of Giffard,[95] which descended in the 13th century to the Marshals, Earls of Pembroke,[96] and later passed to their successors the

[63] Feet of F. Bucks. Trin. 37 Eliz.
[64] P.C.C. 31 Cobham.
[65] P.R.O. *List of Sheriffs,* 9.
[66] Chan. Proc. (Ser. 2), bdle. 263, no. 71.
[67] Feet of F. Bucks. Trin. 41 Eliz.; Chan. Inq. p.m. (Ser. 2), cccxcvi, 135 and 150.
[68] Chan. Inq. p.m. (Ser. 2), cccxcvi, 135.
[69] Ibid. 150.
[70] Feet of F. Bucks. Hil. 21 Jas. I, *bis.*
[71] Ibid. Trin. 22 Jas. I.
[72] Chan. Proc. (Ser. 2), bdle. 412, no. 1.
[73] Feet of F. Bucks. Mich. 4 Chas. I.
[74] *Visit. of London* (Harl. Soc.), ii, 183.

[75] G.E.C. *Complete Baronetage,* ii, 83.
[76] Ibid.   [77] *Cal. Com. for Comp.* 1443.
[78] Willis, op. cit. 205.
[79] G.E.C. *Peerage,* viii, 101.
[80] Willis, loc. cit.; Lipscomb, *Hist. and Antiq. of Bucks.* iii, 25.
[81] Com. Pleas D. Enr. Mich. 10 Geo. III, m. 4; Recov. R. Mich. 10 Geo. III, m. 136.
[82] Lipscomb, loc. cit.
[83] Recov. R. Trin. 33 Geo. III, m. 44.
[84] Com. Pleas Recov. R. Mich. 52 Geo. III, m. 110.
[85] Burke, *Peerage* (St. Albans).

[86] Lewis, *Topog. Dict.*
[87] *V.C.H. Bucks.* i, 250.
[88] Ibid. 259. Suartin could not sell either manor without leave.
[89] Feet of F. case 14, file 15, no. 3.
[90] *Testa de Nevill* (Rec. Com.), 247b, 252, 258.
[91] *Hund. R.* (Rec. Com.), i, 32.
[92] Ibid. ii, 339.
[93] *Feud. Aids,* i, 79.
[94] Ibid. 100, 125; Chan. Inq. p.m. (Ser. 2), dviii, 15.
[95] *Testa de Nevill* (Rec. Com.), 261.
[96] Ibid. 247b.

Valences, Earls of Pembroke.[97] From them it was inherited by the Lords Talbot,[98] who claimed view of frankpledge here in 1371.[99] Their overlordship rights cannot be traced after 1419,[100] but the Earls of Oxford, who held an intermediary lordship under the Marshals in the early 13th century,[1] claimed services in this half fee until the middle of the 17th century.[2]

Yet another intermediary lordship under the Earls of Oxford was exercised by Roger de Missenden and his heirs during the 13th and 14th centuries.[3]

The 3 hides which pertained to Geoffrey de Mandeville in 1086 were later held of his descendants the Earls of Essex and Hereford,[4] but their connexion with Leckhampstead ceases some time after 1279, when an intermediary lordship was held under them by Roger de Missenden, who also occupied the same position with regard to the other fee at that date.[5] Missenden's interest may be represented by Richard Moore of Aylesbury, who in 1606 had overlordship rights in this manor worth 6d. yearly.[6]

The under-tenants of Walter Giffard and Geoffrey de Mandeville in 1086 were Hugh and Osbert respectively.[7]

Richard Fitz Osbert, who received a grant of 8 acres of assart in Leckhampstead in the forest of Whittlewood from Henry II,[8] probably held as successor to the Domesday Osbert, and may have been identical with the Richard Fitz Osbert who was Sheriff of Bedfordshire and Buckinghamshire in 1159, 1160, 1165, 1166.[9] It was doubtless a descendant of the same name who in 1224–5 held both Domesday manors,[10] which he granted to Richard son of Richard, probably his son, to hold at a rent of 12d. for all service, saving the foreign service due.[11] Richard son of Richard was holding as late as 1254,[12] but before 1279 had been succeeded by William son of Roger.[13] It was probably the same William who as William de Leaume was holding the manor in 1284,[14] and who in 1293 purchased certain rents in Leckhampstead from Gregory de Meldeburne and Isabel his wife.[15]

In 1302 this estate, first here called *LECKHAMPSTEAD MANOR*, and later known as *LYMES END*, had passed to Alan de Leaume,[16] who was still in possession in 1316.[17] It was probably a successor of the same name who in 1323–5 was before the justices for an assault on William Chastillon, parson of Bedhampton, Hampshire, of which he, his wife Cecilia, his son John, and Richard, 'Alan's priest of Lenne,' had been guilty at Little Leckhampstead.[18] Alan de Leaume and his sons seem to have carried on

a feud with the Chastillon family, and in 1333 Alan, with his sons John and Thomas and others, had to appear for carrying away the goods of Sir Malcolm Chastillon at Leckhampstead,[19] John son of Alan complaining in 1345 that Richard Chastillon of Great Leckhampstead and Hugh, Richard, John and William, his sons, had maimed and imprisoned him at Little Leckhampstead, so that his life was despaired of, and had mowed and carried away his crops.[20] In 1345 200 marks were owed by John de Wolverton to this son John, and to his father, described as Alan de Leaume of Little Leckhampstead, the elder,[21] and returned in the following year as holding Little Leckhampstead in succession to Alan de Leaume.[22] John's career ended in outlawry in 1347 'for the death of Geoffrey Fraunkleyn and others by him at divers times feloniously slain.'[23] His father, therefore, in 1353 enfeoffed Alan, his younger son, of the manor, which should have passed to John after his own death, and the younger Alan occupied it from that date.[24] After the death of his father, two years later,[25] the manor was seized into the king's hands by reason of John's felony, and was delivered by the king in 1360 to Michael de Ravensdale, parson of Leckhampstead, and Robert de Hornby,[26] but was restored with all issues to Alan as Alan de Leaume the younger in 1362.[27] In July 1384 complaint was made by Alan de Leaume that Henry de Barton and Lettice his wife, Richard Senkler, Roger Doget and others, by night broke his close and houses at Little Leckhampstead, assaulted him, took away six horses, three mares, ten oxen, eight cows, three bullocks and twenty hogs, value £20, felled trees and carried them off, as well as other goods, charters and writings, and assaulted servants.[28] The manor remained in the possession of the Leaumes, and was in 1413 conveyed by William de Leaume for 100 marks to William Pirton, clerk, and others,[29] to whom in the same year and term it was quitclaimed for a like sum by Henry Fraunkleyn and Elizabeth his wife, with warranty against the heirs of Elizabeth.[30] This grant, made apparently to feoffees, seems to have been followed by a lease to William Lacy, who in 1423 released to William Pirton the manor of Little Leckhampstead, which he had held for life by grant from him with remainder to Thomas de Leaume.[31] It had passed from Thomas de Leaume, possibly to a female heir, in 1428, when it was held by William Russell and Margaret his wife, who then granted it for 300 marks to John Morton and Richard English, with warrant against the heirs of Margaret.[32] In 1493 it

[97] *Hund. R.* (Rec. Com.), i, 32; ii, 339; Chan. Inq. p.m. 17 Edw. II, no. 75.
[98] G.E.C. *Peerage*, vii, 359.
[99] Chan. Inq. p.m. 46 Edw. III (1st nos.), no. 66.
[100] Ibid. 20 Ric. II, no. 51; 7 Hen. V, no. 68.
[1] *Testa de Nevill* (Rec. Com.), 247b.
[2] *Hund. R.* (Rec. Com.), ii, 339; *Feud. Aids*, i, 79; Chan. Inq. p.m. 17 Edw. II, no. 35; 20 Ric. II, no. 51; (Ser. 2), dviii, 15; Feet of F. Bucks. East. 26 Eliz.
[3] *Hund. R.* loc. cit.; *Feud. Aids*, i, 79, 125; Chan. Inq. p.m. 34 Edw. III (2nd nos.), no. 35.
[4] *Testa de Nevill* (Rec. Com.), 243b, 252; *Hund. R.* (Rec. Com.), i, 32.
[5] *Hund. R.* (Rec. Com.), ii, 339.

[6] Chan. Inq. p.m. (Ser. 2), ccxciv, 92.
[7] *V.C.H. Bucks.* i, 250, 259.
[8] Cart. Antiq. OO 28.
[9] P.R.O. *List of Sheriffs*, 1.
[10] Feet of F. case 14, file 15, no. 3.
[11] Ibid.
[12] *Hund. R.* (Rec. Com.), i, 32. See also *Testa de Nevill* (Rec. Com.), 243, 247, 252, 258b, 261b.
[13] *Hund. R.* (Rec. Com.), ii, 339.
[14] *Feud. Aids*, i, 79. Variants of the name are Lemes, Leymes, Leames, Leugham, Lealme, Loamme.
[15] Feet of F. case 17, file 52, no. 3.
[16] *Feud. Aids*, i, 100.
[17] Ibid. 108.
[18] *Cal. Pat.* 1321–4, p. 453; 1324–7, pp. 73, 224.
[19] Ibid. 1330–4, pp. 498, 499, 502.
[20] Ibid. 1343–5, pp. 503, 504, 505.

[21] *Cal. Close*, 1343–6, p. 643.
[22] *Feud. Aids*, i, 125.
[23] *Cal. Close*, 1360–4, pp. 370–1. An inquisition as to the killing of Geoffrey and others at Leckhampstead was taken in the previous year (*Cal. Pat.* 1345–8, p. 229).
[24] Chan. Inq. p.m. 34 Edw. III (2nd nos.), no. 35. This inquisition gives the extent: apple trees in garden; fields; oak wood; water-mill; dovecot in ruins.
[25] Ibid.
[26] *Abbrev. Rot. Orig.* (Rec. Com.), ii, 257.
[27] *Cal. Close*, loc. cit.
[28] *Cal. Pat.* 1381–5, p. 500.
[29] Feet of F. case 22, file 116, no. 3.
[30] Ibid. no. 2.
[31] Close, 2 Hen. VI, no. 10, 19.
[32] Feet of F. case 22, file 119, no. 2.

was the property of Mary Middleton, who conveyed it in Easter term of that year for £300 to Richard Empson,[33] to whom in the same year and term it was conveyed by John Maunsell and Margaret his wife.[34] Described as a messuage with meadows, cottages, and copses called Lymeswoods, &c., formerly belonging to Walter Maunsell,[35] it reverted to the Crown on the attainder of Sir Richard Empson in 1512,[36] and was granted in that year to William Tyler.[37] It was held by George Saunders in 1537,[38] and had passed by 1557 into the hands of Thomas Pigott of Loughton, by whom it was then conveyed as the manor of Little Leckhampstead or 'Lemesend' (after its former owners) to George Tyrell,[39] already holding a manor of Leckhampstead, probably Nast End, and lord of Thornton (q.v.), with which it continued to be held until late in the 19th century.[40] An arbitration in 1811 between the Rev. Henry Beauclerk and Sir Thomas Sheppard, bart., which decreed that the former as lord of Leckhampstead Manor was also lord of the manors of Lymes End and Nast End, parcel thereof,[41] cannot have affected the manorial rights of Sir Thomas Sheppard, since his representative, the Hon. Richard Cavendish of Thornton, was lord *circa* 1860.[42]

The property known in the 17th century as the manor of *NAST END* appears to have in part originated in the grant of lands made by Hugh Chastillon in 1280, after the death of his father Richard, to Rose widow of the same Richard.[43] This consisted of one messuage and one-third of the profits of a dovecot belonging to it, but not the garden and fish-stew. She was also to have a third of a wood, and lands in Morsladefield, Longeneham, Sladefield and Northfield, with one-third of Marham Moor. All this was to be held of Hugh for a penny a year and to revert to him after Rose's death.[44] The land, however, afterwards assessed at 2 virgates, remained in Rose's heirs, and continued to be held of the Chastillons of Great Leckhampstead during the 14th century.[45] This estate was augmented by 2½ virgates subinfeudated to the Chastillons by the lords of Little Leckhampstead before 1279,[46] and held of the Leaumes during the 14th century.[47] An intermediary lordship of half a virgate of this part was held in the late 13th and early 14th centuries by Ellis Tingewick,[48] Roger de Missenden standing between him and the lord of Lymes End in 1279.[49] Temporary overlordship rights appear to have been obtained during the 14th century by eight other persons,[50] one of whom, William le Vavasour, owned lands in Great Leckhampstead in 1325.[51]

Rose Chastillon, the holder in fee of this combined estate, immediately after her husband's death married John Tingewick,[52] who was returned as free tenant in Little Leckhampstead in 1279.[53] In 1285 he and Rose acquired additional lands here from Hugh son of Ralf le Clerk and Agnes his wife,[54] and also purchased an estate from Ralf son of William de Plumpton, which at John Tingewick's death in 1304 reverted to William his son and heir by Rose.[55] William also enjoyed the property which had been settled on Rose in 1280 by Hugh Chastillon, but at William's death in 1316, though John Tingewick, his brother, was his heir-at-law, the Chastillon lands went to Malcolm son of Rose by Richard Chastillon.[56] Malcolm Chastillon was lord of Thornton Manor [56a] (q.v.), with which this Leckhampstead property henceforward descends. The name Nast End first appears in 1606, when Sir Edward Tyrell died seised of a newly-built house in Nast End in Great Leckhampstead, which he bequeathed to his wife Margaret.[57] The Tyrells seem to have held their Little Leckhampstead property as Lymes End Manor and their Great Leckhampstead property as Nast End Manor.[58] In the early 19th century Nast End appears to have been absorbed into Lymes End, and is not mentioned separately by name after the arbitration of 1811.[59]

A mill was held with the manor of Great Leckhampstead in 1205,[60] and in 1279 the freeholders of Great Leckhampstead included John the Miller, who held a water-mill at a rent of 20s.[61] A mill was held by Hugh under Walter Giffard at the date of the Domesday Survey,[62] and in 1279 the freeholders of Little Leckhampstead included Richard the Miller, who held a water-mill rented at 26s. 8d. yearly.[63] This water-mill was among the appurtenances of Lymes End Manor in 1360,[64] and was doubtless one of the three or four water corn-mills standing on the Tyrells' Thornton and Leckhampstead estates in the 17th and 18th centuries.[65]

A several fishery in Great and Little Leckhampstead was held with Lymes End Manor in 1557,[66] 1573,[67] and 1606.[68]

The church of the *ASSUMPTION OF THE VIRGIN* consists of a chancel measuring internally 27 ft. by 15 ft., north vestry, nave 56 ft. 6 in. by 19 ft., north aisle 9 ft. wide, south porch, and west tower 11 ft. square; it is built of rubble and roofed with tiles and lead.

The church dates from the early years of the 12th century, and originally consisted of the eastern part of the present nave to within 16 ft. of the west end,

CHURCH

---

[33] De Banco R. East. 8 Hen. VII, m. 21 ; Feet of F. case 22, file 127.

[34] Ibid.

[35] This Walter Maunsell or Mauntell held lands in Leckhampstead about 1460 (Early Chan. Proc. bdle. 28, no. 206).

[36] Chan. Inq. p.m. (Ser. 2), lxxix, 212.

[37] L. and P. Hen. VIII, i, 3492.

[38] Recov. R. Trin. 29 Hen. VIII, m. 123.

[39] Feet of F. Bucks. Hil. 3 & 4 Phil. and Mary.

[40] Ibid. Hil. 30 Geo. II.

[41] Com. Pleas Recov. R. Mich. 52 Geo. III, m. 110.

[42] Sheahan, op. cit. 282.

[43] Feet of F. case 284, file 21, no. 17.

[44] Ibid.

[45] Chan. Inq. p.m. 32 Edw. I, no. 44 ;

[46] Hund. R. (Rec. Com.), ii, 339.

[47] Chan. Inq. p.m. 10 Edw. II, no. 31 ; 11 Edw. III (1st nos.), no. 33.

[48] Hund. R. loc. cit. ; Cal. Chart. R. 1300–26, p. 108.

[49] Hund. R. loc. cit.

[50] Chan. Inq. p.m. 32 Edw. I, no. 44 ; 10 Edw. II, no. 31.

[51] Feet of F. Bucks. 19 Edw. II, no. 14.

[52] Hund. R. (Rec. Com.), ii, 352.

[53] Ibid. 339.

[54] Feet of F. Bucks. 13 Edw. I, no. 18.

[55] Chan. Inq. p.m. 32 Edw. I, no. 44 ; Cal. Close, 1302–7, p. 173.

[56] Chan. Inq. p.m. 10 Edw. II, no. 31 ; 11 Edw. III (1st nos.), no. 33.

[56a] See also Feet of F. Div. Co. Hil.

10 Edw. II, no. 31 ; 11 Edw. III (1st nos.), no. 33.

[46] Hund. R. (Rec. Com.), ii, 339.

[47] Chan. Inq. p.m. 10 Edw. II, no. 31 ; 11 Edw. III (1st nos.), no. 33.

[48] Hund. R. loc. cit. ; Cal. Chart. R. 1300–26, p. 108.

[49] Hund. R. loc. cit.

[50] Chan. Inq. p.m. 32 Edw. I, no. 44 ; 10 Edw. II, no. 31.

[51] Feet of F. Bucks. 19 Edw. II, no. 14.

[52] Hund. R. (Rec. Com.), ii, 352.

[53] Ibid. 339.

[54] Feet of F. Bucks. 13 Edw. I, no. 18.

[55] Chan. Inq. p.m. 32 Edw. I, no. 44 ; Cal. Close, 1302–7, p. 173.

[56] Chan. Inq. p.m. 10 Edw. II, no. 31 ; 11 Edw. III (1st nos.), no. 33.

[56a] See also Feet of F. Div. Co. Hil.

4 & 5 Edw. VI ; Chan. Proc. (Ser. 2), bdles. 8, no. 4 ; 176, no. 60.

[57] Chan. Inq. p.m. (Ser. 2), ccxciv, 92.

[58] Recov. R. Mich. 4 Will. and Mary, m. 113 ; Mich. 35 Geo. III, m. 18.

[59] Com. Pleas Recov. R. Mich. 52 Geo. III, m. 110.

[60] Feet of F. case 14, file 8, no. 1.

[61] Hund. R. (Rec. Com.), ii, 339.

[62] V.C.H. Bucks. i, 250.

[63] Hund. R. loc. cit.

[64] Chan. Inq. p.m. 34 Edw. III (2nd nos.), no. 35.

[65] See Thornton Manor.

[66] Feet of F. Bucks. Hil. 3 & 4 Phil. and Mary.

[67] Chan. Inq. p.m. (Ser. 2), clxiii, 3.

[68] Ibid. ccxciv, 92.

and probably a small chancel ; the nave seems to have been lengthened westward about 1180, when the north aisle was built, the tower was added in the late 13th century, and the chancel was rebuilt and widened about 1350, while the south porch was added late in the 15th century. The whole fabric has been restored at a modern period.

The axis of the chancel does not line with that of the nave, the widening having been effected towards the north only. In the east wall is a modern three-light traceried window and there are two windows in each of the side walls ; that at the south-east, of two lights with flowing tracery, is of about 1350, and opposite to it on the north is a window of similar character, but its tracery has been entirely renewed. The north-west window is also original, and is of two trefoiled lights with tracery in the head composed practically of one large multifoiled opening ; the south-west window, entirely modern except the head, which dates from about 1500, is of three trefoiled lights in a four-centred head. On the north is a narrow 14th-century doorway with an ogee head and a label with head-stops and foliated finial, and on the south are two plain round-headed sedilia, one of which is much wider than the other. The pointed chancel arch and the open timber roof of the chancel are modern.

The nave is lighted by two modern windows in the south wall, each of three pointed lights. The south doorway, which dates from about 1120, has a round head of one order with a large edge roll supported by jamb shafts with carved bird-like capitals and chamfered abaci. Both shafts are enriched with scale and cheveron ornament, that on the east, which terminates below the capital in a monstrous head, having the appearance of a serpent. The tympanum, which rests on a flat lintel with diaper ornament, has a sculptured representation of two dragons which appear to dispute the possession of a long-eared human figure standing between them, and on the infilling above is some mediaeval paint. On the nave wall inside is a large pointed stoup with a modern round bowl. Opening to the aisle on the north is a late 12th-century arcade of four pointed arches supported by square piers and responds with moulded abaci and double-chamfered plinths, the latter extensively repaired. The arches are single chamfered on the side towards the aisle, but on the nave side are recessed in two moulded orders with engrailed labels. There are large grotesque stops at the junctions of the labels over the piers, and carved heads or flower ornament at their apexes, two of the heads having their faces turned towards the altar. Traces of 13th-century painting remain on the piers, including cheveron ornaments and other designs, and two inscriptions, ' Hic sedet Isabella ' on the central pier and ' Ave Maria ' on the easternmost pier, the last four letters being almost obliterated. The late 13th-century pointed tower arch in the west wall is the full width of the tower, and is of three chamfered orders which die into the walls on both sides. At the north-east of the nave is a 15th-century doorway to the rood-loft, and built into the wall below its sill is a piece of 12th-century stonework with diaper ornament.

The north aisle is lighted by three windows in the north wall and one in the west wall, all modern, except perhaps the head of the latter, which is a single trefoiled light. The north doorway, a good example

of late 12th-century work, has a round arch of two moulded orders ; the inner order is enriched with cheveron and foliated ornament, and the jambs are moulded with keeled edge rolls, while the outer order has attached jamb shafts, both rolls and shafts having rudimentary foliated capitals and moulded abaci ; the label has enrichment like that of the inner order of the arch and has head-stops at the springing and the apex. The south porch has an original four-centred entrance archway, which has been repaired, and a restored two-light window in each side wall. A stone over the entrance is inscribed ' W.C. 1688,' and circles have been scratched on the south wall. Standing near the porch is the base of the mediaeval churchyard cross.

The tower is of three stages with buttresses at the angles of the ground stage, and is surmounted by an embattled parapet with a moulded string-course and gargoyles. The west doorway, which dates from about 1280, though slightly restored, has a pointed arch of two richly moulded orders, the inner continuous down the jambs and the outer supported by attached shafts with moulded capitals and bases. Above is a restored round-headed light of about 1180, which has been reset in the wall ; the arch is of two orders, the outer being supported by attached jamb shafts with foliated capitals and moulded bases. The second stage is lighted by loopholes, and the bell-chamber by four windows, each of two lancet lights in an unpierced pointed head, all probably dating from the late 13th century.

The font has an early 14th-century octagonal bowl, four sides of which have sculptured representations of the Crucifixion, the Virgin and Child below a crocketed canopy, St. Catherine, and a bishop ; the other four sides are embellished with conventional foliage, the leaves on the south-east side being connected by a strap-like ornament which might be confounded with earlier work but for the typical 14th-century foliage with which it occurs and in the design of which it obviously forms a part. The stem and base are modern. On the floor at the east end of the north aisle is a brass figure of a man in a fur-lined cloak with the inscription ' Hic jacet Regenoldus Tylney gentylman filius secundus Radulfi Tylney civis et aldermani londinii et unicus heres istius manerii qui obiit tercio die maii anno dñi MCCCCCVI.' Below are small figures of his three daughters and above are the arms of Tylney impaling Gernon ; there is also an early 16th-century brass figure of a lady in a gabled head-dress, which was recently recovered from a house near by, and is now affixed to the south wall. Under the westernmost arch of the arcade is a table tomb, probably commemorating Hugh Chastillon, who died between 1316 and 1323, with the recumbent effigy of a knight in armour wearing a bascinet, cyclas, and long sword, and a shield on the left arm. On the north wall of the chancel is a tablet to Sir Anthony Greenway, who died in 1619. There is a 17th-century carved chair in the chancel.

The tower contains a ring of five bells : the treble and second were added in 1897 ; the third, inscribed ' Gaude Virgo mat(e)r,' dates from the first half of the 16th century ; the fourth is inscribed ' Chandler made me 1664,' and the tenor ' Chandler made me 1662 ' ; there is also a mediaeval sanctus, now in a framework at the west of the north aisle, inscribed ' Crestit me firi fecit.'

The communion plate consists of a beautifully chased cup of 1569 inscribed 'Leckhamstead Parish,' a paten of 1829, and a flagon of 1833.

The registers before 1812 are as follows : (i) all entries 1558 to 1754 ; (ii) baptisms and burials 1756 to 1812, several leaves of this book, some containing earlier entries, have been cut out ; (iii) marriages 1754 to 1823.

ADVOWSON The church is mentioned in 1209–19, when Hugh Chastillon held the advowson,[69] which remained vested in the lord of the manor of Great Leckhampstead [70] until *circa* 1860, when it was held by Henry William Beauclerk. From him it passed *circa* 1882 to Mr. S. Tompkins, who held it until 1899,[71] and has since been again held by the lord of the manor.

The church was valued at £16 in 1291[72] and at £15 13s. 4d. in 1535.[73]

CHARITIES The charity for a schoolmaster, founded by will of John Smith, proved in the P.C.C. 28 August 1806, is endowed with a sum of £315 consols, the annual dividends of which, amounting to £7 17s. 4d., are applied in support of the school.

The charity of the Rev. Heneage Drummond, founded by deed 6 October 1879, now consists of £278 10s. 6d. 2½ per cent. annuities, arising from the sale in 1899 of premises formerly known as 'The Chequers.' By a scheme of the Charity Commissioners of 7 June 1895 the annual dividends, amounting to £6 19s. 4d., are applicable for parochial purposes, such as providing gratuitous lodging for a curate or schoolmaster, or the maintenance of a museum.

The Major Charles Hall Memorial Charity, founded by deed 4 March 1895, is endowed with a sum of £1,737 4s. 9d. India 3½ per cent. stock, purchased with a sum of £2,000, producing £60 16s. yearly, applicable for the benefit of the poor. In 1912 the distribution was made in medicines, food, in the payment of doctor's bills and in subscriptions to hospitals. The sum of £36 8s. 4d. was also distributed in Christmas gifts to about forty recipients.

The several sums of stock are held by the official trustees.

LILLINGSTONE DAYRELL

Lelinchestane (xi cent.) ; Lullingestan, Lyllingstan, Lillingeston Parva (xii–xiii cent.) ; Lillingston Dayerel (xiv cent.).

This parish covers 1,873 acres, of which 1,267 acres are permanent grass, 261 arable, and 74 woods and plantations.[1] The soil is clay. A stream borders the east side of the parish, flowing southward, and is joined about half-way down by a small tributary. The land rises from about 300 ft. above the ordnance datum in the south-east to over 500 ft. in the extreme north-west.

The houses of the village are grouped round the road to Buckingham. Tile House, standing in well-wooded grounds, is the property and residence of the lord of the manor, Mr. Abraham John Robarts. In the park is a large sheet of water, and an avenue leads from the house to the eastern boundary where Tile House Farm stands. Old Tile House, which also stands in the park, is a brick and stone building with a tiled roof. There were five messuages here called the Tile House in 1615,[1a] but the present house was built by Sir Marmaduke Dayrell,[2] a member of a younger branch of the family,[3] between 1693 and 1697, the former date with the Dayrell arms being on a stone over the porch and the latter date on the head of one rain-water pipe, while the initials M.D. occur on another. The house was much altered in the 19th century. It is of two stories with attics, and the original windows have wooden mullions and transoms. Inside some original panelling and other fittings remain. The property descended in the cadet branch of the Dayrell family [3a] until after the death of Marmaduke Dayrell, when, in order to raise portions for his widow and children, his trustees sold it, about 1796, to Abraham Robarts,[4] ancestor of the present owner.

The rectory, formerly called Pondclose House, is a 17th-century building of brick and stone roofed with tiles and slates. It was refronted in the 18th century, and additions were made to it in the 19th century. On the east side of the house are the remains of some fish-ponds.

Near the church was the Old Manor House, which was taken down in 1767.[5] Richard Dayrell, who died in 1704, spent a large sum on the house and estate, at least £4,000 he stated in his will, 'as appears in a book of accounts I have kept for that purpose called the Lillingstone Book which my eldest son may reap the benefit of.'[6] Browne Willis, about 1735, states that the manor-house had 'lately been handsomely fitted up.'[7] A smaller manor-house was built by Richard Dayrell in 1792.[8]

Lillingstone House with a park of about 20 acres is the property of the lord of the manor and the residence of the Hon. Mrs. Archibald Douglas-Pennant.

The site of Luffield Priory exclusive of the church lay in the north-west of the parish, but there is now no trace of the buildings above ground. A little to the east of the site at Chapel Green are the remains of the 15th-century chapel of St. Thomas of Canter-

[69] R. of Hugh of Wells (Cant. and York Soc.), i, 8. The entry is made 'before the 10th year.'
[70] See manor ; also Harl. MS. 6952, fol. 145 ; Inst. Bks. (P.R.O.); Clergy Lists ; Willis, op. cit. 208.
[71] Clergy Lists.
[72] Pope Nich. Tax. (Rec. Com.), 32b.
[73] Valor Eccl. (Rec. Com.), iv, 239.
[1] Statistics from Bd. of Agric. (1905).
[1a] Chan. Inq. p.m. (Ser. 2), cccxlviii, 145.
[2] Browne Willis, Hist. and Antiq. of

Buckingham, 217, 214. In three deeds (Close, 13 Geo. III, pt. xiv, no. 6 ; Recov. R. East. 13 Geo. III, m. 186 ; Feet of F. Bucks. East. 15 Geo. III) Marmaduke Dayrell's property here is referred to as a manor, with the Tile House as its capital messuage. The main manor was, however, held by the elder branch of the family at this date, and it does not appear that the Tile House estate ever had manorial rights. In 1786 it is called a manor or reputed manor (P.C.C. 235 Bishop).

[3] His father, Sir Thomas Dayrell, kt., who died in the spring of 1668–9 (P.C.C. 53 Coke), was son of Francis, who died in January 1614–15 (Chan. Inq. p.m. [Ser. 2], cccxlviii, 145). Francis was the younger son of the Paul Dayrell who died in 1606 (Gen. [New Ser.], xv, 124).
[3a] P.C.C. 91 Auber ; 235 Bishop.
[4] Lipscomb, Hist. and Antiq. of Bucks, iii, 34.   [5] Ibid.
[6] P.C.C. 128 Ash.
[7] Willis, op. cit. 217.
[8] Lipscomb, loc. cit.

bury. This chapel was apparently founded by Robert Dayrell and Ralf his son, who in the 13th century gave to Luffield Priory the piece of land on which it stands.[9] It is built of stone and has now a thatched roof. It was converted into two dwellings and partly rebuilt in the 17th century. There still exist traces of the 15th-century east window of the chapel, the west doorway and west window over it, all now blocked and the east window partially covered by a 17th-century chimney stack.

The royal forest of Whittlewood extended into the parish. At least one member of the Dayrell family was ranger of the forest, and certain hunting rights were held by them from an early date, in token of which they owned a horn known as the ' purlieu horn' that was in the possession of the lord of the manor as late as 1885 and bore the date 1692.[10]

Before the Conquest *LILLING-* MANORS *STONE DAYRELL* and Lillingstone Lovell evidently formed one vill of 10 hides,[11] but by 1086 they had become two vills,

COTTAGE AT CHAPEL GREEN, ONCE THE CHAPEL OF ST. THOMAS OF CANTERBURY

each of 5 hides, the one in Buckinghamshire and the other in Oxfordshire. The 5 hides comprising the manor of Lillingstone Dayrell, formerly held by Syric, a man of Queen Edith, were in 1086 part of the lands of Walter Giffard.[12] As parcel of the honour of Giffard the manor passed to the Earls of Pembroke[13] and so to the Talbots.[14] The overlordship rights, apparently amounting only to a view of frankpledge, were held here by the Talbot family as late as 1419.[15]

Walter Giffard's tenant in 1086 was Hugh,[16] most probably the Hugh de Bolebec whose granddaughter and heir married Robert de Vere, Earl of Oxford,[17] as a mesne lordship was held here by the earl in the 13th century[18] and continued to be held with this title,[19] the last mention of it occurring in 1634.[20] The family whose name was later associated with the parish was settled here in the 12th century and probably earlier, for in 1166–7 Dairel owed half a mark for ' Litlingestan.'[21] In 1194–5 a dispute arose between Richard, brother of Ellis Dayrell, and Maud, who may have been the widow of Ellis, as to whether Richard was seised in demesne as of fee of a messuage in Lillingstone which Maud held.[22] At the same date,[23] and again in 1199,[24] Ralf Dayrell is mentioned in connexion with this county, and was probably lord of Lillingstone, as he certainly held lands here in 1232,[25] and his son Henry was lord of the fee in 1234–5.[26] Henry Dayrell was succeeded before 1254–5 by another Ralf,[27] evidently his son, as in 1262 Ralf granted a messuage in Lillingstone to Richard Grusset and Emma his wife,[28] daughter of Henry,[29] and they, at the instance of the donor, granted it to Henry's widow Jane to hold of them for her life for the yearly rent of a rose.[30] Ralf still held in 1278–9,[31] and was followed before 1284–6 by his son Henry.[32] In 1297 Henry Dayrell quit-claimed the manor to John de Foxley and Constance his wife.[33] In 1301 Henry son of Henry Dayrell, while still a minor, claimed that by reason of that deed he had been unjustly disseised of the manor.[34] Henry, the father, who was still alive, maintained that he was justified in making the conveyance, and added that, as his son had never been in seisin of the manor, the claim of unjust disseisin was impossible, a view which was upheld by the court.[35] John de Foxley was returned as holding the manor in 1302–3,[36] and two years later he recognized the claim of Alice,

[9] Willis, op. cit. 214, quoting registers of Luffield Priory and Cott. MS. Cleop. C. iii, fol. 349. The chapel was included in the leases of Luffield Priory in the early 16th century, and Chapel Green afterwards belonged to the cadet branch of Dayrells.

[10] Dayrell, *Hist. of Dayrells of Lillingstone Dayrell*, 7.

[11] *V.C.H. Bucks.* i, 228.

[12] Ibid. 250.

[13] *Testa de Nevill* (Rec. Com.), 247 ; *Hund. R.* (Rec. Com.), ii, 340 ; Chan. Inq. p.m. 17 Edw. II, no. 75.

[14] Chan. Inq. p.m. 46 Edw. III (1st nos.), no. 66 ; 10 Ric. II, no. 42 ; 20 Ric. II, no. 51 ; *Cal. Pat.* 1396–9, p. 17.

[15] Chan. Inq. p.m. 11 Hen. IV, no. 19 ; 7 Hen. V, no. 68.

[16] *V.C.H. Bucks.* i, 250.

[17] Ibid. 213, 247 ; Dugdale, *Baronage*, i, 451–2.

[18] *Hund. R.* (Rec. Com.), i, 32.

[19] Ibid. ii, 340 ; *Feud. Aids*, i, 79, 125 ; Chan. Inq. p.m. 34 Edw. III (1st nos.), no. 84 ; 45 Edw. III (1st nos.), no. 45 ; *Cal. Inq. p.m. Hen. VII*, i, 244 ; Chan. Inq. p.m. (Ser. 2), cxx, 9 ; Feet of F. Bucks. East. 26 Eliz.

[20] Chan. Inq. p.m. (Ser. 2), dviii, 15.

[21] *Pipe R.* 13 Hen. II (Pipe R. Soc.), 108.

[22] *Rolls of the King's Court* (Pipe R. Soc.), 5.

[23] Ibid. 55.

[24] *Rot. Cur. Reg.* (Rec. Com.), ii, 116.

[25] *Cal. Close*, 1231–4, p. 286.

[26] Ibid. ; *Testa de Nevill* (Rec. Com.), 258, 259, 261.

[27] *Hund. R.* (Rec. Com.), i, 32.

[28] Feet of F. case 16, file 37.

[29] Willis, op. cit. 214.

[30] Feet of F. case 16, file 37.

[31] *Hund. R.* (Rec. Com.), ii, 340.

[32] *Feud. Aids*, i, 79 ; Assize R. 1323, m. 10.

[33] Feet of F. case 17, file 54.

[34] Assize R. 1323, m. 10.

[35] Ibid.

[36] *Feud. Aids*, i, 100.

widow of Henry Dayrell, sen., to a third of the manor as dower.[37] In a further dispute John de Foxley is stated to be the guardian of Henry, the son.[38] The quarrel, however, was finally settled in 1309, when John de Foxley and Constance quitclaimed to Henry Dayrell and Emma his wife all their right in two-thirds of the manor, and their reversionary right in the third held by Alice in dower, on payment by Henry and Emma of £100 sterling.[39] Henry Dayrell still held in 1316.[40] John Dayrell, who presented to the church in 1328,[41] and Jane his wife were seised in 1332–46.[42] Roger, his son,[43] was lord in 1369[44] and member for the county in 1388, 1390, 1393–4 and in 1399.[45] He married Joan Agmondesham, and was succeeded, after 1407, by his son John, who died in 1417, leaving two sons, Paul and Thomas.[46] Nicholas Dayrell, possibly the brother of John,[47] presented to the church in 1441.[48] Paul Dayrell died seised of the manor in 1491, having previously made a settlement of it ; his heir was his son Thomas, aged twenty-four.[49] Thomas married Dorothy Danvers ; his son Paul, who succeeded him in 1524, married as his first wife Margaret daughter of John Cheyne.[50] He died in 1556, leaving a son of the same name,[51] who married Frances Saunders[52] and made various settlements of the manor in 1561,[53] 1573–4[54] and 1602.[55] He died in 1606, and his son and grandson, both called Thomas, were successively lords of the manor.[56] The grandson died in 1628, ten years after his father, without male issue, so that Lillingstone passed to his brother Peter Dayrell,[57] who took an active part in the Civil War as an ardent Royalist.[58] In 1646 he compounded for his delinquency in adhering to the king's cause, and a fine of £788 was imposed.[59] He died in 1667.[60] His two elder sons, Thomas and Peter, died without issue, the latter in 1670, when the third son, Anthony, rector of the parish, became the heir.[61] Anthony's son Thomas died in 1685, his heir being his uncle Paul, who died in 1690, leaving a daughter Frances, and, as male heir, his brother Richard, who married Frances Tucker.[62] He, at his death in 1704, was followed

DAYRELL of Lillingstone. *Argent on three bars sable six cinqfoils argent.*

by his son Peter,[63] who died unmarried in 1725. His brother Thomas, rector of the parish, died in 1729,[64] leaving a son Richard, who was still a minor at this date, but afterwards inherited the property[65] and also held the rectory.[66] After his death in 1767 [66a] his sons Richard and Paul held successively, dying without issue in 1800 and in 1803 respectively.[67] The third son, Henry, who held a commission in the Royal Navy, died in 1823, and his son Richard, captain in the Navy, became lord of the manor, dying in 1841, when his heir was Edmund Francis Dayrell.[68] His son Captain Edmund Marmaduke Dayrell, R.N., was lord of the manor as late as 1885,[69] at about which date the property was sold to Mr. Abraham John Robarts, the present owner.

There was a mill appurtenant to the manor in 1602.[70] In 1610 there were two mills, one of which, called the old mill, was then used as a cottage.[71] A water-mill is again referred to in 1706.[72] In 1628 a rabbit warren and a dovecot were included in the appurtenances.[73]

In 1369 Sir Henry Green, kt., died seised of the manor of *HEYBARNE*, held of the lord of Lillingstone Dayrell, partly in Northamptonshire and partly in this county.[74] The part in this county, which was later said to amount to a toft and a carucate of land, called Heybarnefield, in Lillingstone Dayrell,[75] was worth only 40*d.* per annum at the above date because it was in the forest of Whittlewood, and so had been much harmed by the king's beasts.[76] Sir Thomas Green, kt., son of Sir Henry, died seised in 1391[77], leaving a son Thomas, whose widow Mary, after her husband's death in 1417,[78] held until her death in 1434,[79] when their son Thomas inherited.[80] By the end of the 16th century this property had passed to Peter Wentworth,[81] lord of the manor of Lillingstone Lovell (q.v.), with which it afterwards descended.[82]

The church of *ST. NICHOLAS CHURCH* consists of a chancel measuring internally about 29 ft. 7 in. by 13 ft. 8 in., north organ chamber and vestry, nave 31 ft. 7 in. by 16 ft. 1 in., north and south aisles each 6 ft. 9 in. wide, west tower 9 ft. 2 in. square, and a south porch 7 ft. by 5 ft. 6 in.

The east and west walls of the nave, with the chancel and tower arches, are the only survivals of a late 11th-century aisleless church with a western tower. Early in the 13th century the chancel appears to

[37] De Banco R. 153, m. 53 d.
[38] Ibid.
[39] Feet of F. case 18, file 60.
[40] *Feud. Aids,* i, 108.
[41] Lipscomb, op. cit. iii, 34.
[42] Feet of F. case 19, file 80 ; *Feud. Aids,* i, 125.
[43] Willis, op. cit. 214–16.
[44] Chan. Inq. p.m. 43 Edw. III (1st nos.), no. 48.
[45] *Ret. of Memb. of Parl.* i, 234, 239, 247, 257.
[46] Willis, loc. cit. ; *Cal. Pat.* 1405–8, p. 258 ; Chan. Inq. p.m. 5 Hen. V, no. 39 ; Cott. MS. Cleop. C. iii, fol. 347.
[47] Willis, loc. cit.
[48] Lipscomb, loc. cit.
[49] *Cal. Inq. p.m. Hen. VII,* i, 244. It may be that this Paul was the son of John's son Paul, and a minor in the ward of Nicholas in 1441.
[50] Exch. Inq. p.m. (Ser. 2), file 20, no. 13.

[51] Chan. Inq. p.m. (Ser. 2), cxx, 9.
[52] Willis, loc. cit.
[53] Feet of F. Bucks. East. 3 Eliz.
[54] Ibid. Mich. 16 Eliz.
[55] Ibid. East. 44 Eliz. ; Recov. R. East. 44 Eliz. m. 66.
[56] Chan. Inq. p.m. (Ser. 2), cccxvi, 30 ; ccccxxxiv, 78 ; Feet of F. Bucks. Hil. 10 Jas. I.
[57] Chan. Inq. p.m. (Ser. 2), dccxliii, 12 ; Recov. R. East. 4 Chas. I.
[58] Dayrell, op. cit. 37.
[59] *Cal. Com. for Comp.* 1519.
[60] Lipscomb, op. cit. iii, 33.
[61] Willis, loc. cit. ; Burke, *Hist. of Commoners,* iii, 147 et seq.
[62] Ibid. ; P.C.C. 22 Vere ; 128 Ash. In a dispute, 1697, with Sir Marmaduke Dayrell of the Old Tile House, Richard Dayrell is described as a hosier of London, having recently succeeded his elder brother (Chan. Proc. [Bridges Div.], bdle. 126, no. 13).

[63] Willis, loc. cit. ; Recov. R. Trin. 5 Anne, m. 65 ; Com. Pleas Recov. R. Trin. 5 Anne, m. 8.
[64] Willis, loc. cit. ; P.C.C. 235 Auber.
[65] Ibid.
[66] Lipscomb, op. cit. iii, 33.
[66a] *Musgrave's Obit.* (Harl. Soc.), ii, 159.
[67] Lipscomb, op. cit. iii, 33, 38, 39.
[68] Ibid. 33, 34.
[69] Dayrell, op. cit. 59.
[70] Recov. R. East. 44 Eliz. m. 66.
[71] Chan. Inq. p.m. (Ser. 2), ccxvi, 30.
[72] Recov. R. Trin. 5 Anne, m. 65.
[73] Chan. Inq. p.m. (Ser. 2), dccxliii, 12.
[74] Ibid. 43 Edw. III (1st nos.), no. 48.
[75] Ibid. 5 Hen. V, no. 39.
[76] Ibid. 43 Edw. III (1st nos.), no. 48.
[77] Ibid. 15 Ric. II, pt. i, no. 24.
[78] Ibid. 5 Hen. V, no. 39.
[79] Ibid. 12 Hen. VI, no. 20.
[80] Ibid. [81] Ibid. (Ser. 2), cclviii, 142.
[82] Ibid. cccxxxiii, 46.

have been rebuilt and lengthened, the walls of the western portion following the line of the original walls. The tower, if ever completed, must have been in a ruinous condition at this time, as the window in the west wall of the nave, which now looks into the tower, is of about the same date as the older work in the chancel. About 1240 the tower seems to have been rebuilt, and to the same period may be assigned the coupled lancet windows in the side walls of the eastern half of the chancel. In the last half of the 13th century the aisles were added to the nave and a new east window was inserted in the chancel, the recess on the north and the wall arcade on the south being formed at the same time. The north wall of the chancel is reported to have been in ruins in 1366 [82a]; the 13th-century detail here bears marks of resetting and suggests that the whole wall has been rebuilt, probably a few years after this date. Beyond the addition of the south porch and the insertion of a window in the south aisle in the early 15th century no further structural alterations appear to have been undertaken in the middle ages. At a

Legend:
- c. 1100
- Early 13th Century
- c. 1240
- Late 13th Century
- 14th Cent.
- 15th Cent.
- Modern

VESTRY

NORTH AISLE

ORGAN CHAMBER

TOWER

NAVE

CHANCEL

SOUTH AISLE

PORCH

SCALE OF FEET

PLAN OF LILLINGSTONE DAYRELL CHURCH

later period the north aisle appears to have been pulled down to supply material for the repair of the church; this was probably done at some time in the 17th century, as, according to Browne Willis, there was no north aisle existing in 1735. The uppermost stage of the tower has evidently been rebuilt, perhaps during the 18th century. In 1868 the church was restored by Street, who rebuilt the north aisle and added the north vestry and organ chamber. The walling generally is of limestone rubble, but the south porch has a facing of rough ashlar work. The roofs of the body of the church are tiled.

The late 13th-century east window of the chancel is a fine and interesting example of the transition from plate to bar tracery. The head is two-centred, and it is of three lights, the central light being higher and wider than the side lights; the tracery above is formed by three trefoiled circles with pierced spandrels between them. The mullions are shafted, and the rear-arch also springs from attached shafts with moulded capitals and bases. The coupled lancet at the north-east, originally inserted about 1240 and reset at the

[82a] Linc. Epis. Reg. Memo. Buckingham, fol. 40.

later rebuilding of the wall, has a lozenge ornament between the heads of the lights externally, and a circular flower ornament in a corresponding position internally, now partly covered by the rear-arch. The wide recess to the west of the window has a segmental two-centred head subdivided by forked ribs springing from a central moulded corbel. Both the main head and the ribs are hollow-chamfered, and there are small shafts at the angles of the jambs. The whole work is very rough, and the junction of the ribs with the main head is clumsy in the extreme, the result, doubtless, of unskilful rebuilding. At the west end of the wall is a modern arch opening to the organ chamber. At the east end of the south wall is a late 13th-century piscina with a projecting bowl and credence shelf and a trefoiled ogee head. The label inclosing the head is linked to the label of the contemporary wall arcade which occupies the remainder of the lower part of the wall. Above the arcade are two windows, the eastern a coupled lancet window of the same date as that in the opposite wall, but more elaborately moulded externally, the mullion being shafted and enriched with dog-tooth ornament, while the western window is a lancet of the early 13th century. The end bays of the arcade beneath are narrower than the two middle bays, the easternmost bay having a stilted semicircular head, while the other bays have two-centred segmental heads; all spring from attached shafts with moulded bases and capitals, and the abaci are ornamented with the nail-head. The two eastern bays formed sedilia, and the westernmost bay contains an early 13th-century low-side window rebated for a shutter. The labels are linked horizontally and stopped by a mask-stop on the west. The chancel arch, which is semicircular and of rough workmanship, springs from plain square jambs with chamfered imposts.

The north and south arcades of the nave are each of three bays and are alike in detail; the arches are two-centred and of two chamfered orders, and are supported by octagonal columns with moulded capitals and water-table bases standing on octagonal plinths with square sub-plinths. The outer orders die upon the end walls of the nave, the inner orders being carried by moulded corbels, and the arches are inclosed by labels on both nave and aisle faces. The north arcade, which had been built up, was considerably restored when the north aisle was rebuilt, and the bases are modern. The tower arch is like the chancel arch, but the imposts have been recut; above it is an early 13th-century lancet, now looking into the tower.

The modern north aisle is designed in the style of the 13th century. The south aisle retains no original windows; the east window is an insertion of the 14th century, and is of three trefoiled lights with reticulated tracery in the head, while at the west end of the south wall is a two-light window of the same date and type. The remaining window at the opposite end of the same wall is a square-headed early 15th-

LILLINGSTONE DAYRELL CHURCH FROM THE SOUTH-WEST

LILLINGSTONE DAYRELL CHURCH: THE INTERIOR LOOKING EAST

LILLINGSTONE LOVELL CHURCH FROM THE SOUTH-EAST

century insertion of three cinquefoiled lights. The south doorway, which is contemporary with the aisle, has a two-centred head of two orders, the outer order having shafted jambs, while the inner order is continuous.

The tower rises in three plain stages, the ground and intermediate stages being lighted by plain lancets on the west, and the rebuilt bell-chamber by coupled lancets on all four sides. The early 15th-century south porch has a pointed outer doorway of two chamfered orders, and is lighted from each side by a quatrefoil. The walls rise from a boldly moulded plinth and have small two-stage buttresses on the east and west; the roof is steeply pitched and covered with stone flags.

The font and fittings are modern. In the sanctuary floor are preserved eight early 13th-century tiles with raised designs, and some 14th-century red and yellow 'slip tiles' are placed in the floor on the north and south sides of the chancel. Hung on the north wall of the chancel is a pulpit-hanging embroidered with the Dayrell arms and bearing the inscription '1659 Donum Thomae Dayrelli Armigeri.' Above it are also hung two funeral helms, one probably made up from a 16th-century close helmet, while the other seems to be a modern imitation.

The earliest monument in the church is a table tomb in the third bay of the arcade, on the south side of the chancel, commemorating Paul Dayrell (d. 1491) and his wife Margaret, the date of whose death is not given. In the covering slab are their brass figures, he in the plate armour of the period, and she in a gown trimmed with fur. Below the figures is the inscription, 'Hic jacēt paulus dayrell Armig' et Margareta uxor eius qui quidem | paulus obiit xxix die Marcii A° dñi m°cccc° lxxxxj q̄. aiab3 ppicietr de9.' In the back of the recess in the north wall of the chancel is a brass, with a headless figure, to Richard Blakysley, a former rector (d. 1493). The inscription is as follows : ' Hic sub pede jacet dñs Ricūs blakysley quondm̄ | Rector istius eccl̄ie q̄ obiit sexto die aprilis A° dñi m°cccclxxxxiij° cui9 ām̄e ppicietr de9 amen.' Standing in the middle of the chancel is a fine table tomb to Paul Dayrell (d. 1556) and his third wife Dorothy (d. 1571), widow of William Saunders, with their recumbent effigies. On the sides are shields of arms and the kneeling figures of their nine sons and six daughters. At the angles are small baluster columns supporting a Doric frieze, in the metopes of which are carved elephants' heads and the Saunders coat, alternating with Dayrell cinqfoils. Beneath the altar is a floor slab to William Cave, a former rector (d. 1635). The slab is traditionally said to be the original altar slab, but no

crosses are visible on the exposed side, though they may exist on the underside. The dimensions of the stone render the tradition not improbable. On the south wall of the chancel is a monument to a later Paul Dayrell (d. 1690). There is also a floor slab at the east end of the chancel to Frances, the wife of Matthew Wilkes and daughter of Peter Dayrell (d. 1694).

There are three bells : the treble by John Warner & Sons, 1868, the second by Edward Hall, 1726, and the tenor by Richard Chandler, 1674.

The plate consists of a silver cup of 1604, ornamented with an embossed pattern, and evidently a secular vessel ; a second cup with the date letter partly obliterated, but probably belonging to the 1618–37 cycle ; a standing paten of 1662, a second paten of 1797, presented in 1811 ; and a modern flagon.

The registers begin in 1584.

ADVOWSON In a late 12th-century charter concerning lands in this county the name of Philip, chaplain of Lillingstone, is given as a witness.[83] The church appears to have been in the patronage of the Dayrell family from an early date, and the living is still in the gift of the lord of the manor.[84] In 1366 it appears that the vicar had the right-hand side of the rectory with the hall and a chamber and cellar on the east, the kitchen and brew-house and two-thirds of the garden.[85] In 1278–9 it was found that the church was endowed with 1 virgate of land[86] ; it was valued at £5 in 1291[87] and at £8 in 1535.[88] In 1291 an annual sum of 6s. 8d. was paid to the priory of Newton Longville,[89] to which Walter Giffard had granted certain tithes in Lillingstone in the 11th century.[90]

CHARITIES It appeared from a board in the church that Frances Wilkes in 1674 gave £40 for clothing poor women yearly, and that Elizabeth Dayrell in 1679 gave £50 for apprenticing a boy every five years ; but these charities have been lost sight of.

The Rev. John Langham Dayrell, by his will, proved in the P.C.C. 18 October 1832, bequeathed £300 consols, the annual dividends, amounting to £7 10s., to be laid out in the distribution of clothing at Christmas among the poor.

The sum of stock is held by the official trustees, who also hold a further sum of £63 3s. 1d. consols, representing a sum of money awarded under an Act of 1852–3[91] for disafforesting the forest of Whittlewood, otherwise Whittlebury, as compensation to the poor in lieu of any rights to sere and broken wood. The annual dividends of £1 11s. 4d. are applied in the distribution of coal at Christmas.

LILLINGSTONE LOVELL

Lillingestan (xi cent.) ; Liwngstane (xii cent.) ; Great Lyllingstone (xiii, xiv cent.) ; Lyllingstone Dansey (xiv, xv cent.) ; Lylenstone *alias* Lyllyngstone Lovell (late xiv, xvi cent.).

This parish, which is separated from that of Lilling-

stone Dayrell by a feeder of the River Ouse, extends east and north to the borders of Northamptonshire. It still belongs to the hundred of Ploughley in Oxfordshire, and formed a detached part of that county until 1844, when it was annexed for local government purposes to

---

83 Harl. Chart. 85, A 53.
84 See manor ; R. of Hugh of Wells (Cant. and York Soc.), ii, 90 ; Inst. Bks. (P.R.O.).
85 Linc. Epis. Reg. Buckingham Memo. fol. 40.
86 Hund. R. (Rec. Com.), ii, 340.
87 Pope Nich. Tax. (Rec. Com.), 32.
88 Valor Eccl. (Rec. Com.), iv, 240.
89 Pope Nich. Tax. (Rec. Com.), 32.
90 Cal. Doc. of France, 74, 76.
91 Stat. 16 & 17 Vict. cap. 42.

Buckinghamshire.[1] More than half the area of 1,667 acres is pasture, and the remainder includes 512 acres of arable and 165 acres of woods and plantations.[2] The most important of these are Lovell and Shirehill Woods in the north-west of the parish, and in the north-east, parts of Briary and Cattlehill Woods, both of which extend into Northamptonshire.[3] The level of the land varies from 336 ft. above the ordnance datum to the east of the church to 431 ft. on the Towcester road in the north-west of the parish. The soil is clay, the subsoil principally limestone and marl, the former supplying the material for the building of the church.[4] The village is situated about half a mile to the east of the road from Buckingham to Towcester, and is approached by a by-road which eventually passes eastward through Wicken Wood into Northamptonshire. The main part of the village lies on the east side of a stream which flows into the feeder of the Ouse mentioned above. Here are a few old houses, including a 17th-century farm-house of stone, formerly an inn, on the north side of the road, and some thatched cottages of about the same date on the opposite side of the way. The church, rectory, and schools with a few cottages are grouped together west of the stream. Lillingstone Hall, a plain square stone house with tiled roofs south of the village, was built from the 17th-century materials of part of the old Hall. The remains of a homestead moat and fish-pond in the grounds south of the present house doubtless mark the site of the former building.[5] After their acquisition of the manor in the later 15th century the Wentworths appear to have lived at the house,[6] but later generations evidently resided elsewhere, probably in Essex, from which county the family originally came. Sir Peter Wentworth, who returned to Lillingstone, certainly speaks of himself in February 1635–6 as 'a mere stranger in the county,'[7] i.e., Oxford. The house was then in a ruinous condition, apparently caused by fire in that year,[8] and he evidently repaired and enlarged it. Owing to the money and care he bestowed upon it, the fame of the house spread far.[9] He also laid out extensive grounds and plantations,[10] and inclosed a park which was stocked with ten brace of deer from Whittlewood Forest by a grant of the Commonwealth in 1659.[11] After Major Drake's death in 1788 the estate was neglected; the old timber was cut down and the old mansion ultimately dismantled and demolished, part of the material being re-used for a house at Wicken Park and part for a house at Buckingham.[12]

The Manor House, a comfortable modern building, is situated about a mile to the north-east of the church, with large grounds and a spinney on the south and south-east. It is the residence of Mr. James Bogle Delap, who is both lord of the manor and sole land-owner in the parish.

MANORS In the time of Edward the Confessor Azor held in Lillingstone 2½ hides of land, afterwards LILLINGSTONE DANSEY or LILLINGSTONE LOVELL MANOR, which by 1086 had come to Benzelinus.[13] The holding was later in the St. Martin family, and had passed from Godfrey de St. Martin before 1235 [14] to his son Hugh,[15] who held it of the king in serjeanty by the service of guarding the door of the king's hall at the great feasts.[16] His son Peter succeeded about 1247,[17] and alienated the overlordship soon afterwards to Patrick Chaworth, who leased it to Peter de Chaceporc, Sir Hugh de Chaceporc holding it in 1254.[18] It had reverted to Pain Chaworth before 1279,[19] and passed, through the marriage in 1298 of his niece Maud to Henry, third Earl of Lancaster,[20] to the duchy of Lancaster,[21] and is last mentioned in this connexion in 1613.[22]

William Clifford, tenant of lands in Lillingstone in 1131,[23] was evidently an ancestor of Margery Clifford, who was holding under Sir Hugh de Chaceporc in 1254.[24] Her first husband was Peter de St. Martin,[25] but she was the wife of Peter Dansey in 1260, when Lillingstone Manor was settled on them and their issue with remainder to Margery's right heirs.[26] He was living in 1266 [27] and she in 1284.[28] Her heirs appear to have been Margery Criol (Keriel), Elizabeth wife of John Pabenham, and Margery daughter and heir of Robert and Margaret Hereward,[29] to whom

DUCHY OF LANCASTER. *ENGLAND* with the difference of a label of *FRANCE*.

---

[1] Stat. 7 & 8 Vict. cap. 61.
[2] Statistics from Bd. of Agric. (1905).
[3] The woods in this parish were afforested in the later 12th century and were excluded from the perambulation of the forest of Whittlewood or Whittlebury in Northamptonshire in 1300 (Pat. Suppl. no. 6a, m. 7).
[4] Parker, *Eccl. and Archit. Topog. of Engl.* (Oxon.), pt. iv.
[5] Rutton, *The Family of Wentworth*, 299. The hollows in the soil indicating the site and the terrace walk were still traceable in 1836 (quoting note book of the Rev. William Lloyd, rector from 1826 to 1889).
[6] A reference to the court at the 'manor place' of Nicholas Wentworth occurs about 1530 (Star Chamb. Proc. Hen. VIII, bdle. 20, no. 141). Peter and Paul, sons of Nicholas Wentworth, are both called 'of Lillingstone Lovell' in 1565 (*Hist. MSS. Com. Rep.* x, App. iv, 472).
[7] *Cal. S. P. Dom.* 1635–6, p. 224.
[8] Ibid.
[9] Some idea of its size can be obtained from the inventory of the goods and

chattels (in each room named separately) taken in March 1689–90 (Rutton, op. cit. 295–8, copied from the rector's note-book of 1836).
[10] Three walks of fir trees, averaging 20 ft. in height, are mentioned in 1705 (Plot, *Nat. Hist. of Oxon.* (ed. 2), 175).
[11] *Cal. S. P. Dom.* 1659–60, p. 571.
[12] Rutton, op. cit. 294.
[13] *Dom. Bk.* (Rec. Com.), i, fol. 160a.
[14] *Testa de Nevill* (Rec. Com.), 107b, 118b.
[15] Cur. Reg. R. 120, m. 2; cf. chapel under advowson.
[16] *Testa de Nevill*, loc. cit.; *Cal. Inq. p.m.* (Hen. III), 22. Other references to this serjeanty occur in the 13th century (*Hund. R.* [Rec. Com.], ii, 44, 835; *Feud. Aids*, iv, 157). A fee-farm rent was afterwards substituted.
[17] *Excerpta e Rot. Fin.* (Rec. Com.), ii, 25.
[18] *Hund. R.* (Rec. Com.), ii, 44, 45; *Cal. Chart. R.* 1226–57, p. 345.
[19] *Hund. R.* (Rec. Com.), ii, 835.

[20] See under Lathbury; *Dep. Keeper's Rep.* xxxi, 16.
[21] *Cal. Close*, 1360–4, p. 208; Chan. Inq. p.m. 35 Edw. III, pt. i, no. 122; 13 Edw. IV, no. 33; (Ser. 2), cclviii, 142.
[22] Chan. Inq. p.m. (Ser. 2), cccxxxiii, 46.
[23] Gt. R. of the Pipe 31 Hen. I (Rec. Com.), 85.
[24] *Hund. R.* (Rec. Com.), ii, 44.
[25] Roberts, *Cal. Gen.* 331. She was holding dower in her first husband's lands in Wiltshire in 1283, Patrick Chaworth having the reversionary rights.
[26] Feet of F. Oxon. Hil. 44 Hen. III, no. 19. A clove gillyflower was to be given at Easter to Richard Clifford and his heirs.
[27] *Excerpta e Rot. Fin.* (Rec. Com.), ii, 450. The king remitted 100s. exacted by the Exchequer for relief from lands once Peter de St. Martin's.
[28] *Feud. Aids*, iv, 157.
[29] There were agreements between Margery Criol and John and Elizabeth Pabenham in 1303 and 1304 respecting land in Hinwick (Beds.) (*Cal. Inq. p.m.* [Edw. III], viii, 438).

Richard son and heir of Sir John Clifford quit-claimed in 1313 his rights in Lillingstone and else-where, a special point being made of the lands held by Margery Criol at that date,[30] probably by settle-ment on her marriage. She was the widow of Sir Nicholas Criol, kt.,[31] and was holding this manor in 1316.[32] The Margery, however, who married William Lovel was probably Margery Hereward, and received her purparty of Lillingstone, for in the 14th century there took place a division of the estate into the manors of Overend and Netherend,[33] each appa-rently held for half a fee.[34] This distinction was maintained into the 17th century, though the whole property was then again in one ownership.[35] William Lovel obtained a grant of free warren in Lillingstone in 1346,[36] and was knighted at the siege of Calais the following year.[37] His widow Margery is mentioned in 1348,[38] and Beatrice Lovel, who held this moiety in 1361,[39] was presumably their daughter. The owner of the other moiety was said to be Margery Criol.[40] The re-united manor passed eventually with the Criol-Lovel estate in Irchester (Northamptonshire) to Alice daughter of William Adderbury and Elizabeth Swynford.[41] She married Roger Chamber,[42] called of Lillingstone about 1382,[43] and was in possession of a moiety of Irchester in 1428.[44] Their daughter and heir Mary married Sir John Fitz Simond of North Shoebury (Essex), by whom she had a son and heir Robert Fitz Simond,[45] owner of both Irchester and Lillingstone at his death in 1473.[46] The manors passed to his daughter and co-heir Joan, then wife of Robert Timperley.[47] She afterwards married, as his second wife, Henry Wentworth of Great Codham Hall in Wethersfield (Essex),[48] who died in 1482.[49] About 1509 she was again a widow, when, under the name of Dame Joan Fitz Lewis, she enfeoffed Sir Thomas

Lovel, kt., Sir Richard Fitz Lewis, kt., and Thomas Mansfield in her manor of Lillingstone Lovell to the use, according to directions in her will dated 7 September 1511, of her son Nicholas Wentworth and his issue.[50] About 1519 he asked for a discharge from a relief de-manded, presumably on her death, by the feodary of the duchy of Lancaster, claiming this manor, not by descent, but by purchase in use.[51] He became seised in fee through an Act of Parliament in Feb-ruary 1535-6,[52] and was knighted in or about 1545,[53] shortly before he acquired the other principal manor in Lil-lingstone Lovell (see later). Sir Nicholas Wentworth held the office of Chief Porter of Calais, and died about 1557, in which year his will, dated 7 February 1551-2, was proved.[54] He left his manor of Lilling-stone Lovell in trust for the use of his wife Jane for her life, his son and heir Peter being then a minor.[55] She was buried in Burnham Church in 1569.[56] Peter Wentworth entered Parliament as member for Barnstaple in 1571, and from 1584 was member for the borough of Northampton. He was distinguished for his defence of the House's right to liberty of speech against the queen's attempts to control debate.[57] In 1591 he was imprisoned in the Tower, so closely at first that his health suffered, and some mitigation had to be made,[58] but he appears to have been still under confinement at his death in 1597.[59] His son and heir Nicholas[60] was granted entry into Lillingstone Lovell in 1600,[61] and, dying

Wentworth. *Gules a bend argent with three scallops azure thereon.*

[30] *Coram Rege R.* 214, m. 67.

[31] *Cal. Inq. p.m.* loc. cit. ; *Coram Rege R.* 214, m. 67. She seems to have been the second wife of Sir Nicholas Criol, who in 1302 confirmed the gifts of his ancestor, William Aubervill, to Langdon Abbey, Kent (Dugdale, *Mon.* vi, 897), and died in 1303 (*Cal. Fine R.* 1272–1307, p. 483). He had married in his minority in 1272 Margery daughter of Gilbert Peche (*Cal. Pat.* 1266–72, p. 623).

[32] *Feud. Aids*, iv, 169.

[33] Ct. R. (Gen. Ser.), portf. 155, no. 19.

[34] Chan. Inq. p.m. 35 Edw. III, pt. i, no. 122 ; *Cal. Close*, 1360–4, p. 208. In 1284 the whole manor was held for one fee (*Feud. Aids*, iv, 157).

[35] Chan. Inq. p.m. (Ser. 2), cclviii, 142 ; cccxxxiii, 46.

[36] *Cal. Pat.* 1345–8, p. 477 ; Norman R. 639, m. 19. He also had a grant of free warren in his lands in Irchester (Northants) and in Hunstanton and Wal-pole (Norf.). The Norfolk lands had been settled on him and his lawful issue in 1308 by John second Lord Lovel of Titchmarsh (Feet of F. case 161, file 123, no. 21).

[37] Shaw, *Kts. of Engl.* ii, 7.

[38] *Cal. Close*, 1346–9, p. 603.

[39] Chan. Inq. p.m. 35 Edw. III, pt. i, no. 122. She is presumably the Beatrice who, with her husband Thomas de Aldyn-shelles, conveyed the Hunstanton manor in 1354 to Simon Fransham with warrant against her heirs (Feet of F. case 166, file 161, no. 896).

[40] *Cal. Close*, 1360–4, p. 208.

[41] Wrottesley, *Ped. from Plea R.* 396.

[42] Ibid. Her mother Elizabeth also married as her second husband a Roger Chamber (ibid.) of Spratton (Northants) (*Cal. Pat.* 1385–9, pp. 261, 263, 545 ; 1391–6, p. 292). She was again a widow by November 1401 (ibid. 1401–5, p. 74), and it was evidently her son, Sir John Chamber, and perhaps his son William, both of Lillingstone, whose arrest was ordered in May 1408 (*Cal. Pat.* 1405–8, pp. 474, 483).

[43] Early Chan. Proc. bdle. 68, no. 102.

[44] *Feud. Aids*, iv, 45 ; cf. ibid. 14, 29. Katherine, widow of Sir Thomas Ayles-bury of Drayton Beauchamp (q.v.), held the other moiety of Irchester Manor in 1428. It had come to her as daughter and eventual co-heir of Laurence Paben-ham (*V.C.H. Beds.* iii, 77). She therefore represented the interest of Elizabeth Paben-ham, who is said to have recovered it in 1342 against Sir William and Margery Lovel (Bridges, *Hist. of Northants*, ii, 179).

[45] Wrottesley, loc. cit. ; Morant, *Hist. of Essex*, i (2), 302 ; *Visit. of Essex* (Harl. Soc.), 100. In 1458 this Robert sued his cousin William Chamber for Spratton and other manors, claiming through his grand-mother, Alice Adderbury (Wrottesley, loc. cit.).

[46] Chan. Inq. p.m. 13 Edw. IV, no. 33.

[47] Ibid. Their son, Robert Timperley *alias* Fitz Simond, died in 1494 (P.C.C. 22 Vox).

[48] Le Neve, *Pedigree of the Knights* (Harl. Soc.), 36.

[49] Chan. Inq. p.m. 22 Edw. IV, no. 11.

[50] Duchy of Lanc. Inq. p.m. ii, 30.

Remainder was to the issue of Sir John Fitz Simond and his wife Mary, with final remainder to the latter's right heirs ; cf. Memo. R. (Exch. L.T.R.), Hil. 28 Hen. VIII, m. 24.

[51] Duchy of Lanc. Inq. p.m. ii, 30. About this time he brought a suit against John Mordaunt, afterwards second Lord Mordaunt, who had married Elizabeth, sister and heir of Sir John and only daughter of Sir Richard Fitz Lewis of West Horn-don (Essex) (Morant, op. cit. i [2], 213), for retaining deeds relating to this manor (Early Chan. Proc. bdle. 455, no. 3).

[52] cf. Memo. R. (Exch. L.T.R.), Hil. 1 Mary, m. 24.

[53] Shaw, op. cit. ii, 56.

[54] P.C.C. F. 19 Wrastley. [55] Ibid.

[56] Rutton, op. cit. 219, quoting M.I. on the monument of her younger son Paul Wentworth, and from the parish register.

[57] Rutton, op. cit. 220, 232, 235 ; cf. ibid. 219–44 ; *Dict. Nat. Biog.* under account of Peter Wentworth. In 1565 the Sheriff of Essex received a writ from the justices of the peace to produce Peter and Paul Wentworth, both of Lillingstone Lovell, at the next sessions on an indict-ment 'for transgressions and contempts' (*Hist. MSS. Com. Rep.* x, App. iv, 472).

[58] *Acts of P.C.* 1591, pp. 367, 390, 393, 440.

[59] Chan. Inq. p.m. (Ser. 2), cclviii, 142. His wife Frances, who shared his imprison-ment, had died in the Tower in 1596 (*Dict. Nat. Biog.*).

[60] Chan. Inq. p.m. (Ser. 2), cclviii, 142.

[61] Fine R. 42 Eliz. pt. i, no. 33.

in 1613, was succeeded by his son Peter,[62] who was made a knight of the Bath in February 1625-6.[63] He was Sheriff of Oxfordshire in 1635, meeting with many difficulties in the levying of ship-money in that county, where he had lately settled.[64] He sat in the Long Parliament as member for Tamworth[65] (Staffordshire), and dying at Lillingstone Lovell was buried in the chancel of the church there in 1675.[66] He was succeeded by his brother Paul Wentworth,[67] who died in February 1689–90 and was also buried at Lillingstone Lovell.[68] He left his estates in Oxfordshire and Buckinghamshire to his executors for ten years, for the payment of debts and legacies (including some of his brother's), with remainders to his kinsman John Creswell of Purston in King's Sutton (Northamptonshire) for life and his son John in tail-male.[69] The latter succeeded in 1699, under the name of John Wentworth *alias* Creswell,[70] his father having died two years previously.[71] On his death in 1759[72] he was succeeded by his nephew William Creswell,[73] who took the surname of Wentworth in addition to his own. He was Sheriff of Buckinghamshire in 1768,[74] and died in 1784.[75] By his will Lillingstone Lovell passed to his cousin Major Francis Drake of Frimley, Surrey, and, on his death in 1788,[76] to the Hon. Edward Onslow, second son of the first Earl of Onslow.[77] In 1821 he sold the whole estate to James Bogle Delap of Stoke Park, near Guildford,[78] who died in 1850.[79] On the death of his widow in 1859 it passed to his nephew the Rev. Robert Delap of Monellan, Donegal.[80]

DELAP. *Gules a pile argent with an eagle gules thereon.*

His son Mr. James Bogle Delap, who was sheriff of that county in 1874, succeeded in 1885,[81] and is the present owner.

Two and a half hides in *LILLINGSTONE* were assessed in 1086 among the lands of Richard Engaine.[82] His estate lay chiefly in Northamptonshire[83] and con-stituted the honour of Benefield, held for the service of one fee,[84] of which a quarter was rendered by Lillingstone.[85] The overlordship passed through a later Richard Engaine to his grandson Fulk Lisors,[86] whose granddaughter Alice (daughter and co-heir of Hugh Lisors) married Nicholas de Bassingbourn,[87] overlord of Lillingstone about 1235.[88] Their son Humphrey de Bassingbourn[89] died in or about 1280,[90] and the overlordship was afterwards vested in the Danseys of Dilton, Wiltshire,[91] John Dansey holding it in 1353.[92] It lapsed on the acquisition of the manor by the Crown later in the century.[93]

The Engaine holding in Lillingstone appears to have been subinfeudated in 1131 to Walter Dangerville.[94] In the later 12th century it was in two moieties, of which Sybil Dangerville held one.[95] Her moiety, afterwards called *GREAT LILLINGSTONE, LILLINGSTONE DANSEY* and *LILLINGSTONE LOVELL MANOR* or *KINGSLANDS*, descended with Tattenhoe Manor[96] (q.v.), being confiscated to the Crown with the other lands of William Martel in 1224. In 1225 the king granted his land in Lillingstone during his pleasure to Ralph de Carevill,[97] who appears to have married a daughter of William Martel[98] and was holding in 1231.[99] It was in the king's hands again in 1242, when he granted it to Thomas Barber to hold by the service of a pair of gilt spurs or 6*d.* yearly.[100] Thomas Barber was living in 1254,[1] but his holding had passed before 1276 to James Barber,[2] who in 1284 successfully contested a suit brought against him by Denise de Carevill,[3] Ralph's granddaughter.[4] John Monhaut[5] and his wife Ellen, possibly a daughter of James Barber, were jointly enfeoffed about 1284.[6] Ellen was living in 1294, shortly after her husband's death, but their son Adam[7] had succeeded before 1300.[8] He died about 1306,[9] when the custody of his daughter and heir Elizabeth was granted to Geoffrey de la Lee,[10] who was holding this manor in 1314.[11] Elizabeth Monhaut married Stephen Trafford before 1316,[12] and, surviving her husband, died in 1344, when she was succeeded by their son Stephen Trafford.[13] He granted the manor for life to Thomas Ferrers with reversion to William Baret (whose daughter Margery

[62] Chan. Inq. p.m. (Ser. 2), cccxxxiii, 46.

[63] Shaw, op. cit. i, 162.

[64] Add. MS. 37999, fol. 64 ; Cal. S. P. Dom. 1635, pp. 475, 505 ; 1635–6, p. 224 ; 1637–8, p. 232.

[65] Dict. Nat. Biog.

[66] Le Neve, op. cit. 36.

[67] P.C.C. 26 Bence ; Recov. R. Trin. 28 Chas. II, m. 162.

[68] Le Neve, loc. cit.

[69] P.C.C. 52 Dyke.

[70] Recov. R. Trin. 11 Will. IV, m. 88.

[71] M.I. at Newbottle (Northants) ; cf. Bridges, Hist. of Northants, i, 189, 191.

[72] Rutton, op. cit. 294.

[73] P.C.C. 378 Arran.

[74] P.R.O. List of Sheriffs, 10.

[75] Musgrave's Obit. (Harl. Soc.), vi, 235.

[76] M.I. in church ; Musgrave's Obit. (Harl. Soc.), ii, 210 ; P.C.C. 239 Calvert.

[77] P.C.C. 531 Rockingham.

[78] Sheahan, Hist. and Topog. of Bucks. 286.

[79] Burke, Landed Gent. (1871).

[80] Ibid.

[81] Burke, Landed Gent. of Ireland (1912).

[82] Cal. Dom. Bk. (Rec. Com.), i, fol. 160b,

[83] V.C.H. Northants, i, 356.

[84] Liber Niger (ed. 1771), i, 214 ; Testa de Nevill (Rec. Com.), 28.

[85] Red Bk. of Exch. (Rolls Ser.), 100 ; Testa de Nevill (Rec. Com.), 103, 104.

[86] Liber Niger, loc. cit. ; Red Bk. of Exch. (Rolls Ser.), 333.

[87] Maitland, Bracton's Note Bk. iii, 5 ; cf. Rot. de Oblatis et Fin. (Rec. Com.), i, 41 ; Excerpta e Rot. Fin. (Rec. Com.), i, 96 ; Baker, Hist. of Northants, i, 9 ; Feud. Aids, iv, 448.

[88] Testa de Nevill (Rec. Com.), 117.

[89] Excerpta e Rot. Fin. (Rec. Com.), ii, 145. Humphrey's father is also said to have been called Colin (Gen. [New Ser.], 88 ; cf. Rot. Lit. Claus. [Rec. Com.], ii, 18).

[90] Cal. Inq. p.m. (Edw. I), ii, 199.

[91] cf. Chan. Inq. p.m. Edw. III, files 83, no. 29 ; 130, no. 20.

[92] Chan. Inq. p.m. 27 Edw. III (1st nos.), no. 50.

[93] Misc. Inq. file 213, no. 33.

[94] Gt. R. of the Pipe 31 Hen. I (Rec. Com.), 3.

[95] See under advowson.

[96] Rot. Lit. Claus. (Rec. Com.), i, 234 ; Testa de Nevill (Rec. Com.), 120 ; Maitland, Bracton's Note Bk. ii, 406–7.

[97] Rot. Lit. Claus. (Rec. Com.), ii, 16.

[98] Maitland, loc. cit. ; cf. Red Bk. of Exch. (Rolls Ser.), 799, where Ralph is called Rudolf.

[99] See under advowson ; cf. Testa de Nevill, loc. cit.

[100] Cal. Chart. R. 1226–57, p. 268 ; Abbrev. Rot. Orig. (Rec. Com.), i, 3 (he is called in the second document Thomas, son of John de Malling) ; Abbrev. Plac. (Rec. Com.), 206 ; cf. Testa de Nevill (Rec. Com.), 103, 104.

[1] Hund. R. (Rec. Com.), ii, 44, 45.

[2] Ibid. 31, 835.

[3] Abbrev. Plac. (Rec. Com.), 207.

[4] Roberts, Cal. Gen. 320.

[5] Feud. Aids, iv, 157.

[6] Cal. Inq. p.m. (Edw. I), iii, 105, 127.

[7] Ibid.

[8] Pat. (Suppl.), no. 6a, m. 7.

[9] Chan. Inq. p.m. 34 Edw. I, no. 30 ; cf. Cal. Inq. p.m. (Edw. II), vi, 57.

[10] Cal. Pat. 1301–7, p. 421.

[11] Ibid. 1313–17, pp. 152, 249.

[12] Feud. Aids, iv, 169.

[13] Chan. Inq. p.m. Edw. III, file 73, no. 5.

was Stephen's wife[14]) and his heirs.[15] Thomas Ferrers died in 1353,[16] but the Baret interest, which was acknowledged in the following year,[17] had been purchased by Ferrers and the manor granted in trust to John de Newenham,[18] parson of Cheadle Church (Staffordshire), in addition to Moorend Castle and Manor in Potterspury and other property in Northamptonshire.[19] The king acquired these in 1363 from Thomas le Despencer,[20] who had rights in remainder in 1353,[21] and the Lillingstone Manor in 1364 from John de Newenham.[22] It was held for a time by Sir John de Ypres, kt., and afterwards by Alice Perrers.[23] A grant for life was made in 1398 to Philippa Duchess of Ireland, who was pardoned in the following year for entering upon the manor as parcel of Moorend Castle.[24] In 1516 Sir Thomas Parr and his wife Maud received a grant for life in survivorship,[25] and in 1545 Sir Nicholas Wentworth[26] obtained the manor in fee in exchange for an estate in Towcester (Northamptonshire).[27] He already held by inheritance the other important manor in Lillingstone, into which this estate merged in the 17th century.[28]

The tenant in 1231 of the second moiety of Great Lillingstone was William de Osevill,[29] perhaps the William de Olney whose heirs were holding in mesne in 1254.[30] This overlordship was held by William de Stapelton in 1279,[31] and descended in his family to Robert de Stapelton, who was living in 1361.[32]

Walter de Olney was under-tenant in 1254,[33] and was succeeded by John de Olney before 1276.[34] He was living in 1294,[35] but his estate appears to have passed to Geoffrey de Bradden before 1300.[36] Later in the century it was held by Thomas de Lillingstone, who died seised of it in 1361[37] in addition to his small manor next mentioned, from which it is not afterwards distinguishable.

A small estate known as *LILLINGSTONE MANOR* was held of the king in chief by knights' service.[38] It seems to have descended from Godfrey de Lillingstone, who is mentioned in 1174-6,[39] to Thomas de Lillingstone, who died seised of it in 1361, when a carucate of land, a mill,[40] and 6d. yearly from the pleas and perquisites of the court were included in the extent.[41] His heirs were a nephew, Thomas atte Well, and a great-nephew, Geoffrey Osberne or Thurbarn,[42] against whom Christine, widow of Thomas de Lillingstone and later wife of Hugh de Waltham, recovered seisin, only to be again disseised by the king.[43] In 1390 Thomas atte Well and Geoffrey Osberne granted this manor to Richard II,[44] so that it became parcel of the royal manor[45] granted by Henry VIII to Sir Nicholas Wentworth in 1545.

Another small estate in Lillingstone Lovell was given in the reign of Henry VI by John Mantel to Walter Mantel, Elizabeth his wife, and their heirs.[46] Walter, then Sir Walter Mantel, kt., died in 1487,[47] and in 1492 his grandson and heir John Mantel[48] secured his title against Robert Mantel.[49] This property was afterwards acquired by Sir Richard Empson, and said in 1510 to be mortgaged to John, Earl of Oxford.[50] The king held in 1512, when he granted it to William Tyler.[51] It is probably the property including a close called Hollenden, afterwards claimed by Nicholas Wentworth as purchaser of the leasehold rights held at one time by Thomas Empson.[52] Hollenden Close also appears as one of the contested parcels[53] in the numerous lawsuits in which Wentworth was involved about 1530 in respect of the Clare or Clarell lands, including Herring's Hoo Balk and Hosells,[54] claimed by him as parcel of his manor. His principal opponent, Thomas Poyner, stated that his grandmother Joan had been seised in the lands in dispute in special tail to her and her first husband Thomas Clarell or Clare. She afterwards married John Risley, by whom she had a daughter Jane. After the death of Joan Risley these lands came to her daughter by Thomas Clarell, Isabel (or Elizabeth) wife of Richard Poyner, who in her widowhood gave them

[14] Baker, *Hist. of Northants*, i, 516.
[15] Chan. Inq. p.m. 27 Edw. III (1st nos.), no. 50; *Cal. Close*, 1354-60, p. 5.
[16] Chan. Inq. p.m. 27 Edw. III, file 73, no. 5. References to Ferris Wood (19½ acres) occur until the 17th century (*L. and P. Hen. VIII*, xxi [1], g. 970 [56]; Chan. Inq. p.m. [Ser. 2], cclviii, 142; cccxxxiii, 46).
[17] *Cal. Close*, loc. cit.
[18] Misc. Inq. file 213, no. 33.
[19] *Cal. Close*, 1349-54, p. 559.
[20] *Cal. Pat.* 1361-4, p. 395.
[21] Chan. Inq. p.m. 27 Edw. III, file 73, no. 5.
[22] *Abbrev. Rot. Orig.* (Rec. Com.), ii, 282; *Cal. Pat.* 1364-7, pp. 28, 106.
[23] Misc. Inq. file 213, no. 33.
[24] *Cal. Pat.* 1396-9, pp. 581-2.
[25] *L. and P. Hen. VIII*, ii, 1713.
[26] Lessee under Lady Parr (Star Chamb. Proc. Hen. VIII, bdle. 24, no. 41), who died in 1532 (Chan. Inq. p.m. [Ser.2], liv, 61), her husband having predeceased her in 1518 (ibid. xxxiii, 93).
[27] *Dep. Keeper's Rep.* x, 296; Close, 37 Hen. VIII, pt. ii, no. 3; Add. Chart. 13931; *L. and P. Hen. VIII*, xx (1), g. 970 (56).
[28] Fine R. 42 Eliz. pt. i, no. 33; Chan. Inq. p.m. (Ser. 2), cclviii, 142; cccxxxiii, 46.
[29] See under advowson.
[30] *Hund. R.* (Rec. Com.), ii, 44.

[31] Ibid. 835.
[32] Chan. Inq. p.m. 35 Edw. III, pt. i, no. 117. The service was then a pair of spurs or 6d. yearly.
[33] *Hund. R.* (Rec. Com.), ii, 44.
[34] *Cal. Close*, 1272-9, p. 422; *Hund. R.* (Rec. Com.), ii, 835.
[35] *Cal. Inq. p.m.* (Edw. I), iii, 105; cf. *Cat. Anct. D.* i, 143.
[36] Pat. (Suppl.) 6a, m. 7.
[37] Chan. Inq. p.m. 35 Edw. III, pt. i, no. 117.
[38] Ibid.; (Ser. 2), cclviii, 142.
[39] *Pipe R.* 21 *Hen. II* (Pipe R. Soc.), 13; 22 *Hen. II*, 33. The name of Aylwin de Lillingstone occurs in 1176 (ibid. 22 *Hen. II*, 34).
[40] A mill standing on 3 acres of Margery Dansey's land was held by Richard the Miller in 1279 (*Hund. R.* [Rec. Com.], ii, 835). This land appears to be 'Windmillfield' mentioned about 1530 (Star Chamb. Proc. Hen. VIII, bdle. 19, no. 317). A windmill on the manor formerly Trafford's needed repairs in 1378 (Misc. Inq. file 213, no. 33).
[41] Chan. Inq. p.m. 35 Edw. III, pt. i, no. 117; 6 Ric. II, no. 48.
[42] Ibid.
[43] *Parl. R.* ii, 398. An undated record of the time of Edward III, in which Thomas de Lillingstone is also called Aspelon; cf. Close, 13 Ric. II, pt. ii, m. 24 d. Thomas de Aspelon witnessed

a grant in Lillingstone in 1359 (*Cal. Close*, 1354-60, p. 653). Ato Aspelon, evidently an ancestor, held half a virgate under John de Olney in 1279 (*Hund. R.* [Rec. Com.], ii, 835).
[44] Close, 13 Ric. II, pt. ii, m. 24 d.
[45] Chan. Inq. p.m. (Ser. 2), cclviii, 142.
[46] De Banco R. 924, m. 119.
[47] *Cal. Inq. p.m. Hen. VII*, i, 155.
[48] Ibid.
[49] De Banco R. 924, m. 119.
[50] Exch. Inq. p.m. (Ser. 2), file 784, no. 15.
[51] *L. and P. Hen. VIII*, i, 3492.
[52] Star Chamb. Proc. Hen. VIII, xv, fol. 230. A document of the time of Hen. VIII records a lease by William Roche to Thomas Empson of land here and elsewhere previously purchased from Empson by Roche (*Cat. Anct. D.* iii, 180).
[53] Star Chamb. Proc. Hen. VIII, bdle. 19, no. 317.
[54] Ibid. bdles. 24, no. 41; 19, no. 320. John and Thomas Hosell are mentioned in 1359 (*Cal. Close*, 1354-60, p. 656). Some Clare lands were also claimed from Nicholas Wentworth by Richard Budd and his wife Alice, whose father and mother were enfeoffed by Richard, son and heir of Thomas Clare, in return for taking care of his sister Elizabeth, an idiot (Star Chamb. Proc. Hen. VIII, bdle. 20, no. 133).

to her son, the said Thomas Poyner.[55] The contest appears to have dragged on for at least fourteen years.[56] In 1564 the lands were held by Ralph Redmayn and his wife Bridget, with reversion on her death to Robert son and heir of Richard Poyner, and were sold to Peter Wentworth, owner of the manors of Lillingstone Lovell.[57]

Some land in this parish was held by Luffield Priory as part of its original endowment[58] in the first half of the 12th century.[59] In 1279 it consisted of half a virgate of land held under Margaret (usually called Margery) Dansey, and half a virgate held of John de Olney.[60] This property, mentioned in 1503 on the death of the last prior, Thomas Rowland,[61] was leased in 1505 for forty years to Sir Richard Empson.[62] After his attainder a lease for thirty-four years was obtained in 1512 by William Tyler.[63]

The church of *ST. MARY THE VIRGIN* consists of a chancel 13 ft. 6 in. by 17 ft., a nave 48 ft. by 11 ft. 6 in., north chapel 17 ft. 6 in. by 11 ft., north aisle 6 ft. wide, south aisle 10 ft. wide, western tower 10 ft. square, a south porch and a modern vestry on the north side of the north aisle. The measurements are all internal.

There was apparently a small church here in the early part of the 13th century, of which the lower part of the tower, the reset south doorway, and possibly a part of the western walls of the nave still survive. In the middle of the 14th century the church was rebuilt and considerably enlarged. The retention of the tower and possibly the western part of the nave walls of the 13th-century church necessitated an eastward extension and restricted the width of the nave. The utilisation also of the foundations of the north wall of the north aisle of the earlier and smaller church caused the peculiar narrowness of the 14th-century north aisle. The want of proportion of the nave was still further emphasized by the size of the 14th-century chancel, which exceeds the nave in width and formerly extended considerably further to the east. The north chapel, the south aisle, and the topmost stage of the tower are also of the mid-14th-century. The church remained without alteration in plan for nearly three hundred years. About 1639 all the roofs except that of the chancel were renewed and the south porch was added. In 1777 the church was repaired, and it was at this date apparently that the chancel was shortened to about half its length, the east wall being then built in its present position. In 1892 the north vestry was added and the church was restored.

The chancel is lighted from the east by a 14th-century three-light window with tracery in a pointed head, reset from the older east wall. On the north wall there are indications of the jambs and arch of a blocked window, and on the south is a 14th-century two-light window with tracery in a pointed head. Below this window is a square-headed low-side window

with a modern shutter, and eastward is a 14th-century pointed doorway, now blocked. The pointed chancel arch is of two chamfered orders, the outer continuous and the inner springing from corbels.

The nave arcades of three bays on each side are of 14th-century date and have pointed arches of two chamfered orders springing from octagonal piers with moulded capitals and bases; the western responds have moulded corbels on carved heads, but the corbels on the eastern responds have been destroyed. There are four modern square-headed clearstory windows with trefoil lights on the south side. At the east end of the north wall is an opening possibly to light the rood-loft, and on the south side is the upper doorway to the loft.

The north chapel is lighted from the east by a 14th-century three-light window with tracery in a pointed head which contains some fragments of old glass. On the north side is a two-light window of similar design and in the south-east corner is a 15th-century squint into the chancel. In the south wall at the east end of the chapel are a 14th-century double piscina having two trefoiled arches with tracery in a pointed head and a plain pointed sedile.

The narrow north aisle has a 14th-century two-light window in the north wall corresponding to the window in the north chapel, eastward of which is a moulded doorway with pointed head now leading into the modern vestry.

The south aisle is lighted from the east by a window similar to that in the corresponding position in the north chapel. On the north side of the window is a 15th-century squint to the chancel. In the south wall is an early 13th-century doorway, re-used, which has a pointed head of two moulded orders and shafted jambs with foliated capitals and moulded bases. On the east side of the doorway is a 15th-century stoup and further eastward is a plain three-light window with a four-centred head of a similar date. Beyond this window are a piscina and sedile, the former having two trefoil arches with a quatrefoil in a pointed head and the latter having a plain pointed head. Westward of the south doorway is a 14th-century two-light window, almost wholly restored, with tracery in a pointed head.

The 13th-century tower is surmounted by a modern saddle-back roof, below which is a string-course with heads at the angles. It is of three stages, but is without buttresses or external divisions. The pointed tower arch of two orders springs from square jambs with plain imposts. There is a lancet in the west wall of the tower and above is a smaller lancet on each side except the east. The middle stage has square openings on the north and south sides, and the bell-chamber has on each side a 14th-century window of two lights with tracery in a pointed head.

The porch has a pointed entrance arch of two chamfered orders, over which is a stone with the date 1639, being that of the erection of the porch, and underneath it the date 1892, when a general

[55] Star Chamb. Proc. Hen. VIII, bdle. 20, no. 139. About 1520 Richard and Isabel Poyner sued John Hunt and his wife Jane, half-sister of Isabel, for deeds relating to this property (ibid.; Early Chan. Proc. bdle. 556, no. 3). Thomas Clare is mentioned in connexion with Lillingstone Lovell in 1416 (*Cal. Pat.* 1416–22, p. 17) and Thomas Clarell,

perhaps his son, in 1463 (*Cal. Pat.* 1461–7, p. 326). He is called late of Lillingstone Lovell in 1467 (*Cal. Pat.* 1467–77, p. 7) and died in 1471 (M.I. on brass in the church).
[56] *L. and P. Hen. VIII,* xix (2), 19.
[57] Recov. R. Mich. 6 & 7 Eliz. m. 1146; Com. Pleas D. Enr. Mich. 6 & 7 Eliz. m. 29.

[58] Chan. Inq. p.m. (Ser. 2), xxiii, 214.
[59] *V.C.H. Bucks.* i, 347.
[60] *Hund. R.* (Rec. Com.), ii, 835. Tenants under the priory were respectively Richard Grosset, mentioned in 1294 (*Cal. Inq. p.m.* [Edw. I], iii, 105), and Robert Warin.
[61] Chan. Inq. p.m. (Ser. 2), xxiii, 214.
[62] *L. and P. Hen. VIII,* i, 3297. [63] Ibid.

restoration of the church took place. There is a round sundial in the gable.

The oak pulpit, which is of the time of James I, forms an incomplete octagon in plan and is composed of panels with round-headed arches in two stages.

The font is modern.

There are two brasses in the chancel, one showing two hands rising from conventional clouds holding a pierced heart, below which is an inscription to John de Merston (Marston), rector of the church, who died on 11 February 1446-7. The other brass shows a civilian and his wife in the dress of the period, and an inscription to Thomas Clarell, patron of the church, who died on 20 September 1471, and to Agnes his wife, the date of whose death is left blank. There is a brass in the nave to William Risley, who died on 11 June 1513, and Agnes his wife, with three inverted shields, one bearing the quartered arms of Bradshaw and the others the arms of Risley of Chetwode. The four bells were made by Alexander Rigby in 1693.

The plate comprises an Elizabethan cup and cover paten, the foot of the latter being lost. They are without date letter or hall-mark. There are also a silver almsdish and flagon given by Mrs. Wentworth Creswell in 1761 and 1765 respectively, and a silver paten. The ancient pewter sacramental vessels were presented to the Buckinghamshire Archaeological Society by the Rev. William Lloyd.[64] The registers begin in 1558.

ADVOWSON Half the advowson of the church of Lillingstone Lovell was held in the later 12th century by Sybil Dangerville.[65] Her share was claimed in 1206 by William de Grendon, who derived his right through John de Loreng, who had married his sister Sybil.[66] In 1231 the king recovered the advowson against Ralph de Carevill and William de Osevill.[67] It remained in the Crown [68] until 1354, when it was granted to Nutley Abbey with licence to appropriate the church in lieu of a right to fuel in Bernwood Forest granted by King John.[69] As the abbey had trouble in obtaining the appropriation, a grant was made of 12½ marks yearly until such time as it could be effected.[70] This took place in 1366, when orders were given for the endowment of a vicarage.[71] No other reference occurs to the vicarage, which was apparently never ordained, and the right of presentation which remained with Nutley [72] was to a rectory, valued at £9 yearly at the Dissolution.[73] The advowson remained with the Crown [74] until about 1892,[75] when it was acquired by Mr. James Bogle Delap, the present owner.

There was a chapel at Great Lillingstone to which a presentation was made by Godfrey de St. Martin.[76] His son Hugh gave the advowson to Luffield Priory, which in 1239 sued the parson of Lillingstone for claiming it as appertaining to the mother church.[77] The right of the parson was evidently confirmed by the bishop,[78] but no later reference to the chapel has been found.

CHARITIES Sir Peter Wentworth, who died in 1675, by his will bequeathed £300 for the establishment of a charity for apprenticing.[79] The legacy was laid out in the purchase of a rent-charge of £18 issuing out of property called Keys in the parish of Lillingstone Dayrell, now belonging to Mr. J. B. Delap. One moiety of the rent-charge is applied in the parish of Lillingstone Lovell, and the other moiety is applicable in the parish of Woolstone, but does not appear to have been paid for many years.

The same testator likewise bequeathed for the poor of Lillingstone Lovell the sum of £100, which was laid out in the purchase of a rent-charge of £6 on the property called Keys, above referred to. The income is distributed in coal with that of the charity next mentioned.

The Whittlebury Forest Coal Charity consists of a sum of £63 3s. 1d. consols with the official trustees, arising from compensation for the disafforestation of the forest under an Act of 1852-3.[80] The annual income, amounting to £1 11s. 4d., is applied in the distribution of coal.

The Rev. William Lloyd, by his will proved at London 15 July 1889, bequeathed a legacy, now represented by £136 13s. 1d. consols with the official trustees, the annual dividends of which, amounting to £3 8s. 4d., are distributable among the aged and sick poor and the widows of the parish. In 1913 there were six recipients.

LUFFIELD ABBEY

Luffield covers 216 acres, two-thirds of which are devoted to pasture and one-third to arable land.[1] The soil is clay and gravel and the subsoil various. Luffield was formerly extra-parochial,[2] and considered partly in Buckinghamshire, where it was assessed under Stowe [3] (whose boundaries do not, however, touch it at any point), and partly in Silverstone in Northamptonshire, where the monastic church formerly stood.[4] In 1831 its area was given as 450 acres, of which 60 lay in Northamptonshire.[5]

---

[64] Sheahan, *Hist. and Topog. of Bucks.* 287.

[65] *Abbrev. Plac.* (Rec. Com.), 46.

[66] Ibid. This claim was apparently based on the transfer in 1200 by David de Loreng to William de Grendon of a quarter fee in Lillingstone (Feet of F. case 187, file 2, no. 30).

[67] *R. of Hugh of Wells* (Cant. and York Soc.), ii, 35; *Cal. Pat.* 1225-32, p. 421.

[68] Harl. MS. 6950, fol. 65*b*; *Hund. R.* (Rec. Com.), ii, 44; *Cal. Pat.* 1272-81, p. 329; 1307-13, p. 388; 1340-3, p. 305; 1348-50, p. 321; 1350-4, p. 246.

[69] *Cal. Pat.* 1354-8, pp. 11, 20. The earlier grant on similar terms in 1313

mentioned in a confirmation charter of 1335 (*Cal. Chart. R.* 1327-41, p. 327) and in one of 1398 (*Cal. Pat.* 1396-9, p. 380) was evidently ineffective.

[70] *Cal. Pat.* 1354-8, pp. 519, 540-1; 1364-7, p. 170.

[71] Linc. Epis. Reg. Inst. Buckingham, fol. 412. A vicarage had been ordained by Bishop Grosteste about 1239 (Harl. MS. 6950, fol. 61).

[72] Harl. MS. 6952, fol. 52*b*. Thomas Clarell, called patron of the church in 1471 (M.I. on brass), was evidently so by a grant from Nutley. Richard Empson had a similar grant in 1499 (Harl. MS. 6953, fol. 19*b*).

[73] *Valor Eccl.* (Rec. Com.), ii, 159. It

was assessed at £8 yearly in 1291 (*Pope Nich. Tax.* [Rec. Com.], 31).

[74] Inst. Bks. (P.R.O.); Bacon, *Liber Regis.* 791; Sheahan, op. cit. 287.

[75] *Clergy Lists,* 1890, 1895.

[76] Cur. Reg. R. 120, m. 2.

[77] Ibid.

[78] Harl. MS. 6950, fol. 61.

[79] P.C.C. 26 Bence.

[80] Stat. 16 & 17 Vict. cap. 42.

[1] Statistics from Bd. of Agric. (1905).

[2] Willis, *Hist. and Antiq. of Buckingham,* 225.

[3] *Pop. Ret.* (1831), 26.

[4] Willis, loc. cit.; Sheahan, *Hist. and Topog. of Bucks.* 285.

[5] *Pop. Ret.* loc. cit.

In 1881 it was still reckoned as extra-parochial,[6] but is now rated as a parish extending into both counties. It is still reputed to be extra-parochial for ecclesiastical purposes. The parish consists of a single farm, of which the house occupied in 1831 by the whole population, a family of ten persons,[7] is situated to the north-east, on the site of the old priory. No traces now remain of the former conventual buildings, and even Willis, who visited Luffield on 11 October 1732, found only a piece of the old tower of the church, from which he deduced the supposed dimensions of the church, 80 ft. in length and 30 ft. in breadth.[8]

MANOR The history of the Benedictine priory of *LUFFIELD* down to its acquisition by Westminster Abbey has already been traced elsewhere.[9] The grant of Luffield Priory, manor and advowson to the abbey was confirmed in 1503,[10] and the abbot appears to have leased the estate almost immediately to Sir Richard Empson for forty years.[11] On his attainder a lease for thirty-four years was granted to William Tyler in 1512, with the site and demesne of the priory and lands in Luffield, the chapel of St. Thomas the Martyr in Lillingstone Dayrell and the chapel of St. Nicholas in Evershaw, Biddlesden.[12] At the Dissolution Luffield became Crown property, and as such was attached to the honour of Grafton formed in 1542.[13] In 1551 the manor and site were granted to Sir Nicholas Throckmorton,[14] whose second son Arthur Throckmorton[15] settled the estate by fine in 1580,[16] and again in 1582,[17] 1596,[18] and 1614.[19] Sir Arthur, who died in 1626, had four daughters, of whom the second, Ann, married Sir Peter Temple of Stowe.[20] She had died in January 1619–20, leaving a daughter and heir Ann, who, after the death of her father in 1653,[21] made a settlement of Luffield with her

husband Thomas Roper, Viscount Baltinglass.[22] They were sued for debt in 1658 by Clement Throckmorton and others, who complained that a secret conveyance of Luffield prevented the recovery of the money, and were confined in the Fleet Prison,[23] where Ann died in 1696.[24] A quarrel arose over her inheritance, which included Thornborough (q.v.), between William Temple, of Lillingstone Dayrell, her first cousin once removed on her father's side,[25] and Thomas Lennard, Lord Dacre and Earl of Sussex, her first cousin once removed on her mother's side,[26] the grandson of Sir Arthur Throckmorton's third daughter Elizabeth.[27] In the final division of the property in 1701 Luffield was allotted to William Temple.[28] His son and heir William Temple, who inherited the manor in 1706,[29] gave up his rights in it in 1718 to his cousin Sir Richard Temple, bart., of Stowe, Lord Cobham of Cobham, whom he afterwards succeeded in the baronetcy.[30] It descended with Stowe (q.v.), to which it was still attached in the mid-19th century[31]; but the manorial rights are now vested in Sir Edmund Giles Loder,

LODER. *Azure a fesse between two scallops or with three harts' heads caboshed proper upon the fesse.*

bart., of Leonardslee, Horsham, Sussex, the sole landowner.

In 1230 the prior and monks received a grant of a yearly fair on the feast of the Exaltation of the Holy Cross,[32] of which no mention has been found after 1330.[33]

There do not appear to be any endowed charities subsisting in this parish.

MAIDS' MORETON

Mortone (xi cent.); Morthone (xiii cent.); Maydemorton (xvi cent.).

The parish covers about 1,365 acres, of which 376 are arable, 786 permanent grass and 26 woods and plantations.[1] The ground slopes from a level of about 400 ft. above the ordnance datum in the northwest to about 270 ft. in the south-east. The soil is clay and gravel and the subsoil gravel.

The village lies in the south-west of the parish, along the Buckingham to Towcester road, a mile north-east of Buckingham station on the Bletchley and Banbury section of the London and North Western railway. It contains many 17th-century

houses and cottages of timber frames with brick or plaster filling and thatched roofs. Its most interesting feature is the fine 15th-century church of St. Edmund, said by tradition to have been built by two maiden ladies of the Pever family, whence the name Maids' Moreton.[2] A slab in the nave of the church possibly marks their grave. The church and rectory-house stand at the southern end of the village, high among fine trees. They look down upon Buckingham at the foot of the hill below, the Ouse occupying the foreground. On its banks is a picturesque water-mill, and between it and the town the Grand Junction Canal winds along through

[6] *Lond. Gaz.* 26 Apr. 1881, p. 2013, when by-laws were made regarding school attendance.
[7] *Pop. Ret.* loc. cit.
[8] Willis, loc. cit.
[9] *V.C.H. Northants*, ii, 95; *Bucks.* i, 347.
[10] Pat. 18 Hen. VII, pt. i; *Hist. MSS. Com. Rep.* iv, App. i, 173.
[11] *L. and P. Hen. VIII*, i, 3297.
[12] Ibid. [13] Ibid. xvii, p. 12.
[14] Pat. 5 Edw. VI, pt. iii, m. 31.
[15] Chan. Inq. p.m. (Ser. 2), clvii, 104.
[16] Feet of F. Div. Co. Trin. 22 Eliz.
[17] Ibid. Trin. 24 Eliz.
[18] Ibid. East. 38 Eliz.; Recov. R. East. 38 Eliz. m. 124.

[19] Feet of F. Div. Co. Trin. 12 Jas. I.
[20] Chan. Inq. p.m. (Ser. 2), ccccxxxviii, 126. Sir Arthur left a life interest in all his lands to his wife Ann, who died between 26 July 1628 and 19 October 1629 (P.C.C. 88 Ridley). Katherine Throckmorton, his youngest daughter, was to have the cattle at Luffield (ibid. 106 Hele).
[21] G.E.C. *Baronetage*, i, 82.
[22] Recov. R. Trin. 1654, m. 162.
[23] Chan. Proc. (Ser. 2), bdle. 463, no. 81. [24] G.E.C. loc. cit.
[25] Ibid. [26] G.E.C. *Peerage*, iii, 4–5.
[27] Chan. Inq. p.m. (Ser. 2), ccccxxxviii, 126.

[28] Feet of F. Bucks. Trin. 13 Will. III; Recov. R. Trin. 13 Will. III, m. 208.
[29] G.E.C. *Baronetage*, i, 83.
[30] Ibid.; Feet of F. Bucks. East. 4 Geo. I.
[31] Lipscomb, *Hist. and Antiq. of Bucks.* iii, 112.
[32] *Cal. Chart. R.* 1226–57, p. 114.
[33] *Plac. de Quo Warr.* (Rec. Com.), 520.
[1] Statistics from Bd. of Agric. (1905).
[2] Lipscomb, *Hist. and Antiq. of Bucks.* iv, 210; *N. and Q.* (Ser. 3), xi, 298; (Ser. 4), ii, 521. The last Thomas Pever died in 1429, not in 1449 as stated in *N. and Q.* See Broughton.

the meadows in a course very similar to that of the river, which at one point it joins. About half a mile south-east of the rectory is College Farm, the property of All Souls College, Oxford. The Manor, occupied by its owner, Miss Andrewes, stands west of the church and rectory. A fine avenue, about three-quarters of a mile in length, leads south-west from here through plantations of fir down the hill-side to Buckingham.

Maids' Moreton Manor House, built near the site of the old manor and the residence of Mr. Arthur Lucas, lies off Church Street. It was formerly called Moreton House, and was the early home of the late Bishop Browne of Winchester and of Sir Thomas Gore Browne.[3] From this street Main Street branches north-west through the village, passing the school (built in 1854), the Elms, occupied by Miss Boyd, and at the centre of the village Moreton Lodge, dating from 1715, the property of Baroness Kinloss and residence of Sir A. C. Thornhill, bart. At the

MANORS In 1086 5 hides in *MORETON* were held by Lewin of Nuneham, the pre-Conquest owner.[5] They descended with his chief manors of Mursley and Salden to the Fitz Niels,[6] by whom they were subinfeudated in the early 13th century[7] for three parts of a fee, the Fitz Niels being answerable to the king for scutage and ward to Northampton Castle, assessed at 7s. 6d.[8] From 1300 to 1346, the last date at which the connexion of the Fitz Niels with Moreton is recorded, the service due was returned at half a fee.[9]

Their place as overlords appears to have been taken by the holders of the honour of Gloucester, which had a large interest in Maids' Moreton (see below). Already in 1272, after the death of the tenant, Gilbert de Clare Earl of Gloucester had entered the manor and occupied it for a year.[10] Evidence points to the identity of part of this 5-hide manor with the carucate of land afterwards known

THE VILLAGE, MAIDS' MORETON

northern end of the village is Moreton House, occupied by the owner, Mrs. Henry Bull. Where Main Street joins the Towcester road the Wesleyan chapel, erected in 1869, stands, with Manor Farm, a 16th-century house of stone with modern additions in brick, a little to the south of it. Tradition marks it as once the home of the two maids of Moreton. Upper Farm, according to a date in a chimney stack, was built in 1624, and has later additions. It is of timber and plaster or brick and has tiled and slated roofs. Some of the windows still retain their mullions. The village has in its vicinity the reservoir of the Buckingham Corporation Waterworks.

The parish was inclosed in 1801 by Act of Parliament.[4]

as *GREENHAMS MANOR* in Moreton and held of the honour of Gloucester in the early 15th century.[11]

It is probable that the first tenant under the Fitz Niels was Walter de Morton, about the beginning of the 13th century.[12] His estate, said to be one and a quarter fees in Moreton geldable to the king, passed to Paul Pever, who about 1247, by grant from Henry III, appropriated to himself hidage worth 10s. and suit and view of frankpledge worth 2s. each.[13] He had also acquired Chilton Manor, with which the manor descended for about sixty years.[14] After the death of Emma, widow of Paul Pever's son John, Walter de Morton occupied the manor in succession to Gilbert de Clare, Earl of Gloucester,

[3] *Dict. Nat. Biog.*
[4] Priv. Act, 41 Geo. III, cap. 47.
[5] *V.C.H. Bucks.* i, 275.
[6] *Testa de Nevill* (Rec. Com.), 252. Warine Fitzgerald held in Moreton in the

early 13th century in right of his wife Agnes Fitz Niel.
[7] Chan. Inq. p.m. Hen. III, file 13, no. 2.
[8] *Hund. R.* (Rec. Com.), i, 32; ii, 341; *Feud. Aids*, i, 79.
[9] *Feud. Aids*, i, 100, 125.

[10] *Cal. Inq. p.m.* (Edw. I), ii, 66.
[11] Chan. Inq. p.m. 9 Hen. IV, no. 9; 1 Hen. VI, no. 68.
[12] Harl. Chart. 86, A 17–19.
[13] *Hund. R.* (Rec. Com.), i, 32, 40.
[14] See above, p. 23.

and was in possession in 1274.[15] During his tenure the house had deteriorated to the value of 10 marks, and he had carried away a press and apple-mill worth 20s.[16] This Walter de Morton may be identical with the Walter de Morton whom Paul Pever succeeded, and his descendants appear to have held lands in Moreton as tenants to the Pevers.[17] John Pever, Paul's grandson, had succeeded to the manor by 1279, when he claimed view of frankpledge,[18] and freedom from suit of court and hundred, which his father and grandfather had enjoyed.[19] John Pever was still holding the manor in 1302,[20] but seems to have parted with it before his death in 1315, when he was returned as patron of the advowson only,[21] the manor passing to Richard de Bayhous, who held with Katherine his wife in 1337[22] and was still lord in 1346.[23] Nothing is known of this estate for the next sixty years, but it probably reappears in the carucate of land in Moreton of which Hugh Greenham died seised in 1407.[24] He and his wife Katherine had previously, in 1384, acquired rights in lands here from John Warde of Buckingham.[25] His property passed to his grandson John, son of his son Thomas, who died on 12 November 1408.[26] The heir was Hugh's son William, aged twenty-six, who died on 8 December 1412, leaving a son Thomas to inherit Moreton Manor.[27] The custody of Thomas during his minority was granted to Queen Joan, and by her on 10 April 1413 to Nicholas, Bishop of Bath.[28] Thomas attained his majority on 4 October 1420,[29] and on 4 May 1430, as Thomas Greenham of Ketton (Hunts.), conveyed the manor to Sir John Basynges and others,[30] who released it to him on 1 April 1433. On the same day Thomas Greenham granted lands in Moreton to William Purefoy and others, by whom the manor of Moreton was then granted to John Horwood and Robert Somery.[31]

On 1 April 1442 Robert Somery granted this property as the manor of Moreton called Greenhams to Henry VI,[32] by whom in the following month it was granted to All Souls College, Oxford,[33] the present owners. It was leased by the warden in 1493 as the lordship of Moreton to Robert Woodward, jun., of Buckingham,[34] and in 1518 to John Harris,[35] who in 1535 was paying a rent of £7 6s. 8d. for the manor of Moreton with the mill there called 'Brent Myll.'[36] Old leases existing among the archives of All Souls show that, as the manor of Greenhams, many separate leases were made of it to the Harris

family in the 16th century[37] and to John Easton in the 16th and 17th centuries.[38] It was held with the Christ Church manor in the 18th century on lease by Edward Bate, who died in 1717.[39] In 1801, 1808, and 1815 it was leased to Edwin Oakley Gray of Buckingham by the college.[40] In 1862 the lessee was the Rev. Wm. Andrewes Uthwatt,[41] succeeded by Mrs. Uthwatt about 1883. The manorial rights are now vested in Miss Andrewes.

In 1794 the park belonging to Greenhams was leased to Richard Geast of Blyth Hall, near Coleshill, with assignment thereof to Edwin Oakley Gray.[42]

Two hides of land in Moreton, always reckoned as part of Stowe, to which they appear to have been appurtenant in 1086, were granted with it by Robert Doyley and Roger de Ivry to the college founded by them in the church of St. George in Oxford Castle, and were in the possession of the canons before 1130.[43] With Stowe they passed to Oseney Abbey, which was said to hold them of the fee of Robert Doyley in the 13th century.[44] The abbot enjoyed view of frankpledge, waif and stray and other liberties in this estate,[45] which was assessed at £5 2s. 6½d. in 1535.[46] These 2 carucates were subinfeudated by the abbot for a yearly rent of 3s. 4d. to the Greys of Wilton, and proofs of their tenure exist from 1370 to the mid-15th century.[47] The estate remained in the abbey until the Dissolution,[48] when it formed part of the endowment of the cathedral church of Christ and St. Mary, Oxford.[49] It remained in the possession of the Dean and Chapter of Christ Church, Oxford, who held the manor as late as the early 19th century.[50] Part of their estate in Maids' Moreton was held under them on lease by William Moore at his death in 1600,[51] and came to his son John, at whose death in 1620, without issue, it passed to William's widow Elizabeth, then described as Elizabeth Every, widow, who married John Moore and held these lands with him.[52] In the 18th century Edward Bate, the lessee of All Souls Manor was said to have been tenant also of this manor,[53] of which in 1801 Samuel Churchill was lessee.[54]

In 1086 4 hides in Moreton were held as one manor under Walter Giffard.[55] Alric son of Goding had previously held two of these hides as one manor, Ederic, a man of Asgar the Staller, 1½ hides as one manor, and Saward, a man of Toti, half a hide, all three being able to sell and assign their land.[56] This manor was parcel of the honour of Giffard or Gloucester,[57] of which it was held for one fee[58] until the

[15] Cal. Inq. p.m. (Edw. I), ii, 66.
[16] Ibid.
[17] William son of Walter, who in 1279 held 1 hide for which he paid 9s. to John Pever, by whom it was transferred to the Abbot of Oseney, was apparently son of the Walter of 1274 (Hund. R. [Rec. Com.], ii, 342).
[18] Ibid.
[19] Plac. de Quo Warr. (Rec. Com.), 91.
[20] Feud. Aids, i, 100. See also Assize R. 68, m. 16 d., 21.
[21] Cal. Inq. p.m. (Edw. II), v, 378.
[22] Chan. Inq. p.m. 11 Edw. III (1st nos.), no. 33.
[23] Feud. Aids, i, 125.
[24] Chan. Inq. p.m. 9 Hen. IV, no. 9.
[25] Chas. Trice Martin, Archives of All Souls Coll. Oxon. 53.
[26] Chan. Inq. p.m. 9 Hen. IV, no. 9.
[27] Ibid. 1 Hen. VI, no. 68.
[28] Ibid.
[29] Ibid.

[30] C. T. Martin, loc. cit.
[31] Ibid.
[32] Ibid.
[33] Ibid. 28, 189.
[34] Ibid. 31.   [35] Ibid.
[36] Valor Eccl. (Rec. Com.), ii, 235. All Souls held other lands here of Oseney Abbey, and had for many years refused to pay rent for them.
[37] C. T. Martin, op. cit. 31, 32.
[38] Ibid. 31–3.
[39] Browne Willis, Hist. and Antiq. of Buckingham, 229.
[40] C. T. Martin, op. cit. 33, 34; Priv. Act, 41 Geo. III, cap. 47.
[41] Sheahan, Hist. and Topog. of Bucks. 288.
[42] C. T. Martin, op. cit. 33.
[43] V.C.H. Oxon. ii, 160.
[44] Hund. R. (Rec. Com.), ii, 342, 343. The abbot also held 1½ virgates and 6 acres for 6d. per acre of John Pever (ibid. 341). See also Assize R. 68, m. 17.

[45] Hund. R. (Rec. Com.), ii, 343; Plac. de Quo Warr. (Rec. Com.), 93.
[46] Dugdale, Mon. vi, 256.
[47] Chan. Inq. p.m. 44 Edw. III, no. 30; 15 Ric. II, pt. i, no. 27; 20 Hen. VI, no. 23; Cal. Close, 1369–74, p. 168.
[48] Feud. Aids, i, 108.
[49] Pat. 34 Hen. VIII, pt. vi; 38 Hen. VIII, pt. viii.
[50] Priv. Act, 41 Geo. III, cap. 47.
[51] Chan. Inq. p.m. (Ser. 2), ccccxxxv, 114.
[52] Ibid.
[53] Rec. of Bucks. (Bucks. Arch. and Archit. Soc.), vi, 415; Lysons, Mag. Brit. i (3), 609.
[54] Priv. Act, 41 Geo. III, cap. 47.
[55] V.C.H. Bucks. i, 250.
[56] Ibid.
[57] Testa de Nevill (Rec. Com.), 247, 258.
[58] Hund. R. (Rec. Com.), i, 32; ii, 341.

16th century, when the king claimed to be lord of the honour.[59] In the 13th century the Earls of Gloucester, as overlords,[60] had view of frankpledge in Moreton and all royal rights as from time immemorial.[61] View of frankpledge and a court leet in Moreton are also mentioned in the 14th and 15th centuries.[62] The Temples, who obtained Stowe in Elizabeth's reign, received a grant of free warren here in 1616,[63] and Lord Cobham about 1735, and the Marquess of Buckingham in the early 19th century, put forward a claim to be lords of the paramount manor in Maids' Moreton, as held of the honour of Gloucester, of which they were lords.[64]

The under-tenant in 1086 was Turstin, evidently identical with the Turstin son of Rolf who held Great Missenden at that date.[65] Either he or his successors subinfeudated these 4 hides in Moreton, the intermediary lordship thus created descending with the manor of Great Missenden (q.v.) and, like it, dividing into moieties, after the death of Hugh de Sanford, about 1234, between his two daughters and co-heirs, Christine wife of John de Pleseys and Agnes wife of Walter Husee.[66] These interests in Moreton are last heard of in 1346, when Hugh de Pleseys and Thomas de Missenden were jointly responsible for the fee to the Earl of Gloucester.[67]

The subinfeudation had probably taken place before 1202, when Reynold son of Ascur granted to Richard son of Emma 1 hide in Moreton at a rent of 12s. yearly, excepting from the grant his chief messuage and two assarts at 'Smalethornes' and 'Portgrave,' which he reserved to himself and his heirs.[68] In 1226 there is mention of the wood in Moreton of William son of Reynold,[69] who in 1254 held that moiety of the fee which was dependent on the Husees, the other moiety being then held by Ellis le Drueys.[70] By 1268 they had granted to Matthew de Stratton, Archdeacon of Buckingham, lands which before his death in that year he granted to the abbey of Oseney, by a deed conferring on the abbey in free alms all his court of Moreton which he had of the gift of William son of Reynold, with all its appurtenances within the towns and fields of Moreton, whether of the fee of St. Gregory or of other fees, with a messuage and lands which he had of the gift of John and Robert sons of William de Morton, of Henry son of the said Robert, with all that he had of the gift of Ellis le Drueys and Alina his wife.[71] In 1279 Ellis le Drueys's half-fee was extended at 2 hides and 3 virgates, and Ralf Kam was intermediary between him and Hugh de Pleseys. The bequests of William son of Reynold and of his relatives to Oseney Abbey evidently comprised all his

estate in Moreton, for in 1279 the abbot was answerable to Henry Husee for the half-fee due from William's 2 hides in Moreton.[72] A hide and 3½ virgates were then held of the abbot by John de Morton,[73] who shortly afterwards acquired Ellis le Drueys's portion,[74] and the Walter de Morton holding in 1316 may have been his representative,[75] for during the 14th and 15th centuries the Abbot of Oseney and the heirs of John de Morton are returned as joint lords of this part of Moreton.[76] The Oseney portion was doubtless granted with the rest of the abbey's land in this parish to the Dean and Chapter of Oxford at the Dissolution,[77] and the Mortons' holding may have been represented by the 7 virgates and capital messuage which the Moore family, also lessees of Christ Church (see above), held of the honour of Gloucester in the 17th century.[78]

A 2-hide manor in Moreton, previously held by Ulvric, a man of Alric son of Goding, who could sell, was included in 1386 among the lands of Walter Giffard.[79] It may perhaps be in part accounted for by the lands attached to the honour of Gloucester in the 15th century,[80] and held by the Bartons of Thornton[81] (q.v.). Some of these were granted with other lands in Crendon and Foscott for the foundation of a chantry at Thornton by Isabella Barton.[82] At the Dissolution All Souls College, Oxford, paid 10s. 8d. from its manor in Moreton for the yearly distribution of alms and 6 lb. of corn at Thornton, and were also liable for the stipend of the chaplain celebrating there for the Bartons' souls.[83]

Other Barton lands descended with the Castle House in Buckingham to the Fowlers, of whom Richard Fowler was in possession in 1477,[84] and then to their heirs the Lamberts.[85] They passed to Sir Edward Bagot, bart., by his marriage with Mary daughter and heir of William Lambert, to whom livery of her property was granted in 1639.[86] They are said to have been subsequently held by Sir George Moore, created a baronet as Sir George Moore of Maids' Moreton in 1665,[86a] and sold by him to Dr. George Bate, physician to Charles I, Oliver Cromwell and Charles II.[87] He was born in 1607 at Moreton, where his father, George Bate, was rector until his death in 1643.[88] Edward Bate succeeded his father, the doctor, in 1669, and was described by Browne Willis as 'an excellent, active J.P. . . . . a good neighbour and friend.'[88a] He built a mansion-house near the church, where he died in 1717; the house subsequently passed to Samuel Churchill and Edwin Gray, lessee of Greenhams Manor, to which it was said to belong.[89]

[59] Ct. R. (Gen. Ser.), bdle. 155, no. 13; Chan. Inq. p.m. (Ser. 2), ccccxxxv, 114.

[60] Feud. Aids, i, 79, 98.

[61] Hund. R. (Rec. Com.), i, 32; ii, 343.

[62] Chan. Inq. p.m. 9 Edw. II, no. 68; 10 Ric. II, no. 38; 4 Hen. IV, no. 41; 38 & 39 Hen. VI, no. 59.

[63] Pat. 14 Jas. I, pt. xii, no. 9.

[64] Browne Willis, loc. cit.; Priv. Act, 41 Geo. III, cap. 47; Lysons, loc. cit.; see also Stowe.

[65] V.C.H. Bucks. i, 247.

[66] Ibid. ii, 348; Testa de Nevill (Rec. Com.), 247; Hund. R. (Rec. Com.), i, 32; ii, 341; Feud. Aids, i, 98.

[67] Feud. Aids, i, 123.

[68] Feet of F. Bucks. Mich. 4 John.

[69] Rot. Lit. Claus. (Rec. Com.), ii, 162.

[70] Hund. R. (Rec. Com.), i, 32; see also Testa de Nevill (Rec. Com.), 247.

[71] Cal. Chart. R. 1300–26, p. 425. The Drueys' gift amounted to 1½ virgates 5 acres. See Hund. R. (Rec. Com.), ii, 341.

[72] Hund. R. (Rec. Com.), ii, 341.

[73] Ibid.   [74] Feud. Aids, i, 79.

[75] Ibid. 108.

[76] Chan. Inq. p.m. 10 Ric. II, no. 38; 38 & 39 Hen. VI, no. 59.

[77] See Stowe.

[78] Chan. Inq. p.m. (Ser. 2), ccccxxxv, 114.

[79] V.C.H. Bucks. i, 250.

[80] Chan. Inq. p.m. 38 & 39 Hen. VI, no. 59.

[81] Lansd. Chart. 569, 570, 573.

[82] C. T. Martin, op. cit. 28, 54, 165; Lipscomb, op. cit. iii, 120.

[83] Valor Eccl. loc. cit.

[84] Chan. Inq. p.m. 17 Edw. IV, no. 39; Chan. Proc. (Ser. 2), bdle. 62, no. 62.

[85] Ct. R. (Gen. Ser.), bdle. 155, no. 13.

[86] Fine R. 14 Chas. I, pt. i, no. 54.

[86a] G.E.C. Baronetage, iv, 23.

[87] Dict. Nat. Biog.; Willis, op. cit. 230. His connexion with the Moreton family of Moores has not been established, but he appears to have been a native of Moreton. Lady Moore was living here in 1670 (Cal. S. P. Dom. 1660–70, p. 185).

[88] Willis, op. cit. 236; Cal. S. P. Dom. 1636–7, p. 423.

[88a] Willis, op. cit. 229.

[89] Lipscomb, op. cit. iii, 41; Sheahan, loc. cit.

Lands in Moreton were also held by the abbey of Biddlesden,[90] the convent of Elstow,[91] and the hospital of St. John of Buckingham.[92]

Lewin of Nuneham held a mill worth 10s. with his manor in 1086,[93] probably the water-mill held by John Pever in 1279.[94] The Brend or Brent Mill was held by All Souls College in 1483,[95] and leased by them then and at subsequent dates.

CHURCH The church of *ST. EDMUND* consists of a chancel measuring internally about 25 ft. 11 in. by 15 ft. 11 in., south vestry 6 ft. 8 in. square, with a modern westward extension, nave 40 ft. 3 in. by 23 ft. 11 in., west tower 13 ft. 3 in. by 12 ft. 3 in., north porch 9 ft. by 6 ft. 5 in. and south porch 6 ft. 10 in. by 7 ft.

The present church was entirely rebuilt about 1450, its refoundation being traditionally ascribed to the munificence of the two maiden daughters of the last Thomas Pever, who died in 1429. The only remains from the former church are the late 12th-century font and some 12th-century moulded stones, re-used in the rear arches of the windows of the north porch. As might be expected in the case of a building

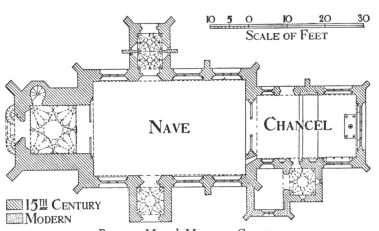

10 5 0 10 20 30
SCALE OF FEET

NAVE   CHANCEL

▨ 15ᵀᴴ CENTURY
▩ MODERN

PLAN OF MAIDS' MORETON CHURCH

erected at a single period, the whole work is carried out in a most complete and elaborate manner, and may challenge comparison with any existing examples of contemporary date in the country. The vestry, porches, and ground stage of the tower are fan-vaulted, and the design of the tower itself is especially remarkable for the boldness and originality displayed in the design of the two upper stages. The walling throughout is of limestone rubble, the south wall of the chancel and the walls of the original vestry being covered with rough-cast. The building was restored in 1882–7, when the vestry was enlarged by the westward extension, which touches the south-east angle of the nave.

The east window of the chancel is of five cinquefoiled lights with transomed vertical tracery in an elliptical head; internally the jambs are brought down to the ground, and the inner fillets of the mullions, interrupted only by a transom-like moulding at the sill, are continued below the foot of the lights and stopped upon a blocking of stone extending

beneath the three middle lights, and probably intended for fixing the high altar. The tracery is set near the middle of the wall, and the jambs are moulded with wide casements on both faces, the casement being stopped internally at the sill level, below which the jambs have a plain splay. The rear arch is concentric with the outer head, and is continuously moulded with the jambs. To the north of the window is a moulded image bracket. A similar treatment is adopted in the case of all the other windows of the chancel and nave, the fillets of the mullions being stopped upon stone benches set back about 3 in. from the internal face of the wall. At the east end of the north wall is a window of three trefoiled lights with floreated cusping and vertical tracery in a segmental two-centred head with almost straight sides. To the west of this window are two narrow recesses with segmental two-centred heads, the western recess, in the lower part of which is the north doorway, extending nearly the whole height of the chancel, while the head of the eastern recess, which is now blocked by a monument, is placed lower to clear the foot of the wall-post of the adjacent roof-truss. At the east end of the wall is a small window of two cinquefoiled lights with quatrefoil tracery in a two-centred head. In the south-east angle of the chancel is a shaft piscina with a moulded semi-hexagonal basin and a shaft of the same form. The south-east window is like the corresponding window in the opposite wall, but the bench in the recess below the sill is divided by buttressed mullions into three sedilia, each having a richly panelled semi-hexagonal projecting canopy with a cinquefoiled and sub-cusped ogee arch in each face and miniature pinnacled buttresses at the angles. The soffits of the canopies have mock vaulting, and the whole work is of great elaboration. It has been a good deal restored, the crowning cornice being apparently modern. To the west of the window are three narrow recesses, the whole height of the chancel, with straight-sided pointed heads and splayed jambs, hollow chamfered at the angles; the middle recess does not descend to the floor level, but is stopped above the head of the vestry doorway, while each of the others has a stone bench with two rectangular panels at the back, stopped at the general sill level to correspond with the treatment of the window recesses. At the west end of the wall, now looking into the vestry, is a window like the corresponding window in the opposite wall. The wide and lofty chancel arch is of two continuously moulded orders, separated by deep, narrow casements. In the east face of the south respond is a squint from the nave having an opening with a trefoiled head. Externally the walls of the chancel rise from a boldly moulded plinth, which is continued round the whole building, and are crowned by a moulded cornice and plain parapet

90 *Harl. Chart.* 86 A, 17–20; *Pope Nich. Tax.* (Rec. Com.), 47; *Valor Eccl.* (Rec. Com.), iv, 237.
91 *Hund. R.* (Rec. Com.), ii, 342; *L. and P. Hen. VIII*, xvi, g. 1226 (30).
92 *Hund. R.* loc. cit.
93 *V.C.H. Bucks.* i, 125.
94 *Hund. R.* (Rec. Com.), ii, 341.
95 C. T. Martin, op. cit. 31 et seq.

with a weathered coping, the east wall having a low-pitched gable. All the windows are labelled, and there is a slight set-back at the level of their sills, capped by a heavy chamfered weather-course, which is utilized to form the label of the north doorway; at the eastern angles and in the centre of the north wall are slender buttresses of two offsets.

The south vestry is lighted by small square-headed windows in the east and south walls, each being of a single trefoiled light, rebated for a shutter, with plain pierced spandrels in the head. At the south-east is a rectangular recess possibly intended for a piscina. An archway on the west opens to the modern extension. The cones of the fan-vault have trefoiled panelling and spring without corbels from the four angles of the vestry, while the centre of the vault is occupied by a multifoiled circle with floreated cusping inclosing a large four-leaved flower.

The nave is divided into four bays by the spacing of the roof trusses, and in each of the first, second, and fourth bays on either side is a tall, finely-proportioned window of three transomed lights, cinquefoiled in both stages, with vertical tracery in a two-centred head. In the third bay on either side are the north and south doorways, each set within a recess of ·the same character as those in the chancel, and rising to the same height as the heads of the windows. The north doorway is of two moulded orders separated by a casement, the head of the outer order being brought to a septfoiled form by pierced cusping with trefoiled sub-cusping. The south doorway is less elaborate and has a four-centred head moulded continuously with the jambs. Placed in the casement mould of the east jamb of the south-east window is a moulded image bracket supported by a carved angel. Though it does not quite fit its position, the presence of a broken piscina in the back of the window recess suggests that it has never been moved, but was probably placed here at some time subsequent to the building of the church as an additional ornament to the altar, which must have occupied this corner of the nave. Immediately to the south of the chancel arch is the squint to the chancel, which has an opening with a cinquefoiled four-centred head towards the nave. The walls are crowned externally by a moulded cornice and plain parapet, and there is a buttress of two off-sets between the two eastern windows on each side, the angles being emphasized by diagonal buttresses of the same number of offsets.

The west tower has an embattled parapet and is of three slightly receding stages with diagonally set buttresses at the angles and a vice at the north-west. The ground stage opens to the nave by a four-centred arch of three orders with continuously moulded jambs towards the nave. The orders are separated by casements, the inner being moulded with a swelled chamfer on each face and the outer orders with hollow chamfers. The fan-vaulted ceiling of the ground stage has a central circular opening and the cones, which have trefoiled panelling with floreated cusps, spring from quarter-circular corbels supported by carved angels and enriched with flowers; the work, though bold and vigorous, is somewhat coarse and the mouldings are heavy. The west doorway has a four-centred head and an elaborate external canopy supported by two richly panelled cones of fan-vaulting springing from roll shafts which form the outermost members of the suite of jamb mouldings. The canopy itself is flat,

and, as the supporting cones do not meet, the intervening portion of the soffit is divided into plain rectangular panels. The cornice of the canopy is enriched with flowers and crowned by an embattled parapet with triangular-headed merlons having trefoiled panels. Immediately above is a window of four cinquefoiled lights with tracery in a two-centred head. A single large recess in each face of the tower includes the windows of the two upper stages, that on the north being made narrower to clear the stair-turret. Each recess has splayed jambs and a two-centred segmental head with pierced septfoil cusping, the cusps terminating in a large trefoiled flower, and is subdivided by a central pier of V-shaped plan rising into the apex of the head; the string-course dividing the stages, with the wall off-set above it, is continued round the recess and the central pier. In each of the two upper compartments thus formed is a single trefoiled light to the bell-chamber (the eastern light on the north side is now blocked), while the ringing chamber is lighted by one smaller trefoiled light only in the lower stage of the recess, the blank compartment containing a trefoiled panel. The crowning cornice has gargoyles at the four angles of the tower, and the merlons of the embattled parapet have circular piercings.

The north porch has a buttress in the centre of each side wall and diagonal buttresses at the northern angles, the walls being crowned by an embattled parapet and moulded cornice with gargoyles at the angles. The outer entrance has a four-centred head continuously moulded with the jambs and rising into the cornice which is lifted to clear it. The ceiling is formed by a fan-vault of elaborate character arranged in two bays and springing from vaulting shafts with moulded capitals and bases placed in the angles and at the centres of the north and south walls. The cones of the vault have trefoiled panelling, and each bay has a sculptured boss, that of the southern bay having vine foliage, while the northern boss has a wreath of roses. The porch is lighted from each side by a pair of trefoiled lights placed on either side of the central shaft; some moulded 12th-century stones from the former church have been re-used in the rear arches of these lights.

The south porch is smaller and less elaborate, being without buttresses and having a plain parapet in place of battlements. In the centre of the parapet, over the outer entrance, which has moulded jambs and a three-centred head inclosed by a label, is a small niche with a trefoiled head under an ogee canopy with flanking pinnacles, crockets and finial. The ceiling has a fan-vault of the same character as that of the vestry, but the cones spring from shafts in the angles.

The original roofs of the chancel and nave remain. The wall-plates are moulded and the trusses are of the king-post type with chamfered tie-beams strutted from moulded wall-posts by curved braces, and all the spandrels are traceried. The chancel roof is of two bays and the wall-posts rest on moulded corbels, those on the north being of stone, while those on the south appear to be of wood. There are carved bosses at the intersections of the main timbers, and under the tie-beam of the central truss is a boss carved with a seated figure of our Lord with one hand raised. The nave roof is of four bays with carved bosses of the same character as those of the chancel roof, and the wall-posts are supported by carved corbels of stone and wood.

The altar table, an elaborate piece of work, bears the date 1623 and the name, presumably of the donor, John Moore (More). The font has a circular bowl of the late 12th century, with a band of acanthus and pellet ornament, and stands on a modern base. The oak chancel screen is of original 15th-century date; it is divided into three bays by buttressed and pinnacled uprights standing on a heavy chamfered sill. The lower portion has cinquefoiled panelling with small piercings in the panels, while in each bay of the upper portion are four open lights with cinquefoiled ogee heads and tracery; the central bay opens in two leaves, and the screen is crowned by a moulded cornice originally surmounted by brattishing, of which the stumps alone remain. Upon the top of the screen, at either end against the jambs of the chancel arch, is placed the half-figure of an angel holding a passion shield; these may have been corbel fronts or bosses from the roof, but if so they had been removed from the church, to which they were restored by Lady Kinloss, into whose possession they had come. The north doorway of the nave retains its original richly traceried door, and the plain door in the north doorway of the chancel is probably also original. In the outer entrance of the north porch is an early 17th-century double door set in a frame with a balustered 'fanlight' in the head, the balusters of which spring from a centre composed of a semi-elliptical block of wood bearing the date 1637 and the initials PR. IA. IN. WA. with a shield of the arms of Pever. In the lights of the tracery of the east window of the chancel is some fragmentary 15th-century glass, including some pieces of scrolls, one inscribed, 'miserere i . . . dns,' a second '[A]ve maria,' while a third has a heart with five wounds upon it. In one of the trefoiled upper lights of the north-east window is a figure with a halo in white and gold upon a blue background, perhaps an angel playing a harp, while in the quatrefoil in the head of the north-west window is a vernicle, also in white and gold. Fragments of figures and canopy work also remain in the west window of the tower. At the back of the sedilia is a late 15th-century painting of the Last Supper, much damaged by a coating of whitewash, and possibly painted over at a later period. Remains of painted decoration are still visible on the east truss of the nave roof, and eight incised consecration crosses contained in circles about 8 in. in diameter and coloured red, remain in the nave between the north and south windows and on either side of the chancel arch.

In the floor of the nave near the north doorway is a slab with three brass shields of the 15th century, charged with the arms, a cheveron with three fleurs de lis thereon, for Pever, and the indents of two female figures and an inscription plate. The indents now contain modern figures designed in the style of the period, and an inscription commemorating the two sisters Pever, whose memorial the slab is traditionally supposed to be. Above the north doorway is a 17th-century painted inscription with the arms of Pever, commemorating the founding of the church in the following terms: 'Sisters and Maids Daughters Of The Lord Pruet (for Pever) The Pious And Munifi-cent Founders of this Church.' On the south wall of the chancel over the vestry doorway is a tablet to Frances daughter of Thomas Attenbury, who died, aged seven years, in 1685. The inscription states that Thomas Attenbury was Alderman of Buckingham and servant to King Charles II and King James. Blocking the recess in the centre of the north wall is an elaborate monument to Edward Bate (d. 1717) and his wife Penelope (d. 1713). The monument is framed by marble columns with gilded bases and composite capitals supporting a curved pediment with a shield of arms. In the nave is a floor slab to John Birtwisle (d. 1697) and his wife Philippa (d. 1696).

There is a ring of six bells, four by Henry Bagley, 1717, and the tenor by John Briant of Hertford, 1806.

The plate is composed of a modern set and another of Sheffield plate.

The registers begin in 1558. The first volume bears at the commencement the title 'The Old Register of Mayde-Moreton ffaythfully transcribed by Matt. Bate, Rector.' Matthew Bate succeeded his father as rector in 1643. An interesting entry under the year 1642 describes the damage done to the church by 'ye souldiers att ye command of one called Colonell Purefoy of Warwickshire,' and goes on to explain, 'we conveighed away what we could, and among other things ye Register was hid and for that cause is not absolutely perfect for divers yeares.'

With the 2 hides of land granted *ADVOWSON* by Robert Doyley and Roger de Ivry to the college founded by them in the church of St. George in Oxford was bestowed the chapel of Moreton,[96] subsequently transferred with this property to the abbey of Oseney.[97] The abbey must have granted the advowson to the owners of the 5-hide manor held by John Pever in 1279, at which date the advowson was in his hands.[98] It continued to be held by the Pevers after they had parted with the manor,[99] following the same descent as Broughton in their descendants the Broughtons,[100] and being sold by Lady Agnes Paulet, Marchioness of Winchester (daughter of William, first Lord Howard of Effingham, by his first wife Katherine, daughter and co-heir of Sir John Broughton [1]), to Richard Blake of Buckland (Berks.), on 22 July 1600.[2] After an intermediate conveyance it came in 1603 to George Bate, rector of Moreton and father of the famous doctor, whose descendants held until 1719, when it was purchased by Thomas Coxed.[3] His widow sold it in 1732 to John Larken, from whom it was acquired in 1733 by Hartley Sandwell.[4] He conveyed it in 1750 to William Hutton,[5] whose relatives, the Hutton Long family, retained it until about 1860,[6] when it was acquired by the Rev. W. A. Uthwatt.[7] His representative, Miss Andrewes, is the present patron.

Walter Giffard bestowed the tithes of his demesne lands in Moreton on the priory of St. Faith, Longueville, Normandy,[8] and they descended with Newton Longville Manor (q.v.), the prior of that place claiming a minute portion of tithes in Moreton Church in the 14th century.[9]

[96] Dugdale, *Mon.* ii, 134.
[97] Ibid. vi, 251.
[98] *Hund. R.* loc. cit.
[99] Chan. Inq. p.m. 9 Edw. II, no. 55.
[100] Willis, op. cit. 233.

[1] G.E.C. *Peerage*, viii, 174.
[2] Willis, op. cit. 230.
[3] Ibid.; Inst. Bks. (P.R.O.).
[4] Ibid.
[5] Feet of F. Bucks. East. 23 Geo. II.

[6] Lipscomb, op. cit. iii, 42; Inst. Bks. (P.R.O.). [7] Sheahan, op. cit. 289.
[8] Round, *Cal. Doc. of France*, 74, 76, 77.
[9] Mins. Accts. (Gen. Ser.), bdles. 1125, no. 1; 1127, no. 18, m. 34.

MAIDSMORTON CHURCH FROM THE SOUTH-EAST

MAIDSMORTON CHURCH: THE INTERIOR LOOKING EAST

Marsh Gibbon Church from the South

Marsh Gibbon Church: The Interior looking East

Lands for the maintenance of a lamp in the church were valued at 2*s*. 4*d*. yearly at the suppression of the chantries,[10] and were granted in 1553 to Sir Edward Bray, John Thornton and John Danby.[11]

CHARITIES The parochial charities have by a scheme of the Charity Commissioners of 20 March 1913 been amalgamated under the title of the United Charities, comprising the charities following, namely :—

1. The charity of John Smart, mentioned on a board in the church dated 1743 ; trust fund, £158 2*s*. 6*d*. consols, with the official trustees, the annual dividends, amounting to £3 19*s*., to be distributed in bread.

2. Charity of William Scott, for apprenticing, founded in or about 1800 by will ; trust fund, £164 3*s*. 9*d*. consols, with the official trustees, producing £4 2*s*. yearly.

3. The poor's allotment, containing 26 a. 1 r. 26 p., allotted to the poor on the inclosure of the parish in 1801, in lieu of common rights. The net income, which in 1912 amounted to £36 6*s*., is distributed in coal.

The church land consists of 1 a. 0 r. 30 p., let at £3 a year, which is applied to church expenses.

This parish is entitled to participate in the charity of William Elmer for clothing. (See under parish of Beachampton.)

MARSH GIBBON

Mersa, Merse (xi cent.) ; Gibbemers[1] (xiii cent.) ; Mershe Gybbewine, Gibwyne, Mershe-juxta-Twyford (xiv cent.) ; Marsh Gibbon (xvi–xx cent.).

This parish, on the Oxfordshire border, covers 2,817 acres, nearly the whole of which is permanent grass.[2] The soil and subsoil are clay ; the principal crops produced are wheat, beans and oats. The parish, which is watered by the River Ray, lies low, varying from 255 ft. above the ordnance datum in the north to 204 ft. in the south.

Marsh Gibbon village is large, its main street extending nearly a mile in length. Many of the cottages date from the middle of the 19th century, when Sir Henry Acland, bart., master of Ewelme, together with the Ewelme trustees, greatly improved the condition of the village. It had suffered from a long suit in Chancery, from the Inclosure Act and non-resident landlords, but under his care the houses were rebuilt, modern sanitation introduced, and a dispensary and reading room started.[2a]

The church and rectory occupy a central position ; the latter, erected in 1846,[3] possibly replaced the Parsonage House of five bays of stone and timber which stood here in 1607.[4] North of the church is a mineral spring known as Stompe or Stump Well, while to the west are traces of entrenchments supposed to have been thrown up by the Parliamentary army when they marched through Marsh Gibbon in June 1645.[5]

The Manor House, belonging to Ewelme almshouses, lies immediately south of the church. It is a stone building of two stories and an attic, dating mainly from the Elizabethan period, but somewhat altered in the early 17th century, when the attic was added, and partially refaced in the 18th century.

THE MANOR HOUSE, MARSH GIBBON

The central block, which faces east, has a wide two-storied bay window with moulded stone mullions and transoms, and the lateral wings are lighted by oak-mullioned windows of the 17th century. The roofs are tiled and have four gables on the east front with 17th-century barge-boards and apex pendants, while rising from the roofs are two groups of diagonal chimney shafts. The hall occupies the ground floor of the central block and is entered through a porch with a stone moulded archway and oak inner doorway, the latter having an original studded door and iron fittings. On the north side of the hall is an original wide stone fireplace with a four-centred arch and moulded jambs, and at the north-east is an early

[10] Chant. Cert. 5, no. 8.
[11] Pat. 6 Edw. VI, pt. ix.
[1] Taken from *Cal. Inq. p.m.* (Rec. Com.), i, 49. This inquisition is now missing.

[2] Statistics from Bd. of Agric. (1905).
[2a] J. B. Atlay, *Henry Acland, a Memoir*, pp. 252–4.
[3] Sheahan, *Hist. and Topog. of Bucks.* 294.

[4] Willis, *Hist. and Antiq. of Buckingham*, 241.
[5] Lysons, *Mag. Brit.* i (3), 603.

17th-century staircase with square newels, bell-shaped finials and turned balusters. The main staircase, constructed in a wing which projects at the south-west and entered from the hall by a 16th-century moulded oak doorway, has square newels with acorn finials, turned balusters and moulded handrails, and is of original 16th-century date to the first floor, but the upper flights are later, and have newels like those of the stairs at the north-east of the hall.

Westbury Manor dates from the 17th century, though it has been considerably altered since. It retains its original staircase, and there are fragmentary remains of a moat near the house.

The village contains several houses of the 16th and 17th centuries, built principally of stone with tiled or thatched roofs ; many of these retain original mullioned windows and brick chimney shafts. A 16th-century inn in Church Street has an original panelled main door with strap hinges. In Clark's Yard, at the bottom of Church Street, is a house dated 1680. Immediately east of the church is an old stone barn, probably a tithe barn, which is lighted by narrow loopholes and has an external stairway.

Townsend is the name given to the west end of the village. Scott's Farm (recently renamed the Priory Farm) and Townsend Farm date from the 16th century, though the former has been largely rebuilt, and Mercia Farm and the Greyhound Inn are of the 17th century. Little Marsh and Summerstown are detached portions on the east side of the village, and now much depopulated.

Marsh Gibbon contains a Congregational chapel built in 1851.

The parish was inclosed by Act of Parliament in 1841, when 5 acres were allotted to a recreation ground.[6] Gubbins Hole Farm, in the east of the parish, still recalls at the present day the Gibbewins, the early holders of Westbury Manor.

MANORS In this parish under Edward the Confessor Ulf son of Borgerete owned land which in 1086 had passed to the Count of Mortain and was assessed at 11 hides.[7] No further mention of overlordship occurs in the manor, which was held in free alms until 1348,[8] and afterwards of the king in chief.[9]

At Domesday the alien monks of Grestein in Normandy were the tenants in *MARSH* of the Count of Mortain, whose father had founded their abbey and who was himself a munificent benefactor to their house.[10] Early in the 13th century the Abbot of Grestein appears to have enfeoffed John de Montague, whom he summoned in 1213 for arrears of a yearly rent of £18 and 1 mark due from the manor of Marsh (Bucks.) and Harrington (Northants). Montague asserted that his lands had long been in the possession of

the king, who had demised them to three knights, Henry Tregoz, Michael de Poynings and Enjuger de Bohun,[11] but late in the year he is found claiming the advowson,[12] and in 1218 he received acknowledgement from William de Dunmear of services due from a hide of land which he, William, held of John in Marsh.[13] Seven years later John de Montague renounced all right to services due from a hide of land held by the rectors of Marsh.[14] John de Montague died in or about the year 1228, and the abbot claimed that before his death John had released the manor to the abbey.[15] Warin Basset and Katherine his wife, who was the daughter of John de Montague, in consequence sued the abbey for the recovery of the manor, here described as 3 carucates of land. They complained that when John de Montague was of unsound mind and on his death-bed the abbot had by undue influence obtained the grant of the manor. The abbot in reply said that John de Montague had been perfectly rational when he made the enfeoffment, his only infirmity having been goitre (*gutturnosus*), and that in return for the enfeoffment he, the abbot, had pardoned him all arrears of service in the manor to the value of 200 marks.[16] Warin Basset and his wife eventually recognized John's charter to the abbot, who retained the manor.[17] Grestein Abbey continued to hold the manor, which in the 14th century was attached to their cell of Wilmington (co. Sussex),[18] until 1348,[19] when the abbot and convent acquired royal licence to demise to the king's merchant Tideman de Lymbergh for 1,000 years Marsh and other manors.[20] Two years later, Tideman having obtained further licence,[21] transferred Marsh to Michael de la Pole and Thomas and Edmund his brothers, whose father William de la Pole obtained in 1354 a release from the abbot and convent of all their rights in the premises,[22] which release was renewed five years later to Thomas de la Pole.[23] His death took place in 1361,[24] and the following year Katherine, his daughter, a minor and a ward of the king, died seised of the manor of Marsh.[25] Her heir was then stated to

DE LA POLE. *Azure a fesse between three leopards' heads or.*

be her uncle Michael de la Pole,[26] who in 1380 acquired licence to grant Marsh to his son Richard de la Pole for life.[27] In 1384 Michael de la Pole made a further settlement with remainder to his sons Thomas, William and Richard de la Pole.[28] The following year he was created Earl of Suffolk,[29] but was attainted for treason in 1388, and fled to France, where he died in 1389.[30] In accordance with the

[6] Priv. Act, 4 & 5 Vict. cap. 14.
[7] *V.C.H. Bucks.* i, 245.
[8] *Feud. Aids*, i, 80.
[9] Chan. Inq. p.m. 36 Edw. III, pt. i, no. 59.
[10] *V.C.H. Sussex*, ii, 122.
[11] *Abbrev. Plac.* (Rec. Com.), 89.
[12] Ibid. 91. It is here suggested that Richard, father of John de Montague, had preceded John in Marsh.
[13] Feet of F. case 14, file 11.
[14] Ibid. file 15. There is a statement as to endowment here which suggests the existence of a rectory manor, of which, however, no further trace has been found.

See also Lipscomb, *Hist. and Antiq. of Bucks.* iii, 54.
[15] *Cal. Pat.* 1225–32, p. 280; Maitland, *Bracton's Note Bk.* ii, 267, 292. Bracton quotes it as an instance of a tenant enfeoffing his lord.
[16] Maitland, op. cit. ii, 293. The abbot had also to prove his case against Andrew de Cancellis acting on the king's writ (ibid. 267).
[17] Ibid. 293.
[18] *V.C.H. Sussex*, ii, 122.
[19] *Pope Nich. Tax.* (Rec. Com.), 47b; *Hund. R.* (Rec. Com.), i, 28; *Feud. Aids*, i, 80, 99, 109, 125.

[20] *Cal. Pat.* 1348–50, p. 221.
[21] Ibid. 513.
[22] Ibid. 1354–8, p. 158.
[23] Close, 33 Edw. III, m. 6 d.
[24] Chan. Inq. p.m. 35 Edw. III, pt. i, no. 61.
[25] Ibid. 36 Edw. III, pt. i, no. 59. The appurtenances included a windmill.
[26] Ibid.
[27] *Cal. Pat.* 1377–81, p. 526.
[28] Ibid. 1381–5, p. 374; Feet of F. Div. Co. 8 Ric. II, no. 34.
[29] G.E.C. *Peerage*, vii, 303.
[30] Ibid.; Chan. Inq. p.m. 11 Ric. II, no. 140.

earlier settlement his son Richard held Marsh till his death in 1403,[31] when, his brother William having died in 1390 without male issue,[32] the manor passed to the other brother, Thomas de la Pole, though the heir male was stated to be the eldest brother, Michael Earl of Suffolk.[33] Thomas was dead by 1411, the year of the death of his widow Elizabeth,[34] and his son Thomas died in 1420 seised of the manor,[35] of which one-third was assigned to his widow Anne in dower. This third included two bays in the west of the 'hall,' with free entry and exit, one bay and half of a large grange there in the north, one-third profits of dove-house, three bays of a certain 'cowshepene,' one-third of 'le Rekeyerd' and 'le Barleycroft,' besides other messuages and crofts.[36] Thomas de la Pole, son and heir of Thomas and Anne,[37] was only three years old at the time of his father's death, and died in 1430 still a ward of the Crown.[38] Though he had a sister Katherine, at this date aged fourteen, in pursuance of the settlement of 1384, Marsh now passed to his cousin William de la Pole, Earl of Suffolk.[39] In 1437 William de la Pole and Alice were given licence to establish an almshouse at Ewelme in Oxfordshire,[40] and by 1442 the foundation, which included in its endowments the manor of Marsh, was complete.[41] A final confirmation was obtained from the earl and his wife in 1447.[42] Ewelme escaped at the Dissolution, doubtless because the king was the immediate patron of the almshouses.[43]

Between 1582 and 1588 leases of the manor were made to Edward Cary, William Tipper, and others,[44] and in 1617 the mastership of Ewelme was granted by James I to augment the stipend of the Regius Professor of Medicine in the University of Oxford, and has since been attached to that professorship.[45] Marsh Manor has thus remained in the possession of the trustees of the Ewelme almshouses, who act as a corporate body as lords of the manor, which they have been in the habit of leasing.[46]

A second manor in Marsh Gibbon parish is known as *WESTBURY MANOR*, and represents the 4-hide manor which William Fitz Ansculf held here in 1086.[47] As the manor was a parcel of the barony of Dudley[48] the overlordship followed the descent of the manor of Newport Pagnell[49] (q.v.). In 1626, when last mention of the overlordship has been found, Westbury Manor was said to be held of the manor of North Marston.[50]

Ailric had held Marsh Manor[51] in the reign of Edward the Confessor, and when dispossessed by William Fitz Ansculf remained as under-tenant in

heaviness and misery (*graviter et miserabiliter*).[52] He was succeeded at some time in the following century by a family of Gibbewin or Gibevin, of whom the earliest known member, Ralph Gibbewin, was living in 1166.[53]

In 1213 Geoffrey son of Ralph Gibbewin is found disputing with John de Montague, who claimed the advowson of Marsh Church. Geoffrey Gibbewin then claimed that his land in Marsh belonged to the barony of Dudley, and that the chancel and the greater part of the church stood within that fee.[54] He further said that in the reign of Henry II Gervase Paynel had brought a suit against Ralph Gibbewin, his father, and had then released the advowson to him. During this suit, which lasted eleven years, Richard father of John de Montague had made no claim to the advowson.[55] Geoffrey Gibbewin did not substantiate his claim to the advowson, but certainly continued to hold his manor. He was justiciar under Henry III,[56] his death taking place previous to 1236, when Robert Lisle (*de Insula*) and Robert son of Brian are stated to be his heirs in a plea against the Abbot of Oseney concerning lands in Marsh.[57] Probably Geoffrey left two daughters as co-heirs. A year or two later Giles Lisle had succeeded Robert Lisle, and held this fee with Robert Brian.[58] Two tenants with these names held 4 hides (the Domesday assessment) in 1254–5.[59] Robert Brian, probably a successor of Robert Brian of 1236, is mentioned in 1278–9,[60] while his widow Jolenta held this manor together with Giles Lisle (who must also be considered a successor to the earlier Giles) in 1284–6.[61] Jolenta Brian had been followed by Robert Brian in 1302–3, who held with Giles Lisle.[62] In 1308 Peter Brian transferred 6 virgates of land, 14 acres of meadow, and 6s. 11d. rent in 'Mershe Gybbewine' to John de Grenstede, parson of Bledlow, and William his brother,[63] while Giles Lisle alienated his share, here given as fifteen messuages, 8 virgates, and 12s. rent, to Richard Damory and Margaret his wife in 1313.[64]

In 1316 Richard Damory and William Mersh (possibly the William of the enfeoffment of 1308 by Peter Brian) are returned as joint owners.[65] The following year Richard Damory obtained a grant of free warren here.[66] William de Bledlow, representing the Brian portion of this estate, is found holding in 1323.[67] Richard Damory died seised of land here in 1330,[68] which was still held by his widow Margaret in 1346,[69] at which date William de Westbury held the other portion of this manor.[70] Nothing more has been found concerning the Damorys in this parish,

[31] Chan. Inq. p.m. 5 Hen. IV, no. 39.
[32] Ibid. 14 Ric. II, no. 40.
[33] Ibid. 5 Hen. IV, no. 39.
[34] Ibid. 13 Hen. IV, no. 34.
[35] Ibid. 8 Hen. V, no. 6.
[36] Ibid. 7 Hen. V, no. 91.
[37] Ibid. 8 Hen. V, no. 56.
[38] Ibid. 9 Hen. VI, no. 45; *Cal. Pat.* 1416–22, p. 412.
[39] Chan. Inq. p.m. 9 Hen. VI, no. 45.
[40] *V.C.H. Oxon.* ii, 156.
[41] *Cal. Pat.* 1441–6, pp. 54, 60; Inq. a.q.d. file 449, no. 6; Feet of F. Div. Co. East. 20 Hen. V; *Hist. MSS. Com. Rep.* ix, App. i, 218a.
[42] Feet of F. Div. Co. 25 Hen. VI, no. 52.
[43] *V.C.H. Oxon.* loc. cit.
[44] Pat. 25 Eliz. pt. iii; 31 Eliz. pt. v.

[45] *V.C.H. Oxon.* loc. cit.
[46] Willis, op. cit. 238; Lysons, op. cit. i (3), 603; *Hist. MSS. Com. Rep.* viii, App. i, 631a; Sheahan, op. cit. 292.
[47] *V.C.H. Bucks.* i, 255.
[48] *Abbrev. Plac.* (Rec. Com.), 91; *Cal. Close*, 1318–23, p. 632; *V.C.H. Worcs.* iii, 90.   [49] *Feud. Aids*, i, 125.
[50] Chan. Inq. p.m. (Ser. 2), dccxl, 125.
[51] The modern name of Westbury does not appear before the 16th century.
[52] *V.C.H. Bucks.* loc. cit.
[53] *Red Bk. of Exch.* (Rolls Ser.), 317.
[54] *Abbrev. Plac.* loc. cit.
[55] Ibid.
[56] Madox, *Hist. of Exch.* (ed. 1769), ii, 43 n.
[57] *Excerpta e Rot. Fin.* (Rec. Com.), 306.

[58] *Testa de Nevill* (Rec. Com.), 249b. The fee is here said to be held of the honour of Bedford, though for what reason cannot be discovered.
[59] *Hund. R.* (Rec. Com.), i, 28.
[60] Ibid. ii, 353.
[61] *Feud. Aids*, i, 80.
[62] Ibid. 99.
[63] Feet of F. Bucks. 1 Edw. II, no. 5.
[64] Ibid. 7 Edw. II, no. 19.
[65] *Feud. Aids*, i, 109.
[66] Chart. R. 10 Edw. II, m. 13.
[67] *Cal. Close*, 1318–23, p. 632; Chan. Inq. p.m. 16 Edw. II, no. 72.
[68] Chan. Inq. p.m. 4 Edw. III (1st nos.), no. 13. The Abbots of Grestein here claimed 20s. 6d. rent and knight service.
[69] *Feud. Aids*, i, 125.
[70] Ibid.

and the name of Westbury, later attached to this manor, shows that it was the Brian share which persisted. Its history during the following century it has not been found possible to trace, but it appears to have formed part of the original endowment of the Mystery or Company of Cooks which was incorporated by charter of Edward IV in 1482.[71] It was retained by the company until 1529, in which year they sold it to Robert Dormer.[72] He shortly after enfeoffed William Howel, who by his will, made 31 November 1557 and proved 20 October 1558, left Westbury Manor to John Howel, his eldest son, with remainder to Henry Howel, a younger son.[73] John Howel died in 1575, whereupon the masters of the Cooks Company trumped up an 'odious suit,' to the effect that the original sale to Robert Dormer had been void because the corporation was misnamed in the indenture. They accordingly put in a tenant of their own, Edmund Croft, against whom Henry Howel brought an action for ejectment.[74] Henry Howel won his case, and is found making a settlement of Westbury Manor in 1587.[75] He survived until 1625, when his son Edward, aged forty years and more, is given as heir, though the widow Margaret was to hold Westbury for her life.[76] She died before 1638, when Edward Howel alienated the property to Richard Francis.[76a] He died in 1659,[77] his widow Elizabeth surviving him two years. She left legacies to the children of her son William Francis by his first wife Martha, Richard, another son, receiving Westbury Manor.[77a] By his will, dated 18 December 1665, Richard left the manor to his nephew Thomas, son of William Francis.[78] Thomas Francis held the manor in 1670 [78a] and died in 1698. His widow Anna Maria Francis conveyed Westbury in 1701 to John Townsend and his heirs.[79] John Townsend settled the property in 1709 [80] and died in 1714,[81] and his descendant Mary Townsend, later wife of William Guy,[82] carried on a lawsuit some years after with the trustees of the Ewelme almshouses, who owned the other manor in this parish. As lady of Westbury Manor she claimed the whole waste and cottages within the larger manor.[83] The litigation extended over the years 1743–7, but her name and that of her husband William Guy are found as late as 1765 in documents recording settlements of the manor.[84] At this latter date their son Townsend Guy [85] is referred to, but the manor was sold in 1777 to John Dixon.[86] It was subsequently in the possession of George Hitchcock, from whom it passed to Richard Ivens. He claimed to be lord of the reputed manor of Westbury in 1841,[87] and was still in possession in 1862.[88] In 1883 it was purchased by Mr. Thomas H. Phipps, in whose family it remains.

The church of *ST. MARY THE VIRGIN* consists of a chancel measuring internally 28 ft. 6 in. by 18 ft., south vestry, nave 50 ft. by 18 ft., north and south tran-

septs each 16 ft. square, north aisle 10 ft. wide, south aisle 6 ft. wide, south porch, and west tower 12 ft. square. It is built of stone rubble.

An aisleless cruciform church, probably without any tower, was built here in the middle of the 13th century. A south aisle was added at the end of that century, and a western tower some twenty years later, while the south porch was built in the 15th century. In the early part of the succeeding century a clearstory was added to the nave, which at the same time was reroofed, and many of the details of the church were renewed. In 1860 the chancel was repaired, and in 1880 the north aisle was added, the tower rebuilt, and the church generally restored.

The chancel has three lancets in each lateral wall, only some internal jamb stones of which are original, and there are three modern lancets in the east wall. A tomb recess on the north contains a late 13th-century coffin-lid, on which is carved an elaborate foliated cross. The pointed chancel arch of two orders is modern.

The eastern part of the nave opens to the transepts by 13th-century pointed arches, which have semi-octagonal responds with foliated capitals of refined design; the eastern capital on the north is further enriched with carved human heads, but both this and the corresponding capital on the south have been partially cut into for the fixing of a later rood-loft, the upper doorway of which remains on the south side, with a small blocked window above it. West of the transept arches are arcades opening to the aisles; that on the south, of two pointed arches supported by an octagonal pillar and responds with moulded capitals and bases, dates from about 1300, and the north arcade is a modern copy of it. The tower arch is modern, but some 14th-century stones have been rebuilt in the responds. The clearstory has two 16th-century windows on the south, each of two plain lights under a square head, and two modern windows on the north. The open timber roof over the nave dates from about 1510, though it has been considerably repaired; its moulded trusses are supported on stone corbels, two of which are plain: one has a carved grotesque figure and the others figures of angels holding shields or scrolls.

The north transept is lighted from the north by two original lancets, which have moulded labels with internal foliated stops, and from the east by a window of three cinquefoiled lights inserted in the 15th century. On the east wall are three plain brackets and two pointed piscinae, the latter evidently marking the positions of two mediaeval altars which stood against the east wall, each having a piscina on the south side. The south transept communicates with the south aisle by a pointed arch, which is probably contemporary with the aisle, and in the south wall is a five-light traceried window of about 1500; a round-headed piscina with a quatrefoil bowl and a double locker in the south wall are probably of this latter period.

[71] Plowden, *Commentaries*, 530 et seq.
[72] Ibid.; Feet of F. Bucks. East. 22 Hen. VIII. [73] P.C.C. 59 Noodes.
[74] Plowden, loc. cit.
[75] Feet of F. Bucks. East. 29 Eliz.
[76] Chan. Inq. p.m. (Ser. 2), dccxl, 125.
[76a] Feet of F. Bucks. Trin. 14 Chas. I; East. 14 Chas. I. [77] P.C.C. 448 Pell.
[77a] Chan. Proc. (Bridges Div.), bdle. 484, no. 26.

[78] Ibid.
[76a] Feet of F. Bucks. Hil. 21 & 22 Chas. II.
[79] Willis, op. cit. 240.
[80] Feet of F. Bucks. Trin. 8 Anne.
[81] Monument in church quoted by Lipscomb, op. cit. iii, 55.
[82] Feet of F. Bucks. Trin. 7 & 8 Geo. II; *Hist. MSS. Com. Rep.* viii, App. i, 630a.

[83] *Hist. MSS. Com. Rep.* loc. cit.
[84] Feet of F. Bucks. Mich. 28 Geo. II; Recov. R. Hil. 5 Geo. III, m. 287.
[85] Monument in church quoted by Lipscomb, loc. cit.
[86] Inf. supplied by the Rev. E. R. Massey; cf. Lysons, loc. cit.
[87] Priv. Act, 4 & 5 Vict. cap. 14.
[88] Sheahan, op. cit. 293.

Both transepts are supported at their external angles by 15th-century diagonal buttresses, and have open timber roofs of the same period and character as that over the nave.

There are two windows in the south aisle, the eastern, of three plain lights under a square head, dating from the 16th century, and the other, of two trefoiled ogee lights with tracery under a square head, dating from about 1350. The south doorway, which has a four-centred head, is of the 15th century, but has been considerably restored. The south porch is lighted by a small window in each lateral wall, both of which are very much restored, and is entered through an original four-centred arch with restored responds. Rebuilt in the walls of the modern north aisle are a 13th-century lancet, similar to those in the north transept, and two 16th-century windows, each of three plain lights under a square head.

The tower is of two stages, with an embattled parapet and corner pinnacles, and western diagonal buttresses; the old material has been re-used in its rebuilding, but the details have been much restored. The ground stage has a west doorway with a pointed arch in a square head, and a three-light window above, both dating from the 15th century, though restored; the bell-chamber is lighted from the north by a pointed window of two trefoiled lights of about 1400, and from the other sides by square-headed two-light windows dating from the 15th century.

On the east wall of the south transept is a monument to the Rev. John Dod, B.D., rector of the parish (d. 1698). There is a 17th-century carved oak chair in the chancel, and a communion table in the vestry is probably of the same period, while incorporated in the seating of the nave are several early 17th-century oak pews. The base and lower part of the octagonal shaft of a 15th-century churchyard cross stand near the south porch.

The tower contains a ring of five bells and a small bell: the treble is by W. Taylor of Oxford, 1848; the second, third and fourth are all by Richard Chandler, 1678, and the tenor is by J. Warner & Sons of London, 1854. The small bell, inscribed 'H. K.,' is doubtless by Henry Knight, cast probably in the early 17th century.

The communion plate includes a cup and cover paten with the London hall-marks for 1674, and both inscribed 'Marsh-Gibbons Bucks. 1675'; a large paten of 1720, given by Robert Clavering, S.T.P.; and a plated flagon.

The registers begin in 1577.

ADVOWSON The early history of the church of Marsh Gibbon is closely connected with the two manors, the lords of both of which claimed the advowson. It was eventually acknowledged to belong to the Abbot of Grestein, and is later found attached to his cell at Wilmington, the advowson being repeatedly in the king's hands on account of war with France.[89] On the grant of the manor to Ewelme in 1442 the advowson of the church was specially exempted,[90] and continued to remain with the de la Pole family until the attainder of Edmund de la Pole in January 1503–4. Charles Brandon Duke of Suffolk presented Andrew Leason in 1533,[91] but the advowson was then resumed by the Crown, with whom the patronage remained[92] until 1853, when it was transferred to the Bishop of Oxford,[93] by whom it is now exercised.

In 1291 the church of Marsh Gibbon was assessed at £16,[94] and at the Dissolution the rectory was worth £22.[95]

At various times the right of presentation was granted for one turn. Thus in 1546 Lord Russell obtained a turn[96]; Richard Hampden in 1689[97] and the Earl of Nottingham in 1691[98] received similar grants.

In 1660 Matthew Bate, brother of the king's physician, and Josiah Howe, who claimed that he and his brothers 'were all eminent sufferers in His Majesty's service,' both petitioned for the living on the death of Dr. Evans,[99] but were put on one side in favour of Dr. Say.[100]

Among the rectors of Marsh Gibbon may be noted Robert Clavering (1671–1747), later Bishop of Peterborough, who was made rector in 1719, and James Douglas Lord Douglas, who was appointed exactly 100 years later.[101]

CHARITIES Unknown Donor's Charity.—This charity consists of 5 a. at Piddington, Oxfordshire, held on a lease for 2,000 years, created in 1628, the rents whereof are applicable for the benefit of aged and infirm poor or in apprenticing. The land is let at £10 a year, which is applied in the maintenance of a poor apprentice.

The poor's allotment, or Tender Land, containing 10 a., was acquired in 1841 under the Inclosure Act. The rent is annually distributed in coal.

Under the same Act 5 a. were set apart as a recreation ground, which is under the control of the Parish Council.

The Church of England school is endowed with a rent-charge of £12 14s. by Sophia Shepherd, by deed dated 16 August 1847. The same donor, by deed dated 6 September 1847, gave a sum of £742 14s. 1d. consols, the annual dividends, amounting to £18 11s. 4d., to be applied for the support of the same school. The stock is held by the official trustees.

PADBURY

Paddebyrig[1] (x cent.); Pateberie (xi cent.).

The parish of Padbury covers 2,013 acres, of which 1,537 are pasture, 9 woodland and 332 arable.[2] The soil is chiefly clay and gravel on a subsoil of Oxford Clay, which is worked for brick-making. The Lovatt River, a tributary of the Ouse, forms the parish

[89] See above under manor; Cur. Reg. R. 105, m. 8; De Banco R. 268, m. 39 d.; 270, m. 5, 120; Cal. Pat. 1324–7, pp. 341, 346.
[90] Cal. Pat. 1441–6, pp. 54, 60; Feet of F. Div. Co. East. 20 Hen. VI.
[91] Willis, op. cit. 243.
[92] Inst. Bks. (P.R.O.); Willis, loc. cit.
[93] Sheahan, loc. cit.
[94] Pope Nich. Tax. (Rec. Com.), 29.
[95] Valor Eccl. (Rec. Com.), iv, 238.
[96] L. and P. Hen. VIII, xxi (2), g. 648 (14).
[97] Cal. S. P. Dom. 1689–90, pp. 178, 350. [98] Ibid. 1690–1, p. 511.
[99] Ibid. 1660–1, p. 230.
[100] Ibid. 1661–2, pp. 89, 96.
[101] Dict. Nat. Biog.
[1] Kemble, Cod. Dipl. no. 1129.
[2] Statistics from Bd. of Agric. (1905).

boundary on the north and west, and its tributary, the Claydon Brook, formerly known as the 'Burn,'[2a] divides Padbury from Steeple Claydon. There is a station at Padbury on the Banbury branch of the London and North Western railway.

The village stands at the meeting of the roads from Buckingham, Thornborough, Winslow and Steeple Claydon. It has the appearance of having been once of more importance than it is now. Although there seems to be no evidence that it was ever a market town, the lay-out of the east end of the main street points to the existence here at one time of an open space suggestive of a market-place or, perhaps, a village green. The buildings upon it, however, show that it must have been encroached upon by the 16th century. The village is principally formed along a single street, and contains several 17th-century half-timber houses and cottages, many of them with thatched roofs and original chimney stacks. The main street is continued as Church Lane north-east-

THE VILLAGE, PADBURY

wards beyond the Buckingham Road and terminates at the church, which stands on a hill overlooking the valley of the Lovatt. In the southern angle between the Buckingham Road and Church Lane is the Manor House, now a farm, which probably occupies the site of the capital messuage of the manor in 1248.[3] The opposite angle contains Padbury Lodge, the residence of Mr. W. F. Gore-Langton. Beyond the Lodge is the present vicarage, but the old vicarage lies further down the main street. It dates from the 16th century, and was described in 1607 as built of timber and thatch, consisting of three bays chambered over and boarded.[3a] It is now divided into two tenements,

and contains an old fireplace and an oak staircase. About the middle of Main Street is the Wesleyan Methodist chapel, built in 1876. The south-west part of the village is called Old End, and here in a by-road are several 17th-century houses and cottages.

Padbury Corn Mill, on the Lovatt, about a mile from the church, probably occupies the site of the mill recorded in 1086. It is an early 17th-century building with later additions. Windmill Furlong may indicate the site of another mill.[4]

The inhabitants of Padbury are chiefly engaged in agriculture, but a few of the women are still employed in lace-making.

The only episode connecting Padbury with national history relates to the Civil War, when Sir Charles Lucas, the Royalist commander, defeated here a force under Col. Middleton on 1 July 1643.[5] The church registers record the burial of eight soldiers on the following day.[6]

In 1602 the Warden and Fellows of All Souls College and the tenants of their manors in Padbury came to an agreement concerning common rights in the parish.[7] The open fields were inclosed in 1796[8] under an Act of the preceding year.[9]

References are found to the curious place-name Prince Hades[10] and to a house called the Town House, which was in lease to Thomas Harris in 1602.[11]

The manor of MANORS PADBURY or OVERBURY was held in 1086 by Manno the Breton,[12] lord of Wolverton (q.v.). His holding, assessed at 20 hides, evidently included not only the manor of Overbury, but also the manor subsequently known as Millbury, the second manor of 'Padbury' and the land afterwards acquired by Bradwell Priory.[13] Elsewhere in the Domesday Survey it is noted[14] that Padbury had formerly been held by Robert Doyley, probably in right of his wife, the daughter of Wigod of Wallingford,[15] and that Robert had exchanged it for Iver with Clarenbold de Maresc. The manor, subsequently styled Overbury, was held by Manno in demesne and remained with his direct male descendants, the Fitz Hamons or Wolvertons,[16] until the middle of the 14th century, after which date they exercised overlordship rights.[17] It was parcel of the barony of Wolverton[18] and owed castle ward at Northampton.[19] It was held by the service of one knight's fee,[20] a moiety of which was assessed on the

[2a] Cal. Rot. Pat. (Rec. Com.), 41.
[3] Chan. Inq. p.m. Hen. III, file 7, no. 3.
[3a] Browne Willis, Hist. and Antiq. of Buckingham, 246–7.
[4] C. Trice Martin, Archives of All Souls, Oxf., 117–20.
[5] Dugdale, View of Troubles in Engl. 186; Dict. Nat. Biog. under Sir Chas. Lucas.

[6] Browne Willis, op. cit. 248.
[7] Martin, op. cit. 104.
[8] A copy of the award is among the college archives (ibid. 106).
[9] Priv. Act, 35 Geo. III, cap. 37.
[10] C. T. Martin, op. cit. 120.
[11] Ibid. 109.   [12] V.C.H. Bucks. i, 270.
[13] See below.   [14] V.C.H. Bucks. i, 258.
[15] Ibid. 214.

[16] For an account of the family see under Wolverton.
[17] Cal. Close, 1349–54, p. 299; Chan. Inq. p.m. 25 Edw. III (1st nos.), no. 6.
[18] Cal. Close, 1272–9, p. 350; Chan. Inq. p.m. 33 Edw. III (1st nos.), no. 5.
[19] Hund. R. (Rec. Com.), i, 27.
[20] Ibid.; Cal. Close, loc. cit.; Feud. Aids, i, 99.

manor of Millbury after its separation from this manor.[21] The lords of Wolverton evidently kept the manor of Padbury Overbury in their own hands. In 1167 Hamon (of Wolverton) paid 1 mark in respect of Padbury.[22] In 1185 it was among the lands of Hamon his son, a minor in the king's custody,[23] and in 1190 Hamon Fitz Hamon is apparently styled 'Hamon of Padbury.'[24] William Fitz Hamon held the manor in demesne,[25] and Alan his brother died seised of it.[26] In 1276, after the death of Alan's son John, it was assigned in dower to his widow Isabel, who married Ralph de Arderne.[27] The heir, John son of John (Wolverton), was a minor, and about 1285 James Cock (Coke) was holding this manor at a rent of 20 marks of Ralph de Bray and John Foliot of Tackley, tenants under John.[28] The latter with his tenants was holding it in 1302–3.[29] It was included under the settlements made in 1313 of Chalfont St. Giles (q.v.), another of the Wolvertons' manors in this county, and was in like manner divided into four parts among the daughters of John de Wolverton after his death in 1349. The moiety which later came into Sir Hugh Wake's possession was retained by him, however, and passed at his death, in April 1360, to his son John,[30] who alienated it in 1370 to John Fitz Richard of Olney.[31] He also acquired another fourth of the manor in 1378 from Adam Basings.[32] The descent of the remaining fourth, the inheritance of Theobald Grossett, cannot be traced after 1359,[33] but it was doubtless conveyed to John Fitz Richard about the same date that the corresponding fourth of Chalfont was alienated to Sir Richard de la Vache. In 1397 Walter Fitz Richard of Olney, evidently the successor of John,[34] had licence for a settlement of 'the manor of Overbury,' so called for the first time, on himself and his wife Margaret with remainder to the heirs of Walter,[35] and Henry Wake, son of the late Sir Hugh Wake, kt., quitclaimed all right in Padbury to Walter Fitz Richard about 1409.[36] In October 1410 a new settlement was made on Walter and his wife Margery in tail-male.[37] This Walter, or another of the same name, with his wife Margery, alienated the manor to John Basings the elder and his wife Joan and John Basings the younger in 1445, reserving to themselves a rent of 10 marks.[38] John Basings the elder released his rights in favour of his son John Basings,[39] who with his wife Margaret sold to the Warden of All Souls College, Oxford, in 1458.[40] The manor is still in the possession of the college.

The manor of *PADBURY* or *MILLBURY*[41] evi-dently originated in the subinfeudation of a portion of the Wolvertons' holding to the family of Etchingham. It consisted of a moiety of the whole vill,[42] including after the middle of the 13th century the whole mill, from which it took its distinctive name. It was held by service of half a knight's fee of the lords of Overbury Manor[43] until 1351, when the service from this half-fee was assigned to Margery wife of John le Hunte, sister of the whole blood to Ralph Wolverton.[44]

ALL SOULS COLLEGE, OXFORD. *Or a cheveron between three cinqfoils gules.*

The subinfeudation had probably taken place before 1201, when Alan de Etch-ingham quitclaimed to the Prior of Bradwell a moiety of the advowson of Pad-bury Church.[45] A moiety of the mill was held of Simon de Etchingham, afterwards Sheriff of Sussex,[46] in 1227, when it fell to the king for a year and a day on account of the conviction and execution of Hugh de Kingsbridge, son and heir of Walter the Miller, for robbery.[47] William Fitz Hamon granted to Simon de Etchingham the whole mill with its meadow and pond.[48] William son of Simon de Etchingham had free warren in Padbury in 1253.[49] He died shortly afterwards, and was succeeded by his brother Simon,[50] whose lands passed to his son[51] William de Etch-ingham.[52] At his death, about 1294, his holding was extended as a messuage, 200 acres of demesne land, the water-mill, rents of free tenants and pleas of court.[53] His heir was his son William, who had married Eva daughter of Ralph de Stop-ham.[54] He had livery of his father's lands in 1294,[55] obtained a grant of free warren in certain other lands in the following year,[56] and granted a life interest in Padbury to his brother Robert.[57] Early in 1316 Robert was distrained for failing to appear and prove his claim to Padbury against Gilbert de St. Owen and his wife Joan, to whom William de Etchingham had granted it by fine,[58] and later in the year a similar action was taken as regards 20 marks

ETCHINGHAM. *Azure fretty argent.*

[21] *Feud. Aids,* i, 81 ; cf. Chan. Inq. p.m. 23 Edw. III, pt. i, no. 35.
[22] *Pipe R.* 13 *Hen.* II (Pipe R. Soc.), 109.
[23] Grimaldi, *Rot. de Dominabus,* 23.
[24] Hunter, *Gt. R. of the Pipe,* 1 *Ric.* I (Rec. Com.), 34.
[25] *Testa de Nevill* (Rec. Com.), 248.
[26] Chan. Inq. p.m. Hen. III, file 7, no. 3.
[27] *Cal. Close,* loc. cit.
[28] *Feud. Aids,* i, 81.   [29] Ibid. 99.
[30] Chan. Inq. p.m. 36 Edw. III, pt. ii (1st nos.), no. 66 ; *Abbrev. Rot. Orig.* (Rec. Com.), ii, 262.
[31] Martin, loc. cit. ; cf. Close, 1 Ric. II, m. 10 d.   [32] Ibid.
[33] Chan. Inq. p.m. 33 Edw. III, no. 5.
[34] Possibly he was heir male, since in 1438 Isabel widow of John Whithill,

daughter and heir of John Fitz Richard the younger, released to him all right in this manor (Martin, op. cit. 98).
[35] *Cal. Pat.* 1396–9, p. 153.
[36] Close, 11 Hen. IV, m. 20.
[37] *Cal. Pat.* 1408–13, p. 241 ; Martin, loc. cit.
[38] *Cal. Pat.* 1441–6, p. 393 ; Martin, loc. cit.
[39] Martin, loc. cit.
[40] Ibid. 99 ; Feet of F. Bucks. 35 Hen. VI, no. 1.
[41] The name 'Millbury' has first been found in 1379 (Martin, op. cit. 94).
[42] *Feud. Aids,* i, 81.
[43] Chan. Inq. p.m. 22 Edw. I, no. 40 ; 25 Edw. III (1st nos.), no. 6.
[44] *Cal. Close,* 1349–54, p. 299.
[45] Hunter, *Pedes Finium* (Rec. Com.), i, 200.

[46] P.R.O. *List of Sheriffs,* 141.
[47] *Rot. Lit. Claus.* (Rec. Com.), ii, 137*b*, 167*b* ; cf. Feet of F. Bucks. 20 Hen. III, no. 54.
[48] Martin, op. cit. 93.
[49] *Cal. Chart. R.* 1226–57, p. 416.
[50] *Cal. Inq. p.m.* (Hen. III), i, 75 ; *Excerpta e Rot. Fin.* (Rec. Com.), ii, 158.
[51] Deed quoted by Spencer Hall, *Echyngham of Echyngham,* 6.
[52] *Testa de Nevill* (Rec. Com.), 248 ; *Feud. Aids,* i, 81.
[53] Chan. Inq. p.m. 22 Edw. I, no. 40.
[54] *Cal. Fine R.* 1272–1307, p. 297. Hall is evidently in error in stating that she married William the elder (loc. cit.).
[55] *Cal. Fine R.* 1272–1307, p. 339.
[56] *Cal. Chart. R.* 1257–1300, p. 461.
[57] De Banco R. 287, m. 196.
[58] Ibid. 214, m. 82 d.

rent payable to Nicholas de la Beche and his wife Joan.[59] To them and their heirs William Etchingham granted his reversionary rights in this manor in the following year.[60] Robert died about 1329,[61] and in 1334 Nicholas and Joan de la Beche made good their rights against Joan widow of Robert Etchingham, who had married Roger Husee and claimed dower in the manor of Padbury.[62] Nevertheless, the manor did revert before 1346 to James Etchingham,[63] nephew and heir of Simon, who was brother and heir of Robert Etchingham.[64] Possibly the conveyance to Nicholas de la Beche was in the nature of a pledge, since Robert Etchingham, and evidently his brother William also, was indebted to him in considerable sums.[65] James Etchingham died in 1349, leaving a son and heir William [66] (afterwards knighted), who in 1377 conveyed the manor to Robert Lindsey, citizen and cutler of London, and other trustees.[67] To these Robert Etchingham and others also released their rights in the same year.[68] They were evidently agents in a sale to Sir John Hawkwood, kt., the famous leader of the 'White Company,' to whom the manor was conveyed in 1379,[69] when he was in the service of Visconti and the Anti-Papal League.[70] The dower of Lady (Elizabeth) Etchingham, widow of Sir William,[71] was evidently reserved, and she was still holding one-third of the manor in 1408,[72] when John son of Sir John Hawkwood by Donnina, illegitimate daughter of Bernabo Visconti,[73] conveyed the remaining two-thirds, and the reversion of this third, to John Barton the younger.[74] Barton subsequently acquired a lease of the remaining third,[75] settled the whole manor upon himself and his wife Isabel,[76] and died in January 1433–4.[77] In 1437 Isabel alienated to Richard and John Forster and to Geoffrey Griffith of Bristol, who subsequently released his rights to Richard Forster. Forster conveyed to John Birkhede, Robert Danvers and John Bold, who agreed to pay a rent of 28 marks to Isabel Barton,[78] and subsequently, in 1442, surrendered the manor to the Crown for the endowment of All Souls College, Oxford.[79] It was thus reunited with the manor of Overbury.

'Millbery Farm,' let on lease 10 March 1493–4,[80] was probably the capital messuage of this manor.

Sir John Hawkwood added to his estate in Padbury lands called Kembell's in Padbury,[81] which evidently included a messuage and lands acquired by William 'de Kenebelle' from Henry Breton in 1320,

and sold by his heirs to Roger and Lettice Skyret, from whom Hawkwood purchased them.[82]

In 1564 it was stated that there had long been two manors called Padbury, one (evidently including both Overbury and Millbury) the property of All Souls College, the other recently purchased from Ferdinand Pulton of Bourton by Thomas Harris and his wife Katherine, and held of Buckingham Castle by fealty and rent of 4d.[83] This second manor of *PADBURY* had been the property of the Cock family, and may therefore have had its origin in the carucate of land and certain rents and rights of pasture which William Fitz Hamon recognized to be the right of Gilbert Cock in 1247.[84] It has been seen that James Cock held half the vill during the minority of John son of John Wolverton.[85] John Cock of Padbury and Ralph his brother were charged as incendiaries in 1316.[86] John acquired additional lands here in 1319,[87] and may be identical with the John, son of Ralph Cock, who disputed the wardship of John grandson of Henry atte Townsend in 1323.[88] He was apparently succeeded after 1329 [89] by his brother Peter, who conveyed his messuage and lands with the services of certain villeins to John de Walton, and to Rose wife of Thomas de Leicester and Elizabeth her sister, the daughters of Ralph Cock.[90] The rights of Rose and Elizabeth were acquired by John and Elizabeth de Walton, and subsequently by Richard and Alice Durrant.[91] Alice outlived her husband and conveyed her rights in 'the manor of Padbury' to William Walton in 1375.[92] It evidently reverted to the heirs of Richard Durrant, and was acquired by Thomas More and Alice his wife, to whom William Savage, heir of Thomas Durrant, made assurance in March 1437–8.[93] Apparently it descended from Thomas and Alice More to Thomas More of Bourton in Buckingham, who suffered recovery of the 'manor of Padbury' in 1536.[94] He was also lord of a manor in Little Woolstone (q.v.), with which Padbury descended, and with which it was conveyed in 1562 to Ferdinand Pulton.[95] In 1564 he sold the manor of Padbury to Thomas Harris and his wife Katherine for £150,[96] and Thomas Harris sold it in 1591 to All Souls College, Oxford.[97] This Thomas Harris was probably the son of another Thomas, who had been bailiff of All Souls College at Padbury. Joan widow of Thomas the elder, with her son Thomas, had a lease of the estate of the college in Padbury 14 June 1560,[98] and the family can be traced in Padbury during the 16th and 17th centuries.[99]

[59] De Banco R. 215, m. 275 d.; 216, m. 375 d.   [60] Ibid. 287, m. 196.
[61] *Cal. Inq. p.m.* (Edw. III), vii, 142. William had died without issue in 1326, his brother Robert inheriting his land. (ibid. [Edw. II], vi, 460; *Cal. Fine R.* 1319–27, p. 403).
[62] De Banco R. 287, m. 196. The plea dragged on from Mich. 5 Edw. III to Mich. 8 Edw. III.
[63] *Feud. Aids*, i, 125.
[64] *Cal. Inq. p.m.* (Edw. III), vii, 142.
[65] *Cal. Close*, 1327–30, pp. 96, 359; cf. ibid. pp. 35, 36.
[66] Chan. Inq. p.m. 25 Edw. III (1st nos.), no. 44.
[67] Close, 1 Ric. II, m. 32 d.; cf. Martin, op. cit. 93.
[68] Close, 1 Ric. II, m. 32 d. Robert Etchingham and his associates were feoffees of Sir William, probably for the purpose of the conveyance (Martin, loc. cit.).

[69] Martin, op. cit. 94; Close, 3 Ric. II, m. 12 d.   [70] *Dict. Nat. Biog.*
[71] Martin, loc. cit.
[72] Close, 10 Hen. IV, m. 7 d.
[73] *Dict. Nat. Biog.*
[74] Close, 10 Hen. IV, m. 7 d., 6 d.; Martin, loc. cit.
[75] Martin, loc. cit.   [76] Ibid. 95.
[77] Chan. Inq. p.m. 11 Hen. VI, no. 35.
[78] Martin, loc. cit.
[79] *Cal. Pat.* 1441–6, pp. 20, 99.
[80] Martin, op. cit. 108.
[81] Ibid. 97; cf. Close, 10 Hen. IV, m. 7 d.
[82] Martin, loc. cit.; for the Breton holding cf. Hunter, *Pedes Finium* (Rec. Com.), i, 223.
[53] Memo. R. (Exch. L.T.R.), East. 6 Eliz. m. 115.
[84] Feet of F. Bucks. 32 Hen. III, no. 24; cf. ibid. no. 25.
[85] *Feud. Aids*, i, 81.
[86] *Cal. Pat.* 1313–17, p. 496.

[87] Feet of F. Bucks. 12 Edw. II, no. 3.
[88] Martin, op. cit. 100.
[89] *Cal. Close*, 1327–30, p. 526.
[90] Martin, loc. cit.; Feet of F. Bucks. 11 Edw. III, no. 1.
[91] Martin, loc. cit.; Feet of F. Bucks. 12 Edw. III, no. 15.
[92] Martin, op. cit. 93.
[93] Ibid. 100, 101.
[94] Recov. R. East. 28 Hen. VIII, m. 358; Feet of F. Div. Co. Hil. 28 Hen. VIII.
[95] Feet of F. Div. Co. Mich. 4 & 5 Eliz.
[96] Feet of F. Bucks. East. 6 Eliz.; Recov. R. East. 6 Eliz. m. 117; Memo. R. (Exch. L.T.R.), East. 6 Eliz. m. 115.
[97] Martin, op. cit. 101.
[98] Ibid. 108.
[99] Ibid. 109 et seq.; Lay Subs. R. bdles. 79, no. 280; 80, no. 305. Thomas Harris *alias* Smith was vicar in 1607 (terrier quoted by Willis, op. cit. 246).

The church of the *NATIVITY OF THE BLESSED VIRGIN* consists of a chancel measuring internally 25 ft. by 14 ft., nave 48 ft. by 20 ft., north aisle 8 ft. 10 in. wide, north-west vestry, south aisle 8 ft. 9 in. wide, south porch, and west tower 12 ft. 2 in. by 11 ft. 4 in. It is built of rubble with stone dressings; the chancel and porch roofs are covered with tiles and the other roofs with lead.

The chancel and nave date from about 1210, and the south aisle and the tower were added about the middle of the 13th century. About 1340 the north aisle was built, a clearstory added to the nave, and the south arcade rebuilt above the capitals of the pillars, while the south doorway was renewed and windows were inserted at the east end of the chancel. Some windows were inserted during the 15th and 16th centuries, and in the 17th century the tower was rebuilt from about 1 ft. 6 in. above the ground level. The whole fabric was restored in 1830 and the chancel was again restored and refitted in 1882. The south porch was built in 1882 and the vestry in 1908, but the former evidently replaced a mediaeval structure, some moulded roof timbers of which remain in the present structure.

In the east wall of the chancel is a three-light traceried window of the 15th century inserted in a 14th-century opening. At the west end of each side wall is a narrow low-side window; that on the south, which has a round rear arch, is of the original date of the chancel, though its trefoiled head, the cusps of which have been cut away, was inserted later, while that on the north, which is rebated for a shutter, was probably inserted in the late 13th century. The north-east window, dating from this latter period, is of two lights with plain tracery in a pointed head, and the window opposite, which was inserted about 1340, is of three trefoiled lights with reticulated tracery in a pointed head. Near this last window, and contemporary with it, is a cinquefoiled piscina with a credence shelf at the back and an octofoil bowl, the projecting part of which has been renewed, and to the east of the piscina are two plain lockers. Between the windows on the south is a narrow doorway with a pointed head, probably of the late 13th century. Circles have been scratched on the stones at the south-east corner of the chancel. The chancel arch is original, dating from about 1210; it is pointed and of two plain orders, now considerably distorted through the deflection of the large segmental responds, which it has thrust out of the perpendicular. The arch springs from heavy plain imposts, and the label on the nave side has been cut flush with the wall. The imposts, originally returned on both sides of the wall, have been cut and repaired. The chancel has an open-timber king-post roof of about 1500 with moulded beams and curved braces; an inscription, ᵀ. ᴹ. ᴬᴺ· ᴰᴼᴹ· ₁₆₅₅ ᵀ. ᶜ. below a carved figure

on the western beam, probably refers to a 17th-century restoration, and the roof has been again restored at a modern period. There is a carved head below the central beam.

The north and south arcades of the nave have each four pointed arches, supported by octagonal pillars, with moulded capitals and bases, and respond-corbels. The pillars and corbels on the south date from about 1250, and have mouldings similar to those found elsewhere in the neighbourhood of this period, though they are more roughly executed. The bases have been considerably repaired, but some of the original moulding remains. On the east and west the arches spring from head corbels upon the responds, now somewhat defaced, which originally formed the capitals of filleted wall-shafts, but the shafts are now cut flush with the faces of the responds, though a part immediately below the head remains on the east corbel. The arches above were rebuilt about 1340 and are of two chamfered orders, with labels on both sides of the wall having head-stops at their junctions. The north arcade is of this latter period and the arches

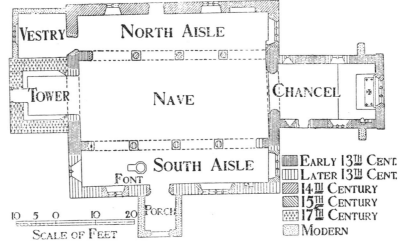

PLAN OF PADBURY CHURCH

VESTRY · NORTH AISLE · TOWER · NAVE · CHANCEL · SOUTH AISLE · FONT · PORCH

EARLY 13ᵀᴴ CENT.
LATER 13ᵀᴴ CENT.
14ᵀᴴ CENTURY
15ᵀᴴ CENTURY
17ᵀᴴ CENTURY
MODERN

10 5 0 10 20
SCALE OF FEET

are precisely similar to those on the south; the pillars, which are repaired in places, have richly moulded capitals and bases and the respond-corbels are moulded, that on the west being carved with a finely-formed head. Above the north arcade, and contemporary with it, are three circular clearstory windows, that in the centre being quatrefoiled and the others sexfoiled; the original lights on the south have been replaced by four 16th-century square-headed windows, which have been considerably restored and the western one entirely renewed at a recent date. The pointed tower arch on the west dates from about 1250; its outer orders die into the responds and the inner springs from head corbels, that on the north having been renewed, probably when the tower was rebuilt.

There are two 14th-century windows in the north wall of the north aisle, the eastern of three trefoiled lights with tracery under a segmental head, and the other of two lights with tracery under a pointed head; in the east wall are a 15th-century square-headed window of three trefoiled lights and a 14th-century trefoiled piscina, and in the west wall is a modern doorway to the vestry. The pointed north doorway is original; it is moulded and has a label with large head-stops, now slightly defaced, and retains an old studded oak door. At the east end of the north wall is a 14th-century tomb recess with a low pointed arch, and above it are some interesting contemporary wall paintings, which were uncovered in 1883 and are now indistinct. These include two scenes from the life of St. Catherine, the upper depicting the saint bound between the wheels which were the instruments of her martyrdom, and the lower the saint with arms extended towards three indistinct figures. Both these scenes are inclosed in a scroll border, and to the west of them is a large circle depicting the expurgation of the seven deadly sins, represented above monsters' heads which terminate in scrolls issuing from various parts of the body of a crowned female figure in the centre of the circle. There are also traces of colouring further west on this wall.

The south aisle has in the west wall an original mid-13th-century window of two pointed lights, which has become somewhat distorted externally through the sinking of the wall at the south, perhaps occasioned by the thrust of the tower; the south doorway retains its original label with nail-head ornament, but the jambs and pointed head, which are continuously moulded, are of the 14th century. There is an early 15th-century window of three trefoiled lights in the east wall, and in the south wall are two windows, both with modern tracery, but old internal jambs, the eastern probably dating from the 15th and the other from the 14th century. Close together at the south-east are a piscina, roughly trefoiled and enriched on the edge with dog-tooth ornament, and a trefoiled locker with rebated edge; these date from the early 13th century, and were probably removed here from the chancel. Both aisles have lean-to roofs of about 1500, that on the south having been extensively repaired, probably in 1764, the date on the easternmost tie-beam.

The tower is of three receding stages, and is surmounted by a plain parapet with corner merlons. A stone seat running round the north, west, and south walls internally probably marks the level from which the tower was rebuilt in the 17th century on all sides except that adjoining the nave. Both the west doorway and the wide single-light window above are plain and have round heads; the second stage has small triangular-headed lights, and the bell-chamber is lighted by larger windows of a similar character.

The present font is modern; it replaced some years since a small round bowl, of doubtful date and origin, which was set on a long shaft, probably that of a churchyard cross; both now lie in the tower. In the chancel are a mural monument with arms to Harris Smith (d. 1690) and Francisca his wife (d. 1705); a mural monument to Anne wife of Thomas Thied, and Mrs. Penelope Smith (d. 1762); and a floor slab

to Richard Smith, son of Harris Smith (d. 1742). The communion table, which is elaborately carved, was given in 1634 by nine persons, whose names are inscribed on the top rail; the panels of a 17th-century pulpit with incised foliated ornament are now incorporated in a large chest, which was constructed in 1908 and stands in the south aisle.

The tower contains a ring of six bells, all by John Briant of Hertford, 1806.

The communion plate consists of a small cup and cover paten of 1574, a paten on stand of 1711, and a large plated flagon.

The registers previous to 1812 are as follows: (i) all entries 1538 to 1671; (ii) all entries 1671 to 1754 (one leaf has been extracted from this book); (iii) baptisms and burials 1764 to 1812; (iv) marriages 1754 to 1810.

ADVOWSON The Priors of Bradwell, a house founded by Meinfelin, son of Manno the Breton, about 1155,[100] were patrons of the church in the 13th century,[1] and probably earlier. Alan de Etchingham released all claim in a moiety of the church to the priory in 1201.[2] In 1524 the endowment of the priory, including the advowson of Padbury, was granted to Wolsey for Cardinal College, Oxford.[3] When the college was deprived of its endowment, the advowson of Padbury was granted to the Carthusian Priory at Sheen.[4] This house surrendered in 1539,[5] and the living has thenceforward been in the gift of the Crown,[6] with the exception of a short period from 1558-9, when under a grant of Queen Mary it was vested in the Bishop of Lincoln.[7]

It is noteworthy that vicars were generally recommended in the late 18th century by the corporation of Buckingham through the Marquess of Buckingham and his family.[8]

A vicarage was ordained shortly before 1274,[9] but in 1455 it was temporarily reunited with the parish church owing to constant disputes between the vicars and the Priors of Bradwell.[10] The rectorial tithes descended with the advowson until February 1577–8, when they were exchanged by the Crown with Edward Earl of Lincoln.[11] Before 1610 they had reverted to the Crown, and were purchased in that year by Sir Anthony Aucher and Sir Thomas Hardres, kts.[12] They subsequently passed to the Temple family,[13] and the rectory-house, together with certain of the tithes, was purchased by the tenant, William Chaplin, from Sir Thomas Temple of Stowe.[14] In 1700 Thomas Gibboard and his wife Elizabeth, William Wheeler and his wife Mary, and Thomas Henshawe and his wife Hannah, conveyed the 'rectory' to Thomas Browne and Robert Robbins.[15] William Baldwin the elder, William Baldwin the younger, John Stanley and his wife Elizabeth, and William Core and his wife Rebecca, made conveyance to William Giles and John Chawke in 1713.[16] The rectory passed by pur-

[100] V.C.H. Bucks. i, 350.

[1] R. of Hugh of Wells (Cant. and York Soc.), i, 93; ii, 72.

[2] Hunter, Pedes Finium (Rec. Com.), i, 200.

[3] V.C.H. Bucks. i, 351; L. and P. Hen. VIII, iv (1), p. 991; Feet of F. Div. Co. Trin. 19 Hen. VIII.

[4] L. and P. Hen. VIII, v, 403.

[5] V.C.H. Surr. ii, 93.

[6] Inst. Bks. (P.R.O.).

[7] Pat. 5 & 6 Phil. and Mary, pt. iv; Willis, op. cit. 245.

[8] Hist. MSS. Com. Rep. xiii, App. iii, 252, 256.

[9] Linc. Epis. Reg. quoted by Willis, op. cit. 247.

[10] Linc. Epis. Reg. Memo. Chedworth, fol. 41; in 1506 a vicar was again presented (Willis, loc. cit.).

[11] Pat. 20 Eliz. pt. vi, m. 1.

[12] Ibid. 8 Jas. I, pt. xliii, no. 5.

[13] Recov. R. Mich. 13 Jas. I, m. 175; Feet of F. Div. Co. Trin. 12 Jas. I.

[14] Lipscomb, Hist. and Antiq. of Bucks. iii, 60; cf. Feet of F. Bucks. Mich. 2 Chas. I; Hil. 8 Chas. I. This house may represent the messuage acquired by the Prior of Bradwell about 1280 (Cal. Close, 1360-4, p. 338; Mins. Accts. [Gen. Ser.], bdle. 762, no. 21).

[15] Feet of F. Bucks. Hil. 11 Will. III.

[16] Ibid. Hil. 11 Anne.

PADBURY CHURCH: THE INTERIOR LOOKING EAST

PADBURY CHURCH FROM THE SOUTH-EAST

chase into the Eyre family in 1768.[17] Other portions of tithes changed hands very frequently during the 17th and 18th centuries.[18] They evidently included the tithe from some 50 acres of land which had been in the possession of Missenden Abbey [19] and were in the occupation of — Andesloe in 1586, when they were the subject of a grant to John Watson and John Cresset, who appear to have been 'fishing grantees.'[20]

The parsonage of Padbury was wrongfully let on a ninety-nine years' lease rent free by John Wells,[21] Prior of Bradwell 1492–1503.[22] The lessee, Thomas Darell, is said to have promised Wells to make him Prior of St. Andrew's, Northampton.[23] Prior Boston obtained from the Crown a reversal of his predecessor's act, which deprived the monastery of the chief part

of its livelihood. Darell refused to be ousted, and forcible entry appears to have been made into the parsonage both by his men and by the servants of the prior, who came in person to the church to bring the king's command to Darell.[24]

CHARITIES

Church Land.—There are about 2 a. 3 r. of land, so called, let at £6 15s. a year, which is carried to the churchwardens' account.

The National school is endowed with a sum of £109 17s. 9d. consols by the will of Mrs. Penelope Hunt, proved in the P.C.C. 9 June 1849, also with a sum of £100 consols by a deed of gift by the Rev. William Thomas Eyre, dated 16 June 1862.

The sums of stock are held by the official trustees, producing £5 4s. 8d. yearly.

PRESTON BISSETT

Prestone (xi cent.); Prestona (xii cent.); Preston Byset (xiii cent.).

This parish covers 1,520 acres, of which 130 are arable and 1,339 permanent grass.[1] The soil is clay and gravel, the subsoil various. The parish is watered by a tributary of the River Ouse. The west of the parish lies low, but the land rises to 357 ft. above the ordnance datum at Cowley in the south-east.

The picturesque village of Preston Bissett is situated in the north of the parish, and is grouped round the parish church, which stands in a churchyard on rising ground. The cottages of which it is mainly composed are thatched, many of them dating from the 17th century, whilst the inn known as 'The Old Hat,' which stands opposite the church, is an ancient building of interest. A house on the south side of the church dates probably from the 16th century, and still retains some of its oak-mullioned windows. The rectory, some little distance to the north of the church, is a brick and stucco house built in the Gothic style in 1840 by the rector. The National schools, in the south of the village, were erected in 1858 and the Methodist chapel in 1853. There are a few modern residences in the east of the village.

The small hamlet of Cowley (Coveleg, Covele, Couele, xiii cent.) lies to the south-east of Preston Bissett, and consists of three farms and two or three cottages. Foundations of the ancient chapel are still to be seen in the field known as Parson's Close.[2] Cowley Farm, built in 1604 according to a date on a frieze inside the house, has been coated with roughcast. Casemore Farm occupies an isolated position in the centre of the parish.

The water in this parish is strongly impregnated

with iron, and one spring has been found, although it is not used.[3]

An Inclosure Award was granted to Preston Bissett in 1781, when a field of 940 acres and a plot of land of 60 acres (which had been granted from Tingewick Common on the inclosure of that parish) were said to be commonable.[4] The rector received an allotment on inclosure in lieu of tithes on land in Preston Bissett.[5] The tithe on the lands in Cowley was commuted at £200 a year, and still remains chargeable on these lands.

The following place-names have been found in records : Patrons Acre [6] (xvi cent.); Gamons Wood, Poole Hooke Meade, and le Wyndmill Hill [7] (xvii cent.).

MANORS

Under the Confessor PRESTON alias PRESTON BISSETT and COWLEY MANOR was held by Wiluf, a man of Earl Lewin, who had power to sell.[8] In 1086, when it was assessed at 15 hides, it had passed to the Bishop of Bayeux.[9] In the middle of the 13th century the overlordship was attached to the honour of 'Chelefeud,' [10] the manor being held by the service of castle ward at Rochester Castle, later commuted to a money payment.[11] No reference to the overlordship has been found after the year 1421.

Ansgot de Ros was the tenant of the Bishop of Bayeux in 1086,[12] and the next owner of the manor was William son of Helte, who held Preston in the reign of Henry II.[13] He appears to have enfeoffed a member of the Bissett family, probably Manasseh Bissett, the well-known *dapifer* of Henry II, for we find the name of Manasseh Bissett in the Pipe Roll of Bedfordshire and Buckingham for the year 1158–9,[14]

[17] Lipscomb, loc. cit.
[18] Feet of F. Bucks. Mich. 13 Chas. I; Hil. 1650; Hil. 1658; Mich. 22 Chas. II; Trin. 35 Chas. II; Trin. 11 Geo. III; Trin. 19 Geo. III; East. 21 Geo. III; East. 24 Geo. III; Trin. 27 Geo. III.
[19] *Pope Nich. Tax.* (Rec. Com.), 47; *Valor Eccl.* (Rec. Com.), iv, 246; Martin, op. cit. 104.
[20] Pat. 28 Eliz. pt. xiv, no. 4.
[21] Early Chan. Proc. bdle. 279, no. 79.
[22] *V.C.H. Bucks.* i, 352.

[23] Star Chamb. Proc. Hen. VIII, bdle. 18, no. 140.
[24] Ibid.; Early Chan. Proc. bdle. 279, no. 79.
[1] Statistics from Bd. of Agric. (1905).
[2] Sheahan, *Hist. and Topog. of Bucks.* 299.
[3] Ibid.
[4] Act Priv. and Loc. 21 Geo. III, cap. 43; 13 Geo. III, cap. 66.
[5] Ibid. 21 Geo. III, cap. 43.
[6] Chan. Inq. p.m. (Ser. 2), cxxii, 12.
[7] Ibid. dccxxv, 28.

[8] *V.C.H. Bucks.* i, 238.
[9] Ibid.
[10] *Testa de Nevill* (Rec. Com.), 243b.
[11] *Hund. R.* (Rec. Com.), i, 29; *Feud. Aids*, i, 87 (here the manor is said to be held of the barony of 'Cancia de Dels'); Anct. Ext. (Exch. K.R.), no. 32 (2); Chan. Inq. p.m. 23 Edw. III (1st nos.), no. 169; 9 Hen. V, no. 58; *Cal. Close, 1349–54*, p. 27.
[12] *V.C.H. Bucks.* i, 238.
[13] Cur. Reg. R. 47, m. 10 d.
[14] *Pipe R. 5 Hen. II* (Pipe R. Soc.), 18,

and also for the year 1162–3 in connexion with 'Prestinton.'[15] Again he may be identified in all probability with the 'Maness' who rendered account of half a mark in Preston in 1166–7.[16] Manasseh's successor was Anselm Bissett, whose name is first found in connexion with Buckinghamshire in 1199,[17] and with Preston Manor in 1205.[18] In that year, and again in 1208, William de Ceriton preferred rights in the manor against Anselm Bissett. His claim was based on his relationship to William son of Helte mentioned above, who had died without issue, leaving three sisters as co-heirs. William de Ceriton was the son of Sibyl, one of these sisters, the other sisters Alice and Emma being represented by a son Anfrid de Caney, and a grandson Robert de Setvans (Septem Vannis) respectively.[19] William de Ceriton's claim appears to have been one of overlordship only, which was recognized in 1284–6.[20] Anselm was succeeded in Preston by Ernald Bissett, who held here in 1254,[21] or even earlier.[22] At the former date his possessions in Preston were extended at 6½ hides.[23] Ernald Bissett appears to have alienated the manor about this date to Laurence de Brok,[24] whose death took place in or about the year 1275,[25] when the executors of his will delivered goods in the manor to his son and heir Hugh.[26] In 1284–6 Hugh de Brok is returned as lord of the vill of Preston and half the hamlet of Cowley.[27] William Bissett is here named as his intermediary lord, but in 1290 Hugh received a final quitclaim from him of the manor.[28] Laurence de Brok succeeded his father Hugh,[29] but some time before 1299 the manor was acquired by Walter, Bishop of Coventry and Lichfield, who in that year received a grant of free warren in this manor.[30] In the following year the bishop alienated to William Tuchet,[31] to whom also free warren was confirmed in Preston Bissett.[32] In 1312 William Tuchet entered into an arrangement with Bartholomew de Badlesmere by which he, William, was to hold Preston Bissett for life, with reversion to Bartholomew if he should die without heir male.[33] Both William Tuchet and Bartholomew de Badlesmere took part in the Earl of Lancaster's rebellion,[34] and in 1322, after Boroughbridge, were executed, Preston Manor escheating to the Crown. Laurence de Brok, its former owner, now claimed possession on the ground that he had been unjustly disseised by the Bishop of Coventry and Lichfield,[35]

and his widow Eleanor claimed and received dower in the manor some years later, her right being last mentioned in 1341.[36] On the other hand when Giles son of Bartholomew de Badlesmere (who had obtained the reversal of his father's attainder in 1328)[37] finally acquired livery of his father's lands in 1333,[38] Preston Bissett was included among them.[39] Giles de Badlesmere married Elizabeth daughter of the Earl of Salisbury, and on his death without issue in 1338 she received in dower two parts of the manor of Preston Bissett.[40] Elizabeth de Badlesmere subsequently married Hugh le Despencer and held Preston with him till his death in February 1348–9.[41] She later married Guy Lord Bryan,[42] retaining the ownership of this manor till her death in 1359.[43] Preston Bissett then passed, in accordance with the settlement made at the time of her first husband's death, to Thomas de Ros de Hamlake, younger surviving son of Margery, wife of William de Ros and eldest sister of Giles de Badlesmere.[44] Thomas de Ros died in 1383, leaving a son and heir John, aged eighteen,[45] but Preston was held in dower for some years by his widow Beatrice,[46] who married Richard de Burley some time previous to 1386.[47] John de Ros predeceased his mother, dying at Paphos in Cyprus on his way to the Holy Land in 1393.[48] He left no issue, so that, on the death of Beatrice de Burley in 1415, Preston Manor passed to her grandson and his nephew John son of William de Ros.[49] John de Ros was slain at Beaugé in March 1420–1,[50] and Preston Manor passed to his brother Thomas, aged fourteen.[51] He died in 1431, and was succeeded by his son Thomas de Ros, a zealous Lancastrian, who was attainted in 1461.[52] In consequence Preston Manor escheated to the Crown. In

Ros. *Gules three water-bougets argent.*

1465 William son of Thomas Fowler had a grant for life for good service,[53] and the reversion was given to Richard Fowler and his heirs male in 1467.[54] Richard Fowler died seised of his interest in the reversion in 1477,[55] and in 1484 Thomas Fowler (whose precise relationship to the preceding members of his family has not been established) and

[15] *Pipe R. 9 Hen. II* (Pipe R. Soc.), 16.
[16] Ibid. 13 Hen. II, 109.
[17] *Rot. Cur. Reg.* (Rec. Com.), i, 264; *Rot. Canc.* (Rec. Com.), 220.
[18] *Rot. de Oblatis et Fin.* (Rec. Com.), 335.   [19] *Cur. Reg. R.* 47, m. 10 d.
[20] *Feud. Aids*, i, 87.
[21] *Hund. R.* (Rec. Com.), i, 29.
[22] *Testa de Nevill* (Rec. Com.), 243*b*.
[23] *Hund. R.* (Rec. Com.), i, 29.
[24] Chan. Misc. Inq. file 88, no. 51.
[25] *Cal. Inq. p.m.* (Edw. II), ii, 76.
[26] Harl. Chart. 46, F 45.
[27] *Feud. Aids*, i, 87.
[28] Feet of F. case 17, file 51, no. 8. In the same year William Bissett and Antigone his wife quitclaimed, on her behalf, lands in Preston to Hugh (ibid. no. 15).
[29] Chan. Misc. Inq. file 88, no. 51.
[30] Chart. R. 28 Edw. I, no. 93.
[31] Feet of F. Div. Co. 29 Edw. I, no. 55.

[32] *Cal. Chart. R.* 1300–26, p. 3.
[33] Feet of F. Div. Co. Hil. 5 Edw. II, no. 59; Chan. Inq. p.m. 4 Edw. III (2nd nos.), no. 111. In 1314 William Tuchet claimed to hold the manor of the bishop (De Banco R. 206, m. 208 d.).
[34] See Chan. Misc. Inq. file 88, no. 51, where William Tuchet is described as a rebel; also G.E.C. *Peerage* (new ed.), ii, 372.
[35] Chan. Misc. Inq. file 88, no. 51.
[36] De Banco R. Mich. 2 Edw. III, m. 215 d.; Chan. Inq. p.m. 12 Edw. III (2nd nos.), no. 54*a*; *Cal. Close*, 1341–3, p. 146.
[37] G.E.C. loc. cit.
[38] Ibid.
[39] Chan. Inq. p.m. files 25, no. 8; 9, no. 10.
[40] *Cal. Close*, 1337–9, p. 498. The remaining third was held by Eleanor de Brok.
[41] Chan. Inq. p.m. 23 Edw. III, pt. ii

(1st nos.), no. 169; see also *Feud. Aids*, i, 124.
[42] G.E.C. loc. cit.
[43] *Cal. Close*, 1349–54, p. 27; Chan. Inq. p.m. 33 Edw. III (1st nos.), no. 42.
[44] Chan. Inq. p.m. 12 Edw. III (2nd nos.), no. 54*a*; *Cal. Close*, 1341–3, p. 146; 1343–6, p. 188.
[45] Chan. Inq. p.m. 7 Ric. II, no. 68.
[46] Ibid.; G.E.C. *Complete Peerage*, vi, 401, gives her name incorrectly as Margaret.
[47] Close, 10 Ric. II, m. 39 d., 23 d.
[48] G.E.C. loc. cit.
[49] Chan. Inq. p.m. 3 Hen. V, no. 44.
[50] Ibid. 9 Hen. V, no. 58; G.E.C. op. cit. vi, 402.
[51] Chan. Inq. p.m. 9 Hen. V, no. 58.
[52] G.E.C. loc. cit.
[53] *Cal. Pat.* 1461–7, p. 440.
[54] Ibid. 1467–77, p. 18.
[55] Chan. Inq. p.m. 17 Edw. IV, no. 39.

Alice (Hulcote) his wife received a further royal confirmation of the manor.[56] In the following year Edmund de Ros obtained a reversal of Thomas's attainder,[57] and Preston Manor, thus restored to his family, was in 1541 in the possession of Thomas Earl of Rutland, whose father was nephew and co-heir of Edmund de Ros.[58] At that date the Earl of Rutland conveyed the estate to Sir John Baldwin, at whose death in 1545 Preston passed to his grandson John, son of Parnel Borlase.[59] The Borlase family (whose descent is given under Little Marlow, q.v.) retained Preston for the next fifty years.[60] In 1594 William Borlase combined with Mary his wife to make a settlement of the manor on John Freestone and William Bridgewater,[61] but no further reference has been found of them in connexion with Preston, which according to Willis passed in 1630 to the Cater family.[62] This is so far confirmed by documentary evidence that in 1631 John Cater is found settling land in Preston Bissett.[63] The same authority states that it next passed to the Gibbs family by the marriage of Alice daughter of John Cater to Robert Gibbs.[64] This statement also receives the confirmation of a fine levied on the manor in 1701–2 between Thomas Gibbs combining with other members of his family and Sir Edmund Denton of Hillesden,[65] who had, however, held the manor for at least three years previously.[66] Preston Bissett now followed the same descent as Hillesden (q.v.) until the 19th century, passing like that manor by descent to the family of Coke,[67] whose representative, Thomas Coke, Earl of Leicester, alienated Preston Bissett in 1824 to John Farquhar.[68] From him it passed almost immediately to the Duke of Buckingham and Chandos,[69] whose descendant, Lady Kinloss, is at the present day lady of the manor.

On the partition of the property of Giles de Badlesmere in 1338 lands in *COWLEY* appear to have been granted to his second sister and co-heir Maud Countess of Oxford.[70] It was stated in 1392 that Maud widow of Thomas de Vere, Earl of Oxford, son of the above Maud de Badlesmere,[71] held the 'manor' of Cowley.[72] In 1407, when Philippa, widow of Robert de Vere, Earl of Oxford and Duke of Ireland, made a settlement of her property in Cowley, it is described as a toft, 15 acres of land, 20 acres of meadow and 20s. rent.[73] No further mention of it has been found.

For more than 100 years previous to their acquisition of the advowson and manor of Preston Bissett the Dentons owned a property in the parish. In 1552 Nicholas Michell and Jacomyne his wife appear to have conveyed their farm or capital messuage in Cowley to Thomas Denton.[74] When his descendant Edmund Denton compounded as a delinquent in 1647 his estate in Preston is mentioned as fined,[75] and is described as the manor of Cowley *alias* Coveley in his will, dated 17 October 1657, empowering his trustees to sell part thereof for the payment of his debts.[76] His son Alexander Denton was stated in 1676 to hold the 'manor' of Cowley,[77] and likewise gave directions to his trustees to sell the same in order to raise money.[78]

A property in the hamlet of Cowley in this parish appears to have included the mill which formed part of Preston Bissett at Domesday.[79] It was attached to Preston Bissett Manor, of which it was held by payment of 3s. towards the ward of Rochester Castle.[80] First mention is found of it in 1252, when John son of Mauger de Cowley received a life grant from John son of John [Mauger] de Cowley[81] of a messuage and lands.[82] In 1258 Mauger de Cowley combined with Henry de Bayworth (who in 1252 had acquired a carucate of land in Cowley from Roger de Gray[83]) to bring an action against the Archdeacon of Buckingham and others regarding the chapel of Cowley.[84] In 1284–6 John de Cowley had succeeded to this property.[85] His name occurs in 1302–3,[86] and that of a descendant, also John de Cowley, in 1346,[87] whilst in 1368 Henry son of Henry de Cowley and Joan his wife were disputing about his mother Agnes's dower in Cowley and elsewhere.[88] No further trace has been found of the name Cowley in connexion with this parish, but the almost immediate appearance of the name Major leads to the inference that the 'Mauger' of the 13th century had always been perpetuated and that the Cowleys of the 13th and 14th centuries may be identified with the Majors, who continued to hold down to the 17th century. In 1377 John Major of Cowley was concerned in an assault made on William la Zouche at Middle Claydon.[89] Again, the water-mill in Preston was held of John Major (Mager) by Thomas Giffard in 1469.[90] Towards the close of the same century (c. 1493–1500) Thomas Benet brought a suit against Thomas Major, who had seized deeds relating to his (Benet's) lands in Preston and Cowley, and had refused to give them up.[91] Thomas was followed by John Major, whose son Richard Major died in 1570 seised of a cottage and 4½ virgates of arable land in Cowley, which passed next to his son Edmund Major.[92] The latter married Anne daughter of

[56] *Cal. Pat.* 1476–85, p. 383.
[57] G.E.C. *Peerage*, vi, 403.
[58] Ibid. ; Recov. R. Hil. 33 Hen. VIII, m. 310.
[59] Chan. Inq. p.m. (Ser. 2), lxxiii, 7.
[60] Recov. R. East. 29 Eliz. m. 27 ; Chan. Inq. p.m. (Ser. 2), ccxxxvii, 121 ; Feet of F. Bucks. Mich. 36 Eliz.
[61] Feet of F. Bucks. Mich. 36 Eliz.
[62] Willis, *Hist. and Antiq. of Buckingham*, 250. Willis has gone rather astray in the history of the manor at this point, for he says it was still in the possession of the Earls of Rutland at the time of the sale to the Caters.
[63] Feet of F. Bucks. Trin. 7 Chas. I.
[64] Willis, loc. cit.
[65] Feet of F. Bucks. Hil. 13 Will. III.
[66] Recov. R. Mich. 10 Will. III, m. 236.

[67] Ibid. East. 32 Geo. III, m. 233 ; Willis, loc. cit. ; Lysons, *Mag. Brit.* i (3), 622.
[68] Feet of F. Bucks. Hil. 4 & 5 Geo. IV.
[69] Sheahan, op. cit. 298 ; Lipscomb, *Hist. and Antiq. of Bucks.* iii, 64.
[70] G.E.C. *Peerage* (new ed.), ii, 373.
[71] Ibid. (ed. 1), v, 164.
[72] Chan. Inq. p.m. 16 Ric. II, pt. ii, no. 34.
[73] *Cal. Pat.* 1405–8, pp. 299, 314.
[74] Com. Pleas D. Enr. Mich. 6 Edw. V, m. 8 d. [75] *Cal. Com. for Comp.* 2878.
[76] P.C.C. 269 Pell.
[77] Recov. R. Hil. 28 & 29 Chas. II, m.133 ; Feet of F. Bucks. Trin. 28 Chas. II.
[78] P.C.C. 57 Pett.
[79] Feet of F. case 16, file 31, no. 9 ; *V.C.H. Bucks.* i, 238 ; Chan. Inq. p.m. 9 & 10 Edw. IV, no. 15.

[80] *Hund. R.* (Rec. Com.), i, 29 ; *Feud. Aids*, i, 87 ; Chan. Inq. p.m. (Ser. 2), clxxxiv, 5.
[81] See *Hund. R.* loc. cit.
[82] Feet of F. case 16, file 31, no. 9.
[83] Ibid. no. 11.
[84] Cur. Reg. R. 160, m. 14.
[85] *Feud. Aids*, i, 87.
[86] Ibid. 99. [87] Ibid. 124.
[88] Chan. Inq. p.m. 42 Edw. III (1st nos.), no. 63.
[89] *Cal. Pat.* 1377–81, p. 91.
[90] Chan. Inq. p.m. 9 & 10 Edw. IV, no. 15.
[91] Early Chan. Proc. bdle. 187, no. 81.
[92] Chan. Inq. p.m. (Ser. 2), clxxxiv, 5. Richard Major held other lands in this parish mentioned elsewhere. Thomas and Robert, brothers of Richard Major, are mentioned.

Edward Ayleworth, whose memorial brass, dated 1613, the year of her death, is still to be seen in the chancel of Preston Bissett Church.[93] Edmund Major was still living in 1631, when with his son Edmund and his grandson Ayleworth Major he made a settlement.[94] Edmund Major, jun., died in 1634, his father surviving, and the 'capital messuage,' cottages and lands in Cowley passed, in pursuance of a previous settlement, to his son Ayleworth Major.[95] Ayleworth Major continued to reside on the family estate at Cowley and had a son Edmund, rector of Turweston, whose death in 1685 is commemorated by a tablet in the parish church.[96] The property, which comprised closes in Cowley called Gibbs Perry Croft and Sea Croft, was left by Edmund's widow Susanna, by her will dated 30 July 1703, to her daughter Susanna, wife of Peter Mourse, D.D.[96a] With her disappears the last trace of this family, who, as has been shown above, had been connected with Cowley for more than 400 years.

PRESTON BISSETT CHURCH FROM THE SOUTH

The monastery of Nutley held lands and rents, valued at 18s., in Preston,[97] which were granted in 1540 to William Risley and Alice his wife,[98] and were still held by his family in 1603.[99]

Land in this parish also belonged to the gild of St. Rumbald of Buckingham, as appears from an inquisition of 1579 on Richard Major, who held a messuage, 2 virgates of land in Cowley bought from William Risley, and 1 virgate bought from Thomas Moyle, all of which had formerly belonged to the gild.[100]

The church of *ST. JOHN BAPTIST CHURCH* consists of a chancel measuring internally 28 ft. by 16 ft., nave 33 ft. 6 in. by 17 ft. 6 in., north aisle 8 ft. wide, south aisle 7 ft.

6 in. wide, south porch, and west tower 11 ft. square; it is built of squared limestone rubble, and all the roofs, except that of the modern porch, are covered with lead.

The chancel, nave and tower were built during the early years of the 14th century,[1] probably on the site of an early 12th-century church, fragments of which, including round window heads and pillar capitals, were found during a modern restoration, and have been built into the east wall of the north aisle. The aisles and the nave clearstory were added about 1350, while a mediaeval south porch and a vestry, which stood on the north side of the chancel, have since been destroyed. The building was considerably restored at various periods during the 19th century, particularly in 1873; an 18th-century gallery has been removed, and the clearstory and the south porch have been rebuilt.

The chancel, which is long in comparison with the nave, has a large east window, inserted about 1350, of three cinquefoiled lights with flowing tracery in a pointed head, and in each side wall are two original two-light windows with tracery in pointed heads, those at the eastern ends being placed high in the walls; the south-west window has flowing tracery in the head and a transom, below which the lights doubtless served the purpose of a low-side window. In the window opposite are some fragments of mediaeval glass. Below the north-east window is a blocked doorway which led to the mediaeval vestry, the roof weather-course of which still remains on the wall outside, and to the west of this is an original moulded doorway with a pointed head. On the south side are two 14th-century sedilia with trefoiled heads, and a pointed piscina with a modern bowl; the sedilia have vaulted canopies and are further enriched by crocketed labels with flanking pinnacles and head-stops. The pointed chancel arch, dating from the 14th century, is of two chamfered orders, the outer continued down the responds and the inner springing from corbels carved as crouching figures; the figure on the south faces outward and has both hands resting on his knees, and that on the north, which is now headless, faces west, one hand resting upon a knee, the other raised to support the abacus.

The nave has 14th-century arcades of three bays on either side with pointed arches, supported by octagonal pillars and pilaster responds; the mouldings of the capitals and bases of both arcades are somewhat

[93] Lipscomb, op. cit. iii, 66.
[94] Feet of F. Bucks. Trin. 7 Chas. I.
[95] Chan. Inq. p.m. (Ser. 2), dccxxv, 28. German and Thomas, sons of Edmund Major, sen., are mentioned in the settlement.
[96] Lipscomb, loc. cit.

[96a] Chan. Proc. (Bridges Div.), bdle. 248, no. 8. Edmund Major was instituted to Turweston Church in 1671 (ibid. bdle. 497, no. 27).
[97] *Valor Eccl.* (Rec. Com.), iv, 232.
[98] *L. and P. Hen. VIII*, xv, g. 831 (58).
[99] Chan. Inq. p.m. (Ser. 2), cclxxx, 47.

[100] Ibid. clxxxiv, 5.
[1] The licence by Bishop Dalderby (1300–20) for the dedication of the high altar in the chancel of the church of Preston in Linc. Epis. Reg. Memo. Dalderby, fol. 257, probably refers to this parish.

unrefined, though elaborate, but there is no evidence of recutting, as the forms used have greater affinity to the 14th century than to any subsequent period. The arches have labels with head-stops of various designs. In the west wall of the nave is a low two-centred drop arch to the tower with a continuous outer order, and an inner order springing from roughly-moulded head corbels, the heads of which are defaced. The clear-story is lighted on either side by three windows, all composed of a large modern octofoil set in an original square framework. On the apex of the gable above the chancel arch is a mediaeval sanctus bellcote formed in a single block of stone and now much weatherworn.

The east window of the north aisle, of three tre-foiled lights, is a charming example of mid-14th-century work with flowing tracery cut from a single block of stone ; near by, but to the south of the respond pilaster of the north arcade, is a contemporary trefoiled piscina, now without its bowl, which doubtless served the altar here. There is a two-light window of the same period on the north and another on the west, both with flowing tracery in their heads, con-taining fragments of mediaeval glass. The original north doorway, which has continuous wave mould-ings and a label with crowned head-stops, is now blocked. The windows of the south aisle are also of the 14th century. On the east is a three-light window with flowing tracery, near which in the south wall is a trefoiled piscina without bowl ; on the south is a two-light window with quatrefoil tracery in the head, and on the west a window of similar design, but more richly moulded. The pointed south doorway, also original, has a deep moulded splay and a label with head-stops, now somewhat weatherworn. The open timber roofs of the chancel and aisles retain mediaeval beams and purlins.

The low tower is of two stages with a straight parapet and string-courses between the stages and below the parapet ; at the western angles are diagonal buttresses, which were added in the 15th century, and rise to the height of the first stage only. The ground stage has a small modern window on the west, and the bell-chamber a single trefoiled light on the north, twin trefoiled lights on the west and south, all of the early 14th century, and a plain light on the east, probably also original.

The font dates from the 15th century and has an octagonal bowl and stem, and a square base with broached stops. On the chancel floor are a mediaeval coffin-lid with a plain cross, and a late 15th-century slab with matrices for a brass figure and four shields. The communion table is of the early 17th century. In the tower are two old plain chests and a late 17th-century bier.

There is a bell, dated 1788, which is probably by W. & T. Mears, and a saunce by Edward Hemins of Bicester, 1728.

The communion plate consists of a cup, paten and flagon, all of 1775.

The registers begin in 1662.

ADVOWSON The church of Preston Bissett does not appear to have been attached in the first instance to the principal manor of Preston Bissett. The earliest patron of whom mention has been found is Henry de Belesby, who in 1252 acknowledged the services due from his tenements in Cowley to Henry de Bayworth (cf. Cowley Manor).[2] He presented to the church in 1262,[3] and was succeeded some time before 1307 by Henry de Greynsby, whose name appears as patron at the latter date.[4] From that time till 1403 the family of Greynsby, called also Reyner de Greynsby, continued to hold the advowson.[5] At the beginning of the 15th century John Langston of Caversfield, who according to Willis married an heiress of the Greynsby family, acquired the right of presentation.[6] The Langstons retained the advowson till the last half of the 16th century,[7] when, like Caversfield Manor (q.v.), it passed by female descent to the Moyles, a member of whom, Walter Moyle, alienated it in 1594 to Edmund Major.[8] He presented in 1604,[9] but in 1621 the advowson was once more alienated, passing from Edmund Major to Walkden Wood, who had held the living since 1604.[10] Elizabeth, widow of Walkden Wood, presented in 1645,[11] and in 1656 the trustees or mortgagees of the Woods, Edward Butterfield, Peter Paxton, and others,[12] conveyed the advowson to John Kersey and Richard Blagrave.[13] The Crown presented to Preston Bissett Church in 1662 'per pravitatem Simonæ,'[14] but John Kersey's name recurs as patron in 1674.[15] Between this date and 1676 it was again alienated, being acquired by Alexander Denton,[16] whose successor Edmund Denton twenty years later acquired the manor of Preston Bissett. It thus follows the same descent as the manor until about the middle of the last century, when it was separated by the assignees of the late Duke of Buckingham (d. 1861) and sold to the Rev. J. S. Bolden.[17] It is now in the gift of and held by the Rev. Charles Bolden.

The church of Preston Bissett was endowed with a messuage, a toft, lands and meadows in Preston, in-cluding a bovate and 6 acres of land in Cowley. This endowment was the subject of a suit between Henry de Greynsby, the patron, and William Tuchet, then lord of Preston Bissett Manor, early in 1306.[18] Henry de Greynsby had presented Robert de Tyring-ton or Westyrington to the living, and he had pro-ceeded to enfeoff William Tuchet for life of the above endowment. Henry de Greynsby then brought an action for unlawful ingress against William Tuchet, who was able to produce satisfactory evidence of his right.[19] Further complications arose, however, on the seizure of William Tuchet's lands for his felony in 1322, for the endowment fell into the possession of the Crown and so remained for some years. It was, however, ultimately proved to be frankalmoign of the church, and accordingly restored to the incum-bent.[20] Traces of this endowment are found in

[2] Feet of F. case 16, file 31, no. 1.
[3] Willis, op. cit. 252, quoting episcopal registers. [4] Ibid.
[5] Ibid. ; Harl. MS. 6951, fol. 118 d.
[6] Willis, op. cit. 253 ; Early Chan. Proc. bdle. 14, no. 29.
[7] Early Chan. Proc. bdle. 145, no. 50 ; N. and Q. (Ser. 5), vii, 373 ; Chan. Inq.

p.m. (Ser. 2), v, 13 ; cxxii, 12 ; Recov. R. East. 4 & 5 Phil. and Mary, m. 151.
[8] Feet of F. Bucks. East. 36 Eliz.
[9] Willis, op. cit. 254.
[10] Feet of F. Bucks. Mich. 19 Jas. I.
[11] Willis, loc. cit.
[12] Lipscomb, op. cit. iii, 64.
[13] Feet of F. Bucks. East. 1656.

[14] Willis, loc. cit.
[15] Inst. Bks. (P.R.O.).
[16] Ibid. ; Feet of F. Bucks. Trin. 28 Chas. II.
[17] Sheahan, op. cit. 298.
[18] Chan. Misc. Inq. file 97, no. 138.
[19] Ibid.
[20] Cal. Close, 1327-30, p. 168.

1558, when John Langston was said to hold 16 acres in Preston called Patron's Acre and the advowson of the church appended to the said meadow.[21]

In the 13th century there was a chapel at Cowley which was subject to the church at Preston and was endowed with 1 virgate and 6 acres of land in the hamlet. Divine service was celebrated here every week.[22] This land was exchanged by the rector in 1847, under the powers of ' An Act for amending the Acts for the commutation of Tithes,' for portions of

land in Preston Bissett and Tingewick, belonging to Sir Edward East and Lord Leigh.

CHARITIES The Rev. William Pearse, a former rector, who died in 1749, by his will bequeathed £100, the interest to be distributed among the poor for ever. The legacy is represented by £106 16s. 2d. consols with the official trustees, the annual dividends of which are paid to the Radcliffe Infirmary, Oxford, whereby benefits are secured for the poor of the parish.

RADCLIVE

Radeclive (xi cent.) ; Radeclyve (xiv cent.).

This parish covers 1,185 acres, of which 370 are arable, 697 permanent grass, and 20 woods and plantations.[1] The slope of the land varies from 396 ft. above the ordnance datum in the north to 276 ft. in the south. The soil is mixed, principally gravel, of

THE MANOR HOUSE, RADCLIVE

which disused pits exist in the north and south of the parish. The chief crops are wheat, barley, and beans. The Ouse flows through the south of the parish. The main road from Buckingham to Brackley runs from east to west, and the avenue between Buckingham and Stowe also passes eastward through this parish.

The village is small and lies in a hollow in the south of the parish. The church and churchyard occupy a central position, with the rectory on the north. This latter is a spacious building with good grounds. The parsonage which it displaced is thus described in a document of 1639 : 'The Parsonage, consisting of 8 Bays, is built of Stone, whereof five Bays Tyled, three Thatcht, and divided into 14 Rooms, above and below ; two Barns, one of Stone

of 6 Bays.'[2] South-west of the church is the manor-house, now used as a farm and for many years in the occupation of the Swain family.[3] It is a gabled building of stone and brick, with a roof of tiles and slates, and bears the date 1621, when probably it was originally built, but it was much altered later, and part of it was demolished in the last century. Many of the windows still retain their wooden mullions and transoms, and some of the doorways are of the 17th century. Within still remain the original staircase and a screen at the south end of the kitchen, which seems to have been part of the hall. The entrance gateway and traces of the garden walls speak of its former importance. The River Ouse runs close by, and on it stands the ancient manorial mill.

The hamlet of Chackmore (Chakemore, xiii cent. ; Jackemor, Chackemore, xiv cent.) in the north-east of the parish contains several old buildings mostly of half-timber with thatched roofs. The post-office is a 17th-century building of stone with an original brick chimney stack. There is a school licensed for divine worship, and also a Wesleyan chapel. Chackmore farm-house is in the adjoining parish of Maids' Moreton.

Radclive was inclosed under an Act of Parliament of 1773.[4]

Roman remains are said to have been found in a field in Radclive called Town Close, and also at Chackmore.[5]

MANORS Under the Confessor, Azor son of Toti held *RADCLIVE MANOR* (with which was included the hamlet of Chackmore), of which the overlordship had passed by 1086 to Roger de Ivri.[6] Like the remainder of Ivri's lands Radclive later became part of the Walery Honour, and the overlordship follows the same descent as the

[21] Chan. Inq. p.m. (Ser. 2), cxxii, 12. It is noteworthy that this endowment was held of the chief manor as stated both here and in 1327.

[22] Cur. Reg. R. 160, m. 14.
[1] Statistics from Bd. of Agric. (1905).
[2] Browne Willis, *Hist. and Antiq. of Buckingham,* 257.

[3] Sheahan, *Hist. and Topog. of Bucks.* 300. [4] Priv. Act, 13 Geo. III, cap. 66.
[5] Sheahan, op. cit. 301.
[6] *V.C.H. Bucks.* i, 269.

adjacent manor of Westbury[7] (q.v.). No mention of the overlordship has been found after 1546, in which year the constable of the honour claimed a 'certain' rent of 13s. 4d. here.[8]

In 1086 Fulk was the mesne tenant of Radclive Manor,[9] which, like Westbury, passed later to the Hareng family, though no reference to their holding has been found earlier than c. 1240, when Ralph Hareng held a fee here.[10] As at Westbury, too, a partition took place in the middle of the same century, by which part of Radclive Manor passed to the family of St. Lys and part to that of Newhall. But whereas in Westbury the Newhalls obtained the greater part of the manor, in Radclive the major portion was assigned to the St. Lys. The latter family, too, had acquired their share as early as 1254–5, when Isabel Hareng still held Westbury in widowhood.[11] Simon de St. Lys, who held Radclive at that date, was also lord of the manor in 1278–9.[12] The name of Simon de St. Lys is returned for the aid of 1284–6,[13] and is followed by that of his son Andrew de St. Lys,[13a] lord of the manor in 1302–3.[14] He obtained a grant of free warren in his manor in 1314,[15] and though his name is not found in connexion with this parish after 1316,[16] probably held this manor for some years longer, for one of his name served as member for the county in the Parliaments of 1325, 1326 and 1328.[17] In 1346 Radclive was divided between John de Wolverton, who held two-thirds, and William Cantelow, who held one-third of the fee which had formerly belonged to Andrew de St. Lys.[18] John de Wolverton presented to the church, which was attached to the manor, in 1349,[19] and in 1361 the advowson was in the possession of Thomas Brember.[20] Shortly after this latter date Radclive Manor was purchased by William de Wykeham,[21] consecrated Bishop of Winchester in 1367,[22] who in 1379 bestowed it as part endowment of his foundation of New College.[23] By New College it has since been leased at various times. According to Willis, the manor-house was held by Sir Thomas Denton in the reign of Charles I and passed from him to Sir William Smyth, member for Buckingham in the Parliament of 1661.[24] He was made a baronet as of Radclive in that year,[25] and inclosed a park here, the pales and bounds of which were still kept up in 1755.[26] He conveyed his right in the estate to Captain John Woodfine, who died in 1693, and whose son-in-law, Mr. Lee, an eminent surgeon, held in 1735.[27] Henry Smith of Charwelton (Northants) was the lessee at the beginning of the last century.[28]

With regard to that minor portion of Radclive which, like Westbury Manor (q.v.), passed to Joan de Somery, it is described in 1278–9 as consisting of 3 virgates in demesne, 2 virgates of land, and 3 virgates in villeinage.[29] After the mention of John Strange's tenancy in 1379[30] no further reference has been found.

An early grant of lands in Radclive appears to have been made to Oseney Abbey,[31] which received a rent of 25s. 7d. from this parish at the Dissolution.[32] This may be the origin of the small titular *RADCLIVE CUM CHACKMORE MANOR* which Sir Richard Temple, lord of Stowe Manor (which had also belonged to Oseney), claimed in 1735.[33] He then claimed to hold a court leet in Chackmore field,[34] and subsequent lords of Stowe are found as 'lords of Radclive cum Chackmore' in 1775,[35] 1803[36] and 1819,[37] while the Baroness Kinloss is returned as a landowner in this parish at the present day.

Mention is made in Domesday of a water-mill worth 5s. belonging to the manor.[38] It was afterwards called West Mill, and as such bestowed by Ralph Hareng in 1243 on St. Michael's chapel.[39] It is occasionally named in later extents, and there is still a water-mill in the village, which is, however, no longer used.

The church of *ST. JOHN THE EVANGELIST* consists of a chancel measuring internally 19 ft. 6 in. by 17 ft. 6 in., nave 33 ft. by 17 ft. 6 in., west tower 9 ft. by 8 ft. 6 in., and a south porch.

The earliest details in the present fabric are the reset jambs of the chancel arch and the south doorway of the nave, both work of c. 1200. The north and east walls of the chancel, which are of limestone rubble, are probably of the same date, but the large coursed masonry of the south wall, approaching almost to ashlar work, shows a subsequent rebuilding, which may be ascribed to the latter part of the first half of the 13th century, the date of the coupled lancets at the north-east and south-west of the chancel. The west tower, the walls of which are of coursed rubble, was added early in the 14th century, when the nave, which is of the same material, was probably rebuilt. Late in the century the two north windows of the nave were reconstructed, a new window being inserted at the same time over the west doorway of the tower. About a hundred years later the south porch was added and the large south-east window of the nave was formed. The church was restored in 1903.

The east window of the chancel is of two cinquefoiled lights with a quatrefoil in a two-centred head. The tracery is of the 15th century, but the jambs and rear-arch with the internal mask-stopped label are made up of 13th-century material re-used. At the sill level, internally and externally, are stringcourses of the earlier date, and above the external head of the window is the head of a 13th-century lancet. At the north-east is a 13th-century coupled lancet window with linked mask-stopped labels, plain internal splays, external glass rebates, and a chamfered semicircular rear-arch. At the east end of the south wall are a modern piscina and sedile designed in the

[7] See mesne descent.
[8] Ct. R. (Gen. Ser.), portf. 212, no. 24.
[9] *V.C.H. Bucks.* loc. cit.
[10] *Testa de Nevill* (Rec. Com.), 244.
[11] *Hund. R.* (Rec. Com.), i, 32.
[12] Ibid. ii, 342.
[13] *Feud. Aids,* i, 79.
[13a] Deeds in the Archives of Magdalen College, Oxford, printed in the Rev. R. Ussher's *History of Westbury,* 116.
[14] *Feud. Aids,* i, 100.
[15] Chart. R. 8 Edw. II, m. 22, no. 57.
[16] *Feud. Aids,* i, 108.

[17] *Ret. of Memb. of Parl.* i, 73, 75, 83, 85. Andrew de St. Lys also founded a chantry in Radclive Church in 1328.
[18] *Feud. Aids,* i, 176.
[19] Willis, op. cit. 258. [20] Ibid.
[21] Ibid. 255 ; Harl. MS. 6952, fol. 22, where he is called lord of the manor in 1364. [22] Stubbs, *Reg. Sacr. Angl.* 223.
[23] *Cal. Pat.* 1377–81, p. 412.
[24] *Ret. of Memb. of Parl.* i, 519.
[25] G.E.C. *Baronetage,* iii, 191.
[26] Willis, op. cit. 257 ; cf. Chan. Proc. (Bridges Div.), bdle. 461, no. 89.

[27] Willis, loc. cit.
[28] Lysons, *Mag. Brit.* i (3), 625.
[29] *Hund. R.* (Rec. Com.), ii, 343.
[30] *Cal. Close,* 1377–81, p. 265.
[31] *Cal. Chart. R.* 1257–1300, p. 69.
[32] *Valor Eccl.* (Rec. Com.), iv, 240.
[33] Willis, op. cit. 256.
[34] Ibid.
[35] Recov. R. Hil. 15 Geo. III, m. 353.
[36] Feet of F. Bucks. Hil. 42 Geo. III.
[37] Recov. R. East. 59 Geo. III, m. 269.
[38] *V.C.H. Bucks.* i, 269.
[39] Linc. Epis. Reg. R. Grosteste.

style of the 14th century. To the west of these is a 13th-century doorway, and at the west end of the wall is a coupled lancet of the same date as that in the north wall, with moulded corbels at the springing of the rear-arch. The chancel arch has reset jambs of c. 1200, but the arch itself, which is pointed, and of two chamfered orders, is evidently a reconstruction of the 15th century. The outer order of the jambs is shafted towards the west, the shafts being overlapped by panelled cheveron moulding. The capital of the northern shaft has leaf enrichment and the vertical face of the abacus is ornamented with circular flowers ; the lower member of the abacus appears to have been cut to an ogee form when the arch was reconstructed. The capital of the southern shaft has vigorous voluted stiff-leaf foliage, and the abacus, which retains its original contour, is enriched with the star ornament. The abaci are continued without enrichment round the two orders of the jambs and back to the side walls of the chancel, but on the west side the abacus is stopped about 9 in. from the present north wall, while on the south side it is cut off to clear a late 15th-century niche with a moulded and cambered head. Above the arch on the same face is a cheveron-moulded voussoir from the original arch, set with other worked stones, doubtless to support a rood-beam. Above these, immediately under the tie-beam of the easternmost truss of the nave roof, are set five more cheveron-moulded voussoirs.

At the east end of the north wall of the nave is a built-up doorway, now flat-headed, but the springing of a two-centred arch can be traced. To the west of this is a late 14th-century window of two trefoiled ogee lights with a quatrefoil in a two-centred head, and at the west end of the wall is a square-headed window of two similar lights, and of about the same date. The heads of both windows are formed of single stones and do not fit the mullions very well. At the south-east is a late 15th-century window of three trefoiled lights with a flat segmental external head and a cambered wood lintel for rear-arch. The south doorway is contemporary with the jambs of the chancel arch and, like it, has been reset. The head is two-centred and of three orders, the two inner orders being moulded with stopped chamfers and the outer with leaf-enriched cheveron moulding, the whole being inclosed by a label with dog-tooth ornament. The two outer orders of the jambs have ringed nook-shafts with stiff-leaved capitals of early type, and the angles of the outermost order have chamfers with dog-tooth ornament at wide intervals. The bases of the shafts are much decayed, but appear to have been of the water-table type. The inner order has angle rolls with a band of water-leaf ornament forming their capitals, and the rear-arch is of the segmental two-centred form. A blocked window, placed high up and probably inserted to light a gallery, can be traced externally at the west end of the wall.

The west tower, a remarkably fine piece of work, is of three slightly receding stages with diagonal buttresses at the western angles, a well-designed south-east vice-turret rising only to the intermediate stage, and an embattled parapet. The walls rise from a boldly moulded plinth, which is continued round the north and south walls of the nave. The tower arch is of three chamfered orders, the outer segmental and continued down the meeting angles of the nave and tower walls, while the inner orders die into the jambs. The west

doorway of the ground stage has a two-centred head of two orders with continuously moulded jambs, and immediately above it is an inserted late 14th-century window of two trefoiled ogee lights with a quatrefoil in a two-centred head. The intermediate stage is lighted from the north and south by small lights with two-centred heads, and the bell-chamber by a larger light of the same character in each face.

The late 15th-century south porch appears to have been originally of timber, but the sides have been encased with masonry and plaster, and portions only of the moulded timbers of the entrance remain.

The chancel roof is of high pitch and is concealed internally by a plastered barrel ceiling. The nave roof has low-pitched king-post trusses with curved tie-beams. They are probably of late 15th-century date, but the wall brackets and corbels are of the Elizabethan period. The altar-table is faced with an elaborately worked early 17th-century chest front. The altar rails are of the same period and have flat pierced balusters, and the moulded stone sanctuary step also belongs to this period. The font is contemporary with the earliest detail in the church ; it is of tub shape with a simply moulded base and stands on a square plinth. Above the head of the opening of the west doorway, immediately under the rear-arch, is a 12th-century sculptured stone, perhaps representing the Agnus Dei. In the north-east window of the nave are some remains of late 14th-century glass ; in the east light is a portion of a bearded figure inclosed by a gabled and crocketed canopy, and in the west light are fragments of the figures of the Virgin and Child with a similar canopy, while in the quatrefoil in the head is a rose with red and green petals. Some black and white pattern quarries of the same date remain in the pierced spandrels of the north-west window. The sounding-board of the modern pulpit is of the 17th century, and in the porch are two 15th-century benches with poppy-head finials brought from elsewhere. In the tower is preserved a very fine Queen Anne brass-bound mahogany chest with two drawers in the lower part.

In the sanctuary floor are slabs to John Norborne, a former rector (d. 1726), and his wife Sarah (d. 1720), and to Mary, daughter of John Norman of Woodford, Essex, who died, so far as can be deciphered, in 1717. There is also a slab to 'C. H.' (d. 1753). On the wall at the north-east of the nave is a tablet commemorating Ann, the wife of Hartley Sandwell and youngest daughter of John Woodfine, 'late of this place' (d. 1729), and her husband (d. 1756).

There is a ring of three bells, the treble uninscribed, but probably of the 17th century, the second inscribed in black letter 'Sancte George Ora KV,'[40] and the third inscribed 'Bartholomewe Attun 1594.'

The plate consists of a silver cup and cover paten of 1603 ; a paten of 1716 ; a plated flagon, and a pewter flagon.

The registers begin in 1594.

ADVOWSON The advowson of Radclive has descended with the manor and is held by New College, Oxford.[41]

[40] Considered by Mr. Cocks to be by a Reading founder of the 16th century (*Church Bells of Bucks.* 554). William Young in 1537 left money for the bells, the high altar, those of St. Mary and St. Katherine and for building the churchyard cross (P.C.C. 10 and 12 Crumwell).
[41] *L. and P. Hen. VIII*, xii (1), 606–7 ; xvii, 791 ; Inst. Bks. (P.R.O.).

RADCLIVE CHURCH: THE INTERIOR LOOKING EAST

RADCLIVE CHURCH FROM THE SOUTH-WEST

In 1279 the endowment of the church included 1 virgate of land,[42] and in 1291 the living was assessed at £5 6s. 8d.[43] At the Dissolution the rectory was worth £9 6s. 8d.[44]

The chapel of St. Michael, situated in the church-yard at Radclive, was in existence before 1243, in which year Ralph Hareng alienated lands to the chaplain daily celebrating there for the souls of him-self and wife Alice, his father and mother Ralph and Isabel and his brother Jordan.[45] 'Dominus' Bartholomew de Capella held in Radclive cum Chackmore in 1254-5,[46] while in 1278-9 Robert 'Capellanus' held 1½ virgates of land in the parish belonging to his chapel.[47] References to St. Michael's Chapel occur in the Lincoln Episcopal Registers in 1276,[48] 1297[49] and 1328.[50] In the latter year Andrew de St. Lys received licence to alienate in mortmain lands and rents here and in Westbury to provide a chaplain to celebrate divine service daily in the chapel of St. Mary, Radclive.[51] William de Wykeham presented to the chantry of the chapel of St. Michael the Archangel in 1364.[52]

When Radclive was inclosed in 1773 the tithes of Radclive were commuted for a rent-charge and those of Chackmore for land.[53]

CHARITIES The Poor's Plot, awarded in 1776 for the benefit of the poor on the inclosure of the parish, consists of 4 a. 3 r. 7 p., which is let in allotments producing £4 10s., the net rents being distributed in coal.

The charities founded by will of the Rev. John Croker, proved at London 4 March 1864: (a) for the distribution of coal, trust fund £104 18s. 4d. consols, and (b) for the benefit of the daily school, trust fund £104 18s. 4d. consols. The sums of stock are held by the official trustees, producing in each case £2 12s. 4d., which is duly applied.

SHALSTONE

Celdestane, Celdestone (xi cent.); Scheldestone, Shaldeston (xiii, xiv cent.); Saldistone (xiv cent.); Shalleston (xvi, xvii cent.).

This parish covers 1,382 acres, of which 355 are arable, 897 permanent grass and 71 acres woodland.[1] The soil is clay and the subsoil clay and limestone. The slope of the ground falls from 442 ft. above the ordnance datum in the north to 319 ft. in the south, where the land is liable to floods from a tributary of the Ouse.

The village stands some little distance off the Buckingham and Banbury road. It is small and irregular, and contains some 17th-century farm-houses built of stone with tiled roofs. The church is situated at the south-east, with the rectory, a good building of stone with a tiled roof, on the north side of the churchyard. It is thus described in 1639, 'The Parsonage, built Part Stone Part Timber and Thatcht, hath a Hall, Parlour, two Butteries, five Chambers boarded, Kitchen and Dairy, and little Room adjoining; a Barn of seven small Bays, a Stable, a Cow House, Hogstye, a Garden and two Orchards and a Close adjoining of an Acre.'[2] The school, which was built in 1852 by Mrs. Fitz Gerald, then lady of the manor, is a white brick building with Bath stone dressings. A spring in the centre of the village serves as a drinking fountain, and was covered in with stone in 1851.[3]

Shalstone House, the residence of the lord of the manor, Rear-Admiral Richard Purefoy Purefoy, M.V.O., R.N., is approached from the south end of the village by an avenue of trees. The house was originally built in the 17th century, probably by George Purefoy, who died in 1661, but was altered and enlarged in the 18th century and later. It is a plastered stone building of two stories with attics. There is an original 17th-century oak staircase, and in a turret is a bell bearing the inscription 'G. Purefoy of Wadley armiger me placet 1656.' The house stands in extensive pleasure grounds running south to the main road. Shalstone was inclosed in 1768 under an Act of Parliament of 1767, when 500 acres of land were found to be commonable.[4]

MANOR There were two holders of land in Shalstone at Domesday, the Bishop of Bayeux, who held a manor of 5 hides,[5] and Robert Doyley, who held one of 4 hides.[6] Both these holdings became subsequently merged in one SHALSTONE MANOR, which was held by knight service of the honour of Wallingford.[7] In 1284-6 Edmund de Salenewe appears as intermediary lord,[8] and in 1330 his descendant John (here called de Aula) conveyed the knight's fee in Shalstone to Ewald Strange and Alice his wife.[9] In 1628 the manor was said to be held of the heirs of William Cauntelow.[10]

Previous to 1086 two thegns called Godric and Wila had held the Bishop of Bayeux's manor, while Azor son of Toti held that of Robert Doyley.[11] At the Survey the bishop himself held Shalstone in demesne, while Robert Doyley's tenant was called Robert.[12] By the beginning of the 13th century both manor and advowson (which throughout follow the same descent) had been acquired by a family called Bainel, of whom William Bainel presented to the church of Shalstone in 1230,[13] and about the same date was said to hold by knight service here.[14] This William Bainel appears to have been succeeded by

[42] Hund. R. (Rec. Com.), ii, 343.
[43] Pope Nich. Tax. (Rec. Com.), 32b.
[44] Valor Eccl. (Rec. Com.), iv, 240.
[45] Linc. Epis. Reg. R. Grosteste.
[46] Hund. R. (Rec. Com.), i, 32.
[47] Ibid. ii, 343.
[48] V.C.H. Bucks. i, 287.
[49] Linc. Epis. Reg. Inst. Sutton, fol. 121 d.
[50] Ibid. Burghersh, fol. 338.
[51] Cal. Pat. 1327-30, p. 266.
[52] Harl. MS. 6952, fol. 22.
[53] Priv. Act, 13 Geo. III, cap. 66.

[1] Statistics from Bd. of Agric. (1905).
[2] Browne Willis, Hist. and Antiq. of Buckingham, 265.
[3] Sheahan, Hist. and Topog. of Bucks. 301.   [4] Blue Bk. Incl. awards, 13.
[5] V.C.H. Bucks. i, 237.
[6] Ibid. 258.
[7] Testa de Nevill (Rec. Com.), 243b.
[8] Feud. Aids, i, 79.
[9] Feet of F. case 19, file 78, no. 9. Ewald was overlord of Stratton Audley, which was also held of this honour.
[10] Chan. Inq. p.m. (Ser. 2), ccccxlv, 54.

It would seem as though Philip la Zouche, who had a lawsuit with the lord of the manor in 1324, in some way represented the overlordship, for the Zouches were certainly the heirs of William Cauntelow (see V.C.H. Beds. iii, 370, where the pedigree of the Zouches is given).
[11] V.C.H. Bucks. i, 237, 258.
[12] Ibid.
[13] R. of Hugh of Wells (Cant. and York Soc.), ii, 79.
[14] Testa de Nevill, loc. cit. The name is here given as Beauvel.

one of the same name, whose widow Alice held a fourth part of the manor in dower in 1280,[15] and whose son and heir Nicholas Bainel [16] at that time made a transfer to William de Aete and Juliana his wife.[17] In 1284–6 William de Aete is returned in the feudal assessment for Shalstone.[18] He was succeeded by John de Aete, presumably his son, who in 1296–7 brought an action for unjust disseisin against Nicholas Bainel.[19] He won his case as heir to Juliana Aete, in whose favour, according to evidence brought forward, the transfer of 1280 was made.[20] John de Aete was succeeded by Laurence de Aete, who was dispossessed, possibly during his minority, by Philip la Zouche, whose name appears as representing Shalstone in 1302 and again in 1316.[21] In or about the year 1313 Laurence de Aete brought an action against Philip la Zouche, William Tuchet, Nicholas le Hundreder, Robert de Dunton, parson of Shalstone, Philip his son and many others for illegal disseisin, and was awarded the manor and 100 marks damages.[22] In 1317 he complained against persons unnamed (but who may be identified with the above) for carrying away his goods by force at Shalstone.[23] In 1324 Laurence appears to have secured his right in the manor,[24] and is found, together with Mariana his wife, making a settlement by fine.[25] In the same year he borrowed from Christina, Elizabeth and Eleanor, daughters of Giles de Lisle, the sum of £200, the non-payment of which was in 1330 the subject of a special inquisition into the value of Shalstone Manor.[26] Laurence de Aete is mentioned in 1335 as patron of the living [27] and in 1346 as holder of a knight's fee here.[28] The next member of this family of whom documentary evidence has been found is Alan Aete,[29] who acted as justice of the peace for the county between 1381 and 1385,[30] while in 1391 'Alan Eyete of Shaldeston' is named as one of the parties concerned in a settlement of the manor of Hanworth in Middlesex.[31] Alan Aete was dead by 1418,[32] in which year William Purefoy, who had married his daughter and heir Marian,[33] presented to the church, the record stating that Alan Aete had presented the last parson in virtue of his lordship of Shalstone.[34] Shalstone Manor passed to the Purefoys, with whom it remained in the direct descent for more than 300 years. William Purefoy died in 1466, leaving a son Philip,[35] who died in 1468,[36] and by

his will, dated 26 March 1468 and proved 18 June 1470, he directed that after suitable provision had been made for his widow Isabel the residue of his estate (not specified) was to go to his son John with remainder settlements on his sons Nicoll and William and his daughter Alice.[37] Isabel widow of Philip Purefoy married again before 1475, in which year, together with her second husband John Denton,[38] she presented to the parish church.[39] She was still alive in 1497,[40] but in 1517 Nicholas Purefoy, who may be taken to be the 'Nicoll' of Philip Purefoy's will, was in possession of Shalstone.[41] Nicholas Purefoy, who was married three times, had a numerous family, of whom Edward, his eldest son by his first wife Alice, daughter of Thomas Denton,[42] succeeded to Shalstone Manor on the death of his father in 1547.[43] Edward Purefoy died and was buried at Shalstone in 1558.[44] John Purefoy, his eldest son and heir, next held Shalstone for twenty years.[45] His death took place in 1579, and by his will, bearing date 4 May 1579 and proved 25 May in the same year, after making suitable provision for his widow Ann, he made his brothers William and Richard his residuary legatees.[46] Shalstone Manor then became the property of William Purefoy, who in the following year, 1580, on the occasion of the marriage of his son Edward Purefoy to Joyce Purefoy, eldest daughter of George Purefoy of Drayton (co. Leic.),[47] made life settlements on Edward and Joyce and Ann widow of John Purefoy, with remainder to the heirs of Edward and Joyce.[48] William Purefoy died in 1595, his son Edward having predeceased him,[49] and Shalstone Manor passed to George son of Edward Purefoy, a child of eleven.[50] Joyce widow of Edward Purefoy, who had a life interest in the manor, died in 1596.[51] Her son George Purefoy is found making settlements in 1605 [52] (probably on attaining his majority), in 1613,[53] in 1617 [54] and in 1619.[55] He married Mary, youngest daughter and co-heir of Sir Valentine Knightley of Fawsley, and after her death in 1617

PUREFOY. *Sable three pairs of mailed and clasped hands argent.*

---

[15] Feet of F. case 17, file 46, no. 11.
[16] Assize R. 1309, m. 50 d.
[17] Feet of F. case 17, file 46, no. 11.
[18] *Feud. Aids*, i, 79.
[19] Assize R. 1309, m. 50 d.
[20] Ibid. Mention is made of one Cecilia de la More, who has not been identified, as holding the manor in 1250.
[21] *Feud. Aids*, i, 100, 108.
[22] *Abbrev. Plac.* (Rec. Com.), 347.
[23] *Cal. Pat.* 1317–21, p. 93.
[24] *Abbrev. Plac.* loc. cit.
[25] Feet of F. case 19, file 75, no. 20.
[26] Chan. Inq. on Debts, 4 Edw. III (1st nos.), no. 44.
[27] Willis, loc. cit.
[28] *Feud. Aids*, i, 126.
[29] *Cal. Close*, 1377–81, p. 103. Willis calls him son of Lawrence, but he is more likely to have been grandson.
[30] *Cal. Pat.* 1381–5, pp. 86, 142, 248, 356, 500, 587.
[31] Ibid. 1388–92, p. 379.
[32] Willis, who had access to family documents, mentions a deed of 1415 by

which Alan Aete secured a pension of 20 marks out of Shalstone Manor with remainder settlement on his daughter and her heirs (Willis, op. cit. 265).
[33] *Visit. of Warws.* (Harl. Soc.), 255.
[34] Harl. MS. 6952, fol. 57. Willis, however, states that it was Alan Aete who presented in 1418 (Willis, loc. cit.).
[35] Chan. Inq. p.m. 6 Edw. IV, no. 5.
[36] Ibid. 8 Edw. IV, no. 29.
[37] P.C.C. 31 Godyn. He left 6s. 8d. to the church of Shalstone.
[38] *Visit. of Warws.* (Harl. Soc.), 97. She was the daughter of John Brome of Baddesley (co. Warw.).
[39] Willis, loc. cit.
[40] Chan. Inq. p.m. (Ser. 2), xii, 42. This inquisition is on John Denton, who held a messuage and 4 virgates here of Isabel Denton as of her manor of Shalstone.
[41] Leadam, *Dom. of Incl.* 1517 (Royal Hist. Soc.), i, 203. The visitation calls him the son of John, a younger brother of Philip Purefoy (*Visit. of Bucks.* [Harl. Soc.], 200).

[42] *Visit. of Bucks.* loc. cit.
[43] Willis, op. cit. 267, quoting parish registers. [44] Ibid.
[45] *Visit. of Bucks.* loc. cit. Willis does not mention him.
[46] P.C.C. 22 Bakon. Ann Purefoy, who was his second wife (*Visit. of Bucks.* loc. cit.), received among other personal effects sixteen milch cows and their calves, a bull, five hundred of the best sheep, twelve best drawing oxen, six best plough horses, 'a grey ambling nagge which she useth to ride on,' a grey trotting gelding, the great white mare's colt, and a dun trotting 'balde nagge.'
[47] Chan. Inq. p.m. (Ser. 2), ccxlv, 91.
[48] Feet of F. Div. Co. Mich. 22 & 23 Eliz.
[49] Chan. Inq. p.m. (Ser. 2), ccxlv, 91.
[50] Ibid.
[51] Ibid. ccxlviii, 19.
[52] Feet of F. Div. Co. Mich. 3 Jas. I.
[53] Ibid. Hil. 10 Jas. I.
[54] Ibid. Trin. 15 Jas. I.
[55] Ibid. East. 17 Jas. I.

took a second wife Dorothy, sister of Lord Denny and widow of William Purefoy or Purvey of Wormley (Herts.).[56] George Purefoy died in 1628 and was succeeded by his son, also George Purefoy,[57] who according to Willis removed his home to Wadley in Faringdon, but 'often retired from thence thither, and exercised great Hospitality and charity at both his seats.'[58] He made a settlement of the manor with his son George Purefoy in 1650,[59] and on his death in 1661 it passed to his third son, Knightley Purefoy,[60] who held it in that year.[61] Knightley died and was buried here in January 1691–2, as appears from a memorial tablet in the chancel of the parish church.[62] Henry Purefoy, his only son, married Elizabeth daughter of Leonard Fish,[63] whose name appears in a recovery of the manor suffered by his son-in-law in 1694.[64] Henry Purefoy died in 1704,[65] and the manor passed to his son Henry Purefoy, 'a Gentleman possessed of many excellent qualities, and fond of Retirement. He conversed more with Books than men.'[66] He died a bachelor in 1762, and under the conditions of his will Shalstone Manor passed, after the death of his mother Elizabeth Purefoy, to George Huddleston Purefoy Jervoise,[67] his cousin, being great-grandson of Mary sister of Knightley Purefoy.[68] His name is given as lord of the manor in the Inclosure Award of 1768.[69] He was a clerk in holy orders, and at the time of his death in 1805 was rector of Shalstone as well as lord of the manor.[70] His eldest son, George Purefoy Jervoise, inherited the estate,[71] and on his death in 1847 Shalstone Manor passed by will to his niece, the wife of Thomas Fitz Gerald, with remainder to her third son, Richard Purefoy Jervoise Fitz Gerald.[72]

Thomas Fitz Gerald died in 1860, aged eighty-two,[73] and his widow is returned as landowner in this parish in 1873.[74] She was alive in 1886,[75] but predeceased Richard Purefoy Fitz Gerald, her son, who died in 1895, and was succeeded by his son Richard, who assumed the name of Purefoy by royal licence in 1900.[76] Rear-Admiral Richard Purefoy Purefoy, M.V.O., is the present lord of the manor.

Luffield Priory owned a small property in Shalstone

in 1291.[77] The prior is named as a tenant here in 1316.[78] After the Dissolution Luffield property is occasionally stated to extend into this parish.[79] This estate may be possibly represented by Oldwick, formerly extra-parochial,[80] but now included in Shalstone parish. It consists of a single farm in the possession of the lord of Shalstone Manor.

The church of *ST. EDWARD THE CONFESSOR* consists of a chancel with vestry, nave with aisles, western tower and south porch.

The church was rebuilt in 1828, the only old detail remaining being the octagonal piers and responds of the arcade of three bays on the north side of the nave, which are of the 15th century. A restoration was undertaken in 1862, and in 1889 the vestry with organ was added by Mrs. Fitz Gerald as a memorial to Captain Keane Fitz Gerald. The fittings are modern. On the east wall of the north aisle is a brass with a figure and inscription commemorating Dame Susan Kingston (d. 1540), 'a vowess,' daughter of Richard

SHALSTONE CHURCH FROM THE SOUTH-EAST

Fettiplace of East Shefford (Berks.) and widow of John Kingston of Childrey (Berks.). She wears a mantle, veil and wimple, and a ring on her right hand. There are other monuments to the Purefoy and Jervoise families.

There is a ring of five bells, all by G. Mears & Co., and dated 1862. The tenor has an inscription stating that the bells were given by the five sons of Thomas and Eliza Fitz Gerald.

[56] *V.C.H. Northants Fam.* 185.
[57] Chan. Inq. p.m. (Ser. 2), ccccxlv, 54.
[58] Willis, op. cit. 263.
[59] Com. Pleas Recov. R. Mich. 1650, m. 11.
[60] P.C.C. 60 May.
[61] Recov. R. Trin. 13 Chas. II, m. 123.
[62] Lipscomb, *Hist. and Antiq. of Bucks.* iii, 73.
[63] Willis, loc. cit.; Lipscomb, op. cit. iii, 71.
[64] Recov. R. Trin. 6 Will. and Mary, m. 82.
[65] Willis, op. cit. 267, quoting parish registers. By his will dated 16 July and proved 9 August 1704 he made his father-in-law, Leonard Fish of Chancery

Lane, and his cousin Richard Jervoise trustees for his son Henry, then under fifteen. His widow Elizabeth was to have Morgan's Farm in Shalstone (P.C.C. 168 Ash).
[66] Lipscomb, op. cit. iii, 75, quoting mural tablet.
[67] Lysons, *Mag. Brit.* i (3), 628. The legatee was son of Richard Jervoise, son of Thomas, son and heir of Mary Purefoy (*The Ancestor*, iii, 7–8). Remainder was to George's brother Tristram Jervoise with contingent remainder to four other people, all to take the name of Purefoy (P.C.C. 24 St. Eloy).
[68] *The Ancestor*, loc. cit.
[69] Priv. Act, 7 Geo. III, cap. 66.

[70] Lipscomb, op. cit. iii, 73; Lysons, op. cit. i (3), 698.
[71] Lipscomb, op. cit. iii, 71. He appears in a settlement of 1791 (Recov. R. East. 31 Geo. III, m. 132).
[72] Sheahan, op. cit. 302. See under charities, below.
[73] Sheahan, loc. cit.
[74] *Ret. of Owners of Land*, 1873, *Bucks.* 8.
[75] Burke, *Landed Gentry* (ed. 7).
[76] Walford, *County Families* (1913), 977.
[77] Pope Nich. Tax. (Rec. Com.), 47.
[78] Feud. Aids, i, 108.
[79] Recov. R. Trin. 13 Will. III, m. 208; Feet of F. Bucks. Trin. 13 Will. III.
[80] Luffield was formerly extra-parochial.

The plate includes a cup of 1571.

The registers begin in 1538.

ADVOWSON The advowson of the parish church has always followed the same descent as the manor, the first mention being found of it in 1230.[81] In 1291 Shalstone is entered at £5 6s. 8d.,[82] and at the Dissolution the rectory was valued at £9.[83] At the dissolution of the chantries an obit was endowed with lands and a tenement in Shalstone.[84] By the Inclosure Award of 1767 the rector received an allotment in lieu of all tithes save those paid by Richard Taylor, whose lands were to continue tithable.[85]

CHARITIES The Jervoise Coal Charity, founded by will of Mary Purefoy Jervoise, proved 18 February 1842, and by will of George Purefoy Jervoise, proved 25 January 1848, is endowed with a sum of £800 consols with the official trustees, the annual dividends of which, amounting to £20, are applicable in the distribution at Christmas in bread, fuel, or money. The distribution is usually made in coal.

STEEPLE CLAYDON

Claindon (xi cent.) ; Stepul Claydone (xiii cent.).

This parish is bounded on the north by the Claydon Brook, and covers 3,329 acres, of which 2,610 are permanent grass, 217 arable, and 64 acres woods and plantations.[1] The land rises from 265 ft. above the ordnance datum at Hog Bridge at the

of Major Wilfred Woodcock. In the house which formerly stood on the site Cromwell slept on the night of 3 March 1644 before advancing to attack Hillesden House. The earthworks from which the house takes its name were probably thrown up at this time to protect the Parliamentary forces.

THE VILLAGE, STEEPLE CLAYDON

The village contains several 17th-century brick and timber houses with thatched roofs and original brick chimneys. The building which contains the public library has been formed by adding to a school-house built by Thomas Chaloner in 1656. The original portion is a rectangular brick building with an old bellcote at the east end. On a stone rebuilt in the gable of the modern porch are the arms of Chaloner and the inscription ' H. SCHOL. FUND. T. C. MDCLVI.' The library comprises a collection of between 3,000 and 4,000 books, to the formation of which Miss Florence Nightingale contributed, and her cheque for £50 hangs on the wall in a stone frame. The

west end of the village to 342 ft. near Claydon Hill Farm in the north-east of the parish. Both soil and subsoil are clay. Crops of wheat and beans are raised, but the land is principally used for grazing. The Great Central railway passes through the south-west of the parish. The Oxford and Bletchley branch of the London and North Western railway crosses its south-east corner and has a station called Claydon.

Half a mile to the north-west of the station is the village of Steeple Claydon, with the church standing in the eastern and higher part. The Manor Farm to the north-east of the church occupies the site of the manor-house of the Chaloners, which was taken down in the early 18th century.[2] West of the church is the Camp, a modern house of brick, the residence

present vicarage was built after the old vicarage was destroyed by fire in 1899.[3] The west end of the village lies in a deep hollow, and the cottages here originally built on the waste belong to a number of small owners, who are gradually replacing them by better houses. There is a Wesleyan chapel in the village. The principal house in the North End is called the Moat. Windmill Hill Farm is in the north-east of the parish. The name of Bull Lane is due to bull-baiting days, and shows the route by which the bulls entered the village. The sport took place as late as 1827 in the Chaloner school yard.[4]

Coins of Carausius and Allectus were found at Steeple Claydon in 1620.[5]

This parish was inclosed in 1795.[6]

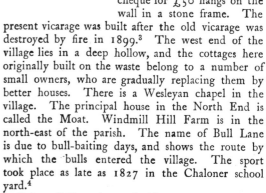

---

81 See manor. See also Inst. Bks. (P.R.O.).

82 *Pope Nich. Tax.* (Rec. Com.), 41.

83 *Valor Eccl.* (Rec. Com.), iv, 239.

84 Chan. Cert. 5, no. 9.

85 Priv. Act, 7 Geo. III, cap. 66.

1 Statistics from Bd. of Agric. (1905).

2 Willis, *Hist. and Antiq. of Buckingham*, 270.

3 *Verney Mem. of 17th Century*, i, 31. It had an oak-panelled parlour with an elaborately ornamented plaster ceiling said

to have been executed in the time of Henry VII.

4 *Verney Mem. of 17th Century*, i, 30.

5 *V.C.H. Bucks.* ii, 10.

6 Priv. Act, 35 Geo. III, cap. 33.

MANORS Steeple Claydon appears to have been always held of the Crown in chief,[7] and was not attached to any particular honour. It later belonged to the group of Crown lands which became queens' dower lands.[8]

STEEPLE CLAYDON MANOR, held at the Conquest by Queen Edith, was assessed in 1086 at 20 hides, and held by Alric the cook.[9] Subsequently it reverted to the Crown, and was given by Henry I about 1120 in marriage with Edith Forne to Robert Doyley the younger.[10] His grandson Henry Doyley (see advowson) granted it to John Fitz Geoffrey[11] about 1230, and his right in it was recognized by the Crown in 1232 after the death of Henry Doyley.[12] Steeple Claydon Manor descended with Whaddon to Richard Earl of Ulster,[13] who was holding in 1302.[14] He alienated it about 1308 to the elder Hugh le Despencer, who soon afterwards granted it to John de Handlo for life.[15] He was holding in 1316,[16] and in 1318 free warren in the manor was granted to Hugh le Despencer, John de Handlo, and the heirs of Hugh.[17] After an inquisition in 1322 John de Handlo was reinstated in Steeple Claydon Manor, which had been besieged and taken by Roger Damory and other opponents of Hugh le Despencer.[18] In 1346 John Mority was holding Steeple Claydon,[19] apparently on lease, during the minority of Lionel Duke of Clarence, who died seised in 1368 in right of his wife Elizabeth[20] Countess of Ulster. This manor must therefore have reverted to the Earls of Ulster and descended with Bierton and Hulcott[21] (q.v.). In 1516 it was leased to John Giffard for sixty-one years, and this lease was inspected and confirmed in 1527.[22] The leasehold rights were granted in 1547 to William Paget,[23] but surrendered by him in the following year to Ralph Giffard and Thomas Damport.[24] Thomas Damport with Richard and George Giffard surrendered rights in this manor to the Crown in 1551,[25] and a fresh lease for forty years was granted to Ralph Giffard in 1554.[26] In 1557 the reversion of the manor was granted in fee to Sir Thomas Chaloner.[27] He died in October 1565, leaving a son and heir Thomas,[27a] afterwards Sir Thomas Chaloner, kt.,[28] who was in possession in 1585.[29] On his second marriage in 1604 he made

a settlement in tail-male on his sons William, Edward, Thomas and James.[30] William Chaloner succeeded in 1615,[31] and became a baronet in 1620.[32] He settled his estates in 1634 on his surviving brothers Thomas and James in trust for his heir Edward Chaloner (son of the second brother Edward), who was still a minor in 1644.[33] Thomas and James Chaloner appear to have renewed the trust of Steeple Claydon Manor to the use of Edward in 1647.[34] At the Restoration, since both had signed the death warrant of

CHALONER. *Sable a cheveron between three cherubs or.*

King Charles, Thomas the survivor was attainted,[35] and died soon afterwards.[36] In 1661[37] Charles II granted Steeple Claydon Manor to Sir Richard Lane, who had helped him to escape after Worcester,[38] but Edward Chaloner bought it from the grantee in 1662,[39] and his son William[40] had succeeded him before 1683.[41] He made a declaration of his title[42] in 1701, and conveyed the manor in 1704 to John Verney, Viscount Fermanagh.[43] It has since descended with Middle Claydon[44] (q.v.), and Sir Harry Calvert Verney, bart., is the present owner.

Richard Fitz John claimed the right of view of frankpledge in 1286.[45] It was included in the lease of 1554, but no later reference to it has been found.[46] Fishing rights appertained to the manor,[47] and were protected under the Inclosure Act of 1795 with express mention of Claydon Great Pond, or Ponds.[48] A note is made in 1254 that Claydon Wood, which had been wasted by Henry Doyley, should be guarded well.[49]

A water-mill in Steeple Claydon is mentioned in the 13th century[50] and again in 1556, together with a windmill.[51] A reference to vineyards on the manor occurs in 1297.[52]

Two and a half hides of land in Steeple Claydon were granted with the church in free alms by Robert Doyley to Oseney Abbey (see advowson). This land became the *RECTORY MANOR*, and was retained

[7] *V.C.H. Bucks.* i, 274; *Testa de Nevill* (Rec. Com.), 260; Chan. Inq. p.m 25 Edw. I, no. 50a; *Feud. Aids,* i, 81, 99, 125; Chan. Inq. p.m. 43 Edw. III, pt. i, no. 23; Pat. 4 & 5 Phil. and Mary, pt. vii, m. 19.

[8] Mins. Accts. Hen. VII, no. 1382; no. 1383–1401; Hen. VIII, no. 158–218.

[9] *V.C.H. Bucks.* loc. cit.

[10] Kennet, *Paroch. Antiq.* i, 119.

[11] Add. MS. 6041, fol. 68b.

[12] *Cal. Close,* 1231–4, p. 164.

[13] *V.C.H. Bucks.* iii, 436–7; *Testa de Nevill* (Rec. Com.), 244; *Hund. R.* (Rec. Com.), i, 28; ii, 352; *Feud. Aids,* i, 81.

[14] *Feud. Aids,* i, 99.

[15] Chan. Inq. p.m. 15 Edw. II, no. 78.

[16] *Feud. Aids,* i, 109.

[17] Chart. R. 11 Edw. II, m. 3, no. 6.

[18] Chan. Inq. p.m. 15 Edw. II, no. 78; *Cal. Close,* 1318–23, p. 464. Roger Damory had interests in this manor which an agreement with the Earl of Ulster and Hugh le Despencer (*Cat. of Anct. D.* i, 44) had apparently failed to adjust.

[19] *Feud. Aids,* i, 125.

[20] Chan. Inq. p.m. 43 Edw. III, pt. i, no. 23.

[21] *V.C.H. Bucks.* ii, 321; *Cal. Pat.* 1381–5, p. 326; Mins. Accts. (Gen. Ser.), bdles. 764, no. 8, 10, 11; 1112, no. 9.

[22] *L. and P. Hen. VIII,* iv, g. 3540 (16).

[23] Pat. 1 Edw. VI, pt. ii, m. 43.

[24] Feet of F. Bucks. Trin. 2 Edw. VI.

[25] Ibid. Hil. 5 Edw. VI.

[26] Pat. 1 & 2 Phil. and Mary, pt. iv, m. 22.

[27] Ibid. 4 & 5 Phil. and Mary, pt. vii, m. 19.

[27a] P.C.C. 47 Bakon. The son Thomas, then a minor, is referred to as 'Thomas, son of Audrey, my wife.'

[28] *Dict. Nat. Biog.*

[29] Recov. R. Mich. 27 Eliz. m. 110.

[30] Chan. Inq. p.m. (Ser. 2), ccclxxv, 73; Feet of F. Div. Co. Trin. 2 Jas. I.

[31] Chan. Inq. p.m. (Ser. 2), ccclxxv, 73.

[32] G.E.C. *Baronetage,* i, 154.

[33] *Lords' Journ.* vii, 113. A conveyance in 1633 was part of the settlement (Feet of F. Div. Co. Trin. 9 Chas. I).

[34] Feet of F. Bucks. Trin. 23 Chas. I.

[35] Exch. Dep. Spec. Com. 13 Chas. II, no. 6149.

[36] *Dict. Nat. Biog.*

[37] *Cal. S. P. Dom.* 1660–1, p. 497.

[38] *Verney Mem. of 17th Century,* i, 30.

[39] Recov. R. East. 14 Chas. II, m. 173.

[40] Lipscomb, *Hist. and Antiq. of Bucks.* ii, 80.

[41] Recov. R. Mich. 35 Chas. II, m. 268; Feet of F. Bucks. Hil. 35 & 36 Chas. II.

[42] Marcham, *Cat. of Bucks. Deeds,* i, 10.

[43] Feet of F. Bucks. Mich. 3 Anne.

[44] See also Priv. Act, 35 Geo. III, cap. 23.

[45] *Plac. de Quo Warr.* (Rec. Com.), 94.

[46] Pat. 1 & 2 Phil. and Mary, pt. iv, m. 22.

[47] Rentals and Surv. (Gen. Ser.), portf. 24, no. 10; Ld. Rev. Misc. Bks. clxxxviii, fol. 42.

[48] Priv. Act, 35 Geo. III, cap. 33.

[49] *Hund. R.* (Rec. Com.), i, 28.

[50] Add. MS. 6041, fol. 68b, no. 4, 5; *Hund. R.* (Rec. Com.), ii, 352.

[51] Ld. Rev. Misc. Bks. clxxxviii, fol. 42.

[52] Chan. Inq. p.m. 25 Edw. I, no. 50a.

by the abbey[53] until its surrender in 1539.[54] Between 1542 and 1589 it was included in the same grants as Abbot's Manor, Princes Risborough.[55] Leasehold rights were obtained by Sir Thomas Chaloner, who by his will dated 13 October 1565 left his 'lease of Rectory and Buisshopps mannor of Steple Claydon' to his son Thomas.[55a] The latter had acquired the freehold before 1604, when he settled the rectory manor in jointure on his second wife Judith Gregory.[56] He afterwards left it by will to their eldest son Henry, and in tail-male to their other sons.[57] Henry Chaloner was fined heavily in 1647 in composition for the sequestration of his property by Parliament.[58] In that year the Rectory Manor was included in

STEEPLE CLAYDON CHURCH FROM THE SOUTH-WEST

the trust to Thomas and James Chaloner.[59] On the attainder of Thomas Chaloner the king in 1660 granted his rights in it to Sir Richard Lane,[60] who shortly afterwards was also grantee of the principal manor, with which the Rectory Manor afterwards descended. Its identity as a manor had lapsed in 1795.[61]

CHURCH The church of ST. MICHAEL consists of a chancel, north vestry, nave, north and south transepts, north aisle, south porch, and west tower ; the transepts are of brick, while the other parts are built of stone rubble, and the roofs are tiled.

The chancel dates from about 1380, but the nave has no detail earlier than the 15th century, when it was widened towards the south ; all the other parts of the building are modern.

In the east wall of the chancel is a three-light traceried window of about 1380, and built into the gable above is the head of a 15th-century cinquefoiled light. In the south wall are two 14th-century windows, each of two trefoiled lights with tracery under a pointed head ; there is a similar window at the east end of the north wall, and at the west end is a single light, mostly modern, opening into the vestry. The sill of the south-east window is carried down to form a sedile, and near it is a pointed piscina with a modern bowl ; the doorway between the south windows was probably inserted in 1631, the date roughly cut on the head. There is a plain locker with rebated edges in the north wall, and at the south-west is a blocked squint from the nave. The lower part of an old window has been re-used in the vestry.

The nave has been considerably modernized and has a modern north arcade. On the south are two square-headed windows of two lights, dating from the 15th century, and a pointed doorway which is probably of the same period. The clearstory windows on the south are late square openings with modern wood frames, and those on the north are entirely modern.

The octagonal font dates from the 15th century and has a 17th-century carved oak cover. The pulpit is made up of early 17th-century panelling reconstructed at a modern period, and incorporated in the nave seating are several 15th-century bench-ends and moulded rails. There are some 18th-century monuments to the Webb family.

The tower contains a ring of five bells : the treble is by Edward Hall, 1737 ; the second is inscribed, 'Phillip Teler gave me, 1620' ; the third is by Bartholomew Atton, 1592 ; the fourth is inscribed, 'Hall made me, 1754,' and is probably by William Hall ; and the tenor is by Taylor & Sons of Oxford, 1828.

The communion plate includes a cup and cover paten of 1569, a stand paten of 1706, and a cup of 1806.

[53] *Hund. R.* (Rec. Com.), i, 28 ; ii, 353 ; *Feud. Aids,* i, 109 ; Leadam, *Dom. Incl.* 1517 (Royal Hist. Soc.), i, 199 ; *Valor Eccl.* (Rec. Com.), ii, 219.
[54] *V.C.H. Oxon.* ii, 92.
[55] *V.C.H. Bucks.* ii, 264.
[55a] P.C.C. 47 Bakon.

[56] Chan. Inq. p.m. (Ser. 2), ccclxxv, 73 ; Feet of F. Div. Co. Trin. 2 Jas. I.
[57] Chan. Inq. p.m. (Ser. 2), ccclxxv, 73.
[58] *Cal. Com. for Comp.* 67, 1608.
[59] Feet of F. Bucks. Trin. 23 Chas. I ; Pat. 12 Chas. II, pt. xvi, no. 12.

[60] Pat. 12 Chas. II, pt. xvi, no. 12.
[61] Priv. Act, 35 Geo. III, cap. 33. Some Court Rolls are extant (Coxe and Turner, *Cal. Chart. in Bodl.* 369, 378, 381), also a survey taken at the Dissolution (Rentals and Surv. [Gen. Ser.], portf. 23, no. 38).

STOWE : VIEW OF THE HOUSE FROM THE PARTERRE

STOWE : VIEW OF THE HOUSE FROM THE EQUESTRIAN STATUE

The registers begin in 1575.

ADVOWSON   Steeple Claydon Church was granted to Oseney Abbey by Robert Doyley in 1129.[62] His grandson Henry, son of Henry Doyley, confirmed the gift,[63] and both charters were inspected and confirmed in 1320.[64] A vicarage had been ordained prior to 1357.[65] The advowson of the church descended with the rectory manor. The advowson was alienated for a period, when it appears to have passed through several hands from the end of the 16th century until before 1683, when William Chaloner owned both.[66] Since 1704 both advowson[67] and rectory have descended with Middle Claydon (q.v.), and are at present owned by Sir Harry Calvert Verney, bart.

In 1821 the vicarage of Steeple Claydon was united to the vicarage of East Claydon (q.v.), but separated from it in 1872.[68]

In 1548 a lamp was maintained in the church from a parcel of meadow worth 3d. yearly.[69] This land, then in the tenure of Robert Hybbote, was granted with other concealed lands in 1571 to Richard Hill and William James.[70]

CHARITIES   A school was built in 1656 by Thomas Chaloner upon land known as the Lord's Waste. In 1901 the school-house and teacher's residence was sold and the proceeds invested in £272 14s. 6d. consols, the annual dividends of which, amounting to £6 16s. 4d., are, under a scheme of the Board of Education of 16 September 1913, applicable in exhibitions and prizes to children attending public elementary schools.

The Female Sick Poor Society, which is understood to have been founded by the late Mrs. Fremantle, the wife of a former Dean of Ripon, is endowed with a sum of £114 19s. 8d. consols, producing £2 17s. 4d. yearly, which is applied in aid of the Claydon Maternity Society.

The sums of stock above-mentioned are held by the official trustees.

This parish also participates in certain of the charities mentioned in the parish of Middle Claydon.[71]

STOWE

This parish covers 3,045 acres, of which 501 are arable, 2,435 permanent grass, and 87 woods and plantations.[1] The soil is gravel and clay, and the subsoil various. Wheat, barley, beans and oats are the principal crops. The land reaches its highest level of 472 ft. above the ordnance datum in the north of the parish.

The greater part of Stowe is taken up by the grounds and park attached to Stowe House, which is approached from Buckingham by a public avenue of elm and beech nearly 2 miles in length, leading up to the entrance lodge known as the 'Corinthian Arch.' Though subject to many alterations and additions throughout the 18th century, Stowe House has preserved a unity and directness of plan which entitle it to a place among the foremost examples of the 'grand manner' of design in England. The walls of the northern side of the central portion, including the hall with the suites of smaller rooms on either side, and parts of the state drawing room, saloon, and music room, are probably those of the house as rebuilt by Sir Richard Temple in the last half of the 17th century. The house must then have consisted of a rectangular building of brick with stone dressings, having four pavilions at the angles; the offices were probably contained in the basement, above which were two principal floors, a third floor being contained in the roof. There are now no means of judging whether the east and west wings containing the kitchen and chapel were part of this scheme, but more probably they form part of the great alterations and additions which were made to the house and grounds by the first Viscount Cobham between 1697 and 1749, when the plan began to assume its present form. The 'orangeries' at the extreme east and west of the house may also belong to this period.

In the set of engravings published by Rigaud and Baron in 1730, and republished in 1739, are good views of the north and south fronts, showing the first stage of transition. The principal alteration to the north front consisted in the addition of the still existing Ionic portico and flight of steps, the wings being connected with the central block by corridors concealed by blank screen walls, each divided into seven bays by pilasters and having a pedimented niche in each bay. The order was continued round the wings, which were each of two stories, and had hipped roofs crowned by small lanterns. The attic windows of the central portion were masked by a stone balustrade, the pavilions at the angles rising one story above the level of the crowning cornice. Low walls following the lines of the present colonnade screened the wings and offices. The view of the south front shows a central pedimented portico in two stages, perhaps a survival of the late 17th-century façade. The wings and connecting corridors appear as on the north front. For these alterations Kent, who painted the ceiling of the hall and designed many of the temples in the gardens, was probably responsible.

The next stage in the development of the house is well illustrated by an engraving of the two elevations published in 1750.[2] The principal additions shown are the galleries connecting the two wings, and the south-eastern and south-western extensions to the wings, which were now transformed to an L shape. To the period between 1730 and 1750 must also be ascribed the lateral additions to the central block containing the two principal staircases, which do not appear in the Rigaud and Baron engravings. By 1763[3] the south elevation, which had till now remained as in the engravings of 1730, was remodelled, the old portico being replaced by a tetrastyle Ionic

[62] V.C.H. Oxon. ii, 90.
[63] Dugdale, Mon. vi, 252, quoting original charter of which only the fragments are now extant (Cott. MS. Vitell. E xv, fol. 6).
[64] Cal. Chart. R. 1300–26, pp. 417, 420.

[65] Cal. Pat. 1354–8, p. 602.
[66] Recov. R. Bucks. Mich. 35 Chas. II, m. 268.
[67] Inst. Bks. (P.R.O.).
[68] Accts. and Papers (1872), xlvi, no. 7.
[69] Chant. Cert. 5, no. 5.
[70] Pat. 14 Eliz. pt. ii, m. 7.

[71] See under the hundred of Ashendon, above.
[1] Statistics from Bd. of Agric. (1905).
[2] B. Seeley, Description of the House and Gardens at Stowe (Buckingham, 1751).
[3] Plan and elevation engraved in Seeley's Descr. of Stowe (ed. of 1763 and 1769).

portico 'approached by a noble flight of steps designed by Signor Barra.'

The magnificent south façade was completed as it now stands in the years between 1769 and 1775, when, with one or two exceptions, the final stage in the evolution of the plan appears to have been reached.[4] The walls of the central block were carried up to include the attic floor, and the whole of the south side was taken down, the original saloon or 'stucco-gallery' being extended southwards to form the present oval saloon, while the former drawing room and dining room were prolonged on either side to form a recessed loggia behind the hexastyle Corinthian portico, which now replaced Barra's Ionic portico. The galleries and wings were refronted, the latter being partially raised to the height of the central portion of the house and given a Corinthian pilaster order to correspond. Internally the eastern gallery was divided into two to form a new drawing room and dining room, the enlarged rooms on either side of the saloon becoming the state drawing room and music room, while the chapel wing was squared up by the addition of a library and ante-library with a bedchamber and dressing room at the north-east. The Ionic colonnades on the north front must also belong to this period of reconstruction.[4a] About 1801 the partition between the two rooms newly formed in the eastern gallery was removed, and the apartment was fitted up as a library,[5] the former library now receiving the name of the Grenville drawing room. A few years later part of the basement beneath was rearranged as the Gothic library and ante-chamber, approach to which was obtained by a new staircase designed in the same manner on the south side of the east corridor; the corridor itself being considerably widened on the north. 'The Egyptian Hall' in the basement beneath the entrance hall on the north front was probably formed about the same time.[5a]

The design of the south front, one of the finest examples of the later Renaissance in England, is said to have been largely due to Lords Temple and Camelford.[6] The elevation of the projecting central block is in three bays corresponding to the internal divisions, the great hexastyle Corinthian portico and recessed loggia, approached by a flight of twenty-three steps, occupying the middle bay. The rooms on either side are each lighted by three grouped windows under an entablature supported by Ionic columns, the group being contained within a large and shallow arched recess, the head of which, filled by a sculptured medallion, serves to mask the blank wall of the upper floor, which is lighted only from the sides. The entablature of the portico is continued upon the front elevation and round the sides, stopping at the outer angles of the staircase projections; it is crowned by a balustrade and supported by Corinthian pilasters flanking the windows. The basement is rusticated, and is lighted by a single arched opening on either side of the portico steps and by a similar opening in each return. The low elevations of the galleries connecting the wings, which are of one story only above

the rusticated basement, have engaged colonnades of the Ionic order with a plain window in each intercolumniation. Both wings have three triple windows like those on either side of the portico, but the central window of the group is sham in every case; the walls are crowned by entablatures supported by Corinthian pilasters of the same height as those of the central block, and are surmounted by balustrades with central panels flanked by allegorical figures. Upon the panel on the west wing is inscribed: 'Richardus comes Temple F.'; on the east wing: 'Anno Salutis 1775.' The facing is of stone, with the exception of the return walls and the galleries, which are cemented, only the basements and dressings on these faces being of stone. Balustrades of iron with stone pedestals surmounted by copper urns inclose flower-gardens extending the whole length of the principal portion of the house on either side of the portico steps. Low ranges of mean design, containing bedrooms and offices, extend from either end of the main building to the 'orangeries.' The Ionic portico, tetrastyle *in antis*, forms the central feature of the north elevation, which has stone dressings, its original brickwork being coated with cement. A somewhat top-heavy appearance is given to this front by the added third story. The windows are all square-headed with moulded architraves, and beneath the steps of the portico is a sunk *porte-cochère* giving entrance to the 'Egyptian Hall.' The wings are screened by the quarter-circular Ionic colonnades which sweep out from either end of the principal block and join the pilastered walls of the office-courts.

The north doorway beneath the portico opens directly into the hall, a rectangular room with a coved and flat painted ceiling representing King William III, as Mars, presenting a sword to the first Lord Cobham. A stone staircase on the east side leads down to the 'Egyptian Hall.' Over a shallow arched recess in the west wall, originally occupied by a fireplace, is a bas-relief of Caractacus before the throne of Claudius, and on the east wall is another, the subject of which is the tent of Darius. At the southern ends of these walls are doorways opening to lobbies communicating with the two principal staircases. The eastern staircase is of stone with wrought-iron balusters, and the ceiling and walls are painted. A doorway in the south wall of the hall, immediately opposite the entrance, leads into the splendid domed saloon or 'marble hall.' The plan is an ellipse 60 ft. by 43 ft., and light is obtained from the glazed eye of the dome. A colonnade of sixteen Doric columns of scagliola in imitation of Sicilian jasper surrounds the walls, and above the entablature, round the drum of the richly coffered dome, is a frieze in bas-relief representing a triumphal procession and sacrifice, the work of Signor Valdré, who modelled the figures from ancient examples. At the four cardinal points are doorways, the other intercolumniations being occupied by semicircular-headed niches, while above the niches and doorways, close under the entablature, are rectangular panels with military trophies modelled in bas-relief. The floor is laid with Carrara marble in squares of 4 ft.

---

[4] Plan and elevations engraved in Seeley's *Descr. of Stowe* (1777), and date inscribed on east wing.

[4a] The chapel wing does not appear to have been finally completed till a few years later. It is shown for the first time in its present form in the plan published in the 1788 edition of Seeley's *Descr. of Stowe*. The colonnades on the north front are not shown before 1777.

[5] Brayley and Britton, *Beauties of Engl. and Wales*, i, 286 et seq. 'The Library, which is nearly finished, occupies the space that was recently the Drawing and Dining Rooms.'

[5a] No description of these rooms appears in Seeley's *Descr. of Stowe* before the 1817 edition.

[6] *Rec. of Bucks.* v, 353; Brayley and Britton, loc. cit.

STOWE HOUSE: THE SOUTH FAÇADE

STOWE HOUSE: THE NORTH FAÇADE

The doorways of all the rooms on either side are placed in an axial line with the east and west doorways of the saloon, so that the whole length of the house can be commanded at one view. The south doorway opens into the loggia beneath the great south portico; above the doorway externally is a frieze representing a sacrifice to Bacchus, and on the sides of the loggia are bas-reliefs of Hercules and Antaeus and Hercules and Cacus, while at the foot of the twenty-three steps ascending to the portico is a pair of lions, modelled from those at the Villa Medici. The west doorway leads directly into the state drawing room, now called simply the drawing room, the decoration of which is contemporary with the saloon. The doorcases and fittings are all of the best type of late 18th-century design, the fireplace being of white marble with panels of porphyry. At the northern end of the room is a semicircular recess with engaged Corinthian columns supporting an entablature with an enriched frieze and cornice, which is continued round the walls of the room. The ceiling has a plain cove and is decorated in the Adam manner. The music room, which opens out of the opposite side of the saloon, corresponds in arrangement with the drawing room, but the decorations, by Valdré, are more elaborate. The Corinthian columns of the recess at the northern end are of scagliola, in imitation of Sienna marble, and have gilded capitals and bases, while the walls are painted after the style of Raphael's Loggia. The ceiling has panels with classical subjects, and the chimneypiece is of white marble with Rosso Antico panels and ormolu ornaments. The 'Egyptian Hall' beneath the entrance hall is a pretty piece of early 19th-century archaeology, the design being founded upon the remains of one of the small temples of Tintyra.

Adjoining the drawing room on the west is the state gallery, now the dining room, a fine apartment measuring 70 ft. 6 in. by 25 ft. It remains as described in the 1763 edition of Seeley's Guide; on the south side is a range of seven windows, while on the north side are two chimneypieces of white and Sienna marble, and above them are carved wood overmantels in the early 18th-century manner, painted in white and gold. These still retain the bas-reliefs in wood described in the Guide as 'a goddess conducting Learning to Truth' and 'Mercury conducting Tragic and Comic Poetry to the hill of Parnassus.' The doorways, which are placed at the northern ends of the east and west walls, have carved architraves and broken pediments supported by consoles, and each is matched by a sham doorway at the opposite end of the wall. The five pieces of tapestry with which the room is hung were made at Brussels for Lord Cobham, and represent the triumphs of Ceres, Bacchus, Venus, Mars, and Diana. A richly ornamented entablature runs round the walls, above which is the elaborately gilded and painted ceiling containing panels with 'emblematical paintings in clare-obscure.' The doorway on the west opens into the small dining room, formerly the state dressing room; the principal feature here is the white marble chimneypiece, above which is a remarkably fine carved wood overmantel framing a portrait of Lord Cobham. The work is of the same date as the state gallery. The tapestries on the walls illustrating Marlborough's campaign in Flanders

were hung in 1763 in the old saloon, or stucco gallery.[7] The last of the suite of rooms on this side of the house, now called the Duchess's drawing room, was originally the state bedchamber. The decorations were designed by Barra, who also designed the state bed now in the state bedchamber at the opposite end of the house. The plan of the room may be described as cruciform, the four corners being filled by small closets. The ceiling of the central portion of the room is ornamented with the star and collar of the order of the Garter and is supported by four engaged Corinthian columns. The lacquered panels and fittings in the Chinese closet at the south-west angle were presented to Lord Cobham in 1747 by Frederick Prince of Wales; they were first placed in a corresponding closet in the east wing, but were removed here when the south front was altered. On the north side of the two dining rooms is a service corridor terminating on the west in a circular staircase belonging to the late 18th-century period of reconstruction.

Returning to the east side of the house, the first room beyond the music room is the library, an excellent example of the restrained and simple style of the early 19th century. The Gothic library in the basement beneath is charmingly designed in the best 'Fonthill' manner. The three rooms on the south front of the east wing are all of the late 18th century, and, though good examples of the period, present no outstanding features of interest. They are now known as the blue drawing room, the green drawing room, and the state bedchamber. The last-named room was used by Queen Victoria when she visited Stowe in 1845.

The chapel on the north side of the wing measures 37 ft. by 20 ft. 10 in., and is lighted by two semi-circular-headed windows in the west wall, a third light being now blocked, and one high up in the north wall. The floor is at the basement level, but the principal seats are placed in a gallery at the south end entered from the service corridor on the principal floor. The walls are lined with cedar panelling in two stages, with Corinthian pilasters and entablatures and applied limewood carvings of fruit, foliage, and flowers, in the Grinling Gibbons manner. The entablature of the lower stage is continued across the front of the gallery, which is supported by Corinthian columns. Above the altar, partly blocking the north window, is a large panel carved with the royal arms as borne by the Stuarts. The communion rails have twisted balusters, and the pulpit bears the date 1707. The panelling was bought by Lord Cobham in 1720 at the sale of Stow, near Kilkhampton in Cornwall, the seat of the Earl of Bath, and the wood is said to have been taken out of a Spanish prize which was brought into Padstow.

Of the celebrated gardens which constitute a small park of 400 acres, a brief description of the more noteworthy features must suffice. They were first laid out by Bridgeman in 1713 under instructions from Richard Viscount Cobham, and beyond the softening down of some of the formality of the original scheme have been little altered since his day. Lancelot Brown, better known as 'Capability Brown,' came into Lord Cobham's service in 1737 and remained

---

[7] These were worked by a subscription of Lord Cobham and other officers serving under the Duke of Marlborough. Similar sets were worked for the Duke of Marlborough at Blenheim, Lord Cadogan at Caversham, Duke of Argyll at Inverary, Lord Orkney at Cliveden, Gen. Lumley at Stanstead, and for Gen. Webb (Seeley's *Descr. of Stowe* [1797]).

till 1750, but it does not appear that he added to the lay-out of the grounds.[8] The principal entrance on the Buckingham side is the lodge known as the Corinthian arch, an uninspired composition said to be due to Lord Camelford, and consisting of a central archway flanked on the south side by Corinthian pilasters, and on the side towards the house by half columns of the same order. The two pavilions on either side of the drive, a little to the north of the Corinthian arch, were originally designed by Kent, but were altered by Barra. The pavilions at the Boycott entrance, though altered by the same hand, remain as good examples of Vanbrugh's ponderous style. The Temple of Bacchus, a rusticated rectangular building coated with stucco, and the domed Rotunda with its circle of Ionic columns, show him in a somewhat lighter mood. Of Kent's designs, the best is the Temple of Concord, an adaptation of the *Maison Carrée* in terms of Ionic. The Temple of Venus, which overlooks the large lake from the head of a glade at the south-west angle of the gardens, is another pleasing composition. About 1790 a portico was added to Kent's building, then known as the Queen's Temple and dedicated to Queen Charlotte in commemoration of the king's recovery. Lord Cobham's pillar was the work of Gibbs, but the pedestal and lions were added by Valdré in the latter half of the 18th century. The Bourbon Tower commemorates the visit of Louis XVIII and the princes of the house of Bourbon who visited Stowe in 1808.[9]

In 1712 Stowe village consisted of thirty-two houses and a population of 180,[10] but owing to the encroachments of the owners of Stowe Park it has practically disappeared, the parish church standing within the park grounds. The greater number of the inhabitants are now to be found at Dadford, formerly Dodford, a prosperous hamlet of some size in the west of the parish. In Dadford are the vicarage and the schools and a few thatched cottages, one or two of which are of the 17th century.

Boycott, which until 1844[11] was in Oxfordshire, is another hamlet in the south-west of Stowe. Lysons speaks of it as depopulated and inclosed in the Marquess of Buckingham's grounds,[12] but it was detached from the park on the acquisition of Boycott Manor by Charles Higgens in the middle of the last century. On a slight eminence in Boycott overlooking a beautiful view of the park he built a house in the Elizabethan style, which is now the residence of Mr. Thomas Close Smith. At the present day there are also brickworks and a smithy in Boycott. A third hamlet, at one time of some importance, is that of Lamport, which gives its name to a few cottages in the east of the parish. The Dayrells had an ancient seat here now used as a farm-house.

The following place-names have been found in 13th-century documents connected with this parish : Akemannedich, Buggerode, Cruchweie, Dolemedes, Ekenstub, Kerswell, Melpethelmull, Rokesmore, Rumhull and Smeyehull[13] ; Le Parrokes in the 14th century[14] ; Anlowefeld, Greystob, Rokesmor, Smethenhull, Wythgonepole, in the 15th century.[15]

The property later to be known as *MANORS STOWE MANOR* was held before the Conquest by Turgis, a man of Baldwin son of Herluin. In 1086 it was assessed at 5 hides under the lands of the Bishop of Bayeux.[16] Robert Doyley and Roger de Ivri held Stowe as tenants of the bishop in 1086.[17] Some years previous to this date they had together founded a college of secular canons in the church of St. George in the castle of Oxford,[18] and Stowe was early added to its endowment, as appears from a confirmation charter of Henry I dated about 1130.[19]

OSENEY ABBEY. *Azure two bends or.*

Within the next twenty years the college was absorbed by Oseney Abbey,[20] which in 1278–9 held 3 hides in Stowe.[21] Oseney Abbey continued to hold the manor, in which it exercised view of frankpledge and full manorial rights down to the Dissolution.[22]

On the suppression of the religious houses a scheme was set on foot to form a bishopric of ' Oseney and Thame,' with a cathedral at Oseney, and in 1542 was carried into effect, the name of the bishopric being altered to Oxford.[23] Stowe Manor, as belonging to Oseney Abbey, formed part of the endowment of the bishopric both at this date[24] and on its reconstruction in 1547.[25] In 1590 the Bishop of Oxford conveyed the manor to Queen Elizabeth,[26] who in the same year granted it to Thomas Crompton and others.[27] They immediately alienated Stowe to John Temple, Susan his wife and their son Thomas Temple.[28] John Temple died in 1603 seised of Stowe Manor, which then passed to his son Thomas Temple.[29] He was knighted in the year of his father's death, and in 1611 was created a baronet, being one of the first four instituted to that order.[30] In 1617 he obtained

TEMPLE of Stowe. *Or an eagle sable, quartered with Argent two bars sable with three martlets or on each bar.*

---

⁸ 'The celebrated Launcelot Brown was originally employed here in a humble situation, whence he arose by degrees to be head gardener, in which situation he continued till 1750. It is generally supposed that his first specimens of landscape gardening were made at Stowe, but we are assured that Lord Cobham restricted him to the kitchen and flower-garden' (Brayley and Britton, loc. cit.).
⁹ Louis XVIII is said to have retained a very grateful recollection of the ale at Stowe, and on his return to Paris sent a request for a cask of it, which was accordingly forwarded to him (*Gent. Mag.* [New Ser.], xi, 309).

¹⁰ Browne Willis, *Hist. and Antiq. of Buckingham*, 280.
¹¹ Stat. 6 & 7 Vict. cap. 61.
¹² Lysons, *Mag. Brit.* i (3), 642.
¹³ Harl. MS. 4714.
¹⁴ Anct. D. (P.R.O.), C 480.
¹⁵ Ibid. D 1038.
¹⁶ *V.C.H. Bucks.* i, 237.
¹⁷ Ibid.
¹⁸ *V.C.H. Oxon.* ii, 160.
¹⁹ Ibid. See also *Hund. R.* (Rec. Com.), i, 32, where Stowe is said to be held of the prebend of St. George in the castle of Oxford.
²⁰ *V.C.H. Oxon.* ii, 90.
²¹ *Hund. R.* (Rec. Com.), ii, 341.

²² *Plac. de Quo Warr.* (Rec. Com.), 93 ; *Testa de Nevill* (Rec. Com.), 243*b*; *Hund. R.* (Rec. Com.), i, 32 ; *Feud. Aids,* i, 108 ; Harl. Chart. 86, A 44 ; 84, F 42 ; *Cal. Chart. R.* 1300–26, pp. 418, 419, 425.
²³ *V.C.H. Oxon.* ii, 29.
²⁴ Pat. 34 Hen. VIII, pt. i.
²⁵ Ibid. 1 Edw. VI, pt. v.
²⁶ Feet of F. Div. Co. Hil. 32 Eliz.
²⁷ Pat. 32 Eliz. pt. ix.
²⁸ Ibid. 32 Eliz. pt. xiv ; Feet of F. Bucks. East. 32 Eliz.
²⁹ Chan. Inq. p.m. (Ser. 2), cclxxxi 93.
³⁰ G.E.C. *Baronetage*, i, 82.

232

a grant of free warren in his manor.[31] Sir Thomas Temple, bart., died in February 1636–7, and was succeeded by his son Peter,[32] who made a settlement of his property in this parish and elsewhere in the year following his father's death.[33]

He took the side of Parliament during the early part of the Civil War,[34] but though appointed one of the judges for the king's trial he did not attend, and on the execution of Charles I threw up his commission in the army.[35] He represented the neighbouring borough of Buckingham in Parliament from 1640 until his death, which took place at Stowe in 1653.[36] Two years before his death he had inclosed a park at Stowe, and stocked it with deer bought from Lord Spencer.[37] His son and heir Sir Richard Temple, bart., made a settlement of the manor in 1655.[38] He was returned as member for the borough in 1659, and represented the county from 1660 till his death in 1697.[39] He was buried at Stowe, his son Sir Richard Temple, bart., inheriting. He, who had greatly distinguished himself in the Flemish wars, was created in 1714 Lord Cobham of Cobham.[40] Four years later he was created Viscount Cobham, with a special remainder (which also applied to his estates in Stowe) to his sisters Hester Grenville and Christian Lyttelton and the heirs male of their bodies.[41] Cobham was the friend and patron of literary men, among whom Pope and Congreve, both of whom were frequent visitors at Stowe, have celebrated him in verse. The latter is distinguished by a funeral monument erected to his memory in Stowe grounds.[42] Lord Cobham died and was buried at Stowe in 1749, and in accordance with the settlement of 1718 his sister Hester became *suo jure* Viscountess Cobham, being created in the same year Countess Temple.[43] She died in 1752, her titles and estates passing to Richard Grenville, her son and heir.[44] Grenville's history, as friend and brother-in-law of Pitt, is closely bound up with the political life of his times. After the death of his brother George Grenville in 1770 he retired from public life, and amused himself with the improvement of his house and gardens at Stowe, 'a sort of mania with the family.'[45] He entertained Princess Amelia here at least three times. On the occasion of her first visit in 1764 'Lady Temple, Sir Richard Lyttelton and the Duchess of Bridgewater are all wheeled into the room in gouty

GRENVILLE. *Vert a cross argent with five roundels gules thereon.*

chairs.'[46] A second visit which she paid in 1770 has been commemorated in the letters of Horace Walpole, who formed one of the party.[47]

Earl Temple died in 1779 as the result of a carriage accident, and as he left no issue George son of his brother George Grenville succeeded him as next Earl Temple, Viscount Cobham and Baron Cobham.[48] In 1784 he was created Marquess of Buckingham, and acted as Lord-Lieutenant of Ireland from 1787 to 1789.[49] On 15 March 1789, when the news of the king's recovery was made public, there were great festivities at Stowe. The Marquess of Buckingham died in 1813, his successor being his son Richard Temple-Nugent-Brydges-Chandos-Grenville, who, in addition to his father's titles, was created Earl Temple of Stowe, Marquess of Chandos and Duke of Buckingham and Chandos in 1822.[50] He was a great personal friend of George IV,[51] and the steward of the household in 1830. On his death in 1839 his son Richard Plantagenet became second Duke of Buckingham and Chandos and inherited the Stowe estates. Queen Victoria, accompanied by the Prince Consort, paid to the duke in August 1845 a three days' visit.[52]

By unfortunate land speculations and other means the duke managed within eight years of his accession to lose the greater part of his fortune, and a sale, in order to satisfy his creditors, was held at Stowe in 1848, and lasted thirty days.[53] His son the Marquess of Chandos also joined with his father at this date in cutting the entails of the estates immediately attached to the dukedom,[54] but though there was a great dispersal of his landed property at this time[55] Stowe itself did not pass away from the family. The Duke of Buckingham and Chandos died in July 1861, and his widow, who had obtained a separation from him in 1850, died on 28 June 1862 at Stowe House,[56] which remained empty for some time after her death.[57] Richard Plantagenet Campbell, the third and last duke, their son and successor, died in 1889. The place was then leased to the Comte de Paris, who died here in 1894.[58] The Baroness Kinloss, daughter and heir of the last Duke of Buckingham and Chandos, in 1912 conveyed it to her son, the Hon. Richard G. G. Morgan-Grenville, who was killed in action in 1914 and was succeeded by his brother Louis.

Two entries relating to Dadford are found in Domesday, but the holdings mentioned were subsequently united to form *DADFORD MANOR*, owned by the Abbot of Biddlesden. Both were assessed at 2 hides, but the more important was that held by Roger de Ivri, which was already styled a manor, and

---

[31] Pat. 14 Jas. I, pt. xi.

[32] Chan. Inq. p.m. (Ser. 2), dlxxv, 142. His wife Hester, daughter of Miles Sandys of Latimer, of whom Fuller relates, 'She had four sons and five daughters which lived to be married, and so exceedingly multiplied that this lady saw 700 extracted from her body,' survived him till 1656.

[33] Feet of F. Div. Co. Trin. 14 Chas. I ; Recov. R. Trin. 14 Chas. I, m. 54.

[34] Cal. Com. for Advance of Money, 554, 712.

[35] G.E.C. Baronetage, i, 82.

[36] Willis, op. cit. 276.

[37] Ibid.

[38] Feet of F. Div. Co. East. 1655.

[39] Ret. of Memb. of Parl. i, 579.

[40] G.E.C. Peerage, ii, 324. He claimed a descent in the female line, but no representation, from the Lords Cobham.

[41] Ibid. ; Feet of F. Bucks. Mich. 6 Geo. I. William Temple, the heir male, renounced his right in these estates in 1718 (Recov. R. East. 4 Geo. I, m. 86).

[42] Dict. Nat. Biog.

[43] G.E.C. Peerage, ii, 325.

[44] Ibid.

[45] Dict. Nat. Biog. ; Gibbs, Local Occurrences, ii, 187.

[46] Clement Shorter, Highways and Byways of Bucks. 267.

[47] Walpole's Letters (ed. Cunningham), v, 245. Though a small 'Vauxhall' was acted for the princess's benefit, it does not appear to have been a very

cheerful visit, for 'the Earl, you know, is bent double, the Countess very lame ; I am a miserable walker, and the Princess, though strong as a Brunswick lion, makes no figure in going down fifty stone stairs.'

[48] Dict. Nat. Biog. ; Gibbs, loc. cit.

[49] G.E.C. Peerage, ii, 60.

[50] Ibid. ; Gent. Mag. xcii (1), 81.

[51] G.E.C. loc. cit.

[52] Gibbs, op. cit. iv, 37.

[53] Annual Reg. 1848, xc, 125.

[54] Ibid.

[55] Gibbs, op. cit. iv, 67, 129.

[56] G.E.C. Peerage, ii, 61.

[57] Sheahan, Hist. and Topog. of Bucks. 304.

[58] Clement Shorter, loc. cit.

had belonged to Lewin, a man of Burgered.[59] Roger de Ivri's lands later became attached to the honour of St. Walery.[60] The second Domesday holder in Dadford was Lewin of Nuneham, who succeeded two thegns, Ravai and Ulward.[61] His land in Dadford was later attached to the honour of Giffard, and the dual overlordship of St. Walery and Giffard is in consequence found exercised in the united manor.[62]

Hamard was Roger de Ivri's tenant in 1086, and Hugh son of Gozer that of Lewin of Nuneham at the same date.[63] Two families are later found making grants to Biddlesden Abbey, and it appears from the cartulary of that abbey that a family called Leigh succeeded Hamard,[64] while another family calling themselves Dadford succeeded Hugh son of Gozer.[65] The grants to Biddlesden of land in Dadford were made as early as the first half of the 12th century,[66] and continued until well into the 13th century,[67] by the middle of which Biddlesden held half the vill of Dadford in free alms,[68] the other half being said to be held by Oseney.[69] In the Hundred Rolls of 1278-9 the abbot's property in Dadford is carefully extended; that portion which he held in pure alms 'of the gift of Thomas of St. Walery' included 4 hides in demesne, 8 acres of assart, 6 acres of wood, while thirteen cottagers on the estate paid rents in money and services.[70] The land held of the Giffard Honour was extended at a hide, of which one half was in demesne, 4½ acres of assart with seventeen cottagers and four free tenants.[71] In 1291 the property (including Gorral Grange in Biddlesden) was assessed at £7 14s. 8d.,[72] and at the Dissolution was returned at £10.[73] It was retained by the Crown for some years, being made the subject of temporary leases.[74] It was finally transferred to Edward Heron and others in 1587,[75] and was by them immediately sold to John Temple,[76] afterwards lord of Stowe Manor, with which it has since descended.

Under Edward the Confessor Suen Suert, a man of Earl Edwin, held 3½ hides in Lamport (Landport, Langport), which by 1086 had passed to Walter Giffard, who then held *LAMPORT MANOR*, valued at 40s.[77] Walter Giffard's lands here became attached later to the honour of Crendon, Crendon manor being the head of the honour of Giffard or Gloucester in this county.[78] In both this and the remaining manor of Lamport the honour of Gloucester claimed the right to a view of frankpledge. Mention is found first of the honour in the early 13th century,[79] and continues to the second quarter of the 17th century.[80]

Berner was the tenant of Walter Giffard in Lamport in 1086[81]; the next tenant of whom mention has been found is John son of Maurice or John Moriz, who in 1227 acquired from William son of Reginald for 5½ marks half a fee in Lamport,[82] which he held in demesne in 1254.[83] His successor, Andrew Moriz, made a grant of this property to the Abbot of Oseney (who already had rights of pasture extending into Lamport)[84] in 1268.[85] In return for 2 carucates of land to be held in pure alms the abbot was to provide Andrew Moriz for life with an annual pension of 2 silver marks and 12 quarters of oats. A suitable lodging was to be provided for him within the abbey, and he was to receive daily the corrodies of two canons, of one free servant and of a groom: to wit, two loaves called great loaves, one brown loaf, one salted loaf and one coarse (*grossum*) loaf, 2 gallons of best ale, one of second quality and one of third quality; from the kitchen he was to have daily what would fall to two canons, one free servant and one groom of the abbot's stable. Andrew Moriz was also to receive yearly 6 cartloads of brushwood, 6 quarters of charcoal, 3 cartloads of straw, 4 cartloads of hay, 1 stone of tallow, and four cheeses worth 1s. After Andrew's death the abbot was released from all claim to the above allowance.[86] Andrew Moriz's grant to Oseney was confirmed at various times,[87] and in 1278-9 the abbot was said to hold 3 hides in Langport, of which 1 hide and 6 acres of wood were held in demesne, 8 virgates were held by ten villeins; there were five cottages, and one tenant of 1 virgate. The manor also owed scutage and hidage.[88] Oseney Abbey continued to hold Lamport Manor down to the Dissolution,[89] from which time onwards its descent follows that of Stowe Manor.

The origin of a second *LAMPORT MANOR* in this parish is to be sought in the 2½ hides of land which Rawen, a man of Wulfwig, Bishop of Dorchester, held here in the reign of the Confessor.[90] It was held in 1086 by Manno the Breton, who was also lord of the manor of Wolverton.[91] Lamport Manor is in consequence later found attached to the barony of Wolverton,[92] of which overlordship last mention is found in 1619.[93]

[59] *V.C.H. Bucks.* i, 269.
[60] *Pipe R.* 9 *Hen. II* (Pipe R. Soc.), 19; *Hund. R.* (Rec. Com.), i, 32; ii, 343; *Feud. Aids,* i, 79; Chan. Inq. p.m. 2 Ric. II, no. 57.
[61] *V.C.H. Bucks.* i, 275.
[62] *Hund. R.* (Rec. Com.), i, 32; ii, 343; *Feud. Aids,* i, 79, 125.
[63] *V.C.H. Bucks.* i, 269, 275.
[64] Ralph Hareng, who represented the St. Walery Honour, is named as overlord of the Leighs (Harl. MS. 4714).
[65] Their charters were confirmed by the Earl of Pembroke, representing the Giffard Honour.
[66] Harl. Chart. 85, C 21, 24, 25.
[67] Harl. MS. 4714; Feet of F. case 16, files 31, no. 16; 33, no. 4.
[68] *Testa de Nevill* (Rec. Com.), 243*b*; *Hund. R.* (Rec. Com.), i, 32.
[69] *Feud. Aids,* i, 79; *Hund. R.* (Rec. Com.), ii, 340, where Oseney is stated to hold 1 hide only.
[70] *Hund. R.* (Rec. Com.), ii, 340.

[71] Ibid.
[72] *Pope Nich. Tax.* (Rec. Com.), 47*b*.
[73] *Valor Eccl.* (Rec. Com.), iv, 235.
[74] Pat. 2 Eliz. pt. xiii; Willis, op. cit. 279.
[75] Pat. 29 Eliz. pt. vi, viii.
[76] Ibid.; Chan. Inq. p.m. (Ser. 2), cclxxxi, 93.
[77] *V.C.H. Bucks.* i, 250.
[78] *Testa de Nevill* (Rec. Com.), 247; *Hund. R.* (Rec. Com.), ii, 343; *Feud. Aids,* i, 79, 125.
[79] *Testa de Nevill* (Rec. Com.), 247.
[80] Chan. Inq. p.m. 8 Edw. II, no. 68; 11 Edw. II, no. 74; 17 Edw. II, no. 75; 21 Edw. III (1st nos.), no. 59; 10 Ric. II, no. 38; 16 Ric. II (pt. i), no. 27; 20 Ric. II, no. 51; 22 Ric. II, no. 46; 4 Hen. IV, no. 41; 7 Hen. V, no. 68; 8 Hen. V, no. 127; 38 & 39 Hen. V, no. 59; *Cal. Inq. p.m. Hen. VII,* i, 362; Chan. Inq. p.m. (Ser. 2), dccxxii, 113; *Cal. Close,* 1313–18, p. 134; *Feud. Aids,* i, 79.

[81] *V.C.H. Bucks,* i, 250.
[82] Feet of F. case 15, file 17, no. 29. In 1236 John Moriz enfeoffed Walter de Morton in 6 acres in Lamport (ibid. file 22, no. 51).
[83] *Testa de Nevill* (Rec. Com.), 247; *Hund. R.* (Rec. Com.), i, 33.
[84] Feet of F. case 14, file 15, no. 2.
[85] Ibid. case 16, file 40, no. 8.
[86] Ibid.
[87] *Cal. Chart. R.* 1300–26, p. 425; *Hund. R.* (Rec. Com.), ii, 341.
[88] *Hund. R.* loc. cit.
[89] *Feud. Aids,* i, 79, 100, 108, 125; *Pope Nich. Tax.* (Rec. Com.), 47*a*.
[90] *V.C.H. Bucks.* i, 270.
[91] Ibid.
[92] *Testa de Nevill* (Rec. Com.), 248*a*; *Cal. Close,* 1272–9, p. 350; *Hund. R.* (Rec. Com.), ii, 343; *Feud. Aids,* i, 79, 125; Chan. Inq. p.m. 23 Edw. III, pt. i, no. 35; 25 Edw. III (1st nos.), no. 6.
[93] Chan. Inq. p.m. (Ser. 2), cccclxxx, 131.

STOWE HOUSE: THE MARBLE SALOON

Girard held of Manno the Breton at Domesday,[94] and his successors took the name of Langport. The earliest of them were Robert de Langport and Jordan his son, benefactors to Luffield Priory, in the 12th century.[95] Ralph de Langport, son of Jordan, flourished c. 1202,[96] and in 1236 John de Langport was making settlements of land here.[97] He was shortly after followed by Ralph de Langport,[98] and for upwards of 200 years this same family continued to hold the manor. It has not been possible to trace the relationship of the various members, but the following names have been found mentioned. Ralph de Langport occurs in 1254, 1278, 1284 and 1302[99]; Richard de Langport occurs over more than one generation in 1314, 1346, 1350 and 1386[100]; Thomas de Langport held between 1392 and 1438.[1] Thomas de Langport appears to have died shortly after this date, leaving two daughters and co-heirs, Eleanor wife of John Dayrell,[2] and Margery wife of William Newnham.[3] Dealing first with that half of Lamport which passed to the Dayrells, we find it descending with Lillingstone Dayrell Manor until the middle of the 16th century, when Francis Dayrell, younger son of Paul Dayrell, removed to Lamport.[4] Edmund son of Francis Dayrell, called Edmund Dayrell of Lamport in 1615,[5] died seised of a capital mansion here in 1633.[6] His son Abel conveyed the half-manor to John and Edmund Dayrell in 1642,[7] and the Dayrell family appears to have remained in the parish until the middle of the 19th century.[8] They built a house on their estate near Stowe House, which in 1862 was in the occupation of James Bennet, farmer.[9]

In 1447 the other half of Thomas de Langport's manor was held by Thomas Wykeham and Agnes his wife, in right of Agnes, who was possibly Thomas de Langport's widow. At that date they granted a twenty-year lease to John Percival at a rent of 43s. 4d.[10] In the same year they conveyed their right in Lamport to Ralph Ingoldsby and Agnes his wife,[11] the latter holding land, which may be taken to represent the half-manor, at her death in March 1492–3.[12] The property reappears in 1531 as the property of Nicholas de Wahull, whose father Fulk had married Anne daughter and co-heir of William Newnham,[13] and of Margery, who was, according to the Harleian visitation, the co-heir of Thomas 'Longports.'[14] The descent of this manor after its acquisition by the Wahulls follows that of Chetwode, no separate mention of it being found later than the 16th century.[15]

The entry for *BOYCOTT MANOR* in Domesday occurs under Oxfordshire, where Reinbald is recorded as holding 1 hide of the king in Boycott which had formerly belonged to Blachemann.[16] This hide went to form part of the original endowment of Cirencester Abbey, founded by Henry I in 1117,[17] the grant being termed the holding of 'Reinbald the Priest.'[18] Cirencester Abbey retained Boycott until the latter half of the 13th century, when the abbot alienated the manor (so described) to the Abbot of Biddlesden. This transfer is recorded in the Biddlesden Cartulary, but is undated.[19] It must, however, have taken place between 1264–5 (in which year the Abbot of Cirencester made a life grant of the mill)[20] and 1276, when the Abbot of Biddlesden was already in possession, for in this latter year he was fined for making a false claim of ancient demesne within the manor.[21] In 1526 the abbot granted a forty-nine years' lease of Boycott to Agnes widow of Lewis Ap Rice,[22] but before 1529 her rent was in arrears and the abbot brought an action against her. The rent was said to be payable on Christmas Day, but not tendered, 'considering the solempnite of the seyd fest,' till St. Thomas's Day.[23] At the Dissolution the manor, of which Agnes Ap Rice still held the unexpired lease, became the possession of the Crown, and was granted in 1543 to Henry Cartwright.[24] He died seised in 1556, his heir being his grandson Henry, son of Thomas Cartwright, a minor.[25] He came of age in 1564,[26] and three years later acquired royal licence to alienate the manor[27] to Thomas Tyringham.[28] He died in 1595, when Boycott Manor was stated to be held by his son Anthony Tyringham and Elizabeth his wife.[29] In 1615 Anthony Tyringham was succeeded by his son Thomas,[30] who made various settlements of Boycott Manor between 1621 and 1627.[31] Its later history is scanty. In 1700 John Miller conveyed the manor by fine to Mary Walford, widow,[32] and in 1718 one of the same name made a similar settlement on Edmund Halsey.[33] When Willis wrote c. 1735 the manor seems already to have been acquired by the lord of Stowe Manor, for he speaks of Boycott as a decayed hamlet, of which part was included in 'the

CIRENCESTER ABBEY.
Argent a cheveron gules with three rams' heads cabossed argent thereon having horns or.

[94] *V.C.H. Bucks.* i, 270.
[95] Willis, op. cit. 278, quoting the Luffield Reg. fol. 118, 119.
[96] Ibid.
[97] Feet of F. Bucks. 20 Hen. III, no. 52, 53.
[98] *Testa de Nevill* (Rec. Com.), 248a.
[99] *Hund. R.* (Rec. Com.), i, 33; ii, 341; *Feud. Aids*, i, 79, 100.
[100] Chan. Inq. p.m. 8 Edw. II, no. 68; 23 Edw. III, pt. i, no. 35; 10 Ric. II, no. 38; *Feud. Aids*, i, 125.
[1] Chan. Inq. p.m. 16 Ric. II, pt. i, no. 27; 22 Ric. II, no. 46; 17 Hen. VI, no. 38.
[2] Lipscomb, *Hist. and Antiq. of Bucks.* iii, 32.
[3] *Visit. of Beds.* (Harl. Soc.), 69.
[4] Com. Pleas D. Enr. East. 4 & 5 Phil. and Mary; Lipscomb, loc. cit.

[5] Chan. Inq. p.m. (Ser. 2), cccxlviii, 145.
[6] Ibid. dccxxii, 113.
[7] Feet of F. Bucks. Trin. 18 Chas. I.
[8] Willis, op. cit. 278; Lipscomb, op. cit. iii, 113. Lipscomb's account of the manor is full of errors and has only been quoted for the date at which he wrote.
[9] Sheahan, op. cit. 310.
[10] Lansd. Chart. 581.
[11] Feet of F. case 293, file 71, no. 58.
[12] *Cal. Inq. p.m. Hen. VII*, i, 362.
[13] *V.C.H. Beds.* iii, 72.
[14] *Visit. of Beds.* (Harl. Soc.), 69.
[15] Chan. Inq. p.m. (Ser. 2), lii, 20; lxv, 6; Feet of F. Div. Co. Trin. 3 Eliz.
[16] *Dom. Bk.* (Rec. Com.), i, 160.
[17] *V.C.H. Gloucs.* ii, 80.
[18] Harl. MS. 4714, fol. 295.
[19] Ibid.

[20] Ibid.
[21] *Abbrev. Plac.* (Rec. Com.), 189, 192. cf. also, as bearing on this case, customs within the manor, and a list of tenants (Harl. MS. 4714, fol. 298, 299 d.).
[22] Harl. Chart. 84, F 20.
[23] Early Chan. Proc. bdle. 460, no. 5.
[24] *L. and P. Hen. VIII*, xviii (2), g. 107 (55).
[25] Chan. Inq. p.m. (Ser. 2), cviii, 90.
[26] Fine R. 6 Eliz. no. 95.
[27] Pat. 9 Eliz. pt. ix.
[28] Feet of F. Div. Co. Hil. 9 Eliz.
[29] Chan. Inq. p.m. (Ser. 2), ccxlvi, 108.
[30] Ibid. cccxlix, 164.
[31] Feet of F. Div. Co. East. 19 Jas. I; Trin. 2 Chas. I; Hil. 2 Chas. I; Recov. R. Mich. 2 Chas. I, m. 67.
[32] Feet of F. Oxon. Trin. 12 Will. III.
[33] Ibid. Mich. 5 Geo. I.

spacious gardens of the Lord Cobham.'[34] It certainly formed part of the Stowe property later,[35] and was retained by the lord of the manor probably till the dispersal of his property in 1848, when it passed to Charles Higgens. A further alienation took place in 1899,[36] the present owner of the Boycott estate being Thomas Close Smith.

The Abbot of Oseney owned an estate in Dadford which formed part of the Domesday holding of Lewin of Nuneham and his tenant Hugh, son of Gozer,[37] for in 1278–9 it is described as being held of the honour of Giffard.[38] It appears to have been granted to the abbey by William son of Ralph de Langport,[39] and consisted of a hide held in demesne, 9 acres of assart, 4 acres of wood, and rents and services of eight cottagers.[40] At the Dissolution these lands were granted to the Bishop of Oxford,[41] with the manor of Stowe, to which they have since remained attached.

The priory of Catesby had a small grant of land in Dadford which was given to the prioress in 1252 by John de la Leigh and Christina his wife.[42] It was leased to Richard son of John March of Dadford in the 15th century,[43] and at the Dissolution was granted to John Giffard.[44] In 1540, together with Gorral Grange in Biddlesden (q.v.), it was confirmed to George Giffard.[45]

BISHOPRIC OF OXFORD. *Sable a fesse argent with three queens' heads in the chief and an ox argent in the foot passing through waves argent and azure.*

Willis, who had an opportunity of examining the Luffield register, quotes numerous grants of land in Lamport by the Langports.[46]

In 1512 William Tyler obtained a grant for thirty-four years of the Luffield property in Lamport, which had been previously leased by the Abbot of Westminster to Sir Richard Empson for forty years.[47] These lands and rents henceforward follow the same descent as Luffield (q.v.), becoming finally merged in Stowe.

Some time early in the 13th century the Prioress of Studley in Oxfordshire acquired 2 virgates of land in Lamport which she held there in 1278–9.[48] In 1577 this land was the property of Laurence Abbott, who had inherited from his father, Thomas Abbott.[49]

The church of the *ASSUMPTION CHURCH OF ST. MARY THE VIRGIN* consists of a chancel measuring internally 29 ft. by 15 ft. 6 in., north chapel 27 ft. by 14 ft. 6 in., nave 39 ft. by 19 ft., north aisle 9 ft. wide, south aisle 8 ft. 6 in. wide, west tower 10 ft. square, and a south porch 8 ft. by 7 ft. 6 in.

The earliest detail in the building is the late 13th-century nave arcade, but the aisle to which it opens appears to have been rebuilt late in the 15th century, when the south aisle, added in the last half of the 14th century, was also rebuilt, the nave clearstory constructed, and the south porch added. The west tower was built in the first half of the 14th century, and the chancel in its present form dates from c.1350. The north chapel was added in the 16th century, when the arcade was pierced in the north wall of the chancel. The church has been restored and the upper stage of the tower has been rebuilt. With this exception the whole of the walls are rough-casted externally; the roofs are covered with copper, that of the chancel being externally of semicircular form.

The east window of the chancel, which is of mid-14th-century date, is of three trefoiled ogee lights with poorly designed reticulated tracery. The north wall is occupied by the arcade of two bays opening to the north chapel. The arches are depressed and the jambs and soffits are divided into panels, in which small shields are set at intervals. The two modern windows in the south wall have each three trefoiled lights with tracery in a flat segmental head. The chancel arch, contemporary with the rebuilding of the chancel, is of three pointed orders, the two inner orders dying into the responds, while the outer order is segmental and continuously moulded with the jambs. The innermost order has plain chamfers, the two outer orders being hollow-chamfered. The north chapel is lighted by five original early 16th-century windows, four in the north wall, and one in the east wall, each being of three plain lights under a depressed head. Beneath the east window is a modern doorway, while a depressed arch of original date opens on the west to the north aisle.

The north and south arcades of the nave are each of three bays with pointed arches of two chamfered orders, and octagonal piers and responds with moulded capitals and bases. The mouldings of the capitals and bases of the piers and responds on the north side, however, show that this arcade is of late 13th-century date, while the mouldings of those on the south side indicate that the south arcade is about a century later. The 15th-century south porch has an outer entrance with an elliptical head within a square containing order. The clearstory windows, six on either side, have depressed four-centred heads and were originally each of three lights, but their tracery has been removed.

The north aisle has a 15th-century north doorway with a window on either side of it. Both are of the 15th century, but are now without tracery; the eastern window has a four-centred head and appears to have been originally of three lights, while the western window, which has a pointed head, was of two lights. At the east end of the aisle is a late 14th-century piscina with a trefoiled head. In the east wall of the south aisle is a pointed 14th-century window of three trefoiled ogee lights with reticulated tracery in the head. The two south windows are like the corresponding windows of the north aisle, and between them is a square-headed 16th-century doorway. At the east end is a piscina like that in the north aisle.

[34] Willis, op. cit. 280.
[35] Recov. R. Hil. 15 Geo. III, m. 353; Lysons, op. cit. i (3), 642; Sheahan, op. cit. 309.
[36] *Land and House Property Year Bk.* 1899. [37] *V.C.H. Bucks.* i, 275.
[38] *Hund. R.* (Rec. Com.), ii, 341.

[39] *Cal. Chart. R.* 1300–26, p. 425.
[40] *Hund. R.* (Rec. Com.), ii, 341; *Feud. Aids,* i, 79, 100, 108, 125.
[41] *L. and P. Hen. VIII,* xvii, g. 881 (25).
[42] Feet of F. case 16, file 31, no. 2.
[43] Anct. D. (P.R.O.), D 1038.

[44] *L. and P. Hen. VIII,* xiii (1), 579.
[45] Ibid. xv, g. 436 (53).
[46] Willis, op. cit. 278.
[47] *L. and P. Hen. VIII,* i, 3297.
[48] *Hund. R.* (Rec. Com.), ii, 341.
[49] Chan. Inq. p.m. (Ser. 2), cclxxv, 332.

STOWE CHURCH FROM THE SOUTH-EAST

STOWE CHURCH: THE INTERIOR LOOKING EAST

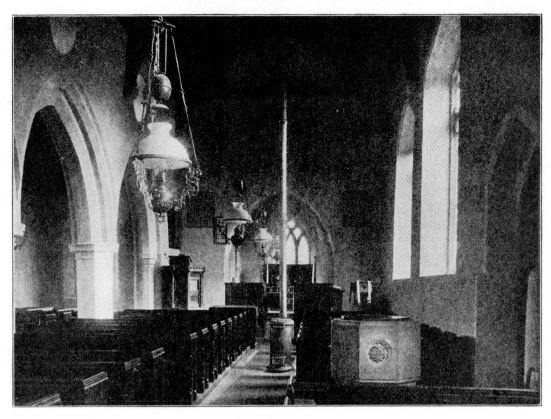

THORNBOROUGH CHURCH: THE INTERIOR LOOKING EAST

THORNBOROUGH CHURCH FROM THE SOUTH-WEST

The tower is of three stages with diagonal western buttresses, and later buttresses against the west wall added to give additional support. The crowning parapet is plain and each stage is slightly recessed. The tower arch is pointed and of three chamfered orders, the innermost order springing from semi-octagonal responds with moulded capitals; it is now covered by a modern gallery and partly blocked. The west doorway has a pointed head inclosed by an external label with head-stops, and is of three orders continuously moulded. Above the doorway externally is a fine and elaborately wrought niche with a trefoiled ogee arch supporting a pyramidal canopy finished with a finial and crockets, the whole being flanked by pinnacled pilasters. The upper part of the niche is sculptured with a crucifix between the figures of St. Mary and St. John, and below are three image brackets. The intermediate stage of the tower is lighted by small square-headed windows on the north and south, while the rebuilt upper stage has pointed two-light windows designed in the style of the 14th century.

Used as a reredos in the chancel is an early 17th-century overmantel carved with the Stuart royal arms. The other fittings are of little interest.

In the chancel is a brass, with figure, to Alice Saunders. The inscription plate is broken, but the date is probably 1461. In the north chapel is an elaborate monument of black and white marble to Martha daughter of Sir Thomas Temple, and wife of Sir Thomas Penyston, bart., who died in 1619. Upon the monument is her recumbent figure, with the effigy of an infant daughter at the feet. This daughter, Hester, who died in 1617, is further commemorated by a floor slab of slate inlaid with marble bearing her figure and a shield of arms. Outside, to the east of the south porch, is a much-decayed 14th-century effigy of a man in civil costume.

There is a ring of five bells: the treble is inscribed, 'James Keene Made This Ring 1654'; the second bears only the date 1660; the third is inscribed, 'William Sptcher (sic) Churchwarden 1654'; the fourth, 'Robart Knight Churchwarden 1654'; and the tenor, 'Richard Keene mad me 1665.' There was a small sanctus bell, now lost, without inscription.

The plate consists of a cup and almsdish given by George Marquess of Buckingham in 1811, a paten and flagon given by Richard Duke of Buckingham in 1837, and a small paten without inscription.

The registers begin in 1568.

ADVOWSON The church of Stowe formed with the manor part of the endowment of the college in St. George's Church, Oxford Castle, first mention being found of it in the confirmation charter of 1130.[50] It has always followed the same descent as the manor of Stowe,[51] the living, which is a vicarage, being at the present day in the gift of the Master of Kinloss.

The rectory also follows the same descent as Stowe Manor.

In 1291 the church of Stowe was assessed at £10,[52] and at the Dissolution at £11 17s. 5d.[53]

CHARITY The Comte de Paris left £60 to the deserving poor of this parish, the interest upon which is distributed annually. The trustees are the vicar and churchwardens.

THORNBOROUGH

Torneberge (xi cent.); Tornburuwe (xiii cent.); Thornborowe (xvi cent.).

The parish of Thornborough covers 2,392 acres on the east bank of the Ouse, which forms its western boundary. Of the total area 1,579 acres are under permanent grass and 580 acres are arable.[1] The soil is clay on a subsoil principally of cornbrash, and the land has an elevation of 300 ft. except in the centre of the parish, where a small stream, called in the 17th century the Cowarde Brook,[2] flows westward into the Ouse. In this valley is the village. Its main street, crossed and re-crossed by the stream, runs east and west; there is a parallel Back Street to the north.

There are many 17th-century stone houses and cottages with thatched roofs. The New Inn is an interesting example of a 17th-century timber-framed house with brick filling of a later date. On the green are the stocks, now much decayed.

The church of St. Mary is in the centre of the village on the south side of the street. To the west of it is Manor Farm, which belongs to Magdalen College, Oxford. This is a two-story Elizabethan house built of stone with a small 17th-century addition at the north-west which was at one time detached. In the old hall on the west is an original wide stone fireplace with moulded jambs, low arch, and sunk spandrels; the 'Court room' above has a heavy collar-beam truss with a carved central boss. The hall is entered through a two-storied porch with original windows and an old studded inner door. On the south gable of the east block is an incised sundial.

On the other side of the street is the Manor House, a 17th-century stone house of two stories with tiled roofs. Its old gateway, flanked by stone posts, still remains; outside the inclosing wall is the old tithe barn.[3] The house has always belonged to the owners of the principal manor and rectory, and in the 18th century was the residence of the Woodnoth family.[4] It is perhaps on the site of that capital messuage which belonged to Robert de Fresne and passed to Luffield Priory in 1303.[5] There must also have been a capital messuage on the manor of the Damorys to account for the domestic chapel mentioned in the 13th century.[6] The foundations of the chapel were found in the pasture land west of the village shortly before 1735.[7] When this manor became the property of Barton's chantry its manor-house was apparently used as the dwelling of the

---

[50] *V.C.H. Oxon.* ii, 160.
[51] Inst. Bks. (P.R.O.).
[52] *Pope Nich. Tax.* (Rec. Com.), 32.
[53] *Valor Eccl.* (Rec. Com.), iv, 240.
[1] Statistics from Bd. of Agric. (1905).

[2] Close, 43 Eliz. pt. xxv.
[3] Apparently the 'barn of three bays' mentioned in a terrier of 1639 (Browne Willis, *Hist. and Antiq. of Buckingham,* 291).

[4] Willis, op. cit. 289.
[5] *Cal. Close,* 1302-7, p. 31. See below.
[6] See below under advowson.
[7] Willis, op. cit. 290.

chantry priest.[8] A capital messuage which the Abbot of Biddlesden acquired from Alan de Fresne in the reign of Henry III [9] is presumably the manor-house of the abbot and convent mentioned in a charter of Sir Richard Damory.[10]

South of the village, on the high road running west to Buckingham, is Windmill Hill. The water-mill of Thornborough is in the north of the parish where the Ouse makes a curve to the east ; it is perhaps on the site of the mill which existed here in 1086.[11] A mill in Thornborough was granted in 1244 [12] to the hospital of St. John, Oxford, and is again mentioned in 1279.[13] It was probably identical with the mill of ‘Stakforde’ mentioned as a boundary mark at about that date.[14] Near the mill the road running north from Thornborough to Leckhampstead crosses the river. Here must have been the ‘Totesbrig’ which was the subject of dispute in the late 14th century between the Master of St. John’s Hospital and the inhabitants of Leckhampstead and Foscott. Judgement was given in

rectangular recess probably for the same purpose. The bridge has been repaired and the parapets are modern. The division between the parishes of Buckingham and Thornborough is marked by a boundary stone in the middle of the bridge. Near the bridge on the north side of the road are Thornborough Mounds, two tumuli in which Roman remains were found in 1839.[16]

In 1268 the freeholders of Thornborough made an agreement with the Abbot of Biddlesden by which they were to have common of pasture in ‘le Breche,’ a ‘culture’ which belonged to the abbot.[17]

The village contains a Baptist chapel dating from 1829, a Wesleyan chapel built in 1832, and a Congregational chapel built in 1872. There are brick and tile works in the south-west of the parish, near a large farm called Coombs.

An Inclosure Act for Thornborough was passed in 1797.[18]

THORNBOROUGH VILLAGE AND STOCKS

MANORS Fourteen hides and 1 virgate in **THORNBOROUGH** were held as one manor by Thori, a thegn of Edward the Confessor. In 1086 they were held by Berner of Manno the Breton, ancestor of the barons of Wolverton.[19] Thornborough represented one knight’s fee in the barony and owed ward to the castle of Northampton.[20] This service in 1254 was rendered by a payment of 15s. 10d. from the whole vill.[21] The lords of Wolverton claimed rights of overlordship in Thornborough as late as 1618.[22]

Hamo son of Meinfelin, probably grandson of Manno,[23] granted the church of Thornborough and a hide of land to Luffield Priory in the reign of Henry II.[24] This hide formed the nucleus of the *LUFFIELD PRIORY MANOR*. The grant was confirmed by Hamo’s grandson William,[25] who in 1242 acquitted the prior of hidage, scutage and suit of court.[26] Further grants to Luffield were made by Hamo Hasteng and Hugh son of William in 1241,[27] by Robert de Westminster in 1255 [28] and by Reynold de Fresne.[29] The holding of the prior in 1279 amounted to 5½ hides, of which 3 hides and 3 virgates were held in demesne.[30] The manor was granted with Luffield Priory, after the dissolution of that house in 1494,[31] to the Abbot of Westminster,[32] and after the general dissolution was given by Edward VI to Sir Nicholas Throck-

1389 that the Master of the Hospital was responsible for half the cost of its repair.[15]

A tributary of the Ouse is crossed on the road to Buckingham by Thornborough Bridge, which is an interesting structure dating from the 14th century. It is 12 ft. wide and spans the river by six low arches, of which all the four middle are moulded and two of them strengthened by ribs ; the two outer arches are plain, and possibly of later date. There are three sterlings on the south side carried up to form refuges, and between the two western arches on the north is a

[8] Pat. 4 Edw. VI, pt. vi, m. 19.

[9] Harl. MS. 4714, fol. 110 d.

[10] Ibid. fol. 128. For the dates of the two Richard Damorys (both knights) see below.

[11] *V.C.H. Bucks.* i, 270.

[12] Feet of F. Bucks. 29 Hen. III, no. 4.

[13] *Hund. R.* (Rec. Com.), ii, 351 ; see also Feet of F. case 17, file 49, no. 37.

[14] Harl. MS. 4714, fol. 107 ; cf. Willis, op. cit. 288.

[15] Willis, op. cit. 288-9.

[16] *V.C.H. Bucks.* ii, 12 ; Sheahan, *Hist. and Topog. of Bucks.* 311.

[17] Harl. MS. 4714, fol. 131 d.

[18] Priv. Act, 37 Geo. III, cap. 49.

[19] *V.C.H. Bucks.* i, 270.

[20] *Hund. R.* (Rec. Com.), i, 27.

[21] Ibid.

[22] *Cal. Close,* 1349-54, p. 169 ; Chan. Inq. p.m. 25 Edw. III (1st nos.), no. 6 ; 17 Hen. VI, no. 38 ; (Ser. 2), dxlii, 131.

[23] See Wolverton.

[24] Dugdale, *Mon.* iv, 350 ; Feet of F. Bucks. 26 Hen. III, no. 2.

[25] Dugdale, loc. cit. See Wolverton.

[26] Feet of F. Bucks. 26 Hen. III, no. 2.

[27] Ibid. 25 Hen. III, no. 33 ; 26 Hen. III, no. 4.

[28] Ibid. 40 Hen. III, no. 7.

[29] Willis, op. cit. 288.

[30] *Hund. R.* (Rec. Com.), ii, 351.

[31] *V.C.H. Bucks.* i, 349.

[32] Pat. 18 Hen. VII, pt. i, m. 23.

morton.[33] It then followed the descent of the manor of Luffield[34] (q.v.) till the second division of the Throckmorton estates in 1701,[35] when Thornborough was allotted to Thomas Lennard, Lord Dacre and Earl of Sussex,[36] a grandson of Sir Arthur Throckmorton's third daughter Elizabeth.[37] The Earl of Sussex sold the manor in 1707 to Benjamin Woodnoth, sen., and Benjamin Woodnoth, jun.,[38] the latter of whom was in possession in 1735 and 1736.[39] In 1747, however, it was conveyed by Alexander Townsend[40] and his wife Elizabeth to Ralph Lord Fermanagh, afterwards Earl Verney.[41] Mary Lady Fermanagh, niece and heir of the last purchaser, was lady of the manor in 1813.[42] It has since followed the descent of Middle Claydon (q.v.), Sir Harry Calvert Verney, bart., being the present owner.

THROCKMORTON.
Gules a cheveron argent charged with three gimel bars sable.

The only important lay tenants of the lords of Wolverton in Thornborough in the 13th century were the family of Fresne (Fraxino).[42a] The Henry de Fresne who held half a knight's fee of Hamo son of Meinfelin in 1166[43] was probably their ancestor. Hugh de Fresne appears to have held land in Thornborough in the late 12th or early 13th century,[44] and Reynold son of his son William[45] was returned as tenant of the knight's fee here between 1232 and 1236.[46] Reynold had a son William,[47] whose services were granted by John son of Alan de Wolverton to Luffield Priory.[48] William's son Robert[49] had nothing in Thornborough in 1279 but a capital messuage and 5 acres of land, held of the Prior of Luffield,[50] the rest of the fee having been alienated by his family and their sub-tenants in part

DE FRESNE. *Gules two bars party fessewise and indented argent and azure.*

to Luffield itself[51] and in part to Biddlesden Abbey.[52] Robert was hanged for felony in 1302,[53] and the remnant of his estate passed to Luffield by grant of the Crown,[54] so becoming part of the priory manor.[55]

The *BIDDLESDEN ABBEY MANOR* consisted of an accumulation of land granted by various donors, for the most part during the 13th century. Alan son of Hugh de Fresne, who gave his dwelling-house and 2 virgates of land,[56] was one of the earliest. His sons Alan and Ralph and his nephew and overlord Reynold confirmed the gift.[57] Roger Foliot and Floria his wife, tenants of the Fresnes, gave 3½ virgates in 1251.[58] Alice daughter of Ralph Moryn and widow of Alan de Fresne gave 1 virgate and John Hasteng gave .4 virgates, also during the reign of Henry III.[59] A more important grant was that of Hugh de Dunster, who gave 2 hides in the fee of Wolverton, probably in the early years of Edward I, and certainly before 1279.[60] This gift was burdened with a rent-charge of 40s. to the nuns of Ivinghoe, which was paid until the Dissolution.[61] In return for a subsequent grant from Hugh of 20 acres the abbot undertook to maintain a priest in the chapel of St. Giles of Littlecote,[62] Stewkley.

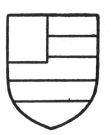

BIDDLESDEN ABBEY.
Argent two bars with a quarter gules.

In 1279 the holding of Biddlesden Abbey amounted to 6 hides and 1 virgate[63]; its annual value in 1291 was £6 4s. 4d.[64] and in 1535 £10 7s. 2d.[65] Courts were held for this manor till the Dissolution.[66] In 1542 evidence was taken as to its customs, the tenants claiming that they held for life, while the late abbot declared that they held at will.[67]

Lands at Thornborough late of Biddlesden were granted for life in 1540–1 to John Joslyn.[68] A similar grant was made to Robert Eton, 'servant of the pantry,' in 1553.[69] From a survey of three years later it appears that the annual value of the manor was £41 16s. 2d.[70] Elizabeth in 1567 granted the reversion to Thomas Newenham for twenty-one years, and in 1573 made a similar grant to Christopher

[33] Orig. R. (Exch. L.T.R.), 5 Edw. VI, pt. i, m. 88.

[34] Chan. Inq. p.m. (Ser. 2), ccccxxxviii, 126 ; Chan. Proc. (Ser. 2), bdle. 463, no. 81.

[35] See Luffield.

[36] Willis, op. cit. 289.

[37] Ibid. ; G.E.C. *Peerage*, iii, 4–5 ; Chan. Inq. p.m. (Ser. 2), ccccxxxviii, 126.

[38] Feet of F. Bucks. Mich. 6 Anne ; Decrees and Orders (Exch. K.R. [Ser. 4]), xxiii, fol. 167b.

[39] Feet of F. Bucks. Hil. 10 Geo. II ; Willis, op. cit. 289.

[40] Sheriff of Berks. 1750, when he was described as 'of Thornborough' (Lipscomb, *Hist. and Antiq. of Bucks.* i, p. xix). Elizabeth was perhaps a Woodnoth.

[41] Feet of F. Bucks. Mich. 21 Geo. II.

[42] Lysons, *Mag. Brit.* i (3), 647.

[42a] Hugh de Dunster (see below) was said to hold his land here partly of John de Beauchamp and partly of Adam de Bernak ; but held of John de Wolverton, and no mesne lordship of the Fresnes is mentioned (*Hund. R.* [Rec. Com.], ii,

350). Beauchamp and Bernak may, however, have held by grant from the Fresnes.

[43] *Red Bk. of Exch.* (Rolls Ser.), 315. Later the Fresnes were said to hold the whole knight's fee of Thornborough (*Testa de Nevill* [Rec. Com.], 248, 259). This was owing to the fact that the other tenants were religious bodies, holding in free alms. From the 14th century onward lists of fees appurtenant to the barony always represent Thornborough as held by the Fresne family (Chan. Inq. p.m. 25 Edw. III [1st nos.], no. 6 ; *Cal. Close*, 1349–54, p. 169 ; Chan. Inq. p.m. 17 Hen. VI, no. 38 ; [Ser. 2], dxlii, 131), though it lost all rights here in 1302 (see below).

[44] Harl. MS. 4714, fol. 110 d.

[45] Ibid. fol. 115.

[46] *Cal. Close*, 1231–4, p. 129 ; *Testa de Nevill* (Rec. Com.), 248, 259.

[47] Harl. MS. 4714, fol. 112, 129.

[48] Dugdale, op. cit. iv, 350.

[49] *Hund. R.* (Rec. Com.), ii, 350.

[50] Ibid.

[51] Willis, op. cit. 288.

[52] See below.

[53] Misc. Inq. file 62, no. 5.

[54] *Cal. Close*, 1302–7, p. 31 ; Dugdale, loc. cit.

[55] See above.

[56] Harl. MS. 4714, fol. 110 d. ; Harl. Chart. 85 E 11.

[57] Harl. MS. 4714, fol. 111–13.

[58] Ibid. fol. 122 d.

[59] Ibid. fol. 116.

[60] Ibid. fol. 107–9 ; *Hund. R.* (Rec. Com.), ii, 350.

[61] *Valor Eccl.* (Rec. Com.), iv, 227.

[62] Harl. MS. loc. cit. ; *Hund. R.* (Rec. Com.), ii, 350.

[63] *Hund. R.* loc. cit.

[64] *Pope Nich. Tax.* (Rec. Com.), 47.

[65] *Valor Eccl.* (Rec. Com.), iv, 237.

[66] Proc. of Ct. of Augm. bdle. 34, no. 13.

[67] Ibid.

[68] *L. and P. Hen. VIII*, xvi, p. 716.

[69] Orig. R. (Exch. L.T.R.), 1 Mary, pt. iv, m. 76.

[70] Ld. Rev. Misc. Bks. clxxxviii, fol. 156–8. Rent called 'Hedsilver' was due from certain premises in the manor to the sheriff.

Edmonds.[71] In March 1590-1 a grant in fee was made to Edward Downing and Roger Rant.[72] They sold their interest soon afterwards to Sir William Spencer, who died seised of the reversion in 1609,[73] leaving authority to his executors to sell it. The purchaser was John Phillips of Foscott.[74] The manor is said to have been acquired later by Sir Richard Temple of Stowe and to have descended with Bartons[75] (q.v.).

The *MAGDALEN COLLEGE MANOR* developed out of grants of land from the Wolverton fee originally made to the hospital of St. John without the east gate of Oxford. The most important of the gifts that are recorded were made between 1243 and 1245, when William de Morton gave 1 hide 1 virgate, Robert son of Alan a virgate and a mill, and John Hasteng 3 virgates.[76] Some of this may perhaps be identified with the land held in Thornborough under Gervase Paynel (c. 1154-94) by Reynold son of Adchur, which was acquired by the hospital before 1291.[77] In 1254 the hospital had 5 hides all but a virgate and view of frankpledge with exemption from suit of county or hundred.[78] The view was claimed under a charter of about 1243, and though in 1279 the warrant was said to be unknown, in 1286 a charter of 1266 was referred to.[79] In 1279 the extent of the holding was given as 4 hides.[80] It was transferred with the other estates of the hospital to the college of St. Mary Magdalen, Oxford, in 1457,[81] and was called a manor in 1595, when John Standish had a lease.[82] This was the only manor in Thornborough for which a court baron was held in 1797.[83] It still belongs to Magdalen College.

MAGDALEN COLLEGE, OXFORD. *Lozengy sable and ermine and a chief sable charged with three garden lilies proper.*

The manor of *BARTONS*, so called after its possessors in the 15th century, belonged in the 12th century to the fee of Doyley. It is not mentioned among the lands of Robert Doyley in 1086, but it seems probable that the omission was accidental. Two-thirds of the tithe of its demesnes were granted by the younger Robert in 1149 to Oseney Abbey with the chapel of St. George in Oxford Castle[84];

probably these tithes were already part of the endowment of the chapel.[85] The Doyley family continued to hold an overlordship here, which about 1245 belonged to the Countess of Warwick, Margaret, niece and heir of the last Henry Doyley.[86] It appears to have been attached to the barony of Hook Norton in Oxfordshire, and the reversion consequently passed by royal grant in 1253 to Margaret's second husband John du Plessis,[87] whose descendants held it during the 13th and early 14th centuries.[88]

The tenants of the Doyleys here as elsewhere were the family of Damory of Bucknell in Oxfordshire, probably the descendants of the Gilbert who held Bucknell of Robert Doyley in 1086.[89] The established pedigree of the family begins with the Robert Damory who made a grant to Godstow Nunnery about 1138.[90] His son and successor Roger[91] had a son Ralph, who confirmed his father's gifts to Godstow about 1150,[92] and also made a grant to Oseney Abbey.[93] Both his charters mention his wife Hawise and son Robert.[94] The latter, who was his heir, had a son also called Robert.[94a] The younger Robert was succeeded before 1245 by Roger called son of Robert,[95] who appears to have held the manor till about 1280.[96] Roger's son Robert[97] survived him by a very few years; in 1284-6 Juliana Damory held a third of Thornborough of his heir as her dower.[98] This heir was Robert's son Richard,[99] tenant in 1302-3.[100] He had a grant of free warren in 1312,[1] and two years later made a grant of the manor to Giles de Lisle and Aline his wife for their lives.[2] He was summoned to Parliament as a baron in 1326,[3] and died in 1330.[4] His son and heir Richard, then a minor, came of age five years later.[5] He granted a life interest in the manor of Thornborough to Adam de Courtenhall,[6] and in 1346 sold the reversion to William son of Laurence de Linford.[7]

DAMORY. *Barry wavy argent and gules.*

William de Linford was succeeded before 1351 by a son Laurence,[8] whose son and heir Thomas settled his lands here in 1385 on his issue by Joan daughter of Esmond de Broke and Margery his wife.[9] By an obscure transaction in 1444 or 1445 the manor appears to have passed from Robert Stafford,

71 *Pat.* 33 Eliz. pt. xi, m. 19-25.
72 *Ibid.* A fee-farm rent of £11 0s. 11d. was reserved on this land and premises in Wick, Thornton, Chalfont and other places in Bucks. It formed part of the queen's dower in Jan. 1663-4 (*Pat.* 15 Chas. II, pt. xiv).
73 Close, 8 Jas. I, pt. xxxiii; *Chan. Inq. p.m.* (Ser. 2), cccxv, 173.
74 Close, 8 Jas. I, pt. xxxiii.
75 Willis, op. cit. 290.
76 *Feet of F. Bucks.* 27 Hen. III, no. 2, 10; 29 Hen. III, no. 4, 10; *Cal. Chart. R.* 1226-57, p. 297.
77 *Pope Nich. Tax.* (Rec. Com.), 47. See below.
78 *Hund. R.* (Rec. Com.), i, 28.
79 *Ibid.* ii, 353; *Plac. de Quo Warr.* (Rec. Com.), 92.
80 *Hund. R.* (Rec. Com.), ii, 351.
81 *V.C.H. Oxon.* ii, 159.
82 Chan. Proc. Eliz. Ss 15, no. 49.
83 Priv. Act, 37 Geo. III, cap. 49.

84 Misc. Bks. (Exch. K.R.), xxvi, fol. 5 d.; Dugdale, op. cit. vi, 252. Oseney Abbey had a portion in the church in 1291 (*Pope Nich. Tax.* [Rec. Com.], 32).
85 *V.C.H. Oxon.* ii, 160; cf. *Cal. Chart. R.* 1257-1300, p. 69.
86 *Topog. and Gen.* i, 369; *Testa de Nevill* (Rec. Com.), 244.
87 *Cal. Pat.* 1247-58, p. 190; *Rôles Gascons*, i, 97, 373, 437; Camden, *Magna Brit.* (ed. Gough), i, 286.
88 *Hund. R.* (Rec. Com.), ii, 351; *Cal. Inq. p.m.* (Edw. III), vii, 202.
89 *Dom. Bk. Fac. Oxf.* fol. 9; Dunkin, *Hund. of Bullingdon and Ploughley*, i, 191.
90 *Godstow Chartul.* (Early Engl. Text Soc.), 214.
91 *Ibid.* 215.
92 *Ibid.* 216.
93 Cott. MS. Vitell. E xv, fol. 12 d.
94 The former mentions also two other sons, Ralph and Richard.

94a Kennett, *Paroch. Antiq.* i, 239; Dunkin, op. cit. i, 192.
95 Cott. MS. Vitell. E xv, fol. 175 d.; *Testa de Nevill* (Rec. Com.), 244.
96 Harl. MS. 4714, fol. 132; *Hund. R.* (Rec. Com.), ii, 351; *Cal. Close*, 1279-88, pp. 32, 86.
97 Kennett, *Paroch. Antiq.* i, 396.
98 *Feud. Aids*, i, 81.
99 *Ibid.* iv, 158; *Cal. Inq. p.m.* (Edw. I), iv, 67.
100 *Feud. Aids*, i, 100.
1 *Cal. Chart. R.* 1300-26, p. 194.
2 *Feet of F. Bucks.* 7 Edw. II, no. 16.
3 G.E.C. *Peerage*, iii, 17.
4 *Cal. Inq. p.m.* (Edw. III), vii, 202.
5 Ibid.
6 *Feud. Aids*, i, 125; *Feet of F. Bucks.* 20 Edw. III, no. 11.
7 *Feet of F. Bucks.* 20 Edw. III, no. 11.
8 De Banco R. 364, m. 1 d.; cf. Jeayes, *Derbyshire Charters*, 214.
9 Close, 9 Ric. II, m. 35.

cousin and heir of Thomas Linford, to Isabel Barton of Thornton, widow of John Barton the younger.[10] Her trustee Richard Fowler[11] conveyed it in 1472 to Thomas Blaklawe, chantry priest of Barton's chantry in Thornton Church,[12] and it appeared as Bartons Manor in Thornborough among the possessions of the chantry at its dissolution.[13] In 1550 it was granted to Edward Chamberlain,[14] who conveyed it six years later to Henry Chytting.[15] Chytting was perhaps a trustee for the sale to William Sargeant, who was in possession when he died in 1561[16]; he had settled the manor on his son Richard and Marion his wife.[17] Richard died less than a year after his father,[18] and William Sargeant his son succeeded.[19] He sold the manor in 1601 to John Temple of Stowe,[20] who gave it to Alexander his younger son.[21] Alexander sold it in 1607 to his elder brother Sir Thomas Temple,[22] and this manor descended with Stowe (q.v.) to the Marquess of Buckingham, who held it in 1813.[23] The Duke of Buckingham was lord in 1862,[24] but the manorial rights have since apparently lapsed.[25]

Gervase Paynel (c. 1154–94) granted to the priory of Tickford all the land of his fee in Thornborough, and the rent of 10s. which was paid by Reynold son of Adchur.[26] This rent was subsequently paid by the Master of St. John's Hospital,[27] and belonged to Tickford at the Dissolution.[28] It appears to have been annexed to the manor of Tickford.[29]

The Prior of St. John of Jerusalem claimed view of frankpledge in 1286 for lands here and elsewhere in Buckinghamshire, but his holding in Thornborough was apparently inconsiderable.[30]

CHURCH The church of *ST. MARY* consists of a chancel measuring internally 27 ft. by 13 ft. 6 in., nave 52 ft. 6 in. by 19 ft., north aisle 10 ft. wide, west tower 12 ft. square, north-west vestry and south porch; it is built of rubble with stone dressings partly coated with cement, and the roofs are covered with slates and tiles.

Some herring-bone masonry in the south wall of the nave indicates the existence of a church here in the 12th century consisting of the present nave and probably a small chancel. A north aisle was added in the mid-13th century, and the chancel was rebuilt about 1290. In the 14th century clearstory windows were inserted above the nave arcade and the aisle was probably widened. The tower was built early in the 15th century and the south porch about 1480, while the lighting of the church was increased by the insertion of large windows in the 15th and early 16th centuries. The fabric has been restored at a modern period and the vestry added.

The chancel is lighted from the east by an original three-light window with interlacing tracery and from the south by three windows with depressed heads, the easternmost being of three lights and dating from about 1520, and the others of two lights with tracery, dating from about 1480. In the tracery of the westernmost window is some contemporary glass including the figure of St. Thomas, part of another figure, and a fragment of an inscription. The lower part of the middle window has been removed to make room for a 17th-century doorway, to the west of which are traces of another doorway, long since blocked. At the west end of the north wall is a small two-light window of the 14th century, the lower part of which has been built up, and in the tracery are some 15th-century quarries and a shield. The chancel arch, doubtless dating from the late 13th century, is acutely pointed, and of one chamfered order. A plastered ceiling conceals an old timber roof, the wall-posts of which protrude below it.

The nave opens to the north aisle by a mid-13th-century arcade of four pointed arches of two chamfered orders, supported by octagonal pillars and responds with moulded capitals and bases. Above the arcade are three circular clearstory windows, the middle window having restored tracery, while the others are quatrefoils. At the east end of the north wall is a rood-loft stairway, which is entered by a four-centred doorway in the north aisle, and provides access to the loft by a pointed doorway placed high in the wall of the nave. On the south side of the nave are three large windows, each of three cinquefoiled lights with perpendicular tracery under four-centred heads; those at the east and west ends have a transom between the lights and the tracery and date from the end of the 15th century, while the other has no transom and is of slightly later date. The south doorway, inserted in the early 15th century, has a wide moulded splay and a four-centred head. The pointed tower arch in the west wall of the nave dates from the 15th century, and is of three chamfered orders supported by responds, the moulded capitals and bases of which were restored in the 17th century. There is a stone bench on both sides of the south porch, and at the north-east corner is the octagonal pedestal of a holy water stoup enriched with trefoiled panels. The square-headed windows in the lateral walls, each of two cinquefoiled lights, and the entrance doorway, which has a pointed arch under a square head, are all original, as is the moulded timber roof. Above the entrance is a cinquefoiled image niche. The porch is supported at the angles by diagonal buttresses and has a plain parapet with a flat gable on the south.

The north wall of the aisle, which has a brick plinth, was considerably repaired in the 18th century. Near the west end is a 14th-century window of two trefoiled lights with flowing tracery under a pointed head, and further east are two windows of about 1500 with tracery under four-centred heads, the eastern of three and the other of two lights. In the

[10] Yeatman, *Feud. Hist. of Derb.* iv, 415, 420. See Thornton.
[11] Nicolas, *Test. Vet.* 344.
[12] Willis, op. cit. 289; cf. *Cal. Pat.* 1467–77, p. 390.
[13] Pat. 4 Edw. VI, pt. vi, m. 19; Feet of F. Bucks. Mich. 3 & 4 Phil. and Mary.
[14] Pat. 4 Edw. VI, pt. vi, m. 19.
[15] Feet of F. Bucks. Mich. 3 & 4 Phil. and Mary.
[16] Chan. Inq. p.m. (Ser. 2), cxxxiv, 189.
[17] Ibid.; Chan. Proc. Eliz. Ss 27, no. 11.

[18] Chan. Proc. Eliz. Ss 27, no. 11.
[19] Ibid.
[20] Feet of F. Bucks. Trin. 43 Eliz.; Close, 43 Eliz. pt. xxv.
[21] Close, 5 Jas. I, pt. iv.
[22] Ibid.; Feet of F. Bucks. Mich. 5 Jas. I; *Visit. of Bucks.* (Harl. Soc.), 212; see also Recov. R. Mich. 13 Jas. I, m. 175.
[23] Feet of F. Div. Co. Trin. 12 Jas. I; East. 1655; Chan. Inq. p.m. (Ser. 2), dlxxv, 142; Priv. Act, 37 Geo. III, cap. 49; Lysons, *Mag. Brit.* i (3), 647.

[24] Sheahan, op. cit. 310.
[25] Lipscomb (op. cit. iii, 115 n.) says that Richard Lord Cobham released this manor to Lord Fermanagh, lord of the Luffield Priory Manor. No record of the release has been found.
[26] Dugdale, op. cit. v, 203.
[27] See above.
[28] *L. and P. Hen. VIII*, xvi, g. 1391 (45); Pat. 21 Jas. I, pt. xviii, no. 1.
[29] Ibid.
[30] *Plac. de Quo Warr.* (Rec. Com.), 90.

east wall is a two-light window of the same character as the last two. The north doorway, which has a four-centred head and continuous mouldings, was also inserted in the 15th century. It is now blocked, but still retains its mediaeval door.

The tower is of three stages divided by string-courses and surmounted by an embattled parapet, the two lower stages being supported by straight buttresses at the western angles. In the west wall of the ground stage is an early 15th-century moulded doorway with a pointed head, above which is a contemporary traceried window of two trefoiled lights; a modern doorway to the vestry has been inserted in the north wall. The second stage is lighted by small trefoiled windows with square heads, and the bell-chamber by windows of two trefoiled lights with tracery under pointed heads; all of these are original.

The font is modern. In the nave is a slab with brass figures of a man and his wife, the former in a long cloak and a hood and the latter in long cloak and veil head-dress, matrices for two brass shields, and the inscription 'Hic jacet Willielmus Barton qui obiit festo Translationis Sancti Benedicti Abbatis anno domini Millesimo cccºlxxxixº et Regni Regis Ricardi Secundi xiii incipiente quando dies dominicalis accidit super literam C hora vesperarum cujus anime propicietur deus amen.' On the sill of the middle window in the aisle is a brass plate with the inscription, 'Hic jacet Johannes Crowche capellanus qui quondam hic celebravit pro animabus Johannis Barton senioris et junioris qui quidem dominus Johannes Crowche obiit viii die maij anno domini mccccºlxxiii litera dominicale C. cujus anime propicietur deus.' On the sill of the east window of the aisle are small brass plates to John Woollhed (d. 1709), Elizabeth his wife (d. 1696), and Dorothy, wife first of John Butcher and afterwards of John Stephens (d. 1685). On the north side of the chancel are two mural monuments with arms, one to Margaret wife of John Corrance of Rendelsham and daughter of Sir John Hare of Stow Bardolph, Norfolk (d. 1715), and the other to Charles Woodnoth (d. 1778) and Ann his sister (d. 1780), while on the south wall is a mural tablet to Elizabeth Townsend (d. 1765). The communion table dates from the 17th century, and there is a chair in the chancel of the same period. Two large oak pews of the 18th century almost entirely occupy the western part of the chancel, leaving only a narrow passage between them. In the vestry are two plain chests, probably of the 16th century, and a small table of the 17th century. On the floors of the nave and aisle are many mediaeval encaustic tiles.

The tower contains a ring of five steel bells by Naylor Vickers & Co., Sheffield, 1860–1. These replaced a ring of four, the inscriptions on which are entered in the marriage register under date 13 June

1861, and, rearranged according to the sizes given, are: treble, 'Assit Principio Sčã Maria Meo'; second, 'Edward Hall made me 1736'; third, 'In multis annis resonet campana Johannis'; tenor, 'Henry Knight made this bell anno Domini 1610. Whose name is called Gabriell.' There is also a small bell without inscription, probably of the 17th century.

The plate consists of a chalice and paten.

The registers begin in 1602.

ADVOWSON The earliest mention of the church of Thornborough is the grant of it made by Hamo son of Meinfelin to Luffield Priory in the reign of Henry II.[31] It was evidently appropriated to the priory at an early date, for a vicarage was ordained before 1223.[32] In 1260 Simon de Boycot, then vicar, made an agreement with the Abbot of Biddlesden about the small tithes from the abbey lands. Without admitting that his lands were liable to tithe the abbot made the vicar a grant of 3 acres of land in satisfaction of his claim.[33] The advowson has followed continuously the descent of the Luffield Priory Manor of Thornborough.[34] The tithes, however, seem to have been alienated between 1786 and 1797 by the lord of this manor to the Marquess of Buckingham.[35]

Robert Damory, probably one of the three Roberts who lived in the 13th century, had licence from the Prior of Luffield to have divine service celebrated in his chapel of St. Laurence.[36] A dispute about this chapel between Luffield Priory and Biddlesden Abbey was settled by the Archdeacon of Buckingham in 1290 in favour of Luffield.[37] The chapel is not afterwards mentioned.

Twenty pence rent from a messuage and yardland in Thornborough maintained an obit in the church.[38]

At the visitation of Bishop Atwater in 1519 it was found that the master of the college of St. Thomas Acon, London, ought to maintain a cantarist in Thornborough Church, but had not done so for twenty years.[39] This was probably the chantry served by John Crowche.[40]

CHARITIES This parish is entitled under the will of William Hill, dated in 1723, to receive an annuity of 20s. for a coat for a poor man, and 20s. for poor attending the sacrament, the annuities being charged upon an estate in Bierton and Hulcott. The annual sum of £2 is usually distributed among five aged poor.

The poor's allotment, acquired under the Inclosure Act, contains 16 a. 1 r. 20 p., which is let in garden allotments producing about £20 a year. The rent is applied in tickets for coal.

The church allotment, acquired under the same Act, containing 5 a. 0 r. 19 p., is let at £7 10s. a year, which is carried to the churchwardens' general account.

31 See above.
32 Willis, op. cit. 290; *Liber Antiq. Hugonis Wells*, 14.
33 Harl. MS. 4714, fol. 133 d.
34 *Pope Nich. Tax.* (Rec. Com.), 32; Pat. 18 Hen. VII, pt. i, m. 22; 34 Hen. VIII, pt. v, m. 5; 2 Eliz., pt. xi; Inst. Bks. (P.R.O.).
35 Bacon, *Liber Regis.* 490; Priv. Act, 37 Geo. III, cap. 49.
36 Willis, op. cit. 290.
37 Ibid. 288.
38 Chant. Cert. 5, no. 1.
39 Bp. Atwater's Visit. in Alnwick Tower, Lincoln, fol. 37.
40 See above.

THORNTON

Ternitone (xi cent.) ; Torentona, Turinton (xii cent.) ; Torintuna, Thorington, Thorenton, Tornton (xiii cent.).

This small parish comprises an area of 1,347 acres, of which 7 are covered by water. There are 129 acres of arable land, 1,033 laid down in permanent grass, and 61 of woods and plantations.[1] The soil is stiff clay with a subsoil of clay, gravel and limestone rock, and wheat, oats, barley and beans are grown. The greatest height, 385 ft. above the ordnance datum, is reached in the south-east, from where the land falls away to 236 ft. in the north-west, where the River Ouse forms the parish and also the county boundary for some distance. It widens out into a small lake where it flows past the lawn of Thornton House, the seat of Mr. H. W. Harris, which stands in a park of 181 acres and is approached from the Beachampton road by an avenue of elm trees. The present house, which was built in 1850 by the Hon. Richard Cavendish[2] from the designs of John Tarring,[3] incloses part of the old building described by Browne Willis, c. 1735, as a quadrangular building of great antiquity with a gallery 125 ft. long.[4] It was afterwards modernized by Dr. Cotton,[5] whose alterations made it the 'spacious and respectable mansion' alluded to by Lipscomb, c. 1847.[6]

The church of St. Michael stands in the grounds to the east of the house at the end of an avenue of pines. There is now no house for the incumbent, as the rector resides at Nash, a chapelry to Thornton since 1854. The former parsonage-house, according to a terrier of 1674, consisted of three and a half bays, and there was a barn of two bays, an orchard, 1 acre of land and half an acre of meadow.[7]

There is no village proper, but a few buildings, among them the Home Farm, lie on the eastern outskirts of the park with one or two houses further south. Blacksfields Farm lies on the eastern boundary of the parish and Tyrrelcote Farm, a 17th-century house of brick and stone, about the centre. The country is very open and chiefly given up to pasture for grazing ; the only woods of any size are Great Wood on the west boundary and Cowpen Wood in the south-east of the parish. The open common was the cause of a dispute in the 16th century between Humfrey Tyrell, the lord of the manor, and the tenants, who accused him of having destroyed on 20 October 1532, and many times since, all the furze on the common. The commissioners heard the case at Northampton on 31 March 1535, when the tenants declared that they had always felled furze and blackthorn by licence of the lord, but were fined for

felling whitethorn. The green, as parcel of the manor, had been formerly inclosed with a stone wall by George Ingleton, but it had lain common for forty years or more ; houses had been built on it and stones from the wall taken to repair the manor-house. Nevertheless, Tyrell had encroached upon the tenants' rights by inclosing with a hedge in the autumn of 1529 2 acres of land used as common for beasts. They admitted, however, that the stone wall at the mill had been injured by the wives washing there and by the course of the common kine, and had also heard that one of Tyrell's servants had been thrown into the water by Robert Wilson's wife and her maid.[8]

MANORS Eight hides in *THORNTON* which had been held as a manor before the Conquest by Azor son of Toti were included in 1086 among the lands of Roger de Ivri.[9] After the death without issue of Geoffrey, his last surviving son,[10] the barony of Ivri, whose 'caput' was at Mixbury, Oxfordshire, was bestowed by the king on Guy de St. Walery or on his son Reynold,[11] from which family it became known as the honour of St. Walery.[12] Reynold's name occurs as owing knight's service for land in Oxfordshire in 1160–1 [13] and in Berkshire and Hampshire in 1166,[14] the year of his death.[15] His son Bernard,[16] who was responsible for this service in 1171–2,[17] was killed at the siege of Acon in 1190,[18] when the honour passed to his surviving son Thomas,[19] who gave 170 marks for relief of his lands in 1193.[20] Three years later they were seized by the king,[21] but Thomas de St. Walery regained his property,[22] and he is returned as a landowner in Bedfordshire and Buckinghamshire about 1212.[23] Shortly afterwards he appears again to have incurred the royal displeasure, as he was restored to favour in 1214, when he had seisin of lands in Hampshire late of his brother Henry.[24] On 13 August 1216 a mandate was issued to the Sheriff of Bedfordshire and Buckinghamshire to give Ralf Hareng the custody of all the lands of Thomas de St. Walery to hold during pleasure for the use of the said Thomas,[25] and about six months later Hareng obtained royal letters 'de conductu' for his lands and those of St. Walery.[26] The first mention of the connexion of the St. Walerys with Thornton occurs in the *Testa de Nevill* and must be presumed to date in or before 1218, since the death of Thomas de St. Walery, whose name is given as lord,[27] took place in that year.[28] In 1219 livery of his lands was given to his daughter and heir, Annora, and her husband, Robert Count of Dreux.[29] The latter forfeited the property, which on 8 March 1224–5 was committed to the custody of

[1] Statistics from Bd. of Agric. (1905).
[2] Sheahan, *Hist. and Topog. of Bucks.* 313.
[3] *Dict. Nat. Biog.*
[4] Willis, *Hist. and Antiq. of Buckingham*, 311–12.
[5] Lysons, *Mag. Brit.* i (3), 648.
[6] Lipscomb, *Hist. and Antiq. of Bucks.* iii, 120.
[7] Willis, op. cit. 300.
[8] Star Chamb. Proc. Hen. VIII, bdles. 29, no. 72 ; 18, no. 97.
[9] *V.C.H. Bucks.* i, 269.
[10] Edmonson, *Baronagium Gen.* i, 173.

[11] Ibid. ; Dugdale, *Baronage*, i, 454–5 ; *Feud. Aids*, ii, 157, 180, 190.
[12] *Red Bk. of Exch.* (Rolls Ser.), 586, 798 ; Mins. Accts. (Gen. Ser.), bdle. 1096, no. 1, 6.
[13] *Red Bk. of Exch.* (Rolls Ser.), 25.
[14] Ibid. 204, 305.
[15] *Gen.* iv, 241.
[16] *Eynsham Cartul.* (Oxf. Hist. Soc.), ii, p. xxv.
[17] *Red Bk. of Exch.* (Rolls Ser.), 51.
[18] Dugdale, loc. cit.
[19] *Eynsham Cartul.* (Oxf. Hist. Soc.), i, 40.

[20] Pipe R. 5 Ric. I, m. 10.
[21] Dugdale, loc. cit. He was, however, in possession of Westbury in that year (Pipe R. 8 Ric. I, m. 17).
[22] Pipe R. 11 John, m. 14 ; *Red Bk. of Exch.* (Rolls Ser.), 99, 128.
[23] *Red Bk. of Exch.* (Rolls Ser.), 138.
[24] *Rot. Lit. Claus.* (Rec. Com.), i, 161.
[25] Ibid. 281.
[26] *Cal. Pat.* 1216–25, p. 24.
[27] *Testa de Nevill* (Rec. Com.), 260.
[28] *Gen.* iv, 241.
[29] *Rot. Lit. Claus.* (Rec. Com.), i, 387.

Ralf Hareng,[30] but a month later Hareng was ordered to restore the fees to the count.[31] Two years later the count lost his lands for good, and their custody was again bestowed upon Ralf Hareng [32] preparatory to a grant to the king's brother Richard Earl of Cornwall, to whom on 21 August 1227 Ralf was ordered to surrender all the lands.[33] The following year the knights and free men formerly of the Count of Dreux were called upon to give competent aid to the Earl of Cornwall to maintain him in the king's service.[34] Ralf Hareng's intermittent possession of Thornton was doubtless instrumental in procuring for him the ownership in fee,[35] the overlordship rights being exercised by the Earls of Cornwall and their heirs in virtue of their tenure of the St. Walery honour, to which Thornton remained attached until the abolition of feudal tenure in the 17th century.[36] Two shillings or a besant was due from the manor to the honour,[37] and it was said to be held in soccage in the early 13th century [38] and later for three parts of a fee.[39] In the later inquisitions the rent service alone was mentioned.[40]

Ralf Hareng was dead by 1230, when he was succeeded by a son and heir Ralf,[41] who is mentioned in 1243.[42] Either the father or son made over some of the property to James Savage, called nephew and heir of Ralf Hareng, who in 1249 acknowledged the right of Gilbert Thornton to 2 virgates subinfeudated by Ralf Hareng for 2s. a year and suit of court to James at Thornton, in a like manner as all the other free tenants of the said James.[43] Ralf Hareng is returned as lord of Thornton in 1254,[44] but died probably four years later, as, though he was appointed Sheriff of Hampshire in 1258, he did not send in any account of the office, James Savage, who had been made sheriff in 1256, continuing in his stead.[45] James Savage may have died in 1275, when Richard Chastillon claimed to be his heir,[46] and made a settlement of Thornton Manor on himself, his wife Rose and their issue.[47] At Richard's death, four years after, Hugh Chastillon, his son and heir, was of full age,[48] but did not inherit Thornton, which passed according to the settlement of 1275 to his step-mother Rose. Immediately after her husband's death she became the wife of John Tingewick,[49] but it was as the widow of Richard Chastillon that her right to Thornton Manor was acknowledged by Hugh Chastillon in 1280.[50] The Thornton property thus passed away from the elder branch of the Chastillon family,

and John Tingewick, Rose's husband, held the lordship rights here in 1284–6.[51] He died in 1304,[52] and the property passed after the death of Rose, still alive in 1315,[53] to Malcolm Chastillon,[54] her son by her first husband,[55] whose name had been given in 1300 [56] and 1308 [57] as responsible for this fee. His feud with the Leaumes of Leckhampstead (q.v.) resulted in his being sued by a member of that family in 1327 for the detention of a horse,[58] and in a complaint lodged by him in 1333 against the Leaumes and others for carrying away his goods at Thornton.[59] He was knight of the shire in five Parliaments from 1327 to 1332,[60] as was his son John, who succeeded him in 1337,[61] in the Parliaments of 1341, 1343 and 1355,[62] as well as Sheriff of Bedfordshire and Buckinghamshire in 1350.[63] Little is known of the Chastillons in Thornton for the next fifty years; their property is referred to as late of John Chastillon both in 1377 [64] and 1399.[65] In 1409 Sir John Chastillon of Thornton was fined 20 marks for not appearing when impanelled on an inquisition,[66] and in 1418 he and his wife Margaret severed the connexion of the family with this parish by transferring the manor to John Barton, jun.[67] He is called of Thornton in 1427 [68] and again in 1433, when he was one of the mainpernors of Joan Beauchamp, Dowager Baroness Bergavenny.[69] He died in January 1433–4,[70] leaving part of his estate to endow anew the chantry, but his executors were sued four years later for Thornton Manor by William Launcelyn of Cople in Bedfordshire, who claimed by inheritance as great-grandson of Margaret, the sister of the last John Chastillon, who died without issue, and granddaughter of Malcolm Chastillon.[71] Further litigation ensued shortly afterwards, when the executors with Isabel, widow of John Barton, jun., were defendants in an action brought by William Fowler to force them to keep an agreement made in 1438 concerning the lands and will of John Barton, sen., Recorder of London.[72] In 1440 the Chastillon family renewed their claim, this time in the person of John Loughton, great-grandson of Elizabeth daughter of Malcolm Chastillon.[73]

William Launcelyn also seized the opportunity this year to plead his rights, but was disposed of by Isabel Barton's assertion that his great-grandmother Margaret was illegitimate,[74] whereupon Launcelyn made a complete renunciation of title to trustees.[75] In 1443 his example was followed by John Loughton,[76] who

[30] *Rot. Lit. Claus.* (Rec. Com.), ii, 22.
[31] Ibid. 26.
[32] *Cal. Pat.* 1225–32, p. 129.
[33] *Rot. Lit. Claus.* (Rec. Com.), ii, 198.
[34] *Cal. Pat.* 1225–32, p. 191.
[35] *Testa de Nevill* (Rec. Com.), 244.
[36] *Red Bk. of Exch.* (Rolls Ser.), 798; *Hund. R.* (Rec. Com.), i, 27; Chan. Inq. p.m. 11 Edw. III (1st nos.), no. 33; Ct. R. (Gen. Ser.), portf. 212, no. 3, 19, 20, 24; Chan. Inq. p.m. (Ser. 2), ccxciv, 92.
[37] Chan. Inq. p.m. Edw. I, file 21, no. 12; *Hund. R.* (Rec. Com.), ii, 352; Mins. Accts. (Gen. Ser.), bdle. 1096, no.1, 6, 14; Chan. Inq. p.m. (Ser. 2), x, 2.
[38] *Testa de Nevill* (Rec. Com.), 244; Chan. Inq. p.m. Edw. I, file 21, no. 12.
[39] *Feud. Aids*, i, 81.
[40] Chan. Inq. p.m. (Ser. 2), clxiii, 3.
[41] *Excerpta e Rot. Fin.* (Rec. Com.), i, 194.
[42] Linc. Epis. Reg. R. Grosteste.
[43] Feet of F. Bucks. 33 Hen. III, no. 4.

[44] *Hund. R.* (Rec. Com.), i, 27; his mother Isabel then held Westbury in dower.
[45] P.R.O. *List of Sheriffs*, 54.
[46] *Cal. Fine R.* 1272–1307, p. 42.
[47] Feet of F. Div. Co. 3 Edw. I, no. 25.
[48] Chan. Inq. p.m. Edw. I, file 21, no. 12.
[49] *Hund. R.* (Rec. Com.), ii, 352.
[50] Feet of F. Div. Co. Mich. 8 & 9 Edw. I, no. 17. Hugh is described as heir of James Savage in 1281 (*Cal. Fine R.* 1272–1307, p. 153).
[51] *Feud. Aids*, i, 81.
[52] Chan. Inq. p.m. 32 Edw. I, no. 44; *Cal. Pat.* 1301–7, p. 332.
[53] Lipscomb, op. cit. iii, 120, quoting episcopal registers.
[54] *Feud. Aids*, i, 109.
[55] Wrottesley, *Ped. from Plea R.* 358.
[56] Chan. Inq. p.m. 28 Edw. I, no. 44.
[57] Mins. Accts. (Gen. Ser.), bdle. 1096, no. 1.

[58] De Banco R. 276, m. 42 d.
[59] *Cal. Pat.* 1330–4, pp. 498, 499.
[60] *Ret. of Memb. of Parl.* i, 78, 83, 91, 95, 98.
[61] Chan. Inq. p.m. 11 Edw. III (1st nos.), no. 33; *Abbrev. Rot. Orig.* (Rec. Com.), ii, 114.
[62] *Ret. of Memb. of Parl.* i, 133, 136; App. p. xiv.
[63] P.R.O. *List of Sheriffs*, 2.
[64] Mins. Accts. (Gen. Ser.), bdle. 1096, no. 6.   [65] Ibid. no. 14.
[66] *Cal. Pat.* 1408–13, p. 100.
[67] Feet of F. case 22, file 117.
[68] Wrottesley, op. cit. 437.
[69] *Cal. Pat.* 1429–36, p. 295.
[70] Chan. Inq. p.m. 11 Hen. VI, no. 35.
[71] Wrottesley, op. cit. 358.
[72] Early Chan. Proc. bdle. 9, no. 136.
[73] Wrottesley, op. cit. 368.
[74] Ibid. 369.
[75] Close, 290, m. 8.
[76] Ibid. 293, m. 15 d.

three years later joined his wife Margaret in quit-claiming any right she might have in half the manor.[77] Isabel Barton had married as her second husband Sir Robert Shottesbrook,[78] who presented to the church in her right in 1453.[79] She died in 1457,[80] and Thornton Manor was sold by the trustees to Sir John Prysot, Thomas Shotbolt, and others to the use of Prysot.[81] He died shortly afterwards, and his widow Margaret about 1460 brought an action against Shotbolt, who refused to make an estate to her and was therefore committed to Newgate.[82] In 1462, however, he released all his right in Thornton to Margaret and her trustees.[83] They were sued two years later by William Gernon, who claimed the manor as a descendant of Richard Chastillon and Rose, but as the pedigree submitted by him gave Hugh as son of Rose instead of stepson the action was easily quashed.[84] In 1467 Gernon renounced any right he might have to Robert Ingleton,[85] to whom the manor had been transferred by the trustees presumably about 1463.[86] Robert Ingleton, who was chancellor of the Exchequer to Edward IV,[87] received a general pardon in 1471 for all offences and unlicensed acquisitions and alienations of land.[88] He is described as of Thornton, late of London and J.P. for Buckinghamshire.[89]

INGLETON of Thornton. *Argent a cheveron between three barrels of pitch sable with fire issuing from them.*

A brass in the church commemorates his death on 15 October 1472,[90] though the inquisition gives the date as 17 October 1473.[91] His son George,[92] Sheriff of Bedfordshire and Buckinghamshire in 1485,[93] died in the early days of 1493–4, leaving a young son Robert,[94] during whose minority Thornton was granted in custody to Sir Richard Empson, minister of Henry VII.[95] He gave his daughter Ann in marriage to his ward, who died in 1503, still under age and leaving an only daughter Jane, nine months old.[96] A few years later the widow Ann, with her second husband John Hugford, sued Robert's trustees in Chancery for failing to pay her jointure from Oakley and other manors.[97] The dispute was settled in 1515, when John and Ann gave up all claim to dower in Oakley, Thornton, and elsewhere for 1,000 marks.[98] Ann was evidently not considered a competent person to have the custody of Jane Ingleton, for the wardship was granted by the king to Dame Joan Bradbury, widow,[99] who held courts at Thornton as guardian of the child.[100] By 1517 Jane Ingleton was the wife of Humfrey son and heir of Sir William Tyrell of Ockendon[1] (Wokendon), Essex, with whom she made a settlement of Thornton in 1526.[2] Humfrey Tyrell died in 1549[3]; his wife surviving him married Alexander St. John, upon whom a rent was settled in 1552 by George son and heir of Humfrey and Jane Tyrell.[4] The first payment was to be made after the death of Jane, which took place in 1557, when Thornton Manor, which had been settled on her in 1550, descended to George Tyrell.[5] He made a settlement of the manor

TYRELL of Thornton, baronet. *Argent two cheverons azure in a border engrailed gules.*

in 1571[6] and died in that year.[7] His son Edward, who succeeded,[8] was sheriff of the county in 1595–6[9] and member for Buckingham borough in 1604.[10] He died in January 1605–6, leaving by will the Thornton property, including the mansion-house, to his son and heir Edward, his widow Margaret receiving an estate in Nast End, Great Leckhampstead, and Oakley Manor[11] (q.v.). Edward was Sheriff of Buckinghamshire in 1612–13[12] and joined with his wife Elizabeth and younger brothers Timothy and Thomas in making a settlement of Thornton in 1626.[13] He had been knighted at Windsor in 1607, and was created a baronet on 31 October 1627.[14] His eldest son Robert joined his father in suffering a recovery of the manor in 1632,[15] but did not take part in a further recovery six years later,[16] as he was disinherited by his father, who on 19 February 1638–9 obtained a new baronetcy, with the former precedency and with special remainder to his two younger sons Toby and Francis.[17] Sir Edward Tyrell, bart., remained in possession of Thornton until his death in 1656,[18] his son Toby, who succeeded to the title and estates, dying in 1671, when Thornton passed to his son Thomas,[19] upon whom a settlement had been made in 1665.[20] He held until 1705,[21] his son Harry, whose right to Thornton had been acknowledged in 1692,[22] inheriting the estate. He died three years

[77] Feet of F. case 22, file 22.
[78] *Cal. Pat.* 1467–77, p. 112.
[79] Willis, op. cit. 308.
[80] Ibid. 296. By her will she left money to Fowler, who was to bestow it on the churches of Thornton, Padbury, &c.; as he failed to do so his son Richard Fowler, Chancellor of the Duchy of Lancaster, bequeathed money for that purpose by his will proved 19 Nov. 1477 (Nicolas, *Test. Vetusta*, 344).
[81] Early Chan. Proc. bdle. 29, no. 99.
[82] Ibid.
[83] Close, 314, m. 26.
[84] Wrottesley, op. cit. 408.
[85] Close, 319, m. 17.
[86] He presented to the church in that year (Willis, op. cit. 308).
[87] Lysons, *Mag. Brit.* i (3), 648.
[88] *Cal. Pat.* 1467–77, p. 267.
[89] Ibid.
[90] See below.
[91] Chan. Inq. p.m. 13 Edw. IV, no. 9.

By this, however, he is said to hold no lands in Northants, Beds., Bucks. or Herts.
[92] Ibid.
[93] P.R.O. *List of Sheriffs*, 2.
[94] Chan. Inq. p.m. (Ser. 2), x, 2.
[95] Exch. Inq. p.m. (Ser. 2), file 6, no. 13.
[96] Chan. Inq. p.m. (Ser. 2), xvi, 113. According to the Visitation of 1634 Robert Ingleton married Sibyl Fiscells (*Visit. of Bucks.* [Harl. Soc.], 118). She is probably identical with Isabel third wife of his grandfather Robert who died in 1472.
[97] Early Chan. Proc. bdle. 141, no. 85.
[98] Feet of F. Div. Co. Hil. 6 Hen. VIII.
[99] Early Chan. Proc. bdle. 539, no. 19.
[100] Star Chamb. Proc. Hen. VIII, bdle. 18, no. 97.
[1] Ibid.; *Visit. of Bucks.* (Harl. Soc.), 118.
[2] Feet of F. Div. Co. East. 18 Hen. VIII.

[3] Chan. Inq. p.m. (Ser. 2), lxxxviii, 56.
[4] Feet of F. Bucks. Mich. 6 Edw. VI.
[5] Chan. Inq. p.m. (Ser. 2), cxii, 137 (1). [6] Feet of F. Bucks. Hil. 13 Eliz.
[7] Chan. Inq. p.m. (Ser. 2), clxiii, 3.
[8] Ibid.
[9] P.R.O. *List of Sheriffs*, 9.
[10] *Ret. of Memb. of Parl.* i, 442.
[11] Chan. Inq. p.m. (Ser. 2), ccxciv, 92.
[12] P.R.O. *List of Sheriffs*, 9.
[13] Feet of F. Bucks. Mich. 2 Chas. I.
[14] G.E.C. *Baronetage*, ii, 34.
[15] Recov. R. Mich. 8 Chas. I, m. 126.
[16] Ibid. Mich. 14 Chas. I, m. 102.
[17] G.E.C. loc. cit.
[18] Ibid.; *Cal. S. P. Dom. Add.* 1625–49, p. 101; 1667–8, p. 150; 1640–1, p. 57.
[19] G.E.C. op. cit. ii, 35.
[20] Recov. R. Hil. 17 Chas. II, m. 9.
[21] *Thornton Par. Reg.* (Bucks. Par. Reg. Soc.), 28.
[22] Recov. R. Mich. 4 Will. and Mary, m. 113.

after his father,[23] leaving three sons, one of them posthumous,[24] of whom the eldest, Thomas, made a settlement of the manor in 1717[25] and died a bachelor the following year.[26] The second son Harry also died unmarried two years later,[27] when Thornton passed to the third son Charles, who held until 1749.[28] He left a daughter and heir Hester Maria under the guardianship of his mother, Hester Lady Tyrell,[29] the title passing to Thomas Tyrell, his cousin and male heir.[30] He is called of Thornton at his death on 11 February 1755 and was buried at Thornton,[31] though his will, dated 28 July 1749, expresses his desire not to be buried in the family vault.[32] He mentions his sisters 'Mrs.' Frances Tyrell and the Hon. Elizabeth Forrester, widow, who proved the will on 13 February 1755.[33] This last Sir Thomas Tyrell was son of Charles, younger brother of Sir Harry who died in 1708. The entry in the parish register relating to the death on 3 May 1752 of Hester, widow of Sir Harry Tyrell, bart., speaks of her as the mother of Sir Thomas, Sir Henry, and Sir Charles, successive baronets and all dead.[34] Her granddaughter, Hester Maria, to whom Sir Charles Tyrell left property at Thornton and Leckhampstead, became the wife of the Rev. William Cotton.[35] She died in 1778[36]; her husband, who survived her until 1782,[37] does not appear to have held Thornton after her death, as in 1779 their daughter and heir Elizabeth with her husband Thomas Sheppard made a settlement of the manor.[38] In 1809 he was made a baronet as Sheppard of Thornton Hall.[39] His elder son William Thomas (who had assumed the name of Sheppard-Cotton by royal licence in 1799[40] in compliance with the will of his grandfather William Cotton)[41] having died without issue in 1803,[42] Thomas was succeeded

Sheppard of Thornton, baronet. *Azure a cheveron or between three fleurs de lis argent with three molets of six points sable on the cheveron.*

at his death in 1821 by his second son Thomas.[43] He had taken the name of Cotton before Sheppard by sign-manual in 1806 on attaining his majority,[44] and had been sheriff of the county in 1813.[45] At his death without issue in 1848 the baronetcy expired,[46] and the property passed to his sister Elizabeth, whose husband Thomas Hart of Uttoxeter also died in that year.[47] Their daughter and heir Elizabeth Maria Margaret, who succeeded her mother in 1854,[48] had

married in 1841 Richard Cavendish,[49] second son of the second Lord Waterpark,[50] who was sheriff for the county in 1851.[51] She died four years after her mother,[52] and her husband held Thornton until his death in 1876,[53] their son William Thomas Cavendish, who succeeded, dying two years later.[54] His son Mr. Henry Sheppard Hart Cavendish, the African traveller and explorer, sold the manor about 1905 to Mr. Whitworth, from whom it was acquired two years later by Mr. Henry W. Harris, the present owner.

On the manor of Thornton in 1086 was a mill worth 10 ores,[55] described in 1278–9 as a water-mill.[56] By 1606 two water-mills are recorded,[57] and throughout the 18th century there were three, called corn-mills, standing on the manor.[58]

A free or several fishery in the Ouse was among the appurtenances of the manor from the 16th century and probably earlier, as was free warren.[59] Reference to the view of frankpledge does not occur until the 17th century.[60] Court Rolls for Thornton are extant dating from 1422 to 1546,[61] and courts leet and baron are included among the manorial privileges in the 18th century.[62]

Under the land of Roger de Ivri in the Domesday Book is included a manor of 1 hide in *HASLEY* (Haselei, Haseleya, Hasle, Haselegh), which had been held before the Conquest by Thori, a man of King Edward, who could sell.[63] The name appears to have been lost after the 14th century, but the place was probably adjacent to, if not actually comprised within, Thornton, which immediately precedes it in the Domesday Book, both places, moreover, being within the hundred of Rovelai. Like the rest of Roger de Ivri's holdings, it formed part of the honour of St. Walery and as such was held of the Earls of Cornwall for a third of a fee in the 13th century.[64] The manorial descent of this property, however, approximates more closely to Radclive, another of Roger de Ivri's manors, than to Thornton, though Radclive is separated from Thornton by Buckingham and lay within a different hundred, that of Mursley, in 1086. Both Radclive and Hasley had the same Domesday tenant Fulk,[65] who had been succeeded in both places by the Hareng family in the 13th century. Of the intermediate holders nothing is known in Radclive, though Humfrey is returned as tenant in Hasley in 1167.[66] Ralf Hareng, who was in possession c. 1235, had subinfeudated Richard Hareng in Hasley.[67] His gift of lands in 1243 to St. Michael's Chapel, Radclive, included an estate in Hasley.[68] In 1251 Hasley Manor was alienated to Simon de

[23] *Thornton Par. Reg.* ut sup. 29.
[24] G.E.C. loc. cit.
[25] Recov. R. Trin. 3 Geo. I, m. 93.
[26] *Thornton Par. Reg.* ut sup. 31. [27] Ibid.
[28] Ibid. 38 ; Willis, op. cit. 299.
[29] P.C.C. 163 Lisle.
[30] Lipscomb, op. cit. iii, 119.
[31] *Thornton Par. Reg.* ut sup. 43.
[32] P.C.C. 60 Paul.
[33] Ibid. She died in 1776 (*Musgrave's Obit.* [Harl. Soc.], ii, 349 ; P.C.C. 457 Bellas). The Rev. William Cotton by his will in 1782 refers to the Cottage Farm in Thornton which he had bought of the late Mrs. Forrester (P.C.C. 484 Gostling).
[34] *Thornton Par. Reg.* ut sup. 39.
[35] G.E.C. loc. cit.
[36] *Thornton Par. Reg.* ut sup. 50.

[37] *Musgrave's Obit.* (Harl. Soc.), ii, 81; P.C.C. 484 Gostling.
[38] Recov. R. Trin. 19 Geo. III, m. 55.
[39] G.E.C. loc. cit.
[40] Phillimore and Fry, *Changes of Name*, 286.
[41] Burke, *Peerage* (ed. 1826).
[42] *Thornton Par. Reg.* ut sup. 52.
[43] Burke, loc. cit.
[44] *Dict. Nat. Biog.*; Phillimore and Fry, op. cit. 74.
[45] P.R.O. *List of Sheriffs*, 11.
[46] *Dict. Nat. Biog.* [48] Ibid.
[47] M.I. in church.
[49] Sheahan, op. cit. 313.
[50] Burke, *Peerage* (ed. 1912).
[51] Sheahan, loc. cit.
[52] M.I. in church.
[53] *Ret. of Owners of Land*, 1873, *Bucks.* 4.

[54] Burke, loc. cit.
[55] *V.C.H. Bucks.* i, 269.
[56] *Hund. R.* (Rec. Com.), ii, 352.
[57] Chan. Inq. p.m. (Ser. 2), ccxciv, 92.
[58] Recov. R. Trin. 19 Geo. III, m. 55.
[59] Chan. Inq. p.m. (Ser. 2), clxiii, 3.
[60] Feet of F. Bucks. Mich. 2 Chas. I.
[61] Ct. R. (Gen. Ser.), portf. 212, no. 3, 19, 20, 24.
[62] Recov. R. Trin. 3 Geo. I, m. 93 ; Trin. 19 Geo. III, m. 55.
[63] *V.C.H. Bucks.* i, 269.
[64] *Testa de Nevill* (Rec. Com.), 244 ; *Abbrev. Plac.* (Rec. Com.), 186.
[65] *V.C.H. Bucks.* i, 269.
[66] *Pipe R.* 13 Hen. II (Pipe R. Soc.), 109.
[67] *Testa de Nevill* (Rec. Com.), 244.
[68] Linc. Epis. Reg. R. Grosteste.

St. Lys by John Hareng, who retained a life interest in it.[69] Simon de St. Lys also acquired Radclive doubtless at this date and certainly before 1254–5, and in 1273 he brought an action against Richard, parson of Buckingham Church, for disseising him of common pasture attached to his free tenement in Radclive and Hasley.[70] He was successful as regards the former place, but failed in Hasley. After 1301, when Hasley was held by Andrew de St. Lys, lord of Radclive,[71] there is no mention of this manor.

Snelshall Priory had a small property in the parish assessed with lands in Beachampton at £2 2s. 5d. in 1291.[72] In 1535 the priory paid 9s. for the rent of a tenement and 4s. for lands in Thornton to Humfrey Tyrell.[73] By 1557 a cottage formerly belonging to Snelshall had come into the possession of Thomas Thomson.[74]

Part of the priory's estate, comprising 1 virgate, 1 acre and a meadow adjoining called Deneaker, was given, with the consent of the priory, to the hospital of St. John without the east gate of Oxford by Henry de Lewknor, parson of Thornton in 1219 (cf. advowson). His patron, Ralf Hareng, likewise bestowed on the hospital 12 acres of land and meadow, and Ellis son of Edmund the miller gave a messuage and 4 acres of land, all these gifts being confirmed to the hospital by Henry III in 1246.[75]

Furzenfield, an outlying farm in the south-east of the parish, was part of the dower of Margery widow of George Tyrell,[76] who by 1577 had married Richard Leigh,[77] and still held the property in 1606, when she was again a widow.[78] The reversion was left by Edward Tyrell at his death in that year to his eldest son Edward,[79] and it descended in the family with the rest of the Thornton property.

The church of *ST. MICHAEL AND ALL ANGELS* consists of a nave measuring internally 39 ft. by 12 ft., north and south aisles each 8 ft. wide, and west tower 10 ft. square. It is built of rubble and the roofs are covered with lead.

Reference to this church occurs as early as 1219,[79a] but the structure of that period was entirely rebuilt in the 14th century, probably by John Chastillon, lord of the manor, who founded a chantry here in 1344. The building then consisted of a chancel, with the adjoining chapel of the Annunciation of the Blessed Virgin Mary for Chastillon's chantry, a nave, north and south aisles and tower. About 1468 the chapel of the Annunciation was rebuilt by Robert Ingleton in accordance with the will of John Barton, who died in 1434.[80] Between 1770 and 1800 the successive patrons, Dr. William Cotton and Thomas Sheppard, carried out drastic restorations. The chancel and chapel were then apparently destroyed and a wall built on the east side of the chancel arch, the roofs were altered, obscuring the clearstory windows, and the present pews inserted. The north aisle was rebuilt in 1850, when the fabric was generally repaired.

At the east end of the nave is the original 14th-century chancel arch, which is now blocked, and a modern three-light window with 14th-century jambs and head, probably taken from the east window of the chancel, has been inserted in the blocking. The north and south arcades, also of the 14th century, are each of four pointed arches, supported by octagonal pillars and responds with moulded capitals of varying detail. At the west end of the nave is an original pointed arch to the tower. A 14th-century clearstory and the nave roof, which retains two 15th-century arched trusses, are hidden by a modern flat ceiling, but the blocked circular windows of the clearstory can be seen from the outside. The three traceried windows in the south wall of the south aisle have been considerably renewed, while the corresponding windows of the north aisle are principally modern, but some old stonework has been re-used in them.

The 14th-century tower is of three stages surmounted by an embattled parapet. The moulded west doorway is original, but the window above only retains the original jambs. The second stage of the tower is pierced by small trefoiled lights, and the bell-chamber by pointed windows of two trefoiled lights, all of which, except the head of the east window of the bell-chamber, are original. The string-course below the parapet is supported at wide intervals by carved heads.

On the south side of the altar is a slab with the brass figures of Robert Ingleton, in plate armour, and his three wives, Margaret, Clemens and Isabel, in horned head-dresses, and groups of six sons and ten daughters. Above are the shields of Ingleton, Dymoke, Cauntelow, and a lion between six crescents for Fiscells (?), and below is the inscription, 'Armiger ecce pius jacet hic tellure Robt9 Ingylton domin9 de Thorneton jur' patron'. In quintodecimo moriens octobr' ab orbe ad celos transit Mil C quat' hec 72 simul adde. Sit sibi ppicia Celi Regina Maria salvet eum x̄p̄i Matris amore deus.' On the north side of the altar is a brass figure of Jane daughter of Robert, grandson of the above-mentioned Robert Ingleton, and Ann, and wife first of Humfrey Tyrell and secondly of Alexander St. John. She died in 1557, and is represented in long gown, puffed and slashed sleeves, and the 'Paris head.' There are four shields, the quartered coat of Tyrell, the quartered coat of Ingleton, Tyrell quartering Ingleton, and Tyrell impaling Ingleton; a marginal inscription, and at the feet of the figure 'Et predicta Jana habuit exit9 Georgiū Terrell filiū suū apparent' et predict' Georgius fuit viginti et septem annos natus die quo predict' Jana obiit.' In the tower are two fine alabaster effigies which now lie one on either side of the west doorway; they are ascribed by Browne Willis to John Barton, jun., who died in 1434, and Isabel his wife,[81] and were in his time below the chancel arch, where they formed part of 'a most elegant monument.' The man, whose feet rest upon the figure of a dog, is in plate armour, and the lady is in a sleeveless gown and long cloak. Some

[69] Feet of F. Bucks. 35 Hen. III, no. 2.
[70] *Abbrev. Plac.* (Rec. Com.), 186.
[71] Chan. Inq. p.m. 28 Edw. I, no. 44.
[72] *Pope Nich. Tax.* (Rec. Com.), 47.
[73] *Valor Eccl.* (Rec. Com.), iv, 228.
[74] Harl. MS. 607, fol. 74.
[75] *Cal. Chart. R.* 1226–57, p. 297.
[76] Chan. Inq. p.m. (Ser. 2), ccxciv, 92.
[77] *Acts of P.C.* 1575–7, p. 223.

[78] Chan. Inq. p.m. (Ser. 2), ccxciv, 92.
[79] Ibid.
[79a] See under advowson.
[80] For references see under advowson.
[81] *Rec. of Bucks.* vii, 53; Lipscomb, op. cit. iii, 121, gives the inscription, 'Orate pro Johanne Barton juniore domino de Thornton conditore istius capelle et pro Isabella uxore eius quorum ani-

mabus propicietur Deus Amen.' Lipscomb also points out that by his will he directed that his body should be buried in the chapel of the Annunciation of B.V.M. in the church of Thornton and that the chapel be newly built at the charge of his estate. He left 10 marks to the fabric of the church and 5 marks for the chancel.

other effigies and brasses described by Browne Willis
have since disappeared. There is an old iron chest
in the tower.

The tower contains a ring of three bells: the
treble, inscribed 'Sint Pro Elya Michael Deus Atque
Maria,' is a 14th-century bell, and 'Elya' probably
refers to Ellis de Tingewick, who was presented to
the rectory in 1315; the second, dated 1635, is
probably by Richard Chandler of Drayton Parslow;
and the tenor, inscribed 'Sum Rosa Pulsata Mundi
Maria Vocata,' is by Richard Hille, and dates from
the early 15th century.

The plate includes a cup and cover paten which
have no hall-marks, but probably date from the 17th
century.

The registers begin in 1562.

ADVOWSON The advowson of Thornton
Church, assessed at £5 6s. 8d. in
1291[82] and at £12 6s. 8d. in 1535,[83]
has always been appendant to Thornton Manor[84]
and is now vested in Col. H. W. Harris. The
first institution of which there is record dates before
1219, when Ralf Hareng presented Henry de Lewknor
(Leukenora).[85] A saving clause was inserted with
regard to the vicarage of Robert the chaplain, which
consisted in all altar offerings (except the tithes of the
parson's cattle), in 2 virgates with their tithes,
and in that messuage which Gilbert formerly held with
the adjacent croft containing 11 selions and 5 buttes
and a certain meadow called Crowelle.[86] Robert was
presented to the vicarage by the said Henry de
Lewknor and was to take possession of the same, but
no further reference to a vicar occurs.

Two parts of the tithes issuing out of the demesnes
of Thornton Manor were claimed by Oseney Abbey
in virtue of a charter of Robert Doyley (erroneously
called lord of Thornton), confirmed by King Henry
and inspected in 1267, giving to the canons of
St. George's Church, founded by Robert in the castle
of Oxford, certain rights in Thornton, Westbury and
Lenborough.[87] This interest in Thornton was
described in 1291 as a pension of 10s. in the
church,[88] but the abbot's title was evidently a little
insecure, for a commission was addressed to the Bishop
of Lincoln by Edward II in 1309 to examine his
claim to what was called one-fourth of Thornton
Church.[89] In despite of this, proceedings against
Walter, the parson of Thornton, were taken by the
Abbot of Oseney in 1312,[90] and were not concluded
by 1314.[91] On 15 June 1319 the court of Canterbury promulgated its sentence as regards the claim of
Oseney Abbey.[92] The decision was probably adverse
to the abbot, for no further payment out of the
Thornton demesnes is recorded. The tithes were
commuted in the first half of the 19th century for
£224 12s. 4d.[93]

The chapelry of All Saints, Nash, a hamlet of
Whaddon, Cottesloe Hundred, was annexed to Thornton for ecclesiastical purposes on 15 April 1854.[94] It
is endowed with £30 a year, payable out of the
Whaddon estate of New College, Oxford, but the
tithes were commuted in 1831 and conveyed to the
vicar of Whaddon.[95]

The chantry founded in Thornton Church by John
Chastillon, lord of the manor, is said to date from
1344,[96] but it was not until four years later that John
Chastillon received licence to alienate in mortmain
two messuages and 100 acres of land in Thornton to a
chaplain to celebrate daily service in Thornton Church
according to an ordinance to be made by him
(Chastillon).[97] The chantry, founded in honour of
the Annunciation of the Blessed Virgin Mary and for
the good estate of the souls of John Chastillon and
his family, was ordained by licence of the bishop in
1356,[98] and Sir Thomas, chaplain of the perpetual
chantry of Thornton, was witness to a charter of
1361.[99] The chantry chapel evidently fell into
decay, for John Barton, jun., a later lord of the
manor, by his will dated 1433, left a legacy for
building it anew and instructions for his burial
there.[100] The royal licence was obtained in 1468
by Robert Ingleton (to whom the manor had passed),
at the request of the feoffees of Barton's widow.
Lands worth £20 yearly were to be alienated to the
chaplain of the chantry, now called St. Mary the
Virgin, for his maintenance and that of six poor feeble
persons of either sex, and a yearly gown was to be
bestowed on six poor boys.[1] Further alienations in
mortmain were made without licence, for which a
general pardon was obtained in 1473 by the chaplain,
Thomas Blaklawe.[2] The presentation to Ingleton's
chantry was vested in the lords of the manor, and a
grant of it was made in 1530 by Humfrey Tyrell.[3]
A distinction, however, was maintained between the
two foundations, that of Barton and that of Ingleton;
both were called Barton's chantry, but Ingleton's was
also known as Our Lady's.[4] It was, moreover, by far
the more important, and was returned as worth
£23 yearly in 1535, of which £8 17s. 4d. was
distributed among poor people, while Barton's proper
was worth only £6, paid, after deduction of 12s. to
the king, to the priest, Reginald Shipley.[5] To prevent confusion the older foundation will henceforward
be called Barton's and the later referred to as Our
Lady's chantry. William Abbott the priest, serving
Our Lady's chantry in 1535,[6] brought an action about
this date against his patron, Humfrey Tyrell, who
on 21 December 1530 ejected Abbott from a house
nigh adjoining the parish church which had belonged
to the chantry from its first foundation, and so
hampered the chaplain from fulfilling his duty to six
poor men and women and six children. Tyrell, who
stigmatized the action as a lying and malicious one,
had suffered the tenement to 'fall and be in extreme
rewen and dekaye,' and had carried away the doors
and windows.[7] The chantry return of 1546 corro-

[82] *Pope Nich. Tax.* (Rec. Com.), 32.
[83] *Valor Eccl.* (Rec. Com.), iv, 240.
[84] See also Inst. Bks. (P.R.O.); *Clergy
Lists*; Bacon, *Liber Regis.* 489.
[85] *R. of Hugh of Wells* (Cant. and York
Soc.), i, 36.
[86] Ibid.
[87] *Cal. Chart. R.* 1257–1300, p. 69;
De Banco R. 195a, m. 278.
[88] *Pope Nich. Tax.* (Rec. Com.), 32.
[89] *Cal. Chart. in Bodl.* 372.

[90] De Banco R. 195a, m. 278.
[91] Ibid. 211, m. 101.
[92] *Cal. Chart. in Bodl.* 372.
[93] Sheahan, op. cit. 314.
[94] Ibid.; *Clergy List* (1915).
[95] Sheahan, loc. cit.
[96] Lipscomb, op. cit. iii, 120.
[97] *Cal. Pat.* 1348–50, p. 47; Inq. a.q.d.
file 285, no. 17.
[98] Linc. Epis. Reg. Memo. Gynewell,
fol. 62.

[99] *Cal. Close*, 1360–4, p. 270.
[100] Willis, op. cit. 301.
[1] *Cal. Pat.* 1467–77, p. 112.
[2] Ibid. 390.
[3] Harl. Chart. 86, F 12.
[4] Chant. Cert. 5, no. 14.
[5] *Valor Eccl.* (Rec. Com.), iv, 240.
[6] Ibid.
[7] Star Chamb. Proc. Hen. VIII, i,
fol. 2, 3.

THORNTON CHURCH FROM THE SOUTH-WEST

THORNTON CHURCH: THE INTERIOR LOOKING EAST

TINGEWICK CHURCH FROM THE SOUTH-EAST

TINGEWICK CHURCH: THE INTERIOR LOOKING EAST

borates Abbott's assertions by stating that Tyrell was at that date in possession of a mansion-house belonging to the chantry, and had deprived the incumbent of the profits for the last fourteen or fifteen years.[8] The ornaments of the chantry were returned in 1546 as worth 33s. 4d., and there was a chalice silver-gilt weighing 18 oz. The priest had an old vestment worth 12d.[9] This chantry of Our Lady was spared at the Dissolution, since there was attached to it a free grammar school, but this seems to have failed to maintain itself for want of funds, and was transferred to Buckingham after 1597.[10]

The priest of Barton's chantry was appointed and paid by All Souls College, Oxford,[11] but his stipend had not been paid for some time previous to 1546, nor were any goods attached to the chantry at that date.[12] This chantry, called Barton's or St. Mary's chantry, with lands in Thornborough and a messuage there called the chantry house, was bestowed by Edward VI in 1550 on Edward Chamberlain, of Fulwell, Oxfordshire, and his heirs.[13] He likewise obtained Bartons manor in Thornborough (q.v.), part of the former possessions of the chantry, with which it descended to Richard Sargeant, who in 1561 leased this property for ninety-six years to William Lee of Thornborough.[14] Together with Bartons it was purchased by John Temple of Stowe in 1601.[15] It figures among the Temples' possessions in 1637,[16] and probably merged later into their Thornborough manor.

There do not appear to be any endowed charities subsisting in this parish.

TINGEWICK

Tedinwiche (xi cent.); Tengewicha (xii cent.); Tingewic, Tyngwyk (xiii–xvi cent.).

This parish covers nearly 2,178 acres, of which 1,215 are pasture, 530 arable, and 181 woods and plantations.[1] The soil is principally gravelly loam with the subsoil various. The general level of the land is well over 300 ft. above the ordnance datum, and reaches 392 ft. on the borders of Oxfordshire. The land falls towards the north and east, where it is liable to floods from the River Ouse and its tributaries.

The village lies along the road from Buckingham to Deddington (Oxon.) and is of a fair size, the irregularly built houses standing on both sides of the High Street. Several of the houses in the village are of the 17th century, and have thatched roofs. At the east entrance to the village a lane leads north to the church, which stands on a slight hill, with the rectory, built in 1854, to the north-west of the churchyard. Browne Willis, the antiquary, writing in 1735, speaks of an arched gateway leading to the rectory-house, conjectured by him to have been built by William of Wykeham, and used by the Oxford scholars in times of pestilence.[2] The rectory-house to which he alludes may be identical with the one described in a terrier dated 22 September 1607, during the incumbency of Erasmus Williams.[3] The house consisted of fifteen bays, ten tiled and five thatched, and among the lands attached to it were Northam and Stratford Howes Meadows, an orchard, two gardens, and Bull Hook Meadow, which was charged with keeping a bull for the use of the parishioners.[4]

Slightly to the north-east of the church is the Manor Farm, lately the residence of Mr. H. Arnatt, J.P., members of whose family were lessees under New College for a considerable period. Sheahan,

about 1860, spoke of it as an ancient building with a mullioned window of four lights in the east front.[5]

Tingewick House, the residence of Mr. G. Robarts, is south of the High Street.

There is a Wesleyan chapel, built in 1863, and a Congregational chapel, dating from 1875.

Little Tingewick, a settlement of a few houses on the Oxfordshire border, is about three-quarters of a mile west of the village on the Buckingham road, which here passes over Sand Pit Hill.

In 1860-2 the remains of a Roman villa were found in Stollidge Field,[6] about a quarter of a mile north-east of the village, and below Tingewick Mill.

The parish was inclosed under an Act of 1773, which included the neighbouring parish of Radclive.[7] The inhabitants of another adjacent parish, Preston Bissett, put in a claim to right of common for sheep and cattle on Preston Hill and Behind Wood in Tingewick.[8] A similar claim on Tingewick Wild or Common, a space of 500 acres, had been made in the early years of the 18th century by the freeholders of Preston Bissett.[9]

MANOR Ten hides in *TINGEWICK*, assessed as a manor in 1086 among the lands of the Bishop of Bayeux, had been held before the Conquest by Alnod, a man of King Edward, who could sell.[10] Ilbert de Laci, the bishop's under-tenant in 1086, shortly afterwards bestowed the manor on the abbey of the Holy Trinity on Mount St. Catherine, above Rouen,[11] and an entry on the Pipe Rolls for 1165 to the effect that 'Tengewicha Abbotis' rendered account of half a mark[12] refers to the abbey's tenancy. Thirty years later the abbot was sued by William son of Gregory for land in Tingewick,[13] and in 1209 he received a quitclaim from Gilbert de Finmere, who claimed to hold Tingewick

---

[8] Chant. Cert. 108.
[9] Ibid. 5, no. 14; 4, no. 10.
[10] See *V.C.H. Bucks.* ii, 145–6.
[11] Chant. Cert. 5, no. 14.
[12] Ibid.
[13] Pat. 831, m. 27.
[14] Chan. Proc. (Ser. 2), bdle. 117, no. 32. After the death of William Lee a quarrel arose over the lease between Richard his eldest son and Joan sister of Richard and her husband Richard Litler, who pleaded on behalf of James Lee, a

minor, son of William Lee by a later wife.
[15] Close, 43 Eliz. pt. xxx.
[16] Chan. Inq. p.m. (Ser. 2), dlxxv, 142.
[1] Statistics from Bd. of Agric. (1905).
[2] Browne Willis, *Hist. and Antiq. of Buckingham,* 313.
[3] Ibid. His will, made 28 March, was proved 7 May 1608 (P.C.C. 40 Windebanck).
[4] Willis, loc. cit.

[5] Sheahan, *Hist. and Topog. of Bucks.* 316.
[6] *Rep. of Roy. Com. on Hist. Monum. North Bucks.* 299; *V.C.H. Bucks.* ii, 12.
[7] Priv. Act, 13 Geo. III, cap. 66.
[8] Ibid.
[9] Exch. Dep. Hil. 5 & 6 Anne, no. 25.
[10] *V.C.H. Bucks.* i, 238.
[11] Ibid. 212.
[12] *Pipe R.* 13 Hen. II (Pipe R. Soc.), 109.
[13] *Rot. Cur. Reg.* (Rec. Com.), i, 44.

Manor of the abbey in fee farm,[14] a further renunciation of rights in 2 carucates of land taking place in 1224.[15] Ralf Dungun, who held the manor in 1254–5,[16] was probably lessee or bailiff of the abbot, to whom John de Littlehill gave some lands in Tingewick in 1268.[17] John de Walemond, keeper of the manor in 1276, was fined £20 for the death of Richard le Tailor, and the goods of the abbot seized for that death were restored by the king.[18] Notwithstanding this pardon, the chests of the abbot at Harmondsworth, a Middlesex manor, were broken into and the deeds carried away.[19] The abbey of the Holy Trinity had a cell at Harmondsworth,[20] and the priors of that house are often returned as lords of Tingewick Manor,[21] Richard, the prior in 1279, complaining that houses and lands in Tingewick, demised to John his predecessor for nine years by Robert de Gibervill, had been re-entered by the said Robert, who broke the locks of the doors and carried away the goods.[22] In 1291 the lands, rents, &c., of the abbot in Tingewick were assessed at £14 10s. 6d., and the fruits, flocks and animals at £1.[23] The trees on the estate were felled and carried away by malefactors in 1316, when the abbot's servants were also assaulted.[24] Roger Sorel, procurator of the abbey of the Holy Trinity, was in possession of the manor in 1340, when an extent was taken. There was then a capital messuage with other houses, old and in bad condition, a garden, dovecote and a water-mill,[25] which had been included in the valuation of 1291,[26] and was perhaps identical with the building assessed at 4s. in 1086.[27] In 1391 licence was obtained by the abbey to alienate Tingewick Manor and other possessions to William of Wykeham, Bishop of Winchester, for the use of Winchester College, Oxford.[28] Ever since that date the manorial rights of Tingewick have been vested in the Warden and Fellows of New College, as it was afterwards called.[29]

The church of *ST. MARY MAGDALENE* consists of a chancel measuring internally 30 ft. by 16 ft., nave 46 ft by 18 ft., north aisle 8 ft. wide, south aisle, west tower 12 ft. by 11 ft. and a south porch.

The three eastern bays of the north arcade of the nave are probably pierced in the wall of a 12th-century church, the nave of which was lengthened westwards and the north aisle added about 1200. This aisle appears to have been considerably altered and perhaps widened at a later period, possibly in the 17th century. The present chancel and west tower were built in the late 15th century, and the south aisle was added in 1830 and the south porch in 1867. The walling is of rubble, and the roofs are covered with slate.

In the east wall of the chancel is a late 15th-century window of three cinquefoiled lights with vertical tracery in a four-centred head. The two windows in each side wall are square-headed and of two lights; the western window on the north side is rather smaller than the others and has tracery, while the eastern

window on the south side has its sill brought down to form a sedile. In the normal position is a piscina with a cinquefoiled head and projecting basin, contemporary, like the windows, with the 15th-century rebuilding of the chancel. The chancel arch, which is the whole width of the chancel, is four-centred and of two chamfered orders springing from corbels. Above it were formerly painted the arms of William and Mary.

The north arcade of the nave is of four bays, the three eastern arches being round-headed, while the westernmost arch is pointed; each is of a single order with chamfered angles, and is inclosed by a label with a serrated moulding on the underside. The east respond has a small impost moulding, and the angles are chamfered. The two eastern piers are round, and have shallow bell capitals with square moulded abaci truncated at the angles; both originally had moulded bases, but that of the second pier has been cut away. The third pier, which probably marks the extent of the original nave, is rectangular, and has a moulded abacus. The modern south arcade has pointed arches supported by octagonal columns.

In the east wall of the north aisle, placed a little to the south of the centre of the wall, is a pointed window of two plain lights with a pierced spandrel in the head. The position of the window suggests that the aisle may have been widened, perhaps in 1634, the date inscribed on a stone now set in the south wall of the modern south aisle, and probably recording some repair or alteration to the fabric. The easternmost window in the north wall is a single light, with a round head inclosed by a roughly pointed label; the window has been made up of fragments from elsewhere, the jambs being of 12th-century moulded stones. The window to the west of this is formed in the pointed head of the blocked north doorway. In the west wall is a window like that at the north-east, but renewed externally. At the east end of the aisle are traces of a former rood doorway. The details of the south aisle are modern.

The 15th-century tower is of three stages, with western diagonal buttresses, a vice turret at the south-east rising only to the intermediate stage, and an embattled parapet. Below the parapet is a moulded cornice, with plain gargoyles at the angles and a grotesque boss in the centre of each face. The tower arch is of two pointed and chamfered orders. In the west wall of the ground stage is a pointed doorway with an outer square inclosing order and unfinished spandrels; above it is a restored window of two lights with tracery in a pointed head. At the south-east is a pointed doorway opening to the vice. The intermediate stage is lighted by a single cinquefoiled light in the south wall, and the bell-chamber has pointed windows of two trefoiled lights on all four sides.

The font is modern. The altar table is of the late 16th century.

---

[14] Pipe R. Beds. and Bucks. 11 John, m. 4.
[15] Feet of F. case 14, file 14, no. 7.
[16] Hund. R. (Rec. Com.), i, 29.
[17] Feet of F. case 16, file 40, no. 1.
[18] Cal. Pat. 1272–81, p. 166.
[19] Ibid. 236.   [20] Tanner, Not. Mon.
[21] Feud. Aids, i, 108; Mins. Accts.

bdle. 1125, no. 1. The abbot is returned as lord in Testa de Nevill (Rec. Com.), 244; Feud. Aids, i, 87.
[22] Cal. Pat. 1272–81, p. 346.
[23] Pope Nich. Tax. (Rec. Com.), 47.
[24] Cal. Pat. 1313–17, pp. 425, 427.
[25] Chan. Inq. p.m. 14 Edw. III (2nd nos.), no. 63.

[26] Pope Nich. Tax. (Rec. Com.), 47.
[27] V.C.H. Bucks. i, 238.
[28] Cal. Pat. 1388–92, pp. 378, 407, 434.
[29] Willis, op. cit. 313; Priv. Act, 13 Geo. III, cap. 66; Lysons, Mag. Brit. i (3), 650; Lipscomb, Hist. and Antiq. of Bucks. iii, 123.

On the north wall of the chancel is an elaborate brass, set in a frame of stone, to Erasmus Williams, a former rector (d. 1608). Upon the brass is his half-figure with a design symbolical of his attainments in music, painting, astronomy and geometry, and below is an epitaph signed by 'R. Haydock.' On the same wall is a monument to Anna, the wife of Thomas Oldys, rector of the parish (d. 1696).

There is a ring of five bells and a sanctus bell: the treble, fourth and sanctus are by Robert Atton, and are dated 1627, 1623 and 1622 respectively; the second is by Bartholomew Atton, 1591; the third is of the 15th century, and is inscribed 'Nomen Magdalene Campana Gerit Melodie'; and the tenor is by Henry Bagley, 1721.

The plate consists of a silver chalice and flagon, a silver paten inscribed E. O., and an electro-plated paten.

The registers begin in 1560.

ADVOWSON The church of Tingewick, valued at £7 6s. 8d. in 1291,[30] and £13 6s. 8d. in 1535,[31] has always descended with the manor,[32] the patronage being now vested in New College, Oxford.

CHARITIES Charles Longland, by his will proved in the P.C.C., in 1688 directed his trustees to purchase a parcel of land called Yard-land, containing about 4½ a., the rent thereof to be distributed among poor widows, possessing certain qualifications. The land is let at £7 12s. 6d. a year, which is distributed among about twenty recipients.

Elizabeth North, by her will, date unknown, bequeathed £40, the trust of which is believed to have been intended for poor maids. The legacy is now represented by £40 11s. 2d. consols with the official trustees, producing £1 a year, which is distributed equally among five poor people.

In 1751 the Rev. Francis Edmonds, a former rector, by deed founded a charity for the education and clothing of six boys and six girls. The endowment consists of a rent-charge of £15 issuing out of lands in the town of Buckingham, which is applied for educational purposes.

The Poor's Plot consists of 22 a., awarded in 1775 for the use of the poor. The land is let in allotments, producing about £13 yearly, which is distributed in money gifts.

TURWESTON

Turvestone (xi cent.); Thurneston, Turnestone (xiv cent.); Turston *alias* Tereweston, Turveston *alias* Tower Weston (xvii cent.); Turson (xviii cent.).

The parish covers 1,295 acres, of which 604 are arable land, 573 permanent grass and 34 woods and plantations.[1] The soil and subsoil are various and the chief crops are wheat, barley and beans. The general level of the ground is well over 400 ft. above the ordnance datum, 430 ft. being reached about the north centre of the parish; on the west border by the River Ouse the land drops to 339 ft.

The road from Brackley to Buckingham throws off a branch leading north to Turweston village, about half a mile distant on the Oxfordshire border. The village is small, but rather straggling, and contains some 17th-century stone cottages. The church is at the east entrance, and to the east of this again, across the road, is the Rectory House, built in 1855.

About 200 yards north of the church is Turweston Manor House, the seat of Sir John Frecheville Ramsden, bart. It is an early 17th-century stone house of two stories, built probably by the Haynes family, who were lessees under the Dean and Chapter of Westminster. Before the west front of the house stretches a park of about 35 acres, the great part of which is in Brackley, the River Ouse, which flows at the foot of the lawn, forming the dividing line. In the grounds is a stone house with mullioned windows, which bears the date 1638. It is now divided into two cottages, and has been considerably restored.

Turweston House, a modern building, was bought from the Dean and Chapter of Westminster by their lessee, Mr. J. Locke Stratton.[2] It is now occupied by his widow.

North-east of the rectory, about half a mile from the village, is Oatlays Hall, a modern house, the residence of the owner, Capt. Spence.

At the north-west end of the village stands Turweston Mill, perhaps on the site of the one worth 7s. 6d. mentioned in Domesday,[3] for which, with half a virgate of land, William the Miller paid 14s. in 1278.[4] William le Muney (Meunier?) brought an action in 1302–3 against William Maunsell for having by night, out of malice aforethought, thrown a great quantity of quicksilver in the mill pond at Turweston, causing damage to the amount of £100.[5] The Haynes family afterwards held the old water-mill on lease from the Dean and Chapter of Westminster, and the removal of a plank bridge leading thereto was the subject of a lawsuit in 1680.[5a] Another 17th-century document refers to arable land called Upper and Lower Wakes Mill and to Old Windmill Hill, together with an existing windmill.[6]

The school stands south of the church, and further beyond is the Wesleyan chapel, built in 1861.

There are a few outlying farms; in the south Turweston Hill Farm and Grove Hill Farm, and about the centre, on the eastern boundary, is the Rectory Farm.

Some 17th-century place-names are Tarriers meadow, Curlockes mead, the Plocke and Cat braines.[7]

The open lands in Turweston were inclosed by an Act of Parliament passed in 1813.[8] Right of common on Wanfordfield, adjoining Westbury, when it should lie fallow, had been claimed in 1566 by Robert Mordaunt, lord of Westbury, by virtue of a grant made to his predecessor Andrew de St. Lys by the Abbot of Westminster in 1313–14. The fields of

---

[30] *Pope Nich. Tax.* (Rec. Com.), 32.
[31] *Valor Eccl.* (Rec. Com.), iv, 239.
[32] See also Inst. Bks. (P.R.O.); Bacon, *Liber Regis.* 489.
[1] Statistics from Bd. of Agric. (1905).

[2] Sheahan, *Hist. and Topog. of Bucks.* 317.
[3] *V.C.H. Bucks.* i, 266.
[4] *Hund. R.* (Rec. Com.), ii, 340.
[5] *Abbrev. Plac.* (Rec. Com.), 246.

[5a] Chan. Proc. Bridges Div. bdle. 410, no. 52.
[6] Close, 3534, m. 5. [7] Ibid.
[8] Loc. and Pers. Act, 53 Geo. III, cap. 144.

the two manors adjoined and were undivided by hedge or ditch. Richard Wygorns, on behalf of the township of Turweston, ejected Mordaunt's cattle about 1562,[9] and no further claim to common rights in Turweston appears to have been put forward by the lords of Westbury.

MANOR Wenesi, the chamberlain of King Edward, held and could sell *TUR- WESTON*, a manor of 5 hides which by 1086 had passed to William de Fougères (Felgeris), and was his only holding in this county.[10] The over-lordship rights afterwards passed to the Mortimers Earl of March, of whom there is record in Turweston from 1278[11] until the 15th century.[12] Holding an inter-mediary lordship under them were the Zouches, whose rights were recognized from the early 13th century[13] until the 15th century.[14] The service rendered was for half a fee, one fee, one-third fee and one and a third fees at varying times, but after the grant to Westminster Abbey the interest of the Mortimers and Zouches must have been purely nominal, and during the 14th century the abbot was said to owe the service of one fee to the king.[15]

Turweston was obtained in fee by the Scovill family before the 13th century. The Humphrey de Scovill who made an arrangement with his father Ralf concerning the manor of Hilperton (Wilts.) in 1205[16] was probably the Humphrey de Scovill against whom Laurentia de Scovill brought an action of novel disseisin in Turweston in 1218.[17] His name is given as lord of the whole 'villata' about 1235,[18] but it was probably a descendant Humphrey who was in possession in 1274.[19] He died shortly after 1278,[20] leaving a widow Florence and four sons, Ralf, Humphrey, Baldwin and William.[21] Florence received Hilperton in dower, but exchanged it for two parts of Turweston with Henry de Mountfort, to whom Ralf de Scovill had transferred his right. After Ralf's death Henry de Mountfort acknowledged the right of Humphrey de Scovill, brother and heir, to Hilperton and a third of Turweston, and Florence bestowed her two parts, in which she had only a life interest, on her son William.[22] In the meantime Humphrey died, about 1281, and the third brother, Baldwin, inherited the third of Turweston, Florence acknowledging his right in return for a rent of 6 marks.[23] Baldwin then proceeded to eject from the other two-thirds of the manor his brother William, and his action was upheld by the court in a suit lasting from 1284[24] to 1286.[25] Simon de Clesworth, whom Baldwin de Scovill apparently enfeoffed of the manor,[26] was said to be responsible for the feudal aid of 1284–6,[27] but Turweston afterwards escheated to the Crown and was bestowed on Queen Eleanor.[28] After her death in 1290 a life grant made by her to Otho de Grandison was confirmed by Edward I in 1291 with reversion to himself.[29] The following year the manor, advowson and liberties, including free warren, were bestowed on Westminster Abbey in free alms for keeping the anniversary of Queen Eleanor,[30] Otho de Grandison receiving the manor of Shenley, Hertfordshire, in compensation.[31] Denham (q.v.) was given at the same time on the same conditions, and the two manors henceforward descend together,[32] the estate at Turweston being augmented in 1340 by 7 messuages 5 virgates of land,[33] in pursuance of a licence granted in 1316.[34] After the Dissolution Turweston was confirmed to the Dean and Chapter of Westminster in 1542,[35] and a further confirmation was obtained from Elizabeth in 1560.[36] Under the Act for abolishing deans and prebends, the trustees of the lands held by them sold Turweston to Nicholas Workman and Henry Lane of Hanslope,[37] but Westminster afterwards regained its possessions, and Turweston continued with the dean and chapter,[38] the Ecclesiastical Commissioners exercising the manorial rights at the present day.

WESTMINSTER ABBEY. *Gules St. Peter's Keys crossed saltirewise with St. Edward's ring in the chief all or.*

Records of leases of the manor exist from the 16th century onwards. A lease for twenty-one years, at a rent of £5 6s. 8d., was obtained in 1534 by Henry Dorell, and at its expiration he remained on the premises as tenant at will of the dean and chapter.[39] In the meantime, however, a lease, evidently in reversion, had been granted in 1550 to Robert Chichester, and by him transferred to Simon Haynes.[40] The latter, when an infant of five, brought an action for trespass against Dorell in the reign of Philip and Mary,[41] and in 1566 had trouble with his neighbour Robert Mordaunt, lord of Westbury, as to pasturage in the common fields of Westbury.[42] A further lease of Turweston was given in 1610 to Simon Haynes for the lives of his wife Anne, son Henry and daughter Joan, the rent of £13 6s. 8d. being reserved to the schools and almshouses at Westminster at the sale of these lands in 1650.[43] Simon Haynes died in April

---

[9] Chan. Proc. (Ser. 2), bdle. 92, no. 35.
[10] V.C.H. Bucks. i, 266.
[11] Hund. R. (Rec. Com.), ii, 340.
[12] Feud. Aids, i, 79 ; Chan. Inq. p.m 32 Edw. I, no. 63b ; 22 Ric. II, no. 34; 3 Hen. VI, no. 32 ; Cal. Close, 1301–7, p. 275.
[13] Testa de Nevill (Rec. Com.), 243b.
[14] Hund. R. loc. cit. ; see also note 12.
[15] Feud. Aids, i, 100, 126.
[16] Rot. de Oblatis et Fin. (Rec. Com.), 328.
[17] Rot. Lit. Claus. (Rec. Com.), i, 367.
[18] Testa de Nevill (Rec. Com.), 243b.
[19] Hund. R. (Rec. Com.), i, 33.
[20] Ibid. ii, 340.
[21] Assize R. 1256, m. 42.
[22] Ibid.
[23] Baldwin is called son and heir of

Humfrey de Scovill in a deed of 1282 (Feet of F. Wilts. 10 Edw. I).
[24] Assize R. 1256, m. 42.
[25] Ibid. 65, m. 2.
[26] Ibid. 1256, m. 42.
[27] Feud. Aids, i, 79.
[28] Mins. Acts. (Gen. Ser.), bdle. 1089, no. 25.
[29] Cal. Pat. 1281–92, p. 417.
[30] Cal. Chart. R. 1257–1300, p. 425.
[31] Cal. Pat. 1292–1301, p. 57.
[32] Cal. Close, 1288–96, p. 436 ; 1296–1302, p. 52 ; Mins. Acts. Hen. VIII, no. 7239. In 1316 the Abbot of Grestein and Henry Turry were said to be the lords of Turweston (Feud. Aids, i, 108).
[33] Cal. Pat. 1340–3, p. 77 ; Inq. a.q.d. file 255, no. 13.
[34] Cal. Pat. 1313–17, p. 522.

[35] L. and P. Hen. VIII, xvii, g. 714 (5).
[36] Pat. 958, m. 15.
[37] Close, 3534, m. 5.
[38] Browne Willis, Hist. and Antiq. of Buckingham, 321 ; Lysons, Mag. Brit. i (3), 652 ; Lipscomb, Hist. and Antiq. of Bucks. iii, 127 ; Sheahan, op. cit. 317.
[39] Ct. of Req. bdle. 22, no. 64.
[40] Ibid. ; Chan. Proc. (Ser. 2), bdle. 92, no. 35.
[41] Ct. of Req. bdles. 22, no. 64 ; 21, no. 60.
[42] Chan. Proc. (Ser. 2), bdle. 92, no. 35.
[43] Close, 3534, m. 5. In 1612 Joan became the wife of Thomas son and heir of John Duncombe of Great Brickhill (Feet of F. Bucks. Mich. 10 Jas. I ; Chan. Inq. p.m. [Ser. 2], ccccxc, 188).

1628,[44] and left as executrix of his will his widow Anne,[45] who died about 1647.[45a] Her son Henry Haynes in 1650 sued in Chancery a neighbour Thomas Yates[46] and claimed four years later to have bought the manor from the Parliamentary trustees.[46a] His infant son, Simon, inherited in 1656.[47] Joseph Haynes held in 1671.[47a] Leases of Turweston in the 18th century were held by Lord Hillsborough, the Weldmans and by Mr. Derbyshire, in whose representatives it was vested in the early 19th century.[47b] By 1813 George Courthope had the leasehold rights,[48] and from about the middle of the 19th century onwards[49] these have been held by the Stratton family.

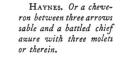

HAYNES. *Or a cheveron between three arrows sable and a battled chief azure with three molets or therein.*

The church of CHURCH the *ASSUMP-TION OF THE BLESSED VIRGIN* consists of a chancel measuring internally 25 ft. 10 in. in length with an average width of 12 ft. 7 in., north vestry and organ chamber, south chancel aisle, nave 32 ft. 3 in. by 16 ft. 6 in., north and south aisles each 11 ft. 8 in. wide, south porch, and west tower 10 ft. by 9 ft. 2 in. It is built of stone rubble, the nave roof being covered with lead and the other roofs with slate.

This church dates from the 12th century and consisted at the end of that period of the nave, north aisle, and probably a small chancel. The south aisle was added early in the 13th century and the chancel rebuilt about 1250, while the west respond of the south arcade was renewed and the arch above it altered at this latter period. In the 14th century a clearstory was added to the nave, and the aisles were widened. During the 19th century the whole fabric was restored and the vestry, chancel aisle, porch and tower were built, the tower probably on old foundations.

The east window of the chancel, which is of three cinquefoiled lights with vertical tracery, was inserted in the 15th century, but there is an original lancet with an external hollow chamfer moulding at the east end of each side wall. The inner jambs of the south lancet were carried down in the 14th century to form a sedile, to the east of which is a large 13th-century piscina with a pointed head, continuous moulded jambs and a quatrefoil bowl, part of which has been cut away. Below the north lancet is an ogee-headed tomb recess of about 1400, which has a moulded edge and crocketed label with a foliated

finial and flanking pinnacles; the sill and part of the moulding of the west jamb have been cut away. At the west end of the chancel are a modern arch to the vestry on the north, and a modern arcade to the chancel aisle on the south. Reset in the east wall of this aisle is a 14th-century traceried window of two trefoiled lights, probably taken from the chancel. The pointed chancel arch, of about 1250, is of two hollow-chamfered orders, the outer dying into the walls on the east side, and the inner supported by half-round shafts with moulded capitals and bases, the latter of which have been considerably cut away. The chancel has a modern timber roof with plastered compartments.

The nave is of two bays and is lighted by a clearstory with two 14th-century pointed windows on both sides, all renewed externally. On the north is a late 12th-century arcade of two bays with round arches of two plain orders, supported by a central pier and responds having engaged half-round shafts and

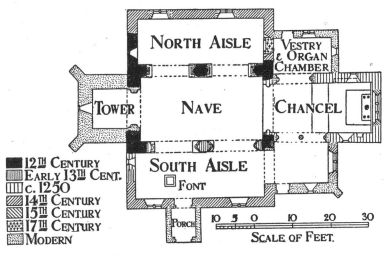

PLAN OF TURWESTON CHURCH

12TH CENTURY
EARLY 13TH CENT.
c. 1250
14TH CENTURY
15TH CENTURY
17TH CENTURY
MODERN

SCALE OF FEET.

edge rolls with moulded capitals and bases. The main capitals of the central pier have rudimentary ornament, but those of the responds are more elaborately treated with rich foliage, that at the west being delicately undercut. The floor of the north aisle has evidently been lowered at some period, as the square plinths of the piers and responds now stand upon rough masonry 12 in. high. The south arcade is also of two bays and has arches of two chamfered orders, the eastern semicircular and the other pointed. Both were originally semicircular, and of the early 13th century, but about 1250 the west respond was rebuilt and the western arch altered to its present form, thus accounting for the break in curvature about 1 ft. 9 in. from the springing line. Both responds of the eastern arch and the east respond of the other are original and have three large rolls with moulded capitals, the central roll being filleted. The bases have been restored in a plain manner and the eastern capital has been entirely renewed. The west respond is similar

[44] M. I. in church.
[45] P.C.C. 40 Barrington.
[45a] Chan. Proc. Bridges Div. bdle. 410, no. 81. See also *Cal. S. P. Dom.* 1634-5, p. 127.

[46] Chan. Proc. Bridges Div. bdle. 410, no. 52.
[46a] Ibid. no. 81.
[47] Ibid. bdle. 28, no. 69.
[47a] Ibid. bdle. 497, no. 27.

[47b] Lysons, loc. cit.
[48] Loc. and Pers. Act, 53 Geo. III, cap. 144.
[49] Sheahan, loc. cit.

to those of the chancel arch and has a half-round shaft with moulded capital and base, and hollow chamfers on both sides with moulded stops. The pointed tower arch in the west wall is modern. The nave has an open timber low-pitched roof with traceried spandrels, which probably dates from the early 16th century.

The north aisle is lighted from the north by two traceried windows of two lights, originally dating from the 14th century, but almost entirely renewed, and from the west by a narrow round-headed light of the late 12th century, now high in the wall, and, owing to the widening of the aisle, much out of centre. A window on the east, similar to those on the north, has been blocked by the Haynes monument. At the south-east are the remains of a piscina. The east wall of the south aisle is pierced by a modern arch opening into the chancel aisle. In the south wall are two windows of about 1350, each of two trefoiled lights, the eastern with running wheel tracery, the other with flowing tracery. Near the north end of the west wall is a 13th-century lancet similar to those in the chancel. The south doorway, which has a round head and plain continuous chamfer, is modern.

The tower is of three stages with western diagonal buttresses and is surmounted by a saddle-back roof covered with slates; reset in the south wall of the second stage is a two-light traceried window, probably of about 1700.

The font and pulpit are modern. On the north side of the chancel is a beautifully drawn brass figure of a priest in mass vestments of the early 15th century, and on the south are two small brass figures of a man and woman of about 1470 with the inscription, ' Orate pro animabus Thome Grene Johanne et Agnetis uxorum eius quorum animabus propicietur deus Amen.' Blocking the east window of the north aisle is a marble monument to Simon Haynes (d. 1628); he is represented with his wife kneeling on either side of a *prie dieu*, in front of which is a child on a low bed, and the monument is flanked by Corinthian columns supporting an entablature and cornice with arms. On the north wall of the tower is a monument to George Harris (d. 1689) and Alice his wife, and on the south wall a monument to William Harris, eldest son of George Harris (d. 1674).

The tower contains two bells by Robert Atton, the treble dated 1626 and the tenor 1625.

The communion plate includes a cup of 1684.

The registers begin in 1695.

ADVOWSON The advowson of the church of Turweston has always descended with the manor, and is now vested in the Dean and Chapter of Westminster.[50] In 1279 there is mention of an endowment of one virgate of land,[51] and in 1291 it was assessed at £8 exclusive of a pension of 4s. paid to Eynsham Abbey[52]; by 1535 the value had increased to £13 6s. 8d.[53] In 1346 a quarrel between the Prior and the Abbot of Westminster as to the exercise of the patronage was decided in favour of the former.[54] The abbot would not accept the verdict[55] and upon complaint by the prior in 1347 that a conspiracy was on foot to prosecute appeals and bring the case into the court of Rome, an order was issued for the arrest of all persons therein concerned.[56]

CHARITIES The Rev. William Fairfax, a former rector, who died in 1762, by his will bequeathed £100 for putting out poor children to learn to read. The endowment now consists of two cottages, presumably purchased out of the trust funds, and £33 14s. 5d. consols with the official trustees. The income of about £7 10s. a year is applied for educational purposes.

On the inclosure of the parish in 1814, 2 r. 32 p. known as the Town Plot were allotted to the churchwardens and overseers, and 3 r. 11 p., known as the Constables Hook, were allotted to the constables of Turweston. The Fuel allotment containing 11 a. 3 r. 32 p. was at the same period allotted in lieu of the right of the poor to cut fuel from the common lands. The land is let at £6 a year, which is distributed in coal.

The Causton Memorial, founded by deed, 12 June 1850. A sum of £102 13s. 11d. consols was raised to perpetuate the memory of the Rev. Thomas Causton, D.D., Prebendary of Westminster, for many years rector of the parish. The sum of stock is held by the official trustees, and the annual dividends amounting to £2 11s. 4d. are applied in the distribution of winter clothing.

TWYFORD with CHARNDON and POUNDON

Toeverde (xi cent.) ; Twiford (xiii cent.) ; Tuyford (xiv cent.).

This large parish on the border of Oxfordshire, with its hamlets of Charndon (1,911 acres) and Poundon (980 acres), covers 4,458 acres, of which 305 are arable, 3,522 permanent grass and 324 woods and plantations.[1] The land rises from 246 ft. above ordnance datum in the south of the parish to 382 ft. on Poundon Hill in the south-west. The soil is chiefly a heavy clay. The Great Central railway crosses the north-east corner of the parish and the Bletchley and Oxford section of the London and North Western railway has a station called Marsh Gibbon and Poundon within the parish.

Two miles north-east of the station is the little

village of Twyford. Near the church is the vicarage, which, although faced with modern brick and tiles, incorporates part of a 15th-century house consisting of a hall, now divided into two floors, with its original roof of three bays and a solar at one end. Considerable alterations and additions were made in the 16th century and many of the fittings, including the staircase and panelling, are of this date. In the village street are several 17th-century houses and cottages, among which is the Red Lion Inn. There are also in the village a school and a Congregational chapel. Twyford House, the residence of Major G. J. Fitz Gerald, is a modern house at the south-west end of the village. Twyford Lodge, a farm-house a little farther to the south-west, stands on the site of a former

[50] Inst. Bks. (P.R.O.) ; Bacon, *Liber Regis.* 489.
[51] *Hund. R.* (Rec. Com.), ii, 340.
[52] *Pope Nich. Tax.* (Rec. Com.), 32.
[53] *Valor Eccl.* (Rec. Com.), iv, 239.
[54] De Banco R. 348, m. 31, 422.
[55] Ibid. 350, m. 15 d ; 351, m. 382 d.
[56] *Cal. Pat.* 1345–8, p. 316.
[1] Statistics from Bd. of Agric. (1905).

TURWESTON CHURCH FROM THE SOUTH-EAST

TURWESTON CHURCH: THE INTERIOR LOOKING EAST

Twyford Church from the South

Twyford Church: The Interior looking East

mansion of the Wenmans.[2] On the removal of that family to Oxfordshire in the early 18th century[3] their Twyford residence was converted into a farm-house which was taken down in 1857.[4] Twyford water-mill is over half a mile north-west from the church. It was settled on Nicholas, son of Henry de Twyford, and his wife Amice in 1321[5] and corresponds to the Nicholas Mill held by the Dayrells of Lillingstone Dayrell in the late 15th and early 16th centuries.[6] The water-mill is named as appurtenant to Twyford Manor in the mid 17th century.[7] The windmill mentioned in 1658[8] was destroyed during a gale in February 1860.[9] The name Windmill Hill still survives.

The hamlet of Charndon (Credendone, xi cent. ; Chardone, Charenendon, xiii cent.) lies about 2 miles south of Twyford. A Congregational chapel was built here in 1825.

Poundon (Powendone, xiv cent.) is a small hamlet about a mile and a quarter south-west of Twyford. Here is a Church of England mission room. The residence of Mr. John Pemberton Heywood Heywood-Lonsdale, the principal landowner, is a modern stone house.

Twyford and Charndon were inclosed by Act of Parliament in 1774.[10]

MANORS Before the Conquest the Countess Goda held *TWYFORD*, a certain man of Earl Harold having there 3 hides as a manor, which he could sell ; by 1086 it had passed as one manor of 17 hides to Ralph de Fougères[11] (Felgeris, Feugeriis).

Twyford Manor was retained for over a century by the lords of Fougères, descending to Ralf's great-grandson, William de Fougères,[12] whose lands were in the king's hands in 1207.[13] It evidently passed with the Fougères estates in Devonshire[14] to Randolph Earl of Chester through his marriage with Clemence daughter of William de Fougères,[15] and on his death without issue in 1232 escheated to the Crown.[16] Twyford Manor was granted during pleasure in the same year to Richard Marshal, Earl of Pembroke,[17] and in the following year to Peter Duke of Brittany and Earl of Richmond.[18] In 1235 he renounced his allegiance to Henry III, who seized his possessions[19] and granted Twyford Manor during pleasure to Walter Marshal.[20] He succeeded to the earldom of Pembroke in 1241 and died in 1245.[21] In 1246

Twyford Manor was granted in fee to Ralf Fitz Nicholas.[22] After 1254[23] he or his son Robert[24] subinfeudated the greater part of the original manor (see later) and the remainder which Simon de Montfort, Earl of Leicester, was holding temporarily in 1254,[25] descended as *TWYFORD MANOR* with Great Linford[26] (q.v.) to James Butler, fourth Earl of Ormond, who made a settlement concerning it in 1430,[27] but appears to have afterwards sold it. It certainly passed before his death in 1452[28] into the hands of Thomas Giffard, owner of the other manor (q.v.), since the two estates coalesced into one manor, of which Giffard died seised in 1469.[29] His son John Giffard[30] died in 1492 and was succeeded by his son Thomas.[31] On his death in 1511 Twyford Manor passed to his son Thomas,[32] and in 1550 to the latter's daughter Ursula, wife of Thomas, after-

GIFFARD. *Gules three lions passant argent.*

WENMAN. *Sable a fesse argent between three anchors or with three lions' heads razed gules upon the fesse.*

wards Sir Thomas Wenman, kt.[33] Their son Richard succeeded his mother in 1558[34] and died in 1572.[35] His son Thomas Wenman[36] settled this manor on his wife Jane in 1574,[37] and she was seised on his death in 1577.[38] Their son Richard,[39] who had succeeded before 1597,[40] made a settlement of Twyford Manor in 1617, on the marriage of his son Thomas with Margaret Hampden,[41] and was created Viscount Wenman of Tuam in 1628.[42] This manor descended with the title[43] to Philip the last viscount, who died in 1800.[44] In the early 19th century it was held in trust for his nephew Philip Thomas Wykeham.[45] The latter's niece Sophia Baroness Wenman[46] was lady of the manor in 1862.[47] Later in the century the manor was split up into freehold

[2] Willis, *Hist. and Antiq. of Buckingham,* 333.
[3] Ibid.
[4] Sheahan, *Hist. and Topog. of Bucks.* 319.
[5] Feet of F. case 18, file 72, no. 11.
[6] Chan. Inq. p.m. (Ser. 2), vi, 5 ; De Banco R. 922, m. 121 ; Exch. Inq. p.m. (Ser. 2), file 20, no. 13.
[7] Recov. R. Trin. 1658, m. 130.
[8] Ibid.
[9] Sheahan, loc. cit.
[10] Priv. Act, 14 Geo. III, cap. 53.
[11] *V.C.H. Bucks.* i, 215, 267.
[12] *Cal. Doc. of France,* i, 586.
[13] *Rot. Lit. Pat.* (Rec. Com.), 70.
[14] *Red Bk. of Exch.* (Rolls Ser.), 620.
[15] G.E.C. *Complete Peerage,* ii, 224.
[16] *Cal. Close,* 1231–4, p. 164.
[17] Ibid.
[18] Ibid. 353, 458.
[19] G.E.C. op. cit. vi, 350.
[20] *Cal. Close,* 1234–7, p. 49 ; *Testa de Nevill* (Rec. Com.), 244.

[21] G.E.C. op. cit. vi, 202–3.
[22] *Cal. Chart. R.* 1226–57, p. 292.
[23] *Hund. R.* (Rec. Com.), i, 28.
[24] *Excerpta e Rot. Fin.* (Rec. Com.), ii, 269.
[25] *Hund. R.* loc. cit.
[26] *Cal. Fine R.* 1272–1307, p. 17 ; Feet of F. case 17, file 49, no. 4 ; *Hund. R.* (Rec. Com.), ii, 353 ; *Feud. Aids,* i, 81, 99, 109, 125 ; Mins. Accts. (Gen. Ser.), bdle. 1121, no. 6. See Great Linford.
[27] *Cal. Pat.* 1429–36, p. 27.
[28] Chan. Inq. p.m. 31 Hen. VI, no. 11.
[29] Ibid. Edw. IV, file 31, no. 15, m. 4.
[30] Ibid.
[31] Ibid. (Ser. 2), vii, 1.
[32] Ibid. xxvi, 89.
[33] Ibid. xciii, 1.
[34] Ibid. cxx, 8.
[35] Ibid. clxiii, 5.
[36] Ibid.
[37] Recov. R. Trin. 16 Eliz. m. 801 ; Chan. Inq. p.m. (Ser. 2), clxxxii, 42.

[38] Chan. Inq. p.m. (Ser. 2), clxxxii, 42.
[39] Ibid.
[40] Chan. Proc. Eliz. Tt 7, no. 51.
[41] Feet of F. Bucks. East. 15 Jas. I ; Chan. Inq. p.m. (Ser. 2), dxciv, 49.
[42] G.E.C. op. cit. viii, 91.
[43] Ibid. 91–3.
[44] Chan. Inq. p.m. (Ser. 2), dxciv, 49 ; Com. Pleas D. Enr. Trin. 1658 ; Willis, op. cit. 340, quoting Twyford Reg. ; Recov. R. Mich. 30 Chas. II, m. 255 ; Trin. 14 & 15 Geo. II, m. 206 ; Hil. 13 Geo. III, m. 363 ; Priv. Act, 14 Geo. III, cap. 53. See also Kingsey Manor.
[45] Lysons, *Mag. Brit.* i (3), 652.
[46] Burke, *Landed Gentry* (1906), under Wykeham-Musgrave.
[47] Sheahan, op. cit. 319. There seems to have been an intermediate transfer, since John and Mary Elizabeth Brown conveyed this manor in 1824 to Henry Ray (Feet of F. Bucks. Hil. 4 & 5 Geo. IV).

estates, the principal landowner in 1873 being Mr. Edward Athawes.[48] His property is now in the hands of trustees.

The greater part of the original manor, amounting to two parts of the vill of Twyford,[49] was subinfeudated, as above said, some time in the second half of the 13th century, and the overlordship was appurtenant to the smaller but more important Twyford Manor [50] until the amalgamation of the two manors, c. 1440.

The enfeoffment, which took place before 1276,[51] was made by Ralf Fitz Nicholas,[52] or more probably by his son Robert, to John Giffard [53] (or Gifford). He was holding in 1290,[54] but seems to have been succeeded before 1300 by John Giffard,[55] surnamed 'le Boef.'[56] He was knighted in 1303 [57] and was living in 1329, when his son John is called the younger.[58] The latter is probably the John Giffard of Twyford who is frequently named between 1333 and 1349.[59] He was succeeded about 1369 by his son Thomas,[60] afterwards Sir Thomas Giffard, who died seised of this manor in 1394.[61] His son and heir Roger Giffard [62] settled it on his wife Isabel and died in 1409, in the minority of their son Thomas.[63] He ratified their estate in Twyford Manor in 1430 to his mother and her second husband John Stokes.[64] They apparently transferred it to John Aston of Somerton, Oxfordshire, who enfeoffed Thomas Giffard in 1437.[65] From the time that he acquired the other manor there is no distinction between the two estates.

A fair at Twyford on the vigil, Feast and the morrow of the Assumption of Our Lady was granted to Ralf Fitz Nicholas and his heirs in 1250.[66]

In 1279 Ralf Pipard and John Giffard held the view of frankpledge for their respective tenants in Twyford.[67] A grant of free warren in Twyford was made to James Butler, Earl of Ormond, and his wife Elizabeth in 1328.[68] The liberties mentioned above with those of courts leet and baron and free fishing were appurtenant to Twyford Manor in 1824.[69]

CHARNDON MANOR was held before the Conquest by Eingar, one of Earl Harold's men.[70] In 1086 it was assessed at 10 hides and held by Ralf de Fougères.[71] It afterwards passed with the Twyford estate [72] to Sophia Baroness Wenman. On her death in 1870 [73] it descended with Hadden-

WYKEHAM-MUSGRAVE.
Argent two cheverons sable between three roses gules.

ham Manor to Mr. Wenman Aubrey Wykeham-Musgrave of Thame Park, Oxfordshire,[74] who is still one of the principal landowners, the other (within the last few years) being Mr. William Smith.

The hamlet of Poundon is named in the early 14th century as forming part of the vill of Twyford.[75] It appears to have descended with the Giffard manor of Twyford during the time of subdivision, since Thomas Giffard ratified in 1430 a transfer of lands there made by John and Isabel Stokes.[76] On the death of the last Viscount Wenman in 1800 the Poundon estate distinguished as *POUNDON MANOR* passed to his elder nephew William Richard Wykeham,[77] and descended with Haddenham Manor to Mr. Wenman Aubrey Wykeham-Musgrave.[78] He has lately sold this property to Mr. John Pemberton Heywood Heywood-Lonsdale.

The church of *THE ASSUMPTION OF THE BLESSED VIRGIN* consists of a chancel measuring internally about 29 ft. 3 in. by 16 ft. 5 in., north organ-chamber, nave 50 ft. 4 in. by 18 ft., north aisle 6 ft. wide, south aisle 15 ft. 7 in. wide, west tower overlapped by the aisles 11 ft. 5 in. square, and a south porch 9 ft. 9 in. by 9 ft.

The reset south doorway and the western jambs of the chancel arch are the only surviving details of a late 12th-century church ; the extent of the nave of this building is probably represented by that of the present nave, and it is possible that the existing north and south arcades are pierced in the original walls. About 1250 the south aisle was added and the chancel arch, and probably the chancel itself, were reconstructed. The aisle is much wider than the normal aisle of the period, but the east wall, which contains the jambs of original lancets, is obviously of 13th-century date, and suggests that the aisle, as first erected, had a chapel at the eastern end, the width of which was adopted for the whole aisle when it was afterwards rebuilt in the 15th century. The north aisle was first added later in the 13th century, and was extended westwards c. 1300 when the west tower was begun. The south aisle must have been similarly extended, as it opens to the ground stage by an arch like that which opens to the north aisle, but all evidence of this has been obscured by the later rebuilding above referred to. Early in the 15th century the clearstory was added and the nave reroofed, and probably at the same time the stairs at the north-east of the north aisle were constructed with the closed passage spanning the east end of the aisle and leading out upon the now destroyed rood-gallery. Late in the century the west tower was completed, the south aisle was brought to its present form, and the south porch was added. The nave, chancel, and tower were restored in 1887,

[48] *Ret. of Owners of Land,* 1873, *Bucks.* 1.
[49] *Plac. de Quo Warr.* (Rec. Com.), 87.
[50] *Feud. Aids,* i, 81, 125 ; Chan. Inq. p.m. 18 Ric. II, no. 16 ; 10 Hen. IV, no. 19.
[51] Feet of F. Div. Co. East. 4 Edw. I, no. 40. See also *Hund. R.* (Rec. Com.), ii, 353 ; *Feud. Aids,* i, 81.
[52] *Parl. R.* i, 49*b.*
[53] *Plac. de Quo Warr.* loc. cit.
[54] *Parl. R.* loc. cit.
[55] Chan. Inq. p.m. Edw. II, file 72, no. 2. This is a reference to the birth of his son John about this time.
[56] De Banco R. 193, m. 142 ; 195*a,*

m. 188 ; *Feud. Aids,* i, 109 ; Feet of F. case 18, file 72, no. 1.
[57] Shaw, *Kts. of Engl.* i, 110.
[58] Chan. Inq. p.m. Edw. III, file 10, no. 25.
[59] *Cal. Pat.* 1330-4, pp. 499, 502 ; 1334-8, pp. 68, 449, 510 ; *Cal. Close,* 1339-41, pp. 55, 436, 448 ; *Feud. Aids,* i, 125 ; *Cal. Pat.* 1345-8, p. 464 ; 1348-50, pp. 294, 383.
[60] *Cal. Close,* 1369-74, p. 22.
[61] Chan. Inq. p.m. 18 Ric. II, no. 16.
[62] Ibid.
[63] Ibid. 10 Hen. IV, no. 19.
[64] Close, 9 Hen. VI, m. 14.
[65] *Cal. Pat.* 1436-41, p. 119.

[66] *Cal. Chart. R.* 1226-57, p. 349.
[67] *Hund. R.* (Rec. Com.), ii, 353. See also *Plac. de Quo Warr.* loc. cit. ; *Parl. R.* loc. cit.
[68] Chart. R. 2 Edw. III, m. 5, no. 13.
[69] Feet of F. Bucks. Hil. 4 & 5 Geo. IV.
[70] *V.C.H. Bucks.* i, 267.
[71] Ibid.
[72] *Feud. Aids,* i, 81, 109 ; Feet of F. Bucks. Hil. 4 & 5 Geo. IV.
[73] G.E.C. op. cit. viii, 93.
[74] *V.C.H. Bucks.* ii, 283.
[75] *Feud. Aids,* i, 109.
[76] Close, 9 Hen. VI, m. 14.
[77] Recov. R. Trin. 40 Geo. III, m. 234.
[78] *V.C.H. Bucks,* ii, 283.

and in 1897 the south aisle and porch were restored. The walling is of rubble, and the north aisle is cemented externally.

In the east wall of the chancel is a late 14th-century window of three cinquefoiled ogee lights with tracery in a pointed head. The middle light rises higher than the side lights, the arrangement recalling the similarly designed windows characteristic of the early years of the same century. At the north-east is a square aumbry rebated for a door, and at the opposite end of the north wall is a modern arch opening to the organ-chamber, in the east wall of which has been reset a two-light 15th-century window removed from the north wall of the chancel when the arch was pierced. Near the centre of the wall is a shouldered doorway of the late 13th century. At the east end of the south wall is a 14th-century piscina with a semi-hexagonal pilaster rising from the floor and supporting a projecting quatrefoil basin, the niche having a trefoiled ogee head inclosed by a label with a restored finial at the apex. Immediately to the west of this is a square-headed early 16th-century window of three plain lights with four-centred heads, and beneath the sill is a range of three 14th-century sedilia which appear to have been reset when the window above was inserted, many of the stones being carelessly misplaced. The central sedile has a trefoiled ogee head, those on either side having semicircular heads; the partitions between them are pierced by rectangular openings and have attached shafts from which the heads spring. At the west end of the wall is a mid-14th-century window of two trefoiled ogee lights with tracery of a simple character in a square head. The chancel arch is two-centred and of two chamfered orders, the inner order springing from large tapering corbels with chamfered angles and small moulded imposts, supported by small attached shafts with moulded capitals and restored bases of the water-table type. The impost moulding of the corbels is continued round the jambs of the outer order on the west side, and back to the side walls of the nave. The jambs of the outer order on this face are made up of re-used late 12th-century stones, the north jamb having an angle roll with overlapping 'dentelles' approaching the beak-head in form, while the southern jamb is enriched by a bold cheveron moulding. Externally the chancel has a low-pitched eastern gable, the walls being crowned by an embattled parapet.

The late 13th-century north arcade of the nave is of four bays with two-centred arches of two chamfered orders supported by clustered piers of quatrefoil plan with moulded bell capitals and restored

bases of late water-table type. The responds repeat the half-plan of the piers; the capital of the west respond differs in section from the other capitals of this arcade and points to the conclusion that the respond was rebuilt when the tower was added. The arches are inclosed by roll-moulded labels intersecting over the piers. The whole arcade has been much restored, the first and second piers having been rebuilt. The south arcade is of the same number of bays, and has arches, piers and responds of the same form, but the capitals and bases are of a different section, the mouldings of the former resembling those of the capitals of the shafts attached to the jambs of the chancel arch. The west respond has a capital like that of the corresponding respond of the north arcade, and, like it, was evidently rebuilt during the construction of the tower. The clearstory has four square-headed windows on either side; those on the north are of the early 15th century and are each of two trefoiled lights, while those on the south are each of two plain lights, and probably assumed their present form in the succeeding century. Over the

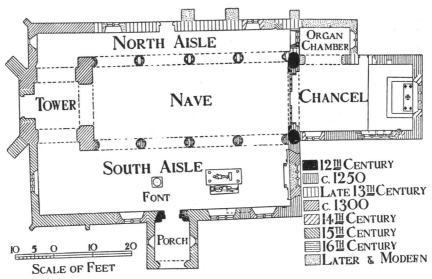

PLAN OF TWYFORD CHURCH

east respond of the north arcade is the rood doorway, which has a four-centred rear-arch towards the nave.

The east window of the north aisle is an early 16th-century insertion of two cinquefoiled lights with vertical tracery in a square head. Above it, spanning the east end of the aisle, is a rough arch carrying the passage to the former rood, and at the east end of the north wall can be seen the east jamb of a doorway leading to the stairs by which the passage was approached. To the west of this is a late 14th-century window of two trefoiled lights with quatrefoil tracery in a two-centred head. The north doorway in the third bay of the aisle is of original 13th-century date, and has a pointed external head inclosed by a label and a segmental rear arch. In the next bay is a modern pointed window of two lights, perhaps a copy of an original window of c. 1300; the extended portion of the aisle overlapping the tower is lighted only by a 15th-century cinquefoiled light in the west wall.

In the east wall of the south aisle, now blocked internally by the Wenman monument, is a 14th-century window of three trefoiled lights with tracery in a two-centred drop head. To the north and south are the outer jambs of a triplet of original 13th-century lancets; no joint is visible externally between this wall and the east wall of the nave. At the east end of the south wall is a pair of small shallow recesses with pointed heads, and to the west of them is a window of two plain lights with a pierced spandrel in a two-centred head, probably an insertion of c. 1300. Immediately to the west of this window is a recess with an ogee head inclosed by a finialled label with a head-stop on the east and a rough block for stop on the west. In the back of the recess is set a stone with a rudely carved figure holding a heart. Partly above this recess is a late 15th-century window of three cinquefoiled lights in a four-centred head, with a plain wood lintel for rear arch. In the third bay of the aisle is the south doorway, reset work of the last half of the 12th century. It is of two round-arched orders externally, the inner order continuously moulded with the cheveron, while the head of the outer order has an angle-roll with beak-head ornament and is supported by nook shafts with sculptured capitals and enriched abaci. The outer order of the jambs on both sides is carved with large eight-rayed suns or flowers. To the west of the doorway is a window of the same type and date as the south-east window; the remainder of the south wall is blank, but in the west wall is a 15th-century window of three trefoiled lights with tracery in a flat segmental head. The walls are crowned externally by a moulded cornice and plain parapet.

The tower rises in two stages with a perceptible batter and has diagonal buttresses at the western angles and an embattled parapet. The ground stage has arches on the east, north and south opening to the nave and aisles. Each of these arches is two-centred and of a single chamfered order springing from jambs with moulded imposts and broach-stopped chamfers at the angles. The arch opening to the nave is larger than those opening to the aisles, and has roll-moulded labels on both faces, while the aisle arches have labels of the same section, but on the inner face of the tower walls only. In the west wall of the ground-stage is a late 15th-century doorway with a four-centred head within an outer square containing order, and above it is a contemporary window of three cinquefoiled lights with vertical tracery in a two-centred head. The bell-chamber is lighted by windows of two cinquefoiled lights on all four sides, those on the west and south having four-centred heads, while the remaining two windows are square-headed. Immediately to the south of the east and west windows are small single trefoiled lights placed with their sills at the level of the springing of the heads of the principal windows.

The south porch has a low-pitched roof with an embattled parapet and is lighted by a single trefoiled light in each side wall. The outer entrance has a two-centred head with an external label, and is of two continuously chamfered orders.

The chancel has an early 16th-century king-post roof of flat pitch with moulded tie-beams and wall-plates. The nave roof, a fine example of early 15th-century carpentry, has trusses of king-post type with foiled struts and traceried wall-brackets resting on carved stone corbels. The font is of the 13th century, but has been very drastically restored. The bowl is circular and stands on a circular moulded stem with a square plinth having a human face carved at the south-west angle and an animal's head at the north-west. The bowl is further supported by four modern shafts encircling the central stem. The communion rails with their turned balusters are of the late 17th century, and the former communion table, now preserved in the vestry, appears to be of the same date. The pulpit is of the early part of the 17th century and has arched panels of the type common at that period. The 15th-century oak chancel-screen has been much restored and in large part renewed; it is divided by the main uprights into three bays, the central bay being open, with tracery in the head, while the side bays have each three open traceried lights in the upper portion, and panels with quatrefoil piercings below. The doors in the north and south doorways, with their original strap hinges, probably date from the 15th century. In the nave is a remarkably interesting series of 15th century benches with desks. The seat backs have boldly moulded top-rails and the ends or standards have large trefoiled finials, with scroll-heads to the elbows and desk-wings, the back and front standards of each set being finished to a buttress form. They average 3 ft. 3 in. in height, 2 ft. in width, and 3 in. in thickness. Three seats of similar type remain in the south aisle, with three other plainer seats of the same date. In the chancel are two 15th-century seats with panelled desks. Fragments of 15th-century glass remain in the two western of the north clearstory windows, and in the west window of the south aisle.

In the recess in the south wall of the south aisle are preserved some carved stones; these include the capital of a late 12th-century shaft, a fragment of a moulded 13th-century label, a broken late 15th-century gargoyle, and a fragment of a cornice from the table tomb containing the Giffard brass described below. In the churchyard is the base and part of the octagonal shaft of a cross of c. 1400. At each angle of the base, which is much worn and decayed, have been small niches with figures, and there are also traces of trefoil enrichment.

At the east end of the north wall of the chancel is a brass with the half-figure of a priest and the following inscription: 'Hic jacet dn̄s Johēs Everdon̄ quondā Rector istius | Ecclīe qui obiit iiijᵗᵒ die Septembris anno dn̄i | mil̄ᵒ. ccccᵒ. xiijᵒ. cuius aīe ꝑpicietur deus Amē.'

On a modern pedestal in the south aisle is a cross-legged stone effigy of a knight of the early 13th century, possibly representing William de Fougères, who held the manor at this time, in chain armour, long surcoat, and pot helm; the right hand rests upon the chest and the left on a sword, while a long shield, reaching to a point below the knees, covers the left side. The upper part of the effigy is in a good state of preservation, but the left leg is mutilated and the lower part of the right leg is broken off. On the north side of this is a 15th-century table tomb, the plain masonry of which is exposed on both sides as the facing has been destroyed, but the ends, each consisting of two cinquefoiled panels containing shields, remain in position, and a fragment of the cornice, as mentioned above, lies in the recess in the south wall. It was possibly erected to commemorate Thomas Giffard, who died in 1469. Placed on the top of the tomb there is now a Purbeck marble slab containing the brass figure of a man in plate armour with an inscription to Thomas Giffard of Twyford, who died in 1550, and Marie (Staveley) his wife ; there are also four shields, two of which are for Giffard, one for Giffard impaling Staveley, and the other for Staveley. The figure and inscription are palimpsest, the reversed sides being composed of fragments of 15th-century brasses, rubbings of which are preserved in the vestry ; they include parts of the figure of a priest in mass vestments and part of an inscription to William Stortford, Treasurer of St. Paul's 1387–93 and Archdeacon of Middlesex 1393–1416 (d. 1416). One of the shields is also palimpsest, the reverse being engraved with canopy work. Blocking the east window of the south aisle is a large monument to Richard first Viscount Wenman (d. 1640), son of Thomas Wenman and Jane (West), and great-grandson of Sir Thomas Wenman and Ursula (Giffard) daughter of the Thomas Giffard commemorated on the above brass. The monument also commemorates Agnes (Fermor) his wife (d. 1617), their son Thomas second Viscount Wenman (d. 1664), who erected the monument, Margaret (Hampden, d. 1658), wife of Thomas, Philip third Viscount Wenman of Tuam (d. 1686), and Ferdinand son of Sir Francis Wenman of Caswell in Witney, Oxfordshire (d. 1671). Over the inscription is an achievement of arms with fifteen quarterings. The monument stands on a base surrounded by iron railings, and the inscription tablet is flanked by Ionic columns supporting a curved pediment. Immediately to the north of this is a mural monument with a shield of ten quarters to Richard Wenman of Twyford, son of Thomas Wenman of Caswell (d. 1672) ; and on the south is a similar monument with a shield of twelve quarters, evidently to a member of the same family, but the inscription is now indecipherable. On the north wall of the north transept is a mural monument with arms to Anne Payne (d. 1624), erected by her daughter Margaret Edmunds in 1641.

The tower contains a ring of six bells : the treble and fourth by W. Blews & Sons of Birmingham, 1872 and 1869 respectively ; the second by T. Mears, London, 1805 ; the third by Lester & Pack, London, 1758 ; the fifth, probably of the late 16th century, is inscribed with the ten initial letters of the alphabet ; and the tenor is by Taylor & Sons, Oxford, 1828 ; there is also a small bell without inscription.

The communion plate consists of a cup of 1569 and two plated patens.

The registers begin in 1558.

Half the church of Twyford seems to have been given by one of the
ADVOWSON
Fougères family to Fougères Priory [79] before 1207, when a presentation was made by King John to the other half.[80] Presentations were made by the priory in 1225 [81] and 1235.[82] In 1260 (an intermediate presentation having been made by the Bishop of Lincoln) [83] Robert Fitz Nicholas secured his right of presentation in a suit against the Prior of Ipplepen (a small cell belonging to Fougères Priory in Devon) [84] by default of the prior.[85] The advowson of Twyford Church, valued at £16 13s. 4d. in 1291,[86] eventually passed to the diocese of Lincoln.[87] In 1475 Bishop Rotherham obtained a licence, provided that a vicarage was ordained and a competent provision made yearly for the poor of the parish, to appropriate this church in mortmain to the rector and scholars of Lincoln College, Oxford.[88] They have since retained both the advowson and the rectory,[89] receiving an allotment in lieu of tithes at the inclosure of the parish in 1774, when their lessee was Viscount Wenman.[90]

William Coleman, by his will,
CHARITIES proved 7 July 1705, charged an estate at Stewkley with an annuity of 11s., whereof 1s. was to be retained by the churchwardens for their trouble, and 10s. to be distributed in bread on Ash Wednesday and Good Friday. The distribution is duly made.

Unknown Donor's Charity, or Church Meadow. A sum of £40 invested in Local Loans 3 per cent. stock is held by the Commissioners for the reduction of the National debt under this title, and would appear to represent a rood of land, the rent of which was formerly claimed by the churchwardens. The interest is now applied to the Churchyard Fund.

The Rev. Richard Hutchins, D.D., a former rector, by a codicil to his will, proved in the P.C.C. 27 August 1781, bequeathed five Oxford Canal shares, vested in Lincoln College, Oxford, one moiety of the income to be applied in augmentation of the stipend of the clergyman at Twyford, and the other moiety in promoting Christian knowledge in the parishes belonging to the churches appropriate to the college, particularly in the parish of Twyford, in distributing Common Prayer Books, putting out children to school, and in such other ways as should seem meet to the rector of the college. In 1910 a moiety of the income amounted to £15 2s. 3d.

Mrs. Elizabeth Perkins, by her will proved at Oxford 21 September 1883, bequeathed £200, the interest to be distributed in coal or blankets in the first week of November in each year. The legacy, less duty, is represented by £176 13s. 8d. consols with the official trustees, producing £4 8s. 4d. yearly.

---

[79] Founded about 1163 (Dugdale, *Mon.* vi, 1114).

[80] *Rot. Lit. Pat.* (Rec. Com.), 70.

[81] *R. of Hugh of Wells* (Cant. and York Soc.), ii, 64. Apparently only to its half of the church, since the right of a certain William the chaplain is reserved. A pension of 6 marks yearly was claimed by the priory from the church.

[82] Harl. MS. 6950, fol. 79. In 1233 a grant of the tithes of the manor which they had been accustomed to have from

the Earl of Chester was made to the canons of Fougères (*Cal. Close*, 1231–4, p. 334), the tithes of hay having been granted to Richard the parson while the manor remained in the king's hands (ibid. 236).

[83] Harl. MS. 6950, fol. 79b.

[84] Dugdale, op. cit. vi, 1046.

[85] Cur. Reg. R. 165, m. 1 d.

[86] *Pope Nich. Tax.* (Rec. Com.), 32b.

[87] Harl. MS. 6952, fol. 64, 69.

[88] *Cal. Pat.* 1467–77, p. 519.

[89] *Valor Eccl.* (Rec. Com.), ii, 241 ; Chan. Proc. Eliz. Cc 19, no. 19 ; Bacon, *Liber Regis.* 490.

[90] Priv. Act, 14 Geo. III, cap. 53. A separate allotment was made in lieu of the tithes of Poundon which were to become part of the rectory at the end of five years if Viscount Wenman did not bring an action within that time in support of a certain interest which he had claimed in these tithes.

WATER STRATFORD

Stradford (xi cent.); Stratforwe, Stratford, Straford, Westratforde (xiii–xv cent.).

Stratford did not acquire its present name until the 15th century, the first reference to Water Stratford occurring about 1436, after which date the name West Stratford seems to have been entirely lost. It is a small parish containing 1,102 acres, of which 763 are permanent grass and 235 arable land.[1] The soil is mixed clay, stone brash and gravel, and the subsoil Oolite. The land falls from about 400 ft. from the ordnance datum in the north to about 300 ft. in the south, where the Ouse forms the boundary, and is joined by a small stream from Stowe. The river is crossed four times by the Banbury branch of the London and North Western railway.

The main road from Brackley to Buckingham runs in a south-easterly direction through the parish, and

WATER STRATFORD MANOR HOUSE

on it is Water Stratford Lodge, one of the entrances to Stowe Park. Near by are Bear Bridge [1a] and Ashmore Hole. Buffler's Holt is a small hamlet to the east. The 'small path,' a footway leading to the Ouse, is said to be part of an ancient street from Alcester and Bicester to Watling Street.[2] There are also said to be traces of a ford at 'Stollidge.'[3] In 1847–8, when digging for the railway viaduct, a number of Roman remains were found.[4]

The village stands on a gentle slope above the river; it is picturesque, with irregular thatched cottages. The church of St. Giles is close to both river and railway, and adjoining the churchyard is

the modern rectory-house. The manor-house is a large substantial stone building of two stories, with tiled roof. On a chimney-stack is the date 1598, which is probably the year in which the house was completed, but it appears to have been much altered about 1669, the date on a stone in the wall of an out-house and on a doorway in the garden wall. In 1650 the house was worth £12 a year, built part with timber and part with stone and rough-cast, and covered with tiles, and consisted of hall, parlour, kitchen, several upstairs chambers, barns, stables and dovehouse.[5] In the garden traces of foundations have been found.[6]

The Town Farm, standing a little to the north of the church, is a 17th-century stone house with roofs of tiles, thatch, and slate.

The following place-names occur: Thadenham, Pukeput,[7] Prestewey, Hanedlond, Shaldambroch, Estmore [8] (xiii cent.); Pyper, Withesgrove, Mixbury Mead, Conyborough Mead [9] (xvii cent.).

There is no Inclosure Award for this parish.

MANOR In the reign of Edward the Confessor *WATER STRATFORD* was held by Azor son of Toti, who could sell it. After the Conquest it was granted to Robert Doyley, and in 1086 was assessed at 8 hides.[10] Robert died in 1090, his heir male being his brother Niel, who was succeeded on his death in 1112 by his son Robert Doyley.[11] This Robert founded the abbey of Oseney,[12] to which he gave two parts of the tithes of Stratford.[13] He died about 1150, and was succeeded by his son Henry, who died about 1168.[14] His son and successor Henry died without issue in 1232, his widow Maud marrying as her second husband William de Cauntelow, who before his death in 1238 was seised of a knight's fee in Water Stratford as part of his wife's dowry.[15] Maud died without issue about 1253. Henry Doyley's lands devolved on his nephew Thomas de Newburgh, sixth Earl of Warwick,[16] who paid relief for his lands in 1232.[17] He died without issue in 1242, and was succeeded in his estates by his sister Margaret, who in 1243 married John du Plessis.[18] Hugh du Plessis, son of John by a former wife,[19] in 1263 did homage for lands formerly belonging to Henry Doyley.[20] Hugh was overlord of Water Stratford in 1284–6,[21] and

[1] Statistics from Bd. of Agric. (1905).
[1a] About 1814 it was the scene of the destruction of a bear which had escaped from a menagerie in Buckingham.
[2] *Rec. of Bucks.* vii, 115.
[3] Ibid.
[4] Ibid.
[5] Parl. Surv. Bucks. no. 19.
[6] *Rec. of Bucks.* vii, 136.

[7] Harl. Chart. R. 86, E 35–8.
[8] Ibid. 85, E 7–10.
[9] Parl. Surv. no. 19, m. 4, 5, 6.
[10] *V.C.H. Bucks.* i, 258.
[11] Nichols, *Topog. and Gen.* i, 368, 369.
[12] Dugdale, *Mon.* vi, 248.
[13] *Cal. Chart. R.* 1257–1300, p. 69.
[14] Nichols, loc. cit.
[15] *Testa de Nevill* (Rec. Com.), 243b.

[16] Nichols, loc. cit.
[17] *Excerpta e Rot. Fin.* (Rec. Com.), i, 231.
[18] G.E.C. *Peerage*, viii, 54.
[19] Ibid. note (a).
[20] *Excerpta e Rot. Fin.* (Rec. Com.), ii, 396; see Thornborough.
[21] *Feud. Aids*, i, 79; *Hund. R.* (Rec. Com.), ii, 342.

died in 1292, in which year his son Hugh had livery of his lands.[22] Hugh the younger granted some of his lands of the Doyley barony to Edward I in exchange,[23] and Water Stratford was perhaps included in this grant, for it was afterwards held by successive Princes of Wales till the overlordship lapsed after 1650.[24]

In 1086 Water Stratford was held of Robert Doyley by Turstin,[25] whose successors took their name from the place. William de Stratford [26] was holder of a knight's fee here about 1235,[27] and William lord of Stratford and William his son were witnesses to a deed in 1240.[28] About this time the 'park of Stratford' is mentioned.[29] William son of William de Stratford granted land here to Biddlesden Abbey early in the reign of Henry III.[30] In 1279–80[31] and again in 1284–6[32] William de Stratford was returned as holder of the vill of Water Stratford, comprising 8 hides, of which one hide was in demesne. Before 1302–3[33] he had been succeeded by his son John,[34] who held in 1316[35] and 1335.[36] He died before 1346,[37] leaving a widow Isabel [38] and three daughters, Elizabeth, Joan and Eleanor.[39] His successor, William de Stratford (son of John, son of John, son of John de Stratford), recovered seisin of the manor against Isabel in 1349.[40] His heir was his brother Thomas,[41] who before 1359 enfeoffed Sir John Giffard of Twyford,[42] probably as trustee. He is said to have settled the manor on himself, with remainder to Thomas Giffard [43] his son.[43a] Roger son and heir of Thomas Giffard [44] was vouchee of the manor of Water Stratford in 1398, when it was claimed by Nicholas de St. Luke, Lucy Ikenam, and John de Stratford, descendants of the three daughters of John and Isabel de Stratford.[45] He was still seised of land here, held of John Giffard, on his death in 1409,[46] but that he no longer held the manor is further shown by the fact that his son Thomas Giffard still held 2 virgates of land on his death in 1469,[47] by which time the manor was in other hands. Before 1409 Thomas de Stratford had enfeoffed John Barton, sen., and John Barton, jun., of the manor.[48] John Barton, jun., in 1433[49] enfeoffed trustees,[50] against whom in 1437 the descendants of two of John de Stratford's three daughters renewed their claim.[51]

From the Bartons the manor passed by enfeoffment before 1452[52] to William Fowler of Lambard's Manor, Buckingham [53] (q.v.), with which it passed to his grandson Richard. He made a settlement of the manor in 1505,[54] and again in 1513 to the use of himself and his wife Julia with remainder to their son John,[55] who in 1533 conveyed it to his brother-in-law,[56] Christopher Wescott of Ludgershall.[57] The latter sold it in 1546 to Sir Edward North,[58] who in turn conveyed it to William Humberston, reserving to himself £11 rent and also a payment

FOWLER. *Azure a cheveron argent between three leopards or with three crosses formy sable on the cheveron.*

of 4s. which had been made to Oseney Abbey.[59] In 1550 Humberston granted his interest to John Frayne,[60] who conveyed the manor in 1553 to John Frankish and Mary his wife.[61] John Frankish died in 1554,[62] and Mary held Water Stratford till her death.[63] Their son and successor Anthony in 1605 settled the manor on his wife Grissel and his eldest son Gerrard.[64] Anthony died in 1615,[65] and his son Gerrard died without issue before 1650. He was succeeded by his half-brother[66] Anthony Frankish,[67] whose daughter and heir probably married Thomas Edgerley.[68] Thomas Edgerley was succeeded in 1659 by his grandson Thomas Edgerley,[69] who in 1670 joined with his wife Frances and Anthony Frankish in a settlement of the manor.[70] Thomas Edgerley was Sheriff of Buckinghamshire in 1678.[71] In January 1698–9 he sold Water Stratford to Thomas Winford.[72] He was created a baronet in 1702, with special remainder to the heirs male of his brother, and died in the same

WINFORD. *Argent a cheveron between three quatrefoils sable.*

[22] *Cal. Inq. p.m.* (Edw. I), iii, 41; *Cal. Fine R.* 1272–1307, p. 313.
[23] Chan. Inq. p.m. 33 Edw. I, no. 194.
[24] Ibid. 17 Edw. IV, no. 39; (Ser. 2), dcxlvii, 42; Parl. Surv. Bucks. no. 19.
[25] *V.C.H. Bucks.* i, 258.
[26] Possibly William son of William de Stratford who in 1228 gave one-fifth part of Elsfield (Oxon.) to the church of St. Frideswide, Oxford (*Cal. Chart. R.* 1226–57, p. 70).
[27] *Testa de Nevill* (Rec. Com.), 243b.
[28] Harl. Chart. 84, D 32.
[29] Ibid. 86, E 38.   [30] Ibid. 35–8.
[31] *Hund. R.* (Rec. Com.), ii, 342. His brothers Richard, Robert and Walter are mentioned here.
[32] *Feud. Aids*, i, 79.   [33] Ibid. 100.
[34] Feet of F. Bucks. Mich. 8 Edw. II, no. 24.   [35] *Feud. Aids*, i, 108.
[36] Feet of F. Bucks. Mich. 9 Edw. III, no. 9.   [37] *Feud. Aids*, i, 126.
[38] De Banco R. 347, m. 85.
[39] Ibid. 551, m. 611 d.
[40] Ibid. 358, m. 156. Nicholas son of John de Stratford is said to have held the manor in 1342 (Willis, *Hist. and Antiq. of Buckingham*, 341, quoting documents belonging to the lord of the manor).

[41] De Banco R. 551, m. 611 d.
[42] Willis, op. cit. 342. He gives the brother's name as Richard.   [43] Ibid.
[43a] *Cal. Close*, 1369–74, p. 22.
[44] Chan. Inq. p.m. 18 Ric. II, no. 16.
[45] De Banco R. 551, m. 611 d.
[46] Chan. Inq. p.m. 10 Hen. IV, no. 19.
[47] Ibid. 9 & 10 Edw. IV, no. 15.
[48] Early Chan. Proc. bdle. 18, no. 64.
[49] Willis, loc. cit. (quoting documents *penes* the lord of the manor of Thornton).
[50] Early Chan. Proc. bdle. 18, no. 64.
[51] De Banco R. 706, m. 107 d.
[52] Willis, loc. cit.
[53] Early Chan. Proc. bdle. 18, no. 64.
[54] De Banco R. 974, m. 431 d.
[55] Close, 10 Hen. VIII. no. 53.
[56] *Visit. of Bucks.* (Harl. Soc.), 165.
[57] Feet of F. Bucks. Hil. 24 and East. 25 Hen. VIII.
[58] Close, 38 Hen. VIII, pt. iii, no. 18.
[59] Willis, loc. cit. He quotes an undated deed (c. 1230) in which the convent of Oseney granted to William de Stratford and his heirs land on payment of 4s. (ibid. 341).   [60] Ibid. 342.
[61] Parl. Surv. Bucks. no. 19; Feet of F. Bucks. Mich. 1 & 2 Phil. and Mary.
[62] Exch. Inq. p.m. (Ser. 2), file 49, no. 2.

[68] Ibid. A grant of this manor of Water Stratford lately in the possession of Henry Pecham, to William Gerrard and others in 1560, was cancelled by surrender of the Patent in 1562 (Pat. 2 Eliz. pt. xiii, m. 13).
[64] Feet of F. Bucks. Mich. 3 Jas. I; Chan. Inq. p.m. (Ser. 2), dcxlvii, 42.
[65] Chan. Inq. p.m. (Ser. 2), dcxlvii, 42.
[66] *Visit. of Bucks.* (Harl. Soc.), 60.
[67] Parl. Surv. Bucks. no. 19.
[68] Willis, op. cit. 342. Anthony appears to have settled the manor on them in 1652 (Recov. R. Mich. 1652, m. 165; Feet of F. Bucks. Mich. 1652).
[69] Willis, loc. cit.; Adm. Act Bk. 1662.
[70] Recov. R. East. 22 Chas. II, m. 134; Feet of F. Bucks. East. 22 Chas. II.
[71] P.R.O. *List of Sheriffs*, 9.
[72] Feet of F. Bucks. Hil. 10 Will. III. An annuity of £30 out of the manor was claimed at this date by Mary wife of John Easton, a jockey or horsedealer. About 1685 she had met Thomas Edgerley, who had persuaded her 'to go by the name of Edgerley as if she were his wife.' He had afterwards carried away her valuables and had her arrested (Chan. Proc. Bridges Div. bdle. 317, no. 4).

year,[73] when he was succeeded by his nephew, Sir Thomas Cookes Winford,[74] who died without issue in 1744. He is said to have given this manor to his nephew Thomas Geers Winford,[75] of whose representatives it was bought by Benjamin Hayes before 1813.[76] His granddaughter Anne Frances, daughter of Treby Hele Hayes,[77] married William, son of William Mackworth-Praed,[78] and she held Water Stratford in her own right about 1862.[79] Their only child Anne Elizabeth married in 1857 Captain, afterwards Rear-Admiral, George Parker and Water Stratford thus passed to that family.[80] Admiral Parker died in 1904 and was succeeded by his eldest son Major William Frederick Parker,[81] the present holder of the manor.

A mill worth 8s. yearly is mentioned in the Domesday Survey.[82] There was a water-mill on the demesne in 1278–9 [83] and a mill is mentioned as having been an appurtenance of the manor, but destroyed by Isabel de Stratford about 1349.[84]

A court leet and court baron were held by the lords of the manor in the 17th century.[85]

CHURCH The church of *ST. GILES* consists of a chancel, nave and western tower.

From the details surviving it would appear that there was a 12th-century church consisting of a chancel and nave. In the 13th century, probably after the grant of this church to Luffield Abbey, new windows were inserted in the chancel, and in the 14th century the tower was added or rebuilt. In the 15th century some repairs were made, and, probably about 1652, the date on a stone over the south door, new windows were inserted in the chancel and nave, including a dormer window on the south side. In the 18th century the tower was cut down and a porch of brick and timber added on the south side.[86] Excepting the tower, the church was practically rebuilt in 1828, but much of the old work was re-used. The church was again restored and altered in 1890.

The east window of the chancel is modern, but a plain 13th-century lancet has been re-used on the south side and another, which forms a low-side window, on the north. In the north wall is a fine reset 12th-century doorway with a round head and a slightly recessed tympanum having a background of a diaper of roses upon which is a representation of the Agnus Dei. On the lintel are two dragons entwined. The chancel arch is of the 13th century and is of two moulded orders.

The nave is lighted by three windows. The eastern of the two in the north wall is of three lights with a round head, and the opposite window in the south wall is of the same character, but of two lights; both are probably of the early 19th-century restoration. The western window on the north, which is square-headed and of two lights, has re-worked 15th-century tracery. The south doorway is a good

example of 12th-century work. It has a semicircular head with zigzag ornament supported by plain columns with scroll-work capitals, billet-moulded abaci and moulded bases. The tympanum is carved with a Majesty having a kneeling angel on each side and the lintel is ornamented with interlaced arcading.

The 14th-century tower is now of two, but was originally probably of three, stages. The west window of the ground stage is of two lights with tracery under a pointed head. The tower arch is of two chamfered orders. The stair to the bell-chamber is in the south-west angle of the nave, which overlaps the tower. The bell-chamber has plain rectangular lights.

On the north wall of the nave is a monument to Mary wife of John 'Franckyshe' who died in child-bed 6 January 1629–30. The monument represents a woman in bed, her husband at the foot and her two sons (Alexander and Anthony) and seven daughters (Grissel, Penelope, Avis, Elizabeth, Mary, Priscilla and Ann) standing round her, and a new-born infant in a cot. A stone in the churchyard commemorates Rev. Joseph Bosworth, D.D., the Anglo-Saxon scholar, who was rector of Water Stratford and died 27 May 1876 aged eighty-eight years.

There are three bells bearing the following inscriptions: treble, 'Marye Cornewell 1594,' by Bartholomew Atton ; second, 'Pro Carolo Newsham hanc resono musam 1669,' by Richard Keene ; tenor, 'Mary Cornwell gave mee 1632. New cast by H. Bagley 1717, Isaac Rushworth, rector, George Crow, C.W.' There is also a sanctus bell inscribed 'E. Hemins fecit 1736, William Fillpott, C.W.'

The plate consists of a silver cup and a plated flagon and plate, bought in 1837. There is a 17th-century wooden alms shovel.

The registers begin in 1596.

ADVOWSON The church of Water Stratford was given by William son of William de Stratford, to Luffield Priory,[87] and confirmed by Bishop Hugh of Wells in 1217.[88] The name of Ralph the rector here occurs about 1245.[89] In 1291 the rectory was valued at 5 marks [90] and at £8 at the Dissolution.[91] The advowson descended with Luffield Priory (q.v.) and with Stowe till about 1850,[92] when it appears to have been sold by the Duke of Buckingham. It passed to the Chawner family, from whom it was acquired about 1877 by W. J. D. Andrew. It was bought of his trustees in 1897 by the Rev. L. E. Goddard, the present patron and rector of the living.[93]

Robert Doyley (d. c. 1150) gave two parts of the tithes of Stratford to the abbey of Oseney, and the gift was confirmed by Henry III in 1267.[94] In 1291 the abbey held a portion of 20s. in this church [95] and had an annual payment of 6s. 8d. till the Dissolution.[96]

Dr. Robert Sipthorpe, presented to the rectory in 1616, was charged by Parliament with having caused

[73] G.E.C. *Baronetage,* iv, 186, 187.
[74] Recov. R. Hil. 2 Anne, m. 92.
[75] Willis, op. cit. 343.
[76] Lysons, *Mag. Brit.* i (3), 645.
[77] Burke, *Extinct Baronetage* ; *Landed Gentry.*
[78] Burke, *Landed Gentry* (1906).
[79] Sheahan, *Hist. and Topog. of Bucks.* 321.
[80] *Ret. of Owners of Land,* 1873, *Bucks.* 15.
[81] Burke, *Peerage* (1907).

[82] *V.C.H. Bucks.* i, 258.
[83] *Hund. R.* (Rec. Com.), ii, 342.
[84] De Banco R. 358, m. 156.
[85] Parl. Surv. Bucks. no. 19.
[86] See an excellent paper on Water Stratford including extracts from Church-wardens' Accounts by John L. Myres in *Rec. of Bucks.* (Bucks. Arch. and Archit. Soc.), vii, 115 et seq.
[87] Dugdale, op. cit. iv, 345, quoting Priory Register, fol. 16b, at Westminster.
[88] *Liber Antiquus Hugonis Wells,* 81.

[89] Harl. Chart. 84, D 37 ; 86, E 38.
[90] *Pope Nich. Tax.* (Rec. Com.), 32.
[91] *Valor Eccl.* (Rec. Com.), iv, 239.
[92] Inst. Bks. (P.R.O.).
[93] *Clergy Lists.*
[94] *Cal. Chart. R.* 1257–1300, p. 69.
[95] *Pope Nich. Tax.* (Rec. Com.), 32.
[96] *Valor Eccl.* (Rec. Com.), iv, 239. All the Oseney lands here were granted to Christ Church, Oxford, in 1542 (*L. and P. Hen. VIII,* xvii, g. 881 [26]).

WATER STRATFORD CHURCH FROM THE SOUTH-EAST

WESTBURY CHURCH FROM THE NORTH-EAST

WESTBURY CHURCH: THE INTERIOR LOOKING EAST

the rupture between them and the king by preaching that the royal prerogative was above the law.[97]

Another rector was John Mason (d. 1694), 'an euthusiastic visionary' who believed he was Elias and appointed to proclaim the second Advent. He also declared that after his death he would rise again in three days. He had a large following who left their homes and filled all the houses and barns near Water Stratford. So great was their belief in his resurrection that his body had to be exhumed to prove his death. For some years after his death his followers continued to assemble at a place they called Holy Ground or at a house in Water Stratford.[98]

In 1325 John de Stratford had licence to grant land and rent in Water Stratford for a chaplain to celebrate divine service daily in the parish church there.[99] The advowson of the chantry at the altar of the Blessed Virgin Mary in the church of Water Stratford was in the hands of John de Stratford in 1335.[100] It is not afterwards mentioned.

CHARITIES Poor's Piece.—There was a piece of land, so called, containing about 5 a., much overgrown with bushes, which it was believed the poor had a right to cut for fuel, and an annual payment of £5, which was regarded as voluntary, was formerly made to the poor.

WESTBURY

Westberie (xi cent.) ; Westbir' (xii cent.).

Westbury is a parish with a large detached portion, amounting to 1,148 acres, separated from it by Shalstone and Biddlesden. The part round the church covers 1,381 acres, of which 654 are arable, 588 permanent grass, and 20 woods and plantations,[1] Westbury Wild in the north of the parish being the only wood of any size. The soil and subsoil are mixed, clay, loam and gravel, and a good building stone is found here. The slope of the land is from north to south and varies from 425 ft. to 313 ft. above ordnance datum. In the neighbourhood of the Ouse, which forms the southern boundary, the land is liable to flood.

The small village, which is situated in the southwest of the parish, contains several 17th-century stone cottages with thatched roofs. The modern manor-house is occupied by Sir Samuel Scott, bart. Southwest of the manor-house is the parish church of St. Augustine standing on low ground and nearly hidden by surrounding trees. Near the church is the vicarage, a 17th-century stone house of two stories with modern brick additions. It was probably built in 1661, the date on a stone reset in the modern work, and retains on the north two original wood-mullioned windows. Westbury has a village green on which stands a remarkably fine elm.[2]

Fulwell and Westbury station, on the Banbury branch of the London and North-Western railway, is in this parish.

Westbury was inclosed by Act of Parliament in 1764,[3] and the detached part was in 1884 transferred to Biddlesden for civil purposes.[4]

Among place-names occur Waterslede, Corhale and Midelcherweie in the early 13th century,[5] and meadow called Winstonslake in the 16th century.[6]

Alnod Cilt, a thegn, held WEST-BURY MANOR in the Confessor's reign,[7] being dispossessed at the Conquest when Westbury was granted to the Bishop of Bayeux.[8] Roger, the tenant in 1086, was probably Roger de Ivri,[9] for after the confiscation of the Bishop of Bayeux's fief, and the erection of the holdings of his chief tenants into baronies,[10] Westbury was attached to the honour of St. Walery, into which Roger de Ivri's lands were absorbed.[11]

Thomas de St. Walery is mentioned as connected with Westbury in 1196,[12] and Gunnora de St. Walery in 1198.[13] The St. Walery Honour was later held by the Earls of Cornwall, and between 1240 and 1335 Westbury Manor is said to be held of the earls as of this honour.[14] After the latter date the St. Walery Honour, as far as this manor is concerned, appears to have become merged in the larger honour of Wallingford.[15] A view for the honour of Wallingford was held at Westbury, Court Rolls being preserved at the Record Office dating from the 15th century. In 1422 a 'certain rent' of 13s. 4d. was paid by the tithing men of Westbury to the honour.

Westbury was subinfeudated to a family which took its name from the parish. Walter de Westbury held here before 1198 [16] and was succeeded by his son, William de Westbury,[17] some time before 1203. In the latter year William conveyed to Ralph Hareng all his land in Westbury, including that held in dower by Eleanor de Westbury, his mother.[18] Seven years later a carucate of land and other appurtenances which William de Fraxino (le Freyne) and Philippa his wife held of William de Westbury were settled by the latter on Ralph Hareng.[19] In 1218 he received licence to impark his wood of Westbury towards the abbey of Biddlesden.[20] His death took place before 1230, in

[97] Lysons, op. cit. i (3), 645 ; Lipscomb, *Hist. and Antiq. of Bucks.* iii, 138.
[98] Ibid. ; *Dict. Nat. Biog.*
[99] *Cal. Pat.* 1324–7, p. 173 ; 1327–30, p. 264.
[100] Feet of F. Bucks. Mich. 9 Edw. III, no. 9.
[1] Statistics from Bd. of Agric. (1905).
[2] Sheahan, *Hist. and Topog. of Bucks.* 323.
[3] Priv. Act, 4 Geo. III, cap. 61.
[4] Local Govt. Bd. Order, no. 15987.
[5] Harl. Chart. 85, F 10.
[6] Anct. D. (P.R.O.), A 12652.
[7] *V.C.H. Bucks.* i, 237.
[8] Ibid.
[9] See Westbury in Shenley for the iden-

tification of Roger with Roger de Ivri as also for the probability of the latter's manor in Westbury, entered under Mursley Hundred in the Domesday Book, being really in Stodfald Hundred and therefore part of the Westbury Manor whose descent is given above.
[10] *V.C.H. Bucks.* i, 211 ; cf. Leckhampstead.
[11] For the descent of the honour see Thornton.
[12] Pipe R. 8 Ric. I, m. 17.
[13] Ibid. 10 Ric. I, m. 1 d.
[14] *Testa de Nevill* (Rec. Com.), 244, 251a ; *Hund. R.* (Rec. Com.), i, 27, 32, 40 ; ii, 342 ; *Feud. Aids*, i, 79 ; Chan. Inq. p.m. 9 Edw. III (1st nos.), no. 42.

[15] *Feud. Aids*, i, 126 ; Chan. Inq. p.m. 2 Ric. II, no. 57 ; 5 Hen. V, no. 16 ; (Ser. 2), cclxviii, 159 ; *Cal. Inq. p.m. Hen. VII*, i, 370 ; Ct. R. (Gen. Ser.), portf. 212, no. 3, 19, 20, 24.
[16] Pipe R. 10 Ric. II, m. 1 d. He may have married a St. Walery heiress (cf. G. H. Fowler in *The Genealogist*).
[17] Add. Chart. 26694.
[18] Feet of F. case 282, file 4, no. 30.
[19] Ibid. no. 57. In 1225–6 William de Westbury made a final release to Ralph of 1 mark from a rent of 9 marks for lands in Westbury and Clanfield probably representing the Westbury estate (Add. Chart. 26694).
[20] *Cal. Pat.* 1216–25, p. 135.

which year Ralph Hareng, his son, paid 50 marks for renewing his father's charter to impark.[21] Ralph Hareng, jun., was returned as holding the vill a few years later,[22] while his mother Isabella [23] held Westbury in dower in 1254–5.[24] Within the next twenty years a partition of Westbury took place between this family and Simon de St. Lys ; the method of acquisition, whether by descent or alienation, has not been discovered. The history of Radclive, however, which runs parallel to that of Westbury, rather points to the former method, for in Radclive (q.v.) Simon de St. Lys is found holding simultaneously with Isabella Hareng.

In 1278–9 Joan de Somery, whose connexion with the Hareng family has not been established, was returned as lady of Westbury. Her property included 2 hides, half a virgate of land, 10 acres of wood and 4 acres of park, of which she held one hide in demesne.[25] Before 1284 she had been succeeded by Edmund de Salenewe, Aula Nova or Newhall, as the name alternatively appears.[26] Edmund was still holding in 1302, when he acquired licence to demise his manor for eight years.[27] Beatrice his widow was assessed for Westbury in 1316,[28] and two years later obtained licence to demise the manor for a period of twelve years.[29] In 1330 John de Newhall, possibly her son, transferred 'two parts of the manor' of Westbury to Ewald Lestrange or Strange,[30] who died seised in 1335.[31] His heir was his kinsman, Roger Strange of Knockin,[32] but his widow Alice, subsequently married to Hugh le Freyne, held Westbury in dower.[33] In 1373 Roger Strange of Knockin, son of the above Roger,[34] granted Westbury Manor to John, son of John Strange of Walton, co. Warwick (perhaps representing a branch of the family), and Mabel his wife and their issue.[35] In 1396 the said

STRANGE. *Gules two lions passant argent.*

John Strange again alienated the manor to another member of the family, Alan Strange, with whose name in the alienation appears that of Margaret his wife, daughter of John Wyard.[36] A remainder settlement here gives the names of Michael, Thomas, John and Baldwin Strange, brothers of Alan Strange, and Philippa and Ida his sisters.[37] Alan Strange died in 1417, but no mention is made of the manor in the inquisition then taken, though he was said to hold by knight service of the honour of Wallingford

2s. annual rent from a messuage and carucate of land held by John Hardwick in Westbury.[38] His heir was stated to be his daughter Eleanor, then aged twelve and more,[39] but Westbury appears to have continued in the male line of the Strange family, for in 1485 Thomas Strange died seised of this estate.[40] His heirs were his daughters Anne and Margaret, aged nine and six respectively.[41] Westbury was assigned to Anne, who carried it in marriage to John Strange of Little Massingham, Norfolk.[42] After his death in 1514[43] she married Sir Edward Knyvett, and, left again a widow in 1528,[44] joined in 1540 with Barbara, wife of Robert Mordaunt, and her daughter and heir by her first husband, in making a settlement of the manor[45] on Robert and Barbara Mordaunt and their heirs. In pursuance of this settlement Westbury passed to their son, Robert Mordaunt, who died in possession in 1602.[46] Lestrange Mordaunt, son of his brother Henry, was his heir,[47] and he in 1621 alienated the manor to Laurence Washington,[48] who had succeeded his father Laurence Washington in 1619.[49] He held until 1639, when he conveyed it to Sir Thomas Littleton, bart.,[50] whose estate in Westbury was assessed at £300 in 1647 as that of a delinquent.[51] His son and heir, Sir Henry Littleton, with his widow Catherine,[52] transferred it in 1650 to Roger Price, sen., and Roger Price, jun.[53] Roger Price, sen., died in Spain in 1677,[54] and Roger Price, jun., Sheriff of Buckinghamshire in 1680,[55] obtained an Act in 1689 empowering him to make a settlement of Westbury Manor on his wife Elizabeth, and a like settlement on his brothers George, Thomas,

PRICE of Westbury. *Argent three Cornish choughs.*

Ingham and Joseph, in respect of their wives.[56] Roger Price died in 1694[57] and was survived by his widow Elizabeth for some years, for in 1709, together with her son Thomas, she made a settlement of Westbury Manor.[58] Thomas Price died in 1733,[59] and the following year Campbell Price, his son,[60] suffered a recovery of the manor.[61] It was probably his daughter and heir who brought Westbury by marriage into the Withers family,[62] of whom Benjamin Price Withers presented to the church in 1753,[63] and by his will dated 1771 settled Westbury Manor on his descendants for ever.[64] One of the same name held

---

[21] *Excerpta e Rot. Fin.* (Rec. Com.), ii, 194.
[22] *Testa de Nevill* (Rec. Com.), 244a, 251a. [23] Harl. Chart. 85, F 10.
[24] *Hund. R.* (Rec. Com.), i, 32.
[25] Ibid. ii, 342.
[26] *Feud. Aids,* i, 79.
[27] *Cal. Pat.* 1301–7, p. 49.
[28] *Feud. Aids,* i, 108.
[29] *Cal. Pat.* 1317–21, p. 75.
[30] Feet of F. case 19, file 78.
[31] Chan. Inq. p.m. 9 Edw. III (1st nos.), no. 42.
[32] Ibid. ; G.E.C. *Complete Peerage,* vii, 273 ; De Banco R. 419, m. 234 d.
[33] *Cal. Close,* 1337–9, p. 25.
[34] G.E.C. loc. cit.
[35] Close, 211, mm. 6 d, 5 d.
[36] Feet of F. case 21, file 109. [37] Ibid.
[38] Chan. Inq. p.m. 5 Hen. V, no. 16.

[39] Ibid.
[40] *Cal. Inq. p.m. Hen. VII,* i, 370.
[41] Ibid.
[42] Chan. Inq. p.m. (Ser. 2), xxix, 82.
[43] Ibid. ; P.C.C. 36 Holder.
[44] Chan. Inq. p.m. (Ser. 2), xlvii, 44 ; l, 139.
[45] Feet of F. Bucks. Hil. 32 Hen. VIII ; *Visit. of Bucks.* (Harl. Soc.), 186.
[46] Chan. Inq. p.m. (Ser. 2), cclxviii, 159. In 1592 a grant of Westbury was made to William Tipper and Robert Dawe, fishing grantees (Pat. 1382, m. 21).
[47] Chan. Inq. p.m. (Ser. 2), cclxviii, 159.
[48] Feet of F. Bucks. Trin. 19 Jas. I ; Recov. R. Trin. 19 Jas. I, m. 75.
[49] P.C.C. 3 Soame.
[50] Willis, *Hist. and Antiq. of Bucks.* 352.
[51] *Cal. Com. for Comp.* 67.
[52] G.E.C. *Baronetage,* i, 117.

[53] Feet of F. Bucks. Trin. 1650.
[54] Willis, op. cit. 357, quoting Par. Reg. His will mentions six younger sons (P.C.C. 26 Reeve).
[55] P.R.O. *List of Sheriffs,* 9.
[56] *Hist. MSS. Com. Rep.* xii, App. vi, 192.
[57] Willis, op. cit. 359, quoting Registers. Lipscomb says he died in 1705 (*Hist. and Antiq. of Bucks.* iii, 143).
[58] Com. Pleas Recov. R. Mich. 8 Anne, m. 4 ; Recov. R. Mich. 8 Anne, m. 112.
[59] Willis, loc. cit. ; *Gent. Mag.* iii, 270.
[60] P.C.C. 206 Price. Thomas Price left his family pictures at Westbury to his son Campbell Price.
[61] Recov. R. East. 7 Geo. II, m. 129.
[62] Lysons, *Mag. Brit.* i (3), 660.
[63] Inst. Bks. (P.R.O).
[64] Lipscomb, op. cit. iii, 142.

the manor in 1789[65] and also exercised patronage in Westbury in 1814.[66] The Price Withers family died out at the beginning of the 19th century. The family of Gurden of Brackley, which succeeded, took the name of Withers, owing to the last Withers being godfather to the heir of the Gurdens.[66a] Westbury was retained by them until 1854, when it passed by purchase to the Hon. Percy Barrington,[67] who succeeded his brother as Viscount Barrington in 1886. After his death in 1901 it

SCOTT, baronet. *Party indented argent and pean a saltire countercoloured.*

was purchased by Sir Samuel Scott, bart., the present owner.

In 1302-3 Simon de Grenehulle was said to hold 'the manor of Westbury' for one fee,[68] and in 1346 William de Cauntelow held two parts of this fee of the honour of Wallingford, Rose widow of Simon de St. Lys holding the third part.[69] No further mention of this fee has been found.

The family of St. Lys, as above stated, had an important holding of the St. Walery Honour in Westbury during the 13th century.[70] First mention is found of them in Westbury c. 1260, when Simon de St. Lys of Radclive made a grant of lands in Westbury which was witnessed by Jordan de St. Lys of Westbury.[70a] In 1274 Simon de St. Lys recovered seisin of 7 acres of wood here.[71] Five years later the same Simon was said to own in this parish 2 virgates in demesne, 10 acres of wood, and 4 of park. He had also one virgate in villeinage and four cottagers.[72] The name of Simon de St. Lys appears under Westbury in the feudal assessment of 1284-6.[73] He died in 1288, leaving a widow Isabel and a son, Andrew, then a minor,[73a] who in 1301[74] and 1316[75] held of the Earl of Cornwall here by knight service. He was contemporaneous with Agnes widow of Roger de St. Lys, who claimed dower in Westbury in 1327,[76] and was succeeded by Ralph de St. Lys,[76a] who conveyed his fee to Ewald Strange, lord of the manor,[77] whose history it henceforth shares.

Part of the Hareng property in Westbury appears to have come to the Chastillon family, who certainly succeeded to the Hareng lands in Thornton (q.v.) with which their estate in Westbury descended. Mentioned in their possession in 1279,[78] it was described as the park of Westbury in the following year,[79] and was

specified in 1440 as 60 acres of wood and the park.[80] These distinctions probably corresponded to the Royes and Makeloms Parks of twenty years later[81] which may perpetuate the names of Rose (Royse) Chastillon and her son Malcolm (Malculmus, Masculinus), the 13th and 14th-century owners. They were still attached to the Thornton estate (q.v.) in the early 17th century as lands and woods in Westbury.[82]

One mill is mentioned in Westbury at Domesday.[83] It was known in the 13th century as Hunt Mill.[84] It remained attached to the honour of Wallingford[85] though separated from the manor, and in the 15th century is found in the ownership of the lords of Shalstone Manor. Philip Purefoy died seised in 1468,[86] and further mention of it in this family occurs during the two following centuries.[87] Hunts Mill still stands at the south-eastern corner of the parish.

Mention is found of a second water-mill in Westbury in the 17th century. In 1608 Thomas Slye died seised of various hereditaments in Westbury,[88] which, on the death of his son William in 1615, were described as a water-mill and lands held of Sir Lestrange Mordaunt bart. as of his manor of Westbury by a rent of 13½d., 2 lb. of wax, and a pair of spurs.[89] This mill is probably to be identified with one standing on the Ouse at the west end of the village at the present day.[90]

In addition to Elstow no fewer than seven religious houses held land in this parish in the 13th century and earlier. The master of St. Thomas Acon held land here as in Buckingham (q.v.).[91] Its extent was said to be in 1278 10 acres of assart not hidated.[92] At the Dissolution two closes of wood called Heremytes Grove or Heremytes Fields in Westbury, containing 28 acres, occupied by John Lambert, lately belonging to St. Thomas Acon, were granted for life to John Josselyn.[93] In 1543 Richard Andrews of Hayles,

ST. THOMAS ACON. *Sable a cross formy party argent and gules.*

Gloucestershire, obtained the reversion in fee of this grant,[94] which was confirmed to him, two years later.[95] Biddlesden Abbey acquired lands in this parish early in the 13th century from a family of Lega, of whom Thomas and John sons of Richard de Lega and Susanna their mother made various

---

[65] Recov. R. Mich. 30 Geo. III, m. 46.

[66] Inst. Bks. (P.R.O.).

[66a] Inform. supplied by the Rev. R. Ussher.

[67] Sheahan, *Hist. and Topog. of Bucks.* 324.

[68] *Feud. Aids,* i, 100.

[69] Ibid. 126.

[70] *Hund. R.* (Rec. Com.), ii, 342, &c.

[70a] Deeds in the archives of Magdalen College, Oxford, published by the Rev. R. Ussher, *Hist. of Westbury,* 102.

[71] *Abbrev. Plac.* (Rec. Com.), 265.

[72] *Hund. R.* (Rec. Com.), ii, 342.

[73] *Feud. Aids,* i, 79.

[73a] R. Ussher, op. cit. 116.

[74] Chan. Inq. p.m. 28 Edw. I, no. 44.

[75] *Feud. Aids,* i, 108.

[76] De Banco R. Hil. 1 Edw. III,

m. 37; 2 Edw. III, m. 56 d.; *Cal. Pat. 1327-30,* p. 266.

[76a] There is mention of a Ralph de St. Lys, rector of Radclive, and brother of the above Andrew, who in 1339 gave lands in Westbury to Rose widow of Simon de St. Lys (R. Ussher, op. cit. 140, quoting old deeds; cf. *Feud. Aids,* i, 126).

[77] *Cal. Close,* 1333-7, p. 452.

[78] Chan. Inq. p.m. Edw. I, file 21, no. 12.

[79] Feet of F. Div. Co. Mich. 8 & 9 Edw. I, no. 17.

[80] Close, 290, m. 8.

[81] Ibid. 314, m. 26; Early Chan. Proc. bdle. 29, no. 99.

[82] Chan. Inq. p.m. (Ser. 2), ccxciv, 92.

[83] *V.C.H. Bucks.* i, 237.

[84] Harl. Chart. 86, D 6.

[85] Chan. Inq. p.m. 10 Edw. II, no. 85;

8 Edw. IV, no. 29. It was possibly included in Simon de Grenehulle's fee mentioned in 1284 and 1346 (*Feud. Aids,* i, 100, 126).

[86] Chan. Inq. p.m. 8 Edw. IV, no. 29.

[87] Ibid. (Ser. 2), ccxlv, 91; ccxlviii, 19; cccxlv, 54; Fine R. 10 Jas. I, no. 19; Feet of F. Bucks. East. 17 Jas. I.

[88] Chan. Inq. p.m. (Ser. 2), cccv, 127.

[89] Ibid. cccxlviii, 108.

[90] It is mentioned in 17th and 18th-century extents of the manor (Recov. R. East. 33 Chas. II, m. 146; Mich. 8 Anne, m. 112).

[91] Chan. Inq. p.m. 18 Edw. I, no. 121, &c.

[92] *Hund. R.* (Rec. Com.), ii, 342.

[93] *L. and P. Hen. VIII,* xvi, p. 716.

[94] Ibid. xviii (1), g. 981 (56).

[95] Ibid. xx (2), g. 496 (29).

grants, confirmed by their overlords Ralph Hareng and his son Ralph.[96] After the Dissolution these lands appear to have been acquired by the Temple family, who were also lords of Stowe (q.v.). Described in 1603 as 'lands' held of the manor of East Greenwich,[97] and in 1638 as lands and view of frankpledge extending into Westbury, late of Biddlesden,[98] this property is in the 18th and 19th centuries erroneously called a manor.[99] The hospital of St. John of Brackley in 1278–9 owned a virgate of land in Westbury for which the master rendered a yearly rent of one pound of cummin.[100] This holding was augmented in 1301, when John le Poer obtained licence to alienate to the hospital a messuage and 35 acres of land and the moiety of an acre of meadow.[1] Roger and Walter Hardel likewise made a grant in 1336.[2]

The Prioress of Catesby, Northants, owned land in Westbury of which mention is first found in 1278–9, when it was assessed at one carucate of assart and 3 acres of wood.[3] In 1309 this property was referred to as a manor in an action for waste brought by the prioress against the lessees.[4] In 1363 she received pardon for acquiring in mortmain from Richard Chastillon of Leckhampstead 18s. rent here.[5] At the Dissolution the priory owned rents in Westbury valued at £4 14s.,[6] and these were leased in 1537 to John Giffard.[7] In 1278–9 Hogshaw Preceptory owned a virgate of land and a water-mill, for which Jordan Bastard paid a yearly rent of 30s.[8]

Luffield Abbey had an early grant of lands in Westbury[9] which were valued in 1291 at 3s.[10] They are mentioned in 1512, when they were leased to William Tyler for thirty-four years.[11] It seems likely that this estate is represented by the view attached to the manor of Luffield and extending into Westbury in 1701.[12] In 1267 an early charter of Robert Doyley to St. George's Chapel, Oxford, was exemplified in favour of the Abbot and canons of Oseney.[13] It contains mention of land in Westbury which was held by Oseney till the Dissolution, when, described as a messuage and 16 acres of land, it was said to be worth 7s.[14] It was granted in 1541 to John Wellesbourne, who also obtained the advowson.[15]

The church of *ST. AUGUSTINE CHURCH* consists of a chancel measuring internally 30 ft. by 17 ft., south vestry and organ chamber, nave 40 ft. by 20 ft. 6 in., north aisle 6 ft. wide, south aisle 7 ft. wide, north porch, and west tower 8 ft. 6 in. square. It is built of rubble with stone dressings, and the roofs are covered with slate and tiles.

The church dates from the 12th century, and consisted then of the present nave and probably a small chancel. In the 13th century the chancel was rebuilt and widened towards the north, and the small tower, which projects some 4 ft. into the west end of the nave, was added. The south aisle was built at the end of the 13th century and the north aisle some twenty-five years later, though the latter was considerably repaired at a subsequent period. The fabric was restored in 1863, and the vestry and porch are modern.

The chancel is lighted by a modern traceried window in the east wall, an original lancet at the east end of each side wall and a 14th-century low-side window at the north-west, the last being of one trefoiled light with a transom, below which the light is blocked. All these windows have modern rear arches. At the west end of the south wall are a modern arch and doorway to the vestry and organ-chamber, and at the east end is a piscina with a cinquefoiled ogee head and modern bowl. The wide chancel arch, dating from the 13th century, is of two chamfered orders, the outer continuous down the jambs and the inner supported by semi-octagonal responds with moulded capitals. Above the capitals the arch has been rebuilt.

The nave is of three bays, and has a modern clearstory with circular cusped windows. Both arcades are of three pointed arches supported by octagonal pillars and responds with moulded capitals and bases. The south arcade dates from the end of the 13th century, and the capitals of its responds are embellished with nail-head ornament. The north arcade is of about 1320, though the mouldings of its capitals and bases seem to have been somewhat altered at a subsequent period. The pointed tower arch in the west wall of the nave is of a single order with an indented label, and dates from the early 13th century; the responds, which are formed of octagonal shafts with moulded capitals and bases, do not appear to be in their original position. There is a square-headed recess to the south of the chancel arch which probably formed the reredos of a nave altar, but its lower part is now built up. At the north-east of the nave is a small ogee-headed piscina of about 1400, without bowl. Both aisles have been extensively restored, and, with the exception of some old jamb stones re-used in the north aisle, the windows and doorways are modern. Several fragments of mediaeval wrought stones have been incorporated in the walling of the south aisle, among them a 15th-century carved head.

The tower, which has been considerably restored, is of three stages, and has a modern saddle-back roof. The windows of the ground stage and bell-chamber are modern, and the ringing chamber is lighted by small loops on the north and south.

The font and pulpit are modern. There are some fragments of old painted glass reset in the south window of the vestry, and on the floor of the chancel are several mediaeval encaustic tiles.

The tower contains a ring of three bells: the second is by Henry Bagley, 1711; the treble, which was also by Henry Bagley, 1711, but had become broken in two parts, was recast in 1898; the tenor,

[96] Harl. MS. 4714, fol. 325; Harl. Chart. 85, G 10, 20; Campbell Chart. xviii, 13.
[97] Chan. Inq. p.m. (Ser. 2), cclxxxi, 93.
[98] Ibid. dlxxv, 142.
[99] Recov. R. East. 4 Geo. I, m. 86; Feet of F. Bucks. Mich. 6 Geo. I; Recov. R. Hil. 15 Geo. III, m. 353; 59 Geo. III, m. 269.
[100] Hund. R. (Rec. Com.), ii, 342.
[1] Cal. Pat. 1292–1301, p. 595; Inq. a.q.d. file 36, no. 3.

[2] Cal. Pat. 1334–8, p. 260; Inq. a.q.d. file 237, no. 6.
[3] Hund. R. loc. cit.
[4] De Banco R. Trin. 3 Edw. II, m. 94.
[5] Cal. Pat. 1361–4, p. 384.
[6] Valor Eccl. (Rec. Com.), iv, 339.
[7] L. and P. Hen. VIII, xiii (1), p. 579.
[8] Hund. R. loc. cit.
[9] Westminster Abbey Deeds; Dugdale, Mon. iv, 349.
[10] Pope Nich. Tax. (Rec. Com.), 47.

[11] L. and P. Hen. VIII, i, 3297.
[12] Recov. R. Trin. 13 Will. III, m. 208.
[13] Cal. Chart. R. 1257–1300, p. 69. A twenty-one years' lease of a portion of tithes in Westbury and also of the 'mese or tenaundry there' made by the abbot in 1525 was afterwards cancelled (Anct. D. [P.R.O.], A 13571).
[14] Valor Eccl. (Rec. Com.), ii, 220.
[15] L. and P. Hen. VIII, xvi, g. 1226 (30).

inscribed with seven letters in Gothic capitals, arranged independently, is of about 1600, and probably from the Bedford foundry.

The communion plate consists of a cup and cover paten of 1592 and a plated flagon and two patens of the 18th century.[16]

The registers begin in 1558.

ADVOWSON The church of Westbury, though not mentioned in the charter of confirmation of Henry II,[17] appears to have been early granted to Elstow Abbey, which some time previous to 1225 had instituted a perpetual vicarage there.[18] In 1278 the endowment of the church included 2 virgates of land and a 'cottage,' for which the abbess paid 20*s.* yearly.[19] In 1291 the abbess was assessed there for rents and heriots worth £1 9*s.* 6*d.*[20] At the Dissolution the rectory was worth 100*s.*[21] and the vicarage £10.[22] The rectory and advowson were granted in 1541 to John Wellesbourne,[23] who died in 1548.[23a] His son and heir John Wellesbourne with Anne his wife made a settlement in 1594 on John Sill,[24] who had married their daughter Elizabeth Wellesbourne.[25] John Sill predeceased John Wellesbourne, who died in 1611, when Elizabeth, then the wife of Edward Mole, inherited the advowson and rectory of Westbury.[26]

Her son Wellesbourne Sill united with herself and husband to make a settlement in 1632.[27] He died in the spring of 1634 leaving his widow Philippa and his son Wellesbourne, then aged sixteen, to survive him.[28] In 1660 Wellesbourne Sill alienated both rectory and advowson to Roger Price,[29] then lord of Westbury Manor. He and his family built the vicarage house c. 1661 and also augmented the vicarage with the great tithes.[30] The advowson has since been retained by the lords of the manor,[31] and is at present the property of Sir Samuel Scott, bart.

In 1328 Andrew de St. Lys obtained licence to alienate land in Westbury in mortmain to a chaplain to celebrate in St. Mary's chapel, Radclive.[32]

Nathaniel Markwick, the divine, was vicar of Westbury 1692–4.[33]

CHARITIES The Poor's Allotment, acquired in 1764, on the inclosure of the parish, contains 21 a. 1 r. 37 p., producing £12 a year, which is applied in the distribution of small sums of money.

The church allotment, also allotted under the same Act in lieu of lands in the common fields belonging to the church, consists of 5 a. 1 r. 27 p., let at about £6 a year, which is carried to the churchwardens' general account.

---

[16] At the visitation of Cardinal Pole in 1556 it appeared that John Morden had taken the chalice and sold it (Strype, *Memorials*, iii (2), 400).
[17] Dugdale, *Mon.* iii, 411.
[18] *R. of Hugh of Wells* (Cant. and York Soc.), ii, 66.
[19] *Hund. R.* loc. cit.
[20] *Pope Nich. Tax.* (Rec. Com.), 47*b*.

[21] *Valor Eccl.* (Rec. Com.), iv, 188.
[22] Ibid. 240.
[23] *L. and P. Hen. VIII*, xvi, g. 1226 (30).
[23a] Chan. Inq. p.m. (Ser. 2), lxxxvii, 56. The heir was then two years old.
[24] Feet of F. Bucks. Mich. 36 Eliz.
[25] Chan. Inq. p.m. (Ser. 2), cccxlix, 156. [26] Ibid.

[27] Feet of F. Div. Co. Trin. 8 Chas. I; Recov. R. Trin. 8 Chas. I, m. 50.
[28] Chan. Inq. p.m. (Ser. 2), dxxxviii, 112.
[29] Feet of F. Bucks. Hil. 1659.
[30] Willis, op. cit. 353.
[31] Inst. Bks. (P.R.O.).
[32] *Cal. Pat.* 1327–30, p. 266.
[33] *Dict. Nat. Biog.*

THE HUNDRED OF NEWPORT

CONTAINING THE PARISHES OF

ASTWOOD
BLETCHLEY with FENNY
    STRATFORD and
    WATER EATON
BRADWELL
BOW BRICKHILL
GREAT BRICKHILL
LITTLE BRICKHILL
BROUGHTON
CALVERTON
CHICHELEY
CLIFTON REYNES
COLD BRAYFIELD
NORTH CRAWLEY
EMBERTON
GAYHURST

HANSLOPE with CASTLE
    THORPE
HARDMEAD
HAVERSHAM
LATHBURY
LAVENDON
GREAT LINFORD
LITTLE LINFORD
LOUGHTON
MILTON KEYNES
MOULSOE
NEWPORT PAGNELL
NEWTON BLOSSOMVILLE
NEWTON LONGVILLE
OLNEY with WARRINGTON
RAVENSTONE
SHENLEY [1]

SHERINGTON
SIMPSON
STANTONBURY
STOKE GOLDINGTON
STOKE HAMMOND
STONY STRATFORD
TYRINGHAM with
    FILGRAVE
WALTON
WAVENDON
WESTON UNDERWOOD
WILLEN
WOLVERTON
GREAT WOOLSTONE
LITTLE WOOLSTONE
WOUGHTON ON THE
    GREEN

Of the places enumerated above, Astwood, Bletchley, Fenny Stratford, Cold Brayfield, Castle Thorpe, Newton Blossomville, Stony Stratford, Filgrave, Walton, Warrington and Willen are not mentioned in the Domesday Survey, while Caldecote and Tickford in Newport Pagnell have separate entries.[2] Newport Hundred includes the hundreds of Sigelai, Bonestou[3] and Moulsoe[4] which were grouped in the latter part of the 13th century as the three hundreds of Newport.[5] Sigelai contained Bletchley, Bradwell, Calverton, Great Linford, Loughton, Newport Pagnell, Newton Longville, Shenley (part of), Simpson, Stantonbury, Stoke Hammond, Stony Stratford, Willen, Great and Little Woolstone, Wolverton and Woughton on the Green. In Bonestou Hundred were Cold Brayfield, Castle Thorpe, Gayhurst, Hanslope, Haversham, Lathbury, Lavendon, Little Linford, Olney, Ravenstone, Stoke Goldington, Tyringham with Filgrave, and Weston Underwood; the remaining parishes were in the hundred of Moulsoe. In 1086 Sigelai Hundred was assessed at 148 hides $2\frac{3}{4}$ virgates (including 7 hides $1\frac{1}{4}$ virgates in Tyringham, $\frac{1}{2}$ virgate in Hardmead, and 2 hides 3 virgates in Wavendon), Bonestou at 9 hides $\frac{1}{4}$ virgate, Moulsoe at 111 hides $2\frac{1}{2}$ virgates (including 5 hides in Tickford afterwards found in Sigelai).[6]

The three royal hundreds of Newport were attached to the honour of Ampthill in the middle 16th century,[7] and payments were made to the bailiff of this honour, instead of to the sheriff of the county.[8] In this and

---

[1] Part of Shenley is in Cottesloe Hundred.   [2] *V.C.H. Bucks.* i, 410–14.
[3] The name survives in Bunsty, now in Gayhurst, but formerly a detached part of Lathbury.
[4] The form which survives in the parish of the name.   [5] *Feud. Aids*, i, 89.
[6] *V.C.H. Bucks.* i, total of hidage under the entries for these hundreds.
[7] Ct. R. (Gen. Ser.), portf. 153, no. 1.   [8] *L. and P. Hen. VIII*, xxi (1), p. 773.

the following century they were usually assessed as a group,[9] but sometimes, as in 1563[10] and 1607,[11] under each hundred separately. These hundreds were leased in 1614 to Sir Francis Fortescue and his sons John and William for their lives in survivorship,[12] and their rights were claimed by John, then Sir John Fortescue, kt., in 1651.[13] In 1663 a lease was granted to Thomas Catesby of Hardmead for twenty-one years.[14] The three Newport hundreds were assigned to Queen Katherine in dower in 1665,[15] and she leased them

in 1682 for thirty-one years to the Earl of Ailesbury.[16] On the expiration of this term no grant was made until 1736, when a lease for a similar term was made to Thomas fourth Duke of Leeds.[17] In 1830 George Thomas Wyndham had the hundredal rights, but by 1855, when the " Manor of the Three Hundreds of Newport " was for sale, all privileges appear to have lapsed.[17a]

An increase in the fee-farm rents of the hundreds of Sigelai, Bonestou and Moulsoe, formerly £5 yearly, was taken by the sheriff after the battle of Evesham.[18] In 1651 these rents, called certainty money, amounted to £23 8s. yearly, the profits of the court and other perquisites yielding an

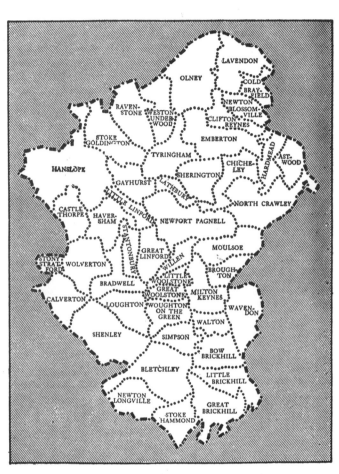

INDEX MAP TO THE HUNDRED OF NEWPORT

additional £14 14s. 4d.[19] At this date the court leet and the three weeks court were held at the customary times.[20] They were usually called at Bunsty, but (the steward being able to adjourn them at will to any place within the hundreds) kept at Newport Pagnell.[21]

[9] Lay Subs. R. bdles. 79, no. 164, m. 6, no. 281 ; 80, no. 325.
[10] Ibid. 79, no. 189.   [11] Ibid. no. 261. See also *V.C.H. Bucks.* i, 225–6.
[12] Pat. 12 Jas. I, pt. xiii, no. 19. A twenty-one years' grant had been obtained by Francis Fortescue in 1594 (information from Mr. F. W. Bull).   [13] Parl. Surv. Bucks. no. 6.
[14] Pat. 15 Chas. II, pt. xi, no. 9.   [15] Ibid. 17 Chas. II, pt. ix, no. 1.
[16] Treas. Crown Lease Bk. iv, 57.   [17] Ibid. 88 et seq.   [17a] Information from Mr. F. W. Bull.
[18] *Hund. R.* (Rec. Com.), i, 37. All the payments made from Bonestou Hundred are given in detail.
[19] Parl. Surv. Bucks. no. 6.   [20] Ibid.
[21] Ibid. Notice for the holding of a court at the Swan Inn, Newport Pagnell, was given in the *Northampton Mercury* for 23 October 1830. Information kindly supplied by Mr. F. W. Bull.

ASTWOOD

Estwod (xii cent.) ; Estwode (xiii, xiv cent.).

This parish covers 1,281 acres, of which 615 are arable and 564 permanent grass.[1] There are 28 acres of woods, Ramacre Wood, Wallace Wood, Snakes Meadow and Jacobs Wood being the names of small woods in the parish. The soil is strong clay, and the subsoil clay, the principal crops being wheat, beans, barley and oats. The slope of the ground varies little, being from 303 ft. to 324 ft. above the ordnance datum.

The village is small, and consists mainly of thatched cottages built round the green. At the west end of the green, in one of the prettiest churchyards in the county, is the parish church. Opposite the church porch is the base of an ancient stone cross. South of the church is the vicarage, an early 19th-century

BURY FARM, ASTWOOD

building. The house which it replaced has been described in a terrier of 1674 as containing 'four Bays of Building covered with Straw.'[2] The Manor Farm, near the Vicarage, stands on the site of the ancient manor-house of Astwood, a large and important building pulled down some fifty years since,[3] which was the seat of John Thurloe in 1674 and of subsequent lords of the manor.[4] A yet more important seat in this parish was that of Astwood Bury in the north, which was pulled down in 1799,

the moat and dovehouse, the latter now a cottage, alone remaining to mark its site at the present day.[5] This building was said to have been begun by the Zouches, continued by the Norwoods, and so improved by William Lowndes that Willis, writing c. 1755, says, ' it may be reported one of the best old seats in the county.'[6] Bury Farm and the old house at Green Valley Farm are 17th-century houses of half-timber, with brick filling and tiled roofs. Besides the homestead moat at Bury Farm, there is also a small quadrangular moat in Astwood.[7]

In 1672 the house of Robert Seabrook of Astwood was licensed for congregational worship.[8] An Independent chapel was erected in the parish in 1826,[9] and the present building dates from 1847.

The following place-names have been found :—Lewenscroft (xv cent.),[10] Bozeats, a messuage (xvi cent.),[11] Windmill field and Claypitts (xvii cent.).[12]

MANORS There is no mention of Astwood by name in the Survey of 1086, but it is likely that *ASTWOOD BURY MANOR* may be included in the unnamed four-hide manor which William Fitz Ansculf then held in Moulsoe Hundred.[13]

He was lord of Newport Pagnell (q.v.), head of the honour of Newport Pagnell, part of the barony of Dudley, of which Astwood Bury was held c. 1240 with Little Crawley.[14] The dependence of Astwood Bury on the manor of Newport Pagnell persisted into the 18th century.[15]

The earliest tenants known of Astwood Bury Manor are a family of Rokele or Rupella, who owned land in Essex[16] as well as in this county. In 1216 Robert de Rokele paid a heavy fine to the Crown to obtain the release of his sons Henry and Richard, and his nephew Colin, son of Nicholas de Tutham.[17] Between 1231 and 1232 one of the same name was disputing the right of Rose de Rokele and Godfrey de Rokele to part of a knight's fee in Astwood.[18] He apparently succeeded in acquiring the fee for which he is returned c. 1240.[19] It was

---

[1] Statistics from Bd. of Agric. (1905).
[2] Add. MS. 5839, fol. 10.
[3] Sheahan, *Hist. and Topog. of Bucks.* 486.
[4] Add. MS. 5839, fol. 7 d.
[5] *V.C.H. Bucks.* ii, 29 ; Lysons, *Mag. Brit.* i (3), 502.
[6] Add. MS. 5839, fol. 8.
[7] *V.C.H. Bucks.* ii, 29.
[8] *Cal. S. P. Dom.* 1672, p. 377.
[9] Sheahan, op. cit. 489.

[10] Add. Chart. 23879.
[11] Chan. Inq. p.m. (Ser. 2), ccxvii, 117.
[12] Chan. Proc. (Ser. 2), bdle. 339, no. 1.
[13] *V.C.H. Bucks.* i, 256. J. H. Round suggests that the entry relates to Crawley, which adjoins Astwood, and with which its history partly runs.
[14] *Testa de Nevill* (Rec. Com.), 248.
[15] *Plac. de Quo Warr.* (Rec. Com.), 88 ; Chan. Inq. p.m. 16 Edw. II, no. 72 ; *Cal. Close*, 1318–23, p. 623 ; Chan. Inq.

p.m. (Ser. 2), ccxxviii, 3 ; Add. MS. 5839, fol. 7 d.
[16] Feet of F. Div. Co. 17 Hen. III, no. 50.
[17] *Rot. de Oblatis et Fin.* (Rec. Com.), 596.
[18] *Cal. Close*, 1227–31, p. 562 ; 1231–4, p. 124 ; Feet of F. Div. Co. 17 Hen. III no. 50. Rose de Rokele also claimed lands in Essex against Robert de Rokele.
[19] *Testa de Nevill* (Rec. Com.), 248.

probably his son Robert de Rokele who in 1281 conveyed a rent-charge of £12 on one messuage, 1 carucate of land, 14 acres of meadow, and 5 marks rent in Astwood to John le Usser for his life.[20] Robert de Rokele still held in 1302–3,[21] but by 1306 had been succeeded by his son and heir Robert de Rokele, who in that year quitclaimed various lands to his tenants in Astwood.[22] Robert de Rokele is returned for the vill in 1316,[23] in 1322 and 1323,[24] but it was probably a descendant of the same name who in 1345 made a settlement of the manor (here so-called for the first time) to the use of Thomas de Shelton and Alice his wife for their joint lives.[25] Thomas de Shelton is accordingly returned in the feudal assessment of the following year.[26] A change occurs in the ownership of this manor between 1346 and 1390, at which date it was the property of Thomas Pever and Margery his wife.[27] They then conveyed it by fine to John de Lincoln, Richard Albon and others, to the use of Richard Albon.[28] Like Lavendon Manor (q.v.), Astwood Bury was retained by the Pever and Zouche families, until John Lord Zouche was attainted after Bosworth, and in 1487 Astwood is described as the property of Philip Curtis.[29] On the reversal of the attainder in 1495,[30] Astwood was restored to the Zouches, and by them retained until 1538, when John, son of the last-mentioned Lord Zouche, alienated the manor to Edward Hazlewood,[31] who two years later transferred it to Thomas Norwood.[32] In 1575 he combined with his sons Nicholas, John, Thomas and William Norwood to make a settlement of the manor on John Norwood, his wife Anne and their children.[33] Thomas Norwood, senior, died in February 1587–8, being predeceased by John, and Astwood Manor then passed to Tyringham, son of John Norwood, twelve years of age.[34] In 1598 Tyringham, together with Thomas Catesby and Anne his wife (possibly widow of John Norwood), settled the manor by fine on Anthony Tyringham and others.[35] Tyringham Norwood received royal licence to enter into the manor in 1606,[36] and retained possession until 1621, when, together with his wife Anne and his son Anthony Norwood,[37] he finally alienated Astwood Bury to Samuel Cranmer,[38] a collateral descendant of the famous archbishop.[39] He died seised of the manor in 1640, having previously settled it on his son Caesar, then only six years of age.[40] Caesar Cranmer, who was knighted in 1677,[40a] acquired considerable

property under the will of his uncle Sir Henry Wood, dated 1676,[41] and took the name of Wood.[42] He made various settlements of the manor between 1683 and 1685,[43] finally mortgaging it to Sarah dowager Duchess of Somerset, wife of Lord Coleraine.[44] She died in 1692,[45] and by her will bequeathed all her right in Astwood to the Honourable Langham Booth, younger son of Henry, first Earl of Warrington.[45a] His trustees foreclosed in or about the year 1704,[46] and Astwood Bury Manor passed to Langham Booth, who in 1715 alienated the property to Charles Hosier and others on behalf of William Lowndes,[47] son of William Lowndes

CRANMER. *Argent a cheveron azure between three pelicans sable with three cinqfoils or on the cheveron.*

of Winslow.[48] William Lowndes, junior, resided at Astwood Bury until his death, which took place in 1775 in the eighty-eighth year of his age.[49] It next passed to his grandson, William Lowndes-Stone,[50] whose descendant, Miss Lowndes-Stone, held in the middle of the 19th century.[51] The property appears to be at present vested in Mr. Benjamin Howkins of Bromham, Bedfordshire.

A second property in Astwood called *ASTWOOD MANOR* was evidently included in 1086 in the $2\frac{1}{2}$ hides $\frac{3}{4}$ virgate belonging to the Bishop of Coutances in Tyringham,[52] of which 'vill' it was reckoned a hamlet in 1284–6, the service of one fee being demanded from both 'vill' and hamlet in conjunction with Lower Filgrave.[53] With Tyringham it was attached to the honour of Newport, the first mention of the overlordship being found in 1274,[54] and the last in 1624.[55]

The Tyringham portion of this holding became the manor of Filgrave (q.v.) with which the Astwood property passed to the Tyringhams, the first John de Tyringham or Giffard dying c. 1274 seised of a messuage, grange, rents and a wood called Pirney in Astwood.[56] Roger his son held here in 1284–6,[57] and another Roger de Tyringham in 1323,[58] but between their ownership the fee seems to have been for some years in possession of Robert Dakeney, who is returned for the aid in 1302–3,[59] and whose name

---

[20] Feet of F. Bucks. Hil. 9 Edw. I, no. 17. In the spring of 1286 Lettice, widow of William de Rokele, called to warrant Robert de Rokele in a dispute over 49 acres and 8s. rent in Astwood, said by William Visdelou to have been held on the day she died by her mother Maud, wife of Humphrey Visdelou (Assize R. 68, m. 9).

[21] *Feud. Aids*, i, 104.

[22] Add. Chart. 23873, 23874.

[23] *Feud. Aids*, i, 110.

[24] Chan. Inq. p.m. 16 Edw. II, no. 72; *Cal. Close*, 1318–23, p. 623.

[25] Feet of F. Bucks. 19 Edw. III, no. 6.

[26] *Feud. Aids*, i, 130.

[27] Browne Willis says a de Rokele heiress married Richard Albon, but documents do not verify his statement (Add. MS. 5839, fol. 7 d.).

[28] Feet of F. Bucks. 13 Ric. II, no. 6.

[29] *Cal. Inq. p.m. Hen. VII*, i, 149.

[30] G.E.C. *Complete Peerage*, viii, 224.

[31] Recov. R. East. 30 Hen. VIII,

m. 100; Feet of F. Bucks. Trin. 30 Hen. VIII.

[32] Com. Pleas D. Enr. Trin. 32 Hen. VIII, m. 14.

[33] Feet of F. Bucks. Hil. 18 Eliz.; Chan. Inq. p.m. (Ser. 2), ccxvii, 117.

[34] Chan. Inq. p.m. (Ser. 2), ccxvii, 117; ccxxxii, 46.

[35] Feet of F. Bucks. Trin. 40 Eliz.

[36] Fine R. 4 Jas. I, pt. iii, no. 8.

[37] *Visit. of Bucks.* (Harl. Soc.), 191.

[38] Feet of F. Bucks. Mich. 19 Jas. I.

[39] Add. MS. 5839, fol. 8, 8d. He is so described on a mural monument to his memory in the parish church.

[40] Chan. Inq. p.m. (Ser. 2), dcxiv, 97.

[40a] Shaw, *Kts. of Engl.* ii, 252.

[41] Le Neve, *Ped. of the Kts.* (Harl. Soc.), 271–2.

[42] Cf. Feet of F. Bucks. Trin. 35 Chas. II, &c.

[43] Feet of F. Bucks. Trin. 35 Chas. II; Recov. R. East. 1 Jas. II, m. 226.

[44] Add. MS. 5839, fol. 8.

[45] G.E.C. *Complete Peerage*, vii, 178.

[45a] G.E.C. op. cit. viii, 51; *Musgrave's Obit.* (Harl. Soc.) i, 216; Burke, *Extinct Peerage*, 61; P.C.C. 22 Ash.

[46] Add. MS. loc. cit.; Feet of F. Bucks. Trin. 3 Anne. Sheahan says later.

[47] Add. MS. loc. cit.; Feet of F. Bucks. Mich. 2 Geo. I.

[48] Lipscomb, *Hist. and Antiq. of Bucks.* iv, 7.

[49] Ibid.; Add. MS. loc. cit.

[50] P.C.C. 146 Alexander; Lysons, op. cit. i (3), 502.

[51] Sheahan, op. cit. 487.

[52] *V.C.H. Bucks.* i, 240.

[53] *Feud. Aids*, i, 73.

[54] Chan. Inq. p.m. 2 Edw. I, no. 39.

[55] Ibid. (Ser. 2), dccxliii, 10.

[56] Ibid. 2 Edw. I, no. 39.

[57] *Feud. Aids*, i, 73.

[58] *Cal. Close*, 1318–23, p. 631.

[59] *Feud. Aids*, i, 104.

appears as witnessing charters in Astwood for the year 1306.[60] In 1346 John Talworth was said to hold this fee in Astwood,[61] and for the next century and more its history is very obscure. It may have been in possession of the Tappe family, who certainly owned land in the parish in the 14th and 15th centuries, and this suggestion is borne out by the fact that there was a small wood called Tappes within the manor in 1610.[62] Thomas Tappe leased lands here to John Breteyn in 1436,[63] and in 1463 Sir John Twe of Bedford quitclaimed land in Astwood to John Asteye *alias* Tappe, son and heir of the above Thomas.[64] It next passed to the Ingleton family, lords of Thornton Manor (q.v.), and by the marriage of Jane daughter and heir of Robert Ingleton to Humphrey Tyrell[65] was acquired by the latter family. Jane Tyrell died in 1557 seised of the manor of Astwood, having previously made various settlements on her son George.[66] At the time of her death she was the wife of Alexander St. John. In 1558 George Tyrell and Eleanor his wife alienated Astwood Manor to Richard Chibnale,[67] whose family had been settled in the parish for at least a generation, as appears from a brass in the church to the memory of Thomas Chibnale and his wives bearing date 1534.[68] Richard Chibnale, possibly son of the above Richard, made a settlement of the manor in 1592,[69] and died seised in 1607, when Astwood passed to Godfrey his son and heir.[70] Godfrey Chibnale was holding the manor in 1620,[71] but died in 1624, when he was succeeded by his son Thomas Chibnale,[72] who held in 1648.[73] In 1665 Thomas Chibnale made a settlement of Astwood on John Trevor and John Upton,[74] according to Willis, in trust for John Thurloe,[75] whose name certainly appears as defendant in a recovery of 1671,[76] and as vouchee in 1674, in which year he appears to have acquired full possession.[77] John Thurloe was not, as stated by Willis and others, Cromwell's celebrated minister of that name, for he died in 1668[78] (before the alienation of Astwood took place), but possibly his son. John Thurloe left a daughter Anne, married to Francis Brace, who held the manor in 1713, when as a widow with her son John Thurloe Brace and other members of the Brace family she settled Astwood on Edward Carteret and John Hamilton.[79] John Thurloe Brace was still holding Astwood in 1735, as various documents testify,[80] but sold it shortly afterwards to the executors of Thomas Trevor, first Baron Trevor of Bromham.[80a] His son Robert

CHIBNALE. *Azure two lions passant or between two flaunches ermine.*

Viscount Hampden was in possession in 1776,[81] and left Astwood to a relative, Robert Trevor, Receiver-General, who inherited in 1783[81a] and held in 1793.[82] In 1803 Astwood Manor[83] was purchased by Thomas David Boswell, M.D.,[84] a representative of whose family, John Irvine Boswell, is at present lord of this manor.

CHURCH The church of *ST. PETER* consists of a chancel measuring internally 24 ft. 6 in. by 14 ft. 3 in., nave 37 ft. by 20 ft. 6 in., south aisle 42 ft. 6 in. by 8 ft. 6 in., west tower 11 ft. by 8 ft. 2 in., and south porch. It is built of rubble with stone dressings and is coated with cement; the roofs of the chancel and porch are covered with tiles and those of the nave and aisle with lead.

The nave probably dates from the 12th century, and must have originally extended to the west wall of the present tower, forming a rectangle completed by the dotted lines on the adjoining plan; the thickness of the original walls would indicate this period, and fragments of moulded stonework of about 1200, including nail-head ornament, are built into the upper part of the tower. During the 14th century the present chancel was built and the south aisle added, and early in the 15th century the tower was constructed at the south-west angle of the nave, into which it projected, cutting off the north-west angle and part of the south arcade. Early in the 16th century the clearstory was added to the nave, and the nave and aisle were reroofed and provided with embattled parapets. The porch is modern, but some old stones have been re-used in the entrance archway.

The east window of the chancel, of three cinquefoiled lights with vertical tracery in a pointed head, was inserted in the 15th century, and at the east end of the south wall is a window of the same period, of two trefoiled lights with tracery in a square head. On the sill of the latter a stone containing a 14th-century piscina bowl has been reset, and immediately to the east of the window is a locker which is probably original. The north wall is pierced only by a modern cinquefoiled light placed near the west end. Opposite to it in the south wall is a similar light, and between this and the eastern window is an original priest's doorway with a pointed head. The pointed chancel arch, which also dates from the 14th century, is of two chamfered orders, the outer continuous and the inner supported by half-round responds with moulded capitals and bases. The trussed rafter roof of the chancel is modern.

The nave opens to the aisle on the south by a mid-14th-century arcade of four pointed arches supported by quatrefoil pillars with moulded capitals and bases; the east respond repeats the half-plan of the pillars, but the west respond and a large portion of the

[60] Add. Chart. 23873, 23874.
[61] *Feud. Aids,* i, 130.
[62] Chan. Inq. p.m. (Ser. 2), dcxlvii, 26. Against this theory must be placed the fact that the Tappes were still tenants in Astwood in the 16th century (Ct. of Req. bdle. 103, no. 52).
[63] Add. Chart. 23926; cf. ibid. 23876.
[64] Ibid. 23928.
[65] *Visit. of Bucks.* (Harl. Soc.), 118.
[66] Chan. Inq. p.m. (Ser. 2), cvii, 2.
[67] Recov. R. Mich. 5 & 6 Phil. and Mary, m. 151; Feet of F. Bucks. East. and Trin. 4 & 5 Phil. and Mary.

[68] Add. MS. 32490, TT 25.
[69] Feet of F. Bucks. Trin. 34 Eliz.
[70] Chan. Inq. p.m. (Ser. 2), dcxlvii, 26.
[71] Recov. R. East. 18 Jas. I, m. 44; Feet of F. Bucks. Hil. 17 Jas. I.
[72] Chan. Inq. p.m. (Ser. 2), dccxliii, 10; P.C.C. 80 Byrde.
[73] Feet of F. Bucks. Mich. 24 Chas. I.
[74] Ibid. Trin. 17 Chas. II.
[75] Add. MS. 5839, fol. 7 d.
[76] Recov. R. East. 23 Chas. II, m. 39.
[77] Ibid. 26 Chas. II, m. 27.
[78] *Dict. Nat. Biog.*
[79] Feet of F. Div. Co. Trin. 12 Anne.

[80] Feet of F. Bucks. Mich. 5 Geo. I; Add. MS. 5839, fol. 7 d.; Recov. R. Trin. 7 Geo. I, m. 107.
[80a] P.C.C. 460 Cornwallis.
[81] G.E.C. op. cit. iv, 154; Com. Pleas Recov. R. Trin. 16 Geo. III, m. 61.
[81a] G.E.C. loc. cit.; P.C.C. 460 Cornwallis.
[82] Recov. R. Trin. 33 Geo. III, m. 238.
[83] The Crawley Grange estate (North Crawley, q.v.) was purchased at the same date from the Lowndes family.
[84] Sheahan, op. cit. 486.

westernmost arch are absorbed by the tower, which projects into the arcade at this point. The only window on the north, which is of two plain lights with a square head, is a 16th-century insertion in a 14th-century opening, the internal jambs and rear-arch of which remain ; at the west end of the wall, and partly encroached upon by the 15th-century work, is a pointed doorway of the 14th century which was blocked not long since. The early 15th-century tower arch at the west end of the nave is pointed and has semi-octagonal responds with moulded capitals and bases. The clearstory has three early 16th-century windows on either side, each of three pointed lights in a four-centred head, and the low-pitched roof of the nave is of the same period : it has heavy cambered beams, intermediate rafters and purlins, all of which are moulded and divide the roof into large plastered panels.

Neither the east nor west wall of the south aisle is pierced, but on the south are three fine and well-preserved windows of the mid-14th century, the eastern of three and the others of two lights, with flowing tracery in pointed heads ; to the east of the large window is a trefoiled piscina with a sexfoil bowl. The south doorway, which retains an old door with mediaeval hinges, has a pointed head of two orders, the inner continuous and the outer supported by shafts ; it has been much defaced and is now coated with cement, while the lower parts of the original jambs have been destroyed. Immediately to the east of the doorway inside is a triangular-headed stoup, now without a bowl. The lean-to roof of the aisle is of similar date and character to the nave roof.

The tower is of three stages with an embattled parapet, and has an unusually large stair turret at the north-west, which, with a diagonal buttress at the south-west, rises through two stages. The south-west angle of the original nave was used for the west and south walls of the lower stage, the other walls being formed within the nave itself, thus cutting off entirely the north-west angle, the stonework of which was doubtless re-used in the new work. A 14th-century window, probably one of two, had been inserted in the west wall of the old nave, and so, while the south wall was strengthened from the foundation, the west wall with its window was retained intact, the necessary additional thickness being procured above the window by a pointed arch of slight projection which spans the space between the turret and buttress. The window is of two trefoiled lights with flowing tracery in a pointed head, and being on the north side of the arched space a cement label has been added at a late date on the south to secure symmetry by suggesting another window. There is a single light in the west wall of the second stage, and the bell-chamber is lighted on each of the north, west, and south sides by an early 15th-century window of two trefoiled lights with tracery in a pointed head and on the east by a square-headed window of two cinquefoiled lights, inserted about 1500.

The font, which dates from the late 14th century, has an octagonal bowl and a square panelled stem with angle shafts ; three sides of the stem are carved and on the south is a representation of the Stafford knot. On the east wall of the aisle are the brass figures of Thomas Chibnale, who died in 1534, in fur-lined gown, and Emma and Alice his wives, with inscription, symbols of the evangelists St. Matthew and St. Luke, and the verse 'Cur caro letatur dum vermibus esca paratur | Terre terra datur caro nascitur ut moriatur | Terram terra tegat demon peccata resumat | mundus res habeat spiritus alta petat' ; the stone slab from which these brasses were taken is on the floor at this end of the aisle. There is also a small brass inscription on the north wall of the nave near the pulpit to Roger Keston (d. 1409). On the north wall of the chancel are marble monuments to William Lowndes of Astwood Bury (d. 1775), who was the son of William Lowndes of Winslow, Bucks., Secretary of the Treasury under William III, Anne, and George I, with a medallion portrait and shield of arms ; to Margaret wife of William Lowndes of Astwood Bury (d. 1764) ; and to Samuel Cranmer (d. 1640), who 'descended in a direct line from Richard Cranmer, second sonn of John Cranmer, elder brother to Thomas Arch Bishop of Canterbury,' his second wife

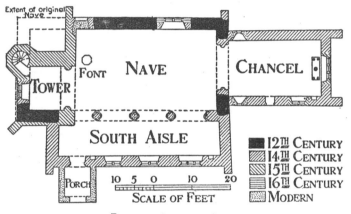

PLAN OF ASTWOOD CHURCH

Mary (Wood) (d. 1684), and Caesar Wood *alias* Cranmer (d. 1685), who erected the monument. On the chancel floor are 18th-century slabs to members of the Lowndes family, and to Thomas Layton (d. 1723) and Elizabeth his wife (d. 1757). The communion table, the communion rails now under the chancel arch, and a carved chair in the chancel all date from the 17th century, while a panelled chest with carved front at the east end of the aisle and some panelling re-used in the aisle pews are of the same period. Four benches and parts of others of about 1500, with moulded rails and panelled ends, are incorporated in the seating of the nave.

The tower contains a ring of three bells : the treble, inscribed 'Sancta Katerina Ora Pro Nobis,' and the second 'Sit Nomen Domini Benedictum,' are both by John Walgrave and date from the early 15th century ; the tenor, inscribed 'God Save Our King 1631. I.K.,' is by James Keene.

The communion plate consists of a cup and cover paten dating originally from the Elizabethan period, though the bowl of the cup and the paten have been altered at a later date, the latter having been restamped in 1827 ; a pewter flagon and paten of the 18th

4
35

century ; a plated cup ; and a knife and fork with silver handles.

The registers before 1812 are as follows : (i) an unbound volume of all entries 1666 to 1688 ; (ii) all entries 1689 to 1712 ; (iii) all entries 1726 to 1758 ; (iv) baptisms and burials 1761 to 1812 ; (v) marriages 1754 to 1775 ; (vi) marriages 1776 to 1824.

ADVOWSON The earliest mention that has been found of Astwood Church concerns the grant by Fulk Paynel, lord of Newport Pagnell, who flourished in the reign of Henry I, of Astwood Church and chapel to Tickford Priory.[85] Numerous references are subsequently found to the prior's exercise of the right of presentation,[86] until Tickford was dissolved in 1524 in order that its revenues might go to the support of Cardinal Wolsey's new college.[87] In 1526 Wolsey received grant of appropriation of Astwood among other spiritualities of the priory,[88] and the advowson appears in the list of endowments conveyed to the dean and canons of the college in the same year.[89] Cardinal Wolsey presented in 1527,[90] but after his fall in 1529 the endowments of the college were forfeited.[90a] In 1532 it was refounded by the king under the name of Henry the Eighth's College,[91] to which in the *Valor* the church is said to owe an annual pension of 40s.[92] The college was once more surrendered to the Crown in 1545[92a] and the advowson of Astwood has remained in royal custody,[93] the living being at the present day in the hands of the Lord Chancellor.

In 1587 the rectory was temporarily granted to Charles Bagehot and Bartholomew Yardley.[94] At the beginning of the 19th century the great tithes were owned by Robert Trevor, lord of Astwood Manor.[95]

CHARITIES It appears from a paper in the custody of the churchwardens that Clara Lowndes by her will dated 17 July 1793 gave £5 per annum for ten poor people. The endowment now consists of £166 13s. 4d. consols with the official trustees, producing £4 3s. 4d. yearly, which is divided equally at Easter among ten poor persons.

BLETCHLEY WITH FENNY STRATFORD AND WATER EATON

Bicchelai (xii cent.) ; Blechelegh (xiii cent.) ; Blecheley (xiv–xvi cent.).

Bletchley, which includes the hamlet of Water Eaton and until 1881–91 also included part of the market town of Fenny Stratford,[1] is a large and low-lying parish, watered on the east by the River Ouzel and the Grand Junction Canal, which run almost parallel through Fenny Stratford and Water Eaton. To the west of the canal the land rises slightly, but its greatest height is 372 ft. above the ordnance datum, reached at Windmill Hill, a little west of Bletchley village. The upper surface is strong clay and the subsoil Oxford Clay.

The London and North Western railway passes almost due south through the parish, and there are important railway works at Bletchley station, the junction of the Bedford and Cambridge and the Banbury and Oxford branch lines with the main line. On the former branch is a station at Fenny Stratford.

Watling Street, which passes south-east through Fenny Stratford, is the chief thoroughfare.

Bletchley has an area of 1,308 acres, of which 970 are permanent grass and 185 arable land.[2] In 1862 it was described as 'scattered and mean-looking—consisting chiefly of poor thatched cottages,' built in two sections, The Green and The Town.[3] The older houses, still for the most part thatched, are half-timbered with brick filling, and date from the 17th century. Bletchley village is about half a mile west of the station. The church stands a little to the north-west of the village, and is approached by a fine avenue of ancient yews ; near it is one of the entrances to Bletchley Park, the seat of Sir Herbert Leon, bart. The park extends as far as the railway. The Rectory Cottages, to the south of the church, incorporate the remains of a small half-timber house of the 15th century. The hall, which is now used as a barn, retains two hammer-beam trusses, one of which is in a comparatively perfect state and has carved heads at the terminations of the hammer-beams. The hall appears to have been originally of three bays, but the easternmost bay has been rebuilt, and now forms part of one of the cottages which occupy the adjoining chamber wing. This portion of the house appears to have been much altered and largely rebuilt in the 17th century, but some moulded beams of original date still remain in the ceiling of the room on the ground floor next the hall. The modern 'town' of Bletchley has grown up round the railway works, and is now practically united to Fenny Stratford. A Wesleyan chapel was built at Bletchley in 1895.

South-east of Bletchley is the hamlet of Water Eaton[4] (Etone, xi cent. ; Eton, Etone, xii–xvi cent.), which has an area of 1,016 acres and a population of 201. Charters were dated from Water Eaton in 1228.[5] In 1725 there was a great flood here.[6] On

[85] Dugdale, *Mon.* vi, 1038 ; *Cal. Doc. of France,* 444.

[86] Mins. Accts. (Gen. Ser.), bdle. 1125, no. 1 ; *Cal. Pat.* 1327–30, p. 277 ; 1340–3, pp. 176, 178, 348 ; 1345–8, pp. 196, 423 ; 1348–50, p. 346 ; 1350–4, pp. 150, 475 ; 1385–9, p. 523 ; 1396–9, p. 118.

[87] *V.C.H. Bucks.* i, 364 ; Chan. Inq. p.m. (Ser. 2), lxxvi, 3.

[88] *L. and P. Hen. VIII,* iv (1), g. 1913 (1), g. 2167 (1) ; (3), p. 3066.

[89] Feet of F. Div. Co. Mich. 18 Hen. VIII.

[90] Add. MS. 5839, fol. 9 d.

[90a] *L. and P. Hen. VIII,* iv (3), g. 6516 (15) ; Chan. Inq. p.m. (Ser. 2), lii, 35.

[91] *L. and P. Hen. VIII,* v, g. 1370 (23).

[92] *Valor Eccl.* (Rec. Com.), iv, 244.

[92a] Tanner, *Not. Mon.*

[93] Inst. Bks. (P.R.O.).

[94] Pat. 29 Eliz. pt. iii, m. 18.

[95] Lysons, op. cit. i (3), 502.

[1] Part of Fenny Stratford was in Simpson parish.

[2] Statistics from Bd. of Agric. (1905).

[3] Sheahan, *Hist. and Topog. of Bucks.* 489. There was formerly a cross on

Bletchley Green with two hillocks used for archery. They were levelled by Browne Willis in 1711 when he built Waterhall, and the iron heads of many arrows were found (Add. MS. 5821, fol. 148 d. ; 6318, fol. 16).

[4] It was known as 'Eton' till 1431 (*Cal. Pat.* 1429–36, p. 183), after which Water Eaton became the more usual name.

[5] *Cal. Chart. R.* 1226–57, p. 67 Possibly Water Eaton in Oxfordshire.

[6] *Rec. of Bucks.* viii, 237.

Astwood : Dove House, now a Cottage

Astwood Church from the South-East

BLETCHLEY CHURCH FROM THE SOUTH-EAST

BLETCHLEY CHURCH: THE INTERIOR LOOKING EAST

the river bank is a corn-mill. There is a Wesleyan Methodist chapel here.

About one and a quarter miles south of Water Eaton, on the bank of the canal, is Waterhall Farm, probably marking the site of the mansion of Waterhall, formerly belonging to the Lords Grey de Wilton.[7] In 1711 Browne Willis, the eccentric Buckingham-shire antiquary, built a house on rising ground by Bletchley Church, which, as William Cole says, 'he very absurdly . . . called . . . Water Hall.'[7a] He never lived there, and in 1780 it was put up for auction.[8] Lipscomb says it was at some time pur-chased by Earl Spencer's steward, who pulled it entirely down.[9] About 1862 there were remaining two portions of what might have been the out offices and a great portion of a moat still full of water. It was approached 'by avenues of elm and lime trees from each side.'[10]

Browne Willis (1682–1760), eldest son of Thomas Willis,[11] was owner of the Bletchley estate from 1699 to 1760. He was M.P. for the borough of Buckingham from 1705 to 1708,[12] and was elected F.S.A. in 1718. 'Through his charitable gifts, his portions to his married children, and the expendi-ture of £5,000 on the build-ing of Waterhall, he ruined his fine estate, and was obliged towards the end of his days to dress meanly and to live in squalor, becoming very dirty and penurious, so that he was often taken for a beggar.' He died at Whad-don and was buried beneath the altar in Fenny Stratford Church; he left a bene-faction for a sermon there every year on St. Martin's Day.[13]

The town of Fenny Strat-ford lies to the north of Water Eaton, on Watling Street; its area is 1,040 acres. The church stands at the junction of Watling Street and Aylesbury Street, and near it are Baptist, Wesleyan and two Primitive Methodist chapels, built in 1800, 1809, 1866 and 1898 respectively. A cemetery with two mortuary chapels was opened in 1859. There are a few 17th-century houses and cottages of half-timber with brick-filling.

Among the rectors presented by Browne Willis to the living of Bletchley were Edward Wells (1716), an 18th-century mathematician and geographer,[14] and

William Cole (1753), the Cambridge antiquary and friend of Horace Walpole.[15]

Lands in Bletchley were inclosed in 1517.[16] In-closures were made in Fenny Stratford and Bow Brick-hill under an Act of 1793.[17] The common lands in Bletchley parish were inclosed under an Act of 1810,[18] the award being made in 1813.[19]

The following place-names occur : 'Le Cok super le Hope,' 'Le Key sur le Hope'[20] (xv cent.), Cot-manfield[21] (xvi cent.), Coketowne End, Madgestewe-hedge,[22] Rickly Close[23] (xvii cent.).

The market town and ancient *BOROUGH* borough of *FENNY STRATFORD* (Fenni Stretford or Venni Stretford, xiii cent.) owed its importance to its position on Watling Street, between Stony Stratford and Dun-stable. Though the site of the Roman station Magio-vintum has now been definitely proved to be at the Auld Fields, Dropshort, Little Brickhill, a short distance to the south of the modern Fenny Stratford

RECTORY COTTAGES, BLETCHLEY

and on Watling Street,[24] yet there is no doubt that Fenny Stratford was afterwards an important place of call on the chief highway between London and the north-west of England. The activity of the towns-people appears to have centred on the bridge over the Ouzel, possibly on the same site as the present three-arched bridge of brick with stone coping, and in 1347 a royal writ was issued to the sheriff of the county to cause as many bridges to be made from Leighton Buzzard to Fenny Stratford as used to be there, and to

[7] Add. MS. 5834, p. 379. This house was pulled down in the time of Elizabeth, the materials being used to build Whaddon (Add. MS. *ut supra*; Sheahan, op. cit. 490, 491). It is noteworthy that the Greys de Wilton held a manor of Water-hall in Cold Brayfield.

[7a] Add. MS. loc. cit.

[8] *Northampton Mercury*, 21 Feb. 1780.

[9] Lipscomb, *Hist. and Antiq. of Bucks.* iv, 11. Perhaps Mr. Harrison, who is said to have pulled it down early in the 19th century (Lysons, *Mag. Brit.* i [3], 512).

[10] Sheahan, op. cit. 491.

[11] *Dict. Nat. Biog.* His parents were both buried in the chancel of Bletchley Church, and out of regard for their memory their son spent £800 on the church between 1704 and 1707.

[12] *Ret. of Memb. of Parl.* ii, 1.

[13] Add. MS. 5821, fol. 149, 155 d., 156 d.

[14] *Dict. Nat. Biog.*

[15] Ibid.

[16] Leadam, *Dom. Incl.* 1517 (Royal Hist. Soc.), i, 178.

[17] Priv. Act, 33 Geo. III, cap. 40.

[18] Loc. and Pers. Act, 50 Geo. III, cap. 66.

[19] *Blue Bk. Incl. Awards*, 10.

[20] *Cal. Pat.* 1422–9, p. 555.

[21] Leadam, loc. cit.; Pat. 11 Eliz. pt. i, m. 45.

[22] Chan. Inq. p.m. (Ser. 2), ccclxxv, 71.

[23] Exch. Dep. Hil. 1651–2, no. 2.

[24] *Arch. Journ.* viii, 45 ; *Rec. of Bucks.* iv, 150, 156 ; Sheahan, op. cit. 25, 532 ; *Proc. Soc. Antiq.* xxiv, 35–7.

compel all those to come who were bound to construct or repair those bridges.[25] The Fenny Stratford Bridge may have been included among those in need of repair, for in 1383 a grant of pontage was made to Richard Candeler and Geoffrey Hall of Fenny Stratford.[26] This was repeated in 1398[27] and again in 1401, when the grant was made to the 'good men of the town.'[28] The town had attained the rank of a borough before 1370, when the burgesses paid 40s. rent to the lord of the manor for half the vill of Fenny Stratford.[29] There is also a mention of burgage tenements in 1429[30] and in 1624.[31] The organization of the burgesses for judicial and administrative purposes appears to have been of the slightest, and their corporate action was exercised solely, so far as is known, in connexion with the gild founded in 1493 (see below). The Patent granting them licence to found the gild constituted it a corporate body with a common seal.[32] There is no record of any attempt on its part to usurp authority in regulating town affairs, and the chief control appears to have vested in the lord of the manor. It was to Roger de Caux, the lord, and not to the townspeople, that a weekly market on Mondays was granted in 1204.[33] The locality specified was the manor of Water Eaton, but it may be safely presumed that the market was held from the first at Fenny Stratford, the position of which on a great thoroughfare with a constant stream of travellers made it a more suitable venue. Moreover, the weekly Monday market at Fenny Stratford is included among the appurtenances of Water Eaton Manor in 1324,[34] when the tolls and stallage fees for a little over one-third of the year amounted to 7s. 6d.[35] An annual fair was also granted to the lord of the manor of Fenny Stratford in 1252, to be held on the vigil and feast of the Nativity of the Virgin (8 September) and six following days.[36]

James I, by charter in 1608, granted to John and Francis Duncombe and the inhabitants of Fenny Stratford a free market on Monday and two fairs on 7, 8 and 9 April and on 12, 13 and 14 October, with tolls and court of pie-powder.[37] Towards the end of the 17th century, 'by the confusion of the Civil Wars and other accidents that followed,'[38] the market fell into disuse. It was revived by Browne Willis in 1702,[39] and was still held in 1792, but by 1888 it had altogether ceased.[40] In 1792 four annual fairs on 19 April, 18 July, 10 October and 28 November were held. By 1888 an additional fair was held on the second and fourth Thursdays in every month, probably identical with the present cattle market held every alternate Thursday. Fairs are still held on 19 April and 11 October. The Market House, the 'sorry little erection' mentioned in 1819,[41] was built by Browne Willis in 1716, but destroyed about 1840.[41a]

In 1436 John Peyntour of Fenny Stratford, 'peyntour' and king's approver, and others were indicted of having in 1419 'sweated and clipped genuine English money, to wit, nobles of choice gold, called "Edwardes" . . . and other nobles, . . . pence called "penyes of topens" and of having coined counterfeit money.'[42] At the same date mention is made of Brabanters, who had settled at Fenny Stratford and taken the oath of fealty.[43]

Fenny Stratford is not mentioned by Leland or Stukeley, but that it maintained its early importance is shown by the frequent references to its inns. The Swan Inn was standing in 1474,[44] and is mentioned in 1624[45]; the George Inn, mentioned in 1459,[46] was taken down in 1681,[47] because it hindered the custom of the 'Red Lion.'[48] The Bull Inn was built before 1609.[49] The Civil War struck the first note of decay.[50] Troops were quartered in the town by Sir William Waller in 1644,[51] and during the war the chapel was destroyed. In 1665 a further disaster befel the town in the shape of a terrible visitation of the plague.[52] The Bletchley registers show a list of 126 burials in that year, mostly of deaths from the plague.[53] The road was temporarily diverted and the inns closed.[54] For many years the market was discontinued. Evidence of the distress occasioned is afforded by a contemporary deed, which, referring to a row of church houses standing in the middle of the town for the poor to dwell in, mentions a messuage much ruined by the poor who inhabited it in the late war and pestilence.[55] The town has never recovered its former status. It is described by Camden in the 18th century as remarkable only for its inns and market.[56] A diary of 1768 refers to it as 'a very small disunited village, not sufficiently considerable to deserve observation.'[57] In 1819 it is described as a small decayed market town, built in the shape of a cross.[58]

Fenny Stratford was still only a chapelry, partly in the parish of Bletchley and partly in Simpson, in 1831,[59] but with the opening of large railway works at Bletchley it has once more acquired a measure of prosperity. It was formed into a separate civil parish between 1881 and 1891, and by Local Government Board Order in 1895 was with Simpson constituted an urban district. The Order was extended in 1898 to include Bletchley.[60] The people are chiefly employed on the railway; brushes are made, and market

[25] Cal. Close, 1346–9, p. 397.
[26] Cal. Pat. 1381–5, p. 236.
[27] Ibid. 1396–9, p. 400.
[28] Ibid. 1399–1401, p. 425. Thomas Searles, by his will in 1573, left £40 towards mending or making the bridge (P.C.C. 30 Peter).
[29] Chan. Inq. p.m. 44 Edw. III (1st nos.), no. 30.
[30] Cal. Pat. 1422–9, p. 554.
[31] Chan. Inq. p.m. (Ser. 2), dccxlvi, 90.
[32] Pat. 9 Hen. VII, m. 26.
[33] Liberate R. 3, m. 6.
[34] Cal. Inq. p.m. (Edw. II), vi, 312.
[35] Mins. Accts. (Gen. Ser.), bdle. 1119, no. 2 ; cf. Add. R. 59370.
[36] Cal. Chart. R. 1226–57, p. 413.
[37] Pat. 6 Jas. I, pt. xxviii, no. 14.
[38] Add. MS. 5821, fol. 151 d.

[39] Ibid. ; Lond. Gaz. 29 June to 2 July 1702.
[40] Rep. of Royal Com. on Market Rts. and Tolls, i, 139.
[41] Hassell, Tour of Grand Junction Canal, 66.
[41a] W. Bradbrook, Hist. of Fenny Stratford.
[42] Cal. Pat. 1422–9, p. 134 ; 1429–36, p. 592. [43] Ibid. 1429–36, p. 559.
[44] Lipscomb, op. cit. iv, 30 ; Lysons, op. cit. i (3), 515.
[45] Chan. Inq. p.m. (Ser. 2), dccxlvi, 90.
[46] Ibid. 36 Hen. VI, no. 36.
[47] Lipscomb, loc. cit. says 1665.
[48] Rec. of Bucks. ix, 206. The 'Red Lion' belonged to John Hatch of Simpson at his death in 1635 (Chan. Inq. p.m. [Ser. 2], dxxv, 115).

[49] Chan. Inq. p.m. (Ser. 2), cccviii, 158 ; ccclxxv, 71.
[50] Add. MS. 5821, fol. 151 d. ; Lond. Gaz. 29 June to 2 July 1702.
[51] Cal. S. P. Dom. 1644, p. 300.
[52] Add. MS. 5821, fol. 155.
[53] Rec. of Bucks. viii, 237.
[54] Add. MS. 5821, fol. 151 d. ; Lond. Gaz. 29 June to 2 July 1702 ; Lysons, op. cit. 515.
[55] Proc. as to Charitable Uses, bdle. 36, no. 20.
[56] Camden, Brit. (ed. Gough), i, 321.
[57] Verulam MSS. (Hist. MSS. Com.), i, 241.
[58] Hassell, Tour of Grand Junction Canal, 66.
[59] Census Rep. 1831.
[60] Ibid. 1901.

gardening is an important industry. Formerly straw-plait and lace were the chief manufactures, but these trades have died out.[61]

Bletchley contains two manors, neither *MANORS* of which is mentioned in the Domesday Survey. At that date the first manor was included in the more important one of Water Eaton. It first occurs as a separate manor in 1499,[62] and has always descended with Water Eaton.

The second manor, known as *OVER*[63] or *WEST*[64] or *OLD*[65] *BLETCHLEY*, or 'le Westmanirade'[66] (xiv cent.), was perhaps included in the adjacent manor of Great Brickhill in the Domesday Survey, for, like Brickhill, it was afterwards attached as half a fee to the honour of Giffard or Gloucester,[67] which descended in the Earls of Gloucester and Stafford, to whom an annual rent of 2s. was paid from this manor.[68] By the early 17th century the tenure was unknown.[69]

Early in the 13th century this manor was held by John Grey,[70] who was accused of withdrawing at Bletchley a hide of land which before was geldable and did suit at the county and hundred courts.[71] He was also lord of Water Eaton, with which place Bletchley formed one vill, the estate being known as the vill of Eaton cum Bletchley in 1284–6[72] and as Bletchley cum membris in 1316.[73] It descended with Water Eaton until the death of John Grey in 1323, when, in accordance with a settlement of 1311, it passed to his younger son Roger,[74] Henry, the elder son, renouncing all claim in 1328.[75] Roger was summoned to Parliament as Baron Grey (de Ruthyn) from 1324.[76] He died in 1353,[77] having settled Bletchley on his son Reynold and Eleanor his wife.[78] Reynold died in 1388[79] and Eleanor held the manor till her death in 1396.[80] Their son Reynold[81] was a privy councillor to Henry IV, with whom he was in great favour. He died in 1440, and, his son John having predeceased him, he was succeeded by his grandson Edmund.[82] He was created Earl of Kent by Edward IV in 1465,[83] having

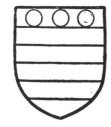

GREY de Ruthyn. *Barry argent and azure with three roundels gules in the chief.*

deserted Henry VI at the battle of Northampton, 1460. He died in 1489, succeeded by his eldest surviving son George,[84] who had been knighted at the coronation of Richard III.[85] On the death of George in 1503 Bletchley descended to his son Richard, who died without issue in 1524, 'when he had greatly wasted his estate.'[86] His half-brother and heir Sir Henry Grey[87] never assumed the title, nor did his grandson Reynold till 1572, ten years after his succession.[88] He died in 1573, succeeded by his brother Henry, who in 1601 dealt with the manor of Bletchley,[89] probably in settlement on his nephew Henry on his marriage with Lady Elizabeth Talbot.[90] Henry Earl of Kent died without issue in January 1614–15,[91] and his brother and heir Charles in 1623.[92] Charles's son Henry sold B' hley in 1630[93] to Katherine dowager Duchess of Buckingham,[94] whose son George sold it to Thomas Willis in 1674.[95] Since that date Bletchley has descended with Water Eaton.

The manor of *FENNY STRATFORD* is first mentioned in 1252, when it was held by John Grey,[96] with whose manor of Water Eaton it has always descended.

The manor of *WATER EATON* was held before the Conquest by Edit'; she could sell it to whom she wished. At the Conquest it was given to Geoffrey Bishop of Coutances, who held in 1086. It was then assessed at 10 hides.[97] The bishop rebelled against William II in 1088,[98] and his estate of Water Eaton is said to have been given to Walter Giffard Earl of Buckingham about 1092.[99] The chief authority for this grant is the confirmation by Walter Giffard, his son,[100] to the priory of Newton Longville of the tithes of the demesne of Bletchley.[1] The younger Walter died without issue in 1164, and this manor is said to have passed to his aunt Rose,[2] wife of Richard Fitz Gilbert, grandfather of the first Earl of Pembroke.[3] The head of the Giffards' Norman honour was Longueville in the Pays de Caux,[4] and it was possibly as the Fitz Gilberts' tenant that Roger de Caux held Water Eaton in 1204.[4a] It may, however, have been granted to Gerard de Caux by Henry I along with land in Ludgershall,[5] as it was held by the same tenure, by a serjeanty of falconry mentioned for the first time in 1210–12.[6] In 1284–6 the kind and number of falcons were stated to be unknown[7]; in 1308 the service was given as that of keeping the king's gerfalcons at the king's expense,[8] and in 1324

[61] Sheahan, op. cit. 489.
[62] Exch. Inq. p.m. (Ser. 2), file 5, no. 9.
[63] Feet of F. Bucks. Mich. 5 Edw. II, no. 24.
[64] Chan. Inq. p.m. 12 Ric. II, no. 23; 19 Ric. II, no. 30.
[65] Ibid. (Ser. 2), cccxlix, 172; ccclxxvi, 144; Feet of F. Div. Co. Trin. 43 Eliz.; Bucks. Mich. 6 Chas. I.
[66] Cal. Inq. p.m. (Edw. II), vi, 312.
[67] Chan. Inq. p.m. 8 Edw. II, no. 68; 21 Edw. III (1st nos.), no. 59; 16 Ric. II, pt. i, no. 27.
[68] Ibid. 22 Ric. II, no. 46; 4 Hen. IV, no. 41; 38 & 39 Hen. VI, no. 59.
[69] Ibid. (Ser. 2), cccxlix, 172.
[70] Testa de Nevill (Rec. Com.), 244b.
[71] Hund. R. (Rec. Com.), i, 40. The like charge was preferred against his son Reynold in 1276 (ibid.).
[72] Feud. Aids, i, 80.
[73] Ibid. 109.
[74] Cal. Inq. p.m. (Edw. II), vi, 313; Feet of F. Bucks. Mich. 5 Edw. II,

no. 24; De Banco R. 187, m. 87; Cal. Close, 1323-7, pp. 76-7, 393-4. This manor was no doubt the 16 virgates in Eaton held of the honour of Gloucester by military service (Anct. Ext. [Exch. K.R.], no. 78 [2]), the other lands being held by serjeanty of falconry.
[75] Cal. Close, 1327-30, p. 399.
[76] G.E.C. Peerage, iv, 105.
[77] Chan. Inq. p.m. 27 Edw. III (1st nos.), no. 58.
[78] Ibid. 12 Ric. II, no. 23.
[79] Ibid.
[80] Ibid. 19 Ric. II, no. 30.
[81] Ibid. 4 Hen. IV, no. 41.
[82] Cal. Pat. 1436-41, 468.
[83] G.E.C. Peerage, iv, 353.
[84] Ibid. 354.
[85] Shaw, Kts. of Engl. i, 141.
[86] L. and P. Hen. VIII, iv, 1309; G.E.C. loc. cit.
[87] Recov. R. Hil. 30 Hen. VIII, m. 544.
[88] G.E.C. op. cit. iv, 355.
[89] Feet of F. Div. Co. Trin. 43 Eliz.

[90] Chan. Inq. p.m. (Ser. 2), ccclxxvi, 144. [91] Ibid. cccxlix, 172.
[92] Ibid. ccclxxvi, 144.
[93] Feet of F. Bucks. Mich. 6 Chas. I.
[94] Add. MS. 5821, fol. 142 d.
[95] Ibid.
[96] Cal. Chart. R. 1226-57, p. 413.
[97] V.C.H. Bucks. i, 240.
[98] Round, Feud. Engl. 133 n.
[99] Sheahan, op. cit. 489; Lipscomb, op. cit. iv, 10; Lysons, op. cit. i (3), 511.
[100] G.E.C. op. cit. ii, 62.
[1] Cal. Doc. of France, 74, 76, 77.
[2] Add. MS. 5821, fol. 142 d.; Sheahan, loc. cit.
[3] G.E.C. op. cit. ii, 62.
[4] Ibid. vi, 199, note (d.).
[4a] Liberate R. 3, m. 6.
[5] Hund. R. (Rec. Com.), i, 35.
[6] Red Bk. of Exch. (Rolls Ser.), 537; Testa de Nevill (Rec. Com.), 260b; Hund. R. (Rec. Com.), i, 30.
[7] Feud. Aids, i, 80.
[8] Cal. Inq. p.m. (Edw. II), v, 19.

of keeping one gerfalcon only.[9] In 1343 Water Eaton was stated to be held by service of keeping one falcon until the time of flight. Upon taking this falcon to the king the tenant received the king's riding horse with trappings, and the table with trestles, linen and all vessels from which the king was served that day, and a tun of wine immediately after the king had tasted it.[10] This service is again mentioned in 1370[11] and in 1511.[12] The last reference occurs in 1563.[13]

The Caux family had an interest here in 1212,[14] and Roger de Caux presented to the church in 1219.[15] Before 1235 John Grey was returned as holder of Water Eaton,[16] and there is no further mention of the Caux family in this place. John Grey was Sheriff of Buckinghamshire in 1238[17]; he is said to have married Helen the daughter of Richard Fitz Gilbert and his wife Rose.[18] In 1243 he had a grant of free warren in his demesne lands of Water Eaton and Bletchley, with licence to hunt the fox, wolf, hare and cat in all the royal forests, except in the king's demesne warrens.[19] His manor of Water Eaton was broken into by malefactors in 1265 and his cattle were carried away.[20] He died in 1266, and was succeeded by his eldest son Reynold,[21] who in 1284–6 was lord of the vill of Water Eaton.[22] From 1295 he was summoned to Parliament as Lord de Grey.[23] He died in 1308[24] and his son John in 1323.[25] John's son Henry in 1337 settled the manor of Water Eaton on his eldest son Reynold,[26] who succeeded him on his death about 1342.[26a]

Reynold died in 1370.[27] His son Henry was summoned to Parliament from 1377 as Lord Grey de Wilton[28] and died in 1396.[29] Richard, son and successor of Henry, mortgaged the manor of Eaton in 1441 to William Burley and others.[30] He died in 1442.[31] His widow Margaret appears to have married Sir Thomas Grey, with whom in 1448 she renounced her life interest in this manor to her first husband's son, Reynold Grey.[32] In 1454 he settled this manor in fee-tail on himself and his wife Tacina[33] and died in 1493, being buried at Bletchley.[34] His son John died in 1499,[35] and in 1501 Elizabeth widow of John, then the wife of Sir Edward Stanley, sued his son Edmund Grey for her dower in Water

Eaton.[36] Edmund settled the manor of Water Eaton on his wife Florence for life,[37] and died in 1511, his will directing his burial to be at Bletchley.[38] As his first three sons George, Thomas and Richard successively died as minors without issue, his fourth son William succeeded to the title in 1520[39] and soon afterwards sued John Abrahull for the retention of deeds relating to Water Eaton,[40] which he inherited on the death of Florence in 1536.[41] He was one of the peers who attempted to place Lady Jane Grey on the throne, and, though pardoned, was attainted and his honours forfeited. They were restored to him in 1559.[42]

GREY de Wilton. *Barry argent and azure with a label gules.*

He died in 1562,[43] having in 1560 quitclaimed this manor for £1,000 to the Marquess of Winchester,[44] to whom it was granted by the queen in 1563[45] and quitclaimed by Arthur son and heir of William Lord Grey in 1564,[46] both grant and quitclaim to be void if Arthur paid £3,000.[47] As he effected this in 1572, Elizabeth regranted the manor to him in that year,[48] and from this date until 1674 Eaton followed the descent of Giffard's Manor in Whaddon.[49] In the spring of 1674–5 it was sold by the Duke of Buckingham[50] to Thomas Willis, M.D.,[51] who died the following November.[52] His son Thomas was in possession in 1681[53]; he died in 1699,[53a] and was succeeded by his son Browne Willis the antiquary.[54] A settlement of Water Eaton was made in August 1735 on the marriage of Thomas, eldest son of Browne Willis, with Anne daughter of John Hulme.[54a] She had a son Thomas, and died sometime before February 1747–8, when Thomas Willis the elder married Frances Robinson, by whom he had a son John.[55] Thomas Willis the elder died in June 1756,[55a] and his elder son Thomas proved the will of his grandfather, Browne Willis, who died in 1760.[56] Thomas Willis took the name and arms of Fleming on inheriting North Stoneham, Hampshire, on the death of a distant cousin, William

[9] *Cal. Inq. p.m.* (Edw. II.), vi, 312.
[10] Chan. Inq. p.m. 16 Edw. III (1st nos.), no. 45.
[11] Ibid. 44 Edw. III (1st nos.), no. 30.
[12] Ibid. (Ser. 2), xxvi, 111.
[13] Ibid. cxxxvi, 1.
[14] Feet of F. Bucks. Mich. 14 John, no. 3.
[15] *R. of Hugh of Wells* (Cant. and York Soc.), i, 169.
[16] *Testa de Nevill* (Rec. Com.), 244b.
[17] P.R.O. *List of Sheriffs*, 1.
[18] Add. MS. 5821, fol. 142 d.; Sheahan, loc. cit.; Lipscomb, loc. cit. This seems improbable, as he is known to have married Emma daughter and heir of Geoffrey de Glanville, and also Joan widow of Paul Pever (*Dict. Nat. Biog.*; Holinshed, *Chron.* [ed. Hooker], iii, 244).
[19] *Cal. Pat.* 1232–47, p. 371.
[20] *Abbrev. Plac.* (Rec. Com.), 158.
[21] G.E.C. op. cit. iv, 111.
[22] *Feud. Aids*, i, 80.
[23] G.E.C. loc. cit.
[24] Chan. Inq. p.m. 1 Edw. II, no. 54.
[25] Ibid. 17 Edw. II, no. 74.
[26] *Cal. Pat.* 1334–8, p. 468.
[26a] Chan. Inq. p.m. 16 Edw. III (1st nos.), no. 45.

[27] Ibid. 44 Edw. III (1st nos.), no. 30.
[28] G.E.C. op. cit. iv, 112.
[29] Chan. Inq. p.m. 19 Ric. II, no. 29.
[30] *Cal. Pat.* 1429–36, p. 183; 1436–41, p. 553.
[31] Chan. Inq. p.m. 20 Hen. VI, no. 23.
[32] Feet of F. Div. Co. Trin. 26 Hen. VI.
[33] *Cal. Pat.* 1452–61, p. 153.
[34] G.E.C. loc. cit.
[35] Exch. Inq. p.m. (Ser. 2), file 5, no. 9.
[36] De Banco R. Hil. 16 Hen. VII, m. 303 d.
[37] Chan. Inq. p.m. (Ser. 2), xxvi, 111.
[38] P.C.C. 38 Bennett.
[39] G.E.C. op. cit. iv, 113.
[40] Early Chan. Proc. bdle. 516, no. 20.
[41] Memo. R. (Exch. L.T.R.), Mich. 33 Hen. VIII, m. 26.
[42] G.E.C. loc. cit.
[43] Chan. Inq. p.m. (Ser. 2), cxxxvi, 1. Only the manor of Bletchley is mentioned here as in the following deeds, but from the service Water Eaton must be included.
[44] Feet of F. Div. Co. Hil. 2 Eliz.
[45] Pat. 1085, m. 9.

[46] Feet of F. Div. Co. Trin. 6 Eliz.
[47] Pat. 1085, m. 9.
[48] Ibid.; Memo. R. (Exch. L.T.R.), East. 14 Eliz. m. 19.
[49] *V.C.H. Bucks.* iii, 439. See also *Hist. MSS. Com. Rep.* xii, App. ii, 103; Feet of F. Div. Co. Hil. 22 Jas. I; *Cal. Com. for Comp.* 324, 376, 390; Recov. R. Mich. 12 Chas. II, m. 133.
[50] The first duke was created Lord Bletchley of Bletchley (G.E.C. *Peerage*, ii, 65, note [b]).
[51] Add. MS. 5821, fol. 143; Lysons, op. cit. i (3), 512; Recov. R. East. 27 Chas. II, m. 23.
[52] *Musgrave's Obit.* (Harl. Soc.), vi, 286.
[53] Feet of F. Bucks. East. 33 Chas. II.
[53a] *Musgrave's Obit.* loc. cit.
[54] *Dict. Nat. Biog.*; Recov. R. Trin. 4 Anne, m. 94.
[54a] Recov. R. Trin. 8 & 9 Geo. II, m. 27; P.C.C. 234 Glazier.
[55] Priv. Act, 1 Geo. III, cap. 45.
[55a] *Musgrave's Obit.* loc. cit.
[56] P.C.C. 176 Lynch. See also Recov. R. Hil. 1 Geo. III, m. 258; Priv. Act, 1 Geo. III, cap. 45.

Fleming.[56a] He is still called Thomas Willis, however, in his will proved after his death in July 1762,[57] but his half-brother John, who inherited under the terms of the will, procured an Act of Parliament in 1767 enabling him to adopt the name of Fleming.[57a] By this John Fleming heretofore Willis the Bletchley and Water Eaton estate was sold to the Rev. Philip Barton of Great Brickhill,[58] with which manor it has since descended to Sir Everard Philip Digby Pauncefort Duncombe, bart., the present owner.

Two parks were included in the extent of the manor of Water Eaton in 1308 : 'there is a park in which are deer . . . and another park of great wood (de grosso bosco), containing 20 acres, in which is no underwood.'[59] Further references to these parks occur during the 14th century.[59a]

A park at Bletchley is first mentioned in 1563.[60] It is said to have been inclosed after Lord Grey removed from Waterhall to Whaddon. 'It had a keeper's lodge in the middle, and was moated about . . . and came down to the great road at Watling Street way.' It was disparked before 1735.[61]

A mill was on the bishop's demesne in Water Eaton in 1086.[62] Browne Willis in his MSS. quotes an undated deed by which Sir John Grey enfeoffed Herman de Eaton and his heirs of the water-mill of Eaton with the whole suit to the mill of the tenants of the honour of Giffard.[63] There was a water-mill on the manor in 1308,[64] while two water-mills are mentioned in 1324[65] and again in 1370.[66] Eaton Mill is mentioned in 1596.[67] There was a water grist-mill here in 1705[68] and two water-mills in 1735.[69] There is a corn-mill at Water Eaton now.

At the British Museum there are Court Rolls for the manor of Eaton for the reigns of Edward III and Richard II.[69a]

In 1308 the lords of the manor had two views of frankpledge on Hock Day and at Michaelmas,[70] pleas and perquisites being assessed at 30s. in 1324[71]; a dovecote and a fishery worth 13d. a year are mentioned at the same time and on other occasions in the 14th century.[72] A free fishery in the Ouzel was among the manorial rights in 1681[73] and 1735.[74]

CHURCHES   The church of ST. MARY consists of a chancel measuring internally 30 ft. 3 in. by 18 ft. 2 in., north chapel 30 ft. 9 in. by 13 ft. 6 in., nave 48 ft. 2 in. by 19 ft., north aisle 13 ft. 6 in. wide, south aisle 10 ft. 6 in. wide, west tower 14 ft. by 12 ft. 9 in., and a south porch 11 ft. 6 in. by 9 ft. 6 in.

The earliest part of the church which can be definitely dated is the late 13th-century chancel, but evidence of an earlier building is afforded by the late 12th-century voussoirs reset over the south doorway of the south aisle. The size of the stones suggests that they formed part of a former chancel arch, and

it is possible that the existing nave walls incorporate those of the structure to which it belonged. The south aisle was built about 1300, when clearstory windows were pierced in the wall over its arcade, and about twenty years later the north chapel was added to the chancel. A north aisle of three bays was thrown out about 1330, and somewhere about this period the original lean-to roof of the south aisle appears to have been superseded by a high-pitched gabled roof, now gone, a new east window being inserted of more lofty proportions than the earlier arrangement would have allowed. Early in the 15th century the west tower was added and the north aisle and arcade were extended one bay westwards. Previous to these alterations it is probable that the west wall of the nave lined with the west wall of the south aisle, as the south-east angle of the tower curtails the westernmost bay of the south arcade, hiding the respond and cutting short the western limb of the arch. Late in the 15th century the chancel and chapel were reroofed and new windows were inserted in the chapel and north aisle, while early in the 16th century a new clearstory was added to the nave and the walls of the south aisle were raised, a new roof being constructed above the old clearstory windows. Between the years 1704 and 1707 the church was 'repaired and beautified' largely at the cost of Browne Willis, the roof of the chancel being ceiled and painted with figures of the twelve Apostles in the Verrio manner. In 1868 the church was restored.

The chancel windows are modern ; a print of 1794[75] shows three windows, apparently of the 15th century, and a doorway of the Browne Willis period in the south wall, but these features have been replaced by two windows and a doorway. At the south-east are three late 13th-century sedilia in range with a fourth recess, doubtless intended for a piscina. The recesses have hollow-chamfered two-centred heads, springing from shafts with moulded capitals and bases attached to the partitions and jambs. At the east end of the north wall, opening to the north chapel, is an early 14th-century doorway with a continuously moulded two-centred head and to the west of it is a small blocked niche with a trefoiled ogee head continuously rebated with the jambs, perhaps originally a locker, but subsequently cut through to open into the piscina recess in the chapel. The remaining portion of the north side of the chancel is occupied by an interesting early 14th-century arcade of two bays, dividing the chancel from the chapel. The arches are two-centred and of two broach-stopped chamfered orders, with labels on both faces, and are supported by a central octagonal column and semi-octagonal responds. The capital of the column has ball-flower ornament, while that of the east respond has a late form of dog-tooth. The late 13th-century chancel

[56a] Burke, *Landed Gentry* (1906) ; *V.C.H. Hants*, iii, 479.

[57] P.C.C. 535 St. Eloy ; *Musgrave's Obit.* loc. cit.

[57a] P.C.C. 535 St. Eloy ; Priv. Act, 7 Geo. III, cap. 67.

[58] Lysons, loc. cit.

[59] Chan. Inq. p.m. 1 Edw. II, no. 54.

[59a] Anct. Ext. (Exch. K.R.), no. 78 (2) ; Mins. Accts. (Gen. Ser.), bdle. 1119, no. 2 ; Chan. Inq. p.m. 44 Edw. III (1st nos.), no. 30.

[60] Chan. Inq. p.m. (Ser. 2), cxxxvi, 1.

[61] Add. MS. 5821, fol. 148 d.

[62] *V.C.H. Bucks.* i, 240.

[63] Add. MS. 5821, fol. 142. This deed was witnessed by Walter de Caux.

[64] *Cal. Inq. p.m.* (Edw. II), v, 19.

[65] Anct. Ext. (Exch. K.R.), no. 78 (2); *Cal. Inq. p.m.* (Edw. II), vi, 312.

[66] Chan. Inq. p.m. 44 Edw. III (1st nos.), no. 30 ; Add. R. 59361-2. Repairs to the mill and water wheel and the mill spindle are mentioned in 1390 (ibid. 59372). There is reference to a horse-mill about this date (ibid. 59366, 59369).

[67] Chan. Inq. p.m. (Ser. 2), ccxlvi, 110.

[68] Recov. R. Trin. 4 Anne, m. 94.

[69] Ibid. Trin. 8 & 9 Geo. II, m. 27.

[69a] Add. Roll, 59361-5, 59368.

[70] *Cal. Inq. p.m.* (Edw. II), v, 19.

[71] Anct. Ext. (Exch. K.R.), no. 78 (2).

[72] *Cal. Inq. p.m.* (Edw. II), vi, 312 ; Mins. Accts. (Gen. Ser.), bdle. 1119, no. 2 ; Chan. Inq. p.m. 44 Edw. III (1st nos.), no. 30 ; Add. R. 59371.

[73] Feet of F. Bucks. East. 33 Chas. II.

[74] Recov. R. Trin. 8 & 9 Geo. II, m. 27.

[75] *Gent. Mag.* lxiv, 305,

arch is two-centred and has an outer order continuously chamfered with the responds, the inner order, which is also chamfered, being carried by moulded corbels. Th is a label on the east face, but only a fragment of the label on the west face remains, the rest having been cut away for the rood beam. The timbers of the roof are probably of the late 15th century, but they are now concealed, with the exception of one tie-beam, by the early 18th-century painted ceiling. Externally an original late 13th-century dwarf buttress with a weathered and gabled head remains at the north end of the east wall, but the diagonal buttress at the south-east angle is probably of the 15th century. The original walling is of neatly worked ironstone rubble where undisturbed, and both here and elsewhere may be distinguished from the limestone rubble of the later alterations. The parapet, like those of the nave and aisles, is embattled.

The east window of the north chapel has jambs of the early 14th century, but the tracery is modern.

a chalice and wafer, probably part of a tomb slab. The low-pitched roof is of the late 15th century.

The north arcade of the nave is of four bays with two-centred arches of three chamfered orders supported by octagonal columns with moulded capitals. The two eastern columns with the three eastern arches, which are of the 14th century, are of limestone; the two outer orders of the easternmost arch die upon the east wall of the nave, the inner order being carried by a moulded corbel supported by a carved head. The westernmost column and arch are contemporary with the early 15th-century west tower, and, with the exception of the base of the column, are of clunch. The semi-octagonal west respond has been moved westwards from its original position in the 14th-century arcade, and, like the other work of that period, is of limestone; the capital is sculptured with four-leaved flowers at the angles and a ball-flower in the centre of each face. The late 13th-century south arcade is of four bays with two-centred arches of two chamfered orders and octagonal columns with moulded capitals and plain splayed bases. The arches have plain labels on both faces, and the chamfers of the inner orders are stopped at their springing. The east respond has a moulded corbel, but the west respond is hidden by the south-east angle of the tower which partially blocks the westernmost bay, cutting short the western limb of the arch. Immediately above the arcade, and now looking into the heightened south aisle, are the three circular quatrefoiled windows of the late 13th-century clearstory. The later clearstory above this level has four

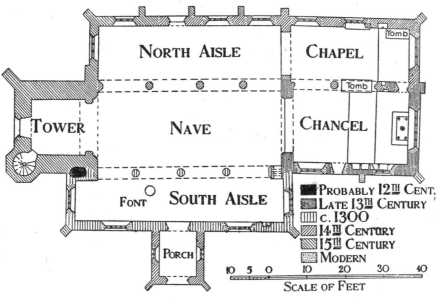

PLAN OF BLETCHLEY CHURCH

Legend in plan:
PROBABLY 12TH CENT.
LATE 13TH CENTURY
c. 1300
14TH CENTURY
15TH CENTURY
MODERN

10 5 0 10 20 30 40
SCALE OF FEET

In the north wall are two late 15th-century windows, each of three cinquefoiled lights under a square head. The sill of the eastern window cuts into the head of a 14th-century tomb recess, leaving only the jambs with a portion of the eastern limb of the arched head and the springing of the western limb. In it is placed a late 13th-century tomb slab carved with a floreated cross and a hunting horn. To the east of this recess is a double locker. On the south side, between the doorway from the chancel and the east respond of the arcade, is the piscina recess, the back of which must have been pierced by the opening in the back of the niche in the chancel above described. It has a trefoiled head and is contemporary with the original building of the chapel. A two-centred arch of two chamfered orders, with moulded corbels supported by heads carrying the inner order, opens into the slightly later north aisle. Externally part of the head of one of the original windows is visible to the west of the eastern window of the north wall. In the parapet of the east wall has been reset a stone carved with

square-headed windows on either side, each of three lights with four-centred heads. Above the east respond of the south arcade, about 9 ft. above the present floor level, the upper doorway to the rood-loft has recently been uncovered and the filling removed, exposing the upper portion of the staircase. The doorway measures about 5 ft. 6 in. by 2 ft., being the full width of the staircase, and the stone-work, which is very rough, appears to have been always plastered. No door seems to have been hung in it, the east jamb, which is flush with the east wall of the nave, having been plastered and painted continuously with the adjoining wall surface. The nave roof, probably of the early 16th century, is low-pitched, and has moulded timbers and carved wall brackets.

In the north wall of the north aisle are three late 15th-century windows like those in the north wall of the chapel, and the west window is of the same date and type. Between the two western windows in the north wall is a good 14th-century doorway, with a two-centred head moulded continuously with the jambs and inclosed by a label with spirited head-stops. The position of the aisle altar is shown by the cutting back of the lower part of the north respond of the arch to the chapel. The lean-to roof must be of the early 15th century, and contemporary with the addition of the western bay to the aisle. It is supported by five trusses with curved braces forming two-centred arches; these spring from wall-posts with moulded feet resting upon stone corbels, some of which have been renewed. With the exception of that at the south-west, the original corbels are carved with grotesque heads. Externally a change in the walling to the west of the north doorway shows the commencement of the 15th-century extension.

The east window of the south aisle, an insertion of c. 1340, is of three trefoiled lights with leaf tracery in a two-centred head. The height of the window, taken in conjunction with indications in the masonry of the external face of the wall, suggests that previous to the raising of the roof in the 16th century a high-pitched gabled roof was constructed over the aisle when this window was inserted, as the head would otherwise have risen considerably above the original lean-to roof, the level of which is shown by a weather-mould below the late 13th-century clearstory. The two windows in the south wall are modern, but the west window is a late 15th-century insertion of the same type as those of the north aisle and chapel. The south doorway is contemporary with the aisle and is of two continuously moulded orders externally, the outer order being inclosed by an arch of reset late 12th-century voussoirs moulded with the beak-head and engrailed ornament. The early 16th-century roof has cambered principal timbers and moulded purlins and wall-plates.

The early 15th-century west tower is of three stages with buttresses at the east ends of the north and south walls, a diagonal buttress at the north-west, and a vice turret at the south-west. The tower arch is of two moulded orders separated by a casement, and springs from responds with well-moulded capitals. Above the west doorway, which has been almost entirely renewed, is a window of four trefoiled lights with vertical tracery in a two-centred head. The ringing-chamber has a single light in the south wall, and the bell-chamber is lighted on all four sides by windows of two lights with traceried two-centred heads, all entirely renewed. The south porch, though much repaired and altered, is substantially of the 14th century. The outer entrance is of two moulded orders, the jambs of the outer order being shafted, and in each side wall is a two-light window, unglazed; that in the west wall is modern, while the lower part of the east window, the lights of which have uncusped segmental heads, has been blocked.

The font, which has a shallow cup-shaped bowl, is probably of the early 17th century, and the pyramidal wooden cover is of the same period. Against the middle column of the south arcade is a poor-box on a baluster stem, bearing the date 1637.

In the east bay of the north arcade of the chancel is the monument of Richard Lord Grey de Wilton (d. 1442), a fine altar tomb with an alabaster effigy of a man in plate armour.[76] The head rests on a helm and the feet on a lion, round the neck is a collar of SS, and the sword and gauntlets hang from the left side. The north and south sides of the tomb have each three quatrefoiled panels containing shields, and between them are narrower cinquefoiled panels. The middle shield on the north side has the arms of Grey of Ruthyn, while the arms in the panels on either side are those of Grey of Wilton; the two eastern shields on the south side bear the same arms, but the western shield is blank. The present inscription seems to have been added by Browne Willis, who had the monument thoroughly restored. On the north wall of the chancel is a marble-framed brass commemorating Dr. Thomas Sparke, a former rector, who died in 1616. The design, which is very delicately engraved, represents a table tomb bearing on the front a portrait of Dr. Sparke in an oval inscribed panel flanked by figures, those on the dexter side representing three sons and two daughters, while those on the sinister side appear to be intended for his congregation. On the top of the tomb is a quaint medley of allegory. Death as a skeleton is filling an urn from which Fame has succeeded in snatching the books written by the doctor, all with their titles inscribed upon them, while above all is an angel with a trumpet; the figures are surrounded by scrolls with inscriptions in Latin verse. On the east wall of the north chapel is a tablet to Rose, the daughter of Andrew Ickforby, and wife of Dr. Sparke, who died in 1615. On the same wall are the coloured alabaster effigies of a man in armour of the late 16th century and those of eight children. The monument, which has no inscription, is said to have been brought by Browne Willis from Deptford Church.[77] At the north-east corner of the chapel is a table tomb commemorating Katherine, the daughter of Daniel Eliot of Port Eliot in the county of Cornwall, and wife of Browne Willis, who died in 1724. In the floor at the east end of the chancel are slabs to Thomas Willis and his wife Alice (Browne), the parents of Browne Willis, both of whom died in 1699.

There is a ring of eight bells: the treble and second cast by Abraham Rudhall in 1717 and 1713 respectively; the third, fourth, and fifth by the same, but bearing the date 1712; the sixth by Robert Stainbank of London, 1867; the seventh by R. Taylor & Sons, 'Oxfod,' 1827; and the tenor by Gillett & Johnson, 1893.

The plate consists of a silver-gilt flagon of 1697, inscribed: 'This Flaggon was Given by Mrs. Katherine Willis to the Church of St. Mary, Blecheley in Buckinghamshire, A.D. 1711'; a silver-gilt stand-paten of 1698, inscribed: 'Ex dono Thō Sparke S Theologiae Professoris et Ecclesiae de Blechlye rectoris'; a large silver-gilt plate of 1710, given, like the flagon, by Mrs. Katherine Willis in 1711; and a silver-gilt cup of 1716, given by Paul Collins and Frances his wife in 1717.

The church possesses a very fine copy of the 1638 Cambridge edition of the Bible, bound up with the Prayer Book and Sternhold and Hopkins's metrical version of the Psalms. The book, which is said to have belonged to Charles I, was given to the church

---

[76] In his will he directed that he should be buried in the church of Bletchley, and that his executors should provide a tomb of alabaster or marble, and find a priest to celebrate divine service daily for four years for his soul in the church of Bletchley (Nicolas, *Test. Vetusta*, 243; Pennant, *Journey from Chester to London*, 285). [77] *Rec. of Bucks.* ix, 202.

by Browne Willis, and received its present binding of red velvet with silver mounting in the early 18th century.[77a]

The registers begin in 1577.

The church of *ST. MARTIN, FENNY STRATFORD*, when erected on the site of the former chapel of St. Margaret in 1730, was a very small building. In 1823 a south aisle was added, which was demolished in 1866, a large new nave and chancel being built in its place, and the former nave became the north aisle. A new south aisle was added in 1908, and the building now consists of chancel, nave, north and south aisles, south porch and tower.[78]

ADVOWSON The church of Bletchley was built before 1212,[79] in which year Gerald de Caux was parson of the church.[80] Roger de Caux held the advowson in the time of Bishop Hugh of Wells,[81] and it descended with the manor of Water Eaton.[82] It was bequeathed with other property by John (Willis) Fleming, who died in 1802, to his cousin John Barton Willis on condition of his taking the name of Fleming.[83] His son John Browne Willis Fleming, who succeeded in 1844, alienated the advowson in 1860 to Joseph Bennitt, by whose family it is still held.

Tithes of the demesne of Bletchley were given to the priory of Newton Longville by Walter Giffard, first Earl of Buckingham, and his son.[84] The priory in 1291 had an annual pension of £1 from the church,[85] and was still in possession of the tithes in the 14th century.[86] Henry VI gave the priory and most of its lands to New College, Oxford, in 1441,[87] and at the Dissolution an annual pension of £1 was still paid to that college.[88]

The chapel of St. Margaret of Fenny Stratford, said to be on the roll of Peter's Pence in 1460,[89] was probably refounded about 1493, in which year it was endowed by the foundation of a gild or fraternity [90] which entirely maintained the chapel for the benefit of the district.[91] Gilbert Ipswell in 1502 left his body to be buried in the chancel of this chapel. His executors were to finish paving the chapel with tiles, work having been begun in the north aisle.[92] It was valued at £6 at the Dissolution.[93] In 1550 the chapel with stones, walls, iron, timber, glass, lead, and bells was granted to Thomas Reeves and others [94] and soon afterwards pulled down.[95] A church which appears to have had parochial rights [96] was built on the same spot and visitations were frequently held in it, but it was destroyed in the Civil War.[97] Browne Willis

bought the site and was instrumental in building on it the new church [98] of which he laid the foundation stone in 1724 and which was consecrated in 1730.[99] The advowson belonged to his family [100] till 1859. It has since passed through a number of hands and is now held by the Bishop of Oxford.[1]

The gild above mentioned, dedicated to St. Margaret and St. Katherine, was founded and endowed by Roger and John Hobbs in 1493. It consisted, besides the brothers and sisters of the gild, of one alderman and two wardens elected yearly on the Sunday after the feast of St. Margaret the Virgin ; the members were a corporate body and had a common seal. They had power to acquire lands to the value of £8 for providing two priests to celebrate divine service daily in the chapel of the gild and for other deeds of charity.[2] In 1547 the fraternity was worth £14 16s. 9d. yearly, of which 15s. was paid to Lord Grey for rent and 5s. 4d. was paid for keeping up the founders' obit. The ornaments and goods were valued at £17 8s., plate '58 once.' There were '2 priests, both well lerned' and with no other living, ministering sacraments and sacramentals.[3] The chantry estate, with the Brotherhood House, was leased in 1569 to Arthur Lord Grey for twenty-one years,[4] and in 1579 to Thomas Wake for a similar term.[5] The Brotherhood House is said to have been converted into the Bull Inn,[6] but they are referred to as two distinct messuages in 1609 and 1616.[7]

CHARITIES The following charities comprised in the Bletchley Inclosure Award, dated 21 January 1813, are regulated by a scheme of the Charity Commissioners, dated 7 May 1901, namely : (1) Fuel allotment, consisting of 24 a. 3 r. 2 p. of land in Bletchley Leys ; (2) Poor's land for ancient township, 2 a. 2 r. 28 p. of land in Bletchley Leys; and (3) Poor's allotment, 2 a. 2 r. 26 p. in Bletchley Leys, and 30 p. in Windmill Field. These properties produce £20 a year, which is distributed in coal to about sixty recipients. (4) Poor's land for the ancient parish, 1 a. 2 r. 33 p. of land in Upper Field in the parish of Shenley, producing £1 15s. yearly, which is distributed in tea among the poor of the ancient parish.

Chapelry of Fenny Stratford.—William Underwood, by his will proved in the P.C.C. 28 February 1798, gave £100, the interest to be distributed in bread in the chapel on New Year's Day. The legacy is represented by £159 7s. 3d. consols with the official trustees, producing £3 19s. 8d. yearly.

[77a] In a book in the handwriting of William Cole, dated 1760, giving an account of the restoration of Bletchley Church by Browne Willis and headed ' An account of what hath been disbursed from June 23, 1704 to Dec. 26, 1709,' is the following entry : ' Paid for a Bible of the best Print which belonged to King Charles the first & for binding it in Crimson Velvet & doing it with Plates of Silver £6 5s.'

[78] Bradbrook, op. cit. ; *Arch. Journ.* viii, 46.

[79] The name of Reginald, parson of Bletchley, is said to occur in 1196 (Add. MS. 5821, fol. 144).

[80] Feet of F. Bucks. Mich. 14 John, no. 3.

[81] *R. of Hugh of Wells* (Cant. and York Soc.), i, 169.

[82] See also *Cal. of Papal Letters*, i, 548 ;

ii, 42 ; vi, 209. In 1616 the next presentation of Bletchley, which had devolved on the Crown by the attainder of Thomas Lord Grey de Wilton, was granted to Henry Rainsford of Orpington, Kent (*Cal. S. P. Dom.* 1611–18, p. 418).

[83] P.C.C. 105 Kenyon.

[84] *Cal. Doc. of France*, 74, 76, 77.

[85] *Pope Nich. Tax.* (Rec. Com.), 34.

[86] Mins. Accts. bdles. 1125, no. 1; 1127, no. 18.

[87] *Cal. Pat.* 1436–41, pp. 516, 558.

[88] *Valor Eccl.* (Rec. Com.), iv, 244.

[89] Add. MS. 5821, fol. 151. 10s. was spent in repairs of a chapel in 1379 (Add. R. 59370).

[90] Pat. 9 Hen. VII, m. 26.

[91] *V.C.H. Bucks.* i, 295.

[92] P.C.C. 17 Blamyr. William Park in 1504 left instructions for his burial in the chapel (ibid. 16 Holgrave).

[93] *Valor Eccl.* (Rec. Com.), iv, 245.

[94] Pat. 4 Edw. VI, pt. vii, m. 23.

[95] Add. MS. 5821, fol. 152 ; *Rec. of Bucks.* i, 198. [96] Add. MS. 5841, p. 43.

[97] Ibid. 5836, fol. 32 d. ; *Rec. of Bucks.* ii, 6 ; iv, 150.

[98] Add. MS. 5836, fol. 33 d., 39 ; *Rec. of Bucks.* iv, 151.

[99] Add. MS. 5821, fol. 149.

[100] Lysons, op. cit. i (3), 514.

[1] *Clergy Lists.*

[2] Pat. 9 Hen. VII, m. 26. The lands were purchased in 1495 (Chan. Inq. p.m. [Ser. 2], xi, 32).

[3] Chant. Cert. 4, no. 13 ; 5, no. 39.

[4] Pat. 11 Eliz. pt. i, m. 45.

[5] Ibid. 21 Eliz. pt. viii, m. 36.

[6] Add. MS. 5821, fol. 152 ; Lysons, op. cit. i (3), 515 ; *Arch. Journ.* viii, 45.

[7] Chan. Inq. p.m. (Ser. 2), cccviii, 158 ; ccclxxv, 71.

It appears from the Parliamentary Returns of 1786 that David Bryne and Browne Willis gave land for the poor. The property was comprised in an indenture dated 25 March 1808, and then consisted of two tenements. The endowment now consists of £33 18s. consols with the official trustees, producing 16s. 8d. yearly, which, together with the dividends from William Underwood's charity, is applied in the distribution of bread.

On the wall of a house called St. Martin's House there is the following inscription : 'This House was settled on the parish Officers of this town for the annual observance of St. Martin's Day, anno Domini 1752.'

This, property given by Browne Willis by deed in 1745, consists of two cottages producing £11 1s. yearly. The net rent is applied in the payment of £1 18s. for a commemoration sermon, and the balance in entertainment to the inhabitants on St. Martin's Day.

In 1864 Sarah Bristow, by deed, gave £657 10s. 8d. stock—now a like amount of consols standing in the names of James Baisley and three others—the annual dividends to be applied in distributing food, blankets and apparel to the fatherless, widows and sick poor of the hamlet of Fenny Stratford and the parish of Simpson. The distribution is made in drapery to about seventy recipients.

BRADWELL

Bradewelle (xi cent.).

This parish covers 917 acres, which are devoted to agriculture, with the exception of about one-sixth.[1] The soil is light clay, the subsoil clay and stone, the chief crops being wheat, oats, barley and beans. The ground falls from about 300 ft. above the ordnance datum in the south and east to about 200 ft. in the north, the land along the Ouse banks being liable to floods.

In the south-west of the parish is the scattered village of Old Bradwell, thus called to distinguish it from the modern red brick railway settlement to the north. The church of St. Lawrence lies at the southern end of Old Bradwell, with the Manor Farm a little to the north. At a short distance to the north-west is the Moat House,[2] formerly the ancient manor-house. The vicarage stands about 300 yards from the church, on a road which leads past the Methodist chapel and Bradwell House (now in the occupation of Mrs. Bellairs-Harries) to the school erected in 1891 by the London and North Western Railway Company.

New Bradwell, though annexed to Stantonbury ecclesiastically, still forms part of the parish for civil purposes. It is chiefly inhabited by the men employed in the London and North Western railway works at Wolverton. The Wolverton and Newport Pagnell branch of this line, which separates this railway settlement from the rest of Bradwell, has a station here, opened in 1867, while at its south-western end the parish is traversed by the main line. The Grand Junction Canal passes through the parish on the north. The church which was erected for New Bradwell and Stantonbury either lost or omitted to obtain the necessary 'instrument' for transferring the rights and privileges of St. Peter's, Stantonbury, to St. James's, and a special Act of Parliament had to be passed in 1909 for this purpose and to legalize 1,000 marriages which had been celebrated there. New Bradwell possesses also a Primitive Methodist chapel in Thomp-

son Street, a Baptist chapel in North Street, a Gospel hall in Caledonian Road, a school, and gasworks, the property of the railway company. The church and school were opened in 1860. At Corner Pin, the extreme north-western corner of New Bradwell, an

THE STOCKS, BRADWELL (NOW REMOVED)

interesting find of bronze implements was made in 1879, on a site now occupied by the County Arms Hotel.[3]

To the north-east of the village are the remains of the earthworks of a small mount and bailey castle, of the history of which nothing is known. It may have been thrown up by a member of the baronial family of Bayeux, who held one of the manors in Bradwell, at the time of the 'anarchy' of Stephen's reign. The castle never had any masonry defences, and its earthworks are now becoming indistinct.

Separated from Bradwell by the railway main line is Bradwell Priory, formerly extra-parochial,[4] but now a parish of 447 acres. It has a soil of cold clay, with subsoil stone and clay, the chief crops grown here being wheat, barley and beans. 'Bradwell Abbey,' a mansion built out of the ruins of the Benedictine monastery of St. Mary, now used as a farm-house,

---

[1] Statistics from Bd. of Agric. (1905).
[2] V.C.H. Bucks. ii, 30.
[3] These have been briefly described in the article on Early Man, V.C.H. Bucks.

i, 183, and more fully in Rec. of Bucks. ix, 431–40.
[4] According to Browne Willis (Add. MS. 5839, p. 23) and Lysons (Mag. Brit.

i [3], 669). Dugdale, however, writes of the priory as being in the extreme part of Wolverton parish (Mon. iv, 508).

contains some wainscoted, spacious and lofty rooms.[5] There are remains of a moat and of the priory fishponds, and an avenue leads to the house, to the northeast of which the small chapel still survives, though now disused and converted into a lumber store for farm purposes.[6] A rental of the priory or manor of Bradwell of some date between 1524 and 1531 describes a considerable range of buildings, the houses of the inner court, the outer court, the gate-house, the hall (55 ft. by 24 ft.), the chamber called the King's Chamber, the prior's chamber, four low parlours, a dorter with five cells, chapter-house, cloisters, and 'a little chapel without the church which may not well be spared.'[7]

The chapel, referred to above, the only trace of the priory buildings left in the time of Browne Willis,[8] is a small rectangular building, measuring 17 ft. by 9 ft. 6 in., built of rubble partly coated with cement and roofed with tiles. The east wall probably dates from the 12th or 13th century, and has on the east face a 14th-century semi-octagonal respond with a moulded capital, and the springers of an arch or arcade which formed part of the conventual buildings running eastward from this point, while a projection at the northern end of the wall probably indicates its original extension in that direction. The chapel built against this wall dates from the mid-14th century, and has in each of the north and south walls a square-headed window, now blocked, of two lights with tracery, and in the west wall a large three-light window with reticulated tracery in a pointed head. The low pointed doorway in the west wall has had a richly moulded head and jamb shafts, all of which are now considerably decayed. In the south wall is a blocked pointed doorway with continuous mouldings enriched with ball-flower ornament, and below the sill of the south window is an ogee-headed piscina, now without a bowl, while high in the wall at the south-west is a row of six quatrefoils which have perhaps been reset. Near the north end of the east wall is a large moulded niche with an ogee head, a label with grotesque stops, flanking pinnacles, and inclosing gable. The building has a semicircular plastered ceiling of the 17th century with paintings of that period now becoming indistinct.

Three hundred acres of land in Bradwell and Wolverton were inclosed by the Prior of Bradwell for pasture on 7 March 1506–7,[9] and 25 acres were inclosed, imparked and stocked for game by Sir John Longville in 1501,[10] probably at a subsequent date being occupied as park lands by the owners of the Abbey Manor. The parish was inclosed by an Act of Parliament of 1788 ; the award, dated 17 March 1789, is in the custody of the clerk of the peace.[11]

Among place-names have been found Stony Hill and Stubborn Hill Closes [12]; Church Lane, Butler's Lane [13] ; Seklo Hill (Close) and Grange Farm [14] (xvi cent.) ; Lingard Pightle, Bear Close, Upper Monks Meadow, Ferries Farm [15] (xviii cent.).

MANORS — Before the Conquest an estate of 1½ hides in *BRADWELL* was held by Alviet, a man of Queen Edith, who could sell.[16] By 1086 this had passed into the possession of Walter Giffard.[17] It was afterwards attached to the honour of Giffard,[18] rights over Bradwell being claimed both by the Earls of Gloucester [19] and their successors the Earls of Stafford [20] and Dukes of Buckingham,[21] and also by the Valences, Earls of Pembroke,[22] and their descendants, the Talbots, Earls of Shrewsbury,[23] their claims being acknowledged as late as 1460 [24] and 1614 [25] respectively.

There is no trace of any holder in fee of this estate after the Domesday tenant Walter Achet until the first quarter of the 13th century, when Peter Barre or Barry, under Alexander de Redham, owned the manorial rights.[26] In the subdivision of the Giffard honour, which took place in 1245,[27] the greater part of Bradwell fell to the Valences, Earls of Pembroke, under whom the Barrys continued to hold, and on the death of Simon Barry before 1318 his son Robert owed 20s. as relief to the Earl of Pembroke.[28] Philip Aylesbury, to whom Robert Barry appears to have transferred the manor, sued the earl for distraining his cattle at Sladefurlong, Bradwell, alleging that the relief had been paid.[29] This Philip Aylesbury, who was returned as lord in 1316,[30] may have been a son of the Walter Aylesbury by whom complaint was made in 1307 that certain persons had forcibly entered his house at Bradwell and carried away his goods.[31] The Aylesburys held this fee,[32] described in 1418 as the manor of Bradwell near Moulsoe,[33] with their manors of Drayton Beauchamp, Milton Keynes, and Broughton (q.v). After the death of Hugh Aylesbury in 1423 it must have passed with the two latter to the Staffords in spite of a quitclaim three years later to the Chaworths, their co-heirs,[34] since it continued to descend with Milton Keynes in the Stafford family [35] until 1571, when Sir Humphrey Stafford sold it to Michael Colles or Collys.[36] In 1603 Michael Colles, described as late of Elmdon (co. Warwick), Mary his wife, and Humphrey his eldest son and heir, sold the manor to Roger Fuller, then of Great Brickhill, for £1,400.[37] Its appurtenances in Bradwell and Stantonbury included six messuages, one of which, adjoining the churchyard, was called Parker's Place or the Over House.[38] Roger Fuller bequeathed the manor to his younger son John in tail-male, with remainder in default to another younger son Roger, and

[5] Ratcliff, *Hist. and Antiq. of Newport Hundred*, 357.

[6] The Bradwell registers contain entries of baptisms of lords of this manor in this chapel in the early 17th century (Add. MS. 5839, p. 24).

[7] Treas. of the Receipt Misc. Bks. clxv, 38. Given in detail by Dugdale, *Mon.* iv, 512.

[8] Add. MS. 5839, p. 23.

[9] Leadam, *Dom. Incl.* 1517 (Royal Hist. Soc.), 181.

[10] Ibid. 182.

[11] *Blue Bk. Incl. Awards*, 10.

[12] Treas. of the Receipt Misc. Bks. clxv, 41.

[13] Ibid. 43.

[14] Ibid. 129–32.

[15] Close, 5091, no. 1.

[16] *V.C.H. Bucks.* i, 251.

[17] Ibid.

[18] *Testa de Nevill* (Rec. Com.), 247 ; *Hund. R.* (Rec. Com.), i, 30.

[19] Chan. Inq. p.m. 21 Edw. III (1st nos.), no. 59.

[20] Ibid. 10 Ric. II, no. 38 ; 16 Ric. II, pt. i, no. 27 ; 22 Ric. II, no. 46 ; 4 Hen. IV, no. 41.

[21] Ibid. 38 & 39 Hen. VI, no. 59.

[22] Ibid. 17 Edw. II, no. 75 ; *Cal. Close*, 1323–7, pp. 267, 274.

[23] Chan. Inq. p.m. 20 Ric. II, no. 51 ; 22 Ric. II, no. 47 ; 6 Hen. V, no. 35.

[24] Ibid. 38 & 39 Hen. VI, no. 59.

[25] Ibid. (Ser. 2), cccxlvii, 73.

[26] *Testa de Nevill* (Rec. Com.), 247.

[27] *V.C.H. Bucks.* ii, 348.

[28] De Banco R. 222, m. 184.

[29] Ibid.   [30] *Feud. Aids*, i, 109.

[31] *Cal. Pat.* 1307–13, p. 41.

[32] Chan. Inq. p.m. 17 Edw. II, no. 75 ; 20 Ric. II, no. 51 ; 21 Ric. II, no. 2.

[33] Ibid. 6 Hen. V, no. 35.

[34] *Cat. of Anct. D.* iii, 402.

[35] Feet of F. Bucks. East. 4 & 5 Phil. and Mary.

[36] Ibid. East. 13 Eliz.

[37] Com. Pleas Recov. R. East. 5 Jas. I, m. 20 ; Feet of F. Bucks. East. 2 Jas. I.

[38] Com. Pleas Recov. R. East. 5 Jas. I, m. 20.

Bradwell Abbey

BRADWELL CHURCH FROM THE NORTH-EAST

BRADWELL CHURCH: THE INTERIOR LOOKING EAST

died on 8 December 1613.[39] In 1656 John Fuller settled the manor on his son Roger,[40] on his marriage with Anne Gilpin,[40a] and they made a further settlement in 1668.[41] Roger Fuller held Bradwell till his death in May 1700, when he was succeeded by his son another Roger.[42] The latter appears to have died without issue sometime after 1707, leaving three sisters as his co-heirs: Elizabeth, married to Thomas Mercer of Hackleton, in the parish of Horton (co. Northampton), and Ann and Mary Fuller,[42a]

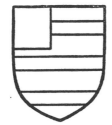

FULLER. *Argent three bars and a quarter gules.*

the two latter dying unmarried between 1732 and 1757.[43] They appear to have been described on a tombstone in the churchyard as ladies of the manor,[44] of which Browne Willis wrote that in 1757 the Mercers, heirs of their sister Elizabeth, were sole owners.[45] In 1776[46] and 1783[47] the manor was held by Thomas Mercer, probably a son or grandson of Thomas Mercer and of Elizabeth Fuller. In 1787 it was sold by Thomas Mercer and Sarah his wife to William Bailey,[48] lord of the manor at the passing of the Inclosure Act for the parish in the following year,[49] and still lord when Lysons wrote, *circa* 1813.[50] Before 1862 it had become the property of William Selby Lowndes of Whaddon,[51] and is still held by the Lowndes family with Whaddon (q.v.).

That part of the original manor which was annexed by the Earl of Gloucester was obtained in fee by a family of Bradwell, Hugh de Bradwell holding in 1386.[52] He had been replaced in 1392 by Thomas de Bradwell,[53] still holding in 1399[54] and 1403.[55] In 1460 the heirs of Hugh de Bradwell were returned as lords of the fee.[56]

A manor of 2 hides and 3 virgates in *BRAD-WELL*, held before 1066 by two thegns, Sibi and Godwin, men of Alric son of Goding, who could sell, was entered in the Domesday Survey among the lands of Miles Crispin,[57] and, as part of the honour of Wallingford,[58] passed to the Earls of Cornwall, who held it in the late 13th[59] and early 14th centuries,[60] and from them to the Princes of Wales, Edward Prince of Wales (the Black Prince) dying seised of a fee in Bradwell in 1376.[61]

This manor was held in 1086 by a sub-tenant William,[62] and part of it was obtained later by the family of Bayeux (Baus, Bauis, Baiois, Beause, Beuhuse). In a charter dating apparently 1151–4 William de Bayeux is referred to as lord of part of this estate.[63] William son of Hugh de Bayeux granted land in Bradwell, part of which was held of the honour of Newport, to the Prior of Tickford and others in 1199[64]

BAYEUX. *Gules two bars and in the chief three scallops argent.*

and 1202,[65] and, with the consent of Maud his wife and William his heir, granted other lands to Bradwell Priory.[66] Avis widow of William de Bayeux claimed land in Bradwell as dower in 1230,[67] and Aumary de Henton, who was responsible for the scutage in 1234,[68] may have been guardian of another William de Bayeux who paid this scutage in the following year.[69] He was perhaps identical with the William de Bayeux who made a grant of land in 1241,[70] and with the William de Bayeux described as heir of his grandfather Hugh in 1274.[71] In 1284 William de Bayeux, probably a son of the last William, was returned as holding 11 virgates of land in Bradwell under the Earl of Cornwall's sub-tenant, Hugh de Filleberd,[72] this intermediary lordship not being recorded, however, in 1302, when the holders in fee were described as the heirs of William de Bayeux.[73] By 1346 a small part of the holding had been obtained by the Prior of Tickford, William de Bayeux being in possession of the rest.[74] An order was issued in 1348 for the arrest and imprisonment in Bedford gaol of William de Bayeux of Bradwell, indicted for many homicides and felonies,[75] and no further record of the Bayeux family in Bradwell exists. This fee was held by John Kimble in 1379,[76] but cannot be further traced.

The remainder of the Domesday manor of Miles Crispin was later acquired in fee by the Bradwell family, Robert de Bradwell exercising the manorial rights *circa* 1151–4.[77] He appears to have succeeded by the Barry (Barre) family, a member of which, Ralph Barry, probably at the end of the 12th century, made a grant of land to Bradwell Priory

[39] Chan. Inq. p.m. (Ser. 2), cccxlvii, 73.
[40] Feet of F. Bucks. Trin. 1656; Add. MS. 5839, p. 24.
[40a] Chan. Proc. (Bridges Div.), bdle. 210, no. 21.
[41] Feet of F. Bucks. Mich. 20 Chas. II.
[42] Recov. R. Trin. 4 Jas. II, m. 40; Chan. Proc. (Bridges Div.), bdle. 335, no. 27.
[42a] Chan. Proc. (Bridges Div.), bdle. 240, no. 43.   [43] Add. MS. 5839, p. 21.
[44] *Char. Com. Rep.* (1834), xxvii, 119.
[45] Add. MS. 5839, p. 21.
[46] Recov. R. Mich. 17 Geo. III, m. 396.
[47] Ibid. East. 23 Geo. III, m. 344.
[48] Feet of F. Bucks. East. 27 Geo. III. Thomas Mercer, solicitor, of Northampton, son of the late lord of the manor, paid 10s. a year up to 1823 in respect of a charity started by his ancestor Roger Fuller. It was stated in 1834 that no payment had been made for the last eleven years (*Char. Com. Rep.* [1834], xxvii, 119).

[49] Priv. Act, 28 Geo. III, cap. 11.
[50] *Mag. Brit.* i (3), 519.
[51] Sheahan, *Hist. and Topog. of Bucks.* 495.
[52] Chan. Inq. p.m. 10 Ric. II, no. 38.
[53] Ibid. 16 Ric. II, pt. i, no. 27.
[54] Ibid. 22 Ric. II, no. 46.
[55] Ibid. 4 Hen. IV, no. 41.
[56] Ibid. 38 & 39 Hen. VI, no. 59.
[57] *V.C.H. Bucks.* i, 263.
[58] *Hund. R.* (Rec. Com.), i, 30; *Testa de Nevill* (Rec. Com.), 261b; see also *V.C.H. Bucks.* i, 213–14. In 1422 the men of Bradwell attended view of frankpledge at Tickford, when a plea of trespass was referred to the court of the honour of Wallingford (Ct. R. [Gen. Ser.], portf. 212, no. 2).
[59] *Feud. Aids*, i, 80.
[60] *Cal. Inq. p.m.* (Edw. I), iii, 481, 482; *Feud. Aids*, i, 106.
[61] Chan. Inq. p.m. 2 Ric. II, no. 57.
[62] *V.C.H. Bucks.* i, 263.
[63] *Cal. Doc. of France*, 444.

[64] *Rot. Cur. Reg.* (Rec. Com.), i, 361; Feet of F. case 14, file 4, no. 5, 7. In the latter grant the prior gave to William in return 7 acres of land which his uncle William de Bayeux had held in the vill. Possibly William the uncle was son of Ranulph de Bayeux and brother of Hugh de Bayeux (Dugdale, *Baronage*, i, 573).
[65] Feet of F. case 14, file 6, no. 7, 8.
[66] Rentals and Surv. (Gen. Ser.), R. 75.
[67] Maitland, *Bracton's Note Bk.* ii, 361. It was contended, however, that her husband was not dead, and, though he had entered religion, was not yet professed.
[68] *Testa de Nevill* (Rec. Com.), 258, 261.
[69] Ibid. 259b.
[70] Feet of F. case 15, file 24, no. 4.
[71] Ibid. case 16, file 43, no. 7; De Banco R. 11, no. 9.
[72] *Feud. Aids*, i, 80.
[73] Ibid. 106.   [74] Ibid. 132.
[75] *Cal. Pat.* 1348–50, p. 75.
[76] Chan. Inq. p.m. 2 Ric. II, no. 57.
[77] *Cal. Doc. of France*, 444.

which was witnessed by a William de Bayeux.[79] The relationship between the early members of this family is obscure. Gerard Barry held land in Bradwell in 1230,[79] and Peter Barry held about the same date under the honour of Giffard (see above). By 1284 the estate had come to Robert Barry, and was held under him by Hugh Barry,[80] who in 1297 complained that he had been assaulted by certain persons who had broken into and burnt his house at Bradwell.[81] The Barrys were lords of the neighbouring manor of Stantonbury (q.v.), with which this holding may have been amalgamated, for there is no trace of it after the early 14th century.[82]

Three virgates in Bradwell held before the Conquest by Alward, a man of Goding, who could sell, and later by William de Celsi, whom Ansculf, when sheriff, unjustly dispossessed of his property, according to the return made by the hundred in the Domesday Survey, were at that date held by William Fitz Ansculf.[83] The only other mention of this property occurs in the middle of the 13th century, when it was described as an eighth of a fee belonging to the honour of Dudley (Newport Pagnell) and held by John Fitz Nicholas.[84]

The property held in Bradwell[85] by the priory which Meinfelin, lord of Wolverton, founded in the parish[86] was conveyed with the site and precincts at the suppression of the priory in 1524 to Cardinal Wolsey,[87] Sir John Longville, lord of Wolverton and patron of the monastery, renouncing all right in the same year.[88] It was soon after bestowed by the cardinal as the manor of *BRADWELL* on the college founded by him at Oxford.[89] After the cardinal's death the possessions of the priory reverted to the Crown, and were granted to the priory of Sheen in exchange for the manors of Lewisham and Greenwich in 1531.[90] A rental for the 'Manor and Town of Bradwell' taken about this time gives Thomas Rowse as tenant at a yearly rental of £24 of the manor-place and its demesnes,[91] the lease of which was later obtained by the instrumentality of Thomas Cromwell for William Wogan.[92]

Bradwell again reverted to the Crown at the surrender of Sheen Priory in 1539 [92a] and a grant in fee of the manor was made in 1543 to Arthur Longville.[93] He was son of Sir John Longville above

mentioned, who had died in 1541.[94] At Arthur Longville's death in 1557 he was succeeded at Wolverton by his eldest son Henry, and at Bradwell by his second son Arthur,[95] who in 1574–5 settled the manor on himself and his wife Judith, with remainder of a moiety to Judith as jointure.[96] He subsequently bequeathed it to his son Thomas and his heirs male, with contingent remainder in tail-male to his own heirs; to his sister, Frances Heydon; and to Richard Ruthall.[97] He died on 26 May 1594, and was succeeded by Thomas,[98] who in July 1598 instituted proceedings against Frances Heydon and George Gascoigne, in connexion with the settlement on his marriage with Nightingale daughter of George Gascoigne,[99] but came to an arrangement with them a few months later.[100] He was certified a lunatic on 10 September 1599 and died on 3 January following.[1] On 3 May 1616 his son Arthur obtained livery of the manor on the attainment of his majority.[2] Eight months later he was attacked with madness,[3] but evidently recovered, for on 10 August 1631 he settled the manor on his wife Alice, and died at Bradwell thirteen days later, being survived by Alice, and by his mother, then Nightingale Windsor, widow, who held a third of the manor in dower.[4] His son Thomas, who had livery of his property on 20 February 1638–9,[5] was knighted by Charles I in 1646.[6] In the same year he petitioned to compound for his estates,[7] having already paid £330 for his delinquency, after being taken prisoner at Grafton House in December 1643. On being informed that the County Committee at Aylesbury 'intended to sequester his estate, he went thither and received a shot in his throat from a soldier of the garrison, which damnified him £500.' On 18 September 1646 his fine was set at the sum of £800.[8] It was doubtless his devotion to the Royalist cause which forced him to part with the manor in 1650 to John Lawrence, jun., and Abraham Cullen,[9] the transaction being completed in 1661 by the quitclaim of rights by William, only son of Thomas Longville, on the attainment of his majority.[10] Sir John Lawrence, the purchaser of Bradwell, sold it in 1666 to Joseph Alston of Chelsea and his son Joseph.[11] The elder Joseph was created a baronet as

[78] Rentals and Surv. (Gen. Ser.), R. 75; cf. *Rot. Cur. Reg.* (Rec. Com.), i, 445.

[79] Maitland, *Bracton's Note Bk.* ii, 361.

[80] *Feud. Aids,* i, 80. Robert Barre or Barry had conveyed messuages, lands and rent in Bradwell to Hugh Barry in 1281 (Feet of F. Div. Co. Hil. 9 Edw. I, no. 27).

[81] *Cal. Pat.* 1292–1301, p. 317.

[82] *Feud. Aids,* i, 109.

[83] *V.C.H. Bucks.* i, 256.

[84] *Testa de Nevill* (Rec. Com.), 248.

[85] Feet of F. case 14, file 11, no. 2; *Pope Nich. Tax.* (Rec. Com.), 47.

[86] *V.C.H. Bucks.* i, 350.

[87] Ibid. i, 351; *L. and P. Hen. VIII,* iv (1), 536.

[88] *Cat. of Anct. D.* i, 80.

[89] *L. and P. Hen. VIII,* iv (1), 650, 697, 1913 (1); (2), 4001 (2, 3); Feet of F. Div. Cos. Trin. 19 Hen. VIII; see also Ct. R. (Gen. Ser.), portf. 155, no. 5.

[90] *L. and P. Hen. VIII,* v, 403, g. 627 (22). In 1535 the manor with rectory of Bradwell was enumerated among the possessions of Sheen as worth £40 (*Valor Eccl.* [Rec. Com.], ii, 52).

[91] Treas. of the Receipt Misc. Bks.

clxv, 38. Printed *in extenso* by Dugdale, *Mon.* iv, 510.

[92] In the month preceding the exchange with Sheen William Wogan wrote to Cromwell: 'I received your letters desiring to know whether I am minded to leave my interest in my farm of Bradwell. I have married an aged gentlewoman, and the living I have by her is only for term of her life; and I have no other place except there where is the best part of my living. I beg I may keep it still as you helped me to it' (*L. and P. Hen. VIII,* v, 385). By his will dated 16 June 1558 William Wogan directed that he should be buried in 'Mr. Stafford's chapel' (in Bradwell Church), and bequeathed a legacy to the vicar to pray for his soul during his lease of Bradwell (Add. MS. 5839, p. 24). He joined with Sir Humphrey Stafford in making a conveyance of the latter's manor in 1558 (Feet of F. Bucks. East. 4 & 5 Phil. and Mary).

[92a] *L. and P. Hen. VIII,* xiv (2), p. 73.

[93] Ibid. xviii (1), g. 346 (38).

[94] Chan. Inq. p.m. (Ser. 2), lxv, 7.

[95] Ibid. cxi, 6; Memo. R. (Exch. L.T.R.), Trin. 13 Eliz. m. 45.

[96] Feet of F. Bucks. Mich. 16 Eliz.; Hil. 17 Eliz.; Chan. Inq. p.m. (Ser. 2), ccxl, 85.

[97] Chan. Inq. p.m. (Ser. 2), ccxl, 85.

[98] Ibid.

[99] Chan. Proc. Eliz. L. 2, no. 60.

[100] Feet of F. Bucks. Mich. 41 Eliz.

[1] Chan. Inq. p.m. (Ser. 2), cclxi, 39, 65. According to Memo. R. East. 9 Jas. I, m. 225, Thomas Longville was alive in 1611.

[2] Fine R. 14 Jas. I, pt. ii, no. 4.

[3] Chan. Inq. p.m. (Ser. 2), ccclx, 86.

[4] Ibid. ccclxxviii, 49.

[5] Fine R. 14 Chas. I, pt. ii, no. 52.

[6] Shaw, *Knights of Engl.* ii, 221.

[7] *Cal. Com. for Comp.* 67, 1293.

[8] Ibid. 1293.

[9] Recov. R. Mich. 1650, m. 113; Notes of F. Bucks. Hil. 1649.

[10] Recov. R. East. 13 Chas. II, m. 184; Feet of F. Bucks. East. 13 Chas. II. See *Dict. Nat. Biog.* for an appreciation of William Longville.

[11] Feet of F. Bucks. East. 18 Chas. II.

of Chelsea and Bradwell Abbey in 1682,[12] and died in May 1688,[13] his son Joseph, who had been sheriff in 1670,[14] and who succeeded him, dying in March of the following year.[15] His son, the third Sir Joseph Alston, who was likewise Sheriff of Buckinghamshire in 1702,[16] made a settlement of the manor on his marriage in 1690 with Penelope Evelyn,[17] with whom he dealt with the manor in 1705,[18] and again in 1713, when their son, the fourth Joseph Alston, was joined with them.[19] The third baronet was succeeded in 1716 by his son, the fourth Sir Joseph,[20] who immediately sold Bradwell to John Fuller,[21] described as of Bradwell Abbey when sheriff of the county in 1723.[22] In that same year John Fuller and his wife Esther sold the manor to Edward Owen,[23] by whom it was conveyed *circa* 1730 to Sir Charles Gounter Nicoll.[24] He was lord of Olney Manor (q.v.), with which Bradwell descended in the Earls of Dartmouth until sold by

ALSTON, baronet.
Azure ten stars or.

LEGGE, Earl of Dartmouth. *Azure a hart's head cabossed argent.*

THE MERCERS. *Gules a demi-virgin coming out of clouds proper clothed or with her hair loose crowned with an eastern crown and wreathed with roses, all in a border of clouds.*

the fifth earl, before 1862,[25] to the Mercers' Company, the present owners.

A free fishery was included among the appurtenances of Bradwell Manor in 1604[26] and 1787.[27]

The rental of the priory manor of Bradwell of 1524–31 enumerates 'a pool called Westmar Hall with a little narrow pool going forth of the same,' and 'divers other pools now wasted and no fish.'[28] A fishery called the Fresh Fishings was granted with this manor to Arthur Longville in 1543.[29]

The Maide Milne, East Milne, and New Milne occur in a rental of the priory of Bradwell of the reign of Henry VI,[30] and the Maide Milne was included among the appurtenances of the priory manor in 1524–31.[31]

The church of *ST. LAWRENCE*
CHURCH consists of a chancel measuring internally 19 ft. 6 in. by 12 ft., nave 30 ft. by 15 ft., south aisle 10 ft. 6 in. wide, north porch, and west tower 10 ft. 6 in. by 10 ft. It is built of rubble with stone dressings, and the roofs are covered with lead and tiles.

The nave, and probably the chancel, date from the early 13th century; the south aisle, though originally added at the same period, appears to have been rebuilt and widened during the second half of the century. The north porch was built in the 15th century, and the tower, added probably about 1380, was rebuilt in the 16th century, when the nave walls were heightened. The whole fabric was restored in 1867–8 and again in 1904.

The east window of the chancel is modern, but its internal label, which was found in the walling when the chancel arch was widened in 1868 and inserted here, dates from the 13th century and is enriched with nail-head ornament. There are two modern windows on the south, and on the north are two 14th-century trefoiled lights, the western a low-side window with an ogee head; the doorway between them is modern. The pointed chancel arch was rebuilt and widened in 1868, but the old stonework, dating from the 13th century, was re-used. It springs from chamfered abaci, upon which are the following inscriptions in Lombardic capitals, 'Viginti : dies : relaxaconis : . . . .,' on the north, and 'H̄ : ecclia : dedicata ē in : honorē Sc̄i : Lavrencii : xi . . . .,' on the south.

The nave opens to the aisle on the south by an early 13th-century arcade of three pointed arches with circular pillars having moulded bases and foliated capitals, and plain responds with chamfered abaci; the eastern capital is carved with plain water-leaf ornament, while the other is more richly foliated and has a carved head on the north side. On the north is a pointed 14th-century doorway between two modern windows, the eastern of which contains some fragments of old glass. In the west wall, opening to the ground stage of the tower, is a pointed arch with very thick stop-chamfered responds, which appears to have been rebuilt in the 16th century. There are three small clearstory windows on either side, all of which are modern. The north porch has been considerably restored.

The south-east window of the aisle, which is of two trefoiled lights with tracery, dates from the second half of the 13th century; immediately to the east of it is a pointed piscina with a circular bowl of the same period. The east window and the other window in the south wall are modern, though their internal jambs are old, while the four-light west window is entirely modern. The round-headed south doorway is of the early 13th century, having been reset when the aisle was rebuilt towards the end of the century.

[12] G.E.C. *Complete Baronetage*, iv, 123.
[13] Ibid. 124.
[14] P.R.O. *List of Sheriffs*, 9.
[15] G.E.C. loc. cit.
[16] P.R.O. *List of Sheriffs*, 10.
[17] Feet of F. Bucks. Trin. 2 Will. and Mary; Recov. R. Trin. 2 Will. and Mary, m. 37.
[18] Feet of F. Bucks. East. 4 Anne.

This was a lease of the manor to Thomas Bendlowes for ninety-nine years.
[19] Ibid. Hil. 11 Anne; Mich. 12 Anne.
[20] Add. MS. 5839, p. 23; G.E.C. loc. cit.
[21] Close, 5091, no. 1.
[22] P.R.O. *List of Sheriffs*, 10; Lipscomb, *Hist. and Antiq. of Bucks.* iv, 44.
[23] Feet of F. Bucks. Trin. 9 Geo. I.
[24] Lipscomb, loc. cit.

[25] Sheahan, op. cit. 495.
[26] Feet of F. Bucks. East. 2 Jas. I.
[27] Ibid. East. 27 Geo. III.
[28] Treas. of the Receipt Misc. Bks. clxv, 38.
[29] Pat. 34 Hen. VIII, pt. iii.
[30] Rentals and Surv. (Gen. Ser.), R. 75.
[31] Treas. of the Receipt Misc. Bks. clxv, 38.

The tower is of two stages surmounted by a saddle-back roof, and has a modern west window in the ground stage, above which is a narrow trefoiled light of the 14th century. The bell-chamber is lighted by a 16th-century window of two transomed lights in a square head in each of the gabled walls and by single lights on the north and south.

The font has an old octagonal bowl, but the stem is modern. In the tower is a floor slab to Sir Joseph Alston of Bradwell Abbey, who died in 1688. The communion table dates from the 17th century.

The tower contains a ring of six bells: the treble and second both date from about 1300, and are inscribed ' Michael : de : Uuymbis : me fecit ' ; the third was inscribed ' Richard Chandler made me 1700,' but was recast in 1909; and the fourth, which is of the early 15th century and is inscribed ' Vox Augustini Sonet In Aure Dei,' is by John Walgrave ; the fifth and tenor, by A. Bowell of Ipswich, were added in 1909. A piece of bell framework dated 1652 and four old clappers now lie in the ground stage.

The communion plate includes a stand paten and flagon of 1688. The registers begin in 1577.

ADVOWSON The advowson when first recorded was shared between William de Bayeux and Robert de Bradwell, by whom it was bestowed about the middle of the 12th century on Newport or Tickford Priory, this grant being confirmed by the Bishops of Lincoln in the 12th and 13th centuries.[32] At the ordination of the vicarage during the episcopate of Hugh of Wells, Bishop of Lincoln (1209–35), the church was described as the property of this monastery,[33] but in 1274 William de Bayeux claimed the right to present, against the prior, on the ground that his grandfather Hugh had presented Robert de Bradwell.[34] In the same year, however, he acknowledged the advowson to be the right of the prior.[35] The Priors of Tickford continued to hold the advowson, which in the 14th century was continually in the king's hands by reason of the war with France and its ownership by an alien priory.[36] After the suppression of Tickford Priory in 1525[37] the advowson was granted by the king to Cardinal Wolsey for his college at Oxford,[38] Anne St. Leger, daughter and co-heir of Thomas, late Earl of Ormond, lord of Newport Pagnell, and George St. Leger, her son and heir, renouncing any claim they might have at the same time.[39] In September 1531 it was included with Bradwell Manor in the exchange with Sheen,[39a] but a ratification of the arrangement in December of that year makes no mention of the advowson.[40] It was probably retained by the king, by whom it was granted in September 1532 to Henry the Eighth's College.[40a] After the dissolution of the college in

1545[41] the advowson reverted to the Crown, by which it has since been held,[41a] save for a temporary grant to Samuel Jones in 1616.[42]

The Giffards bestowed the tithes of their demesnes in Bradwell on the priory of St. Faith, Longueville, in Normandy, this gift being confirmed by their descendant, William Marshal, Earl of Pembroke.[43] The rectory was included in the grant to Samuel Jones in 1616, and has since descended with the advowson.

The tithes were not commuted by the Inclosure Act of 1788,[44] but before the middle of the 19th century had been commuted for £250.[45]

The advowson of St. James's Church in New Bradwell, a vicarage annexed to that of Stantonbury, and which dates from 1860, is the property of Earl Spencer.

CHARITIES The charity of Rev. James Hume, founded by will, proved in the P.C.C. 20 March 1734, is regulated by a scheme of the Charity Commissioners of 5 December 1899. The property consists of 8 acres of land at Hockliffe, Bedfordshire, and £41 6s. 9d. consols with the official trustees, arising from the sale of timber, producing together an income of £15 yearly. By the scheme one-third of the net income is applicable in prizes to school children, under the title of the educational foundation of the Rev. James Hume, another third is distributed among poor deserving members of the Church of England, and the remaining third is applicable for the benefit of poor housekeepers and widows.

The Poor's Allotment.—By an Inclosure Award in 1789, 12 a. 0 r. 35 p. of land in Furnace Corner and 3 a. 2 r. 17 p. on Seekley Hills were allotted in lieu of the rights of the poor of cutting furze for fuel, the income whereof, together with the rent of another piece of land, containing 2 a. 2 r. 26 p., amounting together to about £14 a year, is distributed in coal to about eighty recipients.

About half an acre of land is also let to the poor in allotments, producing £3 yearly, supposed to have been derived from a gift of Alden Fuller in or about 1719. A moiety of the income is applicable in the parish of Newton Longville.

The Public Footpaths Fund, which is regulated by a scheme of the Charity Commissioners of 11 October 1907, consists of £34 5s. 10d. consols, with the official trustees, arising from the sale of an allotment, made under the Inclosure Award of 1789, for a public stone and gravel-pit. The annual dividends of the stock produce 17s., which is applicable for the maintenance of the public footpaths, under the control of the Parish Council of Bradwell.

[32] *Cal. Doc. of France*, 444.
[33] *Liber Antiq. Hugonis Wells* (ed. A. Gibbons), 13.
[34] De Banco R. 11, m. 9.
[35] Feet of F. case 16, file 43, no. 7.
[35] See the Patent Rolls for this century.
[37] Chan. Inq. p.m. (Ser. 2), lxxvi, 3.
[38] Feet of F. Div. Co. Mich. 18 Hen. VIII ; cf. Chan. Inq. p.m. (Ser. 2), lxxvii, 59.

[39] Feet of F. Bucks. Mich. and Hil. 18 Hen. VIII.
[39a] *L. and P. Hen. VIII*, v, 403.
[40] Ibid. g. 627 (22); cf., however, ibid. vi, 299 (ix), and the statement in 1535 that the vicar paid an annual pension of 60s. to Sheen and of 9s. to New College, Oxford (*Valor Eccl.* [Rec. Com.], iv, 245).
[40a] *L. and P. Hen. VIII*, v, g. 1370 (23).
[41] Tanner, *Not. Mon.*
[41a] Inst. Bks. (P.R.O.) ; *Clergy Lists.*

[42] Pat. 14 Jas. I, pt. xxvi, no. 3.
[43] *Cal. Doc. of France*, 76, 77. The gift of tithes in Bradwell to the priory by Roger son of Richard, which was confirmed by Henry I, 1106–9 (ibid. 74), was probably a confirmation of the Giffards' grants made by Roger son of Richard de Clare (cf. G.E.C. *Complete Peerage*, vi, 196).
[44] Priv. Act, 28 Geo. III, cap. 11.
[45] Lewis, *Topog. Dict.*

BOW BRICKHILL

Brichelle (xi cent.); Brichull (xii cent.); Bolle Brichulle, Bellebrikhulle (xiii cent.).

This parish, the northernmost of the three Brickhills, covers about 1,848 acres. Of these only 301 are arable, with wheat, barley and beans the chief crops, 916 permanent grass, and 288 woods and plantations.[1] The surface soil is clay on a subsoil of Lower Greensand. In the village itself and in the woodlands to the east the ground rises from 400 ft. to 500 ft. above the ordnance datum, the average height elsewhere being 300 ft.

The Bletchley and Bedford section of the London and North Western railway, which runs through this parish, has a motor halt here.

The village stands on rising ground to the northeast of Watling Street, and is approached by a by-road from Fenny Stratford. There is a number of whitewashed cottages on either side of the road leading to the church, which stands on higher ground at the southeast end of the village. Some of the houses are of 17th-century date, and are built of half-timber with brick nogging. The Congregational chapel contains some remains of 17th-century work, but was almost entirely rebuilt in 1810. There is also a Wesleyan chapel, built in 1840. The Wheatsheaf Inn is a picturesque half-timber and brick building of about 1600, with a thatched roof.

Caldecott (Caldecote, xi cent.; Calcott, xvi cent.) lies to the east of the River Ouzel. It contains an early 17th-century farm-house with thatched roof and walls of half-timber and brick. To the west is a homestead moat, partly levelled.

THE WHEATSHEAF INN, BOW BRICKHILL

In 1208 a wood in Caldecott bore the name of 'Le Impehey.'[2] Place-names of the 13th century are 'Russesled,' 'Chaldewelleridie' and 'Rielond'[3]; of the 17th century, Bow Close and Grove Close.[4]

Bow Brickhill was inclosed by an Act of Parliament of 1790,[5] the award being dated 16 October 1793.[6]

MANORS   In 1086 two manors in this parish belonged to Walter Giffard. One of these consisted of 5 hides, of which 2 had been held before the Norman Conquest by Goduin, a man of Wulfwig, Bishop of Lincoln, as one manor, the other 3 by Godbold, Alric and Ordric,

each owning a hide and all four having power of sale.[7] The other contained 4 hides. Two belonged to the same Goduin as a manor, the rest to five other thegns, and the right to sell was included in this case also.[8]

This land was later attached to that part of the honour of Giffard afterwards known as the honour of Gloucester, from its descent through the Earls of Gloucester and Hertford.[9] It afterwards passed to the Earls of Stafford, Dukes of Buckingham,[10] after whose attainder it escheated to the Crown, of which Bow Brickhill was held in 1530 as of the honour of Gloucester.[11] It remained attached to the honour, of which it was held by knight service until the abolition of feudal tenure in the 17th century.[12]

From one or both of the tenants of the two manors of Walter Giffard in 1086, of whom Ralph held 5 hides and Robert 4,[13] a manor of BOW BRICKHILL came eventually to the Chaunceys.[14] Geoffrey Chauncey (Cauceis, le Cauchois, Cauceys, Causers), who acquired 2 hides in this parish, which had hitherto been included in Little Brickhill Manor, from Stephen de Thurnham at the close of the 12th century,[15] was dead in 1216, when his 'land of Brickhill' was assigned to his daughter Margaret wife of Geoffrey Martell as her inheritance.[16] The male line of the family, however, had not died out, William Chauncey, a minor, having rights here in 1221.[17] Another member, Robert Chauncey, in the reign of

[1] Statistics from Bd. of Agric. (1905).
[2] Cal. Rot. Chart. 1199–1216 (Rec. Com.), 181.
[3] Feet of F. Bucks. 19 Hen. III, no. 4.
[4] Chan. Inq. p.m. (Ser. 2), dcxxix, 17.
[5] Priv. Act, 30 Geo. III, cap. 40.
[6] Com. Pleas D. Enr. Hil. 34 Geo. III, m. 71.

[7] V.C.H. Bucks. i, 252.
[8] Ibid.
[9] Feud. Aids, i, 83, 103; Cal. Inq. p.m. (Hen. III), i, 158; (Edw. II), v, 343.
[10] Chan. Inq. p.m. 16 Ric. II, pt. i, no. 27; 4 Hen. IV, no. 41; 38 & 39 Hen. VI, no. 59.
[11] Ibid. (Ser. 2), li, 24.
[12] Ct. R. (Gen. Ser.), portf. 155, no. 13;

Chan. Inq. p.m. (Ser. 2), cclv, 156; ccclxxvii, 54; Fine R. 510, no. 20.
[13] V.C.H. Bucks. i, 252.
[14] Possibly Roger Chauncey, living in 1174 (Pipe R. 21 Hen. II [Pipe R. Soc.], 53), was one of the early lords.
[15] Feet of F. Bucks. 9 Ric. I, no. 38.
[16] Rot. Lit. Claus. (Rec. Com.), i, 260b.
[17] See advowson.

Henry III was lord of a knight's fee in Bow Brickhill,[18] part of which, described in the middle of the 14th century as a manor, he had acquired in free marriage with Joan daughter of Robert de Hoo.[19] In 1243, presumably for the sake of Joan, then a nurse in the royal household, the scutage owing for this fee was respited.[20] That Robert had rights in Bow Brickhill apart from his wife seems likely from the renunciation made to him by Margaret daughter of Geoffrey Chauncey and her second husband, Roger de Ibelun, of houses and lands, once her father's, in this parish, and confirmed in 1257 at the instance of the queen and of Robert's wife Joan, 'sometime nurse of Margaret the king's daughter, Queen of Scotland.'[21] Robert, still lord of Bow Brickhill in 1276,[22] and living in 1283,[23] died not long after.[24] The tenure of his son John had ceased in or before 1291, when John son of John, son of Robert Chauncey, sold his lands in Bow Brickhill to Henry Cheval,[25] a member probably of the same family as Roger, Robert and Hugh Cheval, who had owned land here in 1208,[26] 1235,[27] and 1276 respectively.[28] Henry had probably been succeeded before 1301 by his son Robert,[29] who conveyed part of his inheritance here to Nicholas Frembaud,[30] owner of half a knight's fee in this parish in 1302.[31] The occupation of Nicholas was chequered by disputes with the late owners. In 1309 and the three succeeding years he, his wife Annabel and their son John went to law against Robert Cheval to compel him to abide by his agreement made with them concerning the manor of Bow Brickhill, which they held, and claimed to hold, of him.[32] Nicholas Frembaud also recovered 384 acres of land and some rent in this parish from Nicholas Cheval,[33] perhaps a younger brother of Robert, whom he charged about this time and later with trespass and violence.[34] A considerable amount of land still remained in the Cheval family. Osbert Cheval made a settlement of over a hide on his daughter Alice and her husband Robert Maunsel in 1312.[35] Robert Cheval held upwards of 200 acres besides other property in Bow Brickhill in 1315, when they were settled on himself and his wife Alice, with remainders to Nicholas Cheval and his sister Alice.[36] The manor itself, however, was in the hands of Nicholas Frembaud, returned as tenant of the Earl of Gloucester in

1314[37] and as lord of the parish in 1316.[38] In or before 1346 he was succeeded by his son John, who, with his tenants, then held a diminished share of the half fee enjoyed by his father.[39] His right to the manor of Bow Brickhill was challenged in 1347 or 1348 by Robert Noble and his wife Margaret, daughter and heir of the last John Chauncey.[40] Later it possibly passed by marriage to John Woodville,[41] who held here with his wife Katherine in 1366.[42]

The manor remained in the possession of the Woodville family until 1403,[43] and probably afterwards, the heirs of Nicholas Frembaud being described as late tenants in 1460.[44] For the following sixty years its history is obscure.[45]

In 1530 Edward Watson died, leaving his manor of Bow Brickhill (which had been in his possession since 1520, if not earlier) to a younger son Kenelm.[46] In 1587 Kenelm acquired about 100 additional acres from John Richardson,[47] who sued him two years later for non-fulfilment of the contract.[48] At Kenelm's death in 1598 the manor passed to his son and heir Anthony.[49] Anthony, a lunatic in 1601, when an inquiry was made into his condition and possessions,[50] was seised at his death in 1619.[51] A third of the manor came in dower to his widow Elizabeth, who married Sir Francis Browne,[52] and was in her possession nine years later, when Francis, son and heir of Anthony, came of age.[53] In 1632, with his wife Mary, Francis sold Bow Brickhill to Robert Staunton,[54] son and heir-apparent of Sir Francis Staunton of Birchmore in Woburn (Bedfordshire).[55] Robert's son Robert held in 1659[56] and also in 1664 with his wife Elizabeth.[57] Perhaps, like Birchmore, Bow Brickhill remained with the Stauntons until the end of the 17th century.[58] In 1742 a moiety was in the possession of Ann Bartlett, widow, who mortgaged it at that date to William Rhodes.[59] The whole had been acquired before the close of the century by Francis Moore of Hockliffe, Bedfordshire,[60] to whom as lord of the manor compensation was made in 1793 for his manorial rights over certain waste grounds then inclosed.[61]

Bow Brickhill came afterwards, probably through intermarriage with the Hilliers of Stoke Park,[62] to the Delaps of Monellan, Lieut.-Col. James Bogle

18 *Testa de Nevill* (Rec. Com.), 244.
19 De Banco R. 353, m. 98 d.
20 *Excerpta e Rot. Fin.* (Rec. Com.), i, 397. 21 *Cal. Pat.* 1247–58, p. 574.
22 *Hund. R.* (Rec. Com.), i, 41.
23 Assize R. 1247, m. 13 d.
24 *Feud. Aids*, i, 83.
25 *Cal. Close*, 1288–96, p. 200.
26 *Cal. Rot. Chart.* 1199–1216 (Rec. Com.), 181.
27 Feet of F. case 15, file 20.
28 *Hund. R.* (Rec. Com.), i, 41.
29 *Cal. Close*, 1296–1302, p. 492.
30 De Banco R. 179, m. 132.
31 *Feud. Aids*, i, 103.
32 De Banco R. 179, m. 132 ; 183, m. 438 ; 192, m. 33 ; 195a, m. 43.
33 *Abbrev. Rot. Orig.* (Rec. Com.), i, 172.
34 De Banco R. 179, m. 300 ; 187, m. 103 d. ; 201, m. 13. Similar charges were made by him against other inhabitants of Bow Brickhill (ibid. 182, m. 95 ; 187, m. 64).
35 Feet of F. Bucks. 6 Edw. II, no. 26.
36 Ibid. 9 Edw. II, no. 24. The Cheval family retained lands in this parish until

the 17th century at least. In 1401 William Cheval granted his lands here to his cousin and heir Edmund Cheval (Close, 2 Hen. IV, pt. ii, m. 14 d.). Richard and John Cheval were jurors for Bow Brickhill in 1547 (Ct. R. [Gen. Ser.], portf. 155, no. 13), and in 1676 Joan and Anne Cheval, executrices of the late William Cheval, sued John Cheval for lands in Bow Brickhill (Chan. Proc. [Bridges Div.], bdle. 460, no. 145).
37 *Cal. Inq. p.m.* (Edw. II), v, 343.
38 *Feud. Aids*, i, 110.
39 Ibid. 129.
40 De Banco R. 353, m. 98 d.
41 *V.C.H. Beds.* iii, 36.
42 Chart. R. 39 & 40 Edw. III, m. 6, no. 16.
43 Chan. Inq. p.m. 16 Ric. II, pt. i, no. 27 ; 4 Hen. IV, no. 41.
44 Ibid. 38 & 39 Hen. VI, no. 59.
45 See, however, in Caldecott.
46 Chan. Inq. p.m. (Ser. 2), li, 24.
47 Ibid. cclv, 156.
48 Chan. Proc. (Ser. 2), bdle. 228, no. 70. Edward Richardson had formerly held this land.

49 Chan. Inq. p.m. (Ser. 2), cclv, 156.
50 Ibid. cclxii, 177.
51 Ibid. ccclxxvii, 54.
52 Ibid.
53 Fine R. 4 Chas. I, pt. ii, no. 20.
54 Feet of F. Bucks. East. 8 Chas. I.
55 *Visit. of Beds.* (Harl. Soc.), 142.
56 Recov. R. East. 1659, m. 83.
57 Feet of F. Bucks. East. 16 Chas. II.
58 *V.C.H. Beds.* iii, 461. According to Lysons (*Mag. Brit.* i [3], 520) Sir William Boreman died seised of Bow Brickhill in 1697.
59 Feet of F. Bucks. East. 15 Geo. II. Lipscomb (*Hist. and Antiq. of Bucks.* iv, 52) says that a moiety of the manor which belonged to Henry Davis was in the hands of a Mr. Rhodes and another mortgagee in 1757.
60 *V.C.H. Beds.* iii, 384. According to Lipscomb (loc. cit.) and Lysons (loc. cit.) Francis Moore sold Bow Brickhill to the Duke of Bedford in 1792.
61 Com. Pleas D. Enr. Hil. 34 Geo. III, m. 71.
62 See Caldecott Manor.

Delap owning the manor in 1847, his widow in 1854. From her it descended to the Rev. Robert Delap, nephew of the last lord,[63] whose trustees are

DELAP. *Gules a pile argent with an eagle gules thereon.*

RUSSELL, Duke of Bedford. *Argent a lion gules and a chief sable with three scallops argent therein.*

still considerable landowners in the parish, though the manor itself now belongs to the Duke of Bedford.

CALDECOTT MANOR is not mentioned in 1086, but was probably included in Bow Brickhill Manor, as the first mention of the overlordship in 1261 assigns Caldecott to the honour of Gloucester.[64] Though the right of the earl was impugned by the officers of the Crown in 1276,[65] it descended in his heirs and successors, as did the overlordship of Bow Brickhill.

Colour to the supposition that this small manor was comprised within the larger at the Domesday Survey is lent by the fact that the Chaunceys, lords of Bow Brickhill, were also lords of Caldecott. Geoffrey Chauncey owned Caldecott Mill in 1208,[66] and the lands surrendered nearly fifty years later by his daughter Margaret to Robert Chauncey were in Caldecott as well as Bow Brickhill.[67] Robert's knight's fee in this parish was described in 1261 as in Caldecott,[68] in 1276 as in Caldecott and Bow Brickhill,[69] and from that time until the 17th century Bow Brickhill and Caldecott were in the same hands as one knight's fee, but two manors.[70] They descended together until 1628, when Francis Watson and his wife Mary sold the manor of Caldecott to Sir Francis Staunton,[71] who four years later settled it on his second son Francis.[72] At his death in 1639 Sir Francis Staunton was seised only of three messuages and 100 acres of land in Caldecott and Bow Brickhill.[73] No mention of Caldecott has been found in public records from that date until 1798, when, with his wife Mary, Joseph Ager, a landowner here in 1793,[74] sold the manor to Elizabeth Hillier, spinster.[75]

She was probably a relative of Nathaniel Hillier of Stoke Park, whose daughters Harriett and Susan Eliza, with their respective husbands James Bogle Delap and the Hon. Thomas Cranley Onslow,[76] and Susan Hillier, made a settlement of the manor of Caldecott twenty years later.[77] From that time it has followed the descent of Bow Brickhill.

The mill of Caldecott, probably on the site of the mill on the smaller of Walter Giffard's manors in 1086,[78] was granted with some land in 1208 by Geoffrey Chauncey to Robert de Braybrook,[79] from whom this estate descended to Gerard de Braybrook, probably his great-grandson.[80] He alienated it before 1293 to John Grey,[81] who in 1307 settled lands, a mill and rent in Bow Brickhill and Caldecott on himself and his sons.[82] The rent attached to this property appears to have been claimed by the Greys of Wilton, the descendants of the eldest son, who held Water Eaton in Bletchley[83] (q.v.), but the more important part passed to the younger son and his descendants the Greys of Ruthyn who had Bletchley Manor (q.v.), and was held in 1526 by Henry Grey, *de jure* Earl of Kent,[84] as a so-called manor of Bow Brickhill.[85] This younger branch had also held the manor of Brogborough in Ridgmont (Bedford-shire),[86] to which Caldecott Mill was deemed appurtenant in the reign of Elizabeth.[87] The miller, Humphrey Blackshaw,[88] paid a rent of £4 13s. 4d., which was granted to Edward Ferrers and Francis Philipps in 1610, and sold to Andrew Rowley of Birchmore, Woburn (Bedfordshire), in 1650.[89] In 1653 the water-mill with a windmill and messuage in Bow Brickhill and Caldecott were in the possession of Robert Morgan.[90]

Another holding originated in gifts made in the 12th or 13th century by Geoffrey Chauncey and his tenants to Woburn Abbey (Bedfordshire), and confirmed in 1315.[91] The temporalities enjoyed here by this house, valued in 1337 at £6 8s. 4d.,[92] were described in 1346 as a sixth part of the half fee once of Nicholas Frembaud.[93] In 1535 they were leased to William Burre and Edward Staunton,[94] and fourteen years later they were granted as the farm called Bow Brickhill, formerly of the late monastery of Woburn, to William Lord Grey de Wilton, and John Bannester.[95]

At the ecclesiastical taxation of 1291 the rent of £1 was due to Delapré Abbey, near Northampton, for a mill in 'South' Caldecott,[96] so-called in distinction to the hamlet in Newport Pagnell.[97]

From 1166 onwards the nuns of Fontévrault Abbey were paying 32s. a year for lands in Brickhill[98] said to amount to a quarter of this parish and

[63] Burke, *Landed Gentry of Ireland.*
[64] *Cal. Inq. p.m.* (Hen. III), i, 158.
[65] *Hund. R.* (Rec. Com.), i, 41.
[65] Add. Chart. 6014.
[67] *Cal. Pat.* 1247–58, p. 574.
[68] *Cal. Inq. p.m.* (Hen. III), i, 158.
[69] *Hund. R.* (Rec. Com.), i, 41.
[70] See under Bow Brickhill. A release was granted in 1465 by John Hellewell to George Daniel and others of his rights in the manor of Caldecott (Close, 4 Edw. IV, m. 3). In 1619 and 1628 Caldecott was described as a 'manor or grange' (Chan. Inq. p.m. [Ser. 2], ccclxxvii, 54; Fine R. 4 Chas. I, pt. ii, no. 20).
[71] Feet of F. Bucks. Mich. 4 Chas. I.
[72] Ibid. Mich. 8 Chas. I.
[73] Chan. Inq. p.m. (Ser. 2), dccvii, 49.

[74] He was then associated with a Miss Ann Parker of Caldecott Green, described as grantee of a Mr. John Clapham (Com. Pleas D. Enr. Hil. 34 Geo. III, m. 71).
[75] Feet of F. Bucks. Trin. 38 Geo. III.
[76] Burke, op. cit.
[77] Feet of F. Bucks. Trin. 58 Geo. III.
[78] *V.C.H. Bucks.* i, 252.
[79] Add. Chart. 6014; *Cal. Rot. Chart.* 1199–1216 (Rec. Com.), 181.
[80] Clutterbuck, *Hist. and Antiq. o, Herts.* iii, 58.
[81] Add. Chart. 15431; rent alone is mentioned, but the mill must have been included, from its subsequent history.
[82] Feet of F. Div. Co. 35 Edw. I, no. 344.
[83] Chan. Inq. p.m. 19 Ric. II, no. 29.
[84] G.E.C. *Peerage,* iv, 106.

[85] Feet of F. Div. Co. Hil. & East. 17 Hen. VIII.
[86] *V.C.H. Beds.* iii, 321.
[87] Close, 1653, pt. xx, no. 11.
[88] Ct. of Req. bdle. 84, no. 51; Chan. Proc. (Ser. 2), bdle. 157, no. 62.
[89] Close, 1653, pt. xx, no. 11.
[90] Recov. R. Hil. 1652, m. 116.
[91] *Cal. Chart. R.* 1300–26, p. 288.
[92] *Cal. Pat.* 1334–8, p. 493.
[93] *Feud. Aids,* i, 129.
[94] *Valor Eccl.* (Rec. Com.), iv, 212.
[95] Pat. 3 Edw. VI, pt. ix, m. 2.
[96] *Pope Nich. Tax.* (Rec. Com.), 47.
[97] See below, p. 411.
[98] *Pipe R.* 12 *Hen. II* (Pipe R. Soc.), 11; 13 *Hen. II,* 102; 14 *Hen. II,* 7; 15 *Hen. II,* 87, &c.; Hunter, *Gt. R. of the Pipe,* 1 *Ric. I* (Rec. Com.), 30.

called a manor in the 13th century,[99] though only an insignificant rent was ascribed to them in Brickhill in 1291.[100] As a member of their manor of Grovebury, Leighton Buzzard,[1] it descended with Radnage, another of their estates in Buckinghamshire, with which it was bestowed on Eton College in 1444.[2]

A grant of free warren in 1292 to Henry Cheval[3] was renewed in 1366 to John Woodville and his wife Katherine.[4] In 1284 the Abbess of Fontévrault was required to make good her claim to view of frank-pledge in her manor of Bow Brickhill,[5] but this liberty and court leet seem afterwards to have been associated only with the overlordship here.[6]

CHURCH The church of *ALL SAINTS* consists of a chancel measuring internally 25 ft. 6 in. by 11 ft., nave 34 ft. 6 in. by 15 ft., north aisle 9 ft. 6 in. wide, south aisle 9 ft. wide, west tower 12 ft. square, and south porch ; it is built of rubble with stone dressings, and the roofs are covered with tiles.

The nave probably dates from the 12th century, but it was so completely remodelled in the 15th century as to obliterate the earlier details. At this period both aisles and the tower were added and the chancel was probably rebuilt. In 1630 the nave was reroofed. The whole building was restored in 1756–7 by Browne Willis, who rebuilt the east wall of the chancel in brick. The church was again restored in 1883, when the porch was added.

All the windows and other details of the chancel are modern, but the chancel arch, though considerably restored, dates from the 15th century. The nave has a south arcade of three pointed arches, supported by octagonal pillars with moulded capitals and bases, and springing at the responds from moulded corbels. The north arcade is of similar character but without respond corbels ; the western arch on each side is wider than the other two. Both arcades date from the 15th century, and the pointed tower arch in the west wall is of the same period. At the south-east is a pointed niche. The low-pitched king-post roof with plain cambered beams bears the date 1630.

The east window of the north aisle is of two trefoiled lights, and dates from the 15th century, though it has been considerably restored ; all the other windows in this aisle are modern. The south aisle is lighted from the south by three windows, each of two cinquefoiled lights in a square head, from the west by a similar window, and from the east by a window of three trefoiled lights in a four-centred head, all of the 15th century. At the south-east is a pointed piscina of the same period with a round bowl. The south doorway is modern.

The tower is of two stages, with a vice-turret at the south-east, and is surmounted by an embattled parapet. In the west wall of the ground stage is an original window of three plain lights in a three-centred head, and the bell-chamber is lighted by plain windows, also of the 15th century, each of two lights in a pointed head.

The octagonal font has a panelled bowl, below which are figures of angels with outspread wings. It dates from the 15th century. In one of the panels is a shield charged with two implements, perhaps instruments of the Passion. The pulpit, which is of the same period, though considerably restored, is hexagonal and has some traceried panels. On the north wall of the chancel is a tablet to William Watson, rector of the parish, who died in 1608.

The tower contains a ring of four bells : the treble, inscribed 'God Save Ovr King 1634,' is by James Keene ; the second is by Anthony Chandler, 1670 ; the third is of the 16th century and bears the inscription VBGD . ƆꞀꞄ . DEꞀG . EꞀ . W ; the tenor, inscribed 'Soli Deeo Gloria Pax Hominibus 1649' (some letters reversed), is by Henry Bagley. The framework is inscribed '1628 I . I.'

The communion plate includes a cup and paten of 1626, both inscribed 1627.

The registers begin in 1687.

ADVOWSON The church dedicated in honour of All Saints[7] is said to have been given by the Chaunceys to Woburn Abbey in 1185.[8] In 1221, however, the guardian of William Chauncey presented with the consent of the king and the Abbot of Woburn,[9] and the abbot's successor, Roger, fourteen years later surrendered all right in the advowson to Robert Chauncey.[10] The living fell vacant in 1283, when Richard Justin and his wife Alice, who held a considerable amount of land in the parish,[11] after claiming the advowson as Alice's right, agreed, with a reservation of their right to another vacancy, that Robert Chauncey should present on this occasion.[12] From that date until 1628 the advowson descended with the manors of Bow Brick-hill and Caldecott. It passed into other hands soon afterwards, being in the possession of Robert Barker, clerk, at his death in 1632.[13] Christie his son and heir[14] perhaps sold it to Sir William Ashton, who is said to have presented in 1636.[15] Elizabeth Ashton was patron in 1668 or 1669,[16] Mary daughter of William Ashton and widow of Sir John Buck, bart.,[17] in 1671,[18] in which year a later presentation was made by the Crown.[19] Samuel Barker, whose title appears to have been doubtful,[20] presented in 1680,[21] Sir William Buck, son and heir of Sir John Buck and Mary Ashton,[22] in 1681 and 1687.[23] It is said that Sir Charles Buck, son and heir of Sir William,[24] and patron in 1722,[25] sold the advowson of Bow Brickhill in 1726 to Sir John Statham,[26] of whom it was bought in 1735 by David Willaume.[27] David, patron in 1742, 1744, 1751, and 1760,[28]

[99] *Plac. de Quo Warr.* (Rec. Com.), 97.
[100] *Pope Nich. Tax.* (Rec. Com.), 47.
[1] Chan. Inq. p.m. 3 Hen. V, no. 42 ; *V.C.H. Beds.* iii, 403.
[2] *Parl. R.* v, 77*b*.
[3] *Cal. Chart. R.* 1257–1300, p. 423.
[4] *Chart. R.* 39 & 40 Edw. III, m. 6, no. 16.
[5] *Plac. de Quo Warr.* (Rec. Com.), 97.
[6] Mins. Accts. (Gen. Ser.), bdle. 1119, no. 3 ; Ct. R. (Gen. Ser.), portf. 155, no. 13. In 1742, however, they were mentioned amongst the appurtenances of

the manor (Feet of F. Bucks. East. 15 Geo. II).
[7] *Cal. Close,* 1288–96, p. 200 ; P.C.C. 16 Holgrave ; Bacon, *Liber Regis,* 498.
[8] Lipscomb, op. cit. iv, 53.
[9] *R. of Hugh of Wells* (Cant. and York Soc.), ii, 56.
[10] Feet of F. Bucks. 19 Hen. III, no. 4.
[11] Ibid. 18 Edw. I, no. 11 ; 35 Edw. I, no. 2.   [12] Assize R. 1247, m. 13 d.
[13] Chan. Inq. p.m. (Ser. 2), dcxxix, 17.
[14] Ibid.
[15] Lipscomb, op. cit. iv, 54.

[16] Inst. Bks. (P.R.O.).
[17] F. C. Cass, *South Mimms,* 62 ; G.E.C. *Baronetage,* iii, 141–2.
[18] Inst. Bks. (P.R.O.).
[19] Ibid.
[20] Lipscomb, loc. cit. He was probably heir of Robert Barker (see above).
[21] Inst. Bks. (P.R.O.).
[22] G.E.C. loc. cit.
[23] Inst. Bks. (P.R.O.).
[24] G.E.C. loc. cit.
[25] Inst. Bks. (P.R.O.).
[26] Lipscomb, op. cit. iv, 53.
[27] Ibid. iv, 54.   [28] Inst. Bks. (P.R.O.).

was succeeded in or before 1780 by John Williams Willaume,[29] perhaps acting as trustee for David's son Edward,[30] who in 1782 presented himself,[31] in 1783 presented James Bentham, the historian of Ely.[32] The next patron, John Dupré, who presented himself in 1795,[33] took part in a settlement of the advowson on John Ward more than fifteen years later,[34] but was again patron in 1817.[35] John Ward, patron in 1822 and 1829,[36] was succeeded by Mrs. Davis in or before 1836.[37] From 1841 to 1892 the living was in the gift of Queens' College, Cambridge[38]; Mr. R. Knight was patron from 1893 to 1898,[39] and the Rev. Robert Knight, now rector, has been patron since 1899.[40]

Tithes of Brickhill of the gift of Walter Giffard, confirmed to the priory of St. Faith, Longueville, by charters of Henry I and Henry II[41] and valued at £1 in 1291,[42] belonged to the priory of Newton Longville in 1325.[43] At the close of the 14th century these were in the possession of Sir Gilbert Talbot.[44]

In 1384 there is mention of a newly-constructed chapel, as yet unlicensed for divine service.[45]

CHARITIES Charles Parrett, by his will proved in the P.C.C. in 1634, gave £5 yearly for the relief of the poor, £5 towards teaching poor children, £5 for apprenticing poor children and 20s. to a preacher for a sermon on 25 March and another on Michaelmas Day in each year. The several annuities were redeemed in 1863 by the transfer to the official trustees of £533 6s. 8d. consols. Under a scheme of the Charity Commissioners of 14 May 1897 £33 6s. 8d. consols, part thereof, was set aside to form the endowment of the ecclesiastical branch, and the sum of £166 13s. 4d. consols, further part thereof, was, together with £79 7s. 11d. consols, representing accumulations of income, set aside in 1904 to form the endowment of the educational foundation, the annual dividends of which, amounting to £6 3s., are applied in supplying outfits to poor children. The residue of the stock, amounting to £333 6s. 8d. consols, represents the endowment of Parrett's eleemosynary and apprenticing charity, producing £8 6s. 8d. yearly, which is applicable, one moiety for apprenticing and the other moiety for distribution among the poor.

In 1719 Augustus Shaw, by his will, gave £2 10s. yearly, to be applied in putting forth an apprentice to some handicraft trade, issuing out of land at Bow Brickhill belonging to the Duke of Bedford. The annuity is applied, with Parrett's charity, in apprenticing. The premium is usually £25, paid in two instalments.

In 1722 Jane Shaw, by her will, gave £3 yearly for the benefit of the most aged and impotent poor, issuing out of land called Beresteeds. It is distributed among fifteen poor.

Under the Inclosure Award of 1793 land called Black Ground was awarded in trust for the use of the poor for firing. The land was sold in 1896 and the proceeds invested in £101 10s. 8d. consols, with the official trustees. The annual dividends, amounting to £2 10s. 8d., are, together with the income of Parrett's eleemosynary charity, distributed among about seventy poor.

Under the same award 6 a. 0 r. 19 p. of arable land in Bow Brickhill were awarded to the churchwardens and overseers. The land is let at £9. The net income is applied towards church expenses.

The Protestant dissenting chapel and endowment for the minister, chapel and Sunday school are comprised in indentures of lease and release, dated respectively 24 and 25 November 1800. The endowment consists of £1,000 consols, with the official trustees, producing £25 yearly.

GREAT BRICKHILL

Brichella (xi cent.); Magna Brikehille (xii cent.); Magna Brichull (xiii cent.).

This parish contains nearly 2,383 acres, of which the surface is part sand and part clay and the subsoil Lower Greensand. Of this area 444 acres are arable, where wheat, oats and barley are grown, 1,506 are pasture and 130 woods and plantations.[1] The land rises in the west of the parish to 300 ft., and near the village to 400 ft., above the ordnance datum.

The main road of Great Brickhill, called Galley Lane, runs from north to south through the long and straggling village. Near its north-western extremity, in extensive grounds, identical probably with the park of the 13th century and later,[2] stands Brickhill Manor, the seat of Sir Everard Philip Digby Paunce-fort-Duncombe, bt., and the successor probably of more than one ancient manor-house. Robert Bardolf owned a capital messuage in the parish at the close of the 12th century,[3] as did the lords of the house of Grey for the greater part of the 14th century,[4] although in 1396 the site was occupied by buildings of no value.[5] The Duncombes, who were called 'of Great Brickhill,' had a capital messuage here which they and their heirs made their dwelling-house[6] except for a period in which it was leased to the Wallis family.[7] The church and rectory both stand south of the manor-house. There are many picturesque 17th-century houses and cottages in the village with walls of half-timber and brick and roofs mostly of thatch, but some of tiles or slate. The Baptist chapel, at its

---

[29] Inst. Bks. (P.R.O.).
[30] Add. MS. 9408, fol. 306.
[31] Inst. Bks. (P.R.O.).
[32] Ibid.; Dict. Nat. Biog.
[33] Inst. Bks. (P.R.O.).
[34] Feet of F. Bucks. Mich. 51 Geo. III.
[35] Cler. Guide.
[36] Ibid.   [37] Ibid.
[38] Clergy List.
[39] Ibid.
[40] Ibid.

[41] Cal. Doc. of France, 74, 77.
[42] Pope Nich. Tax. (Rec. Com.), 33–4.
[43] Mins. Accts. (Gen. Ser.), bdle. 1125, no. 1.
[44] Chan. Inq. p.m. 22 Ric. II, no. 47.
[45] Linc. Epis. Reg. Memo. Buckingham, fol. 291 d.
[1] Statistics from Bd. of Agric. (1905). There was woodland for 100 swine in 1086 (V.C.H. Bucks. i, 247).
[2] Hund. R. (Rec. Com.), i, 41; Anct.

Extents (Exch. K.R.), no. 78 (1); Chan. Inq. p.m. 19 Ric. II, no. 30; (Ser. 2), ccxlvi, 110; ccccxc, 188.
[3] Feet of F. Beds. 9 Ric. I, no. 14.
[4] Chan. Inq. p.m. Edw. II, files 3, no. 5; 82, no. 9; Anct. Extents (Exch. K.R.), no. 78 (1).
[5] Chan. Inq. p.m. 19 Ric. II, no. 30.
[6] Fine R. 10 Chas. I, pt. iii, no. 23; P.C.C. 266 Norfolk.
[7] Decree R. 1258, no. 7.

south end, dates from 1812, and the Wesleyan Methodist chapel, built in 1877, has succeeded one existing here in 1862.[8]

In the north-west of the parish Orchard Mill preserves the name of a water-mill of the 16th and following century.[9] This was perhaps on the site of one of the two mills standing in 1086 in Great Brickhill,[10] to which a water-mill remained appurtenant until the early 18th century and probably later.[11] The other Domesday mill is probably the Smewnes Mill of 1251[12] or its predecessor, which must have stood in the south-west of the parish, where the Ouzel divides Great Brickhill from Soulbury, in which part of Smewnes lay. This mill in the 13th century associated with the 'water of Novente,'[13] in the 17th described as two mills under one roof,[14] reappears in the 18th as a paper-mill[15] and gave its name to Paper Mill Farm, the name of Smewnes itself having disappeared from modern maps.

'Le lord meadows' of 1634[16] is probably the 'Lord's Mead' of 1771, then held by the rector with 'Swansnest' and 'Half the Parson's Hide.'[17] There was a 'dole meadow' in 1584[18]; 'Eaton leyes' and 'Quydlecott' belong to the 16th and 17th centuries[19]; 'St. Margaret lande,' 'Apenham meade,' 'Achemore field' and 'Barbers' occur in a record of 1596[20]; 'Fosseys farme,' 'Maynard' and 'Conigree Close' in one of 1634.[21] 'Doddes,' 'Bacons,' 'Crowell furlonge,' 'Capon hedges' and 'Otehill,'[22] as also woods called 'Sapgrove' and 'Ladygrove,'[23] and a messuage called 'le White House'[24] were all included in the reputed manor of Smewnes, though the last seems afterwards to have been transferred to the chief manor.[25]

About 1,260 acres in this parish were inclosed by Act of Parliament in 1771.[26]

The manor of GREAT BRICKHILL, MANORS which Earl Tosti held before the Norman Conquest, belonged to Hugh Earl of Chester in 1086, when it was assessed at 9 hides.[27] Randolph Earl of Chester, great-great-grandson of Hugh's sister Margaret,[28] was overlord in 1205.[29] After his death without issue the overlordship of Great Brickhill came to Hugh Earl of Arundel,[30] son and heir of his sister Mabel.[31] He, too, left no child, and the earldom of Chester was annexed to the Crown in 1246.[32] Great Brickhill was still said to form part of the honour of Chester in 1284,[33] but this is the last reference to the connexion of the Earls of Chester with the place, the overlordship rights

having been obtained at that date by Hugh le Despencer,[34] son of Hugh le Despencer and of Alina daughter and heir of Sir Philip Basset of Wycombe,[35] to whom a pair of gilt spurs worth 6d. was owed for this manor.[36] He and his descendants, described as the heirs of Philip Basset, are returned as overlords throughout the 14th century.[37] From 1526 to 1634,

CHESTER. *Azure three sheaves or.*

DESPENCER. *Argent quartered with gules fretty or and over all a bend sable.*

however, the tenure was of the Crown by knight service.[38]

From a certain William, sub-tenant of the Earl of Chester in 1086,[39] or from his heirs the manor of Great Brickhill came to the family of Malbank. It appears to have descended towards the close of the 12th century to the daughters and co-heirs of William, Baron of Nantwich,[40] possibly the William de Malbank who held in Buckinghamshire or Bedfordshire from 1176 to 1184.[41] The number of these ladies is given variously as three[42] and four.[43] Eleanor, described as the second and said to have died unmarried,[44] is by the same authority identified with Aenor Malbank, grantor of part of a Cheshire manor.[45] She is probably the Anor or Annora Malbank who had rights in Great Brickhill in 1205,[46] and who is supposed to have been the wife of Robert Bardolf.[47] The possessions of Robert, a landowner here in 1197 or 1198,[48] were granted as forfeited lands of the Normans to his overlord Randolph Earl of Chester in 1205,[49] but the Malbanks were still in possession of their

MALBANK. *Quarterly or and gules a bend sable.*

---

[8] Sheahan, *Hist. and Topog. of Bucks.* 503.

[9] Chan. Inq. p.m. (Ser. 2), ccxlvi, 110; Fine R. 10 Chas. I, pt. iii, m. 23.

[10] *V.C.H. Bucks.* i, 247.

[11] Chan. Inq. p.m. Edw. II, files 3, no. 5; 82, no. 9; Feet of F. Bucks. Mich. 3 Edw. VI; Mich. 7 Anne. The two water-mills of 1574 (Memo. R. [Exch. L.T.R.], Mich. 17 Eliz. m. 43) and of 1701 (Recov. R. Mich. 13 Will. III, m. 122) were probably under one roof and identical with the mill mentioned in the text.

[12] Feet of F. Bucks. 36 Hen. III, no. 12.

[13] Ibid.

[14] Chan. Inq. p.m. (Ser. 2), cccvi, 143.

[15] Recov. R. Trin. 27 Geo. III, m. 199.

[16] Fine R. 10 Chas. I, pt. iii, no. 23.

[17] Priv. Act, 11 Geo. III, cap. 20.

[18] Ct. of Req. bdle. 74, no. 74.

[19] Fine R. 39 Eliz. pt. i, no. 49; 10 Chas. I, pt. iii, no. 23.

[20] Fine R. 39 Eliz. pt. i, no. 49.

[21] Ibid. 10 Chas. I, pt. iii, no. 23.

[22] Ld. Rev. Misc. Bks. clxxxviii, 309–10.

[23] Memo. R. (Exch. L.T.R.), East. 1 & 2 Phil. and Mary, m. 57.

[24] Chan. Inq. p.m. (Ser. 2), cccvi, 143; Fine R. 14 Jas. I, pt. ii, no. 39.

[25] Fine R. 10 Chas. I, pt. iii, no. 23.

[26] Priv. Act, 11 Geo. III, cap. 20.

[27] *V.C.H. Bucks.* i, 247.

[28] G.E.C. *Peerage*, ii, 222–4.

[29] *Rot. Lit. Pat.* (Rec. Com.), 8b; *Rot. Lit. Claus.* (Rec. Com.), i, 18b.

[30] *Testa de Nevill* (Rec. Com.), 244.

[31] G.E.C. op. cit. 224–5.

[32] Ibid. 225.

[33] *Feud. Aids*, i, 83.

[34] Ibid.

[35] G.E.C. op. cit. iii, 90–1. See below.

[36] *Cal. Inq. p.m.* (Edw. II), v, 19.

[37] *Feud. Aids*, i, 103; Chan. Inq. p.m.

Edw. II, file 82, no. 9; 12 Ric. II, no. 23; 19 Ric. II, no. 30.

[38] Chan. Inq. p.m. (Ser. 2), xlv, 33; ccxlvi, 110; Fine R. 39 Eliz. pt. i, no. 49; 10 Chas. I, pt. iii, no. 23.

[39] *V.C.H. Bucks.* i, 247.

[40] *Genealogist* (New Ser.), vi, 193. A reference to this barony occurs in the *Red Bk. of Exch.* (Rolls Ser.), i, 184.

[41] *Pipe R.* 22 Hen. II (Pipe R. Soc.), 20; 23 Hen. II, 159; 30 Hen. II, 114.

[42] Ormerod, *Hist. of Co. Palat. and City of Chest.* iii, 422.

[43] *Genealogist* loc. cit.

[44] Ormerod, op. cit. iii, 424.

[45] Ibid. 390.

[46] See under advowson.

[47] Lipscomb, *Hist. and Antiq. of Bucks.* iv, 58.

[48] Feet of F. Beds. 9 Ric. I, no. 14.

[49] *Rot. Lit. Pat.* (Rec. Com.), 8b; *Rot. Lit. Claus.* (Rec. Com.), i, 18b.

estate after this date. Ada Malbank, sister of Eleanor or Annora,[50] settled her land in Brickhill on her second son Matthew,[51] and afterwards with her husband Warren de Vernon relinquished her share of the manor to her eldest sister Philippa and her husband Thomas Basset of Headington, Oxfordshire.[52] Philippa, one of the daughters and co-heirs of Thomas and Philippa Basset and wife of the Earl of Warwick,[53] held Great Brickhill as two knights' fees in the reign of Henry III.[54] After her death without issue in 1246,[55] the manor appears to have passed to the third son of her father's younger brother Alan, Sir Philip Basset of Wycombe, and to have been subinfeudated by him to the Grey family, the overlordship thus created having been dealt with above.

John Grey, who was in possession of the manorial rights in 1265,[56] was also lord of Bletchley Manor (q.v.), with which Great Brickhill descended to Richard Earl of Kent.[57] In 1506 he settled the manor, with those of Simpson and Stoke Hammond, on himself for life, with reversion to Sir Charles Somerset, Lord Herbert, whose son and heir Henry was to marry Anne, Richard's sister.[58] The marriage did not take place, and in 1512 a fresh arrangement secured the reversion of Great Brickhill alone to Lord Herbert.[59] In the following year Lord Herbert acquired the

SOMERSET. *FRANCE quartered with ENGLAND in a border gobony argent and azure.*

earl's life interest in return for a yearly rent of £14 6s. 8d.,[60] which was relinquished in 1514 for £400.[61] Lord Herbert, then Earl of Worcester, received the king's pardon in the same year for alienation of the manor without licence,[62] and died seised of it in 1526.[63] He left it to his wife Eleanor, against whom it was claimed in reversion by Henry Grey, half-brother and heir of Richard Earl of Kent, under a settlement made by their father, George Earl of Kent.[64]

In accordance with her husband's will, it passed at Eleanor's death to their younger son Sir George Somerset,[65] who with his wife Mary sold it to William Duncombe in 1549.[66] Another sale by William himself ten years later brought Great Brickhill to his younger son Thomas,[67] on whom it was finally settled

by his father in 1573.[68] In 1574 Thomas Duncombe jun., son of John, William's elder son,[69] surrendered his rights in the manor to his uncle Thomas,[70] who, having soon afterwards accounted for its alienation without licence,[71] remained in possession until his death in February 1595–6.[72] John his eldest son entered into possession the same year,[73] and in 1612, with his wife Lucy, settled this manor on the marriage of their son Thomas with Joan daughter of Simon Haynes of Turweston.[74] Another settlement was made by John, Lucy and Thomas in 1627, in which year Lucy died.[75] John survived her until 1630,[76] and in 1634 Thomas, then aged forty-five, was granted livery of a third of the manor.[77] He was succeeded in or before 1639 by his son and heir John,[78] who in that year leased part of the manor to Richard Sydenham for ninety-nine years, and in 1649 sold the remainder of this term to William Wallis, whose family sued him in Chancery twelve years later.[79] He is said to have been the father of another John Duncombe, whose son of the same name died without issue in 1687, when Great Brickhill descended to his three sisters and co-heirs.[80]

Katherine, the eldest, held a third in 1701, when a settlement was made,[81] probably as a preliminary to her marriage with Thomas Bristowe that year.[82] A further settlement was made in 1708.[83] She died in 1711,[84] her husband, who survived her about thirty years, enjoying a life interest in her share of Great Brickhill.[85] Dr. Duncombe Bristowe, who died in 1758, leaving his property in this parish, then described as a moiety of the manor, to his wife Frances, with remainder to his brother Richard,[86] was probably the elder son of Thomas and Katherine Bristowe. Richard inherited on the death of Frances in 1765,[87] and by his will, made and proved four years later, this moiety came to Philip Barton in 1769.[88]

Philippa, the second sister, then a spinster, owned one-third of Great Brickhill in 1701 and 1708,[89] and afterwards married Dr. Stephen Chase, with whom she was in joint possession in 1720.[90] She died the next year, it would seem without issue, and her husband died in 1740,[91] when this share of the manor reverted to the other co-heirs, who thus each held a moiety.

In 1708 Mary, the youngest sister, held her third with her husband John Barton,[92] afterwards rector of this parish.[93] She died eleven years later,[94] and on

[50] Ormerod, op. cit. iii, 422.
[51] Harl. MS. 1424, fol. 98.
[52] Ibid. 1505, fol. 101 d. See under advowson.
[53] Ibid. ; G.E.C. op. cit. viii, 54.
[54] *Testa de Nevill* (Rec. Com.), 244b.
[55] G.E.C. loc. cit.
[56] *Abbrev. Plac.* (Rec. Com.), 158.
[57] *Cal. Close*, 1272–9, pp. 127, 130 ; *Feud. Aids*, i, 83, 103, 110, 129 ; Anct. Extents (Exch. K.R.), no. 78 (1) ; *Cal. Pat.* 1354–8, p. 334 ; Mins. Accts. (Gen. Ser.), bdle. 1119, no. 4 ; De Banco R. 953, m. 339 d.
[58] De Banco R. 977, m. 138 ; Close, 4 Hen. VIII, no. 21.
[59] Close, 4 Hen. VIII, no. 21.
[60] Ibid. 5 Hen. VIII, no. 27, 28.
[61] Ibid. 6 Hen. VIII, no. 18.
[62] *L. and P. Hen. VIII*, i, 5180.
[63] Chan. Inq. p.m. (Ser. 2), xlv, 33.
[64] Ibid. ; Early Chan. Proc. bdle. 512, no. 31, 32.

[65] Chan. Inq. p.m. (Ser. 2), xlv, 33.
[66] Feet of F. Bucks. Mich. 3 Edw. VI ; Recov. R. Trin. 3 Edw. VI, m. 342.
[67] Memo. R. (Exch. L.T.R.), Mich. 17 Eliz. m. 43.
[68] Ibid. ; Feet of F. Bucks. Mich. 15 Eliz.
[69] Memo. R. (Exch. L.T.R.), Mich. 17 Eliz. m. 43.
[70] Feet of F. Bucks. Trin. 16 Eliz. ; Recov. R. Mich. 18 & 19 Eliz. m. 1213.
[71] Memo. R. (Exch. L.T.R.), Mich. 17 Eliz. m. 43.
[72] Ct. of Req. bdle. 74, no. 74 ; Decree R. 78, no. 21 ; Chan. Inq. p.m. (Ser. 2), ccxlvi, 110.
[73] Fine R. 39 Eliz. pt. i, no. 49.
[74] Feet of F. Bucks. Mich. 10 Jas. I ; Chan. Inq. p.m. (Ser. 2), ccccxc, 188.
[75] Fine R. 10 Chas. I, pt. iii, m. 23 ; Feet of F. Bucks. East. 2 Chas. I.
[76] Chan. Inq. p.m. (Ser. 2), ccccxc, 188.

[77] Fine R. 10 Chas. I, pt. iii, m. 23.
[78] *Cal. S. P. Dom.* 1655–6, p. 60.
[79] Decree R. 1258, no. 7.
[80] Berry, *Bucks. Gen.* 100 ; Lipscomb, op. cit. iv, 62.
[81] Recov. R. Mich. 13 Will. III, m. 122.
[82] Lipscomb, op. cit. iv, 68.
[83] Feet of F. Bucks. Mich. 7 Anne ; Recov. R. Mich. 7 Anne, m. 81.
[84] Lipscomb, op. cit. iv, 67.
[85] Ibid. 67, 69.
[86] P.C.C. 179 Hutton.
[87] Lipscomb, op. cit. iv, 67 ; Recov. R. Mich. 6 Geo. III, m. 465.
[88] P.C.C. 302 Bogg.
[89] Recov. R. Mich. 13 Will. III, m. 122 ; Mich. 7 Anne, m. 81 ; Feet of F. Bucks. Mich. 7 Anne.
[90] Feet of F. Bucks. Mich. 7 Geo. I.
[91] P.C.C. 8 Tremley.
[92] Feet of F. Bucks. Mich. 7 Anne.
[93] Lipscomb, op. cit. iv, 64.
[94] Ibid. 65.

the death of her husband in 1760 [95] the Barton moiety of Great Brickhill descended to their fourth but apparently sole surviving son Philip,[96] who inherited the rest of the manor in 1769.[97]

The Rev. Philip Barton, sole lord of Great Brickhill in 1771,[98] died in 1786, leaving the manor in trust for his godson Philip Duncombe Pauncefort on condition that he should take the name of Duncombe on inheriting.[99] This was done in 1805.[100] In 1849 Great Brickhill descended from the elder Philip to his son of the same name, created a baronet in 1859.[1] He was succeeded in 1890 by his son Philip Henry Pauncefort-Duncombe, whose son and heir Sir Everard

PAUNCEFORT. *Gules three lions argent.*

DUNCOMBE. *Party cheveronwise and engrailed gules and argent three talbots' heads razed and countercoloured with a crosslet or for difference.*

Philip Digby Pauncefort-Duncombe, bart., has been lord of the manor since 1895.[2]

Free warren was an appurtenance of this manor from the 13th to the 17th century.[3] The Earl of Kent complained in 1493 his warren had been broken and hares, coneys, pheasants and partridges taken.[4] A several fishery also belonged to the manor until the 18th century,[5] a quantity of fish being unlawfully taken from it in 1348.[6] It was described in 1596 and 1630 as extending from Stapleford Bridge to Eaton Mill.[7] Liberties that occur in somewhat later records are courts leet and baron and view of frankpledge.[8] From 1323 to 1720 there were dovecotes varying in number from three to one.[9]

A grant of Smewnes Mill and some land in Great Brickhill made by Nicholas de Sanford to Woburn Abbey in 1251 or 1252 [10] was perhaps followed by other gifts before 1337, when the abbot enjoyed temporalities here of considerable value.[11] Together they seem to have formed the manor of *SMEWNES GRANGE*, to which in 1348 John Pessovere or Passe-

lewe of Dunstable, jun., and his wife Margaret had some right for the term of Margaret's life, which they surrendered to the abbot and his successors.[12] The possessions of the abbey in Smewnes were in 1535 held by lease by Edward Staunton, then bailiff,[13] and he was still tenant in 1541, when the king granted them to Sir John Williams in an exchange.[14] Three months later Sir John obtained licence to alienate this property to Henry Terell and Edward Water.[15] A manor of Great Brickhill, however, which appears to be Smewnes, and was annexed to the honour of Ampthill, was in the Crown in 1548,[16] and five years later Edward Staunton, still tenant in 1548,[17] was lord of the 'manor or grange called Smewnes.'[18] He then settled it on trustees for the use of himself and his younger son Edmund, who inherited on his father's death in 1553,[19] and made a settlement in the following year.[20] In 1555 Edmund was called upon to prove his title to his grange of Smewnes,[21] of which he remained lord until 1607.[22] Reginald his son and heir, on whose marriage with Elizabeth Shuckburgh the property had been settled in 1585,[23] entered into full possession in 1617,[24] made a settlement on the marriage of his son Anthony early in 1625,[25] and died seised ten years later.[26] From Anthony, who was granted livery of one-third of Smewnes in 1638,[27] the manor descended through his son and grandson of the same name to Elizabeth, only daughter and heir of the third Anthony Staunton,[28] who with her husband James Stokes[29] in 1718 surrendered her rights in it to John Staunton of Galway,[30] grandson of her great-grandfather's younger brother George.[31] Thomas Staunton, John's son and heir,[32] died in 1784, having survived his sons John and Thomas[33] and his grandson Thomas son of Thomas.[34] In accordance with his will made in 1778, before the death of the third Thomas, Smewnes descended to his daughters Elizabeth Catherine, who

WOBURN ABBEY. *Azure three bars wavy argent.*

STAUNTON. *Argent two cheverons sable.*

[95] Lipscomb, op. cit. iv, 65.
[96] Ibid. 67. There is no mention of any other son of John and Mary Barton in the wills of Duncombe and Richard Bristowe (P.C.C. 179 Hutton ; 302 Bogg).
[97] See above.
[98] Priv. Act, 11 Geo. III, cap. 20.
[99] P.C.C. 266 Norfolk.
[100] Burke, *Peerage and Baronetage* (1912).
[1] Ibid.
[2] Ibid.
[3] *Hund. R.* (Rec. Com.), i, 41 ; Chan. Inq. p.m. (Ser. 2), ccxlvi, 110 ; ccccxc, 188.
[4] De Banco R. 924, m. 103.
[5] Chan. Inq. p.m. 19 Ric. II, no. 30 ; Feet of F. Bucks. Mich. 7 Anne.
[6] De Banco R. 354, m. 60 ; 355, m. 35 ; 356, m. 28 d.

[7] Chan. Inq. p.m. (Ser. 2), ccxlvi, 110 ; ccccxc, 188.
[8] Ibid. ; Feet of F. Bucks. Mich. 7 Anne.
[9] Anct. Extents (Exch. K.R.), no. 78 (1) ; Chan. Inq. p.m. 19 Ric. II, no. 30 ; Memo. R. (Exch. L.T.R.), Mich. 17 Eliz. m. 43.
[10] Feet of F. Bucks. 36 Hen. III, no. 12 ; Div. Co. 36 Hen. III, no. 112.
[11] *Cal. Pat.* 1334–8, p. 493.
[12] Feet of F. Bucks. 22 Edw. III, no. 9.
[13] Dugdale, *Mon.* v, 480.
[14] *L. and P. Hen. VIII*, xvi, g. 779 (21).
[15] Ibid. g. 947 (15).
[16] Ld. Rev. Misc. Bks. clxxxviii, fol. 309–10.
[17] Ibid.
[18] Pat. 7 Edw. VI, pt. iv, m. 27.
[19] Ibid. ; Chan. Inq. p.m. (Ser. 2), c. 7.

[20] Feet of F. Bucks. Mich. 1 & 2 Phil. and Mary.
[21] Memo. R. (Exch. L.T.R.), East. 1 & 2 Phil. and Mary, m. 57.
[22] Recov. R. Trin. 2 & 3 Phil. and Mary, m. 113 ; Trin. 27 Eliz. m. 24 ; Pat. 27 Eliz. pt. ix, m. 15 ; Chan. Inq. p.m. (Ser. 2), cccvi, 143.
[23] Chan. Inq. p.m. (Ser. 2), cccvi, 143.
[24] Fine R. 14 Jas. I, pt. ii, no. 39.
[25] Feet of F. Bucks. Hil. 1 Chas. I.
[26] Chan. Inq. p.m. (Ser. 2), dxlv, 77.
[27] Fine R. 14 Chas. I, pt. ii, no. 35.
[28] G. T. Staunton, *Mem. of Sir George Leonard Staunton, Bart.* 58.
[29] Ibid.
[30] Feet of F. Bucks. Hil. 4 Geo. I.
[31] G. T. Staunton, loc. cit.
[32] Ibid.   [33] Ibid.
[34] Priv. Act, 31 Geo. III, cap. 29.

married John Cumberland Bentley the year after her father's death, and Bettinson Staunton and to his granddaughters Mary and Margaret Staunton, the only surviving children of his son Thomas.[35] The last two being wards in Chancery, an Act of Parliament was passed in 1791 vesting the estates of the late Thomas Staunton in trustees for their sale on behalf of the four co-heirs.[36] It is said that Smewnes was sold the next year to Edward Hanmer of Stockgrove, Soulbury, who owned it about 1813.[37] It passed from him to Colonel H. Hanmer, K.H., M.P., who held in 1862,[38] and appears to have been purchased from his heirs before 1897, together with Grovebury Manor in Leighton Buzzard (Bedfordshire), by Mr. J. T. Mills.[39]

Free fishery was an appurtenance of Smewnes in 1251,[40] a dovecote in 1554.[41]

A farm and lands in Greenend in Great Brickhill, held by William Shepherd in the second half of the 16th century, and disputed between his sons in 1592[42] and 1594,[43] was described as the manor of GREENEND in the latter year, when its court rolls were said to be fraudulently detained by his widow Elizabeth and sons Thomas and Henry.[44]

Land in Great Brickhill, which had belonged to the monastery of St. Mary de Pré in Hertfordshire and came to the Crown on the death of the last prioress, was granted to Cardinal Wolsey in 1528,[45] and afterwards included in grants made to John Penn and his wife in 1531, 1544 and 1545.[46] In 1547 John and his wife Lucy sold it to Sir Robert Dormer,[47] but the claims of the Crown were revived nearly forty years later[48] in a grant to Theophilus Adams and others.[49]

The church of *THE NATIVITY CHURCH OF THE BLESSED VIRGIN*[50] consists of a chancel measuring internally 25 ft. by 13 ft. 6 in., central tower 10 ft. by 14 ft., north and south chapels, nave 49 ft. 6 in. by 15 ft. 6 in., north aisle 13 ft. 6 in. wide, south aisle 12 ft. wide, and south porch. It is built of rubble with stone dressings, and the roofs are covered with tiles.

The chancel, tower, and probably the nave date from the 13th century, but all the original details of the nave have been obliterated by subsequent alterations. The south aisle and chapel were built about 1460, and the north aisle and chapel about thirty years later, the chapels in both cases being formed by the extension of the aisles eastward beyond the tower to the western part of the chancel. The chancel was repaired in 1602. The roofs were heightened and the south porch was added in 1867, when the whole fabric was restored.

The chancel is lighted from the east by a modern window and from each of the lateral walls by a 13th-century lancet with an original moulded rear arch and jamb shafts, but modern external stonework. At the west end of the north wall is a 15th-century segmental arch to the north chapel, and there is a similar arch to the south chapel in the wall opposite. The central tower opens to the chancel and nave by

13th-century pointed arches having semi-octagonal responds with original moulded capitals and restored bases. On the south are a continuously moulded doorway with a much-restored two-light window above it, both probably of about 1390, and a small 15th-century doorway to the stair turret. The larger doorway originally opened to the churchyard, but now leads to the chapel, the roof of which partly covers the window.

The nave arcades are each of four bays with pointed arches supported by octagonal pillars with moulded capitals and bases. Both arcades have semi-octagonal west responds, but die into plain responds on the east. In the west wall is a doorway with a three-light window above, both of which were inserted about 1390, but the tracery of the latter is modern and all the stonework of the doorway has been renewed.

The north chapel and aisle are continuous, and are lighted from the north by three late 15th-century windows, each of three lights in a square head; in the west wall is a three-light window of the same date, though considerably restored, while the east window is modern. There is an original pointed piscina in the east wall. The north doorway, now blocked, is at the west end of the north wall. It has a pointed head, and is continuously moulded. The two eastern windows in the continuous south wall of the south aisle and chapel are modern, and the two western are of the 15th century, but have been much restored; the east and west windows are modern, but the latter retains a few old stones in its external jambs. The south doorway is original, and has a pointed arch in a square head with traceried spandrels.

The central tower rises two stages above the church roof, the upper stage being considerably contracted above offsets on the north and south; it is surmounted by an embattled parapet, and has a projecting stair in a turret on the south. The external stonework has been considerably renewed. On the south side is a clock.

The communion table dates from the 17th century, and there is a chest with incised ornament in the north chapel of the same period. On the internal jambs of the 13th-century lancets in the chancel are traces of original painting. The font is modern. There are many 18th-century monuments to members of the Duncombe, Bristowe, Pauncefort, Barton, and Chase families.

The tower contains a ring of six bells; the second by Thomas Mears, 1840, and all the others by W. & T. Mears, 1789. There is also a small bell by George Chandler, inscribed 'G.C. 1681.'

The plate consists of a silver cup and paten given by John Barton, rector, in 1755; a round silver salver with feet, given in 1756 by the same; a silver flagon given in 1718 by Anne Barton, widow of Samuel Barton, rector; and a rounded hexagonal silver salver with feet, given by Edward Staunton, rector of Tattenhoe, in 1759. Attached to the bottom of the last piece is a silver disc with illegible date mark.

[35] Priv. Act, 31 Geo. III, cap. 29.
[36] Ibid.
[37] Lysons, *Mag. Brit.* i (3), 521.
[38] Sheahan, *Hist. and Topog. of Bucks.* 502.
[39] *Rec. of Bucks.* viii, 96; *V.C.H. Beds.* iii, 404.
[40] Feet of F. Bucks. 36 Hen. III, no. 12.
[41] Ibid. Mich. 1 & 2 Phil. and Mary.
[42] Chan. Proc. Eliz. Ss 19, no. 37.
[43] Ibid. Ss 22, no. 58.   [44] Ibid.
[45] *L. and P. Hen. VIII*, iv (2), 4472.
[46] Ibid. v, g. 457 (1); xix (1), g. 812 (44); xx (1), g. 465 (24).
[47] Feet of F. Bucks. Mich. 1 Edw. VI.
[48] Pat. 27 Eliz. pt. iv, m. 30.
[49] Ibid.
[50] Offerings were made to our Lady of Brickhill in 1523 (*MSS. of Lord Middleton* [Hist. MSS. Com.], 357), and this was the invocation in 1786 (Bacon, *Liber Regis*, 498).

The registers begin in 1558.

The church of Great Brickhill *ADVOWSON* has generally followed the descent of the main manor. Annora Malbank gave a moiety of the church to Dunstable Priory in 1205,[51] but if this grant took effect it can only have been for a short time, Thomas Bassett, who disputed her right[52] and obtained from her sister Ada and her husband Warren de Vernon a renunciation of their claim to a third of the presentation,[53] being acknowledged patron in 1214.[54]

The Prior of Dunstable, however, either through Annora's grant or else in virtue of the gift of the tithe of Brickhill (Brichella) and a villein to the abbey of St. Evroul, Orne, Lower Normandy, by Hugh second Earl of Chester 1071–1101,[55] had some show of right in the tithes of Great Brickhill; 11s. rent, in fact, was due to Dunstable Priory from Walter Cuncus, son of Hugh de Dunstaville, for two parts of the tithe of his demesne of Brickhill, and for half a virgate of land 'de Socheshide' with messuage, and for the messuage next the cemetery, all of which belonged to the church of St. Evroul.[56] This right to the tithes of Great Brickhill the prior exchanged for a pension of 20s. in 1214 by an agreement with the rector,[57] which was renewed and confirmed in 1280.[58] This was paid in 1291.[59]

During the Commonwealth John Duncombe's title to the presentation was disputed on the ground of his alleged delinquency,[60] and the Crown presented in 1660.[61] Anne widow of Samuel Barton, rector of Great Brickhill, was patron for one turn only at his death in 1715.[62] With these exceptions the advowson appears to have been always in the same hands as the manor.

In 1519 Robert Keye obtained licence to build a chapel in honour of the Virgin Mary and St. John the Baptist near the spring called the Maidens' Well.[63]

CHARITIES The following charities are administered under a scheme of the Charity Commissioners of 4 February 1908 under the title of the Parochial Charities, namely :—

1. Charity of Anne Briscoe and William Duncombe, founded by indenture dated 13 July 1631. The endowment consists of a fee-farm rent of £8, issuing out of two water-mills, houses and land at Redbourn, Hertfordshire.

2. The Feoffee's charity, comprised in indenture of 30 September 1640. The property consists of about 14 acres of land at Great Brickhill and £228 13s. 9d. consols, representing accumulations of income. There are also certain almshouses belonging to that charity, occupied by paupers, which are kept in repair by the trustees.

3. Charity of Anthony Holton, will proved 5 May 1725, legacy of £50.

4. Charity of John Newman, will 1700, legacy of £20. These legacies are represented by £100 consols.

5. Charity of John Meade, will 1716, trust fund, £202 5s. 6d. consols, arising from sale of land in 1893, purchased with legacy of £50.

The land belonging to the charities is let at £23 19s. yearly, and the sums of stock, which are held by the official trustees, produce £13 5s. 4d. yearly.

The net income is applied in money payments to about forty poor people and about £8 is distributed in food and fuel.

The Poor's Land, allotted by an Inclosure Award, containing 7 a. 1 r. 7 p. at Partridge Hill, is let in allotments producing £8 17s. yearly, which is applied in the distribution of coal.

A piece of land called the Bell Rope Piece, containing 2 a. 0 r. 11 p., was mentioned on a board in the church. It is let at £2 10s. yearly. One half the income is applied to the ringers and the remaining half towards providing bell-ropes.

It was also stated that Thomas Bust in 1701 left 1s. yearly for the poor. The annuity was paid by the lord of the manor in respect of a cottage belonging to him.

LITTLE BRICKHILL

Brichella, Brichellae (xi cent.) ; Brichel, Brikull, Parva Brychull (xiii cent.) ; Little Brikehill (xv cent.).

This parish, lying between Bow Brickhill on the north and Great Brickhill on the west, contains 1,367 acres, of which the surface is a reddish sand intermixed with clay,[1] the subsoil Lower Greensand. Of this area 199 acres are arable, the chief crops grown being wheat, oats, beans and barley, and 509 acres are permanent grass.[2] Woodland, of which there are now 568 acres,[3] has been abundant here since 1086.[4] At the close of the 13th century there was a park here besides 100 acres of wood,[5] and the records of the 14th century give the same account.[6] Three woods called 'Warrensgrove,' 'le Highfrith' and 'Wolsalewode' or 'Woolfall Wood' were amongst the manorial appurtenances from 1472 to 1708,[7] and the modern Broomhills Wood and Back Wood date from the early years of the 17th century, when the second of the two was also known as 'Ladywood.'[8] The height of the land rises from 300 ft. above the ordnance

---

[51] *Ann. Mon.* (Rolls Ser.), iii, 29 ; Harl. MS. 1885, fol. 30 d.

[52] Cur. Reg. R. 68, m. 11.

[53] *R. of Hugh of Wells* (Cant. and York Soc.), i, 101.

[54] Harl. MS. 1885, fol. 137 d.

[55] *Cal. Doc. of France*, 222–3.

[56] Harl. MS. 1885, fol. 31.

[57] Ibid. 137 d.

[58] *Ann. Mon.* (Rolls Ser.), iii, 285.

[59] *Pope Nich. Tax.* (Rec. Com.), 34. No later mention occurs of the priory's interest in Brickhill, but 'St. John's Close' late of Dunstable Priory belonged to the manor in 1596 (Fine R. 39 Eliz. pt. i, no. 49).

[60] *Cal. S. P. Dom.* 1655–6, pp. 34, 60; Lipscomb, op. cit. iv, 63.

[61] Inst. Bks. (P.R.O.).

[62] Ibid. ; Bacon, loc. cit. ; Lipscomb, op. cit. iv, 64–5.

[63] Linc. Epis. Reg. Memo. Wolsey and Atwater, fol. 88.

[1] Sheahan, *Hist. and Topog. of Bucks.* 503.

[2] Statistics from Bd. of Agric. (1905).

[3] Ibid.

[4] *V.C.H. Bucks.* i, 241, 242.

[5] *Cal. Inq. p.m.* (Edw. I), iii, 234.

[6] Ibid. (Edw. II), v, 329 ; Mins. Accts. (Gen. Ser.), bdle. 1145, no. 5.

[7] Mins. Accts. (Gen. Ser.), bdle. 759, no. 27 ; Hen. VII, no. 1476 ; Hen. VIII, no. 5808 ; Close, 8 Chas. I, pt. xxiii, no. 7 ; 5 Will. and Mary, pt. x, no. 29 ; Com. Pleas D. Enr. Hil. 10 Anne, m. 33.

[8] Exch. Dep. Spec. Com. 11 Jas. I, no. 7114 ; Pat. 13 Jas. I, pt. xviii, no. 6.

datum in the north-west and 400 ft. near the village to 500 ft. in the east of the parish.

Before the advent of the railway Little Brickhill derived importance from its highway, the ancient Watling Street, which runs south-east through the parish. The Roman station Magiovintum is now ascertained to have stood at Dropshort, a hamlet within its borders,[9] and in later times the situation of the village on the main road and at the extreme end of the county made it a convenient spot for the holding of assizes.[10] The village, which is built on a long hill and consists of a single street of inconsiderable houses, was a well-known posting town, and thirty coaches or more are said at one time to have passed daily through it.[11] References to the various inns which once flourished in Little Brickhill are not infrequent. One of these, ' Le Hertishorn,' settled by Humphrey Duke of Buckingham before 1446 on Humphrey Duke of Gloucester and others,[12] seems to reappear as ' the lord's hospice,' called ' le Harteshed ' until 1619,[13] its name surviving in an acre of meadow as late as 1693.[14] A new rent of 2d. paid in 1472 for ' the Bear'[15] was found thirty years later to be due for its licence and fixing a post with the sign.[16] Another inn, known by ' the sign of the White Horse ' in 1520,[17] appears in 1633 and 1708 in company with ' the Black Bull' and ' the Green Tree';[18] ' the Lion' and ' the George,' which gave rise to some litigation near the end of the 16th century,[19] may be ' the Red Lion' of 1640[20] and ' the George' of 1815.[21]

The church stands at the east end of the village. In its registers are preserved the names of certain persons executed on the heath just beyond. The old assize house was newly fronted before 1902, and then faced the sole survivor of the ancient inns of Little Brickhill.[22] The Wesleyan chapel dates from 1840.

In the south of the parish ' Battlehills' probably marks the site of the farm and lands called ' Battels,' which were the subject of a Chancery suit in 1570.[23]

Place-names are plentiful in the records of Little Brickhill. In addition to the woods already mentioned, there was a ' Schereveswode' in 1314,[24] a ' New Coppice' in 1614[25] and 1633,[26] a ' Nunwood' in the latter year and in 1708.[27] Some of many early inclosures made before 1798, when 600 acres of common and waste were inclosed,[28] are ' Backleys,' ' Bullingtons,' ' Lesser Biggins,' ' Buckmasters Biggins,'

and ' Timothies Close '[29] (xvii cent.) ; ' Teggs Close ' and ' Pannells Lane Close '[30] (xvii and xviii cent.) ; ' Bawleys' and ' Turfe Close '[31] (xviii cent.). The ' Cuttedemulne' of 1314[32] seems to reappear in the 17th century under the various forms of ' Cuttmilles,' ' Upper, Bushy, Furzin, and Wheaton Cutmills.'[33] To the 17th century belong ' Lady hills,' a tract of 53 acres with moor adjacent[34]; to the 18th century ' Dole,' ' West Dole' and ' Goose acre.'[35]

BOROUGH Little Brickhill as a settlement on Watling Street was a convenient stage for travellers, and since burgage tenure certainly existed there in the 15th century[36] it is possible that a small borough was formed in the 13th century during the time of John de Gatesden,[37] the king's physician, a considerable buyer and improver of land, or of Philip Lovel, the royal treasurer, whose ill deeds were noted by the Dunstable chronicler.[38] No early rolls are extant, and by the close of the 15th century the borough had been practically absorbed in the manor. The chief industry was that of victualling man and beast on the Chester Road, but we also hear of brick-making and the existence of a tile-house.

Instances of the assembling here of the commissioners for gaol delivery occur about 1284,[39] and in 1491,[39a] 1541 and 1542[40]; pleas of assizes were heard at Little Brickhill in 1432,[41] justices of the peace met in this place in 1452,[42] and in 1535 and 1537 there were sessions and assizes here.[43]

A fair on the vigil, feast and morrow of St. Mary Magdalene (22 July) was granted to John de Gatesden in 1228.[44] In 1257 the date was changed to the festival of St. Giles[45] (1 September), in 1318 to that of the Beheading of St. John the Baptist[46] (29 August). Henry VI granted Humphrey Duke of Buckingham two fairs in Little Brickhill, one on the vigil and feast of SS. Philip and James (1 May), the other on the vigil and feast of St. Luke.[47] (18 October). These, which were afterwards prolonged to the morrow of each feast, remained amongst the appurtenances of the manor from that time,[48] and were still held in 1862.[49] A Thursday market, which was included in all the royal grants of the fair or fairs, has long been discontinued.[50]

The liberties of gallows, pillory and cucking-stool with the assize of bread and ale belonged to this

[9] Proc. Soc. Antiq. xxiv, 35-7.
[10] See below.
[11] Rec. of Bucks. viii, 95 ; Lipscomb, Hist. and Antiq. of Bucks. iv, 70 ; Sheahan, op. cit. 504 ; Berks. Bucks. and Oxon. Arch. Journ. viii, 46 ; MSS. of Lord Middleton (Hist. MSS. Com.), 555.
[12] Chan. Inq. p.m. 38 & 39 Hen. VI, no. 39.
[13] Mins. Accts. (Gen. Ser.), bdle. 759, no. 27 ; Hen. VII, no. 1476 ; Hen. VIII, no. 5808 ; Exch. Dep. Trin. 17 Jas. I, no. 3.
[14] Close, 8 Chas. I, pt. xxiii, no. 7 ; 5 Will. and Mary, pt. ix, no. 29.
[15] Mins. Accts. (Gen. Ser.), bdle. 759, no. 27.
[16] Ibid. Hen. VII, no. 1476; Hen. VIII, no. 5808.
[17] Ibid. Hen. VIII, no. 5808.
[18] Close, 8 Chas. I, pt. xxiii, no. 7 ; Com. Pleas D. Enr. Hil. 10 Anne, m. 33.
[19] Ct. of Req. bdle. 126, no. 48.
[20] Cal. S. P. Dom. 1640-1, p. 177.

[21] Rec. of Bucks. viii, 96.
[22] Berks. Bucks. and Oxon. Arch. Journ. viii, 46.
[23] Chan. Proc. Eliz. Ss no. 10, 26.
[24] Cal. Inq. p.m. (Edw. II), v, 329.
[25] Exch. Dep. Spec. Com. 11 Jas. I, no. 7114.
[26] Close, 8 Chas. I, pt. xxxiii, no. 7.
[27] Ibid. ; Com. Pleas D. Enr. Hil. 10 Anne, m. 33.
[28] Inclosure Awards (Parl. Ret.), 11.
[29] Exch. Dep. Spec. Com. 11 Jas. I, no. 7114 ; Chan. Inq. p.m. (Ser. 2), dcxv, 124.
[30] Close, 5 Will. and Mary, pt. x, no. 29 ; Com. Pleas D. Enr. Hil. 10 Anne, m. 33.
[31] Com. Pleas D. Enr. Hil. 10 Anne, m. 33.
[32] Cal. Inq. p.m. (Edw. II), v, 329.
[33] Exch. Dep. Spec. Com. 11 Jas. I, no. 7114 ; Chan. Inq. p.m. (Ser. 2), dcxv, 124 ; Close, 5 Will. and Mary, pt. x, no. 29.
[34] Close, 8 Chas. I, pt. xxiii, no. 7.

[35] Com. Pleas D. Enr. Hil. 10 Anne, m. 33.
[36] Mins. Accts. (Gen. Ser.), bdle. 759, no. 27 ; cf. ibid. Hen. VII, no. 1476 ; Hen. VIII, no. 5808.
[37] See below as to the grant of a market and fair.
[38] Ann. Mon. (Rolls Ser.), iii, 210.
[39] Assize R. 68, m. 49 d.
[39a] Cal. Pat. 1485-94, p. 356.
[40] L. and P. Hen. VIII, xvi, g. 503 (49) ; xvii, g. 443 (40).
[41] Assize R. 1543, m. 11.
[42] Cal. Pat. 1446-52, p. 571.
[43] L. and P. Hen. VIII, viii, 278 ; xii (2), 275.
[44] Cal. Chart. R. 1226-57, p. 77.
[45] Ibid. 473.
[46] Ibid. 1300-26, p. 395.
[47] Chart. R. 1-20 Hen. VI, no. 19.
[48] L. and P. Hen. VIII, iii (2), g. 2145 (18) ; Chan. Inq. p.m. (Ser. 2), xlviii, 70 ; Pat. 13 Jas. I, pt. xviii, no. 6.
[49] Sheahan, loc. cit.
[50] Ibid.

manor in 1553,[51] and remained amongst its appurtenances for more than a hundred years later.[52] View of frankpledge and courts leet and baron, the former with several tithings, were held on behalf of the lord of the manor from the 14th to the 17th century,[53] and free warren, granted to Philip Lovel in 1257,[54] was still enjoyed by his successors in 1820.[55]

A manor of 5 hides in *BRICKHILL MANOR* which Blacheman, a man of Earl Tostig, had held before the Norman Conquest with power to sell, was owned by the Bishop of Lisieux in 1086.[56] At the same date another manor, consisting of only 1 hide, which had formerly belonged to Alwin, a man of Estan, without right of alienation from Estan's manor of Brickhill, was found amongst the lands of Odo, Bishop of Bayeux.[57] It is probable that after Odo's disgrace this was absorbed in the larger manor, and that the united holding was henceforward held as one fee of the Crown in chief by the service of defence of Dover Castle.[58]

The return of 1284–6, whilst betraying some uncertainty as to the actual tenant of Little Brickhill Manor, made it plain that it had hitherto been held in chief of the honour of Dover.[59] From 1295 until 1460 the overlordship descended with this honour,[60] though the connexion with both honour and castle, for the defence of which a certain annual payment was due,[61] was omitted from the return of 1346,[62] and again four years later.[63] In 1484 Little Brickhill Manor was described as parcel of the honour of Gloucester,[64] in 1523 as held of the king as of Dover Castle.[65] It was held of the Crown by knight service from 1590 to 1641,[66] when the last mention of the overlordship occurs.

The lands in Brickhill which belonged to the Bishops of Lisieux and Bayeux were held of them in 1086 by their sub-tenants Robert and Turstin respectively.[67] In the reign of Henry II Robert de Turnham, lord of the manor of Turnham in Kent,[68] owned Little Brickhill,[69] which afterwards came to his younger son Stephen.[70] Stephen, who was in the king's service in 1212,[71] died in or before 1214, when Mabel, the eldest of his daughters and co-heirs, declared herself willing to undertake the payment of her father's debts to the Crown if she were put in possession of his lands.[72] Her action seems to have induced her sisters to reconsider their refusal to share in this

burden, and in 1216 the lands in Brickhill once of Stephen de Turnham were granted to Adam de Bendeng and his wife Alice, Ralph de Fay and his wife Beatrice, and Mabel de Gatton.[73] In 1218 all the above, with Henry de Braiboef and his wife Clemence, and Roger de Leiburn and his wife Eleanor, were found to owe five palfreys for their shares in the manor of Brickhill, besides the debt to the king of Stephen de Turnham the father.[74] The whole seems to have been afterwards acquired by John de Gatesden, to whom eight years later Thomas de Bavelingham and his wife Mabel, presumably once Mabel de Gatton, sold the fifth of a knight's fee in Brickhill, to be held by him of Mabel and her heirs.[75] The tenure of John, lord until c. 1242,[76] seems to have ceased by 1253, when Nicholas de Wauncy and his wife Alice granted the manor of Little Brickhill to Philip Lovel.[77]

In 1257 or 1258 Philip transferred Little Brickhill to Richard Earl of Gloucester, who at Philip's death in 1258[78] put his son, another Philip Lovel, in possession of the manor for a few months and then took it to farm of him for ten years.[79] The earl had been dead about fifteen years,[80] when Gilbert Earl of Gloucester, his son and heir,[81] became absolute lord of Little Brickhill in 1277 by an exchange with John Lovel,[82] possibly another son of the elder Philip.[83] It was one of the manors which the earl surrendered to Edward I in 1290 and which were regranted in the same year to him and his wife Joan, the king's daughter.[84] At his death in 1295 Little Brickhill descended to his son and heir Gilbert,[85] who was slain at Bannockburn in 1314.[86] In the partition of the last earl's lands between his sisters and co-heirs this manor was assigned to Margaret wife of the younger Hugh Audley.[87] They held together until 1321, when the lands of Hugh Audley, one of the 'contrariants,' were in the king's hands,[88] and Hugh was lord after Margaret died until his death as Earl of Gloucester in 1347.[89]

CLARE. *Or three cheverons gules.*

---

[51] Pat. 6 Edw. VI, pt. v, m. 33.

[52] Close, 8 Chas. I, pt. xxiii, no. 7; Feet of F. Bucks. Trin. 4 Jas. II; Div. Co. Mich. 5 Will. and Mary.

[53] Mins. Accts. (Gen. Ser.), bdle. 1145, no. 5; Hen. VII, no. 1476; Pat. 13 Jas. I, pt. xviii, no. 6.

[54] *Cal. Chart. R.* 1226–57, p. 473.

[55] Recov. R. Mich. 1 Geo. IV, m. 141.

[56] *V.C.H. Bucks.* i, 241, 242.

[57] Ibid. 239. No other mention of Estan's manor of Brickhill occurs in Domesday Book.

[58] *V.C.H. Bucks.* i, 211; Hasted, *Hist. and Surv. of Kent*, ii, 493–4; Lipscomb, op. cit. iv, 70, 71.

[59] *Feud. Aids*, i, 82.

[60] *Cal. Inq. p.m.* (Edw. I), iii, 234; Chan. Inq. p.m. 38 & 39 Hen. VI, no. 59.

[61] *Cal. Inq. p.m.* (Edw. I), iii, 234; Chan. Inq. p.m. 35 Edw. I, no. 47; Mins. Accts. (Gen. Ser.), bdle. 1145, no. 5.

[62] *Feud. Aids*, i, 129.

[63] *Cal. Pat.* 1348–50, p. 570.

[64] Ibid. 1476–85, p. 420.

[65] Chan. Inq. p.m. (Ser. 2), xl, 7.

[66] Ibid. ccxxviii, 90; dcxv, 124; Pat. 13 Jas. I, pt. xviii, no. 6.

[67] *V.C.H. Bucks.* i, 239, 242.

[68] Hasted, op. cit. ii, 494.

[69] Dugdale, *Mon.* vi, 412–13.

[70] Ibid.; Dugdale, *Baronage*, i, 662–3. Probably Stephen inherited directly from his father, as his elder brother Robert was a witness of his confirmation of his father's grant to Combwell Priory (Dugdale, *Mon.* vi, 413).

[71] *Rot. Lit. Claus.* (Rec. Com.), i, 121.

[72] Ibid. 168.

[73] Ibid. 274. Ralph de Fay was husband of one of the daughters of Stephen de Turnham in 1214 (ibid. 141*b*).

[74] Pipe R. 2 Hen. III, m. 6 d.

[75] Feet of F. Bucks. 10 Hen. III, no. 7.

[76] *Testa de Nevill* (Rec. Com.), 244*b*; *Rot. Lit. Claus.* (Rec. Com.), ii, 180; *Cal. Chart. R.* 1226–57, pp. 265–6.

[77] Feet of F. Bucks. 37 Hen. III, no. 7.

[78] *Ann. Mon.* (Rolls Ser.), iii, 210.

[79] *Cal. Inq. p.m.* (Hen. III), i, 161.

[80] G.E.C. *Peerage*, iv, 41.

[81] Ibid.

[82] Feet of F. Div. Co. 5 Edw. I, no. 65.

[83] *V.C.H. Beds.* iii, 422.

[84] *Cal. Chart. R.* 1257–1300, p. 350; *Cal. Fine R.* 1272–1307, p. 275; *Cal. Pat.* 1281–92, pp. 351, 360; *Cal. Close*, 1288–96, p. 151.

[85] *Cal. Inq. p.m.* (Edw. I), iii, 234; Chan. Inq. p.m. 35 Edw. I, no. 47. Robert de la Warde and his tenants held in 1302 (*Feud. Aids*, i, 103).

[86] *Cal. Inq. p.m.* (Edw. II), v, 329; *Cal. Close*, 1313–18, p. 414; G.E.C. *Peerage*, ii, 268.

[87] Chan. Misc. bdle. 9, no. 23; *Cal. Pat.* 1317–21, p. 531.

[88] Mins. Accts. (Gen. Ser.), bdle. 1145, no. 5; Anct. Ext. (Exch. K.R.), no. 32 (2).

[89] *Feud. Aids*, i, 129; Chan. Inq. p.m. 21 Edw. III (1st nos.), no. 59.

The Audleys had also obtained Easington Manor, Chilton parish [90] (q.v.), with which Little Brickhill henceforward descended through the Staffords to Humphrey Duke of Buckingham, killed at the battle of Northampton in 1460.[91] A grant of Little Brickhill to his widow Anne made by Henry VI in the same year [92] was confirmed by Edward IV in 1461.[93] She held alone in 1464,[94] in 1468 with her second husband Sir Walter Blount, Lord Mountjoy.[95] It was perhaps after her death in 1480 [96] that Richard III gave this manor to the Dean and canons of the free chapel of St. Mary of Barking, London,[97] a gift which was never carried into effect.

After the execution in 1483 of Henry Duke of Buckingham, grandson and heir of the last duke,[98] Little Brickhill was forfeited to the Crown, and Richard III made a life grant of its stewardship to his esquire, Thomas Fowler.[99] A receiver was appointed in the following year on behalf of the Crown for this manor,[100] which was afterwards restored to Edward Duke of Buckingham with Easington (q.v.). The two manors passed from the Marnys to the Carys, Henry Cary obtaining royal licence in 1553 to alienate Little Brickhill to Robert Brocas.[1] Four years later he was succeeded by his son Bernard Brocas,[2] who, being in money difficulties, leased the manorhouse to William Hamond and certain lands to other lessees.[3] His lease of the

BROCAS. *Sable a leopard rampant or.*

whole manor to his brother William Brocas, on condition that William should discharge his debts,[4] seems to have been made before or in 1583, in the spring of which year he mortgaged Little Brickhill to Thomas Wren and John Bale.[5] In the following autumn he was sued in Chancery for payment of his debt to the late Peter Tichborne.[6] He and his wife Anne settled Little Brickhill on their son Pexall early in 1585,[7] William Brocas surrendering his rights to his nephew for the sum of £1,000.[8] On Bernard's death in 1589,[9] however, Thomas Cheyne, his son-in-law, who was found to be enjoying the issues of the manor by lease from Bernard and Anne,[10] paid £300 to William Brocas for redemp-

tion of the earlier lease.[11] Thomas was then bought out by William Washborne, husband of Bernard's widow Anne, who died shortly after her second marriage. After her death William Washborne was not only evicted by her son Pexall,[12] who had obtained pardon within six weeks of his father's death for acquiring Little Brickhill without licence,[13] but was arrested for the non-payment of an annuity from the profits of the lease of which he had been deprived to Anne Persey, widowed daughter of his late wife.[14] The history of Pexall Brocas's tenure is another record of debts. In or before 1601 Little Brickhill was extended to satisfy his creditors [15]; it was redeemed by Pexall Brocas, then a knight, in 1611,[16] but was in the king's hands three years later for £500 owing to the Crown.[17] In 1615 the manor was granted to William Jervis in consideration of money paid to him by Pexall,[18] on whose behalf four years later an inquiry was made as to rents raised after that date.[19] Sir Pexall leased Little Brickhill to Sir Robert Cotton and others in 1628 [20] and died seised two years later.[21] His son and heir Thomas,[22] in conjunction with his mother Margaret Brocas [23] and his wife Elizabeth, sold the manor to Anthony Abdy, alderman of London, in 1633.[24] In 1638 Anthony and his wife Abigail settled it on the marriage of their son Thomas with Mary daughter of Luke Corsellis,[25] who entered into possession on Anthony's death in 1640.[26] Thomas, who received a baronetage in 1641,[27] held Little Brickhill until his death in 1686,[28] when he was succeeded by his son and heir Anthony,[29] who with his wife Mary sold Little Brickhill in 1693 to Charles, afterwards Sir Charles, Duncombe.[30] He settled it on himself and his 'first son to be begotten' in July 1708,[31] but died unmarried and intestate three years later.[32] His property descended to his nephews, Anthony son and heir of his brother Anthony Duncombe, and Thomas son and heir of his sister Ursula by her husband Thomas Brown.[33] It would seem that Little Brickhill ultimately fell to the share of Thomas, who assumed the surname of Duncombe, since Thomas his son and heir [34] was lord in 1764.[35] It came afterwards by marriage with Frances daughter of the second Thomas Duncombe [36] to Sir George Henry Rose, lord in 1796 [37] and 1820.[38] He was succeeded in 1855 by his eldest son, Sir Hugh Henry Rose. He was created Lord Strathnairn of Strathnairn and Jhansi in 1866 for his services in the Indian

[90] See also *Cal. Pat.* 1348–50, p. 19.

[91] Chan. Inq. p.m. 38 & 39 Hen. VI, no. 59.

[92] *Cal. Pat.* 1452–61, pp. 639, 645–6.

[93] Ibid. 1461–7, p. 6.

[94] Mins. Accts. (Gen. Ser.), bdle. 1117, no. 11.

[95] *Cal. Pat.* 1467–77, p. 72

[96] G.E.C. op. cit. ii, 63.

[97] De Banco R. Mich. 4 Hen. VII, m. 305.

[98] G.E.C. op. cit. ii, 64.

[99] *Cal. Pat.* 1476–85, pp. 411, 429.

[100] Ibid. 453.

[1] Pat. 6 Edw. VI, pt. v, m. 33 ; Feet of F. Bucks. Hil. 7 Edw. VI.

[2] Chan. Inq. p.m. (Ser. 2), cxi, 2.

[3] Chan. Proc. (Ser. 2), bdle. 219, no. 15.

[4] Ct. of Req. bdle. 93, no. 25.

[5] Feet of F. Bucks. East. 25 Eliz.

[6] Chan. Proc. (Ser. 2), bdle. 219, no. 15.

[7] Feet of F. Div. Co. East. 27 Eliz.

[8] Ct. of Req. bdle. 48, no. 32.

[9] Chan. Inq. p.m. (Ser. 2), ccxxviii, 90.

[10] Ibid.

[11] Ct. of Req. bdle. 93, no. 25.

[12] Ibid.

[13] Pat. 31 Eliz. pt. xiv, no. 26.

[14] Ct. of Req. bdle. 93, no. 25.

[15] Ibid. bdle. 76, no. 40.

[16] Add. Chart. 39946 (13).

[17] Exch. Dep. Spec. Com. 11 Jas. I, no. 7114.

[18] Pat. 13 Jas. I, pt. xviii, no. 6.

[19] Exch. Dep. Trin. 17 Jas. I, no. 3.

[20] Cott. Chart. xxiii, 29a.

[21] Chan. Inq. p.m. (Ser. 2), cccclxxv, 126.

[22] Ibid.

[23] Berry, *Hants Gen.* 91.

[24] Close, 8 Chas. I, pt. xxiii, no. 7 ; Feet of F. Div. Co. Hil. 8 Chas. I ; Recov. R. East. 9 Chas. I, m. 35.

[25] Feet of F. Div. Co. Hil. 13 Chas. I ; Chan. Inq. p.m. (Ser. 2), dcxv, 124.

[26] Chan. Inq. p.m. (Ser. 2), dcxv, 124.

[27] G.E.C. *Baronetage*, ii, 98, 99.

[28] Ibid. See also Feet of F. Div. Co. East. 19 Chas. I ; Mich. 34 Chas. II.

[29] G.E.C. loc. cit. ; Feet of F. Bucks. Trin. 4 Jas. II.

[30] Close, 5 Will. and Mary, pt. x, m. 29 ; Feet of F. Div. Co. Mich. 5 Will. and Mary.

[31] Com. Pleas D. Enr. Hil. 10 Anne, m. 33.

[32] Burke, *Hist. of the Commoners*, i, 151 ; P.C.C. Admon, 1711.

[33] Burke, loc. cit. ; Com. Pleas Recov. R. East. 5 Geo. III, m. 26.

[34] Burke, loc. cit.

[35] Feet of F. Div. Co. East. 4 Geo. III ; Recov. R. East. 4 Geo. III, m. 36.

[36] G.E.C. *Peerage*, vii, 291–2.

[37] Priv. Act, 36 Geo. III, cap. 38.

[38] Recov. R. Mich. 1 Geo. IV, m. 141. George Pitt Rose, who also had rights here in 1820 (Recov. R. Trin. 1 Geo. IV, m. 43), was probably a younger brother of Sir George Henry Rose (Burke, *Landed Gentry* [1871]).

Mutiny, and died unmarried in 1885.[39] Little Brick-hill was inherited by Admiral the Honourable George Henry Douglas and passed in 1888 to Lieut.-Col. Alexander Finlay, the present owner.

A messuage which belonged to the manor from 1277 to 1314[40] may be the capital messuage of 1324,[41] which had probably fallen into decay before 1503, when amongst other houses rebuilt on the site of the manor was one dwelling-house of two bays with two cross chambers at each end, covered with tiles.[42] This was probably the capital messuage, called ' Little Brickhill ' or ' the manor-house ' near the end of the 16th century ;[43] the garden is mentioned in 1633.[44] Dovecotes varying in number from one to three were appurtenances from 1321 to 1820,[45] and there was a horse-mill in 1520.[46]

The church of ST. MARY MAGDA-CHURCH LENE consists of a chancel measuring internally 27 ft. by 17 ft. 6 in., south chapel 15 ft. by 12 ft., nave 48 ft. by 18 ft., south aisle 12 ft. wide, south porch, west tower 7 ft. 6 in. square and small chamber south of the tower. It is built of rubble with stone dressings ; the roof of the porch is covered with tiles and the other roofs are slated.

A church, probably built a little before the middle of the 12th century, when the advowson was granted to the priory of Combwell in Kent, consisted apparently of the present nave and a chancel, but the only detail of that period now remaining is a fragment of the north doorway. A transeptal chapel was added on the north side of the nave about 1330 and a few years later the chancel was rebuilt. At some time in the 15th century the tower was built at the north end of the west wall and towards the end of the century a chamber, roofed continuously with the nave, was added on the south side of the tower, giving it the appearance of being built within the north-west angle of the nave. The south chapel and aisle and the south porch were added about a century later. In 1703 the north transeptal chapel and part of the chancel were blown down ; the former has not been rebuilt, but the arch (now blocked) opening from it to the nave, and a piscina set in what is now the external face of the north wall of the nave, still remain. The fabric of the church was at this time repaired, and a second restoration was undertaken in 1864, when the chancel was practically rebuilt.

All the windows of the chancel are modern ; the only ancient feature is a four-centred arch to the chapel at the west end of the south wall, which probably dates from the end of the 16th century. The pointed chancel arch, however, is of the mid-14th century and has two chamfered orders, the outer continuous and the inner supported by semi-octagonal responds with moulded capitals and bases. The south chapel has been considerably restored ; there is an original four-centred arch to the aisle on the west, a restored doorway and a modern window on the south, and a restored three-light window on the east. A trefoiled piscina, dating probably from the late 13th century and now without a bowl, has been reset very low in the south wall, and in the east wall are a moulded bracket and a locker.

On the south side of the nave there is a late 16th-century arcade of four pointed arches, supported by octagonal pillars and responds with moulded capitals and bases, and at the south-east is a trefoiled piscina of the 14th century with a circular bowl, doubtless for the nave altar. On the east wall are two plain corbels which supported the rood beam, and there is a head corbel at the east end of each of the north and south walls. At the east end of the north wall is the blocked arch to the destroyed north chapel, which now forms a recess. It dates from the first half of the 14th century and has a pointed head and responds with moulded capitals and bases. In the wall outside, formerly inside the chapel, is a trefoiled piscina of the same period. There are three windows in the north wall, a modern one set in the blocking of the chapel arch, and two restored square-headed 15th-century windows, the western of two and the other of three lights. The north doorway, now blocked, has a depressed arch under a square head and dates from the 16th century ; in the walling outside to the west of it is a fragment of a round arch which was probably the head of the original door-way. At the north end of the west wall is a narrow and lofty 15th-century arch opening to the ground stage of the tower, and to the south of it is a pointed doorway to the chamber adjoining the tower on the south, which is lighted by two loopholes on the west.

All the windows of the south aisle are modern, but the pointed south doorway is of about 1280 and has been reset in its present position. A large blocked window with a four-centred head can be traced in the walling west of the doorway. The south porch has a four-centred archway and is lighted from either side by a restored window of two trefoiled lights in a square head.

The tower is of three stages, with massive western buttresses, and is surmounted by an embattled parapet. In the west wall of the ground stage is a partially renewed 15th-century window of two cinquefoiled lights with tracery in a four-centred head. The second stage is lighted from the north by a cinquefoiled light with a square external head and label ; the windows of the bell-chamber are modern.

The font has a plain circular bowl dating probably from the 13th century, and a modern, or possibly recut, stem and base. There is a 17th-century communion table in the south aisle, and an alms shovel dated 1664 is preserved in the south chapel. On the east wall of the aisle is a wood-framed monument to William Benett, who died in 1658.

The tower contains a ring of three bells : the treble, inscribed ' ЯЧCI na an na an an na an,' the smalls in black letter, probably dates from the 16th century ; the second, inscribed ' Ad Convocandum cœtvm 1639 I.K,' is by James Keene ; and the tenor is inscribed ' Chandler made me 1669.' There is also a small bell, probably of the 17th century, but with no inscription.

[39] G.E.C. loc. cit.

[40] Feet of F. Div. Co. 5 Edw. I, no. 65 ; Cal. Inq. p.m. (Edw. I), iii, 234 ; (Edw. II), v, 329.

[41] Anct. Ext. (Exch. K.R.), no. 32 (2).

[42] Mins. Accts. Hen. VII, no. 1476.

[43] Ct. of Req. bdle. 48, no. 32 ; Chan. Proc. (Ser. 2), bdle. 219, no. 15.

[44] See Close, 8 Chas. I, pt. xxiii, no. 7.

[45] Mins. Accts. (Gen. Ser.), bdle. 1145, no. 5 ; Pat. 31 Eliz. pt. xiv, m. 26 ; Recov. R. Mich. 1 Geo. IV, m. 141.

[46] Mins. Accts. Hen. VIII, no. 5808.

LITTLE BRICKHILL CHURCH FROM THE WEST

Broughton Church from the South-East

Broughton Church: The Interior looking East

The plate consists of a silver chalice and paten and a plated flagon and salver.

The registers date from 1559.

ADVOWSON The church, which has probably always been dedicated in honour of St. Mary Magdalene,[47] was given by Robert de Turnham to the priory of Combwell, which he founded in the reign of Henry II.[48] In or before the early years of the 13th century it was appropriated and a vicarage was ordained, which originally consisted of the altarage, lesser tithes, 11 acres of land and a competent manse.[49] This provision seems to have been found insufficient, and in the early years of the reign of Henry VIII the vicar claimed the tithes of corn in accordance with an agreement said to have been made a century before between the predecessors of himself and the present prior, by which the rights of the priory had been commuted for a pension of 20s.[50] The parsonage of Little Brickhill with its glebe lands and rents was reckoned amongst the possessions of this house in 1535,[51] and remained in the Crown after its suppression in that year[52] until 1537, when it was included in a grant of the site of Combwell Priory and its possessions to Thomas Culpepper.[53] In 1542 this advowson with other property once of Combwell, which had reverted to the Crown on the attainder of Thomas, was granted to Sir John Gage, Comptroller of the Household,[54] whose son and heir-apparent Edward, with Sir John Baker, received the reversion rather more than six months later.[55] An exchange shortly afterwards effected between Sir John Gage and Cranmer vested the church of Little Brick-hill in the see of Canterbury,[56] the primate and his successors being afterwards exonerated from the rent reserved,[57] which had been granted to Sir John in 1546.[58] It was a peculiar of the archbishop until 1852,[59] since which year the living has been in the gift of the Bishop of Oxford.[60]

There is said to have been an ancient chantry chapel on the north side of the church.[61] Possibly this was served by the chaplain of the lord of the manor, who in 1503 received 66s. 8d. a year.[62]

CHARITIES The following charities are administered under a scheme of the Charity Commissioners of 24 August 1901, namely :

1. Charity of Anthony Abdy, founded by an indenture 10 April 1699. The property originally consisted of ten cottages with small gardens, situate in Little Brickhill. It was sold in 1872, and the proceeds invested in £150 13s. 4d. consols. The endowment, augmented by accumulations of income, now consists of £333 11s. 5d. consols. The sum of £208 consols, part thereof, was in 1904 set aside to provide £5 4s. a year for bread, to be called 'Abdy's Charity for the Poor.' The remainder of the stock, £125 11s. 5d. consols, entitled 'Abdy's Educational Foundation,' producing £3 2s. 8d. yearly, is applied for educational purposes.

2. The church and poor charity, comprised in an indenture 12 April 1705, trust fund, £906 0s. 4d. consols, arising from the sales in 1873 of a dwelling-house and three cottages and in 1888 of about 6 acres of land. One moiety of the stock, £453 0s. 2d., forms the endowment of the ecclesiastical charity, the income, £11 6s. 4d., being applicable towards the repair and ornaments of the church, and the other moiety constitutes the poor charity, the income of £11 6s. 4d. being distributed in coal.

3. Charity of Charles Penrose, founded by will proved in the P.C.C. 27 October 1856, trust fund, £100 consols. The income of £2 10s. is applied in the gift of blankets.

4. The poor's allotment originally consisted of 15 a. 3 r. 18 p. at Little Brickhill, allotted under the Inclosure Award of 1798. The land was sold in 1901, and the proceeds invested in £739 15s. 7d. Metropolitan 3 per cent. consolidated stock, producing £22 4s. yearly. The income, together with that belonging to the poor charity, is distributed in coal to about thirty-three recipients.

The several sums of stock are held by the official trustees.

An unknown donor's charity, being an annuity of £5, issuing out of land in Great and Little Brick-hill, is applied for the benefit of the school.

BROUGHTON

Brotone (xi cent.) ; Bruchton, Bruhtone, Bruttone, Burwton (xiii cent.).

Broughton lies on the edge of the county, bordering Bedfordshire, and covers 936 acres, of which about three-quarters is grass land.[1] The south and west boundaries are formed by tributaries of the River Ouse. The land is about 200 ft. above the ordnance datum, and is liable to floods along the banks of the streams.

The soil is mixed, the subsoil being gravel and clay. The chief crops grown are wheat, barley, oats and roots.

The road from Newport Pagnell to Woburn runs through the parish from north-west to south-east, and crosses two tributaries of the Ouse by Kingston Bridge and Broughton Bridge. The village lies at the northern end of this road, 3 miles south-east

---

[47] It was given as St. Mary of Brickhill to St. Mary Magdalene of Combwell (Dugdale, *Mon.* vi, 413), and the original fair was on the feast of St. Mary Magdalene (*Cal. Chart. R.* 1226–57, p. 77).

[48] Dugdale, *Mon.* vi, 412–13. At the close of the 13th century the heirs of Stephen de Turnham were said to be the rightful owners of the church (*Feud. Aids*, i, 82).

[49] *Liber Antiquus Hugonis Wells* (ed. A. Gibbons), 12 ; *R. of Hugh of Wells* (Cant. and York Soc.), ii, 70.

[50] Early Chan. Proc. bdle. 583, no. 76. This agreement, if ever made, was not observed. The great tithes belonged to the Archbishop of Canterbury in 1796 (Priv. Act, 36 Geo. III, cap. 38).

[51] *Valor Eccl.* (Rec. Com.), i, 87.

[52] Dugdale, *Mon.* vi, 413.

[53] Ibid. ; *L. and P. Hen. VIII*, xii (2), g. 1150 (31).

[54] *L. and P. Hen. VIII*, xvii, g. 285 (11).

[55] Ibid. g. 1154 (88).

[56] Ibid. xviii (1), 66 (cap. 37) ; Memo. R. (Exch. L.T.R.), East. 14 Eliz. m. 90.

[57] Memo. R. (Exch. L.T.R.), East. 14 Eliz. m. 90.

[58] *L. and P. Hen. VIII*, xxi (1), g. 1537 (24).

[59] *Cal. Com. for Comp.* 67 ; Inst. Bks. (P.R.O.) ; Bacon, *Liber Regis*, 498, 501, 511 ; *Clerical Guide* ; *Clergy List*.

[60] *Clergy List*, 1853–1915.

[61] *Berks. Bucks. and Oxon. Arch. Journ.* viii, 46 ; Lipscomb, op. cit. iv, 75.

[62] Mins. Accts. Hen. VII, no. 1476.

[1] Statistics from Bd. of Agric. (1905).

from Newport Pagnell terminal station on a branch from Wolverton of the London and North Western railway and 3½ miles north-west of Woburn Sands station on the London and North Western railway.

At the northern end of the village are the church, the rectory, and Broughton House, the residence of Lieut.-Col. Arthur William Hervey Good, the lord of the manor. The present house is modern, nothing now remaining of the former manor-house.[2] South of Broughton House is the school, built in 1864, and closed by the Education Department, the children now attending school at Milton Keynes. A messuage or farm-house called the 'Red Lion Inn' was mentioned in the will of Thomas Duncombe dated 13 October 1672.[3] In the north of the parish is Broughton Barn Farm, and in the east Broughton Field Barn Farm. Other farms are Brook Farm, south of the church, King's Head Farm, a little further south, and Broughton Lodge Farm in the extreme north-east.

The parish was inclosed by Act of Parliament in 1748.[4]

Among place-names have been found : the Layes, Wood Hall Holme, Little Fin Meadow, Little Wat Grove, Long Lawrence, Barnard's Fen, Little Horcroft, Amedon's Close, heretofore the Bowling Green,[5] the Taplash, Hither Forge Furlong[6] (xviii cent.).

MANORS In the time of Edward the Confessor 4 hides at BROUGHTON were held as a manor by Oswi, a man of Alric son of Goding, and in 1086 this land was included in the possessions of Walter Giffard.[7] This manor, as that of Great Missenden[8] (q.v.), was appendant to that part of the honour of Giffard which descended in the earldoms of Gloucester, Stafford and Buckingham,[9] a counterclaim being made by Aymer de Valence, Earl of Pembroke, and by the Talbots in the 14th and 15th centuries respectively. At the attainder of the Duke of Buckingham in 1521[10] the manor escheated to the Crown, which, however, had claimed it in 1508.[11] In 1623 the overlordship was unknown.[12]

Hugh de Bolebec, the Domesday tenant,[13] was succeeded here as in Whitchurch by the Earls of Oxford, but the manor was subinfeudated probably soon after the Survey,[14] and the mesne lordship thus created was vested in the earls as late as 1460.[15]

The ownership in fee was obtained by a family which took its name from the place, and a Robert de Broughton and William his son are mentioned as lords of Broughton in a confirmatory charter of

1151–4.[16] Reference to a later William, probably son of the last-named William, occurs in 1211.[17] He had been succeeded by 1245 by his son Robert,[18] whose son Matthew[19] was in possession in 1276.[20] By 1284 the property had passed to his son Ralf,[21] who was still alive in 1302.[22] In 1306 Ralf de Broughton the younger, probably his son,[23] and Joan his wife demised to Robert son of the late Ralf de Mangehoo of Marston Moretaine (Bedfordshire),[23a] for 20 marks sterling and 2 marks yearly, a good and suitable chamber for him to live in in their court in the vill of Broughton, maintenance in food and drink, and the maintenance of a horse in hay and grass.[24] Ralf de Broughton died before 1316, when his widow Joan held alone in Broughton.[25] His son Robert levied a fine of lands in the neighbouring parish of Milton Keynes[26] and with his wife Paulina dealt with lands in Crawley in 1327.[27] He is mentioned in connexion with Broughton in 1331.[28] Three years later he conveyed the reversion of this property, now called BROUGHTON MANOR, after the death of Joan, at that time wife of William Passelewe of Wavendon, to Philip Aylesbury for life, and then to his son Thomas in tail-male.[29] In 1338 Philip Aylesbury acquired Joan Passelewe's life interest in return for a yearly rent of 10 silver marks.[30] He is therefore returned as the lord of Broughton in 1346,[31] and his grandson, Sir John Aylesbury,[32] died seised of the manor in 1409.[33] He was also lord of Drayton Beauchamp Manor (q.v.), with which Broughton descended until the death of Hugh Aylesbury in 1423, when, like Milton Keynes (q.v.), it must have been assigned to Eleanor wife of Sir Humphrey Stafford of Grafton (Northamptonshire), and sister and co-heir of Hugh's father John,[34] since Humphrey Stafford, lord of Milton Keynes, was also seised of Broughton at his death in 1545.[35] His grandson Humphrey sold Broughton in 1573 to Thomas Duncombe,[36] second son of William Duncombe of Great Brickhill.[37] Thomas Duncombe settled the manor on his second son Francis in 1590,[38] and confirmed the settlement by his will, dated 21 November 1595.[39] He died at Great Brickhill on 4 February 1595–6,[40] and was succeeded at Broughton by Francis, who was dealing with the manor in 1599.[41] On 23 November 1619 Francis settled it on his son and heir Thomas on his marriage with Sarah daughter of Thomas Draper, and died on 9 November 1622.[42] Thomas Duncombe, who had joined his father in a settlement of the manor in 1621,[43] settled it on his wife Sarah in 1623,[44] and by his will of 8 May 1632,

---

[2] Sheahan, *Hist. and Topog. of Bucks.* 507. Broughton, the original manorhouse, was occupied by lessees after the purchase in 1748 of the manor by Barnaby Backwell, who lived 'wholly in London,' according to Cole (Add. MS. 5839, p. 78).

[3] P.C.C. 43 Pye.

[4] *Rec. of Bucks.* (Bibliotheca Buckinghamiensis), vi, 72.

[5] Recov. R. D. Enr. Mich. 22 Geo. II, m. 73.

[6] Ibid. Hil. 15 Geo. III, m. 85.

[7] *V.C.H. Bucks.* i, 252.

[8] Ibid. ii, 348.

[9] *Feud. Aids*, i, 83. Chan. Inq. p.m. 38 & 39 Hen. VI, no. 59.

[10] G.E.C. *Peerage*, ii, 64.

[11] Chan. Inq. p.m. (Ser. 2), xxi, 115.

[12] Ibid. ccccvii, 106.

[13] *V.C.H. Bucks.* i, 252.

[14] *Testa de Nevill* (Rec. Com.), 247.

[15] Chan. Inq. p.m. 10 Ric. II, no. 38 ;

4 Hen. IV, no. 41 ; 38 & 39 Hen. VI, no. 59.   [16] *Cal. Doc. of France*, 444.

[17] Feet of F. case 14, file 9.

[18] Ibid. case 15, file 27, no. 8.

[19] *Visit. of Beds.* (Harl. Soc.), 13. A plea of 1380 gives the name of Matthew's father as William, not Robert, living, 1 Edw. I (De Banco R. 480, m. 569 d.).

[20] *Hund. R.* (Rec. Com.), i, 41.

[21] *Feud. Aids*, i, 83 ; *Visit. of Beds.* loc. cit.

[22] *Feud. Aids*, i, 104.

[23] Wrottesley, *Ped. from Plea R.* 140, 192.

[23a] His family evidently had the estate afterwards known as Mangehoo Manor (see *V.C.H. Beds.* iii, 311).

[24] *Cal. Close*, 1302–7, p. 460.

[25] *Feud. Aids*, i, 110.

[26] Feet of F. Bucks. 15 Edw. II, no. 4.

[27] De Banco R. Trin. 1 Edw. III, m. 27.

[28] Feet of F. case 19, file 78, no. 14.

[29] Ibid. file 80, no. 1.

[30] Ibid. file 82, no. 1.

[31] *Feud. Aids*, i, 130.

[32] Chan. Inq. p.m. 15 Hen. VI, no. 50.

[33] Ibid. 11 Hen. IV, no. 9.

[34] Ibid. 2 Hen. VI, no. 21; 15 Hen. VI, no. 50.

[35] Ibid. (Ser. 2), lxxiv, 5.

[36] Feet of F. Bucks. Mich. 15 Eliz.

[37] Memo. R. (Exch. L.T.R.), Mich. 17 Eliz. m. 43.

[38] Chan. Inq. p.m. (Ser. 2), ccxlvi, 110.

[39] P.C.C. 34 Drake.

[40] Chan. Inq. p.m. (Ser. 2), ccxlvi, 110.

[41] Feet of F. Bucks. Hil. 41 Eliz.

[42] Chan. Inq. p.m. (Ser. 2), ccccvii, 106.

[43] Recov. R. Hil. 18 Jas. I, m. 121.

[44] Ibid. East. 21 Jas. I, m. 67 ; Feet of F. Div. Co. Hil. 20 Jas. I ; Chan. Inq. p.m. (Ser. 2), dxxv, 123.

dying four days later.[45] He was succeeded by his son Thomas, who was dealing with the manor in 1657[46] and died in 1672,[47] leaving his manor-house to his wife Margaret for one year and the reversion to Francis, his son and heir by his first wife.[48] Francis suffered a recovery of the manor in 1675[49] and died in 1720.[50] His only son Francis died unmarried on 14 March 1746-7.[51] His sister Anne had married John Robinson of Cransley, Northamptonshire,[52] by whom she had a son John, to whom his uncle left all his real and personal estate in trust to pay debts and legacies.[53] In 1748 John Robinson and his two sisters, Frances wife of Thomas Willis of Walton, and Susan wife of Philip Barton, rector of Sherington, legatees named under the will, with their husbands, conveyed the manor, the manor-house commonly known by the name of Broughton, and all other property of the late Francis Duncombe in Broughton, for £21,200 to Barnaby Backwell, banker, of London and of Tyringham.[54] From Barnaby Backwell the manor passed in 1754 to his only son Tyringham,[55] who in 1775 barred the entail on the manor[56] and died childless. Broughton then passed to his sister Elizabeth, who in 1778 married William Mackworth Praed of Trevethoe in Lelant, Cornwall.[57] The manor was inherited by her son James Backwell Praed,[58] who died on 13 January 1837,[59] and was succeeded by his son William Backwell Praed, J.P. and D.L. for Buckinghamshire and Cornwall, Sheriff of Buckinghamshire in 1860. On 6 August 1859 he assumed by royal licence the surname and arms of Tyringham in lieu of his patronymic.[60] He built the school in Broughton in 1864, and died on 29 November 1870.[61] His son Roger William Giffard Tyringham, born in the year of his father's death, sold the manor in 1909 to Lieut.-Col. A. W. H. Good, the present owner.[62]

PRAED. *Azure six molets argent.*

When Robert de Broughton alienated Broughton Manor to Philip Aylesbury in 1334 he appears to have retained certain lands there which united with the fee held of the honour of Huntingdon (see below) to form *BROUGHTON MANOR*, so called in the early 15th century. References, however, to members of the family in Broughton during the next 150 years are scanty, and chiefly occur in connexion with the advowson, which they retained. John, son of the above Robert, had succeeded his father by 1351,[63] and in 1393 put forward a claim to a messuage in Broughton settled by his great-grandfather Ralf on Simon de Mersheton[64] (? Water Eaton). He was buried in Broughton Church in 1403, his wife Agnes having predeceased him in 1399.[65] His son and heir John married Mary daughter and heir of Thomas Pever of Toddington (Bedfordshire),[66] and after his death, c. 1408, she became the wife of Richard Lord St. Maur, who held this manor in her right at his death early in the following year.[67] John Broughton, the son and heir of Mary Pever by her first husband, in 1410 brought an action to recover lands in the neighbouring parish of Crawley, but the suit was adjourned until 1427-8 on account of his minority.[68] He was twenty-two when he succeeded his maternal grandfather Thomas Pever in 1429,[69] and died in 1489, leaving Robert the son of his deceased son John as his heir.[70] Robert died in 1506, leaving a widow Katherine and a young son John,[71] who did not survive his father many years, and left Broughton at his death in January 1517-18 to his son John, then aged five.[72] The latter died in 1530,[73] and was succeeded by his sisters, Katherine wife of William Lord Howard of Effingham,[74] and Anne, afterwards wife of Sir Thomas Cheney of the Isle of Sheppey.[75] William Lord Howard of Effingham was holding half the manor, evidently in right of his wife, at his attainder in 1542, half the site being leased the next year for twenty-one years to Thomas Garrett at 26s. 8d. rent and 12d. increase.[76] The Howards' daughter Agnes or Ann married William Paulet, Lord St. John,[77] and acquired the Cheneys' interest before 1573, in which year the Paulets conveyed the whole of the manor to Thomas Duncombe.[78] He acquired at the same date the Staffords' manor of Broughton, and the two manors henceforward descend as one.

A hide in Broughton, held as a manor, was included in the Countess Judith's land at the date of the Domesday Survey.[79] Her lands afterwards formed the honour of Huntingdon, to which this hide in Broughton was attached,[80] and which descended in the families of Hastings,[81] Latimer,[82] and Nevill of Raby and Westmorland.[83] The last reference to the honour of Huntingdon in Broughton occurs in 1302,[84] but the connexion of the Nevills, Lords Latimer, continues until 1430.[85]

This manor was held in the time of Edward the Confessor by one Morcar, who could sell, and who was holding it under the Countess Judith at the date

[45] Chan. Inq. p.m. (Ser. 2), dxxv, 123.
[46] Feet of F. Bucks. East. 1657.
[47] M. I. in church.
[48] P.C.C. 43 Pye.
[49] Recov. R. Trin. 27 Chas. II, m. 14.
[50] M. I. on tomb in churchyard quoted by Lipscomb, *Hist. and Antiq. of Bucks.* iv, 82.
[51] Add. MS. 5839, p. 82; *Musgrave's Obit.* (Harl. Soc.), ii, 227.
[52] Add. MS. 5839, p. 82.
[53] P.C.C. 69 Potter.
[54] Recov. R. D. Enr. Mich. 22 Geo. II, m. 73.
[55] *Musgrave's Obit.* (Harl. Soc.), i, 78; P.C.C. 265 Pinfold.
[56] Recov. R. D. Enr. Hil. 15 Geo. III, m. 85.
[57] Burke, *Landed Gentry.*
[58] Lysons, *Mag. Brit.* i (3), 523.

[59] Burke, *Landed Gentry.*
[60] Ibid.   [61] Ibid.
[62] Information kindly supplied by Lieut.-Col. Good.
[63] *Cal. Close,* 1349-54, p. 358.
[64] Wrottesley, op. cit. 192.
[65] M. I. in Broughton Church.
[66] *Visit. of Beds.* (Harl. Soc.), 14.
[67] Chan. Inq. p.m. 10 Hen. IV, no. 38; G.E.C. *Peerage,* vii, 24.
[68] Wrottesley, op. cit. 271.
[69] Chan. Inq. p.m. 8 Hen. VI, no. 21.
[70] Ibid. (Ser. 2), v, 125. He left 8 quarters of 'pesen' to the church (P.C.C. 18 Milles).
[71] Chan. Inq. p.m. (Ser. 2), xxi, 115; P.C.C. 29 Adeane.
[72] Chan. Inq. p.m. (Ser. 2), xxxiii, 108; P.C.C. 17 Ayloffe.
[73] Add. MS. 5839, p. 78.

[74] G.E.C. op. cit. iii, 235.
[75] Close, 31 Hen. VIII, pt. iv, no. 35.
[76] L. and P. Hen. VIII, xviii (1), g. 802 (50).
[77] G.E.C. op. cit. viii, 174.
[78] Recov. R. Mich. 15 Eliz. m. 709; Feet of F. Div. Co. Trin. 15 Eliz.
[79] V.C.H. Bucks. i, 274.
[80] Testa de Nevill (Rec. Com.), 244; Feud. Aids, i, 104.
[81] Testa de Nevill, loc. cit.
[82] Feud. Aids, i, 83; Close, 7 Ric. II, m. 5 d., 7 d., 35 d.; Chan. Inq. p.m. 4 Ric. II, no. 35; Cal. Close, 1377-81, pp. 87, 459.
[83] Chan. Inq. p.m. 12 Ric. II, no. 40; 20 Ric. II, no. 54; 5 Hen. IV, no. 28; Close, 11 Hen. IV, m. 11 d.
[84] Feud. Aids, i, 104.
[85] Chan. Inq. p.m. 9 Hen. VI, no. 24.

of the Domesday Survey.[86] In the 13th century it was held by Ralph Pincerna or Butler,[87] whose heirs were in possession in 1284–6[88] and 1302–3.[89] It is probably they who are referred to under the names of Thomas de Eye, John Campion, and Thomas Quarel, holding in 1346.[90] Shortly after this date this holding appears to have been acquired by the Broughton family, and was joined to the lands retained by Robert de Broughton in 1334 to form the second Broughton Manor, as on the death of Richard Lord St. Maur in 1409 the overlordship of half that manor was ascribed to Lord Latimer.[91]

A mill was held with the principal manor at the date of the Domesday Survey,[92] and there was a water-mill in 1623,[93] when a free fishery was also included in the appurtenances.[94]

The church of *ST. LAWRENCE CHURCH* consists of a chancel measuring internally 25 ft. 6 in. by 14 ft., nave 50 ft. 6 in. by 18 ft. 6 in., west tower 10 ft. 6 in. square, and a south porch.

No detail now remains of an earlier date than the first quarter of the 14th century, when the chancel and nave appear to have been remodelled.[95] Towards the end of the same century new windows were inserted in the nave, and in the early part of the 15th century the west tower was rebuilt, a turret containing a rood-stair being added about the same time at the north-east of the nave. In 1880–1 the church was drastically restored, the tracery of several of the windows being renewed. The walling is of limestone rubble with wrought dressings, and the nave and chancel are crowned by plain parapets.

The east window of the chancel is entirely modern, but the external label and mask-stops and the string-course below the sill appear to be of original early 14th-century date. At the north-east is a recess with original jambs and a modern trefoiled head. At the west end of the north wall is a window with modern tracery in a 14th-century opening with an original rear-arch and an external label with mask-stops. To the east of the window is a modern doorway, the external label of which may be original. At the west end of the south wall is an original 14th-century opening with a labelled rear-arch ; the tracery, which was probably of two lights, has been removed and a modern trefoiled head inserted. The early 14th-century chancel arch is two-centred and of two chamfered orders, the outer order continuous and the inner order carried by moulded corbels supported by carved heads. A change in the character of the masonry to the east of the buttress in the centre of the south wall suggests that the present chancel is an extension of its predecessor.

At the east end of the north wall of the nave are the upper and lower doorways to the rood-turret, each of which has a two-centred head rebated continuously with the jambs. Of the three windows in this wall, the two eastern have late 14th-century two-centred heads and jambs with external casement moulds, but the three-light tracery is modern. The remaining window, which is placed at the west end of the wall, is of original early 14th-century date and is of three trefoiled ogee lights with reticulated tracery in a two-centred head. Between this and the second window is a blocked doorway of about the same date with a two-centred external head and label, and a segmental two-centred rear-arch. In the south wall are three similar windows, the two eastern of the late 14th century with modern tracery and external stone-work and the westernmost of the early 14th century. The south doorway is like the blocked north doorway and occupies a corresponding position.

The tower is of three stages with an embattled parapet and diagonal buttresses of three offsets at the western angles, the junction with the nave being masked by buttresses of two offsets with gabled heads. The tower arch is two-centred and of two chamfered orders continuously moulded with the jambs towards the nave, while on the west face the outer order dies into the side walls of the tower. The west window of the ground stage is of two lights and has original early 15th-century jambs and a two-centred head, but the tracery is modern. At the north-west is a small doorway to the vice, which is only traceable externally by the small loops which light it. The intermediate stage has plain narrow loops on the north and south, and the bell-chamber is lighted from all four sides by restored windows of two lights with traceried two-centred heads. The only ancient detail of the south porch is an original 14th-century window of two trefoiled lights with tracery in a two-centred head in the west wall ; there is a similar light, apparently modern, in the east wall. The low-pitched roof of the chancel is of the late 15th century, but that of the nave is modern.

The chief interest of the church lies in the remarkable series of paintings upon the walls of the nave. The earliest of these is the late 14th-century painting between the two eastern windows in the north wall which represents the dismemberment of the body of Christ. Perhaps the subject is intended to typify the dismemberment of the church by heretics and schismatics, with a possible reference to the Lollard propaganda of the time. The picture has a rectangular engrailed border of a reddish-brown colour, and the figures are drawn with brown outlines upon a plain ground. In the centre is the seated figure of the Virgin, with the mutilated body of our Lord upon her knees. Surrounding her are seven standing figures in the civil costume of the period ; five carry dismembered portions of our Lord's body, while of the remaining figures one is apparently in the act of tearing out His eyes, and the other carries the Host. In the middle foreground are the figures of two men seated on either side of an object which it is difficult to identify. One holds a sword and appears to be threatening the other, who is about to hurl his dagger at him. Over the north doorway, filling the wall surface between the two adjacent windows, is a fine late 15th-century 'doom.' On the dexter side of the picture is represented God the Father seated in majesty, with two orb-crowned towers at His feet. The back of the throne is shown as an embattled wall with flanking turrets, and above the parapet is seen the Son. By the feet of the Father stands the Virgin

[86] *V.C.H. Bucks.* i, 274.
[87] *Testa de Nevill,* loc. cit.
[88] *Feud. Aids,* i, 83.
[89] Ibid. 104.
[90] Ibid. 130.

[91] Chan. Inq. p.m. 10 Hen. IV, no. 38.
[92] *V.C.H. Bucks.* i, 252.
[93] Recov. R. East. 21 Jas. I, m. 67.
[94] Feet of F. Div. Co. Hil. 20 Jas. I.
[95] During the episcopate of Bishop

Dalderby (1300–20) a commission was appointed to dedicate three new altars in the church of Broughton (Linc. Epis. Reg. Memo. Dalderby, fol. 193).

extending her robe to shelter the saved, while with her left hand she gives a favouring touch to the beam of the balance in which a soul is being weighed. Round the beam is entwined a string of beads, and immediately above the balance, which is held by an angel, a figure rising from an open tomb anxiously watches the result. In the centre of the composition is the Angel Gabriel blowing a trumpet, round which is entwined an inscribed scroll no longer decipherable. On the sinister side, represented in the usual manner, is hell mouth, and in the upper portion of this side of the picture is drawn the armed figure of St. Michael. Below the whole is a pattern of white flowers on a bluish ground. The paintings on the south wall of the nave are probably of the middle of the 15th century. Between the two eastern windows is a rectangular compartment with a repainted border, containing figures of St. Helena, and of a bishop, perhaps St. Eloy. St. Helena is represented in a green robe bordered with ermine and holds a tau cross with her right hand and a book in her left. Below this panel are painted a variety of smiths' implements and productions, such as hammers, pincers, horse-shoes, stirrups, keys and padlocks; these surround a representation of a man on horseback, which is almost entirely hidden by a modern memorial tablet. Over the south doorway is a magnificent painting of St. George and the Dragon, now unfortunately much damaged, the head and shoulders of the saint being quite obliterated. He is mounted on a boldly-drawn white horse and wears plate armour; in the bottom dexter corner is the dragon receiving the blow of his lance, while in the background is a female figure, the head of which is no longer visible. The ground is painted a dark green with light green lines upon it to represent grass. A border of red with a white scroll design upon it still remains on the east and west sides and over the head of the doorway. On both north and south walls traces remain of a dado pattern of broad red stripes with a cresting of red squares placed over the spaces between the stripes. On the west wall on either side of the tower arch, and at the west end of the north wall, are painted texts in black letter with circular strapwork borders, probably work of the late 16th century.

The pulpit is of the 18th century. The doors in the north and south doorways are of the 15th century, and both retain their original ironwork, the latter having ornamental strap-hinges and a closing ring with a circular scutcheon. In the chancel is a carved 17th-century chest, and in the tower is a bier bearing the date 1683. Copies of Bishop Jewell's *Apology* (1567) and Erasmus's *Paraphrase* (1632) are chained to desks on either side of the chancel arch. Some fragments of 14th-century glass are preserved in the north-west and south-west windows of the nave.

At the east end of the south wall of the chancel is fixed a brass to John de Broughton, inscribed, 'Hic jacet Johes de Broughton fili' Robti de Broughton qui obiit xxºjºdie mesis decembris Aºdni Mºccccºiijº cui' aie ppiciet' ds amen.' Above it is placed a brass to his wife Agnes, inscribed, 'hic iacet Agnes quondam

ux' Johis de Broughton filii Robti de Broughton que obiit xi die Mensis octobris Aºdni Mºcccºlxxxxºixº cui' aie propiciet' deus Amen.' The figures of both have disappeared. On the north wall of the chancel is a monument commemorating Thomas Duncombe, who died in 1672. The inscription states that he married first, Mary, eldest daughter of Charles Edmonds of Preston Deanery (Northamptonshire), by whom he had one son, Francis, and three daughters, and secondly, Margaret, only daughter of William Norton of Sherington, and relict of Thomas Wiseman of Mayland Hall, Essex, by whom he also had three daughters. His first wife Mary, who died in 1655, is commemorated by a brass at the east end of the chancel. There are also floor-slabs to Sarah, widow of Thomas Duncombe, who died in 1653, and to Mary, the wife of Francis Duncombe, who died in 1686.

There is a ring of four bells: the treble by Anthony Chandler, 1655; the second is inscribed in black letter, 'Sancte Cristine Ora Pro Nobis,' by Henry Jordan, c. 1460–70; the third by James Keene, 1622; and the fourth inscribed ' In Multis Annis Resonet Campana Johannis,' is by the same founder as the second. There is also a sanctus bell, probably by James Keene, bearing the date 1635, the last figure being reversed.[96]

The plate consists of a silver cup of 1720, and a paten and almsdish of the same year, all the gift of Mrs. Ann Bacon, and a flagon of 1721 inscribed ' F. D. to Broughton Church.'

The registers begin in 1720.

ADVOWSON   The church of Broughton, which is a rectory, was originally bestowed on Tickford Priory by Robert de Broughton and William his son, and the gift confirmed by Robert, Bishop of Lincoln 1151–4.[97] For some reason unknown the Broughtons regained possession of the advowson, which was given to Caldwell Priory by William de Broughton, confirmation being made by his son Robert in 1245.[98] In 1318 it was conveyed by the priory to the Dean and Chapter of Lincoln,[99] against whom John de Broughton brought an action in 1380. The dean called the Prior of Caldwell to substantiate his claim to the advowson, and judgement was given against the plaintiff.[100] Some arrangement was evidently arrived at between the two parties, for eight years later the presentation was made by John Broughton.[1] From that date the advowson descended with the secondary manor until 1573, and afterwards with the amalgamated manor,[2] the present patron being Lieut.-Colonel A. W. H. Good.

CHARITIES   The charity of Thomas Duncombe and Francis Duncombe, founded by wills dated respectively 1672 and 1716, is regulated by a scheme of the Charity Commissioners of 14 January 1870. The property consists of the public-house in Loughton called ' The Fountain,' and land containing 16 a. 3 r. 5 p., let at £46 15s. yearly. The official trustees also hold a sum of £27 4s. 3d. consols, producing 13s. 4d. yearly,

[96] A. H. Cocks, *Church Bells of Bucks.* 328.

[97] *Cal. Doc. of France*, 444.

[98] Feet of F. case 15, file 27, no. 8. The church was taxed at £6 in 1291 (*Pope Nich. Tax.* [Rec. Com.], 34).

[99] *Cal. Pat.* 1317–21, p. 67. A messuage and virgate of land in the parish were also included in this grant to the dean and chapter.

[100] De Banco R. 480, m. 569 d.

[1] Add. MS. 5839, p. 79.

[2] Ibid.; Inst. Bks. (P.R.O.); *Clergy Lists*; Feet of F. Div. Co. Trin. 1654; Bucks. Hil. 22 & 23 Chas. II. The presentation was, however, made by John Winter in 1786 and by Sarah Backwell in 1790.

representing residue of proceeds of sale of 2 roods of land, for the purpose of redeeming the land tax on all the property. By an order of the Charity Commissioners, dated 4 September 1903, it was determined that one-third of the income, after payment of £2 12s. to the parish clerk, was applicable to educational purposes. This third is paid to the school; another one-third of the income is applied for the benefit of the poor, chiefly in the distribution of coals, and the remaining one-third for the repair of the church. In 1912 each branch received the sum of £10 3s.

CALVERTON

Calvretone (xi cent.); Calverton or Calveston cum Stony Stratford (xvii cent.).

This parish lies south of Watling Street with a tributary of the Ouse as its western boundary. It has an area of about 1,981 acres, of which the greater part is laid down in grass.[1] The principal crops grown are wheat, oats, beans and barley. The land rises from about 200 to 250 ft. above the ordnance datum in the north and west to nearly 350 ft. in the south and east, the soil being light and stiff clay with a subsoil of clay and stone. The parish formerly included the west side of Stony Stratford, and the Inclosure Act passed in 1782 for Calverton covered this larger area.[2] Later, however, the west side of Stony Stratford was made a separate parish by Act of Parliament. The close connexion between these two places, and the fact that the manorial rights over the west side were held with those of Calverton, led to the manor of Calverton being often called the manor of Calverton with Stony Stratford, and the fair and market of Stony Stratford were included among its appurtenances. A further portion of this parish, a detached part called Stratford Bridge Meadows, was amalgamated with Stratford St. Giles by a Local Government Order dated 25 March 1883. Calverton End, the north part of the parish, is now a suburb of the town of Stony Stratford, and has some good villa residences, as well as the cemetery formed in 1856 at the expense of the parishioners of Stony Stratford. Here are also the water tower and pumping station of Stony Stratford waterworks, lying south of Horsefair Green, which occupies the extreme north-eastern angle of Calverton, this part of the parish being known as Calverton St. Mary.

The village lies on the Calverton road, a continuation of Silver Street in Stony Stratford. At its northern end are All Saints Church and the Manor Farm, formerly the manor-house, an interesting old building of stone.[3] It is of two stories with attics and a tiled roof, and the plan is of the L type, the main block being placed north and south with the entrance front on the west, and a wing at the north-east. The house, it would seem, was originally built during the tenure of the manor by the Earls of Oxford, about 1500, to which date a stone-mullioned two-light window on the ground floor of the west front may be assigned. Probably when the manor came to Henry Earl of Northumberland and Katherine his wife, at the end of the 16th century, an addition was made to the north-east wing, in the south front of

which are two windows of three lights, now blocked, with stone mullions of this date. In 1659 Simon Bennett made considerable alterations to the house. He lengthened the original block southwards, built the attic with its dormer windows, and added the two-storied porch on the west front, which bears in a panel over the entrance this date and his initials, and on either side shields of arms now indecipherable. Alterations were also made to the 16th-century addition about this time. After the sale to William Selby Lowndes, at the beginning of the 19th century, further alterations were made and new windows were added. Inside the house is some good 16th and 17th-century panelling with other fittings of the same periods.

The house is surrounded by a high stone wall inclosing several acres, probably 'the large orchard enclosed with a stately wall' referred to in the lawsuit of 1686 (see under manor[4]). Local tradition places the scene of the murder of Mrs. Grace Bennett in the servants' hall, and the spot at which the murderer climbed over the wall and escaped into Gib Lane, an ancient pack-horse track at the back of the house, was said to be shown by a stone in the wall bearing the date 1693.[4a]

South of the church are the school, built in 1857, and the almshouses, all east of the Calverton road. To the west of the church and of the road is the site of a Roman camp,[5] upon which the present rectory was erected in 1820 by Charles George Lord Arden, then patron.[6]

In addition to Calverton End there are the districts of Lower Weald, which lies south of the village, Middle Weald, south-east of Lower Weald, and Upper Weald, further south-east still. At each of these hamlets there are some 17th-century stone houses or cottages with thatched roofs.

Among place-names have been found Hadley on Culvercroft, Weedeford, Blaken field, Street field,[7] Parsonage Piece, Swans Nest Piece, Round Neale, Pot Yards Piece, the Hop Yards, Crosshill Close, Park Piece,[8] Pochers Piece, Botts Piece[9] (xvii cent.).

In the reign of Edward the Confessor *MANOR CALVERTON* was held by Bisi, a thegn of the king, and in 1086 it was assessed at 10 hides among the lands of Hugh de Bolebec.[10] His possessions, including this manor, afterwards formed the barony of Bolebec, held of the king in chief,[11] and Calverton was described as still so held as late as 1631.[12]

---

[1] Statistics from Bd. of Agric. (1905).
[2] Priv. Act, 22 Geo. III, cap. 22.
[3] It is said to have been bought from the Pigotts of Beachampton (Add. MS. 5839, fol. 43 d.), but there is no evidence that the Pigotts held it.

[4] Exch. Dep. Mich. 2 Jas. II, no. 23.
[4a] Sheahan, *Hist. and Topog. of Bucks.* 510.
[5] Lipscomb, *Hist. and Antiq. of Bucks.* iv, 85.   [6] Ibid.
[7] Add. MS. 5839, fol. 46 d.   Terrier of 1639.

[8] Exch. Dep. Mich. 2 Jas. II, no. 23.
[9] Ibid. Mich. 4 Will. and Mary, no. 9.
[10] *V.C.H. Bucks.* i, 264.
[11] See Whitchurch.
[12] Chan. Inq. p.m. (Ser. 2), cccclxxx, 105.

CALVERTON : THE MANOR HOUSE

CALVERTON CHURCH FROM THE SOUTH

With the exception of a few temporary divergences,[13] Calverton followed the descent of Whitchurch (q.v.) until the death without issue of John Earl of Oxford in 1526.[14] Whitchurch passed with the title, but an Act of Parliament dated 13 March 1531–2 decreed that Ann widow of the late earl should enjoy Calverton Manor for life with remainder to Sir John Nevill, fourth Lord Latimer, the son of the earl's late sister Dorothy (who had died about 1526[15]) and of her husband John Nevill, third Lord Latimer; to the earl's second sister Elizabeth wife of Sir Anthony Wingfield; and to his third sister Ursula wife of Sir Edmund Knightley, serjeant-at-law, and their heirs.[16] Lord Latimer obtained the reversion of a third of the manor in 1541,[17] and with the other co-heirs entered into possession on the death in the spring of 1558–9 of Ann Countess of Oxford.[18]

Lady Ursula Knightley died without issue in the following year, and her share reverted to her nephews Lord Latimer and Sir Robert Wingfield.[19] On 1 January 1561–2 Sir Robert Wingfield received licence to alienate his moiety to John Wingfield and others,[20] to whom it was conveyed at the following Easter by him,[21] and he was dealing with it again in 1576, when with his wife Bridget he conveyed it to Richard and Anthony Wingfield.[22] His cousin Lord Latimer died in the following year,[23] and in 1580 a partition of property among his four daughters and co-heirs and Sir Robert Wingfield assigned Calverton Manor to Katherine the eldest daughter and Henry Earl of Northumberland her husband.[24] This partition was confirmed by Act of Parliament shortly afterwards.[25] The Countess of Northumberland, when a widow, conveyed the manor in 1586, as the manor of Calverton cum Stony Stratford, to Francis Fytton,[26] whom she afterwards married.[26a] In 1592 she settled it on her son Sir Charles Percy for life,[27] and died on 28 October 1596.[28] Her eldest son Henry Earl of Northumberland was holding Calverton in 1615,[29] and in the following year he, with Sir Charles Percy, conveyed it to Sir Thomas Bennett, citizen and alderman of London.[30] Sir Thomas Bennett settled it in 1624 on his second son Simon Bennett of Beachampton, bequeathing by will the remainder to his third son Richard, and died at London in February 1626–7.[31] Richard died in the following April, and his brother, then Sir Simon Bennett, bart., died without issue on 20 August 1631, when he was succeeded by Richard's son Simon,[32] who made a settlement of the manor in 1649.[33] He appears to have been a Roundhead, as in 1660 he made a declaration ' of his laying hold of the King's gracious pardon as granted at Breda, and promise of future obedience.'[34] The death of Simon

Bennett on 30 August 1682 is referred to by Luttrell in these words : ' The great Mr. Bennet of Buckinghamshire is . . . dead, and is said to have left a most prodigious estate behind him.'[35] His widow Grace Bennett continued his policy of inclosing arable land in the common fields and converting it into pasture ground, and was defendant in lawsuits to recover tithes therefrom in 1686[36] and 1692.[37]

The depositions taken in the course of the later suit show the number of ' plow lands ' of about 60 acres each that she kept ' in her owne hands laid downe and untilled so that the parish is almost depopulated and the fields looke like a wildernesse little being mowed and that which was generally so late and kept so long till it was spoyled.' On her own showing her management of the estate was not very fortunate, as she declared that ' shee lost £10,000 by her management of the Lordshipp of Calverton.'[38] She is described as ' a miserable, covetous and wretched

BENNETT. *Gules a bezant between three demi-lions argent.*

CECIL. *Barry of ten pieces argent and azure six scutcheons sable each charged with a lion argent and a crescent for difference.*

LOWNDES. *Argent fretty azure with bezants at the interlacings of the fret and a quarter gules charged with a leopard's head or.*

person,' who ' living by herself in the House at Calverton, and being supposed to have great Store of

---

[13] Cf. *Hund. R.* (Rec. Com.), i, 40; *Feud. Aids,* i, 80, 106, 109, 132; Dugdale, *Baronage,* i, 562 (subinfeudation to a younger son and reversion to the earls); Chan. Inq. p.m. 27 Edw. III (1st nos.), no. 50 (lease to Thomas de Ferar, who died in 1353); *Cal. Pat.* 1361–4, p. 121 (grant in dower); Pat. 2 Ric. III, pt ii, m. 3 (grant to Sir Thomas Bryan); Chan. Inq. p.m. 6 Hen. V, no. 65; *Parl. R.* vi, 228.
[14] G.E.C. *Peerage,* vi, 169.
[15] Ibid. v, 25.
[16] Chan. Inq. p.m. (Ser. 2), cxxvii, 34.
[17] *L. and P. Hen. VIII,* xvi, g. 580 (54).
[18] G.E.C. op. cit. vi, 169.
[19] Chan. Inq. p.m. (Ser. 2), cxxvii, 34.

Elizabeth Wingfield had died about six weeks before the countess (ibid. [Ser. 2], cxix, 175). Lady Ursula's share was the subject of a Chancery suit instituted in March 1562–3 by her niece Elizabeth Nanton, widow, on the ground that it had been bequeathed to her by Lady Ursula for twenty years to perform her will (Chan. Proc. [Ser. 2], bdles. 132, no. 18; 111, no. 21). [20] Pat. 4 Eliz. pt. ix.
[21] Feet of F. Bucks. East. 4 Eliz.
[22] Ibid. Div. Co. Hil. 18 Eliz.; Mich. 18 & 19 Eliz.
[23] G.E.C. op. cit. v, 26.
[24] Chan. Inq. p.m. (Ser. 2), ccxlvi, 116.
[25] Ibid. Sir Robert Wingfield died in 1596 (ibid.).

[26] Feet of F. Div. Co. Trin. 28 Eliz.; Pat. 28 Eliz. pt. iv.
[26a] G.E.C. op. cit. vi, 91.
[27] Feet of F. Div. Co. Trin. 34 Eliz.
[28] Chan. Inq. p.m. (Ser. 2), ccxlviii, 22.
[29] Feet of F. Div. Co. East. 13 Jas. I.
[30] Ibid. Bucks. Hil. 14 Jas. I.
[31] Chan. Inq. p.m. (Ser. 2), ccccxxxv, 116; cccclxxx, 105.
[32] Ibid. cccclxxx, 105.
[33] Feet of F. Bucks. Mich. 1649.
[34] *Cal. S. P. Dom.* 1660–1, p. 38.
[35] Luttrell, *Brief Relation of State Affairs* (ed. 1857), i, 216.
[36] Exch. Dep. Mich. 2 Jas. II, no. 23.
[37] Ibid. Mich. 4 Will. and Mary, no. 9.
[38] Ibid.

Money by her, tempted a Butcher of Stony Stratford to get artfully into the House, and as there was no Body to assist her or call for Help he barbarously murthered her'[39] on 19 September 1694.[40] She left two daughters, co-heirs of their father, of whom Grace, the elder, married John Bennett of Abington, Cambridgeshire,[41] and Frances, the younger, James Earl of Salisbury.[42] Frances's son, James Earl of Salisbury, was dealing with the manor alone in 1714 [43] and in 1720 with Grace Bennett, then a widow.[44] By failure of issue of the elder sister, the sole interest in Calverton devolved on the Earl of Salisbury [45] and descended to his grandson James,[46] afterwards Marquess of Salisbury. He sold the manor in 1806 to William Selby Lowndes [47] of Whaddon (q.v.), whose great-grandson, Mr. William Selby Lowndes of Wh   n Hall, is the present owner.

Two hides in Calverton which had been held as a manor by a man of Queen Edith formed part of Hugh de Bolebec's holding in 1086.[48] They were afterwards subinfeudated by the Earls of Oxford, who retained overlordship rights over Calverton as late as 1632.[49]

Part of this estate was obtained by the Hintes family, and in 1227 Robert d' Hintes held half a virgate in Calverton in right of his wife Sibyl.[50] A successor, Walter de Hintes, is returned as holding 1 hide in 1254.[51]

The remainder of this land was acquired by the Calverton family, a member of which, John de Calverton, had 1 virgate here in 1202, when he bestowed 6 acres of it on Calverton Church.[52] In the following year he acquired 'a cotland' from William son of Aluric [53] and later in the century accounted for one fee in Calverton.[54]

Another hide in Calverton was owned by the Templars, who were accused in 1254 of withholding the suit due.[55] It passed with their other possessions to the Knights Hospitallers, and was attached to their preceptory of Sandford (Oxfordshire).[56] A grant of these lands in fee was obtained in 1564 by Sir Francis Knollys and his wife Catherine,[57] a further grant being made in 1623 to his son William Viscount Wallingford and his wife Elizabeth.[58] They levied a fine of these lands in the following year, under the name of Calverton alias Stony Stratford Manor,[59] which appears to be identical with the second manor held by Sir Simon Bennett in 1631.[60] As there is no further trace of it, the two manors probably coalesced.

View of frankpledge was attached to the manor in 1254 [61] and free warren was claimed in 1275.[62] A fishery in the Ouse was among the appurtenances from the 14th to the 18th century.[63] There was a mill worth 13s. 4d. in 1086,[64] and there is mention of two in 1331 [65] and three in 1586.[66]

CHURCH The church of ALL SAINTS consists of a chancel, nave of three bays, south aisle, western tower and south porch. It was rebuilt in stone in the 12th and 14th-century styles between 1818 and 1824, when some of the old details were re-used. The chancel arch and the nave arcade are apparently 14th-century work reset, and the two-centred tower arch over the modern semicircular arch may be of the 15th century rebuilt. All the fittings are modern.

There is a ring of six bells, all modern.

The plate consists of a chalice, paten, and flagon, probably of the 17th century, and a modern paten.

The registers begin in 1559.

ADVOWSON Richard the clerk of Calverton witnessed a deed with Robert de Whitfield, Sheriff of Oxfordshire 1182–5,[67] thus affording probably an early incidental reference to Calverton Church.[68] It was valued at £14 13s. 4d. in 1291 [69] and at £26 2s. 9d. in 1535.[70]

The advowson of the rectory was held in 1233 by Isabella Countess of Oxford,[71] and descended with the manor until the sale of the latter in 1806.[72] On or about this date [73] the advowson was alienated by the Marquess of Salisbury to Charles George Lord Arden, who presented in 1814,[74] and from whom it has descended to the present owner, the Earl of Egmont.

Lands in Calverton worth 12d. yearly were given for the maintenance of a light.[75]

CHARITIES The charity of Sir Simon Bennett, bart., for Calverton and other parishes, founded by will dated 15 August 1631,[76] is regulated by a scheme of the Charity Commissioners of 19 August 1902. The trust estate consists of the impropriate tithes of the manor of Bourton in the borough of Buckingham, amounting to £100 a year, and £400 Local Loans 3 per cent. stock, producing £12 a year, arising from accumulations of income. By the scheme the income, after deductions for land tax, is divisible into 181 parts, twenty-five of such parts, or about £12 a year, being applicable for the poor of Calverton ; the like proportion for the poor of Beachampton, and ten other of such parts, or about £5 a year, for the church of Beachampton ; forty other parts, or about £20 a year, for the poor of Buckingham ; forty-one other parts for the poor of Stony Stratford, and the remaining forty parts for the repair of the highways in

[39] Add. MS. 5839, fol. 44.
[40] Luttrell, op. cit. iii, 372.
[41] Add. MS. 5839, fol. 43 d. John Bennett presented to the church in 1711 (ibid. fol. 47 d.).
[42] Luttrell, op. cit. i, 269.
[43] G.E.C. op. cit. vii, 42 ; Recov. R. East. 13 Anne, m. 187.
[44] Feet of F. Div. Co. Trin. 6 Geo. I.
[45] Ibid. Trin. 11 Geo. I.
[46] G.E.C. loc. cit. ; Recov. R. Mich. 22 Geo. III, m. 410 ; Priv. Act, 22 Geo. III, cap. 22.
[47] Sheahan, Hist. and Topog. of Bucks. 509.   [48] V.C.H. Bucks. i, 264.
[49] Chan. Inq. p.m. (Ser. 2), dviii, 15.
[50] Feet of F. case 15, file 16, no. 6.
[51] Hund. R. (Rec. Com.), i, 30 ; Testa de Nevill (Rec. Com.), 247b.

[52] Feet of F. case 14, file 6, no. 24.
[53] Ibid. file 8, no. 1.
[54] Testa de Nevill, loc. cit.
[55] Hund. R. (Rec. Com.), i, 30.
[56] Pat. 6 Eliz. pt. iii, m. 21.
[57] Ibid.
[58] Ibid. 20 Jas. I, pt. ix, no. 1 ; G.E.C. Peerage, i, 229.
[59] Feet of F. Div. Co. Trin. 22 Jas. I.
[60] Chan. Inq. p.m. (Ser. 2), ccclxxx, 105.   [61] Hund. R. (Rec. Com.), i, 30.
[62] Ibid. 40.
[63] Chan. Inq. p.m. 5 Edw. III (1st nos.), no. 71 ; Pat. 1274 ; Chan. Inq. p.m. (Ser. 2), ccccxxxv, 116 ; Recov. R. East. 13 Anne, m. 187.
[64] V.C.H. Bucks. i, 264.
[65] Chan. Inq. p.m. 5 Edw. III (1st nos.), no. 71.

[66] Pat. 28 Eliz. pt. iv.
[67] P.R.O. List of Sheriffs, ix, 107.
[68] Cal. Pat. 1313–17, p. 359 ; Add. Chart. 10593, 10595.
[69] Pope Nich. Tax. (Rec. Com.), 34.
[70] Valor Eccl. (Rec. Com.), iv, 245.
[71] R. of Hugh of Wells (Cant. and York Soc.), ii, 89.
[72] Inst. Bks. (P.R.O.). The presentation was, however, made by Thomas Duke of Exeter in 1425, by Sir Thomas Cobham in 1465, Thomas Duke of Norfolk in 1514, and Thomas Pigott in 1577 (Add. MS. 5839, fol. 47 d.).
[73] Lysons, Mag. Brit. i (3), 533.
[74] Lipscomb, op. cit. iv, 86.
[75] Chant. Cert. 5, no. 16.
[76] P.C.C. 100 St. John.

Calverton, Beachampton and Stony Stratford. The proportions for the poor are distributed in clothing.

Ambrose Bennett by his will dated 24 May 1630 gave 20s. yearly issuing out of the manor of Rotherhithe.[77] The annuity is usually applied in paying for the conveyance of poor people to the hospital and in providing boots.

The charity of Simon Bennett, or the Bradwell Estate Charity, was founded by his will, proved 1 February 1682–3,[78] whereby the testator bequeathed £100 for the poor of Calverton, £100 for the poor of the West Side of Stony Stratford, and £50 for the poor of Beachampton. The trust property now consists of 46 a. 1 r. 31 p. of land at Bradwell, acquired at the inclosure of the parish in exchange for other lands originally purchased with the legacies in question, let at £46 10s. a year, and £300 consols, producing

£7 10s. a year, held by the official trustees, who also hold a further sum of £502 7s. 5d. consols, which is being accumulated until 6 April 1929. The stock arises from the sale in 1907 of the Morning Star Inn, subject to a lease for sixty years from 6 April 1869 at a ground rent of £5 5s. In 1911 the share of Calverton amounted to £10 10s., of which 15s. was expended in work on the roads and the remainder in the distribution of coal.

An unknown donor's charity for apprenticing and for poor widows consists of five cottages situate at Lower Weald, Calverton, comprised in a deed of 29 March 1739, and an allotment containing 7 a. 0 r. 32 p., producing an annual income of £37 10s. In 1911 three premiums amounting to £18 were paid, and the sum of £9 was distributed among eighteen widows at Christmas.

CHICHELEY

Cicelai (xi cent.) ; Chichele, Chechele (xiv cent.).

This parish covers 2,070 acres, of which about 70 acres are woodland and the remainder is nearly equally divided between arable land and pasture.[1] Thickthorn Wood in the east of the parish is of some size. The soil and subsoil are both clay, which provides material for the brickworks which exist in the parish. The inhabitants are mainly engaged in agriculture, and the principal crops produced are wheat, beans and roots.

The slope of the ground is from north (where it attains 341 ft. above ordnance datum) to west. The parish is watered by Chicheley Brook, a small tributary of the Ouse. There is in the grounds of Chicheley Hall a never-failing spring, the waters of which formerly supplied the house through the agency of a curious tower three stories high, erected by Sir John Chester, the fourth baronet, in 1725. After serving its purpose for one and a half centuries, the brickwork of the tower gave way and is now an ivy-covered ruin.

The village of Chicheley is small and lies in the centre of the parish on the main road running west from Bedford to Newport Pagnell. It is picturesquely situated in a hollow surrounded by trees. Chicheley Hall, which stands in extensive pleasure grounds, was built at the beginning of the 18th century and replaced a Tudor mansion built by Anthony Cave, of which the foundations may still be traced.[2] The present house is a rectangular structure of brick with stone dressings and is three stories in height with a basement. The centre of the principal front is raised and slightly broken forward, the angles being marked by fluted Corinthian pilasters standing upon pedestals and supporting an enriched entablature at the level of the second floor. The cornice is dropped on either side of the central projection and supported at wide intervals by similar pilasters carrying detached fragments of frieze and architrave. The windows have moulded stone architraves, and the entrance doorway, which is approached by five stone steps, is crowned by a fantastically designed curved pediment.

The main cornice is continued round the other elevations, which are somewhat plainer. Internally some fine 18th-century panelling remains, and in one of the rooms is a beam, brought from the old house, which bears the following inscription : ' Cave ne deum offendas, cave ne proximum loedas, cave ne tua neglentia familiam deseras, 1550.' The date probably marks the completion of the older building.

North-west of Chicheley Hall is the church, with the vicarage, a stuccoed building, adjacent. The vicarage-house is described in 1639 as ' 4 Bays built with Stone and covered with Tyle, chambred over and boarded : the whole Building being contrived into 2 Storys and disposed into 3 Rooms, viz.—the Hall, Parlour, Buttry, Kitchen and Milke House. In the yard a Barn of 3 Bays and Lean-to adjoyning a Close called Baldecroft.'[3] The remainder of the village consists of the school and school-house, red brick buildings erected in 1854 by the Rev. Anthony Chester,[4] a farm-house, inn and a few cottages. Among the farms scattered over the pari may be noted Thickthorn Farm, a modern red brick building, in the east. Traces of fish-ponds are, however, still visible, and the existence of a homestead moat is also indicated.[5] Balney Lodge, or the Grange Farm, which may be identified as the ancient manor-house of the Broughtons and their descendants in this parish, has an Elizabethan south wing with the inscription : ' Sobrie Juste Pie, 1601 ' on the frieze above the lintel of the west front.[6] The east wing seems to be rather later, and the chimney stack bears the date 1773. Sir John Chester, bart., planted an avenue of elms to the house in 1714 'for a view from the great house.'[7] A two-storied gabled house, now divided into three and standing in the hamlet of Bedlam about a quarter of a mile north-west of the church, is possibly of Elizabethan date. Near by are some 17th-century half-timber cottages with thatched roofs.

The following place-names have been found in documents connected with this parish : Portway, Gosland (xiii cent.),[8] Longegosland[9] (xiv cent.),

[77] P.C.C. 29 St. John. He was son and heir of Sir Thomas Bennett and died without issue on 23 March 1630–1 (Chan. Inq. p.m. [Ser. 2], ccclxxx, 105).
[78] P.C.C. 127 Cottle.

[1] Statistics from Bd. of Agric. (1905).
[2] Rec. of Bucks. iv, 331.
[3] Add. MS. 5839, fol. 53.
[4] Sheahan, Hist. and Topog. of Bucks. 519.
[5] V.C.H. Bucks. ii, 30.

[6] Sheahan, op. cit. 517.
[7] Waters, Gen. Mem. of Chesters of Chicheley, ii, 531.
[8] Cat. of Anct. D. i, 5.
[9] Ibid. 1, 4.

Webb Mead (xvi cent.) and Anslowe Close, Butlers, Branons, Grabnooks farm, Dean field, and Jeggs [10] (xvii cent.).

MANORS William Fitz Ansculf held 9 hides 3 virgates in Chicheley in 1086,[11] and his descendants, who held the barony of Newport Pagnell (q.v.), are subsequently found exercising overlordship rights.[12] This property was divided into three manors. The first, of 3 hides, had been held by Baldwin since the time of Edward the Confessor.[13] The second, also of 3 hides, was held by Andrew, who had dispossessed Edestan, a man of Alnod Chentis.[14] The third, of 3 hides 3 virgates, was held by Payn, who succeeded nine thegns with power to sell without licence.[15] Three manors are found later in this parish, but it is impossible to state with certainty the exact origin of each. Two of them are later found belonging to Tickford or Newport Pagnell Priory, founded by Fulk Paynel, lord of Newport Pagnell, at the close of the 11th century,

Newport Pagnell, obtained lands in Chicheley in 1255 [19] and the prior and his tenants are returned for a fee held in perpetual alms in 1302–3.[20] On the suppression of Tickford Priory in 1525 this manor was granted to Cardinal Wolsey for the endowment of his college at Oxford.[21] After the fall of Wolsey Chicheley was resumed by the Crown and granted to the college refounded as Henry the Eighth's College in September 1532.[51a] The college was again surrendered to the Crown in 1545 [22] and in September of that year Anthony Cave, who had acquired wealth as a merchant of the Staple at Calais, petitioned for a grant of Chicheley and Thickthorns Manors, with other property of the dissolved priory of Tickford. His petition states that he was already lessee of the manors for a term of seventy years at a rental of £33 17s. 11½d.,[22a] and he now offered £632 5s. for the purchase of the fee simple.[23] This offer was not accepted, but on 4 December of the same year, in consideration of the sum of £788 18s. 9d.,

THE GRANGE FARM, CHICHELEY

he received a grant in fee of the manors, rectory and advowson to be held by one-twentieth of a knight's fee and £3 10s. 7d. per annum.[24] Anthony Cave lived at Chicheley, where he built a mansion, which was until the 18th century the residence of his descendants.[25] He died without surviving male issue in 1558,[26] and by his will, dated 31 May 1555, his manors in Chicheley were bequeathed to his daughter Judith Cave, subject to his wife Elizabeth's life interest.[27] Elizabeth Cave married shortly after her husband's death John Newdigate,[28] whose son John Newdigate, a well-known 16th-century scholar, married Martha Cave, one of her younger daughters.[29] John Newdigate, sen., died on 16 August 1565,[30] and

the more important being probably *CHICHELEY MANOR*, which takes its name from the parish.[16] Lands in Chicheley granted by Fulk Paynel are mentioned in confirmation charters to Tickford Priory,[17] and in the early 13th century the priory was said to hold a fee here.[18] Oliver, Prior of

the year after his widow married Richard Weston, a judge of Common Pleas.[31] She died in 1577, when the Chicheley property reverted, in pursuance of her husband's will, to Anthony Chester, aged eleven and a-half, son of Judith Cave by her marriage with William Chester.[32] Anthony Chester is said to have

[10] Chan. Proc. (Ser. 2), bdle. 265, no. 20 ; Waters, op. cit. i, 163–4.
[11] *V.C.H. Bucks.* i, 256.
[12] *Plac. de Quo Warr.* (Rec. Com.), 88 ; *Feud. Aids,* i, 83, 104 ; *Cal. Close,* 1318–23, p. 623 ; Chan. Inq. p.m. 16 Edw. II, no. 72 ; 47 Edw. III (1st nos.), no. 27 ; Add. Chart. 11224.
[13] *V.C.H. Bucks.* i, 256.
[14] Ibid. [15] Ibid.
[16] The church appears to have gone with this manor (Dugdale, *Mon.* v, 203), but Thickthorns (see below) certainly had the larger area.
[17] Dugdale, loc. cit.
[18] *Testa de Nevill* (Rec. Com.), 248.
[19] Feet of F. Bucks. 39 Hen. III, no. 13.

[20] *Feud. Aids,* i, 104.
[21] Pat. 17 Hen. VIII, pt. i, m. 21, 22 ; *L. and P. Hen. VIII,* iv (1), g. 2167 (1) ; Feet of F. Div. Co. Mich. 18 Hen. VIII. In 1526 Anne St. Leger, daughter of Thomas late Earl of Ormond, relinquished all her rights in Chicheley to the dean and canons (Feet of F. Bucks. Mich. 18 Hen. VIII).
[21a] *L. and P. Hen. VIII,* v, g. 1370 (23).
[22] Tanner, *Not. Mon.*
[22a] He had obtained a lease from the Dean and canons of Henry the Eighth's College (*L. and P. Hen. VIII,* xvi, g. 1391 [45]).
[23] Waters, op. cit. i, 82, quoting Particulars of Grants (P.R.O.), 37 Hen. VIII.

[24] Ibid. ; *L. and P. Hen. VIII,* xx (2), g. 1068 (10) ; Pat. 37 Hen. VIII, pt. xvii m. 8. A settlement of this quit-rent was made in 1679 (Close, 31 Chas. II, pt. iii, no. 4) and again in 1761 (ibid. 1 Geo. III, pt. iv, no. 4).
[25] Waters, op. cit. i, 83.
[26] Chan. Inq. p.m. (Ser. 2), cxx, 5.
[27] Ibid. ; P.C.C. 37 Mellershe.
[28] *Dict. Nat. Biog.*
[29] Ibid.
[30] Chan. Inq. p.m. (Ser. 2), cxlv, 61.
[31] Waters, op. cit. i, 87.
[32] Chan. Inq. p.m. (Ser. 2), clxxx, 2. Martha Newdigate had predeceased her mother in 1575 (ibid. ccxxxii, 15). The following settlements should be noted. In 1579 Anne wife of Griffith Hampden

CHICHLEY HALL: THE SOUTH-EAST CORNER

CHICHLEY CHURCH FROM THE SOUTH-WEST

CHICHLEY CHURCH: THE INTERIOR LOOKING EAST

CHICHLEY: TOMBS IN CHURCH

raised a troop of horse at his own expense in 1588 to repel the threatened Spanish invasion, and to have accompanied Queen Elizabeth to Tilbury Fort at the head of his troops.[33] He was sheriff of the county in 1602,[34] and in March 1619–20 was created a baronet.[35] He was in 1628 Sheriff of Bedfordshire,[36] where he had recently purchased the Tilsworth estate,[37] and received royal licence to reside outside the county at Chicheley Hall during his year of office.[38] Sir Anthony Chester, bart., died in 1635.[39] He married twice ; by his first wife Elizabeth daughter of Sir Henry Boteler, kt., he had five sons

CHESTER. *Party argent and sable a cheveron engrailed between three rams' heads cut off at the neck and having golden horns all countercoloured in a border gules bezanty.*

and seven daughters,[40] and by his second wife Mary daughter of John Ellis, one son Robert.[41] His eldest son and natural heir Anthony was at this time forty-two years of age,[42] and by his father's will, made on his death-bed and bearing date 26 November 1635, both he and his brothers and sisters were passed over in favour of Henry Chester, their father's third son by the first wife.[43] The Chicheley estates were indeed entailed on Sir Anthony Chester by settlement of 1628,[44] but his father's partial disinheritance appears to have embarrassed his circumstances, for in 1638 he obtained a warrant to admit his son Henry, then thirteen years of age, to levy a fine of these manors in order to enable Sir Anthony to lease the property for twenty-one years, 'whereby to pay his debts of £2,500 and to raise portions for his seven younger children.'[45] Sir Anthony was an ardent Royalist, and greatly distinguished himself for courage and bravery at the battle of Naseby in 1645,[46] in which same year Chicheley Hall was plundered and sacked by Parliamentary troops.[47] He was eventually obliged to take refuge in Holland in 1646, and previous to his departure sold 658 acres in Chicheley to his brother Henry Chester, leaving the remainder of his estate to him in trust in order to secure it from sequestration.[48] There is still extant a letter written by Sir Anthony to his brother on the eve of departure begging him to be 'as a husband to my wife and a father to my children during my absence for I have no friend in the world that I dare trust in as

yourself,' and proceeding to state that if the estate 'be in your hands, then I hope there will be no danger ensue to me or mine.'[49] Sir Anthony Chester returned from exile in 1650 and died the following year at Chicheley.[50] By his wife Elizabeth, daughter of Sir John Peyton, bart., who survived him forty years, he had thirteen children—five sons and eight daughters.[51] Of them Anthony, second and eldest surviving son, succeeded to the Chicheley estates, which were at this time greatly encumbered.[52] He acquired, however, an increase of fortune by his marriage in 1657 with Mary daughter of Samuel Cranmer, a wealthy alderman of London,[53] while on the death of his uncle Henry Chester in 1666 he inherited under his will the 658 acres in Chicheley alienated by the late baronet in 1646, and also the Bedfordshire property.[54] In 1685 Anthony, eldest son of the baronet, died unmarried at the age of twenty-two,[55] and two years later his father made a settlement of Chicheley,[56] which passed on his death in February 1697–8 to John his second son.[57] Sir John Chester did not settle until 1714 at Chicheley, which remained the dower-house of his mother until her death in 1710. Previous to this date he caused the old building to be demolished, and the present house was erected.[58] He died and was buried in February 1725–6 at Chicheley, leaving eleven children by his first wife Ann, daughter of William Wollaston.[59] William, his eldest son, succeeded to the title, but under his father's will, though he acquired the Chicheley estate, should he have no son it was to revert to the testator's favourite son John, who also acquired the more valuable Bedfordshire property.[60] Sir William Chester had six daughters,[61] so that on his death (which took place thirty-two days after his father) not only the title but also the Chicheley estate passed under this will to his heir male, the above John Chester.[62] Penelope, widow of Sir William, thereupon brought a suit in Chancery disputing the terms of her father-in-law's will, but the suit was brought to an unsuccessful close in 1730, the judges being unanimously in favour of Sir John Chester, bart.[63] He married Frances daughter of Sir Edward Bagot, bart., by whom he had two sons and one daughter.[64] He died intestate in February 1747–8, and letters of administration of his estate were granted to his elder son Sir Charles Bagot Chester, bart., in 1748,[65] when he also suffered a recovery of the Chicheley estates.[66] Sir Charles Bagot Chester, bart., is described by Cole as 'a thorough accomplished gentleman and universally

---

and Mary wife of Jerome Weston, also daughters and co-heirs of Anthony Cave (Waters, op. cit. i, 92, 108), made a settlement of two-thirds of the manors (Feet of F. Div. Co. Mich. 21 & 22 Eliz.; Pat. 21 Eliz. pt. vii). John son of Martha Newdigate settled lands in this parish by fine in 1592 (Feet of F. Bucks. Trin. 34 Eliz.), and in 1597 William son of Griffith Hampden died seised of lands here (Chan. Inq. p.m. [Ser. 2], ccxlviii, 39).

[33] Waters, op. cit. i, 111.
[34] P.R.O. *List of Sheriffs*, 9.
[35] G.E.C. *Baronetage*, i, 138.
[36] P.R.O. *List of Sheriffs*, 3. A settlement may be noted at this date (Recov. R. Mich. 3 Chas. I, m. 80).
[37] *V.C.H. Beds.* iii, 434.
[38] *Cal. S. P. Dom.* 1628–9, p. 403.
[39] Chan. Inq. p.m. (Ser. 2), dxli, 94.
[40] Waters, op. cit. i, 111, 119.

[41] Chan. Inq. p.m. (Ser. 2), dxli, 94.
[42] Ibid.
[43] P.C.C. 128 Sadler ; Waters, op. cit. i, 114. With the exception of a few trifling legacies and annuities Henry received all the personal estate. The will was disputed, but upheld by decree of the Ecclesiastical Court.
[44] Chan. Inq. p.m. (Ser. 2), dxli, 94.
[45] *Cal. S. P. Dom.* 1638–9, p. 148. He made a settlement by fine at the same time (Feet of F. Bucks. Trin. 15 Chas. I).
[46] Staines, *Hist. of Newport Pagnell*, 90.
[47] Collins, *The Baronetage of Engl.* (ed. 1720), ii, 132.
[48] Waters, op. cit. i, 162–5, where this arrangement is set forth at full length.
[49] Waters, op. cit. i, 162.
[50] Ibid. 165 ; G.E.C. *Baronetage*, i, 138.
[51] Ibid. ; *Visit. of Bucks.* (Harl. Soc.), 26.

[52] Waters, op. cit. i, 343.
[53] Ibid. See also Astwood.
[54] Ibid. 344. Much of his Bedfordshire estate was in reversion ; for a long period he had to pay the jointures of three Dowager Ladies Chester, who were all living at the same time.
[55] G.E.C. *Baronetage*, i, 139.
[56] Recov. R. Mich. 3 Jas. II, m. 109 ; Feet of F. Bucks. Mich. 3 Jas. II.
[57] Waters, op. cit. ii, 525.
[58] Ibid. 526–30.
[59] Ibid. 533, 535 ; G.E.C. loc. cit.
[60] Waters, op. cit. ii, 533. This will was not proved in the Prerogative Court of Canterbury (G.E.C. loc. cit.).
[61] Waters, op. cit. ii, 608.
[62] Ibid. 612.   [63] Ibid. 607.
[64] Ibid. 612.
[65] Ibid. 613.
[66] Recov. R. Trin. 21 & 22 Geo. II, m. 21.

esteemed by his acquaintance,'[67] but appears to have been a profligate of the worst description, and died in a fit of delirium tremens without legitimate issue in 1755.[68] By his will, dated 21 May 1755, he alienated the whole of the Chester estates, both in Buckinghamshire and Bedfordshire, from that family. Chicheley passed to Charles Bagot, son of his uncle Sir Walter Wagstaffe Bagot, bart., and his heirs in tail-male on condition that he should assume the name and arms of Chester.[69] Charles Bagot accordingly assumed the name of Chester and lived at Chicheley, where he was frequently visited by the poet Cowper, till his death in 1793.[70] Charles Chester, his son and heir, did not live at the Hall, which he leased about this date to Charles Pinfold, lord of Walton.[71] He died unmarried at Hampton Court in 1838,[72] and in accordance with the entail Chicheley passed to Anthony son of his brother Anthony Chester.[73] He died without male issue in 1858, and Chicheley became the property of his first cousin, Charles Montague son of William Chester.[74] The Rev. John Greville Chester, the present lord of the manor, succeeded his father, Charles Montague Chester, on the latter's death in 1879.

A second manor in this parish, known as *THICK-THORNS MANOR*, belonged to Tickford Priory, and is mentioned in the confirmation by Edward II of the founder's gifts. It was then said to be in Chicheley and Hardmead, and to comprise 317 a. 1 r. of land with meadow, pasture and wood.[75] This manor has always followed the same descent as Chicheley, and still gives its name to a farm in the east of the parish.

The right to hold a court every three weeks for both manors of Chicheley and Thickthorns is mentioned in the confirmation by Edward II of the founder's charter to Tickford Priory.[76] The view was held at Thickthorns,[77] and was confirmed by the overlord of the manor in 1310.[78] A grant of free warren in both manors was also obtained in 1311.[79]

Mention of a water-mill here has been found in the 16th century[80] and a windmill in the 14th century.[81]

A third estate in this parish was the titular *BROUGHTONS MANOR*, which appears in the 15th century. In 1420 John Fitz John and Amice his wife received a quitclaim from Richard Hulcote and Agnes his wife (on behalf of the said Agnes) of messuages and land in Chicheley,[82] and in the same year transferred the property to John Andrew and John Webbe.[83] They were probably trustees, for in 1451 John Barley and Agnes his wife[84] made two settlements, in both of which the name of John

Andrew, jun., appears.[85] The second settlement seems to represent a genuine transfer to John Broughton,[86] and this property henceforward follows the same descent as the manor of Broughton (q.v.) (being described as Chicheley Manor in 1504[87]) until 1573, when William Paulet, Lord St. John, transferred Chicheley Manor, called Broughtons, to William Chester,[88] whose son Anthony Chester inherited Chicheley Manor four years later from his grandmother (see above). No further separate mention has been found of Broughtons Manor by name.[89]

Various estates in neighbouring parishes had lands extending into Chicheley, notably the manor of Pateshull or Little Crawley in North Crawley (q.v.), which is indeed sometimes called the manor of Crawley and Chicheley.[90] In 1384 John de Burton, parson of North Crawley, received licence to sue the Prior of Tickford, who had seized tithes and obventions from Little Crawley and lands in Chicheley which John said had been from time immemorial within the metes and bounds of his parish.[91]

Hollowes Manor in North Crawley[92] and Clifton Reynes Manor[93] also both extended into Chicheley.

A younger branch of the family of Mansel or Maunsell, of which Sampson Maunsell was the head in the 13th century, was settled in Chicheley from the 13th to the 17th century. Reference to them is infrequent. In 1273 Sampson Maunsell held of the honour of Newport a fee in Chicheley[93a] which had passed to William Maunsell by 1284–6.[94] It is mentioned a few years later as belonging to the 'heir of Sampson le Maunsel.'[95] In the middle of the 14th century Hugh Maunsell's name occurs in a list of Chicheley jurors.[96] In 1400–1 John Maunsell of Wendlebury (Oxfordshire), smith, and Joan his wife quitclaimed a messuage and land in Chicheley to Richard

MAUNSELL. *Argent a cheveron between three maunches sable.*

Maunsell, belonging to the parish.[97] An old pedigree together with a rhyming chronicle of the family is preserved at Thorpe Malsor, the seat of the Northamptonshire family of Maunsells, who claim descent from the Chicheley branch. According to these ancient records a Maunsell having slain his brother with a longbow, the family suffered reverses and disappeared from this parish until Almighty God

            'of his Grace

Again in Chicheley did us place.'[98]

[67] Add. MS. 5839, fol. 58.
[68] Waters, op. cit. ii, 616; G.E.C. *Baronetage*, i, 140.
[69] Waters, loc. cit.
[70] Ibid. 617; Lysons, *Mag. Brit.* i (3), 540.
[71] Lysons, op. cit. i (3), 690.
[72] Waters, loc. cit.
[73] Ibid.; Burke, *Baronetage* (1912).
[74] Ibid.
[75] Dugdale, op. cit. v, 203.
[76] Ibid.
[77] Ibid.
[78] Add. Chart. 11224.
[79] *Cal. Chart. R.* 1300–26, p. 181.
[80] Chan. Inq. p.m. (Ser. 2), ccxxxii, 15.
[81] Dugdale, op. cit. v, 205.

[82] Feet of F. case 22, file 117, no. 7.
[83] Ibid. no. 44.
[84] Balney Lodge, the old manor-house, is possibly called after this tenant, for 'Balney' certainly goes back to the 16th century.
[85] Feet of F. case 22, file 123, no. 2, 3.
[86] Ibid. no. 3.
[87] *Cal. Inq. p.m.* Hen. VII, i, 238; P.C.C. 29 Adeane; Chan. Inq. p.m. (Ser. 2), xxxiii, 108.
[88] Feet of F. Bucks. Trin. 15 Eliz.
[89] See above for Balney Lodge.
[90] *Hund. R.* (Rec. Com.), i, 41; *Feud. Aids*, i, 110; Chan. Inq. p.m. 37 Hen. VI, no. 19; (Ser. 2), xviii, 29; ccxciii, 30; Pat. 2 Eliz. pt. iv, m. 4; 21 Jas. I, pt. xviii,

no. 4; Ct. of Req. bdle. 77, no. 52; Feet of F. Bucks. Trin. 2 Jas. I; Mich. 3 Jas. I; P.C.C. 14 Stafford.
[91] *Cal. Pat.* 1381–5, p. 445.
[92] Com. Pleas Recov. R. Mich. 39 & 40 Eliz. m. 26; Chan. Inq. p.m. (Ser. 2), dxcii, 87.
[93] Close, 13 Ric. II, pt. ii, m. 9 d.; Feet of F. Bucks. Trin. and Mich. 16 Hen. VIII; Mich. 32 Hen. VIII; Trin. 8 Will. III; Mich. 10 Anne.
[93a] *Cal. Inq. p.m.* (Edw. I), ii, 15.
[94] *Feud. Aids*, i, 83.
[95] Ibid. 104.
[96] *Inq. Nonarum* (Rec. Com.), 337.
[97] Feet of F. case 21, file 111.
[98] *V.C.H. Northants Families*, 227.

There is certainly a gap of nearly 200 years in the history of the family at this date. The name reappears in the person of Thomas son of Richard Maunsell,[99] who by his will, bearing date August 1581, left his lands in Chicheley to his son John.[100] John Maunsell died and was buried at Bromley in Kent in 1625.[1] He had two sons, John and Thomas,[2] who appear to have sold their property in Chicheley shortly after this date to the lord of the manor, for in a schedule of lands belonging to Sir Anthony Chester, bart., lord of the manor, made in 1646, occurs mention of ' all that capitall messuage with the appurtenances called Mansells, situate and being in Berry End in Chicheley aforesaid.'[3] The Maunsell lands have since followed the same descent as the manor, while the family removed to Thorpe Malsor, where it is still established.[4]

A family of Horton was settled in Chicheley for several generations in the 15th century, or possibly earlier. Richard son of John Horton[5] in his will proved in 1461 refers to his grandfather Thomas Horton, whose silver spoons he bequeathed to his sister Joan.[6] Some years after his death his widow Millicent disputed his will with Richard Horton and other trustees.[7]

CHURCH   The church of *ST. LAWRENCE* consists of a chancel 21 ft. by 14 ft., central tower 15 ft. 6 in. by 12 ft., nave 35 ft. by 18 ft., north aisle 52 ft. by 15 ft. 6 in., and south porch ; all the measurements being internal. It is built of rubble, and the roofs are covered with lead.

The plan of the present building appears to be the result of successive additions to a 12th-century church consisting of the existing nave and a small chancel. A north aisle, extending the full length of this building, was added about 1325, while about 1480 the original chancel was replaced by the tower, and a new chancel was built to the east of the tower. In the 16th century the south porch and the nave clearstory were added, and in 1708 the chancel was again rebuilt. The aisle and tower have been recently restored.

The chancel is a pleasing example of the Queen Anne period. At the eastern angles and against the tower are Corinthian pilasters, while the side walls are crowned by a moulded cornice and plain parapet with carved urns at the corners, the east wall being finished with a pediment. Neither the north nor the east wall is pierced, but externally in the east wall are two large semicircular niches with shell heads and carved pedestals. On the south is a square-headed doorway, flanked on either side by a window of two lights with Gothic tracery in a square head. The windows have moulded architraves, which are carried down to inclose blank panels below the sills, and are surmounted by pulvinated friezes and segmental pediments, while above the doorway is a moulded cornice supporting the shield of John Chester, fourth baronet, Chester with Wollaston in pretence. The walls are plastered internally and have a wood-panelled dado ; at the east end, occupying the full width of the wall, is a marble reredos with Corinthian pilasters, supporting a deep richly foliated frieze with a moulded cornice,

above which, in an architectural setting, is a tablet with the inscription 'Gloria in Excelsis.' The fine plaster ceiling has a foliated cornice and a central oval wreath of flowers and fruit. The chancel is entered from the west through an oak screen of three round arches with Roman Doric columns and responds on tall pedestals. The pedestals of the middle arch form posts to a charming wrought-iron gate surmounted by scrollwork and foliation. A lead rain-water head at the north-west corner of the chancel bears the arm of John Chester and the date 1708.

The ground stage of the tower opens to the chancel on the east, to the nave on the west, and to the aisle on the north, by pointed arches of the 15th century, supported by semi-octagonal responds with moulded capitals and bases. Part of the south respond of the western arch has been removed, and the upper part of the arch to the chancel is now blocked. On the south is a tall 15th-century window of three lights with tracery in a pointed head, and at the south-east is a newel staircase to the bell-chamber, the original entrance to which is blocked, a new doorway having been opened externally. High in the wall is a doorway which opened originally from the staircase to the rood-loft, but now admits to an 18th-century gallery forming an upper floor to the ground stage of the tower. The oak rood with figures which now stands upon this gallery was erected in 1904.

On the north side of the nave is an early 14th-century arcade of three pointed arches supported by clustered pillars and responds with moulded capitals and bases. On the south are a three-light window and a plain doorway, both of which were inserted in the 15th century. In the west wall is a three-light traceried window of about 1350. The clearstory is lighted from either side by four 16th-century windows with depressed heads. On the south side of the nave is a 15th-century stoup with a cinquefoiled head, and near the west end of the wall are traces of painting which probably date from the 16th century. The aisle is lighted from the north by two windows, only the jambs and rear arches of which are ancient, and from the west by a modern window. The east window, now blocked, dates from the 14th century, and the pointed north doorway is of the same period. The aisle was reroofed in the 16th century.

The porch is of two stories and has a pointed archway on the south and a square-headed window of two lights in each lateral wall, all of the 16th century. The upper chamber was originally lighted by a small window in the gable, but this is now blocked. The tower rises two stages above the church roof and is surmounted by an embattled parapet. The second stage has two small windows, one of which is partly covered by the clock face, and the bell-chamber is lighted from all sides by long twin windows, each of two trefoiled lights with a transom midway in their height.

On the floor at the east end of the aisle is a brass with the figures of a man in plate armour and his wife in cloak and veil head-dress, and an inscription commemorating Anthony Cave, merchant of the Staple of Calais, who died in 1558 ; two shields

[99] *V.C.H. Northants Families*, 229.
[100] P.C.C. 4 Row. Mention is also made of his sons Richard and Thomas, his wife Agnes, his daughters Elizabeth, Martha and Mary, and his brother John.

[1] Add. MS. 5839, fol. 53, quoting monumental inscription.
[2] Ibid. ; *V.C.H. Northants Families*, 229.
[3] Waters, op. cit. i, 163.
[4] *V.C.H. Northants Families*, 230 et seq.

[5] Early Chan. Proc. bdle. 31, no. 220.
[6] P.C.C. 23 Stokton ; Add. MS. 5839, fol. 56 d.
[7] Early Chan. Proc. bdles. 31, no. 220, 238 ; 39, no. 80 ; 40, no. 226.

A HISTORY OF BUCKINGHAMSHIRE

remain, one of Cave impaling Lovett, and the other of the Staple, while two others are lost. On the east wall of the aisle is a 16th-century brass with the figure of a shrouded skeleton, an inscription in verse, and a shield of Cave. In the nave are a brass inscription with an achievement of arms to William son of Henry Shelley of Patcham, Sussex (d. 1638), and an inscription to Elizabeth Noke[8] (?) (d. 1658). Against the east end of the north wall of the aisle there is also a stone monument to the Anthony Cave mentioned above, erected by Elizabeth (Lovett) his wife in 1576. It consists of a sarcophagus flanked by caryatides standing on pedestals and supporting an entablature and pediment. On the sarcophagus is the recumbent figure of a corpse, above which in high relief are figures of two sons and six daughters; in the pediment is an achievement of the arms of Cave, while above the figures of the children are the shields of Cave and Lovett. At the east end of the aisle is a large monument to Sir Anthony Chester, knight and first baronet (d. 1635), and Dame Elizabeth (Boteler) his first wife (d. 1629). Their kneeling figures are represented below a canopy formed by an entablature and cornice supported by tall Corinthian columns; above the cornice are the shields of Chester, Chester impaling Boteler, and Chester quartering Cave and Boteler. On the north wall of the chancel are two elaborate marble monuments; one, surmounted by the arms of Chester impaling Cranmer, in memory of Sir Anthony Chester, third baronet (d. 1698), and Mary his wife (d. 1710), daughter of Samuel Cranmer, London; and the other, with the arms of Chester impaling Wollaston, to Ann, first wife of Sir John Chester, fourth baronet (d. 1704), daughter of William Wollaston of Shenton, Leicestershire. There are several 17th-century floor slabs in the north aisle. The communion table and rails are

of the 18th century, the former being dated 1755, and the carved ends of a wide seat in the chancel are of the same period. At the west end of the church is some 17th-century panelling, and there is a Bible box of that period in the aisle.

The tower contains a ring of six bells, all by Abraham Rudhall, 1718, and the framework is of the same date.

The communion plate includes a cup and cover paten of 1744 and a flagon of 1735.

The registers begin in 1539.

ADVOWSON The church of Chicheley, which formed part of the original endowment of Tickford Priory, follows the same descent as the manor,[9] and is at present in the gift of the Rev. John Greville Chester. In the taxation of 1291 the vicarage was assessed at £6,[10] and at the Dissolution is entered at £8.[11] The rectory follows the same descent as the advowson.

In 1318 Richard Burgess alienated land in mortmain in Chicheley towards the maintenance of a chaplain in the church of Newport Pagnell.[12]

CHARITIES The charity of John Maunsell, mentioned in the Parliamentary Returns of 1786, consists of an annuity of £2 12s. issuing out of 2 acres of land in the parish which is distributed among poor widows and widowers.

In 1852 the Rev. Henry Cotton by deed gave £100 consols, the dividends to be given to such one, two or three poor inhabitants as the vicar should appoint.

The Rev. Samuel Thomas Townsend by his will in 1874 bequeathed £500, which was invested in £536 3s. 10d. consols, the annual dividends, amounting to £13 8s., to be distributed equally among twelve aged sick or infirm poor.

The sums of stock are held by the official trustees.

CLIFTON REYNES

Cliftone (xi cent.); Clifton next Olneye[1] (xiv cent.).

Clifton Reynes is bounded on the north and northwest by the Ouse, where the land is liable to floods; it rises in the south-east to 273 ft. above ordnance datum. The Bedford and Northampton branch of the Midland railway crosses the north of the parish. The area is 1,454 acres, of which 387 acres are arable, 967 acres permanent grass, and 50 acres woods and plantations.[2] The soil is gravel, stone, and loam, the subsoil chiefly stone; the chief crops are cereals and beans.

The small compact village stands on the hill overlooking the Ouse and the town of Olney, and has St. Mary's Church on the west, with the rectory, a 17th-century stone building incorporating remains of an earlier house, but much altered and restored, to the south of the church. In a terrier of 1639 it is described as of five bays of stone covered with thatch, the whole 'contained in eight rooms.'[3] About 1830

what is said to have been a small 15th-century oratory, which adjoined the house on the east, was pulled down.

North-west of the church stood the house built by Alexander Small on his purchase of the manor c. 1750. It was destroyed about 1850,[4] and nothing now remains to indicate its site save the wall round the garden, orchard, fish-pond and portion of the avenue.[5] The dovecote attached to the manor is still standing in the centre of the village; it is a circular building of 17th-century date with stone walls and a thatched roof.

In the village are some 17th-century houses, among them the Robin Hood Inn.

The common fields were inclosed by Act of Parliament in 1822,[6] and the award is dated 1824.[7] According to Sheahan that part of the parish which belonged to the principal manor (Reynes) was inclosed at a remote and unknown period.[8] One great field

[8] The name is indistinct.
[9] Cf. also Mins. Accts. bdles. 1125, no. 1; 1127, no. 18; De Banco R. Trin. 1 Edw. III, m. 32 d.; Trin. 2 Edw. III, m. 52 d.; Mich. 2 Edw. III, m. 255; Cal. Pat. 1348–50, pp. 288, 338; 1396–9, pp. 27, 531; Inst. Bks. (P.R.O.).

[10] Pope Nich. Tax. (Rec. Com.), 33b.
[11] Valor Eccl. (Rec. Com.), iv, 243.
[12] Cal. Pat. 1317–21, p. 135.
[1] The additional name of Reynes first appears at the end of the 14th century (Close, 13 Ric. II, pt. ii, m. 9 d.).
[2] Statistics from Bd. of Agric. (1905).

[8] Add. MS. 5839, fol. 62.
[4] Sheahan, op. cit. 520.
[5] Wright, The Town of Cowper, 216.
[6] Priv. Act, 3 Geo. IV, cap. 6.
[7] Com. Pleas Recov. R. East. 7 Geo. IV, no. 6.
[8] Op. cit. 519.

CLIFTON REYNES: THE RECTORY

CLIFTON REYNES CHURCH FROM THE SOUTH-EAST

CLIFTON REYNES CHURCH: THE INTERIOR LOOKING EAST

of arable land, in extent about 12 score acres, was inclosed about 1560 by Francis Lowe, then lord of that manor.[9]

Among place-names have been found : Thornydols Close [10] (xvi cent.) ; Water Hills, Revell Mead, Aldridge Wood, Pepies Grove, Long Meadow Dusse,[11] Heirons Grove [12] (xvii cent.).

Osulf, a thegn of King Edward, held *MANORS* and could sell *CLIFTON*, afterwards *CLIFTON REYNES* or *REYNES*, a manor of 4 hides, 1 virgate of which was held by Alric his man.[13] By 1086 this manor had come to Robert de Toeni.[14] He was succeeded by the Daubeneys,[15] whose land passed about 1248 by the marriage of Isabel, daughter and heir of William Daubeney, to Robert de Ros,[16] overlord in 1284–6.[17] The connexion of the Ros family with Clifton existed as late as 1428.[18]

The under-tenants in 1086 were William de Borard (Boscroard, Bosco Roardi, Bosco Rahara, Bosco Roaldi) and his brother, apparently named Roger. They had also taken possession of 3 virgates formerly held by Suert and Turbert, which they had concealed to the king's damage, as the men of the hundred asserted.[19] The Borards also held Stathern in Leicestershire, and a Simon de Borard is mentioned in 1166 as holding three fees in that county of William Daubeney.[20] A late Simon de Borard revolted against King John, but returned to his allegiance in 1217.[21] A son of the same name,[22] who came of age before 1230,[23] held Clifton in the middle of the century,[24] and is said to have died some time after 1260, the latest reference found bearing date October 1261.[24a]

His successor, Richard de Borard, probably his son,[25] is mentioned in 1278,[26] and is returned as lord of Clifton in 1284.[27] He is mentioned in connexion with Stathern in 1290,[28] and in 1293 paid £20 to be exempted for life from bearing the arms of a knight.[29] His sister and heir Joan is said to have married Thomas Reynes,[30] from whose family Clifton received its distinguishing appellation, and their son Ralf Reynes [31] held Clifton in 1302–3.[32] Two wooden figures in the church may commemorate this Ralf and his second wife Mabel, daughter of Sir Richard Chamberlain of Petsoe in Emberton.[33] He must have died before 1310, in which year Sir Roger Tyringham had the custody of his land and heir.[34] This heir, a son Thomas, was in possession of Clifton in 1316,[35] and was knight of the shire for the Parliaments of 1339,

1343, 1344, and 1346.[36] He is mentioned as in possession of the manor in 1344 [37] and in 1346.[38] In 1354 he settled the manor on himself and wife Joan for life, with remainder to Thomas their son and his issue, and contingent remainder to the issue male of Thomas the father, and to Joan, Cecily, and Agnes his daughters.[39] It was probably the son Thomas who was knight of the shire in 1369 and 1377,[40] and made in 1368 a settlement of Clifton Reynes,[41] which he confirmed twenty years later.[42] He appears to have died about this date,[43] and was succeeded by his son John,[44] who is returned as lord in 1394.[45] By his first wife, Katherine Scudamore, who was alive in 1388, John had a son Thomas, who died during his father's lifetime in 1416, leaving a son John,[46] who died an infant five years later,[47] when his grandfather John laid claim to the estate.[48] By his second wife

OLD DOVECOTE, CLIFTON REYNES

he had a son Walter, born in 1403,[49] and by his third wife Alice, on whom he made a settlement of the

[9] Ct. of Req. bdle. 108, no. 30.
[10] Chan. Proc. (Ser. 2), bdle. 115, no. 64.
[11] Close, 25 Chas. II, pt. xix, no. 35, 38.
[12] Chan. Inq. p.m. (Ser. 2), dcxlvii, 33.
[13] *V.C.H. Bucks.* i, 257. [14] Ibid.
[15] Dugdale, *Baronage*, i, 113.
[16] *Excerpta e Rot. Fin.* (Rec. Com.), ii, 42 ; G.E.C. *Peerage*, i, 67.
[17] *Feud. Aids*, i, 82.
[18] Chan. Inq. p.m. 6 Hen. VI, no. 35.
[19] *V.C.H. Bucks.* i, 257.
[20] *Liber Niger* (ed. 2), 208.
[21] *Rot. Lit. Claus.* (Rec. Com.), i, 333*b*.
[22] Lipscomb, *Hist. and Antiq. of Bucks.* iv, 105.

[23] Maitland, *Bracton's Note Bk.* ii, 333.
[24] *Testa de Nevill* (Rec. Com.), 244, 251.
[24a] Assize R. 58, m. 11 d.
[25] Lipscomb, loc. cit.
[26] Chan. Inq. p.m. Edw. I, file 22, no. 2.
[27] *Feud. Aids*, i, 82.
[28] *Cal. Pat.* 1281–92, p. 392 ; Inq. a.q.d. file 15, no. 7.
[29] *Cal. Pat.* 1292–1301, p. 53.
[30] Lipscomb, loc. cit.
[31] Ibid.
[32] *Feud. Aids*, i, 104.
[33] Lipscomb, loc. cit. ; *Rec. of Bucks.* vi, 400.
[34] Add. MS. 5839, fol. 62 d.

[35] *Feud. Aids*, i, 110.
[36] *Ret. of Memb. of Parl.* i, 124, 136, 138, 140.
[37] Inq. a.q.d. file 272, no. 12.
[38] *Feud. Aids*, i, 130.
[39] Feet of F. case 20, file 92, no. 2.
[40] *Ret. of Memb. of Parl.* i, 181, 195.
[41] Close, 231, m. 9 d.
[42] Ibid.
[43] Assize R. 1543, m. 47a.
[44] Ibid.
[45] Chan. Inq. p.m. 18 Ric. II, no. 34.
[46] Ibid. 5 Hen. V, no. 1.
[47] Coram Rege R. 675, m. 111 ; Chan. Inq. p.m. 9 Hen. VI, no. 62.
[48] Coram Rege R. 660, m. 78.
[49] Chan. Inq. p.m. 6 Hen. VI, no. 35.

manor in 1427,[50] he is said to have left a son John.[51] John Reynes died in the following year, and Walter Reynes, his son, was found to be his heir.[52] In 1438 he was sued, unsuccessfully, however, by Joan daughter of Henry Street and of Cecily, daughter of John Reynes by his first wife Katherine, who asserted that in 1388 Clifton Reynes had been settled on John's issue by Katherine, of whom Thomas and Denise his sister had died without issue, leaving Cecily as sole heir.[53] In 1430 Joan's brother,

REYNES. *Checky or and gules a quarter ermine.*

William Street, had laid claim to lands in Hertfordshire as heir to his cousin John Reynes, who died an infant in 1421.[54] As wife of John Anstey, Joan Street renewed her claim in 1440, after the death of Walter Reynes without issue, another claimant being her half-cousin Margaret, wife of John Gibbon and daughter of Margery, sister of the whole blood to the said Walter.[55] It appears, however, that the manor went to John son of John Reynes by his third wife Alice, who is said to have died in 1451,[56] when Clifton passed to Thomas Reynes of Marston Moretaine in Bedfordshire, who had succeeded his father Thomas in that year,[57] the latter being son of Richard, brother of the John Reynes of Clifton who died in 1428.[58] This Thomas Reynes, who was sheriff of the county in 1462,[59] appears to be identical with the Thomas who died in April 1471.[60] He was succeeded by John Reynes, probably his son, alive in March 1498–9,[61] who left a daughter and heir Elizabeth, the wife of Richard Dicons.[62] In 1518 Dicons obtained a quitclaim of rights in half the manor from George Pierpoint,[63] son or grandson and heir by another husband of the Margaret who claimed half the manor in the suit of 1440.[64] The Dicons appear, however, to have renounced their interest in Clifton at an earlier date to Thomas Reynes, clerk, uncle of Elizabeth,[65] who presented to the church in February 1507–8 [65a] and died about the end of 1524.[66] By his will, proved 18 February 1524–5, he left all his household stuff in Marston parsonage to his nieces, the three daughters of his sister.[67] He was succeeded by his brother Richard,[68] during whose tenure of the manor a

renunciation of rights appears to have been made in 1528 by Lawrence Taillard,[69] probably son and heir of Elizabeth wife of William Taillard, and daughter and co-heir of Joan Anstey, the claimant in the suit of 1440.[70] Richard Reynes settled Clifton on his wife Maud,[71] and left three daughters and co-heirs, of whom one married Thomas Lowe, esquire of the body and captain under Henry VIII.[72] In 1540 the Lowes bought up the rights of Sir Robert Dormer,[73] to whom Clifton may have been mortgaged, and in 1544 Thomas Lowe died seised of the manor, which passed to his son Francis.[74] Francis got into debt, and into money difficulties, and repeatedly mortgaged the manor.[75] With his wife Thomasina he was dealing with the manor in 1591.[76] He was succeeded by his son Reynes Lowe,[77] who died in 1618,[78] leaving a son

LOWE. *Argent a bend azure with three wolves' heads razed argent thereon.*

Reynes, a minor, who came of age in 1627.[79] He was living in 1651,[80] but by 1661 had been succeeded by James Lowe,[81] his son,[82] who with his wife Elizabeth was holding the manor in 1668.[83] In 1673 James Lowe and his mother, Mary Lowe, sold Clifton Reynes for £13,500 to Sir John Maynard,[84] Elizabeth wife of John Curtis renouncing any claim to it in the following year for £1,200.[85] This Sir John Maynard was a celebrated Parliamentarian, but also one of the first serjeants called at the Restoration, and termed therefore by Pepys 'a turncoat.' He died in October 1690, and his estate, according to his will, dated 21 March 1689–90, became the right of Elizabeth wife of Sir Henry Hobart, bart., and Mary wife of Thomas second Earl of Stamford, daughters of his son Joseph, who had predeceased him.[86] An Act of Parliament was passed in 1694 for settling the estate,[87] and in 1696 the Hobarts levied a fine of Clifton Reynes.[88] Sir Henry Hobart was killed in a duel in 1698,[89] and his widow died in 1701,[90] leaving an eight year old son, Sir John Hobart.[91] In 1711 Sir John Hobart settled his half of the manor on his eldest son and heirs male.[92] His aunt Mary Countess of Stamford died without issue,[93] and the sole interest in the manor therefore devolved on him. Sir John Hobart as Earl of Buckinghamshire sold it about 1750

50 Feet of F. Bucks. East. 5 Hen. VI.
51 Lipscomb, loc. cit.
52 Chan. Inq. p.m. 6 Hen. VI, no. 35.
53 Assize R. 1543, m. 47a.
54 Coram Rege R. 30, m. 111–13.
55 Wrottesley, *Ped. from Plea R.* 371.
56 Lipscomb, loc. cit.
57 *V.C.H. Beds.* iii, 309, where the name of Dicons (see below) is spelt Decons; brass in Marston Church.
58 Ibid.; Lipscomb, loc. cit.
59 P.R.O. *List of Sheriffs,* 2.
60 Chan. Inq. p.m. 12 Edw. IV, no. 22; cf. *Cal. Pat.* 1467–77, p. 607.
61 Harl. MS. 6953, fol. 57.
62 *Visit. of Beds.* (Harl. Soc.), 140.
63 Feet of F. Bucks. Mich. 10 Hen. VIII.
64 De Banco R. Trin. 15 Edw. IV, m. 101.
65 Lipscomb, loc. cit.
65a Add. MS. 5839, fol. 62 d.

66 He made a settlement of Clifton in that year (Recov. R. East. 16 Hen. VIII, m. 100; Feet of F. Bucks. Trin. and Mich. 16 Hen. VIII).
67 P.C.C. 31 Bodfelde.
68 Lipscomb, loc. cit.
69 Recov. R. Hil. 19 Hen. VIII, m. 125.
70 De Banco R. Trin. 15 Edw. IV, m. 101.
71 Exch. Inq. p.m. (Ser. 2), file 39, no. 10.
72 *Visit. of Bucks.* (Harl. Soc.), 87.
73 Feet of F. Bucks. Mich. 32 Hen. VIII.
74 Exch. Inq. p.m. (Ser. 2), file 39, no. 10.
75 Chan. Proc. (Ser. 2), bdles. 115, no. 64; 132, no. 30; Feet of F. Bucks. Trin. 3 Eliz.
76 Feet of F. Bucks. East. 33 Eliz.
77 *Visit. of Bucks.* loc. cit.
78 Chan. Inq. p.m. (Ser. 2), ccclxxv,

78. In the same year he had made settlement of the manor on his wife Mary, her son Reynes, and her daughters Magdalen, Thomasina, Elizabeth and Margaret.
79 Recov. R. Trin. 3 Chas. I, m. 60.
80 Ibid. Trin. 1651, m. 23.
81 Inst. Bks. (P.R.O.).
82 Close, 25 Chas. II, pt. xix, no. 35.
83 Feet of F. Bucks. Mich. 20 Chas. II.
84 Close, 25 Chas. II, pt. xix, no. 35, 38; Recov. R. East. 25 Chas. II, m. 139.
85 Feet of F. Bucks. Trin. 26 Chas. II.
86 *Dict. Nat. Biog.*; Vernon, *Cases in Chancery* (ed. Raithby, 1829), ii, 644.
87 Vernon, loc. cit.
88 Feet of F. Bucks. Trin. 8 Will. III.
89 G.E.C. *Baronetage,* i, 13.
90 *Musgrave's Obit.* (Harl. Soc.), iii, 224.
91 G.E.C. loc. cit.
92 Feet of F. Bucks. Mich. 10 Anne.
93 G.E.C. *Peerage,* vii, 230.

318

to Alexander Small, surgeon of Chelsea,[94] who died two years later,[95] leaving a legacy to his widow Martha and settling the manor on trustees to the use of his infant son Alexander.[96] The eldest son of this Alexander, another Alexander Small, is mentioned in connexion with Clifton in 1785,[97] when he apparently joined in levying a fine to cut off an entail on the manor. He died in 1794,[98] and his father survived until 1816, when he was succeeded by his daughter Martha Elizabeth Anne Small,[99] to whom he had bequeathed the manor for life, with remainder to an illegitimate son, Arthur Small.[100] This daughter married in 1819 Richard Hurd Lucas, who then became, in right of his wife, lord of the manor.[1] He had been succeeded before 1831 by Arthur George Small, who was then holding it.[2] It was sold some years later by the Smalls to Joseph Robinson,[3] who was still the owner in 1877.[4] By 1899 it had passed into the possession of Mr. James West Scorer, the present lord of the manor.

Two estates in Clifton, one of 1½ hides and the other of 1 hide and half a virgate, which had been held respectively by Alvric, a man of Bishop Wulfwig, and by two thegns, men of Alric son of Goding, were assessed in 1086 among the lands of the Countess Judith.[5] They afterwards formed part of the honour of Huntingdon,[6] the overlordship rights passing from the Hastings[7] to the Greys of Ruthyn,[8] whose interest in Clifton was acknowledged as late as 1475.[9] These two estates, the undertenants of which in 1086 were Niel and Roger de Olney respectively, correspond to the later Butlers and Wakes Manors, which extended into the adjacent parish of Newton Blossomville. *WAKES MANOR*, which owed its distinguishing name to the family who afterwards held it in fee, appears to have passed from Roger de Olney to a descendant, Simon de Olney, who is mentioned in connexion with one-third of a hide in Olney in 1199.[10] He, or a successor of the same name, was said to hold a quarter of a fee in Clifton of the Earl of Arundel in the next century,[11] and is probably identical with the Simon de Breynes holding a quarter of a fee of Henry Hastings in 1241.[11a] His successors in the manor, the Wakes, first appear in Clifton in 1281, when Hugh Wake and Isabel his wife made a life grant of land held in her right to Roger de Stowmarket.[12] Hugh son of the above Hugh Wake[13] was returned as lord of this manor in 1302,[14] and in 1305 he and

his wife Anderina acquired additional land in Clifton.[15] Hugh Wake died before 1313, in which year his widow Anderina held alone,[16] but another Hugh Wake, probably their son, was holding this property in 1318 jointly with Isabel his wife.[17] He was still alive in 1359,[18] but had been succeeded in 1375 by Ralph Basset le Riche,[19] whose widow Joan in 1395 claimed a third of Wakes Manor, first so called, in dower.[20] It descended with the Basset manor of Newton Blossomville[21] (q.v.), but after 1423 lost its distinguishing name of Wakes (except for a single late reference in 1686[22]) and probably coalesced with the manor of Butlers, which had been in the same ownership since 1305, to form the manor of *CLIFTON*. Clifton was retained by the Mordaunts, Earls of Peterborough, when they alienated Newton Blossomville, and descended with the title[23] until 1789, when the fifth and last earl sold it to John Higgins of Turvey House (Bedfordshire) for £1,400.[24] John Higgins died in 1813, and was succeeded by his son Thomas Charles Higgins.[25] He is described in 1822 as holding in his own right, and also as lessee of Queen's College, Oxford.[26] He died at Leamington in 1865,[27] shortly after which date the sole interest in the estate appears to have been acquired by Queen's College, Oxford.[28]

That part of the Countess Judith's lands which afterwards became known as *BUTLERS MANOR* took its name from a family, a member of which, John Butler (Pincerna), held in Clifton in the early 13th century.[29] A William Butler and Alice his wife had lands here in 1275,[30] but the head of the family appears to have been Simon Butler.[31] He was succeeded by Peter Butler, lord in 1284[32] and 1302,[33] who with Margery his wife in 1305 alienated lands here and the reversion of the dower of Joan, the widow of Simon Butler, to Hugh Wake.[34] Butlers, first so called in 1395,[35] henceforward descended with Wakes, but lost its distinguishing name after 1423, probably coalescing with Wakes to form the later Clifton Manor.

Six virgates of land in Newton and Clifton belonged to the honour of Yealmpton (Devon) in

WAKE. *Or two bars gules with three roundels gules in the chief.*

[94] Lysons, *Mag. Brit.* i (3), 544.
[95] *Musgrave's Obit.* (Harl. Soc.), v, 290. Tablet in church.
[96] P.C.C. 107 Bettesworth. By a former wife he had two daughters, both married, one having two children.
[97] Recov. R. Trin. 25 Geo. III, m. 234.
[98] Lipscomb, op. cit. iv, 108.
[99] Tablet in church.
[100] Lipscomb, loc. cit.
[1] Priv. Act, 3 Geo. IV, cap. 6.
[2] Feet of F. Bucks. Hil. 1 Will. IV.
[3] Sheahan, op. cit. 520.
[4] cf. *Ret. of Owners of Lands* (1873), Bucks. 17.
[5] *V.C.H. Bucks.* i, 274.
[6] *Testa de Nevill* (Rec. Com.), 251.
[7] Chan. Inq. p.m. 6 Edw. II, no. 56; 14 Ric. II, no. 9; 21 Ric. II, no. 2.
[8] Ibid. 2 Hen. VI, no. 20.
[9] Ibid. 15 Edw. IV, no. 44.
[10] *Rot. Cur. Reg.* (Rec. Com.), ii, 37.

[11] *Testa de Nevill* (Rec. Com.), 244, 252b.
[11a] *Cal. Close*, 1237–42, p. 370.
[12] Feet of F. Div. Co. Mich. 9 & 10 Edw. I, no. 25.
[13] Ibid. case 17, file 58, no. 14.
[14] *Feud. Aids*, i, 104.
[15] Feet of F. case 17, file 58, no. 13.
[16] Chan. Inq. p.m. 6 Edw. II, no. 56.
[17] Feet of F. case 18, file 70, no. 2.
[18] Harl. Chart. 57, D 29. See also *Feud. Aids*, i, 130; Chan. Inq. p.m. 22 Edw. III (1st nos.), no. 47.
[19] Chan. Inq. p.m. 49 Edw. III (1st nos.), no. 70. There is reference to John Wake of Clifton in 1378 (*Cal. Close*, 1377–81, p. 126).
[20] De Banco R. 538, m. 285 d.
[21] See also Chan. Inq. p.m. 14 Hen. VI, no. 35; Feet of F. Div. Co. Trin. 22 Jas. I; East. 2 Chas. I.
[22] Feet of F. Div. Co. Hil. 1 & 2 Jas. II.

[23] Ibid. Trin. 22 Jas. I; East. 2 Chas. I; Recov. R. Trin. 23 Geo. III, m. 12. See Lavendon for the descent until the middle of the 17th century.
[24] Com. Pleas D. Enr. East. 29 Geo. III, m. 46.
[25] Lipscomb, op. cit. iv, 115.
[26] Priv. Act, 3 Geo. IV, cap. 6.
[27] Harvey, *Hundred of Willey*, 190; cf. Sheahan, loc. cit. The descent of the family as given by Lipscomb loc. cit. is erroneous.
[28] *Rec. of Bucks.* vi, 389.
[29] *Testa de Nevill* (Rec. Com.), 244, 251.
[30] Feet of F. Div. Co. Mich. 3 & 4 Edw. I, no. 35.
[31] Ibid. case 17, file 58, no. 14.
[32] *Feud. Aids*, i, 82.
[33] Ibid. 104.
[34] Feet of F. case 17, file 58, no. 14.
[35] De Banco R. 538, m. 285 d.

the early 13th century.[36] By 1284–6 the overlordship rights had passed to Reynold Grey,[37] and they were held in 1442 by Richard Grey de Wilton.[38] The ownership in fee was vested in the Visdelou family, and in 1188 [Ralf] Moryn paid 1 mark for the farm of Newton which had belonged to Humphrey Visdelou.[39] A later Humphrey Visdelou was in possession in the early 13th century,[40] and in 1227 he claimed land here against Robert de Flurs and Hawise his wife.[41] In 1256 he granted a rent of 2s. in Newton to William de Nottingham and Philippa his wife,[42] and in 1279 they acquired a messuage and half a virgate of land there from Felise, widow of William de Falconberg.[43] John de Nottingham claimed common of pasture in Newton and Clifton in 1307 against John Visdelou and others,[44] and in 1312 Simon de Nottingham and Amice his wife granted land in Newton Blossomville and Clifton to Simon le Bedel of Keysoe (Bedfordshire).[45] This property is mentioned again in 1442, but the names of the tenants are not detailed.[46]

VISDELOU. *Argent three wolves' heads sable.*

A manor of 1½ hides in Clifton was held before the Conquest by Alli, a thegn of King Edward. In 1086 it was held by Morcar of the Bishop of Coutances, who had received it in exchange for Bleadon in Somerset.[47]

Another hide there held in the time of King Edward by Wulfwin, a man of Deus, was held in 1086 by Turbert of the Bishop of Coutances.[43]

There was a mill on the Bishop of Coutances' land in 1086[49] and a moiety of a mill worth 11s. and 125 eels from a fishery on Countess Judith's holding.[50] Two mills were held with Reynes Manor in 1544[51] and in 1627.[52] Three water-mills were held with it in 1673.[53] There is a corn-mill on the Ouse just over the western border.

The church of *ST. MARY THE VIRGIN* consists of a chancel measuring internally about 29 ft. 8 in. by 15 ft. 2 in., north chapel 24 ft. 7 in. by 9 ft. 11 in., nave 31 ft. by 12 ft. 5 in., north aisle 46 ft. by 12 ft., south aisle 45 ft. 8 in. by 11 ft. 6 in., west tower 12 ft. by 11 ft. and a south porch 7 ft. by 8 ft. 6 in.

The lower stage of the tower is the only remaining portion of a 12th-century church, consisting probably of a chancel, nave and western tower. To this church the existing aisles were added in the 13th century. Early in the 14th century the chancel was rebuilt and widened towards the south, and about the same period the present upper stage was added to the tower. Shortly after the completion of the chancel the north chapel was added, and about 1360 the nave arcades were rebuilt, the original proportions of the nave being preserved, and the chancel arch was enlarged to match. The tower arch, which is of the same general

type, was widened a few years later, and early in the 15th century the present clearstory was built, its addition above the tall narrow bays of the arcades giving an unusual height to the somewhat narrow nave. The eastern portion of the south wall of the south aisle, the internal face of which leans outward very considerably, may have been refaced and straightened externally in the same century, when the south-east window was inserted. The south-east angle, however, has been underpinned with headstones from the churchyard, and it is possible that the straightening of the wall is modern. It is difficult to assign a date to the porch, but it may be of the 16th century. The north wall of the north aisle was rebuilt in 1801, but the west wall appears to have been left standing. The portion of the aisle overlapping the tower is divided by a stud partition from the rest of the aisle, being now used as a storehouse, and has a lean-to roof sloping from east to west. The church was restored in 1883–4, and in 1905 an arch was built between the north chapel and aisle in place of a partition which had been inserted at a late period. The walling generally is of limestone rubble, and the nave and aisle roofs are lead-covered, that of the north chapel being tiled.

The chancel is a good example of early 14th-century design, and retains most of its original details. The east window is square-headed and of three cinquefoiled lights; the tracery and head are of the 15th century, but the jambs appear to be of the 14th century. Beneath the sill internally is a partially restored stringcourse, which is dropped on either side of the window, and returned for a short distance upon the side walls. Above the string-course, to the north of the window, is a clumsily moulded image bracket, and beneath it is a smaller bracket, plain and rough, doubtless for a light.[53a] The north side of the chancel is chiefly occupied by an early 14th-century arcade of two bays opening to the chapel. The arches are two-centred and of three orders; the outer order, which projects to allow for the plastering of the wall, now removed, is plain-chamfered, the intermediate order is hollow-chamfered, and the inner order is moulded with a swelled chamfer. The central column is octagonal, and the inner orders are carried on the east and west responds by semi-octagonal pilasters. Of the three windows in the south wall the two eastern are each of two cinquefoiled ogee lights with quatrefoiled tracery in a two-centred head. The rear-arches are moulded, and are inclosed by labels with large head-stops, and there are also labels to the external heads. The westernmost window is a single cinquefoiled light transomed to form a low-side window. Between the two eastern windows is a doorway with a two-centred external head of two orders continuously moulded with the jambs, and a moulded rear-arch inclosed by a label with stops carved as dogs' heads. At the east end of the wall are three graduated sedilia with moulded sills in range with a piscina. The head of the piscina is cinquefoiled, but the sedilia have trefoiled heads with sub-foliated soffit cusps; only the

36 *Testa de Nevill* (Rec. Com.), 244.
37 *Feud. Aids,* i, 82.
38 Chan. Inq. p.m. 20 Hen. VI, no. 23.
39 Pipe R. Beds. and Bucks. 34 Hen. II, m. 9 d.
40 *Testa de Nevill,* loc. cit.
41 *Rot. Lit. Claus.* (Rec. Com.), ii, 212.
42 Feet of F. case 16, file 34, no. 5.

43 Ibid. Bucks. Trin. 7 Edw. I, no. 8.
44 De Banco R. 171, m. 46.
45 Feet of F. case 18, file 64, no. 25.
46 Chan. Inq. p.m. 20 Hen. VI, no. 23.
47 *V.C.H. Bucks.* i, 241.
48 Ibid.
49 Ibid.
50 Ibid. 274.

51 Exch. Inq. p.m. (Ser. 2), file 39, no. 10.
52 Recov. R. Trin. 3 Chas. I, m. 60.
53 Ibid. East. 25 Chas. II, m. 139.
53a Probably the light for the maintenance of which part of the rent arising from Kites Closes was assigned in the first instance (*Bucks. Rec.* vi, 406).

320

head of the westernmost sedile, the cusps of which have leaf-carved spandrels, is original, the heads of the eastern pair having been restored. All spring from circular shafts with moulded capitals and bases and from half shafts against the back of the recess. The late 14th-century chancel arch is of two moulded orders with responds composed of three engaged shafts separated by small rolls, and having moulded capitals of octagonal form with a common upper member to their abaci ; the bases are moulded and stand on octagonal plinths. To the south of the arch, cutting partly into the splay of the low-side window, is a 16th-century squint from the south aisle with a cinquefoiled segmental head. Externally the walls are crowned by a modern embattled parapet.

The east window of the north chapel has a two-centred head and is of two plain lights with a plain spandrel. Most of the stonework is modern, but the internal jambs and rear-arch are of original early 14th-century date. In the north wall, which has no windows, is a fine early 14th-century tomb recess with shafted jambs and an elaborately moulded drop two-centred head having cinquefoiled and sub-foliated soffit-cusping. Inclosing the head is a label with spirited head-stops, and over the apex and the springing are three blank shields.

The nave arcades are each of three bays, with piers and responds similar in detail to the responds of the chancel arch, and sharply pointed two-centred arches of two wave-moulded orders separated by a deep casement. The east responds are nearly continuous with those of the chancel arch, the suite of attached shafts being interrupted only by a narrow swelled chamfer masking the eastern internal angles of the nave. The arches have labels with uncarved stops on the nave face. Over the south-west pier is a square recess with moulded edges ; it appears to have been originally closed by a grille and may possibly have contained relics. The clearstory has two windows on either side, and one in the east gable over the chancel arch, each of two trefoiled lights with vertical quatrefoil tracery in a two-centred head. The walls are crowned externally by an enriched cornice and embattled parapet, the latter having evidently been designed for a roof of lower pitch than the present one.

The rebuilt north aisle has two pointed three-light windows with a plain pointed doorway between them. An inscribed stone let into the wall externally bears the date 1801. The weather-mould of the original roof remains upon the north wall of the tower. The east window of the south aisle is an early 14th-century insertion of three lights with intersecting tracery in a pointed head inclosed by an external label. To the north of the window is the opening of the squint to the chancel, which has a segmental cinquefoiled head like that on the chancel face. At the east end of the south wall, placed too high in the wall to be in its original position, is a rectangular piscina recess with a round basin. To the west of this is a square-headed 15th-century window of three cinquefoiled ogee lights with vertical tracery in the head, inserted

evidently for the better lighting of the aisle altar. The south doorway, opposite the third bay of the south arcade, has been reconstructed, but the label appears to be original 14th-century work. At the west end of the wall is a plain 13th-century lancet with wide internal splays and a flat segmental rear-arch, while in the west wall is a similar but larger lancet with an external label. Externally the walls are crowned by a cornice and embattled parapet like that of the nave.

The tower is of two stages with an embattled parapet, the lower stage containing two stories. The tower arch is two-centred and of three moulded orders, the inner orders springing from responds of a more elaborate plan than those of the nave arcades and chancel arch, but having capitals of the same design. Their bases appear to be made up of 13th-century capitals, perhaps those of the responds of an earlier tower arch. The outer order is continuous on the nave face, but on the west face dies upon the side walls of the tower. In the west wall of the ground stage is a late 15th-century window of three

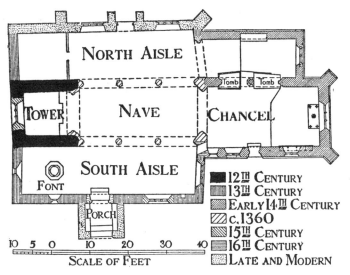

PLAN OF CLIFTON REYNES CHURCH

cinquefoiled lights within a four-centred head. In the east and west walls of the ringing chamber are plain round-headed 12th-century lights, the former now looking into the nave. The early 14th-century bell-chamber is lighted from each side by a large trefoiled light with an external label.

The porch is quite plain, and has stone seats on either side and a pointed outer entrance with chamfered angles.

The nave has a low-pitched king-post roof with wall brackets resting on wooden corbels ; on the tie-beam of the eastern truss is inscribed ' H O R W C 1637.' The roof of the north aisle must certainly be earlier than the date of its rebuilding ; the timbers are probably those of a 16th-century roof re-used.

The font is a fine example of late 14th-century work. The bowl is octagonal and has a small shaft at each angle, from each pair of which springs a segmental arch forming a niche which contains a figure. In the niche on the north face are figures of the Virgin and Child, with St. Margaret and St. Katherine in the niches on either side, and on the south is the

Trinity, with St. Peter and St. Paul in the flanking niches. In the east and west niches are St. Michael and St. Mary Magdalene or, more likely, St. Barbara, as the object held in the hands resembles a tower rather than the box of ointment. The lower edge of the bowl is enriched with heads and foliage, and each face of the octagonal stem, which stands on a moulded base, has a traceried panel. The altar table is of the 17th century. Two chairs of the same period with carved backs and shaped arms also remain in the chancel.

The south-west window of the chancel and the east clearstory window of the nave contain fragments of late 14th-century glass, which are said to have been brought from Emberton Church. In the former window is the figure of a bishop with a border composed of various fragments, and in the head of the window are fragments of canopy work with a leopard's head. In the north light of the east clearstory window is an imperfect figure of a saint holding a book, and in the south light is the head of another saint, both being made up with fragments of canopy work. The main lights of the western of the two north windows of the clearstory contain some good heraldic glass of the early 15th century, evidently contemporary with the clearstory. The west light, which has ornamental quarries and borders, contains a shield of Reynes impaling Reynes, while in the east light, replaced inside out, is a shield of arms— Gules a cheveron between three scallops or—for Chamberlain. In the partition cutting off the west end of the north aisle is set part of the panelled side of a 15th-century table tomb comprising three quatre-foils, in one of which remains a shield charged with two bars. Several other fragments of moulded stone are preserved at the west end of the same aisle. These include two traceried panels of the 14th century, which must have formed part of the side of an altar or tomb, several moulded jamb-stones of 15th-century section, and a fragment of the edge of a moulded slab.

In the recess in the north wall of the north chapel is a pair of wooden effigies representing a knight and his lady, perhaps Sir Ralf Reynes, who held Clifton in 1302–3, and his second wife Mabel,[54] daughter of Sir Richard Chamberlain. The knight has crossed legs and wears a mail coif with a fillet, a hauberk of mail covered by a short surcoat and showing the haketon beneath, hose of mail with knee-cops, and the straps of spurs, which are now gone. With his right hand he grasps his sword, which is suspended from a plain belt hung obliquely, and his feet rest on a dog, the head being supported by two cushions. The lady wears a coverchief and wimple, a kirtle with tight sleeves and a long sleeveless cote. Beneath her head are two cushions and at her feet is a dog.

Upon an elaborate early 14th-century table tomb in the west bay of the chancel arcade is a second pair of wooden effigies of a knight and lady in the costume of c. 1320. These would seem to be Sir Thomas Reynes, son of Ralf Reynes and Mabel, who was living as late as 1354, and his wife Joan, who by the heraldry on the tomb appears to have been a Tyringham. The knight is represented as wearing what may be intended for a bascinet with camail, or possibly a coif of mail with a steel cap beneath it. Over his mail hauberk, which has a pointed skirt, appear to be two garments, a short cyclas-like surcoat

and a pourpoint with an embattled fringe. Beneath the hauberk appears the lower edge of the haketon. His legs are crossed, and are protected by hose of mail and knee-cops. On his left arm is a small heater-shaped shield. The sword has gone, and his right hand has been broken away. The feet rest on a dog and the head on two cushions. The lady wears a wimple and a coverchief, held in place by fillets passing over the crown of her head and round her temples, a kirtle with close-fitting sleeves and a sleeveless cote. At her feet is a dog, and under her head are two cushions. The tomb upon which these effigies are placed has its sides panelled with quatre-foils containing shields. Those on the north side, beginning from the east, are as follows : three arches, for Arches ; a cheveron checky between three scallops, for Chamberlain ; Chamberlain impaling Reynes ; Reynes ; and two lions passant with a label of three points, perhaps for Ekeny. On the south side of the tomb, taking them in the same order, are the follow-ing shields : a cross engrailed, perhaps for Drayton ; ermine a fesse charged with three millrind crosses, for Paynel ; three harts at gaze, for Green ; a saltire engrailed, for Tyringham, impaling Reynes ; and bezanty a quarter ermine, for Zouche.

In the east bay of the arcade is a fine table tomb of the last quarter of the 14th century, with the recumbent effigies in stone of a knight and his lady. The knight wears a pointed bascinet with camail, epaulières and arm-pieces of plate, a tight jupon of the arms of Reynes, beneath which appears the skirt of the mail hauberk, a richly-studded belt with an elaborate clasp, and cuisses and jambs of plate, with sollerets upon his feet. Upon his hands, which are in prayer, are gadded gauntlets ; his sword has been broken away. The head rests on a helm and the feet upon a finely sculptured dog wearing a collar bearing the letters B O, with a cinquefoil flower between them ; the letters probably stand for the dog's name. The lady wears the nebuly head-dress, a kirtle, over which is a sideless cote, cut low at the neck, and decorated with a line of elaborately ornamented buttons extend-ing from the neck to the waist, and a cloak over all fastened by a band with rich clasps. The head rests upon two pillows and the feet upon a pair of small dogs. The sides of the tomb have shallow niches or housings with trefoiled ogee heads, crocketed and finialled, and small gabled and crocketed buttresses between them. The niches contain a fine series of weepers, and the tomb is crowned by a cornice with shields. On the north side are the following shields : a chief with a lion passant therein, for Brok ; three stirrups, for Scudamore ; three crosses fitchy and in chief a demi-lion ; a cross engrailed, perhaps for Drayton ; a scutcheon in an orle of martlets ; Tyring-ham ; and a fesse between six crosses formy. The shields on the south side are as follows : Chamberlain ; Paynel ; Tyringham ; ermine a chief indented, for Morteyne ; Arches ; Green ; an indecipherable shield ; and Zouche. The ends of the tomb abut upon the column and respond of the arcade, and are unsculp-tured. This monument has been ascribed, but with little probability, to Sir John Reynes, who died in 1428, and is commemorated by a brass in the north chapel.[55] The monument in this case would have been erected at the death of his first wife Katherine Scudamore, who was alive in 1388. It is far more

---

[54] See above, p. 317.

[55] *Rec. of Bucks.* vi, 400.

likely that the monument commemorates Thomas, this John Reynes's father, who died between 1388 and 1394. The appearance of the arms of Scudamore would be explained by the supposition that the monument was erected by Sir Thomas's son John, whose first wife was Katherine Scudamore. The later brass affords an interesting commentary on the development of plate armour in the intervening period. The gorget or standard of plate takes the place of the camail, and the jupon has gone out of use, the breastplate, which appears to be worn over mail, being exposed. The armpits are protected by roundels, and the elbow pieces have fan-shaped terminations. The legs and lower taces have disappeared. Beneath is the inscription : ' Hic iacet Joñes Reynes Miles qui obiit xxv° die Marcii anno dñi Mill'imo cccc°xxviij° Cuius aīe ppicietur deus amen.' At the corners of the slab are shields of Reynes. In the floor is a slab with brasses of a man and woman in shrouds, with shields of Reynes, and Reynes impaling Tyringham, at the four corners. The inscription has disappeared, but the brass may be assigned to John Reynes, who was living in 1498.[56]

In the chancel are floor slabs to Ann daughter of Richard Bernar (d. 1639) ; to Elizabeth daughter of Samuel Pepys, rector (d. 1680); to the same Samuel Pepys (d. 1703), and to George Pryer, ' gdson of William Pryer yᵉ Elder ' (d. 1718). In the north aisle are slabs to Mary Dennis (d. 1652) ; to Peter son of Samuel Pepys (d. 1684), and a slab, apparently to a Dennis, bearing the date 1637.

There is a ring of six bells, the treble, a modern addition, and the remaining five by John Hodson, dated 1664. The bells are now hung in a steel frame. The old frame, removed in 1905, was dated 1631, and appears to have been constructed for three larger bells.

The plate consists of a silver cup of 1692, a cover paten without date letter, but bearing the same maker's mark, a large pewter almsdish and a plated flagon and plate, presented between 1805 and 1832.

The registers begin in 1653.

ADVOWSON Clifton Church was bestowed by Simon de Borard in the early 13th century on the Prioress of Stamford, but, as he was then a minor in the custody of Roger Torpel, he recovered the presentation against the prioress in 1229, compensating her with 8s. rent and 1 virgate in Stathern (Leicestershire).[57] The advowson of the church, valued at £8 13s. 4d. in 1291[58] and at £13 6s. 9d. in 1535,[59] henceforward descended with the manor of Clifton Reynes[60] until 1816, when it was bequeathed by Alexander Small in trust for Henry Alexander Small, to whom and his heirs it was conveyed after he had been inducted and instituted rector.[61] He was holding it about 1862,[62] but before 1877 it had passed to the Rev. W. Sutthery, who was also rector. He was still holding in 1883, but in 1895 Mrs. G. G. Sutthery presented the Rev. W. Stanley Sutthery, and at the present day the patron is Mr. A. M. Sutthery.[63]

The rectory was leased in 1565 by the parson, William Astbury, to Ralf Scrope, who transferred his interest to John Studder. The latter in 1571 brought an action against Francis Lowe, lord of the manor, who had deprived him of his rights of common, as lessee of the rectory, for six beasts and forty sheep.[64] Francis Lowe had previously been in trouble for seeking to obtain by persuasion and threat the benefice in farm. He had had a lease of the parsonage, worth £30 a year, and allowed Richard Ellis, the parson, a mere £6.[65]

In 1343 Thomas Reynes received a licence to have an oratory in his house at Clifton Reynes.[66]

CHARITIES Sir Hugh Kite, as appears from the Parliamentary Returns of 1786, gave land then let at £12 per annum for the poor. The land, known as Kite's Closes, contains 19 a. 1 r. 26 p. and is let at £11 14s. yearly. About one-third of the net income is distributed in bread, cheese, tea, &c., the remainder being retained by the rector.[67]

The Church Allotment consists of 3 a. 1 r. 8 p. of pasture land let at £3 10s. yearly, which is applied towards the upkeep of the church.

COLD BRAYFIELD

Branefield, Braunfeld (xii cent.) ; Bramfeld, Braufend (xiii cent.) ; Braumfeld (xiv cent.) ; Brafeld, Britfeld (xv–xvi cent.).

This small parish, first mentioned as ' Cold ' Brayfield towards the end of the 16th century,[1] was formerly included in Lavendon. The River Ouse is on two sides the parish boundary, and the road from Olney to Bedford, after passing through the parish, enters Bedfordshire by Turvey bridge. The area of Cold Brayfield is 744 acres, of which 254 are arable and 424 grass.[2] The soil is various and the subsoil belongs to the Great Oolite series. For the most part the land lies low and is liable to floods, but rises slightly to the north and west.

The small village is in a rather bleak and exposed situation. The church stands near the entrance to Brayfield House, the seat of Mr. Denis Herbert Farrer, which is situated on the hill-side and surrounded by a fine and well-stocked park of about 40 acres.

The common lands in the parishes of Lavendon and Cold Brayfield were inclosed under an Act of Parliament of 1800, the award being made 9 September 1802.[3]

[56] Rec. of Bucks. vi, 402.
[57] Maitland, Bracton's Note Bk. ii, 333 ; Feet of F. Bucks. 14 Hen. III, no. 1 ; R. of Hugh of Wells (Cant. and York Soc.), ii, 79.
[58] Pope Nich. Tax. (Rec. Com.), 33.
[59] Valor Eccl. (Rec. Com.), iv, 243.
[60] See manor ; also Inst. Bks. (P.R.O.); and Add. MS. 5839, fol. 62 d.
[61] Sheahan, op. cit. 521.

[62] Ibid.
[63] Clergy Lists.
[64] Ct. of Req. bdle. 108, no. 30.
[65] Cal. S. P. Dom. 1601–3, p. 521.
[66] Add. MS. 5839, fol. 59 d., quoting Linc. Epis. Reg. Bek.
[67] A grant of this close was made to Nichasius Yatwert and Bartholomew Brokesby in 1570, but it was soon afterwards annexed to the rectory. The

distribution of bread, cheese and ale was originally made on the occasion of beating the parish bounds in Rogation week (Pat. 12 Eliz. pt. x, m. 28 ; Bucks. Rec. vi, 406).
[1] Chan. Proc. (Ser. 2), bdle. 53, no. 13 ; Feet of F. Div. Co. Mich. 15 & 16 Eliz.
[2] Statistics from Bd. of Agric. (1905).
[3] Priv. Act, 41 Geo. III, cap. 100 ; Blue Bk. Incl. Awards, 10.

No mention of *COLD BRAYFIELD* *MANORS* occurs in the Domesday Survey, and until the 13th century the two holdings here were assessed under Lavendon.[4] One of the three fees held there by the Countess Judith in 1086 was a manor assessed at 2 hides 1¼ virgates and held in demesne; twenty years earlier it had been held under Alli by Humman, his man.[5] The Countess Judith, niece of William the Conqueror, was the wife of Waltheof Earl of Huntingdon and Northampton.[6] Their daughter Maud married as her first husband Simon de St. Liz, who died before 1109, and secondly David of Scotland, he being recognized as Earl of Huntingdon in right of his marriage.[7] King David in or about 1136 resigned his earldom to his son Henry, who died in 1152 in his father's lifetime.[8] His son and heir Malcolm was under twelve years of age, and King Stephen gave the earldom to Simon de St. Liz, second Earl of Northampton, son of Simon and Maud.[9] Simon died in the following year, when also Malcolm succeeded to the throne of Scotland.[10] King Malcolm died unmarried in 1165,[11] and the earldom passed to William, his brother. Owing to the war between England and Scotland he was dispossessed in 1174, when Simon de St. Liz, son and heir of Earl Simon, obtained recognition of his claim.[12] On his death without issue in 1183-4 it was secured by David, younger brother of William the Lion. He died in 1219 and was succeeded by John, his son, who, however, died childless in 1237.[13] His lands were then divided among his four co-heirs, Christine, Devorgilla, Isabel, and Ada.[14] The Lavendon lands appear to have fallen to the share of the first and

St. Liz. *Party indented argent and azure.*

Forz. *Gules a cross vair.*

fourth, of whom Christine married William de Forz Earl of Albemarle.[15] A return made in the middle of the 13th century shows that two parts of half a knight's fee in Lavendon were then held under the earl as of the honour of Huntingdon.[16] Ada, the fourth sister of John Earl of Huntingdon, married Henry de Hastings,[17] whose name is given as overlord of part of Brayfield about 1235.[18] On his death in 1250[19] he was succeeded by a son Henry, then a minor.[20] Henry took a leading part in the baronial wars as a follower of Simon de Montfort; he was taken prisoner at the battle of Evesham,[21] held Kenilworth Castle against the Crown, and in 1267 was the leader of the barons in the Isle of Ely.[22] By his wife Joan, sister and co-heir of George de Cauntelow, he had a son John, a minor in the king's wardship at his father's death in 1268.[23] Of this John, claimant to the Scottish throne,[24] half a knight's fee in Lavendon was held in 1284-6.[25] John de Hastings died in February 1312-13, when he was returned as having one quarter of a knight's fee here held by John Grey.[26] No further mention of this overlordship has, however, been found. In the first half of the 12th century a mesne lordship over this fee was held by Sampson le Fort,[27] founder of a priory in the adjoining parish of Harrold (Bedfordshire).[28] His rights descended to Robert son of Pain Brus (Breus, Braos) in the reign of King Malcolm.[29] At a later date Robert son of Nicholas quitclaimed all right in the advowson of Brayfield Church pertaining to the fee of Sampson,[30] but the connexion of the earlier lords with this manor is so far unexplained.

In the time of Sampson the tenancy in demesne seems to have been held by his tenant Robert de Blossomville,[31] lord of what was afterwards known as Newton Blossomville (q.v.) and probably also lord of Harrold.[32] Here, as at Harrold, a feoffment seems to have been made of the family of Moryn.

Ralph Moryn paid the Sheriff of Bedfordshire for half a fee in Harrold in 1194.[33] He was living in 1202,[34] but had probably been succeeded by another Ralph Moryn by 1235.[35] He was mesne lord of certain land of the honour in Brayfield,[36] and was still living in 1253.[37] Before 1262 he was succeeded by John, his son,[38] who was followed by Ralph Moryn, his son, before 1271-2, when he was accused of unjustly distraining some of his free tenants.[39] Ralph was unjustly imprisoned at Oxford about 1274 on suspicion of having stolen the king's gerfalcon,[40] and by 1280 was deeply in debt to the Jews.[41] Before

[4] *Hund. R.* (Rec. Com.), ii, 349.
[5] *V.C.H. Bucks.* i, 273.
[6] *V.C.H. Northants,* i, 293; G.E.C. *Peerage,* iv, 282.
[7] G.E.C. op. cit. iv, 283; Dugdale, *Mon.* v, 190.
[8] Roger of Hoveden, *Chron.* (Rolls Ser.), i, 212-13.
[9] Lawrie, *Annals of the Reigns of Malcolm and William,* 9; G.E.C. loc. cit.
[10] Hoveden, loc. cit.
[11] William of Newburgh, *Hist. Rer. Angl.* (ed. Hearne), i, 166; Gale, *Rerum Anglicarum Scriptores,* i, 169.
[12] Matthew Paris, *Chron. Maj.* (Rolls Ser.), ii, 324; Lawrie, *Annals of the Reigns of Malcolm and William,* 37, 255.
[13] Matthew Paris, op. cit. iv, 491.
[14] *Cal. Doc. of Scotland,* 1108-1272, p. 253; cf. Assize R. 55, m. 9 d.
[15] Ibid.; G.E.C. *Peerage,* i, 56.
[16] *Testa de Nevill* (Rec. Com.), 244.
[17] *V.C.H. Beds.* ii, 210; *Cal. Close,* 1237-42, p. 60.

[18] *Testa de Nevill* (Rec. Com.), 244.
[19] Matthew Paris, op. cit. v, 174.
[20] Ibid. 205; *Cal. Pat.* 1247-58, p. 72.
[21] *Annales Mon.* (Rolls Ser.), ii, 365; iv, 455.
[22] Ibid. iii, 241, 243; iv, 203; cf. *Cal. Pat.* 1258-66, p. 540.
[23] *Annales Mon.* (Rolls Ser.), iii, 257; *Cal. Fine R.* 1272-1307, pp. 18, 179; G.E.C. op. cit. iv, 179.
[24] *Annales Mon.* (Rolls Ser.), ii, 410, 411; iii, 368; iv, 507.
[25] *Feud. Aids,* i, 74.
[26] *Cal. Inq. p.m.* (Edw. II), v, 233.
[27] Lansd. MS. 391 (Harrold Chart.), fol. 4.
[28] *V.C.H. Beds.* i, 387.
[29] Lansd. MS. 391, fol. 4 d. Pain Brus was living in 1130 (Hunter, *Gt. R. of the Pipe,* 31 *Hen. I* [Rec. Com.], 103). Guncod son (*sic*) of Robert Brus gave to Lavendon Abbey a culture in the common field of Harrold (Dugdale, *Mon.* vi,

889). Godeolda or Guntouda Brus and Aubrey her sister inherited land from their mother Aline before 1241; Ralph Moryn was their nephew (Assize R. 695, m. 14 d.).
[30] Lansd. MS. 391, fol. 15 d.
[31] Ibid. For the descent see Newton Blossomville.
[32] *V.C.H. Beds.* iii, 65.
[33] Pipe R. Beds. and Bucks. 6 Ric. I, m. 2 d.
[34] *Select Civil Pleas* (Selden Soc.), 98.
[35] Feet of F. Beds. 18 Hen. III, no. 2; *Testa de Nevill* (Rec. Com.), 242, 251.
[36] *Testa de Nevill* (Rec. Com.), 244.
[37] *Cal. Chart. R.* 1226-57, p. 422.
[38] Ibid.; Feet of F. Beds. 46 Hen. III, no. 12.
[39] Lansd. MS. 391, fol. 9 d.; *Abbrev. Plac.* (Rec. Com.), 180.
[40] *Cal. Close,* 1272-9, p. 142.
[41] Ibid. 1279-88, pp. 38, 269. The debts due to the Crown were to be paid by John Grey.

this date he parted with his manor of Harrold to John Grey,[42] and as Moryn's name does not appear in the returns of landholders made for Lavendon and Brayfield in 1278,[43] it seems probable that the Greys acquired their rights in Brayfield with the Bedfordshire manor. John Grey seems to have enfeoffed Reynold, his son, in this land which Reynold was holding in 1278.[44]

The second fee in Cold Brayfield probably derived its origin from the half hide held by Chetel under the king both before and after the Conquest.[45] In the 13th century *WATERHALL* in this parish was held in chief for half a knight's fee by the family of Rycote,[46] but the intermediate history is obscure. Fulk de Rycote, lord of Rycote (Oxfordshire),[47] was among those on the king's side in 1215,[48] and acted on various commissions[49] before his death in or about 1233.[50] He was succeeded by Fulk son of William de Rycote, then a minor.[51] He came of age before 1247,[52] and about 1260 was coroner for Oxfordshire.[53] He acted as sheriff of that county in 1263,[54] and apparently took the baronial side in the Civil War. Possibly owing to political differences, Fulk was in continual contest with John and Reynold Grey,[55] the latter of whom was his tenant for Waterhall,[56] and lord of Snelston in Lavendon (q.v.). Finally in 1280 Fulk sold to Reynold a messuage and a carucate of land here,[57] apparently releasing to him all his rights, since from this time the Greys held Waterhall in chief[58] by the serjeanty of sending a man armed with hauberk and lance to the wars in Wales.[59]

The two fees in Brayfield were thus united in the hands of the Greys, and retained the name of Waterhall, the composite manor being evidently referred to

under this name in 1308.[60] The manor followed the descent of that of Water Eaton in Bletchley (q.v.) until 1448, when it was granted by Reynold Grey to Robert Olney, Roger, Richard and John Heton.[61] It became the property of John Heton,[62] who died in January 1468-9,[63] and was probably sold, with his manor of Backenho in Thurleigh, Bedfordshire, about 1472 by his son William Heton to John Earl of Wiltshire,[64] whose son Edward[65] in 1497 alienated to John Mordaunt a fishery in the Ouse at Cold Brayfield.[66] The Earls of Wiltshire also held Newton Blossomville Manor (q.v.), with which Waterhall descended to John Lord Mordaunt, created Earl of Peterborough in March 1627-8,[67] by whom it was sold in 1638 to William Bodington, sen., of Turvey, Bedfordshire.[68] He was succeeded by John Bodington, who in 1653 made a settlement on his son John,[69] called lord of Cold Brayfield in 1674.[69a] At his death two years later[70] the estate passed to his son John, who died in 1683, leaving two daughters.[71] Mary, the elder, died without issue, but Martha married Thomas Dymock of Newport Pagnell, who died in 1717.[71a] At the beginning of the following year she conveyed Cold Brayfield to Uriah Ray of Carlton, Bedfordshire, in trust for William Farrer, who acquired possession in 1720.[72] He died before 9 December 1724, when his will was proved by his brother and heir Denis Farrer.[73] Browne Willis speaks of him as resident here in 1735, and as having greatly improved the house.[74] Denis died on 27 January 1746-7, leaving instructions in his will for burial in Cold Brayfield Church next to his late wife.[75] His son and heir William proved his age in that year,[76] and held Cold Brayfield until his death, which

---

[42] *V.C.H. Beds.* iii, 65.

[43] *Hund. R.* (Rec. Com.), ii, 349.

[44] Ibid.

[45] *V.C.H. Bucks.* i, 276.

[46] *Hund. R.* (Rec. Com.), ii, 349.

[47] Cf. *Testa de Nevill* (Rec. Com.), 112.

[48] *Rot. Lit. Pat.* (Rec. Com.), i, 134.

[49] *Cal. Pat.* 1216-25, p. 395 ; 1225-32, p. 349.

[50] *Cal. Close,* 1231-4, p. 275.

[51] Assize R. 699, m. 19. His lands being held of the honour of Wallingford, his custody passed to the Earl of Cornwall, who granted it to Roger Earl of Winchester ; from him it was bought by Geoffrey de Stocwell before 1241 (ibid. 695, m. 14 ; 699, m. 19).

[52] Ibid. 699, m. 19.

[53] Ibid. 701, m. 19.

[54] *Cal. Pat.* 1258-66, p. 327 ; cf. *Cal. Close,* 1272-9, p. 108.

[55] Assize R. 59, m. 6 d. ; cf. ibid. 60, m. 27 ; 68, m. 18 ; *Hund. R.* (Rec. Com.), i, 39.

[56] *Hund. R.* (Rec. Com.), ii, 349.

[57] *Cal. Pat.* 1272-81, p. 416. Fulk died between June 1301 (*Cat. of Anct. D.* ii, 163) and 22 Jan. 1301-2 (*Cal. Fine R.* 1272-1307, p. 448), leaving a son Fulk, a minor (Chan. Inq. p.m. 30 Edw. I, no. 17).

[58] *Feud. Aids,* i, 74.

[59] Chan. Inq. p.m. 1 Edw. II, no. 54. In 1324 the serjeanty was described as that of finding a man armed with haketon, bascinet and lance ; a horse had also to be provided (*Cal. Inq. p.m.* [Edw. II], vi, 312). In 1343 the requirements were a man on a horse without a saddle, price 40d., one bow without a cord, and one arrow without a head

when required by the king (Chan. Inq. p.m. 16 Edw. III [1st nos.], no. 45).

[60] Anct. Ext. (Exch. K.R.), no 78 (1) ; Chan. Inq. p.m. 1 Edw. II, no. 54. This coalescence may account for the fact that the manor of Newton Blossomville (q.v.), originally part of the honour of Huntingdon, was said in the 14th and 15th centuries to be held of Waterhall. The manors of Brayfield and Waterhall were, however, regarded as separate in the 16th and early 17th centuries. At the latter date there is also reference to a manor of Old Layton, which appears as an alternative name for Cold Brayfield in the 18th and 19th centuries.

[61] *Cal. Pat.* 1446-52, p. 163. Waterhall, however, is included among those manors for which William Lord Grey de Wilton sued John Abrahull c. 1525 (Early Chan. Proc. bdle. 516, no. 20).

[62] Chan. Inq. p.m. 38 & 39 Hen. VI, no. 59.

[63] P.C.C. 26 Godyn.

[64] *V.C.H. Beds.* iii, 106.

[65] *G.E.C. Peerage,* viii, 165.

[66] Feet of F. Div. Co. Trin. 12 Hen. VII.

[67] *G.E.C. Peerage,* v, 366.

[68] Close, 14 Chas. I, pt. xviii, no. 22.

[69] Abstract of Title kindly lent by Mr. F. W. Bull.

[69a] Chan. Proc. (Bridges Div.), bdle. 479, no. 54-6.

[70] Lipscomb, *Hist. and Antiq. of Bucks.* iv, 49.

[71] P.C.C. 69 Hare.

[71a] Abstract of Title ut sup. ; cf. Marcham, *Cat. Bucks. Deeds,* no. 160.

[72] Close, 11 Geo. II, pt. xvii, no. 18.

[73] P.C.C. 268 Bolton ; Denis made a

settlement of the rectory in the following year (Feet of F. Bucks. East. 11 Geo. I).

[74] Add. MS. 5839, p. 28. In 1737 a renunciation of rights in the manor was made by William Hamilton and his wife Elizabeth, only daughter and heir of Martha Dymock, then dead (Feet of F. Bucks. Trin. 10 & 11 Geo. II ; Close, 11 Geo. II, pt. xvii, no. 18). In 1725 Denis Farrer married Elizabeth, elder daughter of William Hillersdon of Elstow, Bedfordshire (ob. April 1725, *Musgrave's Obit.* [Harl. Soc.], iii, 217), by Elizabeth daughter of William Farrer of the Inner Temple (P.C.C. 87 Romney ; abstract of Title ut sup.). This William Farrer, whose second wife Elizabeth predeceased him in 1734 at the age of seventy-four (P.C.C. 241 Ockham ; Lipscomb, loc. cit.), died in 1737, aged eighty-one (Lipscomb, loc. cit.). In his will he refers to Denis Farrer as grandson (P.C.C. 223 Wake). He was son of Thomas Farrer of Aylesbury (who died in 1703, aged eighty-three, *Musgrave's Obit.* [Harl. Soc.], ii, 303 ; P.C.C. 166 Degg ; Lipscomb, op. cit. ii, 55) by Helen, eldest daughter of Sir William Boteler of Biddenham, Bedfordshire, which Sir William married in 1641 Sibyl, widow of William Farrer and mother of the said Thomas (Abstract of Title ut sup. ; *Musgrave's Obit.* loc. cit.).

[75] Lipscomb, op. cit. iv, 48 ; P.C.C. 70 Potter.

[76] Recov. R. Mich. 21 Geo. II, m. 338. In 1758 he acquired from Elizabeth Hamilton, widow, above mentioned, and her daughters Mary, Martha and Fitz Willielma Hamilton a messuage in Cold Brayfield and close of pasture called Waterhall (Close, 32 Geo. II, pt. xi, no. 17).

occurred between 19 July 1798 and 12 February 1799, the dates when his will was made and proved.[77] He left three daughters, of whom the eldest, Ann, married the Rev. John Grove Spurgeon, by whom she had a son Farrer Grove Spurgeon, who took the name of Farrer in 1799 according to the terms of his grandfather's will.[78] He inherited Cold Brayfield, but was still a minor in 1801.[79] He died in 1826, and his son William Frederick Farrer was returned as holder of the manor in 1831[80] and later.[81] He was Sheriff of Buckinghamshire in 1856, and died in 1872. His son William Charles Love Farrer held till his death, unmarried, in 1879,[82] and was succeeded in turn by his two uncles, George Denis Farrer (d. 1901) and the Rev. Frederick Farrer.[83] The latter died in 1908, and his only surviving son, Denis Herbert Farrer, is the present holder of the manor.

FARRER. *Argent a bend sable with three horse-shoes or thereon.*

The monastery of Lavendon held lands in Cold Brayfield, which were valued at the Dissolution at 35s. per annum.[84] This estate, sometimes called a manor, was granted with the site of the monastery,[85] and followed the descent of the abbey's manor in Lavendon,[86] to which it probably ultimately became attached.

A virgate of land in Cold Brayfield was given to the priory of Harrold at its foundation (temp. Stephen) by Robert de Blossomville and the gift was confirmed by Sampson le Fort and by William King of Scotland.[87] No lands in Cold Brayfield were included in the priory's possessions at the Dissolution, but it held lands in Lavendon valued at 24s. per annum.[88]

The church of ST. MARY THE VIRGIN consists of a chancel measuring internally 25 ft. 6 in. by 16 ft., nave 31 ft. by 19 ft., west tower 7 ft. 6 in. by 6 ft. 6 in., and north porch ; it is built of rubble with stone dressings and the roofs are covered with tiles.

The church appears to have been built shortly before it was granted to Harrold Priory a little before the middle of the 12th century. The western part of the chancel, and probably the nave, date from this time, but the only remaining details of this period in the nave are a small window in the north wall, now covered by the porch, and the reset doorway below it. The lengthening of the chancel about 1230 is clearly indicated on the north side by the larger stones used in the walling, though the distinction is not so apparent on the south. During the latter part of the 13th century the tower and porch were added and in the 15th century windows were inserted in the chancel and nave. The whole building was restored and reroofed during the latter part of the 19th century.

In the east wall of the chancel is a two-light window which probably dates from the 15th century, though much restored. At the east end of the north wall is a window of similar character, while another window of the same form in the south wall opposite has been entirely renewed. There are also in each lateral wall a 13th-century lancet and, near the west end, a pointed low-side window. A rough pointed piscina at the south-east does not retain sufficient detail to indicate its date. The responds of the chancel arch are of the 12th century, though the arch they support is modern ; they have attached shafts with scalloped capitals and moulded abaci, and the southern shaft is enriched with cheveron ornament.

In the north wall of the nave are a 13th-century lancet and the small round-headed window mentioned above, both considerably repaired ; below the latter is a reset 12th-century doorway with a pointed head of two orders, the outer supported by 13th-century shafts with moulded capitals. On the south are two windows of two lights, the eastern window being of the 15th century with modern tracery and the other entirely modern. Between them there are indications of an early doorway, the defaced impost moulding of which is to be seen on the outside. The plain tower arch in the west wall dates from the 13th century. At the east end of the south wall is a restored piscina, doubtless for the nave altar. There are also two lockers in the east wall and one in the south wall, while at the north-east corner are two niches with conjoined segmental heads.

The porch is lighted by a plain loophole in the west wall and has an original pointed archway of two orders, the outer order supported by jamb shafts with moulded capitals and bases.

The low tower is of two stages, the ground stage lighted by plain loopholes and the bell-chamber by weather-worn lancets, all dating from the 13th century ; it is strengthened by diagonal buttresses and surmounted by a modern parapet.

The font is octagonal, but preserves no detail to indicate its date. There are floor slabs in the chancel to Jane Farrer (d. 1678–9), Ann Farrer (d. 1690), and Ann Farrer (d. 1697); in the nave are floor slabs to Ann Bodington (d. 1696), and Edward Bodington (d. 16—). In a recess at the east end of the nave is a 17th-century chest.

The tower contains a ring of three bells : the treble by John Clark, 1607 ; the second by Alexander Rigby, 1688 ; while the tenor, dated 1828, is evidently by Taylor.

The communion plate includes a late 16th-century cup without any date letter.

The registers begin in 1693.

ADVOWSON The church of Cold Brayfield was built before 1140–50, when it was granted by Sampson le Fort to Gervase, Abbot of St. Nicholas of Arrouaise, for the foundation of Harrold Priory.[89] The grant was confirmed by Robert son of Pain Brus.[90] Gervase bestowed the church on the priory of Harrold, the appropriation taking place before 1168; the grant was confirmed by Robert, Bishop of Lincoln,[91] Robert son of Nicholas

[77] P.C.C. 111 Howe.
[78] Ibid.; Lysons, *Mag. Brit.* i (3), 520.
[79] Priv. Act, 41 Geo. III, cap. 100.
[80] Recov. R. Hil. 1 Will. IV, m. 141.
[81] Sheahan, *Hist. and Topog. of Bucks.* 397.
[82] *Ret. of Owners of Land* (1873), Bucks. 7.
[83] Burke, *Landed Gentry* (1906).
[84] *Valor Eccl.* (Rec. Com.), iv, 241.
[85] *L. and P. Hen. VIII*, xviii (1), g. 981 (108).
[86] Feet of F. Bucks. Mich. 14 Eliz. ;
Mich. and Hil. 16 Eliz. ; Recov. R. Hil. 1 & 2 Jas. II, m. 60.
[87] Dugdale, *Mon.* vi, 330.
[88] *Valor Eccl.* (Rec. Com.), iv, 204.
[89] Lansd. MS. 391, fol. 4.
[90] Ibid. fol. 4 d.
[91] Ibid. fol. 15, 18 d.; *V.C.H. Beds.* ii, 388.

Cold Brayfield Church from the North-East

NORTH CRAWLEY CHURCH FROM THE NORTH

NORTH CRAWLEY CHURCH : THE INTERIOR LOOKING EAST

de Brayfield quitclaiming his right to the advowson.[92] Some disagreement seems to have arisen with the canons of Lavendon concerning the appropriation of the church, for Roger, Bishop of Worcester (1164–79), arbitrated in favour of Harrold.[93] A vicarage was ordained in the time of Bishop Hugh of Wells,[94] but Harrold Priory was probably not able to maintain the vicar and handed over the advowson to Lavendon Abbey, since the vicarage has always descended with that of Lavendon,[95] to which it is still annexed.

There are no references to this living in the Lincoln registers; it has always been considered a donative.

In 1496 it was returned that the chancel was in ruins, the fault of the impropriators, the Prioress and convent of Harrold, but that all the tithes were annexed to Lavendon and did not exceed £5 a year.[96] In return for the tithes Lavendon Abbey paid the priory of Harrold a pension of 24s.[97] For some time after the Dissolution the rectory followed the same descent as the site of Lavendon Abbey[98] (q.v.), but before 1615 it had been acquired by Thomas Farrer,[99]

who made a settlement of it in 1636 on his son Thomas.[100] In 1663 a settlement was made on William son and heir of the younger Thomas Farrer on his marriage with Ann daughter of Henry Parker.[101] William died in February 1706–7, leaving a son William,[102] upon whom the rectory had been settled on his marriage with Elizabeth daughter of Matthew Dennis in 1692.[103] The younger William died in 1712[104] and his son, another William, acquired Cold Brayfield Manor, with which the rectory descended until 1802, when an allotment of land was assigned in lieu of tithe.[105]

The church was endowed by Sampson le Fort with 5 acres of land.[106] John Lovent of Brayfield gave a rood of land and a rood of meadow for finding a lamp burning in the chancel of the church, the gift being confirmed by his son Thomas.[107] At the dissolution of the chantries this endowment was valued at 3s. 8d. a year.[108]

There do not appear to be any endowed charities subsisting in this parish.

NORTH CRAWLEY

Crawele, Craule, Crowle (xiii cent.); Great Craule, Croule juxta Newport Pagnel (xiv cent.); North Crolye (xv cent.).

This parish covers 3,366 acres, of which 1,130 acres are arable, 1,660 permanent grass and only 42 woods and plantations.[1] The soil is strong clay, the subsoil clay, and the chief crops wheat, oats and beans.

It has a general level of 300 ft. to 350 ft. above the ordnance datum, and its northern boundary as well as the western for a considerable distance is formed by the Chicheley Brook.

The division of the parish into Great and Little Crawley had been effected as early as 1197,[2] and the designation of North Crawley was not applied to the more important part until the 15th century. In the early 16th century an attempt was made by the parishioners of Chicheley to attach Little Crawley, just over the border, as a hamlet to their village. The claim may have been motived by the fact that the priory of Tickford had formerly held both Chicheley Church and Little Crawley chapel (see below). This attempt was stoutly resisted by the inhabitants of Little Crawley, who, in proof of their dependence on Great Crawley, instanced their large share in the repair of the church wall there, their right to seats in the church, their contribution towards the tithes, the gifts and bequests made by them, and the register of their burials in the church.[3]

The village of North Crawley, which is large and scattered, lies on a lofty ridge on a road crossing the centre of the parish. At the west end are the church

and the rectory, a fine house, built in 1800. The former rectorial or mansion-house is mentioned in the will, dated 7 March 1767, of William Lowndes, who left £300 in trust to his eldest son William Lowndes-Stone for its repair, should a younger son, Thomas Lowndes, then vicar of Astwood, succeed the rector.[4] The school, which was built in 1844 by the rector and the late Thomas A. Boswell, adjoins the churchyard. There is a Wesleyan chapel north of the church and east of it is a Congregational chapel.

There are some 17th-century cottages at Broadmead, about half a mile east of the church. A house and farm here belonged to Roger Tetlow, lord of Hollowes, who by his will, dated 23 December 1557, left 10s. for repairing the way from thence into the east fields.[5] Broadmead House passed with Hollowes to Ralph Smith, who made a settlement of it in 1631 on his marriage with Elizabeth Claver.[6]

Another half-mile beyond Broadmead is the Manor House at East End, a hamlet mentioned early in the 14th century.[7] The house, which is a 17th-century stone building with a tiled roof, and is surrounded by a moat, is now unoccupied and in a ruinous condition. It was probably the site of Hollowes Manor in Great Crawley. Moat Farm, an early 16th-century house at Little Crawley, a quarter of a mile north of the rectory, appears to have been originally the manor-house of Pateshull or Little Crawley Manor. It is built of stone and half-timber and was originally of L-shaped plan, the wing projecting southwards. In the 17th century a new wing was added at the north-

---

[92] Lansd. MS. 391, fol. 15 d.
[93] Ibid. fol. 15.
[94] Liber Antiquus Hugonis Wells (ed. A. Gibbons), 12.
[95] Recov. R. East. 13 Jas. I, m. 73; Feet of F. Bucks. Trin. 16 Jas. I; Inst. Bks. (P.R.O.).
[96] Lipscomb, op. cit. iv, 48.
[97] Valor Eccl. (Rec. Com.), iv, 242; Dugdale, Mon. vi, 331.
[98] Pat. 15 Eliz. pt. x, m. 11.
[99] Abstract of Title ut sup.
[100] Feet of F. Bucks. Hil. 11 Chas. I;

Recov. R. Hil. 11 Chas. I, m. 73. It was a marriage settlement on Thomas and Sarah daughter and heir of William Goodridge (Abstract of Title ut sup.).
[101] Feet of F. Bucks. Trin. 15 Chas. II; Abstract of Title ut sup.
[102] Lipscomb, op. cit. iv, 49; P.C.C. 61 Poley. His will mentions his son William and grandsons William and Denis.
[103] Abstract of Title ut sup.; Recov. R. Trin. 4 Will. and Mary, m. 26.
[104] Slab in church, quoted by Lipscomb, op. cit. iv, 49.

[105] Priv. Act, 41 Geo. III, cap. 100.
[106] Hund. R. (Rec. Com.), ii, 349.
[107] Lansd. MS. 391, fol. 16.
[108] Chant. Cert. 5, no. 21.
[1] Statistics from Bd. of Agric. (1905).
[2] Feet of F. case 14, file 2, no. 22; cf. file 6, no. 14, 15.
[3] Deed in Crawley Church chest.
[4] P.C.C. 146 Alexander.
[5] Ibid. 22 Noodes.
[6] Chan. Inq. p.m. (Ser. 2), dxcii, 87.
[7] Add. Chart. 23911, 23913.

west of the main block, and subsequent additions have been made on the west and south sides of the house. In the front wall of the 17th-century wing, which contains the entrance, is a stone bearing the inscription 'T G 1661,' and the date 1660 appears on the wall of the entrance internally. On the ground floor of the main block is a hall with rough ceiling beams and doorways with carved spandrels. A third moat, the largest, inclosing four fish-ponds at Up End, a mile north-west of the church and south of Brandon's Wood,[8] probably marks the site of the manor-house of another of the numerous manors in this parish.

About a quarter of a mile north-east of the church, in a park of about 40 acres, is Crawley Grange, the residence of John Irvine Boswell, M.D. It is a much-restored 16th-century building of brick with stone dressings and tiled roofs. The plan is H-shaped, with a porch on the south side of the main block connecting the wings. The stone-mullioned windows

wing, is a carved fireplace bearing the date 1686. In the windows of both these rooms is some foreign heraldic and other glass of the 16th and 17th centuries. The house also contains some panelling of the same periods, and the principal staircase is a good example of Elizabethan design.

In the village are several old timber-framed houses and cottages with tiled or thatched roofs. About half a mile south of the church is Hurst End, with Hurst End Farm. Brook End lies south-west of the church. In the north-east of the parish are Dollarsgrove and Dollarsgrove Farm.

The parish was inclosed under an Act of Parliament of 1772, the award being dated 11 June 1773.[9]

MANORS Though Crawley is not mentioned by name among the numerous Buckinghamshire manors held by Walter Giffard in 1086, three of the more important manors in this parish, Hollowes, Broughtons and Filliols, together with the Crawley Grange estate, were afterwards attached as one fee, one half fee, and one half fee respectively to the honour of Giffard or Gloucester, and the right to hold courts leet and view of frankpledge in Crawley descended to the Clares[10] and Audleys, Earls of Gloucester,[11] and through the Earls of Stafford[12] and Dukes of Buckingham[13] to the Duke of Buckingham attainted in 1521.[14] The honour of Gloucester escheated to the Crown, and the lands in Crawley were among those which went to form the honour of Ampthill in 1542,[15] the king

CRAWLEY GRANGE, NORTH CRAWLEY

are nearly all original, and over the porch entrance are the arms of Boswell and a Latin inscription, both apparently modern. In the hall, which is in the main block, is a fireplace composed of pieces of carved wood of the 17th century and later, in the overmantel of which are the arms of Boswell. A visit of Queen Elizabeth in 1575 is doubtless recorded by the royal arms, with the Tudor rose above and the Plantagenet portcullis below, carved on one of the oak window shutters. In the dining room, situated in the east

being acknowledged as overlord until the abolition of feudal tenures in the 17th century.[16] The honour of Gloucester does not, however, appear to have merged completely into that of Ampthill, for part of Crawley was still referred to in 1628 as appertaining to the honour of Gloucester,[17] and in 1703 John Dormer claimed rights in Crawley as appendant to that honour.[18]

GREAT CRAWLEY MANOR (afterwards Hollowes) was obtained in fee by John Fitz Niel,[19] either

[8] *Rep. of Royal Com. on Hist. Monum. N. Bucks.* 221.

[9] *Blue Bk. Incl. Awards,* 12.

[10] *Testa de Nevill* (Rec. Com.), 247; *Feud. Aids,* i, 82, 83; *Cal. Inq. p.m.* (Edw. II), v, 342.

[11] Chan. Inq. p.m. 21 Edw. III (1st nos.), no. 59.

[12] Ibid. 10 Ric. II, no. 38; 16 Ric. II, pt. i, no. 27; 22 Ric. II,

no. 46; 4 Hen. IV, no. 41; 11 Hen. VI, no. 33.

[13] Ibid. 38 & 39 Hen. VI, no. 59.

[14] G.E.C. *Complete Peerage,* ii, 64. Some confusion exists as to the overlordship of Hollowes Manor in the late 15th century. It was held in 1455 of John Benstede in right of Edith his wife (Chan. Inq. p.m. 33 Hen. VI, no. 28); in 1476 of the honour of Wallingford (ibid. 16 Edw. IV,

no. 73); and in 1489 of the king as of the hundred of Lathbury by fealty and rent (*Cal. Inq. p.m. Hen. VII,* i, 211–12).

[15] *L. and P. Hen. VIII,* xvii, 28 (21).

[16] Chan. Inq. p.m. (Ser. 2), cxx, 7; cccxvi, 6; ccclxix, 164.

[17] Ibid. ccccxlv, 61. See also Ct. R. (Gen. Ser.), portf. 155, no. 13.

[18] Add. MS. 37069, fol. 189–90.

[19] *Cal. Inq. p.m.* (Edw. II), v, 342.

the father, who died about 1289,[20] or the son, who died about ten years later, leaving as heir his daughter Joan, wife of John son of Richard Handlo.[21] This estate appears to have been settled on John Handlo's children by his second wife Maud, sister and heir of Edward Lord Burnell,[22] and was probably identical with the messuage and lands in Crawley which John and Maud Handlo claimed in 1316 as the gift of William Handlo, clerk, and Hugh le Despencer, sen.[23] In 1331 the Handlos made a settlement of Great Crawley and some Essex manors on themselves and their male issue, with contingent remainder as regards the Essex manors to Joan, Elizabeth, and Margaret, daughters of Maud, for life, with remainder in tail-male to John Lord Lovel,[24] son of Maud by her first husband John Lord Lovel of Titchmarsh (Northamptonshire).[25] Nicholas, John Handlo's son by Maud, having assumed the name of Burnell, was summoned to Parliament as Lord Burnell,[26] and his son Hugh Lord Burnell was returned as lord of Crawley during the closing years of the 14th century and the beginning of the 15th.[27] He was succeeded in 1420 by his three granddaughters, of whom the second, Catherine, married Sir John Ratcliff.[28] They conveyed their rights in Crawley Manor to William, seventh Lord Lovel of Titchmarsh,[29] and great-grandson of the John Lord Lovel upon whom the settlement of 1331 had been made.[30] At his death in 1455 William Lord Lovel was seised of the reversion of the manor, then held for life by Thomas Wake.[31] It did not descend to his eldest son, John Lovel, but to a younger son William Lovel, Lord Morley, who settled it on his son Henry Lovel in tail-male, with remainder successively to his own brother Henry Lovel in tail-male, and to the right heirs of his father, William Lord Lovel,[32] and died seised of it in 1476.[33] Henry Lord Morley died without issue in 1489 seised of the manor, his heir being his sister Alice, wife of Sir William Parker,[34] then twenty-two years

HANDLO. *Argent a lion azure sprinkled with drops or.*

LOVEL of Titchmarsh. *Barry wavy or and gules.*

old. Henry, uncle of Lord Morley, having died childless, the manor should have reverted, according to the terms of the settlement, to Francis Lord Lovel, son of John, the eldest son of William, seventh Lord Lovel, but it escheated to the Crown through the forfeiture of Francis Lovel's estates at his attainder in 1485.[35] It appears then to have been granted, as *HOLLOWES MANOR*, to Sir David Philip, at whose death without heirs male in 1504 it escheated to the king,[36] by whom it was given in 1511 to Sir John Nevill to hold during the king's good pleasure,[37] an exemplification of the patent being made in 1522.[38] It was granted in 1537 for thirty years to Robert Latimer[39] of North Crawley,[40] who seems to have obtained the fee simple of the manor before his death in 1548.[41] His daughter and heir Elizabeth became the wife of William Aprice or Aprees,[42] and their daughter Elizabeth married Roger Tetlow.[43] By his will, dated 23 December 1557, Roger Tetlow bequeathed the manor to his parents-in-law, William and Elizabeth Aprice, during the life of Elizabeth Aprice, with remainder to his wife's brothers, Edmund and Lewis and John Aprice, who were to bring up and make provision for his daughters.[44] He died on 23 April 1558,[45] and on 27 April 1570 his daughters Elizabeth and Mary had livery of their thirds of the manor,[46] in which they were to release all right under the provisions of his will. Edmund Aprice, who with his brothers Robert and Lewis, and with Edmund Conquest, had dealt with the manor in 1565,[47] in 1586 with his wife Mary conveyed it to Anthony Tyringham.[48] A further renunciation of rights was made in 1597 to Anthony Tyringham by Edmund Aprice of Wollaston (Northamptonshire), Thomas his son and heir and Robert Aprice of Tansor (Northamptonshire), brother of Edmund.[49] In 1612 the manor was granted by Sir Anthony Tyringham to his second son Arthur in tail-male,[50] and it was sold by the latter in 1616 to Ralph Smith, clerk,[51] Sir Thomas Tyringham, his eldest brother, at the same time renouncing all claim.[52] Ralph Smith died seised of it at North Crawley in 1638, and was succeeded by his son Ralph,[53] who in 1673 conveyed it to George Sedley.[54] It must have passed to John Dormer of Rowsham, Oxfordshire, by whom it was sold in 1704 to Francis Duncombe,[55] and it was conveyed in 1719 by John Robinson and Anne his wife, Francis Duncombe, jun., and Thomas Kilpin to William Lowndes, sen., secretary to the treasury.[56] At his death in January 1723–4 Hollowes passed by will to William Lowndes of Astwood Bury, his son by his third wife.[56a] His son William married in 1744 Catherine daughter

[20] *Cal. Inq. p.m.* (Edw. I), ii, 438.
[21] See Boarstall, *V.C.H. Bucks.* iv, 11.
[22] G.E.C. *Complete Peerage*, ii, 82.
[23] De Banco R. Trin. 10 Edw. II, m. 267.
[24] Feet of F. case 286, file 36, no. 83.
[25] G.E.C. op. cit. v, 164.
[26] Ibid. ii, 82.
[27] Chan. Inq. p.m. 16 Ric. II, pt. i, no. 27 ; 22 Ric. II, no. 46 ; 4 Hen. IV, no. 41.
[28] G.E.C. op. cit. ii, 83.
[29] Chan. Inq. p.m. 33 Hen. VI, no. 28. Catherine is here called Margery in mistake for her sister who married Sir Edmund Hungerford and died in 1486. See *Cal. Inq. p.m.* Hen. VII, i, 55, and P.C.C. 27 Logge.
[30] G.E.C. op. cit. v, 164–5.

[31] Chan. Inq. p.m. 33 Hen. VI, no. 28.
[32] *Cal. Inq. p.m.* Hen. VII, i, 211–12.
[33] Chan. Inq. p.m. 16 Edw. IV, no. 73.
[34] *Cal. Inq. p.m.* loc. cit.
[85] Ibid.
[36] Exch. Inq. p.m. (Ser. 2), file 21, no. 10.
[37] Pat. 3 Hen. VIII, pt. ii, m. 1. The man attainted in the reign of Henry VII is here called James Morley, Lord Morley, but there never was such a person.
[38] *L. and P. Hen. VIII*, iii, g. 2074 (9).
[39] Ld. Rev. Misc. Bks. clxxxviii, fol. 308.
[40] Add. Chart. 23932.
[41] Brass in church.
[42] *Visit. of Bucks.* (Harl. Soc.), 143.
[43] Ibid.
[44] Chan. Inq. p.m. (Ser. 2), cxx, 7 ;

P.C.C. 22 Noodes ; Fine R. 12 Eliz. no. 42.
[45] Chan. Inq. p.m. (Ser. 2), cxx, 7.
[46] Fine R. 12 Eliz. no. 42.
[47] Notes of F. Div. Co. Hil. 7 Eliz.
[48] Pat. 28 Eliz. pt. xiii ; Feet of F. Div. Co. Mich. 28 & 29 Eliz.
[49] Add. Chart. 53731 ; Com. Pleas Recov. R. Mich. 39 & 40 Eliz. m. 26 ; Feet of F. Div. Co. Mich. 39 & 40 Eliz.
[50] Add. Chart. 53746.
[51] Ibid. 23940.
[52] Notes of F. East. 14 Jas. I.
[53] Chan. Inq. p.m. (Ser. 2), dxcii, 87.
[54] Feet of F. Bucks. Mich. 25 Chas. II.
[55] Recov. R. Bucks. 3 Anne, m. 17, 21.
[56] Feet of F. Bucks. Trin. 5 Geo. I.
[56a] P.C.C. 36 Bolton ; *Dict. Nat. Biog.*; Burke, *Landed Gentry*.

of Francis Lowe and took the additional name of Stone.[57] He died in 1773, his son William Lowndes-Stone succeeding his grandfather William Lowndes of Astwood Bury in 1775.[57a] From William Lowndes-Stone the manor passed to his great-granddaughter Catherine Charlotte Lowndes-Stone, who married Captain Robert Thomas Norton in 1862,[58] and held the manorial rights in 1869. By 1877 they had become the property of John Bosworth, and are now vested in his trustees.

A mesne lordship in those parts of Crawley known by the late 15th century as *BROUGHTONS MANOR* and *FILLIOLS MANOR* respectively[59] was held under the Giffard Honour by the Earls of Oxford. Record of their interest in Crawley dates from the early 13th century,[60] and continued until the abolition of feudal tenure in the 17th century,[61] a temporary grant of his prerogatives being made in 1584 by the Earl of Oxford to Peter Palmer.[62]

Broughtons Manor in Crawley was obtained in fee by the Broughton family, from whom it acquired its distinctive name. Their descent has been given under the manor in Broughton parish (q.v.), which, with Crawley, is mentioned as being in their possession in a confirmatory charter of 1151-4.[63] The two manors descended together,[64] and Philip Aylesbury was returned as lord of both in 1346.[65] The Crawley manor did not descend in the Aylesbury family, however, and was evidently retained by the Broughtons, for in 1351 John son of Robert de Broughton conveyed 60 acres of land, 1 acre of meadow, 2s. rent and ½ lb. of pepper to John Bohun of Midhurst and Cecily his wife.[66] Sixty years later John Broughton, grandson of the grantor, claimed this estate against the grantees' son John Bohun, and it was restored to him by order of the court in 1427-8.[67] This property, referred to in 1489 as the 'litell maner in More Craule called Broughtons,'[68] descended with the lands in Broughton parish likewise retained by the Broughton family to Agnes Howard, wife of William Paulet, Lord St. John, by whom it was alienated in 1573 to Richard Morton.[69] Richard Morton died seised of the site of this manor and of 300 acres of land, parcel thereof, in 1595.[70] His son Henry,[71] as Henry Morton, sen., with his wife Anne, in 1625 granted it to Robert Staunton,[72] by whom and his wife Mary it was conveyed in 1634 to William Knight and Brian Harrison.[73] It had

passed before 1704 to John Dormer,[74] and was subsequently held with the manor of Hollowes,[75] the last reference to its distinct identity as Broughtons Manor occurring in 1775.[76]

The part of Crawley afterwards called Filliols Manor was known as such from the Filliol family, of whom William Filliol was fined 5 marks in 1175-6 for breach of the forest law.[77] He was succeeded by Baldwin Filliol, who in 1198 acquired 17 acres in Crawley from William Anketill,[78] and alienated 9 acres in 1202 to Bernard son of Hugh.[79] Baldwin was still alive in 1212,[80] but his heir Richard Filliol,[81] probably his son,[82] was in possession by 1249,[83] and held[84] until his death about 1260.[85] His son John,[86] who was presented by the hundred in 1275 for building a house on the highway,[87] exercised the manorial rights[88] until his death about 1317, when they vested in his nephew and heir John Filliol the elder.[89] He was sued by the Prior of Tickford in 1323,[90] and in 1324-5 settled the manor on himself and his wife Margery.[91] In 1327 the Filliols came to an arrangement with Robert and Paulina Broughton concerning a tenement in Great Crawley.[92] At John Filliol's death *circa* 1333 Richard, his son and heir, aged twelve, inherited some of the family property in Essex, but John, aged seven, his son by Margery (who survived), received the rest of the estate.[93] John Filliol the younger died without issue,[94] and at Margery's

FILLIOL. *Vair a quarter gules.*   BOHUN of Midhurst. *Or a cross azure.*

death in 1346 Cecily, then aged twenty-two, wife of John Bohun of Midhurst, was described as her only child and heir by John Filliol the elder.[95] Philip Aylesbury was returned in this year as lord of the part of Crawley formerly held by John Filliol, but there is doubtless confusion between this and Broughtons

[57] Burke, loc. cit. ; Feet of F. Bucks. Trin. 17 Geo. II ; Priv. Act, 12 Geo. III, cap. 5.

[57a] P.C.C. 146 Alexander; 83 Stevens; Recov. R. East. 15 Geo. III, m. 158; Lysons, *Mag. Brit.* i (3), 545.

[58] Burke, loc. cit.

[59] P.C.C. 18 Milles.

[60] *Testa de Nevill* (Rec. Com.), 247 ; *Feud. Aids,* i, 82, 83.

[61] *Feud. Aids,* i, 104 ; Chan. Inq. p.m. 41 Edw. III (1st nos.), no. 13 ; 5 Ric. II, no. 9 ; 11 Hen. VI, no. 33 ; (Ser. 2), dviii, 15.

[62] Feet of F. Bucks. East. 26 Eliz. Peter Palmer's interest may have been transferred to Richard More, of whom Broughtons was said to be held in 1615 'ut de quodam segnior in gross' by fealty and rent (Fine R. 13 Jas. I, pt. i, no. 40).

[63] Round, *Cal. Doc. of France,* 444.

[64] See also Feet of F. case 14, file 2, no. 29 ; file 3, no. 41.

[65] *Feud. Aids,* i, 129.

[66] *Cal. Close,* 1349–54, p. 358.

[67] Wrottesley, *Ped. from Plea R.* 271.

[68] P.C.C. 18 Milles.

[69] Feet of F. Bucks. Trin. 15 Eliz. ; Recov. R. Mich. 15 & 16 Eliz. m. 746.

[70] Chan. Inq. p.m. (Ser. 2), cccxvi, 6.

[71] Ibid. ; Fine R. 13 Jas. I, pt. i, no. 40.

[72] Feet of F. Bucks. East. 1 Chas. I.

[73] Ibid. Mich. 10 Chas. I.

[74] Com. Pleas Recov. R. Mich. 3 Anne, m. 17, 21.

[75] See also Feet of F. Bucks. Trin. 4 Geo. I.

[76] Recov. R. East. 15 Geo. III, m. 158.

[77] *Pipe R.* 22 *Hen.* II (Pipe R. Soc.), 23.

[78] Feet of F. case 14, file 3, no. 42.

[79] Ibid. file 6, no. 13.

[80] *Red Bk. of Exch.* (Rolls Ser.), 502, 596.

[81] C. Roberts, *Cal. Gen.* 99.

[82] Morant, *Hist. and Antiq. Essex,* ii, 151.

[83] Feet of F. case 16, file 30, no. 6.

[84] Ibid. file 31, no. 5.

[85] *Cal. Inq. p.m.* (Hen. III), i, 134.

[86] Ibid.

[87] *Hund. R.* (Rec. Com.), i, 41.

[88] *Feud. Aids,* i, 82, 104, 110.

[89] *Cal. Inq. p.m.* (Edw. II), vi, 19.

[90] De Banco R. 248, m. 238 ; 255, m. 68.

[91] Ibid. 253, m. 303 d. ; Feet of F. case 19, file 75, no. 2. Robert Filliol of Great Crawley and his wife Alice quitclaimed land in Broughton of her inheritance in 1324 (Feet of F. case 19, file 74, no. 2), and in 1339 they settled 16 acres of land and 2 acres of meadow on Simon de Trewythosa and Cecily his wife and the heirs of Cecily with remainder to Margery Filliol (ibid. file 83, no. 8).

[92] De Banco R. Trin. 1 Edw. III, m. 27.

[93] *Cal. Inq. p.m.* (Edw. III), vii, 317–18.

[94] Wrottesley, op. cit. 229.

[95] Chan. Inq. p.m. 20 Edw. III (1st nos.), no. 45.

Manor.[96] The following year the Bohuns made a settlement on themselves in tail, with remainder to the heirs of Cecily, to Ralph Filliol for life, to William son of John de Sutton, *chivaler*, and to William's brothers Richard and John in tail-male successively.[97] Sir John Bohun, who in 1351 obtained a grant of the Broughtons' estate in Crawley, died seised of the manor in 1367,[98] leaving a son John, to whom the manor descended at the death of Cecily in 1381.[99] Sir John Bohun, who about 1393 leased his manor to John Burton, clerk,[100] and from whom in 1427–8 John Broughton recovered Broughtons Manor, made a settlement of his manor of Great Crawley on 6 January 1432–3,[1] and died on the last day of the same month.[2] He was succeeded by his son Sir Humphrey Bohun,[3] who died in 1468.[4] By him, or by his son Sir John Bohun,[5] the manorial rights appear to have been alienated, the Bohuns retaining some lands and the advowson. Filliols Manor, then so-called for the first time, was certainly in the possession of John Broughton at his death in 1489,[6] and, as there is no further reference to it, it probably coalesced with the larger Broughtons Manor.

A manor in Great Crawley called *MATHIAS* was bequeathed by John Broughton to his heir by his will of 1489,[7] and was possibly identical with the manor of Broughtons granted with Hollowes by Sir Anthony Tyringham in tail-male to his second son Arthur in 1612.[8] At his death in 1614 Sir Anthony Tyringham was seised of the mansion-house within the manor of Broughtons and lands belonging to the same, and of the manor or farm within the manor of Broughtons called *FRANKLYNS FARM*.[9] This was included among lands in North Crawley sold in March 1615–16 by Sir Anthony's son and heir Sir Thomas Tyringham and by Arthur Tyringham to Roger Hackett, D.D.,[10] rector of North Crawley since 1590, whose fame as a preacher was widespread.[11] Roger Hackett died in 1621 seised of the chief messuage called Franklyns Farm held of Henry Morton as of his manor of Great Crawley or Broughtons Manor

HACKETT. *Argent three fleurs de lis bendwise between two bends gules.*

by rent, fealty and suit of court,[12] and of considerable other property acquired by him in North Crawley, which later became known as the *CRAWLEY GRANGE* estate. According to Browne Willis, ' having bought in several Farms and Estates and laid them together,' he built himself

' the principal House in the whole Parish,' and made his 'best and principal' property.[13] His son Roger [14] settled his mansion-house in Crawley on his son and heir Thomas at the marriage of the latter in 1650 with Elizabeth daughter and heir of Augustine Nicholls,[15] and died before 1658.[16] Thomas Hackett died in April 1689,[17] and was succeeded by his son Nicholls,[18] who had made a settlement of this property in the previous year.[19] There is a letter extant of Nicholls Hackett to the Earl of Bridgewater dated 28 January 1704–5, in which he excuses himself from acting as a deputy lieutenant on the ground of not having taken the oaths.[20]

Elizabeth, the only child of Nicholls Hackett, married in 1710 Nicholas, afterwards Sir Nicholas Carew, bart., of Beddington, Surrey,[21] from whom the estate passed to Sir Peter King by the result of successive mortgages.[22] In 1723 it was sold by Sir Peter King to William Lowndes,[23] who settled it on trustees for ninety-nine years with reversion in tail-male to Richard Lowndes, son of his eldest son Robert.[24] It descended with the Winslow and Whaddon estates (q.v.) until purchased in 1803 by Thomas David Boswell, younger brother of Johnson's biographer.[25] He died in 1826,[26] leaving a son Thomas Alexander Boswell,[27] upon whose death without issue in 1852 the Crawley Grange estate passed to Colonel Bruce Boswell, son of his cousin Elizabeth, wife of William Boswell and daughter of James Boswell the biographer.[28] Colonel Boswell died three years later,[29] leaving as heir his sister Elizabeth, widow of John Williams, who was still alive in 1874.[30] By 1883 her property was vested in trustees, but four years later Charles Ware of Crawley Grange, son of her daughter and heir Elizabeth by the Rev. Charles Cumberleye Ware, was said to be one of the principal landowners. The Crawley Grange estate, however, was settled on his sister Edith,[31] and she is apparently the Miss Cumberleye Ware who enjoyed the property during the closing years of the 19th century. It is now in the possession of John Irvine Boswell, M.D., son of the late John Alexander Corrie Boswell.

An estate in Crawley said in 1285 to comprise half the vill [32] was attached in the early 13th century as a quarter fee to that part of the honour of Huntingdon which came to Henry Hastings, under whom it was held in fee by Robert de Hersy (Hurst).[33] In 1197 a quarter virgate had been subinfeudated to him by Richard de Lindesey,[34] who is later returned as holding one quarter fee in Crawley of the fee of Say.[35] From Robert de Hersy the demesne rights passed through Ralf Butler to Robert Burnell, Bishop of Bath and Wells,[36] who in 1282 acquired a few acres

[96] *Feud. Aids*, i, 129.
[97] Feet of F. case 287, file 42.
[98] Chan. Inq. p.m. 41 Edw. III (1st nos.), no. 13 ; *Cal. Close*, 1364–8, p. 415.
[99] Chan. Inq. p.m. 5 Ric. II, no. 9.
[100] *Cat. of Anct. D.* ii, 488.
[1] Chan. Inq. p.m. 11 Hen. VI, no. 33.
[2] Ibid.
[3] Ibid.
[4] G.E.C. *Complete Peerage* (new ed.), ii, 201.
[5] Ibid.
[6] P.C.C. 18 Milles.
[7] Ibid.
[8] Add. Chart. 53746.
[9] Chan. Inq. p.m. (Ser. 3), cccxlix, 164.
[10] Add. Chart. 53748, 53749.

[11] *Dict. Nat. Biog.*
[12] Chan. Inq. p.m. (Ser. 2), ccccxlv, 61.
[13] Add. MS. 5839, p. 129.
[14] Chan. Inq. p.m. (Ser. 2), ccccxlv, 61.
[15] Add. Chart. 23985.
[16] Ibid. 23990.
[17] Brass in church.
[18] Add. Chart. 23960.
[19] Recov. R. Trin. 4 Jas. II, m. 68.
[20] *Hist. MSS. Com. Rep.* xi, App. vii, 165–6. This was in connexion with an order from the Council for searching Papists' houses for horses and arms in pursuance of an Act of Paliament.
[21] Add. Chart. 23965, 23966 ; G.E.C. *Baronetage*, v, 26.
[22] Recov. R. Mich. 10 Geo. I, m. 15, 17.

[23] Ibid. ; Feet of F. Bucks. Mich. 10 Geo. I. [24] P.C.C. 36 Bolton.
[25] Sheahan, op. cit. 525.
[26] *Dict. Nat. Biog.*
[27] Berry, *Bucks. Gen.* 34.
[28] Burke, *Landed Gentry* (1871).
[29] Tablet in church.
[30] Sheahan, op. cit. 525 ; Rogers, *Boswelliana*, 196–7.
[31] Rogers, loc. cit.
[32] *Plac. de Quo Warr.* (Rec. Com.), 96.
[33] *Testa de Nevill* (Rec. Com.), 244 (where he is called Meysy by a scribal error), 251.
[34] Feet of F. case 14, file 2, no. 22.
[35] *Testa de Nevill* (Rec. Com.), 248.
[36] *Plac. de Quo Warr.* (Rec. Com.), 96.

of land in Crawley.[37] The estate was subinfeudated by him before 1285 to Philip Montgomery,[38] who claimed in that year to hold view of frankpledge here.[39] The intermediary lordship lapsed, for in 1302 Philip Montgomery held directly of the honour of Huntingdon,[40] and in 1328 Philip son of Philip Montgomery was sued for 14 acres of land, 8 acres of wood, and 6 marks rent in Great Crawley by John Handlo and his wife Maud Burnell, kinswoman and heir of the bishop, on the ground that the grant had not been in fee simple as Philip Montgomery asserted, but for a term which had expired.[41] The Handlos apparently lost the case, for in 1335 the heirs of Philip Montgomery, names unknown, were returned as lords of the fee.[42] They were then holding of

HASTINGS. *Argent a sleeve sable.* LATIMER. *Gules a cross paty or.*

William Lord Latimer, whose family had succeeded the house of Hastings as overlords, and to whom the manorial rights appear shortly afterwards to have reverted, for in 1346 William Latimer's widow Elizabeth was said to hold this fee, formerly Philip Montgomery's.[43] The Latimers held Isenhampstead Latimer in Chesham (q.v.), with which this manor descended to Richard Nevill, Lord Latimer, who was obliged to part with Isenhampstead Latimer to Sir Robert, Lord Willoughby de Broke. The Crawley manor, which he retained, was carried in marriage by his great-granddaughter Dorothy to Thomas Cecil, first Earl of Exeter,[44] who, towards the end of the 16th century, brought an action against the steward of the manor for detaining the records, court rolls, &c.[45] This estate, which by the early 17th century was called *LATIMERS FEE*,[46] and the importance of which lay in the rights of free fishing, free warren, view of frankpledge, and rights to hold courts leet and baron, only 15 acres of land being appurtenant thereto,[47] remained in the Cecils, Earls of Exeter,[48] and was accounted the paramount manor in Crawley at the inclosure of 1772,[49] the earl receiving rents on alienation or sale of lands.[50] The Marquess of Exeter

still occasionally held a court for the manor at the Cock Inn *circa* 1860,[51] but since then these rights appear to have lapsed.

Four hides in Buckinghamshire which had been held in the time of Edward the Confessor by two thegns, Herald and Alwi, who could sell, were assessed in 1086 among the lands of William Fitz Ansculf, lord of Newport.[52] The locality is not specified, but is in all probability Crawley,[53] as the Paynels, successors of William Fitz Ansculf, gave the chapel of Little Crawley to Tickford Priory before 1150,[54] and by the early 13th century half a fee in Crawley was held of the honour of Dudley,[55] a constituent part of which was the honour of Newport.[56] Later in the century this half fee was divided, both manors continuing to be held of the Somerys, lords of Newport Pagnell,[57] who in 1285 claimed to hold view of frankpledge once a year without the intervention of the king's servant for the tenants of those lands in Crawley which were part of the honour of Dudley.[58] This overlordship is not again recorded in the quarter fee afterwards Tyringhams Manor, the tenure of which was said to be unknown in 1615.[59] Pateshull, the other manor, however, remained attached as a quarter fee to the honour of Newport,[60] and was held of the manor of Newport Pagnell[61] for 2*s.* a year, two barbed arrow heads, and suit at Newport every three weeks.[62] Court Rolls exist for 1544–6 recording the attendance of the tenants at the view of frankpledge held at Newport Pagnell.[63] As chantry land escheating to the Crown it was bestowed upon Sir John Parot in 1559 to hold of the queen in chief for one-twentieth of a fee,[64] the same service being specified in the grant of 1623 (see below).[65]

No mention of any tenant of this holding occurs between Wibert in 1086 [66] and Geoffrey de Beauchamp in the early 13th century.[67] Shortly afterwards it was divided as above said and one moiety was obtained in fee by Simon de Pateshull [68] before 1260, in which year Ida, widow of William de Beauchamp, baron of Bedford, invaded the manor, pulled

PATESHULL. *Argent a fesse sable between three crescents gules.*

down the houses, cut down the trees, and committed other damage.[69] The reason for this conduct may perhaps be found in Simon de Pateshull's refusal to acknowledge her right to the manor and honour of

[37] Feet of F. case 17, file 47, no. 5.
[38] *Feud. Aids*, i, 83.
[39] *Plac. de Quo Warr.* (Rec. Com.), 96.
[40] *Feud. Aids*, i, 104.
[41] De Banco R. Trin. 2 Edw. III, m. 66 d. ; she was sister and heir of Edward son of Philip son of Hugh Burnell, brother of the bishop.
[42] *Cal. Inq. p.m.* (Edw. III), vii, 478 ; *Cal. Close*, 1333–7, p. 547.
[43] *Feud. Aids*, i, 129. The service due to the honour of Huntingdon was rendered in 1388 to the Earl of Pembroke (Chan. Inq. p.m. 12 Ric. II, no. 40), but this estate was afterwards said to be held of the king in chief (ibid. 20 Ric. II, no. 54), of the honour of Wallingford (ibid.

5 Hen. IV, no. 28), and of Lord Grey de Ruthyn (ibid. 9 Hen. VI, no. 24).
[44] G.E.C. *Complete Peerage*, v, 25, 26.
[45] Ct. of Req. bdle. 33, no. 77.
[46] Chan. Inq. p.m. (Ser. 2), dcxlvii, 34.
[47] Recov. R. Trin. 10 Geo. I, m. 54 ; Trin. 21 & 22 Geo. II, m. 152.
[48] Ibid. ; Mich. 13 Geo. III, m. 490 ; East. 16 Geo. III, m. 469–70.
[49] Priv. Act, 12 Geo. III, cap. 5.
[50] Add. MS. 5839, p. 129.
[51] Sheahan, op. cit. 524.
[52] *V.C.H. Bucks.* i, 256.
[53] Ibid. n. 4.
[54] Round, *Cal. Doc. of France*, 444 ; see later.
[55] *Testa de Nevill* (Rec. Com.), 248.
[56] *Cal. Inq. p.m.* (Edw. I), ii, 493.

[57] Ibid. 15 ; *Feud. Aids*, i, 83.
[58] *Plac. de Quo Warr.* (Rec. Com.), 88.
[59] Chan. Inq. p.m. (Ser. 2), cccxlix, 164.
[60] *Cal. Inq. p.m.* (Edw. I), ii, 497 ; (Edw. II), vi, 257 ; *Feud. Aids.* i, 104 ; *Cal. Close*, 1318–22, p. 623.
[61] Chan. Inq. p.m. 3 Hen. VI, no. 20 ; (Ser. 2), xviii, 29.
[62] *Cal. Inq. p.m.* (Edw. III), vii, 196 ; Chan. Inq. p.m. 33 Edw. III (1st nos.), no. 40.
[63] Ct. R. (Gen. Ser.), portf. 155, no. 20.
[64] Pat. 951, m. 4.
[65] Ibid. 2312, no. 4.
[66] *V.C.H. Bucks.* i, 256.
[67] *Testa de Nevill* (Rec. Com.), 248.
[68] *Cal. Inq. p.m.* (Edw. I), ii, 15.
[69] *Ann. Mon.* (Rolls Ser.), iii, 215.

Newport (q.v.). Simon de Pateshull, the supporter of Simon de Montfort and the baronial party, appropriated certain liberties in Crawley[70] before his death in 1274.[71] His son John had seisin of the manor by 1276,[72] and retained it[73] until his death in 1290.[74] His son Simon[75] was seised of Crawley,[76] which passed at his death in 1295 to his son John, then a minor,[77] who is described as the heir of Simon in the feudal aid for 1302–3.[78] A grant of free warren in the demesne lands of Little Crawley was made to him in 1306,[79] and in 1310 he complained that William le Butler of Hardmead and others had broken into his house here, and fished in his stews, &c.[80] This John de Pateshull was known as of Bletsoe, a manor belonging to the family in Bedfordshire,[81] to distinguish him from a relative of the same name to whom he gave a life interest in Crawley Manor, and who was known as of Crawley at his death *circa* 1329.[82] The manor then reverted to John de Pateshull of Bletsoe,[83] who made a settlement of it on himself and his wife Mabel in 1333,[84] and held it[85] until his death in 1349, when it passed to his son William.[86] Ten years later, at William de Pateshull's death,[87] Crawley Manor was assigned to his sister and co-heir, Alice wife of Thomas Wake of Blisworth[88] (Northamptonshire), though she does not appear to have received full seisin until 1368.[89] In 1373 the Wakes settled Crawley on their son Thomas Wake and his wife Maud.[90] Thomas Wake, the father, died before Michaelmas 1382,[91] and his widow Alice held Blisworth at the death of their son Thomas in the following year.[92] His son and heir John Wake, then aged nine,[93] must have died without issue, for at the death of Alice in 1398 the heir was said to be Thomas Wake, son of her deceased son Thomas, a youth of nineteen.[94] He died before his mother Maud, his son, another Thomas, succeeding her in 1425,[95] and settling Crawley on himself and his wife Agnes in the following year.[96] He was succeeded in 1458 by his son Thomas,[97] whose death occurred in 1476.[98] His son Roger, to whom Crawley then passed,[99] was attainted after the battle of Bosworth, and the manor was bestowed in 1486 on Sir John Fortescue and his heirs male.[100] It was restored to Roger Wake before his death in March 1503–4, when it was described as a messuage and 160 acres of land called Pateshull,[1] which he bequeathed for the foundation of a chantry in Blisworth.[2] The

trustees founded the chantry about 1505, and endowed it with Crawley Manor ten years later.[3] After the suppression of the chantries it was granted in 1559 as the manor of Crawley Parva and Chicheley, concealed lands,[4] to Sir John Parot.[5] It was subsequently claimed that the manor had been bequeathed not only to support a chantry priest, but for the maintenance of a school at Blisworth, and by a decree in Chancery, 23 February 1562–3, the grant to Sir John Parot was repealed,[6] and an annual rent of £11 was assured to the school out of the premises.[7] These had been leased as the *MANOR OF PATESHULL* or *LITTLE CRAWLEY* on 18 January 1535–6 to William Johnson by the trustees of Roger Wake for a term of sixty years.[8] Robert Johnson, who succeeded in 1558[9] to his father's interest in the manor, in 1569 sued George Annesley of Tickford,[10] to whom Parot had sold Pateshull for £330 in 1560, Annesley doing homage for the same in 1566.[11] In the earlier suits Annesley is referred to as undertenant of Johnson in part of the manor,[12] but he made good his claim to hold the whole in fee. George Annesley had seven sons,[13] upon three of whom, Matthew, Thomas, and Robert, he made settlements of the manor in 1604 and 1605.[14] Another son, James Annesley, jun., had received in 1600 a messuage, barn, stable and Smythe Wyke close, which descended at his death in January 1605–6 to his son Nicholas.[15] Somerayes Wykes, Pateshull Grove, and other lands amounting to one-fourth of the manor, were settled in 1601 on a son George.[16] Ralph, another son, obtained in 1604 the manor-house and closes called Starkers Croft, Le Motted Close, Wolfie Mead, Le Deane Leyes, &c.[17] The eldest son, James Annesley, sen., aged forty at his father's death in January 1607–8, inherited a fourth of the manor, then in the tenure of Anthony Chester, sen.[18] Some arrangement appears to have been arrived at between the various members of the family, for in 1623 a grant of the manor was made in fee to Anthony Chester, then a baronet, George Annesley of Crawley, and Nicholas Annesley of London.[19] The Chesters probably obtained eventually all the manorial rights, and Pateshull descended with the manor of Chicheley[20] (q.v.), into which it merged, the name of Charles Chester being among those of landowners in Crawley at the inclosure of 1772.[21]

[70] *Hund. R.* (Rec. Com.), i, 41.
[71] *Ann. Mon.* (Rolls Ser.), iii, 260.
[72] *Hund. R.* (Rec. Com.), i, 42.
[73] *Feud. Aids*, i, 83.
[74] *Ann. Mon.* (Rolls Ser.), iii, 365.
[75] Ibid.
[76] *Cal. Inq. p.m.* (Edw. I), ii, 497.
[77] Ibid. iii, 232 ; *Cal. Fine R.* 1272–1307, pp. 356, 367 ; *Ann. Mon.* (Rolls Ser.), iii, 401.
[78] *Feud. Aids*, i, 104.
[79] *Cal. Chart. R.* 1300–26, p. 66.
[80] *Cal. Pat.* 1307–13, p. 309. This complaint was reiterated in 1316 (ibid. 1313–17, p. 500) and in 1322 (ibid. 1321–4, p. 160).
[81] *V.C.H. Beds.* iii, 40–1.
[82] *Cal. Inq. p.m.* (Edw. III), vii, 196. This John, of Crawley, who left a son John, aged five, may be the John to whom reference as lord of Crawley is made in 1316 (*Feud. Aids*, i, 110) and 1322 (Chan. Inq. p.m. 16 Edw. II, no. 72).
[83] *Cal. Close*, 1327–33, p. 515.
[84] Feet of F. case 286, file 37, no. 132.

[85] *Cal. Inq. p.m.* (Edw. III), vii, 478 ; *Feud. Aids*, i, 130.
[86] Chan. Inq. p.m. 23 Edw. III, pt. ii, no. 96.
[87] Ibid. 33 Edw. III (1st nos.), no. 40.
[88] Ibid. ; *Abbrev. Rot. Orig.* (Rec. Com.), ii, 256.
[89] *Cal. Close*, 1364–8, p. 435.
[90] Feet of F. case 288, file 49, no. 100.
[91] Wrottesley, *Ped. from Plea R.* 151.
[92] Chan. Inq. p.m. 8 Ric. II, no. 41.
[93] Ibid.
[94] Ibid. 22 Ric. II, no. 50. See also Wrottesley, op. cit. 268.
[95] Chan. Inq. p.m. 3 Hen. VI, no. 20.
[96] Ibid. 37 Hen. VI, no. 19.
[97] Ibid.
[98] Ibid. 16 Edw. IV, no. 45 ; cf. P.R.O. *List of Sheriffs*, 93.
[99] Nicolas, *Test. Vetusta*, 463.
[100] Pat. 563, m. 21.
[1] Chan. Inq. p.m. (Ser. 2), xviii, 29.
[2] Ibid. ; Ct. of Req. bdle. 107, no. 51.
[3] Ct. of Req. bdle. 107, no. 51.
[4] Ibid.

[5] Pat. 2 Eliz. pt. iv, m. 4.
[6] Chan. Proc. (Ser. 2), bdle. 3, no. 7.
[7] Ct. of Req. bdle. 107, no. 51.
[8] Chan. Proc. (Ser. 2), bdle. 3, no. 7. Pettyshull and Patesills are variants of the name.
[9] Chan. Inq. p.m. (Ser. 2), cxxii, 14.
[10] Ct. of Req. bdle. 77, no. 52.
[11] Memo. R. (Exch. L.T.R.), Hil. 8 Eliz. m. 48.
[12] Ct. of Req. bdle. 107, no. 51.
[13] *Visit. of Bucks.* (Harl. Soc.), 142.
[14] Feet of F. Bucks. Trin. 2 Jas. I ; Mich. 3 Jas. I.
[15] Chan. Inq. p.m. (Ser. 2), ccxciii, 30.
[16] In 1619 closes in Crawley were held of this George as of his manor of Pateshull (Chan. Inq. p.m. [Ser. 2], dcxlvii, 34).
[17] Ibid. ccciv, 91.
[18] Ibid.
[19] Pat. 2312, no. 4.
[20] *Cal. S. P. Dom.* 1638–9, p. 148.
[21] Priv. Act, 12 Geo. III, cap. 5.

The other moiety of the original Dudley fee was acquired before 1272 by John Tyringham,[22] and his son Roger claimed in 1285 that his tenants in Crawley attended the view of frankpledge held once a year at Tyringham, for which he paid his overlord, Roger de Somery, half a mark.[23] The Tyringhams' chief seat was at Tyringham (q.v.), with which this manor descended[24] to Sir Anthony Tyringham, by whom it was granted in 1612 as *TYRINGHAMS MANOR* in North Crawley to his second son Arthur, who received Hollowes at the same time.[25] By him it appears to have been granted, probably in 1616 with Franklyns Farm or Manor, to Roger Hackett of North Crawley, who in 1621 died seised of lands in North Crawley held of Sir Thomas Tyringham as of his manor of Tyringham,[26] these lands doubtless forming part of the later Crawley Grange estate.

Lands in Crawley were held by the abbey of Woburn,[27] and the priories of Tickford,[28] Caldwell[29] and Harrold,[30] grants from which were later made to Lincoln College[31] and to Henry the Eighth's College, Oxford.[32]

years of the 13th century of a south aisle the length of the three eastern bays of the south arcade of the nave. A few years later the original nave was probably extended two bays westwards, the aisle being lengthened to correspond, and a west tower was added, probably at first only three stages in height, as the present bell-chamber appears to be an addition of the late 14th century. At the end of the 13th century the chancel was rebuilt. The date is fixed with fair certainty by an inscription cut in Lombardic capitals beneath the external sill of the east window. Though somewhat weatherworn it can still be clearly read, and runs as follows : ' + PETRUS CANCELLVM TIBI DAT FIRMINE NOVELLVM UT CVM LAVDERIS DEO PETRI MEMORERIS.' This Peter is probably to be identified with Peter of Guildford who was presented to the living of North Crawley in 1294.[36a] Early in the 14th century the north aisle was added, the still existing north arcade being pierced in the north wall of the nave. About 1460 both aisles seem to have been rebuilt, or at any rate, completely remodelled, and the clearstory was added to the nave, the church

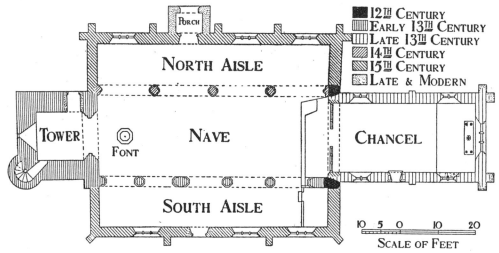

PLAN OF NORTH CRAWLEY CHURCH

12TH CENTURY
EARLY 13TH CENTURY
LATE 13TH CENTURY
14TH CENTURY
15TH CENTURY
LATE & MODERN

There was a mill worth 20s. on William Fitz Ansculf's holding in 1086,[33] and there is mention of a mill in North Crawley in 1202.[34] A windmill was held with the Hackett estates in 1650[35] and 1688.[36]

CHURCH The church of *ST. FIRMIN* consists of a chancel measuring internally about 36 ft. by 17 ft. 6 in., nave 60 ft. 6 in. by 20 ft. 6 in., north aisle 10 ft. 4 in. wide, south aisle of the same width, west tower 12 ft. square, and a modern north porch.

The present building seems to have been developed from a 12th-century church consisting of a chancel and nave, the latter about 20 ft. shorter than the nave in its present form. The first stage in the enlargement of the church was the addition in the early

being reroofed throughout. At the same time the chancel arch was enlarged, the responds being cut back to the side walls of the chancel. The history of the fabric has been somewhat obscured by the coating of cement with which the walls were covered in the early 19th century. The removal of this would throw much light on the date of the walling of the aisles, which may be substantially that of the earlier aisles, repaired and given new windows in the 15th century.

The chancel is a very complete and interesting example of late 13th-century work ; unfortunately the coating of cement hides all the original external wrought detail with the exception of the windows, with their labels, and the inscription on the east wall. A high plinth, extending to the sills of the windows,

[22] *Cal. Inq. p.m.* (Edw. II), ii, 15.
[23] *Plac. de Quo Warr.* (Rec. Com.), 84.
[24] It was held under them in 1284 and 1302 by Hugh de Buckland (*Feud. Aids,* i, 83, 104) and by Hugh's son Thomas in 1346 (ibid. i, 129).
[25] Add. Chart. 53746.
[26] Chan. Inq. p.m. (Ser. 2), ccccxlv, 61.

[27] Feet of F. case 15, file 22, no. 41 ; *Cal. Pat.* 1334–8, p. 493 ; *Valor Eccl.* (Rec. Com.), iv, 212 ; Ct. of Req. bdle. 113, no. 30 ; Add. Chart. 23935, 23941.
[28] Feet of F. case 14, file 4, no. 21 ; case 15, file 19, no. 6 ; Chan. Inq. p.m. (Ser. 2), lxxvi, 3.
[29] *Cal. Pat.* 1340–3, p. 370.
[30] Ibid. 1391–6, p. 343.

[31] *L. and P. Hen. VIII,* iii, g. 1036 (28).
[32] Ibid. v, g. 1370 (23) ; xvi, g. 1391 (45) ; xx (2), g. 1068 (10).
[33] *V.C.H. Bucks.* i, 256.
[34] Feet of F. case 14, file 6, no. 1.
[35] Add. Chart. 23985.
[36] Recov. R. Trin. 4 Jas. II, m. 68.
[36a] *Cal. Pat.* 1292–1301, p. 96.

and stepped upwards at the east end to accommodate itself to the higher level of the east window, runs round the walls, and at the eastern angles are pairs of buttresses, substantially of original 13th-century date, while in the centre of each side wall is a small pilaster buttress resting on the plinth. The walls are crowned by an embattled parapet and cornice of the 15th century. The east window is of three uncusped lights, the central light being higher and wider than the side lights, and in the two-centred main head are three quatrefoiled circles with pierced cusping. The rear-arch, which is ribbed and hollow-chamfered, and is inclosed by a label with mask stops, springs from small attached shafts at the angles of the jambs. On either side of the window is a semi-octagonal image bracket with a supporting cluster of naturalistic foliage. At the east end of each side wall is a window of two uncusped lights with a quatrefoiled circle above in a two-centred head, and a rear-arch and jamb-shafts like those of the east window. A moulded string-course runs along the east wall beneath the sill of the window, and is continued for a short distance along the side walls, where it is dropped to pass beneath the sills of the north-east and south-east windows. The remaining two windows of the chancel are placed at the west ends of the side walls, and correspond exactly in design with the windows at the opposite end of the walls, except that their sills are brought down internally to a lower level. Immediately to the west of the pilaster buttress on the south wall is a small doorway, probably original, the jambs and head of which are covered with cement. Below the south-east window is a double piscina recess, with two-centred moulded heads springing from a central shaft with moulded capital and base, and received upon the jambs by attached shafts of the same design ; the original circular basins still remain, but all the detail is coated with cement. To the west of this is a rectangular recess with moulded edges, probably intended for a credence shelf. Below the north-east window is a second rectangular recess with moulded edges. The chancel arch is of two hollow-chamfered orders, the outer continuous upon the nave side, and the inner order supported by ill-designed 15th-century corbels upon the side walls.

The early 14th-century north arcade of the nave is of four bays with two-centred arches of two hollow-chamfered orders, supported by piers of quatrefoil plan with moulded capitals and bases standing upon rough square sub-plinths. The arches are inclosed by labels with mask stops over each pier, and the inner orders are received upon each respond by semicircular attached shafts.

The early 13th-century south arcade is of five bays, the two western bays being separated from the eastern portion of the arcade by a pier measuring about 3 ft. 10 in. from west to east, against which each of the adjoining arches has an independent respond. The three eastern bays have two-centred arches of two chamfered orders supported by heavy octagonal piers. The capitals of the piers are carved with stiff-leaved foliage, and their abaci are grooved and hollow-chamfered with a small roll below the chamfer ; the bases are of the attic type. The semi-octagonal responds repeat the design of the piers, except that the bell of the capital of the east respond is plain. The abacus of the west respond is continuous with that of the east respond of the western portion of the

arcade, the two bays of which have arches of the same character springing from an octagonal pier and responds with foliated capitals and hollow-chamfered abaci of a slightly later type. The three eastern arches have grooved and chamfered labels on the nave face, and plain chamfered labels on the aisle face, while the western arches have labels of a more advanced section on the nave face only. The lofty 15th-century clearstory has five windows on either side, each of three cinquefoiled lights under a four-centred head. A moulded string-course runs round the walls at the level of the apex of the chancel arch. The nave is crowned externally by a cornice and embattled parapet.

In the north wall of the north aisle are three segmental-headed 15th-century windows, each of three cinquefoiled lights with vertical tracery in the head and casement-moulded external jambs. Between the two western windows is a contemporary doorway with a four-centred head within a square external order with traceried spandrels, the jambs of both orders being shafted. There are no windows in the east and west walls. The walls are crowned by a cornice with grotesque spouts, above which is an embattled parapet. The south aisle has three windows in the south wall like those of the north aisle ; the south doorway, between the two western windows, has been restored with cement, so that the date is difficult to determine ; it is possible, however, that it may be a renewal of a 13th-century doorway, but, as mentioned above, the cement which covers the walls makes it impossible to say whether the 15th-century details here are only insertions or the result of a complete rebuilding of the early aisle. To the west of the easternmost of the three-light windows is a small light with a trefoiled ogee head, placed high up in the wall. The east and west walls are blank, as in the case of the north aisle. The east end of the aisle was partitioned off in the early 19th century, to serve as a vestry. The parapet is embattled, and below the battlements is a cornice with grotesque spouts.

Externally the west tower is of four receding stages and is crowned by an embattled parapet. At the south-west angle is a circular stair turret lighted by small loops, and reaching to the set-off below the third stage, where it is crowned by a pyramidal roof. The tower arch, which is contemporary with the three lower stages, is of three continuously chamfered orders, and has a label with head-stops towards the nave. In the west wall of the ground stage is a tall narrow lancet with wide internal splays. At the east end of the north wall is a round-headed doorway, probably a late insertion. The doorway to the stair-turret has a square head. The second stage is lighted by a 13th-century lancet in the north wall, while the third stage has lancets of the same type on the south and west, and below the clock face on the north are traces of a similar window. The bell-chamber is lighted from all four sides by late 14th-century windows of two cinquefoiled lights with quatrefoil tracery in two-centred heads.

The roofs are all of the 15th century. Those of the chancel and nave are low-pitched and are supported by solid trusses resting on wooden figures placed in the position of wall posts, and standing on corbels carved as birds, while the intermediate rafters have angels holding shields at their feet. The chalice held in the hand of one of the figures supporting the nave roof suggests that the twelve figures here represent the twelve apostles. The purlins, rafters and ridge-pieces are moulded and have carved bosses at their intersections. The aisle roofs are of the lean-to type, and have moulded timbers with carved bosses.

The font is of the 14th century. The bowl is octagonal and has a moulded rim and lower edge ; it is supported by a central octagonal stem and four small clustered shafts with moulded bases but no capitals. The cover is a good example of 17th-century joinery. It is octagonal, and each side has an arched panel with pilasters and carved spandrels ; the whole is crowned by an embattled cresting, above which rises a panelled obelisk. Upon one of the sides of the lower portion is inscribed : 'Anno Domini : 1640 : T.L.' The same workman seems to have been responsible for a seat at the west end of the south aisle bearing the inscription : 'Thomas Nash is at the charge of this seate anno domini 1635—T.L.' The communion table is of oak and dates from the late 17th century. The rood screen, which is complete but for the parapet of the loft, is an unusually interesting example of late 15th-century work. It is divided into eight main bays by uprights moulded on the west side with slender clustered shafts having crested capitals from which spring the ribs of the fan-vaulted cove beneath the loft. The upper part of the screen is open, each bay having a subfoliated trefoiled head with vertical tracery above rising into the space between the cones of the vaulting. The two middle bays are arranged to open as a double door, and a four-centred arch, inclosing the subfoliated trefoiled heads, separates the tracery from the doors. The lower portion of the screen is filled with close panels, each bay being subdivided into two panels, making sixteen in all, and in each panel on the west face is a contemporary painted figure with the name inscribed upon a painted corbel beneath. The figures, taken from north to south, are named as follows :—(1) Jeremy, (2) David, (3) Ysayas, (4) Daniell, (5) Osee, (6) Amos, (7) Sanctus Blas(ius), (8) Sanctus Martin', (9) Sanctus Edward', (10) Sanctus Edmund', (11) Sophanias, (12) Johell, (13) Michias, (14) Malachias, (15) Daniell, (16) Ezechias. With the exception of the figures of St. Blaise, St. Martin, St. Edmund, and St. Edward, each figure has a scroll round it, inscribed with a quotation from the Vulgate. These are now very indistinct, and appear in some cases to have been incorrectly repainted. Several late 15th-century seats remain at the west end of the nave with four desk fronts. The uprights are buttressed, and the panels are carved with the linen pattern. Some 16th-century panels are also worked into the modern seating at the west end of the south aisle. A good Elizabethan chest with enriched panels is preserved in the north aisle. A fragment of 15th-century glass, bearing the inscription 'Petrus' in black letter, remains in the centre light of the east window of the chancel.

At the east end of the south aisle is a brass commemorating Robert Latimer (d. 1548), Katherine his wife, who died in the preceding year, and their daughter and heir Elizabeth. The inscription is remarkable for its defective grammar. On the south wall of the chancel is a brass with a kneeling figure and a death's head and hour-glass, commemorating John Garbrand, a former rector, who died in 1589. The inscription, which is in black letter, is as follows : 'Here lyeth buried John Garbrand doctor | in divinity person of North Crawly and | benefactor to ye poor of the same parish | which departed ye 17 Novem. Aº {aetatis 47, {dm̄i 1589.'

On the same wall are also brass inscriptions to Thomas Hackett (d. 1689), and to Elizabeth daughter of William Middleton and wife of Nicholls Hackett (d. 1690). On the opposite wall of the chancel is a marble tablet to Elizabeth daughter of Edmond Harding of Aspley (Guise), Bedfordshire, and wife of Thomas Giffard of North Crawley, 'by whom she had Francis Giffard, who was buried the 29th day of June 1638.' Her second husband was Thomas White of Caldecot in the parish of Newport Pagnell; she died in 1687, and the monument is stated to have been erected by her grandson, Lewis Atterbury, LL.D., of Highgate, Middlesex. On the south wall of the south aisle is an 18th-century inscription commemorating Robert Latimer, 'The last known lineal Descendant in the male Line from John, 2nd surviving son of William Latimer, 1st Lord Latimer, Baron of Danby, in the County of York: which Robert deceased Anno 1547 (sic), and lyes interred here near this Place ; having left by Catherine, his Wife, who died before him, and also lyes here interred, one sole daughter and Heir, Elizabeth, who married William Ap-Reece, of Washingly, in the County of Huntingdon, Esqʳᵉ.' On the south wall of the chancel is a tablet to Charles Cole, fifty-four years rector of the parish (d. 1771), his wife Mary (d. 1779), and their daughter Mary (d. 1782). At the east end of the nave is a much-decayed 13th-century tomb slab with an incised cross. In the north aisle is a slab with the matrices of four shields and two figures, an inscription below the figures, and a marginal inscription.

There is a ring of five bells: the treble is inscribed '+ God Save Our King 1638 IK' (for James Keene) ; the second is by T. Mears of London, 1813 ; the third, by Anthony Chandler, is inscribed 'Chandler ma de me' ; the fourth is by T. Mears, 1824 ; and the tenor is inscribed 'Newcome of Leicester made me. Aº. 1613.'

The plate consists of a large cup, apparently with the mark of 1669, inscribed ' Eclesiae N. Crawliensi sacravit Ro : Hackett S.T.P.' ; a large paten with foot, having no marks, presented by Thomas Hackett in 1663 ; a flagon of 1710 presented in 1711 by Nicholls Hackett ; and a flagon of 1715, presented in the succeeding year by the same Nicholls Hackett.

The registers begin in 1558.

ADVOWSON The church is referred to in 1086 as a minster (*monasterium*), and there may have been a small community of priests attached to it.[37] Half of it was bestowed by Robert de Broughton and William his son on Tickford Priory, and the grant was confirmed by Robert, Bishop of Lincoln, in 1151–4,[38] and by Hugh, Bishop of Lincoln, as to a quarter of the church, in 1186–1200.[39] The other moiety of the advowson was given by William de Broughton to Caldwell Priory, Bedfordshire, to which it was confirmed early in

---

[37] *V.C.H. Bucks.* i, 257.

[38] Round, *Cal. Doc. of France*, 444.

[39] Ibid.

1244–5 by William's son Robert.[40] In 1249 this moiety was granted by Eudo, Prior of Caldwell, to Richard Filliol,[41] to whom in 1252 the prior's successor Walter confirmed this grant, and conveyed the other half, of which he had then obtained possession.[42] The advowson then descended with the manor of Filliols, though the Bohuns' tenure in the 14th and 15th centuries was by no means secure. In 1351 John son of Robert de Broughton relinquished any right he might have in the advowson, probably as descendant of the original owners, to John and Cecily Bohun.[43] There was also trouble with Tickford, the prior definitely assuming, in a suit about tithes in 1323, that the patronage of Great Crawley Church was in his possession.[43a] Moreover, in 1416 the king was said to be patron, the temporalities of the priory being then in his hands.[44] Finally, in 1430, Sir John Bohun was obliged to sue the Prior of Caldwell in order to establish his right to present to Crawley Church.[45] The Bohuns retained the advowson, together with some land, when they alienated Filliols Manor, and in a deed of Elizabeth's reign Sir John Bohun is referred to as patron in 1480.[46] The right to present to the church, which was an important benefice, assessed at £20 in 1291[47] and at £28 in 1535,[48] devolved at the death of this Sir John Bohun before 26 April 1494[49] on his daughters and co-heirs, Mary wife of Sir David Owen and Ursula wife of Sir Robert Southwell.[50] The presentation appears to have been made by both parties in 1495,[51] and by Sir Robert Southwell in 1505,[52] probably after the death of his wife without issue.[53] The whole interest eventually vested in Sir Henry Owen,[54] son and heir of Sir David and Mary Owen,[55] by whom it was conveyed, together with the land, to Sir Robert Dormer in 1537.[56] It remained in the Dormer family, and in 1566 Sir William Dormer presented to the church John Garbrand or Herks,[57] after whose death in 1589[58] the presentation was made by his father, Garbrand Herks or Herks Garbrand,[59] another son of whom, Thomas Garbrand,[60] had obtained the rectory in 1570 from Sir William Dormer,[61] probably on behalf of his father. Garbrand Herks by his will bequeathed the advowson and rectory of North Crawley to his son Richard Herks and daughters Amy, Martha, Elizabeth, Anne and Judith.[62] Amy, then the wife of John Holloway, sold her interest for £40 in 1604 to Anne Herks, widow, probably the wife of her brother Richard (see later),[63] and in the same year Elizabeth and Anne, wives respectively of John Chippendale of Leicester, LL.D., and of William Paynter of Northampton, LL.B., sold

their shares to Roger Hackett, D.D., who had been presented to the church by their father in 1590.[64] Richard Herks's share was left by him, in his will proved 19 May 1602, to his son Toby Garbrand. His free lands were to be sold by his executors five years after his death,[65] and, after a dispute between Anne, his widow and executrix, and his son, settled in 1605 in favour of the former,[66] these lands and the rectorial estate were doubtless acquired by Hackett, for the advowson and rectory descended with the Crawley Grange estate,[67] with which they were sold in 1723 to William Lowndes.[68] By a codicil to his will 4 January 1723–4 William Lowndes vested the advowson in trustees in perpetuity, they to present such of his sons or grandsons as were suitable.[68a] On the death of the rector, Charles Cole, in 1771, Thomas son of William Lowndes of Astwood Bury was presented, but the living seems to have been afterwards held by members of the Winslow and Whaddon branch alone.[69]

The Lowndes connexion with the advowson was severed about 1895, when the rights were transferred to Mr. S. Smith Harvey, the present patron.[70]

The Priors of Tickford, who were also rectors of Chicheley, asserted that Crawley Church was dependent on Chicheley, and thereupon laid claim to tithes in Crawley[70a] (see above). This claim was renewed by the Dean of Wolsey College, Oxford, to whom a grant of the possessions of the suppressed priory had been made. William Johnson, lessee of Crawley rectory, resisted this assumption of rights and was committed to the Fleet by Wolsey.[71]

A chapel of Little Crawley was granted to Tickford Priory by Fulk Paynel, Ralf his son, and Gervase son of Ralf, and this grant was confirmed by Robert, Bishop of Lincoln, circa 1150.[71a] In the early 13th century the tithes of Little Crawley belonged to the vicarage of Great Woolstone,[72] and in the 14th and 15th centuries tithes from the hamlet of Little Crawley and from 12 virgates of land called Wakesfee in Crawley and Chicheley were in dispute between the rector of Great Crawley and Tickford Priory.[73] An arrangement was arrived at in 1480 by which the prior was to take the tithes of all places beyond Chicheley Brook on the west towards Tickford and Chicheley, and the rector should have the tithes, greater and less, of lambs, &c., of Little Crawley and places east of Chicheley Brook towards Great and Little Crawley, paying to the prior a pension of 10s.,[74] which was duly recorded in the Valor.[75] This composition was cited in a dispute which arose in

[40] Feet of F. case 15, file 27, no. 8.
[41] Ibid. case 16, file 30, no. 6.
[42] Ibid. file 31, no. 5.
[43] Cal. Close, 1349–54, p. 358.
[43a] De Banco R. Mich. 17 Edw. II, m. 238; Hil. 18 Edw. II, m. 68.
[44] Cal. Pat. 1416–22, p. 9.
[45] Wrottesley, op. cit. 343.
[46] Memo. R. (Exch. L.T.R.), Hil. I Eliz. m. 31.
[47] Pope Nich. Tax. (Rec. Com.), 33.
[48] Valor Eccl. (Rec. Com.), iv, 244.
[49] G.E.C. Complete Peerage (new ed.), ii, 201. [50] Visit. of Sussex (Harl. Soc.), 95.
[51] Add. MS. 5839, p. 136. [52] Ibid.
[53] Visit. of Sussex (Harl. Soc.), 95.
[54] Add. MS. 5839, p. 136. He presented in 1509 and his father David in 1510.
[55] Visit. of Sussex (Harl. Soc.), 95.

[56] Feet of F. Berks. Trin. 29 Hen. VII.
[57] Add. MS. 5839, p. 136.
[58] Brass in church; P.C.C. 7 Drury.
[59] Dict. Nat. Biog.; Add. MS. 5839, p. 136. [60] Dict. Nat. Biog.
[61] De Banco R. Trin. 12 Eliz.
[62] Add. Chart. 23939.
[63] Feet of F. Bucks. East. 2 Jas. I.
[64] Add. Chart. 23939; Feet of F. Bucks. Mich. 2 Jas. I.
[65] P.C.C. 32 Montague. His son John was to have Sidlie Close, probably in Crawley. [66] Sentence, P.C.C. 29 Hayes.
[67] Richard Jones was patron in 1630 (Add. MS. 5839, p. 136) and William Cole in 1717 (Inst. Bks. [P.R.O.]).
[68] Com. Pleas Recov. R. Mich. 10 Geo. I, m. 15, 17; Feet of F. Bucks. Mich. 10 Geo. I.

[68a] P.C.C. 36 Bolton.
[69] Inst. Bks. (P.R.O.); P.C.C. 146 Alexander; Priv. Act, 12 Geo. III, cap. 5; Lipscomb, Hist. of Bucks. iv, 130; Add. MS. 37069, fol. 10; Clergy Lists.
[70] Clergy Lists.
[70a] De Banco R. 248, m. 238; Hil. 18 Edw. II, m. 68.
[71] L. and P. Hen. VIII, iv (3), 6075.
[71a] Round, Cal. Doc. of France, 444.
[72] R. of Hugh of Wells (Cant. and York Soc.), i, 198.
[73] Cal. Pat. 1381–5, p. 445; 1388–92, p. 266; 1396–9, p. 173; Cal. of Papal Letters, v, 93; Early Chan. Proc. bdles. 6, no. 240; 43, no. 221.
[74] Memo. R. (Exch. L.T.R.), Hil. I Eliz. m. 31.
[75] Valor Eccl. (Rec. Com.), iv, 244.

1559 on the same subject between Walter Dormer, the rector, and Dorothy, widow of George Wright, receiver for Philip and Mary.[76]

A rent of 5s. 6d. from lands given for the maintenance of a lamp in Crawley Church was recorded at the suppression of the chantries.[77]

CHARITIES The Parochial Charities have by a scheme of the Charity Commissioners of 1 March 1907 been consolidated. They comprise the charities of :

(1) Hester Bryan for apprenticing, will 1688, trust fund, £312 16s. 9d. consols, arising from the sale of land in Marston Moretaine (Bedfordshire). The annual dividends, amounting to £7 16s. 4d., are applied in providing premiums for apprenticing.

(2) John Bryan, will 1655, trust fund, £250 10s. 3d. consols, arising from the sale of land in Marston Moretaine and producing £6 5s. 4d. yearly, which is applied in distributing shoes and gowns to poor widows.

(3) Roger Hackett, D.D., will 1621, being an annuity of £1 issuing out of a field known as Eastfields in North Crawley, one moiety being applicable for the poor and the other moiety towards the repair of the highways.

(4) John Cooper, will proved in the Archdeaconry Court of Buckingham, 11 March 1635, being an annuity of 2s. issuing out of the rectory glebe, applied with the income of the town lands.

(5) The town lands have been in the possession of the parish from time immemorial, the earliest deed extant being dated 1625. The property consists of 6 acres, known as the town lands, 2 a. 1 r. known as the East End Pightle, and 2 roods as the Broad Mead. The lands, which are also supposed to include land given by one Richard Kilpin, are let in allotments producing about £12 10s. yearly. The charity is also possessed of three cottages let at £8 2s. 6d. yearly and of a rent-charge of 2s. 6d.

The net income is applied in the distribution of bread and tea, and a small part in doles of money.

Nonconformist Charity. — In 1895 Tryphena Coales, by her will proved at Oxford 23 August, bequeathed £300, the interest to be applied for the benefit at Christmas time of necessitous persons worshipping at the Congregational chapel at North Crawley. The legacy was invested in £330 11s. 7d. consols, producing £8 5s. yearly. The charity is regulated by a scheme of the Charity Commissioners of 16 October 1906.

The several sums of stock above mentioned are held by the official trustees.

EMBERTON

Ambretone (xi cent.) ; Embirtone (xiv cent.).

The parish of Emberton is well watered by the Ouse and its tributaries. The river divides it from Olney, but connexion with that town is secured by a very low bridge. The compact little village lies about 2 miles south of Olney station on the Bedford and Northampton branch of the Midland railway. There are remains of an abandoned railway near the western boundary. At the south end of the village is the church, to the north of which is the rectory, in its present state mainly of the 18th century, and the school.

Along the road to Olney which forms the village street are some old houses of stone. On the east side is a square house with a slate roof bearing on a plaster panel on the chimney shaft the initials $^P_{TS}$ and date 1699. Next to it is a 17th-century house with a thatched roof. Further north is Manor Farm, originally Emberton Manor, an Elizabethan house with a tiled roof, containing some original fittings. In the centre of the village is a clock tower erected in 1845 to the memory of Margaret wife of the Rev. Thomas Fry, rector. About a quarter of a mile east of the church, off the Newport road, is Emberton House, occupied by Mrs. Savory.

In the east of the parish is Petsoe Manor (Pettesho, Petrosho, xii cent. ; Petisho, Pottesho, xiii cent.), the property of Lincoln College, Oxford, and formerly a separate parish, but now annexed to Emberton for ecclesiastical purposes. The hamlet, called Petsoe End at its western extremity, contains Grange Farm, and the manor-house at the northern end is occupied by Messrs. M. A. Inns & Sons. A free chapel formerly existed at Petsoe and another at Ekeney, the adjoining manor, coupled in the 15th and 16th centuries with Petsoe as the manor or manors of Petsoe and Ekeney. Now no trace remains of Ekeney or of the churches.

Browne Willis wrote in 1733 of Petsoe and Ekeney as 'two small depopulated vills now reduced to one single House . . . left standing at Petsoe . . . there was some Tradition of 17 Tenements having been at Ekeney heretofore, tho' I could see no footsteps of any: . . . the Contents of the two vills did not comprise above 500 acres.'[1] He was unable to ascertain the date of destruction of the chapels, though the site of Ekeney was still very discernible, there being traces of the churchyard bounds in St. Martin's field, about a quarter of a mile south-east of Petsoe manor-house. In the centre of the site of about half an acre was a toft, on which the church had stood, 'a small Fabrick of one single Isle of about 18 Paces in Length and 7 in Bredth.' Some stones were said to have been moved and re-used in a barn at Petsoe manor-house. The tenants frequented Clifton Church for service and burials, though they were nearer to Emberton, in which parish was a small hamlet of about eight or ten cottages called Petsoe End, besides two houses in the grounds belonging to the college, all known as Petsoe.[2] Between Petsoe Manor and the eastern boundary of Emberton is Church Farm.

Emberton has an area of 1,880 acres of land and 7 acres of water, and Petsoe Manor covers 411 acres. The whole area contains 685 acres of arable land,

[76] Memo. R. loc. cit.
[77] Chant. Cert. 5, no. 32.
[1] Add. MS. 5839, fol. 72 d. Elsewhere Browne Willis writes : 'Yet there are still 2 or 3 Grounds which bear the name of Petsoe Grounds, and a Farm House is situate upon them; near which, as may be supposed, stood Petsoe Church or Chapel' (ibid. fol. 71). And again : 'I presume it stood in a mowed Close adjoyning the Maner House equal with the End of it next to Emberton' (ibid. fol. 74).
[2] Ibid. fol. 72 d.

EMBERTON : THE RECTORY

EMBERTON CHURCH FROM THE NORTH-WEST

EMBERTON CHURCH : THE INTERIOR LOOKING EAST

1,387 acres of permanent grass, and 121 acres of woods and plantations.[3] The principal woods are Crossalbans Wood, Parrages Wood, Mulducks, and Hollington Wood, the last of which is mentioned in the 17th century.[4] The soil is gravel and clay, and the chief crops grown are wheat, barley, beans and roots. The land falls from a height of 341 ft. above the ordnance datum in the south-east to 161 ft. on the banks of the Ouse, where it is marshy and liable to floods.

The open fields were inclosed in 1798.[5]

Among the place names occur Gore Acre, Culvers Pightell, Maggotts Furlong, Little Dusse,[6] Cresable Field, and Fluxland[7] (xvii cent.).

Three hides in *EMBERTON* were *MANORS* assessed in 1086 among the possessions of the Bishop of Coutances,[8] and, like his estate in Oving (q.v.), afterwards became part of the honour of Dudley.[9] This belonged in the 12th century to the Paynels,[10] to whose manor of Newport Pagnell, Emberton became attached,[11] the last mention of the overlordship occurring in 1638.[12]

The under-tenants in 1086 were two thegns who had held the land in the time of King Edward, one of these, Godric, holding 2 hides, and the other, Ulric, 1 hide, as one manor. About 1219 the lord of the manor appears to have been William son of Payn, who then presented to the church,[13] and who seems to have been succeeded by Nicholas son of William, or Nicholas de Emberton, who held in the middle of the 13th century.[14] In 1252 he complained of trespass in his free fishery,[15] and in the following year was awarded damages for having been disseised of his common pasture in Middlecroft 'cultura.'[16] Nicholas de Emberton was probably the brother of Eleanor wife of Thomas Furneys, and of Isabel, who claimed the estate as daughters and co-heirs of William le Lord.[17] Roger Furneys held in 1284 Eleanor's part of Emberton,[18] afterwards called *HALL ORCHARD MANOR*. He was dead in 1291,[19] and his heir, doubtless a minor, in whose stead Robert Lathbury is returned as lord of Emberton in 1302,[20] is probably identical with the Thomas Furneys who held the manor in 1316.[21] He was in possession in 1322,[22] but appears to have transferred his rights to the Tolthorp family,[23] as Alice widow of Sir John Tolthorp held Emberton in 1346.[24] Robert Tolthorp, who was later in possession,[25] left a widow Alice[26] and a son John,[27] known as John Olney of Weston Under-

wood.[28] His daughter and heir Katherine married John Chamberlain,[29] and in 1373 they made a settlement of the manor by which the third then held in dower by Alice widow of Robert Tolthorp was to revert to John Olney of Weston.[30] John Chamberlain was dead by 1379, in which year Katherine was the wife of Wakelin Brewes.[31] In 1392 she conveyed Emberton to Thomas, her son by John Chamberlain, and his wife Sarah,[32] who were still in possession in 1413.[33] After this date there is no trace of the manor, which was probably obtained by the Tyringhams, lords of the other moiety, since they acquired sole rights in the advowson at this date, the Chamberlains who held Petsoe Manor in this parish having no connexion, as far as is known, with the Hall Orchard family. The Tyringhams' property, moreover, began to be differentiated about the middle of the 17th century as the manors of Tyringham Higham and Willsheires in Emberton,[34] and this distinction was maintained at least as late as 1720.[35]

The other moiety of Emberton belonging to Isabel, second daughter of William le Lord,[35a] was acquired in the 13th century by Roger Tyringham,[36] from whose family it took the name of *TYRINGHAMS MANOR*, and descended with their manor of Tyringham (q.v.) until the beginning of the 16th century.[37] In 1509 it was held by Richard Higham in right of his wife Anne,[38] probably a Tyringham, and they conveyed it to Henry Edon, merchant of the staple of Calais, and others, evidently trustees.[39] Henry Edon leased Tyringhams at a yearly rent of 11 marks to John Some of Emberton, and Thomas Ellis of Weston Favell (Northamptonshire), from whom Henry's son Thomas Edon, after his father's death, attempted to recover possession.[40] Thomas Edon, jun., with others, obtained in 1524 a renunciation of rights from Edward Bardewell on behalf of his wife Mary,[41] and in 1527 conveyed the manor to Sir Robert Brudenell,[42] uncle and trustee of Thomas Tyringham, who had died in 1526.[43] Emberton remained in the Tyringham family until after the death of Sir Thomas Tyringham in January 1637–8.[44] In 1640 his son and heir John Tyringham and Anne his wife conveyed Tyringhams Manor to Thomas Coppin,[45] who presented to the church in 1661.[46] He died between 8 December 1662 and 19 February following,[47] his son John, who succeeded,[48] dying in 1684, leaving a widow Mary and a son John.[49] He and

[3] Statistics from Bd. of Agric. (1905).
[4] Pat. 3237, no. 20.
[5] Priv. Act, 38 Geo. III, cap. 21.
[6] Exch. Dep. Spec. Com. Mich. 16 Jas. I, no. 14.
[7] Add. MS. 5839, fol. 78.
[8] *V.C.H. Bucks.* i, 241.
[9] *Testa de Nevill* (Rec. Com.), 248.
[10] See Newport Pagnell.
[11] Chan. Inq. p.m. 16 Edw. II, no. 72; 5 Edw. IV, no. 16 ; (Ser. 2), xv, 103.
[12] Ibid. (Ser. 2), dxliii, 19.
[13] *R. of Hugh of Wells* (Cant. & York Soc.), i, 93.
[14] *Testa de Nevill*(Rec. Com.), 244, 248.
[15] Cur. Reg. R. 147, m. 3 d.
[16] Assize R. 1180, m. 1.
[17] Wrottesley, *Ped. from Plea R.* 110 ; De Banco R. Mich. 47 Edw. III, m. 225.
[18] *Feud. Aids,* i, 82.
[19] *Cal. Inq. p.m.* (Edw. I), ii, 496.
[20] *Feud. Aids,* i, 104.
[21] Ibid. 110.
[22] Chan. Inq. p.m. 16 Edw. II, no. 72.

[23] Wrottesley, loc. cit. Robert Tolthorp was dealing with messuages and land in Emberton in 1318 (Feet of F. Bucks. East. 11 Edw. II, no. 11); in 1326 (ibid. Hil. 19 Edw. II, no. 1); and in 1331 (ibid. Mich. 5 Edw. III, no. 10).
[24] *Feud. Aids,* i, 130.
[25] Wrottesley, loc. cit.
[26] Feet of F. case 21, file 101, no. 10.
[27] Wrottesley, loc. cit.
[28] De Banco R. Trin. 1 Hen. V, m. 107, 107 d.
[29] Ibid. ; Wrottesley, loc. cit.
[30] Feet of F. case 21, file 101, no. 10.
[31] Ibid. case 289, file 52, no. 43.
[32] Ibid. file 56, no. 236 ; De Banco R. Mich. 15 Ric. II, m. 527 d.
[33] De Banco R. Trin. 1 Hen. V, m. 107, 107 d.
[34] Chan. Inq. p.m. (Ser. 2), dxliii, 19; Feet of F. Bucks. East. 16 Chas. I.
[35] Close, 5177, no. 13.
[35a] She is perhaps the Isabel, wife of Thomas de Marleberg, who held a con-

siderable estate in Emberton in 1276 (see below).
[36] Wrottesley, loc. cit.
[37] See also *Feud. Aids,* i, 82, 104, 110, 130. Emberton was settled by the John Tyringham who died in 1484 on his younger son Thomas (Chan. Inq. p.m. 2 Ric. III, no. 34), but as John, the elder son, died without issue in 1501, Thomas thus obtained Tyringham also (ibid. [Ser. 2], xv, 103).
[38] Feet of F. Div. Co. Mich. 1 Hen. VIII.
[39] Ibid.
[40] Early Chan. Proc. bdle. 503, no. 10.
[41] Feet of F. Bucks. Hil. 15 Hen. VIII.
[42] Ibid. East. 19 Hen. VIII.
[43] Chan. Inq. p.m. (Ser. 2), xlvi, 57.
[44] Ibid. dxliii, 19.
[45] Feet of F. Bucks. East. 16 Chas. I.
[46] Inst. Bks. (P.R.O.).
[47] P.C.C. 15 Juxon.
[48] *Visit. of Herts.* (Harl. Soc.), 46.
[49] Blaydes, *Beds. N. and Q.* iii, 198. See also Close, 5177, no. 13.

his wife Anne obtained in 1719 a renunciation of all rights in the manor from Francis Coppin,[50] probably a brother,[51] and conveyed it in the following year to John Gore.[52] At the same time he acquired Helsthorpe Manor in Drayton Beauchamp (q.v.), with which Tyringhams Manor descended until *c.* 1797, when it was bought by William Praed.[53] By his marriage with Elizabeth Tyringham Backwell, heiress of the Backwells and Tyringhams, William Praed had acquired Tyringham Manor (q.v.), and the two manors, thus reunited, have since descended together,[54] and are now the property of Mr. F. A. König.

Three hides in Emberton held as a manor in the time of King Edward by Alric, a man of Bishop Wulfwig, were surveyed in 1086 among the lands of the Countess Judith,[55] and afterwards, as *PETSOE MANOR,* formed part of the honour of Huntingdon,[56] passing from the Hastings[57] to the Greys of Ruthyn,[58] the last mention of the overlordship occurring in 1520.[59]

Roger, the under-tenant in 1086, had been succeeded before the middle of the 12th century by Osbert the steward (*dapifer*) and Michael his son, called lords of the estate in a charter of 1151–4, confirming grants made by them.[60] The next name connected with Petsoe is that of Niel, son of Reynold, who in 1197 subinfeudated half a virgate here to Ralf son of Arnulf.[61] This estate afterwards passed to Philip Lengleys (le Angleys, Anglicus), but was forfeited by him as a rebel, and conceded by King John in 1216 to Roger de Gaugy.[62] Philip Lengleys returned to his allegiance the following year,[63] but appears to have again fallen into disfavour, as Petsoe was held about 1235 by Ralph de Kameis (Kameys),[64] who had also revolted against John and returned to his allegiance under Henry.[65] Philip Lengleys, however, was reinstated before 1241,[66] and Joan Lengleys, the heir of the family, carried the manor in marriage to John Lindsey.[67] He conveyed it before 1274[68] in exchange for other lands to William Chamberlain of North Reston, Lincolnshire,[69] whose widow Joan held alone in 1284.[70] In 1286 she proved her right to a view of frankpledge once a year, waif, gallows, tumbril, and quittance of suit of county and hundred.[71] She is still called Joan Chamberlain in 1302[72] and 1304,[73] but before 1310 had married Saer de Raundes,[74] with whom she was defendant in an action brought by Simon Lindsey to recover the manor. He claimed as son and heir of John and Joan Lindsey, his elder

brother Adam having died without issue,[75] but Joan, again a widow, having produced a charter, he renounced all rights in 1313.[76] In the same year she settled Petsoe on herself for life, with reversion to Robert son of her first husband William Chamberlain and his heirs.[77] She was returned as lady of the manor in 1316,[78] and in 1323 she and Robert Chamberlain obtained licence to make, with Richard Chamberlain, a fresh settlement of Petsoe,[79] which took place in the following year, whereby contingent remainder was assigned to Richard, infant son of John Chamberlain, and Margaret his wife.[80] Robert Chamberlain was in possession in 1331,[81] in 1346,[82] and in 1348,[83] but apparently died without issue, since Richard, son of John Chamberlain, known as Sir Richard Chamberlain of Coton (Northamptonshire), upon whom the contingent remainder had been settled in 1324, held in 1375.[84] In 1379 he settled some Bedfordshire estates on his son Richard and the latter's wife Margaret,[85] and died in 1391.[86] Richard the son died in 1396, leaving a son Richard, a minor.[87] His widow Margaret was the wife of Philip St. Clair two years later.[88] She died in 1408, her son Richard Chamberlain being then sixteen.[89] He held Petsoe until his death in 1439,[90] and Richard, his son and heir by his first wife Elizabeth, dying in the same year,[91] Petsoe passed to William, his son by a second wife Margaret.[92] Margaret afterwards married William Gedney, and in 1451 sued the trustees of her first husband for her dower in Petsoe.[93] At her death in 1458 William Chamberlain, then aged twenty-two, entered the manor,[94] but was dead before 1471,[95] leaving a widow Joan,[96] and a son and heir Richard.[97] He and his wife Sibyl Fowler obtained livery of the manor from the trustees in 1471,[98] and at his death in 1496 he was succeeded by his son and heir Edward,[99] Sibyl, his wife, surviving until 1525.[100] In 1520, however, Sir John Mordaunt and others, apparently feoffees of Edward Chamberlain, received a licence in mortmain to grant the manor to Lincoln College, Oxford,[1] money for the purchase having been contributed by Edmund Audley, Bishop of

CHAMBERLAIN. *Gules a cheveron between three scallops or.*

[50] Feet of F. Bucks. Hil. 5 Geo. I.
[51] Blaydes, loc. cit.
[52] Close, 5177, no. 13; Feet of F. Bucks. Trin. 6 Geo. I.
[53] Com. Pleas Recov. R. Trin. 37 Geo. III, m. 13; Priv. Act, 38 Geo. III, cap. 21.
[54] Lysons, *Mag. Brit.* i (3), 556; Sheahan, *Hist. and Topog. of Bucks.* 529.
[55] *V.C.H. Bucks.* i, 274.
[56] *Testa de Nevill* (Rec. Com.), 244, 251; *Plac. de Quo Warr.* (Rec. Com.), 97; *Feud. Aids,* i, 104.
[57] *Feud. Aids,* i, 82; *Cal. Close,* 1237–42, p. 370; Chan. Inq. p.m. 6 Edw. II, no. 56; 22 Edw. III (1st nos.), no. 47; 49 Edw. III (1st nos.), no. 70.
[58] Chan. Inq. p.m. 20 Ric. II, no. 18; 9 Hen. IV, no. 17; (Ser. 2), xi, 102.
[59] Ibid. (Ser. 2), xxxv, 47.
[60] *Cal. Doc. of France,* 44.
[61] Feet of F. case 14, file 2, no. 23.
[62] *Rot. Lit. Claus.* (Rec. Com.), i, 272b.

[63] Ibid. 374.
[64] *Testa de Nevill* (Rec. Com.), 244.
[65] *Rot. Lit. Claus.* (Rec. Com.), i, 320b.
[66] *Cal. Close,* 1237–42, p. 370.
[67] De Banco R. 201, m. 32.
[68] Add. MS. 5839, fol. 73.
[69] De Banco R. 201, m. 32.
[70] *Feud. Aids,* i, 82. The name is erroneously given as 'Johannes.'
[71] *Plac. de Quo Warr.* (Rec. Com.), 97.
[72] *Feud. Aids,* i, 104.
[73] De Banco R. 151, m. 208.
[74] Ibid. 183, m. 81 d.
[75] Ibid. 201, m. 32.   [76] Ibid.
[77] Feet of F. case 18, file 65, no. 14.
[78] *Feud. Aids,* i, 110.
[79] De Banco R. 252, m. 151.
[80] Feet of F. case 19, file 75, no. 18; cf. *Cal. Pat.* 1324–7, p. 2.
[81] *Cal. Inq. p.m.* (Edw. III), vii, 272.
[82] *Feud. Aids,* i, 130.
[83] Chan. Inq. p.m. 22 Edw. III (1st nos.), no. 47.

[84] Ibid. 49 Edw. III (1st nos.), no. 70. The John Chamberlain of Emberton who was pardoned in 1366 for murder was probably Sir Richard's father (*Cal. Pat.* 1364–7, p. 328).
[85] *Cal. Pat.* 1377–81, p. 396.
[86] Gibbons, *Early Lincoln Wills,* 40.
[87] Chan. Inq. p.m. 20 Ric. II, no. 18.
[88] Close, 242, m. 16.
[89] Chan. Inq. p.m. 9 Hen. IV, no. 17.
[90] Ibid. 5 Hen. V, no. 41; 17 Hen. VI, no. 31.
[91] Ibid. 18 Hen. VI, no. 45.   [92] Ibid.
[93] Early Chan. Proc. bdle. 18, no. 18.
[94] Chan. Inq. p.m. 36 Hen. VI, no. 14.
[95] Close, 323, m. 15.
[96] *Cal. Inq. p.m. Hen. VII,* i, 554.
[97] Chan. Inq. p.m. (Ser. 2), xlii, 167.
[98] Close, 323, m. 15.
[99] Chan. Inq. p.m. (Ser. 2), xi, 102.
[100] Ibid. xlii, 167.
[1] *L. and P. Hen. VIII,* iii (1), g. 1036 (28); Chan. Inq. p.m. (Ser. 2), xxxv, 47.

Salisbury, in 1518.[2] In 1600 Robert Chamberlain, probably as descendant of the former owners, renounced all rights in Petsoe to Lincoln College,[3] and in spite of a claim to part of the demesne land by Sir Thomas Tyringham, lord of Emberton Manor, in 1619,[4] Lincoln College has retained Petsoe until the present day.[5]

The manor of *EKENEY* is not mentioned in 1086, but may have been included in the estate of the Bishop of Coutances in Emberton, since it was afterwards held of the honour of Newport,[6] the last reference to the overlordship occurring in 1497.[7]

LINCOLN COLLEGE, OXFORD. *Party palewise in three parts: the middle Argent charged with a scutcheon of the see of Lincoln ensigned with a mitre: between on the dexter side the arms of Bishop Fleming, Barry argent and azure with three lozenges gules in the chief, and on the sinister side the arms of Archbishop Scott, Vert three harts tripping or.*

Ekeney appears to have been held in the early 13th century by John Fitz Nicholas, whose widow Felise in 1248 claimed lands in Emberton against Emma daughter of Parnel, who was first wife of John, and against Adam Fitz Nicholas,[8] who had presented to Ekeney Church in 1246.[9] Robert Fitz Adam, who held in 1278,[10] was probably not only the son of Adam Fitz Nicholas, but also identical with the Robert de Ekeney who presented to Ekeney in 1274,[11] and held in Ekeney in 1291.[12] He, or a successor of the same name, was returned as lord of Ekeney in 1302[13] and 1322,[14] but in 1346 John Talworth held this property.[15] In 1396 it figured among the estates held by Richard Chamberlain at his death,[16] and henceforward descended with Petsoe Manor, with which it was alienated to Lincoln College in 1520.[17] It is not mentioned by name after 1619,[18] and all trace of the hamlet and chapel has likewise disappeared.[19]

In the 13th and early 14th centuries there were three separate estates in Emberton held of different overlords, which united about 1350 to form *EMBERTON* or *GREENS MANOR*, the threefold overlordship continuing till the 15th century. One of these estates appertained to the Hastings' honour of Huntingdon,[20] passing to the Beauchamps of Bergavenny, to whom suit of court once a year at Emberton was owed.[21] The last mention of this interest in Emberton is dated 1476.[22] The second estate was part of the fee of Arundel,[23] and was later attached to Olney Manor,[24] held by Ralf Basset in the 14th century, when suit was due from Emberton every three weeks.[25] There is no reference to this overlordship after 1417, when appearance at the Earl of Warwick's court at Olney once a year was demanded.[26] The third estate was attached to the Chamberlains' manor of Petsoe, and was held in the 14th century for one-thirtieth of half a fee and suit every month at Petsoe court.[27] This overlordship was existing as late as 1417.[28]

The under-tenant of the Hastings fee in 1313 was Edmund de Shakelee,[29] who had been succeeded in 1375 by Henry Green.[30] The Arundel fee was held in the earlier 13th century by Robert Bataille,[31] and a successor, Nicholas Bataille, was living, with Emma and Isabel, his sisters, in 1273.[32] This estate appears to have been held by John de Haversham in 1284,[33] and to have passed by 1302 to Robert Lathbury,[34] who had common pasture here in 1308,[35] and died about 1311, his brother John succeeding.[36] At this date the Lathburys were also tenants of the estate held of the Chamberlains, of which this is the first mention, and which descended with the Arundel fee. In 1314 John Lathbury alienated the property to John Pabenham, jun., and Jane his wife.[37] This transaction was probably a mortgage, which was renewed in 1327 by John Lathbury to the said John Pabenham,[38] who died seised of the estate about 1330.[39] By 1343 these two holdings had come into the possession of Henry Green,[40] afterwards chief justice of the king's bench,[40a] and united with the Hastings fee, held by his son Henry Green,[41] in 1375[41a] to form Greens Manor. It descended in the Green family with their manor of Wavendon (q.v.), with which it was divided into thirds in the 16th century. The third alienated by George Browne to John Lord Mordaunt in 1557 with the third of Wavendon was claimed by his son Wistan Browne in 1568,[42] but evidently unsuccessfully, as in 1590 Lewis Lord Mordaunt made a settlement of his two-thirds of Emberton Manor. Both parts were to be held by George Woodward for six days after Lewis's death with reversion to Thomas Tyringham, lord of Tyringhams Manor, and Anthony his son and heir.[43] As no later deeds for Greens Manor can be found, it was probably merged in Tyringhams Manor in this parish.

[2] Add. MS. 5839, fol. 72.
[3] Feet of F. Bucks. Hil. 42 Eliz.
[4] Exch. Dep. Spec. Com. Mich. 16 Jas. I, no. 14.
[5] Ct. R. (Gen. Ser.), portf. 155, no. 20 ; Ct. of Req. bdle. 124, no. 8 ; Priv. Act, 38 Geo. III, cap. 21.
[6] *Cal. Inq. p.m.* (Edw. I), ii, 497 ; *Feud. Aids,* i, 104 ; Chan. Inq. p.m. 16 Edw. II, no. 72 ; 20 Ric. II, no. 18 ; 9 Hen. IV, no. 17.
[7] Chan. Inq. p.m. (Ser. 2), xi, 102.
[8] Assize R. 177, m. 2.
[9] Harl. MS. 6950, p. 162.
[10] Hund. R. (Rec. Com.), ii, 348.
[11] Add. MS. 5839, fol. 72 d.
[12] *Cal. Inq. p.m.* (Edw. I), ii, 497.
[13] *Feud. Aids,* i, 104.
[14] Chan. Inq. p.m. 16 Edw. II, no. 72.
[15] *Feud. Aids,* i, 130.
[16] Chan. Inq. p.m. 20 Ric. II, no. 18. His father, Sir Richard Chamberlain,

presented to Ekeney Church in 1381 (Add. MS. 5839, fol. 73).
[17] L. and P. Hen. VIII, iii (1), g. 1036 (28).
[18] Exch. Dep. Mich. 16 Jas. I, no. 14.
[19] See description and advowson.
[20] Chan. Inq. p.m. 6 Edw. II, no. 56.
[21] Ibid. 5 Hen. V, no. 41 ; 14 Hen. VI, no. 35.
[22] Ibid. 16 Edw. IV, no. 66.
[23] Testa de Nevill (Rec. Com.), 252b; Feud. Aids, i, 104.
[24] Cal. Close, 1279–88, p. 290 ; Cal. Inq. p.m. (Edw. I), ii, 329–30 ; Feud. Aids, i, 82.
[25] Cal. Inq. p.m. (Edw. III), vii, 272 ; Chan. Inq. p.m. 15 Ric. II, pt. i, no. 24.
[26] Chan. Inq. p.m. 5 Hen. V, no. 41.
[27] Ibid. 5 Edw. II, no. 19 ; Cal. Inq. p.m. (Edw. III), vii, 272 ; Chan. Inq. p.m. 15 Ric. II, pt. i, no. 24.
[28] Chan. Inq. p.m. 5 Hen. V, no. 41.
[29] Ibid. 6 Edw. II, no. 56

[30] Ibid. 49 Edw. III (1st nos.), no. 70.
[31] *Testa de Nevill* (Rec. Com.), 244, 252b.
[32] De Banco R. 3, m. 32.
[33] *Feud. Aids,* i, 82.
[34] Ibid. 104.
[35] *Abbrev. Rot. Orig.* (Rec. Com.), i, 167.
[36] Chan. Inq. p.m. 5 Edw. II, no. 19.
[37] Feet of F. case 18, file 66, no. 28.
[38] Cott. Chart. xxviii, 40.
[39] *Cal. Inq. p.m.* (Edw. III), vii, 272.
[40] Chan. Inq. p.m. 17 Edw. III (1st nos.), no. 59 ; Feud. Aids, i, 130.
[40a] Dict. Nat. Biog.
[41] Chan. Inq. p.m. 43 Edw. III (1st nos.), no. 48.
[41a] Ibid. 49 Edw. III (1st nos.), no. 70.
[42] Feet of F. Bucks. East. 10 Eliz. ; Recov. R. East. 10 Eliz. m. 658.
[43] Feet of F. Bucks. Hil. 32 Eliz. One part was for their lives apparently, the other for 3,000 years.

In 1276 land, wood, and one-third of two mills in Emberton, held by Thomas de Marleberg and Isabel his wife in her right, were granted to Master Roger de Turkelby.[44]

A free fishery was held with the manor of Emberton in 1719.[45]

CHURCH The church of *ALL SAINTS* consists of a chancel measuring internally 35 ft. by 17 ft., south vestry, nave 56 ft. by 17 ft., north aisle 9 ft. wide, south aisle 8 ft. 6 in. wide, north and south porches, and west tower 11 ft. by 10 ft. 6 in. It is built of stone and the roofs are covered with tiles and slate.

The church was built during the first half of the 14th century, and consisted originally of the chancel, nave and aisles. The tower was added about 1400, and the vestry and porches are modern. In 1869 the fabric was considerably restored.

The chancel has a rich traceried east window of the early 14th century, having five trefoiled lights with internal jamb shafts and a moulded rear-arch. In each lateral wall are two windows of three lights with reticulated tracery, and on the north is an original moulded doorway. A four-centred doorway on the south, now opening into the vestry, and a low-side transomed window of one cinquefoiled light at the west end of the south wall, were both inserted in the 15th century. Traces of a squint from the south aisle can be seen in the west jamb of the low-side window. At the south-east are three considerably restored sedilia in range with a piscina with an octofoil bowl ; the recesses are divided from each other by attached shafts with moulded capitals and bases. In the north wall is a plain locker. An original string-course is carried round the walls internally and continued across the transom of the low-side window. Externally the side walls are crowned by a moulded cornice enriched with flowers and grotesques, and there is a string-course at the level of the window sills. In the east wall, below the east window, is a square recess, and in each of the east buttresses is a trefoiled niche. The chancel arch, which is of two moulded orders dying into the wall on each side, probably dates from the early 15th century.

The nave arcades are each of five bays with pointed arches supported by clustered pillars and responds with moulded capitals and bases. Opening to the tower on the west is a sharply pointed arch of about 1400 springing from clustered responds with bell capitals and moulded bases. The clearstory windows are modern. There are three traceried windows, each of three lights, in the north wall of the north aisle, the external stonework of which has been renewed, but the internal jambs and rear-arches are original. Internally, on the north wall, there is an original moulded string-course at the level of the window sills. The moulded north doorway, and a small trefoiled light above it, now opening to the parvise of the modern north porch, are also of the 14th century. West of the doorway is a staircase with a modern doorway to the parvise. The windows and doorway of the south aisle are practically all modern, and of the original piscina only the pointed head remains.

The tower, which retains its original details, is of three stages with a projecting turret at the north-east, and is supported by diagonal buttresses and surmounted by an embattled parapet. The ground stage has a pointed west doorway of three orders with a traceried west window of two trefoiled lights above it. In the south wall of the second stage is a small trefoiled light, and the bell-chamber is lighted from each side by a deeply recessed window of two trefoiled lights with tracery in a pointed head.

The font, which dates from about 1400, has an octagonal bowl with traceried panels, a panelled stem and a moulded base.

On the north wall of the chancel is the brass figure of a priest in mass vestments, with the following inscription : 'Orate pro anima magistri Johannis Mordon alias Andrew quondam Rectoris istius ecclesie qui dedit isti ecclesie portos missale ordinale pars oculi in craticula ferrea manuale processionale et ecclesie de Olney catholicon legendam auream et portos in craticula ferrea et ecclesie de Hullemorton portos in craticula ferrea et alia ornamenta qui obiit die . . . mensis . . . anno domini M^{o}CCCC^{o}X . . . cuius anime propicietur deus amen.' Issuing from the mouth of the figure is a scroll inscribed, 'Jon preyth the sey for hym a pater noster & an ave.' John Mordon probably died in 1413, his successor being instituted in November of that year.[45a] Below the north-east window of the chancel are three cinquefoiled heads of a 15th-century screen with sub-cusping and carved spandrels. There are also in the chancel two elaborately carved chairs of the late 17th century.

The tower contains a ring of five bells, all by W. & J. Taylor of Oxford, 1839, and a small bell, probably of the 18th century, but uninscribed. A former ring of four bells[46] was inscribed (i) 'Ave Maria,' (ii) (modern), (iii) 'In multis annis resonat campana Johannis,' (iv) 'Johes Andrewe Rector de Emberton me fieri fecit.'

The communion plate consists of a 17th-century cup and cover paten without hall-marks ; a large salver of 1671 presented in 1694 ; and a modern chalice and flagon.

The registers begin in 1659.

ADVOWSON The church is mentioned in or before 1219, when the advowson was held by William son of Payn.[47] The advowson descended with the manor, the presentation being made alternately by the lords of each moiety.[48] In 1390 an action was brought against Sir John Tyringham by the Bishop of Salisbury and others, who claimed the right of presentation,[49] and in 1400 Thomas Chamberlain enfeoffed John Olney of Holt in his interest, losing his case when he sought to recover his right in 1413.[50] After this date the Tyringhams secured sole right in the advowson, which descended with their manor of Tyringhams[51] until 1720, when it was not included in the sale

---

[44] Feet of F. case 16, file 44, no. 2.
[45] Ibid. Bucks. Hil. 5 Geo. I.
[45a] Add. MS. 5839, fol. 77. Browne Willis says that John Mordon died in 1410, probably from the date on the brass, but the inscription was evidently made during his lifetime, as the date is

incomplete (cf. De Banco R. Trin. 1 Hen. V, m. 107).
[46] Lipscomb, *Hist. and Antiq. of Bucks.* iv, 140.
[47] *R. of Hugh of Wells* (Cant. and York Soc.), i, 93, 145.

[48] Add. MS. 5839, fol. 77 ; Feet of F. case 289, file 52, no. 43.
[49] De Banco R. 519, m. 121.
[50] Ibid. Trin. 1 Hen. V, m. 107.
[51] See also Add. MS. 5839, fol. 77 ; Feet of F. Div. Co. East. 19 Jas. I ; Inst. Bks. (P.R.O.).

to John Gore.[52] In 1741 the patron was Benjamin Pomfret,[53] whose successor Robert Pomfret was rector in 1798.[54] The advowson changed hands many times in the 19th century,[55] and is now vested in Mr. Campbell A. G. Hutton of Birkdale, Southport.

There was a free or independent chapel of St. James at Petsoe[56] which was bestowed in the 12th century by the lords of Petsoe on Tickford Priory, the gift being confirmed in 1151–4 by Robert, Bishop of Lincoln.[57] The right of presentation had, however, been recovered in 1274 by the lords of Petsoe Manor,[58] with which it descended, the chapel being united to the chapel of Ekeney sometime in the 15th century.[59] The united chapel, the presentation to which was still vested in the lords of Petsoe in the middle of the 16th century,[60] was assessed at 57s. 6d. in 1535.[61] In 1561 a return was made that there was neither church nor congregation, and no more entries of institutions occur. But a stipend of £10 was paid by Lincoln College to persons nominated to the benefice of Ekeney and Petsoe, Samuel Pepys, M.A., rector of Clifton Reynes, becoming minister of the free chapels of Ekeney cum Petsoe on 21 October 1664.[62]

In 1650 Petsoe was accounted a chapelry to Emberton,[63] and it has since been annexed to Emberton for ecclesiastical purposes.

The church or free chapel of St. Martin at Ekeney is mentioned in 1246, when Adam Fitz Nicholas held the advowson,[64] which descended with Ekeney Manor, being united to Petsoe chapel in the 15th century.[65]

Land in Emberton worth 8s. 4d. yearly was given for the keeping of a light, lands and rents for the keeping of obits being worth 9s. 4d.; a rent of 8d. from 2 acres of land was paid for 'keeping of a drinking at Swannes Nest on Rogacion Tuesday.'[66]

CHARITIES The parochial charities have, by a scheme of the Charity Commissioners of 17 January 1911, been consolidated. They comprise the following charities, namely:

(1) The Feoffee estate, comprised in an indenture of 28 January 1805, the property of which consists of a building formerly used as a schoolroom, with the master's house adjoining, 6 a. 1 r. 32 p. and six cottages at Petsoe End, and three cottages near the schoolroom, producing an aggregate income of about £40 a year.

(2) Mary Hughes, founded by a codicil to will proved at London 19 October 1861, trust fund, £48 2s. 3d. consols, producing £1 4s. yearly.

(3) Mrs. Knight Millar, will proved at London 10 December 1852, trust fund, £46 18s. 9d. consols, producing £1 3s. 4d. yearly.

The scheme directs that the school-house be used for a Sunday school, and that the master's house be occupied rent free by a caretaker for the schoolroom; that the income of Mrs. Millar's charity be divided at Christmas among ten poor aged widows, and that the income from the Feoffee estate and Mary Hughes's charity be applied for the benefit of the poor generally.

The sums of stock are held by the official trustees, who also hold £50 17s. 10d. consols, known as 'Hill's Gift to the School,' the annual dividends of which, amounting to £1 5s. 4d., are made applicable, by a scheme of 2 January 1883, towards the support of any efficiently conducted Sunday school in the parish.

GAYHURST

Gateherst (xi cent.); Gaherst (xii, xiii cent.); Goathurst, Gotehurst, Gothurst (xiv–xviii cent.).

Gayhurst is a parish of nearly 1,351 acres. It includes about 360 acres of arable land, 760 of permanent grass and 230 of woods and plantations.[1] The height of the land varies from 263 ft. above the ordnance datum on the eastern boundary to 317 ft. in the west, south of Gayhurst Wood. The soil is various, the subsoil limestone, and the chief crops raised are wheat, barley, oats and turnips. The small village of Gayhurst lies in the valley of the Ouse, on the main road from Newport Pagnell to Northampton. Gayhurst House, an Elizabethan stone mansion, the seat of Mr. William Carlile, stands to the south-west of the village in a well-wooded park of 250 acres, which includes three large fish-ponds. The house, a large E-shaped stone building facing south, is flanked on the west by a long line of ancient yew trees and on the east by a yew hedge, broken at intervals by moulded stone posts with open-work finials, both the trees and hedge being continued on the north side of the house.

The building, which dates from the early 16th century, appears to have been originally of L-shaped plan, with the principal block facing west and a long north-east wing, but it began to assume its present form at the end of the 16th century, when the north-east wing was taken down and extensive additions were made on the east side generally, the original main block being retained as the west arm of the E, and additions made to it on the north and south. This work was probably begun by Sir Everard Digby and continued by his son Sir Kenelm, the latter being responsible for the completion of the flanking wings and for the stone posts in the yew hedge. Sir Kenelm was commissioner of the navy at the beginning of the reign of Charles I, and in 1628 commanded a small squadron under that monarch with considerable address; his connexion with the navy evidently accounts for the anchors which are carved on the stone posts above referred to and on the plinths of the columns before the main entrance. On the acquisition of the property by George Wright, son of Sir Nathan Wright, in 1704 the hall ceiling was raised, some internal alterations were made, and the space between the flanking wings on the north was inclosed, the addition

[52] Sheahan, op. cit. 529.
[53] Inst. Bks. (P.R.O.).
[54] Priv. Act, 38 Geo. III, cap. 21.
[55] Inst. Bks. (P.R.O.); Sheahan, loc. cit.
[56] V.C.H. Bucks. i, 287.
[57] Cal. Doc. of France, 444.

[58] Add. MS. 5839, fol. 73. The fabric of the chapel is mentioned in the will of Sir Richard Chamberlain of Coton, who died in 1391 (Gibbons, loc. cit.).
[59] Add. MS. 5839, fol. 73 d.
[60] Ibid.; Chan. Inq. p.m. (Ser. 2), xi, 102.

[61] Valor Eccl. (Rec. Com.), iv, 245.
[62] Add. MS. 5839, fol. 73 d.
[63] Ibid.
[64] Harl. MS. 6950, p. 162.
[65] Add. MS. 5839, fol. 73 d.
[66] Chant. Cert. 5, no. 18.
[1] Statistics from Bd. of Agric. (1905)

thus formed containing the grand staircase and the dining room with the ballroom above. Further alterations were made in the middle of the 19th century by Robert second Lord Carrington, who during his occupation of the house added the present kitchen, and is said to have filled up the secret chambers.[2] Though somewhat changed internally, however, the house remains one of the most charming examples of Elizabethan architecture in the county.

The south or principal front, like all other parts of the house, with the exception of the 18th-century addition, is of three stories. The central feature is formed by the entrance porch, which extends the full height of the building and is crowned by a curvilinear gable with moulded finials. At the angles made by the projecting wings with the main block are square three-storied bay windows, crowned by gables like that of the porch. Similar gables also surmount the portions of the elevation included between the bay windows and the porch, while the flanking wings have straight parapets, which rise above the main block. All the stories are lighted by mullioned and transomed windows and have horizontal string-courses at the levels of the window lintels. The upper stage of the porch wing projects slightly beyond the general face of the wall, and the projection is supported in the lower stages by a pair of columns of the Ionic order supporting an entablature and superimposed on fluted Doric columns. The entrance doorway has a round head with a moulded archivolt, and above are the arms of George Wright, with Bedford in pretence. The west end of the house, which is now partly obscured by the servants' offices, but was originally the principal front, has a central doorway flanked by small square projections, and a south wing containing the original newel staircase. The central projections are surmounted by gables, which combine with two gabled dormers placed near them to form a very picturesque group against the background of the tiled roof.

The line of the east front is broken by a central square projection, the lower story of which forms an open porch with a round arch in each of the free sides, and by a semi-octagonal bay at either end, all of which rise through the three stories and are surmounted by a continuous straight parapet. This front is also lighted by mullioned and transomed windows; some of the mullions and transoms, however, on the ground story have been removed. The stories are divided by horizontal string-courses.

The north front, which has an unbroken frontage, was completely altered in the early 18th century, when the space between the wings was incorporated in the house and the inclosing wall built flush with the north walls of the wings. This front, the central portion of which is of two stories only, surmounted by a dentil cornice and ball finials, has a central doorway, and is lighted by rectangular windows (those on the first floor having alternate pointed and curved pediments) and two Venetian windows.

The hall, which is entered directly from the south porch, is lighted from the south by wide mullioned windows, and has a moulded stone fireplace on the north; the lofty coved ceiling is the work of the early 18th century. In one of the windows are two shields, both of which have the arms of Digby with five quarterings impaling Mulsho with three quarterings, for Sir Everard Digby, but placed here at a later period. On the east of the hall are the drawing room, anteroom, and billiard room, with the Prince's room, the guardroom, the Digby room, and the peacock room above; on the north are the dining room and the ballroom with the main staircase, and on the west are the servants' offices. Between the hall and anteroom is a moulded stone archway flanked by Corinthian pilasters, and having in the panelled soffit the monogram K.D., doubtless for Kenelm Digby, to whom this work is to be attributed. The main staircase, which dates from the early 18th century, rises by a gentle ascent, and has twisted balusters and a heavy moulded handrail. The ballroom has an 18th-century plastered ceiling with a foliated frieze and dentil cornice. The walls of the billiard room are lined with oak panelling of about 1600 in small squares, and incorporated in the fireplace are some early 17th-century carved panels and a fluted frieze.

The rooms on the first floor of the east wing are of considerable interest. The Digby room, a small apartment over the east porch, is said to have had a second floor at the level of the window transom, thus forming a concealed chamber called Digby's hole,[3] which was lighted by the upper part of the window, and entered from the room in the top story by means of a revolving hearthstone. It is said also that there were secret passages through the walls of this room, but all traces of these arrangements have now been removed. The walls of the peacock room are covered with hand-painted leather, probably of the 17th century, ornamented with designs of peacocks, parrots, and other birds, and branches of trees. The bay window of this room has a rich plastered ceiling of the early 17th century. A chamber in the roof of the house, called the oratory, has a doorway which is said to have led to a secret passage, now filled up.

Below the north-east portion of the house are a series of early 16th-century cellars, which were allowed to remain when the original wing above them was destroyed; these retain two original moulded doorways with four-centred heads, and three mullioned windows. To the south-west of the house are long lines of old stables and outbuildings. In the garden is a sundial bearing the date 1670 and the motto 'Nul que une.' The yew walk known as Digby's Walk preserves the memory of the 17th-century owners, the first of whom, the ill-fated Sir Everard Digby, was executed in 1606 for his share in the Guy Fawkes plot.[4] His son Sir Kenelm Digby, who was born at Gayhurst in 1603, was imprisoned at Winchester House for his loyalty to Charles I in 1642, and subsequently exiled.[5] He is said to have imported from the south of France, for the use of his wife Lady Venetia, who was consumptive, the large edible snail called *Helix pomatia*,[6] which still abounds in the woods at Gayhurst. The church stands within the park to the east of Gayhurst House.

Bunsty (Bunestow, Bonistey, xiii cent.; Bunstead, xix cent.), which gave its name to the hundred of Bonestou, was formerly a detached part of Lathbury.[7]

[2] *Rec. of Bucks.* vi, 443.
[3] Ibid. iv, 45.
[4] *Dict. Nat. Biog.*
[5] Ibid.
[6] Lipscomb, *Hist. and Antiq. of Bucks.* iv, 142.
[7] Ibid.

GAYHURST : HOUSE, EAST FRONT

Gayhurst Church from the South-West

In 1886 it was added to Gayhurst,[8] and lies in the north-west of the parish. Bunsty Farm is a two-storied stone house of the last half of the 17th century, somewhat altered and modernized.

Before the Conquest Siric, one of Earl Lewin's men, held and could sell *GAYHURST MANOR*.[9] In 1086, assessed at 5 hides, it formed part of the lands of the Bishop of Bayeux, who had subinfeudated it to the Bishop of Lisieux.[10] Gayhurst was afterwards held by ward of Dover Castle,[11] the lord of the manor paying in the early 14th century 10s. yearly in lieu of castle ward every thirty-two weeks, to which his tenants contributed 5s. 11¼d.[12] The overlordship descended with that of Leckhampstead[13] (q.v.) to Sir William Heron, kt., who died seised of both in 1404. Gayhurst was afterwards held of the Crown in chief.[14]

In 1086 Robert de Nowers (Noers, Nodariis) was tenant of Gayhurst Manor under the Bishop of Lisieux.[15] Ralf de Nowers was holding in 1166[16] and in 1211,[17] and Aumary,[18] apparently his grandson, before 1219.[19] He was living in 1232.[20] William de Nowers held Gayhurst in the later 13th century,[21] and his son and successor Aumary[22] before 1302.[23] He died in 1308, and was succeeded by his son John.[24] He was jointly enfeoffed with his wife Grace daughter of Robert Fitz Niel by settlements made in 1317 and 1318.[25] He died about 1327[26] and she in 1349, when her heir was her grandson John son of John de Nowers.[27] He made settlements of Gayhurst Manor in 1357,[28] 1368[29] and 1369,[30] the first and last in conjunction with his first wife Maud. He was afterwards knighted, and died in 1396,[31] his second wife Alice receiving dower from all his lands except Stoke Goldington.[32] Their son Aumary[33] was still a minor at his death in 1407, when his heirs were his sisters Grace, Agnes, and Joan wife of Robert, afterwards Sir Robert, Nevill.[34] When

Joan died in 1427 two-thirds of Gayhurst Manor passed to her son John Nevill, then a minor.[35] The next year the other third which Alice de Nowers had held in dower also reverted to him.[36] After his death in 1438 possession was granted to William Tresham, John Loughton and other surviving grantees, to whom he had made a grant of this manor without licence in 1435.[37] In 1453 Thomas Green, Robert Olney and other feoffees granted it for life to Robert Nevill, John's brother,[38] and his wife Joan.[39] The reversion was afterwards granted to their son Robert, his wife Joan and the heirs of their bodies.[40]

Robert Nevill the son died in 1495, his wife Joan

NOWERS. *Argent two bars with three crescents in the chief all gules.*

surviving.[41] A settlement of Gayhurst Manor was made in 1513 by their son Michael[42] on his wife Joan,[43] who was seised at his death in 1521.[44] In 1570 their second son Francis Nevill proved his title

BUNSTY FARM, GAYHURST

[8] Loc. Govt. Bd. Order 18130.
[9] *V.C.H. Bucks.* i, 239.   [10] Ibid.
[11] An Act regulating the ward of Dover Castle was passed in 1523 (*Stat. of the Realm* [Rec. Com.], iii, 279). The latest reference to Gayhurst in this connexion occurs in 1480 (*Cal. Pat.* 1476–85, p. 186).
[12] Chan. Inq. p.m. Edw. II, file 10, no. 7. See also *Hund. R.* (Rec. Com.), ii, 346 ; *Feud. Aids,* i, 105.
[13] *Testa de Nevill* (Rec. Com.), 244*b* ; *Feud. Aids,* i, 73 ; Inq. a.q.d. file 130, no. 9 ; Chan. Inq. p.m. 1 Edw. III (1st nos.), no. 69.
[14] Chan. Inq. p.m. 17 Hen. VI, no. 39 ; (Ser. 2), xi, 5 ; cxciv, 10. The statement in 1408 that Gayhurst was held of the honour of Peverel is doubtless due to confusion with Stoke Goldington, which was so held (ibid. 10 Hen. IV, no. 42).

[15] *V.C.H. Bucks.* i, 239.
[16] *Pipe R.* 12 *Hen. II* (Pipe R. Soc.), 108.
[17] *Red Bk. of Exch.* (Rolls Ser.), 617.
[18] *Testa de Nevill* (Rec. Com.), 244*b* ; *Cal. Close,* 1227–31, p. 213.
[19] Feet of F. case 14, file 11, no. 8.
[20] *Cal. Close,* 1231–4, p. 131.
[21] *Hund. R.* (Rec. Com.), ii, 346 ; *Feud. Aids,* i, 73.
[22] Wrottesley, *Ped. from the Plea R.* 25.
[23] *Feud. Aids,* i, 105.
[24] *Cal. Fine R.* 1307–19, p. 26 ; Chan. Inq. p.m. Edw. II, file 10, no. 7.
[25] Inq. a.q.d. Edw. II, file 130, no. 9 ; De Banco R. 219, m. 300 ; Feet of F. Div. Co. Trin. 11 Edw. II.
[26] Chan. Inq. p.m. Edw. III, file 4, no. 4.
[27] Ibid. file 98, no. 9.
[28] *Cal. Close,* 1354–60, p. 407.
[29] Feet of F. case 20, file 99, no. 5.

[30] *Cal. Close,* 1369–74, p. 76 ; Feet of F. Div. Co. East. 43 Edw. III, no. 50 ; *Cal. Pat.* 1367–70, p. 242.
[31] Chan. Inq. p.m. 20 Ric. II, no. 39.
[32] Close, 238, m. 6.
[33] Chan. Inq. p.m. 20 Ric. II, no. 39.
[34] Ibid. 10 Hen. IV, no. 42.
[35] Ibid. 5 Hen. VI, no. 32.
[36] Ibid. 6 Hen. VI, no. 28.
[37] Ibid. 17 Hen. VI, no. 39 ; *Cal. Pat.* 1436–41, p. 227. An appeal was afterwards made by John Nevill's widow Joan (Early Chan. Proc. bdle. 10, no. 307), but apparently without effect.
[38] *Cal. Pat.* 1452–61, p. 448.
[39] Feet of F. case 22, file 124, no. 1.
[40] Chan. Inq. p.m. (Ser. 2), xi, 5.
[41] Ibid.
[42] Ibid.
[43] *L. and P. Hen. VIII,* i, 3719.
[44] Chan. Inq. p.m. (Ser. 2), xxxvi, 13.

to this manor, his elder brother Nicholas[45] having died without issue before April 1527.[46] Francis Nevill died in 1581, and was succeeded by his sister Mary,[47] wife of Christopher Slingsby.[48] They conveyed Gayhurst Manor in 1581 to William Mulsho,[49] her son by a former marriage,[50] and two settlements were made by him shortly afterwards.[51] On his death in 1602 it passed to his daughter Mary by settlement on her and her male issue on her marriage in 1596 to Sir Everard Digby.[52] He vested his wife's property in trustees,[53] and after his death in 1606 for conspiracy in the Guy Fawkes plot, to which reference has already been made, she was able to secure her inheritance for herself and her young son Kenelm,[54] afterwards Sir Kenelm Digby.[55] As a Papist she was exposed to suspicion on the rumour of a conspiracy at Gayhurst in 1633,[56] and her estates were sequestered under the Commonwealth,[57] a third part being restored in 1651.[58] Mary Lady Digby was buried at Gayhurst in 1653,[59] and in the following year a discharge from the sequestration still remaining on her estates was granted to her grandson John Digby, who claimed them by settlements made in 1646 and 1647 and by her will.[60] This was a temporary arrangement during the exile of his father, Sir Kenelm Digby,[61] who died in 1665.[62] John Digby was buried at Gayhurst in 1673.[63] One of his daughters and co-heirs Mary, sometimes called Margaret Maria,[64] wife of Sir John Conway, bart.,[65] died in 1690[66] and the other, Charlotte wife of Richard Mostyn,[67] in March 1693–4.[68] In 1704 Sir John Conway and Richard Mostyn obtained an Act of Parliament for the sale of the Digby estates, including Gayhurst Manor,[69]

DIGBY. *Azure a fleur de lis argent.*

and they were purchased in that year by George Wright,[70] son of Lord Keeper Sir Nathan Wright.[71] George Wright died in March 1724–5,[72] and was succeeded by his son George,[73] who made a settlement of Gayhurst Manor in 1729.[74] It passed at his death in 1766 to his son George,[75] whose sole heir in 1804 was his daughter Anne Barbara Wright.[76] On her death without issue in 1830 Gayhurst reverted under the terms of her father's will to a distant relative, George Thomas Wyndham of Cromer,[77] who died soon afterwards.[78] His son George, who was allowed to use the surname of Wright before that of Wyndham and to bear the arms of Wright in the second quarter, was still a minor about 1847.[79] The family estates eventually came to his two sisters and co-heirs, Maria Anne, who in 1845 married Godfrey Lord Macdonald of Slate, and Cecilia wife of Lord Alfred Paget. In 1854 Gayhurst and Stoke Goldington were allotted to Lady Macdonald, by whom they were leased a few years later to Lord Carrington[80] and sold in 1882 to Mr. James William Carlile of Ponsbourne Park, Hertfordshire. He was succeeded in 1909 by his son Mr. William Walter Carlile,[80a] the present owner.

WRIGHT of Gayhurst. *Azure two bars argent with three leopards' heads or in the chief.*

In 1229 Aumary de Nowers obtained a licence to impark his inclosed wood at Gayhurst with immunity from forest rights.[81] This immunity was recognized as a manorial liberty in 1279.[82] Another liberty mentioned at this date was that of free fishery.[83] There was a mill on the manor in 1086,[84] and references to a water-mill are found from 1279 to the 17th century.[85] Grants of court leet, the view of frankpledge[86] and free warren in Gayhurst were made to Mary Lady Digby and her heirs in 1620.[87]

[45] Chan. Inq. p.m. (Ser. 2), xxxvi, 13.
[46] Memo. R. (Exch. L.T.R.), Trin. 12 Eliz. m. 32 ; Court R. *penes* Mr. F. W. Bull.
[47] Chan. Inq. p.m. (Ser. 2), cxciv, 10.
[48] Fine R. 23 Eliz. pt. i, no. 40.
[49] Feet of F. Bucks. Trin. 23 Eliz.
[50] *Visit. of Bucks.* (Harl. Soc.), 39.
[51] Feet of F. Bucks. Hil. 24 Eliz.; Harl. Chart. 79, D 20. In 1582 a grant of Gayhurst Manor in the event of its reversion to the Crown was made to Sir Francis Drake (Pat. 24 Eliz. pt. xiii, m. 25).
[52] Chan. Inq. p.m. (Ser. 2), ccclxxxvii, 102.
[53] Feet of F. Bucks. Trin. 44 Eliz.; Trin. 1 Jas. I.
[54] *Cal. S. P. Dom.* 1603–10, p. 553; Chan. Inq. p.m. (Ser. 2), ccclxxxvii, 102.
[55] *Cal. Com. for Comp.* 3170.
[56] *Cal. S. P. Dom.* 1633–4, pp. 26, 27, 29, 74 (2).
[57] *Cal. Com. for Comp.* 67, 2043.
[58] *Ibid.* 2044.
[59] Add. MS. 5839, fol. 86a, quoting Gayhurst Reg.
[60] *Cal. Com. for Comp.* 3171. See also Recov. R. Trin. 1654, m. 6; Feet of F. Bucks. Trin. 1654.
[61] Chan. Proc. (Bridges Div.), bdle. 420, no. 46; *Dict. Nat. Biog.*
[62] *Musgrave's Obit.* (Harl. Soc.), ii, 183.
[63] Add. MS. 5839, p. 86b, quoting Gay-

hurst Reg. In an action brought by Sir Kenelm Digby in 1665 to recover the property from his son the latter is said to have a 'reputed' wife Katherine Howard (Chan. Proc. [Bridges Div.], bdle. 420, no. 46). The mother of John's daughters Mary and Charlotte, however, was either Margaret Longueville or Elizabeth Coates, and the legality of both marriages was denied by Jane wife of Sir Edward Hungerford and daughter and heir of George Digby of Sandon (Staffs.). He was uncle and heir-male of Sir Kenelm Digby, and Jane Hungerford claimed Gayhurst in 1697 against Conway and Mostyn, alleging the insanity of John Digby at the time of the so-called marriages (ibid. bdle. 167, no. 3).
[64] G.E.C. *Baronetage*, iii, 96.
[65] Feet of F. Bucks. Trin. 2 Will. and Mary; Close, 3 Anne, pt. vii, no. 12.
[66] Add. MS. 5839, fol. 82b.
[67] Feet of F. Bucks. Hil. 4 Will. and Mary; Recov. R. East. 5 Will. and Mary, m. 21; Trin. 5 Will. and Mary, m. 22; Close, 3 Anne, pt. vii, no. 12.
[68] *Musgrave's Obit.* (Harl. Soc.), iv, 247.
[69] Priv. Act, 2 & 3 Anne, cap. 47. In 1696 John Digby, apparently the next male heir on the Digby side, surrendered his interest in the manor to Sir John Conway (Feet of F. Bucks. Hil. 7 Will. III).
[70] Close, 3 Anne, pt. vii, no. 12.

[71] *Dict. Nat. Biog.*
[72] *Musgrave's Obit.* (Harl. Soc.), vi, 330.
[73] P.C.C. 103 Romney.
[74] Recov. R. Mich. 3 Geo. II, m. 346; Feet of F. Div. Co. Mich. 3 Geo. II.
[75] P.C.C. 83 Tyndall; Recov. R. Hil. 6 Geo. III, m. 218.
[76] P.C.C. 485 Nelson; Lipscomb, *Hist. and Antiq. of Bucks.* iv, 152.
[77] Ibid.
[78] *Ann. Reg.* lxxii, 251.
[79] Lipscomb, op. cit. iv, 158.
[80] Sheahan, *Hist. and Topog. of Bucks.* 537.
[80a] Burke, *Landed Gentry* (1914).
[81] Cart. Antiq. PP 46; *Cal. Chart. R.* 1226–57, p. 99.
[82] *Hund. R.* (Rec. Com.), ii, 350.
[83] Ibid. 346.
[84] *V.C.H. Bucks.* i, 239.
[85] *Hund. R.* (Rec. Com.), ii, 346; Chan. Inq. p.m. Edw. II, file 10, no. 7; 5 Hen. VI, no. 32; 17 Hen. VI, no. 39. At a Court Baron of April 1628 the tenants were ordered to grind their corn at the mill of the lady of the manor; the water-mill and two houses adjoining, then leased to George Backhouse, were in disrepair, and one of the mill-houses had been converted into a cottage by 1654 (Court Rolls *penes* Mr. F. W. Bull).
[86] Pat. 18 Jas. I, pt. xxi, no. 7.
[87] Ibid. no. 12.

CHURCH The church of *ST. PETER* consists of a chancel measuring internally 17 ft. by 14 ft. 8 in., nave 42 ft. 6 in. by 28 ft., and west tower 15 ft. 10 in. by 13 ft. 5 in. It is built of sandstone ashlar, faced externally and plastered internally, and the roofs are covered with lead.

A mediaeval church existed here which is described in the licence for rebuilding granted by the Bishop of Lincoln to George Wright as consisting of 'church, chancell, and tower,' and as being 'a very old, uncomely, ruinous building.'[88] The licence is dated 23 March 1724–5, and the church was rebuilt about three years afterwards. It was constructed in the prevailing classic Renaissance manner, and is an excellent example of work of that period, retaining practically all its original fittings. The tower and the roof of the church were restored in 1883.

Both the chancel and nave have rusticated quoins and plinths and are crowned by modillion cornices and eastern pediments. The lofty windows are round-headed and have moulded external architraves and original leaded glass with trussed ironwork supports. There is a window in each of the north and south walls of the chancel, and the east wall, although not pierced, is relieved externally by a large semicircular niche with a moulded architrave. The nave is lighted by four windows on either side, and has north and south doorways placed in the middle of the walls. Between the windows externally are Ionic pilasters, and the south doorway is emphasized by Ionic semi-columns supporting a pediment at the level of the cornice which crowns the walls, while the north doorway is contained in a rusticated projection surmounted by a segmental pediment at the same level.

The tower is of two stages, and is surmounted by a moulded cornice, with carved vase finials, and a lead cupola with an arcaded drum. The ground stage is entered by a west doorway with rusticated jambs and a round head, and has a round-headed recess with a moulded architrave on each of the north and south walls, while above the doorway is a round-headed window of two lights. The bell-chamber is lighted by windows similar to that in the west wall of the ground stage, and below the windows are large panels, those on the north and south being hexagonal and the others square; that on the west contains a clock-face.

Internally the chancel has an oak panelled dado, and a plaster ceiling with a coved cornice enriched with foliated and other ornament. Against the east wall is an elaborate oak reredos with large panels, bearing the Commandments, the Lord's Prayer and the Creed, flanked by Corinthian pillars and pilasters which support an entablature and curved pediment, the whole being surmounted by seven candlesticks. The sanctuary is paved with black and white marble and is inclosed by elaborate wrought-iron communion rails arranged on a curved plan; the altar is of plain oak with square legs.

The lateral walls of the nave are enriched between the windows with Corinthian pilasters supporting an entablature, the plain frieze of which is relieved at intervals by mitres and open books. Both the chancel and tower arches are semicircular and have moulded archivolts. Above the chancel arch are the royal arms, the first three quarters of which are those of Anne, but the original fourth quarter has been replaced by that of Hanover, for George I. Over the tower arch are the quartered arms of George Wright, son of Sir Nathan Wright, with Argent three lions' paws in a border engrailed sable in pretence, for his wife Mary, daughter and heir of Thomas Bedford of Doctors' Commons, London. Below the arms is the inscription 'Gloriae Dei Omnipotentis Georgius Wrighte Armiger (Nathan Wrighte Equitis Aurati haud ita pridem Magni Sigilli Angliae Costodis Filius natu maximus) hujus Manerij necnon adjacentis Villae de Stoke Goldington primus ex Genere suo Dominus Ecclesiam hanc quam vivus Instaurari in animo habuit moriens Legavit Anno Dom[ni] 1728.' The nave has a flat plastered ceiling with ribs enriched with egg and dart and foliated ornament, and a large foliated centre-piece.

The font in present use is modern, but an oak pedestal font of the early 18th century, with a lead-lined bowl 7 in. in diameter and a moulded cover, stands below the chancel arch. The nave is entirely seated with oak panelled pews, and at the north-east is an hexagonal oak pulpit with inlaid panels and richly carved canopy; the pulpit was originally a 'three-decker,' but the lower 'deck' has been removed. At the south-east of the nave is a large marble monument, said to be the work of Roubiliac, in memory of Sir Nathan Wright, kt., lord keeper of the great seal of England, and George Wright, his eldest son. Their life-sized figures, Sir Nathan in his robes of office and holding the great seal, stand on a high moulded pedestal, and at the back is an architectural setting with Corinthian pilasters and a broken pediment. In the centre of the pediment are the arms of Sir Nathan, Wright quartered with Or a cheveron vert between three towers gules, for Oneby, impaling Azure a cheveron ermine between three leopards' heads or, for his wife Elizabeth daughter of George Ashby of Quenby, Leicestershire. There is no inscription on the monument, but a large tablet was provided for that purpose in front of the pedestal. Sir Nathan died in 1721 and his son George in March 1724–5, and it is probable that the monument was erected about 1730.

The tower contains a single bell, inscribed 'Anthony Chandler made me 1678.'

The communion plate includes a cup and cover paten of 1569 and a modern chalice.

The registers begin in 1728.

ADVOWSON The earliest reference found to the church of Gayhurst occurs in 1227.[89]

The advowson of the church, which was valued at £5 6s. 8d. in 1291[90] and at £6 10s. 8d. in 1535,[91] has descended with the manor.[92] Mr. William W. Carlile is the present patron.

A settlement of the rectory between George Wright, then lord of the manor, and the rector was made by Act of Parliament in 1711.[93] It was annexed to that of Stoke Goldington in 1736.[94] An allotment to the rector in lieu of tithes was made under the Inclosure Act of Stoke Goldington in 1770.[95]

There do not appear to be any endowed charities subsisting in this parish.

---

[88] Printed in Lipscomb, op. cit. iv, 159, 160.

[89] R. of Hugh of Wells (Cant. and York Soc.), ii, 71.

[90] Pope Nich. Tax. (Rec. Com.), 33.

[91] Valor Eccl. (Rec. Com.), iv, 242.

[92] R. of Hugh of Wells, loc. cit.; Harl. MS. 6950, fol. 80; Cal. Pat. 1399–1401,

p. 10; Bacon, Liber Reg. 499; Inst. Bks. (P.R.O.). [93] Priv. Act, 10 Anne, cap. 16.

[94] Bacon, Liber Reg. 499.

[95] Priv. Act, 10 Geo. III, cap. 61.

HANSLOPE with CASTLE THORPE

Hammescle, Hanslepe, Anslepe (xi cent.); Hameslepe (xiii cent.); Hamslape (xiii, xiv cent.); Hanslopp (xv cent.); Hanslap, Anslope (xvi cent.); Hanslape (xix cent.).

This parish covers 5,800 acres, of which 1,935 are arable, 2,973 permanent grass and 290 woods and plantations.[1] The land varies between 404 ft. above the ordnance datum in the north and 225 ft. in the west of the parish near the River Tove, which here separates it from Northamptonshire. The soil is mixed; the subsoil, stone, gravel and clay, and the chief crops are wheat, barley and roots. In the early 19th century Hanslope was noted for the manufacture of very fine lace,[2] and the making of pillow lace gave employment to about 500 women and children in 1862.[3]

The London and North-Western railway runs through the western part of this parish. The village is fairly central and the church stands in a large churchyard in the south-east end of the village, called Church End.[4] The spire, notable for its height and as being an uncommon feature in Buckinghamshire, fell on 23 June 1804 in 'the most tremendous storm of thunder and lightning ever remembered by the oldest inhabitant.'[5] Rectory Farm, an early 17th-century house much altered and added to in the modern period, with traces of a moat to the south-east, lies to the south of the church with the vicarage to the north-west. There are two Baptist chapels, one of which is now closed, and a Wesleyan chapel. The Green Man Inn and some of the houses and cottages in the main street are of the 17th century. Barnwell's Buildings, on the west of this street, form part of the feoffee estate of which Isabel Barnwell was one of the donors. References to her family in Hanslope occur in the 16th century.[6]

Park Road leads south-east from the church past Ivy Farm, where there is part of a homestead moat,[7] to Hanslope Park, the seat of Mrs. Watts. The house is a large stone mansion, built by Basil Brent at the end of the 17th century,[8] and the park extends over 322 acres and contains two small ponds. There is a quarry in the east of the park and an old gravel-pit to the south. The house on Manor Farm, to the west of Hanslope Park, was built in the 17th century, but the east wing is of the 18th century, and part of the present house is later still. A quarter of a mile south of it is Bullington End. Tathall End (Thotehall, xiii cent.; Tothall, Tothill, xvi cent.) is a mile east from Hanslope Church. The farm-house is a 17th-century building and the dovecote is dated 1602. A short distance to the south of the farm there is another 17th-century house, facing the Greyhound Inn. The stables and outhouses of a mansion which

had formerly stood in Tathall End were taken down in the middle of the 19th century.[9] Green End, where there is a late 16th or early 17th-century farm-house,[10] and Hungate End, other districts in this parish, are respectively a quarter of a mile and a mile west of Hanslope Church. Half a mile north-west of Hungate End is Pindon End with Pindon Manor, a two-storied stone house with the date 1656 on a gable at the back. This house was the seat of the Chapman family in the 17th and 18th centuries.[11] Long Street End, a mile eastward from Pindon End, is a detached part of the village of Hanslope straggling for about a mile along the main road continuous with the High Street and leading north-west to Hartwell in Northamptonshire. Between Long Street End and the village are the Halfway houses and Stocking Green with a farm and school. Salcey Green, formerly part of Salcey Forest, is in the north-east of the parish. It was excluded with Stocking Green and other commons called Blogs and Tipple Greens from the Inclosure Act for Hanslope in 1778.[12] The excluded lands, estimated at 260 acres, were, however, inclosed in 1803[13] and an award made concerning them in 1804.[14]

A small portion of Hanslope parish, extending into Northamptonshire, was transferred to Hartwell parish in that county by an Order of the Local Government Board dated 15 October 1894, in confirmation of an order of a Joint Committee of the Buckinghamshire and Northamptonshire County Councils.

Castle Thorpe (Castelthorp or trop of Hanslope, xiv cent.; Castelthorpe, xvi cent.; Castle Thrupp, xvi, xvii cent.; Thrup, Thurpe, xvii cent.) is a separate civil parish, but ecclesiastically part of Hanslope. Its area is 1,372 acres, nearly half of which is arable, the remainder being laid down in pasture.[15] The village of Castle Thorpe contains some 17th-century stone cottages, a school and a Wesleyan chapel. North of the village is Castle Hill, the site of the castle of Hanslope. The church stands at the south-east corner of this site; near by, to the west, was 'the castle-yard where the castle stood,' included in the lease of 1583 under which Richard Troughton was holding in 1608.[16] The mansion-house occupied by Sir Peter Tyrell in 1703 adjoined the castle-yard,[17] but the greater part had been taken down and the remainder converted into a farm-house before 1799.[18] This building, which is now called Castle Yard and has been converted into tenements, is mainly of early 17th-century date. On the first floor of the gabled south wing is a five-light window with moulded wood mullions and transom.

Castle Thorpe is one of the rare instances in which inclosures were made on Crown lands in the early

[1] Statistics from Bd. of Agric. (1905).
[2] Lysons, *Mag. Brit.* i (3), 573.
[3] Sheahan, *Hist. and Topog. of Bucks.* 539.
[4] Mentioned in 1296 (Add. MS. 28024, fol. 24b).
[5] *Gent. Mag.* lxxiv, 681.
[6] Exch. Inq. p.m. (Ser. 2), file 25, no. 9; Lay Subs. R. bdle. 79, no. 164.
[7] *V.C.H. Bucks.* ii, 30.
[8] Add. MS. 5839, fol. 92a.

[9] Sheahan, op. cit. 540.
[10] A property called the Farm Place in Green End was purchased by the Crown about 1541 from Sir Edmund Knightley of Fawsley, Northamptonshire (*L. and P. Hen. VIII*, xx [1], p. 675; Pat. 2 & 3 Phil. and Mary, pt. v, m. 6).
[11] Thomas, son of Thomas and Elizabeth Chapman, was buried in the north chapel of Hanslope Church in March 1691–2 (Lipscomb, *Hist. and Antiq. of*

Bucks. iv, 178); Add. MS. 5839, fol. 95a.
[12] Priv. Act, 18 Geo. III, cap. 76.
[13] Ibid. 43 Geo. III, cap. 47.
[14] Com. Pleas Recov. R. Trin. 44 Geo. III, m. 338.
[15] Statistics from Bd. of Agric. (1905).
[16] Ld. Rev. Misc. Bks. cc, fol. 25. The kiln-house is also named.
[17] Priv. Act, 2 & 3 Anne, cap. 30.
[18] *Gent. Mag.* lxix, 1025.

16th century.[19] The Inclosure Act for the parish was passed in 1793.[20]

Prehistoric [21] and Romano-British [22] ornaments and coins have been found in Castle Thorpe.

The following place-names have been found in Hanslope: Godwinscroft,[23] Sotesmor [24] (xiii cent.) ; Gayne Stoking, Zeneleys Wykes [25] (xiv cent.) ; Kingewelle Meadow, Ravenesfield in Birchmoreland, Prestescroft [26] (xv cent.) ; London's Close, Dastyns in Tathall End [27] (xvi cent.) ; Palefield in Bullingdon End,[28] Breechfield, Ladyland Close,[29] Haldons and Rubens Closes, Millholmeford,[30] Rothesland, le Breede in Long Street End,[31] Filpotmore, Embersland, Dolemead,[32] Wigland,[33] the Blickside,[34] Syenter's Croft,[35] French Close in Green End,[36] Upstreet,[37] Ruben's Hook [38] (xvii cent.) ; Cocks Grove, Broggsland [39] (xviii cent.).

In Castle Thorpe the following names occur : the Chequer,[40] Bridgefield, the Long Mannells [41] (xvii cent.) ; Little Bullington Ground, Shayling, Tutts, Accridge, Hanwell, Stockings Postern, Blog's Lawn [42] (early xix cent.) ; Grimes' Spinney and Portway Lane (xx cent.).

CASTLE and HONOUR — Hanslope Castle was probably thrown up as a manorial stronghold in the 12th century by William Mauduit, an adherent of the Empress Maud. There are no traces of masonry on the site at Castle Thorpe, but considerable remains exist of the earthworks of a mount and bailey type of castle consisting of a mount with an inner and outer bailey. The plan of the defences is, however, much obliterated. In 1215 the castle was sacked and destroyed by Fawkes de Breauté,[43] to whom it was granted in the following year [44] but was never rebuilt. In 1292 William Beauchamp (see Hanslope Manor) obtained licence to make a wall of stone and lime round a garden court (*viridarium*) within his dwelling-house at Hanslope and to embattle it.[45] This fortified house and garden may have stood on part of the castle site or in the rectangular earthworks to the south-west of the castle mount where the railway station at Castle Thorpe now stands.[46]

Hanslope Castle was the *caput* of the small local honour of Hanslope sometimes called from the 12th and 13th-century holders the Mauduit barony [47] or fee.[48] It represented the Domesday fief of Winemar the Fleming, which lay principally in Hanslope,[49] but extended also into Northamptonshire, where it included small holdings in Cosgrove, Easton Maudit, Strixton, Ashton, and Easton Neston.[50] Winemar was succeeded in all his lands held in chief by Michael de Hanslope,[51] after whose death Henry I granted his honour and lands in marriage with his daughter, Maud de Hanslope, to William Mauduit.[52] They were evidently confiscated in Stephen's reign, but promised by Henry II before his accession to William Mauduit, together with the office of chamberlain of the Treasury [53] or Exchequer, which had been held by him in 1135 in succession to his father William and his elder brother, Robert Mauduit.[54] On the death of William Mauduit, Henry II confirmed Hanslope to his son William, as also the barony and chamberlaincy in England and Normandy.[55] He was holding Hanslope Honour in 1166 by the service of four and a half knights,[56] and presumably late in the century.[57] Robert Mauduit, who succeeded before 1196,[58] joined the barons against King John.[59] In 1215, as already stated, Hanslope Castle was destroyed

MAUDUIT of Hanslope. *Argent two bars gules.*

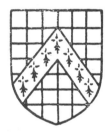

NEWBURGH. *Checky or and azure a cheveron ermine.*

by Fawkes de Breauté, to whom a grant of the site of the castle and of all the lands formerly held by William Mauduit was made in 1216.[60] In 1217

---

[19] Leadam, *Dom. Incl.* 1517 (Royal Hist. Soc.), 209.

[20] Priv. Act, 33 Geo. III, cap. 32.

[21] *V.C.H. Bucks.* i, 192.

[22] Ibid. ii, 5, 6.

[23] Feet of F. Bucks. East. 13 John, no. 4.

[24] Add. MS. 28024, fol. 23a.

[25] Chan. Inq. p.m. 40 Edw. III (2nd nos.), no. 31.

[26] Mins. Accts. bdle. 760, no. 24.

[27] Chan. Proc. (Ser. 2), bdle. 18, no. 86.

[28] Ld. Rev. Misc. Bks. cc, fol. 19.

[29] Ibid. fol. 20.   [30] Ibid. fol. 38.

[31] Ibid. fol. 21.

[32] Ibid. fol. 17.

[33] Ibid. fol. 12.

[34] Ibid. fol. 13.

[35] Ibid. fol. 14.

[36] Ibid.   [37] Ibid. fol. 15.

[38] Ibid. fol. 16.

[39] Close, 12 Will. III, pt. ix, no. 27.

[40] Chan. Proc. (Ser. 2), bdle. 416, no. 135.

[41] Pat. 2 Chas. I, pt. xix, no. 6.

[42] Com. Pleas Recov. R. Hil. 40 Geo. III, m. 108.

[43] Matthew Paris, *Hist. Anglorum* (Rolls Ser.), ii, 170.

[44] *Rot. Lit. Claus.* (Rec. Com.), i, 250b.

[45] *Cal. Pat.* 1281–92, p. 497 ; 1396–9, p. 220.

[46] An ancient rhyme, for which no explanation is forthcoming, runs :—
' If it hadn't been for Cobb-brush Hill,
Thorpe Castle would have stood there still' (*N. and Q.* [Ser. 1], viii, 387).

[47] *Testa de Nevill* (Rec. Com.), 34b.

[48] *V.C.H. Northants,* i, 374, 375 ; *Feud. Aids,* iv, 43, 46.

[49] *V.C.H. Bucks.* i, 272.

[50] *V.C.H. Northants,* i, 342 ; also 3 virgates in Hantone, a name now lost. Winemar is called de Hanslope twice in the Northamptonshire Domesday (ibid. i, 290). Barrowden in Rutland granted by Queen Maud to Michael de Hanslope and afterwards restored by the Empress Maud to William Mauduit (Add. MS. 28024, fol. 21b) was attached to this honour (*Cal. Inq. p.m.* [Edw. II], v, 400).

[51] *V.C.H. Northants,* i, 290, 376.

[52] Add. MS. 28024, fol. 21a. This grant was not earlier than 1123, since William (de Corbeuil), Archbishop of Canterbury (Stubbs, *Reg. Sacr. Angl.* 221), was one of the witnesses. Maud de Hanslope, therefore, did not marry the William Mauduit who held Hartley Mauditt, Portchester (Hants.), in 1086,

but his younger son by his wife Hawise, who received a grant in dower from Henry I early in his reign (see Mr. Round's article on Hartley Mauditt in *Ancestor,* v, 208 et seq.).

[53] This office is often mentioned in connexion with Hanslope (see later under manor), and in 1315 the honour (here called barony) of Hanslope was said to be held by the service of finding a king's chamberlain (*Cal. Inq. p.m.* [Edw. II], v, 400).

[54] Add. MS. 28024, fol. 21b.

[55] Ibid. fol. 22a.

[56] *Liber Niger* (ed. 1771), i, 190–1 ; *Red Bk. of Exch.* (Rolls Ser.), 313. The subdivisions specified make up four fees only, and of these one-quarter of a fee was evidently in Lathbury (Add. MS. 28024, fol. 32a. An entry dated 1338).

[57] *Red Bk. of Exch.* (Rolls Ser.), 36 ; *Pipe R.* 16 Hen. II (Pipe R. Soc.), 28 ; 21 Hen. II, 43 ; 23 Hen. II, 157 ; 24 Hen. II, 93 ; *Anct. Chart.* (Pipe R. Soc.), 97.

[58] *Red Bk. of Exch.* (Rolls Ser.), 109. Later ref. ibid. 536 ; *Testa de Nevill* (Rec. Com.), 260 ; Feet of F. Bucks. 13 John, no. 3, 4.

[59] Dugdale, *Baronage,* i, 398.

[60] *Rot. Lit. Claus.* (Rec. Com.), i, 250b.

Hanslope Honour, formerly Robert Mauduit's, was granted to Henry de Brayboeuf,[61] but seems to have been afterwards restored to Robert Mauduit before his death about 1222.[62] He was succeeded by his son William,[63] who died about 1257, when his heir was his son Sir William Mauduit.[64] In 1263 he succeeded to the earldom of Warwick through his mother Alice, daughter of Waleran de Newburgh, the fourth earl.[65] From this time the fees of the honour of Hanslope are given under those of the earldom, references to the honour occurring until the middle of the 15th century.[66]

MANORS Before the Conquest Aldene, King Edward's housecarl, held and could sell HANSLOPE.[67] In 1086 it was assessed at 10 hides and held by Winemar.[68] Part of it, varying from one fee to a fee and three-quarters, continued to be held in chief as parcel of the honour of Hanslope[69]; the remainder was subinfeudated in part before 1166,[70] and wholly before the middle of the 13th century,[71] among various tenants who held in the vill of Hanslope of the honour but who gradually ceased to differ from free tenants within the manor.[72] The overlordship rights in Hanslope passed to the Crown in 1488 with the manor which in 1542 was attached to the newly-created honour of Grafton.[73] This connexion continued,[74] and is last mentioned in 1663.[75]

That part of the Domesday manor of Hanslope which was not subinfeudated was called Hanslope Manor. It descended with the honour[76] to Sir William Mauduit, who became Earl of Warwick in 1263. He died without issue about 1268, when his heir was William Beauchamp, son of his sister Isabel.[77] He held Hanslope Manor[78] until his death in 1298, when he was succeeded by his son Guy,[79] who died in 1315, leaving as heir an infant son Thomas.[80] Hanslope Manor was assigned in dower to Guy's widow Alice,[81] who died in 1324.[82] Thomas Beauchamp, Earl of Warwick, settled this manor in 1344[83] and died in 1369. He was succeeded by his son Thomas,[84] who was imprisoned in the Tower for high treason in 1396, his estates being forfeited.[85] In 1397 Hanslope Manor was granted to Thomas Duke of Norfolk,[86] and after his forfeiture in 1398 to Edmund Duke of York.[87] Thomas Earl of Warwick was reinstated in all his possessions on the accession of Henry IV,[88] and dying in 1401 was succeeded by his son Richard.[89] In 1423 Hanslope Manor was settled on him and his second wife Isabel le Despencer, Countess of Worcester.[90] He died in April 1439[91] and she a few months later.[92] Their son Henry succeeding,[93] was created Duke of Warwick in 1445,[94] and died in 1446, when the dukedom became extinct, but his other honours passed to his infant daughter Anne.[95] In 1447 Hanslope Manor was granted in dower to the Duke's widow Cecily,[96] who died in 1450, her

BEAUCHAMP. *Gules a fesse between six crosslets or.*

NEVILL. *Gules a saltire argent and a label gobony argent and azure.*

daughter Anne Countess of Warwick having predeceased her.[97]

This manor reverted to Richard Nevill and his wife Anne (sister of Henry Duke of Warwick), who had shortly before been created Earl and Countess of Warwick.[98] They made a settlement concerning part of it in 1466.[99] He, usually known as Warwick the Kingmaker, was slain at the battle of Barnet in 1471,[100] when his widow's rights in Hanslope Manor were ignored in favour of Richard Duke of Gloucester, husband of their daughter Anne.[1] In 1488 Anne

[61] *Rot. Lit. Claus.* (Rec. Com.), i, 304.
[62] *Excerpta e Rot. Fin.* (Rec. Com.), i, 87.
[63] Ibid. 87, 134, 135; *Testa de Nevill* (Rec. Com.), 34b (1½ fees in Northamptonshire), 244b, 252b.
[64] Chan. Inq. p.m. Hen. III, file 20, no. 2.
[65] G.E.C. *Complete Peerage*, viii, 55, 56.
[66] *Feud. Aids*, i, 105, 131; *Cal. Inq. p.m.* (Edw. II), v, 407; Chan. Inq. p.m. 2 Hen. IV, no. 58, m. 58; 8 Hen. IV, no. 68; 24 Hen. VI, no. 43.
[67] *V.C.H. Bucks.* i, 272.
[68] Ibid.
[69] *Red Bk. of Exch.* (Rolls Ser.), 71, 536; *Testa de Nevill* (Rec. Com.), 244b; Chan. Inq. p.m. Hen. III, file 20, no. 2; *Hund. R.* (Rec. Com.), ii, 343; Chan. Inq. p.m. 9 Edw. II, no. 71; *Feud. Aids*, i, 105. Two serjeanties, the offices of chamberlain and usher of the Exchequer (*Cal. Close*, 1369–74, p. 123; Chan. Inq. p.m. 2 Hen. IV, no. 58, m. 6; 24 Hen. VI, no. 43; Feet of F. Div. Co. Hil. 3 Hen. VII), held by the lords of Hanslope Manor in respect of other lands (see under Hanslope Honour), are sometimes named as appendages of their holding in Hanslope (*Testa de Nevill* [Rec. Com.], 260; *Hund. R.* [Rec. Com.], ii, 343; Chan. Inq. p.m. Edw. I,

file 86, no. 1; 9 Edw. II, no. 71; *Cal. Close*, 1369–74, p. 123).
[70] *Red Bk. of Exch.* (Rolls Ser.), 313, 314.
[71] *Testa de Nevill* (Rec. Com.), 244b.
[72] Mins. Accts. bdle. 760, no. 24; Ld. Rev. Misc. Bks. cc, fol. 1; Pat. 4 Chas. I, pt. xi, no. 8.
[73] L. and P. Hen. *VIII*, xvii, 28 (22); *Stat. of Realm* (Rec. Com.), iii, 878.
[74] L. and P. Hen. *VIII*, xxi (1), pp. 780, 785; Ct. R. (Gen. Ser.), portf. 195, no. 34; Add. MS. 6693, fol. 75; Exch. Dep. East. 14 Chas. I, no. 30; *Cal. S. P. Dom.* 1660–1, p. 291.
[75] Pat. 15 Chas. II, pt. vi, no. 2. The fee-farm rents from the manor, £61 6s. 7d., ⅔ lb. of pepper, a red rose and a pair of gilt spurs, were owned in 1729 by Edward Seymour (Recov. R. Mich. 3 Geo. II, m. 179), and in 1775 by Benjamin Isaacs (ibid. East. 15 Geo. III, m. 18).
[76] *Red Bk. of Exch.* (Rolls Ser.), 71, 536; *Rot. Lit. Claus.* (Rec. Com.), ii, 102 (a grant of timber in 1226 to William Mauduit for repairs on his manor); Feet of F. case 16, file 32, no. 3; Add. MS. 28024, fol. 23a, 26b.
[77] Chan. Inq. p.m. Hen. III, file 35, no. 13.
[78] *Hund. R.* (Rec. Com.), ii, 343; *Feud. Aids*, i, 73.

[79] Chan. Inq. p.m. Edw. I, file 86, no. 1. See also Feet of F. Bucks. Mich. 30 Edw. I, no. 7.
[80] Chan. Inq. p.m. 9 Edw. II, no. 71.
[81] *Cal. Close*, 1313–18, p. 255; *Feud. Aids*, i, 111.
[82] Chan. Inq. p.m. Edw. II, file 90, no. 16.
[83] *Cal. Pat.* 1343–5, p. 251; Feet of F. Div. Co. Trin. 18 Edw. III, no. 55.
[84] Chan. Inq. p.m. 43 Edw. III, pt. i, no. 19; *Cal. Close*, 1369–74, p. 123.
[85] Chan. Inq. p.m. 21 Ric. II, no. 137, m. 6.
[86] *Cal. Pat.* 1396–9, p. 220; Chan. Inq. p.m. 22 Ric. II, no. 101.
[87] *Cal. Pat.* 1396–9, pp. 400, 424, 425.
[88] G.E.C. *Complete Peerage*, viii, 58.
[89] Chan. Inq. p.m. 2 Hen. IV, no. 58, m. 6.
[90] Feet of F. Div. Co. Mich. 2 Hen. VI, no. 11.
[91] Chan. Inq. p.m. 17 Hen. VI, no. 54.
[92] Ibid. 18 Hen. VI, no. 3.   [93] Ibid.
[94] G.E.C. *Complete Peerage*, viii, 59.
[95] Chan. Inq. p.m. 24 Hen. VI, no. 43.
[96] *Cal. Pat.* 1446–52, p. 37.
[97] G.E.C. *Complete Peerage*, viii, 60.
[98] Ibid.
[99] Feet of F. Div. Co. Mich. 6 Edw. IV, no. 41.
[100] G.E.C. *Complete Peerage*, viii, 62.
[1] *Parl. R.* vi, 172b.

Hanslope: Rectory Farm

Hanslope Church: The Interior looking East

Hanslope Church from the South

Countess of Warwick, having recovered her rights, surrendered Hanslope Manor, with the other Warwick estates, to the Crown.[2] From this time it is sometimes called *HANSLOPE alias CASTLE THORPE MANOR*. It remained with the Crown,[3] and was in 1550 granted to Princess Elizabeth.[4] It was given in 1603 to Queen Anne.[5] In 1619 Hanslope Manor was leased for ninety-nine years to Sir Henry Hobart and other trustees for Prince Charles.[6] In 1628 the remainder of the term was granted by the trustees to Isaac Pennington and the reversion of the manor was given by the king to Captain John Pennington.[7] The latter sold it to Sir Thomas Tyrell, who obtained a grant of this manor with all reversions and remainders in 1663.[8] He was buried at Castle Thorpe in March 1671-2,[9] and was succeeded by his son Sir Peter Tyrell,[10] who had been created a baronet in 1665.[11] He made a settlement of this manor in 1691,[12] and in 1704 he and his son Thomas were allowed by Act of Parliament to vest it in trustees for sale,[13] reserving certain lands, including the fee-farm rents in Castle Thorpe. It was sold in 1709 to Gervase Lord Pierrepont of Ardglass,[14] who had purchased

PIERREPONT. *Argent powdered with cinqfoils gules a lion sable.*

WATTS. *Azure three arrows or and a chief or with three Moors' heads sable cut off at the neck therein.*

Hanslope Park and other property in Hanslope a few years earlier.[15] He died without issue in 1715, when the barony became extinct.[16] His heir was his nephew Evelyn Duke of Kingston, who died in 1726.[17] In June 1764 his grandson and successor Evelyn, the last duke,[18] sold Hanslope to William Watts, ex-governor of Bengal,[18a] who died the following

August.[19] His son and successor Edward Watts, then a minor,[19a] was lord of the manor in 1778.[20] In 1800 he settled it in favour of his elder son Edward,[21] who died unmarried in the same year.[22] Hanslope Manor passed in 1830 to the second son William, who died in 1847. His son William, who died in 1853, left a son, Edward Hanslope Watts,[23] who was shot by his gamekeeper in July 1912. His widow, Mrs. Watts, is the present owner of the manor.

In 1222 a grant of five stags from Salcey Forest was made to William Mauduit for his park at Hanslope,[24] and in 1278 one of fifteen does and five bucks from Whittlewood Forest to William Beauchamp Earl of Warwick.[25] Trespasses on the deer park[26] are mentioned in the 14th century.[27] Under the Crown the office of keeper of Hanslope Park was combined with those of bailiff and steward of the manor[28] and held by Sir William Forster in 1608.[29] An account of the sales of wood in this park between 1535 and 1536 is extant.[30] Captain John Pennington was negotiating for the purchase of the park estate in reversion in 1628[31] and later,[32] but it was not included in the grant of the manor to him. The leasehold rights in this estate held by Kenelm son of Sir Kenelm Digby[33] of Gayhurst (q.v.), who was living here in 1633,[34] passed on his death in 1649 to his brother John Digby.[35] He was living at Hanslope Park in 1670,[36] but the estate passed later to Basil Brent, who died seised in 1695.[37] In 1697 his creditors obtained a decree in Chancery for the sale of Hanslope Park.[38] It was purchased by Gervase Lord Pierrepont,[39] who shortly afterwards acquired the manor.

The demesne lands of Hanslope Manor in Castle Thorpe, sometimes called *CASTLE THORPE MANOR* in the 16th century,[40] were leased for twenty-one years in 1522 to Thomas Slade,[41] and, on his surrender in 1528, to Christopher Wren and John Knight.[42] A similar lease was granted in 1563 to Thomas Butler and extended to forty-two years in 1569.[43] The lease had passed to Ambrose Butler before 1583, when he obtained a further extension for twenty-one years dating from 1604.[44] He transferred his lease in 1587 to Richard Troughton,[45] who in 1598 obtained a grant of the reversion for thirty years[46] dating from 1626,[47] and was succeeded by his

[2] De Banco R. Hil. 3 Hen. VII, m. 208; Feet of F. Div. Co. Hil. 3 Hen. VII. An Act assuring these estates to the Crown was passed in 1536 (*Stat. of Realm* [Rec. Com.], iii, 677-8).

[3] *L. and P. Hen. VIII*, iii, 3146 (20); 3214 (13); Ct. R. (Gen. Ser.), portf. 155, no. 14; Exch. Spec. Com. no. 448; Ld. Rev. Misc. Bks. cc, fol. 1.

[4] Pat. 4 Edw. VI, pt. iii, m. 25. The reversion was granted in 1553 to John Duke of Northumberland (ibid. 7 Edw. VI, pt. viii, m. 9).

[5] Ibid. 1 Jas. I, pt. xx (second grant from the end).

[6] Ibid. 17 Jas. I, pt. i, m. 17, 19, except the mill and its lands, m. 20.

[7] Ibid. 4 Chas. I, pt. xi, no. 8; *Cal. S. P. Dom.* 1628-9, p. 156. The tenants of the manor petitioned for the right to purchase their estates (ibid. 1629-31, p. 149).

[8] Pat. 15 Chas. II, pt. vi, no. 2.

[9] G.E.C. *Baronetage*, iv, 21.   [10] Ibid.

[11] *Cal. S. P. Dom.* 1664-5, p. 439.

[12] Feet of F. Bucks. East. 3 Will. and Mary.

[13] Priv. Act, 2 & 3 Anne, cap. 30.

[14] Close, 7 Anne, pt. ix, no. 1; Feet of F. Bucks. Hil. 7 Anne.

[15] Close, 12 Will. III, pt. ix, no. 27; pt. xi, no. 8.

[16] G.E.C. *Complete Peerage*, vi, 251.

[17] Ibid. iv, 406.

[18] Ibid. 407.

[18a] Abstract of Title kindly lent by Mr. F. W. Bull.

[19] *Musgrave's Obit.* (Harl. Soc.), vi, 220; P.C.C. 373 Simpson.

[19a] Lysons, *Mag. Brit.* i (3), 572.

[20] Priv. Act, 18 Geo. III, cap. 76.

[21] Com. Pleas Recov. R. Hil. 40 Geo. III, m. 108.

[22] Burke, *Landed Gentry* (1906).

[23] Ibid.; Abstract of Title; Sheahan, op. cit. 513.

[24] *Rot. Lit. Claus.* (Rec. Com.), i, 518b.

[25] *Cal. Close*, 1272-9, p. 440.

[26] Chan. Inq. p.m. 9 Edw. II, no. 71.

[27] *Cal. Pat.* 1292-1301, p. 622; 1321-4, p. 156; 1364-7, pp. 356, 359.

[28] Ibid. 1485-94, p. 4; *L. and P. Hen. VIII*, xx (1), p. 674.

[29] Ld. Rev. Misc. Bks. cc, fol. 54.

[30] Exch. Accts. (Forests), bdle. 141, no. 15.

[31] *Cal. S. P. Dom.* 1628-9, p. 34.

[32] Ibid. 1636-7, p. 324.

[33] *Cal. Com. for Comp.* 2172, 3170.

[34] *Cal. S. P. Dom.* 1633-4, p. 26.

[35] *Cal. Com. for Comp.* 3171; Recov. R. Trin. 1654, m. 6; Feet of F. Bucks. Trin. 1654; Trin. 1659.

[36] *Cal. S. P. Dom.* 1670, p. 574.

[37] Chan. Enr. Decr. no. 1369, m. 9.

[38] Ibid.

[39] Add. MS. 5839, fol. 92b.

[40] Leadam, *Dom. Incl.* 1517 (Royal Hist. Soc.), 209; Pat. 4 Edw. VI, pt. iii, m. 25.

[41] *L. and P. Hen. VIII*, iii, g. 2074 (17).

[42] Ibid. iv, g. 4896 (28).

[43] Pat. 11 Eliz. pt. vii, m. 41.

[44] Chan. Proc. (Ser. 2), bdle. 416, no. 135.

[45] Ibid.

[46] *Cal. S. P. Dom.* 1598-1601, p. 79.

[47] Chan. Proc. (Ser. 2), bdle. 416, no. 135.

son Richard between 1619 and 1625.[48] In 1626 Thomas, afterwards Sir Thomas Tyrell, kt., was granted the reversion of the lease for forty-one years dating from 1658,[49] and in 1627 secured the reversion in fee at the end of his term for Gregory Pratt and others,[50] probably his agents. The grant of Hanslope Manor made to Sir Thomas Tyrell in 1663 included his estate in Castle Thorpe. Upon the sale of the manor in 1709 this estate was reserved for Sir Peter Tyrell's son Thomas and his wife Dorothy in lieu of their marriage settlement in 1696.[51] Thomas Tyrell succeeded his father in 1711, and on his death in 1714 the baronetcy became extinct.[52] He left two daughters and co-heirs Christobella and Harriet.[53] In 1726 they, with their husbands John Knapp and Francis Mann, conveyed the Castle Thorpe estate with free fishing rights in the stream between the mill and Southmead to Matthew Skinner and others.[54] It was purchased soon afterwards by Sarah Duchess of Marlborough,[55] and from 1731 has descended with Dunton Manor.[56] The Marquess of Lincolnshire is the present owner.

TYRELL, baronet.
Argent two cheverons azure and a border engrailed gules.

Balney is named as a park without deer in the extent of Hanslope Manor in 1315.[57] The pasture called Balney land was included in the leases of Castle Thorpe,[58] and Balney Wood, covering 69 acres, in the grants of 1627[59] and 1663.[60] Situated partly in Castle Thorpe, partly in Hanslope, it was retained by the Tyrells in 1709.[61] At the present day Lower Balney grounds are in the parish of Castle Thorpe and Upper Balney grounds in that of Hanslope.

A mill on Hanslope Manor in 1086 was worth 12s. yearly,[62] and was included with it in the grant of Henry I to William Mauduit.[63] Overlordship rights in a mill[64] claimed by the Mauduits earlier in the century[65] had passed before 1279 to Sir John de Wedon[66] and descended to Thomas de Hinton, cousin and heir of Sir Ralph de Wedon, who quit-

claimed to Thomas Beauchamp, Earl of Warwick, in 1363.[67] The Tothalls of Tothall Manor held mesne rights in the mill in the 13th century.[68] These were released by Ralph de Tothall in 1292 to William Beauchamp, Earl of Warwick.[69] Hanslope Mills, included in the grant of the manor to Princess Elizabeth in 1550, were two water-mills under one roof which were leased in 1555 to Robert Matthews.[70] The mills, with a water malt-mill in Church Street which had been included in the Crown leases, were granted in February 1609–10 to Edward Ferrers and Francis Philipps.[71] Thus alienated from the manor they were exempted from the grant of 1619. The corn-mills appear to have passed afterwards with the property of the Lanes[72] in Hanslope (see Tothall Manor). Hanslope or Castle Thorpe Mill is situated in the parish of Castle Thorpe.

The manorial liberties of Hanslope included the court leet with views of frankpledge held twice yearly,[73] the court baron held every three weeks,[74] free warren,[75] and free fishery.[76]

A weekly market on Thursday and a yearly fair on the eve, day and morrow of St. James the Apostle (24, 25, 26 July) and for twelve days following were granted to William Beauchamp, Earl of Warwick, in 1293.[77] They continued into the 18th century,[78] but had been discontinued at its close.[79] At this time a fair for cattle on Holy Thursday had become customary,[80] and was still in existence in 1888.[81]

In the early 17th century the tenants of the manor had common of pasture in part of a forest clearing called Hanslope Green.[82]

A survey of 1608 gives the metes and bounds of Hanslope Manor :

Begin at Hanslope Mill then on west side of River Ouse to ditch called Spereditch north and west for two miles then by ditch on west of Hartwell Park as far as Hanslope Green, north for 1½ miles as far as Lingston's Croft then by Knave way as far as the Cross Way and so by divers streets as far as London gate north for a mile. And then as far as Kelfield gate and then as far as Chaselane end south for a mile. And then south of Gorefields as far as Stoke land end eastward for a mile, then for 3 'stadia' as far as Hanslope Park south for a mile. Then on north of river Ouse as far as Hanslope Mill 1½ miles westward.[83]

One fee in Hanslope, reduced to half a fee before 1346,[84] was known as *TOTHALL MANOR*.[85] It

[48] Chan. Proc. (Ser. 2), bdle. 416, no. 135.
[49] Pat. 2 Chas. I, pt. xix, no. 8.
[50] Ibid. no. 6.
[51] Priv. Act, 2 & 3 Anne, cap. 30 ; 3 & 4 Anne, cap. 53. See also separate settlement of lands in Castle Thorpe only (Feet of F. Bucks. Hil. 7 Anne).
[52] G.E.C. *Baronetage*, iv, 21.
[53] Lipscomb, op. cit. iv, 90.
[54] Feet of F. Bucks. Hil. 12 Geo. I ; Trin. 12 Geo. I.
[55] Add. MS. 5839, fol. 49*a* ; Lysons, *Mag. Brit.* i (3), 533.
[56] *V.C.H. Bucks.* iii, 349 ; Priv. Act, 33 Geo. III, cap. 32 ; *Gent. Mag.* lxix, 1025.
[57] Chan. Inq. p.m. 9 Edw. II, no. 71.
[58] Ld. Rev. Misc. Bks. cc, fol. 25.
[59] Pat. 2 Chas. I, pt. xix, no. 6.
[60] *Cal. S. P. Dom.* 1663–4, p. 188
[61] Close, 7 Anne, pt. ix, no. 1.
[62] *V.C.H. Bucks.* i, 272.
[63] Add. MS. 28024, fol. 21*a*.
[64] Lavendon Abbey had rights in a mill in Hanslope by gift of the founder John de Bidun and Egeline wife of Bertram

Mallore ; these were confirmed in 1227 (Dugdale, *Mon.* vi, 888 ; Chart. R. 11 Hen. III, pt. i, m. 4, no. 38). This abbey received 13s. 6d. rents from Hanslope in 1291 (*Pope Nich. Tax.* [Rec. Com.], 47*b*) and 3s. 6d. in 1535 (*Valor Eccl.* [Rec. Com.], iv, 241).
[65] Add. MS. 28024, fol. 26*b*, 39*a*. Two of the four mills mentioned at this period appear to be Bosenho Mill in Ashton and Cosgrove Mill, both in Northamptonshire.
[66] Hund. R. (Rec. Com.), ii, 345.
[67] *Cal. Close*, 1360–4, p. 550.
[68] Add. MS. 28024, fol. 39*a* ; Hund. R. loc. cit. [69] Add. MS. 28024, fol. 38*a*.
[70] Orig. R. 23 Eliz. pt. v, m. 101.
[71] Pat. 7 Jas. I, pt. xxxiii, no. 7. North of a house at the corner of Newport Road there is an early 17th-century malt-house which is now used as a lumber room (*Rep. Hist. Monum. Com. N. Bucks.* 137). Malt Mill Lane survives as a place-name.
[72] Feet of F. Bucks. Mich. 22 Chas. I ; Recov. R. East. 1 Jas. II, m. 47.
[73] Add. MS. 28024, fol. 29*b* ; Hund. R. (Rec. Com.), ii, 350 ; Chan. Inq. p.m.

Edw. II, file 90, no. 16 ; Ct. R. portf. 155, no. 14 ; Ld. Rev. Misc. Bks. cc, fol. 55 ; Feet of F. Bucks. Hil. 7 Anne.
[74] Chan. Inq. p.m. Edw. II, file 90, no. 16 ; Ld. Rev. Misc. Bks. cc, fol. 55 ; Feet of F. Bucks. Hil. 7 Anne.
[75] *Hund. R.* (Rec. Com.), ii, 350 ; Ld. Rev. Misc. Bks. cc, fol. 55 ; Feet of F. Bucks. Hil. 7 Anne.
[76] Add. MS. 28024, fol. 21*a* ; Chan. Inq. p.m. Edw. I, file 86, no. 1 ; *Cal. Inq. p.m.* (Edw. II), v, 398 ; Chan. Inq. p.m. Edw. II, file 90, no. 16 ; Feet of F. Bucks. Hil. 7 Anne.
[77] Chart. R. 21 Edw. I, m. 4, no. 25.
[78] Ld. Rev. Misc. Bks. cc, fol. 55 ; Feet of F. Bucks. Hil. 7 Anne.
[79] Lysons, *Mag. Brit.* i (3), 571.
[80] Ibid. ; *Rep. of Royal Com. on Market Rts. and Tolls*, i, 139.
[81] *Rep. on Market Rts.* i, 139.
[82] Ld. Rev. Misc. Bks. cc, fol. 55.
[83] Ibid. fol. 56 ; ccx, fol. 148.
[84] The Knights Hospitallers acknowledged that they had no overlordship rights there in 1293 (Add. MS. 28024, fol. 36*a*, 36*b*). [85] *Feud. Aids*, i, 131.

remained subordinate to Hanslope Manor,[86] paying 43*d.* in 1608 in lieu of suit of court,[87] which had been commuted for a money payment before 1359.[88] The family of Tothall were tenants in Tothall in the early 13th century.[89] Robert de Tothall was holding later,[90] and is perhaps the Robert de Tothall, son of Ralph,[91] who was holding Tothall in 1276 and 1279.[92] He was succeeded before 1287[93] by his son Ralph.[94] Ralph's widow Maud was holding dower in lands which Sir Robert de Tothall, his successor,[95] settled in reversion on Simon Barry[96] (Barre), his wife Joan and their son Robert in 1316[97] and 1317.[98] This manor may have been included in Joan's lands in Buckinghamshire, which passed on her death in 1337 to her son Robert Barry,[99] who was holding it before 1346.[100] He went out of his mind about this time, and the custody of his lands was granted to Henry Ewenny and his wife Alice, Robert's sister.[1] The waste with which they were charged in 1363[2] was proved in respect of Tothall Manor in 1366.[3] It was then intrusted to the next heir Robert Barry or de Tothall,[4] on condition that he committed no waste and made suitable provision for his father and the latter's wife and children.[5] In 1385 Joan widow of Robert Barry secured a third of Tothall Manor in dower from Alice Barry,[6] who appears to have brought the whole estate in marriage to William Brampton before 1402.[7] She was holding in 1407,[8] and William Brampton, probably her son, in 1466.[9] There is a break in the descent of the manor, but about 1540 it was settled on William Stone, his wife Alice and their heirs, subject to an annuity to John Rogers and his wife Isabel, and with contingent remainder to them.[10] William Stone died seised of Tothall Manor in 1558, and his son and heir William,[11] attaining his majority in 1568,[12] conveyed this manor in the same year to Robert Lee.[13] He transferred it in 1571 to Roger Andrew,[14] who in 1574 conveyed it to Richard Troughton.[15] He settled Tothall Manor on his son Alexander and his wife Mary on their marriage about 1598.[16] They conveyed it in 1610

to Sir William Romney and his heirs.[17] In 1615 Joseph Romney and others conveyed it to William Atkinson,[18] who transferred it to Richard Lane and his heirs in 1632.[19] He made a settlement of Tothall Manor in 1646 evidently in favour of his son William and his wife Elizabeth daughter of Sir Thomas Tyrell, kt., of Castle Thorpe,[20] and was buried at Hanslope in 1650.[21] Edward son of William Lane[22] entered into possession of this manor in 1685[23] on attaining his majority. His daughter and co-heir Mary married Baldwin son of Sir Baldwin Wake, bart.,[24] and her share of Tothall Manor had passed to their son Sir Charles Wake-Jones, bart.,[25] before 1748.[26] He was succeeded in 1755 by his cousin Sir William

LANE. *Party azure and gules three saltires argent.*

WAKE. *Or two bars with three roundels in the chief all gules.*

Wake of Riddlesworth Hall, Norfolk.[27] His son William Wake agreed in 1763 to bar the entail in Tothall Manor under the will of Sir Charles Wake-Jones,[28] and made a settlement concerning it in 1765.[29] He succeeded his father in the baronetcy in this year,[30] and was one of the landowners in Hanslope in 1778.[31] His elder son William Wake succeeded in 1785,[32] but Tothall Manor was bought by the younger son, the Rev. Richard William Wake, who settled it on the occasion of his marriage in 1798.[33] At the request of himself and his wife it was sold to Edward Watts of Hanslope Park in 1802.[34]

[86] Chan. Inq. p.m. (Ser. 2), cxxxiv, 190.
[87] Ld. Rev. Misc. Bks. cc, fol. 10.
[88] Chan. Inq. p.m. 33 Edw. III (1st nos.), no. 8.
[89] Add. MS. 28024, fol. 32*a.*
[90] *Testa de Nevill* (Rec. Com.), 252*b.*
[91] Add. MS. 28024, fol. 25*b.*
[92] *Hund. R.* (Rec. Com.), i, 38; ii, 344.
[93] *Cal. Close,* 1279–88, p. 488.
[94] Add. MS. 28024, fol. 25*b.*
[95] *Feud. Aids,* i, 105; *Cal. Inq. p.m.* (Edw. II), v, 407.
[96] Also called Simon de Tothall (Chan. Inq. p.m. 36 Edw. III [2nd nos.], no. 46; *Cal. Pat.* 1364–7, p. 223).
[97] Feet of F. case 18, file 67, no. 9.
[98] Ibid. file 70, no. 25.
[99] Chan. Inq. p.m. 36 Edw. III (2nd nos.), no. 46. Inquisition on Hardwick Manor, Huntingdonshire, granted to Simon and Joan and her issue in 1314 (Inq. a.q.d. file 99, no. 3).
[100] *Feud. Aids,* i, 131.
[1] Chan. Inq. p.m. 36 Edw. III (2nd nos.), no. 46.
[2] *Cal. Pat.* 1361–4, p. 450.
[3] Chan. Inq. p.m. 40 Edw. III (2nd nos.), no. 31.
[4] He was eighteen in 1359 and a ward of the Earl of Warwick, who was then receiving the revenues from Tothall Manor

(ibid. 33 Edw. III [1st nos.], no. 8). The father is here called in error son of Robert de Tothall.
[5] *Cal. Pat.* 1364–7, p. 223.
[6] De Banco R. 499, m. 150 d.
[7] Chan. Inq. p.m. 2 Hen. IV, no. 58, m. 58.
[8] Ibid. 8 Hen. IV, no. 68.
[9] Ibid. 24 Hen. VI, no. 43.
[10] Ibid. (Ser. 2), cxxxiv, 190. John Rogers, surviving his wife, died soon after William Stone.
[11] Chan. Inq. p.m. (Ser. 2), cxxxiv, 190.
[12] Fine R. 10 Eliz. no. 64.
[13] Recov. R. Hil. 11 Eliz. m. 558; Feet of F. Bucks. East. and Trin. 10 Eliz.
[14] Feet of F. Bucks. East. 13 Eliz.
[15] Ibid. East. 16 Eliz.
[16] Chan. Proc. (Ser. 2), bdle. 326, no. 23. Alexander Troughton is named as holding under the Crown in 1608 (Ld. Rev. Misc. Bks. cc, fol. 10).
[17] Feet of F. Bucks. Trin. 8 Jas. I. This seems to be the settlement in reference to which Richard Troughton and his son Michael filed a bill in Chancery in 1618 against Alexander and Mary Troughton (Chan. Proc. [Ser. 2], bdle. 326, no. 23).
[18] MS. Cal. of Fines Bucks. Trin. 13 Jas. I. The feet for this term are missing.
[19] Feet of F. Bucks. East. 8 Chas. I. In 1642 Elizabeth, Katherine and Mary

Troughton petitioned the House of Lords in respect of lands in Hanslope, complaining of unfair treatment by their father's executor, Richard Lane (*Hist. MSS. Com. Rep.* v, 65).
[20] Feet of F. Bucks. Mich. 22 Chas. I; Lipscomb, op. cit. iv, 175.
[21] Add. MS. 5839, fol. 93*a*, quoting Reg.   [22] Ibid.
[23] Recov. R. East. 1 Jas. II, m. 47.
[24] *Musgrave's Obit.* (Harl. Soc.), iv, 11; G.E.C. *Baronetage,* i, 180.
[25] G.E.C. loc. cit. He took the surname of Jones from his uncle, Charles Wake-Jones, to whose estates he succeeded in 1740, and afterwards succeeded his grandfather in the baronetcy, his father having died in 1735 (*Musgrave's Obit.* [Harl. Soc.], vi, 180).
[26] Feet of F. Bucks. Hil. 21 Geo. II. The other share in the manor seems to have come eventually to the Wakes.
[27] P.C.C. 48 Paul.
[28] Ibid.; Com. Pleas Recov. R. Hil. 3 Geo. III, m. 20.
[29] Feet of F. Bucks. Trin. 5 Geo. III.
[30] G.E.C. *Baronetage,* i, 181.
[31] Priv. Act, 18 Geo. III, cap. 76.
[32] G.E.C. loc. cit.
[33] P.C.C. 545 Norfolk; Abstract of Title Deeds.
[34] Abstract of Title Deeds; Lysons, *Mag. Brit.* i (3), 572.

This property, known as Tathall End, has remained part of the family estates.

Robert de Tothall had a new park and warren at Tothall in 1276,[35] but neither is mentioned later. In 1366 a vinery called Zedewell, in the manor, had depreciated by 30s., and three vineries had been damaged.[36] At about this date eight dovecotes were stated to be in ruins.[37] There are several references in the 17th century to the dovecote which still stands on Tathall End Farm.[38]

A property called half the manor of Tothall was settled in 1560 on Guy Salisbury, his wife Isabel, daughter of Thomas Pigott, and their heirs.[39] Guy died seised of it without issue in 1586, when his heirs were a sister Mary, wife of John Forster, and two nieces.[40] On the death of Mary Forster in 1615 this property, consisting of a messuage with appurtenances in Tothall, passed to her son Anthony,[41] and does not reappear.

One of the small estates in Hanslope held by service of a quarter fee [42] appears in the 15th century under the name of *STOKES*, later *HANSLOPE alias STOKES MANOR*. It remained subordinate to Hanslope Manor,[43] a connexion which is last mentioned in 1618.[44] This estate derived its name apparently from Thomas Stokes, who married Eleanor daughter of Sir Robert Luton of Hartwell.[45] Their daughter Agnes, having survived her two husbands Sir Thomas Shingleton and — Petite,[46] died seised in 1479.[47] Stokes Manor descended with that of Hartwell to Sir Alexander Hampden.[48] In 1617 he settled it on his niece Margaret Hampden on her marriage with Thomas afterwards Lord Wenman, and on the death of Sir Alexander Hampden in March 1617–18 [49] it came to them as part of her heritage. They evidently gave Stokes Manor to their son Richard,[50] who predeceased his parents about 1646.[51] It was settled in trust on his widow Barbara in 1650,[52] on her marriage with James Earl of Suffolk.[53] He, with his wife and her trustees, conveyed this manor in 1653 to Richard Reeve, jun., and his heirs, with surety against all claimants through Sir Alexander Hampden and Richard Wenman.[54] It afterwards passed to Sir Henry Herbert, younger brother of Edward first Lord Herbert of Chirbury,[55] who in 1673 left it by will to his son Henry.[56] The latter, with his mother Elizabeth, made a settlement concerning it in 1678.[57] The family title was revived

for Henry Herbert in 1694,[58] and Stokes Manor descended with it in 1709 to his son Henry,[59] who sold this manor in 1713 to James Howe.[60] Mary widow of James Howe, and his son John, made a settlement of Stokes in 1741,[61] a further settlement being made in the following year on the marriage of John Howe with Constance Howe, daughter of Mary Sophia Charlotte, dowager Viscountess Howe.[61a] John Howe died without issue in 1769,[62] and in 1774 Richard Viscount Howe, his brother-in-law and

HERBERT of Chirbury. *Party azure and gules three lions or.*

HOWE, Viscount Howe. *Or a fesse between three wolves' heads sable.*

executor, sold Stokes Manor to Edward Watts of Hanslope Park,[63] with whose estate it has since descended.

Some time before 1166 William Mauduit enfeoffed Hugh Wolf of land in Hanslope, owing the service of a quarters fee.[64] It descended to William Wolf before the middle of the 13th century,[65] and before 1315 had come to Nicholas Wolf.[66] He may be the Nicholas Wolf who in 1346 escaped from prison at Aylesbury.[67] It seems to be this Wolf holding, and not the other mentioned later, which passed to the Knight family. Thomas Knight was holding in the early 15th century [68] and William Knight before 1446.[69] A member of the family, John Knight of Hanslope,[70] married Eleanor daughter of Reynburne, third son of Thomas Beauchamp, Earl of Warwick.[71] Their

WOLF. *Gules two wolves passant argent.*

[35] *Hund. R.* (Rec. Com.), i, 38, 45.

[36] Chan. Inq. p.m. 40 Edw. III (2nd nos.), no. 31.

[37] Ibid. 33 Edw. III (1st nos.), no. 8.

[38] Feet of F. Bucks. Trin. 8 Jas. I; East. 8 Chas. I; Mich. 22 Chas. I.

[39] Chan. Inq. p.m. (Ser. 2), ccxi, 157. In February 1569–70 Guy Salisbury claimed that William Stone (see Tothall Manor) had sold him three years before a parcel of land called Dawstyns (Chan. Proc. [Ser. 2], bdle. 163, no. 50), evidently the eighth part of a fee held by Walter Dastyn in Hanslope in the early 15th century (Chan. Inq. p.m. 2 Hen. IV, no. 58, m. 58; 8 Hen. IV, no. 68). A Robert Dastyn was a small tenant in 1316 (*Cal. Inq. p.m.* [Edw. II], v, 402).

[40] Chan. Inq. p.m. (Ser. 2), ccxi, 157.

[41] Ibid. dccxl, 113.   [42] Ibid. clvi, 3.

[43] Ibid.; Ld. Rev. Misc. Bks. cc, fol. 10.

[44] Chan. Inq. p.m. (Ser. 2), ccclxxvi, 96.

[45] *V.C.H. Bucks.* ii, 296.   [46] Ibid.

[47] Chan. Inq. p.m. 19 Edw. IV, no. 34.

[48] *V.C.H. Bucks.* ii, 296; see also De Banco R. 947, m. 130; *L. and P. Hen. VIII*, xvii, g. 1154 (81); *Cal. S. P. Dom.* 1581–90, p. 155.

[49] Chan. Inq. p.m. (Ser. 2), ccclxxvi, 96.

[50] Chan. Proc. (Ser. 2), bdle. 444, no. 60.

[51] G.E.C. *Complete Peerage*, viii, 92.

[52] Feet of F. Bucks. Hil. 1650.

[53] G.E.C. *Complete Peerage*, viii, 92.

[54] Feet of F. Div. Co. Trin. 1653.

[55] G.E.C. *Complete Peerage*, iv, 208.

[56] P.C.C. 59 Pye.

[57] Recov. R. Hil. 29 & 30 Chas. II, m. 18; Feet of F. Bucks. Hil. 29 & 30 Chas. II.

[58] G.E.C. *Complete Peerage*, iv, 209.

[59] Ibid.; Recov. R. Hil. 7 Anne, m. 68; Marcham, *Cat. of Bucks. Deeds*, no. 266.

[60] Close R. 12 Anne, pt. xi, no. 14.

[61] Recov. R. Mich. 15 Geo. II, m. 8; Abstract of Title Deeds.

[61a] Abstract of Title Deeds; G.E.C. *Complete Peerage*, iv, 268–9.

[62] Abstract of Title Deeds.

[63] Ibid. From information supplied to Lysons by a correspondent in 1804, Edward Watts also bought about this time an estate in Hanslope called Singleton Manor. Watts said that his title-deeds did not specify the situation of these manors, but that his gamekeeper acted on his behalf 'for the manors of Hanslope-cum-Castle Thorpe, Stoke, Singleton and Tothall-end' (Add. MS. 9411, fol. 300).

[64] *Red Bk. of Exch.* (Rolls Ser.), 314.

[65] *Testa de Nevill* (Rec. Com.), 244b, 252b.

[66] *Cal. Inq. p.m.* (Edw. II), v, 407.

[67] *Cal. Pat.* 1345–8, p. 201.

[68] Chan. Inq. p.m. 2 Hen. IV, no. 58, m. 58; 8 Hen. IV, no. 68.

[69] Ibid. 24 Hen. VI, no. 43.

[70] A John Knight of Hanslope was living in 1434 (*Cal. Pat.* 1429–36, p. 397).

[71] *Visit. of Bucks.* (Harl. Soc.), 56. Reynburne is mentioned in the settlement of Hanslope Manor in 1344 (*Cal. Pat.* 1343–5, p. 252).

daughter and heir Emma married William Forster, and their great-grandson, Edmund Forster,[72] died seised of *WOLFS PLACE* in 1595.[73] His son and heir Guy,[74] afterwards Sir Guy Forster, made a settlement concerning this estate in 1635 with his wife Frances.[75] In 1663 she with their eldest son William[76] sold Wolfs Place in Bullenden End to Thomas Turner, Dean of Canterbury,[77] who died in 1672.[77a] In 1694 his son and heir, Dr. Francis Turner, then Bishop of Ely, assigned it in trust with other lands principally in Tathall End purchased by himself from Sir Peter Tyrell, bart., or Charles Tyrell in 1672, to Sir William Meredith, bart., of Ashley, Cheshire.[78] In 1695 Sir William Meredith conveyed Wolfs Place (and probably the rest of the trust estate) to William Thursby of Abington (Northamptonshire),[79] who had bought it with the intention of settling it in marriage on Richard Thursby, son of his half-brother Downhall.[80] Vexed by their 'impudent behaviour,' William Thursby, by his will dated 30 July 1700, left only a life interest in Hanslope to Downhall, but by a codicil of the following January the property was settled in tail-male on Richard, who shortly succeeded,[81] but sold the estate in 1751 to William Lowndes of Astwood.[82] Henry Lowndes owned property in Hanslope in 1778,[83] and the house formerly known as Wolfs Place, then a farm-house, belonged in the early 19th century to Mrs. Lowndes.[84]

FORSTER of Wolfs Place. *Sable a cheveron engrailed between three arrows argent.*

A property called Haversham's Place in Church End was also inherited by Sir Guy Forster from his father.[85] In 1635 it was held on lease by his brother Lawrence, his wife Anne and their son Edmund in survivorship[86] and does not reappear.

In 1166 William Wolf (Lupus, Low, le Lou) was holding land in Hanslope by service of half a fee.[87] In 1201 William son of Robert Wolf surrendered it to Robert Mauduit, who assigned him certain specified lands to hold by service of a quarter fee.[88] In 1207 Robert son of Anketill obtained a writ of summons against Robert Mauduit for the custody of the land and heir of William Wolf.[89] Robert Wolf was holding later in the century,[90] and had been succeeded by William Wolf before 1279.[91] He was living in 1295,[92] but in 1302 his holding had passed to Robert[93] and in 1315 to Philip Wolf.[94] By 1346

it was split up between Thomas Butler, Richard Aude and their tenants[95] and does not reappear.

A family called Hanslope, afterwards Fitz John, were evidently tenants in Hanslope in the later 12th century, when references occur to Hugh de Hanslope.[96] In 1279 John Fitz John, sometimes called John Fitz John of Hanslope, was holding 260 acres there for the service of a quarter fee.[97] He was living in 1286, when he levied a fine with Robert Forster de Bayworth concerning certain lands in Hanslope,[98] and there is mention of Roger Fitz John in 1285 and later.[99] John Fitz John was holding in 1315,[100] and Philip Fitz John in 1343, when for an annuity of £10 he granted the estate to his son John and Margaret his wife.[1] It had passed to Edmund Fitz John before 1363,[2] and in 1371 his cousins and heirs, Robert Boteler of Hartwell (Northamptonshire) and William Sparhawk of Hanslope, released all rights in their lands in Hanslope and Hartwell to Sir Thomas Reynes, kt., and other feoffees.[3] The Buckinghamshire property cannot be traced further.

Roger Birchmore, tenant of Hanslope Mill in 1279, also held at that date 70 acres of land in Hanslope by service of an eighth of a fee.[4] Geoffrey de Wythersfield, who held 15 acres by a similar service,[5] had in the previous year with his wife Maud subinfeudated a small estate to Robert Birchmore.[6] The two holdings make up the quarter fee held by Robert Birchmore in 1315.[7] The Birchmore lands were situated in Green End and are mentioned in 1430,[8] but the name of the tenant is not given. References to the Birchmore family in connexion with Hanslope occur in the 16th and 17th centuries. Thomas Birchmore had property here in 1550,[9] and his son Griffin about 1569 claimed some land in Tathall End from the younger William Stone by right of an agreement between their fathers.[10] Griffin's son Thomas Birchmore, who succeeded in 1577,[11] four years later defended his right by heritage from his father and grandfather in Francis Close and other land in Hanslope against John Pen claiming through his mother's father, Richard Birchmore.[12] In 1608 Thomas Birchmore had three small properties,[13] which he was obliged to sell before 1633 to pay his debts, thus severing the long connexion of his family with this parish.[14]

A family connected with Hanslope for 200 years derived its name from Bosenho, the part of Ashton parish, Northamptonshire, in which the mill stands.[15] In 1304 Ralph de Tothall granted Peter Bosenho (Bosno) and his issue a small estate in Hanslope with remainder to Roger Bosenho and his issue and final remainder to Peter, Roger's brother, and his heirs.[16]

[72] *Visit. of Bucks.* (Harl. Soc.), 57, 165.
[73] Chan. Inq. p.m. (Ser. 2), ccl, 76.
[74] Ibid.   [75] Add. Chart. 5376*b*.
[76] Ibid.
[77] Close, 15 Chas. II, pt. iii, no. 28.
[77a] *Musgrave's Obit.* (Harl. Soc.), vi, 136.
[78] Close, 5 Will. and Mary, pt. x, no. 11; G.E.C. *Baronetage*, ii, 439.
[79] Add. MS. 5839, fol. 93*b*.
[80] P.C.C. 40 Dyer.
[81] Ibid.
[82] Add. MS. 5839, fol. 94*a*. Inform. supplied to Cole by William Lowndes.
[83] Priv. Act, 18 Geo. III, cap. 76.
[84] Lysons, *Mag. Brit.* i (3), 572.
[85] Chan. Inq. p.m. (Ser. 2), ccl, 76.
[86] Add. Chart. 5376*b*; *Visit. of Bucks.* (Harl. Soc.), 165.

[87] *Red Bk. of Exch.* (Rolls Ser.), 313.
[88] Hunter, *Pedes Finium* (Rec. Com.), i, 199; Add. MS. 28024, fol. 26*b*.
[89] *Rot. de Oblatis et Fin.* (Rec. Com.), 390.
[90] *Testa de Nevill* (Rec. Com.), 244*b*, 252*b*.
[91] *Hund. R.* (Rec. Com.), ii, 344.
[92] Add. MS. 28024, fol. 25*a*.
[93] *Feud. Aids*, i, 106.
[94] *Cal. Inq. p.m.* (Edw. II), v, 407.
[95] *Feud. Aids*, i, 131.
[96] *Pipe R. 6 Hen. II* (Pipe R. Soc.), 37; 21 Hen. II, 43.
[97] *Hund. R.* (Rec. Com.), ii, 344.
[98] Feet of F. case 17, file 49, no. 32.
[99] *Cal. Close*, 1279–88, p. 375; Add. MS. 28024, fol. 37*b*.
[100] *Cal. Inq. p.m.* (Edw. II), v, 407.

[1] Feet of F. case 19, file 85, no. 15.
[2] *Cal. Close*, 1360–4, p. 548.
[3] Ibid. 1369–74, p. 332.
[4] *Hund. R.* (Rec. Com.), ii, 345.
[5] Ibid.
[6] Feet of F. case 16, file 45, no. 8.
[7] *Cal. Inq. p.m.* (Edw. II), v, 407.
[8] Mins. Accts. bdle. 760, no. 24.
[9] Lay Subs. R. bdle. 79, no. 164.
[10] Chan. Proc. (Ser. 2), bdle. 18, no. 86.
[11] Chan. Inq. p.m. (Ser. 2), clxxxv, 98.
[12] Chan. Proc. Eliz. Pp. 14, no. 34.
[13] Ld. Rev. Misc. Bks. cc, fol. 2.
[14] Chan. Proc. (Ser. 2), bdle. 396, no. 68.
[15] The part of Hanslope nearest to it was called Bosenho End in the middle of the 15th century (Mins. Accts. bdle. 760, no. 24).
[16] Feet of F. case 17, file 57, no. 6.

Roger Bosenho was holding a fortieth part of a fee in 1315 of the Earl of Warwick,[17] and was living in 1336.[18] In 1358 his son Peter with his wife Juliane enfeoffed Thomas Brome of Hanslope in their lands there.[19] It may be possible to identify Thomas Brome's lands with the half fee held of the Earls of Warwick by John Bosenho in right of his wife before 1402[20] and after 1446.[21] This estate seems to have been dispersed during the Wars of the Roses, since in the late 15th and early 16th centuries William son and heir of Thomas Bosenho tried to regain from different owners property in Hanslope which had belonged to his father.[22]

A quarter fee in Hanslope, held by Thomas Chamberlain in right of his wife Isabel, was granted by them to Richard Chamberlain for life in 1257,[23] but seems to have reverted to Thomas Chamberlain before 1279.[24] In 1296 his son Nicholas conveyed this estate to William de Bayworth.[25] It had passed to Henry de Bayworth before 1302[26] and to William de Bayworth before 1315.[27] He died seised about 1325,[28] but his holding had come into the hands of the overlord, Thomas Beauchamp, Earl of Warwick, before 1346,[29] and seems to have remained part of the demesne lands of Hanslope Manor.

Another small estate was held in 1302 by Richard Chamberlain, also by the service of a quarter fee,[30] but what relation he was to the other Chamberlains does not appear. His holding passed to William Newnham before 1346[31] and later in the century to Richard Newnham. He died before 1402,[32] and his heirs were still in possession in 1446,[33] the latest date at which this property is distinguishable.

Before the middle of the 13th century land in Hanslope was held by Peter Blount (Blundus, le Blund) for the service of a quarter fee.[34] This land (60 acres) descended to William Blount before 1279[35] and to Peter Blount before 1302.[36] It was occupied by James Hoddel and his tenants in 1346[37] and does not reappear.

Another quarter fee in Hanslope was held by Ralph Cheyne before the middle of the 13th century,[38] and by a later Ralph Cheyne in 1302.[39] His land had been broken up between William Meriot, Peter de Lyvenden and their tenants before 1346.[40]

Land in Hanslope held by Walter de Tothall by service of a quarter fee before the middle of the 13th century[41] remained in his family for over a century. The heir in 1302[42] was evidently a minor, probably the Walter de Tothall who was holding the property when it is last traceable in 1346.[43]

A property in Hanslope held by Robert Mansell (Mauncel) in 1315 by service of a quarter fee[44] is mentioned in the middle of the 15th century as held by his heirs.[45]

Robert Bellany was holding the twentieth part of a fee in Hanslope under William Mauduit before the middle of the 13th century.[46] Richard Bellany gave up all claim to this land to William Bellany in 1255, in exchange for a small holding in Haversham.[47] It had passed to Robert de Bellow before 1302.[48] John Francis and Richard Hoese (? Hussey) were the tenants later in the century.[49] References in the 15th century until 1446 show that this holding was eventually shared between the heirs of John Francis and Richard Hoese.[50]

Thomas Basset was a small holder in Hanslope before the middle of the 13th century by service of a sixtieth part of a fee.[51] One of the same name was tenant in 1302[52] and John Basset in 1346.[53]

CHURCHES

The church of ST. JAMES consists of a chancel 41 ft. 6 in. by 18 ft. 9 in., a north-east chapel 22 ft. 9 in. by 10 ft. 6 in., nave 63 ft. 6 in. by 25 ft., north aisle 85 ft. by 17 ft. 3 in., south aisle 67 ft. by 14 ft., west tower surmounted by a spire 16 ft. by 15 ft., north porch 9 ft. 3 in. by 10 ft., and south porch 8 ft. 6 in. by 9 ft. These measurements are all internal.

The fine chancel dates from about 1160; the plan and dimensions of a nave of the same period are doubtless preserved in the existing nave, but no detail of an earlier date than the late 15th century now survives. North and south aisles were added in the 13th century. The south aisle was probably built about the middle of the century, and seems to have been originally one bay shorter than at present; the date of the original erection of the north aisle is difficult to determine, as all detail of a period anterior to the 15th century has obviously been reset. Late in the 13th century the east wall of the chancel was rebuilt, and the north chapel, now used as a vestry, was added; the north aisle was at the same time prolonged eastwards to meet it, an arch communicating with the extended portion of the aisle being pierced in the north wall of the chancel. In the 14th century the south aisle appears to have been extended westward to its present length. Early in the 15th century the

[17] *Cal. Inq. p.m.* (Edw. II), v, 407.
[18] *Cal. Close,* 1333–7, p. 691.
[19] Ibid. 1354–60, p. 503. A payment of 20s. yearly was secured to Thomas Brome from Peter Bosenho's lands in Chalk, Kent, in the event of the recovery of the Hanslope lands by the heirs of Peter's body or by the heirs of his uncle, Peter Bosenho.
[20] Chan. Inq. p.m. 2 Hen. IV, no. 58, m. 58; 8 Hen. IV, no. 68.
[21] Ibid. 24 Hen. VI, no. 43. See also Add. Chart. 59303, 59317.
[22] Early Chan. Proc. bdles. 188, no. 2; 120, no. 33; 289, no. 70.
[23] Feet of F. case 16, file 34, no. 7.
[24] *Hund. R.* (Rec. Com.), ii, 344.
[25] Feet of F. Bucks. Hil. 24 Edw. I, no. 4. [26] *Feud. Aids,* i, 105.
[27] *Cal. Inq. p.m.* (Edw. II), v, 407.
[28] *Cal. Inq. p.m.* (Rec. Com.), i, 317. The inquisition is missing.

[29] *Feud. Aids,* i, 131.
[30] Ibid. 105.
[31] Ibid. 131.
[32] Chan. Inq. p.m. 2 Hen. IV, no. 58, m. 58.
[33] Ibid. 24 Hen. VI, no. 43.
[34] *Testa de Nevill* (Rec. Com.), 244b, 252b.
[35] *Hund. R.* (Rec. Com.), ii, 344.
[36] *Feud. Aids,* i, 106.
[37] Ibid. 131.
[38] *Testa de Nevill* (Rec. Com.), 244b, 252b. Muriel, daughter of Peter Cheyne of Furtho, Northamptonshire, and William Cheyne of Hanslope, are named in 1297 (Add. MS. 28024, fol. 22b).
[39] *Feud. Aids,* i, 105.
[40] Ibid. 131.
[41] *Testa de Nevill* (Rec. Com.), 244b, 252b.
[42] *Feud. Aids,* i, 106.
[43] Ibid. 131.

[44] *Cal. Inq. p.m.* (Edw. II), v, 402.
[45] Chan. Inq. p.m. 2 Hen. IV, no. 58, m. 58; 8 Hen. IV, no. 68; 24 Hen. VI, no. 43.
[46] *Testa de Nevill* (Rec. Com.), 244b, 252b.
[47] Feet of F. case 16, file 33, no. 7.
[48] *Feud. Aids,* i, 106.
[49] *Cal. Inq. p.m.* (Edw. II), v, 402; *Feud. Aids,* i, 131. Robert Francis is named as a small tenant in Hanslope in 1279 (*Hund. R.* [Rec. Com.], ii, 345). Richard Hoese also had a life tenancy under the rector (Feet of F. Bucks. Mich. 3 Edw. II, no. 16).
[50] Chan. Inq. p.m. 2 Hen. IV, no. 58, m. 58; 8 Hen. IV, no. 68; 24 Hen. VI, no. 43.
[51] *Testa de Nevill* (Rec. Com.), 244b, 252b.
[52] *Feud. Aids,* i, 106.
[53] Ibid. 131.

lofty and magnificent west tower with its spire was added,[54] and later in the first half of the same century the north aisle was rebuilt. Towards the end of the 15th century both nave arcades were rebuilt, a clearstory being added, and a rood-stair turret was erected at the south-east angle of the nave, while the north and south porches were added to the aisles. The present spire is almost entirely modern, the old spire having been struck by lightning in 1804[55] and ruined nearly to the base. The church was restored in 1904–5. The walling of the body of the church is of limestone rubble, while the tower is faced with ashlar. The stripping of the plaster from the internal face of the walls renders the interior singularly gaunt and bare.

Though somewhat over-zealously restored, the chancel is an extremely fine example of the fully-developed 12th-century style. Externally each side

the original external face of the wall is included within the later north chapel, the projections have been cut away, and only one recess remains complete. The east wall, which was entirely rebuilt in the late 13th century, is flush with the east wall of the contemporary north chapel, and there is a pair of buttresses of this date at the south-east angle of the chancel. Internally there appear to have been string-courses beneath the sills and at the springing level of the heads of the windows. These, where they remain, have been very much restored, but the later piercings of the walls have interrupted them in many places, and on the north side only a short length of the sill-string remains, and this has been almost entirely renewed. The late 13th-century east window has modern five-light tracery, but retains its original jambs and head, with mask-stopped labels on both faces. Beneath the sill internally is a modern string-course.

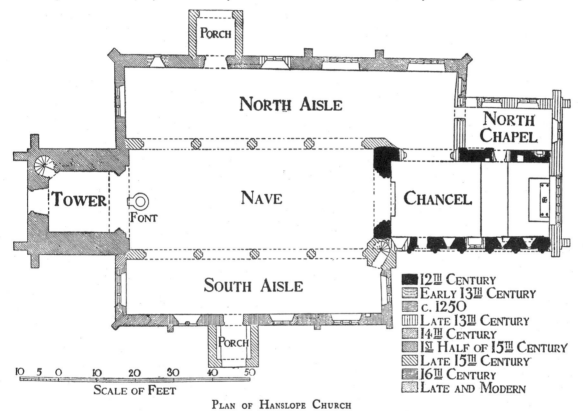

PLAN OF HANSLOPE CHURCH

wall was originally divided into six bays by attached semicircular shafts with variously enriched capitals rising to the corbel table, and in each bay, with the exception of that containing the south doorway, was a semicircular-headed recess with roll-moulded edges extending from the ground to the head of the bay. In the upper thirds of these recesses were placed the small semicircular-headed windows by which the chancel was lighted, a moulded string-course at the sill level of the windows running round the walls and passing like an annulet over the edge rolls and shafts. This arrangement is still nearly complete on the south side, but on the north, where

About 6 ft. from the east end of the chancel, placed high up in the north wall, is a small plain recess or pocket, perhaps intended to house the end of a beam connected with the altar furniture. Nearly under it is an aumbry with rebated jambs, which still retain one of the hooks of the hinges of the original door. To the west of this, opening to the north chapel, is a late 13th-century doorway with a two-centred head inclosed by a restored label and continuously chamfered with the jambs. Above the doorway is the only original window remaining on this side, which now looks into the north chapel. It is a small semicircular-headed window with wide internal splays and a partly renewed rear-arch inclosed by a modern label. The external stonework towards the chapel has been almost entirely renewed; the jambs and head are chamfered, and round the latter are carved three leaves. A little distance to the west is an aumbry with rebated jambs,

[54] Thomas Knight, rector, in his will dated at Leicester, May 1414 (entered in Bishop Repingdon's Register), bequeathed 'fabrice campanilis de Hanslap tantum de bonis suis quantum valent fructus ecclesie sue per unum annum' (Cole MSS., Add. MS. 5839, fol. 93b).

[55] Gent. Mag. lxxiv, 681 ; lxxv, 401.

and above it is a restored length of the 12th-century string-course. The remainder of the wall is occupied by a late 13th-century arch opening into the east end of the north aisle. It is of three chamfered orders and springs from moulded imposts, the jambs having a single chamfer at each angle. There are labels on both faces with mask and broach stops. Three original 12th-century windows remain in the south wall, in the first, second and fourth bays from the east. Each window has an internal label, stopped on the string-course at the springing level of the head by a square stop carved with a flower. The heads are treated externally in the same manner as that of the original light in the north wall. The two eastern windows are half blocked by the sedilia inserted in the wall in the late 13th century. In the third bay the string-courses are interrupted by an inserted two-light window of the same date as the sedilia, the tracery of which has been renewed. In the fifth bay, which has no window, is an original semicircular-headed 12th-century doorway, the internal label of which is formed by the sill-string. Externally the doorway is of two orders, the outer moulded with the cheveron and springing from the enriched capitals of nook-shafts which have now gone, and the inner order moulded continuously with a form of the beak-head ornament overlapping an edge roll. The recess in this bay is curtailed by the doorway, and the jambs, which are unmoulded, start from the external sill-string. In the westernmost bay is a 13th-century low-side lancet window, with a shutter rebate cut in the lower portion of the jambs. The insertion of this window has entirely effaced the external recess in this bay, which is, besides, partly covered by the 15th-century rood-stair turret projecting into the angle between the chancel and nave. The chancel arch is semi-circular, and is recessed in four orders towards the nave. The orders of the arch are all plain; the inner order springs from a pair of semicircular attached shafts on each respond having enriched scalloped capitals with zigzag-moulded and beaded neckings, enriched abaci, and bases of the attic type. The three outer orders are carried by engaged nook shafts with richly carved capitals and attic bases. The abaci of the shafts of the inner and outer orders have been cut to accommodate a rood-loft. The three late 13th-century sedilia at the south-east of the chancel are placed in range with a piscina, the recesses being divided from each other by circular shafts with moulded capitals and bases, and having two-centred trefoiled heads with soffit cusping. The heads are inclosed by labels with mask stops at their inter-sections.

In the east wall of the north chapel, which is now used as the vestry, is a late 13th-century window of three uncusped lights rising into a two-centred main head. In the north wall are two windows of the same date, each of two lights with a plain pierced spandrel in a two-centred head. The lights are pointed and uncusped, those of the eastern window, the tracery of which looks as if it had been reset, having semicircular heads below the pointed heads. At the west end of the wall is a plain doorway with a wood lintel. At the south-east is a piscina recess with a fluted basin, and a re-used 12th-century semi-circular head, richly carved. At the opposite end of the wall on this side of the chapel one nearly complete bay of the external arcading of the chancel

remains; there is no window, but the string-course and corbel table have been left. Half of the bay adjoining on the east, in which is the doorway to the chancel with the original window above it, also remains. The shaft between the bays has been cut off about 2 ft. below the necking of the capital. At the north end of the west wall is a plain square-headed doorway with a wood lintel. Externally the east wall is flush with the east wall of the chancel, and at the north-east angle is a pair of buttresses like those at the south-east angle of the chancel.

The late 15th-century nave arcades are each of four bays with two-centred arches of two hollow-chamfered orders. The inner order springs from semi-octagonal pilasters with moulded capitals and bases, and the outer orders are continuous, but the hollow chamfer changes to a plain chamfer below the springing. The responds repeat the half plan of the piers. The turret containing the rood-stairs projects into the nave at the south-east angle; the doorway which opened on to the loft has a straight-sided four-centred head, and below the doorway is painted a large bear and ragged staff with an inscribed scroll, now illegible. The ground is painted red with yellow foliage, and the bear and staff are white. Above the level of the loft is painted a white figure on a blue ground. The clearstory windows, six on either side, are each of two cinquefoiled lights under a four-centred head with a pierced and foliated spandrel between the heads of the lights. The western piers and responds of the arcades have been much damaged and cut by the insertion of a west gallery.

The east end of the north aisle is largely occupied by a raised burial vault over which is a large private pew. At the north end of the east wall is an early 16th-century square-headed window of two lights with four-centred heads. The external label has shield stops, with charges now almost indecipherable. The southern shield seems to bear a mill-rind, while that on the north bears a cross with indications of other charges. In the eastern portion of the north wall are two large square-headed 15th-century windows, each of five cinquefoiled lights with pierced and foliated spandrels. To the west of these has been reset a fine late 13th-century window of two uncusped lights with a pierced spandrel in a two-centred head. The external label has been much disturbed when the window was reset, two grotesque heads having been placed in the centre of each limb and one at the apex; these heads are probably fragments of 12th-century work. The rear-arch is richly moulded with rolls and hollows and springs from attached shafts at the angles of the jambs with moulded capitals and bases. Adjoining the window on the west is a recess with a two-centred segmental head. To the west of this is the north doorway, which is of the 14th century, and has a two-centred external head moulded continuously with the jambs and a chamfered seg-mental rear-arch. Near the west end of the wall is an early 13th-century lancet with an enriched external label carved with an indented zigzag ornament. There is an external glass rebate and the internal splays are plain, the rear-arch being semicircular and hollow-chamfered. The west window, an insertion of the early 16th century, is square-headed and of three uncusped lights. The external label has shield stops charged with a cross and a saltire respectively. The walls are surmounted by a plain parapet and there are 15th-century buttresses between the three eastern windows and diagonal buttresses of the same date at the angles.

The east window of the south aisle, a square-headed insertion of the same date as the east and west windows of the north aisle, is of three uncusped lights with four-centred heads. The rear-arch and internal jambs are probably of the 13th century. The southern stop of the external label, which is carved with a flower, appears to be a 12th-century fragment. The north-east angle of the aisle is filled by the rood-stair turret ; the doorway to the stairs has a straight-sided four-centred head, the mouldings of which have been cut away, only those upon the jambs remaining. At the east end of the south wall is a 13th-century piscina recess with a plain two-centred head ; the basin no longer exists, but a rough credence shelf remains. The easternmost window in this wall is a 16th-century insertion of three cinquefoiled ogee lights under a square head with plain pierced spandrels. The next window is of the 14th century and is of two trefoiled lights with quatrefoil tracery in a two-centred head. Between this and the easternmost window is a fine mid-13th-century tomb recess with shafted jambs and a trefoiled head, the outer order of which is enriched with the dog-tooth. The south doorway, which is placed nearly opposite the north doorway, is of the 15th century, and has a two-centred external head. The remaining window in this wall is a good coupled lancet of about 1250. The segmental rear-arch, which is inclosed by a label, is elaborately moulded and springs from attached shafts with moulded capitals and bases. The jambs have an external glass rebate and the heads are inclosed by labels intersecting over the wide central mullion. The tracery of the west window is of the same period as that of the east window ; it is square-headed and of three uncusped lights with depressed elliptical heads, but the rear-arch and internal jambs, as in the case of the east window, are of the 13th century. Externally there are buttresses at the east end of the south wall, between the two eastern windows, and immediately to the west of the westernmost window ; a change in the masonry beyond this buttress shows the extent of the 14th-century lengthening of the aisle. At the south-west angle is a diagonal buttress. The walls are surmounted by a plain parapet. The rood-turret, which projects into the angle made by the aisle with the chancel, is divided externally into three stages and rises to a short distance above the parapet of the nave. At the southern angles of the moulded string-course which divides the two upper stages are grotesques.

The west tower rises in five external stages to the base of the spire, where it is crowned by an embattled parapet, and there is a vice in the north-west angle. Each stage is slightly set back and there are pairs of buttresses of five offsets at the western angles and one similar buttress at the east end of each side wall ; these rise to the offset below the top, or bell-chamber stage, and are crowned by crocketed gablets. The angles of the bell-chamber are strengthened by panelled clasping buttresses standing upon the offset. The spire is octagonal with crocketed angles and has flying buttresses at the base, springing from the heavy octagonal shafts of the pinnacles which stand upon the clasping buttresses at the angles of the bell-chamber. The tower arch is of three chamfered orders ; the inner order springs from semicircular

attached shafts with moulded capitals and bases, and the two outer orders are continuous on the nave side, but only the intermediate order is continuous on the west face, the outermost order dying upon the side walls of the tower. The ground stage was originally intended to have been vaulted, and the springers and wall-ribs of the intended vault remain. In the west wall is a doorway with a two-centred head within a square external order with trefoiled spandrels. Above the doorway, in the second external stage, is a wide window of five plain transomed lights under a four-centred head, only the jambs and head of which are of original 15th-century date. The third external stage is lighted by small square-headed windows of two trefoiled lights on the north, west and south, while the stage below the bell-chamber has a small quatre-foiled opening in each wall, that on the north being hidden by the clock face. The bell-chamber is lighted from all four sides by coupled windows ; each is of two transomed and cinquefoiled lights with a vertical-sided quatrefoil in a two-centred head, and each pair of windows has a common square label. Below the embattled parapet is a cornice enriched with grotesques, and having a large carved spout in the centre of each face. The spire itself has two-light dormer windows in the cardinal faces.

The late 15th-century north porch has an outer entrance with a four-centred head moulded continuously with the jambs, and the walls are finished with a plain parapet. The contemporary south porch is of the same character, but the outer entrance, which has been much repaired, has a chamfered two-centred head and plain jambs.

The nave has a late 15th-century roof of low pitch. The trusses are of the king-post type with wall-posts and brackets. An inscription on the truss against the east wall records the repair of the two east bays of the roof in 1770. Three original stone corbels remain beneath the wall-posts : all are carved with angels, one playing a serpentine, another a viol, while the third holds a blank shield. The north aisle roof has been renewed, but one original 15th-century truss remains. The roof of the north porch is original and has moulded timbers. Few old fittings remain ; 15th-century doors remain in the doorways to the rood-stairs and tower vice, and the pew over the burial vault at the east end of the north aisle is approached by an early 18th-century staircase with twisted balusters. Some 15th-century tiles have been set in the sill of the west window of the south aisle, and fragments of original glass remain in the tracery of the two 15th-century windows in the north wall of the north aisle. In the tower are placed two mediaeval stone coffins. A much-decayed 13th-century coffin-lid is placed on the sill of the easternmost window in the south wall of the south aisle, and a fragment of a coffin-lid of the same date, carved with a cross, is set in the west wall of the south porch.

At the east end of the north aisle is a brass with an inscription in verse to the parents of Richard Troughton, the authorship of which is acknowledged in the following words : ' Verses composed in duetye by their beeloved Sonne Richard Troughton.' At the west end of the nave is a brass with the figure of a child, commemorating Mary, daughter of Thomas Birchmore, who died in 1602. At the east end of the nave is a slab with the remains of a fine early 16th-century brass, which originally consisted of the figures of a man in armour with those of his two wives, with an inscription plate beneath, prayer scrolls issuing from the mouths of the female figures, and two shields at the head of the slab. The scrolls and shields are all that remain; the latter are charged with a fesse with three boars' heads thereon, the field being of lead and the fesse of brass. Four slabs with indents now remain in the chancel floor. Two have contained elaborate brasses with marginal inscriptions and figures under canopies, one that of a priest and the other that of a civilian. The other two slabs have indents of figures of priests with inscription plates, one a full-length figure, and the other a half figure. The slab with the latter indent has two 18th-century inscriptions carved upon it. In the chancel are floor slabs commemorating Elizabeth daughter of Thomas Gelding of Poslingford, Suffolk, who died in 1693, and Basil son and heir to Sir Nathaniel Brent, who died in 1695.

There is a ring of six bells. The present treble was added in 1906; the second, the original treble, is by R. Taylor, 'St Neots,' 1815; the third is inscribed 'Hall made me 1752'; the fourth and fifth, each inscribed 'God save Kyng Charls' and dated 1625 and 1626 respectively, are by Robert Atton; and the tenor is by John Briant of Hertford, 1814.

The plate consists of a silver cup of 1621, inscribed 'Hanslop, 1623'; a silver cup of 1732, given by Richard Thursby, and engraved with his arms; a silver flagon of the same year, given by Richard Thursby in 1732; a paten of the same gift, bearing the mark of 1711; and a silver plate without date letter, but having the crowned leopard's head and lion passant.

The registers begin in 1571.

The church of *ST. SIMON AND ST. JUDE*, formerly *OUR LADY*, at Castle Thorpe, consists of a chancel measuring internally 34 ft. 6 in. by 14 ft., nave 30 ft. by 21 ft., north aisle 10 ft. wide, south aisle 8 ft. 6 in. wide, and west tower 9 ft. square. The tower is built of ashlar, and the rest of the church of rubble with stone dressings, the roofs of the nave and aisles being covered with lead and that of the chancel with slate.

The north arcade, which is of the late 12th century, indicates the addition of a north aisle to an already existing church at that period, but no detail of an earlier date survives. About 1350 the nave was apparently widened towards the south and the chancel rebuilt on a larger scale, while in the 15th century the south aisle was added, the north aisle rebuilt, and a clearstory added to the nave. A tower, the date of which is unknown, fell down in 1729, and was replaced by the present structure later in the 18th century, when the fabric was generally repaired.

The chancel, being long and comparatively narrow, presents a strong contrast to the nave, which approximates to a square in shape. In the east wall is a three-light pointed window of about 1350, part of the fine tracery of which, inclosed by what is now a plain circle, has been lost. On the north is a two-light window of the same period, the mullion of which has been removed, though the tracery remains, and opposite to it on the south is a pointed window from which both mullion and tracery have been removed. At the south-west is a two-light low-side window of the 14th century, the sill and mullion of which have been taken away and the opening converted into a doorway, though

the tracery still remains. These alterations were probably made in the 18th century, when the present tower was built and the segmental plastered ceiling placed over the chancel. Below the south-east window is an original piscina with an octagonal bowl, and further west, divided by an attached shaft, are two sedilia, also original, the eastern of which has a low pointed head and the other a segmental head. In the east wall there is a plain locker. The pointed chancel arch is of three orders, all of which die into the north and south walls.

The late 12th-century north arcade of the nave is of two bays with pointed arches supported by a circular pillar with a square foliated capital and moulded base, and plain chamfered responds with moulded abaci. On the south is a lofty 15th-century arcade of two pointed arches with chamfered responds, and an octagonal pillar which is brought to a square form both at the capital and base by broached stops. In the west wall a plain arch, filled by a wooden partition, opens to the ground stage of the tower. There is a rood-loft stairway at the north-east, which is entered through a pointed doorway in the north aisle. The clearstory is lighted from the south only, where there are three small trefoiled windows of the 15th century.

The north aisle was considerably altered in the 18th century, and two wide windows were inserted at that period in the north wall, but one of these has been replaced by a modern window with tracery. On the east is a 15th-century square-headed window, originally of two cinquefoiled lights, from which the mullion with the cusping above it has been removed. In the south wall of the south aisle are two tall 15th-century windows; each is of three cinquefoiled lights and has a square head, but the eastern window is more elaborately moulded than the other. In the east wall is a square-headed two-light window of similar date and type. The low-pitched roof of the nave is of the 15th century, and both aisles have roofs with mediaeval moulded timbers with plastered compartments.

The tower is of three stages with a straight parapet and angle pinnacles and has no buttresses. In the west wall of the ground stage is a plain round-headed doorway with a round-headed window above. The bell-chamber is lighted by windows of similar character. The carved head of a lady with a horned head-dress has been built into the west wall.

The font, which dates from the late 14th century, has a plain octagonal stem and an octagonal bowl with the carved heads of a man and woman on the west side, the latter wearing a *nebulé* head-dress. Against the north wall of the chancel is a large marble monument with arms in memory of Sir Thomas Tyrell, justice of the court of Common Pleas (d. 1671), and Bridget (Harrington) his wife, who erected the monument. Their alabaster effigies, the knight in the robes of a judge, rest on a pedestal under a canopy supported by Ionic columns with alabaster curtains drawn back on the columns on either side. In the chancel floor is a slab to Eyre Tyrell, the date of whose death, first inscribed 1701, has been altered to 1698. The oak pulpit dates from the late 18th century. Below the chancel arch is a low panelled screen of the early 17th century with round-headed carved panels, carved strapwork uprights, and moulded rails. At the south-west corner of the south aisle two sundials are scratched.

CASTLE THORPE: CHURCH AND VILLAGE

CASTLE THORPE CHURCH: THE INTERIOR LOOKING EAST

Castle Thorpe: Castle Yard

Hardmead Church from the South-East

The tower contains one early 15th-century bell, without inscription, but stamped with the cross marks of Joan, widow of Richard Hille.

The communion plate consists of a flagon, two patens and two cups, all plated and probably of 18th-century date ; a silver cup of 1878 elaborately chased with birds and foliage ; and a paten without hall-marks.

The registers previous to 1812 are all contained in one strongly bound volume of entries from 1562 to 1812.

ADVOWSON Hanslope was originally a chapelry[56] of Castle Thorpe, but by a licence granted by Bishop Grosteste (1235–53) it became the parish church in the place of the old mother church, which was thereupon annexed to it as a chapel. The living, which was a rectory,[57] was valued at £40 yearly in 1291.[58] The right of presentation was appendant to the manor until 1522,[59] when the church was granted by the Crown to the Dean and canons of Newark College, Leicester, with licence to appropriate it.[60] The advowson was afterwards resumed by the Crown and granted in 1546 to the corporation of Lincoln, with licence to appropriate the church and to endow a perpetual vicarage after the death of the rector.[61] A confirmation of this grant was obtained in 1593.[62] The advowson remained in the possession of the corporation until 1860,[63] when it was transferred to the Bishop of Oxford,[64] the present owner.

The corporation of Lincoln, as impropriators of the rectory, in 1778 received an allotment in lieu of tithes except in respect of Hanslope Park and Bosenham Field.[65] Lincoln Lodge Farm is in the hands of their lessee.

The chantry chapel of St. Mary, or Keswick's chantry, in Hanslope Church, was founded in 1317 by Thurstan Keswick, rector of Hanslope,[66] and was ordained in 1321.[67] In 1326 licence was granted to Henry Mansell to add to the endowment the reversion of a small property in Roade and Ashton, Northamptonshire.[68] The advowson of the chantry descended with that of the church.[69] The sequestration of Keswick's chantry was ordered by the bishop in 1452,[70] but not carried into effect. Its net value in 1535,[71] and before the Suppression in 1548,[72] was between £7 and £8 yearly. Some land formerly belonging to it, and leased to William Judge, was granted in 1576 to Edward Earl of Lincoln and

Christopher Gough.[73] A messuage, once parcel of this chantry, purchased by Sir Guy Forster from Gabriel Mathew, was included in the settlement of 1635.[74]

The returns of 1548 mention certain lands and rent worth 4s. yearly, for the maintenance of lights in the church, and a quit-rent of 4d. yearly, from a tenement lately William Fox's, for an obit.[75] The former was granted in 1552 to Sir Edward Bray, John Thornton and John Danby.[76] Other property in Hanslope, including 12 acres of land in Castle Thorpe, then or lately in the tenure of Hugh Wren, the last priest appointed to Keswick's chantry,[77] and given for the maintenance of lights and obits, was granted in 1559 to Sir George Howard, kt.[78]

Castle Thorpe Church, as already stated, was originally the mother church of Hanslope, and the presentation made by Sir William Mauduit to Hanslope in 1227[79] was apparently to this church. After the licence granted by Bishop Grosteste the church of Castle Thorpe became a chapel for the Earls of Warwick,[80] and has remained a chapelry annexed to Hanslope. The vicarage of Hanslope (the original endowment of the new church), valued in 1291 at £6 13s. 4d. yearly,[81] passed with the chapel of Castle Thorpe for about sixty years,[82] but was afterwards absorbed into the rectory. The advowson of Castle Thorpe has descended with that of Hanslope,[83] and is now vested in the Bishop of Oxford. The tithes are owned by the corporation of Lincoln.[84]

The Earls of Warwick maintained a chantry in their chapel at Hanslope[85] or Castle Thorpe Church,[86] the last reference occurring in 1488, when it was included in the transfer of the Buckinghamshire lands of the earldom to the Crown.[87]

CHARITIES The Feoffee Estate is regulated by a scheme of the Court of Chancery of 14 February 1868, as varied by schemes of the Charity Commissioners of 1893 and 1898. The estate comprises the charities of Isabel Barnwell, will 1555 ; of William Fox, will (date uncertain), and of an unknown donor, comprised in deeds, 25 September 1739. The trust property now consists of 59 acres, let in allotments, producing about £80 a year, and twenty cottages in Hanslope let at £110 a year. The official trustees also hold a sum of £53 1s. 9d. consols, on an investment account, towards the replacement of a sum of £89 7s. 6d. consols, representing the proceeds of the sale of a messuage in 1877.

[56] The vicarage of Ralph, a chaplain, was reserved in 1227 (*R. of Hugh of Wells* [Cant. and York Soc.], ii, 69).

[57] There were 69 acres of land in 1279 (*Hund. R.* [Rec. Com.], ii, 344) which the rector in the middle of this century had attempted to make into a manor independent of Hanslope Manor (Add. MS. 28024, fol. 29b).

[58] *Pope Nich. Tax.* (Rec. Com.), 33b. The value in 1535 was £48 10s. 7½d. yearly (*Valor Eccl.* [Rec. Com.], iv, 243).

[59] Harl. MSS. 6950, fol. 80b, 123 ; 6952, fol. 57b, 69b ; 6953, fol. 7, 26b, 27b.

[60] *L. and P. Hen. VIII,* iii, g. 2356 (28).

[61] Ibid. xxi (2), g. 648 (24).

[62] *Cal. S. P. Dom.* 1591–4, p. 333.

[63] Inst. Bks. (P.R.O.) ; Bacon, *Liber Reg.* 499.

[64] *Lond. Gaz.* 10 Mar. 1860, p. 1046.

[65] Priv. Act, 18 Geo. III, cap. 76.

[66] Inq. a.q.d. file 123, no. 2 ; *Cal. Pat.* 1313–17, p. 647.

[67] Linc. Epis. Reg. Inst. Burghersh, fol. 326.

[68] *Cal. Pat.* 1324–7, p. 280.

[69] Chan. Inq. p.m. 8 Hen. IV, no. 68.

[70] Linc. Epis. Reg. Memo. Chedworth, fol. 4 d.

[71] *Valor Eccl.* (Rec. Com.), iv, 243.

[72] Chant. Cert. 4, no. 12 ; 5, no. 27.

[73] Pat. 19 Eliz. pt. v, m. 23.

[74] Add. Chart. 53765.

[75] Chant. Cert. 5, no. 27.

[76] Pat. 6 Edw. VI, pt. ix, m. 28.

[77] *Valor Eccl.* (Rec. Com.), iv, 243.

[78] Pat. 2 Eliz. pt. xiii, m. 4.

[79] *R. of Hugh of Wells* (Cant. and York Soc.), ii, 69.

[80] Add. MS. 28024, fol. 23a.

[81] *Pope Nich. Tax.* (Rec. Com.), 41b.

[82] *Hist. MSS. Com. Rep.* xiv, App. viii, 21 ; Linc. Epis. Reg. Memo. Sutton, fol. 15 ; see also list of vicars (Lipscomb, op. cit. iv, 176).

[83] *Hist. MSS. Com. Rep.* xiv, App. viii,

21 ; Bacon, *Liber Reg.* 499. In 1557 the Mayor and burgesses of Lincoln urged the vicar of Hanslope to pay the priest of Castle Thorpe his stipend quarterly (*Hist. MSS. Com. Rep.* xiv, App. viii, 49). In 1569 the Commissioners for Concealed Lands reported that the parsonage was 'ruinous and not well served and therefore must needs be concealed' (*Hist. MSS. Com. Rep.* xiv, App. viii, 64).

[84] Priv. Act, 33 Geo. III, cap. 32 and references as in the case of Hanslope. In 1577 a transfer (apparently of a lease) of the rectory and tithes of Castle Thorpe by Richard Lyster and others to Peter and Edward Grey was licensed by the Crown (Pat. 19 Eliz. pt. vii, m. 23).

[85] *Hund. R.* (Rec. Com.), ii, 344. John the chaplain in 1279 held 30 acres of land and 30s. rents in Hanslope.

[86] Chan. Inq. p.m. 8 Hen. IV, no. 68 ; *Cal. Pat.* 1446–52, p. 37.

[87] Feet of F. Div. Co. Hil. 3 Hen. VII.

In 1904 £500 was borrowed for the purpose of rebuilding two dilapidated cottages. It is being repaid by yearly instalments of £26 and interest.

By an order of the Charity Commissioners of 20 September 1904 five-fifteenths of the entire income and eight-fifteenths of such income, less £80 a year applicable for the benefit of the poor, was constituted as the educational branch of the charity.

In 1912 the sum of £105 9s. was expended in repairs and establishment charges, £38 14s. 5d. in repayment of loans, £11 3s. in scholarships and prizes, £5 2s. 4d. for the library, £16 3s. in distribution in money and articles in kind, £6 6s. to the Northampton Hospital and £8 to the church account. There was a balance at the bank of £207.

The following charities are administered under a scheme of the Charity Commissioners of 16 October 1908, under the title of the United Charities, namely :—

1. Charity founded by will of Richard Miles, who died 25 March 1736, being an annuity of £5 4s., issuing out of lands at Hanslope.

2. Charity of Mary Newman, recorded on the church table as founded by will, date not stated. The property consists of 2 acres of land at Hanslope, let at £2 10s. yearly, and £111 8s. 1d. consols with the official trustees, producing £2 15s. 8d. yearly, arising from the sale in 1901 of land with buildings, situate in Long Street.

3. Serewood Land, otherwise Poor's Allotment, was awarded under an Inclosure Act, passed in 1826,[88] to the poor in lieu of their right of gathering wood; it consists of 6 a. 2 r. 0 p. of land in Long Street, let at £8 18s. 8d. yearly. The scheme directs that the income of the charities shall be applied for the poor, preference being given to widows as regards the charities of Miles and Newman. The distribution is usually made in blankets and bread.

The charity of Lucy Dowager Lady Pierrepont, founded by will in 1721, is regulated by a scheme of the Charity Commissioners, dated 14 November 1890. The endowment, originally £200, consists of 1 a. 0 r. 27 p. of land, let at £4 12s., and messuages let at £6 16s. 6d. yearly. The income is applicable towards the maintenance of the public elementary school at Hanslope, or in granting prizes to children at a public elementary school.[89]

Castle Thorpe.—The Poor's Allotment consists of 18 a. 3 r. 25 p., awarded in 1793 under the Inclosure Act in lieu of lands given by persons unknown for the repair of the church and for the poor. The land is let in allotments to the cottagers, producing about £23 a year.

In 1681 Lady Tyrell, by deed, gave £80 for the poor, now represented by £84 15s. 4d. consols with the official trustees, producing £2 2s. 4d. yearly.

By a scheme of the Charity Commissioners of 12 May 1896 the sum of £1 is made payable to the vicar for a sermon, and 5s. to the parish clerk out of the income of the Poor's Allotment, and, subject thereto, one moiety of the residue is directed to be applied for the repair and maintenance of the parish church, and the other moiety, together with the income of Lady Tyrell's charity, is applicable for the benefit of the poor. In 1912 the sum of £14 15s. 6d. was distributed in coal.

Mary Ann Worley, by her will proved at Oxford 21 October 1859, bequeathed £400, the interest to be applied in keeping in repair the family tomb and tablets to her husband and children, the income not so applied to be distributed among poor widows and old maids. The legacy is represented by £428 7s. 8d. consols, with the official trustees. The annual dividends, amounting to £10 14s., are duly applied under the provisions of a scheme of 2 December 1910.

HARDMEAD

Horelmede, Herulfmede, Herouldmede (xi cent.) ; Harewemede, Haremede (xii cent.) ; Harlemede, Harmede, Hardmed (xiii cent.).

The parish contains about 1,211 acres, of which 498 acres are arable, 702 permanent grass and 6 woods and plantations.[1] The land gradually falls from about 340 ft. above the ordnance datum in the north of the parish to about 255 ft. in the neighbourhood of Chicheley Brook. The soil is Oxford Clay. The village is on a by-road leading north from the high road from Newport Pagnell to Bedford and, with the rectory and schools, lies near the church. The moated site of the old manor-house lies to the north of the church. The house that stood there was for a long time the residence of the Catesbys, who held the manor in the 15th, 16th and 17th centuries, and probably succeeded a capital messuage mentioned in 1325.[2] In a settlement of 1605 certain portions of the house were set apart for the widow's jointure—namely, the great dining chamber and four rooms on the south and west of it on the same floor and places and garrets above them as well as the cellar and store-house below.[3] Browne Willis

states that by his time the biggest part of the manor-house was pulled down and what was left made into a tenant's house. It had ' never been a good one, being Studd Work and lathed and plaistered under the Roof which is tiled ' ; there was ' nothing antique in it.'[4] Even this seems to have been pulled down about the middle of the 19th century, but traces of fish-ponds and a wall, besides the moat, were still to be seen in Sheahan's time.[5] The present Manor Farm is a 17th-century house with very considerable alterations and additions made during the following century and later.

The parsonage-house in the early part of the 17th century was built of timber and plaster, and stood in about an acre of land inclosed with a moat. Besides the house there were two barns and a hay-house. At the back, within the moat, was a garden plot with fruit trees. There were besides about 15 acres of land attached, ten forming a portion called Parsonage Stocking, and two being in the ' Mill Field.'[6]

In the 18th century the parish was said to contain ' about 20 houses and 70 souls.'[7]

[88] Priv. Act, 7 Geo. IV, cap. 16 (for the inclosure of Salcey Forest).
[89] V.C.H. Bucks. ii, 220.
[1] Statistics from Bd. of Agric. (1905).

[2] Chan. Inq. p.m. 19 Edw. II, no. 83.
[3] Ibid. (Ser. 2), dlxxv, 125.
[4] Add. MS. 5839, p. 200.

[5] Hist. and Topog. of Bucks. 545.
[6] Add. MS. 5839, p. 205.
[7] Ibid. p. 200.

Oswi, a man of Alric, held and could

MANORS sell *HARDMEAD MANOR* before the
Conquest.[8] In 1086 it was held as a
manor of 4 hides by·Walter son of Other.[9] The overlordship passed from Walter
to his descendants the Windsors,[10] of whom Hardmead
was held as parcel of their
manor of Stanwell in Middlesex
for one fee, suit every three
weeks, and a rent called ward-
silver, said to be 6s. 8d. every
twenty-four weeks in 1428,[11]
and in 1486,[12] for ward of
Windsor Castle. In 1542
Andrew Lord Windsor ex-
changed Stanwell and his
lands in Hardmead with the

WINDSOR. *Gules a
saltire argent between
twelve crosslets or.*

king,[13] and the services therefrom can be traced as
late as 1638.[14]

Walter's tenant in 1086 was Ralf,[15] and in the
time of Henry III Sarra de Bending held the fee,[16]
which had passed by 1284-6 to William de Bending,[17]
who still held in 1302-3.[18] In 1315 William de
Bending or Bennyng granted about 50 acres of land
and 6s. rent to John de Olney,[19] who was returned
as lord of Hardmead in the next year,[20] and received
a grant of free warren in 1318.[21] He died in 1325,[22]
and his widow Maud, daughter of Nicholas de
Haversham,[23] afterwards held lands in Hardmead
in dower.[24] His son John de Olney, said to be
seventeen years old at the time of his father's death,
made a settlement of the manor in 1329.[25] In 1331,
however, the overlord, Richard de Windsor, brought
a suit against him for having entered the manor while
still a minor.[25a] In 1346 Michael Mynot held the
fee formerly belonging to William de Bending.[26]
Probably he held as guardian or as the husband of John
de Olney's widow, since William de Olney, son of
John,[27] with Isabel his wife, held the manor in 1374.[28]
He died within three years.[28a] In 1418 Thomas
Stutfield and Idonia his wife granted it to John Rose
or Roose,[29] who held in 1428.[30] Before 1452 the
tenant of the Windsors was apparently Thomas Rose.[31]
Hardmead was afterwards held by Richard Maryot,

who granted it before 1485 to his daughter and heir
Joan on her marriage with Humphrey Catesby of
Whiston, Northamptonshire.[32] Humphrey died in
1503, when he held about 200 acres of land in Hardmead.[32a] His son and heir Anthony, who died in
1553, left Hardmead to a
younger son Francis.[33] At his
death four years later Francis
left his estate in Hardmead
to his wife Mary with reversion to his younger son
Anthony.[33a] He appears to
have sold the manor, which
was held in 1580 by Thomas
Ardes,[34] and was purchased of
him before 1583 by Thomas
Catesby,[35] elder brother of
Anthony.[36] A settlement of
the manor was made in 1605

CATESBY. *Argent
two leopards sable having
golden crowns.*

by Thomas on the marriage
of his son Francis Catesby with Susan Brocas.[37]
Thomas died in 1620, his widow Katherine afterwards holding a jointure in the manor.[38] Francis
died in 1636, leaving a son and heir Thomas,[39] who
made a settlement of the manor in the following year.[40]
This Thomas Catesby was sheriff of the county in
1659,[41] and ' by his great Profuseness in his Office and
Equipage ran this Estate (Hardmead) in Debt,' [42] so
that, although he continued to hold the manor for some
time longer,[43] he and his son Thomas were obliged to
join in selling it in 1679 to Sir John Maynard, kt.[44]
Sir John was already possessed of the manor of Clifton
Reynes, with which Hardmead descended until
1792,[45] when Alexander Small, then lord of both
manors, sold Hardmead, then called Hardmead Halfs-
penny, to Robert Earl of Kinnoull.[46] The earl was
succeeded in 1804 by his son Thomas, who sold the
manor to Robert Shedden.[47] He died in 1826, when
Hardmead passed to his son George Shedden. After his
death in 1855 the Buckinghamshire property appears
to have been divided into equal portions between his
sons William George, Roscow Cole, and Edward
Cole, rector of Clapton (Northants),[48] whose names
are given as landowners in 1873.[49] On the death
of the eldest son without issue in that year Roscow

[8] *V.C.H. Bucks.* i, 266 and note.
[9] Ibid.
[10] *Testa de Nevill* (Rec. Com.), 244 ;
Feud. Aids, i, 82, 104 ; Chan. Inq. p.m.
19 Edw. II, no. 83 ; 3 Edw. III (1st
nos.), no. 33; De Banco R. 285, m. 170 d.;
Chan. Inq. p.m. 22 Ric. II, no. 52 ;
9 Hen. V, no. 45 ; 30 Hen. VI, no. 11.
[11] Chan. Inq. p.m. 6 Hen. VI, no. 46.
[12] *Cal. Inq. p.m. Hen. VII*, i, 8, 303.
[13] *L. and P. Hen. VIII*, xvii, g. 285
(18).
[14] Chan. Inq. p.m. (Ser. 2), dlxxv, 125.
[15] *V.C.H. Bucks.* i, 266.
[16] *Testa de Nevill* (Rec. Com.), 244.
[17] *Feud. Aids*, i, 82.
[18] Ibid. 104.
[19] Feet of F. case 18, file 67, no. 14.
The Olney family already owned an estate
here, William son of Simon de Olney
acquiring one messuage, 72 acres, &c., in
1251 (ibid. case 16, file 31, no. 6), and
William son of William de Olney receiving
in 1290 one messuage and 1 carucate from
Roger de Bourt (ibid. case 17, file 51, no. 1).
[20] *Feud. Aids*, i, 110.
[21] *Cal. Chart. R.* 1300-26, p. 391.

[22] *Cal. Inq. p.m.* (Edw. II), vi, 425.
[23] See Haversham.
[24] Chan. Inq. p.m. 3 Edw. III (1st
nos.), no. 33.
[25] Feet of F. case 286, file 35, no. 43.
[25a] De Banco R. 285, m. 170 d.
[26] *Feud. Aids*, i, 130.
[27] See Little Linford.
[28] Feet of F. case 21, file 102, no. 2.
[28a] *Cal. Close* 1377-81, p. 102.
[29] Feet of F. case 22, file 117.
[30] Chan. Inq. p.m. 6 Hen. VI, no. 46.
[31] Ibid. 30 Hen. VI, no. 11. The
name is indistinct in the MS.
[32] *Cal. Inq. p.m. Hen. VII*, i, 8, 303.
[32a] Exch. Inq. p.m. (Ser. 2), file 5, no. 16.
[33] Chan. Inq. p.m. (Ser. 2), ci, 93 ;
Metcalfe, *Visit. of Northants*, 174.
[33a] Chan. Inq. p.m. (Ser. 2), cxiv, 9 ;
P.C.C. 34 Noodes. He died according to
M.I. in church in 1556, but Inq. and
will give 1557.
[34] Feet of F. Bucks. Mich. 22-23 Eliz.
[35] Recov. R. Hil. 25 Eliz. m. 151 ;
Chan. Inq. p.m. (Ser. 2), dlxxv, 125.
[36] P.C.C. 34 Noodes.
[37] Chan. Inq. p.m. (Ser. 2), ccclxxxvi, 94.

[38] Ibid.
[39] Ibid. dlxxv, 125.
[40] Feet of F. Bucks. East. 13 Chas. I ;
Recov. R. East. 13 Chas. I, m. 50.
[41] P.R.O. *List of Sheriffs*, 9.
[42] Add. MS. 5839, p. 199.
[43] Recov. R. Mich. 25 Chas. II, m. 34;
Feet of F. Bucks. Trin. 30 Chas. II.
[44] Close, 31 Chas. II, pt. ix, no. 18 ;
cf. Chan. Proc. (Bridges Div.), bdle. 499,
no. 43.
[45] See under Clifton Reynes.
[46] Lysons, *Mag. Brit.* i (3), 573.
[47] G.E.C. *Complete Peerage*, iv, 414 ;
Recov. R. East. 46 Geo. III, m. 150 ;
Lipscomb, *Hist. and Antiq. of Bucks.* iv,
182. In this statement Lipscomb refers
particularly to the advowson, but it seems
probable that the land was also sold, as
the Sheddens were certainly lords of the
manor afterwards (Sheahan, op. cit. 545)
and are now the landowners.
[48] Sheahan, loc. cit. The second
son Robert John died without issue in
1865.
[49] *Ret. of Owners of Land* (1873),
Bucks. 18.

Cole inherited his portion, which passed at his death four years later to his son George Shedden, the present lord of the manor, the interest of the Rev. E. C. Shedden, who died in 1876, being now vested in his widow.

A windmill is mentioned among the appurtenances of the manor in the 16th and 17th centuries.[50]

A second manor in *HARD-MEAD*, consisting of 1 hide all but half a virgate, was held before the Conquest by Godwin, a man of Ulf, in 1086 by Hervey of William Fitz Ansculf.[51] William was succeeded in his holding by the Paynels,[52] founders of Tickford Priory, and in 1187 a charter of Gervase Paynel,

SHEDDEN. *Azure a cheveron between three griffons' heads razed argent with three cross-lets fitchy gules on the cheveron and a chief argent charged with a scallop azure between two cinq foils gules.*

grandson of Fulk the founder, confirmed to the monks of Tickford the gift of a hide of land at Hardmead.[53] The priory continued to hold this land until the Dissolution,[54] and also received a grant of free warren here in 1311.[55] After the Dissolution it shared the fate of Chicheley, with which manor and that of Thickthorns, partly in Hardmead, it was granted in 1545 to Anthony Cave.[56] Lands here followed the descent of the Chicheley manors in the 17th century,[57] but no record of them appears after that time.

Perhaps the half virgate excepted from this hide of land in 1086, and afterwards apparently restored to it, was that which Godric, a man of Oswi, had held before the Conquest, but which was held of William Fitz Ansculf by Payn in 1086.[58]

Another hide in Hardmead, held as a manor before the Conquest by three brothers, one a man of Tochi and the other two men of Baldwin, was held in 1086 by Baldwin of William Fitz Ansculf.[59] Half a virgate of this land belonged then, as it had in the time of King Edward, to the church of St. Firmin of North Crawley.[60]

Another holding in Hardmead in 1086 was that of 1 hide and 1 virgate which Morcar held of the Countess Judith.[61] This may be the land afterwards held in Hardmead by the Butler family, since they held a manor named after them in Clifton Reynes, which was similarly among the possessions of the Countess Judith in 1086.[62] William Butler and Alice his wife held land here in 1275,[63] and in 1302–3 Isabel, widow of William Salet, recovered seisin of half an acre in Hardmead against William

Butler and Eleanor.[64] There is mention of William Butler in 1316,[65] and William son of William Butler of Hardmead was accused of trespass in 1323.[66] Francis Butler was pardoned for assenting to the counterfeiting of coin in 1326,[67] but there is no further record of their lands here.

A further entry in the Domesday Survey records that Alric son of Godin held a manor assessed at 2½ hides in 1086, and then held by Hugh of Walter Giffard.[68] This Hugh may have been Hugh de Bolebec, the most important of Walter's tenants in this county; he also held half a virgate in Hardmead as his own land which Ulgrim, a man of Earl Lewin, had held before the Conquest.[69]

There is no certain evidence of the descent of this manor, for it does not appear among the lands of the honour of Giffard unless William Marshal, Earl of Pembroke, is meant by the William Marshal, custodian of Gilbert son and heir of Hugh le Heyr, whose widow Avice in 1223 claimed one-third of 12 acres in Hardmead as dower against John le Enfant.[70] Or it may perhaps be traced in the half virgate in 'Harewemede' which Robert son of Anketill exchanged with John son of Hugh in 1194,[71] or in the fee in 'Harewemede' for which William de Willen paid scutage in 1234–5.[72]

CHURCH The church of *ST. MARY* consists of a chancel measuring internally 32 ft. by 14 ft. 6 in., nave 35 ft. by 16 ft. 6 in., north aisle 8 ft. wide, south aisle 8 ft. 6 in. wide, west tower 10 ft. by 9 ft. 6 in. and a south porch 8 ft. square.

Evidence of the existence of a church here in the 12th century is given by the fragments of a font of that date now fixed in the wall on either side of the south doorway, but no other detail of that period survives. The west tower was added to this church about the middle of the 13th century, and some thirty years later a south aisle was built, the arcade opening to which still remains. The north aisle was added early in the 14th century, and towards the middle of the same century the chancel was rebuilt. About 1400 new windows were inserted in the north wall of the north aisle, and a few years later the south aisle was remodelled and the south porch added. Late in the 15th century the clearstory was added to the nave. The east wall of the chancel has been rebuilt, probably during the 19th century, and in 1861 the church was restored. The walling generally is of rubble, and the roofs, with the exception of that of the chancel, which is tiled, are leaded.

The east window of the chancel has modern three-light tracery, but some original 14th-century stones seem to have been used in the rear-arch. There are

---

[50] Feet of F. Bucks. Mich. 22 & 23 Eliz.; Chan. Inq. p.m. (Ser. 2), dlxxv, 125; Recov. R. East. 13 Chas. I, m. 50.

[51] *V.C.H. Bucks.* i, 257.

[52] Ibid. 213.

[53] Dugdale, *Mon.* v, 203.

[54] Ibid. 206 (the entry under Hardmead is 'a close,' value 16s.); *Feud. Aids*, i, 104; Add. Chart. 11224, 23878.

[55] *Cal. Chart. R.* 1300–26, p. 181.

[56] *L. and P. Hen. VIII*, xx (2), g. 1068 (10). The manor of Thickthorns in Chicheley and Hardmead formed part of Fulk Paynel's endowment of the priory (Dugdale, op. cit. v, 203). From the

wording of Gervase's charter, however, it seems that the hide of land forming the second manor of Hardmead was a distinct holding.

[57] Pat. 21 Jas. I, pt. xviii, no. 4; Feet of F. Bucks. Trin. 15 Chas. I. Thomas Catesby, who died in 1620, purchased from Lewis Mordaunt lands in Hardmead (Chan. Inq. p.m. [Ser. 2], dlxxv, 125), which may perhaps have been part of the Tickford Priory estate.

[58] *V.C.H. Bucks.* i, 257.

[59] Ibid.

[60] Ibid.

[61] Ibid. 274.

[62] See Butlers Manor in Clifton Reynes.

[63] Feet of F. Div. Co. Mich. 3 & 4 Edw. I, no. 35.

[64] *Abbrev. Rot. Orig.* (Rec. Com.), i, 129; the Salets are again mentioned as holding small portions of land here in 1315 and 1317 (Feet of F. case 18, file 68, 69).

[65] *Cal. Pat.* 1313–17, p. 500.

[66] Ibid. 1321–4, p. 319.

[67] Ibid. 1324–7, p. 330.

[68] *V.C.H. Bucks.* i, 252.

[69] Ibid. 213, 265.

[70] Maitland, *Bracton's Note Bk.* iii, 456.

[71] *Abbrev. Plac.* (Rec. Com.), 1.

[72] *Testa de Nevill* (Rec. Com.), 258, 262.

two windows in each side wall ; the eastern windows have been almost entirely renewed, but those at the west end are substantially original. Each is of two trefoiled lights with leaf-tracery in a two-centred head, the design of the tracery being very similar to that of the south aisle windows at Haversham Church. In the west jamb of the north-west window is a small rectangular blocked opening, measuring about 14 in. by $2\frac{1}{2}$ in., probably that of a squint from the outside ; no trace of the external opening, however, is now visible. Between the two windows in the south wall is a restored 14th-century doorway with a shouldered rear-arch and a two-centred external head inclosed by an original moulded label with head-stops, one a mitred head and the other that of a man in a liripipe hood. At the east end of the south wall is a modern piscina recess with a trefoiled ogee head, perhaps a copy of an original piscina, and in a corresponding position in the opposite wall is a modern credence table. The 14th-century chancel arch is two-centred and of two chamfered orders dying into the side walls.

The early 14th-century north arcade of the nave is of two bays with two-centred arches of two chamfered orders, supported by a central pier of quatrefoil plan, and responds repeating the half plan of the pier. The capitals and bases of the pier and responds are moulded, and the arches have labels on both faces, those on the north face having a head-stop at their intersection over the pier. The south arcade is of the same number of bays and has similar arches supported by a pier and responds of the same form, but the mouldings of the capitals and bases are of late 13th-century section. The arches have labels with mask-stops on both faces. Above the east respond is the upper doorway of the rood stairs, which are carried up in the thickness of the wall and were entered from a similar doorway at the north-east corner of the south aisle. The late 15th-century clearstory windows, three on either side, are each of two trefoiled lights under a four-centred head.

In the east wall of the north aisle is an early 14th-century window of two trefoiled lights with quatrefoil tracery in a two-centred head. The tracery is of somewhat unusual design, and the heads of the lights are semicircular. The two windows in the north wall are insertions of about 1400. The eastern window, which has been considerably restored, is of two trefoiled lights with a vertical-sided quatrefoil in a two-centred head ; the western is of the same number of trefoiled lights and has a two-centred head with quatrefoil tracery, but the window is much smaller and the lights have ogee heads. The north doorway seems to have been inserted about 1420. It has a two-centred external head continuously moulded with the jambs, and was blocked when the church was restored. To the east of the doorway is a plain pointed stoup recess. The windows of the south aisle, which have escaped renewal, are of the early 15th century. The east window has a four-centred head and is of three cinquefoiled lights, the central light rising into the apex of the opening, while the side lights are acutely pointed. The south-east window is of two cinquefoiled lights with a vertical-sided quatrefoil in a two-centred head. The south doorway is similar in date and design to the north doorway. The south-west window is modern. At the south-east is a 14th-century piscina with a trefoiled ogee head and a basin of sexfoiled form, the projecting portion of which has been cut away.

The west tower is of two receding stages with an embattled parapet. A slight set-off above the windows of the bell-chamber shows that the tower was slightly heightened when the embattled parapet was added in the 15th century. The tower arch is two-centred and of two chamfered orders, the outer order being continuous, while the inner order rests upon modern corbels. The west window of the ground stage is modern, but some original 14th-century stones survive in the inner jambs. Above the head of this window is a small original light with a label and external rebate. The windows of the second or bell-chamber stage afford interesting examples of plate tracery. Each is of two trefoil-headed lights with a foiled piercing under a containing two-centred label brought down nearly to the level of the springing of the heads of the lights. In the case of the windows on the north and south the lights are divided by a shaft with a moulded capital, that of the north window having also a moulded base, but the other windows have only a broad mullion. The early 15th-century south porch has a continuously moulded outer entrance and is lighted from each side wall by a window of two trefoiled lights with quatrefoil tracery in a two-centred head ; at the southern angles of the porch are diagonal buttresses.

The roofs of the chancel and nave are modern, as is also that of the south aisle, though some old timbers have been re-used. The roof of the north aisle is of original late 15th-century date ; it is of the lean-to type and is supported by principals alternately straight and cambered, having carved bosses at their intersections with the purlin. The westernmost boss bears a shield charged with a voided cross between what appear to be four engrailed saltires ; another boss has the crown of thorns.

The octagonal font is of the early 15th century.

At the east end of the south aisle is preserved an early 17th-century communion table. Some original 14th-century glass remains in the tracery of the north-east window of the chancel, and the south-west window of the south aisle contains pieces of 15th-century glass. Nine late 15th-century seats with buttressed uprights and moulded top rails, and three desk-fronts of the same date, are preserved in the nave and north aisle. In the tower is a fine oak bier bearing the following inscription : ROBERD HEARN AND FRANSES PVRNNY CHVRCH WA·RNS T C 1670 W S W C.

At the south-east corner of the north aisle is a brass with figure and inscription commemorating Francis Catesby (d. 1556). The inscription is as follows : 'Of your charyte pray for the soule of Francys | Catesby of hardmeede Gent' the yongest sonne of Antony Catesbye of whyston Esquyer decessyde ; | whyche francys decessyd the xxj day of August in | the yere of oure lord God a Mˡccccclvj On | whose soule and all Christen god have mercy amē.' At the east end of the north wall of the same aisle is an elaborate mural monument of stone and marble, erected in memory of a later Francis Catesby (d. 1636). The design is peculiar and consists of a recess built up of piles of books and containing a small recumbent effigy of Francis Catesby, with kneeling figures of a son and two daughters. The whole is flanked by Corinthian columns supporting a curved broken pediment in which is a shield of arms. Upon a tablet below the recess is inscribed: 'Epitaphium in memoriam Francisci | Catesby armigeri qui decessit die 3° Novembris an° Domini 1636.' A copy of laudatory Latin verse follows. On the west wall of the north aisle is a marble tablet commemorating Elizabeth daughter of Thomas Catesby and wife of Sir Thomas Hanbury, kt. (d. 1665); her father Thomas Catesby (d. 1679); Thomas son of the same Thomas Catesby (d. 1681), and, lastly, Elizabeth, 'Relick' of the elder Thomas Catesby (d. 1699). On the north wall of the chancel is a large marble tablet commemorating Robert Shedden, who sailed in his yacht *Nancy Dawson* to search for Sir John Franklin. He died on board his yacht in 1849, on the Pacific, and was buried in the Protestant burial ground at Mazatlan. A second tablet commemorates his father, William Shedden, who died in 1820.

There are three bells. The treble is inscribed in black letter, 'Vox Augustini Sonet In Aure Dei.' It was probably cast in the first half of the 15th century by Robert Crowch. It is now broken in two and is placed on the floor of the intermediate stage. The second, an early 16th-century bell, is inscribed in black letter, 'Sancta maria ora p̄ nobis.' The tenor is inscribed in Lombardic capitals, 'Vocor Johannes.' It was cast probably in the 14th century by William Rufford.[73]

The plate consists of a silver cup of 1692, a paten of 1658, and a flagon of 1834.

The registers begin in 1556.

ADVOWSON The church of Hardmead was in possession of the priory of Merton in Surrey at an early date, Gilbert, a sub-deacon, being presented by the prior in 1223.[74] The church was valued at £5 6s. 8d. in 1291 and paid a pension of £1 to the prior and also £1 6s. 8d. to the Prior of Tickford.[75] In a fine between the Prior of Merton and G., rector of Hardmead, the latter acknowledged his obligation to pay the pension of £1 at Easter.[76] In after years William de Bending laid claim to the advowson and obliged the prior to establish his right in the law courts in 1316.[77] In 1358 the king presented to the church, owing to 'the temporalities of Merton Priory being lately in his hands.'[78] Some protest was evidently made, as in 1359 the same incumbent was again presented by the Crown,[79] and in 1360 an order was made for the arrest of all persons prosecuting appeals against the decision of the judges whereby the king

lately recovered the said presentation against the prior and John Tybotes, chaplain.[80] Possibly this quarrel is responsible for the subsequent confusion in the descent of the advowson. According to Browne Willis the Priors of Merton continued to present until the Dissolution.[81] At that time, or as late as 1535, they certainly still received their pension from the rector,[82] but in the accounts of their possessions at this date there is no mention of this church. Moreover, in 1374, William de Olney levied a fine of both manor and advowson,[83] while, after the Dissolution, the church was stated to have been a possession of the late monastery of Lavendon,[84] and was granted as such in 1543 to Thomas Lawe in fee.[85] He alienated it in 1545 to Edward Ardes of Sherington,[86] who died in 1570, having settled the advowson on his second son Thomas.[87] Thomas Ardes sold it about 1595 to John Smythe and Thomas Tyllyard or Tyllyer, agents for Mardoch Bownell, clerk, who arranged to pay the purchase money by instalments and gave up his living at Hanwell.[88] In 1598 Bownell brought an action against the agents,[89] stating that he had been deceived as to the age of the then incumbent and the value of the living, and, further, that he had been obliged to make a new purchase from Thomas Ardes's son and heir John. Smythe replied that Bownell had gone to Hardmead, had conferred with the incumbent and satisfied himself about his age and had viewed the parsonage-house and glebe lands, becoming, thereupon, very anxious to purchase. But he seems never to have actually held the living, and shortly afterwards, in 1604, Thomas Catesby, lord of the manor, presented to the church.[90] The advowson then passed with the manor until 1877–8,[91] when it was conveyed to the Rev. R. Hawthorn. His executors sold it to Mr. C. E. Lamplugh, in whose representatives it is now vested.

CHARITIES Town Land.—It is stated in the Parliamentary Returns of 1786 that an unknown donor gave land, then producing £2 a year, to the poor. The land in question was inclosed, and in lieu thereof an annual sum of £2 is now received from the Hardmead estate. This sum is distributed in coal to about ten recipients.

The parish schools were founded by deed poll, 13 December 1861. A cottage belonging to the schools is let for £4, which is applied towards the school expenses.

HAVERSHAM

Havresham (xi cent.); Haveresham, Haversam, Heveresham (xii–xiii cent.); Horsham, Haresham (xvii cent.).

This parish contains about 1,623 acres, of which

about 929 are permanent grass, 584 arable, and 6 woods and plantations.[1] The soil is mixed; the chief crops are wheat, oats and beans. The highest ground is in the north-east, where it is about 332 ft. above

[73] A.H. Cocks, *Church Bells of Bucks.* 412.
[74] *R. of Hugh of Wells* (Cant. and York Soc.), ii, 63; Browne Willis (Add. MS. 5839, p. 198) states that Merton held the church in 1180; there is, however, no certain evidence as to the donor.
[75] *Pope Nich. Tax.* (Rec. Com.), 33.
[76] Cott. MS. Cleop. C vii, fol. 155 d. This fine must be either 1249–52 or 1296–1305.
[77] De Banco R. 213, m. 195.
[78] *Cal. Pat.* 1358–61, p. 107.
[79] Ibid. 171.
[80] Ibid. 420.
[81] Add. MS. 5839, fol. 198.
[82] *Valor Eccl.* (Rec. Com.), iv, 244.
[83] Feet of F. case 21, file 102, no. 2.
[84] Orig. R. 35 Hen. VIII, pt. ii, m. 23; Memo. R. (Exch. L.T.R.), Trin. 13 Eliz. m. 5.
[85] *L. and P. Hen. VIII*, xviii (1), g. 981 (41).
[86] Ibid. xx (2), g. 707 (52).
[87] Chan. Inq. p.m. (Ser. 2), ccxvii, 114.
[88] Chan. Proc. (Ser. 2), bdle. 259, no. 19.
[89] Ibid.
[90] Add. MS. 5839, p. 204; Bownell's name does not occur in the list of rectors.
[91] See under manor; see also Inst. Bks. (P.R.O.).
[1] Statistics from Bd. of Agric. (1905).

the ordnance datum ; but on the borders of the parish, by the Ouse and its tributary, the land is more than 100 ft. lower and liable to floods.

The viaduct of the London and North Western railway crosses the south-west of the parish.

The village, which lies in the south-east, consists of houses scattered along the road from Wolverton to Little Linford. A group of buildings at the south end of the village street comprises the church, rectory and schools. The manor-house with the remains of a moat lies to the south of the church. It is a stone house of two stories with a tiled roof, and dates in part from the last half of the 17th century. A considerable portion of the house was demolished in 1792 [2] and a new wing was added on the north-east two years later. Some of the windows have been blocked and others altered. In the grounds is a square dovecote of stone with a tiled roof which bears the date 1665 and the initials M.T., standing for Maurice Thompson, who purchased the manor in the preceding year. Near the dovecote is a fish-pond. Haversham Grange, about a quarter of a mile north-east of the church, probably represents the grange of the Abbot of Lavendon, who in the 15th century held a grange called 'Grenesden' at the rent of a pound of pepper, payable to the lord of the manor.[3] The present house, a gabled stone building with tiled roofs, seems to have been built in the early 17th century, the date 1628 with the initials $_T{}^T{}_E$ appearing on one of the gables. The plan consists of a block facing north-west, which contains the entrance, and a large wing at the south-west. Some 14th-century details, possibly survivals from the original grange, are incorporated in the structure. These include the pointed entrance doorway on the north-west front, a similar doorway inside between the main block and the south-west wing, a window of two trefoiled lights lighting the ground floor at the north-east end of the house, and a small square-headed window in the ground story of the south-west wing.

Some Roman remains have been found in the parish.[4]

The house of George Martin at Haversham was licensed for Presbyterian worship in 1672.[5]

Old field-names include Ruggemore in the 13th century,[6] Kytlecrofte, Kachewyn, Shurlok in the 15th century,[7] Great and Little Coale Stocking, Woad Stocking, Ffoulkes Stocking, Foddering Yard and Dry Closes, in the 18th century.[8]

An Inclosure Act for the parish was passed in 1764.[9]

MANORS
Before the Conquest the manor of HAVERSHAM was held by Countess Gueth, wife of Earl Ralf of Hereford.[10] In 1086 it was assessed at 10 hides and was held by William Peverel himself.[11] It was afterwards attached as one fee to his honour of Peverel, and so remained, the last mention of this overlordship occurring in 1525.[12]

THE MANOR HOUSE, HAVERSHAM

The tenants who held Haversham in the 12th century took their name from the place. Robert and Nicholas de Haversham are mentioned in 1174–7.[13] In 1190 Hugh de Haversham rendered account of 30 marks for an agreement concerning the wood of Haversham.[14] Hugh held Haversham as late as 1220.[15] His son Nicholas owed 100s. for relief for his father's fee here in 1221.[16] Nicholas de Haversham, who in 1232 was one of the collectors of the one-fortieth in the county,[17] held Haversham until his

[2] Sheahan, *Hist. and Topog. of Bucks.* 547.

[8] Rentals and Surv. (Gen. Ser.), R. 78. John de Haversham, chaplain, gave the abbey 12 acres in Haversham in 1325 (*Cal. Pat.* 1324–7, p. 122) and the abbey still held lands here in 1535 (*Valor Eccl.* [Rec. Com.], iv, 241).

[4] *V.C.H. Bucks.* ii, 7.

[5] *Cal. S. P. Dom.* 1672, pp. 63, 64, 90.

[6] Hunter, *Pedes Finium* (Rec. Com.), 242.

[7] Rentals and Surv. (Gen. Ser.), R. 78.

[8] Close, 3 Geo. II, pt. vi, no. 9.

[9] Priv. Act, 4 Geo. III, cap. 60.

[10] *V.C.H. Bucks.* i, 253.

[11] Ibid.

[12] *Red Bk. of Exch.* (Rolls Ser.), 109, 182 n., 183, 585 ; *Cal. Close,* 1272–9, p. 187; *Feud. Aids,* i, 105; Chan. Inq. p.m. 19 Edw. II, no. 83 ; 3 Edw. III (1st nos.),

no. 33 ; 21 Edw. III (1st nos.), no. 38 ; 6 Edw. IV, no. 30 ; (Ser. 2), xliii, 72.

[13] Pipe R. 21 Hen. II (Pipe R. Soc.), 53, 55 ; 23 Hen. II, 159.

[14] Pipe R. 2 Ric. I, m. 12 d.

[15] Red Bk. of Exch. (Rolls Ser.), 109, 536, 585. Extract from Luffield Priory Register printed in R. Ussher's *Hist. of Westbury Parish,* 129.

[16] Pipe R. 5 Hen. III, m. 13 d.

[17] *Cal. Close,* 1231–4, p. 159.

death about 1251,[18] when he was succeeded by a son of the same name.[19] This Nicholas died in 1274, leaving a daughter and heir Maud, who was then only six months old,[20] and a widow Joan, to whom dower was assigned in the manor.[21] In 1274, during Maud's minority, the bailiff of the king's escheator was accused of selling the timber and destroying a fish-pond there.[22] About this time the custody of the manor was granted to Queen Eleanor.[23] Maud daughter of Nicholas married as her first husband James de la Plaunche, who was seised of the manor in the right of his wife until his death about 1306.[24] He left two sons : John, the elder,[25] who seems to have died young, and William, who afterwards held the manor.[26] His widow married John de Olney [27] before 1309,[28] and in 1324 a settlement was made by which Haversham was to pass after Maud's death to William de la Plaunche and Joan his wife and their issue, with contingent remainders to John son of John de Olney and Maud de Haversham and his issue, to John and James sons of John de Pabenham, the husband of Joan de la Plaunche, daughter of James and Maud, and their issue successively.[29] Maud outlived her second husband,[30] and died about 1329, when William de la Plaunche inherited.[31] He married a second wife, Hawise, and died about 1335, leaving a son William, then aged nearly ten.[32] Roger Hillary

DE LA PLAUNCHE.
Argent billety and a lion sable.

and John Leghe were guardians in 1346.[33] In 1347 William died, leaving two daughters Katherine and Joan, aged four and two, while a third, Elizabeth, was born after his death.[34] By 1356 Joan was dead, Katherine had married William de Birmingham, and Elizabeth five years later was the wife of John son of Fulk de Birmingham.[35] Katherine seems to have died without issue sometime after 1372, when a second inquisition was held as to her father's property,[36] and Elizabeth was seised of the whole by 1389, when she was the wife of John Lord Clinton.[37] She afterwards married Sir John Russell, kt.,[38] and various settlements of the manor were made, it being at this period invariably in the hands of trustees, and known as *PLANCHES* or *PLANKUS MANOR.*[39]

She left no issue at her death in 1423, her heir being William Lucy, the son of Alice, daughter of Margery, daughter of James son of Joan de Pabenham.[40] The manor, however, was claimed under the terms of the settlement of 1324 by Walter de Strickland and Isabel his wife, who was the daughter and heir of John de Olney, son of William, son of John, son of John de Olney and Maud de Haversham.[41] Their claim was upheld, and the manor was quitclaimed to them in 1429 by the trustees of Elizabeth Russell, with reversion, failing Isabel's issue, to Alice Lucy and her issue.[42] Isabel died in 1445.[43] Her son and heir Richard Strickland was a minor, and the manor was again in the hands of trustees.[44] He attained his majority, however, before his death in 1458.[45] Since he left no issue Haversham passed, under the terms of the fine of 1429, to William Lucy,[46] as it was found by inquisition that Alice mother of William Lucy had died in 1430.[47] William died in 1466, and his son William, who succeeded him,[48] also acquired Dagnall Manor in Edlesborough and Great Loughton Manor, with the latter of which Haversham descended. During the tenure of William Lucy, great-great-grandson of the William who died in 1466,[49] Richard

LUCY. *Gules crusilly with three luces argent.*

Ylshaw, who claimed to hold a lease of Haversham lordship, was ordered in 1541 not to molest Thomas Oldney in his possession of the farm of Haversham lordship until the case between the two was decided.[50] William Lucy denied that he had ever promised the farm to Oldney, as the latter maintained, but was advised to reflect that, as the king had written to him in Oldney's favour, it would be well to let him have the farm and recompense Ylshaw some other way, a course which he ultimately followed.[51] Sir Thomas Lucy, kt., son of William, did not alienate Haversham with Loughton Manor in 1557, but, with Thomas his son,[52] made a settlement of the manor in 1580.[53] Sir Thomas's chief claim to fame lies in his alleged prosecution of Shakespeare about 1585 for deer-stealing in the Lucys' park at Charlecote, Warwickshire, which led to the poet's immortalizing Lucy in the character of Justice Shallow.[54] He made a further settlement of Haversham in 1594,[55] and died in 1600,[56]

[18] Feet of F. case 15, file 22, no. 47 ; *Cal. Chart. R.* 1226–37, p. 174 ; *Testa de Nevill* (Rec. Com.), 244, 258, 259, 261 ; *Cal. Inq. p.m.* (Hen. III), 57.
[19] *Cal. Inq. p.m.* (Hen. III), 57.
[20] Chan. Inq. p.m. 2 Edw. I, no. 30.
[21] Ibid. ; *Cal. Close*, 1272–9, p. 267.
[22] *Hund. R.* (Rec. Com.), i, 38, 45.
[23] *Cal. Close*, 1272–9, pp. 109, 267; *Hund. R.* (Rec. Com.), i, 37 ; *Feud. Aids*, i, 73.
[24] *Cal. Close*, 1288–96, p. 11 ; *Feud. Aids*, i, 105 ; *Cal. Close*, 1302–7, p. 414 ; Chan. Inq. p.m. 34 Edw. I, no. 36.
[25] Chan. Inq. p.m. 34 Edw. I, no. 36.
[26] Ibid. 3 Edw. III (1st nos.), no. 33.
[27] *Feud. Aids*, i, 110 ; Chan. Inq. p.m. 19 Edw. II, no. 83 ; *Cat. of Anct. D.* iii, 307.
[28] *Cal. Inq. a.q.d.* (P.R.O. Lists and Indexes), i, 104.
[29] *Abbrev. Rot. Orig.* (Rec. Com.), i,

281 ; Feet of F. Bucks. case 19, file 75 ; De Banco R. Trin. 17 Edw. II, m. 109 d. ; Chan. Inq. p.m. 2 Hen. VI, no. 36 ; Wrottesley, *Ped. from Plea R.* 335.
[30] Chan. Inq. p.m. 19 Edw. II, no. 83.
[31] Ibid. 3 Edw. III (1st nos.), no. 33 ; *Abbrev. Rot. Orig.* (Rec. Com.), ii, 44.
[32] Chan. Inq. p.m. 10 Edw. III (1st nos.), no. 59 ; *Abbrev. Rot. Orig.* (Rec. Com.), ii, 96.   [33] *Feud. Aids*, i, 131.
[34] Chan. Inq. p.m. 21 Edw. III (1st nos.), no. 38 ; *Cal. Close*, 1360–4, p. 233.
[35] *Cal. Close*, loc. cit.
[36] Chan. Inq. p.m. 46 Edw. III (1st nos.), no. 18 ; *Cal. Close*, 1369–74, p. 406.
[37] Feet of F. case 21, file 107 ; Chan. Inq. p.m. 2 Hen. VI, no. 36 ; G.E.C. *Peerage*, ii, 304.
[38] G.E.C. loc. cit.
[39] Feet of F. Div. Co. East. 22 Ric. II ; Trin. 10 Hen. IV ; Chan. Inq. p.m. 2 Hen. VI, no. 36.

[40] Chan. Inq. p.m. 2 Hen. VI, no. 36 ; Wrottesley, op. cit. 336.
[41] Wrottesley, op. cit. 335.
[42] Feet of F. Div. Co. Hil. 7 Hen. VI ; Trin. 20 Hen. VI.
[43] Chan. Inq. p.m. 23 Hen. VI, no. 7.
[44] Ibid. ; *Cal. Pat.* 1441–6, p. 434.
[45] Chan. Inq. p.m. 36 Hen. VI, no. 35b.
[46] Ibid.
[47] Ibid. no. 35a.
[48] Ibid. 6 Edw. IV, no. 30.
[49] See under Dagnall Manor.
[50] *L. and P. Hen. VIII*, xvi, 1002, 1030.
[51] Ibid. 1018.
[52] *Dict. Nat. Biog.*
[53] Feet of F. Div. Co. Mich. 22 & 23 Eliz. ; Pat. 22 Eliz. pt. xii, m. 32.
[54] *Dict. Nat. Biog.*
[55] Feet of F. Div. Co. Hil. 36 Eliz.
[56] W. and L. Inq. p.m. xxvi, 95.

his son Thomas dying in 1605.[57] Thomas, son and heir of the latter, succeeded to Haversham,[58] dying in 1640.[59] He was followed by his eldest son Spenser Lucy, whose widow, with her second husband William Sheldon,[60] quitclaimed the manor in 1653 to Robert Lucy,[61] brother and heir of Spenser.[62] Robert's brother and male heir Richard held in 1660,[63] but appears to have become deeply involved in debt and mortgaged the property to John Corrance, who held with others in 1664.[64] It was apparently sold in that year to Maurice Thompson, 'a Person of mean Extraction,'[65] who was sheriff of the county in 1669,[66] and died in 1671, being succeeded by his son John,[67] upon whom he had settled Haversham Manor in 1668.[68] John Thompson was created a baronet in 1673,[69] and was raised to the peerage as Lord Haversham in 1696.[70] He was member for Gatton, Surrey, in 1685, and was among the heartiest partisans of William of Orange.[71] He

THOMPSON, Lord Haversham. *Or a fesse dancetty azure with three stars argent thereon and a quarter azure charged with a sun or.*

was made a lord of the Admiralty in 1699, but resigned two years later, and went over to the Tory party. As a member of the House of Lords he was instrumental in making that assembly persistently reject the Occasional Conformity Bill. In 1705 he achieved notoriety by moving the address to the queen urging her to call to England Sophia of Brunswick, the heir-presumptive. This was in effect the close of his public career. He died in 1710, and was succeeded by his son Maurice, the second Lord Haversham.[72] He held the Haversham estate [73] until 1729, when he joined with his daughters in selling it for £24,500 to Lucy Knightley,[74] who was descended, on his mother's side, from the Lucy family who had previously held Haversham.[75] He died in 1738, leaving a son and heir Valentine,[76] who was succeeded in 1754 by his son Lucy.[76a] In 1764 he barred the entail,[77] and in the same year sold to the trustees of Alexander Small.[78] In the *Northants Mercury* for September 1764 appeared an advertisement that Small, as owner of the manor of Haversham, 'being desirous to preserve the Game and Fishery in the said Manors (i.e., Clifton, Hardmead and Haversham) for his own and Friends' Amusement, gives this public Notice, that all unqualified Persons who shall hereafter be found guilty of disturbing, killing or destroying the Game . . . shall

be prosecuted by the utmost Rigour of the Law.' [79] He was at this time about seventeen, and was married, having one child. He is described in a contemporary record as 'a great Sportsman and much given up to amorous Dalliances, as reported, so as to occasion great Uneasinesses at Home.' [80] His son Alexander was party to a deed in 1785, the object apparently being to break the entail ; the son, however, died during his father's lifetime.[81] In 1806 Small sold the manor to Roger Radcliffe and William Greaves.[82] By a deed of 1815 it was assigned to the latter,[83] in whose family it has since remained, Mr. Thomas Greaves being now lord of the manor.

The capital messuage of the manor is mentioned in 1273 as being worth, with dovecote, grange, garden and vineyard, 30s. per annum.[84] In 1304 the lord of the manor received licence to crenellate his dwelling-place of Haversham.[85] Part of the dower assigned to Hawise widow of William de la Plaunche in

GREAVES. *Quarterly gules and vert an eagle holding in his beak a slip of oak all or.*

1335 included part of the manor-house—namely, the great chamber with the chapel at the head of it beyond the door of the hall, the maids' chamber with the gallery (*oriola*) leading from the hall to the great chamber, the said door into the hall to be shut at the will of Hawise ; also the painted chamber next the great chamber, with a wardrobe ; a dairy-house with the space between the dairy and the door into the great kitchen, which door could be shut at Hawise's pleasure ; the new stable with the house called the cart-house, a grange called the Kulnhouse, a third part of the dovecote, &c.[86]

A mill was among the appurtenances of the manor in 1086, when it was worth 8s. and seventy-five eels.[87] The water-mill was held with the manor, and is mentioned in many of the deeds and inquisitions relating to that property. Rentals of the manor in the 15th century show that Haversham Mill was then invariably worth 66s. 8d. per annum to the lord.[88] At this time there was also a second water-mill in the parish, called Helwall Mill or the New Mill, where the Prior of Bradwell had a fishery.[89] In 1619 two water grist-mills existed here,[90] but only one is mentioned in 1764.[91]

In 1273 the lord of the manor had a fishery worth 8s.[92] A free fishery in the Ouse belonged to the manor in 1278-9 [93] and so continued, as late as the 17th century.[94]

[57] Chan. Inq. p.m. (Ser. 2), ccxciii, 75 ;
[58] Ibid. ; Pat. 16 Jas. I, pt. ii, no. 13 . Recov. R. East. 17 Jas. I, m. 27 ; Chan. Inq. p.m. (Ser. 2), dccxl, 113.
[59] *Visit. of Warws.* 1682-3 (Harl. Soc.), 94.   [60] Ibid.
[61] Feet of F. Div. Co. Trin. 1653.
[62] *Visit. of Warws.* loc. cit.
[63] Inst. Bks. (P.R.O.) ; Burke, *Commoners,* iii, 100.
[64] Feet of F. Bucks. Trin. 1664 ; Add. MS. 5836, fol. 151.
[65] Add. MS. 5836, fol. 152.
[66] P.R.O. *List of Sheriffs,* 9.
[67] *Dict. Nat. Biog.*
[68] Chan. Proc. (Bridges Div.), bdle. 352, no. 18.
[69] G.E.C. *Baronetage,* iv, 60.

[70] *G.E.C. Peerage,* iv, 193.
[71] *Dict. Nat. Biog.*
[72] Ibid. ; cf. Chan. Proc. (Bridges Div.), bdle. 609, no. 108.
[73] Com. Pleas Recov. R. Mich. 9 Anne, m. 6.
[74] Close, 3 Geo. II, pt. vi, no. 9 ; Feet of F. Bucks. East. 2 Geo. II.
[75] Add. MS. 5836, fol. 152.
[76] P.C.C. 237 Brodrepp.
[76a] Ibid. 138 Pinfold ; *Musgrave's Obit.* (Harl. Soc.), iii, 387.
[77] Close, 4 Geo. III, pt. xv, no. 18 ; Recov. R. Hil. 4 Geo. III, m. 158.
[78] Add. MS. 5836, fol. 151b.
[79] Ibid.   [80] Ibid.
[81] See Clifton Reynes ; Recov. R. Trin. 25 Geo. III, m. 234.

[82] Lipscomb, *Hist. and Antiq. of Bucks.* iv, 189.
[83] Ibid. ; Sheahan, op. cit. 547.
[84] Chan. Inq. p.m. 2 Edw. I, no. 30.
[85] *Cal. Pat.* 1301-7, p. 233.
[86] Chan. Inq. p.m. 10 Edw. III (1st nos.), no. 59.
[87] *V.C.H. Bucks.* i, 253.
[88] Rentals and Surv. (Gen. Ser.), R. 78.
[89] Ibid.
[90] Recov. R. East. 17 Jas. I, m. 27.
[91] Ibid. Hil. 4 Geo. III, m. 158.
[92] Chan. Inq. p.m. 2 Edw. I, no. 30.
[93] *Hund. R.* (Rec. Com.), ii, 346. Robert al Fispond held 9 acres of land in villeinage at this date (ibid.).
[94] See manor ; Pat. 16 Jas. I, pt. ii no. 13.

4

47

A park is mentioned in 1207, when Benedict de Haversham quitclaimed to Hugh de Haversham all common of pasture for his beasts which he had or claimed in Hugh's park.[95] Nicholas de Haversham received a grant of free warren in his demesne lands here in 1233,[96] in virtue of which grant free park and warren were claimed in 1278–9.[96a] In 1309 the park is referred to as having been broken into,[97] but there appears to be no further record of it, although Sir Thomas Lucy received a grant of free warren in 1618.[98]

The estate afterwards known as the manor of BELAUNEY or BOLNEYS consisted of 90 acres in 1278–9, when it was held by Sir John de Haversham of Baldwin de Belauney (Bello Aneto), who held of the main manor.[99] From 1335 to 1342 the fourth part of a knight's fee in Haversham was held by Richard de Belauney and extended at £4 yearly.[100] In 1369 Walter de Miltecoumbe quitclaimed the fourth part of Haversham Manor to Fulk de Birmingham,[1] whose son John married Elizabeth de la Plaunche (vide supra). Elizabeth made a settlement of this manor in

8 ft. by 8 ft. 6 in. These measurements are all internal.

The west wall of the nave, in which is an original window of the latter half of the 12th century, is the only surviving fragment of a church of that period, consisting, doubtless, of a nave and chancel. Before the close of the century the existing west tower was added, and early in the succeeding century the chancel was rebuilt, eastward apparently of the former chancel, and north and south aisles were thrown out on either side of the extended nave. The south chapel seems to have been originally erected at the end of the 13th century, but it was entirely remodelled in the first half of the 14th century, when the south arcade and aisle were rebuilt, the new arcade being placed outside the line of the original south wall of the nave. Later in the same century the north arcade was also rebuilt, and about 1400 the south porch was added. In the 15th century the clearstory was constructed, the pitch of the original roof being lowered. A restoration was undertaken in 1857, and again in 1903, when the tower was thoroughly repaired. The walls are of rubble masonry and the roofs are leaded.

In the east wall of the chancel is a 14th-century window of three trefoiled ogee lights with reticulated tracery in a two-centred head. At the east end of the north wall, and probably contemporary with the late 14th-century tomb recess beneath it, is a window of two cinquefoiled lights with quatrefoil tracery within a two-centred head. At the opposite end of the wall is a window of two elliptical-headed trefoiled

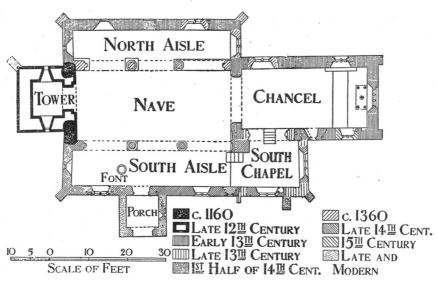

c. 1160	c. 1360
Late 12th Century	Late 14th Cent.
Early 13th Century	15th Century
Late 13th Century	Late and
1st Half of 14th Cent.	Modern

SCALE OF FEET 10 5 0 10 20 30

PLAN OF HAVERSHAM CHURCH

1389,[2] and at her death in 1423 was found to hold the manor called 'Belneys' under the name of a fourth part of Haversham Manor.[3] Under the terms of a settlement Bolneys Manor remained to John Russell, clerk, son of Sir John Russell, kt., her last husband, and his issue.[4] Robert Russell died seised of it in 1502,[5] and his son John sold it to William Lucy in 1533,[6] after which this estate doubtless became again amalgamated with the main manor.

CHURCH The church of ST. MARY consists of a chancel 32 ft. 11 in. by 15 ft. 2 in., south chapel continuous with the south aisle 11 ft. 10 in. wide, nave 40 ft. 3 in. by 17 ft. 9 in., north aisle 7 ft. 9 in. wide, south aisle 8 ft. 9 in. wide, west tower 7 ft. 9 in. by 8 ft. 5 in., and a south porch

lights with a two-centred head filled with leaf tracery; the window is of about 1360 and of the same work as the east and north-east windows of the north aisle. At the south-east is a square aumbry rebated for a door, and immediately to the west of it is a piscina with an acutely pointed chamfered head; the basin appears to have originally projected from the niche, but has been subsequently cut back flush with the wall face. The two windows in the eastern portion of the wall are insertions of the early 15th century; each is square-headed and of two lights with ogee heads, those of the eastern window being cinquefoiled, while the lights of the western window are trefoiled. Below the latter is a 14th-century doorway with a two-centred external head moulded continuously with the jambs.

[95] Hunter, Pedes Finium (Rec. Com.), 242.
[96] Cal. Chart. R. 1226–37, p. 174.
[96a] Hund. R. (Rec. Com.), ii, 350.
[97] Cal. Pat. 1307–13, p. 241.
[98] Pat. 16 Jas. I, pt. ii, no. 13.

[99] Hund. R. (Rec. Com.), ii, 346; Cat. of Anct. D. i, 9.
[100] Chan. Inq. p.m. 10 Edw. III (1st nos.), no. 59; Cal. Pat. 1340–3, p. 368.
[1] Feet of F. case 20, file 99.
[2] Ibid. case 21, file 107.
[3] Chan. Inq. p.m. 2 Hen. VI, no. 36.

[4] Ibid.; Early Chan. Proc. bdle. 16, no. 147.
[5] Chan. Inq. p.m. (Ser. 2), xvi, 107.
[6] Memo. R. (Exch. L.T.R.), Hil. 33 Hen. VIII, m. 16; the fine was not levied until 1541 (ibid.; Feet of F. Bucks. Trin. 33 Hen. VIII).

Haversham Grange

Haversham Church from the South-East

HAVERSHAM CHURCH: TOMB OF LADY

The remainder of the wall is occupied by a late 13th-century arch opening to the south chapel; the arch is two-centred and of two chamfered orders and the responds are formed of three clustered and engaged shafts with moulded capitals. The bases have been cut away, probably for fixing a parclose screen, and the capitals have also been cut into for the same purpose. The chancel arch, which was evidently rebuilt in the 14th century, is two-centred and of two chamfered orders, the outer order segmental and continuous, and the inner order dying into the plain responds. Externally the eastern angles of the chancel are finished with angle rolls, and there are dwarf buttresses, with their outside angles similarly treated, at either end of the east wall, all work of the early 13th century.

The north arcade of the nave dates from about 1360 and is of three bays with two-centred arches of two chamfered orders carried by octagonal columns with moulded capitals and bases. The inner order springs from semi-octagonal responds at either end of the arcade, the outer order being continuous. On the nave face the arches are inclosed by labels terminating in volutes over the east and west responds, and having head-stops over the columns. The south arcade is of the same number of bays, and has arches and columns of the same form, but the capitals and bases are of an earlier and more refined section, and there are no labels. The inner order is carried upon the east respond by a moulded corbel with a 'liripipe'-like termination. To the south of the chancel arch is a large late 14th-century niche with a subfoliated trefoiled head, which probably contained the painted reredos of a nave altar; immediately to the south of it, beneath the respond corbel of the south arcade, is a smaller and narrower niche with a cinquefoiled head and foiled spandrels, doubtless connected with the same purpose. High up in the west wall, above the tower arch, is the 12th-century window above referred to, a small round-headed light with wide internal splays, and a round rear-arch moulded with an angle roll and inclosing cheveron continued upon the edges of the jambs. The 15th-century clearstory windows, three on either side, are all square-headed, and each is of two cinquefoiled lights, the heads of the lights of the south-east window being square.

The east and north-east windows of the north aisle are similar to the north-west window of the chancel, and, like it, are coarse copies of the beautiful south windows of the opposite aisle and chapel. In the middle bay of the north wall, visible only externally, is a blocked early 13th-century doorway with a chamfered two-centred head springing from defaced impost mouldings and inclosed by a label. At the west end of the wall is a small lancet of the same period with an external glass rebate and a flat internal head with widely splayed jambs. In the west wall is a similar but smaller lancet. The diagonal buttresses at the eastern and western angles of the aisle are probably additions of the 14th century.

The east window of the south chapel is square-headed and of three lights; the opening may be of the 14th century, but the head and mullions are evidently late work, probably of the 17th century. The south window, which is of two trefoiled lights with leaf-tracery in a two-centred head, is valuable as an example of the very best type of 14th-century design. The grotesque stops of the external label are specially noteworthy for the delicacy of their carving. In the east jamb is an angle piscina with two ogee-headed trefoiled openings, each inclosed by a moulded label; the basin is now covered by the raised floor upon which the organ stands. The windows in the first and third bays of the continuous south aisle are of the same design, but their labels are without carved stops. Immediately to the west of the buttress which marks the junction of the aisle and chapel is a small blocked 14th-century doorway with a two-centred external head inclosed by a moulded label and moulded continuously with the jambs. The south doorway in the middle bay of the wall has a head of the same form, and is of two continuously moulded orders. In the west wall is an early 13th-century lancet with a moulded external label. The small narrow buttress at the junction of the aisle and chapel is of a different character from those at the east and west angles, and is probably contemporary with the original building of the chapel. The masonry of the walling round the south window of the chapel has been greatly disturbed, probably when the window was inserted, and a large modern buttress has been erected to the east of the window, where the wall bulges considerably.

The south porch appears to have been almost entirely rebuilt at some period with the old materials, as all the detail looks as though reset. The outer entrance has a chamfered two-centred head, and in the east wall is a small trefoiled light with a fragmentary square label above it.

The late 12th-century tower arch is two-centred and is recessed in two plain orders on the nave side. The impost mouldings from which it springs, and the label, are restored. The ground stage is lighted from the north by an original lancet; the window in the south wall now has a square head, but the opening is probably original. Externally the tower rises in three receding stages and is crowned by an embattled parapet. The intermediate stage has no windows, but the bell-chamber is lighted from each side by a window of two round-headed lights contained within an external order with an unpierced head of the same form.

The roofs are modern. The font is of the late 14th century, and has an octagonal bowl and stem with panelled sides. Fifteen 16th-century seats and two desk fronts are preserved in the nave. In the east window of the south chapel are some fragments of 15th-century glass. The pulpit, and a communion table in the south chapel, are of the 17th century.

At the north-east of the chancel is a remarkably fine alabaster tomb and recess of the late 14th century.[7] Upon the tomb, which projects slightly from the recess, is a recumbent female effigy wearing a coverchief upon the head and a pleated widow's barbe; over her dress is a sideless côte covered by a long mantle fastened across the breast by a cord from which hangs a tassel. The hands are joined in prayer, and the head rests upon a pillow held up by angels, while at her feet is a lion. The cornice of the tomb is enriched with four-leaved flowers, and the front has six panels with trefoiled heads, separated from each other by small pinnacled buttresses and having leaf-carved spandrels. The two middle panels contain

[7] It is uncertain to whose memory this tomb was erected, but it probably commemorated one of the daughters and co-heirs of William de la Plaunche, possibly Katherine wife of William de Birmingham, who died between 1372 and 1389 (see p. 368).

male 'weepers' in the civil dress of the period, while in the remaining panels on either side are angels holding blank shields. The head of the recess is formed by a large two-centred arch, continuously moulded with the jambs, and having pierced cinque-foiled cusping, each foil of which is subfoliated. The arch is inclosed by a crocketed ogee canopy, flanked by panelled and pinnacled buttresses, and rising above the sill of the window over the recess. On the south wall of the chancel is a brass, with a figure, commemorating Alice Payn (d. 1427). The inscription is as follows : 'Hic iacet Alicia Payn Nuper uxor Thome Payn | Armigeri que obiit in die Commemoracionis animarum | anno dñi m°cccc°xxvij cujus anime propicietur deus Amen.' In the chancel floor is a brass commemorating John Mansell (d. 1605–6). The brass is engraved with a skeleton lying in a coffin, and two shields, both bearing a cheveron between three maunches with a crescent for difference. The following is the inscription : 'Here resteth the body of Iohn Maunsell Gent : | who departed this life the 25th of Ianuarye | 1605 when he had lived LXVI yeeres fower | moneths and five dayes whose Christian life | and godly end god graunt us all follow.' On the north wall of the chancel is a tablet to Anne Mackerness (d. 1765), and to her husband, John Mackerness, rector of Haversham (d. 1775).

There is a ring of three bells : the treble by Anthony Chandler, 1667 ; the second, inscribed 'God Save Our King 1625 I.K.,' by James Keene ; and the tenor by the same and bearing the same

inscription, but with the date 1638. There is also a sanctus bell dated 1752.

The plate includes a cup and cover paten of 1569, a plated cup and paten and a modern flagon.

The earliest surviving volume of registers contains baptisms from 1665, marriages from 1685, and burials from 1670.

ADVOWSON A presentation to Haversham Church was made in 1221 by the lord of the manor,[8] to which the advowson remained attached until the 19th century.[9] In 1828 Alexander Small's trustees presented Henry Alexander Small,[10] who afterwards obtained the patronage, holding until about 1856. The Rev. A. B. Frazer then became both incumbent and patron, and so remained until 1889, when the Rev. B. L. Symonds obtained the living and is now the patron.

In 1309 the parson of the church complained that the lord of the manor and others had assaulted and imprisoned him, and had forbidden the inhabitants of the parish to give him tithes, fire or water, or to speak to him, and had also greatly damaged his lands, crops and cattle.[11] A later rector, in 1357, received pardon for having killed William Golde, bailiff of Newport Pagnell, in self-defence.[12]

A rent-charge for the support of a light in the church is mentioned as early as the 13th century.[13] In the 16th century it was found that land worth 3s. per annum had been given for this purpose.[14]

There do not appear to be any endowed charities subsisting in this parish.

LATHBURY

Lateberie, Latesberie (xi cent.).

This parish covers nearly 1,055 acres, including 315 acres of arable, 627 of permanent grass and 12 acres of woods and plantations.[1] The slope of the land varies from 178 ft. above the ordnance datum in the south-east of the parish to 210 ft. to the north-west of the village. The soil is gravel, the subsoil limestone, and the chief crops are wheat, barley and roots. The land in the neighbourhood of the River Ouse, which encircles this parish on all sides except the north-west, is liable to floods. Flood Dyke, about 3 ft. high, in the south-east of the parish, follows the course of the Ouse, extending from Woad Farm in a wide semicircle towards the Bedford road. A bridge, built mainly of stone, of four arches, called North Bridge,[2] connects the south end of Lathbury with the parish of Newport Pagnell. Just beyond it, within the parish boundary, is a bridge of brick, consisting of three arches. A mile to the north-east the River Ouse is crossed by Sherington Bridge, also of three arches.

The village of Lathbury occupies a central position. A road leads south-west from it past the rectory and the church to Lathbury Park, the seat of Mr. William

Trevor. The house is of stone and was built in 1801 by Mansel Dawkin Mansel on the site of that erected by Sir William Andrewes, kt., in the early 17th century,[3] and called the Place in 1735.[4] Quarry Hall, in the south-west of the parish, derives its name from an old quarry ; there is a farm of the same name a quarter of a mile to the north-east. Gallard Farm is situated in the north of the parish. The old inn, a large and well-built building, is now used as a farm-house, with nearly 400 acres of land attached.[4a]

James Chelsum, an opponent of Gibbon, was vicar of Lathbury at the end of the 18th century.[5]

The following place-names occur : Ernesden Wood, belonging to Lavendon Abbey[6] (xiii cent.) ; Windmill Post[7] (xvi cent.) ; an inn called the 'Hart's Head'[7a] (xvii cent.) ; Beggars or Hospitalholme[8] (xviii cent.).

MANORS Four hides of land in *LATHBURY* which had been held as two manors before the Conquest by two thegns, Leuric and Olviet, were held as one manor in 1086 by Hugh de Beauchamp.[9] It was attached by the service of half a fee to the barony of Bedford.[10] After the subdivision of that barony in 1265[11] the over-

[8] R. of Hugh of Wells (Cant. and York Soc.), ii, 58–9.
[9] See also Inst. Bks. (P.R.O.) ; Cal. Pat. 1350–4, p. 23 ; Chan. Inq. p.m. 46 Edw. III (1st nos.), no. 18 ; Cal. Close, 1369–74, p. 406 ; Cat. of Anct. D. iv, 446 ; Feet of F. Div. Co. Mich. 9 Geo. I. [10] Lipscomb, op. cit. iv, 192.
[11] Cal. Pat. 1307–13, p. 132.
[12] Ibid. 1354–8, p. 649.
[13] Hund. R. (Rec. Com.), ii, 346.

[14] Chant. Cert. 5, no. 25.
[1] Statistics from Bd. of Agric. (1905).
[2] It was repaired in 1809 at the cost of the inhabitants of Newport Pagnell (Local and Pers. Act, 49 Geo. III, cap. 144).
[3] Lysons, Mag. Brit. i (3), 592. About thirty skeletons were found in digging the foundations. Roman coins have been picked up in the garden.
[4] P.C.C. 137 Anstis.

[4a] F.C.M.B. Some Account of Lathbury, 7. [5] Dict. Nat. Biog.
[6] Dugdale, Mon. vi, 889.
[7] L. and P. Hen. VIII, xix (2), g. 340 (59). [7a] Deeds penes Mr. F. W. Bull.
[8] P.C.C. 137 Anstis ; Com. Pleas Recov. R. Trin. 31 & 32 Geo. II, m. 3.
[9] V.C.H. Bucks. i, 264.
[10] Feet of F. Bucks. Mich. 13 Hen. III, no. 2 ; Testa de Nevill (Rec. Com.), 249b.
[11] V.C.H. Beds. iii, 12.

lordship passed with that portion which descended to the Mowbrays and Brays,[12] and is last mentioned in 1626.[13]

A mesne lordship of this manor was held in 1223 and 1229[14] by Mabel de Bidun, one of the five

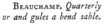

BEAUCHAMP. *Quarterly or and gules a bend sable.*

MOWBRAY. *Gules a lion argent.*

sisters and co-heirs of John de Bidun.[15] Her heir Miles de Beauchamp was living in 1254,[16] and was succeeded about ten years later by his son Richard,[17] mesne lord in the later 13th century.[18] In 1310 this lordship was vested in William Jukel in right of his wife Cecily,[19] apparently one of the daughters and co-heirs of Richard de Beauchamp.[20] William Jukel was still holding in 1317,[21] but his rights in Lathbury had passed before 1324 to Richard Grosset[22] and do not reappear.

William d'Orenge was tenant of the Beauchamp manor of Lathbury in 1086.[23] Ralph d'Orenge and his son and heir William[24] were successive holders in the next century, the latter probably the same William d'Orenge who was holding of Simon de Beauchamp in 1166.[25] Through the marriage of William's daughter Mabel with Simon de Houghton[26] (Hocton) Northamptonshire, who was living in 1199,[27] the Orenge lands in Lathbury came to William de Houghton.[28] He married Isabel daughter and heir of Robert Daubeny of Cainhoe (Bedfordshire),[29] and died about 1235.[30] His widow in 1236 obtained the custody of his lands and heir from John Earl of Chester, to whom it had been previously granted.[31] She held Lathbury[32] for her son William, who, taking the name of Daubeny, attained his majority before his mother's death in 1262[33] and died seised of Lathbury Manor about 1264.[34] His son and heir Simon died

without issue in 1272, leaving as heirs his sisters Isabel, Christine and Joan.[35] Isabel married Hugh de St. Croix; Christine, Peter de la Stane; and Joan, Roger Dakeney.[36] In 1286, after the death of Ellen, widow of William Daubeny,[37] who held Lathbury Manor in dower, the elder co-heirs with their husbands surrendered it with some trifling reservations to Roger and Joan Dakeney.[38] Roger died in 1286,[39] and in the following year Joan's right by inheritance in his lands was acknowledged.[40] Joan survived another husband, Aumary de Nowers, and died in 1310, when her son Robert Dakeney succeeded.[41] On his death in 1316 the custody of his son Roger with two-thirds of Lathbury Manor was granted to Richard de Cave, and the remaining third of the manor was assigned to the widow, Joan Dakeney.[42] Roger Dakeney proved his age in 1324,[43] and continued holding in Lathbury[44] until 1355, when he and his wife Joan surrendered their rights there to Hugh de Sadelyngstanes.[45] He settled Lathbury Manor in 1357 on his wife Isabel and his heirs,[46] and was living in 1361.[47] Before 1409 it had come into the possession of Sir William Thirning, who settled it in that year with Stantonbury Manor on John Fever and other trustees.[48] Sir William Thirning died in 1413[49] and Lady Thirning was holding Lathbury in 1433,[50] but the manor evidently reverted to the Vaux family and descended with Stantonbury[51] (q.v.) until 1535. Thomas Lord Vaux appears to have sold Lathbury Manor in this year to Henry Earl of Essex.[52] His daughter and heir Anne married William Parr, Queen Katherine's brother, who was created Earl of Essex in 1543.[53] He sold Lathbury Manor to Anthony Cave of Chicheley, who died seised in 1558.[54] One moiety of this manor was allotted to his daughter Anne, the other to his daughter Martha, who married John Newdigate.[55] Martha Newdigate died in 1575, and on the death of her husband in 1592 her moiety passed to their son John.[56] He and his wife Anne at once conveyed it to John and Henry Jackman[57] preliminary to its purchase by William Andrews,[58] who was knighted in 1604,[59] and appointed sheriff of the county in 1607.[60] He died seised in 1625, and was succeeded by his son William,[61] who had been knighted in 1618.[62] In 1650 he settled the Lathbury estate in favour of his son

[12] *Hund. R.* (Rec. Com.), ii, 347; *Feud. Aids,* i, 73; Chan. Inq. p.m. 11 Hen. VI, no. 43; 1 Edw. IV, no. 46; (Ser. 2), cxx, 5; ccxxxii, 15; dcxlvi, 19.
[13] Chan. Inq. p.m. (Ser. 2), ccccxxx, 174.
[14] Maitland, *Bracton's Note Bk.* iii, 479; Feet of F. Bucks. Mich. 13 Hen. III, no. 2.
[15] Chan. Inq. p.m. Hen. III, file 16, no. 18.
[16] Ibid.
[17] Ibid. file 36, no. 10.
[18] *Hund. R.* (Rec. Com.), ii, 347; *Feud. Aids,* i, 73; Chan. Inq. p.m. Edw. I, file 46, no. 7.
[19] Chan. Inq. p.m. Edw. II, file 19, no. 16.
[20] Ibid. file 23, no. 18.
[21] Ibid. file 52, no. 1.
[22] Inq. a.q.d. file 163, no. 4.
[23] *V.C.H. Bucks.* i, 264.
[24] They made small grants of land in Lathbury to Tickford Priory (*Cat. of Anct. D.* i, 7), which was probably founded in the early 12th century (*V.C.H. Bucks.* i, 361).
[25] *Red Bk. of Exch.* (Rolls Ser.), 320.

[26] *Cat. of Anct. D.* i, 7.
[27] *Feet of F.* 10 Ric. I (Pipe R. Soc.), 178; *Rot. Cur. Reg.* (Rec. Com.), i, 233.
[28] *Cal. Pat.* 1216–25, p. 395; 1225–32, p. 306; Feet of F. Bucks. Mich. 13 Hen. III, no. 2.
[29] *V.C.H. Beds.* ii, 321.
[30] *Excerpta e Rot. Fin.* (Rec. Com.), i, 259; *Cal. Close,* 1234–7, p. 91.
[31] *Cal. Close,* 1234–7, pp. 213, 327, 358.
[32] *Testa de Nevill* (Rec. Com.), 249b; Feet of F. Bucks. Hil. 25 Hen. III, no. 18.
[33] Chan. Inq. p.m. Hen. III, file 28, no. 1.
[34] *Cal. Inq. p.m.* (Rec. Com.), i, 27. This inquisition was missing in 1806.
[35] Chan. Inq. p.m. Edw. I, file 2, no. 1.
[36] Harl. Chart. 56 E. 9.
[37] Chan. Inq. p.m. Edw. I, file 2, no. 1.
[38] Harl. Chart. 56 E. 9.
[39] Chan. Inq. p.m. Edw. I, file 46, no. 7.
[40] *Cal. Close,* 1279–88, p. 442.
[41] Chan. Inq. p.m. Edw. II, file 19, no. 16; see also *Feud. Aids,* i, 110.

[42] Chan. Inq. p.m. Edw. II, file 52, no. 1; *Cal. Fine R.* 1307–19, p. 294.
[43] *Cal. Close,* 1323–7, p. 231.
[44] *Cal. Pat.* 1324–7, p. 229.
[45] Feet of F. Bucks. Trin. 29 Edw. III, no. 6. [46] Ibid. Hil. 30 Edw. III, no. 1.
[47] *Cal. Pat.* 1361–4, p. 69.
[48] Feet of F. Bucks. Mich. 10 Hen. IV, no. 9.
[49] Gibbons, *Early Linc. Wills,* 140.
[50] Chan. Inq. p.m. 11 Hen. VI, no. 43.
[51] Ibid. 1 Edw. IV, no. 46; De Banco R. 916, m. 102, 103. See under Stantonbury.
[52] Recov. R. East. 27 Hen. VIII, m. 100.
[53] G.E.C. *Complete Peerage,* vi, 69.
[54] Chan. Inq. p.m. (Ser. 2), cxx, 5.
[55] Ibid. ccxlviii, 39.
[56] Ibid. ccxxxii, 15; cf. Add. Chart. 59355.
[57] Feet of F. Bucks. Trin. 34 Eliz.
[58] Close, 34 Eliz. pt. xii.
[59] *Visit. of Bucks.* (Harl. Soc.), 3.
[60] P.R.O. *List of Sheriffs,* 9.
[61] Chan. Inq. p.m. (Ser. 2), ccccxxx, 174.
[62] Shaw, *Knts. of Engl.* ii, 168.

Henry on his marriage with Elizabeth daughter of John Brown of Shingleton, Great Chart, Kent.[63] Henry also acquired the greater part of the other moiety, the Hampdens' interest,[64] shortly before his father's death in 1657.[65] Henry Andrews, who was created a baronet in 1661,[66] made a settlement of the Andrews' moiety of this manor in 1662,[67] and acquired property in 1695 from Brereton Bourchier and others.[68] On the death of Sir Henry Andrews in 1696 the baronetcy became extinct, but his nephew Henry Andrews [69] succeeded to Lathbury Manor.[70] He was

ANDREWS of Lathbury, baronet. *Argent a bend cotised sable with three molets argent on the bend.*

sheriff of the county in 1705[71] and died in 1744.[72] By his will Lathbury Manor passed to his eldest daughter, Elizabeth Uthwatt, for life.[73] In 1753 she gave it to her son Henry for life,[74] and after his death in 1757 [75] she and her sister Jane Symes settled the reversion after their deaths on Jane daughter of Jane Symes.[76] After the death of Elizabeth Uthwatt, in 1764,[76a] a further settlement was made in 1769.[77] Jane Symes, widow, died in 1778, and the younger Jane Symes died unmarried at Lathbury in 1799,[78] leaving the manor to her cousin Margaret Dalway and her friend Mansel Dawkin Mansel for life in survivorship, with a life estate on their death to Elizabeth Brown in the event of her marrying Mansel.[79] The effect of a codicil to the will was to divide the residue in favour of the principal legatees and their heirs.[80] Mansel Dawkin Mansel, who was Sheriff of Buckinghamshire in 1800,[81] married Elizabeth Brown,[82] and they with Margaret Dalway made a settlement in respect of Lathbury Manor in 1801.[83] He retained the principal estate and built a new residence on the site of the old one, dying there in 1823.[84] His widow, surviving him only a fortnight, was also buried at Lathbury.[85] Their sons sold the Lathbury estate to Richard John Tibbits of Barton Seagrave, Northamptonshire, whose daughter and heir Mary Isabella married Samuel third Viscount Hood.[86] He died in 1846, his widow surviving until 1904.[87] Their son, the fourth viscount, imme-

diately sold the manor and a great part of the estate to Mr. Joseph Evans Whiting, the present owner. Lathbury Park with the manor-house was at the same time acquired by Mr. William Trevor.[87a]

Margaret Dalway's moiety of the manor does not reappear after the early 19th century.[88] It is possibly represented in part by Major Long's estate in Lathbury, which has been in his family since 1862 and earlier.[89]

The moiety of Lathbury Manor inherited by Anne Cave in 1558 passed by her marriage to Griffith Hampden.[90] After his death in 1591 [91] she gave it to their son William,[92] and it descended with Great Hampden Manor to his grandson Richard Hampden,[93] who was owner in 1653.[94] Three years later he sold the greater part of this estate to Richard son and heir of John Brown, who in the following year transferred most of the property to his brother-in-law Henry Andrews, owner of the other moiety. In 1664 a further settlement of the estates was made between Sir Henry Andrews and his niece Elizabeth, daughter and heir of Richard Brown, by which an arrangement of 1622 between Sir William Andrews and John Hampden (the patriot) was superseded. In 1677 a settlement of Elizabeth's portion was made on her marriage with Thomas Leigh, Lord Leigh of Stoneleigh, but there is no later reference to this small estate.[95]

A court leet and view of frankpledge were among the manorial liberties in the 18th century,[96] and references to free fishery in the Ouse occur in the 17th and 18th centuries.[97] A several fishery in this river is also mentioned in 1697 [98] and the rights of free warren and toll of the New Bridge in 1758.[99]

A second manor called *LATHBURY MANOR* was held before the Conquest by Edduin, son of Borret, one of King Edward's thegns.[100] In 1086 it was assessed at 5 hides and held by the Bishop of Coutances.[1] The overlordship rights evidently passed later with those of Weston Underwood (q.v.) to the Brewers, and were divided with them in 1233 between the Wakes and Fertes.[2] The Wake interest in a quarter of a fee in Lathbury [3] passed after 1349 to the earldom of Kent,[4] and is last mentioned as held in dower by Joan widow of Thomas Earl of Kent at her death in 1442.[5] The overlordship of the other quarter fee was attached to the honour of Chaworth,[6]

[63] Deed *penes* Mr. F. W. Bull ; Recov. R. East. 1650, m. 50.
[64] Deed *penes* Mr. F. W. Bull.
[65] Add. MS. 5839, fol. 107b.
[66] G.E.C. *Baronetage*, iii, 203.
[67] Feet of F. Bucks. Hil. 14 & 15 Chas. II. [68] Ibid. Mich. 7 Will. III.
[69] G.E.C. loc. cit.
[70] Feet of F. Bucks. East. 9 Will. III ; Recov. R. East. 9 Will. III, m. 192.
[71] P.R.O. *List of Sheriffs*, 10.
[72] G.E.C. loc. cit.
[73] P.C.C. 137 Anstis.
[74] Com. Pleas Recov. R. Hil. 26 Geo. II, m. 2.
[75] M.I. in Lathbury Church. See also under Great Linford.
[76] Com. Pleas Recov. R. Trin. 31 & 32 Geo. II, m. 3. The younger Jane Symes was fourth in the remainders given in her grandfather's will (P.C.C. 137 Anstis).
[76a] P.C.C. 158 Simpson.
[77] Com. Pleas Recov. R. Hil. 9 Geo. III, m. 186.

[78] *Gent. Mag.* lxix, 440.
[79] P.C.C. 685 Howe. Printed in Lipscomb, *Hist. and Antiq. of Bucks.* iv, 199 et seq.
[80] Ibid.
[81] P.R.O. *List of Sheriffs*, 11.
[82] Lipscomb, op. cit. iv, 200.
[83] Feet of F. Bucks. Mich. 41 Geo. III.
[84] Lipscomb, op. cit. iv, 200.
[85] Ibid. 201.
[86] G.E.C. *Peerage*, iv, 254. Information kindly supplied by Mr. F. W. Bull.
[87] Sheahan, *Hist. and Topog. of Bucks.* 551 ; *Ret. of Owners of Land*, 1873, *Bucks.* 11 ; Burke, *Peerage*, 1912.
[87a] Information kindly supplied by Mr. F. W. Bull.
[88] Lysons, op. cit. i (3), 592.
[89] Sheahan, loc. cit.; *Ret. of Owners of Land*, 1873, *Bucks.* 13.
[90] Chan. Proc. Eliz. Pp 6, no. 34.
[91] Chan. Inq. p.m. (Ser. 2), ccxxxii, 67.
[92] Ibid. (Ser. 2), ccxlviii, 39.
[93] *V.C.H. Bucks.* ii, 288, 289.
[94] Recov. R. Mich. 1653, m. 141.

[95] Deeds *penes* Mr. F. W. Bull.
[96] Com. Pleas Recov. R. Hil. 26 Geo. II, m. 2.
[97] Recov. R. East. 1650, m. 50 ; East. 9 Will. III, m. 192 ; Com. Pleas Recov. R. Hil. 26 Geo. II, m. 2.
[98] Feet of F. Bucks. East. 9 Will. III.
[99] Com. Pleas Recov. R. Trin. 31 & 32 Geo. II, m. 3. The bridge was described in 1735 as newly erected on Cook's Close (P.C.C. 137 Anstis).
[100] *V.C.H. Bucks.* i, 240. [1] Ibid.
[2] *Cal. Close*, 1231-4, p. 229.
[3] It was included under two fees chiefly in Northamptonshire and appurtenant to the manor of Bourne in Lincolnshire (Chan. Inq. p.m. Edw. I, file 31, no. 3); cf. *Hund. R.* (Rec. Com.), ii, 347 ; *Feud. Aids*, i, 73.
[4] G.E.C. *Complete Peerage*, iv, 351 ; Chan. Inq. p.m. 26 Edw. III, no. 54 ; *Cal. Close*, 1349-54, p. 553.
[5] Chan. Inq. p.m. 21 Hen. VI, no. 36.
[6] *Testa de Nevill* (Rec. Com.), 244b, 251b.

last mentioned in connexion with Lathbury in the early 14th century.[7] Kempsford, in Gloucestershire, the *caput* of the English barony of Patrick de Chaworth,[8] had by this time come through the marriage in 1298 of Maud or Joan, daughter and heir of his younger son Patrick de Chaworth,[9] to Henry third Earl of Lancaster.[10]

The Bishop of Coutances had subinfeudated his manor in Lathbury before 1086 to William[11] (de Bidun), who was also his tenant in Lavendon, the *caput* of the Bidun holdings in Buckinghamshire.

CHAWORTH. *Burelly argent and gules an orle of martlets sable.*

This manor descended with Lavendon Castle (q.v.) to John de Bidun,[12] and had been allotted before 1225 to one of his five sisters and co-heirs, Ermengarde de Bidun,[13] widow of Andulf de Gatesden.[14] It is represented by the half fee in Lathbury which she was holding in 1235[15] and 1236.[16] In 1241 she subinfeudated part of this land to her younger son Richard, and the remainder, comprising the manorial rights, had passed before 1254 to John son of her elder son John de Gatesden.[17] He conveyed it to his relative Walter de Gatesden,[18] apparently with the advowson in 1269.[19] In this year Walter de Gatesden transferred both to Robert Burnel,[20] who also had a quittance from John de Gatesden.[21] Three years later Burnel bestowed the manor and advowson in free alms upon Lavendon Abbey.[22] Lathbury was retained by the abbey,[23] which, after prolonged lawsuits between 1310 and 1318 with Richard Chamberlain and his wife Joan, daughter and heir of John de Gatesden,[24] and afterwards with their son John Chamberlain, finally secured a verdict against the latter in 1321.[25] Several small properties in Lathbury were acquired by Lavendon Abbey during the 14th century,[26] and it owned a considerable estate there in 1535.[27]

After the Dissolution the manor was leased in 1539 to Thomas Lawe of Olney,[28] and the capital messuage called the Parsonage House or Place was granted to him in fee in 1543.[29] He alienated it, retaining leasehold rights, to Edward Ardes,[30] who transferred it in 1545 to Anthony Cave.[31] He purchased the Lawe interests from Hugh and Thomas Lawe, and died in 1558 seised of all their property in Lathbury which had formerly belonged to Lavendon Abbey.[32] It was divided between his daughters Anne and Martha with the other Lathbury Manor, and part of Martha's share is distinguishable from her moiety of that manor until 1626.[33]

The land which Ermengarde de Bidun granted to her younger son Richard[34] in 1241 was rather less than a carucate of land,[35] equivalent to the quarter fee of the honour of Chaworth which he was holding in Lathbury about this time.[36] John Prude is named as an under-tenant to Richard de Gatesden in 1279,[37] and a Richard de Gatesden held in 1302 the quarter fee which lay partly in Upper Filgrave.[38] Before 1346 it had passed into the hands of the two manorial lords in Lathbury, Roger Dakeney and the Abbot of Lavendon,[39] and does not reappear.

Fishery rights in Lathbury belonged to the manor in 1269,[40] and a dovecote is mentioned in 1291.[41]

A close and pasture called Monwood in Lathbury had been granted by Richard de Beauchamp to Lavendon Abbey before 1227.[42] It seems to be in respect of this land that the abbey owed service to the Dukes of Norfolk, paying a quit-rent of 20*d.* yearly in 1535.[43] Monwood was purchased in 1580 from John Newdigate by Christopher Cotes of Hanslope, who died seised in 1612, leaving a son and heir Henry.[43a]

Lands in Lathbury belonged in 1502 to Edmund Denny,[44] at whose death, in 1520, they passed to Thomas his son.[44a] In 1544 Anthony, younger brother of Thomas Denny, obtained leave to sell this property called *LATHBURY MANOR*, with other lands of the inheritance of John son and heir of Thomas Denny.[45] William Andrews, the next owner recorded, in 1596 sold the estate known as Dennys Lands to Daniel Cage of Layston, Hertfordshire.[45a]

Another manor in Lathbury called *STOCKING MANOR* appears to correspond to a quarter fee held in 1166 by Jordan de Lathbury of the barony of Hanslope.[46] Overlordship rights in Stocking descended

[7] *Feud. Aids*, i, 105.

[8] Chan. Inq. p.m. Hen. III, file 21, no. 12; *Feud. Aids*, ii, 237.

[9] Chan. Inq. p.m. Hen. III, file 21, no. 12; Edw. I, file 22, no. 5; file 35, no. 4; *Cal. Fine R.* 1272–1307, pp. 117, 191, 232.

[10] G.E.C. *Complete Peerage*, v, 6; *Cal. Close*, 1296–1302, p. 274; *Feud. Aids*, ii, 247. [11] *V.C.H. Bucks.* i, 240.

[12] His mother, widow of his father John de Bidun, was holding Lathbury in dower in 1185. One of her five daughters, Maud Visdelou, held 2 hides of land here in dower at this time (Grimaldi, *Rot. de Dominabus*, 22).

[13] Chan. Inq. p.m. Hen. III, file 16, no. 18.

[14] *Cal. Pat.* 1216–25, p. 586. See also Feet of F. Bucks. Mich. 12 Hen. III, no. 31. Andulf held in his wife's right in 1201 (*Rot. de Oblatis et Fin.* [Rec. Com.], 149).

[15] *Testa de Nevill* (Rec. Com.), 262.

[16] Ibid. 259.

[17] Chan. Inq. p.m. Hen. III, file 16, no. 18; De Banco R. 225, m. 99 d.

[18] De Banco R. 240, m. 99 d. See also Feet of F. Bucks. Hil. 25 Hen. III, no. 18.

[19] Feet of F. Bucks. Mich. 53 Hen. III, no. 9.

[20] Ibid. case 16, file 40, no. 1.

[21] De Banco R. 225, m. 99 d.

[22] Feet of F. case 16, file 41, no. 8. Ermengarde de Bidun had granted Bruneswood in Lathbury to Lavendon Abbey before 1227 (Dugdale, op. cit. vi, 889).

[23] *Hund. R.* (Rec. Com.), ii, 347; *Feud. Aids*, i, 73, 110.

[24] De Banco R. 183, m. 9; 184, m. 25; 188, m. 223; 192, m. 10; 195a, m. 289; 201, m. 69; 211, m. 76 d.; 214, m. 52; 216, m. 158 d.; 225, m. 99 d. The last two references are the most important.

[25] Ibid. 230, m. 116 d.; 238, m. 149 d.; 240, m. 99 d.

[26] Inq. a.q.d. files 65, no. 14; 189, no. 1; 272, no. 12; *Cal. Pat.* 1343–5, p. 333; 1364–7, p. 420; *Abbrev. Rot. Orig.* (Rec. Com.), ii, 295.

[27] *Valor Eccl.* (Rec. Com.), iv, 241.

[28] *L. and P. Hen. VIII*, xiv (1), p. 605.

[29] Ibid. xviii (1), g. 981 (41).

[30] Ibid. xx (2), g. 707 (52).

[31] Ibid.

[32] Chan. Inq. p.m. (Ser. 2), cxx, 5.

[33] Ibid. ccxxxii, 15; ccccxxx, 174.

[34] Ibid. Hen. III, file 16, no. 18.

[35] Feet of F. Bucks. Hil. 25 Hen. III, no. 18.

[36] *Testa de Nevill* (Rec. Com.), 251b.

[37] *Hund. R.* (Rec. Com.), ii, 347.

[38] *Feud. Aids*, i, 105.

[39] Ibid. 131.

[40] Feet of F. case 16, file 40, no. 1.

[41] *Pope Nich. Tax.* (Rec. Com.), 48.

[42] Dugdale, op. cit. vi, 889.

[43] Chan. Inq. p.m. 11 Hen. VI, no. 43; *Valor Eccl.* (Rec. Com.), iv, 242.

[43a] Chan. Inq. p.m. (Ser. 2), dcxlvi, 19.

[44] Deeds *penes* Mr. F. W. Bull.

[44a] Chan. Inq. p.m. (Ser. 2), xxxv, 49.

[45] *L. and P. Hen. VIII*, xix (1), 25 (cap. xxiii); *V.C.H. Beds.* iii, 302.

[45a] Deed *penes* Mr. F. W. Bull.

[46] *Red Bk. of Exch.* (Rolls Ser.), 314.

with the principal manor of Lathbury in the 13th and 14th centuries.[47]

Jordan, lord of Stocking, possibly a son of the Jordan de Lathbury mentioned above, was succeeded by John Passelewe,[48] who was holding jointly with his wife Mabel (presumably Jordan's daughter) in her right in 1245, when they acknowledged Ralph Dayrell's right to a carucate in Stocking and Lathbury and to the reversion of the land which Geoffrey de Easton Neston (Northants) and his wife Eustacia were holding of the latter's dower.[49] Ralph Dayrell allowed the Passelewes to retain their holding for life,[50] and in 1247, complaining of waste on the land held by Geoffrey and Eustacia, secured a quitclaim from them for an annuity of 40s. yearly during the latter's life.[51] By 1254 the whole of his interest in Stocking had passed to two heiresses, Sybil and Alice, and their respective husbands William de Merefeld and Peter de Grendon, who quitclaimed it (in subinfeudation which does not reappear) to Robert de Usburn, then holding a lease from Robert de Tothall and Mabel de Stocking (Passelewe).[52] Usburn obtained a licence to impark his wood at Stocking within Salcey Forest in 1257,[53] and evidently married Margery daughter of John de Stocking (John Passelewe). She was holding in 1262,[54] having secured the custody of their son Edmund de Usburn[55] or Stocking, and is the lady of Stocking mentioned in 1275.[56] Edmund was holding in 1279[57] and 1286,[58] but had been succeeded by John de Usburn before 1309, when John settled the property on himself, his wife Alice and their heirs.[59] This estate is apparently identical with that held by John de Stocking in 1355,[60] when it is evident that the disintegration of the former manor of Stocking was nearly complete in the gradual absorption of its sub-tenancies by the owners of Lathbury Manor.

The tenant of one of these small holdings in Stocking in the earlier half of the 13th century was Roger de Stocking,[61] and in 1245 the custody of his land and heir was retained by Ralph Dayrell.[62] His holding appears to be that in which Simon de Stocking and his wife Agnes had a life interest in 1355, when the reversion was transferred with the principal manor of Lathbury to Hugh de Sadelyngstanes.

In 1262 Margery de Stocking quitclaimed a messuage, meadow and 50 acres of land in Lathbury to Adam Franklin,[63] and his holding is mentioned in 1279[64] and 1286.[65] A descendant of his, John Franklin, was a tenant in Lathbury in 1355.[66] A small property there was given in marriage by Nicholas Franklin with his daughter Muriel to John de Usburn,[67] to whom in 1339 Thomas de Beauchamp subinfeudated a carucate of land.[67a] Their son Thomas de Usburn quit claimed the former estate in 1366 to Henry Harlwin of Lathbury, chaplain.[68]

Bunsty, a detached part of Lathbury, which was transferred in 1886 to the parish of Gayhurst (q.v.), is in part identical with the hide of land which Siric, a man of Earl Leofwin, held and could sell before the Conquest.[69] Siric's lands, here and in Gayhurst, were obtained by the Bishop of Bayeux. His tenant in both places in 1086 was the Bishop of Lisieux,[70] and William de Nowers, the descendant of Robert de Nowers, the sub-tenant of the Bishop of Lisieux in Gayhurst (q.v.), was holding one-sixth of a fee in Lathbury as mesne lord in 1279.[71]

The lords of the principal manor of Lathbury were tenants under the Nowers before 1230, when William de Houghton was allowed to impark his wood at Bunsty.[72] Joan (Dakeney) was holding this park with the right of free warren in 1275[73] as one of the heirs of William Daubeny.[74] This part of Lathbury appears to have been surrendered to the mesne lord before the middle of the 14th century,[75] and corresponds to the land there which has since descended with Gayhurst Manor[76] (q.v.).

CHURCH The church of *ALL SAINTS* consists of a chancel measuring internally 30 ft. by 15 ft. 6 in., nave 35 ft. 6 in. by 14 ft. 8 in., north aisle 10 ft. 8 in. wide, south aisle 11 ft. 4 in. wide, west tower 9 ft. 8 in. square, and south porch. It is built of rubble, with stone dressings, and the roofs are covered with lead.

The church dates from the early 12th century, and originally consisted of a small chancel and the present nave, to which a south aisle was added about 1180–90. The tower was erected in the early part of the 13th century and the south aisle was rebuilt about 1280, while the north aisle was added and the chancel rebuilt during the first half of the 14th century. The clearstory was added to the nave, and the nave, aisles and tower were provided with embattled parapets early in the 15th century. The porch is modern, and the whole fabric was restored in 1869.

The chancel is lighted by a large four-light east window, only the jambs of which are old, and by two 14th-century windows on either side, each of two trefoiled lights with tracery in a pointed head. The

[47] *Hund. R.* (Rec. Com.), ii, 347 ; Feet of F. Bucks. Trin. 29 Edw. III, no. 6. Their share in the service of tenants there was excepted from the grant of Lathbury Manor by the other co-heirs to Roger and Joan Dakeney in 1286 (Harl. Chart. 56 E. 9), but this was evidently only a temporary arrangement. William de Nowers (see under Bunsty) arraigned an assize against William de Houghton in respect of a holding in Stocking in 1223 (*Cal. Pat.* 1216–25, p. 395).

[48] Assize R. 68, m. 26. Jordan gave Walter Baych, parson of Lathbury, a virgate of land and some meadow in return for acting as chantry priest three times weekly in his chapel at Stocking, which Baych continued to do while John Passelewe was lord. The chantry was afterwards disallowed by the bishop and the land given up by Richard de Gatesden, then parson, to Robert de Usburn. It was claimed

without success in 1285–6 by Robert de Harlegh as part of his parsonage.

[49] Feet of F. Bucks. Trin. 29 Hen. III, no. 1.

[50] Ibid.

[51] Ibid. Trin. 31 Hen. III, no. 1.

[52] Ibid. Trin. 38 Hen. III, no. 8. Robert de Usburn undertook the annual payment to Eustacia, then widow of Geoffrey de Easton Neston.

[53] *Cal. Pat.* 1247–58, p. 536.

[54] Feet of F. Bucks. East. 46 Hen. III, no. 32.

[55] Assize R. 68, m. 26.

[56] *Hund. R.* (Rec. Com.), i, 38.

[57] Ibid. ii, 347.

[58] Harl. Chart. 56 E. 9 ; see also Assize R. 68, m. 26.

[59] Feet of F. case 18, file 61, no. 21.

[60] Ibid. Bucks. Trin. 29 Edw. III, no. 6. Simon de Usburn is also mentioned as holding two messuages and 12 acres of land for life.

[61] Feet of F. Bucks. Hil. 25 Hen. III, no. 18.

[62] Ibid. Trin. 29 Hen. III, no. 1.

[63] Ibid. East. 46 Hen. III, no. 32.

[64] *Hund. R.* (Rec. Com.), ii, 347.

[65] Harl. Chart. 56 E. 9.

[66] Feet of F. Bucks. Trin. 29 Edw. III, no. 6. There are many references to the Franklin family for the 14th and 15th centuries in Add. Chart. and Mr. Bull's deeds.

[67] Add. Chart. 8124, 59288.

[67a] Add. MS. 28024, fol. 32 d.

[68] Add. Chart. 8124, 59286.

[69] *V.C.H. Bucks.* i, 207 n., 239.

[70] Ibid. 239.

[71] *Hund. R.* (Rec. Com.), ii, 347.

[72] *Cal. Chart. R.* 1226–57, p. 117.

[73] *Hund. R.* (Rec. Com.), i, 38, 45.

[74] Ibid. ii, 347.

[75] *Cal. Close*, 1354–60, p. 408.

[76] Leadam, *Dom. Incl.* 1517 (Royal Hist. Soc.), 196 ; see under Gayhurst Manor.

LATHBURY CHURCH FROM THE SOUTH-EAST

LATHBURY CHURCH : THE INTERIOR LOOKING EAST

tracery of the south-east window is composed of a circle with running trefoils, and below the sill of this window are three sedilia with trefoiled ogee heads and a double piscina with heads of the same form and quatrefoil bowls. At the west end of the north wall is a low blocked opening with a modern lintel, and opposite to it on the south are a window and a low pointed doorway, both of which are also blocked. The chancel arch is of the 14th century, and has semi-octagonal responds with moulded capitals and plain bases; the north respond and both bases have been restored.

The nave opens to the north aisle by a lofty arcade of the early 14th century, consisting of two acutely pointed arches supported by an octagonal pillar and responds, with moulded capitals and restored moulded bases. A moulded abacus of considerable projection is placed on the capital for the reception of the thick 12th-century wall above. On the south is a late 12th-century arcade of two pointed arches, with a circular pillar and plain responds. The pillar has a moulded base with square plinth and leaf-spurs, and the capital is carved with a pair of double-headed dragons on each side. At the angles of the capitals are bunches of foliage upon which the dragons appear to be feeding, while a large grotesque head in the middle of the north face of the capital holds one head of each of the two dragons on that side in its open jaws. The responds have rich foliated capitals. The tower arch, which is now supported by a modern arch, was originally semicircular, but has become distorted. In the west wall above is the jamb of a blocked window, and in the south wall, near the apex of the eastern arch of the south arcade, is the round head of another window, both of which date from the early 12th century. There is a rood-loft stairway at the south-east, which is approached by a pointed doorway in the south aisle, and ascends by steep steps in the thickness of the wall to the upper doorway in the nave. The clearstory has on the south three early 15th-century windows, each of two trefoiled lights with tracery in a pointed head, and on the north are three square-headed windows, originally similar to those on the south, but altered to their present form at a later period. The nave has a low-pitched open-timber roof, the trusses of which are supported by 15th-century angel corbels. The embattled external parapet has the remains of a cross on the east gable.

The walls of the nave are covered with paintings chiefly of the 15th century. On the east wall, and extending partly over the lateral walls, is a painting of the Last Judgement, now indistinct, though our Lord, St. Michael, and small figures rising from their graves can be distinguished. The weighing of souls is depicted on the north wall, where a crowned figure of the Virgin, wearing a red cloak and holding a lily, appears to be placing her hand on the beam of the scales to incline it to the side of mercy; on the south

side. Burial and the Seven Sacraments were represented, but Penance and Extreme Unction are alone visible. On the south wall are also several texts in black letter of the 16th century, and on the soffits of the arches of the south arcade are bands of foliage of the earlier period. Many of these paintings have now become very indistinct, but coloured drawings of them as they appeared when first uncovered are preserved at the rectory.

The north aisle is lighted from the east by a window of three plain lights, with interlacing tracery in a pointed head, from the north by two windows of a similar character, but of two lights, all of early 14th-century date, though very considerably repaired, and from the west by a modern window of two cinquefoiled lights. The north doorway has an original rear-arch, but the external jambs and square head are of the 18th century.

In the east wall of the south aisle is a graceful late 13th-century window of two uncusped lights, with a circle in a pointed head. In the south wall are two early 14th-century windows with interlacing

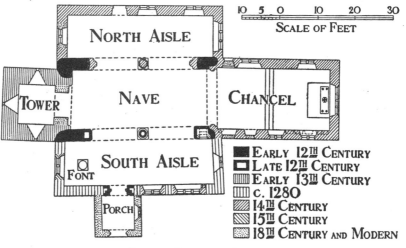

PLAN OF LATHBURY CHURCH

tracery in pointed heads, the eastern window of three lights and the other of two lights. To the east of the larger window, which contains a fragment of 15th-century glass, is a 14th-century pointed piscina with a modern bowl. Below the east window is a small recess, now very much restored. The south doorway, which dates from the late 12th century, was reset when the aisle was rebuilt about a hundred years later. It has a round arch of two chamfered orders, and jamb shafts with foliated capitals and abaci; the shafts and the eastern capital are modern. The two-light west window is of the 15th century, but has been considerably restored. Reset in the wall at the north-east of the aisle is an early 12th-century tympanum, which was found during the repairs of 1869. Upon it is carved a central upright figure of interlacing strapwork, probably representing a serpent, upon which two beasts are making a vigorous attack, while issuing from the figure is some luxuriant foliage. Both aisles have 15th-century parapets with weather-worn gargoyles; at the eastern angles very large and bold figures are carved, that on the north aisle, which represents a fierce creature of half-human form carrying a smaller figure in its right arm, being comparatively well-preserved, but the other is considerably weather-worn.

The tower is of three stages, with an offset between the ground and second stages, and has an original straight parapet with a 15th-century embattled parapet super-imposed upon it. The ground and second stages are lighted by original lancets, while the bell-chamber has windows of two pointed lights with octagonal shafts and unpierced pointed heads ; these are also original, but the east window is now filled with 15th-century tracery, the central shaft having been removed.

The font and pulpit are modern. At the east end of the south aisle is a mediaeval coffin-lid with an incised cross. The chancel is paved with black and white marble slabs of the 17th century, given, as stated by the inscriptions on three of them, by Margaret daughter of Sir Henry Andrews, bart., who died in 1680, at the age of fourteen years ; some of the other slabs have the names of other members of the Andrews family. On the north wall of the chancel is a brass with arms, a lion passant between three fleurs de lis, in memory of Richard Davies of Kynant, Montgomeryshire (d. 1661), whose son Isaiah was vicar of the parish. The inscription is as follows : ' Richard Davies of Kynant in the county of Mont-gomery Gent. hereunder buried. He deceased at the house of his son Isaiah Davies, then minister of this parish, 20th day of November 1661, aged 77 years. His son Thomas Davies Esq., at that time Agent Generall for the English nation upon the coast of Africa caused a scenotaph to be erected in the church of Welch Poole, the place of his birth, to the pious memory of his father, and this small memorial for such Cambria-Brittaines as shall this way travaile.' On the south wall is a brass with arms to Mary wife of Isaiah Davies (d. 1686). On the north wall of the chancel is a mural monument, with arms, to Alice (Pigott) wife of Robert Chandflower, with an incised slab portraying the figures of a woman and child, both kneeling, and two infants, the arms being those of Pigott with a crescent for difference quartering a fesse between three cherubs. In the north aisle is a large mural monument with arms to Henry Uthwatt of Great Linford (d. 1757) and Frances his wife (d. 1800). In the south chapel is a communion table of the 17th century with shaped ends carved with foliage. Two small crosses are incised externally on the north-west corner of the north aisle.

The tower contains a ring of five bells ; the treble was added in 1906, and the others have the following inscriptions : the second, ' Edward Hall made me 1731 ' ; the third, 'Newcome made me 1614 ' ; the fourth, ' God save our King 1627 IK. FC. RP. CW.' ; and the tenor ' God save our King, 1629,' the last two being by James Keene.

The communion plate consists of a silver cup of about 1640, without date letter; a paten of 1683 ; a large flagon of 1648, inscribed ' The gift of Lady Andrews to the parish of Lathbury in memory of her dafter Mrs Margaret Andrews ' ; and a stand paten with embossed bottom.

The registers before 1812 are as follows : (i) all entries 1690 to 1762 ; (ii) baptisms and burials 1763 to 1812 ; (iii) marriages 1754 to 1813.

ADVOWSON John de Bidun, founder of Lavendon Abbey, endowed it with Lathbury Church, and his gift was confirmed in 1227 by Henry III.[77] In 1232, how-ever, Ermengarde de Bidun obtained renunciations of right from the abbot, from William de Houghton, lord of the main manor, and from Robert son of Geoffrey,[78] her nephew.[79] The advowson was soon vested anew in Lavendon Abbey by the acquisition of the Bidun manor, and in 1281 Andrew de Gatesden confirmed the abbot in its possession.[80] Licence was obtained from the pope in 1306 [81] and from Edward II in 1310,[82] to appropriate Lathbury Church, which was endowed with 2¾ virgates of land.[83] After the dissolution of Lavendon Abbey the advowson was granted in 1546 to the Dean and Chapter of Christ Church, Oxford,[84] who have con-tinued in possession until the present time.[85]

In 1528 Lavendon Abbey granted to Thomas Whalley a lease of the rectory, which he surrendered to the Crown in 1545, when a lease for twenty-one years was granted to John Johnson.[86] In 1546 the rectory was included in the grant to the Dean and Chapter of Christ Church, Oxford,[87] and the annual rent for the tithes was released by the Crown in 1554.[88] Various difficulties occurring in the middle of the 17th century about the lease of the rectory, the dean and chapter leased it in perpetuity in 1662 to Isaiah Davies, then vicar, and to his successors,[89] so that the vicar is also rector. The tithes were commuted in 1842.[90]

A suit was brought by Thomas Wellar, vicar of Lathbury, against John Whyte, about 1583, respect-ing a short lease of the vicarage.[91] A terrier of the vicarage dated 1674 is quoted by Browne Willis.[92]

There is reference to a chapel in the churchyard leased in 1553 for ninety-four years by the Dean and Chapter of Christ Church, Oxford, to Anthony Cave for his free school.[93] In 1699 this chapel, then called the school-house, having fallen into decay, was taken down and the materials were used to repair the vicarage.[94] Its site may perhaps be marked by one of the large mounds in the churchyard.

In 1548 5d. yearly was derived from some land and rent given for the maintenance of a light in Lathbury Church.[95] This lamp-land lay in a meadow ' in the western part of Lathbury in a place called the Lord's Dole ' and was granted in 1549 to John Howe and John Broxholme.[96]

CHARITIES The Church Cobs.—It appears from the parish terrier that the rent of certain lands, known as the Church Cobs, was applied for church purposes. Two pieces,

[77] Dugdale, op. cit. vi, 888.

[78] R. of Hugh of Wells (Cant, and York Soc.), ii, 84.

[79] Chan. Inq. p.m. Hen. III, file 16, no. 18.

[80] Cal. Close, 1279–88, p. 176.

[81] Cal. of Papal Letters, ii, 16 ; see also Linc. Epis. Reg. Memo. Dalderby, fol. 100 d.

[82] Inq. a.q.d. file 80, no. 3 ; Cal. Pat. 1307–13, p. 232.

[83] Hund. R. (Rec. Com.), ii, 347.

[84] L. and P. Hen. VIII, xxi (2), p. 335.

[85] Add. MS. 5839, fol. 107a ; Bacon, Liber Regis. 500 ; Clergy List, 1915.

[86] L. and P. Hen. VIII, xx (1), p. 679.

[87] Ibid. xxi (2), pp. 334, 337.

[88] Pat. 2 Mary, pt. i, m. 19.

[89] Add. MS. 5839, fol. 106b, 107a.

[90] Sheahan, op. cit. 551.

[91] Ct. of Req. bdle. 43, no. 98.

[92] Add. MS. 5839, fol. 110a.

[93] Ibid. fol. 106a, quoting from an account of the foundation of this school in a ledger book among the archives of Christ Church. Cf. Chan. Inq. p.m. (Ser. 2), cxx, 5.

[94] Add. MS. 5839, fol. 106b, quoting the licence from the dean and chapter to Robert Creed, then vicar, to do this.

[95] Chant. Cert. 5, no. 24.

[96] Pat. 3 Edw. VI, pt. ii, m. 26

known as Plum Tree Cob and the Church Cob, respectively, were sold in 1870, and the proceeds invested in £179 15s. 2d. consols with the official trustees, producing £4 9s. 2d. yearly. The rest of the land, known as Ozier Cobs, is unlettable. The income is applied to church expenses.

LAVENDON

Lavendene, Lawedene, Lawendene (xi–xiii cent.) ; Launden (xiii–xviii cent.).

The parish of Lavendon covers 2,353 acres on the left bank of the River Ouse, its southern boundary. From the river, which runs at a height of 188 ft. above the ordnance datum, the land slopes gradually upwards towards the north, and, though the village lies for the most part at a height of about 198 ft. to 214 ft., at the extreme northerly point beyond Northey Farm a height of 345 ft. is attained. The soil is mixed. The subsoil varies from Oolite by the river to Oxford Clay in the north, the village and abbey lying upon cornbrash. Of the whole area, 1,046 acres are arable land, 1,167 permanent grass and 114 woods and plantations.[1]

The village lies to the north of the road from Olney to Bedford and is traversed by a branch road to Northampton. It is built about this and a lane running north-east to the site of the castle, which must thus have commanded both highways.

The church is in the western triangle formed by the crossing of these two roads. In Western Lane, leading to Olney, is the Baptist Chapel, founded in 1790 and rebuilt in 1894. The elementary school dates from 1875.

No tradition seems to remain to indicate the spot where once was held the Tuesday market granted to Paul Pever in 1249.[1a] This market had disappeared before the first half of the 18th century, but at that date 'Figg Fair' was still held 'about Palm Eve.'[2] It is not known whether this fair was the successor of that granted to Paul Pever for the vigil, feast and morrow of the Assumption of the Blessed Virgin Mary (15 August).[3]

The older houses are of stone, and with a few exceptions have tiled roofs. The Hit or Miss Inn, a two-storied building with a thatched roof, is probably of the early 17th century. Upon the outhouse is the date 1678 with the initials I.F. The vicarage was described in 1607 as consisting of a parlour, hall, kitchen and dairy ; it had also 'an orchard, a little Backside and a Barn.'[4] The whole was usually let in the 18th century for £20 a year.[5]

East of the village lies the manor-house of Uphoe,

for 400 years the property of the family of Norwich. A circular moat still surrounds the house.

West of the village is Lavendon Grange, the residence of Captain Harold H. Hulse. The house was built by Robert Eccleston,[6] some time after 1626, from the material, it is thought, of the abbey buildings. It is rectangular in plan, with two stories and an attic, and is built of stone, with tiled roofs. Additions were apparently made in 1722, the date on a sundial in a gable on the south side, and the porch was built out of old stones in 1911. Other additions and alterations have been made at different times.

No part remains of the abbey buildings, which

The Hit or Miss Inn, Lavendon

were 'situate hard by the common street and the highway'[7] ; some fragments of the moat surrounding the site exist to the west of the village, and foundations have been discovered to the west of them. According to 18th-century tradition the abbey church 'stood in a Close above the House, where was a Warren of Rabbits, which burrowed among the Ruins.'[8] Under papal indulgence of 1400 penitents visiting this church from the first to the second vespers on Passion Sunday and the feast of St. Augustine of Hippo received special benefits, while a similar licence in 1426 gave release of three years and three quarentines of enjoined penance to those who on Passion Sunday should visit the church and give alms towards its repair.[9] A survey of the abbey lands made soon after the Dissolution mentions the 'grett fyld callyd Colserwell' (Culverwell), containing 75 acres, the Wyndmylhyl Close, land called the

---

[1] Statistics from Bd. of Agric. (1905).
[1a] Cal. Chart. R. 1226–57, p. 341.
[2] Add. MS. 5839, fol. 116.
[3] Cal. Chart. R. loc. cit.

[4] Add. MS. 5839, fol. 117.
[5] Ibid. fol. 115. [6] Ibid. fol. 114 d.
[7] Cal. of Papal Letters, v, 74.
[8] Add. MS. 5839, fol. 118 d. Mention

is here made of a map of the estate of c. 1600 in which there was no trace of the monastic buildings.
[9] Cal. of Papal Letters, v, 376 ; vii, 565.

Laund, and a little wood called Hyghwood.[10] Mention is also made of the Tenoke Fyld,[11] a name reminiscent of the Tynnokeswade of the 12th century, near which was the park given to the house by John de Bidun.[12] The name is now preserved in Tinick Farm in the north of the parish.

In the opposite direction and down by the river is Lavendon Mill, probably on the site of that water-mill which Humphrey held of the Count of Mortain in 1086.[13] The mill is again mentioned in 1246,[14] and in 1534 was the scene of a quarrel between the Throckmortons of the neighbouring parish of Weston Underwood and Thomas Hill, who had obtained leave from the abbot to wash 400 sheep in the mill dam.[15] At the Dissolution it was described as three mills under one roof and was valued at £4 yearly.[16] This was not, however, the only water-mill in the parish, for there was also a mill 'and a moiety' in the chief manor of the Bishop of Coutances in 1086,[17] and this was probably that held at the close of the 13th century by Henry de Norwich of John Pever.[18] In the reign of Edward I a water-mill with a free fishery was appurtenant to the manor of Snelston,[19] and two water-mills are mentioned in an extent of about 1323.[20]

The capital messuage of the manor of Snelston probably occupied the site of the present farm. The herbage and fruit of the gardens were of some value in the 14th century, and a park with two fish-ponds was attached.[21]

Among the early place-names may be mentioned Yerdewere, le Fladehey, and Waldey Wood, all of which were acquired by the family of Norwich.[22]

CASTLE and HONOUR Very little is known of the history of the castle. It was probably built by a member of the baronial family of Bidun, who held the manor in the 12th century, and belonged later to the Pevers. A reference to it in 1231 shows that it then had a chapel.[23] It must have been the head of the small

PEVER. *Argent a cheveron gules with three fleurs de lis or thereon.*

'honour of Lavendon,' of which one mention has been found.[24] The moat and extensive earthworks of the castle may still be seen,[25] but there is now no trace of the wall, 40 ft. long, 10 ft. high and about 5 ft. thick, seen by a writer of the first half of the 18th century.[26] The castle as such seems, indeed, to have disappeared before Leland's time though the park still remained[27] and gave at a later date its name to a farm north of the castle.

MANORS In the reign of Edward the Confessor a manor at *LAVENDON* was held by eight thegns, of whom Alli, a man of the king, was senior over the others.[28] Another manor was held by a man of Borret in the time of the Confessor, and was assessed at 2 hides in 1086.[29] All these lands were in the hands of the Bishop of Coutances in 1086,[30] and with Weston Underwood (q.v.) passed to William Brewer, this overlordship being afterwards divided between the honour of Chaworth and the Wakes of Liddel.[31]

The fee of Alli and his fellows was assessed at 4 hides two-thirds of a virgate in the Domesday Survey, and was held by William, a tenant.[32] It seems probable that William was the progenitor of the family of Bidun, for by the first half of the 12th century Halnath de Bidun was holding William's land in Newton Bromswold (Northamptonshire),[33] and Lavendon was certainly in the possession of this family at a later date. Halnath was succeeded by his son[34] John de Bidun, who was living in 1155.[35] He founded the Premonstratensian abbey of St. John Baptist at Lavendon, and endowed it with certain lands in the surrounding commons and with various other tenements.[36] John was succeeded by a son of the same name,[37] who appears to have died, probably shortly after his father, in 1183–4.[38] The younger John was childless,[39] and his co-heirs were his five sisters, Amice, Mabel, Sarah, Maud and Ermengarde.[40] The fee was apparently divided among them before 1185, when Miles de Beauchamp, husband of Mabel, owed relief for half a knight's fee here.[41]

Amice, the eldest sister, married Henry or Hugh de Clinton; by him she had three daughters and co-heirs[42]—Mabel, who married Luke de Columbars[43] and died before 1254 without issue, Isabel wife of Ralf son of John,[44] and Agnes wife of Warin de

---

[10] Aug. Off. Misc. Bk. ccccii, fol. 17.

[11] The arable commons were Tenocke Field, Cansley Field and Mill Field (Add. MS. 5839, fol. 117). These were inclosed by an Act of 1801 (Priv. Act, 41 Geo. III, cap. 100).

[12] Dugdale, *Mon.* vi, 888. Tynnocks Leys were wrongfully claimed by the bailiff of John Lord Mordaunt as part of Snelston Manor in an action for trespass brought about 1557 by John Waters, lessee of Lavendon Grange Manor (Star Chamb. Proc. Phil. and Mary, bdle. 5, no. 39).

[13] *V.C.H. Bucks.* i, 246.

[14] Assize R. 56, m. 35.

[15] Star Chamb. Proc. Hen. VIII, bdle. 21, no. 193.

[16] Aug. Off. Misc. Bk. ccccii, fol. 17. The mills were included in the sale of the manor in 1671 (see below).

[17] *V.C.H. Bucks.* i, 241.

[18] *Hund. R.* (Rec. Com.), ii, 349.

[19] Ibid.; cf. Lansd. MS. 391, fol. 10 d.; Chan. Inq. p.m. 1 Edw. II, no. 54.

[20] Anct. Extents (Exch. K.R.), no. 78 (1).

[21] Ibid. Here will also be found the service paid by the various classes of tenants.

[22] Feet of F. Bucks. 49 Hen. III, no. 8.

[23] *R. of Hugh of Wells* (Cant. and York Soc.), ii, 86.

[24] *Rot. de Oblatis et Fin.* (Rec. Com.), 145.

[25] A farm-house has been built on the mount (*Hist. Monum. Com. Rep. N. Bucks.* 163).

[26] Add. MS. 5839, fol. 114 d.

[27] Leland, *Itin.* (ed. L. Toulmin Smith), v, 8. The park of Miles de Beauchamp at Lavendon is mentioned in a charter of mid-13th century date (Lansd. MS. 391, fol. 10).

[28] *V.C.H. Bucks.* i, 241.

[29] Ibid. 240.

[30] Ibid.

[31] *Percy Chartul.* (Surt. Soc.), 479; *Hund. R.* (Rec. Com.), ii, 349; *Cal. Inq. p.m.* (Edw. II), vi, 300; Chan. Inq. p.m. 23 Edw. III (1st nos.), no. 75; *Feud. Aids,* i, 105. The overlordship is last mentioned in 1349 (Chan. Inq. p.m. 23 Edw. III [1st nos.], no. 75).

[32] *V.C.H. Bucks.* i, 241.

[33] *V.C.H. Northants,* i, 311, 376. For Halnath (Alnoch, Halenod, Halenald, or Hanelade) see Blomfield, *Norfolk,* v, 475; Dugdale, *Baronage,* i, 599; Stacey Grimaldi, *Rot. de Dominabus,* 27; *Red Bk. of Exch.* (Rolls Ser.), 310.

[34] Maitland, *Bracton's Note Bk.* ii, 498.

[35] Hunter, *Gt. R. of the Pipe 2–4 Hen. II* (Rec. Com.), 23.

[36] Dugdale, *Mon.* vi, 888.

[37] Grimaldi, op. cit. 26, 46.

[38] Pipe R. 30 Hen. II (Pipe R. Soc.), 108.

[39] His widow Maud was aged ten in 1185; she was the daughter of Thomas son of Bernard by Eugenia daughter of Ralf Picot (Grimaldi, op. cit. 26, 29, 46).

[40] *Cal. Inq. p.m.* (Hen. III), i, 86.

[41] Pipe R. 31 Hen. II (Pipe R. Soc.), 140. [42] *Cal. Inq. p.m.* loc. cit.

[43] Assize R. 55, m. 14 d.; Lansd. MS. 391, fol. 10; cf. *Testa de Nevill* (Rec. Com.), 244.

[44] His name occurs in 1227 and 1246 (Assize R. 54, m. 14; 56, m. 7); cf. *Testa de Nevill* (Rec. Com.), 251.

Brakenham or Brageham.[45] In 1254 Agnes was still living, but the rights of Isabel had descended to her son Henry son of Ralf.[46] By 1303 this land was in the possession of Adam Grosset or Grustet and his tenants.[47] No mention of the share of Agnes and Warin de Brageham has been found after 1255.[48]

Sarah, the third sister of John de Bidun, also left three daughters by her husband Richard de Beauchamp—i.e., Isabel, Maud and Philippa[49]—but no record of their descendants' interest in the manor has been found. Equally uncertain is the part played by the descendants of Maud, the fourth sister,[50] and of Ermengarde, the fifth sister, whose heirs in 1254 were her grandson John and her second son Richard de Gatesden.[51] The greatest interest in the manor seems to have been that of Mabel, second sister of John de Bidun.[52] She was married to Miles de Beauchamp before 1185, when he paid relief for half a knight's fee in Lavendon.[53] The name of Miles de Beauchamp occurs in 1201 and 1206,[54] and Mabel seems to have been still holding her half knight's fee in Weston and Lavendon in 1235–6.[55] Possibly she afterwards acquired the share of ano her sister, for in a further return she is said to have three-fourths of a fee in these places.[56] In 1254 the heir of Mabel and Miles was said to be Miles de Beauchamp,[57] who died in or about 1264[58]; some four years later homage was done by Richard his son and heir,[59] who was still living in February 1291–2.[60] Before 1303 this fee had been divided into two portions, one of which was held by Adam Grosset and his tenants,[61] while the second, assessed at half a knight's fee in 1315–16, was inherited by Cecily daughter and co-heir of Richard de Beauchamp, and brought by her in marriage to William Jukel.[62]

The portion of Miles de Beauchamp did not, however, include the castle. This and the advowson of the Biduns' foundation of Lavendon Abbey were held in 1275 and 1278 by John Pever, and had probably been acquired by Paul Pever some twenty-four years previously.[63] Paul was probably already in possession of the Town Manor, which may possibly be identified with that held by Borret's man before the making of the Domesday Survey.[64] It must have been for this manor that he in 1249 obtained grants of a Tuesday market, a fair on the vigil, feast and morrow of the Assumption and free warren in his demesne lands.[65] Paul Pever, steward of Henry III, was, according to Matthew Paris, a self-made man, who acquired wide lands and was an insatiable buyer of manors.[66] However this may be, the only clue to the former history of these Lavendon manors is probably that afforded by the quitclaim in 1288 of one of them to John Pever by Agnes wife of Henry de Hereford.[67] From this time forward the *CASTLE* and *TOWN MANORS*, which apparently became amalgamated, followed the descent of the manor of Chilton (q.v.) until 1;29. In 1537 John Lord Zouche sold the manor of Lavendon *alias* the Castle Manor to John Lord Mordaunt, lord of Turvey in Bedfordshire.[68]

ZOUCHE. *Gules bezanty with a quarter ermine.*   MORDAUNT. *Argent a cheveron between three stars sable.*

Lord Mordaunt, who in 1533 had been summoned to Parliament as a baron,[69] in 1562 was followed by a son John,[70] who, under the terms of his father's will,[71] conveyed the manor of Snelston[72] to Lewis his son. Lewis, who was M.P. for Bedfordshire in 1563–7,[73] died in 1601[74]; his son and successor Henry Lord Mordaunt was suspected of complicity in the Gunpowder Plot and was imprisoned in 1605–6.[75] Before his death in February 1608–9[76] Henry Lord Mordaunt made a conveyance of the Castle Manor.[77] His son and successor John was created Earl of Peterborough in March 1627–8[78]; he was a party to a conveyance of the Castle Manor in 1632[79] and died in 1643.[80] Henry Earl of Peterborough, his son and heir, seems to have mortgaged this manor in 1653[81] to Sir Charles Compton, kt., of Grendon, Northamptonshire,[82] brother of James third Earl of Northampton.[83] Lord Peterborough was still in possession of the manor in

[45] *Cal. Inq. p.m.* loc. cit. Warin and Agnes granted land in Cheselfurlong to Henry de Norwich (Assize R. 55, m. 7 d.).
[46] *Cal. Inq. p.m.* loc. cit. ; Lansd. MS. 391, fol. 10.   [47] *Feud. Aids*, i, 105.
[48] When they with the other co-heirs gave the king a mark for having a writ (*Excerpta e Rot. Fin.* [Rec. Com.], ii, 202).
[49] Grimaldi, op. cit. 23 ; *Cal. Inq. p.m.* loc. cit. In 1254 Isabel was living ; Maud's heir was her daughter Sarah wife of Robert de Walton, and Philippa's rights had descended to her son John de Croxton (ibid.). Isabel was unmarried (*Excerpta e Rot. Fin.* loc. cit.).
[50] *Cal. Inq. p.m.* loc. cit. She is described as Maud Visdelou, a widow, in 1185 (Grimaldi, op. cit. 22) ; in 1254 her heir was her grandson Thomas son of Robert (*Cal. Inq. p.m.* loc. cit.).
[51] *Cal. Inq. p.m.* loc. cit.
[52] Ibid.
[53] Grimaldi, op. cit. 23 ; *Pipe R. 31 Hen. II* (Pipe R. Soc.), 140.
[54] *Rot. de Oblatis et Fin.* (Rec. Com.), 158 ; *Rot. Lit. Pat.* (Rec. Com.), 60.

[55] *Testa de Nevill* (Rec. Com.), 259.
[56] Ibid. 262.
[57] *Cal. Inq. p.m.* loc. cit. ; cf. *Testa de Nevill* (Rec. Com.), 251.
[58] *Cal. Inq. p.m.* (Hen. III), i, 221.
[59] *Excerpta e Rot. Fin.* (Rec. Com.), ii, 487. The judgement by which Lavendon was allotted in 1264 to John, younger son of Miles de Beauchamp (Assize R. 1194, m. 5), was evidently overruled.
[60] *Cal. Pat.* 1281–92, p. 478.
[61] *Feud. Aids*, i, 105 ; Lay Subs. R. bdle. 242, no. 115. Richard Grosset was tenant in 1344 and 1346 (Inq. a.q.d. file 272, no. 2 ; *Feud. Aids*, i, 130).
[62] Chan. Inq. p.m. Edw. II, file 19, no. 16 ; *Cal. Inq. p.m.* (Edw. II), v, 377.
[63] *Hund. R.* (Rec. Com.), i, 37, 45 ; ii, 349. It is here said that Paul Pever had withdrawn the service due for twenty-four years. The purchase, if made by Paul, must have been completed before his death in June 1251 (Matthew Paris, *Chron. Maj.* [Rolls Ser.], v, 242).
[64] See above.
[65] *Cal. Chart. R.* 1226–57, p. 341.

[66] Matthew Paris, loc. cit.
[67] Feet of F. Bucks. 16 Edw. I, no. 2.
[68] Ibid. Trin. 29 Hen. VIII.
[69] Round, *Peerage Studies*, 337.
[70] Chan. Inq. p.m. (Ser. 2), cxxxviii, 6.
[71] P.C.C. 22 Streat.
[72] See below and Recov. R. East. 6 Eliz. m. 450.
[73] *Ret. of Memb. of Parl.* i, 403.
[74] Chan. Inq. p.m. (Ser. 2), cclxviii, 147.
[75] G.E.C. *Complete Peerage*, v, 366.
[76] Chan. Inq. p.m. (Ser. 2), cccix, 200.
[77] Feet of F. Div. Co. Hil. 6 Jas. I.
[78] G.E.C. loc. cit.
[79] Feet of F. Div. Co. Trin. 8 Chas. I.
[80] Chan. Inq. p.m. (Ser. 2), dcxxiv, 64.
[81] Feet of F. Bucks. East. 1653.
[82] Margaret, mother of John first Earl of Peterborough, was the daughter of Henry (Compton), first Lord Compton (G.E.C. loc. cit.). Her half-brother, Sir Henry Compton, K.B., was one of the parties to the conveyance of 1632 (Feet of F. Div. Co. Trin. 8 Chas. I).
[83] G.E.C. *Complete Peerage*, vi, 72 and n. ; Shaw, *Knights of Engl.* ii, 217.

the spring of 1685–6,[84] but in 1698 Hatton, only son of Sir Charles Compton, made a settlement of it on his marriage with Penelope daughter of Sir John Nicholas.[85] Hatton, who was Deputy-Lieutenant of the Tower, was succeeded in 1740 by his son Charles, treasurer of the Society of Antiquaries.[86] He settled the manor to his own use in 1742[87] and died in 1761, when his estates passed to his next brother Edward.[88] William Compton, LL.D., succeeded his father Edward in 1769,[89] and sold Lavendon in 1777 to Thomas Major of Market Harboro', Leicestershire,[90] by whom it was conveyed three years later to Thomas Westcar of Souldern, Oxfordshire. In 1788 he sold it to James and Richard Hale, who transferred their rights ten years later to Thomas Higgins, in trust for William Farrer.[90a] From this time the manor followed the descent of Cold Brayfield (q.v.), and Mr. Denis Herbert Farrer is the present owner.

COMPTON. *Sable a leopard or between three helms argent.*

Before the Conquest a man of Wulfwig Bishop of Leicester and Dorchester (1053–67)[91] held in Lavendon land which he could sell.[92] This holding was assessed at 2 hides 1¼ virgates in 1086, when it was in the hands of Walter Giffard, of whom it was held by one Ralf.[93] The history of this overlordship is obscure, but in the 13th century Lavendon no longer formed part of the honour of Giffard, but was accounted among the fees of the barony of Wahull.[94]

The earliest known under-tenants were members of the family of Grey, and the name of Sir Reynold Grey is given as that of the lord of the manor of *SNELSTON* in 1275–6.[95] Sir Reynold also held the manor of Bletchley (q.v.), with which Snelston descended to Richard Earl of Kent. He in 1506 made a settlement of this and other manors on himself and Elizabeth his wife and their issue.[96] His marriage was, however, childless, and three years later the reversion of the manor of Snelston was sold to John Mordaunt,[97] who in 1512 acquired the whole right of the earl and countess in return for a yearly rent of £8 13s. 4d. payable after the death of Walter Luke of Cople, Bedfordshire.[98] All right in the manor was quitclaimed by Henry, half-brother and heir of the earl, in 1516 and again in 1552.[99] From

this time the manor of Snelston *alias* Grays followed the descent of the Castle Manor [100] into the hands of the family of Farrer.

As early as 1674 Sir Anthony Chester, bart., of Chicheley (q.v.), heir through marriage of the family of Cave,[1] was in possession of Snelston Meadow and other lands here.[2] It was said in the 18th century that the demesne lands of the Mordaunts were sold to the family of Chester, which in 1735[3] and later claimed a reputed manor here. This land for some time followed the descent of the manor of Chicheley (q.v.), but is now in the hands of Mr. Charles Anthony Chester, who does not hold Chicheley.

There were before the Conquest five other holdings described as in Lavendon: one of these possibly formed the nucleus of the abbey fee; three were formed of lands that in later times lay in the parishes of Newton Blossomville and Cold Brayfield, and their descent will be found in

CHESTER of Chicheley. *Party argent and sable a cheveron engrailed between three rams' heads with golden horns all countercoloured and a border engrailed gules bezanty.*

the account of those places.[4] The remaining holding was that held in the time of King Edward by Turbert, a man of the Countess Goda, who could sell his hide if he would.[5] In 1086 it was held by Ralf of the Countess Judith,[6] and afterwards formed part of the honour of Huntingdon.[7]

The earliest known tenant of this fee is Hugh de St. Medard, who gave his church of Lavendon to the abbey, a gift confirmed by John his grandson in 1237.[8] In a return made at or about this time John was said to hold two parts of half a knight's fee of the honour.[9] John, who was also known as St. Mark, was dead by 1246, when Mabel his widow claimed dower against Richard his son and heir and received one messuage and 15 acres.[10] In 1259 Richard de St. Mark and Isabel his wife conveyed another messuage and 15 acres of land in Lavendon, together with Mabel's dower lands and rights in 9 acres held by tenants, to Henry de Norwich,[11] thus augmenting the lands obtained by the family of Norwich at an earlier date, as described below. The whole was afterwards known as the manor of *UPHOE* (Opho, Houpho, xiii cent.).

[84] Feet of F. Div. Co. Hil. 1 & 2 Jas. II.

[85] Edmondson, *Baron. Geneal.* ii, 110; Abstract of Title kindly lent by Mr. F. W. Bull; Recov. R. East. 10 Will. III, m. 19. Sir Charles Compton's will was proved in November 1662 (P.C.C. 138 Laud).

[86] Edmondson, loc. cit.; P.C.C. 6 Spurway; *Musgrave's Obit.* (Harl. Soc.), ii, 50, 51, 52.

[87] Recov. R. East. 15 Geo. II, m. 34.

[88] P.C.C. 426 Cheslyn; *Musgrave's Obit.* (Harl. Soc.), ii, 50.

[89] P.C.C. 335 Bogg; *Musgrave's Obit.* (Harl. Soc.), ii, 51.

[90] Close, 17 Geo. III, pt. xxviii, no. 6; cf. Feet of F. Bucks. Trin. 15 Geo. III.

[90a] Abstract of Title ut sup.; Lysons, *Mag. Brit.* i (3), 593; P.C.C. 111 Howe.

[91] Stubbs, *Reg. Sacrum Angl.* 224.

[92] *V.C.H. Bucks.* i, 252.

[93] Ibid.

[94] *Hund. R.* (Rec. Com.), i, 39; *Feud. Aids,* i, 74; Chan. Inq. p.m. 1 Edw. II, no. 54; 17 Edw. II, no. 74; 27 Edw. III (1st nos.), no. 58; Anct. Extents (Exch. K.R.), no. 78 (1). For the descent of the barony see Ravenstone.

[95] *Hund. R.* (Rec. Com.), i, 41.

[96] S. P. Dom. Hen. VIII, § 34, p. 181.

[97] Ibid. p. 179 d.; cf. Close, 378, m. 7.

[98] S. P. Dom. Hen. VIII, § 34, p. 177; Feet of F. Bucks. Trin. 5 Hen. VIII; *Cat. of Anct. D.* vi, 397.

[99] Com. Pleas D. Enr. Trin. 6 Edw. VI, m. 1; G.E.C. *Complete Peerage,* iv, 354; Feet of F. Bucks. Trin. 6 Edw. VI.

[100] Feet of F. Bucks. Trin. 15 Geo. III; P.C.C. 111 Howe; Priv. Act, 41

Geo. III, cap. 100; Recov. R. Hil. 1 Will. IV, m. 141.

[1] Anthony Cave in 1558 died seised of rents from lands of Lavendon Abbey (Chan. Inq. p.m. [Ser. 2], cxx, 5).

[2] Chan. Proc. (Bridges Div.), bdle. 460, no. 135.

[3] Add. MS. 5839, fol. 114.

[4] See pp. 323, 422.

[5] *V.C.H. Bucks.* i, 273.

[6] Ibid.

[7] For descent see *Feud. Aids,* i, 74. In 1284–6 the tenants were Henry de Norwich, the Abbot of Lavendon and Robert de Northampton (ibid.).

[8] Feet of F. Bucks. Trin. 21 Hen. III, no. 2.

[9] *Testa de Nevill* (Rec. Com.), 244.

[10] Assize R. 56, m. 5 d.

[11] Feet of F. Bucks. 44 Hen. III, no. 12; *Hund. R.* (Rec. Com.), ii, 349.

Roger de Uphoe, who may have been another early tenant of the Huntingdon fee, was followed by his son Robert [12]; he dispersed his lands, selling 13 acres 1 rood to the abbey of Lavendon,[13] and the rest in 1234 [14] to Simon de Norwich, one of the king's clerks.[15] The reason for this Norfolk man's attraction to North Buckinghamshire is obscure, but it will be recalled that the Bidun family had possessions in Tombesland in Norwich [16] and in 1240–1 two of the Bidun co-heirs acknowledged that Simon had obtained land of their fee.[17] Simon also acquired land in the vill before 1234 from William son of Robert de Lavendon and from Ralf son of John.[18] Simon de Abington 'le charter' granted to him all his land with a messuage in Abington (Northamptonshire) and Lavendon,[19] the Lavendon portion being probably the 7 acres quitclaimed to him by Philip son of Simon de Lavendon early in 1235.[20] Simon de Norwich had entered the king's service before 1226,[21] and for the next twenty-two years he was busy with public affairs ; as receiver of the nineteenth, as guardian of the temporalities of various religious houses during vacancies (in 1242 of the issues of the see of London), and as one of the three men responsible for the provisioning of the army in 1245,[22] he was deep in the king's confidence. Henry III rewarded him by extorting from the Abbot of St. Albans in 1236 a yearly gift of 110s.,[23] by giving him a prebend of Lichfield in 1241,[24] and in the following year by ordering the Archbishop of York to provide for him in some church of the king's patronage to the value of 50 marks.[25] In spite of his constant employment at home and abroad Simon seems to have held his Lavendon land in demesne, for in 1246 he sued Simon Druel and Alice his wife [26] who had prevented his fishing and had seized his nets and boat.[27] Simon appears to have retired from the king's service in 1248, and in the autumn of this year he granted his messuage

NORWICH. *Party gules and azure a lion ermine.*

and seven score acres in Lavendon to his kinsman Henry son of Nicholas de Norwich.[28] Simon was to hold them of Henry for life, and after his death Henry was to hold them of Simon's heirs at a yearly rent of 24s.[29] In 1249 Simon bought the mill and three-quarters of a virgate with 6d. rent from Robert le Blund and Mabel his wife,[30] and in 1251 he died.[31] Henry, who was one of Simon's executors,[32] was also in the royal service.[33] He continued Simon's policy of acquiring land in Lavendon,[34] notably the St. Mark fee (see above), and in 1269 he obtained a grant of free warren.[35] Before 1290–1 Henry had been succeeded by another Henry de Norwich,[36] who in 1315 settled messuages and land in Lavendon and elsewhere on himself and Joan his wife for their lives with remainder to Henry's son Simon and his issue.[37] Henry died before the summer of 1327, when the land was in the hands of Simon.[38] Simon seems to have been continually in trouble [39] and quarrelled bitterly with the Abbot of Lavendon over services alleged to be due to him [40] and with some of his neighbours over a fishery.[41] He was still living in 1357.[42] Either this Simon, or more probably his son of the same name, married Margaret sister of John Holt of Brampton (Northamptonshire).[43] Their son Simon, with Simon his son, is mentioned in the will of John Holt made in November 1415.[44] Simon grandson of Margaret and Simon had a son Simon Norwich, aged twenty-three in 1452, when he inherited the lands of his cousin Richard Holt, who had died in 1429.[45] This younger Simon Norwich died in 1468, and was succeeded by John his son, a child eight years old.[46] John settled Uphoe at a later date on Katharine his wife, who held it after his death in March 1503–4,[47] when Simon their son was still under age.[48] Simon settled his manor and mansion of Brampton on Margaret his wife,[49] and, though he died in 1548,[50] she was still in possession in the early years of Elizabeth's reign.[51] John son of Simon and Margaret inherited the rest of the land. He married twice, and on his death, in 1557,[52] quarrels arose between Simon his son and heir and Alice the step-mother, whom Simon accused of being 'wyckedly bente to hinder' him 'by all possible meanes and wayes that she maye devise.' [53]

[12] *Cal. Chart. R.* 1226–57, p. 189.

[13] Assize R. 55, m. 7.

[14] Cur. Reg. R. 115, m. 5 d., where this curious agreement is given in full.

[15] Ibid. ; cf. *Cal. Chart. R.* 1226–57, p. 189.

[16] Maitland, op. cit. iii, 97.

[17] Assize R. 55, m. 7 d.

[18] *Cal. Chart. R.* 1226–57, p. 189.

[19] Ibid. Simon de Norwich had also an interest in the Abington lands of Humphrey Visdelou (*Cal. Close*, 1231–4, p 6 ; *Cal. Chart. R.* 1226–57, p. 151).

[20] Feet of F. Bucks. 19 Hen. III, no. 7.

[21] When he received a Crown presentation to the deanery of Walsingham (*Cal. Pat.* 1225–32, p. 88).

[22] *Cal. Pat., Cal. Close, passim.*

[23] *Cal. Chart. R.* 1226–57, p. 219. Matthew Paris (op. cit. v, 241) makes the sum 100s. and the date twenty years before Simon's death in 1251. He says the gift was made *per extorsionem domini regis satis enormem et impudentem.*

[24] *Cal. Pat.* 1232–47, pp. 268, 272.

[25] Ibid. p. 336.

[26] See Newton Blossomville.

[27] Assize R. 56, m. 5.

[28] *Excerpta e Rot. Fin.* (Rec. Com.), ii, 113.

[29] Feet of F. Bucks. 32 Hen. III, no. 10. Randal le Cunte, brother and heir of Simon, commuted this rent in 1260 for 1d. at Easter for all services (ibid. 45 Hen. III, no. 10).

[30] Ibid. 33 Hen. III, no. 5. To be held of Robert and Mabel and the heirs of Mabel. [31] Matthew Paris, loc. cit.

[32] *Cal. Pat.* 1247–58, p. 164.

[33] Ibid. p. 231 ; 1258–66, p. 55, &c.

[34] See Feet of F. Bucks. 39 Hen. III, no. 28 ; 42 Hen. III, no. 3, 11 ; 49 Hen. III, no. 8 ; cf. Assize R. 1185, m. 2.

[35] *Cal. Chart. R.* 1257–1300, p. 123 ; cf. *Hund. R.* (Rec. Com.), i, 45.

[36] *Cal. Close,* 1318–23, p. 646, a reference to a fine of 1290–1, where mention is made of Iseult widow of Henry. She is first mentioned in 1259 (Feet of F. Bucks. 44 Hen. III, no. 12).

[37] Feet of F. Bucks. 9 Edw. II, no. 22. Contingent remainders were to younger sons, John, Henry and Edmund.

[38] De Banco R. Trin. 1 Edw. III, m. 107.

[39] *Cal. Pat.* 1330–4, p. 48 ; 1338–4°,

pp. 132, 159 ; 1354–8, p. 656 ; *Cal. Close,* 1341–3, p. 370 ; 1343–6, p. 337.

[40] *Cal. Pat.* 1338–40, pp. 281, 283.

[41] De Banco R. 352, m. 560.

[42] *Cal. Pat.* 1354–8, p. 656.

[43] Chan. Inq. p.m. 30 Hen. VI, no. 13.

[44] Gibbons, *Early Linc. Wills,* 124.

[45] Chan. Inq. p.m. 30 Hen. VI, no. 13. See also *Cat. of Anct. D.* i, 459, where mention occurs of Simon in 1462.

[46] Chan. Inq. p.m. 8 Edw. IV, no. 16.

[47] Metcalfe, *Visit. of Northants,* 120.

[48] Chan. Inq. p.m. (Ser. 2), xviii, 105 ; xxvii, 25.

[49] Chan. Proc. (Ser. 2), bdle. 132, no. 8. After the death of Simon Norwich she married Simon Buttry.

[50] Chan. Inq. p.m. (Ser. 2), lxxxix, 99.

[51] Chan. Proc. (Ser. 2), bdle. 132, no. 10.

[52] Chan. Inq. p.m. (Ser. 2), cxii, 115.

[53] Chan. Proc. (Ser. 2), bdle. 132, no. 10. Immediately after his father's death Simon removed his chests containing his title-deeds to the house of a friend, but two years later the friend and Alice broke the locks. See ibid. no. 8–10. Alice was still alive in 1605 (Chan. Inq. p.m. [Ser. 2], cclxxxviii, 119).

Simon Norwich made a conveyance of the manor in 1579,[54] this being possibly for the purpose of the settlement made by him on Bridget his wife and Ascanius his son.[55] Simon died in 1588,[56] but Bridget, who afterwards married Edmund Sands,[57] lived on until the spring of 1611–12.[58] Ascanius seems to have been alive in 1625.[59] Charles son and heir of Simon Norwich included his reversionary interest in the manor in his marriage settlement, made in 1589, on Ann daughter of Edward Watson.[60] Sir Charles[61] died in 1605, leaving a son Simon Norwich, then aged ten years.[62] Simon, who was knighted in February 1617–18,[63] made a conveyance of his manors in Northamptonshire, Buckinghamshire and Leicestershire in 1618,[64] and in 1623 sold Uphoe to John Parker of Duston, Northamptonshire.[65] In 1641 Parker conveyed his interest to William Fitzhugh of London,[65a] who in 1671 released the manor to his son William.[66] He died in 1710, and the following year Robert Fitzhugh conveyed Uphoe to William Carter.[66a] In 1719 it was purchased from Carter by Denis Farrer of Cold Brayfield[67] (q.v.), which manor it subsequently followed in descent.

Before the Conquest a man of Alric son of Goding held land here which was in the hands of Humphrey, tenant of the Count of Mortain, in 1086, when it was assessed as a manor of 2⅓ hides.[68] The subsequent history of this fee is uncertain, but it seems possible that part at least of this land afterwards came to the Premonstratensian abbey founded here by John de Bidun in the reign of Henry II.[69] The abbey may perhaps have also obtained the land held by the Hospitallers in the spring of 1285–6.[70] Other lands were held of the Grossets under the Wakes,[71] but all the possessions of the house, beyond reprises, were in March 1546–7 valued at only £9 14s. 10d.[72]

The abbey was surrendered to the Crown before July 1536,[73] and in 1543 the house and demesne lands were sold to Sir Edmund Peckham of Denham, the king's servant, and Robert Peckham, his eldest son.[74] The second son, Henry Peckham, leased the manor in 1550 to John Waters of Aston Mullins in Dinton for eighty-eight years.[75] On the attainder of Henry Peckham the reversion of the land again passed to the Crown, and in 1558 it was granted to Thomas

White and others.[76] The accession of Elizabeth restored the fortunes of the Peckhams,[77] and in 1573 Sir George, third son of the grantee, obtained royal confirmation of a conveyance of this manor of *LAVENDON*, afterwards *LAVENDON GRANGE*, to Sir Roland Heyward, kt., and Joan his wife.[78] Sir Roland, who was for thirty years an alderman of London and twice lord mayor,[79] died in December 1593.[80] Under a settlement of the manor made in the previous September it passed to his second son, John Heyward,[81] who sold it in 1615 to William and Humphrey Newton.[82] They sold it in 1626 to Robert Eccleston.[83] Robert Eccleston was described as of Lavendon Grange in 1639, when a settlement was made on the marriage of John, his son and heir, with Cecily second daughter of Richard Taylor.[84] John Eccleston, Cecily his wife and Robert his son made a settlement of the manor in 1663.[85] In 1671, after the death of John, Robert and Cecily sold Lavendon Grange to Thomas Newton.[86]

Thomas Newton was succeeded after June 1685[87] by his son Richard Newton,[88] the founder of Hertford College (Oxford) and an educational reformer. He spent much of his spare time at Lavendon, and died there in April 1753.[89] Jane, his only child and heir, married the Rev. Knightley Adams, rector of

NEWTON of Lavendon. *Argent a fesse indented of three points azure with three sheaves or thereon.*

Preston Capes, Northamptonshire,[89a] who barred the entail in 1755.[90] He died in 1769, Jane surviving until 1787 or 1788, when Lavendon passed to her son Simon Adams.[90a] He held until his death in 1806,[91] his son the Rev. Richard Adams, rector of Edingthorpe, Norfolk, succeeding. In 1813 the entail was barred by Richard and his son Samuel Hooper Adams,[91a] the latter dying in 1816, in his father's lifetime.[92] The manor was retained by the family until 1851, when it was sold by the Rev. Richard Newton Adams, D.D., to Mr. Benjamin Sculthorpe Brookes,[92a] who held it for many years.[93]

[54] Feet of F. Bucks. Trin. 21 Eliz.
[55] Chan. Inq. p.m. (Ser. 2), cclxxxviii, 119.
[56] Ibid. ccxxii, 28.
[57] Ibid. cclxxxviii, 119.
[58] Ibid. ccccxx, 88.   [59] Ibid.
[60] Ibid. cclxxxviii, 119.
[61] Charles Norwich was knighted in 1604 (Shaw, *Knights of Engl.* ii, 131).
[62] Chan. Inq. p.m. (Ser. 2), cclxxxviii, 119.
[63] Shaw, op. cit. ii, 167.
[64] Feet of F. Div. Co. East. 16 Jas. I.
[65] Ibid. Bucks. East. 21 Jas. I. The family must have retained some land here, for in 1653 Lewis Norwich of Lavendon was dealing with land in Windmill Field (Marcham, *Cat. of Bucks. Deeds*, no. 383).
[65a] Close, 17 Chas. I, pt. xiii, no. 20.
[66] Abstract of Title *ut sup.*   [66a] Ibid.
[67] Ibid.; cf. Feet of F. Bucks. East. 11 Geo. I; Lysons, op. cit. i (3), 593.
[68] *V.C.H. Bucks.* i, 246. The pre-Conquest holder had power to alienate.
[69] Ibid. 384; Dugdale, *Mon.* vi, 888.
[70] *Plac. de Quo Warr.* (Rec. Com.), 90. At the Dissolution 22s. 4d. was paid yearly

by Lavendon to the hospital of St. John, Northampton, for land and 40s. for 'a certain demesne tenement' (Ld. Rev. Misc. Bk. clxxxviii, fol. 149b; cf. ibid. fol. 36 and cxxiv, fol. 47).
[71] Inq. a.q.d. file 272, no. 12; cf. *Cal. Pat.* 1343–5, p. 333.
[72] Ld. Rev. Misc. Bk. clxxxviii, fol. 149b.
[73] *V.C.H. Bucks.* i, 385.
[74] *L. and P. Hen. VIII* xviii (1), g. 981 (108). See Denham.
[75] Ld. Rev. Misc. Bk. clxxxviii, fol. 36; Feet of F. Bucks. East. 4 Edw. VI; Com. Pleas D. Enr. East. 4 Edw. VI, m. 14.
[76] Add. MS. 5839, fol. 113b.
[77] In 1572 the queen obtained for £800 a renunciation of rights in this manor from John Blunt and Elizabeth his wife, with warrant against Elizabeth's heirs (Feet of F. Bucks. Mich. 14 & 15 Eliz.).
[78] Pat. 15 Eliz. pt. x, m. 11; cf. Memo. R. (Exch. L.T.R.), Hil. 22 Eliz. m. 169.
[79] Add. MS. 5839, fol. 113b.
[80] Chan. Inq. p.m. (Ser. 2), ccxli, 125.
[81] Ibid.
[82] Cal. of F. (P.R.O.), Bucks. East. 13

Jas. I; Recov. R. East. 13 Jas. I, m. 73; cf. Feet of F. Bucks. Trin. 16 Jas. I; Mich. 19 Jas. I.
[83] Feet of F. Bucks. Trin. 2 Chas. I; Hil. 3 Chas. I; Recov. R. East. 2 Chas. I, m. 88.
[84] Marcham, op. cit. no. 379.
[85] Feet of F. Bucks. Mich. 15 Chas. II; Recov. R. Trin. 15 Chas. II, m. 93.
[86] Close, 23 Chas. II, pt. xvii, no. 38; cf. Chan. Proc. (Bridges Div.), bdle. 490, no. 2.
[87] Marcham, op. cit. no. 389.
[88] Katherine, mother of Richard, died in 1680 (M. I. in the church).
[89] P.C.C. 183 Searle.   [89a] Ibid.
[90] Feet of F. Bucks. Mich. 29 Geo. II.
[90a] P.C.C. 403 Bogg; 518 Calvert.
[91] Priv. Act, 41 Geo. III, cap. 100; Add. MS. 9411, fol. 74; Abstract of Title ut sup.
[91a] Recov. R. Trin. 53 Geo. III, m. 168; Abstract of Title ut sup.
[92] Abstract of Title ut sup.
[92a] Sheahan, *Hist. and Topog. of Bucks.* 554.
[93] cf. *Ret. of Owners of Land* (1873), *Bucks.* 3.

Lavendon Grange

LAVENDON CHURCH FROM THE NORTH-EAST

LAVENDON CHURCH · THE INTERIOR LOOKING EAST

It is now in the possession of Captain Harold Hutton Hulse.

The reputed manor of *ADDERSEY* (Adirsey, Addersley) was part of the demesne lands of the Lavendon Abbey manor.[93a] Called in the 16th century a great field pasture of 80 acres [94] it descended for some time with Lavendon Grange.[94a] It later belonged to the last Earl of Halifax,[95] whose daughter and heir Elizabeth married John Montagu, Viscount Hinchinbroke, and died in 1768, in her father's lifetime.[95a] Addersey was purchased from Lord Hinchinbroke before 1792 by Philip Skeen, the owner in the early 19th century.[96] Browne Willis speaks of it as formerly a 'vill,' but consisting in his day of a single house and the estate worth about £50 yearly.[96a] Since then the name appears to have been entirely lost.

The church of *ST. MARY THE VIRGIN* consists of a chancel measuring internally 27 ft. 6 in. by 12 ft. 8 in., nave 48 ft. by 16 ft., north aisle 6 ft. 9 in. wide, south aisle 7 ft. 6 in. wide, north and south porches, and west tower 11 ft. 8 in. square; it is built of rubble, the roofs of the nave and aisles being covered with lead and that of the chancel with tiles.

The nave and tower and the western part of the chancel date from the early 11th century. The church appears to have been left unaltered till early in the 13th century, when the chancel was rebuilt and both aisles were added. No further structural alterations were made until late in the 15th century, when a clearstory was added to the nave, north and south porches were built, several windows were inserted in the aisles, which, with the nave, were reroofed and provided with embattled parapets, and an additional stage was added to the tower. The whole fabric was restored in 1859.

When the chancel was rebuilt the western portion of the original south wall was preserved and still exists, though the window it contained (of which only the round head is now visible) was blocked and a doorway opened out below it. The east window, of three cinquefoiled lights with tracery in a pointed head, was inserted about 1390, and to the south of it is an image bracket of the same period with a well-carved head. On the north are two early 13th-century lancets and a blocked 15th-century low-side window of one wide cinquefoiled light. A 13th-century lancet and the doorway mentioned above, which dates from the same period, have been inserted in the pre-Conquest part of the south wall, and further east is a 15th-century window of three lights in a four-centred head. The external stonework of the lancet, with the exception of the label, has been renewed, and the doorway is blocked. The sill of the south-east window has been carried down to form a sedile, and to the east of it

is a 15th-century cinquefoiled piscina with a circular bowl. There is a square aumbry at the north-east. The timber roof over the chancel and the pointed chancel arch are modern.

The pre-Conquest nave was characteristically lofty in its original state and has been rendered particularly so by the addition of the clearstory. Both lateral walls are pierced by 13th-century arcades which replace all the original windows, except the round head of one near the apex of the easternmost arch of the north arcade. The round tower arch in the west wall, with its plain abaci, and the opening above it, are doubtless original, though, being covered with plaster, the stonework is not visible. The north arcade is of three bays with pointed arches of one plain order supported by circular pillars with square bell capitals and moulded bases, the base of the eastern pillar being modern. The south arcade is also of three bays, and has acutely pointed arches supported by circular pillars with square capitals and bases; the capitals have grotesquely carved heads at their angles

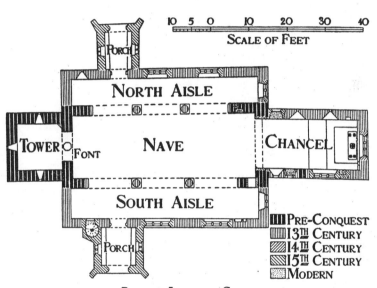

SCALE OF FEET

PLAN OF LAVENDON CHURCH

but no neckings, and the bases large angle spurs but no upper mouldings. The arches of both arcades spring at the responds from chamfered imposts. In a modern recess at the north-east of the nave is a mediaeval piscina bowl. The clearstory is lighted from either side by three square-headed windows of two trefoiled lights dating from the late 15th century, and the low-pitched roof of the nave with its heavy cambered beams is of the same period.

In the east wall of the north aisle is a square-headed window of two trefoiled lights, which was altered in the 15th century, but probably dates from an earlier period. In the north wall are two large windows, inserted late in the 15th century, each of three cinquefoiled lights in a depressed head, and to the west of these is the north doorway, with a small lancet of the early 13th century beyond it. The doorway is of about 1250 and has a pointed head of two richly moulded orders, the outer of which dies into the jambs in a somewhat unskilful

93a *Val. Eccl.* (Rec. Com.), iv, 242.
94 Aug. Off. Misc. Bk. ccccii, fol. 17.
94a Feet of F. Bucks. East. 9 Edw. VI;

Mich. 14 & 15 Eliz. Little Grangefield is also mentioned in these fines.
95 Lysons, loc. cit.

95a G.E.C. *Complete Peerage*, vii, 52–3.
96 Ibid.; Lysons, loc. cit.
96a Add. MS. 5839, fol. 114.b.

manner, while the inner is continuous. In a round-arched plastered recess at the south-east is a 12th-century pillar piscina. The jambs and head of the two-light east window of the south aisle are doubtless original, and the label terminates on the south in a grotesque head, which is very similar to those on the capitals of the south arcade ; the tracery is, however, modern. In the south wall are two late 15th-century windows similar to those in the north aisle, an original doorway with a plain chamfered edge, and a four-centred doorway of the 15th century opening to the parvise stairway, which is now blocked. The east end of this aisle is occupied by the organ, for which an opening has been cut through to the nave on the north. The organ obscures a piscina and a large trefoiled niche on the south. The lean-to roofs of both aisles have rough timbers, probably dating from the late 15th century.

The north porch is lighted from either side by an unglazed square-headed window of two trefoiled lights with plain tracery, and has a pointed entrance arch with a square outer order and foliated spandrels, above which is a cinquefoiled niche, all of the work being original. The pitch of the roof is masked by a straight embattled parapet and the diagonal buttresses are carried up to this level to obviate the awkward appearance which the abrupt drop to the lower level of the side parapets would otherwise have. The south porch was originally of two stages, but the turret stairway at the north-west by which the upper chamber was approached is now blocked, and the floor of the chamber itself has been taken away. The entrance has a four-centred arch under a square outer order with fleurs de lis in the spandrels, and above is a repaired square-headed light which originally lighted the upper chamber. The windows in the lateral walls are similar to those of the north porch. The diagonal buttresses stop below the parapet, which is gabled and has small pinnacles at the southern angles. The lower part of a 13th-century coffin-lid with a foliated cross has been built into the south wall, and some pieces of moulded stonework with nail-head ornament are inserted in the walling to the east of the south doorway.

The tower is a well-preserved example of pre-Conquest work and was originally of three stages, all of which are intact. The two lower stages are lighted by narrow round-headed windows in all the exposed faces, and the third, the original bell-chamber, by larger windows of the same form, the east light being blocked and now partly covered by the clock face. Below the windows of the third stage is a wide course of herring-bone masonry. Upon this bold and simple structure, which has neither string-courses nor buttresses, a late 15th-century bell-chamber has been built with a string-course and slight offset at its base. This is lighted from each side by a traceried window of two cinque-foiled lights and is surmounted by an embattled parapet.

The font is octagonal and dates from the late 15th century ; the bowl has shallow sunk panels enriched with delicate tracery and foliage, while in the panel

at the south-west is a shield of France modern. The panelled oak pulpit dates from the early 17th century, but stands on a modern stone base.

On the north wall of the chancel is a monument with arms to Richard Newton, sometime Canon of Christ Church, Oxford, and Principal of Hertford College (d. 1753). On the south wall is a monument to Katherine Harvey, wife of Thomas Newton of Lavendon Grange (d. 1680). At the east end of the north wall of the north aisle is an incised slab commemorating Nathaniel Waker, a former rector of the parish (d. 1654), and on the south wall is another incised slab commemorating Ephraim Pippen, also rector of the parish (d. 1670). Two brasses, one to the Katherine Newton mentioned above, and the other to James Newton, barrister of the Inner Temple (d. 1690), are preserved at the vicarage. There is a carved mahogany chair of the early 18th century in the chancel, and in the north aisle is an oak chest with three locks of about the same period, while a hatchment of George IV is attached to the east wall of the tower. A mediaeval slab with a raised cross, now considerably weatherworn, has been built into the south wall of the churchyard.

The tower contains a ring of five bells, of which the first three and the tenor are by Alexander Rigby of Stamford, 1689, and the fourth is by R. Taylor & Sons, 1828 ; all have been rehung in the old frame-work, which is inscribed ' IS. RB. C^{H.} W^{D.} 1690.'

The communion plate includes a cup and cover paten of 1569 ; a stand paten of the late 17th century, given by Sir Anthony Chester, bart. ; a modern paten copied from the cover paten of the 1569 cup ; a modern flagon designed in the same manner, and a plated flagon.

The registers begin in 1574.

ADVOWSON Though no mention of the church occurs in the Domesday Survey,[97] it is evident that it was appurtenant to the fee in Lavendon held of the honour of Huntingdon. At the close of the 12th century the advowson of the church of the Blessed Mary was given to the abbey of Lavendon by Hugh de St. Medard, and the gift was confirmed in 1237 by John de St. Medard, his grandson.[98] The vicarage was ordained in the time of Bishop Hugh of Wells,[99] and licence to appropriate in mortmain was afterwards obtained.[100]

The advowson followed the descent of the abbey manor until the spring of 1632–3, when Robert Eccleston and others conveyed the rectory and advowson to Anthony Elcocke,[1] possibly a trustee for Edward (Noel) Viscount Campden In 1670 the dowager Viscountess Campden presented to the living[2]; she died in 1680,[3] and in 1693[4] the patronage was exercised by her great-grandson Baptist (Noel) Earl of Gainsborough.[5] On his death in 1714 it descended to his son Baptist fourth Earl of Gains-borough.[6] He died in 1751 and was succeeded in turn by his sons Baptist (1751–9) and Henry (1759–98), both of whom died unmarried.[7] The last earl bequeathed the advowson to his nephew

[97] The earliest contemporary reference to the church dates from about 1218 (Gibbons, *Liber Antiq.* 12).

[98] Feet of F. Bucks. 21 Hen. III, no. 2. According to *Hund. R.* (Rec. Com.), ii, 349, the donor was William

de St. Medard, but no evidence has been found to support this statement.

[99] *R. of Hugh of Wells* (Cant. and York Soc.), ii, 86.

[100] *Cal. Pat.* 1307–13, p. 232.

[1] Feet of F. Bucks. Hil. 8 Chas. I.

[2] Inst. Bks. (P.R.O.).

[3] G.E.C. *Complete Peerage,* ii, 131.

[4] Inst. Bks. (P.R.O.).

[5] G.E.C. op. cit. iv, 2–3.   [6] Ibid. 3.

[7] Ibid. ; cf. Add. MS. 5839, fol. 114*b*, and Inst. Bks. (P.R.O.).

Sir Gerard Noel Noel, bart., the patron in the early 19th century.[8] By his first wife Diana Lady Barham he had a son Charles, who succeeded his mother as Baron Barham in 1823 and inherited his father's estates in 1838.[9] Charles Lord Barham was created Earl of Gainsborough in 1841,[10] and was returned as patron in 1865,[11] the year before his death.[12] It would seem, however, that he had disposed of his rights in at least one turn, for in 1860–4 the patron was the Rev. William Tomkins.[13] In 1877 the living was in the gift of Mr. Francis Larken Soames, whose trustees are the present patrons.

The chapel in Lavendon Castle is mentioned in 1231, when the abbot, as patron of Lavendon Church, had to provide for services twice a week.[14]

CHARITIES

Church Allotment. — It appears from a tablet in the church that some unknown person or persons gave 9 acres of land adjoining and comprising the poor-house, the rents therefrom to be applied for the repair and ornamentation of the church. By an Inclosure Award 8 a. 3 r. 39 p. of land adjoining the poor-house were awarded in lieu of land in the uninclosed field. The estate is now let at £17 yearly, and two cottages are also let at £6 and £3 8s. respectively. The income is applied to general church expenses.

GREAT LINFORD

Linforda (x cent.) ; Magna Lufford (xiii cent.) ; Mechel Lyngford (xiv cent.) ; Moche Lynforde, Lyndeforde Magna (xvi cent.).

The parish of Great Linford covers 1,835 acres, of which 238 are arable, 1,053 permanent grass and 87 woods and plantations.[1] The soil is mixed, with a subsoil of cornbrash and Great Oolite, producing crops of wheat, barley and oats. The parish is watered by the River Ouse, which forms its north-western boundary. The neighbourhood of the river is liable to floods. The highest point is 369 ft. above the ordnance datum on the southern boundary and the lowest is 199 ft. on the road near Black Horse Farm. There are quarries close to the church, and south-east of the village is a sand-pit.

The village, compact in shape, lies at the northern end of the parish, and south of the main road from Stony Stratford to Newport Pagnell, almost parallel to which is the Newport Pagnell branch of the London and North Western railway ; the station at Great Linford is north-east of the village. The Grand Junction Canal has a wharf between the railway station and the village. Some brickworks lie near it.

The church of St. Andrew lies to the north-west of the village, which also contains a Congregational chapel, built in 1810. The rectory, which stands to the south-east of the church, is a stone building, apparently erected at the close of the 16th century, although there seems to be work of a century earlier in the south-east wing. It is of two stories with an attic, the dormer windows of which belong to the 17th century. North of the modern porch is a late 16th-century four-light window. The 'Nag's Head' and several thatched cottages in High Street are of the 17th century. The almshouses and schoolhouse,

to the east of the church, were built by Sir William Pritchard at the end of the 17th century.[2] The main building is of one story, with a central block of two stories. The original staircase and panelling in the central block are worthy of notice. Adjoining

VILLAGE STREET, GREAT LINFORD

the almshouses is the Manor House, the residence of Mr. Charles Walter Mead. To the south of the village is Great Linford House, and near it is Ivy House, the residence of Captain H. E. Churton Ditmas, R.F.A.

Linford Wood, with Wood House and Wood Farm, are in the south-west of the parish, and Windmill Hill Farm lies in the village. The kennels of the Bucks otter hounds are in the parish.

MANORS

The first reference to Linford occurs in 944, when King Edmund gave to his thegn Aelfheah land at Linforda with liberty to leave it to whom he wished.[3] In 1086 there were two manors, both assessed at 2 hides 1½ virgates. One of these, which had belonged to Alric, son of Goding, at that date formed part of the

[8] Lysons, op. cit. i (3), 593 ; G.E.C. Baronetage, v, 217.
[9] G.E.C. Peerage, iv, 3–4. [10] Ibid.
[11] Clergy List.
[13] Clergy List.
[14] R. of Hugh of Wells, loc. cit.
[12] G.E.C. loc. cit.
[1] Statistics from Bd. of Agric. (1905).
[2] P.C.C. 155 Gee.
[3] Birch, Cart. Sax. ii, 798.

lands of Walter Giffard.[4] As part of the honour of Giffard[5] it descended with Fawley[6] (q.v.), this over-lordship being last mentioned in 1420, when it was assigned to Beatrice, widow of Gilbert Talbot, as part of her dower.[7] It passed in this century to the Crown,[8] by whom the manor was annexed to the honour of Ampthill in 1542,[9] and the overlordship rights retained until the abolition of feudal tenure.[10]

In 1086 Walter Giffard's sub-tenant was Hugh de Bolebec,[11] who was at the same time tenant in chief of the second manor in Great Linford.[12] This manor was held before the Conquest by three thegns, who had the right to assign and sell it. These two manors must have been united to form the manor of *GREAT LINFORD*, as their descent is thenceforward indistinguishable.[13] The Bolebecs later sub-infeudated Great Linford, their overlordship rights passing as in Great Kimble (q.v.) to the Earls of

BOLEBEC. *Vert a lion argent.*

VERE. *Quarterly gules and or with a molet argent in the quarter.*

Oxford,[14] who retained them as one fee until as late as 1632.[15]

The manorial rights of Great Linford were obtained by a branch of the Pipard family which ended in a female heir Alice.[16] Early in the reign of Henry III she was said to be in the gift of the king and married to Geoffrey Marsh (de Marisco, Mareis),[17] who is returned in 1235 as holding Great Linford, worth £20, in right of his wife Alice.[18] Their granddaughter and heir, Alice, was wife of Ralph son of Ralph Fitz Nicholas in 1242, when the manor was granted to Ralph Fitz Nicholas for £18 rent pending inquiries into Alice's claim.[19] The younger Ralph was in possession c. 1255,[20] and was succeeded in 1257[21] by his son Robert Fitz Nicholas.[22] He died about 1273, when his heir was Ralph Pipard,[23] called in the inquisition the son of his brother,[24] but elsewhere said to be the son of his sister, i.e., son of Nichole

a daughter of Ralph, sister of Robert Fitz Nicholas and wife of Henry Pipard.[25] Ralph Pipard complained in 1283 that the deer in his park had been hunted and carried away.[26] He held the manor[27] until his death about 1308.[28] In 1310 his son and heir John conveyed Great Linford to Edmund Butler, reserving a life interest,[29] which he afterwards transferred to Edmund for an annual rent.[30] Five years later, as Edmund had not paid the rent for two years, John Pipard re-entered the manor and held it until Edmund's death in 1321.[31] The manor was then taken into the king's hands, but was restored in 1323 to John Pipard,[32] apparently for life, in accordance

PIPARD. *Argent two bars and a quarter azure with a cinqfoil or in the quarter.*

BUTLER. *Or a chief indented azure.*

with the agreement of 1310. John Pipard was evidently dead in 1328 when James Butler, Earl of Ormond, the son and heir of Edmund Butler, was in possession of Great Linford.[33] The earl died about ten years later seised of the manor, leaving a son and heir James, a child of six.[34] Eleanor, his widow, in January 1343–4 married Thomas Dagworth, Lord Dagworth,[35] who held Great Linford in 1346.[36] He was slain in Brittany in 1359,[37] and Eleanor, who made a settlement of the manor in 1361,[37a] died in 1363, when her life interest devolved on her son James second Earl of Ormond.[38] He was succeeded in 1382 by his son James,[39] who died in 1405, leaving as heir his son, another James, a minor.[40] Before his death in 1452 he had granted the manor to his son and heir James,[41] who had been knighted in 1426, and summoned to Parliament as Earl of Wiltshire in 1449. In 1445 he had acquired Newport Pagnell Manor[42] (q.v.), with which Great Linford escheated to the Crown in 1461.[43] In the following year it was granted to Richard Middleton and his heirs male,[44] a further grant to himself and his wife Maud being made in

⁴ *V.C.H. Bucks.* i, 251.
⁵ *Testa de Nevill* (Rec. Com.), 258.
⁶ Chan. Inq. p.m. 10 Ric. II, no. 42 ; *Cal. Pat.* 1396–9, p. 17.
⁷ Chan. Inq. p.m. 8 Hen. V (Add. nos.), no. 127. The overlordship rights appear to have been temporarily transferred about this time to Thomas Rolfe and Walter Bodelgate (ibid. 7 Hen. V, no. 68).
⁸ *Cal. Pat.* 1461–7, p. 143.
⁹ *L. and P. Hen. VIII*, xvii, 28 (21).
¹⁰ Pat. 3 Eliz. pt. iv, m. 28.
¹¹ *V.C.H. Bucks.* i, 251.
¹² Ibid. 265.
¹³ The grant of the manor in two moieties in 1560 is probably due to its dual origin (Pat. 2 Eliz. pt. iv, m. 25).
¹⁴ Chan. Inq. p.m. 34 Edw. III (1st nos.), no. 84.
¹⁵ Ibid. (Ser. 2), dviii, 15.
¹⁶ Assize R. 62, m. 3.
¹⁷ Ibid.

¹⁸ Ibid. ; *Testa de Nevill* (Rec. Com.), 258, 259 ; *Excerpta e Rot. Fin.* (Rec. Com.), i, 391.
¹⁹ *Excerpta e Rot. Fin.* (Rec. Com.), i, 391 ; *Cal. Close*, 1237–42, p. 515.
²⁰ *Testa de Nevill* (Rec. Com.), 247 ; *Hund. R.* (Rec. Com.), i, 30.
²¹ Matt. Paris, *Chron. Maj.* (Rolls Ser.), v, 616.
²² *Excerpta e Rot. Fin.* (Rec. Com.), ii, 269 ; *Plac. de Quo Warr.* (Rec. Com.), 86.
²³ *Cal. Inq. p.m.* (Edw. I), ii, 22 ; *Cal. Fine R.* 1272–1307, p. 17.
²⁴ *Cal. Inq. p.m.* (Edw. I), ii, 22.
²⁵ Add. MS. 6666, p. 232.
²⁶ *Cal. Pat.* 1281–92, p. 103.
²⁷ *Feud. Aids*, i, 80, 106 ; Feet of F. Div. Co. East. 18 Edw. I.
²⁸ *Cal. Inq. p.m.* (Edw. II), v, 98 ; *Cal. Pat.* 1307–13, p. 135.
²⁹ Feet of F. Div. Co. Hil. 3 Edw. II ; *Feud. Aids*, i, 109.

³⁰ *Cal. Inq. p.m.* (Edw. II), vi, 215.
³¹ Ibid.
³² *Cal. Close*, 1318–23, p. 659.
³³ *Cal. Chart. R.* 1327–41, p. 95 ; Feet of F. Div. Co. Trin. 3 Edw. III.
³⁴ Chan. Inq. p.m. 12 Edw. III (1st nos.), no. 43 ; *Cal. Close*, 1337–9, p. 341.
³⁵ G.E.C. *Peerage*, vi, 140.
³⁶ *Feud. Aids*, i, 132.
³⁷ G.E.C. *Peerage*, vi, 140.
³⁷a Feet of F. Div. Co. Mich. 35 Edw. III.
³⁸ Chan. Inq. p.m. 37 Edw. III (1st nos.), no. 24.
³⁹ Ibid. 6 Ric. II, no. 15 ; Ct. R. (Gen. Ser.), portf. 155, no. 25.
⁴⁰ Chan. Inq. p.m. 7 Hen. IV, no. 19.
⁴¹ Ibid. 31 Hen. VI, no. 11.
⁴² *Cat. of Anct. D.* ii, 337.
⁴³ G.E.C. *Complete Peerage*, viii, 165.
⁴⁴ *Cal. Pat.* 1461–7, p. 143.

1465.[45] In October 1467 the manor was granted for life to the king's daughter, the Princess Elizabeth,[46] afterwards wife of Henry VII,[47] but it was obtained in 1474 by Gerard Caniziani, a merchant of London, and his wife Elizabeth.[48]

On the accession of Henry VII in 1485 the Ormond attainder was reversed and the Butlers were restored to their estates.[49] They were in possession of Great Linford in 1498,[50] and the manor henceforward descends with Newport Pagnell (q.v.) until 1560, when Queen Elizabeth granted it to John Thompson.[51] He died seised of it in 1597,[52] leaving the reversion, after the death of his wife Dorothy, to his son Robert, who at that date had been a lunatic for five years.[53] Robert's son John, then aged eight and afterwards knighted,[54] appears later to have managed his father's estate.[55] Robert died in 1633,[56] and in 1640 Sir John Thompson conveyed the manor to Richard Napier,[57] afterwards Sir Richard Napier, kt.,[58] who died in January 1675–6.[59] His son Thomas Napier[60] alienated Great Linford Manor in 1678 to Sir William Pritchard, kt.,[61] who by his will dated 29 December 1702 left it, after the death of his widow Sarah, to his nephew Richard Uthwatt for life, with remainder to Richard's eldest son John and his male issue.[62] Sir William Pritchard died in February 1704–5[63] and Richard Uthwatt in 1719.[64] His eldest son John died without issue.[65] The second son, Thomas, Sheriff of Buckinghamshire in 1726,[66] who died in 1754,[67] had by his wife Catherine Dalton an only daughter Catherine, wife of Matthew Knapp,[68] who was debarred by Sir William Pritchard's will from inheriting Great Linford. Richard, the third son of Richard Uthwatt, had died before his brother Thomas,[69] and it was his son Henry who inherited the manor in 1754 and broke the entail in that year.[70] Henry, who was sheriff in 1755,[71] died in 1757, and Linford was held by his widow Frances for life.[72] The Knapps appear to have put forward a claim which they renounced in 1760.[73] Frances Uthwatt died in 1800,[74] when the manor, in accordance with the terms of Henry Uthwatt's will, passed to a godson and distant cousin, the Rev. Henry Uthwatt Andrewes,[75] on condition of his taking the name of Uthwatt.[76] He held Great Linford till his death in 1812,[77] and was succeeded by his eldest son Henry Uthwatt, Sheriff of Buckinghamshire in 1831,[78] who died unmarried in

1855, leaving as heir his brother the Rev. William Uthwatt.[79] At his death without issue male in 1879 he was succeeded at Great Linford by his brother Augustus Thomas Uthwatt, from whom the manor passed in 1885 to his nephew and heir, William Francis Edolph Andrewes Uthwatt, the present owner.

Thomas Earl of Ormond appears to have made a temporary alienation or settlement of the manorial rights in the early 16th century, for in 1516 they were settled by Thomas Stafford of Tattenhoe on his illegitimate son William Stafford,[80] who died seised of Great Linford in 1529[81]; it was then held of Lady Anne St. Leger, to whom the manorial rights appear to have reverted, as there is no further trace of this sub-tenancy.

UTHWATT. *Argent a bend between cotises sable and charged with three pierced molets argent.*

The Earls of Pembroke as overlords claimed gallows and assize of bread and ale in Great Linford in the 13th century.[82] View of frankpledge was claimed by the Pipards about the same time,[83] and was held, as also a court baron, as late as the 17th century.[84] Grants of free warren were made to the lords of the manor in 1284,[85] in 1316,[86] and in 1328.[87]

In 1303 a certain William le Waleys and Cecilia his wife owned a messuage, mill and 120 acres of land in Great Linford, the reversion of which they settled on their son John.[88] William was dead four years later, when his widow gave to another son Robert her tenement in Great Linford.[88a] This holding is probably that which became known in the 17th century as *LINFORD* or *WALSHES* or *TYRINGHAM'S* or *PIPARD'S MANOR*.[89] Robert Walsh and Maud his wife, from whose family the manor derived one of the distinctive names, held lands here in 1316,[90] and various references to other members occur as late as 1480,[91] though they are never mentioned in connexion with the manor. In 1465 a grant of a messuage and 160 acres of land, 16 acres of meadow and 20 acres of pasture called 'Walshes' was made to Richard Middelton and Maud his wife on the forfeiture of

[45] Cal. Pat. 1461–7, p. 440; Parl. R. v, 609a.
[46] Cal. Pat. 1467–77, p. 44.
[47] Dict. Nat. Biog.
[48] Cal. Pat. 1467–77, p. 466.
[49] G.E.C. Complete Peerage, vi, 142.
[50] Ct. R. (Gen. Ser.), portf. 177, no. 15, 16.
[51] Pat. 2 Eliz. pt. iv, m. 25. Sir John St. Leger renounced any claim to the manor at the same date (ibid. 3 Eliz. pt. iv, m. 28; Add. Chart. 24917; Feet of F. Bucks. Hil. and East. 3 Eliz.; Recov. R. Trin. 3 Eliz. m. 123).
[52] Chan. Inq. p.m. (Ser. 2), ccxlviii, 34.
[53] Ibid. ccl, 84. [54] Ibid.
[55] Feet of F. Bucks. Mich. 7 Chas. I.
[56] Chan. Inq. p.m. (Ser. 2), dxxv, 118.
[57] Feet of F. Bucks. Mich. 16 Chas. I.
[58] Ibid. Trin. 1650; Hil. 19 & 20 Chas. II.
[59] Dict. Nat. Biog.
[60] Burke, Extinct Baronetage, 378; P.C.C. 94 Bence.
[61] Feet of F. Bucks. Trin. 30 Chas. II.

[62] P.C.C. 155 Gee.
[63] Musgrave's Obit. (Harl. Soc.), v, 89.
[64] P.C.C. 246 Browning.
[65] Com. Pleas Recov. R. Mich. 28 Geo. II, m. 32.
[66] P.R.O. List of Sheriffs, 10.
[67] Musgrave's Obit. (Harl. Soc.), vi, 151.
[68] P.C.C. 240 Pinfold.
[69] Com. Pleas Recov. R. Mich. 28 Geo. II, m. 32.
[70] Ibid.; Recov. R. Mich. 28 Geo. II, m. 229.
[71] P.R.O. List of Sheriffs, 10.
[72] Musgrave's Obit. (Harl. Soc.), vi, 151; P.C.C. 25 Hulton.
[73] Feet of F. Bucks. East. 33 Geo. II.
[74] P.C.C. 69 Abercrombie; mural monument in Lathbury Church.
[75] Berry, Bucks. Gen. 49.
[76] P.C.C. 25 Hulton.
[77] Com. Pleas Recov. R. Trin. 48 Geo. III, m. 103; Lysons, Mag. Brit. i (3), 596; Burke, Landed Gentry (ed. 1912).
[78] P.R.O. List of Sheriffs, 11.

[79] Burke, loc. cit.; Sheahan, Hist. and Topog. of Bucks. 558.
[80] Close, 8 Hen. VIII, no. 1; see also Ct. R. (Gen. Ser.), portf. 177, no. 16.
[81] Chan. Inq. p.m. (Ser. 2), l, 76.
[82] Hund. R. (Rec. Com.), i, 40.
[83] Plac. de Quo Warr. (Rec. Com.), 86.
[84] Feet of F. Bucks. Trin. 30 Chas. II.
[85] Cal. Chart. R. 1257–1300, p. 281.
[86] Ibid. 1300–26, p. 307.
[87] Cal. Chart. R. 1327–41, p. 95.
[88] Feet of F. Bucks. Hil. 31 Edw. I.
[88a] From Mr. Uthwatt's Deeds.
[89] Possibly the Walshes were tenants of the Pipards in the 14th century.
[90] Feet of F. Bucks. Hil. 9 Edw. II.
[91] Var. Coll. (Hist. MSS. Com.), iv, 331; Feet of F. Div. Co. Hil. 12 Edw. II; Cal. Pat. 1391–6, p. 224; 1399–1401, p. 325; 1408–13, p. 301; Ct. R. (Gen. Ser.), portf. 177, no. 14. Many references from 1450 to 1480 to Richard Walsh, Edward his son and heir, and Isabel Osbern, widow, his daughter, are to be found among Mr. Uthwatt's Deeds.

Sir John Fortescue, kt.[92] Nothing further is known of this holding until 1614, when it reappears as the property of Sir Anthony Tyringham, kt.[93] He died in this year, and was succeeded by his son Thomas.[94] In 1621 this holding is first referred to as a manor.[95] Sir Thomas Tyringham died in January 1636–7,[96] and the estate seems to have passed by the marriage of his daughter Anne to Sir Richard Napier,[97] who was seised of it in 1650.[98] From this date it descended with the manor of Great Linford, from which it is not distinguished after 1808.[99]

Before the Conquest two men of Alric son of Goding held 2 hides of land in Great Linford. In 1086 these lands belonged to the Count of Mortain[100]; they eventually passed to the Earl of Cornwall and were held by his tenants of the honour of Berkhampstead,[1] last mentioned in connexion with Great Linford in 1498.[2] Ranulf was the sub-tenant here at the time of the Survey.[3] Ralph Marshall, the next holder, was in possession about the middle of the 13th century,[4] but had subinfeudated John Aynell before 1284–6.[5] Holding with John Aynell in 1302–3 were Peter Basset, Richard Tours and their tenants,[6] and by 1346 this estate had descended to John Aynell, jun.[7] Robert de Luton was the tenant in 1379,[8] but the holding afterwards became merged in Great Linford Manor, which in consequence was said in 1405 to be held in part of the honour of Berkhampstead.[9]

CHURCH The church of ST. ANDREW consists of a chancel measuring internally 30 ft. by 17 ft., nave 47 ft. by 21 ft., north aisle 27 ft. 6 in. by 11 ft. 6 in., north porch, south aisle 6 ft. wide, south porch, and west tower 13 ft. by 12 ft. 6 in It is built of rubble with stone dressings and the roofs are covered with lead and tiles; the clearstory, north aisle and porch, and the tower are coated with cement.

The present church was built about 1250, and to this date belong the nave and the two lower stages of the tower; the chancel and south aisle, though considerably altered, probably date from this time. The north porch was added early in the 14th century, when the chancel arch was rebuilt and the south arcade repaired; the north aisle and the original south porch were built about 1350 and the clearstory was added to the nave late in the 15th century. The fabric appears to have fallen into considerable dilapidation by 1708, when it was very extensively repaired by Sarah, widow of Sir William Pritchard, and her two nephews.[10] This work included the complete remodelling of the chancel and of all the window tracery, the rebuilding of the south porch and the addition of a third stage to the tower. The church was again restored in 1884–5.

The chancel, though remodelled, still probably retains its 13th-century walls, and an original narrow doorway, now blocked, remains at the south-west. In each of the side walls is a two-light pointed window of the 18th century, in which some older material has been re-used. The east window, of three lights

with tracery in a pointed head, is a recent insertion. The early 14th-century chancel arch is pointed, and springs from responds composed of three clustered shafts with richly moulded capitals; the bases are modern.

The nave opens to the south aisle by a late 13th-century arcade of three pointed arches having responds with moulded corbels and carved heads, and octagonal pillars with moulded capitals and bases. The corbels appear to have been inserted in the 14th century, and the abaci of the capitals are modern. On the north is a mid-14th-century arcade of two pointed arches, which also has moulded corbels at the responds, and an octagonal pillar with a moulded capital and base. The east corbel is enriched with ball-flower ornament and an embattled moulding, and the capital of the pillar with five-leaf ornament. The west corbel is modern. West of the arcade is a plain chamfered doorway to the north porch, the round head of which has been considerably defaced. The west tower stands considerably to the south of the axial line of the nave, a disposition common in the neighbourhood (even where, as in this case, the nave does not appear to have been subsequently widened), and doubtless adopted since it admitted of the direct abutment of one of the nave walls. The tower arch, which dates from about 1250, is much distorted and has been built up; it has clustered responds with moulded capitals and bases, the latter being very much defaced. The clearstory is lighted from both sides by four two-light windows of the late 15th century, from all of which the tracery was removed in 1708 and replaced by mullions rising into the heads. Both the chancel and nave have segmental plastered ceilings, that of the nave being intersected by the openings for the clearstory windows.

In its original state the north aisle must have been a rich and charming example of mid-14th-century work. On the north is an original wall arcade of two arches, springing from a circular attached shaft and responds with moulded capitals and bases. Each bay of the arcade is pierced by a large pointed window, the outer orders of which, as well as the capitals of the wall arcades, are enriched with foliated ornament. The original window tracery, however, has been removed and replaced by 18th-century mullions, carried straight up to the head, with transoms at the springing, the windows being now divided into three instead of four lights as formerly. There are some fragments of mediaeval glass in the head of the easternmost window. High in the west wall is an 18th-century doorway to the parvise over the 14th-century north porch. The lower stage of this porch, which is well preserved, is divided into two bays by a sexpartite vault, the chamfered ribs of which spring from head corbels and meet above in a large foliated boss. The entrance on the north is richly moulded and has a pointed ogee head, and at the north-west is a pointed window, the head of which has been restored, while a corresponding window in the east wall is blocked by the aisle. This apartment is now

[92] Cal. Pat. 1461–7, p. 440.
[93] Chan. Inq. p.m. (Ser. 2), cccxlix, 164.
[94] Ibid.
[95] Feet of F. Div. Co. East. 19 Jas. I.
[96] Chan. Inq. p.m. (Ser. 2), dxliii, 19.
[97] Burke, Extinct Baronetage, 378.
[98] Feet of F. Bucks. Trin. 1650.

[99] Com. Pleas Recov. R. Trin. 48 Geo. III, m. 103.
[100] V.C.H. Bucks. i, 246.
[1] Chan. Inq. p.m. 28 Edw. I, no. 44 (20).
[2] Ct. R. (Gen. Ser.), portf. 177, no. 15.
[3] V.C.H. Bucks. i, 246.

[4] Testa de Nevill (Rec. Com.), 244b.
[5] Feud. Aids, i, 77.
[6] Ibid. 107.   [7] Ibid. 133.
[8] Chan. Inq. p.m. 2 Ric. II, no. 57 (23).
[9] Ibid. 7 Hen. IV, no. 19.
[10] Lipscomb, Hist. and Antiq. of Bucks. iv, 223.

used as a vestry, and the old door with strap hinges still retained in the doorway is permanently fastened. In both the north and west walls of the parvise there is a small trefoiled light ; a similar light in the east wall is blocked by the north aisle.

The south aisle, which is particularly narrow, is lighted from the south by two large windows of similar character to those in the side walls of the chancel, but of three lights. The doorway to the west of these windows, which is now coated with plaster, is similar to that in the north wall of the nave. Much of the original material has been re-used in the south porch, including the pointed entrance doorway and the traceried heads of two two-light windows now built into the same opening in the east wall, while a 15th-century corbel, carved as an angel holding a shield, is inserted over the doorway.

The tower is of three stages with western diagonal buttresses and is surmounted by an embattled parapet. The ground stage is lighted by original lancets in the north and south walls, and there is a 15th-century two-light window in the west wall ; the latter has been treated similarly to those of the clearstory, and below it is an 18th-century doorway. The second stage, the original bell-chamber, has two pointed windows of the 13th century on the south. Two corresponding windows formerly existed on the north, the outlines of which can still be traced inside ; these windows, however, were blocked in the 18th century, when an opening to the roof in the east wall was also built up and the south windows were altered externally. The buttresses were added in the 15th century and the present bell-chamber, which is lighted from each side by a large single-light window, was built in 1708.

The font is modern. The painted deal pulpit, with bolection moulded panels, dates from the 18th century. On a slab in the nave are brass figures of Roger Hunt (d. 1473), and Joan his wife, both represented in long gowns, with a marginal inscription, two shields inscribed respectively ' Jhu Mercy,' ' Lady helpe,' and the verses : ' Here lieth I dowen under this stone | Roger hunt and Johane his wiffe | Of whose propre costes alone | This chirche was paved soon aft' ye liffe | Almighty Jhū sittyng in trone | Oñ bothe their soules to have m'cy | As thou camyst from yi fader alone | Wᵗ yi precious blood mañys soule to by.' There are also indents for sons and daughters. In the chancel is a brass with figures of a man and his wife, both wearing ruffs, groups of five sons and three daughters, and an inscription commemorating Anne wife of John Uvedall (d. 1611). In the north aisle is a brass to Thomas Malyn (d. 1536) and Elizabeth his wife, with their figures in fur-trimmed gowns, the lady wearing a gabled head-dress ; there is also a small figure of one daughter and an indent for one son. On the west wall of the north aisle is a monument of white marble commemorating Sir William Pritchard, kt. (1704), his wife Sarah (Coke) (d. 1718), and William, their only son (d. 1685). The inscription states that Sir William Pritchard was ' Alderman,

and sometime since Lord Mayor of London. . . . He was one of the City's Representatives in sevˡ Parliaments, and President of St. Bartholomew's Hospital, where he erected a convenient apartment for cutting of the stone ; and built and endowed a School House and Six Alms Houses in this Parish.' On a shield above are the arms, Ermine a lion sable impaling Party gules and azure three eagles, for Coke. There is a mural monument with arms at the east end of this aisle to Thomas Uthwatt (d. 1754) and Catherine (Dalton) his wife (d. 1769) ; and on the south wall is a monument to Catherine (Uthwatt) daughter of the above and wife of Matthew Knapp (d. 1794). On the chancel floor are slabs commemorating John Coles, for forty-nine years rector of the parish (d. 1748) ; Anne his wife ; Edmund Smyth, also rector of the parish (d. 1789), and Dorothy his wife (d. 1780) ; and Edward Harrison (d. 1676). The altar and altar rails date from about 1700 ; the chancel walls have a deal dado of the 18th century. In the lower stage of the tower is a piece of bell framework of the same period.

The tower contains a ring of six bells, five of which were recast from older bells in 1756, when the treble was added, all by Joseph Eayre of St. Neots, and a small bell dated 1753.

The communion plate consists of a cup and cover paten of 1610, two flagons of 1732, and a large paten of 1754.

There is one register book, which includes all entries 1653 to 1759 and baptisms and burials to 1812, and a book of marriages only 1759 to 1811.

ADVOWSON The advowson of the church descended with the manor[11] until 1560, when Queen Elizabeth granted it to William Button and Thomas Escourt.[12] They immediately sold it to Christopher Troughton,[13] and he or a successor of the same name in 1606 conveyed it to Robert afterwards Sir Robert Napier _alias_ Sandy, bart., of Luton Hoo, Bedfordshire.[14] His brother Richard Napier, the rector since 1590, died in 1634, when the next presentation was made by Richard, younger son of Sir Robert Napier, bart.[15] In 1640 he acquired the manor, with which the advowson has since descended.[16] At the present day it is vested in Mr. Thomas Andrewes Uthwatt, cousin of the lord of the manor.

CHARITIES By his will dated 29 December 1702 Sir William Pritchard gave a yearly rent-charge of £34, £24 thereof to be divided equally among six poor people inhabiting the almshouses built by him, and the other £10 to be paid to a schoolmaster.[17] The rent-charge issues out of a portion of Great Linford estate. The almshouse and school premises consist of a range of buildings containing seven tenements under one roof, also a schoolroom, and residence for the master, and a garden. Under a scheme of the Board of Education of 6 January 1906 it was determined that the old schoolhouse and master's residence with the garden and ten thirty-fourths of the net income in

[11] De Banco R. 240, m. 343 ; 242, m. 151 d. ; 243, m. 61 ; 244, m. 19 ; 245, m. 2 d. ; 246, m. 7 ; 248, m. 16 ; _Cal. Pat._ 1307–13, pp. 135, 140 ; _Cal. Close,_ 1323–7, pp. 238, 242 ; _Cal. Pat._ 1324–7, pp. 89, 152, 182. In 1291 the church was valued at £10 (_Pope Nich. Tax._ [Rec. Com.], 34) ; in 1535 the net

value was £20 0s. 0½d. (_Valor Eccl._ [Rec. Com.], iv, 245).
[12] Pat. 2 Eliz. pt. iii, m. 10 ; 4 Eliz. pt. iii.
[13] Close, 2 Eliz. pt. iv, no. 29.
[14] Ibid. 4 Jas. I, pt. x.
[15] Lipscomb, op. cit. iv, 225 ; _Dict. Nat. Biog._; Burke, _Extinct Baronetage_, 378.

[16] Inst. Bks. (P.R.O.). Sir William Bagot, bart., presented here in 1770 on the nomination of Mrs. Frances Uthwatt. As Lord Bagot he made another presentation in 1786 (Inst. Bks. [P.R.O.] ; Bacon, _Liber Regis_, 500).
[17] P.C.C. 155 Gee.

respect of the rent-charge of £34 should form the endowment of Sir William Pritchard's educational foundation. The almspeople (six in number) received from the charity 1s. 6d. weekly, and £10 is yearly applied to Sir William Pritchard's educational foundation. The alms-people also receive £6 a year from the charity of Dame Sarah Pritchard next mentioned.

Dame Sarah Pritchard, who died in 1718, by her will[18] bequeathed a legacy for charitable purposes, now represented by £645 18s. 2d. consols, with the official trustees, producing £16 2s. 8d. yearly. Under a scheme of the Charity Commissioners of 20 July 1886 the income is applicable as follows : £6 to be divided equally among the inmates of Sir William Pritchard's almshouses, £1 to the rector so long as he shall not permit any cattle to be grazed in the churchyard and burial place, £1 to the parish clerk for keeping clean the pews and windows of the parish church, and the residue, amounting to £8 2s. 8d., in apprenticing, or in the advancement of education under the title of 'Dame Sarah Pritchard's educational foundation.'[19]

Charity of unknown donor.—The earliest reference to this charity is in an account book dated 2 December 1731, in which it is stated that £8 yearly is payable to the poor out of lands belonging to Thomas Uthwatt. The annuity is paid by the lord of the manor, and is distributed in money to about forty-eight recipients.

Miss Ann Cape, by her will, proved at London 7 September 1859, gave a sum of money, now represented by £540 consols, with the official trustees, producing £13 10s. yearly, and directed that five-ninths of the income should be applied towards the support of the Church Sunday school, three-ninths to a master for instructing Sunday school children, girls and boys, in writing and arithmetic in the week, and the remaining one-ninth for the entertainment of children once a year with tea drinking, or some suitable amusement.

Maria Barbara Cape, by her will, proved at London 9 December 1864, gave a sum of money, now represented by £370 15s. 10d. consols, with the official trustees, producing £9 5s. 4d. yearly, the income to be applied at Christmas as follows : £1 to each widow living in Linford on parish allowance and not receiving benefit of an almshouse, £1 to each old man past work and not in an almshouse, and the residue to the poor and needy, in blankets, sheets, flannel, or other useful articles. In 1912 one widow and eight old men received £1 each.

LITTLE LINFORD

Linforde (xi cent.) ; Parva Limford (xiii cent.).

This parish covers 728 acres, of which 143 are arable, 392 permanent grass and 130 woods and plantations.[1] The soil is mixed and the subsoil is Great Oolite. The ground rises from an average of 200 ft. above the ordnance datum in the south to 300 ft. in the north, the highest point, 332 ft., being found on the south-western edge of Linford Wood. The River Ouse forms the southern and eastern boundary of the parish. Between 1320 and 1340 an indulgence was granted for the construction and repair of a bridge at Little Linford.[2] There are now two bridges of three arches each over the river and several footbridges over the streams which run into the river.

To the south-east of the road from Gayhurst to Haversham lies Little Linford Hall, the seat of Mr. John Matthew Knapp, J.P. The house is a three-storied building of stone with a tiled roof and now consists of a principal block with two wings. The building began to assume its present form about 1680, when large additions were made to an earlier manor-house by John Knapp. Considerable alterations were undertaken in the 18th century, and within the last forty years the only remaining portion of the original house was replaced by a modern wing. Some of the 17th-century fittings remain, including a fine fireplace of marble, in the overmantel of which is a large trophy of arms. The house stands at the north-east corner of Little Linford Park, which is well-wooded ; the fish-ponds formerly in the park are now included in the gardens recently laid out by Mr.

J. M. Knapp in a formal style. Outside the park is a quarry.

The church stands close to the Hall on the north side. The vicarage is a modern building situated some distance away, near the road from Gayhurst.

In the north-west of the parish is Linford Wood, mentioned in the 17th century.[3]

LITTLE LINFORD, which had been held by Eddeva wife of Wulfward White,[4] was given to the Bishop of Coutances at the Conquest, Eddeva occupying the 4 hides as tenant in 1086.[5] After the death of the Bishop of Coutances in 1093[6] his nephew Robert de Mowbray inherited, but forfeited his estates for rebellion,[7] and Little Linford was obtained by the Paynels,[8] who already held 1 virgate here as descendants of William Fitz Ansculf, the Domesday holder.[9] They had also inherited his lands in Newport Pagnell, the head in this county of their honour of Dudley, to which Little Linford Manor was thenceforward attached. It was held in free socage at a rent of 6s. and 4s. for view of frankpledge.[10] After the assumption of the manorial rights by the overlords in the 14th century Little Linford was held in chief, and was constituted part of the honour of Grafton or that of Ampthill in 1542.[11]

Eddeva and Robert, the tenants of the two holdings in 1086,[12] had been succeeded by 1205[13] by Henry son of Peter de Northampton, who in 1220[14] conveyed Little Linford to Henry and Ellen de Hauville in trust for their second son Henry, a minor.[15] It does not appear that the grantee was

18 P.C.C. 110 Tenison.
19 See *V.C.H. Bucks.* ii, 218.
1 Statistics from Bd. of Agric. (1905).
2 Linc. Epis. Reg. Memo. Burghersh, fol. 39.
3 Add. Chart. 24045.
4 *V.C.H. Bucks.* i, 216.

5 Ibid. 240.
6 G.E.C. *Peerage*, vi, 82.
7 Ibid. ; *V.C.H. Northants*, i, 288.
8 See advowson ; *Pipe R. 9 Hen. II* (Pipe R. Soc.), 19.
9 *V.C.H. Bucks.* i, 213, 256.
10 *Cal. Inq. p.m.* (Hen. III), i, 205.

11 *L. and P. Hen. VIII*, xvii, 28 (21) (22).
12 *V.C.H. Bucks.* i, 240, 256.
13 *Cal. Rot. Chart.* 1199–1216 (Rec. Com.), 151.
14 Feet of F. Div. Co. East. 4 Hen. III.
15 *Cal. Inq. p.m.* (Hen. III), i, 72–3.

GREAT LINFORD RECTORY

GREAT LINFORD CHURCH FROM THE SOUTH

LITTLE LINFORD CHURCH FROM THE NORTH-WEST

LITTLE LINFORD CHURCH: THE INTERIOR LOOKING EAST

ever in possession of the manor. Henry, the trustee, was sued by the Prior of Newport or Tickford concerning this land in 1224,[16] but held the manor until his death in 1253.[17] His heir was Henry, a minor, son of his eldest son Ralph, who had predeceased him.[18] In 1258 Thomas de Hauville, youngest son of Henry and Ellen, claimed the custody of the manor until his nephew Henry's majority,[19] and died seised of it about 1267,[20] when Henry came of age.[21] In 1277 Henry conveyed the manor to Thomas de Hauville,[22] probably his cousin, who died about 1302.[23] His son and heir Thomas[24] was engaged in a prolonged lawsuit with John de Olney, who in 1314 claimed the manor on behalf of his wife Maud, daughter of Nicholas, described as the son and heir of Hugh de Haversham, who was said to have held it in John's reign.[25] Thomas de Hauville finally mortgaged Little Linford to John de Olney, was unable to redeem it,[26] and was outlawed at Olney's suit in 1316.[27] Thereupon John de Somery, the overlord, seized the manor as an escheat,[28] and made a settlement of it in 1317 on himself for life with remainder to Thomas and Joan de Hauville and their issue.[29] After the death of John de Somery in 1322[30] his widow Lucy claimed her dower in Little Linford,[31] and judgement was given in her favour in 1324.[32] In the meantime John de Olney laid claim to the manor as mortgagee, and it was counted among his possessions at his death in 1325.[33] His son John[34] seems to have made little resistance to the encroachment of the overlords, for Little Linford was included in 1338 among the manors held in demesne by Joan Botetourt,[35] younger sister and co-heir of

John de Somery,[36] and was settled in 1347 by her son John Botetourt on himself and his wife Joyce in tail,[37] a further settlement being made in 1358 on their son John and his wife Maud, daughter of John Grey of Rotherfield.[38] In 1366 the younger John Botetourt and his wife were completely successful in wresting it from their tenant William, son of the aforesaid John de Olney,[39] and John Botetourt died seised of Little Linford in 1369, when it was held by his widow Maud.[40] In 1386 a settlement on her and her second husband, Sir Thomas Harcourt, was made of Newport Pagnell Manor[41] (q.v.), with which Little Linford henceforward descends, and with which it escheated to the Crown in 1461. In 1463 it was granted to George Duke of Clarence,[42] who in 1472 received Newport Pagnell Manor also.[43] The two manors descended together until 1560,[44] when Little Linford continued with Great Linford, but was retained by the Thompsons when they alienated the latter in 1640.[45]

LITTLE LINFORD HALL

In 1655 Little Linford Manor was settled by Sir John Thompson, kt., on St. John Thompson,[46] his son and heir.[46a] In 1659 it was leased by William

[16] Maitland, *Bracton's Note Bk.* ii, 718.
[17] *Testa de Nevill* (Rec. Com.), 248 ; *Cal. Close, 1234–7*, p. 564.
[18] *Cal. Inq. p.m.* (Hen. III), i, 72–3, 97.
[19] Cur. Reg. R. 158, m. 15 d.
[20] *Cal. Inq. p.m.* (Hen. III), i, 205, 216.
[21] Ibid. 206.
[22] Feet of F. Div. Co. Mich. 5 & 6 Edw. I ; cf. *Hund. R.* (Rec. Com.), ii, 346 ; *Feud. Aids*, i, 73.
[23] *Cal. Inq. p.m.* (Edw. I), iv, 71.
[24] Ibid.
[25] De Banco R. 204, m. 181 ; 211, m. 18 ; 212, m. 238 d. ; 214, m. 37 d. The pedigree is faulty, for Nicholas was grandson of Hugh de Haversham, being the son of his son and heir Nicholas (see Haversham).
[26] *Cal. Inq. p.m.* (Edw. II), vi, 425.
[27] De Banco R. 217, m. 196 d.

[28] Ibid. ; *Feud. Aids*, i, 110.
[29] Feet of F. Bucks. Trin. 11 Edw. II, no. 17 ; De Banco R. 222, m. 87 d.
[30] *Cal. Close, 1318–23*, p. 611.
[31] De Banco R. 248, m. 87 ; 253, m. 60.   [32] Ibid. 253, m. 261.
[33] *Cal. Inq. p.m.* loc. cit.
[34] Ibid. (Edw. III), vii, 157.
[35] Chan. Inq. p.m. 12 Edw. III (1st nos.), no. 40.
[36] *Cal. Close, 1318–23*, p. 630.
[37] *Cal. Pat. 1345–8*, p. 351 ; De Banco R. 351, m. 415 ; Feet of F. Bucks. Mich. 21 Edw. III, no. 18.
[38] *Cal. Pat. 1358–61*, p. 125.
[39] De Banco R. 421, m. 3 d. ; 425, m. 273 d. ; *Gen.* (New Ser.), xvii, 119.
[40] Chan. Inq. p.m. 48 Edw. III (1st nos.), no. 11.
[41] *Cal. Pat. 1385–9*, pp. 149, 150.

[42] Ibid. 1461–7, p. 226.
[43] Ibid. 1467–77, p. 345.
[44] See also De Banco R. East. 10 Hen. VII, m. 251, 252 ; Trin. 10 Hen. VII, m. 251 ; Rentals and Surv. (Gen. Ser.), portf. 3, no. 7 ; Ct. R. (Gen. Ser.), portf. 195, no. 27, 29.
[45] Feet of F. Bucks. Mich. 16 Chas. I. John Thompson, the grantee of 1560, had some difficulty in gaining possession of the site of Little Linford Manor, leased by his predecessor Sir John St. Leger to Robert Annesley, whose grandchildren the Mounts claimed the leasehold (Chan. Proc. [Ser. 2], bdle. 128, no. 20).
[46] Recov. R. Hil. 1655, m. 18 ; Mich. 1655, m. 219 ; Feet of F. Bucks. Mich. 1655.
[46a] Feet of F. Bucks. Mich. 11 Chas. I ; Hil. 14 Chas. I.

White, agent for St. John Thompson, to Thomas Hackett and Thomas Kilpin, the former of whom subsequently conveyed his share of the manor to Kilpin,[47] who afterward acquired the freehold rights. This Kilpin, by his will of 4 January 1675–6, bequeathed the manor to his youngest son John,[48] to whom it had passed by 1677, when Thomas and Richard Kilpin, the elder brothers of John, settled it upon him.[49] In 1700 he conveyed it to John Knapp, who was already living in the manor-house.[50]

By his will, dated 13 December 1709 and proved in February 1710–11, John Knapp left the furniture in the Little Linford house to his widow Katherine, with reversion to his son and heir John, to whom the manor was bequeathed.[51] This John made settlements of the manor in 1713[52] and 1729,[53] and died without issue in 1746.[54] He directed that all his real estate after the death of his widow Elizabeth, daughter of Josiah Nicolson, should pass in tail-male to the sons of his brother Matthew Knapp, rector of Shenley.[55] Matthew, the eldest nephew, left daughters only at his death in 1782,[56] and Little Linford was inherited by his brother Primatt Knapp, rector of Shenley.[57] He died in December 1793,

KNAPP. *Party or and sable a lion passant countercoloured holding a broken sword blade downwards and a chief indented also countercoloured charged with three steel helms.*

and his eldest son Nathaniel Matthew,[58] who had suffered a recovery of the manor in 1787,[59] made a further settlement in 1794,[60] probably to the use of his brother and heir Primatt Knapp, rector of Shenley, who inherited Linford the following year.[61] In 1829 he settled the manor on his son and heir Matthew,[62] who succeeded to the remainder of the family estates in 1838.[63] In 1867 they passed to his son Matthew Grenville Samwell,[64] and were inherited in 1896 by his son and heir Mr. John Matthew Knapp, the present lord of the manor.

In 1205 Henry son of Peter de Northampton received a charter granting him leave to inclose his wood at Little Linford and to make a park.[65] In 1278–9 Thomas de Hauville had a free park in Little Linford,[66] described in 1302 as 40 acres in extent and stocked with deer.[66a]

In 1334 free warren here was granted to Joan Botetourt and her heirs,[67] and was appurtenant to the manor in the 18th century.

The mill on the estate in 1086[67a] was probably identical with the water-mill attached to the manor in the 14th century,[68] when mention occurs of a fishpond.[69] Free fishing in the Ouse was also among the rights at that date[69a] and in the 18th century, when courts leet and baron were mentioned.[70]

The church of *ST. LEONARD AND ST. ANDREW* consists of a chancel measuring internally 19 ft. by 14 ft., nave 35 ft. by 12 ft. 6 in., north and south aisles, north porch, and stone bellcote over the west gable. It is built of rubble and the roofs are covered with tiles.

The building dates from the early 13th century, and originally consisted of a chancel, the present nave with its bellcote and a north aisle. The south aisle was added about 1320, but, having probably fallen into decay, was subsequently rebuilt with the original stonework. The north aisle, which had long been destroyed, and the chancel have been rebuilt within recent years, a porch, which had been erected on the north of the nave,[71] being then removed; the present porch is modern.

In the east wall of the chancel is a 13th-century window of two lights with a quatrefoil in a pointed head, and there are two original lancets in the south wall. All have been reset, but a portion of the east wall itself is original. The pointed chancel arch is mostly modern.

The nave opens to the north aisle by an early 13th-century arcade of two pointed arches, which until the rebuilding of the aisle had been walled up for a long period. It has a circular pillar with a moulded capital and base, and moulded corbels at the responds. On the south is an early 14th-century arcade of three bays with pointed arches supported by octagonal pillars with moulded capitals and bases and corbel responds, and in the west wall is a 15th-century window of three lights in a four-centred head. The timber roof over the nave probably dates from the 15th century. The stone bellcote over the west gable, built in the 13th century, is now much weatherworn; it has twin pointed arches for the bells under a high-pitched gable, and is enriched by angle shafts at the responds of the arches and at the external angles.

When the north aisle was rebuilt a pointed doorway and trefoiled stoup, both probably of the 15th century, were reset in the north wall, and an early 14th-century traceried window of two lights was reset in the east wall. A small pointed light has also been rebuilt in the west wall of the porch. The south aisle has an early 14th-century two-light window at the east end, and in the south wall are a 16th-century window of three plain lights in a square head, a pointed doorway of early 13th-century date, enriched with nail-head ornament, which has been reset in a square-headed opening, and further west a cinquefoiled piscina with a quatrefoil bowl, probably of the 15th century, also reset.

The font has a circular bowl, which is probably old, but its detail is obscured by cement. The communion table in the chancel is made up of some late 15th-century tracery, and the altar rails are probably of the 17th century. There is another communion

[47] Add. Chart. 24046. This lease was for forty-two years 'if St. John Thompson . . . should live so long.'
[48] Close, 36 Chas. II, pt. xv, no. 12.
[49] Ibid.; Feet of F. Bucks. East. 29 Chas. II; cf. Feet of F. Bucks. East. 36 Chas. II.
[50] Com. Pleas Recov. R. Mich. 12 Will. III, m. 14, 15.
[51] P.C.C. 30 Young.
[52] Feet of F. Bucks. Trin. 12 Anne.
[53] Recov. R. Mich. 3 Geo. II, m. 343.
[54] *Musgrave's Obit.*(Harl. Soc.), iii, 383.

[55] P.C.C. 54 Strahan.
[56] Admon. Decr. 1782 (P.C.C. Gortling); *Musgrave's Obit.* loc. cit.; Lipscomb, *Hist. and Antiq. of Bucks.* iv, 231.
[57] P.C.C. 54 Strahan.
[58] Ibid. 83 Holman.
[59] Recov. R. Trin. 27 Geo. III, m. 354.
[60] Ibid. Mich. 35 Geo. III, m. 234.
[61] P.C.C. 511 Newcastle; see also Lysons, *Mag. Brit.* i (3), 597.
[62] Recov. R. East. 10 Geo. IV, m. 30.
[63] Lipscomb, loc. cit.; Sheahan, *Hist. and Topog. of Bucks.* 561.

[64] Burke, *Landed Gentry* (1871).
[65] *Cal. Rot. Chart.* 1199–1216 (Rec. Com.), 151.
[66] *Hund. R.* (Rec. Com.), ii, 350.
[66a] *Cal. Inq. p.m.* (Edw. I), iv, 71.
[67] Chart. R. 8 Edw. III, m. 8, no. 19.
[67a] *V.C.H. Bucks.* i, 240.
[68] *Cal. Inq. p.m.* (Edw. I), iv, 71.
[69] Ibid.; Chan. Inq. p.m. 48 Edw. III (1st nos.), no. 75.
[69a] *Cal. Inq. p.m.* (Edw. I), iv, 71.
[70] Recov. R. Mich. 35 Geo. III, m. 234.
[71] Lipscomb, op. cit. iv, 233.

table in the north aisle, which dates from the 17th century, and some panelling in the nave is of the same period. On the wall at the south-west corner of the north aisle are several incised crosses, and there are other crosses at the north-east corner of the nave externally.

The bellcote contains two bells, inscribed 'Ave Maria Gracia Plena' and 'Johannes Vylleby Me Fieri Fecit,' the first probably dating from the 14th century,[71a] and the tenor, which has a shield of Kebyll, from the late 15th century.

The communion plate includes a cup of 1695 and a plated paten.

The registers begin in 1757.

ADVOWSON   The church, which was a chapel to Newport Pagnell,[72] was given by Fulk Paynel to Tickford Priory early in the 12th century, the grant being confirmed by his son Ralph and by his grandson Gervase in 1187.[73] Upon the dissolution of Tickford Priory in 1524 the Crown granted its revenues to Wolsey for the support of his new college at Oxford.[74] Wolsey was attainted in 1529,[75] when Little Linford Chapel reverted to the Crown, who in 1532 refounded Wolsey's College under the name of Henry the Eighth's College.[76] Thirteen years later the college was once more surrendered to the king.[77] In 1590 the queen granted the rectory and church of Little Linford to John Thompson,[78] and from that date to the present time the rectory and advowson have descended with the manor.[79] The living is a vicarage.

There do not appear to be any endowed charities subsisting in this parish.

LOUGHTON

Lochintone (xi cent.); Luhtona, Lutton, Lucton (xiii cent.); Loutone, Loghtone (xiv cent.).

This parish covers 1,536 acres, of which 353 acres are arable, 945 permanent grass and 9 woods and plantations.[1] The level of the land is for the most part about 300 ft. above the ordnance datum, and the soil is Oxford Clay. Limestone is quarried. The chief crops grown are wheat, oats, barley and beans. The London and North Western railway crosses the parish, and the scattered village, 2¾ miles from Bletchley station, lies along a road running north-east from the Watling Street to the railway.

The church of All Saints stands at the north-east end of the village, at the crossroads. A little south of the church are the rectory, a modern house built in 1868, and the school, originally erected in 1867 for forty children, and since enlarged to accommodate seventy children. About a quarter of a mile to the west, on the Green, is Manor Farm, formerly Little Loughton Manor House, and now occupied by Mr. Arthur Fuller. It is a long stone building, with a gabled porch on the south front rising to the full height of the house. The house was originally built about 1500 of half-timber, but about 1580 it was encased with stone by Valentine Pigott, whose initials with those of Anne his wife appear on the porch. Many of the older windows have been blocked, and those which remain have been modernized. The house was altered and enlarged in the 17th century, but contains some curious 16th-century mural paintings. There are several other old houses and cottages of the 17th and 18th centuries in the village, mostly of half-timber, a few of them being thatched. The Baptists had a place of worship here before 1849; the present chapel was enlarged in 1884, and stands in its burial

MANOR FARM, LOUGHTON

ground a short distance to the north of the Memorial Cottages built to commemorate the Diamond Jubilee of Queen Victoria. North-west of the cottages are the Bell and Talbot Inns, and to the south-east are the Plough (in Shenley parish) and Fountain.

The parish is watered by Whaddon Brook, which runs north to the River Ouse, and which formerly separated the two parishes of Great and Little Loughton until their union in 1409, Great Loughton lying to the right of the brook and Little Loughton to the left. The ruins of Little Loughton Church, whose site was near the manor-house, were said to be standing at the beginning of the 19th century. Brook Farm lies on this brook about half a mile south-east of Manor Farm. Cell Farm, immediately south of Manor Farm,

[71a] *V.C.H. Bucks.* ii, 117.

[72] *Pope Nich. Tax.* (Rec. Com.), 33; *Cal. Rot. Chart. et Inq. a.q.d.* (Rec. Com.), 230; *Mins. Accts.* bdle. 1125, no. 1; *Chan. Inq. p.m.* 17 Edw. III (1st nos.), no. 69; *Cal. Pat.* 1354–8, pp. 168,

188; *L. and P. Hen. VIII,* iv (1), 2217 (3).

[73] Round, *Cal. Doc. of France,* 444; Dugdale, *Baronage,* i, 431; *Mon.* v, 203–4.

[74] *V.C.H. Bucks.* i, 363–4.

[75] *L. and P. Hen. VIII,* iv (3), 6129.

[76] Ibid. v, g. 1370 (23); xvi, g. 1391 (45).

[77] Ibid. xx (1), 776.

[78] Pat. 32 Eliz. pt. xxv, m. 11.

[79] Bacon, *Liber Regis,* 502.

[1] Statistics from Bd. of Agric. (1905).

was probably originally the property of Bradwell Priory. It was bought for small holdings in 1914 by the County Council. East of the railway is Rectory Farm, with Old Farm about 700 yards south of it, possibly the site of a Loughton manor-house.

The parish was inclosed by Act of Parliament in 1768, the award being dated 17 June 1769.[2]

Among place-names have been found Wholme End, Eyle Field[3] (xvi cent.) and Curtisse House[4] (xvii cent.). In the 17th century there is also mention of the Church House and a croft abutting upon the church and extending to Church Lane.[5]

MANORS At the date of the Domesday Survey Walter Giffard was holding 4½ hides in LOUGHTON, the manor having been previously held by five thegns who could sell.[6] The overlordship remained vested in the descendants of Walter Giffard, and on the death of Anselm Marshal, Earl of Pembroke, in 1245,[7] it appears to have been at first obtained by his sister and co-heir Isabel, wife of Gilbert de Clare, Earl of Gloucester, since the Earl of Gloucester was overlord in 1284–6.[8] Afterwards

CLARE. *Or three cheverons gules.*

VALENCE. *Burelly argent and azure with an orle of martlets gules.*

these rights were exercised by Aymer de Valence, Earl of Pembroke, son of Joan daughter of Warine de Monchesney by Joan, another sister and co-heir,[9] but they appear to have lapsed during the conflict of claims, as no further trace is found of them. An intermediary lordship in this manor was vested in the Braose family in 1284–6,[10] and continued to be exercised by them as lords of Buckingham during the 14th century.[11] In 1386 it was vested in John Frome of Buckingham, of whom the manor was held by scutage and suit of court of the Earl of Ormond,[12] but a century later he had been replaced by the Abbot of Peterborough,[13] who was also holding in 1525.[14] The Bishop of Peterborough held these rights in 1573 in right of his see,[15] but in 1596 and 1622 the Crown was returned as overlord.[16]

Ivo, the Domesday tenant,[17] was probably the ancestor of the family of Loughton who held Loughton for many generations. Sir John de Loughton is men-

tioned in connexion with Loughton about 1219,[18] and it was probably a son of the same name who was lord

BRAOSE. *Azure crusilly and a lion or.*

PETERBOROUGH ABBEY. *Gules St. Peter's keys crossed saltirewise between four crosslets fitchy or.*

of this fee in 1254–5.[19] In 1270 this John de Loughton granted lands and rent in Loughton to William his son,[20] and in the same year granted to another son, John de Loughton, what was probably GREAT LOUGHTON MANOR,[21] though it was not so known until the early years of the next century. This estate was to be held by the rent of a white glove, and by finding a wax candle of 1 lb. before the altar of the Virgin in the church at the feast of the Assumption.[22] John de Loughton, the son,[23] was holding great Loughton in 1284–6,[24] but was probably dead by 1294, when his son William, rector of Great Loughton, granted to another son Ivo and Cecilia daughter of Robert of Stoke Hammond the principal messuage and lands, &c., which he had of Ivo's gift in Great Loughton.[25] Ivo was holding in 1302–3,[26] but the reversion of the manor after the death of Ivo, who held at a rose rent, was obtained in 1313 by Henry Spigurnel,[27] who in the following year acquired the reversion of lands in Great and Little Loughton from Nicholas de Eure or Iver and Margery his wife.[28] Henry Spigurnel was returned as lord in 1316,[29] and in 1317 obtained from Alexander of Stoke Hammond a renunciation of any right he might have in the manor.[30] He continued to hold Great Loughton[31] until his death circa 1328.[32] He was succeeded by his son Thomas, who is evidently identical with the Thomas de Loughton holding in 1346 the half-fee in Great Loughton formerly Ivo de Loughton's.[33]

SPIGURNEL. *Gules fretty argent a chief or with a lion passant gules therein.*

2 *Blue Bk. Incl. Awards*, 12.
3 Chan. Proc. Eliz. P 2, no. 55.
4 Mentioned at the death of Henry Lane in 1612 (Chan. Inq. p.m. [Ser. 2], cccxliii, 133), sold by his son Thomas to John Hopper in 1618 (ibid. dccxl, 114), and purchased from Hopper by John Farnell, who died-seised in 1624 (ibid. dcxxv, 43).
5 Exch. Dep. Spec. Com. 4 Jas. I, no. 3577 ; 5 Jas. I, no. 3578.
6 *V.C.H. Bucks.* i, 251.
7 *G.E.C. Peerage*, vi, 203.
8 *Feud. Aids*, i, 80.
9 Chan. Inq. p.m. 17 Edw. II, no. 75 ; *Cal. Close*, 1323–7, p. 267.

10 *Feud. Aids*, loc. cit.
11 Ibid. 106 ; *Cal. Inq. p.m.* (Edw. III), vii, 105 ; Chan. Inq. p.m. 40 Edw. III, no. 34.
12 Chan. Inq. p.m. 10 Ric. II, no. 39.
13 *Cal. Inq. p.m. Hen. VII*, i, 361.
14 Chan. Inq. p.m. (Ser. 2), xliii, 72.
15 Ibid. clxviii, 11.
16 Ibid. cclv, 138 ; cccxci, 55.
17 *V.C.H. Bucks.* i, 251.
18 *R. of Hugh of Wells* (Cant. and York Soc.), i, 59.
19 *Hund. R.* (Rec. Com.), i, 30.
20 Feet of F. case 283, file 17, no. 60.

21 Ibid. case 16, file 41, no. 13.
22 Ibid.
23 Ibid. case 17, file 47, no. 11.
24 *Feud. Aids*, i, 80.
25 *Cal. in Bodl. Chart.* 25.
26 *Feud. Aids*, i, 106.
27 Feet of F. case 18, file 65, no. 24.
28 Ibid. no. 10.
29 *Feud. Aids*, i, 109.
30 *Abbrev. Plac.* (Rec. Com.), 328b.
31 Chan. Inq. p.m. 17 Edw. II, no. 75.
32 *Cal. Inq. p.m.* (Edw. III), vii, 105. He held land in Little Loughton of Thomas de Loughton.
33 *Feud. Aids*, i, 132.

William Spigurnel died seised of the manor in 1366,[34] as also of Dagnall Manor in Edlesborough (q.v.), with which Great Loughton henceforward descends until about the middle of the 16th century.[34a] The Lucys then retained Great Loughton while alienating Dagnall, and after the death of William Lucy in 1551 his son and heir Thomas Lucy[35] conveyed it in 1557 to Thomas Hopper.[36] Thomas Hopper died in 1573,[37] leaving his dwelling-house to his wife Audrey for life, with reversion to his son Thomas.[38] On the death of the latter in 1596 Loughton passed to his son, another Thomas,[39] who was succeeded in 1618 by his brother John.[40] He died in March 1621–2, leaving a son Thomas.[41] From these owners the manor seems to have passed to the family of Alston. In 1693 it was held by Edward Alston,[42] who, with his son Joseph, was dealing with it in 1695[43] and 1696,[44] and with whom in 1697 he conveyed it to Thomas Hanslapp.[45] Thomas Hanslapp died seised of it in 1717.[46] It was held by his son John Hanslapp in 1727,[47] and in 1735, at which latter date he had 'new built Part of the Capital House.'[48] John Hanslapp died in May 1746,[48a] after which date little is known of the manor. Before 1813 it had passed from the Hanslapps to Mr. Gee of Newport, who was then holding it.[49]

Mr. Walter Cadman is now lord of the manor.

The moiety of the manor to which Alice Cavendish and Margaret Quadring, probably the granddaughters of John Brecknock, were heirs descended with their moiety of Dagnall Manor until about the middle of the 16th century,[50] after which date it was doubtless acquired by the owners of the other moiety.

The Ivo de Loughton who acquired his brother William's rights in Great Loughton in 1294 does not appear to have succeeded to all the possessions of his father John. An estate was retained by another member of the family with which the sole presentation to Great Loughton Church, and afterwards the alternate presentation to the combined churches of Great and Little Loughton, descended, and it is from deeds relating to the advowson that the history of the holding can for the most part be traced. There is mention of John son of John de Loughton in 1311.[51] He seems to have been succeeded by the Ardres of Turvey (co. Bedford),[52] from whom this estate became known as *ARDRES MANOR*. John de Ardres was alive in 1357,[53] but Iseult his wife held as a widow after his death in 1361.[54] From 1371 to 1395 Alan

Rushley of Turvey appears to have acquired the rights over this manor,[55] but Thomas, the son of the aforesaid John de Ardres,[56] was in possession in 1414.[56a] A Robert Fitz Herbert and Thomas Loughton were apparently joint lords of Ardres about fifty-five years later,[57] Thomas Loughton acquiring the whole interest before 1485.[57a] He was involved in a quarrel over the presentation to the church with the lord of Little Loughton Manor in 1486.[58] Nothing further is known of this holding, unless a presentation in 1625 by the heirs of Loughton, John B——, William Hitcham or Hicks, and John Tresham,[59] was made in right of ownership of Ardres Manor.

In the time of Edward the Confessor 5 hides in Loughton were held as one manor by Alvric, a thegn of the king, who could sell.[60] This manor was given after the Conquest to Manno the Breton,[61] and was afterwards held of his descendants as of their barony of Wolverton,[62] rights in Loughton being claimed as late as 1625.[63]

In the Domesday Survey the manor was entered as held of Manno by two knights.[64] It was next held by a branch of the family known as Loughton, a member of which, Bartholomew, was in possession in 1166.[65] Geoffrey de Loughton held in the first quarter of the 13th century,[66] but by 1254–5 he had been succeeded by William de Loughton,[67] probably identical with the William holding here in 1284–6.[68] He had been succeeded before 1302–3 by Thomas de Loughton,[69] who acquired additional lands here in 1309[70] and 1314,[71] and was returned as lord in 1316.[72] Thomas de Loughton, probably the same, in 1330 settled *LITTLE LOUGHTON MANOR*, first so-called, on himself and his wife Elizabeth for life, with remainder to his sons Thomas, William and Robert and their heirs successively.[73] It was doubtless the son, Thomas de Loughton, who was holding in 1346 Little Loughton, then described as a fee previously held by Ivo de Loughton,[74] but the entry probably shows confusion with Great Loughton. Thomas de Loughton was still alive in 1350[75] and 1351,[76] but appears to have died about 1361, when another Thomas de Loughton obtained livery of the manor.[77] John de Loughton must have been holding the manor at the end of the 14th and beginning of the 15th century, as he presented to Little Loughton Church from 1386 to 1407.[78] There appears to have been a minority in 1418, with Elizabeth Lady Clinton as guardian,[79] probably of John de Loughton,

[34] Chan. Inq. p.m. 40 Edw. III, no. 34.
[34a] See also P.C.C. 22 Horne.
[35] Exch. Inq. p.m. (Ser. 2), file 1151, no. 4.
[36] Feet of F. Bucks. Mich. 4 & 5 Phil. and Mary ; Recov. R. Mich. 4 & 5 Phil. and Mary, m. 340.
[37] Chan. Inq. p.m. (Ser. 2), clxviii, 11.
[38] P.C.C. 34 Peter.
[39] Chan. Inq. p.m. (Ser. 2), cclv, 138.
[40] Ibid. ccclxxvii, 64.
[41] Ibid. cccxci, 55.
[42] Recov. R. Mich. 5 Will. and Mary, m. 197. He was perhaps the Edward Alston whose son Edward was baptized in 1673 (Add. MS. 5839, p. 250).
[43] Feet of F. Bucks. Trin. 7 Will. III.
[44] Ibid. Hil. 8 Will. III.
[45] Ibid. Mich. 9 Will. III.
[46] P.C.C. 210 Whitfield.
[47] Recov. R. East. 13 Geo. I, m. 256.
[48] Add. MS. 5839, p. 248.

[48a] Ibid. p. 250.
[49] Lysons, *Mag. Brit.* i (3), 597.
[50] Feet of F. Div. Co. Hil. 9 Hen. VII ; Chan. Inq. p.m. (Ser. 2), xlii, 171 ; lxv, 8.
[51] Add. MS. 5839, p. 257.
[52] See *V.C.H. Beds.* iii, 112.
[53] Add. MS. 5839, p. 257.
[54] Ibid.   [55] Ibid.
[56] Chan. Inq. p.m. 35 Edw. III, pt. ii (1st nos.), no. 73.
[56a] Add. MS. 5839, p. 259.
[57] De Banco R. Trin. 1 Hen. VII, m. 315 ; Add. MS. 5839, p. 259.
[57a] Add. MS. 5839, p. 259.
[58] De Banco R. Trin. 1 Hen. VII, m. 315.
[59] Add. MS. 5839, p. 259.
[60] *V.C.H. Bucks.* i, 271.   [61] Ibid.
[62] *Testa de Nevill* (Rec. Com.), 248 ; *Cal. Close,* 1272–9, p. 350 ; De Banco R. East. 5 Hen. VI, m. 319 ; Chan. Inq. p.m. 23 Edw. III, pt. i, no. 35 ; 25

Edw. III (1st nos.), no. 6 ; 17 Hen. VI, no. 38 ; (Ser. 2), dxlii, 131.
[63] Chan. Inq. p.m. (Ser. 2), dcxxv, 43.
[64] *V.C.H. Bucks.* i, 271.
[65] *Red Bk. of Exch.* (Rolls Ser.), 314.
[66] *Testa de Nevill* (Rec. Com.), 242a ; *R. of Hugh of Wells* (Cant. and York Soc.), ii, 81.
[67] *Hund. R.* (Rec. Com.), i, 30.
[68] *Feud. Aids,* i, 80.   [69] Ibid. 106.
[70] Feet of F. case 18, file 60, no. 1.
[71] Ibid. file 65, no. 5.
[72] *Feud. Aids,* i, 109.
[73] Feet of F. case 19, file 78, no. 7.
[74] *Feud. Aids,* i, 132.
[75] *Cal. Close,* 1349–54, p. 169 ; Chan. Inq. p.m. 23 Edw. III, pt. i, no. 35.
[76] Ibid. 25 Edw. III (1st nos.), no. 6.
[77] Mins. Accts. (Gen. Ser.), bdle. 1123, no. 10.
[78] Add. MS. 5839, p. 258.
[79] Ibid. 259.

son of the last-mentioned John, who was holding twenty years later,[80] and who refers to his father John and grandfather Thomas in a deed of 1440.[81] This John is referred to with his wife Margaret in 1446,[82] and made a feoffment of the manor to the use of George Loughton, who with Arnetrua his wife conveyed it to trustees in 1461.[83] The trustees transferred their rights to John Edy of Stony Stratford, who, as lord of the manor of Little Loughton, claimed to present to the church in 1486.[84] By his will, proved 12 June 1488, John Edy left Little Loughton Manor to Edmund his second son, with reversion, failing issue, to his eldest son Jakes.[85] Edmund seems to have died shortly afterwards, and Jakes called upon the trustees to make an estate of Loughton to him.[86] They refused, probably at the instigation of Isabel wife of John Pigott of Beachampton, and Margaret wife of William Shirley, sisters of Jakes Edy, who claimed an interest in the manor under the will of their father John.[87] Jakes finally obtained possession of Loughton, which he left at his death in 1493 to his wife Philippa, with reversion to his right heirs, his sisters. If, however, they molested Philippa in any way, the manor was to be sold by his executors and the money spent in good works.[88] Philippa married Francis Catesby, but died before 1500,[89] and John and Isabel Pigott obtained sole rights in the manor, assigning Adstock, the other family estate in Buckinghamshire, to Benedict Lee and his wife Isabel, daughter of Margaret, who was sister of Isabel Pigott, by her husband — Clarell.[90] Robert son of John and Isabel Pigott had succeeded by 1514,[91] and had trouble with Benedict and Isabel Lee.[92] Robert Pigott was dead in 1557.[92a] His son Thomas [93] made a settlement of the manor in 1570

PIGOTT. *Sable three picks argent.*

on his eldest son Valentine, Anne his wife, and Mary their daughter, for sixty years, if any one of them should live so long. The reversion was to Valentine's brothers, Arthur, George, Edmund, Robert, Matthew and Francis, and their heirs male in succession.[94] After the death of Anne, Valentine Pigott married Eleanor daughter of John Fortescue, and a fresh settlement was made in 1585, whereby Eleanor was to hold for the life of Thomas Pigott, the father, with remainder to Valentine and their heirs male.[95] Valentine, as lord of the manor, brought an action against certain freeholders as to rights of common two years later,[96] and died in 1590, leaving three daughters

by his first wife: Ursula wife of Christopher Pigott of Dodershall, a relative; Mary wife of Thomas Waterhouse; and Judith wife of William Tresham.[97] Valentine's brothers, George and Clement Pigott, tried to set aside the will, but it was pronounced valid in the same year.[98] The daughters and their husbands all made settlements of their thirds in the following two years,[99] but George Pigott, the brother of Valentine, and his next heir in Loughton according to the settlement in 1570, Arthur Pigott having died in 1585,[100] attempted to deprive them of their inheritance.[1] Ursula died in December 1592, leaving by Christopher a daughter, Anne Pigott [2]; her grandfather, Thomas Pigott, also died in the same month,[3] leaving all his goods to his wife Alice, who had some trouble in proving the will against her husband's sons, Edmund, Robert, Matthew, Francis, and Clement Pigott.[4] Eleanor, widow of Valentine, was then alive, and as the wife of Edward Huberd brought an action in November 1593 against the husbands of Valentine's daughters to recover the rent from the manor-house, which she had leased to John Mattock.[5] George Pigott, Valentine's brother, still continued to trouble his nieces and their husbands, and with his brothers, the reversionary legatees named in the settlement of 1570, was defendant in an action brought by them in January 1594–5 to prevent him from presenting to the church.[6] About this time, however, he obtained a quitclaim of their interest from Christopher Pigott and William Tresham and Judith,[7] and probably from the Waterhouses also. His brothers renounced their claim in 1596 for £300,[8] and in 1599 George Pigott made a settlement of the manor thus acquired.[9] The next year, however, he transferred his interest to his brother Edmund, another brother Clement at the same time relinquishing any title in the premises.[10] Edmund, by his will, dated 14 August 1612 and proved 12 May 1613, empowered his wife Elizabeth to sell Loughton Manor to John Crane, with whom an agreement had already been arrived at on the 30 July preceding,[11] but the transaction was completed by Edmund Pigott himself in the autumn of 1612.[12] John Crane married Mary daughter of Sir Thomas Tresham of Newton, Northamptonshire, by whom he had eleven sons and five daughters.[13] In 1635 he was chief clerk of His Majesty's kitchen, officer of the Admiralty and marine affairs, and surveyor-general of all victuals for ships.[14] On 21 November 1646, when comptroller of His Majesty's house, he begged to compound for delinquency on the Oxford Articles, having been at Oxford at its surrender, and the 'King's ancient servant during the late unhappy troubles.'[15] He complained in 1647 that he had only a life interest in Loughton, and that he had been

[80] Chan. Inq. p.m. 17 Hen. VI, no. 38.
[81] Wrottesley, *Ped. from Plea R.* 368.
[82] Feet of F. case 22, file 122.
[83] Ibid. file 125.
[84] De Banco R. Trin. 1 Hen. VII, m. 315.
[85] P.C.C. 14 Milles.
[86] Early Chan. Proc. bdle. 92, no. 17.
[87] Ibid.; P.C.C. 28 Dogett.
[88] P.C.C. 28 Dogett.
[89] Early Chan. Proc. bdle. 196, no. 84.
[90] Ibid. bdle. 536, no. 46. William Shirley aforesaid was probably Margaret's second husband.
[91] Add. MS. 5839, p. 259.
[92] Early Chan. Proc. bdle. 536, no. 46.

[92a] Add. MS. 5839, p. 249.
[93] *Visit. of Bucks.* (Harl. Soc.), 196.
[94] Chan. Inq. p.m. (Ser. 2), ccxliii, 81.
[95] Chan. Proc. (Ser. 2), bdle. 252, no. 3; Feet of F. Bucks. Mich. 27 Eliz.
[96] Chan. Proc. Eliz. P 2, no. 55.
[97] Chan. Inq. p.m. (Ser. 2), ccxliii, 81.
[98] P.C.C. 38 Drury.
[99] Feet of F. Bucks. Hil. 33 Eliz.; East. 34 Eliz.
[100] Chan. Inq. p.m. (Ser. 2), ccxliii, 81.
[1] Chan. Proc. (Ser. 2), bdle. 252, no. 3.
[2] Chan. Inq. p.m. (Ser. 2), ccxxxiv, 38.
[3] Ibid.; ccxliii, 2.
[4] P.C.C. 74 Nevell.
[5] Chan. Proc. (Ser. 2), bdle. 241, no. 16.

[6] Ibid. Eliz. W 6, no. 51.
[7] Feet of F. Bucks. Mich. 36 Eliz.; East. 37 Eliz.
[8] Ibid. Mich. 38 & 39 Eliz.
[9] Ibid. Trin. 41 Eliz.
[10] Ibid. East. 42 Eliz.
[11] P.C.C. 37 Capell.
[12] Feet of F. Bucks. Mich. 10 Jas. I.
[13] Add. MS. 5839, p. 252; *Visit. of Bucks.* (Harl. Soc.), 31. For the will of his mother Phyllis Crane, who died in 1622, see P.C.C. 84 Savile.
[14] *Cal. S. P. Dom.* 1636–7, p. 452; cf. *Hist. MSS. Com. Rep.* vi, App. i, 314 a.
[15] *Cal. Com. for Comp.* 1570.

fined as if he held in fee.[16] In 1655, with William Crane his son,[17] he conveyed the manor to Ralph Holt.[18] Ralph Holt died in 1678, and was succeeded by his son Charles,[18a] who in 1722 made a settlement of Loughton with Ralph his son and heir.[19] Ralph succeeded in 1731,[19a] and at his death in 1758 bequeathed the manor to his nephew Thomas Holt of Newport Pagnell,[20] upon whom a settlement had already been made.[20a] He was in possession in 1768,[21] but the estate had passed to the Swans by the beginning of the 19th century, perhaps by the marriage of one of Ralph Holt's daughters.[22] It was later held by Mr. Whitworth, who bequeathed it at his death in 1832 to his two sons, Henry Billington Whitworth and Robert Whitworth of London. The latter's moiety was purchased from him by his brother in 1851.[23]

CRANE of Loughton. *Gules a fesse between three crosses formy fitchy or with three rings azure on the fesse.*

George Loughton, after his sale of the manor to John Edy, appears to have retained a messuage and 80 acres of land in Little Loughton, together with three messuages and 160 acres of land in Great Loughton, which descended to his son Thomas, and from Thomas to his daughter Isabel married to — Knyveton.[24] Their son Humphrey Knyveton died seised of this property about 1587, and was succeeded by his son Matthew,[25] who in 1597 appears to have made a presentation to the church which was set aside.[26] He died in 1610, when his son John succeeded him.[27] John died in 1614, and was succeeded by his brother Charles,[28] who was engaged in a suit as to lands in Loughton in 1625.[29]

Half a hide in Loughton was held at the date of the Domesday Survey by the Count of Mortain.[30] It was afterwards attached to the little fee of Mortain[31] or honour of Berkhampstead,[32] the last reference to the connexion occurring in 1434.[33]

The under-tenant at Domesday was Walter, who had succeeded Elmær, a man of Alvric, son of Goding, who could sell.[34] In the earlier 13th century it was held by Nicholas the Falconer,[35] who was followed by his son John.[36] Alan the Falconer was in possession in 1284–6,[37] and again in 1302–3,[38] but by 1346 Edith de Stoke was holding.[39] Its history then becomes obscure, but it may be identical with the property known as *LOUGHTON MANOR* held at the end of the 15th century by William Saunderson, who died without issue, and whose brother and heir John brought actions against John Broughton and John Edy, the feoffees.[40]

A messuage and 8 acres in Loughton were stated in 1360 to have been appropriated by the Prior of Bradwell without licence,[41] but an inquiry revealed that the appropriation took place before the Statute of Mortmain.[41a] This estate was included in the grant of Bradwell Priory in 1524 to Cardinal Wolsey,[42] and by him transferred immediately to his college at Oxford, the dean and canons holding a court for Bradwell with its members, including Loughton, in 1526.[43] A further grant, probably in confirmation, was made early in 1528 to Wolsey,[44] but after his fall these appurtenances in Loughton were granted by the Crown in 1531 to the priory of Sheen.[45] They were probably comprised in the rent of 9s. in Loughton, formerly of Sheen, which in 1543 was bestowed on Arthur Longville of Wolverton.[46]

In 1535 Snelshall Priory held lands and tenements worth 24s. in Loughton, and paid a rent of 7s. 5d. to Robert Pigott for lands in Beachampton and Loughton.[47]

There was a windmill in Little Loughton Manor in 1361.[48]

There is mention of a mill on the holding of the honour of Berkhampstead in 1497.[49]

A fishery in Loughton Brook was held with the manor of Little Loughton in 1587.[50] James Farnell held fisheries in Loughton with lands and messuages at his death in January 1603–4.[51] This property passed to his son John Farnell, who died seised on 28 September 1624, leaving three daughters as heirs.[52]

The church of *ALL SAINTS* consists **CHURCH** of a chancel measuring internally 20 ft. by 13 ft., nave 40 ft. by 19 ft., continuous south chapel and aisle 36 ft. by 8 ft. 6 in., south porch, and west tower 11 ft. by 9 ft. It is built of rubble with stone dressings and is coated with cement. The chancel has a high-pitched roof covered with tiles, which stands conspicuously above the lead-covered roofs of the other parts of the church.

The chancel and nave probably date from the first years of the 13th century, though all the original details have been removed during subsequent alterations. The east window of the chancel, the blocked north doorway of the nave, and the lower part of

[16] *Cal. Com. for Comp.* 1571.
[17] *Visit. of Bucks.* (Harl. Soc.), 31.
[18] Feet of F. Bucks. Mich. 1655.
[18a] Add. MS. 5839, p. 250.
[19] Recov. R. East. 8 Geo. I, m. 66 ; cf. Exch. Dep. Hil. 4 Geo. II, no. 7.
[19a] Add. MS. 5839, p. 250.
[20] P.C.C. 334 Hutton. Ralph bequeathed to his brother Thomas, father of the said nephew, 1s. only.
[20a] Marcham, *Cat. of Bucks. Deeds*, no. 98.   [21] Priv. Act, 8 Geo. III, cap. 8.
[22] Lysons, op. cit. i (3), 597.
[23] Sheahan, *Hist. and Topog. of Bucks.* 563.
[24] Chan. Inq. p.m. (Ser. 2), ccclxiv, 38.
[25] Ibid. cccxvii, 127.
[26] Hen. Knyveton is the name given, doubtless in error for Matthew. Add. MS. 5839, p. 259.

[27] Chan. Inq. p.m. cccxvi, 25 ; P.C.C. 43 Wingfield.
[28] P.C.C. 40 Cope ; Chan. Inq. p.m. (Ser. 2), ccclxiv, 38.
[29] *Cal. S. P. Dom.* 1623–5, p. 488.
[30] *V.C.H. Bucks.* i, 246.
[31] *Feud. Aids*, i, 107, 133.
[32] Ibid. i, 77 ; *Testa de Nevill* (Rec. Com.), 244 ; Chan. Inq. p.m. 2 Ric. II, no. 57 ; Ct. R. (Gen. Ser.), portf. 177, no. 14.
[33] Ct. R. (Gen. Ser.), portf. 177, no. 14.
[34] *V.C.H. Bucks.* i, 246.
[35] *Testa de Nevill*, loc. cit.
[36] Ibid. 251.
[37] *Feud. Aids*, i, 77.
[38] Ibid. 107.
[39] Ibid. 133.
[40] Early Chan. Proc. bdles. 40, no. 176; 161, no. 53 ; 163, no. 45.

[41] Chan. Inq. p.m. 4 Ric. II, no. 101. The ecclesiastical taxation of 1291 states that a pension of £1 was due to Bradwell Priory from Little Loughton Church (*Pope Nich. Tax.* [Rec. Com.], 33).
[41a] *Cal. Close*, 1360–4, p. 338.
[42] *L. and P. Hen. VIII*, iv (1), 536, g. 1913 (1).
[43] Ct. R. (Gen. Ser.), portf. 155, no. 5.
[44] *L. and P. Hen. VIII*, iv (2), g. 4001 (2, 3).
[45] Ibid. v, 403, g. 627 (22).
[46] Ibid. xviii (1), g. 346 (38).
[47] *Valor Eccl.* (Rec. Com.), iv, 228–9.
[48] Mins. Accts. (Gen. Ser.), bdle. 1123, no. 10.
[49] Ct. R. (Gen. Ser.), portf. 177, no. 15.
[50] Chan. Proc. Eliz. P 2, no. 55.
[51] Chan. Inq. p.m. (Ser. 2), dcxlvi, 3.
[52] Ibid. dcxxv, 43.

the window immediately to the west of the latter are probably insertions of about 1250, altered later ; but these are the earliest details which now remain. During the latter part of the 15th century the south chapel and aisle, the porch and the tower were added and the nave was reroofed. The fabric was restored about 1700 and again in 1851, while in 1886 the seating was renewed.

The chancel is lighted only by its east window, which is of two pointed lights with a round rear-arch and probably dates from the 13th century, though its head was altered at a much later period. Near the west end of the north wall is a low-side window of one square-headed light, now blocked, and on the south, opening to the chapel, is a pointed arch supported by semi-octagonal responds with moulded capitals and bases. This arch is pierced in the north wall of the chapel, which, in order that it might directly abut the nave arcade, was built against but independently of the chancel wall, the western part of the latter being then entirely removed.

At the north-east of the nave is a late 15th-century three-light window with a four-centred head and modern tracery, and further west are the doorway and window mentioned above, the former being completely blocked. The window, which is a tall single light, appears to have been considerably heightened about 1700. Opposite to this on the south is another tall single-light window which has been similarly treated, but was originally of two lights and probably dates from a century later. The south doorway has a two-centred drop arch, and is of about 1400. Opening to the aisle at the south-east is a late 15th-century arcade of two pointed arches with an octagonal pillar and responds of the same details as the arch on the south side of the chancel. The pointed tower arch on the west, which is pierced through a wall of considerable thickness, is of four moulded orders supported by responds composed of three flat segmental shafts divided by fillets, these shafts having coarsely moulded capitals and plain bases. The chancel has a segmental plastered ceiling, and the nave a low-pitched open-timber roof of the late 15th century.

The south chapel and aisle form one rectangular building, which is lighted from the south by three windows of the late 15th century, each of four cinquefoiled lights with tracery in a four-centred head, and from the east by a three-light window of the same character. Between the easternmost windows of the south wall is a small plain doorway. On the east wall are two brackets with carved heads. The moulded lean-to roof is also of the late 15th century and has carved bosses, one of which bears the arms of Boteler. The porch is of slightly earlier date than the aisle and originally had a gable over the entrance, the outline of which is still visible. It is lighted by a plain square-headed window in the west wall, and has an entrance on the south with a depressed arch in a square head. The walls of the chapel, aisle and porch are crowned by a continuous embattled parapet.

The tower is of three stages surmounted by an embattled parapet. Although the walls are 5 ft. 5 in.

thick, and are supported by heavy diagonal buttresses, the structure must have shown signs of weakness soon after its erection, for a strong buttress was placed against the middle of the west wall. This buttress passes through the thickness of the wall, and rises to support the head of the west window, partially blocking it and completely blocking the doorway below. The doorway has a four-centred arch in a square head with traceried spandrels, and its outer mouldings are continuous with those of the window above, so that they form one composition. Two cinquefoiled lights of the window, which originally had a traceried head, are preserved, one on either side of the buttress. The second stage is lighted from the south by a small window with two quatrefoils arranged vertically, and the bell-chamber has on each side a restored window of two trefoiled lights under a pointed head.

The plain octagonal font probably dates from about 1700. On the chancel floor there is a half-length brass of a priest in mass vestments, with the inscription, 'Hic jacet Hugo Parke quondam istius eccłie Rector in artibus magister sacreque theologie bacularius.' Hugh Park died in 1514. On the north wall of the chancel are monuments with arms to Mary (Tresham) wife of John Crane of Loughton (d. 1624), and to Felice [(Phyllis) Moorton], wife first of William Mortoft of Itteringham, and secondly of John Crane of London (d. 1622). On the south wall is a monument to Robert Crane, D.C.L., Fellow of Trinity College, Cambridge (d. 1672), and his father John Crane of Loughton (d. 1660). On the chancel floor are slabs to all of the above, that to Felice Crane having a brass inscription.

In the tower is a large iron-bound poor-box dating probably from the late 16th century, with two holes for money, and in the south chapel are two grotesquely carved wood panels, while some fragments of old glass, mounted in a frame, are placed on the north wall of the nave. At the east end of the chancel is a painting by Gonzales of Christ and the two disciples at the supper at Emmaus. This picture was given to the church by the Rev. John Athawes on his induction to the living in 1833.

The tower contains a ring of six bells : the treble and second are modern ; the third is by Robert Atton, 1631 ; the fourth, inscribed, ' Hec Nova Campana Margareta Est Nominata,' and the fifth, ' Sit Nomen Domini Benedictum,' are both by Henry Jordan, about 1460[5a]; and the tenor is by Bartholomew Atton, 1590.

The communion plate consists of a paten of 1679, given by Dr. Brettell, rector of the parish, two cups of the same gift, but remade in 1865, two plated patens and a plated flagon.

The registers before 1812 are as follows : (i) all entries 1707 to 1755, baptisms and burials to 1778 ; (ii) baptisms and burials 1797 to 1813 ; (iii) marriages 1755 to 1787 ; (iv) marriages 1788 to 1812.

ADVOWSON A church of Great Loughton was recorded as early as 1219,[53] and the advowson was held at first by the lords of the manor of Great Loughton, and then by the holders of Ardres Manor until 1409.[54] At that date the church of Little Loughton, which was also first recorded in 1219,[55] and the advowson of

[52a] A. H. Cocks, *Ch. Bells of Bucks.* 460.
[53] *R. of Hugh of Wells* (Cant. and York Soc.), i, 59.
[54] Add. MS. 5839, p. 257.
[55] *R. of Hugh of Wells* (Cant. and York Soc.), i, 156. The presentation was then made by William son of Hamon, the overlord, probably during the minority of Geoffrey de Loughton.

Loughton Church from the South

MILTON KEYNES CHURCH FROM THE NORTH-WEST

MILTON KEYNES CHURCH: THE INTERIOR LOOKING EAST

which was attached to Little Loughton Manor,[56] was united with Great Loughton,[57] and the presentation was made alternately by the lords of Little Loughton Manor and of Ardres Manor.[58] The right of presentation was a matter of dispute in 1486,[59] and after that date seems to have been vested solely in the lords of the manor of Little Loughton,[60] with the exception of a presentation in 1625 by the heirs of Loughton (of Ardres Manor apparently).[61] It became the right of Clement, younger brother of Valentine Pigott, who, by his will dated 12 December 1615, left it to his wife Frances,[62] and joined with her a year later in conveying it to John Crane,[63] already lord of Little Loughton Manor. It does not appear to have been sold with the manor in 1655, but to have passed to Robert Crane, by whom it was bequeathed to Trinity College, Cambridge. After his death in Feb. 1672–3, it was confirmed to the college by his brother Francis Crane by a deed of gift of 14 November 1678.[64] The advowson has since remained in the possession of Trinity College.[65]

In 1291 the Prior of Longville received a pension of £1 from the church of Loughton,[66] mentioned again in 1327.[67] It was held by Sir Gilbert Talbot at his death in February 1398–9.[68]

Tickford Priory held tithes in Loughton,[69] assessed at 5s. at the Dissolution.[70] These were included in the grants of Tickford Manor in Newport Pagnell[71] (q.v.), with which they were held by Henry Atkins, M.D., in 1623.[72] New College had a pension of 6s. 8d. in Great Loughton Church.[73]

Lands and tenements in Loughton, valued at 52s. 4d. yearly in 1548–9, were given by Richard Stoke, rector of Loughton, for the purpose of giving in Lent to each householder thirty herrings. Five shillings were to be spent in gifts of bread and drink, and 2s. 1d. set aside for an obit.[74]

CHARITIES The charity of Hugh Park, settled by deed dated 1 December 1609, is endowed with two pieces of land containing together 8 a. 3 r. let at £22 a year, and with £757 16s. 2d. consols, arising from sales of land from time to time, producing £18 18s. 8d. yearly. By a scheme of the Charity Commissioners of 3 February 1882 one moiety of the net income is made applicable for the repair of the church and one moiety for the poor, which is applied in the distribution of coal.

In 1721 William Binion, by his will, devised a yearly rent-charge of £5 issuing out of Church Farm for apprenticing a poor boy. The charity is applied as required, a premium of £10 being usually paid.

The Faggot Money.—By the Loughton Inclosure Act, 1768, the allottees of the common lands were required to deliver yearly a certain number of faggots, or a money equivalent, for the poor in lieu of the right of cutting furze on the waste. A sum of £2 9s. 5d. is paid every two years in respect of this charity.

In 1878 Mrs. Whitworth, by deed dated 31 October, gave £104 5s. 11d. consols, the annual dividends, amounting to £3, to be distributed in blankets and flannel to poor widows.

Frederic Wills Bignell, by his will, proved 28 September 1905, bequeathed £95 2s. 3d. India 3½ per cent. stocks, the annual dividends, amounting to £3 6s. 8d., to be distributed on Christmas Eve among the occupants of the four memorial cottages on the London Road. The several sums of stock are held by the official trustees.

MILTON KEYNES

Middeltone (xi cent.) ; Middelton Kaynes, Caynes (xiii cent.) ; Milton Keynes (xv cent.) ; Milton *alias* Middelton Gaynes (xvii cent.).

This parish covers 1,909 acres, of which 479 are arable and 1,339 permanent grass.[1] The soil is clay, the subsoil sand and gravel. The chief crops grown are wheat, beans, barley and oats.

The land has a uniform level of 200 ft. to 250 ft. above the ordnance datum, with a slight slope towards the north ; along the banks of the Ousel and its tributary it is liable to floods.

The village lies somewhat south of the centre of the parish, about a mile west of the London Road. Many of the cottages are of half-timber and brick with thatched roofs, and have in some cases been refronted. The church of All Saints lies at the southern end, and in a field to the west of it are the remains of a moat and traces of fish-ponds,[2] which probably mark the site of the ancient manor-house and its ponds called in 1418 the Pondwykes.[3] At the northern end of the village are the school, built in 1859, and the rectory, a red brick house built by the antiquary, Dr. William Wotton, rector from 1693 to 1726.[4] The former parsonage-house was the birthplace of Francis Atterbury, the famous Jacobite Bishop of Rochester. His father, Lewis Atterbury, predecessor of Dr. Wotton, was drowned on the night of 7 December 1693 when returning home after a visit to London about litigation in which he was engaged with his principal parishioners.[5]

Among place-names are More Close, Chapel Close, Wolston Meadow, Little Hame, Much Dole, King's Bridge Field, Town Field, Bowling Leys, Bares Leys, Bares Meadow.[6]

---

[56] Add. MS. 5839, p. 257.
[57] Ibid. 258 ; Linc. Epis. Reg. Inst. Repingdon, fol. 441.
[58] De Banco R. Trin. 1 Hen. VII, m. 315.
[59] Ibid.
[60] Add. MS. 5839, p. 259.
[61] Ibid.
[62] P.C.C. 98 Byrde.
[63] Feet of F. Bucks. Mich. 14 Jas. I.
[64] Add. MS. 5839, pp. 251, 253 ; Lipscomb, *Hist. and Antiq. of Bucks.* iv, 238.

[65] Inst. Bks. (P.R.O.) ; *Clergy Lists.*
[66] *Pope Nich. Tax.* (Rec. Com.), 33.
[67] Mins. Accts. (Gen. Ser.), bdle. 1127, no. 18.
[68] Chan. Inq. p.m. 22 Ric. II, no. 47.
[69] Mins. Accts. (Gen. Ser.), bdle. 1127, no. 18 ; Chan. Inq. p.m. (Ser. 2), lxxvi, 3.
[70] Treasury of the Receipt, Misc. Bks. clxv, 128 ; *Valor Eccl.* (Rec. Com.), iv, 245.
[71] *L. and P. Hen. VIII,* iv (1), g. 1913 (1) ; v, g. 1370 (23).

[72] Pat. 21 Jas. I, pt. xviii.
[73] *Valor Eccl.* (Rec. Com.), iv, 245.
[74] Chant. Cert. 5, no. 36. Richard Stoke died towards the end of 1545 (Add. MS. 5839, p. 259).
[1] Statistics from Bd. of Agric. (1905).
[2] Sheahan, *Hist. and Topog. of Bucks.* 567.
[3] Chan. Inq. p.m. 6 Hen. V (Add. nos.), no. 60.
[4] Add. MS. 5839, fol. 134 d.; *Dict. Nat. Biog.*   [5] *Dict. Nat. Biog.*
[6] Add. MS. 5836, fol. 123.

MANORS Before the Conquest Queen Edith held this manor, which in 1086 was held of the king by Godric Cratel.[7] The overlordship remained in the Crown until the 17th century,[8] but was said to be unknown in 1645.[9] The service was defined in the 13th century as the serjeanty of finding one horseman with an unbarded horse, a lance, hauberk, haketon and iron cap for forty days in the king's army,[10] but was described in the 16th century as one-thirtieth of a knight's fee.[11]

There is no record of Milton for nearly a century after Domesday, but it appears to have been held by the Berevilles, whose line ended in a daughter and heir Mabel. She and her lands were given in marriage by the king to Hugh de Kaynes (Chahaines, Caaignes, Kahaignes) about 1166,[12] and his name occurs in documents up to the end of this century as the holder of land in Buckinghamshire and the neighbouring counties of Bedfordshire and Berkshire.[13] He appears to have died about the beginning of the 13th century, when Mabel de Bereville was returned as holder of the fee,[14] but she died about 1221, in which year Luke de Kaynes, her son, gave 100s. to have seisin of her land in Milton.[15] What was probably a younger branch of the Bereville family, however, had obtained considerable lands in the parish. An Agnes de Bereville paid scutage for lands in Bedfordshire and Buckinghamshire in 1171[16] and 1186,[17] and in 1219 had a life interest in a virgate of land in Calverton, reverting to the Prior of Bradwell.[18] In 1227 Maud wife of Robert Halebot or Hillebeck, and Ela her sister, afterwards wife of John le Butler, daughters of John de Bereville, claimed a virgate and 2 half virgates in Milton against Adam de Bereville, whom Robert de Homcot, Hugh de Kaynes and Peter de Bereville respectively vouched to warrant.[19] In 1233 the sisters and their husbands claimed a virgate in Milton, then held by Richard de Wing and Eva his wife who called Adam de Bereville to warrant, on the ground that their father, John de Bereville, had died seised

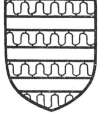

KEYNES. *Vair three bars gules.*

of it. It was found that on the day John died his step-mother Asceline held the virgate in dower, and his daughters therefore lost the case.[20] After this date the Berevilles ceased to be of importance in Milton,[21] and Luke de Kaynes is returned as sole lord of Milton in 1234.[22] In 1239 he settled a half-mark rent on his daughter Sibyl,[23] and in 1246

acquired the reversion of lands from Roger Malvoisin.[24] At his death about 1259 he was succeeded by his son John de Kaynes,[25] who obtained livery of his lands in the same year.[26] In 1275–6 he was accused of having at Milton a house erected by his father Luke in the king's highway, as well as a smithy on the common land.[27] This John de Kaynes was also summoned by Hugh with the Beard about the custody of a messuage in Milton, said in the writ to be held of John by knight service, but in the plea declared to be held for homage and 2s. service yearly.[28] He was further summoned in 1278 for exacting services to which he was not entitled, the plaintiffs alleging that his manor was ancient demesne of the Crown, but search in the Domesday Book proved that Godric Cratel held it at that date of the king.[29]

In the following year John de Kaynes made a settlement of *MIDDLETON KEYNES MANOR*, first so called, on himself and his wife Maud for life, with reversion to his son Robert.[30] John de Kaynes died about 1283, when his heir was said to be his son Nicholas, aged twenty-one,[31] but livery of the manor was given in that year to his widow Maud.[32] Through Robert de Kaynes Milton came to Philip Aylesbury, who had married his daughter and heir Margaret,[33] and who was holding the manor in 1302[34] and 1316.[35] In 1335 he and Margaret settled it on themselves for life with remainder to their only son Thomas,[36] who was already dead at the date of Philip's decease on 14 July 1349.[37] John son of Thomas then succeeded to the manor,[38] of which he died seised on 7 December 1409.[39] He was also lord of Drayton Beauchamp Manor (q.v.), with which Milton Keynes descended in the Aylesbury family. After the death of Sir Thomas Aylesbury in 1418,[40] a third of the manor was assigned in dower to his widow Katherine and included among other rooms one

AYLESBURY. *Azure a cross argent.* STAFFORD. *Or a cheveron gules.*

called the Knight's Chamber.[41] A third of the remaining portion was also assigned in dower after

[7] *V.C.H. Bucks.* i, 276.
[8] *Testa de Nevill* (Rec. Com.), 244; *Feud. Aids,* i, 104; Chan. Inq. p.m. 6 Hen. V, no. 35; (Ser. 2), lxxiv, 5.
[9] Chan. Inq. p.m. (Ser. 2), dcclxxvi, 73.
[10] *Hund. R.* (Rec. Com.), i, 41; Chan. Inq. p.m. Edw. I, file 33, no. 15.
[11] Chan. Inq. p.m. (Ser. 2), lxxiv, 5.
[12] Hearne, *Liber Niger* (ed. 2), 194.
[13] *Red Bk. of Exch.* (Rolls Ser.), 36, 52, 71, 90, 109, 137; *Rot. Cur. Reg.* (Rec. Com.), i, 349; ii, 116.
[14] *Red Bk. of Exch.* (Rolls Ser.), 536.
[15] *Excerpta e Rot. Fin.* (Rec. Com.), i, 68.
[16] *Red Bk. of Exch.* (Rolls Ser.), 52.
[17] Ibid. 59.
[18] Feet of F. case 14, file 12, no. 46.

[19] Ibid. case 15, file 17, no. 31.
[20] Maitland, *Bracton's Note Bk.* ii, 558.
[21] In 1307 there is mention of a Margaret de Bereville holding a small estate in Milton (Feet of F. case 17, file 59, no. 11).
[22] *Testa de Nevill* (Rec. Com.), 262.
[23] Feet of F. case 15, file 23, no. 3. In the following year she and her husband, Ralf Page, alienated half a virgate in Milton to William son of Hugh (ibid. no. 6).
[24] Ibid. case 15, file 27, no. 11.
[25] Chan. Inq. p.m. Hen. III, file 21, no. 20.
[26] *Excerpta e Rot. Fin.* (Rec. Com.), ii, 313, 315.
[27] *Hund. R.* (Rec. Com.), i, 41.

[28] *Abbrev. Plac.* (Rec. Com.), 264, 267.
[29] De Banco R. 27, m. 179.
[30] Feet of F. case 16, file 45, no. 10; *Visit. of Notts.* (Harl. Soc.), 125.
[31] Chan. Inq. p.m. Edw. I, file 33, no. 15.
[32] *Cal. Close,* 1279–88, p. 208.
[33] Dugdale, *Antiq. of Warws.* i, 611; *Visit. of Notts.* (Harl. Soc.), 125.
[34] *Feud. Aids,* i, 104.
[35] Ibid. 110.
[36] *Cal. Pat.* 1334–8, p. 109; Feet of F. Bucks. Mich. 9 Edw. III, no. 7.
[37] Chan. Inq. p.m. 23 Edw. III, pt. ii (1st nos.), no. 170. [38] Ibid.
[39] Ibid. 11 Hen. IV, no. 9.
[40] Ibid. 6 Hen. V, no. 35.
[41] Ibid. (Add. nos.), no. 60.

1422 to Margaret widow of John Aylesbury,[42] and reverted to the Chaworths and Staffords at her death in 1428, when she was the widow of John Skelton.[43] They obtained Katherine's portion at her death in 1436.[44] The Staffords finally obtained the whole of Milton, as they did of Broughton (q.v.). Humphrey Stafford, husband of Eleanor Aylesbury, was slain in Jack Cade's Rebellion in 1450, and was succeeded by a son Humphrey.[45] It was probably the latter's son Humphrey who was attainted as a traitor and executed in 1486.[46] Milton Keynes was granted in 1488 to Sir Edward Poyning and his issue male.[47] He died, without legitimate issue, in 1521,[48] and Milton Keynes was restored to Humphrey, son of the attainted Humphrey, who had obtained a reversal of the attainder in 1503.[49] He made a settlement of the manor in 1532, on his marriage with Joan widow of William Lane,[50] and died in 1545, his son Sir Humphrey succeeding.[51] On his death in 1548 his son, another Humphrey, inherited Milton.[51a] In 1555 he and Elizabeth his wife leased the site of the manor for twenty-one years to Laurence Woodall and his son Richard,[52] an arrangement which later gave rise to a quarrel, one Thomas Digby alleging that Richard Woodall had transferred his interest to him, instead of to his son Thomas Woodall.[53] In 1563 Sir Humphrey Stafford made a settlement of Milton[54] and died in 1574,[55] his brother and heir John dying in 1595.[56] His sons Humphrey of Sudbury in Eaton Socon (co. Bedford) and William of Blatherwycke, Northamptonshire, came to an arrangement by which William took Milton, of which he died seised in 1606.[57] His son William, then a minor, in 1629 settled the manor on his sons Edward, Charles and William respectively,[58] by the first of whom he was succeeded at his death in 1637.[59] Edward Stafford died in the following year, Charles, the second son, then inheriting the estate.[60] The wardship of these minors had been granted to Sir Hatton Farmor, against whose widow Anne Anthony Stafford, great-uncle of Charles, brought an action in 1641 to recover the arrears of an annuity left him by his father John.[61] Charles Stafford was succeeded by his brother William in 1643,[62] but he does not appear to have enjoyed the profits of the estate, which had been mortgaged by his father William for £6,000, in 1634 to Sir Lewis Watson, bart., afterwards Lord Rockingham of Rockingham, and to John Loddington.[63] Rockingham, as a delinquent, compounded for Milton Manor on the Oxford Articles,[64] but Parliament, in

ignorance of this, granted the estate to Sir John Corbett, in recompense of losses caused by the king's troops.[65] Corbett and Rockingham fought out their case in Chancery, and in 1652 it was referred to Parliament, Corbett pleading the Act of Oblivion.[66] Rockingham died early the next year, and his son and heir Edward Watson and John Loddington, the original mortgagee, joined William Stafford in levying a fine of Milton Manor.[67] Henry Stafford, William's son, was sued, when a minor, in 1669, by the rector, Dr. Lewis Atterbury, as to the locality of the glebe lands.[68] In 1677 Henry Stafford and Anne Dawes, widow, conveyed the manor to Daniel Finch,[69] who in 1682 succeeded his father Heneage Finch as second Earl of Nottingham, and became seventh Earl of Winchilsea in 1729.[70] His grandson George, the ninth earl, died unmarried in 1826, when the manor passed to his natural son George Finch of Burley-on-the-Hill, Rutland.[71] From him it descended in 1870 to his son George Henry Finch, whose son Alan George Finch died in 1914, when Milton passed to Mr. Wilfred Finch of Burley-on-the-Hill.[72]

Half a hide in Milton, which had been held in the time of King Edward by Oswi, a man of Alric, who could sell it, was assessed among Walter Giffard's lands in 1086.[73] It descended with the honour of Giffard in the earldoms of Gloucester, Hertford and Stafford,[74] the Duke of Buckingham holding the overlordship rights in 1460.[75]

The under-tenant in 1086 was Hugh,[76] and in 1262 Thomas Toky held.[77] This small estate may be identical with the *MILTON KEYNES MANOR* held by Peter de Campania in 1294 when he complained of assaults on his servants,[78] but the inquisition taken of his lands two years later makes no mention of property in Buckinghamshire.[79]

At the date of the Domesday Survey Otbert held of William Fitz Ansc ulf a hide in Milton which Sawold, a man of Wlward cilt, had previously held, and could sell.[80]

Land in Milton was included among possessions confirmed to the abbey of St. Albans by a charter of King Richard I inspected and confirmed in 1301.[81] A hide of land was also granted to the abbey by John de Kaynes, lord of the manor in the middle of the 13th century.[82] The abbey also received a 40s. pension from Milton Keynes Church.[83] In 1565 a cottage next the churchyard, formerly belonging to St. Albans, was granted to Thomas Sidney and Nicholas Halswell.[84]

---

[42] Chan. Inq. p.m. 7 Hen. VI, no. 55.
[43] Ibid.
[44] Ibid. 15 Hen. VI, no. 50.
[45] Holinshed, *Chron. of Engl.* iii, 634; Chan. Inq. p.m. 28 Hen. VI, no. 7.
[46] Holinshed, op. cit. iii, 764; Chan. Inq. p.m. (Ser. 2), ii, 68; *Parl. R.* vi, 276.   [47] Pat. 569, m. 3.
[48] Chan. Inq. p.m. (Ser. 2), xxxvi, 14; *Dict. Nat. Biog.*
[49] *Parl. R.* vi, 526.
[50] Recov. R. Hil. 23 Hen. VIII, m. 142.
[51] Chan. Inq. p.m. (Ser. 2), lxxiv, 5.
[51a] Ibid. lxxxvii, 77.
[52] Feet of F. Bucks. East. 1 & 2 Phil. and Mary; Mich. 2 & 3 Phil. and Mary; Chan. Proc. (Ser. 2), bdles. 50, no. 37; 51, no. 36.
[53] Chan. Proc. (Ser. 2), bdles. 50, no. 37; 51, no. 36.
[54] Pat. 5 Eliz. pt. v; Feet of F. Bucks. East. 5 Eliz.

[55] Chan. Inq. p.m. (Ser. 2), clxxiii, 84.
[56] Ibid. ccxlvii, 8.
[57] Ibid. ccxciv, 111.
[58] Recov. R. East. 5 Chas. I, m. 37; Chan. Inq. p.m. (Ser. 2), dxlv, 69.
[59] Chan. Inq. p.m. (Ser. 2), dxlv, 69.
[60] Ibid. dlxxvi, 153.
[61] *Cal. S. P. Dom.* 1640–1, p. 590; cf. Chan. Inq. p.m. (Ser. 2), ccxciv, 111.
[62] Chan. Inq. p.m. (Ser. 2), dcclxxvi, 73.
[63] Ibid.; *Cal. Com. for Comp.* 1437.
[64] *Cal. Com. for Comp.* 1436–7.
[65] *Hist. MSS. Com. Rep.* vi, App. 107b, 144b, 145b.
[66] *Cal. Com. for Comp.* 1436–7.
[67] G.E.C. *Complete Peerage*, vi, 384–5; Feet of F. Bucks. Hil. 1652.
[68] Exch. Dep. Mich. 21 Chas. II, no. 4.
[69] Recov. R. East. 29 Chas. II, m. 50; Feet of F. Bucks. Mich. 29 Chas. II.
[70] G.E.C. op. cit. viii, 179.

[71] G.E.C. op. cit. viii, 181; Sheahan, op. cit. 565. See also Marcham, *Cat. Bucks. Deeds*, no. 449; Recov. R. Mich. 15 Geo. III, m. 285; Feet of F. Bucks. Trin. 45 Geo. III.
[72] Burke, *Landed Gentry* (ed. 12).
[73] *V.C.H. Bucks.* i, 252.
[74] Chan. Inq. p.m. Hen. III, file 27, no. 5; 10 Ric. II, no. 38; 16 Ric. II, pt. i, no. 27; 4 Hen. IV, no. 41.
[75] Ibid. 38 & 39 Hen. VI, no. 59.
[76] *V.C.H. Bucks.* i, 252.
[77] Chan. Inq. p.m. Hen. III, file 27, no. 5.
[78] *Cal. Pat.* 1292–1301, p. 111.
[79] Chan. Inq. p.m. Edw. I, file 75, no. 21.
[80] *V.C.H. Bucks.* i, 257.
[81] *Cal. Chart. R.* 1300–26, p. 18.
[82] *Hund. R.* (Rec. Com.), i, 41.
[83] *Pope Nich. Tax.* (Rec. Com.), 33; *Valor Eccl.* (Rec. Com.), iv, 244.
[84] Add. MS. 5839, fol. 133.

A mill was held with the manor in 1086,[85] and one-third of a water-mill was claimed in 1313 by Philip Aylesbury in right of his wife Margaret.[86] In 1349 this was said to be held by grant of Herbert de Broughton of the Earl of Oxford.[87] It was called Foxmilne in 1418, when a fishery in the stream and pond was also included in the appurtenances of the manor.[88]

The church of *ALL SAINTS* consists of a chancel measuring internally 30 ft. 6 in. by 16 ft. 10 in., north chapel 30 ft. 10 in. by 13 ft. 5 in., nave 60 ft. 9 in. by 24 ft. 8 in., north tower about 11 ft. square, and south porch. It is built of stone rubble, faced both internally and externally, and the roofs are covered with tiles.

A church of considerable importance existed here at the end of the 12th century, but the only remains of the original structure are the east wall of the nave, the fine chancel arch, and a lancet reset in the south wall of the nave. Towards the end of the first half of the 14th century the church was almost entirely rebuilt, the nave being widened towards the north and probably lengthened, the chancel enlarged, and the

of three bays below the eastern window on this side. The sedilia are trefoiled and have their seats on different levels; the piscina and credence, which are formed by the subdivision of the eastern bay by a central shaft, are cinquefoiled, and their shafts are carried down below the sills to the level of the seat of the adjacent sedile. On the north side, opening to the chapel, is an arcade of two pointed arches, supported by a circular pillar and filleted responds with moulded capitals and bases. The capitals of the responds were originally enriched by carvings on each side, but these have been cut away. To the east of the arcade is a plain locker recess. The chancel arch, which dates from about 1200, is acutely pointed, and springs from engaged shafts with moulded bases and water-leaf capitals.

The north chapel was probably founded for a chantry by Philip Aylesbury, who died in 1349, or his grandson John who succeeded him. It was endowed apparently by the Chaworths and Staffords in the reign of Henry VI, for masses to be said for the souls of their ancestors the Aylesburys.[89] The chapel is lighted from the east by a window of three cinquefoiled lights with flowing tracery in an ogee head, and from the north by three windows, two of which are of two cinquefoiled lights with graceful tracery in their heads, while the remaining window, at the west end of the wall, is a single light. This last, with the exception of one internal jamb, is entirely modern, but is probably a copy of the original; its lower part is fitted with a small door, and there is a similar opening below the central window, with an original segmental rear-arch formed in the window sill. Assuming that the western light is a faithful copy of the original, this arrangement of two low-side openings near each other in the same wall is most unusual. Between these openings there is a moulded doorway with a pointed head. At the south-east is a large piscina, now without a bowl; it has a trefoiled ogee head with sub-cusping, and a continuous outer moulding enriched with ball-flower ornament. The pointed arch to the nave is moulded on the west side with a large continuous edge roll having broached stops.

The nave has three windows in the south wall, two in the north wall, and one in the west wall, all of three lights with tracery in pointed heads; all these, with the exception of the west window, only the jambs of which are original, date from the 14th century. To the west of the two windows on the north is a doorway similar to that in the chapel, and at the east end of the north wall is a pointed arch, opening to the ground stage of the tower, with moulded

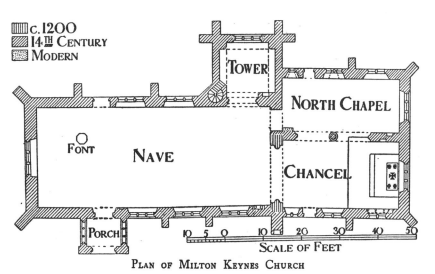

c.1200
14TH CENTURY
MODERN

TOWER

NORTH CHAPEL

FONT

NAVE

CHANCEL

PORCH

SCALE OF FEET

PLAN OF MILTON KEYNES CHURCH

chapel, tower, and porch added. The whole fabric has been restored and reroofed in modern times. Two of the windows and the straight parapets, which are carried round the church, have been substantially renewed, but otherwise the mediaeval stonework is well preserved, and the building, with its fine traceried windows, elaborate south doorway and openwork porch, is one of the finest examples of 14th-century work in the county.

The east window of the chancel is of three trefoiled lights, with reticulated tracery in a pointed head. On the south are two fine traceried windows, each of two cinquefoiled lights, while near the west end of the wall is a two-light low-side window, both lights of which are rebated internally for shutters. Immediately to the east of the low-side window is a small moulded doorway with a pointed head. A piscina, credence niche, and two sedilia, inclosed in a square head with shields in the spandrels, and divided from each other by circular shafts, form one composition

[85] *V.C.H. Bucks.* i, 276.
[86] De Banco R. 201, m. 160 d.
[87] Chan. Inq. p.m. 23 Edw. III, pt. ii (1st nos.), no. 170.
[86] Ibid. 6 Hen. V (Add. nos.), no. 60.
[89] Add M.S. 5836, fol. 122.

responds, the capitals of which are embellished with ball-flower and dog-tooth ornament. The enrichments on the south side of these capitals, like those on the north arcade of the chancel, have been cut away. The south doorway is a particularly rich and well-preserved example of 14th-century work. It has an acutely pointed head with continuous mouldings, the inner member of which develops into a large trefoil with sub-cusping. The label is enriched with a running ball-flower ornament and terminates in carved stops. The bases of the jambs have been restored. Immediately to the east of the doorway inside are the remains of a trefoiled stoup, the projecting bowl of which has been cut away. At the south-east of the nave is a pointed niche formed by the outer stonework of a window of about 1200 reset in the wall and possibly used at one time as a piscina, though there is now no bowl. Externally there is a considerably restored wall arcade of trefoiled arches above the west window, and the buttress supporting the chancel arch on the south side has a tall niche with an ogee head. The angle buttresses both at the east and west ends of the church terminate in crocketed pinnacles. The porch has a moulded entrance archway, partly restored, and each lateral wall is pierced by an arcade of three trefoiled arches with circular pillars and responds and traceried spandrels.

The tower is of three stages, with buttresses at the northern angles, and is surmounted by an embattled parapet. The ground stage was evidently a chapel, and the internal space is considerably increased by wide arched recesses, which on the north and east occupy the full length of the walls. The back of the northern recess is pierced by a three-light window with modern tracery. At the springing level of the arches at the north-east there is a small image bracket with a trefoiled canopy, and a similar bracket with canopy at the north-west has been cut away, while at the south-east there is a large pointed piscina with a cusped head and plain modern sill. The second stage has a small trefoiled window on the west, and the bell-chamber is lighted from the south by a window of two trefoiled lights, and from each of the other sides by a window of three lights with intersecting tracery.

In the north chapel is a plain octagonal 14th-century font, which lay till recently in the churchyard, but has been brought back into the church by the present rector.

On the south wall of the chancel is the brass figure of a priest in mass vestments, with the inscription, 'Hic jacet Adam Badyngtoñ quondam Rector istius ecctíe Qui obiit octavo die mensis Novembr̃ Anno dñi Miłło cccc vicesimo septimo cuius aĩe ppicietur deus Amen.' Two slabs, one with the matrices for this brass and the other for the demi-figure of a knight, are now in the churchyard. On the north

wall of the chapel is a marble tablet to John Lowth, rector of the parish (d. 1761), and Mary his wife (d. 1769) ; on the west wall is a tablet to William Edwards, S.T.P., rector of the parish and Canon of Lincoln (d. 1744). On a desk against the east wall of the nave there is a chained Bible which was 'Imprinted at London by Robert Barker printer to the King's most excellent Maiestie Anno Dom. 1613.' At the west end of the nave is preserved an old table with turned legs. Several encaustic tiles of various patterns, and dating principally from about 1400, have been collected and placed on the sill of the east window of the chapel ; some of these have the shield of Beauchamp, and one is inscribed ' Ricard me fecit.'

The tower contains a ring of five bells : the treble is modern, the second by Newcome, 1614, the third by Anthony Chandler, 1675, the fourth by Richard Chandler, 1704, and the tenor by Gillett of Croydon, 1887, recast from one by Newcome, 1614. There is also a small bell with no inscription, probably dating from the 17th century.

The communion plate consists of a cup, paten and salver of 1715 and a flagon dated 1728, all given by Laurence Smith. The flagon has no hall-marks.

The registers before 1812 are as follows : (i) all entries 1559 to 1653 ; (ii) 1693 to 1727 ; (iii) 1728 to 1812.

The church was first mentioned *ADVOWSON* in 1221, when Luke de Kaynes presented Ralph de Kaynes to the rectory.[90] The advowson descended with the manor, but on the death of Hugh Aylesbury in 1423 the Chaworths and Staffords divided the advowson between them, each taking alternate turns.[91] The Staffords' interest descended with the manor, and the Chaworths' with the Aylesburys' manor of Drayton Beauchamp (q.v.) until *circa* 1543, when it was held in moieties by Thomas Dynham and his cousin Thomas Babington.[92] Their interest seems to have been acquired by John Nurse, George Mace and Michael Coles before 1585, and by them to have been transferred before 1638 to the rector, Ralph Smith.[93] His son or grandson Ralph Smith in 1687 conveyed this moiety of the advowson to Daniel Earl of Nottingham,[94] who had in 1677 acquired the Stafford interest with the manor.[95] The sole right to the advowson has since descended with the manor.[96]

According to Browne Willis, the north chapel was converted into a school in Queen Elizabeth's time.[97] Laurence Ryppington was instituted to the church and chantry of St. Mary in the church in 1444.[98]

By deed, dated 13 June 1684, the *CHARITY* Earl of Nottingham gave an annual fee-farm rent of £2 out of the rectory of Astwood for the poor. The annuity is received from the vicar of Astwood, and applied for the benefit of the school.

[90] *R. of Hugh of Wells* (Cant. and York Soc.), ii, 55. It was valued at £10 in 1291 (*Pope Nich. Tax.* [Rec. Com.], 33), and at £20 in 1535 (*Valor Eccl.* [Rec. Com.], iv, 244).

[91] Add. MS. 5836, fol. 119 d.
[92] Feet of F. Div. Co. Mich. 35 Hen. VIII ; Add. MS. 5839, fol. 133 d.
[93] Add. MS. 5836, fol. 120 d.
[94] Feet of F. Bucks. Trin. 3 Jas. II.

[95] Ibid. Mich. 29 Chas. II ; Recov. R. Mich. 29 Chas. II, m. 231.
[96] Inst. Bks. (P.R.O.) ; *Clergy Lists*.
[97] Add. MS. 5836, fol. 120.
[98] Ibid. fol. 119 d., 120 d.

MOULSOE

Mouleshou (xi cent.); Muleshou (xii cent.); Muselo, Moullesso (xiii cent.).

In the 11th century Moulsoe gave its name to the hundred of Moulsoe, which was later absorbed in the hundred of Newport.[1] It is stated with regard to the parish in an inquisition taken c. 1341 for the purposes of a general taxation throughout the country that Moulsoe was only valued at 7 marks 3 shillings and 4 pence, the low sum being due to the fact that a dry summer had that year spoilt the bean and pea crops, and so deprived the inhabitants of their principal means of livelihood.[2]

At the present day Moulsoe has an area of 1,654 acres, of which 569 acres are arable and 928 acres permanent grass.[3] The soil is mixed, principally strong loam, the subsoil clay and gravel. The principal crops produced are wheat, barley, oats and beans. The slope of the land varies from 354 ft. above the ordnance datum in the north-west to 200 ft. in the south-west. The parish is watered by Claydon Brook, and is well-wooded, containing some 147 acres of woodland; Moulsoe Old Wood in the north and Drake's Gorse in the west may be noted.

The village of Moulsoe in the centre of the parish is small and straggling, and contains a few 17th-century cottages.

A terrier of 1639 thus describes the rectory: 'The parsonage dwelling-house contains six bays tiled, one corn barn of five bays and one lesser of three bays, both thatched, one hay barn of three bays thatched, a stable with a gate house, and other houses for other uses contain five bays; one other little house contains three bays thatched.'[4]

The Civil War, which raged specially in this neighbourhood, did not leave Moulsoe untouched, for it appears from the parish registers that two Parliamentarian soldiers were buried here in 1643.[5] Moulsoe was inclosed by Act of Parliament in 1802.[6]

MANORS In 1086 *MOULSOE MANOR* was among the lands of Walter Giffard, and was assessed at 10 hides.[7] Like other of his lands,[8] this manor became attached to the liberty of the Earl Marshal,[9] and was so held of the Talbots in the 14th and 15th centuries.[10] When the mesne manor fell to the Crown in 1542 Moulsoe became part of the king's honour of Ampthill,[11] and so remained[12] until the grant to Sir John Spencer, Moulsoe being then attached to the manor of East Greenwich.[13] Last mention of the overlordship has been found in 1632.[14]

Eight thegns were tenants of Moulsoe Manor under the Confessor, the 10 hides being subdivided into two manors of 2 hides each, held by Ulf and Alwin respectively; Algar held another manor of 1 hide and a half, the remaining 4½ hides being divided among Elsi, Turchil, Lodi, Osulf, and Elric.[15] By the time of the Survey all these holdings were united in the ownership of one man, Richard.[16] Who were his immediate successors has not been established, but by 1185 the king was guardian to two widows, both owning considerable property in Moulsoe. Emma de Langetot, described as 'de genere illarum de Chedney et Josceline Crispini,' was sixty years old and had land worth £4 per annum. Her heirs were the wife of Alan de Dunstanville and the wife of Alard son of William.[17] The second royal ward was Ida widow of William de Sherington (Schirintone) and daughter of Hugh de Bulli. Her children were three sons and three daughters, the eldest thirty years of age.[18] There must have been some connexion between these very considerable owners of land and the family of Coudray, who are found as lords of the manor barely a generation later, though the missing link has not been discovered. The first of the Coudray family to whom reference has been found in Moulsoe is Peter de Coudray, who is said to have presented to the church in the time of King John.[18a] Fulk de Coudray held a fee here in demesne c. 1240,[19] and died about 1251 seised of Moulsoe Manor, which was then of sufficient importance to have five of the Earl Marshal's knights' fees in Buckinghamshire and one in Bedfordshire attached to it.[20] Peter son of Fulk de Coudray was under age at his father's death.[21]

COUDRAY. *Gules billety or.*

In 1262 Richard de Sifrewast relinquished his right in the manor (obtained by an agreement with Fulk) to Peter de Coudray,[22] who is returned as holding one fee in Moulsoe in 1284–6.[23] Peter de Coudray died about 1303,[24] having leased Moulsoe and other manors in 1297 to his eldest son Thomas de Coudray at an annual rent of £100.[25] Thomas de Coudray's name is found in connexion with Moulsoe in 1302[26] and 1304.[27] In 1310 he made a settlement of the manor on his son Thomas and Lucy, the latter's wife.[28] Thomas de Coudray was part lord of the vill in 1316,[29] but died in 1349, when the manor descended to his 'cousin and heir' Fulk de Coudray, son of Thomas de Coudray,[30] who

[1] *V.C.H. Bucks.* i, 241.
[2] *Inq. Nonarum* (Rec. Com.), 338.
[3] Statistics from Bd. of Agric. (1905).
[4] Add. MS. 5839, fol. 139 d.
[5] Ibid.
[6] Priv. Act, 42 Geo. III, cap. 83.
[7] *V.C.H. Bucks.* i, 252.
[8] See Crendon, the head of this honour in Buckinghamshire.
[9] *Testa de Nevill* (Rec. Com.), 247, 258; *Feud. Aids,* i, 83.
[10] Chan. Inq. p.m. 46 Edw. III (1st nos.), no. 66; 20 Ric. II, no. 51; 8 Hen. V (Add. nos.), no. 127.

[11] *L. and P. Hen. VIII,* xvii, 28 (21).
[12] Pat. 5 Edw. VI, pt. iii, m. 25; 12 Eliz. pt. x, m. 6, 7.
[13] Chan. Inq. p.m. (Ser. 2), cccxviii, 165.
[14] Ibid. ccccxc, 189.
[15] *V.C.H. Bucks.* i, 252.
[16] Ibid.
[17] Stacy Grimaldi, *Rot. de Dominabus,* 21.
[18] Ibid.
[18a] Cur. Reg. R. 147B, m. 37.
[19] *Testa de Nevill* (Rec. Com.), 247.
[20] Chan. Inq. p.m. 36 Hen. III, no. 11.

[21] Ibid. His age is variously stated at thirteen, fourteen, and fifteen.
[22] Assize R. 5, m. 15 d.; *Abbrev. Plac.* (Rec. Com.), 155.
[23] *Feud. Aids,* i, 83.
[24] *Cal. Fine R.* 1272–1307, p. 480.
[25] *Var. Coll.* (Hist. MSS. Com.), iv, 154.
[26] *Feud. Aids,* i, 104.
[27] Inq. a.q.d. file 53, no. 28.
[28] Feet of F. Bucks. 4 Edw. II, no. 15.
[29] *Feud. Aids,* i, 110.
[30] Chan. Inq. p.m. 23 Edw. III, pt. i, no. 49.

held in 1355 with Jane his wife.[31]   Between 1367, in which year the last mention is found of Fulk de Coudray,[32] and 1397 Moulsoe appears to have passed to the Whittingham family, of whom the Bammes and others appear to have held on long leases.   In 1397 Adam Bamme was responsible to the overlord for the fee by which this manor was held,[33] and in 1420 had been followed by Richard Bamme.[34]   In 1452 the will of Sir Robert Whittingham contains mention of Moulsoe Manor, which he bequeathed to his younger son Richard, with remainder to his eldest son Robert.[35]   The manor eventually came to Robert Whittingham, and on his attainder for adherence to the house of Lancaster fell with other of his estates into the possession of the Crown.[36]   Meanwhile a continuance of the interest of the Bammes in the manor is still to be found.   Richard Bamme died in or about the year 1452, when his will was dated.[37]   It contains no mention of Moulsoe by name, but in 1462 his son John acquired licence to enter into the manor, then stated to be under forfeiture on account of Robert Whittingham's attainder.[38]   The Bamme interests had passed by August of the following year to Robert Honyngton, who was declared to have died seised at that date of the manor of Moulsoe,[39] and whose nephew and heir Thomas Honyngton[40] had apparently married Margaret daughter of Richard Bamme.[41] Thomas Honyngton acquired possession of Moulsoe Manor in the same year,[42] but no further reference to his holding has been found.   Moulsoe was still in the king's hands in 1477, being then granted to Thomas Grey, who was to render 2d. yearly at Michaelmas.[43] The Whittinghams appear to have obtained eventually a reversal of the forfeiture of their lands here as elsewhere, for in 1497 Moulsoe Manor is found in the possession of Margaret daughter and heir of Sir Robert Whittingham and wife of Sir John Verney.[44] In that year she transferred the manor to Thomas Heyron.[45]   From him it passed to John Marsh, who sold it to the Crown in 1542.[46]   Princess Elizabeth held it during her brother's reign,[47] and when she came to the throne made it the subject of various grants. Thus Robert Power received a temporary grant in 1550, renewed in 1560,[48] and again in 1577.[49] Finally, in March 1599–1600 Sir John Spencer, kt., received a permanent grant of Moulsoe Manor.[50]   He died in 1610, and the manor next passed to his daughter Elizabeth, wife of William Lord Compton,[51] who was created Earl of Northampton in 1618.[52] He died in 1630,[53] in which year Spencer Earl of Northampton, his son and heir, made a settlement

of Moulsoe Manor[54] which his mother Elizabeth retained till her death in 1632.[55]   Spencer Earl of Northampton was an ardent supporter of Charles I in the Civil War, and was slain at Hopton Heath on 19 March 1642–3 fighting on the Royalist side.[56]   In 1647 his widow compounded for her estate in Moulsoe, James Earl of Northampton, his son and heir, also compounding for his reversionary interest.[57]   He suffered a recovery of the manor in 1658.[58]   He died in 1681, and his eldest surviving son George succeeded to the family title and estates.[59]

CARRINGTON, Marquess of Lincolnshire. *Or a cheveron couple-closed between three demi-griffons sable with a molet gules for difference.*

George, fourth Earl of Northampton, was in turn succeeded in 1727 by his son James,[60] who made a settlement of Moulsoe in 1730.[61]   He died in 1754, when his estates devolved on his brother and heir male George Compton.[62] He also left no direct issue, and in 1758 the title and estates passed to his nephew Charles Compton, who in the year following his accession suffered a recovery of Moulsoe Manor.[63]   In 1781 this manor appears to have been temporarily in the possession of John and Frances Bowater,[64] but it was retained by the Earls of Northampton until 1801, when it was purchased from Charles Earl of Northampton by Lord Carrington,[65] in whose family it has since been retained, the Marquess of Lincolnshire being the present lord of the manor.[66]

Part of Walter Giffard's Domesday property went to form a second MOULSOE MANOR, which follows the same descent as that part of his adjoining manor of Broughton (q.v.) retained by Robert de Broughton in 1334.   Only very occasional reference is found to it. In 1316 Joan widow of Ralph de Broughton held part of Moulsoe,[67] described in 1409 as two cottages.[68] John Broughton died seised of lands and rents here in 1489,[69] while in 1596 Thomas Duncombe died seised of lands in Moulsoe attached to the Broughton manor which he had acquired from William Paulet, Lord St. John, and Ann his wife.[70]   This estate passed with Broughton to a younger son Francis,[71] who in 1599 made a settlement of the property.[72]   The land in Moulsoe is termed a manor in 1635,[73] but it is not mentioned in the will of Thomas Duncombe, who died in 1672,[74] and in 1748 it appears to have been

[31] Feet of F. Bucks. 29 Edw. III, no. 5.

[32] Ibid. 41 Edw. III, no. 11.

[33] Chan. Inq. p.m. 20 Ric. II, no. 51.

[34] Ibid. 8 Hen. V, no. 127.

[35] Add. MS. 5839, fol. 137 d.; Gibbons, *Early Linc. Wills*, 191.

[36] *Cal. Pat.* 1461–7, p. 122.

[37] P.C.C. 17 Rous.

[38] *Cal. Pat.* loc. cit.

[39] Chan. Inq. p.m. 3 Edw. IV, no. 4.

[40] Ibid.

[41] P.C.C. 17 Rous.

[42] Close, 3 Edw. IV, m. 9.

[43] *Cal. Pat.* 1476–85, p. 33.

[44] *Visit. of Bucks.* (Harl. Soc.), 123.

[45] Feet of F. Div. Co. Hil. 12 Hen. VII; De Banco R. 938, m. 21.

[46] Pat. 34 Hen. VIII, pt. vi, m. 9; *L. and P. Hen. VIII*, xviii (1), g. 226 (38).

[47] Pat. 4 Edw. VI, pt. iii, m. 25.

[48] Ibid. 2 Eliz. pt. xii, m. 26.

[49] Ibid. 19 Eliz. pt. ii, m. 15.

[50] Ibid. 42 Eliz. pt. xviii, m. 26.

[51] Chan. Inq. p.m. (Ser. 2), cccxviii, 165.

[52] G.E.C. *Complete Peerage*, vi, 71.

[53] Ibid. vi, 72.

[54] Ibid.; Feet of F. Div. Co. Mich. 6 Chas. I.

[55] Chan. Inq. p.m. (Ser. 2), cccxc, 189.

[56] G.E.C. loc. cit.

[57] *Cal. Com. for Comp.* 67 (bis).

[58] Recov. R. East. 1658, m. 186.

[59] G.E.C. op. cit. vi, 73.

[60] Ibid.

[61] Recov. R. Trin. 3 & 4 Geo. II, m. 174.

[62] G.E.C. op. cit. vi, 74.

[63] Ibid.; Recov. R. Trin. 32 & 33 Geo. II, m. 167.

[64] Recov. R. Trin. 21 Geo. III, m. 383.

[65] Lysons, *Mag. Brit.* i (3), 610; Com. Pleas Recov. R. East. 41 Geo. III, m. 23; Feet of F. Bucks. Hil. 41 Geo. III. Moulsoe occurs in a settlement of the Earl of Northampton's property in 1811 at the coming of age of his son and heir Lord Compton (Recov. R. Hil. 51 Geo. III, m. 46).

[66] Lipscomb, *Hist. and Antiq. of Bucks.* iv, 253; Sheahan, *Hist. and Topog. of Bucks.* 568.   [67] *Feud. Aids*, i, 110.

[68] Chan. Inq. p.m. 10 Hen. IV, no. 38.

[69] *Cal. Inq. p.m. Hen. VII*, i, 238.

[70] Chan. Inq. p.m. (Ser. 2), ccxlvi, 110.

[71] Ibid.

[72] Feet of F. Bucks. Hil. 41 Eliz.

[73] Chan. Inq. p.m. (Ser. 2), dxxv, 123; dxxii, 20.   [74] P.C.C. 43 Pye.

regarded merely as an appurtenance to Broughton Manor.[75]

In 1324 Nicholas de la Husee held by knight's service in Moulsoe of the heirs of the Earl Marshal.[76] In 1346 this fee was said to have formerly belonged to Thomas de Coudray,[77] but nothing further has been heard of it.

The family of Mordaunt appears to have held land in Moulsoe, for at the time of the release of the advowson by Lord Mordaunt to Sir John Spencer in 1602 mention is also made of a manor in Moulsoe.[78] This so-called manor is mentioned in 1610[79] and again in 1632,[80] but after that date becomes absorbed in Moulsoe Manor.

In the 13th century the Abbess of Elstow acquired land from Walter de Cordel[81] worth £1 10s. in 1291.[82] In 1304 Roger Jory and Alice his wife augmented this grant.[83] In 1517 the abbess was said to hold one messuage and 20 acres in demesne there.[84] At the Dissolution the Elstow Abbey lands in Moulsoe were worth 18s.[85] Lavendon Abbey also had a small estate here worth 3s. 3d. in 1291,[86] and 13s. 4d. at the Dissolution,[87] which was granted to William Lloyd and Anthony Gooch in January 1609–10.[88]

CHURCH The church of ST. MARY consists of a chancel 18 ft. by 15 ft., nave 47 ft. by 17 ft., north and south aisles 11 ft. wide, west tower 11 ft. by 10 ft., and a south porch; these measurements are all internal.

The present building has probably been developed from a 12th-century church, consisting of a chancel and nave. The first stage in the evolution of the plan appears to have been the addition of north and south aisles in the 13th century. Considerable alterations were made in the 14th century, when the nave arcades were raised, the aisles rebuilt, and the tower and south porch added. In 1885–90 the chancel and porch were rebuilt and the church restored.

The chancel is entirely modern, except for the chancel arch, which is of the 13th century, rebuilt or recut about 100 years later. It is of two chamfered orders, and rests on semi-octagonal jambs with moulded capitals and bases. Under the arch is a modern oak screen incorporating the moulded principal mullions and two of the traceried panels of a 15th-century screen; the posts at the north and south ends of the screen are also of the 15th century, and the former contain part of a squint of the same date.

The north and south arcades of the nave are each of four bays, with pointed arches of two chamfered orders; the columns are octagonal and with the responds have capitals and bases similar to those of the chancel arch. There are four clearstory windows on the north side and three on the south side, all with plain square openings and wooden lintels, and a few courses of brickwork over the heads outside; they appear to be insertions of the 17th century. The nave roof is hidden by a barrel-vaulted plaster ceiling with wooden cornices. In the south-east corner of the nave is a small square bracket much broken.

The windows of the north aisle are all of the 14th century. In the east wall is a window of three lights, while the two north windows and the west window are each of two lights. Only the inner arch of the north doorway is old. At the east end are traces of a piscina. The remains of a 16th-century screen which formerly inclosed a small chapel at the east end of the aisle are also preserved. The northern portion of the screen up to the sill level, with part of a doorpost, remains; the sill retains its mortises for the upper mullions, and there are plain panels below. There are a few fragments of old tiles on the floor.

The south aisle has a modern east window and two 14th-century windows of two lights in the south wall. The moulded south doorway is of the 14th century, but has been much restored. The east end of this aisle is inclosed by a modern oak screen to form a lady chapel. In the east wall are a trefoil-headed piscina of 14th-century date with a modern basin and a small deep locker with chamfered opening, and to the south of the east window is a chamfered stone bracket much broken. On the modern altar-pace are several much-worn 15th-century tiles of various patterns; one bears the inscription 'Ricard me fecit,' which is also found on a tile at Milton Keynes. Fixed against the west wall of the nave and the south wall of the south aisle are some early 17th-century panels and framing, probably from old pews. At the west end of the south aisle, loose on the floor, is a large stone 16½ in. square and 19 in. high, with chamfered angles, sunk trefoils on the sides, and a bowl sunk in the top. Its use is unknown, but it may have been meant to hold charcoal for burning incense.

The west tower is of two stages, with diagonal buttresses, south-west stair turret, an embattled parapet with a moulded string-course below and stone gargoyles at the angles. The tower arch is chamfered and dies into square jambs, and the ground stage is lighted by two-light windows in the north and west walls. Over the arch is a trefoiled light opening into the nave. The door of the staircase is made of old battens with strap hinges, and the chamfered doorway has an ogee head. The bell-chamber has two-light windows on the north, south, and west sides, the east window being of three lights.

The south porch is a modern rebuilding, but the outer archway of the early 14th century remains; it is similar in design to the inner doorway, but has been much restored.

The font has a modern bowl on a 14th-century octagonal stem, which is moulded at the top and has large rounded stops at the bottom.

In the north aisle are the brass figures of a man and woman; the man is represented in plate armour with a mail skirt and large knee-cops and shoulder-guards, and has a long sword hanging from his belt, while the woman wears a long gown and a pedimental head-dress. A brass shield has the arms: a cross engrailed between four martlets and a quarterly chief charged with two roses for Ruthall of Wolverton, impaling a fesse between three crescents. There are

[75] Com. Pleas Recov. R. Mich. 22 Geo. II, m. 73.

[76] Chan. Inq. p.m. 17 Edw. II, no. 75; cf. also Cal. Close, 1323–7, p. 273.

[77] Feud. Aids, i, 129.

[78] Recov. R. Mich. 44 & 45 Eliz. m. 130; Feet of F. Bucks. Mich. 44 & 45 Eliz.

[79] Chan. Inq. p.m. (Ser. 2), cccxviii, 165.

[80] Ibid. ccccxc, 189.

[81] Abbrev. Plac. (Rec. Com.), 218.

[82] Pope Nich. Tax. (Rec. Com.), 33b.

[83] Cal. Pat. 1301–7, p. 230; Inq. a.q.d. file 49, no. 14.

[84] Leadam, Dom. Incl. 1517 (Royal Hist. Soc.), 179.

[85] Valor Eccl. (Rec. Com.), iv, 188.

[86] Pope Nich. Tax. (Rec. Com.), 48.

[87] Valor Eccl. (Rec. Com.), iv, 241.

[89] Pat. 7 Jas. I, pt. xxx, no. 10.

Moulsoe Church from the South-East

Newport Pagnell : Tickford Abbey

also indents of a marginal inscription, groups of sons and daughters, and three shields. At the north-east corner of the chancel is a stone with the indents of the figure of a priest and an inscription. Partly covered by the altar steps is a slab to George Goodman (d. 1695), and at the east end of the south aisle is a coffin-slab bearing traces of a cross flory on a stepped base, and dating probably from the 14th century.

There are modern wall tablets to Lord and Lady Carrington (d. 1868), Lady Suffield (d. 1850), and members of the Morrell, Cautley, and Levi families.

There are a few small fragments of 14th-century glass in the west window of the tower. At the west end of the north aisle are two chests ; one, of about 1300, has iron bands and two hasps, the other, which is probably of the 17th century, and is smaller, has a fleur de lis strap-hinge. Near the south door is a 17th-century oak poor-box. The modern litany desk in the nave has a front partly composed of two open traceried panels with ogee heads, crockets and finials, probably part of the 15th-century chancel screen. Many of the seats in the nave date from the early 17th century, and have panelled and moulded backs and parts of bench-ends. In the chancel are four 17th-century coffin-stools with turned legs. The oaken bier is a fine dated example, and has turned drop-hinged handles, guilloche ornament carved on the legs, and lettering carved on the rails, which have shaped brackets under each end. The inscription in capitals gives the names of the churchwardens, one of which is partly hidden by a modern iron strengthening band. The legs are worm-eaten in places, but otherwise the bier is in good preservation. The inscription reads : '. . . oughton and William Kent, Churchwardens, 1651, Thomas Larratt,' and concludes with a text.

There are four bells : the treble by James Keene, inscribed '1640 I.K.' ; the second, third and tenor all by W. & J. Taylor, Oxford, 1839.

The communion plate includes a cup and paten of 1783, an almsdish or salver of 1777, and a flagon of 1778, all inscribed 'Given by Henry and Elizabeth Jones, 1783.'

The registers before 1812 are as follows : (i) baptisms and burials 1560 to 1788, marriages 1559 to 1788 ; the parchment covers have an old brass clasp stamped with five fleurs de lis; (ii) marriages 1754 to 1811.

ADVOWSON The advowson of Moulsoe was granted towards the close of the 12th century to the priory of Goring, Oxfordshire, by Geoffrey son of William and by Emma de Langetot.[89] An unsuccessful suit to recover the advowson was brought in 1252 by the guardian of Peter de Coudray,[89a] and the priory remained in possession until the beginning of the 16th century, when a grant was made to John Mordaunt, who presented in 1518.[90] The advowson was retained by the Mordaunt family until 1602, in which year Henry Lord Mordaunt alienated it to Sir John Spencer,[91] lord of Moulsoe Manor, with which its history is henceforward identical, the right of presentation at the present day being vested in the Marquess of Lincolnshire.

About 1536 the rectory of Moulsoe was worth £18.[92]

CHARITIES Mary Countess Dowager of Northampton by her will in 1719 devised a yearly rent-charge of £5 out of lands in Moulsoe to the poor on St. Thomas's Day. The annuity, known locally as St. Thomas's money, is received out of land belonging to the Marquess of Lincolnshire and is distributed equally among about thirty recipients.

The same testatrix directed by her will that land of the clear yearly value of £6 should be purchased and employed towards the maintenance of a schoolmaster. The land purchased in 1721 consists of two closes containing 14 acres.[93]

NEWPORT PAGNELL

Neuport (xi cent.) ; Neuport Paynell or Panell (1220).

The parish of Newport Pagnell is conterminous with the modern urban district and covers 3,396 acres of land with 36 of water. The Ouse and the Lovat (Lovente, xiii cent.) flow from west to east and from south to north respectively through the parish, uniting near its northern boundary. Here the town of Newport Pagnell, cut into two parts by the Lovat, stands on the south bank of the Ouse. The high road from Northampton to London passes through the town, and roads from Stony Stratford, Fenny Stratford and Woburn enter it from various points. There is no tradition of a Roman settlement on this site. Before the Norman Conquest, however, a trading town had sprung up, and by the middle of the 13th century most of its principal features were certainly in existence. The form of the original town is very simple. The long, wide High Street or market-place runs south-west and north-east. From

a point near its centre St. John's Street runs south-east, crossing the Lovat at Tickford Bridge and becoming Tickford Street and then the London road ; and from its north end the Northampton road runs across the Ouse by the North Bridge.

Bridges must have been built at these points at the earliest period of the town's history. The 'Newport Bridge' of Gervase Paynel's charter of 1187[1] is apparently the modern Tickford Bridge, which seems to have been mentioned by the latter name in the foundation charter of Tickford Priory, quoted in a confirmation of charters by Edward II in 1311.[2] The inhabitants had a grant of pontage for the repair of 'North brigge and South brigge' in 1380.[3] The bridges were then in a serious state of decay, and the men of the town were heavily charged for their support.[4] This statement as to the great cost of the bridges occurs again at the end of the 15th century, when a bequest of a messuage was made to relieve it.[5] Other bequests for the same purpose were made at various

[89] V.C.H. Oxon. ii, 103. Emma de Langetot was living in 1185 (Grimaldi, op. cit. 21). [89a] Cur. Reg. R. 147B, m. 37.
[90] Add. MS. 5839, fol. 138. Willis speaks of a long lease to the Mordaunts, which the Crown allowed to expire.

[91] Recov. R. Mich. 44 & 45 Eliz. m. 130 ; Feet of F. Bucks. Mich. 44 & 45 Eliz.
[92] Valor Eccl. (Rec. Com.), iv, 243.
[93] See V.C.H. Bucks. ii, 219.
[1] Dugdale, Mon. v, 203.

[2] Ibid. 202.
[3] Cal. Pat. 1377–81, p. 562.
[4] F. W. Bull, Hist. of Newport Pagnell, 169.
[5] Early Chan. Proc. bdle. 204, no. 80.

times, and it seems that the townsmen in their brotherhood or gild of St. Mary or Our Lady made themselves responsible for the care of the bridges.[6] The gild was presumably dissolved by Edward VI, but its property was held for the maintenance of the bridges by feoffees, who were presented at the manorial court in 1720 and 1721 for not keeping them in repair.[7] In 1809 an Act of Parliament[8] was obtained for their rebuilding, and the present stone bridge over the Ouse and the cast-iron bridge over the Lovat replaced the old stone structures.[9] There was in the 13th century a lepers' hospital 'without the town of Newport Pagnell' dedicated to St. Margaret[10] or St. Margaret and St. Anthony,[11] which perhaps stood on the north side of the North Bridge, just outside the borough and parish boundaries. This site is suggested by two references in 1241 and 1252 to a hospital of St. Margaret in the neighbouring parish of Lathbury.[12] It seems probable that the two were identical. The Newport house was founded probably before 1241[13] and existed in 1272,[14] but is not afterwards mentioned.[15]

The market-place of Newport, in which Gervase Paynel in 1187 granted the monks of Tickford the privilege of buying and selling free of toll,[16] was called by its present name in 1245, when John le Chat had a shop in the High Street.[17] The High Street and North Street both appear in 1543,[18] North Street being probably the street running directly north to the bridge from the north-east end of High Street. In the 16th and 17th centuries eight butchers' shambles stood in the middle of the market-place, apparently at its northern end.[19] In front of the houses along the street, and apparently in the open ground to the south, stalls and booths were erected on market and fair days for the display of the goods of poulterers, glovers, haberdashers and other tradesmen.[20] Part of the market-place was set apart as a 'woman's market,'[21] but it is not clear whether there was any distinction as to wares.

It is as a 'thoroughfare town' that Newport Pagnell has always been most distinguished,[22] and it has always contained a great number of inns.[23] Of these the most important was the 'Saracen's Head,' which existed in the 15th century and was the headquarters of Our Lady's Gild.[24] It seems to have stood in the High Street next to the 'Swan,' and three shambles were attached to it.[25] The Parliamentary Committee for Newport received the rents of sequestered lands here in 1643.[26] The 'Saracen's Head' was still the chief inn in 1830.[27] The George Inn is mentioned in the 16th century,[28] and the Swan Inn, which is now the most important, in 1543.[29] The latter was evidently rebuilt shortly before 1681,[30] and was again very largely rebuilt in the 18th century. Internally a good 17th-century staircase remains. The town hall of Newport, which was adapted from the premises of the British school in 1899,[31] stands in the middle of the High Street towards its southern end. There seems to have been no previous town hall; courts were held in the bailiff's house in the early 17th century.[32] There is now a police station at the southwestern end of the town.

At the north-east end of the High Street is the church of SS. Peter and Paul, surrounded by a graveyard which extends to the banks of the Lovat. The vicarage, which stands on the south side of the High Street a little distance to the west of the church, is a 17th-century building of brick, two stories in height, with an attic. The exterior has been modernized, and additions have been made at the rear of the house. The 17th-century staircase, however, survives with some other fittings of late 17th-century date. Nearer the church, on the opposite side of the street, is a three-storied 17th-century house of brick with a gabled attic. The attic and the floor beneath it oversail the lower stories, which have modern bay windows. An old staircase with twisted balusters communicates with all the floors. Church Passage, a narrow street running in front of the church and down into St. John's Street, is the 'Church Lane' of 1545.[33] Along the edge of the churchyard are seven almshouses, built by John Revis in 1755.[34] The four earlier almshouses, mentioned in the reign of Henry VIII and in 1608, have ceased to exist. There are now six almshouses on the site, which is near the town hall.[35] There was a school-house in or near the churchyard in the 16th century.[36]

Mill Street running west from the northern end of High Street connects it with the manorial mill on the banks of the Ouse. Two mills in Newport are mentioned in the Domesday Survey.[37] In 1480 there were two water corn-mills called North Mill and Gayhurst Mill and two fulling-mills.[38] North Mill was on the present site, Gayhurst Mill on the Ouse opposite Gayhurst House, nearly a mile north-west of the town.[39] Three mills under one roof on the present site were rebuilt shortly before 1622.[40]

---

[6] See below.
[7] F. W. Bull, op. cit. 171. See below under charities.
[8] Local and Pers. Act, 49 Geo. III, cap. 144.   [9] F. W. Bull, op. cit. 172.
[10] Madox, Form. Angl. 424; Cal. Pat. 1247–58, p. 415; 1258–66, pp. 409, 499.
[11] Cal. Pat. 1266–72, p. 682.
[12] Ibid. 1247–58, p. 127; Feet of F. Bucks. 25 Hen. III, no. 18.
[13] Madox, loc. cit. The document quoted, which mentions the hospital, is the will of William de Paveli, dated All Saints Day 'post mortem B. Eadmundi Archiepiscopi.' St. Edmund died in 1240, but was not canonized till 1247, and the form of reference to him is therefore suspicious.
[14] Cal. Pat. 1266–72, p. 682.
[15] A grant of protection made in 1275 to the 'master brethren and sisters of the house of lepers by the bridge' (Cal. Pat. 1272–81, p. 91) was afterwards taken as referring to St. John's Hospital (Char. Proc. Inq. Bucks. bdle. 2, no. 29), though St. John's was a hospital for the poor.
[16] Dugdale, op. cit. v, 204.
[17] Chan. Inq. p.m. 29 Hen. III, no. 50.
[18] Mins. Accts. Hen. VIII, no. 6071.
[19] Ld. Rev. Misc. Bks. cxcvii, fol. 276; F. W. Bull, op. cit. 237.
[20] Exch. Dep. Hil. 1657–8, no. 24; Hil. 36 & 37 Chas. II, no. 19.
[21] Ld. Rev. Misc. Bks. ccx, fol. 348; Exch. Dep. Hil. 1657–8, no. 24.
[22] Chant. Cert. 4, no. 11; Cal. S. P. Dom. 1635–6, p. 217.
[23] Innkeepers were presented in 1545 for excessive charges (Ct. R. [Gen. Ser.], portf. 155, no. 20). 'The Bell' or 'Red Lion,' 'The Angel,' 'The Swan,' and 'The Saracen's Head' are all mentioned in one deed of 1597 (F. W. Bull, loc. cit.).
[24] Pat. 28 Eliz. pt. xiv, m. 12. See below.
[25] F. W. Bull, loc. cit.

[26] Ibid. 165.
[27] Pigott, Dir.
[28] Chan. Proc. (Ser. 2), bdle. 189, no. 15.
[29] Mins. Accts. Hen. VIII, no. 6071.
[30] Hist. MSS. Com. Rep. xiii, App. ii, 274; Guildhall MS. no. 111.
[31] F. W. Bull, op. cit. 206.
[32] See below.
[33] Ct. R. (Gen. Ser.), portf. 155, no. 20.
[34] Char. Com. Rep. (1830), xxvii, 160.
[35] Treas. of the Receipt Misc. Bks. clxv, fol. 88; Char. Proc. Inq. bdle. 1, no. 10; Ld. Rev. Misc. Bks. cxcvii, fol. 277; F. W. Bull, op. cit. 243.
[36] Treas. of the Receipt Misc. Bks. clxv, fol. 89.
[37] V.C.H. Bucks. i, 255.
[38] Mins. Accts. (Duchy of Lanc.), bdle. 643, no. 10438.
[39] Ld. Rev. Misc. Bks. cxcvii, fol. 277; cf. Mins. Accts. Hen. VIII, no. 6071.
[40] Exch. Dep. Trin. 20 Jas. I, no. 12.

The street called St. John's Street is possibly the 'Hawestret' in which Fulk Paynel gave to the priory of Tickford tenements extending 'to the bridge of Tickford on the east side.'[41] It took its present name from the hospital of St. John Baptist and St. John the Evangelist, near Tickford Bridge, founded before 1240[42] and refounded in 1615 as Queen Ann's Hospital. The hospital was rebuilt in 1825 and again in 1891.[43] The only relic of the structure of 1625 is a beam, now built into the wall of the present building, which has the following inscription painted upon it : 'Alyou good Chrystianes that heere dooe pas by give soome thynge to thes poore people that in St. John's Hospital doeth ly An° 1615.' No. 26 in the same street, a two-storied house with an attic, is of early 17th-century date, while No. 3, a plastered two-storied house on the opposite side, bears the inscription : 'This house belongeth to Queen Ann's Hospital and was rebuilt by Madam Tasker, a citizen in St. Giles, Cripplegate, London, Anno Dom. 1690.' From St. John's Street, Silver Street (apparently the 'Little Silver Street' of Henry the Eighth's reign[44]) runs south to the low ground called Marsh End. The 'marsh of Newport' appears to have included most of the land in the parish to the south and west of the town.[45] 'Mables Lane' in Marsh End is mentioned in 1615.[46]

On the other side of the Lovat St. John's Street becomes Tickford Street, and Priory Street runs north from it to where Tickford Abbey stands on the banks of the Ouse and on the site of the old priory. Some fragments of the priory buildings, ranging in date from the 12th to the 15th century, have been reset in the walls of the modern mansion and its outhouses. Priory Street is presumably the 'Monechustret' of the 12th century.[47] The King's Arms Inn in Tickford Street incorporates a late 16th-century building, two moulded ceiling beams of which remain. The brick front bears a panel inscribed : $\begin{smallmatrix} & G \\ I & I \\ & 1690. \end{smallmatrix}$ Tickford Park, a mansion in the south-east of the parish, stands in what was once the deer park of the Paynels[48] and the later lords of the manor of Newport.[49] It was granted in 1592 to Thomas Crompton and others,[50] who seem to

have sold it to Sir John Fortescue.[51] Alice Fortescue his widow and Francis his son and heir sold it, with its deer and the stone walls inclosing it, to Henry Atkins in 1620.[52] It was disparked before 1757.[53] It is now the property of the Marquess of Lincolnshire, and is occupied by Mr. Donald Frazer.

An Inclosure Act was passed for Tickford Fields in 1807.[54] Bury Field,[55] a meadow to the north of the town of Newport, is still uninclosed. The neighbouring Portfield was inclosed in 1795.[56]

South of the town is the farm of Caldecote, about a quarter of a mile from the west bank of the Lovat, and probably on the site of the manor-house which existed here in 1426 and 1750.[57] The sluices for Caldecote Mill still remain, and as in 1543[58] the bridge which here crosses the stream is called the Caldecote Mill Bridge. The mill here was mentioned in the Domesday Survey,[59] and was an important possession of Tickford Priory.[60] It was 'greatly in

TICKFORD PARK, NEWPORT PAGNELL, FROM A PICTURE OF ABOUT 1895

decay' at the Dissolution,[61] but existed down to the 19th century.[62] It was finally destroyed by fire and was not rebuilt.

Newport Pagnell has been associated with few great events in national history. It had several royal visits in the 13th century.[63] During the Civil War it was occupied by the Royalists, who attempted to fortify it by filling trenches from the rivers,[64] and on their retreat in 1643 by Skippon and his forces.[65] A Parliamentary garrison was established here,[66] the

[41] Dugdale, op. cit. v, 202.
[42] Madox, op. cit. 424.
[43] F. W. Bull, op. cit. 227-8.
[44] Treas. of the Receipt Misc. Bks. clxv, fol. 80.
[45] Mins. Accts. Hen. VIII, no. 6071.
[46] Char. Com. Rep. (1830), xxvii, 150.
[47] Dugdale, loc. cit.
[48] Ibid.
[49] Mins. Accts. (Duchy of Lanc.), bdle. 643, no. 10438.
[50] Pat. 34 Eliz. pt. iv, m. 16.
[51] Feet of F. Div. Co. East. 39 Eliz.
[52] Close, 18 Jas. I, pt. xxv, no. 54.

[53] Ibid. 31 Geo. II, pt. xii, no. 14.
[54] Priv. Act, 47 Geo. III (session 1), cap. 30.
[55] See below.
[56] Priv. Act, 34 Geo. III, cap. 86 ; Com. Pleas D. Enr. Trin. 35 Geo. III, m. 148.
[57] Chan. Inq. p.m. 5 Hen. VI, no. 16 ; Com. Pleas D. Enr. Mich. 24 Geo. II, m. 77.
[58] Mins. Accts. Hen. VIII, no. 6071.
[59] V.C.H. Bucks. i, 256.
[60] Chan. Inq. p.m. (Ser. 2), lxxvi, 3 ; Dugdale, op. cit. v, 202, 205.

[61] Treas. of the Receipt Misc. Bks. clxv, fol. 94.
[62] Close, 31 Geo. II, pt. xii, no. 6 ; inform. from Mr. F. W. Bull.
[63] Cal. Chart. R. 1226-57, p. 55 ; Cal. Close, 1279-88, pp. 27-8 ; Cal. Chart. R. 1327-41, p. 326.
[64] Hist. MSS. Com. Rep. xiii, App. i, 145 ; F. W. Bull, op. cit. 155.
[65] Bucks. Rec. (Bucks. Arch. Soc.), ii, 206 et seq.; Dict. Nat. Biog.
[66] Cal. S. P. Dom. 1644, passim ; Hist. MSS. Com. Rep. v, App. i, 117.

governor of which in 1644 was Sir Samuel Luke,[67] the original of Butler's *Hudibras*.[68]

The history of Dissent in the town begins in 1659, when John Gibbs was ejected from the vicarage for refusing to admit the whole parish to communion, and founded the Independent Church.[69] Besides the Independents, the Baptists, Wesleyans and the Society of Friends have chapels at the present day.

In 1814 Newport was connected by a cutting with the Grand Junction Canal at Great Linford.[70] The canal was used until it was purchased in 1864 by the London and North Western Railway Company for the purpose of constructing in its place a branch railway to Wolverton.[71] The station is at the south-west end of the town, where the old wharf stood.

The manufacture of bone lace, which gave the town considerable importance in the 18th century,[72] existed in 1611–12, when various persons are mentioned in the bishop's visitation as having travelled to sell it on the Sabbath Day.[73] It declined greatly about 1830, owing to the introduction of machine-made lace,[74] revived about twenty years later, and became extinct about 1884.[75]

BOROUGH There is no evidence as to the origin of the borough of Newport Pagnell. Burgage tenure existed in 1086, and the name of the vill shows that at that date a market was already in existence.[76] In the time of Fulk Paynel (before 1138) and probably earlier the borough area was marked off from the 'foreign' by boundary crosses.[77] From a document of much later date[78] it appears that there were four of these crosses. The only one of which the site has been definitely fixed was at the junction of Priory Street with Tickford Street.[79] Another stood in the west part of the borough. A natural site for a third would be the North Bridge. Within the area so marked out stood the burgage tenements, of which there were fifty-three in 1245[80] and thirty-four in 1543.[81] The occupiers of the tenements could alienate them at will on payment of a fine to the lord.[82] They owed suit at the borough court or portmote, first mentioned in 1245,[83] though probably much older, and they had certain rights of pasture, probably of very early origin, in the Bury Field, a part of the lord's demesne.[84] They held no land in common, however,[85] and can hardly be said to have had in the 13th century any communal existence. The courts and the administration and profits of the market and fair were in the hands of the lord. By means of his

yearly view of frankpledge and the fortnightly portmote he exercised royal jurisdiction. Newport had been free from suits of counties and hundreds, view of frankpledge and aid of the sheriff since the early 12th century at least. Gervase Paynel lost these privileges by his association with the rebellion of Prince Henry against his father in 1173–4, but they were restored to the custodians of the manor during the minority of Ralph de Somery's heirs.[86] They were confirmed to William de Beauchamp in 1222,[87] and were granted to Walter de Kirkham in 1230,[88] with the additional right of tallaging the manor to his own use whenever the king tallaged his demesnes. In 1255 William de Beauchamp claimed 'the ancient customs of the borough' as Gervase and Hawise Paynel had held them.[89] He had pillory, tumbril, and gallows,[90] and instances of men imprisoned in his gaol and hanged by the order of his court occur in 1262.[91] In 1286 the king's attorney claimed that the view of frankpledge ought to be held twice a year and in the presence of a servant of the king[92]; but Roger de Somery must have succeeded in establishing the independence of his court, which he continued to hold only once a year.[93]

During the 13th century and part of the 14th the profits of the market and fair, the pleas and perquisites of court, and the rent of the burgesses all appear separately among the revenues of the manor,[94] of which the borough was merely the urban part. Between 1338 and 1479, however, some development in the direction of municipal organization took place. In 1380 a grant of pontage was made to Thomas Cowe, Robert Bewes, John Taillour and Simon Swet, evidently principal inhabitants of the town.[95] A similar grant was made to the 'bailiffs and good men' in 1394.[96] The burgesses of Newport Pagnell were evidently responsible as a community for the upkeep of their bridges, and there is evidence to indicate that for this purpose they formed themselves into the gild or fraternity of St. Mary. The burgage called 'The Saracen's Head,' which in February 1483–4 was granted by Richard Read and Ralph Hobbes for the maintenance of the bridges, amendment of the highways, and the relief of the poor,[97] was said in 1543 to be held by the township (*villata*) of Newport,[98] while from a grant of 1586 it appears that, as already stated, this inn was the headquarters of the gild.[99] Other references to the gild occur in 1487 and 1509,[100] but unfortunately they throw no light on its connexion with the other institutions of the town. It is probable, however,

[67] *Hist. MSS. Com. Rep.* xi, App. vii, 39.
[68] *Dict. Nat. Biog.*
[69] T. P. Bull, *Rise of the Independent Church of Newport Pagnell.*
[70] F. W. Bull, op. cit. 17.
[71] Inform. from Mr. F. W. Bull.
[72] *Magna Brit.* (1720–31), i, 211.
[73] F. W. Bull, op. cit. 109.
[74] Pigott, *Dir.* (1830).
[75] F. W. Bull, op. cit. 197.
[76] *V.C.H. Bucks.* i, 255.
[77] Dugdale, op. cit. v, 202.
[78] Ct. R. (Gen. Ser.), portf. 155, no. 20.
[79] Dugdale, loc. cit. ; cf. Add. Chart. 11224.
[80] Chan. Inq. p.m. 29 Hen. III, no. 50. Throughout the account of Newport Pagnell the date 29 Hen. III has been accepted for this important document, which is a survey of the borough representing it as in the possession of Sir

Roger de Somery. The document itself is not dated, and it has been endorsed 29 Hen. III in a much later hand. It is possible, however, for the following reasons, that its true date is between 1270 and 1291 : —(1) It refers to Henry III as 'King Henry son of King John.' (2) It refers to the fair in Newport granted by Henry III. The only known charter granting this fair is dated 1270. (3) It gives the grantee of the fair as Roger de Somery the elder. It is an open question whether there was a Roger de Somery before the Roger living in 1245 (see below). (4) In 1245 the manor was in the hands of Ida de Beauchamp.
[81] Mins. Accts. Hen. VIII, no. 6071.
[82] Ld. Rev. Misc. Bks. cxcvii, fol. 277.
[83] Chan. Inq. p.m. 29 Hen. III, no. 50.
[84] Ld. Rev. Misc. Bks. ccx, fol. 353.
[85] *Hund. R.* (Rec. Com.), i, 28.

[86] Cur. Reg. R. 76, m. 7.
[87] *Rot. Lit. Claus.* (Rec. Com.), i, 520.
[88] Madox, *Hist. of Exch.* i, 418.
[89] *Hund. R.* (Rec. Com.), i, 28.
[90] Chan. Inq. p.m. 29 Hen. III, no. 50 ; *Hund. R.* (Rec. Com.), i, 40.
[91] Assize R. 58, m. 28 d.
[92] *Plac. de Quo Warr.* (Rec. Com.), 88–9.
[93] See below.
[94] Chan. Inq. p.m. 1 Edw. I, no. 15 ; 19 Edw. I, no. 14 ; 12 Edw. III (1st nos.), no. 40.
[95] *Cal. Pat.* 1377–81, p. 562.
[96] Ibid. 1391–6, p. 372.
[97] Chan. Proc. Inq. bdle. 1, no. 10.
[98] Mins. Accts. Hen. VIII, no. 6071.
[99] Pat. 28 Eliz. pt. xiv, m. 12.
[100] F. W. Bull, op. cit. 103 ; see also Treasury of the Receipt Misc. Bks. clxv, fol. 82.

that at about the time of its formation the townsmen acquired the privilege of electing a bailiff of their own to farm the market dues and act as their representative in dealing with the bailiff of the lord. Such an official was certainly in existence in 1479–81, when the tolls of the market were accounted for at £3,[1] the sum for which successive bailiffs farmed them.[2] All the courts of the borough also existed at that date,[3] and it may be assumed that it had already reached that stage of development which is illustrated by the Court Rolls of 1545 and minutely described in a survey of 1608.[4] These documents show that a yearly view of frankpledge for the borough area was held in Pentecost week.[5] To this court all the inhabitants owed suit except those in the fee of Tickford, and here they elected two constables and two 'scrutators' or 'tastators' of the market.[6] The rest of the borough business was done at the court called 'unbodmot,' held four times in the year, on the Mondays after St. Michael the Archangel, the Epiphany, the Annunciation, and St. John the Baptist.[7] At the first of these the bailiff was elected from among the burgesses and sworn in for the coming year. At the Epiphany unbodmot two townsmen [8] were chosen ale-tasters and another townsman constable.[9] All the burgesses were bound to appear at the unbodmot, and the officers of the lord came to deal with offences committed within the borough and to make ordinances for its good government.[10] The assize of bread and ale was proclaimed there and breaches of it were presented by the tasters.[11] The portmote, held once a fortnight on Monday, was in the nature of a police-court. Here breaches of the peace, assaults and bloodshed were punished, and all actions settled which involved a smaller sum than 40s.[12] Any inhabitant who in such an action pleaded in another court than the portmote was subject to a penalty of 40s., payable to the lord.[13] It was only the profits of this court, however, which in 1608 belonged to the lord; it is evident that the burgesses believed the judicial authority to reside in their own body. It was the burgesses, they said, who from time immemorial had been accustomed to hold pleas in the portmote,[14] and the bailiff and burgesses and other inhabitants claimed to have by prescription a supply of timber from the lord's steward for the repair of the pillory, cucking stool, stocks, pinfold and common bushel.[15] Fines and amercements were collected by the bailiff of the borough and paid to the bailiff of the lord.[16] The control of the market and

fair must also have been in the hands of the bailiff of the borough as farmer of the tolls.[17] The yearly value of these must have greatly exceeded the £3 he paid to the lord.[18] It was among the duties of his office, however, to provide dinner for the steward, the jurors and suitors on all the court days, 'taking nothing from the steward and 2d. from each of the others.'[19] All courts were held in his house.[20]

The constitution above described represents the highest point of independence reached by the burgesses. A few years after the date of the survey their position was challenged. The manor had been annexed to the honour of Ampthill in 1542, and during the 16th and early 17th centuries was in the hands of lessees under the Crown and under Ann consort of James I.[21] These lessees were not disposed to reduce their profits by respecting the ancient customs of the town, and about 1615 they began to claim the entire issues of the market and fair, besides any profits arising from the letting of ground for stalls and booths. The inhabitants, 'supposing that the town of Newport was a corporate town consisting of Bailiff and Burgesses, and that they had power to make choice of a Bailiff who was to enjoy the profits of the premises under the yearly rent of £3,' resisted this claim.[22] By an order of 1615 the Court of Exchequer decreed that the waste grounds of Newport Pagnell were the property of the lord of the manor, and that his representatives alone had the right to let them for the erection of stalls. This verdict evaded the question of the election of a bailiff and his right to farm the tolls, and the matter was raised again in 1623, when a bailiff was elected according to custom. Another order was obtained ruling that the tolls belonged to the lord's lessees.[23] The pleadings of an action in Chancery in the following year show that the claims of the burgesses were based entirely on prescription, and that they had no charters to show. Their opponents admitted the custom, but treated its validity as doubtful, and claimed that the matter was disposed of by the Exchequer Decree.[24] Nevertheless, another action of trespass was brought by the burgesses in 1632, under the leadership of their elected bailiff, John Thorpe.[25] Before it was concluded, however, a meeting took place between the counsel of the parties. 'Copies of record' were produced, and the burgesses were convinced that the profits of the fairs and markets had always been the property of the lord and had been included in leases of the manor.[26]

---

[1] Mins. Accts. (Duchy of Lanc.), bdles. 637, no. 10346; 643, no. 10438. It is stated in the latter that the bailiff of the foreign was an elected officer. No statement is made about the borough bailiff.

[2] Mins. Accts. Hen. VIII, no. 6071; Ld. Rev. Misc. Bks. ccx, fol. 352.

[3] Mins. Accts. (Duchy of Lanc.), bdles. 637, no. 10346; 643, no. 10438.

[4] Ct. R. (Gen. Ser.), portf. 155, no. 20; Ld. Rev. Misc. Bks. cxcvii, fol. 277; ccx, fol. 350 et seq.

[5] The day of the week varied, but was finally settled as Monday by 1608.

[6] Ld. Rev. Misc. Bks. ccx, fol. 350, 352. The latter officers presented at the view of frankpledge cases of excessive prices and the sale of bad meat (Ct. R. [Gen. Ser.], portf. 155, no. 20).

[7] Ld. Rev. Misc. Bks. cxcvii, fol. 277.

[8] Not necessarily burgesses.

[9] Ct. R. (Gen. Ser.), portf. 155, no. 20; Ld. Rev. Misc. Bks. ccx, fol. 351. Two constables were elected at the Epiphany unbodmot in 1544–5.

[10] Ld. Rev. Misc. Bks. ccx, fol. 350. In 1545, however, an order that the inhabitants of the borough should repair the street before their houses was made at the view of frankpledge (Ct. R. [Gen. Ser.], portf. 155, no. 20).

[11] Ct. R. (Gen. Ser.), portf. 155, no. 20. Breaches of assize were also presented at the portmote.

[12] Ld. Rev. Misc. Bks. ccx, fol. 350.

[13] Ibid. fol. 353.

[14] Ibid. fol. 350.

[15] Ibid. fol. 352.

[16] Ibid. fol. 354.

[17] A court of pie-powder for actions arising out of the fair was said to exist in 1608. There are no records of it, but it

seems probable that the bailiff presided (ibid. fol. 352).

[18] They brought in £40 in 1624 (Chan. Proc. [Ser. 2], bdle. 386, no. 31).

[19] Ld. Rev. Misc. Bks. ccx, fol. 350. Other customs of the borough mentioned in 1608 are: (1) At the death of a burgess the lord took his best beast as heriot; (2) 16d. relief was paid on the death of a burgess or the alienation of a burgage. This applied also to other freeholders within the borough (ibid. cxcvii, fol. 277).

[20] Ibid. ccx, fol. 350.

[21] See manor.

[22] Decrees and Orders (Exch. K.R. Ser. 3), xii, fol. 360 et seq.

[23] Ibid.

[24] Chan. Proc. (Ser. 2), bdle. 386, no. 31.

[25] Decrees and Orders (Exch. K.R. Ser. 3), xii, fol. 360 et seq.   [26] Ibid.

This decision was presumably the end of any claim on the part of the burgesses to corporate privileges. They were successful, however, in retaining their individual rights to make profit of the ground before their houses by erecting stalls and letting them to traders. In 1657 and 1685 attempts were made to acquire these profits for the representative of the lord.[27] A payment of 2d. for each stall on private property appears about 1812 among the tolls taken by the lord of the manor,[28] so it is evident that his exclusive right to let ground for the erection of stalls had not been maintained.

The officer responsible for the good order of the market-place was still called the bailiff of the town in 1670, when he was presented at the view of frankpledge.[29] It seems certain, however, that after the defeat of 1633 he was appointed by the lord and not elected by the burgesses. No later mention of a bailiff has been found,[30] and the courts of the borough also disappeared. In 1720 Newport Pagnell was described as 'neither a borough nor a corporation, though bigger than many towns that are so.'[31] The yearly view of frankpledge of the manor provided the machinery of government for the town during the 18th century. Here four constables, two ale-tasters, two flesh-tasters, two bread and butter weighers, two leather sealers and a bellman were elected and sworn in. 'Field-tellers' for the Bury Field were also appointed, and orders were made with regard to the repair of the streets and bridges.[32] The town was 'very dirty and ill-paved' in 1768.[33] After 1818 the view was held once every two years till 1830.[34] In 1897 an urban district council was formed under the Local Government Act of 1888. The functions of the portmote passed probably at an early date in the 18th century to the fortnightly petty sessions.

The market day at Newport was Saturday from the earliest date at which there is any record of it.[35] In 1847 there were markets both on Wednesday and Saturday, and the market day is now Wednesday. A fair on St. Luke's Day (18 October) and the six days following was established before 1245.[36] A new fair on the vigil and feast of St. Barnabas (11 June) and the eight days following was granted in 1327,[37] and seems to have been the only one in existence in 1608.[38] In 1720 the fair days were 11 April, 11 June, and 6 November.[39] In the middle of the 19th century there were six fairs: on 22 February, April, June and December, 21 March, and 29 August. Only that on 22 June has survived.

HONOUR In 1086 William Fitz Ansculf held in demesne or in service lands assessed at 103¾ hides in Ellesborough, Hampden, Ditton, Stoke Poges, Hoggeston, Soulbury, Stewkley,

Cheddington, North Marston, Swanbourne, Marsh Gibbon, Newport Pagnell, Caldecote, Little Woolstone, Bradwell, Linford, Tyringham, Chicheley, Tickford, Hardmead, and Milton Keynes, with half a hide in 'Stanes' Hundred, 2 hides in 'Lamva' Hundred, and 4 hides in Moulsoe Hundred, probably representing Great and Little Crawley.[40] His lands in Buckinghamshire became known as the honour of Newport Pagnell, which included fourteen knights' fees in 1210–12.[41] The honour descended with the manor of Newport Pagnell, but as early as 1230 it was regarded as part of the more important barony of Dudley,[42] and it is not separately mentioned after the 14th century. The lords of Newport Pagnell had view of frankpledge in the manors held of them, and records exist of courts held for Chicheley, Crawley, Astwood, Emberton, Little Linford and North Marston in the reign of Henry VIII.[43] Constables for Chicheley, Emberton, Astwood and Caldecote were appointed at the court leet of Newport in the 18th century, and in 1789 the same constabularies were still paying certainty money to Newport Pagnell.[44]

CASTLE The Paynels and Somerys had a castle in this parish of which very little is known.[45] The fortified mount known as the 'battery,' which marks its site, may be seen in the churchyard near the junction of the Lovat with the Ouse.[46] It was probably thrown up in the 12th century as a fortification in that disturbed time, and was afterwards disused. It had apparently no masonry defences, and such buildings as existed were of timber. The meadow on the opposite bank of the Lovat has been known as Castle Mead since the 12th century.[47] In 1272 the lord of Newport Pagnell had a capital messuage here with a dove-house and garden,[48] which probably took the place of the castle. This house was possibly identical with the manorhouse called 'Waterhall,' which belonged to the St. German family in the 15th century, but in 1543 was surveyed with the demesne lands as the capital messuage of the manor.[49]

MANORS The tenant of *NEWPORT* before the Conquest was a thegn of the Confessor called Ulf. In 1086 a manor here assessed at 5 hides and worth £20 was held by William Fitz Ansculf.[50] With his barony of Dudley [51] it passed to Fulk Paynel, who perhaps married his daughter and heir.[52] From the Paynel family the place took its name. Fulk's son Ralph and grandson Gervase [53] successively held the manor; the last-named was in possession from at least 1154,[54] and was dead in 1193–4.[55] His son Robert [56] having predeceased him, his sister Hawise was his heir.[57] Her son Ralph by her husband John de Somery [58]

[27] Exch. Dep. Hil. 1657–8, no. 24; Hil. 36 & 37 Chas. II, no. 19.
[28] F. W. Bull, op. cit. 58.
[29] Ct. R. *penes* Mr. Knapp.
[30] The 'clerks of the market' were presented in 1720 (ibid.).
[31] *Magna Brit.* (1720–31), i, 211.
[32] Ct. R. *penes* Mr. Knapp.
[33] *Verulam MSS.* (Hist. MSS. Com.), i, 229.
[34] Ct. R. *penes* Mr. Knapp.
[35] *Cal. Chart. R.* 1257–1300, p. 131. The market is mentioned in 1245 (Chan. Inq. p.m. 29 Hen. III, no. 50).
[36] Chan. Inq. p.m. 29 Hen. III, no. 50.
[37] *Cal. Chart. R.* 1327–41, p. 12.
[38] Ld. Rev. Misc. Bks. ccx, fol. 352.

[39] *Magna Brit.* loc. cit.
[40] *V.C.H. Bucks.* i, 254–7.
[41] *Red Bk. of Exch.* (Rolls Ser.), 537.
[42] *Testa de Nevill* (Rec. Com.), 248; cf. *Cal. Inq. p.m.* (Edw. I), ii, 493; *Plac. de Quo Warr.* (Rec. Com.), 88. See also *V.C.H. Worcs.* i, 317; iii, 90. The manor of Newport Pagnell itself was annexed to the honour of Ampthill in 1542 (L. and P. Hen. VIII, xvii, 28 [21]).
[43] Ct. R. (Gen. Ser.), portf. 155, no. 20. Emberton became part of the barony after 1086.
[44] Ct. R. *penes* Mr. Knapp.
[45] Leland, *Itin.* (ed. Hearne), i, 26; vi, 56; Camden, *Brit.* (ed. Gough), i, 315.
[46] *Hist. Monum. Com. Rep. N. Bucks.* 209.

[47] Dugdale, op. cit. v, 202.
[48] Chan. Inq. p.m. 1 Edw. I, no. 15.
[49] *Cat. of Anct. D.* ii, 337; Mins. Accts. Hen. VIII, no. 6071; see also Ld. Rev. Misc. Bks. cxcvii, fol. 275.
[50] *V.C.H. Bucks.* i, 255.
[51] *V.C.H. Worcs.* i, 317.
[52] Grazebrook, *Barons of Dudley* (Will. Salt Arch. Soc. ix), 6; *Cal. Doc. of France*, 444.
[53] *Cal. Doc. of France*, 444; Dugdale, op. cit. v, 203.
[54] *Cal. Doc. of France*, 444.
[55] *Coll. for Staffs.* (Will. Salt Arch. Soc.), ii, 33.
[56] Grazebrook, op. cit. 9.
[57] Dugdale, op. cit. v, 204. [58] Ibid.

paid a fine for seisin of his uncle's lands in Stafford-shire in 1198-9.[59] Newport, however, remained in his mother's hands till her death in 1207-8, when Ralph paid £100 for seisin.[60] He died about 1215,[61] his widow being Ida daughter of William Longespee Earl of Salisbury.[62] It was to William Earl of Salisbury that the custody of the son and heir of Ralph was granted.[63] In 1216 a grant was made to Ralph Earl of Chester of the manor of Newport Pagnell to hold as it had been held by the Earl of Salisbury.[64] Soon afterwards,

PAYNEL. *Or two lions passant azure*, which arms were afterwards borne by SOMERY.

however, it must have been assigned as dower to Ida, who with her husband William de Beauchamp, Baron of Bedford, held it from 1220.[65] William died in 1260[66] and Ida before July 1270.[67] On her death the manor reverted to the Somery family.

The son of Ralph de Somery, Ida's first husband, was William, also called Percival, whose son and heir Nicholas died without issue in 1229.[68] The heir of Nicholas was his uncle Roger,[69] to whom a fair in Newport was granted by Henry III before 1245,[70] in spite of the rights of Ida de Beauchamp.[71] In 1245 an extent of the borough was made, in which it was described as the possession of Roger de Somery's son Roger.[72] In 1270 the latter was in full possession, and had a confirmatory grant of his market and fair.[73] He died in 1272-3, when his son Roger was a minor.[74] On the death of the latter in 1291 the manor was granted to Hugh de Vere till John de Somery son of Roger should come of age.[75] John died in possession in 1322,[76] and his inheritance was divided between his sisters Margaret wife of John de Sutton and Joan widow of Thomas Botetourt.[77] Newport Pagnell, which was held by Lucy, widow of John, in dower, became the property of Joan.[78] She had a grant of a new fair in 1327,[79] and was dead in 1338.[80] Her son John paid a fine to have livery, though still under age.[81] He had licence in

1358 to settle the manor on himself and his wife Joyce with remainder to his son John and John's wife Maud, daughter of John de Grey of Rotherfield, and their heirs.[82] The younger John predeceased his father, and on the death of the latter in or about 1386 his heir was Joyce daughter of John and Maud and wife of Sir Hugh Burnell.[83] Maud, who survived and married Sir Thomas Harcourt,[84] held the manor for life under the settlement.[85] In 1386 Sir Hugh Burnell and Joyce executed a new settlement of the reversion, by which Hugh was to have Newport Pagnell and Little Linford in fee simple if after the death of Joyce her heirs disturbed him in the posses-sion of Weoley in Northfield, Worcestershire, and other manors ; otherwise he was to hold for life only.[86] The heirs of Joyce in 1407 were her aunts, Joyce wife of Adam de Peshale, Maud and Agnes Botetourt, and her cousins Maurice Berkeley and Agnes and Joyce Wykes.[87] Adam and Joyce de Peshale settled a third of the manor in 1409 on themselves in tail-male with remainder to William de Birmingham and Joan his wife and the heirs of Joan.[88] Hugh Stranley and his wife Joyce dealt with a third in 1418.[89] Ulti-mately, however, the heirs of Joyce Lady Burnell obtained Weoley,[90] and Hugh Burnell consequently acquired Newport Pagnell in fee ; he granted it in or about 1420 to Joan de Beauchamp Lady Bergavenny and others, apparently to her use.[91] Joan died in 1435, leaving her lands to her grandson James Ormond, subsequently fifth Earl of Ormond and Earl of Wiltshire.[92] The feoffees who had held Newport jointly with Lady Bergavenny delivered seisin to James Ormond in 1445.[93] He was attainted as a Lancastrian and his estates were forfeited in 1461.[94] This manor was granted to Richard Nevill Earl of Warwick in 1462,[95] and to George Duke of Clarence ten years later.[96] The Duke of Clarence died in February 1477-8, and the manor reverted to the Crown.[97] In 1485 Thomas Earl of Ormond, brother of James, was restored to the family estates[98] ; his brother and predecessor John had already been restored in blood.[99] In 1494 Thomas had a release of the manor from Fulk Birmingham.[100] In 1496 William Berkeley and Anne his wife released their claim.[1]

[59] *Coll. for Staffs.* (Will. Salt Arch. Soc.), ii, 73.

[60] Pipe R. 10 John, m. 16 ; cf. *Red Bk. of Exch.* (Rolls Ser.), 537.

[61] Pipe R. 61, m. 2, 4 ; 62, m. 1. The Ralph de Somery whose widow Margaret claimed dower in Berkshire in 1210 (ibid. 56, m. 10) is to be distin-guished from the baron of Dudley.

[62] *Feet of F. Essex* (Essex Arch. Soc.), i, 58. On this point see also *Beds. Hist. Rec. Soc.* i, 15.

[63] *Testa de Nevill* (Rec. Com.), 54 ; Grazebrook, op. cit. 15.

[64] *Rot. Lit. Claus.* (Rec. Com.), i, 286.

[65] Ibid. 441, 458 ; *Cal. Close,* 1231-4, p. 482 ; 1234-7, p. 119.

[66] *Ann. Mon.* (Rolls Ser.), iii, 215.

[67] *Cal. Pat.* 1266-72, p. 102 ; Close, 54 Hen. III, m. 5 d.

[68] *Rot. Lit. Claus.* (Rec. Com.), i, 500 ; *Excerpta e Rot. Fin.* (Rec. Com.), i, 185 ; Grazebrook, op. cit. 15-16.

[69] *Cal. Close,* 1227-31, p. 190.

[70] Chan. Inq. p.m. 29 Hen. III, no. 50.

[71] These had already been disregarded at the death of Nicholas de Somery in 1229, for in 1230 Walter de Kirkham held the manor for life by the king's

grant (Madox, *Hist. of Exch.* i, 418). No more is heard of his tenancy, and William de Beauchamp and Ida probably recovered against him.

[72] Chan. Inq. p.m. 29 Hen. III, no. 50. The fair is here said to have been granted to Roger de Somery 'the elder.' This indicates that the Roger de Somery who died in 1272-3 was the grandson of Ralph, as he is called in Chan. Inq. p.m. 1 Edw. I, no. 15. See Grazebrook (op. cit.) for the view that he was Ralph's son. See also note 80, p. 412, above.

[73] *Cal. Chart. R.* 1257-1300, p. 131.

[74] *Cal. Inq. p.m.* (Edw. I), ii, 14-16.

[75] Ibid. 493 ; *Cal. Pat.* 1281-92, p. 466.

[76] For his tenure of the manor see Add. Chart. 11224 ; *Feud. Aids,* i, 110.

[77] *Cal. Inq. p.m.* (Edw. II), vi, 255.

[78] Ibid. 259.

[79] Chart. R. 1 Edw. III, m. 30 (m i-takenly transcribed as a grant to John Botetourt in *Cal. Chart. R.* 1327-41, p. 12).

[80] *Cal. Close,* 1337-9, p. 522 ; Chan. Inq. p.m. 12 Edw. III (1st nos.), no. 40.

[81] *Cal. Close,* loc. cit.

[82] *Cal. Pat.* 1358-61, p. 124 ; Feet of F. Bucks. 33 Edw. III, no. 2.

[83] Chan. Inq. p.m. 9 Ric. II, no. 4.

[84] Ibid.

[85] Close, 17 Ric. II, m. 18 ; Chan. Inq. p.m. 17 Ric. II, no. 32.

[86] Feet of F. Bucks. 10 Ric. II, no. 10 ; *Cal. Pat.* 1385-9, pp. 149-50.

[87] Chan. Inq. p.m. 8 Hen. IV, no. 64.

[88] Feet of F. Bucks. 10 Hen. IV, no. 2.

[89] Ibid. 6 Hen. V, no. 11.

[90] *V.C.H. Worcs.* iii, 195.

[91] *Cal. Pat.* 1416-22, p. 306 ; Chan. Inq. p.m. 8 Hen. V, no. 116.

[92] Nicolas, *Test. Vetusta,* 226.

[93] *Cat. of Anct. D.* ii, 337.

[94] G.E.C. *Complete Peerage,* vi, 141 ; Chan. Inq. p.m. 1 Edw. IV, no. 29.

[95] *Cal. Pat.* 1461-7, p. 186.

[96] Ibid. 1467-77, p. 345.

[97] G.E.C. *Peerage,* ii, 272 ; *Cal. Pat.* 1476-85, pp. 70, 457.

[98] *Gen.* (New Ser.), iii, 78.

[99] G.E.C. *Complete Peerage,* vi, 142. James seems to have lived till at least 1473 (*Gen.* [New Ser.], iv, 128), though the Inq. p.m. above cited treats him as dead.

[100] *Cat. of Anct. D.* ii, 337 ; Madox, *Form. Angl.* 395-6. Fulk must have claimed through the settlement on William de Birmingham in 1409.

[1] Feet of F. Div. Co. Hil. 11 Hen. VII.

Thomas Ormond died in 1515, leaving daughters and co-heirs Anne and Margaret, of whom the former inherited Newport Pagnell. Her husband was Sir James St. Leger, by whom she had a son George.[2] Anne died in 1533.[3] The manor had been settled in 1519 on John son and heir of George,[4] who before 1542 granted it to the Crown.[5] It was annexed to the honour of Ampthill, and John received lands in Devonshire in exchange.[6] Edward VI granted Newport to his sister Elizabeth, and James I assigned it to his consort Ann.[7] In 1627 it was granted in fee to Sir Francis Annesley, kt. and bart., to hold of the manor of East Greenwich.[8] Sir Francis was created Viscount Valentia in 1622 and Lord Mountnorris in 1629 and died in 1660.[9] His son and successor Arthur was made Earl of Anglesey in 1661.[10] Arthur was succeeded in 1686 by his son James,[11] whose son, another James, succeeded him in 1690 and made a settlement of half the manor in 1701.[12] The second James died in January 1701–2, and his brothers John and Arthur succeeded him in turn.[13] The latter, who held the manor from 1710 to 1737,[13a] was followed by his cousin Richard, who died in 1761.[14] Arthur son of Richard was created Earl of Mountnorris in 1793.[15] He lived till 1816,[16] but must have granted Newport Pagnell to his son George, who was lord of the manor in 1793.[17] In 1810 it was sold to Charles Marius Hardy, the Earl of Mountnorris, as well as his son, being a party to the conveyance.[18] On the death of Charles Marius Hardy in 1827 the manor became the property of his son Charles Henry.[19] The heir of the latter was his sister Maria Newby,[20] on whose death in 1871 it was divided among her three daughters.[21] In 1904, after the death of the survivor, Elizabeth Newby, it was sold by their representatives to Mr. Henry William Whiting, who sold it in 1905 to Mr. J. M. Knapp, the present owner.[22]

There were two fees in Caldecote at the time of

ANNESLEY. *Paly argent and azure a bend gules.*

the Domesday Survey, both of which afterwards went to form the property known as *CALDECOTE MANOR*.[23] The first, consisting of 3 hides and a virgate, had been held by two men of Ulf, and in 1086 was in the hands of William Fitz Ansculf, the tenant of Newport Pagnell.[24] Of that manor it was subsequently held.[25] The mill and some land were granted by Fulk Paynel to the priory of Tickford.[26] The rest was held of Gervase Paynel for a quarter of a knight's fee in 1166 by William de Lovent.[27] Henry de Lovent was the tenant about 1255,[28] Robert son of Adam in 1272,[29] and John de Lovent in 1291.[30] In 1314 this or another John de Lovent released two messuages, four tofts, 50 acres of land, and 8s. 5d. rent to Nicholas de Eure or Iver, who regranted them to him for life.[31] Nicholas de Eure was the tenant of the second Domesday fee, with which this holding was now united. That fee, which had belonged before the Conquest to Gonni, a man of Alvric son of Goding, was held in 1086 by Suerting of Lewin of Nuneham, and was assessed at $2\frac{1}{2}$ hides.[32] It seems to have been annexed during the 12th century to the manor of Meppershall in Bedfordshire, with which it was held by serjeanty of the larder.[33] It was alienated in the early 13th century to Deudo (Deodatus) de Caldecote, who paid 22s. per annum for the serjeanty, did service for a tenth part of a knight's fee, and was quit of a yearly feast which he had owed to Ralph de Meppershall.[34] The fee was henceforth held in chief by these services.[35] In 1251 Deudo conveyed it to Isabel de Eure, receiving in return a grant of it for life.[36] Isabel was perhaps his daughter; one of her descendants subsequently stated that Deudo was his ancestor.[37] She was the widow of Robert de Eure, and her son John was under age in 1247.[38] In 1255 Gilbert de Eure and Isabel de Eure were said to hold Deudo's fee in Caldecote.[39] It seems probable that Isabel had married again, and that Gilbert de Eure was her second husband, the Gilbert de Stratford who held land in Caldecote by serjeanty in 1271.[40] Between 1307 and 1316 the tenant was Nicholas de Eure,[41] whose acquisition of the first fee in the vill has already been mentioned.

Nicholas de Eure was still living in 1322.[42] His son John [43] died in possession of Caldecote in or about

[2] G.E.C. *Complete Peerage*, vi, 143 n. ; Chan. Inq. p.m. (Ser. 2), lv, 19.
[3] Chan. Inq. p.m. (Ser. 2), lv, 19.
[4] Ibid.
[5] *L. and P. Hen. VIII*, xvii, 28 (21) ; xviii (1), g. 802 (37).
[6] Ibid.
[7] Pat. 4 Edw. VI, pt. iii ; 1 Jas. I, pt. xx.
[8] Ibid. 3 Chas. I, pt. xix.
[9] G.E.C. *Complete Peerage*, viii, 13 ; cf. Feet of F. Bucks. Trin. 16 Chas. I.
[10] G.E.C. op. cit. viii, 14 ; cf. Feet of F. Bucks. Trin. 22 Chas. II.
[11] G.E.C. loc. cit.
[12] Recov. R. Trin. 13 Will. III, m. 75 ; G.E.C. loc. cit.
[13] G.E.C. loc. cit. ; cf. Recov. R. East. 1 Anne, m. 60.
[13a] G.E.C. loc. cit.
[14] Recov. R. Trin. 10 & 11 Geo. II, m. 326 ; G.E.C. op. cit. viii, 15.
[15] G.E.C. loc. cit.
[16] Ibid.
[17] Ct. R. *penes* Mr. Knapp ; Com. Pleas D. Enr. Trin. 35 Geo. III, m. 148 ; Priv. Act, 34 Geo. III, cap. 86 ; 47 Geo. III (session 1), cap. 30.

[18] F. W. Bull, op. cit. 61.
[19] Ibid. ; Sheahan, *Hist. and Topog. of Bucks.* 457.
[20] F. W. Bull, loc. cit.   [21] Ibid.
[22] Inform. kindly supplied by Mr. Bull.
[23] A third fee entered under Caldecote in 1086 (*V.C.H. Bucks.* i, 246) has been identified with Willen (q.v.). There appears to have been another Caldecote in Buckinghamshire, the name of which has entirely disappeared. It is described as 'juxta Bibbegrove' (Feet of F. Bucks. 24 Edw. I, no. 6), which is to be identified with Bedgrave in Weston Turville ; the lost Caldecote was probably in that parish or in the adjoining Bierton (ibid. 22 Edw. I, no. 4 ; 19 Edw. II, no. 19 ; Chan. Inq. p.m. 28 Edw. III [1st nos.], no. 58).   [24] *V.C.H. Bucks.* i, 256.
[25] *Red Bk. of Exch.* (Rolls Ser.), 270 ; *Cal. Inq. p.m.* (Edw. I), ii, 15, 497 ; Chan. Inq. p.m. 14 Edw. III (1st nos.), no. 15 ; 30 Edw. III (1st nos.), no. 28. This overlordship is not mentioned after 1356, the tenure in chief (see below) alone appearing in the inquisitions.
[26] Dugdale, op. cit. v, 202.
[27] *Red Bk. of Exch.* loc. cit.

[28] *Hund. R.* (Rec. Com.), i, 30.
[29] *Cal. Inq. p.m.* (Edw. I), ii, 15.
[30] Ibid. 497.
[31] Feet of F. Bucks. 8 Edw. II, no. 20.
[32] *V.C.H. Bucks.* i, 276.
[33] *Testa de Nevill* (Rec. Com.), 257 ; cf. *V.C.H. Beds.* ii, 288.
[34] Pipe R. 3 Hen. III, m. 5 ; *Testa de Nevill*, loc. cit.
[35] *Hund. R.* (Rec. Com.), i, 30 ; Assize R. 60, m. 26 d. ; Chan. Inq. p.m. 14 Edw. III (1st nos.), no. 15 ; 5 Hen. VI, no. 16.
[36] Feet of F. Bucks. 35 Hen. III, no. 7.
[37] Memo. R. (Exch. K.R.) 120.
[38] Assize R. 56, m. 8 d. The Isabel here mentioned in connexion with land in Calverton must be taken to be the Isabel who held Caldecote, for lands in Calverton subsequently belonged to the heirs of the latter (Feet of F. Bucks. 7 Edw. III, no. 16. See below).
[39] *Hund. R.* (Rec. Com.), i, 30.
[40] Assize R. 60, m. 26 d.
[41] *Cal. Pat.* 1301–7, p. 548 ; *Feud. Aids*, i, 109.
[42] *Cal. Inq. p.m.* (Edw. II), vi, 257.
[43] Feet of F. Bucks. 7 Edw. III, no. 16.

1340,[44] leaving a son John, who did homage in that year[45] and settled land in Caldecote on himself and his wife Cecily in 1343.[46] His son and heir was Nicholas, who succeeded him in 1356.[47] The next recorded tenant of Caldecote, here for the first time called a manor, is Thomas Caldecote, who died in 1426 in possession of the holding of the Eures.[48] As he also had their land in Calverton,[49] it is possible that he was himself a Eure who had taken the name of his manor. Thomas had a son and heir William, a minor, who did not live to come of age.[50] His heir in 1439 was his kinswoman Margaret, wife of Thomas Hanchett.[51] Thomas Hanchett, apparently her son,[52] died in possession of the manor in 1509, his heir being his son William.[53] The latter died in March 1514–15 and his son Andrew, a minor, a year later.[54] The heir of Andrew was his brother John,[55] who in 1541 sold Caldecote to John White.[56] John White died in possession in 1572, leaving a son and heir Thomas.[57] Laurence son and heir of Thomas[58] was succeeded on his death in 1600 by his son Thomas.[59] The latter had a son, another Thomas,[60] evidently the Thomas White who died lord of the manor of Caldecote in 1670.[61] His son Thomas made his will in 1678 and was succeeded by a son William.[62] In 1691 William White conveyed the manor to Richard Elborow, a mortgagee.[63] By his will, dated in the following year, he named Sir William Roberts and James Tyrell his executors.[64] From Richard Elborow and James Tyrell the manor was purchased in 1695 by Roger Chapman.[65] Roger died in 1702, and his son Thomas Chapman was the owner in 1734.[66] Thomas sold Caldecote in 1744 to John Pardoe, who in 1747 conveyed it to Sir Edward Turner.[67] The latter sold it three years later to William Backwell, a banker of Pall Mall,[68] who in 1757 acquired from the trustees of Sir Richard Atkins the mill and land in Caldecote which had been granted to Tickford Priory by Fulk Paynel,

WHITE of Caldecote. *Argent a cheveron between three wolves' heads razed sable with three leopards' heads or on the cheveron.*

and had since followed the descent of the priory of Tickford.[69]

William Backwell died in 1770, having left Caldecote to William Harwood,[70] who took the name of Backwell in 1770[71] and died in possession about 1815.[72] The manor then passed to William Adair of Trowse Newton, Norfolk, who had had some interest in it since 1800.[73] His widow Charlotte left it in 1843 to her nephew Charles Hawkins,[74] whose trustees sold it in 1858 to William Whitworth.[75] The present owner is Mr. Henry William Whiting, who purchased the manor from William Whitworth in 1908.[76]

Like Newport Pagnell, *TICKFORD MANOR* belonged to Ulf before the Conquest and to William Fitz Ansculf in 1086, when it was assessed at 5 hides and worth £5.[77] It passed with his other lands to Fulk Paynel, who early in the 12th century[78] founded here a cell to the abbey of Marmoutier, and granted it the site of the house and 'all the land on each side of Monechustret . . . and the lands and tenements in the street called Hawestrete . . . and the lands and tenements before the gate of the house . . . and a meadow called le Castelmede.'[79] This land formed the manor of Tickford, where in 1311 the prior was said to have had view of frankpledge from time immemorial.[80] In that year Edward II granted him in addition the privileges of pillory and tumbril.[81]

The manor remained the property of the priory, which survived the suppression of alien houses by Henry V,[82] and finally surrendered in 1524.[83] It was granted to Wolsey for his college at Oxford,[84] and on his forfeiture was assigned to Henry the Eighth's College.[85] After the surrender of the latter in 1545[86] Tickford remained

ATKINS, baronet. *Azure three bars argent with three bezants in the chief.*

in the possession of the Crown until it was purchased from Elizabeth in 1600 by Henry Atkins, M.D., afterwards king's physician.[87] He died in 1634 seised of the manor, which had been settled on the marriage of his son Henry with Annabel

---

[44] Chan. Inq. p.m. 14 Edw. III (1st nos.), no. 15.

[45] *Abbrev. Rot. Orig.* (Rec. Com.), ii, 136.

[46] *Cal. Pat.* 1343–5, p. 42.

[47] Chan. Inq. p.m. 30 Edw. III (1st nos.), no. 28; *Abbrev. Rot. Orig.* (Rec. Com.), ii, 240.

[48] Chan. Inq. p.m. 5 Hen. VI, no. 16.

[49] Ibid.

[50] Ibid. 18 Hen. VI, no. 22.

[51] Ibid.

[52] Ct. of Req. bdle. 3, no. 111.

[53] Chan. Inq. p.m. (Ser. 2), xxiv, 19.

[54] Ibid. xxxi, 111, 75.

[55] Ibid. 75.

[56] Feet of F. Bucks. Mich. 33 Hen. VIII; Memo. R. (Exch. L.T.R.), East. 34 Hen. VIII, m. 7; Chan. Inq. p.m. (Ser. 2), clxiii, 1.

[57] Chan. Inq. p.m. (Ser. 2), clxiii, 2.

[58] Abstract of Title lent by Mr. F. W. Bull; *Visit. of Bucks.* (Harl. Soc.), 127; cf. Feet of F. Bucks. East. 28 Eliz.

[59] Chan. Inq. p.m. (Ser. 2), cclxvi, 109.

[60] *Visit. of Bucks.* loc. cit.; Chan. Inq. p.m. (Ser. 2), dci, 11.

[61] F. W. Bull, op. cit. 177.

[62] Abstract of Title *ut supra.* An elder son Thomas died without issue before 1688. He may have predeceased his father.

[63] Feet of F. Bucks. Hil. 3 Will. and Mary; Abstract of Title *ut supra.*

[64] F. W. Bull, loc. cit.

[65] Add. MS. 5839, fol. 292; Com. Pleas D. Enr. Mich. 24 Geo. II, m. 77; Abstract of Title *ut supra.*

[66] P.C.C. 24 Degg; Add. MS. 5839, fol. 292.

[67] Com. Pleas D. Enr. Mich. 24 Geo. II, m. 77; Abstract of Title *ut supra.*

[68] Ibid.; Feet of F. Bucks. Hil. 24 Geo. II.

[69] Close, 31 Geo. II, pt. xii, no. 6.

[70] P.C.C. 4 Jenner; *Gent. Mag.* xl, 47.

[71] Phillimore and Fry, *Changes of Name,* 29.

[72] Documents in the possession of Mr. Knapp.

[73] Inform. from Mr. Bull. A rent-

charge on the manor was paid in 1833 by John Andrew Lyon (*Char. Com. Rep.* [1830], xxvii, 155).

[74] P.C.C. 1846 (ccxxxiii, fol. 852). Her maiden name was Harwood, and she was a legatee of William Backwell in 1770 (P.C.C. 4 Jenner).

[75] Inform. from Mr. Bull; Sheahan, op. cit. 457.

[76] Inform. from Mr. Bull.

[77] *V.C.H. Bucks.* i, 257. [78] Ibid. 360.

[79] Dugdale, op. cit. v, 202.

[80] Ibid. 203; cf. Add. Chart. 11224.

[81] Dugdale, loc. cit.

[82] *V.C.H. Bucks.* i, 363.

[83] Ibid.; Chan. Inq. p.m. (Ser. 2), lxxvi, 3.

[84] *L. and P. Hen. VIII,* iv (1), g. 1913 (1); Chan. Inq. p.m. (Ser. 2), lxxvii, 59; Feet of F. Div. Co. Mich. 18 Hen. VIII.

[85] *L. and P. Hen. VIII,* v, g. 1370 (23); xvi, g. 1391 (45).

[86] Tanner, *Not. Mon.*

[87] *Cal. S. P. Dom.* 1598–1601, p. 387; *Dict. Nat. Biog.*

Hawkins.[88] The younger Henry died in 1638, his heir being his son Richard, a minor.[89] Richard was created a baronet in 1660 and died in 1689.[90] His son Sir Richard died in 1696,[91] leaving a son Henry, lord of the manor in 1711.[92] Henry's son and grandson, both called Henry, succeeded him in turn.[93] The last Henry was succeeded in 1742 by his brother Richard,[94] who in 1749 cut off the entail on the estate.[95] He died in 1756,[96] leaving Tickford and other mortgaged premises to Sir William Bowyer and William Stonehouse in trust for sale. They conveyed the manor in 1757 to Henry Uthwatt of Great Linford,[97] who died in that year, leaving this manor to be sold to pay the mortgages on his Linford estate.[98] His devisees sold it in 1764 to Sir William Hart.[99] In 1775 William Nevil Hart, son of Sir William,[100] conveyed it to Joseph Jaques.[1] On the death of Joseph Jaques it became the property of his widow, whose second husband, Frederick Hendrick Van Hagen, held it in her right in 1807,[2] and was presumably the person of that name who died at his seat at Brampton Place, Bexley, Kent, in 1808.[3] Henry Van Hagen was the owner in 1830[4]; he died in 1832.[5] In 1862 Lord Carrington held the estate on lease from Mrs. Van Hagen.[6] It is now the property of his son the Marquess of Lincolnshire.

The site of the priory was sold separately as ' the Abbey Farm' by the trustees of Sir Richard Atkins in 1757 to John Hooton.[7] John Hooton of Tickford Priory died in 1761, leaving sons John and Thomas. John inherited the estates and died in 1764, having devised them to his brother.[7a] Thomas Hooton died in 1804,[8] his heir being his daughter Sarah, wife of Philip Hoddle Ward.[9] Sarah Ward died in 1831,[10] and the estate was sold between that date and 1847 to William Powell.[11] In 1869 Oliver Massey was living at Tickford Abbey, which belonged to his wife in 1877. Mr. P. Butler, the next owner, died in 1898, and his son, Colonel W. J. C. Butler, now holds the estate.

The church of *ST. PETER AND ST. PAUL* consists of a chancel measuring internally 37 ft. by 18 ft. 6 in., north vestries and organ chamber, nave 94 ft. by 25 ft., north aisle 11 ft. wide, south aisle 13 ft. 4 in. wide, north and south porches, and west tower 15 ft. 6 in. square. The tower is built of ashlar and the other parts of the church of rubble, and the roofs are covered with lead and tiles.

The east wall of the nave, which is 5 ft. 4 in. thick, probably incorporates the remains of the central tower of an early cruciform church, but all other parts of the structure were entirely rebuilt in the middle of the 14th century, and the present nave, aisles, and porches are of that period. Early in the 16th century the clearstory was added to the nave, the chancel and

a large part of the north wall of the north aisle were rebuilt, and the whole church was reroofed. At the same time the tower at the west end of the nave was begun, but it appears to have taken a considerable time to complete, for legacies towards the ' Newport steeple' are recorded as late as 1549.[12] The organ chamber was built in 1867 and the vestries were added in 1905. The church was restored in 1828; much of the window tracery has been renewed, particularly in the chancel, where the stone mullions had been removed in the 18th century and replaced by iron frames, and galleries have also been erected in both aisles.

The chancel is lighted from the east by a three-light traceried window with a depressed head; the two windows in the north wall, which are each of two lights, are of the same character, and there are three similar windows in the south wall. All of them are largely modern, though some of the internal jambs and arches, now coated with paint, may date from the early 16th century. Below the middle window on the south is a moulded doorway with a four-centred head, and opposite to it on the north is a similar doorway, now opening into the vestries. At the south-east is an ogee-headed piscina niche of the 14th century, with grooves for a wooden credence shelf; the bowl has been partly broken away. The chancel arch, which is acutely pointed and of three continuous chamfered orders, probably dates from the reconstruction of the chancel in the early 16th century.

The north and south arcades of the nave are each of six bays with moulded arches supported by clustered pillars and responds with moulded capitals and bases, the bases considerably restored. The eastern bay on each side is slightly narrower and more acutely pointed than the others, and is separated from the adjoining bay by a short length of wall; this arrangement is often found in transeptal churches, and may indicate the existence of transepts here before the 14th-century reconstruction and for some time during its progress. At the south-east corner of the nave is a pointed doorway to a turret stairway leading to the roof and forming the only approach to the upper stages of the tower. There are no traces of an entrance to the rood-loft in this stairway, though a large hole in the masonry of the interior suggests an unsuccessful attempt to discover a doorway. It is probable that the rood-loft crossed the nave between the short lengths of wall above referred to, but the approach to it has been obliterated. This assumption is strengthened by the existence here of two head corbels, which occur on the string-courses below the clearstory windows and indicate the position of the rood beam. The clearstory is lighted from either side by a long range of windows, each of three cinquefoiled lights under a four-centred head, and all considerably restored. At the west end of the nave

[88] Chan. Inq. p.m. (Ser. 2), dx, 45.
[89] Ibid. dlxx, 143.
[90] G.E.C. *Baronetage*, iii, 39; Feet of F. Div. Co. Hil. 28 & 29 Chas. II.
[91] G.E.C. loc. cit.
[92] Ibid.; Recov. R. Mich. 10 Anne, m. 295.
[93] G.E.C. op. cit. iii, 39–40.
[94] Ibid. 40; Com. Pleas D. Enr. East. 22 Geo. II, m. 12.
[95] Com. Pleas D. Enr. East. 22 Geo. II, m. 12.

[96] G.E.C. loc. cit.
[97] Close, 31 Geo. II, pt. xii, no. 14.
[98] P.C.C. 25 Hulton.
[99] Close, 4 Geo. III, pt. xviii, no. 2.
[100] Hunter, *Fam. Minorum Gentium* (Harl. Soc.), 429.
[1] Feet of F. Bucks. Hil. 15 Geo. III.
[2] Priv. Act, 47 Geo. III (session 1), cap. 30; Lysons, *Mag. Brit.* i (3), 613.
[3] *Gent. Mag.* lxxviii, 857.
[4] Pigott, *Dir.* (1830).
[5] M. I. in church.

[6] Sheahan, op. cit. 460.
[7] Close, 31 Geo. II, pt. xii, no. 14; Abstract of Title lent by Mr. F. W. Bull.
[7a] P.C.C. 422 St. Eloy; inform. from Mr. F. W. Bull.
[8] Staines, *Hist of Newport Pagnell*, 163 (M. I. at the family burying-place at Tickford).
[9] Ibid.; Lysons, op. cit. 696.
[10] M. I. *ut supra*.
[11] F. W. Bull, loc. cit.
[12] Add. MS. 5839, fol. 146.

NEWPORT PAGNELL CHURCH FROM THE SOUTH

NEWPORT PAGNELL CHURCH: THE INTERIOR LOOKING EAST

is a lofty pointed arch to the tower of early 16th-century date. It is of three chamfered orders continued without break down the jambs to large splayed stops.

The north aisle is lighted from the north by five traceried windows with four-centred heads, the eastern-most of five and the others of three lights. These all date from about 1520, when that part of the wall west of the east bay was rebuilt, and four of them occur in the new part, but the large window was inserted in the older and thicker portion of the wall. The east wall adjoins the modern organ chamber, in which some parts of an old window have been reset. In the west wall of the aisle is a blocked pointed window which is now covered with ivy.

The north porch has a sexpartite vault with hollow-chamfered ribs springing from corbels on which the chamfers die. It is lighted by two small windows, one on either side of the southern bay, that on the west having a pointed head and the other an almost flat head, probably the result of an alteration made when the adjoining aisle wall was reconstructed. The entrance doorway with its two-centred drop arch is original, but the pointed doorway to the aisle is modern. The vault has been slightly repaired. Above the porch is a parvise, which is lighted by a modern square-headed window, but has in each of the east and west walls an original single light now blocked.

The south aisle has been considerably restored, and its tall traceried windows, of which there are five in the south wall and one at each end, are mostly modern. The south doorway is a good example of mid-14th-century workmanship, having a pointed head with elaborate mouldings, some members of which develop into cusping both in the external and rear arches. Much of the stonework of the head, which is inclosed within a square label with plain spandrels, has been renewed. The chapels of our Lady and St. Nicholas, referred to in some early 16th-century wills,[13] probably occupied the east ends of the nave aisles, which were originally built as transepts. It was in the chapel of our Lady, probably that on the south, that the Burgess chantry was founded in 1318.[14] The piscina here has disappeared, but in the south wall between the first and second windows from the east there are three sedilia with cinquefoiled heads and traceried spandrels, all under one square label, which is enriched with ball-flower and four-leaf ornament. These sedilia are divided by clustered shafts, and, though considerably restored, date from the mid-14th century.

The south porch is of one story and has an external doorway similar in character to the south doorway of the aisle, but mostly modern. On the east and west walls is a rich internal wall arcade, with no divisions below the arches. The timber roof of the porch is of the 15th century.

The nave has a richly moulded low-pitched roof of the early 16th century, with foliated bosses at the intersections of the timbers. The wall-posts are connected to the beams by curved brackets and are supported by stone corbels carved as angels holding shields, while in front of each of the posts is a carved wood figure, two of the figures representing angels and the others saints, including the twelve apostles. There are also carved figures of angels at the centres of the tie-beams and at the feet of the intermediate rafters. The lean-to roofs of the aisles are of the same character and period, and have carved wooden figures at the lower corners. Tie-beams and wall-plates of the Tudor period have also been re-used with the modern timbers of the chancel roof.

The tower is of three stages, strengthened by clasping buttresses, and is surmounted by an embattled parapet with pinnacles at the angles and at the centre of each face. The west doorway has a pointed head and continuous mouldings. Above it is a four-light window with modern tracery under a four-centred head. Access to the upper stages is provided by a doorway on the east side of the tower leading from the nave roof, the roof being gained by the turret stairway at the south-east of the nave. The bell-chamber is lighted on each side by two tall windows, each of two trefoiled lights under a pointed head. All this work has been considerably restored, and the parapet and pinnacles are modern.

The font is modern. A brass figure of a civilian of about 1440, now much worn, is nailed to the doorway of the turret stairway at the south-east of the nave. On the wall above this doorway is a tablet to Thomas Jenkins (d. 1705) and Mary his wife. In the south aisle are mural monuments to John Revis, apothecary (d. 1765), 'who did in his life time erect seven alms houses in this churchyard for 4 men & 3 women for ever and at his death gave a generous endowment to this his native Town,' and Elizabeth and Ann his daughters ; Thomas Taylor (d. 1719) ; Chapman Taylor (d. 1705) and Rebecca his sister (d. 1706) ; Roger Chapman (d. 1702), Rebecca his wife (d. 1697) and Felicia Dumas, their daughter (d. 1698), with a shield of arms, a lion standing, impaling a cheveron cut off at the ends, a crescent for difference ; John Rogers (d. 1726), with a shield of arms, a cheveron between three harts ; and Thomas Foster (d. 1775) and T. G. Foster, his son (d. 1792). A floor slab to Sir Richard Atkins of Clapham, Surrey (d. 1696), has been placed against the north wall of the chancel ; it has a shield of arms and the Ulster badge. In the tower are a floor slab to John Barton (d. 1701) and Mary Barton (d. 1699), and an early 16th-century slab with matrices for brasses. In the parvise are preserved an oak iron-bound chest of about 1600 with incised panels, a chest with richly carved panels of about 1650, and an 18th-century chair, and there is a 17th-century table in the vestry. At the east end of the south aisle are two chained books, Foxe's *Actes and Monuments* and *Works of John Jewell*, both 17th-century editions and incomplete.

The tower contains a ring of eight bells, a small bell by Anthony Chandler, inscribed 'A.C. 1671,' and a clock bell, added with the chiming apparatus in 1887. Five of the ring were recast in 1749 by Thomas Lester of London, one was added in 1769, one in 1816, and one in 1819, but the whole ring was again recast in 1911.

The communion plate consists of a cup and cover paten of 1708 ; a paten of 1637, dated 1638 ; and a flagon of 1694 inscribed, 'The Gift of Dame Rebecca Atkins Widdow.'

The registers begin in 1558.

ADVOWSON   The church of Newport Pagnell, with a hide of land, was among the possessions with which Fulk Paynel endowed the priory of Tickford.[15] It was appro-

---

[13] Add. MS. 5839, fol. 146.   [14] See under advowson.   [15] Dugdale, op. cit. v, 202.

priated to the priory, and a vicarage was ordained at the beginning of the 13th century.[16] The prior undertook to provide a dwelling-house for the vicar and a deacon to assist him, besides maintaining him at the table of the priory, paying him a yearly stipend of 20s., and allowing him a certain proportion of the offerings of parishioners.[17] The revenues of the chapel of Little Linford, not mentioned in the ordination, also became part of the endowment of the vicarage ; in 1265 the prior and convent, who had withdrawn these revenues from the vicar, were ordered to restore them.[18]

Except for intervals during which the possessions of Tickford as an alien house were in the king's hands,[19] the priors continued to present till the dissolution of the priory in 1524.[20] The rectory and advowson then followed the descent of the manor of Tickford till the surrender of Henry the Eighth's College in 1545,[21] after which date the advowson remained in the possession of the Crown.[22] It was transferred in 1859 to the Bishop of Oxford, the present patron, in exchange for the advowson of the vicarage of Sutton with Seaford, Sussex.[23]

The rectory followed the descent of the manor of Tickford till the sale of the estates of Sir Richard Atkins.[24] It was purchased in 1758, with the exception of the tithe of certain meadows, by John Dighton.[25] The tithes were in various hands in 1795, when they were largely commuted for allotments under the Inclosure Award.[26]

Richard Burgess had licence in 1318 to endow a chaplain in the church of Newport Pagnell to celebrate daily for his soul and the souls of John de Somery and Lucy his wife.[27] In 1546 the Commissioners for Chantries reported that the assistance of the priest so maintained was very necessary to the vicar.[28] Nevertheless the endowments of the chantry were granted in 1589 to Walter Copinger and Thomas Butler.[29]

A chapel of St. Nicholas existed in the church, probably in connexion with the gild of St. Nicholas mentioned in the 13th century.[30]

A chapel was attached to the hospital of St. John the Baptist, founded here shortly before 1240.[31] The advowson belonged to the lords of the manor.[32] Various grants of the chapel and its endowments were made by Elizabeth.[33] In 1615 it was given to the refounded hospital.[34]

CHARITIES The Town Lands Charities are regulated by a scheme of the Charity Commissioners of 22 March 1898. They include the charities of—

1. William Kitchell, founded by will 1558, consisting of a rent-charge of 13s. 4d. issuing out of Redhouse Close ;

2. Beatrice Holiday, endowments, comprised in deeds of 1499–1500 and 1524–5, now consisting of a house known as the Old Workhouse, two closes in Fishers Wick, a close adjoining Bury Field, let at rents amounting together to £28, and two rent-charges of £6 and £2 issuing respectively out of a house in St. John Street and a messuage now used as a Church Institute and Masonic Hall ;

3. Richard Read and Ralph Hobbs, founded by deed, 3 February 1483–4, endowed with 8 a. 2 r. 18 p., known as Ashway Hill Close, and a rent-charge of £25 5s. issuing out of three houses and shops in the High Street ;

4. Alice Cropthorne, founded by deed, 4 November 1530, included in Ashway Hill Close ;

5. John Sybley, founded by deed 6 February 1504–5, consisting of a close in Fishers Wick containing 1 a. 2 r. let at £8 a year ;

6. Richard Blood, founded by deed 20 April 1599, consisting of two houses in the High Street and a cottage in Church Passage, annual rental value £50 ;

7. A rent-charge of 3s. 4d., stated on a benefaction board in the church to issue out of Goose Half Acre in Water Leys ;

8. Gift for the relief of the poor, and for the amendment of the church, highways and bridges, consisting of 3 a. 0 r. 8 p., known as London Road Land, allotted on the inclosure in 1808 in lieu of lands in Tickford Fields belonging to the trustees from time immemorial. The land is let at £6 a year ;

9. Fifteen almshouses in Bury Street, built from time to time, which are let to various tenants, and produce £10 16s. 8d. yearly.

A sum of £101 4s. 4d. consols, derived from the sales in 1887 and 1888 of two pieces of land, is in course of accumulation by the official trustees.

By the scheme one-fourth part of the net income is made applicable for the repair and maintenance of the parish church, and for the maintenance of the services and furniture, one-fourth part for the repair of North Bridge and Tickford Bridge, one-fourth part for the repair of the highways, and the remaining fourth part for the benefit of the poor. In 1911 a sum of about £90 was divided equally among these objects ; the proportion assigned to the poor was applied in gifts of money and coal, £10 being given to the Good Samaritan and Nursing Society.

Queen Ann's Hospital, formerly the Hospital of St. John the Baptist, was in existence as early as the reign of Henry III, but was re-established by a charter granted by King James I and his consort Queen Ann, dated 29 June 1615. The endowments consist of two houses, four cottages, allotments called Foxgate Piece containing 10 acres, allotments containing 13½ acres, a grass field containing 2½ acres, and a garden containing 2 acres. A sum of £4,300 16s. 2d. consols is also held by the official trustees, representing proceeds of sales from time to time. The aggregate income amounts to about £300 a year. The hospital is divided into three upper tenements occupied by

[16] Apparently in 1215 (R. of Hugh of Wells [Cant. and York Soc.], i, 199).
[17] Liber Antiquus Hugonis Wells, 13.
[18] F. W. Bull, op. cit. 117.
[19] Cal. Pat. 1338–40, p. 51 ; 1343–5, p. 120.
[20] V.C.H. Bucks. i, 364.
[21] L. and P. Hen. VIII, iv (1), g. 1913 (1), 2167 ; v, g. 1370 (23).
[22] Inst. Bks. (P.R.O.). A grant, which does not seem to have become operative, was made to Thomas Bishop of Lincoln

in 1558 (Pat. 5 & 6 Phil. and Mary, pt. iv, m. 27).
[23] Lond. Gaz. 19 July 1859, p. 2801.
[24] Cal. S. P. Dom. 1598–1601, p. 387 ; Chan. Inq. p.m. (Ser. 2), dx, 45 ; Recov. R. East. 22 Geo. II, m. 23. The advowson also is mentioned among the possessions of the Atkins family, but they never exercised the patronage.
[25] Indent. 1758 E 2, no. 3.
[26] Com. Pleas D. Enr. Trin. 35 Geo. III, m. 148.

[27] Cal. Pat. 1317–21, p. 135.
[28] Chant. Cert. 4, no. 11.
[29] Pat. 31 Eliz. pt. vii, m. 31.
[30] Harl. MS. 5839, fol. 146 ; Assize R. 56, m. 14.
[31] Madox, Form. Angl. 424 ; Chan. Inq. p.m. 29 Hen. III, no. 50.
[32] Cal. Pat. 1416–22, p. 306 ; Char. Proc. Inq. bdle. 1, no. 10.
[33] Pat. 30 Eliz. pt. vii, m. 6 ; Pat. 2 Eliz. pt. iv, m. 11 ; 31 Eliz. pt. vii, m. 31.
[34] Pat. 13 Jas. I, pt. xix, no. 9.

three women, and three lower tenements occupied by three men, each inmate receiving 2s. weekly with an allowance of 10s. for firing at Christmas; £5 is expended every other year on a coat for each man and a gown for each woman. After deducting the expenses and medical attendance a moiety of the surplus income is paid to the master.

The four charities next mentioned are also under the administration of the governors of Queen Ann's Hospital.

1. Thomas Kilpin by his will, proved 17 October 1677, devised an annuity of £2 for distribution on 2 February each year among twenty poor families. The annuity is charged on a house in the High Street.

2. Jane Goodman by her will bequeathed to the Rev. John Sharp, afterwards Archbishop of York, £300 to be disposed of for charitable purposes. A sum of £80, part thereof, was expended in 1691 in the purchase of 4 a. 1 r. in Little Crawley, which is let at £10 a year, the rent being applied in apprenticing. There is an alternative trust at the discretion of the governors for the benefit of a minister's widow of Newport Pagnell.

3. Robert Collison by his will, proved at Oxford 25 April 1860, bequeathed £1,845 stock, now consols, with the official trustees, the annual dividends of which, amounting to £46 2s. 6d., are applicable as to £45 in providing food, fuel and clothing for the poor, preference to be given to such as are attentive to their religious duties, and as to £1 2s. 6d. for distribution among the inmates of Queen Ann's Hospital.

4. The Atterbury and Christie Educational Foundation consists of the rent-charge of £10 issuing out of the Delapre estate at Great Houghton, Northamptonshire, devised in 1730 by the will of the Rev. Lewis Atterbury, LL.D., and the rent of the house situate in the Paggs, Newport Pagnell, built by Samuel Christie as a workhouse. The house is let at £9 a year.[35]

The Bread Charities.—Elizabeth Davey by her will, proved in the P.C.C. 3 July 1699, devised land in Tickford Fields for providing £5 4s. yearly for a weekly distribution of bread, in respect of which about 7 a. were allotted on the inclosure; they are now let at £10 a year.

Mark Slingesby by will, dated 2 July 1677, devised an annuity of £5 4s. for providing twenty-four penny loaves weekly for the poor. The annuity was redeemed in 1905 by the transfer of £208 consols to the official trustees.

Edward Whitton by his will, dated in 1766, bequeathed £100, the interest to be expended in bread on 5 July yearly, now represented by £130 2s. 7d. consols.

James Leverett by his will, dated in 1783, bequeathed £300, the interest to be distributed every Sunday in bread, now represented by £300 consols.

William Underwood by his will, dated 1793, bequeathed £200, the interest to be distributed in bread yearly on New Year's Day, now represented by £321 5s. 8d. consols.

The several sums of stock are held by the official trustees, and produce £23 19s. 8d. in yearly dividends, which with the income of Elizabeth Davey's charity are distributed in bread.

35 See V.C.H. Bucks. ii, 220.

Widow's Acre.—There are about 3 acres in Bury Meadow called Widow's Acre, stated in the Parliamentary Returns of 1786 to have been given by a donor unknown for the use of poor widows. The herbage is sold yearly, and realized in 1911 the sum of £4 10s., which was distributed in gifts of 1s. 6d. to poor widows.

A sum of £266 1s. 3d. consols also held by the official trustees, represents a legacy by the will of George Knibb, proved in the P.C.C. 15 December 1826, the annual dividends of which, amounting to £6 13s., are divisible equally among four poor widows of respectable tradesmen, such widows being members of the Church of England.

Mrs. Martha White—as appeared from a tablet in the church—charged a close in Dunton Bassett (co. Leicester) with 20s., of which 10s. was to be given to the vicar for preaching a sermon on Good Friday, 2s. 6d. to the clerk, and 7s. 6d. to fifteen poor persons who should receive the sacrament on that day. The annuity is duly received and applied.

The almshouses founded by John Revis for the accommodation of four poor single men and three poor single women are endowed as follows: A farm at Marston Moretaine, containing 80 a., comprised in deeds, 3 May 1757 and 1 May 1758, let at £67 a year; £1,000 consols, representing a sale in 1866 of two messuages in Newport Pagnell, comprised in the said deed of 3 May 1757; £1,000 consols bequeathed by the founder's will, dated in 1763, for the benefit of the inmates; a further legacy of £350 consols, the interest to be applied in keeping the property in repair and in distributing bread of the value of 10s. weekly for twenty weeks; and a further legacy of £150 consols, the interest to be applied in the payment of £1 1s. to the vicar for a sermon on 13 July yearly, 5s. to the parish clerk, 2s. 6d. to the sexton, and the residue to provide a dinner to the governors on 13 July. The several sums of stock were in 1863 transferred to the official trustees, and in 1910 the sum of £83 9s. 7d. consols was sold and the proceeds invested in the purchase of a fee-farm rent of £2 11s. 4d. charged upon a farm-house, &c., at Marston Moretaine, leaving a sum of £2,416 10s. 5d. consols with the official trustees, producing £60 8s. yearly. The land is subject to tithe amounting in 1912 to £16 15s. 4d. The sum of £10 is distributed to the poor in bread, and £74 4s. was in 1912 paid to the inmates, the fixed payments above mentioned being duly made.

The official trustees also hold a sum of £225 consols, derived under the will of Robert Collison above referred to, the annual dividends, amounting to £5 12s. 4d., being distributable among the inmates of the almshouses on 25 January yearly.

This sum is part of Robert Collison's bequest of £1,125 consols, now held by the official trustees, and producing £28 2s. 6d. yearly, which has been apportioned as directed by the testator as follows:—£225 stock, or £5 12s. 4d. yearly (being one-fifth part), for poor residing in the Feoffee almshouses on 25 January, as mentioned above; £225 stock for the benefit of an organist; £225 stock for the National school, and £450 stock (being two-fifth parts) for Sunday school children. By a scheme of the Board of Education of 9 September 1910 the annual dividend on the last-mentioned sum of stock, amounting to £11 5s., is made applicable in prizes of not more than £1 or less than 2s. 6d. to girls attending a Church of England Sunday school and in attendance at a public elementary school.

Nonconformist Charities.—The charities in connexion with the Congregational Chapel are administered under a scheme of the Charity Commissioners of 4 December 1906. They include (1) the almshouses founded in 1843 by Charlotte Beaty, and endowed by a codicil to her will, proved in the P.C.C. 10 August 1850. The almshouses, four in number, are situate in Union Street, having as endowment two cottages of the yearly rental value of £13 13s., and £1,604 1s. 9d. consols held by the official trustees, producing £40 2s. yearly. The income is directed by the scheme to be applied in the upkeep of the almshouses and in providing stipends for the inmates, who in 1911 received £39 16s. (2) Charlotte Beaty also by her will bequeathed £166 13s. 4d. consols, and (3) Amelia Ann Higgins by her will, proved in the P.C.C. 9 February 1825, bequeathed

£833 6s. 8d. consols. (4) Charities for the minister and poor. The trustees are also possessed of two messuages, being Nos. 75 and 77 High Street, comprised in deeds of lease and release, dated respectively 27 and 28 August 1828, of the yearly rental value of £36 10s., and £658 15s. 8d. consols. The three sums of stock, amounting together to £1,658 15s. 8d. consols, are held by the official trustees. By the scheme the sum of £609 2s. 4d. consols (part thereof), producing £15 4s. 8d. yearly, together with the rents of the two houses in the High Street (subject to a provision of a repair fund) has been apportioned for the benefit of the minister. The balance of the stock, amounting to £1,049 13s. 4d. consols, is by the scheme apportioned for the benefit of the poor, and the annual dividends, amounting to £26 4s. 8d., are made applicable in supplying clothes, fuel, tools, medical aid and food to the poor of the congregation and in augmentation of the stipends of inmates of the almshouses.

NEWTON BLOSSOMVILLE

Neutone (xi cent.); Newenton Blossevill (xiii cent.); Newenton Blossmevill (xiv cent.).

This parish, lying on the borders of Bedfordshire, covers 1,014 acres, of which a little more than half is

OLD HOUSE, NEWTON BLOSSOMVILLE

arable land and the rest, except for some 40 acres of woodland, is pasture. The soil is a strong loam with a subsoil mainly of Oxford Clay, and the principal crops are wheat, beans, oats and roots. The land falls from the south, where it is about 300 ft. above the ordnance datum, towards the north, where the River Ouse forms the northern boundary.

The parish was inclosed by Act of Parliament in 1810.[1]

The small village, which lies in a hollow in the north-east of the parish, is 3 miles west of Turvey

station (Bedfordshire), on the Midland railway. At the eastern end of the village is St. Nicholas's Church, with the school and rectory to the south of it. A little distance to the south-east of the church is a rectangular stone house, now a keeper's lodge, part of which is of the late 16th century. A tablet on a chimney stack has the date 1588, with the initials T.I. and T.A. The school (elementary) was built originally for a Sunday school in 1822 for fifty children.

About half a mile south-east of the church is Newton Park, now a farm. It was formerly the seat of the lords of the manor and extended into Turvey, in the neighbouring county of Bedford.[2] Portions of the wall of the park remain, and a farm-house occupies the site of the earlier house. It is in the occupation of Mr. Richard Quenby.

MANOR Five 'manses' at Newton were released to Sigulf by King Athelstan in 937,[3] but it is not certain whether this Newton was in Buckinghamshire. In the Domesday Survey Newton is not mentioned by name, but may be identified with the 2 hides and 1 virgate held of the Countess Judith in the neighbouring parish of Lavendon,[4] for the descendants of the under-tenant, Gilbert de Blossomville, afterwards held Newton, to which they gave their name. The overlordship rights were attached to the manor of Waterhall[5] in Cold Brayfield, in the possession of the Greys of Shirland and Wilton in the 14th and early 15th centuries.[6] The dependence of Newton Blossomville on Waterhall is last mentioned in 1475.[7]

[1] Local and Pers. Act, 50 Geo. III, cap. 111.

[2] Chan. Inq. p.m. 14 Ric. II, no. 9; 16 Ric. II, pt. i, no. 27; 22 Ric. II, no. 46.

[3] Kemble, *Cod. Dipl.* no. 1114; Birch, *Cart. Sax.* ii, 418.

[4] *V.C.H. Bucks.* i, 273. Lavendon is now separated from Newton Blossomville by Cold Brayfield, but the latter parish was assessed under Lavendon in the Domesday Survey and later.

[5] Chan. Inq. p.m. 19 Ric. II, no. 29; 38 & 39 Hen. VI, no. 59.

[6] Ibid. 16 Ric. II, pt. i, no. 27; 22 Ric. II, no. 46; 4 Hen. IV, no. 41; 2 Hen. VI, no. 20.

[7] It was then held of Richard Middleton. Ibid. 15 Edw. IV, no. 44.

Very little is known of the early history of the Blossomville family, especially in connexion with this parish. Gilbert de Blossomville, the Domesday tenant,[8] appears to have been succeeded by a Robert de Blossomville, who, about 1150, gave lands in Cold Brayfield to Harrold Priory, Bedfordshire.[9] In 1185 William de Blossomville sued Gerin de Charleton for lands in Turvey,[10] but his successor, Robert de Blossomville, is the first mentioned in connexion with Newton, where in 1202 he quitclaimed half a virgate to William Miles.[11] Simon de Blossomville was living in 1232[12]; by 1255, when Gilbert de Blossomville owned land here, the place was already known as Newton Blossomville.[13] The line seems to have ended in a female heir, Alice de Blossomville, who with John Druel, probably her son, in 1265 granted to Simon de Blossomville and Maud his wife for life lands in Newton Blossomville with reversion to the grantors.[14] This Simon de Blossomville was one of the warrantors for the good behaviour of John Druel, who was forgiven in the next year for his share in the rebellion against the king.[15] John Druel, lord in 1302,[16] was probably son of the John Druel of 1265, and identical with the John Druel who with Amice his wife made a settlement of the manor in 1311 on their daughter Nichole for life with remainder to the right heirs of John.[17] In the same year John Druel's lands in Newton Blossomville and Clifton were in the king's hands for his default against John son of Arnald de Buckingham.[18] John Druel was returned as lord of Newton in 1316,[19] and in 1318 granted messuages and land here to Simon le Bedel of Watford[20]; Amice seems to have survived her husband, as she presented to the church in 1323.[21] Their daughter Nichole evidently married Sir Thomas Swinford, who held Newton Blossomville in 1346,[22] and who, with Nichole his wife, conveyed it in 1357 to Sir William de Burgh, clerk of Chancery, and Sir John de Newenham, clerk,[23] to hold at a rent of 28 marks yearly for the life of Nichole, with reversion to Ralph Lord Basset of Drayton.[24] Ralph Basset was in possession of Newton Blossomville by October 1359, when he handed it over to trustees, to hold during his absence in France,[25] and gave them a quitclaim at his return in the following year.[26] He was known as Ralph Basset le Rich, and died in 1390,[27] his widow Joan in 1395 claiming a third of the manor in dower from Elizabeth Beauchamp,[28] to whom he had granted it for the term of her life, with remainder to Nicholas Bradshaw.[29] Ralph Basset died

without issue, and his heir was Thomas Earl of Stafford, who died seised of the reversion in 1392,[30] and was succeeded by his brother William, who died in 1395, leaving as heir his brother Edmund.[31] Elizabeth Beauchamp was holding the manor in 1396[32] and 1397,[33] but granted it soon after to Nicholas Bradshaw,[34] who presented to the church in 1400,[35] and to whom Edmund Earl of Stafford confirmed the grant for the term of his life.[36] The earl died seised of the reversion of the manor in 1403,[37] and was succeeded by his son Humphrey, to whom the manor reverted at the death of Nicholas Bradshaw in 1415.[38] He was dealing with it in 1426,[39] and again after his creation as Duke of Buckingham, with his wife Anne, in 1458.[40] He settled it on himself for life with remainder to John, his third son, and Constance wife of John, daughter of Henry Green of Drayton, Northamptonshire.[41] The Duke of Buckingham was killed at the battle of Northampton on 10 July 1460,[42] his heir being his grandson Henry, son of his son Humphrey, who had been killed in 1455.[43] His son John Stafford with Constance his wife then succeeded him in the manor.[44] John was created Earl of Wiltshire in 1470,[45] and died on 8 May 1473,[46] being survived by his wife Constance, who died in 1475.[47] Their son and heir Edward died without issue in March 1498–9,[48] when his widow Margaret, in obedience to his will, released her right in the manor to Edward Duke of Buckingham,[49] son of her husband's cousin Henry, the second duke, previously mentioned. Edward Duke of Buckingham, with his wife Eleanor, was dealing with it in 1502.[50] He granted it on 27 August 1507 for life to his next brother, Henry Stafford,[51] created in

STAFFORD. *Or a cheveron gules.*

DEVEREUX. *Argent a fesse with three roundels in the chief all gules.*

1510 fifth Earl of Wiltshire,[52] who died in April 1523, the manor then reverting to the Crown, in

[8] *V.C.H. Bucks.* i, 273.

[9] Lansd. MS. 391, fol. 15, 15*b*; Dugdale, *Mon.* vi, 330; *V.C.H. Beds.* i, 387.

[10] Pipe R. Beds. and Bucks. 31 Hen. II, m. 9 d.

[11] Feet of F. case 14, file 7, no. 34.

[12] Ibid. Beds. 16 Hen. III, no. 16.

[13] Ibid. case 16, file 33, no. 24.

[14] Ibid. file 39, no. 7. There is mention of Alice wife of Simon Druel in 1246, when they were accused of trespassing in Simon de Norwich's fishery in Lavendon (Assize R. 56, m. 5).

[15] *Cal. Pat.* 1258–66, p. 572.

[16] *Feud. Aids*, i, 104. John Druel presented to the church in 1291 (Add. MS. 5839, p. 283) and in 1297 (Harl. MS. 6951, fol. 36).

[17] Feet of F. case 18, file 62, no. 5.

[18] *Cal. Close*, 1307–13, p. 355.

[19] *Feud. Aids*, i, 110.

[20] Feet of F. Bucks. Mich. 12 Edw. II, no. 19.

[21] Add. MS. 5839, p. 283.

[22] *Feud. Aids*, i, 130.

[23] Feet of F. Bucks. East. 31 Edw. III, no. 5.

[24] *Cal. Close*, 1354–60, p. 388.

[25] cf. Dugdale, *Baronage*, i, 380.

[26] *Cal. Close*, 1360–4, p. 127.

[27] Chan. Inq. p.m. 14 Ric. II, no. 9.

[28] De Banco R. 538, m. 285 d.; cf. *Cat. of Anct. D.* (P.R.O.), v, 133. She received Olney in satisfaction of her claim, and died in 1402 (Chan. Inq. p.m. 4 Hen. IV, no. 38).

[29] Chan Inq. p.m. 4 Hen. IV, no. 41.

[30] Ibid. 16 Ric. II, pt. i, no. 27.

[31] Ibid. 22 Ric. II, no. 46.

[32] Ibid. 19 Ric. II, no. 29.

[33] Ibid. 21 Ric. II, no. 28.

[34] Ibid. 2 Hen. VI, no. 20.

[35] Add. MS. 5839, p. 283.

[36] Chan. Inq. p.m. 2 Hen. VI, no. 20.

[37] Ibid. 4 Hen. IV, no. 41.

[38] Ibid. 2 Hen. VI, no. 20; Memo. R. (Exch. L.T.R.), 188, m. 10.

[39] Close, 5 Hen. VI, m. 15 d.

[40] Feet of F. Div. Co. Trin. 36 Hen. VI, no. 95.

[41] Chan. Inq. p.m. 38 & 39 Hen. VI, no. 59.   [42] Ibid.

[43] Ibid.; G.E.C. *Peerage*, ii, 63–4.

[44] Mins. Accts. (Gen. Ser.), bdle. 1117, no. 11.

[45] G.E.C. *Peerage*, viii, 165.

[46] Chan. Inq. p.m. 13 Edw. IV, no. 13.

[47] Ibid. 15 Edw. IV, no. 44.

[48] Exch. Inq. p.m. (Ser. 2), file 5, no. 5; G.E.C. *Peerage*, viii, 165.

[49] P.C.C. 31 Horne; Close 360, no. 21.

[50] De Banco R. 961, m. 474; Feet of F. Div. Co. Trin. 17 Hen. VII.

[51] Chan. Inq. p.m. (Ser. 2), lxxviii, 16.

[52] G.E.C. *Peerage*, viii, 166.

consequence of the duke's attainder and execution in 1521.[53] In 1524 it was granted by Henry VIII in tail-male to Walter Devereux, Lord Ferrers,[54] afterwards Viscount Hereford, who was holding it in 1528.[55] The manor descended at his death in 1558 to his grandson Walter, son of his son Richard.[56] He was created Earl of Essex in 1572,[57] and was dealing with the manor in 1573.[58] He died seised of it in 1576, and was succeeded by his son Robert,[59] the favourite of Elizabeth, who in 1596 with his wife Frances conveyed it to the queen.[60] She, at his request, in the same year, granted the manor to Thomas Crompton and Henry Lindley.[61] From them it passed to Henry Lord Mordaunt, who died seised of it in February 1608–9.[62] The Mordaunts also held Lavendon (q.v.), with which Newton Blossomville descended for the next thirty years. In 1639 John Earl of Peterborough transferred his rights in the manor to his younger brother, Lewis Mordaunt,[62a] by whom it was leased in the following year to Humphrey Monoux of Wootton (co. Bedford) and Thomas Butler of Bedford for £500 for thirty-one years at a peppercorn rent.[63] In 1649 Thomas Farrer acquired the ownership in fee and afterwards bought up the remainder of the lease.[63a] Newton Blossomville was sequestered for the recusancy of Lewis Mordaunt, and on 4 November 1651 Thomas Farrer was summoned to prove his title.[64]

FARRER. *Argent a bend sable with three horse-shoes argent thereon.*

The manor has since descended with Cold Brayfield (q.v.), at first with the rectory and from 1720 with the manor, the seat of the Farrers, the present holder being Mr. Denis H. Farrer.

Two flour and three fulling-mills are mentioned in Newton in the 17th century. The course for boats coming from Lavendon Mills was through Costoe water into the lake water, out of that into the Loonde water and so to Newton Mills, but Thomas Bodington and others made a dam of timber, earth, gravel and stones, 300 ft. long and 10 ft. wide, to stop the passage from Costoe water. In September 1676 Thomas Farrer cut through the dam and brought an action to prove the right of way for all renting the waters for fishing or other purposes.[64a] The quarrel probably arose over the respective demarcation of the free fisheries attached to the manor[65] and to the two messuages and lands held by the Bodington family.[66]

CHURCH The church of *ST. NICHOLAS* consists of a chancel 27 ft. 6 in. by 14 ft. 6 in., north chapel 26 ft. 6 in. by 14 ft. 6 in., nave 32 ft. by 15 ft. 6 in. wide, west tower 10 ft. 6 in. square, and south porch. All these measurements are internal.

There was a late 11th-century church on the site, consisting probably of a chancel and nave, of which a few remains exist in the walls of the nave. The chancel was probably rebuilt and a north chapel added to it in the 13th century. In the middle of the 14th century the chancel was enlarged, while a little later the existing north chapel replaced the older one, and the north aisle was added to the nave. The west tower, south porch, and the embattled parapets of the nave and aisle were built early in the 15th century. The church underwent a restoration in 1862.

The chancel has a 14th-century traceried east window of three lights, with moulded jambs, mullions and head, which is central with the nave but not with the chancel. On the north side opening into the north chapel is a late 14th-century arcade of two bays with a central column. The column is quatrefoil on plan, with a moulded capital and base, and appears to be made up of re-used 13th-century material; the responds repeat the half-plan of the column. The south wall has two 14th-century two-light windows with a moulded doorway between them; the westernmost window originally had a low-side light beneath, but this is now blocked. The chancel arch, which is of mid-14th-century date, is pointed and moulded, and the responds have moulded capitals and bases. On the north wall is a plain moulded bracket, and in the south wall is a piscina with a foliated ogee head, a fluted basin, and an original oak shelf. The bracket and piscina are of 14th-century work.

The north chapel has an east window of two lights, and near it is a bracket carved in the shape of a man's head; the top is cut off flat, and it is evidently incomplete. The north window, which is of three lights with tracery under a depressed arch, is an insertion of the 15th century, while the north doorway is probably of the late 14th century. In the same wall is a tall plain locker with edges rebated for a door. An arch of two chamfered orders, with semi-octagonal responds having moulded capitals and bases, opens to the north aisle on the west. In the south wall is a 14th-century piscina similar to that in the chancel, but with a larger basin. The floor and altar-pace are of rough stone flags.

The north arcade of the nave is of two bays with chamfered arches of two orders and an octagonal column with moulded capital and base. On the plain responds are moulded corbels, that at the west end having a grotesque head carved underneath it. In the east respond is a piscina with a plain basin partly mutilated, but otherwise similar to those in the chancel and north chapel. All this work is of 14th-century date. The easternmost window in the south wall, which is of three lights with intersecting tracery, is of the same period. To the west of it is a small light with a wide semicircular rear-arch; this light, which now looks into the porch, is the only surviving window of the 11th-century nave. The pointed external head is, of course, a later repair. Just underneath it outside is a fragment of herring-bone masonry. The remaining window in the south wall is a large lancet of 13th-century date, moulded and rebated outside

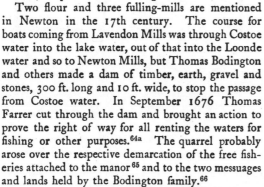

[53] Chan. Inq. p.m. (Ser. 2), lxxviii, 16.
[54] L. and P. Hen. VIII, iv (1), g. 137 (1).
[55] Recov. R. Mich. 20 Hen. VIII, m. 100.
[56] G.E.C. Peerage, iii, 284; Chan. Proc. (Ser. 2), bdle. 53, no. 13.
[57] G.E.C. loc. cit.
[58] Feet of F. Div. Co. Mich. 15 & 16 Eliz.
[59] W. and L. Inq. p.m. xviii, 39.
[60] Feet of F. Bucks. East. 38 Eliz.
[61] Pat. 38 Eliz. pt. xi; cf. Cal. S. P. Dom. 1595–7, p. 62, where the year is given as 1595.
[62] Chan. Inq. p.m. (Ser. 2), ccix, 200.
[62a] Ibid. dcxxiv, 64; Abstract of Title penes Mr. F. W. Bull.
[63] Cal. Com. for Comp. 2869.
[63a] Ibid.; Abstract of Title, loc. cit.; Chan. Proc. (Bridges Div.), bdle. 404, no. 242. [64] Cal. Com. for Comp. 2869.
[64a] Chan. Proc. (Bridges Div.), bdle. 480, no. 78.
[65] Feet of F. Bucks. East. 11 Geo. I.
[66] Ibid. Mich. 9 Will. III.

Newton Blossomville Church from the South

and set high up in the wall. The south doorway is of the 14th century. Just to the east of the doorway inside is a well-preserved stoup dating from the 15th century, with a complete projecting bowl and a pointed hollow-chamfered head.

The north aisle has a plain two-light 14th-century window and a doorway of the same date in the north wall ; the doorway is now blocked. In the west wall is a single trefoiled light of the same period.

The west tower is of three stages, the lower undivided externally, and has a south-east stair-turret, diagonal buttresses, and an embattled parapet. The ground stage has a plain vaulted ceiling with a plain uncarved central boss and moulded corbels in the angles. The tower arch is of two chamfered orders and dies into the walls without imposts. The west window of the ground stage and that of the stage above it are each of two lights, as are also the four bell-chamber windows, but the latter are set in deep external reveals. A modern ringing floor with balustrade has been inserted in the ground stage, and a vestry formed under it.

The south porch has a chamfered outer archway, two stone benches along the sides, and a small opening in the west wall, now blocked. In the gable are the remains of an old dial, above which is a small niche, much decayed, with a foiled ogee head, apparently not original.

The panelled octagonal font is of the early 15th century. Some fragments of old oak benches, probably of the 16th century, are still preserved. The pulpit, which is of the late 17th century, is hexagonal, with moulded panels, cornice and base. It is said to have been brought from another church in the 19th century.

On the floor of the north chapel is an inscription on brass commemorating Bridget wife of John Bodington, clerk (d. 1673), and on the floor of the tower is the indent of another inscription plate. In the north chapel are floor slabs to Elizabeth Garrit (d. 1694), and to William Chibnall and his wife Esther (d. 1772). In the south porch is a much worn slab to Mary wife of Richard Harbird (d. 1709).

Several fragments of early 14th-century glass are fixed in the east window of the north chapel, the best of which represents a censing angel.

There are three bells : the treble by Russell, 1719 ; the second is inscribed, 'John Hodson of Landon made mee 1658' ; and the tenor, dated 1769, which is inscribed with the names of the rector and churchwardens, is probably by Joseph Eayre of St. Neots.[67]

The communion plate includes a chalice, paten, and flagon of 1851, and a pewter flagon and paten, probably of the early 18th century, unmarked.

The registers before 1730 have been lost for many years. From 1730 to 1812 they are contained in one book which includes baptisms, burials, and marriages. There is also a terrier of the glebe, written in 1752 on one sheet of parchment.

ADVOWSON The church of Newton Blossomville, the living of which is a rectory, was assessed at £5 6s. 8d. in 1291.[68] Its value in 1535 was £9 10s. 7d., an annual pension of 12s. being paid to Clifton Reynes.[69] The first presentation recorded is that in 1262 by Alice de Blossomville,[70] lady of the manor, with which the advowson has always descended,[71] the present patron being Mr. Denis H. Farrer.

CHARITIES The Church land, the origin of which is unknown, consists of 2 acres let in allotments, producing £5 5s. yearly, which is applied towards the general church expenses.

The Clerk's allotment, consisting of about 2 acres, is occupied by the parish clerk.

NEWTON LONGVILLE OR NEWNTON LONGUEVILLE

Neutone (xi cent.); Niwentona (xii cent.); Neweton Lungevilers, Neuton Longeville (xiii cent.); Neuuentone Lungeville, Newynton Longevile (xiv cent.).

The parish has an area of 1,734 acres. Of these 373 are arable and 1,206 permanent grass.[1] The soil is light clay and the subsoil clay. The ground falls gradually from about 400ft. above the ordnance datum in the south and west to about 300 ft. in the north. The Oxford and Bletchley branch of the London and North Western railway runs through it from south-west to north-east.

The village, which is 2⅓ miles south-west of Bletchley Junction station, lies at the crossing of the roads from Buckingham to Leighton Buzzard and from Bletchley to Stewkley. The part of the village north of the former road is known as London End and that on the south as Moor End.[2] To the west of Moor End on a by-road connecting the road from Buckingham with that to Stewkley is the hamlet of Westbrook End. It is a curious fact that the majority of the houses and cottages in these three settlements date from about 1575 to 1625, indicating probably a condition of prosperity at that time. The cottages are of half-timber and usually thatched. The church stands at the south-west angle of the crossing, and immediately to the south is the Manor House, generally occupied by the lessee of New College, Oxford, though the present lessee, Mr. Richard Selby-Lowndes, now resides at Shenley Park. The present house, which was built about 1550, or earlier, incorporates part of the buildings of the alien priory at one time existing here. It is of red brick with stone dressings and a tiled roof, and originally consisted of a hall with projecting wings, to which additions were made on the eastern side. Above a reset 15th-century doorway is a moulded panel of the same date containing a 17th-century shield with the arms of New College, Oxford. Not far from the house is an early 16th-century dovecote, now somewhat dilapidated. To the south of the church is the rectory, a modern brick building incorporating fragments of an earlier house. On the eastern side of the Bletchley road, about 100 yards apart, are two farm-houses, one of the early 17th century, with a later wing at the back, while

---

[67] Cocks, *Ch. Bells of Bucks.* 537.
[68] *Pope Nich. Tax.* (Rec. Com.), 34, 41.
[69] *Valor Eccl.* (Rec. Com.), iv, 243.
[70] Harl. MS. 6950, fol. 123.
[71] Feet of F. Div. Co. Trin. 10 Chas. I ;

Add. MS. 5839, p. 283 ; Inst. Bks. (P.R.O.) ; *Clergy Lists.* A presentation was made by the Crown in March 1398-9 (*Cal. Pat.* 1396-9, p. 491).

[1] Statistics from Bd. of Agric. (1905).
[2] In the 18th century there is a reference to a Paradise End (Exch. Dep. East. 2 Geo. II, no. 11).

the other house is of two distinct dates, the southern portion belonging to the late 16th or early 17th century and the northern to a somewhat earlier date.

The school was built in 1838 and rebuilt in 1902, with accommodation for 100 children. A church-house is referred to in 1729.[3]

A little distance north of the church is the Baptist chapel at London End and at about the same distance to the south is the Methodist chapel at Moor End.

Browne Willis, writing in 1732, states that the gallows, the right to which had been held by the lords of the manor, still survived and was maintained 'for peculiarity sake.'[4] Some twelve years later the village was said to consist of seventy-eight houses and seven ale-houses.[4a] The Rev. William Cole described it in 1758 as 'a loose, disorderly, quarrelsome, litigious and drunken Place and so noted in all the country'[5]; but Cole was embittered on account of his liability to pay his predecessor's arrears of a pension due to New College, Oxford, from Bletchley Church.[5a]

An Inclosure Act was passed in 1836, the award being dated 10 November 1841.[6]

Farm House, North-east of the Rectory, Newton Longville

MANOR Ten hides in Newton which had been held in the time of Edward the Confessor by Alward Cilt were assessed in 1086 among the lands of Walter Giffard.[7] He bestowed them before his death (in 1102)[8] on the priory of St. Faith, Longueville, in Normandy, the gift being confirmed by Henry I in 1106-9,[9] by the donor's son, Walter second Earl of Buckingham, *circa* 1150, by Henry II in 1155, and by William Marshal, Earl of Pembroke, in 1200.[10] Soon after the original grant the Norman priory built a cell in

Newton, known as **Newton Longville Priory**, which enjoyed the manorial rights over this land afterwards called *NEWTON LONGVILLE MANOR*. The Prior of St. Faith, Longueville, held the manor in free alms[11] of the honour of Giffard,[12] and it remained attached to that portion of the honour which descended in the earldoms of Gloucester and Stafford.[13] After the dissolution of the priory as an alien house, the interest of the holders of the honour of Giffard became purely nominal,[14] and the grant of 1441 to New College, Oxford, was in free alms, the rent of a red rose at Midsummer being reserved to the Crown.[15] This rent was paid to Charles Earl of Tankerville and Camilla his wife in 1731.[16]

The confirmatory charter of Henry I had given the Prior of Longueville (Normandy) and his men quittance of all tolls and all dues on goods for their own use,[17] and on the strength of this the prior in 1286 claimed soc, sac, toll and theam, infangenthef, and flemensfremth, and all liberties and customs thereto belonging.[18] View of frankpledge, which was not claimed in 1254-5,[19] he asserted in 1286 to have belonged to the manor from time immemorial, as had waif, estray and quittance of suit of court and hundred.[20] The prior was not, however, considered to have made good his claim, and the liberties were taken into the king's hand.[21]

The Norman house seems to have kept in close touch with its English cell, for though the prior of the latter is returned as lord of Newton Longville in 1254-5[22] and in 1316,[23] it was the head of the French priory who appeared in a plea of trespass here against John de Preston and Geoffrey de Hardmead in 1328.[24] The English house was repeatedly in the king's hands on account of wars with France in the 14th and 15th centuries, when various grants were made by the Crown out of the issues. In 1350 a pension of £23 6s. 8d. was granted to Guy de Brian for his good service, especially in the last conflict between the king and his French adversaries at Calais, in carrying the standard against those enemies, and boldly maintaining it erect.[25] Other grants were made to Richard de la Vache in 1356,[26] and to the abbey of Nutley in 1357,[27] but in 1378 Guy de Brian renounced his pension in return for a grant elsewhere.[28] In 1377 a lease of the manor for ten years, during

[3] Exch. Dep. East. 2 Geo. II, no. 11.
[4] Add. MS. 5839, pp. 285-6.
[4a] Ibid. 5830, fol. 91b.
[5] Ibid. fol. 92.
[5a] Ibid. fol. 95.
[6] Blue Bk. *Incl. Awards,* 12.
[7] *V.C.H. Bucks.* i, 251.
[8] G.E.C. *Peerage,* ii, 62.
[9] Round, *Cal. Doc. of France,* 74.
[10] Ibid. 75, 77, 79.
[11] *Plac. de Quo Warr.* (Rec. Com.), 96.
[12] *Hund. R.* (Rec. Com.), i, 30.
[13] *Testa de Nevill* (Rec. Com.), 247;

Chan. Inq. p.m. 21 Edw. III (1st nos.), no. 59; 23 Edw. III (1st nos.), no. 169; 10 Ric. II, no. 38; 16 Ric. II, pt. i, no. 27; 22 Ric. II, no. 46; 4 Hen. IV, no. 41.
[14] The statement that the Duke of Buckingham died seised of the advowson of the priory in 1460 can have no real meaning (Chan. Inq. p.m. 38 & 39 Hen. VI, no. 59).
[15] *Cal. Pat.* 1436-41, pp. 516, 558.
[16] Recov. R. Mich. 5 Geo. II, m. 202.
[17] Round, *Cal. Doc. of France,* 74.

[18] *Plac. de Quo Warr.* (Rec. Com.), 96.
[19] *Hund. R.* (Rec. Com.), i, 30.
[20] *Plac. de Quo Warr.* (Rec. Com.), 96.
[21] Ibid.
[22] *Hund. R.* (Rec. Com.), i, 30.
[23] *Feud. Aids,* i, 109.
[24] De Banco R. Mich. 2 Edw. III, m. 269.
[25] *Cal. Close,* 1349-54, p. 257; *Cal. Pat.* 1350-4, p. 5.
[26] *Cal. Pat.* 1354-8, p. 434.
[27] Ibid. 519.
[28] Ibid. 1377-81, p. 248.

NEWTON LONGVILLE CHURCH FROM THE NORTH-EAST

NEWTON LONGVILLE CHURCH: THE INTERIOR LOOKING EAST

Newton Longville: The Manor House

the war with France, was made to Joan widow of Sir Nicholas Tamworth, and on her marriage with Sir Gilbert Talbot a fresh grant was made to the latter to hold from the end of the said term.[29] On 30 July 1390 Sir Gilbert Talbot and his wife Joan obtained another grant with licence to acquire the manor from the Prior and convent of Longueville during the war, and after the war to hold it from them for their lives at a rose rent. Sir Gilbert and his wife or the heirs of Sir Gilbert should he and his wife die during the war, were to pay £80 yearly to the Exchequer, and to maintain two monks of the Cluniac order if they could be found, otherwise two religious or two secular chaplains in the manor or priory of Newton Longville to celebrate divine service there, paying to each of them 10 marks a year with fuel and lodging, and to the king all tenths, &c.[30] By a later grant of 1411 the number of monks was reduced to one, to be sent from the Norman priory.[31] Sir Gilbert Talbot died on 6 February 1398–9 seised of the manor, leaving an only child Richard, aged forty-seven weeks, his son by Margaret, widow of Constantone de Clifton.[32] During the next forty years grants and leases of varying tenure were made of Newton Longville Manor to Sir Ralph Rocheford.[33] After his death in 1440 the king in 1441 bestowed it on the Warden and fellows of New College, Oxford.[34] This grant was confirmed in the same year and in February 1443–4 the college was successful in proving its title ;[35] the manor was excluded from the Act of Resumption of 1455.[36] Edward IV on 24 July 1461 confirmed the manor to the warden and fellows of the college,[37] by whom it has ever since been held.

In his grant of Newton to Longueville Priory Walter Giffard especially exempted all the fee of Odo there.[38] The overlordship of this part is identical with that of Newton Longville Manor, and is last mentioned in 1460.[39] A similar exemption had been made by Walter Giffard as regards Durands Fee in the parish of Great Horwood (q.v.), and both these portions, the distinction between which was not maintained, were afterwards held by one and the same tenant in the 13th century. This was Bernard de Horwood,[40] and he was succeeded by the Bradwell family, whose descent has been traced under Great Horwood. The

NEW COLLEGE, OXFORD. *Argent two cheverons sable between three roses gules.*

last representatives were the heirs of Hugh de Bradwell, living in 1460.[41]

CHURCH The church of *ST. FAITH* consists of a chancel 26 ft. 6 in. by 14 ft., north chapel 25 ft. by 11 ft. 6 in., nave 34 ft. by 16 ft. 6 in., north and south aisles 10 ft. wide, west tower 10 ft. by 9 ft. 6 in. and north and south porches. All measurements are internal.

The present building incorporates much of the material of a late 12th-century church, consisting of a chancel and aisled nave, which was almost entirely rebuilt in the course of the 14th century. About 1320 a new chancel was erected, the details of the former chancel arch being largely re-used, and a chapel was added on the north side. Some fifty years later the nave and aisles were reconstructed, the materials of the original arcades being made use of in the new work, as in the case of the chancel arch. About 1441 the church was granted to New College, Oxford, and shortly after this date a new series of alterations was entered upon. The present west tower was added, the nave walls were raised to form a clearstory, north and south porches were erected, and the chancel and chapel were altered by the

THE SMITHY, NEWTON LONGVILLE

insertion of new windows. The church was restored in 1881, and the west gallery was then removed.

The east window of the chancel is of the late 15th century ; it is of four lights with tracery under a four-centred head, and the moulded rear arch springs from re-used 14th-century corbels. At the east end of the south wall is a three-light window of about the same date, the head of which is now square, but was originally four-centred. At the opposite end of the wall is a square-headed three-light window of the same period, and between them is a small splayed and moulded mid-16th-century doorway with a four-centred head and carved spandrels. The chancel communicates with the north chapel by a 14th-century pointed arch of two chamfered orders with semi-octagonal responds having a moulded capital on the east side and a re-used angel corbel on the west. A

[29] *Cal. Pat.* 1388–92, pp. 292–3.
[30] Ibid. [31] Ibid. 1408–13, pp. 307–8.
[32] Chan. Inq. p.m. 22 Ric. II, no. 47.
[33] Add. Chart. 12652 ; *Cal. Pat.* 1401–5, pp 47, 244, 488 ; 1405–8, p. 157 ; 1408–13, pp. 307–8, 387 ; 1422–9, pp. 113, 170 ; 1436–41, p. 359.

[34] *Cal. Pat.* 1436–41, pp. 516, 558 ; *Orig. R.* (Exch. L.T.R.), 19 Hen. VI, m. 47.
[35] Memo. R. (Exch. L.T.R.), Hil. 22 Hen. VI, m. 26.
[36] *Parl. R.* v, 304.
[37] Orig. R. 1 Edw. IV, m. 52 ; *Cal. Pat.* 1461–7, p. 54.

[38] Round, *Cal. Doc. of France*, 75.
[39] Chan. Inq. p.m. 38 & 39 Hen. VI, no. 59.
[40] *Testa de Nevill* (Rec. Com.), 247.
[41] Chan. Inq. p.m. 38 & 39 Hen. VI, no. 59.

vertical joint now partially covered by plaster near the chancel arch suggests that part of the original thick east wall of the nave was left by the 14th-century re-builders. To the east of the arch to the chapel is a large locker low down on the floor level with ancient doors and lining of oak, probably of the 15th century. The semicircular attached shafts of the responds of the chancel arch have evidently been re-used from the late 12th-century arch. The northern capital is carved with foliage and grotesque animals, while the southern capital has stiff-leaf foliage. Two carved corbels of the same date have also been reset. The arch itself, which is pointed, has an outer order moulded on the west side and chamfered on the east, at the springing level of the arch on the chancel face of the responds, and an inner hollow-chamfered order with carved leaves and dog-tooth ornament.

The sanctuary within the communion rails is lined with a high modern dado of oak panelling cut away to expose two piscinæ under the sill of the south-east window. The larger piscina has a shallow projecting

chapel is of early 17th-century date. Six brackets are fixed in the wall of the chapel in various positions, one moulded, the others with heads, none probably in their original places. The roof, which is continuous with that of the north aisle, is of late 15th-century date. On the outside of the east wall is a figure in stone of a woman in early 14th-century dress standing on a moulded and carved corbel, which is supposed to represent St. Faith, the patron saint of the church. On the face of the north buttress are two 15th-century traceried panels not in their original position.

The nave arcades are each of two bays with pointed arches supported by circular columns and responds. They were rebuilt in the 14th century with the material of the late 12th-century arcades. On the north side the arches are of two chamfered orders with labels having indented edges and nail-head ornament at the lower ends and head stops. The capital of the pier has a square abacus and is carved with birds, beasts and foliage, and the base is moulded. The arches of the south arcade are moulded on the nave side and have chamfered labels with head-stops. The capital is carved with leaf ornament and the base is moulded. There are three 15th-century clearstory windows on each side, the westernmost of one light and the others of two lights, all much restored. At the north-east of the nave is the rood-loft staircase, now blocked; opposite to it on the south side is a small 14th-century opening about 3 ft. from the floor with a seg-mental pointed head and chamfered jambs, and apparently intended for a monument. It now contains the head of a knight carved in stone with a coif of banded mail of the late 13th or early 14th century, which was brought here from a house in the village. The opening has a modern label towards the nave. The low-pitched nave roof is of the 15th century; five of the stone corbels which have grotesque heads apparently belong to earlier work, but the others are modern. The east bay retains a consider-able amount of its original painted decoration.

The north aisle is lighted from the north by a 15th-century window of three lights with tracery under a pointed head and from the west by a three-light 14th-century window with plain tracery. To the east of the north window is a small locker with rebated jambs. The north doorway is of the 13th century and was evidently reset when the aisle was altered. The doorway to the rood-loft staircase at the south-east of the aisle is rebated and has a four-centred head, and to the east of it is a small trefoiled piscina with a square basin of 13th-century date reset. The south aisle is lighted from the east by a 15th-century window of four lights, and from the south and west by 15th-century windows of three lights with tracery under pointed heads. The pointed south doorway is of the same date. On the east wall is a chamfered bracket, and in the south wall is a 14th-century piscina with a trefoiled head and a fluted circular basin; near it is a small 15th-century locker

PLAN OF NEWTON LONGVILLE CHURCH

basin in a modern recess, which is flanked by three crocketed pinnacles, two on the west and one on the east side, probably reset from destroyed sedilia of the 14th century. The smaller piscina has moulded jambs and tracery of about the same date, and the basin is hidden by a modern oak shelf. The low-pitched chancel roof is of the late 15th century. The tie-beams are moulded and have carved bosses, one displaying the arms of the see of Winchester; under the wall brackets are corbels, two of which at the east end, representing human figures, are ancient, but the others are modern.

The north chapel, now used as a vestry, is lighted from the east by a late 15th-century window of three lights under a four-centred head. The eastern of the two windows in the north wall is of similar date and design, while the western window, which is also of the 15th century, is of the same number of lights, but has tracery in a pointed head. A 14th-century corbel has been reset as one of the stops of the label of the east window. The oak panelled screen sur-mounted by small balusters at the west end of the

with its original oak door. The roof is of 16th-century date.

The 15th-century west tower is of two stages with a plinth and diagonal buttresses. The tower arch is pointed and of two hollow-chamfered orders, both of which die into the side walls of the tower. The west window of two lights, the west door with a four-centred head, and the stair turret doorway, having a four-centred head, are all original. The bell-chamber is lighted by four two-light pointed windows faced with cement.

The north and south porches are both of the 15th century, and have outer doorways with square jambs and chamfered heads.

The font has a tapering circular bowl, which is probably of the 12th century but has been much reworked, and has modern carving upon it; the octagonal base also appears to be old. The oak cover is a good piece of early 17th-century work. It is eight-sided and of pyramidal form, the panels being carved with lions and unicorns, while the counterpoise is carved as a dove with outspread wings. In the north chapel are preserved two chests. The smaller one is of the early 17th century, and the styles and panels are elaborately carved; the other chest dates from the end of the same century and has moulded panels. Incorporated in a modern reading desk in the chancel are two pieces of 14th-century oak tracery, probably from the rood screen. In the north chapel are an oak bench or form and a coffin-stool with carved rails, both dating from the 17th century. A modern brass on the north wall commemorates William Grocyn, rector, the first teacher of Greek at Oxford.

There are eight bells, partly recast from an old ring of five at the expense of Gilbert Flesher of Towcester by W. & J. Taylor of Oxford, 1824. The treble and second were given in 1907 by the Rev. C. Leslie Norris, the rector; the fifth is the original second by John Briant of Hertford, 1800, and the tenor is dated 1826.

The communion plate includes a large flagon of 1638 and a large cup and standing paten of 1685, all given by Margaret Alden in the latter year, with a silk covering with 'M. A. 1685' embroidered upon it, and a small cover paten of the late 16th century.

The registers before 1812 are as follows: (i) mixed entries 1560 to 1719; (ii) baptisms and burials 1719 to 1802; (iii) baptisms and burials 1803 to 1812; (iv) marriages 1719 to 1753; (v) marriages 1754 to 1813.

ADVOWSON The church was given with the manor by Walter Giffard to Longueville Priory.[42] In 1291 it was taxed at £5 6s. 8d. and paid a pension to the Prior of Longueville of £1 6s. 8d.[43] In 1535 it paid the same pension to New College, Oxford.[44]

The patronage of the living, a rectory, has always been held with the manor, and is in the gift of New College, Oxford.

In the course of a dispute as to tithes between the rector and several parishioners in 1729 it was stated that the parsonage had been under sequestration in 1726. About 40 acres of land in the parish were said to be tithe free. Depositions as to common of pasture and custom of tithing and of payment mention the pasturing of old milch cows in Whaddon Chase.[45]

Notable rectors whom the parish owes to its connexion with New College include the Greek scholar Grocyn (rector 1446), commemorated by a tablet recently erected in the church; and Henry Cole, Dean of St. Paul's (rector 1552), who preached at the execution of Cranmer.[46]

CHARITY In connexion with the charity of Alden Fuller[47] a sum of £1 3s. 4d. was received in 1911 from the vicar of Bradwell and distributed among ten poor widows.

OLNEY with WARRINGTON

Ollaneg (x cent.); Olnei (xi cent.); Olnea (xii cent.); Ouneia, Ouneya (xiii cent.); Olneye (xiii–xv cent.).

The ancient parish of Olney covers 3,366 acres[1] on the left bank of the Ouse and contains the township of Olney, the civil parish of Olney Park Farm, and the hamlet of Warrington. The land for the most part lies low, for the River Ouse, which here suddenly bends northwards, forms both the southern and eastern boundaries of the parish. The highest point, 355 ft., is reached at the extreme north of the parish, but the greater portion of the town stands at about 172 ft. to 200 ft. above the ordnance datum and some 12 ft. to 40 ft. above the level of the stream. The parish lies principally on soil of the oolitic series, but cornbrash is found in the north and the subsoil of the higher land is Oxford Clay. Most of the land is laid down in grass, but 1,227 acres are arable and 33 acres woodland.[2] Agriculture absorbs most of the labour, although within recent years a large brewery and tanyard have been established and the making of boots and shoes is also carried on. In 1769 the town was famed for its 'considerable Manufacture of Bone-lace'[3]; the trade greatly decreased in the middle of the 19th century,[4] but has lately been revived.

In the earliest known mention of Olney the boundaries are said to run along a brook to the Ouse and along the river to Wilinford.[5] It is probably to this ford that Olney owes its origin, for the town runs northward from the river along the road from Newport Pagnell to Wellingborough, and the High Street is but a widening of this highway. The river was crossed by a ford at this point until the reign of Queen Anne, when, according to tradition, the bridge of 'wearisome but necessary length'[6] was built across the whole valley, thus making communication with the south possible throughout the year,[7] even when the river was in flood.[8] The bridge was much dilapidated and was rebuilt in 1832. At its northern

---

[42] Round, *Cal. Doc. of France*, 74.
[43] *Pope Nich. Tax.* (Rec. Com.), 33.
[44] *Valor Eccl.* (Rec. Com.), iv, 244.
[45] Exch. Dep. East. 2 Geo. II, no. 11.
[46] *Dict. Nat. Biog.*
[47] See under parish of Bradwell.
[1] This area includes a part of the Ouse.

[2] Statistics from Bd. of Agric. (1905).
[3] Defoe, *A Tour* (ed. 1769), ii, 238.
[4] *Olney and the Lace-Makers, passim.*
[5] Kemble, *Codex Dipl.* no. 621.
[6] Cowper, *The Task*, bk. iv.
[7] Wright, *The Town of Cowper* (ed. 1893), 19.

[8] For a description of Olney in winter, see *The Task*, bk. v; Wright, op. cit. 20. The Rev. Ralph Josselin, curate of Olney, describes how he was nearly drowned in the floods when travelling back from Norfolk to preach at the fair in the spring of 1640 (*Diary* [Camd. Soc.], 8).

end this bridge joined the more ancient one said to have been built in 1619,[9] and itself the successor of a bridge which was out of repair in 1334.[10] Near the five old arches an iron bridge was built in 1894.

The town is entered by Bridge Street. The shrubbery on the left of the bridge was a shallow pool in the 18th century, and across the road was the Anchor Inn, usually kept by the toll-keeper, and perhaps built on the site of the orchard next the bridge mentioned in 1425–6.[11] At its northern end Bridge Street enters the High Street, Church Street running to the east and south, and Weston Road, once Dagnall Street, running west. Still going northward the High Street enters the triangular Market Place at its south-west corner, and then, leaving it at the north, runs straight on for about 600 yds. to an open space, where it divides, one branch going north to Wellingborough, and the other east to Bedford. Modern development, chiefly due to the manufacture of shoes, has occurred in the north of the town, where the station on the Bedford and Northampton branch of the Midland railway stands. Building has also been carried on along East and West Streets, the two 'back lanes' that run parallel with the High Street on either side.

Just north of the open space at the head of the High Street is the Home Close, through which an ancient road running towards Lavendon could still be traced in 1862.[12] Home Close also contains the 'Chrysten Well' mentioned in 1556.[13] Near the Home Close in the High Street is the Castle Inn, a 17th-century house, now much restored. The Duke of York Inn, also in the High Street, bears the inscription $\frac{ME}{1682}$. In 1860 another house at this end of the town contained some interesting reliefs in stucco work wrought at the expense of 'Mr. John Brunt,' one of the king's messengers, in 1624.[14] The northern part of Olney was described in 1862 as having 'a much more ancient aspect than the south end,' many of the houses being thatched and having gable ends.[15] The description is the more remarkable, since a disastrous fire in June 1854 'consumed about 50 houses near the N.E. end of the town, 30 more being damaged.'[16] Some of the older houses, mostly of the 17th century, still stand in this quarter. The footpath that runs past the houses on either side of the High Street is a comparatively modern improvement. Until about 1790 or 1791 a stream ran from the Yardley Road down the western side of the High Street to the High Arch, a bridge now marked by a slight rise in the level of the ground. Here it was met by a second brook flowing north down the street from Spring Lane, and the combined stream then ran east to the Ouse.[17] The road was carried

on a raised causeway in the middle of the street, and this was kept in repair by the Causeway Charity, which was in existence at least as early as 1556, when the 'Cawse house' is mentioned.[18]

Standing back from the middle of the High Street, on the east side, is the Cowper Memorial Congregational Church, built in 1879 to replace the Independent Meeting-house built in 1700.[19] This congregation was formed by a secession from the Baptists, whose old meeting-house, still standing, was built in 1694 and enlarged in 1763.[20] The Baptist chapel occupies the site of Joseph Kent's barn, licensed for Presbyterian meetings in 1672,[21] and used until the revocation of the indulgence in 1678, when meetings were held at Northey in Lavendon, close to the border of both Northamptonshire and Bedfordshire.[22] Nonconformity has always been strong in Olney,[23] and the town was the scene of the labours of John Sutcliff, one of the founders of the Baptist Missionary Society, who in 1799 established a seminary for the training of missionaries in what is now No. 23 High Street.[24] William Bull (1738–1814), the Independent, frequently preached at Olney, both at the meeting-house and at the Great House, where John Newton was always glad of his help.[25] The Wesleyans built an iron chapel here in 1902, and in Silver End is an old meeting-house of the Society of Friends, now used by the Salvation Army. Owing probably to the presence of the Throckmorton family at Weston Underwood, Roman Catholicism has a footing in the neighbourhood, and in 1900 the church of Our Lady, Help of Christians, and St. Laurence was built. Adjoining the church is the convent of St. Joseph, belonging to the congregation of the Holy Ghost.

Around the market-place are several 17th and 18th-century houses of stone with tiled roofs; one on the south side bears on its modern front the date 1622 and the initials $\frac{G}{WE}$, while another on the north side has two stones built into the south-west wall, inscribed $\frac{TS}{1795}$ and $\frac{IG}{1654}$ respectively. It has altered in appearance since Cowper's day, though a few of the old buildings remain. Then as now the Bull Inn stood on the west, while opposite were the 'Royal Oak' and the 'Swan.'[25a] None of these names occur among the inns of the 15th century, but in 1556 there was an inn called the 'Cross Keys,' and mention is also made of the 'Harteshorne.'[26] In the centre of the open space stood the Shïll Hall,[27] a stone building lying north and west with a room approached by a double flight of steps. No building of this name occurs in the mediaeval surveys, but there seems little doubt that it represents the 'Mottehale in the market place' of 1440–1,[28] if not the 'Church House or Town House' of 1556.[29] In the Shill Hall Samuel Teedon

[9] Add. MS. 5839, fol. 157b.
[10] Cal. Pat. 1330–4, p. 517. An indulgence was granted towards its repair at the beginning of the 14th century (Linc. Epis. Reg. Memo. Dalderby, fol. 90 d.).
[11] Rentals and Surv. (Duchy of Lanc.), bdle. 1, no. 9.
[12] Sheahan, *Hist. and Topog. of Bucks.* 580. Potsherds of Roman ware and a bronze Mercury have been found in Ash Close, north of the Home Close (*Rec. of Bucks.* ii, 189).
[13] Ld. Rev. Misc. Bks. clxxxviii, fol. 60b. Olney was the chief manor of the Bishop of Coutances in these parts, the bishop holding it himself (*V.C.H. Bucks.*

i, 240). The Home Close was part of the demesne.
[14] *Rec. of Bucks.* ii, 197.
[15] Sheahan, op. cit. 579.
[16] *Olney Par. Reg.* (Bucks. Par. Reg. Soc.), 504.
[17] Wright, op. cit. 14.
[18] Ld. Rev. Misc. Bks. clxxxviii, fol. 58; cf. ibid. fol. 52 d.
[19] Wright, op. cit. 135–9. The Independent Meeting House was licensed for marriages in 1839 (*Lond. Gaz.* 22 Oct. 1839, p. 1969), its successor in 1881 (ibid. 20 May 1881, p. 2634).
[20] Wright, op. cit. 127.
[21] Ibid. 130; *Cal. S. P. Dom.* 1672, pp. 62, 119.

[22] Wright, op. cit. 132.
[23] *Cal. S. P. Dom.* 1635–6, p. 47; 1636–7, pp. 37, 182; 1637–8, p. 68.
[24] Wright, op. cit. 149. Sutcliff lived in No. 21.
[25] *Dict. Nat. Biog.*
[25a] There is mention of the "White Swan" in 1702 (Chanc. Proc. [Bridges Div.], bdle. 615, no. 102).
[26] Ld. Rev. Misc. Bks. clxxxviii, fol. 58, 57b.
[27] So spelt by Teedon (*Diary* [ed. T. Wright], 2), a spelling which is probably phonetic.
[28] Mins. Accts. (Duchy of Lanc.), bdle. 637, no. 10345.
[29] Ld. Rev. Misc. Bks. clxxxviii, fol. 58.

kept his school, though in 1791 the building was threatened ; in or about 1816 it was destroyed.[30] In the middle of the 18th century it was said that there was no market house here, but good shambles, successors of the 'Flescheshalles' that were repaired in 1440–1.[31]

To the north-east of the Shill Hall stood the Round House or 'lock up,' taken down in 1846.[32]

The south-east corner of the market-place is called Silver End, the inhabitants of which gave William Cowper the poet so much annoyance and amusement. No mention of Silver End has been found in mediaeval records, but it doubtless takes its name from the Silver Street Lane mentioned in 1556.[33] Cowper's house, far from being 'deep in the abyss of Silver End,' stands near the centre of the southern side of the market-place, and in his day was known as Orchard Side. It is an 18th-century building of three stories with a red brick front and slate roof. After varying fortunes, the house was presented to the town by Mr. W. H. Collingridge on 25 April 1900, the centenary of Cowper's death.[34] The day was celebrated with great ceremony, and the building was formally opened as a Cowper and Newton Museum, the property being vested in eight trustees.

On 16 September 1767, two days after Cowper and Mrs. Unwin reached Olney, Newton wrote to Lord Dartmouth that the house was small and cut 'a rueful appearance, having been for a long time empty and in the hands of very poor tenants.'[35] His hopes that when it was furbished up it would be 'tolerable considering the place' do not seem to have been fulfilled, for Unwin was shocked when he saw the house and thought it like a prison.[36] Internally it was comfortable enough. While it was used as the first infants' school certain alterations were made, but some of the rooms have been recently restored. At the back was the greenhouse where Cowper wrote *John Gilpin*,[37] and at the end of the garden the summer-house. The garden ran south, and was separated from that of the vicarage by an orchard, now called the Guinea Field, from the circumstance that Cowper and Newton paid a guinea yearly for right of way between the gardens, thus avoiding a walk through the town.

The vicarage, a building of two stories and attics with a dentil cornice and tiled roof, lies on the north side of Church Street and a short distance from the end of Bridge Street. William Johnson rebuilt the house in the middle of the 17th century, but little of this structure remains. The present vicarage is the 'comfortable habitation' built by Lord Dartmouth for John Newton (1725–1807), the former slaver, who was destined to become one of the leading spirits of the Evangelical revival in the Church of England. Newton was ordained

deacon in April 1764 and priest two months later, having through the influence of Lord Dartmouth secured a title to the curacy of Olney under the non-resident rector, Moses Brown, author of *Angling Sports*.[38] The study in which Newton wrote the *Letters of Omicron* and *Cardiphonia* is an attic at the east end of the house.[39] Over the mantelpiece may still be seen the texts [40] Newton caused to be painted there when he took possession of the house.[41] Newton drew round him a distinguished company of friends and with Cowper's aid organized much parish work and many services.

A little beyond the vicarage is the water-mill, probably on the site of that mill which in 1086 was worth to the lord 40s. and 200 eels.[42] There were two mills appurtenant to the manor in February 1343–4,

COWPER'S SUMMER HOUSE, OLNEY

but only one is mentioned in 1411–12.[43] The mill was let at farm in 1440–1,[44] and this policy was continued by the Crown in the 16th and 17th centuries.

Just across the road from the vicarage and between the mill and the church stood the Great House, an E-shaped building of three stories with stone-mullioned windows, built before 1624.[45] It seems possible that

[30] Teedon, loc. cit. ; T. Wright, op. cit. 12, 14.

[31] Mins. Accts. (Duchy of Lanc.), bdle. 637, no. 10345.

[32] Wright, op. cit. 14.

[33] Ld. Rev. Misc. Bks. clxxxviii, fol. 56.

[34] *Olney Par. Reg.* (Bucks. Par. Reg. Soc.), 506. The house originally had battlements (Wright, op. cit. 2).

[35] *MSS. of Lord Dartmouth* (Hist. MSS. Com.), iii, 183.

[36] Cowper, *Corresp.* (ed. Wright), iii, 63.

[37] Wright, op. cit. 116.

[38] *Dict. Nat. Biog.*

[39] Wright, op. cit. 37.

[40] 'Since thou was precious in my sight, thou hast been honourable' (Isa. xliii, 4). 'But thou shalt remember that thou was a bondman in the land of

Egypt, and the Lord thy God redeemed thee' (Deut. xv, 15).

[41] *MSS. of Lord Dartmouth* (Hist. MSS. Com.), iii, 185. [42] *V.C.H. Bucks.* i, 240.

[43] Chan. Inq. p.m. 17 Edw. III (1st nos.), no. 59 ; Mins. Accts. (Duchy of Lanc.), bdle. 637, no. 10344.

[44] Mins. Accts. (Duchy of Lanc.), bdle. 637, no. 10345.

[45] Wright, op. cit. 33 n.

this occupied the site of 'the old parsonage' mentioned in 1503 [46] and of the tenement of the rector which in 1556 was certainly on this side of the road.[47] The house was enlarged by William Johnson in the middle of the 17th century,[48] and with the rectory came into the hands of Lord Dartmouth,[49] who placed its rooms at Newton's disposal for services and meetings.[50] It was for these services that Cowper and Newton wrote some of the 'Olney Hymns'[51] which include 'How sweet the name of Jesus sounds' and 'God moves in a mysterious way.' Later the house was inhabited by the Rev. Henry Gauntlett, the Evangelical divine, who was vicar here from 1815 to 1833.[52] It was afterwards deserted, and, becoming ruinous, was pulled down before 1857.[53]

Close to the church is a field called The Lordship Close. Though all memory of their origin has been lost, the foundations traceable here are probably those of 'the lordship' which was standing until at least the reign of Charles II.[54] William Byfield was in possession

though formerly extra-parochial,[58] it is now included in the ecclesiastical parish of Olney. It lay on the extreme northern border of the parish, with 'the beastes pasture' on the south-east and the common arable fields to the south and south-west.[59] In the reign of Elizabeth the park was paled, and in 1608 contained 3,854 trees.[60] Sylle woode (Seley wode, xv cent.) lay at the extreme south-west of the park, while 45 acres north of the Lodge were known as the Great Grove.[61] The park came with the manor into the possession of the Crown, and the office of keeper was granted to various distinguished persons, including Arthur Lord Grey de Wilton (1536–93) and Christopher Lord Hatton.[62] In 1640 the Earl of Northampton was staying at the Lodge,[63] which, a few years later, was described as built of timber and stone very strongly and covered with tile.[64] It contained a hall, parlour and small buttery adjoining; 'above stares in the first Storry three chambers and in the second Storry two chambers and a clossett there, and in another Rainge of Buildings standinge on the West side of the sayd Howse.'[65] At the time of the Commonwealth Survey there were no deer, but 'all that game of Conneys beinge in the parke' were valued at £10.[66]

Lying among the fields close to the boundary of Warrington is Olney Hyde.[67] Though now only a farm, it was evidently of more importance in the middle ages, for it was described as a hamlet in 1353,[68] and in 1411–12 there were twelve customary tenants as well as freemen and cottagers.[69]

OLNEY PARK FARM

of a capital messuage in 1302,[55] and in February 1343–4 it was described as having but a dilapidated dovecote and no garden.[56]

The extremely restricted character of the site, hemmed in between the river, the high road and the rectory, probably led to the formation of Olney Park by Ralph Lord Basset under licence obtained in 1374.[57] The tract inclosed now forms the civil parish of Olney Park Farm and contains 206 acres;

The township of Warrington contains 1,008 acres and stretches down to the river; it is well-wooded. The hamlet is small, but contains several cottages of interest. The Earl of Lincoln had a messuage here which was broken into in 1285–6.[70] The house is again mentioned in 1294, when it and its whole inclosure were valued at 13s. 4d.[71] In the 18th century the hall was the residence of a branch of the Throckmorton family.[72]

[46] Mins. Accts. Hen. VII, no. 29.
[47] Ld. Rev. Misc. Bks. clxxxviii, fol. 48.
[48] Wright, op. cit. 32.
[49] See below.
[50] MSS. of Lord Dartmouth (Hist. MSS. Com.), iii, 186, 190.
[51] First published in 1779. Newton had published his Sermons preached in the Parish Church of Olney in 1767.
[52] Dict. Nat. Biog.
[53] Sunday at Home, 1857, p. 696. Wright thinks that it was pulled down in or about 1830 (op. cit. 78).
[54] Lay Subs. R. bdle. 80, no. 349.
[55] Chan. Inq. p.m. 30 Edw. I, no. 45.

[56] Ibid. 17 Edw. III (1st nos.), no. 59.
[57] Inq. a.q.d. file 384, no. 12.
[58] Parl. Surv. Bucks. no. 14.
[59] Duchy of Lancaster Maps and Plans, no. 41. The common fields of Olney were inclosed under an award of February 1768 (Com. Pleas D. Enr. Trin. 8 Geo. III, m. 110).
[60] Rentals and Surv. (Duchy of Lanc.), bdle. 1, no. 10.
[61] Ibid.
[62] Dict. Nat. Biog.
[63] Hist. MSS. Com. Rep. xii, App. ix, p. 491.
[64] Parl. Surv. Bucks. no. 14.

[65] Ibid.   [66] Ibid.
[67] It is mentioned incidentally in 1261–2 (Assize R. 58, m. 30; cf. ibid. 60, m. 27).
[68] Chan. Inq. p.m. 27 Edw. III (1st nos.), no. 43.
[69] Mins. Accts. (Duchy of Lanc.), bdle. 637, no. 10344; cf. ibid. no. 10345.
[70] Assize R. 68, m. 37 d.
[71] Inq. a.q.d. file 21, no. 4. There were 94 a. arable land and 12 a. pasture in demesne; ten customary tenants held 10 virgates and all services had been commuted.
[72] See below.

Very little is known of the mesne *BOROUGH* borough of Olney, the lordship of which followed the descent of the manor.[73] Though possibly in existence at an earlier date, it is first definitely found in 1237,[74] and from this date the vill regularly made separate presentments before the justices in eyre. The number of the early burgage tenements seems to have been fifty-six.[75] Each of these paid 1*s*. in 1302,[75a] but a readjustment of rents was made in 1425 or 1426.[76] In 1440–1 the tenements were usually held as half burgages at 8*d*. or 9*d*. rent, with a further sum of 6*d*. for commuted works.[77] These half burgages were still usual in 1556, but the rents were then very varied and ranged from 3*s*. 4½*d*. to ½*d*.,[78] the amount probably being determined by the quantity of land held beyond the curtilage. The position of these burgages is not known, though they certainly stretched along the High Street, and were also found in Above the Bere Lane, Jeffreys Lane and Silver Street Lane.[79] From the 18th-century evidence[80] it seems probable that the High Arch was the northern limit of the borough. The large number of 13th and 14th-century fines of small quantities of land in Olney would seem to show that the burgesses had power to alienate their holdings[81]; in the 15th century all leases were entered on the rolls of the court of the borough.[82]

The borough courts or portmotes were held on a Tuesday at intervals roughly of three weeks, a fact suggestive of their origin in the manorial court.[83] At this court were heard pleas of debt and trespass. Four great portmotes and sixteen portmotes sat in 1497–8, when the perquisites were 22*s*. 2*d*.[84] A great portmote was held on the Tuesdays following the feasts of St. Denis (9 October), St. Hilary (13 January), St. Ambrose (4 April), and SS. Peter and Paul (29 June).[85] At the first of these courts the officers for the year were elected and sworn in, while as elsewhere presentments were made by each according to his office: thus the constables presented assaults, the ale-tasters presented breaches of the assize of ale, and the tithing men nuisances.[86] At this court also the holders of burgages paid relief and did fealty.[87]

The affairs of the borough were administered by two reeves (*prepositi*),[88] and there was also a body of twelve who on one occasion ordered the reeves to hale an offender from the vill under penalty of 20*s*.[89] The reeves had power to distrain for debt. Two ale-tasters were also appointed as well as two market tasters,[90] six tithing men, three for the vill and three for the fields, and a hayward. Two constables were also sworn in as officers of the king.[91]

Though the fact is not definitely stated, it seems probable that the burgesses were the farmers of the toll of the fair and market-place.[92]

The Monday market was prescriptive and was first mentioned in January 1205–6.[93] It was still held on Monday in the middle of the 18th century,[94] but during the second half of the 19th century it fell into decay and is now held on Thursdays fortnightly. The fair on Easter Monday is also prescriptive, but licence for the fair now known as the 'Cherry Fair' on 29 June[95] was obtained by Ralph Lord Basset in 1316 for the vigil, feast and morrow of St. Peter and St. Paul.[96]

Although the earliest mention of *MANORS OLNEY* occurs in the grant of 10 hides here in 979 by King Ethelred to his kinsman Elfere,[97] the only other fact of its pre-Conquest history that has survived is that in the reign of Edward the Confessor the 'manor' here was held by Borret, an important Northamptonshire thegn.[98] Borret's land here as elsewhere was granted to the Bishop of Coutances before 1086, when it was assessed at 10 hides, of which 3 hides were on the bishop's demesne.[99] The bishop's lands passed as forfeit to the Crown; Olney was in the king's hands in 1162–3 and until at least 1194–5.[100] Between that date and January 1205–6 it was granted to Randal (de Blondevill) Earl of Chester.[1] Randal, who was one of the chief supporters of King John and of Henry III, obtained a quittance of scutage for a fee here in 1214–15,[2] and was returned as holding two fees in Olney in 1217–18.[3] Being childless he resigned his earldom of Lincoln to Hawise his sister at some time between April 1231 and his death in October 1232.[4] His lands were divided among his four sisters[5] or their descendants, Olney being part of the 500 librates of land that formed the share of Hugh (Daubeney) Earl of Arundel,[6] surviving son and heir of Mabel wife of William Earl of Arundel, while Warrington passed to Hawise.[7]

---

[73] Ibid.

[74] Assize R. 56, m. 36.

[75] Chan. Inq. p.m. 30 Edw. I, no. 45, i.e., fourteen to the share of each of the co-heirs.   [75a] Ibid.

[76] Mins. Accts. (Duchy of Lanc.), bdle. 637, no. 10345.

[77] Ibid.

[78] Ld. Rev. Misc Bks. clxxxviii, fol. 48–58.

[79] Ibid.

[80] Cowper, *Corresp.* (ed. Wright), ii, 123.

[81] e.g. Feet of F. Bucks. 4 John, no. 29; 49 Hen. III, no. 9; 55 Hen. III, no. 1; 33 Edw. I, no. 13; 8 Edw. II, no. 28; Assize R. 60, m. 3; De Banco R. Mich. 2 Edw. III, m. 324 d.; Chan. Inq. p.m 5 Edw. III (1st nos.), no. 73.

[82] Mins. Accts. (Duchy of Lanc.), bdle. 637, no. 10345; Ct. R. (Duchy of Lanc.), bdle. i, no. 7.

[83] Ct. R. (Duchy of Lanc.), bdle. i, no. 7. These rolls are assigned in the P.R.O. list by a slip of the pen to the reign of Henry VIII.

[84] Ibid.

[85] Ibid. Four of the lesser portmotes were held on the same day as the great portmotes, but apparently were distinct from them. The lesser portmotes were usually held on the same day as the halmote courts, but not invariably.

[86] Ibid. There are some indications that the great portmote was held by the steward of the manor.

[87] Ibid.

[88] Ibid. i. In October 1497 the reeves were John Wylde, chaplain, and Henry Fermour.

[89] Ibid.

[90] The tasters of bread and ale were sometimes women.

[91] Ct. R. (Duchy of Lanc.), bdle. i, no. 7.

[92] Ibid.; Mins. Accts. (Duchy of Lanc.), bdle. 637, no. 10344, &c.

[93] Rot. Lit. Claus. (Rec. Com.), i, 531.

[94] Add. MS. 5839, fol. 157*b*.

[95] Cf. Cowper, *Corresp.* (ed. Wright), i, 149; Add. MS. 5839, fol. 157 *b*.

[96] Cal. Chart. R. 1300–26, p. 306.

[97] Kemble, *Codex Dipl.* no. 621.

[98] *V.C.H. Bucks.* i, 217, 240; *V.C.H. Beds.* i, 195–6. Under him a sokeman held 1½ virgates, with power to sell.

[99] *V.C.H. Bucks.* i, 240.

[100] Pipe R. 9 Hen. II (Pipe R. Soc.), 18; in 1179–80 the sheriff rendered account of 12*d*. from a knight's fee here (ibid. 26 *Hen. II*, 125); Pipe R. 6 Ric. I, m. 2 d.; Red Bk. *of* Exch. (Rolls Ser.), 39, 63.

[1] Rot. Lit. Claus. (Rec. Com.), i, 531.

[2] Pipe R. 16 John, m. 2.

[3] Ibid. 2 Hen. III, m. 6 d.

[4] Matthew Paris, *Hist. Angl.* (Rolls Ser.), ii, 349; G.E.C. *Complete Peerage*, ii, 224.

[5] G.E.C. *Peerage*, ii, 224, 225 n. (a); Wrottesley, *Ped. from Plea R.* 532. The other sisters were Maud wife of David Earl of Huntingdon and Agnes wife of William Ferrers, Earl of Derby. For Randal's lands here see Mins. Accts. (Gen. Ser.), bdle. 1117, no. 13.

[6] Matthew Paris, loc. cit.

[7] See below.

Hugh Daubeney was holding three-fourths of a fee in Olney in or about 1234–5 [8]; he died childless in 1243,[9] leaving four sisters and co-heirs, Mabel, Nichole, Cecily and Isabel.[10] Olney fell to the share of Nichole wife of Roger de Somery, but was granted to Isabel, Hugh's widow, in dower, and she held it until her death in 1282.[11] Meanwhile both Nichole and Roger had died; their son Ralph predeceased them, his inheritance passing to his four sisters [12]: Margaret widow of Ralph Basset the younger and wife of Ralph de Cromwell, Joan wife of John Lestrange, Mabel (or Elizabeth) wife of Walter de Sully, and Maud wife of Henry de Erdington.[13] The manor was delivered to the co-heirs or their representatives for a season in 1282, but complete livery was delayed perhaps until the full age of all the co-heirs.[14] It is not evident that the Lestranges obtained any permanent interest here,[15] for the manor was apparently held for some years in common by the families of Basset, Sully and Erdington.

Henry de Erdington was dead before December 1282,[16] and by the spring of 1285–6 Maud had married William de Byfield without royal licence.[17] William seems to have survived his wife and lived until about 1302, when Maud's son, Henry de Erdington, was aged twenty-four.[18] Henry may possibly have quit-claimed his interests to the Basset family, for no further mention is found of him in connexion with this place. Short-lived, also, was the interest of Mabel and Walter de Sully. Walter died before the beginning of 1285–6, when her land in the hundred of Bonestou was valued at £16.[19] Before 1310 Mabel and her son Raymond de Sully granted their fourth part of the manor to Philip de Burley for life.[20] Mabel died in or about 1312,[21] and Philip was returned as one of the lords of the vill in 1316.[22] He was still holding at Raymond's death about a year later, when a reversionary interest was inherited by Raymond's daughter Elizabeth, wife of William de Brus (Brewose).[23] William and Elizabeth were in possession of one-fourth of a knight's fee here in 1346.[24]

Margaret, the eldest daughter and co-heir of Roger de Somery,[25] married Ralph Basset, Lord Basset of Drayton, by whom she had a son and heir Ralph.[26] Her husband died in 1265,[27] and she then married Ralph de Cromwell, who was living in the spring of 1285–6.[28] Before June 1293 she had entered the religious life.[29] Ralph Basset, her son and heir, died 31 December 1299, and was succeeded by Ralph his son.[30] Ralph was returned as one of the three joint lords of the vill in 1316,[31] and took a considerable interest in Olney, where he received a grant of free warren in 1330.[32] Olney was one of the manors included in the elaborate marriage settlement made by him in 1339,[33] and from this time it followed the descent of the manor of Hanslope (q.v.), coming into the possession of the Beauchamps, Earls of Warwick. With other manors it was quitclaimed by Anne Countess of Warwick in the spring of 1487–8 to Henry VII,[34] who, however, restored Olney to her for life two years afterwards.[35] She died before 4 December 1492,[36] when it reverted to the Crown.[36a] In 1548 Edward VI granted Olney to the Princess Mary for life,[37] and it was the subject of various leases [37a] until the spring of 1628–9, when it formed part of the vast grant made by Charles I to the citizens of London.[38]

Some ten years later the manor was purchased from the trustees by Richard Nicoll, a Turkey merchant of London, from whom it passed to his son William Nicoll, and was then inherited by his son Richard Nicoll of Norbiton (co. Surrey).[39] Richard left two daughters and co-heirs, of whom Judith married George Gounter of Racton (co. Sussex),[40] and Frances remained a spinster. Judith had one son, Sir Charles Gounter Nicoll, K.B., of Wherwell (Hampshire), but he predeceased his mother in 1733,[41] leaving no male issue. On her death in or about 1737 Judith left all her Buckinghamshire manors to her daughter Catherine, wife of Sir Henry Maynard, bart., of Walthamstow, with remainder to Catherine's son William and his issue and contingent remainder to Elizabeth and Frances Katharine,

[8] *Testa de Nevill* (Rec. Com.), 261; cf. ibid. 259.
[9] G.E.C. *Peerage*, i, 144; Wrottesley, op. cit. 531–2.
[10] Wrottesley, loc. cit. In 1285–6 the co-heirs of Nichole and Roger de Somery claimed to hold the manor in purparty with the remaining co-heirs of Hugh Daubeney, viz., Robert de Tattershall, Roger de Mohaut, and Richard Fitz Alan (*Plac. de Quo Warr.* [Rec. Com.], 91).
[11] *Hund. R.* (Rec. Com.), i, 29; G.E.C. loc. cit.
[12] Wrottesley, op. cit. 532.
[13] Ibid.
[14] *Cal. Fine R.* 1272–1307, pp. 176, 189; *Abbrev. Rot. Orig.* (Rec. Com.), i, 43.
[15] They, with the other co-heirs of the Somerys, claimed to hold view of frank-pledge in 1285–6 (*Plac. de Quo Warr.* [Rec. Com.], 91).
[16] *Cal. Fine R.* 1272–1307, p. 176.
[17] Assize R. 68, m. 37 d. William afterwards paid a fine for this offence.
[18] Chan. Inq. p.m. 30 Edw. I, no. 45.
[19] Assize R. 68, m. 37 d.
[20] *Cal. Pat.* 1307–13, p. 222; cf. *Abbrev. Rot. Orig.* (Rec. Com.), i, 171 Chan. Inq. p.m. 5 Edw. II, no. 12.
[21] Chan. Inq. p.m. 5 Edw. II, no. 12.

[22] *Feud. Aids*, i, 110.
[23] Chan. Inq. p.m. 10 Edw. II, no. 52.
[24] *Feud. Aids*, i, 133.
[25] Wrottesley, op. cit. 531.
[26] *Cal. Close*, 1288–96, p. 288.
[27] *Cal. Pat.* 1258–66, pp. 434, 497.
[28] *Plac. de Quo Warr.* (Rec. Com.), 91.
[29] *Cal. Close*, 1288–96, p. 288.
[30] G.E.C. *Peerage*, i, 257; cf. *Cal. Fine R.* 1272–1307, p. 425.
[31] *Feud. Aids*, i, 110. See below. When going on foreign service in 1323 he appointed the parson of Olney one of his two attorneys (*Cal. Pat.* 1321–4, p. 294).
[32] Chart. R. 4 Edw. III, m. 34.
[33] See Hanslope. The manor of Olney, however, was held in dower by Joan Lady Basset until her death in 1402 (Chan. Inq. p.m. 4 Hen. IV, no. 38) and was soon after the subject of a settlement by Richard Earl of Warwick (*Cal. Pat.* 1401–5, pp. 241, 247). In 1396 Henry Lord Grey de Wilton died seised of one-fourth of the manor (Chan. Inq. p.m. 19 Ric. II, no. 29), and this seems to represent the whole Basset portion, as Joan Lady Basset held one-third of this fourth in dower (ibid.; Close, 20 Ric. II, pt. i, m. 33 d.). Lord Grey was a great-grandson of John Grey and his wife Maud,

daughter of Ralph and Margaret Basset (G.E.C. *Peerage*, iv, 111), but no mention of Olney has been found among the possessions of his predecessors or of his son and heir. Moreover, it was found by an inquisition of 1397 that his right to this fourth part was unknown to the jurors (Chan. Inq. p.m. 21 Ric. II, no. 137, m. 6 b). In 1411–12, however, a fourth part of the market tolls was reserved to Richard Lord Grey (Mins. Accts. [Duchy of Lanc.], bdle. 637, no. 10344).
[34] Feet of F. Div. Co. Hil. 3 Hen. VII.
[35] *Cal. Pat.* 1485–94, p. 298.
[36] Ibid. 410.
[36a] cf. *L. and P. Hen. VIII*, xvi, g. 305 (32).
[37] Pat. 2 Edw. VI, pt. v, m. 32.
[37a] Pat. 34 Eliz. pt. iv; Duchy of Lanc. Misc. Bks. xxv, fol. 43 d., 81 d. Pat. 1 Chas. I, pt. iv, no. 14.
[38] Pat. 4 Chas. I, pt. xxxv; Feet of F. Div. Co. Hil. 4 Chas. I. The reserved rent of £58 17s. 2¾d. was granted by Charles II in March 1662–3 to Edward Earl of Sandwich (Duchy of Lanc. Misc. Bks. xxiv, fol. 164).
[39] Add. MS. 5839, fol. 158; Berry, *Sussex Gen.* 13.
[40] Berry, loc. cit.
[41] *Musgrave's Obit.* (Harl. Soc.), iv, 293.

daughters of Sir Charles Gounter Nicoll.[41a] Catherine survived her husband and died in 1744,[42] when her lands descended to her son Sir William Maynard, bart. Meanwhile Frances Nicoll, by her will proved in 1743, had left her moiety of the manors of Olney, Warrington, &c., to Catherine for life, with remainder to Elizabeth and Frances Katharine Gounter Nicoll and their issue.[43] Elizabeth died shortly afterwards,[44] Frances Katharine being her heir. In 1755 she married William (Legge) second Earl of Dartmouth,[45] who is said to have obtained the remaining moiety of the manors from Sir William Maynard at about the time of the marriage.[46]

LEGGE, Earl of Dartmouth. *Azure a hart's head cabossed argent.*

Lord Dartmouth's great interest in the Evangelical Revival earned him the name of the Psalm Singer,[47] and though Colonial Secretary in 1772–5 and Lord Privy Seal in 1775–82 he found opportunity for interest in the schemes of Newton and for correspondence with the leading members of the seriously-minded society of his day.[48] He died in 1801,[49] and was succeeded by his son George third Earl of Dartmouth, President of the India Board in 1801, and afterwards Lord Warden of the Stannaries. On his death in 1810 the title and estates passed to his son William, on whose death in 1853 they devolved on William Walter, his eldest surviving son.[50] The fifth earl died in 1891, when he was succeeded by his son William Heneage, Earl of Dartmouth, sometime member of Parliament for West Kent and for Lewisham. His son and heir William Viscount Lewisham, who since 1910 has represented West Bromwich in Parliament, is the present lord of the manor.

Olney had its full complement of manorial courts. View of frankpledge was held once a year at the close of the 13th century,[51] and this liberty, together with those of waifs and quittance of suit at the county and hundred courts, was claimed by the lords of the manor in the spring of 1285–6.[52] In 1411–12 the perquisites of the view were said to be usually 64s. 10d.,[53] but the value greatly decreased within the next hundred years.[54] Pleas of debt were heard in the halmote, which sat sixteen times in 1497–8, when the perquisites amounted to 103s. 8d.[55] The number of

courts varied, but in 1440 only four halmotes were held, and there was one court leet held on the feast of the Decollation of St. John Baptist, besides ten courts of freemen.[56] At a later date the courts leet and baron were held once yearly at the Bull Inn.

No mention of *WARRINGTON* (Wardington, Wardyngton, xiii–xvii cent.) is found in the Domesday Survey, and it appears to have been assessed with Olney, which it followed in descent until the death of Randal de Blondevill, Earl of Chester. It then fell to the share of Hawise, the earl's fourth sister. Margaret, only child of Hawise by her husband Robert de Quincy, married John de Lacy, who was created Earl of Lincoln in 1232.[57] He died in 1240, and was succeeded by his son Edmund, a minor. On his death in 1257 Warrington passed to his son Henry Earl of Lincoln,[58] who obtained a grant of free warren in his demesne lands here in 1294.[59] In this same year Henry received licence to lease the manor for life to whomsoever he would.[60] On his death in February 1310–11 he was succeeded by Alice his daughter, who married Thomas, son of Edmund 'Crouchback,' younger son of Henry III.[61] Thomas, who succeeded his father as Earl of Lancaster in 1296,[62] was one of the three joint lords of Olney in 1316.[63] His rebellion cost him his head in March 1321–2, and his lands were then seized by the Crown. His brother

LANCASTER. *ENG-LAND with the difference of a label of FRANCE.*

Henry became Earl of Lancaster in March 1326–7 on the reversal of the attainder,[64] and had a daughter Mary, whose son Henry Percy Earl of Northumberland was in 1390 overlord of at least a portion of Warrington.[65] Henry son of Henry Earl of Lancaster succeeded his father in 1345, and was created Earl of Lincoln in 1349 and Duke of Lancaster in March 1350–1.[66] He died in March 1360–1, when his wide lands passed to Blanche his daughter, wife of John of Gaunt. At some date before 1353,[67] however, the manor of Warrington came into the possession of the Bassets, who remained in possession until the death of Ralph Lord Basset in 1390.[68] It was then seized,[69] unjustly, as it was said, but probably under a writ of formedon or entail by Henry Earl of Derby, evidently in right of his inheritance

[41a] Berry, loc. cit.; cf. Add. MS. 5839, fol. 221.

[42] G.E.C. *Baronetage*, iv, 126; P.C.C. 288 Anstis.

[43] P.C.C. 319 Boycott.

[44] Berry, op. cit. 13.

[45] G.E.C. *Peerage*, iii, 29.

[46] Add. MS. 5839, fol. 156, 221. Sir William had barred the entail in 1747 (Recov. R. East. 20 Geo. II, m. 299).

[47] Wraxall, *Hist. Mem.* (Ed. Wheatley), iii, 268.

[48] See above.

[49] G.E.C. loc. cit.

[50] Ibid. 29–30.

[51] *Hund. R.* (Rec. Com.), i, 29. The administrative officers of the manor included a steward, who held the most important courts and in 1492 received a fee of 40s.; a sub-steward, who held the halmotes, and the bailiff of the manor (Mins. Accts. [Duchy of Lanc.], bdle.

637, no. 10348). There were also a park-keeper and a collector of rents of Olney and la Hyde (ibid. no. 10344). In 1285–6 the bailiff of Olney was accused of having taken a bribe to remove men from the assize (Assize R. 68, m. 37 d.).

[52] *Plac. de Quo Warr.* (Rec. Com.), 91.

[53] Mins. Accts. (Duchy of Lanc.), bdle. 637, no. 10344.

[54] cf. Ibid. no. 10348.

[55] Ct. R. (Duchy of Lanc.), bdle. 1, no. 7.

[56] Mins. Accts. (Duchy of Lanc.), bdle. 637, no. 10345.

[57] G.E.C. *Complete Peerage*, v, 90.

[58] Ibid.

[59] *Cal. Chart. R.* 1257–1300, p. 436.

[60] Inq. a.q.d. file 21, no. 4; *Cal. Pat.* 1292–1301, p. 77.

[61] G.E.C. *Peerage*, v, 91.

[62] Ibid.

[63] *Feud. Aids*, i, 110.

[64] G.E.C. *Peerage*, v, 6.

[65] Ibid. vi, 83; Chan. Inq. p.m. 14 Ric. II, no. 9.

[66] G.E.C. *Peerage*, v, 6–7.

[67] Chan. Inq. p.m. 27 Edw. III (1st nos.), no. 43.

[68] See above. In 1373 Ralph Lord Basset took steps to alienate the manor to Lavendon Abbey (Inq. a.q.d. file 381, no. 11), but the transaction was never completed. Under Ralph's will the manor passed to his nephew, Sir Hugh de Shirley, and it was actually quitclaimed to him by Ralph's heir Edmund Earl of Stafford in 1403 (*Cat. of Anct. D.* v, 133, 135; Chan. Inq. p.m. 14 Ric. II, no. 9), Warrington not being included in the settlement of 1339.

[69] Chan. Inq. p.m. 21 Ric. II, no. 137, m. 6b; cf. Mins. Accts. (Duchy of Lanc.), bdle. 637, no. 10345.

through his mother, the Duchess Blanche.[70] Henry succeeded his father in the duchy of Lancaster in February 1398–9, and in September ascended the throne as Henry IV.[71] From this time Warrington has formed part of the duchy of Lancaster.

In February 1407–8 Henry ordered the manor and vill of Warrington to be delivered to Nicholas Bradshaw, to be held by him for life,[72] and in 1415 it was vested in feoffees.[73] In 1604 the manor was granted in fee to Sir George Throckmorton,[74] lord of Fulbrook in Hogshaw (q.v.). He died seised in 1612, having settled the site of the manor in February 1607–8 on himself for life, with remainder to Raphael his son and Elizabeth his wife for life, with remainder to George their son.[75] Raphael Throckmorton obtained livery in 1618.[76] John Throckmorton was in possession of the manor in 1645,[77] and appears to have been living here in 1675.[78]

THROCKMORTON.
Gules a cheveron argent charged with three gimel bars sable.

He, or another of his name, died at Warrington in 1693,[79] and was apparently succeeded by another John Throckmorton, in possession of the manor in 1710, when a settlement was made.[80] Robert son of John was baptized three years later.[81] The Throckmortons parted with the manor not long afterwards, and in 1767 it was in the hands of Lord Dartmouth.[82] It was apparently again sold, for in 1798 it was the property of William Farrer of Cold Brayfield[82a] q.v.).

The reputed manor of *WHITHILLS* (Wightles, xvii cent.) is first mentioned in the 16th century. It seems to have derived its name from the family of Wighthill, lords of Whitehill in the parish of Tackley (co. Oxon.). Robert Wighthill, the first to be mentioned in connexion with Olney, was in 1474 pardoned for having been concerned in the forgery and publication of a deed relating to land in this parish and in Warrington, Weston Underwood and Sherington.[83] On his second marriage Robert settled the Buckinghamshire lands on Margaret his wife for life, but this arrangement was cancelled in 1523, when the Oxfordshire manor was settled on Margaret, with reversion to Joan wife of Owen Whitton and daughter of Robert and Margaret.[84] Robert died in

the autumn of that year, leaving, by his first marriage, a daughter, Bridget, aged fifty.[85] Bridget and her sister Elizabeth immediately complained of having been wronged by Margaret and Joan, seeing that the Oxfordshire manor was of greater value than the lands in Buckinghamshire.[86] It seems possible that some exchange was afterwards made, for no mention of Bridget or Elizabeth's heirs[87] has been found in connexion with this place, and early in 1569–70 Joan Whitton, widow, conveyed this manor of Whithills to George Whitton.[88] In April 1575 George sued Thomas Osborne and Edward Bromley for the detention of deeds relating to the manor,[89] and in 1602 he settled it on John Whitton *alias* Darling, Mary daughter of John Knottesford, his bride, and their issue.[90] George, who was lord of Hensington (co. Oxon.), died there in 1606.[91] John Whitton *alias* Darling made a conveyance of the manor in 1611, when he was associated with Thomas Parker.[92] Dorothy Parker, widow, with George Parker and Dorothy his wife conveyed it to Robert Fitzhugh in 1629,[93] and in 1667 James Parker cut off the entail.[94] Nothing was known of the manor in 1730,[95] and there is no evidence to connect it with the reputed manor of Dagnall, now represented by Dagnall House in Weston Road,[95a] for which no records exist.

The church of *ST. PETER AND ST. PAUL* consists of a chancel measuring internally 49 ft. by 22 ft. 5 in., nave 75 ft. 6 in. by 22 ft., north aisle 15 ft. 5 in. wide, south aisle 16 ft. wide, west tower 17 ft. 8 in. square, and north porch. It is built of ashlar, faced both internally and externally, and the roofs are covered with tiles, slates and lead.

A church existed in the parish from a very early period, probably long before 1273, the date of the first known reference,[96] but the present structure was built during the middle of the 14th century, the chancel being erected first and the other parts of the building some few years later. As there are no vestiges of earlier work, the local tradition that it was built on a new site is probably correct. By 1556 the chancel had become dilapidated[97] and was probably, with other parts of the building, soon afterwards repaired. A gallery was erected at the west end of the nave in 1723, and another in the north aisle in 1765, but both have been removed. In 1807 the church was extensively restored, particularly on the north side, and the porch was rebuilt, an upper

CHURCH

[70] She had died in 1369 (G.E.C. *Peerage*, v, 9).
[71] Ibid.
[72] Duchy of Lanc. Misc. Bks. xvi, fol. 119 d.
[73] *Cal. Pat.* 1413–16, p. 357.
[74] *Cal. S. P. Dom.* 1603–10, p. 169.
[75] Chan. Inq. p.m. (Ser. 2), cccxxxv, 16 ; P.C.C. 77 Fermer.
[76] Fine R. 16 Jas. I, pt. iii, no. 14.
[77] Recov. R. East. 21 Chas. I, m. 22.
[78] *Olney Par. Reg.* (Bucks. Par. Reg. Soc.), 26.
[79] Ibid. 103.
[80] Ibid. 166 ; Close, 10 Anne, pt. vi, no. 32 ; cf. Feet of F. Bucks. Trin. 11 Anne.
[81] *Olney Par. Reg.* (Bucks. Par. Reg. Soc.), 177 ; for John's younger children see ibid. 182, 194.
[82] Ibid. 485 ; Feet of F. Bucks. Trin. 29 Geo. III.

[82a] P.C.C. 111 Howe.
[83] *Cal. Pat.* 1467–77, p. 420.
[84] Early Chan. Proc. bdle. 390, no. 58.
[85] Chan. Inq. p.m. (Ser. 2), xliii, 35.
[86] Early Chan. Proc. bdle. 390, no. 58.
[87] They had married respectively Nicholas Balby and Gilbert Billingford before 1523 (Early Chan. Proc. loc. cit.). In 1542–58 Whithills was in the possession of Sir William Compton and of his son and heir Peter and his heir (Mins. Accts. Hen. VIII, no. 5890 ; Chan. Inq. p.m. [Ser. 2], lxxiii, 9 ; Ld. Rev. Misc. Bks. clxxxviii, fol. 57, 59b). By a grant in 1511 Sir William Compton was to succeed Robert Wighthill in the rangership of Wychwood Forest, Oxfordshire (*L. and P. Hen. VIII*, i, 1588 ; cf. ibid. 866).
[88] Feet of F. Bucks. Hil. 12 Eliz.
[89] Chan. Proc. Eliz. W 22, no. 11.

[90] Feet of F. Div. Co. Mich. 44 & 45 Eliz. ; Chan. Inq. p.m. (Ser. 2), ccciii, 131.
[91] Chan. Inq. p.m. (Ser. 2), ccciii, 131. His heir was Henry, son of his brother, Thomas Whitton.
[92] Feet of F. Bucks. Mich. 9 Jas. I.
[93] Ibid. Trin. 5 Chas. I.
[94] Com. Pleas D. Enr. East. 19 Chas. II, m. 5.
[95] Add. MS. 5839, fol. 155 b–161.
[95a] This and other local inform. has been kindly supplied by Mr. Thomas Wright.
[96] *Cal. Pat.* 1272–81, p. 30.
[97] A visitation of the diocese of Lincoln in that year for Cardinal Pole, to whom the chancel and rectory belonged, contains this reference to Olney Church: 'Gardiani presentant cancellum fere collapsum esse, ac vix centum marcas sufficere ad reparationem ejusdem.'

OLNEY CHURCH FROM THE SOUTH-WEST

OLNEY CHURCH: THE INTERIOR LOOKING EAST

story being added to it to be used as a schoolroom. 'To cover the expense of these operations,' observed James Storer, writing about 1825,[98] 'it was unfortunately thought necessary to sacrifice a fine carved roof that adorned the interior, and to strip the church of its lead. Accordingly the curiously ornamented work was broken to pieces, and the timber sold by auction in the churchyard. Among the lots were a great variety of figures and heads, some of which are still to be seen in the town as ornaments in gardens or placed upon barns and other buildings. The metal was sold to a Birmingham merchant.' Plaster ceilings were then substituted, and those over the nave and south aisle still remain. The chancel was repaired in 1828 and again in 1832, and the whole building was restored by Sir G. Gilbert Scott between 1870 and 1885. A chapel dedicated in honour of our Lady once stood in the churchyard, but all traces of it have now disappeared.

remain. Below the middle window on the south is a pointed doorway with an original rear-arch but modern external stonework, and further east are three sedilia in range with a piscina, divided from one another by circular shafts; these have been entirely renewed with the exception of the east jamb. On the north, opposite the sedilia, is an original wide tomb recess, which was probably used as an Easter sepulchre, while at the east end of the wall there is a plain aumbry; the former, which has been repaired, has a moulded drop arch and contains a flat tomb with a panelled front. The chancel arch is of three moulded orders, which die into the wall on the north side and into a short projection from the wall on the south, the slight irregularity being probably due to the construction of the nave some few years after the chancel was built; the projection is corbelled off a short distance below the springing of the arch. There is an original straight parapet on each of the north and south sides

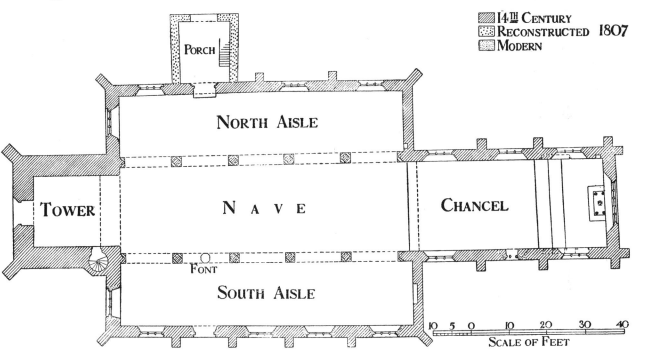

PLAN OF OLNEY CHURCH.

The chancel is a charming example of 14th-century work, and has preserved its original character despite the various restorations it has undergone. In each lateral wall are three tall windows with delicate tracery under pointed heads, the tracery in each window varying from that in the adjacent bay but corresponding to that of the window directly opposite. These have all been repaired, but, with the exception of those in the eastern bay, are mostly original. Both the north and south windows of the western bay have transoms in line with the sills of the other windows, while their own sills are carried to a lower level, thus forming low-side windows of three lights. An arrangement similar to this occurs in the church at Emberton, which in general character closely resembles this building. The large traceried window in the east wall is modern, though its design is probably similar to that of the original window,[99] the jambs of which

of the chancel resting upon a corbel course embellished with grotesques and flowers.

The nave has north and south arcades of five bays with moulded arches acutely pointed and supported by quatrefoil pillars and responds with moulded capitals and bases. In the west wall is the pointed tower arch which spans the full width of the ground-stage, its three orders dying into the walls on either side. The roof of the chancel is modern, and that of the nave is concealed by a segmental plastered ceiling.

The north aisle is lighted by three windows on the north and one on the west, all of three lights with tracery in pointed heads. The north-west window, with its flowing tracery, is original, but the tracery of all the others is modern. Above the two eastern windows on the north side are the outlines of two windows, which were doubtless inserted in 1765 to give light to the north gallery, and have since been blocked. The inner jambs of both the windows of the western bay are enriched with large filleted

[98] *The Rural Walks of Cowper*, 63.
[99] Cf. drawing in *Rec. of Bucks.* vii, 197.

edge rolls which rise to intersect the mouldings of the rear-arches, and the lower parts of the jambs of the north-east window have similar rolls, now considerably hacked for plaster. There is no east window, but at the south end of the east wall is an original cinquefoiled piscina niche with a modern sill, which served the chapel here. The north doorway, which is also original, has a pointed head with a deep outer splay, the mouldings of which are continued to the floor ; the present large label stops date from the late 17th century and represent a bishop and a priest. The south aisle, which has a flat plastered ceiling, has been much restored, and, excepting the jambs of the south-west window, all the openings are practically modern. The north porch, rebuilt in 1807, has a plain entrance doorway with a two-centred drop arch, and against the east wall is a straight flight of stone steps leading to the upper room. A stone reset on the outside, bearing the date 1686, probably records a restoration of the original structure.

The tower is of three diminishing stages with western diagonal buttresses, and is surmounted by a stone broached spire, the sides of which have a very pronounced entasis. Octagonal pinnacles were added at the base of the spire, probably in the 17th century. The ground stage has an original west doorway with a pointed head of three moulded orders dying into plain chamfered jambs. In the north jamb of the doorway is a hole for a heavy oak bolt, and an original west window of two trefoiled lights with flowing tracery. The second stage of the tower is plain and has a clock face on the west. Both these divisions were designed to form one lofty stage with a stone vault at the top, the wall ribs, springers, and moulded corbels of which still remain. The vault, however, has been removed, the present intermediate chamber formed, and a doorway, obviously of late date, cut through the wall from the turret stairway, which originally ascended directly to the bell-chamber. There is an original pointed window of two cinquefoiled lights with tracery in each wall of the bell-chamber, and the spire is pierced by four tiers of spire-lights.

The font in use is modern, but there is an octagonal font in the north aisle which probably dates from the late 16th century and has a plain stem and base, and a panelled bowl, the upper portion of which appears to have been cut away.

On the north wall of the chancel is a mural monument to Catherine daughter of Thomas Johnson (d. 1680), and on the south wall are two tablets, one to the Rev. Moses Browne (d. 1787), who was vicar of the parish for thirty-four years, and the other to Lieut. William Mason and his brother Robert Valentine Mason, 'who were both wrecked in the Æolus Transport near the Isle of Portland in the memorable gale of wind on the 18th of Novr. 1795.' In the north aisle there is a mural monument to William

Gaines (d. 1657). On the west side of the porch is a large iron-bound chest of the 17th century. The Rev. John Newton, who was curate here from 1764 to 1779, and his wife, are buried in the churchyard, where a monument has been erected over their grave. Newton died in 1807 and his wife in 1790, and both were originally buried at St. Mary Woolnoth, London, but their remains were reinterred here in 1893.

The tower contains a ring of eight bells : the treble and second are by Bowell & Sons of Ipswich, 1903 ; the third by Henry Bagley, 1682 ; the fourth is inscribed 'God save the Queen 1599' ; the fifth is by Henry Bagley, 1699 ; the sixth is inscribed 'Robert Atton of Buckingham made me, 1631' ; the seventh is by Thomas Russell, 1733 ; and the tenor probably by one of the Bagleys, 1682.[99a]

The communion plate consists of a cup and cover paten of 1726, a cup and cover of 1796, dated 1797, a standing paten of 1719, and a plated flagon.

The registers to 1812 are as follows : (i) all entries 1665 to 1733 ; (ii) 1734 to 1787 ; (iii) 1787 to 1812.

ADVOWSON The first mention of the church of Olney is found in the 13th century, when the advowson was in the hands of the lords of the vill.[100] It followed the descent of the manor until the spring of 1482–3, when Richard Duke of Gloucester and Anne his wife, by licence of Edward IV,[1] conveyed it to the Dean and canons of the chapel of St. George, Windsor.[2] The conveyance does not, however, appear to have been effectual, possibly owing to the rights of Anne Countess of Warwick, mother of the duchess.[3]

The advowson passed with the manor into the possession of the Crown early in 1487–8, but in 1502 was granted by Henry VII to the abbey of Syon, which at the same time received licence to appropriate.[4] The nuns let the rectory at farm, £13 6s. 8d. being reserved to the vicar as stipend and 6s. 8d. being given as alms.[5] In 1531 the abbey granted a twenty-one years' lease to Thomas Lawe,[6] and the Crown subsequently followed the same policy[7] until 1606, when the rectory and advowson of the vicarage were granted to Sir John Ramsay, kt., in fee.[8] Sir John, a Scot and favourite of James I, was in 1606 created Viscount Haddington and Lord Ramsay of Barnes.[9] In the spring of 1609–10 he conveyed the rectory, advowson and lands here to Michael Throckmorton, Erasmus Cope, Valentine Pigott and Sir Arthur Savage, kt.[10] Valentine Pigott with Cope and Sir Thomas and George Pigott sold the rectory and advowson in the spring of 1623–4 to Sir Robert Gorges, kt., of Redlynch (co. Somerset),[11] who retained them until 1633, when he sold them to William Johnson[12] of Milton Bryant in Bedfordshire.[13] William Johnson was succeeded in 1669 by his son Thomas,[14] who exercised the patronage in 1668 and 1671.[15] His son William Johnson was patron in

[99a] Mr. A. H. Cocks (*Ch. Bells of Bucks.* 153–4) is of opinion that this bell was cast at Bedford by a Newcome and a Watts in partnership.
[100] *Cal. Pat.* 1272–81, p. 30.
[1] Ibid. 1476–85, p. 255.
[2] Feet of F. Bucks. 22 Edw. IV, no. 1.
[3] See above.
[4] Pat. 17 Hen. VII, pt. i, m. 24 ; cf. Mins. Accts. Hen. VII, no. 29.
[5] Mins. Accts. Hen. VIII, no. 225 ; *L. and P. Hen. VIII,* xx (1), p. 678.

[6] *L. and P. Hen. VIII,* xx (1), p. 678.
[7] Ibid. ; Ld. Rev. Misc. Bks. clxxxviii, fol. 127 ; Pat. 20 Eliz. pt. x, m. 20 ; 33 Eliz. pt. ii, m. 38 ; 1 Jas. I, pt. xxi ; cf. Feet of F. Bucks. Trin. 37 Eliz. Olney was among the churches granted by the Crown to the Bishop of Lincoln in 1558 (Pat. 5 & 6 Phil. and Mary, pt. iv, m. 27). This grant was abrogated by Queen Elizabeth.
[8] Pat. 4 Jas. I, pt. viii.

[9] *Dict. Nat. Biog.*
[10] Feet of F. Bucks. Hil. 7 Jas. I.
[11] Ibid. Hil. 21 Jas. I. In 1613 Sir Thomas Pigott and Susan his wife leased the rectory for thirty years or the life of Susan to Henry Throckmorton, gent. (ibid. East. 11 Jas. I).
[12] Ibid. Trin. 9 Chas. I.
[13] Add. MS. 5839, fol. 158.
[14] Ibid. ; Exch. Dep. Mich. 22 Chas. II, no. 11.
[15] Inst. Bks. (P.R.O.).

1732,[16] and died four years later,[17] leaving a son Wolsey Johnson, himself vicar of Olney from 1735 until his resignation in 1753.[17a] He thereupon presented Moses Browne to the church, but as he intended leaving Olney for Lincolnshire,[18] it seems possible that he alienated the advowson to the trustees of Frances Katharine Gounter Nicoll, since the second Earl of Dartmouth was apparently patron in 1764,[19] and held the rectory in the right of his wife.[20] From this time the advowson followed the descent of the manor, the Earl of Dartmouth being the present patron.

By his will made early in 1389–90 Ralph Lord Basset directed that a stipend should be provided for a priest to perform divine service in the chapel of St. Mary in Olney churchyard.[21] In this chapel[22] Richard Earl of Warwick in 1465 obtained licence to found a chantry at the altar of St. Mary for the good estate of the king and his soul after death, and for the welfare of Richard and Anne his wife.[23] This was known as the Earl of Warwick's chantry, and the priest also helped the incumbent.[24] In 1556 the priest of the chantry held land, two burgages, a half burgage, a cottage and a toft,[25] one of these tenements being called the Chapel House and another the Catharine Wheel.[26] Rent from an acre in 'Downefeld' was appropriated to the maintenance of a lamp in the church.[27] In 1516 Sir Thomas Digby, kt., wished to be buried before the image of the Holy Trinity in this church.[28] The fraternity of St. Christopher and St. George is mentioned in 1538.[29]

CHARITIES The Olney feoffee charity, comprising the charity of Richard Pierson, founded by deed 1649, and the Causeway estate, constituted in its present form in 1650, is regulated by a scheme of the Charity Commissioners of 19 February 1886. The property consists of seven cottages on the site of the old churchyard, a cottage in Silver End, two houses in the High Street, a house in Market Place, two cottages and about 8 a. in Weston Road, a close called Fiddle Field containing 5 a. and 9 a. in Olney Pastures, also certain garden grounds. In 1912 the gross income from these sources amounted to about £240. The scheme directs that after providing for the repair and upkeep of the property, and a sum not exceeding £20 yearly towards the repair of the main street, one-third of the net income shall form the endowment of the Olney Educational Foundation, applicable in apprenticing, prizes and scholarships, and the remaining two-thirds to be applied for the general benefit of the poor.

The almshouses founded and endowed by Mrs. Ann Hopkins Smith consist of twelve messuages comprised in deeds of lease and release dated respectively 23 and 24 November 1819, for the accommodation of single women and widows. The donor by her will, dated in 1846, bequeathed £5,200 consols, the dividends to be divided among the inmates, and a further legacy of £700 consols for the insurance and repair of the buildings. The legacies, with accumulations, are now represented by £5,462 8s. 5d. and £942 9s. 3d. India 3 per cent. stock, with the official trustees, producing respectively £163 17s. 4d. and £28 5s. 4d. yearly. In 1910 each of the twelve inmates received 5s. a week and half a ton of coal.

The British school erected by the said Mrs. Ann Hopkins Smith, comprised in a deed of 23 January 1835, was endowed by her will with £1,500 consols now represented with accumulations by a sum of £1,568 0s. 2d. consols, with the official trustees, producing £39 4s. yearly. The school and endowment are regulated by a scheme of the Charity Commissioners of 17 September 1880, providing for the letting of the school buildings and for the application of the income in apprenticing poor children, any surplus to be applied in prizes and exhibitions.

The same testatrix likewise bequeathed £750 consols, the interest to be applied in clothing to be distributed in January to poor persons usually attending the Baptist Meeting. The stock is held by the official trustees, and produces £18 15s. yearly, which appears to be distributed in gifts of money.

The same testatrix further bequeathed £750 consols for clothing for poor persons usually attending the Independent Meeting. The stock is held by the official trustees, and the annual dividends of £18 15s. are applied in the distribution of tickets varying from 2s. 6d. to 10s.

RAVENSTONE

Raunston (xv–xviii cent.).

The parish of Ravenstone lies between the Northamptonshire boundary and the River Ouse, and covers 2,074 acres, of which 784 are arable. There are 120 acres of woodland, nearly all accounted for by the Great Wood on the north-eastern boundary. A piece of waste ground called 'Cokenowebrande,' which was in dispute in 1568, must have been in this part of the parish. It was claimed by the Crown as part of the manor of Ravenstone and by John Cheyne as a detached part of Cogenhoe, in Northamptonshire.[1] To the west of the village, which is near the eastern boundary, is a much smaller plantation called Parkfield Spinney, and near it is Parkfield Farm. Here must have been the 'Great Park' of Ravenstone, mentioned about 1270.[2] 'Tenements called Parkefeld' are mentioned in 1555.[3]

[16] Add. MS. 5839, fol. 158. Richard Snow presented in 1687, apparently for one turn only, as the presentation in 1701 was by William Johnson (Inst. Bks. [P.R.O.]).

[17] Olney Par. Reg. (Bucks. Par. Reg. Soc.), 270.

[17a] Inst. Bks. (P.R.O.); Lipscomb, op. cit. iv, 307.

[18] Lipscomb, loc. cit.; Inst. Bks. (P.R.O.); Add. MS. 5839, fol. 158. For his will, proved after his death in 1756, see P.C.C. 140 Glazier.

[19] When he obtained the appointment of Newton as curate.

[20] Com. Pleas D. Enr. Trin. 8 Geo. III, m. 110; cf. Inst. Bks. (P.R.O.).

[21] Gibbons, Early Linc. Wills, 29.

[22] Chant. Cert. 4, no. 15.

[23] Cal. Pat. 1461–7, p. 462.

[24] Chant. Cert. loc. cit.

[25] Ld. Rev. Misc. Bks. clxxxviii, fol. 57b; cf. Rentals and Surv. (Gen. Ser.), portf. 20, no. 21.

[26] Ld. Rev. Misc. Bks. clxxxviii, fol.

56b; Chant. Cert. 4, no. 15, 108. The cottage was in Bridge Street.

[27] Chant. Cert. 5, no. 37. For the church goods in 1552, see The Edwardian Invent. for Buckinghamshire (Alcuin Club), 19.

[28] Add. MS. 5839, fol. 157.

[29] Ibid.

[1] Exch. Dep. Mich. 10 & 11 Eliz. no. 1.

[2] Cal. Chart. in Bodl. 29.

[3] Ld. Rev. Misc. Bks. clxxxviii, fol. 110.

Limestone was quarried in the parish in 1862.[4] The only industry at the present day appears to be agriculture. Wheat, barley, beans, oats and root crops are raised, the soil being clay on a subsoil of Great Oolite.

The village has a long street running north and south. A lane leading south-west to Stoke Goldington connects it with the Newport Pagnell and Northampton road. Olney, 3 miles away, has the nearest railway station, though the Midland railway cuts across the north-east corner of the parish. The church stands on a little hill at the north end of the street. Below it is the site of the priory, now occupied by Abbey Farm. There are no remains of the building. A large orchard just below the farm is surrounded by a moat,[5] and was probably the site of the old manor-house of Ravenstone. A capital messuage existed here in 1245,[6] and formed part of the endowment of the priory ten years later.[7] The dovecot, which existed in 1291,[8] was probably attached to it. In the 16th century the prior had a 'manor-place' here

THE ALMSHOUSES, RAVENSTONE

with a court in which there were fish-ponds.[9] These were apparently filled by the chalybeate spring from which a little stream now flows south into the Ouse. The existence of the fish-ponds in the orchard already mentioned was still remembered in Lipscomb's time.[10] There are no references to the manor-house later than 1588, but it probably existed as the residence of the Finch family in the 17th and 18th centuries. Sir Heneage Finch, afterwards Lord Chancellor and Earl of Nottingham, was described as of Ravenstone in 1660.[11]

Opposite the Abbey Farm are the almshouses built by him.[12] The buildings are of red and black brick with tiled roofs and wooden cornices at the eaves. They are arranged in two two-storied blocks, each containing six two-roomed houses.

Robinson's Farm, about 150 yards south-west of the church, is a 17th-century stone house of two stories with an attic.

The village also contains a Union chapel, founded in 1790 and rebuilt in 1907.

The only place-names of interest occurring in the records of the parish are 'Thongestoching' (1270, an assart of the Tonge family), 'Scytho' (1331), and 'Wotteny ferme' (1465).[13] It is worthy of note that in the late 15th and early 16th century three messuages in Ravenstone, to each of which 24 acres of land were attached, were destroyed by the prior and George Throckmorton.[14]

MANOR Five hides in *RAVENSTONE* forming one manor were held under the Confessor by a thegn Lewin, who had power to sell. In 1086 this manor belonged to the fee of Walter Giffard, of whom it was held by Hugh (de Bolebec).[15]

The overlordship of the Giffards descended through Rose wife of Richard Fitz Gilbert and sister of Walter Giffard to the Clares, Earls of Hertford and Gloucester.[16] It is last mentioned in 1313.[17] Hugh de Bolebec's lordship followed the descent of Whitchurch (q.v.) to Robert de Vere, third Earl of Oxford, who married Isabel daughter and co-heir of Walter de Bolebec.[18] The Earls of Oxford are mentioned as mesne lords down to the end of the 14th century.[19] Part of the manor was held in 1375 of their manor of Whitchurch by suit of court at Whitchurch every three weeks.[20]

A second fee in Ravenstone, not apparently mentioned in the Survey, belonged in the middle of the 12th century to Osbert Martel.[21] With his land in Edlesborough (q.v.) it was in the king's hands in 1167–8.[22] Three years later part of it had been granted to Adulf de Braci.[23] This fee was always afterwards held in chief.[24]

The two holdings came into the possession of the family of Wahull apparently before the end of the 12th century and formed a single manor. The half which was held of the Bolebecs was given to Walter de Wahull (who flourished 1165–72) in marriage with his wife Rose,[25] probably a Bolebec. The other half Walter or his heirs must have had by grant of the Crown. John de Wahull, son of Walter's successor Simon,[26] was called upon to do homage to the

4 Sheahan, *Hist. and Topog. of Bucks.* 590.
5 *V.C.H. Bucks.* ii, 32 ; *Hist. Monum. Com. Rep. North Bucks.* 252.
6 Feet of F. Bucks. 29 Hen. III, no. 9.
7 *Cal. Close,* 1327–30, p. 345–6.
8 *Pope Nich. Tax.* (Rec. Com.), 47.
9 Pat. 4 & 5 Phil. and Mary, pt. v, m. 52 ; Ld. Rev. Misc. Bks. clxxxviii, fol. 111–12.
10 Lipscomb, *Hist. and Antiq. of Bucks.* iv, 314.
11 G.E.C. *Baronetage,* iii, 30.
12 See below, charities.

13 *Cal. Chart. in Bodl.* 29, 31.
14 Leadam, *Dom. Incl.* 1517 (Roy. Hist. Soc.), 176–7.
15 *V.C.H. Bucks.* i, 252.
16 G.E.C. *Peerage,* vi, 199. See Crendon and *V.C.H. Bucks.* ii, 299.
17 Inq. a.q.d. file 101, no. 13.
18 *Abbrev. Plac.* (Rec. Com.), 87 ; *Red Bk. of Exch.* (Rolls Ser.), 138.
19 *Ann. Mon.* (Rolls Ser.), iii, 150 ; *Cal. Close,* 1237–42, p. 177 ; *Testa de Nevill* (Rec. Com.), 247 ; *Hund. R.* (Rec. Com.), ii, 349 ; *Feud. Aids,* i, 73 ; Inq. a.q.d. file 85, no. 10 ; file 112, no. 4.

20 Chan. Inq. p.m. 50 Edw. III (1st nos.), no. 33a.
21 Pipe R. 14 Hen. II (Pipe R. Soc.), 10.
22 Ibid.
23 Ibid. 17 Hen. II, 57.
24 The mill, which was attached to the Bolebec manor in 1086, subsequently belonged to the priory, which held the Crown fee (*Pope Nich. Tax.* [Rec. Com.], 47). It may have been granted to the priory by the sub-tenants of the Earls of Oxford.
25 *Abbrev. Plac.* (Rec. Com.), 87.
26 Ibid. 46, 87.

Bolebec heirs in 1212[27] and was dead in 1217.[28] Alice his widow, who afterwards married William de Breauté, had rent in Ravenstone as her dower.[29] The heirs of John were his sisters, Rose wife of Robert Lisle and Agnes wife of Robert Basingham,[30] who afterwards married William Fitz Warin.[31] Rose died without issue, and John Basingham, son of Agnes, inherited the family lands in 1238.[32] He died in 1239,[33] when his male heir was Saher de Wahull, evidently a distant cousin.[34] Saher inherited only that half of the manor of Ravenstone which was held of the Crown.[35] He granted it in 1245 to Peter Chaceporc, keeper of the king's wardrobe and a distinguished ecclesiastic, to hold for a rent of one pair of gilt spurs.[36] Peter had a grant of free warren in Ravenstone in 1253[37] and died shortly afterwards.[38] His heir was Hugh Chaceporc, his brother, who at once released the manor to the king.[39] In 1255 it was granted to a community of Augustinian canons, who were called upon to celebrate divine service for the souls of Peter and Hugh de Vivon, his uncle.[40] The prior of the house so founded was said to hold one knight's fee in Ravenstone in 1275.[41] Four years later his holding was described as half a knight's fee, which was probably correct.[42] Its value in 1291 was £10 10s. 10d.[43]

WAHULL. *Or three crescents gules.*

The priory was dissolved in 1525,[44] and in the following year the site and the part of the manor attached to it were granted to Cardinal Wolsey,[45] who also acquired the second half of the manor[46] and devoted the whole to the endowment of his college at Oxford.[47] It came again to the Crown on Wolsey's fall,[48] and in 1535 was granted to Sir Francis Bryan for life.[49] Sir Francis surrendered the manor to Edward VI, who in 1548 made him a new grant for the lives of himself and his wife Joan Countess of Ormond and Ossory.[50] Sir Francis was dead in November 1550.[51] His widow with her third husband Gerald, son and heir of the Earl of Desmond,[52] leased her interest in 1551 to Sir William Herbert and Clement Throckmorton.[53] They sold

the lease to Sir Robert Throckmorton of Weston Underwood,[54] who in 1558 received a grant of the manor for seventy years from the death of Joan at a fee-farm rent of £73 13s.[55] He forfeited his interest through a failure in the payment of his rent,[56] and a lease for twenty-one years was made to Henry Berkeley in 1586.[57] Two years later the queen granted Ravenstone in fee to Sir Moyle Finch and John Audley in trust for Sir Thomas Heneage, afterwards her vice-chamberlain.[58] The trustees conveyed it in the same year to Sir Thomas, who was thereby involved in a dispute with Thomas son of Sir Robert Throckmorton, who had died in 1581,[59] as to the lease of 1558.[60] Throckmorton's claim was finally referred to arbitration,[61] the decision presumably being in favour of Heneage.

Elizabeth daughter and heir of Sir Thomas Heneage, whom she succeeded in 1595,[62] was the wife of Sir Moyle Finch,[63] with whom she made settlements of Ravenstone in 1596 and 1606.[64] She survived her husband, who died in 1614, by twenty years, and was created Viscountess Maidstone in 1623 and Countess of Winchilsea in 1628.[65] She died in possession of Ravenstone, having made in March 1632-3 an elaborate settlement in tail-male on her eldest son, with contingent remainder to John son of her son John, Heneage, Francis and John sons of her son Heneage, and her son Francis.[66] The younger Heneage, who was keeper of the king's seal, Lord Finch of Daventry and Earl of Nottingham, was accordingly holding the manor in 1651 and in 1674.[67] His son and heir Daniel, who inherited Ravenstone in 1682,

FINCH, Earl of Winchilsea. *Argent a cheveron between three griffons passant sable.*

succeeded his second cousin in 1729 as Earl of Winchilsea and died the following year.[68] Daniel's son of the same name died in 1769,[69] and was succeeded by his nephew and heir George,[70] who died unmarried in 1826.[71] By his will the manor passed to George Finch of Burley (co. Rutland), who was still holding it in 1862.[72] George Finch was succeeded in 1870 by his son George Henry, on whose

[27] *Abbrev. Plac.* (Rec. Com.), 87.
[28] *Rot. Lit. Claus.* (Rec. Com.), i, 329.
[29] Ibid. 628 ; *Cur. Reg. R.* 71, m. 13 d ; 79, m. 17.
[30] *Rot. Lit. Claus.* (Rec. Com.), i, 329.
[31] *Excerpta e Rot. Fin.* (Rec. Com.), i, 7.
[32] *Orig. R.* 22 Hen. III, m. 2 d.
[33] *Ann. Mon.* (Rolls Ser.), iii, 150.
[34] Ibid. ; *Cal. Close, 1237-42,* p. 177.
[35] Ibid.
[36] *Feet of F. Bucks.* 29 Hen. III, no. 9.
[37] *Cal. Chart. R.* 1226-57, p. 431.
[38] Ibid. 447.
[39] Ibid.
[40] Ibid. ; *Cal. Chart. in Bodl.* 28 ; *Cal. Close,* 1327-30, p. 345.
[41] *Hund. R.* (Rec. Com.), i, 37.
[42] Ibid. ii, 348.
[43] *Pope Nich. Tax.* (Rec. Com.), 47.
[44] Chan. Inq. p.m. (Ser. 2), lxxvi, 2.
[45] *L. and P. Hen. VIII,* iv, 1913.
[46] See below.
[47] Feet of F. Div. Co. Mich. 18 Hen. VIII.

[48] Chan. Inq. p.m. (Ser. 2), lxxvii, 59.
[49] Pat. 26 Hen. VIII, pt. ii, m. 30. A grant to St. George's Chapel, Windsor, in 1532 does not seem to have become operative (*L. and P. Hen. VIII,* v, 1351).
[50] Star Chamb. Proc. Phil. and Mary, bdle. 10, no. 67 ; Pat. 4 & 5 Phil. and Mary, pt. v, m. 52.
[51] *Acts. of P.C. 1550-2,* p. 158.
[52] G.E.C. *Peerage,* vi, 148.
[53] Ld. Rev. Misc. Bks. clxxxviii, fol. 112.
[54] Star Chamb. Proc. Phil. and Mary, bdle. 10, no. 67.
[55] Pat. 4 & 5 Phil. and Mary, pt. v, m. 52.
[56] Lansd. MS. 106, no. 47.
[57] Pat. 28 Eliz. pt. iii, m. 7.
[58] Ibid. 30 Eliz. pt. xvi, m. 37 ; Chan. Proc. Eliz. W. 11, no. 62.
[59] Chan. Inq. p.m. (Ser. 2), cxciii, 89.
[60] Lansd. MS. 106, no. 47.
[61] Lipscomb, op. cit. iv, 314.
[62] Chan. Inq. p.m. (Ser. 2), ccli, 107.
[63] Ibid ; G.E.C. *Baronetage,* i, 35.

[64] Recov. R. Trin. 38 Eliz. m. 2 ; Feet of F. Bucks. East. 4 Jas. I.
[65] G.E.C. loc. cit. ; Exch. Dep. Spec. Com. no. 5163.
[66] Chan. Inq. p.m. (Ser. 2), dlxxxviii, 86. An earlier settlement was made in 1623 (Feet of F. Div. Co. Hil. 20 Jas. I).
[67] Recov. R. 1651, m. 1 ; Feet of F. Bucks. East. 26 Chas. II. Thomas Earl of Winchilsea, eldest son of the countess, appears to have renounced his claim in 1635 (Feet of F. Bucks. East. 11 Chas. I ; Recov. R. East. 11 Chas. I, m. 57) and other members of the family in 1646 (Feet of F. Div. Co. Trin. 22 Chas. I).
[68] G.E.C. *Peerage,* viii, 179, 181. He made a settlement of the manor in 1694 (Feet of F. Bucks. Trin. 6 Will. and Mary).
[69] G.E.C. *Peerage,* viii, 181.
[70] Ibid; cf. Recov. R. Mich. 15 Geo. III, m. 285 ; Feet of F. Berks. Trin. 45 Geo. III.
[71] G.E.C. *Peerage,* viii, 181.
[72] Sheahan, op. cit. 591.

death in 1907 the manor passed to his son Mr. Alan George Finch.[73]   He was succeeded in 1914 by the present owner, Mr. Wilfred Finch.

That half of the manor which was not inherited by Saher de Wahull in 1239 passed, presumably through female heirs of John Basingham, to William Blancminster and the heirs of Adam de Tyndal,[74] and was held till the end of the 14th century at least in two separate quarters.   William Blancminster had four daughters and co-heirs, of whom Joan the wife of Sir William Barentine seems alone to have had any interest in Ravenstone.[75]   The Hugh Blancminster who was returned as tenant here about 1245 was apparently William's brother, and may have had custody of his heirs.[76]   Joan was still holding land here in 1302–3,[77] and was succeeded by Drew Barentine, probably her son.[78]   Drew was said to hold half a knight's fee in 1316.[79]   In 1330 a settlement of land and rent in Ravenstone was made on William Barentine and Maud his wife and the heirs of William.[80]   Maud survived for more than fifty years and married her second husband Sir Warin Trussel, who is returned as lord of this part of Ravenstone in 1346.[81]   The heir of William Barentine was his brother Philip, who granted the reversion to William Isbrond, ' brouderer,' and his wife Nichole.[82]   They in 1371 conveyed it to John Pykenham, to whom Maud Trussel also granted her interest.[83]   After the death of Maud, John Pykenham gave a life interest in the manor to William Trussel.[84]   Meanwhile Thomas son of John Lovel of Dawley, who claimed the reversion as cousin and heir of William Barentine,[85] made a grant of it in 1381 to Sir Robert Sall,[86] though he had already confirmed the grant to John Pykenham.[87]   The grant to Sall was set aside on the ground that Thomas Lovel was under age[88] ; nevertheless Margaret sister and heir of Sir Robert Sall and her husband Philip Warner conveyed the reversion to Hugh Fastolf and William Snettisham,[89] who in their turn had a confirmation in 1386 from Thomas Lovel.[90]   They conveyed their interest before 1394 to William Thirning and others, who in that year sued William Trussel, the life tenant, for the estate.[91]   The verdict was given for the plaintiffs, but the defendants appealed.   This part of Ravenstone

is next mentioned in 1399, when it belonged to John Baker of Sutton in Holderness (Yorkshire), and was taken into the king's hands for the satisfaction of his creditors, Robert de Garton, Simon Gaunstede, and Henry Maupas, clerks.[92]   Another gap in its history follows, Henry Watford, who was 'late of Raunston' in 1471,[93] being the next tenant whose name is known.   His daughter and heir Joan married William son of William Isham of Pytchley,[94] and with her husband conveyed three messuages and 80 acres in Ravenstone to Robert Throckmorton in 1501.[95] Two years later they made him a further grant of three messuages, 100 acres of land, 20 acres of meadow, 30 acres of pasture, and 10 acres of wood.[96]   Sir Robert died seised of 'the manor' in 1518, leaving a son and heir George, on whom it was settled.[97] In 1528 George Throckmorton sold it to Cardinal Wolsey,[98] and it was joined to that part of the manor which had belonged to the priory.

The remaining fourth part belonged in 1239 to Nicholas de Boltby, who had married Philippa, elder daughter and co-heir of Adam de Tyndal.[99]   Henry de Boltby was said to hold it about 1245,[100] probably in mistake for Nicholas, who lived till 1272.[1] Nicholas' widow Alice held a quarter of the vill in dower for a quarter of a knight's fee in 1279[2] and 1284–6.[3]   In 1302–3 the tenant was Henry de Bray or Gray.[4]   The holding passed before 1316 to Sir William de Muxton (Mokelistone),[5] who had it in right of his wife Joan.[6]   He was in debt to John de Sutton in 1340, and pledged his manor of Ravenstone in payment.[7]   It was forfeit by 1347 to John de Sutton, who mortgaged it in that year to Henry Green.[8]   When next mentioned this part of the manor was held in thirds, one of which Joan Stubbs, who died in 1371, had granted to John Cave and others.[9]   Another was then held by Thomas Bosyate by courtesy of England after the death of Elizabeth his wife, probably a sister of Joan.[10]   On the death of Thomas in 1375 it passed to Thomas Stubbs, son of Joan, as kinsman of Elizabeth.[11]   Thomas granted lands and tenements in Ravenstone in 1390 to trustees,[12] who regranted them to his widow Joan and his daughter Joan nine years later.[13]   The son and heir of Joan the daughter was John Man.[14]

[73] Burke, *Landed Gentry.*
[74] *Cal. Close,* 1237–42, p. 177 ; *Ann. Mon.* (Rolls Ser.), iii, 150.
[75] *Cal. Inq. p.m.* (Edw. I), ii, 226 ; *Feud. Aids,* i, 73 ; *Abbrev. Plac.* (Rec. Com.), 265.
[76] *Testa de Nevill* (Rec. Com.), 247 ; Eyton, *Antiq. of Shrops.* ix, 280.
[77] *Feud. Aids,* i, 105.
[78] Joan settled lands in Dawley, Middlesex, on Gilbert son of William Barentine in 1307 (Feet of F. Middlesex, 35 Edw. I, no. 361).
[79] *Feud. Aids.* i, 110 ; Inq. a.q.d. file 85, no. 10 ; file 112, no. 4.   It is more probable that his holding was a quarter of a knight's fee.
[80] Feet of F. Bucks. 4 Edw. III, no. 8.
[81] Chan. Misc. bdle. 88, file 8, no. 173 ; Close, 10 Ric. II, m. 41 d. ; *Co'l. for Staffs.* (Will. Salt Arch. Soc.), xii, 135 ; *Feud. Aids,* i, 131.
[82] Coram Rege R. Mich. 18 Ric. II, m. 40.   In 1349 Jordan Barentine, whose relationship to William and Philip is not clear, gave Sir Warin Trussel, William Trussel the younger and John

Lowell (Lovel ?) power to receive seisin in his name of his inheritance in Ravenstone and various places in Essex (*Cal. Close,* 1349–54, p. 87).
[83] Coram Rege R. Mich. 18 Ric. II, m. 40 ; Feet of F. Diy. Co. 6 Ric. II, no. 70 ; Close, 6 Ric. II, pt. i, m. 26 d.
[84] Coram Rege R. Mich. 18 Ric. II. m. 40 ; *Cal. Chart. in Bodl.* 31.
[85] Coram Rege R. cit.
[86] Ibid. ; Chan. Misc. bdle. 88, file 8, no. 173.
[87] Close, 6 Ric. II, pt. i, m. 26 d.
[88] Chan. Misc. bdle. 88, file 8, no. 173.
[89] Coram Rege R. Mich. 18 Ric. II, m. 40.
[90] Close, 10 Ric. II, m. 41 d.
[91] Coram Rege R. Mich. 18 Ric. II, m. 40.
[92] Chan. Extents on Debts, file 49, no. 3.
[93] *Cal. Pat.* 1467–77, p. 255.
[94] Early Chan. Proc. bdle. 209, no. 48.
[95] Feet of F. Bucks. East. and Trin. 16 Hen. VII.
[96] Ibid. East. 18 Hen. VII.   He was then a knight.

[97] Chan. Inq. p.m. (Ser. 2), xxxiii, 46.
[98] Close, 20 Hen. VIII, no. 53 ; Ld Rev. Misc. Bks. clxxxviii, fol. 110 ; see also Feet of F. Bucks. Mich. 21 Hen. VIII ; *L. and P. Hen. VIII,* v, 47 (4), 84, 1051.
[99] *Excerpta e Rot. Fin.* (Rec. Com.), i, 244 ; *Cal. Close,* 1237–42, p. 177.
[100] *Testa de Nevill* (Rec. Com.), 247.
[1] *Cal. Inq. p.m.* (Hen. III), i, 286 ; *Excerpta e Rot. Fin.* (Rec. Com.), ii, 588.
[2] *Hund. R.* (Rec. Com.), ii, 349.
[3] *Feud. Aids,* i, 73.
[4] Ibid. 105, 131.   Philip de Castello was a tenant of the Earl of Oxford in 1313 (Inq. a.q.d. file 101, no. 13).
[5] *Feud. Aids,* i, 110 ; see also *Cal. Chart. in Bodl.* 31.
[6] *Cal. Close,* 1346–9, p. 239.
[7] Ibid. 1339–41, p. 489 ; 1346–9, p. 239.
[8] Ibid. 1346–9, p. 239.
[9] Chan. Inq. p.m. 50 Edw. III (1st nos.), no. 33a.
[10] Ibid.   [11] Ibid.
[12] *Cat. of Anct. D.* iv, p. 429.
[13] Ibid. i, p. 19.
[14] Ibid. iv, p. 429.

The further history of this part of the estate is uncertain. John Baker [15] was said to hold 'half the manor' in December 1399, an expression which suggests that both the fourth parts were united in his possession; but Joan Stubbs held this quarter in March 1398–9,[16] and it seems unlikely that John Baker should have acquired land during the intervening months, when he was heavily in debt. Probably this part of the manor was acquired later by Henry Watford or the Throckmortons.

A court baron at Ravenstone in the prior's manor is mentioned in 1525.[17]

CHURCH The church of *ALL SAINTS* consists of a chancel 28 ft. by 15 ft., a south chapel of the same dimensions, nave 39 ft. 6 in. by 21 ft. 6 in., south aisle 11 ft. 6 in. wide, and west tower 10 ft. 6 in. square. All these measurements are internal.

Some herring-bone rubble in the west wall of the nave indicates the former existence of an 11th-century church, consisting probably of a chancel and nave. In the 12th century a short south aisle of two bays was built, and perhaps a north aisle. The present west tower was added about 1250, and some hundred years later the chancel appears to have been rebuilt and the south aisle lengthened westward by one bay and reroofed. A nave clearstory was added in the first half of the 15th century. Considerable restoration and alterations were carried out in 1670, when probably a north aisle was destroyed and most of the windows and doorways were renewed in the style of the time; the walls of the nave and chancel were at the same time lined with oak panelling and oak panelled pews inserted. Probably in 1675 the south chapel was built as a mortuary chapel for the Finch family, and particularly to receive the body of Elizabeth Lady Finch, who died in that year. The church was restored in 1885, and the south chapel in 1892.

The chancel has a modern east window and roof. The chancel arch is of two chamfered orders, which die into plain jambs; the whole of the stonework is coated with modern paint, but probably dates from the 14th century. The walls are lined with oak wainscot having raised moulded panels and a moulded capping, which is continued across the west side to form a low chancel screen with two doors in the middle.

The south chapel with the wall between it and the chancel is of about 1675. It communicates with the chancel by a wide pointed arch of two chamfered orders, the inner order resting on semi-circular shafts which have capitals and bases of Renaissance detail.

The chapel has in the east wall a window of three lights with a transom, under a square head, and a similar window in the south wall; to the west of the latter is a small square-headed doorway. An arch like that to the chancel, but narrower, opens to the south aisle on the west. The openings of both archways are filled in with oak screens, the lower part having raised moulded panels, while the upper part, which is left open, has twisted balusters under a classic entablature. The screens are divided into bays by panelled pilasters and have folding doors with old brass locks. In the middle of the chapel stands a fine monument of black and white marble to Heneage Finch, Earl of Nottingham and Lord Chancellor (d. 1682), and his wife Elizabeth daughter of Daniel Harvey (d. 1675). It consists of a large altar tomb with a moulded top slab of black marble, on which is the life-size effigy of the chancellor in his robes of office, leaning on his right elbow. At the angles are carved and panelled pilasters; on the east and west sides are shields of his arms with coronet and motto, behind which the chancellor's purse and mace are shown in saltire; on the north side is a long inscription in Latin, and on the south side another in English. At each corner of the top slab is a Corinthian column supporting a horizontal canopy with a classic entablature. On the north and south sides are curved and broken pediments inclosing the earl's armorial achievement with crest and supporters; below the entablature on the same sides are white marble curtains twisted round the columns, and at each corner of the canopy is a flaming urn. All the heraldic detail is coloured and gilded, and the whole monument was carefully restored in 1909 by Mrs. Edith Finch, and is in excellent condition. Against the east wall of the chapel is a reredos of four oak panels painted with the Creed, Lord's Prayer and Commandments, and surmounted by a central broken pediment with a flaming urn. This was formerly in the chancel and is of late 17th-century character. A plain oak chest with three locks and iron bands is kept in the chapel and is probably of 17th-century date. The open lean-to roof of the chapel is of flat pitch and has moulded main rafters, purlins and cornices.

The nave has a south arcade of three bays, the two eastern of which date from the latter part of the 12th century, and have plain pointed arches. The east respond has a hollow-chamfered impost, and the eastern column has a moulded base and square plinth and a capital carved with shallow leaf-ornament rising from interlacing arches, the abacus being similar to the impost of the respond. The third and western-most bay was probably added about 1350 and has an arch of two chamfered orders. The western pier has moulded capitals and bases, and the springing stones of the central arch have been cut back to fit the circular capital. The west respond is semicircular. In the wall to the east of the arcade is a plain arched opening, apparently ancient but much plastered. In the north wall is a single light with chamfered jamb and an ogee head, probably of 17th-century date, and to the west of this is a re-set 14th-century doorway with a pointed head. The east end of the wall, which is slightly thicker than the rest, may indicate the position of the east respond of the former north arcade. One of the three buttresses on this side of the nave bears the date 1670. The three pointed clearstory windows on each side of the nave date from the 15th century; each is of two trefoiled lights with quatrefoil tracery in the head. The nave walls are lined with oak wainscot of the same date and detail as that in the chancel; the oak-panelled pews are also of 17th-century date, as well as the hexagonal oak pulpit, which has moulded and inlaid panels, moulded sill and cornice, a panelled wall standard and a large horizontal sounding-board with moulded cornice.

The south aisle has two south windows, both with 15th-century jambs, but the segmental head of the

[15] See above. [16] *Cat. of Anct. D.* i, 19. [17] Chan. Inq. p.m. (Ser. 2), lxxvi, 2.

443

eastern window belongs to the period of the late 17th-century reconstruction, while the head and tracery of the western window are modern. The south doorway is entirely of the late 17th century and has moulded jambs and entablature, above which on the outside is a stone head, probably refixed 15th-century work. The external stonework to the west of the doorway shows signs of alteration. In the west wall is a two-light window of 15th-century date altered in the 17th century. The lean-to roof of three bays has moulded main rafters with curved braces under their southern ends standing on embattled and moulded wooden corbels ; the purlins and lesser principals are chamfered, and all the work dates from the 15th century. Over the nave arcade is a plain chamfered corbel. In the south wall of the aisle are a trefoil-headed piscina, and two sedilia with chamfered heads supported by a small central column and half-columns, attached to the jambs, all with moulded capitals and bases. Both piscina and sedilia are of 14th-century date.

The 13th-century west tower is of three stages, with short angle buttresses at the west corners, and is crowned by a modern parapet, below which are several carved stone heads much decayed. The tower arch is chamfered and has an indented label ; the chamfered jambs have moulded imposts little more than 3 ft. above the floor. The arch is filled in with an oak screen and panelled door of the 17th century. The west doorway is probably of the same date, and just above it is a small ancient lancet. The bell-chamber is lighted by a two-light window in each wall ; that on the east is of 17th-century date. On the north there is a window of the 13th century, with dog-tooth ornament in the heads of the lancet lights, and traces of a moulded capital and base on the mullion. The south window is partially restored, and the west window, which is much decayed, has been repaired with cement.

The early 13th-century font has a tapering circular bowl carved with trefoiled arcading having quatrefoils in the spandrels ; the plain circular base has four volute-like reeded projections near the top, probably intended for foliage. The oak cover is a tall plain pyramid with turned top, and dates from the 17th century.

In the nave is a plain tablet to Robert Chapman, vicar (d. 1785), and on the east side of the church-yard is a head-stone, now illegible, to Thomas Seaton, vicar (d. 1741), founder of the Seatonian Prize for Sacred Poetry at Cambridge University. The communion table is of oak and has a moulded top and rails and twisted legs. The rails have twisted balusters similar to those of the screens in the south chapel. Both table and rails are of 17th-century work.

There is a ring of three bells : the treble is by Newcome, 1616 ; the second, a 14th-century bell, pro-bably by John Rufford, is inscribed 'Ave Maria'[17a] ; the tenor, inscribed 'God Save our King, 1625, I.K.,' is by James Keene.

The plate consists of a cup and cover paten, both without marks, but of 17th-century date. The cup has an engraved shield of the Finch arms surrounded by mantling. There is also a flagon inscribed 'The Gift of Rev. Thos. Seaton, Vicar of Ravenstone in the year 1741.'

The registers down to 1812 are as follows : (i) mixed entries 1568 to 1652 (there is a gap from 1653 to 1700) ; (ii) mixed entries 1701 to 1771 (in this book is a register of briefs with amounts collected, 1726 to 1741) ; (iii) mixed entries 1771 to 1812 ; (iv) marriages 1754 to 1812.

The churchwardens' accounts are contained in two books : (i) 1641 to 1734, (ii) 1767 to 1870. There is also a book of vellum leaves bound in panelled calf, lettered on the outside 'Orders for the Alms-house at Ravenston,' containing carefully written regulations, with a list of deeds and an extract from the will of the Earl of Nottingham, 1682, founder of the charity, and signed on page 17 by his successor and six others of the Finch family. At the end is a register of admissions from 1684 to 1908.

Near the south doorway is the square stone base of a churchyard cross of the 14th or 15th century.

ADVOWSON William Fitz Warin presented a rector to the church of Ravenstone in 1225 in right of his wife Agnes de Wahull.[18] The church was then in the possession of Walter de Ravenstone, who as vicar received its fruits, paying the rector a pension of 40s.[19] The advowson passed with half the manor to the priory of Ravenstone,[20] to which it must have been appro-priated between about 1260, when Richard de Clifford was rector,[21] and 1291, when a vicarage was already ordained.[22] In 1465 the prior agreed to augment the vicar's stipend by £3 14s. from two farms belong-ing to the priory.[23] After the Dissolution the advow-son descended with the manor[24] till the lease in 1558 to Sir Robert Throckmorton, when it was reserved to the Crown.[25] A grant of it was made to Heneage Lord Finch afterwards Earl of Nottingham in 1676,[26] and the lords of the manor have since presented.[27] Mr. Wilfred Finch is the present patron.

The rectory was leased to Sir Robert Throck-morton in 1567 for twenty-one years, and in 1578 was granted to John Goodwin for life with remainder to Thomas Throckmorton for life.[28] In 1604 it was granted to Anthony Crewe and William Starkey,[29] who perhaps sold it to Thomas Throckmorton. In 1610 it was conveyed by Sir Francis Fortescue, Sir William Fortescue and Thomas Throckmorton to Sir Arthur Savage.[30] He sold it two years later to Sir Moyle Finch,[31] and it has since followed the descent of the manor.

At the dissolution of chantries it was found that a

[17a] C. H. Cocks, *V.C.H. Bucks.* ii, 118.

[18] *R. of Hugh of Wells* (Cant. and York Soc.), ii, 67.

[19] Ibid.

[20] Feet of F. Bucks. 29 Hen. III, no. 9 ; *Cal. Chart. R.* 1327–30, p. 345.

[21] *Cal. Chart. in Bodl.* 29.

[22] *Pope Nich. Tax.* (Rec. Com.), 33.

[23] *Cal. Chart. in B*31.

[24] Pat. 17 Hen. VIII, pt. i, m. 21–2 ; 26 Hen. VIII, pt. ii, m. 30.

[25] Pat. 4 & 5 Phil. and Mary, pt. v, m. 52.

[26] *Cal. S. P. Dom.* 1676–7, p. 457. The advowson is mentioned in the fine by which Sir Arthur Savage conveyed the rectory to Sir Moyle Finch, but not in the corresponding Close Roll (see below). The Crown presented in 1660 (Inst. Bks. [P.R.O.]).

[27] Inst. Bks. (P.R.O.) ; Recov. R. East. 2 Jas. II, m. 100. Lord Finch purchased the fee-farm rent of the manor and en-dowed the vicarage with it (Bacon, *Liber Regis,* 500 ; Lysons, *Mag. Brit.* i [3], 626).

[28] Pat. 20 Eliz. pt. ii.

[29] Ibid. 2 Jas. I, pt. xxii, m. 4.

[30] Close, 8 Jas. I, pt. xi.

[31] Ibid. 10 Jas. I, pt. xxv, no. 19 ; Feet of F. Bucks. Mich. 10 Jas. I.

RAVENSTONE CHURCH FROM THE SOUTH-EAST

RAVENSTONE CHURCH: THE INTERIOR LOOKING EAST

rent of 3s. 6d. had been given for an obit in Raven-stone.[32]

CHARITIES The hospital founded in 1682 by Heneage Earl of Nottingham, Lord Chancellor, for six single men and six single women is endowed with certain fee-farm rents in the counties of York and Cambridge, in respect of which £247 11s. 6d. was paid in 1910. The official trustees now (1913) also hold a sum of £1,263 16s. 6d. consols, producing £31 11s. 8d. a year, arising in part from the redemption of fee-farm rents, and a sum of £400 India 2½ per cent. stock is held by the trustees of the hospital, producing £10 a year. The charity is regulated by a scheme of the Charity Commissioners of 20 April 1886, as varied by a scheme of 19 April 1904. The six men hospitallers and the six women hospitallers receive 5s. a week each, amounting to £156 a year, with an allowance for coal, £10. The sum of £84 a year is paid to the vicar of Ravenstone in augmentation of his emoluments, and the sum of £10 a year is paid to the churchwardens for the reparation of the church.

James Ward by his will, 1787, devised a cottage, the rent of which was to be distributed in bread and meat at Christmas. The cottage was sold in 1885, and the proceeds, with accumulations, are now represented by £62 4s. 10d. consols with the official trustees, producing £1 11s. yearly. The income has for some time been accumulated, there being in 1910 a balance in hand of £9.

The Rev. Robert Chapman, a former vicar, by his will proved in the P.C.C. 3 January 1786, bequeathed his residuary personal estate to trustees for investment in the public funds, the interest to be applied for the charitable purposes in his said will specified.[33] The trust fund is now (1913) represented by £5,303 India 3 per cent. stock with the official trustees, producing £159 1s. 8d. a year. The charity was the subject of a scheme of the Court of Chancery, 31 July 1857.

SHENLEY

Senelai (xi cent.) ; Sanleia (xii cent.) ; Senle, Shenlegh (xiii cent.) ; Shendeley (xv cent.).

The parish of Shenley extends into the two hundreds of Newport and Cottesloe, to the south-west of Watling Street. The more important portion, the township of Church End, where St. Mary's Church is, lies in Newport Hundred, and has to the south of it the hamlet of Brook End in Cottesloe Hundred. These names have respectively replaced those of Great and Little Shenley in the 13th and 14th centuries, and of Lower and Upper or of Nether and Over Shenley from the 13th century onwards.

The areas of the township and hamlet have varied considerably during the 19th century. In 1831 there were 1,510 acres in Church End and 1,620 in Brook End, a total of 3,130 acres,[1] which between 1841 and 1851 had decreased to 2,900. A further decrease took place between 1861 and 1871, when the whole parish was assessed at 2,596 acres, of which only 935 were in Brook End. Another change occurred between 1871 and 1881, probably under the Divided Parishes Acts of 1876 or 1879, by which the area of Brook End was increased to 1,659 acres and that of Church End to 1,662 acres, the figures at which they stand at the present day. There are 276 acres of arable land, 933 of permanent grass and 167 of woods and plantations in Church End.[2] A 16th-century survey of Shenley Manor, which lay principally in Church End, speaks of Shenley Park (50 acres), Hangers (38 acres), Redocks Hill (14 acres), and Oakhill (16 acres) as woods 'all well sett with yonge oke.'[3] Howe Park in the south of Brook End was returned at 88 acres in the 17th century,[4] and is referred to in a deed of the 14th century.[5] The woodland in this part of Shenley is now only 65 acres in extent, the greater portion of the land, 1,032 acres, being laid down in grass, while there are 517 acres under cultivation.[5a] The soil is alluvial and clay with a subsoil of stone and clay, producing cereals and beans. It is watered by brooks flowing from the higher land in the west (400 ft. above ordnance datum) to the lower lying fields (300 ft.) in the east of the parish.

Church End is pleasantly situated among trees on a road which crosses Watling Street, and branches west and south at St. Mary's Church and rectory. About a quarter of a mile south-west of the church is the Toot, a moated mound with two large moated inclosures, the whole covering some 7 acres. In the northernmost of the inclosures are traces of the foundations of the old manor-house of Shenley, pulled down in 1774 by Matthew Knapp, then lord of the manor.[6] The present principal landowner, Mr. Richard Selby-Lowndes, lives about a quarter of a mile north at Shenley Park (formerly Shenley House), a stone building which is approached through the park by an avenue of limes.

A short distance to the south of the church are the gabled almshouses of stone with tiled roofs, founded under the will of Thomas Stafford of Tattenhoe, who died in 1607,[7] and to whom there is a monument in the north aisle of Shenley Church.[8] He empowered his son and heir Thomas Stafford, his son-in-law Sir Arthur Savage and other trustees to build an almshouse or hospital for four men and two women in some town in Buckinghamshire 'of their own appointing,' and to endow it with lands worth £30 per annum. Each occupant was to have house-room and a garden plot and was to be given a gown with a red cross on the left sleeve every year, while the men received 3d. and the women 2d. each day.[9] As recorded on a panel in the middle gable of the building, the hospital was erected on land purchased in 1615 by Thomas Stafford the son, who intended to incorporate the

---

[32] Chant. Cert. 5, no. 20.
[33] V.C.H. Bucks. ii, 220.
[1] These and the following figures are taken from the census returns.
[2] Statistics from Bd. of Agric. (1905).
[3] Ld. Rev. Misc. Bks. clxxxviii, fol. 295.
[4] Add. MS. 37069, p. 3, fol. 36 d.
[5] Chan. Inq. p.m. 43 Edw. III, (add. nos.), no. 12.
[5a] Statistics from Bd. of Agric. (1905).
[6] Sheahan, Hist. and Topog. of Bucks. 598.
[7] Chan. Inq. p.m. (Ser. 2), ccclx, 124.
[8] He left £50 to provide a tomb (P.C.C. 47 Huddlestone). Thomas son of the founder, who died in 1629, was likewise buried in Shenley Church (Chan. Inq. p.m. [Ser. 2], ccclix, 50 ; P.C.C. 94 Ridley). Thomas grandson of the founder, to whom there is a mural monument dated 1684, gave directions for burial in the south aisle (P.C.C. 154 Hare).
[9] P.C.C. 47 Huddlestone.

almshouses by a deed poll of 25 February 1626–7. There was, however, no indorsement of enrolment of the deed poll.[10]

Of about the same date is the half-timber farmhouse south of the church. Folly Farm, a mile to the south-west, was built in the same century, but much of the brickwork is modern.

The hamlet of Brook End stands on higher ground about three-quarters of a mile south of the church, and is grouped round a green. To the west of it, in an isolated position surrounded by fields, is Westbury Farm, the site of the manor of that name. Part of the south wing is of the early 17th century, but the greater part of the building seems to have been constructed in 1670, the date inscribed on the south front. Roman remains consisting of part of a tessellated pavement and bricks were found in the neighbourhood at Dovecot Farm in January 1901.

Nether, Middle and Upper Fields in Shenley Brook End and part of East Green Common were enclosed by an Act of 1762, when an allotment was made to the rector in lieu of tithes. The award is dated 2 March 1763.[11] In 1841 Matthew Knapp, lord of Shenley Brook End Manor, was allotted the value of William Selby-Lowndes's chase rights over Shenley Common in part compensation for similar rights over Whaddon Chase relinquished by Matthew Knapp. The said allotment was to be fenced in from the rest of the common.[12] By an award having date 7 November 1851, Shenley Common was still further enclosed under an Act of 1845.[13]

Among place-names have been found : Hartdames, Bushey Bartrams, Fedys, Rowlak's Hill, Tatnyllmill,[14] the Brothered Land, Collet Wyke[15] (xvi cent.) ; Town Street, the Pickle and Calves, Mare Pitts[16] (xvii cent.) ; Fulmore, Bennetty Leys,[17] Carter's Farm[17a] (xviii cent.).

MANORS Two manors in Shenley of 5 and 2 hides respectively, both held in the time of Edward the Confessor by Baurchard, his thegn, were included in 1086 among the lands of Earl Hugh[18] (Earl of Chester). As one fee of the honour of Chester, or, as it was known from its later holders, the honour of Arundel,[19] Shenley was subordinate to Olney Manor, the chief possession from the early 13th century of the Earls of Chester in this county.[20] The descent through the Earls of Arundel, the Bassets of Drayton and Beauchamps and Nevills, Earls of Warwick, has been given under Olney (q.v.), with which the overlordship rights in Shenley were transferred to the Crown in 1488. In 1542 Shenley was included in the honour of Grafton,[21] and was held of the Crown for one-twentieth fee until the 17th century.[22]

From Hugh, the earl's tenant in 1086,[23] these two manors passed as one estate to the family of Maunsell. The William who paid half a mark for Shenley in 1167[24] may be the William Maunsell who in 1183 paid 2 marks for licence to sue John de Caverton for land in Shenley.[25] In 1198 7 virgates in Shenley were quitclaimed by Robert son of Ralph to Thomas Maunsell,[26] to whom Nicholas Maunsell quitclaimed a rent of 40s. in the same year.[27]

In 1223[28] and 1229[29] Thomas Maunsell presented to the church, and he or a successor of the same name paid scutage for Shenley in 1236[30] and was returned as lord of the vill in 1254.[31] Thomas Maunsell supported Simon de Montfort against the king, and it was probably during his absence that John de Grey about 1276 seized the manor, which he wasted, appropriating all he could and selling part.[32] Shenley was forfeited and granted to William de Aette (Ayet or Eyet), in accordance with the 'Dictum of Kenilworth.'[33] It was demised by William to Isabel de Albini, Countess of Arundel, the overlord, and by her granted, together with the custody of the heirs of Thomas Maunsell during their minority, to Richard de la Vache,[34] who was therefore the lord of Shenley in 1278,[35] and who acquired land there in that year.[36] Thomas Maunsell had left two daughters, Mabel, whom Richard de la Vache married to his son Richard, and Alice, who about 1283 married Robert Verdon[37] without her guardian's permission, and entered on certain lands in Shenley which Margery widow of Thomas Maunsell held in dower.[38] This led to trouble with Richard de la Vache the elder, against whom the Verdons brought a suit in 1284 to obtain possession of their moiety of the manor,[39] and both Richard de la Vache the elder and the heirs of Thomas Maunsell laid claim to the manorial rights

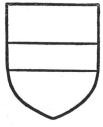 

MAUNSELL. *Gules a fesse argent.*

VACHE. *Gules three lions argent having golden crowns.*

in Shenley that year.[40] In 1285 both sisters and their husbands redeemed their father's lands from William de Aette[41] and divided Shenley between them, the moiety appertaining to the Vaches being settled by them in the following year on Robert de Broughton.[42]

[10] *Char. Com. Rep.* xxvii, 113.
[11] *Priv. Act,* 2 Geo. III, cap. 40 ; *Blue Bk. Inclosure Awards,* 13.
[12] Ibid. 4 & 5 Vict. cap. 23.
[13] *Blue Bk. Inclosure Awards,* 13
[14] *Ld. Rev. Misc. Bks.* clxxxviii, fol. 289, 291.
[15] Add. MS. 37069, fol. 45, 45 d.
[16] Ibid. fol. 39 d. ; *Parl. Surv. Bucks.* no. 18.
[17] *Exch. Dep. Spec. Com. Mich.* 10 Geo. I, no. 13.
[17a] *Chan. Proc.* (Bridges Div.), bdle. 212, no. 4.
[18] *V.C.H. Bucks.* i, 247.

[19] *Testa de Nevill* (Rec. Com.), 244b ; *Hund. R.* (Rec. Com.), ii, 334.
[20] *Cal. Inq. p.m.* (Edw. I), ii, 329 ; *Cal. Close,* 1279–88, p. 289–90 ; *Chan. Inq. p.m.* 17 Edw. III (1st nos.), no. 59.
[21] *L. and P. Hen. VIII,* xvii, 28 (22).
[22] Pat. 987, m. 50 ; *Chan. Inq. p.m.* (Ser. 2), cccv, 100.
[23] *V.C.H. Bucks.* i, 247.
[24] *Pipe R.* 13 *Hen. II* (Pipe R. Soc.), 109.
[25] Pipe R. 29 Hen. II, m. 7 d.
[26] Feet of F. case 14, file 2, no. 36.
[27] Ibid. file 3, no. 50.
[28] *R. of Hugh of Wells* (Cant. and York Soc.), ii, 61.

[29] Ibid. 75.
[30] *Testa de Nevill* (Rec. Com.), 259b ; see also ibid. 244b, 261b.
[31] *Hund. R.* (Rec. Com.), i, 30.
[32] Ibid. 42.
[33] *Cal. Pat.* 1281–92, p. 80.
[34] Ibid.
[35] *Hund. R.* (Rec. Com.), ii, 334.
[36] Feet of F. case 16, file 45, no. 1.
[37] *Abbrev. Plac.* (Rec. Com.), 208.
[38] *Cal. Pat.* 1281–92, p. 81.
[39] *Cal. Close,* 1279–88, p. 305.
[40] *Feud. Aids,* i, 80, 82.
[41] *Abbrev. Plac.* (Rec. Com.), 208.
[42] Feet of F. case 17, file 48, no. 5.

It was seized by the Crown for their default against Thomas Poyle, and an attempt to regain it in 1290 evidently succeeded,[43] for in 1294 Richard de la Vache was dealing with land in Shenley,[44] and in 1308 he settled his Shenley property on himself for life, with remainder successively to his sons Matthew and Richard and his daughter Maud and their heirs.[45] Matthew succeeded to Shenley before 1316,[46] and in 1326 a settlement was made by Walter de la Vache of a messuage and 24 acres of land in Shenley on himself for life, with remainder successively to William son of Wymark of Shenley, to Joan sister of William, to Walter son of Matthew de la Vache, Thomas his brother and Walter's heirs.[47] The Vaches' moiety of *SHENLEY MAUNSELL MANOR,* so-called during the 14th and 15th centuries,[48] descended with their manors in Aston Clinton and Chalfont St. Giles with which it was included in the settlements in the late 14th and early 15th centuries.[49] It passed with Aston Clinton to the Kirkhams, and after the death of Anne Kirkham, then a widow, in 1427[50] was held by a John Kirkham, who is described as of Shenley in 1435.[51]

As in Aston Clinton so also in Shenley, the manorial rights were claimed by Reynold Lord Grey de Wilton on the death in 1442 of his father Richard,[52] to whom Reynold's mother, the Vache heiress, had brought the manor in marriage.[53] After a dispute with his stepmother Margaret,[54] on whom this moiety as well as the other (see later) had been settled,[55] Reynold in 1447 acknowledged her life interest and that of her second husband, Sir Thomas Grey, to *VACHES MANOR* in Shenley, first so-called.[56] She died early in 1451–2, and was survived by Sir Thomas Grey,[57] probably a few years only, as Vaches reverted to Reynold Lord Grey de Wilton, by whom it was alienated in 1456 to Thomas Grey, Lord Richemount, the owner since before 1452 of the other moiety of Shenley called Verdons (q.v.), Reynold's renunciation of right therefore applying to the whole manor of Shenley called Vaches and Verdons.[58] The two manors henceforward remain in the same ownership, but the distinction between them was maintained, the names of Vaches and Verdons being replaced by Nether and Over Shenley after the early 16th century, and occasionally by Church and Brook End in the 18th and 19th centuries. In 1460 Lord Richemount obtained an exemplification of the grant of Verdons,[59] and in the same year granted the whole manor to Henry Duke of Exeter and others.[60] Both Lord Richemount and the Duke of Exeter were attainted as Lancastrians in 1461.[61]

Shenley escheated to the Crown, by whom it was doubtless bestowed on John Lord Grey de Wilton, son of Reynold, who had died in 1493,[69] since at his death in 1499 it was accounted among his possessions.[63] His son and heir Edmund negotiated the sale of the manor in transactions extending from 1506[64] to 1509, in which latter year it was transferred to Hugh Dennis and Thomas Wolverston,[65] who a few weeks later conveyed their interest to Robert Brudenell, justice of the Common Pleas, as trustee for Thomas Pigott of Whaddon, serjeant-at-law.[66] The latter died in 1520,[67] when Shenley passed, in accordance with the terms of his will, to his second son Francis,[68] afterwards called of Stratton (co. Bedford).[69] In 1539 he settled it on his son and heir Thomas, reserving to himself certain acres of wood,[70] for which he did homage the following year.[71] In 1541, however, he was forced to convey the manor to the Crown in exchange for other property.[72] A survey for 1550 mentions a forty years' lease of the manor-place of Shenley made by Francis Pigott to Richard Raven.[73] Edmund Ashfield, who in 1546 had been appointed bailiff and steward of the courts of the manor[74] at a salary of 53s. 4d.,[75] in 1563 obtained a grant of Shenley in fee,[76] Thomas Pigott, the son and heir of Francis, who had died in 1552,[77] releasing all right in the manor to the Crown in the same year.[78] In 1571 Sir Edmund Ashfield[78a] settled the manor on his wife Eleanor, with remainder to John Fortescue, husband of his deceased daughter Cecily, and to their sons Robert, Francis, William and Thomas Fortescue in tail-male.[79] Sir Edmund Ashfield died at Ewelme (co. Oxford) in January 1577–8. His son-in-law, Sir John Fortescue, who succeeded him,[80] purchased before 1573 the manor of Salden in Mursley, with which Shenley descends for the next 100 years.[81] Shenley was sequestered in 1651 for the recusancy of Sir John Fortescue, first baronet,[82]

FORTESCUE of Salden, baronet. *Azure a bend engrailed argent cotised or.*

[43] *Cal. Close,* 1288–96, p. 119.
[44] Feet of F. case 17, file 52, no. 7.
[45] Wrottesley, *Ped. from Plea R.* 376.
[46] *Feud. Aids,* i, 109, 112.
[47] Feet of F. case 19, file 76, no. 3.
[48] The earliest reference to this name is dated 1303 (*Cal. Chart. R.* 1300–26, p. 34) and the latest 1460 (*Cal. Pat.* 1452–61, p. 583).
[49] *V.C.H. Bucks.* ii, 315, iii, 187; see also *Feud. Aids,* i, 132.
[50] Chan. Inq. p.m. 6 Hen. VI, no. 12. A brass in the church to her memory speaks of her as cousin and heir to Sir Philip de la Vache, who died in 1408. She was the daughter and heir of Lucy Spigurnel by William Alberd (Chan. Inq. p.m. 10 Rich. II, no. 39; 14 Rich. II, no. 45).
[51] *Cal. Pat.* 1429–36, p. 438; see also pp. 164–5.
[52] Chan. Inq. p.m. 20 Hen. VI, no. 23.
[53] *V.C.H. Bucks.* ii, 315.
[54] Wrottesley, loc. cit.

[55] Chan. Inq. p.m. 20 Hen. VI, no. 23.
[56] Feet of F. case 293, file 71, no. 55.
[57] Chan. Inq. p.m. 30 Hen. VI, no. 12.
[58] Close, 306, m. 5.
[59] *Cal. Pat.* 1452–61, p. 583.
[60] Close, 311, m. 9.
[61] G.E.C. *Peerage,* vi, 341; iii, 298.
[62] Ibid. iv, 112.
[63] Exch. Inq. p.m. (Ser. 2), file 5, no. 9.
[64] De Banco R. 976, m. 3, 241; 978, m. 7; Feet of F. case 22, file 129, no. 1. Giles Lord Daubeny, king's chamberlain, as tenant of Shenley Manor, received a pardon in 1506, which had the effect of discharging his obligations to the late Lord Grey de Wilton (*Dict. Nat. Biog.*; Pat. 600, m. 16). His name occurs in the negotiations in conjunction with Dennis, &c.
[65] Feet of F. Bucks. East. 1 Hen. VIII.
[66] Pat. 610, m. 28.
[67] Chan. Inq. p.m. (Ser. 2), xxxv, 1.
[68] P.C.C. 26 Ayloffe; Memo. R. (Exch. L.T.R.), Hil. 28 Hen. VIII, m. 7.
[69] *L. and P. Hen. VIII,* xvi, g. 878 (47).

[70] Ibid. xiv (1), g. 191 (9); Feet of F. Div. Co. Hil. 30 Hen. VIII.
[71] Memo. R. (Exch. L.T.R.), East. 32 Hen. VIII, m. 18.
[72] *L. and P. Hen. VIII,* xvi, g. 878 (47).
[73] Ld. Rev. Misc. Bks. clxxxviii, fol. 291. Among the farms leased by Francis Pigott to different tenants were Carters Farm Place, Brokhole's Farm, and Franklyns Place (ibid. fol. 292b–293b).
[74] *L. and P. Hen. VIII,* xxi (1), p. 774.
[75] Ld. Rev. Misc. Bks. clxxxviii, fol. 294b.   [76] Pat. 5 Eliz. pt. i, m. 50.
[77] Chan. Inq. p.m. (Ser. 2), xcv, 1.
[78] Recov. R. Trin. 5 Eliz. m. 559; Feet of F. Bucks. Trin. 5 Eliz.; Hil. 6 Eliz.
[78a] He was knighted in 1570 (Shaw, *Kts. of Engl.* ii, 74).
[79] Pat. 1181, m. 43.
[80] Chan. Inq. p.m. (Ser. 2), clxxx, 1.
[81] Ibid. cccv, 100; Feet of F. Bucks. Mich. 22 Jas. I; Recov. R. Mich. 22 Jas. I, m. 94.
[82] *Cal. Com. for Comp.* 2541.

and in 1652 was held by his two sons Sir John and Edward Fortescue,[83] the elder brother apparently renouncing his rights in it to the younger[84] after the death of their father in 1656.[85] Edward Fortescue was therefore in possession in 1661,[86] possibly as trustee for Elizabeth, the elder brother's daughter,[87] who, with her husband, Thomas Brome Whorwood, held the manor in 1687.[88] They sold it ten years later to John Knapp[89] of Little Linford (q.v.), with which it descended[90] until about 1868, when Matthew Knapp apparently sold the property to Charles Morrell. A writ followed thereupon as to the conveyance. Some twenty years later the Shenley Park estate passed to James Waddell, and with Westbury Farm was purchased about 1900 by Lt.-Col. William Duncan, J.P., for the benefit of his daughter, Mrs. Richard Selby-Lowndes, who is now owner.

The other moiety of Shenley, held by Robert Verdon in 1316,[91] had passed to his son Robert before 1340, in which year another son, William, renounced

VERDON. *Argent a cross azure fretty or.*   BEAUCHAMP. *Gules a fesse between six crosslets or.*

the life interest which the younger Robert had given him.[92] Robert Verdon was still holding in 1346,[93] but before 1397 the manorial rights of this moiety had been acquired by the overlord, Thomas Beauchamp Earl of Warwick,[94] lord of Hanslope (q.v.), with which it descended to Richard Beauchamp Earl of Warwick.[95] In 1408 he released to Thomas Crawe and Robert Huggeford all his right in the manor,[96] probably in process of transferring it to Richard Lord Grey de Wilton, by whom it was settled in the year of his death on his wife Margaret and his issue by her.[97] Margaret conveyed her interest in this moiety of Shenley, now called *VERDONS MANOR*, to Thomas Grey Lord Richemount,[98] William Grey, her son and heir by Richard Lord Grey de Wilton, releasing his title in the manor[99]

immediately after her death in 1452.[100] The two moieties henceforward descend together, and their history has been given under Vaches.

The manorial privileges in the 13th century comprised view of frankpledge, held twice a year, and assize of bread and ale,[1] and were enumerated in the grant of Shenley Manor to Edmund Ashfield in 1563.[2] Free warren bestowed on Richard de la Vache in 1303[3] was still claimed at the end of the 17th century.[4] Courts leet and baron were held from the 16th to the 18th century, and free fishing was among the appurtenances.[5]

Two manors in Shenley of 2½ hides each, held in the time of Edward the Confessor by Wlward, one of his thegns, and Morcar, a man of Earl Harold, were assessed in 1086 as the only holdings in Buckinghamshire of Richard Engaine and Urse de Bersers respectively.[6] The two estates were in Mursley Hundred, afterwards part of Cottesloe Hundred, and united to form the later *WESTBURY MANOR* which lay in the Cottesloe part of Shenley, the amalgamation probably taking place by the marriage of Richard Engaine with the widow of Richard Fitz Urse.[7] Richard Engaine's chief manor in 1086 was Benefield (co. Northampton),[8] the head of an honour to which Westbury was attached[9] and which passed through the families of Lisures[10] and Bassingbourne.[11] In 1278 the overlordship was vested in the heirs of Warner Bassingbourne,[12] but in the assessment of 1284–6 the manor was said to be held of the king,[13] and the Crown was returned as overlord until the 17th century,[14] the service rendered being one-tenth of a fee with 5s. for hidage.[15]

A manor of 2½ hides in Westbury entered in the Domesday Book under Mursley Hundred has been taken to be Westbury Manor in Shenley owing to the hundredal heading.[16] It was then, however, among the possessions of Roger de Ivri, whose lands afterwards went to form the honour of St. Valery.[17] There is no trace of this honour in Shenley, to which, moreover, the other 2½-hide manor of Westbury, in Stodfald, now Buckingham Hundred, was later attached.[18] The owner of this second manor, the Bishop of Bayeux, had as tenant Roger,[19] who may be identical with Roger de Ivri, and it is possible that both these manors, one held in chief and one under the bishop, were in Stodfald Hundred, and that a later amalgamation took place, owing to the manorial rights being held by one and the same lord.[20]

There is no record of the subinfeudation of Westbury

[83] Feet of F. Bucks. Mich. 1652.
[84] Recov. R. Mich. 1657, m. 204.
[85] G.E.C. *Complete Baronetage*, ii, 415.
[86] Feet of F. Bucks. Mich. 13 Chas. II.
[87] Chan. Proc. (Bridges Div.), bdles. 145, no. 156 ; 100, no. 2.
[88] Feet of F. Hil. 3 Jas. II ; Recov. R. East. 3 Jas. II, m. 168.
[89] Feet of F. Bucks. Hil. 8 Will. III ; Recov. R. East. 9 Will. III, m. 40.
[90] Lysons, *Mag. Brit.* i (3), 629 ; Sheahan, op. cit. 597.
[91] *Feud. Aids,* i, 109, 112.
[92] *Cat. of Anct. D.* i, 18.
[93] *Feud. Aids,* i, 132.
[94] Close, 20 Ric. II, pt. ii, m. 9 d.; Chan. Inq. p.m. 21 Ric. II, no. 6b.
[95] The rent from Shenley was held in dower by Agnes daughter of Thomas Fitz Eustace (De Banco R. 575, m. 1) and widow of Robert Verdon, in 1398 (Chan. Inq. p.m. 22 Ric. II, no. 101).

In 1404 Margaret, widow of Thomas Earl of Warwick, received one-third of Shenley in dower (De Banco R. Hil. 5 Hen. IV, m. 210).
[96] Close, 9 Hen. IV, m. 18.
[97] Chan. Inq. p.m. 20 Hen. VI, no. 23.
[98] Ibid. 30 Hen. VI, no. 12.
[99] Close, 31 Hen. VI, m. 22.
[100] Chan. Inq. p.m. 30 Hen. VI, no. 12.
[1] *Hund. R.* (Rec. Com.), ii, 338 ; *Plac. de Quo Warr.* (Rec. Com.), 95.
[2] Pat. 987, m. 50.
[3] *Cal. Chart. R.* 1300–26, p. 34.
[4] Feet of F. Bucks. Hil. 8 Will. III.
[5] Pat. 987, m. 50 ; Recov. R. Mich. 3 Geo. II, m. 343 ; Trin. 27 Geo. III, m. 354.
[6] *V.C.H. Bucks.* i, 269, 271.
[7] *Red Bk. of Exch.* (Rolls Ser.), 333.
[8] *V.C.H. Northants,* i, 356.
[9] *Testa de Nevill* (Rec. Com.), 246.

[10] *V.C.H. Northants,* i, 365.
[11] *Rot. Lit. Pat.* (Rec. Com.), i, 97.
[12] *Hund. R.* (Rec. Com.), ii, 334.
[13] *Feud. Aids,* i, 82.
[14] Chan. Inq. p.m. 35 Edw. III, pt. i, no. 84 ; 8 Hen. V, no. 42 ; Fine R. 6 Chas. I, pt. i, no. 16. In 1530 Westbury was said to be subordinate to Shenley Manor, to which it owed 5s. rent (Chan. Inq. p.m. [Ser. 2], l, 76).
[15] *Cal. Inq. p.m.* (Edw. I), ii, 295 ; *Cal. Close,* 1341–3, p. 432 ; *Feud. Aids,* i, 101, 127.
[16] *V.C.H. Bucks.* i, 269.
[17] See Thornton.
[18] *Hund. R.* (Rec. Com.), i, 32.
[19] *V.C.H. Bucks.* i, 237.
[20] This is borne out by the hidage given for 1278 in *Hund. R.* (Rec. Com.), ii, 342. For the two divisions of Westbury Manor (Buckingham Hundred) it amounts to more than 4 hides.

SHENLEY CHURCH FROM THE NORTH-EAST

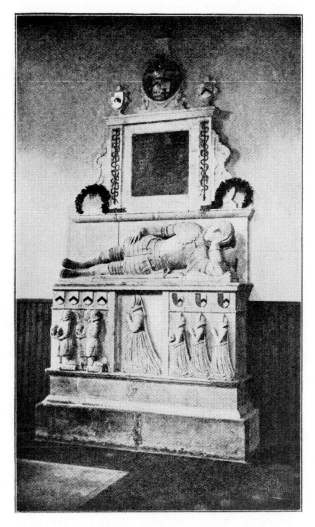

SHENLEY : TOMB OF THOMAS STAFFORD IN CHURCH

Manor in Shenley until the reign of Henry III, when it was held by Joan de Nowers.[21] Thomas son of Stephen had lands in Shenley about 1226,[22] and may have been related to Eustace son of Thomas, after whose death Henry III gave Westbury in custody to Terry (Turricus) Allmain, in possession in 1278.[23] Thomas son of Eustace or Thomas Fitz Eustace, who attained his majority in 1284,[24] received a grant of free warren in Shenley in 1292.[25] In 1320 he obtained licence to have an oratory in his house at Shenley,[26] and in 1327 he settled the manor on himself and his wife Agnes and their issue with remainder to his daughter Joan and her heirs.[27] At his death about 1341 his wife Agnes had the custody of their son Thomas, aged thirteen.[28] He evidently died without issue male, for at Agnes's death in 1361 Shenley Manor passed to her son and heir John Fitz Eustace, aged twenty-two.[29] John Fitz Eustace died in 1369,[30] and this manor was assigned in dower to his widow Christine.[31] She afterwards married Sir William Berland, to whom the marriage of Philip son and heir of John Fitz Eustace was granted in 1385.[32] Philip Fitz Eustace and his wife Blanche enfeoffed Thomas Percy Earl of Worcester and others of Westbury Manor, to the intent that it should be reenfeoffed to them in fee simple, but the Earl of Huntingdon, one of the feoffees, contrary to this order and without the consent of his co-feoffees, enfeoffed Thomas Shelley, kt., at whose execution and forfeiture in 1400 Westbury escheated to the Crown.[33] The Earl of Worcester, however, re-entered the manor without licence and enfeoffed Philip Fitz Eustace and Blanche,[34] who obtained the king's pardon in January 1402-3,[35] and in June of that year they enfeoffed Nicholas Wolbergh, John Whitwell and others,[36] a renunciation of right being made in the following month by Agnes Verdon, daughter of Thomas Fitz Eustace.[37] Notwithstanding the legalization of this transaction by the king,[38] in December of that year he granted Westbury as a forfeiture of Thomas Shelley to John Cope for life.[39] The grant appears to have been ineffective, and in the following February 1403-4 the feoffees' title was strengthened by a renunciation of rights from John Hartshorn, from whom Philip Fitz Eustace had borrowed money.[40] In the following December the feoffees obtained a release of claim to Westbury from Richard brother and heir of Thomas Shelley.[41] The manor was held to the use of Nicholas Wolbergh and

his heirs, and after the death in 1419 of John Whitwell, the surviving feoffee, Westbury passed to Cecily daughter and heir of Wolbergh and wife of William Sydney.[42] In 1430 they settled Westbury on themselves and their sons William and Richard in tail-male,[43] and it was apparently the son William who died seised of the manor in 1462, leaving two infant daughters, Elizabeth and Anne, who afterwards married John Hampden and William Uvedale respectively.[44] The Uvedales before 1512 appear to have renounced their interest in the manor to Thomas Stafford of Tattenhoe, who made a settlement of it that year,[45] and to whom the Hampdens shortly afterwards quitclaimed their rights.[46] Westbury has since descended with Tattenhoe[47] (q.v.) to Mr. W. Selby Lowndes, the present owner, though the manorial rights have long since been obsolete. There are references to a windmill on Westbury Manor in 1278[48] and 1342.[49]

STAFFORD of Tatten-hoe. *Or a cheveron gules and a quarter ermine.*

In 1278 the priory of Snelshall held 1½ virgates in Shenley and half a virgate in Westbury,[50] and paid rent to Woburn Abbey.[51] From this estate 12d. rent each was paid in 1535 to Francis Pigott and to — Hampden,[52] the former of whom received a grant of the property in 1539.[53] Two years later, however, it passed with Shenley Manor to the Crown.

Lands in Shenley belonging to Bradwell Abbey descended with Bradwell Manor (q.v.) to Sheen Priory.[54] The gild of St. Margaret and St. Katherine, Fenny Stratford, had a farm-house with dove-house and 60 acres of land worth £20 yearly in Shenley, to which Sir John Fortescue, bart., of Salden, Mursley, put forward a claim in 1656.[55] This property known as Dovehouse Farm, which was leased by Sir John or his son in 1680, was afterwards bought by John Knapp,[55a] purchaser of the principal manor in Shenley, into which it became absorbed.

The church of *ST. MARY* consists of *CHURCH* a chancel measuring internally 23 ft. 6 in. by 14 ft. 6 in., north vestry, central tower 14 ft. square, north transept 12 ft. by 11 ft.,

[21] *Testa de Nevill* (Rec. Com.), 246.
[22] *Rot. Lit. Claus.* (Rec. Com.), ii, 104; Feet of F. case 15, file 20, no. 7; cf. Maitland, *Bracton's Note Bk.* iii, 539.
[23] *Hund. R.* (Rec. Com.), ii, 334; cf. i, 42.
[24] *Cal. Inq. p.m.* (Edw. I), ii, 295.
[25] *Cal. Chart. R.* 1257–1300, p. 413.
[26] Add. MS. 5839, p. 331.
[27] Feet of F. case 19, file 77, no. 4; De Banco R. East. 1 Edw. III, m. 16 d.; *Abbrev. Rot. Orig.* (Rec. Com.), ii, 14; *Cal. Pat.* 1327–30, p. 17.
[28] *Cal. Close*, 1341–3, p. 432; Chan. Inq. p.m. 15 Edw. III (1st nos.), no. 9.
[29] Chan. Inq. p.m. 35 Edw. III, pt. i, no. 84.
[30] Ibid. 43 Edw. III, pt. i, no. 41.
[31] *Cal. Close*, 1369–74, p. 54; *Abbrev. Rot. Orig.* (Rec. Com.), ii, 304. The assignment of dower included a garden called Chapelyard and another called Holdeculverhouse orchard, three granges, a third of a dovecote, lands called Peche-cheyate, Wuttesbuderwood, Tackenhale,

Goldenhill, Netherdiddeswong (Chan. Inq. p.m. 43 Edw. III [Add. nos.], 12).
[32] *Cal. Pat.* 1381–5, p. 514.
[33] Ibid. 1401–5, p. 453; Chan. Inq. p.m. 1 Hen. IV, no. 5.
[34] *Cal. Pat.* loc. cit.
[35] Ibid. 190.
[36] Harl. Chart. 50, A 36; De Banco R. 570, m. 404; Feet of F. case 21, file 112, no. 8.
[37] De Banco R. 575, m. 1.
[38] *Cal. Pat.* 1401–5, p. 243.
[39] Ibid. 334.
[40] Close, 252, m. 16.
[41] De Banco R. 576, m. 1.
[42] Chan. Inq. p.m. 8 Hen. V, no. 42.
[43] Feet of F. case 22, file 119, no. 10.
[44] Chan. Inq. p.m. 17 Edw. IV, no. 38.
[45] Close, 384, m. 1.
[46] Feet of F. Bucks. Trin. 5 Hen. VIII. A rent of £8 10s. reserved on this sale (Add. MS. 37069, fol. 35) was conveyed in 1608 by Oliver St. John and Elizabeth his wife to Sir Oliver Luke and Thomas Anstell (Feet of F. Div. Co. Trin.

6 Jas. I). In 1610 Francis and Walter Dayrell transferred it to Sir Francis Fortescue (Add. MS. 37069, fol. 36 d.), whose son and grandsons alienated it in 1652 to John Playdell and Ralph Holt (ibid. p. 38; Feet of F. Bucks. Trin. 1652).
[47] See also Recov. R. Trin. 32 Eliz. m. 57; Feet of F. Bucks. Mich. 3 Jas. I; unidentified Co. East. 3 Chas. I; Lysons, *Mag. Brit.* i (3), 629; Sheahan, op. cit. 598.
[48] *Hund. R.* (Rec. Com.), ii, 334.
[49] *Cal. Close*, 1341–3, p. 432.
[50] *Hund. R.* (Rec. Com.), ii, 334.
[51] *Pope Nich. Tax.* (Rec. Com.), 47b; *Cal. Pat.* 1334–8, p. 493; *Valor Eccl.* (Rec. Com.), iv, 229.
[52] *Valor Eccl.* (Rec. Com.), iv, 229.
[53] *L. and P. Hen. VIII*, xiv (1), g. 403 (56).
[54] Ct. R. (Gen. Ser.), portf. 155, no. 5.
[55] Parl. Surv. Bucks. no. 18.
[55a] Chan. Proc. (Bridges Div.), bdles 212, no. 4; 218, no. 30.

south transept 12 ft. by 10 ft., nave 39 ft. 6 in. by 17 ft. 6 in., north and south aisles, both 7 ft. 6 in. wide, and south porch. It is built of rubble, and the roofs are covered with lead and tiles.

The church dates from about 1150, and originally consisted of chancel, nave, north and south transepts, and perhaps a central tower; but both the chancel and tower have been rebuilt, and the only parts of the original structure remaining are the transepts and the west wall of the nave. About 1190 the chancel was rebuilt and the south aisle added; the latter, however, was rebuilt about 1350, when the north aisle and the nave clearstory were also added. The tower was rebuilt about 1490. The porch probably dates from the 17th century, but has been considerably repaired, and the whole fabric was restored in 1888–90. The vestry is modern, but stands on the site of a chapel or sacristy built about 1180 and destroyed when the tower was rebuilt.

The chancel was originally vaulted in two bays, and the richly carved triple corbels which supported the transverse and diagonal ribs are still in position in the middle of the north and south walls, but the vault has been destroyed. Some stones from the moulded ribs have been re-used in the rear arch of the east window, while a sculptured stone lying at the south-west is probably one of the bosses. The eastern bay retains its original windows in the north and south walls, and the western bay has an original window on the south. All these are single pointed lights with moulded external arches of one order and rear-arches of two orders, supported generally by shafts with foliated capitals and moulded bases, most of the shafts having annulets. On the north is an original round-headed doorway, which was evidently designed to open into an adjoining building, probably a sacristy. The east wall is almost entirely occupied by a large five-light window with a four-centred head of about 1490, which has been considerably repaired. A three-light window of the same period has been inserted at the north-west, and opposite to it, at the west end of the south wall, is a low-side window of early 15th-century date, while between the original windows on the south is a round-headed doorway of about 1400. Both the north-west window and the north doorway now open into the vestry. There are two lockers in the chancel, one on the north and the other on the south, and at the south-east is a double trefoiled piscina, probably of the 14th century, with a restored circular bowl, while below the south-east window are two restored sedilia of the 13th century under one segmental arch with a moulded stone seat and dividing arm, the arm being enriched by an attached shaft. The low-pitched moulded roof is of the 16th century.

The ground stage of the tower communicates on all sides with the chancel, nave, and transepts respectively by wide pointed arches of late 15th-century date, each having three orders springing from chamfered responds with moulded capitals and bases. The north transept, which now contains the organ loft, has a restored 14th-century window of two lights with tracery in the north wall, and a small round-headed window of the mid-12th century over a modern doorway in the east wall. A 14th-century pointed arch, the south respond of which has been replaced by the north-west pier of the tower, communicates with the north aisle on the west. The south transept is of

similar character but with slightly different detail; in the east wall is a small 12th-century window, now blocked, while an early 14th-century window of two trefoiled lights with tracery has been inserted in the south wall. The transept opens to the south aisle on the west by a 14th-century arch, which has been treated in the same manner as that on the north. There is a locker on the south, and a rich 12th-century capital has been built into the wall at the north-east.

The nave has north and south arcades of four bays with pointed arches. The south arcade, which dates from the end of the 12th century, is supported by circular piers with crudely formed capitals and square abaci. The north arcade is of about 1350, and the arches rest on octagonal piers with moulded capitals and bases. Both arcades have been repaired. The eastern arches on both sides have been encroached upon by the piers of the tower, which have entirely replaced the east responds. At the west end of the nave is a pointed doorway of the 14th century and above it is a large 15th-century window of five cinquefoiled lights under a four-centred head, both of which have been extensively repaired. The clearstory is lighted from the north by three plain windows of two trefoiled lights, and from the south by three pointed two-light windows with tracery, all of which, though considerably restored, date from the 14th century.

In the north wall of the north aisle are three traceried two-light windows of about 1350 and a moulded doorway, now blocked, of the same period; all the windows have been restored. In the west wall is a modern two-light window. The details of the south aisle are similar in character to those of the north. There are three 14th-century windows of two lights in the south wall, which have also been repaired, and a modern window at the west end. The south doorway is also modern.

The tower rises two stages above the church roof and is surmounted by an embattled parapet; the stair turret at the north-east, which is continued above the parapet, is also embattled. The turret was originally entered by a doorway in the north transept, but this has been blocked and a new doorway opened from the vestry. There is a window of three lights, one glazed and two blind, in each of the north and south walls of the intermediate stage, and the bell-chamber is lighted from all sides by two-light windows with four-centred heads, all being of the late 15th century. On the east and west walls are the weatherings of earlier high-pitched roofs.

The font, which has an octagonal panelled bowl, dates from the 15th century. In the chancel are two slabs, one with a brass inscription to Thomas Thurleby, rector (d. 1432), and the matrix for his figure, and the other with the matrices for a figure and inscription. There is also a marble monument with arms to Sir Edmund Ashfield (d. 1577) and Eleanor his wife. The monument consists of a recess containing a white marble sarcophagus and framed by Corinthian columns supporting an entablature and broken pediment. In the north aisle is a large monument to Thomas Stafford of Tattenhoe (d. 1607), with a reclining alabaster effigy in armour of the period. On the front of the tomb are the kneeling figures of his wife, their four sons and three daughters, each of the sons bearing the arms of Stafford, and the daughters those of their respective husbands, Bernard, Thakeston, and Savage, each impaling Stafford. On the wall above the effigy is an inscription in an architectural setting surmounted by the arms of Stafford of Tattenhoe, quartering Hastang, Burdett and Aylesbury. Some 17th-century carved panels are incorporated in the pulpit, and the legs of the communion table in the south transept are of the same period.

The tower contains a ring of six bells; the treble is modern, while the second and third are by Newcome, 1615 and 1616 respectively, and the fourth and fifth by Bartholomew Atton, 1593 and 1610. The tenor, which bears the inscription 'Missi De Celis Abeo Nomen Amen Gabrelis,' was probably cast by Robert Burford in the early 15th century.[55b] There is also a small bell with no inscription, but probably of the 17th century.

The plate consists of an 18th-century chalice and paten, and a modern flagon.

The registers begin in 1653.

ADVOWSON The advowson of the church of Shenley, mentioned in 1223,[56] descended with the manor until about the middle of the 19th century, since then it

has been held by a succession of owners, incumbents of Shenley.[57] The church was valued at £12 yearly in 1291[58] and at £23 in 1535.[59]

Rents amounting to 11s. 4d. were applied to the keeping of obits and maintenance of a lamp,[60] and the property from which they issued was granted to Sir Edward Bray in 1553.[61] Hugh Earl of Chester bestowed the tithes of Shenley on the abbey of St. Evroul, Normandy, to which Ralph Earl of Chester confirmed them in 1121–9.[62]

CHARITIES The almshouses, erected about 1615, under the will of Thomas Stafford of Tattenhoe, consist of six cottages endowed with a rent-charge of £35 issuing out of an estate at Great Linford; they are regulated by a scheme of the Charity Commissioners of 17 March 1882. By the scheme the inmates are limited to three in number, the remaining cottages being let and the rents applied in augmentation of the income of the charity.

The Bread Charity.—Robert Seeling, by his will proved in the P.C.C. 8 November 1681, devised £3 yearly to the poor in bread. The annuity is paid out of land formerly called Nether Lawn, now the property of Mr. Richard Selby-Lowndes.

SHERINGTON

Serintone (xi cent.); Sirinton, Schirinton (xii cent.); Shyriton (xiii cent.); Shringtone, Scringtone, Sheryngton (xiv cent.); Shryngton (xiv–xv cent.).

This parish covers 1,805 acres, of which 605 are arable, 944 permanent grass and 45 woods and plantations.[1] The soil is various, the subsoil limestone and clay, the principal crops grown being wheat, barley, beans and roots. The ground falls from about 300 ft. above the ordnance datum in the north to about 200 ft. in the west and south, where the River Ouse and Chicheley Brook form the boundary. The river is here crossed by Sherington Bridge, a structure of three large and two small arches [1a] which carries the main road from Olney to Newport Pagnell. This road is joined about a quarter of a mile east of the river by the high road to Bedford.

The village of Sherington, which is large and straggling, lies along the road from Newport Pagnell to Olney, here called High Street. Gun Lane (which ends as Parson's Lane) and Perry Lane branch off to the east and south-east from the High Street, and with it almost encircle the village, the northern and higher end of which is called Church End, this name appearing early in the 16th century.[2] Here the church of St. Laud the Martyr stands on elevated ground, with the rectory about 300 yds. to the south.

The latter is a 17th-century stone house of two stories, built probably about 1607, the date inscribed upon a stone set in the south wall; additions and alterations have been made in modern times. Some original panelling still remains in the hall. Near it is the school. Yew Tree Farm, in the village, is a stone house of the late 16th century, with subsequent additions; a panel on the north front bears the date 1595. Further to the south is another stone house of about the same date, now called the Laurels. It retains some original fittings, including the staircase. At the south end of the village is the Manor House, now occupied by Mrs. Taylor. The present house, which was built probably in the 18th century, is surrounded by a moat. It is uncertain to which manor this house belonged, but as the Umneys, who owned Caves Manor, apparently resided here,[3] it may have been the manor-house of that manor. The principal manor-house, which was occupied by the Linfords, Ardes, Lowes, Adams and Chesters, was situated north of the church, according to Browne Willis.[4] Another manor-house in the parish, which is now known as the Mercers' Farm, is situated to the north of the Manor House.

There is a Methodist chapel north-west of Mercers' Farm, and a Congregational chapel is

[55b] A. H. Cocks, *Ch. Bells of Bucks.* 562.
[56] *R. of Hugh of Wells* (Cant. and York Soc.), ii, 61.
[57] *Clergy Lists* to 1860; Add. MS. 5839, p. 338–40; Inst. Bks. (P.R.O.); Feet of F. Bucks. Mich. 6 Chas. I; Hil. 29 & 30 Chas. II; Trin. 30 Chas. II.
[58] *Pope Nich. Tax.* (Rec. Com.), 33b.
[59] *Valor Eccl.* (Rec. Com.), iv, 245.
[60] Chant. Cert. 5, no. 26.
[61] Pat. 6 Edw. VI, pt. ix.
[62] Round, *Cal. Doc. of France*, 223.
[1] Statistics from Bd. of Agric. (1905).

[1a] Between 1320 and 1342 an indulgence was granted for the repair of the bridge (Linc. Epis. Reg. Memo. Burghersh, fol. 39). Richard Maryot, lord of the manor of Caves and other manors here, in 1490 bequeathed 'to the making of the arches of the brigge of Shiryngton now not vawted with stone with a perpoynt wall upon the seid arches 6 marc if they will not be made with less silver' (P.C.C. 11 Dogett).
[2] In 1520 Humphrey Ardes, son by his second wife Katherine Hamnell (*Visit. of Bucks.* [Harl. Soc.], 144) of

Michael Ardes, lord of the principal manor, died seised of tenements in the Churche End of Sherington, and was succeeded by his year-old son Robert, at whose death the property descended to his sister Elizabeth, aged thirteen in 1530, when she was in possession (Exch. Inq. p.m. [Ser. 2], file 25, no. 10).
[3] Sheahan, *Hist. and Topog. of Bucks.* 601. The capital messuage of Caves Manor, however, was said in 1813 to be divided into two tenements (Recov. R. Trin. 53 Geo. III, m. 63).
[4] Add. MS. 5839, p. 344.

situated north-east of the Manor House and south of Crofts End.

In the west of the parish are parts of an abandoned railway.

About a quarter of a mile south of the village is a district called Chicheley Hill. The north-eastern angle of the parish is occupied by Sherington Wood.

The parish was inclosed by Act of Parliament in 1796,[5] the award being dated 4 July 1797.[6]

Among place-names have been found : Wallecot Furlong, Godescote, Crosfurlong (undated deed)[7]; Longcroft Hale,[8] Pirifurlong, Grenedig, Barndbeg[9] (xiii cent.).

MANORS   In 1086 *SHERINGTON* was included among the lands of the Bishop of Coutances, and was assessed at 10 hides. Six hides of this manor had previously been held as one manor by Edwin son of Borret, 1 hide had been held as one manor by Alwin his man, and 3 hides as one manor by Osulf, a man of King Edward, the last two being able to assign and sell.[10]

THE RECTORY, SHERINGTON

This land owed the service of two knights,[11] each of the three manors, later distinguishable in this parish as Sherington, Cockfield and Fitz Johns, being after-wards answerable for that proportion of the original estate which they represented. This arbitrary division of responsibility seems, however, to have resulted in some confusion, for, though one-third of the whole two fees went to form Fitz John's Manor,[12] the remaining two estates were still said to owe one fee

each.[13]   The tenants of the more important of these, Sherington Manor, owed suit twice yearly at Northampton and at the hundred court, and paid 40d. for ward of La Ho (? Cainhoe Castle, Bedford-shire) and for ward of Northampton Castle.[14] The other fee at that date (1276) was said to be held of the king in chief, but the Abbess of Fontévrault, by gift of the king's ancestors, took the 32s. due.[15] In 1284 the service was unknown, while Sherington Manor was held by the service of two armoured horses in the king's army.[16] The service for the two fees is duly recorded all through the 14th century, but in the 15th the Cockfield portion is returned as owing one-fortieth of a fee only[17] and the chief manor one-third of a fee.[18] An inquisition of 1637, stating that the principal manor was held of the king in chief,[19] corrects a former one of that year whereby the overlordship was ascribed to Newport Pagnell Manor.[20]

After the forfeiture of the lands of the Bishop of Coutances in the reign of William Rufus, Sherington passed to the family of Carun (Karon, Caroun), known also as Sherington. William de Carun, or de Sherington, son of Ralf de Carun or de Sherington, bestowed the church of Sherington on Tickford Priory before 1150.[21] He paid 4 marks scutage in 1160–1,[22] and was paying scutage from that date to 1171–2.[23] He was succeeded, probably in 1188, by his son Richard de Carun,[24] who owed 100 marks fine for land in Sherington in that year.[25] Felicia, widow of William son of Ralf, who claimed a hide of land in Sherington in 1194,[26] was probably the widow of William de Sherington. Richard must have been dead before 1201–2, when Robert Vipount gave the king 20 marks and a palfrey to have the wardship of the lands of Richard de Sherington,[27] for which lands he paid £4 farm in 1202.[28] Richard left a son Ralph,[29] who was succeeded after 1210[30] by his son John, who, as John de Carun, in 1232 claimed two separate properties of 10 acres of land and 2 acres of wood each against John son of Hawise and John de Coveleigh and his wife Scholastica, daughter of John de Carun's grandfather Richard.[31] Some arrangement was concluded in the following

[5] Priv. Act, 36 Geo. III, cap. 66.
[6] Recov. R. D. Enr. Trin. 38 Geo. III, m. 103.
[7] Add. MS. 5836, fol. 140.
[8] Feet of F. case 16, file 44, no. 6.
[9] Ibid. case 15, file 23, no. 7.
[10] *V.C.H. Bucks.* i, 241.
[11] *Red Bk. of Exch.* (Rolls Ser.), 536.
[12] Chan. Inq. p.m. 6 Edw. II, no. 13 ; 1 Hen. V, no. 5.
[13] *Testa de Nevill* (Rec. Com.), 244.
[14] *Hund. R.* (Rec. Com.), i, 41.
[15] Ibid.
[16] *Feud. Aids*, i, 82.
[17] Chan. Inq. p.m. 20 Hen. VI, no. 23.

[18] Ibid. 3 Hen. IV, no. 2.
[19] Ibid. (Ser. 2), dxlvii, 176.
[20] Ibid. dxliii, 19.
[21] Round, *Cal. Doc. of France*, 444 ; Curia Regis R. 102, m. 17.
[22] *Pipe R. 7 Hen. II* (Pipe R. Soc.), 12.
[23] Ibid. 8 *Hen. II*, 42 ; 14 *Hen. II*, 11 ; 18 *Hen. II*, 51.
[24] Wrottesley, *Ped. from Plea R.* 481 ; Maitland, *Bracton's Note Bk.* ii, 672–4.
[25] *Pipe R.* 34 Hen. II, m. 9 d. ; 35 Hen. II, 2 Ric. I.
[26] *R. of the King's Court*, 1194–5 (Pipe R. Soc.), 23.
[27] *Pipe R.* 3 John, m. 22 d. ; cf. *Rot. de Oblatis et Fin.* (Rec. Com.), 106.

[28] Pipe R. 4 John, m. 2.
[29] Maitland, loc. cit. ; Wrottesley, op. cit. 481.
[30] *Red Bk. of Exch.* (Rolls Ser.), 536.
[31] Maitland, loc. cit. This case gives the following pedigree :

William de Carun

Richard — Gervase

Ralf — William — Scholastica = John de Coveleigh

John de Carun — sons

year,[32] and John de Carun was in possession in 1234–5.[33] He was succeeded after 1237[34] by his son Ralph, who died without issue.[35] Martin, brother and heir of Ralph,[36] complained that in 1272 several persons, including Roger Fitz John of Hanslope, probably identical with the Roger Fitz John to whom Martin gave one-third of the manor, had carried off his corn at Sherington.[37] He is returned as lord in 1276[38] and in 1284.[39] A comparison between an extent of the manor taken in 1289[40] and another taken in 1295, after Martin's death,[41] shows a decrease in the number of acres of land, &c., which may be due to the alienation of the third to Fitz John. Martin was succeeded by his son Roger,[42] against whom complaint was brought in 1298 by David le Graunt that, after demising the manor to him for a term of years, Roger de Carun had entered with Simon Spigurnel, before the term was expired, had ejected Graunt's men and carried away corn and other goods.[43] Roger de Carun died before June 1301 seised of the manor, and leaving a daughter Sibyl, then under two years,[44] who, as the heir of Roger de Carun, was returned as holding Sherington in 1302.[45] Three years later Reynold de Grey successfully claimed against her guardian, Richard Golde, one-third of six messuages, 2½ virgates of land, 40 acres of wood, and 6s. 1½d. rent in Sherington as dower of her mother Joan.[46] The custody of the person and lands of Sibyl had been first granted by the king to Edmund Earl of Cornwall, whose executors sold it to Richard Golde. He granted it to his brother Thomas Golde, by whom it was in turn granted to Roger de Pateshull (? Pattishall, Northamptonshire), parson of Bletsoe (co. Beds.).[47] While in his custody Sibyl was in 1311 carried off by John de Burgh, who, with a crowd of armed supporters, broke the hearthstone and windows of the manor-house, and married her against the will of her guardian.[48] Complaint of forcible entry was made in 1313[49]; in the following year John de Burgh and Sibyl, then his wife, having proved her age, had seisin of her father's lands.[50] Her husband had apparently acted with the king's consent,[51] and Sibyl, being deaf and dumb, was unable to hear or to give evidence[52]; the case against John de Burgh was still uncon-

CARUN. *Argent a lion vert holding a cross formy fitchy gules.*

cluded in 1315.[53] In 1316 he was holding the manor,[54] but before 1327 Sibyl was apparently married to Richard Linford, then described as Richard Linford of Sherington.[55] He was returned as lord in 1346,[56] and in 1348, with his wife Sibyl, settled the manor on themselves and their heirs.[57] Richard Linford was succeeded by his son John, who in 1355 acquired a carucate of land in Sherington,[58] and died in 1360,[59] when the wardship of his lands and son and heir John was granted to Roger Grote (or Groton).[60] During the minority of this John Linford a rent of 18 marks was paid out of the manor to Henry Sterky, who assigned this annuity first to John Fitz Richard of Olney and then to Sir Ralph Basset of Drayton.[61] John Linford proved his age on 2 October 1372,[62] and obtained seisin of his lands on 2 February 1373–4.[63] In 1383 he acquired licence to settle the manor on himself and his wife Katherine in tail, with remainder to Roger Groton of Calverton in tail and final remainder to himself in fee simple,[64] the settlement taking place in 1386.[65] In the following year John Linford incurred a debt to John Hende, to whom the manor, of which an extent was taken at that time, was afterwards assigned in security. Linford re-entered the manor and ejected Hende, who thereupon sued him, obtaining a verdict in his favour.[66] John Linford died seised of Sherington in 1401, when he was succeeded by his son, a third John Linford.[67] About 1429 either the same John or a successor of the same name conveyed the manor in fee simple to Walter Fitz Richard and other feoffees,[68] and in 1450 it was settled by Walter Fitz Richard on John Ardes and his wife Isabel,[69] the daughter and heir of John Linford.[70] According to Browne Willis, the last John Linford was buried in the church with his wife Isabel, under a monument bearing the date 1468[71]; but it is more probable that the tomb

ARDES. *Argent a bend between six molets sable.*

was erected to John Ardes, the husband of the Linford heiress Isabel, who may have taken the name of Linford. John Ardes was succeeded by his son Michael, lord in 1491.[72] Michael Ardes was succeeded before 1527[73] by his son Anthony,[74] from whom the manor passed before 1545[75] to his son Edward.[75a] In 1570 Edward Ardes settled the manor on his wife Katherine, daughter of

---

[32] Feet of F. case 15, file 20, no. 1.

[33] *Testa de Nevill* (Rec. Com.), 258b, 259b.

[34] Feet of F. case 15, file 23, no. 3, 7.

[35] Assize R. 68, m. 18 d.

[36] Ibid. Martin de Carun had two brothers, John, who held 10s. rent, and Simon, who held 2 virgates of land of the gift of their father John (*Hund. R.* [Rec. Com.], i, 41).

[37] *Hund. R.* (Rec. Com.), i, 42. This Roger Fitz John of Hanslope owed Martin de Carun 60s. in 1285 (*Cal. Close*, 1279–88, p. 375).

[38] *Hund. R.* (Rec. Com.), i, 41.

[39] *Feud. Aids*, i, 82.

[40] Misc. Inq. file 48, no. 1.

[41] Chan. Inq. p.m. 24 Edw. I, no. 14.

[42] *Cal. Inq. p.m.* (Edw. I), iii, 191.

[43] *Cal. Pat.* 1292–1301, p. 379.

[44] Chan. Inq. p.m. 29 Edw. I, no. 43.

[45] *Feud. Aids*, i, 104.

[46] De Banco R. 155, m. 66 d.

[47] Misc. Inq. file 73, no. 14.

[48] Ibid.; *Cal. Pat.* 1313–17, p. 252.

[49] *Cal. Fine R.* 1307–19, p. 161.

[50] *Cal. Close*, 1313–18, p. 37.

[51] Misc. Inq. file 73, no. 14.

[52] Ibid.

[53] *Cal. Pat.* 1313–17, p. 252.

[54] *Feud. Aids*, i, 110.

[55] De Banco R. East. 1 Edw. III, m. 81 d.

[56] *Feud. Aids*, i, 130.

[57] De Banco R. 356, m. 405; Feet of F. case 20, file 89, no. 18; *Cal. Pat.* 1348–50, p. 99. Sibyl's mother Joan was still holding in dower at this date.

[58] *Cal. Pat.* 1354–8, p. 201.

[59] Chan. Inq. p.m. 34 Edw. III (1st nos.), no. 12. Certain rents were then paid to his brother Richard.

[60] *Cal. Pat.* 1358–61, p. 365.

[61] *Cal. Close*, 1360–4, p. 555.

[62] Chan. Inq. p.m. 46 Edw. III (1st nos.), no. 90.

[63] *Cal. Close*, 1374–7, p. 8.

[64] *Cal. Pat.* 1381–5, p. 227.

[65] Close, 9 Ric. II, m. 13.

[66] Assize R. 1505, m. 2; Chan. Inq. p.m. 11 Ric. II, no. 64.

[67] Chan. Inq. p.m. 3 Hen. IV, no. 2.

[68] *Cal. Pat.* 1422–9, p. 532.

[69] Ibid. 1446–52, p. 336.

[70] *Visit. of Bucks.* (Harl. Soc.), 144.

[71] Add. MS. 5839, p. 343. The monument no longer exists.

[72] *Cal. Inq. p.m. Hen. VII*, i, 302.

[73] Chan. Inq. p.m. (Ser. 2), xlvi, 57.

[74] *Visit. of Bucks.* loc. cit.

[75] *L. and P. Hen. VIII*, xx (2), g. 707 (52).

[75a] *Visit. of Bucks.* loc. cit.

Thomas Lowe of Clifton Reynes, with remainder in tail-male to his sons Richard, Thomas, Israel, Francis, Edward, Andrew, Sherington, Philip and Humphrey respectively.[76] Edward Ardes died in November of that year,[77] and in 1571 his widow was holding the manor,[78] which she and her second husband Raphael Pemberton conveyed in 1588 to her son Richard Ardes.[79] In the following year Richard Ardes conveyed to Thomas Tyringham and Anthony his son, *LINFORDS alias ARDES MANOR*, with the exception of ten messuages, one dovecot and nearly three quarters of the land.[80] The manor descended with Tyringham (q.v.) until sold in 1682 by Sir William Tyringham and others, apparently trustees for Elizabeth Tyringham and her husband John Backwell, to Roger Chapman,[81] attorney of Newport. On his death in 1702 it passed to his eldest son Thomas Chapman,[82] who was holding it in 1734, when, according to Browne Willis, though reputed the principal manor, the demesnes were worth only £50 *per annum*.[83] It was purchased by Barnaby Backwell, who, by his will dated 24 December 1753, left the manor to the use of his wife Sarah for the education of his eldest son.[84] It has since descended with Tyringham,[85] the present owner being Mr. F. A. König of Tyringham.

The land excepted from the sale of Linford's Manor in 1589 appears to have passed to Reynes Lowe, who with John Coles, sen., and John Coles, jun., was holding a manor of *LIN-FORD or LINFORDS* in Sherington in 1611.[86] From Reynes Lowe it passed before 1634[87] to a kinsman Thomas Lowe of Sherington,[88] who was dealing with it in 1650.[89] In 1660, with his wife Anne, Thomas Lowe conveyed it to John Adams,[90] the husband of his daughter Anne.[91] It remained in the Adams family, by whom it was conveyed in 1725 to Sir John Chester, bart., of Chicheley[92] (q.v.), with which manor it was still held late in the 19th century.[93]

LOWE. *Argent a bend azure with three wolves' heads argent thereon.*

According to Browne Willis the manor-house did not pass with the manorial rights to the Tyringhams, but descended with this property.[94]

A property known from the 13th century as a manor of Sherington, and from the 15th as a manor of *CAVES or SHERINGTON*, was held of the principal manor by fealty and rent of 1*d*.[95] It appears to have originated in the amalgamation of numerous small estates in Sherington acquired by John de Cave,

from whose family it took its distinctive name. In 1253 William le Curt and his wife Amphyllis granted him a messuage and 11 acres in Sherington.[96] In the year before he had received a grant of 6½ acres from William Vintner of Stratford and his wife Emma,[97] who in 1255 granted to him a messuage, with the reversion of all the lands in Sherington which Sarah, wife of William le Franceys, and Olive, wife of Ranulph le Franceys, held in dower of the inheritance of Emma, and all other lands belonging to Emma in Sherington, John de Cave paying 60 marks for this grant.[98] In 1257 John le Blake and his wife Felise (apparently one of four co-heirs of a branch of the Sherington family) granted to John de Cave half a messuage, 20 acres of land, and one quarter of a moiety of three mills in Sherington, which they held in right of Felise, together with the reversion of all lands Felise might inherit in Sherington, and one-fourth of all the lands which Beatrice widow of William de Sherington held in dower of her inheritance there, John paying 20 marks for this grant.[99] John de Cave acquired more land from Simon son of Gervase and his wife Agatha in 1260,[100] and in 1261 from Jane daughter of Richard de Newenton, a messuage, one-eighth of a mill, and all Jane's pasture between the Ouse and the arable lands.[1] He was probably dead before 1275, when Geoffrey Kaldsweyn and Lucy his wife, and Eustace le Carpenter and Hawise his wife, granted two parts of a messuage and 18 acres of land in Sherington to Robert de Cave.[2] All this property, now first called a manor, was demised by Robert de Cave for ten years to William de Cave. The latter assigned his term to John de Thorntoft, whose executors in 1291 complained that in spite of this demise, Robert, with his sons John and Nicholas, among others, had entered the manor and ejected them.[3] It was probably the son John here mentioned who in 1318 granted a messuage, land, and rent in Sherington to Richard de Cave, with remainder to Thomas, Robert, and Roger, brothers of Richard, and to his own right heirs.[4] Richard, who appears to have been John's eldest son, was appointed sheriff on 30 May 1319,[5] and in 1322 obtained the restoration of his lands in Sherington which had been forfeited on information that he was in the company of rebels against the Crown at Kingston, though in matter of fact he had been with the Bishop of Ely in the Isle of Ely for its protection. At the same time Roger de Cave, probably his brother, who had been arrested as a rebel, was delivered by the sheriff.[6] There is mention of Richard Cave of Buckinghamshire two years later,[7] and of John Cave in 1363,[8] 1364,[9] 1378 and 1381,[9a] and the manor probably remained for some time in the Cave family, since,

[76] Pat. 1069; Recov. R. Trin. 12 Eliz. m. 560; Chan. Inq. p.m. (Ser. 2), ccxvii, 114.

[77] Chan. Inq. p.m. (Ser. 2), ccxvii, 114.

[78] Memo. R. (Exch. L.T.R.), Trin. 13 Eliz. m. 4.

[79] Feet of F. Bucks. Hil. 30 Eliz.; Pat. 30 Eliz. pt. viii.

[80] Pat. 31 Eliz. pt. vi.

[81] Feet of F. Bucks. Trin. 34 Chas. II.

[82] P.C.C. 24 Degg.

[83] Add. MS. 5839, p. 343.

[84] P.C.C. 265 Pinfold.

[85] See also Priv. Act, 36 Geo. III, cap. 66; Lysons, *Mag. Brit.* i (3), 629; Sheahan, op. cit. 600.

[86] Feet of F. Bucks. Mich. 9 Jas. I.

[87] A rent of two couples of capons and a couple of hens was paid in 1639 for a cottage in Church End in Sherington to Thomas Lowe and Anne his wife, and Thomas Lowe (his son) and Parthenia his wife (Add. Chart. 24051).

[88] *Visit. of Bucks.* (Harl. Soc.), 87.

[89] Recov. R. Mich. 1650, m. 9.

[90] Feet of F. Bucks. Trin. 12 Chas. I.

[91] *Visit. of Bucks.* loc. cit.

[92] Feet of F. Bucks. East. and Trin. 11 Geo. I.

[93] Add. MS. 5839, p. 343; Priv. Act, 36 Geo. III, cap. 66; Lysons, op. cit. i (3), 630; Lipscomb, *Hist. and Antiq. of Bucks.* iv, 334; Sheahan, op. cit. 601.

[94] Add. MS. 5839, p. 344.

[95] *Cal. Inq. p.m.* Hen. VII, i, 302.

[96] Feet of F. case 16, file 32, no. 6.

[97] Ibid. no. 10.

[98] Ibid. file 33, no. 25.

[99] Ibid. file 34, no. 2.

[100] Ibid. file 36, no. 9.

[1] Ibid. no. 8.

[2] Ibid. file 44, no. 6.

[3] *Cal. Pat.* 1281–92, p. 411.

[4] Feet of F. case 18, file 70, no. 14.

[5] *Cal. Fine R.* 1307–19, p. 398.

[6] *Cal. Close*, 1318–23, p. 451.

[7] *Cal. Fine R.* 1319–27, p. 235.

[8] *Cal. Close*, 1360–4, pp. 548, 555.

[9] Ibid. 1364–8, p. 54.

[9a] Ibid. 1377–81, pp. 117, 505.

when it next appears in 1491, it was designated Cave's Manor. Richard Maryot died seised of it on 18 July of that year, leaving a daughter and heir Joan, wife of Humphrey Catesby.[10] The manor appears to have been held by Katherine, widow of Richard Maryot, still alive in 1526,[11] since 15 acres of pasture was all that Humphrey Catesby held in Sherington at his death in 1503,[12] and Katherine was sued for detaining the deeds of the manor of Sherington by Margaret Horsington. She claimed as daughter and eventual heir of Hugh Horsington, after the death of his son John and of the latter's son Randolph without issue.[13] For more than a century all trace of this manor is lost, but in 1627 it was conveyed by Sir Francis Clarke to Sir Richard Norton, bart., and others,[14] probably trustees for William Norton, who was living at Sherington in 1634.[15] His widow Anne, daughter of Sir John Brett, joined with their son Brett Norton and his wife Sarah in a conveyance of the manor in 1655.[16] In 1689 it had passed to Owen Norton,[17] who was holding it in 1697 with Robert Norton and his wife Sarah.[18] It appears to have passed by marriage from the Nortons to the Pargiters, and again by marriage, *circa* 1710, from the Pargiters to the Smiths, being in the hands of John Smith of Passenham (co. Northampton) in 1736, according to Browne Willis, whose account of Sherington, however, is very confused and by no means reliable.[19] At the passing of the Inclosure Act for the parish in 1796 it was held by Dryden Smith,[20] son of Dryden Smith, shipwright of Wapping.[21] He was succeeded by his son James, who in 1813 barred the entail on the manor[22] as a preliminary to its conveyance to Dr. Cheyne,[23] whose trustees in 1857 sold it to Alfred Umney.[24] Mrs. Umney held the manorial rights for about thirty years, but before 1895 they had passed to George Alfred U. Nelson, whose trustees have held since 1907.

The manor of *FITZJOHNS* or *SHERINGTON* had its origin as abovesaid in a grant for life made by Martin de Carun to Roger Fitz John of Sherington of one-third of his manor, this third being quitclaimed for ever to Roger Fitz John in 1297–8 by Martin's son and successor Roger de Carun.[25] Roger Fitz John, the grantee, died before June 1313, when his son Robert was his heir.[26] Robert held in 1316,[27] and in 1351 there is reference to John son and heir of the late Robert Fitz John of Sherington.[27a] John Fitz John of Sherington in 1369 claimed a toft, 30 acres of land, and 2 acres of meadow, as heir of his grandfather Roger, and great-grandfather Roger Fitz John, against Emma, daughter of Thomas Fitz John, and

three other ladies (? apparently co-heirs with her of Roger Fitz John, John's great-grandfather) and their husbands.[28] John Fitz John, or a successor of the same name, died seised of the manor on 31 March 1413.[29] His son John, who then succeeded, appeared in pleas of debt in 1425[30] and 1426.[31] In 1436 John Fitz John granted half of a messuage, many acres of land, a rent of 6s. 5d. (in all apparently a moiety of this manor) to John Chamberlain and Margaret his wife for life[32]; and in 1440 granted the reversion of this moiety together with the other half to Nicholas Wymbyssh, clerk, and others,[33] apparently feoffees. In 1491 the manor, then for the first time called Fitz Johns, was held by Richard Maryot with his other property in Sherington,[34] but after this date its history becomes obscure for more than a century. In 1599 the site of the manor of Fitz Johns was held by William Mountgomery and his wife Margaret,[35] who two years later conveyed this manor, then called Sherington, to their son Sherington Mountgomery.[36] This was possibly the property which in 1623 Sir Anthony Chester, bart., held in Sherington,[37] and which was called the manor of Sherington in 1638, when he obtained leave for his son Henry to levy a fine with him for the purpose of making a twenty-one years' lease.[38] The messuages in Sherington held by Sir Anthony Chester, bart., and his son John in 1687[39] may represent this estate, which may later have merged into the Chesters' manor of Linford in this parish.

One fee, or half of the original estate in Sherington, was obtained in the 13th century by the Cockfield family, by whose name this manor was later distinguished. Though the Caruns do not appear to have subinfeudated this fee, which was held by the Cockfields of the king in chief, yet they evidently had some interest, since it reverted in the 14th century to their successors the Linfords, of whom tenements in the manor were afterwards held.[40] Robert de Cockfield (Cocfeud, Kockefeud) was in possession c. 1235.[41] He was probably identical with the Robert de Cockfield who in 1223 granted a messuage and 5 acres in Sherington to Simon son of Adam in exchange for another messuage and a virgate quitclaimed to himself and to Denis de Cockfield and William de Sherington by Simon.[42] Early in 1240–1 Robert de Cockfield and William de Sherington owed arrears of rent for the mill-pond to Robert le Blund and his wife Mabel, who renounced their claim to the arrears and all future rent.[43] Robert de Cockfield, still alive in 1260,[44] appears to have been succeeded before 1276 by John de Cockfield,[45] probably his son, who by

---

[10] *Cal. Inq. p.m. Hen. VII*, i, 302. That part of the inscription on his tomb dealing with his daughter's marriage runs thus : 'Cujus quidem Ricardi filiam et heredem desponavit Humfridus Catesby armiger' (Add. MS. 5839, p. 347). His will, made in 1490, speaks of his wife Katherine, her mother Dame Elizabeth Tate, and John Tate his brother-in-law (P.C.C. 11 Dogett).

[11] *L. and P. Hen. VIII*, iv, p. 986.

[12] Exch. Inq. p.m. (Ser. 2), file 5, no. 16.

[13] Early Chan. Proc. bdle. 526, no. 47.

[14] Feet of F. Bucks. Trin. 3 Chas. I.

[15] *Visit. of Bucks.* (Harl. Soc.), 96.

[16] Feet of F. Bucks. Mich. 1655.

[17] Ibid. Trin. 1 Will. and Mary.

[18] Ibid. Hil. 9 Will. III.

[19] Add. MS. 5839, p. 344.

[20] Priv. Act, 36 Geo. III, cap. 66.

[21] Com. Pleas Recov. R. Trin. 53 Geo. III, m. 63.

[22] Ibid. See also m. 403 ; Feet of F. Bucks. East. 54 Geo. III. Of the Smiths Lysons wrote, c. 1813, that they had held for nearly a century (op. cit. i [3], 630).

[23] Sheahan, op. cit. 601.

[24] Ibid.

[25] *Cal. Inq. p.m.* (Edw. II), v, 207.

[26] Ibid.

[27] *Feud. Aids*, i, 110.

[27a] Add. Chart. 59280.

[28] De Banco R. 435, m. 387 d.

[29] Chan. Inq. p.m. 1 Hen. V, no. 5.

[30] *Cal. Pat.* 1422–9, p. 250.

[31] Ibid. 312.

[32] *Cal. Pat.* 1429–36, p. 595.

[33] Ibid. 1436–41, p. 367.

[34] *Cal. Inq. p.m. Hen. VII*, i, 302.

[35] Feet of F. Bucks. Mich. 42 Eliz.

[36] Ibid. Mich. 44 Eliz. ; *Visit. of Bucks.* (Harl. Soc.), 183.

[37] Pat. 21 Jas. I, pt. xviii, no. 3.

[38] *Cal. S. P. Dom.* 1638–9, p. 148.

[39] Feet of F. Bucks. Mich. 3 Jas. II.

[40] Chan. Inq. p.m. 19 Ric. II, no. 29.

[41] *Testa de Nevill* (Rec. Com.), 244.

[42] Feet of F. case 14, file 14, no. 5. An Adam de Cockfield was holding land in Sherington in 1237 (ibid. case 15, file 23, no. 7).

[43] Feet of F. case 15, file 25, no. 31.

[44] Cur. Reg. R. 169, m. 68.

[45] *Hund. R.* (Rec. Com.), i, 41,

1284 had subinfeudated this estate to Adam de Cockfield.[46] It was probably the same Adam and his wife Lucy whose confirmation of the gift of 2 virgates of land in Sherington by Robert de Tinchelray and Aveline his wife to the Abbess and nuns of St. Mary (Delapré Abbey), Northampton, was inspected and confirmed in 1328.[47] No later member of the Cockfield family is recorded as tenant, and this fee reverted to the Linfords, who had succeeded the Caruns in the principal manor. It must be this manor which in 1374 was bestowed by John Linford on Henry Lord Grey de Wilton, for although it was then said to be held of the king in chief for 3s. yearly at Northampton Castle and 5s. hidage to the king, a service associated with the principal manor of Linfords, and although it was expressly stated that John Linford had nothing except this manor,[48] yet the Linfords continued to hold the principal manor, and the Greys certainly afterwards owned the manor once held by the Cockfields. In 1380 Henry Lord Grey de Wilton made a settlement on himself and his wife Elizabeth of Sherington Manor,[49] a third of which, at his death in 1396, was said to be held for life by Joan Basset in dower, of the gift of her husband Ralf Basset.[50] The Greys of Wilton also held Water Eaton Manor in Bletchley, but after the death of Richard Grey in 1442 [51] the two manors appear to have diverged, the renunciation of claim by Margaret, Richard's widow, in 1448 [52] evidently not taking effect, since property in Sherington, amongst which were closes called Jurdens and Heynes, was included among Margaret's dower at her death in 1452.[53] It had passed to Edward Grey of Bletchley by 1491, when it was called *COCKFIELD MANOR*,[54] and at his death in 1504 came to his cousin and heir, Edmund Lord Grey de Wilton.[55] It was possibly this property which was acquired by Dean Colet and given to the Mercers' Company in trust for the endowment of St. Paul's School in 1510,[56] and in which the company claimed manorial rights in 1796.[57] It is still held by the company, being known as the Mercers' Farm.

The Bassets of Drayton held lands in Sherington as part of their manor of Olney, and in 1326 [58] and 1331 [59] Ralph Basset of Drayton complained that his free warren, etc., in Sherington had been broken into by Richard Linford and others. These lands descended with the manor of Warrington in Olney. The Bassets about 1359 obtained Newton Blossomville Manor (q.v.), with which this property, described as 50 acres of land, 8 acres of meadow, and 10s. rent,[60] descended through the Earls of Stafford and Dukes of Buckingham, and with which it was granted to Walter Devereux, Lord Ferrers, in 1524.[61]

A property mainly in Sherington, but extending into the neighbouring parish of Lathbury and comprising four messuages, 100 acres of land, 20 acres of meadow, 10 acres of pasture, 6 acres of wood called le Hoo, 15s. assize rent,[62] was known in the 17th century as *LE HOO MANOR*.[63] A Margery Del Hoo is mentioned in connexion with Lathbury in 1278,[64] and about that date Joan Dakeney, lord of the principal Lathbury Manor, claimed warren and a new park at le Hoo.[65] The Tyringhams held rights over this estate in 1405 [66] and probably earlier, for Sir Roger Tyringham and Simon his brother were among those who broke Ralph Basset's closes in 1331.[67] It descended with their manor of Tyringham (q.v.), with which it was held in 1614 by Sir Antony Tyringham.[68]

Two virgates in Sherington were granted to Tickford Priory with the church, to which one of them belonged,[69] and at the dissolution of the priory were bestowed in 1526 on Cardinal Wolsey for the college founded by him in Oxford.[70]

A mill worth 26s. was held with the manor in 1086.[71] The mill pond passed into the possession of Robert de Cockfield and William de Sherington early in 1240-1,[72] and the former had evidently a right to the mills in Sherington in 1260.[73]

An extent of the principal manor of 1301 included two-thirds of a fishery in the Ouse.[74] The remaining third was evidently granted to the Fitz Johns with their third of the manor of Sherington, as the moiety of a third of a fishery in the water of Sherington was held with a moiety of Fitz Johns Manor in 1436.[75] Free fishing in the Ouse and waters of Sherington was attached to the principal manor in the 18th and 19th centuries.[76]

Free fishery in the Ouse was held with the manor of Caves in 1813.[77]

A several fishery in the Ouse was granted with Cockfield Manor to Henry Lord Grey de Wilton by John Linford in 1374.[78]

CHURCH The church of *ST. LAUD* consists of a chancel measuring internally 30 ft. 10 in. in length with a mean width of 16 ft., north vestry, central tower 11 ft. 4 in. by 11 ft., nave 54 ft. 6 in. by 18 ft. 4 in., north and south aisles each 10 ft. wide, and south porch. It is built of large rubble ; the roof of the chancel is covered with tiles and those of the remainder of the church with lead.

A church existed here in the 12th century,[79] but the earliest parts of the present building, consisting principally of the north arcade and the lower stage of the tower, date from about 1250, when the church appears to have consisted of a chancel, central tower,

[46] *Feud. Aids*, i, 82.
[47] Dugdale, *Mon.* v, 212. At the same date was likewise inspected and confirmed the confirmation by Robert de Cockfield of the gift of 3s. rent by his grandmother Lucy de Cockfield to the abbey.
[48] Inq. a.q.d. file 384, no. 19.
[49] *Cal. Pat.* 1377–81, p. 426.
[50] Chan. Inq. p.m. 19 Ric. II, no. 29. Joan Basset died in 1402, holding this third of the manor (ibid. 4 Hen. IV, no. 38).
[51] Ibid. 20 Hen. VI, no. 23.
[52] Feet of F. case 293, file 71, no. 335.
[53] Chan. Inq. p.m. 30 Hen. VI, no. 12.

[54] *Cal. Inq. p.m. Hen. VII*, i, 302.
[55] Exch. Inq. p.m. (Ser. 2), file 5, no. 11.
[56] Chan. Inq. p.m. (Ser. 2), xxv, 160.
[57] Priv. Act, 36 Geo. III, cap. 66.
[58] *Cal. Pat.* 1324–7, p. 292.
[59] Ibid. 1330–4, pp. 205–6.
[60] Chan. Inq. p.m. 22 Ric. II, no. 46.
[61] *L. and P. Hen. VIII*, iv, g. 137 (1).
[62] Chan. Inq. p.m. 2 Ric. III, no. 34 ; (Ser. 2), ccxlvi, 108.
[63] Ibid. cccxlix, 164.
[64] *Hund. R.* (Rec. Com.), ii, 347.
[65] Ibid. i, 38, 45.
[66] De Banco R. 578, m. 362 d.
[67] *Cal. Pat.* 1330–4, p. 205.

[68] Chan. Inq. p.m. (Ser. 2), cccxlix, 164.
[69] *Abbrev. Plac.* (Rec. Com.), 33. A grant of this land was made by the prior in 1254 (Feet of F. case 16, file 33, no. 13).
[70] *L. and P. Hen. VIII*, iv, 1913, 2217.
[71] *V.C.H. Bucks.* i, 241.
[72] Feet of F. case 15, file 25, no. 31.
[73] Cur. Reg. R. 169, m. 68.
[74] Chan. Inq. p.m. 29 Edw. I, no. 43.
[75] *Cal. Pat.* 1429–36, p. 595.
[76] Recov. R. Hil. 15 Geo. III, m. 392 ; Mich. 4 Geo. IV, m. 122.
[77] Ibid. Trin. 53 Geo. III, m. 403 ; Feet of F. Bucks. East. 54 Geo. III.
[78] Inq. a.q.d. file 384, no. 19.
[79] Round, *Cal. Doc. of France*, 444.

Sherington Church from the South-East

SIMPSON : RECTORY FARM

SIMPSON CHURCH FROM THE SOUTH-WEST

nave and narrow north aisle. Both the chancel and north aisle were rebuilt early in the 14th century, and it is probable that the completion of the tower was contemplated at the same time,[80] but little beyond the insertion of the turret stairway was completed at this time. About 1350 the south aisle and the two-storied porch were added, and the nave was widened towards the north, its west wall being rebuilt. The bell-chamber and buttresses were added to the tower late in the 15th century, when the nave clearstory was also added or remodelled, new tracery was inserted in the large west window, and the nave and aisles were re-roofed. In 1870 the whole fabric was restored and a modern vestry has been added.

The chancel widens out towards the east, and was probably begun at that end before the original structure was removed. The head and jambs of the pointed east window, enriched internally with a continuous edge-roll, are of the 14th century, but the tracery is modern. On the south are two three-light windows with vertical tracery, both of which were inserted in

external division between the two lower stages, and they are quite plain except that the second stage has a small pointed window on the south. The bell-chamber is lighted from all sides by twin windows, each of two cinquefoiled lights under a four-centred head; the contrast with the plain walls below is greatly enhanced by the projection of the bell-chamber on all sides on four-centred arches which spring from the upper parts of the buttresses, and, except where interrupted by the stair turret, span the walls between them.

The nave has arcades of four bays with pointed arches on either side. The north arcade, which is supported by circular columns with moulded capitals and bases, dates from about 1250, but it appears to have been reconstructed about 1 ft. further to the north in the mid-14th century, when the south arcade was built. The west respond is formed by a semi-column, but the east respond is of the same plan as those of the tower arches. The south arcade is supported by octagonal piers and responds with moulded

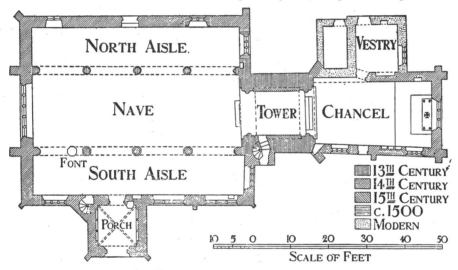

PLAN OF SHERINGTON CHURCH

the late 15th century, and a moulded doorway of the 14th century with a segmental head, while a small low-side window of one trefoiled light pierces the tower buttress at the south-west. There is now no piscina, but on the south are three sedilia of the 15th century, all under one head with chamfered mullions and unpierced vertical tracery. A large recess has been formed at the north-west for the organ, and there is a modern aumbry at the north-east.

The tower is of three stages, with diagonal buttresses extending to the foot of the bell-chamber, and is surmounted by an embattled parapet and slender spirelet. The ground stage opens to the chancel and nave by pointed arches of about 1250, each of three chamfered orders supported by large responds of trefoil plan with moulded capitals and bases. When the bell-chamber was added in the 15th century it was evidently found desirable to reinforce the north and south walls of the tower, in order that the structure should be more accurately square; this was done from the inside. At the south-west is a pointed doorway to the turret stairway, and above it is a four-centred doorway, now blocked, which led to the rood loft. There is no

capitals and bases. There is a large pointed window of five cinquefoiled lights on the west, with jambs and head of the 14th century, but the tracery is of the late 15th century; the nave is further lighted by a clearstory with four windows on either side, each of three uncusped lights under a four-centred head.

The eastern part of the north aisle is lighted by two four-centred windows which were inserted about 1500, one of these, of three lights, being on the east and the other, of two lights, on the north. At the south end of the east wall is a 13th-century piscina, with a trefoiled head and round bowl, now partially covered by the north wall of the nave. The north doorway has a pointed head and elaborate continuous mouldings, but only the east jamb and part of the arch are original. Near the west end of the north wall is an original pointed window of two trefoiled lights with flowing tracery.

The south aisle is lighted by three large windows on the south and one on the east. The east window, with the exception of the label, has been entirely renewed externally, and modern tracery has been inserted in the south-east window, but the adjacent window on the west, with its fine flowing tracery,

[80] Indulgences were granted c. 1305 for the fabric of the church and belfry (Linc. Epis. Reg. Memo. Dalderby, fol. 90 d.).

4   457   58

dates entirely from about 1350; the pointed south doorway, enriched with continuous mouldings, is also of the same period. To the east of the doorway is a low plain recess with a depressed head, and to the west of it is a pointed doorway to the parvise stairway. The south-west window, which has uncusped lights and restored geometrical tracery, dates from the 13th century, and was probably reset here from the nave wall when the aisle was built. At the south-east is a trefoiled piscina of the 14th century with a broken quatrefoil bowl, and on the face of the east respond of the arcade is a trefoiled image niche.

The ground stage of the porch is carried by a stone quadripartite vault with chamfered ribs, and has wall arcades on the east and west, each consisting of three trefoiled arches with traceried spandrels, that on the west being modern; at the north-east is a plain stoup, the bowl of which has been broken away. The entrance archway has been extensively repaired. The parvise has small pointed windows and a straight parapet.

The nave has a low-pitched moulded roof of about 1500, with shields at the feet of the intermediate rafters. The aisles have lean-to roofs of the same period, that of the north aisle having figures at the feet of the principals, one holding a scroll and the others shields.

The font, which dates from the late 14th century, is octagonal and has a panelled bowl and stem, and a moulded base. On each side of the bowl is a defaced figure of a saint under an ogee crocketed label. The figures of St. Paul, St. Andrew and St. Catherine can be easily recognized. On one of the stalls is a leather bound book of Common Prayer 'Printed by the Assigns of John Bill Deceased and by Henry Hills and Thomas Newcomb, Printers to the Kings most excellent Majesty. 1683'; on it is written 'Thomas his Book 1686'

The tower contains a ring of five bells; the second, inscribed 'Gabrel' but not dated, the fourth and the tenor, both dated 1591, were all cast at Bedford by one of the Watts family;[80a] the fourth and tenor are inscribed with the letters of the alphabet, the former in Gothic smalls and the latter in Gothic capitals. The treble is by Pack & Chapman of London, 1773, and the third by Henry Bagley, 1672.

The communion plate consists of a chalice and cover paten of 1733, dated 1735; a flagon of 1769;

a spoon of 1806; and a chalice and standing paten, both of 1843.

The registers begin in 1695.

ADVOWSON The advowson was held by the Caruns or Sheringtons with the principal manor until granted by William de Sherington to Tickford Priory at some date before 1150.[81] An attempt made in 1229 by John de Carun, William's great-grandson, to recover possession of the advowson, in spite of the confirmation of his father Ralph, was unsuccessful,[82] and it remained in the possession of the priory[83] until granted by it in 1293 to the Bishop of Lincoln.[84] It remained the property of the bishops[85] till 1852, when it was transferred to the Bishop of Oxford.[85a]

The church was taxed at £13 6s. 8d. in 1291,[86] and at £20 10s. 8d. in 1535.[87]

A rent of 8d., issuing from land in Sherington held by Gervase de Carun, was devoted by his brother Richard (temp. Richard I) to the maintenance of a lamp before the altar in the church.[87a] At the dissolution of the chantries it was found that land worth 6d. yearly was given for an obit, and other land, worth 11d. yearly, for a lamp.[88]

CHARITIES Edward Fuller, by his will, 1705, devised £5 yearly, to be applied on 27 March as follows: 20s. to the minister for a sermon, 10s. to be expended on the minister and churchwardens, 5s. to the parish clerk, and £3 5s. to be distributed in half-crowns to twenty-six poor. The rent-charge is paid as to £2 10s. out of the Latimer estate belonging to Lord Chesham, £1 5s. out of Gregory's Field, and £1 5s. out of Umney's Close, both in Sherington.

Stonepits Land.—There is a piece of land in the parish containing 2 a. 2 r. 31 p., let at £8 10s. 6d. yearly, which is applied by the Parish Council in lighting the village with street lamps.

Unknown donor's charity or Midsummer Holm consists of a yearly rent-charge of £2 issuing out of Waypost Close, now belonging to Mr. George Fleet, which is applied in aid of church expenses.

Alfred Umney's charity, founded by will proved at London 25 November 1863, consists of £371 14s. 4d. India 3½ per cent. stock with the official trustees, the dividends of which, amounting to £13 yearly, are applicable in aid of the religious and moral instruction of poor children of the parish.

SIMPSON

Siwinestone, Sevinestone (xi cent.), Shiveneston (xiii cent.); Sewenestone (xiv cent.); Sympson, Sympston (xvi cent.); Sewingston (xvii cent.).

This parish has an area of 1,317 acres of land and 19 of land covered by water, and is mostly pasture, 156 acres being arable, and 994 permanent grass.[1] The soil is heavy, some clay, with a subsoil of clay and gravel. The ground falls from about 300 ft. above the ordnance datum in the west to about 200 ft. in the east.

Simpson includes a portion of the town of Fenny Stratford,[2] and is governed by the Bletchley Urban District Council. Watling Street forms the south-west boundary and becomes the High Street of Fenny Stratford in the south. The River Ouzel is the eastern boundary, and the Grand Junction Canal passes through the parish from north to south. The Bedford branch of the London and North Western railway runs through the parish from west to east, and has a station at Fenny Stratford.

[80a] A. H. Cocks, *Ch. Bells of Bucks.* 564.
[81] Round, *Cal. Doc. of France*, 444.
[82] Cur. Reg. R. 102, m. 17.
[83] R. of Hugh of Wells (Cant. and York Soc.), ii, 77.

[84] Linc. Epis. Reg. Inst. Sutton, fol. 114 d.; Cal. Pat. 1313–17, p. 284.
[85] L. and P. Hen. VIII, ix, 117, 349, 453–4, 471, 569; Inst. Bks. (P.R.O.).
[85a] Lond. Gaz. 4 June 1852, p. 1578.
[86] Pope Nich. Tax. (Rec. Com.), 34.

[87] Valor Eccl. (Rec. Com.), iv, 243.
[87a] Maitland, op. cit. ii, 674.
[88] Chant. Cert. 5, no. 31.
[1] Statistics from Bd. of Agric. (1905).
[2] Index to Lond. Gaz. 1830–83, p. 1560.

The village, which contains a number of old cottages, some much altered, lies at the foot of a hill, in the north-east of the parish, east of the Grand Junction Canal, and along a road branching north from Watling Street. At the eastern end of the village is the church of St. Thomas. To the north is the Rectory house, dating from 1872 ; the former house was described by Sheahan about 1860 as an ancient brick building.[3] A little further north is the Rectory Farm, a 17th-century half-timber house of two stories, repaired with later brickwork.

Simpson House, formerly Simpson Villa, lies south-west of the church. It was built about the middle of the 19th century for Mr. C. Warren, and afterwards bought by Mr. Kenet, who renamed it Simpson House. The manor-house, called Simpson Place in the 18th century,[4] was pulled down early in the 19th century, and the Manor Farm, an old farm-house at the south-western end of the village, has since been used as a residence by the Sipthorp family.[5]

A little south of Manor Farm are a wharf and swing-bridge over the canal, with King's Barn about a quarter of a mile west of the wharf. There is a Wesleyan Chapel north-west of the church, originally built in 1842, but rebuilt on a new site in 1870.

The parish contains the Bletchley Urban District and Newport Pagnell Rural District Isolation Hospital, erected in 1907. To the west of the station are Staple Hall and Lodge, and to the north of it are saw-mills west of the swing-bridge over the canal.

The common fields were enclosed by Act of Parliament in 1770, the award bearing date 26 April 1771.[6]

Among place-names has been found Groveway Farm [7] (xviii cent.).

MANOR Before the Conquest Queen Edith held a manor of 8 hides and 3 virgates in SIMPSON, which in 1086 was entered among the lands of the Bishop of Coutances, who held it in pledge of William Bonvaslet.[8] By the 13th century this was annexed as one fee to the barony of Wolverton,[9] of which it still formed part in 1635.[10]

The manor was subinfeudated before the middle of the 13th century, when Geoffrey de Cauz, who presented to the church in 1231,[11] was holding it.[12] Here as in Water Eaton, Bletchley (q.v.), the Cauz family were succeeded by the Greys, probably by marriage, since in 1351, during the Greys' tenure, the lords were described as the heirs of Geoffrey de Cauz.[13] John de Grey, the first of his family mentioned in Simpson, held in 1254.[14] About ten years later Bertram du Sulee sued him for Simpson Manor,[15] a claim which was renewed in 1275 against his son,

Reynold de Grey, by Bartholomew de Sulee.[16] Reynold called to warrant his son John de Grey,[17] who was called lord of Simpson in 1302 in his father's lifetime.[18] In 1307 John made a settlement of the manor on his second son Roger,[19] to whom it passed with Bletchley Manor and Stoke Hammond [20] (q.v.), and was included in the settlement made of the latter at the beginning of the 16th century. By 1551 the manor had passed to Thomas Pigott, senior, of Doddershall, Quainton [21] (q.v.), but was sold by his son Thomas in 1578 to William and Thomas Cranwell.[22]

Thomas Cranwell, with Sir Arthur Wilmot, bart., Robert Saunders and John Hatch, was defendant in 1624 in a suit brought by Robert Dixon of London. He complained that in 1622 Thomas Cranwell had given him the manor as part security for a debt of £165, though it had been previously mortgaged to Sir Arthur Wilmot, who with the other defendants had combined to deprive Dixon of his title in the same by fraudulent conveyances.[23] Settlements of the manor were made by Sir Arthur Wilmot, Thomas Cranwell, and Fitz Hugh Cranwell in 1626 [24] and in 1628.[25] Three years later it was in the hands of Arthur Warren.[26]

It next appears in the possession of the Hatch family, who had held property in Simpson for some generations.[27] In 1574 Thomas Pigott and his wife Mary conveyed to Richard Hatch two messuages, lands, and a weir in Simpson,[28] apparently part of the manor, since this property was like-wise held of Wolverton Barony.[29] The name of Richard Hatch appears in a minute of the Privy Council of 1590–1 as Richard Hatch of Simpson, he having been unlawfully attached by a counterfeit pursuivant.[30] Richard Hatch in 1604 settled

HATCH. *Gules two demi-leopards or.*

a messuage or farm in Simpson and other property on his son and heir John and his heirs, with remainder to his only daughter Joan, widow of Robert Massingberd, and died seised of this property on 9 December 1605, when he was succeeded by his son John.[31] On 2 June 1635 John Hatch died seised of a messuage in Simpson, a farm called Britnells, Pillgrove Wood and land, which he bequeathed to his wife Jane for bringing up his children, until his son Thomas, then aged ten, should be twenty-three years of age.[32] On 1 May 1668 Thomas Hatch and his wife Dorothy, daughter of John Spencer of Windsor,[33] are mentioned in connexion with land in Simpson.[34] Spencer Hatch, pro-

[3] *Hist. and Topog. of Bucks.* 605.
[4] Recov. R. Trin. 16 Geo. III, m. 114.
[5] Sheahan, op. cit. 604.
[6] Priv. Act, 10 Geo. III, cap. 42 ; Blue Bk. Inclosure Awards, 13.
[7] Recov. R. D. Enr. Trin. 16 Geo. III, m. 114. [8] *V.C.H. Bucks.* i, 239.
[9] *Testa de Nevill* (Rec. Com.), 248. See also *Feud. Aids,* i, 106, 132 ; Chan. Inq. p.m. 23 Edw. III, pt. i, no. 35 ; 25 Edw. III (1st nos.), no. 6 ; (Ser. 2), cxxii, 11; dxlii, 131; *Cal. Close,* 1349–54, p. 300. In 1302 and 1346 the service is returned as one quarter of a fee (*Feud. Aids,* loc. cit.).
[10] Chan. Inq. p.m. (Ser. 2), dxxv, 115.

[11] *R. of Hugh of Wells* (Cant. and York Soc.), ii, 81.
[12] *Testa de Nevill,* loc. cit.
[13] Chan. Inq. p.m. 25 Edw. III (1st nos.), no. 6.
[14] *Hund. R.* (Rec. Com.), i, 30.
[15] Assize R. 1195, m. 6.
[16] De Banco R. 11, m. 109 d.
[17] Ibid.
[18] *Feud. Aids,* i, 106; see also ibid. 109.
[19] Feet of F. Bucks. Trin. 35 Edw. I, no. 76 ; *Cal. Close,* 1323–7, p. 77.
[20] See also Feet of F. case 289, file 52 ; Lay Subs. R. bdle. 77, no. 38 ; *Cal. Inq. p.m. Hen. VII,* i, 26.
[21] Feet of F. Bucks. Hil. 4 Edw. VI ;

East. 5 Edw. VI ; cf. Recov. R. Trin. 13 Eliz. m. 148.
[22] Feet of F. Bucks. East. 20 Eliz.
[23] Chan. Proc. (Ser. 2), bdle. 343, no. 5.
[24] Feet of F. Bucks. Mich. 2 Chas. I.
[25] Recov. R. East. 4 Chas. I, m. 17.
[26] Chan. Inq. p.m. (Ser. 2), dxli, 99.
[27] Feet of F. Bucks. East. 16 Eliz.
[28] Ibid.
[29] Chan. Inq. p.m. (Ser. 2), dcxlvi, 23.
[30] *Acts of P.C.* 1590–1, p. 242.
[31] Chan. Inq. p.m. dcxlvi, 23.
[32] Ibid. (Ser. 2), dxxv, 115.
[33] Add. MS. 5839, p. 370.
[34] Marcham, *Cat. of Bucks. Deeds,* no. 551.

bably his son, appears to have succeeded him before 1678,[35] and in 1683 he and his mother Dorothy, William Wellis and Mary his wife, conveyed the manor to John Walden of Coventry.[36] At his death in 1689 it passed by will to his brother Thomas.[37] Thomas Walden died in March 1701-2 in London, when the manor came to his only daughter and heir, Susan.[38] In 1717 she married Job Hanmer,[39] who died in 1739.[40] Of their only son Walden, who succeeded him,[41] Cole wrote in 1760 : 'Job Walden Hanmer was my schole-Fellow at Eton, from thence he removed to Oxford and the Inns of Court, and now practises as a Councillor in this County, living at Broughton, as his mother lives in the house at Simpson.'[42] He was created a baronet in 1774,[43] and in 1776 barred the entail on the manor,[44] of which he died seised in 1783, being buried at Simpson.[45] His son, Sir Thomas Hanmer, who succeeded him, made settlements of the manor in 1785[46] and in 1802.[47] He occasionally resided at the manor-house,[48] which he sold in 1806 to Charles Pinfold with about 210 acres of land.[49] Charles Pinfold pulled down the manor-house, and leased the manor farm to a tenant, William Sipthorp, whose son William Sipthorp purchased this estate before 1860[50]; it is now the property of John Sipthorp. The manorial rights have been for a considerable time in abeyance.

HANMER. *Argent two leopards azure.*

One hide and 1 virgate in *SIMPSON* were held before the Conquest by Lewin Oaura, who could sell, and this property was still held by him in chief in 1086.[51] In 1275 it was in the hands of various owners, including John de Grey, and it was presented by the hundred that 32*s.* rent paid to Henry II had been withdrawn by the Abbess of Fontévrault, but by what warrant was unknown.[52]

A mill worth 10*s.* was held with the manor in 1086,[53] and is mentioned in 1324.[54] Two water-mills under one roof, with the Mill House, Mill-holmes Meadows, fisheries and ferries, were held by the Hatch family in the 17th century,[55] and are probably identical with the water-mill attached to the manor in the 18th and 19th centuries.[56]

CHURCH The church of *ST. THOMAS*[57] consists of a chancel 24 ft. 6 in. by 16 ft., central tower 9 ft. 6 in. by 8 ft. 6 in., north transept 18 ft. by 13 ft., south transept 16 ft. 6 in. by 11 ft., nave 46 ft. 6 in. by 24 ft. 6 in., and a south porch. All these measurements are internal.

No detail of an earlier date than the first half of the 14th century remains in the present structure, which appears to have been almost entirely rebuilt during that period. The somewhat restricted dimen-

sions of the central tower suggest that it was originally designed for a smaller church, and that the reconstruction undertaken in the 14th century consisted in the enlargement of the chancel, transepts and nave of an earlier cruciform building, the existing central tower, the lower portion of which may incorporate work of the previous century, being retained. The arches which pierce the ground stage, however, seem to have been altered in the early years of the 14th century, to which date the responds belong, and again some thirty years later, when the arches themselves were rebuilt. The details of the rest of the church point to the second quarter of the century as the principal period of rebuilding. About 1400 the tower was increased in height, and the nave was re-roofed, the rood stairs built, and several windows altered or inserted in the 15th century. At some time in the same century a north vestry, since demolished, was added on the north side of the chancel. The south porch was built in the 16th century, and the transepts were re-roofed in the 17th century. Restorations of the church were carried out in 1873 and 1904. At this latter date the plaster ceiling of the nave was removed, the east wall of the chancel was rebuilt, and the western archways between nave and transepts were opened out, while the rood-loft staircase was continued up to the belfry in oak, and a new ringers' floor was inserted over the arches of the tower.

The east wall of the chancel, with its window and buttresses, is modern, and there is a modern two-light window in both the north and south walls. In the north wall are a doorway and a window, both blocked, and outside can be seen traces of the vestry wall and a demolished central buttress. The south wall has a buttress in the middle, to the west of which is a high square-headed window, originally of the 14th century, heightened in the 15th or 16th century. It was blocked with brickwork when the Hanmer monument was erected in 1789, and is now visible only from outside.

The tower is three stages in height and has an embattled parapet. Each wall of the ground stage is pierced by a pointed and chamfered arch with semi-circular responds, the shafts having moulded capitals and bases, and dating from the early part of the 14th century, the arches being somewhat later. In the west wall high up is a doorway with a four-centred head opening into the nave. The east and west walls of the upper stages show traces of the position of the old roofs of the chancel and nave. The bell-chamber has four windows, each of two lights, probably of early 15th-century date.

The transepts each have angle-buttresses, and are of the same date as the chancel. In the north and south walls respectively is a three-light window with net tracery, of the first half of the 14th century, and below and to the west of each window is a small low rectangular opening, probably of the 15th century, now

[35] Recov. R. Trin. 30 Chas. II, m. 141.
[36] Feet of F. Bucks. Mich. 35 Chas. II ; Add. MS. 5839, p. 370.
[37] P.C.C. 14 Dyke.
[38] Add. MS. 5839, p. 370; see also Recov. R. East. 12 Anne, m. 129.
[39] Add. MS. 5839, p. 370.
[40] *Musgrave's Obit.* (Harl. Soc.), iii, 139.
[41] Recov. R. Mich. 7 Geo. III, m. 167.
[42] Add. MS. 5839, p. 370.

[43] G.E.C. *Baronetage*, v, 171.
[44] Recov. R. D. Enr. Trin. 16 Geo. III, m. 114.
[45] *Musgrave's Obit.* loc. cit.
[46] Recov. R. Trin. 25 Geo. III, m. 198.
[47] Ibid. East. 42 Geo. III, m. 298.
[48] Lysons, *Mag. Brit.* i (3), 630.
[49] Feet of F. Bucks. Mich. 47 Geo. III ; Sheahan, op. cit. 603.
[50] Sheahan, loc. cit.

[51] *V.C.H. Bucks.* i, 276.
[52] *Hund. R.* (Rec. Com.), i, 40.
[53] *V.C.H. Bucks.* i, 239.
[54] *Cal. Close,* 1323-7, p. 77.
[55] Chan. Inq. p.m. dcxlvi, 23 ; (Ser. 2), dxxv, 115 ; Recov. R. Trin. 30 Chas. II, m. 141.
[56] See under manor.
[57] The invocation is uncertain. It is sometimes given as that of St. Nicholas.

glazed. The north transept has in its east wall an early 15th-century moulded doorway, with an external rear-arch, formerly leading to the demolished vestry. In the west wall is a blocked window, probably of the 15th century, to the south of which are the doorway of the rood-loft staircase and an arched opening giving access to the nave. At the south-east, in the portion of the north wall of the chancel overlapped by the transept, is a trefoil-headed piscina. At the north-east corner of the south transept is a 15th-century squint blocked by the Hanmer monument in the chancel. In the west wall is a blocked window and to the north of it is a skew-arched opening into the nave, having a small inner arch carried on shafts with moulded bell-capitals. The roofs of both transepts have plain trusses with re-cut tie-beams and struts, and were probably rebuilt in the 17th century.

With the exception of the 15th-century west window, all the details of the nave are of 14th-century date. The only window in the north wall is placed at the east end; it is of two trefoiled lights with tracery in a pointed head. In the normal position, a little to the west of the middle of the wall, is the north doorway, which has a moulded head and jambs. In a corresponding position in the south wall is the south doorway, the external label of which has a foliated finial, and to the east of the doorway are two windows, that nearest the doorway being similar to the north window, while the eastern window is of three lights with intersecting tracery. The west window, which has been much restored externally, is of four lights with vertical tracery in the head. The nave roof, a fine piece of work, has three intermediate and two wall-trusses, with moulded wall-plates, tie-beams and purlins, and chamfered wind-braces, struts and collar-beams. The intermediate trusses each have a tie-beam, and two collar-beams carried by struts; the eastern wall-truss has hammer-beams without the lower collar, but with arched struts, while the western wall-truss has hammer-beams and two collars.

The south porch, which is very irregularly set out, has a pointed and chamfered archway of the 16th century, with jamb-shafts having defaced capitals. In the west wall is a small arched light, now blocked, and in the east wall are indications of another blocked window.

The font now in use is modern; the old font is placed in the north transept. It is probably of the 15th century, and has a tapering circular bowl without ornament, standing on a round stem with a stepped base. The font cover is of the 17th century.

In the chancel are four 18th-century mural monuments to members of the Hanmer family, the largest being that which commemorates Sir Walden Hanmer, bart. (d. 1783), by Bacon. Just outside the north transept doorway is a mutilated slab to William Gale (d. 1638).

There are five bells: the treble was added in 1895; the old second was recast in 1896 at the expense of Miss C. Eaton; the second and fifth, the old treble and tenor, and the fourth, the old third, have been recast by Taylor of Loughborough.[57a]

The communion plate includes a cup with long conical bowl and moulded stem; a paten of Sheffield plate, originally with three feet, and a modern plated flagon, neither of which have date-marks.

The registers before the year 1718 have been missing for many years, those up to 1812 are as follows: (i) baptisms and burials 1719 to 1805, marriages 1719 to 1753; (ii) marriages 1754 to 1812; (iii) baptisms 1805 to 1813. There are also two books of accounts: churchwardens' 1778 to 1872, and Feoffees' 1783 to 1873.

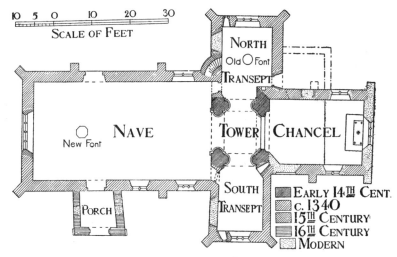

PLAN OF SIMPSON CHURCH

ADVOWSON The advowson was appendant to the manor from the early 13th century and probably before,[58] but was not alienated with it in 1578, being sold by Thomas Pigott and his son Thomas to William Beeley, sen., of Wooburn in 1587.[59] He may have been trustee for George Bury, who presented to the church in 1591,[60] but later conveyed the advowson to Thomas Cranwell, from whom it passed about 1634 to Robert Staunton.[61] He held the right in 1659,[62] but conveyed it in 1663 to George Potter, the rector,[63] doubtless for one turn only, as in 1664 Staunton and his wife were again in possession.[64] It was purchased from the Stauntons by William Cotton,[65] who presented to the church in 1667.[66] According to Browne Willis Cotton sold the advowson about 1690 to John Stannard, then

[57a] The former treble was by Anthony Chandler, 1650, the second by Richard Chandler, 1694, the third by Bartholomew Atton, 1604, and the tenor by James Keene, 1630 (*V.C.H. Bucks.* ii, 124; A. H. Cocks, *Ch. Bells of Bucks.* 565).

[58] *R. of Hugh of Wells* (Cant. and York Soc.), ii, 81; see also manor.
[59] Feet of F. Bucks. Mich. 29 Eliz.; Recov. R. Mich. 29 & 30 Eliz. m. 11.
[60] Lipscomb, *Hist. and Antiq. of Bucks.* iv, 343.
[61] Ibid; Add. MS. 5839, p. 371.

[62] Recov. R. East. 1659, m. 83; cf. Inst. Bks. (P.R.O.).
[63] Feet of F. Bucks. East. 15 Chas. II; Add. MS. 5839, p. 374.
[64] Feet of F. Bucks. East. 16 Chas. II.
[65] Add. MS. 5839, p. 371.
[66] Inst. Bks. (P.R.O.).

incumbent.[67] According to the same authority John Stannard's son about 1712 sold it to Mrs. Elinor Hawes, from whom it passed to her son Matthew, the incumbent.[68] There seems to be some confusion in this statement, since in 1719 Matthew Hawes was presented to the church by his father-in-law Thomas Barrabee, who held in right of his wife Frances,[69] the Barrabees conveying the advowson to Matthew Hawes the same year.[70] Mr. Clobury of Marlow, a later patron, is said to have conveyed his right about 1756 to John Cranwell, clerk,[71] who, with his wife Anne, conveyed it in 1761 to Walden Hanmer.[72] Sir Thomas Hanmer retained the advowson when he sold the manor, and it is now the property of the present baronet, Sir Wyndham Charles Henry Hanmer.

The church was valued at £5 6s. 8d. in 1291,[73] and at £17 6s. 8d. in 1535.[74]

At the suppression of the chantries a tenement and lands worth 6s. 4d. yearly given for an obit in Simpson Church, and a parcel of meadow worth 16d. given for a lamp in Walton Church, were recorded in Simpson.[75]

CHARITIES The charity of Thomas Pigott, founded by deed 25 March 1573, is regulated by a scheme of the Charity Commissioners of 20 October 1908. The trust property consists of a farm at Simpson containing 40 a. let at £45 a year, £1,210 16s. 8d. consols in the High Court and £589 10s. 7d. consols with the official trustees producing in annual dividends £45. The scheme directs that the net income should be applied for the general benefit of the poor in one or more of the modes therein specified. In 1912 the payments included the sum of £10 5s. to the nursing association, £8 16s. to hospitals and travelling expenses of patients, £31 15s. to provident clubs and £13 13s. in the distribution of coal.

The charity of Sir Thomas Hanmer, comprised in a memorandum dated 9 April 1817, consists of a yearly rent-charge of £1 issuing out of a piece of land in the hamlet of Fenny Stratford, now belonging to Mrs. T. Pitkin. By a scheme of the Charity Commissioners of 5 March 1912 the annuity is made applicable in the same manner as the preceding charity.

STANTONBURY

Stantone (xi cent.); Stanton Barry (xiv cent.); Stanton Bury (xviii cent.).[1]; Stantonbury with New Bradwell (xix cent.).

Stantonbury is a small parish of 806 acres,[2] of which 5 acres are arable land, 352 permanent grass, and 25 woods and plantations.[3] The soil is gravel and sand, the subsoil clay. The slope of the ground is from the south, where the highest point is 353 ft. above the ordnance datum, to the north where is the lowest point, 194 ft. above the ordnance datum. The parish is watered by the River Ouse, which forms its northern boundary.

The village of Stantonbury has long since been depopulated, there being only four houses here in 1736.[4] The old church of St. Peter occupies an isolated position near the Ouse in the north-west of the parish, though local tradition says houses formerly stood in the large field north of it. It was restored in 1910, and is now used regularly during the summer.[5] The plan of the house which Sir John Wittewronge built in the 17th century can still be traced near the church, between the river and an artificial mound, which formerly marked the garden boundary and has still hawthorn trees on it.[6] There are a few scattered farms and cottages in the parish, of which Stantonbury Farm in the east is the most important. In 1857 the district known as New Bradwell was added to the ecclesiastical parish of Stantonbury.[7]

In the general inclosure of lands made at the beginning of the 16th century Nicholas Vaux, lord of the manor, turned much of the land in Stantonbury from arable to pasture, and it was complained that at least forty people on his estate were thus deprived of work and home.[8]

MANORS In 1086 Miles Crispin owned the 5-hide manor of STANTON, later known as STANTON BARRY or STANTON BURY.[9] The overlordship passed from him to the honour of Wallingford, of which the manor was held until the 16th century by knight service.[10] After its escheat to the Crown it was subject to a yearly rent of £4 1s. 6½d.,[11] of which mention is found as late as 1688–9.[12]

Bisi, one of the king's thegns, held Stanton Manor under Edward the Confessor, being succeeded before 1086 by Ralph.[13] Ralph de Stanton, who may be regarded as the successor of the Domesday Ralph, is mentioned in the Pipe Roll of 1166–7 [14] and also in that of the year following, when he paid a relief of 100s. for his lands in Stanton.[15] In January 1202–3 Amice daughter of Ralph quitclaimed 2 virgates of land here to Simon de Stanton,[16] in connexion with whom is first found the family surname of Barry or Barre, which has given its distinctive name to the parish. Simon Barry or Simon de Stanton is returned as holding a knight's fee of the honour of Wallingford

[67] Add. MS. 5839, p. 371.

[68] Ibid.

[69] Inst. Bks. (P.R.O.); Add. MS. 5839, fol. 374.

[70] Feet of F. Bucks. Mich. 6 Geo. I.

[71] Add. MS. 5839, pp. 371, 375.

[72] Feet of F. Bucks. Trin. 1 Geo. III.

[73] Pope Nich. Tax. (Rec. Com.), 34.

[74] Valor Eccl. (Rec. Com.), iv, 244.

[75] Chant. Cert. 5, no. 30, 33.

[1] It is said that at the beginning of the 18th century Sir John Wittewronge, bart., lord of the manor, caused the name to be changed from Barry to Bury in consequence of the unearthing of numerous

human remains in the parish (Add. MS. 5839, fol. 179).

[2] This is exclusive of New Bradwell.

[3] Statistics from Bd. of Agric. (1905).

[4] Add. MS. 5839, fol. 179.

[5] Rec. of Bucks. vii, 12.

[6] Ibid.

[7] Sheahan, Hist. and Topog. of Bucks. 606. New Bradwell has been described under Bradwell, to which parish it belongs for civil purposes.

[8] Leadam, Dom. of Incl. 1517 (Roy. Hist. Soc.), 210; Early Chan. Proc. bdle. 452, no. 37.

[9] V.C.H. Bucks. i, 263.

[10] Red Bk. of Exch. (Rolls Ser.), 145, 146,

599; Testa de Nevill (Rec. Com.), 244b. 251a; Hund. R. (Rec. Com.), i, 30; Feud, Aids, i, 80, 106; Chan. Inq. p.m. 28 Edw. I, no. 44; 18 Edw. II, no. 63; 19 Edw. II, no. 41; 6 Edw. III, no. 74; 2 Ric. II, no. 57; (Ser. 2), xliii, 10; Ct. R. (Gen. Ser.), portf. 212, no. 2, 5.

[11] Chan. Inq. p.m. (Ser. 2), xcv, 6.

[12] Feet of F. Div. Co. Hil. 1 Will. and Mary.

[13] V.C.H. Bucks. i, 263.

[14] Pipe R. 13 Hen. II (Pipe R. Soc.), 109.

[15] Ibid. 14 Hen. II, 12.

[16] Hunter, Pedes Finium (Rec. Com.), i, 203.

between the years 1201 and 1212.[17] He died in or about the year 1221, at which date his son and heir Ralph Barry paid a relief of 10 marks for his father's fee.[18] Simon Barry had a second son Peter, who eventually became his brother's heir.[19] The names of both Ralph and Peter Barry are given in the *Testa de Nevill*,[20] and the latter had probably acquired Stanton before the middle of the 13th century. Early in 1280–1 Robert son of Peter Barry [21] confirmed the right of Hugh Barry to 3 acres

BARRY. *Azure two leopards or.*

of meadow in Stanton, which Ralph father of Hugh Barry had held of the fee of Robert Barry.[22] In 1284–6 Robert Barry rendered the feudal aid for Stanton,[23] and various other documentary references are found to his tenure,[24] including a settlement made in 1309 between himself and his son Thomas, by which he secured the manor to himself for life, paying the rent of a rose yearly to Thomas.[25] Robert represented the county in the Parliaments of 1297, 1307 and 1312 [26] and was still alive in February 1316–17, when he and his son Thomas obtained a grant of free warren in their demesne lands of Stanton.[27] Robert died some time before 26 May 1321 ;[28] his widow Maud survived him, and held one-third of the manor in dower till 1326.[29] Thomas Barry held the remaining two-thirds until his own death in 1324–5, when they passed to his son Robert, a minor, fifteen years of age, who also succeeded to his grandmother's third in 1326.[30] At this time the manor (which now begins to be called Stanton Barry) included a garden, a capital messuage, dovecote, a broken-down water-mill, 3 acres of wood, which provided no pannage because it was composed of ash trees, while rents in kind included ten cocks, six capons, 1 lb. of pepper, 1 lb. of cummin, and a pair of spurs.[31]

The wardship of Robert Barry was granted to Richard Blundel,[32] and in 1332, the year of his majority, an inquisition as to proof of his age was made, twelve witnesses coming forward with very varied evidence in his favour.[33] He married a wife Cecilia,[34] who survived him, dying in 1349.[35] Her

heir was then their son William Barry, aged seven years.[36]

In 1377 William Barry and Margaret his wife made a settlement of the manor on themselves and William's issue, subject to a rent to John de Kyngesfold.[37] William Barry's name is given about this time as that of the tenant of the Wallingford Honour in Stanton Barry.[38] He was probably dead before 1399,[39] in which year Hugh Boveton of Yardley Gobion (co. Northampton) (who is said by some historians to have married the daughter and heir of William Barry)[40] and Parnel his wife made a settlement of the manor on Sir William Thirning on behalf of themselves and the heirs of Parnel.[41] Nine years later, in 1408, Sir William Thirning made a further settlement on John Fever and other trustees (including Reynold Boveton, chaplain) [42] probably preliminary to an alienation to William Vaux, who certainly obtained Harrowden (co. Northampton) from Sir William Thirning at this date,[43] and whose descendants are as certainly found in possession of Stanton Barry. William son of William Vaux was attainted in 1461, and this manor became forfeit to

VAUX of Harrowden. *Checky or and gules a cheveron azure with three roses or thereon.*

the Crown,[44] by whom it was granted to Ralph Hastings and later to Richard Fowler, who also received Preston Bissett (q.v.).[45] Nicholas Vaux obtained the reversal of his father's attainder in 1486, and the restoration of Stanton Barry and other of his father's lands.[46] He was created Lord Vaux of Harrowden on 27 April 1523 [47] and died within three weeks in possession of Stanton Barry Manor.[48] Thomas Lord Vaux, his son, made a settlement of Stanton Barry in 1535 [49] preliminary to a sale of much of his property, which took place about this date to Thomas Pope.[50] This sale was confirmed to Thomas Pope by statute of the realm in the same year,[51] but in 1536 there is mention of the purchase of Stantonbury from Thomas Pope by the Crown,[51a] by whom it was granted eleven years later to Sir Thomas Carwardine.[52] He only retained the manor a few years, alienating it in February

[17] *Red Bk. of Exch.* (Rolls Ser.), i, 145, 146 ; ii, 599.
[18] Pipe R. 5 Hen. III, m. 4 d. ; *Excerpta e Rot. Fin.* (Rec. Com.), i, 77.
[19] Baker, *Hist. and Antiq. of Northants.* i, 19. The cartulary of St. James, Northampton, from which Baker seems to have derived the Barry pedigree, unfortunately suffered in the fire of 1731, and the part relating to Great Billing (where the Barrys made grants to the abbey) is indecipherable (cf. Cott. MS. Tib. E. V.).
[20] *Testa de Nevill* (Rec. Com.), 244b, 251a, 258, 259, 261.
[21] Baker, loc. cit.
[22] Feet of F. Div. Co. Hil. 9 Edw. I, no. 27. This Ralph Barry has not been identified, but was possibly a younger son of Peter Barry.
[23] *Feud. Aids*, i, 80.
[24] Ibid. 106 ; Chan. Inq. p.m. 28 Edw. I, no. 44.
[25] Feet of F. case 18, file 61. Simon son of Robert Barry placed a claim on the dorse of this fine.

[26] *Ret. of Members of Parl.* i, 7, 27, 37.
[27] Chart. R. 10 Edw. II, m. 12, no. 27.
[28] Orig. R. 14 Edw. II, m. 11.
[29] Chan. Inq. p.m. 19 Edw. II, no. 41.
[30] Ibid. 18 Edw. II, no. 63.
[31] Ibid.
[32] Chan. Inq. p.m. 6 Edw. III (1st nos.), no. 74.
[33] *Cal. Inq. p.m.* (Edw. III), vii, 344.
[34] Baker (loc. cit.) complains that 'not a single marriage of this family can be retrieved.'
[35] Chan. Inq. p.m. 23 Edw. III, pt. i, no. 24 ; cf. also *Cal. Close*, 1349–54, p. 161.
[36] Chan. Inq. p.m. 23 Edw. III, pt. i, no. 24.
[37] *Cal. Close*, 1377–81, p. 94.
[38] Chan. Inq. p.m. 2 Ric. II, no. 57.
[39] Sir William Thirning in his will proved 21 July 1413 provided masses for Sir William Barry's soul (Gibbons, *Early Linc. Wills*, 140).
[40] Add. MS. 5839, fol. 178 d.

[41] Feet of F. Bucks. East. 22 Ric. II, no. 5.
[42] Ibid. Mich. 10 Hen. IV.
[43] G.E.C. *Peerage*, viii, 18.
[44] Chan. Inq. p.m. 4 Edw. IV, no. 45.
[45] *Cal. Pat.* 1461–7, pp. 195, 369, 437 ; 1467–77, p. 18 ; 1476–85, p. 94 ; Chan. Inq. p.m. 17 Edw. IV, no. 39.
[46] G.E.C. loc. cit.
[47] Ibid.
[48] Chan. Inq. p.m. (Ser. 2), xliii, 10.
[49] Recov. R. Mich. 27 Hen. VIII, m. 333 ; Feet of F. Bucks. Hil. 27 Hen. VIII.
[50] *Stat. of Realm* (Rec. Com.), iii, 627–8. Lord Mordaunt and Elizabeth Tresham his wife and other members of the Tresham family made a conveyance of this manor, among many others, to trustees in 1536 (Feet of F. Div. Co. Hil. 27 Hen. VIII).
[51] *Stat. of Realm*, loc. cit.
[51a] *L. and P. Hen. VIII*, x, 1087 (13).
[52] Pat. 1 Edw. VI, pt. i, m. 37.

1550–1 to John Coke,[53] and his son Robert Coke[54] in 1570 conveyed it to Edmund Ashfield,[55] whose leasehold rights under a grant from Lord Vaux had been specially respected in the sale of 1535.[55a]

Sir Edmund Ashfield died in January 1577–8 and Stanton Barry passed to his daughter and co-heir Avice wife of Edmund Lee.[56] Avice Lee survived her husband, dying in August 1599.[57] Her son and heir Edmund had died the previous March leaving two daughters, Dorothy and Mary, both minors.[58] Dorothy married before 1618 Sir John Temple, kt., bringing him in marriage half the manor of Stanton Barry.[59] Mary Lee and John Claver her husband conveyed her share of the manor in 1621 to Sir Thomas Temple, bart., of Stowe, father of Sir John Temple, kt., on whose behalf the transfer was made.[60] About this date the manor-house is said to have been rented by and in the occupation of Viscount Purbeck, who was then a lunatic under treatment by Dr. Napier, rector of the neighbouring parish of Great Linford.[61] Sir John Temple died in 1632, seised of Stanton Barry Manor, which then passed to his son and heir Peter Temple, aged nineteen.[62] In 1653 Sir Peter Temple made a settlement of his property in Stanton Bury on Sir John Wittewronge, kt.,[63] which was confirmed by his son John Temple in 1658.[64] Four years later Sir John Wittewronge was raised to the title of baronet, being enrolled as of Stanton-bury.[65] His family seat was at Rothamsted in co. Hertford,[66] but he is said to have built a house (which has now disappeared) in this parish for his eldest son John.[67] The first baronet died in 1693 and lies buried at Harpenden.[68] He was succeeded by the above-named son John, who together with his son John is found making a settlement of Stanton Bury Manor in 1695–6.[69] Sir John Wittewronge, bart., died and was buried at Stantonbury in 1697.[70] His son and successor, Sir John Wittewronge, bart., served in the war in Flanders, being colonel of a foot regiment known as 'Wittewronges' which was disbanded in 1717.[71] He sat as member for Aylesbury from 1705–13, and for Wycombe from 1713 until his death in January 1721–2.[72] A few months previous to his death he made a settlement of the manor in con-

WITTEWRONGE of Stantonbury, baronet. *Bendy argent and gules a chief sable charged with a bar dancetty or.*

junction with his son John,[73] who about this date had to flee the country for the murder of Joseph Griffith, a mountebank, at the Saracen's Head in Newport Pagnell.[74] He returned to England some years after his father's death, and in or about the year 1727 sold his Stantonbury property to Sarah Duchess of Marl-borough,[75] the sale being confirmed by Act of Parliament.[76] The Duchess of Marlborough died in possession of the manor in 1744, and under her will it passed under trust to her grandson John Spencer,[77] whose descendant Earl Spencer is now lord of the manor.[78]

SPENCER, Earl Spencer. *Argent quartered with gules fretty or and over all a bend sable charged with three scallops argent.*

A view of frankpledge for the Wallingford Honour was held within this manor,[79] to which was also attached from the 14th to the 17th century the right of free warren and a free fishery.[80]

At Domesday there was a mill in this parish worth 10s. 8d. and fifty eels.[81] It is described as in decay in 1324.[82] There were said to be three water-corn-mills in the parish in 1653[83] and 1695[84] and four in 1721.[85]

Tickford Priory owned a small property in this parish.[86]

CHURCH The old church of *ST. PETER* consists of a chancel measuring internally 29 ft. 4 in. by 13 ft. 3 in., nave 25 ft. 6 in. by 18 ft. and north porch. It is built of rubble and the roofs are covered with tiles.

This small building has been subjected to so many alterations during the course of its history that it is difficult to determine the precise dates of some of its parts, but the chancel probably represents an early church to which a new nave, some 10 ft. longer than at present, was added during the first half of the 12th century. At some period an aisle, or chapel, since destroyed, was built on the south side of the chancel, and in the 13th century the north wall of the chancel was rebuilt and a north aisle added to the nave. The west wall of the nave was rebuilt in its present position in the 15th century. There is no evidence to indicate the date of the destruction of the north aisle and as yet no foundations have been disclosed, but it was probably completed in the 13th century and removed in the late 16th century, when the arcade was blocked and the north porch built.

The south wall of the chancel, which is unusually

[53] Chan. Inq. p.m. (Ser. 2), xcv, 6.
[54] Ibid.
[55] Feet of F. Bucks. Trin. and Mich. 12 Eliz.; Pat. 12 Eliz. pt. ix, m. 26.
[55a] *Stat. of Realm*, loc. cit.; Pat. 1 Edw. VI, pt. i, m. 37.
[56] Add. MS. 5839, fol. 178 d.; Chan. Inq. p.m. (Ser. 2), clxxx, i.
[57] Ct. of Req. bdle. 89, no. 6; Chan. Inq. p.m. (Ser. 2), cclxii, 114.
[58] Ibid. Dorothy was two years and one month old at her father's death. Mary was posthumous.
[59] *Visit. of Bucks.* (Harl. Soc.), 116; Feet of F. Bucks. Hil. 15 Jas. I.
[60] Feet of F. Bucks. East. 19 Jas. I; Chan. Proc. (Ser. 2), bdle. 384, no. 12; (Bridges Div.), bdle. 1, no. 61; *Visit. of Bucks.* (Harl. Soc.), 115–6.
[61] Add. MS. 5839, fol. 179.

[62] Chan. Inq. p.m. (Ser. 2), ccccxc, 158.
[63] Feet of F. Bucks. Hil. 1652; Recov. R. Trin. 1653, m. 34.
[64] *Visit. of Bucks.* (Harl. Soc.), 116; Feet of F. Bucks. Mich. 1658.
[65] *Cal. S. P. Dom.* 1661–2, pp. 333, 346.
[66] *V.C.H. Herts.* ii, 303; Clutterbuck, *Hist. and Antiq. of Herts.* i, 410.
[67] Add. MS. 5839, fol. 178.
[68] G.E.C. *Baronetage*, iii, 248; Clutterbuck, op. cit. i, 411.
[69] Recov. East. 7 Will. III, m. 169; Feet of F. Bucks. East. 8 Will. III.
[70] G.E.C. loc. cit.
[71] Ibid. [72] Ibid.
[73] Recov. Mich. 8 Geo. I, m. 103.
[74] Add. MS. 5839, fol. 178.
[75] Lysons, *Mag. Brit.* i (3), 632.
[76] Priv. Act, 1 Geo. II, cap. 19.

[77] *Gent. Mag.* xiv, 588.
[78] cf. Recov. R. Mich. 20 Geo. III, m. 141; Lysons, loc. cit.; Sheahan, loc. cit.
[79] Ct. R. (Gen. Ser.), portf. 212, no. 2, 5.
[80] Chart. R. 10 Edw. II, m. 12, no. 27; Chan. Inq. p.m. 19 Edw. II, no. 41; Feet of F. Bucks. East. 19 Jas. I; Mich. 1658.
[81] *V.C.H. Bucks.* i, 263.
[82] Chan. Inq. p.m. 18 Edw. II, no. 63.
[83] Recov. R. Trin. 1653, m. 34.
[84] Ibid. East. 7 Will. III, m. 169.
[85] Ibid. Mich. 8 Geo. I, m. 103.
[86] *Pope Nich. Tax.* (Rec. Com.), 47; Inq. a.q.d. file 171, no. 7; *Cal. Rot. Chart. et Inq. a.q.d.* (Rec. Com.), 230; Mins. Accts. (Gen. Ser.), bdles. 1125, no. 1; 1127, no. 18.

STANTONBURY CHURCH: THE INTERIOR LOOKING EAST

STANTONBURY CHURCH: BLOCKED NORTH ARCADE OF NAVE

thick, is probably the oldest part of the building. It was pierced by two openings, now blocked, one a round-headed squint and the other, further west, a

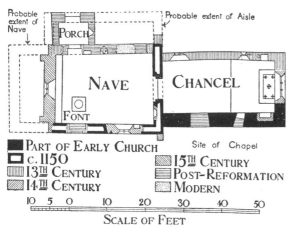

Probable extent of Nave

Probable extent of Aisle

PORCH

NAVE CHANCEL

FONT

■ PART OF EARLY CHURCH   Site of Chapel
□ c. 1150   ▨ 15TH CENTURY
▦ 13TH CENTURY   ▤ POST-REFORMATION
▧ 14TH CENTURY   ▨ MODERN

10 5 0   10   20   30   40   50

SCALE OF FEET

PLAN OF STANTONBURY CHURCH

small archway, the head of which has been removed ; both appear to have opened into a south chapel and probably date from the 12th century, though the material of the former may have been reset. A wide piscina, probably of the 14th century, with a plain pointed head and circular bowl, has been inserted at the east end of the wall. The east window, of three lights with interlacing tracery, dates from the 14th century, and over it is a circular light of the 13th century. On the north are two 13th-century windows, the eastern a single light with a modern external head, and the other of two lights with an external square head of the 16th century. There are two lockers at the east end of the north wall, both rebated for doors, one being square and having a small side recess and the other rectangular. The small chancel arch is a beautiful and fairly well preserved example of Norman work of about 1150. It is of two orders, the outer ornamented with cheveron moulding and the inner with a large roll with beak-head and grotesque ornament at intervals. Both orders are supported by detached shafts with carved capitals and moulded bases, the shafts being enriched with varieties of spiral zigzag and diaper ornament ; one of the capitals is scalloped and the others have grotesque carvings of animals and birds. The arch itself has been strengthened by the insertion (probably in the 14th century) of a third order with a two-centred depressed head moulded in agreement with the original work.

The nave is lighted by two windows, one on the south and the other on the west, both of the 15th century and of two cinquefoiled lights with tracery under pointed heads. The walls of the nave and the roof having been lowered about 2 ft. 6 in., part of the head of the south window has been removed and the tracery blocked, but the west window, being in the gable, is intact, though the tie-beam passes in front of its rear arch. On the west side of the south window are the remains of a small 12th-century light, and on the east side are traces of a window of slightly later date, while near the west end of the wall is a pointed doorway of the 13th century with an indented label ; all three are now blocked. At the

east end of the south wall is a plain piscina with a mediaeval circular bowl, and in the east wall to the south of the chancel arch is a rough pointed image niche.

The north wall contains a mid-13th-century arcade, now built up, of two pointed arches supported by a quatrefoil pillar with moulded capital and base and responds with moulded corbels. The masonry blocking the eastern bay has been pierced by a wide window, now also blocked, and that of the western bay contains a reset pointed doorway, probably of the 13th century, and a stone fragment with two trefoiled panels which has also been reset and forms the west side of a wide recess near the doorway. High in the west gable is a small arched opening which contains a bell. A wide stone bench is carried along the west wall to the full width of the nave. The chancel has an open roof with collar-beam trusses incorporating some old timbers, and the nave an old roof of rough timbers with heavy tie-beams and a central queen-post truss. The porch is lighted by a small pointed window on the east and has a plain entrance with a depressed arch in a square head.

The font has a circular bowl developing below to an octagonal shape, somewhat in the form of a tumbler, an octagonal stem and square base. It probably dates from the 12th century, but the panels were recut in the 17th century. Two 13th-century coffin slabs, each with an incised cross, are now used as benches in the porch.

In the chancel are floor slabs to Clare Wittewronge (d. 1669) ; Sir John Temple (d. 1632) and Dorothy (Lee) his wife (d. 1625) ; Charles Tyrell (d. 1694); and Eleanor (Tyrell) widow of Sir Peter Temple (d. 1671). A slab in the floor against the south wall appears to have supported on the three disengaged sides an iron railing which has been removed, together with everything else indicating the character of the monument inclosed. In the nave is a floor slab to the Rev. William Jenkins (d. 1783) and Ellen his wife (d. 1781). The carved oak pulpit dates from the 17th century, and on the wall near it are a funeral helm with the crest of a Saracen's head,

STANTONBURY CHURCH FROM THE NORTH-EAST

gauntlets and sword, all of the 17th century, though the helm probably incorporates work of an earlier date. At the south-east of the nave is a table with rails and top of the 17th century, but the legs probably date from the 15th century. A 17th-century panelled oak chest has been removed to the new church.

The small bell in the west gable has no inscription, but probably dates from the 16th or 17th century.

The communion plate includes a cup of about 1620, the date mark of which has been obliterated.

The registers begin in 1653.

ADVOWSON The church of Stantonbury formed part of the endowment of Goring Priory in Oxfordshire, as appears from a confirmation charter of 1181, when it was said to be the gift of William and Ralph Barry, brothers.[87] In 1220 the church was appropriated to the priory,[88] to which it continued to belong till the Dissolution,[89] when the vicarage was worth £7 6s. 8d.,[90] the rectory being leased for a rent of 26s. 8d. yearly.[91] The rectory was granted by the Crown to Robert Newdigate of Haynes, Bedfordshire, and others in 1578,[92] and they immediately sold it to Edmund Lee.[93] He apparently also acquired the advowson, since it hereafter descends with the manor in his family.[94] Earl Spencer is the present patron.[95] In 1860 St. James's Church was erected at New Bradwell, and was henceforward used as the parish church, until in 1909 it was discovered that the instrument transferring the rights and privileges of a parish church from the old church of St. Peter to St. James had never been perfected. In consequence the vicar, the Rev. Allan Newman Guest, and the patron, Earl Spencer, obtained a special Act of Parliament for securing legal status for all marriages hitherto solemnized there.

John Mason (1646 ?–94), the enthusiast and poet, was vicar of Stantonbury from 1668 to 1674.[96]

There do not appear to be any endowed charities subsisting in this parish.

STOKE GOLDINGTON

Stoches (xi cent.); Stokes, Stocking, Stók Goldington (xiii cent.).

Stoke Goldington has an area of 2,352 acres, of which about 190 acres are woodland and the remain-

CHURCH FARM, STOKE GOLDINGTON

der equally divided between grass and arable land.[1] The land rises from 175 ft. above the ordnance datum near the River Ouse in the east of the parish to 387 ft. on the western boundary. The soil is chiefly stiff clay and limestone; the subsoil is similar. Brickmaking was carried on here until about ten years ago. The village, in the centre of the parish, lies in a hollow on the road between Newport Pagnell and Northampton. The rectory with its farm is situated near the entrance to Dag Lane. This leads up to the church of St. Peter, which stands on high ground a quarter of a mile north-west of the village. North of the church is Church Farm, a stone house originally built in the early part of the 17th century, but much altered and added to at a subsequent period. The house is surrounded by the remains of a moat, now dry, apparently circular in shape. In the village street there is a late 17th-century stone house with gabled ends. A nearly rectangular moat[2] lies to the west of Stoke Park Wood. The village contains a Congregational chapel; west of the school at the southern end is an old well.

Eakley (Ickele, Gikkele, Jocle, xiii cent.; Icoley alias Ikeley, xvi cent.) is a straggling hamlet with two farms and an old inn, 'The Coach and Horses,' in the north of the parish on the main road from Newport Pagnell to Northampton. It was formerly of much greater importance than at the present day, and seems to have been returned as a hamlet distinct from Stoke Goldington[3] until after the middle of the 16th century, when it was assessed with it.[4] In 1802 Lysons was informed that Eakley had once been a separate parish with a chapel of its own which had been destroyed.[5]

Gorefields, a piece of land of 65 acres without inhabitants in the west of the parish, formerly extra-parochial[6] and mentioned in connexion with Gayhurst in 1848,[7] was annexed to Stoke Goldington in 1865 by an order of quarter sessions.

Ram Alley is a small hamlet to the south-east of the village, comprising a group of 17th-century stone cottages with thatched roofs.

This parish, exclusive of Eakley, was inclosed by Act of Parliament in 1770.[8]

[87] V.C.H. Oxon. ii, 103.
[88] Ibid. ; see also R. of Hugh of Wells (Cant. and York Soc.), i, 197; ii, 67, 78; iii, 94.
[89] L. and P. Hen. VIII, xiii (2), 1098 (3).
[90] Valor Eccl. (Rec. Com.), iv, 245.
[91] Ibid. ii, 205. The rectory was at this date held by William Hyde on an eighty-

one years' lease (Chan. Inq. p.m. [Ser. 2], cclxii, 114).
[92] Pat. 20 Eliz. pt. ii, m. 20.
[93] Chan. Inq. p.m. (Ser. 2), cclxii, 114.
[94] Inst. Bks. (P.R.O.).
[95] Clergy List (1915).
[96] Dict. Nat. Biog.
[1] Statistics from Bd. of Agric. (1905).
[2] V.C.H. Bucks. ii, 32.

[3] Feud. Aids, i, 73. It is mentioned as forming one vill with Haversham in 1316 (ibid. 110).
[4] Lay Subs. R. bdle. 79, no. 189.
[5] Add. MS. 9411, fol. 99. The chapel, if it existed, was probably on the Gore-fields estate.   [6] Pop. Ret. 1831, p. 31 n.
[7] Lond. Gaz. 10 Mar. 1848, p. 967.
[8] Priv. Act, 10 Geo. III, cap. 61.

The following place-names have been found : le Brende Close [9] (xv cent.) ; Cabb yard, Dove House Close[10] (both in Eakley), Storbury Close in Gorefields[11] (xvii cent.) ; Augur's or Orgar's Hill[12] (xix cent.).

STOKE GOLDINGTON MANOR, **MANORS** held before the Conquest by Countess Gueth, was in 1086 assessed at 3 hides 3 virgates, under the lands of William Peverel.[13] The overlordship rights appertaining to the honour of Peverel,[14] last mentioned in this connexion in 1428,[15] gradually merged into those of the Crown.[16]

Drew was tenant of Stoke Goldington under William Peverel in 1086.[17] It was held by Peter de Goldington between 1163 and 1177,[18] and in the early 13th century by Peter de Goldington, presumably a different person.[19] He died about 1218, when the custody of his lands here was given to Walter de St. Owen.[20] Peter de Goldington, who was holding in 1234,[21] died about 1252, leaving three daughters and co-heirs, Denise, Isabel and Maud.[22] Maud may have married William de Grey, whose manor in Stoke Goldington is mentioned in 1265,[23] Denise married Miles Hastings,[24] and Isabel William de Nowers of Gayhurst,[25] and their husbands held Stoke Goldington Manor in two moieties in 1276.[26] The Nowers moiety augmented by one-third of the Hastings moiety was afterwards called Stoke Goldington Manor. Aumary de Nowers was holding in 1279[27] and 1284,[28] in the lifetime of his father William. Grace de Nowers, called lady of Stoke Goldington in 1336,[29] only held one-third of this manor

NOWERS. *Argent two bars gules with three crescents gules in the chief.*

at her death in 1349,[30] the remaining two-thirds reverting to the next heir John de Nowers on the death of Agnes de Nowers between 1357 and 1370.[31] From that date Stoke Goldington Manor descended with Gayhurst[32] (q.v.), which the Nowers had held since the 11th century, to Mr. W. Carlile,[33] the present owner.

The other moiety of Stoke Goldington Manor was held by Miles Hastings[34] until his death about 1305.[35] His grandson and heir Miles,[36] son of Philip Hastings,

died seised of it about 1311.[37] The heirs were Giles Rivel, or Revel, son of Giles Rivel and of Isabel, sister of Miles, and two other sisters Alice wife of Thomas de Furneaux and Margery wife of Roger Boteler,[38] Maud, widow of Miles, receiving dower.[39] The Furneaux portion was acquired later in the century by John son of Aumary de Nowers from William son of Alice de Furneaux.[40] It is mentioned as a distinct part of the Nowers' estate in Stoke Goldington in 1357.[41]

In 1317 Giles Rivel the younger obtained a licence to grant his interests in Stoke Goldington to Simon de Drayton,[42] who also acquired the Boteler portion from William son of Roger and Margery Boteler[43] presumably before 1324,[44] and obtained a grant of free warren in 1327.[45] In 1344 he received licence to alienate his estate here (including the reversion of the land held by Maud Hastings, then widow of John Picard) in mortmain to Ravenstone Priory.[46] This estate[47] augmented by grants to the priory in 1360[48] was afterwards called Stoke Goldington Manor. Under this name it descended with Ravenstone Manor (q.v.) to Daniel second Earl of Nottingham, owner of both manors in 1694, and afterwards seventh Earl of Winchilsea.[49] His estate in Stoke Goldington, into which the Wolf holding in Eakley (see later) had long been apparently absorbed, is presumably that sold in the middle of the 18th century as WOLFSFIELDS MANOR by Daniel eighth Earl of Winchilsea to the trustees of Dr. Busby's charities[50] (cf. Willen). It has since remained in their possession.[51]

A licence was granted to Peter de Goldington in 1214 to inclose his wood at Stoke and to make a park there.[52] Free warren was granted to his son Peter de Goldington in 1251[53] and claimed by the owners of both moieties with rights in the 'new park' in 1276,[54] and a moiety of Stoke Park Wood is mentioned as appertaining to the principal manor in 1495.[55] A grant of court leet and view of frankpledge in this manor was made to Mary Lady Digby in 1620.[56]

Before the Conquest two thegns held a hide and a virgate of land in Stoke Goldington as two manors.[57] Their land in 1086 had passed to the Bishop of Coutances,[58] and was afterwards subordinate to his manor of Olney, the head of the honour of Arundel in Buckinghamshire.[59] John l'Estrange laid claim

[9] Chan. Inq. p.m. (Ser. 2), xi, 5.
[10] Chan. Proc. (Ser. 2), bdle. 447, no. 109.
[11] Chan. Inq. p.m. (Ser. 2), dxvi, 131.
[12] Lipscomb, *Hist. and Antiq. of Bucks.* iv, 351.   [13] *V.C.H. Bucks.* i, 254.
[14] *Testa de Nevill* (Rec. Com.), 244b; *Hund. R.* (Rec. Com.), ii, 347; *Feud. Aids,* i, 105; Chan. Inq. p.m. 33 Edw. I, no. 64; 23 Edw. III (2nd nos.), no. 1; 20 Ric. II, no. 39.
[15] Chan. Inq. p.m. 6 Hen. VI, no. 28.
[16] Ct. R. (Duchy of Lanc.), bdle. 1, no. 7; Chan. Inq. p.m. (Ser. 2), xi, 5; Pat. 24 Eliz. pt. xiii, m. 25.
[17] *V.C.H. Bucks.* loc. cit.
[18] *Pipe R.* 9 Hen. II (Pipe R. Soc.), 18; 13 Hen. II, 107; 24 Hen. II, 95.
[19] *Red Bk. of Exch.* (Rolls Ser.), 585.
[20] *Rot. Lit. Claus.* (Rec. Com.), i, 351b.
[21] *Testa de Nevill* (Rec. Com.), 258.
[22] Chan. Inq. p.m. Hen. III, file 14, no. 9.
[23] *Abbrev. Plac.* (Rec. Com.), 158.
[24] Chan. Inq. p.m. 33 Edw. I, no. 64.

[25] *Excerpta e Rot. Fin.* (Rec. Com.), ii, 254.   [26] *Hund. R.* (Rec. Com.), i, 38.
[27] Ibid. ii, 347.
[28] *Feud. Aids,* i, 73.
[29] *Cal. Close,* 1333–7, p. 632.
[30] Chan. Inq. p.m. Edw. III, file 98, no. 9.
[31] *Cal. Close,* 1354–60, p. 407; Chan. Inq. p.m. 44 Edw. III (2nd nos.), no. 15.
[32] In 1403 one-third of two parts of the manor was claimed against the guardians of Aumary de Nowers by John Bosenho and Eleanor his wife as her dower from her former husband John Stokes (De Banco R. 571, m. 543).
[33] See under Gayhurst Manor; Priv. Act, 10 Geo. III, cap. 61.
[34] *Hund. R.* (Rec. Com.), ii, 347; *Feud. Aids,* i, 73, 105. There was a settlement in 1287 (*Cal. Close,* 1279–88, p. 488).
[35] Chan. Inq. p.m. 33 Edw. I, no. 64.
[36] Ibid.
[37] Ibid. Edw. II, file 24, no. 24.
[38] Ibid.; *Cal. Fine R.* 1307–19, p. 104.

[39] *Cal. Close,* 1307–13, p. 379.
[40] De Banco R. 463, m. 37.
[41] *Cal. Close,* 1354–60, p. 407.
[42] *Cal. Pat.* 1317–21, p. 47.
[43] De Banco R. 463, m. 37.
[44] *Feud. Aids,* i, 133.
[45] Chart. R. 1 Edw. III, m. 29, no. 51.
[46] Inq. a.q.d. file 258, no. 18; *Cal. Pat.* 1343–5, p. 215.
[47] *Feud. Aids,* i, 131.
[48] Inq. a.q.d. file 332, no. 18; *Cal. Pat.* 1358–61, pp. 334, 369.
[49] See under Ravenstone Manor.
[50] Add. MS. 9411, fol. 99.
[51] cf. Sheahan, *Hist. and Topog. of Bucks.* 610.
[52] *Pipe R.* (Bucks. and Beds.), 16 John, m. 2.
[53] *Cal. Chart. R.* 1226–57, p. 351.
[54] *Hund. R.* (Rec. Com.), i, 38, 45.
[55] Chan. Inq. p.m. (Ser. 2), xi, 5.
[56] Pat. 18 Jas. I, pt. xxi, no. 7.
[57] *V.C.H. Bucks.* i, 249.
[58] Ibid.
[59] *Hund. R.* (Rec. Com.), ii, 347.

to the overlordship rights in 1284,[60] and in 1343 they were vested in Ralph Lord Basset of Drayton.[61]

The bishop's holding in Stoke Goldington was held under him by an Englishman in 1086.[62] Part of it, possibly the messuage and 40 acres of land quitclaimed by Thomas son of William de Woolaweston and Beatrice his wife to Roger son of William de More-well in 1271,[63] appears in 1279 in the tenure of John de Morewell,[64] who was holding a carucate of land in 1284 [65] and is mentioned in 1287 with his brother Roger.[65a] A reference to John de Morewell occurs in 1313.[66] His land in Stoke Goldington was held for life by Robert de Morewell and his wife Lucy in 1317, when Giles Rivel the younger granted the reversion to Simon de Drayton [67] with his interests in the Hastings moiety of Stoke Goldington Manor into which this small holding eventually merged.

A property in Stoke Goldington called in the late 16th century *GERVEYS PLACE MANOR* derived its name from the family of John Gerveys, who held land here in the late 14th century.[68] In 1392 he leased it to John Smart, his wife Joan, and their son John in survivorship.[69] In January 1569–70 Thomas son of William Astry stated that his father (whose death occurred in 1542) [70] had died seised of this manor, and that the deeds were detained by Robert Willoughby,[71] then owner of Eakley Manor. The latter probably secured the property, of which no later mention has been found. The name perhaps survives in Jarvis's Wood.

Delapré Abbey in Northamptonshire had a small holding in Stoke Goldington in the later 13th century,[72] possibly *LA GARE*, originally granted by Richard de Bosvile and included in the confirmation grant of 1328.[73] This corresponds to the close of pasture called *GOREFIELD alias MARYMAWDE-LYN alias CHAPELFIELD*,[74] afterwards *GORE-FIELDS*, which in 1536 was reserved to the Crown in a re-grant of its possessions to the abbey.[75] In 1540 Gorefields was leased for twenty-one years to Arthur Longville,[76] and in 1545 granted in fee to George Tresham.[77] He shortly afterwards transferred his rights to Thomas and Isabel Pigott.[78] In the next century Thomas son of Christopher Winkles was seised of Gorefields and died there in 1633, when he was succeeded by his nephew Thomas, son of Richard Winkles.[79] In the later 18th century this property, subject to a quit-rent of 8s. 7d. yearly to

Wolfsfields, was purchased from a family named Wilkinson [80] by the last George Wright of Gayhurst [81](q.v.) and added to his Stoke Goldington estate.

The hamlet of Eakley is first mentioned in the early 13th century as forming part of a knight's fee, including Plumpton and Harpole in Northamptonshire, which was held of the honour of Peverel.[82] The overlordship of Eakley, which was held by the service of one-sixth of a fee in the 13th and 14th centuries, continued in the Peverel fee,[83] afterwards annexed to the honour of Gloucester [84] and last mentioned in this connexion in 1615.[85]

Baldwin Wake,[86] and afterwards Edmund Mortimer, held mesne rights in one-half of Eakley in the later 13th century.[87]

References occur from 1182 to Robert Saucey [88] (de la Salceto, Sausere), who was holding Eakley in 1211.[89] This property is called *EAKLEY MANOR* in 1218, when Hugh son of Gwalerat quitclaimed to him certain rights there.[90] In 1230 it was agreed that Robert Saucey was to hold the park of Eakley of Robert son of Hugh for life at a rent of a pair of white gauntlets, with reversion to Robert son of Hugh and his heirs, who were to hold of the heirs of Robert Saucey at a rent of a pair of gilded spurs.[91] In 1235, on the death of Robert Saucey, Robert son of Hugh surrendered all claims in the manor, park and mill of Eakley to his heirs.[92] These heirs were four nephews and two sisters, two of the nephews Waleran Mortimer [93] and Robert Wolf (le Lup, Lou or Lowe) [94] evidently succeeding to Eakley. Waleran's estate passed to William Mortimer, who died about 1273.[95] Another William Mortimer followed, who was holding of Waleran Mortimer in 1279 [96] and was succeeded by him or another of the same name between 1287 [97] and 1302.[98] Edmund Mortimer was holding in 1316 and 1346 [99] and

MORTIMER. *Argent two bars and a chief gules with three sexfoils argent in the chief.*

John Mortimer before 1439, when he received a grant of free warren in Eakley.[100] In 1458 a settlement of Eakley Manor was made on Baldwin Willoughby with reversion to Agnes daughter and heir of John Mortimer the younger of Grendon

[60] *Feud. Aids*, i, 73.
[61] Chan. Inq. p.m. 17 Edw. III (1st nos.), no. 59.
[62] *V.C.H. Bucks*. loc. cit.
[63] Feet of F. case 15, file 42, no. 13.
[64] *Hund. R.* loc. cit.
[65] *Feud. Aids*, i, 73.
[65a] *Cal. Close*, 1279–88, p. 488.
[66] Ibid. 1307–13, p. 563; see also p. 355.
[67] Inq. a.q.d. file 126, no. 12. The statement that John de Morewell was holding in 1343 is probably inaccurate (Chan. Inq. p.m. 17 Edw. III [1st nos.], no. 59).
[68] *Cal. Pat.* 1381–5, p. 580.
[69] Add. Chart. 19921.
[70] Chan. Inq. p.m. (Ser. 2), lxix, 80. A Kent inquisition.
[71] Chan. Proc. (Ser. 2), bdle. 4, no. 69.
[72] *Hund. R.* (Rec. Com.), i, 38 ; ii, 348.
[73] Dugdale, *Mon.* v, 212.
[74] There seems to have been a small cell here dedicated in honour of St. Mary Magdalene. Gore chapel is noted in

1787 as having been destroyed (Tanner, *Not. Mon.* [ed. Nasmith], Bucks. no. 11).
[75] *L. and P. Hen. VIII*, xi, g. 1417 (12). Gorefields is here (erroneously) said to be in Hanslope, the adjoining parish.
[76] Ibid. xv, p. 556.
[77] Ibid. xx (1), g. 1335 (21).
[78] Ibid. p. 672.
[79] Chan. Inq. p.m. (Ser. 2), dxvi, 131.
[80] John Wilkinson was assessed for Gore chapel about 1659 (Lay Subs. R. bdle. 80, no. 325).
[81] Add. MS. 9411, fol. 99.
[82] *Red Bk. of Exch.* (Rolls Ser.), 585.
[83] *Excerpta e Rot. Fin.* (Rec. Com.), i, 296 ; *Testa de Nevill* (Rec. Com.), 244b ; *Hund. R.* (Rec. Com.), ii, 348 ; *Feud. Aids*, i, 105, 131.
[84] Chan. Inq. p.m. (Ser. 2), cxviii, 9.
[85] Ibid. cccxlviii, 147.
[86] *Hund. R.* (Rec. Com.), ii, 348.
[87] *Feud. Aids*, i, 73.
[88] *Pipe R. 29 Hen. II* (Pipe R. Soc.), 82 ; Hunter, *Pedes Finium*, i, 187.

[89] *Red Bk. of Exch.* (Rolls Ser.), 585.
[90] Feet of F. case 14, file 11, no. 21 ; see also *R. of Hugh of Wells* (Cant. and York Soc.), i, 95.
[91] Feet of F. Bucks. East. 14 Hen. III, no. 3.
[92] Ibid. case 15, file 22, no. 31. (The Mortimer heir is called John in this document. No reference to park or mill after 1279 has been found) ; *Hund. R.* (Rec. Com.), ii, 348, 350).
[93] *Testa de Nevill* (Rec. Com.), 244b.
[94] *Excerpta e Rot. Fin.* (Rec. Com.), i, 296.
[95] *Hund. R.* (Rec. Com.), i, 38, 45.
[96] Ibid. ii, 348.
[97] *Feud. Aids*, i, 73 ; *Cal. Close*, 1279–88, p. 488.
[98] *Feud. Aids*, i, 105.
[99] Ibid. 110, 131.
[100] Chart. R. 1–20 Hen. VI, no. 42. This right is mentioned in the 17th century (Chan. Inq. p.m. [Ser. 2], cccxlviii, 147).

(co. Northampton),[1] whom he afterwards married.[2] At the end of the century Baldwin Willoughby, and after him his son and successor John Willoughby, had to defend their rights in Eakley against William and John Holdenby.[3] These were finally secured to the aforesaid John Willoughby and Richard Willoughby by an award in 1513.[4] In the following year E l i z a b e t h Giles, her son George Hatton, and John Holdenby[5] q u i t c l a i m e d Eakley Manor to Richard Willoughby,[6] and his son and successor Edward died seised in 1558.[7] On the death of his son and heir Robert Willoughby[8] in February 1614–15 it passed by marriage settlement to his widow Mary.[9] She was living in 1621, at the death of Robert's brother and heir Richard Willoughby.[10] His son and heir Philip[11] was in possession before 1630,[12] and in 1636 he and his wife Mary conveyed Eakley Manor to Robert, Richard and William Hocknell,[13] subject to an annuity of £110 to Mary Willoughby, who died in 1657.[14] The Hocknells mortgaged Eakley to Richard Lane and complained in 1658 that his sons William, Charles and Henry Lane refused to accept the repayment of the principal without interest, the Lanes having agreed to forgo the interest during the Civil Wars and Mrs. Willoughby's lifetime.[15] The Lanes, however, who based their right upon their father's will, evidently proved their title, and in November 1671, shortly before his death, Charles Lane settled two cottages called the Dovehouse and the Tollhouse, parcel of Eakley Manor, on his wife Mary and his younger children, who sued the son and heir Henry Lane in the following year.[15a] A settlement was made by Henry and William Lane in 1681.[16] Charles Lane was owner in 1766,[17] and Charles Burton Lane and his wife Grace made a settlement of the manor in 1784.[18] He died before 1802, when his executor was in possession.[19] Lysons states that the estate known as *EAKLEY LANES*, chargeable with repairs to the chancel of Stoke Goldington Church, was sold in 1804 to Sir Robert Gunning, bart.,[20] but it has not been found possible to trace its later descent.

Tolls from fairs in Eakley were appurtenant to the manor in the 17th century.[21] No grant of these fairs has been found, nor any particulars as to their discontinuance.

WILLOUGHBY. *Or on two bars gules three water bougets argent.*

The estate in Eakley inherited from Robert Saucey by Robert Wolf passed in 1262[22] to his son and heir John,[23] who is called Sir John Wolf in 1276.[24] He granted it in 1280 to his son Robert and his heirs to hold of himself for £10 and of his heirs for 1d. yearly.[25] This Robert Wolf, or possibly his son of the same name, was holding in Eakley[26] apparently into the middle of the 14th century.[27] The absence of documentary evidence as to the later descent of the Wolf estate[28] points to the conclusion that it was absorbed, as already stated, into the Stoke Goldington Manor belonging to Ravenstone Priory.[29]

CHURCH

The church of *ST. PETER* consists of a chancel 29 ft. 6 in. by 13 ft., south chapel 29 ft. 6 in. by 11 ft., nave 38 ft. by 18 ft. 6 in., north aisle 7 ft. wide, south aisle 8 ft. wide, west tower 11 ft. square and a south porch. All these measurements are internal.

The earliest part of the structure is the nave, which is shown by the chancel arch to be of the early 12th century. North and south aisles were added about the middle of the 13th century, and in the first half of the succeeding century the chancel was rebuilt with the addition of a south chapel, and the south porch was erected. In the early part of the 15th century considerable alteration was made to the church, the north aisle being rebuilt, while a little later the tower was added. The north aisle was shortened and the nave clearstory added in the 16th century. During the restoration of the church in 1897 the south wall of the south chapel and the north wall of the chancel were rebuilt.

The chancel is lighted from the east by a window of three cinquefoiled lights, the tracery of which is of the 15th century, and has evidently been inserted in a 14th-century opening. In the north wall are two square-headed 14th-century windows of three cinquefoiled lights. The south wall is chiefly occupied by an arcade of two bays opening into the south chapel; the arches are chamfered, the column is circular and the responds semicircular. This work has been entirely rebuilt, partly with the old stonework. The semicircular chancel arch dates from the early part of the 12th century and is of a single plain order. Most of the arch stones and the chamfered abaci have remains of a carved diaper pattern. The jambs are plastered. In the south wall of the chancel, in the usual position, is a 15th-century piscina with a trefoiled head and circular basin.

The south chapel, now used as a vestry, is lighted from the east by a 14th-century pointed window of two cinquefoiled lights with quatrefoil tracery, and from the south by a small reset window of the same date of two

[1] Feet of F. case 22, file 124, no. 98.
[2] Early Chan. Proc. bdles. 97, no. 80 ; 179, no. 5.
[3] Ibid.   [4] Close 449, no. 21.
[5] Ibid.
[6] Feet of F. Div. Co. Hil. 5 Hen. VIII.
[7] Chan. Inq. p.m. (Ser. 2), cxviii, 9.
[8] Ibid.
[9] Ibid. cccxlviii, 147 ; see also Feet of F. Div. Co. East. 11 Jas. I.
[10] Chan. Inq. p.m. (Ser. 2), ccclxxxvi, 99.
[11] Ibid.
[12] Feet of F. Bucks. Mich. 6 Chas. I.
[13] Ibid. East. 12 Chas. I.
[14] Chan. Proc. (Ser. 2), bdle. 447, no. 109.

[15] Ibid.
[15a] Ibid. (Bridges Div.), bdle. 513, no. 61.
[16] Feet of F. Bucks. East. 33 Chas. II ; Recov. R. Trin. 33 Chas. II, m. 158.
[17] Feet of F. Bucks. Trin. 6 Geo. III ; Recov. R. Trin. 6 Geo. III, m. 335.
[18] Feet of F. Bucks. Hil. 24 Geo. III.
[19] Add. MS. 9411, fol. 99.
[20] Ibid. ; Lysons, *Mag. Brit.* i (3), 698.
[21] Chan. Inq. p.m. (Ser. 2), cccxlviii, 147 ; Feet of F. Div. Co. East. 11 Jas. I ; Bucks. East. 33 Chas. II.
[22] *Excerpta e Rot. Fin.* (Rec. Com.), ii, 369.
[23] Chan. Inq. p.m. Hen. III, file 45, no. 10.

[24] *Hund. R.* (Rec. Com.), i, 38.
[25] Feet of F. case 17, file 46, no. 7 ; *Feud. Aids*, i, 73 ; cf. *Hund. R.* (Rec. Com.), ii, 348.
[26] *Feud. Aids*, i, 105, 110 ; Feet of F. case 18, file 64, no. 20.
[27] *Feud. Aids*, i, 131.
[28] John Wolf of Harpole is named in connexion with Stoke Goldington in 1359 (*Cal. Pat.* 1358–61, p. 276), and Wolfsfield occurs as a place-name in 1427, but with no certain reference to this holding (Chan. Inq. p.m. 5 Hen. VI, no. 32).
[29] Some land in Eakley was alienated in mortmain to this priory in 1350 (*Cal. Pat.* 1348–50, p. 511).

uncusped lights. Towards the west end of the south wall is a doorway with a few old stones in the jambs. In this wall has also been reset a piscina with a trefoiled head and large circular basin of the 15th century.

The nave has north and south arcades, each of three bays, dating from the middle of the 13th century, the south arcade being a few years earlier than the north. The arches are pointed and of two chamfered orders springing from circular columns ; the responds of the north arcade have moulded abaci, and, like the arches, are of two chamfered orders, while the responds of the south arcade are semicircular. The capitals and bases are moulded, except those of one column on the north, which are chamfered. There are three plain rectangular windows on the south side of the clearstory. The nave has a plastered ceiling with 17th-century tie-beams.

The north aisle is lighted from the east by a window of two cinquefoiled lights under a square head, the mullion of which is badly broken and decayed, from the north by a late 14th-century traceried window of two lights with an internal rebate for a wooden frame, and from the west by a 16th-century window of two lights under a square head. The north doorway is of 13th-century date ; the external label is mostly modern, but incorporates some old stones carved with nail-head ornament. On the inside of the door, which has a modern casing, are the letters SK with the date 1716 in nail-heads. The south aisle is lighted by two windows in the south wall; the eastern, a 16th-century insertion, is of two uncusped lights under a square head, and has an internal rebate for a wooden frame; the western is modern. Between them is the 13th-century north doorway. Both aisles have 17th-century lean-to roofs.

The 15th-century west tower is of two stages and has diagonal western buttresses, a vice in the south-west angle and an embattled parapet. The tower arch is of three chamfered orders, the innermost order resting upon semi-octagonal responds with moulded capitals and bases. In the west wall of the ground stage, above the moulded west doorway, is a two-light window, with tracery in a pointed head, and there are small lancet lights high up in the north and south walls. The bell-chamber is lighted from all four sides by two-light windows like the west window of the ground stage. The south porch has a much-restored outer archway with a 14th-century label.

The font is quite plain, and has a tapered circular bowl of the 12th or 13th century. In the cusping of the east window of the north aisle is a piece of 15th-century glass, now broken, with IHS in yellow on white. Under the modern communion table is a smaller table of late 17th-century date with turned legs. A 17th-century chest with a carved front, much restored, stands in the vestry. In the nave and north aisle are several fragments of oak pews and moulded framing of early and late 17th-century work.

On the north side of the chancel are four floor slabs to Ann widow of Robert Howard (d. 169–) ; Edmund Butt, rector (d. 1701) ; John Hillersdon,

rector and Archdeacon of Buckingham (d. 1684); and John Deane, rector (d. 1759). At the south-east of the nave is a marble tablet to Thomas Hodgkins (d. 1720), his wife Sarah (d. 1710) and daughter Sarah (d. 1738). In the south aisle is an early 14th-century slab with a much defaced marginal inscription in Lombardic capitals, and indents of two shields. Only the name ' Alianora ' can now be deciphered. In the vestry is a much-worn late 17th-century carved slab.

In the churchyard, against the east wall of the porch, is a 13th-century stone coffin-lid, much worn, with a hollow-chamfered edge and an eight-pointed foliated cross carved upon it.

There are five bells : the treble is by Henry Penn, 1707 ; the second, third, fourth and tenor, by Robert Atton,[29a] are inscribed, 'God save Kyng Charles 1625.' The bell-cage is dated 1625.

The plate consists of a standing paten inscribed ' Ex dono Johan. Hillersdon Archd. Bucks. 1673 ' ; a large cup with curved bowl, the top edge defective, and moulded stem and base, probably of the 18th century, unmarked ; and a modern electro-plated chalice.

The registers begin in 1538.

ADVOWSON The advowson of the rectory of Stoke Goldington, valued at £13 6s.8d. yearly in 1291 [30] and at £14 6s. 8d. in 1535,[31] has descended with certain exceptions with the principal manor.[32] During the minority of the younger Peter de Goldington it came into the possession of Huntingdon Priory, and a presentation was made by the prior before 1220.[33] In 1234, however, Peter de Goldington used his right of presentation, having sued the prior and recovered the advowson.[34] When the manor was divided into moieties the holder of each presented alternately.[35] The disintegration of the Hastings moiety in the early 14th century eventually gave the Nowers family a greater share in the advowson, and John de Nowers in 1376 nullified a presentation made by Ravenstone Priory.[26] The latter seems to have presented for one turn in every three until the Dissolution, when this right lapsed to the lord of the principal manor.[37] The present owner of the advowson is Mr. W. W. Carlile.

The rectory of Stoke Goldington was united with that of Gayhurst in 1736,[38] and an allotment in lieu of tithes except of those in Eakley was made in 1770.[39]

In 1548 an obit in the church was maintained by 17s. 10d. and a light by 9d. yearly from certain lands and tenements in Stoke Goldington.[40]

CHARITIES Parish Houses, otherwise known as Widows' Money.—It appears from the Parliamentary Returns of 1786 that a person unknown gave some houses for six poor widows and for apprenticing children. The property formerly consisted of thirteen houses let by the overseers. The houses having been destroyed by fire, the site was sold in 1891, and the proceeds invested in £103 9s. 2d. India 3 per cents., the dividends of which, amounting to £3 2s., are applied for the benefit of poor widows.

[29a] A. H. Cocks, *Ch. Bells of Bucks*, 574.
[30] *Pope Nich. Tax.* (Rec. Com.), 34.
[31] *Valor Eccl.* (Rec. Com.), iv, 243.
[32] cf. Bacon, *Liber Regis*, 501 ; Inst. Bks. (P.R.O.).
[33] *R. of Hugh of Wells* (Cant. and York Soc.), i, 95. A vicarage was ordained at

this time allowing the appropriation by the priory of half the rectory and the tithes of sheaves from Robert Saucey's fee in Eakley. This arrangement lapsed with the loss of the advowson by the priory.
[34] Ibid. ii, 89.

[35] De Banco R. 463, m. 37.
[36] Ibid.
[37] See Lipscomb's list of presentations (op. cit. iv, 354–5).
[38] Bacon, *Liber Regis*, 501.
[39] Priv. Act, 10 Geo. III, cap. 61.
[40] Chant. Cert. 5, no. 22.

STOKE GOLDINGTON CHURCH FROM THE SOUTH-EAST

STOKE GOLDINGTON CHURCH: THE INTERIOR LOOKING EAST

STOKE HAMMOND CHURCH FROM THE SOUTH-EAST

STOKE HAMMOND

Stoches (xi cent.); Stokes (xii, xiii cent.); Stokes Hamund (xiii cent.).

The parish of Stoke Hammond derives its distinguishing name from Hamon son of Meinfelin, a 12th-century holder. It covers 1,566 acres, including 1,080 acres of permanent grass and 343 of arable.[1] The land rises from 238 ft. above the ordnance datum near the Grand Junction Canal to 340 ft. in the west of the parish. The soil is light clay, the subsoil clay and gravel, and the chief crops are wheat, oats, beans and barley. The River Ouzel forms the eastern boundary, and the main line of the London and North Western railway runs through the middle of the parish. The somewhat scattered village is situated in the south-east. It contains many half-timber 17th-century cottages, some of which have thatched roofs. The Bell Inn is a 17th-century brick building rearranged internally.

The church, standing on high ground at the north end of the village, is approached through an avenue of lime trees. In the churchyard there are two yew trees planted in 1687. The rectory is on the south-west of the church and the school a short distance east of it.

Stoke Lodge, to the south of the road between the Bell Inn and the post office, is the residence of Mr. Percival Lovett. It was built before the middle of the 19th century by one of the Bernard Fountaines,[2] members of an old yeoman family which has been connected with Stoke Hammond from the 17th century.[3] There is a Wesleyan chapel in the village.

Tyrell's Manor, so called from the 16th-century owners, lies about a quarter of a mile south-east from the church. Stoke House, the property and residence of Mrs. Percival, stands in the north-east of the parish, east of the Fenny Stratford road. A short distance eastward from the dairy farm is the corn-mill known as the Orchard Mill. The Rectory Farm is in the north-west of the parish.

Inclosures for turning arable land into pasture were being made here in the 15th century,[4] but the general inclosure of the common lands including Cow Common was made by Act of Parliament in 1774, the award being dated 25 March 1775.[5]

The following place-names occur: Levedene-made[6] (xii cent.); Saddeston,[7] Hollond[8] (xvi cent.); Coyes, Herring leyes,[9] the Tiled House Pools,[10] Docky Hooke[11] (xvii cent.).

MANORS Before the Conquest *STOKE HAMMOND MANOR* was held by eight thegns, one of them holding 6 hides less half a virgate as one manor.[12] In 1086 it was assessed at 10 hides among the lands of Manno the Breton,[13] and was afterwards attached to his barony of Wolverton,[14] paying in the middle of the 16th century £1 3s. 4½d. for castle ward.[15] Stoke Hammond is mentioned as one of the fees of Wolverton Manor in 1619,[16] but the idea of feudal tenure was then lost and the manor had been granted in socage in 1607.[17]

Stoke Hammond descended with Wolverton (q.v.) to William son of Hamon,[18] who subinfeudated it in 1247 to Alan son of Robert[19] [de Stoke]. He was perhaps a descendant of Owen de Stoke, who in 1166 held by recent enfeoffment of Hamon son of Meinfelin[20] a quarter fee corresponding to the hide of land which his successor Owen quitclaimed in 1198 to the aforesaid William son of Hamon in return for a virgate.[21] Alan was holding Stoke Hammond in 1254,[22] but his son Robert had succeeded before 1284[23] and Alexander de Stoke before 1302.[24] In 1311 John de Stoke, parson of Strixton (co. Northampton), granted two parts of this manor to John Grey, Lord de Grey, with the reversion of the remaining part which John de Eton and Lettice his wife held for life of her dower.[25] John Grey's share of Stoke Hammond Manor,[26] and the whole manor when the reversion fell in (Lettice was still living in 1327),[27] descended with Bletchley Manor (q.v.) to Richard Earl of Kent.[28] In 1506 he settled this manor with those of Great Brickhill and Simpson,[29] and it was again settled with Simpson in 1512 on John Huse, who was about to marry Richard's sister Anne.[30] In 1514 John and Anne Huse conveyed Stoke Hammond Manor to Sir Henry Wyatt and others, trustees[31] for Richard Wyatt, and the legality of this transfer was acknowledged in 1518 by Sir Henry Grey,[32] half-brother and heir of Richard Earl of Kent.[33] This manor passed to Sir John Williams, who in 1541 exchanged it for other lands with the Crown,[34] the transaction being completed

[1] Statistics from Bd. of Agric. (1905).
[2] Sheahan, *Hist. and Topog. of Bucks.* 612.
[3] Monumental inscriptions in church from 1636 to 1709. Inscription on family tomb in the churchyard between 1802 and 1908.
[4] Leadam, *Dom. Incl.* 1517 (Roy. Hist Soc.), 180.
[5] Priv. Act, 14 Geo. III, cap. 76; Blue Bk. *Inclosure Awards*, 13.
[6] Hunter, *Pedes Finium* (Rec. Com.), i, 172.
[7] Ld. Rev. Misc. Bks. clxxxviii, fol. 29a.
[8] Ibid. fol. 30a.
[9] Com. Pleas Recov. R. East. 28 Chas. II, m. 3.
[10] Chan. Inq. p.m. (Ser. 2), cccxxiii, 39.
[11] Add. MS. 5830, fol. 139b.
[12] *V.C.H. Bucks.* i, 270.
[13] Ibid.
[14] *Liber Niger* (ed. 1771), 192; *Testa*

de Nevill (Rec. Com.), 248; Anct. Extents (Exch. K.R.), no. 78 (1); Chan. Inq. p.m. 27 Edw. III, no. 58; 17 Hen. VI, no. 38, m. 4. In 1388 this manor was said to be held of the heirs of Philip Basset (Chan. Inq. p.m. 12 Ric. II, no. 23), apparently by some confusion with Great Brickhill (q.v.).
[15] Ld. Rev. Misc. Bks. clxxxviii, fol. 30a, 32b, 33a, taking the total for the entries under this head; 13s. 4d. was also paid from the manor to the fee of Richard Blacknall.
[16] Chan. Inq. p.m. (Ser. 2), dxlii, 131.
[17] Pat. 5 Jas. I, pt. xix, m. 28; see also Chan. Inq. p.m. (Ser. 2), cccxlii, 123.
[18] *Testa de Nevill* (Rec. Com.), 258, 259b, 262; Maud, widow of Hamon son of Meinfelin, held it in dower in 1185 (Grimaldi, *Rot. de Dominabus*, 21).
[19] Feet of F. case 15, file 29, no. 29.
[20] *Liber Niger* (ed. 1771), 192.

[21] Hunter, op. cit. i, 172.
[22] *Hund. R.* (Rec. Com.), i, 30.
[23] *Feud. Aids*, i, 80.
[24] Ibid. 106.
[25] Feet of F. case 18, file 63, no. 18; see also De Banco R. 187, m. 87; 189, m. 30.
[26] *Feud. Aids*, i, 109; Anct. Extents (Exch. K.R.), no. 78 (1).
[27] Lay Subs. R. bdle. 242, no. 85. She is here called Lettice de Stoke.
[28] *Feud. Aids*, i, 132; see also under Bletchley.
[29] De Banco R. 977, m. 138; Close, 4 Hen. VIII, no. 21.
[30] Close, 4 Hen. VIII, no. 21; see also no. 20, 24; Feet of F. Div. Co. Hil. 4 Hen. VIII.
[31] Feet of F. Bucks. Mich. 6 Hen. VIII, no. 44.
[32] Close, 10 Hen. VIII, no. 36.
[33] G.E.C. *Complete Peerage*, iv, 354.
[34] *L. and P. Hen. VIII*, xvi, g. 779 (21).

in 1542.[35] Stoke Hammond Manor was retained by the Crown[36] until 1607, when it was granted to Robert Earl of Salisbury.[37] He died in 1612, when he was succeeded by his son William.[38] He sold this manor to William Ashton, who with his wife Anne transferred it in 1619 with warranty against claimants through Robert Earl of Salisbury to Levinus Monke.[39] He was one of the Clerks of the Signet and died in 1623.[40] His widow Elizabeth was holding in 1625, during the minority of their son Robert.[41] Later in the century Stoke Hammond Manor fell into moieties. A settlement of one moiety was made in 1648[42] on the marriage of Jane daughter of Richard Bennet by his first wife Jane, daughter of Levinus Monke,[43] with James Scudamore, son of John first Viscount Scudamore of Sligo.[44] Their son John, who succeeded his grandfather as viscount in 1671,[45] made a settlement of his moiety in 1682.[46] His son James succeeding in 1697[47] also made a settlement respecting it in 1706.[48] He died in 1716 and his only daughter and heir Frances in 1750.[49] A settlement

SCUDAMORE. *Gules three stirrups or with their leathers and buckles.*

HOWARD. *Gules a bend between six crosslets fitchy argent with the augmentation for Flodden on the bend.*

of her moiety was made in 1771[50] on the marriage of her only daughter Frances Fitzroy Scudamore[51] to Charles Howard the younger.[52] The manorial rights of the Smiths, owners of the other moiety, were purchased in trust for her in 1773,[53] and she was sole lady of the manor in 1774.[54] Her husband, who succeeded to the dukedom of Norfolk in 1786,[55] made a settlement of Stoke Hammond property in 1811[56] and died in 1815, his widow, then a lunatic, surviving until 1820.[57] His cousin Bernard, the next Duke of Norfolk,[58] sold the Stoke Hammond estates

chiefly to members of the Fountaine family,[59] and Bernard Fountaine was lord of the manor in 1862.[60] It remained in his family[61] until recently. Mrs. Percival is the present owner.

The other moiety of Stoke Hammond Manor passed by the marriage about 1630 of Mary daughter of Levinus Monke to Thomas, younger brother of Richard Bennet.[62] They made a settlement concerning it in 1653,[63] on the marriage of their son Levinus to Judith daughter of William Boevey.[64] Thomas Bennet was made a baronet in 1660 and was buried at Babraham (co. Cambridge) in 1667.[65] In 1672 his widow and son conveyed their estate in Stoke Hammond to Sir John Pye, bart., and Sir Michael Heneage.[66] A moiety of this, equivalent to a quarter of the whole manor (the remaining quarter cannot be traced), was conveyed in 1682 by Sir John Pye to Harris Smith of Padbury,[67] father of Richard Smith, who owned it in 1736.[68] It appears to have been his widow Penelope,[69] who made a settlement respecting it in 1752 with the heir Richard Smith.[70] He was probably the Mr. Smith[71] who sold his manorial rights to Charles Howard in 1773, so that the whole manor, as already said, became vested in his wife Frances. The land previously owned by the Smiths passed through various hands before 1802 and does not reappear.[72]

An estate including the site and capital messuage of the manor, a messuage called White House and Lord's Close, was leased for twenty-two years by Sir John Williams in 1539 to Thomas Golsew.[73] It was held later by Edmund Atkinson, and granted in 1569 to Henry Fowler, his wife Alice and their son John for their lives in survivorship.[74] An additional term of twenty-one years was granted in 1585 to John Fowler.[75]

A mill at Stoke Hammond worth 8s. yearly in 1086[76] descended with the manor to Sir John Williams,[77] and was included in his lease of the site of the manor, but excepted from the Crown leases. The mill-house with some 70 acres of land was held in chief of the Crown by William Turney at his death in 1610, when it passed to his son John.[78] John Hillersdon held a piece of land in the neighbourhood of Orchard Mill (the name of the present mill) in 1637,[79] and Browne Willis states in 1735 that the Turney property in Stoke Hammond was acquired by the Hillersdons.[80]

[35] Feet of F. Div. Co. Trin. 34 Hen. VIII, no. 15.
[36] Ct. R. (Gen. Ser.), portf. 155, no. 23; Ld. Rev. Misc. Bks. clxxxviii, fol. 29–34; Exch. Spec. Com. 460.
[37] Pat. 5 Jas. I, pt. xix, m. 28.
[38] Chan. Inq. p.m. (Ser. 2), cccxlii, 123.
[39] Close, 17 Jas. I, pt. iv, no. 23; Feet of F. Bucks. Mich. 17 Jas. I.
[40] Chan. Inq. p.m. (Ser. 2), ccccvi, 27; P.C.C. 36 Swann.
[41] Ibid.
[42] Feet of F. Div. Co. Mich. 24 Chas. I.
[43] Add. MS. 5839, fol. 185b; Burke, *Extinct Baronetage.*
[44] G.E.C. *Peerage,* vii, 93.
[45] Ibid.
[46] Feet of F. Div. Co. Hil. 33 & 34 Chas. II.
[47] G.E.C. loc. cit.
[48] Recov. R. Hil. 4 Anne, m. 13.
[49] G.E.C. *Peerage,* i, 282.
[50] Recov. R. East. 11 Geo. III, m. 276.
[51] G.E.C. *Peerage,* vi, 57

[52] *Marriage Reg. of St. George, Hanover Square* (Harl. Soc.), i, 207.
[53] Lysons, *Mag. Brit.* i (3), 634.
[54] Priv. Act, 14 Geo. III, cap. 76.
[55] G.E.C. *Peerage,* vi, 57.
[56] Com. Pleas Recov. R. Trin. 51 Geo. III, m. 39.
[57] G.E.C. loc. cit.
[58] Ibid. p. 58.
[59] Lipscomb, *Hist. and Antiq. of Bucks.* iv, 361. Two branches of the Fountaine family in addition to the one holding the manor occupied their own farms later in the century (Sheahan, op. cit. 612; *Ret. of Owners of Land* [1873], *Bucks.* 8).
[60] Sheahan, loc. cit.
[61] *Ret. of Owners of Land* (1873), *Bucks.* 8.
[62] G.E.C. *Baronetage,* iii, 130.
[63] Feet of F. Div. Co. Trin. 1653; Recov. R. Trin. 1653, m. 51.
[64] G.E.C. loc. cit.
[65] Ibid.; M. I. in Babraham Church; P.C.C. 144 Carr.

[66] Feet of F. Bucks. Hil. 23 & 24 Chas. II.
[67] Close, 4588, no. 21.
[68] Add. MS. 5830, fol. 135b.
[69] Browne Willis is somewhat confused as to the generations of this family. Ibid. 5839, fol. 185b.
[70] Recov. R. Hil. 25 Geo. II, m. 227.
[71] Add. MS. 9411, fol. 111 (Letter to Lysons dated 20 July 1802).
[72] Ibid.
[73] Ld. Rev. Misc. Bks. clxxxviii, fol. 32a.
[74] Pat. 11 Eliz. pt. iii; see also Pat. 27 Eliz. pt. vii, m. 12.
[75] Ibid. 27 Eliz. pt. vii, m. 12.
[76] *V.C.H. Bucks.* i, 270.
[77] Anct. Extents (Exch. K.R.), no. 78 (1); Chan. Inq. p.m. Edw. II, file 3, no. 5; 17 Edw. II, no. 74; Ld. Rev. Misc. Bks. clxxxviii, fol. 32a.
[78] Chan. Inq. p.m. (Ser. 2), cccxxiii, 39.
[79] Ibid. dcxiv, 94.
[80] Add. MS. 5839, fol. 135b; see under Tyrell's Manor. A messuage called

A dove-house on the manor is named in 1323[81] and 1619,[82] and references to it occur later in both moieties.[83] The right of free fishery is mentioned in the 17th century.[84]

A second manor called *STOKE HAMMOND MANOR* belonged to Dunstable Priory, which in 1245 acquired about 2 virgates from Adam de London and his wife Alice.[85] The priory built a great barn at Stoke in 1246 and a hall and a cattle shed in 1249,[86] and in 1284 Robert son of Alan de Stoke cleared for it another virgate of land belonging to his fee and given by John Hastings.[87] This manor was leased by Dunstable Priory for £3 6s. 8d. yearly until the Dissolution.[88] Thomas Page was lessee in 1535,[89] but in 1538 a sixty years' lease was granted by the priory to Sir John Williams,[90] then apparently lord of the principal manor. In 1543 he exchanged his leasehold interest for a grant from the Crown,[91] but some compromise must have been effected, since the priory lands, including two messuages, were comprised in the survey of the Crown manor in 1555.[92] Both messuages, one under the name of Pervaunts, were granted by the Crown in 1564 to John Somer and Thomas Kerry.[93] The second messuage is apparently that of which John Fowler above mentioned died seised about 1609.[94] This property, which his widow Alice and her second husband Thomas Voggett were holding for life in 1610, was acquired from the son and heir Henry Fowler[95] by Levinus Monke before 1623.[96] It is not afterwards distinguishable from the manorial estate of Stoke Hammond.

The right of the Prior of Dunstable to view of frankpledge and assize of bread and ale in Stoke was called in question in 1286,[97] and evidently established from general charters in his favour.[98] The view of frankpledge and court baron were included in the priory lease to Sir John Williams, but do not reappear.

An estate in Stoke Hammond known as *INGLETONS*, originally a freehold of the principal manor,[99]

DUNSTABLE PRIORY.
Argent a pile sable with a horse-shoe fixed thereto by a staple or.

appears in the late 15th century as *STOKE HAMMOND MANOR*, held of the king in chief by service of one-thirtieth part of a fee,[100] for which tenure in socage was afterwards substituted.[1] George Ingleton held this estate at his death in January 1493–4,[2] and it descended with Thornton Manor (q.v.) to George Tyrell,[3] who sold it in 1557 to Edward Kirke of Bow Brickhill, yeoman.[4] He was pardoned for acquiring it without licence in 1558, but had to prove his title in the following year.[5] Edward Kirke died in 1573, leaving his estate to be divided equally between his sons William and Kenelm.[6] William Kirke obtained livery of Stoke Hammond Manor in 1574,[7] and later in the year he and his wife Joan surrendered it to Kenelm.[8] Difficulties arose with the Crown, which were finally adjusted in 1579.[9] In 1598 Kenelm Kirke and his wife Joyce conveyed this manor to Thomas Cripps,[10] who in 1608 settled it on himself and his wife Joan for life with reversion as to one half to Frances wife of John Hillersdon of Ampthill (co. Bedford). He was to enjoy all the manorial privileges after his wife's death with remainder to their son and heir Thomas Hillersdon.[11] Joan was living when Thomas Cripps died in 1611.[12] John Hillersdon, styled of Stoke Hammond in 1634,[13] died seised of some property there in 1637.[14] His son and heir Thomas[15] was fined in 1646 for the discharge of his estate in Stoke Hammond, valued at £130 yearly, which had been sequestered for delinquency.[16] He died in 1658,[17] and in 1676 his son John[18] cut off the entails and remainders on the estate entitled *TYRELLS MANOR*, then partly in the tenure of his mother Elizabeth and partly in that of William Abwell.[19] Elizabeth Hillersdon died in 1705[20] and John Hillersdon in 1729.[21] His family held property in Stoke Hammond later in the century,[22] but there is no mention of it or of Tyrell's Manor in the Inclosure Act of 1774. It is perhaps included in the estate owned before 1862 by Baron Lionel

HILLERSDON. *Argent a cheveron and a border engrailed sable with three bulls' heads cabossed argent on the cheveron.*

'Mills house' among other property was, however, claimed in February 1685–6 by John Turney, claiming through his father John (who died about 1671) son of the John of 1610. William, great-grandfather of the claimant, was said to have bought the premises in March 1593–4 of Kenelm Kirke (Chan. Proc. [Bridges Div.], bdle. 84, no. 32).

[81] Mins. Accts. bdle. 1119, no. 2.

[82] Feet of F. Bucks. Mich. 17 Jas. I.

[83] Ibid. Hil. 23 & 24 Chas. II; Recov. R. Hil. 25 Geo. II, m. 227; East. 11 Geo. III, m. 276.

[84] Feet of F. Bucks. Mich. 17 Jas. I; Hil. 23 & 24 Chas. II.

[85] *Ann. Mon.* (Rolls Ser.), iii, 169; Feet of F. case 15, file 27, no. 4, 5.

[86] *Ann. Mon.* (Rolls Ser.), iii, 171, 179.

[87] Ibid. 314.

[88] *Pope Nich. Tax.* (Rec. Com.), 47b; Inq. a.q.d. file 231, no. 7. In 1298 a lease was made to Henry Spigurnel (*Ann. Mon.* [Rolls Ser.], iii, 358), afterwards lord of Great Loughton, who was assessed

in Stoke in 1327 (Lay Subs. R. bdle. 242, no. 85).

[89] *Valor Eccl.* (Rec. Com.), iv, 207.

[90] Mins. Accts. Hen. VIII, no. 12.

[91] *L. and P. Hen. VIII*, xviii (1), g. 226 (79).

[92] Ld. Rev. Misc. Bks. clxxxviii, fol. 34a.

[93] Pat. 6 Eliz. pt. iii, m. 8.

[94] Chan. Inq. p.m. (Ser. 2), dcxlvii, 28.

[95] Ibid.

[96] Ibid. ccccvi, 27.

[97] *Plac. de Quo Warr.* (Rec. Com.), 96.

[98] *Ann. Mon.* (Rolls Ser.), iii, 323.

[99] Ld. Rev. Misc. Bks. clxxxviii, fol. 29a.

[100] Chan. Inq. p.m. (Ser. 2), x, 2.

[1] Memo. R. (Exch. L.T.R.), Mich. 21 Eliz. m. 129.

[2] Chan. Inq. p.m. (Ser. 2), x, 2.

[3] See also Ld. Rev. Misc. Bks. clxxxviii, fol. 29a.

[4] Com. Pleas D. Enr. Mich. 3 & 4 Phil. and Mary; Feet of F. Bucks. East. 3 & 4 Phil. and Mary.

[5] Memo. R. (Exch. L.T.R.), Trin. 1 Eliz. m. 2.

[6] Chan. Inq. p.m. (Ser. 2), clxviii, 10.

[7] Fine R. 16 Eliz. no. 58.

[8] Feet of F. Bucks. Mich. 16 & 17 Eliz.

[9] Memo. R. (Exch. L.T.R.), Hil. 17 Eliz. m. 56; Mich. 21 Eliz. m. 129; Pat. 22 Eliz. pt. v, m. 29.

[10] Feet of F. Bucks. Trin. 40 Eliz.

[11] Chan. Inq. p.m. (Ser. 2), dcxlvi, 12.

[12] Ibid.; P.C.C. 43 Wood.

[13] *Visit. of Bucks.* (Harl. Soc.), 74.

[14] Chan. Inq. p.m. (Ser. 2), dcxiv, 94.

[15] Ibid.

[16] *Cal. Com. for Comp.* 947–8.

[17] M. I. in church; P.C.C. 23 Pell.

[18] Ibid.

[19] Com. Pleas D. Enr. East. 28 Chas. II, m. 3.

[20] Inscription on slab in church.

[21] *Musgrave's Obit.* (Harl. Soc.), iii, 217.

[22] Add. MS. 5839, fol. 135b.

Nathan de Rothschild,[23] which has since descended to his third son Mr. Leopold de Rothschild.

A small property in Stoke Hammond confirmed to Missenden Abbey by Pope Innocent IV in 1253,[24] and described as 2 virgates of land worth £2 yearly in 1291,[25] was again confirmed to this abbey by papal authority in 1401.[26] The rents were valued at £1 6s. 8d. yearly in 1535.[27] After the Dissolution this property appears to have passed with other possessions of Missenden Abbey to the Dormers,[28] since in 1615 Robert Lord Dormer sold some land here to Henry Fowler.[29] He transferred it in 1616 to William Ashton, who sold it with the principal manor of Stoke Hammond to Levinus Monke in 1619.[30] This land, worth £5 yearly in 1625,[31] is not afterwards distinguishable from the manor.

CHURCH
The church of *ST. LUKE* consists of a chancel 23 ft. by 16 ft., central tower 9 ft. by 8 ft., north and south transepts each 10 ft. by 8 ft. 6 in., nave 33 ft. 6 in. by 20 ft., south porch and small modern north vestry. All these measurements are internal.

There was apparently an early church here consisting of a chancel and nave, the eastern angle of the south

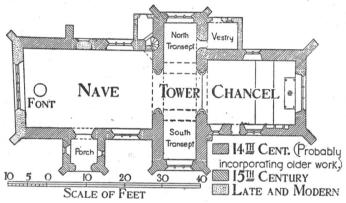

PLAN OF STOKE HAMMOND CHURCH

wall of the latter being still visible in the east wall of the south transept. In the middle of the 14th century the church assumed its present cruciform plan, the chancel being rebuilt and enlarged, and the central tower and transepts added. Repairs were effected in the 15th century, when the north and south walls of the transepts were rebuilt, the nave walls heightened, the roofs renewed, and the south porch added. Some work seems to have been done to the nave roof in 1703, as that date appears on one of the tie-beams, and it is said that the tower was raised and embattled in the same year, a former saddle-back roof being then removed. To the same date must probably be assigned the brick gable of the south porch. The west wall of the nave was rebuilt and the whole building restored in 1852. The church is built of stone; the mullions and tracery of many of the windows have been patched with cement.

The east window of the chancel is of the late 15th century and has three cinquefoiled lights under a three-centred head. In the north wall is a 14th-century window of two cinquefoiled lights with tracery

in a pointed head, and opposite to it in the south wall is a similar window. At the south-west is a low-side window, much restored externally. This window contains an oval quarry dated 1682, with an armorial achievement. The shield is quarterly, 1 and 4 Argent a fesse gules with three fleurs de lis gold thereon; 2 and 3 Argent three leopards passant gules, with a sable martlet on the centre point for difference. The crest is a lion gules standing on a helmet with wreath and mantling, and the motto 'Deus scutum meum' on a scroll below the shield. The priest's doorway between the windows is of 14th-century date, with head and jambs moulded in two orders. Near the east end of the wall are two sedilia with cinquefoiled ogee heads and foliated spandrels in range with a piscina having a trefoiled head and sexfoil basin. The eastern sedile communicates with the piscina niche by a small trefoil-headed piercing on a level with the seat. The 15th-century tie-beams of the roof are still in position, though the roof has been much restored.

The tower is of two stages and is carried by four 14th-century pointed arches, each of two chamfered orders. Those opening to the chancel and nave have their outer orders continuous, while the inner orders rest on semi-octagonal pilasters with moulded capitals and bases. The two orders of the arches opening to the transepts die into the walls at their springing. The bell-chamber is lighted by four pointed windows, each of two trefoiled ogee lights with tracery; the east and west windows are at a higher level than the others, owing to the former higher pitch of the roofs, the weatherings of which are visible.

In the end wall of each transept is a 15th-century window of three cinquefoiled lights under a four-centred head. The east and west walls are probably of the same date as the tower, as they are of the same thickness as the tower arches between them, but the windows are of late 15th-century work. Each transept has a late 15th-century roof of two bays with central and wall trusses; each truss consists of a cambered tie-beam with a modern carved boss in the middle of the soffit, and curved brackets resting on stone corbels carved as demi-angels holding plain shields. In the east wall of the north transept is a small modern door leading to the vestry.

The nave has a three-light window towards the east end of the north wall and another opposite to it on the south side, both late 15th-century work, and of three cinquefoiled lights with tracery in a four-centred head. The north window contains some contemporary 15th-century glass consisting of six small figures, more or less perfect. These are as follows: a bishop in mitre and mass vestments holding a staff, on a diapered background; a man in a cap and loose robe holding a book, with a scroll inscribed 'Johel' in black letter, much discoloured and imperfect; the half-figure of a man in a cap and a white robe over an elaborate undergarment holding a book, with a scroll inscribed 'Osee' in black letter;

[23] Sheahan, *Hist. and Topog. of Bucks.* 612. [24] *Cal. of Papal Letters*, v, 435. [25] *Pope Nich. Tax.* (Rec. Com.), 47b.

[26] *Cal. of Papal Letters*, v, 435. [27] *Valor Eccl.* (Rec. Com.), iv, 246. [28] *V.C.H. Bucks.* ii, 350.

[29] Close, 17 Jas. I, pt. iv, no. 23. [30] Ibid. [31] Chan. Inq. p.m. (Ser. 2), ccccvi, 27.

a man in a robe similar to the last, but smaller, and holding a book, with a scroll inscribed 'Sofonias' in black letter, the background diapered ; a man similar to the foregoing, but holding a scroll instead of a book inscribed 'Ezekiel' in black letter, the background diapered; and fragments of the figure of an archbishop in vestments and pallium, holding a crozier. In the north-east corner is a narrow doorway with rebated jambs and pointed head and two hooks for hinges; some of the jamb stones on the west side have diagonal tooling, and may be earlier material reset. This doorway formerly opened into the tower staircase, but is now blocked, and access is at present gained through a small chamber entered from outside in the corner between the nave and north transept, and apparently of much later date. The north doorway of the nave, which is blocked with modern masonry, has chamfered external jambs with a label, probably of the late 15th century. The west wall, window and buttresses are modern, but a few old stones have been re-used. The south doorway has moulded jambs and head, and is of the same date as the south porch ; the door is modern, but has ancient strap hinges on the inside. The nave roof, which is of three bays, is late 15th-century work, but, as mentioned above, appears to have been reconstructed in 1703 ; the tie-beams are cambered and hollow-chamfered and have modern carved bosses ; one beam has the date 1703 cut upon it. The ridge and purlins are moulded and the rafters chamfered ; the wall-plates, brackets and corbels are modern.

The south porch has a plinth and angle buttresses and a late 15th-century outer archway repaired with cement. The gable has been rebuilt in brick in the early 18th century, and the weathering of the former roof is visible in the nave wall; the brickwork is covered with cement and has a sunk panel with a lead slab bearing the words 'Reverence my sanctuary' between two cherubs' heads and surrounded by a moulded frame, all cast in relief. In each side wall of the porch is a small single light with a deep internal splayed opening.

There are remains of ancient sundials on the south doorway of the chancel, the outer archway of the porch, and the south-east buttress of the south transept; the last has a small iron gnomon.

The 14th-century font has a circular bowl supported by a stem surrounded by four circular shafts with moulded capitals which die into the bowl ; the shafts, originally detached, are now joined to the stem by modern cement. The communion table is of oak, with six turned legs, and bears on its upper rail the date 1619 in four small panels. In the south transept is a 17th-century oak coffin-stool with carved legs and rails. In the nave is an oak poor-box dated 1618 with a turned baluster stem. The hinged lid is secured by three iron fastenings and a padlock.

On the north wall of the chancel is a marble tablet with a pediment and two columns, commemorating the following members of the Disney family : Mary daughter of Thomas Disney (d. 1658), Thomas son of Sir Henry Disney of Norton Disney and Swinderby (co. Lincoln), rector of Stoke Hammond (d. 1686), Joan daughter of Edward Wilks and wife of Thomas Disney (d. 1680), and Mark son of Edward Wilks (d. 1678). In the pediment are five kneeling figures in relief, and below them an hourglass with a skull and cross-bones between two shields : the dexter quarterly, 1 and 4 three fleurs de lis on a fesse, 2 and 3 three leopards ; the sinister, paly a chief charged with three roses. Adjoining this tablet is a smaller one with an inscription to Mary daughter of Thomas Disney (d. 1658), above are a skull and cross-bones and a lozenge charged with three fleurs de lis on a fesse. On the west wall of the north transept is a slab divided into eight compartments commemorating Mary wife of Thomas Fountaine (d. 1650), Joanna wife of William Fountaine (d. 1680), Thomas son of Thomas Fountaine (d. 1636), Thomas Fountaine (d. 1668), Thomas son of William Fountaine (d. 1656), Bernard Fountaine (d. 1690), Agnise wife of Bernard Fonntaine (d. 1703), and William their son (d. 1709). In the west jamb of the transept window close by is a small tablet inscribed T.F. 1704. On the north wall of the nave is a tablet to Trimnell (d. 1765) and Catherine (d. 1743), son and daughter of Hillersdon Frank. In the chancel are floor slabs to Thomas Hillersdon (d. 1658) and his widow Elizabeth (d. 1705), and in the nave are floor-slabs to Richard Wigg (d. 1701), his daughters Frances (d. 1689) and Elizabeth (d. 1701), his widow Frances (d. 1728), Elizabeth daughter of John Frank (d. 1709) and another daughter of the same, whose name and the date of her death are no longer legible, and John Pettingall, D.D., rector (d. 1781).

There is a ring of three bells and a sanctus : the treble is by Bartholomew Atton, 1590 ; the second, a 14th-century bell inscribed ' Ave Maria,' is probably by John Rufford [31a] ; the third was recast by John Taylor & Co. of Loughborough in 1882 and is inscribed ' Sancta Trinitas Ora Pro Nobis.' The sanctus is inscribed I.S. (for John Sturdy) and is of the 15th century.

The plate consists of a parcel-gilt cup of Elizabethan type, the marks on which have been destroyed by modern alterations, a small parcel-gilt cover paten unmarked, a larger paten with a foot inscribed ' Tho. Disney minister Barnerd Fountaine Tho. Fountaine Churchwardens 1686,' a Sheffield-plate flagon with the date 1827 scratched on the foot, and a modern flagon of 1897.

The registers down to 1812 are as follows : (i) baptisms and burials 1537 to 1758, with a gap from 1723 to 1728 in the burials, marriages 1538 to 1756, with two entries of 1534 ; (ii) baptisms and burials 1724 to 1807, marriages 1724 to 1759 ; (iii) marriages 1760 to 1807 ; (iv) baptisms and burials 1807 to 1812, marriages 1808 to 1812.

ADVOWSON The rectory of the church of Stoke Hammond formed part of the original endowment of Bradwell Priory in the 12th century,[32] and a presentation was made by the prior between 1209 and 1220.[33] In 1254 Alan son of Robert unsuccessfully claimed the right of presentation against the prior,[34] who in 1259 granted this church with that of Chalfont St. Giles to the Bishop of Lincoln.[35] The advowson of Stoke

---

[31a] V.C.H. Bucks. ii, 118.

[32] Dugdale, Mon. iv, 508 ; V.C.H. Bucks. i, 351. A correspondent of Lysons stated in 1802 that an account of the endowment of the church in the 12th century and a list of incumbents from that time were preserved in the old parish register (Add. MS. 9411, fol. 111).

[33] R. of Hugh of Wells (Cant. and York Soc.), i, 103. The vicarage of a chaplain was reserved and an ancient pension to the priory of 20s.

[34] Assize R. 1181, m. 6.

[35] Dugdale, op. cit. iv, 50 ; Bucks. i, 351.

Hammond, valued at £8 yearly in 1291[36] and at £20 in 1535,[37] descended with the diocese of Lincoln[38] until 1852, when it was transferred to that of Oxford.[39] It was acquired by the Rev. John Hart, the rector, in 1860,[40] and has since remained in his family,[41] Mr. Edward Hart being the present owner.

John Chedworth was rector of Stoke Hammond in 1452, when he was elected Bishop of Lincoln,[42] and John Hacket, who was rector here between 1621 and 1624, became Bishop of Coventry and Lichfield in 1661.[43]

A terrier of the rectory dated 1639 is quoted in full by Willis in 1735.[44] An allotment in lieu of tithes was made to the rector in 1774.[45]

In 1548 1 acre in the west field called 'parsonage land,' yielding 10d. yearly for the maintenance of a light in the church, was claimed by the rector as part of his land.[46] This acre with another acre in Wodiche Furlong was included in a grant to Sir Edward Bray, John Thornton and John Danby in 1552.[47]

CHARITY   For the charity of John Hillersdon for a schoolmaster, see article on Schools.[48]

STONY STRATFORD

Straford, Stoni Strafford, Stani Stratford, Stony-Stretteford (xiii cent.).

The market town and ancient borough of Stony Stratford · stands midway between Towcester and Fenny Stratford on Watling Street, which divides it into two portions corresponding to the ecclesiastical parishes of St. Giles and St. Mary Magdalen respectively. The West side was formerly in the parish of Calverton, and the common lands here, with the exception of Horse Fair Green, were inclosed under the Act dealing with Calverton in 1782.[1] The suburb of Calverton End is still included in that parish. The East side lay in Wolverton, which still contains the suburb of Wolverton End, formed into the ecclesiastical parish of Wolverton St. Mary in 1870.[2] These two portions were made independent parishes by Act of Parliament towards the end of the 18th century, and by a Local Government Board Order of 25 March 1883 a detached portion of Calverton called Stratford Bridge Meadows was amalgamated with Stratford St. Giles.

The area of the West side is 84 acres, of which 15 acres are grass land and 1 acre arable land.[3] The population in 1901 was 1,395.[4] The East side is smaller, having an area of 69 acres, 20 of it being grass, and a population of 958. The inhabitants were formerly chiefly engaged in the manufacture of lace, but that industry has now practically died out. Mr. Edward Hayes's engineering works employ a number of people.

Stony Stratford lies low, varying only from 220 ft. to 240 ft. above the ordnance datum; it is almost encircled by the River Ouse, which here forms the county boundary.

The town is small, consisting mainly of one narrow street, Watling Street, which here becomes the High Street for about three-quarters of a mile, crossed near the market-place by a road leading to Calverton and Wolverton respectively. From its position on

Watling Street, Camden and many others suggested Stony Stratford as the site of the Roman station Lactodorum,[5] and numerous Roman remains have been found in the neighbourhood,[6] but later research has almost conclusively assigned the Roman station to Towcester.[7] North of the junction of Watling Street and Calverton Road lies the Market Square, near which is the church of St. Giles. Almost opposite, on the east side, are the remains of the church of St. Mary Magdalen. Though spared in a fire which swept the town in 1736, when fifty-three houses were destroyed, the church, together with 113 houses, was burnt six years later, when the damage was estimated at £10,000.[7a] The tower is the only part now standing. Probably by reason of these fires few ancient houses survive. The 'King's Head' in the Market Square dates from the early part of the 17th century, and there are some other houses, mostly built of rubble with tiled roofs, of this date in the High Street. Two shops on the west side of this street, now numbered 95 and 97, may perhaps have been originally built in the 15th century, but have been much altered subsequently. To the north of the church is St. Paul's College, founded in 1863 as a middle class school, and used since 1900 as a home for orphan boys. There is incidental reference in the middle of the 14th century to a 'Scolhous' in Stony Stratford which was to be used for the chapel of St. Thomas the Martyr.[8] In this part of Stony Stratford, called Bridge End in the 16th century from its proximity to the bridge spanning the Ouse,[9] stood the leper hospital of St. John the Baptist without Stony Stratford. It was described in the 14th century as situated near 'le Shrob' and the causeway leading to the bridge.[10] It was in existence probably before about 1240, in which year William de Paveli bequeathed 12d. 'infirmis de Straford,'[11] and certainly before 1257.[12] In 1329, however, the master and brethren were found to be

36 Pope Nich. Tax. (Rec. Com.), 34.
37 Valor Eccl. (Rec. Com.), iv, 244.
38 De Banco R. 208, m. 3; Cal. S. P. Dom. 1580–1625, p. 442; Inst. Bks. (P.R.O.); Priv. Act, 14 Geo. III, cap. 76; Bacon, Liber Reg. 501. The advowson is mentioned in connexion with the principal manor in the early 16th century and in a few 17th-century documents (Close R. 4 Hen. VIII, no. 20; Feet of F. Bucks. Mich. 17 Jas. I; Div. Co. Trin. 1653; Bucks. Hil. 23 & 24 Chas. II).

39 Lond. Gaz. 4 June 1852, p. 1578.
40 Ibid. 10 Mar. 1860, p. 1046
41 Clergy Lists (1861–1915).
42 Dict. Nat. Biog.
43 Ibid.
44 Add. MS. 5839, fol. 139b.
45 Priv. Act, 14 Geo. III, cap. 76.
46 Pat. 6 Edw. VI, pt. ix, m. 28; Chant. Cert. 5, no. 34.
47 Pat. 6 Edw. VI, pt. ix, m. 28.
48 V.C.H. Bucks. ii, 218.
1 Local & Personal Act, 22 Geo. III, cap. 22.

2 Lond. Gaz. 29 Nov. 1870, p. 5409.
3 Statistics from Bd. of Agric. (1905).
4 Census Ret. (1901).
5 Camden, Brit. (ed. Gough), i, 321.
6 V.C.H. Bucks. ii, 11.
7 Ibid. 3.
7a Lysons, Mag. Brit. i (3), 644.
8 Cal. Pat. 1345–8, p. 43.
9 Cal. S. P. Dom. 1591–4, p. 381.
10 Cal. Pat. 1350–4, p. 303.
11 Madox, Form. Angl. 424.
12 Cal. Pat. 1247–58, p. 544; cf. ibid. 1258–66, p. 538.

'without the means of living unless others come to their aid,'[13] and in 1352 their chapel was 'for the most part in ruins.'[14]

The old bridge across the Ouse, which here separates Stony Stratford from Old Stratford in Northamptonshire, was partly destroyed in the Civil War and became very dilapidated,[15] so that in 1801 an Act was passed for repairing it.[16] In 1835 a new bridge was built under an Act of Parliament of 1834[17]; it is on an enlarged plan, and consists of three stone arches with a long raised causeway for carrying off floods. On the bank of the Ouse, not far from the Market Square, is a corn-mill, perhaps standing on the site of the one which with the capital messuage called Malletts, held of Henry Longville of Wolverton Manor, was bought by John Penn from Thomas Pigott in 1581. On his death in 1587 he bequeathed the mill to his son Thomas Penn,[18] who died in 1618.[19] At Calverton End on the West side, near the Stony Stratford Waterworks, is the cemetery with two mortuary chapels opened in 1856 at Galley Hill. To the south of the market square is a Methodist chapel built in 1844, and near it, on Horsefair Green, is the Baptist chapel on the site of the one founded in 1656. Some fittings of the 17th-century building remain, and also a wooden window frame, preserved in the vestry. There is another chapel, dating from 1823, on the Wolverton road.

Nonconformists were active here in the 17th century, and in 1661 John Crook, a Quaker minister, was arrested with seven others for attempting to hold an illegal meeting in the neighbourhood.[20] In 1672 the house of Edmund Carter was licensed for Presbyterian worship.[21] On the other hand Thomas Smith of Stony Stratford was apprehended in 1652 on suspicion of being a Jesuit,[22] and in 1666 the house of John Digby, son of Sir Kenelm Digby, a strong Papist, was searched and 300 arms found. 'They were not

taken away, but he took it so ill that he went away in his coach and six horses.'[23]

Stony Stratford was once a place of considerable importance, owing to its position on Watling Street. Letters Patent were dated from here by King John in 1215[24] and by Henry IV in 1409,[25] Letters Close and writs in 1309[26] and 1329.[27] It was one of the resting-places of the body of Queen Eleanor, and the Cross stood until the Civil War, when it was destroyed.[28] From its proximity to the Northamptonshire Salcey Forest, Stocking Wood, near Stony Stratford, being deemed part of that forest in the 13th century,[29] it was a good hunting centre, and Edward IV hunted in Wychwood Forest in this neighbourhood in 1464.[30] Many references to the forester of Stony Stratford occur.[31] Edward V slept here with his half-brother Lord Richard Grey on his journey to London in 1483, when the latter, along with Lord Rivers and Sir Thomas Vaughan, was taken prisoner by Richard Duke of Gloucester.[32] Shakespeare alludes

THE 'KING'S HEAD,' STONY STRATFORD

to this in *Richard III*,'[33] where the lines 'Last night I heard they lay at Stony Stratford' occur. Margaret of Scotland dated from here a letter in 1516 to Henry VIII,[34] who himself sent letters from Stony Stratford on 8 and 20 September 1525.[35] Hungarian ambassadors sent on an embassy to him were here in 1531,[36] and the king appears to have been at Stony Stratford again in 1540, as one of the tapsters, who

[13] *Cal. Pat.* 1327–30, p. 417.
[14] Ibid. 1350–4, p. 303.
[15] Sheahan, *Hist. and Topog. of Bucks.* 618.
[16] Local and Pers. Act, 41 Geo. III, cap. 130.
[17] Ibid. 4 & 5 Will. IV, cap. 83.
[18] Chan. Inq. p.m. (Ser. 2), ccxvi, 77.
[19] Ibid. dccxl, 128.
[20] *Dict. Nat. Biog.*
[21] *Cal. S. P. Dom.* 1672, pp. 61, 64, 90.
[22] Ibid. 1651–2, p. 321.
[23] Ibid. 1666–7, p. 238.
[24] *Rot. Lit. Pat.* (Rec. Com.), 129.
[25] *Cal. Pat.* 1408–13, pp. 136, 150.

[26] *Cal. Close*, 1307–13, pp. 117, 119, 160; *Cal. Fine R.* 1307–9, pp. 38, 43, 50.
[27] *Cal. Close*, 1327–30, pp. 500, 502, 503, 573, 578.
[28] *Rec. of Bucks.* iii, 157. Browne Willis, who wrote about 1735, said that the cross stood at the lower end of the town by the Horse Shoe Inn. William Hartley, then nearly eighty, remembered having seen the base still standing (Add. MS. 5839, fol. 194).
[29] *Cal. Pat.* 1216–25, p. 395; 1247–58, p. 536.
[30] Holinshed, *Chron.* (ed. Hooper), iii, 668.

[31] Feet of F. Northants, Easter, 15 John, no. 243; Harl. Chart. 84 E, 15, 55; 85 D, 47, 56; 86 C, 2; 86 G, 1, 2; *Cal. Pat.* 1317–21, p. 194; 1324–7, p. 40; 1334–8, p. 292; Chan. Inq. p.m. 30 Edw. III (1st nos.), no. 50.
[32] Holinshed, op. cit. iii, 715. According to tradition the king lodged at the 'Swan,' afterwards the Three Swans Inn (Add. MS. 5839, fol. 194).
[33] Act i, Sc. iv.
[34] *L. and P. Hen. VIII*, ii (1), 1829.
[35] Ibid. iv, 1628, 1649.
[36] Ibid. v, p. 756.

vagrantly followed the court and enhanced the price of victuals, was condemned to sit in the pillory at Stony Stratford with a paper on his head.[37] The plague was virulent in this part of the country in 1537 ; the unemployment and discontent arising therefrom probably accounted for the affray which took place at that time between the shoemakers and organ player of the town, resulting in the appearance of six shoemakers at the assizes at Little Brickhill.[38]

The 16th and 17th centuries probably saw the height of prosperity of the town ; its situation on the great road to Ireland by way of Chester was a cause of much enrichment.[39] It was a noted rendezvous for pack-horses and a baiting station for travellers,[40] whose accommodation was provided for by several good inns. The 'Cock,' the most celebrated, is mentioned in 1500–15[41]; it was left in 1520 by Thomas Pigott of Beachampton, serjeant-at-law, for the maintenance and repair of the bridges.[42] The 'Rose and Crown,' another important inn, was left by the will of Michael Hipwell in 1609 to found a grammar school,[43] and though it was at first used for that purpose the school later found another house, and the old building was let by the proprietors, the Church of England school managers, who devoted the rent to the upkeep of the school. The 'White Horse,' which belonged to the gild, was the subject of a dispute between the wardens and their lessees in the reign of Henry VIII.[44] It afterwards came into the possession of William Matthew, whose son and heir inherited it in March 1608–9.[44a] The 'Swan,' a 15th-century inn,[45] appears perhaps as the 'Swan with Two Necks' in 1609,[46] the 'Three Swans' in 1667,[47] again as the 'Swan with Two Necks' in 1691,[48] and the 'Three Swans' the following year.[49] The 'Red Lion' was the cause of a quarrel between William Edy's heirs in 1529[50]; there is mention of the 'George' in 1609,[51] and of the 'White Hart' in 1625.[52] The innkeepers were not always above suspicion, Greathead, one of them, being accounted 'a notable bad fellow' in 1596, both he and Thomas Car, another innkeeper, being common receivers.[53] Troops were frequently in the neighbourhood of Stony Stratford in the Civil War,[54] and the Earl of Cleveland maintained a station here for the king, who himself passed through on his way to Woburn.[55] The town, however, appears to have suffered in no way and remained a 'populous and much frequented market town.'[56] The descriptions given by 17th and

18th-century travellers are by no means flattering. Baskerville, who was in Stony Stratford in May 1681, calls it 'a town of very ordinary building,'[57] while another writer nearly a century later is no kinder : 'a small straggling town, not remarkable in any shape.'[58] Hassell in 1819 complained that it was 'most vilely paved with stones of various dimensions,'[59] and that after an Act had been passed in 1801 for paving the streets.[60]

Theophilus Eaton, the first governor of New Haven, was born at Stony Stratford about 1590.[61] Benjamin Holloway, an 18th-century divine, was also born here about 1691.[62]

The following place-names occur : Le Shrob[63] (xiv cent.) and Bozardes[64] (xvii cent.).

BOROUGH There are no borough records extant for Stony Stratford, and the incidental references to the borough are few, but to a large extent it presents the same features as Fenny Stratford. Both towns occupy important positions on Watling Street and were interested in the maintenance of their bridges in a state of good repair, that of Stony Stratford spanning the important waterway of the Ouse. The organization of the burgesses of Stony Stratford appears to be in as elementary a state as that of the burgesses of the sister town. The towns were linked together by the traders passing along Watling Street, and both were centres of commerce, focussing the industrial and agricultural activities of the surrounding country in their weekly markets and periodical fairs. It was therefore essential that the bridge which afforded access to the west and north of England should not be allowed to fall in decay, and Hugh de Vere Earl of Oxford paid half a mark for bridge vigil in 1254.[65] The bridge of Stratford mentioned in 1276[66] probably refers to this one, for which pontage grants were made in 1349,[67] 1352[68] and 1380.[69] The first of these grants was partly, and the second wholly, for repair of the causeway adjacent to the bridge, and in 1391 a grant of pavage for four years to repair the highway between the two Stratfords was made to John Lughton and John Haywood, 'ermyte.'[70] The ancient tolls taken at the bridge served as a model, among others, for those to be levied on Bow Bridge in the 17th century.[71]

These grants of pontage were generally made to individuals by name, but that of 1349 was to the bailiff and good men of Stony Stratford.[72] The order in September 1380 to lay in a store of provisions against the coming of the king's lieges on their way

[37] L. and P. Hen.. VIII, xvi, 10.
[38] Ibid. xii (2), 275.
[39] Cal. S. P. Dom. 1648–9, p. 420.
[40] Sheahan, loc. cit. MSS. of the Duke of Rutland (Hist. MSS. Com.), iv, 571; MSS. Ld. Middleton (Hist. MSS. Com.), 354.
[41] Early Chan. Proc. bdle. 375, no. 36.
[42] Lipscomb, Hist. and Antiq. of Bucks. iv, 367. It is not mentioned in the actual will (P.C.C. 26 Ayloffe) and was probably left by deed.
[43] Chan. Inq. p.m. (Ser. 2), dcclxv, 32; V.C.H. Bucks. ii, 212.
[44] Star Chamb. Proc. Hen. VIII, i, fol. 6–14; see also Chan. Proc. Eliz. m. 6, no. 16.
[44a] Chan. Inq. p.m. (Ser. 2), dcxlvii, 30.
[45] Add. MS. 5839, fol. 194; Ct. R. (Gen. Ser.), portf. 155, no. 5; Chan. Proc. (Ser. 2), bdles. 112, no. 18; 62, no. 26.
[46] Chan. Inq. p.m. (Ser. 2), dcclxv, 32.

[47] Cal. S. P. Dom. 1667, pp. 417, 453.
[48] Petty Bag Inq. Charitable Uses, bdle. 44, no. 3.
[49] Exch. Dep. Mich. 4 Will. and Mary, no. 9.
[50] Ct. of Req. bdle. 2, no. 186; Feet of F. Bucks. Mich. 21 Hen. VIII.
[51] Chan. Inq. p.m. (Ser. 2), dcclxv, 32.
[52] Chan. Proc. (Ser. 2), bdle. 398, no. 37.
[53] MSS. of Duke of Buccleuch, Montagu House (Hist. MSS. Com.), i, 232.
[54] MSS. of Lord Montagu of Beaulieu (Hist. MSS. Com.), 159; Hist. MSS. Com. Rep. xiii, App. i, 144; Leyborne Popham MSS. (Hist. MSS. Com.), 208; Cal. S. P. Dom. 1644, pp. 64, 69, 310; 1644–5, p. 580.
[55] Lipscomb, loc. cit. quoting confirmation of Parl. Scouts and Weekly Account, 30 May 1643.

[56] Hassell, Tour of the Grand Junction Canal, 78.
[57] Hist. MSS. Com. Rep. xiii, App. ii, 274.
[58] Verulam MSS. (Hist. MSS. Com.), i, 241.
[59] Hassell, loc. cit.
[60] Local and Pers. Act, 41 Geo. III, cap. 130.
[61] Dict. Nat. Biog.   [62] Ibid.
[63] Cal. Pat. 1350–4, p. 303.
[64] Chan. Inq. p.m. (Ser. 2), dcclxxix, 29.
[65] Hund. R. (Rec. Com.), i, 30.
[66] Ibid. 41. The name of William atte Brigge of Stony Stratford occurs in 1293 (Feet of F. Bucks. East. 21 Edw. I).
[67] Cal. Pat. 1348–50, p. 263.
[68] Ibid. 1350–4, p. 303.
[69] Ibid. 1377–81, p. 559.
[70] Ibid. 1388–92, p. 432.
[71] Cal. S. P. Dom. 1634–5, p. 423.
[72] Cal. Pat. 1348–50, p. 263.

Stony Stratford East : No. 48, High Street

STONY STRATFORD EAST: 48 HIGH STREET (BACK)

to the Parliament at Northampton was likewise addressed to the bailiff and true men of Stony Stratford.[72a] At a court held there in 1420 by the steward one of the witnesses in a case about injury to horses was Thomas Brasyer, bailiff and burgess of Stony Stratford.[73] The bailiff and the constable of the place were together indicted in 1573 for stealing a horse from Robert Jonson.[74] These officers were probably appointed by the lord of the manor, and not elected by the commonalty. The chief corporate action of the burgesses appears to have been the regulation of the gild of St. Mary and St. Thomas the Martyr, a corporate body with a common seal with power of pleading and being impleaded. Licence to found this gild was given to John Edy and others in 1476. It was to consist of two wardens elected yearly, who could be removed and others appointed at pleasure, and a number of brothers and sisters who could dress themselves in one suit of gowns or hoods. They had power to acquire land to the value of 20 marks a year, in order to find two chaplains to celebrate divine service (in the chapel of St. Mary Magdalen and St. Giles) and for other works of piety.[75] In 1547 the gild was known as the fraternity of our Lady and was valued at £13 4s.[76] There were two priests, who had no other living and who doubtless officiated in the chapels of St. Mary Magdalen and St. Giles (see below). There must have been a flourishing business community in the 15th century, when references occur to the trades of ironmonger,[77] chapman,[78] woolman[79] and brewer,[80] and in the 16th century there were many shoemakers engaged in business here.[81] The Flemish refugees of the 15th century probably brought new industries to Stony Stratford,[82] though the only one specified when the oaths of fealty were taken was that of a wheelwright.[83]

An outlet for the goods produced by the townspeople was provided by the weekly market. No grant has been found conferring this privilege, nor is the day of the week on which it was held mentioned, but it was probably granted to Hugh de Vere Earl of Oxford about the time he obtained the fair, and was located on the west side of Stony Stratford, towards Calverton. It was given in dower to Anna wife of Aubrey de Vere, ratified to her in 1462,[84] and is mentioned regularly as an appurtenance of the manor of Calverton in the 16th and 17th centuries.[85] The town unsuccessfully petitioned for a market on the east side of Stony Stratford in 1657,[86] and the weekly Friday market granted in 1662 by Charles II to Simon Bennett and his heirs[87] was doubtless held as of old on the west side. By 1792 the market had ceased to be held, but had been revived in 1888.[88] There is still a corn market on Friday, and also a cattle market on the first Monday in every month.

An annual fair on the vigil, the feast and the morrow of St. Giles (1 September) was granted to Hugh de Vere in 1257.[89] In 1290 he had a grant of an additional fair on the vigil and feast of St. Mary Magdalen[90] (22 July). John de Vere in 1334 sued Simon Gobion and others for carrying away his goods at Stony Stratford and Calverton and for assaulting his servant John Dagenham while collecting toll and other profits belonging to his fair and market at Stony Stratford, as well as merchants and others offering their wares there, compelling them to withdraw.[91] The fair was held with the market in the 16th and 17th centuries. In 1662 Charles II granted four annual fairs in the west part of Stony Stratford, the first on Friday before the feast of St. Michael the Archangel (29 September), the second on the feast of All Saints (1 November), the third on 9 April and the fourth on Wednesday before the feast of Pentecost.[92]

In 1792 there were three annual fairs, 2 August, Friday before 10 October and 12 November. In 1888 there was only one fair, on 2 August,[93] which is still held on that day and the day following.

MANORS Neither of the manors in *STONY STRATFORD* is recorded in the Domesday Survey. The west side was then part of Calverton, with which it has always descended. It first occurs as a separate manor in 1257,[94] and was subinfeudated by the Earls of Oxford. It was held by Robert Broughton, who died seised of it in 1506.[95] His son John in 1516 made a settlement of the manor in view of the proposed marriage of his infant son John with Dorothy, one of the daughters of Thomas Earl of Norfolk, one of the trustees named being Thomas Wolsey, Archbishop of York.[96] John Broughton died in January 1517-18, and was succeeded by his son,[96a] but the manor evidently reverted to the Earls of Oxford shortly afterwards.

VERE. *Quarterly gules and or with a molet argent in the quarter.*

A fishery in the Ouse occurs as an appurtenance of this manor from the 16th century.[97]

The east side formed part of the manor of Wolverton,[98] with which it has always descended. It appears to have ranked as a separate manor in the 16th century.[99]

CHURCHES The church of *ST. GILES*, consisting of a chancel, nave, north and south aisles, vestries and west tower, was built originally in the late 15th century as a chantry chapel, but having become dilapidated[100] was, with the exception of the tower, entirely rebuilt in

[72a] *Cal. Close*, 1377–81, p. 406.
[73] Harl. Chart. 84, H 22.
[74] *Acts of P.C.* 1571–5, p. 130.
[75] *Cal. Pat.* 1467–77, p. 584.
[76] Chant. Cert. 5, no. 15.
[77] *Cal. Pat.* 1416–22, p. 353.
[78] Ibid. 1422–9, p. 148.
[79] Ibid. p. 368.
[80] Ibid. 1436–41, p. 12.
[81] *L. and P. Hen. VIII*, xii (2), 275.
[82] *Cal. Pat.* 1429–36, p. 582; 1436–41, p. 37.   [83] Ibid. 1429–36, p. 550.
[84] *Cal. Pat.* 1461–7, p. 76.

[85] See under Calverton Manor.
[86] *Cal. S. P. Dom.* 1657–8, pp. 238, 322.
[87] Pat. 14 Chas. II, pt. vii, no. 19.
[88] *Rep. of Royal Com. on Mkt. Rts. and Tolls*, i, 139.
[89] *Cal. Chart. R.* 1226–57, p. 475.
[90] Ibid. 1257–1300, p. 351.
[91] *Cal. Pat.* 1330–4, p. 571.
[92] Pat. 14 Chas. II, pt. vii, no. 19.
[93] *Rep. on Market Rts.* i, 139.
[94] *Cal. Chart. R.* 1226–57, p. 475.
[95] Chan. Inq. p.m. (Ser. 2), xxi, 115.

[96] Ibid. xxxiii, 108; Nicolas, *Test. Vet.* 557.
[96a] Chan. Inq. p.m. (Ser. 2), xxxiii, 108.
[97] Pat. 28 Eliz. pt. iv; Chan. Inq. p.m. (Ser. 2), ccxlviii, 22; ccccxxxv, 116; Recov. R. East. 13 Anne, m. 187; Mich. 22 Geo. III, m. 410.
[98] *Cal. Close*, 1323–7, p. 293; Chan. Inq. p.m. (Ser. 2), xiv, 63; Ct. of Req. bdle. 11, no. 89.
[99] *L. and P. Hen. VIII*, iv, p. 986; Feet of F. Div. Co. Hil. 40 Eliz.
[100] Add. MS. 5839, fol. 191.

1776. It is constructed in the Gothic style, as understood at that period, and has a lofty nave with north and south arcades and a groined plastered ceiling, the clustered pillars of the arcades being composed of iron encased in wood. The pointed tower arch in the west wall of the nave dates from the late 15th century, and is of two moulded orders with shafted responds.

The tower, which is built of squared stone, is of four stages with clasping buttresses and surmounted by an embattled parapet. In the west wall of the ground stage is a four-centred doorway with a modern window above, while the third stage has a square moulded panel and a narrow light on the west. The bell-chamber is lighted from each side by a traceried window of two lights.

The font is modern. At the east end of the north aisle is a marble monument in memory of Barbara

CHURCH OF ST. GILES, STONY STRATFORD, FROM THE SOUTH-WEST

Ripington of Armington (d. 1775), and at the east end of the south aisle is a monument commemorating Leonard Sedgwick, vicar of the parish and Prebendary of Lincoln (d. 1747). There is a 15th-century traceried chest in the north aisle with a lid of later date, and in the vestry is an early 17th-century desk enriched with carved dragons and arabesque work.

The tower contains a ring of six bells, all by

W. & J. Taylor of Oxford, 1837–8, and a small bell, uninscribed, but evidently by the same makers.

The communion plate includes two pewter plates, dated 1696, which originally belonged to the church of St. Mary Magdalen.

The registers begin in 1738.

The church of *ST. MARY MAGDALEN* has never been rebuilt since its destruction by fire in 1742, but by the efforts of Browne Willis the west tower was repaired and the arches of the ground stage built up soon after the disaster 'in order to preserve it, to have the Church rebuilt again to it.'[1] In the 19th century an elder tree grew out of the walls at the top of the tower and became a menace to that part of the fabric,[2] but in 1893 the tree was removed and the structure was again repaired. The tower is of three stages with clasping buttresses to the two lower stages and is surmounted by an embattled parapet with small gables on the north and south. It is built of limestone, and dates from about 1450.[2a] On the east and south sides of the ground stage are pointed arches, now blocked, which opened to the nave and south aisle respectively, the aisle evidently having extended to the west wall of the tower, and on the west is a blocked two-light window. The second stage has on the west a square moulded panel and a narrow light, and the bell-chamber has on each side a transomed window of two lights with tracery under a pointed head. Boldly carved gargoyles occupy the angles of the string-course below the parapet.

There was apparently a church *ADVOWSON* at Stony Stratford before 1202 and 1203, in which years references are made to Richard the clerk,[3] Peter the clerk,[4] Roger the clerk[5] and William the priest.[6] There is no mention of either of the present churches by name till 1476,[7] in which year a chantry was founded 'in the chapel of St. Mary Magdalen and St. Giles.'[8] They were chapels of ease to the mother churches of Wolverton and Calverton respectively.[9] In the early 16th century there was trouble between the vicar of Wolverton and the parishioners of St. Mary Magdalen, who were supported by the Prior of Bradwell, patron of Wolverton. It was settled by an order of the Bishop of Lincoln that there was to be one chaplain for the said chapel, the vicar of Wolverton taking the mortuary fees, oblations and tithes of milk, &c.[10] At the dissolution of the chantries a few years later St. Mary Magdalen was referred to as a free chapel, half a mile distant from Wolverton Church, with two priests, to one of whom was allotted a portion of the tithes belonging to Wolverton vicarage, while the other was maintained by the gild of Stony Stratford.[11] Shortly after 1641 the two chapels in Stony Stratford were united, and services were held in them alternately.[12] This arrangement proved inadequate for the needs of the

[1] Add. MS. 5839, fol. 194 d.
[2] Sheahan, op. cit. 620.
[2a] By his will dated 1487 John Edy left £8 for the repair of the chancel roof, the money to be used for St. Ann's aisle, Bradwell, if the work was not done within two years. He also left 40s. for the gable window of the chancel (P.C.C. 14 Milles).
[3] Feet of F. Bucks. Mich. 4 John, no. 38. He received 3 acres in Calverton

from John de Calverton, on which he erected a building (ibid. no. 24).
[4] Ibid. no. 39.
[5] Ibid. Trin. 5 John, no. 6.
[6] Ibid. Mich. 4 John, no. 40.
[7] St. Giles is said by some county historians to have been founded about 1450 (Lysons, *Mag. Brit.* i [3], 644; Lipscomb, op. cit. iv, 371); Sheahan, op. cit. 620. 40s. towards the steeple was left by the will of John Edy, 1487

(Lipscomb, loc. cit. note 3; P.C.C. 14 Milles).
[8] *Cal. Pat.* 1467–77, p. 584.
[9] Bacon, *Liber Regis* (1786), p. 502; *Cal. S. P. Dom.* 1641–3, p. 172.
[10] Rentals and Surv. (Gen. Ser.), R. 75, chart. 83; Linc. Epis. Reg. Memo. Wolsey and Atwater, fol. 72 d.
[11] Chant. Cert. 5, no. 17.
[12] *Cal. S. P. Dom.* 1641–3, p. 172; 1648–9, p. 420.

people: 'the inhabitants were forced to build a great gallery in St. Giles, and many people were forced to remain at home for want of accommodation.'[13] Before 1648 two separate parishes were created, each with its own chapel,[14] the parishioners of St. Mary Magdalen complaining in 1651 that through neglect they were prevented from enjoying a grant of £50 a year from the rectory of Wolverton, sequestered for the Earl of Northampton's delinquency.[15] St. Mary's Church being burnt down in 1742, St. Giles became the only church, and as it was then 'too small and ancient and decayed building,' briefs were issued for its repair and enlargement in 1774-5 and 1779-80.[16] In 1852 the advowson was transferred from the Bishop of Lincoln to the Bishop of Oxford.[17]

By his will in 1534 William Bystocke desired to be buried on the south side of the Lady Chapel in St. Giles, and gave a legacy to the making of St. Catherine's vestry.[18]

In 1346 licence was granted to the good men of Stony Stratford to found a chapel in honour of St. Thomas the Martyr in a place called 'Scolhous' in Stony Stratford, and to endow it and ordain a chantry in it for a chaplain to celebrate divine service daily.[19] There is no further mention of this chapel, but its name suggests that it may have been connected with the chief gild of the town, licence to found or refound which, as the gild or fraternity of St. Mary and St. Thomas, was granted in 1476.[19a]

CHARITIES

The Grammar School, founded by Michael Hipwell.—The official trustees hold a sum of £416 19s. under the title of 'The Rose and Crown Charity,' representing sales of certain lands belonging to the school, producing £12 10s. yearly.

Sir Simon Bennett's Charity.—In 1911 the share of this parish for the poor amounted to £19 13s., which was applied in the distribution of clothing and coal, and the sum of £12 18s. was paid to the Stony Stratford and Wolverton Rural District Council for the repair of the highways. (See under parish of Calverton.)

Charity of Simon Bennett, or the Bradwell Estate Charity.—The share of this parish in 1911 amounted to £17 10s., which was applied in the distribution of clothing and coal among widows and aged persons. (See under parish of Calverton.)

Whitnell's bread charity is endowed with 14 a. in the hamlet of Denshanger in Passenham (Northants), purchased in 1692 with a legacy of £50, by the will of Silvester Whitnell, dated 2 February 1684-5,[19b] and a gift of £40 by Mrs. Elizabeth Collins. The land is let at £14 a year, the net income of which is distributed in bread.

The bell-rope charity, formerly consisting of an acre of land in Calverton, is now represented by £180 16s. 10d. consols in the individual names of the churchwardens, the annual dividends of which, amounting to £4 10s. 4d., are carried to the churchwardens' accounts for providing bell-ropes, &c.

The charity of John Whalley, founded by will, proved in the P.C.C. 15 February 1670-1, and comprised in an order of the High Court of Chancery,

1834, is endowed with a farm at Hartwell (co. Northampton), containing 179 a. 1 r. 29 p., let at £140 a year, and 2 a. 0 r. 39 p. of land and four cottages at Cosgrove (co. Northampton), producing £22 11s. 8d. yearly. The charity is regulated by schemes of the Charity Commissioners of 1866, 1899 and 1904. The income is subject to the payment of £4 a year to the curate of Hartwell. In 1912 the sum of £25 was applied towards school expenses, £85 for apprenticing in Stony Stratford and Cosgrove generally, and £20 was applied specifically for apprenticing duly qualified boys at the railway carriage works at Wolverton in pursuance of the scheme of 1904. There was a balance at the bank of £322.

The charity of Edmund Arnold, or the Furthoe charity, founded in 1689.—In 1911 the sum of £52 18s. 9d. was apportioned by the trustees of Arnold's general charity for apprenticing and education in Stony Stratford, and the sum of £13 4s. 8d. was apportioned out of the same charity for the benefit of the poor, the recipients to be members of the Church of England. The sum of £20 is also paid annually to the vicar of Stony Stratford.

The bridge and street charities, originally founded by John Pigott, serjeant-at-law, who died in February 1519-20,[20] by John White in 1674, by John Mashe and other donors unknown, are endowed with a farm at Loughton, known as the Manor Farm, containing 144 a., let at £200 a year, purchased under an Act of 1801[21] with the proceeds of sale of the original property belonging to the charities, and 1 a. 2 r. in Stony Stratford, known as the Town Close, let at £4 10s. a year, and manorial rights in Market Square and Horse Fair Green, the income therefrom being variable. In 1911 the sum of £17 9s. 6d. was received from tolls. The net income is applied in lighting and paving and cleaning. By an order of the Charity Commissioners of 8 July 1913 the trustees were authorized to borrow a sum of £1,400 at 4¼ per cent. for effecting improvements on the Manor Farm and for paying off certain existing debts, the sum to be repaid within thirty years.

John Oliver by his will, proved at London in 1862, bequeathed £500, now represented by £534 1s. consols, the annual dividends of which, amounting to £13 7s., are applicable in the payment of £3 3s. to the Northampton Hospital, and the surplus to be divided on Christmas Day amongst ten of the poorest of the parish.

A sum of £2 a year was formerly paid out of a cottage situate on the east side of the town and applied for the benefit of the poor under a codicil to the will of Thomas Oliver, proved at Westminster 7 April 1657.

William Parrott by deed dated 22 July 1881 declared the trusts of a sum of £297 14s. consols, the dividends of £7 8s. 8d. a year to be applied in January in the distribution of coats, cloaks and bonnets to widows and spinsters under sixty years of age. The two sums of stock above mentioned are held by the official trustees, who also hold a further sum of £151 10s. 4d. consols, producing £3 15s. 8d. yearly, which is payable under the will of Thomas Smith to the Baptist minister.

[13] Cal. S. P. Dom. 1648-9, p. 420.
[14] Ibid.
[15] Cal. Com. for Comp. 1247, 1251.
[16] Church Brief, B. xv, 3; xx, 1.
[17] Lond. Gaz. 4 June 1852, p. 1578.
[18] Add. MS. 5839, fol. 191 d.
[19] Cal. Pat. 1345-8, p. 43.
[19a] Ibid. 1467-77, p. 584.
[19b] P.C.C. 111 Lloyd.
[20] Chan. Inq. p.m. (Ser. 2), xxxv, 1.
[21] Local and Pers. Act, 41 Geo. III, cap. 130.

By an order of the Charity Commissioners of 10 September 1888 a residence for the Baptist minister, situate upon the Green, was purchased partly with the proceeds of the sale of the minister's residence, formerly held by the trustees, and partly from private sources.

TYRINGHAM with FILGRAVE

Telingham, Tedlingham (xi cent.) ; Tyrengham-cum-Philegrave, Tyringham-cum-Filegrave (xiii cent.).

Tyringham with Filgrave is a parish covering nearly 1,792 acres, including 652 acres of arable, 1,004 acres of permanent grass and 73 acres of woods and plantations.[1] It is encircled on all sides except the east by the River Ouse and is liable to floods in the north and south. The level of the land varies between 164 ft. above the ordnance datum in the north of the parish and 292 ft. in the west on the road leading from Filgrave to the neighbouring parish of Emberton. The soil is mixed, the subsoil oolite and clay. The chief crops are wheat, barley, beans and oats. The cultivation of woad for dyeing was introduced into this parish among other places in the early 18th century by a company of Manchester manufacturers and Yorkshire clothiers with a view to breaking the heavy monopoly in this article.[2] The industry was still carried on here in the middle of the last century.[3] A large brick and tile works was also established about 1859,[4] but is no longer in existence.

Tyringham House, the old manor-house of the Tyringhams, was described by Pennant in 1782 as 'neglected . . . but not wholly unfurnished.'[5] The present house, the seat of Mr. F. A. König, was built by William Praed[6] after plans by Sir John Soane dated 1793, which are preserved in the Soane Museum, Lincoln's Inn Fields. It is a fine stone building standing in the south-west of the parish in a well-wooded park of 100 acres sloping down to the River Ouse. The public road through the park leads over a one-arched stone bridge and joins the main road from Newport Pagnell to Northampton a little below the river. The small church of St. Peter stands on rising ground in the park about a quarter of a mile south-east of Tyringham House. Most of the few parishioners live at Filgrave, more than 1½ miles north-east of the church by the road. In a disused graveyard south of some allotments in the north-east of Filgrave is the site of the former parish church of St. Mary of Filgrave.[7] Near

it to the south-east the Rectory House, formerly that of Filgrave only,[8] stands on high ground commanding beautiful views.

Some small inclosures made by Thomas Tyringham in this parish in 1509 had been removed by 1520.[9] About this date he was sued by the Abbot of Lavendon for not keeping his agreement in an interchange of an acre of land in Filgrave which he had required for his inclosure there.[10] Thomas son of the above-mentioned Thomas Tyringham was pardoned in 1578 for inclosing 480 acres in Tyringham and Filgrave.[11]

The following place-names occur : Mortons[12] (xvi cent.) ; Broadgreen, Colewort or Calliworth, Hobb's Beanfield and Portway[13] (xvii cent.).

MANORS In 1086 *TYRINGHAM MANOR* was held by William Fitz Ansculf, and assessed at 7 hides 1¼ virgates.[14] The overlordship afterwards passed to the barony of Dudley,[15] and descending with the honour and manor of Newport Pagnell[16] (q.v.) is last mentioned in 1638.[17]

Acard was sub-tenant of Tyringham Manor in 1086.[18] Richard de Tyringham held here between 1209 and 1220, and was succeeded by Giffard[19] (of Tyringham). John Giffard of Tyringham or John de Tyringham died seised about 1274, during the minority of his son and heir Roger,[20] and the custody of his lands was granted to Roger de Thurkelby.[21] Roger de Tyringham, who was holding in 1279,[22] is called Giffard in 1284,[23] but the latter surname did not survive in his family. He was succeeded by his son Roger, whose son, another Roger,[24] in 1342 settled the reversion of Tyringham Manor on his son John, his wife Isabel and John's heirs.[25] John son of John de Tyringham was in the king's wardship in 1373,[26] and he is apparently the Sir

TYRINGHAM. *Azure a saltire engrailed argent.*

---

[1] Statistics from Bd. of Agric. (1905).

[2] Add. MS. 9411, fol. 101.

[3] Lipscomb, *Hist. and Antiq. of Bucks.* iv, 372.

[4] Sheahan, *Hist. and Topog. of Bucks.* 626.

[5] *Journey from Chester to London*, 456.

[6] Lysons, *Mag. Brit.* i (3), 653 ; *Rec. of Bucks.* iv, 44.

[7] Part of the former cemetery was ploughed up during the vacancy in the living before 1863. This was restored as far as possible by the next rector, who had the whole properly fenced from the adjoining glebe (*Rec. of Bucks.* ii, 203–4).

[8] In 1637 the rectory-house of Tyringham had long been uninhabitable, and that of Filgrave was in a like condition. John Tyringham petitioned that the amount both rectory-houses would have cost to rebuild should be expended upon one of them only (*Cal. S. P. Dom.* 1636–7, p. 423 ; 1637–8, pp. 274–5).

[9] Leadam, *Dom. of Incl.* 1517 (Roy. Hist. Soc.), 195.

[10] Early Chan. Proc. bdle. 536, no. 15.

[11] Pat. 20 Eliz. pt. xi, m. 45.

[12] Leadam, loc. cit.

[13] Lipscomb, op. cit. iv. 379, quoting rectory terriers from parish register.

[14] *V.C.H. Bucks.* i, 256. It included five pre-Conquest holdings. Three are called manors, one of which (1½ hides) was held by Alveva independently of her husband Herold.

[15] *Testa de Nevill* (Rec. Com.), 248.

[16] Chan. Inq. p.m. Edw. I, file 7, no. 6 ; *Hund. R.* (Rec. Com.), ii, 348 ; Chan. Inq. p.m. 5 Edw. IV, no. 16 ; *Cat. of Anct. D.* ii, 337 ; Chan. Inq. p.m. (Ser. 2), xlvi, 57 ; liv, 47.

[17] Chan. Inq. p.m. (Ser. 2), dxliii, 19.

[18] *V.C.H. Bucks.* loc. cit.

[19] *Testa de Nevill*, loc. cit.

[20] Chan. Inq. p.m. Edw. I, file 7, no. 6.

[21] *Cal. Pat.* 1272–81, p. 87 ; see also *Cal. Fine R.* 1272–1307, p. 24.

[22] *Hund. R.* (Rec. Com), ii, 348 ; see also *Plac. de Quo Warr.* (Rec. Com.), 84.

[23] *Feud. Aids*, i, 73.

[24] Wrottesley, *Ped. from Plea R.* 110. The following references to Roger de Tyringham give no information as to succession : *Cal. Close*, 1288–96, p. 521 ; *Cat. of Anct. D.* iii, 360 ; *Feud. Aids*, i, 110 ; Chan. Inq. p.m. 16 Edw. II, no. 72 ; *Cal. Close*, 1318–23, pp. 239, 631 ; 1323–7, p. 200 ; *Cal. Pat.* 1330–4, p. 205. A Roger de Tyringham was Sheriff of Bedfordshire and Buckinghamshire in 1318 and 1323 (P.R.O. *List of Sheriffs*, 1), and member for the county in 1321 and 1328 (*Ret. of Memb. of Parl.* i, 62, 80), as an earlier one had been in 1295 and 1305 (*Ret. of Memb. of Parl.*), 4, 18).

[25] Feet of F. case 19, file 84, no. 10.

[26] Wrottesley, loc. cit.

John de Tyringham whose widow Alice claimed dower in this manor in 1405.[27] At the death in January 1415–16 of the next heir John de Tyringham, John Reynes and other feoffees were seised both of the reversion of Alice's portion and of the remaining two-thirds of the manor[28] for the payment of John de Tyringham's debts. They leased this manor to Roger Tyringham,[29] who received a grant of the marriage of the heir[30] John, son of the above John Tyringham and his wife Eleanor.[31] He attained his majority in 1432,[32] was exempted from attendance on juries in 1459,[33] and died in March 1464–5.[34] His son and successor, another John,[35] died in 1484.[36] His lands were granted to his widow Elizabeth during the minority of their son John.[37] The latter was holding Tyringham in 1492,[38] and was succeeded on his death in 1501[39] by his brother Thomas.[40] He died in 1526, and his son Robert[41] died under age in 1532.[42] The wardship of the next heir, Robert's brother Thomas,[43] was granted to Sir Francis Brian.[44] Thomas Tyringham, who was sheriff of the counties of Bedford and Buckingham in 1560,[45] died seised of Tyringham Manor in 1595.[46] His son and successor Anthony,[47] afterwards Sir Anthony Tyringham,[48] was sheriff of the county in 1596[49] and died in 1614.[50] His son and heir Thomas,[51] also knighted,[52] made settlements of this manor in 1621[53] and 1628,[54] and died at Tyringham in January 1636–7.[55] His son John, afterwards Sir John Tyringham,[56] succeeded,[57] and was buried at St. Mary's, Oxford, in 1645.[58] His estates passed to his brother William,[59] who, after much delay, obtained a discharge in 1652 from liability for delinquency.[60] He took legal steps to secure his title to Tyringham Manor in 1653,[61] but continued to be treated as a suspect during the Commonwealth.[62] He was made a Knight of the Bath at the coronation of Charles II[63] and in 1670 conveyed this manor to John Morris and Richard Mounteney, jun.[64] They were presumably agents for Edward Backwell, the London goldsmith and banker, who acquired Tyringham about this time and in 1675 made a presentation to the church.[65]

On his death in 1683[66] Tyringham Manor passed to his son John Backwell,[67] who in 1678 had married Elizabeth daughter and heir of Sir William Tyringham.[68] She was buried at Tyringham in 1688.[69] Their son Tyringham Backwell[70] made settlements of the manor in the early 18th century,[71] in the lifetime of his father,[72] who was buried at Tyringham in 1708.[73] Tyringham Backwell died in 1754, a few months before his son Barnaby.[74] The next heir, Barnaby's son Tyringham Backwell, an infant at his father's death,[75] entered into possession of Tyringham Manor in 1775[76] and died unmarried in 1777.[77] The manor passed in marriage with his sister Elizabeth in 1778[78] to William Mackworth Praed,[79] who was member of Parliament for St. Ives from 1781 to 1806[80] and died in 1833.[81] His son and successor James Backwell Praed[82] had been Sheriff of Buckinghamshire in 1807[83] and represented the county in Parliament from 1835 until his death in 1837.[84] He was succeeded by his son William Backwell Praed, who, by royal licence in 1859, substituted for Praed the surname and arms of Tyringham.[85] His son Mr. Roger William Giffard Tyringham succeeding in 1870, owned Tyringham Manor in 1906,[86] but it has since been acquired by Mr. F. A. König, the present owner.

A second estate called *TYRINGHAM MANOR* in 1086 was then assessed at 2½ hides and three-quarters of a virgate, and formed part of the lands of the Bishop of Coutances.[87] By the early 13th century it was included with the main manor in the Tyringham fee held of the barony of Dudley. Part of it afterwards became one of the manors in Astwood parish (q.v.), and the remainder constituted *FILGRAVE MANOR.*

PRAED. *Azure six molets argent.*

[27] De Banco R. 578, m. 362 d.
[28] Chan. Inq. p.m. 3 Hen. V, no. 35.
[29] Early Chan. Proc. bdle. 5, no. 75.
[30] Memo. R. (Exch. L.T.R.), Mich. 5 Hen. V, m. 14.
[31] Ibid.; Chan. Inq. p.m. 3 Hen. V, no. 35.
[32] Chan. Inq. p.m. 10 Hen. VI, no. 55.
[33] Cal. Pat. 1452–61, p. 484.
[34] Chan. Inq. p.m. 5 Edw. IV, no. 16.
[35] Ibid.; cf. Add. Chart. 59388.
[36] Chan. Inq. p.m. 2 Ric. III, no. 34.
[37] Cal. Pat. 1476–85, pp. 503, 505.
[38] Cat. of Anct. D. ii, 337.
[39] Chan. Inq. p.m. (Ser. 2), xv, 103.
[40] Ibid. xlvi, 57.   [41] Ibid.
[42] Ibid. liv, 47.
[43] Ibid.
[44] L. and P. Hen. VIII, vi, g. 105 (23).
[45] P.R.O. List of Sheriffs, 3.
[46] Chan. Inq. p.m. (Ser. 2), ccxlvi, 108; see also M.I.
[47] Ibid.
[48] Shaw, Kts. of Engl. ii, 111.
[49] P.R.O. List of Sheriffs, 9.
[50] Chan. Inq. p.m. (Ser. 2), cccxlix, 164.
[51] Ibid.
[52] Shaw, op. cit. ii, 110.
[53] Feet of F. Div. Co. East. 19 Jas. I.
[54] Ibid. Bucks. East. 4 Chas. I.
[55] Chan. Inq. p.m. (Ser. 2), dxliii, 19.
[56] Shaw, op. cit. ii, 215.

[57] Chan. Inq. p.m. (Ser. 2), dxliii, 19; Recov. R. Hil. 13 Chas. I, m. 23.
[58] Add. MS. 5839, fol. 196a, quoting register.
[59] Cal. Com. for Comp. 935. An autograph letter from Charles I dated 1648 asking for an immediate remittance of £500 from William Tyringham is preserved at Tyringham House (Rec. of Bucks. iv, 45).
[60] Cal. Com. for Comp. 936; Chan. Proc. (Bridges Div.), bdle. 390, no. 31.
[61] Recov. R. East. 1653, m. 208.
[62] Cal. S. P. Dom. 1657–8, p. 382; 1659–60, p. 112.
[63] Shaw, op. cit. i, 165; see also Cal. S. P. Dom. 1663–4, p. 3.
[64] Feet of F. Bucks. Trin. 22 Chas. II; Recov. R. Trin. 22 Chas. II, m. 116. In a lawsuit of 1679 Sir William Tyringham refers to 1668 as the year in which he alienated the estate inherited from his brother (Chan. Proc. [Bridges Div.], bdle. 459, no. 30).
[65] Inst. Bks. (P.R.O.).
[66] Dict. Nat. Biog.
[67] Pat. 35 Chas. II, pt. iii, no. 20.
[68] Burke, Landed Gentry (1906), under Tyringham.
[69] Add. MS. 5839, fol. 196a, quoting register.
[70] Lipscomb, op. cit. iv, 376.

[71] Recov. R. Hil. 12 Will. III, m. 164; Hil. 2 Anne, m. 33.
[72] Feet of F. Div. Co. Hil. 12 Will. III.
[73] Add. MS. 5839, fol. 196a, quoting register.
[74] Musgrave's Obit. (Harl. Soc.), i, 78.
[75] P.C.C. 265 Pinfold. His mother was to hold during her son's minority, and is the Mrs. Backwell mentioned in 1760 (Add. MS. 5839, fol. 196a; see also under Advowson).
[76] Com. Pleas Recov. R. Hil. 15 Geo. III, m. 85.
[77] Lipscomb, op. cit. iv, 376. Letters of administration were granted in November 1777 (P.C.C. Collier).
[78] Burke, loc. cit.
[79] cf. Verulam MSS. (Hist. MSS. Com.), 146; Hist. MSS. Com. Rep. xiv, App. v, 656.
[80] Burke, loc. cit.
[81] Mon. tablet in Tyringham Church; Gent. Mag. ciii (2), 381.
[82] Burke, loc. cit. See also Recov. R. Mich. 4 Geo. IV, m. 122.
[83] P.R.O. List of Sheriffs, 11.
[84] Burke, loc. cit.   [85] Ibid.
[86] Ibid. See also Ret. of Owners of Lands (1873), Bucks. 20.
[87] V.C.H. Bucks. i, 240. The three-quarters of a virgate was a separate estate before the Conquest.

Anschitil was sub-tenant of the bishop's manor of Tyringham in 1086.[88] By the early 13th century the whole of Tyringham had passed to the Giffards.[89] John Giffard's manor[90] evidently included Filgrave,[91] since his estate a few years later appears as Tyringham with Filgrave.[92] The descent of Filgrave Manor has been identical with that of Tyringham,[93] and Mr. König's estate of Tyringham with Filgrave includes the whole parish.

View of frankpledge in Tyringham and Filgrave was held by Roger de Tyringham,[94] who claimed the right by inheritance, but was deprived of it in 1286.[95] The right of warren appropriated by John de Tyringham shortly before his death[96] is not mentioned after 1279.[97] References to the manorial right of free fishery in the Ouse occur from 1274.[98]

In the later 13th century there were three water-mills on the Tyringham with Filgrave estate, one of which was a fulling-mill.[99] Mills here are mentioned from time to time into the 17th century,[100] but only one in 1700.[1] The mill-house in Tyringham was the only house there in 1730 in addition to the manor-house.[2]

The overlordship of half a fee in Filgrave is attributed in the middle 13th century to the honour of Chaworth,[3] and the Wakes had an interest in half of this as in the case of Weston Underwood. Their rights in this quarter fee in Filgrave held under the heirs of the Biduns ('de Bydoneys') in 1279[4] are traceable until 1442,[5] and descended with similar rights in the second manor of Lathbury (q.v.).

William de Sherington held the half fee in Filgrave of the honour of Chaworth c. 1235.[6] Part of this holding appears to have been comprised in the endowment of Filgrave Church confirmed by William son of Alexander de Sherington.[7] One virgate certainly passed in marriage with William de Sherington's daughter Hawise to Robert Curtfaluz.[8] It descended with the Curtfaluz manor in Weston Underwood (q.v.) to John Pever, who was sued for the same in 1261–2 by Hawise.[9]

Part of the half fee came to William son of Roland, who in 1222 subinfeudated a small estate in Filgrave to Simon Curtfaluz, father of the Robert aforesaid,[10] in return for a pair of gauntlets at Easter.[11] Before 1227 this was granted by Gervase de —— with William's consent to Lavendon Abbey,[12] of which it was held by John son of John the clerk in the later 13th century as a half virgate.[13] Lavendon Abbey also obtained the remainder of the half fee, amounting in all to the quarter fee held under the Wakes, and its estate in Filgrave, assessed at 2 hides in 1279,[14] appertained to its property in Lathbury, with which it formed one vill in the 14th century.[15]

Some land in Filgrave was included by the later 13th century among the possessions of Tickford Priory,[16] and was comprised in the grants of the site of the priory (Newport Pagnell, q.v.) following upon the Dissolution.[17]

CHURCH The church of ST. PETER consists of a chancel, north chapel, nave, south transept, north porch and west tower. It is built of rubble and the roofs are covered with tiles.

A church existed here from the 12th century, but the only part of the old structure now remaining is the tower, the lower stages of which date from the end of the 12th century and the bell-chamber from about 1500. All the other parts were entirely rebuilt in the Gothic manner in 1871.

The chancel terminates in an apse and is lighted by lancet windows, while the nave has pointed windows of two lights with plate tracery. At the west end of the nave is the original tower arch, which dates from about 1200; it is semicircular and of two plain orders springing from hollow-chamfered imposts, and above the arch are traces of a blocked window of the same period.

The tower is of four stages with diagonal buttresses and is surmounted by an embattled parapet. The ground stage has a blocked light on the north and a 17th-century window of two plain lights under a square head on the west. The third stage has a lancet window on the south and a blocked round-headed window on the west, while the bell-chamber is lighted from all sides by transomed windows of two plain lights, that on the west having label stops carved with the shields of Tyringham and Howard. Below the string-course immediately under this window is another shield bearing Tyringham impaling Howard.

Affixed to the east wall of the transept are several brasses which have become detached from their original slabs. A man in armour and an inscription commemorating John Tyringham, Elizabeth (Catesby) and Elizabeth (Brudenell) his wives, probably belong to one memorial, the other figures having been lost. The man wears a helmet and a tabard bearing the arms of Tyringham, and is represented in the attitude of prayer, slightly inclined to the right and his feet resting on a dog. The figure of a woman in gabled head-dress, an inscription commemorating Mary (Tyringham) wife of Anthony Catesby (d. 1508) and two shields, one of Tyringham and the other of Catesby, doubtless formed another complete brass. Besides these there also remain an inscription, partly cut away, commemorating Thomas Tyringham (d. 1595) and Parnell (Goodwin) his wife (d. 1594), and a label of about 1500 inscribed 'domine accipe spiritum meum.'

[88] V.C.H. Bucks. i, 240.
[89] Testa de Nevill (Rec. Com.), 248.
[90] Chan. Inq. p.m. Edw. I, file 7, no. 6.
[91] As John de Tyringham he held in Filgrave in 1258 (Feet of F. case 16, file 35, no. 2).
[92] Hund. R. (Rec. Com.), ii, 348.
[93] See also Feet of F. Bucks. Trin. 23 Chas. I; Hil. 30 & 31 Chas. II; Trin. 13 Will. III; Hil. 2 Anne.
[94] Hund. R. (Rec. Com.), ii, 350.
[95] Plac. de Quo Warr. (Rec. Com.), 84.
[96] Hund. R. (Rec. Com.), i, 38.
[97] Ibid. ii, 350.
[98] Chan. Inq. p.m. Edw. I, file 7, no. 6; Hund. R. (Rec. Com.), ii, 348; Feet of F. Bucks. East. 4 Chas. I; Recov. R.

Trin. 22 Chas. II, m. 116; Hil. 12 Will. III, m. 164; Hil. 2 Anne, m. 33; Hil. 15 Geo. III, m. 392.
[99] Chan. Inq. p.m. Edw. I, file 7, no. 6.
[100] Hund. R. (Rec. Com.), ii, 348, naming one only; Early Chan. Proc. bdle. 5, no. 76; Chan. Inq. p.m. (Ser. 2), cccxlix, 164; Recov. R. Hil. 13 Chas. I, m. 23.
[1] Recov. R. Hil. 12 Will. III, m. 164.
[2] Add. MS. 5839, fol. 196b.
[3] Testa de Nevill (Rec. Com.), 244b.
[4] Hund. R. (Rec. Com.), ii, 348.
[5] Chan. Inq. p.m. 21 Hen. VI, no. 36; cf. Feud. Aids, i, 73.
[6] Testa de Nevill, loc. cit.
[7] Chart. R. 2 Edw. III, m. 14, no. 47.

[8] Assize R. 58, m. 11 d.
[9] Ibid.
[10] Ibid. 68, m. 9 d.
[11] Feet of F. Bucks. Trin. 6 Hen. III.
[12] Dugdale, Mon. vii, 889.
[13] Hund. R. (Rec. Com.), ii, 348.
[14] Ibid.
[15] Feud. Aids, i, 73, 110, 131.
[16] Pope Nich. Tax. (Rec. Com.), 47b; cf. Mins. Accts. bdle. 1127, no. 18, m. 17.
[17] In 1527 Anne daughter and co-heir of Thomas Earl of Ormond and her son George St. Leger quitclaimed any interest in this land as overlords of Filgrave to Cardinal's College, Oxford (Feet of F. Bucks. Mich. and Hil. 18 Hen. VIII).

Tyringham Church from the North

WALTON: THE MANOR HOUSE

WALTON CHURCH FROM THE SOUTH

The tower contains a ring of five bells : the treble, inscribed 'Ecce Quam Bonum Et Quam Jucundum 1629,' is by James Keene [17a]; the second and the tenor are by Richard Chandler, 1720 and 1708 respectively ; the third, inscribed 'Sicut Ros Hermon In Monte Sion 1629,' is also by James Keene ; and the fourth is by Thomas Russell of Wootton, 1735.

The communion plate includes a chalice of 1570 and a paten dated 1707.

The registers begin in 1629.

ADVOWSON A presentation to Tyringham Church was made by Richard de Tyringham between 1209 and 1220.[18] The advowson of the rectory, valued at £13 6s. 8d. yearly in 1291 [19] and at £13 17s. 4d. in 1535,[20] has always been appurtenant to Tyringham Manor.[21] The advowson of the rectory of Filgrave coming under the same ownership before 1614,[22] the union of the rectories was recognized in 1639.[23] The present owner of the advowson of Tyringham with Filgrave is Mr. F. A. König.

Filgrave Church with 2½ virgates 2 acres of land and four dwelling-houses was given by Hugh, clerk of Filgrave, to Delapré Abbey, Northamptonshire, and confirmed to that house by William son of Alexander de Sherington.[24] William de Sherington surrendered his claim to the advowson in 1230.[25] A vicarage was ordained at Filgrave before the inquiry by Bishop Hugh of Wells.[26] The advowson was retained by the abbey until the Dissolution,[27] when its value had increased from £4 13s. 4d. yearly in 1291 [28] to £7.[29] It was granted in 1551 to Sir Nicholas Throckmorton with the site of Luffield Priory (q.v.) and nominally descended with it until 1701.[30] Filgrave Church, although still in use in 1585,[31] was allowed to fall into decay, and the advowson, as already stated, had, in fact, passed under the same ownership as that of Tyringham before 1615. A Commission [32] having reported that the churches had been so long under one incumbent that the glebe lands could not be exactly determined, a settlement of the glebe as suggested by John Tyringham [33] was made in 1639.[34]

In 1637 Filgrave Church was without a roof and trees were growing on its walls.[35] According to Browne Willis the ruined walls of the church were still standing in 1730, the tower being in a good state of preservation.[36] Cole says in 1760 that Mrs. Backwell gave orders in 1758 that the tower should be pulled down and the stones used for the repair of a mill.[37] He also states, on the authority of the then rector, that the latter had soon afterwards used the foundations of the church for the repair of his parsonage.[38]

In 1548 12d. yearly from a rood of meadow land in Ludney was used for the maintenance of a light in Tyringham Church.[39]

There do not appear to be any endowed charities subsisting in this parish.

WALTON

Wauton (xiii cent.).

Walton is a small parish of 772 acres, of which 202 acres are arable land, 5 acres woods and plantations and the rest permanent grass.[1] The land lies low, and in the neighbourhood of the Ouzel, which forms the western boundary, is liable to flood. The highest point attained above the ordnance datum is 294 ft. in the east. The soil is light clay, the subsoil gravel and clay. The principal crops produced are wheat, beans, barley and oats.

Cole, writing c. 1760, speaks of Walton as ' a most dirty, detestable village,' but notes that the pastures were remarkable for the goodness of their produce.[2]

The village is situated off the main road from Newport Pagnell to Fenny Stratford. It contains a few cottages and two farm-houses, one of which, the Manor House, formerly inhabited by the Gilpins, is an ancient building dating from the 16th century, with additions made about 1701 by Sir Thomas Pinfold.[3] It was thoroughly restored in 1855,[4] and is built partly of stone, half-timber and brick, and has tiled roofs. Many of the windows have wooden mullions, and inside is an original open fireplace. The old manor-house of the Beales, pulled down by Sir Thomas Pinfold when he moved to the Gilpins' house on the Green,[5] stood north-west of the church,[6] which is some distance north-west of the village within the park of Walton Hall. Near the church is the rectory, which is described in 1639 as ' a Dwelling house of 3 bays, a Barn of 4 bays, a Stable of 1 bay.' [7] The present building is principally modern, but incorporates part of a 17th-century house now rough-casted. Walton Hall, the seat of Mr. Vaughan Harley, M.D., lord of the manor, is a spacious brick and stucco mansion built in 1830 by Charles Pinfold.[8] It stands in 60 acres of well-wooded park.

Walton is famous for the growth of walnuts, of which many hundreds of trees flourish in the parish.[9] These trees give their name to the farm with a half-timber house built towards the close of the 16th

[17a] A. H. Cocks, *Ch. Bells of Bucks.* 603.
[18] *R. of Hugh of Wells* (Cant. and York Soc.), i, 38.
[19] *Pope Nich. Tax.* (Rec. Com.), 34.
[20] *Valor Eccl.* (Rec. Com.), iv, 243.
[21] See also Inst. Bks. (P.R.O.); Bacon, *Liber Regis*, 499. William Beauchamp presented in 1252 (*Rolls of Robert Grosseteste* [Cant. and York. Soc.], 383).
[22] Chan. Inq. p.m. (Ser. 2), cccxlix, 164.
[23] *Cal. S. P. Dom.* 1639, p. 424.
[24] These charters, with one from John son of John the clerk of Tyringham, giving up his right in the advowson and another from Giffard of Tyringham granting half a virgate of land in Filgrave to the abbey, were inspected and confirmed in 1328 (Chart. R. 2 Edw. III, m. 14, no. 47).
[25] Feet of F. case 15, file 18, no. 6.
[26] *V.C.H. Bucks.* i, 284.
[27] *Valor Eccl.* (Rec. Com.), iv, 243, 321. A yearly pension of 10s. from this church to the abbey was payable to the lord of the manor in 1775 (Recov. R. Hil. 15 Geo. III, m. 392).
[28] *Pope Nich. Tax.* (Rec. Com.), 34, 41.
[29] *Valor Eccl.* (Rec. Com.), iv, 243.
[30] See under Luffield Abbey.
[31] *V.C.H. Bucks.* i, 318.
[32] *Cal. S. P. Dom.* 1636-7, p. 423.
[33] Ibid. 1637-8, pp. 274-5.
[34] Ibid. 1639, p. 424.
[35] Ibid. 1636-7, p. 423.
[36] Add. MS. 5839, fol. 79b.
[37] Ibid.
[38] Ibid. fol. 80a.
[39] Chant. Cert. 5, no. 38.
[1] Statistics from Bd. of Agric. (1905).
[2] Add. MS. 5830, fol. 153.
[3] Ibid. 5839, fol. 199.
[4] Sheahan, *Hist. and Topog. of Bucks.* 628.
[5] Add. MS. 5839, fol. 199.
[6] Ibid.
[7] Ibid. 5830, fol. 152 d.
[8] Sheahan, loc. cit.
[9] Sheahan, op. cit. 627.

century and added to in later times. It is of timber framing with brick filling coated with plaster and has tiled roofs.

The following place-names have been found in documents connected with this parish: Hickson's Croft in the 16th and 17th centuries,[10] Abels, Margarets pasture, Peatelys (a farm), Portway,[11] Gabriel Thorn and Windmills Closes in the 17th century.[12]

There is no mention of *WALTON MANORS* in Domesday, and it has been assumed that it was included in the land which Walter Giffard held in the neighbouring parish of Bow Brickhill.[13] On its first appearance by name at the beginning of the 13th century it certainly appears as attached to the Giffard honour of Crendon[14] (q.v.). The overlordship was attached to the manor of Moulsoe, whose lords, the Coudrays, appear as intermediaries in the 13th and 14th centuries.[15] The overlordship passed to that branch of the honour vested in the Earls of Shrewsbury; the latest mention of it occurs in 1458.[16]

The first reference to Walton has been found in 1201, when the manor was already divided into moieties. In that year Hugh Richepaut, or Rixbaud as it more usually appears, and Juliana his wife paid 1 mark for a writ of summons against Roger de Bray and Margaret his wife for lands in Walton and elsewhere,[17] but whether Juliana and Margaret were co-heirs has not been established. By 1231 Hugh Rixbaud was succeeded by William Rixbaud, who then made a presentation to the church.[18] William was followed by another Hugh Rixbaud, whose daughter Margery was in the guardianship of Richard de Hemington in 1262.[19] Before 1284 Margery married Nicholas de Hemington,[20] possibly a son of the above Richard, but obtained a divorce from him some time before 1291, in which year, described as his divorced wife, she combined with him in making a presentation to the church.[21] Roger de Brailsford, who is assumed by Willis to be her second husband, presented with Margery Rixbaud in 1292.[22] He held by knight service in Walton in 1302-3,[23] and his name again occurs with that of Margery in 1311, when they together made a settlement of the advowson and lands on Ralph de Hatle.[24] John Brailsford had succeeded before 1324,[25] but some time during the next twenty years the property had passed from this family, being held in 1346 by Nicholas Hunt.[26] In 1348 the presentation was made in the names of Nicholas Hunt of Fenny Stratford, Agnes his wife and William his son,[27] the last-named of whom made the presentation in 1361,[28] but Walton passed eventually to John, another son of Nicholas Hunt,[29] whose daughter Joan married John Longville,[30] and together with her husband obtained a quitclaim of this estate in 1399 from Robert Craven and Isabel his wife on behalf of Isabel and her heirs.[31] The half manor, as it is usually termed, thus acquired by the Longvilles was retained by them and follows the same descent as their principal manor of Wolverton[32] (q.v.) until the year 1622, about which date a transfer appears to have taken place to John Beale and Bartholomew Beale.[33] Bartholomew Beale died and was buried at Walton in 1660,[34] and his son, also Bartholomew,[35] combined with another son Charles Beale,[36] Richard Gilpin and others to make a settlement of the manor on George and Thomas Gilpin in 1668.[37] Bartholomew Beale died in 1674,[38] and his son and successor of the same name[39] made settlements of Walton Manor in 1676, 1677 and in 1690.[40] In the last settlement the names of Richard and Thomas Gilpin are again mentioned, appearing as deforciants with Bartholomew Beale,[41] and, according to Willis, Richard Gilpin definitely acquired Walton Manor at this date.[42] He did not long retain it, alienating it in March 1700-1 to Sir Thomas Pinfold, kt.,[43] to whom he had already sold the advowson and some land in 1698.[44] Sir Thomas Pinfold, kt., was chancellor of the diocese of Peterborough, and died and was buried here in 1701.[45] He was succeeded by his elder son and heir Dr. Charles Pinfold, LL.D., Provost of Eton, who died in 1754.[46] His son, also Charles Pinfold, was for ten years Governor of the Barbadoes (1756-66).[47] On his death, unmarried, in 1788, at the advanced age of eighty-one,[48] Walton Manor passed to his nephew

[10] Chan. Inq. p.m. (Ser. 2), xc, 9; dcclxix, 43.
[11] Add. MS. loc. cit.; Chan. Inq. p.m. (Ser. 2), dccxli, 161; Chan. Proc.(Ser. 2), bdle. 377, no. 7.
[12] P.C.C. 70 Dyer.
[13] *V.C.H. Bucks.* i, 252b; Add. MS. 5839, fol. 198 d.
[14] *Testa de Nevill* (Rec. Com.), 247a.
[15] Ibid. 259, 262; *Feud. Aids,* i, 83, 103; Chan. Inq. p.m. 17 Edw. II, no. 74; 27 Edw. III (1st nos.), no. 58.
[16] *Feud. Aids,* i, 83; Chan. Inq. p.m. 17 Edw. II, no. 75; 20 Ric. II, no. 51; 7 Hen. V, no. 68; 8 Hen. V (Add. nos.), no. 127; 17 Hen. VI, no. 38; 36 Hen. VI, no. 36; 37 Hen. VI, no. 28; *Cal. Close,* 1323-7, p. 267.
[17] *Rot. de Oblatis et Fin.* (Rec. Com.), 137; *Rot. Canc.* (Rec. Com.), 352.
[18] *R. of Hugh of Wells* (Cant. and York Soc.), ii, 82.   [19] Add. MS. loc. cit.
[20] *Feud. Aids,* i, 83.
[21] Add. MS. 5839, fol. 199 d.
[22] Ibid.   They also presented in 1304.
[23] *Feud. Aids,* i, 103.
[24] Feet of F. Div. Co. 5 Edw. II, no. 52.
[25] Chan. Inq. p.m. 17 Edw. II, no. 75.
[26] *Feud. Aids,* i, 129.
[27] Add. MS. loc. cit.

[28] Ibid.
[29] *Cal. Close,* 1354-60, p. 325.
[30] *Her. and Gen.* vi, 49; Chan. Inq. p.m. 17 Hen. VI, no. 38. Joan is generally supposed to be the daughter of John Hunt by Margery daughter of the last John Wolverton.
[31] Feet of F. case 21, file 110. Isabel was probably a sister.
[32] See Wolverton; also *Cal. Pat.* 1452-61, p. 595; Leadam, *Dom. Incl.* 1517 (Royal Hist. Soc.), 180.
[33] Recov. R. Mich. 20 Jas. I, m. 101. A good deal of litigation occurred at this date owing to a lease extending over forty-one years made of the manor in 1608 by Sir Henry Longville, kt., to William Seabrooke (Feet of F.Bucks. East. 6 Jas. I; East. 8 Jas. I; Chan. Proc. [Ser. 2], bdle. 377, no. 7). In 1622 William Seabrooke made a settlement in trust on John and Robert Beale (Feet of F. Div. Co. Trin. 20 Jas. I), but in the same year his sons Robert and Gilbert repudiated their father's liabilities (Chan. Proc. [Ser. 2], bdle. 377, no. 7). Bartholomew Beale was defendant in this suit.
[34] Add. MS. 5830, fol. 153 d. quoting parish registers.   [35] Ibid.
[36] P.C.C. 2 Bunce. Charles Beale is

described in the *Dict. Nat. Biog.* as lord of Walton Manor about this date. He married Mary Cradock, the portrait painter.
[37] Feet of F. Bucks. Trin. 20 Chas. II. The manor ceased to be called 'half' after the 16th century.
[38] P.C.C. 2 Bunce.
[39] Ibid.
[40] Feet of F. Bucks. Trin. 28 Chas. II; Trin. 2 Will. and Mary; Recov. R. Trin. 29 Chas. II, m. 57; Trin. 2 Will. and Mary, m. 173.
[41] Feet of F. Bucks. Trin. 2 Will. and Mary; Recov. R. Trin. 2 Will. and Mary, m. 173.
[42] Add. MS. 5839, fol. 199.
[43] P.C.C. 70 Dyer.
[44] Feet of F. Bucks. East. 10 Will. III; Close, 10 Will. III, pt. x, no. 21.
[45] Lysons, *Mag. Brit.* i (3), 657. His will dated 11 Aug. 1699 and proved 22 May 1701 makes provision for his two sons Charles and William (P.C.C. 70 Dyer).
[46] Add. MS. 5830, fol. 154; P.C.C. 175 Pinfold.
[47] Add. MS. 5830, fol. 153; Burke, *Landed Gentry* (5th ed.).
[48] Sheahan, op. cit. 629; P.C.C. 613 Calvert.

Captain Charles Pinfold, son of Joseph Pinfold.[49] He died in 1857, when Walton became the property of his granddaughter Fanny Maria Pinfold.[50] She was described in 1871 as lady of the manor,[51] and so remained till the close of the last century. The manor next became the property of Miss Seagrave, a connexion of Miss Pinfold on her mother's side.[52] She held Walton in 1903, but between that date and 1907 alienated it to Vaughan Harley, M.D., the present lord of the manor.

PINFOLD of Walton. *Azure a cheveron or voided azure and charged with three roundels azure between three doves proper.*

With reference to the second half of Walton Manor, the earliest tenants of whom mention has been found are the family of Bray, whose holding dates from the 12th century.[53] In 1201 Hugh Rixbaud, lord of the other half of the manor, obtained a writ of summons against Roger de Bray and Margaret his wife for lands in Walton and elsewhere.[54] In 1225 their turn of the advowson was exercised by Godfrey de Limhoud, who then presented Roger de Bray (evidently a member of the family) to a moiety of the parsonage.[55] In 1249 the patronage was vested in Stephen de Bray.[55a] In the 13th century Robert del Hoo is stated to have 'wardam' in Walton.[56] Peter de Coudray as guardian of Hugh de Brabeu (? Bray) presented in 1278,[57] after which date no further reference has been found to the Brays, though at Silsoe, Bedfordshire, where they were also settled, they continued to hold for some time.[58] The fact that the next owners of the Walton property, the Grey family, appear about the same time in Silsoe suggests that a Grey may have intermarried with the Brays. Sir John Grey certainly held this moiety of Walton in 1302–3,[59] and presented to the church in 1307.[60] The Greys had Water Eaton and Bletchley Manors in this county (q.v.), Walton, like Simpson Manor (q.v.), passing with Bletchley to the younger branch, the Greys of Ruthyn.[61] The descent of Walton Manor diverges from that of Bletchley in 1524, when, like Brogborough in Ridgmont, Bedfordshire, it became Crown property.[62] It was annexed to the honour of Ampthill formed in 1542,[63] and was granted by Elizabeth in 1602 to Robert Morgan and Thomas Bradford, being then termed a messuage and lands in Walton part of Brogborough Manor.[64] It would appear to have passed

shortly after this date to Richard Gilpin, lord of Redcote Manor, who at his death in 1616 held Kent House and Kent Farm,[65] with which may be identified the property anciently held here by the Greys.[66] In 1690, like Redcote Manor, it became once more united to the other moiety of Walton by the alienation of the latter to Richard Gilpin, a member of this family.

A titular manor in this parish known as *WALTON MANOR alias REDCOTE MANOR* probably takes its name from a family of Redcote who owned land in this parish in the 13th century. John de Redcote, the first member of whom mention has been found, in 1285 conveyed a messuage, land and rents here to William Cheltenham.[67] In 1307 William son of Robert de Battlesden acknowledged John's claim to a messuage and a virgate in Walton.[68] Finally William de Redcote's name appears in the middle of the 14th century as one of the assessors in a levy of the ninth in Walton.[69]

The Redcote property reappears in 1542, when Edward Taylor transferred land in Walton, with which, as will be seen below, it may be regarded as identical, to Robert Chernock of Holcot (co. Bedford).[70] He died seised in February 1548-9 of a messuage and land in Walton described as formerly belonging to John Redcote.[71] It then passed to his son Richard Chernock,[72] who in 1589 together with Mary his wife and others transferred the manor of Redcote in this parish to Thomas Anglesey.[73] The latter in 1600 sold this estate to Richard Saunders,[74] by whom it was dispersed by sale, the greater part going to Thomas Gilpin.[75] No further mention has been found of Redcote Manor, but it may be identified with the White House of which Richard Gilpin died seised in 1616,[76] and henceforward follows the same descent as the Grey moiety of Walton Manor.

CHURCH The church of *ST. MICHAEL* consists of a chancel measuring internally 22 ft. 6 in. by 13 ft., north vestry, nave 39 ft. 6 in. by 20 ft., west tower 10 ft. 6 in. square, and south porch. It is built of rubble, partially coated with cement, and the roofs are covered with lead and tiles.

A church existed here in 1225,[77] but the structure of that period was entirely rebuilt about the middle of the 14th century, the date of the present chancel and nave. The tower was added in the 15th century, and it is probable that the porch, with its pointed doorway and unglazed windows, though it has been considerably

[49] Add. MS. 5830, fol. 152, 153; Burke, loc. cit.; Sheahan, op. cit. 628.
[50] Burke, loc. cit. [51] Ibid.
[52] Ibid. Miss Pinfold's father married Anna Maria daughter of the Rev. John Seagrave.
[53] See *V.C.H. Beds.* ii, 330, where there is a reference in 1199 to the holding of Roger de Bray in Silsoe.
[54] *Rot. de Oblatis et Fin.* (Rec. Com.), 137.
[55] *R. of Hugh of Wells* (Cant. and York Soc.), ii, 66.
[55a] *R. of Robert Grosseteste* (Cant. and York Soc.), 377.
[56] *Testa de Nevill* (Rec. Com.), 247a.
[57] Add. MS. 5839, fol. 199 d.
[58] *V.C.H. Beds.* ii, 330.
[59] *Feud. Aids,* i, 103.
[60] Add. MS. loc. cit.

[61] See also *Feud. Aids,* i, 110, 129.
[62] *V.C.H. Beds.* iii, 321.
[63] *L. and P. Hen. VIII,* xvii, 28 (21).
[64] Pat. 44 Eliz. pt. ix, m. 16. In 1624 James I devised rents in Walton *inter alia* to Prince Charles (Pat. 22 Jas. I, pt. xvi, no. 9), who demised them to the Lord Mayor and citizens of London (ibid. 4 Chas. I, pt. xxxv).
[65] Chan. Inq. p.m. (Ser. 2), dccxli, 161. Kent House and Farm were held of the Crown as of the manor of East Greenwich, but other lands in Walton were attached to Brogborough Manor, which included appurtenances in Walton in 1702 (Feet of F. Div. Co. East. 1 Anne).
[66] Kent House and Farm may, however, have derived their name from Robert, Thomas and Richard Kent to whom Elizabeth leased a farm and 200 acres of land in

Walton. This interest was conveyed to William Seabrooke in November 1600 (Chan. Proc. Eliz. S 17, no. 33).
[67] Feet of F. case 17, file 47, no 4.
[68] Ibid. file 59, no. 9.
[69] *Inq. Nonarum* (Rec. Com.), 337.
[70] Com. Pleas D. Enr. East. 34 Hen. VIII, m. 13.
[71] Chan. Inq. p.m. (Ser. 2), xc, 9.
[72] Ibid.
[73] Feet of F. Bucks. Trin. 31 Eliz.
[74] Ibid. East. 42 Eliz.
[75] Chan. Inq. p.m. (Ser. 2), dcclxix, 43. John Allen bought one cottage.
[76] Ibid. dccxli, 161. Thomas was brother and heir of Richard Gilpin. Their father John Gilpin died in January 1629-30 (ibid [Ser. 2], dcxxxvi, 92).
[77] *R. of Hugh of Wells* (Cant. and York Soc.), ii, 66; cf. ibid. 82,

restored with cement, is of the same period. The vestry, now used as a store room, was probably added at the time of the general restoration of the church in 1861.

The chancel, which inclines towards the south, has one window on the east, one on the north, and three on the south side. All of them are of the mid-14th century except that at the west end of the south wall, a square-headed low-side window of two cinquefoiled lights, which was inserted a century later. The east and south-east windows are each of three lights with tracery in a pointed head, and the other windows are of similar character but of two lights with more simple tracery. A pointed priest's doorway below the middle window on the south is also of the 14th century, and a cinquefoiled piscina at the south-east, though considerably restored, probably dates from the same period. The pointed chancel arch is of three orders, and has semi-octagonal respond shafts with moulded capitals and bases.

The nave has two windows on the north and two on the south, all of two lights with tracery under pointed heads, and of mid-14th-century date. There is also an original pointed doorway at the west end of each lateral wall. Near the south doorway is a restored stoup with a round bowl. A trefoiled piscina at the south-east marks the position of the nave altar, which probably stood against the east wall. This corner of the nave is further distinguished by the more elaborate character of the window tracery. A turret-stair with a narrow blocked light, which projects at the north-east of the nave, formerly gave access to the rood-loft. The 15th-century tower arch is of three chamfered orders dying into plain responds. The nave has a low-pitched timber roof of about 1600, the king-post trusses of which have moulded and carved timbers and rest upon moulded stone corbels. Traces of a black-letter inscription and colour-painting remain on one of the tie-beams. The high-pitched collar-beam roof of the chancel probably dates from the early 16th century.

The tower is of two stages divided by a string-course and surmounted by an embattled parapet. It is constructed with very thick walls and supported by diagonal buttresses at the west and straight buttresses at the east. In the west wall of the ground stage is a three-light window with modern tracery, and on each side of the bell-chamber is a two-light window, the tracery of which is original, though considerably restored with cement. Below the north and south windows of the bell-chamber are small square-headed cinquefoiled lights.

The font is modern. On the north wall of the chancel is a marble monument in memory of Bartholomew Beale, who died in 1660, and Katherine his wife (d. 1657), with their two busts flanked by Corinthian columns and surmounted by a broken pediment and achievement of arms. There is also on the north wall a brass inscription in verse in memory of Elizabeth daughter of William Pyxe

(d. 1617). In the nave is a mural monument with a medallion portrait and arms commemorating Sir Thomas Pinfold, kt., LL.D., king's advocate and Chancellor of Peterborough, who died in 1701, Elizabeth (Suckley) his wife and Elizabeth his mother. There is also a tablet to Charles Pinfold, LL.D., Governor of Barbadoes 1756–66, who died in 1788, and Ann his sister (d. 1805). In the tower is a panelled chest of the early 17th century.

The tower contains two bells, the treble by Anthony Chandler, 1679, and the tenor by Richard and George Chandler, 1709.[77a] They are set in an old frame dated 1639.

The plate consists of a silver cup of 1814 inscribed 'For the town of Walton'; a silver paten of the same date; a plated flagon with the same inscription; and a plated flagon without date or inscription.

The registers begin in 1598.

ADVOWSON In the early 13th century the church was attached to the manor of Walton and, like it, was divided into moieties, the lord of each moiety of the manor having the right to present a rector to his moiety of the church.[78] This system of two rectors persisted until 1458, when, at the request of the two patrons, the unification of the moieties took place.[79] Probably by mutual arrangements made at that date the lords of the manor have since made alternate presentations.

That moiety of the advowson which went with the Rixbauds' share of the manor (see above) follows the same descent as that property until its transfer to Sir Thomas Pinfold, kt., in 1698, when he purchased the advowson in trust for John Harrison, who owned it c. 1735.[80] The right of presentation belonged to William Ellis, rector 1790–1821, at the close of the century.[81] In 1851 it belonged to the Rev. G. W. Pearse, who was instituted rector at that date and so remained for nearly fifty years. His trustees have the right of alternate presentation at the present day.[82]

The moiety of the advowson which with the Greys' share of the manor escheated to the Crown has so remained vested, an alternate presentation being made at the present day by the Lord Chancellor.[83]

In 1291 the church of Walton is returned at £5 6s. 8d.,[84] and at the Dissolution the rectory was worth £9.[85] In 1495 lands in Walton were granted to the gild at Fenny Stratford[86] (q.v.). In 1598 these lands were granted by the Crown to Henry Best and Robert Holland.[87] In 1589 a messuage and land in Walton and Simpson given in pre-Reformation times to provide obits were granted to Walter Coppinger and Thomas Butler.[88]

CHARITIES Unknown donor's charity.—In the Parliamentary Returns of 1786 some land is stated to have been given by an unknown donor for the use of the parishioners. The charity is now represented by a sum of £532 2s. 2d. consols, with the official trustees, and is regulated by a scheme of the High Court of Chancery of 26 February 1862. By an order of the Charity Commissioners of 20 January 1905 one

[77a] A. H. Cocks, Ch. Bells of Bucks. 607.
[78] R. of Hugh of Wells (Cant. and York Soc.), ii, 66, 82.
[79] Linc. Epis. Reg. Memo. Chedworth, fol. 32 d.; Add. MS. 5839, fol. 199.
[80] Add. MS. 5830, fol. 153 d.; 5839, fol. 199. John Waller presented for a turn in 1711 (Inst. Bks. [P.R.O.]).
[81] Inst. Bks. (P.R.O.); Bacon, Liber Regis, 501. He was succeeded by his son Valentine Ellis in 1821 on presentation by the king (Lipscomb, Hist. and Antiq. of Bucks. iv, 387). [82] Clergy List, 1915.
[83] Ibid.; Inst. Bks. (P.R.O.); Lipscomb, loc. cit.; Lysons, Mag. Brit. i (3), 657.
[84] Pope Nich. Tax. (Rec. Com.), 41b.
[85] Valor Eccl. (Rec. Com.), iv, 244.
[86] Chan. Inq. p.m. (Ser. 2), xi, 32.
[87] Lipscomb, op. cit. iv, 384, quoting patent.
[88] Add. MS. 5839, fol. 198 d., quoting Pat. 31 Eliz. pt. ii.

moiety of the stock, namely, £266 1s. 1d., was appropriated as the educational foundation, the annual dividends, amounting to £6 13s., being applicable towards the salary of master or mistress of the infants' or Sunday school, and the other moiety as the eleemosynary charity, the dividends being applicable in the distribution of coals and clothing.

The Church Land consists of 2 a. 1 r. in the adjoining parish of Milton let at £4 10s. a year, which is carried to the churchwardens' accounts.

WAVENDON

Wafanduninga[1] (x cent.) ; Wavendone (xi cent.) ; Wauenden (xii–xvi cent.) ; Wavyngdon, Warnden (xiv cent.) ; Wandon (xviii cent.).

The parish of Wavendon has an extent of 2,192 acres, and of these 1,285 are permanent grass, 682 arable land and 190 woods and plantations.[2] The soil is stiff loam and sand, the subsoil clay and gravel. The chief crops are wheat, oats, beans and barley. The parish is bordered on the north and east by Bedfordshire, the boundary on the north being formed by a tributary stream, flowing westward, of the Ouzel River. The land in this district is about 220 ft. above the ordnance datum ; it rises steadily towards the south until the high ground and hilly district of Wavendon Heath is reached, the height here being from 400 ft. to 500 ft. This part of the parish, open heath and woodland, forms a great contrast to the thickly populated district on its eastern border. Further north, again, in Wavendon village, the land is fairly well built over ; in the extreme north, save for a few farms, there is practically nothing but open fields. In the village are several 17th-century cottages of half-timber, many of them having thatched roofs. In 1740 the Rev. W. Cole mentioned the following districts or hamlets in Wavendon—Church End, Cross End, Duck End, In the Heath, Hogsty End, Longslade, East End and Green End,[3] and some of the names are still preserved.

The manor-house in Cross End is probably that acquired in 1653 by James Selby from the Worrall family.[4] It is an E-shaped Elizabethan house, built of timber framing with brick filling, now coated with rough-cast, and has tiled roofs. It underwent considerable alterations at the beginning of the 18th century, and many of the existing fittings were inserted at that date. James Selby's chief property here appears to have been the mansion at Green End, now Wavendon House.[5] This he partly rebuilt, and his son in the 18th century greatly enlarged it, making gardens, canals and fish-ponds and planting orchards and avenues of trees.[6] The Hoare family, subsequent possessors, again enlarged it.[7] At present it is owned by Sir H. H. A. Hoare, bart., and is the residence of Mr. Francis Edward Bond.

The Manor Farm, opposite the church, in the centre of the village, is thought to have been built on the site of the house belonging to the Passelewe family in the 14th century.[8] It was sold about 1907.[9] There are Wesleyan and Primitive Methodist chapels in Wavendon.

It is not evident when the fuller's earth pits in the south-east of the parish first began to be worked. What appears to be the earliest mention of these pits occurs in 1539, when they were leased to John Sheppard, who later held the Earl of Devonshire's manor, as a parcel of the lands called the 'Clay pits' in which the 'Fullers erthe' is.[10] A suit heard in January 1578–9 between Henry Charge, lord of Mordaunts Manor, and Thomas Wells, part owner of the Earl of Devonshire's manor, is interesting as throwing light on the conditions under which the pits were held.[11] Charge, as lessee of Richard Moreton, brother-in-law of Wells, claimed half the profits of those earth pits of which Moreton and Wells were tenants in common, stating that the earth sold out of the pits was 'very profitable and commodious for fulling.' Wells, not allowing the justice of Charge's plea, had claimed for himself alone the earth pit, which he would have opened by himself had he not been persuaded by the other owners and leaseholders to conform to the usual custom and to enjoy the joint advantages of co-operation. Their method of work was to open only one pit yearly out of the total five, whereby a £10 profit was assured to every owner. The final decision in the suit is not known. The pits were originally worked by removing the upper layers of sand, but in Lipscomb's time they were 'subjected to the usual operation of miners,' a shaft being driven into the hill.[12] Lysons, about 1813, stated that at that time only one pit was occasionally worked, as the sale of the earth had greatly diminished, owing to the practice of the dealers of procuring inferior earth from elsewhere and selling it as the product of this neighbourhood.[13]

Among place-names are Hardwick Wood and Maggott's Close in the 17th century.[14]

An Act for inclosing lands in the parish was passed in 1788,[15] the award bearing date 9 March 1791.[15a] Wavendon at that time included in its bounds the district called Hogsty End, now known as Woburn Sands, which was formed into a civil parish in Bedfordshire in 1907. In the 17th and 18th centuries it was one of the most important[16] centres of the Society of Friends in Buckinghamshire. The Quakers had a meeting-house and a burial ground here. The earliest notice of them occurs in the parish register under 1658, when 'a child of George Cooper was born and not baptized he being a Quaker, died, & he buried where he pleased.' Soon after the wife of a Quaker died and was 'putte into the ground by him a Quaker' ; another Quaker who died was 'buried in his garden.' In 1659 there is a record that 'Friends riding to a meeting at

---

[1] A charter of 969 concerning land in the neighbourhood mentions 'Wafanduninga gemaere' (Add. Chart. 19793).

[2] Statistics from Bd. of Agric. (1905).

[3] *Rec. of Bucks.* ix, 44.

[4] Add. Chart. 53886.

[5] Lipscomb, *Hist. and Antiq. of Bucks.* iv, 395.

[6] Add. MS. 5839, pp. 402, 404.

[7] Sheahan, *Hist. and Topog. of Bucks.* 630.

[8] Add. MS. 5839, p. 400.

[9] *Land and House Property Year Bk.* 1907.

[10] *L. and P. Hen. VIII*, xiv (1), g. 1056 (22).

[11] Ct. of Req. bdle. 66, no. 29.

[12] Lipscomb, op. cit. iv, 391.

[13] Lysons, *Mag. Brit.* i (3), 477-8.

[14] Chan. Inq. p.m. (Ser. 2), ccclxxv, 72.

[15] Priv. Act, 28 Geo. III, cap. 12.

[15a] *Blue Bk. Incl. Awards*, 13.

[16] *Rec. of Bucks.* ix, 41-2.

Wandon had their horses confiscated as a punishment for Sunday travelling.' Frequent references to burials in the Hogsty End ground occur in the 18th century, it being often added that the dead were 'buried in woollen according to law.'

MANORS　In the time of Edward the Confessor Golnil, a house carl of the king, held a manor here, assessed at 2 hides, which belonged to the Count of Mortain in 1086.[17] A second manor of 2 hides, which also belonged to the count, had been held by Brictuin, a man of Earl Harold, before the Conquest.[18] Chentis, a man of Leventot son of Osmund, had held 3 virgates which in 1086 formed the Count of Mortain's third holding in Wavendon.[19] The count's tenant in the last-named portion was Humfrey,[20] but the land was probably amalgamated with one of the larger portions.

It seems probable that the first of the two manors was the manor of Wavendon known in the 16th and 17th centuries as *MORDAUNTS MANOR*. The manor was afterwards attached to the honour of Berkhampstead, and was held of it as of the manor of Langley Chenduit,[21] the overlordship being last mentioned in 1640.[22] Ralf, the count's tenant in Wavendon in 1086, was therefore probably identical with the Ralf of Langley, the ancestor of the Chenduit family, who held the Hertfordshire manor afterwards.[23]

Paul Pever had obtained the manor of Wavendon before 1243, in which year he was granted free warren.[24] About the same date he also acquired Chilton (q.v.), with which manor, and with Marsworth (q.v.) later belonging to the Pever family, Wavendon descended until about the middle of the 14th century.[25]

The Pever holding in Wavendon was augmented in 1314 by the acquisition by that family of Passelewes manor, and the two estates were thenceforth held as 'the manor of Wavendon' until they were again separated in the 15th century. The overlordship rights are, however, always distinguished. The Pevers' original moiety consisted of a capital messuage and a carucate of land, while the other formerly held by the Passelewes comprised a carucate of land and the church.[26] In 1359 Wavendon was

alienated by Nicholas Pever to Sir Henry Green,[27] afterwards of Drayton (co. Northampton), at whose death ten years later it passed by settlement to his second son Henry.[28] Henry died in 1399, when Wavendon descended to his son and heir Ralph,[29] at whose death without issue in 1417 his brother John inherited.[30] Henry Green succeeded his father John in 1433,[31] and by his wife Constance[32] had a daughter and heir Constance, who inherited Wavendon at her father's death in 1468, when she was the wife of John Stafford, third son of the first Duke of Buckingham.[33] He was created Earl of Wiltshire in 1470, a

GREEN. *Azure three harts tripping or.*

title inherited in 1473 by Edward, his son by Constance.[34] Edward died without issue in 1499,[35] and Wavendon passed to his cousins the daughters of Henry Vere of Great Addington, Northamptonshire, who had died in 1493,[36] and to whom the reversion had descended from his mother Isabel Green, wife of Richard Vere and aunt of Constance Green.[37]

These co-heirs, Elizabeth wife of Sir John Mordaunt, kt., afterwards first Lord Mordaunt, Anne wife of Sir Humphrey Browne, and Audrey, brought an action in 1505 to recover seisin of the manor.[38] Audrey afterwards married John Browne, a nephew of Sir Humphrey,[39] and their son and heir George Browne succeeded his father in 1550.[40] In 1557 George Browne conveyed the reversion of his third of the manor, after his mother's death, to John Lord Mordaunt,[41] who thus became seised of two-thirds. John, his son by Elizabeth Vere, succeeded to the title in 1562,[42] but the Wavendon estate passed by settlement to Lewis Mordaunt, son of the younger John, who proved his right to the acquired third in 1563[43] and in 1571, when Lord Mordaunt, sold both portions to Henry Charge.[44] Meanwhile Sir Humphrey Browne made a settlement of his third in 1562 on George his son by Anne Vere and on Mary, Christine and Katherine his daughters by another wife, Agnes Richer, widow,

[17] *V.C.H. Bucks.* i, 246.
[18] Ibid.　[19] Ibid. 247.
[20] Ibid.
[21] *Testa de Nevill* (Rec. Com.), 244; *Feud. Aids*, i, 77, 107; Chan. Inq. p.m. 17 Edw. II, no. 67; 7 Edw. III (1st nos.), no. 33; 5 Hen. V, no. 41; Ct. R. (Gen. Ser.), portf. 177, no. 14; Memo. R. (Exch. L.T.R.), Hil. 5 Eliz. m. 40.
[22] Chan. Inq. p.m. (Ser. 2), dcclxviii, 10. In this it is said to be held of the manor of Langley Regis.
[23] *V.C.H. Herts.* ii, 240.
[24] *Testa de Nevill* (Rec. Com.), 244; *Cal. Chart. R.* 1226–57, p. 276.
[25] *Hund. R.* (Rec. Com.), i, 41; *Feud. Aids*, i, 77, 103, 132; *Plac. de Quo Warr.* (Rec. Com.), 91. Wavendon was held in dower by Mary widow of John Pever, who died in 1315 (*Cal. Inq. p.m.* [Edw. II], v, 378). At her death about 1333 it reverted to the head of the family (Chan. Inq. p.m. 7 Edw. III [1st nos.], no. 33).
[26] *Cal. Inq. p.m.* (Edw. II), v, 378; Chan. Inq. p.m. 7 Edw. III (1st nos.), no. 33; see also later inquisitions on the Greens.

[27] Feet of F. case 20, file 94, no. 10.
[28] Chan. Inq. p.m. 43 Edw. III (1st nos.), no. 48; *Cal. Close*, 1369–74, p. 48.
[29] Chan. Inq. p.m. 1 Hen. IV, pt. ii, m. 6; Close, 3 Hen. IV, m. 24; Feet of F. Div. Co. East. 4 Hen. V.
[30] Chan. Inq. p.m. 5 Hen. V, no. 41. Both Ralph and his father held the manor of Thomas, Sir Henry Green's eldest son, and of Thomas's son Thomas (ibid. 15 Ric. II, pt. i, no. 24; 1 Hen. IV, pt. ii, m. 6; 5 Hen. V, no. 39).
[31] Ibid. 11 Hen. VI, no. 32.
[32] *Cal. Pat.* 1436–41, p. 264.
[33] Chan. Inq. p.m. 7 Edw. IV, no. 1; G.E.C. *Peerage*, viii, 165.
[34] G.E.C. loc. cit.; Chan. Inq. p.m. 13 Edw. IV, no. 13.
[35] Exch. Inq. p.m. (Ser. 2), file 5, no. 5. Wavendon is not mentioned by name among his lands.
[36] Ibid. file 292, no. 1.
[37] Chan. Inq. p.m. 20 Edw. IV, no. 11; De Banco R. 973, m. 509 d.
[38] De Banco R. 973, m. 509 d. A fourth sister, Constance, aged four in 1493 (Exch. Inq. p.m. [Ser. 2], file 292, no. 1), seems to have died in infancy.

[39] Feet of F. Div. Co. Hil. 31 Hen. VIII; *Visit. of Essex* (Harl. Soc.), 166.
[40] Chan. Inq. p.m. (Ser. 2), xciii, 45.
[41] Memo. R. (Exch. L.T.R.), Hil. 5 Eliz. m. 40. The fine referred to in this document was levied in Easter Term 3 & 4 Philip and Mary (1557). It was not recorded, however, until 1561 (Feet of F. Div. Co. East. 3 Eliz.), after the death of George Browne, the deforciant, who died early in 1559 (Chan. Inq. p.m. [Ser. 2], cxx, 94).
[42] G.E.C. *Peerage*, v, 366; Chan. Inq. p.m. (Ser. 2), cxxxviii, 6. George Browne at his death in February 1558-9 left a son and heir Wistan (Chan. Inq. p.m. [Ser. 2], cxx, 94), who was sued by his step-mother Elizabeth, formerly wife of Sir Henry Hublethorne, for her dower in Wavendon Manor, which had been assured her by a deed of 1557 (Chan. Proc. [Ser. 2], bdle. 82, no. 15).
[43] G.E.C. loc. cit.; Memo. R. (Exch. L.T.R.), Hil. 5 Eliz. m. 40.
[44] Com. Pleas D. Enr. Trin. 13 Eliz. m. 12 d.; Feet of F. Bucks. Trin. 13 Eliz.

and died the same year.[45] George, who was aged fifty at his father's death, seems to have died soon afterwards,[46] as in 1571 Mary and her husband Thomas Wilford conveyed a ninth part of the manor to Henry Charge,[47] and some five years later Christine wife of John Tufton and Katherine Browne (later Roper) conveyed their two-thirds of the third to the same person.[48] Henry Charge, thus seised of the whole manor, died towards the end of 1594 and his daughter Elizabeth and her husband Richard Saunders succeeded him.[49] Saunders died seised of Mordaunts Manor, now so called, in 1639, having settled it in 1621 on his second son William.[50] William Saunders was holding in 1650[51] and was still alive in 1653.[52] The manor was sold by the Saunders family to John Cullen,[53] who obtained other property here in 1672 (see Passelewes Manor). He was sheriff in 1682.[54] Cullen's granddaughter and heir Mary married Robert Isaacson,[55] who was lord here in 1727[56] and 1735.[57] At his death he left two daughters and co-heirs, Arabella, afterwards wife of the Rev. William Denison, Principal of Magdalen College, Oxford,[58] and Mary, who married Roger Altham in 1746.[59] A moiety of the manor was held by each of the heirs.[60] By the Denison marriage settlement of 1759 the children of the marriage were to hold the property as tenants in common,[61] and in 1794 Arabella, a widow since 1786,[62] with her children Anna Maria, Frances, the Rev. William, the Rev. Robert and Thomas, suffered a recovery of their moiety of the manor.[63] The other moiety was similarly settled, and after the death of Mary Altham in 1781[64] and of her husband in 1788[65] was held by their five daughters and heirs, Frances wife of James Heseltine, Arabella wife of John Graham Clarke, Mary wife of Aubone Surtees, Jane wife of Nathaniel Bishop and Charlotte wife of Thomas Lewis.[66] These

SAUNDERS. *Party cheveronwise sable and argent three elephants' heads razed and countercoloured.*

heirs appear to have conveyed their share of the manor to the Denison family. Lysons states that Mrs. Denison held the manor about 1813,[67] and in 1862 William Henry Denison was lord of it.[68] Henry G. Denison held the estate in 1869, but after 1873[69] it passed to Thomas Gadsden, who was returned as lord of the manor in 1877, and until after 1884. The manorial rights disappear after this date, but the greater part of the property was purchased by Messrs. Eastwood & Company, Limited.

The origin of the manor afterwards known as *PASSELEWES* or *PASLOWS MANOR* is obscure. It was held in the 13th century and afterwards of the honour of Clare, which passed through the Earls of Gloucester and the Earls of Stafford[70] to the Duke of Buckingham, who died seised of the overlordship rights in 1460.[71] The last mention of this overlordship occurs in 1619.[72]

There is no Domesday entry for Wavendon to which this holding can be definitely traced.

In 1166 William Passelewe held three fees in the county of Walter Giffard.[73] William appears to have been succeeded by Gilbert Passelewe, who paid relief for three fees in 1170–1[74] and was still alive in 1189–90.[75] Simon Passelewe in 1199 made a life grant to Nicholas Passelewe, his uncle, of a knight's fee in Wavendon with certain reservations, the grant to have effect after the death of Liveva, Simon's mother, who held in dower.[76] Simon was still lord in 1221.[77] Gilbert Passelewe held a fee here as heir to Simon in 1228.[78] Gilbert was succeeded after 1262[79] by William Passelewe, who held this fee in 1314[80]; but he seems to have held only a mesne lordship, which is again mentioned as being held by William Passelewe, described as 'of Bromham' or 'of Holcutt' in 1316[81] and in 1333.[82] Another branch of the same family appears to have been subinfeudated here before 1314[83] and possibly as early as 1275–6.[84] In 1314 Peter Passelewe held the manor in demesne and conveyed it in that year to John Pever,[85] who already held another estate in Wavendon, with which, as has been already stated, the Passelewe manor then descended. They were held together as late as 1417,[86] but appear to have been separated before 1505.[87]

[45] Feet of F. Div. Co. East. 4 Eliz.; Chan. Inq. p.m. (Ser. 2), cxxxvii, 18.

[46] The settlement on him was for ninety-nine years with reversion to his step-sisters and their issue.

[47] Feet of F. Bucks. East. 13 Eliz.

[48] Ibid. East. 18 Eliz.; Trin. 18 Eliz., cf. Recov. R. East. 14 Eliz. m. 1067.

[49] P.C.C. 11 Scott. From her uncle John Charge, who died in June 1594, she inherited part of Lord Mordaunt's *alias* Charge's Wood. He also left 10s. each to the repair of Annot Lane, the church, the bells and the church 'cawsey' (ibid. 2 Scott; Chan. Inq. p.m. [Ser. 2], ccxliii, 23).

[50] Chan. Inq. p.m. (Ser. 2), dcclxviii, 10; c.f. Feet of F. Bucks. East. 17 Jas. I.

[51] Recov. R. Trin. 1650, m. 76.

[52] Add. Chart. 53886.

[53] *Rec. of Bucks.* ix, 51.

[54] P.R.O. *List of Sheriffs*, 9.

[55] Add. MS. 5839, fol. 401.

[56] Recov. R. Hil. 13 Geo. I, m. 266; Feet of F. Bucks. Hil. 13 Geo. I.

[57] Add. MS. 5839, fol. 401.

[58] Com. Pleas Recov. R. East. 34 Geo. III, m. 2.

[59] P.C.C. 468 Calvert.

[60] Recov. R. Mich. 33 Geo. II, m. 412; Trin. 4 Geo. III, m. 20; Feet of F. Bucks. Trin. 4 Geo. III; Recov. R. Hil. 17 Geo. III, m. 41.

[61] Com. Pleas Recov. R. East. 34 Geo. III, m. 2.

[62] *Gent. Mag.* lvi (2), 1000.

[63] Com. Pleas Recov. R. East. 34 Geo. III, m. 2; Recov. R. Hil. 34 Geo. III, m. 182.

[64] *Gent. Mag.* li, 147; cf. Priv. Act, 28 Geo. III, cap. 12.

[65] P.C.C. 468 Calvert; *Gent. Mag.* lviii (2), 937.

[66] Com. Pleas Recov. R. Trin. 41 Geo. III, m. 131; Feet of F. Bucks. Trin. 41 Geo. III.

[67] Lysons, op. cit. i (3), 658.

[68] Sheahan, op. cit. 639.

[69] *Ret. of Owners of Lands* (1873), *Bucks.* 6. W. H. Denison, who was still living at Woburn Sands in 1877, had 41 acres here in 1873, Henry G. Denison owned 132 and K. T. Denison of Emberton had 83.

[70] *Testa de Nevill* (Rec. Com.), 244; *Cal. Inq. p.m.* (Hen. III), i, 152; (Edw. II), v, 342; Chan. Inq. p.m. 11 Edw. II, no. 74; 46 Edw. III, pt. i, no. 62; 10

Ric. II, no. 38; 16 Ric. II, pt. i, no. 27; 22 Ric. II, no. 46; 4 Hen. IV, no. 41.

[71] Chan. Inq. p.m. 38 & 39 Hen. VI, no. 59.   [72] Ibid. (Ser. 2), ccclxxv, 72.

[73] *Red Bk. of Exch.* (Rolls Ser.), 312.

[74] *Pipe R.* 17 Hen. II (Pipe R. Soc.), 60

[75] Hunter, *Gt. R. of the Pipe* 1 Ric. I (Rec. Com.), 32.

[76] Hunter, *Pedes Finium* (Rec. Com.), 186.

[77] *R. of Hugh of Wells* (Cant. and York Soc.), ii, 53.

[78] Ibid. 74; *Testa de Nevill* (Rec. Com.), 244.

[79] *Cal. Inq. p.m.* (Hen. III), i, 158.

[80] Ibid. (Edw. II), v, 342.

[81] Ibid. 378.

[82] Chan. Inq. p.m. 7 Edw. III (1st nos.), no. 33.

[83] Feet of F. case 18, file 65, no. 7.

[84] *Hund. R.* (Rec. Com.), i, 41. At this date Peter held land in Wavendon of John de Wedon, who held of the Earl of Cornwall' (see later under Wahull holding).

[85] Feet of F. case 18, file 65, no. 7; De Banco R. 193, m. 19.

[86] Chan. Inq. p.m. 5 Hen. V, no. 41.

[87] De Banco R. 973, m. 509 d.

In 1560 the manor of Passelewes, first so-called, was held by William Fitz Hugh, who settled it in that year on Robert Fitz Hugh,[88] his son.[89] Robert died seised of the manor in February 1609–10, leaving as heirs his daughter Anne wife of Thomas Cranwell, his grandson Robert Saunders, son of another daughter Frances and of Richard Saunders, and a third daughter Mary wife of William Astrey.[90] Mary died without issue in January 1610–11 [91] and her husband died in 1615, leaving will all his right in Passelewes Manor to his nephew Robert Saunders.[92] In 1622, after the death of Anne Cranwell, Robert Saunders agreed to sell his moiety to Thomas Cranwell and Fitzhugh his son for £625, payable in two instalments before Midsummer 1624.[93] Cranwell, however, was by that time so deeply in debt that he had for the past eighteen months concealed himself from his creditors and could not be found.[94] One of these, Robert Dixon, suing for a debt of £165, stated that Cranwell had conspired with Robert Saunders, John Hatch and Sir Arthur Wilmot, bart., to defraud him.[95] How the matter was settled is uncertain, but Fitzhugh Cranwell appears to have finally inherited the manor, which he sold to Giffard Beale, who held it in 1656.[96] From him it passed in 1672 to John Cullen, and descended to the Denisons and Althams, with the manor formerly Mordaunts, with which it probably became amalgamated, although it is mentioned by its distinctive name of Passelewes as late as 1801.[97]

In connexion with the Passelewe family in this parish it must be noted that in the 13th century Gilbert and Peter successively had another holding here belonging to the honour of Wahull.[98] In 1284–6 William Passelewe held 4 virgates of John Pever, who held of John de Wahull.[99] William held half a fee here in 1316, when he is distinguished by the name of 'William Passelewe of Wavendon' from the 'William Passelewe of Bromham' [100] who at that time was the mesne lord in the Passelewes' chief holding, as explained above.

William Passelewe of Wavendon and Jane his wife dealt with five messuages and 2 carucates of land here in 1325[1] and he is mentioned in 1340 and 1341.[2] He received licence from the bishop to celebrate divine service in an oratory in his house at Wavendon in 1344.[3] In 1346 William Passelewe, jun., held part of a fee here which William Passelewe, sen., had previously held,[4] and which was still held by a William Passelewe in 1387.[5] In 1390 John Passelewe of Wavendon was pardoned for having killed two men and for having broken into a house at Milton Keynes.[6] He held this estate in 1392 [7] and in 1399,[8] while William Passelewe was holding in 1460.[9] There is no further trace of this holding, unless it may be identified with the otherwise unexplained manor of Wavendon which was held between 1485 and 1500 by Thomas Lucas, of Woburn, Bedfordshire, whose daughters Mary and Joan inherited it at his death.[10]

Suen, a man of Earl Harold, had a manor here before the Conquest. In 1086 it was held as 3 hides except 1 virgate of Hugh de Bolebec.[11] This was the manor afterwards known as *THE EARL OF DEVONSHIRE'S FARM* or *MANOR*. From Hugh de Bolebec the overlordship passed to the Earls of Oxford, who at one time held in chief [12]; but a mesne lordship, vested in the holders of the honour of Clare, existed between the Earls of Oxford and the Crown in the 13th and 14th centuries.[13] These overlordships lapsed in the 15th century,[14] and in 1542 Wavendon was attached to the newly created honour of Ampthill.[15] It was stated to be held in chief as late as 1575.[16]

Ansel was tenant here at the time of the Survey.[17] In the latter part of the 13th century Isabel daughter of Hugh de Vere, Earl of Oxford, brought the manor in marriage to her husband John de Courtenay of Okehampton, who died in 1273.[18] The Courtenays, Earls of Devon, continued to hold this manor in demesne with those of Waddesdon and Hillesden (q.v.) until the attainder and forfeiture of Thomas Courtenay fifteenth Earl in 1461.[19] In 1462 a grant of the manor was made by the Crown to William Nevill, Earl of Kent,[20] and, after his death, to George Duke of Clarence and his issue, in

COURTENAY. *Or three roundels gules with a label azure.*

[88] Feet of F. Div. Co. East. 2 Eliz.; cf. Recov. R. Hil. 10 Eliz. m. 103; Chan. Proc. Eliz. B 22, no. 22.

[89] *Visit. of Bucks.* (Harl. Soc.), 164. Thomas Fitz Hugh, who died in 1552 (Chan. Inq. p.m. [Ser. 2], xcvi, 31), left his estate in Wavendon after the death of his wife Jane to his brother, the above William, and the latter's son William. Other property was left to another brother Richard and his son Richard (P.C.C. 26 Powell). By her will dated 16 Aug. 1558, and proved 3 June 1559, Jane left 40s. to the repair of the church or steeple, and made her son Henry Blackwall executor (P.C.C. 24 Chaynay; see also Chan. Proc. Eliz. B 3, no. 27).

[90] Chan. Inq. p.m. (Ser. 2), ccclxxv, 72; P.C.C. 30 Dorset; Chan. Proc. (Ser. 2), bdle. 343, no. 5.

[91] Chan. Inq. p.m. (Ser. 2), ccclxxv, 72.

[92] P.C.C. 96 Rudd.

[93] Chan. Proc. (Ser. 2), bdle. 343, no. 5.

[94] Ibid.   [95] Ibid.

[96] Add. MS. 5839, p. 401; Recov. R. East. 1656, m. 154.

[97] Add. MS. 5839, p. 401; Feet of F. Bucks. Trin. 41 Geo. III.

[98] *Testa de Nevill* (Rec. Com.), 244, 251; *Hund. R.* (Rec. Com.), i, 41.

[99] *Feud. Aids,* i, 83, cf. ibid. 103.

[100] *Cal. Inq. p.m.* (Edw. II), v, 378; William Passelewe of Wavendon had land in Bromham in 1302–3 (*Feud. Aids,* i, 11).

[1] Feet of F. case 19, file 75, no. 8.

[2] *Cal. Pat.* 1340–3, pp. 58, 118.

[3] Add. MS. 5839, p. 400.

[4] *Feud. Aids,* i, 129.

[5] Chan. Inq. p.m. 10 Ric. II, no. 38.

[6] *Cal. Pat.* 1388–92, p. 181.

[7] Chan. Inq. p.m. 16 Ric. II, pt. i, no. 27.

[8] Ibid. 22 Ric. II, no. 46.

[9] Ibid. 38 & 39 Hen. VI, no. 59.

[10] Early Chan. Proc. bdle. 212, no. 38.

[11] *V.C.H. Bucks.* i, 265.

[12] *Testa de Nevill* (Rec. Com.), 247.

[13] Ibid. 251; *Feud. Aids,* i, 83; Chan. Inq. p.m. 51 Edw. III (1st nos.), no. 6.

[14] Chan. Inq. p.m. 7 Hen. V, no. 75; 10 Hen. V, no. 29b. Overlordship rights in Wavendon were, however, claimed by the Earl of Oxford, who died in 1632. (Chan. Inq. p.m. [Ser. 2], dviii, 15).

[15] *L. and P. Hen. VIII,* xvii, 28 (21).

[16] Chan. Inq. p.m. (Ser. 2), clxxii, 147.

[17] *V.C.H. Bucks.* i, 265.

[18] Chan. Inq. p.m. 2 Edw. I, no. 27; see Hillesden. Tenants under the Veres here earlier in the century were the Pevers. Paul Pever (*Testa de Nevill* [Rec. Com.], 251), and afterwards Emma, widow of John Pever, held, but their tenancy appears to have ceased after her death in 1272 (Chan. Inq. p.m. 2 Edw. I, no. 65).

[19] *Hund. R.* (Rec. Com.), i, 41; *Feud. Aids,* i, 110, 129; Feet of F. Div. Co. Mich. 15 Edw. III; *Cal. Pat.* 1340–3, p. 282; Chan. Inq. p.m. 49 Edw. III, pt. i, no. 27; G.E.C. *Peerage,* iii, 104. In 1284–6 William de Bratton held the Courtenays' fee here, as did Nichole de Bratton in 1302–3, but it had returned to the Courtenays by 1316 (*Feud. Aids,* i, 83, 103, 110, 129).

[20] *Cal. Pat.* 1461–7, p. 225.

1463.[21] In 1468, after the duke's rebellion, the king granted Wavendon for life to Hugh Hernage, or Harnage,[22] who died in 1471.[23] In 1472 a life grant of it was made to John Hulcote, the manor being extended at the annual value of £7.[24] In January 1482–3 Hulcote's widow Alice received a life grant,[25] and on her marriage with Thomas Fowler a grant to both in survivorship was made.[26]

Like Waddesdon and Hillesden, Wavendon was later restored to the Courtenays and likewise estreated to the Crown in 1539 on the attainder of the Marquess of Exeter. In that year John Sheppard obtained the site of the manor on a twenty-one years' lease,[27] which was renewed by Edward VI in 1552.[28] In the next year Edward Courtenay, son and heir of the Marquess of Exeter, was created Earl of Devon and restored to his estates by Queen Mary, to whom Wavendon again reverted on his death without issue in 1556.[29] In February 1557–8 a grant in fee was made to John Sheppard, the lessee of 1539.[30] He died in 1561, leaving a widow Joan, who survived him about sixteen months, and four daughters and co-heirs, Jane wife of Thomas Wells, Agnes who afterwards married Richard Moreton, Sibyl wife of William Doggett, and Elizabeth wife of Bernard Turney.[31] Each of these heirs received a fourth of the manor,[32] but the shares of the Turney and Doggett families do not again appear. Agnes Moreton died seised of a third in 1568, leaving two daughters and heirs, Joan and Agnes,[33] who afterwards married Edward Basse and Thomas Fountayne respectively.[34] Agnes Fountayne died in 1592, three years before her father, Richard Moreton, leaving as heir a daughter Olive,[35] who with her husband John Vintner received livery of a moiety of a third of the manor in 1617,[36] a similar portion having been obtained by Joan Basse, widow, in 1611.[37] The main part of Sheppard's manor and the manor house, however, eventually came into the possession of George Wells, aged four at the death of his mother, Jane Wells, in 1564[38]; he received livery of this manor in 1590.[39] He was succeeded by his son John Wells,[1] whose house in Wavendon is referred to in a deed of 1653.[2] John was succeeded by his son George, who died in February 1713–4, leaving his house and lands in

this parish to a brother, Lionel Wells,[3] from whom they passed four years later to his son John,[4] lord in 1735.[5] The property seems afterwards to have come to daughters and co-heirs of the Wells family, as in 1788 Dixie Gregory and his sister-in-law, Ellen Wells, spinster, together claimed manorial rights in Wavendon.[6] This was on the occasion of the passing of the Inclosure Act, but the commissioners appointed afterwards found that the Denison property was the only one in the parish to which manorial rights were still attached.[7]

Lysons states that Mr. Dixie (? Gregory) held this estate in the early 19th century.[8] Possibly it formed part of the lands bought here about this time from several different owners by Henry Hugh Hoare,[9] who succeeded his half-brother in the baronetcy in 1838 and died at Wavendon House in 1841.[10] His Wavendon estates did not pass with the title, as Henry Charles Hoare, his younger son, afterwards held them. He died in 1852.[11] Upon the succession to the baronetcy of his son Henry Ainslie Hoare in 1857, the Wavendon estate passed to Henry Ainslie's uncle, Henry Arthur Hoare,[11a] youngest son of Sir Henry Hugh Hoare, who died in 1873. His son Sir Henry Hugh Arthur Hoare, bart., who succeeded his cousin in the title in 1894, is now one of the chief landowners in the parish.

Some of the Bolebec lands in *WAVENDON* became the property of Woburn Abbey before 1208 by grant of Aubrey de Vere, Earl of Oxford, and Isabel de Bolebec.[12] The abbots continued to hold here of the Earls of Oxford and of other overlords (see below) until the Dissolution.[13] In January 1559–60 the late abbey's manor of Wavendon was granted to Richard Champion and John Thompson and their heirs,[14] and descended with Great Linford (q.v.) in the Thompson family to Sir John Thompson,[15] by whom it was conveyed in 1641 to Henry Chester, William Stone, Arthur Claver and William Smyth.[16]

WOBURN ABBEY.
Azure three bars wavy argent.

[21] *Cal. Pat.* 1461–7, p. 226.
[22] Ibid. 1467–77, pp. 116, 155.
[23] Chan. Inq. p.m. 11 Edw. IV, no. 37.
[24] *Cal. Pat.* 1467–77, p. 327.
[25] Ibid. 1476–85, p. 332. A grant to the Duke of Clarence of the manor of Wavendon was made in 1474 (ibid. 1467–77, p. 457, cf. ibid. p. 529), but appears to have been withdrawn in favour of John Hulcote's widow.
[26] Ibid. 1476–85, pp. 352, 417.
[27] *L. and P. Hen. VIII*, xiv (1), g. 1056 (22).
[28] Pat. 4 & 5 Phil. and Mary, pt. viii, m. 18.
[29] Ibid.; G.E.C. *Peerage*, iii, 107, 109.
[30] Pat. 4 & 5 Phil. and Mary, pt. viii, m. 18.
[31] Chan. Inq. p.m. (Ser. 2), cxxxiv, 188; ccxvi, 73.
[32] Memo. R. (Exch. L.T.R.), Mich. 4 Eliz. m. 74; Fine R. 4 Eliz. m. 32, 34, 35, 53.
[33] Chan. Inq. p.m. (Ser. 2), ccxvi, 73.
[34] Ibid. ccxliii, 55.
[35] Ibid.

[36] Fine R. 15 Jas. I, pt. iii, no. 11.
[37] Ibid. 9 Jas. I, pt. ii, no. 36.
[38] Chan. Inq. p.m. (Ser. 2), clxxii, 147.
[39] Fine R. 32 Eliz. pt. ii, no. 6. William Astrey of Passelewes Manor at his death in 1615 bequeathed to George Wells called of Wavendon, senior, his estate in that part of Holders purchased of Thomas Vintner, John and Olive Vintner, evidently part of the Earl of Devonshire's manor (P.C.C. 96 Rudd).
[1] Add. MS. 5839, p. 402. He appears to have been a younger son, if his father, the George Wells of Wavendon, the elder, above mentioned, is identical with the George Wells the elder who died in 1616 (P.C.C. 110 Cope).
[2] Add. Chart. 53886.
[3] P.C.C. 80 Aston; Add. MS. 5839, p. 402; *Rec. of Bucks.* ix, 51.
[4] P.C.C. 49 Tenison.
[5] Add. MS. 5839, p. 402.
[6] Priv. Act, 28 Geo. III, cap. 12.
[7] Lysons, op. cit. i (3), 658.
[8] Ibid.
[9] It is improbable that the property

sold by Gregory to H. H. Hoare was the Grange as Lipscomb states (iv, 395). The Gregorys were a well-known family in the parish (*Selbyana* [1825], 9; Add. MS. 5839, p. 404), and John Gregory of Wavendon was one of the attorneys empowered by John Style in 1653 to give seisin of the Grange to James Selby (Add. Chart. 53886).
[10] G.E.C. *Baronetage*, v, 256.
[11] Ibid.
[11a] Sheahan, op. cit. 630.
[12] Add. Chart. 6026.
[13] *Testa de Nevill* (Rec. Com.), 258, 262; *Feud. Aids*, i, 104, 129; *Abbrev. Plac.* (Rec. Com.), 258; *Cal. Pat.* 1334–8, p. 493; *Pope Nich. Tax* (Rec. Com.), 48; *Valor Eccl.* (Rec. Com.), iv, 212.
[14] Pat. 2 Eliz. pt. iv, m. 23.
[15] By an agreement of 1584 with her father-in-law, John Thompson, the grantee, Jane wife of Robert Thompson held Wavendon for life (Chan. Inq. p.m. [Ser. 2], dxxv, 118).
[16] Feet of F. Bucks. East. 17 Chas. I. Probably the whole property was not so conveyed (see below).

The last-named appears to have been the William Smyth of Radclive who was created a baronet in 1661, and at whose death in 1696 the baronetcy and lands in Akeley (q.v.) descended to his son Thomas.[17]

SMYTH of Radclive. *Sable a cheveron between six crosses formy fitchy argent with three fleurs de lis azure on the cheveron.*

Wavendon Manor, however, was bequeathed by Sir William Smyth to his godson William, son of his brother John,[18] who appears to have assumed the title on the death without issue in 1732 of his cousin Sir Thomas Smyth, bart., as in his will of 1741 he is described as Sir William Smyth of Warden (co. Bedford), kt. and bart.[19] He left a niece, Martha Lane, and various cousins as heirs.[20] In 1775 one of the original devisees and the heirs of two others suffered a recovery of this manor with a view to barring the entail.[21] They were William Smyth King of Warden (co. Bedford), son of John, son of Margaret, wife of Peregrine King, and sister of Sir Thomas Smyth, bart.; George Pitt Hurst, son of John Hurst and Dorothy, sister of William Smyth King, and, in 1738, wife of Henry Longville; and William Howard of King's Cliffe (co. Northampton) son of Ann King by the Rev. Thomas Howard.[22] By this deed the manor was settled on Smyth King in tail-male with remainder in moieties to Hurst and Howard,[23] who were in possession in 1788.[24] There is no further evidence of this property, but it may have become parcel of the lands bought by H. H. Hoare, and still held by his descendant Sir H. H. A. Hoare, bart.

The grange at Wavendon, the site of the abbey's manor here, and some of the fuller's earth pits, were leased to Richard Hull in 1544 for twenty-one years at £6 5s. per annum.[25] This property was included in the grant to John Thompson,[26] but seems to have been conveyed by him or his heirs to the Worrall family. In 1653 John Style of Steppingley (co. Bedford) and Jane his wife, Jane Worrall of Steppingley, widow, and others sold to James Selby the 'Grange or manor house or messuage in Wavendon in a certain endshippe there called Crosse End.'[27]

James Selby also obtained other lands of this manor.[28] Possibly the third of a manor of Wavendon conveyed to Selby and others in 1660 by John Collins and Lidea his wife[29] represented part of this estate. He married Margaret daughter of John Wells of Wavendon, and was succeeded at his death in 1688 by his son James Selby, serjeant-at-law.[30] This second James died in 1724, leaving an only son Thomas James, who inherited the house and lands at Wavendon.[31] Thomas James Selby, who also held Whaddon (q.v.), died unmarried in 1772. Shortly before his death, in 1767, the Rev. William Cole, in writing of this neighbourhood, described him as a very shy and reserved man, given up to fox-hunting.[32] He added, in reference to his unmarried condition : 'No one can tell where his large Estate will descend. The Alstons are his nearest Relations, but they are half mad.'[33] Nevertheless, by his will, dated 1768, Selby left his Wavendon property, in reversion after the death of Elizabeth Vane, his mistress, to Temperance Bedford, his cousin, whose mother had been a Miss Alston.[34] Miss Bedford married the Rev. Daniel Shipton, rector of Wavendon, who alienated the estate, which passed successively to Robinson Shuttleworth, Lord Charles Fitzroy, and H. H. Hoare.[35]

A survey made in 1549 of the late abbey's property here includes, among the free tenants of the manor, the villagers of Wavendon who held freely a piece of land called 'garden grownde plot' with a messuage called the Townhouse by charter to them and their successors for ever for a rent of 4s. 4½d.[36]

In the 18th century it was stated that the abbey lands were held of the royalty of Brogborough, Bedfordshire, belonging about 1630 to members of the Stone family. They conveyed it about 1702 to the Duke of Bedford, whose family in consequence inherited a quit-rent of £3 per annum.[37] In the Inclosure Act of 1788 the duke claimed, as lord of Brogborough, to be entitled to certain parts of the heath in Wavendon, a claim also put forward by George Pitt Hurst and William Howard.[38]

In 1086 another small manor in a locality not named, consisting of 1 hide and 1 virgate, which Suenihc, a man of Earl Harold, had owned before the Conquest, was in possession of Walter the Fleming and held of him by Fulcuin.[39] The overlordship was afterwards vested in Walter's heirs, the Wahulls, who in their turn held of the Earls of Cornwall.[40]

The tenants in part of this fee were the Abbots of Woburn,[41] with whose other land in Wavendon this doubtless became amalgamated. The holding of the Passelewe family under the honour of Wahull has been already noticed.

---

[17] G.E.C. *Baronetage*, iii, 191.

[18] P.C.C. 40 Pyne ; Wavendon Heath, about 500 acres, on which were pits for fuller's earth, was included in the bequest.

[19] P.C.C. 319 Spurway; G.E.C. *Baronetage*, iii, 191 and note.

[20] P.C.C. 319 Spurway.

[21] Ibid. ; Com. Pleas Recov. R. 770, m. 57 ; Recov. R. Mich. 16 Geo. III, m. 137. A fourth party to the deed of 1775 was Gravely Hurst of London, possibly the son of George.

[22] P.C.C. 40 Pyne ; Com. Pleas Recov. R. 770, m. 57.

[23] Com. Pleas Recov. R. 770, m. 57.

[24] Priv. Act, 28 Geo. III, cap. 12.

[25] *L. and P. Hen. VIII*, xx (1), p. 682 ; Ld. Rev. Misc. Bks. clxxxviii, fol. 315 d.

[26] Pat. 2 Eliz. pt. iv, m. 23. The reversion had already been granted by Edward VI in February 1549–50.

[27] Add. Chart. 53886. Willis states (Add. MS. 5839, pp. 402, 404) that the grange 'belonged to the Gregorys who purchased it of the Thompsons, as did also the Family of Wells.' Lipscomb (iv, 395) says the grange was purchased of Gregory by H. H. Hoare in 1805.

[28] Add. MS. 5839, pp. 402, 404.

[29] Feet of F. Bucks. Trin. 12 Chas. II ; Recov. R. Trin. 12 Chas. II, m. 46.

[30] *Selbyana*, 8–9.

[31] P.C.C. 177 Bolton.

[32] Add. MS. 5839, p. 404.   [33] Ibid.

[34] *Selbyana*, 29 ; P.C.C. 459 Taverner.

[35] *Selbyana*, 29

[36] Ld. Rev. Misc. Bks. clxxxviii, fol. 314. The Townhouse is mentioned seventy years later as separated from the garden of the manor place of Passelewes

by Waldrons *alias* Priest's close (Chan. Inq. p.m. [Ser. 2], ccclxxv, 72).

[37] Add. MS. 5839, p. 402 ; Feet of F. Bucks. East. 1 Anne.

[38] Priv. Act, 28 Geo. III, cap. 12.

[39] *V.C.H. Bucks*. i, 266. Mr. Round, in a note, suggests that this entry refers to Bow Brickhill, owing to subsequent entries in the *Testa de Nevill* and in *Feud. Aids*. In the *Testa de Nevill*, however, the preceding entry refers to Wavendon. In the *Feud. Aids*, although the preceding entry refers to Bow Brickhill, the next parish named, after this and other unnamed holdings have been enumerated, is Wavendon, and the rest of these intervening entries most certainly refer to Wavendon (*Feud. Aids*, i, 83).

[40] *Feud. Aids*, i, 83.

[41] *Testa de Nevill* (Rec. Com.), 244 ; *Feud. Aids*, i, 83.

WAVENDON CHURCH: THE INTERIOR LOOKING EAST

WAVENDON CHURCH FROM THE SOUTH

A family called Bray also held of the Wahull honour in the 13th century, Thomas de Bray and William de Bray in the reign of Henry III,[42] and Nicholas de Bray under the heir of Hugh de Bray in 1284–6.[42a]

Possibly the origin of the manor or reputed manor called *WARDS* in the 16th century may be found in the land, probably the glebeland[43] (see advowson), inherited at the death of Sir Henry Green in 1369 by his eldest son Thomas, called of Greens Norton (co. Northampton).[43a] He also held Heyborne Manor (q.v.) in Lillingstone Dayrell with which this small property descended to the Thomas Green who succeeded in 1417. He died in 1462, leaving a son and heir Thomas,[44] by whom this land was conveyed in 1482 to Thomas Stafford of Tattenhoe[44a] (q.v.). His illegitimate son William Stafford died in 1529 seised of a manor of Wavendon, which he left to his son Thomas.[45] The manor of Wards was held in 1578 by Thomas Stafford and Elizabeth his wife.[46] In 1645 Thomas Hopper and Rose his wife conveyed it to John and James Worrall.[47] James Worrall and Elizabeth his wife held in 1650.[48] There is no further trace of it, but it may be noted that other Worrall property in this parish passed about this time to the Selby family (see above).

Lewin Chava, the king's bailiff, before the Conquest held a hide of land in Wavendon, which he continued to hold of King William in 1086, and a virgate of land was held by Goduin the priest of Lewin of Nuneham.[49]

CHURCH The church of *ST. MARY* consists of a chancel 28 ft. 6 in. by 15 ft. 6 in., nave 53 ft. by 16 ft., north and south aisles, west tower 13 ft. by 12 ft. 6 in., south porch and north vestry. All these measurements are internal.

The nave and chancel show no detail earlier than the 13th century ; the nave was extended westward and aisles thrown out towards the close of that century, and the west tower was built in the 15th century. In 1848–9 there was a complete restoration of the church, and much of the walling was refaced and in places possibly rebuilt ; at the same time the porch and vestry were added.

The chancel has been much modernized. The east window is of four lights with tracery under a pointed head, and the windows and other details in the north and south walls are also modern. The only ancient feature is the chancel arch, which is of late 13th-century date, and is of two chamfered orders with a moulded label on the west side ; the jambs are octagonal with moulded capitals and bases.

The nave arcades are each of four bays ; the arches are pointed, and of two chamfered orders, and have moulded labels on the nave sides ; the columns are of quatrefoil plan, and with the exception of the east respond of the south arcade, which is semi-octagonal, the responds repeat the half-plan of the piers. The two-light clearstory windows are modern. The roof is also modern, but is supported by stone corbels of the 15th century carved with angels holding shields and scrolls. The north and south aisles have modern two-light windows with tracery in pointed heads, and the other details exhibit no points of interest except some pieces of 15th-century glass in the westernmost windows of the north wall of the north aisle and of the south wall of the south aisle. The former is merely a floral design, but the latter has the head of a saint.

The tower is of four stages and has diagonal buttresses at the western angles and plain buttresses at the eastern angles and a staircase in the south-west angle. The tower arch is of three moulded orders, the innermost order resting on semicircular jambs with moulded capitals and bases. The west doorway and window over it belong to the 19th-century restoration. The bell-chamber has a window in each wall of two lights with tracery in a pointed head.

The font is modern. The fine oak pulpit is of late 17th-century date, and is said to have been brought from the church of St. Dunstan-in-the-West, London. It is hexagonal and has cherubs' heads and pendants of fruit and flowers carved at the angles, and the panels are inlaid. In the tower is a large plain oak chest of the 15th or 16th century, with three locks, the middle lock having a carved scutcheon. At the west end of the south aisle is a small oak table of the 17th century in a neglected condition, with legs carved as small Doric columns supporting an entablature.

On the west wall of the modern vestry is a rectangular brass plate with inscription to Richard Saunders (d. 1639), ' whose Ancestors are inter'd at Badleston and Potsgrave in ye County of Bedford,' who married four wives and had twenty-seven children. Above is a lozenge-shaped plate with an achievement of his arms and elephant's head crest. This brass was originally in the chancel. In the south aisle is a plain wall tablet to the memory of William Fisher, captain in the 10th Foot Regiment, who fell at Waterloo ; there are also several memorials to members of the Hoare family, 1841–73.

There is a ring of five bells : the treble is by the Newcomes, 1616, the second by Edward Arnold of Leicester, 1799, the third is inscribed ' Chandler made me 1705,' and the tenor ' Richard Chandler made me 1705,'[49a] while the fourth is by John Briant of Hertford, 1815.

The plate was given by Anne Penelope Hoare in 1849, and consists of two chalices, two patens, two glass cruets, an offertory basin, and a small credence paten.

The registers before 1812 are as follows : (i) baptisms and burials 1567 to 1720, marriages 1569 to 1720 ; (ii) baptisms 1722 to 1811, burials 1722 to 1813, marriages 1722 to 1754 ; (iii) marriages 1754 to 1812. There is also a book of mixed entries of various dates from 1679 to 1753, which was apparently a rough note-book kept by the parish clerk.

ADVOWSON The advowson of the church is mentioned in 1199, when Simon Passelewe excepted it from a grant made to Nicholas his uncle.[50] The patronage

[42] *Testa de Nevill* (Rec. Com.), 250, 251. Hugh de Chastillon held a fee here some time during the same reign (ibid. 258, 262). Unless he held in the right of his wife, Gunnora de Bray (see Leckhampstead), it is not evident what land this was.

[42a] *Feud. Aids*, i, 83 ; a Walter de Bray

dealt with a small portion of land here in 1236 (Feet of F. case 15, file 21), no. 17.

[43] Chan. Inq. p.m. 5 Hen. V., no. 39.

[43a] Ibid. 43 Edw. III. (1st. no.), no. 48 ; Bridges, *Hist and Antiq. of Northants*, i, 240.

[44] Chan. Inq. p.m. 4 Edw. IV., no. 21.

[44a] Close, 334, m. 21.

[45] Chan. Inq. p.m. (Ser. 2), l, 76.

[46] Feet of F. Bucks. Trin. Mich. 20 Eliz.

[47] Ibid. East. 21 Chas. I.

[48] Ibid. Mich. 1650.

[49] *V.C.H. Bucks.* i, 275.

[49a] See *V.C.H. Bucks*, ii, 124.

[50] Hunter, *Pedes Finium* (Rec. Com.), i, 186.

remained in the lords of Passelewes Manor [50a] until 1369, when it passed to Thomas Green with the glebeland afterwards Wards Manor.[51] With Wards it came into the possession of Thomas Stafford,[51a] by whom it was conveyed in 1595 to William Stone, clerk.[52] He was patron in 1602,[53] but afterwards sold the advowson to Robert Norton, who held in 1608.[54] A daughter and heir of William Norton married John Deyos, whose heir sold it to — Gilpin, from whom it was conveyed to John Jeffreys, who became rector of the parish in 1647.[55] It was purchased in 1678 of Jeffrey's heirs by Thomas Stafford, with whose estate at Tattenhoe it passed to the Selby family.[56] Thomas James Selby bequeathed it with his other property here to Temperance Bedford,[57] by whom it appears to have been sold soon afterwards, as William Hampson claimed to be patron in 1788.[58] Robert Gatty and Mary his wife made a conveyance of the rectory in 1806 to John Fisher,[59] whom Gatty had presented the previous year.[60] The next incumbent was presented in 1847 by H. A. Hoare,[61] whose father had obtained the patronage some years before.[62] It is now the property of Sir H. H. A. Hoare.

A vicarage existed here in the early years of the 13th century. In 1221 William son of Robert was presented to it by Gilbert Passelewe 'persona' with the consent of Simon Passelewe, the patron.[63] He was allotted the vicarage-house which Gilbert son of Gilbert Passelewe confirmed to the church, and was to pay synodals, the 'parson' being, however, responsible for all other church expenses.[64] Seven years later another vicar was presented by Gilbert Passelewe, 'parson and patron.'[65] In 1230 Hamo de Stokton was presented by Gilbert Passelewe to the church, 'vacant by the resignation of the said Gilbert, who held it last.'[66] The new incumbent was enjoined to study and to attend schools.[67] Apparently, on the above resignation, the vicarial and rectorial tithes were amalgamated, as no further presentation to a vicarage is found.[68] The church was valued at £10 in 1291[69] and at £26 17s. 4d. in 1535.[70]

In 1721 Peter Gally obtained a grant of the presentation from Selby and presented his son Henry Gally, a classical scholar of some note.[71] Henry Gally resigned, however, and the cure was served until 1742 by the father, Peter, described as 'an old miserable French refugee.'[72]

A quit-rent was paid for an obit here in the 16th century.[73]

CHARITIES   The charity of George Wells, founded by will proved in the P.C.C. 28 April 1714,[74] is endowed with a house at Wavendon let at £9 a year, with two cottages occupied as a schoolmaster's residence, and with a farmhouse and 99 a. 2 r. 3 p. in the parish of Husborne Crawley (co. Bedford), let at £75 a year. The net income is applied in scholarships for children of Wavendon and Woburn Sands and in apprenticing the same. The official trustees also hold a sum of £183 1s. 5d. consols, which is being accumulated until a sum of £245 11s. 4d. consols shall have been attained. (See article on 'Schools.'[75])

The town lands consist of about 10 a. and cottages comprised in a deed of 12 July 1646, producing £25 a year or thereabouts, the objects of the trust being the repairs of the church and highways, and otherwise the benefit of the poor.

The charity founded by will of John Farr consists of an annuity of £1 charged on 3 a. of land in Wavendon, distributable in bread.

James Anderson by his will, proved 4 September 1872, bequeathed £100, the interest to be given to the poor on Christmas Day. The legacy is represented by £107 13s. 5d. consols with the official trustees, producing £2 13s. 8d. yearly. These charities are administered together. In 1912 out of the net income £5 was paid to the church offertory, £5 to the District Council, and £8 was distributed in bread.

The Poor's Coal.—By articles of agreement, entered into by John Duke of Bedford, and carried into effect by an Act of Parliament in 1810, certain lands were vested in the said duke and his heirs, and charged perpetually with a certain quantity of coals of the value of £150, including the carriage, to be yearly placed at the disposal of the parish officers for the use of the poor. In 1911 167 tons of coal were distributed among 115 recipients.

Surveyor's Allotment.—By the Inclosure Act of 1788 two pieces of land containing together about 6 a. were awarded to the surveyor of the highways. In 1883 part of the allotment was sold to the London and North Western Railway Company and the proceeds invested in £136 9s. 4d. consols with the official trustees, producing £3 8s. a year. The remainder of the land, containing 2 a., is let at £8 a year.

The Ecclesiastical District of Woburn Sands, now transferred to Bedfordshire.—The Literary and Scientific Institution was founded by statutory grant, 4 February 1875, by the Rev. Hay Macdowall Erskine. By an order of the Charity Commissioners of 15 December 1891, trustees were appointed and the legal estate was vested in 'the official trustee of Charity Lands.'

[50a] R. of Hugh of Wells (Cant. and York Soc.), ii, 53, 74, 78 ; see under Passelewes Manor.

[51] Cal. Close, 1369–74, p. 48.

[51a] Cf. Early Chan. Proc. bdle. 567, no. 75. A deed of March 1481–2 (Cat. Anct. D, V, 75) records the grant by William Catesby and four others of the next presentation to Richard Maryet and John Brewster, the said Catesby and others being in possession of the manor (i.e. Wards) and advowson of Wavendon by grant of John Palady and Robert Barker, clerks, who had the same of Sir Thomas Billing, chief justice. Billing and other feoffees had presented to Greens Norton church in 1471 (Bridges, op. cit. i, 241).

[52] Feet of F. Bucks. Trin. 37 Eliz.

[53] Add. MS. 5839, p. 404.

[54] Ibid. p. 401.

[55] Ibid. ; Hist. MSS. Com. Rep. vi, App. i, 214b.

[56] Add. MS. 5839, p. 401 ; Inst. Bks. (P.R.O.).

[57] P.C.C. 459 Tavernor.

[58] Priv. Act, 28 Geo. III, cap. 12.

[59] Feet of F. Bucks. Trin. 46 Geo. III.

[60] Inst. Bks. (P.R.O.).

[61] Clergy List.

[62] Ibid. 1841.

[63] R. of Hugh of Wells (Cant. and York Soc.), ii, 53.

[64] Ibid.

[65] Ibid. 74.

[66] Ibid. 78.

[67] Ibid.

[68] In 1308 Adam de Osgodby, parson of Wavendon, sued the Abbot of Woburn for common of pasture in 11 acres called Thiggethorn croft and 7 acres called Eastcroft, of which he said Hamo Passelewe, parson in 1266 (Cal. Pat. 1258–66, p. 539), had been disseised by a former abbot. Eastcroft had been held by Hugh de Bolebec, and both places were inclosed before they came to the abbot (De Banco R. 169, m. 72 ; 173, m. 458 ; 180, m. 116 d).

[69] Pope Nich. Tax. (Rec. Com.), 34.

[70] Valor Eccl. (Rec. Com.), iv, 244.

[71] Add. MS. 5839, p. 404 ; Dict. Nat. Biog.

[72] Add. MS. 5839, p. 404.

[73] Chant. Cert. 5, no. 35.

[74] P.C.C. 80 Aston.

[75] V.C.H. Bucks. ii, 219.

WESTON UNDERWOOD

Westone (xi cent.) ; Weston by Launden, Weston by Olney, Weston Underwode (xiv cent.).

The parish of Weston Underwood has an area of 1,873 acres, of which 477 are arable land, 1,150 permanent grass and 115 woods and plantations.[1] The soil is loam, in places rich, but elsewhere very poor ; the subsoil is clay. The chief crops are wheat, barley, beans and oats. There is a gradual fall in the level of the ground from about 300 ft. in the north to 200 ft. in the south, where the land is liable to floods along the banks of the Ouse.

The Bedford and Northampton branch of the Midland railway runs through the northern end of the parish.

The small but extremely pretty village of Weston Underwood is situated on the road from Northampton to Olney, at the centre of the parish, and lies along a high ridge of ground overlooking the river. It consists principally of stone-built and thatched cottages, and has been frequently described owing to the residence here of the poet Cowper from 1786 to 1795. His house, Weston Lodge, which stands halfway up the street, is a good-sized 17th-century building of stone with a tiled roof, having a small garden in front and a larger one behind, and has been practically unaltered since his day. A low wall and railings separate it from the street. It was at one time occupied by the curate in charge, who paid a rent of a basket of pears from an old pear tree, which gave the house the name of Pear Tree House.[2]

At the south-west end of the village is the church of St. Laurence. To the south of it is a moat, possibly once surrounding the chief messuage which the Pevers had here in 1315.[3] The Manor House, the residence of Lieut.-Col. W. G. Bowyer, R.E., lies at the north-eastern end of the village, about a quarter of a mile up the road leading to Olney and on its south side. It is a stone house with newly added wings, and has to the north of it the school, endowed in 1826 by the lord of the manor.[4] Near by is the site of the old manor-house of the Throckmortons, who resided here for nearly six centuries. The house was partially rebuilt by Robert Throckmorton, who died here in 1721.[5] When it was

pulled down in 1827 it was in a dilapidated condition, and the south part had been uninhabited for over 200 years. The extensive and valuable library, numerous family portraits, and many coats of arms in painted glass were removed to the family's Warwickshire home at Coughton.[6] Nothing now survives of the old house except a small 17th-century building adjoining the stables of Lieut.-Col. Bowyer's house and a pair of stone gate-posts which stand to the north of the house. The former is crowned by a cupola, which contains a good clock.

The Roman Catholic chapel built by the Throckmortons in 1838, after the collapse of a chapel contrived out of a portion of the old building, has a black and white marble pavement which came from the entrance hall of the old Weston House, and occupies

COWPER'S HOUSE, WESTON UNDERWOOD

a portion of its site. The old park belonging to the Throckmortons' house, about 75 acres in extent, contains fine avenues of lime, beech, elm and chestnut trees. It commands varied and extensive views over the Ouse and surrounding country, and its beauties are celebrated in Cowper's verse. It stretches away to the north of the site, from which it is separated by the road leading to Olney. This road was formerly a private one, and was closed at night by the shutting of the iron gates at the Olney and Weston entrances ; only the stone posts of the latter gate are now standing. The old public road passed to the south of the house, but it is now disused except where it joins the village street near where the base of the 15th-century village cross stands.

Noteworthy personalities connected with the parish are George Anderson, Accountant-General to the Board of Control, born here in 1760, and Thomas

---

[1] Statistics from Bd. of Agric. (1905).
[2] Oliver Ratcliff, *Hist. and Antiq. of Newport Hund.* 81.
[3] Chan. Inq. p.m. 9 Edw. II, no. 55.

[4] Lewis, *Topog. Dict.*
[5] Lipscomb, *Hist. and Topog. of Bucks.* iv, 401.
[6] A description of the old mansion, with its priest's hole and attic chapel,

is to be found in Sheahan's *Hist. and Topog. of Bucks.* 637, 641-2, and there is a plate of the building, a quadrangle inclosing a court, in Ratcliffe, *op. cit.* 78.

Scott, commentator on the Bible, curate from 1773 to 1781 at Weston.

MANORS Before the Conquest ten thegns, who could sell, men of Borret, held a manor of 7½ hides in *WESTON*, a man of Alric, also able to sell, holding 3 virgates there. This manor was held in 1086 by the Bishop of Coutances,[6a] after whose rebellion in 1088 it was forfeited to the Crown. Weston Underwood was afterwards divided into two portions, corresponding to the manors held by the Nowers and Pevers,[7] each owing half a fee, in the 12th and 13th centuries,[8] though in the later 13th century and during the 14th century the service rendered varied from one-fourth to one-tenth fee.[9] The overlordship rights over both portions were obtained by William Brewer,[10] whose son William succeeded him about 1227[11] and died five years later without issue. The interest in Weston Underwood devolved on his sisters, Margaret wife of William de Ferte and Isabel wife of Baldwin Wake.[12] Gundred, daughter and heir of the Fertes, married Payn de Chaworth (Churches, Chaorciis, Cadurcis),[13] and their son Patrick[14] claimed rights in both manors in Weston Underwood, as part of the honour of Chaworth, in the middle of the 13th century.[15] The Wakes' interest was confined to the Pevers' manor, Baldwin Wake, the overlord in 1279,[16] dying in 1282,[17] when his son, John Wake of Liddell, succeeded.[18] He was summoned to Parliament as a baron in 1295 and died in 1300.[19] His son Thomas Wake exercised these rights until his death in 1349,[20] after which the connexion of the Wakes with Weston appears to have ceased.

An intermediary lordship was held under the Brewers and their successors by the Bidun family, of whom John de Bidun is mentioned in the reign of Henry I.[21] After the death of the last John de Bidun without issue the barony was divided among his five sisters and co-heirs,[22] of whom the eldest, Amice wife of Henry de Clinton,[23] obtained the rights in Weston Underwood which she was exercising as early as 1222.[24] Her interest devolved on the Clintons[25] and the connexion of the honour of Bidun with both manors was maintained until the early 14th century at least,[26] the John de Beauchamp of Wotton who

held under the Wakes in the Pevers' manor in 1279[27] probably representing a younger branch of the Biduns.[28] After 1300 the overlordship of the Nowers' manor is obscure ; it was held of Baldwin Nevill in 1309,[29] of Geoffrey de Say in 1317,[30] and of William Eydon in 1327.[31] By 1518 the two manors appear to have amalgamated, and were then held of Lord Zouche,[32] to whom the Pevers' portion had come partly by inheritance and partly by purchase. By 1615 the king had replaced the Zouches as overlord, and Weston Underwood was then attached to his manor of Hampstead.[33]

Half of the Domesday manor was granted by John de Bidun in the reign of Henry I to Ralf de Nowers, who was still holding in 1166.[34] His descendant Aumary de Nowers was sued in 1222 by Amice de Clinton, mesne lord between Nowers and William Brewer, for service in the king's army at Bytham Castle in Lincolnshire, which was raised to suppress forces of William de Albemarle in 1220.[35] The Nowers were lords of Gayhurst (q.v.), with which this manor descended[36] to the last John de Nowers, against whom John Barker of Olney, merchant, obtained judgement in 1361 for the recovery of £20.[37] The sequel is probably to be found in the transfer of the manor two years later to Barker for the yearly rent of 8 marks,[38] which rent was quitclaimed to him in the following year by John de Nowers.[39] John Barker of Olney, who appears to be identical with John de Olney, described in 1371 as 'marchaunt' of Weston,[40] in 1375 obtained permission for himself and his wife Denise to have a portable altar and to choose their confessor.[41] John Olney had died before 1396,[41a] and had been succeeded by his son John, then holding the manor with his mother Denise, Sir Richard Abburbury and John Olney of London, the reversion belonging to himself.[42] On 11 May 1420 he made his will, which was proved on 2 December 1422.[43] He was survived by his wife Margery, to whom in 1439 Robert Nevill of Gayhurst, son of one of the Nowers heirs (see Gayhurst), released all right in the manor.[44] John Olney's successor was Robert Olney, probably his son, who in 1434, as Robert Olney of Weston, was required to take the oath not to maintain peace-breakers.[45] In 1446 Robert Olney's daughter

---

[6a] *V.C.H. Bucks.* i, 240.
[7] In 1279 each manor was assessed at 3 hides (*Hund. R.* [Rec. Com.], ii, 349, 350).
[8] *Red Bk. of Exch.* (Rolls Ser.), 332 ; *Testa de Nevill* (Rec. Com.), 244, 251, 259 ; *Hund. R.* (Rec. Com.), ii, 349, 350.
[9] *Feud. Aids,* i, 74, 105, 131 ; *Cal. Inq. p.m.* (Edw. II), v, 63, 377 ; Chan. Inq. p.m. 1 Edw. III (1st nos.), no. 69 ; Inq. a.q.d. file 130, no. 9.
[10] Maitland, *Bracton's Note Bk.* ii, 165.
[11] Dugdale, *Baronage,* i, 702.
[12] Ibid. ; *Cal. Close, 1231–4,* pp. 228, 229.
[13] *Excerpta e Rot. Fin.* i, 239.
[14] Dugdale, op. cit. i, 517.
[15] *Testa de Nevill* (Rec. Com.), 244, 251 ; cf. *Feud. Aids,* i, 105.
[16] *Hund. R.* (Rec. Com.), ii, 350.
[17] *Cal. Inq. p.m.* (Edw. I), ii, 262.
[18] G.E.C. *Peerage,* viii, 35 ; *Feud. Aids,* i, 74.
[19] G.E.C. loc. cit. ; Chan. Inq. p.m. Edw. I, file 94, no. 3.
[20] *Cal. Inq. p.m.* (Edw. II), v, 377 ; Chan. Inq. p.m. 17 Edw. II, no. 67 ; 23 Edw. III (1st nos.), no. 75.

[21] *Red Bk. of Exch.* (Rolls Ser.), 332.
[22] Chan. Inq. p.m. Hen. III, file 16, no. 18.
[23] Maitland, *Bracton's Note Bk.* ii, 498 ; iii, 316.
[24] Maitland, op. cit. ii, 165 ; *Testa de Nevill* (Rec. Com.), 258, 259.
[25] *Hund. R.* (Rec. Com.), ii, 349 ; *Feud. Aids,* i, 74.
[26] *Feud. Aids,* i, 105.
[27] *Hund. R.* (Rec. Com.), ii, 350.
[28] Maitland, op. cit. ii, 498 ; Chan. Inq. p.m. Hen. III, file 16, no. 18. The Earl of Gloucester laid claim to the overlordship of this and most of the other Pever manors in 1272 (Chan. Inq. p.m. 2 Edw. I, no. 65), but had apparently no legal title.
[29] *Cal. Inq. p.m.* (Edw. II), v, 63.
[30] Inq. a.q.d. file 130, no. 9. He was also overlord of the Nowers' manor of Gayhurst.
[31] Chan. Inq. p.m. 1 Edw. III (1st nos.), no. 69.
[32] Ibid. (Ser. 2), xxxiii, 46.
[33] Ibid. ccclxvii, 100.
[34] *Red Bk. of Exch.* (Rolls Ser.), 332.
[35] Maitland, op. cit. ii, 165.

[36] Assize R. 68, m. 37 ; *Testa de Nevill* (Rec. Com.), 251 ; *Hund. R.* (Rec. Com.), i, 38 (where Lady Joan de Nowers is said to hold 20 acres of land of the assart of wood of Chemenhey) ; ibid. ii, 349 ; *Feud. Aids,* i, 74, 105, 110 ; see also p. 131, which gives Joan widow of John de Nowers as lady of Weston in 1346. Grace, however, was the name of the widow of the John de Nowers who died in 1327 (Chan. Inq. p.m. Edw. III, file 98, no. 9), and Agnes that of the widow of her son John, who was dead by 1349. (Ibid. 44 Edw. III. (2nd nos.) no. 15).
[37] *Cal. Close,* 1360–4, p. 257.
[38] Ibid. 548.   [39] Ibid. 1364–8, p. 54.
[40] Ibid. 1369–74, p. 332.
[41] *Cal. of Papal Letters,* iv, 204, 216.
[41a] See M. I.
[42] Close, 20 Ric. II, pt. i, m. 31 d. As John Olney the younger of Weston he appeared in 1400 as executor of the will of John Olney the elder, late citizen and woolman of London (*Cal. Pat.* 1399–1401, p. 314).
[43] P.C.C. 55 Marche.
[44] Close, 17 Hen. VI, m. 9.
[45] *Cal. Pat.* 1429–36, p. 397.

Margaret married Thomas Throckmorton,[46] who died in 1472.[47] Their son Robert, who succeeded,[48] died abroad on a pilgrimage to the Holy Land in 1518 and was succeeded by his son Sir George Throckmorton.[49]

OLNEY. *Argent a battled fesse between six crosslets fitchy gules with three crescents argent on the fesse.*

THROCKMORTON. *Gules a cheveron argent charged with three gimel bars sable.*

Sir George bequeathed the manor to his son Robert and the latter's second wife Elizabeth, widow of Lord Hungerford, on 20 July 1552, and died at the Throckmortons' Warwickshire seat at Coughton on 6 August following.[50] His son Sir Robert, whose wife Lady Elizabeth was buried at Weston in January 1553–4,[51] was dealing with the manor in 1567.[52] He was succeeded in February 1580–1 by his son Thomas,[53] who with Margaret his wife and John his son and heir-apparent was dealing with the manor in 1598.[54] John Throckmorton died in February 1603–4, leaving a son and heir Robert, upon whom his grandfather Thomas made a settlement.[55] Thomas died in March 1614–15 and was succeeded by Robert,[56] to whom licence to travel for three years had been granted on 25 March 1608,[57] the Throckmortons being Papist recusants. He petitioned in 1629 for confirmation to himself and his heirs of courts leet, view of frankpledge and other privileges enjoyed by him in his manor of Weston Underwood,[58] and in 1637, as a recusant, obtained a licence to grant and lease any part of the manor (then stated to be of the clear yearly value of £40, the king's two parts thereof being worth £26 13s. 4d.) for forty-one years.[59] On 1 September 1642 he was created a baronet.[60] He 'kept a bountiful house at Weston,'[61] which was sequestered in 1647,[62] and suffered much for his loyalty to the king. He died in 1650 and was succeeded by his son Sir Francis Throckmorton, who was dealing with the manor in 1670[63] and at his death in 1680 was buried at Weston.[64] His eldest son Francis had died four

years before, at the age of sixteen, at Bruges, his heart being buried at Weston.[65] His younger brother Robert, who succeeded to the manor, was admitted to Gray's Inn in 1683[66] and was dealing with Weston in 1684.[67] He was a Roman Catholic nonjuror, distinguished for his great charity and benevolence. His son Sir Robert succeeded him in March 1720–1 and made a settlement of the manor in 1723[68] and again in 1748 on the marriage of his only son and heir George with Anne Maria Paston.[69] George died in the lifetime of his father, and his second but eldest surviving son John Courtenay Throckmorton, then of Weston Underwood and the heir-apparent of his grandfather, was dealing with the manor in 1782[70] and succeeded his grandfather in 1791. John Courtenay Throckmorton, who was the friend of Cowper and the Benevolus of *The Task*, died childless in 1819.[70a] He was succeeded by his brother Sir George Courtenay Throckmorton, who seems to have held the manor during his brother's lifetime.[71] He died here in 1826, also childless, and was succeeded by his brother Sir Charles Throckmorton, the seventh baronet.[71a] Sir Charles pulled down the old manor-house shortly after his succession to the property,[72] and made a settlement of the manor in 1826 on his nephew Robert George Throckmorton,[73] by whom he was succeeded in the baronetcy at his death without issue in 1840.[74] Sir Robert George Throckmorton was succeeded in 1862 by his son Sir Nicholas William George Throckmorton. The manor was sold by him in 1898 to Lieut.-Col. Wentworth Grenville Bowyer, who now holds it.[75]

A windmill was included among the appurtenances of the Nowers Manor in 1278[76] and in 1309,[77] and rights to a free fishery were claimed by the lords of the manor in 1723[78] and 1782.[79]

The other half of the Domesday Manor was sub-infeudated by John de Bidun in the reign of Henry I to Robert Curtfaluz (Curifale, Curtfelun, Curcefalur), who was in possession in 1166,[80] and was fined 2 marks in 1176 for a breach of the forest law.[81] His descendant, Simon Curtfaluz, left a son Robert,[82] who held about 1235.[83] He transferred 1 carucate to Peter de Mora, from whom it was obtained in 1244 for 100 marks by Paul Pever, Robert Curtfaluz confirming the grant, and bestowing upon Pever the reversion of the land then held by Olive widow of his father Simon.[84] Paul Pever was to render all services due, but this clause notwithstanding it was said in 1275 that suit of court and hundred had been abstracted

[46] Add. MS. 5839, p. 405.
[47] Chan. Inq. p.m. 12 Edw. IV, no. 33.
[48] Court R. (Duchy of Lanc.), bdle. 1, no. 7.
[49] Chan. Inq. p.m. (Ser. 2), xxxiii, 46. A letter from Sir Geo. Throckmorton to Thomas Cromwell was dated at Weston in 1535 (*L. and P. Hen. VIII*, viii, 90).
[50] Chan. Inq. p.m. (Ser. 2), xcviii, 75.
[51] Add. MS. 5839, p. 410.
[52] Feet of F. Bucks. East. 9 Eliz.
[53] Chan. Inq. p.m. (Ser. 2), cxciii, 89.
[54] Feet of F. Bucks. Mich. 41 Eliz.
[55] Chan. Inq. p.m. (Ser. 2), ccclxvii, 100 ; Feet of F. Bucks. East. 1 Jas. I.
[56] Chan. Inq. p.m. (Ser. 2), ccclxvii, 100.
[57] Cal. S. P. Dom. 1603–10, p. 418.
[58] Ibid. 1625–49, p. 345.
[59] Pat. 13 Chas. I, pt. xxiii, m. 7.

[60] G.E.C. *Complete Baronetage*, ii, 197.
[61] Ibid.
[62] Cal. Com. for Comp. 68.
[63] G.E.C. op. cit. ii. 198 ; Feet of F. Div. Co. Hil. 21 & 22 Chas. II.
[64] M.I. in church.
[65] Ibid.
[66] G.E.C. *Complete Baronetage*, ii, 198.
[67] Feet of F. Div. Co. Hil. 36 & 37 Chas. II ; Recov. R. Trin. 36 Chas. II, m. 226. See also Chan. Proc. (Bridges Div.) bdle. 163, no. 41.
[68] G.E.C. loc. cit. Recov. R. Mich. 10 Geo. I, m. 236.
[69] Com. Pleas Recov. R. Trin. 21 & 22 Geo. II, m. 118, 120.
[70] Recov. R. East. 22 Geo. III, m. 151 ; Com. Pleas Recov. R. Trin. 22 Geo. III, m. 280.
[70a] G.E.C. loc. cit.

[71] Lysons, *Mag. Brit.* i (3), 661.
[71a] G.E.C. loc. cit.
[72] Sheahan, op. cit. 637.
[73] Com. Pleas Recov. R. 974, m. 28 ; Recov. R. Trin. 7 Geo. IV, m. 184 ; Mich. 7 Geo. IV, m. 262.
[74] G.E.C. op. cit. ii, 199.
[75] Ratcliff, op. cit. 77. Many documents dealing with the manor are among the Throckmorton documents at Coughton (*Hist. MSS. Com. Rep.* iii, App. 256).
[76] Hund. R. (Rec. Com.), ii, 349.
[77] Chan. Inq. p.m. 2 Edw. II, no. 70.
[78] Recov. R. Mich. 10 Geo. I, m. 236.
[79] Ibid. East. 22 Geo. III, m. 151.
[80] Red Bk. of Exch. (Rolls Ser.), 332.
[81] Pipe R. 22 Hen. II (Pipe R. Soc.), 23.
[82] Feet of F. case 15, file 27, no. 6.
[83] Testa de Nevill (Rec. Com.), 244.
[84] Feet of F. case 15, file 27, no. 6.

and 9s. hidage unpaid for the last twenty-four years,[85] and a similar complaint was made in 1276.[86] There was considerable dissension between the Pevers and the former owners, and in 1261–2 Hawise daughter of William de Sherington and widow of Robert Curtfaluz brought an unsuccessful action to recover dower in Weston[87]; in 1275 the land was taken into the king's hand for default against Henry Curtfaluz.[88] The Curtfaluz claim was renewed in 1286 in the person of Alice wife of Simon son of John, and heir of Robert Curtfaluz, her uncle. She contended that Peter de Mora had a lease only of the estate, here extended at a messuage, 24 acres land, 7 acres meadow and 4s. rent.[89] The Pevers successfully contested these suits and claimed view of frankpledge in 1279 and 1286 as held from the time of Paul Pever, the purchaser of the manor.[90] He had also obtained Chilton (q.v.), with which Weston Underwood descended[91] to the John Broughton who succeeded his grandfather Thomas Pever in 1429.[92] A settlement of half the manor had been made by the latter in 1389,[93] apparently on his daughter Mary, mother of John Broughton, who by her second husband Richard Lord St. Maur had a daughter Alice, wife of William Lord Zouche.[94] In 1430 Alice obtained from her half-brother John Broughton, here called John Pever, a renunciation of rights in this half manor.[95] It remained in the Zouche family, as did Chilton, and the other half was doubtless acquired by them after the death in 1489 of John Broughton, who alludes to it in his will as 'my manor called Yongis in Weston.'[96] It appears to be the whole manor with which the Zouches were dealing in 1501,[97] but it had passed before 1518 to the Throckmortons, lords of the Nowers' manor (q.v.), the Zouches retaining merely a nominal interest.[98]

Three virgates and two-thirds of a virgate held before 1086 by two thegns, men of Borret, and a virgate held at that date by another thegn, a man of Alric son of Goding, were included among the lands of the Count of Mortain in 1086,[99] and were later held of that part of the honour of Berkhampstead[100] known as the little fee of Mortain,[1] in virtue of which the Earl of Cornwall claimed view of frankpledge here in 1279.[2] The last mention of the connexion with the honour of Berkhampstead occurs in 1649.[3]

In 1086 the count had an under-tenant, Ivo.[4] A 13th-century successor was Hugh son of Walter, whose holding in Weston amounted to a hide of land.[5] Another son of Walter, Adam, to whom William de Fering quitclaimed half a virgate of land in Weston in 1238,[6] may have been identical with Adam de Furtho who held 40 acres in Weston of the honour of Berkhampstead in 1279,[7] perhaps by inheri-

tance from his brother. Adam de Furtho remained in possession of this estate, returned at 4 virgates in 1284,[8] until some time after 1316,[9] when he was succeeded by William de Furtho, who held in 1346.[10]

Three virgates in Weston which had been held before the Conquest by Ulvric, a man of Earl Waltheof, who could sell, were assessed in 1086 among the lands of the Countess Judith and held of her by Anschitil.[11] Her possessions afterwards became known as the honour of Huntingdon, to which half a virgate in Weston in the tenure of Ellis son of Richard of Weston was appurtenant in 1279.[12]

The third part of half a fee in Weston was held in the 13th century by Simon de Ravenstone of the Earl of Albemarle.[13] It was possibly part of this property which Adam de Ravenstone and his wife Alice held in Weston in 1250.[14]

Sir William Andrews, bart., of Denton (co. Northampton) held property in Weston Underwood in 1647, which was sequestered for his delinquency, two-thirds of it being leased to Thomas Tripp of Olney for £73 6s. 8d.[15] This was held by his son, Sir John Andrews, bart., in 1649.[16]

The priory of Ravenstone held messuages and rents in Weston, which at the Dissolution were given to Cardinal Wolsey, and after his attainder were granted to the Dean and Canons of St. George's Chapel, Windsor, in 1532,[17] the king also granting rent from the same property to Sir Francis Bryan in 1535.[18]

In 1279 property in Weston was held by the hospital of St. John, Northampton, and by Lavendon Abbey,[19] the latter acquiring further property in 1344[20] and 1367.[21]

The church of *ST. LAURENCE CHURCH* consists of a chancel 28 ft. 6 in. by 15 ft., nave 44 ft. by 17 ft., north aisle 9 ft. wide, south aisle 10 ft. wide, west tower 10 ft. 6 in. square, and a north porch. All these measurements are internal.

The nave probably incorporates part of the walling of a 12th century church to which aisles were added about the middle of the 13th century. The chancel arch was rebuilt in the first half of the 14th century, but by the middle of the century the condition of the fabric must have become very unsatisfactory, as its restoration was undertaken by John Olney, lord of the manor, about 1368, in which year the church was refounded.[22] The rebuilding of the chancel was probably the only work accomplished by this date, but the reconstruction of the rest of the building appears to have been continued during the next twenty years, the nave arcades being rebuilt, largely with the old material, the clearstory added, and new windows inserted in both aisles. The tower and

[85] *Hund. R.* (Rec. Com.), i, 37.
[86] Ibid. 45 ; cf. also Assize R. 68, m. 37.
[87] Assize R. 58, m. 11 d., 16 d.
[88] *Cal. Close*, 1272–9, p. 230.
[89] Assize R. 68, m. 9 d.
[90] *Hund. R.* (Rec. Com.), ii, 350 ; *Plac. de Quo Warr.* (Rec. Com.), 91.
[91] See also *Feud. Aids*, i, 74, 105, 110, 131.
[92] Chan. Inq. p.m. 8 Hen. VI, no. 21.
[93] Feet of F. case 21, file 107.
[94] G.E.C. *Peerage*, vii, 24.
[95] Close, 8 Hen. VI, m. 1.
[96] P.C.C. 18 Mills.
[97] De Banco R. 958, m. 118.

[98] Chan. Inq. p.m. (Ser. 2), xxxiii, 46.
[99] *V.C.H. Bucks.* i, 246.
[100] *Testa de Nevill* (Rec. Com.) 244 ; *Hund. R.* (Rec. Com.), ii, 350 ; *Feud. Aids*, i, 74, 77 ; Chan. Inq. p.m. 28 Edw. I. no. 44 ; Court R. (Gen. Ser.), ptf. 177, no. 14.
[1] *Feud Aids*, i, 107, 133.
[2] *Hund. R.* (Rec. Com.), ii, 350.
[3] Ct. R. (Gen. Ser.), portf. 177, no. 21.
[4] *V.C.H. Bucks.* i, 246.
[5] *Testa de Nevill* (Rec. Com.), 244b.
[6] Feet of F. Bucks. 12 Hen. III, no. 40.
[7] *Hund. R.* (Rec. Com.), ii, 350.
[8] *Feud. Aids*, i, 74.
[9] Ibid. 107, 110.

[10] Ibid. 133.
[11] *V.C.H. Bucks.* i, 273.
[12] *Hund. R.* (Rec. Com.), ii, 350.
[13] *Testa de Nevill* (Rec. Com.), 244, 252.
[14] Feet of F. case 16, file 30, no. 7.
[15] *Cal. Com. for Comp.* 67, 1739, 1740.
[16] Feet of F. Bucks. Mich. 1649.
[17] *L. and P. Hen. VIII*, v, 1351.
[18] Ibid. viii, g. 481 (31).
[19] *Hund. R.* (Rec. Com.), ii, 350.
[20] *Cal. Pat.* 1343–5, p. 333.
[21] *Abbrev. Rot. Orig.* (Rec. Com.), ii, 295.
[22] See under advowson and M. I. in the church.

Weston Underwood Church from the North-West

WESTON UNDERWOOD CHURCH: THE INTERIOR LOOKING EAST

north porch were added about the middle of the 15th century. The church was restored in 1891.

All the details of the chancel are of about 1368. The east window is of three cinquefoiled lights with elaborate tracery under a pointed head and is a typical example of the period. In the tracery is a considerable quantity of old glass comprising the following subjects : a bishop with nimbus ; St. Peter ; St. John Baptist ; St. John Evangelist with a chalice and serpent ; St. Lawrence with a gridiron ; St. Paul with a sword ; the Ascension ; a piece with a censing angel on either side of the last subject, one probably modern ; and two pieces, each painted with a yellow and white rose with a blue band on a red background with white and yellow borders. In each side wall are two pointed windows, both of two cinquefoiled lights with quatrefoiled tracery in the head. The western windows are transomed and prolonged downwards to form low-side lights, now blocked, and the sill of the south-east window is lowered internally to form a sedile. The north-east window contains some original glass with canopy work, while the two south windows have foliated and floral designs. There is a contemporary doorway between the windows on the north side and in the north-east corner is a plain aumbry of uncertain date. Near the sedile is a large piscina with a pointed and cinquefoiled head and a basin of eight foils. The early 14th-century chancel arch, which is of two chamfered orders, probably contains re-used material from an earlier arch. The jambs are chamfered, and the inner order rests on triple shafts with moulded bases and capitals.

The nave has on each side an arcade of four bays, with chamfered arches and circular columns, with moulded capitals and bases. The westernmost columns and the chamfered west responds are of 13th-century date, but the remainder, with the semicircular eastern responds, are Olney's work of 1368 and are partly built of earlier material. The capitals and bases are moulded. At the north-east of the nave is the upper doorway to the rood-loft, the stairs to which have been removed. The late 14th-century clearstory windows, three on each side, are each of two trefoiled lights, with quatrefoil tracery in a pointed head. Both the chancel and nave have flat plastered ceilings.

The north aisle is lighted from the north by two square-headed late 14th-century windows, each of three trefoiled lights with vertical tracery in the head, and the south aisle has two corresponding windows of the same date and design. Both aisles have doorways between the windows, the north doorway being of the late 14th century, while the south doorway is of the 13th century. The aisle roofs contain some old timbers.

The 15th-century tower is of two stages and has diagonal buttresses, a north-west staircase, and an embattled parapet. The tower arch is of two chamfered orders. In the west wall of the ground stage is a restored doorway with a pointed head, and above it is a pointed window of two cinquefoiled lights with tracery, also much restored. The bell-chamber is lighted by four two-light windows of the same character.

The north porch has a moulded entrance archway, and in each side wall is a single trefoiled light.

The font is of the 15th century and has an elaborate octagonal tapering bowl. In each face of the octagonal stem is a trefoiled ogee-headed panel containing a shield of arms : (1) a cheveron with three fleurs de lis thereon, for Pever ; (2) a chief indented ; (3) an embattled fesse between six crosslets fitchy with three crescents on the fesse, for Olney ; (4) a plain fesse ; (5) an embattled fesse with three crosslets fitchy in the chief ; (6) a plain cross, for Hussey ; (7) an embattled fesse with a pierced molet thereon ; (8) two bars with three roundels in chief, for Hungerford. The pyramidal wooden cover is of the 17th century.

The late 17th-century communion table has twisted legs, and the communion rail of the same date is moulded and has twisted balusters. At the east end of the north aisle is a plain iron-bound chest with the initials IH on the top and the date 1662 on the front marked in nail-heads.

Nailed to the modern boarded floor of the chancel is an inscription on strips of brass to John Olney, kt., and his wife Denise, 1395. The inscription is in Latin but very defective,[23] and the strips are fixed in the wrong order. At the four corners are the symbols of the Evangelists. There were probably brass figures within the inscription, but they have disappeared, and the only remaining portion is a brass shield bearing an embattled fesse. At the east end of the floor of the south aisle is the brass figure of a lady in an embroidered gown with slashed sleeves, the head missing ; beneath is an inscription to Elizabeth (d. 1553) daughter of Lord Hussey, wife of (1) Walter Lord Hungerford, and (2) Robert Throckmorton. There are also a group of five daughters and four shields of arms : (1) Throckmorton ; (2) Hussey ; (3) Throckmorton with six quarterings impaling Hussey and Fortescue ; (4) Hungerford impaling Hussey ; and the indent for a fifth shield now missing. On the east wall of the same aisle is a large monument of marble to (1) Thomas Throckmorton, 1614 ; (2) Sir Francis Throckmorton, kt. and bart., 1680 ; (3) Francis son of the last (d. at Bruges, his heart buried here, 1676) ; (4) Robert son of Sir Robert Throckmorton, bart., 1688 ; (5) Sir George Throckmorton, bart., 1826 ; and (6) his wife Catherine, 1839. In the same aisle are mural tablets to members of the Higgins, Chapman and Ruck families, 1726 to 1819 ; in the north aisle are three Higgins tablets, 1792 to 1802, and a floor slab to Dorothy wife of John Frasie, 1709. In the north porch are two slabs to Ann Butcher, 1729, and Mary wife of Charles Bennet, 17—. In the chancel is a tablet to the Rev. John Buchanan, friend of the poet Cowper (d. 1826).

There are six bells : the first five by Henry & Matthew Bagley, 1687 ; the tenor by William Emerton of Wootton, 1779. The bells were rehung in 1914.

The plate includes a cup and paten of 1700.

The registers previous to 1812 are as follows ; (i) baptisms and burials 1681 to 1775, marriages 1681 to 1753 ; (ii) baptisms 1782 to 1812 ; (iii) marriages 1754 to 1812.

ADVOWSON The chapel of Weston Underwood, which was annexed to the parish church of Olney, was founded anew in

[23] The full inscription is given in Lipscomb, op. cit. iv, 405. The Latin is obscure, but the date is rather 1395 than 1405. The inscription records that he made the old chapel into a parish church. Cf. Add. MS. 5839, p. 409.

1368. The parishioners thereupon refused to attend the church at Olney, claiming that the rector, then one Adam, was bound to provide them at his own cost with a priest in their chapel at Weston. The official of the court of Canterbury had decided against the rector and excommunicated him for non-compliance with the order, notwithstanding an appeal of Adam to Rome.[24] The dissension continued until 1376, when a papal bull was obtained according to the right of burial to the chapel, in which all the other sacraments were administered.[25] The successful petitioners were the parishioners and John Olney, then lord of the manor, to whom is due the rebuilding of the chapel, he having found it small and in ruins.[26] The right of presentation remained in the rectors of Olney, who were responsible for the stipend of the priest,[27] but the appointment of the latter was reserved in the 16th and early 17th-century leases of Olney rectory.[28] The Pigotts, who obtained Olney rectory in the spring of 1610, appear to have retained Weston chapel when they alienated Olney,[29] but by 1670 the advowson of this perpetual curacy was vested in the lord of Weston Underwood Manor,[30] with which it has since descended.[31]

The will, dated 1420, of John Olney, lord of the manor, and son of the re-founder of 1368, directed that his body should be buried in the chapel of our Lady in the church of Saint Nicholas of Weston,[32] but the dedication is now to St. Laurence.

At the suppression of the chantries lands and rents worth 8d. yearly given for the keeping of a lamp, and a rent of 6d. from a tenement, given for an obit, were recorded.[33] In 1552 the land formerly devoted to the maintenance of the lamp was bestowed on Sir Edward Bray.[34]

A messuage called the Chapel House lately belonging to the chantry in Olney Church was granted to Sir George Howard in 1560.[35]

CHARITIES

The parochial charities were amalgamated by a scheme of the Charity Commissioners of 24 January 1893, comprising the following charities, namely :—

1. The Feoffee Estate Charity, endowed with 6 a. and cottages purchased in 1695 with legacies by will of Thomas Porter and Mrs. Elizabeth Tripp and by will of John Derry, 1674.

2. Town Dudley charity, consisting of 20 a. 2 r. 30 p., formerly known as common land, the origin of which appears to be unknown.

The lands of the two charities are let to various tenants, producing about £40 a year, and the official trustees also hold a sum of £107 4s. 9d. consols, producing £2 13s. 4d. yearly, arising from the sale in 1902 of 20 p. and two cottages thereon belonging to the Feoffee Estate.

3. Unknown donor's charity, consisting of 1 a. of land called Maids' Meadow, part of a field called Near Town, let at £2 a year.

These three charities are administered under the provisions of a scheme of the Court of Chancery of 6 March 1860. In 1912–13 the sum of £9 was distributed among widows, £15 was distributed in coal, and £5 applied in apprenticing, in respect of which there was a balance in hand of £27.

4. Charles Higgins's charity, founded by will dated 15 May 1792, proved in the P.C.C., trust fund, £592 5s. 3d., producing £14 16s. yearly, applicable in the distribution of clothing to ten poor women in December annually.

5. Sarah Spink's charity, founded by will proved 8 October 1833, trust fund, £355 4s. 9d. consols, the annual dividends, amounting to £8 17s. 8d., to be applied in the distribution of clothing among the poor on St. Thomas's Day.

The several sums of stock are held by the official trustees, and the dividends therefrom are duly applied.

WILLEN

Wilinges (xii cent.) ; Wylie, Wilies (xiii cent.) ; Wilne, Wylyene (xiv cent.) ; Wyllyen, Wyllyn (xv cent.).

Willen has an area of 669 acres of land and 9 acres covered by water ; about a third is arable land, about two-thirds permanent grass, and there are 6 acres only of woods and plantations.[1] The soil is mixed, the subsoil gravel and stone. The chief crops grown are wheat, barley, oats and roots.

The parish has an undulating surface of from 200 ft. to 250 ft., the land on the east along the Ouzel banks being liable to floods.

The road from Newport Pagnell to Fenny Stratford runs through the middle of the parish from north to south, and is crossed about a quarter of the way by another road, along the east fork of which lies the village of Willen, pleasantly situated on rising ground. At its northern end is the church, standing on an

eminence commanding beautiful views. On the west side of the church is the vicarage, an 18th-century building of red brick, approached by an avenue of elm trees. The school, built in 1847, and Brook Farm, occupied by Mr. John Nelson Payne, lie to the east.

A short distance south of the church is Manor Farm, formerly the manor-house, an old building with modern additions, occupied by Mr. Joseph Bennett Whiting.

In the early 16th century 80 acres of arable land were inclosed and converted into pasture,[2] and further extensive inclosures were made about 1650.[3]

MANORS

WILLEN is not recorded by name in the Domesday Survey, but it can be identified with the 4 hides 1 virgate assessed under Caldecote, part of the neighbouring parish of Newport Pagnell, and held under the Count of Mortain by Alvered.[4] These two parishes were

[24] Cal. of Papal Letters, iv, 75. See also Linc. Epis. Reg. Memo., Buckingham, fol. 68, 62.
[25] Cal. of Papal Letters, iv, 224 ; V.C.H. Bucks. i, 295 ; Linc. Epis. Reg. Memo., Buckingham, fol. 205 d.
[26] M. I. in church.
[27] Pat. 4 Jas. I, pt. viii.
[28] Ibid. 33 Eliz. pt. ii, m. 38 ; 1 Jas. I,

pt. xxi ; L. and P. Hen. VIII, xx (1), p. 678.
[29] Cf. Feet of F. Bucks. Mich. 9 Jas. I ; Hil. 18 Jas. I.
[30] Ibid. Div. Co. Hil. 21 & 22 Chas. II ; the lord of the manor in 1567 claimed the right of presentation (ibid. Bucks. East. 9 Eliz.).
[31] Bacon, Liber Regis, 503; Clergy Lists.

[32] P.C.C. 55 Marche.
[33] Chant. Cert. 5, no. 19.
[34] Pat. 6 Edw. VI, pt. ix.
[35] Ibid. 2 Eliz. pt. xiii.
[1] Statistics from Bd. of Agric. (1905).
[2] I. S. Leadam, Dom. Incl. 1517 (Royal Hist. Soc.), i, 177.
[3] Add. MS. 5839, p. 411.
[4] V.C.H. Bucks. i, 246.

described as one vill as late as the 14th century.[5] The estate was afterwards divided, and a portion which remained attached to the honour of Berkhampstead as one-sixth of a fee was later held by the Abbot of Lavendon,[6] who continued to hold till the Dissolution.[7] These lands were doubtless then dispersed, as there is no further record of them.

The more important part, assessed at 2 hides, included the Domesday mill.[8] The overlordship rights over this appear to have been acquired by the Crown during one of the periods when the honour of Berkhampstead was in its possession,[9] and from 1284–6 onwards this manor was said to be held of the Crown for one-sixth of a fee.[10] Philip de Kaynes is mentioned as tenant c. 1150,[11] but the property had passed before 1196 to Roger de Salford.[12] He was succeeded, probably in 1204, by Hugh de Salford, who then paid 1 mark for a writ of *mort d'ancestor* of 2 hides in Willen.[13] In the following year 7 virgates were apparently successfully claimed against him, possibly as heir male, by Rose de Verdon,[14] who was possibly the daughter of Roger de Salford. In 1208–9 Rose held 8 virgates in Willen, of which she granted to Hugh 3 virgates and a chief messuage to hold by the service of one knight, the residue being quitclaimed to her by Hugh. Half a virgate which Hugh Grimbald held by enfeoffment of Hugh de Salford was to be held of Rose and her heirs by the service of 2s. 6d. yearly.[15] These 3 virgates must have reverted to Rose, since no later record of the Salfords or their descendants exists in Willen, and the whole 2-hide manor descended with Farnham Royal (q.v.), which was held by Rose as widow of Bertram de Verdon.[16] The Verdons subinfeudated Willen to another branch of the family, retaining overlordship rights until the 14th century.[17] Nicholas de Verdon occurs as their tenant in 1284,[18] and it may have been his son Nicholas, a minor, for whom the Abbot of Lavendon answered in 1302.[19] In 1316 John de Verdon was returned as holding Willen,[20] and in 1327 he received a grant of free warren in his demesne lands at Willen at the request of Robert de Staunton.[21] Alice widow of Nicholas de Verdon was answerable for Willen in 1346,[22] but the descent of the manor for the next 150 years has been lost. In 1499 the manor was held by Thomas Malyns of Blunham (co. Bedford), and conveyed by him to John Mordaunt of Turvey (co. Bedford).[23] It was held by the Mordaunts with Turvey[24] and with the Castle Manor in Lavendon (q.v.) until conveyed in 1637 by John Earl of

Peterborough to his sisters Elizabeth, Margaret and Anne Mordaunt.[25] In 1640 they united with their brother Lewis Mordaunt[25a] in conveying it to Roger Nicholls and others,[26] to whom in the following year the earl relinquished his claim.[27] Nicholls and his trustees transferred their interest in 1653 to John Trevor and Richard Knightley,[28] and the manor was sold not long after to Col. Robert Hammond of Chertsey (Surrey), the custodian of Charles I in the Isle of Wight.[29] He died in 1654, leaving three daughters, Elizabeth, Mary and Letitia, as his co-heirs.[30] His widow Mary, the sixth daughter of John Hampden, the 'Patriot,' to whom Hammond left Willen for life,[31] married in 1656 Sir John Hobart, third baronet,[32] and with him conveyed the manor in 1672 to Herbert Thornedicke, clerk, and Barnabas Clay, clerk,[33] as a preliminary to its sale by Elizabeth Hammond, Sir Edward and Mary Massie, Phineas and Letitia Preston (the daughters of Col. Hammond and their husbands), to the celebrated Dr. Richard Busby, of Westminster School, later in the same year.[34] Dr. Busby died in 1695, and by his will, proved in February 1697–8, bequeathed the manor to trustees for the foundation of a lectureship in divinity.[35] It is still held by Dr. Busby's trustees.

A several fishery in the water of Willen was appurtenant to the manor from the 15th[36] to the 17th century.[37] One mill was held with the manor in 1499,[38] and two water-mills are mentioned in 1641.[39]

Lands and rents in Willen were granted with the advowson to Tickford Priory, and were held under the priory in 1489 by John Broughton with Broughton.[40] After the Dissolution this property was leased in 1541 by King Henry the Eighth's College to Anthony Cave for seventy years.[41]

In 1228 Henry III confirmed to Snelshall Priory a tenement given by Geoffrey Gibbewin, who had held it of Hugh de Salford.[42]

The church of *ST. MARY MAG-CHURCH DALENE* consists of a small apsidal chancel, nave measuring internally 44 ft. 6 in. by 24 ft., west tower 8 ft. 6 in. by 6 ft., and two vestries, one on the north and the other on the south side of the tower. It is built of brick with limestone dressings, the brickwork having now acquired a rich brown tone, and the roofs are covered with lead.

A church has existed here from the 12th century,[43] but the ancient structure, having probably fallen into decay,[44] was removed in 1680, and the present nave

[5] *Feud. Aids*, i, 109; *Hund. R.* (Rec. Com.), i, 30.
[6] *Testa de Nevill* (Rec. Com.), 244.
[7] *Pope Nich. Tax.* (Rec. Com.), 48; *Valor Eccl.* (Rec. Com.), iv, 241.
[8] De Banco R. Hil. 15 Hen. VII, m. 375.
[9] *V.C.H. Herts.* ii, 165–6.
[10] *Feud. Aids*, i, 80.
[11] Round, *Cal. Doc. of France*, 444.
[12] Pipe R. 7 Ric. I, m. 2 d.
[13] Pipe R. 6 John, m. 2; *Rot. de Oblatis et Fin.* (Rec. Com.), 207.
[14] *Rot. de Oblatis et Fin.* (Rec. Com.), 335; Pipe R. 8 John, m. 4 d.
[15] Feet of F. Bucks. case 14, file 9, no. 2.
[16] Dugdale, *Baronage*, i, 472.
[17] *Feud. Aids*, i, 80, 106.
[18] Ibid. 80.   [19] Ibid. 106.
[20] Ibid. 109.
[21] *Cal. Chart. R.* 1327–41, p. 12.
[22] *Feud. Aids*, i, 132.

[23] De Banco R. Chart. Enr. Hil. 15 Hen. VII, m. 2. John Mordaunt agreed to pay an annuity of £1 to Robert Malyns of Linford.
[24] *V.C.H. Beds.* iii, 110; see also Recov. R. Mich. 1560, m. 942; Feet of F. Div. Co. Hil. 6 Jas. I; Chan. Inq. p.m. (Ser. 2), cccix, 200.
[25] Feet of F. Bucks. East. 13 Chas. I.
[25a] Chan. Inq. p.m. [Ser. 2], dcxxiv, 64.
[26] Feet of F. Bucks. Trin. 16 Chas. I.
[27] Recov. R. Trin. 17 Chas. I, m. 29. See also Chan. Proc. (Bridges Div.), bdle. 404, no. 14.
[28] Feet of F. Bucks. East. 1653.
[29] Add. MS. 5839, p. 411.
[30] Ibid. p. 412.
[31] P.C.C. 438 Alchin.
[32] G.E.C. *Complete Baronetage*, i, 13.
[33] Feet of F. Bucks. East. 24 Chas. II.
[34] Ibid. Mich. 24 Chas. II.

[35] P.C.C. 30 Lort.
[36] De Banco R. Hil. 15 Hen. VII, m. 375.
[37] Feet of F. Bucks. Trin. 16 Chas. I; East. 24 Chas. II.
[38] De Banco R. Hil. 15 Hen. VII, m. 375.
[39] Recov. R. Trin. 17 Chas. I, m. 29.
[40] *Cal. Inq. p.m.* Hen. VII, i, 238.
[41] *L. and P. Hen. VIII*, xvi, g. 1391 (45). In 1545 he obtained a grant of tithes in Willen (Pat 37 Hen. VIII, pt. xvii, m. 8), which descended through his daughter and co-heir Judith, wife of William Chester, to her son Anthony Chester who inherited them in 1577 upon the death of his grandmother, then Elizabeth Weston (Chan. Inq. p.m. [Ser. 2], clxxx, 228).
[42] Dugdale, *Mon* iv, 235.
[43] Round, *Cal. Doc. of France*, 444.
[44] The walls of the church were reported defective in 1519 (Bp. Atwater's

tower and vestries were built by Dr. Richard Busby, head master of Westminster School, from designs, it is said, by his former pupil, Sir Christopher Wren. No traces are now left to indicate the character of the earlier structure [45] The apse was added in 1862, and the whole church was then restored.

The nave is lighted from each side by three tall round-headed windows, with moulded external architraves, and there are three similar but narrower windows in the modern semicircular apse. A moulded cornice and plinth are carried round the walls of the nave, the angles of which have rusticated quoins, and there is a pediment at the east end with a circular opening in the centre. The walls are plastered internally, and an oak panelled dado, reaching to the window sills about 7 ft. 9 in. above the floor, is continued all round the church. The nave roof is concealed by an original plastered ceiling having the form of a segmental vault intersected by the round arches over the windows. It is divided into large blue-tinted panels by wide foliated bands, and is further enriched with cherubs and foliated bosses. On the bands inclosing the central panel are two open Bibles and the date 1680. The large windows are filled with good modern glass having subject panels on white grounds. At the west end of the nave is a round-headed doorway to the tower set in a wide recess, above which is a shield inscribed with the name Jehovah in Hebrew. A shield over the modern chancel arch is charged with a hexagram.

The tower is of three stages, the lowest of limestone and the others of brick with limestone dressings, and is surmounted by a deep moulded cornice and pineapple-shaped pinnacles. The lowest stage is entered by a tall round-headed doorway on the west, the effect of which is enhanced by being set back near the inner face of the wall within a deep hollow splay, made continuous in arch and jambs, and having before it a semicircular platform approached by five steps. The second stage is lighted by a large circular window on the west, and the bell-chamber by two tiers of two-light windows on all sides, the lower having segmental heads and the upper round heads. Both the lowest stages have rusticated quoins, upon which stand tall Corinthian pilasters rising through the full height of the bell-chamber and clasping the angles. Access to the second stage is gained from the ground floor by a narrow stairway with a barrel vault constructed in the thickness of the north wall.

The tower is flanked on the north and south by brick vestries, which are entered by doorways in the ground stage and lighted by square-headed windows. A moulded cornice is continued round both vestries and across the west face of the tower, and the west walls have curved half gables with foliated ornaments against the tower at the top and pineapple pinnacles at the feet.

The internal fittings, including the oak seating of the nave with panelled doors and shaped ends, and the organ case, date from the late 17th century and are good examples of the period. The font has an octagonal bowl of white marble enriched on the upper edge with cherubs' heads and conventional scrolls connected by festoons of drapery, and at the bottom with acanthus leaves ; both the baluster-shaped stem and the square base are of black marble. The elaborate oak cover has a band of cherubs' heads at the base, a domical top with floral enrichments, and an urn-shaped finial. The altar stands upon twisted legs, and the altar rails, now placed in front of the quire stalls, are supported alternately by solid panels and twisted balusters. The hexagonal pulpit with bolection-moulded panels and moulded cornice stands at the south-east of the nave, and against the north wall opposite is the organ, the upper portion of which, enriched with Corinthian pilasters, foliated carving and deep cornice, overhangs the keyboard and is supported at the outer corners by modern twisted columns. The western entrance doors and the doors to the vestries are all of oak and date from the late 17th century. There is a chest of the same period in the south vestry, and in the chancel is a carved chair of about 1620.

A collection of books, principally of a theological character, dating from the 16th to the 18th century and formerly housed in the south vestry, is now preserved at the vicarage. They were presented by Dr. Richard Busby, patron of the living, in 1695, and by the Rev. James Hume, rector of Bradwell, about 1730, and number 620 volumes.

The churchyard is inclosed by a 17th-century brick wall with gateways on the east and west, the gateways having tall brick posts with stone cornices and ball finials.

The tower contains a ring of three bells, all by Richard Chandler, 1683.

The communion plate includes a cup, paten, flagon and salver, all of 1683, inscribed as given by Dr. Busby in 1682.

The registers begin in 1665–6.

ADVOWSON The church was bestowed before 1150 by Philip de Kaynes on Tickford Priory.[46] A perpetual vicarage had been appointed before 1223, and its endowments included land and a toft belonging to the church.[47]

The advowson was held by the priory [48] until its dissolution in 1524, when the patronage reverted to the Crown.[49] In 1526 rights in it were quitclaimed by Anne St. Leger, daughter and co-heir of Thomas late Earl of Ormond, and by Sir George St. Leger, kt., her son and heir-apparent, to Cardinal Wolsey[50] to whom it had been given for his college at Oxford by the king earlier in the same year.[51] After the cardinal's attainder, it was assigned to the refounded college called Henry the Eighth's College.[52] The presentation was made by the college in 1544,[53] but on its surrender in 1545,[53a] the advowson reverted to the Crown by which it was retained until 1676 when a grant was made to Heneage, Lord

Visit. [Alnwick Tower, Lincoln], fol. 39).
[45] Browne Willis compares the ancient church to that at Great Woolstone, but the latter was itself rebuilt in 1839.
[46] Round, Cal. Doc. of France, 444.
[47] Liber Antiquus Hugonis Wells (ed.

A. Gibbons), 13 ; R. of Hugh of Wells (Cant. R. of Robert Grosseteste (Cant. and York Soc.) 358, and York Soc.), ii, 63.
[48] Cal. Pat. 1348–50, pp. 367, 370 ; 1381–5, p. 15 ; 1388–92, pp. 94, 504 ; Add. MS. 5839, p. 414.
[49] Chan. Inq. p.m. [Ser. 2], lxxvi, 3.

[50] Feet of F. Bucks. Mich. and Hil. 18 Hen. VIII ; Div. Co. Mich. 18 Hen. VIII.
[51] L. and P. Hen. VIII, iv (1), 1913 (1) ; 2167 (1).
[52] Ibid. v, g. 1370 (23).
[53] Add. MS. 5839, p. 414.
[53a] Tanner, Not. Mon.

WILLEN CHURCH FROM THE SOUTH-WEST

Finch.[54] He was to convey the advowson to Dr. Richard Busby, the purchaser of the manor, with which it has since descended.[55]

The rectory has always descended with the advow-

son, save for a temporary alienation to Charles Bagehot and Bartholomew Yardley in 1587.[56]

There do not appear to be any endowed charities subsisting in this parish.

WOLVERTON

Wlverintone (xi cent.) ; Wolfrington (xii cent.) ; Wulvrinton, Wlvregton (xiii cent.).

The parish of Wolverton covers an area of 2,324 acres, and is bounded on the north by the Ouse, on the east by a small tributary of that river flowing from Calverton, and on the south-west by the Roman road called Watling Street. Where Watling Street becomes the main street of Stony Stratford the boundary leaves it and turns north so as to exclude the town from Wolverton. The ancient boundary evidently ran straight down Watling Street to the banks of the Ouse, for till the 16th century at least the 'east end' of Stony Stratford was part of Wolverton.[1] The ground slopes downwards from a height of about 300 ft. in the south of the parish to 200 ft. on the banks of the Ouse.

The parish is crossed from west to east by the Grand Junction Canal, which is carried across the Ouse valley by a cast-iron aqueduct,[2] and from north to south by the London and North Western railway. At the opening of the railway in 1838 the company established its engine works at Wolverton,[3] and a colony of railway workers sprang up round the station and works, which stand on the Grand Junction Canal near the eastern boundary of the parish. There is now a town of more than 4,000 inhabitants called Wolverton or New Wolverton, with the railway works, where the carriages for the line are now made,[4] on the north. Its streets are regularly arranged at right angles to each other. The church of St. George the Martyr, opened in 1844,[5] is at its eastern end. A Science and Art Institute was opened in 1864 and a Church Institute in 1908. The town has Roman Catholic, Congregational, Primitive Methodist and Wesleyan chapels.

New Wolverton in 1844 was separated by the canal from the main highway between Stony Stratford and Newport Pagnell. A new road was therefore begun in that year,[6] which runs west for three-quarters of a mile from the town and joins the original road at the south end of the old village, thus providing direct communication with Stony Stratford. A tramway now runs between the two towns.

The village of Old Wolverton, now in its turn standing just off the most important highway, has a wharf on the canal at its north end. To the west is the church of Holy Trinity adjoining the site of the manor-house. The castle here of the mount and

bailey type was built probably by the lords of the manor, possibly Meinfelin or Hamon, in the 12th century. Its site is to the north-east of the church.[7] It was probably never defended by masonry walls, and there is no documentary evidence as to its history. A capital messuage, with a court and garden, existed here in 1248,[8] and continues to be mentioned during the 14th century.[9] Two ruinous dove-houses were attached to it in 1349.[10] The Longville family evidently rebuilt the manor-house when they came into possession, for Leland states that they lived here and 'buildid fairly.'[11] A fresh reconstruction is said to have taken place in 1586.[12] The house was described as a 'fine seat' in 1720,[13] but a few years later it was pulled down by order of the Radcliffe trustees.[14] The vicarage-house, near by, was built partly out of its materials[15] and preserves two early 17th-century doorways ; one of them, now the principal entrance, is flanked by Corinthian columns supporting a broken pediment containing the arms of Longville, while the other, which is inside the house, is surmounted by a pediment with the Longville crest of a talbot. Sir John Longville had a park at Wolverton in 1501, which he had increased by inclosing land in 'Barreclose' and elsewhere.[16] Wolverton Park and Warren Farm, two houses to the south-west of the village, mark its position. Possibly the Longvilles made further additions to its area at the inclosure of the parish about 1654.[17] The park, which was noticed by the topographer Baskerville in 1681,[18] was 20 acres in extent in 1713, while the 'Low Park' was 30 acres.[19] The inclosure of about 1654 is said to have been accompanied by oppressive acts on the part of the Longville family,[20] whose arbitrary behaviour with regard to the common lands caused more than one dispute with the inhabitants of Wolverton. Sir John Longville (c. 1486-1541) was said to have wrongfully inclosed land 'next the east side of Ardwell.'[21] His grandson Henry turned 140 beasts on to the pasture called 'The Furzes,' so that there was no grass left for the cattle of the inhabitants, who claimed the immemorial right of pasture there.[22] Other pasture land in dispute was on Stratford Moor, Wolverton Moor and 'Stacey Buskes.'[23] The last must have been near the modern Stacey Hill Farm, called in the 19th century Stacey Bushes Farm.[24]

---

[54] Pat. 28 Chas. II, pt. ii, no. 7.
[55] Add. MS. 5839, p. 413 ; Inst. Bks. (P.R.O.)
[56] Pat. 29 Eliz. pt. iii, m. 18.
[1] See Stony Stratford ; Chant. Cert. 5, no. 17.
[2] It replaced before 1819 a similar aqueduct of wood (Hassell, *Tour of the Grand Junction Canal*, 75).
[3] *V.C.H. Bucks.* ii, 126.
[4] The engine works were gradually removed to Crewe between 1865 and 1877 (ibid. 127).
[5] Lipscomb, *Hist. and Antiq. of Bucks.*

iv, 420 ; Sheahan, *Hist. and Topog. of Bucks.* 648.
[6] Lipscomb, op. cit. iv, 419.
[7] *Hist. Monum. Com. Rep. N. Bucks.* 345.
[8] Chan. Inq. p.m. Hen. III, file 7, no. 3.
[9] Ibid. 15 Edw. III (1st nos.), no. 25 ; 23 Edw. III, pt. i, no. 35.
[10] Ibid. 23 Edw. III, pt. i, no. 35 ; 25 Edw. III (1st nos.), no. 6.
[11] Leland, *Itin.* (ed. L. Toulmin Smith), ii, 23.
[12] *Her. and Gen.* vi, 50.
[13] *Magna Brit.* (1720-31), i, 210-1.

[14] Add. MS. 5839, p. 428.
[15] Ibid. 5836, fol. 126.
[16] Leadam, *Dom. Incl.* 1517 (Royal Hist. Soc.), i, 182.
[17] Exch. Dep. Mich. 5 Geo. I, no. 7 ; Add. MS. 5839, p. 434.
[18] *Hist. MSS. Com. Rep.* xiii, App. ii, 274.
[19] Close, 12 Anne, pt. xi, no. 15.
[20] Add. MS. 5839, p. 434.
[21] Chan. Proc. Eliz. W 23, no. 55. See also Ct. of Req. bdle. 11, no. 189.
[22] Chan. Proc. Eliz. W 23, no. 55.
[23] Ibid.   [24] Plan 36307 C (B.M.).

In the north of the parish between the Grand Junction Canal and the Ouse is the Manor Farm. As a field near this farm was known as the Grange and contained in 1862 the remains of an old dovecot,[25] it seems probable that it marks the site of the manor or grange held here by Chicksand Priory.[26] A branch of the Ouse just north of it seems to have formed a mill race, perhaps for that 'Mead Mill' which belonged to the Priors of Bradwell.[27] John son of Alan in the 13th century granted to Bradwell all the fishery between its mill called Mead Mill and 'Stanebrige,'[28] the second of these landmarks being represented by the bridge on the eastern boundary opposite the station, close to which is Stonebridge House Farm. There were two mills in Wolverton in 1086,[29] the second of which was called in the 13th century West Mill.[30] It seems probable that it occupied the site of the present Wolverton Mill, which stands on the Ouse to the west of the village and to the north of a mansion called Wolverton House. West Mill [31] seems to have belonged continuously to the lords of the manor.[32] In 1342 there were two mills on the manor, only one of which would grind.[33] The two mills attached to it in 1689 [34] were probably Mead Mill and West Mill.[35]

Only a fifth of the area of the parish is under cultivation. Most of its inhabitants find employment on the railway. There are disused brickworks in the southern corner, and in 1903 New Wolverton had a manufactory of postal registered envelopes.

MANOR AND BARONY WOLVERTON was held under Edward the Confessor in a free tenure by three thegns: Godvin, a man of Earl Harold, Tori, a house carl of King Edward, and Alvric, a man of Queen Edith.[36] In 1086 it was an important manor assessed at 20 hides, the head of the fief of Manno the Breton, who also held land in Ellesborough, Chalfont St. Giles, Aston Sandford, Drayton Beauchamp, Helsthorpe (in Drayton Beauchamp), Lamport in Stowe, Thornborough, Padbury, Stoke Hammond and Loughton.[37] All these vills had been freely held before the Conquest by various thegns. The whole of Manno's fief in Buckinghamshire,[38] with his land

in Wicken, Maidwell, Draughton and Thenford (co. Northampton), and Lutterworth,[39] (co. Leicester), formed the barony of Wolverton,[40] which was held of the Crown for fifteen knights' fees and the service of defending the castle of Northampton.[41] Wolverton itself is generally said to account for two knights' fees.[42]

Manno's successor was Meinfelin,[43] called in one place 'Meinfelin Brito,' [44] and probably his son. He was the founder of the priory of Bradwell,[45] and was appointed Sheriff of Bedfordshire and Buckinghamshire in 1125.[46] His son Hamon succeeded him before 1155.[47] Hamon owed £20 for scutage in 1160–1 and £10 in 1167–8,[48] and owed £100 for a forest fine in 1176.[49] He died in 1184 or 1185, leaving four daughters, of whom one was a nun, and a son Hamon. His widow was Maud, apparently a sister of William Mauduit.[50] The younger Hamon was under age in 1185 and had taken a wife at the king's command.[51] This was perhaps Agatha, daughter and co-heir of William Trusbut, a share of whose lands Hamon claimed in 1195.[52] His son and heir was William,[53] who confirmed the gifts of his father to Luffield Priory.[54] William was disseised by King John in 1215 and paid 50 marks in the next year to recover his lands.[55] He forfeited them again under Henry III for omitting to perform his service with the army in Wales, but was reseised in 1223.[56] He died in or shortly before 1248,[57] when his brother and heir Alan owed the relief proper to a baron of £100.[58] His widow was Hawise.[59] Alan survived his brother by two years at most. His son John in 1249 owed not only his own relief but half of his father's which was still unpaid.[60] By 1255, when John son of Alan was still lord of Wolverton, the service of ward of Northampton Castle had been commuted for a payment of £7 10s. towards the defence of the castle from the whole barony.[61] Wolverton was then said to pay 40s. of this,[62] though in the 14th century it only paid 25s.[63] Loughton paid 10s., Stoke Hammond 17s. 2d.,[64] Aston Sandford 10s.[65] John son of Alan de Wolverton was dead in 1274, when his widow Isabel, subsequently wife of Ralph de Arden, had dower assigned to her.[66] His son and heir

[25] Sheahan, op. cit. 645.
[26] See below.   [27] See below.
[28] Rentals and Surv. (Gen. Ser.), R. 75, cart. 74.
[29] V.C.H. Bucks. i, 271.
[30] Feet of F. Div. Co. 39 Hen. III, no. 98; Dugdale, Mon. iv, 350.
[31] Mills in Wolverton were sold by Richard son of John to John son of Alan shortly before 1252 (Feet of F. Bucks. 36 Hen. III, no. 8). It is uncertain which mills these were.
[32] Dugdale, loc. cit. Feet of F. Div. Co. 39 Hen. III, no. 98.
[33] Chan. Inq. p.m. 15 Edw. III (1st nos.), no. 25.
[34] Recov. R. East. 1 Will. and Mary, m. 162.
[35] The Prior of Bradwell leased two 'Mead Mills' in 1491 (De Banco R. East. 8 Hen. VII, m. 154 d.), but they were probably both in one mill-house. Only one is mentioned at the Dissolution (Dugdale, Mon. iv, 511).
[36] V.C.H. Bucks. i, 271.
[37] Ibid. 269–71.
[38] Chenies in Burnham Hundred (q.v.) belonged to the barony in 1165, though

it is not mentioned in the Survey. Simpson was also annexed to it in the early 13th century.
[39] V.C.H. Northants, i, 349; V.C.H. Leics, i, 332.
[40] Red Bk. of Exch. (Rolls Ser.), 314; Cal. Close, 1272–9, p. 350.
[41] Red Bk. of Exch. (Rolls Ser.), 71, 314, 535; Rot. Lit. Claus. (Rec. Com.), i, 154.
[42] Testa de Nevill (Rec. Com.), 258; Hund. R. (Rec. Com.), i, 30; Feud. Aids, i, 80, 106, 132. In 1276 it was said to be held for two and a half fees (Cal. Close, 1272–9, p. 350). In one place (Chan. Inq. p.m. Hen. III, file 7, no. 3) the whole barony was said to be held for twenty fees.
[43] V.C.H. Northants, i, 368, 374, 385.
[44] Rentals and Surv. (Gen. Ser.), R. 75, cart. 76.
[45] Ibid.
[46] P.R.O. List of Sheriffs, 1.
[47] Rentals and Surv. (Gen. Ser.), R. 75, cart. 80; Gt. R. of the Pipe 2–4 Hen. II (Rec. Com.), 22.
[48] Pipe R. 7 Hen. II (Pipe R. Soc.), 12; 14 Hen. II, 11.

[49] Ibid. 22 Hen. II, 22; 23 Hen. II, 160.
[50] Rot. de Dominabus, 20, 21.
[51] Ibid.
[52] Stapleton, Mag. Rot. Scacc. Norman. ii, pp. lxxvi, lxxviii. In 1189–90 Hamon owed £62 6s. 8d. as relief for his father's lands (Gt. R. of the Pipe 1 Ric. I [Rec. Com.], 34).
[53] Rot. Lit. Claus. (Rec. Com.), i, 154.
[54] Dugdale, Mon. iv, 350.
[55] Rot. Lit. Claus. (Rec. Com.), i, 235; Rot. de Oblatis et Fin. (Rec. Com.), 568.
[56] Rot. Lit. Claus. (Rec. Com.), i, 629.
[57] Cal. Inq. p.m. Hen. III, i, 23.
[58] Pipe R. 32 Hen. III, m. 11 d.
[59] Cal. Inq. p.m. Hen. III, i, 31.
[60] Ibid; Excerpta e Rot. Fin. (Rec. Com.), ii, 59; Pipe R. 34 Hen. III, m. 10 d.
[61] Hund. R. (Rec. Com.), i, 31; cf. Thornborough.
[62] Hund. R. loc. cit.
[63] Chan. Inq. p.m. 23 Edw. III, pt. i, no. 35; Inq. a.q.d. file 392, no. 5.
[64] Hund. R. (Rec. Com.), i, 31.
[65] Cal. Inq. p.m. Edw. III, vii, 100.
[66] Cal. Fine R. 1272–1307, pp. 29, 51; De Banco R. 6, m. 69.

John was still under age in 1284–6.[67] His marriage was granted by Queen Eleanor to the Bishop of Bath and Wells, but John declined to accept the wife chosen for him by the bishop.[68] The name of his wife is unknown. John was summoned in 1297 and 1301 to perform military service in person beyond the sea and against the Scots, but was exonerated on one occasion after payment of a fine.[69] He was summoned to Parliament in 1324,[70] and was sent on foreign service in the next year.[71] In 1328 he claimed exemption as a tenant in chief holding by barony from being empanelled on an assize.[72]

WOLVERTON. *Azure an eagle or with a baston gules athwart him.*

This John was apparently the last lord of Wolverton to retain the status of a baron. No later lord of the manor was summoned to Parliament,[73] and there are very few subsequent references to the barony,[74] the only relic of which was the rent paid to Northampton Castle. John died in or about 1341, when his son John was over forty years old.[75] The younger John had married first Joan daughter of Bartholomew Pecche, by whom he had four daughters, Joan, Sarah, Cecilia and Constance.[76] She was dead in 1331, when he was married to his second wife, also called Joan,[77] by whom he had a son Ralph and two daughters, Margery and Elizabeth.[78] At his death in 1349 the heir of Wolverton was Ralph, then aged two.[79] Two years later, however, he died in the king's wardship, and the manor and appurtenant knights' fees were divided between his two sisters of the whole blood.[80] Margery was betrothed at her brother's death to John Hunt, whom she married within the year.[81] She was the wife of Roger de Louth in 1365,[82] and of Richard Imworth in 1377,[83] when her moiety of the manor was settled on herself and her third husband.[84] He also seems to have predeceased her, for in 1382, as Margery Wolverton, she had licence to settle her estate on herself and John Hewes for their lives, with remainder to the heirs and executors of John Hewes for ten years longer, and finally to her own right heirs.[85] In 1393 Margery was dead and John

Hewes had licence to grant his interest to John Longville, the husband of her daughter and heir Joan.[86] John Longville died holding this moiety of the manor by courtesy of England in 1439, and was succeeded by his son and heir George.[87] Before 1448 George succeeded also to the second moiety of the manor.[88] This had passed to the Cogenhoe family of Cogenhoe (co. Northampton) through the marriage of Elizabeth Wolverton with William Cogenhoe.[89] William and Elizabeth granted a life interest in their moiety to John Cheyne of Chenies in 1378, with remainder to themselves in tail and to the right heirs of Elizabeth.[90] In 1389 William Cogenhoe died seised, leaving a son and heir William,[91] who died ten years later still a minor.[92] The heir of the younger William was his sister Agnes, who married John Cheyne of Chenies [93] (q.v.), and was dead in 1421.[94] It seems that her only son Alexander died without issue,[95] and on the death of John Cheyne, which took place before November 1445,[96] the estate would naturally pass to George Longville. He settled the whole manor in 1448 on his younger son George,[97] with remainder to Richard son of his elder son Richard [98] in tail-male and further remainder to his daughters.[99] The younger George had livery of the manor from Edward IV in 1461,[100] his father having died in 1458.[1] In 1485 or 1486 his cousin John Longville, son and heir of Richard son of Richard, and therefore holder of the reversion on the failure of heirs to George,[2] made a forcible entry on the manor.[3] He apparently succeeded in ousting his kinsman or in buying him out, for on the death of George in July 1499 [4] he held only tenements in Stony Stratford and Wolverton of Sir John Longville as of his manor of Wolverton,[5] and immediately afterwards (7 August) Sir John had a release from Richard son and heir of George of all his claim on the manor.[6]

Sir John Longville lived to be eighty-three,[7] and left one legitimate daughter Anne and several illegitimate sons [8] on whom he settled the manor. The eldest son Thomas predeceased his father, and the settlement which came into operation gave the manor to Arthur, the second son, and his heirs male.[9] In 1542 Arthur had a release of all claim on the manor from John Cheyne, son and heir of Drew Cheyne and Anne Longville.[10] He died in 1557, and his widow

[67] *Feud. Aids,* i, 80.
[68] *Cal. Close,* 1288–96, p. 36.
[69] *Parl. Writs* (Rec. Com.), i, 911; ii (3), 1632.
[70] Ibid. ii (3), 1632.   [71] Ibid.
[72] *Parl. R.* ii, 19.
[73] Dugdale, *Baronage,* i, 543.
[74] See Chan. Inq. p.m. (Ser. 2), v, 20; Chan. Proc. Eliz. C 24, no. 9.
[75] Chan. Inq. p.m. 15 Edw. III (1st nos.), no. 25.
[76] Inq. a.q.d. file 91, no. 19; Chan. Inq. p.m. 23 Edw. III, pt. i, no. 35.
[77] Inq. a.q.d. file 212, no. 20.
[78] Chan. Inq. p.m. 23 Edw. III, pt. i, no. 35; *Cal. Close,* 1364–8, p. 241.
[79] Chan. Inq. p.m. 23 Edw. III, pt. i, no. 35. The manors of Padbury and Chalfont St. Giles, which had been settled on John and his first wife, passed to their four daughters and co-heirs (*Cal. Close,* 1349–54, p. 546).
[80] Chan. Inq. p.m. 25 Edw. III (1st nos.), no. 6; *Cal. Close,* 1349–54, p. 299. Their mother Joan, then wife of John Chastillon, held one-third of Wolverton in dower.

[81] Ibid.
[82] *Cal. Close,* 1364–8, p. 101.
[83] Inq. a.q.d. file 392, no. 5.
[84] Ibid.; Feet of F. Bucks. 1 Ric. II, no. 4.
[85] *Cal. Pat.* 1381–5, p. 155. In 1381 John Wake, grandson of the last John Wolverton by his first wife Joan Pecche (see Chalfont St. Giles), quitclaimed all right in Wolverton Manor to Margery Wolverton (Close, 5 Ric. II, m. 33 d.).
[86] *Cal. Pat.* 1391–6, p. 224; Chan. Inq. p.m. 17 Hen. VI, no. 38. Joan is generally said to have been the daughter of John Hunt (*Her. and Gen.* vi, 49; Baker, *Hist. and Antiq. of Northants,* i, 27).
[87] Chan. Inq. p.m. 17 Hen. VI, no. 38.
[88] *Cal. Pat.* 1446–52, p. 151.
[89] Inq. a.q.d. file 362, no. 10; *Cal. Close,* 1364–8, p. 101.
[90] *Cal. Pat.* 1377–81, p. 235.
[91] Chan. Inq. p.m. 12 Ric. II, no. 8.
[92] Ibid. 22 Ric. II, no. 15.
[93] Ibid.; Fine R. 22 Ric. II, m. 9.
[94] *Cal. Papal Letters,* vii, 208.
[95] Close, 18 Hen. VI, m. 22; Bridges, *Hist. and Antiq. of Northants,* i, 348.

[96] Close, 24 Hen. VI, m. 41 d.
[97] Son of his second wife Margaret.
[98] By his first wife Elizabeth.
[99] *Cal. Pat.* 1446–52, p. 151. The daughters were Elizabeth wife of James Swetenham, Elizabeth wife of John Dyve, and Anne wife of John Mortimer.
[100] Close, 1 Edw. IV, m. 2.
[1] Chan. Inq. p.m. 36 Hen. VI, no. 36.
[2] Ibid.; Pat. 19 Edw. IV, m. 17. The younger Richard had died in 1458 (Chan. Inq. p.m. 37 Hen. VI, no. 28).
[3] Early Chan. Proc. bdle. 77, no. 92.
[4] P.C.C. 37 Horne.
[5] Chan. Inq. p.m. (Ser. 2), xiv, 63.
[6] Close, 15 Hen. VII, no. 39.
[7] Leland says 103 (*Itin.* [ed. L. Toulmin Smith], ii, 23), but his age in 1458 was thirty weeks and he died in 1541.
[8] Chan. Proc. Eliz. C 24, no. 9.
[9] Ibid.; Memo. R. (Exch. L.T.R.), Hil. 37 Hen. VIII, m. 36; Chan. Inq. p.m. (Ser. 2), lxv, 7; Leland, loc. cit.
[10] Com. Pleas D. Enr. East. 35 Hen. VIII, m. 7.

Anne held Wolverton for life.[11] His son and heir Henry Longville,[12] who was sheriff for the county in 1592 and 1606,[13] married Elizabeth Cotton[14] and died in 1618.[15] The heir was Sir Henry Longville, his son, on whose marriage with Katherine daughter of Sir Edward Cary the manor had been settled in tail-male in January 1597–8.[16] He died in 1621,[17] leaving a son and heir Edward, created a baronet seventeen years later.[18] Sir Edward died in 1661, and was succeeded by his son Thomas, who lived till 1685.[19] Sir Edward, son of Sir Thomas,[20] sold the manor of Wolverton in 1713 to John Radcliffe, the famous doctor [21] and benefactor of Oxford University. Dr. Radcliffe died in the next year, leaving his Buckinghamshire estates, subject to annuities to his family and to a charge of £100 for the maintenance of his library at Oxford, to trustees for charitable purposes.[22] The Radcliffe trustees are still lords of the manor.

LONGVILLE of Wolverton. *Gules a fesse dancetty ermine between six crosslets fitchy argent.*

The Priors of Chicksand had land in Wolverton in 1291, probably by grant of the lords of the manor.[23] In 1325 the manor of the priory was granted to John de Puisaquil of Genoa and Joan his wife for their lives, free of all service. They were to keep the manor in repair and were to have timber from the prior's wood at Chicksand for the purpose.[24] At the Dissolution this manor was worth £4 a year.[25] It was granted in 1543 to Arthur Longville,[26] who left it to his younger son Arthur in 1557.[27] It subsequently followed the descent of the manor of Bradwell Abbey in Bradwell parish (q.v.), and seems to have been known as the Grange.[28]

The priory of Bradwell acquired various possessions in Wolverton from the lords of the manor, besides Meinfelin's initial grant of the church.[29] The most important were the mill called Mead Mill [30] and 31 acres of land next Watling Street granted by William son of Hamon.[31] In 1272 Henry Hyntes and Amice his wife added a messuage and a virgate and 10 acres of land.[32] In the early 16th century some of this land was inclosed and turned to pasture.[33] The whole of the possessions of the priory in Wolverton, except the church and rectory, were given to Sir John Longville just before the dissolution of the house

in exchange for a farm which he held within its precincts.[34]

Michael Rote, a tenant of William son of Hamon, granted half a virgate in Wolverton to Biddlesden Abbey.[35] An acre of meadow was given to the same house by William Visdelou.[36] No possessions here appeared among the lands of Biddlesden at the Dissolution.

The Prior of Luffield received from Hamon son of Meinfelin a grant of the tithe of the bread of his house, wherever he might be, in exchange for a claim on the priory of Bradwell.[37] William son of Hamon subsequently gave in exchange for this tithe a rent of 10s. from West Mill in Wolverton.[38] The rent was still paid at the Dissolution.[39]

A small amount of land here belonged to the gild of St. Mary and St. Thomas at Stony Stratford.[40]

The church of the *HOLY TRINITY* consists of a chancel, nave, transepts and west tower. The tower dates from the 14th century and the rest of the structure from 1815, when the church was rebuilt and the tower encased, the work being carried out in the Norman style. The chancel and nave were redecorated in 1903.

The ancient church dated from the 12th century,[41] but had doubtless undergone various later alterations. It was described in the mid-18th century as consisting of a chancel, central tower, nave and south aisle.[42] At the rebuilding of the church the tower was preserved at the west of the new structure, a third stage was added, and the pointed arches on the north and south sides of the ground stage, originally intended to communicate with transepts, were blocked. These arches were completely hidden till 1903, when they were exposed internally. An incised cross has been rebuilt in one of the tower arches and a grotesque head, perhaps of the 12th century, in the stair turret. The internal walls of the second stage bear traces of having had a gabled roof.

Refixed on the north side of the chancel is a large marble monument with a recumbent effigy in memory of Sir Thomas Longville of Wolverton, second baronet (d. 1685). He married first Mary daughter and co-heir of Sir William Fenwick of Northumberland (d. 1683), and secondly Katherine daughter and co-heir of Sir Thomas Peyton of Knowlton (Kent); on the monument are the arms of Longville impaling Fenwick and Longville impaling Peyton. A 17th-century stool is preserved inside the church, and some

---

[11] Chan. Inq. p.m. (Ser. 2), cxi, 6 ; Chan. Proc. (Ser. 2), bdle. 112, no. 18.
[12] Ibid.
[13] P.R.O. *List of Sheriffs*, 9. Other members of the family who occupied that position were John, 1507; Thomas, 1536; Arthur, 1554 ; Edward, 1687 (ibid. 3. 9).
[14] See Feet of F. Div. Co. Hil. 40 Eliz.
[15] *Visit. of Bucks.* (Harl. Soc.), 83 ; *Misc. Gen. et Her.* i, 65 ; Chan. Inq. p.m. (Ser. 2), dxlii, 131.
[16] Chan. Inq. p.m. (Ser. 2), ccclxxxvi, 93 ; Feet of F. Div. Co. Hil. 40 Eliz.
[17] *Misc. Gen. et Her.* i, 65 ; Chan. Inq. p.m. (Ser. 2), ccclxxxvi, 93.
[18] Chan. Inq. p.m. (Ser. 2), ccclxxxvi, 93 ; G.E.C. *Baronetage*, ii, 437. He seems to have leased Wolverton to Sir Thomas Temple, bart. (Feet of F. Div. Co. Trin. 4 Chas. I ; *Cal. S. P. Dom.* 1628–9, p. 467), but made a settlement of it in

1636 (Recov. R. Trin. 12 Chas. I, m. 32).
[19] G.E.C. loc. cit. See also Feet of F. Bucks. Hil. 23 & 24 Chas. II ; Hil. 29 & 30 Chas. II.
[20] G.E.C. loc. cit. ; Recov. R. East. I Will. and Mary, m. 162.
[21] Close, 12 Anne, pt. xi, no. 15 ; Feet of F. Bucks. Trin. 12 Anne.
[22] Pittis, *Life of Dr. Radcliffe*, 92–4.
[23] *Pope Nich. Tax.* (Rec. Com.), 47.
[24] *Cal. Close*, 1323–7, p. 293.
[25] Dugdale, *Mon.* vii, 951.
[26] *L. and P. Hen. VIII*, xviii (1), g. 346 (38).
[27] Chan. Inq. p.m. (Ser. 2), cxi, 6.
[28] Ibid. ccxl, 85 ; ccclx, 86 ; Feet of F. Bucks. Mich. 41 Eliz. ; Trin. 2 Will. and Mary; Trin. 9 Geo. V.
[29] See below.
[30] See above.

[31] Rentals and Surv. (Gen. Ser.), R. 75, cart. 1, 63.
[32] Feet of F. Bucks. 56 Hen. III, no. 17.
[33] Leadam, op. cit. i, 181.
[34] Treas. of the Receipt Misc. Bks. clxv, fol. 42 ; cf. Leadam, op. cit. i. 211. The mill appears among the possessions given in exchange to Sir John Longville (Treas. of the Receipt Misc. Bks. clxv, fol. 42), and therefore it was probably in error that it was included among Cardinal Wolsey's possessions late of Bradwell Priory in 1530 (Chan. Inq. p.m. [Ser. 2], lxxvii, 59).
[35] Harl. Chart. 86, D. 27 ; 85, D. 42.
[36] Ibid. 86, F. 17.
[37] Dugdale, *Mon.* iv, 350.
[38] Ibid. [39] Ibid. 351.
[40] *Cal. Pat.* 1476–85, p. 330.
[41] See Advowson.
[42] Add. MS. 5839, p. 430.

508

old floor slabs with matrices for small brass plates have been relaid outside the south doorway.

The tower contains a ring of six bells, all by John Briant of Hertford, 1820.

The plate consists of a chalice of 1867 made from a cup given in 1686 by Catherine Longville, and a paten and flagon of 1837 given by the trustees of Dr. Radcliffe.

The registers begin in 1535.

The church of *ST. GEORGE THE MARTYR* was built in 1843–4, and a district was assigned to it in 1846.[43] It is a building of stone in the 13th-century style, and now consists of a chancel, nave, south porch and north-east tower with spire containing one bell. The living is a vicarage in the gift of the Radcliffe trustees.

The church of *ST. MARY THE VIRGIN*, Wolverton End, was built in 1864, and a district was assigned to it in 1870.[44] It is a stone building in the 13th-century style, designed by Sir Gilbert Scott, and now consists of an apsidal chancel, nave with aisles, south porch and bell-turret. The living is a vicarage in the same gift.

ADVOWSON The church of Wolverton was granted to the priory of Bradwell by Meinfelin the Breton,[45] and a vicarage was ordained in the 12th or early 13th century.[46] The presentation belonged to the priors till the dissolution of the house in 1526,[47] when it was granted to Cardinal Wolsey.[48] He gave it to his new college at Oxford,[49] the possessions of which were taken into the king's hands on his fall. In 1531 the advowson was granted with Bradwell Priory in exchange to the priory of Sheen,[50] which appropriated the church two years later.[51] After the general dissolution it was granted to Arthur Longville,[52] and subsequently descended with the manor of Wolverton.[53]

The rectory followed the descent of the advowson till the dissolution of Sheen Priory,[54] after which it was retained by the Crown till 1568. In that year it was granted to Anthony Rotsey to farm for twenty-one years.[55] He transferred his interest to Michael Coles, who had a new lease for twenty-one years in 1577,[56] and in 1583 a grant for the lives of himself, Mary his wife and Humphrey their son.[57] The Coles conveyed their life interest in 1601 to Henry Longville.[58] Meanwhile the rectory had been granted in

fee in 1599 to Sir John Spencer,[59] whose daughter and heir Elizabeth was the wife of William Compton, afterwards Earl of Northampton.[60] It was sequestered in 1647 for the delinquency of James Earl of Northampton, her grandson,[61] who was directed by the committee for compounding to settle its revenues on the ministry.[62] The Earls of Northampton continued to own it till the middle of the 18th century, but it was held from them on a continuous lease by the lords of the manor.[63] Sir Edward Longville sold his interest along with the manor to Dr. Radcliffe.[64] The rent-charge reserved was sold by the Earl of Northampton about 1737 to Brasenose College, Oxford.[65]

About 1661 the stipend paid to the vicar by Sir Thomas Longville, then lessee of the rectory, was £40 a year. Some of the parishioners were dissatisfied with this sum and claimed that his due was £50.[66] The Radcliffe trustees augmented the vicarage in 1757 by a gift of £2,000.[67]

In 1345 the Bishop of Lincoln granted John Wolverton licence to have an 'oratory' in his manor-house.[68] No further reference to a domestic chapel has been found.

CHARITIES The charity of Catherine Featherstone, founded by will dated in 1711, consists of 4 a. 1 r. 15 p. in the parish of Whaddon, allotted on the inclosure of that parish in lieu of lands purchased with the original legacies. The land produces about £5 a year, which is applicable in the distribution of coal, blankets, clothing, etc., among the poor attending church, a proportion being payable to the parish clerk.

The charity of Mrs. Elizabeth Miles, founded by will proved at London, 22 January 1872, is endowed with £247 19s. 6d. consols with the official trustees, the annual dividends of which, amounting to £6 4s., are applied in the distribution of blankets and clothing in the week preceding Christmas among the agricultural poor, a preference being given to widows.

The Congregational chapel and trust property comprised in indentures of 30 April 1875 and 10 November 1880 were, by an order of the Charity Commissioners of 7 November 1890, vested in the administering trustees thereby appointed upon the trusts of a scheme thereby established.

An account of the county school has already been given.[69]

GREAT WOOLSTONE

Ulsiestone (xi cent.) ; Wulsistone, Wolston, Wolleston, Great Woulstone (xiii cent.).

Great Woolstone has an area of 508 acres of land with 6 acres covered by water ; about one-third of the parish is arable land and the remainder consists of

permanent grass.[1] The soil is light clay and gravel, with some rich meadow land, the subsoil clay and gravel. The chief crops grown are wheat, beans, barley and oats.

The ground falls from about 300 ft. above the

[43] *Lond. Gaz.* 29 May 1846, p. 1979.
[44] Ibid. 29 Nov. 1870, p. 5409.
[45] Rentals and Surv. (Gen. Ser.), R. 75, cart. 76.
[46] *Liber Antiquus Hugonis Wells* (ed. A. Gibbons), 12.
[47] *Cal. Pat.* 1348–50, p. 347 ; 1354–8, pp. 168, 188 ; Exch. Inq. p.m. (Ser. 2), file 22, no. 8.
[48] *L. and P. Hen. VIII*, iv (1), p. 991.
[49] Ibid. p. 986 ; (2), g. 4001 (2, 3) ; Feet of F. Div. Co. 19 Hen. VIII.
[50] *L. and P. Hen. VIII*, v, 403.
[51] Ibid. vi, 299 (ix).
[52] Chan. Inq. p.m. (Ser. 2), cxi, 6.

Apparently it was included in the grant of Bradwell (*L. and P. Hen. VIII*, xviii [1], g. 346 [38]).
[53] Inst. Bks. (P.R.O.).
[54] *L. and P. Hen. VIII*, iv, p. 991 ; vi, 299 (ix).
[55] Pat. 10 Eliz. pt. v, m. 34.
[56] Ibid. 19 Eliz. pt. viii, m. 23.
[57] Ibid. 25 Eliz. pt. vi, m. 42.
[58] Feet of F. Bucks. Mich. 43 Eliz.
[59] Pat. 41 Eliz. pt. xxii, m. 36, 38.
[60] Chan. Inq. p.m. (Ser. 2), cccxviii, 165 ; G.E.C. *Peerage*, vi, 72.
[61] G.E.C. loc. cit.
[62] *Cal. Com. for Comp.* 1249, 1251,

2266. Sir Robert Bannister, another delinquent, had also a claim upon it (ibid. 67), presumably through a grant made by William Earl of Northampton and Elizabeth his wife to Henry Bannister in 1627–8 (Feet of F. Bucks. Hil. 3 Chas. I).
[63] Add. MS. 5839, p. 425.
[64] Close, 12 Anne, pt. xi, no. 15.
[65] Add. MS. 5839, p. 425.
[66] Exch. Dep. Mich. 5 Geo. I, no. 7.
[67] Bacon, *Liber Regis*, 502.
[68] Add. MS. 5839, p. 426.
[69] See *V.C.H. Bucks.* ii, 218.
[1] Statistics from Bd. of Agric. (1905).

ordnance datum in the west to about 200 ft. in the east, where the River Ouzel forms the boundary.

The village lies in the east of the parish, along the road from Newport Pagnell to Fenny Stratford. It has at its southern end the church and the rectory ; Hill Farm, in the occupation of Mr. F. Clarke, lies a little further north, with the smithy beyond. The Cross Keys Inn, at the south end of the village, is a picturesque 17th-century building of stone, two stories in height, with a thatched roof. The lord of the manor, Mr. W. Clarkson, resides at the Manor House.

In 1675 an agreement was come to between the rector and parishioners as to the inclosing of lands in the open and common fields.[2] The parish was inclosed by Act of Parliament in 1796.[3]

Henry Tattam, D.D., the Coptic scholar (1789–1868), was rector of the parish from 1831 to 1849.[4]

Among the lands held by the Dudley and Gilpin or Kilpin families, important freeholders here,[5] occur the following place-names : the Berryes, Ryfurlong

The more important overlordship rights were, however, exercised by the Bolebecs and their successors, Hugh de Bolebec having bestowed the manor on the abbey.[13] The grant was said in the 13th century to be in free alms,[14] but the service recorded a century later was that of a pair of gilt spurs or 6d.[15] The interest of the Earls of Oxford continued until the abolition of feudal tenures in the 17th century.[16]

The abbey of La Couture sold the manor in 1243, to Paul Pever of Toddington in Bedfordshire [17] the Earl of Oxford's stewards, Peter de la Mare and William de Bikeling, in vain asserting the illegality of the transfer to lay hands, the original gift having been in free alms.[18] Paul Pever also acquired about this date Chilton Manor (q.v.), where the early history of this family has been traced. From the end of the 13th century it has been given under Marsworth (q.v.), which they then obtained. Their property in Great Woolstone descended with Chilton and Marsworth until the middle of the 14th century, with a few divergences which are noted below. After the death in March 1271–2 of Emma, widow of Paul's son, John Pever, the Earl of Gloucester entered upon the manor, which he held for some time, when he was followed by the Earl of Oxford,[19] both apparently with the object of enforcing their overlordship rights. One mark for hidage and suit was due from Woolstone to the king, but it was stated in 1254 [20] and again in 1276 [21] that this had been withdrawn from the date of purchase. Ten years later the 'vill' of Woolstone, John grandson of Paul Pever, and Gilbert de Clare Earl of Gloucester were attached for the payment of this mark and of arrears amounting to £5, the earl's father, Richard de Clare, being accused of having

THE CROSS KEYS INN, GREAT WOOLSTONE.

Leyes, Tom's Leyes[6] (xvii cent.); Odells Field, Elbow Field, Meareslade, Jenkins' Close [7] (xviii cent.).

In the time of King Edward Alric son *MANOR* of Goding, who could sell, held a manor of 5 hides in *WOOLSTONE*, entered in 1086 among the lands of Walter Giffard, and held under him by the abbey of La Couture, Le Mans, Maine.[8] Rights in Great Woolstone consisting of a leet and rent were afterwards attached to the honour of Gloucester, passing through the Clares[9] and Audleys, Earls of Gloucester,[10] to the Staffords.[11] In 1547 they pertained to the king as part of the honour.[12]

first seized this rent to his own use.[22] John Pever and his wife Beatrice in 1305 made a settlement of the manor on Robert Durival and his wife Parnel,[23] and Durival was accordingly returned as lord of Woolstone in 1316.[24] At his death about 1332 his wife was called Margaret, daughter of the John Pever who made a settlement in 1305, to whose grandson and heir Nicholas the manor reverted.[25] In 1356 Nicholas Pever alienated Great Woolstone to Sir Henry Green [26] ; the grant was for life only, but Green must afterwards have obtained the fee simple, as it thenceforward descended with his manor of Wavendon

[2] Exch. Dep. Mich. 2 Anne, no. 2.
[3] Priv. Act, 36 Geo. III, cap. 12.
[4] Dict. Nat. Biog.
[5] Chan. Inq. p.m. (Ser. 2), cclxxxvii, 90 ; dcxxxvi, 92 ; Chan. Proc. (Bridges Div.), bdles. 155, no. 61 ; 474, no. 19 ; 603, no. 95.
[6] Chan. Inq. p.m. (Ser. 2), dcclxviii, 7.
[7] Exch. Dep. Mich. 2 Anne, no. 2.
[8] V.C.H. Bucks. i, 251. There was a mill worth 6s. 4d.
[9] Cal. Inq. p.m. (Edw. II), v, 329.

[10] Chan. Inq. p.m. 11 Edw. II, no. 74 ; 21 Edw. III (1st nos.), no. 59.
[11] Ibid. 10 Ric. II, no. 38 ; 16 Ric. II, pt. i, no. 27 ; 4 Hen. IV, no. 41 ; 38 & 39 Hen. VI, no. 59.
[12] Ct. R. (Gen. Ser.), portf. 155, no. 13.
[13] Cur. Reg. R. 131, m. 12d.   [14] Ibid.
[15] Cal. Inq. p.m. (Edw. II), vi, 300.
[16] Chan. Inq. p.m. 6 Edw. III (1st nos.), no. 44 ; 43 Edw. III (1st nos.), no. 48 ; 15 Ric. II, pt. i, no. 24 ; 5 Hen. V, no. 41 ; (Ser. 2), dviii, 15.

[17] Cur. Reg. R. 131, m. 12 d. ; Plac. de Quo Warr. (Rec. Com.), 84.
[18] Cur. Reg. R. 131, m. 12 d.
[19] Cal. Inq. p.m. (Edw. I), ii, 66.
[20] Hund. R. (Rec. Com.), i, 30.
[21] Ibid. 40.
[22] Plac. de Quo Warr. (Rec. Com.), 84.
[23] Inq. a.q.d. file 55, no. 15.
[24] Feud. Aids, i, 109.
[25] Chan. Inq. p.m. 6 Edw. III (1st nos.), no. 44.
[26] Feet of F. case 20, file 93, no. 5.

(q.v.), with which it was divided into thirds in the 16th century.[27] In 1589 one-third was conveyed by John Tufton and Christine his wife, William Roper and Katherine his wife, and Thomas Wilford, husband of Mary Browne, deceased, to Robert Staunton,[28] Lewis Lord Mordaunt transferring his right in the remaining two-thirds in the following year.[29] Great Woolstone had passed before 1704 to John Dormer of Rowsham, Oxfordshire, who was then holding it with his manor of Hollowes, North Crawley.[30] It shared the history of this manor (q.v.) until about the end of the 18th century,[30a] but appears to have been then acquired by the elder branch of the Lowndes family, the Selby-Lowndes of Whaddon,[31] W. S. Lowndes of Whaddon holding about 1860.[32] In 1869 it was the property of Henry Emerson Westcar of Strode Park, Herne, Kent, from whom it had passed between 1871 and 1877 to Eliza, widow of Sir George William Prescott, 3rd bart. At her death in 1887 Woolstone was inherited by her second son Charles William Prescott of Strode Park, Herne, Kent, who in that year assumed the additional surname and arms of Westcar. After his death in 1910 it was sold by his elder son Charles Henry Beeston Prescott-Westcar to Mr. Walter Clarkson, the present lord of the manor.

The small church of the HOLY TRINITY CHURCH consists of a chancel and nave with a bellcote on the west gable. It is built of stone in the Tudor style and dates from 1839, but stands on the site of an ancient structure, to which reference is found early in the 13th century.[33] Scanty evidence exists as to the character of this early building, but Browne Willis refers to the church as existing in his day as 'a small mean Fabrick consisting of a Body and Chancel, which are leaded. At the end is a wooden Turrit, supported by the Walls of the Church, and 2 Props or Posts withinside the Church, in which hang 3 small modern Bells.'[34]

The font, which was removed from the old church of St. Cuthbert, Bedford, has a 12th-century round bowl, the face of which is relieved by four engaged shafts with scalloped capitals. At the west end of the nave is a 16th-century bench with a carved end, and on the nave floor are several floor slabs of the late 17th century to the Dudley and Gilpin families.

The bellcote contains one bell by Anthony Chandler, 1679.[34a]

The plate consists of an Elizabethan cup of 1569; a large paten inscribed, 'This piece of Plate was bought for the use of Woolston Church

Octo[r] 21st 1755'; a large modern two-handled cup, unmarked; a silver-gilt flagon, Jubilee Memorial, 1897, and a Sheffield or electro-plate alms-dish, unmarked.

The registers before 1812 are as follows : (i) mixed entries 1538 to 1776—the vellum cover appears to be part of a service-book with musical notation, (?) late 15th or early 16th century ; (ii) baptisms and burials 1777 to 1810 ; (iii) marriages 1754 to 1811.

ADVOWSON Reference to the church occurs in 1222, when Garnerius was presented by the abbey of La Couture to the perpetual vicarage[35] which had been ordained after the Council of Oxford.[36] The advowson descended with the manor, with which, however, it was not alienated to Robert Durival for life in 1305.[37] Between 1562[38] and 1576 it was conveyed to Henry Charge, who presented in the latter year.[39] It was then held by a succession of owners[40] until acquired by the Neild family, of whom James Neild of Stoke Hammond, sheriff in 1804,[41] was in possession in the early 19th century.[42] His son John Camden Neild of Cheyne Walk, Chelsea, barrister, at his death in 1852 bequeathed the advowson with his immense fortune to Queen Victoria.[43] The advowson remains the property of the Crown under the patronage of the Lord Chancellor.

The church was valued at £5 yearly in 1291[44] and at £9 6s. 8d. in 1535.[45] The living was consolidated with that of Little Woolstone in 1854.

Tithes in Great Woolstone held by Tickford Priory were granted with the priory's other possessions to Cardinal Wolsey in 1526,[46] and after his attainder were confirmed by the king in 1532 to Wolsey's college at Oxford founded at that date as King Henry the Eighth's College.[47]

CHARITIES Richard Bludd alias Blood, who died in 1602, by his will proved in the P.C.C.,[48] bequeathed 5 marks to be put forth for a stock by the minister and churchwardens of Great Woolstone, the increase thereof to be distributed by them yearly upon the Thursday next before Easter amongst the poor there for ever. This legacy was recorded, together with a gift of a tenement for the use of the poor of Newport Pagnell (see under Newport Pagnell Town Lands), on a brass plate affixed to the north side of the chancel in the parish church. The legacy, however, appears to have been lost sight of.

---

[27] Feet of F. Bucks. Mich. 18 Eliz. ; Recov. R. East. 18 Eliz. m. 1106.

[28] Recov. R. D. Enr. Mich. 31 & 32 Eliz. m. 20.

[29] Feet of F. Bucks. Trin. 32 Eliz.

[30] Recov. R. East. 3 Anne, m. 263 ; Mich. 3 Anne, m. 76.

[30a] Recov. R. East 15 Geo. III. m. 158.

[31] Lysons, Mag. Brit. i (3), 672.

[32] Sheahan, Hist. and Topog. of Bucks. 650. The trustees of Mr. Westcar, a minor, then owned one of the two farms which constituted nearly all the parish, Mr. Bolding being owner of the other.

[33] R. of Hugh of Wells (Cant. and York Soc.), ii, 59.

[34] Add. MS. 5839, p. 416.

[34a] A. H. Cocks, Ch. Bells of Bucks. 638.

[35] R. of Hugh of Wells (Cant. and York Soc.), ii, 59.

[36] Ibid. i, 198 ; Liber Antiquus Hugonis Wells (ed. A. Gibbons), 12. It consisted among other things of the tithes of sheaves of the demesne of the monks and their tenants in Woolstone, all altar offerings, an acre in 'utroque' field in Woolstone and a suitable house.

[37] Chan. Inq. p.m. 9 Edw. II, no. 55 ;

Cal. Inq. p.m. (Edw. II), vi, 300 ; Feet of F. case 18, file 73, no. 15.

[38] Feet of F. Div. Co. East. 4 Eliz.

[39] Lipscomb, op. cit. iv, 422.

[40] Ibid. ; Feet of F. Bucks. East. 9 Geo. I ; Add. MS. 5839, p. 417 ; Inst. Bks. (P.R.O.).

[41] P.R.O. List of Sheriffs, 11.

[42] Inst. Bks. (P.R.O.).

[43] Sheahan, op. cit. 650 ; cf. ibid. 404.

[44] Pope Nich. Tax. (Rec. Com.), 34.

[45] Valor Eccl. (Rec. Com.), iv, 245.

[46] L. and P. Hen. VIII, iv, 1913.

[47] Ibid. v, g. 1370 (23).

[48] P.C.C. 40 Bolein.

LITTLE WOOLSTONE

Wlsiestone (xi cent.); Wolfeston, Wulsiston, Parva Wolstone, Wolstone Coudray (xiii cent.).

Little Woolstone has an area of 631 acres (623 acres of land and 8 acres covered by water), of which 147 are arable land, 1½ are covered by woods and plantations and the remainder laid down in permanent grass.[1] The ground falls from the west, where it rises to 363 ft. above the ordnance datum, to about 200 ft. in the east, where the River Ouzel forms the boundary, and the land is liable to floods.

The village lies in the south-east of the parish on the high road from Newport Pagnell to Fenny Stratford and on a road branching east from it. At their junction stands the Manor Farm occupied by Mr. John Sharman.

At the eastern end of the village is the church,

THE MILL HOUSE, LITTLE WOOLSTONE.

described in 1755 as a poor mean building, with a wooden turret at the west end.[2] West of the church is the farmhouse which was for many years the residence of the Smith family. It is a 17th-century red brick building, considerably altered and modernised.[3] The school was built in 1861 on land given by William Smith. 'Sister Dora,' the celebrated sister of Mark Pattison, was schoolmistress here from 1861 to 1864.[4] The Mill House on the River Ouzel, is a 17th-century stone house with an upper story of half-timber and a thatched roof.

The Grand Junction Canal passes through the centre of the parish from north to south.

Little Woolstone was inclosed by Act of Parliament in 1791,[5] the award being dated in the following year, when £5 (now £5 5s.) worth of fuel per annum was allotted to the poor of the parish.[6]

MANORS In the reign of Edward the Confessor Edward, a thegn of the king, held 3½ hides in WOOLSTONE as one manor.[7] This was included in 1086 among the lands of Walter Giffard,[8] from whom it descended as half a fee held of the honour of Giffard,[9] through the Clares, Marshals, and Valences, Earls of Pembroke,[10] to the Talbots,[11] who leased their view of frankpledge here for life to John Wyche of Hereford, by whom it was conveyed in 1409 to Robert Chidwall and others.[12] During the 15th century the overlordship of Little Woolstone is confused with that of Broughton,[13] but the heirs of William de Valence were given as overlords in 1630, when the service was said to be unknown.[14]

Under Walter Giffard the manor was held in 1086 by Ralf,[15] from whom it had passed by the early 13th century to Hugh de Chislehampton.[16] In 1254 Ralf son of Nicholas is given as the holder,[17] but the Chislehamptons evidently retained their rights, which they transferred to the Coudrays, since in 1262 Peter de Coudray granted a messuage and a carucate of land in Little Woolstone to Hugh de Chislehampton and Rosamund his wife for life.[18] Peter de Coudray, jun., who may have been a younger son, held Little Woolstone in 1284,[19] but had been succeeded before 1302-3[20] by Thomas, the eldest son of Peter,[21] who died about this date.[22] Thomas de Coudray was still lord in 1316,[23] and settled the reversion of this half fee, extended at eighteen messuages, a mill, a carucate and 8½ virgates of land in Little Woolstone, on his daughter Margery and her husband Roger, son of Roger de Tyringham.[24] Richard de Woodhill, probably the husband of Peter de Coudray's widow, held for life at this date[25] and in 1325,[26] but by 1346 Roger de Tyringham was in possession.[27] By 1397 Little Woolstone had

---

[1] Statistics from Bd. of Agric. (1905).
[2] Add. MS. 5836, fol. 158.
[3] Sheahan, *Hist. and Topog. of Bucks.* 651.
[4] *Dict. Nat. Biog.*, Dorothy Wyndlow Pattison.
[5] Priv. Act, 31 Geo. III, cap. 21.
[6] Recov. R. Mich. 33 Geo. III, m. 87.
[7] *V.C.H. Bucks.* i, 251.   [8] Ibid.
[9] *Testa de Nevill* (Rec. Com.), 247; *Hund. R.* (Rec. Com.), i, 31; *Feud. Aids,* i, 132.

[10] *Feud. Aids,* i, 80, 106; Chan. Inq. p.m. 17 Edw. II, no. 75; *Cal. Close,* 1323-7, p. 273.
[11] Chan. Inq. p.m. 20 Ric. II, no. 51.
[12] Close, 11 Hen. IV, m. 19.
[13] Chan. Inq. p.m. 10 Hen. IV, no. 38.
[14] Ibid. (Ser. 2), dccxlii, 174. Thomas Hanchet, who was returned as overlord in 1489, may have had a grant for life (*Cal. Inq. p.m. Hen. VII*, i, 238).
[15] *V.C.H. Bucks.* i, 251.
[16] *Testa de Nevill* (Rec. Com.), 247.

[17] *Hund. R.* (Rec. Com.), i, 31.
[18] Feet of F. case 16, file 39, no. 1.
[19] *Feud. Aids,* i, 80.
[20] Ibid. 106.
[21] *Var. Coll.* (Hist. MSS. Com.), iv, 154.
[22] *Cal. Fine R.* 1272-1307, p. 480.
[23] *Feud. Aids,* i, 109.
[24] Feet of F. case 18, file 67, no. 19.
[25] Ibid.
[26] *Cal. Close,* 1323-7, p. 273.
[27] *Feud. Aids,* i, 132.

passed from the Tyringhams to the Broughtons,[28] and was held with their manor of Broughton (q.v.) until it was conveyed in 1575 by Thomas Duncumbe and Isabel his wife to George Bury.[29]

In 1596 the manor was granted by George Bury and his wife Mary to Roger Nicholls,[30] who in April 1597 settled it on his son and heir George in tail-male, and died seised of it on 20 November 1629.[31] George Nicholls succeeded his father in the manor,[32] and in 1637 with his wife Elizabeth and others conveyed it by fine to Roger Nicholls.[33] Roger Nicholls and his wife Anne granted the manor in the spring of 1641-2 to Hugh Smith,[34] in whose family it has since remained[35] though the manorial rights seem to have been in abeyance by the end of the 18th. Hugh Smith the elder and his wife Ruth were holding the manor in 1701,[36] and it was held by Hugh Smith in 1735[37] and 1739.[38] No lord of the manor was given in the Inclosure Act of 1791, but William Smith was returned among the principal proprietors of lands.[39] Sheahan wrote about 1862 of William Smith as a principal landowner, whose family had been in occupation for over 250 years.[40] He was the inventor of the 'Steam Cultivator,' and of the mode of cultivation called the Woolstone system.[41] The present representative of the family is the Rev. H. W. Smith, who is also rector.

In 1086 1½ hides in Woolstone were entered among the lands of William Fitz Ansculf, and had been previously held by Ulf, a thegn of King Edward, who could sell.[42] This property continued to be held as a quarter of a fee pertaining to the manor of Newport Pagnell (which had been held by William Fitz Ansculf at Domesday) as late as 1322.[43]

The first under-tenant recorded was William de Newport, clerk, holding 6 virgates in Little Woolstone in 1254.[44] He or his descendants took the name of Clerk. William's son Henry was holding this quarter fee in 1273,[45] and it had descended to Henry's son Richard in 1291.[46] He may be identical with Richard de Tours, by whom it was held in 1322,[47] for it remained in the Clerk family until conveyed to John Comyn by his marriage with Margaret daughter of John Clerk.[48] The Comyns made a settlement of it in 1415 on themselves and the heirs of Margaret, with remainder to John's children John, Thomas, William, Alice and Katherine, and their heirs, and to John Tyringham, John Mortimer and Robert Atteford and the heirs of Robert successively.[49] For the next century the history of this manor remains obscure.

In 1537 it was held by Thomas More of Bourton, Buckingham,[50] who was dead by 1557,[51] leaving two daughters and co-heirs, Jane wife of Thomas Brooke and Alice wife of Giles Pulton.[52] Alice married as her second husband Richard Neale of Nether Dean in Bedfordshire,[53] to whom in 1557 the Brookes conveyed a moiety of the manor.[54] The two sisters and their husbands joined in 1562 in quitclaiming their rights in the manor to Ferdinand Pulton,[55] son of Alice by her first husband,[56] but Richard Neale afterwards acquired sole possession of Little Woolstone, and by his will made 14 February 1574-5

NEALE. Party sable and gules a leopard argent.

and proved 13 June 1575 bequeathed it to his second son Richard in tail-male, with remainder in tail-male to his elder son Thomas, to his godson Richard Neale, son of John Neale of Yelden, Bedfordshire, the elder, and to John second son of the said John Neale, successively.[57] Richard Neale apparently died without issue male, and under his will proved in March 1617, immediately after his death the manor passed to his brother Thomas, of Nether Dean,[58] who in the same year sold it to his second son, Peter Neale of Shelton, Bedfordshire.[59] This Peter was dealing with the manor in 1649,[60] and died in 1661, when he was succeeded by a son and heir Noah.[60a] The manor remained in the Neale family, who appear to have migrated to St. Martin, Stamford Baron, Northamptonshire, until after the death of Noah Neale in January 1769.[61] In 1771 it was alienated by his widow Elizabeth Neale and Noah Neale, presumably his son, to Ambrose Reddall.[62] At the inclosure of the parish in 1791 no lord of this manor was given, but Ambrose Reddall was described as a considerable owner of lands.[63] He died in June of that year, and in his will mentions his widow Sarah, his son Henry and his kinsman Richard Ambrose Reddall of Woburn, Bedfordshire, whom he made executor.[64] The estate was subsequently held by Sir John Riddell, bart., and had passed to Mr. Hanscomb of Newport before 1803.[65]

A mill worth 10s. was held by Walter Giffard with his manor in 1086,[66] and remained among the appurtenances,[67] being leased in 1564 by Sir William Paulet and Dame Agnes his wife to Richard Banes of Woolstone.[68]

[28] Chan. Inq. p.m. 20 Ric. II, no. 51. It was left by Sir Robert Broughton by his will proved 10 July 1507 to his brother William (P.C.C. 29 Adeane).
[29] Feet of F. Bucks. East. 17 Eliz.
[30] Ibid. Mich. 39 Eliz.
[31] Chan. Inq. p.m. (Ser. 2), dccxlii, 174.
[32] Ibid.
[33] Feet of F. Bucks. Mich. 13 Chas. I.
[34] Ibid. Hil. 17 Chas. I.
[35] P.C.C. 88 Drax. Sheahan, loc. cit.
[36] Feet of F. Bucks. Trin. 13 Will. III.
[37] Add. MS. 5839, p. 420.
[38] Feet of F. Bucks. Trin. 13 Geo. II.
[39] Priv. Act, 31 Geo. III, cap. 21.
[40] Loc. cit.
[41] Ibid.
[42] V.C.H. Bucks. i, 256.
[43] Cal. Inq. p.m. (Edw. I), ii, 15, 497; (Edw. II), vi, 257; Cal. Close, 1288-96, p. 220.

[44] Hund. R. (Rec. Com.), i, 31.
[45] Cal. Inq. p.m. (Edw. I), ii, 15.
[46] Ibid. 497; Cal. Close, 1288-96, p. 220.
[47] Cal. Inq. p.m. (Edw. II), vi, 257. Cf. Feet of F. case 19, file 74, no. 19.
[48] Feet of F. case 22, file 116, no. 8.
[49] Ibid.
[50] Recov. R. East. 28 Hen. VIII m. 358; Feet of F. Div. Co. Hil. 28 Hen. VIII.
[51] Feet of F. Bucks. Trin. 3 & 4 Phil. and Mary.
[52] Chan. Inq. p.m. (Ser. 2), dxiv, 47.
[53] Visit. of Beds. (Harl. Soc.), 126.
[54] Feet of F. Bucks. Trin. 3 & 4 Phil. and Mary.
[55] Ibid. Div. Co. Mich. 4 & 5 Eliz.
[56] Chan. Inq. p.m. (Ser. 2), dxiv, 47.
[57] P.C.C. 24 Pickering.
[58] Ibid. 24 Weldon.

[59] Com. Pleas Recov. R. Trin. 15 Jas. I, m. 3.
[60] Feet of F. Bucks. Mich. 1649.
[60a] Blaydes, Gen. Beds., 90, 370. Noah's son was also called Noah and was an infant at the Visitation of 1634 (Visit. of Beds. [Harl. Soc.], 126).
[61] Musgrave's Obit. (Harl. Soc.), iv, 272; P.C.C. 98 Bogg. The Noah Neale who died in Nov. 1734 (Musgrave's Obit. loc. cit.) was probably the father of the Noah who died in 1769.
[62] Recov. R. Hil. 11 Geo. III, m. 417.
[63] Priv. Act, 31 Geo. III, cap. 21.
[64] Musgrave's Obit. (Harl. Soc.), v, 123; P.C.C. 536 Bevor.
[65] Lysons, Mag. Brit. i (3), 672; add MS. 9411, fol. 118d.
[66] V.C.H. Bucks. i, 251.
[67] Feet of F. case 18, file 67, no. 19.
[68] Add Chart 58629.

A free fishery was also attached to this manor in the 17th century.[69] A messuage and land in Little Woolstone, with free fishery in the water of Little Woolstone, was granted in 1701 by John Perry and Susan his wife to John Parrett and Mary Parrett, widow, to hold for 5,000 years at a rent of 2*d*.[70]

The church of the *HOLY TRINITY CHURCH* consists of a chancel 20 ft. 6 in. by 13 ft. 6 in., nave 49 ft. by 23 ft. with bellcote at the west end, a south porch and a north vestry. All these measurements are internal.

There was probably a church on the site, consisting of a chancel and nave, in the latter part of the 12th century, but nothing of it now remains except the font. Towards the end of the 13th century the chancel was probably rebuilt; the chancel arch of that date still survives. The present nave with its bellcote was built in the middle of the 14th century, and the west jamb of an arched opening in the north wall suggests that there was an intention to build a transept on that side, which was never carried into effect. In the 16th century the south porch was added, though it may have succeeded an earlier structure. There was a restoration in 1854. In 1861 the chancel was rebuilt and the north vestry added, while a further restoration was made in 1866.

The chancel, which is wholly modern, is designed to match the 14th-century work of the nave, but there is a lancet in the north wall with some old stones re-used in the jambs. The 13th-century chancel arch is of three chamfered orders and rests on triple clustered respond shafts with moulded capitals, but no visible bases.

The nave is lighted by one window on the north side, two on the south side, and one at the west end, all of the 14th century and having three lights with tracery in pointed heads inclosed by external labels with head-stops. In the west window are several fragments of 14th-century glass, including part of a winged lion, a sitting animal, a fish, the hinder part of a leopard and some other pieces. The north and south doorways are pointed and continuously moulded, that on the north being blocked. In the south wall is a piscina with a trefoiled head and ogee cusps, without a basin. The hearth for the stove at the west end is laid with several old tiles, each containing a quarter of a circular pattern. On the north side of the chancel arch is a plain square corbel which possibly held one end of the rood-beam, while a set-off in the wall on the south side may have supported the other. There is also a corbel set in the east jamb of the south-east window. The nave roof is of four bays and unusually steep pitch. The rafters and collar-beams are concealed by plaster, but the naturally-cambered tie-beams are visible and carry rough octagonal king-posts with moulded capitals and bases which support four-way struts. On the outside a moulded string-course extends for some distance along the south and east walls of the nave and round the buttresses at the south-east angle, but is apparently unfinished.

The bellcote is constructed of ancient oak timbers covered with modern weather-boards and stands on four posts with gallows-bracing between those on the east. The bell-frame forms part of the construction of the cote. The south porch has a moulded but much-weathered plinth; the outer doorway has an innermoulded three-centred arch under a square outer order. Over the arch are two small lights, now blocked, of similar design to that of the doorway. In the side walls are two-light openings of the same character, the mullions of which are now gone. In the north-east corner are the remains of a stoup.

In the window of the modern vestry are some fragments of 14th-century glass, including a bird standing in a trefoiled niche, two human heads issuing from quatrefoils and some tracery.

The font is of the late 12th century and has a moulded base and a circular bowl carved with interlacing semicircular arches and dog-tooth ornament below.

There are three bells, all by Anthony Chandler, 1662.

The plate includes a cup of 1569, similar to that at Great Woolstone and of the same date but smaller; a large paten of 1755, similar to one of the same date at Great Woolstone; and a small modern flagon and paten, unmarked.

The registers previous to 1812 are as follows: (i) mixed entries 1596 to 1771, the title is dated 1558; (ii) baptisms and burials 1772 to 1812, marriages 1774 to 1810.

The advowson of Little Woolstone *ADVOWSON* was obtained by the priory of Combwell in Kent, which presented to the church in 1231[71] and retained the advowson until the Dissolution.[72] It seems then to have been held for one turn by Sir John Gage, by whom it was conveyed in 1550 to Anthony Cave,[73] who presented in 1557.[74] In 1562 the presentation was made by John Newdigate,[75] and in 1677 by the Crown, in whom the advowson has since been vested.[76]

The church was valued at £4 6s. 8d. in 1291[77] and at £8 16s. 8d. in 1535.[78] The living was united to that of Great Woolstone in 1854.

The priory of Tickford held tithes in Little Woolstone[79] which at the Dissolution were granted to Cardinal Wolsey for his college at Oxford, and after his attainder confirmed to that college refounded as King Henry the Eighth's College, by the king.[80] These tithes were held in January 1607-8 by Henry Berry at his death, and in 1613 were in the hands of his son George.[81]

A quit-rent and lands given for the maintenance of the sepulchre light in the church, worth 12*d*. yearly, were recorded at the suppression of the chantries.[82]

For the charity of the Rev. Robert *CHARITIES* Chapman see under parish of Ravenstone.

Poor's rent-charge.—On the inclosure of the parish an allotment was made to the then owner of an

[69] Feet of F. Bucks. Hil. 17 Chas. I; Trin. 13 Will. III.

[70] Feet of F. Bucks. East. 13 Will. III.

[71] *R. of Hugh of Wells* (Cant. and York Soc.), ii, 81.

[72] Harl. Roll V, 13; Add. MS. 5839 p. 421.

[73] Feet of F. Bucks. East. 4 Edw. VI.

[74] Add. MS. 5839, p. 421.

[75] Ibid.

[76] Inst. Bks. (P.R.O.); *Clergy Lists*.

[77] *Pope Nich. Tax.* (Rec. Com.), 33.

[78] *Valor Eccl.* (Rec. Com.), iv, 245.

[79] Chan. Inq. p.m. (Ser. 2), lxxvi, 3.

[80] *L. and P. Hen. VIII*, v, g. 1370 (23).

[81] Chan. Inq. p.m. (Ser. 2), cccxxxvi, 42.

[82] Chant. Cert. 5, no. 28.

GREAT WOOLSTONE CHURCH FROM THE SOUTH-WEST

LITTLE WOOLSTONE CHURCH FROM THE SOUTH

WOUGHTON-ON-THE-GREEN CHURCH FROM THE WEST

estate, now belonging to Mr. J. Sharman, charged with a payment of £5 5s. for fuel for the poor in lieu of the common rights formerly enjoyed by them. The annuity is applied in the distribution of coal.

Church property.—A rent-charge of £1 11s. 6d. issuing out of a farm near the church is annually paid by the owner, the present rector, to the churchwardens and carried to their account.

WOUGHTON ON THE GREEN

Ulchetone (xi cent.); Woketon (xiii cent.); Woketon, Wocton (xiv cent.); Woughton on the Green (xvi cent.); Woughton *alias* Wokington super the Green (xvii cent.); Wokington *alias* Aston super le Greene (xvi and xviii cent.).[1]

The parish of Woughton has an area of 1,224 acres, of which 333 acres are arable land and 806 permanent grass.[2] The soil is various, mostly clay, and the sub-soil clay and gravel. The principal crops grown are wheat, beans and barley. The parish is watered by the River Ouzel, which forms its eastern boundary. The slope of the land is from 345 ft. above ordnance datum in the west to 216 ft. above ordnance datum in the east, where the Ouzel is liable to overflow its banks. Until the end of the 18th century the river here was crossed by a bridge, known as Monxton's Bridge, connecting Walton and Woughton parishes.[3] This name is supposed to commemorate William de Mokelestone, at one time lord of a manor in Woughton, to whom the priest's effigy in the church was wrongly ascribed by Browne Willis.[4]

The village of Woughton on the Green stands on low ground in the east of the parish, and, as its name implies, has grown up around a large central green. On the east side of the green is St. Mary's Church and near by are the entrance gates of Woughton House, a modern building standing in a park of 43 acres. It is the property and residence of Mr. W. J. Levi, J.P. The older houses are mostly of half-timber with brick filling and thatched roofs. The old Swan Inn is a 17th-century house with later additions. The present rectory stands to the south of the church; an older and moated building, situated some distance westward in the neighbourhood of the canal, was formerly used as the rectory. This is probably the house referred to in a terrier of 1639 as a 'homestall' with a moat, a mansion-house containing five bays—namely, a kitchen, buttery, hall, two parlours and a study. There were also a stable of two little bays, a milk-house over the moat containing two bays, a garden plot and orchard of half a rood with a little house standing in the orchard. Without the moat was a barn of six bays, a hay-house of two bays, and

land scattered over the common fields.[5] There is a Wesleyan chapel in the village, erected in 1867. Woughton was inclosed by private Act of Parliament in 1768,[6] when it was provided that proprietors of inclosed lands should deliver yearly to the poor a certain number of faggots in lieu of the right to cut furze on the waste lands.[7]

MANORS There were two manors in *WOUGHTON* at Domesday, of which the more important, assessed at 5½ hides, belonged to Martin who had succeeded Azor son of Toti, a thegn of King Edward.[8] The overlordship of this manor is found later attached to the earldom of Arundel,[9] until Richard Fitz Alan, Earl of Arundel,

THE SWAN INN, WOUGHTON ON THE GREEN

a Lord Appellant, was executed in 1397 as a political traitor, his honours being forfeited to the Crown.[10] The overlordship of Woughton appears to have been permanently alienated from the earldom, and is found in the possession of John Nowers in 1458,[11] 1459,[12] and 1470,[13] after which date no further reference has been found to its exercise.

The descent of the mesne manor of Woughton presents considerable difficulties, which have not hitherto been very successfully handled by Willis and other historians of Buckinghamshire. The lord of this, the principal manor, also owned the advowson of the church, and only by working together two sets of documents, those relating to the manor itself and those relating to the church, has it been found possible to disentangle, as far as may be, the descents. Martin held the land in demesne in 1086,[14] and

[1] This alternative of 'Aston' has only been found in reference to the de Grey property (q.v.) in this parish.

[2] Statistics from Bd. of Agric. (1905).

[3] Add. MS. 5839, fol. 223.

[4] Ibid.

[5] Add. MS. 5839, fol. 225

[6] Acts Priv. and Loc. 8 Geo. III, cap. 25.

[7] Lysons, *Mag. Brit.* i (3), 674; see under charities.

[8] *V.C.H. Bucks.* i, 272.

[9] *Testa de Nevill* (Rec. Com.), 244, 252; *Cal. Close,* 1237–42, p. 478; *Feud.*

Aids, i, 80, 106; Chan. Inq. p.m. 17 Ric. II, no. 32. [244.

[10] G.E.C. *Complete Peerage* (new ed.), i,

[11] Chan. Inq. p.m. 36 Hen. VI, no. 36.

[12] Ibid. 37 Hen. VI, no. 28.

[13] Close, 10 Edw. IV, m. 14.

[14] *V.C.H. Bucks.* i, 272.

the next holders of whom mention has been found are members of the Verly family. Roger de Verly was holding in 1162–3, when he paid half a mark for the king's pardon.[15] His name occurs again in 1175–6, when he was fined 10 marks for a breach of forest law,[16] and it is probably the same Roger against whom Avice wife of Robert de Cleies brought a plea of dower in 1200.[17] In 1221 and again in 1232 one of the same name presented Robert de Haia and William de Haia respectively to the parsonage of Woughton.[18] In 1234 the lands of Roger de Verly and of Hugh his son in Buckinghamshire and Norfolk were said to be mortgaged to the Jews.[19] Roger de Verly died about 1235, in which year Hugh was answerable for his father's debts,[20] and about the same date he was said to hold a fee in Woughton.[2] Hugh de Verly, of whom no later mention has been found than 1242,[22] left a daughter and heir Clarice.[23] His mother, Hawise de Verly,[24] however, held Woughton in dower, as appears from a suit which she brought in 1258–9 against trespassers on her free fishery there,[25] and also from the fact that she presented to the church in 1263.[26] The actual date of Clarice de Verly's occupation of Woughton has not been established ; she was succeeded by her daughter and heir Agnes,[27] who died at some time before 1287,[28] when Sibyl wife of Robert de Cave and Alice wife of Robert de Brangwyn, sisters of Hugh de Verly,[29] claimed equal rights in her inheritance. At this date the Brangwyns sued the Caves for the right of presentation to the church, which fell vacant during the minority of Thomas son of Roger de Nikelfield.[30] Thomas de Nikelfield, whose identity has not been established, was still a minor in 1287.[31] No further mention of him has been found, and Roger de Tyringham, whose connexion with the lords of Woughton Manor has not been established, presented to the church in 1301.[32] About this date there seems to have been a partition of the manor into two unequal divisions.[33] The more important share is found in 1316 in the possession of William de Mokelstone,[34] who held three parts of Woughton Manor and the advowson in right of Joan his wife.[35] Together with her he alienated it in 1347, to

Sir John de Pulteney, kt.,[36] who appears to have alienated it almost immediately to John de Botetourt, for he is found presenting to the church in 1349.[37] In 1358 John de Botetourt and Joyce his wife settled the manor and advowson of Woughton on their son John on the occasion of his marriage with Maud daughter of John de Grey of Rotherfield.[38] John de Botetourt, jun., died seised in 1369, when his son John, aged seven, was declared to be his heir.[39] At this date the manor was said to be worth 100s. and the church 10 marks.[40] Maud de Botetourt married a second husband, Thomas Harcourt, and held this manor in dower till her death in January 1393-4.[41] Her son John predeceased her, and her heir was then her daughter Joyce, wife of Sir Hugh Burnell, kt.,[42] who had already made a settlement of the manor in favour of Thomas Harcourt in 1386.[43] Sir Hugh Burnell held the advowson in 1394,[44] between which date and 1417 an alienation took place to Sir Thomas Green, kt., who then died seised.[45] His heir was his son Thomas Green, who did not long retain the Woughton property, for in 1424 the feoffees of Richard Fox had acquired it.[46] A gap here occurs in the descent of the manor, which is next found in the family of Vavasour, who are described in the bishop's register as dwelling ' in Partibus Borealibus.'[47] This description helps to identify them with the Vavasours of Hazlewood, Yorkshire, more especially as names of the Vavasours connected with Woughton fit in with the known pedigree of this family.[48] In 1490 Sir John Vavasour, justice of the King's Bench, presented to Woughton Church,[49] and in 1518 one of the same family had the patronage.[50] Finally, in 1553 Peter Vavasour conveyed both manor and advowson to Edmund Mordaunt.[51] They were retained by the Mordaunts (later Earls of Peterborough) with the Castle Manor in Lavendon and with Willen (q.v.) till about the middle of the 17th century.[52] In 1637 Woughton Manor and advowson were conveyed, together with Willen, by John Earl of Peterborough to his sisters, Elizabeth, Margaret and Ann Mordaunt.[53] In 1640 they and their brother Lewis Mordaunt[54] transferred Willen to Roger Nicholls,[55] the conveyance probably comprising Woughton, since the Earl re-

[15] *Pipe R. 9 Hen. II* (Pipe R. Soc.), 17.

[16] Ibid. 22 *Hen. II*, 22.

[17] *Rot. Cur. Reg.* (Rec. Com.), ii, 58 ; Feet of F. Div. Co. 1 John, no. 10.

[18] *R. of Hugh of Wells* (Cant. and York Soc.), ii, 55, 86. The vacancy of 1221 was on account of the marriage and consequent resignation of Luke de Kaynes, the recent parson.

[19] *Cal. Close*, 1231–4, p. 502.

[20] *Excerpta e Rot. Fin.* (Rec. Com.), i, 285.

[21] *Testa de Nevill* (Rec. Com.), 244, 247, 251a, 252b.

[22] *Cal. Close*, 1237–42, p. 478. *Rolls of Robert Grosseteste* (Cant. and York Soc.) 356, 361.

[23] De Banco R. 65, m. 2.

[24] Ibid.

[25] Assize R. 1188, m. 12. Luke de Kaynes, the ex-parson of Woughton, was one of the trespassers.

[26] Add. MS. 5839, fol. 224.

[27] De Banco R. loc. cit.

[28] In 1284–6 the heirs of Hugh de Verly were said to hold Woughton (*Feud. Aids*, i, 80).

[29] De Banco R. loc. cit.

[30] Ibid. ; *Cal. Pat.* 1281–92, p. 264.

The Caves won the case, being able to prove that the Brangwyns had transferred to them their interest during the minority of Thomas.

[31] Agnes (de Verly) is expressly stated to have left no heir (De Banco R. loc. cit.).

[32] Add. MS. loc. cit.

[33] In documents quoted in the ensuing paragraphs the property is variously described as moiety or whole of the manor, and it has been thought better to quote in the text in each instance the actual term employed. There seems to be no doubt about the property being the same.

[34] *Feud. Aids*, i, 109.

[35] Feet of F. case 20, file 88, no. 12.

[36] Ibid. ; De Banco R. 350, m. 314.

[37] Add. MS. loc. cit.

[38] Feet of F. case 20, file 94, no. 14 ; *Cal. Pat.* 1358–61, p. 127.

[39] Chan. Inq. p.m. 48 Edw. III (1st nos.), no. 11.

[40] Ibid.

[41] Ibid. 17 Ric. II, no. 32.

[42] Ibid.

[43] Feet of F. Div. Co. 10 Ric. II, no. 149 ; Close, 17 Ric. II, m. 21.

[44] Add. MS. loc. cit.

[45] Chan. Inq. p.m. 5 Hen. V, no. 39.

It is doubtful, however, if the Greens ever held Woughton. Wokketon, as it is written in the inquisition, is probably an error for (Great) Woolstone, for it appears in conjunction with Wavendon and Emberton, all which three manors were held by the Greens in the 14th and 15th centuries. This deed is the only one in which Wokketon appears, and is precisely the only one in which Woolstone is not mentioned.

[46] Add. MS. loc. cit.

[47] Ibid. fol. 224.

[48] *Visit. of Yorks.* (Harl. Soc.), 329.

[49] Add. MS. 5839, fol. 224. By his will dated 11 Jan. 1493–4, and proved 21 Dec. 1506, he decreed that all lands purchased by him, save Woughton, were to be sold (P.C.C. 16 Adeane). His heir was Peter Vavasour, son of his brother William (Chan. Inq. p.m. [Ser. 2], xx, 96).

[50] Add. MS. 5839, fol. 224.

[51] Feet of F. Bucks. Trin. 7 Edw. VI.

[52] Add. MS. 5839, fol. 223 ; Feet of F. Div. Co. Hil. 6 Jas. I ; Chan. Inq. p.m. [Ser. 2], cccix, 200.

[53] Feet of F. Bucks. East. 13 Chas. I.

[54] Chan. Inq. p.m. [Ser. 2], dcxxiv, 64.

[55] Feet of F. Bucks. Trin. 16 Chas. I.

nounced all rights in the same in the following year.[56] In 1656 Roger Nicholls made a settlement on William Nicholls.[57] In 1678 Richard Nicholls and Elizabeth his wife combined with William Nicholls and others in a further settlement.[58] Roger Nicholls, the next lord of the manor, presented to the church in 1704,[59] and finally, in 1717, disposed of the whole estate to William Troutbeck.[60] Of this latter family Edward Troutbeck, who was vicar of Westbury, presented to Woughton Rectory in 1746,[61] and Thomas Troutbeck and Lucy his wife made a settlement of the manor in 1781.[62] Thomas Troutbeck died in 1782,[63] in which year his widow Lucy presented to the church.[64] The name of William Troutbeck, a beneficiary under the will of Thomas, occurs between 1793 and 1800,[65] but shortly after that date changes in ownership took place, the Rev. Mr. Dreyer being patron and incumbent about 1813,[66] while Francis Rose acquired Woughton from him before 1823.[67] Sheahan gives the name of the Rev. Maurice Farrell, who died in 1888, as lord of the manor and patron of the rectory,[68] while since the end of the 19th century the advowson has been held by Mr. Henry Carrington Bowles, who is also one of the principal landowners.

TROUTBECK. *Azure three trout argent interlaced in a triangle.*

Returning to the history of the second moiety of Woughton Manor, after its partition between the Verly co-heirs, we find very little detail of its descent in the 14th century. Walter de Cheriton appears to have been in possession in 1346,[69] and forty years later had given place to John Longville.[70] This family, whose seat was at Wolverton (q.v.), was destined to retain their estate in Woughton for upwards of 400 years.[71] In 1732 the Longvilles were said still to retain the third of the advowson[72] and presumably the moiety of the manor. They must have parted with them shortly after this date to the Troutbecks, lords of the other moiety, for four consecutive presentations were made in 1782, 1793, 1796 and 1800 by members of the Troutbeck family,[73] and no further trace of division of the manor has been found.

In 1086 a second property known as *WOUGHTON MANOR* was assessed at 4 hides, and attached to the lands of the Count of Mortain.[74] He was half-brother of the Conqueror, and was usually considered Earl of Cornwall,[75] to which earldom the overlordship is later found attached. The manor was held by knight's service, ranging from two fees about 1235[76] to a quarter of a fee in 1302–3.[77] At the latter date it was part of the earl's honour of Berkhampstead.[78] The overlordship was held by the Prince of Wales (also Duke of Cornwall) in 1376,[79] but in 1388 was said to be exercised by Thomas Pever.[80]

Overlordship rights in Woughton were attached to the Honour of Berkhampstead as late as 1649.[80a]

Eight thegns, whose names are given, held this manor under the Confessor, and had been succeeded in 1086 by Ralph.[81] His successors took the surname of de Wocheton, Woketon or Woughton. Of them may be noted Robert de Woketon, who in 1166–7 paid half a mark to the sheriff of the county,[82] and whose name also occurs as a juror in the first year of King John's reign.[83] Walter de Woketon appears in 1225, when he was engaged in a dispute with the parson of Woughton as to whether $26\frac{1}{2}$ acres of land were of his lay fee or belonged to the church.[84] His name occurs for the last time about 1235,[85] and was followed by that of Hugh de Woketon, holding here in 1255.[86] His death occurred in or about the year 1279, when a division of his estates took place between his daughters and co-heirs, Joan wife of William de Jarpenville and Sibyl wife of Hugh de Bray.[87] In that year Hugh de Bray and Sibyl came to the king's court and complained that an unfair division had been made of Hugh's inheritance, and after what they wished to propound had been heard, it was found that the chief messuage that belonged to Hugh de Woketon in Woughton remained to be divided between Hugh and Sibyl and William de Jarpenville and Joan his wife, elder daughter and co-heir of Hugh de Woketon, and it was considered in the same court that William and Joan should have the hearth and the things that pertain to hearth-heir (*astrarium*), and that Hugh and Sibyl should have their purparty within the said messuage.[88]

With regard to the history of that moiety of Woughton Manor which fell to William and Joan de Jarpenville, William de Jarpenville's name is returned

[56] Recov. R. Trin. 17 Chas. I, m. 29. Lewis Mordaunt, however, retained an estate in Woughton, on which he was fined £20 as a Papist in 1647 (*Cal. Com. for Comp.* 67).

[57] Feet of F. Bucks. Hil. 1656.

[58] Ibid. Mich. 30 Chas. II.

[59] Inst. Bks. (P.R.O.). It should be noted that in 1664 Richard Barnwell acquired the right of presentation to the church for one turn. He was son-in-law of Roger Nicholls, the purchaser of 1640, whom he sued in 1652 for non-payment of his wife's marriage portion from the projected sale of Willen Manor. (Chan. Proc. [Bridges Div.], bdle. 404, no. 14.)

[60] Feet of F. Bucks. Mich. 4 Geo. I.

[61] Inst. Bks. (P.R.O.).

[62] Feet of F. Bucks. Hil. 21 Geo. III.

[63] P.C.C. 204 Gostling. His will was proved 3 Apr. 1782.

[64] Inst. Bks. (P.R.O.).

[65] Ibid.

[66] Lysons, *Mag. Brit.* i (3), 674.

[67] Lipscomb, *Hist. and Antiq. of Bucks.* iv, 428.

[68] Sheahan, *Hist. and Topog. of Bucks.* 653. He held 211 acres in Woughton in 1873 (*Ret. of Owners of Land* [1873], *Bucks.* 7). Cf. also Charities.

[69] Add. MS. 5839, fol. 224.

[70] Ibid.

[71] In 1458, 1541, and 1557 their estate is called 'one quarter' of the manor and advowson (Chan. Inq. p.m. 36 Hen. VI, no. 36; Feet of F. Div. Co. Trin. 33 Hen. VIII; Chan. Inq. p.m. [Ser. 2], cxi, 6), in 1618 the manor and one-third of the advowson (Chan. Inq. p.m. [Ser. 2], dxlii, 131), and in 1621 a moiety of the manor (ibid. ccclxxxvi, 93). For other references see also Add. MS. 5839, fol. 223; Chan. Inq. p.m. 37 Hen. VI, no. 28; Inst. Bks. (P.R.O.); Leadam, *Dom. Incl.* 1517 (Royal Hist. Soc.), 179–180.

[72] Add. MSS. 5839, fol. 223. Lysons says an alienation was made to Dr. Radcliffe c. 1712 (Lysons, loc. cit., ibid. 668).

[73] Inst. Bks. (P.R.O.).

[74] *V.C.H. Bucks.* i, 246.

[75] G.E.C. *Complete Peerage*, ii, 360.

[76] *Testa de Nevill* (Rec. Com.), 258b.

[77] *Feud. Aids*, i, 107.

[78] Ibid. 106.

[79] Chan. Inq. p.m. 2 Ric. II, no. 57.

[80] Ibid. 12 Ric. II, no. 23.

[80a] Ct. R. (Gen. Ser.), portf. 177, no. 21.

[81] *V.C.H. Bucks.* i, 246. The number of thegns is said to be eight, but ten names are given, and two of the ten holdings enumerated, totals 4 hides $2\frac{1}{2}$ virgates.

[82] *Pipe R.* 13 Hen. II (Pipe R. Soc.), 108.

[83] *Rot. Cur. Reg.* (Rec. Com.), ii, 15.

[84] *Cal. Pat.* 1216–25, p. 582.

[85] *Testa de Nevill* (Rec. Com.), 258b.

[86] Feet of F. Bucks. Mich. 39 Hen. III. Dower in Woughton was claimed from Hugh by Mabel, wife of Walter de Blossomville and widow of Walter de Woketon.

[87] *Cal. Close*, 1272–9, p. 537.

[88] Ibid.

in the Feudal Aid for 1284–6,[89] and in 1302–3 that of Robert de Jarpenville associated with him.[90] In 1321 he acknowledged a debt of £500 to Henry de Jarpenville, to be levied in default of payment on his goods and chattels in Bedfordshire.[91] In 1335 William de Jarpenville, probably a son of the first-named, levied a fine with Hawise Luke on nine messuages, 138 acres of land, 7s. 10d. rent and one-third of a messuage in Woughton, a settlement of this property being made on William, Hawise, Hugh son of Hawise and William his brother, with remainder to the right heirs of William de Jarpenville.[92] In 1346 Hugh de Croft [93] held William de Jarpenville's land, while Hugh de Jarpenville held the fee which Robert de Jarpenville held in 1302–3,[94] but after 1346 nothing further has been ascertained of the Jarpenville moiety.

With reference to the moiety which passed to Hugh and Sibyl de Bray, a settlement is found in 1283, by which Hugh and Sibyl recognized the right of Ralph son of Philip de Woketon (evidently a younger branch of the family resident in the parish) to a messuage and three parts of a virgate in Woughton, Ralph paying a yearly rent and suit of court in return.[95] Hugh de Bray's name occurs as connected with Woughton in 1284.[96] and again in 1291,[97] but shortly after the latter year he appears to have alienated his property in Woughton to Peter de Flitton.[98] The only evidence that has been found of any composition between them is in 1293, when Hugh and Sibyl acknowledged the right of Alice wife of Peter de Flitton to half a virgate in Woughton.[99] Peter de Flitton held Hugh de Bray's fee in 1302,[100] between which date and 1316 it had been alienated by Alice de Flitton to Roger Grey on behalf of his father, John Grey, Lord de Grey.[1] The Greys (afterwards Earls of Kent) owned the manor of Bletchley (q.v.), and this part of Woughton follows the same descent as that manor until its alienation in the 17th century. Woughton, however, remained with the Greys until certainly the 18th century, and was attached to their manor of Brogborough, Bedfordshire.[2] Several individual references to Woughton may be noted in accounts of Grey property. In 1323 the total value of Woughton, arising from free tenants, bondmen and rents of assize, was 69s. 11¾d.[3] In 1324 Roger son of John Lord de Grey was said to hold Woughton Manor,[4] and in 1388 and again in 1396 the property was described as one-fourth of the manor.[5] In the middle of the 16th century it is called 'certain lands and tenements . . . parcel of the manor of Brokborowe,' and then included one tenant holding in free soccage, four customary tenants and three paying rents of assize.[6] After the 17th century casual mention is found of appurtenances in Woughton attached to Brogborough Manor.[7]

The Abbot of Woburn owned a small property in Woughton, which was taxed, together with Crawley, at 59s. 11d. in 1337.[8] A messuage and 15 acres in Woughton belonged to the abbot in 1366.[9] At the Dissolution the abbey's rents in Woughton were demised to Richard Potte, and were worth 13s. 4d.[10] In 1579 Edmund Downing and John Walker received a royal grant of these lands.[11]

The church of the *ASSUMPTION CHURCH OF THE BLESSED VIRGIN* consists of a chancel 38 ft. by 17 ft., north vestry, south organ chamber, nave 46 ft. 6 in. by 19 ft., south aisle 9 ft. 6 in. wide, west tower 10 ft. square, and south porch. A north vestry and south organ chamber are modern additions.

The church appears to have been reconstructed and enlarged in the first half of the 14th century, when the south aisle and porches were added, but the chancel and nave incorporate in their north walls remains of a 13th-century building, and the stones of the chancel arch, which was widened when the church was rebuilt, belong to the middle of that century. The west tower was built early in the 15th century. The north vestry was added in 1867 and the organ chamber in 1891.

The chancel is lighted by a modern window at the east end, by a two-light window with modern tracery on the north, and on the south by a two-light 14th-century window, the sill of which has been carried down to form a seat with traceried back. At the east end of the north wall is a 14th-century recess much restored, with an elaborately moulded ogee arch and a carved finial; two roughly carved heads are set in the imposts, while at the west end of the wall is a modern doorway to the vestry. To the west of the window in the south wall is the entrance to the modern organ chamber. The chancel arch was originally of mid-13th-century date, but the enlargement of the chancel in the 14th-century required increased width of the arch, which does not now fit on to the jambs. The square jambs have half-octagonal pilasters with moulded capitals and bases. There is a 15th-century piscina with a cinquefoiled head having crockets and buttresses, much of which is modern. In the modern organ chamber are two 14th-century windows, that in the east wall was taken from the east wall of the south aisle. A similar window and a door in the south wall have been reset from the chancel.

The nave is lighted from the north by two 15th-century windows, the eastern of which has modern tracery, and in the same wall is a contemporary moulded doorway. On the south side is an arcade of four bays of early 14th-century date. The arches are pointed and of two chamfered orders, and spring from quatrefoil columns and responds with moulded capitals and bases. In the wall to the east of the arcade is a small arched opening, nearly all modern, but with an old sill about 3 ft. above the floor, in which is the bowl of a piscina. Above the arch is a partly

[89] *Feud. Aids*, i, 77.
[90] Ibid. 107.
[91] *Cal. Close*, 1318–23, p. 478; cf. *Feud. Aids*, i, 109.
[92] Feet of F. Bucks. Trin. 9 Edw. III, no. 4.
[93] Possibly Hugh son of Hawise Luke quoted in the above settlement.
[94] *Feud. Aids*, i, 133.
[95] Feet of F. Bucks. Trin. 11 Edw. I, no. 2.
[96] *Feud. Aids*, i, 77.
[97] *Cal. Close*, 1288–96, p. 200.

[98] Peter seems to have had some prior interest in Woughton, for his name appears in the aid for 1284–6 (*Feud. Aids*, i, 77).
[99] Feet of F. Bucks. Mich. 21 Edw. I, no. 8. [100] *Feud. Aids*, i, 107.
[1] Chan. Inq. p.m. 17 Edw. II, no. 74; *Feud. Aids*, i, 109.
[2] Ld. Rev. Misc. Bks. clxxxviii, fol. 303; *V.C.H. Beds.* iii, 321. Their pedigree is given in full under Wrest in Flitton (ibid. ii, 327), and is also to be found in G.E.C. *Complete Peerage*, iv, 105 et seq.

[3] Anct. Ext. (Exch. L.T.R.), no. 78 (1).
[4] *Cal. Close*, 1323–7, p. 77.
[5] Chan. Inq. p.m. 12 Ric. II, no. 23; 19 Ric. II, no. 30.
[6] Ld. Rev. Misc. Bks. clxxxviii, fol. 303.
[7] Feet of F. Div. Co. East. 1 Anne.
[8] *Cal. Pat.* 1334–8, p. 493.
[9] *Cal. Close*, 1364–8, p. 244.
[10] *Valor Eccl.* (Rec. Com.), iv, 212.
[11] Pat. 21 Eliz. pt. vi, m. 1; Add. MS. 5839, fol. 222 d.

broken grotesque head with curled hair. In the east wall is a 14th-century niche with a trefoiled head partly cut back to the wall. In the modern external cornice of the north wall are set several small carved grotesques, apparently of the 13th century, which were found during restoration buried in the wall. The different character of the masonry in the western bay points to a lengthening of the 13th-century nave in the 14th century.

The south aisle is lighted from the south by two windows and from the west by one window; the openings of both appear to be original but the tracery is modern. Between the windows in the south wall is a 14th-century moulded and chamfered doorway. At the south-east is a double piscina of the 15th century with flanking buttresses and a crocketed and finialled main head of ogee form inclosing two trefoiled heads with a pierced quatrefoil between them. Only the eastern recess has a bowl, and the central mullion is gone. The rood-loft staircase at the north-east corner of the aisle is intact and retains its upper and lower square-headed doorways. Over the latter is a 15th-century canopy resting on grotesque corbels.

The tower is of three stages. The tower arch is four-centred, with moulded capitals and bases. The two-light west window of the ground stage has modern tracery in original jambs. Above it is a small square-headed window, and in the bell-chamber are four windows of two lights under pointed heads, all badly repaired in cement.

The 14th-century south porch has an outer archway with chamfered jambs having half-octagonal pilasters and moulded capitals, but no bases. Over the arch is an image niche with a trefoiled head. At the sides are square openings containing two lights with trefoiled heads.

The font has a tub-shaped bowl of the 13th century. The communion table is of late 16th-century date, and has large turned baluster legs. It has a modern top and two new legs, and has been much enlarged. There is a chair in the chancel of about the same date with a carved back, turned legs, and curved arms.

In the recess in the chancel is a 14th-century effigy of a priest in mass vestments, his feet resting on an animal. It lies on a slab raised above the floor with a panelled front of tracery of the same date. North of the chancel in the churchyard is a ridged coffin lid with remains of an incised cross of the 13th or 14th century. In the chancel is a marble wall tablet to David James, rector (d. 1746), and his wife Martha (d. 1735). In the tower floor is a slab to the same persons, but not in its original position. Another marble tablet in the chancel is to David James (d. 1789), his wife Catherine (d. 1780), and widow Ann (d. 1791).

There are four bells: the treble and second, formerly dated 1653 and 1717 respectively, were recast in 1887; the third is inscribed 'Chandler made me 1701,' and the fourth is by Pack & Chapman of London, 1771.

The plate consists of a fine 15th-century paten; a flagon inscribed 'Ex dono Mary James 1738,' but without date-mark; a plain cup with moulded stem of 17th-century date, unmarked; a paten inscribed 'The Gift of Da. James Rector of Woughton 1732,' with the date-mark of 1720; and a modern chalice. The 15th-century paten is silver-gilt, and has a central sexfoil sinking inscribed with the sacred monogram, the cusps and foils being engraved with foliated ornament. Round the rim is a black-letter inscription, 'Miserere mei Deus secundum magnam misericordiam tuam,' with foliated stops between the words. The metal shows signs of wear.

The registers previous to 1812 are as follows: (i) mixed entries 1558 to 1652, in very bad condition, has been printed by the Bucks Parish Register Society; (ii) mixed entries 1692 to 1718; (iii) baptisms and burials 1718 to 1812; (iv) marriages 1755 to 1812. The entries from 1653 to 1692 have been lost.

ADVOWSON The descent of the advowson of the church of Woughton has already been traced under the history of the manor. In 1291 the church was assessed at £6 13s. 4d.,[12] and at the Dissolution the rectory was said to be worth £17.[13]

By the Inclosure Act of 1768 an allotment of land was assigned to the rector in lieu of tithes.[14]

CHARITIES Church and Poor's Allotment.— Under the Inclosure Award of 1769[15] an allotment of 13 a. 3 r. 2 p. was made to the feoffees of Woughton in lieu of lands formerly belonging to them. The property of the charity consists of this allotment, also of five cottages and two gardens, producing a gross income of about £20. The net income is divided into moieties, one moiety being applied for church purposes and the other, together with the fuel money next mentioned, is distributed in coal.

Fuel for Poor.—Under the Inclosure Act above referred to provision was made for delivery at the church gate of a certain number of faggots for the use of the poor. The sum of £2 2s. 4d. is now paid annually in respect of this charity.

The Rev. Maurice Farrell by his will, proved at London 2 August 1888, bequeathed £100 consols (with the official trustees), the annual dividends of £2 10s. being applicable under the provisions of a scheme of 17 February 1891 for the benefit of the poor in such way as the trustees should consider most conducive to the formation of provident habits.

[12] *Pope Nich. Tax.* (Rec. Com.), 34, 41.

[13] *Valor Eccl.* (Rec. Com.), iv, 245.

[14] Lysons, *Mag. Brit.* i (3), 674.

[15] *Blue Book of Inclosures*, 13.

POLITICAL HISTORY

THE earliest entry in the chronicle[1] connecting the Anglo-Saxon folk with Buckinghamshire falls under the year 571 and tells the story of the incursion of Cuthwulf, one of the royal house of Wessex, when he fought the Bretwalas at Bedcanforda, taking four towns, Lygeanburg, Ægelesburg, Baenesingtun and Egonesham, and died that year. A problem is presented by the very statement, though of the identities of the place of battle, Bedford, and of three of the towns there is no sort of doubt—Aylesbury, Benson and Eynsham, and of the fourth there need not have been any. Benson and Aylesbury are so near to the track of Icknield Way, the trackway from Wessex leading north-eastwards beyond the Thames at Wallingford, that Lygeanburg might be naturally looked for on it; and close by the source of the Lea[2] where Icknield Way crosses in the neighbourhood of mysterious earthworks is Limbury, and near is also the escarpment from which the plains towards Bedford lie stretched before the beholder's view. The problem is caused by the order in which the names were fossilized in the entry of the chronicle. Bedford, Limbury, Aylesbury and Benson and the Thames at Wallingford are a quite easily intelligible route to one who knows the district, but the order is the reverse of that which one might expect a raid to take. Still it feels safer to keep to the traditional order given. Conjectures about the reason of it can be practically limited to two: either a march by Cuthwulf along the Portway past the Oxfordshire Dorchester towards Towcester and across the watershed and by the Ouse to Bedford, followed by his subjugation of the tract between this and the Thames, by advancing first from Bedford to the Chilterns and then taking the Icknield Way as the route home; or else a pursuit of British forces beginning at Benson, by the same Icknield Way past Aylesbury and Limbury and thence to Bedford, and then a making secure by conquest of the three towns on the return. Perhaps the former is the more likely. Eynsham must in either case have been a separate matter.[3]

But the utmost effect of Cuthwulf's raid so far as it concerns the county must have been the gaining possession of less than two-thirds of it, the part north-west of the Chilterns. The distinctly West Saxon remains[4] do not mount the escarpment. The remains found at Taplow, well within the line of heights but down near the Thames, were of a more south-eastern character,[5] but these were too near the easier water-way of the Thames to allow of arguing from them that the uplands of the Chilterns, the district of the 'Ciltern sætna,' were peopled from the south-east. To get light on this we have to work from other data. The East Saxon diocese of London only touched the county where it borders upon Middlesex, and the Liberty of St. Albans, which did not belong to Wessex but to Mercia, was, like the whole county of Buckingham, included in the diocese of Lincoln till after the 12th century.[6] Then again the long rampart or boundary earthwork called

---

[1] *Angl.-Sax. Chron.* (Rolls Ser.), i, 32.

[2] Lige, Lyge, Lygean (Angl.-Sax.). Cf. *Place-Names Soc.* ii, p. xii.

[3] As associated with the Anglo-Saxon, or rather West Saxon, occupation of the Thames valley, a discovery of remains ought not to be passed over, though it cannot be proved to be connected with this particular raid. About 100 yards from the eastern track of the Icknield Way in Pitstone parish, on a knoll close under the Chilterns, in 1900, the writer helped to dig out the remains of a skeleton buried about 2 ft. below the surface. The body lay north-west and south-east, the head to the north-west. Over one knee was a shield boss of iron of the conoid form with shoulder rim and spike and stud. The total height of the boss, including the spike, was $7\frac{6}{8}$ in., the spike itself was $1\frac{5}{16}$ in., the shoulder rim was $\frac{6}{8}$ in. The diameter at the base, not counting the rim, was $4\frac{6}{8}$ in. The rim to the shoulder of the base (the part where the wooden shield had been fitted in) was $\frac{3}{4}$ in. The sword, of iron, straight, and broken as usual in heathen burials, was of 2-in. blade. Its total length was $32\frac{1}{2}$ in., one fragment being 22 in.—5-in. handle and 17 in. part of blade—the other $12\frac{1}{2}$ in. This was about the usual length of Anglo-Saxon swords. No fibula was found, but a fragment of an iron plate, evidently part of the shield brace, and seven fragments of cutlery. The bones were placed afterwards by the Rev. G. W. R. Kent, then vicar, in the churchyard of Pitstone.

[4] *V.C.H. Bucks.* i, 195–205. [5] Ibid.

[6] Robert de Gorham, Abbot of St. Albans, procured in 1161 from Pope Adrian IV freedom from diocesan control (Walsingham, *Gesta Abbat.* [Rolls Ser.], i, 128).

Grimsdyke[7] has its ditch on its south-eastern side, and from that side accordingly were its possibilities of being carried. Scattered here and there outside it at a little distance are earthworks (camps) certainly not Roman. It could hardly be other than the last defence of a people driven back on the sloping uplands almost to the summit of the escarpment. The Chiltern uplands are to this day a difficult region for a stranger to find his way about in. When they were chiefly forest the conquest and occupation of them must have taken generations to accomplish, and if we take the evidence of diocesan boundaries into account were only completed after Essex was under the hegemony of Mercia, and then the final strip of heights between the dyke and the slope of the escarpment could be carried, perhaps not before Mercia had come into possession of the lower lands of the Thame valley. To this combined occupation by Mercia and Essex somewhat agrees the witness of the dialect, which is—or was—distinct from that of the rest of the county[8]; and added to this is the long-continued rivalry between the hill districts and the vale, of which we hear something in connexion with 17th-century assessments,[9] and which continued till after the 19th century began.[10]

Thus Buckinghamshire has the characteristics of a county with parts of separate origin that were with some difficulty welded. It is not one of the counties of original West Saxon origin, nor one of those of Mercian foundation. It was a frontier district and had the vicissitudes of such districts. Some of these we may with advantage follow up.

In 628, when Penda[11] of Mercia fought with Cynegils of Wessex and an agreement was made between them, the district of the diocese of Dorchester which included the county must have been left to Wessex; for its bishop, Birinus,[12] baptized the West Saxons in 634. What happened in the three years of Cenwalh's expulsion from Wessex by the Mercian king we cannot say. Cenwalh's grant to Cuthrede in 648 of 3,000 'londes be Æscesdune'[13] (Ashdown, co. Berks.) taken into consideration with the hidage of that county, in 1065 given as 2,502,[14] suggests the making of Berkshire into a frontier state, and this might mean that Mercia was already encroaching on Oxfordshire and Buckinghamshire. In 661 Wulfhere, Penda's son, was ravaging as far as Ashdown, and he even gave Wight to the South Saxon king.[15] In 705 Waldhere, Bishop of London, held a meeting to settle disputes between Wessex and Essex at Brentford[16]; but close up to this time Surrey was evidently under Wessex; and the conference need not imply a conterminous boundary more than that of Middlesex and Surrey. But in Ethelbald's days and all through Offa's (c. 718–96) Mercia rose to a great height of power, and Kent, Surrey and Middlesex, and therefore Essex, fell before it. The two kings, Ethelred of Mercia and Cuthred of Wessex, appear in alliance in 743.[17] In 752 Cuthred overcame[18] his rival. But divisions evidently arose in the West Saxon kingdom and in 777 Offa took possession of Benson.[19]

From that date onwards the district became permanently a part of Mercia, a kingdom which seems, from study of the charters, to have been the dominion of a paramount lord who had half-independent rulers under him called with little distinction of terms 'duces,' 'subreguli' or 'principes.' Of these there were at least twelve contemporaneous in Offa's time as witnesses to his charters. But though these separate principalities were doubtless the originals of Mercian counties—of those, at least, outside of the Danelaw—there is no traceable connexion between any of them and Buckinghamshire.

From Offa's time to the days of Ethelred I of Wessex history is silent about the county, but in 871,[20] when the Danes, after the defeat and slaughter of St. Edmund in East Anglia, made an incursion into Wessex, their route must have been along the Icknield Way, and this their first ravage of the county. Twice before 873 Mercia made peace with them. In 877, after Alfred[21]

---

[7] *V.C.H. Bucks.* ii, 34. Ploughing and filling in has destroyed much of this dyke. The writer had the good fortune to interest one farmer sufficiently in it to cause him to desist.

[8] A. J. Ellis, *Philolog. Soc. Trans.* ii (1885–7) and maps. The dialect there is given as like that of North London and Middlesex. The author was making observations for Mr. Ellis till his death. London was of course after Offa's time practically a Mercian city.

[9] *Verney Papers* (Camd. Soc.), 127.

[10] The late Mr. Benjamin Fuller, J.P., in 1880, an aged man at the time, told the writer of the difficulty he had when a young man in the early 19th century in keeping the peace between the militia of the Chilterns and that of the other part of the county in their musters at Aylesbury.

[11] *Angl.-Sax. Chron.* (Rolls Ser.), i, 44.   [12] Ibid.   [13] Ibid. 48.

[14] F. H. Baring, *Domesday Tables*, 51.   [15] *Angl.-Sax. Chron.* loc. cit.

[16] Birch, *Cart. Sax.* i, 169–70.   [17] *Angl.-Sax. Chron.* (Rolls Ser.), i, 78.   [18] Ibid.

[19] Ibid. 92. In 795 Offa gave land in Swanbourne and Horwood (Little) to St. Alban (Birch, op. cit. i, 367), and just before his death the manor of Winslow, where he was living (Matt. Paris, *Chron. Maj.* [Rolls Ser.], i, 361).

[20] The dates henceforward given are those which are decided for by Plummer in *Two Saxon Chronicles* (1892), i, 70.   [21] Ibid. 75.

had baffled them at Exeter, the Danes left Wessex for Mercia and there made Ceolwulf the king partition his kingdom by surrendering to them a portion. But the county, as it would seem, was not given up to them, and remained in English Mercia. In 879, after [22] the defeat of the Danes by Alfred at Ethandune, when they were forced to make peace with him, those of the Danish army who adhered to Guthrum settled in East Anglia and Essex, but Buckinghamshire still remained in English Mercia, for a witenagemot was held under Ethelred of Mercia at Princes Risborough in 884.[23] Two years later Alfred occupied [24] London, and the boundary of the East Anglian kingdom as settled between Alfred and Guthrum after 885 shows that in this part of English Mercia which Ethelred seems to have held till his death in 912 were included Hertfordshire south and west of the Lea, South Bedfordshire west of the sources of the Lea to a line drawn straight to Bedford, and thence, south of the Ouse, to the borders of Buckinghamshire, and all the county of Buckingham except the very small portion north of the Ouse and north-east of Watling Street where that river crosses it.[25] But some years before 912 the rebellion of Ethelwold, son of Ethelred I, must have inflicted much damage on the county, since the Danes he brought from East Anglia passed through it on their way to Cricklade [26] in 904. After this campaign was over peace was made by Edward with the Danes of East Anglia and those of Northumbria, which must have included terms made with the 'Five Boroughs' at Yttingford. This Mr. Stevenson in his map places near Linslade. With Edward's taking into his own hands after Ethelred's death the lands that belonged to Oxford and London together with those cities, and so relieving his sister of the burden of a boundary conterminous with East Anglia, we begin to see preparations for the division of this district into counties; for in 913 he built a fortress borough at Hertford,[27] and in 915 another at Buckingham,[28] where he spent four weeks while it was being fortified. Both at Buckingham and Hertford it is noticeable that Edward built and fortified on both sides of the streams on which they lay, and when we study his campaigns it becomes very clear that these two boroughs were established for frontier purposes and also as centres for the assembling of the 'fyrde'—the local militia of each county. Swifter mobilization was a necessity in the face of the new Danish strongholds settled at Bedford and Northampton. This appears to be the origin of these two counties Hertfordshire and Buckinghamshire, though, except for the needs of the frontiers, St. Albans in the one case and Aylesbury in the other would have been the more natural county towns.

These arrangements made, Edward could advance in 916 to take possession of Bedford.[29] After this he had London, Hertford, Buckingham and Oxford, and the newly captured stronghold Bedford to defend the whole of the south-eastern part of English Mercia—that is, the region which included the south-western quarter of Essex, Middlesex, Hertfordshire, at first only to the Lea, Buckinghamshire, and the south of Bedfordshire and Oxfordshire—and to keep back East Anglian Danes and those of the 'Five Boroughs.' Then with these fortresses and those in Mid and North Essex in his hands he began to move his general frontier northwards to subdue the Danelaw. But this was not unchecked. In 918 the Danes of Northampton and Leicester and of parts more northerly broke [30] in upon Towcester, which Edward had just been fortifying, much as in 914 they had broken in upon Hook Norton (Oxon) and Leighton (Beds.). They spent a whole day in trying to capture Towcester, but being foiled in this sent out a band at night and ravaged Bernwood (round Brill) and the county as far as Aylesbury. Edward erected stone fortifications at Towcester in consequence, instead of earth and timber, reduced Northamptonshire as far as the Welland, and rebuilt Huntingdon, which the Danes had forsaken to fortify Tempsford (Beds.).[31] As a result at his death he left Buckinghamshire far within his boundary. No loss of territory was incurred by Athelstan, but we gather from his laws that there was still a difference between the jurisdiction of Mercia and that of Wessex south of the Thames. For a time in 939 at the beginning of Edmund's reign the county was separated from Wessex by the revolt of the Northumbrian Danes and their incursion, but Edmund soon recovered his dominion over the Danelaw. Again in 959 the revolt of Mercia against Edwin seems to have separated it.[32] But this was over when, a few months later, Edgar succeeded to both kingdoms.

[22] Plummer, *Two Saxon Chronicles* (1892), i, 77.

[23] Birch, op. cit. ii, 174–5.   [24] Plummer, op. cit. i, 80 ; ii, 99.

[25] A part of Essex may, and probably must, have been included, for Chron. A mentions under 897 (=896) amongst the chief losses by death of King Alfred's most valuable men Beorhtulf, Ealdorman of Essex. Hertfordshire seems to have been in English Mercia in 888 (Birch, op. cit. ii, 194).

[26] *Angl.-Sax. Chron.* (Rolls Ser.), i, 180 ; Plummer, op. cit. i, 92.

[27] Plummer, op. cit. i, 96.   [28] Ibid. 100 ; cf. ibid. ii, 116.

[29] Ibid. i, 100.   [30] Ibid. 101 ; cf. ibid. ii, 116.

[31] Chron. A 94 (918) ; cf. Plummer, op. cit. i, 101 ; ii, 116. This is incidental evidence that these counties, Huntingdon and Bedford, were not yet distinctly formed, though they seem to have been marked out on the lines of Danish districts.   [32] Plummer, op. cit. i, 113.

Thence we have no history to record until towards the end of the reign of Ethelred II and the different whirlwinds of Sweyn's incursions : that of 1009, when he led [33] his men from London, through 'Chiltern to Oxford,' and ravaged also on his return journey ; that of 1010, first on somewhat the same track, and then north-eastwards towards Bedford, 'burning ever as he went' ; that of 1013, when, after reaching Watling Street in his advance from the north, he and his army wrought the 'greatest evils that any army could.' [34] In these the county must have been thoroughly wrecked. And to the devastations wrought by the invaders were added the expenses of raising bodies of men (the fyrde) used to ineffective purpose, and of contributing to build ships, one from each hundred, to help to form a fleet, which by the same bad management was frittered away in internecine strife.

Then in 1016 came the contest between Cnut and Edmund Ironside ; once again the county was plundered, and upon that followed the last struggle, when the English nobility fell at Assandun [35] (Ashingdon), in Essex, in a desperate battle. A settlement was then reached by the partition of the realm between Cnut, who held England north of the Thames, and Edmund, who held the south. But this was only for a year. At Edmund's deat.. on 30 November 1016 all fell into the hands of Cnut.

During the time between the middle of the 10th century and this, the county seems to have been included in the greater ealdormanry of Essex ; for one of these ealdormen, Leofsige, is found reversing a decision of the reeves of Buckinghamshire and Oxfordshire.[36] The succession of these ealdormen given by Napier and Stevenson [37] is as follows : Ælfgar, who died in 951 ; Byrhtnoth, the hero of the fight at Maldon, from 956 to 990 ; Leofsige, 994 to 1002.

Though the frontier county, as it then was, suffered so many vicissitudes and such frequent devastations, yet examination of the Domesday record reveals on the whole an amount of comparative prosperity which may excite surprise. Perhaps the silence between 1016 and 1066 is the best record of its recovery, for the county in that period has practically no history. In 1017 Cnut divided England into four great earldoms ; and for the fifty succeeding years these were continued with many modifications in their number and extent, but whether Buckinghamshire remained in one of these for all that time or was transferred from one to another is uncertain.[38]

In 1066, after Hastings and the collapse of the English resistance, William passed through Buckinghamshire on his way to Westminster. At Wallingford, where he crossed the Thames, he seems to have made friends with Wigod the thane there, whose post and possessions on both sides of the river, extended afterwards as the honour of Wallingford, appear to mark him out as the custodian of the ford, a position which in the old divided state of the country, when raids were many, was important to the Anglo-Saxon kings in England as well as to the Kings of Wessex. William's track through the county has been traced with great probability by the Hon. F. H. Baring through careful examination of the lines of depressed values of manors when 'received,' as the Domesday record has it, by the Norman owners.[39] These reduced values show three lines of devastation, probably the lines of a divided march, through Bledlow, Risborough, Ellesborough, Stoke Mandeville, Weston Turville, Aston Clinton, Waddesdon, Hardwick, Claydon, Padbury, Tingewick and Thornborough, and thence eastward to Beachampton, Wolverton, Loughton, Linford, Hanslope, Sherington, Olney and Lavendon ; from Aston Clinton another line is traceable, as if from a parting of the army near there, through Buckland, Aston Abbots, Cublington, Mentmore, Linslade, Simpson and Brickhill ; and the line of march of a detachment, covering the London side of the main march, Mr. Baring tracks through Iver (from Harmondsworth), Stoke Poges, Burnham, Taplow, Hitcham and Wooburn. These all united later in Hertfordshire for William's march on London.

Walter Giffard, owner of forty-seven manors and holdings in the county in 1086, and afterwards earl—if it was not his son of the same name—took in 1090 and in 1095 the part of William Rufus against Robert of Normandy, and in 1102 the part of Robert against Henry I, and this is almost all we hear politically of Buckinghamshire till we come to the Angevin kings. The areas of private jurisdiction in which courts were held for pleas separate from the courts of the hundreds, producing revenues and fees to the baronial owners which were thus lost to the Crown, were for this reason amongst others found by the Plantagenets prejudicial to their interests. The early arrangements of the shrievalties, as we find them in the reign of Henry II, show the beginning of a movement towards vesting all jurisdiction in the Crown which Edward I systematically worked for. In 1154–5 three men, Richard Basset, Aubrey de Vere and Robert Carun, were appointed as a body of sheriffs over the six counties of Bedford, Buckingham, Hertford, Essex, Huntingdon and Cambridge, but in the next year

[33] Plummer, op. cit. i, 139.   [34] Ibid. 143.   [35] Ibid. 153.   [36] Kemble, *Cod. Dipl.* no. 1289.
[37] Napier and Stevenson, *Crawford Charters*, 85, 86, 102, 135.
[38] Freeman, *Norman Conquest*, ii, note 9; *V.C.H. Bucks.* i, 210.   [39] F. H. Baring, op. cit. 207 et seq.

the district was divided up, and Buckinghamshire placed with Bedfordshire in one shrieval area, and this arrangement remained in force till 1575.[40] The greatest barony of the county which held these rights was the honour of Wallingford, the lord of which in Stephen's time, Brian Fitz Count, had taken part against Stephen. But, as is the case also all through Plantagenet times with most of the great owners, his history belongs to other counties more than to this. Remembrance of an older state of things is shown by the entry in the Hundred Rolls about Marsworth, one of the fifty-six manors of the county included in the honour, in which it is shown that the people there used to be under the jurisdiction of the hundred, though at the time of the return they made their suit only to the honour court at Wallingford.[41] Gradually, like some others of these franchises which had been incontestably granted, this was got into the king's hands by being given to scions of the royal house. In 1217 the honour of Wallingford was given to Richard, called King of the Romans, who was made Earl of Cornwall; from him it descended to his son. But his son dying without issue made the king his heir. Then the honour was held for short periods by different grantees till it was given to John of Eltham, who was made Earl of Cornwall; when he died in 1336 it reverted to the Crown. On the occasion of creating Edward the Black Prince Duke of Cornwall it was made an appanage of this duchy as the inheritance of the eldest sons of the kings.[42]

Up to the time of Edward I the kings had a palace at Brill, and a forest was attached thereto, but the royal visits have no record of anything of political importance happening there. Edward I kept his Christmas at Ashridge in 1290,[43] and held his Parliament at that college in the following year.[44] Castle Thorpe (Hanslope) was razed by Falkes de Breauté in December 1215 during the war between John and the barons. Alan Basset, lord of Wycombe, was one of the barons whose names John associated with his own in the granting of the Great Charter. But the centres of political activity as well as the greater possessions of the baronial houses lay elsewhere in other counties.

The rising of the Commons in 1380, widespread as it was, does not seem to have reached Buckinghamshire. In 1400, after the imprisonment of Richard II, we come upon an incidental notice of something that happened within its borders. This is in the conspiracy to restore Richard II, related by various chronicles with differences in particulars and places.[45] The main lines seem clear, however, that the Earls of Rutland, Huntingdon and Kent, all of the royal blood, and others, some of them only just released from the prisons in which Henry IV had placed them, arrayed a cleric named Magdelain, a former royal chaplain, in voice and figure somewhat like to Richard II, in kingly robes, and made for Windsor to capture or slay Henry IV. Rutland was not with them at this juncture, but was to meet them at Colnbrook on 6 January 1399–1400. They were there on the 4th on their way to London, and there as elsewhere on their journey they got many to join them in the belief that Richard was with them. Rutland did meet them, but only to tell them that the king knew all and was advancing to attack them. They had gathered together some thousands of men, but they did not stay to be attacked. They retired apparently through Maidenhead, where their rearguard kept the king's forces at bay for a few hours. But the conspiracy collapsed and most of the leaders were put to death.

Thomas Chaucer, son of Geoffrey the poet, Speaker of the House of Commons in 1407, 1410, 1411 and 1414, who maintained the privileges and freedom of the Speaker when they were assailed

---

[40] The assizes during the 13th and 14th centuries were usually held at Newport Pagnell for the convenience of the northern hundreds, and High Wycombe for that of the Chiltern district, and occasionally at Aylesbury or elsewhere.

The Gaol Delivery Rolls show that the prisons were at Wycombe and Aylesbury in the times of Edward I, Edward II and Edward III, and at Aylesbury in the time of Henry IV. In 1534 there was still a county prison at Aylesbury. In 1543–4 the commission of gaol delivery to John Baldwin and others shows that there was then a gaol in Buckingham Castle, and this may possibly have been the case since the time of Henry VI. The king's session-house, or at any rate one of them, was at Aylesbury in the reign of Henry VIII, for we are told that it needed a new roof of lead. It would seem from these particulars that the process of making Aylesbury the centre for assize and judicial administration was only gradual, that Buckingham was seldom used for this purpose, and that Wycombe was a more important centre.

Some names amongst those of the mediaeval sheriffs may be mentioned here. In 34 Hen. III Alexander de Hammeden, 52 Hen. III Edward son of the king, 31 Edw. III John de Hampden, 14 Ric. II Edmund Hampden, 2 Hen. V Edward Hampden, 13 Hen. VI John Hampden, 7 Edw. IV John Hampden, 21 Edward IV John Verney, 22 Edw. IV Thomas Hampden, 3 Hen. VIII Ralph Verney, 20 Hen. VIII John Hampden, 32 Hen. VIII Ralph Verney.

[41] *Hund. R.* (Rec. Com.), i, 44.

[42] In 1540 it was separated from the duchy and its privileges gradually died away (*L. and P. Hen. VIII,* xv, p. 213).

[43] *V.C.H. Bucks.* i, 387.   [44] *V.C.H. Herts.* ii, 209.

[45] e.g. Froissart, *Chron.* iv, 80 ; *Chronique de la traison et mort de Richart deux* (anonymous).

by Henry IV was connected with the county by owning a manor in Edlesborough and by being bailiff of the Chiltern Hundreds and custodian of the castle of Wallingford,[46] but he was really of Ewelme (Oxfordshire).

We have now a period of silence again till the very pathetic scene at Stony Stratford in the year 1483. Edward IV had died on 9 April, and his son was but thirteen years old. From Ludlow, where he was with the guardians and court appointed by his father, he set out for London, the council refusing him more than 2,000 men as escort. Richard Duke of Gloucester hurried southwards from the Scottish borders on hearing of his brother's death, and took the oath of allegiance to Edward V at York, but as he proceeded further increased his escort. He contrived to be only a few miles behind when Edward's retinue reached Stony Stratford. The Duke of Buckingham met Richard at Northampton, and, as counsellor, helped him to form his plans. Edward, learning of Richard's approach, sent Anthony Lord Rivers, his mother's brother, and Sir Richard Grey, his mother's son, to meet and greet him in his name. Richard received them with a traitor's pleasant manners, saw the young king safely housed in his lodgings at Stony Stratford, made himself again agreeable to Rivers and Grey that night, and then next day arrested them for conspiring, he said, to estrange his nephew from him and to cause variance amongst the barons.[47] The officers of Edward's retinue he also seized, and ordered the troops, who were from the Welsh marches, to disperse. He then dispatched the prisoners to Yorkshire, while the boy king wept bitterly at being separated from his relatives, and over and over again vouched for the loyalty of his uncle Anthony and for the innocence of his half-brother Grey.

There is little more to record during Plantagenet times. It is a point of interest that Sir Edmund Hampden, ancestor of John Hampden, was chamberlain to Edward, son of Henry VI, and lost his life in the Lancastrian cause.[48] It is another that William Catesby, owner of Hardmead, of ill fame as one of the evil advisers of Richard III, was chosen as Speaker of the Commons in the Parliament of 1484—a Parliament that had some awkward work to do in having to consent to alleged reasons invented to show that Richard was most rightfully and legitimately king, and to make their memories oblivious of facts which they could not but know well. But Catesby was capable of giving right advice upon occasion, as when he helped to dissuade [49] Richard from his strange proposal to marry his own niece, Elizabeth, daughter of Edward IV, advice perhaps given more to stave off complete unpopularity than for any better reason. Catesby was buried at Hardmead in 1485.

Even in early Tudor times there is little to record. The great days of the county were yet to come. In 1525, when Wolsey as chancellor called for a subsidy, under the name of benevolence, of one-sixth from laymen and one-fourth from ecclesiastics for the invasion of France, most of those in this county, as many in other counties liable to assessment for it, refused, and the attempt caused so much ill feeling throughout the country that for once it was not enforced.

Cromwell, Earl of Essex, who succeeded to Wolsey's methods, and surpassed them, was able to dictate who should be elected in this county for the Parliament summoned to sanction the king's marriage with Jane Seymour, just as a former Parliament had been expected to sanction his divorce from Catherine and his marriage with Anne Boleyn. Something of the methods of that tyranny of Henry, which reduced his later Parliaments to almost household service, remained during the government of the Protector Somerset. Land inclosures had commenced—a necessary step through the growth of population and the increased needs of agriculture, and not ill-judged when rights and claims have been properly adjusted. But this adjustment seems to have been insufficiently attended to in some cases, and there were just outcries as well as unnecessary complaints. Somerset, without waiting for an Act of Parliament to remedy what was wrong, issued a dictatorial order for the laying open of lands that had been inclosed. The order was not obeyed, and he could not enforce it without a sanction from the Parliament which perhaps it was impossible to get. In consequence the discontented took matters into their own hands. Agrarian tumults began, in which, if Holinshed [50] is right, Buckinghamshire was among the counties which took the lead. Fences were removed and destruction wrought, but Lord Grey of Wilton and Russell, lord privy seal, suppressed the disorder. The economic distress had various causes, and among them the opportunity given not long before to alienate estates,[51] the extinction of villeinage, which altered the conditions of labour,[52] and the suppression of the monasteries, which could not be

[46] *Dict. Nat. Biog.* ; see note at the end on the stewardship of the Chiltern Hundreds.

[47] Ramsay, *Lancaster and York*, ii, 478.   [48] Warkworth, *Chron. of Edw. IV* (Camd. Soc.), 18.

[49] Ramsay, op. cit. ii, 531.

[50] 'First they began to plaie these parts in Summersetshire, Buckinghamshire, Northamptonshire, Kent, Essex and Lincolneshire' (*Chron.* 1002).

[51] By judgement in the case of 'Taltarum,' limited, however, to some extent by Statute of Fines, 4 Hen. VII, cap. 24, and Statute of Uses, 27 Hen. VIII, cap. 16.

[52] On this, however, see Stubbs, *Constitutional Hist.* iii, 623–5.

carried out without causing great changes in the county : these all combined to bring about a want of employment and consequent distress.

When Dudley attempted to set Lady Jane Grey upon the throne, supported in Buckinghamshire by the preaching of John Knox at Amersham, where Lollardism had been notoriously strong, both in the town itself and the surrounding manors, efforts were made to gain support for her elsewhere in the county. The prompt action, however, of William second Lord Windsor of Bradenham, Sir Edward Peckham of Denham and Sir Francis Hastings, who lost no time in declaring Mary queen and raising troops, to hang upon the rear of Northumberland's forces, settled the question for this county. Indeed, when Mary left Framlingham for London she was accompanied by 1,000 men, many of whom came from Buckinghamshire, and these escorted her to the City on 3 August 1553. The queen showed her gratitude by granting charters of incorporation to Buckingham and Aylesbury, and to Aylesbury in addition the right of being represented in Parliament. Sir Edward Peckham was rewarded by being made a privy councillor as well as by being kept in office in the Treasury of the Mint. On the outbreak of Sir Thomas Wyatt's revolt Elizabeth was at Ashridge, and the council intercepted a letter from Wyatt recommending her retirement further from London to Donnington Castle. In consequence the queen on 26 January 1554 wrote inviting [53] the princess to return to the court, mentioning also the spread of ' lewd and untrue rumours,' no doubt of Elizabeth's complicity in the rebellion. Fearing danger to her person, she excused herself on the ground of illness. On 10 February the queen sent Elizabeth's great-uncle, Lord William Howard, and other commissioners, with two physicians, one of whom had known the princess from childhood, to interview her, and if she was well enough to escort her to London. Two days after she set out, travelling in the queen's own litter and with so little haste that five days were spent between Ashridge and Highgate. About a month later, on 16 March, Elizabeth was lodged in the Tower. While she was there imprisoned Wyatt was executed on 11 April 1554, and trials of his accomplices followed. The most remarkable of these was that of Sir Nicholas Throckmorton (or Throgmorton) of Weston Underwood, whose able pleading in defence caused his acquittal by the jury. They were reproved by the lord chief justice, still maintained their verdict, and the matter ended by his ordering Throckmorton to be taken back to the Tower on pretence of his having to meet other charges, and the imprisonment of the jury—eight of whom remained incarcerated for some months—and the amercing of them all. Throckmorton was released on payment of £2,000. When, two years later, the queen had become more unpopular than before, a relative of Nicholas, John Throckmorton, Henry Peckham of Denton, son of Mary's early adherent, and Edmund and Francis Verney, brothers, of the Claydon family, and Edmund the last Lord Bray—who protested that he was innocent—were charged with being implicated in the somewhat obscure conspiracy of Henry Dudley. These Buckinghamshire men, implicated or accused, were neighbours or connexions. The plan seems to have been to get help from France, to bring home from the Continent the refugees proscribed by Mary's government, to arm these and others and to set Elizabeth on the throne ; the actual achievement was an attempt on the Exchequer Treasury in the Tower, made futile apparently through Peckham's disclosure of the plan. He at any rate gave evidence in court against his fellow conspirators. John Throckmorton, though tortured, would reveal nothing against his fellows in conspiracy, and was executed. Peckham's execution followed. Francis Verney was found guilty and condemned on 18 June 1556. Edmund Verney, for some reason not revealed to us, was not tried, and was pardoned on 12 July 1556. Lord Bray—who belonged to Bedfordshire more than to Buckinghamshire— remained in the Tower for twelve months, and then was pardoned on the intercession of his wife.[54] Sir Nicholas Throckmorton rose into favour under Queen Elizabeth. In 1560 he was ambassador in France ; in 1565 he was sent to Edinburgh to express the queen's displeasure at the proposed marriage of Mary of Scots with Henry Darnley, and he was again sent as special envoy from Elizabeth to Scotland, where the lords confederate, led by Morton, calling themselves the lords of the Secret Council, had confined Queen Mary. He comes into view again at the time of the intrigue between Queen Mary and the Duke of Norfolk in 1572. To the idea of marriage with her Norfolk, if he really was committed, seems to have been committed only after pressure by the Earl of Leicester and Throckmorton, who had attached himself to Leicester. There was an intrigue going on to undermine Cecil, and this was an obscure part of that intrigue. Norfolk suggested Leicester for the proposed marriage as against himself. At the end of the business and before his execution he seems to have realized that Throckmorton had been playing a part in it for his own purposes only. Throckmorton's record may be one of loyalty to Elizabeth, for Wyatt's insurrection was in her favour, but beyond that his is no noble history.

[53] Tytler, *England under Edw. VI and Mary*, ii, 422 et seq. ; Mumby, *Girlhood of Queen Elizabeth*, 99 et seq.
[54] *Verney Papers* (Camd. Soc.), 75.

527

There were changes in the county administration in the reign of Queen Elizabeth. In 1572 an Act was passed for ' Keeping of the Assizes at Aylesbury.' [55] In 1575 the union of Buckinghamshire with Bedfordshire in the same shrievalty, which had existed since the beginning of the reign of Henry II, if not longer, was broken by the appointment of separate sheriffs.[56]

The treatment which Mary Queen of Scots received stirred up the chivalrous feelings of at least one band of men whose early manhood, not vitiated by intrigue, was capable of feelings of devotion. This was in 1586. The result was what was known as the Babington conspiracy, in which Edward Windsor, brother of Lord Windsor of Bradenham, was implicated. The Windsor family had not been disloyal to Elizabeth, who in 1566 had been entertained at Bradenham with ovation on her return from visiting the university of Oxford. The conspiracy quickly came to grief, by treachery as usual, and all implicated, except Edward Windsor, who escaped, were tortured and then executed.

At the crisis of the Spanish Armada in 1588 the force officially levied in Buckinghamshire for the defence of the country consisted of 25 lances, 83 light horse and 500 foot,[57] and the list of those who contributed money contains fifty-two names, five persons giving £50 each and the rest £25.[58] Later in the same year the county was one of those to which application was made for volunteers for service against Spain in the Low Countries.[59]

The remainder of Elizabeth's reign has no interest as regards the county, except that two Buckinghamshire men were rising into prominence—Sir John Croke of Chilton, who became Speaker of the Commons and a judge of the King's Bench, and Sir John Fortescue of Salden, chancellor of the Exchequer. Sir Edward Coke, who together with Francis Bacon took so unsatisfactory a part as Crown lawyer in the trial of Essex in 1600, did not belong to the county till the favour of James I granted him Stoke Poges, and he was soon figuring in his characteristic fashion in the trial of Sir Walter Raleigh.

In this king's reign began the first mutterings of that storm which, before the 17th century was out, had changed for the time the constitution of the realm. This storm of contest, in which men of the county were destined to take a large part, began almost by accident in conditions favourable for its awakening. In elections to Parliament the Tudor sovereigns had interfered when interference suited them, but this was as a sort of bullying, and done without pretence of constitutional right. James, with notions of his own about the divine rights of kings and the divinely intended subjection of subjects, claimed, not simply the absolute ruling of a Parliament, but the ruling of the elections, and issued orders stating what sort of persons were to be elected, under pain of fines to be inflicted on electors and elected, and imprisonment of the elected if he disapproved of them. His instructions were for the most part disregarded or evaded. The Parliament which was summoned for 19 March 1604 met him at the very outset with a question about privilege. As member for the county had been elected Sir Francis Goodwin[60] in opposition to Sir John Fortescue (chancellor of the duchy of Lancaster and a privy councillor),[61] the candidate who was supported by the king. To make the matter more marked, Goodwin had been outlawed some years before. This gave a convenient reason for the sheriff to reject the election as contrary to the king's proclamation. A second election was ordered, and this time Fortescue had most votes. But the House was in no acquiescent mood. After debate they resolved that Goodwin was lawfully elected and ought to take his seat. When the Lords, to support the king, desired a conference on the matter with the Commons, the Commons rejected that idea at once, refusing to give account of their proceedings. Coke was used as intermediary, and was instructed to insist on a conference, which the king thought necessary, as the matter ' touched his honour.' The Commons sent the Speaker and a deputation to the king refusing and explaining why. James, in reply, insisted that the House should not ' meddle ' with the returns, and bade them confer with the judges on the matter. This also the House refused, but they sent up a written statement of their objections through the Lords, whom they requested to mediate on their behalf. The king sent for the Speaker in private, and, while he professed that he was in doubt about the rights of the case, gave him an absolute command to deliver to the Commons, that they were to have a conference with the judges. The Commons on their part, doubtful what to do, agreed to appoint a select committee to confer with the judges in the presence of the king and council. After three weeks

[55] *Commons Journ.* i, 99, 101.
[56] The last sheriff of the two counties was Ralph Astrey, appointed 15 Nov. 1574. The first of Buckinghamshire alone was John Croke (Crooke).
[57] *Acts of P.C.* 1588, pp. 169, 171.
[58] *The names of those Persons who subscribed . . . at the time of the Spanish Armada* (1886), 4–6.
[59] *Acts of P.C.* 1588, p. 297.
[60] Goodwin had been elected as member for the county in 1586 and 1597 and for Wycombe in 1588 ; Fortescue for the county in 1592–3 (*Ret. of Memb. of Parl.* i, 417, 422, 432, 427).
[61] Camden, *Brit.* (ed. 1610), 396.

of debating, the matter was ended by a compromise which James suggested. Goodwin and Fortescue were both to be rejected and a fresh writ for election issued.[62] Goodwin did not, however, remain long out of Parliament, for he was elected for the borough of Buckingham on a vacancy occurring in February 1606. The king was practically defeated, and his defeat was followed up by attacks made in this Parliament on the abuses of purveyance and of wardships, by the instruction which they offered to the king, as well in their later meetings as in their earlier, on the limits of an English monarch's power, and by the limited supplies they voted.

All this was constitutionally well; less well was the increased severity their measures wrought against Roman Catholics, which brought on an episode very different from constitutional resistance to oppression, the Gunpowder Plot, of 1605, a plot in which some of the more ardent enthusiasts, among them Robert Catesby, whose family still belonged to Hardmead, and in a lesser degree Sir Everard Digby of Gayhurst, but not the great body of Roman Catholics, were implicated. Catesby, on learning from a fellow-conspirator that the scheme was probably revealed, rode off with one of his accomplices to join Digby at Dunchurch, in Warwickshire; at Brickhill he was overtaken by Rookwood, one of the band, who had stayed on in London till Fawkes had been arrested. From Dunchurch the chief conspirators rode to Holbeach on the Staffordshire and Worcestershire borders, fear keeping any Roman Catholic from even giving them shelter. At Holbeach Catesby was shot, and died clasping an image of the Virgin found there in the vestibule. Digby was overtaken near Dudley, and was one of the eight arrested who were condemned to the barbarities of 'the traitor's death.' Coke's conduct on one of the consequent trials (that of Henry Garnet, superior of the Jesuits) has been severely commented on.

The Parliament, in the session of 1606, was no more tractable than in that of 1604. The king had a scheme for the union of the two kingdoms, the only scheme of foresight which he seems ever to have had, but it was premature and was opposed in unmeasured language by Christopher Pigot. His words, when noised abroad, enraged the Scots so much that they talked of war, which frightened James, and he rebuked the Commons and threatened them, and this time to some purpose. They expelled Pigot, making him a scapegoat, and sent him to the Tower.

In the remaining constitutional struggles of this reign Coke took conspicuous part as well as in the various intrigues surrounding the trial of Somerset. His worst effort at influence at court was the almost incredible sacrifice of his own daughter, Lady Hatton's child and Burghley's grandchild, whom, against her own will and her mother's, he married to John Villiers, brother of the Duke of Buckingham, created Baron Villiers of Stoke Poges (her inheritance), and then Viscount Purbeck, an imbecile confined as incapable eighteen months after marriage; Coke's daughter was then juggled out of her mother's property by Buckingham. The proceedings to prevent the marriage brought on by Lady Hatton were effectual only in causing ill blood between Coke and Bacon. The record of both these men shows how little the study of law and keen ability in law bring of themselves a sense of justice, and how little philosophical ability can of itself produce exalted character and strength of mind.

From surroundings so unhappy it is an intense relief to make our way to the pure patriotism and pure loyalty to principle of Sir Edmund Verney of Claydon and of John Hampden of Hampden, who are now to come upon the scene, the one losing his life in devotion to his king, and in no less devotion to his country, the other in devotion to his country, but in opposition to his king. But we may pause at the opening of that iron age to examine the reason why so small a county had so great a share in its events. The character of the people of the county could not have worked to such effective purpose except for the possibilities afforded by the county representation—this will be understood when it is made clear.

After 1290, for many generations, two knights of the shire elected at Buckingham were sent up, and two members from Wycombe, first returned in 1300-1, elected by the mayor, bailiffs and burgesses not in receipt of alms. This arrangement continued till 1529, when Buckingham sent up two members for the borough, elected by the bailiff and twelve burgesses, making the representation from the county six. In 1554 Queen Mary's grant to Aylesbury added two more, and until the end of the reign of James I eight members were regularly returned. Just when the Stuart methods of government were causing the need for representation to be felt, the discovery was made by William Hakewell, who belonged to Wendover, while he was making researches amongst the Parliamentary writs in the Tower, that Wendover, Amersham and Marlow[63]—all towns among the Chilterns—had been granted the right of representation in 1300-1, but that none of these towns had returned members since 1309. When the expenses of members had to be paid, represen-

[62] Christopher Pigot was accordingly returned on 16 May to fill the vacant seat. For the contested return for Bucks. in 1604 see Howell, *State Trials*, ii, 91.

[63] In Amersham, as in Marlow, the electors were the householders paying 'scot and lot'; this did not include all householders in either parish.

tation was a burden to the places represented, which was sometimes gladly dropped; but ceasing to elect did not annul the right. Petitions to the House sent by means of Hakewell resulted in the establishment of the claims of these three towns. King James demurred. He thought he had a sufficiency of members to contend with, but he could not prevent the Speaker's warrant from being issued for elections to be held. Members were returned for these three boroughs as well as for the county and for the other three boroughs, to the first Parliament of Charles I, in May 1625,[64] and thus three towns in the Chilterns, not distant from each other, were added to Wycombe in being represented in the House, bringing up the total of the county to fourteen.[65] In days when these Chiltern towns, with interests keeping them together, peopled by a race whose characteristic is to work well in opposition, when minor rivalries are sunk, could by themselves outvote some whole counties,[66] and when united with the remainder of the county could outvote even some groups of two counties, the influence of such men as Hampden, who was also a relative of Cromwell, was able to create of them a phalanx difficult to deal with.

Loyalty to a sovereign has one of its noblest examples in Sir Edmund Verney of Claydon.[67] His connexion with the king began in King James's time, but it is convenient to introduce him now. Born in 1590, he was in the household, first, of Henry, Prince of Wales, and afterwards in that of Prince Charles. He was knighted in 1610, and in 1613 was made by Buckingham keeper of Whaddon Chase, and used his position to represent grievances that were very real there. In Spain, as one of the retinue of Prince Charles, in 1623, when the prince was wooing the Infanta, Sir Edmund Verney, angered by a Roman Catholic priest who was disturbing the death hour of a Buckinghamshire man, his neighbour and fellow retainer, Thomas Washington, struck him. The refusal of Charles to have Verney punished caused Philip of Spain, who was not over-pleased with the prince otherwise, to require him to dismiss all his Protestant attendants, if he wished to stay on in Madrid, but Charles, for his own reasons, came away. Sir Edmund Verney, after his return, was elected for the borough of Buckingham for the Parliament of 1624. The death of James next year left to his son the legacy of his use of the prerogative in extorting money, the methods of his extortions, and his dislike of Parliaments. Charles had anticipated all grants by what was called a loan, when his first Parliament, of which both Verney and Coke were members, met and the House granted, to his surprise, a more limited supply than had been the custom at the accession of a sovereign, and showed themselves unwilling to agree to more subsidies or more tonnage and poundage, either to help the king to spend money or to pay his father's debts. Coke, now thoroughly in opposition, denounced at once the multiplication of useless offices and officials about the court, and also the vesting of several offices in one person—aiming in both points at the Duke of Buckingham. In the end the House decided to let supplies depend on the reforms of grievances and abuses. Charles dissolved the Parliament, and, by the encouragement of Buckingham, turned to illegal means of raising money, enforcing the tonnage and poundage which had not been granted, and exacting more forced loans. The two subsidies granted by the Parliament had taken from the county £3,052, and the sheriffs were required almost immediately afterwards to send in the names of men of the county to whom privy seals could be sent for a loan in addition, amounting to £1,805 6s. 8d. The assessment was not easily agreed to. That of John Hampden [68] and also that of his mother, Elizabeth Hampden, were higher than they should have been, but the county was galled throughout. Charles was left in arrears, and as a bid for favour in the Parliament which he saw he must summon began harassing his Roman Catholic subjects,[69] thereby breaking through his marriage treaty. This step he followed up by annoyance of those whom he sought to please, by crossing out of the list of sheriffs presented for his approval seven names, and inserting in their place those of seven of his most determined opponents in the Commons, a sheriff, according to custom, not being eligible for election. Two of those thus cut out were Buckinghamshire men, Sir Edward Coke and Sir William Fleetwood (of Missenden). Coke maintained, on legal grounds, that though a sheriff could not be elected for the county in which he was sheriff, he could be returned for some other constituency, and he got himself elected for Norwich, though he did not take his seat. This Parliament, in which Hampden sat for Wendover, was dismissed in the midst of its proceedings, after the impeachment of the Duke of Buckingham, in order to save the duke from the result which the king foresaw; and yet he allowed himself to be persuaded by Buckingham

[64] The discoverer, Hakewell, had the satisfaction of being returned for Amersham in 1628.

[65] In this Parliament first occurs the name of Drake as member for Amersham. The family represented Amersham almost continuously till it was disfranchised in 1832 (see *Ret. of Memb. of Parl. passim*).

[66] Bedfordshire sent up four members, Berkshire nine, Northamptonshire nine, Oxford nine, Warwickshire six, Northumberland nine, London and Middlesex together eight, Nottinghamshire eight, Surrey ten.

[67] *Mem. of Verney Family* and Gardiner, *Hist. of Gt. Rebellion*, also *Verney Papers*, all through the Civil War, have been consulted, and are the authorities where not otherwise stated.

[68] *Mem. of Verney Family*, i, 89.   [69] Ibid. 88.

530

into further illegal extortion. More forced loans were exacted and the request to have the amounts not repaid of the past loans deducted from the amount of the new was refused ; men were impressed from each hundred for service in the Low Countries or the Isle of Rhé, equipped at so much per man by the hundreds from which they came, 100 men in all being required from Buckinghamshire. Individuals who refused extortions were imprisoned, towns and townships not compliant had troops quartered on them. Half a regiment from Berkshire, for instance, was billeted on the parts of the county which are near the Berkshire border. This fell heavily on the hundred of Ashendon, where we are told that Ludgershall and Boarstall refused all contributions, and resistance to the demand was shown by individuals in Chilton, Ilmer, Brill and Chearsley. The Court of Wards and Liveries, founded for the protection of the undefended, was also turned into a means of exaction, and its action fell heavy on some of the county families, and though this oppression was not felt directly by the mass of the people it still added to the discontent. Worst of all, the idea was spreading that the king was arranging to have foreign mercenaries brought over, and this suspicion was deepened when Charles, after issuing writs for the new Parliament of 1628 to meet on 17 March, appointed commissioners to raise war taxes, giving to all the intimation that if the tax was paid he would meet the Parliament, and if not he would find some more speedy way with them. The storm roused caused the recall of the commission, but the error had been made, and its consequences could not be recalled. As Charles just then had more troops than before at his command, men faced the outlook sternly.

The country in 1628 sent up a House of determined men,[70] who, after an irritating speech from the king, and a thinly-veiled threat, through the lord keeper, granted five subsidies, but required that infringements on the ancient liberty of the country should first be stopped, and that the king should pledge himself to redress the grievances of his subjects ; and, led by Sir John Eliot, they drew up the Petition of Right, a statement of the constitutional rights of the subject, founded on old charters and statutes of the kings, and laid it before the king for his assent. The king's answer was evasive, except that the Commons, through their Speaker, were forbidden to censure any official of his government, and were told that the Parliament would be prorogued in six more days. A tempest of excitement followed. After more trouble and demur, Charles gave his assent to the Petition of Right, the Commons passed the five subsidies, and prorogation followed. Charles quickly afterwards broke his compact, and in contravention of it continued his illegal demands for poundage and tonnage and the loans. A little more than two months later Buckingham was stabbed, and the prorogation prolonged till the next year. Meanwhile the king published an edition of the Petition of Right, not as assented to by him, but with alterations and additions, and with his first answer appended. In the mood roused by this, Charles had his Parliament to meet. Of his threats disguised in conciliatory words they took but little notice ; they discussed, first, burning points of the religious question, deferred all sanctioning of grants till illegal levying of taxes was stopped, and summoned the customs officers to answer for their exactions. On 10 March they somehow learnt that the king's messenger was on his way to announce dissolution, and their work was yet unfinished. Sir Miles Hobart, member for Marlow, locked the door and placed the key in his pocket, while they brought the session to an end by a resolution that whoever should bring in innovations in religion or endorse the levying of subsidies not granted by Parliament was a chief enemy of the realm, and that all subjects who paid an illegal subsidy were betrayers of liberty. Then Hobart gave up the key, and the king's message was received. Besides Hobart the men of the county who in or out of Parliament chiefly resisted the king in this were Coke, Bulstrode Whitelocke, Sir Peter Temple,[71] Sir John Fortescue of Salden, Ralph Verney, son of Sir Edmund, and John Hampden. When Parliament was over Sir John Eliot, one of Hampden's chief friends, Sir Miles Hobart and some others were imprisoned by the king. After eighteen months in prison, all except Eliot were released. Eliot was retained to die in his imprisonment, during the length of which Hampden kept up correspondence with him, and after the prisoner's death was a father to his sons.

Ten years went by before another Parliament was summoned. Before those years had passed, Hampden's house was made desolate by his wife's death. He spent those years of sorrow in the study of constitutional history and law and in frequent communications with Lord Falkland (Henry Carey). They were years which brought seeds of future trouble to Hampden's country as well as present desolation to Hampden. Petty wars with France and Spain were ignobly ended; agitation about religious questions grew greater in the county as well as elsewhere in the country. Fear of Romanism, carried to unreasoning excess, produced unreasonable dislike to decent ritual, and even to decent condition of the church buildings, which, despoiled of treasures and adornments and even of necessary equipments, were reduced to conditions almost incredible.

[70] Sir Edmund Verney sat in this Parliament for Aylesbury.
[71] Imprisoned at the time in his own house at Stowe for refusing to pay ship-money.

The Visitation Records [72] show the disgraceful state of things which Bishop Laud, unfortunately in a despotic fashion, sought to remedy. It was too easy for this method to develop a spirit of persecution.

Charles permitted many tyrannies, the evil effects of which he did not personally come in contact with, so as to bring them home to his feelings of sympathy; and in Laud, rewarded by being made archbishop after his attempt to force high ritual on the Scottish church, he found a helper. Illegal extortion increased. Obsolete feudal usages bringing in fees and revenues were revived—those, for instance, who were rated at £40 were fined if they did not take up knighthood. Defendants in cases at law against the king, and they were many, lost heavily through law expenses, even if they won. A society for purchasing lay impropriations and advowsons and presenting incumbents was prosecuted, its leaning being Puritanical. The funds subscribed, as at High Wycombe in 1637, were forfeited to the Crown, and the appeal of the subscribers against this, that they had simply attempted to secure a revenue for a vicar there, was refused by Laud. Authority was given to gamekeepers and bailiffs—as, for instance, to William Roades of Middle Claydon and Ralph Hill of Wendover—to seize greyhounds for the king's use; and to all this was added the continued extortion of ship-money. On 4 August 1635 the county was assessed for this at £4,500, and another writ for the same amount was issued in 1636. In September 1637 the total arrears amounted to £2,985, and the sheriff was summoned to London and ordered to get in the money by Michaelmas. But on 31 October there still remained arrears of £278 on the writ of 1635 and £2,230 on that of 1636. There was much dissatisfaction with the individual assessment for the tax, and on the occasion of a fresh levy of £4,500 in the same month the Privy Council warned Sir Alexander Denton, who was sheriff, to take care to prevent complaints of inequality of assessment 'wherewith the Council was much troubled last year,' [73] and in February 1637–8 Denton wrote, hoping that there would be no complaints, as the assessment had taken up his whole time 'in that county that has been so often troublesome to the Lords (of the Privy Council) to regulate the just complaints of the inhabitants.' About the same time, however, information was sent to the council that Denton and the other officials 'privately listen very much to their kindred and friends near them, who, to speak very modestly, are known to be hollow-hearted to the king.' [74] Denton did not succeed in getting the business finished before his term of office expired. In May 1639 the bailiffs of the three hundreds of Newport, the three hundreds of Aylesbury and the Chiltern Hundreds were ordered to 'perfect their accounts' with him, and in September a serjeant-at-arms was sent to take him into custody, and attend him from place to place while he collected the arrears.[75] Next year the trouble continued. Thomas Archdale, the sheriff, was pressed in June to send up the money due on a writ of 1639, as the inhabitants had all 'in a manner' paid their assessments; and in August he reported that he had gathered in about £50, and 'pressed the service as far as I durst for fear of raising a mutiny.' [76]

John Hampden in 1637, together with thirty other parishioners of Great Kimble, had refused to pay. In consequence the king proceeded against him in the Court of Exchequer for default. His trial before the whole bench of judges lasted till 11 June 1638, when two of the judges decided in favour of Hampden, a third temporized, and the rest, a majority, decided for the legality of the tax. But resistance to it was encouraged by even this result, though Hampden's own prudence kept him from imprisonment—and worse. In such a state of things emigration to America went on apace, Lords Say and Brooke getting advice from Hampden and others about it, and giving it encouragement; but its frequency caused a royal proclamation (30 April 1637) forbidding men who were of standing to pay subsidy to emigrate 'without reason,' and this was followed by the prohibition of any emigration without licence of the king.[77]

In the short war with the Scots in 1639 Sir Edmund Verney, his knight marshal, accompanied the king in loyalty but in sadness, dragged two ways at the heart between attachment to the king and disapproval of his doings. He made his will under the impression that he would never return home. From the county also 200 men were levied, and by 11 April were ready to be conveyed to the rendezvous at Selby. A few poor skirmishes with the Scots were all the engage-

---

[72] See *V.C.H. Bucks.* i, 323–6. Visitation reports, many of them duplicates of those mentioned there, exist in the Archidiaconal Registry at Aylesbury and were examined by the writer, who also examined some of these in S. P. Dom. Chas. I.

[73] *Cal. S. P. Dom.* 1637, pp. 408, 460, 504.   [74] Ibid. 1637–8, pp. 237, 357.

[75] Ibid. 1639, pp. 134, 491. There is a discrepancy of date between this and ibid. 1638–9, p. 137, where the claim of the serjeant for his expenses is dated November 1638.   [76] Ibid. 1640, pp. 367–8, 578.

[77] The amounts uncollected on the various writs for ship-money in the county are given as follows by Miss C. D. Gordon in *Roy. Hist. Soc. Trans.* (Ser. 3), iv : on writ of 1635, for £4,500, £188 1s. 11d.; of 1636, for £4,500, £1,030; of 1637, for £4,500, £852 6s.; of 1638, for £1,650, £335 4s. 9d.; of 1639, for £4,500, £4,500—the whole.

ments in this war; unprovisioned and ill-clad the English recruits sank in the shelterless northern spring. Sir Edmund, sent to treat with the Scots, gained their consent to a conference of six of the Scottish lords and six English to settle differences. The king surprised the conference by coming in while they were deliberating, and made no easier the conclusion of a treaty which for a time patched things up. Set free from the campaign by this treaty, Sir Edmund Verney went to Bath, where he stayed for some months in the attempt to obtain release from the physical suffering which he had been enduring while he was on campaign.

In the Short Parliament, which met on 18 April 1640, Sir Edmund Verney and Thomas Lane sat for Wycombe, Ralph Verney, son of Sir Edmund, for Aylesbury, John Hampden for Buckinghamshire. Coke had died in 1634. The Commons, not noticing a lecture, long and wordy, of Lord Keeper Finch, turned quietly at once to the discussion of grievances, referred the cases of Sir John Eliot and Mr. Hollis to a committee, and ordered the record in the case of Hampden to be brought into the House. A month was not out before Finch in the presence of the king administered another lecture. The reply of the Commons, led by Edmund Waller,[78] lord of the manor of Beaconsfield, was a resolution, passed with the utmost calmness, that former kings had redressed grievances or had promised to redress them before they asked assistance, and that Charles must restore to them their own before they could grant support to him. The king in a close conference with the Lords persuaded the Upper House to vote precedence to supply, to the great indignation of the Commons, who maintained that this was a violation of their privilege. In the end Charles offered to do without ship-money if they would grant him twelve subsidies at once. No resolution was passed and Parliament was dissolved next day (6 May). War with the Scots broke out again, and a fresh levy was made. The Earl of Northumberland, writing on 13 June, included Buckinghamshire among the counties which were 'so restive that we shall not get nearly our number of men from them.' Chesham, for instance, was ordered to press eight men, and at first sent only two; the constables were brought to account, and the required number was then made up. The Earl of Carnarvon, lord-lieutenant of the county, writing in July to the Earl of Northumberland, was hopeful that the soldiers would be well clothed, but saw no possibility of procuring draught horses, 'the county was so averse to paying ready money.'[79] Several men were arrested for refusing to pay 'coat and conduct' money, but the king, who was then at York, ordered their release at the end of September in order to conciliate the country with a view to the election of a new Parliament[80]; it was his last.

In this, the famous Long Parliament, Sir Edmund Verney, Alexander Denton, Francis Goodwin, Ralph Verney, Robert Croke, Bulstrode Whitelocke, John Hampden, William Drake, Francis Drake, Thomas Founteyn and Peter Hoby were among those who represented the constituencies of the county. In its memorable beginning, marked by the impeachments of Laud and Strafford—executed not long after—by the amercement of the judges who had upheld the legality of ship-money, and by the wholesale sweeping away of old engines of oppression, this Parliament showed its attitude towards the king, and then made its grant—six subsidies.[81] On a committee in July 1641, formed to debate whether Queen Henrietta Maria was to be allowed to go to Spa for her health, John Hampden and Ralph Verney sat. The committee objected to the proposal, divining, as they did, under the plea of health a purpose of obtaining means abroad to support the king against the Parliament; and when Charles went to Scotland, intending there to form schemes against them, Hampden with others was appointed to go north ostensibly to ensure a good understanding between the Scottish and the English Parliaments, really to keep watch over the king's movements. During his sojourn there a plot against the lives of the three chief covenanting lords—planned or imagined only as planned—in Edinburgh caused actual panic when the news spread. It was interpreted as part of a wide conspiracy against prominent opponents of the king.[82] The Commons refused to pay the expenses of garrisons in the north, and in November issued the ominous Grand Remonstrance, an appeal to the country and not to the Crown against the subversions of the laws and principles of government by 'papists, bishops and evil councillors,' and urging conformity in religion. In the debate on this Falkland objected to the inclusion of all bishops in the accusation; Hampden, Pym and Hollis were for passing it as it stood, and this was carried by 189 to 148. Then Hampden proposed the publication of it in print, to which Hyde and Palmer objected unless the Peers should consent. Thereupon followed

---

[78] Waller was related to Hampden and connected with Cromwell.

[79] *Cal. S. P. Dom.* 1640, pp. 294, 498, 537.   [80] Ibid. 1640–1, pp. 111, 128, 138.

[81] Lord Paget was nominated by this Parliament as Lord-Lieutenant of Buckinghamshire 10 Feb. 1640–1 (*Commons' Journ.* ii, 424).

[82] Buckinghamshire was one of the counties warned on 16 Nov. 1641 that the 'Popish recusants' had appointed the 18th for assembling, and care was to be taken to suppress unlawful assemblies but there is no record of measures having been taken (*Cal. S. P. Dom.* 1641–3, p. 166).

an uproar which, we are told, would have ended in bloodshed on the floor of the House except for the influence of Hampden.

On the 4th of the next January the attempted arrest of the five members, of whom Hampden was one, caused an excitement which very quickly spread and caused rapid action. On the 11th petitions were sent up to the Lords by the 'knights, esquires, captains and gentlemen with a very great number of freeholders' of the county against 'Popish lords, bishops and others,' demanding that the king's 'wicked councellors' should be brought to justice,[83] and asking for co-operation of the Lords with the Commons. This petition was taken up by 3,000 men, who rode up with it to London and carried with them a petition to the king, the procession reaching, we are told, 'from the Exchange to Newgate three and four in a rank' as they made their way from Bishopsgate to Westminster.[84] They received the thanks of both Houses for their petition to them, and the Commons selected some six or eight of their own members to deliver their petition to the king. With it they went to Hampton Court, and thence followed the king, who had left, to Windsor. The petition, besides complaining of the breach of privilege of Parliament, pointed out that the arrest of Hampden was a reflection on the 'judgement and care' of the men of Buckinghamshire in electing him to the House. The king replied that he intended to proceed against the members 'in an unquestionable way,' he would much rather they were proved innocent than guilty, and he could not see how the arrest could reflect in any way on the electors.[85] The effect of the excitement in the Chiltern Hundreds is told by a letter of 18 January sent from Beaconsfield, written by a Prebendary of Worcester, who says that the justices and their trained bands and supplies were to concentrate there from the several hundreds, and that the order was eagerly and officiously obeyed, 'every countryman's mouth almost is full of the breach of the privilege of Parliament.'[86] The mustering of troops which was going on Charles forbade, except by his consent. It was too late. Lord Paget had appointed as his deputies Hampden, Goodwin, Grenville, Winwood and Whitelocke. On 23 May he wrote to the Earl of Holland that the county showed great readiness to obey the militia ordinance,[87] but on receiving the king's proclamation of forbiddal he resigned his office, and on 17 June the members of the trained bands which had assembled at Aylesbury along with nearly 1,000 volunteers petitioned Parliament to appoint a lord-lieutenant 'in whom we may confide,' and Lord Wharton was appointed.[88]

Contributions for the expenses of the Irish war, with a view to further securing safety in England, were forthcoming. Among the members of the Commons, where subscriptions began, Hampden's name is down for £1,000 and Whitelocke's for £600. In April 1642 the gentlemen of Buckinghamshire offered a loan of £6,000 for these expenses. This offer was gratefully accepted by Parliament, which ordered that the loan should be repaid out of the county's contribution to the sum of the £400,000 which it had been settled to raise. The loan was not repaid for some years. As late as 1647 it still remained as a charge on the arrears due from Buckinghamshire towards the £400,000. Another method of raising money was to call in the money still remaining in the collector's hands on account of the loans imposed 'about sixteen years since,' the county having agreed that these sums should be used for the militia.[89] On 5 July Hampden, Goodwin, Winwood and Whitelocke were sent to the county 'to further the proposition for the raising of horse' in the county, and on 8 July it was ordered that the county should retain £1,000 out of the money subscribed by it, in order to provide arms for its cavalry; and officers were sent down at the public expense to train them.[90] The war was no longer Irish, it was now beginning against the king. The army was raised by the Parliament, and Essex appointed its commander 'for the safety of the king's person and the defence of the country and Parliament.' In artillery the country was deficient; and it was a matter of some concern when the king's force removed the artillery from Banbury. The 'Parliamentary gentlemen of Buckinghamshire[91] were moved to a serious carefulness to recover the same,' but failed (9 August 1642). But these 'Parliamentary gentlemen' did other work. Whitelocke joined, amongst others, and Hampden raised a regiment of his tenants, friends, and neighbours, a marked regiment, known by its green uniform, its admirable order, and the motto 'God with us' on its flag.

We have a vivid description of the conduct of the Parliamentary muster in a series of letters, written to the master to whom he had been apprenticed, by Nehemiah Wharton, one of the volunteers from London sent to join the troops of Essex.[92] They seem to have had a particular animosity to altar rails, and surplices, which they took to make handkerchiefs of; one was worn in mockery on the march before being torn up. Passing through Amersham they found the people favourable

[83] B.M. Pamphlets, E 131 (21), Rushworth.   [84] Wallington, *Hist. Notices*, ii, 1–2.
[85] B.M. Pamphlets, E 131 (21).   [86] *Cal. S. P. Dom.* 1641–3, p. 260.
[87] B.M. Press mark, 669 f. 6 (22).   [88] B.M. Press mark 669 f. 5 (50); *Commons' Journ.* ii, 648.
[89] *Commons' Journ.* ii, 519, 562, 611; v, 150.   [90] Ibid. ii, 654, 660.
[91] *Cal. S. P. Dom.* 1641–3, p. 367.   [92] Ibid. 372 et seq.

to their cause; for Wharton describes the country as the sweetest he ever saw, 'and as is the country so is the people.' At Great Missenden they had 'noble entertainment from the whole town.' At Wendover they burnt the altar rails, as usual, and one of the company, 'forgetting that he was charged with a bullet,' shot a maid through the head and 'she immediately died.' Two miles further on, after marching 'very sadly,' they found Colonel Hampden, who with great joy saluted and welcomed them, and conducted them into Aylesbury. He was accompanied 'with many gentlemen well horsed.' In Aylesbury their welcome 'was such' that they 'wanted nothing but a good Lieutenant Colonel.' The day after their arrival, 15 August, was 'the Sabbath.' From a pulpit erected in the market-place they heard two 'worthy' sermons. There was friction between the men and their 'ungodly' lieutenant-colonel, and his orders were not obeyed. How they employed themselves at Aylesbury the next words show: 'Every day our soldiers by stealth do visit Papists (i.e., Churchmen's) houses and constrain from them both meat and money, they give them whole great loaves and cheeses which they triumphantly carry upon the points of their swords.' On 17 August the company received six field pieces, and were joined by two troops of horse at Aylesbury and had a skirmish in the afternoon. They were ordered to be ready to march by 4 o'clock the next morning, and both officers and men refused. On the 20th, however, their 'ungodly' lieutenant-colonel was superseded and they willingly marched to Buckingham in the rear of Colonel Cholmley's regiment, which took up all the available quarters in the town. So the company of the London volunteers had to find quarters in the country round, and Nehemiah Wharton was hospitably entertained by Sir Richard Ingoldsby. There it occurred to him that as Sir Alexander Denton was a 'malignant' it would be well to relieve him of some of his big game. He therefore shot a fat buck in Sir Alexander's park and had it taken to Buckingham, where he feasted two captains and the son of Colonel Hampden on it, and others also, and received their thanks. In less than a month after this they met Rupert, and learnt, at Worcester, that pillage and battle are not quite the same, but before this fight Wharton gives another specimen of the kind of discipline maintained amongst the musters, mentioning that the troopers with them pillaged their own foot soldiers.[93]

The first movement of Hampden's regiment, of 400 musketeers and 100 horse, would seem to have been against the Earl of Berkshire, who was attempting to seize munitions stored at Watlington. The earl was captured and sent as prisoner to the Parliament, 17 August 1642. The regiment next marched to help to form the garrison at Coventry, which the king's forces had in vain attempted to secure. But the ceremonial opening of the war was the raising of the standard on 25 August at Nottingham, the interest of which to the county is the appointment of Sir Edmund Verney as the standard-bearer. His words on receiving the honour and responsibility have been handed down, that by the grace of God they that would wrest the standard from his hand must first wrest his soul from his body. It was not long, 23 October, at Edgehill, before his vow was fulfilled. The standard to which his dead hand clung was captured, but recovered in the night following the battle by the daring of a Captain Smith. Verney's body was buried somewhere among the unknown corpses on the field of fight. His hand and the ring on it containing a miniature of Charles, the king's gift, was found and taken to Claydon, where his ghost, so legend says, wandered for generations through his house seeking for his severed hand. The king's army drew off by Banbury to Oxford, whence early in the morning of 1 November Prince Rupert's troops occupied Aylesbury, and remained there in 'indifferent peaceble disposition' until Sir William Balfour approached with a considerable force of horse and foot. Rupert went out to meet him and made a vigorous attack, but was beaten off by the Parliamentary troops, which were drawn up in the form of a wedge and had the advantage of wind and sun.[94] He retreated to Oxford, plundering the villages on his way. Later in November the king's army made for London, passing Fawley Court, Whitelocke's house, which they sacked, and Colnbrook, which Rupert plundered,[95] and at Brentford, which they attempted to slip through in a thick November fog, they were held at bay by the remains of Hollis's regiment till the regiments of Hampden and Lord Brooke came up. These were able to force the Royalists back, when Essex arrived with a considerable number of horse; at first he ordered Hampden's men to make a detour and fall on the king's rear, while the rest attacked the royal forces in front and on the flank, but soon, to the sorrow of the Buckinghamshire men, recalled his orders. They thus lost a chance of capturing the king early in the war and bringing it to a rapid close. On 1 December, according to a Parliamentary pamphlet, a body of cavaliers under Wilmot came to Aylesbury, and on beginning to plunder next morning were chased out of the town by the inhabitants

---

[93] *Cal. S. P. Dom.* 1641–3, p. 386.

[94] 'Good and joyful News out of Bucks,' B.M. Pamphlets, E 126 (9). This account puts Rupert's force at 10,000 and Balfour's at 1,500, and claims that Balfour lost 90 men, killed 600 and took 200. Most certainly some of the figures must be wrong. [95] B.M. Pamphlets, E 127 (2).

with considerable loss. Five days later there was an engagement in the neighbourhood of the town, the Royalist commander on this occasion being Lord Wentworth, son of the Earl of Cleveland.[96] A week later (7 December) 'the gentry and commonalty' of the counties of Buckingham, Bedford, Hertford and Cambridge joined in a 'Remonstrance and Protestation' justifying their having taken up arms on the ground that religion was 'in imminent danger to be altered to Popery,' and demanding that 'blasphemous and plundering Rupert' should be banished and the 'notorious Papists' who were said to be in command of the royal army brought to 'a due course of justice.'[97] In the same month of December Grafton House in Northamptonshire was taken by a force from Newport Pagnell, and Sir John Digby among others was captured[98]; and on 15 December an ordinance of Parliament formed the counties of Leicester, Derby, Nottingham, Rutland, Northampton, Huntingdon, Bedford and Buckingham into the Midland Association for the maintenance of defence and the raising of territorial forces. The members of the association for Buckinghamshire were Sir Peter Temple, Sir William Drake, Sir John Borlase, Sir William Andrews, Sir Richard Pigot, Sir Richard Ingoldsby, Sir Henry Proby, Sir John Parsons, Sir Thomas Sander, John Hampden, Arthur Goodwin, Edmund Waller, Richard Winwood, Bulstrode Whitelocke, Thomas Terrill, Henry Bulstrode, Richard Grenville, Edmund West and Richard Sargeant.[99] This association did not attain the importance of the Eastern Association, which included the counties in which Parliamentary influence was supreme. Throughout the war Buckinghamshire was a frontier county between the Eastern Association and the Royalist territory of the West Midlands.[100]

Towards the end of January 1642–3 Colonel Goodwin, who is described as commanding in chief at Aylesbury, made an attempt to seize Brill, where a position naturally strong had been fortified by the Royalists as an outpost guarding Oxford; the Parliamentary troops were repulsed, after a vigorous assault, and pursued 4 miles.[1] On the cessation of hostilities, 28 February, for the purpose of negotiations it was agreed that the king's forces should not advance beyond Brill nor the Parliamentary forces beyond Aylesbury.[2]

On the commission which went to Oxford to negotiate with the king were Bulstrode Whitelocke, Edmund Waller and Richard Winwood. Waller had a reception more gracious than the others on the commission. The negotiations failed, and that too in spite of a separate effort silently carried on by Pym and Hampden together with three peers in communication with the queen, who had landed from Holland, to persuade her to induce the king to listen. They discovered that while she was negotiating with them she was hurrying up supplies to Charles, and they desisted from further attempt. Meantime the county committee had raised money for the support of the garrison of Aylesbury, and when a tax of £425 per week was imposed on Buckinghamshire for the general expenses of the army it was arranged that £200 of this should be allotted to that purpose.[3] The burden of this, therefore, was not altogether new (30 March 1642–3). But later in the spring the committee at Aylesbury complained of the defenceless state of the county and described the plunder and burning of Swanbourne, which the Aylesbury garrison was unable to hinder for want of horse. Their letter was read in Parliament and ordered to be printed and circulated as an incentive to the activity of the associated counties.[4] In the same month, May, a plot was revealed by one of its accomplices in which Edmund Waller and others were planning to hand London over to Charles and to seize the leading members of the Commons. They were tried, some were executed and some spared, amongst whom was Waller, who after imprisonment and a fine of £10,000 was conditionally set free.[5]

The head quarters of Essex were at that time at Thame, his outposts and detachments scattered. Those covering the roads to London were at Wycombe, Chinnor and Postcombe, and the country was left too open to the sudden raids of Rupert. In an attempt to gain possession of Islip so as to command the road from Oxford across the Cherwell Essex failed; of Hampden's urgent advice to concentrate more he took insufficient notice. While things were thus a deserter from the army of Essex, Colonel Hurry or Urry, accepted as an officer by Rupert, revealed to the prince that a convoy of money of £21,000 was on its way to Thame from London.[6] Rupert dashed

---

[96] B.M. Pamphlets, E 128 (33), 129 (17). There is the usual exaggeration of numbers, and it is possible that some of these Parliamentary successes are fictitious.

[97] Ibid. E 129 (22).   [98] *Cal. S. P. Dom.* 1641–3, p. 508.   [99] *Lords' Journ.* v, 493.

[100] The maps in Gardiner, *Hist. of Gt. Civil War*, show the boundary of the Royalist and Parliamentary territories as at first running from a point east of the town of Buckingham due south to the west of Aylesbury; from November 1644 Buckingham is included in the Parliamentary territory.

[1] B.M. Pamphlets, E 88 (3). The Royalist *Mercurius Aulicus* and Clarendon, *Hist. of Rebellion* (Clarendon Press ed.), ii, 495, say erroneously that Hampden was in command (*Dict. Nat. Biog.*).

[2] Clarendon, op. cit. ii, 498.   [3] *Commons' Journ.* iii, 24.

[4] Letter dated 16 May 1643; *Lords' Journ.* vi, 52; *Commons' Journ.* iii, 91.

[5] Clarendon, op. cit. vi, 52; Nugent, *Mem. of Hampden* (ed. 4), 369 et seq.

[6] Clarendon, op. cit. vi, 53 et seq.

out of Oxford on 17 June with 2,000 horse and foot, and crossing the Thame at Chislehampton made his way towards High Wycombe, but he could never move without the noise of storm, and when he passed towards the steep incline of the Chilterns not far from Watlington the news reached Hampden, who was there, that night. Wycombe, Rupert did not reach, nor did he find the convoy, which had time to conceal itself in the woods, and apparently he was in retreat when he came upon the detachment at Chinnor, of whom he slaughtered some fifty and carried away half naked, dragging them by the horses, about 120 more. Hampden, immediately he learnt that Rupert had passed, sent a trooper to Essex urging him to occupy Chislehampton bridge and to be ready, and he himself with a troop of horse rode up past Lewknor to the Beacon hill to take observations where to confront the raiders. At sunrise they were near to Chinnor, hardly 4 miles away, and he could see which way they were moving. Past Watlington and Pirton—for the last time—he and his troop pressed on to come up with Rupert and keep him occupied and prevent his reaching Chislehampton before Essex should appear from Thame. At Chalgrove he found Rupert, hardly 4 miles from Chislehampton, hardly 10 from Thame. No Essex there, but a detachment under Colonel Gunter coming from Thame by Easington—three troops of horse, one of dragoons—that threw themselves upon Rupert's right. His left wing folded in upon them, the strife was fierce and Gunter fell, and his men were being scattered. Where was Essex tarrying ? Hampden dashed up with a squadron to rally Gunter's men, and had not reached them when his right arm fell shattered by a bullet, and the reins dropped loose. Leaning his head upon his horse's neck he tried to ride away to Pirton, where his young days had been made bright by his first wife's love—to die there. But Rupert's horsemen occupied the plain and it was useless to attempt it. He turned his horse to the left and made for Thame, which he reached overdone with agony. From there he sent to Essex imploring him to concentrate and cover London, and actually wrote to head quarters urging the correction of the errors of campaign. Six days he lingered on in suffering, and a few hours before he died received the sacrament at the hands of his old friend Dr. Giles, the rector of Chinnor. The chaplain of his regiment, an Independent, was also ministering at his bedside. On Saturday, 24 June, he died, praying for his country and his king. A few days afterwards they bore him home to rest. From Thame across the lowlands to the steep slope of the Chilterns and their summit, whence the view stretched wide behind them to the blue distance and the field of sorrow they had left, the mourning procession took its way to the secluded church of Great Hampden standing inside its ring of forest trees close by the home of his long descended race. There to the beat of muffled drums, with the banner of the regiment and its motto veiled, rolled forth from stern lips the Psalm 'Lord, Thou hast been our refuge,' and when the words of prayer and committal to the grave had died away, and the body lay at rest within that chancel, the slow tramp of the regiment in departing march was accompanied by the singing of Psalm xliii, inculcating hope and trust in God : the last command, as it were, of their dead leader this, though uttered not by lip and living voice, but by the wordless influence of his noble spirit when he could be heard and seen no more.[7]

Urry had been knighted on the field at Chalgrove, and a week later he swept round the rear of Essex and plundered Wycombe,[8] possibly still hoping to find the stray convoy in the Chilterns somewhere. Sir Philip Stapleton opposed him without success. On 2 July an unimportant engagement took place at Padbury between a Parliamentary force of 500 horse and dragoons commanded by Colonel Middleton and a regiment of the king's horse under Sir Charles Lucas, which resulted, after 'more blood drawn than was usual upon such actions,' in a victory for the Royalists, who killed 100 of the enemy and took some important prisoners.[9] Essex fell back on Aylesbury, 3 July, where he was joined by the forces of the associated counties.[10] He had summoned the men of Buckinghamshire to meet him there at the end of June—was he obeying the last injunction of the dead Hampden ? He tried in vain to draw Rupert near Buckingham into fight, and at the end of July, leaving six regiments of foot and forty troops of horse at Aylesbury, retreated with the rest, going through Stony Stratford to Brickhill, there to keep open his communications with London by Watling Street. His army seems to have been at the time in a terrible condition, many sick and many so weak that in a march of 8 miles a day, which was all that they could accomplish, thirty to forty dropped exhausted ; weaponless and almost naked many of them dragged themselves along, and they were all in such condition that fresh recruits refused to join.[11] On the whole, the king's side seemed to be gaining ground. But Rupert spoilt all. Men of capacity could not obey such a headstrong youth, and his careless pillaging of friend and foe alike led only to a desperation fatal to the king. Essex, on his way to relieve Gloucester, passed

[7] Particulars of Hampden's death and burial are given in Nugent, op. cit. 379 et seq.

[8] He is said to have carried off £3,000 worth of goods, 'most of it from the Parliament's' friends (*Parliament Scout*, no. 2 [29 June–6 July]).

[9] Clarendon, op. cit. iii, 106.   [10] Ibid. 169.   [11] *Mercurius Aulicus*, 23 July 1643.

through Colnbrook and Aylesbury in September; troops and trained bands for the Parliamentary army on the way to Newbury—where Falkland, the friend of Hampden, found the death he longed for, fighting for his king—also passed through Aylesbury, and some were quartered at Claydon. Both sides were plundering. In October Rupert, having Urry with him, occupied Newport Pagnell, where he left Sir Lewis Dyve to entrench while he went on to Northamptonshire. On 28 October Dyve abandoned Newport Pagnell owing, says Clarendon, to his mistaking the orders received from Oxford,[12] and the town was at once occupied by a detachment of the army of Essex. Skippon was there in November,[13] and on 18 December Newport was constituted a garrison by an ordinance of Parliament. Sir Samuel Luke of Bedfordshire, an able soldier, was made governor, the garrison consisting of 2,000 men, and £400 per month was raised for its support.[14] The burden of supplying men and money rested almost entirely on the counties of the Eastern Association, which were themselves free from military operations, and of which Newport was 'so considerable a frontier.' It remained throughout the war a position of great importance, and, though never seriously threatened by the king's forces, gave much anxiety to the authorities in London. These often had to remonstrate with the counties responsible for its support because of their slackness in contributing. An attack on Olney was made by a Royalist force, said to be under the command of Rupert, early in November, and a skirmish took place on the long causeway leading to the bridge over the Ouse. 'Some of our men ran away,' says the Parliamentary reporter, 'and Harvey (their commander) fired at them,' but they finally drove off the assailants.[15]

On 23 December 1643, the Commons being informed that the garrison of Aylesbury, 'a place of great consequence,' was in much distress, resolved that £1,500 should be sent for its relief. The Independents and the Peace Party had been opening negotiations with the king, and Ogle, the intermediary, gave Charles the hope that Colonel Mosley, an officer of the garrison there, was prepared to hand over Aylesbury. But Mosley was only leading Ogle on and transmitting the information gained to the Parliamentary leaders, who allowed Ogle, then in prison for some reason not recorded, to escape in order to further the plot and be entrapped, and only revealed it to Parliament when the plot had come to nothing on 26 January 1643–4. On 21 January Rupert, sent to surprise Aylesbury, failed to obtain possession or admittance. The snow was deep, and prevented Essex from getting round his rear and intercepting his retreat, but the rapid thaw of the night following did the work as effectually as fighting. Rupert lost more than 400 men in his retreat, left exhausted in the Buckinghamshire mud or drowned in the swollen brooks.

In the early part of this year Cromwell was occupied round Newport Pagnell, and while his head quarters were there, happened the destruction of Hillesden House. This, one of the finest houses in the county at the time, was the home of Sir Alexander Denton, brother-in-law of Verney the king's standard-bearer, and a kinsman of the Temples and the Hampdens. He had begun at any rate to fortify the house, which was placed upon a hill in the chain of communication between Oxford and Newport Pagnell, had a wide view, and was a strong position. According to Sir William Dugdale, who was at Oxford at this time and kept a careful diary, Captain Waldron, of the Earl of Northampton's regiment, was sent to Hillesden with 100 foot on 10 January, and on the 13th he withdrew, and the house was occupied by the Parliamentary forces, who quitted it on 2 February. Thereupon a Royalist garrison was sent in under the command of Captain Bekman, a Swedish officer of the queen's regiment, and the place was fortified.[16] We must take it that the fortifications were not altogether completed even then. The entrenchments inclosed the house and the parish church, but the command of the garrison seems to have been in the hands of Colonel Smith, by one of whose raids attention was turned to Hillesden. An attempt to surprise it from Aylesbury failed, and Sir Samuel Luke at Newport Pagnell made ready for a second attack at the head of 2,000 men. Command was taken by Cromwell, and the assault made on two sides on 4 March, one from Steeple Claydon under Cromwell in person, the other from another side under Luke. Before 9 o'clock that morning they had surrounded Hillesden. Summoned to surrender at discretion, Colonel Smith sought to obtain terms which were refused. The entrenchments were carried, being not yet complete; the garrison was forced back, some to the church, some to the house. The church was speedily carried, and Colonel Smith seeing defence was hopeless offered to surrender on the promise of quarter. The promise was given. Denton and his brother, Colonel Smith and others were marched on foot to Padbury, and next day to Newport Pagnell, but several others of the prisoners, the promise of quarter notwithstanding, were put to death. Treasure discovered next day behind wainscoting and under the lead of the

---

[12] Clarendon, op. cit. iii, 232.   [13] Gardiner, op. cit. i, 286.

[14] *Lords' Journ.* vi, 344–5. The three hundreds of Newport furnished seventy-five men for the garrison and paid £250 a month. A later ordinance, Sept. 1645, provided for the support of Newport and other garrisons by a monthly charge of £3,756, of which £80 was allotted to Bucks.

[15] B.M. Pamphlets, E 76 (3).   [16] Dugdale, *Diary*, 58, 60.

roof stimulated to a general sack, in which the house was wrecked, and on report of an advance of Royalist troops from Oxford burnt and left.[17] The history of Sir Alexander brings home to us in most pathetic manner the sufferings caused by the war. He had lost his wife and mother in the same month just before it began. His nearest relatives took opposite sides. His house was sacked and burnt, and he was a prisoner. In the following August his eldest son was killed in battle near Abingdon, pierced with thirty wounds. His heart was broken, and he died and was buried at Hillesden in the January following, aged only forty-seven.[18]

Cromwell, whose eldest son, Oliver, is said to have died of small-pox at Newport Pagnell in this spring, went from Hillesden by Buckingham to Cambridge. On his arrival there he found Lieut.-Col. Warner, who had been sent by Crawford from Buckinghamshire under arrest as an Anabaptist, and therefore unfit for military service. Cromwell sent him back with a letter, in which he vigorously expressed the need for the toleration of religious differences as a matter of expediency : ' Sir, the State, in choosing men to serve it, takes no notice of their opinions ; if they be willing faithfully to serve it, that satisfies.'[19] His sense of the need of toleration does not seem to have extended to English Churchmen and to Roman Catholics, and he was that much wanting in the element of greatness.

In the next month (April 1644), when it was found that the Parliamentary forces were gathering in the neighbourhood of Buckingham and Stony Stratford, Secretary Nicholas wrote (16 April) that if the Royalists had in Buckinghamshire a reasonably strong party of horse it would ' spoil the rebels drawing together in those parts.' The Earl of Manchester was at this time at Newport Pagnell with 2,000 or 3,000 Parliamentary horse and foot,[20] and the ' spoiling ' of the ' drawing together ' of the rebels seems not to have been effected ; indeed, Charles ordered the withdrawal of the garrison of Boarstall House and the destruction of the fortifications, whereupon the place was at once seized by a detachment from the Parliamentary garrison at Aylesbury. The mistake was then only too apparent, and on 10 June Colonel Gage was sent out from Oxford with 1,000 men to retake it, which he did on the 12th, allowing the garrison to march out with their arms.[21] For two years thereafter it was held for the king, and the garrison almost supported itself by raids on the country round, sometimes approaching very near to Aylesbury. The fortification of the house is thus described by Richard Symonds in 1645 : ' A pallasado, or rather a stockado, without the graffe,[22] a deepe graffe and wide, full of water ; a palisado above the false bray, and another six or seven foot above that, neare the top of the curten.'[23]

The king's manœuvres brought him to Buckingham on 22 June (1644) with Waller ' toiling heavily after him.' He remained there for four days, sending to Oxford for advice as to his next move. Rupert urged him to march to Yorkshire and join Newcastle there ; another proposal made was to raid the Eastern Associated Counties, and while the alternatives were being discussed it was suggested that a move should be made on London itself. Meantime Charles sent out bodies of cavalry to plunder the country round. The Earl of Cleveland advanced to Newport Pagnell, ' hoping to draw his old acquaintance, Sir Samuel Luke,' but without result, and another party seized, at Brickhill, 16 cartloads of wine, grocery and tobacco, which were intended for Coventry and Warwick, ' but it was better disposed amongst the Horse.'[24] The royal forces were also reported to be playing off their great guns against Aylesbury.[25] The king was kept in anxiety at this time by the jealousy between his civil and military advisers, which frequently disturbed his council. Wilmot (afterwards Earl of Rochester) fomented among the cavalry officers distrust of Colepepper and Digby, who were sent to Oxford to consult the lords as to the wisdom of the proposed advance on London.[26] This scheme was put an end to by the advance of Waller, whom the king moved to Cropredy to meet. But the news of the king's raids on Buckinghamshire and Befordshire had caused alarm in London, and Browne was dispatched with a force drawn from the City and the counties of the Eastern Association to protect the country between Buckingham and London. Browne was too late to co-operate with Waller before the battle of Cropredy Bridge, but joined him in Northamptonshire early in July, and was then ordered to proceed to

---

[17] Accounts of the siege and surrender are conflicting. The paper by Rev. H. Roundell in *Rec. of Bucks.* (Bucks. Arch. and Archit. Soc.), ii, 93–8, may be consulted. The *Mercurius Civicus* (7 Mar. 1643–4) allows a slaughter of 30 men and claims the capture of 450 prisoners and of many stores. The *Mercurius Aulicus* of 9 March gives the number of prisoners as 100 only and describes a scene of barbarity. The official report of Luke gives details of the garrison and states the number killed.

[18] Rev. H. Roundell, ' Hillsden House in 1644,' ut sup.

[19] Carlyle, *Letters and Speeches of Cromwell* (ed. S. C. Lomas), i, 170. Carlyle wrongly identified the anonymous officer with Packer, who was also in trouble about this time, and his mistake is corrected by Mrs. S. C. Lomas.

[20] *Cal. S. P. Dom.* 1644, p. 121.　　[21] Clarendon, op. cit. iii, 361 ; Dugdale, *Diary*, 69.

[22] i.e., outside ; graffe is of course moat.　　[23] *Diary* (Camd. Soc.), 231.

[24] Walker, *Hist. Disc.* 29.　　[25] *Cal. S. P. Dom.* 1644, p. 279.　　[26] Clarendon, op. cit. iii, 364.

the siege of Greenland House, which had been fortified by the king, in the south of the county, on the Oxfordshire border.[27] This had given great trouble to the Parliamentarians of the neighbourhood, and had already been under siege for a month by the Hertfordshire regiment, and on 8 July was relieved by the Royalists. On the 11th Browne arrived, and the garrison surrendered on condition of being allowed to march away to Oxford.[28] The Royalist writers say that further defence was hopeless, since the house was almost destroyed by cannonade.[29] Browne had great difficulty in keeping his troops together. When he was at Northampton with Waller they attacked him personally, and struck him in the face; 'such men,' wrote Waller, 'are only fit for a gallows here and a hell hereafter,' but he demolished the fortifications of Greenland House with the help of the country people, and then moved off to Abingdon. Waller himself was soon in Buckinghamshire in the course of his marchings, and on 20 July he reported that he had summoned Boarstall House to surrender, but had been unable to attack it for want of guns. He had lost these at Cropredy. The garrison of Newport Pagnell had been ordered to supply him with 400 men if required; he reported that they were unwilling. Captain Middleton, indeed, flatly refused to join him and went off to Cambridge.[30]

By this time a new organization had come into existence, the 'committee of the three counties,' Oxfordshire, Buckinghamshire and Berkshire, to which frequent reference is made in the State Papers. Thus on 3 July it was arranged that the Hertfordshire regiment should continue to serve at the siege of Greenland House, and that after a fortnight its pay should be provided by the three counties, and a similar arrangement was made in September regarding the troops who were engaged in besieging Banbury.[31] These arrangements do not seem to have worked well. Three days after the capture of Greenland House Browne informed the Committee of Both Kingdoms that most of the Hertfordshire men were gone, and six months later he wrote from Abingdon: 'It will not be believed how many men run away daily to Aylesbury, where they are constantly paid.'[32]

In the winter of 1644–5 the posts occupied by the Royalists in the county were at Buckingham, Winslow, Brill, Boarstall and Haddenham, while the Parliamentary troops held Newport Pagnell, Waddesdon, Eythorp, Hartwell, Aylesbury, Bierton, Wing, Wendover, Stoke Mandeville, Ellesborough, Missenden, Amersham, Lee and Chesham.[33] A Parliamentary newspaper complained that 'the king's forces there plunder and play such reaks that the poore country is like to bee utterly undone by them.'[34] The support of the many bodies of Parliamentary troops was a heavy burden also. This was taken into consideration on the establishment of the New Model army in January 1644–5. No new contribution was required from Buckinghamshire, as it was included among the counties partly in the possession of the Parliamentary party, which were expected to maintain their own garrisons and forces as far as they could.[35] The New Model was a fresh organization, meant for conquest, and intended to lessen such miseries as the counties in the field of operations were enduring. Besides those already alluded to, Buckinghamshire was suffering from Major-General Crawford's troop living at free quarters, and Waller's cavalry settling themselves down in mutiny at Beaconsfield and refusing to return to duty except they had six weeks' pay.

The capture of Leicester on 31 May 1645 made the Committee of Both Kingdoms anxious for the safety of Newport Pagnell.[36] Luke had complained that he had only 600 men, whereas its defence required 2,000, and the place was badly provisioned for a siege.[37] Fairfax abandoned the siege of Oxford, and on his way north to engage the king's army he attacked Boarstall House, defended by Sir William Campion. Campion held Fairfax at bay, and the attempt to capture it was given up, Fairfax, anxious to lose no time, advancing to join Vermuyden at Sherington, and Cromwell afterwards. The disaster of Naseby, 14 June, caused Charles to retreat to the west, whence in August he marched to Doncaster, and thence turned south, once more passing through Bedfordshire into Buckinghamshire. On 27 August he stayed at the Earl of Carnarvon's house at Wing, where he had a soldier hanged for stealing a chalice from the church, and the next day he moved on by Boarstall to Oxford.

Meanwhile Sir Kenelm Digby of Gayhurst—whose trunk, heavy as was supposed with 'papists'' money, had been seized and sent to head quarters of the Parliament on 7 August 1642— was dispatched to Rome by the queen to negotiate for an advance of money, and was employed in the attempt to gain support in Ireland for the king by means of articles of arrangement which Charles did not sign. Though peace was made in Ireland, no help came for the king's cause in

[27] Col. Hawkins was sent there from Oxford with his regiment on 15 May (*Cal. S. P. Dom.* 1644, p. 163).
[28] Ibid. 184, &c.   [29] Walker, op. cit. 38; Clarendon, op. cit. iii, 411.
[30] *Cal. S. P. Dom.* 1644, pp. 324, 326, 333–4, 346–53, 362–3.   [31] Ibid. 304, 472, 531.
[32] Ibid. 1644–5, p. 233.
[33] *Weekly Account*, 1–8 Jan. 1644–5.   [34] *Perfect Occurrences*, 27 Dec.–3 Jan. 1644–5.
[35] *Lords' Journ.* vii, 204–9.   [36] *Cal. S. P. Dom.* 1644–5, p. 554.   [37] *Dict. Nat. Biog.*

England from the negotiations. Boarstall, the last Royalist hold in Buckinghamshire, yielded on 10 June 1645, followed by the surrender of Oxford on 24 June.

So far as Buckinghamshire was concerned the war was now over. Only a small body of eighty horse was ordered to be maintained in the county. The garrison of Newport Pagnell was disbanded after two and a half years' service, and its men, with others from the county and from Berkshire and Oxfordshire, numbering in all 700 horse and 12,000 or 13,000 foot, were sent to Ireland. In January 1645–6 the Committee of Both Kingdoms wrote to Colonel Whalley with reference to the quartering of his horse in the two counties of Buckinghamshire and Bedfordshire, ' whereby places wholly in our power are wasted and rendered unable to pay taxes,' and bidding him quarter his troops in ' the enemy's country.' In February 1646–7 it was decided that no garrisons need any longer be maintained in the county.[38] Charles was once more within its borders, in the summer of 1647, as a prisoner in the hands of the army, and was domiciled for a time at Stoke Poges, while the army head quarters were at Colnbrook.

In September 1647 there was sent up a petition from the county against tithes and free quarters, and another from the three counties of Oxford, Buckingham and Hertford, demanding that ill-affected persons should be removed from Parliament as ' obstructors of all that really tends to the people's good.'[39] Having promised to consider the matter, the House of Commons, in December, sent Edmund West, member for the county, and Simon Mayne, member for Aylesbury, to see to the disbandment of supernumerary soldiers and the relief of the inhabitants from free quarter. They had also laid upon them the duty of ' quickening ' the assessment for the county's share of the monthly tax of £60,000, which had been imposed a little time before for general purposes.[40] On the renewal of war in 1648 the three counties of Buckingham, Bedford and Hertford entered into an engagement to raise forces for their own defence, and on the failure of the rising of the Earl of Holland at Kingston in July they were ready for action.[41] It was to Bedfordshire, however, that Holland turned his flight, and no fighting took place within the Buckinghamshire borders.

The end alone remains. Two of those who signed the king's death-warrant belonged to Dinton, Simon Mayne, member for Aylesbury, and Sir Richard Ingoldsby, afterwards one of Cromwell's second chamber; three others of the county were Thomas Chaloner of Claydon, George Fleetwood of Chalfont St. Giles, and Sir Peter Temple of Stowe. Then followed the tragedy witnessed by Buckinghamshire eyes as the trial had been listened to by Buckinghamshire ears—those of Whitelocke; and tradition persistently has it that the actual executioner was John Bigg, a Dinton man, who lived there afterwards as a hermit in concealment, protected for years by the two regicides of Dinton.

Before continuing the narrative, we turn to the fines and sequestrations which were consequences of the hostilities, leaving the history of Sir Ralph Verney's case to be told by itself, because of its especial interest and the light it throws on the condition of things under the Long Parliament and the Commonwealth.

Much severity was exercised towards the Royalist inhabitants of those counties where the Parliamentary influence was predominant, as a means at once of punishment for any aid, active or passive, given to the king, and of raising money for the expenses of the war. Buckinghamshire, as a frontier county, was difficult to deal with. In April 1644 G. Palmer wrote to London that nothing had hitherto been done in the county because of the presence of the king's forces, who imposed contributions on the inhabitants. He took advantage of the strength of the Parliamentary forces at that time to sequester the estates of ' delinquents,' and to secure the rents, if the tenants could be got to pay them; they were, however, liable to be plundered by the Royalists if they obeyed the commands of the Parliamentary committee.[42] At the surrender of Oxford terms were arranged by which most of those who had been with the king ' came in ' and compounded, as others had done before them, for their ' delinquency.' A committee was appointed to deal with those belonging to Buckinghamshire, and it had also work to do in composing certain ' differences ' which had arisen ' between the (Parliamentary) gentlemen of the county.'[43] On 29 May 1647 the county committee, in compliance with the order of the House of Commons of 10 November 1646, sent in a list of the estates of ' all Papists and delinquents sequestered in this county,' explaining that they could not send it earlier ' because many estates lying under the power of the enemy were not fully discovered till the delinquents, by the articles of Oxford, were allowed to enjoy their estates.' The list includes about one hundred persons, of whom thirty-three are marked as ' Papists,' three as ' Papists and delinquents,' and the rest simply as ' delinquents.' Four of the estates were of value exceeding £1,000 per annum—those of the late Sir Alexander Denton, £2,750, the Earl of Antrim and his wife, the Duchess of Buckingham, £2,101, Sir Edmund Pye, £1,050, and Sir Ralph

---

[38] *Commons' Journ.* v, 96.   [39] B.M. Pamphlets, E 407 (29).
[40] *Commons' Journ.* v, 400–1.   [41] B.M. Pamphlets, E 452 (1).   [42] *Cal. S. P. Dom.* 1644, p. 96.
[43] Letter of Col. Bulstrode, Governor of Aylesbury, in *Commons' Journ.* iv, 625.

Verney, £1,002. At the other extreme was Edward Tomkins, 'Papist,' of Hanslope, £4.[44] The list is by no means exhaustive, for sequestration of estates was only one method of procedure. Most of the Royalists compounded for their ' delinquency ' by payment of fines varying from one-half to one-tenth of the capital value of their property, and the records of the Committees for the Advance of Money and for Compounding contain many Buckinghamshire names besides those appearing in the list described above. In many cases the negotiations for the payment of the fine or assessment went on for years, and it was not till the government of the Long Parliament had given place to Cromwell's protectorate that the final settlements took place. The administration of the sequestered estates caused endless trouble with tenants and claimants to rent-charges, and the full value was seldom received. Thus, in 1650, the London committee complained to the Buckinghamshire commissioners that out of £1,961 due at Lady Day, besides arrears, only £921 had been paid in. Either there had been remissness in enforcing payment or detention of money by the commissioners. Sir John Pakington of Aylesbury (and Westwood, Worcestershire) was fined in 1646 the enormous sum of £13,595, being half the value of his estates. The proportion was next year reduced to one-third, which was valued at £7,670, and he paid £500. Two years later he made another payment of £3,000, and £2,670 was remitted, on his making over to the inhabitants of Aylesbury the rights of common of Heydon Hill. In 1650 he was discharged on paying the balance of £1,500. But his troubles were not over, for in 1651 he was charged with assisting Charles II at Worcester and fined £2,000, of which he paid down £1,000 and gave security for the remainder, which was apparently paid in 1654 after he had been, as he said, ' prosecuted for three years and imprisoned for seven months.' Once again, in 1659, his estate was ordered to be seized for his suspected complicity in Sir George Booth's rising, and he filed his former payment of £1,000 to widow Guise, whose husband was hanged by the Scots.

Other notable Royalists of the county who suffered for various degrees of ' delinquency ' were Sir John Borlase of Medmenham, Sir Thomas Longville of Bradwell, Sir James Palmer of Burnham and Dorney, one of the gentlemen of the king's bed-chamber, and Sir Richard Minshull of Bourton. Sir Thomas Ashfield of Chesham was heavily fined as a recusant, and in 1653 was imprisoned in the Fleet, whence he petitioned the committee after eight months' durance, begging them to provide him ' either a grave or a bedlam,' his misery in incarceration was so great. The case of Sir Thomas Hampson of Taplow is an example of what fate those had who tried to live a quiet life without active participation in the war. In 1642–3 he lent Parliament £600, and furnished two men and horses, and for this the king declared his estate sequestered. In February 1644 the king demanded a loan of £500. He had previously lent him £200, and on his refusal to give any more his house and barns were burnt by the king's soldiers, the damage being reckoned at £2,000 or £3,000. Yet in 1647 he was accused of ' delinquency,' and it was not till 1650 that he was finally cleared of the charge after a full debate. The Duke of Buckingham's estate at Whaddon Chase furnished considerable spoil. In 1650 the trees were ordered to be cut down to the value of £3,000, half of which was to be sent to the garrison at Windsor and the other half was given to the support of the Parliamentary forces in Buckinghamshire and Berkshire.[45]

After the execution of the king Sir Peter Temple resigned his commission, and was accused of using seditious language.[46] The Englishman's after-thoughts of doubt came perhaps to him, and that sooner than to most of his contemporaries, though many who, like him, had been active in the war did the same. To the Executive Council of State which was soon formed, on which Whitelocke sat, John Milton, son of a Buckinghamshire woman, and himself in after years denizen of the county, was appointed secretary.

The Levellers, who were naturally to be found in a county so penetrated with democratic feeling, had issued a pamphlet in 1648 or 1649 entitled *Light Shining out of Bucks*, in which was demanded ' the removall of the kingly power ' in order ' to free all alike out of slavery.' ' Rich men cry for a king,' it says, ' the horseleech lawyer cries for a king '. . . ' the Lords Barons do cry for a king, else their tyrannical House of Peers falls down.' [47] To these belonged no doubt the ' several gentlemen of Buckingham ' who a fortnight after the execution of the king brought to Parliament ' a Representation of the Grounds of their Bondage and Slavery.' [48] Their eyes were opened by the arrest of Lilburn and his associates. They found ' both the Parliament and Army to break their promises and to be as arbitrary as those that were before them '; and in this new light entered a general protest against ' all Arbitrary Courts, Terms, Lawyers, Impropriators, Lords of Mannors, Patents, Priviledges,' &c., against ' the whole Norman power,' and against paying ' Tythes, Tolls, Customs, &c.' This pamphlet professed to represent the views of ' the

---

[44] *Cal. Com. for Comp.* 66–8.

[45] Ibid. ; *Cal. Com. for Advance of Money*, see indexes.

[46] *Commons' Journ.* vii, 76, 79, 108. Sir Peter died in 1653.

[47] B.M. Pamphlets, E 475 (11).   [48] *Commons' Journ.* vi, 140.

middle sort of men within the three Chiltern Hundreds of Disborough, Burnum and Stoke, and part Alisbury Hundred.' [49]

Campaigns followed, in which Cromwell broke down with actual barbarity the Royalist opposition. He passed through Aylesbury on his way back to London after the victory of Worcester and was met near the town by the four members, of whom Whitelocke was one, sent to convey to him the congratulations of the House.[50] What Cromwell was half proposing to himself is told by Whitelocke's record of a conversation which he had with him apparently after the campaigns were over, and his dissuading him from the idea of making himself king.[51] Cromwell dissolved the 'Long Parliament' in 1653, and called another, 'the little Parliament,' derisively known as 'Barebones,' in which the county was represented by George Fleetwood and George Baldwin. When this, after its five months of existence, was persuaded by him to dissolve itself, and by the Instrument of Government he was made Protector and supreme, the number of the House of Commons for England was fixed at 400. In the allotment the counties gained somewhat at the expense of the boroughs. Five members were given to Buckinghamshire as county members, and one each to the boroughs of Buckingham, Aylesbury and Wycombe. Fleetwood had joined in the debate which led to all this, and Whitelocke was made keeper of the Great Seal in that year (1653). The members for the county in the Parliament of 1654 were Whitelocke, Sir R. Pigot, Richard Ingoldsby, Richard Grenville and G. Fleetwood; the boroughs were represented by Francis Ingoldsby, H. Phillips and T. Scott. Francis Drake, most probably of Amersham, sat for Surrey. In 1656 Richard Hampden took the place of Fleetwood.[52] Cromwell's position of Chief Magistrate of the Commonwealth was a position of suspicion and anxiety. He was continually finding, fearing or suspecting plots to upset and perhaps to murder him. This made still heavier the new tyranny which had begun with the Long Parliament, that supposed itself to be a bar to tyranny, and not even under the kings were things more desperate. Sir Ralph Verney, one of the members of that Parliament, had been expelled the House for non-attendance on 22 September 1645. If he could not support the tyranny of a king, he could as little agree with the despotic actions of a Parliament. He could only retire in sorrow and dismay, and take no action on either part. He could not consent to sign the Covenant, and beyond this, except that he was not present at debates in the House, there was nothing to be brought against him. When sequestration was threatened and compounding was allowed he could not compound for his estates, simply because the compounder had to admit having given assistance to the king, and this he had not given. His estates were placed under sequestration on 14 October 1646, and he only escaped arrest by going into exile. By persistent efforts carried on with the noblest patience his wife, Mary Blacknell of Wasing, coming back to England when her husband and children had to remain in exile, secured the removal of the sequestration. But this was only accomplished on 5 January 1648, after hard journeyings to and fro in England, disappointments and delays, frequent appeals and applications to those who had influence, and in the end an *inducement* offered to the Speaker of the House. Severe illnesses which she had during all this in absence from the husband whom she loved so tenderly, and for whom she was working so devotedly, had not daunted her, while in the midst of it all she bore a child. No wonder that her days were shortened, and that Ralph Verney had bereavement added to the bitterness of exile, nor did his subsequent return home to what his wife's self-sacrificing efforts had won, bring him security. On 13 June 1655 he was arrested [53] at Claydon as a suspected Royalist, and conveyed by way of Northampton to a London prison. His friends, pleading his past work for the Parliament, tried to obtain his release; other men arrested in the same way gained theirs by entering into bonds for good conduct. Ralph's spirit refused for some time to sign any bond which implied having done what he had never done, but in the miseries of imprisonment on 8 October he gave reluctant consent to such a bond, and he was then released,[54] but not to be exempt from further trouble.

The insurrection of 1655 did not directly affect the county, but an important enemy of Cromwell was allowed to escape from Aylesbury, namely Wilmot, Earl of Rochester. He and Nicholas Armorer arrived there on 20 March, and were arrested on suspicion, though their identity was not known. The constable committed them to the charge of an innkeeper, who allowed Wilmot and Armorer to escape. He was bribed, if Clarendon is right, with some 30 jacobuses and a 'fair gold chain' worth over £100. This innkeeper Clarendon speaks of as 'of unquestionable fidelity.' The government regarded him, on the contrary, as a 'very untoward fellow,' and he was committed to prison.[55] The discomfort to Cromwell of plots and imagined

---

[49] A Declaration, &c., B.M. Pamphlets, E 555 (1).   [50] Whitelocke, *Mem.* 509.
[51] Ibid. 549.   [52] Cobbett, *Parl. Hist.* iii, 1407, 1418, 1428, 1479.
[53] *Mem. of Verney Family*, iii, 233.   [54] Ibid. 251.
[55] Thurloe, *State Papers*, iii, 281, 335–6 ; Clarendon, op. cit. v, 381 ; *Clarke Papers* (ed. C. H. Firth, Camd. Soc.), iii, 32–3.

plots and insurrections led to the parcelling out of the country into eleven districts presided over by officials called major-generals, chiefly to act with the militia to keep down all such attempts, but also to do more, to gather revenue for the rapidly rising national expenditure. Refusal to contribute and mere complaint were punished by brutal usage—even to the boring of complaining tongues with red-hot iron. The new plan gave a wide field for the exercise of cupidity by unprincipled officials and for the indulgence of private hatreds. The country gentlepeople, who had been some of the worst sufferers throughout the war, were an especial object of this pillage. Buckinghamshire formed part of the district assigned to Major-General Fleetwood; George Fleetwood and Packer acted as his deputies, and twenty-one commissioners were associated with them in the government of the county.[56] Before these some forty of the men of position in the county were summoned on 11 March 1656 to furnish particulars of their estates on pain of sequestration. The mere accusation of delinquency was ground for the intended decimation of possessions. Sir Ralph, one of the forty summoned, appealed to Cromwell himself, as one who was no delinquent, and he gave particulars of the removal of sequestration from his estates in 1648. Cromwell referred his petition back to the committee acting under Fleetwood, and, as would be expected, Sir Ralph had to suffer the extortion, to enforce which the new sequestration had been threatened, and he was in addition forbidden to go to London for six months.[57] The disposition in the county of those who had not much to lose is disclosed by the suggestion which, in September 1656, Packer made to Cromwell that a 'good regiment' might be raised in the county, and he mentioned Colonel Fletcher, Major Browne and Major Theed as capable officers.[58]

The new Parliament of March 1657 [59] put an end to these military tribunals of exaction, but by that time a more than sufficient amount of injustice, suffering and impoverishment had been wrought as well in the county as elsewhere. By this time, 1657, a Second Chamber was felt to be a necessity, single-chamber government proving unworkable, and Cromwell was petitioned to call this. He was even pressed to take the title of king by a committee of the House headed, after a strange change of sentiment, by Whitelocke, when they were sent on 16 April to learn his mind. He had the sense to refuse, and received the title of Protector, and the 'other House' was called, the formation of which out of his chief supporters in the Commons weakened his position there. Men of the county who were in the 'other House' were Fleetwood, Whitelocke and Lord Wharton; of the whole body of the hereditary peers only two deigned to join it.

On 3 September 1658 Cromwell died. Though his private life, so far as it could be, had been quiet and unostentatious, yet he entertained at Hampton Court; and among his guests there were included Waller the poet, Milton and Sir Kenelm Digby, all belonging to the county. His death let loose the forces of reaction. There was an incapable successor, an ineffectual Parliament soon dissolved, premature risings of Royalists,[60] and then a second military supremacy, in which Fleetwood of the army and Sir Richard Temple and Francis Ingoldsby of the Commons played their part, and Whitelocke also, who was accused of carrying on a treasonable correspondence with 'Charles Stuart.' Everything in the end fell under the power of Monck, commander in the North—the new constitution of 1659, the remains of the Long Parliament, and the dissentient officers of the army also. On 2 February 1659–60 the 'knights, divines, freeholders and others' of the county of Buckingham, like those of so many other counties, presented a congratulatory address to him and petitioned for the restoration of the ejected members of the Long Parliament and for free election to vacancies without oath or engagement of any kind.[61] So astutely and with such concealment of his purposes had Monck worked them out, that though some suspected him none knew how to hinder. Sir Ralph Verney again showed his independent judgement. Unlike most of his neighbours, he refused to wait on Monck upon his way to London

[56] The list of these is as follows : T. Walmesley, John Deverell, W. Grange, Richard Biscoe, G. Baldwin, W. Theed, C. Egleton, John Stace, W. Theede, H. Gould, John Theede, Richard Beke, J. Biscoe, T. White, H. Whitehead, W. Foskett, J. Browne, Richard Ingoldesby, Edmund West, Cornelius Holland and Simon Mayne (Thurloe, op. cit. iv, 583).

[57] *Mem. of Verney Family*, iii, 283.   [58] Thurloe, op. cit. v, 409.

[59] This Parliament was elected on the old franchise, Cromwell's reforms being abolished. Most of those who had sat for the county in the last two Parliaments were again returned, and Sir Richard Temple for the first time represented the borough of Buckingham, for which his father had sat in the Short and Long Parliaments (Cobbett, op. cit. iii, 1580–1).

[60] The leader of one of these in Cheshire, Sir George Booth, after its failure, escaped with two or three companions and arrived at the Red Lion Inn of Newport Pagnell disguised in female dress. The size of his feet aroused suspicion, and when his companions bought a razor and soap from the barber whom they had called in to shave them suspicion grew to conviction. The innkeeper gathered some 'well affected' neighbours together and burst into the room. Sir George confessed who he was and was arrested and sent to London (B.M. Pamphlets, E 995 [4]; *Clarke Papers, ut supra,* iv, 47).

[61] B.M. Press mark, 669 f. 23 (24).

or to invite him to his house at Claydon.[62] The House of Lords was re-established, and almost without conditions 'Charles Stuart' was accepted as the king. The unthinking readiness shown in his restoration was the result of the tyranny of the government of the people and of the severity of religious intolerance combined, and the disastrous consequences rapidly appeared.

With the Restoration there was naturally a great reaction. Buckinghamshire, like other counties, sent up an address of laudation and congratulation to the king and petitions from those of the royalist party who had suffered during the interregnum poured in to the king and council. In many of these petitions a special point is made of the oppression of the Committee for Buckinghamshire. Trouble was expected from the Anabaptists and Fifth Monarchy men who had their agents in most counties and had raised much money. Buckinghamshire was particularly mentioned as a county where trouble from this source might arise. Although Charles expressed a desire for oblivion his treatment of some of the regicides did not show the tolerance he expressed. The Buckinghamshire regicides seem to have come off better than the others, for Mayne, though convicted, was only confined in the Tower, where he died in 1661, and Ingoldsby, who had taken the side of Charles II, was pardoned and lived till 1685. Sir Richard Temple became member for the borough of Buckingham in 1661, and continued as member till his death in 1697, except in the Short Parliament of March 1678-9, when he was defeated by the influence of the Duke of Buckingham.[63] But all the best energies of the county, politically speaking, seem to have been expended before the Restoration; and during the reign of Charles II there is little to show, and part of that little in those times, when the king on the one side and members of Parliament on the other stooped to take the pay of the King of France, forms a record one would wish to forget. Even John Hampden, grandson of the hero, took 500 guineas of French gold in 1678-9. The Commons of 1681, in the unreasonable fear which followed a supposed Roman Catholic plot, and in their reasonable fear of James Duke of York, withheld supplies; and Hampden was one of the chief movers of the resolution to withhold, unless the duke should be excluded from the succession to the throne. As against York, Hampden also, in conjunction with Lord Shaftesbury and others, was concerting schemes for bringing Monmouth in, but the king would not consent to proclaim him legitimate, and their attempts only succeeded in the inception of the Rye House Plot. To this plot Edmund Waller of Beaconsfield (son of the poet) and Carleton Whitelocke were accused of being privy, while Hampden, amongst others, for complicity in it was imprisoned in the Tower, and in 1684 was brought to trial on a charge of misdemeanour, and not high treason; simply, however, because misdemeanour needed only one witness for prosecution and high treason needed two, and only one witness was forthcoming—Lord Howard of Escrick, a man of doubtful veracity. Hampden was fined £40,000, and was ordered to find sureties for good behaviour for life. The reign of Charles was followed by that of his even less statesmanlike brother, James II, in which, however, Hampden, though still in prison, got off a further charge, that of high treason, by paying £6,000. An honourable part was played by Sir Ralph Verney. He had been rewarded for his persecution under the Commonwealth by being made a baronet, but he was not a member of the 'Pensionary Parliament.' In 1680-1 he stood for the borough of Buckingham, and was one of the few Whigs returned. In the election of the only Parliament of James II in 1685 he helped to save the county representation and kept his own seat, while he supported the burgesses of Buckingham against the attack made on their electoral rights by Judge Jeffreys, who had acquired the manor of Bulstrode, and in 1687 was appointed lord-lieutenant of the county with a view to the packing of a Parliament.[64] From a pamphlet published after the Revolution we learn that the official bailiff, James Child, was compelled by Jeffreys to give up the exemplification of the ancient charter of the town, which had been made in 1665-6,[65] whereupon it was 'vacated' on pretence of forgery. The next move was to have some twenty poor men put on the list as burgesses and to levy a rate, nominally for church repairs, but in reality to enable these sham electors to pay their 'scot and lot' at the expense of the real burgesses. Child and others who refused to pay the rate were prosecuted in the Ecclesiastical Court.[66] Fortunately the Parliament for which such preparations were made was never to meet. The reign of James, so far as the county is concerned, has one solitary redeeming record on the king's part, his tolerance towards William Penn, though the Society of Friends did not reap from it much advantage. Penn had been acquitted in 1670 by jury when tried for recusancy, and the jury were fined for their verdict—the last time in English history that a jury were so fined. Hampden was very naturally one of those who met at Hurley House (*alias* Lady Place), on the Thames, to promote the bringing over of William III. There was a scare[67] with

[62] *Dict. Nat. Biog.*   [63] *Ret. of Memb. of Parl.* i, 519-72 ; *Dict. Nat. Biog.*
[64] *Dict. Nat. Biog.* Sir R. Verney and George Jeffreys.
[65] The original charter, the pamphlet states, was granted in 9 Hen. IV.
[66] 'Grievances and oppressions of James Child,' B.M. Press mark 717, m. 19 (71).
[67] Defoe, *Tour* (ed. 1742), ii, 67.

some real foundation at Colnbrook, which must have happened after the landing of William, though Defoe, who tells us of it, does not give the date. James's Irish dragoons had been driven out of Reading by the Dutch, and they fled towards London, threatening massacre, and were approaching Colnbrook. The people of Colnbrook appealed for protection to the colonel of a regiment of the king's Scots guards that happened to be there. The colonel was in difficulty what do to, but decided to stop all plundering, and disposed his men so as to resist any attempt at it. At 10 p.m. on a wet winter night the Irish troops approached and were challenged by the picket of the Scots guards, saying that they were commanded to prevent any troops from entering the town till their colonel gave further orders. This caused an uproar among the dragoons, whereon the lieutenant in command of the Scots' picket closed up his men and placed them across the road, and forbade the dragoons to advance or he would fire. The picket was all the time in touch with the main body of their regiment, and at this moment the drums beating the Scots' march were heard, and the Irish dragoons were quieted. The major then came up with the colonel's orders. If the Irish could show written orders from their general for quartering in the town or for marching by that way he would admit them, but otherwise he would keep out everybody, and especially at night. After more bluster the dragoons retreated towards Staines.

Hampden was in the chair in the Convention Parliament called together in the interregnum to consider how to act,[68] and when William and Mary were enthroned as king and queen, 12 February 1689, he was made one of their first privy councillors.

Little of importance connected with the county occurred before King William's death except Lord Haversham's attack on the Commons in the conference between the two Houses which took place when the Lower House wanted a joint committee to discuss the impeachment of Lord Somers, who was attacked by Tories and malcontent Whigs, ostensibly because of his share in advising King William to agree to the treaty for division of the Spanish monarchy, actually, however, from party animosity. John Thompson, Lord Haversham of Haversham, was son of one and nephew of another member of government under Cromwell; he had been in the Lower House, was a strong Whig at the time and a lord of the Admiralty. He had been created baron in 1696. He used vigorous language about the partiality of the Commons shown in accusing some of the king's advisers, and omitting to notice others who were parties to the same transaction, but were of the Tory side. The Commons showed great resentment at his words. Somers was tried by his peers and acquitted, no accuser presenting himself, and the Commons doing nothing more effective than making a ludicrous objection to the proceeding.

The friction between the two Houses caused by this had scarcely passed away when early in the next reign another cause of friction came. At Aylesbury at the end of 1700 a certain Matthew Ashby legally possessed of the franchise found his vote rejected by the returning officer.[69] It was not unusual in those days, it appears, for one side, when a chance was found, to ignore votes given to the other. Ashby had voted for Sir Thomas Lee and Simon Mayne. Mayne was defeated, and lodged a petition in the House. Sir Thomas had votes sufficient recorded, but the Commons voted him not duly elected, and Robert Dormer was declared as returned instead of him. The majority in power happened to be Tory, the country having grown weary of the Whigs whom William III had favoured. An election was easily declared void by the predominating party on either side, when convenient, under pretext of corruption. The returning officers at Aylesbury were believed to be acting in collusion with some candidates against others. To discount votes given for their opponents Q (= query) was placed against names of sundry voters on some pretext of illegality of claim, and the votes of such, called technically ' Qd men,' were not allowed. Ashby, one of the men thus disfranchised by means of the ' Q,' determined to resist, and settled on action at law. But this took time. Meanwhile Sir Thomas Lee had been elected in December 1701, and died as member in 1702. Disputes arose about the Wendover and Wycombe elections on the same grounds. At Wendover Richard Crawley gained his point; at Wycombe Lord Shelburne lost his. Ashby meanwhile persisted in his attempt to prosecute the returning officers.[70] A committee of the whole House in January 1703 resolved that the qualification of any elector and the right of any person elected would be determined only by the House itself except as Acts of Parliament had otherwise provided, and they resolved that Matthew Ashby was guilty of breach of privilege of the House by his prosecution of the returning officers at common law. Ashby's action, however, resulted in his obtaining a verdict of £5 damages against the returning officers in the county assizes. Appeal to Queen's Bench made by the defendants resulted in the judge-

[68] This was the last Parliament in which Sir Ralph Verney sat. He had been member since 1680.

[69] This was of course in King William's reign, but the action taken by Ashby and its legal consequences did not come before the committee of the whole House of Commons till the next reign (Gibbs, *Local Occurrences*, ii, 6).

[70] Gibbs, *Bucks. Local Records*, ii, 1–8 ; Hallam, *Const. Hist.* (ed. 1876), iii, 273 ff.

ment, given by three judges against the opinion of the fourth—Lord Justice Holt—that the plaintiff had no cause of action (April 1703). The discontent at Aylesbury was not to be thus satisfied, however, and by the October following five fresh actions were brought against the returning officers. The Commons in anger ordered the five prosecutors to be committed to Newgate, and their attorney, Robert Mead, to be taken into the custody of the serjeant-at-arms. Writs of *habeas corpus* were moved for in the Queen's Bench, and were refused to the five prosecutors, who were John Paty, John Oviatt, John Paton, Henry Basse and Daniel Horne; and in November, from Newgate, John Paty and John Oviatt petitioned the queen for writ of error so that the case might be brought before the Lords. Against this the Commons also petitioned the queen, after removing the prisoners from Newgate to the custody of the serjeant-at-arms, lest the queen should grant the petition of the prosecutors. The Commons next interfered still further with the liberties of the subject by attaching six men of law who had defended the cases of the prosecutors. Here the House of Lords interfered and issued prohibition of these arrests, but in one case the Commons were not baulked. Then came the storm, the Lords maintaining the rights of the people, the Commons their imagined privilege. The judgement of Queen's Bench in the preceding April was upset by the House of Lords, and the Commons losing dignity issued a set of resolutions against the judgement of the Lords, and fixed them up on the gates of Westminster Hall. The Peers persisted in their judgement, maintaining that it was the right of Englishmen to have redress from any wrong in the courts of justice. Queen Anne, not remarkable for grip, chose the line of weakest resistance, and first prorogued the Parliament, a step which by custom released the prisoners, and then dissolved it, but practically the Commons were defeated, and though petitions against returns of members were sent up all through Queen Anne's reign there were no further actions for breach of privilege by the Commons. A point of interest at this juncture is that Browne Willis the antiquary sat for Buckingham in 1705, though he made no figure in the House. Lord Haversham resigned the office of lord of the Admiralty in 1701, and from being a strong Whig became a leading member of the Tories. He three times persuaded the Lords to reject the 'Occasional Conformity' Bill, a Bill framed to allow Nonconformists to be placed in office by complying, when convenient for that purpose, with the Test Act. In 1709 he opposed the impeachment of Sacheverell, and in 1710 he appears to have left his speeches written out for printing.[71] In 1709 Richard Hampden joined himself to some of the extreme Whigs, the Tories and the Scots, in the now United Parliament of Great Britain, in the attempt to bring about a moderation of cruelty in punishing persons convicted of treason, and succeeded, after much debate in both Houses, in the attempt.

An interesting light on a past state of things is given by the petition lodged in the Commons in 1713 against the return of Thomas Chapman and Dr. John Radcliffe in the election for the borough of Buckingham. The body of electors consisted of a bailiff and twelve burgesses. One of the burgesses was absent, and the votes were given as follows:—for T. Chapman 8, for Dr. Radcliffe 7, for Sir Richard Temple 5, for Sir Edmund Denton 4. The defeated candidates in their petition claimed that four burgesses who would have supported them had been deprived unjustly of their franchise for an alleged failure to qualify by taking the sacrament in the course of the last year, and that their places had been filled by others, and accordingly that the votes should rightly have gone thus:—for Temple 9, for Denton 4, for Radcliffe 4, for Chapman 3.[72] The Commons resolved that Chapman and Radcliffe were duly elected, and for a time the influence of the Temple family was broken in the borough, to be restored, however, by 1721, when Richard Grenville, heir of the Temples through marriage with Sir Richard Temple's daughter, sat for the borough and was member till he died; he had before that represented Wendover, when he was succeeded by Richard Steele of *Tatler* fame in 1722. Other petitions against returns—indeed, these continued till nearly the end of the century—included one in March 1715, when John Deacle, who was elected for Aylesbury, retired and was replaced by Trevor Hill, afterwards Lord Hillsborough,[73] and one in 1717, when Henry Lord Shelburne, notwithstanding the petition against him, was resolved by the House to have been duly elected for Marlow. The Verney family still continued in Parliament, representing the county or one of its boroughs. In 1725 the election of Henry Waller for Wycombe was declared void by the Commons on a petition sent up against him, but the Mayor of Wycombe, Richard Shrimpton, persisted in returning him until the business was ended by his being committed to Newgate[74] by the Commons for illegal practices in the election.

[71] These were published in a memoir of him in the next year and are the first speeches of a member of the Upper House so printed (*Dict. Nat. Biog.*).

[72] 'Case of Borough of Buckingham,' B.M. Press mark G 999 (1).

[73] Gibbs, *Bucks. Local Rec.* ii, 31. Lord Hillsborough was in the ministry later, but he did not then belong to the county. [74] Ibid. 52.

In 1718 Richard Hampden, who had sat in several Parliaments,[75] was made paymaster of the Navy, an office which afforded great chances for private gain. It was but two years after this when a deficiency of £73,000 in his accounts was found. Sequestration of his estates was ordered, against which he petitioned. The petition was considered in committee in March 1725, and a suggestion to pardon him for the sake of his great-grandfather was opposed on public grounds by Walpole. The case ended in the following May, when his whole estates and possessions were placed in the hands of trustees, who were to pay the debt and to provide out of the remainder for the Hampden family.[76] The £73,000 had been lost in the South Sea Scheme. He was elected again, notwithstanding, for Wendover (1721), and for the county in 1727. He died in July 1728.

Till the last part of the reign of George II there is little of interest as regards the county, and that little is hardly pleasant reading. In 1732 a member for Marlow, George Robinson, was expelled the House charged with breach of trust in the management of funds of a corporation called the Charitable Corporation, of which he was cashier, and a most enlightened proposition made in 1753 by Potter, member for Aylesbury, son of John Potter, Archbishop of Canterbury, to introduce a census and registration scheme, was passed through the Commons with much difficulty and rejected by the Lords.

The 18th century is marked for the county by the rise of the great families belonging to it, which for some seventy years—from the middle of that century to close on 1820—almost held the destinies of the United Kingdom in their hands. These were (1) the Grenville family of Wotton Underwood, after the marriage of Sir Richard Grenville,[77] in 1710, with Hester daughter and heir of Sir Richard Temple of Stowe. Three sons of this marriage became prominent in Parliament, a daughter, Hester, was married to William Pitt the elder, and was mother of the younger Pitt, and other members of the family, grandchildren, held offices in different administrations, (2) the family of the Earl of Shelburne, afterwards Marquess of Lansdowne (Lord Wycombe), and (3) the Portland family of Bulstrode. These all played their parts in political history in those crowded decades wherein Great Britain, through extremities of vicissitude and struggle with her formidable enemies, rose from a second-rate to a first-rate power, to the empire of the seas and to a controlling influence on continents. It is the misfortune of a county historian that he has to refrain from relating, though he keeps in mind, those parts of the political service of the county which belong to the wider area of the kingdom, and to confine himself almost entirely to recording the under play of the lesser men and the lower tone of the subordinate figures. But the reader as well as the writer may preserve in the background of his thoughts the remembrance that the merely local record is not all, and that the county had a preponderating share in the grandeur of the Imperial history concurrent with the trivial local history.

Almost at the beginning of Pitt's career there was a sharp encounter between him and John Hampden, the last of the direct line, member for Wendover, in a debate on the Mutiny Bill, which except for the interference of the Speaker would have ended in a duel. Sir Francis Dashwood of West Wycombe (afterwards Lord le Despencer), of notoriety otherwise as chief of the Franciscan or Hell Fire Club of Medmenham, was a prominent political figure, and his was almost the only voice to urge the mercy which would have been justice in the case of Admiral Byng. In the much more confined area of local administration there was excitement in the county about the town which should be its local capital wherein assizes should be held. The fact of the county having two centres, Aylesbury and Buckingham, and a third quasi-centre, Wycombe, has been already mentioned.[78] Aylesbury as the most central had the gaol and county hall. The undertone of rivalry between this town and Buckingham was roused to open vociferation and a pamphlet war in 1748,[79] when Lord Cobham [80] obtained an Act of Parliament for holding the summer assizes at Buckingham till for any reason that town should prove unfit. The summer assizes had been held there from 1720 onwards with the exception of the preceding year, and the Act really did no more than enforce the practice.[81] The Act of 1748 remained in force till 1849.

Great excitement, not confined to the county, was stirred up in 1762 by John Wilkes, who was member for Aylesbury and colonel of the Militia of the county, by his publication of the *North Briton*. When he was prosecuted for issuing the famous No. 45, Temple, lord-lieutenant of the county, was ordered by Lord Egremont on the king's behalf to dismiss Wilkes from his colonelcy.

[75] He had been returned for Wendover, 1700–2 and 1705, for the county 1708, for Berwick-upon-Tweed 1713. [76] Gibbs, *Bucks. Local Rec.* ii, 51–2.

[77] He was a descendant of Richard Grenville, sheriff of the county in 1642, who commanded a troop in the army of the Parliament. [78] Cf. *V.C.H. Bucks.* iii, 1–2.

[79] B.M. Press mark 357 d. 3 (41), 816 m. 16 (1), G 3764 ; Gibbs, *Hist. of Aylesbury*, 502.

[80] Lord Cobham was husband of Christian daughter of Sir Richard Temple of Stowe.

[81] Assizes between 1666 and 1717 in winter and summer had been held seventy-four times at Aylesbury, nineteen times at Buckingham and eleven times at Wycombe ; the summer assizes between 1666 and 1720, twenty-five times at Aylesbury, twenty-one at Buckingham and nine at Wycombe.

Lord Temple's expressions of regret in doing this caused his own dismissal from the lord-lieutenant's office and the Privy Council. In 1764 Wilkes was expelled the House.[82] The war against him went on afterwards, especially after he proposed himself for election in Middlesex. He had left sympathizers, however, amongst his old constituents, for a petition was got up in the county in his favour in April 1768 signed by 1,800 freeholders who belonged to it. Rockingham's Ministry (1765) is noticeable from the county point of view for the first speech made by Edmund Burke in the House in the attempt to get a hearing for the American colonies. He was member for Wendover, where he had obtained the seat at a by-election in 1765 under the patronage of Ralph Earl Verney, whose peerage was an Irish one and who could therefore himself sit in the Commons.[83] Verney was the great opponent in the county of the Grenvilles and Temples, and on succeeding to Claydon in 1752 he added a new wing to the house in the hope of rivalling Stowe. He sat for Wendover from 1753 to 1761, and for the county from 1768 to 1784.[84] Extravagance in expenditure brought his affairs into hopeless confusion, but he made a show as spirited as ever at the election of 1784, when the polling went on for sixteen days, and William Grenville was in front of him by twenty-four votes. Six years later, when he was on the verge of ruin, another general election came on, and, though seventy-eight, he plunged into the contest. This time his agent hoped to limit his expenses to £12,000 or £13,000. He was returned, but his financial ruin was now complete. He died in March 1791, and his title ended with him.

In the Session of 1782 a motion for putting an end to the war with the American colonies was carried by a majority of nineteen (on 29 February). The votes of members belonging to the county on this division are recorded. Against continuing the war were Earl Verney and Thomas Grenville (county), James Grenville and William Grenville (Buckingham), Lord Mahon [85] (Wycombe), Richard Smith and J. M. Smith (Wendover), William Drake the elder and William Drake the younger (Amersham); and for continuing the war Robert Waller (Wycombe), Anthony Bacon and Thomas Ord (Aylesbury) and John Borlase (Marlow).[86]

After the parties of North and Fox coalesced and overthrew Shelburne in 1783, under Portland nominally chief, when the proposition to place the East India Company under commissioners was defeated, practically by the king, the sympathy in the county was clearly on the side of the king and the Opposition. Addresses were sent up to the king from Aylesbury, Buckingham, High Wycombe and other places within its borders thanking him for dismissing the Ministry who were 'encroaching on the royal and other rights.' Pitt was then called by the king, and the corporation of Wycombe elected him a burgess in the next year 'for his patriotic endeavours at reform.' In January 1789 William Wyndham Grenville, joint paymaster of the forces, was elected Speaker of the House; in June of the same year he vacated the chair, being made home secretary; in November 1790 he was created Baron Grenville to lead Pitt's party in the Lords. He was next transferred to the Foreign Office, at that time a most difficult position. In 1800 George Canning sat for Wendover, but the distinguished part of his Parliamentary career does not belong to the county.

At the election of 1802 a West India merchant named Bent was elected for Aylesbury with Dupré and a petition against the return was lodged by the defeated candidate. At the subsequent inquiry one witness said he thought that 400 out of the 450 electors took money, while the remaining 50 gave it away. It was stated that the bribery was open and shameless, and that the representatives of the candidate sat with two bowls before them, one containing punch, the other guineas. As soon as an elector had proved his right to vote he received a glass of punch from one and three guineas from the other bowl. As a result of the inquiry an Act was passed in 1804 to enlarge the constituency so as to include the three hundreds of Aylesbury as well as the borough in it, and the number of electors was raised from 450 to 1,000. This was developed later into the constituency of Mid-Bucks. Next year the Marquess of Buckingham created fifty freeholds of the value of 40s. on his Hartwell estate and the occupants of these were qualified to vote both for the county and the borough.[87] In 1806 Lord Henry Petty, son of the Marquess of Lansdowne, though not effective as chancellor of the Exchequer, did good service by introducing measures to prevent officials from making profit from public moneys, and by instituting a better audit. He was one who supported Wilberforce and his fellow workers for the abolition of the slave trade. For this abolition they had been working against odds for years, and as far back as 1799 it had been opposed with vehemence by Drake, member for Amersham, amongst others.

[82] *Dict. Nat. Biog.*; Massey, *Hist. of Engl. during Reign of Geo. III* (ed. 1865), i, 135.

[83] Burke was elected again in 1768. In 1774 Verney asked him to find another seat, as he could no longer afford the election expenses. Verney apparently advanced him £6,000 for the purchase of Gregories in Beaconsfield, and they continued friends.

[84] Between 1761 and 1768 he represented Caermarthen boroughs.

[85] Husband of Hester daughter of William Pitt.   [86] Gibbs, *Bucks. Local Rec.* ii, 197.

[87] Gibbs, *Hist. of Aylesbury*, 254–7, 276–7.

The end of the predominance of the county in politics came in the coalition of the Grenville party with that of Lord Liverpool in 1821; it had been gradually dwindling, and the centre of political activities for some time after this was transferred to the manufacturing counties and only comes back to Buckinghamshire just before the Reform Bill passed. The rick-burning epidemic of 1830 spread into the county and caused desperate anxiety and tribulation. The cry for Parliamentary reform, however, drew the attention of agitators to other matters. Reform was wanted badly, in representation in Parliament, in the civil list and in the poor law. This was the juncture in which a new candidate not in any way a scion of any of the old ruling families came into the arena of representation in the county, and before he passed away had once more brought Buckinghamshire politics into the wider field of imperial history. This was Benjamin Disraeli, who came forward as candidate for High Wycombe, opposed by the son of the Prime Minister (Colonel Grey). All that seemed to be understood at that time of his wide and deep political views was his distrust of the Whigs, and the reason for this was not grasped. He was defeated. After the passing of the Reform Bill in 1832 [88] he once more came forward. His views were, if not more developed, more clearly enunciated. He attacked the useless places and undeserved pensions and reversions which were in existence as a Whig monopoly. He spoke strongly on the condition of the poor and the position of trade, expressed sympathy with Romilly in his desire to reform the criminal law, was bent on the abolition of slavery in the West Indies, had doubts about the corn laws and denounced the Whigs as a tyrannical and rapacious party who had taken sufficient care of their family interests in managing the Reform Bill. His ideal was a new party, a fusion of Tory and the Reform party called Radical—though he disliked the names of Whig and Tory—a National Party embracing the best views of Radical and Tory. This was too much in advance of the time to be understood. By some he was attacked as a Radical in disguise, by others accused of being a Tory nominee. The family interest in the county, reduced though it was, was against him, and his descent was sneered at. He was again rejected. Then came the end of Earl Grey's Reform Ministry in 1834 and dissolution. He was candidate once more and for the third time defeated. After this he does not appear again as candidate for any constituency in the county till 1847, when he had been some years in Parliament and had made his mark there.

During the campaigns of the 'Free Trade' agitation Cobden visited Aylesbury in 1843, and at his meeting there [89] succeeded in getting a resolution passed approving of its principles with very few dissentients. In 1850, when he went again, the farmers showed that it had no attraction for them; his hearers were chiefly artisans and mechanical labourers and there was a free fight during his address. Disraeli showed himself throughout against the new policy and in favour of Fair Trade. When he spoke at Newport Pagnell in May 1847 the windows of the room were broken by the crowd outside, that for want of space could not obtain admittance, in order that they might hear him speak. He was supporting the union between Church and State, condemning a permanent income tax and setting forth his views that moderate customs-duties were the only stable plan to defray national expenses. His onslaught on Liberals as those who have opinions that ensure enjoyment to themselves and are opposed to self-sacrifice was sharp and incisive; his pleas for proper care for the poor and regard to sanitation brought a sneer from one of the Ministry, but it was a noble plea. County influence was again brought against him, but he was returned without opposition, after all. In 1850 Protectionist meetings were held in Aylesbury as well as in other parts of the county, and a petition from 200 of the owners and occupiers of land praying for relief from local burdens and for equality of privilege with foreign agriculturists went up, but Disraeli's proposition of a committee of the whole House to consider such revision of the poor laws as might alleviate agricultural distress was defeated. To the Parliament of 1857 Disraeli was returned without opposition. He had already been chancellor of the Exchequer, but Layard was replaced

---

[88] The Reform Bill reduced the county representation from fourteen to eleven. Amersham and Wendover were disfranchised, reducing the number by four, but one knight of the shire was added. Since 1625 Amersham had often been represented by a member of the Drake family. At the election of December 1832 Sir Harry Verney of Claydon was returned at the head of the poll for the borough of Buckingham. He was not of the old family, though he bore its name. He was son of Sir Harry Calvert and took the Buckinghamshire name when he succeeded, by the will of his cousin Mrs. Verney, to the estate of Claydon in 1827. He lost his seat in 1834, held it again from 1837 to 1841, and then from 1857 represented the borough continuously till its disfranchisement in 1885. He carried on, as he thought his duty, the better traditions of the Verney name. One of the clauses in the Bill was the noted Chandos Clause, carried by the Marquess of Chandos, son of the Duke of Buckingham, ensuring the right to vote to tenants at will in the counties who occupied tenements at a yearly value of £50. In 1835 the same Lord Chandos proposed the repeal of the malt tax, which fell very heavily on the farming interest. This was against his own party (Peel's), but all sides seem to have had a majority against its repeal.

[89] Morley, *Life of Cobden*, i, 274.

POLITICAL HISTORY

at Aylesbury by Sir Richard Bethell, afterwards Lord Westbury. By June 1859, when Palmerston[90] was called for the second time, old boundary marks of party had disappeared. Disraeli preferred to consider his the Constitutional Party. Against the abolition of church rates which came up he contended in vain. It was the church-rate question, and not that of race, which seems to have been the chief objection raised against Mr. N. M. de Rothschild (later Lord Rothschild), who was elected, in spite of objections, for Aylesbury in 1865 for what had been a Conservative seat, the general feeling being that on most questions of change he would not be on the side of extremes. To the new Parliament which met on 1 February 1866 Disraeli and his two coadjutors were returned unopposed. In 1868 he introduced the Act for reform of Parliamentary representation, arranging for it by reducing the value of the qualifying tenements and adding other franchises, a plan which required redistribution. This Act reduced the constituencies of the county from eleven to eight by depriving Buckingham, Wycombe and Great Marlow of one each of their members. In 1885 all the boroughs of the county lost their members, and since then the three divisions of the county have returned one member each.

Disraeli was raised to the peerage as Earl of Beaconsfield in 1876 to the great rejoicing of the county. But the elections after dissolution in 1879 turned against him. His last cabinet was held on 29 April 1880 and he died on 19 April 1881. In the county whose interests he had so long upheld, where men had come to understand him and to love him well, in that upland vale of Hughenden he sleeps, near the trees that he cherished. Since 1881 the county has shown no special prominence in politics, though one more Prime Minister, Lord Rosebery, has his seat within the county. But it remained steadfast to the principles which Beaconsfield upheld till 1906, when only its Mid-Division remained true. Since then, however, there have been plain and indubitable signs of its return to them, and two out of the three constituencies hold his tenets fast.

MILITARY HISTORY

The control of the Militia, a main point in dispute between the Parliament and the king at the beginning of the Civil War, passed without any question at the Restoration into the king's hands, and was exercised in each county by the lord-lieutenant. The amount expended annually upon it was in Buckinghamshire not to exceed £320.[91] This arrangement seems to have continued till 1756, when Pitt felt reorganization needful. The Militia Act was passed in 1757, and the number of men to be levied in the county was 560; in 1796 there was an additional levy, under the feeling of insecurity caused by the political situation on the Continent, and Buckinghamshire had to furnish 662 men for the Supplementary Militia.

Two regiments have borne for a time the county title, the 16th and the 14th. The 16th Regiment of Foot, originally formed in 1688, was ordered in 1782 to take the title of 16th or Buckinghamshire Regiment and to cultivate connexion with the county for the purpose of recruiting there. In the next year it was placed on a peace establishment, and from 1784 to 1790 was stationed in Ireland. Thence it was moved to Nova Scotia and in 1791 to Jamaica, where it remained till 1796. In the last part of its time there it was occupied in difficult operations against the Maroons, descendants of slaves who had escaped and were asserting their independence and harassing the colonists. Brought home in 1796, it was stationed towards the end of that year in Scotland, then removed to Ireland, and then in 1804 was moved again to the West Indies and was engaged in the capture of Surinam. While still in the West Indies in May 1809 its name was changed to that of the 'Bedfordshire Regiment' by exchange with the 14th.[92]

The 14th [93] was originally formed in 1685. The title of 'Bedfordshire Regiment' was given to it in 1782. The first battalion was sent in 1807 to India, and it was there till 1831. The second battalion distinguished itself at the battle of Corunna and when brought home was stationed at Buckingham and Aylesbury. Its title was changed in May 1809 to 'Buckinghamshire,' at the request of Major-General Sir Harry Calvert, who had been appointed colonel of the regiment in 1806, and it received drafts of 370 volunteers from the Royal Bucks and other Militia regiments. It was engaged in the Walcheren expedition and was mentioned in General Orders for gallant behaviour at the capture of Flushing in August 1809. After being brought back home in September it was sent out again to Walcheren at the end of the year to destroy the naval works at Flushing and to bring away the survivors of the expedition. Then till the end of the war it was at Malta, and in 1814 it was transferred to Genoa. The first battalion meanwhile took part in the capture

[90] It is interesting to remember that Lord Palmerston was a scion of the Temple family and was descended from the first owner of Stowe of the name in the 16th century.

[91] Grose, *Military Antiq.* i, 27–8. The amount was one-fourth of the county's proportion (£1,283 6s. 8d.) of the tax assessed under the Commonwealth.

[92] Cannon, *Hist. Rec. 16th Regt.* 23–8.

[93] The account following is compiled from Captain H. O'Donnell's *Hist. Rec. of 14th Regt.*

of Java in 1811. This is commemorated on the regimental colours. A third battalion [94] was formed at Weedon Barracks in 1813, composed of volunteers from the Militia. This was intended for service in America and was on the point of being disbanded, peace being concluded with the United States, when Napoleon's return from Elba caused it to be sent to Belgium. There it formed part of Sir Charles Colville's Fourth Division, and was engaged at Waterloo. According to the late Earl of Albemarle, who had just joined as junior ensign in his sixteenth year, fourteen of the officers and 300 of the men were under twenty years of age. ' These last, consisting principally of Buckinghamshire lads fresh from the plough, were called at home " the Bucks," but their un-buckish appearance procured for them the nickname of the " Peasants." ' [95] These ' boys ' were at first condemned to garrison duty at Antwerp, but Lieut.-Col. Tidy, by a personal appeal to the Duke of Wellington, saved them from this fate, and his confidence was justified. Stationed on the extreme right of the British line ' the very young 3rd battalion of the 14th displayed a steadiness and gallantry becoming of veteran troops.' [96] Its losses were not heavy : seven of the rank and file were killed and an ensign, four sergeants and sixteen rank and file wounded. [97] The battalion was the first to enter Cambrai on 23 June, and thence it marched to Paris. On its return to England it was disbanded in February 1816; some of the officers and all the effective non-commissioned officers and men were transferred to the other battalions of the regiment, and the ' Waterloo ' which it had earned was placed on their colours. The second battalion, together with other British and some foreign troops, for a time occupied Marseilles and helped to restore calm after the anarchy of the 'White Terror,' then was sent back to Malta and thence to the Ionian Islands. In 1817, on its return home, it also was disbanded, and 420 rank and file were transferred to the first battalion, which now constituted the whole regiment. Its next work was in the campaign against the Ghoorkas, 1814–15, and the destruction of the fortress of Hatrass in the province of Agra, then it had a long time of inactivity in cantonments at Meerut. Towards the end of 1825, when the rights of the young Rajah of Bhurtpore needed defending against a usurping kinsman, the 14th formed part of the force which on 5 January 1826 stormed the rock fortress of Bhurtpore, from which, twenty years before, Lord Lake had been repulsed with heavy loss. The regiment lost in this 36 killed and 108 wounded out of a total strength of 900. ' Bhurtpore ' was inscribed on the colours and ' Bhurtpore day ' was long kept as one of the regimental anniversaries. The regiment returned to England in 1831, after twenty-three years' service in India, for which in 1838 it received the right to place a royal tiger with ' India ' on its colours and appointments. Its next time of active service was during the Crimean war ; it was dispatched to Malta first and did not reach the seat of war till February 1855, where it served in the trenches before Sebastopol. ' The regiment,' however, ' had kept up no local connection in England, and for long previous to the war, as well as for some time after, was largely recruited in Ireland,' [98] and a second battalion formed in 1858 had its head quarters at Naas. In 1873 a rearrangement of the military districts transferred the head quarters of the 14th to Bradford. In 1876 the Prince of Wales presented the 1st battalion with new colours on his visit to India, where it was then serving, and the name was altered to ' 14th (Buckinghamshire) Prince of Wales's Own Regiment,' and the prince's plume was placed on the colours of the regiment. The second battalion had its first fighting in New Zealand, 1860–6, and in 1880 kept up in the Afghan war the traditions of the ' old and bold ' 14th. In 1881 the new territorial scheme altered its name to ' West Yorkshire Regiment,' and its nominal connexion with the county came to an end. After that the county formed part of the recruiting district of the Oxfordshire Light Infantry, and the Royal Bucks Militia (Lieut.-Col. W. Terry) constituted the 3rd battalion. To this were also attached the 1st Bucks Volunteer Rifle Corps (Lieut.-Col. Hon. T. F. Fremantle, V.D.), with its head quarters at Great Marlow, [99] and the 2nd Bucks Volunteer Rifle Corps (Major-Commandant R. S. de Havilland), Eton College. [100]

There was also a regiment of Imperial Yeomanry (Lieut.-Col. Hon. M. L. Lawson), which served in the South African war and took part in the capture of Cronje and the relief of Mafeking ; and in that war some 400 Militia reservists joined the 1st battalion of the Oxfordshire Light Infantry, and a volunteer battalion was recruited from the Territorial volunteer battalions. [101]

---

[94] The unusual number of three battalions procured for the regiment the nickname of ' Calvert's Entire.'

[95] Earl of Albemarle, *Fifty Years of my Life* (1877), 132.

[96] Sir Charles Colville's Divisional Orders, quoted by O'Donnell, op. cit. 118.

[97] Sir John Burgoyne, *Reg. Rec. Beds. Militia*, 66. He says that some of the men wore the uniform of the Beds. Militia. The battalion was composed of drafts from various Militia regiments and doubtless had men in it from Bedfordshire as well as from Buckinghamshire. [98] O'Donnell, op. cit.

[99] Under the new Territorial scheme, which came into force on 1 April 1908, this corps is controlled by the Buckinghamshire County Association.

[100] See for the history of this corps the account of Eton College under ' Schools.' For staff colleges at High Wycombe and Marlow see vol. iii, pp. 66, 114.

[101] Rudolf, *Territ. Regts. of Brit. Army*, 436.